THE STATESMAN'S YEAR-BOOK

1983–1984

Man hat behauptet, die Welt werde durch Zahlen regiert: das aber weiss ich, dass die Zahlen uns belehren, ob sie gut oder schlecht regiert werde.

GOETHE

Editors

Frederick Martin	1864–1883
Sir John Scott-Keltie	1883–1926
Mortimer Epstein	1911/27–1946
S. H. Steinberg	1946–1969
John Paxton	1963/69–

THE STATESMAN'S YEAR-BOOK

STATISTICAL AND HISTORICAL ANNUAL
OF THE STATES OF THE WORLD
FOR THE YEAR

1983–1984

EDITED BY

JOHN PAXTON

ST. MARTIN'S PRESS
NEW YORK

First published in 1864
120th edition 1983

For information, write:
ST. MARTIN'S PRESS, INC.
175 Fifth Ave., New York, N.Y. 10010

Typeset in Great Britain by
MB GRAPHIC SERVICES LIMITED
Leighton Buzzard, Bedfordshire

Printed in Great Britain by
RICHARD CLAY (THE CHAUCER PRESS), LTD
Bungay, Suffolk

Library of Congress Catalog Card No. 4–3776

ISBN 0–312–76096–5

This edition published United States of America 1983

PREFACE

THE STATESMAN'S YEAR-BOOK was first published in 1864 when the original sub-title read 'A Statistical, Genealogical and Historical Account of the States and Sovereigns of the Civilized World', and has been published annually since. The editor has been looking back at that 1864 edition and comparing it with the present one hundred and twentieth edition and finds that the basic plan devised by the first editor still runs through the pages. Great political, economic and social upheavals have taken place and two world wars have been fought, but THE STATESMAN'S YEAR-BOOK has recorded with impartiality these momentous events. During these one hundred and twenty years there have only been five editors, but all would have agreed that THE STATESMAN'S YEAR-BOOK would not have survived and improved each year without the informed and constructive criticism of its readers. The editor is now looking into the future to see how THE STATESMAN'S YEAR-BOOK can best serve its readers in the decades to come and will welcome ideas.

This year there are two specially prepared maps; the first of 'Antarctica' and the second an entirely new map showing the 'World's Changing Wealth'. There have been many interesting elections this year, some taking place just as this edition was going to press. One, in Albania, in Nov. 1982 claimed a 100% turnout of the electorate of 1,627,968 for the 250 candidates on the single list of the Albanian Democratic Front. There were 8 spoiled papers and 1 vote against.

The editor's mail has been particularly heavy and he is grateful to all his correspondents. Some of the suggestions have been incorporated this year and others will be used in future editions.

The second edition of THE STATESMAN'S YEAR-BOOK WORLD GAZETTEER is available for those who need more details about individual towns.

J.P.

THE STATESMAN'S YEAR-BOOK OFFICE,
THE MACMILLAN PRESS LTD,
LITTLE ESSEX STREET,
LONDON, WC2R 3LF

WEIGHTS AND MEASURES

On 1 Jan. 1960 following an agreement between the standards laboratories of Great Britain, Canada, Australia, New Zealand, South Africa and the USA, an international yard and an international pound (avoirdupois) came into existence. 1 yard = 91·44 centimetres; 1 lb. = 453·59237 grammes.

The abbreviation 'm' signifies 'million(s)' and tonnes implies metric tons.

LENGTH	
Centimetre	0·394 inch
Metre	1·094 yards
Kilometre	0·621 mile
LIQUID MEASURE	
Litre	1·75 pints
Hectolitre	22 gallons
SURFACE MEASURE	
Square metre	10·76 sq. feet
Hectare	2·47 acres
Square kilometre	0·386 sq. mile

DRY MEASURE	
Litre	0·91 quart
Hectolitre	2·75 bushels
WEIGHT—AVOIRDUPOIS	
Gramme	15·42 grains
Kilogramme	2·205 pounds
Quintal (= 100 kg)	220·46 pounds
Tonne (= 1,000 kg)	0·984 long ton 1·102 short tons
WEIGHT—TROY	
Gramme	15·43 grains
Kilogramme	32·15 ounces 2·68 pounds

BRITISH WEIGHTS AND MEASURES

LENGTH	
1 foot	0·305 metre
1 yard	0·914 metre
1 mile (= 1,760 yds)	1·609 kilometres
SURFACE MEASURE	
1 sq. foot	9·290 sq. decimetres
1 sq. yard	0·836 sq. metre
1 acre	0·405 hectare
1 sq. mile	2·590 sq. kilometres

WEIGHT	
1 ounce (= 437·2 grains)	28·350 grammes
1 lb. (= 7,000 grains)	453·6 grammes
1 cwt. (= 112 lb.)	50·802 kilogrammes
1 long ton (= 2,240 lb.)	1·016 tonnes
1 short ton (= 2,000 lb.)	0·907 tonne
LIQUID MEASURE	
1 pint	0·568 litre
1 gallon	4·546 litres
1 quarter	2·909 hectolitres

CONTENTS

Part II: Countries of the World A–Z

WHEAT

Countries	Area (1,000 hectares) Average 1969-71	1978	1979	1980	1981	Production (1,000 tonnes) Average 1969-71	1978	1979	1980	1981
Afghánistán	2,199	...	2,400*	2,400	2,600	2,150	...	2,663	2,700	3,000
Algeria	2,214	1,864	1,946	2,071	2,000*	1,359	1,083	1,080	1,511	1,400*
Argentina	4,402	4,685	4,787	5,023	5,757	5,873	8,100	8,100	7,780	8,100
Australia [1]	7,695	10,249	11,153	11,292	12,041	9,014	18,086	16,483	11,176	16,773
Bulgaria [1,2]	1,022	935	958	968	1,032	2,898	3,466	3,355	3,847	4,429
Canada	7,669	10,579	10,489	11,098	12,230	13,901	21,146	17,185	19,157	24,519
Chile [1]	737	580	560	546	432	1,296	893	995	966	686
China [1]	25,422	26,501	29,358	28,841	29,201	29,687	52,002	62,733	54,158	57,003
Czechoslovakia [2]	1,076	1,270	1,092	1,189	1,125	3,436	5,601	3,736	5,386	4,400
Egypt [1]	551	585	584	557	585*	1,509	1,943	1,856	1,796	1,850*
France	3,892	4,167	4,087	4,582	4,753	14,112	20,970	19,522	23,683	22,782
Germany, Fed. Rep. of [2]	1,511	1,619	1,627	1,668	1,632	6,268	8,118	8,061	8,156	8,314
Greece	1,010	954	991	1,003	987	1,867	2,660	2,407	2,951	2,750
Hungary [1,3]	1,289	1,324	1,135	1,276	1,150	3,410	5,677	3,709	6,077	4,800
India	16,941	21.456	22,641	22,172	22,104	20,859	31,749	35,508	31,830	36,460
Iran	5,370	5,600	5,000*	5,500	5,500	3,946	5,700	5,500*	5,700*	5,800*
Iraq	1,216	1,496	1,750*	1,500*	861	1,080	910	1,492	1,300	1,100*
Italy	4,089	3,472	3,452	3,405	1,200*	9,756	9,332	8,980	9,150	8,921
Japan [1]	227	112	149	191	3,260	557	367	541	583	612
Mexico	781	...	599	739	861	2,278	...	2,339	2,785	3,189
Morocco	1,952	1,754	1,656	1,715	900*	1,819	1,876	1,796	1,811	892*
Pakistan [1]	6,122	6,360	6,687	6,912	6,914	6,796	8,367	9,950	10,805	11,340
Poland [1]	2,004	1,852	1,549	1,609	1,418	4,924	6,029	4,187	4,175	4,229
Romania [1]	2,527	2,284	2,105	2,244	2,111*	4,433	6,243	4,676	6,427	5,800
S. Africa, Republic of	1,330	1,792	1,900*	1,620*	1,790*	1,461	1,690	2,086	1,470	2,090
Spain [2]	3,727	2,752	2,551	2,694	2,623	4,734	4,806	4,101	5,849	3,356
Turkey [2]	8,732	9,346	9,380	9,061	9,400*	11,423	16,764	17,569	16,554	17,040
USSR [1]	65,230	62,898	57,682	61,475	59,232	92,804	120,824	90,207	98,185	88,000
UK	980	1,257	1,371	1,441	1,491	4,140	6,613	7,168	8,470	8,465
USA	18,669	22,863	25,275	28,727	32,759	40,034	48,322	58,081	64,619	76,026
Yugoslavia [2]	1,928	1,715	1,524	1,516	1,386	4,760	5,355	4,512	5,091	4,270
World total	212,884	226,957	228,972	236,883	239,381	327,922	449,372	428,777	444,603	458,195

* Unofficial figures. [1] Sown area. [2] Includes spelt. [3] Field crops and other crops.

RYE

Countries	Area (1,000 hectares) Average 1969–71	1978	1979	1980	1981	Production (1,000 tonnes) Average 1969/71	1978	1979	1980	1981
Argentina	440	260	225	210	245*	271	210	202	155	200*
Austria	143	109	106	109	101	417	410	278	383	320
Belgium	23	17	14	12*	9*	82	64	51	41*	36*
Bulgaria [1]	22	13	16	20	27	27	19	25	28	35
Canada	356	318	330	310	449	474	605	525	448	964
China	1,200	...	800	1,000	900	1,233	...	1,400	1,200	1,000
Czechoslovakia [2]	243	185	164	177	171	586	630	486	570	500
Denmark	42	84	70	56	51	136	315	257	199	200
Finland	67	38	37	53	41	130	74	77	124	64
France	139	138	116	130	117	297	435	355	408	342
German Demo. Rep.	679	652	678	678	670	1,594	1,895	1,830	1,917	1,800
Germany, Fed. Rep. of	868	651	564	547	484	2,862	2,457	2,114	2,098	1,729
Hungary [1, 3]	155	78	69	73	70	193	138	93	141	120
Netherlands	60	17	12	10	7	196	68	49	39	29
Poland [1]	3,766	3,030	2,868	3,039	3,002	7,143	7,434	5,201	6,566	6,789
Portugal	227	213	209	206	173	164	123	120	138	125
Romania [1]	45	40*	35*	35*	30*	52	57	40	40*	35*
Spain	320	228	223	222	216	292	251	220	292	216
Sweden	78	81	59	67	52	239	298	195	226	195
Turkey	663	469	470	443	420*	781	620	620	525	500
USSR [1]	9,588	7,719	6,476	8,645	7,551	12,235	13,607	8,117	10,205	8,500
USA	603	375	352	273	282	984	611	569	419	473
Yugoslavia	115	64	59	55	54	132	81	81	79	75
World total	20,046	16,362	14,118	16,532	15,302	30,782	32,448	23,127	26,452	24,473

* Unofficial figures. [1] Sown area. [2] Includes mixture of wheat and rye. [3] Field crops and other crops.

BARLEY

Countries	Area (1,000 hectares) Average 1969–71	1978	1979	1980	1981	Production (1,000 tonnes) Average 1969–71	1978	1979	1980	1981
Australia [1]	2,024	2,785	2,482	2,452	2,775	2,372	4,006	3,703	2,711	3,320
Austria	286	...	373	374	362	954	...	1,129	1,514	1,220
Belgium	174	...	176	171	173*	608	...	842	865*	823*
Bulgaria [1]	416	473	468	426	382	1,108	1,488	1,536	1,375	1,401
Canada	4,483	4,259	3,724	4,634	5,390	10,024	10,387	8,460	11,258	13,384
Czechoslovakia	810	906	1,017	911	996	2,543	3,642	3,604	3,575	3,500
Denmark	1,342	1,570	1,622	1,577	1,545	5,175	6,301	6,662	6,044	6,010
Finland	395	...	633	533	570	943	...	1,650	1,534	1,080
France	2,825	2,813	2,803	2,650	2,578*	8,865	11,321	11,196	11,716	10,180*
German Demo. Rep.	646	1,038	945	969	1,050	2,093	4,135	3,323	3,979	3,800
Germany, Fed. Rep. of	1,456	1,951	1,989	2,002	2,044	5,219	8,608	8,184	8,826	8,687
Greece	335	...	384	334	321	655	...	861	892	790
Hungary [1, 2]	322	225	262	246	280	749	763	710	929	950
India	2,693	2,001	1,828	1,771	1,821	2,642	2,311	2,142	1,624	2,242
Iran	1,532	1,300*	1,250*	1,300	1,300	1,042	1,000*	1,000*	1,100	1,300*
Ireland	216	...	324	332	330	854	...	1,439	1,370*	1,495*
Italy	180	...	308	330	338	326	...	813	947	993
Japan [1]	224	96	116	122	122	629	326	406	385	390*
Korea, South [1]	723	554	473	331	320	1,589	1,348	1,508	811	771
Morocco	2,003	2,415	2,193	2,150	920*	2,190	2,238	1,888	2,210	1,039*
Poland [1]	861	1,203	1,470	1,322	1,294	2,182	3,635	3,731	3,420	3,575
Romania [1]	309	722	773	809	920*	615	2,307	2,043	2,466	2,500
Spain	2,235	3,519	3,424	3,443	3,415	3,922	8,068	6,153	8,435	4,709
Sweden	602	...	704	648	678	1,836	...	2,346	2,172	2,510
Syria	784	1,033	1,102	1,210	1,346	375	729	396	1,587	1,406
Turkey	2,611	2,577	2,790	2,800	2,900*	3,720	4,750	5,240	5,300	5,900
USSR [1]	21,782	32,690	37,005	31,583	31,781	35,132	62,077	47,954	43,450	43,000
UK	2,317	2,348	2,343	2,330	2,329	8,257	9,848	9,623	10,326	10,149
USA	3,963	3,743	3,044	2,944	3,703	9,476	9,901	8,334	7,859	10,414
World total	66,775	84,256	83,855	78,588	79,751	125,229	181,487	157,554	159,567	158,488

* Unofficial figures. [1] Sown area. [2] Field crops and other crops.

OATS

Countries	Area (1,000 hectares) Average 1969–71	1978	1979	1980	1981	Production (1,000 tonnes) Average 1969–71	1978	1979	1980	1981
Argentina	328	500	410	349	400	420	676	522	433	515*
Australia	1,390	1,359	1,123	1,090	1,582	1,378	1,763	1,411	1,129	1,520
Austria	101	89	95	92	92	281	304	273	316	304
Belgium	89	40	44	45	41*	331	192	178	162*	161*
Canada	2,834	1,829	1,541	1,515	1,754	5,508	3,620	2,978	3,028	3,570
Chile	76	...	79	92	80	106	...	150	173	131
China	1,000	900	400	500	400	833	1,000	700	600	600
Czechoslovakia [2]	372	132	127	121	160	882	454	401	421	400
Denmark	192	61	39	40	44	699	206	163	159	165*
Finland	516	446	451	448	434	1,297	1,082	1,283	1,258	1,008
France	829	611	540	534	500	2,317	1,865	1,845	1,927	1,754
German Demo. Rep.	237	153	136	155	130	735	595	532	582	500
Germany, Fed.Rep.of	840	749	728	691	682	2,832	3,202	2,994	2,658	2,678
Ireland	68	31	28	26	24	222	124	105	96*	85*
Italy	297	228	222	227	222	488	468	432	450	429
Netherlands	61	25	21	18	21	243	140	109	94	115
Norway	69	...	95	112	1,156	215	...	361	400*	417*
Poland [1]	1,409	1,030	1,094	997	472	3,156	2,491	2,186	2,245	2,768
Spain	481	442	428	441	463	504	553	449	658	454
Sweden	505	453	457	452	472	1,561	1,550	1,524	1,567	1,732
Turkey	326	225	220	197	190*	446	370	370	355	300
USSR [1]	9,394	12,097	12,239	11,770	12,470	13,974	18,507	15,162	15,544	15,000
UK	375	180	136	148	144	1,300	706	542	601	622
USA	7,051	4,503	3,917	3,501	3,809	13,350	8,443	7,643	6,652	7,375
Yugoslavia	273	...	209	194	194	310	...	283	294	311
World Total	30,358	27,563	25,949	24,935	26,810	54,494	50,040	43,658	42,912	44,024

* Unofficial figures. [1] Sown area. [2] Includes mixture of oats and barley. [3] Field crops and other crops.

MAIZE

Countries	Area (1,000 hectares) Average 1969–71	1978	1979	1980	1981	Production (1,000 tonnes) Average 1969–71	1978	1979	1980	1981
Argentina	3,880	2,630	2,800	2,490	3,500	8,717	9,500	8,700	6,400	13,500
Austria	122	...	188	193	189	677	...	1,347	1,293	1,374
Brazil	10,021	11,315	11,319	11,438	11,491	13,680	13,569	16,306	20,374	21,098
Bulgaria	623	601	666	585	571	2,436	2,236	3,223	2,256	2,477
Canada	490	...	893	958	1,058	2,487	...	4,983	5,434	6,214
China	15,965	19,037	20,167	20,035	20,537	32,376	53,107	60,149	61,105	61,601
Egypt	634	797	791	800	714*	2,370	3,117	2,938	3,231	2,700*
France	1,436	1,803	1,995	1,757	1,570	7,394	9,531	10,413	9,358	9,100
Greece	162	120	123	170	159	498	537	711	1,158	1,250
Hungary	1,272	1,296	1,367	1,253	1,350	4,542	6,655	7,396	6,673	6,500*
India	5,794	5,760	5,721	5,983	5,800	6,087	6,199	5,603	6,804	7,000
Indonesia	2,667	3,025	2,594	2,771	2,735	2,575	4,029	3,606	4,012	3,991
Italy	986	928	937	937	991	4,601	6,221	6,197	6,403	7,250
Kenya	1,383	...	1,400	1,120	1,200	2,060	...	1,800	1,768	2,250
Malawi	1,039	...	1,000	1,100	1,100*	1,066	...	1,200*	1,100	1,600*
Mexico	7,412	7,191	5,502	6,955	8,150	9,025	10,930	8,124	12,383	14,766
Nigeria	1,398	...	1,665	1,710	1,746	1,215	...	1,500	1,550	1,580
Philippines	2,356	3,222	3,327	3,281	3,319	1,915	2,855	3,167	3,117	3,176
Portugal	432	389	394	394	388	599	499	506	534	417
Romania	3,170	3,179	3,311	3,288	3,150*	7,354	10,208	12,425	11,153	11,200
S. Africa, Republic of	5,290	6,000	5,000	6,000	7,000	6,691	9,930	8,240	10,790	14,650
Spain	526	443	460	448	430	1,804	1,969	2,205	2,208	2,151
Thailand	771	...	1,509	1,562*	1,716*	1,979	...	3,300	3,150	3,700*
Turkey	646	580	585	583	580*	1,058	1,300	1,350	1,240	1,100
USSR[1]	3,617	2,535	2,667	2,977	3,545	9,993	8,951	8,373	9,454	8,000
USA	23,749	29,109	29,300	29,555	30,200	122,649	184,614	201,655	168,787	208,314
Yugoslavia	2,391	2,129	2,251	2,161	2,275	7,399	7,585	10,084	9,317	9,800*
Zimbabwe	914	931*	800	1,146	1,350	1,366	1,616*	1,200	1,539	2,880
World total	114,485	127,142	125,796	128,764	134,024	283,031	390,104	418,357	394,056	451,704

* Unofficial figures. [1] For dry grain only.

RICE (Paddy)

Countries	Area (1,000 hectares) Average 1969–71	1978	1979	1980	1981	Production (1,000 tonnes) Average 1969–71	1978	1979	1980	1981
Bangladesh	9,842	10,102	10,160	10,309	10,100	16,540	19,582	19,599	20,822	20,000
Brazil	4,788	5,624	5,452	6,208	6,066	6,847	7,296	7,595	9,748	8,261
Burma	4,748	5,011	4,442	5,040	5,500	8,107	10,500	10,448	13,107	14,636*
Cambodia	2,074	1,400	853	1,200*	1,200	3,016	1,500	850*	1,000	1,160*
China	33,341	33,752	34,594	33,887	34,480	109,853	138,202	146,959	142,338	146,087
Colombia	260	...	442	416	413	756	...	1,932	1,798	1,799
Egypt	487	435	439	408	462*	2,566	2,358	2,517	2,350	2,500*
India	37,677	38,980	39,414	39,773	40,000	62,861	80,660	63,476	79,930	82,000
Indonesia	8,158	8,929	8,804	9,018	9,005	19,136	25,781	26,283	29,774	33,000
Iran	362	315	300	300	320	1,041	1,280	1,420	1,212	1,400*
Italy	172	191	183	176	173	858	979	1,107	950	931
Japan	2,968	2,548	2,497	2,377	2,278	16,280	16,349	14,948	12,189	12,824
Korea, South	1,204	1,230	1,224	1,220	1,224	5,574	8,352	7,881	5,311	7,032
Madagascar	992	1,037	1,164	1,178	1,175*	1,894	1,914	2,045	2,109	1,999*
Malaysia	708	583	738	764	762	1,696	1,498	2,095	2,171	2,147
Mexico	152	121	149	132	180	390	402	500	456	644
Nepal	1,185	...	1,250	1,270	1,270	2,297	...	2,060	2,464	2,407*
Nigeria	272	...	400	550*	600*	352	...	750	1,090*	1,241*
Pakistan	1,527	2,026	2,035	1,935	1,989	3,431	4,908	4,824	4,679	5,093
Philippines	3,157	3,469	3,500	3,503	3,500	5,225	7,198	7,504	7,840	7,720
Sri Lanka	579	839	790	824	800	1,463	1,890	1,917	2,133	2,020
Thailand	6,919	8,288	8,651	9,145*	9,140	13,475	17,530	15,758	17,366	19,000*
USSR	356	580	610	666	634	1,272	2,096	2,394	2,791	2,400
USA	777	1,202	1,161	1,340	1,539	3,953	6,040	5,985	6,629	8,408
Vietnam	4,916	5,486	5,483	5,544	5,615	9,918	10,040	10,758	11,679	12,570
World total	132,876	140,527	141,052	143,534	144,915	309,791	385,885	377,394	397,597	413,785

* Unofficial figures.

MILLET

Countries	Area (1,000 hectares) Average 1969–71	1978	1979	1980	1981	Production (1,000 tonnes) Average 1969–71	1978	1979	1980	1981
Argentina	160	244	238	182	187	168	330	310	188	238
Australia	39	50	32	19	27	37	33	36	14	13*
Cameroon	477	490	497	450	450	343	409	414	400	400
Chad	925	1,140	1,140	1,150*	1,150	615	580	550	600	580
Egypt	206	183	171	172	168*	847	686	635	636*	643*
Ethiopia	197	...	249*	267*	260	117	...	191*	193*	190
Ghana	218	238*	250	240*	230	120	72*	149	66	73*
India	19,618	18,500	17,196	17,866	18,000	10,182	10,661	8,094	9,461	10,500
Kenya	75	...	81	81	82	127	...	110	130	130
Korea, North	423	...	415	420	420	407	...	440	440	450
Korea, South	59	6	3	3	3	47	7	3	4	4
Mali	953	1,400	1,400	1,400	1,420	784	1,035*	922*	750	930
Nepal	109	...	121	120	120	128	...	119	122	135
Niger	2,313	2,747	2,883	3,072	3,038*	974	1,123	1,246	1,371	1,117*
Nigeria	5,022	5,000*	5,000*	5,030*	5,050*	2,792	3,100*	3,130*	3,130*	3,230*
Pakistan	713	659	561	407	650	339	317	277	214	315*
Senegal	996	950*	968	1,089	850*	539	803	521	531*	750*
Sudan	750	1,270	1,293	1,300	1,250	424	507	550	450	500*
Tanzania	211	...	220	220	220	140	...	160	160	140*
Togo	190	170	170	170	170	121	130	136	128	107*
Uganda	739	550	313	279	300	721	480	481	459	480*
USSR	2,821	2,924	2,784	2,907	2,692	2,477	2,196	1,553	1,873	1,500*
Upper Volta	843	910*	900	800	900	352	406*	431	330	400*
Zimbabwe [1]	380	390	400	380	380	190	200	140	180	180*
World total	46,794	44,147	42,613	43,267	43,203	33,180	30,720	27,441	28,335	29,653

* Unofficial figures. [1] On farms and estates.

SORGHUM

Countries	Area (1,000 hectares) Average 1969–71	1978	1979	1980	1981	Production (1,000 tonnes) Average 1969–71	1978	1979	1980	1981
Argentina	1,979	2,254	2,044	1,279	2,100	3,823	7,200	6,200	2,960	7,550
Australia	374	394	469	519	649	759	714	1,125	922	1,090
China	5,411	...	3,174	3,103	3,004	8,607	...	7,656	7,410	7,510
Colombia	64	...	221	206	231	153	...	501	431	532
Ethiopia [1, 2]	950	763	726	763*	763*	827	708	680	689*	687*
France	55	...	84	71	66	203	...	339	336	320
India	17,585	16,140	16,674	15,610	16,000	8,516	11,436	11,648	10,504	11,500
Mexico	930	1,399	1,456	1,579	1,767	2,573	4,193	3,917	4,812	6,296
Niger	589	796	716	768	982*	262	371	346	380	273*
Nigeria	5,572	6,000*	6,000*	6,000*	6,025*	3,632	3,760*	3,785*	3,800*	3,835*
S. Africa, Republic of	358	...	280	450	400*	376	...	354	695	557
Sudan	1,828	2,798	3,025	3,000	3,106	1,525	2,017	2,408	2,200	2,800
Thailand	45	...	230*	270*	270*	123	...	260*	350*	380*
Uganda	299	350	174	350	380	337	520	316	450	500
USA	5,820	5,427	5,221	5,068	5,555	19,314	18,575	20,546	14,712	22,360
Upper Volta	1,054	1,030*	900	850	1,200	528	610*	610	559	750*
Venezuela	4	...	215	335	343*	5	...	429	584	578*
Yemen Arab Republic	1,235	...	673*	681*	697*	878	...	632*	636*	635*
World total	48,064	46,509	46,243	44,993	47,762	55,629	64,129	65,171	55,839	71,984

* Unofficial figures. [1] Includes teff. [2] Unspecified millet and sorghum.

CENTRIFUGAL RAW SUGAR
(in 1,000 tonnes)

Countries	*Average 1969–71*	*1976*	*1977*	*1978*	*1979*	*1980*	*1981*
Argentina	985	1,599	1,666	1,397	1,411	1,716	1,624
Australia [1]	2,511	3,296	3,318	2,902	2,963	3,329	3,450
Barbados [2]	146	106	124*	101	114	135	96*
Brazil	5,161	7,598*	8,760*	7,767*	7,027*	8,547*	8,500*
Canada	130	163	149	123	106	89	125*
China	2,234	4,652	3,076	3,213	3,587	3,615	4,031
Cuba	6,388	6,279*	6,607*	7,457	8,048	6,787	7,359*
Czechoslovakia	731	620*	939*	885*	910*	830*	870*
Dominican Rep.	1,010	1,287*	1,258	1,199	1,200	1,039*	1,032*
Egypt	564	668	668	635	668	662	679
France	2,873	2,974	4,268	4,065	4,332	4,253	5,600*
Fiji [1]	329	296	362	347	473	396	450
German Demo. Rep.	487	560*	780*	780*	679*	600*	740*
Germany, Fed. Rep.of	2,158	2,733	3,075	2,997	3,088	2,994	3,600*
Guyana	361	343	253*	342	316	286	320*
India [3]	4,188	4,632	5,261	7,018	6,367	4,191	5,587
Indonesia [4]	760	1,033	1.106	1,105	1,307	1,403*	1,449
Italy	1,271	1,675	1,359	1,620	1,707	1,932*	2,170*
Jamaica	383	369	295	292	283	232	203*
Mauritius [4]	659	731	705	705	730	504	610
Mexico	2,486	2,720*	2,728	3,072	3,078*	2,765*	2,518*
Pakistan [3]	557	631	800	936	663	624	928
Peru	782	959	926	856	716	552	493*
Philippines	1,859	2,514	2,688	2,335	2,342	2,343	2,394
Poland	1,581	1,801	1,850*	1,763*	1,762	1,186	1,872
Puerto Rico	383	279	239	185*	174	158	137
S. Africa, Rep. of	1,629	2,042	2,084	2,082	2,079	1,606	2,050
Spain	891	1,491	1,213	1,143	750	1,010*	1,054*
Sweden	233	302*	343	327	350	327	374*
Trinidad	229	207	179	148*	144	114	90*
USSR	8,722	7,350*	8,825*	9,100*	7,700*	7,150*	6,100*
UK	1,033	746	1,015	1,111	1,255	1,202	1,200*
USA [5]	5,258	6,257	5,254	5,353	5,061	5,331	5,771
World total	70,699	85,342	89,747	90,258	88,984	84,212	92,046

[1] 94° net titre.
[2] Includes the sugar equivalent of fancy molasses.
[3] Includes sugar (raw value) refined from gur.
[4] Tel quel.
[5] Includes Hawaii.
* Unofficial figures.

WORLD ESTIMATED CRUDE OIL PRODUCTION[1]

(in 1,000 tonnes)

	1960	*1970*	*1981*	*1982*
North America				
USA	384,080	533,677	477,645	480,000
Canada	27,480	69,954	75,645	73,000
Caribbean Area				
Venezuela	148,690	193,209	111,320	99,500
Trinidad	6,075	7,225	9,845	9,500
Colombia	8,100	11,071	6,927	7,400
Other Latin America				
Mexico	14,125	21,877	127,660	148,000
Argentina	9,160	19,969	25,173	24,750
Brazil	390	8,009	10,980	13,500
Ecuador	2,680	191	10,695	9,750
Peru	450	3,450	9,527	10,000
Bolivia	990	1,128	1,008	1,200
Chile		1,620	2,300	2,500
Middle East				
Saudi Arabia	61,090	176,851	490,270	325,000
Iran	52,065	191,663	65,190	98,000
Iraq	47,480	76,600	44,935	48,000
Kuwait	81,860	137,397	56,595	42,000
Abu Dhabi	—	33,288	54,470	42,000
Qatar	8,210	17,257	19,495	16,000
Syria	—	4,350	8,500	8,500
Turkey	350	3,461	2,413	2,450
Bahrain	2,250	3,834	2,307	2,200
Sharjah	—	—	475	330
Africa				
Nigeria	880	53,420	71,165	64,000
Libya	—	159,201	54,270	54,500
Algeria	8,630	47,253	37,420	32,000
Gabon	850	5,460	7,635	7,400
Angola	70	5,066	7,158	6,500
Tunisia	—	4,151	5,407	5,400
Congo	—	—	3,090	3,900
Zaïre	—	—	993	1,000

[1] Excluding small scale production in Afghánistan, Bangladesh, Cuba, Guatemala, Israel, Mongolia, Morocco, New Zealand, Taiwan and Thailand.

WORLD ESTIMATED CRUDE OIL PRODUCTION
(contd.)

(in 1,000 tonnes)

	1960	*1970*	*1981*	*1982*
Western Europe				
UK	90	84	89,396	102,500
Norway	—	—	23,549	24,000
Germany, Fed. Rep. of	5,560	7,536	4,442	4,250
Austria	2,440	2,798	1,337	1,335
Spain	—	156	1,227	1,370
Netherlands	1,920	1,919	1,606	1,700
France	2,260	2,308	1,712	1,650
Italy	1,990	1,408	1,480	1,500
Denmark	—	—	758	1,800
Far East				
Indonesia	20,560	42,102	78,640	65,000
Australia	—	8,292	18,625	17,500
Brunei	4,690	6,916	8,700	8,500
India	440	6,809	14,920	19,000
Malaysia	—	—	12,560	14,450
Burma	530	750	1,250	1,450
Japan	510	750	392	375
Pakistan	360	486	463	600
USSR and Eastern Europe				
USSR	148,000	352,667	609,000	612,400
Romania	11,500	13,377	11,600	12,000
Yugoslavia	1,040	2,854	4,376	4,500
Albania	600	1,199	3,800	4,000
Hungary	1,215	1,937	2,024	2,050
Poland	195	424	300	300
German Dem. Rep.	—	60	60	60
Bulgaria	200	334	300	300
Czechoslovakia	140	203	88	90
China	5,000	20,000	101,220	101,700
World Total	1,090,080	2,336,153	2,904,320	2,755,625

ENERGY

Europe's Nuclear Capacity

	% nuclear electricity in 1981	*Reactors under construction*
Belgium	25·3	4
Finland	35·8	–
France	37·7	26
Germany, Federal Republic of	14·6	10
Italy	1·5	3
Netherlands	5·7	–
Spain	8·6	11
Sweden	35·3	3
Switzerland	28·1	1
UK	12·7	10
Yugoslavia	–	1

Proven Oil Reserves

Jan. 1982

	1m. tons	*%*
North America	5,000	5·5
Latin America	11,400	12·7
Middle East	48,700	54·1
Asia-Pacific	2,600	2·9
Africa	7,500	8·3
Western Europe	3,300	3·7
Centrally Planned Economies	11,500	12·8
Antarctica	–	–
Total	*90,000*	*100·0*

TERRITORIAL SEA LIMITS (IN MILES)

State	*Territorial Sea*	*Jurisdiction over fisheries (measured from the baseline of the territorial sea)*
Albania	15 (1976)	—
Algeria	12 (1963)	—
Angola	20 (1976)	200 (1976)
Antigua and Barbuda	12 (1982)	200 (1982) [1]
Argentina	200 (1967)	—
Australia	3 (1878)	200 (1979)
Bahamas	3 (1878)	200 (1977)
Bahrain	3	—
Bangladesh	12 (1974)	200 (1974) [1]
Barbados	12 (1977)	200 (1978) [1]
Belgium	3	up to median line (1978)
Belize	3 (1878)	12 (1978)
Benin	200 (1976)	—
Brazil	200 (1970)	—
Bulgaria	12 (1951)	—
Burma	12 (1968)	200 (1977) [1]
Cambodia	12(1969)	200 (1979) [1]
Cameroon	50 (1974)	—
Canada	12 (1970)	200 (1977)
Cape Verde	12 (1978)	200 (1978) [1]
Chile	3	200 (1952) [1]
China	12 (1958)	—
Colombia	12 (1970)	200 (1978) [1]
Comoros	12 (1976)	200 (1976) [1]
Congo	200 (1977)	—
Costa Rica	12 (1972)	200 (1975) [1]
Cuba	12 (1977)	200 (1977) [1]
Cyprus	12 (1964)	—
Denmark (including Faroe Islands and Greenland)	3 (1966)	200 (1977)
Djibouti	12 (1971)	200 (1979) [1]
Dominica	12 (1981)	200 (1981) [1]
Dominican Republic	6 (1967)	200 (1977) [1]
Ecuador	200 (1966)	—
Egypt	12 (1958)	—
El Salvador	200 (1950)	—
Equatorial Guinea	12 (1970)	—
Ethiopia	12 (1953)	—
Fiji	12 (1976)	200 (1981) [1]
Finland	4 (1956)	12 (1975)
France	12 (1971)	200 (1977) [1] (except Mediterranean)
Gabon	100 (1972)	—
Gambia	12 (1969)	200 (1978)
German Democratic Republic	3	up to median line (1978)
Germany, Federal Republic of	In accordance with international law	200 (1977)
Ghana	200 (1977)	—
Greece	6 (1936)	—
Grenada	12 (1978)	200 (1978) [1]
Guatemala	12 (1934)	200 (1976) [1]
Guinea	12 (1980)	200 (1980) [1]
Guinea-Bissau	12 (1978)	200 (1978) [1]
Guyana	12 (1977)	200 (1977)
Haiti	12 (1972)	200 (1977) [1]
Honduras	12 (1965)	200 (1951) [1]

[1] Economic zone.

TERRITORIAL SEA LIMITS (IN MILES)—*contd.*

State	*Territorial Sea*	*Jurisdiction over fisheries (measured from the baseline of the territorial sea)*
Iceland	12 (1979)	200 (1979) [1]
India	12 (1967)	200 (1977) [1]
Indonesia	12 (1957) [2]	200 (1980) [1]
Iran	12 (1959)	[3]
Iraq	12 (1958)	—
Ireland	3 (1959)	200 (1977)
Israel	6 (1956)	—
Italy	12 (1974)	—
Ivory Coast	12 (1977)	200 (1977) [1]
Jamaica	12 (1971)	—
Japan	12 (1977)	200 (1977)
Jordan	3 (1943)	—
Kenya	12 (1969)	200 (1979) [1]
Kiribati	3 (1878)	200 (1979)
Korea (North)	12	200 (1977) [1]
Korea (South)	12 (1978)	20–200 (1952–54)
Kuwait	12 (1967)	—
Lebanon	—	6 (1921)
Liberia	200 (1976)	—
Libya	12 (1959)	—
Madagascar	50 (1973)	—
Malaysia	12 (1969)	200 (1980) [1]
Maldive, Republic of	3–55 [3]	(1976) [1, 4]
Malta	12 (1978)	25 (1978)
Mauritania	70 (1978)	200 (1978) [1]
Mauritius	12 (1970)	200 (1977) [1]
Mexico	12 (1969)	200 (1976) [1]
Monaco	12	—
Morocco	12 (1973)	200 (1981) [1, 5]
Mozambique	12 (1976)	200 (1976) [1]
Namibia	3	12 (1964)
Nauru	12 (1971)	200 (1978) [1]
Netherlands	12	200 (1977)
New Zealand	12 (1977)	200 (1978) [1]
Nicaragua	3	200 (1980) [1]
Nigeria	12 (1967)	200 (1978) [1]
Norway	4 (1812)	200 (1977) [1]
Oman	12 (1977)	200 (1981) [1]
Pakistan	12 (1966)	200 (1976) [1]
Panama	200 (1967)	—
Papua New Guinea	12 (1978)	200 (1978) (offshore waters)
Peru	200 (1947) [6]	200 (1947) [6]
Philippines	[7]	200 (1979) [1]

[1] Economic zone.

[2] The territorial sea of Indonesia is measured by straight lines surrounding the archipelago.

[3] Outer limits of the superjacent waters of the continental shelf. Median line in the Sea of Oman (1973).

[4] Territorial limits and economic zone defined by geographical co-ordinates.

[5] Limits with opposite or adjacent states to be fixed by agreement, failing which median line principle to apply.

[6] Sovereignty and jurisdiction over the sea, its soil and subsoil up to 200 miles (1947).

[7] The territorial sea of the Philippines is determined by straight base-lines joining appropriate points of the outermost islands forming the Philippine archipelago in accordance with Treaties of 1898, 1900 and 1930 (1961).

TERRITORIAL SEA LIMITS (IN MILES)—*contd.*

State	*Territorial Sea*	*Jurisdiction over fisheries (measured from the baseline of the territorial sea)*
Poland	12 (1977)	up to median line (1978)
Portugal	12 (1977)	200 (1977) [2]
Qatar	3	[1]
Romania	12 (1951)	—
St Lucia	3 (1878)	—
St Vincent	3 (1878)	—
São Tomé	12 (1978)	200 (1978) [2]
Saudi Arabia	12 (1958)	[1]
Senegal	150 (1976)	200 (1976)
Seychelles	12 (1977)	200 (1977) [2]
Sierra Leone	200 (1971)	—
Singapore	3 (1878)	—
Solomon Islands	12 (1978)	200 (1978)
Somalia	200 (1972)	—
South Africa, Republic of	12 (1977)	200 (1977)
Spain	12 (1977)	200 (1978) [2] (except Mediterranean)
Sri Lanka	12 (1971)	200 (1977) [2]
Sudan	12 (1960)	—
Suriname	12 (1978)	200 (1978) [2]
Sweden	4 (1779)	200 (1978)
Syria	35 (1981)	—
Tanzania	50 (1973)	—
Thailand	12 (1966)	—
Togo	30 (1977)	200 (1977) [2]
Tonga	[3]	—
Trinidad and Tobago	12 (1969)	—
Tunisia	12 (1973)	—
Turkey	6 (1964)	12 (1964)
Tuvalu	3 (1878)	200 (1976)
USSR	12 (1909)	200 (1977)
United Arab Emirates	3 [4]	[5]
UK	3 (1878)	200 (1977)
USA	3 (1793)	200 (1977)
Uruguay	200 (1969)	—
Vanuatu	3 (1978–82)	200 (1978–82) [2]
Venezuela	12 (1956)	200 (1978) [2]
Vietnam	12 (1977)	200 (1977) [2]
Western Samoa	12 (1977)	200 (1981)
Yemen, Peoples Dem. Rep. of	12 (1970)	200 (1978) [2]
Yemen, Republic of	12 (1967)	—
Yugoslavia	12 (1979)	—
Zaïre	12 (1974)	—

[1] Outer limits of the superjacent waters of the continental shelf (1974).
[2] Economic zone.
[3] Territorial limits defined by geographical co-ordinates (173–177° W. and 15–23° 30′ S.) (1887).
[4] Sharjah, 12 miles.
[5] Limits to be defined by agreement, failing which median line to apply (1980).

The table above, reproduced from a survey prepared by the FAO of the UN shows: *(a)* the territorial sea limit, and *(b)* jurisdiction over fisheries.

Books of Reference

Buzan, B., *Seabed Politics.* New York, 1976
Janis, M. W., *Sea Power and the Law of the Sea.* Lexington, 1977
Luard, E., *The Control of the Sea-Bed.* London, 1974
Moore, G., *Legislation on Coastal State Requirements for Foreign Fishing. FAO Legislative Study No. 21.* Rev. ed. Rome, 1983

ADDENDA

AUSTRALIA. Result of March 1983 general elections:

Party	House of Representatives	Senate
Labor	75	30
Liberal	33	24
National	17	4
Democratic	–	5
Independent	–	1

AUSTRIA. Results of April 1983 general elections:

	Seats	
Party	1983	1979
Social Democrats	90	95
People's Party	81	77
Freedom Party	12	11

On 26 April Chancellor Bruno Kreisky resigned.

CZECHOSLOVAKIA. Vaclav Hula, Deputy Premier died on 1 April 1983.

EL SALVADOR. *Ambassador to UK:* Dr Alfonso Moises Breatrix.

FINLAND. Results of March 1983 general elections:

	Seats	
Party	1983	1979
Social Democrats	57	52
Communists	27	35
Conservatives	44	46
Centre-Liberal	38	40
Rural Party	17	7
Christians	3	9
Swedish Party	11	10
Constitutional	1	0
Greens	2	–

GHANA. *UK High Commissioner:* Kevin Burns (also *Ambassador to Togo*).

GREENLAND. Results of the April 1983 general elections: Atassut, 12 seats; Siumut, 12; Inuit, 2.

ICELAND. Results of April 1983 general elections: Independent Party, 23 seats; Progressive Party, 14; People's Alliance, 10; Social Democrats, 6; New Social Democrats, 4; Feminists, 3.

MAURITIUS. The Cabinet in March 1983 was composed as follows: *Prime Minister and Finance:* Aneerood Jugnauth. *Information and Co-operatives:* Harish Boodhoo. *Agriculture:* Kilshore Deerpalsingh. *Works:* Rohit Beedassy. *Minister for Rodrigues Island:* Serge Clair. *Industry and Trade, Attorney-General:* Kader Bhayat. *Foreign Affairs, Tourism:* Anyl Gayan. *Youth and Sports:* Sylvio Michel. *Social Security and Employment:* Diwakar Bundhun. *Education, Arts and Culture:* Armoogum Parsooramen. *Labour, Industrial Relations:* Satteanund Peerhum. *Housing, Land, Environment:* Dwarkanath Gungah. *Planning and Economic Development:* Karl Offman. *Regional Administration:* Lutchmeepardadising Ramsahok. *Energy, Communications:* Hahyendra Utchanan. *Health:* Jugdish Gobordhun.

POLAND. *UK Ambassador:* John Morgan.

PORTUGAL. Provisional results of April 1983 general elections: Socialists, 99 seats; Social Democrats, 72; Christian Democrats, 29; Communists, 55.
Six results unknown at the time of going to press.

REPUBLIC OF SOUTH AFRICA. Voting will take place in Oct. 1983 by the white electorate in a referendum on constitutional reforms.

THAILAND. Gen. Prem Tinsulanonda announced on 26 April 1983 that he would be retiring from politics and would not become Prime Minister in the new cabinet being formed following indecisive elections.

PART I

INTERNATIONAL ORGANIZATIONS

THE UNITED NATIONS

The United Nations is an association of states which have pledged themselves, through signing the Charter, to maintain international peace and security and to co-operate in establishing political, economic and social conditions under which this task can be securely achieved. Nothing contained in the Charter authorizes the organization to intervene in matters which are essentially within the domestic jurisdiction of any state.

The United Nations Charter originated from proposals agreed upon at discussions held at Dumbarton Oaks (Washington, D.C.) between the USSR, US and UK from 21 Aug. to 28 Sept., and between US, UK and China from 29 Sept. to 7 Oct. 1944. These proposals were laid before the United Nations Conference on International Organization, held at San Francisco from 25 April to 26 June 1945, and (after amendments had been made to the original proposals) the Charter of the United Nations was signed on 26 June 1945 by the delegates of 50 countries. Ratification of all the signatures had been received by 31 Dec. 1945. (For the complete text of the Charter *see* THE STATESMAN'S YEAR-BOOK, 1946, pp. xxi–xxxii.)

The United Nations formally came into existence on 24 Oct. 1945, with the deposit of the requisite number of ratifications of the Charter with the US Department of State. The official languages of the United Nations are Arabic, Chinese, English, French, Russian and Spanish; the working languages are English, French and (in the General Assembly) Arabic, Chinese, Spanish and Russian.

The headquarters of the United Nations is in New York City, USA.

Flag: UN emblem in white centred on a light blue ground.

Membership. Membership is open to all peace-loving states whose admission will be effected by the General Assembly upon recommendation of the Security Council. The table on pp. 10–11 shows the member states of the United Nations.

The Principal Organs of the United Nations are: 1. The General Assembly. 2. The Security Council. 3. The Economic and Social Council. 4 The Trusteeship Council. 5. The International Court of Justice. 6. The Secretariat.

1. **The General Assembly** consists of all the members of the United Nations. Each member has only 1 vote. The General Assembly meets regularly once a year, commencing on the third Tuesday in Sept.; the session normally lasts until mid-December and is resumed for some weeks in the new year if this is required. Special sessions may be convoked by the Secretary-General if requested by the Security Council, by a majority of the members of the United Nations or by 1 member concurred with by the majority of the members. The Assembly also meets in emergency special session. The General Assembly elects its President for each session.

The first regular session was held in London from 10 Jan. to 14 Feb. and in New York from 23 Oct. to 16 Dec. 1946.

Special sessions have been held on Palestine (1947, 1948), Tunisia (1961), Financial Situation of UN (1963), South West Africa, Peace-Keeping, Postponement of Outer Space Conference (1967), Raw Materials and Development (1974), New International Economic Order (1975), Peace-keeping force in the Lebanon, Namibia, Disarmament (1978, 1982), Economic Issues (1980); Emergency Special sessions were held on Suez, Hungary (1956), Lebanon-Jordan-United Arab Republic dispute (1958), Congo (1960), Middle East (1967), Afghánistán, Palestine (1980) and Namibia (1981).

The work of the General Assembly is divided between 6 Main Committees and the Special Political Committee, on each of which every member state is represented. I. Political Security. II. Economic and Financial. III. Social, Humanitarian and Cultural. IV. Trust and Non-Self-Governing Territories. V. Administrative and Budgetary. VI. Legal.

In addition there is a General Committee charged with the task of co-ordinating the proceedings of the Assembly and its Committees; and a Credentials Committee which verifies the credentials of the delegates. The General Committee consists of 25 members, comprising the President of the General Assembly, its 17 Vice-Presidents and the Chairmen of the 7 Main Committees. The Credentials Committee consists of 9 members, elected at the beginning of each session of the General Assembly. The Assembly has 2 standing committees—an Advisory Committee on Administrative and Budgetary Questions, and a Committee on Contributions. The General Assembly establishes subsidiary and *ad hoc* bodies when necessary to deal with specific matters. These include: Special Committee on Peace-keeping Operations (33 members), Commission on Human Rights (32 members), Commission for the unification and rehabilitation of Korea (7 members), Committee on the peaceful uses of outer space (28 members), Conciliation Commission for Palestine (3 members), Committee on Disarmament (40 members), International Law Commission (25 members), Scientific Committee on the effects of atomic radiation (15 members), Special Committee on the implementation of the declaration on the granting of independence to colonial countries and peoples (24 members), Special Committee on the policies of Apartheid of the Government of the Republic of South Africa (11 members), UN High Commissioner for Refugees, UN Relief and Works Agency for Palestine Refugees in the Near East, Peace Observation Commission (14 members), UN Commission on International Trade Law (29 members) and Committee on the Peaceful Uses of Sea-bed and Ocean Floor Beyond the Limits of National Jurisdiction (91 members), Governing Council for Environmental Programmes (54 members).

The General Assembly may discuss any matters within the scope of the Charter, and, with the exception of any situation or dispute on the agenda of the Security Council, may make recommendations on any such questions or matters. For decisions on important questions a two-thirds majority is required, on other questions a simple majority of members present and voting. In addition, the Assembly at its fifth session, in 1950, decided that if the Security Council, because of lack of unanimity of the permanent members, fails to exercise its primary responsibility for the maintenance of international peace and security in any case where there appears to be a threat to the peace, breach of the peace or act of aggression, the General Assembly shall consider the matter immediately with a view to making appropriate recommendations to members for collective measures, including in the case of a breach of the peace or act of aggression the use of armed force when necessary, to maintain or restore international peace and security.

The General Assembly receives and considers reports from the other organs of the United Nations, including the Security Council. The Secretary-General makes an annual report to it on the work of the Organization.

2. **The Security Council** consists of 15 members, each of which has 1 vote. There are 5 permanent and 10 non-permanent members elected for a 2-year term by a two-thirds majority of the General Assembly.

Retiring members are not eligible for immediate re-election. Any other member of the United Nations will be invited to participate without vote in the discussion of questions specially affecting its interests.

The Security Council bears the primary responsibility for the maintenance of peace and security. It is also responsible for the functions of the UN in trust territories classed as 'strategic areas'. Decisions on procedural questions are made by an affirmative vote of 9 members. On all other matters the affirmative vote of 9 members must include the concurring votes of all permanent members (in practice, however, an abstention by a permanent member is not considered a veto), subject to the provision that when the Security Council is considering methods for the peaceful settlement of a dispute, parties to the dispute abstain from voting.

For the maintenance of international peace and security the Security Council can, in accordance with special agreements to be concluded, call on armed forces, assistance and facilities of the member states. It is assisted by a Military Staff Committee consisting of the Chiefs of Staff of the permanent members of the Security Council or their representatives.

The Presidency of the Security Council is held for 1 month in rotation by the member states in the English alphabetical order of their names.

The Security Council functions continuously. Its members are permanently represented at the seat of the organization, but it may meet at any place that will best facilitate its work.

The Council has 2 standing committees of Experts and on the Admission of New Members. In addition, from time to time, it establishes *ad hoc* committees and commissions such as the Truce Supervision Organization in Palestine.

Permanent Members: China, France, USSR, UK, USA.
Non-Permanent Members: Malta, Netherlands, Nicaragua, Pakistan, Zimbabwe (until 31 Dec. 1984); Guyana, Jordan, Poland, Togo, Zaïre (until 31 Dec. 1983).

3. **The Economic and Social Council** is responsible under the General Assembly for carrying out the functions of the United Nations with regard to international economic, social, cultural, educational, health and related matters.

By Nov. 1977, 15 'specialized' inter-governmental agencies working in these fields had been brought into relationship with the United Nations. The Economic and Social Council may also make arrangements for consultation with international non-governmental organizations and, after consultation with the member concerned, with national organizations; by Sept. 1978, 231 non-governmental organizations had been granted consultative status and a further 534 were on the register.

The Economic and Social Council consists of 54 Member States elected by a two-thirds majority of the General Assembly. Nine are elected each year for a 3-year term. Retiring members are eligible for immediate re-election. Each member has 1 vote. Decisions are made by a majority of the members present and voting.

The Council nominally holds 2 sessions a year, and special sessions may be held if required. The President is elected for 1 year and is eligible for immediate re-election.

The Economic and Social Council has the following commissions:

Regional Economic Commissions: ECE (Economic Commission for Europe. Geneva); ESCAP (Economic and Social Commission for Asia and the Pacific. Bangkok); ECLA (Economic Commission for Latin America. Santiago, Chile); ECA (Economic Commission for Africa. Addis Ababa). ECWA (Economic Commission for Western Asia. Baghdad). These Commissions have been established to enable the nations of the major regions of the world to co-operate on common problems and also to produce economic information.

(1) Six functional Statistical Commissions; with subcommission on Statistical Sampling. (2) Commission on Human Rights; with subcommission on Prevention of Discrimination and Protection of Minorities; (3) Social Development Commission; (4) Commission on the Status of Women; (5) Commission on Narcotic Drugs; (6) Population Commission.

The Economic and Social Council has the following standing committees: The Economic Committee, Social Committee, Co-ordination Committee, Committee on Non-Governmental Organizations, Interim Committee on Programme of Conferences, Committee for Industrial Development, Advisory Committee on the Application of Science and Technology to Development, Committee on Housing, Building and Planning.

Other special bodies are the International Narcotics Control Board, the Interim Co-ordinating Committee for International Commodity Arrangements and the Administrative Committee on Co-ordination to ensure (1) the most effective implementation of the agreements entered into between the United Nations and the specialized agencies and (2) co-ordination of activities.

Membership: Austria, Benin, Brazil, Colombia, France, Federal Republic of

Germany, Greece, Japan, Liberia, Mali, Pakistan, Portugal, Qatar, Romania, St Lucia, Swaziland, Tunisia (until 31 Dec. 1984). Argentina, Bangladesh, Burundi, Byelorussia, Cameroon, Canada, China, Denmark, Fiji, India, Kenya, Nicaragua, Norway, Peru, Poland, Sudan, USSR, UK (until 31 Dec. 1983): Algeria, Botswana, Bulgaria, Congo, Djibouti, Ecuador, German Democratic Republic, Lebanon, Luxembourg, Malaysia, Mexico, Netherlands, New Zealand, Saudi Arabia, Sierra Leone, Suriname, Thailand, USA (until 31 Dec. 1985).

4. **The Trusteeship Council.** The Charter provides for an international trusteeship system to safeguard the interests of the inhabitants of territories which are not yet fully self-governing and which may be placed thereunder by individual trusteeship agreements. These are called trust territories.

All of the original 11 trust territories except one, the Pacific Islands (Micronesia), administered by the USA, have become independent or joined independent countries. The Trusteeship Council consists of the 1 member administering trust territories: USA; the permanent members of the Security Council that are not administering trust territories: China, France, USSR and UK. Decisions of the Council are made by a majority of the members present and voting, each member having 1 vote. The Council holds one regular session each year, and special sessions if required.

5. **The International Court of Justice** was created by an international treaty, the Statute of the Court, which forms an integral part of the United Nations Charter. All members of the United Nations are *ipso facto* parties to the Statute of the Court.

The Court is composed of independent judges, elected regardless of their nationality, who possess the qualifications required in their countries for appointment to the highest judicial offices, or are jurisconsuls of recognized competence in international law. There are 15 judges, no 2 of whom may be nationals of the same state. They are elected by the Security Council and the General Assembly of the United Nations sitting independently. Candidates are chosen from a list of persons nominated by the national groups in the Permanent Court of Arbitration established by the Hague Conventions of 1899 and 1907. In the case of members of the United Nations not represented in the Permanent Court of Arbitration, candidates are nominated by national groups appointed for the purpose by their governments. The judges are elected for a 9-year term and are eligible for immediate re-election. When engaged on business of the Court, they enjoy diplomatic privileges and immunities.

The Court elects its own President and Vice-Presidents for 3 years and remains permanently in session, except for judicial vacations. The full court of 15 judges normally sits, but a quorum of 9 judges is sufficient to constitute the Court. It may form chambers of 3 or more judges for dealing with particular categories of cases, and forms annually a chamber of 5 judges to hear and determine, at the request of the parties, cases by summary procedures. Taslim O. Elias (Nigeria) and José Sette-Camara (Argentina) are, respectively, President and Vice-President of the Court until 1985.

Competence and Jurisdiction. Only states may be parties in cases before the Court, which is open to the states parties to its Statute. The conditions under which the Court will be open to other states are laid down by the Security Council. The Court exercises its jurisdiction in all cases which the parties refer to it and in all matters provided for in the Charter, or in treaties and conventions in force. Disputes concerning the jurisdiction of the Court are settled by the Court's own decision.

The Court may apply in its decision: *(a)* international conventions; *(b)* international custom; *(c)* the general principles of law recognized by civilized nations; and *(d)* as subsidiary means for the determination of the rules of law, judicial decisions and the teachings of highly qualified publicists. If the parties agree, the Court may decide a case *ex aequo et bono*. The Court may also give an advisory opinion on any legal question to any organ of the United Nations or its agencies.

Procedure. The official languages of the Court are French and English. At the request of any party the Court will authorize the use of another language by this party. All questions are decided by a majority of the judges present. If the votes are equal, the President has a casting vote. The judgment is final and without appeal, but a revision may be applied for within 10 years from the date of the judgment on the ground of a new decisive factor. Unless otherwise decided by the Court, each party bears its own costs.

Judges. The judges of the Court, elected by the Security Council and the General Assembly, are as follows: (1) To serve until 5 Feb. 1985: Manfred Lachs (Poland), Taslim Olawale Elias (Nigeria), Hermann Mosler (Federal Republic of Germany), Shigeru Oda (Japan), Abdallah Fikri El-Khani (Syria). (2) To serve until 5 Feb. 1988: Platon D. Morozov (USSR), Roberto Ago (Italy), Bedjaoui (Algeria), José Sette-Camara (Brazil), Stephen Schwebel (USA). (3) To serve until 5 Feb. 1991: Nagendra Singh (India), José Maria Ruda (Argentina), Sir Robert Jennings (UK), Guy Ladreit de Lacharrière (France), Kéba Mbaye (Senegal).

Judges. If there is no judge on the bench of the nationality of the parties to the dispute, each party has the right to choose a judge. Such judges shall take part in the decision on terms of complete equality with their colleagues.

The Court has its seat at The Hague, but may sit elsewhere whenever it considers this desirable. The expenses of the Court are borne by the UN.

Registrar: Santiago Torres Bernárdez (Spain).

6. **The Secretariat** is composed of the Secretary-General, who is the chief administrative officer of the organization, and an international staff appointed by him under regulations established by the General Assembly. However, the Secretary-General, the High Commissioner for Refugees and the Managing Director of the Fund are appointed by the General Assembly. The first Secretary-General was Trygve Lie (Norway), 1946–53; the second, Dag Hammarskjöld (Sweden), 1953–61; the third, U. Thant (Burma), 1961–71; the fourth, Kurt Waldheim (Austria), 1972–81.

The Secretary-General acts as chief administrative officer in all meetings of the General Assembly, the Security Council, the Economic and Social Council and the Trusteeship Council.

Secretary-General: Javier Perez de Cuellar (Peru), appointed 1 Jan. 1982 for a 5-year term.

The Secretary-General is assisted by about 20 Under-Secretaries-General and nearly 20 Assistant Secretaries-General.

The *UN Development Programme*, created on 22 Nov. 1965, is an amalgamation of the programme of Technical Assistance and the Special Fund. *Administrator:* Bradford Morse (USA).

The *UN Conference on Trade and Development* was established in 1964. It comprises those states which are members of the UN, its specialized agencies or the International Atomic Energy Agency. Its permanent organ, the Trade and Development Board (55 members), meets twice a year. Its 4 subsidiary organs meet annually: these are the Committees on Commodities, Manufactures, Shipping, and Invisibles and Financing Related to Trade. The first UNCTAD was held in Geneva in 1964, the second in New Delhi in 1968, the third in Santiago (Chile) 1972, the fourth in Nairobi (Kenya) 1976 and the fifth in Manila (Philippines) 1979. *Secretary-General:* Gamani Corea (Sri Lanka, appointed May 1974). *Headquarters:* Geneva, Switzerland.

The *UN Industrial Organization* (UNIDO) has worked as an autonomous body with the UN to promote industrialization and co-ordinate activities undertaken by the UN family in this field since 1967. Principal body is the 45-member Industrial Development Board, which formulates UNIDO's policy and its programme of activities. UNIDO tries to help the urgent need of developing countries to accelerate their promotional and operational activities and supports them by relevant studies and research. UNIDO will become a Specialized Agency of the UN system. *Executive Director:* Abderraham Khane (Algeria). *Headquarters:* Wagramerstrasse 5, Vienna XXII, Austria.

Office of the United Nations High Commissioner for Refugees (UNHCR) was established by the UN General Assembly with effect from 1 Jan. 1951, originally for 3 years. Since 1954, its mandate has been renewed for 5-year periods. Under General Assembly resolution 32/67 adopted in Nov. 1977 the Office was prolonged until 31 Dec. 1983.

The task of UNHCR is of a purely humanitarian and non-political character.

The main functions of the Office of the High Commissioner are to provide international protection for refugees, to seek permanent solutions to their problems through voluntary repatriation, resettlement in other countries or integration into the country of present residence. UNHCR may also be called upon to provide emergency relief and supplementary aid where necessary.

UNHCR concerns itself with refugees who have been determined to come within its mandate under the Statute, and with persons in analogous circumstances whom it assists under the terms of the good offices resolutions adopted by the General Assembly.

The High Commissioner is elected by the General Assembly and follows policy directives given him by the General Assembly or the Economic and Social Council. He reports to the Third Committee of the General Assembly (Social and Humanitarian Affairs), through the Economic and Social Council. The Executive Committee of the High Commissioner's Programme gives the High Commissioner guidance in respect of material assistance programmes and advises him at his request in the exercise of his functions under the Statute. It meets normally once a year at Geneva. It includes representatives of 40 states, members and non-members of the UN. Its annual sessions are normally held in October in Geneva. In recent years it has been customary for the High Commissioner to invite representatives of member states to meet with him informally at least once between sessions to keep them abreast of important developments.

International protection is the primary function of UNHCR. Its main objective is to promote and safeguard the rights and interests of refugees. In so doing UNHCR devotes special attention to promoting a generous policy of asylum on the part of governments and seeks to improve the status of refugees in their country of residence. It also helps them to cease to be refugees through the acquisition of the nationality of their country of residence when voluntary repatriation is not applicable. UNHCR pursues its objectives in the field of protection by encouraging the conclusion of intergovernmental legal instruments in favour of refugees, by supervising the implementation of their provisions and by encouraging governments to adopt legislation and administrative procedures for the benefit of refugees. The main instrument in this field is the 1951 Convention Relating to the Status of Refugees. It prescribes a minimum standard of treatment for refugees in such important matters as employment, social security and freedom of movement, and provides for the issuance, by contracting states, of travel documents in lieu of national passports. The most important provision of the Convention is embodied in Article 33 which forbids the return of a refugee to a country where his life or liberty would be in danger because of persecution for reasons of race, religion, nationality or political opinion *(refoulement)*.

A protocol relating to the status of refugees came into force in 1967 and had the effect of extending the provisions of the 1951 Convention (which applies to persons who have become refugees as a result of events prior to that date) to new groups of refugees.

On 1 Nov. 1982, 93 member states had acceded to the 1951 Convention and/or the 1967 Protocol.

The thirty-third session of the Executive Committee of the High Commissioner's Programme, held in Oct. 1982 expressed the belief that the mandate of UNHCR was sufficiently flexible and adaptable to changing requirements and adequate in the evolving refugee situation; most delegates believed that the mandate should remain unchanged when the question of the continuation of the Office came before the General Assembly in Nov. The Committee noted with deep concern that problems in the field of international protection had increased in seriousness, and was particularly alarmed over the recurrence of military attacks, acts of piracy and forcible return of refugees and asylum-seekers.

During 1982, Bolivia, the People's Republic of China, and Japan acceded to the 1951 Convention relating to the Status of Refugees, thus bringing the total number of states party to the Convention to 93.

About half of the world's refugees are located in Africa where their presence, in some of the least developed countries, constitutes a serious economic burden. The refugee problem in the Horn of Africa and the Sudan, while remaining the largest in the continent, stabilized considerably during 1982. The Special Programme for returnees in Ethiopia, initiated in 1980, was expanded, while the number of refugees assisted in 35 camps in Somalia have been assessed at some 700,000. In Zaïre, the UNHCR programme for 70,000 Ugandans has continued to develop. In Chad, the voluntary repatriation of some 150,000 refugees from neighbouring countries was successfully completed by mid-1982. UNHCR assistance was also extended to some 50,000 internally displaced persons. The revised estimates for 1982 expenditure in Africa amounted to some $140m.

In Pakistan, Afghan refugees continued to arrive. By mid-1982, Pakistani authorities estimated their number at 2·7m. Assistance requirements planned for the most needy cases totalling 2·1m. persons was put at some $72m.

The problem of refugees and displaced persons from the Indo-Chinese peninsula continued to be the main focus of attention in South-East Asia. Although refugee numbers decreased by 73,000 during 1981, new arrivals brought the net decrease to only 15,000 by mid-1982. Some 218,000 persons still remained in camps, mostly in Thailand, awaiting resettlement. By the end of June 1982, some 835,000 Indo-Chinese refugees had been resettled mostly in Australia (63,000), Canada (80,000), China (265,000), France (74,000) and the USA (450,000).

In Central America and Mexico, refugee needs increased sharply throughout 1981 and 1982. By 31 Dec. 1981, the total refugee population in the region had reached an estimated 205,000 persons of whom 181,000 were from El Salvador. Others were mostly from Guatemala and Nicaragua. The situation in Honduras, where the refugee population grew from 24,500 to 29,000 in the first half of 1982 called for an expanded programme of assistance valued at US$12·9m.

In Oct. 1982, the Executive Committee of the High Commissioner's Programme approved a revised financial target of US$430m. for all UNHCR programmes in 1982 and also approved the figure of US$425m. for projected requirements in 1983.

For its work on behalf of refugees around the world, UNHCR was awarded the Nobel Peace Prize in 1955 and again in 1981.

Headquarters: Palais des Nations 1211, Geneva 10, Switzerland.
UK Office: 36 Westminster Palace Gardens, London, SW1P 1RR.
High Commissioner: Poul Hartling (Denmark).

UNHCR reports. Geneva, 1966 ff.
UNHCR Bulletin. Geneva, 1968–74
UNHCR Tabloids. Geneva, 1974 ff.
UNHCR *Refugee Update.* Geneva, 1979 ff.
UNHCR *The Last Ten Years.* Geneva, 1980
Forty Years of International Assistance to Refugees. Geneva, 1962
The Red Cross and the Refugees. Geneva, 1963
A Mandate to Protect and Assist Refugees. Geneva, 1971
The Refugee Problem Isn't Hopeless Unless You Think So. Geneva, 1975
Habitat: Refugees in Human Settlements. Geneva, 1976

The United Nations Relief and Works Agency for Palestine Refugees in the Near East (UNRWA) was established by the General Assembly in Dec. 1949. It is supported by private contributions and by governmental pledges made each year at the General Assembly. UNRWA's operations, direct relief, long-term rehabilitation and vocational training, cover the Gaza Strip, Jordan, Lebanon and Syria, where over 1m. refugees were living before the war of June 1967.

Headquarters: Storchengasse 1, A-1150 Vienna, Austria.
Commissioner-General: Olof Rydbeck (Norway).

The United Nations' Children's Fund (UNICEF), established by the General

Assembly on 11 Dec. 1946, functions under the supervision of the Economic and Social Council. It assists child health, nutrition and welfare programmes in 116 countries and territories. Its work is financed through voluntary contributions from governments and donations from the public. UNICEF received the Nobel Peace Prize for 1965.

Headquarters: United Nations Headquarters, New York City.
Executive Director: James P. Grant (USA).

The International Narcotics Control Board (INCB)

Origin. The INCB was established by the Single Convention on Narcotic Drugs, 1961, and assumed the functions of the Permanent Central Board and the Drug Supervisory Body, which were themselves treaty organs created by the narcotics Conventions of 1925 and 1931 respectively. The 1961 Convention came into force on 13 Dec. 1964. The INCB entered upon its duties on 2 March 1968. Its functions and membership were enlarged by the 1972 Protocol amending the 1961 Convention.

Functions. The functions of the Board under the Treaties are to work with governments to ensure that the aims of the drug control treaties are not seriously endangered by reason of the failure of any country or territory to carry out the provisions of such treaties; to limit the cultivation, production, manufacture and use of drugs to an adequate amount required for medical and scientific purposes; to prevent the illicit cultivation, production and manufacture of, and illicit trafficking in and use of, drugs; to ensure the availability of drugs for medical and scientific purposes; to encourage universal co-operation in the field of drug control. The 1971 Convention on Psychotropic Substances broadens the scope of the Board's activities to include the supervision of national control over these substances.

Organization. The INCB is composed of 13 members, elected by the Economic and Social Council in their individual capacities and not as representatives of governments, who, by their competence, impartiality and disinterestedness, will command general confidence. During its sessions held at least twice a year, the Board reviews the drug situation throughout the world and supervises the implementation of the various drug control treaties. The INCB is assisted by a permanent secretariat which is in continuous dialogue with national authorities. Information received from over 170 governments is analysed by the secretariat and submitted for the Board's attention during its sessions.

Headquarters: Vienna International Centre, Vienna, Austria.
President: Professor Paul Reuter.
Secretary: Abdelaziz Bahi.

Publications. Report of the International Narcotics Control Board. 1968 ff.—*Estimated World Requirements of Narcotic Drugs.* With supplements. 1969 ff.—*Statistics on Narcotic Drugs* 1967 ff.—*Comparative Statement of Estimates and Statistics on Narcotic Drugs.* 1967 ff.—*List of Narcotic Drugs under International Control.* 1968 ff. *Statistics on Psychotropic Substances.* 1977 ff.—*List of Psychotropic Substances under International Control.* 1980 ff.

The Budget of the United Nations. The financial year coincides with the calendar year; accountancy is in US$. Budget for 1982–83, $1,506,241,800.

Membership and percentage scale of contributions to UN budget, 1980–82:

Afghánistán	0·01	Belgium	1·22	Canada	3·28
Albania	0·01	Benin	0·01	Cape Verde	0·01
Algeria	0·12	Bhután	0·01	Central African Rep.	0·01
Angola	0·01	Bolivia	0·01	Chad	0·01
Argentina	0·78	Botswana	0·01	Chile	0·07
Australia	1·83	Brazil	1·27	China	1·62
Austria	0·71	Bulgaria	0·16	Colombia	0·11
Bahamas	0·01	Burma	0·01	Comoros	0·01
Bahrain	0·01	Burundi	0·01	Congo	0·01
Bangladesh	0·04	Byelorussia	0·39	Costa Rica	0·02
Barbados	0·01	Cameroon	0·01	Cuba	0·11

Cyprus	0·01
Czechoslovakia	0·83
Denmark	0·74
Djibouti	0·01
Dominica	0·01
Dominican Republic	0·03
Ecuador	0·02
Egypt	0·07
El Salvador	0·01
Equatorial Guinea	0·01
Ethiopia	0·01
Fiji	0·01
Finland	0·48
France	6·26
Gabon	0·02
Gambia	0·01
German Demo. Rep.	1·39
Germany, Federal Rep.	8·31
Ghana	0·03
Greece	0·35
Grenada	0·01
Guatemala	0·02
Guinea	0·01
Guinea-Bissau	0·01
Guyana	0·01
Haiti	0·01
Honduras	0·01
Hungary	0·33
Iceland	0·03
India	0·60
Indonesia	0·16
Iran	0·65
Iraq	0·12
Ireland	0·16
Israel	0·25
Italy	3·45
Ivory Coast	0·03
Jamaica	0·02
Japan	9·58
Jordan	0·01
Kampuchea, Demo.	0·01
Kenya	0·01
Kuwait	0·20
Laos	0·01
Lebanon	0·03
Lesotho	0·01
Liberia	0·01
Libya	0·23
Luxembourg	0·05
Madagascar	0·01
Malawi	0·01
Malaysia	0·09
Maldive, Republic of	0·01
Mali	0·01
Malta	0·01
Mauritania	0·01
Mauritius	0·01
Mexico	0·76
Mongolia	0·01
Morocco	0·05
Mozambique	0·01
Nepál	0·01
Netherlands	1·63
New Zealand	0·27
Nicaragua	0·01
Niger	0·01
Nigeria	0·16
Norway	0·50
Oman	0·01
Pakistan	0·07
Panama	0·02
Papua New Guinea	0·01
Paraguay	0·01
Peru	0·06
Philippines	0·10
Poland	1·24
Portugal	0·19
Qatar	0·03
Romania	0·21
Rwanda	0·01
St Lucia	0·01
St Vincent	0·01
São Tomé	0·01
Saudi Arabia	0·58
Senegal	0·01
Seychelles	0·01
Sierra Leone	0·01
Singapore	0·08
Solomon Islands	0·01
Somalia	0·01
South Africa, Rep. of	0·42
Spain	1·70
Sri Lanka	0·02
Sudan	0·01
Suriname	0·01
Swaziland	0·01
Sweden	1·31
Syria	0·03
Tanzania	0·01
Thailand	0·10
Togo	0·01
Trinidad and Tobago	0·03
Tunisia	0·03
Turkey	0·30
Uganda	0·01
Ukraine	1·46
USSR	11·10
United Arab Emirates	0·10
UK	4·46
USA	25·00
Upper Volta	0·01
Uruguay	0·04
Venezuela	0·50
Vietnam	0·03
Western Samoa	0·01
Yemen Arab Republic	0·01
Yemen, People's Dem. Rep.	0·01
Yugoslavia	0·42
Zaïre	0·02
Zambia	0·02
Zimbabwe	0·02

Books of Reference

Yearbook of the United Nations. New York, 1947 ff. Annual

United Nations Chronicle. Quarterly

Monthly Bulletin of Statistics

General Assembly: Official-Records: Resolutions

Reports of the Secretary-General of the United Nations on the work of the Organization. 1946 ff.

Documents of the United Nations Conference on International Organization, San Francisco, 1945. 16 vols.

Charter of the United Nations and Statute of the International Court of Justice. Text in English, French, Chinese, Russian and Spanish.

Repertory of Practice of UN's Organs. 5 vols. New York, 1955

Official Records of the Security Council, the Economic and Social Council, Trusteeship Council and the Disarmament Commission

Demographic Yearbook, 1948 ff. New York, 1969

Everyman's United Nations. New York. 1958 ff. Annual

Statistical Yearbook. New York, 1947 ff.

Yearbook of International Statistics. New York, 1950 ff.

World Economic Survey. New York, 1947 ff.

Economic Survey of Asia and the Far East. New York, 1946 ff.

Economic Survey of Latin America. New York, 1948 ff.

Economic Survey of Europe. New York, 1948 ff.

Economic Survey of Africa. New York, 1960 ff.

Bailey, S. D., *The General Assembly.* London, 1960

Boyd, A., *Fifteen Men and a Powder Keg.* London, 1971

Foote, W., *Dag Hammarskjöld—Servant of Peace.* London, 1962
Forsythe, D., *United Nations Peacemaking: The Conciliation Commission for Palestine.* Johns Hopkins Univ. Press, 1973
Hiscocks, R., *The Security Council: A Study in Adolescence.* New York, 1974
Lie, Trygve, *In the Cause of Peace.* London, 1954
Luard, E., *A History of the United Nations.* Vol. 1. London, 1982
Meron, T., *The United Nations Secretariat.* Lexington, 1977
Ogley, R., *The United Nations and East–West Relations.* Univ. of Sussex, 1972
Rikhye, I. J., Harbottle, M., Egge, B., *The Thin Blue Line.* London, 1974
Symonds, R., and Carder, M., *The United Nations and the Population Question.* London, 1973
Thant, U., *Towards World Peace.* New York, 1964
Urquhart, B., *Hammarskjöld.* London, 1973
Walters, F. P., *A History of the League of Nations.* 2 vols. London, 1952
Winton, H. N. M. (comp. and ed.), *Man and the Environment. A Bibliography of Selected Publications of the United Nations System 1946–1971.* New York, 1972
Witthauer, K., *Die Bevölkerung der Erde: Verteilung und Dynamik.* Gotha, 1958.—*Distribution and Dynamics Relating to World Population.* Gotha, 1969
Her Majesty's Stationery Office. *Sectional List 23* (currently revised) and *International Organizations Publications* contain a full list of publications on UN and Specialized Agencies, issued by HMSO.

United Nations Information Centre. 14–15 Stratford Place, London W1N 9AF

MEMBER STATES OF THE UN

(as in 1982)

Afghánistán	19 Nov. 1946	Democratic Kampuchea	14 Dec. 1955
Albania	14 Dec. 1955	Democratic Yemen	14 Dec. 1967
Algeria	8 Oct. 1962	Denmark [1]	24 Oct. 1945
Angola	1 Dec. 1976	Djibouti	20 Sept. 1977
Antigua and Barbuda	11 Nov. 1981	Dominica	18 Dec. 1978
Argentina [1]	24 Oct. 1945	Dominican Republic [1]	24 Oct. 1945
Australia [1]	1 Nov. 1945	Ecuador [1]	21 Dec. 1945
Austria	14 Dec. 1955	Egypt [1]	24 Oct. 1945
Bahamas	18 Sept. 1973	El Salvador [1]	24 Oct. 1945
Bahrain	21 Sept. 1971	Equatorial Guinea	12 Nov. 1968
Bangladesh	17 Sept. 1974	Ethiopia [1]	13 Nov. 1945
Barbados	9 Dec. 1966	Fiji	13 Oct. 1970
Belgium [1]	27 Dec. 1945	Finland	14 Dec. 1955
Belize	25 Sept. 1981	France [1]	24 Oct. 1945
Benin	20 Sept. 1960	Gabon	20 Sept. 1960
Bhután	21 Sept. 1971	Gambia	21 Sept. 1965
Bolivia [1]	14 Nov. 1945	German Democratic Rep.	18 Sept. 1973
Botswana	17 Oct. 1966	Germany, Federal Rep. of	18 Sept. 1973
Brazil [1]	24 Oct. 1945	Ghana	8 Mar. 1957
Bulgaria	14 Dec. 1955	Greece [1]	25 Oct. 1945
Burma	19 April 1948	Grenada	17 Sept. 1974
Burundi	18 Sept. 1962	Guatemala [1]	21 Nov. 1945
Byelorussia [1]	24 Oct. 1945	Guinea	12 Dec. 1958
Canada [1]	9 Nov. 1945	Guinea-Bissau	17 Sept. 1974
Cape Verde	16 Sept. 1975	Guyana	20 Sept. 1966
Central African Rep.	20 Sept. 1960	Haiti [1]	24 Oct. 1945
Chad	20 Sept. 1960	Honduras [1]	17 Dec. 1945
Chile [1]	24 Oct. 1945	Hungary	14 Dec. 1955
China [1]	24 Oct. 1945	Iceland	19 Dec. 1946
Colombia [1]	5 Nov. 1945	India [1]	30 Oct. 1945
Comoros	12 Nov. 1975	Indonesia	28 Sept. 1950
Congo	20 Sept. 1960	Iran [1]	24 Oct. 1945
Costa Rica [1]	2 Nov. 1945	Iraq [1]	21 Dec. 1945
Cuba [1]	24 Oct. 1945	Ireland	14 Dec. 1955
Cyprus	20 Sept. 1960	Israel	11 May 1949
Czechoslovakia [1]	24 Oct. 1945	Italy	14 Dec. 1955

Ivory Coast	20 Sept. 1960
Jamaica	18 Sept. 1962
Japan	18 Dec. 1956
Jordan	14 Dec. 1955
Kenya	16 Dec. 1963
Kuwait	14 May 1963
Laos People's Dem. Rep.	14 Dec. 1955
Lebanon [1]	24 Oct. 1945
Lesotho	17 Oct. 1966
Liberia [1]	2 Nov. 1945
Libyan Arab Jamahiriya	14 Dec. 1955
Luxembourg [1]	24 Oct. 1945
Madagascar	20 Sept. 1960
Malawi	1 Dec. 1964
Malaysia	17 Sept. 1957
Maldives	21 Sept. 1965
Mali	28 Sept. 1960
Malta	1 Dec. 1964
Mauritania	27 Oct. 1961
Mauritius	24 Apr. 1968
Mexico [1]	7 Nov. 1945
Mongolia	27 Oct. 1961
Morocco	12 Nov. 1956
Mozambique	16 Sept. 1975
Nepál	14 Dec. 1955
Netherlands [1]	10 Dec. 1945
New Zealand [1]	24 Oct. 1945
Nicaragua [1]	24 Oct. 1945
Niger	20 Sept. 1960
Nigeria	7 Oct. 1960
Norway [1]	27 Nov. 1945
Oman	7 Oct. 1971
Pakistan	30 Sept. 1947
Panama [1]	13 Nov. 1945
Papua New Guinea	10 Oct. 1975
Paraguay [1]	24 Oct. 1945
Peru [1]	31 Oct. 1945
Philippines [1]	24 Oct. 1945
Poland [1]	24 Oct. 1945
Portugal	14 Dec. 1955
Qatar	21 Sept. 1971
Romania	14 Dec. 1955
Rwanda	18 Sept. 1962
St Lucia	18 Sept. 1979
St Vincent and the Grenadines	16 Sept. 1980
Samoa, Western	15 Dec. 1976
São Tomé and Principe	16 Sept. 1975
Saudi Arabia [1]	24 Oct. 1945
Senegal	28 Sept. 1960
Seychelles	21 Sept. 1976
Sierra Leone	27 Sept. 1961
Singapore	21 Sept. 1965
Solomon Islands	19 Sept. 1978
Somalia	20 Sept. 1960
South Africa [1]	7 Nov. 1945
Spain	14 Dec. 1955
Sri Lanka	14 Dec. 1955
Sudan	12 Nov. 1956
Suriname	4 Dec. 1975
Swaziland	24 Sept. 1968
Sweden	19 Nov. 1946
Syrian Arab Rep. [1]	24 Oct. 1945
Thailand	16 Dec. 1946
Togo	20 Sept. 1960
Trinidad and Tobago	18 Sept. 1962
Tunisia	12 Nov. 1956
Turkey [1]	24 Oct. 1945
Uganda	25 Oct. 1962
Ukrainian Soviet Socialist Rep. [1]	24 Oct. 1945
USSR [1]	24 Oct. 1945
United Arab Emirates	9 Dec. 1971
UK [1]	24 Oct. 1945
United Rep. of Cameroon	20 Sept. 1960
United Rep. of Tanzania	14 Dec. 1961
USA [1]	24 Oct. 1945
Upper Volta	20 Sept. 1960
Uruguay [1]	18 Dec. 1945
Vanuatu	15 Sept. 1981
Venezuela [1]	15 Nov. 1945
Vietnam	20 Sept. 1977
Yemen	30 Sept. 1947
Yugoslavia [1]	24 Oct. 1945
Zaïre	20 Sept. 1960
Zambia	1 Dec. 1964
Zimbabwe	25 Aug. 1980

[1] Original member.

SPECIALIZED AGENCIES OF THE UN

INTERNATIONAL ATOMIC ENERGY AGENCY (IAEA)

Origin. The International Atomic Energy Agency came into existence on 29 July 1957. Its statute had been approved on 26 Oct. 1956, at an international conference held at UN Headquarters, New York. A relationship agreement links it with the United Nations. The IAEA had 110 member states in 1982.

Functions. (1) To accelerate and enlarge the contribution of atomic energy to peace, health and prosperity throughout the world, and (2) to ensure that assistance provided by it or at its request or under its supervision or control is not used in such a way as to further any military purpose.

The IAEA gives advice and technical assistance to developing countries on nuclear power development (provides a series of training courses on nuclear power project planning), on health and safety, on radioactive waste management, on legal aspects of the use of atomic energy, and on prospecting for and exploiting nuclear raw materials; in addition it promotes the use of radiation and isotopes in agriculture, industry, medicine and hydrology through expert services, training courses and fellowships, grants of equipment and supplies, research contracts, scientific meetings and publications. Since 1958 the Agency has provided assistance totalling over $127m. More than 6,000 persons have been trained in nuclear science subjects through the award of fellowships, and over 5,500 through participation in training courses and study tours; more than 2,500 experts have been sent into the field as advisers and training course lecturers; and equipment worth more than $45m. has been provided. The IAEA has research laboratories in Austria and Monaco. At Trieste, the International Centre for Theoretical Physics was established in 1964 which is now operated jointly by UNESCO and IAEA.

The IAEA applies safeguards in 39 States pursuant to NPT and in 14 States under other agreements to 130 power reactors, 4 conversion plants, 38 fabrication plants, 4 enrichment plants, 6 reprocessing plants, 176 research reactors and critical assemblies, 24 separate storage facilities, 40 locations containing more than 1 effective kg of nuclear material, 422 locations containing 1 or less than 1 effective kg of nuclear material. The above figures include facilities safeguarded under agreement with the European Atomic Energy Community and its non-nuclear-weapon States.

Organization. The Statute provides for an annual General Conference, a Board of Governors of 34 members and a Secretariat headed by a Director-General.

Headquarters: Vienna International Centre, PO Box 100, A-1400 Vienna, Austria.

Director-General: Hans Blix (Sweden).

INTERNATIONAL LABOUR ORGANISATION (ILO)

Origin. The ILO, established in 1919 as an autonomous part of the League of Nations, is an intergovernmental agency with a tripartite structure, in which representatives of governments, employers and workers participate. It seeks through international action to improve labour conditions, raise living standards and promote productive employment. In 1946 the ILO was recognized by the United Nations as a specialized agency. In 1969 it was awarded the Nobel Peace Prize. In 1982 it numbered 150 members.

Functions. One of the ILO's principal functions is the formulation of international standards in the form of International Labour Conventions and Recommendations. Member countries are required to submit Conventions to their competent national authorities with a view to ratification. If a country ratifies a Convention it agrees to bring its laws into line with its terms and to report periodically how these regulations are being applied. More than 5,000 ratifications of 158 Conventions had been deposited by mid-1982. Machinery is available to ascertain whether Conventions thus ratified are effectively applied.

Recommendations do not require ratification, but member states are obliged to consider them with a view to giving effect to their provisions by legislation or other action. By the end of 1982 the International Labour Conference had adopted 166 recommendations.

Organization. The ILO consists of the International Labour Conference, the Governing Body and the International Labour Office.

The Conference is the supreme deliberative organ of the ILO; it meets annually at Geneva. National delegations are composed of 2 government delegates, 1 employers' delegate and 1 workers' delegate.

The Governing Body, elected by the Conference, is the executive council. It is composed of 28 government members, 14 workers' members and 14 employers' members.

Ten governments hold permanent seats on the Governing Board because of their industrial importance, namely, Brazil, Canada, China, Federal Republic of Germany, France, India, Italy, Japan, USSR and UK, with the addition in 1980 of US. The remaining 18 government seats were, at the end of 1982, held by Australia,

Bahrain, Bangladesh, Barbados, Bulgaria, Colombia, Ecuador, Egypt, German Democratic Republic, Kenya, Mali, Mexico, Mozambique, Netherlands, Nigeria, Philippines, Senegal and Venezuela.

The Office serves as secretariat, operational headquarters, research centre and publishing house.

The ILO budget for 1982–83 amounted to US$230m.

Activities. In addition to its research and advisory activities, the ILO extends technical co-operation to governments under its regular budget and under the UN Development Programme and Funds-in-Trust in the fields of employment promotion, human resources development (including vocational and management training), development of social institutions, small-scale industries, rural development, social security, industrial safety and hygiene, productivity, etc. Technical co-operation also includes expert missions and a fellowship programme. Some $100m. was spent on technical co-operation in 1981. Projects were in progress in some 115 countries and about 900 experts involved.

Major emphasis is being given to the ILO's World Employment Programme, launched in 1969 with the purpose of stimulating national and international efforts to increase the volume of productive employment, and so to counter the problem of rising unemployment in developing countries. Employment strategy missions were carried out under the Programme in Colombia, the Dominican Republic, Egypt, Iran, Kenya, Sri Lanka, Sudan and the Philippines. The work of these missions was complemented by an ILO programme of research designed to provide policy-makers with the information to promote employment. A World Employment Conference was held in June 1976.

The International Labour Conference (Geneva, June 1982) adopted a Convention concerning the maintenance of rights in social security and a Convention and Recommendation on termination of employment at the initiative of the employer. It also revised the Plantations Convention (No. 110) and prepared the way for new Recommendations in 1983 on maintenance of rights in social security and on vocational rehabilitation of the disabled.

In 1960 the ILO established in Geneva the International Institute for Labour Studies. The Institute specializes in advanced education and research on social and labour policy. It brings together for group study experienced persons from all parts of the world—government administrators, trade-union officials, industrial experts, management, university and other specialists.

A training institution was opened by the ILO in Turin, Italy, in 1965—the International Centre for Advanced Technical and Vocational Training. The Centre provides opportunities for technical, vocational and management training for individuals who have advanced beyond the facilities available in their own countries. Courses are geared particularly to the needs of developing countries.

Headquarters: International Labour Office, CH-1211 Geneva 22, Switzerland.
Director-General: Francis Blanchard (France).
Chairman of the Governing Body: Aída Gonzales Martinez (Mexico).
London Branch Office: 96/98 Marsham St., SW1.

ILO received the Nobel Peace Prize for 1969.

The ILO has regional offices in Addis Ababa (for Africa), Bangkok (for Asia and the Pacific), Lima (for Latin America and the Caribbean) and Beirut (for Arab States).

Publications: Regular periodicals in English, French and Spanish include the *International Labour Review, Legislative Series, Bulletin of Labour Statistics, Year Book of Labour Statistics, Official Bulletin* and *Labour Education. Women at Work* and the *Social and Labour Bulletin* are issued in English and French.

The Practice of Entrepreneurship. Workforce Reductions in Undertakings. Agrarian Policies and Rural Poverty in Africa. Workers' Management in Yugoslavia. Negotiating Development: Labour Relations in Southern Asia. Deterrence and Compensation: Legal Liability in Occupational Safety and Health. Working Conditions and Environment. Employment Opportunities and Equity in a Changing Economy: Egypt in the 1980s. International Labour Conventions and Recommendations, 1919–1981. New Technologies: Their Impact on Employ-

ment and the Working Environment. Safety and Health in the Construction of Fixed Offshore Installations in the Petroleum Industry. (All 1982).

FOOD AND AGRICULTURE ORGANIZATION OF THE UNITED NATIONS (FAO)

Origin. The UN Conference on Food and Agriculture in May 1943, at Hot Springs, Virginia, set up an Interim Commission in Washington in July 1943 to plan the Organization, which came into being on 16 Oct. 1945.

Aims and Activities. The aims of FAO are to raise levels of nutrition and standards of living; to improve the production and distribution of all food and agricultural products from farms, forests and fisheries; to improve the living conditions of rural populations; and, by these means, to eliminate hunger.

In carrying out these aims, FAO promotes investment in agriculture, better soil and water management, improved yields of crops and livestock, and the transfer of technology to, and the development of agricultural research in, developing countries. FAO promotes the conservation of natural resources and the rational use of fertilizers and pesticides. The Organization combats animal diseases, promotes the development of marine and inland fisheries, and encourages the rational use of forest resources. Technical assistance is provided in all these fields and others such as nutrition, agricultural engineering, agrarian reform, development communications, remote sensing for natural resources, and the prevention of food losses.

Special FAO programmes help countries prepare for, and provide relief in the event of, emergency food situations, in particular through the setting up of food reserves. The Global Information and Early Warning System provides current information on the world food situation and identifies countries threatened by shortages to guide potential donors. Assistance is given to set up national and regional early warning systems.

The Organization also has a major rôle in the collection, analysis and dissemination of information on natural resources and agricultural production.

The second World Food Day, on 16 Oct. 1982 was marked in more than 130 countries by tens of thousands of activities – evidence of the growing concern by people worldwide that the time has come to apply lasting solutions to the problems of hunger and malnutrition.

FAO sponsors the World Food Programme (WFP) with the UN; WFP uses food commodities, cash and services contributed by member States of the UN to back programmes of social and economic development, as well as for relief in emergency situations.

Finance and Administration. The General Conference of FAO, composed of all member States, meets every other year to determine the policy and approve the budget and work programme of FAO. The Council, consisting of 49 member nations elected by the Conference serves as the governing body of FAO between sessions of the Conference. At its 21st session in Nov. 1981, it admitted five new states: Bhutan, Equatorial Guinea, Saint Vincent and the Grenadines, Tonga and Zimbabwe, to bring total membership to 152 countries. The Conference also approved a Regular Programme budget of $366·6m. for 1982–83. The Regular programme, which is financed by contributions from member governments, covers the cost of the Organization's secretariat, its Technical Co-operation Programme and part of the cost of several Special Action Programmes.

FAO provides advice and assistance in the field through its Field Programme, funded largely from external sources such as the UN Development Programme (UNDP) and various trust funds provided by donor governments. Funds available from UNDP were expected to drop from $182m. in 1981 to around $145m. in 1982, a reduction in real terms of about 25%. UNDP's share of FAO's Field Programme costs declined from 87% in 1972 to less than 50% in 1982. The fall in funds from UNDP was partially offset by increases in trust funds and in funds available through the Technical Co-operation Programme, funded from FAO's own Regular Programme budget. Trust fund delivery in 1982 was expected to be about

$130m., an increase of 8% over the previous year's figure. Delivery under the Technical Co-operation Programme in 1982 accounted for about $19m., an increase of about 20% over the previous year. The total Field Programme delivery in 1982 was about $294m., a decrease of 7·5% in real terms.

Budget for 1982–83: $366·6m.

Headquarters: Viale delle Terme di Caracalla, Rome, Italy.
Director-General: Dr Edouard Saouma (Lebanon).

FAO publications include: FAO Books in Print 1980-81: The State of Food and Agriculture (annual), 1974 ff.; *Animal Health Yearbook* (annual), 1957 ff.; *Production Yearbook* (annual), 1947 ff.; *Trade Yearbook* (annual), 1947 ff.; *FAO Commodity Review* (annual), 1961 ff.; *Yearbook of Forest Products Statistics* (annual), 1947 ff.; *Yearbook of Fishery Statistics* (in two volumes). *Ceres* (bi-monthly). *Food and Nutrition* (bi-annual), *FAO Fertilizer Yearbook, FAO Plant Protection Bulletin* (quarterly), *World Animal Review* (quarterly).

UNITED NATIONS EDUCATIONAL, SCIENTIFIC AND CULTURAL ORGANIZATION (UNESCO)

Origin. A Conference for the establishment of an Educational, Scientific and Cultural Organization of the United Nations was convened by the Government of the UK in association with the Government of France, and met in London, 1–16 Nov. 1945. UNESCO came into being on 4 Nov. 1946.

Functions. The purpose of UNESCO is to contribute to peace and security by promoting collaboration among the nations through education, science and culture in order to further universal respect for justice, for the rule of law and for the human rights and fundamental freedoms which are affirmed for the peoples of the world, without distinction of race, sex, language or religion, by the Charter of the United Nations. The UNESCO budget for 1980 was $115·5m.

Activities. The education programme has four main objectives: the extension of education; the improvement of education; and life-long education for living in a world community.

To train teachers specialized in the techniques of fundamental education UNESCO is helping to establish regional and national training centres. A centre for Latin America was opened in Mexico in 1951, one for the Arab States was set up in Egypt in 1953. UNESCO seeks to promote the progressive application of the right to free and compulsory education for all and to improve the quality of education everywhere.

In the natural sciences, UNESCO seeks to promote international scientific co-operation, such as the International Hydrological Programme which began in 1966. It encourages scientific research designed to improve the living conditions of mankind. Science co-operation offices have been set up in Montevideo, Cairo, New Delhi, Nairobi and Jakarta.

In the field of communication, UNESCO endeavours, by disseminating information, carrying out research and providing advice, to increase the scope and quality of press, film and radio services throughout the world.

Organization. The organs of UNESCO are a General Conference (composed of representatives from each member state), an Executive Board (consisting of 45 government representatives elected by the General Conference) and a Secretariat. UNESCO had 153 members and 1 associate member in 1980.

National commissions act as liaison groups between UNESCO and the educational, scientific and cultural life of their own countries.

Budget for 1981: $200,133,700.

Headquarters: UNESCO House, 9 Place de Fontenoy, Paris (7eme).
Director-General: Amadou Mahtar M'Bow (Senegal).

Periodicals. Museum (quarterly, English and French); *International Social Science Journal (quarterly, English and French); Impact of Science on Society* (quarterly, English and French); *Unesco Courier* (monthly, English, French and Spanish); *Fundamental and Adult Education*

Bulletin (quarterly, English, French and Spanish); *Copyright Bulletin* (twice-yearly, English and French); *Unesco News* (English, French and Spanish); *Unesco Bulletin for Libraries* (monthly, English, French and Spanish).

WORLD HEALTH ORGANIZATION (WHO)

Origin. An International Conference, convened by the UN Economic and Social Council, to consider a single health organization resulted in the adoption on 22 July 1946 of the constitution of the World Health Organization. This constitution came into force on 7 April 1948.

Structure. The principal organs of WHO are the World Health Assembly, the Executive Board and the Secretariat. Each of the 158 member states and 1 Associate Member (1980) has the right to be represented at the Assembly, which meets annually usually in Geneva, Switzerland. The 30-member Executive Board is composed of technically qualified health experts designated by as many member states elected by the Assembly. The Secretariat consists of technical and administrative staff headed by a Director-General. Health activities in member countries are carried out through regional organizations which have been established in Africa (regional office, Brazzaville), South-East Asia (New Delhi), Europe (Copenhagen), Eastern Mediterranean (Alexandria) and Western Pacific (Manila). The Pan American Sanitary Bureau in Washington serves as the Regional Office of WHO for the Americas.

Functions. WHO's objective, as stated in the first article of the Constitution is 'the attainment by all peoples of the highest possible level of health'. As the directing and co-ordinating authority on international health it establishes and maintains collaboration with the UN, specialized agencies, government health administrations, professional and other groups concerned with health. The Constitution also directs WHO to assist governments to strengthen their health services, to stimulate and advance work to eradicate diseases, to promote maternal and child health, mental health, medical research and the prevention of accidents; to improve standards of teaching and training in the health professions, and of nutrition, housing, sanitation, working conditions and other aspects of environment health. The Organization also is empowered to propose conventions, agreements and regulations and make recommendations about international health matters; to revise the international nomenclature of diseases, causes of death and public health practices; to develop, establish and promote international standards concerning foods, biological, pharmaceutical and similar substances.

Methods of work. Co-operation in country projects is undertaken only on the request of the government concerned, through the 6 regional offices of the Organization. Worldwide technical services are made available by headquarters. Expert committees whose members are chosen from the 47 advisory panels of experts meet to advise the Director-General on a given subject. Scientific groups and consultative meetings are called for similar purposes. To further the education of health personnel of all categories, seminars, technical conferences and training courses are organized and advisors, consultants and lecturers are provided. WHO awards fellowships for study to nationals of member countries.

Activities. The main thrust of WHO's activities in 1981–82 was towards promoting national, regional and global strategies for the attainment of the main social target of the Member States for the next two decades: 'Health for All by the Year 2000', or the attainment by all citizens of the world of a level of health that will permit them to lead a socially and economically productive life.

Almost all countries indicated a high level of political commitment to this goal, and guiding principles for formulating corresponding strategies and plans of action were prepared.

The 34th World Health Assembly, meeting in May 1981, adopted 'The Global Strategy for Health for All by the Year 2000'. Based on primary health care approach to health as outlined in the Declaration of Alma-Ata (named after the city in the Soviet Union where the International Conference on Primary Health Care was held in 1978), the Global Strategy reflects the national and regional strategies as seen from a global perspective and responds to the UN General Assembly Resolution concerning health as an integral part of development. It describes broad lines of action to be undertaken at policy and operational levels, nationally and internationally, in the health and other social and economic sectors to attain 'Health for All by the Year 2000'.

Member States were invited to enter into this 'contract for health' of their own volition, and to enlist the involvement of people in all walks of life, including individuals, families, communities, all categories of health workers, non-governmental organizations and other associations of people concerned. They were urged to allocate adequate resources for health and in particular for primary health care and for the supporting levels of the health system.

Among milestones set as countries strive for the goal of health for all are these: Ensuring enough of the right kind of food for all by 1985; providing essential drugs for all by 1986; providing an adequate supply of safe drinking water and basic sanitation for all by 1990; and immunizing all children against six common diseases – measles, whooping cough, tetanus, polio, tuberculosis and diptheria – also by 1990.

The Assembly invited the relevant agencies, programmes and funds of the UN system, as well as other bodies concerned, to provide financial and other support to developing countries for the implementation of national strategies to achieve health for all by the year 2000.

The Global Strategy was presented to the 1981 UN General Assembly by the Director-General of WHO. The unique role conferred on the WHO in international health work was stressed. This rôle comprises in essence the inseparable and mutually supportive functions of acting as the directing and co-ordinating authority in the field of health and of international health work, and of ensuring technical co-operation between the WHO and its Member States. These functions are essential for the attainment of health for all by the year 2000.

The Organization's working budget for 1982–83 is $484·3m.

Meeting in May 1982, the 35th World Health Assembly approved the plan of action for implementing the Global Strategy for Health for All and requested the Director-General and the Executive Board to monitor progress. It called on Member States 'to fulfil their responsibilities as partners in the solemnly agreed Strategy for Health for All by carrying out in their countries as well as through inter-country co-operation, the activities devolving on them in the plan of action for implementing the strategy'. Once again, the Assembly emphasized that the strategy is not a 'WHO exercise', but rather an expression of individual and collective national responsibilities fully supported by WHO, which offers a unique opportunity for international co-operation in an important area of basic human needs.

The Assembly approved the Seventh General Programme of Work covering the period 1984–89 which constitutes a 'satisfactory response' of the Organization to the Global Strategy.

Patents: The Assembly decided that WHO should enter the fields of patents to encourage research in areas where it is needed and to ensure that new discoveries in the field of health are placed within reach of all. A resolution ('Policy on Patents', Resolution WHA 35/14), says that 'it shall be the policy of WHO to obtain patents, inventors' certificates or interests in patents on patentable health technology developed through projects supported by WHO, where such rights and interests are necessary to ensure development of the new technology'. This will be done to promote the 'development, production, and wide availability of health technology in the public interest'.

WHO will thus be able to induce pharmaceutical companies, for example, to develop useful drugs by helping to protect them whilst a large, potential market is assured. Also, by controlling patent rights WHO can insist that the price at which the process or product is sold remains low enough to be available to developing countries that need it most. Examples of health technology funded wholly or in part by WHO are in the field of malaria vaccine and low-dose, long-acting hormone preparations for fertility control.

Action Programme on Essential Drugs: Member States wishing to carry out national programmes aimed at making essential drugs available to all their people have been promised WHO's technical co-operation and support.

An Assembly resolution invited other agencies, programmes and funds of the UN system, bilateral agencies, non-governmental and voluntary organizations and the pharmaceutical industry to collaborate in their respective fields of interest in carrying out the Action Programme. WHO has already drawn up model lists of around 200 of the basic drugs and vaccines that are required within any one country's health services; these lists can then be adapted to the specific needs of each Member State.

Health implications of development schemes: The Assembly noted that many development projects carry major potential health hazards and dangers to the health of populations and the environment has deteriorated as a result of development projects, especially those associated with water resources. The resolution pledges WHO's total commitment to work with Member States, international and national agencies and financial institutions to incorporate the necessary preventive measures into development projects so as to minimize health and environment risks.

Marketing of breast-milk substitutes: The Assembly noted that, while many Member States had taken some measures related to improving infant and young child feeding, few countries had yet adopted and adhered to the International Code of Marketing of Breast-milk Substitutes drawn up at last year's Assembly. Member States were urged to give fresh attention to the need for national legislation, regulations or other suitable measures to give effect to the Code. Meanwhile WHO will undertake prospective surveys, including statistical data of infant and young child feeding practices in the various countries, particularly with regard to the incidence and duration of breast-feeding.

Health care of the elderly: WHO is asked to continue to collaborate closely with the UN in the field of aging, in a role that goes beyond traditional medical concerns and involves the health sector in the larger context of improving the quality of life for the elderly.

World Health Day: World Health Day, 7 April 1982, was devoted to the theme 'Add Life to Years'. The theme chosen for World Health Day 1983 is 'Health for All: the Count-down has begun!'.

New Members: Saint Lucia and Bhután were admitted to membership of the Organization, making total membership 158.

The Assembly reiterated its appeal to Member States to multiply their efforts to consolidate peace in the world, reinforce detente and achieve disarmament so as to release resources for the development of public health in the world.

Headquarters: 1211 Geneva 27. *Regional Offices:* Alexandria, Brazzaville, Copenhagen, Manila, New Delhi, Washington.

Director-General: Dr Halfdan T. Mahler (Denmark).

Basic Documents. 30th ed., 1980 (English, French, Russian, Spanish)
Handbook of Resolutions and Decisions. Vol. I, 1973 and Vol. II, 1979 (Arabic, English, French, Russian, Spanish)
WHO Chronicle (bi-monthly from 1947; English, French, Russian and Spanish)
Bulletin of WHO (quarterly, 1947–51; 6 issues a year from 1978; English and French)
International Digest of Health Legislation (quarterly, from 1948; English)
World Health, the Magazine of WHO. 1957 ff. (10 issues a year; Arabic, English, French, German, Italian, Persian, Portuguese, Russian and Spanish)
WHO Technical Report Series, 1950 ff. (English, French, Russian, Spanish)
WHO Monograph Series, 1951 ff. (English, French, Russian, Spanish)
Public Health Papers, 1959 ff. (English, French, Russian, Spanish)
World Health Statistics Annual (from 1939; English, French and Russian)
World Health Statistics Quarterly (monthly, 1947–76 then quarterly; English and French)
Weekly Epidemiological Record (from 1926; English and French)
Publications of the WHO, 1947–57: a bibliography (1958).—*1958–62* (1965).—*1963–67* (1969).—*1968–72* (1974)
World Directories:

Dental Schools, 1963 (1967); *Medical Schools, 1979; Post-Basic and Post-Graduate Schools of Nursing* (1965); *Schools of Pharmacy, 1963* (1966); *Schools of Public Health, 1971* (1972); *Venereal Disease Treatment Centres at Ports* (1972); *Veterinary Schools, 1971* (1973). *Schools for Medical Assistants, 1973* (1976); *Auxiliary Sanitarians 1973* (1978); *Dental Auxiliaries 1973* (1977); *Medical Lab. Technicians and Assistants, 1973* (1977)

The International Pharmacopoeia. 3rd. ed., 1979 (English, French and Spanish)

Manual of the International Statistical Classification of Diseases, Injuries and Causes of Death. 9th rev. (1977; English, French, Russian, Spanish)

IARC Monographs on the Evaluation of Carcinogenic Risk of Chemicals to Humans. 1967 *ff.* (English)

International Histological Classification of Tumours. Books and slides, from 1967, No. 25, 1980 (English, French, Russian and Spanish)

Report on the World Health Situation. 1959 ff. (English, French, Russian, Spanish); Sixth report 1973–77 (1979)

INTERNATIONAL MONETARY FUND (IMF)

The International Monetary Fund was established on 27 Dec. 1945 as an independent international organization and began operations on 1 March 1947; its relationship with the UN is defined in an agreement of mutual co-operation which came into force on 15 Nov. 1947. The first amendment to the Fund's articles creating the special drawing right (SDR) took effect on 28 July 1969 and the second amendment took effect on 1 April 1978.

The Fund is authorized under its Articles of Agreement to supplement its resources by borrowing. In Jan. 1962, a 4-year agreement was concluded with 10 industrial members (Belgium, Canada, France, Federal Republic of Germany, Italy, Japan, Netherlands, Sweden, UK, USA) who undertook to lend the Fund up to $6,000m. in their own currencies, if this should be needed to forestall or cope with an impairment of the international monetary system. Switzerland subsequently joined the group as an associate. These agreements, which have now been extended until Oct. 1985, were used to finance drawings made by the UK in 1964, 1965, 1968, 1969 and 1977, by France in 1969 and 1970 and by USA in 1978. The Fund has also borrowed from member countries and official institutions for a supplementary financing facility, and, more recently, from the Saudi Arabian Monetary Agency (SAMA).

Purposes: To promote international monetary co-operation, the expansion of international trade and exchange rate stability; to assist in the removal of exchange restrictions and the establishment of a multilateral system of payments; and to alleviate any serious disequilibrium in members' international balance of payments by making the financial resources of the Fund available to them, usually subject to conditions to ensure the revolving nature of Fund resources.

Activities. Each member of the Fund undertakes a broad obligation to collaborate with the Fund and other members to ensure the existence of orderly exchange arrangements and to promote a system of stable exchange rates. In addition, members are subject to certain obligations relating to domestic and external policies that can affect the balance of payments and the exchange rate. The Fund makes its resources available, under proper safeguards, to its members to meet short-term or medium-term payments difficulties. The first allocation of special drawing rights was made on 1 Jan. 1970 with five SDR allocations since then. SDRs in existence now total SDR 21,400m. On 24 Sept. 1978 the Fund's Interim Committee agreed on a 50% increase in quotas under the 7th general review of quotas; such reviews are required at least every five years. Total quotas now amount to SDR 61,000m., and the 8th general review of quotas is proceeding. To further enhance its balance of payments assistance to its members the Fund established a compensatory financing facility on 23 Feb. 1963, temporary oil facilities in 1974 and 1975, a trust fund in 1976, and an extended facility for medium term assistance to members with special balance of payments problems on 13 Sept. 1974 with additional financing now provided through a policy of enlarged access.

A Report on Reform of the International Monetary System was submitted to the Board of Governors at the 1972 annual meeting. During the meeting the Committee on Reform of the International Monetary System and Related Issues, generally known as the Committee of Twenty, held its first session, with the mandate to advise and report to the Board on all aspects of the international monetary system, including proposals for any amendments of the Articles of Agreement. The Committee of Twenty disbanded after submitting its final report in 1974. An Interim Committee of the Board of Governors on the International Monetary System and a Joint Ministerial Committee of the Boards of Governors of the World Bank and the Fund on the Transfer of Real Resources to Developing Countries (Development Committee) were established and held their initial meetings in Jan. 1975 and since then have met on a semi-annual basis.

Organization. The highest authority in the Fund is exercised by the Board of Governors on which each member government is represented. Normally the Governors meet once a year, although the Governors may take votes by mail or other means between annual meetings. The Board of Governors has delegated many of its powers to the executive directors in Washington, of whom there are 22, of which 6 are appointed by individual members and the other 16 elected by groups of countries. Each appointed director has voting power proportionate to the quota of the government he represents, while each elected director casts all the votes of the countries which elected him. The 6 appointed executive directors represent the US, UK, France, Federal Republic of Germany, Saudi Arabia and Japan.

The managing director is selected by the executive directors; he presides as chairman at their meetings, but may not vote except in case of a tie. His term is for 5 years, but may be extended or terminated at the discretion of the executive directors. He is responsible for the ordinary business of the Fund, under general control of the executive directors, and supervises a staff of about 1,500.

Headquarters: 700 19th St. NW, Washington, D.C., 20431. Offices in Paris and Geneva.

Managing Director: Jacques de Larosière (France).

Publications. Summary Proceedings of Annual Meetings of the Board of Governors.—Annual Report of the Executive Board.—Financial Statement (quarterly).—*International Financial Statistics* (monthly).—*IMF Survey* (bi-weekly).—*Balance of Payments Statistics.* Washington, monthly.—*IMF Staff Papers* (four times a year). Washington, from Feb. 1950.—*IMF Occasional Papers.—Annual Report on Exchange Arrangements and Exchange Restrictions.* Washington, 1950 ff.—*Finance and Development.* Washington, from June 1964 (quarterly).—*Direction of Trade.* Washington (monthly). *World Economic Outlook.* Washington (annual). *Government Finance Statistics Yearbook.*

de Vries, M. G., *The International Monetary Fund 1966–1971.* Washington D.C., 1976

INTERNATIONAL BANK FOR RECONSTRUCTION AND DEVELOPMENT (IBRD)

Conceived at the Bretton Woods Conference, July 1944, the Bank began operations in June 1946. Its purpose is to provide funds and technical assistance to facilitate economic development in its poorer member countries.

The Bank obtains its funds from the following sources: Capital subscribed by member countries; sales of its own securities; sales of parts of its loans; repayments; and net earnings. The subscribed capital of the Bank amounted to $36,614m. at 30 June 1981. On 4 Jan. 1980, the Board of Governors adopted a resolution that increased the authorized capital stock of the Bank by 331,500 shares. This represented an increase of approximately $40,000m. The resolution provides that the paid-in portion of the shares authorized to be subscribed under it will be 75%, compared with the 10% paid-in portion of existing capital stock. Borrowing in the market had reached more than $50,000m. by 30 June 1981, of which $27,797m. was outstanding, and sales of portions of Bank loans from portfolio had totalled $2,980m. The Bank is self-supporting. Its net earnings for year ending 30 June 1980 amounted to $588m.; in addition, the Bank had reserves of $3,995m.

By 30 June 1981 the Bank had made 2,015 loans totalling $68,150·3m. in 102 of its 139 member countries. Lending was for the following purposes: Agriculture and rural development, $14,383m.; Development Finance Companies, $7,027m.; education, $2,473m.; energy, $14,535m.; industry, $5,156m.; non-project, $2,516m.; population, health and nutrition, $239m.; small-scale enterprises, $833m.; telecommunications, $1,264m.; tourism, $364m.; transportation,

$13,665m.; urban development, $1,596m.; water supply and sewerage, $3,216m., and technical assistance, $91·1m. In order to eliminate wasteful overlapping of development assistance and to ensure that the funds available are used to the best possible effect, the Bank has organized consortia or consultative groups of aid-giving nations for the following countries: Bangladesh, Colombia, Egypt, Korea, Nepál, Pakistan, the Philippines, Sudan, Uganda, Zaïre and the Caribbean Group for Co-operation in Economic Development. The Bank furnishes a wide variety of technical assistance. It acts as executing agency for a number of pre-investment surveys financed by the UN Development Programme. Resident missions have been established in 23 developing member countries as well as 3 regional missions in East and West Africa and Thailand primarily to assist in the preparation of projects. The Bank helps member countries to identify and prepare projects for the development of agriculture, education and water supply by drawing on the expertise of the FAO, WHO, UNIDO and UNESCO through its co-operative agreements with these organizations. The Bank maintains a staff college, the Economic Development Institute in Washington, D.C., for senior officials of the member countries.

To help the poorest member countries the INTERNATIONAL DEVELOPMENT ASSOCIATION (IDA) was established in 1960. IDA grants development credits on a long-term, interest-free basis. By 30 June 1981 IDA had extended 1,079 credits to 73 countries, totalling $24,052m. for the same general purpose as bank loans. IDA's primary lending resources have been the subscriptions and supplementary contributions of member countries, chiefly its 21 wealthiest. The World Bank has made grants to IDA out of its net income; the Association also has a small flow of net income of its own.

Headquarters: 1818 H St., NW, Washington, D.C., 20433, USA. *European office:* 66 avenue d'Iéna, 75116 Paris, France. *London office:* New Zealand House, Haymarket, SW1Y 4TE, England. *Tōkyō office:* Kokusai Building, 1-1, Marunouchi 3-chome, Chiyoda-ku, Tōkyō 100, Japan.

2 President: Alden W. (Tom) Clausen (USA).

Publications. Annual Reports. 1946 ff.—*Summary Proceedings of Annual Meetings.* 1947 ff.—*The World Bank Group.* 1971.—*The World Bank Atlas.* 1967 ff.—*The World Bank, Group Policies and Operations.* 1974.—*Catalog of Publications,* 1982.—IDA, 1979.—*World Development Report.* 1978 ff.

INTERNATIONAL DEVELOPMENT ASSOCIATION (IDA)

A lending agency which came into existence on 24 Sept. 1960. Administered by the World Bank, IDA is open to all members of the Bank.

IDA concentrates its assistance on those countries with an annual *per capita* gross national product of less than $520 (1975 rate). Its resources consist mostly of subscriptions, general replenishments from its more industrialized and developed members, special contributions, and transfers from the net earnings of the Bank. IDA credits are made to Governments only. It had committed over $16,730m. for development projects by 30 June 1979.

INTERNATIONAL FINANCE CORPORATION (IFC)

The Corporation, an affiliate of the World Bank, was established in July 1956. Paid-in capital at 30 June 1982 was $497·3m., subscribed by 122 member countries. In addition, it has accumulated earnings of $181m. IFC supplements the activities of the World Bank by encouraging the growth of productive private enterprises in less developed member countries. Chiefly, IFC makes investments in the form of subscriptions to the share capital of privately owned companies, or long-term loans, or both. The Corporation will help finance new ventures, and it will also assist established enterprises to expand, improve or diversify their operations.

At 30 June 1982 IFC had approved investments amounting to $4,467m., in 80 countries. The total amount of loans and equity which IFC had sold or agreed to sell to other investors as of that date was $1,747m.

President: Alden W. (Tom) Clausen (USA).
Executive Vice-President: Hans A. Wuttke (Germany).

Publications. Annual Reports. 1956 ff.—*General Policies.* 1982

INTERNATIONAL CIVIL AVIATION ORGANIZATION (ICAO)

Origin. The Convention providing for the establishment of the International Civil Aviation Organization was drawn up by the International Civil Aviation Conference held in Chicago from 1 Nov. to 7 Dec. 1944. A Provisional International Civil Aviation Organization (PICAO) operated for 20 months until the formal establishment of ICAO on 4 April 1947.

The Convention on International Civil Aviation superseded the provisions of the Paris Convention of 1919, which established the International Commission for Air Navigation (ICAN), and the Pan American Convention on Air Navigation drawn up at Havana in 1928.

Functions. It assists international civil aviation by establishing technical standards for safety and efficiency of air navigation and promoting simpler procedures at borders; develops regional plans for ground facilities and services needed for international flying; disseminates air-transport statistics and prepares studies on aviation economics; fosters the development of air law conventions. As part of the UN Development Programme it provides technical assistance to States in developing civil aviation programmes.

Organization. The principal organs of ICAO are an Assembly, consisting of all members of the Organization, and a Council, which is comprised of 33 states elected by the Assembly, for 3 years, and meets in virtually continuous session. In electing these states, the Assembly must give adequate representation to: (1) states of major importance in air transport; (2) states which make the largest contribution to the provision of facilities for the international civil air navigation; (3) those states not otherwise included whose election will ensure that all major geographical areas of the world are represented. The main subsidiary bodies are: the Air Navigation Commission, composed of 15 members appointed by the Council; Air Transport Committee, open to council members; and the Legal Committee, on which all members of ICAO may be represented. There are 150 members. Budget for 1981: $28,096,476.

Headquarters: 1000 Sherbrooke St. West, Suite 400, Montreal, Quebec, Canada H3A 2R2.
President: Dr Assad Kotaite (Lebanon).
Secretary-General: Yves Lambert (France).

Annual Report of the Council. 1981 (English, French, Russian, Spanish).

UNIVERSAL POSTAL UNION (UPU)

Origin. The UPU was established on 1 July 1875, when the Universal Postal Convention adopted by the Postal Congress of Berne on 9 Oct. 1874 came into force. The UPU was known at first as the General Postal Union, its name being changed at the Congress of Paris in 1878. In 1980 there were 158 member countries.

Functions. The aim of the UPU is to assure the organization and perfection of the various postal services and to promote, in this field, the development of international collaboration. To this end, the members of UPU are united in a single postal territory for the reciprocal exchange of correspondence.

Organization. The UPU is composed of a Universal Postal Congress which usually meets every 5 years, a permanent Executive Council consisting of 40 members, a consultative Committee, which consists of 35 members elected on a geographical basis by each Congress, and an International Bureau, which functions as the permanent secretariat.

Since 1 July 1948 the Union has been governed by the revised Convention adopted by the twelfth Congress in Paris on 5 July 1947.
Budget for 1981: $9·5m.

Headquarters: Weltpoststrasse 4, 3000, Berne 15, Switzerland.
Director-General: Mohamed Ibrahim Sobhi (Egypt).

Publications. Documents of the Lausanne Congress 1974. Bern, 1975.—*Universal Postal Convention: Paris, 5 July, 1948.* (Cmd. 7435).—*The Postal Union* (monthly, Arabic, Chinese, English, French, German, Spanish, Russian).—*The UPU: Its Foundation and Development.* Bern, 1959.

INTERNATIONAL TELECOMMUNICATION UNION (ITU)

Origin. The International Telegraph Union, founded in Paris in 1865, and the International Radiotelegraph Union, founded in Berlin in 1906, were merged by the Madrid Convention of 1932 to form the International Telecommunication Union. ITU came into being on 1 Jan. 1934. The ITU has been governed since 1 Jan. 1975 by the revised International Telecommunication Convention adopted on 23 Oct. 1973.

Functions. The ITU: (1) allocates radio frequencies and registers radio-frequency assignments; (2) seeks to establish the lowest rates possible, consistent with efficient service and taking into account the necessity for keeping the independent financial administration of telecommunication on a sound basis; (3) promotes the adoption of measures for ensuring the safety of life through telecommunicion; and (4) makes studies and recommendations and collects and publishes information for the benefit of its members.

Organization. The ITU consists of the Plenipotentiary Conference, Administrative Conferences, the Administrative Council of 36 members, the General Secretariat, the International Frequency Registration Board, and 2 international consultative committees (radio, telephone and telegraph).
Budget for 1975: $62·32m.

Headquarters: Place des Nations, Geneva, Switzerland.
Secretary-General: Mohamed Mili (Tunisia).

Publications: International Convention on Telecommunications, Malaga-Torremolinos, 1973.—*Yearbook of Common Carrier Telecommunication Statistics (1964–73),* 1975. —*Telecommunication Journal* (monthly).—*Radio Regulations.* 1971.

WORLD METEOROLOGICAL ORGANIZATION (WMO)

Origin. A Conference of Directors of the International Meteorological Organization (set up in 1873), meeting in Washington in 1947, adopted a Convention creating the World Meteorological Organization. The WMO Convention became effective on 23 March 1950, and WMO was formally established on 19 March 1951, when the first session of its Congress was convened in Paris. An agreement to bring WMO into relationship with the United Nations was approved by this Congress and came into force on 21 Dec. 1951 with its approval by the General Assembly of the United Nations.

Functions. (1) To facilitate world-wide co-operation in the establishment of networks of stations for the making of meteorological observations as well as hydrological or other geophysical observations related to meteorology, and to promote the establishment and maintenance of meteorological centres charged with the provision of meteorological and related services; (2) to promote the establishment and maintenance of systems for the rapid exchange of meteorological and related information; (3) to promote standardization of meteorological and related observations and to ensure the uniform publication of observations and statistics; (4) to further the application of meteorology to aviation, shipping, water problems, agriculture and other human activities; (5) to promote activities in operational hydrology and to further close co-operation between meteorological and hydrological services; and (6) to encourage research and training in meteorology and, as appropriate, to assist in co-ordinating the international aspects of such research and training.

Organization. WMO is an inter-governmental organization of 151 member states and 5 member territories responsible for the operation of their own meteorological services. Constituent bodies of WMO are the World Meteorological Congress which meets every 4 years, the executive committee composed of 29 members elected in their personal capacity and including the President and 3 Vice-Presidents of the Organization, 6 regional associations of members and 8 technical commissions established by the Congress. A permanent secretariat is maintained in Geneva.

Budget for 1982: $17,516,800.

Headquarters: Case postale 5, CH-1211, Geneva 20, Switzerland.
Secretary-General: A. C. Wiin-Nielsen (Denmark).

Publications. WMO Bulletin. 1952 ff.—*Meteorological Services of the World.* 1982. —*Publications of the World Meteorological Organization, 1951–1980.*

INTERNATIONAL MARITIME ORGANIZATION (IMO)

Origin. The International Maritime Organization was established as a specialized agency of the UN by a convention drawn up at the UN Maritime Conference held at Geneva in Feb./March 1948. The Convention became effective on 17 March 1958 when it had been ratified by 21 countries, including 7 with at least 1m. gross tons of shipping each. The International Maritime Organization started operations in Jan. 1959.

Functions. To facilitate co-operation among governments on technical matters affecting merchant shipping, especially concerning safety at sea; to prevent and control marine pollution caused by ships; to encourage abolition of discriminatory and restrictive practices affecting merchant shipping. The International Maritime Organization is responsible for convening international maritime conferences and for drafting international maritime conventions.

Organization. The International Maritime Organization had 122 members (and 1 associate member) in 1982. The Assembly, composed of all member states, normally meets every 2 years. The Council of 24 member states acts as governing body between Assembly sessions. The Maritime Safety Committee deals with all technical questions. It can establish specialized sub-committees to deal with specific problems and like the Marine Environment Protection Committee, Legal Committee, Facilitation Committee and Committee on Technical Co-operation is open to all International Maritime Organization members. The Secretariat is composed of international civil servants.

The International Maritime Organization is depositary authority for the International Convention for the Safety of Life at Sea, 1960, and the Regulations for Preventing Collisions at Sea, 1948 and 1960; the International Convention for the Prevention of Pollution of the Sea by Oil, 1954, as amended in 1962 and 1969; the Convention on Facilitation of International Maritime Traffic, 1965; the International Convention on Load Lines, 1966; the International Convention on Tonnage Measurement of Ships, 1969; the International Convention relating to Intervention on the High Seas in cases of Oil Pollution Casualties 1969; the International Convention on Civil Liability for Oil Pollution Damage, 1969; Convention on International Compensation Fund for Oil Pollution Damage, 1971; Special Trade Passenger Ships Agreement, 1971; Convention on International Regulations for Preventing Collisions at Sea, 1972; the International Convention for Safe Containers, 1972; the International Convention on Prevention of Pollution from Ships, 1973; the International Convention for the Safety of Life at Sea, 1974; Athens Convention relating to the Carriage of Passengers and their Luggage by Sea, 1974; Convention on the International Maritime Satellite Organization, 1976; Convention on Limitation of Maritime Claims, 1976; Torremolinos International Convention for the Safety of Fishing Vessels, 1977; International Convention on

Standards of Training, Certification and Watchkeeping for Seafarers, 1978; International Convention on Maritime Search and Rescue, 1979.

Headquarters: 4 Albert Embankment, London SE1 7SR.
Secretary-General: C. P. Srivastava (India).
Secretary, Maritime Safety Committee: Capt. G. Kostylev (USSR).

IMCO and its Activities. 1979
Imo News

GENERAL AGREEMENT ON TARIFFS AND TRADE (GATT)

Origin. The General Agreement on Tariffs and Trade was negotiated in 1947 and entered into force on 1 Jan. 1948. Its 23 original signatories were members of a Preparatory Committee appointed by the UN Economic and Social Council to draft the charter for a proposed International Trade Organization. Since this charter was never ratified, the General Agreement, intended as an interim arrangement, has instead remained as the only international instrument laying down trade rules accepted by countries responsible for most of the world's trade. In Nov. 1982 there were 88 contracting parties, with a further 31 countries participating under special arrangements.

Functions. GATT functions both as a multilateral treaty that lays down a common code of conduct in international trade and trade relations and as a forum for negotiation and consultation to overcome trade problems and reduce trade barriers. Key provisions of the Agreement guarantee most-favoured-nation treatment (exceptions being granted to customs unions and free trade areas, and for certain preferences in favour of developing countries); require that protection be given to domestic industry only through tariffs (apart from specified exceptions); provide for negotiations to reduce tariffs (which are then 'bound' against subsequent increase) and other trade distortions; and lay down principles (particularly in Part IV of the Agreement, added in 1965) to assist the trade of developing countries. The Agreement also provides for consultation on, and settlement of, disputes, for 'waivers' (the grant of authorization, when warranted, to derogate from specific GATT obligations) and for emergency action in defined circumstances.

Seven 'rounds' of multilateral trade negotiations, including the Kennedy Round of 1964–67, took place in GATT up to 1979. The latest in this series, the Tōkyō Round, although held in Geneva, was so called because it was launched at a Ministerial meeting in the Japanese capital in Sept. 1973.

Ninety-nine countries participated in the Tōkyō Round. In Nov. 1979, the negotiations were concluded with agreements covering: an improved legal framework for the conduct of world trade (which includes recognition of tariff and non-tariff treatment in favour of and among developing countries as a permanent legal feature of the world trading system); non-tariff measures (subsidies and countervailing duties; technical barriers to trade; government procurement; customs valuation; import licensing procedures; and a revision of the 1967 GATT anti-dumping code); bovine meat; dairy products; tropical products; and an agreement on free trade in civil aircraft. The agreements contain provisions for special and more favourable treatment for developing countries.

Participating countries also agreed to reduce tariffs on thousands of industrial and agricultural products, for the most part over a period of 7 years beginning on 1 Jan. 1980. As a result of these concessions, industrialized countries will reduce the average level of their import duties on manufactures by about 34%, a cut comparable to that achieved in the Kennedy Round.

The agreements providing an improved framework for the conduct of world trade took effect in Nov. 1979. The other agreements took effect on 1 Jan. 1980, except for those covering government procurement and customs valuation, which took effect on 1 Jan. 1981, and the concessions on tropical products which began as early as 1977. Committees were established to supervise implemention of each of the Tōkyō Round agreements. Negotiations continued on the one major unresolved Tōkyō Round issue of whether to revise GATT rules on emergency safeguard action against imports.

GATT's member governments met in Geneva 24–29 Nov. 1982. The purpose of the meeting was to 'examine the functioning of the multilateral trading system, and to reinforce the common efforts of the contracting parties to support and improve the system for the benefit of all nations'. They adopted by consensus a joint Ministerial declaration which included: (i) An agreement on the problems facing the world economy and international trade; (ii) reaffirmation of the member governments' commitment to the GATT rules and to the multilateral trading system; (iii) an undertaking to refrain from taking or maintaining any trade measures inconsistent with GATT; (iv) an undertaking to ensure the effective implementation of GATT rules and provisions concerning developing countries, thereby furthering the dynamic role of these countries in international trade; (v) an undertaking to bring agriculture more fully into the multilateral trading system; to this end a Committee on Trade in Agriculture is to be established to carry out a major two-year work programme in this area; (vi) an undertaking to bring into effect quickly a comprehensive understanding on safeguards to be based on the principles of the General Agreement.

The Ministerial declaration also included decisions to improve the GATT procedures for settling trade disputes between members, to study such issues as trade in certain natural resource products, and to exchange information through GATT on international trade in services.

To assist the trade of developing countries, GATT established in 1964 the International Trade Centre (since 1968 operated jointly with the UN Conference on Trade and Development) to provide information and training on export markets and marketing techniques. Other GATT action in favour of developing countries includes training courses on trade policy questions.

Budget for 1982: Sw. Frs. 45·5m.

Headquarters: Centre William Rappard, 154 rue de Lausanne, 1211 Geneva 21, Switzerland.

Director-General: Arthur Dunkel (Switzerland).

Publications. Basic Instruments and Selected Documents. 4 vols. and 28 supplements 1952–82.—*International Trade* [i.e., annual review], 1952 ff. Annually from 1953.—*GATT, What It Is, What It Does* (1982).—*GATT Activities,* 1960 ff. Annually from 1972.—*GATT Focus.* Monthly from Feb. 1981.—*GATT Studies in International Trade.* 1971 ff. (irregular series).—*The Tokyo Round of Multilateral Trade Negotiations.* Report of the Director-General, 2 vols., 1979

Casadio, G. P., *Transatlantic Trade: USA–EEC Confrontation in the GATT Negotiations.* Farnborough, 1973

Dam, K. W., *The GATT: Law and International Economic Organization.* Chicago and London, 1970

Golt, S., *The GATT Negotiations, 1973–75: A Guide to the Issues.* London, 1974

Hudec, R. E., *The GATT Legal System and World Trade Diplomacy.* New York, 1975

Jackson, J. H., *World Trade and the Law of GATT: A Legal Analysis of the General Agreement on Tariffs and Trade.* New York, 1969

WORLD INTELLECTUAL PROPERTY ORGANIZATION (WIPO)

Origin. The Convention establishing WIPO was signed at Stockholm in 1967 by 51 countries, and entered into force in April 1970. In Dec. 1974 WIPO became a specialized agency of the UN.

Objectives. The objectives of WIPO are to promote the protection of intellectual property throughout the world through co-operation among States and, where appropriate, in collaboration with any other international organization, and to ensure administrative co-operation among the Unions established by various treaties for the protection of intellectual property. The Convention provides expressly for the encouragement of the conclusion of international agreements designed to promote the protection of intellectual property, and for the provision of legal-technical assistance at the request of States.

Intellectual property includes the rights relating to: literary, artistic and scientific works; performances of performing artists, phonograms and broadcasts; inventions in all fields of human endeavour; scientific discoveries; industrial designs; trademarks, service marks and commercial names and designations; protection against unfair competition and all other rights resulting from intellectual activity in the industrial, scientific, literary or artistic fields.

Membership in WIPO is open to any State which is a member of at least one of the Unions and to other States which are members of the organizations of the United Nations system, are party to the Statute of the International Court of Justice, or are invited to join by the General Assembly of WIPO. Membership of the Unions is open to any State. The total combined membership of WIPO and of the Unions on 31 Dec. 1982, was 120 states.

Organization. The bodies of WIPO are: The *General Assembly* consisting of all States members of WIPO which are members of any of the Unions. Among its other functions, the General Assembly appoints and gives instructions to the Director General, reviews and approves his reports and adopts the biennial budget of expenses common to the Unions. The *Conference,* consisting of all States members of WIPO whether or not they are members of any of the Unions. Among its other functions, the Conference adopts its biennial budget and establishes the biennial programme of legal-technical assistance. The *Co-ordination Committee,* consisting of the States members of WIPO which are members of the Executive Committees of the Paris or Berne Unions.

In addition, the Paris and Berne Unions have Assemblies and Executive Committees, with functions similar to those of the WIPO bodies in respect of the biennial and annual budgets and programmes of the Unions.

Headquarters: 34, chemin des Colombettes, 1211 Geneva 20, Switzerland.
Director General: Arpad Bogsch (USA).

Principal publications. Industrial Property (monthly, in English and French).—*Copyright* (monthly, in English and French).—*Les Marques internationales* (monthly, in French).—*Manuals and Brochures of Conventions and Agreements.*—*Collections of Laws and Treaties.*—*Model Laws for Developing Countries on Inventions, on Marks Trade Names and Acts of Unfair Competition on Designs on Copyright and on Neighbouring Rights* (in English, French and Spanish).—*Licensing Guide for Developing Countries* (in Arabic, Chinese, English, French and Spanish).—*Glossaries – industrial property and copyright* (multilingual).—*Guide to the Berne Convention* (in Arabic, English, French, German, Hindi, Japanese, Portuguese, Russian, Spanish).—*Guide to the Rome and Phonograms Convention* (in English, French and Spanish).

INTERNATIONAL FUND FOR AGRICULTURAL DEVELOPMENT (IFAD)

The establishment of IFAD was one of the major actions proposed by the 1974 World Food Conference. The agreement for IFAD entered into force on 30 Nov. 1977 following attainment of initial pledges of $1,000m. and the agency began its operations the following month. IFAD's purpose is to mobilise additional funds for agricultural and rural development in developing countries through projects and programmes directly benefitting the poorest rural population. In line with the Fund's focus on the rural poor, its resources are being made available in highly concessional loans.

Organization. The Governing Council, consisting of the entire membership, directs the Fund's operations. The chief executive is the President, who is also the Chairman of the 18-member Executive Board.

President: Abdelmuhsin Al-Sudeary (Saudi Arabia)
Headquarters: 107 Via del Serafico, Rome, Italy.

THE COMMONWEALTH

The Commonwealth is a free association of sovereign independent nations, numbering 47 at the end of 1983. There is no charter, treaty or constitution; the association is expressed in co-operation, consultation and mutual assistance for which the Commonwealth Secretariat is the central co-ordinating organization.

The Commonwealth was first defined by the Imperial Conference of 1926 as a group of 'autonomous communities within the British Empire, equal in status, in no way subordinate one to another in any aspect of their domestic or foreign affairs, though united by a common allegiance to the Crown, and freely associated as members of the British Commonwealth of Nations'. The basis of the association changed from one owing allegiance to a common Crown, and the modern Commonwealth was born in 1949, when the member countries accepted India's intention of becoming a republic at the same time continuing 'her full membership of the Commonwealth of Nations and her acceptance of the King as the symbol of the free association of its independent member nations and as such the Head of the Commonwealth'. There are now (1983) 17 Queen's realms, 26 republics, and 4 other monarchies in the Commonwealth. All acknowledge the Queen symbolically as Head of the Commonwealth.

The Queen's legal title rests on the statute of 12 and 13 Will. III, c. 3, by which the succession to the Crown of Great Britain and Ireland was settled on the Princess Sophia of Hanover and the 'heirs of her body being Protestants'. By proclamation of 17 July 1917 the royal family became known as the House and Family of Windsor. On 8 Feb. 1960 the Queen issued a declaration varying her confirmatory declaration of 9 April 1952 to the effect that while the Queen and her children should continue to be known as the House of Windsor, her descendants, other than descendants entitled to the style of Royal Highness and the title of Prince or Princess, and female descendants who marry and their descendants should bear the name of Mountbatten-Windsor. The Royal Style and Titles of Queen Elizabeth are: In *Antigua and Barbuda* 'Elizabeth the Second, by the Grace of God, Queen of Antigua and Barbuda and of Her other Realms and Territories, Head of the Commonwealth'. In *Australia*: 'Elizabeth the Second, by the Grace of God Queen of Australia and Her other Realms and Territories, Head of the Commonwealth'. In the *Bahamas*: 'Elizabeth the Second, by the Grace of God, Queen of the Commonwealth of the Bahamas and of Her other Realms and Territories, Head of the Commonwealth'. In *Barbados*: 'Elizabeth the Second, by the Grace of God, Queen of Barbados and of Her other Realms and Territories, Head of the Commonwealth'. In *Belize*: 'Elizabeth the Second, by the Grace of God, Queen of Belize and of Her other Realms and Territories, Head of the Commonwealth'. In *Canada*: 'Elizabeth the Second, by the Grace of God of the United Kingdom, Canada and Her other Realms and Territories Queen, Head of the Commonwealth, Defender of the Faith'. In *Fiji*: 'Elizabeth the Second, by the Grace of God, Queen of Fiji and of Her other Realms and Territories, Head of the Commonwealth'. In *Grenada*: 'Elizabeth the Second, by the Grace of God, Queen of the United Kingdom of Great Britain and Northern Ireland and of Grenada and Her other Realms and Territories, Head of the Commonwealth'. In *Jamaica*: 'Elizabeth the Second, by the Grace of God of Jamaica and of Her other Realms and Territories Queen, Head of the Commonwealth'. In *Mauritius*: 'Elizabeth the Second, Queen of Mauritius and of Her other Realms and Territories, Head of the Commonwealth'. In *New Zealand*: 'Elizabeth the Second, by the Grace of God Queen of New Zealand and Her Other Realms and Territories, Head of the Commonwealth, Defender of the Faith'. In *Papua New Guinea*: 'Elizabeth the Second, Queen of Papua New Guinea and Her other Realms and Territories, Head of the Commonwealth'. In *Saint Lucia*: 'Elizabeth the Second, by the Grace of God, Queen of Saint Lucia and of Her other Realms and Territories, Head of Commonwealth'. In *Saint Vincent and the Grenadines*: 'Elizabeth the Second, by the Grace of God, Queen of Saint Vincent and the Grenadines and of Her other Realms and Territories, Head of the Commonwealth'. In *Solomon Islands*: 'Elizabeth the Second by the Grace of God Queen of Solomon Islands and of Her other Realms and Territories, Head of the Commonwealth'. In *Tuvalu*: 'Elizabeth the Second by the Grace of God, Queen of Tuvalu and of Her other Realms and Territories, Head of the Commonwealth'. In the *United Kingdom*: 'Elizabeth the Second, by the Grace of God of the United Kingdom of Great Britain and Northern

Ireland and of Her other Realms and Territories Queen, Head of the Commonwealth, Defender of the Faith'.

A number of territories, formerly under British jurisdiction or mandate did not join the Commonwealth: Egypt, Iraq, Transjordan, Burma, Palestine, Sudan, British Somaliland, South Cameroons, and Aden. Two countries, the Republic of South Africa in 1961 and Pakistan in 1972, have left the Commonwealth.

Maldives, Nauru, Tuvalu and Saint Vincent and the Grenadines are special members, with the right to participate in all functional Commonwealth meetings and activities but not to attend meetings of Commonwealth Heads of Government.

Member States. The following are the member countries, with their dates of independence, and, where appropriate, the date on which they became republics: *United Kingdom*; *Canada* 1 July 1867; *Australia* 1 Jan. 1901; *New Zealand* 26 Sept. 1907; *India* 15 Aug. 1947 and became a Republic on 26 Jan. 1950; *Sri Lanka* 4 Feb. 1948 (Republic on 22 May 1972); *Ghana* 6 March 1957 (Republic on 1 July 1960); *Malaysia* 31 Aug. 1957 as Federation of Malaya, 16 Sept. 1963 as Federation of Malaysia; *Cyprus* 16 Aug. 1960 (Republic on independence); *Nigeria* 1 Oct. 1960 (Republic on 1 Oct. 1963); *Sierra Leone* 27 April 1961 (Republic 19 April 1971); *Tanzania*–Tanganyika 9 Dec. 1961 (Republic 9 Dec. 1962), Zanzibar 10 Dec. 1963 (Republic on independence), United Republic of Tanganyika and Zanzibar 26 April 1964; renamed Tanzania 29 Oct. 1964; *Western Samoa* 1 Jan. 1962; *Jamaica* 6 Aug. 1962; *Trinidad and Tobago* 31 Aug. 1962 (Republic on 1 Aug. 1976); *Uganda* 9 Oct. 1962 (Republic 8 Sept. 1967, second republic 25 Jan. 1971); *Kenya* 12 Dec. 1963 (Republic on 12 Dec. 1964); *Malawi* 6 July 1964 (Republic on 6 July 1966); *Malta* 21 Sept. 1964 (Republic on 13 Dec. 1974); *Zambia* 24 Oct. 1964 (Republic on independence); *The Gambia* 18 Feb. 1965 (Republic on 24 April 1970); *Singapore* 16 Sept. 1963 as a state in the Federation of Malaysia, 9 Aug. 1965 as an independent state and republic not part of Malaysia; *Guyana* 26 May 1966 (Republic on 23 Feb. 1970); *Botswana* 30 Sept. 1966 (Republic on independence); *Lesotho* 4 Oct. 1966; *Barbados* 30 Nov. 1966; *Nauru* 31 Jan. 1968 (Republic on independence); *Mauritius* 12 March 1968; *Swaziland* 6 Sept. 1968; *Tonga* 4 June 1970; *Fiji* 10 Oct. 1970; *Bangladesh* seceded from Pakistan 16 Dec. 1971, recognized by United Kingdom 4 Feb. 1972; *Bahamas* 10 July 1973; *Grenada* 7 Feb. 1974; *Papua New Guinea* 16 Sept. 1975; *Seychelles* 29 June 1976 (Republic on independence); *Solomon Islands* 7 July 1978; *Tuvalu* 1 Oct. 1978; *Dominica* 3 Nov. 1978 (Republic on independence); *Saint Lucia* 22 Feb. 1979; *Kiribati* 12 July 1979 (Republic on independence); *Saint Vincent and the Grenadines* 27 Oct. 1979; *Zimbabwe* 18 April 1980 (Republic on independence); *Vanuatu* 30 July 1980 (Republic on independence); *Belize* 21 Sept. 1981; *Antigua* and *Barbuda* 1 Nov. 1981; Maldives (Republic on Independence) July 1982.

Associated States. The Caribbean islands of Antigua, St Christopher–Nevis–Anguilla, Dominica, Grenada and Saint Lucia entered into a new form of association with Britain in Feb. 1967. St Vincent became an associated state on 27 Oct. 1969. Each had control of its internal affairs, with the right to amend its own constitution (including the power to end the associated status and declare itself independent). Britain continued to be responsible for external affairs and defence. Grenada became independent, within the Commonwealth, on 7 Feb. 1974, Dominica on 3 Nov. 1978, Saint Lucia on 22 Feb. 1979, Saint Vincent and the Grenadines on 27 Oct. 1979 and Antigua and Barbuda on 1 Nov. 1981, which means that there is (Dec. 1981) one remaining associated state, *viz.* St Christopher–Nevis due for independence in Sept. 1983. The Cook Islands and Niue are similarly associated with New Zealand.

An Act of the UK Parliament, the Anguilla Act (which came into effect on 19 Dec. 1980, formally separated Anguilla from the Associated State of St Christopher–Nevis–Anguilla, Anguilla thus now has *de jure* the status of a separate dependency which it has enjoyed *de facto* since 1969.

Dependent Territories. There are 13 British dependent territories, 6 Australian dependent territories and 2 New Zealand dependent territories. A dependent territory is a territory belonging by settlement, conquest or annexation to the British, Australian or New Zealand Crown.

United Kingdom dependent territories administered through the Foreign and Commonwealth Office comprise, in the Far East: Hong Kong; in the Indian Ocean: British Indian Ocean Territory; in the Mediterranean: Gibraltar; in the Atlantic Ocean: Bermuda, Falkland Islands and dependencies South Georgia and South Sandwich Islands, British Antarctic Territory, St Helena and dependencies of Ascension and Tristan da Cunha; in the Caribbean: Montserrat, British Virgin Islands, Cayman Islands, Turks and Caicos Islands, Anguilla *(see above)*; in the Western Pacific: Pitcairn. The Australian dependent territories are: Coral Sea Islands Territory, Cocos (Keeling) Islands, Christmas Island, Heard and McDonald Islands, Norfolk Island and the Australian Antarctic Territory. The New Zealand dependent territories are: Tokelau Islands and Ross Dependency.

While constitutional responsibility to Parliament for the government of the British dependent territories rests with the Secretary of State for Foreign and Commonwealth Affairs, the administration of the territories is carried out by the Governments of the territories themselves.

Brunei is a sovereign state in treaty relationship with Great Britain, whereby Great Britain is responsible for the conduct of external affairs and has a consultative responsibility for defence. It has never been a dependent territory, and in 1971 ceased to be a protected state. A Treaty of Friendship and Co-operation was signed on 7 Jan. 1979, becoming effective on 31 Dec. 1983 when Brunei will assume her full international responsibilities and Britain will give up her consultative commitment over defence matters.

British Government Department. With effect from 17 Oct. 1968, the Secretary of State for Foreign and Commonwealth Affairs is responsible for the conduct of relations with members of the Commonwealth as well as with foreign countries, and for the administration of British dependent territories.

Commonwealth Secretariat. The Commonwealth Secretariat is an international body at the service of all 47 member countries. It provides the central organization for joint consultation and co-operation in many fields. It was established in 1965 by Commonwealth Heads of Government and has observer status at the UN General Assembly.

The Secretariat disseminates information on matters of common concern, organizes and services meetings and conferences, co-ordinates many Commonwealth activities, and provides expert technical assistance for economic and social development through the multilateral Commonwealth Fund for Technical Co-operation. The Secretariat is organized in divisions and sections which correspond to its main areas of operation: International affairs, economic affairs, food production and rural development, youth, education, information, applied studies in government, science and technology, law and health. Within this structure the Secretariat organizes the biennial meetings of Commonwealth Heads of Government, annual meetings of Finance Ministers of member countries, and regular meetings of Ministers of Education, Law, Health, and others as appropriate.

To emphasize the multilateral nature of the association, meetings are held in different cities and regions within the Commonwealth. Heads of Government decided that the Secretariat should work from London as it has the widest range of communications of any Commonwealth city, as well as the largest assembly of diplomatic missions.

The Commonwealth Secretary-General, who has access to Heads of Government, is the head of the Secretariat which is staffed by officers from member countries and financed by contributions from member governments.

Headquarters: Marlborough House, Pall Mall, London, SW1Y 5HX.
Secretary-General: Shridath S. Ramphal (Guyana).

Books of Reference

Year-Book of the Commonwealth, HMSO, 1983
The Cambridge History of the British Empire. 8 vols. CUP, 1929 ff.

Economic Survey of the Colonial Territories. 7 vols. HMSO. 1952 ff.
Ball, M., *The Open Commonwealth.* Duke Univ. Press, 1971
Bradley, K. (ed.), *The Living Commonwealth.* London, 1961
Burns, Sir Alan, *In Defence of Colonies.* London, 1957
Chadwick, J., *The Unofficial Commonwealth,* London, 1982
Garner, J., *The Commonwealth Office, 1925–1968.* London, 1978
Grierson, E., *The Imperial Dream.* London, 1972
Griffiths, Sir P., *Empire into Commonwealth.* London, 1969
Hailey, Lord, *An African Survey.* Rev. ed. Oxford, 1957.—*Native Administration in the British African Territories.* 5 vols. HMSO, 1951 ff.
Hall, H. D., *Commonwealth: A History of the British Commonwealth.* London and New York, 1971
Holland, R. F., *Britain and the Commonwealth Alliance 1918–39.* London, 1981
Ingram, D. T., *The Commonwealth at Work.* London, 1969.—*The Imperfect Commonwealth.* London, 1977
Keeton, G. W. (ed.), *The British Commonwealth: Its Laws and Constitutions.* 9 vols. London, 1951 ff.
McIntyre, W. D., *The Commonwealth of Nations: Origins and Impact 1869–1971.* Univ. of Minnesota Press and OUP, 1978
Mansbergh, N., *The Commonwealth Experience.* Rev. ed. London, 1982
Maxwell, W. H. and L. F., *A Legal Bibliography of the British Commonwealth of Nations.* 2nd ed. London, 1956
Roberts-Wray, K., *Commonwealth and Colonial Law.* London, 1966
Smith, T. E., *Commonwealth Migration: Flows and Policies.* London, 1981
Wade, E. C. S., and Phillips, G. G., *Constitutional Law: An Outline of the Law and Practice of the Constitution, Including Central and Local Government and the Constitutional Relations of the British Commonwealth and Empire.* 8th ed. London, 1970
Walker, A., *The Modern Commonwealth.* London, 1976.—*A New Look at the Commonwealth.* Oxford, 1977
Wheare, K. C., *The Statute of Westminster and Dominion Status.* 5th ed. Oxford, 1953.—*Constitutional Structure of the Commonwealth.* Oxford, 1960

WORLD COUNCIL OF CHURCHES

The World Council of Churches was formally constituted on 23 Aug. 1948, at Amsterdam, by an assembly representing 147 churches from 44 countries. By 1980 the member churches numbered nearly 300, from over 100 countries.

The basis of membership (1975) states: 'The World Council of Churches is a fellowship of Churches which confess the Lord Jesus Christ as God and Saviour according to the Scriptures and therefore seek to fulfil together their common calling to the glory of the one God, Father, Son and Holy Spirit.' Membership is open to Churches which express their agreement with this basis and satisfy such criteria as the Assembly or Central Committee may prescribe. Today 271 Churches of Protestant, Anglican, Orthodox, Old Catholic and Pentecostal confessions belong to this fellowship.

The World Council was founded by the coming together of several diverse Christian movements. These included the overseas mission groups gathered from 1921 in the International Missionary Council, the Faith and Order Movement founded by American Episcopal Bishop Charles Brent, and the Life and Work Movement led by Swedish Lutheran Archbishop Nathan Söderblom.

On 13 May 1938 at Utrecht a provisional committee was appointed to prepare for the formation of a World Council of Churches. It was under the chairmanship of William Temple, then Archbishop of York.

Assembly. The governing body of the World Council, consisting of delegates specially appointed by the member Churches. It meets every 6 or 7 years to frame policy and to consider some main theme. The Assembly has no legislative powers and depends for the implementation of its decisions upon the action of the member Churches. Assemblies have been held in Amsterdam (1948), Evanston (1954), New Delhi (1961), Uppsala (1968), and Nairobi (1975). The next is to be held in Vancouver, Canada in 1983 under the theme 'Jesus Christ: the Life of the World'. In between assemblies, a 134-member Central Committee meets annually to carry out the assembly mandate, with a smaller 26-member Executive Committee meeting twice a year.

Presidents. Hon. President: The Rev. Dr W. A. Visser't Hooft. *Presidium:* Mrs Justice A. R. Jiagge (Ghana), Prof. José Miguez-Bonino (Argentina), Dr T. B. Simatupang (Indonesia), Most Rev. Olof Sundby (Sweden), Dr Cynthia Wedel (USA), His Holiness Ilyia II (USSR).

WCC programmes are organized from headquarters in Geneva, Switzerland by a staff of 300 and a range of supervisory committees drawn from member churches. The 3 programme units are:

(i) Justice and Service which includes Inter-Church Aid, Refugee and World Service (channelling over $30m. from member churches to areas of need); the Commission on the Churches' Participation in Development; the Commission of the Churches on International Affairs, the Programme to Combat Racism and the Christian Medical Commission.

(ii) Education and Renewal includes sections dealing with renewal and congregational life, women, youth, church-related education, biblical studies, family ministry and the Programme on Theological Education.

(iii) Faith and Witness includes the Commission on Faith and Order, World Mission and Evangelism, Church and Society and the sub-unit on Dialogue with People of Living Faiths and Ideologies.

A General Secretariat with a Communication Department, finance and central services co-ordinates the work of these 3 units.

Since 1975 the WCC has held several major world conferences on such diverse themes as 'Faith, Science and the Future', 'Your Kingdom Come', 'Family Power and Social Change', 'Strategies for Churches Combating Racism in the 1980's', 'The Community of Women and Men in the Church' and 'Giving an Account of the Hope that is in Us'.

Officers of the Central and Executive Committees: *Moderator:* The Most Rev. Edward W. Scott (Canada). *Vice-Moderators:* His Holiness Karekin II (Lebanon); Jean Skuse (Australia). *General Secretary:* The Rev. Dr Philip A. Potter.

Office: PO Box 66, 150 route de Ferney, 1211 Geneva 20, Switzerland.

The British Council of Churches, which is an associated national council of the World Council, acts as agent for the WCC in the UK.

Books of Reference

Official Reports: The First [. . . *etc.*] *Assembly* (London, 1948, 1955, 1962, Geneva, 1968)
New Delhi to Uppsala 1961–68. Geneva, 1968
Uppsala to Nairobi 1968–75. Geneva, 1975
Official Reports of the Faith and Order Conferences at Lausanne 1927, Edinburgh 1937, Lund 1952, Montreal 1963, Meeting of Faith and Order Commission, Louvain 1971, Accra 1974, Bangalore 1978
Official Reports of the Life and Work Conferences at Stockholm 1925 and Oxford 1937; World Conference on Church and Society 1966
Minutes of the Central Committee. Geneva, 1949 to date
Howell, L., *Acting in Faith: The World Council of Churches since 1975.* London, 1982
Hudson, D., *The World Council of Churches in International Affairs.* Leighton Buzzard, 1977
Paton, D. M., *Breaking Barriers—Nairobi 1975.* London, 1976
Potter, P., *Life in all its Fullness.* Geneva, 1981
van der Bent, A. J., *What in the World is the World Council of Churches?* Geneva, 1978.—*Handbook of Member Churches of the World Council of Churches* (annual)

INTERNATIONAL TRADE UNIONISM

There are three main international trade union confederations *(i)* the International Confederation of Free Trade Unions (ICFTU) which has in membership most of the national trade union confederations in the Western industrialized countries as well as democratic organizations in Asia, Africa, and Latin America; *(ii)* the World

Federation of Trade Unions (WFTU) which draws its support mainly from Eastern Europe, but which also has affiliates in France and in several developing countries; and *(iii)* the World Confederation of Labour (WCL) which has affiliates in Western Europe, Latin America and a small number of African and Asian countries. In addition, national trade unions are frequently members of international trade union federations, set up to protect the interests of working people in particular industries or trades, which are associated with the international confederations. The International Trade Secretariats (ITS) are associated with the ICFTU; Trade Union Internationals (TUI) with the WFTU; and the International Trade Federations (ITF) with the WCL.

Coldrick, A. P., and Jones, P., *International Directory of the Trade Union Movement.* London, 1979

History. The international trade union structure in 1982 was shaped mainly by developments since 1945. In that year the WFTU was set up with world-wide membership. Attempts by trade unions in Eastern Europe to turn the WFTU into an organization voicing unquestioning support for the policies of the USSR led to most of the affiliates in the Western European countries to break away from the WFTU and from the ICFTU in 1949.

EUROPEAN TRADE UNION CONFEDERATION. In Feb. 1973 the European Trade Union Confederation was formed by trade unionists in 15 Western European countries to deal with questions of interest to European working people arising inside and outside the EEC. All the founding organizations were ICFTU affiliates but subsequently they accepted into membership European WCL affiliates, the Irish Congress of Trade Unions and the Italian Communist trade union centre (CGIL) and other national organizations. The ETUC Congress meets every 3 years and the Executive Committee 6 times a year. The membership is now about 40m. from 34 centres in 18 countries.

General Secretary: Mathias Hinterscheid.
Headquarters: Rue Montagne aux Herbes Potagères 37, 1000 Brussels.

INTERNATIONAL CONFEDERATION OF FREE TRADE UNIONS. The first congress of ICFTU was held in London in Dec. 1949. The constitution as amended provides for co-operation with the United Nations and the International Labour Organization and for regional organizations to promote free trade unionism, especially in less-developed countries.

Organization. The Congress meets every 4 years. It elects the Executive Board of 29 members nominated on an area basis for a 4-year period; the Board meets at least twice a year. Various committees cover policy *vis-à-vis* such problems as those connected with Atomic Energy and also the administration of the International Solidarity Fund. There are joint ICFTU–ITS committees for co-ordinating activities and also for women workers' problems.

Headquarters: 37–41, rue Montagne aux Herbes Potagères, Brussels 1000, Belgium.

General Secretary: Otto Kersten.

Regional organizations exist in America, offices in Mexico City and Caracas; Asia, offices in New Delhi and Singapore.

Membership. The ICFTU has 126 affiliated organizations in 94 countries, which together represent about 85m. workers. The biggest groups were the American Federation of Labor and Congress of Industrial Organizations (13·5m.), the British Trades Union Congress (11·6m.), the Federal German Deutscher Gewerkschaftsbund (7·8m.), the Confederazione Italiana Sindacati Lavoratori (2·1m.), the Swedish Landsorganisationen (2m.), the Canadian Labour Congress (1·3m.), the Österreichischer Gewerkschaftsbund (1·6m.), the Belgian General Federation of Labour (900,000), the Indian National Trade Union Congress (3·2m.), Australian

Council of Trade Unions (2m.), Japanese Confederation of Labour, Domei (1·4m.).

Publications (in 4 languages). *Free Labour World* (bi-monthly); *International Trade Union News* (fortnightly); *Economic and Social Bulletin* (bi-monthly).

THE WORLD FEDERATION OF TRADE UNIONS. The WFTU formally came into existence on 3 Oct. 1945, representing trade-union organizations in more than 50 countries of the world, both Communist and non-Communist, excluding Federal Republic of Germany and Japan, as well as a number of lesser and colonial territories. Representation from the USA was limited to the Congress of Industrial Organizations, as the American Federation of Labor declined to participate.

In Jan. 1949 the British, USA and Netherlands trade unions withdrew from WFTU, which had come under complete Communist control; and by June 1951 all non-Communist trade-unions, and the Yugoslavian Federation, had left WFTU.

Organization. The Congress meets every 4 years. In between, the General Council, of 134 members (including deputies), is the governing body, meeting (in theory) at least once a year. The Bureau controls the activities of WFTU between meetings of the General Council; it consists of the President, the General Secretary and members from different continents, the total number being decided at each Congress. The Bureau is elected by the General Council.

General Secretary: I. Zakaria (Sudan).

Membership. A total membership of 180m. from 71 national centres is claimed. The biggest groups are the Soviet All-Union Central Council of Trade Unions (107m.), the German Democratic Republic Free German Trade Union Federation (8m.), the Czechoslovak Central Council of Trade Unions (6m.), the Romanian General Confederation of Labour (6·4m.), the Hungarian Central Council of Trade Unions (4·5m.) and the French Confederation of Labour (CGT, 2m.).

Publications. World Trade Union Movement (monthly, in 9 languages); *Trade Union Press* (fortnightly, in 6 languages).

WORLD CONFEDERATION OF LABOUR. The first congress of the International Federation of Christian Trade Unions (IFCTU), as the WCL was then called, met in 1920; but a large proportion of its 3·4m. members were in Italy and Germany, where affiliated unions were suppressed by the Fascist and Nazi régimes, and in 1940 IFCTU went out of existence. It was reconstituted in 1945, and declined to merge with WFTU and, later, with ICFTU. The policy of IFCTU was based on the papal encyclicals *Rerum novarum* (1891) and *Quadragesimo anno* (1931), but in 1968, when the Federation became the WCL, it was broadened to include other concepts. The WCL now has Protestant, Buddhist and Moslem members as well as its mainly Roman Catholic members.

Organization. The WCL is organized on a federative basis which leaves wide discretion to its autonomous constituent unions. Its governing body is the Congress, which meets every 4 years. The Congress appoints (or re-appoints) the Secretary-General at each 4-yearly meeting. The General Council which meets at least once a year, is composed of the members of the Confederal Board (at least 22 members, elected by the Congress) and representatives of national confederations, international trade federations, and trade union organizations where there is no confederation affiliated to the WCL. The Confederal Board is responsible for the general leadership of the WCL, in accordance with the decisions and directives of the Council and Congress. Headquarters: 71 rue Joseph II, Brussels 1040, Belgium.

Secretary-General: Jan Kulakowski.

There are regional organizations in Latin America (office in Caracas), Africa (office in Banjul, Gambia) and Asia (office in Manila) There is also a liaison centre in Montreal.

Membership. A total membership of 14m. in about 90 countries is claimed. The biggest group is the Confederation of Christian Trade Unions of Belgium (1·1m.).

Publication. Labour Press and Information (11 each year, in 5 languages).

ORGANISATION FOR ECONOMIC CO-OPERATION AND DEVELOPMENT (OECD)

History and Membership. On 30 Sept. 1961 the Organisation for European Economic Co-operation (OEEC), after a history of 14 years (*see* THE STATESMAN'S YEAR-BOOK, 1961, p. 32), was replaced by the Organisation for Economic Co-operation and Development. The change of title marks the Organisation's altered status and functions: with the accession of Canada and USA as full members it ceased to be a purely European body; while at the same time it added development aid to the list of its other activities. The member countries are now Australia, Austria, Belgium, Canada, Denmark, Federal Republic of Germany, Finland, France, Greece, Iceland, Ireland, Italy, Japan, Luxembourg, the Netherlands, New Zealand, Norway, Portugal, Spain, Sweden, Switzerland, Turkey, UK and USA. Yugoslavia participates in the Organisation's activities with a special status. The Commission of the European Communities generally takes part in OECD's work.

Objectives. To promote economic and social welfare throughout the OECD area by assisting its member governments in the formulation of policies designed to this end and by co-ordinating these policies; and to stimulate and harmonize its members' efforts in favour of developing countries.

Organs. The supreme body of the Organisation is the Council composed of one representative for each member country. It meets either at Heads of Delegations level (about once a week) under the Chairmanship of the Secretary-General, or at Ministerial level (usually once a year) under the Chairmanship of a Minister elected annually. Decisions and Recommendations are adopted by mutual agreement of all members of the Council.

The Council is assisted by an Executive Committee composed of 14 members of the Council designated annually by the latter. The major part of the Organisation's work is, however, prepared and carried out in numerous specialized committees and working parties and sub-groups, of which there exist over 200. Thus, the Organisation comprises Committees for Economic Policy; Economic and Development Review; Development Assistance (DAC); Trade; Capital Movements and Invisible Transactions; Financial Markets; Fiscal Affairs; Restrictive Business Practices; Maritime Transport; International Investment and Multinational Enterprises; Tourism; Energy Policy; Industry; Steel; Scientific and Technological Policy; Information, Computer and Communications Policy; Education; Manpower and Social Affairs; Environment; Agriculture; Fisheries, etc. Moreover there exists a High-Level Group on Commodities and a Group on North-South Economic Issues.

Four autonomous or semi-autonomous bodies also belong to the Organisation: the International Energy Agency (IEA); the Nuclear Energy Agency (NEA); the Development Centre and the Centre for Educational Research and Innovation (CERI). Each one of these bodies has its own governing committee.

The Council, the committees and the other bodies are serviced by an international Secretariat headed by the Secretary-General of the Organisation.

All member countries have established permanent Delegations to OECD, each headed by an Ambassador.

Chairman of the Council (ministerial): Elected annually.
Chairman of the Council (official level): The Secretary-General.
Chairman of the Executive Committee: Hervé Robinet (Belgium).
Secretary-General: Emile van Lennep (Netherlands).

Deputy Secretaries-General: Jacob M. Myerson (USA), Paul Lemerle (France).

Executive Director of the International Energy Agency: Ulf Lantzke (Federal Republic of Germany).

Headquarters: Château de la Muette, 2, rue André Pascal, 75775 Paris Cedex 16, France.

OECD publishes numerous reports and statistical papers. Regular features include:
Activities of OECD. Annual, from 1972
News from OECD. Monthly
Main Economic Indicators. Monthly, from 1965
The OECD Observer. Bi-monthly, from 1962
The OECD Economic Outlook. 1966 ff.
OEEC/OECD Economic Surveys of Member Countries. 1954 ff.
European Nuclear Energy Agency, Activity Report. 1959 ff.
The Flow of Financial Resources to Countries in Course of Economic Development. 1960 ff.
Development Assistance Efforts and Policies. 1962 ff.
Tourism Policy and International Tourism in OECD Member Countries. 1955 ff.
Energy Policies and Programmes of the IEA Member Countries. 1977 ff.

NORTH ATLANTIC TREATY ORGANIZATION (NATO)

Western perceptions of the political situation in Europe following World War II gave rise, in 1947, to 2 major US initiatives – the Truman Doctrine and the Marshall Plan. These policies were designed to increase the ability of Western European countries to resist outside pressure and to assist them in bringing about their economic recovery. By 1948, on the initiative of the Foreign Secretary of the UK Ernest Bevin, 5 Western European nations had also entered into a treaty of mutual assistance in which they pledged themselves to come to each other's aid in the event of armed aggression against them (Brussels Treaty, 17 March 1948). The idea of a single mutual defence system involving North America as well as the European signatories of the Brussels Treaty was put forward by the Canadian Secretary of State for External Affairs in April 1948. It led, *via* the Vandenberg Resolution which enabled the US constitutionally to participate, to the creation of the Atlantic Alliance.

On 4 April 1949 the foreign ministers of Belgium, Canada, Denmark, France, Iceland, Italy, Luxembourg, the Netherlands, Norway, Portugal, the UK and the USA met in Washington and signed a treaty, the main clauses of which read as follows:

Article 1. The parties undertake, as set forth in the Charter of the United Nations, to settle any international disputes in which they may be involved by peaceful means in such a manner that international peace and security and justice are not endangered, and to refrain in their international relations from the threat or use of force in any manner inconsistent with the purposes of the United Nations.

Article 2. The parties will contribute toward the further development of peaceful and friendly international relations by strengthening their free institutions, by bringing about a better understanding of the principles upon which these institutions are founded, and by promoting conditions of stability and well-being. They will seek to eliminate conflict in their international economic policies and will encourage economic collaboration between any or all of them.

Article 3. In order more effectively to achieve the objectives of this treaty, the parties, separately and jointly by means of continuous and effective self-help and mutual aid, will maintain and develop their individual and collective capacity to resist armed attack.

Article 4. The parties will consult together whenever, in the opinion of any of them, the territorial integrity, political independence or security of any of the parties is threatened.

Article 5. The parties agree that an armed attack against one or more of them in Europe or North America shall be considered an attack against them all and consequently they agree that, if such an armed attack occurs, each of them, in exercise of the right of individual or collective self-defence recognized by article 51 of the Charter of the United Nations, will assist the party or parties so attacked by taking forthwith, individually and in concert with the other parties, such action as it deems necessary, including the use of armed force, to restore and maintain the security of the North Atlantic area. Any such armed attack and all measures taken as a result thereof shall immediately be reported to the Security Council. Such measures shall be terminated when the Security Council has taken the measures necessary to restore and maintain international peace and security.

Article 6. For the purpose of Article 5 an armed attack on one or more of the parties is deemed to include an armed attack *(i)* on the territory of any of the parties in Europe or North America, on the Algerian Departments of France, on the territory of Turkey or on the islands under the jurisdiction of any of the parties in the North Atlantic area north of the Tropic of Cancer; *(ii)* on the forces, vessels or aircraft of any of the parties, when in or over these territories or any other area in Europe in which occupation forces of any of the parties were stationed on the date when the treaty entered into force or the Mediterranean Sea or the North Atlantic area north of the Tropic of Cancer.

Article 8. Each party declares that none of the international engagements now in force between it and any other of the parties or any third state is in conflict with the provisions of this treaty, and undertakes not to enter into any international engagement in conflict with this treaty.

Article 10. The parties may, by unanimous agreement, invite any other European state in a position to further the principles of this treaty and to contribute to the security of the North Atlantic area to accede to this treaty. Any state so invited may become a party to the treaty by depositing its instrument of accession with the government of the United States of America. The government of the United States of America will inform each of the parties of the deposit of each such instrument of accession.

Article 12. After the treaty has been in force for 10 years, or at any time thereafter, the parties shall, if any of them so requests, consult together for the purpose of reviewing the treaty, having regard for the factors then affecting peace and security in the North Atlantic area, including the development of universal as well as regional arrangements under the Charter of the United Nations for the maintenance of international peace and security.

Article 13. After the treaty has been in force for 20 years, any party may cease to be a party one year after its notice of denunciation has been given to the government of the United States of America, which will inform the governments of the other parties of the deposit of each notice of denunciation.

The treaty came into force on 24 Aug. 1949. Greece and Turkey were admitted as parties to the treaty in 1952, the Federal Republic of Germany in 1955 and Spain in 1982.

NATO is an organization of sovereign states equal in status. Decisions taken are expressions of the collective will of member governments arrived at by common consent.

The North Atlantic Council is composed of representatives of the 16 member countries. At Ministerial Meetings of the Council, member nations are represented by Ministers of Foreign Affairs. These meetings are held twice a year. The Council also meets on occasion at the level of Heads of State and Government. In permanent session, at the level of Ambassadors, the Council meets at least once a week.

The Defence Planning Committee is composed of representatives of the 15 member countries taking part in NATO's integrated military structure. Like the Council, it meets both in permanent session at the level of Ambassadors and twice a year at Ministerial level. At Ministerial Meetings member nations are represented by Defence Ministers.

The Council and Defence Planning Committee are chaired by the Secretary General of NATO at whatever level they meet. Opening sessions of Ministerial Meetings of the Council are presided over by the President, an honorary position held annually by the Foreign Minister of one of the member nations.

Nuclear matters are discussed by the Nuclear Planning Group in which 13 countries now participate. It meets regularly at the level of Permanent Representatives (Ambassadors) and twice a year at the level of Ministers of Defence.

The Permanent Representatives of member countries are supported by the National Delegations located at NATO Headquarters. The Delegations are composed of advisors and officials qualified to represent their countries on the various committees created by the Council. The Committees are supported by the International Staff responsible to the Secretary General.

Headquarters: 1110 Brussels, Belgium.
Secretary-General: Joseph Luns (Netherlands), appointed Oct. 1971.
Flag: Dark blue with a white compass rose of 4 points in the centre.

The *Military Committee* is responsible for making recommendations to the Council and the Defence Planning Committee on military matters and for supplying guidance to the Allied Commanders. Composed of the Chiefs-of-Staff of all member countries except France and Iceland (which has no military forces), the Committee is assisted by an International Military Staff. It meets at Chiefs-of-Staff level at least twice a year but remains in permanent session at the level of national military representatives. Liaison between the Military Committee and the French High Command is effected through the French Mission to the Military Committee. The permanent chairman of the Military Committee is elected by the Chiefs-of-Staff for a period of 2–3 years. The present chairman is Gen. Cornelis De Jager (Netherlands), appointed July 1983.

The area covered by the North Atlantic Treaty is divided among three commands: The Atlantic Ocean Command, the European Command and the Channel Command. Defence plans for the North American area are developed by the Canada–US Regional Planning Group.

The NATO commanders are responsible for the development of defence plans for their respective areas, for the determination of force requirements and for the deployment and exercise of the forces under their command.

The *Allied Command Europe* (ACE) covers the area extending from the North Cape to the Mediterranean and from the Atlantic to the eastern border of Turkey, excluding the UK and Portugal, the defence of which does not fall under any one major NATO Command. The European area, which is subdivided into a number of subordinate commands, is under the Supreme Allied Commander Europe (SACEUR) whose Headquarters, near Mons in Belgium, are known as SHAPE (Supreme Headquarters Allied Powers Europe).

SACEUR has also under his orders the ACE Mobile Force, composed of both land and air force units from different member countries, which can be ready for action at very short notice in any threatened area. The present SACEUR is Gen. Bernard W. Rogers (USA).

Under the Supreme Allied Commander Atlantic (SACLANT) the *Atlantic Command* extends from the North Pole to the Tropic of Cancer and from the coastal waters of North America to those of Europe and Africa, but excludes the Channel and the British Isles. SACLANT, who would have the primary task in wartime of ensuring the security of the sea lanes in the whole Atlantic area, is an operational rather than an administrative commander. Under his direct command is the Standing Naval Force Atlantic (STANAVFORLANT) which is a permanent international squadron of ships drawn from NATO Navies which normally operate in the Atlantic.

The present SACLANT, whose Headquarters are in Norfolk (USA), is Admiral Wesley L. McDonald (US), appointed Sept. 1982.

The *Channel Command* covers the English Channel and the southern North Sea. Under the Allied Commander-in-Chief Channel (CINCHAN) its mission is to control and protect merchant shipping in the area, co-operating with SACEUR in the air defence of the Channel. The forces earmarked to the Command in emergency are predominantly naval but include maritime air forces. CINCHAN has also under his command the NATO Standing Naval Force Channel (STANAVFORCHAN) a permanent mine counter measures force comprising ships drawn from the navies of Belgium, the Netherlands and the UK. The present CINCHAN, with Headquarters at Northwood (UK), is Admiral Sir William Staveley (UK), appointed Oct. 1982.

The *Canada–US Regional Planning Group*, which covers the North American area, develops and recommends to the Military Committee plans for the defence of this area. It meets alternately in Washington and Ottawa.

The NATO Handbook.—NATO: Facts and Figures.—The NATO Review (bi-monthly).—*Aspects of NATO.—NATO Pocket Guide.—NATO Folder.—NATO and the Warsaw Pact.—Economic and Scientific Publications.*

Hill-Norton, P., *No Soft Options: The Politico-Military Realities of NATO.* London, 1980
Kaplan, L. S., and Clawson, R. W., *NATO After Thirty Years.* Wilmington, 1981
Myers, K. A. (ed.), *NATO: The Next Twenty Years.* Boulder, 1980

WESTERN EUROPEAN UNION

On 17 March 1948 a 50-year treaty 'for collaboration in economic, social and cultural matters and for collective self-defence' was signed in Brussels by the Foreign Ministers of the UK, France, the Netherlands, Belgium and Luxembourg. (*See* THE STATESMAN'S YEAR-BOOK, 1954, pp. 32 f.)

On 20 Dec. 1950 the functions of the Western Union defence organization were transferred to the North Atlantic Treaty command, but it was decided that the reorganization of the military machinery should not affect the right of the Western Union Defence Ministers and the Chiefs of Staff to meet as they please to consider matters of mutual concern to the Brussels Treaty powers.

After the breakdown of the European Defence Community on 30 Aug. 1954 a conference was held in London from 28 Sept. to 3 Oct. 1954, attended by Belgium, Canada, France, the Federal Republic of Germany, Italy, Luxembourg, the Netherlands, the UK and the USA, at which it was decided to invite the Federal Republic of Germany and Italy to accede to the Brussels Treaty, to end the occupation of Western Germany and to invite the latter to accede to the North Atlantic Treaty; the Federal Republic agreed that it would voluntarily limit its arms production, and provision was made for the setting up of an agency to control the armaments of the 7 Brussels Treaty powers; the UK undertook not to withdraw from the Continent her 4 divisions and the Tactical Air Force assigned to the Supreme Allied Commander against the wishes of a majority, *i.e.*, 4 of the Brussels Treaty powers, except in the event of an acute overseas emergency.

At a Conference of Ministers held in Paris from 20 to 23 Oct. 1954 these decisions were embodied in 4 Protocols modifying the Brussels Treaty which were signed in Paris on 23 Oct. 1954 and came into force on 6 May 1955.

The *Council of WEU* consists of the Foreign Ministers of the 7 powers or their representatives; it is so organized as to be able to exercise its functions continuously. An *Assembly,* composed of representatives of the Brussels Treaty powers to the Consultative Assembly of the Council of Europe, meets twice a year, usually in Paris. An *Agency for the Control of Armaments* and a *Standing Armaments Committee* have been set up in Paris. The social and cultural activities were transferred to the Council of Europe on 1 June 1960.

After the breakdown of the negotiations for Britain's entry into the Common Market in 1963 the 6 EEC countries proposed to the UK that the WEU Council (the Six and the UK) should meet every 3 months 'to take stock of the political and economic situation in Europe'. The UK welcomed this proposal, and regular meetings took place. Following the re-opening of negotiations in 1970 which led to the signing of the Treaty of Accession in Jan. 1972 this arrangement has been discontinued.

Headquarters: 9 Grosvenor Place, London, SW1.
Secretary-General: Edouard F. T. Longerstaey.

COUNCIL OF EUROPE

In 1948 the 'Congress of Europe', bringing together at The Hague nearly 1,000 influential Europeans from 26 countries, called for the creation of a united Europe, including a European Assembly. This proposal, examined first by the Ministerial Council of the Brussels Treaty Organization, then by a conference of ambassadors, was at the origin of the Council of Europe, which is, with its 21 member States, the widest organization bringing together all European democracies. The Statute of the Council was signed at London on 5 May 1949 and came into force 2 months later. The founder members were Belgium, Denmark, France, Ireland, Italy, Luxembourg, the Netherlands, Norway, Sweden and the UK. Turkey and Greece joined in 1949, Iceland in 1950, the Federal Republic of Germany in 1951 (having been an associate since 1950), Austria in 1956, Cyprus in 1961, Switzerland in 1963, Malta in 1965, Portugal in 1976, Spain in 1977 and Liechtenstein in 1978.

Membership is limited to European States which 'accept the principles of the rule of law and of the enjoyment by all persons within [their] jurisdiction of human rights and fundamental freedoms'. The Statute provides for both withdrawal (Art. 7) and suspension (Arts. 8 and 9). Greece withdrew from the Council in Dec. 1969 and rejoined in Nov. 1974.

Structure. Under the Statute two organs were set up: an inter-governmental *Committee of* [*Foreign*] *Ministers* with powers of decision and of recommendation to governments, and an inter-parliamentary deliberative body, the *Parliamentary Assembly* (referred to in the Statute as the *Consultative Assembly*)—both of which are served by the Secretariat. In addition, a large number of committees of experts have been established, two of them, the Council for Cultural Co-operation and the Committee on Legal Co-operation, having a measure of autonomy; on municipal matters the Committee of Ministers receives recommendations from the Conference of Local and Regional Authorities of Europe.

The Committee of Ministers meets usually twice a year, their deputies 10 times a year.

The Parliamentary Assembly normally consists of 170 parliamentarians elected or appointed by their national parliaments (Austria 6, Belgium 7, Cyprus 3, Denmark 5, France 18, Federal Republic of Germany 18, Greece 7, Iceland 3, Ireland 4, Italy 18, Liechtenstein 2, Luxembourg 3, Malta 3, Netherlands 7, Norway 5, Portugal 7, Spain 12, Sweden 6, Switzerland 6, Turkey 12, UK 18); it meets 3 times a year for approximately a week. For domestic reasons Cyprus is not at present represented in the Assembly. The work of the Assembly is prepared by parliamentary committees.

The *Joint Committee*, which acts as an organ of co-ordination and liaison between representatives of the Committee of Ministers and members of the Parliamentary Assembly and gives members an opportunity to exchange views on matters of important European interest.

The European Convention on Human Rights, signed in 1950, set up special machinery to guarantee internationally fundamental rights and freedoms. A *European Commission* investigates alleged violations of the Convention submitted to it either by States or, in most cases, by individuals. Its findings can then be examined by the *European Court of Human Rights* (set up in 1959), whose obligatory jurisdiction has been recognized by 19 States, or by the Committee of Ministers, empowered to take binding decisions by two-thirds majority vote.

For questions of national refugees and over-population, a Special Representative has been appointed, responsible to the governments collectively.In 1956 the Resettlement Fund for National Refugees and Over-Population was created on the initiative of the special representative. With 19 member countries, the main purpose of the Fund is to give financial aid, particularly in the spheres of housing, vocational training, regional planning and regional development. Since its foundation, the total amount of loans thus granted comes to over US$1,403m. at 31 Dec. 1981.

In 1970 the Council set up a European Youth Centre where young people can discuss their own approach to international co-operation. More recently, a European Youth Foundation was created, administered by the Secretary-General, and which provides money to subsidize activities by European Youth Organizations.

Aims and Achievements. Art. 1 of the Statute states that the Council's aim is 'to achieve a greater unity between its members for the purpose of safeguarding and realising the ideals and principles which are their common heritage and facilitating their economic and social progress'; 'this aim shall be pursued . . . by discussion of questions of common concern and by agreements and common action'. The only limitation is provided by Art. 1 *(d)*, which excludes 'matters relating to national defence'.

Although without legislative powers, the Assembly acts as the power-house of the Council initiating European action in key areas by making recommendations to the Committee of Ministers. As the widest parliamentary forum in Western Europe, the Assembly also acts as the conscience of the area by voicing its opinions on important current issues. These are embodied in resolutions. The Ministers' rôle is to translate the Assembly's recommendations into action, particularly as regards lowering the barriers between the European countries, harmonizing their legislation or introducing where possible common European laws, abolishing discrimination on grounds of nationality and undertaking certain tasks on a joint European basis.

In May 1976 the first plan of intergovernmental co-operation to be undertaken by the Council of Europe was adopted by the Committee of Ministers. The second one, adopted in Dec. 1980, will run until Dec. 1986, subject to a mid-term revision in 1983. The plan takes account of political developments and progress achieved, and covers 8 key areas: human rights, social and socio-economic questions, education and culture, youth, public health, environment and regional planning, local and regional government, and legal co-operation.

More than 100 Conventions and Agreements have been concluded covering such matters as social security, patents, extradition, medical treatment, training of nurses, equivalence of degrees and diplomas, innkeepers' liability, compulsory motor insurance, the protection of television broadcasts, adoption of children, transportation of animals and *au pair* placement. In the legal field, of particular significance in 1977, was the adoption of the European Convention on the Suppression of Terrorism, as well as the European Convention on the Legal Status of Migrant Workers. In 1980 the Committee of Ministers adopted a European Convention for the protection of individuals with regard to the automatic processing of personal data. A Social Charter which came into force in 1965 sets out the social and economic rights which all member governments agree to guarantee to their citizens.

The official languages are English and French.

Chairman of the Committee of Ministers: (held in rotation).

President of the Parliamentary Assembly: José Maria de Areilza (Spain).

President of the European Court of Human Rights: Gérard J. Wiarda (Netherlands).

President of the European Commission of Human Rights: Carl Aage Nørgaard (Denmark).

Secretary-General: Franz Karasek (Austria).

Headquarters: Palais de l'Europe, 67006, Strasbourg, CEDEX, France.

Flag: Dark blue with a ring of 12 gold stars in the centre.

European Yearbook. The Hague, from 1955
Forum. Strasbourg, from 1978, 4 times a year
Guide to the Council of Europe. Strasbourg, 1982
Manual of the Council of Europe. London, 1970
Yearbook on the Convention on Human Rights. Strasbourg, from 1958
Cook, C., and Paxton, J., *European Political Facts, 1918–73.* London, 1975

EUROPEAN COMMUNITIES

In May 1950 Belgium, France, the Federal Republic of Germany, Italy, Luxembourg and the Netherlands started negotiations with the aim of ensuring continual peace by a merging of their essential interests. The negotiations culminated in the signing in 1951 of the Treaty of Paris creating the European Coal and Steel Community (ECSC). After it was found impossible to create European Communities covering Defence and Foreign Affairs, two more communities with the aims of gradually integrating the economies of the 6 nations and of moving towards closer political unity, the European Economic Community (EEC) and the European Atomic Energy Community (EAEC or Euratom) were created in 1957 by the signing of the Treaties of Rome.

On 30 June 1970 membership negotiations began between the Six and the UK, Denmark, Ireland and Norway. On 22 Jan. 1972 those 4 countries signed a Treaty of Accession, although this was rejected by Norway in a referendum in Nov. 1972. On 1 Jan. 1973 the UK, Denmark and Ireland became full members. On 28 May 1979 the Greek Treaty of Accession was signed, and Greece joined the Community on 1 Jan. 1981. Negotiations for accession were in progress in 1983 with Spain and Portugal.

The institutional arrangements of the Communities provide an independant executive with powers of proposal (the Commission), various consultative bodies, and a decision-making body drawn from the Governments (the Council). Until 1967 the 3 Communities were completely distinct, although they shared some non-decision-making bodies: from that date the executives were merged in the European Commission, and the decision-taking bodies in the Council. The institutions and organs of the Communities are as follows:

The *Commission* consists of 14 members appointed by the member states to serve for 4 years; the President and Vice-Presidents are appointed initially for 2 years, but are generally re-appointed for the rest of their term. The Commission acts independently of any country in the interests of the Community as a whole, with as its mandate the implementation and guardianship of the Treaties. In this it has the right of initiative (putting proposals to the Council for action); and execution (once the Council has decided); and can take the other institutions or individual countries before the Court of Justice (see below) should any of these renege upon its responsibilities.

President: Gaston Thorn.
Address: 200 rue de la Loi, 1049, Brussels.

The *Council of Ministers* consists of foreign ministers from the 10 national governments and represents the national as opposed to the Community interests. It is the body which takes decisions under the Treaties. Although legally most of its decisions should be made by majority, it has since 1966 sought unanimity wherever possible, using majority votes only rarely. Specialist Councils (*e.g.* the Agriculture Council) meet to discuss matters related to individual policies. Since 1974 the Heads of State and Government have met 3 times a year as the *European Council* to discuss Community, and also Foreign Policy, affairs. The Foreign Ministers also meet in Political Co-operation to discuss Foreign Policy matters. The Presidency of the Council is held for a 6-month term in the following order: Belgium, Denmark, Federal Republic of Germany, Greece, France, Ireland, Italy, Luxembourg, Netherlands, UK. From 1 Jan.–30 June 1983: Federal Republic of Germany.

Address: 170 rue de la Loi, 1048, Brussels.

The *European Parliament* consists of 434 members of whom all but the Greek members were elected by direct universal suffrage on 7 and 10 June 1979; the Greek elections were held on 18 Oct. 1981. France, the Federal Republic of Germany, Italy and the UK each returned 81 members, the Netherlands 25, Belgium and Greece 24, Denmark 16, Ireland 15 and Luxembourg 6. Party representation in the new Parliament was as follows: Socialists and Allies 124, European People's Party—Christian Democratic Group 117, European Democratic Group (formerly European Conservative Group) 63, Communists and Allies 48, Liberal and Democratic Group 39, European Progressive Democratic Group 22, Others 21. Elections are next due in June 1984. The Parliament has a right to be consulted on a wide range of legislative proposals, and forms one arm of the Communities' Budgetary Authority.

President: Piet Dankert.
Address: Centre européen du Kirchberg, Luxembourg.

The *Economic and Social Committee* has an advisory role and consists of 156 representatives, employers, trade unions, consumers, etc. The *Consultative Committee*, of 84 members, performs a similar role for the ECSC.

President: François Ceyrac.
Address: 2, rue Ravenstein, 1000 Brussels.

The *European Court of Justice* is composed of 11 judges and 5 advocates-general, is responsible for the adjudication of disputes arising out of the application of the treaties, and its findings are enforceable in all member countries.

President: Josse Mertens de Wilmars.
Address: Palais de la Cour de Justice, Kirchberg, Luxembourg.

The *Court of Auditors* was established by a Treaty signed on 22 July 1975 which took effect on 1 June 1977. It consists of 10 members, and replaced the former *Audit Board*. It audits all income and current and past expenditure of the European Communities.

President: Pierre Lelong.
Address: 29 Rue Aldringen, Luxembourg.

Annual Report of the Court of Auditors, from 1977

The *European Investment Bank* (EIB) was created by the EEC Treaty to which its statute is annexed. Its governing body is the Board of Governors consisting of ministers designated by member states. Its main task is to contribute to the balanced development of the common market in the interest of the Community by financing projects: developing less-developed regions; for modernizing or converting undertakings; or developing new activities, or those of common interest to several member states.

Address: 100, Boulevard Konrad Adenauer, Plateau du Kirchberg, Luxembourg.

Annual Report of the European Investment Bank

Community Law. Provisions of the Treaties and secondary legislation may be either directly applicable in Member States or only applicable after Member States have enacted their own implementing legislation. Secondary legislation consists of: regulations, which are of general application and binding in their entirety and directly applicable in all member states; directives which are binding upon each Member State as to the result to be achieved within a given time, but leave the national authority the choice of form and method of achieving this result; decisions, which are binding in their entirety on their addressees. In addition the Council and Commission can issue recommendations and opinions, which have no binding force.

The Community's Legislative Process starts with a proposal from the Commission (either at the suggestion of its services or in pursuit of its declared political aims) to the Council. The Council generally seeks the views of the European Parliament on the proposal, and the Parliament adopts a formal Opinion, after consideration of the matter by its specialist Committees. The Council may also (and in some cases is obliged to) consult the Economic and Social Committee, which similarly delivers an opinion. When these opinions have been received, the Council will decide. Most decisions are taken on a majority basis, but will take account of reserves expressed by individual member states. The text eventually approved may differ substantially from the original Commission proposal.

Community Finances. The general budget of the European Communities for 1981 was (in ECUm.; 1EUA=US$0·93 or £0·55 on 1 Oct. 1982):

Receipts		*Expenditure*	
Agricultural levies	2,685	Agriculture	14,532
Import duties	6,939	Social	1,022
VAT	11,998	Regional	2,948
Miscellaneous	362	Industry, energy, research	436
	21,984	Development Aid	817
		Administration and miscellaneous	2,229
			21,984

The resources of the Community (the levies and duties mentioned above, and up to a 1% VAT charge) have been surrendered to it by Treaty. The Budget is made by the Council and the Parliament acting jointly as the Budgetary Authority. The Parliament has control, within a certain margin, of non-obligatory expenditure (*i.e.*, expenditure where the amount to be spent is not set out in the legislation concerned), and can also reject the Budget totally (this has only been done once, for the 1980 Budget). Otherwise, the Council decides. ECSC operations are separately funded by a turnover levy (1982: 0·31%) on the coal and steel industries of the Community. The ECSC operating budget for 1982 was ECU268m.

THE EUROPEAN COAL AND STEEL COMMUNITY. The ECSC was the first of the 3 Communities, coming into existence on 10 Aug. 1952 following the signature of the Treaty of Paris on 18 April 1951. Its aim was to contribute towards economic expansion, growth of employment and a rising standard of living in Member States, through common action in the coal and steel sector, in a Community open to other nations. Since 1957 it has had the same membership as the other Communities.

The Common Market for Coal and Steel. This first aim of the ECSC was achieved for coal, iron ore and scrap in Feb. 1953, for steel in May 1953 and for special steels in Aug. 1954. The Common External Tariff on ECSC products is between 4-8%. Rules for fair competition within the Common Market, based on non-discrimination by nationality and the free movement of goods, have been established. The ECSC also gives readaptation and retraining grants to former workers in these industries, and makes capital grants for new industrial investment in former coal and steel areas.

The Commission has to approve take-overs and mergers of coal or steel undertakings, and has the power in the case of crisis (and with the approval of the Council) to set production quotas and minimum prices by product, with fines for non-observance. This power was first used in 1980.

THE EUROPEAN ECONOMIC COMMUNITY (EEC) or COMMON MARKET

Based on the Treaty of Rome of 25 March 1957 the EEC came into being on 1 Jan. 1958 with the same original members as the ECSC. The Treaty guarantees certain rights to the citizens of all Member States (*e.g.,* the outlawing of economic discrimination by nationality, and equal pay for equal work as between men and women) and sets out certain other areas where secondary legislation is to fill in the details. The most important policy areas are as follows:

Freedom of movement for persons, goods and capital. Under the Treaty individuals or companies may establish themselves in another country (for the purposes of economic activity) or sell goods or services there on the same basis as nationals of that country. With a few exceptions, restrictions on the movement of capital have also been ended.

Customs Union and External Trade Relations. Goods or Services originating in one Member State have free circulation within the EEC, which implies common arrangements for trade with the rest of the world. Member States can no longer make bilateral trade agreements with third countries: this power has been ceded to the Community. The Customs Union was achieved in July 1968, with the abolition of internal customs tariffs (or equivalents) and quantitative restrictions, and the establishment of the Common External Tariff. Denmark, Ireland and the UK adopted these from July 1977; Greece is due to do so by Jan. 1986.

Following the 1973 accessions the Community made a series of agreements with the member states of EFTA to form an industrial free trade zone and to start the liberalization of agricultural trade. Association agreements which could lead to accession or customs union have been made with Cyprus, Malta and Turkey; and commercial, industrial, technical and financial aid agreements with Algeria, Egypt, Israel, Jordan, Lebanon, Morocco, Syria and Tunisia. In 1976 Canada signed a framework agreement for co-operation in industrial trade, science and natural resources.

In the *Development Aid* sector, the Community has an agreement (the Lomé Convention, originally signed in 1975 but renewed and enlarged in 1979) with some 60 African, Caribbean and Pacific countries which removes customs duties without reciprocal arrangements for most of their imports to the Community, and under which ECU5,600m. of aid will be granted between 1980–84. An economic and commercial agreement has also been signed with ASEAN.

The Common Agricultural Policy (CAP). The objectives set out in the Treaty are to increase agricultural productivity, to ensure a fair standard of living for the agricultural community, to stabilise markets, to assure supplies, and to ensure reasonable consumer prices. In Dec. 1960 the Council laid down the fundamental principles on which the CAP is based: a single market, which calls for common prices, stable currency parities and the harmonising of health and veterinary legislation; Community preference, which protects the single Community market from imports; common financing, through the European Agricultural Guidance and Guarantee Fund (EAGGF), which seeks to improve agriculture through its Guidance section, and to stabilise markets against world price fluctuations through market intervention, with levies and refunds on exports. At present common market organizations cover over 95% of EEC agricultural production. Greece will bring its agricultural prices into line with the Community over a period of up to 7 years.

Following the disappearance of stable currency parities, artificial currency levels have been applied in the CAP. This factor, together with over-production due to high producer prices, means that the CAP consumes about two-thirds of the Communities' budget.

The European Monetary System (EMS), whose immediate objective is to create a zone of monetary stability in Europe by closer monetary co-operation, began operating in March 1979. All Member States (except Greece and the UK, 1982) limit fluctuations in the exchange rates of their currencies against a central rate denominated in ECU. The Greek drachma will join the EMS by 31 Dec. 1986.

Competition. The Competition (anti-trust) law of the Community is based on 2 principles: that businesses should not seek to nullify the creation of the common market by the erection of artificial national (or other) barriers to the free movement of goods; and against the abuse of dominant positions in any market. These two principles have led among other things to the outlawing of prohibitions on exports to other Member States, of price-fixing agreements and of refusal to supply; and to the refusal by the Commission to allow mergers or take-overs by dominant undertakings in specific cases. Increasingly heavy fines are imposed on offenders.

THE EUROPEAN ATOMIC ENERGY COMMUNITY (EURATOM)

Like the EEC, Euratom came into being on 1 Jan. 1958 following a Treaty signed in Rome on 25 March 1957, and it had the same Member States as the EEC. Its task is to promote common efforts between its members in the development of nuclear energy for peaceful purposes, and for this purpose it has monopoly powers of acquisition of fissile materials for civil purposes. It is in no way concerned with military uses of nuclear power; indeed, its members are forbidden under the Treaty to use nuclear materials obtained through Euratom for such purposes.

The execution of the Treaty now rests with the European Commission, which is advised by the Scientific and Technical Committee (28 members). Major decisions rest with the Council. Euratom has 1 substantial research institute of its own, at Ispra, in Italy; it does other work in co-operation with research institutes in the Member States, or in joint and international undertakings.

A common market for nuclear materials and equipment came into force, and external tariffs were suspended, in Jan. 1959. Although a recent Court of Justice decision has confirmed that Member States have ceded to Euratom the right to make supply contracts with outside suppliers (*e.g.* Australia, Canada or the USA), Euratom has generally been growing less effective in recent years, and most major new nuclear energy projects within the Member States have been undertaken outside its framework.

European Community Delegation to the US: 2111 M Street NW (Suite 707), Washington DC 20037.
Head of Delegation: Sir Roy Denman.
US Delegation to the European Community: 40 Boulevard du Régent, 1000 Brussels.
Head of Delegation: George S. Vest.

European Community Delegation to the United Nations: 1 Dag Hammarskjöld Plaza, 245 East 47th Street, New York NY 10017.
Head of Delegation: Michael Hardy.

Books of Reference

Official Journal of the European Communities.—General Report on the Activities of the European Communities (annual, from 1967).—*The Agricultural Situation in the Community.* 1982.—*Twelfth Report of Competition Policy.* 1982.—*Report on the Development of the Social Situation in the Community in 1982.—Basic Statistics of the Community* (annual).—*Bulletin of the European Community* (monthly)

Europe (monthly), obtainable from the Information Office of the European Commission, 20 Kensington Palace Gdns, London, W8 4QQ

Arbuthnott, H. and Edwards, G., (eds.), *A Common Man's Guide to the Common Market.* London, 1979

Coffey, P., *The External Economic Relations of the E.E.C.* London, 1976

Cook, C., and Francis, M., *The First European Elections.* London, 1979

Drew, J., *Doing Business with the European Community.* London, 1979

Dyas, G. P., and Thanheiser, H. T., *The Emerging European Enterprise.* London, 1976

Fennell, R., *The Common Agricultural Policy of the European Community.* London, 1979

Fitzmaurice, J., *The European Parliament.* London, 1982

Goodhart, P., *Full-hearted Consent.* London, 1976

Hallstein, W., *Europe in the Making.* London, 1973

Herman, V., and Lodge, J., *The European Parliament and the European Community.* London, 1978

Korah, V., *An Introductory Guide to EEC Competition Law and Practice.* Oxford, 1979

Palmer, D. M., *Sources of Information on the European Communities.* London, 1979

Parry, A., and Hardy, S., *EEC Law.* London, 1973

Paxton, J., *The Developing Common Market.* London, 1976.—*A Dictionary of the European Communities.* 2nd ed. London, 1982

Shanks, M., *European Social Policy, Today and Tomorrow.* Oxford, 1977

Swann, D., *The Economies of the Common Market.* 4th ed. Harmondsworth, 1978

Twitchett, C. C., *Harmonisation in the EEC.* London, 1981

Wallace, W., and Herreman, I. (eds.), *A Community of Twelve?* Bruges, 1978

Walsh, A. E., and Paxton, J., *Competition Policy.* London, 1975

EUROPEAN FREE TRADE ASSOCIATION (EFTA)

The European Free Trade Association has 6 member countries: Austria, Iceland, Norway, Portugal, Sweden and Switzerland. A seventh country, Finland, is an associate member. The Stockholm Convention establishing the Association entered into force on 3 May 1960 and Finland became associated on 27 March 1961. Iceland joined EFTA on 1 March 1970 and was immediately granted duty-free entry for industrial goods exported to EFTA countries, while being given 10 years to abolish her own existing protective duties. Two founder members of EFTA, the UK and Denmark, left EFTA on 31 Dec. 1972 to join the EEC.

When the Association was created it had three objectives: to achieve free trade in industrial products between member countries, to assist in the creation of a single market embracing the countries of Western Europe, and to contribute to the expansion of world trade in general.

The first objective was achieved on 31 Dec. 1966, when virtually all inter-EFTA tariffs were removed. This was 3 years earlier than originally planned. Finland removed her remaining EFTA tariffs a year later on 31 Dec. 1967 and Iceland removed her tariffs on 31 Dec. 1979.

The fulfilment of the second aim was secured in 1972. On 22 Jan. 1972 the UK and Denmark signed the Treaty of Accession to the EEC whereby they became members of the enlarged Community from 1 Jan. 1973. On 22 July 1972, 5 other EFTA countries, Austria, Iceland, Portugal, Sweden and Switzerland signed Free Trade Agreements with the enlarged EEC. A similar agreement negotiated with Finland was signed on 5 Oct. 1973. Norway, whose intention of joining the EEC was reversed following a referendum, signed a similar agreement on 14 May 1973.

Through these agreements virtually complete free trade in industrial goods was achieved in 16 Western European countries from July 1977. The free trade agreements apply also to Greece since its accession to the EEC on 1 Jan. 1981. A multilateral free trade agreement between the EFTA countries and Spain, a candidate for EEC membership, came into force on 1 May 1980 and the first tariff cuts were applied on 1 June 1980.

The third objective was to contribute to the expansion of world trade. In 1959 trade between the countries now in EFTA amounted to US$759m. and total exports from these countries were US$6,852m. In 1981 the respective figures were US$15,966m. and US$108,194m. More than half EFTA trade is with the EEC.

EFTA tariff treatment applies to those industrial products which are of EFTA origin, and these are traded freely between member countries. Each EFTA country remains free, however, to impose its own rates of duty on products entering from outside EFTA or the EEC.

Generally, agricultural products do not come under the provisions for free trade, but bilateral agreements have been negotiated to increase trade in these products.

The operation of the Convention is the responsibility of a Council assisted by a small secretariat. Each EFTA country holds the chairmanship of the Council for 6 months.

Secretary-General: Per Kleppe (Norway).

Headquarters: 9–11 rue de Varembé, 1211 Geneva 20, Switzerland.

Convention Establishing the European Free Trade Association
EFTA Bulletin (Four issues a year)
EFTA What it is, What it does
The European Free Trade Association

THE WARSAW PACT

On 14 May 1955 the USSR, Albania, Bulgaria, Czechoslovakia, the German Democratic Republic, Hungary, Poland and Romania signed, in Warsaw, a 20-year treaty of friendship and collaboration, after the USSR had (on 7 May) annulled the 20-year treaties of alliance with the UK (1942) and France (1944).

The main provisions of the treaty are as follows:

Article 4. In case of armed aggression in Europe against one or several States party to the pact by a State or group of States, each State member of the pact . . . will afford to the State or States which are the object of such aggression immediate assistance . . . with all means which appear necessary, including the use of armed force . . . These measures will cease as soon as the Security Council takes measures necessary for establishing and preserving international peace and security.

Article 5. The contracting Powers agree to set up a joint command of their armed forces to be allotted by agreement between the Powers, at the disposal of this command and used on the basis of jointly established principles. They will also take over agreed measures necessary to strengthen their defences.

Article 9. The present treaty is open to other States, irrespective of their social or Government regime, who declare their readiness to abide by the terms of the treaty in order to safeguard peace and security of the peoples.

Article 11. In the event of a system of collective security being set up in Europe and a pact to this effect being signed—to which each party to this treaty will direct its efforts—the present treaty will lapse from the day such a collective security treaty comes into force.

It is estimated (1981) that the armed forces of the Warsaw Pact countries total 4·82m., including 3·71m. Russians, compared with 4·99m. NATO forces.

Marshal Grechko was from July 1960 to April 1967 C.-in-C. of the united Armed Forces, with headquarters in Moscow. He was succeeded by Marshal I. I. Yakubovsky in 1967 and by Marshal V. G. Kulikov in Jan. 1977.

In 1962 Albania was no longer invited to the Warsaw Pact meetings without being formally expelled.

Two Soviet divisions are stationed in Poland, 20 divisions in German

Democratic Republic, 4 divisions in Hungary and 5 in Czechoslovakia.

Clawson, R. W. and Kaplan, L. S. (eds.), *The Warsaw Pact: Political Purpose and Military Means*. Wilmington, 1982

COUNCIL FOR MUTUAL ECONOMIC ASSISTANCE [1]

Membership. Founder members were USSR, Bulgaria, Czechoslovakia, Hungary, Poland and Romania. Later admissions were Albania (1949; ceased participation 1961), German Democratic Republic (1950), Mongolia (1962), Cuba (1972), Vietnam (1978). In 1964 Yugoslavia concluded an agreement with CMEA whereby Yugoslavia would participate in the work of some CMEA bodies (at present 21). Afghánistán, Angola, Ethiopia, Laos, Mozambique and the People's Democratic Republic of Yemen attend CMEA sessions as observers.

External relations. There are co-operation agreements with Finland, Iraq and Mexico. Talks with the EEC at expert level on possible commercial co-operation were resumed in July 1980.

The Charter. The charter consists of a preamble and 18 articles. Extracts (in the language of the official English version) are as follows:

Article 1. Aims and Principles: 1 'The purpose of the Council is to promote, by uniting and co-ordinating the efforts of the member countries, the further extension and improvement of co-operation and the development of socialist economic integration, the planned development of their national economies, the acceleration of economic and technical progress in these countries, higher level of industrialization of the less industrialized countries, a continuous increase in labour productivity, a gradual approximation and equalization of economic development levels and a steady improvement in the wellbeing of the peoples. 2 The Council is based on the principles of the sovereign equality of all member countries.'

Article 2. Membership 'open to other countries which subscribe to the purposes and principles of the Council'.

Article 3. Functions and Powers to (a) 'organize all-round . . . co-operation of member countries in the most rational use of natural resources and acceleration of the development of their productive forces'; (b) 'foster the improvement of the international socialist division of labour by co-ordinating national economic development plans, and the specialization and co-operation of production in member countries'; (c) to assist in . . . carrying out joint measures for the development of industry and agriculture . . . transport . . . principal capital investments . . . [and] trade'.

Article 4. Recommendations and Decisions '. . . shall be adopted only with the consent of the interested member countries.'

The Structure. The supreme authority is the 'Session' of all members held (usually annually) in members' capitals in rotation under the chairmanship of the head of the delegation of the host country; all members must be present, and decisions must be unanimous. Delegations are usually led by prime ministers.

The *Executive Committee* is made up of 1 representative from each member state of deputy premier rank. It meets at least once every 3 months.

The administrative organ is the *Secretariat.*

Headquarters: Prospekt Kalinina, 56, Moscow, G-205.
Secretary: N. V. Faddeev (appointed 1958).

There is a *Committee for Co-operation in the Field of Planning* and a *Committee for Scientific and Technical Co-operation* set up in 1971 and a *Committee for Material and Technical Supply* set up in 1974. There are *Permanent Commissions* on: Statistics, Foreign Trade, Currency and Finance, Electricity, Peaceful Uses of Atomic Energy, Geology, Coal Industry, Oil and Gas Industry, Chemical Industry, Iron and Steel Industry, Non-Ferrous Metals Industry, Engineering Industry,

[1] Abbreviations and Foreign Names. CMEA is the official abbreviation. Other unofficial abbreviations are COMECON and CEMA. The working language of the organization is Russian. The Russian form is *Sovet Ekonomicheskoi Vzaimopomoshchi* (SEV).

Radio Engineering and Electronics Industries, Light Industry, Food Industry, Agriculture, Construction, Transport, Posts and Telecommunications, Standardization, Civil Aviation, Public Health.

There are 7 *Standing Conferences:* for Legal Problems; of Ministers of Internal Trade; of Chiefs of Water Resources Authorities; of Chiefs of Patent Authorities; of Chiefs of Pricing Authorities; of Chiefs of Labour Authorities, and of Representatives of Freight and Shipping Organizations.

There are 3 semi-autonomous bodies within CMEA: The Institute of Standardization, The Bureau for the Co-ordination of Ship Freighting and The International Institute of Economic Problems of World Socialist System.

In 1983 there were over 20 technical and economic agencies associated with CMEA.

Also associated with CMEA are:

The **International Bank for Economic Co-operation** was founded in 1963 with a capital of 300m. roubles and started operating on 1 Jan. 1964. It undertakes multilateral settlements in 'transferable roubles' (*i.e.*, used for intra-CMEA clearing accounts only) and advances credits to finance trading and other operations. The transferable *rouble* is a unit of account: gold content 0·987412 gramme.

The **International Investments Bank** was founded in 1970 and went into operation on 1 Jan. 1971 with a capital of 1,713m. roubles (70% transferable and 30% convertible or in gold).

Banking and Sources of Finance in Comecon. London, 1978
Charter of the Council for Mutual Economic Assistance. Moscow, 1980
Council for Mutual Economic Assistance: Thirty Years. Moscow, 1979
Comprehensive Programme for the Further Extension and Improvement of Co-operation and the Development of Socialist Economic Integration by the CMEA-member Countries. Moscow, 1971 (The official English-language version. This document also frequently referred to as the *Complex Programme,* etc.)
Ekonomicheskoe Sotrudnichestvo Stran-Chlenov SEV. Moscow, 6 a year
Multilateral Economic Co-operation of Socialist States: A Collection of Documents. Moscow, 1977
Statistical Year Book of CMEA Member Countries. Moscow, annual
Survey of CMEA Activities. Moscow, annual
Bautina, N. V., *CMEA Today: from Economic Co-operation to Economic Integration.* Moscow, 1975
Bystrický, R., *Le Droit de l'Intégration Économique Socialiste.* Geneva, 1979
Schiavone, G., *The Institutions of Comecon.* London, 1981
Shaeffer, H. W., *Comecon and the Politics of Integration.* New York and London, 1972
Szawlowski, R., *The System of the International Organizations of the Communist Countries.* Leyden, 1976
van Brabant, J. M. P., *Essays on Planning, Trade and Integration in Eastern Europe.* Rotterdam Univ. Press, 1974
Wilcox, H., *Comecon and the Politics of Integration.* New York and London, 1972
Wilczynski, J., *Technology in Comecon.* London, 1974

COLOMBO PLAN

History: Founded in 1950 to promote the development of newly independent Asian member countries, the Colombo Plan has grown from its modest beginning as a group of seven Commonwealth nations into an international organization of 26 countries.

Originally the Plan was conceived for a period of six years. Its life has since been extended from time to time, generally at five-year intervals. The Consultative Committee, the Plan's highest deliberative body, at its meeting in Jakarta in 1980, gave the Plan an indefinite span of life; its need and relevance will henceforth be examined only if considered necessary.

The Plan is multilateral in approach but bilateral in operation: multilateral in that it takes cognizance of the problems of development of member countries in the Asia and Pacific region and endeavours to deal with them in a co-ordinated way;

bilateral because negotiations for assistance are made direct between a donor and a recipient country.

Aims: The aims of the Colombo Plan are: *(a)* to promote interest in and support for the economic and social development in Asia and the Pacific; *(b)* to keep under review economic and social progress in the region and help accelerate development through co-operative effort; and *(c)* to facilitate development assistance to and within the region.

Member Countries: Afghánistán, Australia, Bangladesh, Bhutan, Burma, Cambodia, Canada, Fiji, India, Indonesia, Iran, Japan, Republic of Korea, Lao People's Democratic Republic, Malaysia, Maldives, Nepal, New Zealand, Pakistan, Papua New Guinea, Philippines, Singapore, Sri Lanka, Thailand, UK and USA.

Development Assistance: Colombo Plan aid covers all fields of socio-economic development but it takes two principal forms:

(i) *Capital Aid* takes the form of grants and loans for national projects mainly from the six developed member countries to the developing member countries of the Plan.
From 1950 to 1981 the total amount of aid from the major donors was as follows:

	US$1m.
USA	39,610·8
Japan	11,639·8
UK	5,275·8
Australia	4,112·1
Canada	3,430·1
India	791·4
New Zealand	222·0
Total	65,082·0

(ii) *Technical Co-operation:* Technical assistance is provided in the form of services of experts and technicians, fellowships, and equipment for training and research. From 1950 to Dec. 1981, 160,397 trainees and students had received technical training and 46,028 experts and 2,101 volunteers and equipment to the value of US$865,096m. had been provided.
During 1981, 7,105 trainees and students received training, 1,603 experts and 209 volunteers were sent out, value of equipment supplied was $32·8m.; total value of co-operation activities from the inception of the Plan to Dec. 1981 was nearly $4,400m. Disbursements in 1981 totalled $419·5m.

Structure: There are four organs which give focus to the Plan:

Consultative Committee: The Committee consists of Ministers of member Governments who meet once in two years. The Ministerial meeting is preceded by a meeting of senior officials who are directly concerned with the operation of the Plan in various countries.

Colombo Plan Council: The Council is also a deliberative body which meets two or three times a year in Colombo, where most member countries have resident diplomatic missions, to review the economic and social development of the Asia-Pacific region and promote co-operation among member countries.

Colombo Plan Bureau: This is the only permanent organ of the Colombo Plan with headquarters in Colombo. Its functions include servicing the meetings of the Colombo Plan Council and the Consultative Committee, carrying out research, and dissemination of statistical and other information relating to activities under the Plan. Since 1973 the Bureau has been operating a Drug Advisory Programme to assist national and regional efforts to eliminate the causes and ameliorate the effects of drug abuse.

Colombo Plan Staff College: The Colombo Plan Staff College for Technician Education, located in Singapore, was opened in March 1975 to help member countries in developing their system of technician education. The College conducts training courses for senior technician educators and planners both at the College and in regional member countries.

Headquarters: Colombo Plan Bureau, 12 Melbourne Avenue, PO Box 596, Colombo 4, Sri Lanka.

The Colombo Plan (Cmd. 8080). HMSO, 1950; reprinted 1952.—*Annual Report.* HMSO, 1952 to 1971 followed by Colombo Plan Bureaux, Sri Lanka, 1972 to date
Reports of the Council for Technical Co-operation. HMSO annually until 1966–67 followed by the Colombo Plan Bureau, Sri Lanka, 1967–68 to date

ASSOCIATION OF SOUTH EAST ASIAN NATIONS (ASEAN)

History and Membership. The Association of South East Asian Nations is a regional organization formed by the governments of Indonesia, Malaysia, the Philippines, Singapore and Thailand through the Bangkok Declaration which was signed by the Foreign Ministers of ASEAN countries on 8 Aug. 1967.

Objectives. The main objectives are to accelerate economic growth, social progress and cultural development, to promote active collaboration and mutual assistance in matters of common interest, to ensure the stability of the South East Asian region and to maintain close co-operation with existing international and regional organizations with similar aims. Principal projects concern economic co-operation and development, with the intensification of Intra-ASEAN trade and trade between the region and the rest of the world; joint research and technological programmes; co-operation in transportation and communications; promotion of tourism and south-east Asian studies; including cultural, scientific, educational and administrative exchanges.

Organs. The highest authority in ASEAN are the Heads of Government of the Member Countries who meet as and when necessary to give directions to ASEAN. The highest policy-making body is the Meeting of Foreign Ministers, commonly known as the Annual Ministerial Meeting, which convenes in each of the ASEAN members countries on a rotational basis in alphabetical order. The Standing Committee, comprising the Foreign Minister of the country hosting the Ministerial Meeting in that particular year and the accredited ambassadors of the other member countries, carries out the work of the Association in between the Ministerial Meetings and handles the routine matters to ensure continuity and to make decisions which can not wait for the Ministerial Meetings and submit for the consideration of the Foreign Ministers all reports and recommendations of the various ASEAN committees. There are 4 specialized committees under the Standing Committee and five others under the ASEAN Economic Ministers that recommend and draw up programmes of ASEAN co-operation. These committees are responsible for the operation and implementation of ASEAN projects in their respective fields. Each ASEAN capital has an ASEAN National Secretariat. The central secretariat for ASEAN is located in Jakarta, Indonesia, and is headed by the ASEAN Secretary General, a post that revolves among the member states in alphabetical order every 2 years. Bureau directors and other officers of the ASEAN Secretariat remain in office for 3 years.

Secretary-General: Chan Kai Yau (Singapore).

Book of Reference

Wong, J., *ASEAN Economics in Perspective.* London, 1979

ORGANIZATION OF AMERICAN STATES

On 14 April 1890 representatives of the American republics, meeting in Washington at the First International Conference of American States, established an 'International Union of American Republics' and, as its central office, a 'Commercial Bureau of American Republics', which later became the Pan American Union. This international organization's object was to foster mutual understanding and co-operation among the nations of the western hemisphere. Since that time, successive inter-American conferences have greatly broadened the scope of work of the organization.

This led to the adoption on 30 April 1948 by the Ninth International Conference of American States, at Bogotá, Colombia, of the Charter of the Organization of American States. This co-ordinated the work of all the former independent official entities in the inter-American system and defined their mutual relationships. The purposes of the OAS are to achieve an order of peace and justice, promote American solidarity, strengthen collaboration among the member states and defend their sovereignty, territorial integrity and independence. The OAS is a regional organization of the United Nations for the maintenance of peace and security.

Membership is on a basis of absolute equality. Each country has one vote in the Council of the Organization and its organs. The member countries were (1980): Antigua and Barbuda, Argentina, Bahamas, Barbados, Bolivia, Brazil, Chile, Colombia, Costa Rica, Cuba, Commonwealth of Dominica, Dominican Republic, Ecuador, El Salvador, Grenada, Guatemala, Haiti, Honduras, Jamaica, Mexico, Nicaragua, Panama, Paraguay, Peru, Saint Lucia, Saint Vincent and the Grenadines, Suriname, Trinidad and Tobago, USA, Uruguay, Venezuela.

The OAS has been concerned increasingly in recent years with programmes to promote Latin American economic and social development. The OAS provides specialized training for thousands of Latin Americans each year in a wide variety of development-related fields. It also carries out several missions projects each year in response to requests from member governments.

On 27 Feb. 1967 the Third Special Inter-American Conference in Buenos Aires approved the Protocol of Amendment to the Charter of the OAS, which contained new standards for inter-American co-operation and a number of structural changes in the Organization.

On 14 April 1967 the Declaration of the Presidents of America, signed in Punta del Este, Uruguay, expressed the commitment of the American chiefs of state to promote Latin American economic integration; to join in efforts to increase substantially Latin American foreign-trade earnings; to modernize the living conditions of the rural population and raise agricultural productivity; and to expand programmes in education, science, technology and health.

On 22 Feb. 1968, in the Resolution of Maracay, the Inter-American Cultural Council launched new regional programmes for educational development and for scientific and technological development.

On 27 Feb. 1970, by ratification of more than the mandatory two-thirds of the OAS member states, the Protocol of Buenos Aires, modifying the 1948 Charter, entered into effect.

Under the amended Charter, the OAS accomplishes its purposes by means of:

(a) The *General Assembly*, which meets annually in various countries of the member states.

(b) The *Meeting of Consultation of Ministers of Foreign Affairs*, held to consider problems of an urgent nature and of common interest.

(c) Three councils of equal rank: the *Permanent Council*, which replaces the old OAS Council; the *Inter-American Economic and Social Council*; and the *Inter-American Council for Education, Science and Culture*. Functions are to direct and co-ordinate work in the areas of their competence and render the governments such specialized services as they may request. Each council is composed of 1 representative from each member state, appointed by his government.

(d) The *Inter-American Juridical Committee* which acts as an advisory body to

the OAS on juridical matters and promotes the development and codification of international law. Eleven jurists, elected every 4 years by the General Assembly, represent all the American States.

(e) The *Inter-American Commission on Human Rights* which oversees the observance and protection of human rights. Seven members represent all the OAS member states.

(f) The *General Secretariat* is the central and permanent organ of the OAS.

(g) The *Specialized Conferences*, meeting to deal with special technical matters or to develop specific aspects of inter-American co-operation.

(h) The *Specialized Organizations*, inter-governmental organizations established by multilateral agreements to discharge specific functions in their respective fields of action, such as women's affairs, agriculture, child welfare, Indian affairs, geography and history, and health.

Secretary-General: Alejandro Orfila (Argentina).

Assistant Secretary-General: Valerie McComie (Barbados).

The Secretary-General and the Assistant Secretary-General are elected by the General Assembly for 5-year terms. The General Assembly approves the annual budget for the Organization, which is financed by quotas contributed by the member governments.

General Secretariat: Washington, D.C., 20006, USA.
Flag: Light blue with the OAS seal in colour in the centre.

Books of Reference

Publications of the OAS General Secretariat include:

Charter of the Organization of American States. 1948.—*As Amended by the Protocol of Buenos Aires in 1967*
Americas. Illustrated monthly, from 1949 (Spanish, Portuguese and English edition)
Organization of American States, a Handbook. Rev. ed. 1977
Organization of American States. Directory. Quarterly, from 1951
Report on the Tenth Inter-American Conference, Caracas 1954. 1955
Inter-American Review of Bibliography. Quarterly, from 1951
Annual Report of the Secretary-General
Status of Inter-American Treaties and Conventions. Annual
The Alliance for Progress: The Charter of Punta del Este. 1962
The Americas in the 1980s: An Agenda for the Decade Ahead. 1982
Human Rights in the American States. 1960
Report of Inter-American Commission on Human Rights. From 1970

Publications on Latin America (*see also* the bibliographical notes appended to each country):

Revenue, Expenditure and Public Debts of the Latin American Republics. Division of Financial Information, US Department of Commerce. Annual
Fortnightly [from July 1960 also *Quarterly*] *Review of Business and Economic Conditions in South and Central America.* Bank of London and South America. London, 1935–66; restyled *B.O.L.S.A. Review,* from Jan. 1967
Boundaries of the Latin American Republics: An Annotated List of Documents, 1493–1943. Department of State, Office of the Geographer. Washington, 1944
Burgin, M. (ed.), *Handbook of Latin American Studies.* Gainesville, Fla., 1935 ff.
Davies, H. (ed.), *The South American Handbook.* London, 1924 to date
Hirschman, Albert O., *Latin American Issues:* [11] *Essays and Comments.* New York, 1961
Humphreys, R. A., *Latin American History: A Guide to the Literature in English.* London, 1958
Munro, D. G., *The Latin American Republics; A History.* London, 1961
Nehemkis, P., *Latin America: Myth and Reality.* New York, 1964
Plaza, G., *The Organization of American States: Instrument for Hemispheric Development.* Washington, 1969.—*Latin America Today and Tomorrow.* Washington, 1971
Steward, J. H. (ed.), *Handbook of the South American Indian.* 7 vols. Washington, 1946–59
Szulc, T., *Winds of Revolution.* New York, 1965
Thomas, A. V. W. and A. J., *The Organization of American States.* Southern Methodist Univ. Press, 1963
Ureña, P. H., *A Concise History of Latin American Culture.* London, 1966

LATIN AMERICAN ECONOMIC GROUPINGS

The Economic Commission for Latin America, an organ of the United Nations, with headquarters in Santiago, Chile, has facilitated the co-operation of two groups of countries concerning production, tariffs and trade.

Latin American Free Trade Association was concluded in Montevideo on 18 Feb. 1961 by Argentina, Boliva, Brazil, Chile, Mexico, Paraguay, Peru and Uruguay. Colombia (3 Oct. 1961), Ecuador (20 Oct. 1961) and Venezuela (1 Sept. 1966) have joined the ALALC/LAFTA Treaty. The permanent secretariat is at Montevideo. The 11 signatories held the 19th Extraordinary Conference at Acapulco, 16–27 June 1980. A Constitution was drawn up for a new Latin American Integration Association (LAIA) to take over after LAFTA expired on 31 Dec. 1980.

Central American Common Market (ODECA). On 13 Dec. 1960, at Managua, El Salvador, Guatemala, Honduras and Nicaragua concluded a general treaty on Central American integration; a protocol on the equalization of import duties and charges; and an agreement establishing the Central American Bank for Economic Integration. Costa Rica acceded in 1962 and in Sept. 1963 ratified the charter of the Banco Centroamericano de Integración Económica (in Tegucigalpa), whose capital was thereupon increased to US$20m.

The San Salvador Charter, signed on 14 Dec. 1962, expanded these provisions, envisaging permanent political, economic, educational, defence, etc., councils. The permanent secretariat is at Guatemala City.

Total intra-ODECA trade increased from US$8·6m. in 1960 to US$176m. in 1966. Total USA investments in the area are about $400m.

The Andean Group (Grupo Andino). On 26 May 1969 an agreement was signed by Bolivia, Chile, Colombia, Ecuador and Peru creating the Andean Group. Venezuela was initially actively involved but did not sign the agreement. The Group signed a further agreement on 31 Dec. 1970 on common regulations controlling foreign investments. Under the Cartagena Agreement of 1975 the development of an integrated petrochemical industry in each of the member countries was established.

Sistema Económico Latinoamericano (SELA) was created by 25 countries (not including USA) meeting at Panama, 17 Oct. 1975. Its Permanent Secretary is Jaime Moncayo, former Finance Minister of Ecuador. It held an 'extraordinary' technical meeting at Caracas, 5 Jan. 1976, to prepare for other activities, such as UNCTAD, at Nairobi in May 1976.

Britain and Latin America. Latin America Bureau, London (annual)
British Bulletin of Publications on Latin America, the Caribbean, Portugal and Spain. London, from June 1949 (half-yearly)
Hispanic and Luso–Brazilian Councils, Portuguese and Spanish Dictionaries. London, 1971
Instruments of Economic Integration in Latin America and the Caribbean. New York, 1975
Libre Comercio. Revista oficial de la Associación de Empresarios participantes de la ALALC. Montevideo, from June 1964 (monthly)
Committee on Latin America (COLA), *Latin American Serials.* 3 vols. London, 1969, 1973, 1977
Brooks, J. (ed.), *The South American Handbook.* Bath (Annual)
Einaudi, L., R. (ed.), *Beyond Cuba: Latin America Takes Charge of its Future.* New York, 1974
Furtado, C., *Economic Development of Latin America.* London, 1970
Griffin, K., *Financing Development of Latin America.* London, 1971
Jaguaribe, H., *Political Development: A General Theory and a Latin American Case Study.* New York, 1973
Loveman, B., and Davies, T. M., *The Politics of Antipolitics: The Military in Latin America.* Univ. of Nebraska Press, 1978
Milenky, E. S., *The Politics of Regional Organization in Latin America. The Latin American Free Trade Association.* New York, 1973
Morawetz, D., *The Andean Group: A Case Study in Economic Integration Among Developing Countries.* MIT Press, 1974

Sánchez-Albornoz, N., *The Population of Latin America: A History.* Univ. of Calif. Press, 1974
UN Economic Commission for Latin America. *The Latin America Economy.* Washington (annual)

CARIBBEAN COMMUNITY (CARICOM)

Establishment and Functions. The Treaty establishing the Caribbean Community, including the Caribbean Common Market, and the Agreement establishing the Common External Tariff for the Caribbean Common Market, was signed by the Prime Ministers of Barbados, Guyana, Jamaica and Trinidad and Tobago at Chaguaramas, Trinidad, on 4 July 1973, and entered into force on 1 Aug. 1973. Six less developed countries of CARIFTA signed the Treaty of Chaguaramas on 17 April 1974. They were Belize, Dominica, Grenada, Saint Lucia, St Vincent and Montserrat, and the Treaty came into effect for those countries on 1 May 1974. Antigua acceded to Membership on 4 July 1974 and on 26 July the Associated State of St Kitts–Nevis–Anguilla signed the Treaty of Chaguaramas in Kingston, Jamaica, and became a member of the Caribbean Community.

The Caribbean Community has 3 areas of activity: economic integration (that is, the Caribbean Common Market which replaces CARIFTA); co-operation in non-economic areas and the operation of certain common services; and co-ordination of foreign policies of independent member states.

The Caribbean Common Market provides for the establishment of a Common External Tariff, a common protective policy and the progressive co-ordination of external trade policies; the adoption of a scheme for the harmonization of fiscal incentives to industry; double taxation arrangements among member countries; the co-ordination of economic policies and development planning; and a special regime for the less developed countries of the community.

Membership: Antigua, Barbados, Belize, the Commonwealth of Dominica, Grenada, Guyana, Jamaica, Montserrat, St Kitts–Nevis, Saint Lucia, St Vincent and the Grenadines, and Trinidad and Tobago.

Structure: The *Heads of Government Conference* is the principal organ of the Community, and its primary responsibility is to determine the policy of the Community. It is the final authority of the Community and the Common Market, and for the conclusion of treaties and relationships between the Community and international organizations and States. It is responsible for financial arrangements for meeting the expenses of the Community.

The *Common Market Council* is the principal organ of the Common Market and consists of a Minister of Government designated by each member state. Decisions in both the Conference and the Council are in the main taken on the basis of unanimity.

The *Secretariat*, successor to the Commonwealth Caribbean Regional Secretariat, is the principal administrative organ of the Community and of the Common Market. The Secretary-General is appointed by the Conference on the recommendation of the Council for a term not exceeding 5 years and may be reappointed. The Secretary-General shall act in that capacity in all meetings of the Conference, the Council, and of the institutions of the Community.

Institutions of the Community, established by the Heads of Government Conference, are: Conference of Ministers responsible for Health; Standing Committees of Ministers responsible for Education, Industry, Labour, Foreign Affairs, Finance, Agriculture, Mines and Transport, respectively.

Associate Institutions: East Caribbean Common Market Council of Ministers; Organization of East Caribbean States; Caribbean Development Bank; Caribbean Examinations Council; Caribbean Investment Corporation; Council of Legal Education; University of the West Indies; University of Guyana.

Field Projects: Caribbean Agricultural and Rural Development Advisory and Training Service; Caribbean Agricultural Research and Development Institute; Caribbean Food Corporation; Caribbean Tourism Research Centre; West Indies Shipping Corporation; Small Vessel Shipping Project; LIAT 1974 Ltd. and Caribbean Aviation Training Institute.

Secretary-General: Dr Kurleigh King.
Deputy Secretary-General: Roderick Rainford.
Headquarters: Bank of Guyana Building, PO Box 10827, Georgetown, Guyana.

The language of the Community is English.

Books of Reference

CARICOM Perspective. (Bi-monthly). *CARICOM Bibliography* (Bi-annual)
Axline, A. W., *Caribbean Integration: The Politics of Regionalism.* London and New York, 1979
Payne, A. J., *The Politics of the Caribbean Community 1961–79.* Manchester Univ. Press, 1980

THE LEAGUE OF ARAB STATES

Origin. The formation of the League of Arab States in 1945 was largely inspired by the Arab awakening of the 19th century. This movement sought to re-create and reintegrate the Arab community which, though for 400 years a part of the Ottoman Empire, had preserved its identity as a separate national group held together by memories of a common past, a common religion and a common language, as well as by the consciousness of being part of a common cultural heritage. The leaders of the Arab movement in the 19th century and of the Arab revolt against Turkey in the First World War sought to achieve these aims through secession from the Ottoman Empire into a united and independent Arab state comprising all the Arab countries in Asia. However the 1919 peace settlement divided the Arab world in Asia (with the exception of Saudi Arabia and the Yemen) into British and French spheres of influence and established in them a number of separate states and administrations (Syria, Lebanon, Iraq, Jordan and Palestine) under temporary mandatory control.

By 1943, however, 7 of these countries had substantially achieved their independence. An Arab conference therefore met in Alexandria in the autumn of 1944; it formulated the 'Alexandria Protocol', which delineated the outlines of the Arab League. It was found that neither a unitary state nor a federation could be achieved, but only a league of sovereign states. A covenant, establishing such a league, was signed in Cairo on 22 March 1945 by the representatives of Egypt, Iraq, Saudi Arabia, Syria, Lebanon, Jordan and Yemen. There were (1980) 21 members of the League: Algeria, Bahrain, Iraq, Jibuti, Jordan, Kuwait, Lebanon, Libya, Mauritania, Morocco, Oman, Palestine L.O., Qatar, Saudi Arabia, Somalia, Sudan, Syria, Tunisia, United Arab Emirates, P.D.R. of Yemen and Yemen Arab Republic.

Egypt's membership of the League was suspended, in accordance with a resolution passed at the Baghdad summit, in March 1979, at which time it was also agreed that the League secretariat should be moved from Cairo to Tunis. This action was taken in response to the signing of a bilateral peace treaty between Egypt and Israel.

Organization. The machinery of the League consists of a Council, a number of Special Committees and a Permanent Secretariat. On the Council each state has one vote. The Council may meet in any of the Arab capitals. Its functions include mediation in any dispute between any of the League states or a League state and a country outside the League. The Council has a Political Committee consisting of the Foreign Ministers of the Arab states.

The Permanent Secretariat of the League, under a Secretary-General (who enjoys, along with his senior colleagues, full diplomatic status), has its seat in Tunisia.

The League considers itself a regional organization within the framework of the United Nations at which its secretary-general is an observer.

Secretary-General: Chedli Klibi (Tunisia).

Flag: Dark green with the seal of the Arab League in white in the centre.

Arab Common Market. The Arab Common Market came into operation on 1 Jan. 1965. The agreement, reached on 13 Aug. 1964 and open to all the Arab League states, has been signed by Iraq, Jordan, Syria and Egypt. The agreement provides for the abolition of customs duties on agricultural products and natural resources within 5 years, by reducing tariffs at an annual rate of 20%. Customs duties on industrial products are to be reduced by 10% annually. The agreement also provides for the free movement of capital and labour between member countries, the establishment of common external tariffs, the co-ordination of economical development and the framing of a common foreign economic policy.

Books of Reference

Arab Maritime Data, 1979–80. London, 1979
Atlas of the Arab World and the Middle East. London and New York, 1960
Oxford Regional Economic Atlas: The Middle East and North Africa. OUP, 1960
Glubb, Sir John, *Britain and the Arabs.* London, 1956
Gomaa, A. M., *The Foundation of the League of Arab States.* London, 1977

ORGANIZATION OF THE PETROLEUM EXPORTING COUNTRIES

Aims. The Organization was founded in Iraq in 1960 with the following founder members, Iran, Iraq, Kuwait, Saudi Arabia and Venezuela. The principal aims are unifying the petroleum policies of member countries and determining the best means for safeguarding their interests, individually and collectively; to devise ways and means of ensuring the stabilization of prices in international oil markets with a view to eliminating harmful and unnecessary fluctuations; and to secure a steady income for the producing countries, an efficient, economic and regular supply of petroleum to consuming nations, and a fair return on their capital to those investing in the petroleum industry.

Membership (1981). Algeria, Ecuador, Gabon, Indonesia, Iran, Iraq, Kuwait, Libya, Nigeria, Qatar, Saudi Arabia, United Arab Emirates and Venezuela. Membership is open to any other country having substantial net exports of crude petroleum, which has fundamentally similar interests to those of member countries.

OPEC Fund. The Fund was established in 1976 to provide financial aid to developing countries, other than OPEC members, on advantageous terms.

Secretary-General: Dr Marc S. Nan Nguema (Gabon).
Deputy Secretary-General: Dr Fadhil J. Al-Chalabi (Iraq).

Headquarters: Obere Donaustrasse 93, A–1020 Vienna, Austria.

Books of Reference

OPEC publications include: *Annual Statistical Bulletin. Annual Report. Proceedings of the OPEC Seminar 1977. OPEC Bulletin* (monthly). *OPEC Review* (quarterly). *OPEC Papers* (bi-monthly).
Al-Chalabi, Dr F., *OPEC and the International Oil Industry: A Changing Structure.* OUP, 1980
Abolfathi, F., *The OPEC Market to 1985.* Lexington, 1977
Ghadar, F., *The Evolution of OPEC Strategy.* Lexington, 1977

ORGANIZATION OF AFRICAN UNITY

On 25 May 1963 the heads of state or government of 32 African countries, at a conference in Addis Ababa, signed a charter establishing an 'Organization of African Unity' *(Organisation de l'Unité Africaine)*.

Its chief objects are the furtherance of African unity and solidarity; the co-ordination of the political, economic, cultural, health, scientific and defence policies and the elimination of colonialism in Africa.

The organs of the Organization are: (1) the assembly of the heads of state and government; (2) the council of foreign ministers; (3) the general secretariat; (4) a commission of mediation, conciliation and arbitration. Arabic, French and English are recognized as working languages.

Chairman: President Daniel Arap Moi (Kenya).
Secretary-General: Edem Kodjo (Togo).
Headquarters: Addis Ababa.
Flag: Horizontally green, white, green, with the white fimbriated yellow, and the seal of the OAU in the centre.

DANUBE COMMISSION

The Danube Commission was constituted in 1949 based on the Convention regarding the regime of navigation on the Danube, which was signed in Belgrade on 18 Aug. 1948. The Belgrade Convention reaffirmed that navigation on the Danube from Ulm to the Black Sea, with access to the sea through the Sulina arm and the Sulina Canal, is equally free and open to the nationals, merchant shipping and merchandise of all states as to harbour and navigation fees as well as conditions of merchant navigation.

The Danube Commission is composed of representatives from the countries on the Danube (1 for each of these countries), namely, Austria, Bulgaria, Hungary, Romania, Czechoslovakia, USSR and Yugoslavia. Since 1957, representatives of the Ministry of Transport from the Federal Republic of Germany have attended the meetings of the Commission as guests of the Secretariat.

The functions of the Danube Commission are to check that the provisions of the Convention are carried out, to establish a uniform buoying system on all the Danube's navigable waterways and to establish the basic regulations for navigation on the river. The Commission co-ordinates the regulations for river, customs and sanitation control as well as the hydrometeorological service and collects statistical data concerning navigation on the Danube.

The Danube Commission enjoys legal status. It has its own seal and flag. The members of the Commission and elected officers enjoy diplomatic immunity. The Commission's official buildings, archives and documents are inviolable. French and Russian are the official languages of the Commission.

Since 1954 the headquarters of the Commission have been in Budapest.

Flag: Blue, with a red strip fimbriated white along the bottom edge, and the initials of the Commission within a wreath in the canton—Latin letters on obverse Cyrillic on reverse.

Books of Reference

Danube Commission's publications include: *Summary Records and Documents Adopted by the Sessions of the Danube Commission. Rules of Procedure of the Danube Commission. Basic Regulations for Navigation on the Danube. Reports on the Maintenance of the Navigability of the Danube. Guidebook for Sailors. Hydrological Yearbooks. Statistical Yearbooks. Mileage Chart of the Danube. Ice Control on the Danube. Collection of Internal Laws Concerning Navigation on the Danube. Collection of International Agreements Relating to Navigation on the Danube. Radio-Codes for Navigation on the Danube.*

PART II

COUNTRIES OF THE WORLD

A—Z

AFGHÁNISTÁN

De Afghanistan Democrateek Jamhuriat

Capital: Kábul
Population: 16·28m. (1981)
GNP per capita: US$170 (1979)

HISTORY. A military *coup* on 17 July 1973 overthrew the monarchy of King Záhir Shàh. The *coup* was led by the King's cousin and brother-in-law Mohammad Daoud who declared a Republic. King Záhir abdicated on 24 Aug. 1973. President Daoud was killed in a military *coup* in April 1978 which led to the establishment of a pro-Soviet government of the People's Democratic Party of Afghánistán.

AREA AND POPULATION. Afghánistán is bounded north by the USSR, east and south by Pakistan and west by Iran.

The area is 251,773 sq. miles (652,090 sq. km). Population, according to the (1979) census, is 15,551,358, of which some 2·5m. are nomadic tribes. Estimate (1981) 16,276,000 of whom 2m. are living in Pakistan and Iran as refugees. Annual population growth rate (1981) 2·6%; infant mortality rate (1979) 182 per 1,000 live births.

Census (1979), Kábul 913,164; Kandahár, 178,409; Herát, 140,323; Mazár-i-Sharif, 103,372; Jalálábád, 53,915; Kunduz, 53,251; Baghlan, 39,228; Charikar, 22,424; Shiberghan, 18,955; Gardez, 9,550; Faizabad, 9,098; Qala-i-nau, 5,340; Uiback, 4,938; Meterlam, 3,987; Cheghcherán, 2,974.

The main ethnic group are the Pathans. Other ethnic groups include the Tajiks, the Hazaras, the Turkomans and the Uzbeks.

CONSTITUTION AND GOVERNMENT. The 1964 Constitution was abolished by Presidential decree in 1973 and on 14 Feb. 1977 a new Constitution was adopted by the *Loya-Jirgah* (Grand Assembly). The 1977 Constitution was abrogated in April 1978 by the new Head of State, Noor Mohammad Taraki. On 16 Sept. 1979 President Taraki was ousted in a *coup* and replaced by Hafizullah Amin. In Dec. 1979 Soviet troops invaded Afghánistán and Hafizullah Amin was deposed and replaced by Babrak Karmal. The pretext for the airlift of combat troops to Kábul was the Treaty of Friendship signed in Dec. 1978 between USSR and Afghánistán. In Oct. 1982 there were up to 100,000 Soviet troops in Afghánistán.

President: Babrak Karmal.
Prime Minister: Sultan Ali Kishtmand.
National flag: Three equal horizontal stripes of red, black and green, with the national arms in the canton.

The official languages are Pushtu and Dari (Persian).

DEFENCE

Army. The Army is based on conscription with a regular cadre of officers and n.c.o.s. Call-up begins at the age of 19, and is for 3 years. Reserve liability is up to the age of 42.

The strength of the Army (1982) was about 40,000. It was organized in 3 armoured and 10 infantry divisions, 3 mountain infantry brigades and 1 artillery brigade. Equipment is almost entirely Russian and includes T-62, T-54/55 and T-34 tanks and surface-to-air missiles. Transport is mainly mechanized.

The Army has the following training establishments: a military academy (formed 1932), a school for each principal arm, a technical school, an n.c.o.s' school and a military high school (Kábul), which takes boys from the age of 10, and from which the regular element in the armed forces is mainly drawn. Selected officers receive training abroad, chiefly in USSR. In 1982 it was well below strength, largely as a result of desertions.

Air Force. The Air Force, which is Russian-equipped, has about 125 combat aircraft and 6,000 officers and men. Nominal strength comprises 1 squadron of Su-17 attack aircraft, 3 squadrons of MiG-21 interceptors (about 25 aircraft), 4 squadrons of MiG-17s (about 50 aircraft), 2 bomber squadrons each with about 10 twin-jet Il-28s, a helicopter attack force of about 30 Mi-24s, a transport wing with 15 twin-turboprop An-26s, about 10 piston-engined An-2s, 30 Mi-8 and 14 Mi-4 helicopters and 1 or 2 turboprop Il-18s, and Yak-18, Aero L-39 and MiG-15UTI trainers. The main fighter station is Bagram, with facilities for the largest jet airliners and bombers. A Russian-built bomber station was completed at Shindand in 1963. There is a training station at Mazár-i-Sharif and an air academy at Sherpur with about 400 cadets. Large numbers of 'Guideline' and 'Goa' surface-to-air missiles are operational in Afghánistán. Strong Soviet forces in Afghánistán in 1982 included Su-25 attack aircraft, and large numbers of Mi-8 assault helicopters and Mi-24 helicopter gunships.

Police and Militia. In addition to the Army and Air Force there are police troops (formerly the gendarmerie, pre-1979 strength about 30,000) and an armed militia of 'Defence of the Revolution' troops.

INTERNATIONAL RELATIONS

Membership. Afghánistán is a member of UN and of the Colombo Plan.

ECONOMY

Planning. The first two 5-year plans ran 1956–61 and 1962–67. The third plan (1967–72) envisaged expenditures of Afs. 33,000m. (compared with actual expenditures of 25,000m. during the second plan), but was never approved by Parliament. It was later tacitly abandoned, although some of the projects mentioned in the plan were implemented. The Minister of Planning then prepared a series of 1-year rolling plans but abandoned these in favour of a third 7-year plan which was in preparation in 1976. Later, an economic and social growth plan for 1979–83 was approved.

Budget. In 1980–81 the budget envisaged expenditure of Afs. 33,759m. and revenue of Afs. 33,759m.

Currency. The monetary system is on the silver standard. The unit is the *afgháni*, weighing 10 grammes of silver 0·900 fine, which is subdivided into 100 *puls*. Rates of exchange fluctuate round Afs. 100 = £1; Afs. 50 = US$1.

Banking. The Afghán State Bank *(Da Afghánistán Bank)* is the largest of the 3 main banks and also undertakes the functions of a central bank, holding the exclusive right of note issue. Total assets of the 3 main banks were: Da Afghánistán Bánk (1967), Afs. 28,074·4m.; Pashtany Tejaraty Bánk (1980), Afs. 5,682m.; Bánk-i-Milli (1967), Afs. 1,410·29m.

Weights and Measures. Weights and measures used in Kábul are: Weights: 1 *khurd* = 0·244 lb.; 1 *pao* = 0·974 lb.; 1 *charak* = 3·896 lb.; 1 *sere* = 16 lb.; 1 *kharwár* = 1,280 lb. or 16 maunds of 80 lb. each. Long measure: 1 yard or *gaz* = 40 in. The metric system is in increasingly common use. Square measures: 1 *jarib* = 60 × 60 kábuli yd or ½ acre; 1 *kulbá* = 40 jaríbs (area in which 2½ kharwárs of seed can be sown); 1 jaríb yd = 29 in.

Local weights and measures are in use in the provinces.

ENERGY AND NATURAL RESOURCES

Minerals. Mineral resources are scattered and little developed. Coal is mined at Karkar in Pul-i-Khumri, Ishpushta near Doshi, north of Kábul and Dar-i-Suf south of Mazar (total production, 1975–76, 150,000 tonnes). Natural gas is found in northern Afghánistán around Shiberghan and Sar-i-Pol; over 2,000m. cu.

metres, about 90% of production, is piped to the USSR annually. Rich, but as yet unexploited, deposits of iron ore exist in the Hajigak hills about 100 miles west of Kábul; beryllium has been found in the Kunar valley and barite in Bamian province. Other deposits include gold; silver (now unexploited, in the Panjshir valley); lapis lazuli (in the Panjshir valley and Badakhshán); asbestos; mica; sulphur (near Maimana); chrome (in the Logar valley and near Herát); and copper (in the north).

Agriculture. Although the greater part of Afghánistán is more or less mountainous and a good deal of the country is too dry and rocky for successful cultivation, there are many fertile plains and valleys, which, with the assistance of irrigation from small rivers or wells, yield very satisfactory crops of fruit, vegetables and cereals. It is estimated that there are 14m. hectares of cultivable land in the country, of which 7,844,000 hectares are being cultivated (5·34m. hectares of this being irrigated land). Before 1979 Afghánistán was virtually self-supporting in foodstuffs (including wheat in 1973), apart from sugar. The USSR now provides wheat, sugar and other foodstuffs.

The castor-oil plant, madder and the asafœtida plant abound.

Fruit forms a staple food (with bread) of many people throughout the year, both in the fresh and preserved state, and in the latter condition is exported in great quantities. The fat-tailed sheep furnish the principal meat diet, and the grease of the tail is a substitute for butter. Wool and skins provide material for warm apparel and one of the more important articles of export. Persian lambskins (Karakuls) are one of the chief exports.

Cotton production, 1981, was estimated at 65,000 tonnes; wheat, 2·75m.; barley, 321,000; maize, 798,000; rice, 461,000.

Livestock (1981): Cattle, 3·8m.; horses, donkeys and mules, 1·7m.; sheep, 18·7m.; goats, 2·9m.; poultry, 6·5m.

INDUSTRY AND TRADE

Industry. At Kábul there are factories for the manufacture of cotton and woollen textiles, leather, boots, marble-ware, furniture, glass, bicycles, prefabricated houses and plastics. A large machine shop has been constructed and equipped by the USSR, with a capability of manufacturing motor spares. There is a wool factory and there are several cotton-ginning plants; a small cotton factory at Jabal-us-Seráj and a larger one at Pul-i-Khumri; a cotton-seed oil extraction plant at Lashkargah; a cotton textile factory at Gulbahar, and a cotton plant at Balkh.

An ordnance factory manufactures arms and ammunition, boots and clothing, etc. for the Army. There is a beet sugar plant at Baghlan (equipped with Soviet machinery) and a fruit-canning factory in Kandahár. Hydro-electric plants have been constructed at Sarobi, Nangarhár, Naghlu, Mahipár, Pul-i-Khumri and Kandahár; more hydro and thermal plants are projected.

Industries include cement, coalmining, cotton textiles, small vehicle assembly plants, fruit canning, carpet making, leather tanning, footwear manufacture, sugar manufacture, preparation of hides and skins, and building. Most of these are relatively small and, with the exception of hides and skins, carpets and fruits, do not meet domestic requirements.

Commerce. Trade is supervised by the Government through the Ministries of Commerce and Finance and the Da Afghánistán Bánk. The Association of Afghán Chambers of Commerce works in close liaison with the Ministry of Commerce. The Government monopoly controls the import of petrol and oil, sugar, cigarettes and tobacco, motor vehicles and consignment goods from bilateral trading countries. The principal surface routes for imports to Afghánistán are *via* the Soviet rail system and the border posts at Torghundi and Hairatan; and from Karachi *via* the border post at Torkham.

In the year ended 20 March 1981 Afghán imports totalled US$551·7m. and exports US$705·2m.

Main export commodities were karakul skins (US$33·3m.), raw cotton (US$ 39·7m.), dried fruit and nuts (US$169·5m.), fresh fruit (US$39·8m.) and natural gas (US$233·1m.). Main items imported were petroleum products (US$124m.), textiles (US$60·3m.).

Total trade between Afghánistán and UK (in £1,000 sterling, British Department of Trade returns):

	1978	*1979*	*1980*	*1981*	*1982*
Imports to UK	17,927	20,276	20,174	22,822	20,855
Exports and re-exports from UK	17,524	9,567	6,818	7,725	9,344

Tourism. Owing to internal political instability there has been negligible tourism since 1979.

COMMUNICATIONS

Roads. There were in 1978 over 2,500 km of asphalted road. The Americans asphalted the Kandahár–Chaman and Kábul–Torkham roads. The Russians constructed a road and tunnel through the Salang pass (over 11,000 ft) which was opened in Sept. 1964 and cut 120 miles off the old road from Kábul to the north; they continued this road to Kunduz and Sherkhan Bandar (Qizil Qala) on the Oxus. In addition, the Americans in 1966 completed the road between Kábul and Kandahár and the Russians constructed a concrete road between Kandahár and Herát. In 1968 the Americans completed an asphalt road from Herát to the Iranian frontier at Islam Qala. With Soviet assistance a metalled road from Pul-i-Khumri to Mazár-i-Sharif was completed in 1969 and Mazár-i-Sharif to Shiberghán in 1971. A Soviet-built road and rail bridge across the Oxus (Amu Darya) River was opened in May 1982.

Railways. There are no railways in the country, but a rail and road bridge over the Amadarya river near Termez was opened in 1982, bringing Soviet Railways' track into the country. A 200 km line has been authorized from Termez to Puli-Khumri.

Aviation. On 29 June 1956 Afghánistán signed an agreement with the USA for the development of civil aviation, including the construction of the international airport at Kandahár, comprising a loan of $5m. and a grant of $9·56m. Kábul airport has been expanded with Russian assistance. New runways at Kábul and Kandahár airports have been completed. Provincial all-weather airports have been constructed at Herát, Qunduz, Jalálábád and Mazár-i-Sharif.

Ariana Afghan Airlines (a national airline) operates regular services to New Delhi, Tashkent and Moscow.

Bakhtar Afghan Airlines (the domestic national airline) began operations on 8 Feb. 1968 and regularly serves the main internal airfields.

Shipping. There are practically no navigable rivers in Afghánistán, and timber is the only article of commerce conveyed by water, floated down the Kunar and Kábul rivers from Chitral on rafts. A port has been built at Qizil Qala on the Oxus; barge traffic is increasing on the Oxus. Three river ports on the Amu Darya have been built at Sherkhan Bandar, Tashguzar and Hairatan, linked by road to Kábul.

Post and Broadcasting. Telephones, installed in most of the large towns, numbered 31,200 in 1978. There is telegraphic communication between all the larger towns and with other parts of the world. Kábul Radio broadcasts in Pushtu, Persian, Urdu, English, French, Russian and German. The first TV colour transmissions in Kábul began in mid-1978. An agreement was signed in 1981 under which the USSR undertook to assist with the development of communications. The agreement covered radio and television, telephones, telegraphs and the modernization of the postal system.

JUSTICE, RELIGION, EDUCATION AND WELFARE

Justice. A Supreme Court was established in June 1978. If no provision exists in the Constitution or in the general laws of the State, the courts follow the Hanafi jurisprudence of Islamic law.

Religion. The predominant religion is Islam, mostly of the Sunni sect, though there is a minority of about 1m. Shiah Moslems.

Education. There are elementary schools throughout the country, but secondary schools exist only in Kábul and provincial capitals. Both elementary and secondary education are free. In 1981 there were 1·04m. pupils (32,938 teachers) in primary education and 123,000 pupils (6,170 teachers) in secondary education. There are 3 teacher-training institutions in Kábul and 11 elsewhere; UNESCO is supporting an expansion programme. Technical, art, commercial and medical schools exist for higher education. Kábul University was founded in 1932 and has 9 faculties (medicine, science, agriculture, engineering, law and political science, letters, economics, theology, pharmacology). The University of Nangarhar in Jalálábád was founded in 1963. A Polytechnic in Kábul was completed in 1968. In 1981 there were 13,797 students in higher education, 7,449 in teacher-training schools and 1,538 in technical schools.

Health. In 1981 there were 1,121 doctors and 4,285 hospital beds. Two-thirds of the doctors and half the beds were in Kabul.

DIPLOMATIC REPRESENTATIVES

Of Afghánistán in Great Britain (31 Prince's Gate, London, SW7 1QQ)
Chargé d'Affaires: Mohammad Azam Shahim.

Of Great Britain in Afghánistán (Karte Parwan, Kábul)
Chargé d'Affaires: J. D. Garner, MVO.

Of Afghánistán in the USA (2341 Wyoming Ave., NW, Washington, D.C., 20008)
Chargé d'Affaires: Salem M. Spartak.

Of the USA in Afghánistán (Wazir Akbar Khan Mina, Kábul)
Chargé d'Affaires: Charles F. Dunbar.

Of Afghánistán to the United Nations
Ambassador: Farid Zarif.

Books of Reference

Arnold, A., *Afghanistan: The Soviet Invasion in Perspective.* Oxford and Stanford, 1981
Chaliand, G., *Rapport sur la résistance afghane.* Paris, 1981.—*Report from Afghanistan.* New York, 1982
Dupree, L., *Afghanistan.* Princeton Univ. Press, 1974
Fraser-Tytler, Sir W. K., *Afghanistan.* Rev. ed. OUP, 1967
Gilbertson, G. W., *Pakkhto Idiom Dictionary.* 2 vols. London, 1932
Gregorian, V., *The Emergence of Modern Afghanistan.* Stamford, 1970
Griffiths, J. C., *Afghanistan: Key to a Continent.* London, 1981
Hammond, T. T., *Red Star over Afghanistan.* Boulder, 1982
Hanifi, M. J., *Historical and Cultural Dictionary of Afghanistan.* Metuchen, 1976
Humlum, J., *La Géographie de l'Afghanistan.* Copenhagen, 1959
Klimburg, M., *Afghanistan.* Vienna, 1966
Male, B., *Revolutionary Afghanistan.* London, 1982
Misra, K. P., *Afghanistan in Crisis.* London, 1981
Newell, N. P. and Newell, R. S., *The Struggle for Afghanistan.* Cornell Univ. Press, 1981
Sykes, P. M., *A History of Afghanistan.* 2 vols. New York, 1975
Wilber, D. N. (ed.), *Afghanistan.* 2nd ed. New Haven, 1962.—(ed.), *Afghanistan, A Bibliography.* 2nd ed. New Haven, 1963

ALBANIA

Capital: Tirana
Population: 2·75m. (1982)
GNP per capita: US$840 (1979)

Republika Popullore Socialiste e Shqipërisë

HISTORY. After the death of Gjergi Kastrioti Skënderbeu (Skanderbeg), Albania's national hero, in 1468 Albania passed under Turkish suzerainty until 1912. Independence was proclaimed at Vlonë on 28 Nov. 1912, and the London conference of ambassadors decided upon its frontiers and nominated as its ruler Prince William of Wied, who arrived at Durrës on 7 March 1914, but on 3 Sept. 1914 left the country, which fell into a state of anarchy. By the secret Pact of London of 26 April 1915 provision was made for the partition of Albania; but this arrangement was repudiated on 3 June 1917, when the Italian C.-in-C. in Albania proclaimed at Gjirokastër the independence of Albania. In Jan. 1925 a republic was proclaimed and on 1 Sept. 1928 a monarchy. Ahmed Beg Zogu, President since 31 Jan. 1925, reigned as King Zog till April 1939, when, on the occupation of the country by the Italians, he fled to England. After the liberation he was deposed *in absentia* on 2 Jan. 1946. During the years 1939–44 the country was overrun by Italians and Germans. The official Albanian date of the liberation is 29 Nov. 1944.

On 10 Nov. 1945 the British, US and USSR Governments recognized the Provisional Government under Gen. Enver Hoxha, on the understanding that it would hold free elections. The elections of 2 Dec. 1945 resulted in a Communist-controlled assembly, which on 11 Jan. 1946 proclaimed Albania a republic.

In 1946 Great Britain and the USA broke off relations with Albania and vetoed its admission to the United Nations. Albania was finally admitted on 15 Dec. 1955.

Because of Albania's Stalinist and pro-Chinese attitudes diplomatic relations with USSR were broken off in 1961. In 1977 Albania terminated its special relationship with China. In Dec. 1981 the Prime Minister, Mehmet Shehu committed suicide. Later Hoxha alleged that Shehu had been a foreign agent. Massive purges of Shehu's associates in the leadership took place in 1982.

AREA AND POPULATION. The area of the country is 28,748 sq. km (11,101 sq. miles). By the peace treaty Italy restored the island of Sazan (Saseno) to Albania. At the census of Jan. 1979 the population was, 2,590,600 (34% urban; density, 90 per sq. km). Population in 1982, 2·75m. The capital is Tirana (1978 population (in 1,000), 198); other large towns are Shkodër (Shkodra, Scutari) (62·5), Durrës (Durrsi, Durazzo) (61), Vlorë (Vlona, Vlonë, Vlora, Valona) (58·4), Korçë (Korça, Koritza) (50·9), Elbasan (50·7). Other towns (1975): Berat (30), Fier (28), Gjirokastër (Argyrocastro) (22), Lushnjë (21), Kavajë, 1971 (18), Qytet Stalin (formerly Kuçovë) (14).

There is a small Greek minority (1977 estimate, 50,000).

Vital statistics, 1980 (per 1,000): Births, 26·5; deaths, 6·4; marriages, 8·1; divorces, 0·8; natural increase, 20·1 per thousand. Population density, 93 per sq. km. Growth rate, 1945–79, 2·5%. Life expectancy in 1979 was 69 years.

The country is administratively divided into 26 districts (*rreth*, pl. *rrethët*) (*see* map in THE STATESMAN'S YEAR-BOOK, 1962. N.B. The district of Ersekë has been renamed Kolonjë). Districts are subdivided into *lokaliteteve*.

Districts	*Area (sq. km)*	*Population (in 1,000) (1973)*	*Districts*	*Area (sq. km)*	*Population (in 1,000) (1973)*
Berat	1,026	124·3	Gramsh	695	29·4
Dibrë	1,569	106·8	Gjirokastër	1,137	53·5
Durrës	859	182·4	Kolonjë	805	19·2
Elbasan	1,466	154·7	Korçë	2,181	175·4
Fier	1,191	171·5	Krujë	607	75·6

Districts	Area (sq. km)	Population (in 1,000) (1973)	Districts	Area (sq. km)	Population (in 1,000) (1973)
Kukës	1,564	71·4	Pukë	969	32·8
Lezhë	479	40·5	Sarandë	1,097	66·5
Librazhd	1,013	48·5	Skrapar	775	30·8
Lushnjë	712	94·1	Shkodër	2,528	178·5
Mat	1,028	53·5	Tepelenë	817	37·8
Mirditë	698	29·4	Tirana	1,222	272·0
Përmet	930	31·7	Tropojë	1,043	30·5
Pogradec	725	49·3	Vlorë	1,609	133·5

The districts are for the greater part named after their capitals; exceptions: Tropojë, chief town, Bajram Curri; Mat, Burrel; Mirditë, Rrëshen; Skrapar, Çorovodë.

The Albanian language is divided into two dialects—Gheg, north of the river Shkumbi, and Tosk in the south. Many places therefore have two forms of name: Vlonë (Gheg), Vlorë (Tosk), etc., and many are known also by an Italian name, *e.g.*, Valona. Since 1945 the official language has been based on Tosk.

CLIMATE. Mediterranean-type, with rainfall mainly in winter, but thunderstorms are frequent and severe in the great heat of the plains in summer. Winters in the highlands can be severe, with much snow. Tirana. Jan. 44°F (6·8°C), July 75°F (23·9°C). Annual rainfall 54″ (1,353 mm).

CONSTITUTION AND GOVERNMENT. The political structure derived from the Constitution of 14 March 1946 as amended in 1950, 1955, 1960 and 1963. In Dec. 1976 a new Constitution was adopted, by which Albania became a 'Socialist People's Republic'. The supreme legislative body is the single-chamber People's Assembly of 250 deputies, which meets twice a year, and delegates its day-to-day functions to a Presidium composed of a chairman, 3 deputy chairmen, a secretary and 10 members. Election to the People's Assembly is by universal suffrage (at 18) every 4 years.

In the elections of 14 Nov. 1982 a 100% turnout of the electorate of 1,627,968 was claimed to vote for the 250 candidates on the single list of the Albanian Democratic Front. (There were 8 spoiled papers and 1 vote against).

The Government consists of a prime minister (Chairman of the Council of Ministers), 3 deputy prime ministers, 13 ministers and the chairman of the State Planning Commission. Effective rule is exercised by the Albanian Labour (*i.e.*, Communist) Party, founded 8 Nov. 1941, whose governing body is the Politburo.

In 1979 the Party had 88,000 full members and 13,500 candidates (37·5% workers, 29% farmers, 27% women).

Titular Head of State: Chairman of the Presidium of the People's Assembly: Ramiz Alia, elected Nov. 1982. In March 1983 the chief Party and Government posts were filled as follows: Full members of the Politburo:

First Secretary of the Central Committee of the Party: Enver Hoxha. *Chairman of the Council of Ministers:* Adil Çarçani, Ramiz Alia. Hekuran Isai *(Minister of the Interior)*, Pali Miska, Manush Myftiu,[1] Rita Marko. Muho Asllani; Hajreddin Celiku *(Ministry of Industry)*; Simon Stefani; Lenka Çuko. Candidate members: Llambi Gegprifti; Qirjako Mihali *(Minister of Finance)*. Besnek Bekteshi [1]; Prokop Murra *(Minister for Energy)*. Not in the Politburo: *Foreign Minister:* Reis Malile *(Minister of Foreign Trade):* Shane Korbeci. *Minister of Agriculture:* Themie Thomai. *Chairman, State Planning Commission:* Harilla Papajorgji.

[1] Deputy Chairman, Council of Ministers.

Local Government is carried out by People's Councils at village, *lokalitet*, town and district level. Councillors are elected for 3 years.

National flag: Red, with a black double-headed eagle and a red, gold-edged 5-pointed star above it. *Mercantile flag:* red, black, red (horizontal) with a red yellow-edged star in the centre.

National anthem: Rreth Flamurit te per bashkuar (The flag that united us in the struggle).

DEFENCE. Albania withdrew from the Warsaw Pact in 1968 in protest against the invasion of Czechoslovakia. Albania's military equipment was largely supplied by China before 1978.

Ranks were abolished in March 1966 and political commissars re-introduced.

Army. Army service is 2 years. Strength in 1981, 30,000 in 8 infantry and 1 armoured brigade, with about 100 T-34, T-54 and T-59 tanks. Security police ('SSSh') had a strength of 13,000, divided into 4 security battalions (5,000 personnel), and 5 battalions of frontier-guards (8,000).

Navy. The Navy consists of 3 submarines, 2 fleet minesweepers, 3 patrol vessels, 4 inshore minesweepers, 44 torpedo boats, 6 fast gunboats, 11 minesweeping boats, 1 degaussing ship, 4 oilers, 2 diving tenders, 2 torpedo recovery craft, 4 tugs and 12 small auxiliaries and service tenders. Navy personnel in 1983 exceeded 3,000 officers and ratings, including 300 coastal frontier guards. Service for ratings is 3 years. There are naval bases at Durrës and Vlorë.

Air Force. The Air Force, controlled by the Army, has about 10,000 officers and men, and operates the serviceable survivors of more than 125 combat aircraft received before relations with China were broken. The original force included 20 Chinese-built MiG-21s and 36 MiG-19s, some Il-28 twin-jet light bombers and 2 ground attack squadrons of MiG-15s and MiG-17s. Transport and training types include 3 Il-14s, 10 An-2s, Mi-4 helicopters, Yak-11s, Yak-18s and MiG-15UTIs.

INTERNATIONAL RELATIONS

Membership. Albania is a member of UN.

ECONOMY

Planning. For the first five 5-year plans *see* THE STATESMAN'S YEAR-BOOK, 1982–83. The sixth 5-year plan ran from 1976 to 1980. Annual average increases: national income, 5%; industrial production, 6·8%; agricultural production, 21·4%. The seventh 5-year plan covers 1981–85. Target increases: agricultural production, 32%, industrial, 34%. Emphasis is laid on industrial expansion, especially in the oil, mining and chemical industries. It is now stated that economic policy is founded on 'the revolutionary principle of self-reliance'.

Budget. Budget figures for 1979: Revenue, 7,800m. leks (7,200m. leks from enterprises and agricultural co-operatives); expenditure, 7,750m. leks (industry, 4,800m. leks; social, 1,800m. leks; defence, 885m. leks).

Currency. The monetary unit is the *lek* of 100 *qintars.* It replaced the gold franc *(franc ar)* in July 1947. In Aug. 1965 a new *lek* was introduced: 10 old *leks* = 1 new *lek.* There are 5, 10, 20 and 50 *qintar* coins and a 1 *lek* coin; notes are for 1, 3, 5, 10, 25, 50 and 100 *leks.* Exchange rates, March 1983: US$1 = 6·68 *leks*; £1 = 10·14.

Banking. The Albanian State Bank was founded in 1925 with Italian aid. In 1970 savings deposits amounted to 572m. leks. In 1970 the Agricultural Bank was set up as a credit institution for agricultural co-operatives.

Weights and Measures. The metric system is in force.

ENERGY AND NATURAL RESOURCES

Electricity. There are 6 hydro-electric power plants operational and one under construction. Electric power production in 1973 was 1,603m. kwh., of which 1,127m. was hydro-electric.

Oil. The oil industry is being rapidly expanded. Output in 1973: Crude, 2,107,000 tonnes; refined, 1,596,000 tonnes. Refining capacity in 1970 was over 1m. tonnes. Oil is produced chiefly at Qytet Stalin which a pipeline connects to the port of Vlorë. Natural gas is extracted.

Minerals. The mineral wealth of Albania is considerable but is only recently being developed. In 1971 there were 8 coal, 7 chromium (1977 output 9,000 tonnes) and 6 copper mines. Ferro-nickel ores are mined and output is increasing. In 1969 extensive coal deposits were discovered at Valias, near Tirana. There is no bituminous coal. Salt is extracted near Vlorë and bitumen mined at Selenicë. Production in tonnes (1973): Chrome ore, 611,000; copper ore, 435,000; ferro-nickel ore, 384,000; brown coal, 811,000; phosphate, 110,000; nitrogenous fertilizer, 106,000; bitumen (1964), 242,000; cement (1965), 133,600.

Agriculture. The country for the greater part is rugged, wild and mountainous, the exceptions being along the Adriatic littoral and the Korçë (Koritza) Basin, which are fertile. In 1973 a programme of land reclamation and anti-erosion measures was instituted. In 1970 arable land comprised 599,000 hectares and pasture 623,000 hectares. 283,200 hectares were irrigated.

Land is held by the State (largely forests and non-agricultural), state farms (33 in 1970 holding 100,700 hectares of arable land) and co-operatives (423 in 1980 producing 77% of agricultural output). Co-operatives are divided into 'advanced' and 'ordinary'. A pension plan for collective farmers was enacted in 1972. Tractors in 1980 numbered 17,300 (in 15-h.p. units).

The yield of the main crops in 1981 was (in 1,000 tonnes): Wheat, 510; sugar-beet, 270; maize, 250; potatoes, 140; fruit, 132; grapes, 62; oats, 30; sorghum, 30; cotton, 26; barley, 25; sunflower seeds, 25; wine, 23; rice, 17; beans, 16; tobacco, 15.

Livestock, 1981: Cattle, 476,000; sheep, 1·17m.; goats, 670,000; pigs, 125,000; horses and mules, 65,000; poultry, 2·48m.

Forestry. 47% of the territory of Albania is forest land, of which 38% is oak forest, 26% elm and 18% pine and birch. Timber reserves reach 44·5m. cu. metres. In 1967 forests covered 1,242,100 hectares; 6,784 hectares were afforested, 10,000 hectares improved in 1967.

Fisheries. The catch in 1964 was 3,600 tonnes.

INDUSTRY AND TRADE

Industry. All industry is nationalized down to the smallest workshop. Output is small, and the principal industries are agricultural product processing, textiles, oil products and cement. Chemical and engineering industries are being built up. The metallurgical combine at Elbasan is being extended.

Labour. In 1973, 462,900 persons worked in the socialist sector of the national economy, of whom 34·7% were employed in industry. In 1976, 46% of wage-earners were women.

Minimum wages may not fall below one-third of maximum. A new labour code was introduced in 1980 normalizing an 8-hour day and 6-day week and 12 days yearly paid holiday. Retirement age is 60 for men and 55 for women.

Commerce. Between 1954 and 1978 Chinese aid amounted to US$5,000m., but economic relations were then broken off. There are 1981–5 trade agreements with Bulgaria, Czechoslovakia, North Korea, Poland, Vietnam and Yugoslavia; and Albania also trades with Italy, France, Czechoslovakia and India. The establishment of joint companies with, and the acceptance of credits from, capitalist firms is forbidden by the constitution. In 1980 indebtedness to the West was US$100m.

Exports include crude oil, bitumen, chrome, nickel, copper, tobacco, fruit and vegetables.

Total trade between Albania and UK (British Department of Trade returns, in £1,000 sterling):

	1977	*1978*	*1979*	*1980*	*1981*	*1982*
Imports to UK	61	52	62	107	110	45
Exports and re-exports from UK	222	255	701	1,478	2,445	4,453

COMMUNICATIONS

Roads. There were, in 1960, 3,100 km of roads suitable for motor traffic. The mountain districts of the north are still mostly inaccessible for wheeled vehicles, and communications are still by means of pack ponies or donkeys. Registered motor vehicles in 1960: Cars, 1,900; lorries and buses, 3,400. Road traffic carried 8·6m. passengers in 1970; goods carried, 34m. tonnes.

Railways. Total length, in 1983 was 253 km. They comprise the lines Durrës–Tirana, Durrës–Kavajë–Pegin–Elbasan, Vlorë–Memaliaj, Vlorë–Milot, Perrenjas–Pogradec, Durrës–Tirana-Shkodër. In 1974 a railway was opened from Elbasan to the iron mines at Pishkash and a line is under construction from Fier to Balkh. In 1981 the Laç–Shkodër section of the Tirana–Shkodër line opened. In April 1982 Albania and Yugoslavia signed an agreement for the construction of a line from Shkodër to Titograd to be opened in 1984. Goods carried in 1970 amounted to 2,324,000 tonnes; passengers (1971), 6·4m.

Aviation. There are regular scheduled flights from Tirana (Rinas Airport) to Belgrade, Bucharest, Budapest and East Berlin. Olympic Airways operate a weekly flight from Athens to Tirana.

Shipping. The ports are Shëngjin (San Giovanni di Medua), Durrës (Durazzo), Vlorë (Valona) and Sarandë (Santi Quaranta). 567,000 tonnes of freight were carried in 1970.

Post and Broadcasting. Number of post and telegraph offices (1970), 292; telephones (1963), 10,150. There are 17 broadcasting stations, including Tirana and Korçë. Radio Tirana operates a foreign service in 18 languages. Radio receiving sets (1978), 200,000; television sets, 5,000. Regular television broadcasting began in 1971.

Cinemas and Theatres (1973). There were 105 cinemas with an attendance of 7·9m. and 27 theatres with an attendance of 1·6m.

Newspapers. In 1976 there were 25 newspapers with an annual circulation of 47m. The Party paper is *Zëri i Popullit* (Voice of the People) (daily circulation, 105,000).

JUSTICE, RELIGION, EDUCATION AND WELFARE

Justice is administered by People's Courts. Judges of the Supreme Court are elected by the People's Assembly for 4-year terms. The Office of the Procurator-General oversees the administration of justice. In 1966 the Ministry of Justice was incorporated into the Ministry of the Interior. In 1968 tribunals were set up in towns and villages to try minor crimes which had previously been dealt with by courts.

Religion. Albania is constitutionally an atheist state. In 1967 the Government closed all mosques and churches. For details of the situation before 1967 *see* THE STATESMAN'S YEAR-BOOK, 1969–70. The population had been mainly Moslem.

Education. Primary education is free and compulsory in 8-year schools from 7 to 15 years. Secondary education is available in 12-year (general), technical-professional or lower vocational schools. Periods of productive work and military service are intermingled with full-time education. There were, in 1973–74, 1,615 kindergartens with 52,899 pupils and 2,790 teachers; 1,470 primary schools with 569,600 pupils and 22,686 teachers; 39 secondary schools with 32,900 pupils; 116 technical–professional schools with 69,700 pupils (the last two categories had 3,990 teachers taken together); and (in 1969–70) 36 institutes of higher education with 36,525 students and 941 teachers, including a university in Tirana (founded 1957), a polytechnic, an agricultural college, a medical school, 5 teachers' training colleges and an institute of science. In 1969–70 there were 382 teachers and 12,783 full-time students at Tirana University. An Albanian Academy was founded in 1973.

Health. Medical services are free, though medicines are charged for. In 1982 there were 4,476 doctors and dentists, and 70 hospital beds per 1,000 inhabitants. In 1982 there were 730 maternity hospitals or hospital sections.

DIPLOMATIC REPRESENTATIVE

Of Albania to the United Nations
Ambassador: Abdi Baleta.

Books of Reference

Vjetari Statistikor (Statistical Yearbook). Tirana, irregular, 1959–72
35 vjet Shqipëri socialiste (statistical handbook). Tirana, 1979
History of the Labour Party of Albania. Tirana, 1971
History of the Labour Party of Albania 1966–1980. Tirana, 1981
Bertolino, J., *Albanie: la Citadelle de Staline.* Paris, 1979
Duro, I., and Hysa, R., *Albanian-English Dictionary.* Tirana, 1981
Hoxha, E., *Réflexions sur la Chine.* Paris, 1979.—*Speeches, Conversations and Articles, 1969–1970.* Tirana, 1980.—*The Khrushchevites: Memoirs.* Tirana, 1980
Logoreci, A., *The Albanians: Europe's Forgotten Survivors.* London, 1977
Marmullaku, R., *Albania and the Albanians.* London, 1975
Martin, N., *La Forteresse Albanaise: un Communisme National.* Paris, 1979
Pano, N. C., *The People's Republic of Albania.* Baltimore, 1968
Pollo, S. and Arben, P., *The History of Albania.* London, 1981
Prifti, P. R., *Socialist Albania since 1944.* Cambridge, Mass., 1978
Russ, W., *Der Entwicklungsweg Albaniens.* Meisenheim-am-Glan, 1979
Schnytzer, A., *Stalinist Economic Strategy: The Case of Albania.* OUP, 1982
Tönnes, B., *Sonderfall Albanien: Enver Hoxhas 'Eigener Weg und die Historischen Ursprünge seiner Ideologie.* Munich, 1980

ALGERIA

Capital: Algiers
Population: 21m. (1982)
GNP per capita: US$1,920 (1980)

El Djemhouria El Djazaïria Eddemokratia Echaabia

HISTORY. On 1 Nov. 1954 the National Liberation Front (FLN) went over to open warfare against the French administration and armed forces. For details of history 1958–62 *see* p. 76 THE STATESMAN'S YEAR-BOOK, 1982–83. A cease-fire agreement was reached on 18 March 1962, and Gen. de Gaulle declared Algeria independent on 3 July 1962; the Republic was declared on 25 Sept. 1962.

On 25 Sept. the National Assembly met and elected Ferhat Abbas President of the Assembly and Ben Bella President of the Council of Ministers.

A national referendum held on 15 Sept. 1963 elected Ben Bella, the only candidate, as President of the new Democratic People's Republic of Algeria.

The Government was overthrown by a junta of army officers which, on 19 June 1965, established a Revolutionary Council under Col. Houari Boumédienne.

AREA AND POPULATION. Algeria is bounded west by Morocco and Western Sahara, south-west by Mauritania and Mali, south-east by Niger, east by Libya and Tunisia, and north by the Mediterranean Sea. It has an area of 2,381,741 sq. km. Population (census 1977) 17,273,000; estimate (1982) 21m.

The 31 departments are as follows:

Departments	*Area (sq. km)*	*Population (1980)*	*Departments*	*Area (sq. km)*	*Population (1980)*
Adrar	422,498	146,815	Médéa	8,704	511,070
Alger (Algiers)	786	2,159,573	Mostaganem	7,024	791,688
Annaba	3,489	544,519	M'Sila	19,825	477,614
Batna	14,882	633,723	Ouahran (Oran)	1,820	795,405
Béchar	306,000	156,107	Ouargla	559,234	226,728
Béjaia	3,444	590,979	Oum el Bouaghi	8,123	429,296
Biskra	109,728	585,403	Saida	106,177	469,348
Blida	3,704	962,664	Sétif	10,350	1,061,161
Bouira	4,517	401,419	Sidi-Bel-Abbès	11,648	546,377
Constantine	3,562	929,213	Skikda	4,748	520,359
Djelfa	22,905	722,927	Tamanrasset	556,000	60,702
El Asnam	8,677	384,694	Tébessa	16,575	403,278
Guelma	8,624	589,120	Tiaret	23,456	676,467
Jijel	3,704	529,651	Tizi-Ouzou	3,756	931,071
Laghouat	112,052	354,959	Tlemcen	9,284	618,856
Mascara	5,846	455,314			

The chief towns (estimates, 1974) are as follows: Algiers, 1,503,720; Oran, 485,139; Constantine, 350,183; Annaba, 313,174; Tizi-Ouzou, 223,702; Blida, 158,947; Sétif, 157,065; Sidi-Bel-Abbès, 151,148; Skikda, 127,968; Batna, 115,138; Tlemcen, 115,054; Al Asnam, 114,327; Bejaia, 103,996; Médéa, 102,336; Mostaganem, 101,780.

Arabic is spoken by 80·4% of the population and Berber by 18·7%.

CONSTITUTION AND GOVERNMENT. A new Constitution was approved by referendum on 19 Nov. 1976 and came into effect 3 days later. It provides for a single Party, the *Front de Libération Nationale,* working in parallel with state organs.

The President of the Republic is Head of State, Head of the Armed Forces, and

Head of Government. He is nominated by the FLN Congress and elected by universal suffrage for 5-year terms (renewable).

Former Presidents of the Republic:

Ferhat Abbas, 25 Sept. 1962–15 Sept. 1963.
Ahmed Ben Bella, 15 Sept. 1963–19 June 1965 (deposed).
Col. Houari Boumediénne, 19 June 1965–27 Dec. 1978 (died).
Rabah Bitat (interim), 27 Dec. 1978–9 Feb. 1979.

President of the Republic, General Secretary of the FLN, Minister of Defence: Col. Bendjedid Chadli (sworn in 9 Feb. 1979).

The President appoints a Prime Minister and other Ministers, and presides over meetings of the Council of Ministers.

The Council of Ministers, as in Jan. 1983, consisted of:

Prime Minister: Col. Mohammed Benahmed Abdelghani.

Foreign Affairs: Dr Ahmed Taleb Ibrahimi. *Interior:* Mohammed Hadj Yalla. *Finance:* Boualem Ben Hamouda. *Agriculture and Agrarian Revolution:* Lieut.-Col. Selim Saâdi. *Irrigation:* Brahim Brahmia. *Public Works:* Mohammed Kortebi. *Energy and Petrochemicals:* Belkacem Nabi. *Light Industry:* Said Ait Messaoudène. *Heavy Industry:* Mohammed Liassine. *Planning and Territorial Organization:* Abdelhamid Brahimi. *Health:* Abderrazak Bouhara. *Higher Education and Scientific Research:* Abdelhak Brehri. *Primary and Secondary Education:* Mohammed Kharroubi. *Labour:* Mouloud Oumeziane. *Vocational Training:* Mohammed Nabi. *Commerce:* Abdelaziz Khallaf. *Posts and Telecommunications:* Bachir Rouis. *Housing, Construction and Town Planning:* Ahmed Ali Ghazali. *Veterans:* Bakhti Nemiche. *Religious Affairs:* Abderrahman Chibane. *Youth and Sport:* Adennour Bekka. *Tourism:* Col. Abdelmadjid Allahoum. *Transport:* Salah Goudjil. *Justice:* Baki Boualem. *Information:* Boualem Bessaiah. *Culture:* Abdelmadjid Meziane.

Legislative power is held by the National People's Assembly, whose 261 members are elected for a 5-year term by universal suffrage from the single list of the FLN who nominate 3 candidates for each single-member seat.

National flag: Vertically green and white, a red crescent and star over all in centre.

The official language is Arabic, French being the principal foreign language.

DEFENCE

Army. The Army in 1983 had a strength of 150,000 men, organized in 1 armoured, 1 mechanized and 4 motorized brigades, 3 tank battalions, 2 parachute, 11 air defence, 4 engineer and 63 independent battalions. Equipment includes Soviet T-54, T-55, T-62 and T-72 tanks.

Navy. The Navy, almost entirely supplied from the USSR, consists of 2 new frigates, 2 missile-armed corvettes, 2 fleet minesweepers, 6 patrol vessels, 22 fast missile boats, 4 torpedo boats, 18 coastguard fast gunboats, 1 landing vessel, 1 diving tender, 2 training craft, 1 torpedo recovery vessel, 1 degaussing ship, 1 survey ship, 6 fishery protection craft and 18 coastguard cutters (16 Italian-built). Naval personnel in 1983 totalled 300 officers and cadets and 3,500 ratings.

The French naval base of Mers el Kebir was taken over by the Algerian army and navy in Feb. 1968.

Air Force. Five MiG-15 jet-fighters were delivered in 1962 as the nucleus of an Algerian Air Force. Since then many more aircraft of Soviet design have followed, and the Air Force now has about 300 combat aircraft and 12,500 personnel. Training and technical assistance have been given by Egypt and the Soviet Union. There are 3 squadrons of MiG-21s, 3 squadrons of MiG-23 variable-geometry interceptors and fighter-bombers, 2 squadrons of MiG-17 fighter-bombers, 2 squadrons of Su-7 and Su-20 variable-geometry attack aircraft, 1 squadron of Il-28 twin-jet bombers, 2 squadrons with MiG-25 fighter and reconnaissance aircraft, more than 30 Mi-24 helicopter gunships, 14 C-130H Hercules and An-12 transports, an

Il-18 and a variety of smaller transports, a wing of 4 Mi-6, 12 Mi-8, about 10 Mi-4, 5 Puma and 6 Hughes 269 helicopters, and training units equipped with CM.170 Magister armed jet counter-insurgency/trainers (26), 3 Beech Queen Air twin-engine/instrument trainers, MiG-15s and -15UTIs, and two-seat versions of operational types. Surface-to-air missile units have Soviet-built 'Guidelines', 'Gainfuls' and 'Gaskins'.

INTERNATIONAL RELATIONS

Membership. Algeria is a member of UN, OAU, the Arab League, OAPEC, OPEC and the Maghreb Organization.

ECONOMY

Planning. The second 4-year development plan (1974–77) envisaged investment of DA 110,000m. The third development plan (1980–84) gives priority to education, housing, water supply and agriculture.

Currency. The Algerian currency is the *dinar* (DA). There are in circulation banknotes of DA 5, 10, 50 and 100 and coins of 1, 2, 5, 20 and 50 centimes and DA 1, 5 and 10. In March 1983, £1 = 7·049 DA; US$1 = 4·647.

Budget. The budget (including extraordinary budget) was as follows in calendar years (in DA 1m.):

	1976	*1977*	*1978*	*1979*	*1980*
Revenue	26,215	33,479	36,782	46,429	59,344
Expenditure	20,118	25,472	29,946	33,514	43,214

Banking. The Banque Centrale d'Algérie is the government emission bank. Other banks operating in Algeria are Banque National d'Algérie, Crédit Populaire d'Algérie, Banque Extérieure d'Algérie, Caisse Algérienne de Développement, Banque Algérienne de Développement, Banque de l'Agriculture et du Développement.

Weights and Measures. The metric system is in use.

ENERGY AND NATURAL RESOURCES

Electricity. Production of energy in 1980 totalled 7·1m. kwh.

Oil. Two large oilfields went into production in 1957 around Edjélé and Hassi Messaoud and in 1959 at El Gassi. In 1960 about 200 wells were productive. Natural gas was discovered at Djebel Berga in 1954 and at Hassi-R'Mel in 1956. Oil pipelines from Edjélé to Skirra (Tunisia) and from Hassi Messaoud to Bougie, and a gas pipeline from Hassi Messaoud *via* Hassi-R'Mel to Mostaganem–Oran–Algiers, have been completed. Oil production in 1980, 51·5m. tonnes. Production of natural gas in 1980 was 14,823m. cu. metres.

Minerals. Algeria possesses deposits of iron, zinc, lead, mercury, copper and antimony. Kaolin, marble and onyx, salt and coal are also found. Mineral output in 1980 (1,000 tonnes): Ferrous metals, 3,500; zinc, 7·6; copper, 0·8; lead, 2·7; phosphates, 1,025.

Agriculture. There exists a small area of highly fertile plains and valleys near the coast, mainly owned by self-management committees and some Europeans, which is cultivated scientifically, and where profitable returns are obtained from vineyards, cereals, etc. Self-management groups supplied 60% of revenue from agriculture in 1970, and held 80% of cultivated land. The greater part of Algeria is of limited value for agricultural purposes. In the northern portion the mountains are generally better adapted to grazing and forestry than agriculture, and a large portion of the native population is quite poor. In spite of the many excellent roads built by the Government, a considerable area of the mountainous region is without adequate means of communication and is accessible only with difficulty. There were an estimated 7·5m. hectares of agricultural land in 1978–79, of which 6·8m. hectares were arable; 200,000 hectares under vine and 31·7m. hectares pastures and brushlands.

The chief crops in 1980 were (in 1,000 tonnes): Wheat, 1,512; barley, 794; dates, 201; potatoes, 591; oranges, 281; wine, 284; tomatoes, 182; olives, 103; onions, 118; oats, 110.

Livestock, 1981: 134,000 horses, 727,000 mules and asses, 1·37m. cattle, 1·36m. sheep, 2,723,000 goats and 149,000 camels.

Forestry. The greater part of the state forests are mere brushwood, but there are very large areas covered with cork-oak trees, Aleppo pine, evergreen oak and cedar. The dwarf-palm is grown on the plains, alfa on the table-land. Timber is cut for firewood, also for industrial purposes, for railway sleepers, telegraph poles, etc., and for bark for tanning. Considerable portions of the forest area are also leased for tillage, or for pasturage for cattle and sheep.

Fisheries. There are extensive fisheries for sardines, anchovies, sprats, tunny fish, etc., and also shellfish. In 1977, 692 boats were employed in fishing. Fish taken in 1980 amounted to 33,615 tonnes, value DA 311m.

INDUSTRY AND TRADE

Industry. The main industries are iron and steel, plastics and fertilizers.

Commerce. The foreign trade of Algeria was as follows (in DA 1m.):

	1977	*1978*	*1979*	*1980*
Imports	29,534	34,439	32,378	41,545
Exports	25,356	25,037	36,505	52,418

In 1980 imports came chiefly from France (22%), Federal Republic of Germany (14%), Italy (12%), USA (7%). Exports went mainly to USA (49%), Federal Republic of Germany (11%), France (15%).

Crude oil amounted to 70% and petroleum products 14%, of exports.

Total trade between Algeria and UK (British Department of Trade returns, in £1,000 sterling):

	1977	*1978*	*1979*	*1980*	*1981*	*1982*
Imports to UK	49,762	37,930	87,526	114,054	159,470	176,304
Exports and re-exports from UK	98,655	120,642	115,016	142,552	172,964	199,234

Tourism. In 1976, 184,800 tourists visited Algeria.

COMMUNICATIONS

Roads. There were in 1978, 19,157 km of national highway. Motor vehicles in 1980 included 472,483 passenger cars and 283,966 commercial vehicles.

Railways. In 1982 there were 3,890 km of which 2,632 km is of standard gauge (256 km electrified) and 1,258 km of 1,055mm gauge railway open for traffic. In 1979 the railways carried 1,900m. passengers-km and 3,853m. tonne-km of freight.

Aviation. There are 65 airfields controlled by government and 135 owned by petroleum companies. Air Algeria serves the main Algerian cities, and an international network. Algeria is also served by Swissair, Royal Air Maroc, United Arab Airline, Tunis Air, SABENA, Aeroflot, Interflug, Alitalia and Air France. In 1980 the airports handled 2·84m. passengers and 22,479 tonnes of freight.

Shipping. In 1980, 63·2m. tonnes of goods were handled at Algerian ports.

A state shipping line, Compagnie Nationale Algérienne de Navigation, was formed in Jan. 1964 and comprises (1980) 1·2m. gross tonnes.

Post and Broadcasting. There were, in 1980, 1,534 post offices; number of telephones (1981), 484,973, of which 161,879 were in Algiers and 42,184 in Oran. In 1974 there were some 3·5m. radio receivers and 500,000 TV licences issued.

Newspapers (1980). There were 4 daily newspapers, 1 in French and 3 in Arabic, with a combined circulation of 350,000.

JUSTICE, RELIGION, EDUCATION AND WELFARE

Justice. There are appeal courts at Algiers, Constantine and Oran; and in the *arrondissements* are 17 courts of first instance. There are also commercial courts and justices of the peace with extensive powers. Criminal justice is organized as in France.

The Supreme Court is at the same time Council of State and High Court of Appeal.

Religion. The overwhelming part of the population are Moslems. The Roman Catholic Church has an archbishop and 2 bishops, with some 400 officiating clergymen. Jews number about 150,000.

There are 13 Protestant pastors and 6 Jewish rabbis sharing in government grants.

Education. About 80% of children attended primary school in 1979. Primary schools had 3,918,827 pupils in 1981; secondary schools had 999,937 pupils and technical schools, 12,903. In 1979 there were 13,315 students in teacher-training establishments. In 1981 there were 72,200 students in higher education including universities at Algiers, Oran, Constantine and Annaba. There are also university centres at Tlemcen, Tizi-Ouzou, Sétif, Batna and Tiaret.

Health. There were in 1980, 182 general and specialized hospitals with together 45,160 beds; there were 6,081 doctors, 1,183 dentists, 778 pharmacists. There were also 1,422 dispensaries and consulting rooms, 747 health centres and 175 specializing centres for tuberculosis, venereal disease and trachoma.

DIPLOMATIC REPRESENTATIVES

Of Algeria in Great Britain (54 Holland Park, London, W11 3RS)
Ambassador: Redha Malek.

Of Great Britain in Algeria (Résidence Cassiopée, 7 Chemin des Glycines, Algiers)
Ambassador: B. L. Strachan, CMG.

Of Algeria in the USA (2118 Kalorama Rd., NW, Washington, D.C., 20008)
Ambassador: Layachi Yaker.

Of the USA in Algeria (4 Chemin Cheikh Bachir Brahimi, Algiers)
Ambassador: Michael H. Newlin.

Of Algeria to the United Nations
Ambassador: Mohammed Bedjaoui.

Books of Reference

Statistical Information: The Service de Statisque Générale (12, rue Bab-Azoun, Alger) publishes the annual *Statistique Générale de l'Algérie, Documents statistiques sur le commerce de l'Algérie* (from 1902). *Tableaux de l'économie algérienne* (1960).

Gordon, D. C., *The Passing of French Algeria.* OUP, 1965
Hensissart, P., *Wolves in the City: The Death of French Algeria.* New York, 1970
Horne, A., *A Savage War of Peace: Algeria 1954–1962.* London, 1977
Ministère de l'Information et de la Culture, *La Révolution Algérienne: Réalités et Perspectives,* Algiers, 1972.—*Dix années de réalisations 19 juin 1965–19 juin 1975.* Algiers, 1976.—*Statistiques 1967–78.* Algiers, 1980
Lawless, R. I., *Algeria.* [Bibliography] Oxford and Santa Barbara, 1981
Ottaway, D., *Algeria: The Politics of a Socialist Revolution.* Berkeley, 1970
Quandt, W. B., *Revolution and Political Leadership: Algeria, 1954–68.* Cambridge, Mass., 1970
Verlaque, C., *Le Sahara pétrolier.* Paris, 1964

ANDORRA

Capital: Andorre-la-Vieille
Population: 38,051 (1982)

Principat d'Andorra

HISTORY AND CONSTITUTION. The political status of Andorra was regulated by the *Paréage* of 1278 which placed Andorra under the joint suzerainty of the Comte de Foix and of the Bishop of Urgel. The rights vested in the house of Foix passed by marriage to that of Bearn and, on the accession of Henri IV, to the French crown. The sovereignty is exercised jointly by the President of the French Republic and the Bishop of Urgel.

The co-princes are represented in Andorra by the *'Viguier français'* and the *'Viguier Episcopal'*. Each co-prince has set up a Permanent Delegation for Andorran affairs; the Prefect of the Eastern Pyrenees is the French Permanent Delegate.

The valleys pay every second year a due of 960 francs to France and 460 pesetas to the bishop.

A 'General Council of the Valleys' submits motions and proposals to the Permanent Delegations. Its 28 members are elected for 4 years; half of the council is renewed every 2 years.

The council nominates a First Syndic *(Syndic Procureur Général)* and a Second Syndic from outside its members.

First Syndic: Francesc Cerqueda-Pascuet.

National flag: Three vertical strips of blue, yellow, red, with the arms of Andorra in the centre.

AREA AND POPULATION. The co-principality of Andorra is situated in the eastern Pyrenees on the French–Spanish border. The country consists of gorges, narrow valleys and defiles, surrounded by high mountain peaks varying between 1,880 and 3,000 metres. Its maximum length is 30 km and its width 20 km; it has an area of 465 sq. km (190 sq. miles) and a population of (1982) 38,051, scattered in 7 villages.

Catalan is the official and spoken language.

ECONOMY

Budget. The 1979 budget balanced at 3,209m. pesetas.

Currency. French and Spanish currency are both in use.

Tourism. Tourism is the main industry, and over 6m. people visited Andorra in 1982.

COMMUNICATIONS

Roads. A good road connects the Spanish and French frontiers by way of Sant Julià, Andorre-la-Vieille, les Escaldes, Encamp, Canillo and Soldeu: it crosses the Col d'Envalira (2,400 metres). Another road connects Andorre-la-Vieille with La Massana and Ordino. Motor vehicles (1980) 28,630.

Aviation. The nearest airports are at Barcelona and Perpignan.

Post and Broadcasting. Number of telephones (1981) 15,785. Radio Andorra is a private commercial broadcasting company. Number of receivers (1977), radio, 7,000; TV, 3,000.

JUSTICE, RELIGION AND EDUCATION

Justice. Judicial power is exercised in civil matters in the first instance, according to the plaintiff's choice, by either the *Bayle Français* or the *Bayle Episcopal*, who are nominated by the respective co-princes. The judge of appeal is nominated alternately for 5 years by each co-prince; the third instance *(Tercera Sala)* is either the supreme court of Andorra at Perpignan or the supreme court of the Bishop at Urgel.

Criminal justice is administered by the *Corts* consisting of the 2 Viguiers, the judge of appeal, 2 *rahonadors* elected by the general council of the valleys, a general attorney and an attorney nominated for 5 years alternatively by each of the co-princes. The accused may be assisted by a barrister.

Religion. The prevailing religious denomination is Roman Catholic.

Education. In 1979–80 there were 1,761 pupils at infant schools, 3,318 at primary schools, 2,380 at secondary schools and 181 at technical schools.

Books of Reference

Brutails, *La Coutume d'Andorre.* Paris, 1904
Corts Peyret, J., *Geografia e Historia de Andorra.* Barcelona, 1945
Llobet, S., *El medio y la vida en Andorra.* Barcelona, 1947
Vidally Guitart, J. M., *Institutiones politicas y sociales de Andorra.* Madrid, 1949

ANGOLA

República Popular de Angola

Capital: Luanda
Population: 7·08m. (1982)
GNP per capita: US$470 (1980)

HISTORY. The first Europeans to arrive in Angola were the Portuguese in 1482, and the first settlers arrived there in 1491. Luanda was founded in 1575. Apart from a brief period of Dutch occupation from 1641 to 1648, Angola remained a Portuguese colony until 11 June 1951, when it became an Overseas Province of Portugal. On 11 Nov. 1975 Angola became fully independent as the People's Republic of Angola.

AREA AND POPULATION. Angola is bounded by Congo on the north, Zaïre on the north and north-east, Zambia on the east, South West Africa/Namibia on the south and the Atlantic ocean on the west. The area is 1,246,700 sq. km (481,351 sq. miles) including the 7,270 sq. km province of Cabinda, an enclave of territory separated by 30 km of Zaïre. The most important towns (with 1970 populations) are Luanda, the capital (480,613), Huambo (61,885), Lobito (59,258), Benguela (40,996), Lubango (31,674) and Malange (31,559). The population at census, 1970, was 5,673,046, of whom 300,000 were white. Estimate (1982) 7·08m., of whom 38% speak Umbundu, 27% Kimbundu, 13% Lunda and 11% Kikongo. Portuguese remains the official language. There were (1978) about 40,000 whites in Angola.

CONSTITUTION AND GOVERNMENT. Under the Constitution adopted at independence, the sole legal party is the *Movimento Popular de Libertação de Angola – Partido de Trabalho.* The supreme organ of state is the unicameral National People's Assembly, whose 203 members were first elected in Aug. 1980 for a 3-year term and a further 20 members appointed by the 75-member Central Committee of the MPLA–PT. There is an executive President, who appoints a Council of Ministers to assist him.

The Council of Ministers in Jan. 1983 was as follows:

President: José Eduardo dos Santos.

Planning: Lopo Fortunato do Nascimento. *Defence:* Col. Pedro Maria Tonha (Pedalé). *Foreign Relations:* Paulo Teixeira Jorge. *Justice:* Diogenes de Assis Boavida. *Education:* Augusto Lopes Teixeira (Tutu). *Health:* Agostinho Mendes de Carvalho. *Finance:* Augusto Teixeira de Matos. *External Trade:* Ismael Gaspar Martins. *Internal Trade:* Adriano Perreira dos Santos Junior. *Industry:* Maj. Alberto do Carmo Bento Ribeiro. *Transport and Communications:* Fernando Faustino Muteka. *Labour and Social Security:* Horacio Perreira Brás da Silva. *Agriculture:* Artur Vidal Gomes. *State Security:* Col. Julião Mateus Paulo (Dino Matross). *Interior:* Manuel Alexandre Rodrigues (Kito). *Petroleum and Energy:* Pedro Castro Van-Dúnem (Lou). *Construction:* Manuel Alves dos Passos Mangueira. *Housing:* Lourenço Ferreira (Diandengue). *Provincial Co-ordination:* Maj. Evaristo Domingos (Kimba). *Fisheries:* Emílio Guerra. There are 4 Secretaries of State.

Flag: Horizontally red over black, with a star and an arc of cogwheel crossed by a machete, all yellow over all in the centre.

Local government: Angola is divided into 18 provinces – (Cabinda, Zaïre, Uíge, Luanda, Cuanza Norte, Cuanza Sul, Malange, Lunda Norte, Lunda Sul, Benguela, Huambo, Bié, Moxico, Cuando-Cubango, Moçâmedes, Huíla, Cunene and Bengo) each under a Provincial Commissioner, appointed by the President and an elected legislative of from 55 to 85 members.

DEFENCE

Army. The Army has 2 armoured, 17 infantry, and 4 air defence brigades. Total strength (1983): 35,000.

Navy. Twenty Portuguese naval craft were transferred on independence in 1975 and 9 vessels were acquired from the Soviet Navy in 1977-79, when 8 merchant ships were taken over from local trade for naval use. There are 4 fast torpedo boats, 2 fast gunboats, 5 patrol craft, 7 coastal patrol boats, 17 landing craft, 1 survey ship and 8 auxiliary vessels. Naval personnel in 1983 totalled 1,500.

Air Force. The Angolan People's Air Force (FAPA) was formed in 1976. Combat equipment is mainly of Soviet origin, comprising about 25 MiG-21 and 15 MiG-17 fighters, supported by 3 MiG-15UTI two-seat trainers. FAPA also has 1 F.27 Maritime overwater reconnaissance aircraft, 1 Noratlas, 1 Tu-134A, 1 F.27 Friendship, 4 Nord 262, 2 L-100-20 Hercules, 5 An-26 and 3 C-47 transports, 13 Islander twin-engined light transports, 2 Turbo-Porter liaison aircraft, 12 PC-7 Turbo Trainers, 24 L-39 jet trainers, and 13 Alouette III and 15 Mi-8 helicopters.

INTERNATIONAL RELATIONS

Membership. Angola is a member of UN and OAU.

ECONOMY

Budget. The 1981 budget balanced at 108,874m. Kwanza.

Currency. The currency is the *kwanza* divided into 100 *lwei*. Coins are of 50 *lwei*, 1, 2, 5 and 10 *kwanza*; notes are of 20, 50, 100, 500 and 1,000 *kwanza*. In March 1983, £1 = 47 *kwanza*; US$1 = 30 *kwanza*.

Banking. All banking was nationalized in 1975. The *Banco Nacional de Angola* is the central bank and bank of issue, while the *Banco Popular de Angola* handles all commercial activities throughout the country.

Weights and Measures. The metric system is in force.

ENERGY AND NATURAL RESOURCES

Electricity. Production (1977) totalled 1,360 m. kwh, mainly hydro-electricity.

Oil. Total production (1980) 7·4m. tonnes.

Minerals. The country possesses valuable diamond deposits. Production of diamonds during 1981 totalled 1·4m. carats (1978, 650,000). Production (1973) of salt, 96,717 tonnes. There has been no production of iron ore since 1975, but the mines at Kassinga were restarted in 1980 and a second project near Dondo started production in early 1981. Manganese and copper deposits exist.

Agriculture. The principal cash crops (with 1979 production, in 1,000 tonnes) were coffee (60), bananas (300), palm oil (40), palm kernels (12), cotton (11); others include sugar, tobacco, citrus fruit and sisal. Food crops comprise cassava (*c.* 1,700), maize (300), sweet potatoes (170) and beans (55).

Livestock (1981): 3·2m. cattle, 230,000 sheep, 940,000 goats, 420,000 pigs.

Fisheries. Total catch (1978) 118,600 tonnes.

Forestry. Mahogany and other hardwoods are exported, chiefly from the tropical rain forests of the north, especially Cabinda. Production (1979) 8·56m. cu. metres.

COMMERCE. Imports (1979, in 1m. kwanza), 28,093; exports, 39,531. The chief imports are textiles, transport equipment, foodstuffs, pig-iron and steel; chief exports are crude oil, coffee, diamonds, sisal, fish, maize, palm-oil. Oil represented 68% of exports, coffee 14% and diamonds 11%.

Total trade between Angola and UK for calendar years (British Department of Trade returns, in £1,000 sterling):

	1979	*1980*	*1981*	*1982*
Imports to UK	49,469	83,125	6,388	7,368
Exports and re-exports from UK	30,561	27,811	39,507	25,781

COMMUNICATIONS

Roads. There were, in 1973, 72,323 km of roads, and in 1978, 143,100 cars and 42,600 commercial vehicles.

Railways. The length of railways open for traffic in 1982 was 2,798 km. The Benguela Railway runs from Lobito to the Zaïre border at Dilolo where it connects with the National Railways of Zaïre. Other lines link Luanda with Malange; Gunza with Gabela; and Moçâmedes with Menongue. In 1979 Angola's railways carried 7·6m. passengers and 876,000 tonnes of freight.

Aviation. Luanda has international air links to Lisbon, Rome, Paris, Moscow, Budapest, Brazzaville, Saõ Tomé, Lusaka, Maputo, Sal (Cape Verde Islands), Havana, Kinshasa, Libreville, Berlin, Tripoli, Lagos, Algiers, Niamey, and Sofia.

Shipping. In 1973, 6,500 vessels of 16,256,322 net tons entered Angolan ports. In 1975, 2·85m. tonnes were discharged and 16m. tonnes loaded in Angolan ports.

Post and Broadcasting. Angola is connected by cable with east, west and south African telegraph systems. There were, in 1973, 1,808 km of telegraph lines, 77 telephone stations (with 29,796 instruments in 1978), 162 telegraph stations and 31 wireless stations.

Emissora Oficial de Angola is the largest of the 18 stations operating on medium- and short-waves. *Emissora Oficial* transmits 3 programmes as well as operating 2 regional stations. Number of radio receivers (1981)125,000 and television receivers 20,000.

Cinemas. There were, in 1972, 47 cinemas with seating capacity of 35,142.

Newspaper. The national daily newspaper is *Jornal de Angola*, with a circulation of 41,000.

RELIGION, EDUCATION AND WELFARE

Religion. Article 7 of the Constitution of the People's Republic of Angola states that: 'The People's Republic of Angola is a lay state, where there is a complete separation of religious institutions from the state. All religions will be respected and the State will give protection to churches and religious places and objects so long as they accept the laws of the State'.

In 1979 46% of the population were Roman Catholic, 12% Protestant and 42% animist.

Education. In 1983 there were 2·4m. pupils in primary schools, 153,000 in secondary schools and 4,746 students in higher education. The *Universidade de Angola* (founded 1963) at Luanda with faculties at Huambo and Lubango, had 3,500 students in 1982.

Health. In 1972 there were 4 state, 14 regional and 70 rural hospitals and about 260 health centres and dispensaries, with a total of 18,011 hospital beds. In 1973 there were 383 doctors, 87 pharmacists, 284 midwives and 3,115 nursing personnel.

DIPLOMATIC REPRESENTATIVES

Of Great Britain in Angola (Rua Diogo Cao, 4, Luanda)
Ambassador: F. Kennedy, CBE.

Of Angola to the United Nations
Ambassador: Elisio de Figueiredo.

Books of Reference

Anuário Estatistico de Angola. Luanda, from 1897

Araújo, A. Correia de, *Aspectos do desenvolvimento económico e social de Angola.* Lisbon, 1964
Bender, G. J., *Angola under the Portuguese.* London, 1979
Davidson, B., *In the Eye of the Storm.* London, 1972
Dias, G. de Sousa, *Os portugueses em Angola.* Lisbon, 1959
Klinghoffer, A. J., *The Angolan War.* Boulder, 1980
Pelissier, R., *Les guerres grises.* Montamets, 1980—*La Colonie du Minotaure.* Montamets, 1980.—*Le naufrage des coravelles.* Montamets, 1980
Wheeler, D. L., and Pélissier, R., *Angola.* London, 1971
Zirka, A. K., *Angola Libre?* Paris, 1975

ANGUILLA

Capital: The Valley
Population: 6,500 (1980)

HISTORY. Anguilla was probably given its name by the Spaniards because of its eel-like shape. After British settlements in the 17th century, the territory was administered as part of the Leeward Islands. From 1825 it became more closely associated with St Kitts and ultimately incorporated in the colony of St Kitts-Nevis-Anguilla. Opposition to this association grew and finally in 1967 the island seceded unilaterally. Following direct intervention by the UK in 1969 Anguilla became *de facto* a separate dependency of Britain; and this was formalized on 19 Dec. 1980 under the Anguilla Act 1980.

AREA AND POPULATION. Anguilla is the most northerly of the Leeward Islands, some 70 miles (112 km) to the north-west of St Kitts and 5 miles (8 km) to the north of St Martin/St Maarten. The territory also comprises the island of Sombrero (on which there is an important lighthouse) and several other off-shore islets or cays. The total area of the territory is about 60 sq. miles (155 sq. km). Census population (1974) was 6,500. The capital is The Valley.

CONSTITUTION AND GOVERNMENT. The House of Assembly consists of a Speaker, 7 elected members, 2 nominated members and 2 official members.

Executive power is vested in the Governor who is appointed by HM The Queen. Apart from his special responsibilities (External Affairs, Defence, Internal Security, including the Police, and the Public Service) and his reserve powers in respect of legislation, the Governor discharges his executive powers on the advice of an Executive Council comprising a Chief Minister, 3 Ministers and 2 official members: Attorney-General and Permanent Secretary, Finance.

Governor: Charles Henry Godden, CBE.
Chief Minister and Minister of Finance: James Ronald Webster.

ECONOMY

Budget. In 1982, the recurrent budget was: Expenditure EC$10,759,868; Local Revenue EC$9,899,301; Grant-in-Aid EC$1,081,000.

Currency. The currency is the Eastern Caribbean *dollar.*

NATURAL RESOURCES

Agriculture. Because of low rainfall agriculture potential is limited. Main crops are pigeon peas, corn and sweet potatoes. Livestock consists of sheep, goats, cattle and poultry.

Fisheries. Fishing is a thriving industry with exports to neighbouring islands.

TOURISM. There are some unpretentious hotels, guest houses and apartments. Several new hotels of international standard are under construction. These are expected to come on stream in 1983 and 1984 offering some 200-300 beds.

COMMUNICATIONS

Roads. There are about 32 miles of tarred roads and 25 miles of secondary roads.

Aviation. There is a 3,600 ft surfaced runway at Wallblake Airport. Apart from regular air taxi and charter flights WINAIR (subsidiary of ALM) provides daily scheduled services between Juliana International Airport, St Maarten and Anguilla.

Shipping. The main seaports are Road Bay and Blowing Point, the latter serving passenger and cargo traffic to and from St Martin.

Post and Telecommunications. There is a modern internal telephone service with (1982) 800 exchange lines shortly to be increased to 1,200; and international telegraph, telex and telephone services, all operated by Cable & Wireless.

EDUCATION AND WELFARE

Education. There are 6 government primary schools and 1 secondary school. Tertiary education is provided at regional universities and similar institutions.

Health. There is a 24-bed cottage hospital, clinics and a modern dental clinic.

ANTIGUA AND BARBUDA

Capital: St John's
Population: 74,000 (1981)
GNP per capita: US$ 1,270 (1980)

HISTORY. Antigua was discovered by Colombus in 1493 and named by him after a church in Seville (Spain). It was first colonized by English settlers in 1632; nearby Barbuda was colonized in 1661 from Antigua. Formed part of the Leeward Islands Federation from 1871 until 30 June 1956, when Antigua became a separate Crown Colony, which was part of the West Indies Federation from 3 Jan. 1958 until 31 May 1962. It became an Associated State of the UK on 27 Feb. 1967 and obtained independence on 1 Nov. 1981.

AREA AND POPULATION. Antigua and Barbuda comprises 3 islands of the Lesser Antilles situated in the Eastern Caribbean with a total land area of 442 sq. km (171 sq. miles); it consists of Antigua (280 sq. km), Barbuda, 40 km to the north (161 sq. km) and uninhabited Redonda, 40 km to the southwest (1 sq. km).

The population at the Census of 7 April 1970 was 65,525; the latest estimate (1981) is 74,000. The chief towns are St John's, the capital on Antigua (24,000 inhabitants in 1975) and Codrington, the only settlement on Barbuda.

Vital statistics (1974): Birth rate, 18·3 per 1,000; death rate 7·1 per 1,000.

CONSTITUTION AND GOVERNMENT

Governor-General: Sir Wilfred Ebenezer Jacobs, KCVO, OBE, QC.

Premier: Right Hon. Vere C. Bird, Sen., PC.

Flag: Red, with a triangle based on the top edge, divided horizontally black, blue, white, with a rising sun in gold on the black portion.

ECONOMY

Budget. The budget for 1979 was EC$57,173,624.

Currency. The Eastern Caribbean $. In March 1983, £1 = EC$4·10; US$1 = EC$2·70.

Banking. In government savings bank, 4,917 depositors on 31 Dec. 1971, $432,277 deposits. Barclays Bank International, Royal Bank of Canada, Canadian Imperial Bank of Commerce, the Virgin Islands National Bank, the Antilles International Trust Co. and the Bank of Nova Scotia have branches at St John's. The Antigua Co-operative Bank was opened in Jan. 1965.

AGRICULTURE. Sugar, cotton and fruits are the main crops. There were 178,804 lb. of cotton produced in 1976.

INDUSTRY AND TRADE

Commerce. Imports in 1975 amounted to EC$145·14m. (of which 19% came from the UK and 19% from the US) and exports to EC$59·92m. of which the major amount came from bunkering provided to ships.

Tourism. There were 67,412 tourists (excluding cruise passengers) in 1978.

COMMUNICATIONS

Roads. There are 600 miles of roads (150 miles main road).

Shipping. The main harbour is the St John's deep water harbour. There are 2 tugs for the berthing of ships and all modern and efficient general cargo handling equipment. The harbour can also accommodate 3 large cruise ships simultaneously.

Post and Broadcasting. Telephone lines, 720 miles; 3,104 telephones.

RELIGION, EDUCATION AND WELFARE.

Religion. The vast majority of the population are Christian, preponderantly Anglican.

Education. In 1977 there were 13,285 pupils and 477 teachers in primary schools and 6,458 pupils and 271 teachers in secondary schools.

Health. There is a general hospital (Holberton) with 215 beds, a mental hospital with 200 beds, a geriatric unit with 150 beds, 4 health centres and 16 dispensaries.

DIPLOMATIC REPRESENTATIVES

Of Antigua and Barbuda in Great Britain (10 Kensington Ct., London, W8)
High Commissioner: Dr Claudius C. Thomas, CMG.

Of Great Britain in Antigua and Barbuda (38 St Mary's St., St John's)
High Commissioner: Viscount Dunrossil, CMG.

Of Antigua and Barbuda in the USA (2000 N. St., NW, Washington, D.C., 20036)
Ambassador: Edmund Hawkins Lake.

Of the USA in Antigua and Barbuda
Ambassador: Milan D. Bish (resides in Bridgetown).

Of Antigua and Barbuda to the United Nations
Ambassador: Lloydston Jacobs.

ARGENTINA

República Argentina

Capital: Buenos Aires
Population: 27·95m. (1980)
GNP per capita: US$2,390 (1980)

HISTORY. In 1515 Juan Díaz de Solis discovered the Río de La Plata. In 1534 Pedro de Mendoza was sent by the King of Spain to take charge of the 'Gobernación y Capitanía de las tierras del Rio de La Plata', and in Feb. 1536 he founded the city of the 'Puerto de Santa María del Buen Aire'. In 1810 the population rose against Spanish rule, and in 1816 Argentina proclaimed its independence. Civil wars and anarchy followed until, in 1853, stable government was established.

AREA AND POPULATION. The Argentine Republic is bounded in the north by Bolivia, in the north-east by Paraguay, in the east by Brazil, Uruguay and the Atlantic Ocean and the west by Chile. The republic consists of 22 provinces, 1 federal district and the National Territories of Tierra del Fuego, the Antarctic and the South Atlantic Islands (census of 1980) as follows:

Provinces	*Area: sq. km. 1960*	*Population: census, 1980*	*Capital*	*Population census, 1980 (1,000)*
Litoral				
Federal Capital	200	2,922,829	Buenos Aires	2,908
Buenos Aires	307,804	10,865,408	La Plata	455
Corrientes	88,199	661,454	Corrientes	180
Entre Ríos	76,216	908,313	Paraná	160
Chaco	99,633	701,392	Resistencia	218
Santa Fé	133,007	2,465,546	Santa Fé	287
Formosa	72,066	295,887	Formosa	95
Misiones	29,801	588,977	Posadas	140
Norte				
Jujuy	53,219	410,008	San Salvador de Jujuy	124
Salta	154,775	662,870	Salta	260
Santiago del Estero	135,254	594,920	Santiago del Estero	148
Tucumán	22,524	972,655	San Miguel de Tucuman	497
Centro				
Córdoba	168,766	2,407,754	Córdoba	969
La Pampa	143,440	208,260	Santa Rosa	52
San Luis	76,748	214,416	San Luis	71
Andina				
Catamarca	99,818	207,717	Catamarca	88
La Rioja	92,331	164,217	La Rioja	67
Mendoza	150,839	1,196,228	Mendoza	597
San Juan	86,137	465,976	San Juan	118
Neuquén	94,078	243,850	Neuquén	90
Patagonia				
Chubut	224,686	263,116	Rawson	52
Rio Negro	203,013	383,354	Viedma	24
Santa Cruz	243,943	114,941	Rio Gallegos	43
Tierra del Fuego [2]	20,912	29,392	Ushuaia	11
Grand total	2,777,815 [1]	27,949,480		

[1] Total area claimed was 2,808,602 sq. km (1,084,120 sq. miles).
[2] The official census including the 'Antarctic Sector', and stated to comprise the 'Malvinas' (Falklands), South Orcadas (Orkneys), South Georgias, South Sandwich Islands and the 'sovereign territories of Argentina in the Antarctic': population 3,300.

Other large towns (1970 Census): Rosario (750,455), Mar del Plata (302,282), Bahia Blanca (182,158).

CONSTITUTION AND GOVERNMENT. Military leaders supported by the Navy and Air Force staged a *coup d'état* on 27 June 1966, and the temporary Revolutionary Junta of the Commanders-in-Chief of the three Armed Services deposed Dr Illia and his Government elected in 1963. A former Commander-in-Chief of the Army, Lieut.-Gen. Onganía, was appointed President and the Junta dissolved. The previous Constitution remained in force in so far as it was consistent with the statutes and objectives of the Revolution. For details of earlier Constitutions *see* THE STATESMAN'S YEAR-BOOK, 1982–83.

Presidential, congressional and municipal elections will take place on 30 Oct. 1983 and a return to civilian rule is envisaged on 30 Jan. 1984.

The following is a list of Presidents from 1966 onwards:

Gen. Juan Carlos Onganía. 29 June 1966–8 June 1970. (Deposed.)
Brig.-Gen. Robert Marcelo Levingston. 18 June 1970–22 March 1971. (Deposed.)
Gen. Alejandro Agustin Lanusse. 26 March 1971–May 1973.
Dr Hector Cámpora. 27 May 1973–13 July 1973.
Gen. Juan Domingo Perón. 12 Oct. 1973–1 July 1974.
Maria Estela (Isabel) Martinez Perón. 1 July 1974 (*a.i.* from 29 June 1974)–23 March 1976. (Deposed.)
Gen. Jorge Rafael Videla. 29 March 1976–29 March 1981.
Gen. Roberto Viola, 29 March–22 Dec. 1981.
Gen. Leopoldo Fortunato Galtieri, 22 Dec. 1981–17 June 1982.

President of the Republic: Gen. Reynaldo Benito Antonio Bignone (sworn in 1 July 1982).

Membership of the *Junta Militar* (Jan. 1983): Lieut.-Gen. Cristino Nicolaides (Army), Brig.-Gen. Augusto Hughes (Air Force), Vice-Adm. Ruben Oscar Franco (Navy).

The Cabinet at 2 July 1982 comprised: *Foreign Affairs:* Juan Ramón Aguirre Lanari. *Interior:* Maj.-Gen. Llamil Reston. *Treasury and Finance:* Dr José Maria Dagnino Pastore. *Labour:* Héctor Francisco Villaveiran. *Defence:* Julio Martinez Vivot. *Justice:* Dr Jaime Lucás Lennon. *Public Health and Environment:* Dr Horacio Rodriguez Castells. *Education:* Dr Cayetano Antonio Licciardo. *Public Works:* Conrado Ernesto Bauer. *Social Welfare:* Adolfo Navajas Ataza. *Secretary-General to the Presidency:* Brig.-Gen. Jorge Alberto Márquez.

National flag: Three horizontal stripes of light blue, white and light blue, with the gold Sun of May in the centre.

National anthem: Oid, mortales, el grito sagrado Libertad (words by V. López y Planes, 1813; tune by J. Blas Parera).

Local Government. From June 1966 the governors have been appointed by the President and are responsible to him.

DEFENCE

Army. The Army is a National Militia, service in which is compulsory for all citizens from their 20th to their 45th year. Naturalized citizens are exempt for a period of 10 years. For the first 10 years the men belong to the 'active' Army, or first line. After completing 10 years in the first line the men pass to the National Guard, and serve in it for another 10 years, finishing their service with 5 years in the Territorial Guard; the latter is mobilized only in case of war. The period of continuous service, or training in the ranks with the permanent forces, is for 1 year for the Army or Air Force, and 14 months for the Navy. The reservists can be called out for training periodically.

The territory of the republic is divided into 5 military districts for administrative purposes. The Army is organized in 4 army corps; it consists of 2 armoured and 6 infantry brigades, 3 mountain brigades, 1 airborne brigade, 1 aviation and 6 air defence battalions.

In 1983 the Army was 125,000 strong, of whom 90,000 were National Service men and the remainder, an officer corps of 5,000 and 15,000 n.c.o.s, all of whom were career regulars.

The trained reserve numbers about 250,000, of whom 200,000 belong to the National Guard and 50,000 to the Territorial Guard.

Navy. Principal ships of the Argentine Navy:[3]

Completed	*Name*	*Standard displacement Tons*	*Aircraft*	*Guns*	*Shaft horse-power*	*Speed Knots*
		Aircraft Carrier [1]				
1945	Veinicinco de Maya [2]	15,892	18 fixed-wing, 4 helicopters	9 40mm guns	40,000	24·0

[1] The aircraft carrier *Independence*, ex-*Warrior*, purchased from the UK in 1958 was withdrawn from service in 1971.

[2] Ex-*Karel Doorman*, purchased from the Netherlands in 1968, ex-*Venerable*, purchased from UK in 1948.

[3] The cruiser *General Belgrano, ex-Phoenix*, purchased from the USA in 1951 was sunk by the British fleet submarine *Conqueror* in May 1982. Sister ship *Nueve de Julio* (ex-USS *Bloise*) was withdrawn from service in 1980. The cruiser *La Argentina* was stricken from the list in 1975.

There are 2 modern German-built submarines, 1 old *ex*-US submarine, 2 new German-built destroyers, 2 new British-built destroyers (Type 42), 5 old *ex*-US destroyers, 3 new French-built small frigates, 2 old training frigates, 1 corvette (*ex*-fleet minesweeper), 4 coastal minesweepers, 2 minehunters, 5 patrol vessels (armed ocean tugs), 2 fast patrol vessels, 2 torpedo boats, 6 patrol craft, 2 survey ships, 2 survey launches, 1 training ship, 5 transports, 3 oilers, 1 tank landing ship, 12 minor landing craft, 58 auxiliary landing craft, polar ships, 20 auxiliary vessels and service craft and 12 tugs.

The new construction programme includes 6 diesel-powered patrol submarines, 2 destroyers, 6 fast frigates, 5 corvettes and 20 coastal patrol craft.

The submarine *Sante Fe,* ex-USS *Catfish,* was damaged and beached during the Falklands invasion in April 1982. A corvette was sunk.

The active personnel of the Navy in 1983 comprised 31,000 (2,900 officers and 28,100 men, including 12,000 conscripts, who serve 12 months). The Marine Corps numbered 6,000 including coast artillery.

The Naval Aviation Service, formed on 17 Oct. 1919, has some 122 fixed-wing aircraft and helicopters with 2,000 personnel, in 4 wings. Aircraft include 10 A-4Q Skyhawk attack bombers, 8 Aermacchi M.B. 326 and 10 M.B.339A light jet armed trainers, 5 P-2H Neptune and 10 S-2A/S-2E ship-based Tracker anti-submarine aircraft, navalized Harvard trainers, and North American armed T-28s bought from France, and a dozen types of training, transport and general purpose aircraft, plus 7 types of helicopters. Skyhawks, Trackers and Sea King and Alouette helicopters were operated from the aircraft carrier. Skyhawks are being replaced by Super Entendards.

Air Force. The Air Force, founded on 10 Aug. 1912 and autonomous since 4 Jan. 1945, is organized into Air Operations, Air Regions, Materiel and Personnel Commands. Air Operations Command, responsible for all operational flying, is made up of air brigades, each with 1 to 4 squadrons, usually operating from a single base. No. I Air Brigade is a military air transport service, with responsibility also for LADE (state airline) operations into areas of Argentina not served by civilian companies. Before the Falklands campaign in 1982, its equipment included 7 C-130E/H Hercules and 10 F.27 Friendship/Troopship turboprop transports, 2 KC-130H Hercules tanker/transports, 5 twin-turbofan F.28 Fellowship freighters, 6 Twin Otters, 15 Guarani IIs, the Presidential Boeing 707-320B and 707-320C, 2 VIP Fellowships, and many older or smaller types. No. II Air Brigade had 7 Canberra twin-jet bombers and 2 Canberra trainers; a photographic squadron with Guarani IIs. No. III Air Brigade had 2 squadrons of IA 58 Pucara twin-turboprop COIN aircraft. No. IV Air Brigade comprised 2 ground attack squadrons equipped with about 20 A-4P Skyhawks and 25 Paris light jet combat and liaison aircraft. No. V Air Brigade comprised 2 squadrons with a total of about 40 A-4P Skyhawk strike aircraft. No. VI Air Brigade had 42 Dagger (Israeli-built Mirage III) fighters, equipping 2 squadrons. No. VII Air Brigade had 2 COIN, general-purpose, and search and rescue squadrons with 14 armed Hughes 500M, 6 Lama, 5 Sikorsky S-58T/S-61, 8 Bell 212 and 9 Bell UH-1 helicopters; and a COIN/training squadron of T-34 Mentors. No. VIII Air Brigade had 1 squadron with 16 Mirage IIIE fighter-bombers and 2 Mirage IIID trainers. Estimated losses total 45 Skyhawks, 27 Mirages and Daggers, 21 Pucaras, 4 Mentors, 3 Canberras, 1 Hercules and 1 Learjet; some have been replaced subsequently, reported orders including 32 Mirages and Daggers. There is a flying school at Córdoba, equipped with piston-engined T-34 Mentors and Paris jets. There are about 19,500 personnel and 300 aircraft.

INTERNATIONAL RELATIONS

Membership. Argentina is a member of UN, OAS and LAIA (formerly LAFTA).

ECONOMY

Budget. The financial year commences on 1 Nov. Budget receipts in 1980 33,459,261m. pesos and expenditure 37,248,461m. pesos.

Currency. The monetary system is on a gold-exchange standard, the unit for foreign transactions being, nominally, the *peso oro* (gold peso) and for domestic transactions, the *peso moneda nacional* (paper peso), legal tender for all domestic debts.

The gold peso weighs 1·6129 grammes of gold 0·900 fine; it is divided into 100 *centavos*, but gold is not in circulation. Circulation consists chiefly of paper notes (issued since 1897) ranging from 100,000 down to 50 pesos. The coins actually circulating, 1968, were steel-nickel, 25, 10, 5, 1 peso and 50 centavos. In March 1983, US$1 = 57,000 *pesos*; £1 = 93,301 *pesos*.

Banking. A law promulgated 25 March 1946 nationalized the Central Bank (established in 1935), originally as an autonomous institution, but later, in Oct. 1949, placed under the Minister of Finance, who became president. Six decree-laws of Oct. 1957 have brought back a greater elasticity to the structure, especially as regards the deposits and loans of the private banks, which have regained their autonomy.

In 1980 there were 29 government banks, 160 private banks and 22 foreign banks. There are 6 Stock Exchanges.

Weights and Measures. Since 1 Jan. 1887 the use of the metric system has been compulsory.

ENERGY AND NATURAL RESOURCES

Electricity. Electric power production (1972) was 25,319 kwh.

Oil and gas. Crude oil production (1980) 179·8m. bbls. Investment of US$10,000m. is envisaged by 1985 in the oil industry with the aim of achieving self-sufficiency. Natural gas production (1980) 9,900,000m. cu. metres.

Minerals. Argentina produced 726,900 tonnes of washed coal in 1979. Gold, silver and copper are worked in Catamarca, where there are also 2 tin-mines, and gold and copper in San Juan, La Rioja and the south-western territories. Iron ore (102,000 tonnes in 1972), tungsten, beryllium, mica, uranium (25 tonnes in 1972), lead (39,000 tonnes in 1972), barites, zinc (43,500 tonnes in 1972), tin (1·8m. tonnes in 1972), manganese and limestone are produced.

Agriculture. Argentina has an area of about 670,251,000 acres, of which about 41% is pasture land, 32% woodland and 11% (73·73m. acres) cultivated.

Livestock (1981): Cattle 54,235,000; sheep, 30m.; pigs, 3·9m.; horses, 3m. The Province of Buenos Aires has 38% of the cattle. Wool production, 1972, was 194,000 tonnes.

Crop statistics with area (in 1,000 hectares) and production (in 1,000 tonnes) are shown as follows:

	1976–77		*1977–78*[1]		*1978–79*[1]	
	Area	*Output*	*Area*	*Output*	*Area*	*Output*
Wheat	7,192	11,000	4,600	5,300	5,230	7,800
Linseed	722	617	950	810	900	630
Maize	2,980	8,300	3,100	9,700	3,300	9,000
Oats	1,471	530	1,480	570	1,545	676
Barley	962	650	890	353	761	554
Rye	2,300	330	2,140	170	1,722	210
Sunflower seed	1,460	900	2,200	1,600	1,745	1,270
Sugar-cane	360	16,000	356	13,600	350	14,100

[1]Provisional.

Argentina's meat exports are calculated in terms of actual weight; not 'carcase weight', as is the international practice.

Cotton, potatoes, vine, tobacco, citrus fruit, olives, rice, soya, and yerba maté (Paraguayan tea) are also cultivated. There are 36 cane-sugar mills and 1 beet-sugar factory; production, 1979, 14·12m. tonnes. Potato harvest, 1979, amounted to 1,694,000 tonnes. The area under tobacco, 1979, was 76,000 hectares; output 68,000 tonnes.

Sunflower seed, first grown by Russian immigrants in 1900, now furnishes the country's most popular edible oil. There are more than 10m. olive trees, of which 48% are in Mendoza. 672,000 tonnes of groundnuts were produced in 1979 (mainly in Córdoba). Argentina is the world's largest source of tannin.

Fisheries. Fish landings in 1979 amounted to 658,688 tonnes.

INDUSTRY AND TRADE

Industry. Production (1979 in tonnes) Paper, 39,000; sulphuric acid, 279,066; cement, 6·7m. Motor vehicles produced (1981) totalled, 172,350; television receivers, 262,000.

Commerce. Import values include charges for carriage, insurance and freight; export values are on a f.o.b. basis. Real values of foreign trade (in US$1m.), exclusive of coin and bullion:

	1974	*1975*	*1976*	*1977*	*1978*	*1979*	*1980*
Imports	3,216	3,510	2,766	4,162	3,834	6,300	10,400
Exports	3,930	2,961	3,916	5,652	6,400	7,750	8,000

Total trade between Argentina and UK (British Department of Trade returns, in £1,000 sterling):

	1977	*1978*	*1979*	*1980*	*1981*	*1982*
Imports to UK	120,040	153,191	145,064	114,286	136,892	58,728
Exports and re-exports from UK	130,271	113,826	128,278	172,830	161,192	37,349

Tourism. In 1976, 1,303,000 tourists visited Argentina.

COMMUNICATIONS

Roads. In 1974 there were 309,086 km of national and provincial highways. The 4 main roads constituting Argentina's portion of the Pan-American Highway were opened to traffic in 1942. In 1978 there were 2·87m. cars and 1·24m. lorries and buses.

Railways. The system based on the 1949 amalgamation of 18 government, British and French-owned railways, comprises 6 railways with a total route-km in 1981 of 33,807 km (116 km electrified) on metre, 1,435 mm and 1,676 mm gauges. In 1980 railways carried 16m. tonnes of freight and 394m. passengers.

Aviation. There were (1980) 10 international airports. Commercial airlines flew a total of 82m. km in 1979, carrying 5m. passengers and 46,900 tonnes of freight.

Shipping. The merchant fleet, 31 Dec. 1973 (registered with Lloyd's), consisted of

1,453,000 GRT; traffic during 1971: vessels of 13·27m. GRT entered ports; 14m. tonnes of goods were unloaded and 10·6m. tonnes were loaded.

Post and Broadcasting. In 1949 the telephone service was nationalized; instruments numbered 2,880,754 in 1981. In 1980 there were 7·5m. radio receivers and 5·6m. television receivers.

Cinemas (1972). Cinemas numbered 1,650, with seating capacity of 611,400.

Newspapers (1976). Daily newspapers numbered 297. Buenos Aires had (1980) 8 daily newspapers with a circulation of 1·55m.

JUSTICE, RELIGION, EDUCATION AND WELFARE

Justice. Justice is administered by federal and provincial courts. The former deal only with cases of a national character, or in which different provinces or inhabitants of different provinces are parties. The chief federal court is the Supreme Court, with 5 judges at Buenos Aires. Other federal courts are the appeal courts, at Buenos Aires, Bahía Blanca, La Plata, Córdoba, Mendoza, Tucumán and Resistencia. Each province has its own judicial system, with a Supreme Court (generally so designated) and several minor chambers. Trial by jury is established by the Constitution for criminal cases, but never practised, except occasionally in the provinces of Buenos Aires and Córdoba.

The death penalty was re-introduced in 1976 for the killing of government, military police and judicial officials, and for participation in terrorist activities.

The police force is centralized under the Federal Security Council.

Religion. The Roman Catholic religion is supported by the State and membership was 23·67m. in 1976.

In 1888, civil marriage was established in the republic. Divorce was made legal in Dec. 1954 but ceased to be so by a decree of 1 March 1956. On 10 Oct. 1966 Argentina returned to the Vatican the right to appoint bishops and archbishops, who had been nominated by the Argentine Government since 1853.

Education. In 1977 the primary schools had 199,384 teachers and 3,680,185 pupils; secondary schools had 60,199 teachers and 441,907 pupils; secondary technical schools had 113,515 teachers and 846,200 pupils; higher schools had 39,970 teaching staff and 619,950 students.

There are National Universities at Buenos Aires (2), Córdoba (2), La Plata, Tucumán, Santa Fé (Litoral), Rosario, Corrientes (Nordeste,), Mendoza (Cuyo), Bahía Blanca (Sur), Catamarca, Tandil, Neuquén (Comahue), San Salvador de Jujuy, Salta, Santa Rosa (La Pampa), Mar del Plata, Comodoro Rivadavia (Patagonia), Río Cuarto and Santiago del Estero. There are also private universities in Buenos Aires (6), Mendoza (3), Córdoba, Comodoro Rivadavia, La Plata, Morón, Tucumán, Salta, Santa Fé and Santiago del Estero.

Health. Free medical attention is obtainable from public hospitals. Many trade unions provide medical, dental and maternity services for their members and dependants. A Ministry of Social Welfare was set up in 1966. In 1971 there were 2,864 hospitals with 133,847 beds and in 1975 there were 48,693 doctors.

DIPLOMATIC REPRESENTATIVES

Diplomatic links with Argentina were broken by Great Britain in April 1982 following the invasion of the Falkland Islands.

Of Argentina in the USA (1600 New Hampshire Ave., NW, Washington, 20009)
Ambassador: Lucio Garcia del Solar.

Of the USA in Argentina (4300 Colombia, Palermo, Buenos Aires)
Ambassador: Harry W. Shlaudeman.

Of Argentina to the United Nations
Ambassador: Dr Eduardo A. Roca.

Books of Reference

Boletin del comercio exterio Argentino y estadisticas económicas retrospectivas. Annual
Anuario de comercio exterior de la República Argentina. Annual
Economic Review, Banco de la Nación. Buenos Aires
Sintesis Estadistica Mensual. Dirección General de Estadistica. Buenos Aires, 1947 ff.
Boletin Internacional de Bibliografia Argentina. Ministry of Foreign Relations. Buenos Aires. Monthly
Geografia de la República Argentino. Ed. by the Sociedad Argentina de Estudios Geográficos. 7 vols. Buenos Aires. 1945–53
Bridges, E. L., *Uttermost Part of the Earth* [*Tierra del Fuego*]. New York, 1949
Ferns, H. S., *Britain and Argentina in the 19th Century.* OUP, 1960.—*The Argentine Republic 1516–1971.* Newton Abbot, 1973
Graham-Yooll, A., *The Forgotten Colony: A History of the English-Speaking Communities in Argentina.* London, 1981
Santillán, Diego A. de (ed.), *Gran Enciclopedia Argentina.* 9 vols. 1956–64
Snow, P. G., *Political Forces in Argentina.* Rev. ed. New York and London, 1979

AUSTRALIA

Capital: Canberra
Population: 14·92m. (1981)
GNP per capita: US$9,820 (1980)

HISTORY. On 1 Jan. 1901 New South Wales, Victoria, Queensland, South Australia, Western Australia and Tasmania were federated under the name of the 'Commonwealth of Australia', the designation of 'colonies' being at the same time changed into that of 'states'—except in the case of Northern Territory, which was transferred from South Australia to the Commonwealth as a 'territory' on 1 Jan. 1911.

In 1911 the Commonwealth acquired from the State of New South Wales the Canberra site for the Australian capital. Building operations were begun in 1923 and Parliament was opened at Canberra on 9 May 1927 by HRH the Duke of York (afterwards King George VI). A further area at Jervis Bay was acquired in 1915.

Territories under the administration of Australia in Jan. 1977, but not included in it, comprise Norfolk Island, the territory of Ashmore and Cartier Islands, and the Australian Antarctic Territory (24 Aug. 1936), comprising all the islands and territory other than Adélie Land, situated south of 60° S. lat. and between 160° and 45° E. long.

The British Government transferred sovereignty in the Heard Island and McDonald Islands to the Australian Government on 26 Dec. 1947. Cocos (Keeling) Islands on 23 Nov. 1955 and Christmas Island on 1 Oct. 1958 were also transferred to Australian jurisdiction.

AREA AND POPULATION. Area and resident population, preliminary estimate 30 June 1981:

States and Territories (capitals in brackets)	*Area (sq. km)*	*Males*	*Females*	*Total*	*Per 100 sq. km*
New South Wales (Sydney)	801,600	2,607,900	2,629,200	5,237,100	653
Victoria (Melbourne)	227,600	1,960,100	1,988,500	3,948,600	1,735
Queensland (Brisbane)	1,727,200	1,179,100	1,166,300	2,345,300	136
South Australia (Adelaide)	984,000	654,700	664,600	1,319,300	134
Western Australia (Perth)	2,525,500	656,400	642,700	1,299,100	51
Tasmania (Hobart)	67,800	212,400	214,900	427,300	630
Northern Territory (Darwin)	1,346,200	65,600	57,300	122,800	9
Aust. Cap. Terr. (Canberra)	2,400	113,500	113,700	227,300	9,471
Total	7,682,300	7,449,600	7,477,200	14,926,800	194

Resident population in State capitals and other major cities, preliminary estimate 30 June 1981:

Statistical division	*State*	*Persons*
Sydney	NSW	3,280,900
Melbourne	Vic.	2,803,600
Brisbane	Qld	1,086,500
Adelaide	SA	952,700
Perth	WA	918,000
Newcastle [1]	NSW	402,300
Canberra [1] [2]	ACT	246,100
Wollongong [1]	NSW	231,000
Hobart	Tas.	170,900
Gold Coast [1] [3]	Qld	164,100
Geelong [1]	Vic.	142,100

[1] Statistical District of 100,000 persons or more.
[2] Includes Queanbeyan.
[3] Includes Tweed Heads.

The number of occupied dwellings in Australia (at 1981 census) was 4,691,425, distributed as follows: New South Wales, 1,669,596; Victoria, 1,243,453; Queensland, 703,964; South Australia, 433,841; Western Australia, 405,999;

Tasmania, 136,269; Northern Territory, 29,563; Australian Capital Territory, 68,740. There were also 469,742 unoccupied dwellings. Total completed new dwellings numbered 129,268 in 1979–80.

Vital statistics for 1981:

States and Territories	*Marriages*	*Divorces*	*Births*	*Deaths* [1]	*Infant deaths* [1]
New South Wales	40,679	14,512	81,530	39,959	809
Victoria	28,648	9,769	59,513	29,034	562
Queensland	18,305	6,470	38,834	17,175	425
South Australia	10,252	4,132	19,351	9,706	157
Western Australia	10,111	3,481	21,877	7,993	193
Tasmania	3,515	1,139	7,188	3,320	86
Northern Territory	719	393	3,080	854	70
Aust. Cap. Terr.	1,676	1,516	4,469	962	45
Total	13,905	41,412	235,842	109,003	2,347
Rate [2]	7·6	2·8	15·8	7·3	10·0

[1] Provisional.
[2] Rate per 1,000 mean population.

Overseas arrivals during 1981 numbered 2,330,803 and departures 2,203,287. Of these 212,689 were long-term and permanent arrivals and 85,612 were long-term and permanent departures. Of these 118,735 came to Australia intending to settle. There were 19,856 Australian residents departing permanently.

Australian Bureau of Statistics, *Australian Demographic Statistics.* Quarterly. Canberra, June 1979 to date

National Population Inquiry, Population and Australia, A Demographic Analysis and Projection. Canberra, 1975

National Population Inquiry, Population and Australia: Recent Demographic Trends and their Implications. Canberra, 1978

CONSTITUTION AND GOVERNMENT. *Federal Government:* Under the Australian Constitution legislative power in Australia is vested in a Federal Parliament, consisting of the Queen, represented by a Governor-General, a Senate and a House of Representatives. Under the terms of the constitution there must be a session of parliament at least once a year.

The Senate comprises 64 Senators (10 for each State voting as one electorate and as from Aug. 1974, 2 Senators respectively for the Australian Capital Territory and the Northern Territory). Senators representing the States are chosen for 6 years. The terms of Senators representing the Territories expire at the close of the day next preceding the polling day for the general elections of the House of Representatives. In general, the Senate is renewed to the extent of one-half every 3 years, but in case of disagreement with the House of Representatives, it, together with the House of Representatives, may be dissolved, and an entirely new Senate elected. The House of Representatives consists, as nearly as practicable, of twice as many Members as there are Senators, the numbers chosen in the several States being in proportion to population as shown by the latest statistics, but not less than 5 for any original State. The numerical size of the House after the election in 1980 was 125, including the Members for Northern Territory and the Australian Capital Territory. The Northern Territory has been represented by 1 Member in the House of Representatives since 1922, and the Australian Capital Territory by 1 Member since 1949 and 2 Members since May 1974. The Member for the Australian Capital Territory was given full voting rights as from the Parliament elected in Nov. 1966. The Member for the Northern Territory was given full voting rights in 1968. The House of Representatives continues for 3 years from the date of its first meeting, unless sooner dissolved. Every Senator or Member of the House of Representatives must be a British subject, be of full age, possess electoral qualifications and have resided for 3 years within Australia. The franchise for both Houses is the same and is based on universal (males and females aged 18 years) suffrage. Compulsory voting was introduced in 1925. If a Member of a State Parliament wishes to be a candidate in a federal election, he must first resign his State seat.

Executive power in Australia is vested in the Governor-General, who is advised by an Executive Council. This is presided over by the Governor-General, and its members hold office at his pleasure. All Ministers of State, who are members of the party or parties commanding a majority in the lower House, are members of the Executive Council under summons. A record of proceedings of meetings is kept by the Secretary to the Council. At Executive Council meetings the decisions of the Cabinet are (where necessary) given legal form, appointments made, resignations accepted, proclamations, regulations and the like made.

The policy of a ministry is, in practice, determined by the Ministers of State meeting without the Governor-General under the chairmanship of the Prime Minister. This group is known as the Cabinet. The Cabinet of the Liberal–National Country Party Coalition Government comprises the 14 senior Ministers. Other Ministers attend meetings of Cabinet only when required. Meetings of the full Ministry are held when necessary. There are 11 Standing Committees of the Cabinet comprising varying numbers of Cabinet and non-Cabinet Ministers. In Labor Governments all Ministers have been members of Cabinet. Cabinet meetings are private and deliberative and records of meetings are not made public. The Cabinet does not form part of the legal mechanisms of Government; the decisions it takes have, in themselves, no legal effect. The Cabinet substantially controls, in ordinary circumstances, not only the general legislative programme of Parliament but the whole course of Parliamentary proceedings. In effect, though not in form, the Cabinet, by reason of the fact that all Ministers are members of the Executive Council, is also the dominant element in the executive government of the country.

The legislative powers of the Federal Parliament embrace trade and commerce, shipping, etc.; taxation, finance, banking, currency, bills of exchange, bankruptcy, insurance; defence; external affairs, naturalization and aliens, quarantine, immigration and emigration; the people of any race for whom it is deemed necessary to make special laws; postal, telegraph and like services; census and statistics; weights and measures; astronomical and meteorological observations; copyrights; railways; conciliation and arbitration in disputes extending beyond the limits of any one State; social services; marriage, divorce etc.; service and execution of the civil and criminal process; recognition of the laws, Acts and records, and judicial proceedings of the States. The Senate may not originate or amend money bills; and disagreement with the House of Representatives may result in dissolution and, in the last resort, a joint sitting of the two Houses. No religion may be established by the Commonwealth. The Federal Parliament has limited and enumerated powers, the several State parliaments retaining the residuary power of government over their respective territories. If a State law is inconsistent with a Commonwealth law, the latter prevails.

The Constitution also provides for the admission or creation of new States. Proposed laws for the alteration of the Constitution must be submitted to the electors, and they can be enacted only if approved by a majority of the States and by a majority of all the electors voting.

The 33rd Parliament was elected in March 1983.

The results of the elections to the House of Representatives and to the Senate held in March 1983 were not available when THE STATESMAN'S YEAR-BOOK went to press but they do appear in the ADDENDA.

Governor-General: Sir Ninian Stephen, GCMG, GCVO, KBE, PC.

The following is a list of Governors-General of the Commonwealth:

Earl of Hopetoun	1901–02	HRH the Duke of Gloucester	1945–47
Lord Tennyson	1902–04	Sir William McKell	1947–53
Lord Northcote	1904–08	Viscount Slim	1953–60
Earl of Dudley	1908–11	Viscount Dunrossil	1960–61
Lord Denman	1911–14	Viscount De L'Isle	1961–65
Viscount Novar	1914–20	Lord Casey	1965–69
Lord Forster	1920–25	Sir Paul Hasluck	1969–74
Lord Stonehaven	1925–31	Sir John Kerr	1974–77
Sir Isaac Isaacs	1931–36	Sir Zelman Cowen	1977–82
Earl Gowrie	1936–45	Sir Ninian Stephen	1982–

National flag: The British Blue Ensign with a large star of 7 points beneath the Union Flag, and in the fly 5 stars of the Southern Cross, all in white.

The cabinet of the Labour administration was announced on 10 March 1983.

Prime Minister: Robert Hawke.
Deputy Prime Minister and Minister for Trade: Lionel Bowen.
Industry and Commerce: John Button.
Social Security: Don Grimes.
Employment and Industrial Relations: Ralph Willis.
Treasurer: Paul Keating.
Special Minister of State: Mick Young.
Immigration and Ethnic Affairs: Stewart West.
Resources and Energy: Peter Walsh.
Foreign Affairs: Bill Hayden.
Education and Youth Affairs: Susan Ryan.
Attorney General: Gareth Evans.
Defence: Gordon Scholes.
Transport: Peter Morris.
Primary Industry: John Kerin.
Aviation: Kim Beazley.
Housing and Construction: Chris Hurford.
Sport, Recreation and Tourism, and Administrative Services: John Brown.
Finance: John Dawkins.
Health: Neal Blewett.
Science and Technology: Barry Jones.
Communications: Michael Duffy.
Home Affairs and the Environment: Barry Cohen.
Aboriginal Affairs: Clyde Holding.
Veterans' Affairs: Arthur Gietzelt.
Territories and Local Government: Tom Uren.
Defence Support: Brian Howe.

The Acts of the Parliament of the Commonwealth of Australia Passed from 1901 to 1973. 12 vols. Annual volumes, 1974 to date
Parliamentary Handbook of the Commonwealth of Australia. Canberra, 1915 to date
Commonwealth of Australia Directory [1921–1958 The Federal Guide; 1961–72 *Commonwealth Directory;* 1973–75 *Australian Government Directory*]. *Prime Minister's Department.* Canberra, 1924 to date
Crisp, L. F., *Australian National Government.* 3rd ed. Melbourne and London, 1975
Hughes, C. A., and Graham, B. D., *A Handbook of Australian Government and Politics.* Canberra, 1968
Odgers, J. R., *Australian Senate Practice.* 5th ed. Canberra, 1976
Paton, Sir George (ed.), *The Commonwealth of Australia: its Laws and Constitution.* London, 1952
Pettifer, J. A., *House of Representatives Practice.* Canberra, 1981
Sawer, G., *Australian Federal Politics and Law 1901–1929, 1929–1949.* 2 vols. Melbourne, 1974.—*Australian Government To-day.* 11th ed. Melbourne, 1973
Spann, R. N. (ed.), *Public Administration in Australia.* 3rd ed. Sydney, 1973
Wynes, W. A., *Executive and Judicial Powers in Australia.* 5th ed. Sydney, 1976

State Government: In each of the 6 States (New South Wales, Victoria, Queensland, South Australia, Western Australia, Tasmania) there is a State government whose constitution, powers and laws continue, subject to changes embodied in the Australian Constitution and subsequent alterations and agreements, as they were before federation. The system of government is basically the same as that described above for the Commonwealth—*i.e.*, the Sovereign, her representative (in this case a

Governor), an upper and lower house of Parliament (except in Queensland, where the upper house was abolished in 1922), a cabinet led by the Premier and an Executive Council. Among the more important functions of the State governments are those relating to education, health, hospitals and charities, law, order and public safety, business undertakings such as railways and tramways, and public utilities such as water supply and sewerage. In the domains of education, hospitals, justice, the police, penal establishments, and railway and tramway operation, State government activity predominates. Care of the public health and recreative activities are shared with local government authorities and the Federal Government, social services other than those referred to above are now primarily the concern of the Federal Government, and the operation of public utilities is shared with local and semi-government authorities.

Administration of Territories. Since 1911, responsibility for administration and development of the Australian Capital Territory has been vested in Federal Ministers and Departments. In 1930, the ACT Advisory Council was established, with both elected and appointed Members, to advise the Minister on administration of the Territory.

Late in 1974 the Government replaced the ACT Advisory Council with a Legislative Assembly of eighteen Members all of whom are elected and on 29 June 1979 the Legislative Assembly became the House of Assembly. While the Assembly has been accorded the forms of a legislature, it continues to perform an advisory function for the Minister for the Capital Territory.

On 1 July 1978 the Northern Territory of Australia became a self-governing Territory with expenditure responsibilities and revenue-raising powers broadly approximating those of a State, although the Territory is not a State under the Constitution.

Under self-government the Legislative Assembly and Ministers of the Northern Territory have responsibility in the areas of insurance, banking, taxation, provision of credit and assistance; Public Service of the Territory; maintenance of law and order and the administration of Justice etc.; civil liberties; markets and marketing; inquiries and administrative reviews; consumer affairs; sales and leases of goods and supply of services etc.; prices and rent control; industry and regulation of businesses and professions; tourism; printing and publishing; labour relations and industrial safety; mining and minerals; land and land use; transport; environment protection and conservation; fire prevention; water resources; energy planning, public utilities and public works; local government; housing, education, health, welfare etc.; censorship; Supreme Court, agreements between the Territory and the Commonwealth, State or States.

Local Government. The system of municipal government is broadly the same throughout Australia, although local government legislation is a State matter.

Each State is sub-divided into areas known variously as municipalities, cities, boroughs, towns, shires or district councils, totalling about 900. Within these areas the management of road, street and bridge construction, health, sanitary and garbage services, water supply and sewerage, and electric light and gas undertakings, hospitals, fire brigades, tramways and omnibus services and harbours is generally part of the functions of elected aldermen and councillors. The scope of their duties, however, differs considerably, for in all States the State Government, either directly or through semi-government authorities, also carries out some or all of these types of services.

In some instances, *e.g.*, in New South Wales, a number of local government authorities combine to conduct a public undertaking such as the supply of water or electricity.

DEFENCE. The Minister for Defence has responsibility under legislation for the control and administration of the Defence Force. The Chief of Defence Force Staff is vested with command of the Defence Force. He is the principal military adviser to the Minister. The Secretary, Department of Defence is the Permanent Head of the Department. He is the principal civilian adviser to the Minister and has statutory responsibility for financial administration of the Defence outlay. The Chief of Defence Force Staff and the Secretary are jointly responsible for the administration of the Defence Force except with respect to matters falling within the command of the Defence Force or any other matter specified by the Minister.

The Chief of Naval Staff, the Chief of the General Staff and the Chief of the Air Staff command the Navy, Army and Air Force respectively. They have delegated authority from the Chief of Defence Force Staff and the Secretary to administer matters relating to their particular Service.

The structure of Defence is characterized by 3 organizational types: *(i)* A Central Office comprising 5 groups of functional orientated Divisions: Strategic Policy and Force Development; Supply and Support; Manpower and Financial Services; Management and Infrastructure Services; and, Defence Science and Technology; *(ii)* the 3 Armed Services of the Defence Force, each having a Service Office element in addition to the command structure; and *(iii)* a small number of outrider organizations concerned with such specialist fields as intelligence and natural disasters.

Defence Support. A separate Department of Defence Support was formally established on 7 May 1982, and draws together elements previously located in the Departments of Administrative Services, Defence, and Industry and Commerce.

The Department: Undertakes the purchase of goods and services for defence purposes; undertakes and sponsors research and deployment relevant to defence needs, supporting both the Defence Force and the defence industry base in this regard; provides technical expertise and other forms of assistance to encourage defence industry initiatives and the acquisition of modern techniques and technologies; ensures that Australian industry participates in the procurement and support of defence equipment to the maximum practical extent; administers the Australian Offsets Program so as to stimulate technological advancement and broaden the capabilities of Australian industries of significance to this country's strategic and overall manufacturing needs; manages the Government's defence oriented facilities including munitions and aircraft factories, and dockyards; and consistent with the Government's defence and foreign affairs policies, markets defence and allied products and services to help maintain industrial capabilities of strategic significance.

Army. Overall organization and financial control of the Australian Army is vested in the Chief of General Staff. Under the Defence Force Re-organisation Act, which received the Royal Assent on 9 Sept. 1975, the Military Board, which was previously the controlling body of the Army, was abolished. The Act became effective on 1 Feb. 1976. A functional command structure, Headquarters Field Force Command, Headquarters Logistic Command, and Headquarters Training Command, with Headquarters in military districts, was introduced in 1973.

The strength of the Army was 33,053 as at 30 June 1982. There is emphasis in the field force organization on the combat element and high-priority logistic units to meet the requirements for limited war and tropical warfare with light air-portable formations. The Field Force is organized on the divisional structure, on the basis of 6 battalions organized in 3 brigades each with combat and logistic support.

The effective strength of the Army Reserve at 30 June 1982 was 30,036.

Training for commissioned rank is carried out at the Royal Military College and the Officer Cadet School. The Royal Military College was established in Canberra in 1911, to train young men from Australia and New Zealand for the Regular Armies of those two countries. The college, which is affiliated with the University of New South Wales, accepts young men between the ages of 17 and 20 who are qualified to enter university. The course covers 4 years and leads to the award of the university's degrees of Bachelor of Arts, Bachelor of Science and Bachelor of Engineering.

The Officer Cadet School was established at Portsea, Victoria, in 1952. The course there takes 11 months.

Staff and command training is carried out at the Command and Staff College, Queenscliff, Victoria and the Land Warfare Centre, Canungra, Queensland.

Navy. The overall control of the Royal Australian Navy is vested in the Chief of Naval Staff assisted by the Deputy Chief of Naval Staff with the Chief of Naval Personnel, the Chief of Naval Technical Services and the Chief of Naval Material. Under the Defence Re-organisation Act effective from 1 Feb. 1976 the Naval Board was abolished. The command, operation and administration of the Fleet is the responsibility of the Flag Officer Commanding HM Australian Fleet. The Flag Officer Naval Support Command, formerly the Flag Officer Commanding East Australia area, is responsible for the material support for the fleet.

Aircraft carrier of the Royal Australian Navy:

Completed	*Name*	*Displacement, tons*	*Aircraft*	*Guns*	*Shaft horse-power*	*Speed, knots*
1955	Melbourne (*ex*-Majestic)[1]	16,000	12 fixed-wing 5 helicopters	4 40-mm AA	40,000	23

[1] Sister ship *Sydney* (ex-*Terrible*), completed as an aircraft carrier in 1949, converted to a fast military transport in 1961, officially announced for disposal on 20 July 1973, left Sydney for shipbreakers on 23 Dec. 1975.

There are also 6 British-built 'Oberon' class submarines, *Onslow, Otway, Ovens* and *Oxley* (completed in 1967–69) and *Orion* and *Otama* (completed in 1977–78), 3 US-built guided-missile destroyers, *Brisbane, Hobart* and *Perth* (completed in 1965–68), 1 'Daring' class destroyer, *Vampire* now used as a training ship, 4 US-built guided missile frigates, *Adelaide, Camberra* and *Sydney* (completed in 1981–83) and *Darwin* (completing in 1984), 6 destroyer escorts or 'Type 12' fast anti-submarine frigates, 4 oceanographic research and survey ships, 2 mine-hunters, 1 minesweeper, a destroyer tender, 20 attack class patrol craft, 1 landing ship, 6 landing craft, 1 fleet oiler, 14 auxiliary vessels, 8 service craft and 55 work-boats, etc. HMAS *Jervis Bay* (formerly the ANL ro-ro vessel *Australian Trader*) was commissioned in 1977 as the RAN's training ship.

Naval dockyards are at Garden Island, Sydney, and Williamstown, Victoria. Naval shipbuilding is carried out at Williamstown, at Cockatoo Dock and Engineering Company, Sydney, or by private contract. The main repair base and store depots are at Sydney.

The main training establishments are HMAS *Cerberus* in Victoria, HMAS *Watson*, HMAS *Penguin* and HMAS *Nirimba* at Sydney, HMAS *Albatross* (Naval Air Station) at Nowra, NSW, and HMAS *Creswell* (Royal Australian Naval College) at Jervis Bay, ACT. Training for junior recruits is carried out at HMAS *Leeuwin* in Fremantle, WA, and Reserve training in naval establishments in all major seaboard capital cities.

The Fleet Air Arm was established in 1948. At 30 June 1982 it had 70 aircraft and consisted of 6 squadrons the operational elements of which were 1 Skyhawk, 1 Tracker and 1 Sea King squadrons embarked in HMAS *Melbourne*. The Wessex, Iroquois and Bell 206B helicopters are used in the utility/search and rescue rôle. The 2 HS 748 aircraft are now employed in the electronic warfare training rôle.

The serving strength at 30 June 1982 totalled 17,630 personnel including 1,040 WRANS.

Navy estimates 1981–82, $A1,164,665,000; 1982–83, $A1,097,566,000.

Air Force. Command of the Royal Australian Air Force is vested in the Chief of the Air Staff (CAS) assisted by the Deputy Chief of the Air Staff, Chief of Air Force Development, Chief of Air Force Material, Chief of Air Force Personnel, Chief of Air Force Technical Services, Director-General Supply—Air Force and Assistant Secretary Resources Planning.

The CAS administers and controls RAAF units through two commands: Operational Command and Support Command. Operational Command is responsible to the CAS for the command of operational units and the conduct of their operations within Australia and overseas. Support Command is responsible to the CAS for training of personnel, and the supply and maintenance of service equipment.

Flying establishment comprises 15 squadrons, of which 2 are equipped with 24 F-111 strike/reconnaissance aircraft. Of the others, 3 are equipped with missile-armed Mirage III-O Mach 2 fighters, 2 with Orion maritime reconnaissance aircraft. There are eight transport squadrons, two with Hercules turboprop transports,

1 with Caribou STOL transports, 1 with a mix of fixed-wing Caribou and Iroquois helicopters, 1 with Boeing Vertol CH-47C medium lift helicopters, 2 with Iroquois helicopters, and a special transport squadron equipped with BAC One-Eleven, Mystère 20 and HS 748 aircraft. There is also one flight operating B707 aircraft. Training aircraft include piston-engined Airtrainers, built in New Zealand, Aermacchi MB 326H jets for pilot training, and HS 748 aircraft for navigator training.

Training for commissioned rank is carried out at the RAAF Academy and Officers' Training School, both located at Point Cook, Victoria. Other major training activities which lead to commissioned rank include basic aircrew training and technical and commercial cadet schemes. Basic ground training to tradesman level is conducted at RAAF technical training schools. Higher command and staff training is, in the main, carried out at the RAAF Staff College, Fairbairn, ACT.

The authorized service manpower ceiling for the Permanent Air Force was 22,707 at 30 June 1982. Combat aircraft totalled about 100.

Long, G. (ed.), *Australia in the War of 1939–45.* 22 vols. Canberra, 1952 ff.

INTERNATIONAL RELATIONS

Membership. Australia is a member of the UN, the Commonwealth, OECD, Colombo Plan, the South Pacific Commission and the South Pacific Bureau for Economic Co-operation.

ECONOMY

Budget. In 1929, under a financial agreement between the Federal Government and States, approved by a referendum, the Federal Government took over all State debts existing on 30 June 1927 and agreed to pay $A15–17m. a year for 58 years towards the interest charges thereon, and to make substantial contributions towards a sinking fund on State debt. The sinking fund arrangements were revised under an amendment to the agreement in 1976. The Federal Government arranges all borrowings, with minor exceptions, for both the Federal and States Governments through a Loan Council which consists of representatives of these governments. Since 1942 the Federal Government alone has levied taxes on incomes. In return for vacating this field of taxation, the States are reimbursed by a grant from the Federal Government out of revenue received.

Receipts, Financing Transactions and Outlays of the Federal Government for years ending 30 June (in $A1m.):

Receipts:	*1977–78*	*1978–79*	*1979–80*	*1980–81*
Income taxes	15,313	15,913	18,541	22,343
Estate duty	96	82	48	17
Gift duty	7	1	1	—
Customs duties	1,232	1,457	1,629	1,884
Excise duties	2,733	3,845	4,965	5,834
Sales tax	1,758	1,770	1,865	2,102
Primary production taxes	179	283	278	353
Stevedoring industry charge	29	19	20	19
Payroll tax	20	13	12	11
Other taxes, fees, fines, etc.	135	151	193	212
Total taxes, fees, fines	21,501	23,534	27,552	32,775
Income from public enterprises	819	1,011	993	1,014
Property income	1,376	1,457	1,609	1,838
Total receipts	23,696	26,002	30,154	35,627
Financing Transactions:	4,368	4,194	3,047	2,152
Total funds available	28,064	30,197	33,201	37,779
Outlay:				
General public services	1,811	1,907	2,141	2,467
Defence	2,377	2,606	3,008	3,537
Education:				
University	781	810	875	953
Primary and Secondary	788	830	818	947
Other	819	883	915	1,032
Total education	2,388	2,523	2,608	2,932

Outlay (cont.):	1977–78	1978–79	1979–80	1980–81
Health				
Hospital and clinical services	1,761	1,802	1,972	2,314
Other	932	1,097	1,190	1,329
Total health	2,693	2,897	3,162	3,643
Social security and welfare				
Care of and assistance to				
Aged persons	3,042	3,344	3,643	4,077
Incapacitated and handicapped persons	689	795	901	1,006
Unemployed and sick	942	1,061	1,105	1,241
Ex-servicemen	835	896	1,006	1,239
Families and children	1,077	1,038	1,055	1,001
Other	834	958	1,085	1,344
Total social security, etc.	7,419	8,092	8,795	9,909
Housing and community amenities	661	442	369	372
Recreation and culture	263	279	318	400
Economic services				
Agriculture, forestry and fishing	375	308	386	489
Mining, manufacturing and construction	52	138	369	220
Transport and communication	1,943	1,801	2,030	2,325
Other	489	560	560	783
Total economic services	2,858	2,808	3,345	3,817
Other purposes	7,594	8,643	9,454	10,704
Total outlay	28,064	30,197	33,201	37,779

The following table shows Government securities on issue on account of the Commonwealth Government and States, at 30 June 1982:

Currency in which repayable	*Australian Government*	*States*	*Total*
Australian Dollar ($A1,000)	12,580,448	15,656,981	28,237,428
Sterling (£1,000)	7,311	4,402	11,713
United States Dollar (US$1,000)	1,447,353	8,999	1,456,352
Swiss Francs (SW.F.1,000)	2,570,000	—	2,570,000
Netherlands Guilders (fl.1,000)	940,000	—	940,000
Deutsche Marks (DM 1,000)	2,935,138	—	2,935,138
European Units of Account (EUA1,000)	—	—	—
Japanese Yen (Yen 1m.)	311,000	—	311,000
Total ($A1,000 equivalents) [1]	17,916,115	15,673,291	33,589,406

[1] Converted at rate of exchange ruling at 30 June 1982.

Debt per head of population at 30 June 1982 was $A2,215, while the annual interest charge amounted to $A209 per head.

States: The following table presents a summary of the receipts and outlay of State and local authorities during 1979–80 (in $A1m.).

	NSW	*Vic.*	*Qld*	*SA*	*WA*	*Tas.*	*NT*	*All States*
Receipts and Financing Transactions								
Taxes, fees, fines, etc.	3,011	2,264	963	559	598	181	38	7,613
Income from public enterprises	173	343	192	80	38	79	–39	865
Grants from Commonwealth Government	3,739	2,790	1,947	1,227	1,304	507	469	11,983
Advances from Commonwealth Government (net)	308	220	77	110	83	56	83	937
All other	1,975	1,423	818	304	417	136	75	5,149
Total funds available	9,206	7,040	3,997	2,280	2,440	958	626	26,547

	NSW	Vic.	Qld	SA	WA	Tas.	NT	All States
Outlay								
Final consumption expenditure	5,000	3,870	2,079	1,402	1,406	513	366	14,690
Interest paid	938	827	508	273	229	138	22	2,935
Gross fixed capital expenditure on new assets	2,909	2,131	1,329	538	735	275	170	8,086
All other	359	212	81	67	16	32	68	836
Total outlay	9,206	7,040	3,997	2,280	2,440	958	626	26,547

Finance (5 parts), Australian Bureau of Statistics, Canberra, 1907–1962/63
Australian National Accounts. Australian Bureau of Statistics. 1953–54 to date
Public Authority Finance, No. 1. Australian Bureau of Statistics, 1972
Public Authority Finance: Commonwealth Government Finance, Australia. Australian Bureau of Statistics, 1962–63 to date
Public Authority Finance: State and Local Government Finance, Australia. Australian Bureau of Statistics, 1971–72 to date
Public Authority Finance: Government Financial Estimates. Australian Bureau of Statistics, 1975–76 to date
National Income and Expenditure. Australian Bureau of Statistics. Canberra, 1946 to date
Australia's Committee of Economic Enquiry. Report. Canberra, 1965
Treasury Information Bulletin (and Supplements). Canberra Treasury Dept., 1956 to date (quarterly)
Karmel, P. H., *The Structure of the Australian Economy.* Melbourne, 1962
Maxwell, J. A., *Commonwealth–State Financial Arrangements in Australia.* Melbourne Univ. Press

Currency. On 14 Feb. 1966 Australia adopted a system of decimal currency. The currency unit, the *dollar* ($) is divided into 100 *cents.* The transition period ended on 31 July 1967. Decimal system notes have been issued in denominations of $1, 2, 5, 10, 20 and 50. Coins have been issued in denominations of 50, 20, 10, 5, 2 and 1 cent.

Australian notes, issued by the note-issue department of the Reserve Bank, are legal tender throughout Australia. The total value of notes in circulation on 30 June 1982 was $A5,837·5m., of which $A5,160·1m. were held by the public. In March 1983, US$1 = 1·17 *dollars*; £1 = 1·76 *dollars.*

Banking. The banking system in Australia comprises:

(a) The Reserve Bank of Australia. This is the central bank which in addition to its central banking business (including the note-issue department) provides special financing facilities through the rural credits department for the processing, manufacture and marketing of primary produce.

(b) Six major trading banks: (i) The Commonwealth Trading Bank of Australia; (ii) 5 private trading banks: The Australia and New Zealand Banking Group Ltd, the Bank of New South Wales, The Commercial Bank of Australia Ltd, The Commercial Banking Company of Sydney Ltd and The National Bank of Australasia Ltd.

(c) Other trading banks: (i) 3 State Government banks—The State Bank of New South Wales, The State Bank of South Australia, and the Rural and Industries Bank of Western Australia; (ii) one joint stock bank—The Bank of Queensland Ltd, formerly The Brisbane Permanent Building and Banking Co. Ltd, which has specialized business in one district only; (iii) The Australian Bank Ltd; (iv) branches of 2 overseas banks—the Bank of New Zealand and the Banque Nationale de Paris, which are mainly concerned with financing trade, etc., between Australia and overseas countries.

(d) The Commonwealth Development Bank of Australia.

(e) Savings Banks.

(f) The Australian Resources Development Bank Ltd opened on 29 March 1968. Its main objective is to assist Australian enterprises in the development of Australia's natural resources, through direct loans and equity investment or by re-financing loans made by trading banks. The bank is jointly owned by the 6 major Australian trading banks.

(g) The Primary Industry Bank of Australia Ltd commenced operations on 22 Sept. 1978. The equity capital of the bank consists of eight shares. Seven shares are held by the Australian Government and the 6 major trading banks while the eighth share is held equally by the 4 State banks. The main objective of the bank is to facilitate the provision of loans to primary producers on longer terms than are otherwise generally available. The role of the bank is restricted to re-financing loans made by banks and other financial institutions.

The Reserve Bank's functions and responsibilities derive from the Reserve Bank Act 1959 and the Banking Act 1959, which came into effect in 1960. They had their origins, however, in the development of the central banking role of the Commonwealth Bank, which was established in 1911 as a Government savings and trading bank.

Control of the Australian note issue was transferred from the Commonwealth Treasury to a Notes Board in 1920 and, in 1924, to the Bank. The Commonwealth Bank Act 1945 formally constituted the Bank as a central bank, and these powers were carried through into the 1959 Act establishing the Reserve Bank.

The Acts of 1959 provided for: (i) the separation of the central bank from the Commonwealth group of banking institutions and its reconstitution as the Reserve Bank of Australia; (ii) the establishment of an entirely separate Commonwealth Banking Corporation, with responsibilities for the non-central-banking elements that had developed from within the original Commonwealth Bank—namely the Commonwealth Trading Bank, the Commonwealth Savings Bank and the Commonwealth Development Bank, the latter being basically an amalgamation of the Mortgage Bank and Industrial Finance Department of the Commonwealth Bank.

At 30 June 1982 the capital of the Reserve Bank totalled $A49·4m. and reserve funds (including a special reserve for IMF special drawing rights) $A2,860m. The capital was distributed as follows: Central banking business, $A40m.; rural credits department, $A9·4m. Reserve funds held were: Central banking business, $A1,472m.; rural credits department, $A80m.; note issue department, $A1,308m. Profits for the year ended 30 June 1982 (including all departments) amounted to $A442m.

Particulars as at 30 June 1982 for the banks under the control of the Commonwealth Banking Corporation: Commonwealth Trading Bank, capital, $A15m.; reserve fund, $A162m.; profits for the year, $A26m. Commonwealth Development Bank, capital, $A62m.; reserve fund, $A136m.; profits for the year, $A7m. Commonwealth Savings Bank, reserve fund, $A356m.; profits for the year, $A53m.

At 30 June 1982 the 13 trading banks operating in Australia provided full banking facilities at 5,164 branches and 1,051 agencies all over Australia.

The weekly average of deposits in Australia with all trading banks (under *(b)* and *(c)* above) during June 1982 amounted to $A33,486m.; the average of advances owing to the banks was $A26,213m.; the average of total assets was $A48,153m.

At 30 June 1982, 12 savings banks were operating in Australia. These are the 6 major savings banks being wholly owned subsidiaries of the trading banks; the Bank of New Zealand Saving Bank Ltd; and operating, with certain exceptions, in all States and Territories; the State Bank in Victoria and the State Savings Bank of South Australia; the Rural and Industries Bank of Western Australia, and 2 Trustee Savings Banks in Tasmania. At 30 June 1982 these savings banks provided savings facilities at 5,703 branches and 12,011 agencies throughout Australia. At end of June 1982 they held deposits in Australia amounting to $A25,030m.

In 1982 there were 45 companies registered under the Life Insurance Act, 1945, transacting life insurance business in Australia; in addition there were 3 State government institutions. During 1981–82 premiums received were $A2,635m. and claims, etc., paid were $A1,822m.

The following table is a summary of banking and insurance business (in $A1m.) in the several States of the Commonwealth:

Particulars	*NSW*	*Vic.*	*Q'ld*	*SA*	*WA*	*Tas.*	*Australia (including A.C.T. and N.T.)*
All trading banks:[1]							
Fixed deposits	9,292	4,976	3,660	1,272	1,731	344	21,592
Current deposits	5,139	2,797	1,931	629	905	199	11,868
Advances	11,400	5,386	3,309	2,390	2,417	499	26,207
Savings bank deposits [2]	6,887	9,475	3,460	2,594	1,514	759	25,030
Life insurance:[3]							
New policies issued (sum insured)							
Ordinary and industrial	3,151	3,256	2,447	973	1,114	315	14,134
Superannuation	1,145	4,833	1,927	1,032	1,374	264	22,086
Policies existing [2] (sum insured)							
Ordinary and industrial	15,377	19,481	13,425	6,104	6,534	1,778	77,698
Superannuation	3,394	15,929	5,504	3,541	3,786	975	68,625

[1] Weekly averages for June 1982. [2] At June 1982. [3] Year ended 30 June 1982.

Treasury Information Bulletin. Department of the Treasury. Canberra, 1956 to date (quarterly)
Reserve Bank of Australia. *Statistical Bulletin.* Sydney, 1937 to date (monthly)

Weights and Measures. Conversion to the metric system is in progress.

ENERGY AND NATURAL RESOURCES

Electricity. Total production 1981–82, 104,499m. kwh. (of which hydro, 14,545m.).

Minerals. The mineral output was valued ex-mine as follows (in $A1,000):

Mineral	*1979–80*	*1980–81*
Copper concentrate	327,471	288,768
Gold bullion [1]	203,337	184,434
Iron ore [2]	1,004,308	1,007,307
Lead concentrate	623,973	375,018
Tin concentrate	166,674	143,343
Zinc concentrate	174,065	188,075
Black coal	1,760,095	2,392,460
Brown coal [3]	91,821	107,052
Total (value of minerals and construction materials)	7,207,971	8,094,049

[1] Includes alluvial gold.
[2] Includes iron ore for pellet production.
[3] Excludes value of brown coal used in making briquettes.

Gold production (kg), in 1976–77, 15,608; 1977–78, 21,047; 1978–79, 19,584; 1979–80, 18,273; 1980–81, 16,672.

Black coal (1,000 tonnes) mined in 1976–77, 75,982; 1977–78, 79,338; 1978–79, 81,197; 1979–80, 81,249; 1980–81, 96,074.

Agriculture. In 1982, of a total Australian area of 768m. hectares, 633·6m. hectares (82·5%) were Crown lands; private lands formed the remainder, of which 134·7m. hectares (17·6%) were alienated or in the process of alienation.

Area and production of the principal crops in 1981–82[2]:

Crops	*Total area (1,000 hectares)*	*Total production (1,000 tonnes)*
Wheat (grain)	11,880	16,330
Oats (grain)	1,387	1,619
Barley (grain)	2,677	3,511
Maize (grain)	59	...
Hay (cereal)	380	...
Potatoes (ordinary)	34	...
Sugar-cane (for crushing)	316	25,054
Vineyards	70	...
		(1,000 litres)
Wine made	...	394,738
Fruit	102	...

The following summary shows the production and gross value of the most important items or classes of production, classified by States:

1981–82 [2]	*NSW*	*Vic.*	*Q'ld*	*SA*	*WA*	*Tas.*	*Aust.*[1]
Area of crops (1,000 hectares)	5,721	2,166	2,751	2,881	5,955	91	19,567
Production of wheat (1,000 tonnes)	5,910	2,466	1,485	1,695	4,771	2	16,330
1981–82 [2]							
Total wool production (1,000m. tons)	227·8	146·3	59·9	104·3	149·9	22·0	710·7
1980–81 [2]							
Factory butter (1,000 kg)	1,371	67,765	2,791	...	...	4,235	79,182
Non-processed cheese (1,000 kg)	11,292	78,629	11,142	16,982	3,342	13,907	135,294
All meat (tonnes, carcase weight)							
1979–80	679,737	563,824	589,851	183,653	211,191	56,931	2,332,505
1980–81	606,455	637,929	507,757	193,125	226,290	59,999	2,280,671
1981–82 [2]	542,750	622,040	644,239	194,673	208,425	65,078	2,317,980
Total Agriculture (value $A1m.)							
1979–80	3,504·0	2,587·0	2,352·6	1,341·6	1,581·9	268·2	11,768·2

[1] Includes Northern Territory and Australian Capital Territory.
[2] Preliminary, subject to revision.

Livestock (in 1,000) at 31 March 1982 (preliminary):

	NSW	*Vic.*	*Q'ld*	*SA*	*WA*	*Tas.*	*N. Terr.*	*ACT*	*Australia*
Cattle	5,379	4,137	9,765	1,010	1,935	628	1,622	14	24,490
Sheep	48,400	25,152	12,283	16,724	30,242	4,500	1	110	137,412
Pigs	759	407	503	373	263	47	3	—	2,354

Forestry. At 31 March 1980 there were 718,000 hectares of coniferous plantations.

INDUSTRY AND TRADE

Industry. Statistics of the manufacturing industries in Australia in 1980–81: Number of establishments, 27,681; workers employed, 1,149,838; salaries and wages paid, $A14,911m.; value-added, $A28,530m. (excludes small single-establishment enterprises employing less than 4 persons).

Estimated gross value (in $A1,000) of the products of Australia:

Products	*1977–78*	*1978–79*	*1979–80*	*1980–81*	*1981–82*[1]
Crops	3,046,953	4,912,513	5,540,828	5,394,707	6,127,112
Livestock slaughtering and other disposals	1,954,393	3,097,729	3,658,802	3,447,098	3,264,265
Livestock products	1,970,440	2,214,463	2,568,026	2,801,534	3,028,363
Forestry, fishing and hunting	523,925	594,627	712,950	...	...
Mining and quarrying	4,902,640	5,646,937	7,207,712	8,094,049	...

[1] Preliminary, subject to revision.

Labour. The majority of wage and salary earners in Australia have their minimum wages and conditions of work prescribed in awards of industrial arbitration authorities established under federal and State legislation. However, in some States, some conditions of work (*e.g.*, normal weekly hours of work, long-service leave, annual leave) are set down in State legislation. Practically all employees in Australia have a standard working week of 40 hours or less; paid annual leave of at least 4 weeks; and paid long-service leave (*i.e.*, leave granted to workers who remain with one employer over an extended period of time and in certain other areas) of at least 13 weeks after 15 years' continuous service. For most occupations equal pay for males and females has been granted.

In addition to the minimum rates of pay for a standard working week prescribed in awards of industrial arbitration authorities, many wage-earners are in receipt of over-award pay and payments for overtime. At the end of Oct. 1981 it was estimated that the average weekly earnings of adult males (other than managerial, professional and higher supervisory staff) in full-time private and government employment was $A311·40 and average weekly hours 40·9.

Employees in all States are covered by workers' compensation legislation and by certain industrial award provisions relating to work injuries.

During 1981 industrial disputes involving stoppages of work of 10 man-days or more accounted for 4,192,200 working days lost. In these disputes 1,251,800 workers were involved.

The following table shows estimates (in 1,000) of the civilian population, by labour force status. The estimates are derived by the ABS from the population survey which is based on a sample of dwellings, carried out by personal interview, covering about two-thirds of 1% of the population of Australia. Prior to Feb. 1978, when monthly surveys were introduced, the surveys were conducted quarterly. The labour force estimates for Feb. 1978 and subsequent months are based on population estimates derived from the 1976 Population Census, adjusted for under-enumeration and were obtained using a new sample and revised questionnaire. Estimates for earlier periods have been revised to make them comparable with current surveys.

	May 1978	*May 1979*	*May 1980*	*May 1981*	*May 1982*
In the labour force	6,394·0	6,439·9	6,651·4	6,752·7	6,854·7
Employed	5,998·7	6,043·3	6,237·8	6,377·2	6,404·8
Unemployed	395·3	396·6	413·6	375·5	449·9
Not in the labour force	4,051·7	4,193·6	4,167·7	4,280·5	4,408·7
Civilian population aged 15 years and over	10,445·7	10,633·5	10,819·1	11,033·2	11,263·3

The following table shows population survey estimates (in 1,000) of employed persons in Australia classified by industry:

Industry [1]	*May 1979*	*May 1980*	*May 1981*	*May 1982*
Agriculture and services to agriculture	361·8	382·2	394·6	377·2
Forestry and logging, fishing and hunting	29·3	25·2	30·9	32·7
Mining	85·1	80·3	91·1	96·1
Manufacturing	1,216·9	1,257·4	1,262·3	1,244·9
Food, beverages and tobacco	188·7	190·8	174·9	182·9
Metal products	203·0	200·0	236·1	223·2
Other manufacturing	825·3	866·6	851·3	838·8
Electricity, gas and water	116·0	129·9	129·1	124·9
Construction	485·4	476·3	488·9	469·8
Wholesale trade	361·7	371·7	396·1	389·0
Retail trade	878·4	914·8	869·7	882·2
Transport and storage	340·7	329·4	345·3	366·6
Communication	128·5	121·5	122·7	141·4
Finance, property and business services	484·9	512·1	559·2	573·2
Public administration and defence	275·0	281·3	287·1	286·5
Community services	901·1	968·0	1,005·3	1,020·5
Recreation, personal and other services	373·6	387·7	394·7	399·8
Total employed	6,043·3	6,237·8	6,377·2	6,404·8

[1] Australian Standard Industrial Classification.

The following table shows the number of unemployed persons (from the population survey), job vacancies (from the ABS Job Vacancies survey) and the number of persons in receipt of unemployment benefit:

	May 1978	*May 1979*	*May 1980*	*May 1981*	*May 1982*
Persons unemployed	395,300	396,600	413,600	375,500	449,900
Job Vacancies	32,200 [1]	34,300	29,800	35,700	25,300
Unemployment benefit recipients [2]	286,100	312,000	311,200	314,500 [3]	390,700

[1] Not directly comparable with results from later surveys.
[2] Data relates to the month of June.
[3] Estimate.

Trade Unions. At the end of 1981 there were 324 trade unions reporting in Australia with an estimated membership of 2,994,100. About 55% of wage and salary earners were estimated to be members of unions. In 1981 there were 36 unions with fewer than 100 members and 7 unions with 80,000 or more members. Many of the larger trade unions are affiliated with central labour organizations, the oldest and by far the largest being the Australian Council of Trade Unions formed in 1927.

Labour Statistics. Australian Bureau of Statistics. Canberra, 1980
Foenander, O. de R., *Industrial Conciliation and Arbitration in Australia.* Sydney, 1959.—*Trade Unionism in Australia.* Sydney, 1962.—*Shop Stewards and Shop Committees.* Melbourne Univ. Press, 1965
Huntly, P., *Inside Australia's Top 100 Trade Unions.* Sydney, 1976
Isaac, J. E., and Ford, G. W., *Australian Industrial Relations.* Melbourne, 1971
O'Dea, R., *A Guide to Industrial Relations in Australia.* Sydney, 1967
Portus, J. H., *The Development of Australian Trade Union Law.* Melbourne, 1958
Rawson, D. W., *A Handbook of Australian Trade Unions and Employees' Associations.* Canberra, 1977
Walker, K. F., *Australian Industrial Relations Systems.* Cambridge, Mass., 1970

Commerce. Throughout Australia there are uniform customs duties, and trade between the States is free. For 1980–81[1] the gross revenue collected from customs duties amounted to $A1,826·1m. and from excise $A5,818·4m.

Value of the total imports and exports for years ending 30 June, in $A1,000:

	Imports	*Exports (excluding ships' and aircraft stores) Australian produce*	*Re-exports*	*Total*
1979–80	16,217,505	18,202,526	667,553	18,870,079
1980–81	18,964,266	18,353,692	815,551	19,169,243
1981–82 [1]	23,003,215	18,737,946	847,945	19,585,891

[1] Preliminary, subject to revision.

The Australian customs tariff provides for preferences to goods produced in and shipped from certain specified countries such as UK, Canada, New Zealand and Ireland. Preferences occur as a result of reciprocal trade agreements between Australia and these countries.

Australia also has bilateral agreements with a number of other countries guaranteeing reciprocal treatment in matters of trade.

The Australia–New Zealand free-trade agreement came into force on 1 Jan. 1966 in certain scheduled goods.

In addition, Australia is a signatory to the multilateral General Agreement on Tariffs and Trade (GATT).

Principal commodities exported and imported from Australia (in $A1,000) in 1981–82 [1]:

	Exports	*Imports*
Live animals	227,627	33,308
Meat	1,381,044	10,148
Dairy products	300,464	45,604
Fish	308,348	213,201
Cereals	2,503,703	31,157
Fruit and vegetables	205,582	147,537
Sugar, etc., and honey	793,725	14,149
Coffee, tea, etc.	31,379	187,134
Food for animals	40,538	21,646
Miscellaneous food	13,736	28,265
Beverages	39,458	104,491
Tobacco	10,635	69,447
Hides, skins, etc.	217,474	2,979
Oil-seeds, nuts, kernels	14,870	13,552
Crude rubber	2,136	56,857
Wood, timber and cork	184,304	206,931
Pulp and waste paper	1,437	97,521
Textile fibres and their waste	1,888,884	90,426
Crude fertilizers and minerals	84,464	223,532
Metalliferous ores and metal scrap	3,372,126	33,935
Crude animal & vegetable materials, n.e.s.	56,098	44,733
Coal, coke & briquettes	2,295,015	2,011
Petroleum and products	557,387	2,988,394
Petroleum gases	316,719	653
Animal oils and fats	82,095	482
Fixed vegetable oils and fats	7,550	53,477
Animal and vegetable oils and fats	5,736	26,069
Organic chemicals	44,283	495,087
Inorganic chemicals	44,957	260,840
Dyeing, tanning and colouring materials	18,798	88,592
Medicinal and pharmaceutical products	88,469	155,402
Essential oils and perfumes, etc.	30,803	102,007
Fertilizers, manufactured	4,522	56,752
Explosives and pyrotechnic products	7,837	13,038
Plastic materials	90,757	430,425
Chemical materials and products, n.e.s.	73,866	224,660
Leather manufactures, n.e.s.	34,195	43,770
Rubber manufactures, n.e.s.	10,954	287,229
Wood and cork manufactures (except furniture)	6,838	106,208
Paper and paperboard	51,082	556,833
Textile yarn, fabrics, etc.	138,951	1,097,275
Non-metallic mineral manufactures, n.e.s.	114,461	409,224
Iron and steel	440,866	577,785
Non-ferrous metals	994,618	136,695
Manufactures of metal, n.e.s.	193,842	640,849

	Exports	*Imports*
Power generating machinery and equipment	98,371	747,266
Machinery specialized for particular industries	170,205	1,480,962
Metalworking machinery	23,502	227,281
General industrial machinery and equipment, n.e.s. and machine parts, n.e.s.	154,968	1,212,899
Office machines and automatic data processing equipment	71,453	732,511
Telecommunications and sound recording and reproducing apparatus and equipment	39,838	710,636
Electrical machinery, apparatus and appliances, n.e.s. and electrical parts thereof (including non-electrical counterparts n.e.s., of electrical household type equipment)	111,396	995,847
Road vehicles (including air cushion vehicles)	196,705	1,969,036
Other transport equipment	236,190	1,277,674
Sanitary, plumbing, heating and lighting fixtures and fittings, n.e.s.	5,249	41,938
Furniture and parts thereof	13,715	128,942
Travel goods, handbags and similar containers	834	78,683
Articles of apparel and clothing accessories	13,355	392,366
Footwear	3,742	143,596
Professional, scientific and controlling instruments and apparatus, n.e.s.	110,310	437,879
Photographic apparatus, equipment and supplies and optical goods, n.e.s.; watches and clocks	103,527	391,891
Miscellaneous manufactured articles, n.e.s.	151,273	1,066,487
Commodities and transactions of merchandise trade, not elsewhere classified [2]	469,296	292,427
Total merchandise trade	19,306,326	22,758,629
Commodities and transactions not included in merchandise trade	279,572	236,199
Total recorded trade	19,585,898	22,994,829

[1] Preliminary. [2] Industrial petroleum gases.

Total trade in ($A1,000) with the more important countries, according to origin (imports) and consignment (exports):

From or to	*1980–81* Imports	*1980–81* Exports	*1981–82*[1] Imports	*1981–82*[1] Exports
Belgium–Luxembourg	119,300	171,516	135,247	128,968
Canada	500,192	434,120	584,925	366,621
China–excl. Taiwan Province	269,789	671,201	284,767	606,205
Egypt, Arab Republic of	172	393,514	153	294,794
France	305,229	366,305	628,031	400,033
Germany, Fed. Republic of	1,079,380	473,677	1,355,778	465,319
Hong Kong	394,947	309,252	500,422	431,526
India	108,682	176,859	123,559	311,822
Indonesia	416,875	358,582	515,885	416,986
Iran	33,418	196,471	58,738	145,078
Italy	427,656	393,976	506,879	391,877
Japan	3,628,928	5,227,118	4,527,083	5,385,802
Kuwait	350,768	182,539	263,062	117,028
Malaysia	186,741	442,425	187,718	438,234
Netherlands	198,988	208,048	357,799	210,646
New Zealand	636,193	915,543	726,204	1,039,517
Pakistan	14,334	36,558	40,788	58,000
Papua New Guinea	73,641	433,430	70,538	420,557
Saudi Arabia	1,032,219	276,305	1,193,137	362,868
Singapore, Republic of	507,289	513,025	652,293	515,394
Sri Lanka	11,153	53,061	12,217	34,426
Sweden	294,618	56,775	321,208	57,408
Switzerland	177,538	17,147	213,441	20,887
USSR	8,974	831,758	8,637	669,159
UK	1,584,605	715,329	1,649,138	725,811
USA	4,168,673	2,147,012	5,249,356	2,154,507

[1] Preliminary.

Imports and exports for particular State ($A1,000):

States, etc.	*1980–81* Imports	*1980–81* Exports	*1981–82*[1] Imports	*1981–82*[1] Exports
New South Wales	7,951,738	4,466,489	9,232,219	4,203,519
Victoria	5,929,278	3,989,429	7,169,661	3,899,387
Queensland	1,882,815	4,501,290	2,179,733	4,349,547
South Australia	1,072,425	1,400,028	1,337,311	1,280,871
Western Australia	1,663,378	3,781,114	2,535,102	3,901,823
Tasmania	172,456	658,013	166,032	646,739
Northern Territory	282,138	359,569	373,895	373,928
Aust. Cap. Terr.	10,038	3,341	9,262	2,666
Total	18,964,266	19,169,243	23,003,215	19,585,891

In this table the value of goods sent from one state to another for transhipment abroad has been included in the State from which the goods were finally dispatched.

[1] Preliminary, subject to revision.

Overseas Trade. Australian Bureau of Statistics. Canberra, 1906 to date

Total trade between UK and Australia (British Department of Trade returns, in £1,000 sterling):

	1978	*1979*	*1980*	*1981*	*1982*
Imports to UK	349,068	474,902	484,112	395,387	493,196
Exports and re-exports from UK	856,317	839,871	815,652	863,636	1,043,615

Tourism. During 1981, 936,727 overseas visitors arrived in Australia intending to stay for less than 12 months, and international tourism receipts were $A1,028m.

Australian Bureau of Statistics, Canberra: *Rural Industries.* 1962–63 to date.—*Manufacturing Establishments: Details of Operations.* 1968–69 to date.—*Non-rural Primary Industries.* 1967–68 and 1968–69.—*Value of Production.* 1964–65 to 1968–69.—*Manufacturing Industry.* 1963–64 to 1967–68.—*Manufacturing Commodities.* 1963–64 and 1964–65.—*Building and Construction.* 1964–65 to date

Quarterly Review of Agricultural Economics. Bureau of Agricultural Economics. Canberra, 1948 to date

Developments in Australian Manufacturing Industry. Department of Trade. Melbourne, 1954–55 to date (annual)
The Australian Mineral Industry Review. Department of National Development—Bureau of Mineral Resources, Geology and Geophysics. Canberra, 1948 to date
Australian Economy. Department of the Treasury. Canberra, 1956 to date
Australasian Institute of Mining and Metallurgy. *Proceedings: New Series.* Melbourne, 1912 to date

COMMUNICATIONS

Roads. The length of roads in Australia for general traffic is about 817,000 km, of which approximately 238,000 is sealed, 211,000 of gravel, crushed stone or other improved surface, and 368,000 of cleared or formed surface only.

At 30 June 1981, 7,917,600 motor vehicles, including 6,021,000 cars and station wagons, 956,700 utilities and panel-vans, 587,500 truck type vehicles and buses and 352,300 motor cycles, were registered in Australia. The revenue derived from registration fees and motor tax for the year 1978–79 was $A506·3m., drivers' and riders' licences, $A75·4m., and miscellaneous, $A213·8m. New motor vehicle registration figures for 1981–82 include 471,255 cars and station wagons, 100,044 utilities and panel-vans, 50,943 truck type vehicles and buses and 71,691 motor cycles.

Railways. Government railways for the year ended 30 June 1980:

System	*Route-km open* [4]	*Revenue train-km run, 1,000*	*Passenger journeys, 1,000*	*Goods and livestock, carried, 1,000 tonnes*	*Gross earnings, $A1,000*	*Working expenses, $A1,000*
State:						
New South Wales	9,773	59,356	208,821	39,685	495,833	757,555
Victoria	6,184	30,795	88,962	13,454	230,549	392,586
Queensland	9,904	32,589	29,482	38,440	352,700	422,503
South Australia [3]	142	3,977	73,210	...	26,943	74,391
Western Australia	5,773	11,759	233 [5]	21,388	174,258	180,280
Australian National [1] [2]	7,687	12,392	585	12,704	157,971	222,799

[1] The Australian National Railways operates services of the former Commonwealth Railways, the non-metropolitan South Australian Railways and the Tasmanian Railways.
[2] Excludes Adelaide metropolitan rail passenger services and the Tasmanian Region.
[3] The South Australian State Transport Authority operates services in the Adelaide metropolitan area.
[4] Inter system traffic is included in the total for each system over which it passes.
[5] Excludes details of Western Australian suburban rail operations.

The State railway gauges are: New South Wales, 1,435 mm; Victoria, 1,600 mm (325 km 1,435 mm); Queensland, 1,067 mm (111 km 1,435 mm); South Australia, 1,600 mm for 2,533 km, 1,824 km 1,435 mm and the rest 1,067 mm; West Australia, 137 km, 1,435 mm and the rest 1,067 mm, and Tasmania, 1,067 mm. Of the Australian National Railways, the gauge of the Trans-Australian and Australian Capital Territory is 1,435 mm, for the Central Australia 1,067 mm for 869 km and 1,435 mm for 350 km and for North Australia, 1,067 mm. Under various Commonwealth–State standardization agreements Brisbane, Sydney and Melbourne are linked by a standard 1,435 mm gauge line and Sydney is linked with Perth, *via* Broken Hill to Port Pirie (South Australia), from Port Pirie to Kalgoorlie (Western Australia) and from Kalgoorlie to Perth. The overall length of the Sydney–Perth railway is 3,961 km. The Central Australia railway extends as far north as Alice Springs (now standard gauge on new alignment from Tarcoola to Alice Springs).

Aviation. Civil flying in Australia and Territories is subject to legislative control by the Australian Government. The administration of the Air Navigation Act and Regulations is a function of the Commonwealth Department of Aviation under the Minister for Aviation.

Operations of regular internal air services in Australia include flights of all

Australian-owned airlines, except Qantas Airways. During 1981 hours flown numbered 269,929. The total distance flown was 136m. km. Paying passengers carried numbered 11,302,772; weight of goods carried was 130,198 tonnes, and gross weight of mail was 17,097 tonnes.

During 1981 hours flown by Australian regular overseas services numbered 74,375; km flown, 59m.; paying passengers, 1,891,449; freight, 69,906 tonnes; mail, 4,018 tonnes.

Expenditure by the Australian Government on air transport for the year 1980–81 was $A329·4m. (including $A51·4m. on capital works).

At 30 June 1982 there were 368 licensed aerodromes and 77 governmental aerodromes in Australia.

Shipping. As at 30 June 1981 the Australian merchant marine (vessels of 150 tons gross and over) consisted of 84 coastal vessels of 1,333,115 tons gross and 21 overseas vessels of 620,450 tons gross.

Entrances and clearances of vessels (with cargo and in ballast) engaged in overseas trade:

	Entrances		*Clearances*	
	No.	*DWT*	*No.*	*DWT*
1979–80	11,967	360,747,938	12,063	364,080,024
1980–81	11,949	360,940,597	12,090	363,543,269

The following summary shows shipping activity by States, 1980–81:

Particulars	*NSW*	*Vic.*	*Q'ld*	*SA*	*WA*	*Tas.*	*N.T.*	*Unsp.*	*Aust.*
Overseas vessel arrivals									
Calls	2,992	2,431	2,270	865	2,540	394	283	174	11,949
DWT (1,000 tonnes)	80,808	50,980	65,828	17,528	125,992	10,073	7,766	1,964	360,941
Overseas cargo:									
Discharged: 1,000 tonnes	6,289	3,148	2,666	2,715	5,376	252	1,195	945	22,586
Discharged: 1,000 cu. metres	3,774	3,457	901	428	643	57	56	578	9,894
Overseas vessel departures									
Calls	2,927	2,499	2,333	849	2,531	410	281	290	12,090
DWT (1,000 tonnes)	79,573	52,492	66,735	17,280	125,006	10,072	7,709	4,675	363,543
Overseas cargo									
Loaded: 1,000 tonnes	29,783	7,673	34,223	4,143	90,317	5,148	4,672	1,644	177,604
Loaded: 1,000 cu. metres	459	705	705	65	93	26	1	347	1,809

Post and Broadcasting. Business, year ended 30 June 1982. Number of post offices, 4,906. Earnings: Postal, $A887·4m. Working expenses: $A906·6m.

At 30 June 1982, there were 5,356,572 telephone services, 59,196 data services, 37,802 telex services and 5,411 telephone exchanges.

Radio broadcasting stations are in operation in all State capitals and in other areas throughout Australia. The National Broadcasting Service is provided by the Australian Broadcasting Commission, which at 30 June 1982 operated 94 medium-wave, 15 frequency modulation and 6 high-frequency stations, and 11 high-frequency stations for overseas services. In addition, 128 medium-wave, and 7 frequency modulation, commercial broadcasting stations plus 28 public radio stations (both MW and FM) were operating.

Television services are conducted in each State, the Northern Territory and the Australian Capital Territory by the National Television Service and by the Commercial Television Service. There were 251 national stations (including translators) and 50 commercial television stations in 1981.

The Overseas Telecommunications Commission (OTC), established by the Overseas Telecommunications Act 1946, is responsible for the establishment, maintenance, operation and development of all public telecommunications' services between Australia and other countries, between Australia and its external territories and with ships at sea. In co-operation with Telecom and communications carriers in other countries, OTC provides ISD, other international telephone, telegram, facsimile, phototelegram, telex, leased circuit, audio broadcast and data transmission services to countries throughout the world by means of submarine cables, communications satellites and, in a decreasing number of cases, short wave radio. Television relay is provided to and from countries with access to satellite communications' facilities.

Cinemas (1971). There were 976 cinemas including 241 drive-in cinemas, with a total seating capacity of about 478,000.

Newspapers (1979). There was 1 national newspaper (average daily circulation 126,000) and 14 metropolitan daily newspapers in Australia with a combined daily circulation of 3·6m. Of these, 3 papers published in Melbourne accounted for 1·3m. and 4 published in Sydney for 1·2m.

Australian Transport 1974–75. Annual Report. Department of Transport, Canberra
Australian Transport. Sydney, Institute of Transport, 1937 to date (quarterly)

JUSTICE, RELIGION, EDUCATION AND WELFARE

Justice. The judicial power of the Commonwealth of Australia is vested in the High Court of Australia (the Federal Supreme Court), in the Federal courts created by the Federal Parliament (the Federal Court of Australia, the Family Court of Australia, the Federal Court of Bankruptcy and the Australian Industrial Court) and in the State courts invested by Parliament with Federal jurisdiction.

High Court. The High Court consists of a Chief Justice and 6 other Justices, appointed by the Governor-General in Council. The Constitution confers on the High Court original jurisdiction, *inter alia*, in all matters arising under treaties or affecting consuls or other foreign representatives, matters between the States of the Commonwealth, matters to which the Commonwealth is a party and matters between residents of different States. Federal Parliament may make laws conferring original jurisdiction on the High Court, *inter alia*, in matters arising under the Constitution or under any laws made by the Parliament. It has in fact conferred jurisdiction on the High Court in matters arising under the Constitution and in matters arising under certain laws made by Parliament.

The High Court may hear and determine appeals from its own Justices exercising original jurisdiction, from any other Federal Court, from a Court exercising Federal jurisdiction and from the Supreme Courts of the States. It also has jurisdiction to hear and determine appeals from the Supreme Courts of the Territories. No appeal from the High Court to the Privy Council is permitted on questions as to the limits *inter se* of the constitutional powers of the States or the Commonwealth and the States except on the certificate of the High Court. No appeal to the Privy Council, whether special or otherwise, is permitted from a decision of Federal Courts (not being the High Court) or of the Supreme Court of a Territory. Appeal from the High Court to the Privy Council by special leave of the Privy Council is possible only in a matter in which the decision of the High Court was a decision that *(a)* was given on appeal from a decision of a Supreme Court of a State given otherwise than in the exercise of Federal jurisdiction and *(b)* did not involve the interpretation of the Constitution, a law made by the Federal Parliament or an instrument (including an ordinance, rule, regulation or by-law) made under a law made by the Parliament.

Other Federal Courts. Since 1924, 4 other Federal courts have been created to exercise special Federal jurisdiction, *i.e.* the Federal Court of Australia, the Family Court of Australia, the Australian Industrial Court and the Federal Court of Bankruptcy. The Federal Court of Australia was established in 1977. It exercises jurisdiction in matters previously dealt with by the Australian Industrial Court and the Federal Court of Bankruptcy, and in some matters previously invested in either the High Court or State and Territory Supreme Courts. The Federal Court also acts as a court of appeal from State and Territory courts in relation to Federal matters. Appeal from the Federal Court to the High Court will be by way of special leave only. The State Supreme Courts have also been invested with Federal jurisdiction in bankruptcy.

State Courts. The general Federal jurisdiction of the State courts extends, subject to certain restrictions and exceptions, to all matters in which the High Court has jurisdiction or in which jurisdiction may be conferred upon it. In matters of non-Federal jurisdiction a right of appeal is still possible, as a matter of law, from the State courts direct to the Privy Council.

Industrial Tribunals. The major Federal industrial tribunal in Australia is the Australian Conciliation and Arbitration Commission, constituted by presidential members (with the status of judges) and commissioners. The Commission's functions include settling industrial disputes, making awards, determining the standard hours of work, wage fixation, etc. Questions of law, the judicial interpretation of awards, imposition of penalties, etc., in relation to industrial matters, are now dealt with by the Federal Court.

Australian Digest of Reported Decisions of the Australian Courts and of Australian Appeals to the Privy Council. 2nd ed. Sydney, Law Book Co. 1963—Supplements 1964 ff.
Baalman, J., *Outline of Law in Australia.* 3rd ed. Sydney, 1969
Benjafield, D. G., and Whitmore, H., *Principles of Australian Administrative Law.* 3rd ed. Sydney, 1966
Cowen, Z., *Federal Jurisdiction in Australia.* 2nd ed. Melbourne, 1978
Fleming, J. G., *The Law of Torts.* 5th ed. Sydney, 1977
Gunn, J. A. L., *Australian Income Tax Law and Practice.* 9th ed. by F. C. Bock and E. F. Mannix, Sydney, 1969, and *Butterworth's Taxation Service* to date
Howard, C., *Criminal Law.* 3rd ed. Sydney, 1975
Joske, P. E., *Matrimonial Causes and Marriage and Practice of in Australia and New Zealand.* 2 vols. 5th ed. Sydney, 1969
Mills, C. P., and Sorrell, G. H., *Federal Industrial Law. (Nolan and Cohen.)* 5th ed. Sydney, 1975
O'Connell, D. P. (ed.), *International Law in Australia.* Sydney, 1966
Paterson, W. E., and Ednie, H. H., *Australian Company Law.* 2nd ed. Sydney, 1976, and *Butterworth's Company Service* to date
Wynes, A., *Legislative, Executive and Judicial Powers in Australia.* 5th ed. Sydney, 1976
Yorston, R. K., and Fortescue, E. E., *Australian Mercantile Law.* 14th ed. Sydney, 1971

Religion. Under the Constitution the Commonwealth cannot make any law to establish any religion, to impose any religious observance or to prohibit the free exercise of any religion, nor can it require a religious test as qualification for office or public trust under the Commonwealth. The figures in the table refer to those religions with the largest number of adherents at the census of 1981. The census question on religion was not obligatory, however.

Religion	*Persons*	*Religion*	*Persons*
Christian		Non-Christian	
Baptist	190,259	Hebrew	62,126
Brethren	21,489	Muslim	76,792
Catholic [1]	3,786,505	Other	23,577
Churches of Christ	89,424		
Church of England	3,810,469	Total Non-Christian	197,568
Congregational	23,017		
Jehovah's Witness	51,815	Indefinite	73,551
Orthodox	421,281	No religion	1,576,718
Lutheran	199,760	No reply	1,595,195
Methodist, inc. Wesley	490,767		
Presbyterian	637,818	Grand Total	14,576,330
Salvation Army	71,570		
Seventh-day Adventist	712,609		
Protestant (undefined)	220,679		
Other (including Christian undefined)	250,188		
Total Christian	11,133,298		

[1] Includes 'Catholic' and 'Roman Catholic'.

Education. The Governments of the Australian States and the Northern Territory have the major responsibility for education, including the administration and substantial funding of primary, secondary and technical and further education. In most States, a single Education Department is responsible for these three levels of education, but in New South Wales and South Australia there is a separate department responsible solely for technical and further education and in Victoria, a Technical and Further Education Board. Furthermore, in New South Wales an Education Commission advises the Minister on primary, secondary and further education.

The Australian Government is directly responsible for education services in the Australian Capital Territory, administered through an education authority, and for services to Norfolk Island, Christmas Island and the Cocos (Keeling) Islands. The Australian Government provides supplementary finance to the States and is responsible for the total funding of universities and colleges of advanced education. It also has special responsibilities for student assistance, education programmes for Aboriginal people and children from non-English-speaking backgrounds, and for international relations in education.

The Australian Constitution empowers the Australian Government to make grants to the States and to place conditions upon such grants. This power has been used to provide financial assistance to the States specifically for educational purposes. There are two national Education Commissions which advise the Australian Government on the needs of educational institutions throughout Australia for the purpose of financial assistance. The Commonwealth Schools Commission, established in 1973, advises on the provision of financial assistance to the States for government and non-government schools. The Commonwealth Tertiary Education Commission, which was established in 1977 to replace three former commissions (the Universities Commission, the Commission on Advanced Education and the Technical and Further Education Commission), advises on the provision to the States of total funding for universities and colleges of advanced education and of supplementary financial assistance for their institutions of technical and further education.

School attendance is compulsory throughout Australia between the ages of 6 and 15 years (16 years in Tasmania), at either a government school or a recognized non-government educational institution. Many Australian children attend pre-schools for a year before entering school (usually in sessions of 2-3 hours, for 2-5 days per week). Government schools are usually co-educational and comprehensive. Non-government schools have been traditionally single-sex, particularly in secondary schools, but there is a developing trend towards co-education. Tuition is free at government schools, but fees are normally charged at non-government schools.

The following is a summary at July 1981 of primary and secondary school education:

	Schools		*Teachers*		*Pupils*	
States and Territories	*Government*	*Non-government*	*Government schools*	*Non-government schools*	*Government schools*	*Non-government schools*
New South Wales	2,236	804	45,248	12,663	790,393	237,853
Victoria	2,149	632	40,462	12,411	595,042	221,611
Queensland	1,268	349	19,719	4,952	360,424	100,503
South Australia	638	163	14,472	2,527	213,033	43,312
Western Australia	695	206	11,691	2,719	207,126	48,507
Tasmania	261	61	4,947	853	70,932	14,917
Northern Territory	130	13	1,486	222	23,271	4,215
Aust. Cap. Terr.	95	33	2,500	878	39,182	17,078
	7,472	2,261	37,225	37,225	2,299,403	687,996

Opportunities to pursue post-secondary education are available in universities, colleges of advanced education, technical and further education institutions and some more specialized post-school institutions. Tuition fees were abolished in 1974 and student allowances are provided for full-time students subject to a means test. Universities are autonomous institutions, as are the substantial majority of colleges of advanced education. While both offer degree courses, colleges also offer diploma and associate diploma courses and in general their courses have a more applied emphasis and are more vocationally oriented.

Universities and colleges of advanced education at 30 April 1981:

	Universities[2]			*Colleges of advanced education*		
States and Territory	*Number*	*Students*	*Staff*[1]	*Number*	*Students*	*Staff*[1]
New South Wales	6	63,532	5,072	23	39,907	2,416
Victoria	4	44,219	3,550	22	56,566	3,628
Queensland	3	22,392	1,822	10	23,418	1,321
South Australia	2	12,811	1,149	6	17,558	1,093
Western Australia	2	12,620	1,006	5	20,237	1,097
Tasmania	1	5,082	386	1	2,082	132
Aust. Cap. Terr.	1	5,955	1,221	1	5,299	307
	19	166,611	14,206	68	165,067	9,995

[1] Full-time academic staff plus the full-time equivalent of part-time academic staff.
[2] Preliminary.

Technical and Further Education institutions offer a wide variety of courses of study which are classified into the following six streams: professional, para-professional, trades, other skilled, preparatory and adult or further education. The majority of TAFE courses are part-time, concurrent with employment, but there is also provision for full-time and external study. A network of over 900 government-run institutions facilitates access to these courses. Enrolments in 1980 numbered 983,262 (57,619 full-time, 860,553 part-time and 65,090 external enrolments).

Teacher education usually takes place in colleges of advanced education, though a substantial number of secondary teachers and a few primary teachers receive their pre-service education in a university. Government school teachers are recruited by the State and Northern Territory departments of education, and in the Australian Capital Territory by the ACT Schools Authority and the Public Service Board. Non-government schools recruit their own teachers.

The Australian Government provides a number of schemes of assistance for students to facilitate access to education. The Secondary Allowances Scheme aims to help parents with a limited income to keep their children at school for the final 2 years of secondary education. The Assistance for Isolated Children Scheme provides special support to families whose children are isolated from schooling or are handicapped. The Adult Secondary Education Assistance Scheme provides assistance for mature-age students undertaking full-time a one-year matriculation level programme or a two-year programme if studies beyond the tenth year in the Australian secondary school system have not previously been undertaken. The Tertiary Education Assistance Scheme is a means-tested scheme to assist students enrolled for full-time study in approved courses at post-secondary institutions. Allowances are also available for post-graduate study and overseas study. Aboriginal students are eligible for assistance under the Aboriginal Secondary Grants Scheme and the Aboriginal Study Grants Scheme. The States also offer various schemes of assistance, principally at the primary and secondary levels.

There are a number of bodies at the national level which have an important co-ordinating, planning or funding rôle. These include: the Australian Education Council, comprising the Federal and State Ministers of Education, the Conference of Directors-General of Education and an advisory body, the National Aboriginal Education Committee.

Total expenditure on education in Australia in 1980–81 was estimated at $A8,042m.

Austin, A. G., *Australian Education 1788–1900.* Melbourne, 1961
Australian Education Directory. Canberra, 1978
Directory of Higher Education Courses 1979. Canberra, 1979
Education in Australia. Canberra, 1977
Jones, P. E., *Education in Australia.* Melbourne, 1974
Primary and Secondary Schooling in Australia. Canberra, 1977
Schools Commission, *Triennium 1982–84. Report for 1982.* Canberra, 1981
Tertiary Education Commission, *Report for 1982–84, Triennium Vol. 2: Recommendations for 1982.* Canberra, 1981

Social Security. The National Welfare Fund finances all Federal Government social and health benefits except repatriation and certain other payments primarily of a capital nature. Total expenditure from the Fund during 1981–82 was $A11,305m.

The following summarizes the rates and conditions of the major benefits provided at June 1979. For expenditure on these benefits during 1978–79, *see* table on p. 103.

Age and invalid pensions—men 65 years of age or more and women 60 years of age or more may receive an age pension. Persons 16 years of age or more who are permanently blind or permanently incapacitated for work to the extent of at least 85% may receive an invalid pension. To be paid an age pension, a person must have lived in Australia for a specified period and, unless permanently blind or over 70 years of age, also satisfy an income test. There is no residence qualification for an invalid pension if the incapacity of permanent blindness occurred within Australia or during temporary absence from Australia. An income test must be satisfied for an invalid pension unless permanently blind or over 70 years of age. The maximum rates are $A61.05 a week in the case of the 'standard' rate pension, and in the case of the 'married' rate pension, $A101.70 a week ($A50.85 each). These amounts are subject to income tax. Additional amounts, subject to an income test, are paid to pensioners with dependent children. Pensions, free of the income test, are paid to permanently blind persons and to persons 70 years of age and over. Supplementary assistance of up to $A5 a week for the 'standard' rate pension and $A2.50 for the 'married' rate pension may be paid to a pensioner paying rent or for lodging. Supplementary assistance and additional pension for children are not taxable.

Widows' pensions—widows, divorcees, certain deserted wives, women who have been the dependant of a man for 3 years immediately prior to his death and women whose husbands are in mental hospitals or prison may, if they satisfy a residence requirement and a means test, receive a widow's pension. Such women with at least one dependent child may be paid a pension of up to $A61.05 a week plus a mother's allowance of $A4 a week ($A6 if she has an invalid child requiring full-time care or a child under 6 years) plus $A7.50 a week for each child. Persons who pay rent may also receive supplementary assistance of up to $A5 a week. Pensions, but not mothers' allowances, additional pension for children or supplementary assistance, are subject to income tax.

Supporting parents benefit—unmarried mothers or fathers and parents who are deserted *de facto* partners, *de facto* wives of prisoners and separated spouses ineligible for widow's pension may, if they satisfy a residence requirement and a means test, receive supporting parents benefit. It is payable at the same rate as the widow's pension payable to a widow with one or more children in her care and is subject to the same income test.

Family allowance—is paid without income test to families with children under 16 years or eligible student children aged 16 years or more but under 25 years. It is not subject to income tax. Monthly rates payable are: 1 child, $A15.20; 2 children, $A21.70; 3 children, $A26; 4 children, $A26 and $A30.35 for each subsequent child. For each child or eligible student in an approved institution, the rate is $A21.70 per month.

Handicapped child's allowance—payable to parents or guardians of severely physically or mentally handicapped children in the family home and needing constant care and attention. The allowance is $A65 per month and is free of an income test but is subject to a residence qualification similar to that for family allowance.

Double orphan's pension—the guardian of a child under 16 years of age or of a full-time student under 21, both of whose parents are dead, or one of whose parents is dead and the whereabouts of the other parent unknown, may receive double orphan's pension of $A47.70 a month. The payment is not subject to an income test.

Unemployment and sickness benefits—are paid, subject to an income test, to persons between the ages of 16 and 65 (males) and 16 and 60 (females) who are unemployed, or temporarily incapacitated for work. The maximum weekly rates of benefit are for unemployment benefits $A36 (single, under 18 years), $A51.45 (single, 18 and over), $A61·05 (single, 18 and over with dependents), $A101.70 (married); and for sickness benefits $A36 (single, under 18 years), $A61.05 (single, 18 and over), $A61.05 (single, 18 and over with dependants), $A101.70 (married). To be granted benefit a person must have resided in Australia for at least 12 months preceding his claim or intend to reside permanently in Australia. For unemployment benefit purposes unemployment must not be due to direct participation in a strike.

Health Insurance. The health costs of eligible pensioners (i.e. Pensioner Health Benefits cardholders) and those who qualify under the Commonwealth definition as being in special need, and the dependants of those people, are covered by the Government under the special assistance schemes. These people are entitled to free public hospital accommodation and treatment, and bulk billed medical services. People in special need, as defined, comprise migrants during their first six months in Australia, unemployment and special beneficiaries, and people on low incomes.

All other people must meet their health care costs either through health insurance or by way of personal payments. For those people with basic medical insurance with a registered medical benefits fund, the Commonwealth pays Commonwealth medical benefits at the rate of 30% of the Schedule fee for each medical service.

Basic medical insurance provides benefits, when combined with the 30% Commonwealth medical benefit, at 85% of the Schedule fee or the Schedule fee less $A10, whichever is the greater amount. Other medical benefits tables may provide cover up to 100% of the Schedule fee and/or ancillary services.

Basic hospital insurance provides benefits equal to the standard fees for shared ward accommodation in recognised public hospitals, professional service fees and outpatient charges. Additional insurance may provide benefits to cover private room accommodation charges in recognized hospitals or fees in private hospitals and/or ancillary services.

Hospitals. In respect of recognized public hospitals, cost-sharing arrangements expired on 30 June 1981 for all States other than South Australia and Tasmania. Funds are now provided to non-cost-sharing States through general revenue grants for recognized public hospitals and services previously funded under the Community Health Program and the School Dental Scheme. General revenue grants also provide Commonwealth funds for community and School Dental services in South Australia and Tasmania, while the agreed net operating costs of public hospitals in those States continue to be shared between the Commonwealth and the States under the cost-sharing arrangements. For private hospitals a bed day subsidy of $A28 is paid for patients receiving prescribed surgical procedures in private hospitals. A bed day subsidy of $A16 is payable in respect of all other patients.

Nursing Home Type Patients in Hospitals. During 1980 some States and Territories introduced new arrangements whereby after 60 days of hospitalization non-acute patients are required to make a personal, uninsurable contribution towards their care and accommodation in hospital in the same manner as similar patients in nursing homes.

Nursing Homes. The Commonwealth pays benefits in respect of all qualified patients in nursing homes approved under the National Health Act. As at 5 Nov. 1981 the maximum amount of basic nursing home benefit payable per day in each State was: New South Wales $A23.00; Victoria $A31.65; Queensland $A20.40; South Australia $A27.60; Western Australia $A18.55 and Tasmania $A20.65. For eligible nursing homes approved under the Nursing Homes Assistance Act the Commonwealth meets the approved operating deficit of the home. All nursing home patients are required to make a minimum contribution towards the cost of their care and accommodation. At 5 Nov. 1981 the minimum patient contribution was $A9.30 per day.

Domiciliary Nursing Care Benefit. This benefit of $A42 per fortnight can be paid to any persons who provide nursing care in their own home for eligible patients. A person may not receive benefits for the care of more than two patients at any one time.

Eligible patients must be 16 years of age or more, have a certificate from their doctor that they have a continuing need for nursing care, and be receiving this care by a registered nurse on a regular basis involving at least two visits each week.

This requirement for two visits a week may be relaxed where a registered nurse has certified as to the competence of the caring peson. This benefit is not subject to a means test and is payable under the National Health Act, in addition to any entitlements that persons may have under the Social Services Act or the Repatriation Act for pensions or other supplementary allowances. The benefit cannot be paid in respect of any period prior to the date on which an application is received in the Department of Health. The benefit is not subject to taxation.

Pharmaceutical Benefits. A comprehensive range of drugs and medicinal preparations is available. In general, a fee of $A4 is charged for each prescription.

Service Pension. is a social welfare-type payment similar to age and invalid pensions payable by the Department of Social Security. Service pension may be granted, subject to an income test, to a veteran who has theatre of war experience, at 60 years on the ground of age, which is five years earlier than the age pension, or at any age if a veteran is permanently unemployable for medical reasons. Wives of service pensioners are also eligible provided that they do not receive a pension from the Department of Social Security.

Disability Pension. is a compensatory payment in respect of incapacity attributable to war service. It is paid at a rate commensurate with the degree of incapacity suffered from service-related disabilities and is free of any income test. A separate allowance may be paid to dependants.

Department of Territories, *Progress Towards Assimilation.* Canberra, 1958
Bilton, J., *The Royal Flying Doctor Service of Australia.* Sydney, 1961
Henderson, R., *People in Poverty.* Melbourne, 1970
Scott, D., *Leisure: A Social Enquiry into Leisure Activities and Needs in an Australian Housing Estate.* Melbourne, 1962

DIPLOMATIC REPRESENTATIVES

Of Australia in Great Britain (Australia House, Strand, London, WC2B 4LA)
High Commissioner: Sir Victor Garland, KBE.

Of Great Britain in Australia (Commonwealth Ave., Canberra)
High Commissioner: Sir John Mason, KCMG.

Of Australia in the USA (1601 Massachusetts Ave., NW, Washington, D.C., 20036)
Ambassador: Sir Robert Cotton.

Of the USA in Australia (Moonah Pl., Canberra)
Ambassador: Robert D. Nesen.

Of Australia to the United Nations
Ambassador: H. D. Anderson, AO, OBE.

Books of Reference

Statistical Information: The Australian Bureau of Statistics (Cameron Offices, Belconnen, A.C.T., 2616) was established in 1906. All the activities of the Bureau are covered by the Census and Statistics Act, which confers authority to collect information and contains secrecy provisions to ensure that individual particulars obtained are not divulged. Under the provisions of the Statistics (Arrangements with States) Act which became law on 12 May 1956, the statistical services of all the States have been integrated with the Australian Bureau. An outline of the development of statistics in Australia is published in the *Official Year Book*, No. 51, 1965. *Australian Statistician:* Dr R. J. Cameron.

The principal publications of the Bureau are:

Official Year Book of Australia. 1907 to date
Pocket Year Book Australia. 1913 to date
Monthly Summary of Statistics Australia. Oct. 1937 to date
Digest of Current Economic Statistics Australia. Aug. 1959 to date
Catalogue of Publications. 1976 to date

Other Official Publications

Atlas of Australian Resources. Dept. of National Development, Melbourne, 1955 ff.
Climatological Atlas of Australia. Bureau of Meteorology. Melbourne, 1940
Norfolk Island—Annual Report. Government of New South Wales and Commonwealth of Australia. From 1896
Cocos (Keeling) Islands—Annual Report. Dept. of Administrative Services, Canberra
Christmas Island—Annual Report. Dept. of Administrative Services, Canberra. From 1958
Australian Books: Select List of Works About or Published in Australia. National Library of Australia, Canberra, 1934 to date
Australian National Bibliography. Canberra, 1936 to date
Historical Records of Australia. 34 vols. National Library, Canberra, 1914–25
Australia: Official Handbook. Dept. of the Capital Territory, Canberra, 1961 to date
Annual Report. Dept. of Foreign Affairs, Canberra, 1932 to date
Australian Foreign Affairs Record. Dept. of Foreign Affairs, Canberra, 1936 to date
Australian Treaty List. Dept. of Foreign Affairs, Canberra, consolidated volume from Federation to 1970 with supplements to date
Coxon, H., *Australian Official Publications.* Oxford, 1981
Documents on Australian Foreign Policy 1937–49. Vol. 1: 1937–38, Vol. 2: 1939, Vol. 3 in preparation. Dept. of Foreign Affairs, Canberra
Diplomatic List. Dept. of Foreign Affairs, Canberra. 1949 to date
Consular and Trade Representatives. Dept. of Foreign Affairs, Canberra. 1936 to date

Non-Official Publications

Australian Quarterly: A Quarterly Review of Australian Affairs. Sydney, 1929 to date
Chipman, E., *Australians in the Frozen South.* Melbourne, 1978
Chisholm, A. H. (ed.), *Australian Encyclopædia.* 10 vols. Sydney, 1962
Clark, C. M. H. (ed.), *Select Documents in Australian History, 1788–1900.* 2 vols. Sydney, 1950–55
Ferguson, Sir John, *Bibliography of Australia, 1784–1850.* 4 vols. Sydney, 1941–55; vol. 5 (1851–1900), Part 1, 1963. Parts 2 and 3 in preparation
Grant, B., *The Crisis of Loyalty: A Study of Australian Foreign Policy.* Sydney, 1972
Hancock, Sir Keith, *Australia.* Brisbane, 1961
Horne, D., *The Australian People.* Sydney, 1972
Menzies, Sir Robert, *Speech is of Time.* London, 1958
Noble, N. S. (ed.), *The Australian Environment.* 3rd ed. Melbourne, 1960
Serle, P., *Dictionary of Australian Biography.* 2 vols. Sydney, 1949
Taylor, T. G., *Australia: A Study of Warm Environments and their Effect on British Settlement.* 7th ed. London, 1959
Who's Who in Australia. Melbourne, 1906 to date

National Library: The National Library, Canberra, A.C.T. *Director-General:* Dr G. Chandler.

AUSTRALIAN TERRITORIES

AUSTRALIAN CAPITAL TERRITORY

HISTORY. The area, now the Australian Capital Territory, was first visited by white men in 1820 and settlement commenced in 1824. Until its selection as the seat of government it was a quiet pastoral and agricultural community.

AREA AND POPULATION. The area of the Australian Capital Territory is 2,432 sq. km (including Jervis Bay area). The population (estimate) at 30 June 1980 was 226,600. Previous census population:

	Males	Females	Total		Males	Females	Total
1911	992	722	1,714	1961	30,858	27,970	58,828
1921	1,567	1,005	2,572	1966	49,991	46,041	96,032
1933	4,805	4,142	8,947	1971	73,589	70,474	144,063
1947	9,092	7,813	16,905	1976	100,103	95,519	197,622
1954	16,229	14,086	30,315	1981	110,415	111,194	221,609

(Figures before 1961 exclude particulars of full-blood Aborigines.)

CONSTITUTION AND GOVERNMENT. The Constitution of Australia provided (Sec. 125) that the seat of government should be selected by parliament and that it should be within New South Wales but at least 161 km from Sydney. The present area was surrendered by New South Wales and accepted by the Australian Government from 1 Jan. 1911. In 1915 an additional 73 sq. km at Jervis Bay was transferred from New South Wales to the Commonwealth. In 1911 an international competition was held for the city plan. The plan chosen was that of W. Burley Griffin, of Chicago. Construction was delayed by the First World War, and it was not until 1927 that, with the transfer of parliament and certain departments, Canberra became in fact the seat of government. Most Australian Government departments now have their headquarters in Canberra.

The general administration of the Territory is in the hands of the Minister for the Capital Territory, but certain specific services are undertaken by other Federal Government Departments and Authorities. Since June 1979 the Minister has been advised on matters of local concern by the ACT House of Assembly consisting of 18 elected members. Prior to that date this function was performed by the ACT Legislative Assembly (from 1974), replacing the ACT Advisory Council which had been in existence since 1930 and consisted of both nominated and elected members.

The Australian Capital Territory Representation (House of Representatives) Act, 1973, provided for the representation of residents of the Territory by 2 elected members in the House of Representatives. The Senate (Representation of Territories) Act 1973 provided for the election of 2 Senators from the Territory. Elections took place in Nov. 1980.

FINANCE. The receipts and outlay of the Australian Capital Territory cover the transactions of the Australian Government in the Consolidated Revenue and other funds. They also include details of the ACT public corporations.

Receipts and outlay ($A1,000) for years ended 30 June:

		Outlay		
	Receipts	*Capital*	*Current*	*Total*
1978	106,529	215,572	220,164	435,736
1979	99,986	158,757	235,891	394,648
1980	86,756	119,414	265,240	384,572
1981[1]	94,331	50,775	330,799	381,572

[1]Preliminary.

The chief sources of receipts in 1980–81 were taxes, fees and fines, $A58m.; and interest and rent, $A32m. Capital outlay comprised gross capital formation, $A385m., and net advances to other sectors, $A3m.

PRODUCTION. The Territory is predominantly pastoral. Livestock, 31 March 1980: 13,559 cattle, 98,359 sheep. A considerable amount of reafforestation (mostly pine) has been undertaken, the total area of commercial plantations at 30 June 1981 being 14,119 hectares. There is no secondary industry of any importance.

EDUCATION. In 1974 education in government schools became the direct responsibility of the Commonwealth Government. A Schools Authority has been established to administer the Australian Capital Territory government school system. In July 1981 there were 95 government schools comprising 67 primary schools, 25 secondary schools and colleges and 3 schools with both primary and secondary enrolments. Non-government schools numbered 33 in total of which there were 22 primary schools, 4 secondary schools and 7 schools with both primary and secondary enrolments. Students enrolled in government schools in 1981 numbered 24,480 and 14,702 at primary and secondary school levels respectively. Enrolments at non-government schools comprised 9,765 primary school students and 7,313 secondary school students. Pre-school education is provided at 74 centres with a total enrolment of 4,845 (Nov. 1980). There are also 33 non-government schools, 11 of which provide secondary education; total enrolment

(July 1981) 17,078. The Canberra Technical College and Bruce College of Technical and Further Education with a total enrolment of about 17,000 in 1980 provide training in commercial and special courses.

The Canberra School of Music, opened in 1965, had 639 students in 1981.

The Canberra College of Advanced Education commenced operation in 1970. Enrolments (1981) 5,299.

The Australian National University is situated in Canberra. Enrolments (1981) 5,955.

Books of Reference

A.C.T. Statistical Summary. Australian Bureau of Statistics. From 1960
Annual Report. National Capital Development Commission. From 1958
Tomorrow's Canberra. National Capital Development Commission, 1970
Wigmore, L., *Canberra: A History of Australia's National Capital.* 2nd ed. Canberra, 1971

NORTHERN TERRITORY

HISTORY. The Northern Territory, after forming part of New South Wales, was annexed on 6 July 1863 to South Australia and in 1901 entered the Commonwealth as a corporate part of South Australia. The Commonwealth Constitution Act of 1900 made provision for the surrender to the Commonwealth of any territory by any state, and under this provision an agreement was entered into on 7 Dec. 1907 for the transfer of the Northern Territory to the Commonwealth, and it formally passed under the control of the Commonwealth Government on 1 Jan. 1911. For details of Constitutional development until 1978 *see* THE STATESMAN'S YEAR-BOOK 1980–81 pp. 123–24. The Commonwealth Government retained responsibility until Self-Government was granted on 1 July 1978.

AREA AND POPULATION. The Northern Territory is bounded by the 26th parallel of S. lat. and 129° and 138° E. long. Its total area is 1,346, 200 sq. km. The coastline is about 6,200 km in length, the principal port being Darwin. The greater part of the interior consists of a tableland rising gradually from the coast to a height of about 700 metres. On this tableland there are large areas of excellent pasturage. The southern part of the Territory is generally sandy and has a small rainfall, but water may be obtained by means of sub-artesian bores. The climate is tropical, but varies considerably over the whole Territory.

In the coastal region, there are two main climatic divisions—the wet season, Nov. to April, and the dry season, May to Oct. Farther south the climate is of a continental type, showing a great variation between the hottest and coldest months.

The capital and seat of Government, Darwin is situated on the north coast. Darwin had a population of 50,612 in July 1979. The total population of the Territory is about 129,000. Other main centres include Katherine (3,200), 330 km south of Darwin; Alice Springs (16,500), in Central Australia; Tennant Creek (2,400), a rich mining centre 500 km north of Alice Springs; Nhulunbuy (3,500), a bauxite mining centre on the Gove Peninsula in eastern Arnhem Land; and Jabiru, a model town being built to serve the rich Uranium Province in eastern Arnhem Land with a planned population of 6,000. There also are a number of large self-contained Aboriginal communities.

Vital statistics for 1980: Births, 2,843; deaths, 603; marriages, 622; divorces, 289.

CONSTITUTION AND GOVERNMENT. The Northern Territory (Self-Government) Act 1978 established the Northern Territory as a body politic as from 1 July 1978, with Ministers having control over and responsibility for Territory finances and the administration of the functions of government as specified by the Federal Government by regulations made pursuant to the Act. Regulations have been made conferring executive authority for the bulk of administrative functions. Responsibility for health services was transferred on 1 Jan. 1979, and for education on 1 July 1979. Proposed laws passed by the Legislative Assembly in relation to a transferred function require the assent of the Administrator. Proposed laws in all other cases may be assented to by the Administrator or reserved by the Administrator for the Governor-General's pleasure. The Governor-General may disallow any law assented to by the Administrator within 6 months of the Administrator's assent.

The Northern Territory has federal representation electing 1 member to the House of Representatives and 2 members to the Senate.

FINANCE. Since the introduction of self-government in 1978, the Northern Territory Budget had almost doubled by 1980–81 from the $A350m. appropriated in the first self-government Budget.

	1980–81
Revenue	$A656,053,692
Expenditure	$A655,489,319

The revenue available in 1980–81 comprised $A554m. in payments to the Northern Territory from the Commonwealth, as established by agreement at the time of self-government, together with $A102m. raised by the Northern Territory which included $A29m. through state-like taxes.

Expenditure during 1980–81 included $A92.1m. for education; $A72.8m. for lands and housing; $A79.5m. for health; $A49.5m. for community development and $A88m. on the capital works programme.

ENERGY AND NATURAL RESOURCES

Oil. In 1979–80, 7 new offshore permits were granted and applications were invited for a further 6 in the Arafura Sea. On 30 June 1980 there were 14 offshore permits covering 2,698 blocks and 7 onshore oil permits totalling 111,150 sq. km. There are 12 onshore oil permits and three oil leases under application.

Minerals. The mining industry is the Northern Territory's main industry. The main minerals produced are bauxite ore, manganese ore, copper, gold and bismuth ore. The value of all mineral production in 1979–80 was $A369·6m.

In the Gove area of Arnhem Land a bauxite/alumina project has been completed. Development costs were in excess of $A310m. Exports of bauxite commenced in June 1971 and in 1979–80, 4·9m. tonnes of bauxite were mined (2·3m. exported). Exports of alumina totalled 1·1m. tonnes.

Manganese ore is produced on Groote Eylandt. Northern Territory production in 1979–80 was 3·7m. tonnes. The ore is shipped to Tasmania, Japan, Europe and the USA.

Shipments of iron ore from Frances Creek through the port of Darwin ceased in Dec. 1975, after the bulk loading facilities at the wharf had been badly damaged by cyclone 'Tracy'.

Mines in the Tennant Creek area are the principal producers of gold, copper and bismuth in the Northern Territory. In 1977–78 the Northern Territory production of these minerals was bismuth concentrate, 5,650 tonnes; copper, 14,911 tonnes; silver (1974–75), 1,876,974 grammes; and gold, 4,263 kg.

In the Alligator River region 250 km east of Darwin, rich deposits of uranium have been discovered at Narbarlek, Jabiru (Ranger), Koongarra and Jabiluka. This area is considered to be a uranium province of world importance. Mining has commenced at Ranger where the estimated annual output of uranium oxide is 3,000 tonnes.

Agriculture. General agriculture is conducted on a small scale in the Northern Territory. Small quantities of fruit, vegetables, eggs, dairy produce, poultry and pasture are produced. Seeds were produced in areas adjacent to the principal population centres. The total gross value of agricultural production for 1979–80 was $A812,633. However the beef cattle industry is the main rural activity in the Northern Territory, and production depends almost entirely on export markets. The value of beef production for the year 1979–80 was $A93,621,570. Buffalo production realized $A6,027,271 (1979–80). A recent development has been an increase in the export of live cattle and buffalo to overseas countries which has provided alternative markets to producers.

Despite the depressed state of the industry, the accelerated eradication programme for tuberculosis and brucellosis is progressing satisfactorily and compensation payments are now extended to include cattle slaughtered as brucellosis reactors.

Livestock (31 March 1977): 1·7m. cattle; 1,000 sheep; 2,700 breeding sows.

Forestry. A forest development programme which commenced in 1970 has continued the multiple use management of Northern Territory forested areas; this programme included a softwood programme of 400 hectares per year, the introduction of additional suitable tree species in both arid and higher rainfall areas, conservation and management of native forests for production and recreational purposes, survey and assessment of resources, fire control activities and the creation of training opportunities for Aboriginals in forestry and allied sawmilling activities.

Local production of sawn timber, mainly Cypress pine, amounted to 870 cu. metres of pine in 1975–76. This was supplemented by 35,500 cu. metres of timber imported from interstate and overseas.

Local production of treated poles and rails amounted to 115 cu. metres. Only 280 hectares of plantation were established during the year because of complications arising from cyclone 'Tracy'.

During 1975–76 the Forestry Section of the Department of the Northern Territory redeveloped parks and open-space areas on behalf of the Darwin Reconstruction Commission.

Fisheries. The fishing industry is second only to beef cattle in Northern Territory primary industries. During 1978–79 the industry employed over 1,600 people and used 406 vessels and equipment worth in excess of $A82m. The major fishery is prawning, and for 1978–79 over 900 tonnes (processed weight) of prawns were exported. This represented 10% of the total Australian prawn exports and was valued at $A11m.

The other main fishery in the Territory is scale fish, particularly Barramundi (Giant Perch). Total scale fish production for 1978–79 was 920 tonnes live weight, valued at $A2m.

A major review of Northern Territory fisheries was carried out between 1973 and 1975 with assistance of a consultant resource economist and the final report contains several specific recommendations designed to increase the economic stability of fisheries.

INDUSTRY AND TRADE. In 1979–80 value added in the manufacturing industry, from 101 factories (with 4 or more persons employed) was $A77m. 2,512 persons were employed in these factories. In 1980, 70 trade unions had 19,600 members.

Tourism. In 1980–81, there were 363,000 tourists contributing about $A106m. to the economy.

National Parks and Reserves. About 43,000 sq. km have been set aside as wildlife sanctuaries under the Wildlife Conservation and Control Ordinance. They are controlled by the Chief Inspector of Wildlife who is an officer of the Department of the Northern Territory. 236,000 sq. km of Aboriginal reserves are also wild-life protected areas.

The Northern Territory Reserves Board administers some 37 national parks and reserves covering an area of over 249,926 hectares. The Board is responsible under the National Parks and Gardens Ordinance for the care, control and management of these reserves, and its functions include the preservation and protection of natural and historical features and the encouragement of public use and enjoyment of land set aside in such reserves.

COMMUNICATIONS

Roads. There are now 5,598 km of sealed road within the Northern Territory. They include three major interstate links: the Stuart Highway from Darwin to the South Australian border, the Barkly Highway, Tennant Creek to Mt. Isa, 447 km of which is in the Northern Territory, and the Victoria Highway, Katherine to the Western Australian border, a distance of 452 km. In addition to this there are 4,123 km of gravel roads, 4,975 km of formed roads and 6,651 km of unformed roads or tracks, totalling approximately 21,347 km of roads within the Northern Territory. In 1979–80 registrations of new motor vehicles included 1,656 cars, 1,550 utilities etc., 207 trucks, 48 buses and 486 motor cycles.

Railways. Alice Springs is linked to the Trans-continental network by a new standard (1,435 mm) gauge railway to Tarcoola (831 km), opened in 1980. This replaced the largely narrow gauge line to Port Augusta. The standard gauge railway is to be extended to Darwin by 1988, providing Australia with its first north-south rail link.

Aviation. Darwin is the first port of arrival in Australia for some aircraft from Europe and Asia. In 1976–77, 237,411 passengers were carried and 6,389 tonnes of freight. There are regular inland services connecting Darwin with all the State capitals and many inland towns.

Shipping. Regular freight shipping services connect Darwin with Western Australia, the eastern States and overseas. Passenger vessels also call at Darwin at irregular intervals.

The ports of Melville Bay (Gove) and Milner Bay (Groote Eylandt) are connected with Darwin, the eastern States and overseas by regular shipping freight services.

The inland and coastal communities around the coast are provided with regular freight barge services from Darwin. Some of these communities also receive a barge freight-transhipment service out of a Brisbane vessel which calls at Melville and Milner Bays, where the transhipment is effected.

EDUCATION AND WELFARE

Education. In 1981 there were 143 schools. Teachers totalled 1,579 and pupils 30,707.

Health. In 1980 there were 6 hospitals with 756 beds. Community health services are provided from 9 urban Health Centres and 62 rural Health Centres including mobile units.

AUSTRALIAN EXTERNAL TERRITORIES

AUSTRALIAN ANTARCTIC TERRITORY. An Imperial Order in Council of 7 Feb. 1933 placed under Australian authority all the islands and territories other than Adélie Land situated south of 60° S. lat. and lying between 160° E. long. and 45° E. long. The Order came into force with a Proclamation issued by the Governor-General on 24 Aug. 1936 after the passage of the Australian Antarctic Territory Acceptance Act 1933. The boundaries of Adélie Land were definitively fixed by a French Decree of 1 April 1938 as the islands and territories south of 60° S. lat. lying between 136° E. long. and 142° E. long. The Australian Antarctic Territory Act 1954 declared that the laws in force in the Australian Capital Territory are, so far as they are applicable and are not inconsistent with any ordinance made under the Act, in force in the Australian Antarctic Territory.

In 1968 responsibility for the administration of this Act was transferred from the Minister for External Affairs to the Minister for Supply; in 1972 responsibility was transferred to the Minister for Science.

On 13 Feb. 1954 the Australian National Antarctic Research Expeditions (ANARE) established a station on MacRobertson Land at lat. 67° 37′ S. and long. 62° 52′ E. The station was named Mawson in honour of the late Sir Douglas Mawson. Meteorological and other scientific research is conducted at Mawson, which is the centre for coastal and inland survey expeditions.

A second Australian scientific research station was established on the coast of Princess Elizabeth Land on 13 Jan. 1957 at lat. 68° 34′ S. and long. 77° 58′ E. The station was named Davis in honour of Capt. John King Davis, Mawson's second-in-command on 2 expeditions. The station was temporarily closed down in Jan. 1965 and re-opened in Feb. 1969.

In Feb. 1959 the Australian Government accepted from the US Government custody of Wilkes Station, which was established by the US on 16 Jan. 1957 on the Budd Coast of Wilkes Land, at lat. 66° 15′ S. and long. 110° 32′ E. The station was named in honour of Lieut. Charles Wilkes, who commanded the 1838–40 US expedition to the area, and was closed in Feb. 1969. Operations were then transferred to the new station, Casey. Construction commenced on Casey station in Jan. 1965 and was continued, mainly during summer visits, until Feb. 1969, when it was opened. The station, specially designed to withstand blizzard winds and prevent inundation by snow, is situated 2·4 km south of Wilkes at lat. 66° 17′ S. and long. 110° 32′ E. The Antarctic Division has also operated a station, since March 1948, at Macquarie Island, about 1,370 km south-east of Hobart. Macquarie Island is a dependency of the State of Tasmania.

On 1 Dec. 1959 Australia signed the Antarctic Treaty with Argentina, Belgium, Chile, France, Japan, New Zealand, Norway, South Africa, the USSR, the UK and the USA. Poland, Czechoslovakia, German Democratic Republic, Netherlands, Romania, Brazil, Denmark, Bulgaria, Federal Republic of Germany, Italy, Papua New Guinea, Peru and Uruguay have subsequently acceded to the Treaty. Poland became a full member of the Antarctic Treaty in 1977 and the German Democratic Republic in 1981. The Treaty reserves the Antarctic area south of 60° S. lat. for peaceful purposes, provides for international co-operation in scientific investigation and research, and preserves, for the duration of the Treaty, the *status quo* with regard to territorial sovereignty, rights and claims. The Treaty entered into force on 23 June 1961. Since then the Antarctic Treaty powers have held 11 consultative meetings. The 12th is to be held in Canberra in Sept. 1983.

COCOS (KEELING) ISLANDS. The Cocos (Keeling) Islands are 2 separate atolls comprising some 27 small coral islands with a total area of about 14·2 sq. km, and are situated in the Indian Ocean at 12° 05′ S. lat. and 96° 53′ E. long. They lie 2,768 km north-west of Perth and 3,685 km west of Darwin, while Colombo is 2,255 km to the north-west of the group.

The main islands in this Australian Territory are West Island (the largest, about 10 km from north to south) on which is an airport and an animal quarantine station, and most of the European community; Home Islands, occupied by the Cocos Malay community; Direction, South and Horsburgh Islands, and North Keeling Island, 24 km to the north of the group.

Although the islands were discovered in 1609 by Capt. William Keeling of the East India Company, they remained uninhabited until 1826, when the first settlement was established on the main atoll by an Englishman, Alexander Hare. Hare left the islands in 1831, by which time a second settlement had been formed on the main atoll by John Clunies-Ross, a Scottish seaman and adventurer, who landed with several boat-loads of Malay seamen to begin commercial development of the islands' coconut palms.

In 1857 the islands were annexed to the Crown; in 1878 responsibility was transferred from the Colonial Office to the Government of Ceylon, and in 1886 to the Government of the Straits Settlement. By indenture in 1886 Queen Victoria granted all land in the islands to George Clunies-Ross and his heirs in perpetuity (with certain rights reserved to the Crown). The head of the family had semi-official status as resident magistrate and representative of the Government. In 1903 the islands were incorporated in the Settlement of Singapore and in 1942–46 temporarily placed under the Governor of Ceylon. In 1946 a Resident Administrator, responsible to the Governor of Singapore, was appointed.

On 23 Nov. 1955 the Cocos Islands were placed under the authority of the Australian Government as the Territory of Cocos (Keeling) Islands. An Administrator, appointed by the Governor-General, is the Government's representative in the

Territory and is responsible to the Minister for Home Affairs and Environment. The Cocos (Keeling) Islands Council, established as the elected body of the Cocos Malay community in July 1979, advises the Administrator on all issues affecting the Territory.

In 1978 the Australian Government purchased the Clunies-Ross family's entire interests in the islands, except for the family residence. A Cocos Malay co-operative has been established to take over the running of the Clunies-Ross copra plantation (323 tonnes of copra were exported in 1979) and to engage in other business with the Commonwealth in the Territory, including construction projects.

The population of the Territory at 30 June 1982 was 546, distributed between Home Island (320) and West Island (226).

The islands are low-lying, flat and thickly covered by coconut palms, and surround a lagoon in which ships drawing up to 7 metres may be anchored, but which is extremely difficult for navigation.

The climate is equable and pleasant, being usually under the influence of the south-east trade winds for about three-quarters of the year. However, the winds vary at times, and meteorological reports from the Territory are particularly valuable for those engaged in forecasting for the eastern Indian Ocean. The temperature varies between 21° and 32° C, the rainfall is moderate and there are occasional violent storms.

The Cocos (Keeling) Islands Act 1955–1975 is the basis of the Territory's administrative, legislative and judicial systems. The laws of the Colony of Singapore which were in force in the islands immediately before the transfer have, with certain exceptions, been continued in force. They can be amended, repealed or substituted by ordinances made by the Governor-General.

The *Singapore Ordinances Application Ordinance* 1979 had the effect of repealing all Singapore Ordinances in force in the Territory and applying the provisions of 95 selected Singapore Ordinances only to be laws of the Territory.

Administrator: E. H. Hanfield.

CHRISTMAS ISLAND is in the Indian Ocean, lat. 10° 25′ 22″ S., long. 105° 39′ 59″ E. It lies 360 km S., 8° E. of Java Head, and 417 km N. 79° E. from Cocos Islands, 1,310 km from Singapore and 2,623 km from Fremantle. Area about 135 sq. km. The climate is moderate. The island was formally annexed by the UK on 6 June 1888, placed under the administration of the Governor of the Straits Settlements in 1889, and incorporated with the Settlement of Singapore in 1900. Sovereignty was transferred to the Australian Government on 1 Oct. 1958. The population (estimate, 1982), 3,018 (Europeans, 352; Chinese, 1,818; Malays, 753 and 95 others).

The legislative, judicial and administrative systems are regulated by the Christmas Island Act, 1958–73, which is administered by the Minister for Home Affairs and Environment with an Administrator, responsible for the local administration. The laws of Singapore which were in force before the transfer have been continued but can be amended, repealed or substituted by ordinances made by the Governor-General.

Extraction and export of rock phosphate and phosphate dust is the island's only industry. In Dec. 1948 Australia and New Zealand bought the lease rights of the Christmas Island Phosphate Co. and set up the Christmas Island Phosphate Commission, for which the Phosphate Mining Co. of Christmas Island (PMG) act as managing agents. The export of phosphate rock during 1981–82 was 1,526,282 tonnes, which is shipped to Australia and New Zealand; in addition, 133,851 tonnes of phosphate dust was shipped to Singapore, Malaysia and Australia and 2,000 tonnes of citraphos and calciphos was shipped to Australia and South East Asian ports.

There is direct radio communication with Australia and Singapore. Regular air charter flights commenced in 1974 to Australia.

At 30 June 1981 there were 602 primary and secondary pupils at the Christmas Island Area School. There is a technical school which provides commercial, apprenticeship and adult education courses, with (1979) some 701 students.

Medical, dental and hospital services are provided free of charge by the British Phosphate Commission.

Administrator: W. Yates.

NORFOLK ISLAND. 29° 04′ S. lat. 167° 57′ E. long., area 3,455 hectares, population, approximately 1,700. The island was formerly part of the colony of New South Wales and then of Van Diemen's Land. It has been a distinct settlement since 1856, under the jurisdiction of the state of New South Wales; and finally by the passage of the Norfolk Island Act 1913, it was accepted as a Territory of the Australian Government. The Norfolk Island Act 1957 is the basis of the Territory's legislative, administrative and judicial systems. An Administrator, appointed by the Governor-General and responsible to the Minister for Home Affairs and Environment, is the senior government representative in the Territory.

The Norfolk Island Act 1979 equips Norfolk Island with responsible legislative and executive government to enable it to run its own affairs to the greatest practicable extent. Wide powers are exercised by the Norfolk Island Legislative Assembly and by an Executive Council, comprising the executive members of the Legislative Assembly who have ministerial-type responsibilities. The Act preserves the Commonwealth's responsibility for Norfolk Island as a Territory under its authority, with the Minister for Home Affairs and Environment being the responsible Minister, and indicates the Parliament's intention that consideration will be given to an extension of the powers of the Legislative Assembly and the political and administrative institutions of Norfolk Island within 5 years.

The Executive Council has executive authority over a prescribed range of matters.

The island's Supreme Court sits as required and a Court of Petty Sessions exercises both civil and criminal jurisdiction.

The Territory Administration is financed from local revenue which for 1980–81 totalled $A3,288,338. A further $A286,000 was provided by the Commonwealth during the year for the restoration and maintenance of historic structures.

Public revenue is derived mainly from the sale of postage stamps, customs duties, liquor sales and company registration and licence fees. Residents are not liable for income tax on earnings within the Territory, nor are death and personal stamp duties levied. In 1980–81 imports totalled $A13·4m. and exports $A1·8m.

An estimated 23,000 visitors travelled to Norfolk during 1980–81. Descendants of the *Bounty* mutineer families constitute the 'original' settlers and are known locally as 'Islanders', while later settlers, mostly from Australia, New Zealand and UK, are identified as 'mainlanders'. Over the years the Islanders have preserved their own lifestyle and customs, and their language remains a mixture of West Country English and Tahitian.

The Administration subsidises a public hospital and dispensary, and health services, together with free dental services for children, are provided by qualified government officers.

Norfolk Island's public school is staffed by the New South Wales Department of Education and follows the State's education system. A bursary scheme is available to provide students with secondary education on the mainland.

A radio telephone service between the island and Sydney is maintained by the Overseas Telecommunications Commission, and there is a local automatic telephone service.

Administrator: Air Vice-Marshal R. E. Trebilico, DFC.

HEARD AND McDONALD ISLANDS. These islands, about 2,500 miles south-west of Fremantle, were transferred from UK to Australian control as from 26 Dec. 1947. Heard Island is about 43 km long and 21 km wide; Shag Island is about 8 km north of Heard. The total area is 412 sq. km (159 sq. miles). The McDonald Islands are 42 km to the west of Heard.

TERRITORY OF ASHMORE AND CARTIER ISLANDS. By Imperial Order in Council of 23 July 1931, Ashmore Islands (known as Middle, East and West Islands) and Cartier Island, situated in the Indian Ocean, some 320 km off the north-west coast of Australia, were placed under the authority of the Commonwealth.

Under the Ashmore and Cartier Islands Acceptance Act, 1933, the islands were accepted by the Commonwealth under the name of the Territory of Ashmore and Cartier Islands, and the effective date was proclaimed by the Governor-General to be 10 May 1934. It was the intention that the Territory should be administered by the State of Western Australia, but owing to administrative difficulties the Territory was annexed to and deemed to form part of the Northern Territory of Australia (by amendment to the Act in 1938) with relevant laws of the Northern Territory, applying to the Territory of Ashmore and Cartier Islands. From 1 July 1978, responsibility for the administration of Ashmore and Cartier Islands became a direct responsibility of the Commonwealth.

The islands are uninhabited but Indonesian fishing boats, which have traditionally plied the area, fish within the Territory and land to collect water in accordance with an agreement between the governments of Australia and Indonesia.

Periodic visits are made to the islands by ships of the Royal Australian Navy, and aircraft of the Royal Australian Air Force make aerial surveys of the islands and neighbouring waters.

TERRITORY OF CORAL SEA ISLANDS. The Coral Sea Islands became a Territory of the Commonwealth of Australia under the Coral Sea Islands Act 1969. It comprises scattered reefs and islands over a sea area of about 1m. sq. km. The Territory is uninhabited apart from a manned meteorological station on Willis Island.

Books of Reference

The Northern Territory: Annual Report. Dept. of Territories, Canberra, from 1911. Dept. of the Interior, Canberra, from 1966–67. Dept. of Northern Territory, from 1972

Australian Territories, Dept. of Territories, Canberra, 1960 to 1973. Dept. of Special Minister of State, Canberra, 1973–75. Department of Administrative Services, 1976

Northern Territory Statistical Summary. Australian Bureau of Statistics, Canberra, from 1960

Prospects of Agriculture in the Northern Territory. Dept. of Territories, Canberra, 1961

Northern Territory Scientific Liaison Conference, Darwin, 1961, *Conference Papers.* Melbourne, 1961

Holmes, J. M., *Australia's Open North.* Sydney, 1963

Lockwood, D. W., *Fair Dinkum.* London, 1960

NEW SOUTH WALES

HISTORY. New South Wales became a British possession in 1770; the first settlement was established at Port Jackson in 1788; a partially elective Council was established in 1843, and responsible government in 1856. New South Wales federated with the other Australian states to form the Commonwealth of Australia in 1901.

AREA AND POPULATION. New South Wales is situated between the 28th and 38th parallels of S. lat. and 141st and 154th meridians of E. long., and comprises 309,433 sq. miles (801,428 sq. km), inclusive of Lord Howe Island, 6 sq. miles (17 sq. km), but exclusive of the Australian Capital Territory (911 sq. miles, 2,359 sq. km) at Canberra and 28 sq. miles (73 sq. km), at Jervis Bay.

Lord Howe Island, 31° 33′ 4″ S., 159° 4′ 26″ E., which is part of New South Wales, is situated about 702 km north-east of Sydney; area, 1,656 hectares, of which only about 120 hectares are arable; resident population, estimate (30 June 1981), 300. The island, which was discovered in 1788, is of volcanic origin. Mount Gower, the highest point, reaches a height of 866 metres.

The Lord Howe Island Board manages the affairs of the Island and supervises the Kentia palm-seed industry.

Census population of New South Wales (including full-blood Aboriginals from 1966):

	Males	*Females*	*Persons*	*Population per sq. km*	*Average annual increase % since previous census*
1881	410,211	339,614	749,825	1	4·07
1891	609,666	517,471	1,127,137	1	4·16
1901	710,264	645,091	1,355,355	2	1·86
1911	857,698	789,036	1,646,734	2	1·97
1921	1,071,501	1,028,870	2,100,371	3	2·46
1933	1,318,471	1,282,376	2,600,847	3	1·76
1947	1,492,211	1,492,627	2,984,838	4	0·99
1954	1,720,860	1,702,669	3,423,529	4	1·98
1961	1,972,909	1,944,104	3,917,013	5	1·94
1966	2,126,652	2,111,249	4,237,901	5	1·58
1971	2,307,210	2,293,970	4,601,180	6	1·66
1976	2,380,149	2,396,953	4,777,102	6	0·75
1981	2,548,566	2,577,117	5,125,683	6	1·42

At 30 June 1981 the resident population (estimate) of New South Wales was 5,237,100 (1976, estimate, 4,959,600). Sydney (Statistical Division), 3,280,900 (3,143,750); Newcastle (Statistical District), 1,402,250 (379,950); Wollongong (Statistical District), 230,950 (222,250). Population of principal country municipalities: Albury, 37,350 (34,000); Armidale, 19,000 (19,250); Bathurst, 23,050 (21,150); Broken Hill, 27,850 (28,800); Casino, 10,450 (10,250); Dubbo, 28,850 (23,950); Goulburn, 22,050 (22,400); Grafton, 17,250 (17,100); Hastings, 34,500 (25,200); Lake Macquarie, 153,500 (139,150); Lismore, 34,700 (30,450); Lithgow, Greater, 20,350 (19,850); Orange, 31,300 (29,950); Queanbeyan, 20,000 (19,900); Shellharbour, 43,450 (39,400); Shoalhaven, 48,800 (39,000); Tamworth, 32,550 (30,350); Greater Taree, 32,000 (27,400); Wagga Wagga, 48,150 (44,150).

Vital statistics for calendar years:

	Live births	*Marriages*	*Divorces*	*Deaths (excluding still-births)*	*Infantile mortality per 1,000 live births*	*Estimated net migration*[1]
1978	77,773	35,904	13,797	40,394	12·9	8,300
1979	77,134	36,906	12,606	38,817	11·4	21,100
1980	79,455	38,965	13,449	40,282	10·7	30,600
1981	81,530	40,679	14,532	39,959	9·9	24,900

[1] Includes an adjustment for intercensal discrepancy.

The annual rates per 1,000 of mean resident population (estimate) in 1981 were: Births, 15·57; deaths, 7·63; marriages, 7·77.

CONSTITUTION AND GOVERNMENT. Within the State there are three levels of government: the Commonwealth Government, with authority derived from a written constitution; the State Government with residual powers; the local government authorities with powers based upon a State Act of Parliament, operating within incorporated areas extending over seven-eighths of the State.

The Constitution of New South Wales is drawn from several diverse sources; certain Imperial statutes such as the Colonial Laws Validity Act (1865) and the Commonwealth of Australia Constitution Act (1900); the Australian States Constitution Act (1907); the Letters Patent and the Instructions to the Governor; an element of inherited English law; amendments to the Commonwealth of Australia Constitution Act; the (State) Constitution Act and certain other State Statutes; numerous legal decisions; and a large amount of English and local convention.

The Parliament of New South Wales may legislate for the peace, welfare and good government of the State in all matters not specifically reserved to the Commonwealth Government.

The State Legislature consists of the Sovereign, represented by the Governor, and two Houses of Parliament, the Legislative Council (upper house) and the Legislative Assembly (lower house).

Under legislation passed in 1978, the Legislative Council is to consist of 45 members elected by popular vote for a term of office equivalent to three terms of the Legislative Assembly, with 15 members retiring at the same time as the Legislative Assembly elections. In Oct. 1982, the Council consisted of the following parties: Labor, 24; Liberal and National Party, 18; Australian Democrats, 1; Independent, 1.

Australian citizens, and British subjects who were enrolled before 1983, men and women aged 18 years and over, are entitled to the franchise. Voting is compulsory.

The President of the Legislative Council has an annual salary (1982) of $A41,282; the Leader of the Opposition members, $A39,888; the Chairman of Committees, the Deputy Leader of the Government members (if not a Minister) and the Deputy Leader of the Opposition members (when a leader of a party), $A27,922 each; the Deputy Leader of the Opposition members (when not a leader of a party) and Government and Opposition Whips, $A26,060 each. The President is paid an annual expense allowance of $A5,728; the Leader of the Opposition members, $A4,197; the Chairman of Committees, the Deputy Leader of the Government members (if not a Minister) and the Deputy Leader of the Opposition members (when a leader of a party), $A2,938 each; the Deputy Leader of the Opposition members (when not a leader of a party) and Government and Opposition Whips, $A1,387 each. Other members who are not Ministers receive an annual salary of $A22,400. All members receive an annual electoral allowance of $A7,146. Special expenses allowances ($A3,669 or $A4,585) are paid to members who are not Ministers and reside in outlying electorates.

The Legislative Assembly has 99 members elected by popular vote for a maximum period of 3 years. (Subsequent parliaments maximum period will be 4 years.) The Legislative Assembly, elected on 19 Sept. 1981, consisted in Oct. 1982 of the following parties: Labor, 69; Liberal and National Party, 27; Independents, 3.

The Speaker of the Legislative Assembly and the Leader of the Opposition members receive a salary of (1982) $A55,042 each; the Chairman of Committees, Deputy Leader of the Opposition members and Leader of the Country Party, $A39,888 each; Government and Opposition Whips, $A37,228 each. The Speaker and the Leader of the Opposition members also receive an expense allowance of $A7,637 each; the Chairman of Committees, Deputy Leader of the Opposition members and Leader of the Country Party, $A4,197 each; Government and Opposition Whips, and Deputy Leader of the Country Party, $A1,982 each. Members who are not Ministers receive an annual salary of $A32,000. All members receive an annual electoral allowance ranging from $A10,208 to $A18,233 according to the location of their constituencies. Special expenses allowances are paid to members who represent outlying electorates, $A6,140 each to the Speaker, the Leader of the Opposition members and the Leader of the Country Party; and to other members who are not Ministers, a sum of $A4,077 or $A5,094, according to the location of their electorate.

The executive is in the hands of a Governor, appointed by the Crown, and an Executive Council consisting of members of the Cabinet. Ministers receive the following annual salaries: Premier, $A69,880; Deputy Premier, $A62,618; the Leader of the Government members in the Legislative Council, $A63,373; Deputy Leader of Government members in the Legislative Council, $A60,170; other Ministers, $A58,892. Ministers also receive an expense allowance (Premier, $A16,347; Deputy Premier, $A8,173; other Ministers, $A7,637 each). Ministers also receive an electoral allowance ranging from $A10,208 to $A18,233 to members of the Legislative Assembly, according to the location of their electorate; and $A7,146 to each member of the Legislative Council. A special expenses allowance of $A6,140 is paid to Ministers who represent (in the case of the Legislative Assembly) or reside in (in the case of the Legislative Council), outlying electorates.

Governor: Air Marshal Sir James Anthony Rowland, KBE, DFC, AFC, KStJ (sworn in 20 Jan. 1981).

The Labor Party Cabinet, in Oct. 1982, was as follows:

Premier and Minister for Mineral Resources: The Hon. Neville Wran, QC, MP. *Deputy Premier, Minister for Public Works and Minister for Ports:* The Hon. L. J. Ferguson, MP. *Minister for Transport:* The Hon. P. F. Cox, MP. *Attorney-General, Minister of Justice and Minister for Aboriginal Affairs:* The Hon. F. J. Walker, QC, MP. *Minister for Industrial Relations and Minister for Technology:* The Hon. P. D. Hills, MP. *Minister for Energy, Minister for Water Resources and Vice-President of the Executive Council:* The Hon. D. P. Landa, LLB, MLC. *Treasurer:* The Hon. K. G. Booth, MP. *Minister for Industrial Development and Minister for Decentralization:* The Hon. Donald Day, MP. *Minister for Corrective Services:* The Hon. R. F. Jackson, MP. *Minister for Planning and Environment:* The Hon. E. L. Bedford, BA, MP. *Minister for Youth and Community Services:* The Hon. K. J. Stewart, MP. *Minister for Education:* The Hon. R. J. Mulock, LLB, MP. *Minister for Local Government and Minister for Lands:* The Hon. A. R. L. Gordon, MP. *Minister for Agriculture and Fisheries:* The Hon. J. R. Hallam, MLC. *Minister for Housing, Minister for Co-operative Societies and Minister Assisting the Premier:* The Hon. T. W. Sheahan, BA, LLB, MP. *Minister for Health:* The Hon. L. J. Brereton, MP. *Minister for Police and Emergency Services:* The Hon. P. T. Anderson, MP. *Minister for Leisure, Sport and Recreation and Minister for Tourism:* The Hon. M. A. Cleary, MP. *Minister for Consumer Affairs and Minister for Roads:* The Hon. P. F. P. Whelan, LLB, MP.

Agent-General in London: R. F. Watson, CMG (66 Strand, WC2N 5LZ).

Local Government. A system of local government extends over most of the State, including the whole of the Eastern and Central land divisions and more than two-thirds of the sparsely populated Western division. At 30 June 1982 there were 62 municipalities, and 113 corporate bodies called shires. A number of the municipalities and shires have combined to form 43 county councils, which administer electricity or water supply undertakings or render other services of common benefit.

ECONOMY

Budget. State Consolidated Revenue Fund: statement of receipts and payments (in $A1,000) for financial years ending 30 June:

	1978–79	*1979–80*	*1980–81*	*1981–82*
Revenue	3,569,625	4,089,282	4,741,568	5,480,120
Working Expenditure	3,293,933	3,791,995	4,416,750	5,147,637
Debt Charges	275,388	301,746	354,486	401,826
Total	3,569,321	4,093,740	4,771,236	5,549,463
Surplus/deficit	+ 304	− 4,458	− 29,668	− 69,343

State Government revenue in 1981–82 included (in $A1,000) receipts from the Commonwealth Government of 2,277,686; namely, towards public debt charges, 5,835; general financial assistance, 2,034,575; health, etc., 5,530; education, 182,222; other purposes, 49,524. State Government expenditure in 1981–82 included (in $A1,000) expenditure on education, 1,951,044; health etc., 869,713; law, order and public safety, 569,672; state resources, 344,475, and social amelioration, 236,099.

Public Debt. In terms of the financial agreement between the Commonwealth and State Governments, the Commonwealth Government has assumed responsibility for debts of the Australian States, and contributes towards the interest thereon and sinking funds established for redemption of the debts. Loans for the States are raised by the Commonwealth Government in accordance with decisions of the Australian Loan Council.

The public debt of New South Wales at 30 June 1982 (overseas loans converted to Australian currency equivalent at current rates of exchange) comprised the following (in $A1,000): Repayable in Australia, 5,104,381; in New York, 3,682. Interest liability for 1981–82 amounted (in $A1,000) to 505,502, of which 202 was in respect of the external debt. Contributions to the sinking fund for New South Wales debt, 71,839, include 13,767 contributed by the Commonwealth Government. The net cost of securities redeemed in the year was 72,388.

Banking. There were 10 trading banks operating in New South Wales at 30 June 1982, including the Commonwealth Trading Bank and State Bank (Government banks) and 1 New Zealand bank. The trading bank business is transacted chiefly by the Commonwealth Trading Bank, the State Bank and 5 private banks, all of which have their head offices in Australia. At 30 June 1982 the 10 banks operated 1,887 branches and 324 agencies in New South Wales.

The weekly average amount of deposits held in New South Wales by the 10 banks was $A14,430·7m. in June 1982, consisting of $A9,887·1m. bearing interest and $A4,543·6m. not bearing interest. Bank advances, overdrafts, bills discounted, etc., amounted to $A11,399·7m. A statement of other assets and liabilities of the banks in New South Wales is of little significance, as banking business is conducted on an Australia-wide basis.

Savings bank deposits at the end of June 1982 amounted to $A6,889·5m., representing $A1,303 per head of population.

ENERGY AND NATURAL RESOURCES

Minerals. New South Wales contains extensive mineral deposits. The most important minerals mined are: Coal (which accounts for 68% of the value of the State's mineral production); silver–lead–zinc (14%); construction materials (sand, gravel, stone, etc., 10%); and mineral sands (rutile, zircon, etc., 2%). At 30 June 1981, there were 633 mining establishments with an average employment of 28,798. During 1980–81, wages and salaries paid were $A619m., and value added was $A1,263m. Mine production of coal and metallic minerals (gross content) is shown below:

	1978–79	*1979–80*	*1980–81*	*1981–82*
Antimony (tonnes)	1,588	1,435	1,207	1,233
Cadmium (tonnes)	1,053	1,174	1,156	1,345
Coal (1,000 tonnes)	50,517	48,975	58,549	60,172
Cobalt (tonnes)	86	84	74	73
Copper (tonnes)	17,675	19,043	17,162	23,453
Gold (kg)	469	518	572	599
Lead (tonnes)	244,665	237,189	224,938	248,115
Silver (kg)	314,925	291,017	283,667	300,688
Sulphur (tonnes)	223,952	243,216	236,244	270,182
Tin (tonnes)	2,588	2,424	2,053	1,652
Titanium dioxide (tonnes)	142,192	111,057	111,021	82,831
Zinc (tonnes)	297,454	322,173	309,181	355,536
Zircon (tonnes)	141,275	106,477	113,009	89,063

The value of output in mining and quarrying in 1980–81 was $A1,941,972,553.

Land settlement. The total area of land alienated, virtually alienated or in process of alienation from the Crown on 30 June 1981 was 29,979,975 hectares, exclusive of the Australian Capital Territory; 42,947,128 hectares (including 30,814,582 hectares of the Western Division) were held under lease from the Crown; the total area of land neither alienated nor leased (including roads, reserves for public purposes, etc.) was 7,215,676 hectares.

Agriculture. The area under cultivation in New South Wales during 3 years (ended 31 March) and the principal crops (in tonnes) produced were as follows:

	1979	*1980*	*1981*
Hectares under cultivation	5,253,281	5,400,333	5,376,115
Value (farm) of all crops	$A1,231m.	$A1,395m.	$A1,108m.

Principal crops		1979 Hectares	1979 Produce	1980 Hectares	1980 Produce	1981 Hectares	1981 Produce
Wheat	Grain	3,162,108	6,640,401	3,415,027	6,000,000	3,345,000	2,865,000
	Hay	11,989	38,350	13,547	40,611	33,081	67,830
Maize	Grain	15,216	55,398	12,133	49,922	13,031	45,486
Barley	Grain	467,638	675,937	445,195	686,330	455,481	413,325
	Hay	1,438	3,382	1,379	2,600	3,451	6,190
Oats	Grain	431,466	594,251	348,743	460,652	363,250	309,867
	Hay	28,474	84,300	28,128	75,870	42,716	90,151
Potatoes		8,256	124,156	7,443	102,408	6,262	86,526
Lucerne (hay)		51,090	227,213	40,506	191,905	41,858	197,469
Tobacco		768	1,366	690	1,297	644	1,043
Rice		105,864	674,440	110,431	585,980	98,824	703,530
Cotton		35,400	115,664	54,480	188,329	53,743	173,428

In 1980–81, 14,018 hectares of sugar-cane were cut for crushing, the production being 1,435,287 tonnes. The total area under grapes was 14,257 (including 978 not bearing) hectares; the production of table grapes was 5,006 tonnes; of wine, 115,733 tonnes; of dried vine fruits, 11,696 tonnes.

In 1980–81, 5,422 hectares of banana plantations; production from 4,938 hectares, 62,836 tonnes; there were 26,716 hectares of orchard fruit.

At 31 March 1981 the State had 46m. sheep and lambs, 5,459,087 cattle and 786,953 pigs. The production of wool in 1980–81 was 198·2m. kg (greasy). In the year ended 30 June 1981 production of butter was 1,388,333 kg; cheese, 10,823,000 kg, and bacon and ham, 25,643,996 kg.

Forestry. The estimated area of Crown and private lands is 16·3m. hectares. The total area of State forests amounts to 3·3m. hectares, and 315,000 hectares have been set apart as timber reserves.

The revenue from royalties, licences, etc., amounted in the year ended June 1980 to $A20,044,000. At 30 June 1980 there were 651 saw-mills, employing 7,082 persons. The value of forestry production for 1979–80 was $A103·4m.

INDUSTRY AND TRADE

Industry. Approximately 20% of employed persons in New South Wales are employed in manufacturing industries.

A very wide range of manufacturing activities is undertaken in the Sydney area, and there are large iron and steel works and associated metal fabrication works in operation in proximity to the coalfields at Newcastle and Port Kembla.

The following table shows a summary of manufacturing industries' statistics for 1980–81:

Industry	Establishments [1] No.	Employment [2] Males (No.)	Employment [2] Females (No.)	Wages and salaries [3] ($A1m.)	Value added ($A1m.)
Food, beverages and tobacco	999	41,743	16,998	788·9	1,563·3
Textiles	222	6,045	4,796	134·7	247·6
Clothing and footwear	747	5,376	19,571	242·0	388·7
Wood, wood products and furniture	1,382	22,470	4,265	300·7	567·9
Paper, paper products, printing and publishing	1,194	26,016	12,117	538·5	986·8
Chemical, petroleum and coal products	426	20,247	9,258	462·4	1,218·9
Non-metallic mineral products	576	14,996	1,987	263·1	531·4
Basic metal products	213	52,286	3,753	912·1	1,561·3
Fabricated metal products	1,679	34,319	8,190	543·4	951·8
Transport equipment	451	31,788	3,505	469·6	706·6
Other machinery and equipment	1,601	52,344	19,507	926·0	1,584·7
Miscellaneous manufacturing	844	15,487	9,050	302·5	556·6
Total manufacturing	10,334	323,117	112,997	5,883·9	10,865·4

[1] Operating at 30 June 1981. Excludes single-establishment manufacturing enterprises with less than 4 persons employed.

[2] Persons employed—average over whole year, including working proprietors.

[3] Excludes drawings of working proprietors.

Some of the principal articles manufactured in 1981–82 were:

Article	*Quantity*	*Article*	*Quantity*
Flour (1,000 tonnes)	530	Raw steel (1,000 tonnes)	6,354
Cloth: cotton, wool, rayon, synthetic (1,000 sq. metres)	67,758	Electric motors (1,000)	1,994
Ale, beer and stout (1,000 litres)	645,094	Clay bricks (1 m.)	872
		Electricity (1 m. kwh.)	37,841

During 1981–82 the value of all building jobs commenced in New South Wales was $A3,582m. (of which jobs valued at $A338m. were being built for government ownership), jobs completed were valued at $A3,862m. ($A423m. for government ownership), and jobs under construction at the end of the period were valued at $A2,982m. ($A663m. for government ownership).

Labour. Two systems of industrial arbitration and conciliation for the adjustment of industrial relations between employers and employees are in operation—the State system which operates within the territorial limits of the State, and the Commonwealth system, which applies to industrial disputes extending beyond State borders.

The industrial tribunals are authorized to fix minimum rates of wages and other conditions of employment. Their awards may be enforced by law, as may be industrial agreements between employers and organizations of employees, when registered.

The principal State tribunal is the Industrial Commission of New South Wales. The Commission is empowered to exercise all the arbitration and conciliation powers conferred on subsidiary tribunals, and has in addition authority to determine any widely defined 'industrial matter', to adjudicate in case of illegal strikes and lockouts, etc., to investigate union ballots when irregularities are alleged and to hear appeals from subsidiary tribunals. Subsidiary tribunals are Conciliation Committees for various industries, each having an equal number representing employers and employees and a Conciliation Commissioner as chairman.

The chief industrial tribunals of the Commonwealth are the Industrial Division of the Federal Court of Australia, composed of judges, and the Australian Conciliation and Arbitration Commission, composed of presidential members, and commissioners.

Most State awards and agreements prescribe a basic wage and, for each industry, margins assessed on skill, etc. Since May 1974, the State Industrial Commission has also specified a minimum wage in line with Commonwealth awards. In Sept. 1982, the minimum wage payable in Sydney for a full week's work by an adult male or female was $A146.10 under both State and Commonwealth awards. The average weekly earnings of all employees in the June quarter 1982 was $A299·60.

A standard working week of 40 hours is prescribed for employees in most industries. Overtime is permitted under prescribed conditions.

Trade Unions. Registration of trade unions is effected under the New South Wales Trade Union Act, 1881, which follows substantially the Trade Union Acts of 1871 and 1876 of England. Registration confers a quasi-corporate existence with power to hold property, to sue and be sued, etc., and the various classes of employees covered by the union are required to be prescribed by the constitution of the union. For the purpose of bringing an industry under the review of the State industrial tribunals, or participating in proceedings relating to disputes before Commonwealth tribunals, employees and employers must be registered as industrial unions, under State or Commonwealth industrial legislation respectively.

Commerce. The external commerce of New South Wales, exclusive of interstate trade, is included in the statement of the commerce of Australia (*see* pp. 110–12). The overseas commerce of the State is given in $A1,000 ending 30 June:

	Imports	*Exports* [1]		*Imports*	*Exports* [1]
1976–77	4,278,450	2,718,352	1979–80	6,704,649	4,558,301
1977–78	4,635,018	3,114,401	1980–81	7,952,051	4,697,316
1978–79	5,760,063	3,770,509	1981–82	9,232,219	4,810,501

[1] Includes non-Australian produce ($A607m. in 1981–82).

The main exports from New South Wales of Australian produce in 1981–82 were coal (25%), cereal grains (13·8%), wool (9·6%), iron and steel (6·9%), meat (5·3%), machinery (6%), non-ferrous metals (3%). Principal imports were machinery and transport equipment (38·8%), chemicals (9%), petroleum and petroleum products (9·6%), textiles (4·6%), paper and paperboard (2·7%), photographic apparatus and optical goods (2·3%), precision instruments and apparatus (2·3%).

Principal destinations of all exports from New South Wales in 1981–82 were Japan (24·6%), EEC countries (9·1%), ASEAN countries (8·1%), New Zealand (6·5%), USA (5%), Papua New Guinea (2·9%), China (2·3%). Major sources of supply were USA (23·8%), EEC countries (21%), Japan (20·6%), Saudi Arabia (5·6%) and New Zealand (3·7%).

COMMUNICATIONS

Roads. At 30 June 1978 there were 204,571 km of roads and streets in New South Wales, comprising 424 km cement concrete, 7,462 km bituminous concrete, 62,595 km other bitumen surface, 66,413 km gravel, 39,188 km earth formed and 28,490 km natural surface.

The principal bus services in Sydney and Newcastle are operated by the State Government.

The number of registered motor vehicles (excluding tractors and trailers) at 30 June 1982 was 2,769,500, including 2·11m. cars and station wagons, 162,700 utilities, 161,400 panel vans, 189,300 trucks, 15,900 buses and 129,900 motor cycles.

Railways. At 30 June 1981, 9,773 km of government railway were open. The revenue (including supplements) in 1980–81 was $A902·3m.; the expenditure from revenue, $A902·1m.; the number of passengers carried, 213m. Also open for traffic are 324 km of Victorian Government railways which extend over the border; 68 km of private railways (mainly in mining districts) and 47 km of Commonwealth Government-owned track.

Aviation. Sydney is the major airport in New South Wales and Australia's principal international air terminal. During the year ended 31 Dec. 1980 aircraft movements at Sydney totalled 105,291. Passengers totalled 5,999,925 on domestic services and 2,412,152 on international services. Freight handled on domestic and international services was 53,935 tonnes and 84,011 tonnes respectively.

Shipping. The number of vessels engaged in overseas trade which entered the ports of New South Wales in 1980–81 was 2,992 and the clearances numbered 2,927. The gross weight tonnage of cargo discharged and loaded was 8·1m. and 30m. respectively. Sydney Harbour is the principal port of Australia. The number of overseas vessels which entered in 1980–81 was 1,501.

JUSTICE, RELIGION, EDUCATION AND WELFARE

Justice. Legal processes may be carried on in Lower or Magistrates' Courts, or in the Higher Courts presided over by judges. There is also an appellate jurisdiction. Persons charged with the more serious crimes must be tried before the Higher Courts.

Children's Courts have been established with the object of removing children as far as possible from the atmosphere of a public court. There are also a number of tribunals exercising special jurisdiction, *e.g.*, the Industrial Commission and the Workers' Compensation Commission.

In 1981 there were 3,910 distinct persons convicted at the Higher Courts. At 30 June 1979 there were 3,591 persons (including 126 females) held under sentence in prison.

Religion. There is no established church in New South Wales, and freedom of worship is accorded to all.

The following table shows the statistics of the religious denominations in New South Wales at the census, and of ministers of religion registered for the celebration of marriages, in 1981:

Denomination	*Ministers*	*Adherents*	*Denomination*	*Ministers*	*Adherents*
Church of England	938	1,569,374	Hebrew	25	25,176
Roman Catholic	1,693	1,424,499	Moslem	10	38,527
Presbyterian	211	252,725	Other Non-Christian	13	25,408
Uniting Church	563	148,992	Others	...	954,564 [1]
Baptist	342	64,663			
Lutheran	90	31,696	Total	5,094	5,126,217
Other Christian	1,209	590,593			

[1] Includes 443,159 'no religion' and 491,146 'religion not stated' (this is not a compulsory question in the census schedule).

Education. The State Government maintains a system of primary and secondary education, and attendance at school is compulsory from 6 to 15 years of age. In all government schools education is free. Non-government schools are subject to government inspection.

In July 1981 there were 2,236 government schools, comprising 1,695 primary and infant schools, 64 combined primary and secondary schools, 363 secondary schools and 114 special-purpose schools. In July 1981 the effective enrolment was 790,393 students, comprising 506,877 receiving primary instruction and 283,516 receiving secondary instruction. There were 45,248 teachers (including the full-time equivalent of part-time teachers) in 1981.

In July 1981 there were 804 non-government schools with 12,663 teachers (including the full-time equivalent of part-time teachers) and an effective enrolment of 237,853 students, including 609 Roman Catholic schools, having 9,735 teachers and 195,773 students, and 31 Anglican schools with 1,099 teachers and 16,454 students.

The University of Sydney, founded in 1850, had 17,805 students in 1981. There are 6 colleges providing residential facilities at the university. The University of New England at Armidale, previously affiliated with the University of Sydney, was incorporated in 1954, and in 1981 had 8,914 students.

The University of New South Wales was established in 1949. Enrolments in 1981 numbered 18,844. There are 8 colleges providing residential facilities at the university. The University of Newcastle, previously affiliated with the University of New South Wales, was granted autonomy from 1965, and in 1981 had 4,391 students. The University of Wollongong, also previously associated with the University of New South Wales, became autonomous in 1975, and in 1981 had 3,089 students. The Macquarie University in Sydney, established in 1964, had 10,489 students in 1981.

Colleges of Advanced Education were first established in 1971 to provide tertiary training with a vocational emphasis. In 1981 there were 39,907 students (including 21,549part-time students) enrolled at 23 colleges.

Post-school technical and further education is provided at State technical colleges. Students enrolled in 1981 totalled 314,042 (including 23,236 correspondence students).

State Government expenditure (including loan expenditure) on education in 1980–81 was $A1,634m.

Social Welfare. The Commonwealth Government makes provision for social benefits, such as age and invalid pensions, widows' pensions, supporting parents' benefits, family allowances, and unemployment, sickness and special benefits.

The number of age and invalid pensions (including wives' pensions) current in New South Wales on 30 June 1982 was: Age, 508,852 (males, 164,761; females, 344,091; invalid, 96,524 (males, 53,729; females, 42,795). Expenditure for the year ended 30 June 1982 was $A1,674m. for age pensions and $A356m. for invalid pensions.

Commonwealth Government widows' pensions current in New South Wales at 30 June 1982 numbered 60,363, the expenditure for 1981–82, $A274m. Supporting parents' benefits at 30 June 1982 numbered 45,197; expenditure in 1981–82 was $A228m.

Under the Family Allowance scheme, which commenced in 1976, payments to families and approved institutions for children under 16 years and full-time students under 25 years (1,444,453 such children or students) during 1981–82 amounted to $A375m.

Unemployment, sickness and special benefits commenced in 1945. During the year 1981–82 claims totalling $A581m. were paid in New South Wales. At 30 June 1982 unemployment benefit was being paid to an estimated 142,098 persons, and sickness and special benefits to 31,302 persons.

Direct State Government social welfare services are limited, for the most part, to the assistance of persons not eligible for Commonwealth Government benefit and the provision of certain forms of assistance not available from the Commonwealth Government. The State also subsidizes many approved services for needy persons. During 1981–82, expenditure on social amelioration and war obligations was $A238m.

Books of Reference

Statistical Information: The NSW Government Statistician's Office was established in 1886, and in 1957 was integrated with the Commonwealth Bureau of Census and Statistics (now called the Australian Bureau of Statistics). *Acting Deputy Commonwealth Statistician:* T. J. Skinner. Its principal publications are:

New South Wales Year Book (1886/87–1900/01 under the title *Wealth and Progress of NSW):* latest issue, 1982
New South Wales Handbook of Local Statistics: latest issue, 1982
New South Wales Principal Subject Bulletins (previously published under the title *Statistical Register* (since 1858); latest issue of separate bulletins, 1980–81 and 1982
New South Wales Pocket Year Book. Published since 1913; latest issue, 1982
Monthly Summary of Statistics. Published since May 1931
New South Wales in Brief. 1982

New South Wales Dept. of Tourism, *New South Wales–Australia.* Sydney, 1981
New South Wales Dept. of Industrial Development and Decentralisation, *New South Wales Handbook for Industrialists.* 1982
State Planning Authority, *Sydney Region, 1970–2000 A.D.: Outline Plan.* Sydney, 1968
New South Wales Planning and Environment Commission, *Review: Sydney Region Outline Plan.* Sydney, 1980
New South Wales Government Information Service, *The Government of New South Wales: Directory of Administration and Services.* Sydney, 1979 (as amended)

State Library: The State Library of NSW, Macquarie St., Sydney. *State Librarian:* R. F. Doust, BA, M.Lib, FLAA.

QUEENSLAND

AREA AND POPULATION. Queensland comprises the whole north-eastern portion of the Australian continent, including the adjacent islands in the Pacific Ocean and in the Gulf of Carpentaria. Estimated area 1,727,000 sq. km.

The increase in the population as shown by the censuses since 1901 has been as follows:

	Census counts			*Intercensal increase*	
Year	*Males*	*Females*	*Total*	*Numerical*	*Rate per annum %*
1901	277,003	221,126	498,129	—	—
1911	329,506	276,307	605,813	107,684	1·98
1921	398,969	357,003	755,972	150,159	2·24
1933	497,217	450,317	947,534	191,562	1·86
1947	567,471	538,944	1,106,415	158,881	1·11
1954	676,252	642,007	1,318,259	211,844	2·53
1961	774,579	744,249	1,518,828	200,569	2·04
1966	849,390 [1]	824,934 [1]	1,674,324 [1]	144,857	1·84
1971	921,665 [1]	905,400 [1]	1,827,065 [1]	152,741 [1]	1·76 [1]
1976	1,024,611 [1]	1,012,586 [1]	2,037,197 [1]	210,132 [1]	2·20 [1]
1981	1,153,404 [1]	1,141,719 [1]	2,295,123 [1]	257,926 [1]	2·41 [1]

[1] Including Aboriginals.

Since the 1981 census, official population estimates are according to place of usual residence and are referred to as "estimated resident population", Estimated resident populations at the census dates of 1971, 1976, and 1981 were 1,851,500; 2,092,400; and 2,345,300; respectively.

Statistics on birthplaces from the 1981 census are as follows: Australia, 1,932,810 (84·2%); UK and Ireland, 147,083 (6·4%); other countries, 183,068 (8%); at sea and not stated, 32,165 (1·4%).

Vital statistics (including Aboriginals) for calendar years:

	Total births	*Marriages*	*Divorces*	*Deaths*
1979	35,195	16,082	5,811	16,388
1980	34,972	17,157	6,219	16,497
1981	38,834	18,305	6,470	17,175

The annual rates per 1,000 population in 1981 were: Marriages, 7·8; births, 16·6; deaths, 7·3. The infant death rate was 10·9 per 1,000 births.

Brisbane, the capital, had on 30 June 1981 a resident population of 1,086,470 (Statistical Division). The resident populations of the other chief towns at the same date were: Gold Coast, 104,620; Townsville, 82,760; Toowoomba, 73,260; Rockhampton, 54,780; Cairns, 36,930; Bundaberg, 32,550; Mount Isa, 25,760; Gladstone, 23,960; Maryborough, 22,470; Mackay, 21,130; Hervey Bay, 12,330; Gympie, 11,420.

CONSTITUTION AND GOVERNMENT. Queensland, formerly a portion of New South Wales, was formed into a separate colony in 1859, and responsible government was conferred. The power of making laws and imposing taxes is vested in a Parliament of one House—the Legislative Assembly, which comprises 82 members, returned from 4 electoral zones for 3 years, elected for single-member constituencies at compulsory ballot. Members are entitled to $A37,695 per annum, with individual electorate allowances for travelling, postage, etc., of from $A9,540 to $A24,620.

At the general election of 29 Nov. 1980 there were 1,341,365 persons registered as qualified to vote under the Elections Act 1915–1976. This Act provides franchise for all males and females, 18 years of age and over, qualified by 6 months' residence in Australia and 3 months in the electoral district.

The Legislative Assembly, following the elections of 29 Nov. 1980, was composed of the following parties: National, 35; Liberal, 22; Australian Labor, 25; total, 82.

Governor of Queensland: Cde Sir James Maxwell Ramsay, KCMG, CBE, DSC (assumed office April 1977).

The Executive Council of Ministers, at 31 Dec. 1981, consisted of the following members:

Premier: Johannes Bjelke-Petersen (National).

Treasurer and Deputy Premier: Llewellyn Roy Edwards (Liberal). *Commerce and Industry:* Victor Bruce Sullivan (National). *Justice and Attorney-General:* Samuel Sydney Doumany (Liberal). *Employment and Labour Relations:* Sir William Knox (Liberal). *Local Government, Main Roads and Police:* Russell James Hinze (National). *Water Resources and Aboriginal and Island Affairs:* Kenneth Burgoyne Tomkins (National). *Northern Development and Maritime Services:* Valmond James Bird (National). *Works and Housing:* Claude Alfred Wharton (National). *Mines and Energy:* Ivan James Gibbs (National). *Primary Industries:* Michael John Ahern (National). *Environment, Valuation and Administrative Services:* William Douglas Hewitt (Liberal). *Transport:* Donald Frederick Lane (Liberal). *Education:* William Angus Manson Gunn (National). *Lands and Forestry:* William Hamline Glasson (National). *Tourism, National Parks, Sports and the Arts:* Jannion Anthony Elliott (National). *Health:* Brian Douglas Austin (Liberal). *Welfare Services:* Terrence Anthony White (Liberal).

Each Minister has a salary of $A61,963, the Premier receives $A78,725, the Deputy Premier, $A67,513, and the Leader of the Opposition, $A53,471.

Agent-General in London: J. H. Andrews (392 Strand, WC2).

Local Government. Provision is made for local government by the subdivision of the State into cities, towns and shires. These are under the management of aldermen or councillors, who are elected by all persons 18 years and over. Local Authorities are charged with the control of all matters of a parochial nature, such as sewerage, cleansing and sanitary services, health services, domestic water supplies, and roads and bridges within their allotted areas. In addition to Government grants and subsidies, Local Authority revenue is derived from general rates, paid by landowners on the unimproved capital value of land, and by charging for some specific services.

For the year ended 30 June 1980, the receipts and expenditure (including loans) for the 134 Local Authorities were $A851m. and $A821·5m. respectively and their rateable values amounted to $A6,080·3m.

ECONOMY

Budget. Revenue and expenditure of the Consolidated Revenue Fund of Queensland during 5 years ending 30 June (in $A1,000):

	1978–79	*1979–80*	*1980–81*	*1981–82*	*1982–83*[1]
Revenue	1,947,444	2,206,954	2,604,036	3,276,756	3,668,690
Expenditure	1,946,867	2,207,893	2,604,010	3,276,926	3,668,947

[1] Estimates.

Total funds available to the Queensland Government in 1980–81 were $A2,932·9m., of which Taxation and Federal Government grants amounted to $A2,668·7m. Expenditure from these funds included: Education, $A947m.; economic services (roads, electricity, etc.), $A565·6m.; health, $A508·2m.

Revenue and expenditure of Commonwealth Government departments on account of Queensland are not included.

Debt. The gross public debt of the State at par rates of exchange amounted, on 30 June 1982, to $A2,112·1m. The debt was domiciled as follows (in $A1,000): Australia, 2,110,171; UK, 1,094; USA, 63; European countries, 742. The annual interest charge on the public debt at 30 June 1982 was $A192·8m.

Banking. There were 9 trading banks operating in Queensland at 30 June 1982, including the Commonwealth Trading Bank of Australia, the 5 larger Australian trading banks, a Queensland bank with head office in Brisbane, the Bank of New Zealand and the Banque Nationale de Paris. The Commonwealth Trading Bank had 157 branches and 63 agencies; the other banks had 678 branches and 128 agencies in the State. Queensland deposits of all trading banks, including the Commonwealth Trading Bank of Australia, amounted to $A5,590·3m.; and loans, advances and bills discounted in Queensland were $A3,308·7m. At 30 June 1982 savings bank business was conducted in Queensland by 7 banks, the Commonwealth Savings Bank with 166 branches and 1,176 agencies, and 6 other banks with 653 branches and 1,079 agencies. Depositors' balances amounted to $A3,460m. in 3·27m. accounts.

ENERGY AND NATURAL RESOURCES

Electricity. The State Electricity Commission, established in 1938 and under a single Commissioner since 1948, co-ordinates the electricity industry in Queensland.

Electricity generated by the principal stations in the year ended 30 June 1981 was 11,156m. kwh. Natural gas is being used for electric generation at Roma. Black coal was used to generate 93% of the power; hydro-electric stations generated 7%.

Minerals. Principal minerals produced during 1980–81 were: Copper, 170,000 tonnes; coal, 32,356,000 tonnes; lead, 139,000 tonnes; zinc, 115,000 tonnes; silver, 405,285 kg; tin, 2,999 tonnes; gold, 1,579 kg; bauxite, 7,937,000 tonnes; mineral sands concentrates, 160,000 tonnes; uranium, 836 tonnes. Value of output, at the mine, was $A1,918m. The chief mines are Mount Isa (copper, silver, lead, zinc), Weipa (bauxite), Mount Morgan (copper, gold), Moreton and Bowen Basin (coal), Greenvale (nickel) and Mary Kathleen (uranium).

Land Settlement. Of the total area of the State, 13·1m. hectares had been alienated at 31 Dec. 1980; in process of alienation, under deferred payment system, were 20·3m. hectares, leaving 139·3m. hectares, still the property of the Crown, or 80·7% of the total area. A large proportion of the area is leased for pastoral purposes (96·3m. hectares at 31 Dec. 1980).

In the western portion of the State water is comparatively easily found by sinking artesian bores. At 30 June 1980, 3,423 such bores had been drilled, of which 2,336 were flowing.

Agriculture. Livestock on farms and stations at 31 March 1981 numbered 9·92m. cattle, 10·62m. sheep and 502,000 pigs. The wool production (greasy) was, in 1980–81, 47m. kg, valued at $A117m. The total area under crops during 1980–81 was 2·57m. hectares.

	Area (hectares)		*Yield (tonnes)*	
Crop	*1979–80*	*1980–81*	*1979–80*	*1980–81*
Sugar-cane, crushed	255,358	274,259	19,859,591	22,540,367
Wheat	733,287	726,964	845,959	485,255
Maize	41,205	42,566	97,914	123,190
Sorghum	368,698	528,394	711,315	1,050,177
Barley	194,775	159,686	346,519	170,339
Oats	12,458	14,268	8,742	5,932
Potatoes	6,514	5,751	127,441	113,339
Pumpkins	3,801	4,102	24,191	32,195
Tomatoes	3,117	3,361	45,705	55,660
Peanuts	31,273	26,773	38,466	42,386
Tobacco	3,523	3,454	7,679	7,592
Apples [1]	3,557	3,423	30,265	23,086
Grapes [1]	1,390	1,411	5,257	5,391
Citrus [1]	2,069	2,041	41,743	44,303
Bananas [1]	2,174	2,414	44,746	53,761
Pineapples [1]	4,075	4,085	123,050	123,220
Green fodder [2]	351,208	399,297	...	...
Hay (all kinds)	31,803	39,157	169,750	196,214
Cotton (raw)	20,550	24,182	19,786	22,548

[1] Bearing area only. [2] Excluding lucerne.

Forestry. A considerable area consists of natural forest, eucalyptus, pine and cabinet woods being the timbers mostly in evidence; a large quantity of ornamental woods is utilized by cabinet makers. The amount of native timber processed in 1980–81 was (in cu. metres): Conifers, 599,982; hardwoods, structural timbers and cabinet woods, 804,713.

INDUSTRY AND TRADE

Industry. The 1970s created a milestone in the State's industrial progress when the value added in production by the manufacturing sector exceeded the value of production in the agriculture, forestry, fishing and hunting sector. In 1980–81, there were 3,291 establishments, with four or more workers, employing 94,319 males and 21,796 females, and producing goods and services worth $A9,667m. The value added was $A3,075m. The manufacturing establishments contributing most to the overall production during 1980–81 were those predominantly engaged in the processing of food, beverages and tobacco.

The gross value of Queensland agricultural commodity production (in $A1,000) during 1980–81, amounted to 2,411,436, which included crops, 1,452,137; livestock disposals, 711,720; livestock products, 247,578.

Labour. Of the total population of 2·4m., 975,700 were in employment in Aug. 1982, 130,800 in manufacturing. Industrial wages and conditions are controlled partly by Federal and State authorities. A State Industrial Commission is empowered to determine all industrial matters in relation to employers and employees, to fix minimum wage-rates and other conditions of employment. An Industrial Court hears appeals and decides points of industrial law. The Australian Industrial Court, Conciliation and Arbitration Commission are superior within their jurisdictions. In Queensland most employees (67%) work under State awards; 25% under Federal awards.

Rates of wages for each occupation are prescribed by these courts. The minimum weighted average award wage for adult males was $A218·91 and for adult females $A198·40, at 31 March 1982, while for the March quarter 1982, average weekly earnings were $A337·40 for full-time adult males and $A312·80 for full-time adult females. (Average earnings include award, over-award and overtime payments.) A standard working week of 40 hours is prescribed for most awards.

Trade Unions. Unions both of employees and employers must be registered with the State or Australian Commission. There were 74 employees' and 39 employers' unions registered with the State Commission at 31 Dec. 1981, the former comprising 374,013 and the latter 36,854 members.

Commerce. The overseas commerce of Queensland is included in the statement of the commerce of Australia (*see* pp. 110–12).

Total value of the direct overseas imports and exports of Queensland (in $A1,000) f.o.b. port of shipment for both imports and exports:

	1976–77	*1977–78*	*1978–79*	*1979–80*	*1980–81*	*1981–82*
Imports	835,771	887,179	1,028,010	1,321,214	1,882,815	2,179,733
Exports	2,815,608	2,821,362	3,285,778 [1]	4,265,101 [1]	4,501,290 [1]	4,349,547 [1]

[1] State of origin.

In 1981–82 interstate exports totalled $A1,786·9m. and imports $A4,497·9m. The chief exports overseas are minerals including alumina, coal, meat (preserved or frozen), sugar, wool, cereal grains, copper and lead, and manufactured goods. Principal overseas imports are machinery, motor vehicles, mineral fuels (including lubricants, etc.), chemicals and manufactured goods classified by material. Chief sources of imports in 1981–82 were Japan ($A592m.), USA ($A521·9m.), Indonesia ($A149·2m.); exports went chiefly to Japan ($A1,535·3m.), USA ($A680·9m.), UK ($A263·6m.), EEC, excluding UK ($A390·3m.).

COMMUNICATIONS

Roads. At 30 June 1981 there were 160,981 km of roads; of these, 138,405 km were formed roads, of which 47,562 km were surfaced with concrete sealed pavement.

At 30 June 1981 motor vehicles registered in Queensland totalled 1,355,631, comprising 946,159 cars and station wagons, 178,412 utilities, 68,249 panel vans, 5,877 buses, 65,643 trucks and 91,291 motor cycles.

Railways. Practically all the railways are owned by the State Government. Total length of line at 30 June 1981 was 9,932 km. In 1980–81, 31,873,000 passengers and 41·5m. tonnes of goods and livestock were carried.

Aviation. Queensland is well served with a network of air services, with overseas and interstate connexions. Subsidiary companies provide planes for taxi and charter work, and the Flying Doctor Service operates throughout western Queensland.

Shipping. In 1980–81, cargo discharged was 3·6m. revenue tonnes and cargo loaded was 34·3m. revenue tonnes.

Broadcasting. At 30 June 1981, 56 broadcasting and 43 television stations were in operation throughout Queensland.

JUSTICE, RELIGION, EDUCATION AND WELFARE

Justice. Justice is administered by a Supreme Court, District Courts, Magistrates' Courts and Children's Courts. The Supreme Court comprises a Chief Justice, a senior puisne judge and 13 puisne judges; the District Court, 17 district court judges. Stipendiary magistrates preside over the Lower Courts, except in the smaller centres, where justices of the peace officiate. A parole board may recommend prisoners for release.

The total number of persons convicted of serious offences by the superior courts in 1980–81 was 1,243; summary convictions in lower courts numbered 100,782. There were, at 30 June 1981, 5 prisons, 2 gaols for short-term prisoners, 2 prison farms conducted on the honour system and 1 prison for mentally-ill prisoners, with 1,733 male and 49 female prisoners. The total police force, was 4,557 at 30 June 1981.

Religion. There is no State Church. Membership, census 1981: Anglican, 601,537; Roman Catholic and Catholic (not further defined), 554,912; Uniting Church, 146,898; Presbyterian, 132,525; Methodist, 86,750; Lutheran, 50,401; Baptist, 34,323; other Christian, 166,611; Buddhist, 2,967; Muslim, 2,457; Hebrew, 2,021; all others (including not stated and no religion), 513,721.

Education. Education in Queensland ranges from pre-school level through to tertiary level. In addition, child care, kindergarten and adult education facilities are available. Education is compulsory between the ages of 6 and 15 years and is provided free in government schools. Expenditure on education by government authorities for 1979–80 was $A832·2m.

At 1 July 1981, pre-school education and child care was provided at 1,077 centres with 3,257 staff and 58,214 children.

Primary and secondary education comprises 12 years of full-time formal schooling and is provided by both the government and non-government sectors. At 1 July 1981, the State administered 1,041 primary, 85 primary/secondary, and 142 secondary schools with 251,819 primary students, 108,605 secondary students and 19,627 teachers. Special education, which is included in the above figures, was provided to 4,837 children at 60 special schools and 37 primary schools with special classes. Non-government enrolments at 1 July 1981 were 56,989 primary students and 43,514 secondary students taught by 4,952 teachers at 220 primary, 55 primary/secondary and 74 secondary schools.

Post-secondary education in Queensland involves technical and further education, advanced education and university education. Tertiary education in 1980 involved 431 full-time and 333 part-time students at technical colleges, 10,501 full-time and 12,771 part-time students at colleges of advanced education and 12,012 full-time and 10,237 part-time students at universities.

Sub-tertiary education in 1980 involved 42,273 students at technical colleges, 1,099 students at colleges of advanced education and 431 students at rural training schools.

Social Welfare. Public hospitals are maintained by State and Federal Government endowment, supplemented by fees from patients not in standard wards. Welfare institutions providing shelter and social care for the aged, the handicapped, and children, are maintained or assisted by the State. A maternal and child welfare service is provided throughout the State. Age, invalid, widows', disability and war service pensions, family allowances, and unemployment and sickness benefits are paid by the Federal Government. Age pensioners in the State at 30 June 1981 numbered 207,089; invalid pensioners, 35,555; disability pensioners, 123,339 (including dependants).

There were 21,437 widows' pensions current at 30 June 1981, and at the same date family allowances were being paid to 321,193 families in respect of 663,046 children under 16 years or students aged 16 or more but under 25. In addition, family allowances were paid to 1,936 children and students in institutions.

Housing. In 1981–82, 38,123 dwellings valued at $A1,635m. were approved for construction. This total comprised 23,689 houses and 14,434 individual other dwelling units contained in flats, semi-detached units, home units, villa units, town houses, etc. In 1980–81, 29,960 new dwellings were completed and 15,898 were being built at 30 June 1981. The Queensland Housing Commission, financed by Federal and State Government loans, builds dwellings for sale and for rental. Building and co-operative housing societies are assisted by Federal and State Government loans.

Books of Reference

Statistical Information: The Statistical Office (345 Ann St., Brisbane) was set up in 1859.

Deputy Commonwealth Statistician: O. M. May. *A Queensland Official Year Book* was issued in 1901, the annual *ABC of Queensland Statistics* from 1905 to 1936 with exception of 1918 and 1922. Present publications include: *Queensland Year Book.* Annual, from 1937 (omitting 1942, 1943, 1944).—*Queensland Pocket Year Book.* Annual from 1950.—*Monthly Summary of Queensland Statistics.* From Jan. 1961

Australian and New Zealand Association for the Advancement of Science, *Introducing Queensland.* Brisbane, 1961
Queensland Department of Agriculture and Stock, *The Queensland Agricultural and Pastoral Handbook.* 2 vols. Brisbane, 1962
Australian Sugar Year Book. Brisbane, from 1941
Bolton, G. C., *A Thousand Miles Away! A History of North Queensland to 1920.* Brisbane, 1963
Cilento, R., and Lack, C., *Triumph in the Tropics.* Brisbane, 1959
Greenwood, G., and Laverty, J., *Brisbane 1859–1959.* Sydney, 1959
Greenwood, R. H., *Queensland, City, Coast and Country.* London, 1959
Lack, C., *Queensland, Daughter of the Sun.* Brisbane, 1959.—*Three Decades of Queensland Political History.* Brisbane, 1962

State Library: The State Library of Queensland, William St., Brisbane. *State Librarian:* S. L. Ryan.

SOUTH AUSTRALIA

AREA AND POPULATION. The total area of South Australia is 380,070 sq. miles (984,377 sq. km). The settled part is divided into counties and hundreds. There are 49 counties proclaimed, covering 23m. hectares, of which 19m. hectares are occupied. Outside this area there are extensive pastoral districts, covering 76m. hectares, 46m. of which are under pastoral leases.

Census population (exclusive of full-blood Aboriginals before 1966):

	Males	*Females*	*Total*		*Males*	*Females*	*Total*
1901	180,485	177,861	358,346	1961	490,225	479,115	969,340
1911	207,358	201,200	408,558	1966	550,196	544,788	1,094,984
1921	248,267	246,893	495,160	1971	586,051	587,656	1,173,707
1933	290,962	289,987	580,949	1976	620,162	624,594	1,244,756
1947	320,031	326,042	646,073	1981	635,696	649,337	1,285,033

The number of Aboriginals (as reported on Census schedules) in the State at the Census of 30 June 1981 was 9,476.

Vital statistics for calendar years:

	Births	*Marriages*	*Divorces*	*Deaths*
1979	18,478	9,778	3,797	9,661
1980	18,499	10,064	4,203	9,582
1981	19,351	10,252	4,132	9,706

The infant mortality rate in 1981 was 8·11 per 1,000 live births.

CONSTITUTION AND GOVERNMENT. South Australia was formed into a British province by letters patent of Feb. 1836, and a partially elective Legislative Council was established in 1851. The present Constitution bears date 24 Oct. 1856. It vests the legislative power in an elected Parliament, consisting of a Legislative Council and a House of Assembly. The former is composed of 22 members. Every 3 years half the members retire, and the resulting vacancies are filled at a general election on the basis of proportional representation with the State as one multi-member electorate. The qualifications of an elector are, to be a natural born or naturalized British subject of at least 18 years of age and to have lived continuously in Australia for at least 6 months, in South Australia for at least 3 months and in the sub-division for which he is enrolled for at least 1 month. War service may substitute for residential qualifications in some cases. By the Constitution Act Amendment Act, 1894, the franchise was extended to women, who voted for the first time at the general election of 25 April 1896. The qualifications for election as a member of both Houses are the same as for an elector. Certain persons are ineligible for election to either House.

The House of Assembly consists of 47 members elected for 3 years, representing single electorates. Election of members of both Houses takes place by preferential secret ballot. Voting is compulsory for those on the Electoral Roll.

The House of Assembly, elected on 6 Nov. 1982, consists of the following members: Liberal Party of Australia, 21; Australian Labor Party, 24; National Party of Australia, 1; Independent, 1. The Legislative Council consists of 11 Liberal Party of Australia, 9 Labor and 2 Australian Democrat members.

Each member of Parliament receives $A31,530 per annum with allowances of $A6,105–22,590 according to location of electorate, a free pass over government railways and superannuation rights. Electors enrolled (June 1982) numbered 858,295.

The executive power is vested in a Governor appointed by the Crown and an Executive Council, consisting of the Governor and the Ministers of the Crown. The Governor has the power to dissolve the House of Assembly but not the Legislative Council unless that Chamber has twice consecutively with an election intervening defeated the same or substantially the same Bill passed in the House of Assembly by an absolute majority.

Governor: Lieut.-Gen. Sir Donald Dunstan, KBE, CB.

The South Australian Labour Ministry, in Jan. 1983 was as follows:

Premier, Treasurer, Minister of State and Development and Minister for the Arts: John Charles Bannon, MP.

Deputy Premier, Minister of Labour and Minister of Public Works: John David Wright, MP. *Attorney-General, Minister of Consumer and Corporate Affairs and Minister of Ethnic Affairs:* Christopher John Sumner, MLC. *Minister for Environment and Planning, Minister of Lands and Minister of Repatriation:* Donald Jack Hopgood, MP. *Minister of Agriculture, Minister of Fisheries and Minister of Forests:* Brian Alfred Chatterton, MLC. *Minister of Transport and Minister of Marine:* Roy Kitto Abbott, MP. *Minister of Health:* John Robert Cornawall, MLC. *Minister of Education and Minister for Technology:* Lynn Maurice Arnold, MP. *Chief Secretary and Minister of Tourism:* Gavin Frances Keneally, MP. *Minister of Mines and Energy:* Ronald George Payne, MP. *Minister of Community Welfare and Minister of Aboriginal Affairs:* Gregory John Crafter, MP. *Minister of Water Resources and Minister of Recreation and Sport:* John William Slater, MP. *Minister of Housing and Minister of Local Government:* Terence Henry Hemmings, MP.

Ministers are jointly and individually responsible to the legislature for all their official acts, as in the UK.

Agent-General in London: J. L. Rundle (50 Strand, WC2).

Local Government. The closely settled part of the State (mainly near the sea-coast and the River Murray) is incorporated into local government areas, and subdivided into district councils (rural areas only), municipal corporations (mainly metropolitan, but including larger country towns) and cities (more densely populated areas with a qualification of 15,000 residents in the Adelaide metropolitan area, and 10,000 in the country). The main functions of councils are the construction and maintenance of roads and bridges. Other functions include health, welfare, recreation and garbage disposal.

The number and area of the sub-divisions, together with expenditure (in $A1,000) for the year ended 30 June 1981, were:

	No.	*Area (1,000 hectares)*	*Roads and bridges*	*Recreation and Culture*	*All other*	*Total expenditure*
Adelaide statistical division	32	185·2	33,044	28,338	91,143	152,525
Other municipal corporations and district councils	95	14,967·2	27,047	8,144	53,939	89,130
Total	127	15,152·4	60,091	36,482	145,082	241,655

ECONOMY

Budget. Revenue and expenditure (in $A1,000) for years ended 30 June:

	1977	*1978*	*1979*	*1980*	*1981*	*1982*
Revenue	1,174,025	1,167,196	1,264,705	1,384,589	1,548,299	1,705,499
Expenditure	1,183,180	1,192,063	1,258,252	1,384,589	1,554,884	1,766,772

The public debt of the State amounted, on 30 June 1982, to $A1,962·6m.

Banking. There were 9 trading banks at 30 June 1982, including the Federal and State Government Banks. In June 1982 their average deposits were $A1,900·7m. and average loans and advances $A2,390m.

The 8 savings banks on 30 June 1982 had deposits amounting to $A2,595·3m. or $A1,967 per head of population.

NATURAL RESOURCES

Minerals. The value of minerals produced in 1980–81 was $A226·4m. The principal minerals produced are opals, natural gas, iron ore, copper, gypsum, salt, talc, clays, limestone, dolomite and sub-bituminous coal.

Agriculture. Of the total area of South Australia (984,377 sq. km), 74,249 sq. km were alienated, 549,164 sq. km were held under lease and 360,964 sq. km were unoccupied. Area under cultivation, at 31 March 1981, was 59,596 sq. km.

Soil Conservation. Under the direction of special officers in the Department of Agriculture, determined efforts are made to deal with the problems of erosion and soil conservation. Included in the programme are the planting of cereal rye, perennial rye and other grasses to check sand drifts; contour-furrowing and contour banking; contour planting with vines and fruit trees and several water-diversion schemes.

Irrigation. For the year ended 31 March 1981, 79,474 hectares were under irrigated culture, being used as follows: Vineyards, 20,253; orchards, 12,627; vegetables, 5,676, and other crops and pasture, 40,918. Most of these areas are along the river Murray.

Gross value of agricultural production (in $A1,000), 1980–81: Crops, 693,592; livestock slaughtering, 306,896; livestock products, 321,053. Total gross value, 1,321,540; local value (*i.e.* less marketing costs), 1,202,651.

	1979–80		*1980–81*	
Chief crops	*Hectares*	*Tonnes*	*Hectares*	*Tonnes*
Wheat	1,424,219	2,348,694	1,445,287	1,650,390
Barley	983,615	1,527,546	988,504	1,158,077
Oats	129,015	144,055	105,486	96,054
Hay	159,545	509,198	161,312	440,049
Vines	...	234,323,000 [1]	...	220,384,000 [1]

[1] Litres of wine.

Fruit culture is extensively carried on, and in 1980–81, 246,832 tonnes of fresh fruit were produced. Other products, in addition to all kinds of root crops and vegetables, are grass seeds and oil seeds. Livestock, March 1981: 1,091,301 cattle, 17,055,849 sheep and 393,516 pigs. In 1980–81, 102,561 tonnes of wool and 319·4m. litres of milk were produced.

INDUSTRY AND TRADE

Industry. The turnover for manufacturing industries for 1980–81 was $A6,067m. The following statistics for 1980–81 are not comparable with factory statistics for years prior to 1968–69.

Industry sub-division	*Establishments (No.)*	*Persons employed (No.)*	*Wages and salaries ($A1m.)*	*Turnover ($A1m.)*	*Value added ($A1m.)*
Food, beverages and tobacco	372	17,238	194	1,219	423
Textiles, clothing and footwear	117	6,746	69	280	114
Wood, wood products and furniture	304	7,806	87	380	148

Industry sub-division	*Establishments (No.)*	*Persons employed (No.)*	*Wages and salaries ($A1m.)*	*Turnover ($A1m.)*	*Value added ($A1m.)*
Paper, paper products, printing and publishing	195	7,664	93	336	173
Chemical, petroleum and coal products	50	2,927	45	248	94
Non-metallic mineral products	131	3,562	49	257	115
Basic metal products	36	9,465	143	887	246
Fabricated metal products	353	8,791	99	443	188
Transport equipment	114	18,085	239	958	427
Other machinery and equipment	287	16,566	194	769	337
Miscellaneous manufacturing	172	5,905	71	290	122
Total	2,131	104,755	1,283	6,067	2,387

Practically all forms of secondary industry are to be found, the most important being smelting, motor vehicle manufacture, saw-milling and the manufacture of household appliances, basic iron and steel, meat and meat products, and wine and brandy.

Labour. Two systems of industrial arbitration and conciliation for the adjustment of industrial relations between employers and employees are in operation—the State system, which operates when industrial disputes are confined to the territorial limits of the State, and the Federal system, which applies when disputes involve other parts of Australia as well as South Australia.

The industrial tribunals are authorized to fix minimum rates of wages and other conditions of employment, and their awards may be enforced by law. Industrial agreements between employers and organizations of employees, when registered, may be enforced in the same manner as awards. The Commission fixed the minimum wage in July 1981 at $A145.70.

Commerce. The commerce of South Australia, exclusive of inter-state trade, is comprised in the statement of the commerce of Australia given under the heading of the Commonwealth, *see* pp. 110–12.

Overseas imports and exports in $A1,000 (year ending 30 June):

	1976–77	*1977–78*	*1978–79*	*1979–80*	*1980–81*	*1981–82*
Imports	629,309	628,568	865,554	882,457	1,072,449	1,337,301
Exports [1]	789,872	661,887	922,754	1,599,199	1,417,811	1,275,938

[1] From 1978–79 exports are recorded by 'State of Origin', whereas details prior to this are by 'State of Lodgment of Documents'.

Principal exports in 1981–82 were (in $A1,000): Wheat, 211,362 (1,291,241 tonnes); barley, 109,550 (668,717 tonnes); wool, 213,084 (77,781 tonnes); lead, 101,671 (168,344 tonnes); meat, 89,712 (56,164 tonnes); live sheep and lambs, 58,630 (2,157,941 head).

Principal imports in 1981–82 were (in $A1,000): Transport equipment, 190,738; petrol and products, 431,823; machinery, 274,852.

In 1981–82 the leading suppliers of imports were (in $A1m.): Saudi Arabia (388·6), Japan (284·1), USA (178·9), Federal Republic of Germany (95·5); main exports went to USSR (152), Japan (141·3), Saudi Arabia (101·9), USA (92·7), New Zealand (74·8), Iraq (63·6), Singapore (53·4).

Tourism. In June 1982 there were 270 hotels and guest houses with 6,820 rooms; 159 caravan parks had a total of 18,191 sites.

COMMUNICATIONS

Roads. At 30 June 1981, of the roads customarily used by the public, there were 2,604 km of national roads, 10,823 km of arterial roads and 88,695 km of local roads, totalling 102,122 km. Lengths of road classified by surface were as follows: Sealed, 20,586 km; unsealed, 81,536 km. Costs of construction and maintenance are shared by the State and Federal governments and by the councils of the local areas. Motor vehicles registered at 30 June 1982 include 494,062 cars, 85,090 station wagons, 128,997 commercial vehicles and 36,555 cycles.

Railways. At June 1981, there were more than 5,900 km of railway, including the South Australian portion of the Transcontinental Railway from Port Pirie in South Australia to Kalgoorlie in Western Australia, which, in connexion with various State lines, completes a through rail connexion between Brisbane on the north-east coast and Fremantle on the west coast. It also includes the South Australian portion of the Australian National Railways from Tarcoola to the Northern Territory and private railways from Iron Knob to Whyalla and Coffin Bay to Port Lincoln. In June 1981 the State Transport Authority operated 141 km of railway in the metropolitan area of Adelaide.

Aviation. For the year ended 30 June 1981 there were 1,930,219 passengers and 19,157 tonnes of freight handled at Adelaide, South Australia's principal airport. On 30 June 1981 there were 8 government and 21 licensed aerodromes.

Shipping. There are several good harbours, of which Port Adelaide is the principal one. In 1980–81, 822 vessels entered South Australia with 2,684,513 import tonnes of cargo and left with 4,364,838 export tonnes.

Post and Broadcasting. At 30 June 1981, there were 645 post offices. Telephone services connected totalled 480,873 on 30 June 1981 and there were 25 radio and 13 television stations.

JUSTICE, RELIGION, EDUCATION AND WELFARE

Justice. There is a Supreme Court, which incorporates admiralty, civil, criminal, land and valuation, and testamentary jurisdiction; district criminal courts, which have jurisdiction in many indictable offences; local courts and courts of summary jurisdiction. Circuit courts are held at several places. In the year ended 30 June 1982, 1,541 cases were heard in higher courts and 185,784 cases in courts of summary jurisdiction. During the year ending 30 June 1982 there were 860 sequestrations and schemes under the Bankruptcy Act. There were 810 prisoners in custody on 1 July 1982, of whom 127 were on remand.

Religion. At the Census of 1981 the religious distribution of the population (as reported on Census schedules) was as follows: Church of England, 260,919; Roman Catholic and Catholic (so described), 255,332; Uniting Church, 108,857; Methodist, 85,935; Lutheran, 63,860; Baptist, 22,287; Presbyterian, 21,725; other Christians, 138,350; non-Christian, 7,128; indefinite, 6,529; no religion, 178,136; no reply, 135,970.

Education. Education is secular and is compulsory for children 6–15 years of age. Primary and secondary education at government schools is free. In 1981 there were 638 government schools, comprising 447 primary, 67 primary and secondary, 99 secondary schools and 25 special schools. There were 213,033 full-time students. The Department of Further Education is responsible for technical, adult and vocational education. In 1981 there were 13 metropolitan and 15 country colleges of further education, 1 college of external studies and a language and migrant education centre. Tertiary education, including teacher education, is provided by the 2 universities and 6 colleges of advanced education. There were 163 non-government schools and colleges, most of which are associated with religious denominations (43,312 students) and 491 day care and pre-school centres with a total enrolment of 29,600 pre-school children.

Social Welfare. Age, invalidity, war, etc., pensions are paid by the Federal Government. The number of pensioners in South Australia at 30 June 1981 was: Disability and service, 67,728; age, 132,578; invalid, 20,632. There are schemes for family allowances, widows, unemployment and sickness and hospital and pharmaceutical benefits.

Books of Reference

Statistical Information: The State branch of the Australian Bureau of Statistics is in City Mutual Centre, 10–20 Pulteney St., Adelaide (GPO Box 2272). *Deputy Commonwealth Statistician:* J. F. Wilson. Although the first printed statistical publication was the *Statistics of South Australia, 1854* with the title altered to *Statistical Register* in 1859, there is a written volume for each year back to 1838. These contain simple records of trade, demography, production, etc. and were prepared only for the use of the Colonial Office; one copy was retained in the State.

The publications of the State branch include the *South Australian Year Book*, the *Pocket Year Book of South Australia* and a *Monthly Summary of Statistics*, a quarterly bulletin of building activity, a quarterly bulletin of tourist accommodation and approximately 50 special bulletins issued each year as particulars of various sections of statistics become available.

South Australia: Development. Dept. of Industry and Commerce, Adelaide, 1977
Best, R. J. (ed.), *Introducing South Australia.* Cambridge, 1959
Crowley, F. K., *South Australian History: A Survey for Research Students.* Adelaide, 1965
Douglas, J., *South Australia from Space.* Adelaide, 1980
Finlayson, H. H., *The Red Centre: Man and Beast in the Heart of Australia.* 2nd ed. Sydney, 1952
Gibbs, R. M., *A History of South Australia.* Adelaide, 1969
Whitelock, D., *Adelaide, 1836–1976: A History of Difference.* Univ. of Queensland Press, 1977

State Library: The State Library of S.A., North Terrace, Adelaide. *State Librarian:* R. K. Olding, BEc., FLAA.

TASMANIA

HISTORY. Abel Janzoon Tasman discovered Van Diemen's Land (Tasmania) on 24 Nov. 1642. The island became a British settlement in 1803 as a dependency of New South Wales; in 1825 its connexion with New South Wales was terminated; in 1851 a partially elective Legislative Council was established, and in 1856 responsible government came into operation. On 1 Jan. 1901 Tasmania was federated with the other Australian states into the Commonwealth of Australia.

AREA AND POPULATION. Tasmania is an island separated from the mainland by the Bass Strait with an area (including islands) of 68,330 sq. km, or 6·83m. hectares, of which 6,441,000 hectares form the area of the main island. The population at 10 consecutive censuses was:

	Population	Increase % per annum		Population	Increase % per annum
1911	191,211	1·04	1961	350,340	1·82
1921	213,780	1·12	1966	371,436	1·18
1933	227,599	0·52	1971	398,100 [1]	0·99
1947	257,078	0·87	1976	412,300 [1]	0·70 [2]
1954	308,752	2·65	1981	427,300 [1]	0·72 [2]

[1] Resident population. [2] Not comparable with previous censuses.

The resident population (estimate) on 30 June 1981 consisted of 212,400 males and 214,900 females. At the census of 30 June 1981, 2·8% were born in the British Isles, 5·5% in other European countries and 88·7% in Australia. The last full-blooded Tasmanian Aboriginal died in 1876.

Vital statistics for calendar years:

	Marriages	Divorces	Births	Deaths	Natural increase
1978	3,148	1,131	6,788	3,311	3,477
1979	3,254	1,167	6,757	3,167	3,590
1980	3,433	1,285	6,735	3,392	3,343
1981	3,515	1,139	7,188	3,320	3,868

CONSTITUTION AND GOVERNMENT. Parliament consists of the Governor, the Legislative Council and the House of Assembly. The Council has 19 members, elected by adults with 6 months' residence. Members sit for 6 years, 3 retiring annually and 4 every sixth year. There is no power to dissolve the Council.

Vacancies are filled by by-elections. The House of Assembly has 35 members; the maximum term for the House of Assembly is 4 years. Members of both Houses are paid a basic salary of $A28,621 (1981–82), plus an electorate allowance, according to the division represented. The annual allowance payable is calculated as a percentage of basic salary. The amounts vary from $A3,148 (11%) to $A10,017 (35%). Women received the right to vote in 1903. Proportional representation was adopted in 1907, the method now being the single transferable vote in 7-member constituencies. Casual vacancies in the House of Assembly are determined by a transfer of the preference of the vacating member's ballot papers to consenting candidates who were unsuccessful at the last general election.

A Minister must have a seat in one of the two Houses; all present Ministers are members of the House of Assembly.

In addition to the salary paid to Ministers as members of either House, the following allowances are payable: Premier, in conjunction with a ministerial office, $A35,776; Deputy Premier, in conjunction with a ministerial office, $A24,328; other Ministers, $A20,034. The Leader of the Opposition in the House of Assembly receives an allowance of $A20,034. The holders of some other offices receive allowances ranging from $A1,717 to $A9,540.

An election, precipitated by the House of Assembly wanting vote of confidence in the minority Labor Government, in May 1982 resulted in the Liberal Party forming a government in its own right. The composition of the new House of Assembly was Liberal, 19 seats, Labor, 14, Australian Democrats, 1 and 1 Independent.

The Legislative Council is predominantly independent without formal party allegiance; 2 members are Labor-endorsed.

Governor: Sir James Plimsoll, CBE.

The Liberal Party Cabinet is composed as follows:

Premier, Treasurer, Minister for Energy, Racing and Gaming: R. Gray.

Deputy Premier, Attorney-General, Education, Industrial Relations, Police and Emergency Services: M. Bingham. *Tourism, National Parks and Recreational Lands, Environment, Licensing:* G. Pearsall. *Industry and Small Business, Inland Fisheries:* N. Robson. *Health, Community Welfare and the Elderly, Ethnic Affairs:* J. Cleary. *Housing, Construction, Main Roads, Local Governments, Lands:* I. Braid. *Primary Industry, Forests, Sea Fisheries, Water Resources:* J. Beswick. *Mines, Transport, Administrative Services:* R. Groom.

Local Government. For the purposes of local government, the State is divided into 49 municipal areas comprising the cities of Hobart, Launceston, Glenorchy and Devonport and 45 municipalities. The cities and municipalities are managed by elected aldermen and councillors, respectively, with reference to local matters such as sanitation and health services, domestic water supplies and roads and bridges within each particular area. The chief source of revenue is rates (based on improved values) levied on owners of property.

Tasmanian Islands. Three inhabited Tasmanian islands (Bruny, King and Flinders) are organized as municipalities. Nearly 1,600 km south-east lies Macquarie Island, part of the State, and used only as an Australian research base and meteorological station.

ECONOMY

Budget. The revenue is derived chiefly from taxation (pay-roll tax, motor, land, stamp and death duties), and from grants and reimbursements from the Federal Government. Customs, excise, sales and income tax are levied by the Federal Government, which makes grants to Tasmania for both revenue and capital purposes. Federal Government grants to Tasmania in 1981–82 totalled $A559m. These included Financial Assistance Grants, $A322m.; specific purpose payments, $A202m.; Capital Grants, $A31m.; and Health Grants, $A5m.

Specific purpose payments are mainly used to provide essential services such as housing, roads and schools, while Financial Assistance Grants have been paid since 1942 to compensate the State for the loss of income tax to the federal government.

Consolidated Revenue Fund receipts and expenditure, in $A1,000, for financial years ending 30 June:

	1976–77	*1977–78*	*1978–79*	*1979–80*	*1980–81*	*1981–82*
Revenue	396,617	444,263	495,822	560,192	620,307	683,231
Expenditure	395,033	450,706	492,961	563,917	627,441	717,628

The public debt at current exchange rates amounted to $A1,071m. at 30 June 1982.

In 1981–82 State taxation receipts amounted to $A152·5m., of which pay-roll tax provided $A56·2m.; motor vehicles, $A18·9m.; death duties, $A3·3m.; land tax, $A6·4m., and stamp duties, $A32·5m.

Banking. Trading bank activity in Tasmania is divided between 6 private banks and the Commonwealth Bank of Australia. For the month of June 1982 liabilities represented by depositors' balances averaged $A548m. and assets represented by advances, $A449m. The 9 savings banks operating in Tasmania are the Commonwealth Savings Bank, 2 trustee savings banks and 6 private savings banks operated by trading banks. At 30 June 1982 total savings bank deposits were $A759m.

ENERGY AND NATURAL RESOURCES

Electricity. Tasmania has good supplies of hydro-electric power because of assured rainfall and high level water storages (natural and artificial). The Hydro-Electric Commission, Tasmania's sole commercial supplier of electricity, has been surveying water power resources of the State for many years and it is estimated that about 3m. kw. can be economically developed. By mid-1981, 1,780,400 kw. of generating plant was in commission. In 1980–81 the peak loading was 1,225,400 kw. Two major projects are currently in progress; the Pieman River Power Development, comprising 3 stations, scheduled for completion in 1986, and the Gordon River Power Development Stage 2 (the Gordon-below-Franklin scheme) scheduled for completion in 1991.

Minerals. The assayed content of principal metallic minerals contained in locally produced concentrates for 1980–81 was (in tonnes): Zinc, 53,500; iron, 1,503,189; copper, 24,532; lead, 16,775; tin, 7,059; gold, 1,445 kg; silver, 58,337 kg. Coal production, 304,727 tonnes.

Primary Industries. The estimated gross value of recorded production from agriculture in 1980–81 was (in $A1,000): Livestock products, 100,219; livestock slaughterings and other disposals, 94,080; crops, 80,324; total gross value, 274,623. Estimated gross value of fisheries was $A26·5m.

Agriculture. The area occupied by the 6,188 holdings in 1980–81 totalled 2,220,336 hectares, of which 985,882 were devoted to crops and sown pasture. The following table shows the area and production, in tonnes, of the principal crops:

	1978–79		*1979–80*		*1980–81*	
	Hectares	*Production*	*Hectares*	*Production*	*Hectares*	*Production*
Wheat	1,366	2,867	1,972	3,727	1,614	2,545
Barley	11,938	26,971	10,558	17,304	10,056	18,307
Oats	8,564	11,826	7,489	7,955	8,781	11,146
Green peas, ex-shell	6,483	30,179	7,004	25,615	7,107	26,552
Potatoes	3,646	124,385	4,115	136,197	4,335	155,965
Hay	68,035	304,847	59,661	249,766	64,088	249,348
Hops (bearing) (dry)	578	1,457	620	1,183	672	1,558

Livestock at 31 March 1981: Sheep, 4·4m.; cattle, 658,500; pigs, 54,500.

Wool produced during 1980–81 was 20m. kg, valued at $A51m. In 1980–81 butter production was 4,234 tonnes; cheese, 13,905 tonnes.

Forestry. Indigenous forests cover a considerable part of the State, and the sawmilling industry is very important. Production of sawn timber in 1981–82 was 327,200 cu. metres. 862,600 cu. metres of logs were used for milling in 1981–82 and a further 3·1m. cu. metres were used for chipping, grinding or flaking. Newsprint and paper are produced from native hardwoods, principally eucalypts.

INDUSTRY AND TRADE

Industry. The most important manufactures for export are refined metals, newsprint and other paper manufactures, pigments, woollen goods, fruit pulp, confectionery, butter, cheese, preserved and dried vegetables, sawn timber, iron ore pellets and processed fish products. The electrolytic-zinc works at Risdon near Hobart treat large quantities of local and imported ore, and produce zinc, sulphuric acid, superphosphate, sulphate of ammonia, cadmium and other by-products. At George Town, large-scale plants produce refined aluminium and manganese alloys. During 1981–82, 3·1m. tonnes (green weight) of woodchips were produced. In 1980–81 the average employment in manufacturing establishments employing 4 or more persons was 26,528; wages and salaries (excluding proprietors drawings), $A346·6m.; turnover, $A1,867·1m.; value added, $A713·4m.; and number operating at 30 June, 558.

Labour. The Commonwealth Industrial Court (judicial powers) and Commonwealth Conciliation and Arbitration Commission (arbitral powers) have jurisdiction over federal unions, *i.e.*, with interstate membership. Most Tasmanian employees are covered by federal awards.

State Industrial Boards, established for the various trades by resolution of Parliament or proclamation of the Governor, cover most of the remaining employees. Each Board consists of a Chairman appointed by the Governor with equal representation of employers and employees. The Boards have authority over minimum rates for wages or piecework, number of working hours for which the wage is payable, conditions of apprenticeship, annual leave and adjustment of wage and piecework rates. Industrial Boards follow to a large extent the wage rates fixed by the Conciliation and Arbitration Commission.

Commerce. Trade by sea and air in $A1m. for years ending 30 June:

	1974–75	*1975–76*	*1976–77*	*1977–78*	*1978–79*
Imports	529·5	607·6	689·8	750·0	836·8
Exports	637·8	728·3	859·7	1,027·0	1,180·2

In 1978–79 exports by sea and air totalled $A1,180m.; comprising $A667m. to other Australian states and $A513m. to overseas countries. The principal countries of destination (with values in $A1m.) for overseas exports were: Japan, 163; USA, 65; Malaysia, 53; Federal Republic of Germany, 23; and Indonesia, 19. Imports totalled $A837m.; comprising $A696m. from other Australian states and $A141m. from overseas countries. The principal countries of origin (with values in $A1m.) for overseas imports were: Japan, 23; USA, 19; New Zealand, 15; Canada, 14; and UK, 12.

The main commodities by value (with values in $A1m.) exported during 1978–79 were: Ores and concentrates (iron, copper, lead, tin and tungsten), 199; refined zinc, 122; vegetables, 46; textiles, 44; and greasy wool, 39. Other main exports, for which details are not available for separate publication were woodchips, newsprint, printing and writing papers, refined aluminium, ferro-alloys and chocolate confectionery. The main imports (with values in $A1m.) were: Petroleum products, 119; ores and concentrates, 91; new motor vehicles, 87; machinery, 86; and clothing, cocoa beans and wood-pulp.

Tourism. In 1981 (estimate) 306,671 adult visitors spent at least one night in Tasmania.

COMMUNICATIONS

Roads. The total road length at 30 June 1981 was 22,489 km, consisting of a classified road system of 3,907 km maintained by the State Department of Main Roads, and the remainder maintained by local government authorities, the Forestry Commission and the Hydro-Electric Commission. Motor vehicles registered at 30 June 1982 comprised 190,000 cars, 48,800 other vehicles and 5,800 motor cycles.

Railways. There is an 851-km network of 1,067-mm gauge lines linking Hobart and Launceston with coastal and country areas, formerly operated by Tasmanian Government Railways, but since 1 July 1975 worked by the Australian National Railways Commission. A private railway of 134 km, operated by the Emu Bay Railway Co. Ltd, connects Burnie with the mining settlements on the west coast.

Aviation. Regular daily passenger and freight air services connect the south, north and north-west of the State with the mainland of Australia. In the year ending 30 June 1981 there was a total of 28,586 scheduled aircraft movements at Tasmanian airports; a total of 1,025,969 passengers and 33,548 tonnes of freight, including mail, was carried.

Shipping. In 1977–78 a total of 1,528 vessels (6,992,000 net tons), from overseas and other Australian states, arrived at ports in Tasmania. These vessels discharged 2·13m. tonnes and 1,731,000 cu. metres of cargo and shipped 5,328,000 tonnes and 1,513,000 cu. metres.

For posts and telegraphs, *see* p. 114.

JUSTICE, RELIGION, EDUCATION AND WELFARE

Justice. The Supreme Court of Tasmania, with civil, criminal, ecclesiastical, admiralty and matrimonial jurisdiction, established by Royal Charter on 13 Oct. 1823, is a superior court of record, with both original and appellate jurisdiction, and consists of a Chief Justice and 5 puisne judges. There are also inferior civil courts with limited jurisdiction, licensing courts, mining courts, courts of petty sessions and coroners' courts.

During the year 1980, 35,999 persons were summarily convicted in lower courts (23,973 for traffic offences) and 237 persons were convicted in the Supreme Court. The total police force on 30 June 1981 was 1,029. There was 1 gaol, with 262 inmates at the end of June 1981.

Religion. There is no State Church. At the census of 1981 the following numbers of adherents of the principal religions were recorded:

Anglican Church	151,207	Other religions	32,213
Roman Catholic	78,143	No religion	36,222
Methodist	19,906	Not stated [1]	64,058
Uniting Church	17,668		
Presbyterian	11,575	Total [1]	418,957
Baptist	7,965		

[1] 'As counted' Census results.

Education. Education is controlled by the State and is free, secular and compulsory between the ages of 6 and 16. At 1 July 1981 government schools had a total enrolment of 70,932 pupils, including 29,311 at secondary level; private schools had a total enrolment of 14,917 pupils, including 6,598 at secondary level.

Technical and further education is conducted at technical and community colleges in the major centres throughout the state. In 1980 there were 1,604 full-time, 14,320 part-time and 1,180 external students. Teaching staff was made up of 474 full-time and 1,481 part-time teachers.

Tertiary education is offered at the University of Tasmania in Hobart and the Tasmanian College of Advanced Education in Launceston. The University (established 1890) had (1981) 3,189 full-time and 1,893 part-time students, and 373 full-time teachers. There were 957 full-time and 1,125 part-time students at the College and a full-time teaching staff of 123.

Social Welfare. Old Age, Invalid, War Service and Widows' Pensions are paid by the Federal Government. The number of pensioners in Tasmania on 30 June 1981 was: Age, 40,000; invalid, 6,487; war (disability), 16,944; widows, 5,230. Benefit payments totalled $A185·4m. (including payments to wives).

Books of Reference

Statistical Information: The State Government Statistical Office (Commonwealth Government Centre, Hobart), established in 1877, became in 1924 the Tasmanian Office of the Australian Bureau of Statistics, but continues to serve State statistical needs as required. *Deputy Commonwealth Statistician and Government Statistician:* D. N. Allen.

Main publications: *Annual Statistical Bulletins (e.g., Demography, Agricultural Industry, Finance, Manufacturing Establishments* etc.).—*Pocket Year Book of Tasmania.* Annual (from 1913).—*Tasmanian Year Book.* Annual (from 1967).—*Monthly Summary of Statistics* (from July 1945)

Department of Planning and Development, *Tasmanian Manufacturers Directory.* Hobart. Annual.
Premier's Dept., *Tasmania–Australia.* Hobart, 1979
Angus, M., *The World of Olegas Truchanas.* Hobart, 1975
Clark, C. I., *The Parliament of Tasmania.* Hobart, 1947
Davies, J. L. (ed.), *Atlas of Tasmania.* Hobart, 1965
Green, F. C. (ed.), *A Century of Responsible Government.* Hobart, 1956
Mercury-Walch Pty. Ltd, *The Tasmanian Almanac.* Hobart. Annual
Townsley, W. A., *The Government of Tasmania.* Univ. of Queensland Press, 1976
Wettenhall, R. L., *A Guide to Tasmanian Government Administration.* Hobart, 1968

State Library: The State Library of Tasmania, Hobart. *Librarian:* W. L. Brown, FLA, ALAA.

VICTORIA

AREA AND POPULATION. The State has an area of 227,600 sq. km, and a census population of 3,948,555 at 30 June 1981.

The population (estimate) of the Melbourne Statistical Division at 30 June 1981 was 2,803,600 or 71% of the population of the State. The population of each Statistical District in Victoria was: Ballarat, 74,220; Bendigo, 60,550; Geelong, 142,080; Morwell, 17,030; Shepparton-Mooroopna, 35,960.

The census population (exclusive of full-blood aboriginals prior to 1961) was:

Date of census enumeration	*Population* Males	*Population* Females	*Population* Total	*On previous census* Numerical increase	*On previous census* Increase %
5 April 1891	598,222	541,866	1,140,088	278,522	32·33
31 March 1901	603,720	597,350	1,201,070	60,982	5·35
3 April 1911	655,591	659,960	1,315,551	114,481	9·53
4 April 1921	754,724	776,556	1,531,280	215,729	16·40
30 June 1933	903,244	917,017	1,820,261	288,981	18·87
30 June 1947	1,013,867	1,040,834	2,054,701	234,440	12·88
30 June 1954	1,231,099	1,221,242	2,452,341	397,640	19·35
30 June 1961	1,474,536	1,455,830	2,930,366	478,025	19·49
30 June 1966	1,614,240	1,605,977	3,220,217	289,851	9·89
30 June 1971	1,799,486	1,801,866	3,601,352	381,135	11·84
30 June 1976	1,900,488	1,909,398	3,810,426	209,074	5·81
30 June 1981	1,960,052	1,988,503	3,948,555	202,574	5·41

The population of urban Melbourne (capital city) on 30 June 1981 was 2,578,759. The population of urban Geelong was 125,279; urban Ballarat, 62,641; urban Bendigo, 52,741. Other urban centres: Shepparton-Mooroopna, 28,373; Warrnambool, 21,414; Moe-Yallourn, 18,159; Wangaratta, 16,202; Morwell, 16,491; Traralgon, 18,057; Mildura, 15,763; Sale, 13,968; Horsham, 12,034; Colac, 10,587; Hamilton, 9,751; Bairnsdale, 9,459; Benalla, 8,151; Portland, 9,353; Ararat, 8,336; Swan Hill, 8,398; Castlemaine, 7,583; Maryborough, 7,858; Warragul, 7,712.

Vital statistics for calendar years:

	Births	*Marriages*	*Divorces*	*Deaths*
1978	58,861	27,178	10,821	29,096
1979	57,767	27,019	9,471	29,078
1980	58,206	27,724	9,207	29,374
1981	59,521	28,648	9,769	29,044

The annual rates per 1,000 of the estimated mean population in 1981 were: Marriages, 7·25; births, 15·07; deaths, 7·35; divorces, 2·47.

CONSTITUTION AND GOVERNMENT. Victoria, formerly a portion of New South Wales, was, in 1851, proclaimed a separate colony, with a partially elective Legislative Council. In 1855 responsible government was conferred, the legislative power being vested in a parliament of two Houses, the Legislative Council and the Legislative Assembly. At present the Council consists of 44 members who are elected for 6 years, one-half retiring every third year. The Assembly consists of 81 members, elected for 3 years from the date of its first meeting unless sooner dissolved by the Governor. Members and electors of both Houses must be aged 18 years and natural born or naturalized British subjects. Women are fully enfranchised. No property qualification is required, but judges, members of the Commonwealth Parliament and undischarged bankrupts may not be members of either House. Single voting (one elector one vote) and compulsory preferential voting apply to Council and Assembly elections. Enrolment for Council and Assembly electors is compulsory. The Council may not initiate or amend money bills, but may suggest amendments in such bills other than amendments which would increase any charge. Any Minister, with the consent of the House of which he is not a member, may sit and speak in that House to explain a bill relating to the department administered by him, but may not vote in that House. A bill shall not become law unless passed by both Houses, except that, in the event of a continued disagreement between the two Houses as to a bill passed by the Assembly, other than certain constitutional bills, the Governor having dissolved the Assembly may subsequently dissolve the Council, and if the disagreement still continues he may convene a joint sitting of the members of the Council and the Assembly; if at such joint sitting the bill in dispute is passed by an absolute majority of all members it shall become law.

Private members of both Houses receive salaries of $A32,513 per annum, additional allowances rising from $A10,080 to $A14,720 (outer electorates), and a living-away-from-home allowance of $A57·15 for each day of attendance for each member (not being a responsible Minister or a metropolitan member).

Members holding the following offices receive the salaries and allowances specified: The President of the Council, $A56,898 salary and $A3,576 expense allowance; the Speaker of the Assembly, $A56,898 salary and $A3,576 expense allowance; the Chairman of Committees of the Council, $A42,917 salary and $A1,301 expense allowance; the Chairman of Committees of the Assembly, $A42,917 salary and $A1,301 expense allowance; the Leader of the Opposition in the Assembly, $A56,898 salary and $A5,852 expense allowance; the Deputy Leader of the Opposition in the Assembly, $A42,917 salary and $A1,951 expense allowance; the Leader of the Third Party, $A42,917 salary and $A1,951 expense allowance; a member of either House who is the Parliamentary Secretary of the Cabinet, $A42,917 salary and $A1,951 expense allowance; the Government Whip in the Assembly, $A38,365 salary; the Whip of any recognized Party which consists of at least 12 members of Parliament, of which Party no member is a responsible Minister, $A36,089 salary. All members have free passes over the Victorian Railways; country members are also entitled to certain allowances for air travel.

The Legislative Assembly, elected on 3 April 1982, is composed as follows: Labor Party, 49; Liberal Party, 24; National Party, 8.

Governor: Rear-Adm. Sir Brian Stewart Murray, KCMG.

In the exercise of the executive power the Governor is advised by a Cabinet of responsible Ministers. Section 50 of the Constitution Act 1975 provides that the number of responsible Ministers shall not at any one time exceed 18, of whom not more than 6 may sit in the Legislative Council. No responsible Minister may hold office for more than 3 months unless he is or becomes a member of the Council or the Assembly.

Responsible Ministers receive the following amounts: The Premier, $A65,026 salary and $A13,655 expense allowance; the Deputy Premier, $A60,149 salary and

$A6,828 expense allowance; 16 other responsible Ministers, $A56,898 salary and $A5,852 expense allowance. Each responsible Minister also receives an electorate allowance, an electorate office allowance, a residential allowance (where applicable) and, when travelling on business of the State, a travelling allowance. The President, Speaker, Chairman of Committees in the Assembly and in the Council, Parliamentary Secretary of the Cabinet, Leader and Deputy Leader of the Opposition in the Assembly, Leader of the Opposition in the Council and Leader in the Assembly of the Third Party, also receive a travelling allowance when travelling on official business. Members of Committees receive attendance fees and certain travelling expenses when on Committee duties.

The Labor Party Government (first appointed 8 April 1982) is as follows:

Premier, Attorney-General and Minister for Federal Affairs: John Cain, MP.

Deputy Premier, Minister of Education and Educational Services: R. C. Fordham, MP. *Economic Development and Tourism:* W. A. Landeryou, MLC. *Conservation and Planning:* E. H. Walker, MLC. *Housing:* I. R. Cathie, MP. *Transport:* S. M. Crabb, MP. *Treasurer, Labour and Industry:* R. A. Jolly, MP. *Agriculture:* D. E. Kent, MLC. *Forests, Lands and Soldier Settlement:* R. A. Mackenzie, MLC. *Arts, Police and Emergency Services:* C. R. T. Mathews, MP. *Health:* T. W. Roper, MP. *Employment and Training:* J. L. Simmonds, MP. *Public Works, Property and Services:* J. H. Simpson, MP. *Community Welfare Services:* P. T. Toner, MP. *Youth, Sport and Recreation:* N. B. Trezise, MP. *Minerals and Energy, Mines and Water Supply:* D. R. White, MLC. *Local Government:* F. N. Wilkes, MP. *Consumer Affairs, Immigration and Ethnic Affairs:* P. C. Spyker, MP. *Parliamentary Secretary of the Cabinet:* Dr K. A. Coghill, MP.

Agent-General in London: The Hon. J. A. Rafferty (Victoria House, Melbourne Place, Strand, London, WC28 4LG).

Local Government. With the exception of Yallourn Works area (269 sq. km) and the unincorporated areas—French Island (154 sq. km), Lady Julia Percy Island (1·3 sq. km), the Bass Strait Islands and part of Gippsland Lakes (312·8 sq. km) and Tower Hill Lake Reserve (5 sq. km), the State is divided (at 30 June 1980) into 211 municipal districts, namely 65 cities, 6 towns, 7 boroughs and 133 shires. The constitution of cities, towns, boroughs and shires is based on statutory requirements concerning population, rate revenue and net annual value of rateable property.

ECONOMY

Budget. The receipts and payments (in $A1m.) of the Consolidated Fund in the years shown (ended 30 June) were:

	1978–79	*1979–80*	*1980–81*	*1981–82*	*1982–83* [1]
Receipts	3,544	3,986	4,482	5,466	7,343
Payments	3,544	3,953	4,502	5,473	7,349

[1] Estimates.

The principal receipt items (in $A1m.) during 1980–81 were: Taxation, 2,977 (including Federal Government reimbursement, 1,355, but excluding 187 paid to special funds); railways, 252; other Federal Government payments, 327, and mining royalties, 173. The principal heads of expenditure were: Interest and public debt charges (including railways), 361; railways, 441; education, 1,294; health, hospitals and charities, 566.

The amount raised by taxation (exclusive of taxes collected by the Federal Government or paid to special funds but inclusive of the Federal Government reimbursements under the uniform taxation scheme), as shown in the above paragraph, was approximately $A776.86 per head of population.

The public debt of Victoria (in $A1m.) on 30 June 1980 was 4,582. During the year ending 30 June 1981, an amount of 436 was expended on capital works. Of this amount, 149 was spent on education, 54 on railways, 31 on water supply, irrigation and drainage, 5 on protection of the environment (including sewerage), 17 on forestry, 60 on health services, 6 on agricultural, pastoral, etc., services, 43 on culture and recreation, 16 on law, order and public safety, 11 on legislature and general administration, 7 on development and decentralization, and 37 on all other purposes. In addition to the public debt noted above, Victoria had other liabilities due to the Federal Government at 30 June 1981. These included 1,111·6 advances for housing, 11·1 special assistance loans for soldier settlement, 73·2 advance for sewerage, 63·6 for rural and dairy reconstruction, 98·6 for growth centres and 44 for land acquisition.

Banking. On 30 June 1982 there were 7·7m. operative accounts (excluding school bank accounts) in savings banks in Victoria. The total credit due to depositors amounted to $A9,474·9m., made up of State Savings Bank, $A4,780·8m.; Commonwealth Savings Bank, $A1,879·3m.; private savings banks, $A2,814·8m.

The weekly average of deposits and advances of trading banks operating in Victoria during June 1982 were as follows: Deposits, not bearing interest, $A2,485·9m.; deposits, bearing interest, $A5,287·8m.; total deposits, $A7,773·7m.; loans, advances, and bills discounted, $A5,387·3m. The weekly average of debits to customers' accounts (excluding debits to Federal and State Government accounts at City branches in State capitals) for the same period totalled $A13,027·4m.

ENERGY AND NATURAL RESOURCES

Electricity. All electricity in this State for public supply is generated by the largest electricity supply authority in Australia—the State Electricity Commission of Victoria. Its supply network serves over 99% of the entire Victorian population and some New South Wales municipalities as well as irrigation settlements bordering the Murray River.

The major base load generating stations are located in the Latrobe Valley on top of a large brown coal field with estimated geological resources of 107,847m. tonnes. Burning raw brown coal on site and with an installed generating capacity of 2,991,000 kw., these stations produce over 80% of Victoria's electricity. The chief one is Hazelwood, which was completed in 1971 with a capacity of 1·6m. kw. The total installed generating capacity of all thermal stations in Victoria is 4,282,000 kw. including the base load stations in the Latrobe Valley and smaller ones in Melbourne, and some provincial cities.

The total installed capacity of the Commission's system at 30 June 1980 was 5·79m. kw.; it includes Victoria's share of about one-third (1,084,000 kw. at 30 June 1981) of the Snowy Mountains hydro-electric scheme in New South Wales and its half share (25,000 kw.) of the Hume hydro-electric station, shared with New South Wales. Excluding the Snowy and Hume schemes in New South Wales the installed hydro-electric capacity totalled 469,000 kw. at 30 June 1981, with Kiewa (3 stations totalling 184,000 kw.) being the chief undertaking.

Total power generated and purchased in 1980–81 was 23,255 gwh.

Oil and Natural Gas. Crude oil in commercially recoverable quantities was first discovered by the Esso/BHP partnership in 1967 in 2 large fields offshore in East Gippsland in Bass Strait between 65 and 80 km from land. These fields, Halibut and Kingfish, with 10 other fields since discovered—Marlin, Snapper, Barracouta, Mackerel, Tuna, Cobia, Flounder, Fortescue, Bream and Seahorse have been assessed as containing initial recoverable reserves of more than 2,930m. bbls of treated crude oil. Total production since 1969 from the producing fields to the end of Sept. 1980 has amounted to 1,288m. bbls, leaving a balance of recoverable reserves of 1,642m. bbls.

Gippsland crude now supplies approximately 71% of Australia's refinery requirements, and during 1980 a total of 129m. bbls were produced. Depletion of production from the 2 major fields, Kingfish and Halibut and the smaller Barracouta field, is now expected to occur in the late-1980s.

Natural gas was discovered offshore in East Gippsland in 1965. The initial recoverable reserves of treated gas are 7,783,000m. cu. ft. Reserves are sufficient for 30 years. Following an extensive development and distribution programme, natural gas was first connected to homes and industry in Victoria in April 1969. All gas consumers in Melbourne, Geelong, Ballarat, Bendigo, Shepparton, Euroa, Benalla, Wangaratta, Wodonga, Albury and a number of towns near Melbourne, in the Latrobe Valley and in East Gippsland, are now using natural gas. At 30 June 1981 a total of 872,786 consumers were being supplied with it. During the period 1 July 1979 to 30 June 1980 a total volume of 4,262m. cu. metres of gas was consumed in Victoria, including commercial sales and plant usage.

Natural gas and crude oil are conveyed from the producing fields to a large treatment plant at Longford in East Gippsland from where both hydrocarbons are distributed by a network of transmission lines to tank farms and city gate distribution points.

The crude oil is then distributed to refineries in Victoria by pipeline and to other States by seagoing tankers. Natural gas is distributed to residential and industrial consumers through a network of approximately 18,600 km of mains.

Liquefied petroleum gas is now being produced after extraction of the propane and butane fractions from the untreated oil and gas. For the year ended June 1981, approximately 1·8m. tonnes was exported by Esso and BHP, mainly to Japan.

Brown Coal. Major deposits of brown coal are located in the Central Gippsland region and comprise approximately 94% of the total resources in Victoria. In the Latrobe Valley section of this region the thick brown coal seams underlie an area from 10–30 km wide and extend over a length of approximately 70 km from Yallourn in the west to the south of Sale in the east. Small fields have also been found at Stradbroke in the ranges on the southern flank of the Valley and in the Gelliondale–Welshpool area near the coast. On a geological basis the brown coal resources in Central Gippsland are estimated to be in the order of 108,000 megatonnes, of which about 65,000 megatonnes are proven and the remaining 43,000 megatonnes are inferred.

About 54% of the resources occur in areas where the overburden over the uppermost seam is less than 30·5 metres while 95% is in areas with less than 91·4 metres of overburden. The current primary use of these reserves is to fuel the major base load electricity generating stations located at Morwell and Yallourn, and larger cuts have been opened for this purpose at these localities.

Land Settlement. Of the total area of Victoria (22·76m. hectares), 14,029,892 hectares on 30 June 1981 were either alienated or in process of alienation. The remainder (8,730,108) constituted Crown land as follows: Perpetual leases, grazing and other leases and licences, 2,311,649; reservations including forest and timber reserves, water, catchment and drainage purposes, national parks, wildlife reserves, water frontages and other reserves, plus unoccupied and unreserved including areas set aside for roads, 6,418,459. Rural establishments at 31 March 1981 numbered 49,958.

Agriculture. The following table shows the area under the principal crops and the produce of each for 3 seasons (in 1,000 units):

	Total crop area	*Wheat*		*Oats*		*Barley*		*Potatoes*		*Hay*	
Season	*Hectares*	*Hectares*	*Tonnes*	*Hectares*	*Tonnes*	*Hectares*	*Tonnes*	*Hectares*	*Tonnes*	*Hectares*	*Tonnes*
1978–79	2,215	1,337	2,998	291	446	365	519	11	280	510	2,012
1979–80	2,247	1,457	3,250	256	390	325	494	13	334	412	1,615
1980–81	2,184	1,431	2,538	219	322	303	418	13	349	496	1,893

In 1980–81 there were 20,756 hectares of vines, yielding 65,076 tonnes of grapes for wine-making and 196,927 tonnes of grapes for drying or for table use. Green fodder covered 65,468 hectares, and orchards and vegetables, including potatoes and onions, occupied 47,017 hectares.

At March 1981 there were in the State 4·3m. head of cattle, 25,486,993 sheep and 400,179 pigs. In 1980–81, 637,178 tonnes of fresh meat was produced. The wool produced in the season 1980–81 amounted to 149m. kg, valued at $A334m. The quantity of butter produced in 1980–81 was 67·8m. kg.

The gross value of Victorian primary production in (rural and non-rural) 1980–81 was $A2,740m.

Minerals. The recorded production of certain metals and minerals raised in Victoria for the year 1980–81 was: Gold, 62,000 grammes, value $A829,000; coal, brown, 32·1m. tonnes, value $A107·1m.

INDUSTRY AND TRADE

Industry. From the 1975–76 Census of Manufacturing Establishments onwards only a limited range of data—employment and wages and salaries—has been collected from single-establishment manufacturing enterprises with less than 4 persons employed. This procedure significantly reduces the statistical reporting obligations of small businesses. Data in respect of the larger manufacturers provides reliable information for the evaluation of trends in the manufacturing sector of the economy. From the 1977–78 census, the classification of census units to industry is based on the 1978 edition of the Australian Standard Industrial Classification. The following data relates to manufacturing establishments owned by multi-establishment enterprises, and single-establishment manufacturing enterprises with 4 or more persons employed.

The total number of manufacturing establishments in Victoria in 1980–81 (figures for 1979–80 in brackets) was 8,726 (8,902). Persons employed, including working proprietors, on the last pay day in June were males 277,744 (281,959) and females 113,745 (115,354). Salaries and wages paid were $A5,032m. ($A4,563m.), excluding drawings of working proprietors. The cost of purchases, transfers in, and selected expenses was $A14,814m. ($A13,353m.) and sales, transfers out and other operating revenue were $A23,856m. ($A21,233m.).

The preceding figures exclude gas and electricity producing and distributing establishments. In terms of persons employed the most important manufacturing activities were: Basic and fabricated metal products including transport equipment, other machinery and equipment, 160,265 (165,455); textiles, clothing and footwear, 63,325 (64,436); food, beverages and tobacco, 55,349 (54,477).

Trade Unions. There were 173 trade unions with a total membership of 771,700 operating in Victoria in Dec. 1981.

Commerce. The commerce of Victoria, exclusive of inter-state trade, is included in the statement of the commerce of Australia, *see* pp. 110–12.

The total value of the overseas imports and exports of Victoria, including bullion and specie but excluding inter-state trade, was as follows (in $A1,000):

	1976–77	*1977–78*	*1978–79*	*1979–80*	*1980–81*	*1981–82*[1]
Imports	3,665,914	3,855,619	4,694,481	5,506,400	5,929,278	7,169,661
Exports	2,216,237	2,505,768	2,702,452	3,782,993	3,993,482	3,899,387

[1] Preliminary.

The chief exports[1] in 1981–82 were: Cereals and cereal preparations, petroleum products and gases, vegetables and fruit, dairy products, meat, textile fibres and their wastes and road vehicles.

[1] From 1 July 1978 state export figures changed from 'State of Lodgement of documents with the Bureau of Customs' to 'State of Origin'.

COMMUNICATIONS

Roads. At 30 June 1981 there were 158,075 km of road open for general traffic consisting of 63,196 km of bituminous seal, etc., 48,197 km of waterbound macadam, gravel, etc., 24,183 km formed, but not paved, and 22,499 km not formed. The number of registered motor vehicles (other than tractors) at 30 June 1981 was 2,035,900.

Railways. All the railways are the property of the State and are under the management of a 9-member governing board, appointed by, and responsible to, the Victorian Government.

At 30 June 1981, 6,184 km of government railway were open. During the year

1980–81 the gross revenue amounted to $A256,258,700 and the total working expenses to $A448,278,345. 88,538,076 (estimate) passengers, 12,616,183 tonnes of freight and 104,597 tonnes of livestock were carried.

Aviation. During the year ended 31 Dec. 1981 there were 76,218 aircraft movements at Melbourne (Tullamarine) airport. Passengers totalled 5m. on domestic flights (international, 955,784). Freight handled, 74,377 tonnes, domestic flights (35,189 international).

JUSTICE, RELIGION, EDUCATION AND WELFARE

Justice. There is a Supreme Court with a Chief Justice and 20 puisne judges. There are magistrates' courts, county courts, a court of licensing, and a bankruptcy court.

Criminal statistics for 1978: 378,054 convictions (in addition approximately for 209,349 driving and traffic offences) in magistrates' courts; 1,210 convicted persons in higher (judges') courts.

There are 11 gaols in Victoria. At 30 June 1981 there were confined in these prisons, 1,841 persons.

Religion. There is no State Church in Victoria, and no State assistance has been given to religion since 1875. At the date of the 1981 census the following were the enumerated numbers of each of the principal religions: Catholic,[1] 524,612; Church of England, 371,873; Uniting, 97,611; Orthodox, 87,119; Presbyterian, 83,223; Protestant (undefined), 46,403; Methodist, 43,030; other Christian, 34,361; Moslem, 15,666; Hebrew, 14,668; no religion, 258,249; no reply, 231,821.

[1] So described on individual census schedules.

Education. Education establishments in Victoria consist of 4 universities, established under special Acts and opened in 1855, 1961, 1967 and 1977; Colleges of Advanced Education; government schools (primary, primary-secondary, high and secondary technical, and further education colleges), and non-government schools.

The University of Melbourne, founded in 1853, had, in 1980, 16,214 students (including 6,420 females) and 1,489 teaching and research staff.

Monash University, founded in 1958 in an eastern suburb of Melbourne, had, in 1980, 14,096 students (including 6,066 females) and 1,148 teaching and research staff.

La Trobe University, founded in 1964 in a northern suburb of Melbourne, had 8,770 students (including 4,297 females) and 552 teaching and research staff in 1980.

Deakin University (1974) near Melbourne had 4,799 students and 251 staff in 1980.

Primary education of children of the ages of 6 to 15 years inclusive is free, secular and compulsory. At 1 July 1980 there were 1,676 government primary schools and 70 special schools with 19,472 full-time and 711 part-time teachers and an enrolment of 370,089 pupils; 20 government primary-secondary schools had 508 full-time and 65 part-time teachers and an enrolment of 6,875 pupils. There were also 392 government secondary schools, including junior technical schools and high schools with 18,440 full-time and 3,104 part-time teachers and an enrolment of 229,183 pupils. In 1980 there were 196,719 students enrolled in technical and further education schools and colleges.

Non-government Schools. There were at 1 July 1980, 633 non-government schools, excluding commercial colleges, with 10,706 full-time and 2,328 part-time teachers and 216,125 pupils enrolled. Of these schools, 490 were Roman Catholic.

Social Services. Victoria was the first State of Australia to make a statutory provision for the payment of Age Pensions. The Act providing for the payment of such pensions came into operation on 18 Jan. 1901, and continued until 1 July 1909, when the Australian Invalid and Old Age Pension Act came into force. The Social Services Consolidation Act, which came into operation on 1 July 1947, repealed the various legislative enactments relating to age (previously old-age) and invalid pensions, maternity allowances, child endowment, and unemployment, and sickness benefits and while following in general the Acts repealed, considerably liberalized many of their provisions: it has since been amended. On 30 June 1981 there were 369,767 aged and 73,080 invalid pensioners in Victoria, and the amount paid in pensions, including payments to wives of invalid pensioners, during 1980–81 was $A1,259·5m.

The number of disability pensions (members of the forces and their dependants) payable in Victoria on 30 June 1981 was 105,576, and the number of service pensions was 59,252. The amount paid in war and service pensions by the Federal Government during 1980–81 was $A291·8m.

Under the Australian Unemployment and Sickness Benefit Act 1944, there were 87,109 persons receiving benefits at June 1981 (excluding migrants in accommodation centres) and the amount paid in benefits totalled $A293·9m. in the year ended 30 June 1981.

The number of widows' pensions in force in Victoria at 30 June 1981 was 45,663, and the total amount paid in allowances during the year was $A172·1m.

The number of family allowances in force in Victoria at 30 June 1981 was 1,141,803 (including students). In addition (in 1981), endowment was being paid in respect of 2,541 children who were being maintained in approved institutions. The total amount paid in endowment in Victoria during the year ended 30 June 1981 was $A258·4m.

State Housing. The various State housing authorities were consolidated under the control of the Ministry of Housing early in 1973. The authorities include the Housing Commission, the Government Employee Housing Authority and the Co-operative Housing Registry. The Co-operative Housing Registry administers distribution of finance to the co-operative building societies from loan moneys advanced by the Federal Government.

On the coming into operation of amending legislation on 24 Jan. 1979, the Housing Commission, as it was constituted, ceased to exist and was replaced by a Commission consisting of a full-time Chairman and 3 part-time members. The Director of Housing (the Permanent Head of the Ministry of Housing) is, *ex officio*, Chairman of the Commission. The Housing Advisory Council was also created under that legislation, its functions being to advise on and investigate matters affecting housing and to consult with all sections of the housing industry. The Council consists of the Director and 6 part-time members appointed by the Minister of Housing.

Since its inception in 1938, the Housing Commission had built and purchased, to 30 June 1982, 93,437 housing units, of which 50,604 had been sold. Approximately 40% of all construction since 1938 is located outside the Melbourne metropolitan area.

Rental charges for the year ended 30 June 1981 were $A82,322,250, against which $A17,027,592 was allowed in rent rebates to tenants on low incomes, including pensioners.

Books of Reference

Statistical Information: Australian Bureau of Statistics (Commonwealth Banks Building, corner of Elizabeth and Flinders Streets, Melbourne, 3000). *Deputy Commonwealth Statistician:* I. M. Cowie, B.Com.

Victorian Year Book. (Annually since 1873)
Victorian Pocket Year Book. (Annually since 1956)
Victorian Statistical Register. (Annually from 1854 to 1916)
Monthly Summary of Statistics (from Jan. 1960)

Victoria: The First Century. Official History of Victoria. Melbourne, 1934
Victorian Municipal Directory. Melbourne, (From 1866). Melbourne, Arnall and Jackson
Grant, J., and Serle, G., *The Melbourne Scene 1803–1956.* Melbourne Univ. Press, 1956
Pratt, A., *The Centenary History of Victoria.* Melbourne, 1934

State Library: The State Library of Victoria, 328 Swanston St., Melbourne, 3000. *State Librarian:* W. Horton, BA, ALAA.

WESTERN AUSTRALIA

HISTORY. In 1791 Vancouver, in the *Discovery*, took formal possession of the country about King George Sound. In 1826 the Government of New South Wales sent 20 convicts and a detachment of soldiers to King George Sound and formed a settlement then called Frederickstown. In 1827 Captain (afterwards Sir) James Stirling surveyed the coast from King George Sound to the Swan River, and in May 1829 Captain (afterwards Sir) Charles Fremantle took possession of the territory. In June 1829 Captain Stirling, newly appointed Lieut.-Governor, founded the colony now known as the State of Western Australia. On 1 Jan. 1901 Western Australia became one of the 6 federated States within the Commonwealth of Australia.

AREA AND POPULATION. Western Australia lies between 113° 09′ and 129° E. long. and 13° 44′ and 35° 08′ S. lat.; its area is 2,525,500 sq. km.

The population at each census from 1933 was as follows [1]:

	Males	*Females*	*Total*		*Males*	*Females*	*Total*
1933	233,937	204,915	438,852	1966	432,569	415,531	848,100
1947	258,076	244,404	502,480	1971	534,100	509,000	1,043,100
1954	330,358	309,413	639,771	1976	596,800	573,100	1,169,800
1961	375,452	361,177	736,629	1981	656,400	642,700	1,299,100

[1] 1961 and earlier exclude full-blood Aboriginals; from 1966 figures refer to total population (*i.e.*, including Aboriginals).

Of the census population in 1981, 910,666 were born in Australia. Married persons numbered 585,465 (285,224 males and 283,241 females); widowers, 10,088; widows, 45,465; divorced, 16,180 males and 19,171 females; never married, 318,273 males and 267,761 females. The number of males under 21 was 240,210 and of females 228,155.

Perth, the capital, had an estimated population of 918,000 at June 1981. Of this, the area administered by the City of Perth had a population of 80,960 while the population in the area for which the City of Fremantle is responsible (which includes the chief port of the State) was 23,780.

Principal urban centres outside the metropolitan area, with population at the census of 30 June 1981: Bunbury, 21,749; Geraldton, 20,895; Kalgoorlie–Boulder, 19,848; Albany, 15,222; Port Hedland, 12,948; Mandurah, 10,978; Collie, 7,667; Northam, 6,791; Busselton, 6,463; Esperance, 6,375; Carnarvon, 5,053; Narrogin, 4,969.

Vital statistics for calendar years [1]:

	Births	*Ex-nuptial births*	*Marriages*	*Divorces*	*Deaths*
1979	20,469	2,783	9,239	3,397	8,020
1980	20,607	2,833	9,594	3,073	8,166
1981	21,877	3,300	10,111	3,481	7,993

[1] Including Aboriginals.

CONSTITUTION AND GOVERNMENT. In 1870 partially representative government was instituted, and in 1890 the administration was vested in the Governor, a Legislative Council and a Legislative Assembly. The Legislative Council was, in the first instance, nominated by the Governor, but it was provided that in the event of the population of the colony reaching 60,000, it should be elective. In 1893 this limit of population being reached, the Colonial Parliament amended the Constitution accordingly.

The Legislative Council consists of 32 members, 2 members representing each of the 16 electoral provinces. Each member is elected for a term of 6 years, one-half of the members retiring every 3 years.

There are 55 members of the Legislative Assembly, each member representing one of the 55 electoral districts of the State. Members are elected for the duration of the Parliament, normally 3 years. The qualifications applying to candidates and electors are identical for the Legislative Council and the Legislative Assembly. A candidate must have resided in Western Australia for a minimum of 12 months, be at least 18 years of age and free from legal incapacity, be a British subject, and be enrolled, or qualified for enrolment, as an elector. A judge of the Supreme Court, the Sheriff of Western Australia, an undischarged bankrupt or a debtor against whose estate there is a subsisting order in bankruptcy may not be elected to Parliament. No person may hold office as a member of the Legislative Assembly and the Legislative Council at the same time. An elector must be at least 18 years of age, be a British subject free from legal incapacity, must have resided in the Commonwealth of Australia for 6 and in Western Australia for 3 months continuously and in the electoral district for which he claims enrolment for a continuous period of 1 month immediately preceding the date of his claim. Enrolment is compulsory for all qualified persons except Aboriginal natives of Australia, who are entitled but not required to enrol. Voting at elections is on the preferential system and is compulsory for all enrolled persons.

Ordinary members of the legislature are paid a salary of $A31,935 a year, with an additional electorate allowance, ranging from $A9,000 to $A20,650 according to location of electorate. Members are entitled to free travel on Western Australian government railways and on the Metropolitan (Perth) Passenger Transport Trust omnibus and ferry services, and, by arrangement, once every year on government railways in other States. All members of Parliament contribute to superannuation benefits.

The Premier receives a salary, including an electorate allowance, of $A76,135, the Deputy Premier $A69,480, the Leader of the Government in the Legislative Council $A65,405, and all other Ministers $A60,830—70,230 according to location of electorate.

The Legislative Assembly, elected on 23 Feb. 1980, is composed as follows: Liberal Party, 26; Australian Labor Party, 23; National Country Party, 4; National Party, 2. The Legislative Council, one-half of which was elected on the same day, is composed of 18 Liberal Party, 10 Australian Labor Party, 3 National Country Party, 1 National Party.

Governor: Rear-Admiral Sir Richard Trowbridge, KCVO, KStJ.

The Liberal-National Country Party coalition Cabinet was, at 16 Aug. 1982:

Premier, Treasurer, and Minister Co-ordinating Economic and Regional Development: Hon. Raymond James O'Connor, MLA.

Deputy Premier, Minister for Transport, and Emergency Services: Hon. Edgar Cyril Rushton, MLA. *Minister for Primary Industry and Agriculture, and Fisheries and Wildlife:* Hon. Richard Charles Old, MLA. *Attorney-General, Minister for Federal Affairs, and Leader of the Government in the Legislative Council:* Hon. Ian George Medcalf, ED, QC, MLC. *Minister for Works, Water Resources, and Minister Assisting the Minister Co-ordinating Economic and Regional Development:* Hon. Andrew Mensaros, MLA. *Minister for Resources Development, Mines, and Fuel and Energy:* Hon. Peter Vernon Jones, MLA. *Minister for Health:* Hon. Raymond Laurence Young, FCA, MLA. *Minister for Police and Prisons, and Minister Assisting the Minister for Emergency Services:* Hon. William Ralph Boucher Hassell, LLB, MA, MLA. *Minister for Labour and Industry, and Immigration:* Hon. Gordon Edgar Masters, MLC. *Minister for Local Government, and Urban Development and Town Planning:* Hon. Margaret June Craig, MLA. *Minister for Lands, Forests, and Conservation and the Environment:* Hon. Ian James Laurance, BA, MLA. *Minister for Industrial, Commercial and Regional Development, the North West, and Tourism:* Hon. Barry John MacKinnon, BEc, AASA, MLA. *Chief Secretary, Minister for Cultural Affairs, and Recreation:* Hon. Robert Gerald Pike, MLC. *Minister for Education:* Hon. James George Clarko, AE, BA, Dip Ed, MACE, JP, MLA. *Minister for Community Welfare, Housing, and Consumer Affairs:* Hon. Richard Steel Shalders, MLA.

Agent-General in London: R. Douglas (Western Australia House, 115 Strand, WC2R 0AJ).

Local Government. The only unincorporated area in mainland Western Australia is King's Park, a public reserve of about 403 hectares in Perth. Including the lord-mayoralty of Perth there were 12 cities, 12 towns and 114 shires at 30 June 1981. The executive body in each of these districts is normally an elective council, presided over by a mayor (city and town) or a president (shire), but in certain circumstances it may be a commissioner appointed by the Governor. Their functions include road construction and repair, the provision of parks and recreation grounds, the administration of building controls and local services such as health and, in some country districts, traffic. Finance is derived largely from rates levied on property owners as well as charges for services and government grants (mainly for road construction).

ECONOMY

Budget. The revenue and expenditure (in $A) of Western Australia in years ended 30 June, are given as follows:

	1980	*1981*	*1982*	*1983* [1]
Revenue	1,641,191,281	1,860,548,032	2,061,893,781	2,335,500,000
Expenditure	1,641,191,281	1,862,006,834	2,061,893,781	2,335,500,000

[1] Estimates.

Main items of revenue in 1981–82: Railways ($A196,318,202), taxation ($A431,732,812), lands, timber and mining ($A109,709,620), public utilities other than railways ($A47,505,059), from Federal funds ($A1,038,687,825). Western Australia had a net loan liability of $A1,485,788,284 on 30 June 1982, the charge for the year being $A155,873,845.

Banking. There are 10 trading banks in Western Australia including the Commonwealth Trading Bank and The Rural and Industries Bank of Western Australia. In the June quarter, 1982, the average of customers' balances was $A2,725·6m. and average advances $A2,446·9m.

At 30 June 1982, the 8 savings banks held deposits of $A1,514·2m., in 1,741,114 accounts.

ENERGY AND NATURAL RESOURCES

Minerals. The mining industry has been for many years of considerable significance in the Western Australian economy. Until the mid-1960s the major mineral produced was gold. However, in recent years gold has been displaced by iron ore and nickel concentrates in terms of value.

The total ex-mine value of minerals from mining and quarrying in the State in 1980–81 was $A1,857·8m. Principal minerals produced in 1980–81 were: Iron ore and pellets, 89m. tonnes, value $A953·8m.; crude oil, 1·53m. cu. metres, value $A124·7m.; gold bullion, 12·4m. grammes, value $A161·5m.; construction materials (excluding sand and gravel), value $A32·6m.; mineral sands, 1·62m. tonnes, value, $A84·4m.; black coal, 3·13m. tonnes, value $A63·1m.; salt, 5·74m. tonnes, value $A57·5m.; tin concentrates, 730 tonnes, value $A6·84m.; nickel concentrates, 403,943 tonnes; bauxite, 12·2m. tonnes, and natural gas, 883m. cu. metres, value $A28·1m.

Land Settlement. Up to 31 Dec. 1980, of the entire area of the State (252·55m. hectares) 16,807,226 hectares had been alienated; on that date 2,150,947 hectares were in process of alienation; the area alienated and in process of alienation thus amounting to 18,958,173 hectares. There were in force leases comprising an area of 98,138,655 hectares, of which 95,066,304 hectares were pastoral, 832,970 hectares were timber, 131,369 hectares mining leases, 10,932 hectares miners' homestead leases and 2,097,080 hectares for reserves, residential lots, special and perpetual leases.

Agriculture.

Crop	1979–80 Area Hectares	1979–80 Production Tonnes	1980–81 Area Hectares	1980–81 Production Tonnes
Wheat	4,120,784	3,739,139	4,333,144	3,315,248
Oats	369,553	399,272	381,971	383,570
Barley	522,855	631,644	534,757	504,019
Hay	207,694	636,425	240,231	702,747
Potatoes	2,039	66,184	1,920	64,308
Cauliflower	510	11,241	555	13,110

Crop	1979–80 No. Trees Bearing	1979–80 Production Cases	1980–81 No. Trees Bearing	1980–81 Production Cases
Apples	749,029	2,831,637	721,327	2,692,487
Pears	70,321	281,613	70,814	279,617
Oranges	209,558	369,556	196,700	331,938

Irrigation has been established by the Government along the south-western coastal plain and in the north of the State. Reservoirs with an aggregate capacity of 6,137m. cu. metres provided irrigation water for 24,392 hectares in 6 districts during 1980–81.

The livestock at 31 March 1981 consisted of 2,033,770 cattle, 30,763,684 sheep and 289,395 pigs.

The wool clip in 1980–81 was 159,317 tonnes; the overseas exports for 1980–81, greasy wool, 115,542 tonnes; degreased wool, 19,987 tonnes.

Forestry. The area of State forests and timber reserves at 31 Dec. 1980 was 2,231,449 hectares; 1980–81 production of sawn timber was 353,817 cu. metres, principally Jarrah and Karri hardwoods.

Fisheries. The catch of fish, crustaceans and molluscs in Western Australia in 1980–81 totalled 26,288 tonnes for a gross value of $A82·8m. Of this, rock lobsters, with a total catch of 9,956 tonnes accounted for $A57·2m.

Value of Agricultural Commodities Produced. The estimated gross value of Western Australian agricultural commodities during 1980–81 was as follows: Crops and pastures, $A778·25m.; livestock slaughterings and other disposals, $A422·84m.; livestock products, $A485·49m.

INDUSTRY AND TRADE

Industry. Up to the early 1950s most of the factories in Western Australia were small and medium sized establishments supplying the local market and carrying out some processing of the State's primary products for export. Development of heavy industry and large-scale operations since the early 1950s has been associated with the establishment of a large oil refinery at Kwinana in 1954 which provided the basis for an integrated industrial complex adjacent to Perth; more recent developments have been associated with the processing of the State's vast deposits of iron ore, nickel, bauxite and mineral sands.

The following table shows manufacturing industry statistics for 1980–81 [1]:

Industry sub-division	*Number of establishments operating at 30 June*	*Persons employed* [2]	*Wages and salaries $A1,000*	*Turnover $A1,000*	*Value added $A1,000*
Food, beverages and tobacco	334	12,237	146,146	1,075,259	305,535
Textiles	29	757	9,357	42,231	14,342
Clothing and footwear	61	1,525	12,661	32,159	17,736
Wood, wood products and furniture	444	7,749	79,474	327,035	155,637
Paper, paper products, printing and publishing	197	6,454	79,254	252,816	133,560
Chemical, petroleum and coal products	72	3,139	51,894	378,721	139,268
Non-metallic mineral products	216	4,987	67,855	332,736	146,709
Basic metal products	33	6,181	107,788	1,203,499	421,567
Fabricated metal products	425	9,327	110,530	493,664	193,788
Transport equipment	162	5,727	69,669	194,588	96,444
Other machinery and equipment	283	8,290	107,040	432,856	194,677
Miscellaneous manufacturing	170	2,497	27,554	136,674	57,399
Total	2,426	68,870	869,223	4,902,236	1,876,664

[1] Excludes single establishment enterprises with less than 4 persons employed.
[2] Annual average. Includes working proprietors.

Labour. A Court of Arbitration was established in Western Australia in 1901 under the provisions of the 'Industrial Conciliation and Arbitration Act 1900'. The Court of Arbitration was replaced, with effect from 1 Feb. 1964, by the Western Australian Industrial Appeal Court and The Western Australian Industrial Commission, authorities constituted in terms of the *Industrial Arbitration Act 1912–1977*. These authorities continue to operate under the provisions of the *Industrial Arbitration Act 1979–81*.

The Western Australian Industrial Appeal Court consists of 3 Judges, one of whom is the Presiding Judge. The members are nominated by the Chief Justice of Western Australia. An appeal lies to the Court from decisions of the President of the Western Australian Industrial Commission, the Full Bench or the Commission in Court Session but only on the ground that the decision is erroneous in law or is in excess of jurisdiction.

The Western Australian Industrial Commission consists of a President, a Chief Industrial Commissioner, a Senior Commissioner, and 'such number of other Commissioners as may, from time to time, be necessary'. There were 5 'other Commissioners' at 1 March 1982. A person shall not be appointed as President unless he is qualified to be a Judge, and on appointment he is entitled to the status of a Puisne Judge. The President or a Commissioner sitting or acting alone constitutes the Commission and may exercise the appropriate powers of the Commission.

The Commission can inquire into any industrial matter and make an award, order or declaration relating to such matter. 'Industrial matter' means any matter affecting or relating to the work, privileges, rights, or duties of employers or employees in any industry and includes any matter relating to the wages, salaries, allowances, or other remuneration of employees or the prices to be paid in respect of their employment; the hours of employment, sex, age, qualification or status of employees and the mode, terms and conditions of employment including conditions which are to take effect after the termination of employment. The Commission may also make inquiries where industrial action has occurred or is likely to occur.

The Commission in Court Session is constituted by not less than 3 Commissioners sitting or acting together, and may make General Orders, hear matters referred by the Commission, and hear appeals from decisions of Boards of Reference.

The Full Bench is constituted by not less than 3 members of the Commission, 1 of whom is the President, and may hear matters referred by the Commission on questions of law, and appeals from decisions of the Commission and Industrial Magistrates.

The following table shows details of the number of industrial awards, unions and members registered with The Western Australian Industrial Commission.

At 30 June	*1978*	*1979*	*1980*	*1981*	*1982*
Awards in force	393	355	494	459	483
Consent agreements in force [1]	205	135	... [2]	... [2]	... [2]
Unions of workers:					
Number	77	77	74	68	69
Membership	184,578	192,056	181,409	170,414	171,912
Unions of employers:					
Number	15	14	14	14	14
Membership	2,156	2,102	2,040	2,139	2,142

[1] Named as 'Industrial agreements' prior to 1980. [2] Included in 'Awards in force'.

Commerce. The external commerce of Western Australia, exclusive of interstate trade, is comprised in the statement of the commerce of Australia, *see* pp. 110–12.

The total value of the imports and exports, including interstate trade, but excluding interstate value of horses, in 5 years (30 June) is, in $A, as follows:

	1976–77	*1977–78*	*1978–79*	*1979–80*	*1980–81*
Imports	2,470,955,480	2,765,860,023	3,205,610,959	3,787,501,582	4,504,299,867
Exports[1]	2,901,942,796	2,944,104,696	3,266,342,542	4,489,434,258	4,604,110,266

[1] Excluding ships' stores.

Selected overseas exports (in $A) for 1980–81 (excluding ships' stores): Iron ore, 1,069,086,589; wheat, 422,442,739; wool, 398,467,478; transport equipment, 160,513,154; live sheep and lambs, 100,339,684; petroleum and petroleum products, 89,857,237; beef and veal, 87,668,549; mutton and lamb, 57,515,100; barley, 45,675,376; salt, 44,575,832; rock lobster tails, 42,479,503; iron and steel, 42,423,264; machinery, 37,295,506; gold, 31,340,196; ilmenite and leucoxene, 23,725,639; rutile, 22,568,861; rock lobster, whole, 19,563,024; zirconium, 19,384,666; hides and skins, 17,598,730; animal oils and fats, 17,224,228; prawns, 15,624,742; fruit and nuts (fresh or dried), 9,670,287; oats, 7,635,917; timber, 7,050,488; inorganic chemicals, 3,944,754.

Selected overseas imports (in $A) for 1980–81: Petroleum and petroleum products, 668,088,924; machinery, 323,138,220; transport equipment, 153,498,905; iron and steel, 79,018,431; chemicals, 66,997,108; textiles and apparel, 31,172,629; crude fertilizer, 30,244,348; food, 28,187,056; rubber manufactures, 26,326,270; paper and paperboard, 24,564,861.

The chief countries exporting to Western Australia in 1980–81 were (in $A): Japan, 274,887,901; USA, 263,717,362; Kuwait, 177,510,613; UAE, 152,555,940; Singapore, 129,436,223; Indonesia, 107,166,870. Western Australian exports in 1980–81 (in $A) went chiefly to: Japan, 1,374,926,943; USA, 538,698,433; China, People's Republic of, 134,449,808; Singapore, 109,073,322; Korea, Republic of, 95,831,929; USSR, 93,249,138.

Tourism. In 1981, 461,900 (estimate) visitors contributed about $A264m. to the economy; interstate tourists, 4,157,000 (estimate) contributed $A478m. to the economy.

COMMUNICATIONS

Roads. At 30 June 1979 there were 120,684 km of prepared and formed roads in Western Australia, namely, 35,344 km of bituminous surface, 39,214 other constructed surfaces and 46,126 formed but not metalled or otherwise prepared. In addition, there are approximately 40,788 km unprepared except for clearing which are used for general traffic.

New motor vehicles registered in Western Australia during the year ended 30 June 1982 were 64,243.

Railways. At 30 June 1981 the State had 5,773 km of State government railway and 731 km of Federal line, the latter being the western portion of the Trans-Australian line (Kalgoorlie–Port Pirie), which links the State railway system to those of the other States of the Commonwealth. At 30 June 1981, mining companies operated 1,160 km of private railways for the transport of ore to ports on the north-west coast.

Aviation. An extensive system of regular air services operates in Western Australia for the transport of passengers, freight and mail. During the year ended 30 June 1981, Perth Airport handled a total of 16,403 aircraft movements, 19,999 tonnes of freight and 1,278,912 passengers on domestic and international services.

Shipping. In 1980–81, the number of overseas direct vessels through the major ports was: Port of Fremantle, 589 entered, 692 cleared; Dampier, 383 entered, 394 cleared; Port Hedland, 362 entered, 324 cleared; Port Walcott, 122 entered, 119 cleared. The gross weight (in tonnes) of overseas cargo through those ports was: Port of Fremantle, 4,615,510 discharged, 4,183,294 loaded; Dampier, 234,295 discharged, 34,396,480 loaded; Port Hedland, 173,684 discharged, 29,473,491 loaded; Port Walcott, 36,031 discharged, 13,902,175 loaded.

Post and Broadcasting. Postal, telephone and telegraph facilities are afforded at 487 offices. An additional 27 offices provide only telephone and telegraph facilities. Telephones connected totalled 609,781 at 30 June 1981.

There were 43 wireless broadcasting and 51 television stations, including translator stations, in operation at 30 June 1981.

JUSTICE, RELIGION, EDUCATION AND WELFARE

Justice. In Western Australia justice is administered by a Supreme Court, consisting of a Chief Justice and 6 puisne judges at 30 June 1982, a District Court comprising a chairman of judges and 6 district court judges and Magistrates' Courts exercising both civil and criminal jurisdiction. The lower courts are presided over by justices of the peace, except in the more important centres, where the court is constituted by a stipendiary magistrate. There are special Magistrates' Courts for juvenile offenders.

Offences against law	*1977*	*1978*	*1979*	*1980*	*1981*
Charges [1]	108,756	117,408	122,419	126,012	122,176
Lower Court convictions [2]	94,823	105,136	111,864	115,787	116,541
Higher Court convictions	1,154	1,204	1,584	...	1,759

[1] In the case of concurrent offences each offence is included.

[2] Includes convictions for traffic offences: 44,176 in 1977; 50,235 in 1978; 56,310 in 1979; 54,734 in 1980; 55,325 in 1981. In addition, small fines were imposed for minor traffic offences as follows: 1977, 306,885; 1978, 307,396; 1979, 333,545; 1980, 332,754; 1981, 348,452.

Persons in prison at 30 June 1981 numbered 1,312 males and 59 females.

Religion. There is no State Church, and freedom of worship is accorded to all. At the census, 30 June 1981, the principal denominations were: Church of England, 375,848; Roman Catholic and Catholic, 316,337; Methodist, 51,225; Presbyterian, 32,033; Baptist, 15,859; Church of Christ, 14,163; other Christian, 131,637; Hebrew, 3,156; all other, including not stated and no religion, 333,368.

Education. School attendance is compulsory from the age of 6 until the end of the year in which the child attains 15 years. Pre-school education is provided by a kindergarten system partly financed from government subsidy. In 1981 there were 695 government primary and secondary schools providing free education to 220,098 pupils and 206 non-government primary and secondary schools providing education, for which fees are charged, to 50,026 pupils.

Technical education is available at a number of technical colleges, schools and centres, which are staffed and controlled by the Education Department.

In 1981 the full-time teaching and research staff of the University of Western Australia was 727 and the number of students enrolled was 9,835. Murdoch University enrolled 2,785 students in 1981. Full-time teaching and research staff numbered 176.

Tertiary education is also offered by the Western Australian Institute of Technology and the Western Australian College of Advanced Education.

State Government expenditure from consolidated revenue on education, including financial assistance to the Universities, during the year ended 30 June 1981, amounted to $A462,500,269.

Social Welfare. At 30 June 1981 there were 48 general hospitals and 8 nursing homes maintained wholly by public funds and 50 general hospitals and 9 nursing homes partly assisted therefrom. In addition, there are numerous private hospitals. Government mental health services comprise 4 approved hospitals, 18 clinics, 7 rehabilitation units, 37 units concerned with the intellectually handicapped, 1 after-care hostel and 1 in-patient unit for children.

The Department for Community Welfare is responsible for the provision of welfare services throughout the State. There are 28 district offices, 7 country divisional offices, 8 metropolitan divisional offices and 4 metropolitan sub-offices.

The Department runs 9 facilities for the care, assessment, training and support of children who have behavioural problems or are emotionally disturbed. It also provides accommodation at 28 hostels, mainly for Aboriginal children.

There are specialized units working in the areas of child abuse, drug abuse, adoptions and youth activities, and the Department offers help for parents having difficulties looking after their families and supervises all day care centres in the State. There is a homemaker service, a psychological service and a counselling and welfare service attached to the Family Court.

The Department administers the Children's Courts and the Children's (Suspended Proceedings) Panels.

Through the Department, the State Government makes financial assistance available to people in necessitous circumstances.

During the year ended 30 June 1981, 15,977 persons or families received assistance.

Age, invalid, widows' and war and service pensions are paid by the Federal Government. The number of pensioners in Western Australia at 30 June 1981 was: Age, 101,042; invalid, 16,352; widows, 12,526; and disability, service, 54,949.

Housing. In 1980–81, a total of 10,120 new houses and 4,531 new other dwellings were completed in Western Australia. Of these, the State Housing Commission provided 1,114 new dwelling units for sale and for rental.

The value of the total number of dwellings completed during this period was $A483·4m. Additions and alterations valued at $A10,000 or more to dwellings, were valued at $A37·5m.

Books of Reference

Statistical Information: The State Government Statistician's Office was established in 1897 and now functions as the Western Australian Office of the Australian Bureau of Statistics (1–3 St George's Tce, Perth). *Deputy Commonwealth Statistician and Government Statistician:* W. M. Bartlett. Its principal publications are: *Western Australian Year Book* (new series, from 1957). *Western Australian Pocket Year Book* (from 1919). *Monthly Summary of Statistics* (from 1958)

Battye, J. S., *Western Australia: A History from its Discovery to the Inauguration of the Commonwealth.* Oxford, 1924.—*The Cyclopedia of Western Australia.* Adelaide, Vol. 1 (1912), Vol. 2 (1913)
Third. London, 1960
Crowley, F. K., and De Garis, B. K., *A Short History of Western Australia.* Melbourne, 1969
Gentilli, J., *Atlas of Western Australian Agriculture.* Perth, 1941
Kerr, Alex, *The South-West Region of Western Australia.* Perth, 1965.—*Australia's North-West.* Perth, 1967
Kimberley, W. B., *History of Western Australia: A Narrative of Her Past.* Melbourne, 1978
Metropolitan Region Planning Authority, *The Corridor Plan for Perth.* Perth, 1970
Stannage, C. T. (ed.) *A New History of Western Australia.* Perth, 1980
Stephenson, G., and Hepburn, J. A., *Plan for the Metropolitan Region: Perth and Fremantle.* Perth, 1955

State Library: The State Library of Western Australia, Perth. *State Librarian:* R. C. Sharman, BA, FLAA.

AUSTRIA

Republik Österreich

Capital: Vienna
Population: 7·56m. (1981)
GNP per capita: US$10,230 (1980)

HISTORY. On 27 April 1945 a provisional government restored the Republic of Austria and was recognized by the Allied Control Council on 20 Oct. 1945.

AREA AND POPULATION. For the boundaries of Austria according to the Treaty of St Germain, signed in Sept. 1919, *see* THE STATESMAN'S YEAR-BOOK, 1920, pp. 674–75.

Federal States	*Area sq. km*	*Population (census 12 May 1981)*	*Percentage of population*	*Population per sq. km*
Vienna (Wien)	415	1,515,666	20·1	3,652
Lower Austria (Niederösterreich)	19,171	1,439,137	19·0	75
Burgenland	3,966	272,274	3·6	69
Upper Austria (Oberösterreich)	11,979	1,270,426	16·8	106
Salzburg	7,154	441,842	5·8	62
Styria (Steiermark)	16,387	1,187,512	15·7	72
Carinthia (Kärnten)	9,533	536,727	7·1	56
Tirol	12,647	586,139	7·8	46
Vorarlberg	2,601	305,615	4·0	117
Total	83,853 [1]	7,555,338	100·0	90

[1] 32,375 sq. miles.

Vital statistics for calendar years:

	Live births	*Still births*	*Deaths* [1]	*Marriages*	*Divorces*	*Emigration Austrians*	*Emigration Others*
1978	85,402	562	94,617	44,573	12,400	10	2,071
1979	86,388	561	92,012	45,445	13,042	11	2,597
1980	90,872	602	92,442	46,435	13,327	15	3,818
1981	93,942	511	92,693	47,768	13,369	9	6,909

[1] Excluding still births.

The population of the principal towns (excluding Vienna), according to the census of 12 May 1981 (area, 12 May 1981) was as follows:

Graz	243,405	Steyr	38,967	Feldkirch	23,876	Mödling	19,333
Linz	197,962	Dornbirn	38,663	Klosterneuburg	23,307	Lustenau	17,404
Salzburg	138,213	Wiener Neustadt	35,050	Baden	23,235	Braunau am Inn	16,192
Innsbruck	116,100	Leoben	32,006	Krems a.d.D.	23,123	Ternitz	16,154
Klagenfurt	86,303	Wolfsberg	28,182	Amstetten	22,015	Hallein	15,404
Villach	52,744	Kapfenberg	25,719	Traun	21,524	Bruck an der Mur	15,086
St Pölten	51,102	Bregenz	24,683	Leonding	19,402		
Wels	51,024						

CLIMATE. Climate ranges from cool temperate to mountain type according to situation. Winters are cold, with considerable snowfall, but summers are very warm. The wettest months are May to August.

Vienna, Jan. 28°F (–2°C), July 67°F (19·5°C). Annual rainfall 25·6″ (640 mm). Graz, Jan. 28°F (–2°C), July 67°F (19·5°C). Annual rainfall 34″ (849 mm). Innsbruck, Jan. 27°F (–2·7°C), July 66°F (18·8°C). Annual rainfall 34·7″ (868 mm). Salzburg, Jan. 28°F (–2·0°C), July 65°F (18·3°C). Annual rainfall 50·6″ (1,266 mm).

CONSTITUTION AND GOVERNMENT. Austria recovered its sovereignty and independence on 27 July 1955 by the coming into force of the Austrian State Treaty between the UK, the USA, the USSR and France on the one part and the Republic of Austria on the other part (signed on 15 May).

On 12 March 1938 Austria was forcibly absorbed in the German Reich until it was liberated by the American, British, French and Soviet armies in spring 1945. Already in the Moscow Declaration of Oct. 1943, UK, the USA and the USSR had resolved upon the re-establishment of a free and independent Austria.

On 27 April 1945 Dr Karl Renner set up a provisional government which restored the Republic of Austria in the spirit of the Constitution of 1920–29, and was recognized by the Four-Power Allied Control Council on 20 Oct. 1945. The last occupation forces left Austria in Oct. 1955.

President of the Republic: Dr Rudolf Kirchschläger, former Minister of Foreign Affairs, elected on 23 June 1974 and re-elected on 18 May 1980.

On 6 March 1979 the elections were held for the National Assembly, which returned 95 Socialists, 77 People's Party, 11 Freedom Party.

The government of the Socialist Party which was formed in Oct. 1971 was composed Oct. 1982 as follows:

Chancellor: Dr Bruno Kreisky.

Vice-Chancellor and Education and the Arts: Dr Fred Sinowatz. *Finance:* Dr Herbert Salcher; Elfriede Karl *(Minister of State)*; Hans Saidd *(Minister of State). Social Welfare:* Alfred Dallinger; Franziska Fast *(Minister of State). Foreign Affairs:* Dr Willibald Pahr. *Interior:* Erwin Lanc. *Agriculture and Forestry:* Günther Haiden; Albin Schober *(Minister of State). Transport:* Karl Lausecker. *Justice:* Dr Christian Broda. *Trade, Commerce and Industry:* Dr Josef Staribacher; Anneliese Albrecht *(Minister of State). Defence:* Otto Rösch. *Construction and Technology:* Karl Sekanina; Dr Beatrix Eypeltauer *(Minister of State). Science and Research:* Dr Hertha Firnberg. *Health and Environment:* Dr Kurt Steyrer. *Federal Chancellory:* Dr Adolf Nussbaumer *(Minister of State).* Dr Franz Löschnak *(Minister of State).* Johanna Dohnal *(Minister of State).*

The Federal Council *(Bundesrat)* which represents the federal provinces has 58 members and (1980) the Socialist Party had 29 members and the People's Party 29. The *Nationalrat* and *Bundesrat* together form the National Assembly.

National flag: Three horizontal stripes of red, white, red.

National anthem: Land der Berge, Land am Strome (words by Paula Preradovic; tune by W. A. Mozart).

The official language is German.

Local Government. The Republic of Austria comprises 9 Federal States (Vienna, Lower Austria, Upper Austria, Salzburg, Styria, Carinthia, Tirol, Vorarlberg, Burgenland). There is in every province an elected Provincial Assembly.

Every commune has a Council, which chooses one of its number to be head of the Commune (burgomaster) and a committee for the administration and execution of its resolutions.

DEFENCE

Army. The Army consists of an alert force *(Bereitschaftruppe)* of 15,000 regulars and a militia *(Landwehr)* of 6-month conscripts and reservists (186,000). The country is divided into 2 corps areas, I (Graz) and II (Salzburg). The aim is to deploy 1 mechanized division, 3 ordnance regiments and 28 *Landwehrregimenter* of local defence battalions and companies. Strength (1983) 44,950 (conscripts, 32,000).

Air Force. The Air Force is an integral part of army command and comprises 14 squadrons with about 4,300 personnel and 180 aircraft, divided among 3 Flight Regiments each of which includes air defence battalions of anti-aircraft guns. About 30 Saab-105Oe jet light attack aircraft equip a surveillance wing of 2 squadrons with responsibilty for defence of Austrian airspace; a fighter-bomber wing of 2 squadrons. Helicopters equip 7 squadrons for transport/ support, communications, observation and search and rescue duties, in addition to training units; types in service include Alouette III, armed Kiowa, JetRanger, and Agusta-Bell 212. Fixed-wing transports comprise 2 Skyvans and 12 Turbo-Porters.

INTERNATIONAL RELATIONS

Membership. Austria is a member of UN and EFTA.

External debt. The external debt was (1979) 63·7m. schilling.

ECONOMY

Budget. The budget for calendar years provided revenue and expenditure (ordinary and extraordinary) as follows (in 1m. schilling):

	1976	*1977*	*1978*	*1979*	*1980*	*1981*	*1982*[1]
Revenue	177,904	194,782	214,949	237,620	259,028	287,791	309,134
Expenditure	221,901	236,656	266,136	288,134	306,492	339,456	368,349

[1] Provisional.

Currency. The Austrian unit of currency is the *schilling* of 100 *groschen*. The rate of exchange in March 1983, £1 = 26·48 *schilling*, US$1 = 17·05 *schilling*. Exchange rates since 24 Aug. 1971 have been floating.

Banking. The National Bank of Austria, opened on 2 Jan. 1923, was taken over by the German Reichsbank on 17 March 1938. It was re-established on 3 July 1945. At 31 Dec. 1981 foreign exchange amounted to 65,601m. and note circulation to 77,731m. schilling.

Weights and Measures. The metric system of weights and measures is in use.

ENERGY AND NATURAL RESOURCES

Electricity. Electric energy produced (1m. kwh.): 1980, 41,966; 1981, 42,891.

Oil. The commercial production of petroleum began in the early 1930s. Production of crude oil (in tonnes): 1960, 2,448,391; 1971, 2,798,237; 1981, 1,337,679.

Minerals. The mineral production (in tonnes) was as follows:

	1980	*1981*		*1980*	*1981*
Lignite	2,864,967	3,061,262	Pig-iron	3,485,161	3,477,257
Iron ore	3,200,000	3,050,000	Raw steel	4,623,751	4,655,503
Lead and zinc ore[1]	694,545	797,654	Rolled steel	3,677,094	3,673,022
Raw magnesite[1]	1,318,156	1,158,852			

[1] Including recovery from slag.

Austria is one of the world's largest sources of high-grade graphite. Production, which averaged 20,000 tonnes yearly from 1929 to 1944, dropped to 246 in 1946, but rose to 102,237 in 1964, and fell again to 23,992 in 1970, 40,501 in 1978, 40,519 in 1979, 37,199 in 1980 and 23,807 in 1981.

Agriculture. In 1981 the total area sown amounted to 1,479,869 hectares.

The chief products (area in hectares, yield in tonnes) were as follows:

	1979		*1980*		*1981*	
	Area	*Yield*	*Area*	*Yield*	*Area*	*Yield*
Wheat	270,188	849,921	268,753	1,200,599	274,286	1,025,011
Rye	105,542	277,974	109,234	382,801	101,109	320,215
Barley	373,205	1,128,714	373,912	1,514,491	362,202	1,219,816
Oats	95,032	272,732	91,989	315,896	91,544	303,898
Potatoes	58,048	1,493,706	52,569	1,263,922	49,639	1,309,779

Production of raw sugar in 1949, 66,700; 1955, 219,300; 1960, 308,000; refined sugar: 1970, 298,000; 1979, 377,400; 1980, 419,800; 1981, 446,900 tonnes.

Livestock (1981): Cattle, 2,530,232; pigs, 4,009,535; sheep, 194,390; goats, 32,534; horses, 41,514; poultry, 15,987,126.

Forestry. Felled timber, in cu. metres: 1960, 10,015,925; 1970, 11,122,896; 1980, 12,732,507; 1981, 12,168,535.

INDUSTRY AND TRADE

Industry. On 26 July 1946 the Austrian parliament passed a government bill, nationalizing some 70 industrial concerns. As from 17 Sept. 1946 ownership of the 3 largest commercial banks, most oil-producing and refining companies and the principal firms in the following industries devolved upon the Austrian state: River navigation; coal extraction; non-ferrous mining and refining; iron-ore mining; pig-iron and steel production; manufacture of iron and steel products, including structural material, machinery, railroad equipment and repairs, and shipbuilding; electrical machinery and appliances. Six companies supplying electric power were nationalized in accordance with a law of 26 March 1947.

In 1981, 6,802 industrial establishments employed 616,125 persons, producing a gross output of 526m. schillings.

Commerce. Imports and exports are as follows (excluding coined gold):

	Imports			*Exports*		
	1979	*1980*	*1981*	*1979*	*1980*	*1981*
Quantity (1,000 tonnes)	36,090	36,825	35,848	14,564	15,085	15,317
Value (1m. sch.)	269,862	315,846	334,510	206,253	226,169	251,769

The total trade between Austria and UK (British Department of Trade returns, in £1,000 sterling):

	1978	*1979*	*1980*	*1981*	*1982*
Imports to UK	324,132	345,446	307,267	347,971	404,318
Exports and re-exports from UK	240,127	259,251	279,681	246,877	251,032

Tourism. Tourism is an important industry. In 1981, 21,661 hotels and boarding-houses had a total of 671,295 beds available; 14,241,392 foreigners visited Austria; of these 552,764 came from the UK and 440,965 from the USA.

COMMUNICATIONS

Roads. On 1 Jan. 1977 federal roads had a total length of 10,140 km, 743·2 km autobahn; provincial roads, 22,996 km. On 31 Dec. 1981 there were registered 3,494,065 motor vehicles, including 2,312,932 passenger cars, 190,296 lorries, 339,506 tractors and 208,332 trailers.

Railways. Austrian railways have been nationalized since before the First World War. Length of track (Dec. 1981), 5,857 km, of which 3,233 km were electrified. Twenty private railways have a total length of 602 km. Passengers in 1981 numbered 170m. and 50m. tonnes of freight.

Aviation. Austria has 6 airports in Vienna (Schwechat), Linz, Salzburg, Graz, Klagenfurt and Innsbruck. In 1981, 79,315 aircraft arrived and departed at Austrian airports on commercial air transport.

Shipping. Austria has no sea frontiers, but the Danube is an important waterway. Goods traffic (in tonnes): 5,883,596 in 1978; 6,583,433 in 1979; 6,587,190 in 1980; 6,108,263 in 1981. Coal and coke, mineral oil products and iron ore comprise in bulk more than two-thirds of these cargoes. The Danube Steamship Co. (DDSG) is the main Austrian shipping company.

Post and Broadcasting. All postal, telegraph and telephone services are run by the State. On 1 Jan. 1982 there were 2,395,037 telephones.

Österreicher Rundfunk transmits 3 regional and 10 local programmes, including one in English and one in French; there is also a 24 hours overseas service. All broadcasting is financed by licence payments and advertisements. There were 2·3m. registered listeners in Sept. 1980. Television was inaugurated in autumn 1955 and 2 programmes are transmitted, both in colour.

Cinemas (1981). There were 496 cinemas.

Newspapers (1981). There were 31 daily newspapers (6 of them in Vienna) with a combined circulation of 2,663,120.

JUSTICE, RELIGION, EDUCATION AND WELFARE

Justice. The Supreme Court of Justice *(Oberster Gerichtshof)* in Vienna is the highest court in the land. Besides there are 4 higher provincial courts *(Oberlandesgerichte)*, 20 provincial and district courts *(Landes- und Kreisgerichte)* and 205 local courts *(Bezirksgerichte)*.

Religion. In 1971 there were 6,540,294 Roman Catholics (87·7%), 446,307 Protestants (6%), 111,558 others (1·5%), 320,031 without religious allegiance (4·3%) and

38,213 (0·5%) unknown. The Roman Catholic Church has 2 archbishoprics and 7 bishoprics.

Education (1981–82). There were in Austria 5,171 elementary and special schools with 64,596 teachers and 799,261 pupils. Of all kinds of secondary schools there were 1,445 with 567,050 pupils.

There were also 103 commercial academies with 33,805 students and 4,301 teachers. There were 195 schools of technical and industrial training (including schools of hotel management and catering) with 5,701 teachers and 53,511 pupils; 41 schools of women's professions (secondary level) with 11,437 pupils; 8 training colleges of social workers with 618 pupils. 132 trade schools had 26,142 pupils.

Austria has 12 universities and 6 colleges of arts maintained by the State: Universities at Vienna (3,979 teachers, 45,128 students), Graz (1,368 teachers, 17,266 students), Innsbruck (1,519 teachers, 15,688 students) and Salzburg (693 teachers, 8,336 students). There are also technical universities at Vienna (1,168 teachers, 9,828 students) and Graz (590 teachers, 5,550 students), a mining university at Leoben (230 teachers, 1,126 students), an agricultural university at Vienna (266 teachers, 3,206 students), a veterinary university at Vienna (192 teachers, 1,538 students), a commercial university at Vienna (258 teachers, 8,972 students), a university for social and economic sciences at Linz (379 teachers, 5,566 students) and a university for educational sciences at Klagenfurt (199 teachers, 1,327 students). There is an academy of fine arts at Vienna (142 teachers, 511 students), a college of applied arts at Vienna (158 teachers, 670 students), 3 colleges of music and dramatic art at Vienna (410 teachers, 2,000 students), Salzburg (259 teachers, 1,081 students) and Graz (226 teachers, 883 students); the college for industrial design at Linz (95 teachers, 361 students).

Health. In 1981 there were 19,157 doctors, 327 hospitals and 84,313 hospital beds.

DIPLOMATIC REPRESENTATIVES

Of Austria in Great Britain (18 Belgrave Mews West, London, SW1X 8HU)
Ambassador: Dr Reginald Thomas (accredited 10 March 1982).

Of Great Britain in Austria (Reisnerstrasse 40, 1030 Vienna)
Ambassador: M. O'D. B. Alexander, CMG.

Of Austria in the USA (2343 Massachusetts Ave., NW, Washington, D.C., 20008)
Ambassador: Dr Thomas Klestil.

Of the USA in Austria (IX Boltzmangasse, 16, A-1091 Vienna)
Chargé d'Affaires: Sol Polansky.

Of Austria to the United Nations
Ambassador: (Vacant).

Books of Reference

Statistical Information: The Austrian Central Statistical Office was founded in 1863. *Address:* Neue Burg, Heldenplatz, A-1014 Vienna. *President:* Dr Josef Schmidt. Main publications:
Statistisches Handbuch für die Republik Österreich. New Series from 1950. Annually
Statistische Nachrichten. Monthly
Beiträge zur österreichischen Statistik (585 vols.)
Ergebnisse der Volkszählung vom 12 Mai 1981
Ergebnisse der Häuser- und Wohnungszählung vom 12 Mai 1971
HA-Taschenbuch 75. Annually from 1971
Statistiches Handbuch auch der Republik Österreich. Annual.

Bobek, H. (ed.), *Atlas der Republik Österreich.* 3 vols. Vienna, 1961 ff.
Österreich Lexikon. Wien-Munchen, 1966
Scheidl, L. G., and Lechleitner, H., *Österreich—Land, Volk, Wirtschaft.* Vienna, 1967
Sotriffer, K., *Greater Austria: 100 Years of Intellectual and Social Life from 1800 to the Present Time.* Vienna, 1982

National Library: Österreichische Nationalbibliothek, Vienna. *Librarian:* Dr Zessner-Spitzenberg.

THE COMMONWEALTH OF THE BAHAMAS

Capital: Nassau
Population: 209,505 (1981)
GNP per capita: US$3,300 (1980)

HISTORY. The Bahamas were discovered by Colombus in 1492 but the Spanish did not make a permanent settlement. British settlers arrived in the 17th century and it was occupied by Britain, except for a short period in the 18th century, until it gained independence.

AREA AND POPULATION. The Commonwealth of the Bahamas consists of 700 islands and more than 1,000 cays off the south-east coast of Florida. They are the surface protuberances of two oceanic banks, the Little Bahama Bank and the Great Bahama Bank. Land area, 5,353 sq. miles (13,864 sq. km). Average winter temperature, 69·9°F. (21·1°C.); average summer temperature, 82·8°F. (28·2°C.).

Principal islands with census population in 1980: New Providence (135,437, containing capital, Nassau), Abaco (7,324), Andros (8,397), Cat Island (2,143), Eleuthera (10,600), Grand Bahama (33,102), Inagua (939), Long Island (3,358). Total census population, with other islands and cays, 209,505.

Vital statistics, 1977: Births, 4,871; deaths, 1,067 (excluding still-births); marriages, 1,297.

CONSTITUTION AND GOVERNMENT. Internal self-government with cabinet responsibility was introduced 7 Jan. 1964.

Qualification for membership of the House of Assembly, under the 1973 Independence Constitution requires that a member shall be a citizen of the Bahamas of the age of 21 years or upwards, and shall have been ordinarily resident in the Bahamas for a period of not less than 1 year immediately before the date of his nomination for election. The Representation of the People's Act provides for adult suffrage. Women are eligible for election to the House of Assembly.

The Constitution of the Commonwealth of the Bahamas (1973) establishes the Bahamas as a free and democratic sovereign state. The constitution is the supreme law of the Bahamas and where any other law is inconsistent with it, the Constitution shall prevail and the other law shall, to the extent of the inconsistency be void.

The Constitution created the office of Governor-General, the holder of which is appointed by Her Majesty. There is a Senate of 16 members, 9 appointed by the Governor-General on the advice of the Prime Minister, 4 appointed by the Governor-General on the advice of the Leader of the Opposition and 3 appointed by the Governor-General on the advice of the Prime Minister after consultation with the Leader of the Opposition. The House of Assembly consists of 43 members. The life of a Parliament is 5 years, but it may be prorogued or dissolved at any time by the Governor-General on the advice of the Prime Minister.

At the elections of 11 June 1982 the Progressive Liberal Party obtained 32 seats and the Free National Movement 11 seats.

Independence from Britain took place on 10 July 1973.

Governor-General: Sir Gerald Cash, GCMG, KCVO, OBE.

The Cabinet in Nov. 1982 was composed as follows:

Prime Minister and Minister of Economic Affairs: Rt. Hon. Lynden O. Pindling. *Deputy Prime Minister and Minister of Finance:* Arthur D. Hanna. *Labour and Home Affairs:* Clement T. Maynard. *Health:* Livingston N. Coakley. *Works and Utilities:* A. Loftus Roker. *Education:* Darrell E. Rolle. *External Affairs and Attorney-General:* Paul L. Adderley. *Agriculture, Fisheries and Local Government:* George A. Smith. *Economics:* Alfred T. Maycock. *Tourism:* Perry G.

Christie. *Transport:* Philip M. Bethel. *Youth, Sports, Culture and Community Affairs:* Kendal W. Nottage. *National Insurance and Housing:* Hubert Ingraham.

National flag: Three horizontal stripes of aquamarine, gold, aquamarine, with a black triangle on the hoist.

INTERNATIONAL RELATIONS

Membership. The Commonwealth of the Bahamas is a member of UN, the Commonwealth and an ACP state of EEC.

ECONOMY

Budget (in B$):

	1979	*1980*	*1981*
Revenue	212,405,423	255,257,167	295,923,300
Expenditure	248,227,193	287,408,577	336,339,638

The main sources of revenue were customs duties and receipts from fees, post office and public utilities.

Currency. A decimal system of currency was introduced in 1966. Bahamian $1.52 = £1 sterling (March 1983). Notes: $0.50, 1, 3, 5, 10, 20, 50, 100; coins: 1, 5, 10, 15, 25, 50 cents, $1, 2, 5. Sterling currency has been withdrawn. American currency is generally accepted.

Bank of England and Canadian notes are not accepted, except at the banks from travellers from the UK.

Banking. The Central Bank of the Bahamas was established in June 1974 with assets (Dec. 1980) of B$154·95m. and capital and reserves of B$29·98m. Among these were the Royal Bank of Canada, the Bank of Nova Scotia, the Bank of Montreal, Chase Manhattan Bank, Barclays Bank International, the Canadian Imperial Bank of Commerce and Citibank. While the majority of banks are located in Nassau, there are branches on several of the other islands. The Bahamas Development Bank was established in 1974 and began operations in Jan. 1978; at Dec. 1980 it had total assets of B$7·45m. and paid-up capital of B$6m.

On 31 Dec. 1980 there were 314 institutions licensed to carry on banking and/or trust business under the Banks and Trust Companies Regulations Act. There were 17 designated institutions by the Exchange Control Department as authorized dealers and agents.

The post office savings bank, 31 Dec. 1980, had deposits of B$2·2m.

Weights and Measures. The UK (Imperial) system is in force.

ENERGY AND NATURAL RESOURCES

Electricity. Electricity for lighting and power is available in New Providence, Grand Bahama and the Family Islands. Total units generated in New Providence/Paradise Island and Family Islands in 1979–80, 390m. kwh.

Agriculture. There were (1978) 4,246 agricultural holdings or parcels of farm land in the Bahamas, totalling 89,565 acres. About 40% of these holdings are cultivated with temporary and permanent crops. Livestock operations within the Bahamas are predominantly sheep and goat enterprises.

Several agricultural programmes exist to further stimulate agricultural production. Some of these programmes are subsidized by government and include land clearing and duty free importation of trucks and other farm implements. Farmers also have access to 2 credit programmes: a) The Agricultural Credit Guarantee Fund; b) The Stores on Credit Programme.

Total agricultural production including fisheries was valued at about B$30m. in 1980.

Livestock (1981): Cattle, 4,000; sheep, 36,000; goats, 17,000; pigs, 19,000; poultry, 795,000.

Forestry. Production of cascarilla bark and pulp-wood in 1976 was B$1·8m., all of which was exported.

Fisheries. Total production was valued at B$10·5m. in 1976.

INDUSTRY AND TRADE

Industry. Tourism is the major industry. Several light industries have been established on Grand Bahama and New Providence in response to special encouragement legislation; these include garment manufacturing, ice, furniture, purified water, plastic containers, perfumes, industrial gases, jewellery and others. Larger industrial activities in the Bahamas include oil refining, oil transhipment, manufacture of alcoholic beverages, pharmaceuticals, aragonite mining, solar salt production and cement. Two industrial sites, one in New Providence and the other in Grand Bahama, have been developed as part of the industrialization programme.

Commerce. The principal exports in 1980 were hormones, rum, salt, crawfish, cement, aragonite and plywood.

The principal imports in 1977 were: Food, drink and tobacco, raw materials and articles mainly unmanufactured, articles wholly or mainly manufactured, animals not for food.

Imports and exports (excluding bullion and specie) for 6 calendar years in B$:

	Imports	*Exports*		*Imports*	*Exports*
1975	2,482,108	2,216,018	1978	2,482,235	2,117,938
1976	2,892,555	2,616,029	1979	3,985,034	3,495,043
1977	2,787,943	2,597,352	1980	5,506,577	4,836,366

The Bahamas became affiliated with CARIFTA (now CARICOM) in 1968.

Total trade between Bahamas and UK, in £1,000 sterling (British Department of Trade returns):

	1977	*1978*	*1979*	*1980*	*1981*	*1982*
Imports to UK	13,960	12,650	21,758	59,123	30,915	18,273
Exports and re-exports from UK	21,995	104,204	79,851	77,366	171,347	26,364

Tourism. Tourism is the most important industry in the Bahamas. It accounts for approximately 58% of government revenue and 66% of employment. In 1981 there were 1·7m. foreign arrivals in the Bahamas.

COMMUNICATIONS

Roads. There are 240 miles of paved roads in New Providence, and 426 miles in Grand Bahama. The other major islands have 400 miles of motorable roads. In 1978, 51,290 motor vehicles were registered. There are no railroads.

Aviation. Nassau international airport is located on the island of New Providence, about 10 miles from the city of Nassau. There is another international airport at Freeport. Scheduled flights—Air Canada: 3 times weekly from Toronto and once weekly from Montreal to Nassau; twice weekly from Toronto to Freeport and once weekly from Montreal to Freeport. Delta: twice daily from New York to Nassau; once daily from Boston and Newark. Eastern Airlines: 3 flights daily from New York, 3 times daily from Miami, once daily from Fort Lauderdale, twice weekly from Baltimore, Washington and Philadelphia, once daily from Boston and Newark, once daily from New York *via* Miami and Fort Lauderdale to Nassau; 3 times daily from Miami, once daily from Baltimore and Philadelphia to Freeport: Lufthansa: 3 times weekly from Frankfurt and Mexico and once weekly from Merida to Nassau. Air Jamaica: once daily from Chicago, Kingston and Montego Bay to Nassau. American Airlines: once daily from New York to Nassau and 4 times weekly from New York to Freeport. British Airways: 4 times weekly from London and Bermuda, twice weekly from Kingston and Panama and once weekly from Mexico City, all to Nassau; once weekly from London, Bermuda, Kingston and Panama to Freeport. There are numerous domestic schedules to the Family Islands and Florida. There are 53 airstrips on the various Family Islands and numerous water alighting areas. During 1977, 494,263 passengers landed at Nassau and 38,840 aircraft arrivals. At Freeport in 1977, 407,772 passengers landed from 41,799 aircraft arrivals.

Shipping. In 1980, 678 cruise liners cleared Nassau carrying 499,527 passengers; 653 cargo vessels discharged 268,477 tons of cargo at Nassau. There are indirect cargo services with UK and Canada *via* the USA and passenger services with the USA only.

Telecommunications. New Providence and all the major islands have automatic telephone systems of the latest type in operation, together with an extensive system of underground cables. The total number of telephones in use at 1 Jan. 1981 was 71,883; 170 radio-telephone channels provide service *via* the USA to any part of the world. In 1971 direct dialling was introduced to the USA and in 1973 to Canada. All the important islands are connected with Nassau by means of radio-telegraphy, and in most cases radio-telephony is also available. Connexion through Nassau to the UK, the USA, Canada and Central America can be provided. Radio-teletype to Bermuda and Florida and ship-shore radio-telephone services are also available. Radio-teletype service is provided from Nassau to Freeport and West End in Grand Bahama. In 1976 a fully automated Telex exchange came into service. The Bahamas broadcasting station operates on 1,540, 1,240 and 810 kc.

Cinemas (1977). There are 16 cinemas and 3 drive-ins.

Newspapers (1977). There are 2 daily and 1 weekly newspapers in Nassau.

JUSTICE, EDUCATION AND WELFARE

Justice (1977). 9,655 cases (traffic, 3,550; criminal, 3,218; civil, 1,880; domestic, 1,007) were dealt with in the magistrates' court, and civil, 816; divorce, 256 in the Supreme Court. The strength of the police force (1973) was 932 officers and other ranks.

Education. Education is under the jurisdiction of the Ministry of Education and Culture. In 1980–81 there were 227 schools, and of these, 187 are fully maintained by Government and 40 are independent schools. Total school enrolment, 61,160. There are 38 government-owned schools in New Providence and 149 on the Family Islands. 24 independent schools are located on New Providence and 12 on the Family Islands. 181 students attended 4 special schools, 3 on New Providence and 1 on Grand Bahama; total staff, 38. Free education is available in ministry schools in New Providence and the Family Islands. Courses lead to the Bahamas Junior Certificate and the General Certificate of Education (GCE).

Independent schools provide education at primary, secondary and higher levels. Several schools of continuing education offer secretarial and academic courses. The Government-operated Princess Margaret Hospital offers a nursing course at two levels. The College of the Bahamas was established in 1974. It provides a 2- or 3-year programme leading to an associate degree in any of the 7 academic divisions. Several college degree programmes are offered in conjunction with the University of the West Indies and the University of Miami. The Hotel Training College offers a wide range of subjects up to middle management level in aspects of hotel work. Enrolment in this institution includes Bahamian as well as regional and international students.

Health. In 1980 there was a government general hospital in Nassau (460 beds) and 1 in Freeport (50). Grand Bahama has 4 clinics, 3 staffed by district medical officers and 1 by a nurse and the Family Islands have about 50 health centres. There are 2 private hospitals. Dental treatment is provided for smaller islands by a flying dentist service. There are 122 doctors, 387 nurses, 8 midwives and 5 dentists in the government service. There are many private doctors, dentists, nurses and midwives providing health care on a fee basis.

DIPLOMATIC REPRESENTATIVES

Of the Bahamas in Great Britain (39 Pall Mall, London, SW1Y 5JG)
High Commissioner: R. F. Anthony Roberts.

Of Great Britain in the Bahamas (Bitco Bldg., East St., Nassau)
High Commissioner: Peter William Heap.

Of the Bahamas in the USA (600 New Hampshire Ave., NW, Washington, D.C., 20037)
Ambassador: Reginald L. Woods, CBE.

Of the USA in the Bahamas (Queen St., Nassau)
Chargé d'Affaires: Andrew F. Antippas.

Of the Bahamas to the United Nations
Ambassador: Dr Davidson L. Hepburn.

Books of Reference

Bahamas Handbook and Businessman's Annual (Annual)
Albury, P., *The Story of the Bahamas.* London, 1975
Craton, M. A., *A History of the Bahamas.* London, 1962
Hughes, C. A., *Race and Politics in the Bahamas.* Univ. of Queensland Press, 1981
Hunte, G., *The Bahamas.* London, 1975

Library: Nassau Public Library.

BAHRAIN

Capital: Manama
Population: 350,798 (1981)
GNP per capita: US$5,560 (1980)

HISTORY. Treaties with Britain of 1882 and 1892 were replaced by a treaty of friendship which was signed on 15 Aug. 1971. Under the earlier treaties Britain had been responsible for Bahrain's defence and foreign relations. On the same day Bahrain declared its independence.

AREA AND POPULATION. The Bahrain islands form an archipelago in the Arabian Gulf, between the Qatar peninsula and the mainland of Saudi Arabia. The total area is about 255 sq. miles. Bahrain ('Two Seas'), largest island, is 30 miles long and 10 miles wide. Muharraq, to the north-east, 4 miles long and 1 mile wide, is connected with Bahrain by a causeway, nearly 1·5 miles long, carrying a motor road. Other islands are Sitra, to the east, 3 miles long and 1 mile wide; Umm An-Nassan, to the west, 3 miles by 2 miles; Jidda, also to the west, 1 mile by 0·5 mile, the Hawar group off Qatar and several islets, some uninhabited. From Sitra oil pipelines and a causeway carrying a road extend out to sea for 3 miles to a deep-water anchorage. The islands are low lying, the highest ground being a hill in the centre of Bahrain, 450 ft high.

The population in 1981 (census) was 350,798. The majority of the people are Moslem Arabs.

Manama, the capital of the state and the commercial centre, is situated at the northern end of the largest island and extends for 1·5 miles along the shore. It has a population of 121,986 (1981 census). Electricity from the government power-station in Manama supplies light and power in Manama, Muharraq (61,853, 1981 census), Hidd (7,111), Rifa'a (28,150) and Isa Town (21,275) and the villages. Water is obtained from artesian wells and desalination plants, and there is a piped supply in Manama, Muharraq, Isa Town, Rifa'a and most villages.

CONSTITUTION AND GOVERNMENT. A Constituent Assembly met in Dec. 1972 to draft a Constitution and this was published in 1973. A National Assembly with a proposed 4-year life met for the first time in 1973 but was dissolved at the end of 1975. Bahrain is administered by a cabinet, which was formed in 1971 to succeed the Council of State.

Reigning Amir: The ruling family, the Al Khalifa, an Arab dynasty, who have been in power since 1782. The present Amir, HH Shaikh Isa bin Sulman Al-Khalifa (born 1933) succeeded on 2 Nov. 1961. *Crown Prince and Minister of Defence:* Shaikh Hamed bin Isa Al-Khalifa.

Prime Minister: Shaikh Khalifa bin Sulman Al-Khalifa.

Defence: Shaikh Hamed bin Isa Al-Khalifa. *Transport:* Ibrahim Mohammed Hassan Homaidan. *Housing:* Shaikh Khalid bin Abdulla Al-Khalifa. *Information:* Tariq Abdulrahman Almoayyed. *Education:* Dr Ali Fakhro. *Health:* Jawad Salim Al-Arrayed. *Justice and Islamic Affairs:* Shaikh Abdullah bin Khalid Al-Khalifa. *Labour and Social Affairs:* Shaikh Khalifa bin Salman bin Mohammed Al-Khalifa. *Works, Power and Water:* Majid Jawad Al Jishi. *Interior:* Shaikh Mohammed bin Khalifa Al-Khalifa. *Foreign Affairs:* Shaikh Mohammed bin Mubarak Al-Khalifa. *Finance and National Economy:* Ebrahim Abdul-Karim. *Development and Industry:* Yusuf Ahmed Al-Shirawi. *Commerce and Agriculture:* Habib Ahmed Qassim. *Acting Minister of State for Cabinet Affairs:* Dr Ali Fakhro. *Minister of State for Legal Affairs:* Dr Hussain Al Baharna.

Flag: Red, with white serrated vertical strip on hoist.

DEFENCE

Army. The Army consists of 1 infantry battalion and 1 armoured car squadron with a personnel strength of 2,300 (1983).

Air Wing. Formed in 1977, the Air Wing ordered 4 F-5E Tiger IIs and 2 two-seat F-5Fs in May 1982 to equip its first combat unit. Other equipment comprises 3 BO 105 and 2 Hughes 500D light helicopters.

INTERNATIONAL RELATIONS

Membership. Bahrain is a member of UN, the Arab League and OAPEC.

ECONOMY

Budget. The revenue of the State is derived from oil royalties and from customs duties, which are 10% *ad valorem* for luxury goods and 5% for essential goods. The exceptions are liquor (75%) and tobacco (30%). Total revenues in 1977, BD 249m.; 1978, BD 280m.; 1979, BD 311m.; 1980, BD 329m.; 1981, BD 351m.

On 2 Jan. 1958 Manama was declared a free transit port and the former 2% transit duty was abolished, but storage charges are levied.

Currency. The Bahrain *dinar* is divided into 1,000 *fils*. The Bahrain currency board issues notes of 10, 5, 1 and ½ *dinars*, and coins of 100, 50, 25 and 5 *fils*. £1 = BD 0·570 in March 1983; US$1 = BD 0·377.

Banking. The Bahrain Monetary Agency has central banking powers. Other banking facilities are provided by the National Bank of Bahrain, the Bank of Bahrain and Kuwait and branches of the Chartered Bank, the British Bank of the Middle East, the Arab Bank, Habib Bank (Overseas), United Bank, Citibank, Banque du Caire, Chase Manhattan, Grindlays Bank, Bank Melli, Algemene Bank, Bank Saderet, Bank de Paris et des Pays-Bas, National Bank of Abu Dhabi, Rafidain Bank, Barclays International, Al-Ahli Commercial Bank.

Weights and Measures. The metric system of weights and measures is officially in use.

NATURAL RESOURCES

Oil. In 1931 oil was discovered. Operations are being conducted by the Bahrain Petroleum Co., registered in Canada but owned by US interests, under a concession granted by the Shaikh. Production of crude oil in 1981 was 16.9m. bbls. A large oil refinery on Bahrain Island, besides treating crude oil produced locally, also processes oil from Saudi Arabia transported by pipeline.

In 1975 the Bahrain Government assumed a direct 60% interest in the Bahrain oilfield and related crude oil facilities of BAPCO. Bahrain's gas reserves are 100% government-owned.

Under the terms of the agreement signed between Bahrain and Saudi Arabia in 1958, Bahrain will receive 25% of the profits on any oil produced in the Abu Saafa area of sea between Bahrain and Saudi Arabia. Aramco, which is responsible for the development of this field, began production in 1966.

Gas. There is an abundant supply of natural gas with known reserves of 9,000,000m. cu. ft. Production, 1981, 163,101m. cu. ft.

INDUSTRY AND TRADE

Industry. Bahrain is being developed as a major manufacturing state, the first important enterprise being the Aluminium Bahrain Smelter, a company whose original shareholders included the Bahrain Government and British, Swedish, Federal German and US interests. In 1975, the government acquired a majority shareholding in the enterprise. The aluminium operation is the largest non-oil industry in the Gulf. Ancillary industries developed around aluminium smelting include the production of aluminium powder. Other projects at present under consideration include the further development of marine industries. The Arab Shipbuilding and Repair Yard (ASRY), commissioned in 1977, is now in service. The dry dock can handle up to 50 tankers (550,000 DWT each) annually. A US$400m. petrochemical complex will go on stream in 1984. The construction of the Saudi-Bahrain causeway begun in 1982 and which should be completed in 1986, is the largest project in the history of the Gulf. Total cost of the 25 km project is US$800m. and the cost is being borne by Saudi Arabia.

In addition to the traditional minor industries such as boat-building, weaving, pottery, etc., other modern industries have developed, which include the manufacture of building materials, soft drinks, drinking straws, paper bags, woollen garments, plastic and other consumer goods. There is also an important fishing industry and a fairly large farming community. The most important crops are dates and vegetables, and there is also poultry farming.

Livestock (1981): Cattle, 6,000; sheep, 7,000; goats, 15,000; poultry, 790,000.

The pearling industry for which Bahrain used to be famous has considerably declined. Only about 10 boats visit the pearl banks each year, as compared with the 600–1,000 that were employed 30 years ago.

Commerce. In 1981 imports totalled BD 429,607,000; exports and re-exports, non-oil, BD 40,728,000. Chief imports were manufactured goods, machinery and transport equipment, food and live animals, chemicals.

Import of arms and ammunition and telecommunication equipment is subject to special permission; the sale of alcoholic liquor is restricted and the import of cultured pearls is forbidden.

Total trade between Bahrain and UK (British Department of Trade returns, in £1,000 sterling):

	1978	*1979*	*1980*	*1981*	*1982*
Imports to UK	34,704	23,780	25,063	16,713	35,459
Exports and re-exports from UK	119,855	123,467	115,569	102,337	152,272

COMMUNICATIONS

Aviation. The airport, situated at Muharraq, can take the largest aircraft. British Airways, Gulf Air, Middle East Airlines, Pakistan International Airways, Qantas, Kuwait Airways, Air India International, Singapore Airlines, UTA, Saudi Arabian Airlines, KLM, Air Lanka, Cathy Pacific Airways, Iraqi Airways, Korean Airways, Philippine Airlines, Thai Airways International, Trans-Mediterranean Airways, Egyptair, Alia, Cyprus Airways, Ethiopia Airlines and Sudan Airways also operate to and from Bahrain. Bahrain International Airport is the Arabian Gulf's main air communication centre.

Shipping. Bahrain's traditional position as the entrepôt of the Southern Gulf has been supplemented by the development of Mina Sulman—the new modern harbour—as a free transit and industrial area. Local and international companies have developed industries in this area, which is also used as a storage centre for firms selling elsewhere in the Gulf. The facilities offered by Mina Sulman include engineering and ship repairing yards; the Basrec slipway is probably the largest between Rotterdam and Hong Kong.

Post and Broadcasting. There were, at 1 Jan. 1981, 84,593 telephones. There is a state-operated radio and television station.

EDUCATION. There were, in 1980–81, 125 state schools for boys and girls with 3,405 teachers and 69,083 pupils. Six boys' general and commercial schools had 3,132 pupils; 2 boys' industrial schools at secondary level, had 1,071 pupils. In addition there were 7 private schools. The Men's Teacher Training College (established 1966) and the Women's Teacher Training College (established 1967) give 2-year courses. In 1980–81, 2,626 Bahrainis were in higher education abroad. The Gulf Technical College opened in Bahrain in Sept. 1968 and Bahrain University in 1978. In 1980–81, 40 adult literacy centres were opened throughout Bahrain.

HEALTH. There is a free medical service for all residents of Bahrain. In 1980–81, there were 46 government hospitals and health centres with 1,071 beds, an American mission hospital, an oil company hospital, a military hospital and an international hospital.

DIPLOMATIC REPRESENTATIVES

Of Bahrain in Great Britain (98 Gloucester Rd., London, SW7 4AU)
Ambassador: Shaikh Abdul-Rahman Faris Al-Khalifa (accredited 17 Dec. 1980).

Of Great Britain in Bahrain (21 Government Rd., Manama)
Ambassador: W. R. Tomkys.

Of Bahrain in the USA (2600 Virginia Ave., NW, Washington D.C., 20037)
Chargé d'Affaires: Ahmed Mahdi Al-Haddad.

Of the USA in Bahrain (Shaikh Isa Road, Manama)
Ambassador: Peter A. Sutherland.

Of Bahrain to the United Nations
Ambassador: (Vacant).

Books of Reference

Statistical and General Information: Ministry of Information, PO Box 253, Manama.
Statistical Abstract 1981. Directorate of Statistics (annual).

Belgrave, J. H. D., *Welcome to Bahrain.* 9th ed. Manama, 1975
Rumaihi, M. G., *Bahrain: Social and Political Change since the First World War.* New York and London, 1976

BANGLADESH

People's Republic of Bangladesh

Capital: Dacca (Dhaka)
Population: 89m. (1981)
GNP per capita: US$120 (1981)

HISTORY. The state was formerly the Eastern Province of Pakistan. In Dec. 1970 Sheikh Mujibur Rahman's Awami League Party gained 167 seats out of 300 at the Pakistan general election and immediately made known their wish for greater independence for the then Eastern Province. Martial law was imposed following disturbances in Dacca, and civil war developed in March 1971. The war ended in Dec. 1971 and Bangladesh was proclaimed an independent state.

AREA AND POPULATION. Bangladesh is bounded west and north-west by West Bengal (India), north by Assam and Meghalaya (India), east by Assam, Tripura (India) and Burma, south by the Bay of Bengal. The area is 55,598 sq. miles (144,020 sq. km). The small island of South Talpatty in the estuary of the river Hariabhanga was annexed by India in May 1981. Bangladesh's population (1974 census), 71,316,517 (36,949,033 male, 34,367,484 female), an increase of 40·27% since 1961. Population estimate, 1982, 92m. Growth rate (1974–82), 2·6%. The capital is Dacca or Dhaka (population, 1981, 3,458,602) and its ports are Chittagong (1,388,475) and Khulna (623,184). Other large cities are Narayanganj (298,400), Rajshahi (171,600) and Barisal (166,680). There are 20 districts:

	Area (sq. km)	*Population 1981*		*Area (sq. km)*	*Population 1981*
Dinajpur	6,757	3,198,000	Kushtia	3,551	2,273,000
Rangpur	9,593	6,490,000	Jessore	6,597	4,016,000
Bogra	3,890	2,718,000	Khulna	12,049	4,353,000
Rajshahi	9,464	5,263,000	Barisal	6,757	4,668,000
Pabna	4,861	3,418,000	Patuakhali	4,224	1,840,000
Rajshahi division	*34,565*	*21,087,000*	Khulna division	*33,178*	*17,150,000*
Tangail	3,370	2,444,000	Sylhet	12,393	5,650,000
Mymensingh	13,105	6,543,000	Comilla	6,718	6,880,000
Jamalpur	3,405	2,445,000	Noakhali	4,804	3,813,000
Dacca	7,464	10,049,000	Chittagong	7,006	5,476,000
Faridpur	6,977	4,768,000	Chittagong Hill Tracts	13,191	746,000
Dacca division	*30,916*	*26,249,000*	Chittagong division	*44,112*	*22,565,000*

The language is Bengali.

GOVERNMENT AND CONSTITUTION. Bangladesh is a republic. The Constitution came into force on 16 Dec. 1972 and provided for a parliamentary democracy. On 25 Jan. 1975 Sheikh Mujibur Rahman took on the office of President, with an advisory Parliament. All political parties were abolished, and replaced by the new Bangladesh Krisha Sramik Awami League. On 15 Aug. 1975 Sheikh Mujibur Rahman and his family were killed; martial law was introduced on 20 Aug. and political parties were banned (including the new BKSAL) on 30 Aug. K. M.Ahmed was installed as President on 15 Aug. and replaced on 7 Nov. by former Chief Justice A. M. Sayem. Elections to parliament were promised for Feb. 1977 but postponed indefinitely in 1976. Political parties were made legal once again and requested to apply for registration in Aug. 1976.

On 29 Nov. 1976 Maj.-Gen. Ziaur Rahman became Chief Martial Law Administrator, with the Chiefs of Naval and Air Staff as his deputies. On 21 April 1977 President Sayem resigned and Maj.-Gen. Ziaur Rahman was sworn in as President.

On 22 April 1977 the constitution of 1972 was amended to establish 'absolute trust and faith in Allah' as the first fundamental principle of state and to provide for a Supreme Judicial Council which would prescribe a code of conduct for judges and advise the President. Three political parties (JSD, Bangladesh Communist Party (pro-Soviet) and Democratic League) were dissolved in Oct. 1977. The President was confirmed in office by general election. Martial law ended in April 1979. President Ziaur Rahman was murdered by a group of army officers on 30 May 1981. Mr Justice Abdus Sattar was installed as Acting President and elected president in Nov. 1981.

A Presidential election was held on 15 Nov. 1981, resulting in a victory for Mr Justice Abdus Sattar.

On 23 March 1982 there was a bloodless military *coup*, by which Lieut.-Gen. Hossain Mohammad Ershad became head of state and chief martial law administrator. President Sattar was deposed. The Constitution was suspended and parliament ceased to function. Lieut.-Gen. Ershad, the commander of the army, said that a temporary military government was necessary to restore economic and social order and democratic civilian government would return as soon as possible. Assanuddin Chowdhury was sworn in as civilian president on 27 March.

Parliament has one chamber of 300 members directly elected every 5 years by citizens over 18. There are 30 seats reserved for women members elected by Parliament. A general election is planned for 1984.

The government in autumn 1982 was composed as follows:

Prime Minister: Lieut.-Gen. Hossain Mohammad Ershad.

Special Adviser to the Prime Minister: Maj.-Gen. M. I. Karim. *Foreign Affairs:* A. R. Shams-ud Doha. *Home Affairs:* Maj.-Gen. V. M. K. Choudhury. *Finance and Planning:* A. M. A. Muhith. *Industry:* S. M. Shafiul Azam. *Transport and Communications:* Rear-Adml. M. A. Khan. *Flood Control, Energy and Mineral Resources:* Air-Vice-Marshal Sultan Mahmud. *Law, Land Administration, Land Reform, Attorney General:* K. A. Bakr. *Health and Population Control.* Maj.-Gen. M. Shamsul Haq. *Food and Relief:* Air Vice-Marshal A. G. Mahmud. *Public Works and Urban Development:* Maj.-Gen. Abdul Mannan Siddique. *Labour and Manpower:* Air Vice-Marshal Aminul Islam. *Information and Broadcasting:* S. N. Hashim. *Local Government and Rural Development:* M. Rahman. *Agriculture:* A. Z. M. Obaidullah Khan. *Social Welfare and Women's Affairs:* S. Katun. *Education and Religious Affairs:* A. Majid Khan.

National flag: Bottle green with a red disc in the centre.

National anthem: Amar Sonar Bangla, ami tomay bhalobashi (My golden Bengal, I love you). Words by Rabindranath Tagore.

DEFENCE

Army. There are 5 infantry divisions with 27 battalions and 2 tank regiments, 12 artillery regiments, 6 engineer battalions and supporting arms. Strength (1983) 70,000. There are 66,000 paramilitary militia volunteers.

Navy. Naval bases are at Chittagong (handed over by India on 14 Feb. 1972), Kaptai, Khulna and Dacca.

The fleet comprises 3 former British frigates (*Ali Hyder, ex*-HMS *Jaguar*, 2,520 tons full load, transferred in July 1978; and *Lincoln* and *Umar Farooq, ex*-HMS *Llandaff*, each 2,408 tons full load, transferred in Feb. 1982 and Dec 1976); 2 *ex*-Yugoslav 200-ton patrol vessels, 4 *ex*-Chinese fast gunboats, 2 *ex*-Indian 150-ton patrol craft, 1 British-built 140-ton patrol craft, 5 indigenously built 70-ton river gunboats, 1 support ship, 1 repair vessel and 1 training ship of 710 tons.

The manpower of the Navy in 1983 was 5,300, comprising 300 officers and 5,000 ratings.

Air Force. Deliveries, from the Soviet Union and China successively, have built up a current strength of about 32 J-6 (MiG-19) fighter-bombers; 6 MiG-21MF fighters; 3 An-12, 1 An-24 and 3 An-26 turboprop transports; about 16 Mi-8, Bell

212 and Alouette III helicopters; 12 Chinese CJ-6 piston-engined primary trainers, 8 Magister armed jet trainers and some light aircraft, including 4 Otters. Personnel strength, 3,000.

INTERNATIONAL RELATIONS

Membership. Bangladesh is a member of the UN and all its related agencies, of the Colombo Plan and of the Islamic Conference.

External Debt. Estimated debt, Dec. 1981, US$4,000m. Most of this was in loans from the Western aid group through the World Bank.

Treaties. Bangladesh signed an economic and technical co-operation agreement with China on 4 Jan. 1977. The amended constitution of 1977 states that Bangladesh seeks fraternal relations with Moslem countries based on Islamic solidarity.

ECONOMY

Planning. The development budget for 1982–83 was Tk.27,000m., of which the highest proportion is for agriculture, irrigation, flood control and rural development.

The second 5-year plan was launched in 1980, as part of a 20-year perspective plan. There was a 2-year interim plan 1978–80, with an envisaged investment of Tk.36,700m. mainly for rural development.

Budget. Details were as follows for two financial years (Tk.1m.):

	1980–81	*1981–82*
Revenue receipts	23,430	25,538
Revenue expenditure	14,816	18,497
Foreign assistance	15,330	20,814

Money supply (June 1979) stood at Tk.15,150·6m. and foreign exchange reserves (June 1977) at Tk.4,561·6m.

Currency. A new currency, the *Taka*, was floated in 1976 (Tk.36·40 = £1 and Tk.24·10=US$1 in March 1983).

Banking. The former private banking system, except for foreign banks, has been nationalized. In June 1978 there were 2,756 bank branches (1,594 rural).

Weights and Measures. Imperial measures are in use. Weight is in the *seer* (1 *seer* = 2 lb.); the *maund* (1 *maund* = 40 *seers*) and the ton. The metric system was to be introduced from July 1982.

ENERGY AND NATURAL RESOURCES

Electricity. There is a hydro-electric power station at Kaptai on Karnafulli and other power stations at Siddhirganj (80 mw), Ashuganj (120), Ghorasal (110), Shahjibazar (1,000), Khulna (60) and Bheramara (40). Installed capacity for electric power (1976) 755,000 kw (of which 80,000 kw are from hydro-electric plants). Production (1975), 1,378m. kwh., of which 355m. kwh. are hydro-electricity.

Water. On 5 Nov. 1977 India and Bangladesh signed an agreement on sharing the water of the river Ganges. The flow will be monitored daily at the Farakka barrage and two other points. By a further agreement of 1982 the waters of the Brahmaputra will be diverted to the Ganges to augment the flow.

Oil. Supplies have been located in the Bay of Bengal. Drilling is in progress.

Gas. Natural gas from Titas is piped to Dacca; drilling is in progress at other sites, and reserves are considered sufficient for 200 years. Production, 1981, 145m. cu. ft. per day.

Minerals. Coal has been found at Jamalpur (about 700m. tons). Other minerals include salt (750,000 tonnes in 1975), limestone, white clay, glass sand. The Rajshahi area has known reserves of deep-lying coal. In 1979 the Saudi fund for Development invested US$30m. for a limestone and cement project at Jaipurhat.

Agriculture. Agriculture contributes about 54% of GDP (Tk. 37,512m. in 1981–82) and employs about 80% of the economically active population; 64% of the total area is under cultivation; 80% of that is under rice and 9% under jute. Cultivable waste is about 1·5m. acres. About 3·6m. acres (1977–78) is irrigated. Rice is the most important food crop; food grain production (90% rice) in 1980–81, 15m. tonnes. Other crops in 1979 (1,000 tonnes): Sugar-cane, 6,900; wheat (1980), 800; tobacco, 49; tea (1980), 87·5m. lb. There were 2,250 tractors in use in 1974.

Livestock in 1980 (1,000): Poultry, 71,500; cattle, 33,000; goats, 11,500; sheep, 1,061; buffalo, 1,550; horses, 45.

Bangladesh produces about 70% of the world production of raw jute which is the principal foreign exchange earner. Production, 1981–82, 4·7m. bales.

Forestry. The total area under forests (1977) is 9,283 sq. miles, of which 5,105 sq. miles are Reserved Forests. The output of timber in 1975 was 15·9m. cu. metres of roundwood (broad-leaved timber) and 410,000 cu. metres of sawn wood. Among minor forest products are 76·5m. stems of bamboos, 415,000 canes, 6,500 maunds of honey annually.

Fisheries. Being bounded on the south by the Bay of Bengal and having numerous rivers, streams, khals and bils, the state is pre-eminently a fish-producing area and possesses great possibilities for the manufacture of various oils and fish products. Fish production, 1978–79, 850,000 tonnes.

INDUSTRY AND TRADE

Industry. Out of the existing industries, the textile-mills, sugar factories, match factories, glass works, hosiery factories, a paper-mill, jute-mills, aluminium works and a cement factory, with a capacity of 2m. tons per annum, are the most prominent. New government policy in 1982 aimed to restore public-sector jute and textile mills to private ownership and encourage the private sector. Arms and ammunition, atomic energy, forestry, air transport, communications and electrical industries would remain in the public sector.

Refinery distillation capacity, 1·68m. tonnes. There is a steel mill at Chittagong with a capacity of 250,000 ingot-tons per annum. There is also a newsprint factory, 4 fertilizer factories, a shipyard, a dockyard and a liquified natural gas plant. Jute products, 1981–82, 581,000 tons. Industry employs about 7% of the active population and provides 8·8% (1981–82) of the GNP. Industrial output grew by about 5% in 1982.

Labour. In 1974–75, 1,417 firms (employing more than 10 people) had 293,200 paid employees earning Tk.1,298·7m.; value added, Tk.3,781m.

Commerce. The main export commodities are jute goods, hide, skins, leather and tea. Bangladesh has resumed trade with Pakistan. In 1981-82 exports were valued at Tk.12,000m., of which Tk.7,720m. was from jute and jute products. Principal imports (Tk.47,780m.) are machinery, transport equipment, food grains, mineral fuels, chemicals, drugs, medicines and consumer goods.

Total trade between Bangladesh and UK (British Department of Trade returns, in £1,000 sterling):

	1979	*1980*	*1981*	*1982*
Imports to UK	60,421	73,084	15,063	25,558
Exports and re-exports from UK	90,071	110,408	45,210	58,179

Tourism. In 1980 there were 64,162 visitors to Bangladesh. They spent TK.238m.

COMMUNICATIONS

Roads. The State is backward in the matter of road communications, but there are some 2,500 miles of paved and 2,000 miles of unpaved road. In 1976 there were 66m. motor vehicles.

Railways. In 1980 there were 2,883 km of railways, comprising 973 km of 1,676 mm gauge and 1,910 km of metre gauge. In 1980–81 the railways carried 2·9m. tonnes of freight and 89·3m. passengers.

Aviation. Bangladesh Biman (Bangladesh Airways) has domestic flights from

Dacca and international services to Calcutta, Kathmandu, Bombay, Dubai, Abu Dhabi, Jeddah, Bangkok, Singapore, London, Doha, Kuwait, Amsterdam, Rome, Karachi, Kuala Lumpur, Dahrain, Tripoli, Athens and Muscat.

Shipping. Bangladesh possesses important natural advantages in her navigable channels which give valuable service in carrying produce by 5,000 miles of cheap water routes. There are 3 principal waterways, the Padma, Brahmaputra and Meghna. These are freely used by inland steam vessels, which serve areas where railways cannot be economically constructed. The Bangladesh Shipping Corporation owns 24 ships including a 93,000-ton oil tanker *(Banglar Noor)*. The Corporation has the capacity to carry 20% of imports and 12% of exports.

Post and Broadcasting. There were 129,000 telephones in 1981. Dacca and Islamabad were linked by telephone in Oct. 1976 and a second telephone circuit was agreed on 11 April 1977. International communications are by satellite, Chittagong being linked to the Indian Ocean Intelsat IV satellite.

Newspapers. In Nov. 1981 there were 53 daily newspapers, 200 weeklies, 34 fortnightlies, 194 monthlies and 43 quarterly periodicals. Most papers are published in Dacca. The Government has set up a paper *(Dainik Barta-at Rajshahi)* to stimulate a regional press. Most papers are privately owned. There is a Press Institute.

JUSTICE, RELIGION, EDUCATION AND WELFARE

Justice. The amended constitution in 1977 set up a Supreme Judicial Council to establish a code of conduct for Supreme Court and High Court judges, who may be removed from office by the President on the Council's recommendation.

Religion. Islam is the official religion, about 80% of the people being Muslim and the rest Hindus, Buddhists and Christians.

Education. In 1980 (estimate) under 24% of the population was literate. The compulsory primary education scheme has been replaced by model primary education. The Government has dissolved the District School Boards and taken over school administration.

In 1980 there were 43,634 primary schools, 8,946 secondary schools and about 600 intermediate and degree colleges. Primary schools had 8m. students, secondary schools about 2m. and technical colleges about 16,000. There were 6 universities including those at Dacca, Rajshahi, Mymensingh and Chittagong (founded 1964); one university is for engineering and one for agriculture. Universities had about 28,000 students in 1977. There are 14 teacher-training colleges, 47 primary training institutes, 16 polytechnics and 26 vocational institutes.

Health. In 1979 there were 405 hospitals, 1 mental and 5 tuberculosis and chest hospitals, 8 medical colleges and nursing training centres which train about 1,200 nurses annually. In 1979 the number of beds was 17,494.

DIPLOMATIC REPRESENTATIVES

Of Bangladesh in Great Britain (28 Queen's Gate, London, SW7)
High Commissioner: Fakhruddin Ahmed (accredited 11 June 1982)

Of Great Britain in Bangladesh (Aku Bakr Hse., Plot 7, Road 84, Gulshan Dacca, 12)
High Commissioner: F. Mills, CMG.

Of Bangladesh in the USA (3421 Massachusetts Ave., NW, Washington, D.C., 20007)
Ambassador: Humayun Rasheed Choudbury.

Of the USA in Bangladesh (Adamjee Court Bldg., Motijheel, Dacca)
Ambassador: Jane A. Coon.

Of Bangladesh to the United Nations
Ambassador: (Vacant).

Books of Reference

Bangladesh Bureau of Statistics, *Statistical Digests.—Statistical Pocket Book of Bangladesh.*
Bangladesh Planning Commission, *The First Five Year Plan—The Second Five Year Plan.*
Ministry of Finance. *Bangladesh Economic Survey.* 1979–80
Abdullah, T., and Zeidenstein, S., *Village Women of Bangladesh: Prospects for Change.* Oxford, 1981
Chen, L. C. (ed.), *Disaster in Bangladesh, Health Crisis in a Developing Nation.* OUP, 1973
Chowdhury, R., *The Genesis of Bangladesh.* London, 1972
Dutt, K., *Bangladesh Economy: An Analytical Study.* New Delhi, 1973
Franda, M., *Bangladesh: The First Decade.* New Delhi, 1982
Kamal, K. A., *Sheikh Mujibur Rahman.* 2nd ed. Dacca, 1970
Kashyap, S. C. (ed.), *Bangla Desh: Background and Perspectives.* New Delhi, 1971
Khan, A. R., *The Economy of Bangladesh.* London, 1972
Oliver, T. W., *The United Nations in Bangladesh.* Princeton Univ. Press, 1978
Rahman, M., *Bangladesh Today: An Indictment and a Lament.* London, 1978
Robinson, E. A. G., and Griffin, K. (ed.), *The Economic Development of Bangladesh.* London, 1974

BARBADOS

Capital: Bridgetown
Population: 250,500 (1981)
GNP per capita: US$3,040 (1980)

HISTORY. Barbados was occupied by the British in 1627 and during its colonial history never changed hands. Full internal self-government was attained in 1961. Barbados became an independent sovereign state within the Commonwealth on 30 Nov. 1966.

AREA AND POPULATION. Barbados lies to the east of the Windward Islands. Area 166 sq. miles (430 sq. km). The hot and rainy seasons last from June to December, and the average rainfall is 56 in. per year. In 1980 the census population was 248,983. Bridgetown is the principal city: population, 7,552.

CONSTITUTION AND GOVERNMENT. The Legislature consists of the Governor-General, a Senate and a House of Assembly. The Senate comprises 21 members appointed by the Governor-General, 12 being appointed on the advice of the Prime Minister, 2 on the advice of the leader of the opposition and 7 in the Governor-General's discretion. The House of Assembly comprises 27 members elected every 5 years. In 1963 the voting age was reduced to 18.

The Privy Council is appointed by the Governor-General after consultation with the Prime Minister. It consists of 12 members and the Governor-General as chairman. It advises the Governor-General in the exercise of the royal prerogative of mercy and in the exercise of his disciplinary powers over members of the public and police services.

In the general election of June 1981 the Barbados Labour Party held 17 seats and the Democratic Labour Party 10 seats.

Governor-General: Sir Deighton Ward, GCMG, CVO.

The Cabinet, appointed in June 1981, was:

Prime Minister, Finance and Planning: Rt Hon. J. M. G. M. ("Tom") Adams, PC.

Deputy Prime Minister, Trade, Industry, Tourism and Caribbean Affairs: H. Bernard St John. *Foreign Affairs and Attorney-General:* Louis R. Tull. *Parliamentary Affairs:* Lionel S. Craig. *Education:* Miss Billie A. Miller. *Health:* Lloyd B. Braithwaite. *Information and Culture:* Nigel A. Barrow. *Transport and Works:* Dr Donald G. Blackman. *Housing and Lands.* Delisle Bradshaw. *Prime Minister's Office:* O'Brien Trotman. *Labour and Social Security:* Victor L. Johnson. *Agriculture, Food and Consumer Affairs:* Dr R. L. Johnny Cheltenham.

National flag: Three vertical strips of blue, gold, blue, with a black trident in the centre.

INTERNATIONAL RELATIONS

Membership. Barbados is a member of UN, OAS, CARICOM, the Commonwealth and an ACP state of EEC.

ECONOMY

Budget. The fiscal year runs from 1 April to 31 March; accounts in BD$:

	1978–79	*1979–80*	*1980–81*	*1981–82*
Revenue	315,664,759	362,800,000	452,900,000	454,000,000
Expenditure	357,434,970	427,400,000	565,100,000	648,300,000

Currency. The monetary unit is the *Barbados dollar* (BD$) divided into 100 *cents*. In March 1983, £1 = BD$3.04; US$1 = 2.01.

Banking. Seven main commercial banks operate in Barbados including Barclays

Bank International, the Royal Bank of Canada, Canadian Imperial Bank of Commerce, the Bank of Nova Scotia, Chase Manhattan Bank, First National Bank of Chicago and Citibank, The Barbados National Bank.

Barbados is headquarters for the Caribbean Development Bank. It is a member of the Caribbean Common Market (CARICOM). The Barbados Development Bank opened on 15 April 1969 and Barbados became a member of the Inter-American Development Bank on 19 March 1969.

NATURAL RESOURCES

Agriculture. Of the total area of 106,240 acres, about 54,932 acres are arable land. The land is intensely cultivated, and sugar-cane occupies 64,000 acres, 39,178 were reaped in 1977. The agricultural sector accounted for 9·6% of GDP in 1980 (1946, 45%; 1967, 24%). In 1981, 9,500 persons were employed in agriculture. In 1980, 135,000 tons of sugar were produced. There are 12 sugar factories, 1 syrup plant and a rum distillery in production.

Livestock (1981): Cattle, 19,000; sheep, 53,000; goats, 29,000; pigs, 50,000; poultry, 848,000.

Fisheries. There are about 544 powered boats and many men and women are employed during the flying-fish season. Large numbers of these boats are laid up from July to Oct. The fish catch in 1981 was 4,297 tonnes.

INDUSTRY AND TRADE

Industry. Industries operating in Barbados in 1977 numbered 178 and ranged from the manufacture of processed food to small specialized products such as garment manufacturing, furniture and household appliances, electrical components, plastic products and electronic parts.

Commerce. Total trade for calendar years in BD$1,000:

	1977	*1978*	*1979*	*1980*	*1981*
Imports [1]	545,110	628,221	852,446	1,064,107	1,126,854
Exports [1]	151,055	187,815	234,794	337,592	306,958

[1] Exclusive of bullion and specie.

In 1981 the principal imports (BD$1m.) were: Machinery and transport equipment, 278·3; manufactured goods, 211·8; lubricants, mineral fuels, etc., 193·8; food, 162·3; chemicals, 100·2; crude minerals, 27; animal and vegetable oils, 13·5. In 1981 the principal domestic exports (BD$1m.) were: Sugar, 74·6; clothing, 51·9; electrical parts, 56·2; miscellaneous, 99·8.

Total trade between Barbados and UK (British Department of Trade returns, in £1,000 sterling):

	1978	*1979*	*1980*	*1981*	*1982*
Imports from UK	11,765	8,414	7,630	9,390	14,887
Exports and re-exports to UK	24,367	27,253	29,860	35,409	26,886

Tourism. In 1981, 352,555 visitors came to Barbados, spending BD$526·9m. The industry employs over 10,000 people.

COMMUNICATIONS

Roads. There are 1,020 miles of road open to traffic, of which 840 miles are all-weather roads. In 1977 there were 22,000 private cars, 2,000 taxis, 266 buses and 4,000 other vehicles.

Aviation. There is an international airport at Seawell, Christ Church, Barbados, served by British Airways, BWIA, Leeward Islands Air Transport, PANAM, Air Canada, SAS, Caribbean Airways and Eastern Airlines, Cubana Airlines, Venezuelan Airlines. In 1976, 360,170 passengers arrived by air; 217,729 were in transit.

Shipping. A deep-water harbour opened in 1961 at Bridgetown provides 8 berths for ships 500–600 ft in length, including one specially designed for bulk sugar loading. The number of merchant vessels entering in 1972 was 1,381 of 4,067,500 net tons.

Post and Telephone. There is a general post office in Bridgetown and 13 branches on the island. In Jan. 1981 there were 66,679 telephones and stations in service.

Cinemas. There were (1981) 6 cinemas with a seating capacity of 5,040, and 2 drive-in cinemas for 600 cars.

Newspapers. In 1981 there were 2 daily newspapers.

JUSTICE, RELIGION, EDUCATION AND WELFARE

Justice. Justice is administered by the Supreme Court and by magistrates' courts. All have both civil and criminal jurisdiction. There is a Chief Justice and 3 puisne judges of the Supreme Court and 8 magistrates.

Religion. The majority (about 70%) of the population are Anglicans, the remainder mainly Methodists, Moravians and Roman Catholics.

Education. In 1981–82 children in 115 government primary schools numbered 33,395; in 21 secondary schools, 21,457; in 7 vocational centres, 595; in 15 private approved secondary schools, 4,289. There are 25 independent primary schools with 3,101 pupils and a number of independent schools for which no accurate figures are available. Education is free in all government-owned and maintained institutions from primary to university level.

In 1963 Erdiston College became one of the constituent Colleges of the University of the West Indies Institute of Education. The College of Arts and Sciences of the University of the West Indies in Barbados was opened in Sept. 1963 and Cave Hill campus in 1967. In 1979–80, 1,399 students attended the Cave Hill campus. The Barbados Community College for higher education at pre-university level was opened in 1969; in 1979–80, 1,800 students (full- and part-time) were enrolled. In 1980–81, 1,610 students (mainly part-time) attended the Samuel Jackman Prescod Polytechnic which was opened in Nov. 1969 to give training in, among other things, construction, electrical and engineering trades. In 1972–73, 74 government scholars, bursars and exhibitioners were attending universities overseas. Government expenditure on education during 1981–82 was estimated at BD$101,261,267.

Health. In 1972 there were 2,220 hospital beds and (1973) 160 doctors.

DIPLOMATIC REPRESENTATIVES

Of Barbados in Great Britain (6 Upper Belgrave St., London, SW1X 8AZ)
High Commissioner: A. W. Symmonds.

Of Great Britain in Barbados (147/9 Roebuck St., Bridgetown)
High Commissioner: Viscount Dunrossil, CMG.

Of Barbados in the USA (2144 Wyoming Ave., NW, Washington, D.C. 20008)
Ambassador: Charles A. T. Skeete.

Of the USA in Barbados (PO Box 302, Bridgetown)
Ambassador: Milan Bish.

Of Barbados to the United Nations
Ambassador: Harley S. L. Moseley.

Books of Reference

Statistical Information: The Barbados Statistical Service (NIS Bldg, Fairchild St, St Michael) produces selected monthly statistics and annual abstracts. *Government Statistician:* Selwyn Straughn.
Barbados Economic Survey, 1978
Barbados Development Plan, 1979–83

Chandler, M. J., *A Guide to Records in Barbados.* Univ. of the West Indies, 1965
Hoyos, F. A., *Barbados, Our Island Home.* London, 1970.—*Barbados: A History from the Amerindians to Independence.* London, 1978
Starkey, O. P., *Commercial Geography of Barbados.* Indiana Univ. Press, 1961

Library: The Barbados Public Library, Bridgetown. *Acting Chief Librarian:* Betty Carrillo.

BELGIUM

Capital: Brussels
Population: 9·8m. (1981)
GNP per capita: US$12,180 (1980)

Royaume de Belgique—Koninkrijk België

HISTORY. The kingdom of Belgium formed itself into an independent state in 1830, having from 1815 been part of the Netherlands. The secession was decreed on 4 Oct. 1830 by a provisional government, established in consequence of a revolution which broke out at Brussels, on 25 Aug. 1830. A National Congress elected Prince Leopold of Saxe-Coburg King of the Belgians on 4 June 1831; he ascended the throne 21 July 1831.

By the Treaty of London, 15 Nov. 1831, the neutrality of Belgium was guaranteed by Austria, Russia, Great Britain and Prussia. It was not until after the signing of the Treaty of London, 19 April 1839, which established peace between King Leopold I and the King of the Netherlands, that all the states of Europe recognized the kingdom of Belgium. In the Treaty of Versailles (28 June 1919) it is stated that as the treaties of 1839 'no longer conform to the requirements of the situation', these are abrogated and will be replaced by other treaties.

AREA AND POPULATION. Belgium is bounded north by the Netherlands, north-west by the North Sea, west and south by France, east by Federal Republic of Germany and Luxembourg. Belgium has an area of 30,519 sq. km (11,778 sq. miles). The Belgium exclave of Baarle-Hertog in the Netherlands has an area of 7 sq. km, and a population (1 Jan. 1981) of 1,100 males and 1,019 females.

By an agreement, 23 Sept. 1956, the frontier with Germany was slightly readjusted.

Census	*Population*	*Increase % per annum*	*Census*	*Population*	*Increase % per annum*
1900	6,693,548	1·03	1947	8,512,195	0·36
1910	7,423,784	1·09	1961	9,189,741	0·52
1920	7,465,782	0·06	1970	9,650,944	0·55
1930	8,092,004	0·84			

Provinces	*Provincial capitals*	*Area (hectares)*	*Estimated population (31 Dec.)* 1970[1]	1979	1980	1981
Antwerp (Anvers)	Antwerp	286,725	1,533,249	1,573,647	1,575,530	1,571,092
Brabant	Brussels	335,811	2,176,373	2,220,699	2,221,782	2,222,974
Flanders West	Bruges	313,439	1,054,429	1,078,239	1,080,400	1,296,719
Flanders East	Ghent	298,167	1,310,117	1,330,134	1,331,043	998,007
Hainaut	Mons	378,669	1,317,453	1,308,931	1,305,163	720,766
Liège	Liège	386,213	1,008,905	1,005,947	1,004,034	222,437
Limbourg	Hasselt	242,231	652,547	710,715	716,059	408,134
Luxembourg	Arlon	444,114	217,310	222,317	223,396	1,332,547
Namur	Namur	366,501	380,561	404,481	405,967	1,081,943
Total		3,051,871	9,650,944	9,855,110	9,863,374	9,854,589

[1] Census.

In 1980 there were 4,821,395 males and 5,041,979 females.

Foreigners numbered 903,736 on 1 Jan. 1981.

Vital statistics for calendar years:

	Births	*Deaths*	*Marriages*	*Divorces*	*Immigration*	*Emigration*
1977	121,523	112,208	69,109	13,031	55,298	55,076
1978	121,983	115,060	67,206	13,645	52,594	58,495
1979	123,658	112,156	65,476	13,499	54,854	59,552
1980	124,794	114,364	66,413	14,538	54,694	58,212
1981	124,827	113,308	65,011	15,704	49,298	60,191

	1979	*1980*	*1981*
Of the total births including still-born	*123,658*	*124,794*	*124,827*
Boys	63,905	63,917	64,295
Girls	59,753	60,877	60,532

The most important towns, with estimated population on 1 Jan. 1982:

Brussels and suburbs [1]	994,774	Seraing	63,749
Ghent (Gand)	237,687	Genk	61,643
Charleroi	219,579	Verviers	54,800
Liège (Luik)	211,528	Mouscron (Moeskroen)	54,562
Antwerp (Anvers)	183,025	Roeselare (Roulers)	51,866
Brugge (Bruges)	118,048	Berchem	45,128
Namur (Namen)	102,075	Borgerhout	43,556
Mons (Bergen)	93,377	Wilruyck	42,349
Leuven (Louvain)	84,914	Merksem	41,782
Aalst (Alost)	78,707	Herstal	38,189
Mechelen (Malines)	77,067	Turnhout	37,567
Deurne	76,744	Hoboken	34,505
Kortrijk (Courtrai)	75,731	Lokeren	33,534
Oostende (Ostende)	69,331	Vilvoorde (Vilvorde)	33,007
St Niklass (St Nicolas)	68,208	Lier (Lierre)	31,300
Tournai (Doornik)	67,576	Ronse (Renaix)	24,287
Hasselt	65,100		

[1] The suburbs comprise 18 distinct communes, viz., Anderlecht, Etterbeek, Forest Ixelles, Jette, Koekelberg, Molenbeek St Jean, St Gilles, St Josse-ten-Noode, Schaerbeek, Uccle, Woluwe-St Lambert, Auderghem, Watermael-Boitsfort, Woluwe-St Pierre, Berchem, Ste Agathe, Evere and Ganshoren.

CLIMATE. Cool temperate climate, influenced by the sea. From Dec. to April, conditions are relatively cool (32–43°F, 0–6°C). Warm weather begins in May and continues until Sept. (54–72°F, 12–22°C) and in this period, sunshine averages 200–300 hours per month. Annual rainfall in Brussels, 28·5″ (724 mm); Bruges 34″ (854 mm).

KING. Baudouin, born 7 Sept. 1930, succeeded his father, Leopold III, on 17 July 1951, when he took the oath on the constitution before the two Chambers: married on 15 Dec. 1960 to Fabiola de Mora y Aragón, daughter of the Conde de Mora and Marqués de Casa Riera.

Father of the King. Leopold III, born 3 Nov. 1901, son of the late King Albert (died 17 Feb. 1934) and of Queen Elisabeth, Duchess of Bavaria (died 23 Nov. 1965); married (1) on 4 Nov. 1926 to Princess Astrid of Sweden, died 29 Aug. 1935, and (2) on 11 Sept. (civil marriage, 6 Dec.) 1941, to Mlle Mary Lilian Baels, Princess de Rethy, daughter of Hendrik Baels, formerly Minister of Agriculture. Leopold III succeeded to the throne on 23 Feb. 1934; on 20 Sept. 1944 parliament elected Prince Charles, Count of Flanders, Leopold's brother as Regent of the Kingdom. The Regency ended on 22 July 1950; but King Leopold delegated his powers to Prince Baudouin on 11 Aug. 1950, and abdicated on 16 July 1951.

Brother and Sister of the King. (1) Josephine Charlotte, Princess of Belgium, born 11 Oct. 1927; married to Prince Jean of Luxembourg, 9 April 1953; (2) Albert, Prince of Liège, born 6 June 1934; married to Paola Ruffo di Calabria, 2 July 1959; *offspring:* Prince Philippe, born 15 April 1960; Princess Astrid, born 5 June 1962; Prince Laurent, born 19 Oct. 1963. *Half-brother and half-sisters of the King.* Prince Alexandre, born 18 July 1942; Princess Marie Christine, born 6 Feb. 1951; Princess Maria-Esmeralda, born 30 Sept. 1956.

Uncle and Aunt of the King. (1) Prince Charles, Count of Flanders, born 10 Oct. 1903. (2) Princess Marie-José, born 4 Aug. 1906, married to Prince Umberto (King Umberto II of Italy in 1946) on 8 Jan. 1930.

BELGIAN SOVEREIGNS

Leopold I	1831–65	Leopold III	1934–44, 1950–51
Leopold II	1865–1909	Regency	1944–50
Albert	1909–34	Baudouin	1951–

CONSTITUTION AND GOVERNMENT. According to the constitution of 1831, Belgium is a constitutional, representative and hereditary monarchy. The legislative power is vested in the King, the Senate and the Chamber of Representatives. The royal succession is in direct male line in the order of primogeniture. By marriage without the King's consent, however, the right of succession is forfeited, but may be restored by the King with the consent of the two Chambers. No act of the King can have effect unless countersigned by one of his Ministers, who thus becomes responsible for it. The King convokes, prorogues and dissolves the Chambers. In default of male heirs, the King may nominate his successor with the consent of the Chambers. If the successor be under 18 years of age the two Chambers meet together for the purpose of nominating a regent during the minority.

National flag: Three vertical strips of black, yellow, red.

National anthem: Après des siècles d'esclavage (La Brabançonne; words by Jenneval, 1830; tune by F. van Campenhout, 1930).

French, Dutch and German are official languages.

Those sections of the Belgian Constitution which regulate the organization of the legislative power were revised in Oct. 1921. For both Senate and Chamber all elections are held on the principle of universal suffrage.

The Senate consists of members elected for 4 years, partly directly and partly indirectly. The number elected directly is equal to half the number of members of the Chamber of Representatives. The constituent body is similar to that which elects deputies to the Chamber; the minimum age of electors is 18 years, and the minimum length of residence required is 6 months. Women were given the suffrage at parliamentary elections on 24 March 1948. In the direct elections of members of both the Senate and Chamber of Representatives the principle of proportional representation was introduced by law of 29 Dec. 1899.

Senators are elected indirectly by the provincial councils, on the basis of 1 for 200,000 inhabitants. Every addition of 125,000 inhabitants gives the right to 1 senator more. Each provincial council elects at least 3 senators. There are at present 50 provincial senators. No one, during 2 years preceding the election, must have been a member of the council appointing him. Senators are elected by the Senate itself in the proportion of half the preceding category. The senators belonging to these two latter categories are also elected by the method of proportional representation. All senators must be at least 40 years of age. They receive 900,000 francs per annum. Sons of the King, or failing these, Belgian princes of the reigning branch of the royal family, are by right senators at the age of 18, but have no voice in the deliberations till the age of 25 years; this prerogative is hardly ever used.

The members of the Chamber of Representatives are elected by the electoral body. Their number, at present 212 (law of 3 April 1965), is proportional to the population, and cannot exceed one for every 40,000 inhabitants. They sit for 4 years. Deputies must be not less than 25 years of age, and resident in Belgium.

Each deputy has an annual allowance of 900,000 francs. Senators and deputies have also free railway passes.

The Senate and Chamber meet annually in October and must sit for at least 40 days; but the King has the power of convoking extraordinary sessions and of dissolving them either simultaneously or separately. In the latter case a new election must take place within 40 days and a meeting of the chambers within 2 months.

An adjournment cannot be made for a period exceeding 1 month without the consent of the Chambers.

After the revision of the Constitution by the laws of 24 Dec. 1970 and 28 July 1971 establishing three regions and two cultural councils, legislation on 'preparatory regionalization' was enacted in July 1974.

Parliament was dissolved on 6 Oct. 1981 and general elections were held on 8 Nov. 1981.

Parties in the Senate after the election: *Christelijke Volkspartij,* 22; *Parti social chrétien,* 8; *Socialistische Partij,* 13; *Parti Socialiste Belge,* 18; *Partij voor Vrijheid en Vooruitgang,* 14; *Parti Reformateur Libéral (PRL),* 11; *Other parties,* 20.

Parties in the Chamber of Representatives after the election: *Christelijke Volkspartij*, 43; *Parti social chrétien*, 18; *Parti Socialiste*, 35; *Socialistische Partij*, 26; *Partij voor Vrijheid en Vooruitgang*, 28; *Parti Reformateur Libéral*, 24; *Other parties*, 38.

A 4-party coalition government was formed in Dec. 1981 and in March 1982 was composed as follows:

Prime Minister: Dr Wilfried Martens (CVP).

Deputy Prime Ministers: Jean Gol, PRL (*Justice and Institutional Reform*); Willy de Clercq, PVV (*Finance and Foreign Trade*); Charles-Ferdinand Nothomb, PSC (*Interior and Public Works*). *Foreign Affairs:* Léo Tindemans (CVP). *Economic Affairs:* Mark Eyskens (CVP). *Public Works:* Louis Olivier (PRL). *Posts and Telecommunications:* Herman de Croo (PVV).*Labour and Employment:* Michel Hansenne (PSC). *Education (Flemish):* Daniel Coens (CVP). *Budget, Scientific Policy and Research:* Philippe Maystadt (PSC). *Brussels Regional Affairs and the Middle Classes:* Albert Demuyter (PRL). *Defence:* Freddy Vreven (PVV). *Education (French-language):* Michel Tromont (PRL). *Social Affairs and Institutional Reform:* Jean-Luc Dehaene (CVP).

There are ten Secretaries of State.

Local Government. Belgium has 9 provinces and since the so-called 'Amalgamation Law' of 30 Dec. 1975, 589 communes (instead of 2,359). They have a large measure of autonomous government. According to the law of 15 April 1920, changed by law, 1 July 1969, all Belgians over 18 years of age without distinction of sex, who have been domiciled for at least 3 months, have the right to vote in communal elections. Proportional representation is applied to the communal elections, and communal councils are to be renewed every 6 years. In each commune there is a college composed of the burgomaster as the president and a certain number of aldermen.

DEFENCE. Belgium is a full member of NATO since 1949 and of the Eurogroup since 1968. The need to extend European armaments co-operation led to the formation of the Independent European Program Group (IEPG) in 1976. Its members include Belgium.

According to the Military Law of 30 April 1962, the Belgian Army is recruited by annual calls to the colours and by voluntary enlistments.

Compulsory service lasts 8 or 10 months for private soldiers, 13 months for voluntary reserve officers and 15 for the paracommando regiment. Duration of military obligation is 8 years for most soldiers called for compulsory service.

Army. The Army comprises as major units 1 armoured and 3 mechanized brigades (2 of which are deployed as the Belgian divisions in the Belgian corps area in the Federal Republic of Germany) and 1 paracommando regiment. There are also 3 reconnaissance battalions. Total strength about 62,500. *Gendarmerie*, 15,750.

Equipment includes nearly 330 LEOPARD Main Battle Tanks, 135 SCORPION Light Tanks, 150 SCIMITAR Armoured Fighting Vehicles, 1,150 Armoured Personnel Carriers and 80 JPK 90mm Self-Propelled Anti-Tank Guns; Artillery Battalions are equipped with 105mm, 155mm and 203mm Self-Propelled Howitzers, LANCE Surface-to-Surface Missiles, HAWK Surface-to-Air Missiles and GEPARD Armoured Vehicles with 35mm Anti-Aircraft Guns.

Other equipment in use: MILAN Anti-Tank Guided Weapon, STRIKER Armoured Fighting Vehicle with SWINGFIRE Anti-Tank Guided Weapon, Islander aircraft, Alouette II helicopters, Epervier Remotely Piloted Vehicle.

Navy. The naval forces include 4 frigates (Navy designed and built) completed in 1978, 7 ocean minehunters, 2 command and logistic support ships, 2 coastal minehunters, 4 coastal minesweepers (4 in reserve), 14 inshore minesweepers, 2 research ships, 6 river patrol boats, 5 tugs, 1 degaussing ship, 1 ammunition transport and 5 miscellaneous craft. A tripartite minehunter is being built and nine others are projected. Naval personnel in 1983 totalled 4,720 officers and ratings.

The naval air arm comprises 3 Alouette III general utility helicopters.

Air Force. The Air Force has a strength of about 20,000 personnel and more than 270 aircraft in 14 operational squadrons and support units. There are 2 all-weather fighter wings (each 2 squadrons), of F-16s; 2 tactical wings with 3 squadrons of Mirage 5Bs, including Mirage 5BD two-seat trainers, and 1 squadron of Mirage 5BR photo-reconnaissance aircraft; and 1 wing (2 squadrons) equipped with 12 C-130H Hercules turboprop transports, 2 light twin-jet Falcons, 3 HS 748 twin-turboprop transports, 5 Swearingen Merlin III light turboprop transports and 2 Boeing 727. Two wings, based in Germany, have Nike surface-to-air missiles. Other types in service include Sea King Mk 48 search and rescue helicopters, SIAI-Marchetti SF.260M and Alpha Jet training aircraft.

INTERNATIONAL RELATIONS

Membership. Belgium is a member of UN, EEC, Benelux Economic Union, Council of Europe, NATO, OECD and WEU.

ECONOMY

Budget. Revenue and expenditure for calendar years (in 1m. francs):

	1977	*1978*	*1979*	*1980*	*1981*	*1982*
Receipts						
Current	747,509	877,324	941,484	979,239	1,010,200	1,146,300
Capital	159,515	167,769	175,687	197,867	157,200	...
Total	907,024	1,045,093	1,171,171	1,177,106	1,167,400	...
Expenditure						
Current	865,733	1,012,521	1,092,766	1,107,082	1,300,400	1,397,800
Capital	85,225	113,351	119,212	168,088	186,400	185,000
Total	950,958	1,125,872	1,211,978	1,275,170	1,486,800	1,582,800

On 31 Aug. 1982 the Belgian public debt consisted of (in 1m. francs): Internal debt consolidated, 1,392,500; short and middle terms, 845,700; at sight, 92,125. External debt, 587,000.

Currency. The *franc*, containing 0·01826 gramme of fine gold, is the unit of currency.

No gold has been minted since 1882 (save only 5m. francs struck in 1914). New silver coins of 250 francs have been issued since 16 March 1976. Note circulation 31 Dec. 1980, 371,796m. francs.

The official rate of exchange in March 1983 was US$1 = 47·81 francs; £1 = 71·45 francs.

Banking. The bank of issue in Belgium is the National Bank, instituted in 1850. It is the cashier of the State, and is authorized to carry on the usual banking operations. The note circulation on 31 Dec. 1981 amounted to 382,225m. francs. The articles of association of the National Bank of Belgium were modified on 13 Sept. 1948 so as to strengthen public control.

The savings banks are mainly operated by the *Caisse Générale d'Epargne et de Retraite* and by the private savings banks. *The Caisse Générale d'Epargne et de Retraite* (CGER), a state institution, consists of 2 parts: *the Caisse d'Epargne* which performs the whole range of banking activities and a further unit which embodies the funds engaged in social security and insurance activities; the CGER operates under the authority of the Minister of Finance. The *Commission bancaire* (bank commission) supervises the financial situation and the activities of the Caisse d'Epargne. It co-operates with the Belgian postal service, thus obviating any need of a postal-savings system. The savings deposits and savings bonds of the Caisse d'Epargne amounted to 543,252m. francs on 31 Dec. 1980. The private savings banks, whose liabilities expressed in savings accounts and bonds amounted to 597,084m. francs on 31 Dec. 1981, are controlled by the 'Commission bancaire'.

Weights and Measures. The metric system is in force.

ENERGY AND NATURAL RESOURCES

Electricity. The production of electricity (1m. kwh.) amounted to 48,357 in 1978; 49,648 in 1979; 51,015 in 1980; 48,179 in 1981.

Gas. Production of gas (in 1m. cu. metres): 703 in 1978; 730 in 1979; 675 in 1980; 690 in 1981.

Minerals. Output (in tonnes) for 5 calendar years:

	1977	*1978*	*1979*	*1980*	*1981*
Coal	7,068,041	6,590,268	6,124,503	6,324,034	6,136,446
Briquettes	126,080	124,496	152,492	81,597	53,981
Coke	5,568,703	5,747,192	6,450,359	6,047,504	6,003,730
Cast iron	8,910,532	10,127,996	10,775,843	9,844,629	9,786,077
Wrought steel	11,261,005	12,604,240	13,444,799	12,323,519	12,285,083
Finished steel	8,631,802	9,696,177	10,364,011	9,517,357	8,888,253

Agriculture. Of the total area of 3,051,871 hectares, there were, in 1981, 1,408,993 hectares under cultivation, of which 371,731 were under cereals, 22,995 vegetables, 139,469 industrial plants, 118,005 root crops, 697,104 pastures and meadows.

Chief	*Area in hectares*			*Produce in tonnes*		
crops	*1979*	*1980*	*1981*	*1979*	*1980*	*1981*
Wheat	182,478	179,160	166,092	953,429	852,765	875,426
Barley	155,670	152,732	152,403	766,675	807,057	751,885
Oats	28,091	28,284	26,418	118,826	108,892	108,842
Rye	12,236	10,175	8,349	46,742	38,157	31,978
Potatoes	36,263	38,132	34,272	1,178,830	1,181,470	1,195,291
Beet (sugar)	115,716	117,165	130,326	5,867,937	5,314,597	6,935,934
Beet (fodder)	18,248	17,276	16,201	1,710,063	1,541,871	1,547,953
Tobacco	524	436	481	1,796	1,059	1,604

In 1981 there were 31,489 horses, 2,858,901 cattle, 79,232 sheep, 6,227 goats and 5,075,973 pigs.

Forestry. In 1970 the forest area covered 19·7% of the land surface. In 1970, 2·85 cu. metres of timber were felled.

Fisheries. The total quantity of fish landed amounted to 35,873 tons valued at 1,861m. francs in 1980. The fishing fleet had a total tonnage of 21,588 gross tons at 31 Dec. 1981.

INDUSTRY AND TRADE

Industry. In 1981 there were 14 sugar factories, output 168,069 tonnes of raw sugar; 3 sugar refineries, output 260,833 tonnes; 7 distilleries, output 109,767 hectolitres of potable and industrial alcohol; 134 breweries, output 13,811,076 hectolitres of beer; margarine factories, output 149,927 tonnes.

Six trusts control the greater part of Belgian industry: the Société Générale (founded in 1822) owns about 40% of coal, 50% of steel, 65% of non-ferrous metals and 35% of electricity; Brufina-Confinindus operates in steel, coal, electricity and heavy engineering; the Groupe Solvay rules the chemical industry; the Groupe Copée has interests in steel and coal; Empain controls tramways and electrical equipment; the Banque Lambert owns petroleum firms and their accessories.

Commerce. By the convention concluded at Brussels on 25 July 1921 between Belgium and Luxembourg and ratified on 5 March 1922 an economic union was formed by the two countries, and the customs frontier between them was abolished on 1 May 1922. Dissolved in Aug. 1940, the union was re-established on 1 May 1945. On 14 March 1947, in execution of an agreement signed in London on 5 Sept. 1944, there was concluded a customs union between Belgium and Luxembourg, on the one hand, and the Netherlands, on the other. The union came into force on 1 Jan. 1948, and is now known as the Benelux Economic Union. A joint tariff has been adopted and import duties are no longer levied at the Netherlands frontier, but import licences may still be required. A full economic union of the three countries came into operation on 1 Nov. 1960.

Benelux information is supplied by the Secrétariat Général de l'Union Douaniére Néerlando-Belgo-Luxembourgeoise, Rue de la Régence, 39, 1000 Brussels. It publishes *Benelux. Bulletin Trimestriel de Statistique; Statistisch Kwartaalbericht* (1955 ff.).

Trade by selected countries (in 1,000 Belgian francs):

	Imports from			*Exports to*		
	1979	*1980*	*1981* [1]	*1979*	*1980*	*1981* [1]
France	279,300,766	303,328,230	315,952,138	317,583,534	367,103,921	395,582,544
USA	119,082,380	161,130,425	165,939,976	61,854,060	63,336,344	87,152,270
UK	141,495,571	169,453,710	171,442,793	134,539,118	160,281,547	177,660,091
Netherlands	297,400,606	344,508,752	394,397,768	268,249,807	287,019,767	305,357,063
German Dem. Rep.	3,912,928	4,230,277	6,053,009	4,043,475	3,774,302	3,156,944
Germany, Fed. Rep.	394,186,010	413,045,898	435,354,580	373,254,153	401,531,524	414,123,911
Argentina	5,105,069	4,558,478	4,727,455	3,435,497	3,601,825	2,877,342
Italy	72,427,994	75,336,177	11,346,684	87,717,898	104,281,448	104,735,092
Switzerland	35,656,681	57,756,719	80,538,132	47,637,810	72,287,115	64,787,862
Zaïre	28,073,599	36,156,375	35,989,008	5,778,421	7,654,771	7,304,624
Denmark	8,149,148	9,738,732	9,982,649	19,770,083	22,492,972	27,157,142
USSR	17,401,055	32,543,225	36,318,716	13,822,083	18,117,926	21,884,703
India	7,053,144	6,633,042	7,807,996	11,651,516	10,702,620	20,039,004
Rep. of S. Africa	12,498,774	12,967,088	14,535,344	5,077,193	7,421,713	11,159,909
Canada	14,263,764	15,642,112	19,822,425	5,283,084	5,255,669	8,982,712
Brazil	8,205,556	9,066,873	13,168,019	4,414,375	4,333,550	4,557,981
Australia	6,051,544	6,444,824	6,094,337	3,347,777	4,288,391	4,589,326

[1] Provisional.

Imports and exports for 6 calendar years (in 1,000 Belgian francs):

	Imports	*Exports*		*Imports*	*Exports*
1976	1,368,961,214	1,266,457,241	1979	1,784,353,190	1,661,244,397
1977	1,447,981,180	1,344,704,149	1980	2,100,807,473	1,890,359,149
1978	1,526,044,142	1,410,257,630	1981 [1]	2,309,761,017	2,062,315,689

[1] Provisional.

The total trade between Belgium and Luxembourg and UK was as follows (British Department of Trade returns, in £1,000 sterling):

	1978	*1979*	*1980*	*1981*	*1982*
Imports to UK	1,831,278	2,324,561	2,596,962	2,448,605	2,861,809
Exports and re-exports from UK	2,201,820	2,467,631	2,624,108	2,092,011	2,298,118

Principal Belgian-Luxembourg exports to UK in 1981 [1] (tonnes; francs): Textiles (94,154; 1,456,101m.); metals (469,444; 13,401m.); chemical and pharmaceutical products (509,176; 16,311m.); precious stones and manufactures thereof (573; 40,745m.).

Principal Belgian-Luxembourg imports from the UK in 1981[1] (tonnes; francs): Machinery and electrical apparatus (44,759; 15,871m.); vehicles, chiefly motor cars, and aircraft (93,357; 15,459m.); textiles (37,313; 6,312m.); precious stones (81; 48,011m.); base metals and manufactures thereof (163,994; 6,663m.).

[1] Provisional.

Tourism. In 1981 receipts totalled 27m. francs, comprising 20m. francs from Belgian tourists and 7m. francs from overseas visitors.

COMMUNICATIONS

Roads. The total length of the roads in Belgium on 31 Dec. 1980 was as follows: State roads (including 1,252 km of motorway), 12,969 km; provincial roads, 1,362 km; communal roads, 108,671 km. The majority of roads are metalled. Number of motor vehicles in Belgium, 1 Aug. 1982, 3,827,004, including 3,230,951 passenger cars, 18,744 buses, 257,068 lorries, 28,003 non-agricultural tractors, 133,953 agricultural tractors, 121,959 motor cycles and 36,326 special vehicles.

Railways. The main Belgian lines were a State enterprise from their inception in 1834. In 1926 the *Société Nationale des Chemins de Fer Belges (SNCB)* was formed to take over the railways. The State is sole holder of the ordinary shares of SNCB, which carry the majority vote at General Meetings. The length of railway operated on 31 Dec. 1981 was 3,930 km. Revenue (1981), 47,700m. francs; expenditure, 53,570m. francs. SNCB is to absorb the Belgian National Light Railway (SNCV has 205 km of electrified, metre gauge) under a plan announced in 1980.

Aviation. The national Belgian airline SABENA (*Société anonyme belge d'exploitation de la navigation aérienne*) was set up in 1923. Its capital is 750m. francs. In addition to its European network, SABENA operates different routes to North and South America, to North, Central and South Africa and to the Near, the Middle and the Far East. In 1981 its airfleet comprised 26 aircraft. In 1981 SABENA flew 51m. km, carrying 2,052,996 revenue passengers, 441·5m. ton-km of freight and 12·54m. ton-km of mail.

Shipping.[1] On 1 Jan. 1981 the Belgian merchant fleet was composed of 99 vessels of 1,887,076 tons. There were 50 shipping companies, of which the most important were the Compagnie Maritime Belge, with 24 ships, and the Belgian Fruit Lines, SA, with 6 ships.

[1] Belgian shipping returns are given in the official 'Moorsom tons', which may be converted into net tons by deducting 19·85% from the Moorsom total.

The navigation at the port of Antwerp in 1981 was as follows: Number of vessels entered, 16,802; tonnage, 104,610,692. Number of vessels cleared, 16,731; tonnage, 104,864,074.

The total length of navigable waterways (rivers and canals) was 1,573·7 km in 1981.

Post and Broadcasting. On 31 Dec. 1981 there were 2,309 post offices. The gross revenue of the post office in the year 1981 amounted to 20,954m. francs.

A régie of telegraphs and telephones for running the services on business lines was created in 1930. Telegraph offices for dispatching and receiving wires numbered 106; for dispatching only, 26. Receipts for 1980 were 4,325·14m. francs; expenditure, 3,969,709,000 francs.

In 1980 the telephone service comprised 656 exchanges, connecting 7,040 public telephone stations and 2,441,993 subscribers. Number of telephones, 1 Jan. 1980, 3,636,074. Receipts in 1980, 33,382,830m. francs; expenditure, 34,029,254m. francs.

Radiodiffusion-Télévision Belge de la Communauté Culturelle Française (RTBF)–Belgische Radio en Televisie (BRT) is a public service broadcasting on medium- and short-waves and on FM. There are 3 programmes in each network including regional broadcasts. The short-wave service is mainly intended for Africa and it is broadcast in French (RTBF), Dutch, English and Spanish (BRT) languages. RTBF broadcasts TV programmes in French and BRT in Dutch. The programmes are financed by state grants in aids. Colour programmes are broadcast by PAL system. Number of receivers (1981), radio, 4,596,365; TV, 2,963,126 (including 1,943,082 colour sets).

Cinemas (1981). There were 479 cinemas, with a seating capacity of 160,607.

Newspapers (1982). There are 38 daily newspapers (some of them only regional or local editions of larger dailies), of which 23 are in French, 14 in Dutch and 1 in German.

JUSTICE, RELIGION, EDUCATION AND WELFARE

Justice. Judges are appointed for life. There is a court of cassation, 5 courts of appeal, and assize courts for political and criminal cases. There are 26 judicial districts, each with a court of first instance. In each of the 222 cantons is a justice and judge of the peace. There are, besides, various special tribunals. There is trial by jury in assize courts.

Religion. Of the inhabitants professing a religion the majority are Roman Catholic, but no inquiry as to the profession of faith is now made at the censuses. There are, however, statistics concerning the clergy, and according to these there were in 1980: Roman Catholic higher clergy, 130; inferior clergy, 6,956; Protestant pastors, 83; Anglican Church, 10 chaplains; Jews (rabbis and ministers), 26. The State does not interfere in any way with the internal affairs of any church. There is full religious liberty, and part of the income of the ministers of all denominations is paid by the State.

There are 8 Roman Catholic dioceses subdivided into 260 deaneries.

Estimated number of Protestants, 24,000; of Jews, 35,000.

The Protestant (Evangelical) Church is under a synod. There is also a Central Jewish Consistory, a Central Committee of the Anglican Church and a Free Protestant Church.

Education. On 8 Nov. 1962/2 Aug. 1963 a linguistic frontier was fixed between the Dutch-speaking, French-speaking and German-speaking parts of Belgium. In the north, Dutch is recognized as the official language, in the south, French, and along the eastern border, German. The city and *arrondissement* of Brussels are bilingual. The percentage of the population in the Flemish, French, German and bilingual regions was 57·1, 32·1, 0·7, 10·1 on 1 Jan. 1981. (*See* map in THE STATESMAN'S YEAR-BOOK, 1967–68.)

Higher Education (1980–81). Higher education is given in state universities: Ghent (12,378 students), Liège (9,517 students), Mons (1,455 students), the Polytechnic Faculty in Mons (498 students), the Antwerp State University Centre (1,949 students), the Gembloux Faculty of Agronomical Sciences (784 students), the Royal Military School in Brussels (732 students) and in the private universities: Catholic University of Louvain (38,714 students), the Free University of Brussels (19,087), University Institution Antwerp (1,402 students), St Ignatius Antwerp (2,705 students), Our Lady of Peace in Namur (2,898 students), Catholic University Faculty in Mons (618 students), St Lewis in Brussels (1,532 students), the Limbourg University Centre (842 students) and the Protestant Faculty of Theology in Brussels (136 students). The total number of students in university colleges, faculties and institutes was 95,246.

There are 5 royal academies of fine arts and 5 royal conservatoires at Brussels, Liège, Ghent, Antwerp and Mons.

Secondary Education. 1,050 (1977–78) middle schools, 2,353 (1974–75) technical schools and 515 (1974–75) schools of the new system had a total of 199,167 (1980–81) pupils in the general classes and 264,911 in the technical classes in the traditional system and 384,639 pupils in the new system.

Elementary Education. There were 5,648 (1977–78) primary schools, with 857,418 pupils in 1980–81 and 4,607 (1977–78) infant schools, with 384,694 pupils in 1980–81.

Normal Schools. Under the French and German linguistic systems there were 26 (1975–76) schools for training secondary teachers (4,374 students) in 1980–81; 44 (1975–76) for training elementary teachers (3,578 students) in 1980–81, 63 technical normal schools in 1974–75 with (1980–81) 1,212 students and 19 (1975–76) normal infant schools with 1,087 students in 1980–81. The pedagogical education under the Dutch linguistic system is differently organized and totalled 14,306 students in 1980–81.

Health. In 1981 there were 25,629 physicians (including 546 dentists), 4,690 other dentists, 9,942 pharmacists and (1978) 3,593 midwives. Hospital beds numbered 92,436 on 1 Jan. 1981.

Social Security. Social security is based on the law of Dec. 1944. It applies to all workers subject to an employment contract, and is administered by the Central

National Office of Social Security (ONSS), which collects from employers and employees all contributions referring to family allowances, health insurance, old age insurance, holidays and unemployment. These sums are distributed by the Central Office to the various institutions concerned with these benefits. Insurance against unemployment is organized through a common fund, which also undertakes to re-train the unemployed for another employment while providing for their families. Since 1944 further laws have increased allowances, made fresh provisions for housing (1945), injuries while working, professional illnesses, etc. (1948).

Apart from private charity, the poor are assisted by the communes through the agency of the *Centre Public d'Aide Sociale* in French-speaking parts of the country and *Openbaar Centrum voor Maatschappelijk Welzijn* in Dutch-speaking areas. Provisions of a national character have been made for looking after war orphans and men disabled in the war. Certain other establishments, either state or provincial, provide for the needs of the deaf-mutes and the blind, and of children who are placed under the control of the courts. Provision is also made for repressing begging and providing shelter for the homeless.

DIPLOMATIC REPRESENTATIVES

Of Belgium in Great Britain (103 Eaton Sq., London, SW1W 9AB)
Ambassador: Robert Vaes, KCMG (accredited 17 Feb. 1977).

Of Great Britain in Belgium (Britannia Hse., rue Joseph II 28, 1040 Brussels)
Ambassador: J. E. Jackson, CMG.

Of Belgium in the USA (3330 Garfield St., NW, Washington, D.C., 20008)
Ambassador: J. Raoul Schoumaker.

Of the USA in Belgium (Blvd. du Régent 27, 1000 Brussels)
Ambassador: Charles H. Price, II.

Of Belgium to the United Nations
Ambassador: Edmonde Dever.

Books of Reference

Statistical Information: The Institut National de Statistique (44 rue de Louvain, Brussels) was set up on 24 Jan. 1831, under the designation of Bureau de Statistique Générale; after several changes, it received its present name on 2 May 1946. *Director-General:* Dr P. van Landeghem. *Main publications:*

Bulletin du Commerce Extérieur
Bulletin de Statistique. Monthly
Annuaire Statistique de la Belgique (from 1870).—*Annuaire statistique de poche* (from 1965)
Statistiques Agricoles. Monthly
Recensement général de la population au 31 déc. 1970. 13 vols.
Recensement de l'agriculture au 15 mai 1970. 3 vols.
Recensement de l'industrie et du commerce au 31 déc. 1970. 10 vols.

Annuaire administratif et judiciaire de Belgique. Annual. Brussels
L'économie belge. Ministère des Affaires Economiques. Annual (from 1947)
Belgium, Investment Guide. Ministère des Affaires Economique, 1974
Guide des Ministères: Revue de l'Administration Belge. Brussels, Annual
Belgique: Un Panorama. Institut Belge d'Information et de documentation, Brussels, 1969
Molitor, A., *L'Administration de la Belgique.* Brussels, 1974.

BELIZE

Capital: Belmopan
Population: 144,353 (1980)
GNP per capita: US$1,080 (1980)

HISTORY. The early settlement of the territory was probably effected by British woodcutters about 1638; from that date to 1798, in spite of armed opposition from the Spaniards, settlers held their own and prospered. In 1780 the Home Government appointed a superintendent, and in 1862 the settlement was declared a colony, subordinate to Jamaica. It became an independent colony in 1884. Self-government was attained in 1964. Independence was achieved on 21 Sept. 1981.

AREA AND POPULATION. Belize is bounded north by Mexico, west by Guatemala and south and east by the Caribbean sea. Area, 22,963 sq. km. There are 6 districts:

	Sq. km	*Population census, 1980*		*Sq. km*	*Population census, 1980*
Corozal	1,860	22,902	Cayo	5,338	22,837
Belize	4,204	50,801	Stann Creek	2,176	14,181
Orange Walk	4,737	22,870	Toledo	4,649	11,762

Total population (census, 1980) 145,353. Voters on the roll numbered 71,740 in 1980. In 1980 the birth rate per 1,000 was 43·1 and the death rate 4·9; infantile mortality 30 per 1,000 births; there were 907 marriages.

Main city, Belize City; population, census 1980, 39,771. Following the severe hurricane which struck the territory on 31 Oct. 1961 the capital Belmopan (population, 1980, 2,932) has been moved to a new site 50 miles inland; construction began in Jan. 1967 and it became the seat of government on 3 Aug. 1970. *See* map in the 1978–79 edition of THE STATESMAN'S YEAR-BOOK.

CONSTITUTION AND GOVERNMENT. Having achieved self-government in Jan. 1964 delays occurred in achieving independence because of the outstanding territorial claim by Guatemala. Attempts to reach agreement on the claim finally failed prior to independence being granted, but guarantees were given by Britain that a military force would remain.

The Constitution, which came into force on 21 Sept. 1981, provided for a National Assembly, with a 5-year term, comprising an 18-member House of Representatives elected by universal adult suffrage, and a Senate consisting of 5 members appointed by the Governor-General on the advice of the Prime Minister and 3 other nominated members.

Governor-General: Elmira Minita Gordon.

Prime Minister and Minister of Foreign Affairs: Rt. Hon. George Cadle Price PC.

Deputy Prime Minister, Minister of Defence and Home Affairs: Carl L. B. Rogers.

Flag: Blue with red band along the top and bottom edges. In the centre a white disc containing the coat of arms surrounded by a green garland.

DEFENCE. The Air Wing of the Belize Defence Force has two twin-engined BN-2B Defenders for maritime patrol and transport duties. RAF aircraft based temporarily in Belize include a detachment of Harrier V/STOL ground attack/reconnaissance aircraft.

ECONOMY

Budget. Revenue and expenditure (in $B1,000) for calendar years:

	1977	*1978*	*1979*	*1980-81*	*1981-82*
Revenue	54,439	65,359	75,828	88,977	86,687
Expenditure	63,526	66,990	76,850	91,935	71,049

Public debt, 31 March 1980, $B25,739,358; sinking fund, $B961,978.

Currency. There was (29 April 1980) a paper currency of $B17,695,000 in government notes of $B100, 20, 10, 5 and 1, and a subsidiary mixed metal coinage of 1-, 5-, 10-, 25- and 50-cent pieces.

Banking. The Royal Bank of Canada took over the business of the local bank in 1912; it has 8 branches. There are 7 government savings banks; depositors, about 10,000; deposits, $B82·3m. on 31 Dec. 1979.

Barclays Bank International have 7 branches, Bank of Nova Scotia have 5 branches and Atlantic Bank 3 branches.

NATURAL RESOURCES

Agriculture. The main agricultural export is sugar, followed by citrus fruit, chiefly grapefruit and oranges, whole, canned, juice and concentrates. Citrus production, 1981, 1,649,000 boxes. Sugar production in 1981 was 970,000 tonnes. Banana production began in 1973, and first shipments began in 1974; exports, 1981, 549,300 boxes. [Ed. note: Box of grapefruit, 80 lb., oranges, 90 lb., bananas, 42 lb.]

Livestock (1981): Cattle, 50,000; sheep, 3,000; pigs, 16,000; poultry, 348,000.

Forestry. 2,964 sq. miles, 49% of the total land area, are under forests which include mahogany, cedar, Santa Maria, pine and rosewood, and many secondary hardwoods of known or probable market value, as well as woods suitable for pulp production. Exports of forest produce in 1981 amounted to $B2·6m.

Fisheries. Food and game fish are plentiful, and domestic consumption is heavy. The total exported in 1981 was valued at $B13·3m. Turtles—Hawksbill, Loggerhead and Green—are plentiful but as yet are not exported.

LABOUR. The labour market alternates between full employment, often accompanied by local shortages in the citrus and sugar-cane harvesting (Jan.–July), and under-employment during the wet season (Aug.–Dec.), aggravated by the seasonal nature of the major industries.

COMMERCE. In 1981 total imports amounted to $B323·9m. Total domestic exports, $B149·5m. The principal domestic exports were timber, sugar, fish products, garments, bananas and citrus fruit.

Total trade between Belize and UK (British Department of Trade returns, in £1,000 sterling):

	1977	*1978*	*1979*	*1980*	*1981*	*1982*
Imports to UK	13,300	13,120	13,515	13,168	15,050	13,326
Exports and re-exports from UK	8,129	10,807	10,347	11,824	9,995	10,455

COMMUNICATIONS

Aviation. In 1981, 169,200 passengers and 1,821 tonnes of freight arrived and departed on international flights.

Shipping (1981). Registered shipping, 55 sailing vessels, 1,348 net tons, and 323 motor vessels, 745,197 net tons.

Post. Telephone lines connect Belize City with Corozal Town and Consejo on the coast, Orange Walk Town on New River, San Antonio on the Rio Hondo and other stations in the north, San Ignacio and Benque Viejo Towns in the west, Dangriga and Punta Gorda Town and other points in the south. Number of telephones (1981), 6,250. The Belize Telecommunication Authority has instituted a country-wide fully automatic telephone dialling facility. There are 6 post offices and 45 rural sub-post offices.

Cinemas (1979). There were 13 cinemas with seating capacity of 10,000.

Newspapers. There were 4 weekly newspapers and 4 monthly magazines in 1979.

JUSTICE, EDUCATION AND WELFARE

Justice. There are 3 magistrates' courts in Belize and 1 in each district town. The police force contained (1978) 30 officers and 470 n.c.o.s and constables.

Education. In 1981, 198 primary schools had a total enrolment of 35,113 pupils; 22 secondary schools, 6,298 pupils; and 5 other technical schools with 525 students. In Sept. 1979 the Belize College of Arts, Science and Technology was opened for post-sixth form courses. The Teachers' College offers courses for primary school teachers. The 3-year course leads to a teachers' diploma granted by the University of the West Indies.

Health. In 1982 there was 1 general hospital and 6 district hospitals with 55 doctors and 536 hospital beds.

DIPLOMATIC REPRESENTATIVES

Of Great Britain in Belize (Belize Hse., Belmopan)
High Commissioner: F. S. E. Trew.

Of the USA in Belize (Gabourel Lane, Belize City)
Chargé d'Affaires: Malcolm R. Barneby.

Books of Reference

Annual Report, 1972. Government Printer, Belize City, 1974
Abstract of Statistics 1981. Government Printer, Belize City, 1982
Anderson, A. H., *Brief Sketch of the British Honduras.* 7th ed. Belize, 1958
Bianchi, W. J., *Belize: The Controversy Between Guatemala and Great Britain.* New York, 1959
Dobson, D., *A History of Belize.* Belize, 1973
Floyd, B., *Focus on Honduras.* Univ. of West Indies, Jamaica, 1970
Grant, C. H., *The Making of Modern Belize.* CUP, 1976
Romney, D. H., (ed.), *Land in British Honduras.* HMSO, 1959
Setzekorn, W. D., *Formerly British Honduras: A Profile of the New Nation of Belize.* Ohio Univ. Press, 1981
Woodward, R. L., Jr, *Belize.* [Bibliography] Oxford and Santa Barbara, 1980

BENIN

Capital: Porto Novo
Population: 3·72m. (1982)
GNP per capita: US$300 (1980)

République Populaire du Benin

HISTORY. The territory of the present State was occupied by France in 1892 and was constituted a division of French West Africa in 1904 under the name of Dahomey. It became an independent republic within the French Community on 4 Dec. 1958, and acquired full independence on 1 Aug. 1960.

In the sixth *coup* since independence, Maj. Mathieu (now Ahmed) Kerekou came to power on 26 Oct. 1972 and proclaimed a Marxist–Leninist state, whose name was altered from Dahomey to Benin in Dec. 1975.

AREA AND POPULATION. Benin is bounded east by Nigeria, north by Niger and Upper Volta and west by Togo. The area is 112,622 sq. km, and the population, census 1979, 3,338,240. Estimate (1982) 3·72m. The seat of government is Porto Novo (132,000 inhabitants in 1979); the chief port and business centre is Cotonou (327,600); other important towns are Natitingou (50,800), Abomey (41,000), Kandi (31,000), Ouidah (30,000) and Parakou (23,000).

French is the official language, while 47% of the people speak Fon, 12% Adja, 10% Bariba, 9% Yoruba, 5% Somba and 5% Aizo.

CONSTITUTION AND GOVERNMENT. Under a *Loi fondamentale* adopted in Aug. 1977, the sole political party is the *Parti de la Revolution Populaire du Bénin;* its Congress held in Nov. 1979 elected a Central Committee of 45 members to direct Party policy and to appoint the 13-member Political Bureau.

There is a unicameral legislature, the National Revolutionary Assembly of 336 People's Commissioners elected on 20 Nov. 1979 from the sole list of the PRPB. On 4 Feb. 1980 this took over the responsibility for state policy from the former National Council of the Revolution.

The Assembly elects the President, who appoints and leads a National Executive Council of (1982) 21 Ministers.

President, Minister of National Defence: Lieut.-Col. Ahmed Kerekou.
Foreign Affairs: Simon Ifede Okouma.

National flag: Green with a red star in the canton.

Local Government. The 6 provinces, Atakora, Borgou, Zou, Ouémé, Atlantique and Mono, each governed by an appointed Prefect and a Provincial Revolutionary Council, are divided into 84 districts.

DEFENCE

Army. The Army consists of 1 engineer and 2 infantry battalions and support units; strength (1983), 3,000. There is a paramilitary *gendarmerie* of about 1,100.

Navy. A naval force was formed in 1979 with 2 fast gunboats, 2 fast torpedo boats and 2 coastal patrol craft transferred from the USSR, constituting a somewhat over-ambitious navy for such a short coastline. Personnel in 1983 was upwards of 200.

Air Force. The Air Force has a strength of about 100 officers and men, 2 twin-turboprop An-26, 1 F.27 and 2 C-47 transports, 1 Cessna Skymaster, 1 Aero Commander 500, 2 Broussard communications aircraft, up to 6 L-39 jet trainers, an Agusta-Bell 47G and an Alouette II helicopter. A twin-turbofan Corvette is operated by the Air Force on VIP missions for government agencies.

INTERNATIONAL RELATIONS

Membership. Benin is a member of UN, OAU and is an ACP country of EEC.

ECONOMY

Planning. A 10-year development plan (1980–90) envizages an expenditure of 958,800m. francs CFA.

Budget. The 1982 recurrent budget balanced at 46,863m. francs CFA and the investment budget at 96,730m. francs CFA.

Currency. The monetary unit is the *franc CFA (Communauté financière africaine)*, with a parity value of 50 *francs CFA* to 1 French *franc.* There are coins of 1, 2, 5, 10 and 25 *francs CFA*, and banknotes of 50, 100, 500, 1,000 and 5,000 *francs CFA*.

Banking. The *Banque Centrale des Etats de l'Afrique de l'Ouest* is the bank of issue and the central bank. The *Banque Commerciale du Bénin*, in Cotonou, conducts all government business.

ENERGY AND NATURAL RESOURCES

Electricity. The national electricity and water company, *Société Béninoise d'Electricité et d'Eau*, produced 5m. kwh in 1978 from generating plants at Cotonou, Porto-Novo and Parakou. Major development of hydro-electric resources along the Mono river are being conducted jointly with Togo.

Oil. The Semé oilfield, located 10 miles offshore, was discovered in 1968. Production is expected to commence in 1981–82 and should reach 150,000 bbls a day.

Agriculture. 90% of the population subsist by agriculture. The chief products, 1981 (in 1,000 tonnes) were: Cassava, 975; yams (1979), 650; maize, 349; sorghum, 80; groundnuts, 60; beans, 50; rice,16; and sweet potatoes, 14, while cash crops were palm kernels, 75, and palm oil, 34. Cotton cultivation has been successfully introduced in the north; coffee cultivation has given good results in the south.

Livestock (1981 in 1,000): Cattle (770), sheep (964), goats (930), pigs (460), poultry (4·15m.), horses (6), asses (1).

Fisheries. Total catch in 1979 was 25,500 tonnes (80% from inland and lagoon waters).

Forestry. There are about 16,000 sq. km of classified forest, mainly in the north. Roundwood production in 1978 was 2·53m. cu. metres.

INDUSTRY AND TRADE

Industry. Industrial plants are few, limited mainly to palm-oil processing and brewing. Under the 1977–80 Plan, a sugar complex was built at Savé and a cement plant at Onigbolo. There are textile mills at Cotonou and Parakou.

Labour. In 1973 the small trade unions were amalgamated to form a single body, now named the *Union Nationale des Syndicats des Travaillers du Bénin.*

Commerce. Imports in 1978, 60,210m. francs CFA; exports, 5,780m. francs CFA. The principal imports in 1975 (in 1m. francs CFA): Textiles, 5,744; machinery, 5,415; motor vehicles and parts, 3,852; clothing and footwear, 2,877. The principal exports were: Cotton lint, 1,542; palm-oil, 828; cocoa beans, 642; cement, 556. In 1977, France provided 23% and the UK 13% of imports, while of exports (1978) the Netherlands took 28%, Japan 27% and France 24%.

Total trade between Benin and UK (British Department of Trade returns, in £1,000 sterling):

	1978	*1979*	*1980*	*1981*	*1982*
Imports to UK	566	2,558	2,856	896	1,227
Exports and re-exports from UK	11,463	12,480	13,119	18,611	14,941

Tourism. There were 23,033 foreign tourists in 1977.

COMMUNICATIONS

Roads. There were 6,937 km of roads in 1974. There were 17,000 motor cars and 9,500 goods vehicles in 1974.

Railways. There are 579 km of metre-gauge railway. One line connects Cotonou with Parakou (438 km) and is to be extended to Dosso (in Niger); the second runs from Cotonou via Porto-Novo Pobé (107 km); and the third from Cotonou via Ouidah to Segboroué on the Togo frontier (34 km), continuing to Lomé.In 1979 carried 1·6m. passengers and 322,00 tonnes of freight.

Aviation. In 1980, 75,100 passengers used Cotonou airport. There are other airports at Abomey, Natitingou, Kandi and Parakou.

Shipping. In 1979, 144m. tonnes were unloaded and 1m. tonnes loaded at the port of Cotonou. There were (1979) 8 vessels of 1,074 GRT registered in Benin.

Post and Broadcasting. There were, in 1975, 9,624 telephones. Telegraph lines connect Cotonou with Togo, Niger and Senegal. In 1981 there were 65,000 radios and 12,500 television receivers.

Cinemas. In 1976 there were 4 cinemas with a seating capacity of 4,400.

Newspapers. In 1980 there was 1 daily newspaper with a circulation of 10,000.

JUSTICE, RELIGION, EDUCATION AND WELFARE

Justice. The Supreme Court is at Cotonou. There are Magistrates Courts in Cotonou, Porto-Novo, Natitingou, Abomey, Kandi, Ouidah and Parakou, and a *tribunal de conciliation* in each district. Judges at provincial and district level are appointed by and responsible to the Executive Council.

Religion. 66% of the population follow animist beliefs, 17% are Christian and 15% Moslem.

Education. There were, in 1979, 357,348 pupils in primary schools, 64,275 in secondary schools and (1977) 3,239 students in technical schools. The University of Benin (Cotonou) had 3,041 students in 1978.

Health. In 1976 there were 361 hospitals and dispensaries with 4,394 beds, 93 doctors, 10 dentists, 34 pharmacists and 243 midwives.

DIPLOMATIC REPRESENTATIVES

Of Benin in Great Britain
Chargé d'Affaires: Alexandre Ladipo (resides in Paris).

Of Great Britain in Benin
Ambassador: Sir Mervyn Brown, KCMG, OBE (resides in Lagos).

Of the USA in Benin (Rue Caporal Anami Bernard, Cotonou)
Chargé d'Affaires: James R. Bullington.

Of Benin to the United Nations
Ambassador: Thomas Setondji Boya.

Book of Reference

Ronen, D., *Dahomey: Between Tradition and Modernity.* Cornell Univ. Press, 1975

BERMUDA

Capital: Hamilton
Population: 54,670 (1980)
GNP per capita: US$11,050 (1980)

HISTORY. The Spaniards visited the islands in 1515, but, according to a 17th-century French cartographer, they were discovered in 1503 by Juan Bermudez, after whom they were named. No settlement was made, and they were uninhabited until a party of colonists under Sir George Somers was wrecked there in 1609. A company was formed for the 'Plantation of the Somers' Islands', as they were called at first, and in 1684 the Crown took over the government.

AREA AND POPULATION. Bermuda consists of a group of some 150 small islands (about 20 inhabited), situated in the western Atlantic (32° 18′ N. lat., 64° 46′ W. long.); the nearest point of the mainland, about 570 miles distant, is Cape Hatteras, N.C., and 690 miles from New York; noted for its climate and scenery; a favourite resort for Americans.

The area is 20·59 sq. miles (53·3 sq. km), of which 2·3 sq. miles were leased in 1941 for 99 years to the US Government for naval and air bases. The civil population (*i.e.*, excluding British and American military, naval and air force personnel) in 1980 (Census) was 54,670.

Chief town, Hamilton; population, about 3,000.

In 1981 there were 783 live births, 579 marriages and 452 deaths; infantile mortality rate was 14 per 1,000 live births.

CONSTITUTION AND GOVERNMENT. Bermuda is a colony with representative government. Under the constitution of 8 June 1968 the Governor, appointed by the Crown, is normally bound to accept the advice of the Cabinet in matters other than external affairs, defence, internal security and the police, for which he retains special responsibility. The Cabinet is appointed from among members of the bicameral legislature, on the recommendation of the Premier. The Senate, of whom one or two members may serve on Cabinet, consists of 11 members. As a result of a Constitutional Conference held in Feb. 1979, it was decided that 5 Senators would be appointed by the Governor on the recommendation of the Premier, 3 by the Governor on the recommendation of the Opposition Leader and 3 by the Governor in his own discretion. The 40 members of the House of Assembly are elected 2 from each of 20 constituencies under full universal, adult suffrage. The general election on 18 May 1976 resulted in the return of 26 members of the United Bermuda Party and 14 members of the Progressive Labour Party. A by-election was held on 21 Sept. 1976 resulting in a total of 25 members of the United Bermuda Party and 15 members of the Progressive Labour Party. A general election was held on 6 Feb. 1983, which resulted in the United Bermuda Party being returned to power. The United Bermuda Party won 26 seats and the Progressive Labour Party, 14.

Governor: (Vacant).
Premier: John W. D. Swan.
Flag: The British Red Ensign with the badge of the Colony in the fly.

DEFENCE. The Bermuda Regiment had 630 men and women in 1981.

ECONOMY

Budget. Revenue and expenditure in $B for years ending 31 March:

	1978–79	*1979–80*	*1980–81*	*1981–82* [1]	*1982–83*
Revenue	91,392,263	105,207,166	125,232,000	131,966,000	155,129,150
Expenditure	85,901,549	101,224,172	122,936,000	129,821,000	154,858,550

[1] Estimate.

Expenditure in $B1,000 (excluding capital items) was earmarked as follows:

	1978–79	*1979–80*	*1980–81*	*1981–82*[1]	*1982–83*
Education	15,862	19,189	24,717	21,928	25,919
Health and Social Services	15,619	18,189	21,353	28,478	30,386
Public Works	11,303	12,011	15,284	14,817	13,333
Police	7,034	8,006	9,244	10,623	12,427
Tourism	6,234	7,136	8,124	8,880	10,851
Marine and Air Services	3,301	4,539	8,028	8,312	3,794
Public Transportation	3,430	4,222	4,707	1,496	4,307
Agriculture and Fisheries	3,112	3,874	4,080	4,452	5,077
Post Office	2,923	2,939	3,429	3,404	4,169
All Other Expenditure	17,084	21,119	23,971	27,341	...

[1] Estimate.

Chief sources of revenue in 1981–82 were: Customs duties, $65,650,500; employment tax, $13·65m.; companies tax, $8,107,500; land tax, $7,387,000; hotel occupancy tax, $8·03m.; hospital levy, $14·43m.; vehicle licences, $5·15m.; stamp duties, $4·5m.; passenger taxes, $4,385,000.

Public debt, as at 31 March 1981, was $4·3m.

Currency. Decimal currency based on a *Bermuda dollar* of 100 *cents* was introduced 6 Feb. 1970. In March 1983 £1 = 1.52 Bermuda dollars and US$1 = 1 Bermuda dollar. The Bermuda Monetary Authority issues notes in denominations of $100, $50, $20, $10, $5 and $1, and coins in values of 50c, 25c, 10c, 5c and 1c.

Banking. There are 3 banks, the Bank of Bermuda, Ltd, the Bank of N. T. Butterfield and Son, Ltd, and the Bermuda Provident Bank, Ltd.

Weights and Measures. British, except that US instead of Imperial fluid measures are used.

AGRICULTURE. The chief products are fresh vegetables, bananas and citrus fruit. In 1980–81, 708 acres were under cultivation. In 1980 about 5% of the work force were engaged in agriculture, fishing and horticulture.

In 1980, total value of agricultural products was $B5·2m.

Livestock (1981): Cattle, 1,000; pigs, 2,000; poultry, 45,000.

TRADE UNIONS. Legislation providing for trade unions was enacted in Oct. 1946, and there are 9 trade unions with a total membership (1981) of 8,806.

COMMERCE. Imports and exports in $B:

	1978	*1979*	*1980*	*1981*
Imports	211,622,000	234,000,000	311,468,000	322,732,859
Exports	41,177,000	31,290,000	36,489,000	29,383,399

The visible adverse balance of trade is more than compensated for by invisible exports, including tourism and off-shore insurance business.

Imports in 1981 from USA, $171m.; UK, $35m.; Canada, $23m.; Japan, $12m.; West Indies, $5m.; Hong Kong, $5m.; France, $4m.; Federal Republic of Germany, $3m.; Netherlands, $2m.; Italy, $2m.

In 1980 the principal imports were food, drink and tobacco ($65m.), finished manufactures ($62m.), mineral fuels ($54m.), chemicals ($31m.); the principal local exports were beauty preparations ($443,000). The bulk of exports comprise sales of fuel to aircraft and ships, and re-exports of pharmaceuticals.

Total trade between Bermuda and UK, in £1,000 sterling (British Department of Trade returns):

	1977	*1978*	*1979*	*1980*	*1981*	*1982*
Imports to UK	5,780	11,259	3,794	2,900	5,652	5,128
Exports and re-exports from UK	19,686	22,200	17,209	24,499	17,492	18,222

TOURISM. In 1981, 535,247 tourists visited Bermuda including 429,802 arriving by air and 105,445 cruise ship visitors. Tourism represents 41% of GDP.

COMMUNICATIONS

Roads. In 1948 the railway service was discontinued and a government-operated bus service introduced.

Between 1908 and Aug. 1946 the use of motor vehicles, with the exception of ambulances, fire engines and other essential services, was prohibited. With the passing of the Motor Car Act in 1946, the use of motor vehicles, subject to certain limitations on size and horse-power, became lawful. In 1981, out of 40,402 registered vehicles 14,442 were private cars.

Aviation. American Airlines, Pan American, Delta Airlines and Eastern Airlines maintain regular services between Bermuda and the USA. British Airways also have regular flights through Bermuda linking London with Mexico and the Caribbean. Air Canada Airlines call at Bermuda on their service between Canada, Barbados, Antigua and Trinidad; they also operate services between Bermuda, Toronto, Montreal and Halifax.

Shipping. At 31 Dec. 1981, 71 commercial vessels of 490,996 gross tons and 213 pleasure yachts of 12,140 gross tons were registered at Hamilton. In 1981 the gross tonnage of 544 vessels entered and cleared was 4,494,572 tons.

Post and Broadcasting (1981). There are 15 post offices. The telephone company is privately owned and operated 46,290 telephones in 1981. Cables connect the islands with the USA, Halifax (N.S.) and Tortola, providing connexion with the world.

Radio and television broadcasting is commercial.

Cinemas. There was (1981) 1 cinema with a seating capacity of 1,054.

JUSTICE, EDUCATION AND WELFARE

Justice. There are 4 magistrates' courts, a Supreme Court and a court of appeal. The police had a strength of 415 men and women in 1981.

Education. Education is compulsory between the ages of 5 and 16, and government assistance is given by the payment of grants, and, where necessary, of school fees. Free elementary education was introduced on 1 May 1949 and free secondary education in Sept. 1965. In 1981, there were 11 government nurseries, 6 special units for the handicapped, 18 government primary schools, 9 government secondary schools, the Bermuda College and 4 private, fee-paying schools. Total enrolment was 11,312 pupils.

Health. In 1981 there were 65 doctors.

Books of Reference

Annual Report, 1971. HMSO, 1972
Bermuda Historical Quarterly. 1944 ff.
Baron, S., *Your Guide to Bermuda.* London, 1965
Bell, E. Y., *Beautiful Bermuda.* 10th ed. New York and Bermuda, 1947
Dyer, H. T., *The Next 20 Years: A Report on the Development Plans for Bermuda.* Hamilton, 1963
Hayward, S. J., Holt-Gomez, V., and Sterrer, W., *Bermuda's Delicate Balance: People and the Environment.* Hamilton, 1981
Warwick, J. B., (ed.), *Who's Who in Bermuda 1980–81.* Hamilton, 1982
Wilkinson, H. C., *Bermuda from Sail to Steam.* OUP, 1973
Zuill, W. S., *The Story of Bermuda and Her People.* London, 1973

National Library: The Bermuda Library, Hamilton. *Head Librarian:* Mrs M. Skiffington.

BHUTÁN

Druk-yul

Capital: Thimphu
Population: 1·1m. (1979)
GNP per capita: US$80 (1980)

HISTORY. In 1774 the East India Company concluded a treaty with the ruler of Bhután. Under a treaty signed in Nov. 1865 the Bhután Government was granted an annual subsidy. By an amending treaty concluded in Jan. 1910 the British Government undertook to exercise no interference in the internal affairs of Bhután, and the Bhután Government agreed to be guided by the advice of the British Government in regard to its external relations.

The Government of India concluded a fresh treaty with Bhután on 8 Aug. 1949. Under this treaty the Government of Bhután continues to be guided by the Government of India in regard to its external relations, and the Government of India have undertaken not to interfere in the internal administration of Bhután. The subsidy paid to Bhután has been increased to Rs 500,000, and the Government of India agreed to retrocede to Bhután an area of about 32 sq. miles in the territory known as Dewangiri, which was annexed in 1865.

AREA AND POPULATION. Bhután is situated in the eastern Himalayas, between 26° 45′ and 28° N. lat. and between 89° and 92° E. long., bordered on the north and east by Tibet and India, on the west by Sikkim and on the south by India. Extreme length from east to west 190 miles: extreme breadth 90 miles. Area about 18,000 sq. miles (46,600 sq. km); population estimated at approximately 1m. (1979). Life expectancy (1977) was 46 years. The capital is at Thimphu. There are 17 districts.

KING. Jigme Singye Wangchuck, succeeded his father Jigme Dorji Wangchuck who died 21 July 1972.

GOVERNMENT. In 1907 the Tongsa Penlop (the governor of the province of Tongsa in eastern Bhután), Sir Ugyen Wangchuk, GCIE, KCSI, was elected as the first hereditary Maharaja of Bhután. The Bhutánese title is Druk Gyalpo, but his successor is now addressed as King of Bhután. From Oct. 1969 the absolute monarchy was changed to a form of 'democratic monarchy'. The National Assembly (*Tshogdu*) was reinstituted in 1953. It has approximately 150 members and meets twice a year. Two-thirds are representatives of the people and are elected for a 3-year term. All Bhutánese over 25 years may be candidates. Ten monastic representatives are elected by regional ecclesiastical bodies, while the remaining members are nominated by the King, and include members of the Council of Ministers and the Royal Advisory Council.

The official languages are Dzongkha, Nepali and English.

National flag: Diagonally yellow over orange, over all in the centre a white dragon.

DEFENCE. Bhután has an army of about 4,000 men.

ECONOMY

Planning. The Government of Bhután has drawn up five 5-year development plans (1961–65, 1966–70, 1971–76, 1977–81, 1982–86), with the active co-operation and financial support of the Government of India. Educational facilities are being expanded and medical facilities are being provided. Forest and mineral wealth is to be exploited. About 1,900 km of new roads have been built.

Budget. The budget for 1982–83 envisaged expenditure of N635m. and revenue of N165m.

Currency. Paper currency has been introduced, known as the *Ngultrum*. Silver currency is known as *Tikchung*. Indian currency is also legal tender.

Banking. The Bank of Bhután was established in 1968. The headquarters are at Phuntsholing with 14 branches throughout the country.

ENERGY AND NATURAL RESOURCES

Electricity. In 1974 construction work began on the Chukha hydro-electric project at a cost of US$92m. and in 1979, 15 towns and 97 villages had electricity.

Minerals. Large deposits of limestone, marble, dolomite, graphite, lead, copper, slate, coal, talc, gypsum, beryl, mica, pyrites and tufa have been found.

Agriculture. The area under cultivation in 1978 was 5,534 sq. km. The chief products are rice, millet, wheat, barley, maize, cardomom, potatoes, oranges, apples, handloom cloth, timber and yaks. Extensive and valuable forests abound.

Livestock (1981): Horses, 20,000; asses, 18,000; cattle, 306,000; pigs, 55,000; sheep, 43,000; poultry, 186,000.

INDUSTRY AND TRADE

Industry. In 1980 there were about 40 small-scale industrial units and also a cement plant, a fruit processing factory, a tea-chest ply veneer factory, a resin and turpentine factory and 3 distilleries.

Commerce. Trade with India is considerable but timber, cardomom and liquor are also exported to the Middle East, Singapore and Western Europe. Bhután imported from the UK in 1982 goods valued at £89,000.

Tourism. The country has been opened for tourism since 1974 and it is the largest source of foreign exchange. In 1979–80, 1,500 tourists visited Bhután.

COMMUNICATIONS

Roads. In 1978 there were about 1,775 km of roads. In 1979, there were 2,179 vehicles, of which 1,432 were private cars and 747 buses and trucks.

Post. A modern postal system was introduced in 1962. There are 53 general post offices and 28 branch post offices. In 1979 there were 1,086 km of telephone lines, 15 automatic exchanges and (1978) 1,355 telephones.

Newspapers. There is a government weekly newspaper published in 3 languages (English, Dzongkha and Nepali). Total circulation (1979) about 5,000.

RELIGION, EDUCATION AND WELFARE

Religion. The majority of the people are Mahayana Buddhists of the Drukpa subsect of the Karyud School which was first introduced from Tibet during the 12th century.

Education. In 1980 there were 144 state schools, 1 college and 2 technical schools with 31,892 pupils. There were 1,206 teachers. Many students were receiving training under the Colombo Plan in Australia, New Zealand, Japan, Singapore and UK in 1979.

Health. There were (1980) 12 general hospitals, 39 dispensaries, 43 basic health units, 4 indigenous dispensaries, 3 leprosy hospitals, 1 mobile hospital, 1 health school and 15 malaria eradication centres. In 1979 beds totalled 536 and there were 52 doctors.

DIPLOMATIC REPRESENTATIVE

Of Bhután to the United Nations
Ambassador: Om. Pradhan.

The Government of Bhután is in diplomatic relations with Bangladesh and India at ambassadorial level. Honorary Consuls have also been appointed in Singapore and Hong Kong.

Books of Reference

Bhutan, Himalayan Kingdom. Bhutan Government, Thimphu, 1979
Das, N., *The Dragon Country.* New Delhi, 1973
Labh, K., *India and Bhutan.* New Delhi, 1974
Mehra, G. N., *Bhutan: Land of the Peaceful Dragon.* New Delhi, 1974
Olschak, B. C., *Bhutan: Land of Hidden Treasures.* New Delhi, 1971
Rahul, R., *Modern Bhutan.* New Delhi, 1971
Rathore, L. S., *The Changing Bhutan.* New Delhi, 1974
Ronaldshay, the Earl of, *Lands of the Thunderbolt.* 2nd ed. London, 1931
Rose, L. E., *The Politics of Bhutan.* Cornell Univ. Press, 1977
Rustomji, N., *Bhutan: The Dragon Kingdom in Crisis.* OUP, 1978
Singh, N., *Bhutan.* New Delhi, 1972

BOLIVIA

Capital: La Paz
Population: 6·08m. (1983)
GNP per capita: US$570 (1980)

República de Bolivia

HISTORY. Until 1884, when Bolivia was defeated by Chile, she had a strip bordering on the Pacific which contains extensive nitrate beds and at that time the port of Cobija (which no longer exists). She lost this area to Chile; but in Sept. 1953 Chile declared Arica a free port and, although it is no longer a free port for Bolivian imports, Bolivia still has certain privileges.

AREA AND POPULATION. Bolivia is a landlocked state with an area of some 424,160 sq. miles (1,098,580 sq. km). In the series of disastrous wars in the 19th and early 20th centuries its territorial losses to each of 5 neighbouring nations reduced its area from an estimated 1·16m. sq. miles.

The following table shows the area and population of the departments (the capitals of each are given in brackets):

Departments	*Area (sq. km)*	*Census Aug.-Sept. 1950*	*Census 1976*	*Per sq. km 1975*
La Paz (La Paz)	133,985	948,446	1,456,078	12·50
Cochabamba (Cochabamba)	55,631	490,475	720,952	15·57
Potosí (Potosí)	118,218	534,399	657,743	7·98
Santa Cruz (Santa Cruz)	370,621	286,145	710,724	1·36
Chuquisaca (Sucre)	51,524	282,980	358,516	9·69
Tarija (Tarija)	37,623	126,752	186,704	5·95
Oruro (Oruro)	53,588	210,260	310,409	6·93
Beni (Trinidad)	213,564	119,770	168,367	0·99
Pando (Cobija)	63,827	19,804	34,493	0·55
Total	1,098,581	3,019,031 [1]	4,687,718	4·85

[1] An official estimate allowing for under-enumeration; the total actually recorded was 2,704,165.

Total population (estimate 1983) 6,081,722.

Population (census 1976) of the principal towns: La Paz, 654,713; Santa Cruz, 255,568; Cochabamba, 204,414; Oruro, 124,414; Potosí, 77,233; Sucre, 63,259; Tarija, 38,500.

Crude birth rate, 1968, 42 per 1,000 population; crude death rate (1978), 17·4; crude marriage rate (1958), 4; infantile mortality, 140 (1978) per 1,000 live births.

The language of the educated classes is Spanish, that of the majority of Indians, Aymará (25·2%) or Quechua (34·4%).

CONSTITUTION AND GOVERNMENT. The Republic of Bolivia was proclaimed on 6 Aug. 1825; its first constitution was adopted on 19 Nov. 1826.

La Paz is the actual capital and seat of the Government, but Sucre is the legal capital and the seat of the judiciary.

The following is a list of presidents since 1931 and the date on which they took office:

Dr Daniel Salamanca, 5 March 1931 (resigned Nov. 1934).
Luis Tejada Sorzano, 27 Nov. 1934 (deposed 17 May 1936).
Col. José David Toro, 17 May 1936 (deposed 13 July 1937).
Lieut.-Gen. German Busch, 13 July 1937 (committed suicide 23 Aug. 1939).
Gen. Carlos Quintanilla (provisional), 23 Aug. 1939–12 March 1940.
Gen. Enrique Peñaranda, 12 March 1940 (deposed 20 Dec. 1943).

Maj. Gualberto Villaroel, 20 Dec. 1943 (deposed and lynched 21 July 1946).
Dr Néstor Guillén (provisional) 27 July–1 Aug. 1946.
Chief Justice Monje Gutiérrez, 15 Aug. 1946–9 March 1947.
Dr Enrique Hertzog, 10 March 1947–23 Oct. 1949.
Dr Mamerto Urriolangoitia, 24 Oct. 1949–15 May 1951.
Gen. Hugo Ballivián Rojas, 15 May 1951–8 April 1952.
Dr Victor Paz Estenssoro, 16 April 1952–6 Aug. 1956.
Dr Hernán Siles Zuazo, 6 Aug. 1956–6 Aug. 1960.
Dr Victor Paz Estenssoro, (deposed) 6 Aug. 1960–4 Nov. 1964.
Gen. René Barrientos Ortuño, 4 Nov. 1964–26 May 1965 (Head of Military Junta).
Gen. René Barrientos Ortuño and Gen. Alfredo Ovando Candia (joint Presidents), 26 May 1965–Jan. 1966.
Gen. Alfredo Ovando Candia, Jan. 1966–6 Aug. 1966.
Gen. René Barrientos Ortuño (Constitutional President killed in air accident), 6 Aug. 1966–27 April 1969.
Dr Luis Adolfo Siles Salinas (deposed), 27 April 1969–26 Sept. 1969.
Gen. Alfredo Ovando Candia, 26 Sept. 1969–6 Oct. 1970.
Gen. Juan José Torres, 7 Oct. 1970–21 Aug. 1971.
Gen. Hugo Banzer Suarez, 21 Aug. 1971–21 July 1978.
Gen. Juan Pereda Asbun, 21 July 1978–24 Nov. 1978.
Gen. David Padilla A, 24 Nov. 1978–8 Aug. 1979.
Dr Walter Guevara A, 8 Aug. 1979–1 Nov. 1979.
Lidia Gueiler, 20 Nov. 1979–17 July 1980.
Gen. Luis García Meza, 18 July 1980.

Following elections in July 1979 which were inconclusive an interim President was chosen with the agreement of the three parties who had polled most votes. For details of political history 1970–78 *see* THE STATESMAN'S YEAR-BOOK, 1980–81. On 1 Nov. 1979, Dr Guevara was overthrown by Col. Alberto Natusch Busch who failed to become President and Congress named Lidia Gueiler as the first woman president and was sworn in on 20 Nov. 1979. Presidential and congressional elections took place in June 1980. Dr Siles Zuazo won about one-third of the votes but on 17 July Lidia Gueiler was overthrown by a military junta led by Gen. García Meza.

A military uprising in Santa Cruz led by Gen. Alberto Natusch Busch and Gen. Lucio Añez Rivero forced the resignation of Gen. Luis García Meza from the Presidency on 4 Aug. 1981. He handed over power to a junta of the commanders of the armed forces who exercised the power of president until 4 Sept. 1981 when they nominated one of their number, the army commander Gen. Celso Torrelio Villa, as sole president.

Gen. Celso Torrelio Villa resigned on 20 July 1982, and on 21 July the Junta of Commanders appointed Gen. Guido Vildoso Calderon as President with a mandate to hold elections in April 1983. Gen. Calderon succumbed to political and economic pressure and announced the reconstitution of the Congress elected in 1980, which then elected Dr Siles Zuazo as Constitutional President.

The Cabinet consists of the President and 18 Ministers of State.

President: Dr Siles Zuazo (sworn in 10 Oct. 1982).

Vice-President: Lic Jaime Paz Zamora. *Foreign Affairs and Worship:* Mario Velarde Dorado. *Interior, Migration and Justice:* Mario Roncal Antezana. *Defence:* José Ortiz Mercado. *Aviation:* Gen. Oscar Villa Urioste. *Finance:* Flavio Machicado. *Planning:* Arturo Nuñez del Prado. *Education and Culture:* Enrique Melgar. *Transport and Communications:* Hernando Poppe Martínez. *Industry, Commerce and Tourism:* Javier Lupo Gamarra. *Labour:* Roberto Arnez Villarroel. *Mining and Metallurgy:* Carlos Barragán Vargas. *Health:* Javier Tórrez Goitta. *Agriculture:* Zenón Barrientos Mamani. *Energy:* Jorge Medina Pinedo. *Housing:* Vacant. *Secretary-General to the Presidency:* Horacio Tórrez Guzmán. *Secretary-General of Integration:* Jorge Gonzáles Roda. *Information:* Mario Rueda Peña.

National flag: Three horizontal stripes of red, yellow, green, with the arms of Bolivia in the centre.

National anthem: Bolivianos, el hado propicio (words by I. de Sanjinés; tune by B. Vincenti).

Local Government: The republic is divided into 9 departments, established in

Jan. 1826, with 98 provinces administered by sub-prefects, and 1,272 cantons administered by corregidores. The supreme authority in each department is vested in a prefect appointed by the President.

DEFENCE. Bolivia is divided into 8 military districts, with divisional headquarters in Viacha, Oruro, Villa Montes, Camiri, Roboré, Riberalta, Santa Cruz, Cochabamba; regional HQ are located at La Paz, Sucre, Tarija, Potosí, Trinidad and Cobija.

Army. The law of 1943 provided for a permanent force of 15,000 men, including the police force and the frontier carabineers, but the standing army in 1983 numbered 20,000 men. Military service is compulsory for all males from the 19th to the 49th year. The Army consists of 13 infantry regiments, 1 motorized regiment, 1 mechanized and 4 cavalry regiments, 3 artillery regiments, a paratroop battalion (CITE) and 2 ranger regiments specially trained in anti-guerrilla warfare.

Navy. A small Navy exists for river and lake patrol comprising 36 patrol craft operating in Lake Titicaca and the Bolivia-Paraguay 6,000-mile river systems, 1 transport (a gift from Venezuela for use to and from Bolivian free zones in Argentina and Uruguay) and 2 hospital ships (one a gift from USA).

Personnel in 1983 totalled 4,000 officers and men including marines. Most training of officers and petty officers is carried out in Argentina. The junior ratings are almost entirely converted soldiers.

Air Force. The Air Force, established in 1923, has 3 combat-capable squadrons, equipped with 12 Canadian-built T-33 armed jet trainers, 10 T-6G armed piston-engined trainers, and 12 Hughes 500M armed helicopters, for counter-insurgency operations. A search and rescue helicopter squadron has 6 Brazilian-assembled Gaviãos (Lamas). Other types in service include Brazilian T-23 Uirapuru and American T-41 primary trainers, Italian SF.260M and Swiss turboprop-powered Pilatus PC-7 basic trainers, 16 PC-6 Turbo Porter utility aircraft, 1 Electra four-turboprop transport, 6 Fokker F.27 and 5 Israeli-built Arava twin-turboprop light transports, 3 Convair 580 twin-turboprop transports, 2 C-130H/L-100-30 Hercules, 1 DC-6B, 6 C-47 and 3 Convair 440 piston-engined transports with which a military airline service is operated, about 30 Cessna single- and twin-engined light aircraft and helicopters. Personnel strength is about 4,000.

INTERNATIONAL RELATIONS

Membership. Bolivia is a member of UN, OAS, LAIA (formerly LAFTA), the Andean Group and the Amazon Pact.

External Debt. The contracted external debt was US$3,641m., Dec. 1980.

ECONOMY

Budget. Revenue and expenditures in 1m. *pesos bolivianos* balanced as follows: In 1981 there was a projected budget deficit of US$1,200m. Aid from USA in 1971 was about US$20·2m.

Currency. On 1 Jan. 1963 the *peso boliviano* ($b.) was introduced. Exchange rates were $b.44 = US$1 and $b.66 = £1 in March 1983.

Banking. The Banco Central de Bolivia was established in 1911 as Banco de la Nacion Boliviana and re-organized in 1928. The Bank was nationalized in 1939. At 30 June 1980 the Bank's gross gold and foreign exchange reserves amounted to US$222·43m. and Bolivia's net reserves stood at US$83·3m.

Weights and Measures. The metric system of weights and measures is used by the administration and prescribed by law, but the old Spanish system is also employed.

ENERGY AND NATURAL RESOURCES

Electricity. Electric power production is expanding. Installed capacity was estimated at 428,595 kw. at the end of 1978. Estimated production from all sources (1978), 1,340,996 Mwh.

Oil and Gas. There are petroleum and natural gas deposits in the Santa Cruz-Camiri areas. A pipeline for crude oil connects Caranda (Santa Cruz) with the Pacific coast at Arica (Chile) and a natural gas pipeline to Argentina was inaugurated in May 1972. All production, refining and internal distribution is now in the hands of *Yacimientos Petrolíferos Fiscales Bolivianos* (the State Petroleum Organization). Total production of petroleum and condensates in 1981 was estimated at 8·1m. bbls. Production of natural gas in 1981 was estimated at 175,478m. cu. ft.

Minerals. Mining is the most important industry, accounting for about 69% of the foreign-exchange earnings. About half the mineral mined is tin. Tin mines are at altitudes of from 12,000 to 18,000 ft, where few except native Indians can stand the conditions; transport is costly. Bolivian tin is extracted by shaft-mining, frequently very deep; the ore yields only 0·7% or less of tin and is very refractory; tin is exported in concentrates called *barrilla,* through Pacific ports for refining. Smelting capacity was increased in 1980 and it is planned to smelt all the ores from the State Mining Co. but complex ores still have to be exported for smelting. Tin production in 1981 was 27,562 tonnes.

The state industry is being run by the *Corporación Minera de Bolivia* (COMIBOL) employing about 23,000 in mining and administrative capacities.

Alluvial gold deposits in the Alto Beni region are being exploited. Co-operative mines at Tipuani produced 770 kg in 1978.

Foreign firms are seeking exploration rights for uranium and a small uranium processing plant was opened in Oct. 1980 at Cotaje (Potosí province). Large deposits of salt are found near Lake Poopó and in the south of Bolivia.

Agriculture. The extensive and still largely undeveloped region east of the Andes comprises about three-quarters of the entire area of the country, and since the agrarian reform of 1952 sugar-cane, rice and cotton have been grown in this *Oriente* in increasing abundance, reaching self-sufficiency in all these products. Output in tonnes in 1980 was: Sugar-cane, 2·83m.; rice, 87,700; coffee, 19,600; maize, 327,700; potatoes, 720,000; wheat, 50,000; cotton (lint), 7,500; cocoa, 25,200.

The public lands of the State have an area of about 245,000 sq. miles, of which 104,000 sq. miles are reserved for special colonization.

A colony of Jewish refugees was established in 1940 at Buena Tierra, 60 miles east of La Paz and, more recently, Japanese and Okinawan settlements in the region of Santa Cruz. The Bolivian Development Corporation has a programme for relief of over-population on the barren altiplano and in 1964 resettled 1,217 families in tropical areas.

Livestock: In 1981 there were 4·1m. head of cattle, mostly in the Santa Cruz and Beni departments; some are exported to Peru; horses, 410,000; asses, 780,000; pigs, 1·5m.; sheep, 8·9m.; goats, 3·05m.; poultry, 8·8m.

Forestry. Tropical forests with woods ranging from the 'iron tree' to the light *palo de balsa* are beginning to be exploited. In 1962 the Forestry Service announced proved reserves of 46·3m. hectares, plus a similar amount available for immediate development.

INDUSTRY AND TRADE

Industry. There are few industrial establishments and the country relies on imports for the supply of many consumer goods. However a new investment law passed in 1971 provides incentives and protection for new investment, both foreign and domestic, and for reinvestment in various fields including manufacturing industry, mining, agriculture, construction and tourism.

Labour. The Ministry of Planning estimated economically active population in 1970 at 1·48m., of whom 1m. were employed in agriculture, 118,300 in industrial manufacture, 35,100 in construction, 74,000 in commerce and finance, 65,000 in central and local government, 47,800 in mining and 41,900 in transport. The ban on trade unions, imposed in 1974, was lifted in 1978 but re-imposed in 1980.

Commerce. The value of imports and exports in US$1,000 has been as follows:

	1975	*1976*	*1977*	*1978*	*1979*	*1980*
Imports	510,000	536,000	552,000	848,200	984,000	833,160
Exports	449,000	545,000	556,000	640,300	793,000	942,000

Tin ore remains the principal export. Total exports, 1980, of all minerals, in concentrates, ingots or solder, were valued at US$641m.

Bolivia having no seaport, imports and exports pass chiefly through the ports of Arica and Antofagasta in Chile, Mollendo-Matarani in Peru, through La Quiaca on the Bolivian-Argentine border and through river-ports on the rivers flowing into the Amazon. The chief imports are lard, flour, cooking oil, iron and steel products, mining machinery, pharmaceuticals, paper products and textiles.

Total trade between Bolivia and UK for 5 years (British Department of Trade returns in £1,000 sterling):

	1978	*1979*	*1980*	*1981*	*1982*
Imports to UK	32,202	37,619	33,179	36,800	20,899
Exports and re-exports from UK	16,493	9,594	8,684	12,676	4,943

COMMUNICATIONS

Roads. A highway, in poor condition, 497 km long, runs from Cochabamba to the lowland farming region of Santa Cruz. La Paz and Oruro are also connected by a metalled road. Of other main highways (unmetalled) there is one from La Paz through Guaqui into Peru, another from La Paz, *via* Oruro, Potosí, Tarija and Bermejo, into Argentina, with branches to Cochabamba, Sucre and Camiri, passable throughout the year except at the height of the rainy season, and others from Villazón to Villa Montes *via* Tarija, passable during the dry season. The total length of the road system is 37,708 km (1977). Motor vehicles in use in 1980, 134,790, including 65,540 cars, 69,250 heavy goods vehicles and buses and 1,133 agricultural tractors.

Railways. In 1964 Bolivian National Railways (ENFE) was formed by the amalgamation of the Bolivian Government Railways, Bolivian Railway Co. and the Bolivian section of the Antofagasta (Chile) & Bolivia Railway. The Guaqui-La Paz Railway, formerly operated by Peru, became part of ENFE in 1973. Access to the Pacific is by 3 routes: to Antofagasta and Arica in Chile, and to Mollendo in Peru via Guaqui, the Lake Titicaca train ferry to Puno (Peru), then rail to the coast. Construction began in 1978 of a 150-km line linking Puno with Desaguadero on the Bolivian border which would by-pass the train ferry, though gauge difference would still prevent through running to Peru. Current network totals 3,538 km of metre gauge, comprising unconnected Eastern (1,386 km) and Western (2,152 km) systems. In 1980 the railways carried 1·7m. passengers and 1·3m. tonnes of freight.

Aviation. The national airline is Lloyd Aéreo Boliviano; in 1978 a total of 20,620 hours were flown, carrying 1,060,044 passengers. The airline runs regular services between La Paz and Lima, São Paulo, Buenos Aires, Miami, Caracas, Salta and Arica as well as many internal services. Braniff International Airways runs regular flights between La Paz, Lima, Buenos Aires, Santiago and Asunción linking Bolivia (*via* Lima) to the USA. Lufthansa links Bolivia with Europe. Other airlines serving Bolivia are Aerolineas Argentinas, Cruzeiro, Aero Peru, Lan Chile and Avianca.

Shipping. Traffic on Lake Titicaca between Guaqui and Puno is carried on by the steamers of the Peruvian Corporation. About 12,000 miles of rivers, in 4 main systems (Beni, Pilcomayo, Titicaca-Desaguadero, Mamoré), are open to navigation by light-draught vessels.

Post and Broadcasting. In Bolivia there were, in 1978, 458 post offices, of these, 205 provided telegraph and telephone services together with a further 245 offices for telegraph and telephone service only. There is telephone service in the cities of La Paz, Cochabamba, Oruro, Sucre, Potosí, Santa Cruz, Tarija, Camiri, Tupiza,

Villazon, Riberalta and Trinidad with (1981), 135,100 telephones. There are about 119 broadcasting stations, of which 7 are state-owned. There is a commercial government television service.

Newspapers. There are 6 daily newspapers in La Paz, 2 in Oruro, and 2 in Cochabamba. Several other towns have regular newspapers devoted to local news, but most of them appear only a few times a week. An economic monthly journal *Revista Economica* and 4 daily newspapers are produced in Santa Cruz.

JUSTICE, RELIGION, EDUCATION AND WELFARE

Justice. Justice is administered by the Supreme Court, superior district courts (of 5 or 7 judges) and courts of local justice. The Supreme Court, with headquarters at Sucre, is divided into two sections, civil and criminal, of 5 justices each, with the Chief Justice presiding over both. Members of the Supreme Court are chosen on a two-thirds vote of Congress.

Religion. The Roman Catholic is the recognized religion of the state; the free exercise of other forms of worship is permitted. The Catholic Church is under a cardinal (in Sucre), an archbishop (in La Paz), 6 bishops (Cochabamba, Santa Cruz, Oruro, Potosí, Riberalta and Tarija) and vicars apostolic (titular bishops resident in Cueva, Trinidad, San Ignacio de Velasco, Riberalta and Rurrenabaque).

By a law of 11 Oct. 1911 all marriages must be celebrated by the civil authorities. Divorce is permitted by a law enacted on 15 April 1932.

Education. Primary instruction is free and obligatory between the ages of 6 and 14 years. Estimates for 1974 show that 989,858 children between 6 and 14 years attended school. All illiterates between 15 and 50 years are obliged to attend literacy classes and in 1977 this represented 40% of the population.

At Sucre, Oruro, Potosí, Cochabamba, Santa Cruz, Tarija, Trinidad and La Paz are universities; La Paz is the most important of them while the San Francisco Xavier University at Sucre is one of the oldest in America, founded in 1624.

Health. In 1972 there were 2,143 doctors.

DIPLOMATIC REPRESENTATIVES

Of Bolivia in Great Britain (106 Eaton Sq., London, SW1W 9AD)
Chargé d'Affaires: Carlos Quintanilla.

Of Great Britain in Bolivia (Avenida Arce 2732–2754, La Paz)
Ambassador: S. F. St C. Duncan.

Of Bolivia in the USA (3014 Massachusetts Ave, NW, Washington, D.C. 20008)
Ambassador: Mariano Baptista Gumucio.

Of the USA in Bolivia (Banco Popular Del Peru Bldg, La Paz)
Ambassador: Edwin G. Carr.

Of Bolivia to the United Nations
Charge d'Affaires: Alvaro Gálvez.

Books of Reference

There is a weekly official gazette.

Anuario Geográfico y Estadístico de la República de Bolivia
Anuario del Comercia Exterior de Bolivia
Boletín Mensual de Información Estadistica
Baptista Gumucio, M., *Cultural Policy in Bolivia.* UNESCO, 1978
Fifer, J. V., *Bolivia: Land, Location and Politics Since 1825.* CUP, 1972
Guillermo, L., *A History of the Bolivian Labour Movement 1848–1971.* CUP, 1977
Klein, H., *Bolivia: The Evolution of a Multi-Ethnic Society.* OUP, 1982
Mitchell, C., *The Legacy of Populism in Bolivia.* New York, 1977

BOTSWANA

Capital: Gaborone
Population: 936,600 (1981)
GNP per capita: US$910 (1980)

HISTORY. In 1885 the territory was declared to be within the British sphere; in 1889 it was included in the sphere of the British South Africa Company, but was never administered by the company; in 1890 a Resident Commissioner was appointed, and in 1895, on the annexation of the Crown Colony of British Bechuanaland to the Cape of Good Hope, the British Government was in favour of transferring the Protectorate to the BSA Company, but the three major chiefs of the Bakwena, the Bangwaketse and the Bamangwato went to England to protest against this proposal, and agreement was reached that their country should remain a British Protectorate if they ceded a strip of land on the eastern side of the country for railway construction. This railway was built in 1896–97.

On 30 Sept. 1966 the Bechuanaland Protectorate became an independent and sovereign member of the Commonwealth under the name of the Republic of Botswana.

AREA AND POPULATION. Botswana comprises the territory lying between the Molopo River on the south and the Zambezi on the north, and extending from the Transvaal Province and Zimbabwe on the east to South-West Africa on the west. The climate is on the whole sub-tropical and the atmosphere throughout the year is very dry. Area about 222,000 sq. miles (582,000 sq. km); population, according to the census of 1971, was 630,379 (census, 1981, preliminary, 936,600).

The main business centres (with estimated population, 1980) are Gaborone (1981, 59,700), Francistown (32,000), Selebi-Pikwe (29,000), Kanye (22,000), Lobatse (20,000), Mochudi (20,000), Molepolole (19,000), Mahalapye (19,000), Maun (16,000).

The seat of government is at Gaborone.

The official language is English; the national language is Setswana.

CONSTITUTION AND GOVERNMENT. The Constitution of the republic is based on the Constitution which came into effect in March 1965, with some minor alterations.

The executive rests with the President of the Republic who is responsible to the National Assembly.

The National Assembly consists of 36 members (32 elected by universal suffrage, 4 nominated by the President, the Attorney-General and the Speaker *ex-officio*). The general election, held in Oct. 1979, returned 33 members of the Botswana Democratic Party, 1 Botswana People's Party and 2 Botswana National Front.

The President is an *ex-officio* member of the Assembly. If the President is already a member of the National Assembly, a by-election will be held in the constituency of that member.

There is also a House of Chiefs to advise the Government. It consists of the Chiefs of the 8 tribes who were autonomous during the days of the British protectorate, and 4 members elected by and from among the sub-chiefs in 4 districts.

The first President of Botswana, who was re-elected 3 times, was Sir Seretse Khama, KBE, who died 13 July 1980.

President of the Republic: Dr Quett Ketumile Joni Masire.

In March 1983 the Cabinet was as follows:

Vice President and Minister of Local Government and Lands: (Vacant). *Finance and Development Planning:* P. S. Mmusi. *Public Service and Information:* D. K. Kwelagobe. *External Affairs:* A. M. Mogwe. *Health:* L. Makgekgenene. *Agriculture:* W. Meswele. *Works and Communications:* C. Blackbeard. *Commerce and Industry:* M. P. K. Nwako. *Mineral Resources and Water Affairs:* Dr G. K. T.

Chiepe. *Education:* K. P. Morake. *Home Affairs:* K. L. Disele. *Assistant for Finance and Development Planning:* O. I. Chilume. *Assistant for Local Government and Lands:* J. L. T. Mothibamele. *Assistant for Agriculture:* G. U. S. Matlhabaphiri. *Attorney-General:* Moleleki Mokama. *Speaker of the National Assembly:* J. G. Haskins.

National flag: Light blue with a horizontal black stripe, edged white, across the centre.

Local Government. Local government is carried out by 9 district councils and 4 town councils. Revenue is obtained mainly from local income tax, levied on all inhabitants in the area; from rates in the towns and from central government subventions in the districts.

DEFENCE

Army. A defence force has been created for border control and comprises 2 infantry battalions; strength, total armed forces (1983) 2,850. Paramilitary forces number 1,260.

Air Force. Equipment includes 5 Britten-Norman Defender armed light transports for border patrol, counter-insurgency and casualty evacuation duties, 6 Bulldog piston-engined basic trainers, 2 Skyvan turboprop passenger/cargo transports and 2 Cessna 152 light aircraft. Personnel total about 150.

INTERNATIONAL RELATIONS

Membership. Botswana is a member of UN, OAU, the Commonwealth and is an ACP state of EEC.

ECONOMY

Planning. The National Development Plan 1979–85 envisages a total capital expenditure of P530m., GDP growth of 10·1% per annum, employment growth of 7% and a strong balance of payments.

Budget. Revenue and expenditure (in 1m. Pula) for financial years ending 31 March:

	1977–78	*1978–79*	*1979–80*
Revenues and grants	118	167	220
Expenditure and net lending	123	172	227

Chief items of revenue, 1978–79: Minerals, P38·8m.; customs pool, P49·8m.; non-mineral, income tax, P20·9m.

Chief items of expenditure, 1978–79: Education, P21·9m.; works and communications development projects, P22·9m.

Public debt, on 31 March 1980, amounted to P112·8m.

Currency. The currency was formerly the South African Rand but in Aug. 1976 a new currency, the *pula*, was introduced (P1·610 = £1 sterling in March 1983).

Banking. The Standard Bank Ltd and Barclays Bank International have branches in Francistown, Lobatse, Mahalapye, Maun and Gaborone and about 46 agencies throughout the country. A government-financed National Development Bank was founded in 1964.

The post office savings bank had deposits of about P1·6m. from 11,000 depositors in mid-1976.

NATURAL RESOURCES

Minerals. An important part of government revenue comes from the diamond mine at Orapa (production started in 1971, 821,914 carats; 1980 (estimate), P223,623,000) and the nickel–copper complex at Selebi-Pikwe (production started in 1974) with production (1980, estimate) valued at P83,258,000. An open-pit coalmine has been developed at Morupule, and produced (1978) 315,000 tonnes valued at P4·3m. A new diamond mine at Jwaneng is expected to come into production in 1982.

Mineral resources in north-east Botswana are being investigated, including salt and soda ash on the Sua Pan of the Makgadikgadi Salt Pans, nickel–copper at Selkirk and Phoenix, copper south of Maun and close to Ghanzi, and coal at Mmamabula.

Agriculture. Cattle-rearing is the chief industry, but the country is more a pastoral than an agricultural one, crops depending entirely upon the rainfall. Increasing numbers of boreholes are being established where underground supply is adequate. However the rural economy is particularly vulnerable to drought and foot and mouth disease. The abattoir at Lobatse, opened in Oct. 1954, is of great importance to the country's economy. In 1981 the number of cattle was 2·95m.; goats, 680,000; sheep, 180,000; poultry, 870,000.

LABOUR. In 1977, 68·8% of the labour force were engaged in agriculture, 12% was employed outside Botswana, mainly in the Republic of South Africa in the mining industry and 2·9% was engaged in domestic service. Total labour force was 384,000.

COMMERCE. In 1978 imports were valued at P258·5m. including (1977): Food, beverages and tobacco, P45,996,000; machinery and electrical equipment, P30·33m.; textiles and footwear, P24,759,000; fuels, P24,523,000; vehicles and transport equipment, P23,415,000; metal and metal products, P22,119,000. Exports (1978) were P186·7m. including: Diamonds, P75m.; meat and meat products, P27m. (a large decrease owing to foot and mouth disease); copper–nickel matte, P49m.

Botswana is a member of the South African customs union with Lesotho, the Republic of South Africa and Swaziland.

Total trade between Botswana and UK (British Department of Trade returns, in £1,000 sterling):

	1978	*1979*	*1980*	*1981*	*1982*
Imports to UK	5,378	26,264	4,044	13,026	19,140
Exports and re-exports from UK	3,256	3,845	2,644	3,397	5,163

TOURISM. The infrastructure for tourism is being developed and there were 97,260 tourists in 1981.

COMMUNICATIONS

Roads. On 31 Dec. 1981, 1,202 km of road were bitumen-surfaced, 1,626 km gravel and over 5,199 km earth. In 1979 there were 21,800 registered motor vehicles.

Railways. 714 km of the Cape Town to Zimbabwe railway line lie within Botswana. The railway is owned and operated by the National Railways of Zimbabwe but the Government of Botswana is preparing to take over the line of rail in Botswana and has formed the Botswana Railway Corporation.

In addition there are 2 Government owned branch lines which serve the coalmine at Morupule and the copper and nickel mining complex at Selibi Pikwe.

Aviation. There are 3 airports and many airstrips. Regular international flights are flown by Air Botswana, Air Zimbabwe and SAA into Gaborone.

Post and Broadcasting. The telegraph, telephone and railway lines from Cape Town to Zimbabwe traverse Botswana. Wireless communication has been established between headquarters at Gaborone and various district offices and police stations. There are 39 post offices and 42 agencies. There were 10,833 telephones installed in 1978. A new earth station giving independent access to the international telecommunications system, was completed in 1980.

Newspapers. In 1981 there was 1 daily newspaper.

JUSTICE, EDUCATION AND WELFARE

Justice. The Botswana Court of Appeal succeeded the Court of Appeal for

Basutoland, Bechuanaland and Swaziland, which was established in 1954. It has jurisdiction in respect of criminal and civil appeals emanating from the High Court of Botswana. Further appeal lies in certain circumstances to the Judicial Committee of the Privy Council.

The High Court for Botswana succeeded the High Court for Bechuanaland, which was established in 1938. It has jurisdiction in all criminal and civil causes and proceedings. Subordinate courts and African courts are in each of the 12 administrative districts.

Police. The police force consisted of 286 officers and subordinate officers, 234 n.c.o.s and 1,434 other ranks in 1980.

Education (1978). There were 336 primary, 15 secondary, 15 governmental aided, 14 private secondary and continuation, 26 vocational training schools and 3 teacher-training colleges. The great majority of the primary schools and the junior secondary schools are controlled, under the Chief Education Officer, by school committees with district-council and mission representatives. Three secondary schools and the homecraft centre are run by missions with Government support; Moeng College by a governing council; the remaining schools by the Government. District-council schools are financed by district-council treasuries and assisted with grants from the Central Government. Enrolment in primary schools in 1980 was 172,000; government secondary, 13,424; private secondary (1979), 4,561; vocational, 1,741; in teacher-training colleges, 844. University students on the Botswana campus of the University of Botswana and Swaziland 928 and university students abroad numbered 558.

In 1981, an estimated 66% of the total population were literate. In 1975, 71% of children of primary school age were receiving instruction.

Welfare (1981). There were 13 general hospitals, 21 maternity centres, a mental home, 7 health centres, 104 clinics and 533 health posts. Total number of beds, 1,871 (1977). There were 113 registered medical practitioners, 8 dentists, and 1,157 nurses. The health facilities are the concern of central and local government, medical missions, mining companies and voluntary organizations. Government expenditure on medical services was P6·5m. for the year ended 31 March 1977.

DIPLOMATIC REPRESENTATIVES

Of Botswana in Great Britain (162 Buckingham Palace Rd., London, SW1)
High Commissioner: Samuel Akana Mpuchane (accredited 18 Feb. 1982).

Of Great Britain in Botswana (Private Bag 0023, Gaborone)
High Commissioner: W. Jones, CMG.

Of Botswana in the USA (4301 Connecticut Ave., NW, Washington, D.C., 20008)
Ambassador: Dr M. J. Melamu.

Of the USA in Botswana (PO Box 90, Gaborone)
Chargé d'Affaires: William L. Jacobsen, Jr.

Of Botswana to the United Nations
Ambassador: Joseph Legwaila.

Books of Reference

General Information: The Director of Information and Broadcasting, PO Box 0060, Gaborone, Botswana publishes *Facts About Botswana*, the monthly *Kutlwano, The Botswana Daily News* and *Botswana Magazine*.
Statistical Bulletins. Quarterly. Central Statistical Office, Gaborone
Report on the Population Census, 1971. Government Printer, Gaborone, 1972
Campbell, A. C., *The Guide to Botswana.* Gaborone, 1980
Colclough, C. and McCarthy, S., *The Political Economy of Botswana.* OUP, 1980
Jones, D., *Aid and Development in Southern Africa.* London, 1979
Selwyn, P., *Industries in the Southern African Periphery.* London, 1975
Sillery, A., *Botswana: A Short Political History.* London, 1974
Stevens, C., *Food Aid and the Developing World.* London, 1979

BRAZIL

Capital: Brasília
Population: 119m. (1980)
GNP per capita: US$2,050 (1980)

República Federativa do Brasil

HISTORY. Brazil was discovered on 22 April 1500 by the Portuguese Admiral Pedro Alvares Cabral, and thus became a Portuguese settlement; in 1815 the colony was declared 'a kingdom', and on 13 May 1822 Dom Pedro, eldest surviving son of King João VI of Portugal, was chosen 'Perpetual Defender' of Brazil by a National Congress. He proclaimed the independence of the country on 7 Sept. 1822, and was chosen 'Constitutional Emperor and Perpetual Defender' on 12 Oct. 1822. He resigned in 1831 and 9 years later, his 14-year-old son Pedro, became the second Emperor of Brazil.

AREA AND POPULATION. Brazil is bounded east by the Atlantic and on its north-west and southern borders by all the South American countries except Chile and Ecuador. Population as at 1 Sept. 1970 (census) and 1 Sept. 1980 (census):

State and Capital	*Area (sq. km)*	*Census 1970*	*Census 1980* [10]
North	3,581,180	3,603,860	5,885,536
Rondônia [1] (Porto Velho [2])	243,044	111,064	490,153
Acre (Rio Branco)	152,589	215,299	302,662
Amazonas [3] (Manaus)	1,564,445	955,235	1,427,784
Roraima (Boa Vista [2])	230,104	40,885	79,407
Pará (Bélem) [3]	1,250,722	2,167,018	3,410,088
Amapá (Macapá[2])	140,276	114,359	175,442
North-east	1,548,672	28,111,927	34,855,469
Maranhão (São Luis)	328,663	2,992,686	4,000,083
Piauí (Teresina)	250,934	1,680,573	2,138,790
Ceará (Fortaleza) [4]	150,630	4,361,603	5,297,750
Rio Grande do Norte (Natal)	53,015	1,550,244	1,901,745
Paraíba (João Pessoa)	56,372	2,382,617	2,769,521
Pernambuco (Recife)	98,281	5,160,640	6,147,080
Alagoas (Maceió)	27,731	1,588,109	1,989,703
Fernando de Noronha [5]	26	1,241	1,323
Sergipe (Aracajú)	21,994	900,744	1,136,951
Bahia (Salvador)	561,026	7,493,470	9,472,523
South-east:	924,934	39,853,498	51,746,318
Minas Gerais (Belo Horizonte)	587,172	11,487,415	13,389,605
Espírito Santo [6] (Vitória)	45,597	1,599,333	2,019,877
Rio de Janeiro (Rio de Janeiro) [7]	44,268	8,994,802	11,300,665
São Paulo (São Paulo)	247,898	17,771,948	25,036,171
South	577,723	16,496,493	19,038,935
Paranâ (Curitiba)	199,554	6,929,868	7,629,405
Santa Catarina (Florianópolis)	95,985	2,901,734	3,631,368
Rio Grande do Sul (Pórto Alegre)	282,184	6,664,891	7,778,162
Central West	1,879,455	5,073,259	7,544,607
Mato Grosso (Cuiabá) [8]	881,001	998,211	1,138,866
Mato Grosso do Sul (Campo Grande) [8]	350,548	598,879	1,367,197
Goiás (Goiânia)	642,092	2,938,677	3,864,629
Distrito Federal (Brasília)	5,814	537,492	1,173,915
Total	8,511,965[9]	93,139,037	119,070,865

For notes *see* p. 229.

Density of census population, 1980, was about 14 per sq. km.

The 1980 census showed 59,146,099 males and 59,924,766 females. The urban and suburban population comprised 45·1% in 1960, 55·9% in 1970 and 67·6% in 1980.

The language is Portuguese.

The new capital, Brasília, was inaugurated 21 April 1960. The federal district (5,814 sq. km) was detached from the west-central state of Goiás, about 1,000 km north-west of Rio de Janeiro.

Population of principal cities (1980 census [10]):

São Paulo	7,033,529	Campinas	566,517
Rio de Janeiro	5,093,232	Santo André	549,278
Salvador	1,496,276	Nova Iguaçu	491,802
Belo Horizonte	1,442,483	Osasco	473,856
Recife	1,184,215	Brasília	411,305
Porto Alegre	1,108,883	Santos	411,023
Curitiba	843,733	Guarulhos	395,117
Belém	758,117	Niterói	386,185
Goiânia	703,263	São Bernardo do Campo	381,261
Fortaleza	648,815	Natal	376,552
Manaus	613,098	Maceió	376,479

CONSTITUTION AND GOVERNMENT. On 15 Nov. 1889 Dom Pedro II (1825–91) was dethroned by a revolution, and Brazil declared a republic.

Presidents since the establishment of the republic:

Marshal Manuel Deodoro da Fonseca, 15 Nov. 1889–23 Nov. 1891 (resigned).
Marshal Floriano Peixoto (Acting), 23 Nov. 1891–15 Nov. 1894.
Dr Prudente José de Moraes Barros, 15 Nov. 1894–15 Nov. 1898.
Dr Manuel Ferraz de Campos Salles, 15 Nov. 1898–15 Nov. 1902.
Dr Francisco da Paula Rodrigues Alves, 15 Nov. 1902–15 Nov. 1906.
Dr Affonso Augusto Moreira Penna, 15 Nov. 1906–14 June 1909 (died).
Dr Nilo Peçanha (Acting), 14 June 1909–15 Nov. 1910.
Marshal Hermes Rodrigues da Fonseca, 15 Nov. 1910–15 Nov. 1914.
Dr Wenceslau Braz Pereira Gomes, 15 Nov. 1914–15 Nov. 1918.
Dr Francisco da Paula Rodrigues Alves.[1]
Dr Delphim Moreira da Costa Ribeiro (Acting), 15 Nov. 1918–28 July 1919.
Dr Epitácio da Silva Pessoa, 28 July 1919–15 Nov. 1922.
Dr Arthur Bernardes, 15 Nov. 1922–15 Nov. 1926.
Dr Washington Luiz Pereira de Souza, 15 Nov. 1926–25 Oct. 1930 (deposed).
Dr Getúlio Dornelles Vargas, 26 Oct. 1930–29 Oct. 1945 (resigned).
Dr José Linhares (Provisional President), 30 Oct. 1945–31 Jan. 1946.
Gen. Eurico Gaspar Dutra, 31 Jan. 1946–31 Jan. 1951.
Dr Getúlio Dornelles Vargas, 31 Jan. 1951–died 24 Aug. 1954.
Dr João Café Filho, 24 Aug. 1954–8 Nov. 1955 (resigned).
Carlos Coimbra da Luz (Acting), 8 Nov. 1955–11 Nov. 1955 (deposed).
Nereu de Oliveira Ramos (Acting), 11 Nov. 1955–31 Jan. 1956.
Juscelino Kubitschek de Oliveira, 31 Jan. 1956–31 Jan. 1961.

---

[1] The name 'Território Federal do Guaporé' was changed to 'Território Federal de Rondônia' on 17 Feb. 1956 and became a state in 1981.

[2] Raised to the status of territorial capitals in 1943; previously, Pôrto Velho and Boa Vista belonged to the state of Amazonas and Macapá to the state of Pará.

[3] Including 2,680 sq. km in dispute with the state of Amazonas.

[4] Includes an area of 2,614 sq. km to be demarcated between states of Piauí and Ceará.

[5] Territory created in 1942 includes 8 sq. km of islets.

[6] Including the islands of Trindade and Martim Vaz.

[7] According to Complementary Law no. 20 1 July 1974, the States of Rio de Janeiro and Guanabara were consolidated, since 15 March 1975, into a single political unit, the State of Rio de Janeiro with the City of Rio de Janeiro as its capital city.

[8] On 1 Jan. 1979, the former state of Mato Grosso was divided into Mato Grosso (capital, Cuiabá) and Mato Grosso do Sul (capital, Campo Grande).

[9] 3,286,000 sq. miles.

[10] Preliminary figures.

Jânio da Silva Quadros, 31 Jan. 1961–25 Aug. 1961 (resigned).
João Belchior Marques Goulart, 7 Sept. 1961–31 March 1964 (deposed).
Marshal Humberto de A. Castelo Branco, 15 April 1964–15 March 1967.
Marshal Artur da Costa e Silva, 15 March 1967–31 Aug. 1969 (resigned).
Gen. Emilio Garrastazu Medici, 30 Oct. 1969–15 March 1974.
Gen. Ernesto Geisel, 15 March 1974–15 March 1979.
Gen. João Baptista de Oliveira Figueiredo, 15 March 1979–

[1] Owing to illness did not take office; died 10 Jan. 1919.

On 24 Jan. 1967 both houses of Congress in joint session approved the new Constitution and press law which came into force on 15 March. An amendment to the Constitution, which came into force on 30 Oct. 1969, was issued on 17 Oct. The present Constitution provides for the indirect election of the President and Vice-President by an electoral college, comprising the members of Congress and delegates from the state legislatures; it grants powers to the President to issue decree-laws on matters connected with the economy and national security; it gives the President authority to intervene in any of the 22 states without consultation with Congress and the right to declare a state of siege and to rule by decree. President and Vice-President are elected for a 6-year term and are not immediately re-eligible. The Senate is elected for 8 years, the Chamber of Deputies for 4 years.

Under the 1969 Constitution, Congress consists of a 67-member Senate and a 420-member Chamber of Deputies. The Senate is two-thirds directly elected (50% of these elected for 8 years in rotation) and one-third indirectly elected. The Chamber of Deputies is elected by universal franchise (with a literacy qualification) for 4 years.

The name of the country was changed from 'Estados Unidos do Brasil' to 'Brasil' and later to 'República Federativa do Brasil'.

Freedom of speech and press are not absolute: war propaganda, the teaching of 'subversive doctrines' and the dissemination of race or class prejudices are banned, as also are political parties opposed to democracy or to 'fundamental human rights' which include the right to own private property. The Supreme Electoral Court on 7 May 1947 declared the Communist Party illegal and on 20 Dec. 1979 the Political Parties Statute of 1965 was amended to allow for the formation of new political parties.

The Institutional Act No. 5 issued on 13 Dec. 1968 was incorporated into the new Constitution through an amendment on 17 Oct. 1969. It was repealed by the Constitutional Amendment Number 11 of 13 Oct. 1978. The Congress renewed its session on 22 Oct. 1969 and elections were held on 15 Nov. 1970, 1974, 1978 and 1982.

Voting is compulsory for men and women between the ages of 18 and 65 and optional for persons over 65. Enlisted men and illiterates (who comprise about 40% of the adult population) may not vote.

President of the Republic: Gen. João Baptista de Oliveira Figueiredo, assumed office 15 March 1979.

Vice-President: Aureliano Chaves.

Minister of Foreign Affairs: Ramiro Elysio Saraiva Guerreiro.

There are Secretaries of State at the head of the following Ministries: Finance; Justice; Interior; Foreign Affairs; Transport; Communications; Agriculture; Labour; Education and Culture; Health; Industry and Commerce; Mines and Power; Welfare and Social Security; and the Ministries of Army, Marine and Air. There is a Secretariat of Planning and General Co-ordination established in 1974 as an agency of the Presidency of the Republic and equivalent to a Ministry in charge of general co-ordination of planning in the country. There are also two other Ministries without portfolio with the same 'status' as the others: the Ministry of Debureaucratization (created in 1979) and the Ministry for Land Reform Affairs (created in 1982).

National flag: Green, with yellow lozenge on which is placed a blue sphere, containing 23 white stars and crossed with a band bearing the motto *Ordem e Progresso.*

National anthem: Ouviram do Ipiranga . . . (words by J. O. Duque Estrada; tune by F. M. da Silva).

Local Government. Brazil consists of 23 states (Rondônia became a state in 1981), 3 federal territories (Roraima, Amapá, Fernando de Noronha) and 1 federal district. Each state has its distinct administrative, legislative and judicial authorities, its own constitution and laws, which must, however, agree with the constitutional principles of the Union. The states may unite or split or form new states. Taxes on interstate commerce, levied by individual states, are prohibited. The governors and members of the legislatures are elected, but magistrates are appointed and are not removable from office save by judicial sentence. Rio de Janeiro and Guanabara became one state in 1975.

DEFENCE

Army. Under the constitution military service is compulsory for every Brazilian man from 21 years of age to 45. The terms of service are 9 years (from the 21st to the 30th years of age) in the Army 'first line' (1 in the ranks, the rest in the reserve) and 14 years (from the 30th to the 45th years of age) in the Army 'second line' (7 in the 'second line' and 7 in the reserve of the same). The men in the Territorial Army also have an annual training of 2 to 4 weeks. The Army is organized in 8 divisions, each with up to 6 armoured, 4 mechanized or motorized infantry brigades; in addition there are 5 light 'jungle' infantry battalions, 2 independent infantry and 1 independent parachute brigades; total strength (1983) 182,750.

Navy. The principal ship of the Brazilian Navy:

Completed	*Name*	*Standard displacement Tons*	*Aircraft*	*Guns*	*Shaft horsepower*	*Speed Knots*
		Aircraft Carrier				
1945	Minas Gerais [1]	15,890	16 fixed-wing, 4 helicopters	10 40mm AA	40,000	24·0

[1] Ex-*Vengeance*, purchased from Great Britain in 1956.

There are also 8 diesel-powered submarines (3 modern built in Britain and 5 old *ex*-US), 6 new destroyer leaders (or large frigates), the *Constituição, Defensora, Liberal* and *Niteroi*, built in Britain, and the *Independencia* and *Uniao*, built in Brazil, 12 old *ex*-US destroyers, 10 fleet tug type corvettes, 6 coastal minesweepers, 1 river monitor, 5 river patrol ships, 6 coastal gunboats, 1 submarine rescue ship, 2 tank landing ships, 4 transports, 18 local transports, 4 oilers, 1 repair ship, 8 survey ships, 1 helicopter-carrying navigation tender, 6 survey launches, 35 minor landing craft, 4 buoy tenders, 20 auxiliaries and 13 tugs. There are also 3 floating docks.

Rather a static navy for such a large country which is apparently suffering from financial stringency. A considerable replacement programme is needed but this has been delayed.

The new construction programme has been revised to replace old *ex*-US submarines and destroyers. A training ship (frigate) and a river support ship were projected.

Among the 50 new units planned are a carrier, guided missile leaders, frigates and amphibious ships.

Naval bases are at Rio de Janeiro, Aratu (Bahia), Belém, Natal, Recife, Salvador, with a river base at Ladario.

The Fleet Air Arm was formed on 26 Jan. 1965. Aircraft obtained from the USA for service on the carrier include 5 Sikorsky SH-3D helicopters and 8 S-2A/E Tracker anti-submarine aircraft, the latter being operated by the Air Force. Nine Wasp light helicopters were obtained from Britain, and are operated on utility and search and rescue duties with 3 turbine-powered Whirlwind, 8 Bell Jet Ranger and 6 Brazilian-assembled Esquilo (AS 350) helicopters. Nine Westland Lynx helicopters were provided for the destroyer leader/frigates of the 'Niteroi' class. Ten Jet Rangers are used for training.

The active personnel in 1983 totalled 46,000 (4,100 officers and 41,900 men), including 14,500 marines and auxiliary corps.

Air Force. The Air Force, formed in 1918, has been independent of the Army and Navy since 1941. It is organized in 6 zones, centred on Belém, Recife, Rio de Janeiro, São Paulo, Porto Alegre and Brasília. The 1a ALADA (air defence wing) has 13 Mirage IIIE fighters and 2 Mirage IIID trainers, integrated with Roland mobile short-range surface-to-air missile systems deployed by the Army, and a radar/communications/computer network. One fighter group has 2 squadrons of F-5E Tiger II supersonic fighter-bombers and two-seat F-5Bs; 2 others operate AT-26 (Aermacchi MB 326G) Xavante light jet attack/trainers, licence-built in Brazil. Counter-insurgency squadrons are equipped with AT-26 Xavantes for reconnaissance and attack, and with Neiva Regente lightplanes, Universal armed piston-engined trainers, and UH-1D/H Iroquois and armed JetRanger helicopters for liaison and observation. There is an ASW group of S-2A/E Trackers for shore-based and carrier-based operations; a maritime patrol group (2 squadrons) with 12 EMB-111 (P-95) twin-turboprop aircraft developed from the Brazilian-designed Bandeirante transport; and 3 air-sea rescue units with RC-130E Hercules reconnaissance transports, SC-95B Bandeirantes, SA 330L Puma and SH-1D Iroquois helicopters. Equipment of transport units includes 1 group of C-130E/H Hercules transports and KC-130H Hercules tankers; 1 group made up of a squadron of HS 748 and C-95 Bandeirante turboprop transports and a second squadron of HS 748s with large freight doors; 1 troop-carrier group with DHC-5 Buffaloes; and 6 independent squadrons with Bandeirantes and Buffaloes. Light aircraft for liaison duties include 32 Embraer U-7s (licence-built Piper Senecas). The VIP transport group has 2 Boeing 737s, 8 HS 125 twin-jet light transports, some Bandeirantes, 6 Embraer Xingu (VU-9) twin-turboprop pressurized transports and 6 JetRanger helicopters. Training is performed primarily on locally-built Aerotec T-23 Uirapuru *ab initio* trainers (being replaced by T-17 Tangarás), T-25 Universal and turboprop T-27 Tucano (EMB-312) basic trainers, and AT-26 Xavante armed jet basic trainers.

Personnel strength (1982) about 42,800, with more than 600 aircraft of all types.

INTERNATIONAL RELATIONS

Membership. Brazil is a member of UN, OAS and LAIA (formerly LAFTA).

ECONOMY

Budget. Receipts and expenditures for the federal government (excluding states, federal district and municipalities) for calendar years have been as follows in 1m. Cr$:

	1977	*1978*	*1979*	*1980*
Revenue	252,605	357,705	544,244	1,230,018
Expenditure	247,467	356,000	521,136	1,190,994

Chief items of revenue were in 1980 as follows (in Cr$1m.): Taxes, 1,002,704; government property, 20,484. Principal items of expenditure: Transport, 62,191; education, 73,896; army, 50,886; aviation and navy, 64,677; welfare and security, 25,252; finance, 19,199.

The foreign debt (including states and municipalities) of Brazil on 31 March 1982 amounted to US$62,882m. Internal federal debt, May 1982 was Cr$4,765,266m. Internal states and municipalities (main securities outstanding), May 1982, Cr$551,341m.

Currency. The *cruzeiro* (Cr$) is the monetary unit, and is divided into 100 *centavos*. The exchange rate was in March 1983 US$1 = Cr$380·50; £1 = Cr$587·32.

Banking. The Bank of Brazil (founded in 1808 and reorganized in 1906, with an authorized capital of NCr$60m. from 1967) is not a central bank of issue but a closely controlled commercial bank; it had 1,137 branches in 1980 throughout the republic. On 31 Dec. 1980 deposits were Cr$434,420m.

On 31 Dec. 1964 the Banco Central da República do Brasil was founded.

The country's currency held by the public on 31 Dec. 1981 was Cr$500,463m. Since Sept. 1939 gold and dollar supply has risen from US$40m. to US$420m., of which the government's gold was US$288m. in May 1961. All banks had on 31 Dec. 1980 deposits of Cr$1,635,328m. and loans of Cr$6,034,808m.

Weights and Measures. The metric system has been in use in all official departments since 1862. It was made compulsory in 1872, but the ancient measures are still partly employed in remote districts. They are: *libra* = 1·012 lb. avoirdupois; *arroba* = 32·98 lb.; *quintal* = 129·54 lb.; *alqueire* (of Roi) = 1 Imperial bushel, or 40 litres; *oitava* = 55·34 grains.

ENERGY AND NATURAL RESOURCES

Electricity. Brazil's hydraulic potential capacity for electric power production was estimated at 106,499 mw. in 1980, one of the largest in the world, of which 34% belongs to the Amazon hydrographic basin. Installed electric power in 1980 was 31,735 mw.; gross production, 137,023 gwh.; consumption, 120,726 gwh.

Oil. There are 13 oil refineries, of which 11 are state owned. Crude oil output was 10,497,028 tonnes in 1981, of which 45% was from the continental shelf. Promising results have been obtained with the exploration of that area which in 1974 represented only 9% of all the national oil production.

The country imported substantial amounts of oil in 1981: 42,209,325 tonnes (value US$10,604m.) representing 48% of total value of all Brazilian imports. Imports come mainly from Iraq and Saudi Arabia.

The government created the National Alcohol Program in 1975 with the aim of a gradual replacement of the consumption of petroleum by combustible alcohol specially produced from sugar-cane and cassava. About US$5,000m. will be invested by 1985. By May 1980, 281 sugar-cane alcohol distillery projects had been approved and their authorized capacity represents 61% of the national aim for 1985 (about 11m. cu. metres). An agreement between the automotive industry and the government was signed in Sept. 1979 and it is hoped that by 1982–83 about 900,000 vehicles utilizing 100% alcohol-combustive will be produced.

Minerals. Brazil is the only source of high-grade quartz crystal in commercial quantities; output, 1980, 133,068 tonnes; exports in 1981, 5,147 tonnes. It is the first largest western producer of chrome ore (reserves of 4m. tonnes; output, 1980, 833,935 tonnes); fifth in the output of mica (10,995 tonnes in 1980); third in zirconium, 4,420 tonnes in 1980; it is the largest producer of beryllium, output, raw beryllium (1980) 21 tonnes; graphite (1980), 234,883 tonnes; titanium ore (1980), 18,686 tonnes, and magnesite (1980), 788,365 tonnes. Along the coasts of the states of Rio de Janeiro, Espírito Santo and Bahia are found monazite sands containing thorium; output, 1980, 2,532 tonnes; reserves are estimated at 30,212 tonnes. Manganese ores of high content are important (reserves in the Amapá region alone are estimated at 16m. tonnes); output, 1980, 3,044,320 tonnes. Output of tungsten ore, 1980, totalled 485,970 tonnes, unrough, 1,897 tonnes. Mine production of lead (1980), 327,515 tonnes. Asbestos production, 1980, 2,602,501 tonnes. Coal deposits exist in Rio Grande do Sul, Santa Catarina, Paraná and São Paulo. Total reserves are estimated at 404m. tonnes; output (1980), 16,006,235 tonnes.

Iron is found chiefly in Minas Gerais, notably the Cauê Peak at Itabira. The Government is now opening up what is believed to be one of the richest iron-ore deposits in the world, situated in Carajás, in the northern state of Pará, with estimated reserves of 18,000m. tonnes, representing the largest concentration of high-grade (66%) iron ore in the world. Total output of iron ore, 1980, mainly from the Cia. Vale do Rio Doce mine at Itabira, was 139,696,561 tonnes. The National Iron and Steel Co. at Volta Redonda, State of Rio de Janeiro, furnishes a substantial part of Brazil's steel. Brazil's total output, 1981: Pig-iron, 10,791,213 tonnes; crude steel ingots castings, 13,226,128 tonnes.

Production of aluminium was started in Minas Gerais in 1945; output of bauxite, 1980, 6,688,015 tonnes. Production of tin ore (cassiterite, processed) was 13,119 tonnes in 1980. Output of barytes (processed) in 1980, 108,015 tonnes;

exports of barytes, 1981, was 24,255 tonnes. Cement output, 1981, was 24,866,636 tonnes. Output of phosphate rock (processed), 1980, was 2,561,889 tonnes.

Gold in large-scale mining was confined to a single mine in Minas Gerais; the production in 1981, 4,058 kg. Large-scale gold deposits have been discovered at Serra Pelada in Pará; production, 1981, 13,752 kg. Roraima silver output, 1980, 24,394 tonnes. Salt output (1980), 3,136,066 tonnes. Diamond districts are Minas Gerais, Mato Grosso, Rotaima, Bahia and São Paulo; output in 1980 was 158,205 carats (80,547 carats from Minas Gerais, 37,701 carats from Mato Grosso).

Agriculture. 32·43% of Brazil's population is rural. Production (in tonnes):

	1980	*1981* [1]		*1980*	*1981* [1]
Bananas (1,000 bunches)	448,046	446,380	Cocoa	319,141	304,000
Beans	1,968,165	2,338,718	Coffee	2,122,391	3,755,320
Cassava	23,465,649	25,050,215	Cotton, raw	1,675,884	1,730,348
Castor beans	280,688	278,006	Jute	27,680	38,909
Oranges	10,891,814	11,429,713	Maize	20,372,072	21,098,300
Potatoes	1,939,537	1,079,251	Soya	15,155,804	14,977,972
Rice	9,775,720	8,260,547	Sugar-cane	148,650,563	153,858,357
Sisal	234,981	243,432	Tobacco	404,860	362,250
Grapes	445,961	661,405	Wheat	2,701,613	2,206,518

[1] Preliminary.

The 4 states of São Paulo, Paraná, Espírito Santo and Minas Gerais are the principal districts for coffee-growing. Output, 1981, from 2,337,200 hectares, 3,755,320 tonnes; exports (1981), 825,443 tonnes.

Bahia furnishes 95% of the cocoa output; in 1981 total output was 304,000 tonnes from 500,102 hectares; exports (1981), 125,228 tonnes. Two crops a year are grown. Castor-bean output usually exceeds 250,000 tonnes; output, 1981, 278,006 tonnes from 433,308 hectares.

Tobacco output was 362,250 tonnes in 1981. In 1981, 131,690 tonnes were exported.

Brazil now ranks second only to the US in production of oranges, output 1980, 10,891,814 tonnes; 1981, 11,429,713. Output of bananas (1,000 bunches), 1980, 448,046; 1981, 446,380. Output of cotton, raw, 1980, 1,675,884 tonnes; 1981, 1,730,348. Exports of cotton wool (raw), 1980, 8,651 tonnes; 1981, 30,266. Brazil formerly furnished only 10% of her own requirements in wheat (average output, 1934–38, 144,000 tonnes); output, 1980, 2,701,613 tonnes; 1981, 2,206,518; imports, 4,360,034 tonnes in 1981. Rice is important; output (rough rice), 1980, was 9,775,720 tonnes; 1981, 8,260,547.

Rubber is another natural product of the country, chiefly in the states of Acre, Amazonas and Pará. Output, 1981, 253,128 tonnes (natural and synthetic); peak reached in 1912 (when rubber realized US$3 a lb.) was 42,510 gross tons. Output of tyres in local factories has risen from 421,765 units (tyres and tubes) in 1940 to 48,542,320 in 1981. Brazilian consumption of rubber in 1981, was 275,681 tonnes. Brazil is the chief source of carnaúba wax, used for electric insulation and gramophone records, exporting 10,088,791 kg in 1981. Caroá fibre is grown as a substitute for Indian jute; production, 1980, 253 tonnes. Jute output, 1981, 38,909 tonnes. Plantations of tung trees established in 1930 (4m. trees in 1946) are beginning to yield tung oils in commercial quantities; output of tung, 1980, 7,981 tonnes.

Livestock (in 1,000): 1981, 93,000 cattle, 35,000 swine, 18,000 sheep, 8,000 goats, 6,300 horses, 1,500 asses and 1,600 mules. In 1980, 10m. cattle, 10m. swine, 0·8m. sheep and lambs, 0·3m. goats and 616m. poultry were slaughtered for meat.

Fisheries. The fishing industry totalled a fleet of 154,695 vessels in 1968; the catch in 1979 was 858,183 tonnes.

INDUSTRY AND TRADE

Industry. The total number of persons engaged in industry (1978) was 4,274,323 and the value of production Cr$2,638,842m.

A paper-mill, reported to be the largest pulp-and-paper mill in South America, is at Monte Alegre, Paraná. Brazil's output of paper, 1980, was 3,361,697 tonnes.

Commerce. Imports and exports for calendar years in Cr$1,000:

	1977	*1978*	*1979*	*1980*	*1981*
Imports	181,479,538	264,988,521	500,134,047	1,228,628,361	2,145,425,789
Exports	167,101,643	224,114,456	393,531,168	1,038,083,296	2,054,524,562

Exports in 1981, 123,994,487 tonnes; 1980, 109,100,450. Imports in 1981, 64,066,069 tonnes; 1980, 71,885,402 tonnes.

Principal imports in 1981 were (in US$1m.): Crude petroleum, 10,597; wheat, 832; coal, 279; soybeans, 246; oil, 233; copper wire, 217.

Principal exports in 1981 were (in US$1m.): Soybean bran, 2,136; coffee (green), 1,517; pig-iron, 1,147; concentrated orange juice, 659; iron ore, 601; sugar, 578.

Of exports (in US$1m.) in 1981, USA took 4,111; Netherlands, 1,470; Germany (Fed. Rep.), 1,317; Japan, 1,220; Italy, 961; Argentina, 880; France, 851; Niger, 770; UK, 735; Mexico, 643. Of 1981 imports, Saudi Arabia furnished 3,792; USA, 3,504; Iraq, 1,896; Japan, 1,240; Germany (Fed. Rep.), 1,076; Venezuela, 968; Mexico, 784; Niger, 729; Italy, 605; France, 597.

Total trade between Brazil and UK (according to British Department of Trade returns, in £1,000 sterling):

	1977	*1978*	*1979*	*1980*	*1981*	*1982*
Imports to UK	300,576	282,574	400,378	269,340	389,898	443,956
Exports and re-exports from UK	245,405	221,423	286,481	218,159	174,361	158,837

Tourism. In 1980, 1,271,465 tourists visited Brazil, spending US$182,346m. 590,258 were Argentinian, 203,360 Uruguayan, 91,897 US citizens, 66,448 Paraguayan, 37,839 German, 29,613 Chilean, 26,275 Italian, 15,628 British and 13,592 Japanese.

COMMUNICATIONS

Roads. There were (1980) 1,398,557 km of highways. In 1980 Brazil had 10,649,533 motor vehicles, including 8,155,707 passenger cars, 1,784,888 commercial vehicles, 119,428 buses and minibuses. 1,210,480 motor vehicles of all types were produced in 1980.

Railways. Public railways are operated by two administrations, the Federal Railways (RFFSA) formed in 1957 and São Paulo Railways (FEPASA) formed in 1971, which is confined to the state of São Paulo. RFFSA had a route-length of 23,591 km in 1981 and FEPASA 5,054 km. Principal gauges are metre and 1,600 mm. The share of the freight market declined to a low of 15% in 1967, but subsequent heavy government investment in reconstruction and new lines, coupled with a policy of forcing bulk commodities on to rail, had raised the share to over 20% in 1974. Continued investment in new wagons, electrification, gauge-conversion, and 'export corridor' routes to the ports will further improve this figure, and some new lines are planned up to the year 2000. Except in the urban areas of Rio de Janeiro and São Paulo, passenger traffic moving by rail is negligible. Traffic moved by RFFSA in 1981 amounted to 66m. tonnes of freight and 394m. passengers. FEPASA carried 19·6m. tonnes and 60·4m. passengers.

There are several important independent freight railways, including the Vitoria à Minas (773 km and (1980) 88m. tonnes of freight) and the Amapa (194 km). São Paulo has a rapid transit railway, and a similar system opened in Rio de Janeiro in 1979.

Aviation. There were 36 regular airlines (27 foreign) operating in 1980. The 4 largest Brazilian companies cover the whole territory and in 1980 they carried 12,439,000 passengers (10,607,000 in domestic traffic) and 2,114m. tonne-km of freight. Their commercial fleet consisted of 119 aircraft on 31 Dec. 1980. There were 126 taxiplane companies on 31 Dec. 1980. The chief airline is Viação Aérea Rio Grande do Sul, (VARIG).

Shipping. Inland waterways, mostly rivers, are open to navigation over some 21,944 miles; number of vessels in 1980, 849. Rio de Janeiro and Santos are the 2 leading ports; there are 18 other large ports. Bolivia and Paraguay have been given free ports at Santos. During 1980, 41,174 vessels entered and cleared the Brazilian ports.

The Lloyd Brasileiro is owned and operated by the Government; its fleet comprised (1980), 48 vessels of 553,769 DWT. Brazilian shipping, 1980 (registered with Lloyds) amounted to 1,165 vessels of 8,069,279 DWT. Petrobrás, the government oil monopoly, took over the government tanker fleet of 26 vessels in 1958; total tanker fleet in 1980 was 181 vessels of 4,578,055 DWT.

Post and Broadcasting. Of the telegraph system of the country, about half, including all interstate lines, is under control of the Government. There were 4,565 post and telegraph offices in 1980. There were 7,496,000 telephones in Jan. 1981 (São Paulo, 1,467,697; Rio de Janeiro, 955,893; Brasilia, 205,988). In 1979 there were 1,159 broadcasting and 108 television stations.

Cinemas (1977). Cinemas numbered 2,356 with a seating capacity of 1,505,620.

Newspapers (1979). There were 344 daily newspapers with a total yearly circulation of 1,587,087,000. Foreigners and corporations (except political parties) are not allowed to own or control newspapers or wireless stations. The press law of 1967 prohibits anonymous journalism and the publication of material defamatory to the armed forces and other public institutions.

JUSTICE, RELIGION, EDUCATION AND HEALTH

Justice. There is a Supreme Federal Court of Justice at Brasília. It has 11 judges; all are appointed by the President with the approval of the Senate. There are also federal courts in each state and the federal district and in the Territories, as well as 'electoral courts' to protect the elections, and labour tribunals. Justice is administered in the states in accordance with state law, by state courts, but in Brasília federal justice is administered. Judges are appointed for life. There are also 3,074 magistrates and 5,634 justices of the peace. In Dec. 1977 the Senate approved laws for allowing marriages to be dissolved. Brazilian citizens can apply for one divorce only during their lifetime. In the case of a marriage partner becoming mentally ill, divorce proceedings cannot begin until 5 years after the illness has been proved. The death penalty was re-introduced in Sept. 1969.

Religion. The population is overwhelmingly Roman Catholic (89% at the census, 1980). In 1889 connexion between Church and State was abolished; it was restored by the 1934 constitution, but again abolished in 1946.

In 1980 (census, preliminary) Catholics numbered 106,154,966; Protestants, 7,856,272, and Spiritualists, 1,625,361.

Education. Elementary education is compulsory. In 1980 (census, preliminary) there were 70,387,991 persons 5 years of age or over who could read and write; this was 68·72% of that age group; 69·36% of the literates were men.

There were, in 1979, 192,723 first degree school units, with 22,025,449 pupils and 862,282 teachers; 7,140 second degree establishments (not school units), with 2,658,078 pupils and 183,352 teachers; 4,398 third degree units, with 1,311,799 pupils and 108,821 teachers.

There were, in 1980, 65 universities (including 20 private) and 817 faculties not belonging to universities (662 private), including the University of Rio de Janeiro (founded on 7 Sept. 1920), the University of Bahia (founded in 1946), the University of Recife (1946), the University of Paraná (1946), the Rural University (1948, State of Rio de Janeiro), the University of São Paulo (1934), the University of Minas Gerais (1927), the University of Rio Grande do Sul (1934), the University of Brasília (1960) and the University of Mato Grosso (1971). There are also 12 Catholic universities (all private) in Rio de Janeiro (1946), São Paulo (1946), Rio Grande do Sul (1948), Pernambuco (1951), Minas Gerais (1958), Bahia, Paraná, Campinas, Petrópolis and Pelotas. Students in 1976 totalled 1,096,727.

Health. In 1979 there were 17,079 health establishments of which 6,036 were for inpatients; total number of beds, 488,323 (369,860 in private institutions).

DIPLOMATIC REPRESENTATIVES

Of Brazil in Great Britain (32 Green St., London, W1Y 3FD)
Ambassador: Mario Gibson Alves Barboza (accredited 10 Dec. 1982).

Of Great Britain in Brazil (Setor de Embaixadas Sul, Quadra 801, Conjunto K, Brasília, D.F.)
Ambassador: G. W. Harding, CMG, MVO.

Of Brazil in the USA (3006 Massachusetts Ave., NW, Washington, D.C., 20008)
Ambassador: Antonio Francisco Azeredo da Silveira.

Of the USA in Brazil (Ave das Nocões, Lote 3, Brasília, D.F.)
Ambassador: Langhorne A. Motley.

Of Brazil to the United Nations
Ambassador: Sérgio Corrêa Da Costa.

Books of Reference

Amazônia Mineração. *Projeto Carajás.* Belém
Anuário do Transporte Aéreo. Departamento de Aviação Civil. Rio de Janeiro, 1980
Anuário Estatístico do Brasil. Vol. 42. Fundação Instituto Brasileiro de Geografia e Estatística, Rio de Janeiro, 1981
Anuário Estatístico das Ferrovias do Brasil. Vol. 4. Rede Ferroviária Federal. Rio de Janeiro, 1980
Anuário Estatístico dos Transportes. Vol. 11. Empresa Brasileira de Planejamento de Transportes. Brasília, 1981
Anuário Estatístico Embratur. Vol. 12. Empresa Brasileira de Turismo. Rio de Janeiro, 1981
Anuário Mineral Brasileiro. Departamento Nacional da Produção Mineral. Brasília, 1981
Atlas do Brasil. Instituto Brasileiro de Geografia. 2nd ed. Rio de Janeiro, 1959
Boletim do Banco Central do Brasil. Banco Central do Brasil. Brasília. Monthly
Bulletin of the British Chamber of Commerce in Brazil. Rio de Janeiro. Monthly
Sinopse Estatística do Brasil. Vol. 7. Fundação Instituto Brasileiro de Geografia e Estatística. Rio de Janeiro, 1981
Azevedo, Aroldo de., *Geografia do Brazil.* 2 vols. Rio de Janeiro, 1960
Banco do Brasil, *Boletim Trimestral.* Brasília, D.F. From 1966
Burns, E. B., *A History of Brazil.* 2nd ed. Columbia Univ. Press, 1980
Calogeras, João Pandiá, *A History of Brazil.* Chapel Hill, North Carolina, 1939
Campbell, G., *Brazil Struggles for Development.* London, 1973
Cowell, A., *The Tribe that Hides from Man.* London, 1973
Dickenson, J. P., *Brazil.* Folkestone, 1978
Fiechter, G.-A., *Brazil Since 1964: Modernisation Under a Military Regime.* London, 1975
Hanbury-Tenison, R., *A Question of Survival for the Indians of Brazil.* London, 1973
McDonough, P., *Power and Ideology in Brazil.* Princeton Univ. Press, 1981
Moraes, R. Borba de., *Bibliographia Brasiliana (1504–1900).* 2 vols. 1958
Raine, P., *Brazil: Awakening Giant.* Washington, 1974
Roiter, F., *Brazil.* London, 1971
Saunders, J., *Modern Brazil: New Patterns and Developments.* Univ. of Florida Press, 1971
Schuh, G. E., and Alves, E. R., *The Agricultural Development of Brazil.* New York, 1970
Selcher, W. E. (ed.), *Brazil in the International System: The Rise of a Middle Power.* Boulder, 1981
Smith, P. B., *Oil and Politics in Modern Brazil.* Toronto, 1975
Tyler, W. G., *The Brazilian Industrial Economy.* Aldershot, 1981
Wellington, R. A., *The Brazilians.* Newton Abbot, 1974

National Library: Biblioteca Nacional Avenida Rio Branco 219–39, Rio de Janeiro, G.B. *Director:* Célia Ribeiro Zaher.

BRITISH INDIAN OCEAN TERRITORY

HISTORY. This territory was established on 8 Nov. 1965, consisting then of the Chagos Archipelago (formerly administered by Mauritius) and the islands of Aldabra, Desroches and Farquhar (all formerly administered by the Seychelles). The latter islands being returned to the Seychelles when that country achieved independence on 29 June 1976, the territory now comprises the Chagos Archipelago, lying 1,180 miles (1,899 km) north-west of Mauritius.

AREA AND POPULATION. The group, with a total land area of 20 sq. miles (52 sq. km) comprises 5 coral atolls (Diego Garcia, Peros Banhos, Salomon, Eagle and Egmont) of which the largest and southern-most, Diego Garcia, covers 14 sq. miles (36 sq. km). The transient Mauritian population of some 1,400 on Diego Garcia was repatriated in 1972 to facilitate the construction of British-US defence installations, and service personnel now form the only population.

Commissioner: W. N. Wenhban-Smith (non-resident).
Administrator: D. H. Doble.

BRUNEI

Capital: Bandar Seri Begawan
Population: 191,770 (1981)
GNP per capita: US$11,890 (1980)

HISTORY. The Sultanate of Brunei was a powerful state in the early 16th century, with authority over the whole of the island of Borneo and some parts of the Sulu Islands and the Philippines. At the end of the 16th century its power had begun to decline and various cessions were made to Great Britain, the Rajah of Sarawak and the British North Borneo Company in the 19th century to combat piracy and anarchy. By the middle of the 19th century the State had been reduced to its present limits.

In 1847 the Sultan of Brunei entered into a treaty with Great Britain for the furtherance of commercial relations and the suppression of piracy, and in 1888, by a further treaty, the State was placed under the protection of Great Britain. Brunei was the only former British dependency inhabited by a Malay people that did not join the Federation of Malaysia in 1963.

AREA AND POPULATION. Brunei, on the northwest coast of Borneo, is bounded on all sides by Sarawak territory, which splits the State into two separate parts. Area, about 2,226 sq. miles (5,800 sq. km), with a coastline of about 100 miles. Population (1981 census) was 191,770. The 4 districts are Brunei/Muara (114,310), Belait (49,590), Tutong (21,640), Temburong (6,230). The capital is Bandar Seri Begawan, 9 miles from the mouth of Brunei River. The climate is of tropical marine type, hot and moist, with cool nights.

CONSTITUTION AND GOVERNMENT. On 29 Sept. 1959 the Sultan promulgated a constitution. There is a Privy Council, an Executive and a Legislative Council. On 6 Jan. 1965 the constitution was amended to provide for general elections to the Legislative Council; at the same time the Executive Council was renamed Council of Ministers. The Legislative Council consists of 20 members and a Speaker appointed by the Sultan. The Council of Ministers is presided over by the Sultan and consists of 6 *ex-officio* members and 4 other members, all of whom except one are members of the Legislative Council. The Mentri Besar, who is one of the *ex-officio* members of the Legislative Council and the Council of Ministers, is responsible to the Sultan for the exercise of executive authority in the State. As a result of negotiations in June 1978, the Sultan and the British Government signed a new treaty on 7 Jan. 1979 under which Brunei will become a fully sovereign and independent State at the end of 1983.

The official language is Malay, but English may be used for other purposes.

Sultan of Brunei: Duli Yang Maha Mulia Paduka Seri Baginda Sultan and Yang di-Pertuan Negeri Brunei Sir Muda Hassanal Bolkiah Mu'izzaddin Waddaulah ibni Duli Yang Teramat Mulia Paduka Seri Begawan Sultan Sir Muda Omar Ali Saifuddin Sa'adul Khairi Waddin, DK, PGGUB, DPKG, DPKT, PSPNB, PSNB, PSLJ, SPMB, PANB, GCMG, DMN, DK (Kelantan), DK (Johore), DK (Negeri Sembilan). The Sultan was crowned on 1 Aug. 1968.

General Adviser to HH The Sultan: The Most Hon., Pehin Orang Kaya Laila Setia Bakti Di-Raja Dato Laila Utama Awang Haji Isa bin Pehin Datu Perdana Mentri Dato Laila Utama Haji Ibrahim, DK, SPMB, DSNB, CVO, OBE, PHBS, PBLI, PJK.

Mentri Besar (Chief Minister, Acting): The Rt Hon. Pehin Orang Kaya Laila Wijaya Dato Seri Setia Haji Abdul Aziz bin Begawan Pehin Udana Khatib Dato Seri Paduka Haji Umar, PSNB, DPMB, SLJ, PJK

Flag: Yellow, with 2 diagonal strips of white over black with the national arms in red placed over all in the centre.

DEFENCE

Army. The Royal Brunei Malay Regiment, whose strength at 28 Feb. 1981 was

243 officers and 2,873 other ranks. The Regiment is equipped with modern sophisticated Western weapons and equipment. The Regiment main elements comprise the following: (a) Two Infantry Battalions; (b) An armoured squadron of Scorpion tanks; (c) A squadron of Bell 212 medium-lift helicopters and armed BO 105; (d) A battery of Rapier Air Defence missiles with 105mm light-guns combined; (e) A Flotilla of 3 new fast gunboats armed with Exocet Missile and three coastal patrol boats and 2 landing crafts; (f) Special Boat Squadron of 3 river patrol craft (ROTORK) and 24 Fast Assault boats; (g) Combat Engineer Squadron equipped with engineering capabilities.

Navy. The First Flotilla of the Royal Brunei Malay Regiment comprises 3 fast missile-armed attack craft of 150 tons (completed by Vosper, Singapore in 1978–79), 3 coastal patrol boats (built by Vosper-Thornycroft (Singapore)), 2 landing craft and 3 small patrol boats. Special Boat Squadron operates 24 fast assault boats. Personnel in 1983 numbered 336 (36 officers and 300 ratings) in the First Flotilla (for offshore work) plus 120 (6 officers and 114 men) in the Special Boat Squadron (for riverine affairs), all under a Commander, Royal Navy.

Two coastal patrol craft built by Vosper, Singapore, were supplied in 1979 for the Brunei Police.

Air Wing. The Air Wing of the Royal Brunei Malay Regiment was formed in 1965. Current equipment includes up to 6 MBB BO 105, 3 Bell 205A, 3 Bell 206B JetRanger and 7 Bell 212 helicopters, a twin-turboprop HS 748 transport used also for VIP passenger and search and rescue duties, SF.260M and 2 Cherokee piston-engined trainers. Delivery has begun of 7 Sikorsky S-76 transport helicopters. In 1982 there were about 100 personnel.

Police. Establishment provides over 1,750 officers and men (1980). In addition, there is a small auxiliary force mostly employed on static guard duties.

ECONOMY

Planning. A fourth Five-Year National Development Plan was announced in 1980 to further improve the economic, social and cultural life of the people.

Budget. In mid-1979 the actual revenue was B$1,882m. and expenditure was B$1,048m. The main sources of revenue in 1979 were: Taxes, B$1,350m.; royalties, B$282m.; interest on investments, B$250m. The main heads of expenditure in 1979 were: Defence, B$372m.; education, B$92m.; public works, B$83m.; medical, B$40m.; police, B$39m.; other current expenditure, B$297m.; transfer to development fund, B$100m.

Currency. The currency is the *Brunei dollar* with a par value of 0·290 299 gramme of gold.

ENERGY AND NATURAL RESOURCES

Oil. The Seria oilfield, discovered in 1929, has passed its peak production. The high level of crude oil production is maintained through the increase of offshore oilfields production, which exceeds onshore oilfields production. Production is about 240,000 bbls a day. The crude oil is exported directly, and only a small amount is refined at Seria for domestic uses.

Gas. Natural gas is also produced at one of the biggest liquefied natural gas plants of its kind in the world and is exported to Japan.

Agriculture. The chief agricultural products in 1981 were rice (10,000 tonnes) and bananas (3,000 tonnes).

Livestock in 1981: Cattle, 4,000; buffaloes, 14,000; pigs, 14,000; chickens, 1·2m.

Forestry. Most of the interior is under forest, containing large potential supplies of serviceable timber.

INDUSTRY AND TRADE

Industry. Brunei depends primarily on its oil industry, which employs more than 7% of the entire working population. Crude oil accounts for 62% of the total value of the exports and re-exports. The second main export is liquefied natural gas, which contributes 31% and petroleum products 6%.

Other minor products are rubber, pepper, sawn timber, gravel and animal hides. Local industries include boat-building, cloth weaving and the manufacture of brass-and silverware.

Commerce. In 1980 imports totalled B$1,230m.; exports, B$9,853m.

Total trade between Brunei and UK (British Department of Trade returns, in £1,000 sterling):

	1977	*1978*	*1979*	*1980*	*1981*	*1982*
Imports to UK	454	408	419	889	2,757	2,434
Exports and re-exports from UK	17,429	16,265	22,763	23,118	24,165	41,804

COMMUNICATIONS

Roads. The State has about 916 miles of road, of which 451 miles are bituminous surfaced. The main road connects Bandar Seri Begawan with Kuala Belait and Seria. Considerable work is being undertaken for development of secondary roads and a coastal road between Muara and Tutong is being constructed. The number of motor vehicles (1980) was 60,751.

Aviation. Royal Brunei Airlines (RBA) and Singapore Airlines provide daily services linking Brunei and Singapore. RBA also operates services to Bangkok, Manila, Kuala Lumpur, Kuching, Kota Kinabalu and Hong Kong. Cathay Pacific Airways also operates to Brunei and on to Western Australia from Hong Kong. British Airways provides a weekly service between Brunei and UK. Malaysian Airlines System has air connections from neighbouring regions.

Shipping. Regular shipping services operate from Singapore, Hong Kong, and from ports in Sarawak and Sabah to Bandar Seri Begawan. Private companies operate a passenger ferry service between Bandar Seri Begawan and Labuan, Sabah, 7 days a week.

Post and Broadcasting. There were 8 post offices (1980) and a telephone network (17,930 telephones in 1981) linking the main centres. Radio Brunei is operated by the Department of Radio and Television and operates on medium- and short-waves in Malay, Iban, Dusun, English and Chinese. Number of radio receivers, 38,000 and television sets, 32,000.

A satellite communications earth station provides easy and quick long-distance external communication and a feasibility study has been undertaken to establish a second earth satellite station.

RELIGION AND EDUCATION

Religion. The official religion is Islam.

Education (1979). Free education in the Malay language is provided in government primary schools (29,934 pupils) and 4 government secondary Malay schools (1,218 pupils). Free education in English was provided in 30 government preparatory schools (8,546 pupils) and 7 government secondary schools (7,344 pupils) and one 6th form centre (819 pupils). The government also provided one Arabic preparatory school (203 pupils) and 2 Arabic secondary schools (251 pupils). Teacher-training was provided in 2 government teachers' colleges, in both Malay and English for 601 students. Eight non-government Mission schools provided education in English at kindergarten, primary and secondary level for a total of 6,745 pupils; 8 non-government Chinese schools provided education in Chinese at the same levels for a total of 5,813 pupils. One private kindergarten and primary school, administered by the Brunei Shell Petroleum Co., provided education in either English or Dutch for a total of 986 pupils, and there was also 1 private vocational school administered by the Brunei Shell Petroleum Co. (140 artisan-trainees). Two government vocational schools provided full training courses to 274 students in the engineering and building trades.

DIPLOMATIC REPRESENTATIVE

Of Great Britain in Brunei (Jalan Residency, Bandar Seri Begawan)
High Commissioner: A. C. Watson, CMG.

BULGARIA

Capital: Sofia
Population: 8·89m. (1981)
GNP per capita: US$4,150 (1980)

Narodna Republika Bulgaria

HISTORY. The Bulgarian state was founded in 681, but fell under Turkish rule in 1396. By the Treaty of Berlin, which followed the Russo-Turkish war of 1878, the Principality of Bulgaria and the Autonomous Province of Eastern Rumelia, both under Turkish suzerainty, were constituted. In 1885 Rumelia was reunited with Bulgaria. On 5 Oct. 1908 Bulgaria declared her independence of Turkey. *Rulers:* Prince Alexander I of Battenberg, 1879–86; Prince (after 1908, Tsar) Ferdinand, 1887–1918 (abdicated); Tsar Boris III, 1918–43; Tsar Simeon II, lost his throne as a result of a referendum held on 8 Sept. 1946 (3,801,160 votes for a republic, 197,176 for the monarchy, 119,168 invalid).

In 1941 Bulgaria signed the Three Power Pact and the Anti-Comintern Pact. In 1944 Bulgaria asked the UK and the USA for an armistice. The USSR declared war on Bulgaria on 5 Sept. 1944. The Fatherland Front government (established 9 Sept.) asked the USSR for an armistice, which was signed on 28 Oct. 1944 by the USSR, the UK and the USA. The peace treaty was signed in Paris on 10 Feb. 1947.

AREA AND POPULATION. On 8 Sept. 1940 by the treaty of Craiova, Romania ceded to Bulgaria the Southern Dobrudja, fixing the new frontier on the 1912 line.

In April 1941 Bulgaria occupied the Yugoslav part of Macedonia, and the Greek districts of Western Thrace, Eastern Macedonia, Florina and Castoria. The peace treaty of 1947 restored the frontiers as on 1 Jan. 1941.

The area of Bulgaria is 110,911·5 sq. km (42,823 sq. miles) and is bounded in the north by Romania, east by the Black Sea, south by Turkey and Greece and west by Yugoslavia.

The country is divided into 28 provinces (*okrŭg,* plur. *okrŭzi).* Area and population in 1980:

Province	*Area (sq. km)*	*Pop. 1,000*	*Province*	*Area (sq. km)*	*Pop. 1,000*	*Province*	*Area (sq. km)*	*Pop. 1,000*
Blagoevgrad	6,464	334	Pleven	4,184	373	Sofia (City)	1,038	1,139
Burgas	7,605	430	Plovdiv	5,591	745	Stara Zagora	4,902	407
Gabrovo	2,068	177	Razgrad	2,646	191	Tolbukhin	4,689	251
Khaskovo	4,029	294	Ruse	2,624	294	Tŭrgovishte	2,754	172
Kŭrdzhali	4,020	281	Shumen	3,374	250	Varna	3,820	464
Kyustendil	3,002	199	Silistra	2,876	173	Veliko Tŭrnovo	4,690	349
Lovech	4,129	212	Sliven	3,729	234	Vidin	3,110	171
Mikhailovgrad	3,585	235	Smolyan	3,518	171	Vratsa	4,186	293
Pazardzhik	4,379	319	Sofia	7,385	310	Yambol	4,162	206
Pernik	2,355	174						

The population at the census of 2 Dec. 1975 was 8,727,771 (males, 4,357,820; urban, 5,061,087). Population in June 1981 was 8·89m. (4·4m. males; 5·5m. urban). Population density 80 per sq. km.

Ethnic minorities are estimated to total 1·2m. The language estimates are: Bulgarian 88%, Turkish 8·6%. The remainder include Gipsies, Jews, Romanians and Armenians. Some Turks have been repatriated.

Population of principal towns (1980): Sofia, 1,056,945; Plovdiv, 350,438; Varna, 291,224; Ruse, 172,782; Burgas, 168,412; Stara Zagora, 136,177; Pleven, 127,716; Sliven, 97,714; Gabrovo, 78,349; Pernik, 92,653; Tolbukhin, 95,672; Shumen, 94,765; Yambol, 82,523; Khaskovo, 84,117; Pazardzhik, 73,402.

Vital statistics, 1980: Live births, 126,577; deaths, 95,000; marriages, 68,592; divorces, 12,756; crude birth rate, 15·5 per 1,000 population; crude death rate, 10·5; infant mortality, 22·2 per 1,000; growth rate, 5.

Expectation of life in 1980 was: men, 68·7 years, women 73·9.

CLIMATE. The southern parts have a Meditterranean climate, with winters mild and moist and summers hot and dry, but further north the conditions become more continental, with a larger range of temperature and greater amounts of rainfall in summer and early autumn. Sofia, Jan. 28°F(–2·2°C), July 69°F (20·6°C). Annual rainfall 25·4" (635 mm).

CONSTITUTION AND GOVERNMENT. A People's Republic was proclaimed by the National Assembly on 15 Sept. 1946, and the existing 'Tŭrnovo' Constitution of 1879 was replaced by the 'Dimitrov' Constitution in 1947. This was in turn replaced by a new constitution on 18 May 1971. This provides for a single-chamber National Assembly *(Narodno Sŭbranie).* The highest permanently operating organ of the state is the Council of State which consists of a chairman, 2 first vice-chairmen, 4 vice-chairmen, a secretary and 17 members; it is elected by the National Assembly from its members. Supreme power is vested in the National Assembly, which consists of 400 deputies elected from areas of equal population by direct, secret and universal suffrage (everybody at age of 18 being eligible to vote and hold office) for a term of 5 years; it is to meet at least three times every year. The National Assembly also elects the Council of State and the ministers who are responsible to it.

A general election was held on 27 Oct. 1946. The Fatherland Front, composed of the Workers (Communist), Agrarian, Socialist and Zveno Parties, and non-party independents, obtained 364 seats (277 of which went to the Communists) and the opposition 101. On 26 Aug. 1947 the oppositional Agrarian Union was dissolved; its leader, Nikola Petkov, was sentenced to death and hanged on 23 Sept. The Socialist Party was merged with the Workers' Party in Aug. 1948, and the Zveno Party dissolved itself.

The Fatherland Front became, in 1948, a unified mass organization with individual memberships. Inside the Fatherland Front, there remain two political parties, the Bulgarian Communist Party and the Bulgarian People's Agrarian Union. Petŭr Tanchev *(1st Vice-Chairman, Council of State)* is Secretary of the Agrarian Union and Pencho Kubadinski Chairman of the Fatherland Front's National Council.

In 1981 the membership of the Communist Party was 825,876; Young Communist League, (1976) 1·3m.; Agrarian Union, 120,000; Fatherland Front, 3,770,080.

At the elections of 7 June 1981, 99·96% of the electorate voted, and 99·93% of the votes were cast for the 400 candidates (87 women) of the Fatherland Front; there were no other candidates. The list comprised 271 Communists, 99 Agrarians and 30 independents. The President of the National Assembly is Stanko Todorov.

There is no constitutional single Head of State, but Todor Zhivkov *(Chairman of the Council of State, Secretary-General of the Communist Party)*, performs some of the functions of a Head of State.

The highest policy-making and executive body of the Bulgarian Communist Party is its Politburo, consisting of 11 full members and 3 candidate members. The Politburo is elected by and from the Central Committee.

The Politburo was in March 1983 composed as follows: FULL MEMBERS: Todor Zhivkov, Grisha Filipov *(Chairman, Council of Ministers, i.e. Prime Minister)*, Todor Bozhinov *(1st Deputy Chairman, Council of Ministers, Minister of Metallurgy)*, Stanko Todorov, Pencho Kubadinski, Milko Balev, Tsola Dragoicheva, Aleksandŭr Lilov, Gen. Dobri Dzhurov *(Defence Minister)*, Petŭr Mladenov *(Foreign Minister)*, Ognian Doinov. CANDIDATE MEMBERS: Petŭr Dyulgerov; Andrei Lukanov *(Deputy Chairman, Council of Ministers)*, Georgi Yordanov *(Deputy Chairman, Council of Ministers, Chairman, Committee for Culture)*.

Ministers not in the Politburo include: Kiril Zarev *(Deputy Chairman, Council of Ministers)*, Stanish Bonev *(Deputy Chairman, Council of Ministers, Chairman, State Planning Committee)*, Georgi Karamanev, *(Deputy Chairman, Council of*

Ministers, Minister of Internal Trade), Khristo Khristov *(Foreign Trade)*, Dimitŭr Stoyanov *(Internal Affairs)*, Belcho Belchev *(Finance)*.

In May 1967 a second 20-year treaty of friendship, co-operation and mutual assistance with the Soviet Union was signed.

National flag: Three horizontal stripes of white, green, red, with the national emblem in the canton.

National anthem: An arrangement of Mila Rodino (Dear Fatherland), a popular patriotic song, was declared the national anthem in 1964.

Local Government. People's Councils at province and commune level are elected for terms of 30 months, to deal with all economic, social and cultural problems of their area. They also supervise the management of state and publicly owned enterprises. The Council's executive organs are Permanent Committees. 52,712 councillors and 3,960 mayors were elected on 7 June 1981.

DEFENCE. There is a compulsory service of 2 years in the Army and Air Force (3 years in the Navy).

Army. In 1983 the Army had a strength of 105,000 men, organized in 8 motorized divisions and 5 tank brigades. There are 3 Army Commands (Military Regions), Sofia, Plovdiv, Sliven. Tanks, mainly T-34s and some T-54s and T-55s, numbered 1,900. Security police numbered 22,500 (5 brigades of border guards, 8 regiments of security forces).

Navy. The Navy consists of 2 *ex*-Soviet 'R' class submarines, 2 *ex*-Soviet 'Riga' class frigates, 3 *ex*-Soviet 'Poti' class corvettes, 4 *ex*-Soviet 'Osa' class missile boats, 6 *ex*-Soviet patrol vessels, 10 *ex*-Soviet torpedo boats, 2 fleet minesweepers, 4 coastal minesweepers, 12 minesweeping boats, 27 landing craft, 3 oilers, 3 survey ships, 2 salvage craft, 8 tugs and 28 auxiliaries and service craft. Personnel in 1983 totalled 10,000 officers and ratings of whom 4,000 were afloat.

Air Force. The large tactical Air Force has about 250 Soviet-built combat aircraft and 34,000 personnel. There are 6 squadrons of MiG-21 interceptors; about 6 squadrons of fighter/ground attack MiG-23s and MiG-17s; 2 reconnaissance squadrons of MiG-17s; some Mi-24 helicopter gunships; a total of about 20 Tu-134, Il-14 and An-24/26 transport aircraft; 40 Mi-4, 30 Mi-2 and a few Mi-6, Mi-8 and Mi-14 helicopters; and L-29 Delfin, MiG-15UTI and MiG-21UTI trainers. Soviet-built 'Guideline', 'Goa' and 'Gainful' surface-to-air missiles have also been supplied to Bulgaria.

INTERNATIONAL RELATIONS

Membership. Bulgaria is a member of UN, Comecon and the Warsaw Pact.

External Debt. Agreements of 1955 and 1963 settled outstanding financial claims by the UK and USA respectively.

ECONOMY

Planning. State economic planning started in 1947. After 1964 there was a limited decentralization in planning, culminating in the economic reform of 1 Jan. 1969. A new economic mechanism was introduced on 1 Jan. 1982. This provides for direct linking of production to the market, a shift from extensive to intensive development, the establishment of profit as the sole criterion of success, the widening of enterprises' powers to make their own plans and the election of managerial staff (except the chief) by the workforce.

For the first seven 5-year plans *see* THE STATESMAN'S YEAR-BOOK for 1980–81 and 1981–82. The eighth 5-year plan (1981–85) envisages a rise in national income of 20%, in industrial production of 28% and in agriculture of 18%.

Prices of consumer goods rose by 25–30% in 1979.

Budget. The revenue and expenditure of Bulgaria for calendar years were as follows (in 1m. leva):

	1972	*1973*	*1974*	*1975*	*1976*	*1977*	*1980*	*1981*	*1982*[1]
Revenue	6,355	7,055	8,060	9,321	8,778	9,498	13,187	15,385	15,824
Expenditure	6,261	7,036	8,044	9,223	8,758	9,477	13,167	15,370	15,809

[1] Estimate.

Of the 1982 revenue 92% came from the national economy. 1980 expenditure was: National economy, 5,777m. leva; social and education, 5,265m.; administration, 291m.

Currency. The unit of currency is the *lev* (pl. *leva*) divided into 100 *stotinki* (sing. *stotinka*). It has been linked to the Soviet rouble since May 1952. A new *lev*, equalling 10 old leva, was introduced on 1 Jan. 1962. The parity (clearing value) is 1 rouble = 1·30 *leva*. Official rate of exchange (March 1983) was £1 = 1·485 *leva*; US$1 = 0·965 *leva*. Rate of exchange for non-commercial transactions: £1 = 2·40 leva; US$1 = 1·65 *leva*.

Banking. In 1947 banks were nationalized and the National Bank gained autonomy, freeing it from responsibility for state debts. In 1969 the banking system was reorganized. The National Bank became the central bank and was made responsible for issuing currency. It also plays an important part in the management of the economy: its chairman has ministerial rank. There is also a Foreign Trade Bank, a Mineral Bank and a State Savings Bank. In 1980, 8·8m. depositors had savings totalling 8,442m. leva. The State Savings Bank has advanced personal loans up to 500 leva at 3·5% interest to some 500,000 users. Interest on deposits is from 1% to 3%.

Weights and Measures. The metric system is in general use. On 1 April 1916 the Gregorian calendar came into force in Bulgaria.

ENERGY AND NATURAL RESOURCES

Energy. Bulgaria has little oil, gas or high-grade coal and energy policy is based on the exploitation of its low-grade coal and limited water resources. Local fuels account for 32% of the power balance and water resources for 10%. The first nuclear power plant went into action in 1974 and nuclear power accounts for 20% of electric power generation. Geothermal and solar energy sources are being developed.

Electricity. A joint Romanian-Bulgarian hydroelectric station is being built on the Danube at Turnu-Magurele-Nikopol.

Oil and Natural Gas. Oil is extracted in the Balchik district on the Black Sea, in an area 100 km north of Varna and at Dolni Dubnik near Pleven. Crude oil production was 129,000 tonnes in 1977. There are refineries at Burgas (annual capacity 5m. tonnes) and Dolni Dubnik (7m. tonnes). 190m. cu. metres of natural gas were produced in 1980.

Minerals. Ore production 1980: Manganese, 14,200 tonnes; iron, 590,000 tonnes. 31·6m. tonnes of coal including 446,000 tonnes of hard coal and 24·1m. tonnes of lignite were mined in 1980. 82 tonnes of salt were extracted in 1980.

Agriculture. In 1979 the National Agro-Industrial Union was formed, replacing the Ministry of Agriculture. It comprises state and collective organizations, and is responsible for agriculture, the food industry and agricultural machine building. In 1980 cultivated agricultural land covered 6,184,800 hectares, of which 4,665,100 hectares are arable.

Size of private plots (maximum, 1 hectare) is based on the number of members of a household. Total area of private plots in 1980 was 598,000 hectares. In 1978 these accounted for 23% of all agricultural production. There were, in 1980, 19 co-operative farms. There were 34 machine-tractor stations. 153,341 tractors (in 15-h.p. units) were in use and 21,171 combine harvesters. Collective and state farms have been incorporated into 'agricultural-industrial complexes'. There were 283 of these in 1980 with 4,843,694 hectares.

In 1980, 26 irrigation systems and 151 dams irrigated 1,197,300 hectares.

Yield in 1980 (in 1,000 tonnes): Wheat, 3,847; rye, 28; maize 2,256; barley, 1,375; oats, 54; rice, 67; sunflower seed, 380; unginned cotton, 12; tobacco, 119; tomatoes, 834; potatoes, 301; grapes, 952. Bulgaria is the world's principal supplier of attar of roses; annual production, 1,200 kg.

Other products (in 1,000 tonnes) in 1980: Meat, 1,116; wool, 35; sugar, 341; 2,434m. eggs were produced and 2,151m. litres of milk.

Livestock (1981): 119,732 horses, 1,795,669 cattle, including 698,776 milch cows, 10,432,646 sheep, 3,807,621 pigs, 41,635,971 poultry and 619,362 beehives.

Forestry. The forest area, 1980, was 3,845,000 hectares, of which 1·25m. were coniferous. 47,274 hectares were afforested in 1980. 8·5m. cu. metres of timber were cut in 1980.

Fisheries. The catch of sea fish was 89,500 tonnes in 1979.

INDUSTRY AND TRADE

Industry. All industry was nationalized in 1947.

Industrial production	*1975*	*1976*	*1977*	*1978*	*1979*	*1980*
Electricity (1m. kwh.)	25,232	27,742	29,707	31,486	32,484	35,500
Crude steel (1,000 tonnes)	2,265	2,460	2,589	2,470	2,482	2,565
Pig-iron (1,000 tonnes)	1,560	1,612	1,664	1,538	1,501	1,588
Cement (1,000 tonnes)	4,358	4,362	4,665	5,149	5,401	5,429
Sulphuric acid (1,000 tonnes)	853	857	860	974	998	852

In 1980 there were also produced (in 1,000 tonnes): Coke, 1,348; rolled steel, 3,213; artificial fertilizers, 1,836; calcinated soda, 1,479; cotton fabrics, 347 sq. metres; silk fabrics, 40m. metres.

Labour. There is 42½-hour 5-day working week. The average wage (excluding peasantry) was 182 leva per month in 1980. Retiring age is 60 for men and 55 for women. The labour force (excluding peasantry) in 1980 was 3,997,615 (2,560,529 female), of whom 1,369,680 worked in industry, 341,213 in building and 944,723 in agriculture and forestry.

Commerce. Foreign trade is controlled by the Ministry of Foreign Trade. Bulgarian trade has developed as follows (in 1m. leva):

	1975	*1976*	*1977*	*1978*	*1979*	*1980*
Imports	5,236	5,436	6,061	6,801	7,363	8,283
Exports	4,541	5,200	6,022	6,650	7,667	8,905

Structure of imports and exports in 1980: Producers' goods, 86%, 73%; consumer goods, 14%, 27%; industrial products, 98%, 76%; agricultural products, 2%, 24%.

Main exports are food products, tobacco, non-ferrous metals, cast iron, leather articles, textiles and (to Communist countries) machinery; main imports are machinery, oil, natural gas, steel, cellulose and timber.

75% of Bulgaria's trade is with the Communist countries (54% with USSR). Agreements with USSR envisage the co-ordination of the Soviet and Bulgarian 5-year plans in the spirit of 'socialist internationalism'. In 1979 a 10-year plan of economic specialization and co-operation was signed with the USSR. Greece is Bulgaria's biggest non-Communist export market, Federal Republic of Germany her major non-Communist supplier.

Indebtedness to the West was some US$2,300m. in 1982.

Total trade between Bulgaria and UK (British Department of Trade returns, in £1,000 sterling):

	1978	*1979*	*1980*	*1981*	*1982*
Imports to UK	15,096	12,082	14,425	13,353	21,009
Exports and re-exports from UK	26,636	27,324	35,242	33,838	46,104

Joint Western-Bulgarian industrial ventures are permitted under laws of June 1974 and March 1980. In 1979 there were 40 in operation. Western share participation may exceed 50%.

On 13 May 1974 Bulgaria and the UK signed a 10-year economic, scientific and technological co-operation agreement.

COMMUNICATIONS

Roads. In 1980 there were 32,417 km of roads, including 108 km of motorways and 2,352 km of main roads. 816m. tonnes of freight and 1,950m. passengers were carried.

Railways. In 1982 Bulgaria had 4,045 km of standard gauge railway, including 1,650 km electrified. 100m. passengers and 77·8m. tons of freight were carried in 1980.

Aviation. BALKAN (Bulgarian Airlines) operates internal flights from Sofia (airport: Vrazhdebna) to Burgas, Khaskovo, Pleven, Plovdiv, Ruse, Silistra, Stara Zagora, Tŭrgovishte, Veliko Tŭrnovo, Varna, Vidin and Yambol and international flights to Algiers, Amsterdam, Athens, Baghdad, Bratislava, Belgrade, Benghazi, Berlin, Brussels, Bucharest, Budapest, Cairo, Casablanca, Copenhagen, Damascus, Dresden, Frankfurt, Istanbul, London, Madrid, Moscow, Nicosia, Paris, Prague, Rome, Stockholm, Syktyvkar, Tunis, Vienna, Warsaw and Zurich. There are also flights from Burgas to Leningrad and Kiev, and from Varna to Leningrad, Kuwait, Athens and Stockholm. In 1972 BALKAN had 234 planes and in 1980 it carried 2·2m. passengers and 24,585 tonnes of freight. British Airways opened a service from London to Sofia in 1970.

Shipping. Ports, shipping and shipbuilding are controlled by the Bulgarian United Shipping and Shipbuilding Corporation. The mercantile marine in 1982 possessed 194 ocean-going vessels and tankers with a total loading capacity of 1·6m. DWT. Burgas is a fishing and oil-port open to tankers of 20,000 tons. Varna is the other important port. In Nov. 1978 a rail ferry, with an initial capacity of 4·5m. tonnes of freight a year, was opened between Varna and Ilitchovsk (USSR). In 1980, 699,000 passengers and 24·7m. tonnes of cargo were carried.

Post and Broadcasting. In 1980 there were 2,857 post offices, 1,255,792 telephones, 56 broadcasting stations and 24 television stations. Radio Sofia, the government broadcasting station, transmits 2 programmes on medium- and short-waves. There is also a special tourist service, broadcast *via* the Varna II transmitter on 1,124 kHz. Advertisements are broadcast for half an hour a day. Bulgaria participates in the East European TV link 'Intervision'. Colour programmes by SECAM system. Radio receiving sets licensed in 1980, 2,148,811; television, 1,651,906.

Cinemas and Theatres (1980). There were 37 theatres, 12 puppet theatres, 8 opera houses, 1 operetta house and 3,453 cinemas. 513 films were made (31 full-length).

Newspapers and Books. In 1980 there were 14 dailies with a circulation of 2·2m. The Party newspaper is *Rabotnicheskoto Delo* ('The Workers' Cause') with a circulation of 800,000 in 1982. 4,681 book titles were published in 1980.

JUSTICE, RELIGION, EDUCATION AND WELFARE

Justice. A law of Nov. 1982 provides for the election (and recall) of all judges by the National Assembly. The lower courts include lay assessors as well as professional judges. There are a Supreme Court, 28 provincial courts (including Sofia), 105 regional courts and 'Comrades' Courts' for minor offences.

New Family and Penal Codes were approved by the National Assembly in April 1968. The maximum term of imprisonment is now 20 years except for 'exceptionally dangerous crimes' which carry the death penalty.

The Prosecutor General, elected by the National Assembly for 5 years and subordinate to it alone, exercises supreme control over the correct observance of the law by all government bodies, officials and citizens. He appoints and discharges all Prosecutors of every grade. The powers of this office were extended and redefined by a law of 1980 to put a greater emphasis on crime prevention and the rights of citizens.

Religion. 'The traditional church of the Bulgarian people' (as it is officially described), is that of the Eastern Orthodox Church. It was disestablished under the 1947 Constitution. On 10 May 1953 the Bulgarian Patriarchate was revived and Metropolitan Kiril was elected the first Bulgarian Patriarch since 1393. Upon the death of Kiril Metropolitan Maksim of Lovech was enthroned as the new Patriarch in July 1971. The seat of the Patriarch is at Sofia. There are 11 dioceses, each under a Metropolitan, 10 bishops, 2,600 parishes and 1,500 priests. In 1976 there were 3,720 churches, 500 chapels and some 20 monasteries and nunneries.

The Constitution provides for freedom of conscience and belief but forbids propaganda against the Government. The State provides 17% of Church funds.

Churches may not maintain schools or colleges, except theological seminaries, or organize youth movements.

In 1976 there were some 50,000 Roman Catholics in 3 bishoprics with 40 priests and 30 churches, and 16,000 Protestants with 101 churches and 265 priests. There were 80,000 Moslems under a Grand Mufti and 6 regional mufti boards with 1,180 mosques.

Education. Education is free, and compulsory for children between the ages of 7 and 16. The gradual introduction of unified secondary polytechnical schools offering compulsory education for all children from the ages of 7 to 17 was begun in 1973–74. Complete literacy is claimed. Schools are classified according to which years of schooling they offer: Elementary (1–4), primary (1–7), preparatory (5–8), secondary (9–11), complete secondary (1–11).

Educational statistics for 1980–81: 6,185 kindergartens (420,804 children, 28,996 teachers); 800 elementary schools; 2,386 primary schools; 69 preparatory schools; 112 secondary schools; 210 complete secondary schools. Numbers of teachers and pupils: School years 1 to 4, 17,200 and 392,374; 5 to 8, 34,448 and 602,836; 9 to 11, 7,419 and 97,089. There were also 3 vocational-technical schools (63 teachers, 1,514 students), 234 technical colleges (9,415 teachers, 97,575 students), 24 post-secondary institutions (1,790 teachers, 14,024 students) and 28 institutes of higher education (12,622 teachers, 85,330 students). There are 3 universities: the Kliment Ohrid University in Sofia (founded 1888) had 1,195 teachers and 12,616 students (in 1977–78); the Kirill i Metodii University in Veliko Tŭrnovo (founded 1971) had 240 teachers and 5,046 students and the Paisi Hilendarski University in Plovdiv (founded 1972) had 265 teachers and 3,921 students.

The Academy of Sciences was founded in 1869.

Social Welfare. Retirement and disablement pensions and temporary sick pay are calculated as a percentage of previous wages (respectively 55–80%, 35–100%, 69–90%) and according to the nature of the employment.

Monthly family allowances for children under 16: 15 leva for 1 child, 25 leva for 2 children and 45 leva for 3 children.

In 1979, 1·99m. persons received pensions totalling 1,393m. leva.

All medical services are free. In 1979 there were 185 hospitals (including 16 mental hospitals and addiction treatment centres) with 73,033 beds. There were 21,249 doctors and 4,641 dentists.

DIPLOMATIC REPRESENTATIVES

Of Bulgaria in Great Britain (186 Queen's Gate, London, SW7 5HL)
Ambassador: Kiril Shterev (accredited 26 Nov. 1980).

Of Great Britain in Bulgaria (Blvd. Marshal Tolbukhin 65–67, Sofia)
Ambassador: G. L. Bullard, CMG.

Of Bulgaria in the USA (1621–22nd St., NW, Washington, D.C., 20008)
Ambassador: Stoyan I. Zhulev.

Of the USA in Bulgaria (1 Stamboliiski Blvd., Sofia)
Ambassador: Robert L. Barry.

Of Bulgaria to the United Nations
Ambassador: Boris Tsvetkov.

Books of Reference

Kratka Bŭlgarska Entsiklopediia (Short Bulgarian Encyclopaedia), 5 vols. Sofia, 1963–69
Statisticheski Godishnik (Statistical Yearbook). Sofia from 1956
Constitution of the People's Republic of Bulgaria. Sofia, 1971
Modern Bulgaria: History, Politics, Economy, Culture. Sofia, 1981
Atanasova, T., *et al.*, *Bulgarian-English Dictionary.* Sofia, 1975
Brown, J. F., *Bulgaria under Communist Rule.* London, 1970
Dobrin, B., *Bulgarian Economic Development Since World War II.* New York, 1973
Feiwel, G. R., *Growth and Reforms in Centrally Planned Economies: the Lessons of the Bulgarian Experience.* New York, 1977
Markov, M., *System of Social Administration in Bulgaria.* Sofia, 1969
Oren, N., *Communism Administered: Agrarianism and Communism in Bulgaria.* Baltimore, 1973
Pundeff, M. V., *Bulgaria: A Bibliographic Guide.* Library of Congress, 1965
Spasov, B., *La Bulgarie.* Paris, 1973
Todorov, N., and others, *Bulgaria: Historic and Geographical Outline.* Sofia, 1965
Zhivkov, T., *Modern Bulgaria: Problems and Tasks in Building an Advanced Socialist Society,* New York, 1974

BURMA

Capital: Rangoon
Population: 33m. (1979)
GNP per capita: US$180 (1980)

Pyidaungsu Socialist Thammada Myanma Naingngandaw

HISTORY. The Union of Burma came formally into existence on 4 Jan. 1948 and became the Socialist Republic of the Union of Burma in 1974. In 1948 Sir Hubert Rance, the last British Governor, handed over authority to Sao Shwe Thaike, the first President of the Burmese Republic, and Parliament ratified the treaty with Great Britain providing for the independence of Burma as a country not within His Britannic Majesty's dominions and not entitled to His Britannic Majesty's protection. This treaty was signed in London on 17 Oct. 1947 and enacted by the British Parliament on 10 Dec. 1947.

For the history of Burma's connexion with Great Britain *see* THE STATESMAN'S YEAR-BOOK, 1950, p. 836.

AREA AND POPULATION. Burma is bounded east by China, Laos and Thailand, west by the Indian ocean, Bangladesh and India. The total area of the Union is 261,789 sq. miles (678,000 sq. km). Some small rectifications of the border with China were agreed upon in 1960 and with Pakistan in 1964. The population in 1973 (census) was 28,172,936. Estimate (1979) 33m. Birth rate (1977 estimate), 29·1; death rate, 10·4 per 1,000 population; infant deaths, 56·3 per 1,000 live births. The leading towns are: Rangoon, the capital (1973), 3,662,312; Mandalay, 417,266; Bassein, 355,588; Henzada, 283,658; Pegu, 254,761, Myingyan, 220,129; Moulmein, 202,967; Prome, 148,123; Akyab, 143,215; Tavoy, 101,536.

	Area in sq. km	*Population 1973 census*	*Chief town*
Kachin State	87,808	687,218	Myitkyina
Sagaing Division	99,150	3,119,054	Sagaing
Mandalay Division	34,253	3,668,493	Mandalay
Shan State	158,222	2,640,170	Taunggyi
Magwe Division	44,799	2,634,757	Magwe
Chin State	36,009	318,112	Haka
Arakan State	36,762	1,710,506	Akyab
Irrawaddy Division	35,167	4,156,673	Bassein
Pegu Division	49,787	3,177,464	Pegu
Rangoon Division	518	3,188,783	Rangoon
Kayah State	11,670	107,342	Loikaw
Karen State	28,726	660,244	Panan
Tenasserim Division	43,328	716,440	Tavoy
Mon State	11,831	1,387,680	Moulmein
	678,030	28,172,936	

The Burmese belong to the Tibeto-Chinese (or Tibeto-Burman) family.

CONSTITUTION. A new Constitution was approved by referendum in Dec. 1973. On 2 March 1974 military rule ended and Burma became a one-party socialist republic. Elections to the People's Assembly took place in Jan. and Feb. 1974. U Ne Win became President under the new Constitution and in Jan. 1978 his term of office was extended for 4 years. For earlier Constitutions *see* THE STATEMAN'S YEAR-BOOK, 1981–82, p. 252.

In Nov. 1981, U San Yu was elected Head of State by the People's Assembly.

The State Council has 27 members with U San Yu as Chairman and U Aye Ko as secretary.

In Nov. 1981 the Council of Ministers consisted of:

Prime Minister: U Maung Maung Kha.

Deputy Prime Minister, Planning and Finance: U Tun Tin. *Deputy Prime Minister, Defence:* Gen. Thura Kyaw Htin. *Agriculture and Forests:* U Ye Goung. *Co-operatives:* U Sein Tun. *Transport and Communications:* Thura U Saw Pru. *Foreign Affairs:* U Chit Hlaing. *Industry:* U Tint Swe, U Maung Cho. *Construction:* U Hla Tun. *Mines:* U Than Tin. *Trade:* U Khin Maung Ghi. *Education:* U Kyaw Nyein. *Information and Culture:* U Aung Kyaw Myint. *Home and Religious Affairs:* Col. Bo Ni. *Labour and Social Welfare:* U Ohn Kyaw. *Health:* U Tun Wai.

National flag: Red with a blue canton bearing 2 ears of rice within a cog-wheel and a ring of 14 stars, all in white.

Language: The official language is Burmese; the use of English is permitted.

Local government: Burma is divided into 7 states and 7 administrative divisions; these are sub-divided into townships and thence into villages and wards. At each level is a directly-elected People's Council which appoints an executive committee to administer its decisions.

DEFENCE

Army. The strength of the Army (1983) was 163,000. The Army is organized into 9 regional commands comprising approximately 110 independent infantry battalions. Three operational divisions are directly under the Ministry of Defence and contain 30 infantry battalions. In addition there are 2 armoured and 3 artillery battalions.

Navy. The Navy includes 1 very old escort minesweeper (*ex*-British), 2 old escort patrol vessels (*ex*-USA PCE and MSF types), 2 small indigenously built corvettes, 3 support gunboats (*ex*-landing craft), 13 coastal gunboats, 20 river gunboats, 40 small river patrol craft, 1 support ship, 2 survey vessels, 10 fishery protection cutters and 9 landing craft. Personnel in 1983: 10,000 including 800 marines.

Air Force. The Air Force is intended primarily for internal security duties. Its combat force comprises about 6 T-33A jet fighter/trainers supplied under MAP, supplemented by 9 SIAI-Marchetti SF.260W light piston-engined attack/trainers. Other training aircraft include 10 piston-engined SF.260Ms, 16 turboprop Pilatus PC-7s and 10 jet-powered T-37Cs. Transport and second-line units are equipped with small numbers of FH-227, Turbo-Porter and Cessna 180 aircraft, and Japanese-built Bell 47 (H-13) and Vertol KV-107-II, Bell UH-1, and Alouette III helicopters. Personnel about 9,000.

INTERNATIONAL RELATIONS

Membership. Burma is a member of the UN and Colombo Plan.

ECONOMY

Planning. The economy has been controlled since 1972 through a series of 4-year plans. The third plan began in 1978–79 and aims to increase average *per capita* output by 6·6%, and net output value by 5·9%, distributed as follows: Construction, 23·2%; financial institutions, 21·4%; power, 16·8%; mining, 13·4%; processing and manufacturing, 13·4%; transport, 8·6%; communications, 8·5%; agriculture, 5%; livestock and fish, 4·7%; forestry, 4·1%; trade, 3%; social development and administration, 2·3%.

Budget. The budget estimates (in K.1m.) for fiscal year 1 April 1980–31 March 1981 was revenue K.24,968m. and expenditure K.27,104m.

The largest items, in 1980–81, of revenue were commodities and service tax (K.2,360·1m.) and customs (K.590m.); of expenditure, processing and manufacturing (K.8,769m.); trade (K.5,222·3m.); transport and communication (1,736·2m.).

The internal public debt was K.3,084m. at the end of March 1979.

Currency. The currency unit is now the *kyat* divided into 100 *pyas*. There are notes of *kyat* 25, 20, 10, 5 and 1, and coins of *kyat* 1; *pyas* 50, 25, 10, 5 and 1.

Currency in circulation at 31 March 1980 was valued at K.7,172m.

Banking. The Union of Burma Bank is being reconstituted into 4 banks and an insurance corporation with effect from 1 April under the 1975 Bank Law and the 1975 Insurance Law.

The banks being formed in reconstitution are the Union of Burma Bank, the Myanma Economic Bank, the Myanma Foreign Trade Bank and the Myanma Agricultural Bank and the corporation is the Myanma Insurance Corporation. Work now being carried out by the Union of Burma Bank will be continued by the 4 banks and the Corporation.

ENERGY AND NATURAL RESOURCES

Electricity. In 1979 the total installed capacity of power plants was 642,230 kw., of which 168,500 was hydro-electricity and 158,850 gas turbine; there were 264 towns and 709 villages with electricity.

Oil. Production (1980–81, provisional) of crude oil was 11·18m. bbls; natural gas (1979–80), 12,846m. cu. ft.

Minerals. Production in 1977–78 (provisional): Silver, 410,000 oz.; zinc, 6,000 tons; copper matte, 90 tons; refined lead, 5,198 tons; nickel speiss, 75 tons; antimony, 1,455 tons; tin, 866 tons; tungsten, 568 tons; tin tungsten-scheelite, 500 tons; coal, 27,000 tons; gypsum, 28,000 tons; limestone, 1m. tons.

Agriculture. The area sown in 1979–80 (provisional) was 23·8m. acres; matured acreage, 22·1m. acres.

Acreage (1,000) and production (1,000 tons) of principal crops:

	1979–1980			*1979–1980*	
	Acreage	*Production*		*Acreage*	*Production*
Paddy	12,395	10,493	Cotton	481	54
Maize	250	100	Groundnuts	1,494	486
Pulses	1,868	422	Tobacco	139	100
Sesamum	2,652	134	Jute	261	92
Sugar-cane	243	1,449	Wheat	206	73

Livestock (1981): Cattle, 8·6m.; buffaloes, 1·9m.

In 1979–80 the area irrigated by government-controlled irrigation works was 2,417,769 acres.

Forestry. The area of reserved forests in 1977–78 was 23,477,000 acres; other forests, 55,986,000 acres. Teak extracted in 1979–80 (provisional), 400,250 cu. tons; hardwood, 1,049,000 cu. tons. All the teak and about 50% of the hardwood is from the state sector. Other forest produce (1977–78) included 13m. tons of firewood and 680,000 bamboo canes. 2,780 elephants are at work on extraction.

Fisheries. In 1979 sea fishing produced 413,000 tonnes and freshwater fisheries 153,000 tonnes. The contribution of state-owned fishing vessels (32 trawlers and 43 other craft) is about 3%.

INDUSTRY AND TRADE

Industry. The main manufacturing groups (with value (1978) of production in K. lakhs): Food and beverages, 97,157; clothing, 15,066; minerals, 11,196; industrial raw materials, 7,712; construction materials, 6,583; transport vehicles, 3,303; electrical goods, 1,528; agricultural equipment, 1,423. Production (1,000 tons): Cement, 365; salt, 198; fertilizer, 131·8; sugar, 36; cotton yarn, 13·5; shirting and poplin, 17·2m. yd; bricks and tiles, 154m. units; diesel oil, 75·7m. gallons; motor spirit, 61·2m. gallons; kerosene, 51·7m. gallons; radios, 22,000 units; cars, 1,884 units; bicycles, 19,000 units; tractors, 1,300 units; cigarettes, 2,440m. units.

Labour. In 1977–78 (provisional, 1,000) the workforce numbered 12,640: Agriculture, 8,212 (state sector 73); trade, 1,206 (45); processing and manufacturing, 929

(160); administration, 483 (459); transport and communication, 420 (104); social services, 246 (174); construction, 184 (124); livestock and fisheries, 167 (8); forestry, 152 (73); mining, 67 (65); power, 15 (15).

Trade Unions. Labour disputes are dealt with by the government labour sub-committees.

Commerce. All foreign trade is handled by the government trading organizations.

Imports and exports (in K. 1m.) for the calendar years.

	1978	*1979*	*1980*
Imports	3,638·5	4,189·9	3,965·2
Exports	1,608·4	2,548·8	3,122·6

Total trade between Burma and UK (British Department of Trade returns, in £1,000 sterling):

	1977	*1978*	*1979*	*1980*	*1981*	*1982*
Imports to UK	3,652	5,773	6,000	5,379	3,613	5,342
Exports and re-exports from UK	12,314	26,439	18,641	20,494	28,036	44,242

Tourism. There were 23,845 tourists in 1980.

COMMUNICATIONS

Roads. There were 13,948 miles of road in 1977–78, of which 2,452 miles were union highway.

Railways. The Burma Railways were nationalized in 1948 and the present Burma Railways Corporation took over in 1972. In 1980 there were 3,137 km of route on metre gauge. In 1977–78 the railway carried 2·29m. tons of freight and 64·2m. passengers.

Aviation. Union of Burma Airways started its internal service in Sept. 1948 and its external service in Nov. 1950. International services were in 1963 maintained between Rangoon and Bangkok and Calcutta. The routes were extended to Hong Kong in 1969 and to Dacca and Káthmándu in 1970. There were, in 1971, 43 civil aerodromes and landing grounds. In 1977-78 internal flights carried 609,000 passengers and 6,400 tons of freight; external flights, 42,000 passengers and 2,100 tons of freight.

Shipping. Burma has 60 miles of navigable canals. The Irrawaddy is navigable up to Myitkyina, 900 miles from the sea, and its tributary, the Chindwin, is navigable for 390 miles. The Irrawaddy delta has nearly 2,000 miles of navigable water. The Salween, the Attaran and the G'yne provide about 250 miles of navigable waters around Moulmein. The Inland Water Transport Board runs services from Bhamo to Myitkyina. The Burma Five Star Line Ltd operates coastal steamer services to the major ports in Burma, India, Bangladesh, Malaya, Japan, Europe and UK.

The port of Rangoon in 1974–75 handled 1·19m. tons of seaborne trade.

Post and Broadcasting. There were 1,101 post offices in 1977. Number of telephones was 32,616 in 1978, of which 22,456 are in Rangoon.

Cinemas. In 1971 there were about 418 cinemas.

Newspapers. In 1978 there were 7 daily newspapers.

JUSTICE, RELIGION, EDUCATION AND WELFARE

Justice. Since March 1974 the highest judicial authority has been the Council of People's Justices, appointed by the People's Assembly from its own members, which serves as the Supreme Court and Central Criminal Court. At lower levels courts are appointed by the local People's Councils from among their own membership.

Religion. The Revolutionary Government, having repealed the amendment of 1961 which made Buddhism the state religion, recognizes 'the right of everyone freely to profess and practise his religion'.

Education. The medium of instruction in all schools is Burmese; English is taught as a compulsory second language from kindergarten level.

Education is free in the primary, junior secondary and vocational schools; fees are charged in senior secondary schools and universities.

In 1977–78 there were 586 state high schools with 189,146 pupils, 1,262 state middle schools with 825,195 pupils and 21,999 state primary schools with 3,841,687 pupils; the total teaching staff was 111,339, of which 80,343 were in primary schools.

The Higher Education Law 1964 has decentralized the University of Rangoon. Beside the Arts and Science University, there are independent degree-giving institutes of engineering, education, medicine, agriculture, economics and commerce, and veterinary sciences. The University of Mandalay has been similarly decentralized. A foreign-languages institute in Rangoon has about 800 students learning English, French, German, Russian, Japanese, Chinese and Italian.

There are intermediate colleges at Taunggyi, Magwe, Akyab and Myitkyina, and degree colleges at Moulmein and Bassein, and several technical and agricultural institutes at higher and middle level. 4,656 school teachers were being trained in 15 training colleges in 1977–78. Technical high schools had 2,488 students; agricultural schools, 1,077; other vocational colleges, 1,438, and university colleges, 63,292.

A correspondence course for universities and colleges was introduced in 1976.

Health. In 1977 there were 5,787 doctors and 512 hospitals with 22,755 beds. There were 1,459 health centres.

DIPLOMATIC REPRESENTATIVES

Of Burma in Great Britain (19A Charles St., London, W1X 8ER)
Ambassador: U Myo Aung (accredited 16 Dec. 1981).

Of Great Britain in Burma (80 Strand Rd., Rangoon)
Ambassador: N. M. Fenn, CMG.

Of Burma in the USA (2300 S St., NW, Washington, D.C., 20008)
Ambassador: U Kyee Myint.

Of the USA in Burma (581 Merchant St., Rangoon)
Ambassador: Patricia M. Byrne.

Of Burma to the United Nations
Ambassador: Saw Hlaing.

Books of Reference

Burma: Treaty between the Government of the United Kingdom and the Provisional Government of Burma. (Treaty Series No. 16, 1948.) HMSO, 1948
Cornyn, W. S., and Musgrave, J. K., *Burmese Glossary.* New York, 1958
Lehman, F. K., *The Structure of Chin Society.* Univ. of Illinois Press, 1963
Silverstein, J., *Burma: Military Rule and the Politics of Stagnation.* Cornell Univ. Press, 1978.
—*Burmese Politics: The Dilemma of National Unity.* Rutgers Univ. Press, 1980
Smith, D. E., *Religion and Politics in Burma.* Princeton Univ. Press, 1965
Steinberg, D. I., *Burma.* Boulder, 1982
Stewart, J. A., and Dunn, C. W., *Burmese–English Dictionary.* London, 1940 ff.

BURUNDI

Capital: Bujumbura
Population: 4·38m. (1979)
GNP per capita: US$200 (1980)

HISTORY. Tradition recounts the establishment of a Tutsi kingdom under successive Mwamis as early as the 16th century. German military occupation in 1890 incorporated the territory into German East Africa. From 1919 Burundi formed part of Ruanda-Urundi administered by the Belgians, first as a League of Nations mandate and then as a United Nations trust territory. Elections supervised by the United Nations in Sept. 1961 resulted in a large majority for the Unité et Progrès National party (UPRONA). Internal self-government was granted on 1 Jan. 1962, followed by independence on 1 July 1962. An agreement, signed with Rwanda under United Nations auspices at Addis Ababa in April 1962, provided for a monetary and customs union. This union and all organizations operated jointly by the two governments were dissolved by 30 Sept. 1964.

On 8 July 1966 Prince Charles Ndizeye deposed his father Mwami Mwambutsa IV, suspended the constitution and made Capt. Michel Micombero Prime Minister. On 1 Sept. Prince Charles was enthroned as Mwami Ntare V. On 28 Nov., while the Mwami was attending a Head of States Conference in Kinshasa (Congo), Micombero declared Burundi a republic with himself as president.

On 31 March 1972 Prince Charles returned to Burundi from Uganda and was placed under house arrest. On 29 April 1972 President Micombero dissolved the Council of Ministers and took full power; that night heavy fighting broke out between rebels from both Burundi and neighbouring countries, and the ruling Tutsi, apparently with the intention of destroying the Tutsi hegemony. Prince Charles was killed during the fighting and it was estimated that up to 120,000 were killed. On 14 July 1972 President Micombero reinstated a Government with a Prime Minister. On 1 Nov. 1976 President Micombero was deposed by the Army. A Supreme Revolutionary Council of the Armed Forces was established which appointed Col. Jean-Baptiste Bagaza president.

AREA AND POPULATION. Burundi extends from lat. 2½° to 4½° S. and long. 29° to 31° E., and has an area of 27,834 sq. km (10,759 sq. miles). It lies astride the main Nile–Congo dividing crest (6,000–7,000 ft) bounded on the west by the narrow plain of the Ruzizi River and Lake Tanganyika (2,534 ft). The interior is a broken plateau at an average height of about 5,000 ft, sloping eastwards down to Tanzania and the valley of the Maragarazi River. The southernmost tributary of the Nile system, the Luvironza, rises in the south of the country.

The population at the last census in 1959 was 2,213,280; but was 4·38m. in 1979. There are three ethnic groups—Hutu (Bantu, forming the great majority): Tutsi (Nilotic, less than 15%); Twa (pygmoids, less than 1%). There are some 3,500 Europeans and 1,500 Asians. In 1974 some 49,000 Tutsi refugees from Rwanda were living in Burundi.

Bujumbura, the capital, had (1976 estimate) 157,100 inhabitants. Kitega (10,000 inhabitants) was formerly the royal residence.

CONSTITUTION AND GOVERNMENT. A new Constitution was promulgated on 21 Nov. 1981 and provides for a one-party state. The first national Congress of National Progress and Unity Party (UPRONA) was held in Dec. 1979 when a Party Central Committee was elected to take over the functions of the Supreme Revolutionary Council in Jan. 1980, with President Bagaza as Party Chairman and Head of the Central Committee for a 5-year term.

President of the Republic: Col. Jean-Baptiste Bagaza.
Foreign Affairs: Edouard Nzambimana.

The administrative divisions are: 8 provinces, each under a military governor

(Bujumbura, Bubanza, Muramvya, Ngozi, Gitega, Muhinga, Ruyigi and Bururi); 18 arrondissements; and 78 communes.

Flag: White diagonal cross dividing triangles of red and green, in the centre a white disc bearing 3 red green-bordered 6-pointed stars.

DEFENCE. The national armed forces total (1981), 6,000 (there are also about 1,500 in paramilitary units) and include a small naval flotilla and air force flight of 3 SF 260, 2 Cessna 150 and 2 Do 27 liaison aircraft and 4 Alouette III helicopters. On order are 4 SF. 260 TP turboprop trainers. The army comprises 2 infantry battalions with supporting units.

INTERNATIONAL RELATIONS

Membership. Burundi is a member of UN and OAU and is an ACP state of EEC.

ECONOMY

Budget. The 1980 budget envisaged receipts of 14,600m. Burundi francs.

Currency. The currency is administered by the Bank of the Republic of Burundi. The rate was 139·12 *Burundi francs* = £1 and 90 *Burundi francs* = US$1 in March 1983.

Weights and Measures. The metric system operates.

ENERGY AND NATURAL RESOURCES

Electricity. Electricity generation capacity was 6 mw in 1976.

Minerals. Mineral ores such as bastnasite and cassenite were formerly mined but output is now insignificant. Deposits of nickel (280m. tonnes) remain to be exploited.

Agriculture. The main economic activity and the main source of employment of the country is subsistence agriculture, which accounts for well over half of the gross national product. Beans, kassava, maize, sweet potatoes, groundnuts, peas, sorghum and bananas are grown according to the climate and the region.

The main cash crop is coffee, of which about 95% is arabica. It accounts for 90% of exports and taxes and levies on coffee constitute a major source of revenue. A coffee board (OCIBU) manages the grading and export of the crop. Production (1981) 41,000 tonnes. Cotton production is falling; 8,000 tonnes 1981. Plantations of good-quality tea are being developed. Production (1981) 1,540 tonnes.

Cattle play an important traditional role, and there were about 872,000 head in 1981. The quality is poor, but efforts are being made to improve it. There were (1981) some 1,018,000 goats and sheep and 37,000 pigs.

Fisheries. There is a small commercial fishing industry on Lake Tanganyika which produced 7,941 tonnes in 1973 and is undergoing further development.

INDUSTRY AND TRADE

Industry. Industrial development is rudimentary. In Bujumbura there are plants for the processing of coffee and by-products of cotton, a brewery, cement works, a textile factory, a soap factory, a shoe factory and small metal workshops.

Commerce. The total value of exports 1981 was 6,260m. Burundi francs, and of imports, 14,559m. Burundi francs. Main exports in 1981 were coffee, (5,352m. Burundi francs); cotton, (188m.); tea, (181m.). Main imports, petrol products, food, vehicles and textiles.

Total trade between Burundi and the UK (British Department of Trade returns, in £1,000 sterling):

	1977	*1978*	*1979*	*1980*	*1981*	*1982*
Imports to UK	1,817	812	710	1,881	6,329	8,737
Exports and re-exports from UK	1,645	1,710	1,158	583	1,479	1,522

Tourism. Tourism is developing and there were 13,000 visitors Jan.–June 1976.

COMMUNICATIONS

Roads. There is a road network of 6,400 km connecting with Rwanda, Congo and Tanzania but in 1982 only 310 km were macadamized.

Aviation. Bujumbura has an airport of international standard and there are regular services to Europe, Zaïre and East Africa.

Shipping. There are lake services from Bujumbura to Kigoma (Tanzania). The main route for exports and imports is *via* Kigoma, and thence by rail to Dar es Salaam.

Post and Broadcasting. Number of telephones (1978), 4,995.

JUSTICE, RELIGION, EDUCATION AND WELFARE

Justice. There is a Supreme Court, an appeal court and a *tribunal de première instance* at Bujumbura.

Religion. Over half the population is Roman Catholic; there is a Roman Catholic archbishop and 3 bishops. The Anglican Missions under a bishop fall within the archdiocese of Uganda.

Education. In 1981 the number of children in primary school was 180,290 and 18,000 pupils were receiving secondary education. The university of Bujumbura had (1981) about 1,000 students.

The local language is Kirundi, a Bantu language. French is also an official language. Kiswahili is spoken in the commercial centres.

Health. In 1979 there were about 130 doctors and 21 hospitals.

DIPLOMATIC REPRESENTATIVES

Of Burundi in Great Britain
Ambassador: Cyprien Mbonimpa (resides in Brussels).

Of Great Britain in Burundi
Ambassador: J. M. O. Snodgrass, CMG (resides in Kinshasa).

Of Burundi in the USA (2233 Wisconsin Ave., NW, Washington, D.C., 20007)
Ambassador: Simon Sabimbona.

Of the USA in Burundi (Chaussée Prince Louis Rwagasore, Bujumbura)
Ambassador: Frances D. Cook.

Of Burundi to the United Nations
Ambassador: Melchoir Bwakira.

Books of Reference

Lemarchand, R., *Rwanda and Burundi.* London, 1970
Melady, T. P., *Burundi: The Tragic Years.* Maryknoll, New York, 1974
Mpozapara, G., *La République du Burundi.* Paris, 1971
Weinstein, W., *Historical Dictionary of Burundi.* Metuchen, 1976

CAMBODIA

Democratic Kampuchea

Capital: Phnom Penh
Population: 5·76m. (1981)
GNP per capita: No accurate estimate available (1981)

Since April 1975 the situation in Cambodia has been such that it has been impossible to obtain reliable statistical and other information.

HISTORY. The recorded history of Cambodia starts at the beginning of the Christian era with the Kingdom of Fou-Nan, whose territories at one time included parts of Thailand, Malaya, Cochin-China and Laos. The religious, cultural and administrative inspirations of this state came from India. The Kingdom was absorbed at the end of the 6th century by the Khmers, under whose monarchs was built, between the 9th and 13th centuries, the splendid complex of shrines and temples at Angkor. Attacked on either side by the Vietnamese and the Thai from the 15th century on, Cambodia was saved from annihilation by the establishment of a French protectorate in 1863. Thailand eventually recognized the protectorate and renounced all claims to suzerainty in exchange for Cambodia's north-western provinces of Battambang and Siem Reap, which were, however, returned under a Franco-Thai convention of 1907, confirmed in the Franco-Thai treaty of 1937. In 1904 the province of Stung Treng, formerly administered as part of Laos, was attached to Cambodia. For history to 1969 *see* THE STATESMAN'S YEAR-BOOK, 1973–74, p. 1112.

Following a period of increasing economic difficulties and growing indirect involvement in the Vietnamese war Prince Sihanouk was deposed in March 1970 and on 9 Oct. 1970 the Kingdom of Cambodia became the Khmer Republic. From 1970 hostilities extended throughout most of the country involving North and South Vietnamese and US forces as well as Republican and anti-Republican Khmer troops. During 1973 direct American and North Vietnamese participation in the fighting came to an end, leaving a civil war situation which continued during 1974 with large-scale fighting between forces of the Khmer Republic supported by American arms and economic aid and the forces of the United National Cambodian Front including 'Khmer Rouge' communists supported by North Vietnam and China.

After unsuccessful attempts to capture Phnom Penh in 1973 and 1974, the Khmer Rouge ended the 5-year war in April 1975, when the remnants of the republican forces surrendered the city.

From April 1975 the Khmer Rouge instituted a harsh and highly regimented régime. They cut the country off from normal contact with the world and expelled all foreigners. All cities and towns were forcibly evacuated and the population were set to work in the fields.

The régime had difficulties with the Vietnamese from 1975 and this escalated into full-scale fighting in 1977–78. On 7 Jan. 1979, Phnom Penh was captured by the Vietnamese, and the Prime Minister, Pol Pot, fled. In March 1982 Pol Pot still commanded 30,000 guerrillas fighting the Vietnamese in Kampuchea.

In June 1982 the Khmer Rouge (who claim to have abandoned their Communist ideology and to have disbanded their Communist Party) entered into a coalition with Son Sann's Kampuchean People's National Liberation Front and Prince Sihanouk's group. This government is recognized by the UN.

President of the Coalition Government: Prince Norondom Sihanouk. *Deputy President:* Khieu Samphan. *Prime Minister:* Son Sann.

AREA AND POPULATION. Cambodia is bounded north by Laos and Thailand, in the west by Thailand, east by Vietnam and south by the Gulf of

Thailand. It has an area of about 181,000 sq. km (71,000 sq. miles), divided into 17 provinces: Kompong Thom (population, 322,000), Kompong Cham (820,000), Battambang (551,860), Kampot (337,879), Siem Reap (313,000), Kompong Chhang (273,000), Kompong Speu (307,000), Takeo (467,000), Kratié (136,000), Stung Treng (136,000), Svay Rieng (287,000), Prey Veng (492,000), Pursat (180,000), Kandal (population, excluding Phnom Penh, 706,000), Ratanakiri (49,400), Mondolkiri (14,300), Koh Kong (38,700).

The total population of 5,756,141 (1981) included Chinese and Chams. In the uplands and in the north-east live various groups of hillmen, known as Khmer-Loeu.

The chief towns are Phnom Penh, the capital located at the junction of the Mekong and Tonle Sap rivers, and Battambang. Populations of major towns have fluctuated greatly since 1970 by flows of refugees from rural areas and from one town to another. Phnom Penh formerly had a population of at least 2·5m. but a 1981 estimate puts it at 400,000. Khmer is the official language.

CONSTITUTION AND GOVERNMENT. Following the ousting of the Khmer Rouge régime, the Vietnamese-backed Kampuchean National United Front for National Salvation (KNUFNS) on 8 Jan. 1979 proclaimed a People's Republic and established a People's Revolutionary Council to administer the country. A 117-member National Assembly was elected on 1 May 1981 for a 5-year term; in June 1981 it ratified a new Constitution under which it appointed a 7-member Council of State and a 16-member Council of Ministers, replacing the Revolutionary Council.

President of the Council of State: Heng Samrin.
Prime Minister: Chan Si.

National flag: Red with a five-towered silhouette of the temple of Angkor Wat in the centre in yellow.

DEFENCE. Since the end of the war in April 1975 there has been no accurate data on defence and the three sections below should be treated with severe reserve.

Army. No accurate data was available in early 1983.

Navy. The Marine Royale Khmer was established on 1 March 1954 and became Marine Nationale Khmer on 9 Oct. 1970. It includes, 15 coastal patrol craft, 25 river patrol boats and 20 small craft, converted junks, etc. Less than a third of this force is operational and the residual navy has little fighting value. Two patrol vessels and 2 support (landing) gunboats escaped from Khmer Rouge, and 2 torpedo boats were believed to have sunk. Units since stricken include 7 amphibious vessels, 8 coastal patrol craft and 55 river patrol boats and service craft.

Naval active personnel in 1983 did not exceed 4,000. In addition there is a battalion of marines.

Air Force. In 1974 the Air Force had a strength of about 7,000 officers and men, including 120 pilots, with about 200 aircraft, none of them jets. Combat squadrons operated approximately 60 T-28 piston-engined light attack aircraft. The remaining equipment comprised C-123 and C-47 transports, UH-1H and Alouette helicopters, and U-1A, O-1A/D and AU-24A light aircraft. It is not known how many of these aircraft remain serviceable.

ECONOMY

Currency. Under the Paris agreements of 29 Dec. 1954, between the Associate States and France, the parity of the Cambodian *piastre* (henceforth to be known as a *riel*) was to be maintained for the time being at 10 francs=1 *riel.* In 1978 money was officially abolished and no wages or salaries were paid, but in 1980 the use of money was restored.

Banking. In 1964 all bank functions were taken over by government banks. In 1972 legislation permitted the re-opening of foreign banks but by the end of Dec. 1973 only a few representational offices had opened. In 1979 there was no longer anything that could be called a normal banking system.

NATURAL RESOURCES

Minerals. A phosphate factory, jointly controlled by the State and private interests, was set up in 1966 near a deposit of an estimated 350,000 tons. Another deposit of about the same size is earmarked for exploitation. High-grade iron-ore deposits (possibly as much as 2·5m. tons) exist in Northern Khmer, but are not exploited commercially because of transportation difficulties. Some small-scale gold panning (6,687 troy oz. in 1963) and gem (mainly zircon) mining is carried out at Pailin where there is potential for considerable expansion.

Agriculture. The overwhelming majority of the population is normally engaged in agriculture, fishing and forestry. Of the country's total area of 44m. acres, about 20m. are cultivable and over 20m. are forest land. In 1980, 1·5m. hectares were cultivated. Before the spread of war the high productivity provided for a low, but well-fed standard of living for the peasant farmers, the majority of whom owned the land they worked. A relatively small proportion of the food production entered the cash economy. The war and unwise pricing policies have led to a disastrous reduction in production to a stage in which the country had become a net importer of rice in 1972 and 1973 and continued to be so in 1974. Since April 1975 a vigorous agricultural programme has been implemented to meet food shortages.

A crop of about 635,000 tonnes of paddy were produced in 1974. Rubber production in 1968 amounted to 49,000 tonnes but less than 10,000 tonnes in 1972.

Other products are maize, and, in usual order of value, livestock, timber, pepper, haricot beans, soybeans and fish.

Livestock (1981) FAO estimate: Cattle, 986,000; buffaloes, 404,000; sheep, 1,000; pigs, 223,000; horses, 8,000; poultry, 6·6m.

Forestry. Much of Cambodia's surface is covered by potentially valuable forests, 3·8m. hectares of which are reserved by the Government to be awarded to concessionaires, and are not at present worked to an appreciable extent. The remainder is available for exploitation by the local residents, and as a result some areas are over-exploited and conservation is not practised. There are substantial reserves of pitch pine.

Fisheries. Cambodia has the greatest freshwater fish resources in South-East Asia but production in 1970 (30,000 tons) was about a third of that for 1966.

INDUSTRY AND TRADE

Industry. Some development of industry had taken place before the spread of open warfare in 1970. Industry established and in operation in Jan. 1970 included a motor-vehicle assembly plant, 3 cigarette manufacturing concerns, a modern factory, several metal fabricating concerns, a distillery, a saw-mill, textile, fish canning, plywood, paper, cement, sugar sack, tyre, pottery and glassware factories and a cotton-ginnery. In the private sector there are about 3,200 manufacturing enterprises, producing a wide range of goods; most of them are small family concerns. An oil refinery at Kompong Som came into production in 1969 but was put out of action by an attack in early 1971. Since April 1975 a programme for repairing factories has been started and some 70 are back in production.

Commerce. Principal imports by order of value (1972) were petroleum products, metals and machinery (including vehicles), general foodstuffs and chemicals.

The only recorded export in 1972 was 7,328 tonnes of rubber. Much of the country's trade is with Hong Kong and Singapore.

Total trade between Cambodia and UK (British Department of Trade returns, in £1,000 sterling):

	1977	*1978*	*1979*	*1980*	*1981*	*1982*
Imports to UK	86	120	83	73	91	92
Exports and re-exports from UK	92	52	401	825	645	479

COMMUNICATIONS

Roads. There were, in 1970, 2,574 km of asphalt roads (including the 'Khmer-American Friendship Highway' from outside Phnom Penh to close to Kompong Som, built under the US aid programme and opened in July 1959), 359 km of macadamized roads, and about 1,213 km of improved dirt roads. Since 1970 many road bridges have been destroyed and long stretches of highway closed to traffic or open only to escorted convoys.

Railways. A line of 385 km (metre gauge) links Phnom Penh to Poipet (Thai frontier). In 1969 traffic amounted to 170m. passenger-km and 76m. ton-km. Work was completed during 1969 on a line Phnom Penh-Kompong Som *via* Takeo and Kampot. Total length, 649 km but by 1973 only a short stretch between Battambang and the Thai border remained in operation, the remainder having been closed by military action. Passenger and freight trains were running over about 80% of the network in 1980.

Aviation. The Pochentong airport is 10 km from Phnom Penh.

Shipping. The port of Phnom Penh can be reached by the Mekong (through Vietnam) by ships of between 3,000 and 4,000 tons. In 1970, 97 ocean-going vessels imported 51,300 tons of cargo at Phnom Penh and exported 86,400 tons.

A new ocean port has been built under the French aid programme at Kompong Som (formerly Sihanoukville) on the Gulf of Siam and is being increasingly used by long-distance shipping.

Post. There were 58 post offices functioning in 1968 but in 1979 it was doubtful if any offices operate. There are telephone exchanges in all the main towns; number of telephones in 1968, 6,325. There is an International Telex network in Phnom Penh and direct telephone and telegraphic links with Singapore.

RELIGION. The majority of the population practised Theravada Buddhism before 1975. The Constitution of 1976 ended Buddhism as the State religion. There are small Roman Catholic and Moslem minorities.

EDUCATION (1970–71). There were 1,490 primary schools (337,290 pupils) compared with 5,699 and 989,464 in 1969-70, 95 secondary schools (81,611 pupils) and 12,453 students in higher education. These figures show the disruption caused by the spread of war in 1970 which led to the concentration of all university education in Phnom Penh and closed many schools in rural areas and provincial towns. In 1980 there were 1·3m. pupils in all types of school.

DIPLOMATIC REPRESENTATIVES

Of Cambodia in Great Britain (26 Townsend Rd., London, NW8 6LE)
Embassy closed.

Of Great Britain in Cambodia (96 Moha Vithei, Phnom Penh)
All staff temporarily withdrawn from post.

Of Cambodia in USA (4500-16th St., NW, Washington, DC., 20011)
Embassy closed.

Of the USA in Cambodia
Embassy closed on 12 April 1975.

Books of Reference

Annuaire Statistique Retrospectif du Cambodge. Vol. I, 1937–57; vol. II, 1958-60. Ministry of Planning, Phnom-Penh

Indo-China: Geographical Appreciation. Department of Mines and Technical Surveys. Ottawa, 1953

Barron, J., and Paul, A., *Murder of a Gentle Land.* New York, 1977.—*Peace with Horror.* London, 1977

Debré, F., *La Révolution de la Forêt.* Paris, 1976

Kirk, D., *Wider War.* London, 1971
Leifer, M., *Cambodia: The Search for Security.* London, 1967
McDonald, M., *Angkor.* London, 1958
Migozzi, J., *Cambodge.* Paris, 1973
Ponchaud, F., *Cambodia, Year Zero.* London, 1978
Shawcross, W., *The Sideshow: Nixon, Kissinger and the Destruction of Cambodia.* London, 1979

CAMEROON

Capital: Yaoundé
Population: 8·85m. (1982)
GNP per capita: US$670 (1980)

République Unie du Cameroun

HISTORY. The former German colony of Kamerun was occupied by French and British troops in 1916. The greater portion of the territory (422,673 sq. km) was in 1919 placed under French administration, excluding the territory ceded to Germany in 1911, which reverted to French Equatorial Africa. The portion under French trusteeship was granted full internal autonomy on 1 Jan. 1959 and complete independence was proclaimed on 1 Jan. 1960.

The portion assigned to British trusteeship consisted of 2 parts where separate plebiscites were held in Feb. 1961. The northern part decided in favour of joining Nigeria, while the southern part decided to join the Cameroon Republic. This was implemented on 1 Oct. 1961 with the formation of a Federal Republic of Cameroon.

As a result of a national referendum, the creation of a unitary, bilingual and pluricultural state, came into force on 2 June 1972.

AREA AND POPULATION. Cameroon is bounded west by the Gulf of Guinea, north-west by Nigeria and east by Chad, with Lake Chad at its northern tip, and the Central African Republic, and south by Congo, Gabon and Equatorial Guinea. The total area is 465,054 sq. km (179,558 sq. miles). Population (1976 census) 7,663,246 (28·5% urban). Estimate (1982) 8·85m.

The areas, census populations and chief towns of the 7 provinces were:

Province	*Area sq. km*	*Census 1976*	*Chief town*	*Census 1976*
Centre-Sud	116,036	1,491,945	Yaoundé (capital)	313,706
Est	109,011	366,235	Bertoua	18,450
Littoral	20,239	935,166	Douala	458,426
Nord	163,513	2,233,257	Garoua	69,285
Nord-Ouest	17,810	980,531	Bamenda	67,184
Ouest	13,872	1,035,597	Bafoussam	62,239
Sud-Ouest	24,471	620,515	Buea	13,000

Other large towns (1976 census): Nkongsamba (71,298), Maroua (67,187), Foumban (59,701), Kumba and Nimbe (formerly Victoria) (31,222).

The population is composed of Sudanic-speaking people in the north (Sao, Fulani and Kanuri) and Bantu-speaking groups in the rest of the country.

CONSTITUTION AND GOVERNMENT. The 1972 Constitution, amended 1975, provides for a President as chief of state and commander of the armed forces, who is elected for a 5-year term, and a cabinet whose members must not be members of parliament.

The National Assembly, elected by universal adult suffrage for 5 years, consists of 120 representatives. Elections took place on 28 May 1978. Since 1966 the sole legal party is the *Union National Camerounaise.*

The Economic and Social Council consists of 85 members appointed for 5 years by the President of the Republic to represent various social and economic interests; its chairman, appointed by decree, is assisted by a board appointed for 1 year.

President: Paul Biya (assumed office 4 Nov. 1982).

Prime Minister: Bello Bonba Maigari.

National flag: Three vertical strips of green, red, yellow, with a gold star in the centre.

National anthem: O Cameroun, berceau de nos ancêtres.

Local Government: The 7 provinces are each administered by a governor appointed by the President. They are sub-divided into 40 *départements* (each under a *préfet*) and then into 131 *arrondissements* (each under a *sous-préfet*).

The official languages are French and English.

DEFENCE

Army. The Army consists of infantry battalions and support units; total strength (1983), 6,600.

Navy. The Navy operates 2 fast attack craft, 1 patrol vessel, 2 small patrol craft, 6 coastal patrol launches and 24 auxiliaries. Personnel in 1983, 350.

Air Force. The Air Force has 3 C-130H Hercules turboprop transports, 2 HS.748 twin-turboprop freight transports, 4 Buffalo and 2 Caribou STOL transports, 4 C-47s and 2 Dornier Do 28s for transport and communications duties, 4 Broussard liaison aircraft, 4 Magister armed jet basic trainers, 6 Alpha Jet basic/advanced trainers, and 2 Alouette II helicopters. Some of 4 Gazelle light helicopters are armed with anti-tank missiles. A small VIP transport fleet, maintained in civil markings, comprises 1 Boeing 727 jet aircraft, 1 Alouette III helicopter and a twin-engined Puma helicopter. Radar-equipped Do 128-6 twin-turboprop aircraft were acquired in 1982 for offshore oilfield patrol. Personnel total about 350.

INTERNATIONAL RELATIONS

Membership. Cameroon is a member of UN, OAU and is an ACP state of EEC.

ECONOMY

Planning. The Fourth 5-year Development Plan, 1976–81 envisaged expenditure of 725,232m. francs CFA.

Budget. The budget for 1981-82 balanced at 310,000m. francs CFA.

Currency. The unit of currency is the *franc CFA*, with a parity rate of 50 *francs CFA* to 1 French *franc*.

Banking. The Banque des Etats de l'Afrique Centrale is the sole bank of issue. The main banks are Banque Internationale pour l'Afrique Occidentale, Société Camerounaise de Banque, Société Générale de Banques au Cameroun and Cameroon Bank. Most of the banks operate in all the large cities and towns throughout the United Republic.

ENERGY AND NATURAL RESOURCES

Electricity. There are 3 hydro-electric power stations at Edéa on the Sanaga river with a capacity of 180,000 kW, and another on the Wouri river near Douala. Total production (1980) 1,340m. kwh.

Oil. Production (1981) from Kole oilfield was over 4m. tonnes.

Minerals. There are considerable deposits of bauxite and kyanite around Ngaoundéré. Further deposits of bauxite and cassiterite remain to be exploited in the Adamawa plateau.

Agriculture. At the 1976 Census, 80% of the working population were engaged in agriculture. The main food crops (with 1979 production in 1,000 tonnes): Cassava, 864; millet, 390; maize, 480; plantains, 955; yams, 173; groundnuts, 285. Cash crops include sugar, 720; bananas, 110;cocoa, 115; coffee, 102 in 1980; rubber, 16; cotton, 26.

Livestock (1981): 3·3m. cattle, 2·2m. sheep, 2·4m. goats, 1·3m. pigs.

Fisheries. In 1979 the total catch was 69,400 tonnes.

Forestry. Over a third of Cameroon consists of forests, ranging from tropical rain forests in the south (producing hardwoods such as mahogany, ebony and sapele) to semi-deciduous forests in the centre and wooded savannah in the north. Production in 1979 amounted to 9.8m. cu. metres.

INDUSTRY AND TRADE

Industry. There is a major aluminium smelting complex at Edéa; aluminium production in 1979 amounted to 53,000 tonnes. Production of cement totalled 278,000 tonnes in 1977. There are also factories producing shoes, soap, oil and food products, cigarettes.

Commerce. Imports and exports in 1m. francs CFA were as follows:

	1976	*1977*	*1978*	*1979*	*1980*
Imports	145,963	192,391	237,247	271,160	337,602
Exports	127,283	179,319	196,064	243,699	290,614

In 1979, 25% (by value) of exports went to France, 21% to the Netherlands and 21% to the USA, while France provided 44% of imports; the main exports were coffee (25%), cocoa (24%), crude oil (23%) and timber (9%).

Total trade between Cameroon and UK (British Department of Trade returns, in £1,000 sterling):

	1978	*1979*	*1980*	*1981*	*1982*
Imports to UK	9,940	16,278	9,798	24,022	9,108
Exports and re-exports from UK	19,087	18,811	17,470	24,014	22,462

Tourism. There were an estimated 1,206,337 foreign visitors in 1979. There are 13 National Parks and reserves, with a total area of nearly 20,000 sq. km.

COMMUNICATIONS

Roads. There were (1977) 2,155 km of tarred roads, 9,284 km earth roads and 15,482 km of secondary roads. In 1976 there were 110,700 vehicles in use.

Railways. Cameroon Railways (1,168 km in 1983) link Douala with Nkongsamba and Ngaoundére, with branches M'Banga–Kumba and Makak–M'Balmayo.

Aviation. Douala is the main international airport; other airports are at Yaoundé and Garoua. In 1976, 342,000 passengers and 20,000 tonnes of freight passed through the airports.

Shipping. The merchant-marine consisted (1980) of 44 vessels (over 100 GRT) of 62,080 GRT. The major port of Douala handled (1975) 1·33m. tonnes of imports and 718,000 tonnes of exports. The second port is now Kribi (162,496 tonnes exports, of which timber amounted to 146,850 tonnes; and 10,006 tonnes imports), while another 50,000 tonnes of timber was exported through nearby Campo. The ports of Bota and Tiko (at Nimbe) handled 26,305 tonnes and Garoua on the river Benue 21,041 tonnes (comprising 6,022 tonnes fertilizer imports and 15,019 tonnes cotton exports).

Post and Broadcasting. There were (1975) 150 post offices supplemented by a mobile postal service; telephone lines, 2,677 km; main telephones (1978), 14,321; radio stations, 36 with (1980) 760,000 receivers.

Cinemas. There were (1977) 45 cinemas with a capacity of 25,000 seats.

Newspapers. There were (1975) 2 daily newspapers with a circulation of 25,000.

JUSTICE, RELIGION, EDUCATION AND WELFARE

Justice. The Supreme Court sits at Yaoundé, as does the High Court of Justice (consisting of 9 titular judges and 6 surrogates all appointed by the National Assembly). There are magistrates' courts situated in the provinces.

Religion. 21% of the population is Roman Catholic, 20% Moslem, 14% Protestant, while 45% follow traditional (animist) religions.

Education (1978–79). There were 1,254,056 pupils and 25,248 teachers in primary schools, 147,073 pupils and 5,112 teachers in secondary schools, 45,051 students and 1,804 teachers in vocational schools and 1,677 students and 168 teachers in teacher-training colleges. The University of Yaoundé (established 1962) had (1977–78) 10,001 students and other university centres have been opened at Douala, Buea, Dschang and Ngaoundére.

Health. In 1976 there were 85 hospitals with 16,734 beds, and 347 dispensaries and health centres. In 1977 there were 477 doctors, 19 dentists, 93 pharmacists, 1,805 midwives and 3,533 nursing personnel.

DIPLOMATIC REPRESENTATIVES

Of the United Republic of Cameroon in Great Britain (84 Holland Pk., London, W11 3SB)
Chargé d'Affaires: Jean-Hilaire Mbea Mbea.

Of Great Britain in the United Republic of Cameroon (Ave. Winston Churchill, BP 547, Yaoundé)
Ambassador: B. Sparrow.

Of the United Republic of Cameroon in the USA (2349 Massachusetts Ave., NW, Washington, D.C., 20008)
Ambassador: Vincent Paul-Thomas Pondi.

Of the USA in the United Republic of Cameroon (Rue Nachtigal, BP 817, Yaoundé)
Ambassador: Hume A. Horan.

Of the United Republic of Cameroon to the United Nations
Ambassador: Ferdinand Léopold Oyono.

Books of Reference

Statistical Information: The Service de la Statistique Générale, at Douala, set up in 1945, publishes a monthly bulletin (from Nov. 1950)

Debel, A., *Cameroon Today.* Paris, 1977
Le Vine, V. T., *The Cameroon Federal Republic.* Cornell Univ. Press, 1971
Ndongko, W. A., *Planning for Economic Development in a Federal State: The Case of Cameroon, 1960–71.* New York, 1975
Rubin, N., *Cameroon.* New York, 1972

CANADA

Capital: Ottawa
Population: 24·6m. (1982)
GNP per capita: US$10,130 (1980)

HISTORY. The territories which now constitute Canada came under British power at various times by settlement, conquest or cession. Nova Scotia was occupied in 1628 by settlement at Port Royal, was ceded back to France in 1632 and was finally ceded by France in 1713, by the Treaty of Utrecht; the Hudson's Bay Company's charter, conferring rights over all the territory draining into Hudson Bay, was granted in 1670; Canada, with all its dependencies, including New Brunswick and Prince Edward Island, was formally ceded to Great Britain by France in 1763; Vancouver Island was acknowledged to be British by the Oregon Boundary Treaty of 1846, and British Columbia was established as a separate colony in 1858. As originally constituted, Canada was composed of Upper and Lower Canada (now Ontario and Quebec), Nova Scotia and New Brunswick. They were united under an Act of the Imperial Parliament, 'The British North America Act, 1867', which came into operation on 1 July 1867 by royal proclamation. The Act provided that the constitution of Canada should be 'similar in principle to that of the United Kingdom'; that the executive authority shall be vested in the Sovereign, and carried on in his name by a Governor-General and Privy Council; and that the legislative power shall be exercised by a Parliament of two Houses, called the 'Senate' and the 'House of Commons'.

On 30 June 1931 the British House of Commons approved the enactment of the Statute of Westminster freeing the Provinces as well as the Dominion from the operation of the Colonial Laws Validity Act, and thus removing what legal limitations existed as regards Canada's legislative autonomy. A joint address of the Senate and the House of Commons was sent to the Governor-General for transmission to London on 10 July 1931. The statute received the royal assent on 12 Dec. 1931.

Provision was made in the British North America Act for the admission of British Columbia, Prince Edward Island, Newfoundland, Rupert's Land and Northwest Territory into the Union. In 1869 Rupert's Land, or the Northwest Territories, was purchased from the Hudson's Bay Company. On 15 July 1870, Rupert's Land and the Northwest Territory were annexed to Canada and named the Northwest Territories, Canada having agreed to pay the Hudson's Bay Company in cash and land for its relinquishing of claims to the territory. By the same action the Province of Manitoba was created from a small portion of this territory and they were admitted into the Confederation on 15 July 1870. On 20 July 1871 the province of British Columbia was admitted, and Prince Edward Island on 1 July 1873. The provinces of Alberta and Saskatchewan were formed from the provisional districts of Alberta, Athabaska, Assiniboia and Saskatchewan and originally parts of the Northwest Territories and admitted on 1 Sept. 1905. Newfoundland formally joined Canada as its tenth province on 31 March 1949.

In Feb. 1931 Norway formally recognized the Canadian title to the Sverdrup group of Arctic islands. Canada thus holds sovereignty in the whole Arctic sector north of the Canadian mainland.

In Nov. 1981 the Canadian government agreed on the provisions of an amended constitution, to the end that it should replace the British North America Act and that its future amendment should be the prerogative of Canada. These proposals were adopted by the Parliament of Canada and were enacted by the UK Parliament as the Canada Act of 1982.

AREA AND POPULATION. Population of the area now included in Canada:

1851	2,436,297	1901	5,371,315	1951	14,009,429
1861	3,229,633	1911	7,206,643	1961	18,238,247
1871	3,689,257	1921	8,787,949	1971	21,568,311
1881	4,324,810	1931	10,376,786 [1]	1981	24,343,181
1891	4,833,239	1941	11,506,655 [1]		

[1] From 1951 figures include Newfoundland.

Population (estimated), 1 July 1982, was 24·6m.

Areas of the provinces, etc. (in sq. km) and population at recent censuses:

Province	*Land area*	*Fresh water area*	*Total land and fresh water area*	*Population, 1971*	*Population, 1976*	*Population, 1981*
Newfoundland	371,690	34,030	405,720	522,104	557,725	567,681
Prince Edward Island	5,600	—	5,660	111,641	118,229	122,506
Nova Scotia	52,840	2,650	55,490	788,960	828,571	847,442
New Brunswick	72,090	1,350	73,440	634,557	677,250	696,403
Quebec	1,356,790	183,890	1,540,680	6,027,764	6,234,445	6,438,403
Ontario	891,190	177,390	1,068,580	7,703,106	8,264,465	8,625,107
Manitoba	548,360	101,590	649,950	988,247	1,021,506	1,026,241
Saskatchewan	570,700	81,630	652,330	926,242	921,323	968,313
Alberta	644,390	16,800	661,190	1,627,874	1,838,037	2,237,724
British Columbia	929,730	18,070	947,800	2,184,621	2,466,608	2,744,467
Yukon	478,970	4,480	483,450	18,388	21,836	22,135
Northwest Territories	3,293,020	133,300	3,426,320	34,807	42,609	45,471
Total	9,215,430	755,180	9,970,610	21,568,311	22,992,604	24,343,181

Of the total population in 1971, 18,272,780 were Canadian born, 933,040 other British born and 2,362,490 foreign born, 309,640 of the latter being USA born.

The population born outside Canada in the provinces was in the following ratio (%): Newfoundland, 1·7; Prince Edward Island, 3·3; Nova Scotia, 4·7; New Brunswick, 3·7; Quebec, 7·8; Ontario, 22·2; Manitoba, 15·3; Saskatchewan, 12; Alberta, 17·3; British Columbia, 22·7.

In 1971, figures for the population, according to origin, were:

British Isles		Netherlands	425,945	Danish	75,725
English	6,245,970	Polish	316,430	Russian	64,425
Scottish	1,720,390	Indian and Eskimo	312,760	Finnish	59,215
Irish	1,581,730	Hebrew	296,945	Belgian	51,135
Other	76,030	Norwegian	179,290	Austrian	42,120
Total, British	9,624,115	Hungarian	131,890	Japanese	37,260
French	6,180,120	Greek	124,475	Negro	34,445
German	1,317,200	Chinese	118,815	Icelandic	27,905
Italian	730,820	Yugoslav	104,955	Romanian	27,375
Ukrainian	580,660	Swedish	101,870	Lithuanian	24,535
		Czech and Slovak	81,870	Not stated	171,645

The native Indian registered population numbered 288,938 in 1976 and the Eskimo population was 17,550 in 1971.

Populations of Census Metropolitan Areas (CMA) and Cities (proper), 1976 census:

	CMA	*City proper*		*CMA*	*City proper*
Toronto	2,998,947	559,217	Halifax	277,727	114,594
Montreal	2,828,349	980,354	Windsor	246,110	192,083
Vancouver	1,268,183	414,281	Victoria	233,481	64,379
Ottawa-Hull	717,978	295,163	Regina	164,313	162,613
Edmonton	657,057	532,246	St John's	154,820	83,770
Calgary	592,743	592,743	Oshawa	154,217	117,519
Winnipeg	584,842	564,473	Saskatoon	154,210	154,210
Quebec	576,075	166,474	Sudbury	149,923	91,829
Hamilton	542,095	306,434	Chicoutimi-Jonquiere	135,172	—
St Catharines-Niagara	304,353	—	Chicoutimi	—	60,064
St Catharines	—	124,018	Jonquiere	—	60,354
Niagara Falls	—	70,960	Thunder Bay	121,379	112,486
Kitchener	287,801	139,734	Saint John	114,048	80,521
London	283,668	254,280	Trois Rivieres	111,453	50,466

The total 'urban' population of Canada in 1981 was 18,435,927, against 17,366,970 in 1976.

While the registration of births, marriages and deaths is under provincial control, the statistics are compiled on a uniform system by Statistics Canada.

The following table gives the results for the year 1981, estimate:

Province	Living births Number	Marriages Number	Deaths Number
Newfoundland	11,310	3,450	3,070
Prince Edward Island	1,970	810	970
Nova Scotia	12,000	6,110	6,440
New Brunswick	10,910	5,160	5,320
Quebec	95,790	43,380	43,440
Ontario	123,240	67,030	63,390
Manitoba	16,920	7,670	8,870
Saskatchewan	16,920	7,000	7,160
Alberta	39,810	18,710	12,260
British Columbia	39,700	21,790	19,680
Yukon Territory	520	220	140
N.W. Territories	1,060	280	170
	370,150	181,610	170,910

Immigrant arrivals by country of last permanent residence:

Country	1980	1981
UK	18,890	10,602
France	1,890	1,084
Germany	1,642	1,066
Netherlands	1,864	963
Greece	1,091	479
Italy	1,544	1,045
Portugal	4,219	1,073
Other Europe	9,713	5,787
Asia	71,453	48,830
Australasia	1,555	1,317
USA	9,900	10,557
West Indies	7,187	8,632
All other	11,491	36,550
Total	142,439	128,615

Dawe, A., *Profiles of a Nation: Canadian Themes and Styles.* Toronto, 1970
Jenness, D., *The Indians of Canada.* 5th ed. Ottawa, 1960
Park, J., *The Culture of Contemporary Canada.* Toronto, 1970
Porter, J., *The Vertical Mosaic.* Toronto, 1965
Rosenberg, S. E., *The Jewish Community in Canada: A History.* Toronto, 1970
Wade, M., *The French Canadians, 1760–1967.* 2 vols. 2nd ed. Toronto and London, 1968

CONSTITUTION AND GOVERNMENT. The members of the Senate are appointed until age 75 by summons of the Governor-General under the Great Seal of Canada. Members appointed before 2 June 1965 may remain in office for life. The Senate consists of 104 senators, namely, 24 from Ontario, 24 from Quebec, 10 from Nova Scotia, 10 from New Brunswick, 4 from Prince Edward Island, 6 from Manitoba, 6 from British Columbia, 6 from Alberta, 6 from Saskatchewan, 6 from Newfoundland, 1 from the Yukon Territory and 1 from the Northwest Territories. Each senator must be at least 30 years of age, a born or naturalized subject of the Queen and must reside in the province for which he is appointed and his total net worth must be at least $4,000. The House of Commons is elected by the people, for 5 years, unless sooner dissolved. Women have the vote and are eligible. From 1867 to the election of 1945 representation was based on Quebec having 65 seats and the other provinces the same proportion of 65 which their population had to the population of Quebec. In the General Election of 1949 readjustments were based on the population of all the provinces taken as a whole. Generally speaking, this format for representation has prevailed in all subsequent elections with readjustments made after each decennial census. However, on 31 Dec. 1974, the law was changed so that it has reverted somewhat to the type of system that had prevailed initially. That is to say, Quebec is to be assigned a fixed number of seats in the House of Commons and the representation of the other provinces calculated by a quotient which reflects this fact.

The thirty-second Parliament, elected on 19 Feb. 1980, comprises 282 members and the provincial and territorial representation are: Ontario, 95; Quebec, 75; Nova Scotia, 11; New Brunswick, 10; Manitoba, 14; British Columbia, 28; Prince Edward Island, 4; Saskatchewan 14; Alberta, 21; Newfoundland, 7; Yukon Territory, 1; Northwest Territories, 2.

State of parties in the Senate (Nov. 1982): Liberals, 60; Progressive Conservatives, 24; Independent, 2; Social Credit, 1; Independent Liberal, 1; Vacant, 16; total 104.

State of the parties in the House of Commons (Nov. 1982): Liberals, 146; Progressive Conservatives, 102; New Democratic Party, 33; Independent, 1; total, 282. Elections took place on 19 Feb. 1980.

The following is a list of Governors-General of Canada:

Viscount Monck	1867–1868	Viscount Byng of Vimy	1921–1926
Lord Lisgar	1868–1872	Viscount Willingdon	1926–1931
Earl of Dufferin	1872–1878	Earl of Bessborough	1931–1935
Marquess of Lorne	1878–1883	Lord Tweedsmuir	1935–1940
Marquess of Lansdowne	1883–1888	Earl of Athlone	1940–1946
Lord Stanley of Preston	1888–1893	Field-Marshal Viscount Alexander of Tunis	1946–1952
Earl of Aberdeen	1893–1898	Vincent Massey	1952–1959
Earl of Minto	1898–1904	Georges Philias Vanier	1959–1967
Earl Grey	1904–1911	Roland Michener	1967–1974
HRH the Duke of Connaught	1911–1916	Jules Léger	1974–1979
Duke of Devonshire	1916–1921		

Governor-General: Edward Schreyer (sworn in Jan. 1979).

National flag: Vertically red, white, red with the white of double width and bearing a stylized red maple leaf.

The office and appointment of the Governor-General are regulated by letters patent, signed by the King on 8 Sept. 1947, which came into force on 1 Oct. 1947. In 1977 the Queen approved the transfer to the Governor-General functions discharged by the Sovereign. He is assisted in his functions, under the provisions of the Act of 1867, by a Privy Council composed of Cabinet Ministers.

The following is the list of the Liberal Cabinet in March 1982, in order of precedence, which in Canada attaches generally rather to the person than to the office:

Prime Minister: Rt Hon. Pierre Elliott Trudeau.
Deputy Prime Minister and Secretary of State for External Affairs: Allan MacEachen.
Transport: Jean-Luc Pépin.
Energy, Mines and Resources: Jean Chrétien.
Indian Affairs and Northern Development: John Munro.
Leader of the Government in the Senate: Senator Bud Olson.
President of the Treasury Board: Herb Gray.
Agriculture: Eugene Whelan.
Consumer and Corporate Affairs: André Ouellet.
Finance: Marc Lalonde.
Minister responsible for fitness and Amateur Sport: Raymond Perreault.
Public Works: Roméo Leblanc.
Environment: John Roberts.
Health and Welfare: Monique Bégin.
Supply and Services: Jean-Jacques Blais.
Communications: Francis Fox.
Defence: J. Gilles Lamontagne.
Fisheries and Oceans: Pierre de Bane.
Minister Responsible for Canadian Wheat Board: Senator Hagen Argue.
Minister of State, International Trade: Gerald Regan.
Attorney-General, Justice: Mark MacGuigan.
Solicitor-General: Bob Kaplan.
Minister of State Responsible for Multiculturalism: Jim Fleming.
Minister of State, Small Business and Tourism: Bill Rompkey.
National Revenue: Pierre Bussières.

Minister of State, External Relations: Charles Lapointe.
Industry, Trade and Commerce, Regional and Economic Expansion: Ed Lumley.
Government House Leader: Yvon Pinard.
Minister of State, Economic Development, Science and Technology: Donald Johnston.
Employment and Immigration: Lloyd Axworthy.
Minister of State, Finance: Paul Cosgrove.
Minister of State, Mines and Minister of State for the Status of Women: Judy Erola.
Minister of State, Social Development: Jack Austin.
Minister of Labour: Charles Caccia.
Secretary of State for Canada: Serge Joyal.
Minister of Veterans' Affairs: Bennett Campbell.

The salary of a member of the House of Commons is $43,800 with a tax-free allowance of $14,700. The salary of a senator is $43,800 with a tax-free allowance of $7,200. The salary and allowances of the Prime Minister total $108,500. The salary of the Speaker of the House of Commons is $77,400; the salary of the Speaker of the Senate is $77,400; the salary of the Opposition Leader is $77,400 and that of the National Democratic Party Leader, $64,000; all these also have tax-free allowances of $14,700, except the Speaker of the Senate who has $7,200.

Future increases are to be pegged at 1% less than increases in the consumer price index or industrial composite index, whichever is lower.

An Act to provide retiring allowances, on a contributory basis, to members of the House of Commons was given the Royal Assent on 4 July 1952. This Act was amended in July 1963; a member can now opt for a reduced retiring allowance in favour of an additional allowance for the widow; and provision has been made for retiring allowance for former Prime Ministers and their widows.

The Canadian Parliamentary Guide. Annual. Ottawa
Report of the Royal Commission on Dominion–Provincial Relations, Canada 1867–1939. 3 vols. Ottawa, 1940
Byers, R. B. (ed.), *Canada Challenged: The Viability of the Confederation.* Toronto, 1979
Information Canada, *Organization of the Government of Canada.* Loose-leaf service. Ottawa, 1970
Kennedy, W. F. M., *Statutes, Treaties and Documents of the Canadian Constitution, 1713–1929.* Toronto, 1930
Kernaghan, N. (ed.), *Bureaucracy in Canadian Government, Selected Readings.* Toronto, 1969
Morton, W. L., *The Kingdom of Canada; A General History From Earliest Times.* Toronto, 1969
Olmsted, R. A., *Decisions of the Judicial Committee of the Privy Council Relating to the British North America Act, 1867, and the Canadian Constitution, 1867–1954.* Ottawa, Queens' Printer, 1954
Russell, P. H. (ed.), *Leading Constitutional Decisions; Cases on the British North America Act.* Toronto, 1968
Stanley, F. G., *A Short History of the Canadian Constitution.* Toronto, 1969
Trudeau, P. E., *Federalism and the French Canadians.* London, 1968

DEFENCE. The Department of National Defence was created by the National Defence Act, 1922, which established one civil Department of Government in place of the previous Departments of Militia and Defence, Naval Service and the Air Board. The Minister of National Defence has the control and management of the Canadian Forces and all matters relating to national defence establishments and works for the defence of Canada. He is the Minister responsible for presenting before the Cabinet, matters of major defence policy for which Cabinet direction is required. Until Oct. 1973, he was responsible for the Canada Emergency Measures Organization which was renamed 'Emergency Planning Canada' in 1976, and given wider responsibilities for the co-ordination of civil emergency planning. This organization now reports to the President of the Privy Council, but the Minister of National Defence continues to be responsible for certain civil emergency powers, duties and functions as outlined in Order-in-Council P.C.1. 1965–1041 dated 8 June 1965, as amended.

In Dec. 1976, the Minister of National Defence was named as minister responsible for all aspects of air Search and Rescue in the areas of Canadian SAR responsibility, and for the overall co-ordination of marine search and rescue including provision of air resources for marine SAR within Canadian territorial waters and in designated oceanic areas off the Pacific and Atlantic Coasts in accordance with agreements made with the United States Coast Guard.

Command Structure. The Canadian forces are organized on a functional basis to reflect the major commitments assigned by the Government. All forces devoted to a primary mission are grouped under a single commander who is assigned sufficient resources to discharge his responsibilities. Specifically, the Canadian forces consist of National Defence Headquarters and the following major commands reporting to the Chief of the Defence Staff:

1. *Mobile Command* provides units trained and equipped to support the United Nations or other peacekeeping operations; provides ground forces for the protection of Canadian territory; maintains combat formations in Canada for support of overseas commitments. It is comprised of 3 airportable combat groups in Canada; the United Nations force in Cyprus; the Canadian Airborne Regiment, and 1 combat training centre. The Militia and Air Reserve components are also controlled by Mobile Command. Strength (1980), 12,675.

2. *Maritime Command.* All maritime forces are under the Commander, Maritime Command, with headquarters in Halifax, Nova Scotia. In addition, he also exercises operational control of aircraft assigned to him by the commander Maritime Air Group for Maritime operations. The Commander Maritime Forces (Pacific), who is the Deputy Commander, has his headquarters in Esquimalt, British Columbia. Maritime Command is to defend Canada against attack from the sea; provide anti-submarine defence in support of NATO; provide sea transport in support of Mobile Command. Composition of the maritime forces includes 3 submarines, 4 destroyers, 19 smaller destroyer-escorts, 3 supply ships, 6 patrol craft, 7 small support ships, 6 training vessels (*ex*-coastal minesweepers), 4 research ships and 30 auxiliaries and service craft. There are 16 naval reserve units in major Canadian cities which form an essential component of Maritime Command.

Active naval personnel strength in Maritime Command ships and shore establishments in 1983 was about 18% of the Regular Forces, *i.e.*, some 14,000 comprising 2,000 officers and 12,000 ratings (men and women).

3. *Air Command.* On 2 Sept. 1975, the aviation units administered by Mobile Command and Maritime Command were withdrawn and allocated to a newly-formed Air Command, which now controls all Canadian military aviation units through a single senior commander. Air Command responsibilities include maintenance of operationally-ready regular and reserve air forces to meet Canada's sovereignty requirements, participation with the USA in the air defence of North America through NORAD, and support of overseas commitments including NATO responsibilities in Europe and elsewhere. It is organized in 4 operational groups: Air Defence Group, Maritime Air Group, Air Transport Group and Fighter Group; has reinforcement and training responsibilities to 1 Canadian Air Group (1 CAG with 3 squadrons of CF-104s) in Europe; and exercises command and control over Air Training Schools and the Air Reserve.

Air Defence Group, through NORAD, has entire responsibility for control of Canadian airspace. It comprises 3 squadrons of CF-101 Voodoo all-weather interceptors, armed with nuclear and conventional missiles, with replacement by CF-18 Hornets scheduled to begin in 1984; an electronic warfare squadron with 9 CC-117 (Falcon) and 16 T-33A aircraft and 1 operational training squadron with Voodoos; eastern and western control centres and a trans-continental radar chain, integrated in NORAD through the semi-automatic ground environment (SAGE) network.

Maritime Air Group's primary responsibilities include coastal and anti-pollution patrol, fishery protection and Arctic surveillance. Its equipment includes 3 operational squadrons of CP-140 Aurora and 1 of Tracker maritime patrol aircraft, and 2 ASW helicopter squadrons with CH-124 Sea Kings.

Air Transport Group has 3 squadrons of C-130E/H turboprop transports; 1

squadron of 5 CC-137 (Boeing 707) jet transports, of which 2 can operate as flight refuelling tankers; a VIP squadron with 2 CC-132 Dash 7 four-turboprop and 7 CC-109 Cosmopolitan twin-turboprop transports and 2 twin-jet CC-144 Challengers; and 4 dual-role transport/search and rescue squadrons with 11 twin-turboprop CC-115 Buffalo and 8 CC-138 Twin Otter aircraft and helicopters. Fighter Group has 2 squadrons of CF-5 fighters and 6 squadrons of CH-147 Chinook, CH-135 (Bell UH-1N) and CH-136 (Kiowa) helicopters.

Training aircraft include Beech CT-134A Musketeer IIs and JetRanger helicopters for basic instruction, CT-114 Tutor advanced trainers, and CC-130E Hercules for navigator training.

4. *Training Command* plans and conducts all recruit and individual trades and classification training that is common to more than one command. The Command is also responsible for the Prairie Region, one of 6 military regions into which Canada is divided. The Command headquarters is in Winnipeg and the 9 bases within the Command are located in 7 provinces. A total of 24,239 students attended one or more of 1,258 courses conducted by the Command during 1973.

5. *Canadian Forces Communications Command (CFCC)* manages, operates and maintains strategic communications for the Canadian Forces and, in the event of emergencies, for the federal and provincial governments. The Command also provides points for interconnecting strategic and tactical networks and CFCC manages, operates and maintains the major DND automatic data processing centres.

6. *The Reserves* are composed of the Naval Reserve, the Militia and the Air Reserve.

Projected National Defence expenditures for 1982–83 were $6,941m. at 31 Oct. 1982. Strength of the Regular Forces in 1982 was about 82,000.

7. *Canadian Forces Europe.* The Canadian Forces allocated to support NATO in Europe are part of Canadian Forces Europe. The land element is No. 4 Canadian Mechanized Brigade Group operationally responsible to the Central Army Group. The air element, No. 1 Canadian Air Group, consisting of 3 CF-104 Starfighter squadrons, is operationally assigned to No. 4 Allied Tactical Air Force. These elements are located in the Baden-Baden area of Federal Republic of Germany and are supported administratively by CFB Europe at Lahr.

Police Forces. The police forces of Canada are organized in three groups: (1) the federal force, which is the Royal Canadian Mounted Police; (2) provincial police forces—the Provinces of Ontario and Quebec have their own provincial police forces, but all other provinces engage the services of the Royal Canadian Mounted Police to perform parallel functions within their borders, and (3) municipal police forces—each urban centre of reasonable size maintains its own police force or engages the services of the provincial police, under contract, to attend to police matters.

In addition, the Canadian National Railways, the Canadian Pacific Railway Company and the National Harbours Board have their own police forces.

Royal Canadian Mounted Police. The Royal Canadian Mounted Police is a civil force maintained by the federal government. It was established in 1873, as the North-West Mounted Police for service in what was then the North-West Territories and, in recognition of its services, was granted the use of the prefix 'Royal' by King Edward VII in 1904. Its sphere of operations was expanded in 1918 to include all of Canada west of Thunder Bay. In 1920 the force absorbed the Dominion Police, and its headquarters was transferred from Regina to Ottawa, and its title was changed to Royal Canadian Mounted Police. The force is responsible to the Solicitor-General of Canada and is controlled and managed by a Commissioner who holds the rank and status of a Deputy Minister. The Commissioner is empowered under the Royal Canadian Mounted Police Act to appoint members to be peace officers in all provinces and territories of Canada.

The responsibilities of the Royal Canadian Mounted Police are national in scope. The administration of justice within the provinces, including the enforcement of the Criminal Code of Canada, is part of the power and duty delegated to the provincial governments.

All provinces except Ontario and Quebec have entered into contracts with the Royal Canadian Mounted Police to enforce criminal and provincial laws under the direction of the respective Attorneys-General. In addition, in these 8 provinces the Force is under agreement to provide police services to 191 municipalities, thereby assuming the enforcement responsibility of municipal as well as criminal and provincial laws within these communities. The Royal Canadian Mounted Police is also responsible for all police work in the Yukon and Northwest territories enforcing federal law and territorial ordinances. The 15 Operational Divisions, alphabetically designated, make up the strength of the Force across Canada; they comprise 48 sub-divisions which include 710 detachments. Headquarters Division, as well as the Office of the Commissioner, is located in Ottawa. The Force maintains liaison officers in 31 countries and represents Canada in the International Criminal Police Organization which has its headquarters in Paris.

Thorough training is emphasized for members of the Force. Recruits receive 6 months of basic training at the Royal Canadian Mounted Police Academy in Regina. This is followed by a further 6 months of supervised on-the-job training. The RCMP also operates the Canadian Police College at which its members and selected representatives of other Canadian and foreign police forces may study the latest advances in the fields of crime prevention and detection.

Many of these advances have been incorporated into the operation of the Force. A teletype system links the widespread divisional headquarters with the administrative centre at Ottawa and a network of fixed and mobile radio units operates within the provinces. The focal point of the criminal investigation work of the Force is the Directorate of Laboratories and Identification; its services, together with those of divisional and sub-divisional units, and of 8 Crime Detection Laboratories, are available to police forces throughout Canada. The Canadian Police Information Centre at RCMP Headquarters, a duplexed computer system, is staffed and operated by the Force. Law Enforcement agencies throughout Canada have access *via* a series of remote terminals to information on stolen vehicles, licences and wanted persons.

In Oct. 1982, the Force had a total strength of 20,748 including regular members, special constables, civilian members and Public Service employees. It maintained 6,071 motor vehicles, 76 police service dogs and 144 horses.

The Force has 13 divisions actively engaged in law enforcement, 1 Headquarters Division and 2 training divisions. In addition it maintains Marine Services and Air Services with headquarters at Ottawa. The Marine Services is comprised of 12 patrol vessels and 350 smaller craft which operate on the east and west coasts, the Great Lakes and the St Lawrence River. The Air Directorate has stations throughout Canada and maintains 36 aircraft.

Dornbusch, C. E., *The Canadian Army 1855–1958; Regimental Histories.* Cornwailville, N.Y., 1959
Eayrs, J., *In Defence of Canada: Growing up Allied.* Univ. of Toronto Press, 1980
Feasby, W. R. (ed.), *Official History of the Canadian Medical Services, 1939–45.* 2 vols. Dept. of National Defence. Ottawa, 1953–56
Swettenham, J., *Canada and the First World War.* Toronto, 1970

INTERNATIONAL RELATIONS

Membership. Canada is a member of UN, the Commonwealth, OECD, NATO and Colombo Plan.

ECONOMY

Budget. Budgetary revenue and expenditure of the Government of Canada for years ended 31 March (in Canadian $1m.):

	1978–79	*1979–80*	*1980–81*	*1981–82* [1]	*1982–83* [1]
Revenue	35,215	40,159	45,200	54,068	55,660
Expenditure	46,934	51,534	59,350	67,674	79,210

[1] Not comparable to earlier years, adjustment to Canada Post revenues and expenditures.

Budgetary revenue, main items, 1982–83 (estimates in Canadian $1m.):

Income tax, personal	24,046	Non-resident tax	1,018
Income tax, corporation	8,118	Oil export charge	519
Sales	6,185	Natural gas tax	998
Customs duties	3,439	Non-tax revenue	6,113

Details of budget estimates[1], 1982–83 (in Canadian $1m.):

Energy	3,039	External affairs	2,167
Economic development	7,559	Defence	7,000
Social affairs	30,150	Parliament	156
Justice and legal affairs	1,541	Services to government	3,448
Public debt charges	16,765		

[1] The Department of Finance now manages expenditure under a new system of broad categories (listed above) called 'envelopes'.

On 31 March 1981 the net debt was $94,869m.

Canadian Tax Foundation. *The National Finances: An Analysis of the Revenues and Expenditures of the Government of Canada.* Toronto. Annual

Currency. The denominations of money in the currency of Canada are dollars and cents. The cent is one-hundredth part of a dollar. Subsidiary coins of the denominations of 1, 5, 10, 25 and 50 cents and $1 are in use. The monetary standard is gold of 900 millesimal fineness (23·22 grains of pure gold equal to 1 gold dollar). The Currency Act provides for gold coins in the denominations of $5, $10 and $20, which are legal tender. The British and US gold coins are also legal tender, at the par rate of exchange. The legal equivalent of the British sovereign is $4.86⅔.

The Bank of Canada has the sole right to issue paper money for circulation in Canada. Restrictions introduced by the 1944 revisions of the Bank Act cancelled the right of chartered banks to issue or re-issue notes after 1 Jan. 1945; and in Jan. 1950 the chartered banks' liability for such of their notes as then remained outstanding was transferred to the Bank of Canada in return for payment of a like sum to the Bank of Canada. On 31 May 1970 the Canadian dollar which was stabilized at 92·50 US cents was allowed to fluctuate. The value of the US$ in Canadian funds was $1·23 and £1 sterling = Canadian $1·86 in March 1983.

The Bank of Canada issues notes, which are legal tender, in denominations of $1, $2, $5, $10, $20, $50, $100, $500 and $1,000. Under the terms of the Bank of Canada Act, the bank is required to sell gold in bars of 400 oz. to any person tendering legal tender. This obligation is at the present time suspended by Order-in-Council. The exportation of gold from Canada is prohibited except by licence issued by the Minister of Finance to the Bank of Canada or a chartered bank.

The Ottawa Mint was established in 1908 as a branch of the Royal Mint, in pursuance of the Ottawa Mint Act, 1901. In Dec. 1931 control of the Mint was passed over to the Canadian Government, and since that time has operated as the Royal Canadian Mint. The Mint issues silver, nickel, bronze and steel coins for circulation in Canada. In 1967, in celebration of Canada's Centennial of Confederation, a $20 gold piece was minted, the first gold coin struck since 1919. In 1935, on the occasion of His Majesty's Silver Jubilee, the Royal Canadian Mint issued the first Canadian silver dollars. Commemorative dollars were also issued in 1939 on the occasion of the visit of King George VI and Queen Elizabeth to Canada; in 1949, when Newfoundland became the tenth Province of Canada; in 1958, the one-hundredth anniversary of the establishment of the Colony of British Columbia; in 1964, the centennial of the Charlottetown and Quebec Conferences which paved the way to confederation. The silver dollar bearing the design of the canoe manned by an Indian and a Voyageur has been issued in the years 1935–38, 1945–48, 1950–57, 1959–63, 1965, 1966 and 1972. For centennial year the Canada goose replaced the usual canoe design on the silver dollar. Because of a world-wide shortage of silver, the Government, in Aug. 1967, authorized the Mint to change the metal content of the 25-cent and 10-cent coins. Commencing in Sept. 1968, the 10-cent, 50-cent and $1 coins were minted in pure nickel. Gold refining is one of the principal activities of the Mint. In 1981, 1,140,358 troy oz. of rough bullion were received for treatment, containing 933,396 oz. of fine gold and 128,152 oz. of fine silver. Coin issued: Bronze, $109,396,805·11; nickel, $524,110,236·25; silver, $695,400; gold, $275,025,400.

Banking. Commercial banks in Canada are known as chartered banks and are incorporated under the terms of the Bank Act, which imposes strict conditions as to capital, notes in circulation, returns to the Dominion Government, types of lending operations and other matters. In Oct. 1982 there were 70 chartered banks (13 domestic banks and 57 foreign bank subsidiaries) incorporated under the provisions of the Bank Act; the 13 had 7,300 branches serving 2,000 communities in all provinces in Canada and nearly 300 branches in other countries. There was also one bank incorporated under the Quebec Savings Bank Act. The foreign bank subsidiaries operate 190 offices in Canada including 57 head offices. The Bank Act is subject to revision by Parliament every 10 years. Bank charters expire every 10 years and are renewed at each decennial revision of the Bank Act. The chartered banks make detailed monthly and yearly returns to the Minister of Finance and are subject to periodic inspection by the Inspector-General of Banks, an official appointed by the Government.

The following are some particulars of the 12 chartered banks at 30 Sept. 1982: assets of gold coin and bullion, $516,902,000; Canadian currency, $1,691,371,000; Bank of Canada deposits and notes, $4,467,732; deposits with banks, $38,262,723,000; cheques and other items in transit, $1,539,509; ordinary personal loans, (Oct. 1982) $31,722m.; business and farming loans, (Oct. 1982) $81,034m.; total assets, $351,195,708,000.

The Bank of Canada Act, passed on 3 July 1934, provided for the establishment of a central bank for the Dominion. This bank commenced operations on 11 March 1935 with a paid-up capital of $5m. By reason of certain changes introduced into the composition of stockholders of the bank (for which *see* THE STATESMAN'S YEAR-BOOK, 1944 pp. 322–23), the Minister of Finance on behalf of Canada is the sole registered owner of the capital stock of the bank. The revised Bank Act, which came into force on 1 May 1967, requires the chartered banks, beginning Feb. 1968, to maintain a statutory cash ratio of 12% on demand deposits and 4% on other deposits, in the form of reserves with and notes on the Bank of Canada. A secondary reserve of 7% in treasury bills, government bonds, etc., is also required. All gold held in Canada by the chartered banks was transferred to the Bank of Canada along with the gold held by the Government as reserve against Dominion notes outstanding at the time of the commencement of operations of the Bank of Canada. The liability of the Dominion notes outstanding at the commencement of business of the Bank of Canada was assumed by the bank.

In 1975 the Industrial Development Bank was succeeded by the Crown corporation, the Federal Business Development Bank, which was proclaimed in force on 2 Oct. 1975. In the year ending 31 March 1982, the Federal Business Development Bank authorized 4,630 loans for a total of $476m.

Weights and Measures. The legal weights and measures are in transition from the Imperial to the International system of units. The Metric Commission, established in June 1971, co-ordinates Canada's conversion to the metric system.

ENERGY AND NATURAL RESOURCES

Electricity. The net generation of electricity in 1980 was 367,305,670 mwh., of which utilities accounted for 328,636,136 mwh. Of the total, 251,217,245 mwh. was from hydro-electricity, 114,312,847 mwh. from conventional steam plants and 35,863,378 mwh. from nuclear plants. Demand (1980) was 340,072,879 mwh.

Oil and Natural Gas. With the discovery of large oilfields in Alberta, the production of petroleum became a major Canadian industry. The Interprovincial Pipeline, Canada's longest oil pipeline, moves crude oil from Edmonton, Alberta, to Montreal, Quebec. The pipeline serves Canadian refineries from Edmonton to Montreal and many in the USA. Another pipeline, Trans-Mountain, extends from

Edmonton to Vancouver. Nine refineries, 5 in Canada and 4 in Washington State, are served by the pipeline. At the end of 1980 Canada's oil pipeline system had 35,662·6 km of line in operation. Net oil deliveries in 1980 were 148,921,906 cu. metres. The Trans-Canada natural gas line is the longest in the world (10,389 km). It brings natural gas from the Alberta–Saskatchewan border across the prairies, through northern Ontario to Toronto, then eastward to Montreal. Natural gas pipeline mileage totalled 155,291 km in 1980. Total gas received from fields and processing plants at June 1982, 5,969·8m. cu. metres; total gas supplied to gas utilities, 4,564·7m. cu. metres.

Minerals. Alberta, Ontario, British Columbia, Quebec and Saskatchewan are the chief mining provinces. Total value of minerals produced in 1981 was $33,084,291,000. Principal minerals produced in 1981 (preliminary) were as follows:

	Quantity (1,000)	*Value ($1,000)*
Metallics		
Copper (kg)	718,082	1,590,841
Nickel (kg)	155,175	1,414,743
Zinc (kg)	995,049	1,193,477
Iron ore (tonnes)	49,844	1,917,614
Gold (grammes)	49,500	881,116
Lead (kg)	272,920	207,937
Silver (kg)	1,203	487,254
Molybdenum (kg)	14,134	317,207
Total metallics	...	9,397,976
Non-metallics		
Asbestos (tonnes)	1,133	589,163
Potash (K_2O) (tonnes)	6,815	1,050,513
Salt (tonnes)	7,283	135,103
Sulphur, elemental (tonnes)	8,320	695,900
Gypsum (tonnes)	7,800	46,410
Total non-metallics	...	2,832,668
Fuels		
Crude petroleum (cu. metres)	74,763	9,411,247
Natural gas (cu. metres)	82,186	6,156,901
Natural gas by-products (cu. metres)	18,988	2,398,151
Coal (tonnes)	39,250	1,045,500
Total fuels	...	19,011,799
Structural materials		
Cement (tonnes)	10,368	680,587
Sand and gravel (tonnes)	287,468	547,096
Stone (tonnes)	94,577	345,518
Clay products (bricks, tiles, etc.)	...	120,174
Lime (tonnes)	2,463	148,473
Total structural materials	...	1,841,848

Value (in Canadian $1,000) of mineral production by provinces:

Provinces	*1980* [1]	*1981* [2]	*Provinces*	*1980* [1]	*1981* [2]
Newfoundland	1,035,653	1,104,494	Saskatchewan	2,314,616	2,409,912
Pr. Ed. Island	2,340	2,575	Alberta	16,378,970	17,571,382
Nova Scotia	246,738	261,916	British Columbia	2,795,338	2,971,723
New Brunswick	372,522	534,569	Yukon Territory	361,257	298,173
Quebec	2,466,795	2,383,441	N.W. Territories	424,501	467,171
Ontario	4,640,453	4,317,611			
Manitoba	802,575	671,324	Total	31,841,758	33,084,291

Agriculture. Though the manufacturing industries now predominate, agriculture is still very important to the Canadian economy. It contributes about 2·6% of the net value of production and in 1981 accounted for about 11·5% of the value of commodities exported.

According to the census of 1981 the total land area is 2,278·6m. acres of which 162·8m. acres are agricultural land.

Grain growing, dairy farming, fruit farming, ranching and fur farming are all carried on successfully. Total farm receipts (1981) $18,597m.

The following table shows the estimated value of selected agricultural production for 1981, in Canadian $1,000:

Wheat	3,249,417	Tobacco	380,641
Oats and barley	861,577	Cattle and calves	3,524,587
Rapeseed	592,646	Hogs	1,626,843
Potatoes	304,289	Sheep and lambs	26,256
Other vegetables	383,998	Dairy products	2,373,918
Fruit	223,794	Poultry and eggs	1,236,349

Number of occupied farms (census of 1981) was 318,361.

Field Crops. In 1981, 72,653,100 acres were under principal field crops. The most valuable field crops are wheat, tame hay, oats, barley, rye, corn for grain, flaxseed, mixed grains, rapeseed, fodder corn, soybeans and sugar-beet.

The estimated acreage and yield of the principal field crops, by provinces, 1981 were:

	Wheat		*Tame hay*		*Oats for Grain*	
Provinces	*1,000 acres*	*1,000 bu.*	*1,000 acres*	*1,000 tons*	*1,000 acres*	*1,000 bu.*
Prince Edward Island	8·1	332	124	260	33	1,881
Nova Scotia	7·1	312	176	422	16·6	913
New Brunswick	9	369	171	359	37	1,998
Quebec	101	4,391	2,386	5,440	371	17,280
Ontario	527	26,931	2,600	7,765	330	17,483
Manitoba	3,900	122,200	1,250	2,500	600	30,000
Saskatchewan	19,350	525,000	1,700	2,100	1,100	53,000
Alberta	6,700	228,600	3,500	6,700	1,300	81,000
British Columbia	106	3,200	717	2,000	68	3,200
Total, Canada	30,708	911,335	12,624	27,546	3,855·6	206,755

	Barley		*Rye*		*Maize for Grain*	
Provinces	*1,000 acres*	*1,000 bu.*	*1,000 acres*	*1,000 bu.*	*1,000 acres*	*1,000 bu.*
Prince Edward Island	53	2,756	—	—	—	—
Nova Scotia	8·6	430	5·3	255	—	—
New Brunswick	9·6	451	—	—	—	—
Quebec	262	11,804	8·2	165	400	41,140
Ontario	470	26,802	90	3,322	2,170	206,120
Manitoba	2,350	107,000	190	6,900	225	17,000
Saskatchewan	3,700	153,000	500	13,000	—	—
Alberta	6,450	320,000	300	12,600	11	1,200
British Columbia	230	8,100	9·2	275	—	—
Total, Canada	13,533·2	630,343	1,102·7	36,517	2,806	265,460

	Flaxseed		*Mixed grains*		*Soybeans*	
Provinces	*1,000 acres*	*1,000 bu.*	*1,000 acres*	*1,000 bu.*	*1,000 acres*	*1,000 bu.*
Prince Edward Island	—	—	85	4,930	—	—
Nova Scotia	—	—	5·4	281	—	—
New Brunswick	—	—	5	255	—	—
Quebec	—	—	126	6,369	—	—
Ontario	—	—	785	48,770	690	22,297
Manitoba	700	10,300	120	5,400	—	—
Saskatchewan	350	5,900	65	2,700	—	—
Alberta	100	2,200	150	8,000	—	—
British Columbia	—	—	4·4	180	—	—
Total, Canada	1,150	18,400	1,345·8	76,885	690	22,297

Provinces	Fodder corn 1,000 acres	Fodder corn 1,000 tons	Rapeseed 1,000 acres	Rapeseed 1,000 bu.	Sugar-beet 1,000 acres	Sugar-beet 1,000 tons
Prince Edward Island	6·3	92	—	—	—	—
Nova Scotia	8	108	—	—	—	—
New Brunswick	4	60	—	—	—	—
Quebec	209	3,171	—	—	9·6	176
Ontario	645	8,567	—	—	—	—
Manitoba	50	390	600	13,500	29	380
Saskatchewan	—	—	1,350	33,000	—	—
Alberta	25	470	1,450	33,500	35	788
British Columbia	29	480	63	140	—	—
Total, Canada	976·3	13,338	3,463	81,000	73·6	1,344

Livestock. In parts of Saskatchewan and Alberta stockraising is still carried on as a primary industry, but the livestock industry of the country at large is mainly a subsidiary of mixed farming. The following table shows the numbers of livestock (in 1,000) by provinces in July 1982:

Provinces	Milch cows	Other cattle	Sheep and lambs	Swine
Newfoundland	2·6	4·3	7·2	23·1
Prince Edward Island	23·9	70·1	7·5	113
Nova Scotia	35·7	105·3	44	145
New Brunswick	28·2	81·8	12·2	111
Quebec	695	952	120	3,140
Ontario	560	2,202	247	3,320
Manitoba	80·5	1,044·5	38·4	865
Saskatchewan	86	2,214	75	500
Alberta	162	3,859	205	1,150
British Columbia	91	687	61	235
Total	1,764·9	11,226	816·9	9,602·1

Net production of farm eggs in 1980, 488m. doz. ($410·1m.); 1981, 487·9m. doz. ($479·7m.).

Wool production (in tonnes), 1967, 1,618; 1968, 1,469; 1969, 1,460; 1970, 1,483; 1971, 1,623; 1972, 1,574; 1973, 1,482; 1974, 1,410; 1975, 1,266; 1976, 1,095; 1977, 938; 1978, 885; 1979, 1,147; 1980, 1,209; 1981, 1,300.

Dairying. The dairy products industry has shown a marked tendency towards centralization; the number of establishments decreased between 1961 and 1977 from 1,710 to 466 (72·8%), whereas the number of employees has decreased only 16·9%. Production, 1981: Creamery butter, 113,348 tonnes; cheddar cheese, 98,543 tonnes; concentrated whole milk products, 189,474 kl; skim milk powder, 136,688 tonnes.

Fruit Farming. The value of fruit production (excluding apples) in 1981 was (estimated in $1,000): Ontario, 54,465; British Columbia, 16,107 ; Quebec, 13,141; Nova Scotia, 9,271; New Brunswick, 3,849; Prince Edward Island, 776. Total apple production in Canada in 1981 was 461,354 tonnes.

Tobacco. Commercial production of tobacco is confined to Ontario and Quebec. Farm cash receipts in 1981 totalled $381m.

Forestry. The total area of land covered by forests is estimated at about 3,417,000 sq. km, of which 3,141,000 sq. km are classed as production forest land.

Lumber production (in 100 cu. ft) 1976, 49,132,000; 1977, 51,299,000; 1978, 55,054,000; 1979, 57,124,000; 1980, 55,151,000.

The volume of lumber shipments from sawmills and planing mills in 1980 was 17,098,365 bd ft valued at $4,004·8m. Pulp production was 19·9m. tonnes in 1980 and 20·73m. tonnes in 1979. In 1980 mill shipments of paper amounted to 13·1m. tonnes valued at $6,218,134,000.

Fur Trade. In 1980–81 (year ended 30 June), 5,517,633 pelts valued at $119,390,381, were taken. In wild-life pelt production beaver led in total value, followed by muskrat, fox, lynx and raccoon. The most important animal raised on fur farms is mink, with 99% of the total production. The value of pelts from fur farms in 1981 was $49,087,354, of which mink accounted for $44,450,500. There were, in 1981, 415 fur farms reporting fox and 679 mink.

Fisheries. During 1980, landings in Canadian commercial fisheries reached 1,340,311 tonnes. The landed value was $740·7m. and the estimated market value was $1,651·4m. The landed value of principal fish in 1980 was (in $1,000): Salmon, 125,967; cod, 150,962; lobster, 80,012; herring, 69,684; scallops, 68,496; freshwater fish, 48,352; halibut, 14,042. Shipment of fisheries' products, 1980, were valued at $1,274·9m.

Canadian Mines Handbook. Annual. Toronto, from 1931

INDUSTRY AND TRADE

Industry. Industry groups ranked by value of shipments, survey of 1980:

Industry	*Production workers*	*Wages ($1,000)*	*Cost of materials ($1,000)*	*Value of shipments ($1,000)*
Food and beverages	158,981	2,446,324	19,634,947	28,314,437
Tobacco products	5,407	99,016	644,179	1,212,249
Rubber and plastics	45,584	655,757	2,135,011	4,093,448
Leather industries	21,256	231,108	561,215	1,083,792
Textile industries	53,490	709,916	2,417,711	4,423,248
Knitting mills	18,682	198,228	506,100	944,703
Clothing industries	83,452	893,301	1,934,235	3,867,139
Wood industries	98,839	1,797,955	4,865,230	8,397,175
Furniture and fixtures	42,826	543,140	1,112,669	2,322,482
Paper and allied industries	99,071	1,986,629	6,785,485	14,502,818
Printing, publishing and allied industries	63,646	1,059,086	2,097,857	5,623,229
Primary metal industries	97,885	1,980,423	7,342,167	13,417,834
Metal fabricating industries	123,923	2,064,096	6,348,635	11,718,220
Machinery industries	73,356	1,277,807	4,038,160	7,649,222
Transport equipment	137,004	2,570,316	13,025,645	18,993,253
Electrical products industries	80,157	1,246,098	3,863,689	7,765,311
Non-metallic mineral products	40,775	743,007	1,723,592	4,225,184
Petroleum and coal products	8,277	203,685	12,975,221	14,530,329
Chemical and chemical prods.	45,603	831,782	5,785,917	11,218,598
Miscellaneous manufacturing	48,216	623,820	1,982,313	3,748,575
All industries	1,346,160	22,161,504	99,779,987	168,051,258

Value of shipments ($1m.) in 1981: Food and beverages, 32,153·3; Transport equipment, 22,478; Machinery, 8,211·7; Petroleum and coal products, 19,240·1; Paper and allied industries, 15,168·3; Primary metals, 14,245·5; Chemicals and chemical products, 12,661·3; Wood industries, 8,356; Electrical products, 8,497·3; Printing, publishing and allied industries, 6,281·6; Non-metallic mineral products, 4,741·2; Textiles, 4,916; Clothing, 3,966·7; Rubber and plastics, 4,435·2; Miscellaneous manufacturing, 4,085·6; Furniture and fixtures, 2,650·3; Tobacco products, 1,459·3; Leather industries, 1,246·3; Knitting mills, 938·8.

Labour. In Sept. 1982 the industrial distribution of the employed was estimated as follows (in 1,000): Service, 7,235; manufacturing, 1,906; trade, 1,795; transport, communication and other utilities, 865; construction, 623; public administration, 764; finance, insurance and real estate, 585; agriculture, 515; other primary industries, 265; total employed, 10,474; unemployed, 1,458.

Union returns filed for 1980 in compliance with the Corporations and Returns Act (1962), show 182 labour organizations reporting on 13,107 local union branches in Canada. Union membership in 1980 was 3·09m. 32·2% of the wage and salary workers in major industry groups were members of reporting labour organizations, with about 73·2% of the organized workers members of unions affiliated with the Canada Labour Congress. Over 1·55m. of the union members were in international unions, which have branches both in Canada and the USA and in most cases belong to central labour organizations in both countries.

It is generally established by legislation, both federal and provincial, that a trade union to which the majority of employees in a unit suitable for collective bargaining belong, is given certain rights and duties. An employer is required to meet and negotiate with such a trade union to determine wage-rates and other working conditions of his employees. The employer, the trade union and the employees affected are bound by the resulting agreement. If an impasse is reached in negotiation conciliation services provided by the appropriate government board are available. Generally, work stoppages may not take place until an established conciliation procedure has been carried out and are prohibited while an agreement is in effect. Almost 28% of the workers affected by collective agreements are in the manufacturing industry.

Freedom of association is a civil right in Canada, and under common law workers are at liberty to join unions and participate in their activities. This right has also been guaranteed by statutes which make it an offence to interfere with freedom of association.

Certain specific minimum standards in regard to working conditions are set by law, for the most part by provincial labour legislation. Minimum wages, maximum hours of work or an overtime rate of pay after a specified number of hours, minimum weekly rest periods and annual vacations with pay are established for the majority of workers.

Workmen injured in the course of employment or disabled by industrial disease are required to receive compensation under workmen's compensation laws which apply to most employees except agricultural workers. Benefits during the period of disability for work are set by law at a proportion (now 75%) of the workman's average earnings, subject to a maximum established in each province. Benefits (which also include monthly allowances to dependants in the case of the death of a workman caused by an accident or disease arising out of his employment) are paid out of an accident fund administered by a government board in each province. The fund is made up of contributions from employers according to an annual assessment rate, varying from a few cents to several dollars per $100 of payroll according to the hazards of the industry.

Dept. of Labour, *Working Conditions in Canadian Industry.* Annual. Ottawa

Commerce. In the past the custom tariff of Canada has been protective, with a preferential tariff in favour of the UK, the Dominions, a number of Crown Colonies, and the Irish and South African Republics. At the Imperial Economic Conference of 1932, held in Ottawa, the UK developed further the policy of preferential tariffs to the Dominions, and on the part of the latter there was a general lowering of the existing tariffs against certain lines of UK manufacturers. Canada is one of the signatories of the General Agreement on Tariffs and Trade (GATT) and of the Kennedy Round agreements.

Imports for home consumption and domestic exports (in Canadian $1,000) for calendar years (merchandise only):

	Imports	*Exports*		*Imports*	*Exports*
1960	5,842,695	5,255,575	1978	49,605,912	51,681,380
1970	13,951,903	16,820,098	1979	62,724,100	65,514,400
1975	34,690,714	32,466,068	1980	69,127,659	74,259,343
1976	37,444,389	37,575,693	1981 [1]	78,665,049	80,895,244
1977	42,155,973	43,505,799			

[1] Estimate

Exports (domestic) by countries in 1981 (in Canadian $1,000):

Australia	827,618
Bahamas	31,594
Bahrain	5,344
Bangladesh	56,589
Barbados	42,585
Belize	3,717
Bermuda	38,830
Britain	3,346,963
British Oceania	445
Cyprus	3,544
Falkland Islands	1
Fiji	2,787
Gambia	43
Ghana	21,463
Gibraltar	165
Guyana	19,136
Hong Kong	190,604
India	348,218
Ireland	138,379
Jamaica	82,831
Kenya	28,037
Leeward and Windward Islands	34,900
Malaysia	127,086
Malawi	1,310
Malta	3,105
Mauritius and Dependencies	1,076
New Zealand	140,797
Nigeria	101,669
Pakistan	92,045
Qatar	13,555
Sierra Leone	1,177
Singapore	149,280
South Africa, Republic of	261,641
Sri Lanka	34,471
Tanzania	17,960
Trinidad and Tobago	109,559
Uganda	491
Zambia	3,831
Afghánistán	171
Albania	1
Algeria	380,170
Angola	2,289
Argentina	177,664
Austria	60,992
Belgium and Luxembourg	856,302
Benin	2,567
Bolivia	10,412
Brazil	690,113
Bulgaria	12,178
Burma	2,869
Cameroon Republic	80,683
Chile	124,191
China	1,006,822
Colombia	201,823
Costa Rica	22,468
Cuba	452,787
Czechoslovakia	28,238
Denmark	95,059
Dominican Republic	49,432
Ecuador	96,265
Egypt (UAR)	132,022
El Salvador	19,705
Ethiopia	37,390
Finland	102,577
France	1,004,120
French Africa	12,866
French Guiana	59
French Oceania	5,644
French West Indies	3,322
Gabon	4,256
German Democratic Rep.	4,455
Germany, Fed. Rep. of	1,321,144
Greece	76,198
Greenland	5,408
Guatemala	18,553
Guinea	734
Haiti, Republic of	21,871
Honduras	21,251
Hungary	11,936
Iceland	9,839
Indonesia	95,463
Iran	22,325
Iraq	321,364
Israel	132,022
Italy	928,386
Ivory Coast	21,225
Japan	4,521,694
Jordan	16,954
Korea, North	—
Korea, South	446,874
Kuwait	83,339
Lebanon	53,325
Liberia	12,534
Libya	112,221
Madagascar	16,414
Mauritania	2,961
Mexico	734,185
Morocco	104,114
Mozambique	19,675
Netherlands	1,208,535
Netherlands Antilles	27,529
Nicaragua	16,813
Norway	428,149
Panama	52,413
Paraguay	3,017
Peru	93,685
Philippines	84,681
Poland	333,050
Portugal	93,233
Portuguese Africa	514
Puerto Rico	105,872
Romania	9,372
Saudi Arabia	460,661
Senegal	13,901
Somalia	3,590
Spain	207,693
Spanish Africa	22,180
St Pierre and Miquelon	20,980
Sudan	10,763
Suriname	5,822
Sweden	233,011
Switzerland	271,784
Syria	5,887
Taiwan	236,996
Thailand	117,602
Togo	818
Tunisia	74,306
Turkey	74,974
USSR	1,866,805
United Arab Emirates	52,969
USA	55,378,174
US Oceania	1,927
US Virgin Islands	39,646
Uruguay	18,416
Venezuela	829,193
Vietnam (South)	1,002
Yemen	1,309
Yugoslavia	84,631
Zaïre	51,689
Zimbabwe	6,862

Imports (for consumption) by countries in 1981 (in Canadian $1,000):

Australia	499,184
Bahamas	53,504
Bahrain	179
Bangladesh	7,459
Barbados	9,279
Belize	3,239
Bermuda	1,768
Britain	2,376,588
British Oceania	25
Cyprus	1,463
Fiji	12,312
Ghana	4,906
Gibraltar	76
Guyana	22,637
Hong Kong	674,535
India	107,011
Ireland	117,898
Jamaica	97,531
Kenya	12,898
Leeward and Windward Islands	1,824
Malaysia	100,031
Malawi	672
Malta	2,125
Mauritius and Dependencies	65
New Zealand	145,740
Nigeria	112,011
Pakistan	17,474
Singapore	174,629
South Africa, Republic of	402,723
Sri Lanka	17,467
Tanzania	5,103
Trinidad and Tobago	75,402
Uganda	455
Zambia	3,748

Afghánistán	187
Albania	1,260
Algeria	424,339
Argentina	79,389
Austria	90,471
Belgium and Luxembourg	297,089
Benin	16
Bolivia	18,493
Brazil	430,779
Bulgaria	3,239
Burma	164
Cameroon Republic	492
Chile	110,551
China	220,013
Colombia	83,394
Costa Rica	38,993
Cuba	192,219
Czechoslovakia	72,890
Denmark	159,448
Dominican Republic	17,796
Ecuador	47,094
Egypt (UAR)	6,604
El Salvador	25,135
Ethiopia	1,654
Finland	97,273
France	878,587
French Africa	674
French Oceania	521
French West Indies	104
Gabon	12,653
German Democratic Rep.	12,790
Germany, Fed. Rep. of	1,611,460
Greece	54,148
Greenland	552
Guatemala	35,985
Guinea	20,369
Haiti, Republic of	7,573
Honduras	35,464
Hungary	31,225
Iceland	6,511
Indonesia	36,961
Iran	2,702
Iraq	1,031
Israel	51,402
Italy	702,177
Ivory Coast	8,731
Japan	4,038,388
Korea, North	132
Korea, South	608,183
Kuwait	164,598
Lebanon	426
Liberia	772
Libya	149,629
Madagascar	347
Mexico	996,354
Morocco	15,242
Mozambique	842
Netherlands	295,763
Netherlands Antilles	45,801
Nicaragua	52,090
Norway	169,137
Panama	25,226
Paraguay	1,389
Peru	51,099
Philippines	108,682
Poland	73,956
Portugal	53,005
Puerto Rico	123,415
Romania	46,466
Saudi Arabia	2,272,750
Senegal	1,786
Spain	237,770
Spanish Africa	63
St Pierre and Miquelon	165
Sudan	444
Suriname	8,880
Sweden	445,164
Switzerland	424,013
Syria	130
Taiwan	729,194
Thailand	33,067
Tunisia	1,436
Turkey	10,946
USSR	77,669
United Arab Emirates	63,760
USA	54,350,280
US Oceania	60
US Virgin Islands	577
Uruguay	10,094
Venezuela	2,385,295
Vietnam, South	657
Yemen	114
Yugoslavia	30,870
Zaïre	606
Zimbabwe	2,176

Categories of imports in 1981, estimate (in Canadian $1m.):

Live animals	201·9	Fabricated materials, inedible	14,529·0
Food, feed, beverages and tobacco	4,979·2	End products, inedible	45,801·5
Crude materials, inedible	12,149·9	Special transactions	1,003·4

Categories of exports (Canadian produce) in 1981, estimate (in Canadian $1m.):

Live animals	228·7	Fabricated materials, inedible	30,534·6
Food, feed, beverages and tobacco	9,176·1	End products, inedible	25,129·0
Crude materials, inedible	15,168·2	Special transactions	658·6

Total trade of Canada with UK (British Department of Trade returns, in £1,000 sterling):

	1978	*1979*	*1980*	*1981*	*1982*
Imports to UK	1,088,897	1,260,057	1,412,156	1,508,756	1,439,619
Exports and re-exports from UK	740,508	766,430	758,367	844,978	851,703

Tourism. The number of visitors to Canada in 1981 was 41,953,000 (1980, 40,664,000). In 1981, 39,808,000 came from USA (1980, 38,501,000).

COMMUNICATIONS

Roads. The total highway mileage in Canada in 1976 was 549,462 (884,273 km). Of this total 442,615 miles (712,319 km) were surfaced and 106,453 miles (171,336 km) improved and other earth roads. Expenditure (1976) on roads, bridges, ferries, etc., reached a total of $4,449m. Federal and provincial governments supplied $2,905m., with the remainder contributed by municipal and other sources. Federal expenditure was chiefly devoted towards the upkeep of national-park roadways and nationally owned bridges and ferries, although for the 'Mackenzie Highway' from Grimshaw, Alberta, to Hay River, Northwest Territories, the federal government paid about 68% of the total cost. In general, however, highways are provincially controlled and maintained, and the responsibility of assisting municipalities and townships falls directly on the provinces.

The Alaska Highway is part of the Canadian highway system. For the Trans-Canada Highway *see* map in THE STATESMAN'S YEAR-BOOK, 1962.

Registered motor vehicles totalled 13,851,482 in 1981 (preliminary); they included 10,199,388 passenger cars and taxis, 3,137,987 trucks and buses and 406,871 motor cycles.

Urban Transit. In 1980 urban transit systems (motor bus, trolley coach, street car and subway operations) carried 1,307,199,000 fare passengers 653,276,722 km for an operating revenue of $1,060,568,834. In 1980, intercity and rural bus operations carried 33,282,000 fare passengers 3,622,933 vehicle-km, earning revenues of $3,946,127,000.

Railways. The total length of main track railways in Canada on 31 Dec. 1980 was 67,067 km. The total route km, including route duplicate, yardtrack and sidings, was 93,361.

Canada has 2 great trans-continental systems: the Canadian National Railway system (CN), a government-owned body which operates 34,830 km (1980) of the total first maintrack, and the Canadian Pacific Railway, a joint-stock corporation operating 24,410 km (1980). From 1 April 1978, a government funded organization known as Via Rail took over passenger services formerly operated by CP and CN.

Selected statistics of Canadian railways for 1980: Income from passengers carried $478,327,089; freight revenue, $4,134,073,877; total railway operating revenues, $5,333·8m.

Aviation. Civil aviation in Canada is under the jurisdiction of the federal government. The technical and administrative aspects are supervised by the Administrator of Air Transportation, while the economic functions are assigned to the Canadian Transportation Commission.

In 1980 Canadian airports handled 51,516,087 passengers, 131,208 kg of mail and 510,280 kg of cargo. Operating revenue (1980) was $3,984·7m.; operating expenditure, $3,797·5m.

Shipping. The registered shipping in Jan. 1982, including vessels for inland navigation, totalled 34,103 with a gross tonnage of 5,148,471. A total of 56,463 vessels (international shipping) visited Canadian ports in 1980, loading and unloading 218m. tonnes of cargo.

The major canals in Canada are those of the St Lawrence–Great Lakes waterway with their 7 locks, providing navigation for vessels of 25·75-ft draught from Montreal to Lake Ontario; the Welland Canal by-passing the Niagara River between Lake Ontario and Lake Erie with its 8 locks; and the Sault Ste Marie Canal and lock between Lake Huron and Lake Superior. These 16 locks overcome a drop of 582 ft from the head of the lakes to Montreal. The St Lawrence Seaway was opened to navigation on 1 April 1959 (*see* map in THE STATESMAN'S YEAR-BOOK, 1957). In 1981, traffic on the Montreal–Lake Ontario Section of the Seaway numbered 4,628 vessels carrying 50·6m. cargo tonnes; on the Welland Canal Section, 5,960 vessels with 58·9m. gross tonnes. Value of fixed assets was $666,555,842 and investments, $40,506,888 at 31 March 1982.

Coast Guard. The Canadian Coast Guard (formed in 1962) is responsible to the Minister of Transport. In 1982 it comprised 7 heavy icebreakers; a heavy icebreaker/cable repair vessel; 7 medium icebreakers; 3 light icebreakers; 25 aid tenders; 3 special shallow draft vessels; 60 search and rescue vessels (all types and sizes); 4 hovercraft and 34 helicopters.

Post. In May 1982 there were 8,285 postal facilities in operation and 6,500m. pieces of mail were processed. Gross revenue (estimate 1982–83) was $2,275m.; gross expenditure, $2,675m.

There were 919,143 miles (1,479,216 km) of telegraph wire in Canada in 1979 (including external cable landed in Canada). There were 16,449,825 telephones on 1 Aug. 1982.

Broadcasting. There were 706 originating stations operating in Canada at 31 March 1982, of which 94 were Canadian Broadcasting Corporation stations, 115 were CBC affiliates and 461 were privately owned and operated. Included were 396 AM radio stations, 198 FM radio stations, 112 television stations and 15 shortwave stations. Radio and television licence fees were abolished in 1953.

Wireless 'beam' stations are operated at Montreal for direct communications with Great Britain and Australia, and a station at Louisburg, N.S., provides a long-distance service to ships.

Cinemas (1980). There were 1,037 cinemas with a seating capacity of 615,346 and 287 drive-in theatres with a capacity of 141,266 cars.

Newspapers (1981). There were 121 daily newspapers, of which 107 were in English, 11 in French and 3 others.

JUSTICE, RELIGION, EDUCATION AND WELFARE

Justice. There is a Supreme Court in Ottawa, having general appellate jurisdiction in civil and criminal cases throughout Canada. There is an Exchequer Court, which is also a Court of Admiralty. There is a Superior Court in each province and county courts, with limited jurisdiction, in most of the provinces, all the judges in these courts being appointed by the Governor-General. Police, magistrates and justices of the peace are appointed by the provincial governments.

For the year ended 31 Dec. 1981, 2,168,201 Criminal Code Offences were reported and 393,573 persons were charged.

Canadian Legal and Directory. Toronto. Annual

Religion. Membership of the leading denominations in 1971:

Province	Roman Catholic	United Church of Canada	Anglican Church of Canada	Presbyterian	Lutheran
Newfoundland	190,960	101,805	144,445	3,055	515
Prince Edward Island	51,215	27,830	6,905	13,050	95
Nova Scotia	286,320	162,885	135,695	40,380	11,570
New Brunswick	331,290	85,185	69,260	13,155	1,875
Quebec	5,226,150	176,825	181,875	51,785	23,845
Ontario	2,568,695	1,682,820	1,220,535	540,035	267,225
Manitoba	242,855	256,560	123,015	30,825	64,735
Saskatchewan	258,630	274,285	87,210	20,805	90,850
Alberta	391,390	456,925	170,230	57,185	133,045
British Columbia	408,330	537,565	386,670	100,940	120,335
Yukon	4,670	3,110	4,645	690	925
Northwest Territories	14,385	3,005	12,685	445	725
Total, Canada	9,974,895	3,768,805	2,543,175	872,330	715,740

Other denominations: Baptist, 667,245; Greek Orthodox, 316,605; Jewish, 276,025; Ukrainian (Greek) Catholic, 227,730; Pentecostal, 220,390; Mennonite, 168,150; other, 1,817,220.

Education. The various provincial legislatures have power over education. These powers are subject to certain qualifications respecting the rights of denominational and minority language schools. Newfoundland and Quebec legislations provide for Roman Catholic and Protestant school boards. School Acts in Ontario, Saskatchewan and Alberta provide tax support for both public and separate schools. School board revenues derive from local taxation on real property and government grants from general provincial revenue.

Except in Quebec the number of private elementary and secondary schools is small; their enrolments in 1981–82 were less than 5% of the total elementary-secondary population. Indian and Northern Affairs Canada finances schools for Indian and Inuit children; the enrolment in 1981–82 was 35,658.

In 1980–81, 382,600 full-time regular students were enrolled in universities. In 1980 some 27,000 took first degrees in social sciences, commerce, economics, law, political science and geography; 17,000 in education; 9,500 in humanities; 7,300 in engineering and applied sciences; 5,500 in agriculture; 5,800 in health subjects; 4,400 in mathematics and physical sciences and 2,700 in fine and applied arts.

The following statistics give information, for 1981–82, about all elementary and secondary schools, public, federal and private:

Province	Schools	Teachers	Pupils
Newfoundland	657	7,801	145,574
Prince Edward Island	72	1,358	26,314
Nova Scotia	620	10,816	184,986
New Brunswick	477	7,736	151,169
Quebec	2,832	72,570	1,193,110
Ontario	5,297	94,383	1,890,235
Manitoba	821	12,007	219,167
Saskatchewan	1,066	11,326	211,460
Alberta	1,578	23,771	455,161
British Columbia	1,866	28,066	534,358
Yukon	25	270	5,121
Northwest Territories	71	690	12,581
National Defence (overseas)	10	240	3,232
Total	15,392	271,034	5,032,468

Association of Canadian Universities & Colleges. *Canadian Universities & Colleges.* Ottawa. Annual

Health. Canada achieves national health insurance through a series of interlocking provincial plans which qualify the provinces for federal financial support if they meet the minimum criteria of the federal legislation with respect to comprehensiveness of coverage with regard to services, universality of coverage with regard to people, accessibility to services uninhibited by excessive user charges, portability of benefits and non-profit administration by a public agency. There are also related, unconditional, federal contributions made by yielding income-tax from the provinces. The federal contributions to the provinces cover about 50% of the provincial costs for the insured services of the national Hospital Insurance and Medical Care Program. (In the health field the federal government also furnishes the provinces with *per capita* cash contributions towards the cost of extended health care services; *e.g.*, nursing home care, certain home care services; these are unconditional except that the provinces must provide appropriate information.

The Canadian approach to the development of a national health programme has been to progressively provide major segments of personal health care on a publicly financed basis to virtually the whole population, and this is achieved with the co-operation of the provinces, which exercise the primary constitutional prerogative in health matters.

The insurance programmes are designed to ensure that all residents of Canada have reasonable access to needed medical and hospital care on a prepaid basis. The insured services of the Hospital Insurance Programme, which commenced in 1958, include in-patient care (including necessary drugs, diagnostic tests, etc.); out-patient services, although optional under the national programmes, are insured in all provinces. Complementing the protection of the Hospital Insurance Programme is the Medical Care Programme, inaugurated in 1968, which covers all medically required services rendered by medical practitioners no matter where the services are rendered, and certain surgical–dental procedures undertaken by dental surgeons in hospital. All 10 provinces and the 2 northern territories are participating in both programmes, which provide health insurance coverage for over 99% of the population (or over 24m. people).

The approach taken by Canada is one of state-sponsored health insurance. Accordingly, the advent of the programmes produced little change in the ownership of hospitals, almost all of which are owned by non-governmental non-profit corporations, or in the rights and privileges of private medical practice. Patients are free to choose their own general practitioners and/or specialists without losing their insured benefits (there is a minor exception in Quebec involving the non-emergency services of a few physicians). Except for 0·5% of the population whose care is provided for under other legislation (such as serving members of the Canadian Armed Forces), all residents are eligible, regardless of whether they are in the work force. Benefits are available without upper limit so long as they are medically necessary, provided any registration or premium payment obligations are met. Benefits are also portable during any temporary absence from Canada anywhere in the world—subject to any limitation a province may impose upon treatment electively sought outside the particular province without prior approval. Provinces may prescribe limits on benefits payable for out-of-province care.

In addition to the benefits qualifying for federal contributions, provinces are free to provide additional benefits at their own discretion. Most provinces provide such benefits, which cover a variety of services (*e.g.*, optometric care, children's dental programme, drug benefits) depending upon the province. Most provinces fund their portion of health insurance costs out of general provincial revenues. Three provinces levy premiums which meet part of the provincial costs, 2 provinces impose a levy on employers, and 1 province utilizes part of its sales tax revenues for this purpose. Three provinces have nominal co-charges for short-term hospital care. Several provinces have charges for long-term hospital care geared, approximately, to the room and board portion of the OAS–GIS payments mentioned under Social Welfare.

Social Welfare. The Department of National Health and Welfare administers a number of social security programmes. Most notable among them are the Family Allowances programme, introduced in 1945 and amended in 1974; the Old Age Security programme, introduced in 1952 and to which were added the Guaranteed Income Supplement in 1966 and the Spouse's Allowance in 1975; the Canada Pension Plan which came into being in 1966 and the Child Tax Credit implemented in 1979. Social assistance and services programmes which are provided by the provinces and territories and (in some cases) by municipal governments, are cost-shared by the federal government under the Canada Assistance Plan, which was introduced in 1966.

The 1973 federal Family Allowances Act provides for the payment of a monthly Family Allowance ($26.91 in 1982) in respect of a dependent child under the age of 18 who is a resident of Canada, who is wholly or substantially maintained by a parent or guardian. At least one parent must be a Canadian citizen, or admitted to Canada as a permanent resident under the Immigration Act, or admitted to Canada for a period of not less than 1 year, if during that time his or her income is subject to Canadian Income Tax. Benefits are also paid under certain prescribed circumstances to Canadian citizens living abroad. A Special Allowance ($37·65 in 1982) is paid on behalf of a child under the age of 18 who is maintained by a welfare agency, a government department or an institution. In some cases, payment is made directly to a foster parent. The Special Allowance was paid on behalf of some 40,000 children across Canada in March 1982.

Family Allowances are considered as income for income-tax purposes for the parent who claims an exemption for the child. During the month of March 1982, over 3·5m. Canadian families (including 6·7m. eligible children) received Family Allowances from the Federal Government; the total FA bill for the 1981–82 fiscal year was just over $2,000m.

Family Allowance benefits are raised each year in Jan. in accordance with the Consumer Price Index; for 1983 and 1984, however, indexation will be limited to 6% and 5% respectively, in accordance with the federal policy on fiscal restraints announced in late 1982. The Family Allowances Act specifies that a provincial government may request the federal government to vary the allowance rates payable within that province subject to the fulfilment of stipulated conditions. Only the provinces of Alberta and Quebec have exercised this option.

In addition to Family Allowances, parents may receive a Child Tax Credit (CTC), administered through the Income Tax System by Revenue Canada. The CTC programme is designed to provide additional assistance in meeting the costs of raising children in low to middle income families. The maximum credit payable in 1982 (in respect of the 1981 taxation year) was $261 for each eligible child (*i.e.,* entitled to Family Allowances), where the net annual family income for the 1981 taxation year was less than $23,470; CTC entitlement is reduced by 5% of the amount by which the family's income exceeded this level. The credit and basic income levels are raised each year to reflect changes in the Consumer Price Index; for the 1982 taxation year, however, the maximum annual benefit, which would have been $293 per eligible child (in accordance with CPI increases), has increased by $50 per child to compensate for the limited indexing of Family Allowances for the next two years. The Child Tax Credit is paid in a single, non-taxable annual lump sum. It is estimated that approximately $1,000m. was paid out to approximately 2·5m. Canadian families in 1982 for the 1981 taxation year.

The Canada Pension Plan (CPP) is designed to provide workers with a basic level of income protection in the event of retirement, disability or death. Benefits are determined by the contributor's earnings and contributions made to the Plan, and are adjusted annually to reflect cost of living increases. Contribution is compulsory for most employed and self-employed Canadians 18 to 65 years of age. The Canada Pension Plan does not operate in Quebec, which has exercised its constitutional prerogative to establish a similar plan, the Quebec Pension Plan (QPP), to operate in lieu of CPP; there is reciprocity between the two to ensure coverage for all adult Canadians in the labour force.

CPP/QPP contributions are deductible for income tax purposes, while benefits are taxable. Benefits are adjusted annually to fully reflect increases in the Consumer Price Index.

Both CPP and QPP are funded by equal contributions of 1·8% of pensionable earnings from the employer and 1·8% from the employee (self-employed persons contribute the full 3·6%), in addition to the interest on the investment of excess funds. In 1982, the range of yearly pensionable earnings was from $1,600 to $16,500; a person who earned and contributed at less than the maximum level receives monthly benefits at rates lower than the maximum allowable under CPP/QPP.

For CPP, an advisory committee representing employers, employees, self-employed persons and the public regularly reviews the operation of the plan, the state of investments and the adequacy of coverage and benefits, and reports to the Minister of National Health and Welfare. CPP authorizes reciprocal agreements with other countries to achieve portability of pensions. Such agreements have been made with Italy, France and Portugal, and agreements with the US and Greece have been signed, but are not yet (1982) in force. In general, parallel provisions apply under QPP. In March 1982, close to 1·5m. Canadians received Canada Pension Plan benefits; an additional 400,000 persons received Quebec Pension Plan benefits. Total expenditures during 1981–82 were just under $2,500m. for CPP and approximately $850m. for QPP.

The Old Age Security (OAS) pension is payable to persons 65 years of age and over who satisfy the residence requirements stipulated in the Old Age Security Act. The amount payable, whether full or partial, is also governed by stipulated conditions, as is the payment of an OAS pension to a recipient who absents himself from Canada. OAS pensioners with little or no income apart from OAS may, upon application, receive a full or partial supplement known as the Guaranteed Income Supplement (GIS). Entitlement is normally based on the pensioner's income in the preceding year, calculated in accordance with the Income Tax Act. The spouse of an OAS pensioner, aged 60 to 64, meeting the same residence requirements as those stipulated for OAS, may be eligible for a full or partial Spouse's Allowance (SA). SA is payable, on application, the annual combined income of the couple being subject to an income test which does not include the OAS pension, the Guaranteed Income Supplement or the Spouse's Allowance.

The OAS pension is taxable; GIS and SA are not taxable. However, they must be included in computing the net income of a dependant for income-tax purposes. OAS, GIS and SA are subject to an increase every Jan., April, July and Oct. to reflect increases in the Consumer Price Index. In 1983 and 1984 adjustments will be limited to 6% and 5% respectively.

In Oct. 1982, the basic OAS pension was $246·92 monthly; the maximum Guaranteed Income Supplement was $247·89 monthly for a single pensioner or a married pensioner whose spouse was not receiving a pension or a Spouse's Allowance, and $191·12 monthly for each spouse of a married couple where both are pensioners. The maximum Spouse's Allowance for the same quarter was $438·04 monthly (equal to the basic pension plus the maximum GIS married rate). Total OAS expenditure for the 1981–82 financial year was $8,500m.

Under the Canada Assistance Plan, the federal government pays 50% of the cost, to the provinces, of assistance to persons in need; welfare services provided to persons who are in need or likely to become in need if they do not receive such services (welfare services means services having as their object the lessening, removal or prevention of the causes and effects of poverty, child neglect or dependence on public assistance); and work activity projects which are designed to improve the employability of persons who have unusual difficulty in finding or retaining jobs or in undertaking job training.

'Need' is defined by each province and is determined by the 'budget deficit' method, that is, the difference between an applicant's requirements and his income and resources. The rates of assistance payable are also determined by provincial authorities and are non-taxable. Provinces generally adjust social assistance rates once a year in accordance with certain economic indicators.

In addition to persons in need as defined in the Plan, federal contributions may be made towards agency costs of providing welfare services to persons who are likely to become in need, if such services are not provided. The amount of federal subsidy is dependent on the proportion of eligible persons as determined by the use of an income test or a pre-determined income level for different sized families.

In March 1982, close to 1·5m. Canadians (representing 770,000 households) were in receipt of direct financial assistance from provincial programmes shareable under the Canada Assistance Plan. Total payments to the provinces under the Plan (including General Assistance, Homes for Special Care, Child Welfare, Health

Care, Welfare Services and Work Activity) for the 1981–82 financial year were over $2,600m.; this amount includes the estimated value of income tax points transferred to the province of Quebec by the Department of Finance under the Interim Arrangements Act.

Unemployment Insurance covers about 95% of workers. To be insurable, workers must be employed by the same employer for at least 15 hours a week or make at least $70·00 a week (1982). Neither the self-employed nor workers over 65 may insure their earnings. Benefit rate is 60% of average weekly insurable earnings. Maximum weekly benefit (1982) $210.

Workers' compensation coverage is compulsory for employees in specified trades and industries. Maximum compensation is 75% of gross earnings except in Quebec, Alberta and New Brunswick where it is 90% of net earnings.

The New Horizons Program, established in 1972 and administered by the Department of National Health and Welfare, is designed to encourage the self-determination and community involvement of retired Canadians. From inception late in 1972 until March 1982, close to $102m. had been approved for over 16,000 projects.

DIPLOMATIC REPRESENTATIVES

Of Canada in Great Britain (Macdonald House., Grosvenor Sq., London, W1X 0AB)
High Commissioner: Donald C. Jamieson.

Of Great Britain in Canada (80 Elgin St., Ottawa, K1P 5K7)
High Commissioner: Lord Moran, KCMG.

Of Canada in USA (1746 Massachusetts Ave., NW, Washington, D.C., 20036)
Ambassador: Allan Gotlieb.

Of the USA in Canada (100 Wellington St., Ottawa)
Ambassador: Paul H. Robinson, Jr.

Of Canada to the United Nations
Ambassador: Gérard Pelletetier.

Books of Reference

Statistical Information: Statistics Canada, Ottawa, has been the official central statistical organization for Canada since 1918. The Bureau, which reports to Parliament through the Minister of Industry, Trade and Commerce, serves as the statistical agency for federal government departments; co-ordinates the statistics of the provincial governments along national lines; and channels all Canadian statistical data to internal organizations. *Statistician Chief of Canada:* Dr Peter G. Kirkham.

Publications of Statistics Canada are classified as periodical (issued more frequently than once a year), annual, biennial and occasional publications. The occasional publications frequently supplement the annual reports and usually contain historical information. A complete list is contained in the 1978–79 edition of the Statistics Canada catalogue and supplements, available on request. Official publications include:

The Canada Year Book. Annual, from 1905
Canada, Official Handbook. Annual, from 1930
Canadian Statistical Review. Monthly, with weekly supplements, from 1948
1966 Census of Canada. Ottawa, 1967
1976 Census of Canada. Ottawa, 1977
Tenth Decennial Census of Canada, 1961. Ottawa, 1962
Eleventh Decennial Census of Canada, 1971. Ottawa, 1972
Atlas and Gazetteer of Canada. Dept. of Energy, Mines and Resources. Ottawa, 1969
Cambridge History of the British Empire. Vol. VI. Canada and Newfoundland. Cambridge, 1930
Canadian Almanac and Directory. Toronto. Annual
Canadian Annual Review. Annual, from 1960
Canadian Dictionary: French–English. Toronto, 1970
Canadiana; A List of Publications of Canadian Interest. National Library, Ottawa. Monthly, with annual cumulation. 1951 ff.
National Reference Book on Canadian Business Personalities. 11th ed. Montreal, 1969

Cook, R., *French-Canadian Nationalism; An Anthology*. Toronto, 1970.—*The Maple Leaf Forever; Essays on Nationalism and Politics in Canada*. Toronto, 1971
Creighton, Donald G., *Dominion of the North: A History of Canada*. New ed. Toronto, 1957.—*The Empire of the St Lawrence*. Toronto, 1956.—*Canada's First Century*. Toronto, 1970.—*Towards the Discovery of Canada*. Toronto, 1974
Dictionnaire Bélisle de la langue française au Canada; dictionnaire oxford. 1970
Dictionnaire canadien; français–anglais–français. Toronto, 1962
Encyclopedia Canadiana. 10 vols. Rev. ed. Ottawa, 1967
Hardy, W. G., *From Sea to Sea; Canada, 1850–1920: The Road to Nationhood*. Toronto, 1960
Hawkins, F., *Canada and Immigration*. Montreal and London, 1972
Hockin, T. A., *Government in Canada*. London, 1976
Keenleyside, H. L., *Canada and the United States*. Rev. ed. New York, 1952
Kerr, D. G. G., *Historical Atlas of Canada*. Toronto, 1960
Lower, A. R. M., *Colony to Nation: A History of Canada*. 4th ed. Toronto, 1964
Lumsden, I. (ed.), *Close the 49th Parallel, etc.; The Americanization of Canada*. Toronto, 1970
Mallory, J. R., *The Structure of Canadian Government*. Toronto, 1971
McInnis, E., *Canada: A Political and Social History*. Rev. ed. Toronto, 1959
MacLennan, Hugh, *Seven Rivers of Canada: the Mackenzie, the St Lawrence, the Ottawa, the Red, the Saskatchewan, the Fraser, the St John*. Toronto, 1961
Moir, J., and Saunders, R., *Northern Destiny: A History of Canada*. Toronto, 1970
Morton, W. L., *The Kingdom of Canada; A General History from Earliest Times*. Toronto, 1969
Putnam, D. F., *Canadian Regions. A Geography of Canada*. 2nd ed. Toronto, 1954.—*Canada: A Regional Analysis*. Toronto, 1970
Urquhart, M. C., and Buckley, K. A. H. (ed.), *Historic Statistics of Canada*. Toronto, 1965

National Library: The National Library of Canada, Ottawa, Ontario. *Librarian:* J. Guy Sylvestre.

CANADIAN PROVINCES

The 10 provinces have each a separate parliament and administration, with a Lieut.-Governor, appointed by the Governor-General in Council at the head of the executive. They have full powers to regulate their own local affairs and dispose of their revenues, provided only they do not interfere with the action and policy of the central administration. Among the subjects assigned exclusively to the provincial legislatures are: the amendment of the provincial constitution, except as regards the office of the Lieut.-Governor; property and civil rights; direct taxation for revenue purposes; borrowing; management and sale of Crown lands; provincial hospitals, reformatories, etc.; shop, saloon, tavern, auctioneer and other licences for local or provincial purposes; local works and undertakings, except lines of ships, railways, canals, telegraphs, etc., extending beyond the province or connecting with other provinces, and excepting also such works as the Dominion Parliament declares are for the general good; marriages, administration of justice within the province; education.

Local Government. Under the terms of the British North America Act the provinces are given full powers over local government. All local government institutions are, therefore, supervised by the provinces, and are incorporated and function under provincial acts.

The acts under which municipalities operate vary from province to province. A municipal corporation is usually administered by an elected council headed by a mayor or reeve, whose powers to administer affairs and to raise funds by taxation and other methods are set forth in provincial laws, as is the scope of its obligations to, and on behalf of, the citizens. Similarly, the types of municipal corporations, their official designations and the requirements for their incorporation vary between provinces. The following table sets out the classifications as at 1 Jan. 1977.

Type and size of group	*Nfld.*	*PEI*	*NS*	*NB*	*Que.*	*Ont.*	*Man.*
Type:							
Regional municipalities	—	—	—	—	75	39	—
Metropolitan and regional municipalities[1]	—	—	—	—	3	12	—
Counties and regional districts	—	—	—	—	72	27	—
Unitary municipalities	129	36	65	112	1,500	784	185
Cities	2	1	3	6	64	45[2]	5
Towns	127[3]	8	38	21	195	144	35
Villages	—	27	—	85	242	120	40
Rural municipalities[4]	—	—	24	—	999	475	105
Quasi-municipalities[5]	171	—	—	—	—	13	17
Total	300	36	65	112	1,575	836	202
Population size group (1976 census):							
Unitary municipalities—							
Over 100,000	—	—	1	—	4	17	1
50,000 to 99,999	1	—	2	2	14	14	—
10,000 to 49,999	5	1	17	5	72	76	3
Under 10,000	123	35	45	105	1,410	677	181
Total	129	36	65	112	1,500	784	185

Type and size of group	*Sask.*	*Alta.*	*BC*	*YT*	*NWT*	*Canada*
Type:						
Regional municipalities	—	—	28	—	—	142
Metropolitan and regional municipalities[1]	—	—	—	—	—	15
Counties and regional districts	—	—	28	—	—	127
Unitary municipalities	783	327	140	3	7	4,071
Cities	11	10	33	2	1	183
Towns	135	102	10	1	4	820
Villages	344	167	59	—	2	1,086
Rural municipalities[4]	293	48	38	—	—	1,982
Quasi-municipalities[5]	7	22	—	4	10	244
Total	790	349	168	7	17	4,457
Population size group (1976 census):						
Unitary municipalities—						
Over 100,000	2	2	3	—	—	30
50,000 to 99,999	—	—	9	—	—	42
10,000 to 49,999	6	14	26	1	—	227
Under 10,000	775	311	102	2	7	3,772
Total	783	327	140	3	7	4,071

[1] Includes urban communities in Quebec; and Metropolitan Toronto, regional municipalities and the district municipality in Ontario.
[2] Includes the 5 boroughs of Metropolitan Toronto.
[3] Includes 11 rural districts.
[4] Includes municipalities in Nova Scotia; parishes, townships, united townships and municipalities in Quebec; townships in Ontario; rural municipalities in Manitoba and Saskatchewan; municipal districts and counties in Alberta; and districts in British Columbia.
[5] Includes local government communities, local improvement districts and the metropolitan area in Newfoundland; improvement districts in Ontario and Alberta; local government districts in Manitoba; local improvement districts in Saskatchewan and the Yukon Territory; and hamlets in the Northwest Territories.

ALBERTA

HISTORY. The southern half of the province of Alberta was part of Rupert's land which was granted by royal charter in 1670 to the Hudson's Bay Company. The intervention by the North West Company in the fur trade after 1783 led to the establishment of trading posts. In 1869 Rupert's land was transferred from the Hudson's Bay Company (which had absorbed its rival in 1821) to the new

Dominion, and in the following year this land was combined with the former Crown land of the North Western Territories to form the Northwest Territories.

In 1882 'Alberta' first appeared as a provisional 'district', consisting of the southern half of the present province. In 1905 the Athabasca district to the north was added when provincial status was granted to Alberta.

Four parties have held office: the Liberals 1905–21; the United Farmers 1921–35; Social Credit 1935–71, and Progressive Conservative since Sept. 1971.

AREA AND POPULATION. The area of the province is 661,188 sq. km; 644,392 sq. km being land area and 16,796 sq. km water area. The population (estimate 1 June 1982) was 2,315,100; the urban population, centres of 1,000 or over, was 1,727,545 and the rural 510,179. Population of the principal cities (1 June 1982): Calgary, 623,133; Edmonton, 551,314; Lethbridge, 56,500; Red Deer, 48,562; Medicine Hat, 40,380; Fort McMurray, 33,576; St Albert, 32,982 and Grande Prairie, 24,263.

Vital statistics, *see* p. 269.

Religion, *see* p. 286.

CONSTITUTION AND GOVERNMENT. The constitution of Alberta is contained in the British North America Act of 1867, and amending Acts; also in the Alberta Act of 1905, passed by the Parliament of the Dominion of Canada, which created the province out of the then Northwest Territories. All the provisions of the British North America Act, except those with respect to school lands and the public domain, were made to apply to Alberta as they apply to the older provinces of Canada. On 1 Oct. 1930 the natural resources were transferred from the Dominion to provincial government control. The province is represented by 6 members in the Senate and 21 in the House of Commons of Canada.

The executive is vested nominally in the Lieut.-Governor, who is appointed by the federal government, but actually in the Executive Council or the Cabinet of the legislature. Legislative power is vested in the Assembly in the name of the Queen.

Members of the Legislative Assembly are elected by the universal vote of adults over the age of 18 years.

There are 79 members in the legislature (elected 2 Nov. 1982): 75 Progressive Conservative, 2 New Democratic Party, 2 Independent.

Lieut.-Governor: His Hon. Frank Lynch-Staunton (sworn in 4 Oct. 1979).
Flag: Blue with the shield of the province in the centre.

The members of the Ministry (all Progressive Conservative) are as follows:

Premier, President of Executive Council: Hon. Peter Lougheed.

Provincial Treasurer: Hon. L. D. Hyndman. *Attorney-General and Government House Leader:* Hon. N. Crawford. *Hospitals and Medical Care:* Hon. D. J. Russell. *Transportation:* Hon. M. E. Moore. *Municipal Affairs:* Hon. J. G. J. Koziak. *Federal and Intergovernmental Affairs, Deputy Government House Leader:* Hon. J. D. Horsman. *Economic Development:* Hon. H. Planche. *Advanced Education:* Hon. D. Johnston. *Education:* Hon. D. King. *Labour:* Hon. L. G. Young. *Public Works, Supply and Services:* Hon. T. W. Chambers. *Tourism and Small Business:* Hon. J. A. Adair. *Energy:* Hon. J. B. Zaozirny. *Agriculture:* Hon. E. L. Fjordbotten. *Utilities and Telecommunications:* Hon. R. J. Bogle. *Social Services and Community Health:* Hon. Dr P. N. Webber. *Housing:* Hon. L. R. Shaben. *International Trade:* Hon. H. A. Schmid. *Consumer and Corporate Affairs:* Hon. C. E. Osterman. *Environment:* Hon. F. D. Bradley. *Solicitor-General:* Hon. G. L. Harle. *Culture:* Hon. M. J. LeMessurier. *Recreation and Parks:* Hon. P. Trynchy. *Minister responsible for Native Affairs:* Hon. M. G. Pahl. *Manpower:* Hon. E. D. Isley. *Associate Minister of Public Lands and Wildlife:* Hon. D. Sparrow. *Minister responsible for Workers' Health, Safety and Compensation:* Hon. B. W. Diachuk. *Minister responsible for Personnel Administration:* Hon. G. P. Stevens. *Minister without Portfolio:* Hon. W. E. Payne.

Local Government. The local government units are City, Town, New Town,

Village, Summer Village, County, Municipal District and Improvement District.

There are 12 cities in Alberta, namely: Calgary, Camrose, Drumheller, Edmonton, Fort McMurray, Grande Prairie, Lethbridge, Lloydminster, Medicine Hat, Red Deer, St Albert and Wetaskiwin. These cities operate under the Municipal Government Act. The governing body consists of a mayor and a council of from 6 to 20 members. A city can be incorporated by order of the Lieut.-Governor-in-Council. A population of 10,000 is required.

There are no limits of area specified in the statutes for any of the different local government units. The population requirement for a Town as specified in the Municipal Government Act is 1,000 people, and the area at incorporation is that of the original village.

A Village must contain 75 separate and occupied dwellings. The Municipal Government Act requires each dwelling to have been occupied continuously for a period of at least 6 months. A Summer Village must contain 50 separate dwellings.

A rural county area is an area incorporated through an order of the Lieut.-Governor-in-Council under the provisions of the County Act. One board of councillors deal with both municipal and school affairs.

A rural Municipal District is an area which has been incorporated under the Municipal Government Act. In Municipal Districts separate boards control municipal and school affairs.

Areas not incorporated as counties or Municipal Districts are termed Improvement Districts or Special Areas. Sparsely populated, such districts are administered and taxed by the Department of Municipal Affairs of the provincial government. There are no requirements as to the minimum number of residents of a County or Municipal District.

FINANCE. The budgetary revenue and expenditure (in Canadian $) for years ending 31 March were as follows:

	1978–79 [1]	*1979–80*	*1980–81*	*1981–82*	*1982–83* [1]
Revenue	4,801,000,000 [2]	5,668,000,000 [2]	6,578,000,000 [2]	6,367,000,000 [2]	7,961,000,000 [2,3]
Expenditure	3,704,000,000	4,665,000,000	5,561,000,000	6,703,000,000	8,719,000,000

[1] Estimates. [2] Excludes funds allocated to Alberta Heritage Savings Trust Fund.
[3] Excludes funds allocated to Natural Gas Rebates Fund.

Personal income *per capita* (1981), $12,346.

ENERGY AND NATURAL RESOURCES

Oil. In 1981, 64,476,000 cu. metres of crude oil and condensate were produced with gross sales value of $8,225,022,000. Alberta produced 86·2% of Canada's oil output in 1981. Production of natural gas by-product was 18,605,000 cu. metres, valued at $2,357,686,000.

Major deposits of oil sands are found in areas totalling 105,320 sq. km in northern and eastern Alberta. There are 4 major deposits of oil sands, the Athabasca, Cold Lake, Peace River and Buffalo Head Hills deposits; total area, 105,320 sq. km. A limited part of the deposits along the Athabasca River can be exploited through open-pit mining. The rest of the Athabasca, and all the deposits in the other areas, are deeper reserves which must be developed through in situ techniques. These reserves reach depths of 760 metres.

One recovery plant, situated 25 miles north of Fort McMurray, began production in 1967. The deposit being produced is sufficiently close to the surface to permit strip mining. A second plant, to produce 20,000 cu. metres per day of synthetic crude oil, began production in 1978.

Gas. Natural gas is found in abundance in numerous localities. In 1981, 72,451m. cu. metres valued at $5,728,039,000 were produced.

Minerals. In 1981 the ultimate remaining recoverable coal resources of Alberta were estimated at 14,700m. tonnes; the proved remaining recoverable reserves were estimated at 47,000m. tonnes.

Value of total mineral production increased from $16,378·97m. in 1980 to $17,571,382,000 in 1981.

Agriculture. Of the surveyed area of the province (about 85m. acres) approximately 80m. acres may be classed as capable of agricultural development. Up to the present, however, only 40% of this area has been brought under cultivation.

For particulars of agricultural production and livestock, *see under* CANADA, pp. 278–80. Farm cash receipts in 1981 totalled $3,876,253,000, of which crops contributed $2,106,657,000; livestock and products, $1,708,844,000, and other sources, $65,292,000.

Forestry. Alberta has an estimated net merchantable volume of 1,700m. cu. metres of timber comprised of 700m. cu. metres of hardwood and 1,000m. cu. metres of softwood. In 1980–81, 3,901,113 cu. metres of lumber were produced.

Fisheries. The lakes of the province contain whitefish, pike and tullibee. Commercial catches are marketed through the Freshwater Fish Marketing Corporation which was inaugurated in May 1969 as the result of an agreement between the federal government and the provinces for the buying and exporting of freshwater fish. Marketed value of commercially caught fish 1981–82 was $3,172,156. This value includes fish not marketed through the corporation.

INDUSTRY. The leading manufacturing industries are food and beverages, petroleum refining, metal fabricating, wood industries, primary metal, chemical and chemical products and non-metallic mineral products industries. There were in 1979 approximately 2,305 manufacturing establishments, in which were employed about 77,345 persons, who earned in salaries and wages $1,321,102,000.

Manufacturing shipments had a total value of $12,958·1m. in 1981. Chief among these shipments were: Food and beverages, $3,363·2m.; petroleum and coal products, $2,841·3m.; chemicals and chemical products, $1,383·2m.; primary metals, $821·1m.; metal fabricating, $841·3m.; non-metallic mineral products, $710·2m.; machinery, $577·6m.; wood, $556·4m.; other, $1,728·1m.

Total retail sales (1981) $10,906·4m.

Tourism is of increasing importance and in 1981 contributed $1,350m. to the economy.

COMMUNICATIONS

Roads. In 1981 there were 150,862 km of roads and highways, including 99,165 km gravelled and 14,076 km paved.

At 31 March 1982 there were 2,026,990 motor vehicles registered, including 1,199,582 passenger cars, 531,849 public and commercial vehicles, 239,920 trailers and 55,639 motor cycles.

Railways. In 1981 the length of main railway lines was 10,857 km. In 1982 there was a rail rapid transit network in Edmonton (9·4 km) and Calgary (13 km).

Post and Telecommunications. Alberta's modern telephone system is owned and operated by the provincial government, except in the city of Edmonton (owned and operated by Edmonton) and some rural lines. There were 1,851,325 telephones in service in April 1982.

JUSTICE AND EDUCATION

Justice. The Supreme Judicial authority of the province is the Court of Appeal. Judges of the Court of Appeal and Court of Queen's Bench are appointed by the Dominion Government and hold office until retirement at the age of 75. There are courts of lesser jurisdiction in both civil and criminal matters. The Court of Queen's Bench has full jurisdiction over civil proceedings. A Provincial Court which has jurisdiction in civil matters up to $1,000 is presided over by provincially appointed judges. Juvenile Courts have power to try boys and girls 16 and under for offences against the Juvenile Delinquents Act.

The jurisdiction of all criminal courts in Alberta is enacted in the provisions of the Criminal Code. The system of procedure in civil and criminal cases conforms as nearly as possible to the English system.

Education. Schools of all grades are included under the term of public school (including those in the separate school system which are publicly supported). The same board of trustees controls the schools from kindergarten to university entrance. In 1980–81 there were 417,016 pupils enrolled in elementary, junior high schools and high schools. The University of Alberta (in Edmonton), organized in 1907, had, in 1981–82, 19,571 full-time students. The University of Calgary, formerly part of the University of Alberta and autonomous from April 1966, had in 1981–82, 12,106 full-time students. The University of Lethbridge, organized in 1966, had in 1981–82, 1,771 full-time students. The full-time enrolment at Alberta's 10 public colleges totalled 11,652 students in 1981–82.

Books of Reference

Statistical Information: The Alberta Bureau of Statistics (Dept. of Treasury, Edmonton), which was established in 1939, collects, compiles and distributes information relative to Alberta. *Director:* Harvey W. Ford. Among its publications are: *Alberta Statistical Review* (Annual).—*Alberta Statistical Review* (Quarterly).—*Alberta Economic Accounts* (Annual).—*Alberta Pay and Benefits Survey* (Annual).—*Retail and Service Trade Statistics, Alberta* (Annual).—*Alberta Fact Sheet* (Annual).—*Principal Manufacturing Statistics, Alberta* (Annual).—*Population Projections, Alberta* (Occasional).—*Quarterly Population Growth, Alberta* (Quarterly).—*Place-to-Place Price Comparisons for Selected Alberta Communities* (Annual).

Dept. of Economic Development and Dept. of Federal and Intergovernmental Affairs, *Alberta Profile.* Edmonton, 1980

Hardy, W. G., *Alberta Golden Jubilee Anthology.* Toronto, 1955
Irving, J. A., *The Social Credit Movement in Alberta.* Toronto, 1959
Kroetsch, R., *Alberta.* Toronto, 1968
Macpherson, C. B., *Democracy in Alberta.* 2nd ed. Toronto, 1962
Nesbitt, L. D., *Tides in the West [history of the Alberta Wheat Pool].* Saskatoon, 1962

BRITISH COLUMBIA

HISTORY. Vancouver Island was organized as a colony in 1849; the mainland as far as the watershed of the Rocky Mountains was organized as a colony following a gold rush on the Fraser River in 1858. The two were united as the colony of British Columbia in 1866; this became a Canadian Province in 1871.

AREA AND POPULATION. British Columbia has an area of 948,596 sq. km. The capital is Victoria. The province is bordered westerly by the Pacific ocean and Alaska Panhandle, northerly by the Yukon and Northwest Territories, easterly by the Province of Alberta and southerly by the USA along the 49th parallel. A chain of islands, the largest of which are Vancouver Island and the Queen Charlotte Islands, affords protection to the mainland coast.

The June 1981 census population was 2,744,467.

The principal cities and their populations (1981) are as follows: Greater Vancouver, 1,268,183; Greater Victoria, 233,481; Prince George, 67,559; Kamloops, 64,048; Kelowna, 59,196; Nanaimo, 47,069; Penticton, 23,181; Vernon, 19,987; Port Alberni, 19,892; Prince Rupert, 16,197; Cranbrook, 15,915; Dawson Creek, 11,373.

Vital statistics, *see* p. 269.

Religion, *see* p. 286.

CONSTITUTION AND GOVERNMENT. British Columbia (then known as New Caledonia) originally formed part of the Hudson's Bay Company's concession. In 1849 Vancouver Island and in 1858 British Columbia were constituted Crown Colonies; in 1866 the two colonies amalgamated. The British North America Act of 1867 provided for eventual admission into Canadian Confederation, and on 20 July 1871 British Columbia became the sixth province of the Dominion.

British Columbia has a unicameral legislature of 57 elected members. Government policy is determined by the Executive Council responsible to the Legislature. The Lieut.-Governor is appointed by the Governor-General of Canada, usually for a term of 5 years, and is the head of the executive government of the province.

Lieut.-Governor: The Hon. Henry P. Bell-Irving, DSO, OBE.

Flag: A banner of the arms, *i.e.*, blue and white wavy stripes charged with a setting sun in gold, across the top of a Union Flag with a gold coronet in the centre.

The Legislative Assembly is elected for a maximum term of 5 years. Every male or female Canadian citizen 18 years and over, having resided a minimum of 6 months in the province, duly registered, is entitled to vote. Representation of the parties at 20 Oct. 1981: Social Credit Party, 31; New Democratic Party, 26; total, 57.

The province is represented in the Federal Parliament by 28 members in the House of Commons, and 6 Senators.

The Executive Council was composed as follows, Sept. 1982:

Premier: William Richards Bennett.

Deputy Premier and Human Resources: Grace McCarthy.

Agriculture and Food: Harvey W. Schroeder. *Attorney-General:* Allan Williams. *Consumer and Corporate Affairs:* James J. Hewitt. *Education:* William Vander Zalm. *Energy, Mines and Petroleum Resources:* Brian Smith. *Environment:* Stephen Rogers. *Finance:* Hugh A. Curtis. *Forests:* Thomas M. Waterland. *Health:* James Nielsen. *Industry and Small Business Development:* Donald M. Phillips. *Intergovernmental Relations:* Garde B. Gardom. *Labour:* Robert H. McClelland. *Lands, Parks and Housing:* Anthony J. Brummet. *Municipal Affairs:* John H. Heinrich. *Provincial Secretary:* James R. Chabot. *Tourism:* Claude Richmond. *Transportation and Highways:* Alexander V. Fraser. *Universities, Science and Communications:* Patrick L. McGeer.

Agent-General in London: Alexander H. Harte, QC (British Columbia House, 1 Regent St., London, SW1Y 4NS).

Local Government. Vancouver City was incorporated by statute and operates under the provisions of the Vancouver Charter of 1953 and amendments. This is the only incorporated area in British Columbia not operating under the provisions of the Municipal Act. Under this Act municipalities are divided into the following classes: *(a)* a village with a population between 500 and 2,500, governed by a council consisting of a mayor and 4 aldermen; *(b)* a town with a population between 2,500 and 5,000, governed by a council consisting of a mayor and 4 aldermen; *(c)* a city where the population exceeds 5,000 governed by a council consisting of a mayor and 6 or 8 aldermen depending on population; *(d)* a district where the area exceeds 810 hectares and the average density is less than 5 persons per hectare, governed by a council consisting of a mayor and 6 or 8 aldermen depending on population.

There are two other forms of local government: the regional district covering a number of areas both incorporated and unincorporated, governed by a board of directors; and the improvement district governed by a board of 3 trustees.

Revenue for municipal services is derived mainly from real-property taxation, although additional revenue is derived from licence fees, business taxes, fines, public utility projects and grants-in-aid from the provincial government.

ECONOMY

Budget. Current provincial revenue and expenditure, including all capital expenditures, in Canadian $1m. for fiscal years ending 31 March:

	1978–79	*1979–80*	*1980–81*	*1981–82*[1]
Revenue	4,568·9	5,515·4	5,802·7	6,868·4
Expenditure	4,429·0	5,327·0	6,060·0	7,042·0

[1] Provisional.

The main sources of current revenue are the income taxes, sales and fuel taxes, contributions from the federal government, and privileges, licences and natural resources taxes and royalties.

The main items of expenditure in 1981–82 are as follows: Health and social services, $2,963·7m.; education, $1,537·1m.; transport and communication, $596·1m.; natural resources and primary industry, $447·6m.; general government, $307·2m.

Banking. Cheques cashed (in $1m.): 1977, 207,854; 1978, 233,387; 1979, 286,902; 1980, 382,836; 1981, 519,386.

ENERGY AND NATURAL RESOURCES

Electricity. Generation in 1981 totalled 51,008m. kwh. of which a net 8,987m. kwh. were exported. Consumption within the province was 43,180m. kwh.

Minerals. Copper, coal, natural gas, crude oil, molybdenum and silver are the most important minerals produced. The 1981 total of mineral production was estimated at $3,011·8m. Total value of fuels produced in 1981 was estimated at $1,441·9m.

Agriculture. Only 2·4m. hectares or 3% of the total land area is arable or potentially arable. Farm cash receipts, in 1981, reached $854m.

Forestry. About 55% of British Columbia's land is forest land, with 47·8m. hectares bearing commercial forest. Over 94% of the forest area is owned or administered by the provincial government. The total cut from forests in 1981 was 60m. cu. metres.

Fisheries. In 1981 the wholesale market value of fish products reached $519m., a 29% increase on the 1979 figure. Increased catches in the salmon and roe herring fisheries largely accounted for this.

INDUSTRY AND TRADE

Industry. The selling value of factory shipments from all manufacturing industries reached an estimated $16,415m. in 1981.

Commerce. Exports through British Columbia customs ports during 1981 totalled $15,959m. in value, while imports amounted to $7,943m.

Principal export commodity groups through British Columbia customs ports (1981): Forest products, $4,006·7; coal, crude petroleum and natural gas, $3,900·1m.; metal ores, concentrates, non-ferrous metals and crude non-metallic minerals, $1,525·4m.; grain and cereal products, $2,170·1m.; fish and marine animals, $311m. About 40% of exports through British Columbia customs ports are products from other provinces, primarily grains, potash and fuels from the Prairie Provinces. USA is the largest market for products exported through British Columbia customs ports ($6,123m. in 1981) followed by Japan ($3,791m.) and the EEC ($1,835·1m.).

COMMUNICATIONS

Roads. At 31 March 1982 there were 43,071 km of provincial roads and rights of way in the province, of which 18,119 km were paved and 24,952 km were gravelled.

Railways. The province is served by two transcontinental railways, the Canadian Pacific Railway and the Canadian National Railway. British Columbia is also served by the publicly owned British Columbia Railway, the Railway Freight Service of the B.C. Hydro and Power Authority, the Northern Alberta Railways Company and the Burlington Northern Inc. The combined route-mileage of mainline track operated by the CPR, CNR and BCR totals 7,4004 km. The system also includes CPR and CNR railcar barge connections to Vancouver Island, between Prince Rupert and Alaska, and interchanges with American railways at southern border points.

Aviation. International airports are located at Vancouver and Victoria. Daily interprovincial and intraprovincial flights serve all main population centres. Small public and private airstrips are located throughout the province.

Shipping. The major ports are Vancouver, New Westminster, Victoria, Nanaimo and Prince Rupert. The volume of domestic and international cargo handled during 1981 was 67m. tonnes and 45m. tonnes respectively.

The British Columbia Ferries connect Vancouver Island with the mainland and also provide service to other coastal points. Service by other ferry systems is also provided between Vancouver Island and the USA. The Alaska State Ferries connect Prince Rupert with centres in Alaska.

Post and Broadcasting. The British Columbia Telephone Company had (1981) 2m. telephones in service. There were 13 television stations and 226 radio stations operating in the province in 1981. Many of these are repeater stations.

EDUCATION AND WELFARE

Education. Education, free up to Grade XII levels, is financed jointly from municipal and provincial government revenues. Attendance is compulsory from the age of 6 to 15. There were 504,000 pupils enrolled in public schools from kindergarten to Grade XII in Sept. 1981.

The universities had a full-time enrolment of 32,772 for 1981–82. They include University of British Columbia, Vancouver; University of Victoria, Victoria; Simon Fraser University, Burnaby, and the David Thompson University Centre, Nelson. The regional colleges are Camosun College, Victoria; Capilano College, North Vancouver; Cariboo College, Kamloops; College of New Caledonia, Prince George; Douglas College, New Westminister; East Kootenay Community College, Cranbrook; Fraser Valley College, Chilliwack/Abbotsford; Kwantlen College, Surrey; Malaspina College, Nanaimo; North Island College, Comox; Northern Lights College, Dawson Creek/Fort St John; Northwest Community College, Terrace/Prince Rupert; Okanagan College, Kelowna with branches at Salmon Arm and Vernon; Selkirk College, Castlegar; Vancouver Community College, Vancouver.

There are also the British Columbia Institute of Technology, Burnaby; Emily Carr College of Art and Design, Vancouver; Justice Institute of British Columbia, Vancouver; Open Learning Institute, Richmond; Pacific Marine Training Institute, North Vancouver; Pacific Vocational Institute, Burnaby/Maple Ridge/Richmond. A televised distance education and special programmes through KNOW, the Knowledge Network of the West is provided.

Health. The Government operates a hospital insurance scheme giving universal coverage after a qualifying period of 3 months' residence in the province. The province has come under a national medicare scheme which is partially subsidized by the provincial government and partially by the federal government.

Books of Reference

Statistical Information: Information Services (Ministry of Industry and Small Business Development, Hon. Don Phillips—Minister, Parliament Buildings, Victoria, B.C.V8V 1 × 4), collects, compiles and distributes information relative to the Province.

Publications include *British Columbia Business Bulletin; Economic Review and Outlook* (Annual); *Manufacturers' Directory; External Trade Report* (Annual); *B.C. Manual of Facts and Statistics* (Annual).

Ministry of Finance, *British Columbia Financial and Economic Review.* Victoria, B.C. (Annual)

Fifteenth British Columbia Natural Resources Conference, *Inventory of the Natural Resources of British Columbia,* 1964

MANITOBA

HISTORY. The Hudson's Bay Company formed a colony on the Red River in 1812. This being part of territory annexed to Canada in 1870. The Metis colonists (part-Indian, mostly French-speaking, Catholic) objected to the arrangements for the purchase of the Company territory by Canada and the province of Manitoba was created to accommodate them. It was extended northwards and westwards in 1881 and to Hudson Bay in 1912.

AREA AND POPULATION. The area of the province is 250,946 sq. miles (649,046 sq. km), of which 211,721 sq. miles are land and 39,225 sq. miles water. From north to south it is 793 km and the widest point is 493 km.

The population (June 1981) was 1,017,323. Population of the principal cities (census 1981): Winnipeg (capital), 560,028; Brandon, 35,894; Thompson, 14,102; Portage la Prairie, 12,959; Flin Flon, 7,819.

Vital statistics, *see* p. 269.

Religion, *see* p. 286.

CONSTITUTION AND GOVERNMENT. Manitoba was known as the Red River Settlement before its entry into the Dominion in 1870. The provincial government is administered by a Lieut.-Governor and a legislative assembly of 57 members elected for 5 years. Women were enfranchised in 1916. The Electoral Division Act, 1955, created 57 single-member constituencies and abolished the transferable vote. The Electoral Divisions Act, 1979, created 27 rural electoral divisions, and 30 urban electoral divisions. The province is represented by 6 members in the Senate and 14 in the House of Commons of Canada.

Lieut.-Governor: Pearl McGonigal (sworn in 23 Oct. 1981).

Flag: The British Red Ensign with the shield of the province in the fly.

State of parties in the Legislative Assembly (sworn in 30 Nov. 1981): New Democratic Party, 34; Progressive Conservative, 23.

The members of the New Democratic Party Ministry are as follows (Sept. 1982):

Premier, President of the Council, Minister of Federal Provincial Relations: Howard Russell Pawley.

Health, Recreation and Sport, Minister responsible for the administration of The Lotteries and Gaming Control Act: Laurent Louis Desjardins. *Highways and Transportation:* Samuel Uskiw. *Community Services and Corrections:* Leonard Salusbury Evans. *Agriculture:* Billie Uruski. *Municipal Affairs:* A. R. Adam. *Northern Affairs, Environmental Management, Minister responsible for the administration of The Clean Environment Act, The Workplace Safety and Health Act, The Workers Compensation Act, The Communities Economic Development Fund Act:* Jay Marine Cowan. *Energy and Mines, Crown Investments, Minister responsible for the administration of The Manitoba Hydro Act, Manitoba Forestry Resources Act:* Wilson Dwight Parasiuk. *Finance, Minister responsible for the administration of The Manitoba Data Services Act, Chairman of Treasury Board:* Victor Schroeder. *Education:* Maureen Lucille Hemphill. *Cultural Affairs and Historical Resources, Urban Affairs, Minister responsible for the administration of The Public Printing Act and the Office of the Queen's Printer:* Eugene Michael Kostyra. *Attorney-General, Keeper of the Great Seal, Minister responsible for the administration of The Liquor Control Act:* Roland Penner. *Economic Development and Tourism, Minister responsible for the administration of The Development Corporation Act:* Muriel Ann Smith. *Natural Resources:* Alvin Henry Mackling. *Labour and Manpower, Minister responsible for the administration of The Civil Service Act, The Civil Service Superannuation Act, The Pension Benefits Act, The Public Servants Insurance Act, Minister responsible for the Status of Women:* Mary Elisabeth Dolin. *Housing, Minister responsible for the administration of The Landlord and Tenant Act, The Residential Rent Regulation Act, The Housing and Renewal Corporation Act and The Elderly and Infirm Persons' Housing Act:* Jerry Thomas Storie. *Consumer and Corporate Affairs, Co-operative Development,*

Minister responsible for the administration of The Manitoba Public Insurance Corporation Act: John Bucklaschuk. *Government Services, Minister responsible for the administration of The Manitoba Telephone System Act:* John S. Plohman.

Local Government. Rural Manitoba is organized into rural municipalities which vary widely in size. Some have only 4 townships (a township is 36 sq. miles), while the largest has 22 townships. The province has 105 rural municipalities, as well as 35 incorporated towns, 40 incorporated villages and 5 incorporated cities.

On 1 Jan. 1972, the cities and towns comprising the metropolitan area of Winnipeg were amalgamated to form the City of Winnipeg. A mayor and council are elected to a central government, but councillors also sit on 'community committees' which represent the areas or wards they serve. These committees are advised by non-elected residents of the area on provision of municipal services within the community committee jurisdiction. Taxing powers and overall budgeting rest with the central council. The mayor is elected at the same time as the councillors in a city-wide vote. Revisions to the City of Winnipeg Act came into effect with the municipal elections held in Oct. 1977.

Since Jan. 1945, 17 Local Government Districts have been formed in the less densely populated areas of the province. They are administered by a provincially appointed person, who acts on the advice of locally elected councils.

In the extreme north, many communities have locally elected councils, while others are administered directly by the Department of Northern Affairs. This department provides most of the funding in all these northern settlements.

FINANCE. Provincial revenue and expenditure (current account) for fiscal years ending 31 March (in Canadian $):

	1978–79	*1979–80*	*1980–81*[1]	*1981–82*[1]	*1982–83*[1]
Revenue	1,550,819,062	1,805,982,583	1,965,137,000	2,161,200,533	2,495,234,300
Expenditure	1,635,142,056	1,850,737,379	2,057,913,000	2,381,015,800	2,829,756,600

[1] Estimated.

ENERGY AND NATURAL RESOURCES

Electricity. The total generating capacity of Manitoba's power stations is 3·6m. kw. The Manitoba Hydro system, owned by the province, provides most of this power, while the city-owned Winnipeg Hydro provides about 190,000 kw. The systems have about 397,000 customers and consumption was 11·5m. kwh. in 1981.

Oil. Crude oil production in 1980 was valued at $54·9m. for the 3·5m. bbls produced.

Minerals. Total value of minerals in 1981 was about $680m. Principal minerals mined are nickel, zinc, copper, and small quantities of gold and silver. Manitoba has the world's largest deposits of caesium ore and also produces tantalite concentrates.

Agriculture. Rich farmland is the main primary resource, although the area of Manitoba in farms is only about 14% of the total land area. In 1981 the total value of agricultural production in Manitoba was $2,000m., with $1,450m. from crops, $535m. from livestock and about $15m. from the sale of other products including furs, hides and honey.

Forestry. About 40% of the land area is wooded, of which 53,700 sq. miles is productive forest land. Total sales of wood-using industries (1980) $400m.

Fur Trade. Value of fur production to the trapper was $8·2m. in 1981–82.

Fisheries. From 22,000 sq. miles of rivers and lakes fisheries production was about $18·6m. in 1981–82. Whitefish, sauger, pickerel, pike, trout and perch are the principle varieties of fish caught.

INDUSTRY AND TRADE

Industry. Manufacturing, the largest industry in the province, encompasses almost every major industrial activity in Canada. Estimated shipments in 1981 totalled $4,860m. Manufacturing employed about 65,000 persons. Due to the agricultural base of the province, the food and beverage group of industries is by far the largest, accounting for about 34% of the total value. The next largest segments are machinery at about 9%, metal fabricating at 12% and transportation equipment at about 7%.

Trade. Products grown and manufactured in Manitoba find ready markets in other areas of Canada, in the USA, particularly the upper midwest region, and in other countries. Export shipments to foreign countries from Manitoba in 1980 were valued at about $1,161·5m., with about 76·2% going to the US. Of these, about 33% are raw materials and about 66% are processed and manufactured products.

Tourism. In 1981, Canadian, US and Manitoba tourists numbered 3,063,000 contributing about $486m. to the economy.

COMMUNICATIONS

Roads. Highways and provincial roads had a total mileage of 12,300 in 1980.

Railways. At 31 Dec. 1980 the province had 4,027 miles of railway, not including industrial track, yards and sidings.

Aviation. A total of 102 licensed commercial air carriers operate from bases in Manitoba, as well as major national and international airlines.

Post. All of the province's 733,000 telephones are dial-operated.

EDUCATION. Education is controlled through locally elected school divisions. There are about 200,000 children enrolled in the province's elementary and secondary schools. The University of Manitoba, founded in 1877, in Winnipeg, had an enrolment of 20,000, the University of Winnipeg, 2,444, and Brandon University, 1,032, during the 1980–81 year. Expenditure (estimate) on education in the 1981–82 fiscal year was $644m.

Three community colleges, in Brandon, The Pas and Winnipeg, offer 2-year diploma courses in a number of fields, as well as specialized training in many trades. They also give a large number and variety of shorter courses, both at their campuses and in many communities throughout the province.

Books of Reference

General Information: Inquiries may be addressed to the Information Services Branch, Room 29, Legislative Building, Winnipeg, R3C OV8.

The Department of Agriculture publishes: *Year Book of Manitoba Agriculture*
Information Services Branch publishes: *Manitoba Facts*
Manitoba Statistical Review. Manitoba Bureau of Statistics, Quarterly
Tenth Census of Canada: Manitoba. Statistics Canada, 1971

NEW BRUNSWICK

HISTORY. Touched by Jacques Cartier in 1534, New Brunswick was first explored by Samuel de Champlain in 1604. It was ceded by the French in the Treaty of Utrecht in 1713 and became a permanent British possession in 1763. It was separated from Nova Scotia and became a province in June 1784, as a result of the great influx of United Empire Loyalists. Responsible government came into being in 1848, and consisted of an executive council, a legislative council (later abolished) and a House of Assembly.

AREA AND POPULATION. The area of the province is 28,354 sq. miles (73,000 sq. km), of which 27,633 sq. miles (71,569 sq. km) are land area. The population (census 1976) was 677,250. Of the total population (1971) about 58%

are of British origin, 37% French and the remainder are principally of Netherlands, German and Scandinavian descent, and in 1980 there were about 5,300 Indians. Census population of urban centres: Saint John, 85,956; Moncton, 55,934; Fredericton (capital), 45,248; Bathurst, 16,301; Edmundston, 12,710; Campbellton, 9,282.

Vital statistics, *see* p. 269.
Religion, *see* p. 286.

CONSTITUTION AND GOVERNMENT. The government is vested in a Lieut.-Governor and a Legislative Assembly of 58 members each of whom is individually elected to represent the voters in one constituency or riding. A simultaneous translation system is used in the Assembly. Any Canadian subject of full age and 6 months' residence is entitled to vote. As a result of the provincial election held on 23 Oct. 1978 and subsequent by-elections, the Assembly is composed of 30 Progressive Conservatives and 28 Liberals. The province has 10 members in the Canadian Senate and 10 members in the federal House of Commons.

Lieut.-Governor: George F. S. Stanley (appointed 23 Dec. 1981).

Flag: A banner of the Arms, *i.e.*, yellow charged with a black heraldic ship on wavy lines of blue and white; across the top a red band with a gold lion.

The members of the Progressive Conservative Ministry are as follows (Dec. 1982):

Premier and President of the Executive Council: Richard Hatfield.

Attorney-General and Justice: Fernand Dube, QC. *Finance and Minister Responsible for New Brunswick Housing Corporation:* John B. M. Baxter, QC. *Chairman of the Treasury Board:* Harold N. Fanjoy. *Supply and Services:* Edwin G. Allen. *Transportation:* Wilfred G. Bishop. *Natural Resources and Minister Responsible for Energy Policy:* Gerald Merrithew. *Agriculture and Rural Development:* Malcolm N. MacLeod. *Health:* Charles G. Gallagher. *Social Services:* Nancy E. Clark Teed. *Labour and Manpower:* Joseph W. Mombourquette. *Education:* Mabel M. DeWare. *Municipal Affairs:* Yvon R. Poitras. *Commerce and Development:* Paul W. Dawson. *Fisheries:* Jean Gauvin. *Environment:* C. W. (Bill) Harmer. *Tourism:* Omer Leger. *Youth and Recreation:* Leslie I. Hull. *Cultural and Historical Resources:* Jean-Pierre Ouellet.

Local Government. Under the reforms introduced in 1967 the province has assumed complete administrative and financial responsibility for education, health, welfare and administration of justice. Local government is now restricted to provision of services of a strictly local nature. Under the new municipal structure, units include existing and new cities, towns and villages. Counties have disappeared as municipal units. Areas with limited populations have become local service districts. The former local improvement districts have become towns, villages or local service districts depending on their size.

FINANCE. The ordinary budget (in Canadian $) is shown as follows (financial years ended 31 March):

	1979	*1980*	*1981*	*1982*
Gross revenue	1,268,924,745	1,449,457,490	1,534,897,829	1,772,232,788
Gross expenditure[1]	1,198,129,445	1,321,661,738	1,505,252,819	1,795,554,444

[1] Excluding sinking fund instalment.

Funded debt and capital loans outstanding (exclusive of Treasury Bills) as of 31 March 1982 was $1,822m. Sinking funds held by the province at 31 March 1982, $480m. The ordinary budget excludes capital spending.

ENERGY AND NATURAL RESOURCES

Electricity. Hydro-electric and thermal power plants of the New Brunswick Electric Power Commission had an installed capacity of 2,526,576 kw. at 31 March 1981, consisting of 13 generating stations. This includes 6 units with a capacity of over 600,000 kw. at the Mactaquac hydro-electric development near Fredericton. Three units (1m. kw.) are in operation at Coleson Cove in the Lorneville area near Saint John. The 630,000 kw. nuclear plant at Point Lepreau will be operational in 1982. An additional 200,000 kw. of hydro and thermal capacity have been installed at Mactaquac and Dalhousie respectively. The Commission is interconnected with the neighbouring provinces of Nova Scotia, Quebec, Prince Edward Island and the New England states, USA. Hook-up permits exchange of power including large blocks from Churchill Falls in Labrador through Hydro-Quebec as well as with the state of Maine, USA.

Minerals. A considerable variety of metals, industrial minerals, fuels and structural materials occur in the province. These include zinc, lead, copper, cadmium, bismuth, nickel, gold, silver, cobalt, tungsten, tin, molybdenum, antimony, potash, salt, glauberite, limestone, dolomite, gypsum, oil, gas, coal, uranium, oil shale, sand, gravel, clay, peat, diatomite and marl. Not all have been explored sufficiently. 51% of the value of minerals produced in 1982, which totalled $517m., was attributed to zinc produced from 2 mines in the Bathurst–Newcastle area: Brunswick Mining and Smelting, Heath Steele Mines Ltd. New Brunswick is the third largest producer of zinc in Canada. A lead smelter, fertilizer plant and port facilities have been constructed at Belledune. Numerous other discoveries have been made in the area and several deposits are now in the final stages of exploration. Canada's only primary antimony producer is located at Lake George, near Fredericton, and a large low-grade tungsten–molybdenum–bismuth deposit exists at Mount Pleasant. Exploration and development is also in process near Sussex and Salt Springs, where potash and salt deposits have been found. Limestone and gypsum are quarried at Havelock and Hillsborough and small quantities of oil and natural gas are produced from the Stoney Creek Field south of Moncton. Coal is mined at Grand Lake and exploration is underway for other deposits of this important energy resource.

Agriculture. The total area under crops is estimated at 322,538 acres, exclusive of improved pasture land (102,497 acres). Farms numbered 4,063 and averaged 266 acres each (census 1981). Mixed farming is common throughout the province. Dairy farming is centred around the larger urban areas, and is located mainly along the Saint John River Valley and in the south-eastern sections of the province. For particulars of agricultural production and livestock, *see under* CANADA, pp. 278–79. Farm cash receipts in 1981 were approximately $198,365,000.

Forestry. New Brunswick contains some 27,000 sq. km of productive forest lands. The combined value of primary and secondary forest production was about $1,108m. in 1979, of which wood and paper and allied industries accounted for about $880m. Timber-using plants employ about 14,600 men for all aspects of the forest industry, including harvesting, processing and transportation. Practically all forest products are exported from the province's numerous ports and harbours near which the mills are located or sent by road or rail to the USA.

Fisheries. Commercial fishing is one of the most important basic industries of the province. Nearly 50 commercial species of fish and shellfish are landed, of which lobster, crab, herring and cod are the most valuable. Landings in 1982 (108,000 tonnes) amounted to $65·5m. In 1982 there were 120 fish processing plants employing more than 11,000 people in peak periods. The total market value of fish products in 1981 was approximately $250m.

INDUSTRY. In 1981 there were 1,258 manufacturing and processing establishments, employing about 40,900 persons. New Brunswick's location, with deep-water harbours open throughout the year and container facilities at Saint John, makes it ideal for exporting. Industries include food and beverages, paper and allied industries, timber products. About 20% of the industrial labour force work in Saint John.

TOURISM. Tourism is a major industry. During 1982, more than 4m. tourists spent approximately $330m.

COMMUNICATIONS

Roads. There are about 2,133 km of arterial highways and 2,322 km of collector roads, 95% of which are hard-surfaced. 12,845 km of local roads provide access to most areas in the province. The main highway system, including 616 km of the Trans-Canada Highway, links the province with the principal roads in Quebec and Nova Scotia, as well as the Interstate Highway System in the eastern seaboard states of the USA. Passenger vehicles, 31 March 1979, numbered 250,388; commercial vehicles, 95,010; motor cycles, 10,869.

Railways. New Brunswick is served by main lines of both Canadian Pacific and Canadian National railways.

Post and Broadcasting. In 1980 the New Brunswick Telephone Co. Ltd had 389,466 telephones in service. The province is served by 16 radio stations. Twelve are privately owned and 4 owned by the Canadian Broadcasting Corporation. Three stations broadcast in the French language, 1 is bilingual and the CBC International Service broadcasts in several languages from its station at Sackville. The province is served by 3 television stations, 1 of which broadcasts in French.

Newspapers. New Brunswick had (1983) 5 daily newspapers, and 23 weekly newspapers, 7 in French or bilingual.

EDUCATION. Public education is free and non-sectarian. There are 4 universities. The University of New Brunswick at Fredericton (founded 13 Dec. 1785 by the Loyalists, elevated to university status in 1823, reorganized as the University of New Brunswick in 1859) had 5,657 full-time students at the Fredericton campus and 754 full-time students at the Saint John campus (1981–82); Mount Allison University at Sackville had 1,547 full-time students; the Université de Moncton at Moncton, 2,619 full-time students; St Thomas University at Fredericton, 889 full-time students. During the period 1 July 1981 to 30 June 1982, there were 9,943 students enrolled full-time at 10 Community College campuses and at various campus training centres.

There were, in Sept. 1980, 152,141 students and 7,829 full-time teachers in the province's 466 schools. Large new regional schools are absorbing numbers of small country schools; there are 37 school districts.

Books of Reference

Industrial Information: Dept. of Commerce and Development, Fredericton. *Economic Information:* Dept. of Finance, Economics and Statistics Branch. Fredericton. *General Information:* NB Information Service, Fredericton.

New Brunswick and Its People. Fredericton, 1962

Department of Commerce and Development, *Annual Report.* Fredericton, 1973.—*New Brunswick in Profile.* Fredericton

NEWFOUNDLAND AND LABRADOR

HISTORY. Archaeological finds at L'Anse-au-Meadow in northern Newfoundland suggest that the Vikings had established a colony there at about A.D. 1000. Newfoundland was discovered by John Cabot 24 June 1497, and was soon frequented in the summer months by the Portuguese, Spanish and French for its fisheries. It was formally occupied in Aug. 1583 by Sir Humphrey Gilbert on behalf of the English Crown, but various attempts to colonize the island remained unsuccessful. Although British sovereignty was recognized in 1713 by the Treaty of Utrecht, disputes over fishing rights with the French were not finally settled till 1904. By the Anglo-French Convention of 1904, France renounced her exclusive fishing rights along part of the coast, granted under the Treaty of Utrecht, but retained sovereignty of the offshore islands of St Pierre and Miquelon.

AREA AND POPULATION. Area, 156,185 sq. miles (383,300 sq. km). In March 1927 the Privy Council decided the boundary between Canada and Newfoundland in Labrador. This area, now part of the Province of Newfoundland and Labrador, is 112,826 sq. miles. The coastline is extremely irregular. Bays, fiords and inlets are numerous and there are many good harbours with deep water close to shore. The coast is rugged with bold rocky cliffs from 200 to 400 ft high; in the Bay of Islands some of the islands rise 500 ft, with the adjacent shore 1,000 ft above tide level. The interior is a plateau of moderate elevation and the chief relief features trend north-east and south-west. Long Range, the most notable of these, begins at Cape Ray and extends north-east for 200 miles, the highest peak reaching 2,673 ft. Approximately one-third of the area is covered by water. Grand Lake, the largest body of water, has an area of about 200 sq. miles. The principal rivers flow towards the north-east. On the borders of the lakes and water-courses good land is generally found, particularly in the valleys of the Terra Nova River, the Gander River, the Exploits River and the Humber River, which are also heavily timbered.

Census population, 1981, was 567,681.

The capital of Newfoundland is the City of St John's (154,820, metropolitan area). The only other city is Corner Brook (24,339); important towns are Labrador City (11,538), Gander (10,404), Stephenville (8,876), Grand Falls (8,765), Happy Valley–Goose Bay (7,103), Channel-Port aux Basques (5,988) Windsor (5,747), Carbonear (5,335), Bonavista (4,460), Wabana (4,254), Wabush (3,155).

Vital statistics, *see* p. 269.

Religion, *see* p. 286.

CONSTITUTION AND GOVERNMENT. Until 1832 Newfoundland was ruled by the Governor under instructions of the Colonial Office. In that year a Legislature was brought into existence, but the Governor and his Executive Council were not responsible to it. Under the constitution of 1855, which lasted until its suspension in 1934, the government was administered by the Governor appointed by the Crown with an Executive Council responsible to the House of Assembly of 27 elected members and a Legislative Council of 24 members nominated for life by the Governor in Council. Women were enfranchised in 1925. At the Imperial Conference of 1917 Newfoundland was constituted as a Dominion.

In 1933 the financial situation had become so critical that the Government of Newfoundland asked the Government of the UK to appoint a Royal Commission to investigate conditions. On the strength of their recommendations, the parliamentary form of government was suspended and Government by Commission was inaugurated on 16 Feb. 1934.

A National Convention, elected in 1946, made, in 1948, recommendations to H.M. Government in Great Britain as to the possible forms of future government to be submitted to the people at a national referendum. Two referenda were held. In the first referendum (June 1948) the three forms of government submitted to the people were: commission of government for 5 years, confederation with Canada and responsible government as it existed in 1933. No one form of government received a clear majority of the votes polled, and commission of government, receiving the fewest votes, was eliminated. In the second referendum (July 1948) confederation with Canada received 78,408 and responsible government 71,464 votes.

In the Canadian Senate on 18 Feb. 1949 Royal assent was given to the terms of union of Newfoundland and Labrador with Canada, and on 23 March 1949, in the House of Lords, London, Royal assent was given to an amendment to the British North America Act made necessary by the inclusion of Newfoundland and Labrador as the tenth Province of Canada.

Under the terms of union of Newfoundland and Labrador with Canada, which was signed at Ottawa on 11 Dec. 1948, the constitution of the Legislature of Newfoundland and Labrador as it existed immediately prior to 16 Feb. 1934 shall, subject to the terms of the British North America Acts, 1867 to 1946, continue as the constitution of the Legislature of the Province of Newfoundland and Labrador until altered under the authority of the said Acts.

The franchise was in 1965 extended to all male and female residents who have attained the age of 19 years and are otherwise qualified as electors.

The House of Assembly (Amendment) Act, 1979, established 52 electoral districts and 52 members of the Legislature.

At 6 April 1982 there were 44 Progressive-Conservatives and 8 Liberals.

The province is represented by 6 members in the Senate and by 7 members in the House of Commons of Canada.

Lieut.-Governor: Hon. Dr W. A. Paddon (assumed office 10 July 1981).

Flag: White, in the hoist 4 solid blue triangles; in the fly 2 red triangles voided white, and between them a yellow tongue bordered in red.

The Progressive-Conservative Executive Council was, at 6 April 1982, composed as follows:

Premier and Intergovernmental Affairs: Brian Peckford.

President of the Executive Council and Minister of Energy: W. Marshall. *Finance:* J. Collins. *Justice:* G. R. Ottenheimer. *Development and Mines:* N. Windsor. *Health:* W. House. *Fisheries:* J. Morgan. *Rural, Agricultural and Northern Development:* J. Goudie. *Labour and Manpower:* J. Dinn. *Social Services:* T. Hickey. *Forest Resources and Lands:* C. Power. *Public Works and Services:* H. Young. *Municipal Affairs:* H. Newhook. *Education:* L. Verge. *Transportation:* R. Dawe. *Environment:* H. Andrews. *Culture, Recreation and Youth:* L. Simms. *Minister responsible for Communications:* N.Doyle. *Speaker of the House of Assembly:* J. Russell. *Clerk of the Executive Council:* D. Vardy.

Agent-General in London: H. Watson Jamer (60 Trafalgar Sq., WC2).

FINANCE. Budget [1] in Canadian $1,000 for fiscal years ended 31 March:

	1977–78	*1978–79*	*1979–80*	*1980–81*	*1981–82* [2]	*1982–83* [3]
Gross revenue	964,235	1,084,083	1,215,697	1,359,209	1,510,584	1,724,136
Gross expenditure	955,834	1,062,244	1,174,091	1,310,018	1,506,059	1,718,730

[1] Current amount only. [2] Revised estimates. [3] Estimates.

Public debenture debt as at 31 March 1982 (preliminary) was $2,235·7m.; sinking fund, $420·4m.

ENERGY AND NATURAL RESOURCES

Electricity. The electrical energy requirements of the province are met mainly by hydro-electric power, with petroleum fuels being utilized to provide the balance. The total amount of energy generated in the province in 1981 (preliminary) was 44,665,056 mwh., of which approximately 99% was derived from hydro-electric facilities. The greater part of the energy produced in 1981 (preliminary) came from Churchill Falls, of which 36,039,280 mwh. was sold to Hydro-Quebec under the terms of a long-term contract. Energy consumed in the province during 1981 (preliminary) totalled 8,625,776 mwh., with approximately 8,172,266 mwh., or 95%, coming from hydro-electric facilities.

At 31 Dec. 1980 total electrical generating capacity in the province was 7,194,675 kw., with hydro-electric plants accounting for 6,444,256 kw., or 90%. A 75 mw hydro project started in 1978 at Hind's Lake in central Newfoundland and was completed in 1981. It is estimated that potential additional hydro-electric generating capacity of up to 4·5m. kw. can be developed at various sites in the Labrador part of the province.

Oil. In 1979 the province consumed refined petroleum at the rate of 42,000 bbls a day with 30% of this being refined in the province. While the refining capacity of the province is 114,000 bbls per day, there is presently only one refinery being operated, a 13,000 bbls-per-day refinery at Holyrood.

Since 1965, 82 wells have been drilled on the Continental Margin of the Province. In 1982 it is estimated that offshore exploration expenditures would be $316m.

In Oct. 1974, two natural gas finds off the coast of Labrador were announced. Tests of these two wells resulted in rates of flow of 13–20m. cu. ft per day respectively, with some condensate and no water present. Additional natural gas finds with flows of 9·8m. cu. ft per day and 32m. cu. ft per day, with significant condensates and no water present, were announced in 1976 and 1978 respectively.

In 1979, a discovery of oil was made on the Hibernia geological structure located 164 nautical miles east of Cape Spear. The discovery well, Hibernia P–15, tested medium gravity, sweet crude from several intervals with a reported total producing capability in excess of 20,000 bbls of oil per day.

Minerals. The mineral resources are vast but only partially documented. Large deposits of iron ore, with an ore reserve of over 5,000m. tons at Labrador City, Wabush City and in the Knob Lake area are supplying approximately half of Canada's production. Other large deposits of iron ore are known to exist in the Julienne Lake area.

There are a variety of other minerals being produced in the province in more limited amounts.

Uranium deposits in the Kaipokak Bay area near Makkovik in Labrador are presently being studied by Brinex. The Central Mineral Belt, which extends from the Smallwood Reservoir to the Atlantic coast near Makkovik, holds uranium, copper, beryllium and molybdenite potential.

Production in 1981 (preliminary): Iron ore, 26,008,000 tonnes ($1,058,275,000); copper, 5,583,000 kg ($12·35m.); zinc, 40,504,000 kg ($48,604,000); asbestos, 57,000 tonnes ($39·33m.); lead, 3,178,000 kg ($3·12m.); silver, 8,000 kg ($3,107,000); gold, 241 kg ($4,263,000); cadmium, 88,000 kg ($441,000); gypsum, 669,000 tonnes ($4,683,000); pyrophyllite, soapstone and talc ($959,000); cement ($7,388,000); clay products ($957,000); sand and gravel, 3,607,000 tonnes ($6,889,000); stone, 1·1m. tonnes ($3·3m.); quartz ($828,000).

Agriculture. The estimated value of agricultural products sold, including livestock, 1981, was $30·1m.

Forestry. The forestry economy in the province is mainly dependent on the operation of 3 newsprint mills. In 1980 the value of newsprint exported from these 3 mills totalled $344·5m. Lumber mills, saw-log operations produced 39m. f.b.m.

Fisheries. The principal fish landings are cod, flounder, redfish, Queen crabs (in shell), lobster, salmon and herring. In 1981 a yearly average of some 9,700 persons were employed by the fish-processing industry and there were 28,495 licensed full-, part-time and casual fishermen engaged in harvesting operations. Approximately 200 processing operations were active in 1981. The production of fresh and frozen fish products was $405m. in 1980.

The total catch in 1981 was 496,570 tonnes valued at $167·2m., of which the main items were: Cod, 245,159 tonnes ($83·4m.); flounder, 78,644 ($20·1m.); herring, 24,754 tonnes ($5·4m.); redfish, 32,624 ($5·7m.); lobster, 2,376 ($10·7m.); salmon, 1,910 ($6·7m.).

The seal fishery in 1981 had 5 large licensed and 146 small licensed vessels with 720 men who landed 112,475 pelts. The number of pelts landed by landsmen totalled 40,510.

INDUSTRY. The total value of manufacturing shipments in 1981 was $1,214·4m. This consists largely of first-stage processing of primary resource products with two of the largest components being paper and fish products.

TRADE UNIONS. There were (1980) 368 unions representing 66,419 members of international and national unions, government employee associations as well as 16 local independent unions.

COMMUNICATIONS

Roads. In 1981 there were 8,713 km, of which 5,367 were paved.

Railways. In 1980 there were 1,517 km of railway, of which the Canadian National Railways operated 1,130·6 (3 ft 6 in.), the Quebec North Shore and Labrador Railway 384 (4 ft 8½ in.) and there were 2·4 km of private line. Car and passenger ferries operate from Port aux Basques and Argentia to North Sydney, Nova Scotia. On the island of Newfoundland, the Canadian National Railways operates a trans-island bus and rail freight service in addition to a coastal service for both passengers and freight. In the months that the Labrador coast is ice-free, usually from June to Nov., the Canadian National Railways operates a scheduled coastal steamer service every week.

Aviation. The province is linked to the rest of Canada by regular air services provided by Air Canada, Eastern Provincial Airways, Quebecair and a number of smaller air carriers.

Shipping. In 1981 there were 1,546 ships registered in Newfoundland.

Post. There were 483 post offices open in 1980, and (1981) 2 telegraph offices in the Newfoundland and Labrador postal district. Telephone connexions in the province numbered 258,617 in 1980.

EDUCATION. The number of schools in 1981–82 was 657. The enrolment was 145,454; teachers numbered 7,801. The Memorial University, offering courses in arts, science, engineering, education, nursing and medicine, had approximately 11,400 full- and part-time students. Total expenditure for education by the Government in 1981–82 was $439m.

Books of Reference

Blackburn, R. H. (ed.), *Encyclopaedia of Canada: Newfoundland Supplement.* Toronto, 1949
Bruet, E., *Le Labrador et le Nouveau-Québec.* Paris, 1949
Horwood, H., *Newfoundland.* Toronto, 1969
Loture, R. de, *Histoire de la grande pêche de Terre-Neuve.* Paris, 1949
Mercer, G. A., *The Province of Newfoundland and Labrador: Geographical Aspects.* Ottawa, 1970
Perlin, A. B., *The Story of Newfoundland, 1497–1959.* St John's, 1959
Tanner, V., *Outlines of Geography. Life and Customs of Newfoundland–Labrador.* 2 vols. Helsinki, 1944, and Toronto, 1947
Taylor, T. G., *Newfoundland: A Study of Settlement.* Toronto, 1946

NOVA SCOTIA

HISTORY. The first permanent settlement was made by the French early in the 17th century, and the province was called Acadia until finally ceded to the British by the Treaty of Utrecht in 1713.

AREA AND POPULATION. The area of the province is 21,425 sq. miles (55,000 sq. km), of which 20,401 sq. miles are land area, 1,024 sq. miles water area. The population (census 1981) was 847,442; estimate (1982) 582,800.

Population of the principal cities and towns (census 1981): Halifax, 114,594; Dartmouth 62,277; Sydney, 29,444; Glace Bay, 21,466; Truro, 12,552; New Glasgow, 10,464; Amherst, 9,684; Sydney Mines, 8,501; North Sydney, 7,820; Yarmouth, 7,475.

Vital statistics, *see* p. 269.
Religion, *see* p. 286.

CONSTITUTION AND GOVERNMENT. Under the British North America Act of 1867 the legislature of Nova Scotia may exclusively make laws in relation to local matters, including direct taxation within the province, education and the administration of justice. The legislature of Nova Scotia consists of a Lieut.-Governor, appointed and paid by the federal government, and holding office for 5 years, and a House of Assembly of 52 members, chosen by popular vote not more than every 5 years. The province is represented in the Canadian Senate by 10 members, and in the House of Commons by 11.

The franchise and eligibility to the legislature are granted to every person, male or female, if of age (19 years), a British subject or Canadian citizen, and a resident in the province for 1 year and 2 months before the date of the writ of election in the county or electoral district of which the polling district forms part, and if not by law otherwise disqualified. State of parties in March 1982: 37 Progressive Conservatives, 13 Liberals, 1 New Democrat, 1 independent.

Lieut.-Governor: John E. Shaffner.

Flag: A banner of the Arms, *i.e.*, white with a blue diagonal cross, bearing in the centre the royal shield of Scotland.

The members of the Progressive Conservatives Ministry are as follows:

Premier, President of the Executive Council, Chairman of the Policy Board, Minister of Intergovernmental Affairs: John M. Buchanan, QC.

Finance: Joel Matheson. *Development and Minister in Charge of Administration of the Research Foundation Corporation Act:* Roland J. Thornhill. *Attorney-General, Provincial Secretary and Minister in Charge of Administration of the Regulations Act:* Harry W. How. *Education and Minister in Charge of Administration of the Advisory Council on Status of Women Act:* Terence Donahoe. *Lands and Forests:* George Henley. *Health, Minister in Charge of Administration of the Drug Dependency Act and Registrar-General:* Gerald Sheehy. *Mines and Energy and Minister in Charge of the Nova Scotia Energy Council:* Ronald Barkhouse. *Agriculture and Marketing:* Roger S. Bacon. *Fisheries:* Kenneth Streatch. *Tourism:* Bruce Cochran. *Municipal Affairs:* Thomas McInnis. *Labour and Manpower:* Jack MacIsaac. *Chairman of the Management Board, Minister in Charge of Administration of the Civil Service Act and Minister in Charge of Administration of the Liquor Control Act:* Ronald Russell. *Transportation, Minister in Charge of Office of Communication Policy:* Ronald Giffin. *Social Services:* Edmund Morris. *Government Services, Minister in Charge of Administration of Communication and Information Act:* Jerry Lawrence. *Environment, Minister in Charge of Administration of the Nova Scotia Emergency Measures Act and Regulations (EMO) and Chairman of Resources Development Cabinet Policy Board:* Greg Kerr. *Culture, Recreation and Fitness, Minister in Charge of the Nova Scotia Heritage Property Act and Minister Responsible for Lotteries:* Fisher Hudson. *Consumer Affairs, Minister in Charge of Administration of Human Rights Act, Minister in Charge of Administration of the Residential Tenancies Act and Chairman of Social Development Cabinet Policy Board:* Laird Stirling. *Minister Without Portfolio in Charge of Administration of the Housing Development Act:* Michael Laffin.

Agent-General in London: Donald M. Smith (14 Pall Mall, SW1Y 5LU).

Local Government. The main divisions of the province for governmental purposes are the 3 cities, the 39 towns and the 24 rural municipalities, each governed by a council and a mayor or warden. The cities have independent charters, and the various towns take their powers from and are limited by The Towns Act, and the various municipalities take their powers from and are limited by The Municipal Act as revised in 1967. The majority of municipalities comprise 1 county, but 6 counties are divided into 2 municipalities each. In no case do the boundaries of any municipality overlap county lines. The 18 counties as such have no administrative functions.

Any city (of which there are 3) or incorporated town (of which there are 39) that lies within the boundaries of a municipality is excluded from any jurisdiction by the municipal council and has its own government.

FINANCE. Revenue is derived from provincial sources, payments from the federal government under the Federal-Provincial Fiscal Arrangements and Established Programs Financing Act (the '1977 Act'). Recoveries consist generally of amounts received under various federal cost-shared programmes. Main sources of provincial revenues include income and sales taxes.

Revenue, expenditure and debt (in Canadian $1m.) for fiscal years ending 31 March:

	1979	*1980*	*1981*	*1982*	*1983*[1]
Budgetary Transactions					
Current Expenditure	1,425·2	1,524·3	1,769·6	2,117·7	2,395·1
Current Revenues and Recoveries	1,393·4	1,565·2	1,750·1	1,937·4	2,265·8
Operating Deficit (Surplus)	31·8	(40·9)	19·5	180·3	129·3
Sinking fund Installments and Serial Retirements	29·4	30·9	32·2	34·3	45·4
Net Capital Expenditures	124·1	122·7	160·9	249·6	199·5
Net Budgetary Transactions	185·3	112·7	212·6	464·2	374·2
Non-Budgetary Transactions					
Capital Expenditures	9·1	2·5	10·2	3·2	3·2
Net Increase in Advances and Investments	34·3	86·4	108·5	75·6	9·4
Net Other Transactions	27·7	23·8	21·9	25·1	11·2
Non-Budgetary Transactions	71·1	112·7	140·6	103·9	23·8
	256·4	225·4	353·2	568·1	398·0

[1] Estimate.

NATURAL RESOURCES

Minerals. Principal minerals in 1981 were: Coal, 2·5m. tons, valued at $126m.; gypsum, 5·6m. tonnes, valued at $29m.; salt, 1·1m. tonnes, valued at $30·1m.; sand and gravel, 10m. tonnes, valued at $26m. Total value of mineral production in 1981 was about $261,916,000.

Agriculture. Dairying, poultry and egg production, livestock and fruit growing are the most important branches. Farm cash receipts for 1981 were estimated at $218·8m., with an additional $5·2m. going to persons on farms as income in kind.

Cash receipts from sale of dairy products was $62·7m., with total milk production of 173,163,000 litres.

The production of poultry meat in 1981 was 16,604 tonnes, of which 13,486 tonnes were chickens, 1,395 tonnes were fowls and 1,723 tonnes were turkeys. Egg production was 18·8m. dozen.

The main 1981 fruit crops were apples, 47,627 tonnes; blueberries, 5,889 tonnes; and strawberries, 1,588 tonnes.

Forestry. The estimated forest area of Nova Scotia is 15,555 sq. miles (40,298 sq. km), of which about 25% is owned by the province. The principal trees are spruce, balsam fir, hemlock, pine, larch, birch, oak, maple, poplar and ash. 3,689,213 cu. metres of round and sawn forest products were produced in 1981.

Fisheries. The fisheries of the province in 1981 had a landed value of $263·7m. of sea fish including scallop fishery, $88·3m., and lobster fishery, $41·3m. In 1980 there were about 6,805 employees in the fish processing industry; the value of shipment of goods was $376·4m.

INDUSTRY. The number of manufacturing establishments was 815 in 1980; the number of employees was 40,260; wages and salaries, $626·1m.; value of shipments was $3,454·4m. The value of shipments in 1981, was $3,744·2m., and the leading industries were petroleum and coal products, food and beverages, paper and allied industries and transportation equipment.

TRADE UNIONS. Total union membership during 1982 was 104,057 belonging to 98 unions comprised of 605 individual branches. The largest percentage of the total union membership was in the public administration and defence sector followed closely by the Service sector. An estimated 47,045 members in 357 branches were affiliated with the Canadian Labour Congress.

COMMUNICATIONS

Roads. In March 1982 there were 25,432 km of highways; 2,587 km of paved arterial highways; 4,650 km of collector highways (of which 4,328 km are paved); 18,195 km of local highways (of which 4,039 km are paved). The figures are exclusive of highways within cities and towns.

Railways. The province is covered with a network of railways, 1,223 miles in extent.

Aviation. There is a direct air service to major Canadian and USA cities, London and Bermuda.

Shipping. Ferry services connect Nova Scotia with Newfoundland, Prince Edward Island, New Brunswick and Maine. Direct service by container vessels is provided from the Port of Halifax to ports in Europe, Asia and the Caribbean.

JUSTICE AND EDUCATION

Justice. There is a Supreme Court which is a Court of common law and equity possessing original and appellate jurisdiction in civil and in criminal cases. The Supreme Court consists of an appeal division of 7 judges and a trial division of 12 judges. There are also county courts, family courts, probate courts, magistrates' courts, municipal and justices' courts. Bodies, sometimes referred to as courts, are established for the revision of assessment rolls, voters' lists and like purposes. Juvenile courts under the auspices of the family courts throughout the province have power to try boys and girls under the age of 16 years.

For the year ending 31 Dec. 1981 there were 4,327 admissions to provincial jails, of these, 2,854 were sentenced. The Adult Probation Service handled 6,639 cases during 1981.

Education. Public education in Nova Scotia is free, compulsory and undenominational through elementary and high school. Attendance is compulsory to the age of 16. In addition to over 600 public schools there are the Atlantic Inter-provincial Resource Centres for the Hearing Handicapped and for the Visually Impaired; the Nova Scotia School for Boys and the Nova Scotia School for Girls for delinquent children; and the Nova Scotia Youth Training Centre for mentally handicapped children. The province has 14 universities and colleges of which the largest is Dalhousie University in Halifax. The Nova Scotia Agricultural College and the Nova Scotia Teachers' College are located at Truro. The Technical University of Nova Scotia at Halifax grants degrees in engineering and architecture.

The Adult Education programme of the Nova Scotia Department of Education administers 2 institutes of technology and a nautical institute. It also provides in-school training for the Department of Labour Apprenticeship programme.

The Continuing Education Activity of the Department of Education offers financial support and organizational assistance to local school boards for provision of weekend and evening courses in academic and avocational subjects, and citizenship for new Canadians. It also provides local authorities with specialist support services to assist them in providing community workshops and it operates a correspondence study service for children and adults.

Occupational courses at the high school level are provided by 14 regional vocational schools under the jurisdiction (except in 3 amalgamated school areas) of the Department of Education.

Total expenditure on public education for the year 1980–81 was $456·9m., of which 72·1% was borne by the provincial government. In 1980–81, classrooms operated in 615 school houses, with 11,444 teachers and 190,478 pupils, of whom

96,970 were in elementary school grades and junior auxiliary classes and 93,500 in junior and senior high school grades.

Books of Reference

Atlantic Provinces Economic Council. *The Atlantic Vision, 1990.* Halifax, 1979
Nova Scotia, Today's Economy. Nova Scotia Dept. of Development. Halifax, 1980
Public Archives of Nova Scotia. *Place Names and Places of Nova Scotia.* Halifax, 1967
Beck, Murray, *The Government of Nova Scotia.* Toronto, 1957.—*Joseph Howe. The Voice of Nova Scotia.* 1964.—*The Evolution of Municipal Government in Nova Scotia, 1749–1973.* 1973
Elliott, S. B., *Nova Scotia Book of Days: A Calendar of the Province's History.* Halifax, 1979
Fergusson, C. B., *Nova Scotia in Encyclopedia Canadiana,* Vol. VII. Toronto, 1968
Raddall, T. H., *Halifax, Warden of the North.* Toronto, 1972
Vaison, R., *Nova Scotia Past and Present: A Bibliography and Guide.* Halifax, 1976

ONTARIO

HISTORY. The French explorer Samuel de Champlain explored the Ottawa River from 1613. The area was governed by the French, first under a joint stock company and then as a royal province, from 1627 and was ceded to Great Britain in 1763. A constitutional act of 1791 created there the province of Upper Canada, largely to accommodate loyalists of English descent who had immigrated after the United States war of independence. Upper Canada entered the Confederation as Ontario in 1867.

AREA AND POPULATION. The total area is about 412,600 sq. miles (1,068,630 sq. km), of which some 344,100 sq. miles (891,220 sq. km) are land area and some 68,500 sq. miles (177,420 sq. km) are fresh water.

The province extends 1,000 miles from east to west and 1,050 miles from north to south.

Ontario is bounded on the north by the waters of Hudson and James Bay, on the east by Quebec, on the west by Manitoba, and on the south by the states of New York, Pennsylvania, Ohio, Michigan, Wisconsin and Minnesota.

The population of the province (census, 1 June 1981) was 8,625,107. Census population of the principal cities (1981): Toronto (provincial capital), 599,217 (city), 2,998,947 (census metropolitan area); Hamilton, 306,434 (city), 542,095 (census metropolitan area); Ottawa (federal capital), 295,163 (city), 547,399 (census metropolitan area); London, 254,280 (city); Windsor, 192,083 (city), Kitchener, 139,734 (city), 287,801 (census metropolitan area); Sudbury, 89,773 (city), 159,779 (regional municipality).

Vital statistics, *see* p. 269.
Religion, *see* p. 286.

CONSTITUTION AND GOVERNMENT. The provincial government is administered by a Lieut.-Governor, a cabinet and one chamber elected by a general franchise for a period of 5 years. Women have the vote and can be elected to the chamber. The minimum voting age is 18 years.

In Oct. 1981 the provincial legislature was composed as follows: Progressive Conservatives, 70; Liberals, 34; New Democrats, 21; total 125.

Lieut.-Governor: Hon. John B. Aird, QC, BA, LLD (appointed 15 Sept. 1980).
Flag: The British Red Ensign with the shield of Ontario in the fly.

The members of the Executive Council in Oct. 1980 were as follows (all Progressive Conservatives):

Premier and President of the Council: William G. Davis, QC.
Energy and Deputy Minister: Robert Welch, QC. *Provincial Secretary for Justice:* Norman Sterling. *Provincial Secretary for Resources Development:* Lorne

Henderson. *Provincial Secretary for Social Development:* Margaret Birch. *Agriculture and Food:* Dennis Timbrell. *Attorney General:* Roy McMurtry, QC. *Citizenship and Culture:* Bruce McCaffrey. *Community and Social Services:* Frank Drea. *Consumer and Commercial Relations:* Dr Robert Elgie. *Correctional Services:* Nick Leluk. *Education and Colleges and Universities:* Dr Bette Stephenson. *Environment:* Keith Norton. *Government Services:* Douglas Wiseman. *Health:* Larry Grossman. *Industry and Trade Development:* Gordon Walker. *Intergovernmental Affairs:* Thomas Wells. *Labour:* Russell Ramsay. *Management Board of Cabinet (Chairman):* George McCague. *Municipal Affairs:* Claude Bennett. *Natural Resources:* Alan Pope. *Northern Affairs:* Leo Bernier. *Revenue:* George Ashe. *Solicitor General:* George Taylor, QC. *Tourism and Recreation:* Reuben Baetz. *Transportation and Communications:* James Snow. *Treasury and Economics:* Frank Miller. *Without Portfolio:* Bud Gregory, Robert Eaton.

Local Government. Local government in Ontario is divided into two branches, one covering municipal institutions and the other education.

The present municipal system dates from The Municipal Corporations Act enacted by The Province of Canada in 1849. It has been considerably modified in recent years with the creation of the Municipality of Metropolitan Toronto in 1954 and the launching of the Government of Ontario's local government restructuring programme in 1968. Generally, there are two levels of municipal government in Ontario. The upper level consists of 27 counties plus 12 restructured regional municipalities. The local level comprises more than 800 cities, towns and townships. Cities in the traditional county system function independently of the county in which they lie, as do 5 towns which have been separated for municipal purposes. There are no separated municipal units in regional governments.

Ontario's local municipalities are governed by councils elected by popular vote.

A city council usually consists of a mayor, aldermen and, sometimes, an executive committee known as a board of control.

Councils of towns, villages and townships usually consist of a mayor, reeve, deputy reeve, councillors and, in the case of the newer regional municipalities, one or more regional councillors who represent the area municipalities on the regional council.

County and regional government councils are federated assemblies.

A county council consists of the reeves and deputy reeves of the towns, villages and townships. The head of the county council is the warden, who is elected by the council from among its own members.

A regional council consists of the heads of council of the local municipalities, as well as a varying number of regional councillors, who are elected on the basis of representation, either directly or indirectly. The head of the regional council is the chairman who is elected by council but who, unlike a county warden, need not have been a council member.

No municipality in Ontario may incur long-term debts without the sanction of the tribunal created by the Provincial Legislature and known as the Ontario Municipal Board. Debenture obligations incurred by municipalities for utility undertakings (water-works and electric light and power systems) are discharged ordinarily out of revenues derived from the sale of utility services and do not fall upon the ratepayers.

Municipal councils have no jurisdiction for education beyond the collection of taxes for school purposes. Responsibility for providing, operating and maintaining school facilities, and for the supply of teachers, rests with local education authorities known as boards of education or school boards. These boards are now generally organized on a county or regional basis. Apart from some of the larger cities, local municipal school boards no longer exist.

Municipal institutions come under the jurisdiction of the Provincial Ministry of Intergovernmental Affairs. One of the principal functions of the Ministry is to advise and assist municipalities on such matters as accounting, reporting, auditing, budgeting and planning. Educational support and guidance at the provincial level is the responsibility of the Ministry of Education, which deals with the training of teachers and the formulation of curriculum. (At the university and community college level, education support services are provided by the Ministry of Colleges and Universities.)

There are considerable areas in the northernmost parts of Ontario where as yet there is little or no settlement of population. In such areas no municipal organization exists, and control for all purposes over such areas remains in the hands of the Provincial Government.

FINANCE. The gross revenue and expenditure and the net cash requirements (in Canadian $1,000) for years ending 31 March were as follows:

	1977–78	*1978–79*	*1979–80*	*1980–81*	*1981–82*
Gross revenue	11,782	13,233	15,246	16,470	18,886
Gross expenditure	13,544	14,413	15,830	17,273	20,389
Net cash requirement	1,762	1,180	584	803	1,503

Gross revenue and expenditure figures include all non-budgetary transactions, *i.e.*, the lending and investment activity of the Government to Crown corporations, agencies and municipalities as well as the repayment of these loans or recovery of investments. Transactions on behalf of Ontario Hydro are excluded.

ENERGY AND NATURAL RESOURCES

Electricity (1981). Ontario Hydro recorded for the calendar year a dependable peak capacity of 24·6m. kw. and a net energy output generated and purchased of 113,500m. kwh.

Minerals (1980, estimate). The value of shipments (in $1m.) in the mineral products industry were: Nickel, 1,159·7; copper, 504·7; iron ore, 247·2; gold, 292·6. The total value of mineral production was estimated at $4,317·6m. in 1981. The mining industry employed about 47,000 people.

Agriculture. In 1981, 3·5m. hectares were under field crops with total farm receipts of $4,901·5m.

Forestry. According to the most recent inventory (1963) the total area of productive forested land is 46,644,872 hectares, comprising: Softwoods, 23,591,147; hardwoods, 5,537,313; mixed woods, 14,270,428; reproducing forests, 3,245,983. The growing stock equals 4,266,868m. cu. ft. The estimated value of shipments by the forest products industry (including logging) was (1980 census) $6,857m.

INDUSTRY AND TRADE

Industry (1979). Ontario is Canada's most highly industrialized province. About 73% of value added in commodity-producing industries is accounted for by manufacturing. Construction is next with 13%.

In 1980, the labour force was 4,481,000. Total labour income was $73,986m. The Gross Provincial Product (GPP) was $124,800m.

The leading manufacturing industries are motor vehicles and parts, iron and steel, meat and meat preparations, dairy products, paper and paperboard, chemical products, petroleum and coal products, machinery and equipment, metal stamping and pressing and communications equipment.

Trade. In 1981 Ontario exported 35% ($29,493·8m.) of Canada's total foreign trade.

COMMUNICATIONS

Roads. There were, in 1980, 160,141·8 km of roads. Motor licences numbered approximately 5·3m., of which 3·7m. were passenger cars, 813,890 trucks and tractors, 20,620 buses, 520,602 trailers, 98,425 motor cycles and 143,980 snow vehicles.

Railways. The provincially-owned Ontario Northland Railway has about 550 miles of track and the Algoma Central Railway 325 miles. The Canadian National and Canadian Pacific Railways operate a total of about 9,500 miles in Ontario.

Post (1981). Telephone service is provided by 31 independent systems (270,035 telephones) and Bell Canada (about 6m. telephones).

EDUCATION. There is a complete provincial system of elementary and secondary schools as well as private schools. In 1981 publicly financed elementary and secondary schools had a total enrolment of 1,793,515 pupils.

In 1965 Ontario established Colleges of Applied Arts and Technology (CAATS). There are now 22 of these publicly owned colleges with full-time enrolment of over 75,813 in academic courses.

The University of Toronto, founded in 1827 (full-time enrolment, 1981, 34,808), and 14 other major universities, all receive provincial grants. The net general expenditure of the provincial ministries of education and colleges and universities for the fiscal year ending 31 March 1981 was $4,146m.

Books of Reference

Statistical Information: Annual publications of the Ontario Ministry of Treasury and Economics include: *Ontario Statistics; Ontario Budget; Public Accounts; Financial Report.*

PRINCE EDWARD ISLAND

HISTORY. The earliest discovery of the island is not satisfactorily known, but the first recorded visit was by Jacques Cartier in 1534, who named it Isle St-Jean; it was first settled by the French, but was taken from them in 1758. It was annexed to Nova Scotia in 1763, and constituted a separate colony in 1769. Prince Edward Island entered the Confederation on 1 July 1873.

AREA AND POPULATION. The province, which is the smallest in Canada, lies in the Gulf of St Lawrence, and is separated from the mainland of New Brunswick and Nova Scotia by Northumberland Strait. The area of the island is 2,184 sq. miles (5,656 sq. km). Total population (census, 1981), 124,200. Population of the principal cities (1980): Charlottetown (capital), 17,063; Summerside, 8,532.

Vital statistics, *see* p. 269.

Religion, *see* p. 286.

CONSTITUTION AND GOVERNMENT. The provincial government is administered by a Lieut.-Governor-in-Council (Cabinet) and a Legislative Assembly of 32 members who are elected for up to 5 years. In Oct. 1982, parties in the Legislative Assembly were: Progressive Conservatives, 21; Liberals, 11.

Lieut.-Governor: Joseph Aubin Doiron (sworn in 14 Jan. 1980).

Flag: A banner of the arms, *i.e.*, a white field bearing 3 small trees and a larger tree on a compartment, all green, and at the top a red band with a golden lion; on 3 sides a border of red and white rectangles.

Premier, President of the Executive Council: James M. Lee.

Finance and Tourism: Lloyd G. MacPhail. *Justice, Labour and Attorney-General:* George R. McMahon, QC. *Fisheries and Industry:* Patrick G. Binns. *Agriculture:* Prowse G. Chappell. *Energy and Forestry:* Frederick L. Driscoll. *Health and Social Services:* Albert Fogarty. *Transportation and Public Works:* R. B. (Roddy) Pratt. *Education:* Leone Bagnall. *Community and Cultural Affairs:* Gordon Lank.

Local Government. The Village Service Act, 1954, provides for the incorporation of villages. The city of Charlottetown and the town of Summerside have been incorporated under Special Acts. The Town Act, 1951, provides for the incorporation of all towns. The Community Improvement Act, 1968, provides for the establishment of Community Improvement Committees in the unincorporated areas of the province.

FINANCE. Revenue and expenditure (in Canadian $) for 6 financial years ending 31 March:

	1977–78	*1978–79*	*1979–80*	*1980–81*	*1981–82*	*1982–83*
Revenue	216,817,800	242,274,000	273,375,400	307,566,300	352,556,900	380,883,900
Expenditure	216,708,700	242,488,500	273,074,300	306,789,900	351,486,200	386,878,700

ENERGY AND NATURAL RESOURCES

Electricity. Electric power is supplied to 98% of the population. The province's net generated and purchased consumption of electricity dropped during 1981 from 515m. kwh. to 514m. kwh. In 1981, peak demand for electricity was 96·6 mw. In 1977 the province completed the laying of an undersea power cable which links the island with New Brunswick and the Maritime Power Grid. In 1980, 30 miles of additional 138 kv transmission line was added to the PEI system. In 1981, about 94% of power requirements were supplied through this system.

Agriculture. Improved farm land occupies about 774,630 acres out of a total of 1,399,040 acres. Potatoes provided about 41·7% of total farm cash receipts in 1981, with dairy products, cattle, calves and hogs following in importance. Farm cash receipts in 1981 were $184·2m. The land in natural forest covers 920 sq. miles, producing annually about 17m. bd ft of lumber and 35,000 cords of pulpwood. For particulars of agricultural production and livestock, *see under* CANADA, pp. 277–79.

Fisheries. The fishery of the province in 1981 had a landed value of $31·9m. Lobsters accounted for 58·5% of the total. The famous 'Malpeque' oyster industry had a landed value of $1·4m. in 1981, an increase of 34% over 1980. Seaplant landings were valued at $1·9m.; bluefin tuna landings were valued at $525,000; scallops were valued at $1·6m.; and groundfish at $5·4m.

INDUSTRY AND TRADE

Industry. Industrial establishments produced goods to a shipment value of $260·3m. in 1979.

Commerce. Average personal income rose from $7,154 in 1980 to $7,829 in 1981. The average wage rose from $230·03 per week in 1980 to $250·13 in 1981. The labour force averaged 54,000 in 1981. Total employment was 48,000 in 1981.

Value added in manufacturing, 1979 was $85·2m. and the value added in the construction industry was $84m.

Continued growth in trade, commerce, finance and transport and other services is reflected by retail trade valued at $400,745,000 (1981).

Tourism. The value of the tourist industry was estimated at $49·4m. in 1981 with 214,909 tourist parties.

COMMUNICATIONS

Roads. The province has a total of 5,278 km of road, including 3,592·76 km of paved highway.

Railways. Rail service is provided over 274 miles of track within the province and connects with the national railways system *via* the New Brunswick–Prince Edward Island ferry service.

Aviation. Air service for passengers, mail and cargo is scheduled to provide 8 flights daily in each direction between the province and various points in eastern Canada. A daily bus service operates between various centres in the province as well as to Nova Scotia during the summer months.

Shipping. A ferry service provides rail and highway communication with New Brunswick by means of 4 large ferries, 2 of which are powerful ice-breakers. Another ferry service employing 2 ferries plus an additional 2 for summertime operates between the province and Nova Scotia throughout the season of open navigation. A third ferry service employing 1 ferry operates between the province and Magdalen Islands, Quebec, during the open navigation season.

Post. In 1982 there were approximately 71,959 telephones.

EDUCATION (1981–82). Under the regional school boards there are 68 public schools, 1,408 teachers, 25,968 students. Vocational school enrolment, 845 students. There is one undergraduate university (1,390 full-time students), and a college of applied arts and technology (750 full-time post-secondary students), both in Charlottetown. Total expenditure in education in the year ending 31 March 1983 is forecast to be $96,063,800.

Books of Reference

Clark, A. H., *Three Centuries and the Island.* Toronto, 1959
Hocking, A., *Prince Edward Island.* Toronto, 1978
MacKinnon, F., *The Government of Prince Edward Island.* Toronto, 1951

QUEBEC—QUÉBEC

HISTORY. Quebec was formerly known as New France or Canada from 1534 to 1763; as the province of Quebec from 1763 to 1790; as Lower Canada from 1791 to 1846; as Canada East from 1846 to 1867, and when, by the union of the four original provinces, the Confederation of the Dominion of Canada was formed, it again became known as the province of Quebec (Québec).

The Quebec Act, passed by the British Parliament in 1774, guaranteed to the people of the newly conquered French territory in North America security in their religion and language, their customs and tenures, under their own civil laws.

In the referendum held 20 May 1980, 59·5% voted against and 40·5% for 'separatism'.

AREA AND POPULATION. The area of Quebec (as amended by the Labrador Boundary Award) is 594,860 sq. miles (1,540,668 sq. km), of which 523,860 sq. miles is land area and 71,000 sq. miles water. Of this extent, 351,780 sq. miles represent the Territory of Ungava, annexed in 1912 under the Quebec Boundaries Extension Act. The population (census 1981) was 6,438,403.

Principal cities (1981): Quebec (capital), 166,474; Montreal, 980,354; Laval, 268,335; Sherbrooke, 74,075; Verdun, 61,287; Hull, 56,225; Trois-Rivières, 50,466.

Vital statistics, *see* p. 269.
Religion, *see* p. 286.

CONSTITUTION AND GOVERNMENT. There is a Legislative Assembly consisting of 122 members, elected in 122 electoral districts for 4 years. There were, 13 April 1981, 80 *Parti Québecois*, 42 Liberals.

Lieut.-Governor: The Hon. Jean Pierre Côté.

Flag: The Fleurdelysé flag, blue with a white cross, and in each quarter a white fleur-de-lis.

The members of the Executive Council as on 8 March 1982, are as follows:

Prime Minister and President of the Council: René Lévesque.

Vice-Prime Minister and Minister of Intergovernmental Affairs: Jacques-Yvan Morin. *Education:* Camille Laurin. *Finance, Financial Institutions and Co-operatives:* Jacques Parizeau. *Treasury:* Yves Bérubé. *Parliamentary Leader and Minister of Communications:* Jean-François Bertrand. *Justice:* Marc-André Bédard. *Economic Development:* Bernard Landry. *Social Development:* Denis Lazure. *Planning:* François Gendron. *Women's Affairs:* Pauline Marois. *Work and Manpower:* Pierre Marois. *Municipal Affairs:* Jacques Léonard. *Agriculture and Fisheries:* Jean Garon. *Environment:* Marcel Léger. *Recreation and Sport:* Lucien Lessard. *Energy and Resources:* Yves Duhaime. *Consumer Affairs:* Guy Tardif. *Social Affairs:* Pierre-Marc Johnson. *Transport:* Michel Clair. *Cultural*

Affairs: Clément Richard. *Immigration:* Gérald Godin. *Public Functions:* Denise Leblanc-Bantey. *Public Works:* Alain Marcoux. *Industry, Commerce and Tourism:* Rodrigue Biron. *Revenue:* Raynald Fréchette.

General-delegate in London: Vacant (59 Pall Mall, SW1).

General-delegate in New York: Raymond Gosselin (17 West 50th St., Rockefeller Center, New York 10020).

General-delegate in Paris: Yves Michaud (66 Pergolèse, Paris 75116).

ECONOMY

Budget. Ordinary revenue and expenditure (in Canadian $1,000) for fiscal years ending 31 March:

	1976–77	*1977–78*	*1978–79*	*1979–80*	*1980–81*
Revenue	9,217,265	10,742,609	11,928,343	13,306,680	14,718,305
Expenditure	10,208,430	11,503,008	13,402,830	15,123,200	17,596,659

The total net debt at 31 March 1981 was $12,059,002,000.

ENERGY AND NATURAL RESOURCES

Electricity. Water power is one of the most important natural resources of the province of Quebec. Its turbine installation represents about 40% of the aggregate of Canada. At the end of 1980 the installed generating capacity was 20,531 mw. Production, 1981, was 102,904 gwh.

Minerals (1981). The estimated value of the mineral production (metal mines only) was $1,351,189,000. Chief minerals: Iron ore, $588,009,000; copper, $200,477,000; gold, $298,294,000; zinc, $64,614,000.

The second major iron-ore development in northern Quebec is, like the one at Knob Lake which gave birth to Schefferville, based on the Quebec–Labrador Trough which extends from Lac Jeannine to the northern tip of Ungava peninsula. The port of Sept-Iles and the railway connecting it with Schefferville allow easy shipment to the furnaces and steel mills of Canada, the USA and Europe. The setting-up of a steel industry is being explored.

Non-metallic minerals produced include: Asbestos ($471,443,000; about 87% of Canadian production), titane-dioxide ($114,754,000), industrial lime, dolomite and brucite, quartz and pyrite. Among the building materials produced were: Stone, $154,143,000; cement, $128,973,000; sand and gravel, $83,047,000; lime, $20,589,000.

Agriculture. In 1981 the total area of the principal field crops was 2,149,700 hectares. The yield of the principal crops was (in 1,000 tonnes):

Crops	*Yield*	*Crops*	*Yield*
Tame hay	5,463	Fodder corn	3,706
Oats for grain	366	Maize for grain	620
Potatoes	377	Barley	177
Mixed grains	129	Buckwheat	7

The farm cash receipts from farming operations in 1981 amounted to $2,670,968,000. The principal items being: Livestock and products, $2,110,626,000; crops, $301,505,000; dairy supplements payments, $135,132,000, forest and maple products, $65,412,000.

Forestry. Forests cover an area of 684,480 sq. km. About 490,693 sq. km are classified as productive forests, of which 611,625 sq. km are provincial crown land and 70,912 sq. km are privately owned. Quebec leads the Canadian provinces in pulpwood production, having nearly half of the Canadian estimated total.

In 1980 production of lumber was softwood and hardwood, 8,059,120 cu. metres; woodpulp, 6,356,079 tonnes; paper and paperboard, 5,494,563 tonnes.

Fisheries. The principal fish are cod, herring, red fish, lobster and salmon. Total catch of sea fish, 1981, 79,114·26 tonnes, valued at $46,790,433.

INDUSTRY AND TRADE

Industry. In 1980 there were 10,740 industrial establishments in the province; employees, 391,374; salaries and wages, \$5,914,006; cost of materials, \$25,727,023; value of shipments, \$44,586,552. Among the leading industries are petroleum refining, pulp and paper mills, smelting and refining, dairy products, slaughtering and meat processing, motor vehicle manufacturing, women's clothing, saw-mills and planing mills, iron and steel mills, commercial printing.

Commerce. In 1981 the value of Canadian exports through Quebec custom ports was \$18,053·1m.; value of imports, \$16,223,042,000.

COMMUNICATIONS

Roads. In 1976 there were 49,072 miles of roads and (1980) 4,370,598 registered motor vehicles.

Railways. There were (1980) 8,322 km of railway.

Aviation. In 1979 Quebec had 2 international airports, Dorval (Montreal) with landing runway of 27,600 ft and Mirabel (Montreal) with 24,000 ft.

Post and Broadcasting. Telephones numbered 4,130,712 in 1980 and there were 24 television and 119 radio stations in 1981.

Newspapers (1981). There were 10 French- and 2 English-language daily newspapers.

EDUCATION. The province has 7 universities: 3 English-language universities, McGill (Montreal) founded in 1821, Bishop (Lennoxville) founded in 1845 and the Concordia University (Montreal) granted a charter in 1975; 4 French-language universities: Laval (Quebec) founded in 1852, Montreal University, opened in 1876 as a branch of Laval and became independent in 1920, Sherbrooke University founded in 1954 and University of Quebec founded in 1968.

In 1980–81 there were 87,259 full-time university students and 101,810 part-time students.

In 1980–81, in pre-kindergartens, there were 7,082 pupils; in kindergartens, 87,772; primary schools, 500,442; in secondary schools, 521,930; in colleges (post-secondary, non-university), 135,319; and in classes for children with special needs, 96,624. The school boards had a total of 68,509 teachers.

Expenditure of the Department of Education for 1980–81 (Canadian \$1,000), 5,047,962 net. This included 792,941 for universities, 3,096,286 for public primary and secondary schools, 203,460 for private primary and secondary schools and 595,477 for colleges.

Books of Reference

Statistical Information: The Quebec Bureau of Statistics was established in 1912. The Bureau, which reports to the Executive council since Sept. 1981, collects, compiles and distributes statistical information relative to Quebec. *Director:* M. Yvon Fortin.

A statistical information list is available on request. Among the most important publications are: *Annuaire du Québec* (Quebec Yearbook), *Statistiques* (quarterly), *Comptes économiques du Québec* (annual), *Perspectives démographiques* (annual), *Situation démographique* (annual), *Exportations internationales du Québec* (annual), *Statistiques du travail et de la main-d'oeuvre* (annual), *Investissements privés et publics* (annual), *Eléments de prévisions économiques* (quarterly), *Statistiques manufacturières* (annual).

Atlas du Québec: L'Agriculture. Ministère de l'Industrie et du Commerce, Quebec, 1966
Baudoin, L., *Le Droit civil de la province de Québec.* Montreal, 1953
Blanchard, R., *Le Canada-français.* Paris, 1959
Cook, R., *Canada and the French-Canadian Question.* Toronto, 1966
Hamelin, J., *Histoire du Québec.* St-Hyacinthe, 1978
Jacobs, J., *The Question of Separatism: Quebec and the Struggle for Sovereignty.* London, 1981
McWhinney, E., *Quebec and the Constitution.* Univ. of Toronto Press, 1979
Ouellet, F., *Histoire de la Chambre de Commerce de Québec, 1809–1959.* Québec, 1959
Raynauld, A., *Croissance et structure économiques de la province de Québec.* Québec, 1961

Trofimenkoff, S. M., *Action Française.* Univ. of Toronto Press, 1975
Wade, F. M., *The French Canadians, 1760–1967.* Toronto, 1968.—*Canadian Dualism: Studies of French–English Relations.* Quebec–Toronto, 1960

SASKATCHEWAN

HISTORY. Saskatchewan derives its name from its major river system, which the Cree Indians called 'Kis-is-ska-tche-wan', meaning 'swift flowing'. It officially became a province when it joined the Confederation on 1 Sept. 1905.

In 1670 King Charles II granted to Prince Rupert and his friends a charter covering exclusive trading rights in 'all the land drained by streams finding their outlet in the Hudson Bay'. This included what is now Saskatchewan. The trading company was first known as The Governor and Company of Adventurers of England; later as the Hudson's Bay Company. In 1869 the Northwest Territories was formed, and this included Saskatchewan. In 1882 the District of Saskatchewan was formed. By 1885 the North-West Mounted Police had been inaugurated, with headquarters in Regina (now the capital), and the Canadian Pacific Railway's transcontinental line had been completed, bringing a stream of immigrants to southern Saskatchewan. The Hudson's Bay Company surrendered its claim to territory in return for cash and land around the existing trading posts. Legislative government was introduced.

AREA AND POPULATION. Saskatchewan is bounded on the west by Alberta, on the east by Manitoba, to the north by the Northwest Territories; to the south it is bordered by the US states of Montana and North Dakota. The area of the province is 220,121 sq. miles (570,113 sq. km), of which 220,182 sq. miles is land area and 31,518 sq. miles is water. The population (1981 census) was 968,313. Population of principal cities (1981 census): Regina (capital), 162,613; Saskatoon, 154,210; Moose Jaw, 33,941; Prince Albert, 31,380; Yorkton, 15,339; Swift Current, 14,747; North Battleford, 14,030; Estevan, 10,359; Weyburn, 9,523; Lloydminster, 6,034; Melfort, 6,010; Melville, 5,092.

Vital statistics, *see* p. 269.

Religion, *see* p. 286.

CONSTITUTION AND GOVERNMENT. The provincial government is vested in a Lieut.-Governor, an Executive Council and a Legislative Assembly, elected for 5 years. Women were given the franchise in 1916 and are also eligible for election to the legislature. State of parties in May 1982: Progressive Conservative, 56; New Democratic Party, 8.

Lieut.-Governor: C. Irwin McIntosh.

Flag: Green over gold, with the shield of the province in the canton, and a green and red prairie lily in the fly.

The Progressive Conservative Ministry in Jan. 1983 was composed as follows:

Premier: Grant Devine.

Deputy Premier, Agriculture and House Leader: Eric Berntson. *Finance:* Bob Andrew. *Mineral Resources:* Vacant. *Attorney-General, Intergovernmental Affairs and Communications:* Gary Lane. *Industry and Commerce:* Paul Rousseau. *Health:* Graham Taylor. *Government Services and Revenue, Supply and Services:* Joan Duncan. *Environment:* Neal Hardy. *Northern Saskatchewan and Tourism and Renewable Resources:* George McLeod. *Social Services:* Pat Smith. *Rural Affairs:* Bob Pickering. *Highways and Transportation:* Jim Garner. *Labour:* Lorne McLaren. *Education:* Gord Durrie. *Consumer Affairs and Co-operative Development:* Jack Sandberg. *Culture and Youth and Urban Affairs:* Paul Schoenhals.

Agent-General in London: W. M. Johnson, 14–16 Cockspur St., SW1 5BL.

Local Government. The organization of a city requires a minimum population of

5,000 persons; that of a town, 500; that of a village, 100 people. No requirements as to population exist for the rural municipality and the local improvement district.

Cities, towns, villages and rural municipalities are governed by elected councils, which consist of a mayor and 6–20 aldermen in a city; a mayor and 6 councillors in a town; a mayor and 2 other members in a village; a reeve and a councillor for each division in a rural municipality (usually 6). Local improvement districts are administered by the Department of Municipal Affairs.

FINANCE. Budget and net assets (years ending 31 March) in Canadian $1,000[2]:

	1976–77	*1977–78*	*1978–79*	*1979–80* [1]	*1980–81* [1]
Budgetary revenue	1,340,636	1,459,979	1,613,470	1,807,160	2,019,345
Budgetary expenditure	1,364,142	1,503,112	1,676,322	1,856,556	2,018,303
Net assets	55,919	56,871	21,424	...	...

[1] Estimate.
[2] Excludes Consolidated Fund, Community Capital Fund, Saskatchewan Heritage Fund, Energy and Resource Development Fund and The Marketing Development Fund.

ENERGY AND NATURAL RESOURCES. Agriculture used to dominate the history and economics of Saskatchewan, but the 'prairie province' is now a rapidly developing mining and manufacturing area. It is a major supplier of oil; has the world's largest deposits of potash; is the only source of helium in the 'free world' outside the USA, which limits production to internal use; and net value of non-agricultural production account for (1979 estimate) 60% of the provincial economy.

Electricity. The Saskatchewan Power Corporation generated 8,982m. kwh. in 1979.

Minerals. The 1979 mineral production was valued at $1,835·1m., including (in $1m.): Petroleum 720; natural gas, 15·5; coal, 22; gold, 4; silver, 3; copper, 13·8; zinc, 3·5; potash, 695·3; salt, 11; uranium, 258.

Agriculture. Saskatchewan produces normally about two-thirds of Canada's wheat. Wheat production in 1979 (in 1,000 tonnes), was 10,179 (374m. bu.) from 17m. acres; oats, 632 (41m. bu.) from 1m. acres; barley, 1,960 (90m. bu.) from 2·6m. acres; rye, 203 (80m. bu.) from 360,000 acres; rapeseed, 1,281 (57m. bu.) from 3·3m. acres; flax, 259 (10m. bu.) from 800,000 acres. Livestock (Jan. 1980): Cattle, 2·17m.; swine, 660,000; sheep, 60,000. Poultry in 1979: Chickens and turkeys 11·4m. Cash income from the sale of farm products in 1979 was $2,905,193,000. At the June 1976 census there were 66,258 commercial farms in the province, each being a holding having agricultural sales of $2,500 or more.

The South Saskatchewan River irrigation project, whose main feature is the Gardiner Dam, was completed in 1967. It will ultimately provide for an area of 200,000 acres of irrigated cultivation in Central Saskatchewan. In 1979–80, 32,199 acres were under development.

Forestry. Half of Saskatchewan's area is forested, but only 115,000 sq. km are of commercial value at present. Forest products valued at $162m. were produced in 1978–79. The province's first pulp-mill, at Prince Albert, went into production in 1968; its daily capacity is 1,000 tons of high-grade kraft pulp.

Fur Production. In 1978–79 wild fur production was estimated at $10,099,490. Ranch-raised fur production amounted to $410,586.

Fisheries. The lakeside value of the 1978–79 commercial fish catch of 2·6m. lb. was $538,000.

INDUSTRY. In 1979 Saskatchewan had 676 manufacturing establishments, employing 23,000 persons. The net value of non-agricultural production was $3,460m. Manufacturing accounted for $718m., construction for $1,058m.

TOURISM. An estimated 1,051,000 tourists spent $104m. in 1978.

COMMUNICATIONS

Roads. In 1979 there were 19,561 km of provincial highways, 180,647 km of municipal roads (including prairie trails). Motor vehicles registered totalled (1979) 682,821. Bus services are provided by 2 major lines.

Railways. There were (1979) approximately 12,342 km of main railway track in operation.

Aviation. Saskatchewan had 2 major airports, 176 airports and landing strips in 1976.

Post and Broadcasting. There were (1979) 716 post offices (excluding sub-post offices), 68 TV and re-broadcasting stations and 35 AM and FM radio stations. 584,456 telephones were connected to the Saskatchewan Telecommunications system.

EDUCATION. The University of Saskatchewan was established at Saskatoon on 3 April 1907. In 1978–79 it had about 10,313 (day-time) degree students, 1,116 (part-time) and 2,528 full-time and part-time teaching staff at Saskatoon and 3,342 (full-time) and 716 (part-time) students and 947 full- and part-time faculty members at the University of Regina which was established 1 July 1974. The Saskatchewan public education system in 1978–79 consisted of 120 school units and districts serving 143,456 elementary pupils, 30,629 high-school students and 3,306 students enrolled in special classes. In addition, 3 provincial technical and vocational schools provided training for approximately 14,561 technical and 2,943 trade students. There are also 17 Roman Catholic separate school districts and 2 separate high-school districts. In addition there are 15 community colleges with an enrolment of over 100,000 registrations per year.

Books of Reference

Tourist and industrial publications, descriptive of the Government's programme, are obtainable from the Department of Industry and Commerce; other government publications from Government Information Services (Legislative Building, Regina).
Saskatchewan Economic Review. Executive Council, Regina. Annual
Archer and Derby, *The Story of a Province.* Toronto, 1955
McCourt, E. A., *Saskatchewan.* Toronto, 1968
Morton, A. S., *Saskatchewan, the Making of a University.* Toronto, 1959
Richards, J. S., and Fung, K. I. (eds.), *Atlas of Saskatchewan.* Univ. of Saskatchewan, 1969
Wright, J. F. C., *Saskatchewan, the History of a Province.* Toronto, 1955

THE NORTHWEST TERRITORIES

HISTORY. The Territory was developed by the Hudson's Bay Company and the North West Company (of Montreal) from the 17th century. The Canadian Government bought out the Hudson's Bay Company in 1869 and the Territory was annexed to Canada in 1870. The Arctic Island lying north of the Canadian mainland was annexed to Canada in 1880 by Queen Victoria.

AREA AND POPULATION. The total area of the Territories is 1,304,903 sq. miles (3,379,700 sq. km), divided into 5 districts, namely, Inuvik, Fort Smith, Keewatin, Baffin and Kitikmeot. The population in June 1981 was 45,741, about 55% of whom were Indians or Inuit (Eskimo). Main centres (census 1980): Inuvik (2,918), Fort Smith (2,265), Hay River (3,322), Frobisher Bay (2,444), Fort Simpson (981). When the transfer of governmental responsibility from Ottawa to the Territorial capital at Yellowknife took place in 1967, the population of Yellowknife increased by the influx of civil servants from 3,741 in 1966 to 9,731 in 1980.

CONSTITUTION AND GOVERNMENT. The Northwest Territories comprises all that portion of Canada lying north of the 60th parallel of N. lat.

except those portions within the Yukon Territory and the Provinces of Quebec and Newfoundland: it also includes the islands in Hudson Bay, James Bay and Ungava Bay except those within the Provinces of Manitoba, Ontario and Quebec.

The Northwest Territories is governed by a Commissioner and a Legislative Assembly. The Council is composed of 22 members elected for a 4-year term of office. The seat of government was transferred from Ottawa to Yellowknife when it was named territorial capital on 18 Jan. 1967.

Commissioner: J. H. Parker.

Flag: Vertically, blue, white, blue, with the white of double width and bearing the shield of the Territory.

Legislative powers are exercised by the Commissioner-in-Council on such matters as taxation within the Territories in order to raise revenue, maintenance of justice, licences, solemnization of marriages, education, public health, property, civil rights and generally all matters of a local nature.

TheTerritorial Government has now assumed responsibility for the administration of the entire Northwest Territories. In May 1982 the legislature voted to request the Federal Government to divide the territories into two parts and to establish a Commission to determine a boundary.

ENERGY AND NATURAL RESOURCES

Oil and Gas. As of March 1982, 2,068 permits for oil and gas exploration were held for 54·18m. hectares, of which 110 leases were on the mainland, 1,508 were on the arctic islands and 440 on the marine coast.

Crude oil, discovered in 1920, is produced and refined at Norman Wells on the Mackenzie River. In 1981, oil production was 181·989 cu. metres.

Minerals. Mineral production for the year 1981, from 8 producing mines, was valued at $540,866,401, of which zinc accounted for $331·7m.; lead, $83·5m.; gold, $66·9m.; tungsten, $40m.; silver, $18·2m.; copper, $440,920 and cadmium, $881·000.

Yellowknife continues to be the centre of goldmining activity and Canada's Cominco Ltd has completed construction of a lead-zinc mine, the Polaris Project, on Little Cornwallis Island in the central high arctic. Production is expected to start in 1982.

Trapping and Game. Fur produced during the 1981–82 season was valued at $5,029,000, primarily in muskrat, fox, lynx and marten. A herd of some 6,500 buffalo is protected in Wood Buffalo National Park. Barren ground caribou are increasing, due to more effective management techniques.

Forestry. The principal trees are white and black spruce, jack-pine, balsam, poplar and birch. In 1981, 45,850 cu. metres measure of lumber, 2,833 cu. metres of round timber and 5,540 cu. metres of fuelwood were cut.

Fisheries. Commercial fishing, principally on Great Slave Lake, in 1981–82 produced fish valued at $1·3m., principally trout, char and whitefish.

CO-OPERATIVES. There are 36 active co-operatives in the Northwest Territories. They are active in handicrafts, furs, fisheries, retail stores, print shops, provision of housing, contracting for services, etc. Total sales in 1980–81 were more than $20m.

COMMUNICATIONS

Roads. The Mackenzie Route connects Grimshaw, Alberta, with Hay River, Pine Point, Fort Smith, Fort Providence, Rae-Edzo and Yellowknife. The Mackenzie Highway extension to Fort Simpson and a road between Pine Point and Fort Resolution have both been opened.

Clearing began in 1972 for extending the Mackenzie Highway north of Fort Simpson to the arctic coast. Highway service to Inuvik in the Mackenzie Delta was opened in spring 1980, extending north from Dawson, Yukon as the Dempster

Highway. The Liard Highway connecting the communities of the Liard River valley to British Columbia is expected to open in 1983.

Railways. The Great Slave Lake Railway runs from Pine Point and Hay River, on the south shore of Great Slave Lake, 435 miles south to Grimshaw, Alberta, where it connects with the CN Rail's main system.

Aviation (1979). Fourteen licensed and 1 unlicensed airports are operated by the federal Ministry of Transport and there are 17 licensed and 18 unlicensed airports operated by the Government of the Northwest Territories. Two licensed and 10 unlicensed airports are operated by private owners. Regular mail,passenger and express services are maintained throughout the Territories. A seaplane base is operated by the Ministry of Transport and there are 17 private seaplane bases. Scheduled services join major points with centres in southern Canada.

Shipping. A direct inland-water transportation route for about 1,700 miles is provided by the Mackenzie River and its tributaries, the Athabasca and Slave rivers. Subsidiary routes on Lake Athabasca, Great Slave Lake and Great Bear River and Lake total more than 800 miles.

Post and Broadcasting (1982). There were 54 post offices. The CBC northern service operated radio stations at Yellowknife, Inuvik, Frobisher Bay and Rankin Inlet. Virtually all communities of 150 or over were receiving television in 1982 *via* satellite. Telephone service is provided by common carriers to nearly all communities in the Northwest Territories. Those few communities without service have high frequency or very high frequency radios for emergency use.

EDUCATION AND WELFARE

Education. In 1981–82 the Government of the Northwest Territories operated 71 schools with 719 teachers. In addition, one public school district operated at Yellowknife, one Roman Catholic separate school district at Yellowknife, and one school society operated a school at Rae-Edzo. The total enrolment was 12,581 in 1982, of whom about 65% were Inuit (Eskimos) and Indians. Four large and 4 small residences accommodate 400 students. Free correspondence courses are available to any pupil in a settlement where appropriate instruction is not available. There is a full range of courses available in the school system: academic, industrial arts, home economics, commercial, technical and occupational training. The continuing and special education programme provides courses and financial assistance to residents who have left the school system or are taking post high school training.

Health. In 1980 there were 7 hospitals in the Territories, 3 operated by the territorial government (Yellowknife, Hay River and Fort Smith) and 4 operated by the federal government. Thirty-nine nursing stations, 6 health stations and 8 health centres were in operation.

Welfare. Welfare services are provided by professional social workers. Facilities included (1978) 5 children's receiving homes, 2 homes for the aged and 1 transient centre.

Books of Reference

Annual Report of the Department of Indian Affairs and Northern Development, 1974–75
Annual Report of the Government of the Northwest Territories, 1980
Boyle, E., and Sprudz, A., *Arctic Cooperatives, Canada 1965–68*
Dawson, C. A., *The New North-West.* Toronto, 1947
MacKay, D., *The Honorable Company.* Toronto, 1949

YUKON TERRITORY

HISTORY. Formerly part of the North-West Territory, Yukon was joined to the Dominion as a separate territory in 1898.

AREA AND POPULATION. The Yukon Territory is situated in the extreme north-western section of Canada and comprises 531,843 sq. km. The census population in 1981 was 22,153. Principal centres are Whitehorse (capital), 14,814; Faro, 1,652; Watson Lake, 748; Dawson City, 697; Mayo-Elsa, 398.

Vital statistics, *see* p. 269.
Religion, *see* p. 286.

CONSTITUTION AND GOVERNMENT. The Yukon Territory was constituted a separate territory in June 1898. It is governed by a 5-member Executive Council (Cabinet) appointed from among the 16-member elected Legislative Assembly. The members are elected for a 4-year term. The seat of government is at Whitehorse. A federally appointed Commissioner has the final signing authority for all legislation passed by the Assembly.

Commissioner: Doug Bell.

Flag: Vertically green, white, blue, in the proportions 2 : 3 : 2, charged in the centre with the arms of the Territory.

The legislative authority of the Assembly includes direct taxation, education, property and civil rights, territorial civil service, municipalities and generally all matters of local or private nature. All other major administration including Crown lands, income tax, natural resources and particularly that which requires the spending of large sums of money, is federally controlled.

ECONOMY

Planning. Proposed economic development of the Yukon Territory into the 1980s envisages a total expenditure of about $5,000m. Confirmed development projects include the construction of a natural gas pipeline through the territory to deliver Alaskan natural gas from Prudhoe Bay to the continental 48 states. Another confirmed project is the reconstruction and paving of 482 km of highways through south-western Yukon. Roads subject to this are the Haines Road and the Alaska Highway. In 1981 the opening of 5 new mines in eastern Yukon, the extension of railways from southern Canada and Alaska and a proposed aluminium smelter were under consideration but by 1982 many of these plans were shelved, because of the recession..

Finance. The territorial revenue and expenditure (in Canadian $) for fiscal years ended 31 March was:

	1977–78	*1978–79*	*1979–80*	*1980–81*
Revenue	84,483,715	98,904,000	88,442,000	143,195,000
Expenditure	78,340,311	95,228,000	103,839,000	135,725,000

ENERGY AND NATURAL RESOURCES

Minerals. Mining remains the main industry. Lead, zinc, copper, silver and gold are the chief minerals. Production figures for year ending 31 Dec. 1978 were: Lead, 78,250 kg; zinc, 113,573 kg; silver, 130 kg; copper, 7,778 kg; gold, 1,190 grammes. The value of mining production sales in 1979 was approximately $300m.

There were 209 land use permits issued during the 1979–80 fiscal year including 93 for government projects, 62 private road construction, 20 campsite and staging areas, 17 for quarrying, 13 for woods operations and 4 for research projects.

Forestry. The forests are part of the great Boreal forest region of Canada which stretches from the east coast of Canada into Alaska and north well above the Arctic Circle. Vast areas are covered by coniferous stands in the southern portion of Yukon with white spruce and lodgepole pine forming pure stands on wet sites and in northern aspects. Deciduous species form pure stands or occur mixed with conifers throughout forest areas.

The forest industry is small with approximately 18 active saw-mills and timber operations. Most are portable 'bush' mills although a few semi-permanent mills have been established. There are also 33 commercial cutters of fuelwood the production of which ranges from 10 cords (36 cu. metres) to 200 cords (724·9 cu. metres). Production in 1979–80 was 4,083,000 cu. metres (20·44m. bd ft) of lumber, 1,394,000 cu. ft (17,432 cords) of cordwood and 143,000 cu. ft of round timber including poles, pilings, building logs, mine timbers and fenceposts.

Game and Furs. The country abounds with big game, such as moose, goat, caribou, mountain sheep and bear (grizzly and black). In 1978–79, 41,580 pelts were taken for a market value of $927,814. Lynx was the most valuable fur and made up 46% of the total harvest bringing in $430,613 in revenues.

TOURISM. In 1980, 340,000 tourists visited Yukon and spent $38m.

COMMUNICATIONS

Roads. The Alaska Highway and its side roads connect Yukon's main communities with Alaska and the provinces and with adjacent mining centres. Interior roads connect the mining communities of Elsa (silver–lead–zinc–cadmium), Faro (lead–zinc). Cantung (tungsten) and mineral exploration properties (lead–zinc–iron ore–tungsten) north of Ross River. The Dempster Highway north of Dawson City connects with Inuvik, on the Arctic coast; this highway, the first public road to be built to the Arctic ocean, was opened in Aug. 1979. The Carcross–Skagway road was opened in May 1979, providing a new access to the Pacific ocean. There are 4,230 km of roads in the Territory, of which about 380 km are paved. The rest are all-weather gravel.

Railways. The 176-km White Pass and Yukon Railway connected Whitehorse with year-round ocean shipping at Skagway, Alaska but was suspended in 1982.

Aviation. Commercial airlines provide services every day between Whitehorse, Watson Lake, Yellowknife, Edmonton and Vancouver. Regularly scheduled air services extend from Whitehorse to interior communities of Faro, Mayo, Dawson City, Old Crow, Ross River, Haines Junction and Beaver Creek. There are several commercial bush plane operations for charter service.

Shipping. Some goods are shipped into the Territory by air or *via* the Alaska Highway, but most are containerized in Vancouver and brought up the coast by ship to Skagway, Alaska. The containers are then taken by train from Skagway to Whitehorse, and then hauled by truck to the outlying communities. Many of these trucks then return to Whitehorse hauling ore to be shipped out. Some goods are transported within the Territory by air. Although navigable, the rivers are no longer used for shipping.

Post and Broadcasting. There are 2 radio stations in Whitehorse and 14 low-power relay radio transmitters operated by CBC. There are also 8 cable-TV channels in Whitehorse, TV channels in Whitehorse and private cable operations in Faro, Dawson City and Watson Lake. Live CBC national television is provided by the Anik satellite to virtually every community in the Territory. All telephone and telecommunications in the Territory are provided by NorthwesTel, a subsidiary of Canadian National Telecommunications. Almost all pole lines have been replaced with microwave transmission.

Newspapers. In 1981 there were 2 newspapers, each 3 days a week, in Whitehorse. Faro has a two-monthly newspaper.

EDUCATION AND WELFARE

Education (1981–82). The Territory had 25 schools with 5,080 pupils. In addition to the courses given in the Yukon Vocational and Technical Centre, the Yukon offers a limited number of post-secondary courses through the University of Alberta. A Yukon Teacher Education Programme started in 1977 to train local residents to obtain Bachelor of Education degrees in Education and a Teaching Certificate. The course is conducted by the University of British Columbia. The Government provides financial assistance to students requiring further education elsewhere.

Health. The health care system provides all residents with the care demanded by illness or accident. The federal government operates 1 general hospital at Whitehorse, 3 cottage hospitals, 2 nursing stations, with a total of 150 beds, and 9 health centres. The territorial government also operates a medical evacuation programme to send patients to Edmonton or Vancouver for specialized treatment not available in the Territory.

Books of Reference

Publications of the Department of Northern Affairs and National Resources, Ottawa: *The Yukon Act, Chapter 53, Statutes of Canada, 1953,* as amended.—*Mining in the North.* 1962.—*The Yukon Today.* 1968

Annual Report of the Commissioner. 1972–73
Yukon Territorial Government, *Statistical Review.* 1970–74
Berton, P., *Klondike.* Toronto, 1963
McCourt, E., *The Yukon and Northwest Territories.* Toronto, 1969

CAPE VERDE

Capital: Praia
Population: 296,093 (1980)
GNP per capita: US$300 (1980)

República de Cabo Verde

HISTORY. The Cape Verde Islands were discovered in 1460 by Diogo Gomes, the first settlers arriving in 1462. In 1587 its administration was unified under a Portuguese governor. The colony became an Overseas Province in 1951.

On 30 Dec. 1974 Portugal transferred power to a transitional government headed by the Portuguese High Commissioner. Full independence was granted on 5 July 1975.

AREA AND POPULATION. Cape Verde is situated in the Atlantic Ocean 620 km WNW of Senegal and consists of 10 islands and 5 islets. Praia is the capital. The islands are divided into 2 groups, named Barlavento (windward) and Sotavento (leeward). The total area is 4,033 sq. km (1,557 sq. miles). The population (census, 1980) was 296,093.

The areas and populations (1976) of the islands are:

	Sq. km	*Population*		*Sq. km*	*Population*
Santo Antão	779	48,480	Maio	269	3,970
São Vicente [1]	227	37,634	São Tiago	991	145,115
São Nicolau	388	18,164	Fogo	476	32,956
Sal	216	6,815	Brava	67	8,881
Boa Vista	620	4,031			
			Sotavento	1,803	190,922
Barlovento	2,230	115,124			
			Total	4,033	306,046

[1] Includes Santa Luzia which is uninhabited.

The main towns (with populations at the 1970 census) are Mindelo on São Vicente (28,797) and Praia on São Tiago, the capital (21,494).

CONSTITUTION AND GOVERNMENT. The Constitution adopted on 12 Feb. 1981 removed all reference to possible future union with Guinea-Bissau, and the *Partido Africano da Independencia de Cabo Verde*, founded 20 Jan. 1981, became the sole legal party. The legislature consists of a unicameral People's National Assembly of 56 members elected for 5 years by universal suffrage; it elects the President, who appoints and leads a Council of Ministers. Elections were held on 7 Dec. 1980.

President: Aristides Maria Pereira.
Prime Minister: Maj. Pedro Verona Rodrigues Pires.
Foreign Minister: Col. Silvino Manuel da Luz.

National flag: Horizontally yellow over green, with a vertical red strip in the hoist charged slightly above the centre with a black star surrounded by a wreath of maize, and beneath this a yellow clam shell.

Local government: The 2 *distritos* (Barlovento and Sotavento) are sub-divided into 14 *conçelhos* – Ribeira Grande, Paúl, Porto Novo (these 3 covering Santo Antão island), São Vicente (including Santa Luzia), São Nicolau, Sal, Boa Vista, Maio, Praia, Santa Catarina, Tarrafal, Santa Cruz (these 4 covering Sao Tiago island), Fogo and Brava.

INTERNATIONAL RELATIONS

Membership. Cape Verde is a member of UN, OAU and an ACP state of EEC.

ECONOMY

Budget. The budget (1979) balanced at 1,327m. escudos Caboverdianos.

Currency. *Escudo Caboverdianos.* In March 1983, 95·05 *Escudo*=£1.

ENERGY AND NATURAL RESOURCES

Electricity. Production in 1972 amounted to 6m. kwh.

Minerals. Salt is obtained on the islands of Sal, Boa Vista and Maio. Volcanic rock (pozzolana) is mined for export.

Agriculture. Mostly confined to irrigated inland valleys, the chief crops (production, 1981, in tonnes) are: Sugar-cane, 15,000; bananas, 9,000; cassava, 6,000, sweet potatoes, 5,000; maize, 3,000 and coffee. Bananas and coffee are mainly for export.

Livestock (1981): 68,000 goats, 12,000 cattle, 23,000 pigs and 6,000 asses.

Fisheries. Fish (mainly tunny) and shellfish formed (1976) 29% of exports.

COMMERCE. Imports in 1976 totalled 911·4m. escudos Caboverdianos, of which 58% came from Portugal; exports in 1976 totalled 480·3m. escudos Caboverdianos, of which 63% went to Portugal and 14% to Angola. In 1976 29% by value of exports were fish, 19% bananas and 9% salt.

Total trade of Cape Verde with UK (British Department of Trade returns, in £1,000 sterling):

	1979	*1980*	*1981*	*1982*
Imports to UK	81	207	22	49
Exports and re-exports from UK	1,596	1,047	1,260	2,068

COMMUNICATIONS

Roads. There were 1,287 km of roads in 1976, 2,889 cars and 826 commercial vehicles.

Aviation. Amilcar Cabral International Airport, on Sal, is a major refuelling point on flights to Africa and South America, with 31,000 passengers in 1977.

Shipping. The main ports are Mindelo and Praia. In 1977 the ports handled 195,000 tonnes of imports and 27,000 tonnes of exports.

Broadcasting. The private broadcasting stations are operating on shortwaves. There were (1976) 36,000 radio receivers and (1981) 1,739 telephones.

Cinemas. In 1972 there were 6 cinemas with 2,800 seats.

RELIGION, EDUCATION AND WELFARE

Religion. The vast majority of the population are Roman Catholic.

Education. In 1978 there were 55,406 pupils and 1,269 teachers at 655 primary schools, 6,045 pupils and 256 teachers at secondary schools, and 782 pupils and 43 teachers at technical schools, as well as 198 students in teacher training and about 500 students at foreign universities.

Health. In 1977 there were 23 hospitals and dispensaries with 640 beds; there were also 43 doctors, 2 dentists, 6 pharmacists and 148 nursing personnel.

DIPLOMATIC REPRESENTATIVES

Of Great Britain in Cape Verde
Ambassador: P. L. O'Keeffe, CVO (resides in Dakar).

Of Cape Verde in the USA (3415 Massachusetts Ave., NW, Washington, D.C., 20007)
Ambassador: José Luis Fernandes Lopes.

Of the USA in Cape Verde (Rua Hoji Ya Yenda 81, Praia)
Ambassador: Peter Jon De Vos (resides in Bissau).

Of Cape Verde to the United Nations
Ambassador: Dr Amaro Alexandre da Luz.

Books of Reference

Annuario Estatistico de Cabo Verde. Praia. Annual
Andrade, E., *The Cape Verde Islands: From Slavery to Modern Times.* Dakar, 1973
Lobban, R., *The Cape Verde Islands.* New York, 1974

CAYMAN ISLANDS

Capital: George Town
Population: 17,955 (1981)

HISTORY. The Caymans were a dependency of Jamaica until 1959 when they became a separate dependent territory of UK.

AREA AND POPULATION. Cayman Islands consist of Grand Cayman, Little Cayman and Cayman Brac. Situated in the Caribbean Sea, about 200 miles NW of Jamaica, the islands were discovered by Columbus on 10 May 1503. Area, 100 sq. miles (260 sq. km). Census population of 1979, 16,677. Grand Cayman (population 15,074), 22 miles long, 4–8 miles broad; capital: George Town (population 7,617). Little Cayman, 10 miles long, 1 mile broad. Cayman Brac, 12 miles long and 1¼ miles wide. Total population of the lesser islands, 1,677. Vital statistics (1981): Births, 347; marriages, 204; deaths, 106.

CONSTITUTION AND GOVERNMENT. A new Constitution came into force in Aug. 1972. The Legislative Assembly consists of the Governor, not less than 2 nor more than 3 official members, and 12 elected members.

The Executive Council consists of 3 official members appointed from among the official members of the Legislative Assembly, and 4 elected members elected by the elected members of the Assembly with the Governor as Chairman.

Governor: G. Peter Lloyd, CMG.

Flag: British Blue Ensign with the arms of the Colony on a white disc in the fly.

ECONOMY

Budget. Revenue 1981, CI$43,760,731; expenditure, CI$38,930,190. Public debt (31 Dec. 1981), CI$7·4m.; Total reserves, CI$21.93m.

Banking. Thirty commercial banks and trust companies hold category 'A' licences, which permit the holders to offer services to the public. Barclays Bank International has branches at George Town.

INDUSTRY AND TRADE

Industry. Finance and tourism are the main industries.

Commerce. Exports (estimate), 1981 (f.o.b.), totalled CI$3m. and included turtle shell, tropical fish and dried turtle meat. Imports, estimate (c.i.f.), CI$109m.; principally foodstuffs, textiles, building materials, automobiles and petroleum products.

Tourism. Tourism is now the chief industry of the islands and in recent years 19 hotels have been completed. There were 202,611 visitors in 1981.

COMMUNICATIONS

Roads. There were (1981) about 110 miles of road and over 7,645 motor vehicles.

Aviation. Cayman Airways provide regular services between Grand Cayman and Miami, Houston and Jamaica. Republic Airways provide a daily service between Miami and Grand Cayman. CAL provides a regular inter-island service. Aerosun provides a twice-weekly service from Tampa, Florida, to the Cayman Islands.

Shipping. Motor vessels ply regularly between the Cayman Islands, Jamaica and Florida. Shipping registered at George Town, 615 vessels of 143,360 net tons (31 Dec. 1981).

Post and Broadcasting. There were 8,156 telephones in 1981 and there are 2 broadcasting stations in the islands.

EDUCATION AND WELFARE

Education. In 1982 there were 9 government primary schools with 1,150 pupils, 6 private elementary schools with 945 pupils and 4 private secondary schools with 222 pupils. Post-primary education at the Government High School and the Middle School was attended by 1,748 pupils. There was also a private institution for further education and a school for special educational needs with 23 pupils.

Health. In 1982 there was a fully-equipped general hospital with 8 doctors, a dental clinic, 6 district clinics and a hospital in Cayman Brac.

Book of Reference

Annual Report, 1981. Cayman Islands Government, 1982

CENTRAL AFRICAN REPUBLIC

Capital: Bangui
Population: 2·48m. (1982)
GNP per capita: US$300(1980)

République centrafricaine

HISTORY. Central African Republic became independent on 13 Aug. 1960, after having been one of the 4 territories of French Equatorial Africa (under the name of Ubangi Shari) and from 1 Dec. 1958 a member state of the French Community. In Jan. 1959 the 4 republics formed an 'economic, technical and customs union'. A new Constitution was adopted by a special congress of the *Mouvement pour l'évolution sociale de l'Afrique noire* on 4 Dec. 1976. It provided for the country to be a parliamentary democracy and to be known as the Central African Empire. President Bokassa became Emperor Bokassa I. The Emperor was overthrown in a *coup* on 20–21 Sept. 1979 and the empire was abolished. On 15 March 1981 David Dacko was again elected President but was deposed on 1 Sept. 1981 by General Kolingba.

AREA AND POPULATION. The Central African Republic is bounded north by Chad, east by Sudan, south by Zaïre and west by Cameroon. The area covers 624,977 sq. km; its population in 1982 was 2·48m. (35% urban). The capital is Bangui (301,793 inhabitants in 1975): other towns, Berberati (95,000) and Bouar (51,000).

The principal ethno-linguistic groups are the Banda (27·4% of the population), Baya (24·4%), Mandja (21·2%), Ubangi (12·2%), Sara (7%), Mbum (6%) and Fertit (2·4%).

CONSTITUTION AND GOVERNMENT. Following the bloodless *coup* of 1 Sept. 1981, all legislative and executive power was held by a 23-member Military Committee for National Recovery (CMRN), ruling through an appointed Council of Ministers. The constitution and political parties were suspended.

In Aug. 1982 the leading cabinet posts were held as follows:

Chairman of CMRN, Head of State and Government, Minister of Defence and Veterans' Affairs: Gen. André Kolingba (assumed office 1 Sept. 1981).
Justice: Brig. Xavier Sylvestre Yangongo.
Economy and Finance: Quartermaster Alphonse Kongole.
Interior: Lieut.-Col. Sebastien Guipi.

National flag: Four horizontal stripes of blue, white, green, yellow; over all in the centre a vertical red strip, and in the canton a yellow star.

Local Government: Central African Republic is divided into 14 prefectures, 2 'economic prefectures' and the autonomous commune of Bangui (the capital).

The national language is Sango, used as a *lingua franca* throughout the country; French is also an official language.

DEFENCE

Army. The Army consists of an infantry battalion of about 2,000 men.

Air Force. The Air Force has 2 Rallye Guerrier armed light aircraft, 1 twin-jet Caravelle, 1 DC-4 and 4 C-47 transports, 2 Reims-Cessna 337, 10 Aermacchi AL.60 and 6 Broussard liaison aircraft, 1 Alouette and 4 H-34 helicopters. It also maintains and operates the Corvette twin-jet VIP aircraft. Personnel strength (1983) about 300.

INTERNATIONAL RELATIONS

Membership. Central African Republic is a member of UN, OAU and an ACP state of EEC.

ECONOMY

Planning. The third 5-year development plan (1976–80) provided for expenditure of 23,623m. francs CFA.

Budget. The budget for 1980 balanced at 25,447m. francs CFA.

Currency. The unit of currency is the *franc CFA* with a parity of 50 *francs CFA* to 1 French *franc.*

Banking. The *Banque des Etats de l'Afrique Centrale* is the bank of issue.

ENERGY AND NATURAL RESOURCES

Electricity. Production in 1980 totalled 64m. kwh (94% hydro-electric).

Minerals. 250,000 carats of gem diamonds were mined in 1980.

Agriculture. Over 90% of the working population is occupied in subsistence agriculture. The main crops (production 1981, in 1,000 tonnes) are cassava, 1,021; groundnuts, 125; bananas, 82; plantains, 62; millet, 50; maize, 40; cotton, 23; coffee, 17; rice, 15.

Livestock (1981): Cattle, 1·27m.; goats, 951,000; sheep, 86,000; pigs, 135,000.

Forestry. The extensive hardwood forests, particularly in the south-west, provide mahogany, obeche and limba for export. Production (1979) 2·9m. cu. metres.

INDUSTRY AND TRADE

Industry. The small industrial sector includes factories producing cotton fabrics (3m. metres in 1978) and radios.

Commerce. Imports and exports in 1m. francs CFA:

	1978	*1979*	*1980*
Imports	12,776	14,816	17,009
Exports	16,182	16,937	24,384

In 1979, France took 46% of exports and provided 63% of imports. Of all exports, coffee comprised 25% (by value), diamonds 44%, timber 12% and cotton 7%.

Total trade of Central African Republic with UK (British Department of Trade returns, in £1,000 sterling):

	1977	*1978*	*1979*	*1980*	*1981*	*1982*
Imports to UK	278	798	954	1,466	782	878
Exports and re-exports from UK	868	553	808	738	373	576

COMMUNICATIONS

Roads. In Dec. 1976 there were 21,950 km of roads and (1974) there were 9,100 passenger cars and 3,900 commercial vehicles in use.

Railways. There are no railways, but a proposal exists (1979) for an 800 km line (1,435 mm gauge) from Bangui through Cameroon and Congo to connect with the Trans-Gabon railway at Belinga.

Aviation. There is an international airport at Mpoko, near Bangui, and Air Centrafrique operates extensive internal services to several airstrips.

Post and Broadcasting. There were (1977) 200 television and 80,000 radio receivers and (1973) 5,000 telephones.

Cinemas. In 1971 there were 8 cinemas.

JUSTICE, RELIGION, EDUCATION AND WELFARE

Justice. The Criminal Court and Supreme Court are situated in Bangui. There are 7 civil courts throughout the country.

Religion. About 57% of the population follow animist beliefs, 20% are Roman Catholic, 15% Protestant and 8% Moslem.

Education. The University of Bangui was founded in 1970 and had 1,489 students in 1980. In 1978 there were 241,201 pupils at primary schools and 46,084 at secondary schools; technical schools held 2,523 students, while (1976) 615 were at the 2 teacher-training establishments.

Health. In 1977 there were 61 hospitals and dispensaries with 2,983 beds and 106 doctors, 3 dentists, 16 pharmacists, 142 midwives and 1,200 nursing personnel.

DIPLOMATIC REPRESENTATIVES

Of Central African Republic in Great Britain
Ambassador: Dr Firmin Jean-Marie Frisat (resides in Paris).

Of Great Britain in Central African Republic
Ambassador: B. Sparrow (resides in Yaoundé).

Of Central African Republic in the USA (1618 22nd St., NW, Washington, D.C. 20008)
Ambassador: Christian Lingama-Toleque.

Of the USA in Central African Republic (Ave. President Dacko, Bangui)
Ambassador: Arthur H. Woodruff.

Of Central African Republic to the United Nations
Ambassador: Simon Pierre Kibanda.

CHAD

Capital: N'djaména
Population: 4·75m. (1982)
GNP per capita: US$120 (1980)

République du Tchad

HISTORY. France proclaimed a protectorate over Chad on 5 Sept. 1900, and in July 1908 the territory was incorporated into French Equatorial Africa. It became a separate colony March 1920, and in 1946 one of the four constituent territories of French Equatorial Africa. On 1 Jan. 1959 Chad became an autonomous republic within the French Community and achieved full independence on 11 Aug. 1960, although the northern prefecture of Borkou-Ennedi-Tibesti remained under French military administration until 1965.

Conflicts between the central government of President François (later Ngarta) Tombalbaye and secessionist groups, particularly in the Moslem north and centre of Chad, began in 1965 and continued despite attempts at reconciliation. President Tombalbaye was assassinated on 13 April 1975 following an Army *coup d'etat.* A Supreme Military Council of 9 members, under the Presidency of Gen. Felix Malloum, ruled until 29 Aug. 1978, when the Council was dissolved and Malloum formed a new government of 'national unity'.

Fighting continued between the differing groups and, following further peace conferences, Gen. Malloum resigned on 23 March 1979. An accord was finally signed in Lagos on 21 Aug. between representatives of 11 warring factions. A 22-member Transitional Government of National Unity (GUNT) was formed on 10 Nov. under the Presidency of Goukouni Oueddei. The reconciliation agreement broke down on 25 April 1980, and civil war continued until June 1982 when the *Forces Armées du Nord* (FAN) led by Hissène Habré gained control of the country.

AREA AND POPULATION. Chad is bounded west by Cameroon, Nigeria and Niger, north by Libya, east by Sudan and south by Central African Republic. Area, 1,284,000 sq. km; its population in 1982 was estimated at 4·75m. (census 1975, 4,029,917). The capital is N'djaména, formerly Fort Lamy with 303,000 inhabitants in 1979, other large towns being Moundou (66,000), Sarh (65,000) and Abéché (54,000).

Préfecture	*sq. km*	*Population 1979*	*Capital*
Borkou-Ennedi-Tibesti	600,350	88,000	Faya-Largeau
Biltine	46,850	175,000	Biltine
Ouaddaï	76,240	347,000	Abéché
Batha	88,800	354,000	Ati
Kanem	114,520	200,000	Mao
Lac	22,320	139,000	Bol
Chari-Baguirmi	82,910	676,000	N'djaména
Guéra	58,950	207,000	Mongo
Salamat	63,000	107,000	Am Timan
Moyen-Chari	45,180	524,000	Sarh
Logone Oriental	28,035	307,000	Doba
Logone Occidental	8,695	295,000	Moundou
Tandjilé	18,045	302,000	Laï
Mayo-Kabbi	30,105	684,000	Bongor

More than 100 different languages and dialects are spoken. The largest ethnic group is the Sara of southern Chad, forming 30% of the population. Arabic serves as a common language throughout the semi-tropical (Sahelian) centre and the Saharan north.

CONSTITUTION AND GOVERNMENT. From June 1982 a State Council administered the country until 21 Oct. 1982, when Hissène Habré was sworn in as President and a 31-member government appointed as follows:

President: Hissène Habré.

Foreign Affairs: Idriss Miskine. *Interior and Security:* Tahar Guinassou. *Defence and Veterans' Affairs:* Capt. Rotouang Yoma. *Justice:* Oudalbaye Naham. *Agriculture and Rural Development:* Djidingar Dono Ngardoum. *Economy and Trade:* Ali Djalbord Diar. *Natural Disasters:* Taher Abeldjelil. *Animal and Water Resources:* Adoum Moussa Seif. *Finance and Equipment:* Elie Romba. *Planning and Reconstruction:* Joseph Yodeyman. *Works, Mines and Petroleum:* Hassan Djamous. *Transport:* Lol Mohammed Shawa. *Information:* Soumalia Mahamat. *Posts and Telecommunications:* Assileck Halata. *Further Education and Research:* Capt. Gouara Lassou. *Establishments:* Ngartokete Tatola. *Education, Youth and Sports:* Dr Abba Sidick. *Labour and Women's Advancement:* Doubangar Doregim. *Health and Social Affairs:* Koibla Djimasta. *Tourism, Crafts, Forests and Game Parks:* Kolbassia Vouna.

There are also 12 Secretaries of State. A National Consultative Council was also formed on 21 Oct., comprising 2 representatives from each of the 14 prefectures and 2 from the capital, N'djaména.

The official language is French.

National flag: Three vertical strips of blue, yellow, red.

Local Government: The 14 *préfectures* are divided into 53 *sous-préfectures.*

DEFENCE

Army. A new national army, the Forces Armées Nationales Tchadiennes (FANT) was formed in Dec. 1982. Other forces loyal to elements of the former GUNT remained in remote districts, particularly in the far north.

Air Force. The Air Force has at least 1 Noratlas, 1 VIP Caravelle, 3 C-54 and 9 C-47 transports, 4 Reims-Cessna F337 light aircraft, 2 Turbo-Porters, 2 Broussard communications aircraft and about 14 Puma and Alouette III helicopters. Personnel about 200.

INTERNATIONAL RELATIONS

Membership. Chad is a member of UN, OAU and is an ACP state of EEC.

ECONOMY

Budget. The budget for 1978 balanced at 17,084m. francs CFA.

Currency. The unit of currency is the *franc CFA* with a parity value of 50 *francs CFA* to 1 French *franc.*

Banking. The *Banque des Etats de l'Afrique Centrale* is the bank of issue, and the principal commercial banks are the *Banque de Développement du Tchad* and the *Banque Tchadienne de Crédit et de Dépôts.*

ENERGY AND NATURAL RESOURCES

Electricity. Production (1980) amounted to 64m. kwh.

Oil. The oilfield in Kanem préfecture has been linked by pipeline to a new refinery at Laï (in Tandjilé).

Minerals. Salt (about 4,000 tonnes per annum) is mined around Lake Chad, and deposits of uranium, gold and bauxite are to be exploited.

Agriculture. In 1981, 82·7% of the 1,738,000 work force were occupied in agriculture, forestry and fishing. Cotton growing (in the south) and animal husbandry (in the central zone) are the most important industries. Production (1981, in 1,000 tonnes) was: Millet, 580; unginned cotton, 195; groundnuts, 110; cassava, 51.

Livestock (1981): Cattle, 3·8m.; sheep, 2·3m.; goats, 2·3m.; chickens, 3·3m.

Fisheries. Fish production from Lake Chad and the Chari and Logone rivers, was estimated at 115,000 tonnes in 1979.

TRADE (in 1m. francs CFA):

	1974	*1975*	*1976*	*1977*
Imports	20,859	28,325	27,593	28,111
Exports	9,053	10,103	14,861	...

In 1976 main imports: Petroleum products, textile yarn, sugar and machinery. Exports were raw cotton (80%) and meat.

The main sources of imports are France (37% in 1976) and Nigeria and main destinations of exports Nigeria (20%), France and Congo.

Total trade with UK (British Department of Trade returns, in £1,000 sterling):

	1978	*1979*	*1980*	*1981*	*1982*
Imports to UK	291	240	279	12	3
Exports and re-exports from UK	5,284	612	361	375	1,082

COMMUNICATIONS

Roads. In 1976 there were 30,725 km of roads, of which only 240 km are surfaced. In 1977 there were 7,636 private cars and 9,668 commercial vehicles.

Aviation. There is an international airport at N'djaména, from which UTA and Air Afrique run 4 flights per week to Paris; there are also flights to Douala, Bangui and Kinshasa. Air Tchad operates internal services to 12 secondary airports.

Post and Broadcasting. In 1978 there were 3,850 telephones and (1981), 70,000 radios in use.

Cinemas. In 1977 there were 13 cinemas with 12,400 seats.

JUSTICE, RELIGION, EDUCATION AND WELFARE

Justice. There are criminal courts and magistrates courts in N'djaména, Moundou, Sarh and Abéché, with a Court of Appeal situated in N'djaména.

Religion. The northern and central parts of the country are predominantly Moslem (52% of the total population) and the southern part is mainly animist (43%) or Christian (5%).

Education. In 1977 there were 229,191 pupils in primary schools, 18,382 in secondary schools, 649 in technical schools and 549 students in teacher-training establishments. The University of Chad (founded 1971) at N'djaména had (1980) 800 students.

Health. There were 33 hospitals with 3,353 beds in 1977; 100 doctors, 4 dentists, 13 pharmacists, 98 midwives and 1,000 nursing personnel.

DIPLOMATIC REPRESENTATIVES

Of Chad in Great Britain
Chargé d'Affaires: Issa Abbas Ali.

Of Great Britain in Chad
Ambassador: A. C. D. S. MacRae.

Of Chad in the USA (2002 R. St., NW, Washington, D.C., 20009)
Chargé d'Affaires: Mahamat Ali Adoum.

Of the USA in Chad (Ave., Felix Eboue, N'djaména)
Chargé d'Affaires: Peter Moffat.

Of Chad to the United Nations
Ambassador: Ramadane Barma.

Books of Reference

Aperçu sur le Tchad. Publication of the President. 2nd ed. N'djaména, 1973
L'essentiel sur le Tchad. Publication of the President. 2nd ed. N'djaména, 1972
Thompson, V., and Adloff, R., *Conflict in Chad.* London and Berkeley, 1981
Westebbe, R., *Chad: Development Potential and Constraints.* Washington, D.C., 1974

CHILE

República de Chile

Capital: Santiago
Population: 11·5 (1982)
GNP per capita: US$2,160 (1980)

HISTORY. The Republic of Chile threw off allegiance to the crown of Spain, constituting a national government on 18 Sept. 1810, finally freeing itself from Spanish rule in 1818.

AREA AND POPULATION. Chile is bounded north by Peru, east by Bolivia and Argentina, and west by the Pacific ocean.

Many islands to the west and south belong to Chile, including Easter Island (Isla de Pascua; 63·9 sq. miles), discovered in 1722. The coastline is about 2,650 miles in length; the average width of the country, 120 miles. Area, 751,626 sq. km or 292,135 sq. miles.

In 1940 Chile declared, and in each subsequent year has reaffirmed, its ownership of the sector of the Antarctic lying between 53° and 90° W. long.; and asserted that the British claim to the sector between the meridians 20° and 90° W. long. overlapped the Chilean by 27°. Five Chilean bases were established in Antarctica in 1947, 1948, 1951 and 1962. A law promulgated 21 July 1955 put the Intendente of the Province of Magallanes in charge of the 'Chilean Antarctic Territory'.

Three thinly-settled southern provinces of Magallanes, Chiloé and Aysén and the northern provinces of Arica and Iquique are known as 'free zones', which implies that all commodities imported into those areas from abroad are not subject to all national import duties.

The total population at the census in 1970 was 8,884,768. Estimate (1982) 11,493,000. Density per sq. km, 1972, was 13·54.

The areas of the 13 regions and their populations (estimates, 1978) were as follows:

Region	*Sq. km*	*Population 1978*	*Capital*	*Population 1978*
Taracapá	58,073	229,824	Iquique	63,600[1]
Antofagasta	125,306	302,294	Antofagasta	157,000
Atacama	78,268	191,155	Copiapó	39,942[2]
Coquimbo	39,647	401,931	La Serena	61,889[2]
Aconcagua	16,109	1,181,638	Valparaíso	248,200[3]
Metropolitan	13,808	4,111,823	Santiago	3,448,700[4]
Liberador	18,193	570,052	Rancagua	122,500
Maule	30,518	707,047	Talca	129,100
Bíobío	36,823	1,466,627	Concepción	172,800[5]
Araucanía	31,760	663,325	Temuco	156,900
Los Lagos	67,090	862,003	Puerto Montt	62,748[2]
Aisén	108,998	61,998	Coihaique	...
Magallanes	132,033	107,411	Punta Arenas	67,600[1]

[1] 1975. [2] 1970. [3] Metropolitan Area 620,180 including Viña del Mar (262,100).
[4] Metropolitan Area 3,691,548.
[5] Metropolitan Area 518,950 including Talcahuano (204,100).

Vital statistics (1971): Revised birth rate 27·6 per 1,000 population; death rate, 8·4; marriage rate, 8·6; infantile mortality rate, 70·9 per 1,000 live births.

The great majority of the population is mixed or *mestizo*, due to the free inter-marriage between the early Spaniards and women of indigenous tribes; language and culture remain of European origin. The indigenous inhabitants are of 3 branches: The *Fuegians*, mostly nomadic, living in or near Tierra del Fuego; the *Araucanions* in the valleys or on the western slopes of the Andes; the

Changos, who inhabit the northern coast region and work as labourers and fishermen.

Other large towns (1978) are Arica (118,500), Chillán (111,800), Valdivia (106,800) and Osorno (71,000 in 1975). Punta Arenas, on the Strait of Magellan, with a population of 67,600, is the southernmost city in the world. The Antarctic Territory proper is now stated to be 484,800 sq. miles.

There are 4 geographical zones in Chile—the arid 'desert' zone in the north, which for many years furnished the world's entire supply of natural nitrate of soda, 90% of its iodine and 18% of copper consumed; the agricultural 'Mediterranean' zone in the centre; the 'forest' zone to the south; and the 'Atlantic' zone in the extreme south, barren on the Pacific side, but with rich sheltered pampa on the Atlantic side.

CONSTITUTION AND GOVERNMENT. The Marxist coalition government of President Salvador Allende Gossens was ousted on 11 Sept. 1973 by the 3 Armed Services and the *Carabineros* (para-military police). These forces formed a government headed by a Junta of the 4 Commanders-in-Chief. Gen. Augusto Pinochet Ugarte, Commander-in-Chief of the Army, took over the presidency. President Allende was killed on the day of the *coup.*

Marxist parties were outlawed and all political activities banned. The new Government assumed wide-ranging powers but the 'state of siege' ended in March 1978. A new Constitution was approved by 67·5% of the voters on 11 Sept. 1980 and came into force on 11 March 1981. It provided for a return to democracy after a minimum period of 8 years. Gen. Pinochet would remain in office during this period after which the Junta would nominate a single candidate for President.

For details of the 1925 Constitution and earlier political history *see* THE STATESMAN'S YEAR-BOOK 1975–76, p. 808.

The capital is Santiago, founded on 12 Feb. 1541.

National flag: Two horizontal bands, white, red, with a white star on blue square in top sixth next to staff.

National anthem: Dulce patria, recibe los votos (words by E. Lillo, 1847; tune by Ramón Carnicer, 1828).

The following is a list of the presidents since 1927:

Gen. Carlos Ibáñez (Acting, then elected 6 May 1927–26 July 1931 (resigned).
Pedro Opazo (Acting), 26–27 July 1931 (resigned).
Juan Esteban Montero (Acting), 27 July–18 Aug. 1931 (resigned).
Manuel Trucco (Acting), 18 Aug.–15 Nov. 1931.
Juan Esteban Montero, 15 Nov. 1931–4 June 1932 (deposed).
Socialist Junta (Carlos Dávila, Col. Marmaduke Grove, Gen. Arturo Puga), 4 June–8 July 1932.
Carlos Dávila (Acting), 8 July–13 Sept. 1932 (deposed).
Gen. Bartolomé Blanche (Acting), 13 Sept.–1 Oct. 1932 (resigned).
Abraham Oyanedel (Acting), 1 Oct.–24 Dec. 1932.
Arturo Alessandri, 24 Dec. 1932–24 Dec. 1938.
Pedro Aguirre Cerda, 24 Dec. 1938–25 Nov. 1941 (died).
Geronimo Méndez (succeeded as Vice-President), 25 Nov. 1941–1 April 1942.
Juan Antonio Rios, 1 April 1942–27 June 1946 (died).
Alfredo Duhalde (Acting), 27 June–3 Aug. 1946 (resigned).
Vice-Admiral Vicente Merino Bielech (Acting), 3 Aug.–3 Nov. 1946.
Gabriel González Videla, 3 Nov. 1946–3 Nov. 1952.
Carlos Ibáñez del Campo, 3 Nov. 1952–3 Nov. 1958.
Jorge Alessandri Rodriguez, 3 Nov. 1958–3 Nov. 1964.
Eduardo Frei Montalva, 3 Nov. 1964–3 Nov. 1970.
Salvador Allende Gossens, 3 Nov. 1970–11 Sept. 1973 (deposed).

President of the Republic: Gen. Augusto Pinochet Ugarte.

Local Government. For the purposes of local government the Military Junta in pursuance of its policy of administrative decentralization, has divided the republic into 13 regions (12 and Greater Santiago). Each Region is presided over by a *Governador,* while the provinces (40) included in it are in charge of an *Intendente* who represents the central government. The provinces are divided into municipalities under an *alcalde* (mayor). All these officials are appointed by the President.

DEFENCE. Chile on 9 April 1952 signed the Military Assistance pact with the US, promising access to raw materials and armed support in defence of the Western Hemisphere.

Army. The Chilean Army is a national militia in which all able-bodied citizens are obliged to serve. Liability extends from the 20th to the 45th year, inclusive. In many cases exemption can easily be obtained, as the supply exceeds the number that can adequately be trained. The annual intake has varied up to 30,000. Recruits are called up in their 20th year, and are trained for 24 months. After this training they pass into the reserve, which is estimated at 160,000.

Army aviation operates 6 CASA Aviocar transports.

The Army is organized in 21 infantry, 7 cavalry (3 armoured, 1 heliborne and 3 horsed), and 6 artillery regiments. Total strength (1983), about 53,000 men.

Navy. The principal ships of the Chilean Navy are as follows:

Completed	*Name*	*Standard displacement Tons*	*Armour Belt In.*	*Armour Turrets In.*	*Guns*	*Shaft horse-power*	*Speed Knots*
			Cruisers				
1943	Latorre [2]	8,200	3–4	3–5	7·6 in.	100,000	33·0
1938	O'Higgins [1]	10,000	4	3–5	15·6 in.;8·5-in.	100,000	32·5

[1] Ex-*Nashville* and ex-*Brooklyn*, respectively, purchased from USA in 1951 with sister ship *Prat* (ex-*Nashville*) discarded in 1981. *O'Higgins* used as an alongside accommodation ship since she was damaged by grounding in Aug. 1974 was refitted during 1978 and later recommissioned.

[2] Ex-*Göta Lejou*, purchased from Sweden in 1971.

The British guided missile armed destroyer *Norfolk*, 5,440 tons standard, completed in 1970, was purchased in 1982 and re-named *Prat* on transfer.

There are 2 modern diesel powered patrol submarines (British 'Oberon' class), 1 old *ex*-US submarine, 6 destroyers (2 British built and 4 old *ex*-US), 5 frigates (2 modern British 'Leander' class, *Condell* and *Lynch*, and 3 old *ex*-US destroyer escort transports), 2 fast missile craft, 4 torpedo boats, 6 patrol vessels, 12 coastal patrol craft, 2 amphibious transports, 2 landing ships, 13 landing craft, 1 survey ship, 4 transports, 1 training ship, 1 antarctic patrol ship, 3 oilers, 3 floating docks and 4 tugs.

Naval personnel in 1983 totalled 28,600 (2,000 officers, 24,000 ratings, 2,600 marines).

Air Force. Approximate current strength is 15,000 personnel, with 85 first-line and 150 second-line aircraft, divided among 12 groups, each comprising 1 squadron, within 4 combat and support wings. Groups 1 and 12 have twin-jet A-37Bs, from a total of 34 acquired for light strike/reconnaissance duties. Group 3 is equipped for general duties with about 12 UH-1H Iroquois and Puma helicopters. Group 4 has 20 Mirage 50 fighters. Group 5 has 14 Twin Otters for light transport and survey duties. Group 6 operates 3 civil-registered Learjet 35 and King Air 100 aircraft on photo survey duties. Group 7 received 15 F-5E Tiger II fighter-bombers and 3 F-5F trainers. Groups 8 and 9 are also fighter-bomber units, with a total of 30 Hunter F.71s, *ex*-RAF FGA.9s, and T.72s. Group 10 is a transport wing, with 2 C-130H Hercules and 5 DC-6Bs. Group 11 has 9 twin-turboprop Beech 99A instrument/navigation trainers. Three *ex*-RAF Canberra PR.9s have been acquired for reconnaissance duties. Training aircraft include piston-engined Piper T-35 Pillan primary trainers and T-37 jets. The A-37Bs and T-37s are being replaced by 60 CASA C-101BB/CC Aviojets ordered from Spain.

INTERNATIONAL RELATIONS

Membership. Chile is a member of the UN, OAS and LAIA (formerly LAFTA).

ECONOMY

Budget. In 1980 revenue was US$3,448·22m. and expenditure, US$3,371·79m.

Currency. In Jan. 1960 a system came into force based on the *escudo* (equivalent of 1,000 *pesos*), the *centésimo* (10 *pesos*) and the *milésimo (1 peso)*. On 29 Sept. 1975 the currency reverted to *pesos* with a value of 1,000 escudos to the new peso.

In March 1983 there were 109·08 *pesos* = £1 and 75·37 *pesos* = US$1.

Banking. Notes in circulation and deposits in currency were 60,709m. pesos at 31 Dec. 1981; total deposits in the commercial banks stood at 406,569m. pesos (1981).

Commercial banks, since July 1979, must maintain cash reserves of 40% of all sight deposits and 20% of time deposits over 30 days.

Inflation is decreasing; 38·9% in 1979 and 31·2% in 1980.

Weights and Measures. The metric system has been legally established in Chile since 1865, but the old Spanish weights and measures are still in use to some extent.

ENERGY AND NATURAL RESOURCES

Electricity. In 1980 production of electricity was 12,363·4m. gwh.

Oil. Petroleum was discovered in 1945 in the southern area of Magallanes with an output of 1,933·2m. cu. metres in 1980. Production of liquified gas amounted to 5,395·6m. cu. metres in 1980.

Minerals. The wealth of the country consists chiefly in its minerals, especially in the northern provinces of Atacama and Tarapacá.

Copper is the most important source of foreign exchange (about 48% of exports) and government revenues (over 30%). The copper industry, which is state-owned since July 1971, manages 5 large mines which in 1980 had proceeds returned to Chile amounting to US$1,839·4m. On the same basis the medium and small-sized companies recorded US$361m. Copper production for 1980 was1,067,700 tonnes. Exports during 1979 were valued at US$1,800m.

Nitrate of soda is found in the Atacama deserts. Exports were US$85m. in 1980. Production was 620,400 tonnes in 1980. Iodine is a by-product: 1980 production totalled 2,601 tonnes. The use of solar evaporation as a means of reducing costs has developed the production of potassium salts as an additional by-product.

Iron ore, of which high-grade deposits estimated at over 1,000m. tons exist in the provinces of Atacama and Coquimbo, has overtaken nitrate as Chile's second mineral. Production in 1980 was 8,834,577 tonnes.

Coal reserves exceed 2,000m. tons, partially low in thermal unit. Net 1980 production was 995,561 tonnes.

In 1977 other minerals include molybdenum (10,940 tonnes, pure), zinc (2,826 tonnes), manganese (27,000 tonnes), lead (122 tonnes).

Agriculture. Agriculture and forestry contribute one-twelfth of the national product, although one-third of the population take part in it. Total area of land being exploited (census of 1968) was 52·4m. hectares; 14·9% for agriculture, 26·7% for pasture, 28·8% for forest; 29·6% is desert or unproductive.

Chile used to import annually about two-thirds of the foodstuffs needed, a quarter of the total imports, but this has now been reduced, by stimulating local production, to about 12% of total imports.

Some principal crops were as follows:

Crop	*Area sown, 1,000 hectares 1979–80*	*Production, 1,000 quintals 1979–80*	*Crop*	*Area sown, 1,000 hectares 1979–80*	*Production, 1,000 quintals 1979–80*
Wheat	546	9,660	Potatoes	89	9,031
Oats	92	1,726	Beans	111	842
Barley	49	1,050	Lentils	53	268
Maize	116	4,052	Peas	18	136
Rice	41	952	Sugar-beet	11	4,502

There were in 1955 over 300 large farms, each with more than 12,250 acres, while 500,000 peasants live on less than 4 acres per family. The military government has opted in most cases to increase the number of settlements with access to individual property. The process was completed in early 1979 with some 24,000 property titles issued, a large proportion of which were in co-operative schemes.

Production of animal products in 1980 was (in 1,000 tonnes): Cattle, 162·3; sheep, 15·4; pork, 49·7; poultry, 102. Eggs, 1,425m.; milk, 1,080m. litres.

Livestock (1981): Cattle, 3·74m.; horses, 450,000; asses, 29,000; sheep, 6·2m.; goats, 600,000; pigs, 1·1m.; poultry, 25m.

Forestry. According to the Forestry Institute, by late 1978, there were 277,944 hectares of artificial forests from Maule to Magallanes, the most important species being the pine (*pinus radiata*) which covers 640,000 hectares. Eucalyptus and poplar cover some 72,000 hectares. Native species of importance amounted to 9m. hectares in 1978.

Production during 1980 amounted to about 124m. in. of sawn timber. Exports in 1980 were valued at US$75m.

Fisheries. Chile's catch of fish in 1980 was 2·05m. tonnes, including shellfish, 145,000 tonnes. Exports of seafood in 1980 were US$136m., of which fishmeal accounted for US$95m.

INDUSTRY AND TRADE

Industry. A nationally-owned steel plant operates from Huachipato, near Concepción. Output, 1980, 695,000 tonnes of steel ingots. Cellulose and wood-pulp are two industries which are rapidly developing; in 1979, 1,456 tonnes of cellulose were produced.

Labour. In Sept. 1981 the 'economically active' numbered 3·8m. in the Santiago area. Professional and 'white-collar' workers numbered 820,000; agriculture employed 603,000; manufacturing, 514,000; mining, 73,000; construction, 224,700, and transport, 233,700.

Trade unions began in the middle 1880s.

Commerce. Imports and exports in US$1m.:

	1976	*1977*	*1978*	*1979*	*1980*	*1981*
Imports	1,594	2,221	2,917	4,200	5,821	7,368
Exports	2,069	2,171	2,480	3,800	4,818	4,000

In 1980 imports (in US$1m.) from USA, were valued at 1,583; Japan, 608; Brazil, 476; Federal Republic of Germany, 316; Venezuela, 280; Argentina, 246; France, 190; Spain, 172; Italy, 126; UK, 123.

In 1980 the principal imports were (in US$1m.): Fuels, 960; chemicals, 801; industrial equipment, 612; transport equipment, 600; spares, 340, and live animals and foodstuffs, 250. The principal exports in 1980 were (in US$1m.): Copper, 2,200; timber, 286; paper and pulp, 280; iron ore, 158; nitrate, 89.

Total trade between Chile and UK for 5 years (British Department of Trade returns, in £1,000 sterling):

	1978	*1979*	*1980*	*1981*	*1982*
Imports to UK	82,269	131,218	126,273	87,939	111,206
Exports and re-exports from UK	37,571	45,640	55,741	62,227	56,897

Tourism. There were 326,415 foreign visitors in 1980.

COMMUNICATIONS

Roads. In 1978 there were in Chile 75,420 km of highways. There were in 1974, 235,335 automobiles, 149,642 goods vehicles, 15,682 buses and 28,833 motor cycles and scooters.

Railways. The total length of state railway lines was (1981) 6,302 km, including 907 km electrified, of broad- and metre-gauge. Further electrification is in progress between Concepción and Puerto Montt (600 km). An underground railway in Santiago was opened in Sept. 1975.

Aviation. There are 7 international airports, 16 domestic airports and about 300 landing grounds. Chile is served by 19 commercial air companies (2 Chilean). In 1980, 325,800 passengers were carried into and out of Chile on international services; 265,400 passengers were carried on internal routes.

Shipping. The mercantile marine had, in 1979, 154 ships of over 100 tons (536,616 DWT) but most of the fleet operates under flags of convenience. Valparaíso is the chief port. The free ports of Magallanes, Chiloé and Aysén serve the southern provinces. Chilean ports handled 21·9m. tons in 1974. There are 2,185 km of navigable rivers.

Post and Broadcasting. There are 1,486 post offices and agencies. The length of telegraph lines in 1971 was 12,870 km. In 1981 there were 569,969 (Santiago, 359,721) telephones in use.

A chain of wireless stations along the coast for shore-to-ship transmission is operated by the Navy. At the end of 1974 there were some 150 commercial broadcasting stations. Three television stations are operated by the Universities and there is a national television station using NTSC 525 line colour standards. On 9 Aug. 1968 the satellite station at Longovilo, 50 miles south-west of Santiago, was inaugurated to cover transmissions (including colour) from the USA and Europe. In 1977 there were 2m. radio receivers and (1976) 710,000 television receivers.

Cinemas (1975). Cinemas numbered 196; 61 of them are in Santiago.

Newspapers (1975). There were 80 daily newspapers.

JUSTICE, RELIGION, EDUCATION AND WELFARE

Justice. There are a High Court of Justice in the capital, 12 courts of appeal distributed over the republic, tribunals of first instance in the departmental capitals and second-class judges in the sub-delegations. The police force had (1975) about 27,000 officers and men; it is organized and regulated by the Ministry of Defence.

Religion. The Roman Catholic religion was disestablished in 1925; it remains, however, a national Church in a state wherein 89·5% of the population are Catholics. There are 1 cardinal-archbishop, 5 archbishops, 22 bishops and 2 vicars apostolic. Latest estimates show 6·7m. Roman Catholics, 880,500 Protestants and 25,000 Jews.

Education. Education is in 3 stages: Basic (6–14 years), Middle (15–18) and University (19–23). Enrolment (1970): Pre-school (a new programme initiated in 1970), 60,360 children; primary school, 2,043,032; secondary school, 302,064.

University education is provided in the state university (founded in 1842), the Catholic University at Santiago (1888), the University of Concepción (1919), the Catholic University at Valparaíso (1928), the Universidad Técnica Federico Santa María at Valparaíso (1930), the Universidad Técnica del Estado (1952), Universidad Austral, Valdivia (1954) and Universidad del Norte, Antofagasta (1957) with a total student population of 96,000 in 1970. A decree of 30 Dec. 1980 laid down new regulations for universities including a restriction of the number of courses offered to 12. New private universities are envisaged.

Health. A national health service covered some 1·5m. employees (1977) and there are plans for an extension of the service to a further 1·5m.

DIPLOMATIC REPRESENTATIVES

Of Chile in Great Britain (12 Devonshire St., London, W1N 2FS)
Ambassador: Miguel Schweitzer (accredited 26 March 1980).

Of Great Britain in Chile (La Concepción 177, Casilla 72-D, Santiago)
Ambassador: J. K. Hickman, CMG.

Of Chile in the USA (1732 Massachusetts Ave., NW, Washington, D.C., 20036)
Ambassador: Enrique Valenzuela.

Of the USA in Chile (Agustinas 1343, Santiago)
Ambassador: James D. Theberge.

Of Chile to the United Nations
Ambassador: Manuel Trucco.

Books of Reference

Statistical Information: The Instituto Nacional de Estadística (Santiago), was founded 17 Sept. 1847. *Director General:* Sergio Chaparro Ruiz. Principal publications: *Anuario Estadística* and the bi-monthly *Estadística Chilena*.

Other sources are: *Geografía Económica,* by the Corporación de Fomento de la Production, and *Boletín Mensual*, by the Banco Central de Chile.

Allende, S., *Chile's Road to Socialism.* Harmondsworth, 1973
De Vylder, S., *Allende's Chile.* CUP, 1976
Empresa Periodística, *Diccionario biográfico de Chile.* 8th ed. Santiago, 1952
Horne, A., *Small Earthquake in Chile. A Visit to Allende's South America.* London, 1972
Lasaga, M., *The Copper Industry in the Chilean Economy. An Econometric Analysis.* Aldershot, 1981
MacEoin, G., *No Peaceful Way: Chile's Struggle for Dignity.* New York, 1974
Petras, J., and Merino, H. Z., *Peasants in Revolt: A Chilean Case Study.* Univ. of Texas Press, 1972
Pinochet de la Barra, O., *La Antártido Chilena.* Santiago de Chile, 1948
Porteous, J. D., *The Modernization of Easter Island.* Victoria, B.C., 1981

PEOPLE'S REPUBLIC OF CHINA

Capital: Peking (Beijing)
Population: 1,008m. (1982)
GNP per capita: US$290 (1980)

Zhonghua Renmin Gonghe Guo

HISTORY. In the course of 1949 the Communists obtained full control of the mainland of China, and in 1950 also over most islands off the coast, including Hainan.

On 1 Oct. 1949 Mao Zedong (Tse-tung) proclaimed the establishment of the People's Republic of China.

AREA AND POPULATION. China is bounded north by the USSR and Mongolia, east by Korea, the Yellow Sea and the East China Sea, with Hong Kong and Macao as enclaves on the south-east coast; south by Vietnam, Laos, Burma, India, Bhután and Nepál; west by India, Pakistan, Afghánistán and the USSR. China is composed of 22 provinces (this figure includes Taiwan), 5 autonomous regions originally entirely or largely inhabited by national minorities (owing to the immigration of Han Chinese the original nationality is sometimes outnumbered, *e.g.,* by 10 to 1 in Inner Mongolia), namely Inner Mongolia, Xinjiang–Uygur, Guangxi–Zhuang, Ningxia–Hui, Tibet and 3 centrally controlled municipalities (Peking, Shanghai, Tianjin).

The capital is Peking (Beijing).

See map in THE STATESMAN'S YEAR-BOOK, 1968–69.

The total area is estimated at 9,597,000 sq. km (3,704,400 sq. miles).

The latest census took place in July 1982 and it is reported that the population was 1,007·6m.

Population densities vary from 10 per sq. km in the West to over 100 per sq. km in the East.

Estimates of persons of Chinese race outside China, Taiwan and Hong Kong in 1980 varied from 15m. to 20m. China permits the emigration of a limited number of persons to Hong Kong annually. There were 70,456 in 1979.

A number of widely divergent varieties of Chinese are spoken. The official 'Modern Standard Chinese' is based on the dialect of North China, and the Government is promoting its use generally. The ideographic writing system is uniform throughout the country, and has undergone systematic simplification. In 1958 a phonetic alphabet (*Pinyin*) was devised to transcribe the characters, and on 1 Jan. 1979 this was officially adopted for use in all texts in the Roman alphabet (*see also* Post and Broadcasting, p. 355). The decision of press agencies to use the *Pinyin* transcription led to the supersession of the system previously widely used in English-speaking countries (Wade). Starting with THE STATESMAN'S YEAR-BOOK, 1979–80 new names were introduced in *Pinyin.* In this edition with a few exceptions *Pinyin* forms are used for all names. *Pinyin* forms are not used in Taiwan.

From 1949 to 1955 the country was divided into 6 large administrative regions. This system was terminated in 1955, but in 1961 was revived in the form of 6 regional Party Bureaux. These ceased to function during the Cultural Revolution. The table below shows the Provinces, Autonomous Regions and Government-controlled Municipalities grouped regionally. The cities shown in brackets are the seats of the former regional Party Bureaux.

	Area (in 1,000 sq. km)	*Population Census 1953 (in 1,000)*	*Population Estimate 1980 (in 1m.)*	*Capital*
North-Eastern Region (Shenyang)				
Heilongjiang [1]	710·0	11,897	31·69	Harbin
Jilin [1]	290·0	11,290	21·85	Changchun
Liaoning [1]	230·0	18,545	34·43	Shenyang
Northern Region (Peking)				
Hebei	202·7	35,985	51·04	Shijiazhuang
Inner Mongolia (Aut. Region) [1]	450·0	6,100	18·51	Hohhot
Peking (municipality) (Beijing)	17·8	2,768	8·70	—
Shanxi	157·1	14,314	24·47	Taiyuan
Tianjin (municipality)	4·0	2,694	7·39	
Eastern Region (Shanghai)				
Shandong	153·3	48,877	72·31	Jinan
Jiangxi	164·8	16,773	32·29	Nanchang
Jiangsu	102·2	41,252	58·93	Nanking (Nanjing)
Shanghai (municipality)	5·8	6,204	11·32	—
Anhui	139·9	30,344	48·03	Hefei
Zhejiang	101·8	22,866	37·92	Hangzhou
Fujian	123·1	13,143	24·80	Fuzhou
Taiwan	36·0	7,591	17·48	Taibei
Central-Southern Region (Wuhan)				
Henan	167·0	44,215	71·89	Zhengzhou
Hubei	187·5	27,790	46·32	Wuhan
Hunan	210·5	33,227	52·23	Changsha
Guangdong	231·4	34,770	56·81	Canton (Guangzhou)
Guangxi–Zhuang (Aut. Region)	220·4	19,561	34·70	Nanning
South-Western Region (Chongqing)				
Sichuan	569·0	62,304	97·74	Chengdu
Guizhou	174·0	15,037	27·31	Guiyang
Yunnan	436·2	17,473	31·35	Kunming
Tibet (Aut. Region)	1,221·6	1,273	1·83	Lhasa
North-Western Region (Xian)				
Shaanxi	195·8	15,881	28·07	Xian
Gansu [1]	530·0	12,928 (Gansu and Ningxia–Hui combined)	18·94	Lanzhou
Ningxia–Hui (Aut. Region) [1]	170·0		3·64	Yinchuan
Qinghai	721·0	1,677	3·72	Xining
Xinjiang–Uygur (Aut. Region)	1,646·8	4,874	12·56	Urumqi

[1] Boundaries restored to approximately the pre-1970 position in 1979.

Large towns, with population in 1977: Chongqing, 6m.; Canton (Guangzhou), 5m.; Shenyang, 4·4m.; Wuhan, 3·5m.; Nanjing, 3m.; Harbin, 2·1m.

Manchuria, a term not used by the Chinese, is roughly identical with the 3 provinces of the N.E. Region.

Tibet. For events before the revolt of 1959 *see* THE STATESMAN'S YEAR-BOOK, 1964–65, under TIBET. After the revolt was suppressed the Preparatory Committee for the Autonomous Region of Tibet (set up 1955) took over the functions of local government, led by its Vice-Chairman, the Banqen Lama, in the absence of its Chairman, the Dalai Lama, who had fled to India in 1959. In Dec. 1964 both the Dalai and Banqen Lamas were removed from their posts and on 9 Sept. 1965 Tibet became an Autonomous Region. 301 delegates were elected to the first People's Congress, of whom 226 were Tibetans and in 1968 a Revolutionary Committee was established to administer the Region. This gave way to a People's Government in Aug. 1979. The Banqen Lama was re-elected to the Standing Committee of the Chinese People's Political Consultative Conference in March 1978—he became one of its Vice-Chairmen in July 1979—and has made several appeals to the Dalai Lama to return to China. In 1982 the population was reported to be 1,892,393. 4·25m. Tibetans live outside Tibet, in China, and in India and Nepál. Chinese efforts to modernize Tibet include irrigation, road-building and the establishment of light industry: more than 260 small and medium-sized factories and mines have been set up producing electric power, coal, building materials, lumber, textiles, chemicals and animal products.

In 1979, 1·6m. were engaged in agriculture, including 0·5m. nomadic herdsmen.

Agricultural communes were first introduced in 1965; by 1975 it was announced that 99% of villages had formed them. In 1975 Tibet became self-sufficient in grain for the first time. There are now 21,000 km of highways, and air routes link Lhasa with Chengdu and Xian.

It was officially admitted in Peking in 1980 that the administration of Tibet had been badly conducted hitherto. The borders were opened for trade with neighbouring countries, and agricultural reforms allowing for more individual autonomy within the commune system were announced.

Efforts are being made to revive Tibetan culture as part of China's new liberal policy towards minorities. Buddhist monasteries, closed in the Cultural Revolution, are now re-opening. Circulation of the Tibetan-language *Xizang Daily* now totals 38,000. In 1980 there were 6,000 primary schools, about 100 secondary schools and 4 colleges. There were more than 6,000 medical workers and nearly 500 hospitals, with a total of 4,000 beds.

The Dalai Lama, *My Land and My People* (ed. D. Howarth). London, 1962
Dawa Norbu, *Red Star Over Tibet.* London, 1974
Jäschke, H. A., *A Tibetan–English Dictionary.* London, 1934
Mele, F., *Tibet.* Paris, 1975
Richardson, H. E., *Tibet and its History.* OUP, 1962
Shakabpa, T. W. D., *Tibet: A Political History.* Yale Univ. Press, 1967
Thubten, J. N., and Turnbull, C., *Tibet: Its History, Religion and People.* Harmondsworth, 1972

CONSTITUTION AND GOVERNMENT. On 21 Sept. 1949 the 'Chinese People's Political Consultative Conference' met in Peking, convened by the Chinese Communist Party. The Conference adopted a 'Common Programme' of 60 articles and the 'Organic Law of the Central People's Government' (31 articles). Both became the basis of the Constitution adopted on 20 Sept. 1954 by the 1st National People's Congress, the supreme legislative body. The Consultative Conference continued to exist after 1954 as an advisory body. Both bodies stopped functioning in the Cultural Revolution. The People's Congress was revived in 1975 and the Consultative Conference in 1978, when Deng Xiaoping was elected as its head. In 1979 it had 1,734 members.

The 1954 Constitution was both a political and an organizational document. It indicated the steps to be taken to build a 'socialist' society, defined the structure and functions of government organs and the rights and duties of citizens appropriate in the period of transition to 'socialism'.

In Jan. 1975 the 4th National People's Congress approved a constitution, under which China was defined as a 'socialist state of the dictatorship of the proletariat'. The 1975 Constitution was a simpler document than its predecessor emphasizing the role of politics in society, especially the thought of Mao, but giving fewer organizational details. In March 1978 the 5th National People's Congress adopted a new constitution of 60 articles which revives several of the provisions of the 1954 constitution dropped in the 1975 document and eliminates much of the latter's innovatory radicalism. More administrative detail is given. Provisions (Art.45) for freedom of speech and publication were withdrawn in 1980.

A new draft Constitution was published in April 1982 was adopted in 1983. It defines 'socialist modernisation' as China's basic task. Its most striking change is the restoration of the post of State Chairman (*i.e.* Head of State).

The National People's Congress is the highest organ of state power. It can amend the Constitution, elects and has power to remove from office the highest State dignitaries, decides on the national economic plan, etc. The Congress elects a *Standing Committee* which supervises the State Council and whose chairman is the equivalent of head of state. The present chairman (elected March 1978) is Ye Jianying.

The Constitution provides that the Congress be elected for a 5-year term and should meet once a year. It is composed of deputies elected on a constituency basis by direct secret ballot. Any voter, and certain organizations, may nominate candidates. Nominations may exceed seats by 50–100%. 3,497 deputies were elected to the 5th Congress in March 1978.

Under the streamlining of the government structure which is currently taking place (1983), the number of Ministries, Commissions and other agencies of the State Council has been reduced from 98 to 52. There are now 33 Ministries and 7 Commissions under the State Council. Zhao Ziyang remains Premier. The number of Vice-Premiers has been reduced from 13 to 2 (Wanhi, Yao Yilin). Many of the former Vice-Premiers have taken the newly-created post of State Councillor, of which there are 10. Some of these are also Ministers, *i.e.* Huang Hua *(Foreign Affairs),* Chen Muhua *(Foreign Trade and Economic Relations),* Geng Biao *(Defence)* and one, Zhang Jingfu, heads the Economic Commission.

Since 1970 when China began to emerge from the isolation of the Cultural Revolution, her diplomatic relations have expanded considerably. On 25 Oct. 1971 the UN voted for the People's Republic to take over the China seat from the Nationalists by 76 votes to 35 with 17 abstentions. US President Nixon visited China in Feb. 1972 and in 1973 'liaison offices' were opened in the capitals of the two countries. On 1 Jan. 1979 the US recognized the Peking government as the sole legal government of China and diplomatic relations were established. In Jan.–Feb. 1979 Deng Xiaoping paid an official visit to USA. On 12 Aug. 1978 China and Japan signed a 10-year treaty of peace and friendship (ratified 22 Oct. 1978). China has announced that it will not renew its treaty of friendship with the USSR which expired in 1980.

State emblem: 5 stars above Peking's Gate of Heavenly Peace, surrounded by a border of ears of grain entwined with drapings, which form a knot in the centre of a cogwheel at the base; the colours are red and gold.

National flag: Red with a large star and 4 smaller stars all in yellow in the canton.

National anthem: 'March of the Volunteers' (composed 1935 by Tien Han. (Replacing the 1978 version).

De facto power is in the hands of the Communist Party of China, which had 39·6m. members in 1982. There are 8 other parties, all members of the United Front headed by Deng Xiaoping. Communist Party officials hold key positions in government organs and most social, economic and cultural organizations. In mid-1966 the Party Chairman, Mao Tse-tung, launched the 'Great Proletarian Cultural Revolution' to eradicate 'revisionism' and numerous Party and State officials were dismissed. The Cultural Revolution can be taken to have terminated by April 1969 when the long-delayed 9th Party Congress was convened, although it was not officially declared to have been brought to a 'victorious conclusion' until Aug. 1977. The 9th Congress adopted a new Party Constitution which proclaimed the leading rôle of the Party in the State and designated Lin Biao as Chairman Mao's successor. A factional dispute developed, however, centred on Lin Biao (killed in an air crash in Mongolia in Sept. 1971) and in Aug. 1973 the 10th Party Congress adopted amendments to the Party Constitution, removing references to Lin Biao and the succession to Chairman Mao, and electing a new Central Committee which appointed a new Politburo and Standing Committee. In Jan. 1975 the Central Committee appointed as a vice-chairman of the Politburo Deng Xiaoping, former Party Secretary-General dismissed during the Cultural Revolution. In April 1976 a 'radical' faction in the Politburo engineered a second dismissal of Deng from all his posts, and Hua Guofeng was appointed First Party Vice-Chairman as well as Premier. On the death of Mao Tse-tung on 9 Sept. 1976 Hua became Party Chairman. In Oct. 1976 the 'radical' faction (now identified and excoriated as the 'Gang of Four': Mao's widow, Jiang Qing, Zhang Chunqiao, Wang Hongwen and Yao Wenyuan) were placed under arrest. At the 11th Party Congress in Aug. 1977 a new Party Constitution was adopted, and a new Central Committee was elected. Changes in the leadership saw the elimination of the 'radical' faction and a second reinstatement of Deng to his Party and government posts. In Feb. 1980 Liu Shaoqi, former head of state denounced by Mao as a traitor, was posthumously reinstated, and 4 Politburo members of Maoist persuasion were dismissed. Hua Guofeng was replaced as Premier by Zhao Ziyang in Sept. 1980. The 'Gang of Four', along with Chen Boda (a former secretary of Mao), were brought to trial only on 20 Nov. 1980. At the same time the trial opened of five generals accused of complicity with Lin Biao in an attempt to seize power. All 10 accused were found guilty on 25 Jan. 1981. Suspended death sentences were passed on Jiang Qing and Zhang Chunqiao. Hua Guofeng was removed from the Party Chairmanship in June 1981 and replaced by Hu Yaobang. At the 12th Party Congress (Sept. 1982), the posts of Chairman and Vice-Chairman of the CPC were abolished, and greater stress laid on the position of General Secretary of the Central Committee. The members of the Standing Committee of the Politiburo elected at the 12th Party Congress are Hu Yaobang *(General Secretary)*, Ye Kanying, Deng Xiaoping *(Chairman of the Military Commission of the Central Committee)*, Zhao Ziyang, Li Xiannian and Chen Yun *(Chairman of the Central Commission for Discipline Inspection)*. Other members of the Politiburo are: Wan Li, Xi Zhongxun, Wang Zhen, Wei Guoqing, Ulanhu, Fang Yi, Deng Yingchao, Li Desheng, Yang Shangkun, Yang Dezhi, Yuqiuli, Song Renqiong, Zhang Tingfa, Hu Qiaomu, Nie Rongzhen, Ni Zhifu, Xu Xiangwian, Peng Zhen, Liao Chengzhi. A new central Party body—the Central Advisory Commission, chaired by Deng Xiaoping—was elected by the Congress.

Local Government. There are 4 administrative levels: (1) Provinces, Autonomous Regions and the municipalities directly administered by the Government; (2) prefectures and autonomous prefectures (*zhou*); (3) counties, autonomous counties and municipalities; (4) towns and rural communes. Local government after 1968 was in the hands of Revolutionary Committees. From 1 Jan. 1980 these were replaced by elected People's Congresses and People's Governments. These exist at provincial, county and commune levels and in national minority autonomous prefectures, but not in ordinary prefectures which are just agencies of the provincial government. Up to county level Congresses are elected directly.

DEFENCE. China is divided into 11 military regions. The military commander also commands the air, naval and civilian militia forces assigned to each region.

Conscription is compulsory but for organizational reasons selective: only some 10% of potential recruits are called up. Service is 3 years with the Army, 4 years with the Air Force and 5 years with the Navy.

Marks of rank were abolished in 1965 but uniforms distinguish officers from other ranks.

Army. The Army (PLA: 'People's Liberation Army') is divided into main and local forces. Main forces, administered by the military regions in which they are stationed but commanded by the Ministry of Defence, are available for operation anywhere and are better equipped. Local forces concentrate on the defence of their own regions. The Army consists of 185 divisions including 40 artillery, 11 armoured, 118 infantry, 3 airborne and 85 local divisions. Total strength in 1983 was 3·15m.

The security forces, including the armed police, number some 300,000.

The People's Militia consists of the Armed Militia of up to 6m. strength, the Ordinary Militia of several million, unarmed but with some basic military training, and which includes the Urban Militia, and the Civilian Production and Construction Corps of 4m.

Navy. The steady new construction programme of all classes of warships in modernized yards, all with advanced nuclear and missile capability, has been maintained. Chinese naval strength is an important factor in the present and future balance of power east of Suez.

Present strength comprises 2 nuclear powered submarines, 1 submarine with ballistic missile tubes, 105 other submarines, 14 destroyers, 20 frigates, 14 patrol escorts, 210 missile boats, 21 large patrol boats, 30 fast patrol craft, 380 fast gunboats, 260 fast torpedo boats, 23 ocean minesweepers, 80 mine warfare craft, 120 coastal patrol craft, 27 survey and research ships, 40 supply and support ships, 25 oilers, 6 boom defence vessels, 2 repair ships, 40 landing ships, 470 landing craft, 3 salvage ships, 2 icebreakers, 40 tugs and 900 coast and river defence craft and vessels of the Maritime Militia.

Active personnel in 1983 exceeded 300,000 officers and men, including 30,000 in the naval air force and over 28,000 marines.

Main naval bases: Qingdao (North Sea Fleet); Shanghai (East Sea Fleet); Tsamkong (Zhanjiang) (South Sea Fleet).

The largely land-based naval air force of over 700 aircraft, primarily for defensive and anti-submarine surface, includes MiG-17, MiG-19 and MiG-21 fighters, some 150 Il-28 torpedo bombers, Madge flying boats, Hound M14 helicopters and communications and transport aircraft.

Air Force. In 1982 the Air Force was estimated at 5,300 front-line aircraft, organized in over 100 regiments of jet-fighters and about 12 regiments of tactical bombers, plus reconnaissance, transport and helicopter units. Each regiment is made up of 3 or 4 squadrons (each 12 aircraft), and 3 regiments form a division.

Equipment is predominantly Russian in design and includes about 250 J-7 (MiG-21), 3,000 J-6 (MiG-19) and 300 J-5 (MiG-17) home-defence interceptors, with about 550 H-5 (Il-28) jet-bombers, more than 100 H-6 Chinese-built copies of the Soviet Tu-16 twin-jet strategic bomber, and a few piston-engined Tu-4 (Soviet copy of Boeing B-29) strategic bombers, plus several hundred Q-5 twin-jet fighter-bombers (known in the west as 'Fantan'), evolved from the MiG-19. Entering service is a new fighter designated J-8 (known in the west as 'Finback'). Transport aircraft include about 300 Y-5 (An-2), Y-8 (An-12), An-24/26, 100 Li-2, 30 Il-14, 10 Il-18 and a few three-turbofan Trident fixed-wing types, plus 300 Mi-4 and Mi-8 helicopters and 13 French-built Super Frelon heavy transport helicopters. The MiG fighters and Antonov transports have been manufactured in China, initially under licence, and other types have been assembled there, including several hundred JT-5 (2-seat MiG-17) trainers.

Total strength (1982) about 490,000, including 220,000 in air defence organization.

INTERNATIONAL RELATIONS

Membership. The People's Republic of China is a member of UN.

ECONOMY

Planning. For planning history 1953–73 *see* THE STATESMAN'S YEAR-BOOK, 1973–74, p. 817.

The long-term aim of the present leadership is to transform China by the year 2000 into a modern developed economic power by the implementation of 'the 4 modernizations', *i.e.,* of agriculture, industry, defence and science and technology. In 1978, as a first step to the realization of the '4 modernizations', a 10-year plan (1976–85) was introduced. However this proved in practice to be over-ambitious; many of the planned targets were too high and the scale of capital construction was too great. The pursuit of the plan caused serious imbalances in the economy. Since 1979 a policy of 'readjusting, restructuring, consolidating and improving' the economy has been followed.

The more rational approach adopted to China's material and financial limitations embodied in the readjustment programme remains the foundation of Chinese economic policy. Agriculture and light industry will receive higher priority in investment compared to heavy industry. The growth rates in 1980 were lower and the 1981 targets were twice revised downwards in an effort to balance the budget. (The total value of industrial and agricultural production in 1981 rose by 4%.)

Budget. 1981 revenue was 106,430m. yuan; expenditure, 108,970m. yuan.

Communes pay an agricultural tax, and this accounts for almost 10% of budgetary revenue. Since 1981 state-owned enterprises have paid a business tax instead of turning over their profits to the state. Income tax was introduced in 1980; it affects mainly foreigners. China will pay off US claims of US$80·5m. before 1 Oct. 1984, and USA will unblock Chinese assets of the same value. Registration of British claims for loss of assets in 1949 was requested by the Foreign Compensation

Commission in Jan. 1981. A credit of 450m. SDF was granted by IMF in March 1981.

China's reserves at 31 Dec. 1980 were US$2,361m. of foreign exchange and 12·8m. troy oz. of gold.

Currency. The currency is called Renminbi (RMB, *i.e.,* People's Currency). The unit of currency is the *yuan* which is divided into 10 *jiao*, the *jiao,* into 10 *fen*. The official rate of exchange is £ = 3·35 *yuan*; US$1 = 1·83 *yuan*; Hong Kong $1 = 0·983 *yuan*; 1 rouble = 2·222 *yuan* (non-commercial, 1 rouble = 1·29 *yuan*).

Notes are issued for 1, 2 and 5 *jiao* and 1, 2, 5 and 10 *yuan* and coins for 1, 2 and 5 *fen*.

Banking. Banking is controlled by the People's Bank which has 30,000 branches. It is both the bank of issue and the principal commercial and domestic bank. It is also the major instrument of economic policy through which enterprises are controlled or supervised by the Government. Its president has ministerial rank.

There are 2 specialized banks: the Construction Bank and the Bank of Communications. The Bank of China, which has branches abroad (including 1 in London) is an agency of the People's Bank.

Weights and Measures. The metric system is in general use. For older units of measurement, *see* THE STATESMAN'S YEAR-BOOK, 1975–76, p. 826 and 1954, pp. 877–88.

ENERGY AND NATURAL RESOURCES

Electricity. In 1979 coal provided over 60% of China's energy, although there is a large hydro-electric potential in the centre and south. Generating is not centralized; local units range between 30 and 60 mw of output. Output in 1981: 309,300m. kwh.

Oil. China has made rapid progress in oil extraction and refining. There are probably about 100 oilfields, of which the largest are at Daqing, Shengli, Dagang and Karamai. Offshore resources in Bohai Bay are also being exploited. Refining capacity is estimated at 80m. tons per annum. Oil reserves may be as much as 10,000m. tonnes. Crude oil production was 101·22m. tonnes in 1981.

Gas. Natural gas is available from fields near Canton and Shanghai and in Sichuan province. Production was 14,890m. cu. metres in 1981, but is only used locally.

Minerals. *Coal.* Most provinces contain coal, and there are 70 major production centres, of which the largest are in Hebei, Shanxi, Shandong, Jilin and Anhui. Coal reserves are estimated at 200,000m. tonnes. Coal production was 620m. tonnes in 1981.

Iron. Iron ores are abundant in the anthracite field of Shanxi, in Hebei, in Shandong and other provinces, and iron (found in conjunction with coal) is worked in Manchuria. 300m. tons of ore are estimated to be in Shanxi; the principal iron-ore reserves total about 44,000m. tons. The Daye iron deposits, near Wuhan, are among the richest in the world. Estimated output of iron ore in 1972, 75m. tonnes. The biggest steel bases are at Anshan (in Manchuria) with a capacity of 6m. tons, Wuhan (capacity 3·5m. tonnes), Baotou and Maanshan (both 2·5m. tonnes).

Tin. Tin ore is plentiful in Yunnan, where the tin-mining industry has long existed. Tin production was 15,000 tonnes in 1978.

Tungsten. China is the world's principal producer of wolfram (tungsten ore), producing 9,000 tonnes in 1978. Mining of wolfram is carried on in Hunan, Guangdong and Yunnan.

Production of other minerals in 1978 (in tonnes): Phosphate rock, 4·5m.; aluminium, 225,000; copper, 200,000; lead, 120,000; zinc, 125,000; antimony, 9,000; manganese, 2m.; (1973) sulphur, 130,000; (1967) bauxite, 350,000; (1973) salt, 18,000; (1969) asbestos, 160,000. Other minerals produced: barite, bismuth, gold, graphite, gypsum, mercury, molybdenum, silver.

Agriculture. China remains essentially an agricultural country. Some 11% of the total land area is under cultivation. Intensive agriculture and horticulture have been practised for millennia. Present-day policy aims to avert the traditional threats from floods and droughts by soil conservancy, afforestation, irrigation and drainage projects, and to increase the 'high stable yields' areas by introducing fertilizers, pesticides and improved crops. Crop priorities: food grains; raw materials for industry (especially cotton); crops for export (especially oil seeds). Among livestock, priority is given to pig production.

Since 1958 modifications have been made in the commune system, including size reductions. There were some 50,000 in 1977. Small private plots account for 20% or more of the peasant income which averaged 83·40 yuan in 1979.

Since 1978 more flexible methods of management have been adopted comprising 'responsibility systems', whereby individual households or other small units are contracted to supply to the commune or government purchasing agency a quantity of crops to be produced from an alloted area of commune land. Any surplus is at the disposal of the household, to be consumed or marketed.

In 1974 there were estimated to be 127m. hectares of arable land. In 1977 there were 43m. tractors (15 h.p. units).

Agricultural production, 1981 (in 1m. tonnes). Total grain, 325; tea, 0·34; cotton, 2·97; rice, 143·2; oilseed crops, 10·2.

Livestock, 1981: Horses and cattle, 64·5m.; sheep and goats, 187·5m.; pigs, 310·25m. Meat production in 1980 was 12·06m. tonnes.

Forestry. Forests cover some 12m. hectares. The chief forested areas are in Heilongjiang, Sichuan and Yunnan. Timber output in 1981 was 49·4m. cu. metres.

The most important timber product is teak. It is estimated that some 1·3m. hectares are afforested each year.

INDUSTRY AND TRADE

Industry. 'Cottage' industry is very old in the economy and persists into the 20th century. Modern industrial development began with the manufacture of cotton textiles, and the establishment of silk filatures, steel plants, flour-mills and match factories. Expanding sectors of manufacture are: steel, chemicals, cement, agricultural implements, plastics and lorries.

1981 production (in tonnes): Chemical fertilizer, 12·39m.; chemical fibres, 527,000; pig-iron. 34·2m.; cement, 84m.; cotton cloth, 14,270m. metres; 176,000 motor vehicles were produced, 53,000 tractors and 17·5m. bicycles.

35·6m. tonnes of steel and 5·4m. tonnes of paper were produced in 1981.

Labour. Number employed in state and collective urban enterprises in 1981: 109·4m. with an average wage of 772 yuan. Wage increases affecting 40% of the non-agricultural workforce were introduced in Oct. 1977 and in Nov. 1979. There is a 6-day 48-hour working week.

Commerce. Foreign trade, formerly conducted exclusively through national corporations under the Ministry of Foreign Trade, is now being decentralized. Trade authorities are being established in the main cities, to date Beijing (Peking), Shanghai and Tianjin, and in selected provinces, to date Guangdong and Fujian. The quasi-governmental China International Trust and Investment Corporation also handles foreign trade. Duty-free zones have been set up in the latter. Foreign firms pay a profits tax of 15%. In 1978 China reversed its policy of not accepting foreign credit and aid. A law of July 1979 permits the establishment of joint ventures with foreign firms. There is no maximum limit on the foreign share of the holdings; the minimum limit is 25%. Foreign indebtedness was about £1,400m. in 1980.

Imports include grain, raw materials and semi-manufactured products for agriculture (primarily chemical fertilizers), light industry and textiles, advanced equipment, particularly whole plants and consumer goods. Exports include heavy industrial goods including petroleum, chemicals, minerals, machinery and equipment, light industrial goods and agricultural products.

Trade in 1981: Imports, 36,770m. yuan; exports, 36,760m. yuan.

Some 85% of China's trade is with non-Communist countries. Japan is China's biggest trading partner, and an 8-year trade agreement was signed in Feb. 1978 and extended for 5 years in March 1979. Other major trading partners are Hong Kong, Federal Republic of Germany, USA and Australia. Imports from USA totalled US$1,720m. in 1979; exports to USA were US$551m. Customs duties on imports and exports between Taiwan and the mainland were abolished in April 1980. Trade with USA is increasing rapidly.

Total trade between China and UK (British Department of Trade returns, in £1,000 sterling):

	1978	*1979*	*1980*	*1981*	*1982*
Imports to UK	110,624	137,891	153,433	184,069	193,231
Exports and re-exports from UK	91,093	213,039	169,500	120,048	103,051

In April 1978 a most-favoured-nation agreement was signed with EEC, and in 1980 the EEC extended preferential tariffs to China.

On 15 Nov. 1978 a science and technology agreement was signed by UK and China and on 4 March 1979 an agreement on economic co-operation. In July 1979 the USA and China signed a 3-year trade agreement which accords China most-favoured-nation status from 1980.

On 17 April 1980 China gained representation in the IMF, and on 15 May 1980 in the IBRD.

COMMUNICATIONS

Roads. The total road length was 897,200 km in 1981. 83% of communes could be reached by road in 1976. Highways are well graded but mostly unmetalled. In 1969 there were some 409,000 lorries, 60,000 cars and 30,000 buses.

In 1978, 27,900m. tonne-km of freight were transported by road.

Railways. Chinese railway history begins in 1876, when the Wusong–Shanghai line was opened. In 1982 there were some 52,000 km of railway including 2,100 km electrified.

The principal railways are:

(1) The great north–south trunk lines: (*a*) Peking–Canton Railway (over 2,300 km), *via* Zhengzhou–Wuhan–Zhuzhou–Hengyang.

(*b*) Tianjin–Shanghai Railway (1,500 km), *via* Pukow and Nanjing (double-tracked in July 1976).

(*c*) Baoji–Chongqing Railway, *via* Chengdu (1,174 km). Chongqing with the east–west route from Hengyang to the Vietnam border, and to Kunming, connecting there with the Yunnan Railway to the Vietnam border. Two further lines connect Baoji.

(2) Great east–west trunk lines: (*a*) Longhai Railway; Lianyungkang–Xuzhou–Zhengzhou (on the Peking–Canton line) –Xian–Baoji–Tianshui–Lanzhou (1,500 km). The Baoji–Lanzhou section was upgraded in 1978. (*b*) Lanzhou–Xinjiang Railway: Lanzhou–Yumen–Hami–Turfan–Urumqi (1,800 km); (c) Shanghai–Youyiguan (Vietnam border) *via* Hangzhou, Nanchang, Hengyang (on the Peking–Canton line), Guilin, Liuzhou and Nanning. (*d*) Peking–Lanzhou *via* Xining (from which a branch connects with the lines through Mongolia to the Trans-Siberian Railway), Dadong (from which a branch serves the province of Shanxi), Baotou and Yinchuan (Ningxia). (*e*) Zhuzhou–Guiyang (632 km). A new east–west line was opened in 1978 between Xiangfan and Chongqing.

Branches link coastal areas (*e.g.*, Fujian province) and the smaller inland centres with the main parts of the system. Surveys have been made for a new 500-km railway, linking the trunk line with the oilfield of Karamai in Xinjiang.

(3) The Manchurian system: (*a*) Chinese Eastern (Changchun) Railway (2,370 km), from Manzhouli on the Soviet border through northern Inner Mongolia and Manchuria *via* Qiqihar, Harbin and Mudanjiang to the Soviet border near Vladivostok. (*b*) South Manchuria Railway (705 km, 1,120 km with branches), Changchun–Shenyang–Luda. (*c*) Peking–Shenyang Railway, with branches in Manchuria (854 km, 1,350 km with branches).

Branches give connexions with outlying parts of Manchuria and Inner Mongolia as well as international links with Korean railways. Chinese railways are all constructed to the standard gauge except for some 600 km of metre gauge in Yunnan. Trunk routes are being converted from single to double track. The route between Baoji and Chengdu (676 km) was electrified in 1975 and that between Yangpingguan (on the Baoji–Chengdu route) and Ankang in 1977.

Capacity is being expanded under the 1976–85 development plan: 6 new lines are to be built by 1985. Lines are planned to link Tibet with the Chinese network (opened as far as Golmud in 1979) and to bridge gaps in the system such as Liuzhou–Canton, Kantang–Taiyuan and southern Xinjiang.

In 1980 the railways carried 1,202m. tons of freight.

Aviation. The Civil Aviation Administration of China (CAAC) flies routes to Pyongyang, Hanoi, Rangoon, Karachi, Tōkyō, Moscow, Teheran, Addis Ababa, Bucharest, Belgrade, Zürich, Paris, Frankfurt, Manila, New York, San Francisco, London and Hong Kong. It also provides services to Hong Kong. Its inventory includes 3 Boeing 747s, 10 Boeing 707s, 16 Tridents and 5 Il–62s. British Airways have a direct flight London-Beijing. Japan Airlines have a route from Tōkyō to Beijing (*via* Osaka and Shanghai), Air France Paris to Beijing (*via* Athens and Karachi), Pakistan Airlines Karachi to Beijing, Aeroflot Moscow to Beijing, Ethiopian Airlines Addis Ababa to Shanghai, Tarom (Romania) Bucharest to Beijing, Swissair Geneva to Peking and Shanghai, Iran Air Paris to Peking and PANAM Peking *via* Tōkyō.

In 1979 there were 160 internal routes with over 500 weekly flights.

Air services agreements have been signed with Bangladesh, Canada, the Federal Republic of Germany, Greece, Iraq, Italy, Japan, Laos, Nepál, the Netherlands, the Philippines, Spain, Sweden, Thailand, UK and USA.

Shipping. In 1980 the ocean-going merchant fleet consisted of 431 vessels with a total DWT of 7·92m.

The major ports are at Tianjin, Shanghai, Qingdao, Luda and Canton. New ports are under construction at Changchiang, Huangpu, Qinhuangdao, Yantai and Lienyunkang. Ports cannot accommodate vessels over 100,000 GRT and most harbours have a draught limitation of 35 ft. 217m. tonnes of cargo was handled in 1980.

Inland waterways total about 136,000 km. Plans were announced in 1978 for a national transport waterway network.

Pipeline. A pipeline links the Daqing oilfield to the port of Luda and to refineries in Peking. There is a pipeline from Lanzhou to Lhasa.

Post and Broadcasting. Number of post offices of all kinds in 1958 was 67,000. The use of *Pinyin* transcription of place names has been requested for mail to addresses in China (*e.g.*, 'Beijing' *not* 'Peking'; 'Tianjin' *not* 'Tientsin'; 'Guangzhou' *not* 'Canton', etc.).

In 1980 there were 106 radio broadcasting stations. In 1964 there were some 7m. radio receivers. In 1980 there were 38 television stations and 9·02m. TV receivers. Most are communally owned.

Cinemas. Cinemas numbered 1,386 in 1958.

Newspapers. In 1980 newspaper production totalled 14,040m. copies, and journals, 1,120m. copies. The Party newspaper is *Renmin Ribao* (People's Daily). In 1979 it had a daily circulation of 7m.

JUSTICE, RELIGION, EDUCATION AND WELFARE

Justice. Six new codes of law (including criminal and electoral) came into force in Jan. 1980, which, it is claimed, will regularize the legal unorthodoxy of recent years. The new codes specify a process of repentance as a precondition for a possible reduction of sentence. There is no provision for *habeas corpus*. The death penalty is prescribed for murder and treason. Courts will no longer be subject to the intervention of other state bodies, and their decisions will be reversible only by higher courts. 'People's courts' are divided into some 30 higher, 200 intermediate and 2,000 basic-level courts, and headed by the Supreme People's Court. The latter tries cases, hears appeals and supervises the people's courts. The Ministry of Justice, abolished in 1959, was re-established in 1979.

People's courts are composed of a president, vice-presidents, judges and 'people's assessors' who are the equivalent of jurors. 'People's conciliation committees' are charged with settling minor disputes.

There are also special military courts.

Procuratorial powers and functions are exercised by the Supreme People's Procuracy and local procuracies.

Religion. Confucianism, Buddhism and Taoism have long been practised. Confucianism has no ecclesiastical organization and appears rather as a philosophy of ethics and government. Taoism—of Chinese origin—copied Buddhist ceremonial soon after the arrival of Buddhism two millennia ago. Buddhism in return adopted many Taoist beliefs and practices. It is no longer possible to estimate the number of adherents to these faiths. A more tolerant attitude towards religion had emerged by 1979, and the Government's Bureau of Religious Affairs was reactivated.

Ceremonies of reverence to ancestors have been observed by the whole population regardless of philosophical or religious beliefs.

Moslems are found in every province of China, being most numerous in the Ningxia–Hui Autonomous Region, Yunnan, Shaanxi, Gansu, Hebei, Honan, Shandong, Sichuan, Xinjiang and Shanxi. They totalled 10m. in 1980.

Roman Catholicism has had a footing in China for more than 3 centuries. In 1979 there were about 2m. Catholics who are members of the Patriotic Catholic Association, which declared its independence of Rome in 1958, and about 1,000 priests. In 1977 there were 78 bishops and 4 apostolic administrators, not all of whom were permitted to undertake religious activity. This figure included 46 'democratically elected' bishops not recognized by the Vatican. A Catholic bishop of Peking was consecrated in Dec. 1979 without the consent of the Vatican.

Protestants are members of the All-China Conference of Protestant Churches.

Education. During the Cultural Revolution and the 'Gang of Four' period the educational system was in a turmoil of radical reformation involving a reduction in the length of courses at all levels, the substitution of class background for academic achievement as a criterion for entry to higher education, a heavy emphasis on political education, and lengthy periods of manual labour sandwiched between courses. 1977 marked the beginning of a return to a more conventional system, and by 1978 3 out of every 4 children were attending school. University entry now normally follows from secondary schooling and is dependent upon entrance examinations in which political reliability tests are accompanied by tests in academic subjects. Obligatory manual labour has been reduced to 1 month per year. In 1978 a system of 'key' schools for the best-performing pupils was set up, and it was announced that new universities and colleges would be established. It was also announced that several thousand students would be sent to Western universities. In 1980 there were 675 universities and institutes of higher education, with some 1·14m. students. In 1979 there were some 146m. pupils in 1m. primary schools, and 65m. pupils in 200,000 secondary schools.

The Academy of Sciences had in 1964 some 20 provincial branches and an Academy of Social Sciences was established in 1977.

Among the universities are the following: People's University of China, Peking (founded 1912 by Dr Sun Yat-sen; reorganized 1950; about 3,000 students); Peking University, Peking (1898, enlarged 1945; about 10,000 students); Xiamen University, Fujian (1921 and 1937); Fudan University, Shanghai (1905); Inner Mongolia University, Hohhot; Lanzhou University, Lanzhou (Gansu Prov.); Nankai University, Tianjin (1919); Nanjing University, Nanjing (1888 and 1928); Jilin University, Changchun (Jilin Prov.); North-West University, Xian (Shanxi Prov.); Shandong University, Qingdao (1926); Sun Yat-sen University, Canton (founded 1924 by Dr Sun Yat-sen); Sichuan University, Chengdu (1931); Qinghua University, Peking, Wuhan University, Wuhan (Hubei Prov.; 1905 and 1928); Yunnan University, Kunming. In 1958 a university of science and technology was set up by the Academy of Sciences.

Chen, T. H., *Chinese Education since 1949.* Oxford, 1981.

Health. Medical treatment is free only for certain groups of employees, but where costs are incurred they are partly borne by the patient's employing organization. In 1980 there were 891,000 Western-style doctors and 262,000 doctors of Chinese medicine. In rural areas there were also 1·5m. 'bare-foot doctors', who receive 3 months' training and remain in the community treating simple ailments and implementing public health directives.

80% of production brigades have co-operative medical services. There were 1·98m. hospital beds in 1980.

DIPLOMATIC REPRESENTATIVES

Of China in Great Britain (31 Portland Place, London, W1N 3AG)
Ambassador: Ke Hua (accredited on 7 Nov. 1978).

Of Great Britain in China (11 Guang Hua Lu, Jian Guo Men Wai, Peking)
Ambassador: Sir Percy Cradock, KCMG.

Of China in the USA (2300 Connecticut Ave., NW, Washington, D.C., 20008)
Ambassador: Chai Zemin.

Of the USA in China (Guang Hua Lu 17, Peking)
Ambassador: Arthur W. Hummel, Jr.

Of China to the United Nations
Ambassador: Ling Qing.

Books of Reference

Beijing Review. Peking, weekly
The China Quarterly. London, from 1960
China Reconstructs. Peking, monthly
China's Foreign Trade. Bimonthly. Peking, from 1966
Bartke, W., *Who's Who in the People's Republic of China.* New York, 1981
Bennett, G. (ed.), *China's Finance and Trade: a Policy Reader.* London, 1978
Bettelheim, C., and Burton, N. G., *China Since Mao.* New York, 1978
Boardman, R., *Britain and the People's Republic of China, 1949–1974.* London, 1976
Bonavia, D., *The Chinese.* New York, 1980.—*The Chinese: A Portrait.* London, 1981
Boorman, H. L., and Howard, R. C. (eds.), *Biographical Dictionary of Republican China.* 5 vols. Columbia Univ. Press, 1967 ff.
Brugger, B. (ed.), *China since the Gang of Four,* London, 1980
The Cambridge History of China. 14 vols. CUP, 1978 ff.
Cheng, C., *China's Economic Development.* Boulder, 1982
Cheng, P., *China.* [Bibliography] Oxford and Santa Barbara, 1982
China: A General Survey. Peking, 1979
Fairbank, J. K., *The United States and China.* 4th ed. Cambridge, Mass., 1979
Fung, K. K., (ed.) *Current Economic Problems in China.* Boulder, 1982
Garside, R., *Coming Alive: China after Mao.* New York, 1980
Gittings, J., *The World and China, 1922–1972.* London, 1974
Hinton, H. C., (ed), *The People's Republic of China: A Handbook.* Boulder, 1979.—*The Peoples Republic of China 1949–1979.* 5 vols. Wilmington, 1980
Hook, B., (ed.) *The Cambridge Encyclopaedia of China.* CUP, 1982.
Houn, F. W., *A Short History of Chinese Communism.* 2nd ed. Englewood Cliffs, N.J., 1973
Howe, C., *China's Economy: A Basic Guide.* London, 1978
Hsieh, C. M., *Atlas of China.* New York, 1973
Hsu, R. C., *Ford for One Billion.* Boulder, 1982
Hsüeh, C.-T. (ed.), *Dimensions of China's Foreign Relations.* New York, 1977
Jingrong, W., (ed.), *The Pinyin-Chinese Dictionary.* Beijing and San Francisco, 1979
Kallgren, J., (ed.), *The People's Republic of China after 30 years.* Berkeley, 1979
Kaplan, F. M. (ed.), *Encyclopedia of China Today.* 3rd ed. London, 1982
Kim, S. S., *China, the United Nations and World Order.* Princeton, 1979
Klein, D. W., and Clark, A. B., *Biographic Dictionary of Chinese Communism, 1921–1965.* Harvard U.P., 1971
Lardy, N. R., *Economic Growth and Distribution in China.* CUP, 1978
Mao Tse-tung, Selected works. 5 vols. Peking, 1965–77
Mathews, R. H., *Chinese-English Dictionary.* Cambridge, Mass., 1943–47
Meyer, C., *China Observed.* London, 1981

Middleton, D., *The Duel of the Giants: China and Russia in Asia.* New York, 1978
O'Leary, G., *The Shaping of Chinese Foreign Policy.* London, 1980
Qi Wen, *China: a General Survey.* Peking, 1979
Rodzinski, W., *A History of China.* Vol. 1. Oxford, 1981
Schaller, M., *The United States and China in the Twentieth Century.* OUP, 1979
Scott, G. L., *Chinese Treaties: The Post-revolutionary Restoration of International Law and Order.* New York, 1975
Skinner, G. W. (ed.), *Modern Chinese Society: An Analytical Bibliography.* 3 vols. Stanford U.P., 1974
Szuprowicz, B. O. and M. R., *Doing Business with the People's Republic of China.* New York, 1978
The Times Atlas of China. London, 1974
Thornton, R. C., *China: A Political History, 1917–1980.* Boulder, 1982
US Congress Joint Economic Committee. *Chinese Economy, Post-Mao.* Washington, 1978
Yahuda, M. B., *China's Role in World Affairs.* London, 1978

TAIWAN

'Republic of China'

Capital: Taipei
Population: 18·27m. (1982)
GNP per capita: US$1,869 (1979)

HISTORY. The island of Taiwan (Formosa) was ceded to Japan by China by the Treaty of Shimonoseki on 8 May 1895. After the Second World War the island was surrendered to Gen. Chiang Kai-shek in Sept. 1945 and was placed under Chinese administration on 25 Oct. 1945. USA broke off diplomatic relations with Taiwan on 1 Jan. 1979 on establishing diplomatic relations with the Peking Government. Relations between the USA and Taiwan are maintained through the American Institute on Taiwan and the Taiwan Co-ordination Council for North American Affairs, set up in 1978 and accorded diplomatic status in Oct. 1980.

AREA AND POPULATION. Taiwan lies between the East and South China Seas about 100 miles from the coast of Fujian province. The total area of Taiwan Island and the Penghu Archipelago is 13,895 sq. miles (35,989 sq. km). Population (1982), 18·27m., of whom some 2m. are mainland Chinese who came with the Nationalist Government. There are also some 260,000 aboriginals. Population density: 503·7 per sq. km.

In 1981, birth rate was 2·29%; death rate, 0·48%; rate of growth, 1·81% per annum.

Taiwan is divided into two special municipalities (Taipei, the capital, population 2·27m. in 1981 and Kaohsiung, population 1·2m. in 1981), 5 municipalities (Keelung, Taichung, Tainan, Chiayi and Hsinchu) and 16 counties (*hsien*): Changhua, Chiayi, Hsinchu, Hualien, Ilan, Kaohsiung, Miaoli, Nantou, Penghu, Pingtung, Taichung, Tainan, Taipei, Taitung, Taoyuan, Yunlin.

CONSTITUTION AND GOVERNMENT. Taiwan is controlled by the remnants of the Nationalist Government. On 1 March 1950, Chiang Kai-shek resumed the presidency of the 'Republic of China', and was re-elected for his fifth 6-year presidential term in March 1972. He died 5 April 1975 and was succeeded by Dr Yen Chia-kan who was replaced in the presidential elections of 21 March 1978 by Chiang Kai-shek's eldest son Chiang Ching-kuo. There are 3 political parties: the ruling Kuomintang (1·5m. members in 1976), which has a youth movement (China Youth Corps) of over 1m. members, the Young China Party and the China Democratic Socialist Party.

The National Assembly was elected in 1947. In 1979 it had 1,185 delegates. The

National Assembly operates through 5 *yuan* or councils. The highest administrative organ is the Executive Yuan, headed by the premier, which includes a number of ministers. The highest legislative body is the Legislative Yuan, elected in 1948, which at the end of 1979 numbered 373 members. The National Assembly, Legislative Yuan and Control Yuan are elected bodies. Their terms of office have been extended indefinitely. As the number of original delegates dwindled, regulations introduced in 1966 and 1972 provided for the election of additional members to the National Assembly and Legislative Yuan, and elections were held in 1969, 1972, 1975 and 1980. There is also a Provincial Assembly of which the current Seventh Assembly with 77 members was elected on 14 Nov. 1981.

A political campaign by the journal *Mei-li Tao* and others calling on the Kuomintang to abandon its claim to represent all China and hold representative elections resulted in the sentencing of the prime movers at a court-martial in March 1980.

State emblem: A 12-pointed white sun in a blue sky.
National flag: Red with a blue first quarter bearing the state emblem in white.
National anthem: 'San Min Chu I', words by Dr Sun Yat-sen; tune by Cheng Mao-yun.

Prime Minister: Sun Yun-hsuan.
Vice-Premier: Chiu Chuang-huan. *Foreign Minister:* Chu Fu-sung. *Minister of National Defence:* Adm. Soong Chang-chih. *Minister of the Interior:* Lin Yang-kang. *Minister of Finance:* Hui Li-teh. *Governor of Taiwan:* Lee Teng-hui

DEFENCE. Army. The Army, which embodies the remnants of the forces which escaped to Taiwan with Chiang Kai-shek at the end of the civil war in 1949, numbered about 310,000 in 1983. It was reorganized, re-equipped and trained by the USA and now consists of 2 armoured, 12 infantry, 6 light infantry divisions, 2 armoured cavalry regiments and 2 airborne brigades. There is a conscription system for 2 years and reserve liability. Strong garrisons (about 80,000 men) are maintained on the Penghu islands (Pescadores) and the offshore islands of Quemoy and Matsu. US supplies of military equipment were resumed in 1980 after a moratorium in 1979. US forces were withdrawn by 1 May 1979.

Navy. Most of the 200 vessels in naval service are former US Navy ships now well over 30 years old and overdue for replacement. There are 2 diesel powered patrol submarines, 23 destroyers, 10 frigates, 3 escort vessels, 2 fast missile craft, 9 torpedo boats, 14 coastal minesweepers, 1 coastal minelayer, 9 minesweeping boats, 10 coastal patrol craft, 2 dock landing ships, 1 amphibious flagship, 26 landing ships, 22 landing craft, 2 repair ships, 4 surveying ships, 12 support ships, 2 transports, 7 oilers, 1 supply ship, 10 tugs, 5 floating docks and 25 service craft. There are also 7 coastguard cutters (customs).

Active personnel in 1983 exceeded 7,100 naval officers and 28,000 ratings; 3,000 marine officers and 26,000 men.

The Navy has 12 anti-submarine torpedo helicopters and operational control of 2 squadrons of Air Force anti-submarine warfare Tracker aircraft; and the Marine Corps operates a number of observation aircraft and helicopters.

Air Force. The Nationalist Air Force is equipped mainly with aircraft of US design, including F-5E fighters built in Taiwan. It has 13 squadrons of F-104G Starfighter, F-5A/B/E/F and F-100 Super Sabre fighter-bombers, 1 interceptor squadron of F-104S Starfighters, and 1 tactical reconnaissance squadron of RF-104G Starfighters. The 6 transport squadrons are equipped with a VIP Boeing 720, 5 C-54s, 20 C-47s, about 40 C-119Gs and 10 C-123 Providers. There is a naval co-operation squadron with S-2A/E Trackers and an ASW squadron with Hughes 500 MD helicopters. Search and rescue units operate Albatross amphibians and Iroquois helicopters, and there are other helicopter and large training elements. Total strength in 1982: 77,000 personnel and 485 combat aircraft.

INTERNATIONAL RELATIONS. By a treaty of 1 Dec. 1954 the USA was pledged to protect Taiwan, but this treaty lapsed 1 year after the USA established diplomatic relations with the People's Republic of China on 1 Jan. 1979. In April 1979 the US Congress approved a law to maintain commercial, cultural and other relations between USA and Taiwan.

The People's Republic took over the China seat in the UN from the Nationalists on 25 Oct. 1971.

ECONOMY

Planning. Government policy is to 'develop industry through agriculture and expand agriculture through industry'. Regional planning was carried out through a series of 4-year plans, of which the sixth (1973–76) was terminated in 1975 because of difficulties arising from the international economic situation. The 6-year programme (1976–81) envisaged a GNP annual growth rate of 8·5% and a 4-year plan (1982–85) envisages a GNP annual growth rate of 8%.

Budget. There are 2 budgets, the national together with a special defence budget (partly secret) and the provincial (*i.e.,* for Taiwan proper). For the fiscal year 1983 (July 1982–June 1983) tax revenue was NT$536,228m.; expenditure, NT$535,198m.

Currency. In 1945 the existing currency was converted into notes of the Bank of Taiwan. Taiwan dollars were linked to Chinese national currency at a fixed rate of exchange. When the Gold Yuan entered upon its last phase in early 1949, the Taiwan currency was detached and linked to the US$. Exchange rates (March 1983): £1 = NT$60·50; US$1 = NT$39·87.

Banking. The Central Bank of China (reactivated in 1961) regulates the money market, manages foreign exchange and issues currency. The former Bank of China, a foreign exchange bank with branches in New York, Chicago, Tōkyō, Osaka, Panama and Bangkok, was reorganized in 1972 as a private bank for export financing and renamed the China International Commercial Bank (capital NT$1,000m.).

The Bank of Taiwan is the largest commercial bank and the fiscal agent of the Government.

Other banking institutions include the China Development Corporation.

ENERGY AND NATURAL RESOURCES

Electricity. Output of electricity in 1981 was 40,149m. kwh.; total generating capacity was 10·2m. kw. One nuclear power-station (capacity 0·7m. kw.) came into use in 1977, two more are under construction and a fourth envisaged.

Minerals. There are reserves of coal (202·9m. tonnes), gold (6·1m. tonnes), copper (12·5m. tonnes), sulphur (2·4m. tonnes), oil (1·8m. kl.) and natural gas (25,921 cu. metres). In 1976 an offshore gas-field south-west of Taiwan was discovered with an annual capacity of 500m. cu. metres. In 1981, coal production was 2·4m. tonnes; petroleum, 182,812 kl.; natural gas, 1,501·9m. cu. metres.

Agriculture. The cultivated area was 900,062 hectares in 1981, of which 502,822 hectares were paddy fields. Production in 1,000 tonnes, in 1981: Rice, 2,375 (2,354 in 1980); tea, 25; bananas, 185; pineapples, 181; sugar-cane, 8,422; sweet potatoes, 834; wheat, 2·7; soybeans, 15·9; peanuts, 81·7.

Livestock (1979): Cattle, 40,000; pigs, 7,276,000; goats, 45,000.

Forestry. Forest area, 1981: 1,865,141 hectares; forest reserves, 326,421,000 cu. metres; timber production, 595,140 cu. metres.

Fisheries. The fleet comprised 4,412 vessels over 20 GRT in 1981; the catch was 911,678 tonnes in 1981.

INDUSTRY AND TRADE

Industry. Output (in tonnes) in 1981 (and 1980): Steel, 5,844,066 (5,685,479); pig-iron, 184,906 (271,644); aluminium, 30,532 (63,549); shipbuilding, 776,195 (572,224); sugar, 1,130,983 (981,072); cement, 14·3m. (14·1m.); fertilizers, 1·4m. (1·5m.); paper, 471,369 (490,278); cotton fabrics, 822m. metres (807m.).

In 1981, 19,419m. litres of crude oil were refined; the main refinery at Kaohsiung has an annual capacity of 18,833m. litres.

Labour. In 1981 the labour force was 6·7m., of whom 1·3m. worked in agriculture, forestry and fisheries, 2·8m. in industry (including 2·2m. in manufacturing and 0·6m. in building), 1·1m. in commerce, 0·4m. in transport and communications, and 1·1m. in other services. 92,000 were registered unemployed.

Commerce. Foreign trade affairs are handled by the China External Trade Development Council (founded 1970), which operates branches in 28 countries under the name of Far East Trade Service. Principal exports: textiles, electrical machinery, foodstuffs, agricultural products, machinery, plastic products. Principal imports: minerals, oil, agricultural products, metal products, machinery. Total trade, in US$1m.:

	1975	*1976*	*1977*	*1978*	*1979*	*1980*	*1981*	*1982*
Imports	5,952	7,599	8,511	11,027	14,774	19,733	21,200	193,231
Exports	5,309	8,166	9,361	12,678	16,103	19,811	22,611	103,051

The USA, Japan and Hong Kong are Taiwan's major trade partners followed by the Federal Republic of Germany and Malaysia and Singapore.

Total trade between Taiwan and UK (British Department of Trade returns, in £1,000 sterling):

	1977	*1978*	*1979*	*1980*	*1981*	*1982*
Imports to UK	138,730	46,879	217,736	253,915	321,082	335,537
Exports and re-exports from UK	61,607	92,542	103,044	92,386	120,038	125,183

COMMUNICATIONS

Roads. In 1981 there were 17,521·8 km of roads (12,743 km surfaced). 5,413,407 motor vehicles were registered in 1981 including 506,291 passenger cars, 18,790 buses, 277,866 trucks and 4,591,547 motor cycles. 2,055m. passengers and 183m. tons of freight were transported (excluding urban buses).

Railways. Total route length in 1981 was 3,082 km (1,067 mm to 762 mm gauge), of which a large proportion is owned by the Taiwan Sugar Corporation and other concerns. The state network consists of 1,091 km. Taiwan railways have various gauges, ranging from 3 ft 6 in. to 2 ft. Electrification of the west trunk line of the state network from Keelung and Kaohsiung was completed in 1979. Freight traffic in 1981 amounted to 31·7m. tons and passenger traffic to 131·7m.

Aviation. There are 2 international airports: Taoyuan and Kaohsiung. There are 6 domestic airlines, including China Airlines (CAL), which also operates international services to Bangkok, Hong Kong, Kuala Lumpur, Manila, Seoul, Singapore, South Africa, Saudi Arabia, Japan and USA.

Shipping. The merchant marine in 1981 comprised 8,144 vessels over 20 GRT, totalling 2,666,651 GRT; it included 28 passenger ships and 382 freighters. Ocean-going freight-traffic was 23·1m. tonnes.

The 4 international ports, Kaohsiung, Keelung, Hualien and T'aichung, are being extensively redeveloped. The first two are container centres. The lesser ports of Suao and Wuchi are also being built up.

Post and Broadcasting. In 1981 there were 11,827 postal establishments. Number of telephones in 1981, 3,166,169. In 1978 there were 8m. radio receivers and 3m. TV receivers. There are 3 TV networks.

Cinemas (1982). Cinemas numbered 621.

Newspapers (1982). There were 31 daily papers and 2,400 periodicals.

RELIGION, EDUCATION AND WELFARE

Religion. The predominant faith is Confucianism, and there were 5,000 temples in 1976. There were 1·15m. Taoists in 1981 with 6,088 temples and 17,973 priests, and 0·8m. Buddhists with 1,157 temples and 3,471 priests. There are some 600,000 Christians, mainly in Hualien, of whom there were 286,088 Catholics and 305,200 Presbyterians in 1981.

Education. Since 1968 there has been free compulsory education for 9 years (6–15). In that year the curriculum was modernized to give more emphasis to science while retaining the traditional basis of Confucian ethics. There were, in 1981–82, 2,444 primary schools with 69,613 teachers and 2,213,179 pupils; 1,034 secondary schools with 71,099 teachers and 1,627,652 students; 104 schools of higher learning, including 27 universities and colleges, with 17,452 full-time teachers and 358,437 students.

Health. In 1981 there were 103,642 registered medical personnel, including 20,779 doctors, 4,406 dentists and 4,562 'herb doctors', and 11,186 health and medical care facilities, including 1,028 public health and medical care facilities and 10,158 private hospitals and clinics.

Books of Reference

Statistical Yearbook of the Republic of China. Taipei, annual
China Yearbook. Taipei, annual
Taiwan Statistical Data Book. Taipei, annual
Chiu, H. (ed.), *China and the Taiwan issue.* New York, 1979
Clough, R. N., *Island China.* Cambridge, Mass., 1978
Goddard, W. G., *Formosa: A Study in Chinese History.* London, 1966
Ho, S. P. S., *Economic Development of Taiwan, 1860–1970.* Yale Univ. Press, 1978
Hsiung, J. C., (ed.), *Contemporary Republic of China.* New York, 1981
Li, K. T., *The Experience of Dynamic Economic Growth on Taiwan.* Taipei, 1976
Lin, C.-Y., *Industrialization in Taiwan, 1946–72.* New York, 1973
Mendel, D., *The Politics of Formosan Nationalism.* California Univ. Press, 1970
Tierney, J. (ed.), *About Face: The China Decision and its Consequences.* New Rochelle, 1979

COLOMBIA

Capital: Bogotá
Population: 27·5m. (1981)
GNP per capita: US$1,180 (1980)

República de Colombia

HISTORY. The Vice-royalty of New Granada gained its independence of Spain in 1819, and was officially constituted 17 Dec. 1819, together with the present territories of Panama, Venezuela and Ecuador, as the state of 'Greater Colombia', which continued for about 12 years. It then split up into Venezuela, Ecuador and the republic of New Granada in 1830. The constitution of 22 May 1858 changed New Granada into a confederation of 8 states, under the name of Confederación Granadina. Under the constitution of 8 May 1863 the country was renamed 'Estados Unidos de Colombia', which were 9 in number. The revolution of 1885 led the National Council of Bogotá, composed of 2 delegates from each state, to promulgate the constitution of 5 Aug. 1886, forming the Republic of Colombia, which abolished the sovereignty of the states, converting them into departments, with governors appointed by the President of the Republic, though they retained some of their old rights, such as the management of their own finances. A decree of May 1928 abolished their right to borrow abroad without the sanction of the central government.

AREA AND POPULATION. Colombia is bounded north by the Caribbean sea, north-west by Panama, west by the Pacific ocean, south-west by Ecuador and Peru, north-east by Venezuela and south-east by Brazil. The estimated area of the republic as given to the United Nations is 1,138,914 sq. km (456,535 sq. miles). It lies between lat. 12° 30′ N. and 4° 30′ S., and between long. 67° and 79° W. of Greenwich. It has a coastline of about 2,900 km, of which 1,600 km are on the Caribbean sea and 1,300 km on the Pacific ocean. The area 1,138,914 sq. km (as estimated by the census bureau) and population 26·5m. according to the estimate of 24 Oct. 1978, were as follows:

Départmentos	*Area (sq. km)*	*Population 1978*	*Capital*	*Population 1978*
Antioquia	63,612	3,556,058	Medellín	1,442,244
Atlántico	3,382	1,227,319	Barranquilla	825,487
Bolívar	25,978	1,049,223	Cartagena	418,953
Boyacá	23,189	1,179,350	Tunja (M.E.)	125,700 [1]
Caquetá	88,965	88,920 [1]	Florencia	—
Caldas	7,888	754,381	Manizales	246,036
Cauca	29,308	813,937	Popayán	107,800 [1]
César (El)	22,905	492,328	Valledupar	161,500 [1]
Chocó	46,530	253,968	Quibdó	48,800 [1]
Córdoba	25,020	894,279	Montería	173,100 [1]
Cundinamarca	22,623	1,219,406	—	—
Huila	19,890	545,603	Neiva	129,700 [1]
Guajira (La)	20,848	262,056	Riohacha	56,900 [1]
Magdalena	23,188	684,704	Santa Marta	174,200 [1]
Meta	85,635	328,077	Villavicencio	83,700 [1]
Nariño	33,268	993,050	Pasto	140,700 [1]
Norte de Santander	21,658	862,829	Cúcuta	358,240
Quindío	1,845	355,328	Armenia	196,500 [1]
Risaralda	4,140	497,122	Pereira	251,861
Santander	30,537	1,284,035	Bucaramanga	387,886
Sucre	10,917	475,637	Sincelejo	77,800 [1]
Tolima	23,512	1,024,184	Ibagué	263,669
Valle del Cauca	22,140	2,775,142	Cali	1,255,198

[1] 1973.

Intendencias	*Area (sq. km)*	*Population 1978*	*Capital*
Arauca	23,818	27,497 [1]	Arauca
Casanare	44,640	[2]	El Yopal
Putumayo	24,885	29,137 [1]	Mocoa
San Andrés y Providencia	44	22,719 [1]	San Andrés
Comisarías			
Amazonas	109,665	12,962 [1]	Leticia
Guainía	72,238	3,602 [1]	Puerto Inírida
Guaviare	42.327	—	—
Vaupés	65,268	13,403 [1]	Mitú
Vichada	100,242	12,330 [1]	Puerto Carreño
Total	1,141,748	26,500,000	

[1] 1973. [2] Included in figure for Boyacá.

The bulk of the population lives at altitudes of from 4,000 to 9,000 ft above sea-level. It is divided broadly into: 68% mestizo, 20% white, 7% Indio and 5% Negro.

The language spoken is Spanish.

CONSTITUTION AND GOVERNMENT. The legislative power rests with a Congress of 2 houses, the Senate, of 112 members, and the House of Representatives, of 199 members, both elected for 4 years. In 1968 a congressional committee unanimously approved a constitutional amendment providing for progressive reductions in the membership of Congress to 90 senators and 162 representatives by 1974. Congress meets annually at Bogotá on 20 July. Women were given the vote, which is now open to citizens of either sex, over 18 years of age, on 25 Aug. 1954.

The President is elected by direct vote of the people for a term of 4 years, and is not eligible for re-election until 4 years afterwards. Congress elects, for a term of 2 years, one substitute to occupy the presidency in the event of a vacancy during a presidential term. There are 13 Ministries. The Governors of Departments and the Mayor of Bogotá are nominated by the national government.

A National Economic Council, functioning since May 1935, went through several transformations, becoming in 1954 a Directorate of Planning.

National Flag: Three horizontal stripes of yellow, blue, red with the yellow of double width.

National anthem: Oh! Gloria inmarcesible (words by R. Núñez; tune by O. Síndici).

The following is a list of presidents since 1945:

Dr Alberto Lleras Camargo, 7 Aug. 1945–7 Aug. 1946.
Dr Mariano Ospina Pérez, 7 Aug. 1946–7 Aug. 1950.
Dr Laureano Gómez, 7 Aug. 1950–13 June 1953.
Gen. Gustavo Rojas Pinilla, 13 June 1953–10 May 1957.
Military Junta, Maj.-Gen. Gabriel París and 4 others, 10 May 1957–7 Aug. 1958.
Dr Alberto Lleras Camargo (Lib.), 7 Aug. 1958–7 Aug. 1962.
Dr Guillermo León Valencia (Cons.), 7 Aug. 1962–7 Aug. 1966.
Dr Carlos Lleras Restrepo (Lib.), 7 Aug. 1966–7 Aug. 1970.
Dr Misael Pastrana Borrero (Cons.), 7 Aug 1970–7 Aug. 1974.
Dr Alfonso López Michelsen (Cons./Lib.), 7 Aug. 1974–7 Aug. 1978.
Dr Julio Cesar Turbay Ayala (Lib.), 7 Aug. 1978–7 Aug. 1982.

President: Dr Belisario Betancur. He was elected on 30 May 1982 and took office on 7 Aug. 1982.

Minister of Foreign Affairs: Dr Rodrigo Lloreda Caicedo.

DEFENCE. On 17 April 1952 Colombia signed the Military Assistance pact with the USA.

Army. Military service is compulsory between the years of 18 and 30. Service with the colours is for 1 year. From 30 to 45 years of age the citizens are on the reserved lists, classified in 1st, 2nd and 3rd classes, with the obligation of presenting themselves on being called up. The permanent Army consists of 10 infantry and 1 training brigades, artillery, cavalry, engineer and motorized troops and the usual services. The peace effective is 57,000 men; reserves 70,000. Number of national police, about 50,000.

Navy. Colombia has new Federal German-built 1,200-ton diesel-electric powered patrol submarines completed in 1975, 2 Italian-built midget submarines; 2 destroyers completed in Sweden in 1958; 1 old (1944) *ex*-US destroyer; 1 old *ex*-US frigate (small DE type); 3 old patrol vessels (*ex*-US fleet tugs); 4 river gunboats; 5 surveying vessels; 9 coastguard patrol vessels; 10 patrol motor launches; 1 oiler; 4 small transports, 1 training ship, 5 service craft, and 12 tugs. Personnel in 1983 exceeded 700 officers and 6,500 men. The Navy has also a brigade of marines with 2,500 officers and men.

Air Force. Formed in 1922, the Air Force has been independent of the Army and Navy since 1943, when its reorganization began with US assistance. In 1982 it had about 300 aircraft, including a squadron of Mirage 5-COA fighter-bombers, 5-COR reconnaissance aircraft and 5-COD two-seat operational trainers; a squadron of Israeli-built Kfir-C2 fighters, a squadron of AT-33A jets for counter-insurgency duties, a transport group equipped with 2 C-130s, 17 C-47s, 3 C-54s and a small number of Arava, Beaver and Porter light transports; a presidential F-28 Fellowship jet transport; UH-1B/H utility helicopters; and a reconnaissance unit with Hughes OH-6A helicopters. Eleven more C-47s, 1 C-54 and 2 HS.748 transports are flown by the Air Force operated airline SATENA. Thirty Cessna T-41D primary trainer/light transports were delivered in 1968 and were followed by 10 T-37C jet advanced trainers to supplement piston-engined T-34s and T-33A armed jet trainers. Latest deliveries include 6 T-38A jet trainers for operation by the Military Air Academy. Total strength is about 3,800 personnel.

INTERNATIONAL RELATIONS

Membership. Colombia is a member of the UN, OAS, the Andean Group and LAIA (formerly LAFTA).

ECONOMY

Budget. Ordinary revenue and expenditure for calendar years in 1m. paper pesos:

	1980	*1981*
Revenue	192,200	196,500
Expenditure	192,200	196,500

Currency. Coins include 50, 20 and 10 *centavos* (90% steel and 10% nickel) and 5, 2 and 1 *centavos* of various combinations of copper–nickel–bronze–steel. There are also notes representing 1, 5, 10, 20, 50, 100 and 500 *gold pesos*. Exchange rate March 1983, 107·83 *pesos* = £1 sterling; 72·81 *pesos* = US$1.

Banking. On 23 July 1923 the Banco de la República was inaugurated as a semi-official central bank, with the exclusive privilege of issuing bank-notes in Colombia; its charter, in 1951, was extended to 1973. Its note issues must be covered by a reserve in gold of foreign exchange of 25% of their value.

There are 25 domestic commercial banks of importance and 5 foreign banks (English, Canadian, American, French and Franco-Italian); but a high percentage of all commercial bank deposits are with the 4 largest domestic banks, which have branches throughout the country. External debt (1979) US$4,026m.

Weights and Measures. The metric system was introduced in 1857, but in ordinary commerce Spanish weights and measures are generally used; according to new definitions by the Ministry of Development, *e.g., botella* (750 grammes), *galón* (5 *botellas*), *vara* (70 cm), *arroba* (25 lb., of 500 grammes; 4 *arrobas* = 1 quintal).

ENERGY AND NATURAL RESOURCES

Electricity. Capacity of electric power (1973) is 2,795,000 kw. Electric power produced in 1976, 13,717,170 kwh. There is increasing utilization of natural gas.

Oil. Petroleum production in 1981 was 146,000 bbls (of 42 gallons) a day.

Minerals. Colombia is rich in minerals; gold is found chiefly in Antioquia and moderately in Cauca, Caldas, Tolima, Nariño and Chocó; output in 1979, 265,600 troy oz., highest in South America.

Other minerals are silver (99,300 troy oz. in 1979), copper, lead, mercury, manganese, emeralds and platinum (first discovered in Colombia in 1735 and the largest deposit in the world); production of platinum, 1977, 26,000 troy oz. The chief emerald mines are those of Muzo and Chivor.

The Government holds the monopoly, which is leased to the Banco de la República, for extracting salts from the outstanding Zipaquirá mines (several hundred feet in depth and several hundred square miles in area) and for evaporating many sea salt pans; salt production in 1977 was 180,890 tons of land salt from the Zipaquirá mines and 435,542 tons of sea salt from Manaure and Galerazamba on the Caribe coast. Colombia's coal reserves are estimated at 4,100m. tonnes; production (1975) 10m. short tons.

Agriculture. Very little of the country is under cultivaton, but much of the soil is fertile and is coming into use as roads improve. The range of climate and crops is extraordinary; the agricultural colleges have different courses for 'cold-climate farming' and 'warm-climate farming'. Some 6m. acres are described as arable, 96m. pasture and 148m. forest.

Coffee covers an area (1980) of 1·01m. hectares. Crops are grown by smallholders, and are picked all the year round. Production (1980, in tonnes): Cotton seed, 300,000; rice, 1,892,000; barley, 72,000; maize, 813,000; potatoes, 2,038,000; soybean, 155,000; wheat, 41,000; bananas, 1·2m.; cacao, 41,000.

The rubber tree grows wild, and its cultivation has begun; output is a few hundred tons. Fibres are being exploited, notably the 'fique' fibre, which furnishes all the country's requirements for sacks and cordage; output about 12,000 tons. Tolú balsam is cultivated, and copaiba trees are tapped but are not cultivated. Tanning is an important industry, 12m. sq. ft of hides being exported in 1965.

Livestock (1981): 24·25m. cattle, 2·2m. pigs, 2·43m. sheep, 30·65m. poultry.

Fishery. In Sept. 1963 a *Sección de Caza y Pesca* was set up in the Ministry of Agriculture. It extended territorial waters to 200 nautical miles.

INDUSTRY AND TRADE

Industry. There are 69 reassembly plants, apart from the motor industry. At the end of 1965 the 101 firms with more than 50% US control equalled an investment of US$510m.; they employed over 29,000 Colombians.

Commerce. For the 'Charter of Quito' trading agreement in 1948 between Colombia, Ecuador, Panama and Venezuela, *see* THE STATESMAN'S YEAR-BOOK, 1956, p. 882. Colombia's entry into the Latin American Free Trade Area (ALALC) was ratified on 29 Sept. 1961. A fresh impulse to this effort was given by the Bases for an Immediate Action Programme under the 'Charter of Bogotá' signed by Colombia, Chile, Equador, Peru and Venezuela on 16 Aug. 1966.

Imports (c.i.f. values) and exports (f.o.b. values) (excluding export tax) for calendar years (in US$1m.):

	1979	*1980*	*1981*
Imports	2,558	3,504	3,863
Exports	3,044	3,394	2,926

Important articles of export in 1980 (in US$1m.) were coffee (2,329), cotton (102), sugar (175), fuel oil (239), clothing and textiles (258), bananas (108). The chief imports are machinery, vehicles, tractors, metals and manufactures, rubber, chemical products, wheat, fertilizers and wool.

Total trade between Colombia and UK (British Department of Trade returns, in £1,000 sterling).

	1978	*1979*	*1980*	*1981*	*1982*
Imports to UK	24,974	21,874	34,289	32,951	34,502
Exports and re-exports from UK	50,841	52,258	41,920	45,145	50,328

Tourism. Foreign visitors totalled 1·4m. in 1980.

COMMUNICATIONS

Roads. Owing to the mountainous character of the country, the construction of arterial roads and railways is costly and difficult. Total length of highways, 51,253 km in 1972. Of the 2,300-mile Simón Bolívar highway, which runs from Caracas in Venezuela to Guayaquil in Ecuador, the Colombian portion is complete. Buena ventura and Cali are linked by a highway (Carreterra al Mar). Motor vehicles numbered 550,293, of which 258,526 were passenger cars and 54,730 lorries in 1977.

Railways. There are 5 divisions of the State Railway with a total length of 2,912 km in 1978 and a gauge of 3 ft. The Pacific Railway connects Bogotá with the port of Buenaventura. The Atlantic line from Bogotá to Sta. Marta was opened in July 1961. Three connecting links are planned to improve the operating efficiency of the network. Total railway traffic, 1976, was 4m. passengers and 2,411,372 tonnes of freight.

Aviation. In civil aviation Colombia ranks perhaps second, after Brazil, among South American countries. There are 675 landing grounds of all kinds. In 1977 the national airports moved 8,071,882 passengers and 169,474 tonnes of cargo.

Shipping. Vessels entering Colombian ports in 1977 unloaded 8·07m. tonnes of imports and loaded 1·95m. tonnes of exports. The Colombian merchant fleet in 1966 owned 23 vessels of 187,906 net tons, and leased 20 of 164,360 net tons; in 1965 it carried 1·9m. tonnes.

The Magdelena River is subject to drought, and navigation is always impeded during the dry season, but it is an important artery of passenger and goods traffic. The river is navigable for 900 miles; steamers ascend to La Dorada, 592 miles from Barranquilla. In 1977 they carried 2,326,000 tonnes of cargo, of which 88·2% was manufactured goods.

Post and Broadcasting. The length of telephone lines in service is 705,852 km (Bogotá only); instruments in use, 1 Jan. 1981, 1,1,623,105, of which 537,000 were in Bogotá in 1980. The cable company is government owned. Television was established in 1954 and in 1978 there were 1·75m. sets in use. In 1979 there were 350 radio stations.

Cinemas (1973). There were 352 cinemas.

Newspapers (1973). There were 36 daily newspapers, with daily circulation totalling 1,448,467. There were 388 periodical publications.

JUSTICE, RELIGION, EDUCATION AND WELFARE

Justice. The Supreme Court, at Bogotá, of 20 members, is divided into 3 chambers—civil cassation (6), criminal cassation (8), labour cassation (6). Each of the 61 judicial districts has a superior court with various sub-dependent tribunals of lower juridical grade. Communism was outlawed by government decree on 5 March 1956.

Religion. The religion is Roman Catholic, with the Cardinal Archbishop of Bogotá as Primate of Colombia and 7 other archbishops in Cartagena, Manizales, Medellín, Pamplona, Popayán, Cali and Tunja, 26 bishops, 1,546 parishes and 4,020 priests. Other forms of religion are permitted so long as their exercise is 'not contrary to Christian morals or to the law'.

Education. Primary education is free but not compulsory, and facilities are limited. Schools are both state and privately controlled. In 1974 there were 30,558 primary schools with 3,844,257 pupils and 123,139 teachers. In 4,200 secondary schools there were 1,159,996 pupils with 62,000 teachers. In the 176 industrial schools, there were 27,808 pupils with 2,855 teachers. 178 night schools had 11,504 pupils with 1,668 teachers. 81 agricultural schools catered for 7,930 pupils with 815 teachers. There were 638 commercial schools catering for 69,233 pupils with 7,844 teachers. 110 art schools had 8,681 pupils and 709 teachers. Theological institutes (all private) numbered 22 with 674 students and 180 tutors. In *normalista* schools, of which there were 239, 54,198 pupils had 5,407 teachers.

The National University in Bogotá was founded in 1867 and there are 97 other universities with 171,002 students and 17,963 lecturers.

Health. In 1976 there were 670 hospitals and clinics. There were also 1,499 health centres.

DIPLOMATIC REPRESENTATIVES

Of Colombia in Great Britain (3 Hans Crescent, London, SW1X 0LR)
Ambassador: Dr Augusto Espinosa (accredited 15 Dec. 1982).

Of Great Britain in Colombia (Calle 38, No. 13–35, Bogotá)
Ambassador: J. A. Robson.

Of Colombia in the USA (2118 Leroy Pl., NW, Washington, D.C., 20008)
Ambassador: Fernando Gaviria.

Of the USA in Colombia (Calle 37, 8 40, Bogotá)
Ambassador: Thomas D. Boyatt.

Of Colombia to the United Nations
Ambassador: Dr Carlos Sanz de Santamaria.

Books of Reference

Anuario General de Estadística de Colombia. Bogotá. Annual
Anuario de Comercio Exterior de Colombia. Annual
Anuario Estadístico Bogotá D. E. Annual
Boletín Mensual de Estadística. Monthly
Economía y Estadística. Occasional
Informe Financiero del Contralor General. Annual
Informe del Gerente de la Caja de Crédito Agrario, Industrial y Minero. Annual
Memorias (13) de los Ministros al Congreso Nacional. Annual
McGreevey, W. P., *An Economic History of Colombia, 1845–1930.* CUP, 1970
Morairetz, D., *Why the Emperor's New Clothes are not made in Colombia.* OUP, 1982
Wurfel, S. W., *Foreign Enterprise in Colombia: Laws and Policies.* Univ. of N. Carolina Press, 1965

COMOROS

Capital: Moroni
Population: 356,000 (1980)
GNP per capita: US$300 (1980)

Republique fédérale islamique des Comores

HISTORY. The 3 islands forming the present state became French protectorates at the end of the 19th century, and were proclaimed colonies on 25 July 1912. With neighbouring Mayotte they were administratively attached to Madagascar from 1914 until 1947, when the 4 islands became a French Overseas Territory, achieving internal self-government in Dec. 1961.

In referenda held on each island on 22 Dec. 1974, the 3 western islands voted overwhelmingly for independence, while Mayotte voted to remain French. The Comoran Chamber of Deputies unilaterally declared the islands' independence on 6 July 1975, but Mayotte remained a French dependency.

The first government of Ahmed Abdallah was overthrown on 3 Aug. 1975 by a *coup* led by Ali Soilih (who assumed the Presidency on 2 Jan. 1976), but Ahmed Abdallah regained the Presidency after a second *coup* ousted Ali Soilih in May 1978.

AREA AND POPULATION. The Comoros consists of 3 islands in the Indian ocean between the African mainland and Madagascar. The majority of the population throughout the islands speak Kiswahili, but a small proportion speak French or Arabic.

	Area sq. km	*Population census 1966*	*Population census 1980*	*Chief town*
Njazídja (Grande Comore)	1,148	126,205	189,000	Moroni
Mwali (Mohéli)	290	10,300	19,000	Fomboni
Nzwami (Anjouan)	424	80,082	148,000	Mutsamudu
	1,862	216,587	356,000	

Population of the capital, Moroni (1977) 16,000; Fomboni, 4,500; Mutsamudu, 10,000.

CONSTITUTION AND GOVERNMENT. Under the new Constitution approved by referendum on 1 Oct. 1978, the Comoros are a Federal Islamic Republic. Mayotte has the right to join when it so chooses.

The President is Head of State, directly elected for a 6-year term (renewable once). He appoints a Prime Minister and up to 9 other Ministers to form the Council of Government, on which each island's Governor has a non-voting seat. There is a 39-member unicameral Federal Assembly, directly elected for 5 years. Each of the 3 islands is administered by a Governor (directly elected for a 5-year term), up to 4 Commissioners whom he appoints to assist him, and a Legislative Council directly elected for 4 years.

President: Ahmed Abdallah Abderemane.

The Council of Government, as re-organized 15 Feb. 1982, comprised:

Prime Minister: Ali Mroudjae.

Foreign Affairs, Co-operation and External Trade: Saïd Kafe. *Equipment, Environment and Town Planning:* Mohamed Moumine. *Justice:* Mohamed Saïd Turqui. *Agriculture, Industry and Handicraft:* Mohamed Chaher Ben Saï Massoundé. *Economy and Finance:* Ali Nassor. *National Education:* Ahmed Ali Mohamed. *Secretaries of State:* Antoy Abdou *(Transport and Tourism)*, Yahaya Djamadar *(Civil Service)*, Abdillah Mbae *(Posts and Telecommunications)*.

National flag: Green with a crescent and 4 stars all in white in the centre.

DEFENCE

Navy. An *ex*-British landing craft built in 1945 was transferred from France in 1976.

Air Arm. Equipment, acquired since 1977–78, comprises 3 SIAI-Marchetti SF.-260W Warrior armed trainers built in Italy and a Cessna 402B communications aircraft.

INTERNATIONAL RELATIONS

Membership. Comoros is a member of UN and an ACP state of EEC.

ECONOMY

Budget. The ordinary budget for 1979 balanced at 3,200m. francs CFA.

Currency. The unit of currency is the *franc CFA,* with a parity value of 50 *francs CFA* to 1 French *franc.*

Banking. The Institut d'émission des Comores was established as the new bank of issue in 1975. The chief commercial bank is the Banque des Comores, established in 1974 by the separation of the former Comoran section of the Banque de Madagascar et des Comores.

Weights and Measures. The metric system is in force.

NATURAL RESOURCES

Agriculture. The chief product was formerly sugar-cane, but now vanilla, copra, cacao, sisal, coffee, cloves and essential oils (citronella, ylang, lemon-grass) are the most important products.

Livestock (1981): Cattle, 79,000; sheep, 9,000; goats, 87,000; asses, 4,000.

Forestry. Njazídja has a fine forest and produces timber for building.

COMMERCE. Imports in 1977 amounted to 4,055m. francs CFA, exports to 2,205m. francs CFA. In 1977 France provided 41% of imports and (in 1978) took 71% of exports. The main exports (1978) were vanilla (735m. francs CFA), essential oils (640m.), cloves (460m.) and copra (205m.).

Trade between Comoros and UK (British Department of Trade returns, in £1,000 sterling):

	1979	*1980*	*1981*	*1982*
Imports to UK	21	40	188	108
Exports and re-exports from UK	52	155	212	258

COMMUNICATIONS

Roads. In 1973 there were 750 km of classified roads, of which 262 km were tarmac. There were 3,600 registered vehicles.

Aviation. The new international airport at Hahaya (on Njazídja) came into service in 1975. Air Comores have twice-weekly flights to Antanarivo, Dar es Salaam and Mombasa. Air France and Air Madagascar also have twice-weekly flights to Antanarivo. Air Comores has daily internal flights between Moroni and Nzwami, and 5 per week between Moroni and Mwali.

In 1973 nearly 16,000 passengers landed and 900 tonnes of freight were carried.

Shipping. In 1973, 279 vessels entered Comoran ports (excluding internal traffic) to discharge 54,391 tonnes and load 8,700 tonnes.

Post and Broadcasting. There were 1,035 telephones in 1977. *Comores-Inter* broadcasts in French and Comorian on short-wave and FM for approximately 8 hours a day. Number of radios (1975): 36,000.

Cinemas. In 1973 there were 2 cinemas with a seating capacity of 800.

RELIGION, EDUCATION AND WELFARE

Religion. Islam is the official religion, adhered to by the vast majority of the population.

Education. In 1979, 130 primary classes had 934 teachers and 49,940 pupils, secondary schools had 499 teachers and 8,932 pupils and a teacher-training college has 3 teachers and 45 students.

Health. In 1975 there were 3 hospitals and a number of clinics.

CONGO

Capital: Brazzaville
Population: 1·63m. (1982)
GNP per capita: US$730 (1980)

République Populaire du Congo

HISTORY. First occupied by France in 1882, the Congo became (as 'Middle Congo') a territory of French Equatorial Africa from 1908 until 28 Nov. 1958, when it became a member state of the French Community. It became an independent Republic on 15 Aug. 1960.

The first President, Fulbert Youlou, was deposed on 15 Aug. 1963 by a *coup* led by Alphonse Massemba-Débat, who became President on 19 Dec. Following a second *coup* in Aug. 1968, the Army took power under the leadership of Major Marien Ngouabi, whose colleague, Major Alfred Raoul, was appointed President from 3 Sept. until 1 Jan. 1969, when Ngouabi himself became President.

The country's present name was established on 3 Jan. 1970, when a Marxist-Leninist state was introduced. Ngouabi was assassinated on 18 March 1977, and succeeded by Col. Joachim Yhombi-Opango, who in turn was replaced on 5 Feb. 1979 by Col. Denis Sassou-Nguesso.

AREA AND POPULATION. The Congo is bounded by Cameroon and the Central African Republic in the north, Zaïre to the east and south, the Cabinda province of Angola and the Atlantic to the south-west and Gabon to the west, and covers 342,000 sq. km; census population (1974), 1,300,120. Estimate (1982) 1·63m. The main towns (population in 1980) are Brazzaville, the capital (422,402) and Pointe-Noire, the main port and oil centre (185,105); other large towns (Census 1974) are Louboma (28,941) and Jacob (28,326).

In 1974, 45% spoke Kongo dialects, 15% Téké, 15% Sanga, 12% Ubangi; there are also about 12,000 pygmies and 12,000 Europeans (mainly French). French is the official language.

CONSTITUTION AND GOVERNMENT. In July 1979 a new Constitution was approved by referendum. Executive power was vested in the President, elected for a 5-year term by the National Congress of the *Parti congolais du travail* (the sole legal party since 1969). The President is assisted by a Council of Ministers, appointed and led by him. At its Congress (March 1979), the PCT elected a Central Committee of 60 members and a Political Bureau of 5 to administer it; it nominated all candidates for the 153-member People's National Assembly and for the regional, district and local councils, all of which were elected on 8 July 1979.

President: Col. Denis Sassou-Nguesso.
Prime Minister: Col. Louis-Sylvain Goma.
Foreign Affairs: Pierre Nze.

National flag: Red, in the canton the national emblem of a crossed hoe and mattock, a green wreath and a gold star.

Local Government: The republic is divided into the capital district of Brazzaville and 9 regions (each under an appointed Commissioner and an elected Council), which are sub-divided into 46 districts.

DEFENCE

Army. The Army consists of 5 battalions, 1 armoured, 1 artillery, 1 infantry, 1 engineering, and 1 paracommando. Total personnel (1983) 8,000.

Navy. The Navy has 1 *ex*-Soviet torpedo boat, 3 *ex*-Chinese gunboats, 4 *ex*-

Chinese river patrol craft, 1 new tug, French built, and 12 small river patrol boats, 3 fast patrol craft are being completed in Spain. Personnel in 1983 totalled 250 officers and men.

Air Force. The Air Force has about 500 personnel, 10 MiG-15/17 jet fighters, 1 twin-turbofan F28 Fellowship and 1 Corvette for VIP transport, 1 Frégate and 5 Antonov An-24 turboprop transports, 2 C-47 and 5 Il-14 piston-engined transports, 3 Broussard communications aircraft, 6 L-39 jet trainers, 1 Puma and 4 Alouette II and Alouette III light helicopters.

INTERNATIONAL RELATIONS

Membership. Congo is a member of UN, OAU and is an ACP state of EEC.

ECONOMY

Planning. The National Plan runs 1982–86.

Budget. The ordinary budget in 1982 balanced at 279,930m. francs CFA. Oil revenues finance 70% of the operational budget.

Currency. The unit of currency is the *franc CFA* with a parity value of 50 *francs CFA* to 1 French franc.

Banking. The *Banque des États de l'Afrique Centrale* is the bank of issue. There are 4 commercial banks situated in Brazzaville, including the *Banque Commerciale Congolaise* and the *Union Congolaise de Banques.*

ENERGY AND NATURAL RESOURCES

Electricity. Production in 1978 was 126m. kwh from a hydro-electric plant at Djoué near Brazzaville and from about 6 thermal plants.

Oil. Oil reserves are estimated at 500–1,000m. tonnes. Output in 1982 was almost 5m. tonnes from the 26 offshore oil platforms operated by Elf Congo and Agip Congo. Oil receipts furnished 70% of the 1981 budget revenue.

Minerals. Lead, copper, zinc and gold (16 kg in 1978) are the main minerals.

Agriculture. Production (1981, in tonnes): Cassava, 530,000; sugar-cane, 225,000; pineapples, 107.

Livestock (1981): Cattle, 75,000; pigs, 53,000; sheep, 69,000; goats, 133,000; poultry, 1·15m.

Forestry. Equatorial forests cover 20m. hectares (60% of the total land area) from which (in 1980) 800,000 cu. metres of timber were produced, mainly okoumé from the south and sapele from the north. Hardwoods (mainly mahogany) are also exported.

Fisheries. In 1977 the catch amounted to 16,400 tonnes.

INDUSTRY AND TRADE

Industry. There is a growing manufacturing sector, located mainly in the 4 major towns, producing processed foods, textiles, cement (61,000 tonnes in 1978), metal industries and chemicals.

Commerce. Imports in 1978 totalled 58,860m. francs CFA (mainly machinery) and exports 31,160m. (of which petroleum 21,065m.). 50% of imports were from France; 31% of exports were to Italy and 24% to France.

Total trade between the Congo and UK (British Department of Trade returns, in £1,000 sterling):

	1977	*1978*	*1979*	*1980*	*1981*	*1982*
Imports to UK	1,822	4,520	3,339	3,416	3,670	2,393
Exports and re-exports from UK	3,478	2,072	3,391	2,943	4,434	9,766

COMMUNICATIONS

Roads. There were (1980) 8,246 km of all-weather roads. In 1976 there were 20,000 cars and 13,000 commercial vehicles.

Railways. A railway (517 km, 1,067 mm gauge) and a telegraph line connect Brazzaville with Pointe-Noire and a 200 km branch railway links Mont-Belo with Mbinda on the Gabon border.

Aviation. The principal airports are at Maya Maya and Pointe-Noire. In addition there are 22 airfields served by the local airline, Lina-Congo.

Shipping. Pointe-Noire handled (1979) 2·4m. tonnes of goods including manganese from Gabon. There were (1979) 16 vessels of 6,942 GNT registered.

Post and Broadcasting. Telephones (1978) numbered 13,376, of which 6,990 were in Brazzaville. In 1977 there were 88,000 radios and 3,500 TV sets in use.

Cinemas. In 1973 there were 7 cinemas with a seating capacity of 5,100.

JUSTICE, RELIGION, EDUCATION AND WELFARE

Justice. The Supreme Court, Court of Appeal and a criminal court are situated in Brazzaville, with a network of *tribunaux de grande instance* and *tribunaux d'instance* in the regions.

Religion. In 1977, 50% of the population were Christian (40·5% Roman Catholic and 9·5% Protestant), 47% followed animist beliefs and 3% were Moslem.

Education. In 1979 there were 358,761 pupils and 6,832 teachers in primary schools, 138,525 pupils and 3,009 teachers in secondary schools, 9,633 students with 505 teachers in technical schools and 1,228 students with 102 teachers in teacher-training establishments. The Université Marien-Ngouabi (founded 1972) in Brazzaville had 4,336 students in 1980.

Health. There were (1976) 121 hospitals with 6,912 beds; and 190 doctors, 4 dentists, 25 pharmacists, 152 midwives and 1,734 nursing personnel.

DIPLOMATIC REPRESENTATIVES

Of the Congo in Great Britain
Ambassador: Jean-Pierre Nonault (resides in Paris).

Of Great Britain in the Congo
Ambassador: J. M. O. Snodgrass, CMG (resides in Kinshasa).

Of the USA in the Congo (PO Box 1015, Brazzaville)
Ambassador: Kenneth L. Brown.

Of Congo to the USA and United Nations
Ambassador: Nicolas Mondjo.

COSTA RICA

Capital: San José
Population: 2·34m. (1982)
GNP per capita: US$1,730 (1980)

República de Costa Rica

HISTORY. The republic of Costa Rica (the 'Rich Coast') has been independent since 1821, although it formed, from 1824 to 1838, part of the Confederation of Central America.

AREA AND POPULATION. The area is estimated at 51,100 sq. km (19,344 sq. miles). The population at the census of 14 May 1973 was 1,871,780, compared with 800,875 shown in the 1950 census.

The area and official estimate of population for 1 Jan. 1982 (2,339,828) was as follows:

Province	*Population*	*Area (sq. km)*	*Capital*	*Population*
San José	867,025	4,957·09	San José	265,445
Alajuela	403,005	9,718·10	Alajuela	41,502
Cartago	253,520	3,031·14	Cartago	27,148
Heredia	166,868	2,673·49	Heredia	28,728
Guanacaste	222,833	10,199·58	Liberia [1]	13,931
Puntarenas	277,930	11,302·21	Puntarenas [1]	30,577
Limón	148,647	9,218·39	Limón [1]	36,615

[1] 1 Jan. 1980.

Vital statistics for calendar years:

	Marriages	*Births*	*Deaths*
1978	16,453	67,659	8,625
1979	17,048	69,992	9,268
1980	17,527	69,992	9,273

The population of European descent, many of them of pure Spanish blood, dwell mostly around the capital of the republic, San José, and in the principal towns of the provinces. Limón, on the Caribbean coast, and Puntarenas, on the Pacific coast, are the chief commercial ports. The United Fruit Co., who in 1941 abandoned their banana plantations on the Atlantic coast in favour of large new plantations on the Pacific coast, have constructed ports at Quepos and Golfito. The Standard Fruit Co. and others have cleared land since 1958 in the Atlantic coast area and now have 2,325 acres producing some 4·2m. stems a year. There are some 15,000 West Indians, mostly in Limón province. The indigenous Indian population is dwindling and is now estimated at 1,200.

Spanish is the language of the country.

CONSTITUTION AND GOVERNMENT. The Constitution, promulgated on 7 Dec. 1871, has been modified very frequently, last in 1949. The Constitution forbids the establishment or maintenance of an army. The legislative power is normally vested in a single chamber called the Legislative Assembly, which since 1962 consists of 57 deputies, 1 for every 25,214 inhabitants, elected for 4 years. The President is elected for 4 years; the candidate receiving the largest vote, provided it is over 40% of the total, is declared elected, but a second ballot is required if no candidate gets 40% of the total. By the election law of 18 Jan. 1946 all citizens who are 20 years of age are entitled to vote; married men and teachers, from the age of 18. Women over 21 were enfranchised in 1949. Elections are normally held on the first Sunday in February. Voting for President, Deputies and Municipal Councillors is secret and compulsory for all men under 70 years of age. Independent non-party candidates are barred from the ballot.

President: Luis Alberto Monge, elected 7 Feb. 1982.

Elections for the Legislative Assembly took place on 7 Feb. 1982; Preliminary results show that Partido de Liberacíon won 33 and Partido Unidad 19 of the 57 seats.

The administration is carried on by 13 ministers, appointed by the President. The powers of the President are limited by the constitution, which leaves him the power to appoint and remove at will members of his cabinet. All other public appointments are made jointly in the names of the President and of the minister in charge of the department concerned.

National flag: Five unequal stripes of blue, white, red, white, blue, with the national arms on a white disc near the hoist.

National anthem: Noble patria, tu hermosa bandera (words by J. M. Zeledón, 1903; tune by M. M. Gutiérrez, 1851).

DEFENCE

Army. The Army was abolished in 1948, and replaced by a Civil Guard reputed to be 5,000 strong. There has never been compulsory military service or training.

Navy. The republic has 1 fast patrol craft and 1 armed tug on the Atlantic coast and 5 small coastal patrol craft for revenue purposes and 3 smaller craft on the Pacific coast. Personnel (1983) 90 officers and men.

Air Wing. The Civil Guard operates a small air wing equipped with 3 Otter STOL utility transports, plus a few lightplanes and helicopters.

INTERNATIONAL RELATIONS

Membership. Costa Rica is a member of UN and OAS.

ECONOMY

Budget. The budget for 1980 balanced at 8,029m. colones. Of the 1980 total, 33% will be used for repayment of the public debt.

The income-tax law of 10 March 1972 raised the maximum rate to 50% for personal incomes of 350,000 colones and over, and to 40% for corporate incomes of 1m. colones and over.

External government debt on 31 Dec. 1981 was 2,900m. colones.

Currency. The unit of currency is the *colone* (₡). The official rate in March 1983 was ₡40·25 = US$1; 60·70 = £1. The official rate is used for all imports on an essential list and by the Government and autonomous institutions and a free rate is used for all other transactions.

The currency is chiefly notes. The Banco Central issue notes for 5, 10, 20, 50, 100, 500 and 1,000 colones. Silver coins of 1 colone, 50 centimos and 25 centimos were in 1935 replaced by coins (2 and 1 colones and 50 and 25 centimos) made up of 3 parts copper and 1 part nickel, and given the same value as the subsidiary silver currency. There are copper coins (and chromium stainless steel coins) of 10 and 5 centimos.

Banking. By a law passed on 28 Jan. 1950 a Central Bank was established for the organization and direction of the national monetary system and of dealings in foreign exchange, the promotion of facilities for credit and the supervision of all banking operations in the country. The bank has a board of 7 directors appointed by the Government, including *ex officio* the Minister of Finance and the Planning Office Director.

The National Insurance Institute *(Instituto Nacional de Seguros)* is a Government organization, created in 1924, which has a monopoly of new insurance business.

Weights and Measures. The metric system is legally established; but in the country districts the following old Spanish weights and measures are found: *libra* = 1·014 lb. avoirdupois; *arroba* = 25·35 lb. avoirdupois; *quintal* = 101·40 lb. avoirdupois, and *fanega* = 11 Imperial bushels.

ENERGY AND NATURAL RESOURCES

Electricity. Electricity, derived from water power in the highlands, is increasingly used as motive power. Output, 1975, was 1,263m. kwh.

Minerals. Gold output is about 3,000 troy oz. per year. Salt production from sea water is about 10,000 tonnes annually. Haematite ore was discovered on the Nicoya Peninsula late in 1960 and sulphur near San Carlos in 1966. The United Nations have offered US$1m. towards a 3-year mining survey.

Agriculture. Agriculture is the principal industry. The cultivated area is about 1m. acres; grass lands cover 1·8m. acres; forests and woodlands, 9,855,000 acres. There are thousands of square miles of public lands that have never been cleared on which can be found quantities of rosewood, cedar, mahogany and other cabinet woods. The principal agricultural products are coffee, bananas, sugar and cattle. Coffee normally accounts for about half the country's foreign-exchange earnings. Cocoa, maize, sugar, tobacco, rice and potatoes are commonly cultivated. The distillation of spirits is a government monopoly.

Coffee production in 1980–81 was 120,000 tonnes. Sugar production (1980–81) 2,522,000 tonnes.

Dairy-farming and cattle-raising are substantial pursuits. In 1981 cattle numbered 2·3m. and pigs 240,000.

Costa Rica is the seat of the Inter-American Institute of Agricultural Sciences, with headquarters at Turrialba.

INDUSTRY AND TRADE

Industry. The main manufactured goods are foodstuffs, textiles, fertilizers, pharmaceuticals, furniture, cement, tyres, canning, clothing, plastic goods, plywood and electrical equipment.

Industrial production was valued at 25·1m. colones in 1980, compared with 1·499m. in 1972.

Labour. As Costa Rica is still essentially an agricultural country, the organization of labour has made progress only in the larger centres of population, and even there it is not a strong movement. There are two main trade unions, *Rerum Novarum* (anti-Communist) and *Confederación General de Trabajadores Costarricenses* (Communist). It is estimated that they have under 10,000 members each. In addition there were (1963) 284 other trade unions and 34 employers' organizations.

Commerce. The value of imports into and exports from Costa Rica in 5 years was as follows in US$ (8·60 colones = US$1):

	1977	*1978*	*1979*	*1980*	*1981*
Imports	1,021,430,406	1,165,730,038	1,396,812,332	1,523,797,000	1,208,529,000
Exports	828,163,886	864,906,915	934,391,357	1,001,742,230	1,030,203,040

The value (in US$1m.) of the principal imports in 1981 were: Machinery, including transport equipment, 283·3; manufactures, 339·5; chemicals, 237·4; fuel and mineral oils, 205·3; foodstuffs, 92·3.

Chief exports (in US$1m.) in 1980 were: Manufactured goods and other products, 403·8; coffee, 247·8 (mostly to Federal Republic of Germany and USA); bananas, 207·5 (to USA); sugar, 40·7; cocoa, 4·2.

Total trade between Costa Rica and UK (British Department of Trade returns in £1,000 sterling):

	1978	*1979*	*1980*	*1981*	*1982*
Imports to UK	1,801	3,123	5,424	6,433	15,068
Exports and re-exports from UK	11,799	9,752	8,302	4,791	5,455

Tourism. There was a total of 345,470 visitors in 1980.

COMMUNICATIONS

Roads. In 1978 there were about 26,993 km of all-weather motor roads open. On the Costa Rica section of the Inter-American Highway it is possible to motor to

Panama during the dry season. The Pan-American Highway into Nicaragua is metalled for most of the way and there is now a good highway open almost to Puntarenas. Motor vehicles, 1978, numbered 179,941.

Railways. The nationalized railway system *(Ferrocarriles de Costa Rica)*, totalling 785 km (228 km electrified) of 1,067 mm gauge, connect San José with Limón, the Atlantic port, and San José with Puntarenas, the Pacific port.

Aviation. Passenger movement in and out of Costa Rica is almost entirely by air *via* the local company, LACSA, PANAM and TACA. LACSA links San José by daily services with all the more important towns. The international airport at Juan Santamaría was opened in June 1955.

Shipping. In 1978, 1,473 ships entered and cleared the ports of the republic (Puerto Limón, Puntarenas and Golfito); combined cargo, 1,918,500 tonnes.

Post and Broadcasting. There were 236,132 telephones in 1981.

The commercial wireless telegraph stations are operated by *Cia Radiográfica Internacional de Costa Rica.* The stations are located at Cartago, Limón, Puntarenas, Quepos and Golfito. The Government has 19 wireless telegraph stations in its local network. The principal or central station at San José also maintains international radio-telegraph circuits to Nicaragua, Honduras, San Salvador and Mexico. The Government has 202 telegraph offices and 88 official telephone stations. The official list of broadcasting stations shows 28 long-wave stations and 7 short-wave stations. Television was inaugurated in May 1960; there were 5 stations and 155,000 receivers in 1976.

Cinemas (1979). Cinemas numbered 106, with seating capacity of 105,000.

Newspapers (1979). There were 6 daily newspapers all published in San José.

JUSTICE, RELIGION, EDUCATION AND WELFARE

Justice. Justice is administered by the Supreme Court, 4 appeal courts and the Court of Cassation. There are also subordinate courts in the separate provinces and local justices throughout the republic. Capital punishment may not be inflicted.

Religion. Roman Catholicism is the religion of the State, which contributes to its maintenance but controls the Church Patronage and insists on lay instruction in history, economics and similar subjects; there is entire religious liberty under the constitution, but religious appeals are forbidden in current political discussions. The Archbishop of Costa Rica has 4 bishops at Alajuela, Limón, San Isidro el General and Tilarán.

Protestants number about 40,000.

Education. Costa Rica has a very low illiteracy rate. Elementary instruction is compulsory and free; secondary education (since 1949) is also free. Elementary schools are provided and maintained by local school councils, while the national government pays the teachers, besides making subventions in aid of local funds. In 1980 there were 2,907 public primary schools with 10,536 teachers and administrative staff and 377,645 enrolled pupils; there were 228 public and private secondary schools with 173,067 pupils. The University of Costa Rica, founded in San José in 1843, has 2,337 professors in 13 faculties and 38,629 students. A medical school was opened in 1961. The budget for 1971 provides ₡250m. for public education. Since 1944 English has been taught in all secondary schools.

Social Welfare. The labour code of 1943 provides considerable protection for the workers, while a system of social insurance against sickness covering 756,347 workers in 1968, old age and death covering 68,949 is gradually being extended throughout the country.

DIPLOMATIC REPRESENTATIVES

Of Costa Rica in Great Britain (225 Cromwell Rd., London SW5)
Ambassador: Jorge Borbon Zeller (accredited 20 July 1982).

Of Great Britain in Costa Rica (Edificio Centro Colon, Apartado 815, San José)
Ambassador and Consul-General: Peter Wayre Summerscale.

Of Costa Rica in the USA (2112 S St., NW, Washington D.C., 20008)
Ambassador: Fernando Soto-Harrison, CBE.

Of the USA in Costa Rica (Avenida 3, Calle 1, San José)
Ambassador: Francis J. McNeil.

Of Costa Rica to the United Nations
Ambassador: Rodolfo Piza Escalante.

Books of Reference

Statistical Information: Official statistics are issued by the Director General de Estadística (Ministerio de Industria y Comercio, San José) as they become available. The compilation of statistics was started in 1861.

Bell, J. P., *Crisis in Costa Rica.* London and Austin, USA, 1971
Biesanz, R., *(et al), The Costa Ricans.* Hemel Hempstead, 1982
Fernandez Guardia, L., *Historia de Costa Rica.* 2nd ed., 2 vols. San José, 1941
Seligson, M. A., *Peasants of Costa Rica and the Development of Agrarian Capitalism.* Univ. of Wisconsin Press, 1980
Trejos, Juan, *Geografía ilustrada de Costa Rica.* San José, 1948

CUBA

Capital: Havana
Population: 9·71m. (1981)
GNP per capita: US$1,410 (1979)

República de Cuba

HISTORY. Cuba, except for the brief British occupancy in 1762–63, remained a Spanish possession from its discovery by Columbus in 1492 until 10 Dec. 1898, when the sovereignty was relinquished under the terms of the Treaty of Paris, which ended the struggle of the Cubans against Spanish rule. Cuba thus became an independent republic, but the United States stipulated under the 'Platt Amendment' (abrogated by Roosevelt in 1934) that Cuba must enter into no treaty relations with a foreign power, which might endanger its independence. A convention which assembled on 5 Nov. 1900 adopted the first constitution of the republic on 21 Feb. 1901.

The revolutionary movement against the Batista dictatorship, led by Dr Fidel Castro, started on 26 July 1953 (now a national holiday). It achieved power on 1 Jan. 1959 when Batista fled the country.

An invasion force of émigrés and adventurers landed in Cuba on 17 April 1961; the main body was defeated at the Bay of Pigs (Las Villas province) and mopped up by 20 April.

The US Navy blockaded Cuba from 22 Oct. to 22 Nov. 1962.

AREA AND POPULATION. The island of Cuba forms the largest and most westerly of the Greater Antilles group and lies 135 miles south of the tip of Florida, USA. It has an area of 44,206 sq. miles (114,524 sq. km); the Isle of Youth (formerly Isle of Pines) has 1,180 sq. miles, and other islands about 1,350 sq. miles. Estimated population in 1978 was 9·73m.

The area, population and density of population of the 14 provinces and their capitals were as follows (1981 census):

	Area sq. km	*Population*	*Capital*	*Population*
Pinar del Rió	10,860	640,740	Pinar del Río	312,614
La Habana	5,671	586,029	Güira de Melena	429,090
Ciudad de La Habana	740	1,924,886	La Habana	1,924,886
Isla de la Juventud	2,199	57,879	—	—
Matanzas	11,669	557,628	Matanzas	421,272
Cienfuegos	4,149	326,412	Cienfuegos	235,293
Villa Clara	8,069	764,743	Santa Clara	525,402
Sancti Spíritus	6,737	399,700	Sancti Spíritus	249,092
Ciego de Avila	6,485	320,961	Ciego de Avila	213,913
Camagüey	14,134	664,566	Camagüey	480,620
Las Tunas	6,373	436,341	Victoria de las Tunas	217,177
Holguín	9,105	911,034	Holguín	456,595
Granma	8,452	739,335	Bayamo	375,446
Santiago de Cuba	6,343	909,506	Santiago de Cuba	563,455
Guantánamo	6,366	466,609	Guantánamo	246,739
Total	110,922 [1]	9,706,369		

[1] 42,827 sq. miles, includes outlying islands and cays not within any province.

CONSTITUTION AND GOVERNMENT. The previous Constitution was suspended in Jan. 1959. The first socialist Constitution came into force on 24 Feb. 1976.

Since the last representative in Cuba of the King of Spain, Gen. Don Adolfo Jiménez Castellanos, handed over the island on 1 Jan. 1899 the following have been at the head of the administration:

US Military Governors

	Took office
Maj.-Gen. John R. Brooke	1 Jan. 1899
Maj.-Gen. Leonard Wood	23 Dec. 1899

President of the Republic

Tomas Estrada Palma	20 May 1902

US Provisional Governors

William Howard Taft	29 Sept. 1906
Charles Edward Magoon	13 Oct. 1906

Presidents of the Republic

	Took office
Gen. José Miguel Gómez	28 Jan. 1909
Gen. Mario García Menocal	20 May 1913
Dr Alfredo Zayas y Alfonso	20 May 1921
Gen. Gerardo Machado y Morales	20 May 1925
Dr Carlos Manuel de Céspedes	12 Aug. 1933
Dr Ramón Grau San Martín	10 Sept. 1933
Col. Carlos Mendieta	Jan. 1934
Dr José A. Barnet	12 Dec. 1935
Dr Miguel Mariano Gómez y Arias	20 May 1936
Dr Federico Laredo Bru	24 Dec. 1936
Gen. Fulgencio Batista y Zaldívar	10 Oct. 1940
Dr Ramón Grau San Martín	10 Oct. 1944
Dr Carlos Prío Socarrás	10 Oct. 1948
Gen. Fulgencio Batista y Zaldívar	10 March 1952
Dr Manuel Urratia Lleo	2 Jan. 1959
Osvaldo Dorticos Torrado	17 July 1959

President: Dr Fidel Castro Ruz became President of the Council of State on 3 Dec. 1976. He is also President of the Council of Ministers, First Secretary of the Cuban Communist Party and C.-in-C. of the Revolutionary Armed Forces. From Jan. 1980 he took overall charge of Defence, Interior, Health and Culture.

Dr Castro on 2 Dec. 1961 proclaimed 'a Marxist–Leninist programme adapted to the precise objective conditions existing in our country'. The provisional *Organizaciones Revolucionarias Integradas* (ORI) were established as an intermediate stage towards a single (communist) party, and gave way to the *Partido Unido de la Revolución Socialista* (PURS). This brought together the *Partido Socialista Popular, Movimiento de 26 Julio* and (Students') *Directorio Revolucionario*. The PURS in turn became (3 Oct. 1965) the *Partido Comunista de Cuba*. The Communist Party had been outlawed by Batista in 1954, but legally reinstated after the revolution.

National flag: 3 blue, 2 white stripes (horizontal); a white 5-pointed star in a red triangle at the hoist.

National anthem: Al combate corred bayameses (words and tune by P. Figueredo, 1868).

Local Government. The country is divided into 14 provinces and 169 municipalities. Local Government is the responsibility of the organizations of Peoples' Power. Elections were held in 1976, 1979 and 1981 for delegates to the provincial and municipal assemblies and to the national assembly.

DEFENCE. On 13 Nov. 1963 conscription was introduced for all men between the ages of 16 and 45, later raised to 50 (3 years); women of the 17–35 age groups may volunteer (for 2 years).

Army. The strength was 100,000 officers and men in 1983. Reserves are estimated at 190,000.

The Army is organized in 15 infantry brigades, 3 armoured brigades and 8 independent battalions. It has over 600 Russian-built tanks. Para-military forces total 15,000 and the new Territorial Militia, more than 500,000.

Navy. The Navy consists of 3 *ex*-Soviet diesel-powered submarines, 1 *ex*-Soviet guided missile-armed frigate, 28 missile boats, 6 hydrofoil attack craft, 13 patrol vessels, 18 torpedo boats, 22 fast gunboats, 12 inshore minesweepers, 12 motor launches, 14 coastguard vessels, 13 survey vessels, 7 landing craft and 10 service craft. The large majority of these 160 craft are former units of the Soviet Navy. Personnel in 1983 exceeded 6,000 officers and ratings. One of the 3 old *ex*-US patrol frigates still exists as a harbour hulk. The USA is still in possession of the Guantanámo naval base, but the Cuban Government refuses to accept the nominal rent of US$5,000 per annum.

Air Force. The Air Force has been extensively re-equipped with aircraft supplied by USSR and in 1981 had a strength of some 16,000 officers and men and 190 combat aircraft. About 8 interceptor and 3 ground-attack squadrons fly MiG-23, MiG-21 and MiG-17 jet fighters. There is a squadron of An-26 twin-turboprop transports, some An-24 twin-turboprop transports, piston-engined Il-14s, and about 100 Mi-24, Mi-8 (some armed) and Mi-4 helicopters, Zlin 326 piston-engined trainers and MiG-15UTI, MiG-21U and MiG-23U jet trainers. Many An-2M biplanes are operated by the Air Force, mainly on agricultural and liaison duties. Soviet-built surface-to-air ('Guideline' and 'Goa') and coastal defence ('Samlet') missiles are in service.

INTERNATIONAL RELATIONS

Membership. Cuba is a member of the UN and COMECON.

ECONOMY

Planning. The Cuban economy is now centrally planned. Since July 1972 Cuba has been a member of the Council for Mutual Economic Assistance (COMECON) and, since Jan. 1974, of the two COMECON international banks. Cuba has very large reserves of nickel and a guaranteed market in the USSR; output is currently some 36,000 tons per annum but it is to be increased to 60,000 tons after 1980. Sugar remains the mainstay of the economy. Investment in this and other agricultural sectors (rice, coffee, and dairy products) has recently been relatively high but output generally has failed to respond. Some items of food and clothing are rationed.

Budget. Revenue in 1981 was 11,201·3m. pesos and expenditure, 11,197·4m. pesos.

Currency. The Cuban *peso* has been tied to the French franc since early 1972. In March 1983, the sterling-peso rate was £1 = 1·25 *pesos*. The gold content is 0·888671 gramme of fine gold, thus 1 troy oz. of fine gold = 35 *pesos*. The law of 7 Nov. 1914, established that the monetary unit was a gold *peso* (equal to the US gold dollar) of 1·6718 grammes (1·5046 grammes fine) divided in 100 *centavos*. The old gold *pesos* and all US currency are no longer legal tender.

Copper-nickel coins of 40, 20, 5 and 1 *cent* are issued. Notes are for 100, 50, 20, 10, 5 and 1 *peso*.

Banking. On 23 Dec. 1948 the president signed the law creating a central bank (with capital of US$10m.) and which began operating 27 April 1950.

On 14 Oct. 1960 all banks were nationalized, except the Royal Bank of Canada and the Bank of Nova Scotia, which were bought out later. All banking is now carried out by the National Bank of Cuba through its 250 agencies. In 1964, 1·6m. small savings accounts totalled US$738m.

All insurance business was nationalized in Jan. 1964.

Weights and Measures. The metric system of weights and measures is legally compulsory, but the American and old Spanish systems are much used. The sugar industry uses the Spanish long ton (1·03 tonnes) and short ton (0·92 tonne). Cuba sugar sack = 329·59 lb. or 149·49 kg. Land is measured in *caballerías* (of 13·4 hectares or 33 acres).

ENERGY AND NATURAL RESOURCES

Electricity. Installed capacity 1979 was 2,052 mw. Production in 1981 was 9,264m. kwh.

Minerals. Iron ore abounds, with deposits estimated at 3,500m. tons, of which 90% were held as reserves by American steel interests but are now controlled by the Cuban Mining Institute; output (tonnes), wrought iron (1980), 1,180; steel (1981), 329,835.

Output of copper (1981) was 1,443 tonnes; refractory chrome (1980), 28,457 tonnes. Other minerals are nickel and cobalt (1981, 40,255 tonnes), silica and barytes. Gold and silver are also worked. Cuba has a small output of petroleum

(1978: 6·4m. tonnes). Salt output from the solar evaporation of sea water was 130,453 tonnes in 1980.

All mineral resources were nationalized in 1960.

Agriculture. In May 1959 all land over 30 *caballerías* was nationalized and has since been turned into state farms. In Oct. 1963 private holdings were reduced to a maximum of 5 *caballerías* (approximately 67 hectares). By 1960, 764 co-operative farms had been formed, and by late 1966 almost 65% of farm land was state-owned; the balance being in private hands.

In Sept. 1982 there were 1,402 co-operatives comprising 47,357 *caballerías* of land. The total cultivated land included state-owned, 3,398,200 hectares, and in the private sector, 475,400 hectares.

The staple products are tobacco and sugar, of which latter Cuba is the world's second largest producer; with its by-products it furnishes nearly 80% by value of the national exports. The 1981–82 crop was 8·2m. tonnes. There are 151 mills, including 40 of the largest, which were taken over from US interests, and which represent 39% of total capacity. Coffee, cotton, maize, rice and potatoes are grown.

Production of other important crops in 1981 was (in tonnes): Tobacco, 54,598; rice, 460,886; maize (1980), 15,839; coffee (1980), 19,168.

Tobacco is grown mainly in the Vuelta–Abajo district, near Pinar del Río. Coffee is grown chiefly in the province of Oriente.

Output of henequén fibre in 1964 was 233,919 tons. A fast-growing fibre, *kenaf*, originally from India, soft in texture, is replacing jute for sacking; the tobacco industry uses *majagua*, another local fibre, while a third fibre, *yarey*, from palms is also used. 208,540 tonnes of potatoes were produced in 1980. A nitrate plant has been built at Nuevitas and a large British-built urea plant at Cienfuegos. The principal fruits exported are pineapples, citrus fruit, tomatoes and pimentos. A rice cultivation plan began in 1967 in the south of Havana province. Cultivation is highly mechanized and the area so far sown produces two crops a year.

In 1981 citrus fruit production was 459,100 tonnes.

In 1962, 2,105 *caballerías* were allocated to cotton; cotton produced, 1964, was 2,653 tons against 13,000 tons in 1962.

In 1981 the livestock included 1·95m. pigs; 829,000 horses; 365,000 sheep; 100,000 goats; 5·9m. head of cattle.

Forestry. Cuba has extensive forest lands. These forests contain valuable cabinet woods, such as mahogany and cedar, besides dye-woods, fibres, gums, resins and oils. Cedar is used locally for cigar-boxes, and mahogany is exported. During the re-forestation campaign of 1959–60, 34,000 eucalyptus saplings were planted over 1,120 *caballerías*. Cedars, mahogany, *majagua*, teca, etc., are also being raised and planted out. In 1980 saplings planted included: Eucalyptus, 2,110; pine, 34,732; majagua, 4,187; mahogany, 1,729; cedar, 1,722; casuarina, 9,671.

INDUSTRY AND TRADE

Industry. Production in 1981 was: Textiles, 174·4m. sq. metres; cement, 3,292,200 tonnes; wheat flour, 354,000 tonnes; gasoline (1980), 816,036 tonnes; 326,400 tyres; 360,400 tubes; shoes (1980), 12,927,400 pairs; paint (1980), 149,420 hectolitres; soft drinks (1980), 1,867,100 hectolitres; cigars, 239m.; cigarettes, 15,000m.; fertilizers (1980), 1,059,152 tonnes.

Trade Unions. All workers have a right to join a trade union. The Workers' Central Union of Cuba, to which 23 unions are affiliated, had 2m. members in 1978.

Commerce. Imports and exports (including bullion and specie) for calendar years (in 1m. pesos):

	1978	*1979*	*1980*	*1981*
Imports	3,574	3,687	4,059	5,081
Exports	3,440	3,500	3,967	4,259

Cuba's principal exports are sugar, minerals, tobacco and fish, which in 1974 were planned to furnish 86%, 6·4%, 2·7% and 2·3% respectively by value. The main imports from non-Communist countries are chemicals and engineering and electrical machinery and transport equipment.

Sugar accounts for approximately 80% of the exports. In 1980 over 2,207,000 tons were sold in free world markets, the balance going mainly to Eastern Europe under long-term guaranteed price contracts. Tobacco, fish and nickel are the other major exports. Most trade is with Eastern Europe, particularly with the USSR which supplies approximately 50% of total Cuban imports.

Total trade between Cuba and UK (British Department of Trade returns, in £1,000 sterling):

	1977	*1978*	*1979*	*1980*	*1981*	*1982*
Imports to UK	9,732	7,960	14,970	26,208	16,829	17,688
Exports and re-exports from UK	27,455	27,625	36,112	35,272	27,656	64,835

COMMUNICATIONS

Roads. There are 31,204 km of highways open to traffic, including the Central Highway, traversing the island for 760 miles from Pinar del Río to Santiago. In 1980 there were 32,662 hire cars (including coaches and buses).

Railways. There were (1980) 5,196 km of public railway (mainly 1,435 mm gauge) of which 199 km is electrified. In 1980 it carried 20m. passengers and 14·1m. tonnes of freight. In addition, the large sugar estates have 9,441 km of lines on 1,435, 914 and 760 mm gauges.

Aviation. The state airline CUBANA operates all internal services, and from Havana to Mexico City, Madrid, Berlin, Montreal, Prague, Tripoli and Baghdad, and also to Lima, Panama, Kingston, Bridgetown, Port of Spain, Georgetown. The other regular foreign services are Mexican, Spanish, Soviet, Czech, East German, Canadian and Angolan. In Dec. 1977 the first charter flights since 1960 started operating between USA and Cuba.

Shipping. The coastline is over 3,500 miles long and has many fine harbours. The merchant marine, in 1981, consisted of 93 sea-going vessels of 953,700 DWT.

Post and Broadcasting. There are 3,545 miles of public and 8,902 miles of private telegraph wires. Cuba has 103 broadcasting stations and 2 television stations. Radio receiving sets, 1974, numbered 909,000; television sets, 300,000. The national telephone system (1980) had 390,000 instruments.

Cinemas. In 1980 there were 692 cinemas.

Newspapers. In 1980 there were 29 newspapers of which 14 were daily newspapers.

JUSTICE, RELIGION, EDUCATION AND WELFARE

Justice. There is a Supreme Court in Havana and 7 regional courts of appeal. The provinces are divided into judicial districts, with courts for civil and criminal actions, with municipal courts for minor offences. The civil code guaranteed aliens the same property and personal rights as are enjoyed by nationals.

The 1959 Agrarian Reform Law and the Urban Reform Law passed on 14 Oct. 1960 have placed certain restrictions on both. Revolutionary Summary Tribunals have wide powers.

Religion. There is no state Church, though Roman Catholics predominate. There is a bishop of the American Episcopal Church in Havana; there are congregations of Methodists in Havana and in the provinces. Protestants numbered 265,000 in 1962; they have been organized as the Cuban Council of Evangelical Churches.

Education. Education is compulsory (between the ages of 6 and 14) and free, and now available everywhere. In 1964 illiteracy was officially declared to have been completely eliminated.

In 1977 the 4 universities had 122,546 students and 9,934 teaching staff. There were (1980–81) 1,468,538 pupils and (1977) 82,250 teachers at primary schools; 1,177,813 pupils at intermediate schools; 151,733 students at higher schools;

277,003 students at adult primary and intermediate schools; and 169,326 students at other schools.

The Camilo Cienfuegos school city in the Sierra Maestra was designed for 12,000 boys and 8,000 girls by 1970 (1965: 4,000, total). In 1974 the V. I. Lenin vocational school opened as a forerunner of 6 such schools.

Health (1981). There were 16,193 posts for doctors and 266 hospitals. The 1982 health and education budget was 2,040·3m. pesos.

Free medical services are provided by the state polyclinics, though some doctors still have private practices. All serious tropical diseases are effectively kept under control, and virtually all children under the age of 15 have been vaccinated against poliomyelitis.

DIPLOMATIC REPRESENTATIVES

Of Cuba in Great Britain (167 High Holborn, London, WC1)
Ambassador: Hermes Herrera (accredited 16 Feb. 1982).

Of Great Britain in Cuba (Edificio Bolivar, Carcel 101–103, Havana)
Ambassador: David C. Thomas, CMG.

Of Cuba to the United Nations
Ambassador: Dr Raúl Roa Kouri.

The USA broke off diplomatic relations with Cuba on 3 Jan. 1961 but the first steps towards normal relations were taken in Sept. 1977 when missions were opened in both capitals.

Books of Reference

Anuario Estadístico de a República de Cuba. Havana, 1914, 1953, 1957, 1972, 1973, 1979
Boletín Oficial, Ministerio de Comercio. Monthly
Estadística General: Commercio Exterior. Quarterly and Annual.—*Movimiento de Población.* Monthly and Annual. Havana
Anuario azucarero de Cuba. Havana, from 1937
Aguilar, L. E., *Cuba 1933.* Cornell Univ. Press, 1972
Canet, G., and Raisz, E., *Atlas de Cuba.* Cambridge, Mass., 1949
Carpentier, A., *Reasons of State.* London, 1976
Caute, D., *¿Cuba, Yes?* London, 1974
Chaderick, L., *A Cuban Journey.* London, 1975
Domínguez, J. I., *Cuba: Order and Revolution.* Harvard Univ. Press, 1978
Guerra y Sánchez, R., and others, *Historia de la Nación Cubana.* 10 vols. Havana, 1952
Gonzalez, E., *Cuba Under Castro: The Limits of Charisma.* Boston, 1974
MacEwan, A., *Revolution and Economic Development in Cuba.* London, 1981
Mesa-Lago, C., *The Economy of Socialist Cuba: A Two-Decade Appraisal.* Univ. of New Mexico Press, 1981
Meyer, K. E., and Szulc, T., *The Cuban Invasion.* New York, 1962
Miller, W., *The Lost Plantation.* London, 1961
Montaner, C. A., *Informe secreto sobre la revolución cubana.* Madrid, 1975
Nelson, L., *Cuba: The Measure of the Revolution.* Univ. of Minnesota Press, 1972
O'Connor, J., *The Origins of Socialism in Cuba.* London, Cornell Univ. Press, 1970
Ritter, A. R. M., *The Economic Development of Revolutionary Cuba: Strategy and Performance.* New York, 1974
Suchlicki, J. (ed.), *Cuba, Castro, and Revolution.* Univ. of Miami Press, 1972.—*Cuba: From Columbus to Castro.* New York, 1974
Thomas, H., *Cuba: Or the Pursuit of Freedom.* London, 1971
Vives, J., *Les Maîtres de Cuba.* Paris, 1981

CYPRUS

Kypriaki Dimokratia—Kıbrıs Cumhuriyeti

Capital: Nicosia
Population: 637,000 (1981)
GNP per capita: US$3,560 (1980)

HISTORY. About the middle of the 2nd millennium B.C. Greek colonies were established in Cyprus and later it formed part of the Persian, Roman and Byzantine empires. In 1193 it became a Frankish kingdom, in 1489 a Venetian dependency and in 1571 was conquered by the Turks. They retained possession of it until its cession to England for administrative purposes under a convention concluded with the Sultan at Constantinople, 4 June 1878. On 5 Nov. 1914 the island was annexed by Great Britain and on 1 May 1925 given the status of a Crown Colony.

For the history of Cyprus from 1931 to 1958 *see* THE STATESMAN'S YEAR-BOOK, 1958, pp. 237–38, and 1959, p. 236.

On 1 April 1955 the Greek Cypriots embarked on a guerrilla struggle against the British. On 19 Feb. 1959, following discussions in Zürich between the Greek and Turkish Foreign Ministers, an agreement was signed in London by the Prime Ministers of Great Britain, Greece and Turkey, and by the representatives of the Greek Cypriots and Turkish Cypriots. This agreement was implemented on 16 Aug. 1960, when Cyprus became an independent republic. By treaties between the Republic of Cyprus, Great Britain, Greece and Turkey both Enosis and partition are precluded; and Britain retains sovereignty over the areas containing her military bases in the island.

When President Makarios proposed some incisive modifications of the Zürich–London agreements, violent clashes between Greek and Turkish Cypriots broke out on 22 Dec. 1963. First, a joint force of British, Greek and Turkish troops and later a UN peace force were sent to Cyprus. A UN mediator on 26 March 1965 submitted proposals for a settlement of the Cyprus problem. These were accepted by Greece and the Greek Cypriots, but rejected by Turkey; thereupon the mediator, Dr Galo Plaza (Ecuador), resigned. The UN General Assembly on 17 Dec. 1965 called upon all states to respect the sovereignty, unity, independence and territorial integrity of Cyprus and to refrain from any intervention.

In June 1968 representatives of the Greek and Turkish Cypriots started talks in Cyprus aimed at finding a solution to the Cyprus problem but without success.

On 15 July 1974 a *coup* was staged in Cyprus by the men of the Greek ruling junta, for the overthrow of President Makarios. The President left the island and the *coup* was short-lived. On 23 July power was handed over to the President of the House of Representatives, Glafcos Clerides, in accordance with the Constitution. He acted as President until the return of President Makarios on Dec. 7.

Turkey invaded the island on 20 July, eventually landing 40,000 troops supported with heavy armament and tanks. In two military operations 20–30 July and 14–16 Aug. the Turkish troops managed to occupy 40% of the northern part of Cyprus. As a result 200,000 Greek Cypriots fled to live as refugees in the south. The Cyprus crisis was raised in the UN and the General Assembly unanimously adopted resolutions calling for the withdrawal of all foreign troops from Cyprus and the return of refugees to their homes, but without result.

On 13 Feb. 1975 at a special meeting of the executive council and legislative assembly of the Autonomous Turkish Cypriot Administration a Turkish Cypriot Federated State was proclaimed. Rauf Denktash was appointed President and he declared that the state would not seek international recognition. The proclamation was denounced by President Makarios and the Greek Prime Minister but welcomed by the Turkish Prime Minister.

AREA AND POPULATION. The island lies in the eastern Mediterranean, about 50 miles off the south coast of Turkey and (at the nearest points) 65 miles off the coast of Syria. Area 3,572 sq. miles (9,251 sq. km); about 150 miles is greatest length from east to west, and about 60 miles is greatest breadth from north to south. Populations by religions:

Religion	*1946*	*1956*	*1960*	*1973*	*1980*
Greek Orthodox	361,199	416,986	441,656	498,511	514,700
Turkish Moslem	80,548	92,642	104,942	116,000	118,800
Others	8,367	19,251	26,968	17,267	...
Total	450,114	528,879	573,566	631,778	...

Population estimate (1981) 637,000, of which 77% are Greek Cypriot (Armenian, Maronite and Latin minorities included) and 18% Turkish Cypriot. Principal towns with populations (1980 estimate): Nicosia (the capital), 161,200 (Greek Cypriots); Limassol, 105,200; Famagusta, 39,400 (1975); Larnaca, 34,700.

As a result of the Turkish invasion and the occupation of part of Cyprus, 200,000 Greek Cypriots were displaced and forced to find refuge in the south of the island. The urban centres of Famagusta, Kyrenia and Morphou were completely evacuated.

Vital statistics. The birth rate per 1,000 population in 1980 was 21·7%; death rate, 9·1%; infantile mortality per 1,000 live births, 17·2%.

CONSTITUTION AND GOVERNMENT. The legislative power is exercised by the House of Representatives of 50 members, of whom 35 were elected by the Greek community and 15 by the Turkish community. As from Dec. 1963 the Turkish members have ceased to attend.

On 13 Dec. 1959 Archbishop Makarios was elected President of the Republic, having received 144,501 votes (against 71,753 cast for the candidate sponsored by the Left). Dr Fazil Kuchuk was elected Vice-President unopposed; he resigned on 4 Jan. 1964. On 13 Feb. 1975, Rauf Denktash the Turkish-Cypriot leader announced the formation of a Turkish-Cypriot state within a federal republic.

When President Makarios died in Aug. 1977 Spyros Kyprianou became acting President and was proclaimed President on 31 Aug. 1977 and was elected for a 5-year term on 26 Jan. 1978 and re-elected 13 Feb. 1983.

Flag: White with a copper-coloured outline of the island with 2 green olive-branches beneath.

The elections held on 25 May 1981 returned 8 Democratic Party, 12 Akel Party (Communists), 3 EDEK (Socialist Party), 12, Democratic Rally. The Turks have not participated in the proceedings of the House since Dec. 1963.

The President reshuffled the Council of Ministers in Sept. 1980:

Foreign Affairs: Nicos A. Rolandis. *Interior and Defence:* Christodoulos Veniamin. *Finance:* Afxentis Afxentiou. *Minister to the President:* Stelios Katsellis. *Commerce and Industry:* Constantinos Kittis. *Education:* Nicolaos Konomis. *Communications and Works:* George Hadjicostas. *Agriculture and Natural Resources:* Nicos Pattichis. *Labour and Social Insurance:* George Stavrinakis. *Health:* George Tombazos. *Justice:* Andreas Demetriades. *Deputy Minister of the Interior:* Petros Stylianou.

DEFENCE

Army. Total strength (1983) 10,000 organized into 20 battalions and 15 artillery and support units. There is also a para-military force of 3,000 armed police.

The Turkish-Cypriot Security Force consisted of about 4,500 men supported by some T-34 tanks.

INTERNATIONAL RELATIONS

Membership. Cyprus is a member of UN, the Commonwealth and the Council of Europe.

ECONOMY

Planning. Under the Emergency Action Plan of 1977–78 the Government invested about £C45m. in restoring and building up manufacturing, agriculture, housing, transport and communications. The resulting budget deficit was met mainly from external aid, foreign and domestic borrowing. Private sector investment at £C127m. met 130% of its required achievement. The Plan aimed at turning output towards foreign markets.

A third plan was launched in 1979 for 3 years; expenditure, 1979, £C34·8m. Agriculture and irrigation have been emphasized (expenditure, 1977–78, £C20·3m.; 1979 (planned) £C15·2m.).

Budget. Revenue and expenditure for calendar years (in £C):

	1976	1977	1978	1979	1980
Ordinary					
Revenue	76,957,000	87,012,000	102,388,322	123,577,963	151,487,049
Expenditure	69,727,000	81,145,000	92,670,326	117,997,560	168,243,726
Development					
Expenditure	18,433,000	19,866,000	24,299,017	32,229,929	34,791,114

Main sources of ordinary revenue in 1980 (in £C) were: Import duties, 34,899,589; excise duties, 29,797,776; income tax, 28,587,359; rents, royalties and interest, 11,935,628; sales of goods and services, 9,310,363; other duties and taxes, 14,061,881.

Main divisions of ordinary expenditure in 1980 (in £C): Personal emoluments, 60,995,000; pensions and gratuities, 5·39m.; commodity subsidies, 10m.; subventions and contributions, 17,889,000; public debt charges, 18,701,000; refunds and drawbacks, 7,002,999.

Development expenditure for 1980 (in £C) included 8,575,000 for water development, 5,755,111 for agriculture, forests and fisheries, 1,812,000 for rural development, 5,210,898 for roads, 717,414 for airports and 613,500 for tourism. (An independent Ports Authority with its own funds was set up in 1977.)

The outstanding public debt as at 31 Dec. 1980 was £C114,022,532, excluding sinking fund reserves, and accumulated sinking funds totalled £C12,547,925. Outstanding loans as at 31 Dec. 1979 totalled £C49,084,112; including £C7,884,000 to the Electricity Authority of Cyprus and £C2,956,000 to the Cyprus Telecommunications Authority.

Currency. The *Cyprus £* is divided into 1,000 *mils*. Notes of the following denominations are in circulation: £10, £5, £1, 500 *mils*, 250 *mils*. Coins in circulation: Cupro-nickel: 100, 50, 25 *mils*; bronze and aluminium: 5 *mils*. Rate of exchange, March 1983: £1 = £C0·765; US$1 = £C1·946.

Banking. There is a Central and Issuing Bank exercising monetary functions, and the Cyprus Development Corporation created by the Government as a major source of loan funds for industrial development. Commercial banks carrying on business in Cyprus are: Bank of Cyprus Ltd, Turkish Bank Ltd, Cyprus Popular Bank Ltd, Barclays Bank International, The Chartered Bank, National Bank of Greece, Hellenic Bank Ltd, Cyprus Turkish Co-operative Central Bank Ltd, Mortgage Bank of Cyprus Ltd, Turkiye Ish Bankasi, The Co-operative Central Bank, Grindlays Bank and Lombard Banking (Cyprus) Ltd.

The Central Bank of Cyprus, established in 1963, is responsible for the issue of currency, the regulation of money supply and credit, administration of the exchange control law and the foreign-exchange reserves of the republic. The Bank also acts as a banker of the banks operating in Cyprus and of the Government.

At the end of Dec. 1980 total deposits in banks were £C464m. The country's foreign exchange reserves at the end of Dec. 1980 were £C150·9m.

Weights and Measures. Cyprus weights and measures follow the standard weights and measures of Great Britain. The metric system may also be lawfully used. In internal trade the following special Cyprus weights and measures are in use: 1 *pic* = ⅔ yd; 1 *oke* = 2·8 lb.; 1 *kilé* = 8 Imperial gallons. The Cyprus *donum* is approximately ⅓ acre.

ENERGY AND NATURAL RESOURCES

Water resources. Since 1960, £C85m. has been spent on water dams, water supplies, hydrological research and geophysical surveys. Existing dams have (1982) a capacity of 116m. cu. metres as against 6m. cu. metres before independence.

Minerals. The principal minerals exported during 1980 were (in tonnes): Iron pyrites, 88,000; cupreous concentrates, 7,400; asbestos, 29,965; clay (bentonite), 22,905; gypsum, 5,519; umber, 5,300. Mining provided about 5% of all exports in 1980. Total value of minerals exported in 1980 was £C8m. No figures for copper cement at the Xeros mines as this is in the Turkish occupied area.

Agriculture. Chief agricultural products in 1980 (tonnes): Grapes, 205,000; potatoes, 188,000; milk, 70,750; barley, 80,000; grapefruit, 47,200; oranges, 32,000; meat, 32,600; water melons, 18,000; carobs, 12,500; lemons, 16,500; wheat, 13,000; olives, 15,000; carrots, 7,300; melons, 4,800; wines including commandaria, 11·5m. gallons.

Of the island's 2·3m. acres, approximately 1m. are cultivated. 21·4% of the economically active population are engaged in agriculture.

Livestock in 1981 (in 1,000): Cattle, 41; sheep, 525; goats, 360; pigs, 183.

Forestry. Reforesting the areas burnt during the Turkish invasion is continuing and by Dec. 1981 12,037 hectares of burnt forests were reforested and/or cultivated. Total forest area, 1,734 sq. km.

In 1981 the chief forest products were timber, valued at £C456,521; firewood, £C12,590; figures relate to the area of Cyprus not occupied by Turkey.

INDUSTRY AND TRADE

Industry. Cyprus has no heavy industry, but a wide variety of light manufacturing industries. The establishment of a Development Bank in 1963 has given further impetus to industrial activity. Manufacturing industry in 1980 contributed about 17·9% to the GDP and gave employment to 22% of the economically active population. The GDP of manufacturing industries in 1980 was estimated at £C124·6m.

The highest increases in output in 1980 were production of paper and paperboard products, chemicals, footwear and clothing. Industrial exports rose by 24·3% to £C107·3m. in 1980.

Trade Unions and Associations. Registration of trade unions and employers' associations is compulsory and freedom of association is constitutionally and statutorily guaranteed. At the end of 1976 the trade unions were distributed as follows: Pancyprian Federation of Labour ('old' trade unions), 46,080 members in 12 unions; Cyprus Workers Confederation ('free' labour syndicates), 32,775 members in 49 unions; Pancyprian Federation of Independent Trade Unions, 654 members in 7 unions; Cyprus Turkish Trade Unions Federation, 5,668 members in 13 unions (1973); Cyprus Democratic Labour Federation, 193 members in 4 unions; Civil Service Trade Union, 9,926 members.

The 'old' trade unions are affiliated to the World Federation of Trade Unions, the 'free' labour syndicates and the Turkish Federation are affiliated to the International Confederation of Free Trade Unions.

In Dec. 1976 the total number of employers' associations was 24 with a total membership of 3,071. Some of the employers' associations are members of the Cyprus Employers' Federation, an organization with 11 trade associations consisting of 320 members.

Commerce. The commerce and the shipping, exclusive of coasting trade, for calendar years were (in £C):

	1977	*1978*	*1979*	*1980*	*1981*
Imports [1]	362,868,184	375,972,000	357,602,505	424,292,466	489,535,744
Exports [2]	185,359,554	170,732,000	161,870,504	188,035,504	234,772,708

[1] Excluding Naafi imports of about £C4m. in 1981.
[2] Including re-exports and ships' stores of about £C41m. in 1981.

Chief civil imports, 1981 (in £C1,000):

Fuels and lubricants	105,360	Feeding stuff for animals	8,296
Textile yarn and fabrics made up	42,279	Beverages and tobacco	7,567
Iron and steel	17,814	Meat and meat preparations	6,157
Cereals and cereal preparations	30,540	Household electrical and non-electrical equipment	6,228
Transport equipment	27,903	Medicinal and pharmaceutical products	5,991
Paper, paperboard and pulp and articles thereof	17,483	Fertilizers	2,534
Raw materials for plastics	10,747	Dairy products and eggs	4,970
Road vehicles	27,688		

Chief domestic exports, 1981 (in £C1,000):

Grapes	3,878	Minerals, mainly asbestos	8,221
Grapefruit	4,229	Cigarettes	8,834
Lemons	3,085	Paper products	9,780
Oranges	3,692	Travel goods	4,572
Fruit and vegetables, preserved	2,434	Cement	12,832
Potatoes	16,063	Clothing	39,507
Wine	6,302	Footwear	16,287

In 1981 UK supplied 14·19% of the imports; other EEC countries, 35·13%; Arab countries, 13·49%; Eastern Europe, 6·43%; others, 30·76%. Of the exports (1981), 52·5% went to Arab countries; 21·5% to the UK; 9·7% to other EEC countries; 7·2% to Eastern Europe and 9·1% to other countries.

Total trade between Cyprus and UK (British Department of Trade returns, in £1,000 sterling):

	1977	*1978*	*1979*	*1980*	*1981*	*1982*
Imports to UK	79,749	112,014	115,636	128,386	80,580	89,908
Exports and re-exports from UK	82,906	111,183	120,101	153,754	115,597	111,882

Tourism. Foreign tourists (1980), 353,375 and 145,829 excursionists.

COMMUNICATIONS

Roads. In 1979 the total length of roads was 10,012 km, of which 4,936 km were paved and 5,076 km were earth or gravel roads. The main roads which are maintained by the Ministry of Communications and Works (Public Works Department) totalled 2,657 km, of which 2,582 km were paved. The total of urban streets was 1,616 km, of which 1,118 were paved. Village roads and streets totalled 3,832 km, of which 1,236 km were paved, the rest being of earth or gravel surface. There were also 1,906 km of unpaved forest roads.

The area controlled by the Government of the Republic and that occupied by Turkey are now served by separate transport systems, and there are no services linking the two areas.

Aviation. Nicosia airport has been closed since Aug. 1974. During 1979, 838,339 persons travelled and 28,657,000 kg of commercial air-freight was handled through Larnaca airport.

Shipping. In 1979, 3,660 ships of 5·3m. net tons entered Cyprus ports. Ships under Cyprus registry (1979) numbered 1,200 of 2·5m. tons. Famagusta has been closed to international traffic since Aug. 1974.

Post and Broadcasting. In 1979 there were 52 post offices and 535 postal agencies. There are 17 post offices and 368 postal agencies in the Turkish occupied area. Telephones (1981) 113,437. Wireless licences issued (1978) were 222,470, including television licences.

Cyprus Broadcasting Corporation broadcasts mainly in Greek, but also in Turkish, English, and Armenian on medium-waves. The corporation also broadcasts one TV programme.

Cinemas (1976). In the Greek part of Cyprus there were 66 winter cinemas (38,500 seats) and 17 open-air cinemas (9,700 seats).

Newspapers (1980). There are 11 Greek, 4 Turkish and 1 English daily newspapers and 11 Greek, 6 Turkish and 1 English weeklies.

JUSTICE, RELIGION, EDUCATION AND WELFARE

Justice. Under the Constitution and other legislation in force the following judicial institutions are established: The Supreme Court of the Republic, the Assize Courts and District Courts.

The Supreme Court is composed of 10, one of whom is the President. The Supreme Court adjudicates exclusively and finally: on all constitutional and administrative law matters, including any recourse that any law or decision of the House of Representatives or the budget is discriminatory against either of the two Communities; on any conflict of competence between state organs, questions of unconstitutionality of any law or decisions on any question of interpretation of the Constitution in case of ambiguity, as well as recourses for annulment of administrative acts, decisions or omissions. The Supreme Court is the highest appellate court in the republic and has jurisdiction to hear and determine all appeals from any court. It has exclusive jurisdiction to issue orders in the nature of *habeas corpus, mandamus,* prohibition, *quo warranto* and *certiorari* and in admiralty and matrimonial matters.

There are 6 assize courts and 6 district courts, 1 for each district. The assize courts have unlimited criminal jurisdiction and power to order compensation up to £C800. The district courts exercise original civil and criminal jurisdiction, the extent of which varies with the composition of the Bench. In civil matters (other than those within the original jurisdiction of Supreme Court) a District Court composed of not less than 2 and not more than 3 judges has unlimited jurisdiction. A President or a Senior District Judge sitting alone has jurisdiction up to £C3,000, and a District Judge sitting alone up to £C1,000, and is also empowered to deal with any action for the recovery of possession of any immovable property, and certain other specified matters. In criminal matters the jurisdiction of a District Court is exercised by its members sitting singly and is of a summary character. A President, a Senior District Judge or a District Judge sitting alone has power to try any offence punishable with imprisonment up to 3 years, or with a fine up to £C500 or with both, and may order compensation up to £C500.

Religion. *See* Area and Population, p. 386.

Education. Until 31 March 1965 each community in Cyprus managed its own schooling through its respective Communal Chamber. Intercommunal education had been placed under the Minister of the Interior, assisted by a Board of Education for Intercommunal Schools, of which the Minister was the Chairman. In 1965 the Greek Communal Chamber was dissolved and a Ministry of Education was established to take its place. Intercommunal education has been placed under this Ministry.

Greek-Cypriot Education. Elementary education is compulsory and is provided free in 6 grades to children between 6 and 13 years of age. In some towns and large villages there are separate junior schools consisting of the first three grades. Apart from schools for the deaf and blind and the Lambousa School for juvenile offenders, there are also 7 schools for handicapped children. The Ministry runs 88 kindergartens for children from low-income families; most pre-primary education is privately run. There were 439 primary schools (including privately run institutions) with 54,309 pupils and 2,260 teachers in 1978–79.

Secondary education is free for the first 3 years and is fee-paying for the rest, although senior pupils can be wholly or partially exempt from payment. The secondary school is 6 years, 3 years at the gymnasium followed by 3 years at the lykeion. There were 3 types of lykeia: classical, science, economic. There are 5- to 6-year technical schools. In 1980–81 there were 91 secondary schools with 2,910 teachers and 47,599 pupils.

Post-secondary education is provided at the Pedagogical Academy, which organizes 3-year courses for the training of pre-primary and primary school teachers, and at the Higher Technical Institute, which provides 3-year courses for technicians in civil, electrical and mechanical engineering. There is also a 2-year Forestry College (administered by the Ministry of Agriculture), a Hotel and Catering Institute and a 3-year Nurses' School and 1-year School for Health Inspectors (Ministry of Health). Adult education is conducted through youth centres in rural areas, foreign language institutes in the towns and private institutions offering courses in business administration and secretarial work.

In 1978–79, 12,112 students were studying in universities abroad, mainly in Greece and the UK.

Turkish-Cypriot Education. The Office of Education of the Turkish Community of Cyprus caters for some 18% of the island's population and (1976) administered 10 kindergartens, 167 elementary schools (16,014 pupils), 18 secondary schools (7,190 pupils), 6 technical schools (735 pupils) and 1 teacher-training college (13 students). There were 43 evening institutes for adult education.

Greek is the language of 80% of the population and Turkish of 18%. English is widely spoken. English and French are compulsory subjects in secondary schools. Illiteracy is largely confined to older people.

Social Security. The administration of the social-security services in Cyprus is in the hands of the Ministry of Labour and Social Insurance, with the Ministry of Health providing medical services through public clinics and hospitals on a means test, except medical treatment for employment accidents, which is given free to all insured employees and financed by the Social Insurance Scheme.

Social Insurance. The island's Social Insurance Scheme, which covers compulsorily both employees and self-employed persons, provides, in the case of employees, cash benefits for sickness, unemployment, maternity, marriage (females only), old-age, widowhood and death and cash benefits with free medical treatment for employment accidents and occupational diseases as well as for invalidity cases.

Annual Holiday Scheme. An Annual Holidays with Pay Law, introduced in 1967, provides for a minimum of 9 days paid leave to all workers in the island. The law is implemented by means of regular contributions by employers into a fund administered by Government. Employers offering more than 9 days' paid leave by collective agreement or otherwise may be exempted from paying contributions into the fund.

Termination of Employment Scheme. A Termination of Employment Law also enacted in 1967 provides for the establishment of a Redundancy Fund to which all employers contribute 0·5% of their pay-roll. The law provides for a minimum period of notice to employees, from 1 to 6 weeks according to length of service; for compensation on arbitrary dismissal; for redundancy payments.

DIPLOMATIC REPRESENTATIVES

Of Cyprus in Great Britain (93 Park St., London, W1Y 4ET)
High Commissioner: Tasos Panayides.

Of Great Britain in Cyprus (Alexander Pallis St., Nicosia)
High Commissioner: W. J. A. Wilberforce, CMG.

Of Cyprus in the USA (2211 R. St., NW, Washington, D.C., 20008)
Ambassador: Andrew J. Jacobvides.

Of the USA in Cyprus (Therissos St., Nicosia)
Ambassador: Raymond C. Ewing.

Of Cyprus to the United Nations
Ambassador: Dinos Moushoutas.

Books of Reference

Statistical Information: Statistics and Research Department, Nicosia.
Alastos, D., *Cyprus in History.* London, 1955.—*Cyprus Guerilla.* London, 1960
Bitsios, D. S., *Cyprus: The Vulnerable Republic.* Thessaloniki, 1975
Christodoulou, D., *The Evolution of the Rural Land use Pattern in Cyprus.* Bude, 1960
Crawshaw, N., *The Cyprus Revolt: An Account of the Struggle for Union with Greece.* London, 1978

Crouzet, F., *Le Conflit de Chypre 1946–1959.* Brussels, 1973
Denktash, R., *The Cyprus Triangle.* London, 1982
Emilianides, A., *Histoire de Chypre.* Paris, 1962—*The Zurich and London Agreements and the Cyprus Republic.* Athens, 1962
Halil, K., *The Rape of Cyprus.* London, 1982
Hill, Sir George F., *A History of Cyprus.* 4 vols. Cambridge, 1940–52
Hunt, D., *Footprints in Cyprus.* London, 1982
Kitromilides, P. M., and Evriviades, M. L., *Cyprus,* [Bibliography]. Oxford and Santa Barbara, 1982
Kosut, H., *Cyprus 1946–68.* New York, 1970
Loizos, P., *The Heart Grows Bitter: A Chronicle of Cypriot War Refugees.* CUP, 1982
Luke, Sir Harry, *Cyprus.* Rev. ed. London, 1965
Markides, K. C., *The Rise and Fall of the Cyprus Republic.* Yale Univ. Press, 1977
Mayes, S., *Makarios.* London, 1981
Polyviou, P. G., *Cyprus: The Tragedy and the Challenge.* London, 1975.—*Cyprus in Search of a Constitution.* Nicosia, 1976.—*Cyprus: Conflict and Negotiation, 1960–1980.* London, 1980
Salih, H. I., *Cyprus: The Impact of Diverse Nationalism on a State.* Univ. of Alabama Press, 1979
Stavrinides, Z., *The Cyprus Conflict.* Nicosia, 1976
Vanezis, P. N., *Makarios: Faith and Power.* New York, 1972

CZECHOSLOVAKIA

Československá Socialistická Republika

Capital: Prague
Population: 15·28m. (1980)
GNP per capita: US$5,820 (1980)

HISTORY. The Czechoslovak State came into existence on 28 Oct. 1918, when the Czech *Národní Výbor* (National Committee) took over the government of the Czech lands upon the dissolution of Austria–Hungary. Two days later the Slovak National Council manifested its desire to unite politically with the Czechs. On 14 Nov. 1918 the first Czechoslovak National Assembly declared the Czechoslovak State to be a republic with T. G. Masaryk as President (1918–35).

The Treaty of St Germain-en-Laye (1919) recognized the Czechoslovak Republic, consisting of the Czech lands (Bohemia, Moravia, part of Silesia) and Slovakia. To these lands were added as a trust the autonomous province of Subcarpathian Ruthenia.

This territory was broken up for the benefit of Germany, Poland and Hungary by the Munich agreement (29 Sept. 1938) between UK, France, Germany and Italy.

In March 1939 the German-sponsored Slovak government proclaimed Slovakia independent, and Germany incorporated the Czech lands into the Reich as the 'Protectorate of Bohemia and Moravia'. A government-in-exile, headed by Dr Beneš, was set up in London in July 1940.

Liberation by the Soviet Army and US Forces was completed by May 1945.

Territories taken by Germans, Poles and Hungarians were restored to Czechoslovak sovereignty. Subcarpathian Ruthenia was transferred to the USSR.

Elections were held in May 1946, at which the Communist Party obtained about 38% of the votes.

A coalition government under a Communist Prime Minister, Klement Gottwald, remained in power until 20 Feb. 1948, when 12 of the non-Communist ministers resigned in protest against infiltration of Communists into the police.

In Feb. a predominantly Communist government was formed by Gottwald. In May elections resulted in an 89% majority for the government and President Beneš resigned.

In the first months of 1968 mounting pressure for liberalization culminated in the overthrow of the Stalinist President and Party Secretary, Antonín Novotný, and his associates. Under a new leadership the Communist Party introduced in April 1968 an 'Action Programme' of far-reaching political and economic reforms.

Soviet pressure to abandon this programme was exerted between May and Aug. 1968, and finally, Warsaw Pact forces occupied Czechoslovakia on 21 Aug. The enforced Moscow agreement of 26 Aug. bound the Czechoslovak government to a policy of 'normalization' (*i.e.*, abandonment of most reforms) and to the stationing of Soviet forces on Czechoslovak soil. This situation was confirmed by the Czechoslovak–Soviet 'Status of Forces Agreement' of 16 Oct. In 1969–1970 Soviet pressure led to extensive changes in the Party and Government. In Oct. 1969 Czechoslovakia repudiated its condemnation of the Warsaw Pact invasion.

A Czechoslovak–Soviet 20-year Treaty of Friendship, Co-operation and Mutual Assistance was signed in May 1970. Since 1977 a dissident civil rights movement 'Charter 77' has been active despite official efforts to supress it.

On 11 Dec. 1973 the German Federal Republic and Czechoslovakia signed a treaty normalizing relations and annulling the Munich agreement of 1938. This was ratified by both countries' parliaments in July 1974.

AREA AND POPULATION. At the census of 11 Nov. 1980 the population was 15,276,799 (4,987,853 in Slovakia; 7·8m. females. There are 12 administrative regions, one of which is the capital, Prague (Praha) and one the capital of Slovakia, Bratislava.

Region	*Chief city*	*Area in sq. km*	*Population 1980*
Czech			
Prague	—	495	1,182,862
Středočeský	Prague (Praha)	11,004	1,151,354
Jihočeský	České Budějovice	11,344	688,795
Západočeský	Plzeň (Pilsen)	10,876	879,640
Severočeský	Ústí nad Labem	7,809	1,166,002
Východočeský	Hradec Králové	11,240	1,247,976
Jihomoravský	Brno	15,028	2,040,260
Severomoravský	Ostrava	11,067	1,931,877
Slovak			
Bratislava	—	368	380,248
Západoslovenský	Bratislava	14,491	1,682,591
Středoslovenský	Banská Bystrica	17,977	1,524,238
Východoslovenský	Košice	16,182	1,400,776

The area of Czechoslovakia is 127,871 sq. km (49,365 sq. miles) (Slovakia, 49,018 sq. km). Population density in 1980: 119 per sq. km. Growth rate in 1980, 4·1 per 1,000. Expectation of life in 1973 was 66·3 (males); 73·3 (females).

Ethnic minorities have equal political and cultural rights. In 1980 there were (in 1,000): Czechs, 9,819; Slovaks, 4,664; Hungarians, 580; Poles, 68; Germans, 62; Ukrainians and Russians, 55. There were 250,000 gipsies in 1980.

Official languages are Czech and Slovak.

The population of the principal towns in 1980 was as follows (in 1,000):

Prague (Praha)	1,182	Hradec Králové	96	Nitra	77
Bratislava	381	Pardubice	92	Prešov	72
Brno	371	České Budějovice	90	Kladno	71
Ostrava	322	Havířov	90	Banská Bystrica	66
Košice	203	Ústí nad Labem	88	Trnava	64
Plzeň	171	Gottwaldov	84	Karlovy Vary	61
Olomouc	102	Žilina	83	Most	60
Liberec	98	Karviná	78	Frýdek-Místek	60

Vital statistics for calendar years:

	Live births	*Marriages*	*Divorces*	*Deaths*
1977	281,722	137,488	31,163	173,006
1978	278,250	134,509	33,222	174,416
1979	271,824	126,984	32,241	174,832
1980	248,048	117,841	33,863	185,116

CLIMATE. A humid continental climate, with warm summers and cold winters. Precipitation is generally greater in summer, with thunderstorms. Autumn, with dry, clear weather and spring, which is damp, are each of short duration.

Prague, Jan. 29·5°F (–1·5°C), July 67°F (19·4°C). Annual rainfall 19·3″ (483mm).

CONSTITUTION AND GOVERNMENT. For details of previous constitutions, *see* THE STATESMAN'S YEAR-BOOK, 1968–69, pp. 927–28.

Since 1 Jan. 1969 Czechoslovakia has been a federal socialist republic consisting of two nations of equal rights: the Czech Socialist Republic (the Czech lands, previously Bohemia, Moravia and part of Silesia), and the Slovak Socialist Republic (Slovakia). Each Republic is governed by a National Council (the Czech with 200 deputies, the Slovak with 150), which delegates to an overall Federal Assembly responsibility for constitutional and foreign affairs, defence and important economic decisions. The Federal Assembly consists of the Chamber of Nations, which has 75 Czech and 75 Slovak delegates elected by their respective National Councils, and the Chamber of the People, which has 200 deputies elected by national suffrage.

The previous constitution (1960) remains in force as amended by Constitutional Acts 143 and 144 of 1968. Since 1971 deputies are elected for a 5-year term so as to coincide with Communist Party congresses. Minimum age of voters is 18, of deputies, 21 years. At the elections of 5–6 June 1981 a single list of National Front candidates was presented. Turnout was 10,736,312 from an electorate of 10,789,574 (99·5%). 99·96% of the votes were cast for the official candidates.

President of the Republic: Gustáv Husák (born 1913), *President of the Federal Assembly:* Alois Indra.

The *de facto* primary source of power is the Communist Party of Czechoslovakia, of which the Communist Party of Slovakia (*First Secretary:* Josef Lenárt) is a constituent part. Communists head the National Front, which incorporates the remaining political parties (Czechoslovak Socialist Party, Czechoslovak People's Party, Slovak Reconstruction Party, Slovak Freedom Party) and the trade unions and youth organizations. The Communist Party had 1,458,000 members and 123,000 candidate members on 1 Jan. 1982. In March 1983 the Presidium consisted of Gustáv Husák *(General Secretary)*; Vasil Bil'ak; Peter Colotka *(Deputy Prime Minister)*; Karel Hoffmann *(Chairman, Central Council of Trade Unions)*; Václav Hůla *(Deputy Prime Minister)*; Alois Indra; Miloš Jakeš; Antonín Kapek; Josef Kempný; Josef Korčák *(Deputy Prime Minister)*; Josef Lenárt; Lubomír Štrougal *(Prime Minister)*. Candidate members: Jan Fojtík, Josef Hamán, Miloslav Hruškovič.

In March 1983 members of the government not mentioned above included: *(Deputy Prime Ministers)* Ladislav Gerle; Karol Laco; Matej Lúčan; Svatopluk Potač *(Chairman, State Planning Commission)*; Rudolf Rohlíček; Josef Šimon; (other ministers) Bohumil Urban *(Foreign Trade)*; Martin Dzúr *(Defence)*; František Ondřich *(Chairman, Czechoslovak Control Committee)*; Bohuslav Chňoupek *(Foreign)*; Leopold Lér *(Finance)*; Michal Štancel' *(Labour)*; Jaromír Obzina *(Interior)*; Vlastimir Ehrenberger *(Minister of Fuel and Power)*.

The Czech Prime Minister is Josef Korčák; the Slovak, Peter Colotka.

Local government is carried on by National Committees consisting of deputies elected for 5-year terms. There are 10 regional Committees, 2 City Committees with the same status for Prague and Bratislava, 108 district Committees and 7,979 town and community Committees. Elections were held in 1981.

National flag: White and red (horizontal), with a blue triangle of full depth at the hoist, point to the fly.

National anthem: Kde domov můj (words by J. K. Tyl; tune by F. J. Škroup, 1834); combined with, Nad Tatru sa blyska (words by J. Matuška, 1844).

DEFENCE. Defence is the responsibility of the Defence Council set up in Feb. 1969 and headed by the First Secretary of the Party. Army service lasts 2 years. There are 2 military districts. The security forces and frontier guards are organized in regiments and brigades respectively; total strength, 36,000.

The Warsaw Pact invasion of Aug. 1968 brought an estimated 500,000 occupation troops into the country. By early 1970 this number had been reduced to 80,000 Soviet troops, the presence of which is legalized by the Czech–Soviet 'Status of Forces' Agreement of Oct. 1968.

In Feb. 1969 the government announced an increase in defence capacity, and Czechoslovakia resumed participation in Warsaw Pact meetings.

Army. The Army is organized in 10 divisions (5 tank and 5 motorized divisions). The regular army had, in 1983, a total strength of about 142,500 men and 3,400 tanks, mainly T-55s, with some T-54s.

Air Force. The Air Force is organized as a tactical force, under overall army command, and has a strength of some 54,000 personnel and 500 combat aircraft. Six interceptor regiments (each 3 squadrons of 14 aircraft) are equipped with MiG-23 and MiG-21 jets, and there are 4 regiments of Su-7, Su-20, MiG-23 and MiG-21 ground attack aircraft, as well as Mi-24 gunship helicopters. MiG-21s and adapted L-29 Delfin jet trainers are used for tactical reconnaissance. Transport units have a total of about 50 Let L-410, An-24/26, Il-14, Tu-134, and Tu-154 aircraft and Mil Mi-2 (armed), Mi-4 and Mi-8 helicopters. Training units are equipped with 2-seat

MiG-23s and MiG-21s and Czech-built aircraft, including L-29 Delfin and L-39 Albatros jet advanced trainers. Surface-to-air ('Guideline', 'Goa', 'Ganef' and 'Gainful') missile units are operational.

INTERNATIONAL RELATIONS

Membership. Czechoslovakia is a member of UN, COMECON and the Warsaw Pact.

ECONOMY

Planning. For the first five 5-year plans *see* THE STATESMAN'S YEAR-BOOK, 1978–79, p. 385. Economic reforms of the period 1965–68 were abandoned after the Soviet intervention of 1968, and the economy reverted to the traditional communist centrally planned type. In 1978 and 1980 some rationalizations in the planning system, economic levers (profits, prices, wages) and organization of labour were applied. Food prices were raised in Jan. 1982.

The sixth 5-year plan for 1976–80 saw an increase of 3% in national income, 3·2% in industrial, and 6% in agricultural, production. Targets were not met. The 7th 5-year plan is running from 1981 to 1985. National income is to rise by 2·8%, industrial production by 2·7%, agricultural by 2·6%.

Budget. Budgets for calendar years (in Kčs. 1m.):

	1974	*1975*	*1976*	*1977*	*1978*	*1979*	*1980*
Revenue	263,755	278,113	292,165	280,786	286,267	294,638	306,262
Expenditure	259,185	273,774	290,071	278,301	283,912	292,403	304,182

Main items of the 1980 budget were (in Kčs. 1,000m.): Revenue: from the economy, 250; direct taxes, 41. Expenditure: national economy, 131; culture, health and social services, 144; defence, 23; administration, 6.

Currency. The monetary unit in the Czechoslovak Republic is the *koruna* (Kčs.) or crown of 100 *haler*. Notes in circulation: Kčs. 10, 20, 50, 100, 500. Coin: 5, 10, 20, 50 *halers*, and Kčs. 1, 2, 5. The *koruna* is based on a gold content of 0·123426 gramme of pure gold and pegged on the rouble at Kčs. 1·80 = R.1. The International Monetary Fund did not approve this change of the par value, and Czechoslovak membership was terminated in 1954, and ceased to be a member of the International Bank. The official rates of exchange are £1 = Kčs. 9·80; US$1 = Kčs. 5·64; 1 Soviet rouble = Kčs. 8. Tourist rate: £1 = Kčs. 17·06.

The return of 18·4 tonnes of gold seized by Nazi Germany and held in London and New York since the nationalization of Western assets in 1948 was agreed in Jan. 1982 by the Czech, British and US governments in exchange for compensation of the asset-holders.

Banking. For previous banking history *see* THE STATESMAN'S YEAR-BOOK, 1971–72, pp. 858–59. The central bank and bank of issue is the State Bank (Statní Banka), which controls foreign exchange reserves, and is a savings bank and a commercial credit bank to enterprises, except foreign trade enterprises. These are financed by the Commercial Bank (Obchodní Banka) which carries out all foreign trade transactions. The Trade Bank (Živnostenská Banka, provides banking services for private foreign clients, and maintains branches abroad. There is also an Investment Bank (Investiční Banka), one of whose functions is to manage foreign securities. 'Foreign exchange points' (*e.g.*, hotels) have partial foreign exchange authorization.

Weights and Measures. The metric system is in force.

ENERGY AND NATURAL RESOURCES

Energy. There is an oil pipeline from the USSR with branches to Bratislava and Zaluzi and a natural gas pipeline which supplies the German Federal and Democratic Republics, Austria and Italy as well as Czechoslovakia. A second is under construction. Production of electricity in 1980: 72,732m. kwh.

Minerals. Czechoslovakia is not rich in minerals. There are hard and soft coal reserves (chief coalfields: Most, Chomutov, Kladno, Ostrava and Sokolov). There is also uranium, glass sand and salt, and small quantities of iron ore, graphite, copper and lead. Production in 1980 (in tonnes): Coal, 27,680,000; lignite and brown coal, 95,529,000.

Agriculture. In 1980 there were 6·9m. hectares of agricultural land (4·9m. hectares arable, 0·9m. meadow, 0·8m. pasture), of which 4·3m. were held by collective farms, 2·1m. by state farms and 102,000 as private plots (maximum size 1 hectare).

In 1980 there were 1,722 collective farms with 978,474 members and 200 state farms with 165,806 employees. Crop production in 1980 (in 1,000 tonnes): Sugar-beet, 7,255; wheat, 5,386; potatoes, 2,695; barley, 3,575; maize, 745; rye, 570.

Livestock. In 1979 the number of livestock was: Cattle, 4·92m. (including 1·9m. milch cows); horses, 47,000; pigs, 7·6m.; sheep, 875,000; poultry, 48·4m. In 1979 production of meat was 1,656,109 tonnes (live weight); milk, 5,493m. litres; 4,732m. eggs. In 1980 there were 136,661 tractors.

Forestry. Czechoslovakia is a richly wooded country, and the timber industry is important. Forest area in 1981 was 4,578,354 hectares (50% spruce, 16% beech and pine, 7% oak). The area reafforested in 1980 was 74,062 hectares. The timber yield was 19·5m. cu. metres in 1980.

INDUSTRY AND TRADE

Industry. Industrialization is well developed and antedates the Communist régime. All industry is nationalized.

Output in 1980 (in 1,000 tonnes): Pig-iron, 9,819; crude steel, 15,225; coke, 10,323; rolled-steel products, 10,760; cement, 10,546; paper, 893; sulphuric acid, 1,284; nitrogenous fertilizers, 618; phosphate fertilizers, 361; plastics, 894; synthetic fibres, 152; sugar, 779; beer, 23·4m. hectolitres; cars, 183,746 (no.).

Textile production (in 1m. metres) in 1980: Cotton, 562; linen, 91; woollen, 59; shoes, 127m. pairs (69·5m. leather).

Labour. There were 8,709,825 persons of employable age in 1980 (*i.e.*, males, 15–59; females 15–54), of whom 7,215,811 were employed (3·3m. women), 5·6m. in production (industry, 2·8m.; agriculture, 953,311; building, 640,898; commerce, 652,314); and 1·7m. in services.

A 5-day 42-hour week with 4 weeks annual holiday is standard. Average monthly wage in 1980: Kčs. 2,640. In 1979 the trade union movement had 6·5m. members.

Commerce. Total trade (in Kčs. 1m.) for calendar years:

	1976	*1977*	*1978*	*1979*	*1980*	*1981*
Imports	55,996	63,213	68,074	75,760	81,540	86,276
Exports	52,137	58,246	63,609	70,156	80,163	87,689

In 1981, trade with Communist countries amounted to 125,174m. Kčs. (67,468m. Kčs. with the USSR, 16,951m. Kčs. with the German Democratic Republic, 11,418m. Kčs. with Poland). The UK is Czechoslovakia's fourth biggest non-Communist trade partner after the Federal German Republic, Austria and Switzerland.

Major exports in 1980 (percentage of total): Machinery, 51·9; industrial consumer goods, 16·7; raw materials and fuel, 27·5. Imports: Machinery, 34·6; raw materials and fuel, 52·7. Oil imports in 1980, 19·3m. tonnes, 98% from USSR.

There are 11 foreign trade agencies (independent legal entities with their own capital run by state-appointed managers). Western firms are permitted to set up their own offices on Czechoslovak soil. Enterprises must obtain agreement from the Ministry of Foreign Trade before trading with foreign firms. Foreign indebtedness was US$1,400m. in 1982; US$3,500m. (1981).

In 1972 an Anglo-Czech Agreement on Co-operation was signed. Under this an Anglo-Czech Joint Commission was established to further the development of trade and industrial and scientific co-operation.

UK-Czechoslovak trade has been conducted since 1 Jan. 1975 on the basis of autonomous EEC measures.

Total trade between Czechoslovakia and UK for calendar years (British Department of Trade returns, in £1,000 sterling):

	1977	*1978*	*1979*	*1980*	*1981*	*1982*
Imports to UK	86,179	85,439	96,577	87,812	70,503	82,007
Exports and re-exports from UK	65,183	73,167	73,801	81,026	70,686	70,105

Tourism. In 1980, 12,769,072 tourists visited Czechoslovakia (684,955 from the West) and 9,244,327 Czechoslovak tourists made visits abroad (266,311 to the West).

COMMUNICATIONS

Roads. In 1980 there were 73,791 km of motorways and first-class roads and 2,273,931 passenger cars. In 1980 state road transport carried 2,063m. passengers and 337m. tonnes of freight.

Railways. In 1982 the length of railway track was 13,131 km. Of this, 3,034 km was electrified. In 1980, 416m. passengers and 286m. tonnes of freight were carried.

Aviation. Air transport is run by ČSA (Czechoslovak Airlines). The main airports are: Prague (Ruzyně), Brno (Cernovice), Bratislava (Vajnory), Olomouc (Holice), Košice (Barca). In 1980, 1·7m. passengers and 25,235 tonnes of freight were flown. There are direct flights from Prague to some 50 cities, including most European capitals, Havana, Jakarta, Conakry, New York and Montreal. British Airways operates air traffic London–Prague, Air France Paris–Prague–Bucharest.

Shipping. In 1983 Czechoslovak Maritime Shipping *(Československá námorní plavba)* (founded 1959) had 14 freighters totalling 264,000 DWT, based on Szczecin. In 1980, 1,711m. tonnes of cargo were carried. Freight transport within Czechoslovakia totalled 8·78m. tonnes. There are fleets on the Danube and Elbe.

Czechoslovak Danube Shipping *(Československá plavba dunajská)* operate 5 ships in the Mediterranean from the port of Bratislava.

Post and Broadcasting. Number of telephones in service in 1980 was 3,150,477. *Československý Rozhlas*, the governmental broadcasting station, broadcasts on 2 networks; 1 from Prague with 3 programmes in Czech and Slovak and 1 from Bratislava with 2 programmes in Slovak and additional broadcasts in Hungarian and Ukrainian. *Československá Televise* broadcast 2 television programmes nation-wide, including colour broadcasts. In 1981, 4·1m. people held wireless and 4·3m. TV licences.

Cinemas and Theatres (1980). There were 3,084 cinemas and 80 theatres. 48 full-length films were made.

Newspapers (1980). There were 30 daily newspapers, including 12 in Slovak. The party daily *Rudé Právo* ('Red Justice') has a circulation of about 1m.

JUSTICE, RELIGION, EDUCATION AND WELFARE

Justice. The criminal and criminal procedure codes date from 1 Jan. 1962, as amended in April 1973.

Police powers were strengthened in July 1974.

There is a Federal Supreme Court and federal military courts, with judges elected by the Federal Assembly. Both republics have Supreme Courts and a network of regional and district courts whose professional judges are elected by the republican National Councils. Lay judges are elected by regional or district local authorities. Local authorities and social organizations may participate in the decision-making of the courts.

Religion. Churches are under the control of the State Secretariat for Church Affairs and the organization Pacem in Terris. In 1977 there were 18 different faiths with 4,860 clergy and 8,228 churches. The largest single church is the Roman Catholic (10m. members, 1983): its main support is in Slovakia. Cardinal

František Tomášek was installed as archbishop of Prague in 1978. The archbishoprics of Trnava and of Olomouc were vacant in 1983. In 1983 there were 5 bishops (the remaining 8 dioceses are directed by Government-appointed capitulary vicars) and 1 archbishop and 5 bishops working among émigrés. There were 3,200 priests in 1983 and 2 seminaries.

In 1981 there were 600,000 Hussites in 5 dioceses, 270,000 Czech Brethren with 272 parishes, 450,000 Slovak Lutherans with 326 parishes, 46,700 Silesian Lutherans and 180,000 Reformed Christians with 310 parishes. In 1981 there were 15,000 Jews (mainly in Prague, where there is a synagogue). The Uniate Church was suppressed in 1950.

Education. In 1980–81 there were 11,119 kindergartens for children from 3 to 6 years of age, with 47,290 teachers and 694,720 pupils. All children receive free education from the ages of 6 to 15, where possible remaining at a single school for the whole 9 years. In 1980–81 there were 6,753 schools with 1,904,476 pupils and 90,380 teachers.

Subsequent education is of 3 types. First, 3 final years of secondary school (in 1980–81, 341 schools with 8,730 teachers and 147,738 pupils). Secondly, technical, teachers' training and other vocational schools (1980–81, 578 schools with 331,334 students). Thirdly, higher education (1980–81, 147,862 full-time students, and 45,138 part-time and correspondence students); academic staff numbered 18,320 in 1980–81. There are 36 institutions of higher education, with 110 faculties. These include 5 universities—the Charles University in Prague (founded 1348); the Purkyně (formerly Masaryk) University in Brno (1919); the Comenius University in Bratislava (1919); the Palacký University in Olomouc (1573); the Šafárik University in Košice (1959); and 12 technical universities or institutes.

Welfare. Medical care is free. In 1980 Kčs. 25,613m. were spent on health insurance benefits. There were, in 1980, 226 hospitals with a total of 119,376 beds, and 49,826 doctors and dentists. Family allowances (Kčs. per month): 1 child, 140; 2 children, 530; 3, 1,030. Old age pensions averaging 67% of salary are paid at the age of 60 (men), 53–57 (women).

DIPLOMATIC REPRESENTATIVES

Of Czechoslovakia in Great Britain (25 Kensington Palace Gdns., London, W8 4QY)
Ambassador: Dr Zdeněk Černík (accredited on 16 Nov. 1977).

Of Great Britain in Czechoslovakia (Thunovská 14, Prague 1)
Ambassador: J. R. Rich, CMG.

Of Czechoslovakia in the USA (3900 Linnean Ave., NW, Washington, D.C., 20008)
Ambassador: Jaroslav Zantovsky.

Of the USA in Czechoslovakia (Tržiste 15–12548 Praha, Prague)
Ambassador: J. F. Matlock, Jr.

Of Czechoslovakia to the United Nations
Ambassador: Dr Stanislav Suja.

Books of Reference

The Constitution of the Czechoslovak Socialist Republic [English ed.]. Prague, 1960
Statistická ročenka ČSSR [Statistical Yearbook]. Prague, annual since 1958
Czechoslovak Foreign Trade. Prague, monthly
Socialist Czechoslovakia. Prague, 1976
Bradley, J. F. N. *Politics in Czechoslovakia, 1945–1971.* Lanham, 1981
Czechoslovak Chamber of Commerce and Industry. *Facts on Czechoslovak Foreign Trade.* Prague, annual since 1967.—*Your Trade Partners in Czechoslovakia.* Prague, 1979
Demek, J., and others, *Geography of Czechoslovakia.* Prague, 1971
Eidlin, F. H. *The Logic of 'Normalization': The Soviet Intervention in Czechoslovakia of 21*

August 1968 and the Czechoslovak Response. Columbia Univ. Press, 1980
Hermann, A. H., *A History of the Czechs.* London, 1975
Hejzlar, Z., and Kusin, V. V., *Czechoslovakia, 1968–1969.* New York, 1975
Jičinský, J., and Skála, J. *The Czechoslovak Federation,* Prague, 1969
Kalvoda, J., *Czechoslovakia's Role in Soviet Strategy.* Washington, 1981
Kolafová, V., and Slaba, D. *Czech-English and English-Czech dictionary.* Prague, 1979
Korbel, J., *Twentieth-Century Czechoslovakia: The Meanings of its History.* Columbia Univ. Press, 1977
Krejčí, *Social Change and Stratification in Postwar Czechoslovakia.* London, 1972
Krystufek, Z., *The Soviet Régime in Czechoslovakia.* Columbia Univ. Press, 1981
Kusin, V. V., *From Dubček to Charter 77.* Edinburgh, 1978
Littell, R. (ed.), *The Czech Black Book; prepared by the Institute of History of the Czechoslovak Academy of Sciences.* London, 1969
Mamatey, V. S., and Luža, R. (eds.), *A History of the Czechoslovak Republic 1918–1948.* Princeton Univ. Press, 1973
Mlynař, Z., *Night Frost in Prague: the End of Humane Socialism.* New York, 1980
Oxley, A., Pravda, A., Richie, A., *Czechoslovakia: The Party and the People.* New York, 1973
Procházka, J., *English–Czech and Czech–English Dictionary.* 16th ed. London, 1959
Sejna, J. *We will bury you.* London, 1982
Šik, O., *Czechoslovakia: The Bureaucratic Economy.* New York, 1972
Sperling. W., *Tschechoslowakei: Beiträge zur Landeskunde Ostmitteleurapas.* Stuttgart, 1981
Suda, Z. L., *Zealots and Rebels: A History of the Communist Party in Czechoslovakia.* Stanford, 1980
Teplý, J., *Economie Nationale de la Tchécoslovaquie Contemporaine.* Paris, 1977
Ulč, O., *Politics in Czechoslovakia.* San Francisco, 1974
Wallace, W. V., *Czechoslovakia.* London, 1977

DENMARK

Kongeriget Danmark

Capital: Copenhagen
Population: 5·12m. (1982)
GNP per capita: US$12,950 (1980)

HISTORY. First organized as a unified state in the 10th century, Denmark acquired approximately its present boundaries in 1815, having ceded Norway to Sweden and its north German territory to Prussia. Denmark became a constitutional monarchy in 1849.

AREA AND POPULATION. According to the census held on 9 Nov. 1970 the area of Denmark proper was 43,075 sq. km (16,631 sq. miles) and the population 4,937,579. Population, Jan. 1982: 5,119,155.

Administrative divisions		*Area (sq. km) 1982*	*Population 1970*	*Population 1982*	*Population 1982 per sq. km*
København (Copenhagen)	(city)	88	622,773	490,587	5,570
Frederiksberg	(borough)	9	101,874	88,047	10,040
Københavns	(county)	522	615,343	622,504	1,192
Frederiksborg	,,	1,347	259,442	329,815	245
Roskilde	,,	891	153,199	203,975	229
Vestsjællands	,,	2,984	259,057	278,117	93
Storstrøms	,,	3,398	252,363	259,624	76
Bornholms	,,	588	47,239	47,357	81
Fyns	,,	3,486	432,699	453,799	130
Sønderjyllands	,,	3,930	238,062	250,409	64
Ribe	,,	3,131	197,843	214,104	68
Vejle	,,	2,997	306,263	326,760	109
Ringkøbing	,,	4,853	241,327	263,880	54
Aarhus	,,	4,561	533,190	576,705	127
Viborg	,,	4,122	220,734	231,428	56
Nordjyllands	,,	6,173	456,171	482,044	78
Total		43,080	4,937,579	5,119,155	119

The population is almost entirely Scandinavian; in July 1976, of the inhabitants of Denmark proper, 97·2% were born in Denmark, including Faroe Islands and Greenland.

On 1 Jan. 1982 the population of the capital, Copenhagen (comprising Copenhagen, Frederiksberg and Gentofte municipalities), was 645,198 (including suburbs, 1,377,064); Aarhus, 246,679; Odense, 170,189; Aalborg, 154,218; Esbjerg, 80,053; Randers, 62,134; Kolding, 56,321; Helsingør, 56,163; Herning, 55,905; Horsens, 54,565.

Vital statistics for calendar years:

	Living births	*Still births*	*Marriages*	*Divorces*	*Deaths*	*Emigration*	*Immigration*
1977	61,878	369	32,174	13,383	50,485	26,906	32,740
1978	62,036	364	28,763	13,072	52,864	26,735	32,059
1979	59,464	309	27,842	13,044	54,654	27,731	33,183
1980	57,293	253	26,448	13,593	55,939	29,913	30,311
1981	53,089	281	25,411	14,425	56,359	29,719	27,874

Illegitimate births: 1978, 27·9%; 1979, 30·7%; 1980, 33·2%; 1981, 35·8%.

REIGNING QUEEN. Margrethe II, born 16 April 1940; married 10 June 1967 to Prince Henrik, born Count de Monpezat; *offspring:* Crown Prince Frederik, born 26 May 1968; Prince Joachim, born 7 June 1969. She succeeded to the throne on the death of her father, King Frederik IX, on 14 Jan. 1972.

Mother of the Queen: Queen Ingrid, born Princess of Sweden, 28 March 1910.

Sisters of the Queen: Princess Benedikte, born 29 April 1944 (married 3 Feb. 1968 to Prince Richard of Sayn-Wittgenstein-Berleburg); Princess Anne-Marie, born 30 Aug. 1946 (married 18 Sept. 1964 to King Constantine of Greece).

The crown of Denmark was elective from the earliest times. In 1448 after the death of the last male descendant of Swein Estridsen the Danish Diet elected to the throne Christian I, Count of Oldenburg, in whose family the royal dignity remained for more than 4 centuries, although the crown was not rendered hereditary by right till 1660. The direct male line of the house of Oldenburg became extinct with King Frederik VII on 15 Nov. 1863. In view of the death of the king, without direct heirs, the Great Powers signed a treaty at London on 8 May 1852, by the terms of which the succession to the crown of Denmark was made over to Prince Christian of Schleswig-Holstein-Sonderburg-Glücksburg, and to the direct male descendants of his union with the Princess Louise of Hesse-Cassel, niece of King Christian VIII of Denmark. In accordance with this treaty, a law concerning the succession to the Danish crown was adopted by the Diet, and obtained the royal sanction 31 July 1853. Linked to the constitution of 5 June 1953, a new law of succession, dated 27 March 1953, has come into force, which restricts the right of succession to the descendants of King Christian X and Queen Alexandrine, and admits the sovereign's daughters to the line of succession, ranking after the sovereign's sons.

Subjoined is a list of the kings of Denmark, with the dates of their accession, from the time of election of Christian I of Oldenburg:

House of Oldenburg

Christian I	1448	Christian IV	1588	Frederik V	1746
Hans	1481	Frederik III	1648	Christian VII	1766
Christian II	1513	Christian V	1670	Frederik VI	1808
Frederik I	1523	Frederik IV	1699	Christian VIII	1839
Christian III	1534	Christian VI	1730	Frederik VII	1848
Frederik II	1559				

House of Schleswig-Holstein-Sonderburg-Glücksburg

Christian IX	1863	Christian X	1912	Margrethe II	1972
Frederik VIII	1906	Frederik IX	1947		

CONSTITUTION AND GOVERNMENT. The present constitution of Denmark is founded upon the 'Grundlov' (charter) of 5 June 1953.

The legislative power lies with the Queen and the *Folketing* (Diet) jointly. The executive power is vested in the Queen, who exercises her authority through the ministers. The judicial power is with the courts. The Queen must be a member of the Evangelical-Lutheran Church, the official Church of the State. The Queen cannot assume major international obligations without the consent of the *Folketing*. The *Folketing* consists of one chamber. All men and women of Danish nationality of more than 18 years of age and permanently resident in Denmark possess the franchise and are eligible for election to the *Folketing*, which is at present composed of 179 members; 135 members are elected by the method of proportional representation in 17 districts. In order to attain an equal representation of the different parties, 40 *tillægsmandater* (additional seats) are divided among such parties which have not obtained sufficient returns at the district elections. Two members are elected for the Faroe Islands and 2 for Greenland. The term of the legislature is 4 years, but a general election may be called at any time.

The *Folketing* must meet every year on the first Tuesday in October. Besides its legislative functions, it appoints every 6 years judges who, together with the ordinary members of the Supreme Court *(Højesteret)*, form the *Rigsret*, a tribunal which can alone try parliamentary impeachments. The ministers have free access to the House, but can vote only if they are members.

Folketing, elected 8 Dec. 1981: 59 Social Democrats, 9 Radical Liberals, 26 Conservatives, 21 Socialist People's Party, 15 Centre Democrats, 4 Christian People's Party, 20 Liberals, 5 Left Socialists, 16 Progress Party, 2 Faroe Islands and 2 Greenland representatives.

The executive (called the State Council *(Statsraadet)* when acting with the Queen presiding) is a minority non-Socialist coalition government, consisting of the Conservatives, the Liberals, the Centre Democrats and the Christian People's Party; it was in Jan. 1983 as follows:

Prime Minister: Poul Schlüter.

Foreign Affairs: Uffe Ellemann-Jensen. *Finance:* Henning Christophersen. *Economy:* Anders Andersen. *Industry:* Ib Stetter. *Greenland:* Tom Høyem. *Social Affairs:* Palle Simonsen. *Agriculture:* Niels Anker Kofoed. *Fisheries:* Henning Grove. *Education:* Bertel Haarder. *Culture:* Mimi Stilling Jakobsen. *Defence:* Hans Engell. *Labour:* Grethe Fenger Møller. *Housing:* Niels Bollman. *Inland Revenue:* Isi Foighel. *Energy:* Knud Enggaard. *Interior:* Britta Schall Holberg. *Justice:* Erik Ninn-Hansen. *Environment and Nordic Affairs:* Christian Christensen. *Public Works:* Arne Melchior. *Ecclesiastical Affairs:* Elsebeth Kock-Petersen.

The ministers are individually and collectively responsible for their acts, and if impeached and found guilty, cannot be pardoned without the consent of the *Folketing.*

In 1948 a separate legislature *(Lagting)* and executive *(Landsstyre)* were established for the Faroe Islands, to deal with specified local matters and in 1979 a separate legislature *(Landsting)* and executive *(Landsstyre)* were established for Greenland, also to deal with specified local matters.

National flag: Red with white Scandinavian cross (Dannebrog).

National anthems: Kong Kristian stod ved højen Mast (words by J. Ewald, 1778; tune by J. E. Hartmann, 1780) and Der er et yndigt land.

Local Government. For administrative purposes Denmark is divided into 275 municipalities *(kommuner)*; each of them has a district council of between 5 and 25 members, headed by an elected mayor. The city of Copenhagen forms a district by itself and is governed by a city council of 55 members, elected every 4 years, and an executive *(magistraten)*, consisting of the chief burgomaster *(overborgmesteren)* and 6 burgomasters, appointed by the city council for 4 years. There are 14 counties *(amtskommuner)*, each of which is administered by a county council *(amstråd)* of between 13 and 31 members, headed by an elected mayor. All councils are elected directly by universal suffrage and proportional representation for 4-year terms. A third council, the Metropolitan Council, with a constitution similar to the counties was established 1 April 1974. The Metropolitan Council is responsible for overall development within Metropolitan Copenhagen.

The counties and Copenhagen are superintended by a ministry of interior affairs. The municipalities are superintended by 14 local supervision committees, headed by a state county prefect *(statsamtmand)* who is a civil servant appointed by the Queen.

DEFENCE. The Danish military defence is organized in accordance with the Defence Act of May 1982 and the overall organization of the Danish Armed Forces comprises the Defence Command, the Army, the Navy, the Air Force and inter-service authorities and institutions. To this should be added the Home Guard, which is an indispensable part of Danish military defence. The Home Guard is based on the Home Guard Act of May 1982.

In accordance with the Defence Act the Chief of Defence has full command of the three services: the Army, the Navy and the Air Force. The Chief of Defence, and the Defence Staff constitute the Defence Command. The Inspector Generals of the Army, the Navy and the Air Force are members of the Defence Staff.

The Minister of Defence is assisted by a Defence Council consisting of the Chief of Defence, the Chief of Defence Staff, the Chief of Danish Operational Forces, the Inspector Generals of the Army, the Navy and the Air Force and the Chief of the Home Guard.

The Constitution of 1849 declared it the duty of every fit man to contribute to the national defence, and this provision is still in force. According to the Personnel Act of May 1982, the military personnel comprises officers, n.c.o.s and privates. Private personnel are provided by enlistment and by recruiting of volunteers. Selection of conscripts takes place at the age of 18–19 years, and the conscripts are normally called up for 9 months service ½–1½ years later. Afterwards conscripts may be recalled for refresher training or musters.

Army. The peace-time Army strength is about 22,000. The Army comprises field army formations and the local defence forces. The field army formations are organized in an operationally balanced covering force and in reserve units. The covering force numbers about 13,000 men and comprises a standing force, and a supplementary force consisting of men newly released from service. This force is part of the field army reserve which numbers 41,000. The standing force number about 7,000 men organized in standing brigade units, headquarters units and support units. The brigade units are organized in 5 mechanized infantry brigades. The field army is equipped with 200 medium battle tanks and about 650 armoured personnel carriers as well as artillery including 72 self-propelled howitzers. The local defence units consist of about 24,000 men organized in 21 infantry battalions and 7 artillery battalions. The men of the latest annual service groups form the troops of the line, while those of the previous years form the local defence, the reserve and the reserve for the Home Guard. The mobilization units of the field army and the local defence force will total about 59,000 men.

Navy. The Navy comprises the fleet and coast-defence which includes several permanent fortifications. The fleet includes 5 submarines, 2 frigates, 5 ocean escorts (for fishery protection and surveying duties), 3 corvettes, 10 fast missile craft, 6 fast torpedo boats, 4 ocean minelayers, 3 coastal minelayers, 6 coastal minesweepers, 2 torpedo recovery vessels, 22 patrol vessels, 8 coastal patrol launches, 2 oilers and the royal yacht. The Naval Air Arm comprises 8 helicopters (one is carried in each of the ocean escorts).

Total strength of the Navy is about 8,400 officers and men, and the mobilization force about 4,000 men.

Air Force. The operational units of the Air Force comprise 6 surface-to-air missile squadrons and 6 flying squadrons with a total of 104 aircraft.

The air defence force consists of the 6 surface-to-air missile squadrons and 2 all-weather air-defence squadrons with a unit establishment of 20 CF-104G/F-104G Starfighters.

The fighter bomber force comprises 3 squadrons with a unit establishment of 16 F-16 and F 35 Drakens, and 1 reconnaissance squadron with a unit establishment of 16 RF 35 Drakens.

In addition the Air Force has a number of supplementary units, including 1 transport squadron (C-130 Hercules and Gulfstream III), 1 helicopter rescue squadron (S-61As), and a control and warning system.

Total strength of the Air Force is about 9,800, and the mobilization force about 9,000 men.

Home Guard. The overall Home Guard organization comprises the Home Guard Command, the Army Home Guard, the Navy Home Guard and the Air Force Home Guard.

The personnel of the Home Guard is recruited on a voluntary basis. The personnel establishment of the Home Guard is at present about 77,000 persons (59,300 in the Army Home Guard, 5,300 in the Navy Home Guard and 12,400 in the Air Force Home Guard).

INTERNATIONAL RELATIONS

Membership. Denmark is a member of UN, NATO, OECD and EEC.

ECONOMY

Budget. The budget *(Finanslovforslag)* must be laid before the Parliament *(Folketing)* not later than 4 months before the beginning of a new fiscal year.

The following shows the actual revenue and expenditure as shown in central government accounts for the calendar years 1979, 1980 and 1981, the approved budget figures for 1982 and the budget for 1983 (in 1,000 kroner):

	1979	*1980*	*1981*	*1982*	*1983*
Revenue	98,199,458	106,707,623	111,997,031	119,489,309	117,089,166
Expenditure	111,259,378	124,602,838	145,863,972	167,100,097	190,805,896

Receipts and expenditures of special government funds and expenditures on public works are included.

The 1982 budget envisages revenue of 62,327m. kroner from income and property taxes and 78,193m. from consumer taxes.

The central government debt on 31 Dec. 1981 amounted to 190,271m. kroner.

Currency. The monetary unit is the *krone* of 100 *øre*. In 1931 Denmark went off the gold standard, as established in 1873.

Small change: 10-kroner and 5-kroner pieces of copper-nickel, 1-krone pieces of copper-nickel; 25-øre and 10-øre pieces of copper-nickel, and 5-øre pieces of copper–steel–copper clad. In March 1983, £1 = 13·02 *kroner*; US$1 = 8·64 *kroner*.

Banking. On 31 Dec. 1981 the accounts of the National Bank balanced at 98,275m. kroner. The assets included 5,741m. kroner in gold bullion. The liabilities included 14,018m. kroner note issue, 12,384m. kroner general capital fund and reserve fund. On 31 Dec. 1981 there were 157 savings banks, with 6·4m. accounts and deposits of 53,922m. kroner. Their advances amounted to 42,673m. kroner.

On 31 Dec. 1981 there were 73 other banks for commercial, agricultural and industrial purposes; their deposits amounted to 125,183m. kroner; advances were 93,936m. kroner.

Weights and Measures. The use of the metric system of weights and measures has been obligatory in Denmark since 1 April 1912.

ENERGY AND NATURAL RESOURCES

Electricity. Owing to the concentration of power production, the number of generating power stations has declined from 371 in 1949–50 to 23 in 1980, while the net power production (in 1m. kwh.) has risen from 1,689 in 1949–50 to 23,520 in 1980.

Agriculture. Land ownership is widely distributed. In 1981 the total number of farms was 115,465. There were 34,309 small holdings (with less than 10 hectares), 68,922 medium sized holdings (10–50 hectares) and 12,234 holdings with more than 50 hectares.

The number of agricultural workers declined from 120,442 in July 1961 to 24,942 in June 1981, while the index of production was 100 in 1975 and 114 in 1979.

In June 1981 the cultivated area was utilized as follows (in 1,000 hectares): Grain, 1,787; peas and beans, 4; root crops, 245; other crops, 203; green fodder and grass, 656; fallow, 2; total cultivated area, 2,897.

	Area (1,000 hectares)			*Production (in 1,000 tonnes)*		
Chief crops	*1979*	*1980*	*1981*	*1979*	*1980*	*1981*
Wheat	114	139	150	589	652	835
Rye	70	56	50	257	199	208
Barley	1,622	1,577	1,541	6,662	6,044	6,044
Oats	39	40	42	163	159	176
Mixed grain	5	4	4	19	16	14
Potatoes	32	34	36	844	842	1,053
Other root crops	215	207	209	10,110	9,261	10,277

Livestock, 1981: Horses, 44,000; cattle, 2,914,000; pigs, 9,799,000; sheep, 55,000; poultry, 15,339,000.

Production (in 1,000 tonnes) in 1981: Milk, 5,037; butter, 109; cheese, 243; beef, 255; pork and bacon, 1,049; eggs, 79.

In June 1981 farm tractors numbered 181,349 and harvester-threshers, 38,362.

Fisheries. The total value of the fish caught was (in 1m. kroner): 1950, 156; 1955, 252; 1960, 376; 1965, 650; 1970, 854; 1975, 1,442; 1979, 2,888. The fishing fleet in 1977 consisted of 7,340 motor boats, 182 sailing boats and 2,761 rowing boats.

INDUSTRY AND TRADE

Industry. The following table sets forth the gross factor income (in 1m. kroner) by industrial origin in 3 calendar years:

	1979 Current Prices	1979 1975 Prices	1980 Current Prices	1980 1975 Prices	1981 Current Prices	1981 1975 Prices
Agriculture, fur-farming, forestry, etc.	14,563	10,718	15,358	10,916	18,021	12,038
Fishing	1,507	955	1,575	872	1,778	1,006
Total	16,070	11,673	16,933	11,788	19,799	13,044
Mining and quarrying	599	405	418	184	1,482	905
Manufacturing	56,984	44,173	61,135	44,167	66,606	44,404
Electricity, gas and water	4,589	3,838	5,058	4,250	5,784	3,594
Construction	21,314	15,871	19,745	13,818	19,058	11,490
Total	83,486	64,286	86,357	62,718	92,931	59,893
Wholesale and retail trade	42,817	34,248	46,298	32,895	51,149	32,643
Restaurants and hotels	3,853	2,381	4,230	2,419	4,420	2,366
Transport and storage	20,594	16,039	22,073	15,963	25,298	16,145
Communication	4,073	3,749	4,239	3,881	4,665	3,911
Financing and insurance	10,289	7,359	10,558	7,036	11,189	6,925
Dwellings	27,811	17,307	30,027	17,139	33,600	18,118
Business services	12,024	8,480	13,349	8,871	15,320	8,946
Market services of education, health	4,189	3,435	4,614	3,559	5,356	3,610
Recreational and cultural services	2,703	2,022	2,909	2,113	3,171	2,038
Household services, incl. auto repair	8,117	5,830	8,422	5,480	9,722	5,664
Total	136,471	100,849	146,719	99,356	163,890	100,365
Other producers, excl. government	1,998	1,299	2,303	1,379	2,570	1,386
Producers of government services	64,160	47,478	72,828	49,771	83,360	51,572
Total	66,158	48,777	75,132	51,150	85,930	52,958
Imputed bank service charges	÷ 9,868	÷ 7,043	÷ 9,816	÷ 6,432	÷ 11,048	÷ 6,533
Gross domestic product at factor cost	292,317	218,542	315,325	218,279	351,502	219,727
Plus indirect taxes	65,759	30,175	69,827	27,729	75,123	26,467
Less subsidies	11,184		11,855		12,516	
Gross domestic product at market prices	346,892	248,717	373,297	246,009	414,109	246,193

According to the registration of business units for VAT settlement there were in 1979 a total of 36,000 manufacturing enterprises. In the following table 'number of wage-earners' refers to 6,900 establishments with 6 employees or more, while 'gross-output' and 'value-added' cover 3,100 kind-of-activity units of enterprises with 20 employees or more.

Branch of industry	*Number of wage-earners (1,000)*	*Gross output in factor values (1m. kroner)*	*Value added in factor values (1m. kroner)*
Mining and quarrying	1·1	339	262
Food products	47·6	46,182	11,304
Beverages	9·0	3,897	2,493
Tobacco	2·5	1,056	557
Textiles	11·2	4,177	1,909
Wearing apparel	10·4	2,128	1,118
Leather and products	1·2	314	147
Footwear	2·3	585	284
Wood products	7·9	2,680	1,180

Branch of industry	Number of wage-earners (1,000)	Gross output in factor values (1m. kroner)	Value added in factor values (1m. kroner)
Furniture and fixtures	10·1	2,633	1,427
Paper and products	6·7	3,253	1,552
Printing, publishing	15·8	6,635	4,481
Industrial chemicals	6·8	5,621	2,713
Other chemical products, petroleum refineries and petroleum coal products	6·3	14,031	3,434
Rubber products	2·2	665	378
Plastic products	6·4	2,321	1,236
Pottery, china, etc.	3·2	498	431
Glass and products	2·4	805	476
Non-metal products	12·8	5,305	3,173
Iron and steel	4·5	1,874	848
Non-ferrous metals	1·7	1,132	354
Metal products	23·8	7,768	3,964
Machinery	40·8	14,219	7,861
Electrical machinery	17·2	6,766	3,735
Transport equipment	21·1	6,938	3,249
Professional goods	5·3	2,238	1,410
Other industries	4·2	1,477	908
Total manufacturing	284·1	145,197	60,622

Labour. In 1981, 7% of the working population lived on agriculture, forestry and fishery, 25% on industries and handicrafts, 8% on construction, 15% on commerce, etc., 7% on transport and communication, and 38% on administration, professional services, etc.

Commerce. The following table shows the value, in 1,000 kroner, of special trade imports and exports (including trade with the Faroe Islands and Greenland) for calendar years:

	1976	1977	1978	1979	1980	1981[1]
Imports	75,010,879	79,636,962	81,405,158	96,838,868	109,388,313	124,675,712
Exports	55,034,147	60,436,289	65,307,647	77,361,446	95,670,845	113,802,452

[1] Preliminary.

Imports and exports (in 1,000 kroner) for calendar years:

Leading commodities	1980 Imports	1980 Exports	1981[1] Imports	1981[1] Exports
Live animals, meat, etc.	124,720	13,521,884	156,680	16,607,827
Dairy products, eggs	449,074	4,838,310	735,939	5,945,120
Fish and fish preparations	1,831,661	4,520,125	2,123,780	5,401,518
Cereals and cereal preparations	896,514	2,017,789	1,215,494	1,732,143
Sugar and sugar preparations	470,302	1,139,612	509,158	1,312,191
Coffee, tea, cocoa, etc.	1,746,067	352,069	1,812,573	443,083
Feeding stuff for animals	2,958,357	1,238,331	4,072,656	1,471,959
Wood, lumber and cork	1,730,172	335,027	1,366,753	390,298
Textiles, fibres, yarns, fabrics, etc.	4,092,610	2,474,208	4,393,599	2,702,449
Fuels, lubricants, etc.	24,138,633	2,804,845	23,471,547	3,187,008
Pharmaceutical products	1,157,913	2,082,930	1,386,558	2,643,050
Fertilizers, etc.	1,376,037	498,976	1,593,877	636,912
Metals, manufactures of metals	10,107,393	5,202,563	10,342,416	5,417,847
Machinery, electric, equipment, etc.	16,755,173	19,113,440	17,810,357	21,805,767
Transport equipment	5,698,280	3,664,411	8,158,644	6,087,018

[1] Preliminary.

Distribution of Danish foreign trade (in 1,000 kroner) according to countries of origin and destination, for calendar years:

Countries	Imports 1979	Imports 1980	Imports 1981[1]	Exports 1979	Exports 1980	Exports 1981[1]
Belgium	3,562,935	3,757,608	4,446,723	1,462,125	1,831,793	1,972,551
Finland	3,680,824	4,151,943	4,602,208	1,485,067	2,034,863	2,336,552
France	4,588,115	4,739,490	5,039,312	3,785,120	4,919,660	5,464,901
Germany (Fed. Rep.)	19,134,648	20,127,384	23,095,245	13,510,004	18,054,729	18,926,173
Norway	4,019,432	4,501,863	5,332,014	4,660,440	5,984,759	7,040,851

[1] Preliminary.

	Imports			Exports		
Countries	*1979*	*1980*	*1981* [1]	*1979*	*1980*	*1981* [1]
Sweden	12,318,620	13,969,307	14,952,582	10,394,318	11,927,330	13,037,417
Switzerland	1,664,146	1,846,237	2,033,911	1,519,726	2,119,119	2,637,154
UK	11,500,165	13,262,568	14,671,365	11,523,793	13,693,651	15,877,792
USA	5,055,238	6,988,269	11,122,911	3,697,386	4,262,046	6,013,884
Allied forces in Fed. Rep. Germany	—	—	—	119,873	139,772	146,581

[1] Preliminary.

Total trade between Denmark (without the Faroe Islands) and UK (British Department of Trade returns, in £1,000 sterling):

	1978	*1979*	*1980*	*1981*	*1982*
Imports to UK	962,464	1,081,247	1,103,590	1,179,065	1,335,640
Exports and re-exports from UK	841,377	1,016,403	1,032,525	2,812,957	1,096,642

Tourism. In 1981, foreigners visiting Denmark spent some 8,948m. kroner. In 1981 foreigners spent 4·48m. nights in hotels and 4·07 nights at camping sites.

Industrial Statistics. Danmarks Statistik. Copenhagen (annually)
Quarterly Statistics for the Industry: Commodity Statistics. Danmarks Statistik, Copenhagen
Statistics on Agriculture, Horticulture and Forestry. Danmarks Statistik. Copenhagen (annually)
Agriculture in Denmark. Agricultural Council of Denmark. Copenhagen, 1972
Agricultural Statistics 1900–1965. Vol. I: *Agricultural Area and Harvest and Utilization of Fertilizers.*—Vol. II: *Livestock and Livestock Products, and Consumption of Feeding Stuffs.* Danmarks Statistik. Copenhagen, 1968–69
External Trade of Denmark. Danmarks Statistik, Copenhagen
Danish Industry in Facts and Figures. Federation of Danish Industries. Copenhagen (annually)
Energy Supply of Denmark, 1900–58 and *1948–65.* Danmarks Statistik. Copenhagen, 1959, 1967. Annual Supplements 1966–75 have been published in Statistical News
Report on Fisheries. Ministry of Fisheries, Copenhagen (annually)
Nash, E. F., and Attwood, E. A., *The Agricultural Policies of Britain and Denmark.* London, 1961
The 1,000 Largest Companies in Denmark. 8th ed. Copenhagen, 1975

COMMUNICATIONS

Roads. Denmark proper had (1 Jan. 1980), 464 km of motorways, 4,199 km of other state roads, 6,840 km of provincial roads and 56,691 km of commercial roads. Motor vehicles registered at 31 Dec. 1980 comprised 1,379,085 passenger cars, 251,801 lorries, 10,462 taxicabs (including 3,118 for private hire), 7,351 buses and 34,362 cycles.

Railways. There were in 1980 railways of a total length of 2,556 km open for traffic. Of this total, 2,015 km belong to the State. In 1980 the state railways carried 7m. tonnes of freight and 129m. passengers.

Aviation. On 1 Oct. 1950 the 3 Scandinavian airlines, Det Danske Luftfartsselskab, ABA and DNL, combined in Scandinavian Airlines System. In 1980 SAS flew 118·6m. km and carried 8,301,200 passengers.

SAS inaugurated its transpolar routes Copenhagen–Los Angeles on 15 Nov. 1954 and Copenhagen–Tōkyō on 25 Feb. 1957, and its trans-Asian express route Copenhagen–Bangkok–Singapore *via* Tashkent on 4 Nov. 1967.

Shipping. On 31 Dec. 1980 the Danish merchant fleet consisted of 2,967 vessels (above 20 GRT) of 5,213,838 GRT.

In 1980, 43,188 vessels of 33m. NRT entered the Danish ports, unloading 46m. tonnes and loading 15m. tonnes of cargo; traffic by passenger ships and ferries is not included.

Post and Broadcasting. There were, in 1980, 1,321 post offices. On 31 Dec. 1980 the length of telephone circuits of private companies was 11,353,117 km. On 31 Dec. 1980 there were 3,316,709 telephone subscribers (including those in the

Faroe Islands and Greenland). Postal revenues, 1980, 4,504m. kroner; expenditure, 4,818m. kroner.

Danmarks Radio is the government broadcasting station and is financed by licence fees. Television is broadcast by *Danmarks Radio* with colour programmes by PAL system. Number of receivers: Radio, 1·95m.; television, 1·86m., including 1·27m. colour sets.

Cinemas. In 1981 there were 471 cinemas with a seating capacity of 102,953.

Newspapers. In 1981 there were 48 daily newspapers with a combined circulation of 1·88m. on weekdays; 10 of them (905,000) appeared in Copenhagen.

JUSTICE, RELIGION, EDUCATION AND WELFARE

Justice. The lowest courts of justice are organized in 84 tribunals *(byretter)*, where cases are dealt with by a single judge. The tribunals at Copenhagen have 34 judges, Aarhus 13, Odense 10, Aalborg 9, and the other tribunals have 1 to 4. Cases of greater consequence are dealt with by the superior courts *(Landsretterne)*; these courts are also courts of appeal for the above-named cases. Of superior courts there are two: *Østre Landsret* in Copenhagen with 46 judges, *Vestre Landret* in Viborg with 23 judges. From these an appeal lies to the Supreme Court *(Højesteret)* in Copenhagen, composed of 16 judges. Judges under 70 years of age can be removed only by judicial sentence.

In 1978, 10,953 men and 867 women were convicted of crimes and delicts, fines not included. In 1981, the daily average population in penal institutions, local prisons, etc, was 3,352 men and 145 women, of whom 971 men and 67 women were on remand.

Religion. At the Reformation in 1536 the Danish Church ceased to exist as a legally independent unit, a part of the Roman Catholic Church, and became instead a Lutheran Church under the direction of the State. Since that time the State has, in one form or another, continued to exercise supreme authority in the affairs of the Church, and has regulated these by the passing of laws, by royal decree, or other appropriate means. The great majority of Danish citizens (about 90%) belongs to the National Church. Administratively, Denmark is divided into 10 dioceses each with a Bishop who, within the framework of the law, is the supreme diocesan authority in ecclesiastical affairs. The Bishop together with the Chief Administrative Officer of the county make up the diocesan governing body, responsible for all matters of ecclesiastical local finance and general administration. Bishops are appointed by the Crown after an election at which the clergy and parish council members of the diocese have had the opportunity of voting for the candidates nominated. Each diocese is divided into a number of deaneries (about 107 in the whole country) each with its Dean and Deanery Committee, who have certain financial powers. Local government at parish level (there are about 2,200 parishes in all) is in the hands of Parish Councils, who are elected for a 4-year period of office.

Since the Constitution of 1849 complete religious toleration is extended to every sect, and no civil disabilities attach to Dissenters.

Kjær, J. C., *History of the Church of Denmark.* Blair, Nebr., 1945
Roesen, August, *Religion in Denmark.* Copenhagen, 1963

Education. Education has been compulsory since 1814. The *folkeskole* (public primary and lower secondary school) comprises a pre-school class *(børnehaveklassen)*, a 9-year basic school corresponding to the period of compulsory education and 1-year voluntary tenth form. Compulsory education may be fulfilled either through attending the *folkeskole* or private schools or through home-instruction, the only requirement being that the instruction given should be comparable to that offered in the *folkeskole. Folkeskolen* are mainly municipal and no fees are paid. In the year 1981–82, 2,288 primary and lower secondary schools had 776,781 pupils and employed 65,234 teachers. Approximately 12% of the total number of schools were private schools and they were attended by 8% of the total number of pupils. The 9-year basic school is in practice not streamed. However, a certain differentiation may take place in the eighth and ninth forms.

After the completion of the eighth and ninth forms the pupils may sit for the leaving examination of the *folkeskole (folkeskolens afgangsprøve)*. After the completion of the tenth form the pupils may sit for either the leaving examination of the *folkeskole (folkeskolens afgangsprøve)* or the advanced leaving examination of the *folkeskole (folkeskolens udvidede afgangsprøve)*.

Under certain conditions the pupils may continue their education either in a 3-year gymnasium ending with *studentereksamen* or in the 2-year higher preparatory school ending with the *højere forberedelseseksamen*. There were (1981–82) 143 of these upper secondary schools with 75,879 pupils and 7,368 teachers.

Youth and leisure-time education: 278 schools (continuation schools, youth residential schools, home economics schools, folk high schools, youth high schools and agricultural schools) with 24,313 pupils.

Vocational education and training consists of Basic Vocational Training in trade and commerce with 47,600 students, and 30,000 receive training in technical education. There are 10,000 apprentices who receive training in the field of trade and commerce, and 46,900 trainees in the technical branches. Finally, 11,800 students are admitted to the diploma courses for trade and commerce, and 6,900 students are admitted to the technical diploma courses. In 1981–82, vocational education and training totalled 153,300 students.

There were 29 teacher-training colleges with 10,766 students and 26 colleges for training of teachers for kindergartens and leisure-time activities with 6,588 students.

Degree-courses in engineering: The Technical University of Denmark had 3,502 students. The Engineering Academy had 1,344 students and 8 engineering colleges with 3,440 students.

Universities: The University of Copenhagen (founded 1479) 24,852 students. The University of Aarhus (founded in 1928) 12,263 students. The University of Odense (founded in 1964) 4,851 students. Roskilde University Centre (founded in 1972) 2,196 students. Aalborg University Centre (founded in 1974) 3,066 students.

Other types of post-secondary education: The Royal Veterinary and Agricultural College had 2,176 students. The two dental colleges had 1,217 students. The Danish School of Pharmacy had 713 students. The 11 colleges of economics and business administration had 14,896 students. The 2 schools of architecture had 2,082 students. Five academies of music had 758 students. The Danish School of Librarianship had 960 students. The Royal Danish School of Educational Studies had 2,023 students. The Danish State Institute of Physical Education had 185 students. The 4 schools of social work had 880 students. The Danish School of Journalism had 405 students. Six colleges of physical therapy had 941 students. One School of Midwifery Education had 158 students.

Andresén, A., *The Danish Folk High School To-day.* Copenhagen, 1981
Struve, K., *Schools and Education in Denmark.* Copenhagen, 1981
Thomsen, O. B., *Some Aspects of Education in Denmark.* Toronto, 1976
Thorsen, L., *Public Libraries in Denmark.* English and French eds., Copenhagen, 1972
Trane, E., *Education and Culture in Denmark.* Copenhagen, 1958

Social Security. The main body of Danish social welfare legislation is consolidated in 9 acts concerning (1) health insurance, (2) daily cash benefits, (3) disablement pensions, (4) old age pensions, (5) widows pensions, (6) employment injuries insurance, (7) employment services and unemployment insurance, (8) social assistance including assistance to handicapped, rehabilitation, child and juvenile guidance, care of the aged and sick, and (9) family allowances.

Health insurance, covering the entire population, provides free medical care, substantial subsidies for certain essential medicines together with some dental care and a funeral allowance. Hospitals are primarily municipal and the hospital treatment is normally free. Wage-earners are granted daily sickness allowances, others can have limited daily sickness allowances. Daily cash benefits are granted in the case of temporary incapacity for work because of illness, injury or childbirth to all persons who earn an income derived from personal work. The benefit is paid at the rate of 90% of the average weekly earnings. There was a maximum rate of 2,008 kroner a week (Oct. 1982).

Disablement and old-age pensions cover the entire population. Entitlement to benefits at the full rates is subject to the condition that the beneficiary has been ordinarily resident in Denmark for a number of years (40). For a shorter period of residence, the benefits are reduced proportionally. The basic amount of the old-age pension in Oct. 1982 was 57,072 kroner to married couples and 31,068 to single persons. Various supplementary allowances, depending on age and income, may be payable with the basic amount. Persons over 67 years of age are entitled to the basic amount. The pensions to a married couple are calculated and paid to the husband and the wife separately. Invalidity pension is payable, having regard to the degree of disability, at a rate of up to 71,028 kroner to a single person. The rate of the widow's pension corresponds more or less to that of the old-age pension. Invalidity and widow's pensions may be subject to income regulation.

Employment injuries insurance provides for disablement or survivors' pensions and funeral allowances. The scheme covers practically all employees.

Employment services are provided by regional public employment agencies. The insurance against unemployment provides daily allowances. The unemployment insurance funds had at 31 Dec. 1981 a membership of 1,705,400, of which 1,482,400 were full-time insured and 223,000 part-time.

The *Social Assistance Act* applies to the field of social legislation which rules the individually granted benefits in contrast to the other fields of social legislation which apply to fixed benefits.

Total social expenditure, including hospital and health services, statutory pensions, etc, amounted in the financial year 1980 to 104,407m. kroner.

Bibliography of Foreign Language Literature on Industrial Relations and Social Services in Denmark. Ministries of Labour and Social Affairs, Copenhagen, 1975

Social Conditions in Denmark. Vols. 1–8. Ministries of Labour and Social Affairs, Copenhagen

Marcussen, E., *Social Welfare in Denmark.* 4th ed. Copenhagen, 1980

THE FAROE ISLANDS

Færøerne

HISTORY. A Norwegian province 1380–1709, the islands secured the restoration of their Parliament in 1852 and full self-government in 1948.

AREA AND POPULATION. Area, 1,399 sq. km (540 sq. miles); population (31 Dec. 1980), 43,609. Capital, Thorshavn. Population (31 Dec. 1980) 13,757.

GOVERNMENT. The parliament *(Lagting)*, elected on 8 Nov. 1980, consists of 32 members: 8 Samband Party, 7 Social Democrats, 6 Folkeflok, 2 Progressive Party, 3 Home Rule Party, 6 Republicans.

Flag: White with a red blue-edged Scandinavian cross.

From 1 Jan. 1972 the Faroe Islands were no longer members of EFTA.

COMMERCE. The main industries are fisheries and crafts. Exports, mainly fresh, frozen, filleted and salted fish, amounted to 757·7m. kroner in 1979; imports to 1,082·9m. kroner.

Total trade with UK (British Department of Trade returns, in £1,000 sterling):

	1977	*1978*	*1979*	*1980*	*1981*	*1982*
Imports to UK	9,791	7,342	10,669	10,559	12,530	8,925
Exports and re-exports from UK	3,277	4,357	4,189	2,434	2,568	2,397

BROADCASTING. *Utvarp Føroya* is the broadcasting station and the number of receivers 16,000.

EDUCATION. In 1980–81 there were 5,879 primary and 2,837 secondary school pupils with 484 teachers.

Books of Reference

Årbog for Færøerne. 1980
Faroes in Figures. Thorshavn, annual, from 1956
West, J. F., *Faroe.* London, 1973
Williamson, K., *The Atlantic Islands: A Study of the Faroe Life and Scene.* London, 1970

GREENLAND
Grønland/Kalaallit Nunaat

AREA AND POPULATION. Area 2,175,600 sq. km (840,000 sq. miles), made up of 1,833,900 sq. km of ice cap and 341,700 sq. km of ice-free land. The population, 1 Jan. 1982, numbered 51,435; West Greenland, 46,106; East Greenland, 3,246; North Greenland (Thule), 770, and 1,313 not belonging to any specific municipality. Of the total, 9,279 were born outside Greenland. Capital, Godthaab (Nuuk) (1982), 9,717.

CONSTITUTION. On 5 June 1953 Greenland became an integral part of the Danish Realm with the same rights as other counties in Denmark and with a democratically elected council *(landsråd).* A referendum held in Jan. 1979 approved of home rule from 1 May 1979. At the elections held on 4 April 1979 for the new 21-member Parliament, *Landsting*, the *Siumut* gained 13 seats and the *Atassut*, the remaining 8 seats. The Premier, Jonathan Motzfeldt, formed a 5-member administration, *Landsstyre.*

INDUSTRY. Until the beginning of this century, the hunting of land and sea mammals, especially seals, was the main occupation of the population; now fishing is most important. Fish-processing industries, construction and trade are also important occupations.

Coal production ceased in 1972. A deposit of the valuable mineral cryolite has been mined at Ivigtut. The mine is now worked out, but exports from stock will continue for some years. In 1973 the Danish company Greenex A/S began producing lead and zinc concentrate near Umanak. Annual production of lead and zinc concentrates is about 40,000 tonnes and 150,000 tonnes respectively. In 1975, 6 groups of oil companies were granted 13 oil concessions off the west coast. These concessions were terminated by 31 Dec. 1978.

Public authorities are investigating uranium and coal deposits in Greenland as well as possibilities of hydro-electric power and there are other private prospectors for various minerals.

COMMERCE. Imports (c.i.f. Greenland) (in 1,000 kroner): 1976, 777,911; 1977, 964,579; 1978, 980,292; 1979, 1,447,904; 1980, 1,847,877; 1981 (provisional), 2,129,522. Exports (f.o.b. Greenland) (in 1,000 kroner): 1976, 516,519; 1977, 555,172; 1978, 559,274; 1979, 866,926; 1980, 1,199,301; 1981 (provisional), 1,480,356. Trade is mainly with Denmark.

Total trade with UK (British Department of Trade returns, in £1,000 sterling):

	1977	*1978*	*1979*	*1980*	*1981*	*1982*
Imports to UK	2,211	714	348	282	270	1,095
Exports and re-exports from UK	5,329	3,975	2,283	5,930	2,502	288

BROADCASTING. *Grønlands Radio* broadcasts in Greenlandic and Danish. The short wave transmitters are located at Godthaab. Several towns have local television stations.

EDUCATION. There were (1981–82) 11,165 pupils in primary comprehensive schools, of whom 8,574 were in the course of compulsory education (9 years). There were 328 students in upper secondary schools. On 1 Jan. 1981, 1,487 students were enrolled in vocational training.

Books of Reference

Greenland. R. Danish Ministry of Greenland. Copenhagen. Annual from 1968
Meddelelser om Grønland. Ed. Kommissionen for videnskabelige undersøgelser i Grønland. Copenhagen, 1899 ff. Since 1979 issued in 3 separate series: 'Bioscience', 'Geoscience' and 'Man and Society'
Birket-Smith, K. (ed.), *Grønlandsbogen.* 2 vols. Copenhagen, 1950
Gad, F., *A History of Greenland.* Vol. 1. London, 1970.—Vol. 2. London, 1973
Hertling, K. (ed.), *Greenland Past and Present.* Copenhagen, 1970

DIPLOMATIC REPRESENTATIVES

Of Denmark in Great Britain (55 Sloane St., London, SW1X 9SR)
Ambassador: Tyge Dahlgaard (accredited 28 Feb. 1981).

Of Great Britain in Denmark (36–40 Kastelsvej, DK-2100, Copenhagen)
Ambassador: James Mellon.

Of Denmark in the USA (3200 Whitehaven St., NW, Washington, D.C., 20008)
Ambassador: Otto R. Borch.

Of the USA in Denmark (Dag Hammarskjolds Alle 24, Copenhagen)
Ambassador: John Langeloth Loeb, Jr.

Of Denmark to the United Nations
Ambassador: Wilh. Ulrichsen.

Books of Reference

Statistical Information: Danmarks Statistik (Sejrøgade 11, 2100 Copenhagen Ø.) was founded in 1849 and reorganized in 1966 as an independent institution; it is administratively placed under the Minister of Economic Affairs. *Chief:* N. V. Skak-Nielsen. Its main publications are: *Statistisk Årbog* (Statistical Yearbook). From 1896; *Statistiske Efterretninger* (Statistical News). From 1909; *Statistiske Meddelelser* (Statistical Reports). From 1852; *Handelsstatistiske Meddelelser* (Reports on Foreign Trade). From 1910; *Statistiske Tabelværker* (Statistical Tables). From 1850; *Statistiske Undersøgelser* (Statistical Inquiries).

Ministry of Foreign Affairs, *Danish Foreign Office Journal. Commercial and General Review.—Denmark.* 1961.—*Economic Survey of Denmark* (annual).—*Facts About Denmark.* 1959.—Hæstrup, J., *From Occupied to Ally: the Danish Resistance Movement.* 1963
Atlas over Danmark. R. Danish Geog. Society. Copenhagen, 1963
Bibliografi over Danmarks Offentlige Publikationer. Institut for International Udveksling, Copenhagen. Annual
Dania polyglotta. Annual Bibliography of Books ... in Foreign Languages Printed in Denmark. State Library, Copenhagen. Annual
Kongelig Dansk Hof og Statskalender. Copenhagen. Annual
Brynildsen, F., *A Dictionary of the English and Dano-Norwegian Languages.* 2 vols. Copenhagen, 1902–07
Danstrup, J., *History of Denmark.* 2nd ed. Copenhagen, 1949
Jones, N. G., *Denmark.* London, 1970
Krabbe, L., *Histoire de Danemark.* Copenhagen and Paris, 1950
Lauring, P., *A History of Denmark.* Copenhagen, 1960
Nielsen, B. K., *Engelsk–Dansk Ordbog.* Copenhagen, 1964
Trap, J. P., *Kongeriget Danmark.* 5th ed. 11 vols. Copenhagen, 1953 ff.
Vinterberg, H., and Bodelsen, C. A., *Dansk-Engelsk Ordbog.* Copenhagen, 1966

National Library: Det Kongelige Bibliotek, Copenhagen. *Librarian:* P. Birkelund.

DJIBOUTI

Capital: Djibouti
Population: 350,000 (1981)
GNP per capita: US$480 (1980)

Jumhouriyya Djibouti

HISTORY. At a referendum held on 19 March 1967, 60% of the electorate voted for continued association with France rather than independence and the new statute for the territory came into being on 5 July 1967. In Jan. 1976, following discussions between Ali Aref and President Giscard d'Estaing, it was announced that the French Government affirmed that the Territory of the Afars and the Issas was destined for independence but no date was fixed. Legislative elections were held on 8 May and independence as the Republic of Djibouti was achieved on 27 June 1977.

AREA AND POPULATION. Djibouti is bounded north-east by the Gulf of Aden, south-east by Somalia and all other sides by Ethiopia.

Djibouti has an area of 23,000 sq. km (8,880 sq. miles). The population was estimated in 1981 at 350,000, of whom 47% were Somali, 37% Afar, 8% European and 6% Arab. There were (1982) about 40,000 refugees from Ethiopia. Djibouti, the seat of government, had (1981) 150,000 inhabitants; other towns are Tadjoura and Obock.

CONSTITUTION AND GOVERNMENT. The 65-member Chamber of Deputies, elected 8 May 1977 and comprising 33 Somali, 30 Afar and 2 Arab members, became a Constituent Assembly at independence, charged with drawing up a new Constitution. Under an organic law approved by the Assembly on 10 Feb. 1981, the President is directly elected for a 6-year term (renewable once). In Oct. 1981, the Assembly declared Djibouti a one-Party state, the ruling Party being the *Rassemblement Populaire pour le Progrès*.

President: Hassan Gouled Aptidon (elected 1977 and re-elected 1981).
Prime Minister and Ports: Barkat Gourad Hamadou.

National flag: Horizontally blue over green, with a white triangle based on the hoist charged with a red star.

DEFENCE

Army. The army comprises 1 infantry battalion. The armed forces, all services, number (1983), 2,600.

Navy. The nucleus of a naval force was acquired in 1977 with the commissioning of a coastal patrol craft.

Air Force. As the nucleus of an air force, the French *Armée de l'Air* transferred to the Djibouti Government 2 Noratlas piston-engined tactical transport aircraft. These have since been supplemented by a twin-jet Mystère 20 for VIP duties, 2 light aircraft and an Alouette helicopter. A Boeing 737 has been ordered for VIP use.

INTERNATIONAL RELATIONS

Membership. Djibouti is a member of UN, OAU, the Arab League and an ACP State of the EEC.

ECONOMY

Budget. The ordinary budget for 1981 envisaged an expenditure of 15,730m. Djibouti francs.

Currency. The *Djibouti franc* was introduced on 17 March 1949. The currency is covered 100% by a US dollar fund. In March 1983, £1 = 250 *Djibouti francs*; US$1 = 177·72 *Djibouti francs*.

Banking. The Banque Nationale de Djibouti is the bank of issue. There are 6 commercial banks.

NATURAL RESOURCES

Minerals. Minerals supposed to exist are gypsum, mica, amethyst and sulphur.

Agriculture. Mainly market gardening at the oasis of Ambouli and near urban areas. Livestock (1981): 34,000 cattle, 330,000 sheep, 530,000 goats, 5,000 donkeys, 26,000 camels.

Fisheries. Fishing has only been partially exploited. Catch is 300–400 tonnes per annum with a workforce of 350.

INDUSTRY AND TRADE

Industry. Industry provides employment for 1,500 and the main industry is a bottling plant opened in 1981.

Commerce. The main economic activity is the operation of the port. The chief imports are cotton goods, sugar, cement, flour, fuel oil and vehicles; the chief exports are hides, cattle and coffee (transit from Ethiopia). Trade in 1m. Djibouti francs:

	1979	*1980*	*1981*
Imports	28,436	33,782	36,654
Exports	14,147	19,171	20,348

In 1977 France provided 55% of imports and took 74% of exports.

Total trade between Djibouti and UK (British Department of Trade returns, in £1,000 sterling):

	1978	*1979*	*1980*	*1981*	*1982*
Imports to UK	14	328	303	227	53
Exports and re-exports from UK	7,145	6,499	6,682	6,555	6,521

COMMUNICATIONS

Roads. There were (1978) 1,650 km of roads, of which 75 km were hard-surfaced. In 1977 there were 11,800 passenger cars and 3,300 lorries.

Railway. For the line Djibouti–Addis Ababa *see* p. 450. In 1969–70 the railway carried goods traffic of 411,460 tons and 457,000 passengers.

Aviation. Air Djibouti provides services to Addis Ababa, Nairobi, Jidda and the Gulf. Other airlines serving Djibouti airport are Ethiopian Airlines, Air France, Air Tanzania and Yemen Airways Corporation.

Shipping. In 1970 there entered at Djibouti 1,217 vessels, unloading 232,866 tons and loading 88,092 tons of merchandise. In 1981 the merchant marine comprised 8 vessels of 3,185 GRT.

Post and Broadcasting. Number of telephones (1980), 4,348. *Radiodiffusion-Télévision de Djibouti* broadcasts on medium- and short-waves in French, Somali, Afar and Arabic. There is a television transmitter in Djibouti, broadcasting for 19 hours a week. Number of receivers (1979): radio, 16,000; TV, 10,000.

Cinemas. In 1975 there were 4 cinemas with a seating capacity of 5,800.

JUSTICE, RELIGION, EDUCATION AND WELFARE

Justice. The judicial system is based on Islamic law.

Religion. The vast majority of the population is Moslem, with about 12,000 Roman Catholics.

Education. In 1981 there were 16,841 pupils and 375 teachers at primary schools, 3,812 pupils and 174 teachers at secondary schools, and 1,279 pupils with 88 teachers in technical schools.

Health. There were (1975) 11 hospitals and dispensaries with 1,028 beds; 52 physicians.

DIPLOMATIC REPRESENTATIVES

Of Djibouti in Great Britain
Ambassador: Ahmed Ibrahim Abdi (resides in Paris).

Of Great Britain in Djibouti
Ambassador: J. F. Walker, CMG, MBE (resides in Sana'a).

Of the USA in Djibouti (Villa Plateau du Serpent Blvd., Djibouti)
Chargé d'Affaires: Eugene D. Schmiel.

Of Djibouti to the United Nations and in the USA
Ambassador: Saleh Haji Farah Dirir.

Books of Reference

Poinsot, J.-P., *Djibouti et la Côte française des Somalis.* Paris, 1965
Thompson, V., and Adloff, R., *Djibouti and the Horn of Africa.* Stanford Univ. Press, 1967

COMMONWEALTH OF DOMINICA

Capital: Roseau
Population: 74,089 (1980)
GNP per capita: US$620 (1980)

HISTORY. Dominica was discovered by Columbus. It was a British possession from 1805, a member of the Federation of the West Indies 1958–62, an Associated State of the UK, 1967–78 and became an independent republic as the Commonwealth of Dominica on 3 Nov. 1978.

AREA AND POPULATION. Dominica is an island in the Windward group of the West Indies situated between Martinique and Guadeloupe. It has an area of 751 sq. km (290 sq. miles) and a population at the 1980 Census of 74,089. The chief town, Roseau, had about 16,800 inhabitants in 1978.

The population is mainly of Negro and mixed origins, with small white and Asian minorities. There is a Carib settlement of about 500, almost entirely of mixed blood.

CONSTITUTION AND GOVERNMENT. The House of Assembly has 21 elected and 9 nominated members, 1 *ex-officio* member. The Speaker is elected from among the members of the House or from outside. The Cabinet is presided over by the Prime Minister and consists of 5 other Ministers and the Attorney-General (official member). Elections were held in July 1980. The Dominica Freedom Party won 17 seats, Dominica Democratic Labour Party, 2 seats and Independents 2 seats.

President: Aurelius Marie.

The Cabinet in Jan. 1983 was composed as follows:

Prime Minister and Minister of Finance, Foreign Affairs, Trade, Development and Industry: Mary Eugenia Charles.

Attorney-General and Minister of Legal Affairs: Roland David. *Home Affairs, Women's Affairs, Industrial Relations and Housing:* Brian G. K. Alleyne. *Agriculture, Lands, Co-operatives and Fisheries:* Heskeith Alexander. *Communications and Works:* Henry Dyer. *Education, Health, Youth Affairs, Sports and Culture:* Charles Maynard.

National flag: Green with a cross over all of yellow, white, and black pieces, and in the centre a red disc charged with a Sisserou parrot in natural colours within a ring of 11 green stars.

INTERNATIONAL RELATIONS

Membership. The Commonwealth of Dominica is a member of UN, OAS, CARICOM, the Commonwealth and is an ACP state of EEC.

ECONOMY

Budget. A deficit for 1981–82 of EC$8·9m. is envisaged.

Currency. The French *franc,* the £ sterling and the East Caribbean *dollar* are legal tender. In March 1983, EC$2·7025 = US$1 and EC$4·10 = £1.

Banking. Savings bank (1974), 2,954 depositors, with $571,794 deposits. There are branches of Barclays Bank International, Royal Bank of Canada and Dominica Co-operative Bank in Roseau, a branch of Barclays at Portsmouth and agencies of Barclays at Marigot and Grand Bay. The National Commercial and Development Bank was opened in 1977 and Banque Française Commerciale opened in 1979.

NATURAL RESOURCES

Agriculture. Hurricanes in 1979 and 1980 devastated large agricultural areas and damaged infrastructure. Production (1981): Bananas, 34,000 tonnes; coconuts, 9,565,000 nuts; beef, 450,000lb; pork, 500,000 tonnes.

Livestock (1981): Cattle, 4,000; pigs, 8,000; sheep, 4,000; goats, 6,000; poultry, 112,000.

INDUSTRY AND TRADE

Industry. The main industries are agriculture and tourism. A freeport is planned, to be called New Hong Kong.

Commerce (1980). Imports, EC$128,730; exports, EC$25,212. Chief products: Bananas, soap, fruit juices, essential oils, coconuts, vegetables, fruit and fruit preparations, and alcoholic drinks.

Total trade between Dominica and UK (British Department of Trade returns, in £1,000 sterling):

	1980	*1981*	*1982*
Imports to UK	9,146	14,462	11,376
Exports and re-exports from UK	12,868	7,924	7,423

Tourism. Tourists (1982) totalled 10,419.

COMMUNICATIONS

Roads. In 1976 there were 467 miles of road and 282 miles of track. Vehicles totalled (1976) 3,574.

Post and Broadcasting. Telephone lines, 136 route miles; number of telephones, 2,972 (1982). Radio receivers (1982) 13,405.

Cinemas. In 1970 there were 3 cinemas with a seating capacity of 1,500.

JUSTICE, RELIGION, EDUCATION AND WELFARE

Justice. There are 4 magistrates' courts. They dealt with 11 civil and 3,274 criminal cases in 1973. The police force consists of 10 officers and 361 other ranks.

Religion. 80% of the population is Roman Catholic.

Education. In 1982 there were 18,780 primary and 6,195 secondary school pupils and 4 colleges of higher education with 500 students.

Health. In 1982 there were 3 hospitals with 237 beds, 25 doctors, 4 dentists, 11 pharmacists and 131 nursing personnel.

DIPLOMATIC REPRESENTATIVES

Of Dominica in Great Britain (10 Kensington Ct., London, W8).
High Commissioner: Arden Shillingford, MBE (accredited 13 Dec. 1978).

Of Great Britain in Dominica
High Commissioner: Viscount Dunrossil, CMG (resides in Bridgetown).

Of Dominica to the USA and the United Nations
Ambassador: Franklyn A. M. Baron.

Book of Reference

Commonwealth of Dominica. HMSO, 1979

Library: Public Library, Roseau. *Librarian:* Miss C. Henry.

DOMINICAN REPUBLIC

Capital: Santo Domingo
Population: 5·2m. (1980)
GNP per capita: US$1,140 (1980)

República Dominicana

HISTORY. On 5 Dec. 1492 Columbus discovered the island of Santo Domingo, which he called La Española; for a time it was called Hispaniola. The city of Santo Domingo, founded by his brother, Bartholomew, in 1496, is the oldest city in the Americas. The western third of the island—now the Republic of Haiti—was later occupied and colonized by the French, to whom the Spanish colony of Santo Domingo was also ceded in 1795. In 1808 the Dominican population, under the command of Gen. Juan Sánchez Ramirez, routed an important French military force commanded by Gen. Ferrand, at the famous battle of Palo Hincado. This battle was the beginning of the end for French rule in Santo Domingo and culminated in the successful siege of the capital. Eventually, with the aid of a British naval squadron, the French were forced to capitulate and the colony returned again to Spanish rule, from which it declared its independence in 1821. It was invaded and held by the Haitians from 1822 to 1844, when they were expelled, and the Dominican Republic was founded and a constitution adopted. Independence day 27 Feb. 1844. Great Britain, in 1850, was the first country to recognize the Dominican Republic. The country was occupied by American Marines from 1916 until 1924. In 1936 the name of the capital city was changed from Santo Domingo to Ciudad Trujillo; and back again in 1961.

AREA AND POPULATION. The Dominican Republic occupies the eastern portion (about two-thirds) of the island of Hispaniola, Quisqueya or Santo Domingo, the western division forming the Republic of Haiti. It consists of the National District (containing the capital, Santo Domingo; population, census 1970, 817,067), and 26 provinces.

Area is 48,442 sq. km (18,700 sq. miles) with 870 miles of coastline, 193 miles of frontier line with Haiti (marked out in 1936).

The populations of the 26 provinces at the 1970 census were:

La Altagracia	87,180	Puerto Plata	185,800
Azua	91,511	La Romana	56,995
Bahoruco	66,572	Salcedo	89,773
Barahona	112,914	Samaná	53,893
Dajabón	50,780	Sánchez Ramírez	106,177
Duarte	200,813	San Cristóbal	324,395
Espaillat	139,579	San Juan	191,065
La Estrelleta	53,228	San Pedro de Macorís	105,490
Independencia	32,580	Santiago	386,269
María Trinidad Sánchez	97,043	Santiago Rodríguez	49,958
Montecristi	69,276	El Seibo	132,795
Pedernales	12,547	Valverde	76,608
Peravia	127,587	La Vega	293,694

Census population of 1970 was 4,009,458 (2,000,824 males and 2,008,734 females) with 48% of population under 15 years and only 2% over 65. Estimate (1980) 5·2m.

Population of the principal municipalities (1978): National District (including Santo Domingo) 1,103,425; Santiago de los Caballeros, 241,955; San Pedro de Macoris, 74,693; San Francisco de Macoris, 66,303; Barahona, 59,808.

The population is partly of Spanish descent, but is mainly composed of a mixed race of European and African blood.

CONSTITUTION AND GOVERNMENT. A new Constitution was promulgated on 28 Nov. 1966.

The President is elected for 4 years, by direct vote. In case of death, resignation or disability, he is succeeded by the Vice-president. There are 12 secretaries of state, a judicial adviser with secretary-of-state rank and 2 ministers without portfolio in charge of departments. Citizens are entitled to vote at the age of 18, or less when married. Elections will be held on 16 May 1982.

Recent Presidents have been: Dr Joaquín Balaguer, 4 Aug. 1960–62; Lic. Rafael Bonnelly, 18 Jan. 1962; Professor Juan Bosch, 27 Feb.–25 Sept. 1963 (deposed); Dr Héctor Gracía Godoy, 3 Sept. 1965–1 July 1966; Joaquín Balaguer, 1 July 1966–15 Aug. 1978; Antonio Guzan, 26 May 1978–4 July 1982.

President: Salvador Jorge Blanc. (assumed office 14 Aug. 1982).

The country's first free elections for nearly 40 years were held in Dec. 1962 when Juan Bosch was elected President with a clear majority, after which a new Constitution was approved on 29 April 1963. Bosch was overthrown by a military *coup d'état* in Sept. 1963 and the declared aim of the Constitutionalist side in the Civil War of April–Sept. 1965 was the restoration of Bosch as President and a return to the 1963 Constitution.

On 29 April 1965 USA landed a force of 44,000 Marine and Army, later assisted by Organization of American States contributions. The capital remained divided between these forces and various rival factions of nationals. A provisional government was eventually installed on 3 Sept. 1965.

Until elections on 1 June 1966 there was government by decree. The voting on 16 May 1974 was 924,779 votes for Dr Joaquín Balaguer (Reformist Party).

National flag: Blue, red; quartered by a white cross.

National anthem: Quisqueyanos valientes, alzemos (words by E. Prud'homme; tune by J. Reyes, 1883).

DEFENCE. The armed forces are under the command of the President of the Republic, acting through the Secretary of State for the Armed Forces.

Army. The Army has a strength (1983) of about 14,000 all ranks. It is organized in 3 infantry brigades, 1 artillery regiment and support battalions, and has some light tanks and armoured cars.

Navy. The Navy, largely comprising former US vessels, consists of 1 very old frigate acting as the operational flagship (former training ship, *ex*-presidential yacht), 2 escort (*ex*-fleet) minesweepers, 3 patrol vessels (*ex*-netlayers), 1 medium landing ship, 2 landing craft, 5 coastguard vessels, 8 patrol cutters, 4 small training craft, 2 oilers, 4 survey craft and 10 tugs. Personnel in 1983 totalled 4,000 officers and men.

Air Force. The Air Force, with HQ at San Isidoro, has 3 operational squadrons, each with 6–15 first-line aircraft. One is equipped with F-51D Mustang piston-engined interceptors; another with jet-powered Vampire Mk. 1 and Mk. 50 fighter-bombers. The third squadron, with 6 T-28Ds, has a joint counter-insurgency/training rôle. There are also transport (C-46, C-47 and Beaver) helicopter and training units. Total strength (1983) was about 5,000.

INTERNATIONAL RELATIONS

Membership. The Dominican Republic is a member of UN and OAS.

ECONOMY

Budget. The 1981 budget balanced at RD$1,233m.

Income tax, established in 1949, was replaced in 1950 by an identity-card tax, known as the 'cédula tax', but re-introduced in 1962.

Currency. In Oct. 1947 the *peso oro*, equal to the US$, was formally made the unit of currency, replacing the US gold dollar, which had been the standard since 1 July 1897. In March 1983, £1 = RD$1·518; US$1 = RD$1.

There are silver coins for 50, 25 and 10 centavos, a copper-nickel 5-centavo piece and a copper 1-centavo piece.

Banking. On 24 Oct. 1941 a law was passed for the creation of a Dominican commercial bank (government controlled) to be known as the Banco de Reservas de la República Dominicana, with a capital of RD$1m., now increased to RD$68,877,000. This bank, starting with branches purchased from the National City Bank of New York, opened for business on 27 Oct. 1941 and now has 30 branches covering the country. It is authorized to perform all customary banking transactions. On 31 Oct. 1966 its assets and liabilities totalled RD$142,126,322. There are 4 foreign banks—the Royal Bank of Canada with 12 branches, the Bank of Nova Scotia with 11 branches, the Citibank with 6 branches, the Chase Manhattan Bank with 7 branches and the Bank of America with 4 branches. An agricultural and mortgage bank, with paid-up capital of RD$500,000, was established in 1945; in 1950 its capital was increased to RD$5m.; in 1952 steps were begun to raise it to cover a 5-year programme of agricultural expansion; it stood at RD$100m. in Nov. 1962.

In 1947 the Central Bank of the Dominican Republic was launched. Chief liability was note circulation, chiefly bank-notes of 1, 5 and 10 pesos (RD$104·5m. in 1966); total assets and liabilities were RD$215·8m. The net reserve of foreign exchange was US$32m. at 31 Aug. 1966.

A new Banco Popular Dominicano, with an authorized capital of RD$5m., opened in Jan. 1964.

Weights and Measures. The metric system was nominally adopted on 1 Aug. 1913, but English and Spanish units have remained in common use in ordinary commercial transactions; on 17 Sept. 1954 a more drastic law requiring the decimal metric system was passed.

ENERGY AND NATURAL RESOURCES

Electricity. Hurricane 'David' (Aug. 1979) damaged 3 of the hydro-electric plants which produce 30% of electricity supply. 1,943·4m. kwh. of electricity was generated in 1977.

Minerals. The Aluminium Co. of America sent its first shipment of bauxite for smelting, to Texas, on 13 Jan. 1959. Output in 1977 was 574,966 tonnes. Silver and platinum have been found, and near Neiba there are several hills of rock salt (production 1977, 48,592 tonnes). Copper production (1969) 1,200 tonnes. The Rosario Dominicana goldmines were nationalized in Oct. 1979. Exports of Doré, a gold and silver alloy, (1980) US$180m.

Agriculture. Agriculture is the chief source of wealth, sugar cultivation being the principal industry. Of the total area, 9,900 sq. miles are cultivable, and about 3,700 are under cultivation.

Livestock in 1981: 2·15m. cattle, 50,000 pigs, 55,000 sheep.

The largest sugar estates are in the south-eastern part of the republic. Sugar production, 1980–81, was 1·25m. tonnes. Two companies produce four-fifths of the total, but in all there are 16 sugar 'centrals'.

Coffee is exported mainly to USA. Output, 1976, 31,851 tonnes. Production of rice for home consumption and export is fostered; output, 1977, 288,959 tonnes. Cocoa is the second principal crop and covers 2m. *tareas* (340,000 acres); output in 1977, 25,755 tonnes. Other principal exports are leaf tobacco and molasses (17,673 tonnes in 1977). There are useful crops of yucca (1977: 162,287 tonnes) and beans (1977: 38,792 tonnes) for local consumption. Scientific growing of bananas (1977: 290,837 tonnes) and of tobacco (1977: 34,918 tonnes) is progressing.

INDUSTRY AND TRADE

Industry. In 1975, 1,286 industrial establishments employed 130,000 men and women, who earned RD$157·57m. Output was valued at RD$205·1m. There were 1,036 establishments in 1970. Important manufactures are sugar (1,342,000 tonnes in 1977), textiles (7m. metres of cotton fabric in 1972), cement (678,000 tonnes in 1972), glass bottles, paper and matches. Oil refining capacity was 1·5m. tonnes in 1972, and chemical plants produced 57,000 hectolitres of ethyl alcohol.

Commerce. Total imports and exports in RD$1m. (equal to US$1m.):

	1975	*1976*	*1977*	*1978*	*1979*	*1980*
Imports	893·4	763·6	847·8	859·7	1,054·6	1,430·0
Exports	893·8	716·4	780·4	675·5	868·6	960·0

The principal exports in 1980 were (in RD$1m.): Sugar and by-products, 242·9; coffee, 48·5; ferronickel, 92·7; Doré, 184.

Total trade between the Dominican Republic and UK (British Department of Trade returns, in £1,000 sterling):

	1978	*1979*	*1980*	*1981*	*1982*
Imports to UK	971	5,174	4,788	7,013	5,752
Exports and re-exports from UK	9,660	9,627	11,514	10,860	10,161

Tourism. 395,699 tourists visited the Dominican Republic in 1977.

COMMUNICATIONS

Roads. Three main trunk highways, with branches, extend from Santo Domingo eastward to Higuey (106 miles), northward to Santiago and Montecristi and Dajabón (204 miles) and westward to San Juan (128 miles) and Elías Piña on the Haitian border (161 miles). At Elías Piña the road joins the Haitian road to Port-au-Prince. Total highway system in 1977 was 5,224 km first-, 1,538 km second- and 2,505 km third-class roads; there were 647 bridges. Road transport is the chief means of travel. There were 82,001 cars, 40,626 commercial vehicles and 34,967 motor cycles in 1977.

Railways. Some 100 km of the Dominican Government Railway remains in use between La Vega and the port of Sánchez. Other lines, including the Central Romana Railway, exist to serve the sugar industry.

Aviation. The country is reached from the American continent and the Caribbean islands by 8 international airlines. Two local aviation companies provide interior services and connect Santo Domingo with San Juan in Puerto Rico, Curaçao, Aruba and Miami.

Shipping. Santo Domingo is the leading port; Puerto Plata ranks next. In 1971, vessels of 9,833,000 tons entered the ports to discharge 3,009,000 tonnes of cargo, and vessels of 5,276,000 tons cleared the ports having loaded 1,986,000 tonnes.

Post and Broadcasting. Number of telephone instruments (1981), 165,253, of which 130,562 in Santo Domingo. The telephone system is mainly operated by an American company. The telegraph has a total length of about 500 km, privately owned; they have been leased to All-America Cables, Inc., which also controls submarine cables connecting, in the north, Puerto Plata with Puerto Rico and New York, and in the south, Santo Domingo with Puerto Rico, Cuba and Curaçao.

There are 151 broadcasting stations in Santo Domingo and other towns; this includes the 2 government stations. There are 4 television stations.

Cinemas (1978). Cinemas numbered 72, with seating capacity of about 40,000.

Newspapers (1978). There were 7 daily newspapers with a circulation of 155,000.

JUSTICE, RELIGION, EDUCATION AND WELFARE

Justice. The judicial power resides in the Supreme Court of Justice, the courts of appeal, the courts of first instance, the communal courts and other tribunals created by special laws, such as the land courts. The Supreme Court consists of a president and 8 judges chosen by the Senate, and the procurator-general, appointed by the executive; it supervises the lower courts. Each province forms a judicial district, as does the *Distrito Nacional*, and each has its own procurator fiscal and court of first instance; these districts are subdivided, in all, into 72 municipalities and 18 municipal districts, each with one or more local justices. The death penalty was abolished in 1924.

Religion. The religion of the state is Roman Catholic; other forms of religion are permitted.

Education. Primary instruction (5,245 schools) is free and obligatory for children between 7 and 14 years of age; there are also secondary, normal, vocational and special schools, all of which are either wholly maintained by the State or state-aided; in 1975, primary schools had 15,216 teachers and 833,439 pupils; 997 intermediate and secondary schools had 4,950 teachers and 142,501 pupils. The campaign against adult illiteracy dates from 1941, but in 1964 about 65% of the population were still illiterate.

The University of Santo Domingo (founded 1538) had (1975) 27,675 students; 5 other universities had 14,573 students.

Health. In 1978, 18 towns had complete waterworks. There were, in 1975, 1,310 doctors, 121 hospitals, health centres and polyclinics with 8,389 beds.

DIPLOMATIC REPRESENTATIVES

Of the Dominican Republic in Great Britain (4 Braemar Mansions, London, SW7 4AG)
Ambassador: Alfredo A. Ricart.

Of Great Britain in the Dominican Republic (Ave. Independencia 506, Santo Domingo)
Ambassador: M. A. Cafferty.

Of the Dominican Republic in the USA (1715–22nd St., NW, Washington, D.C., 20008)
Ambassador: Carlos Despradel.

Of the USA in the Dominican Republic (Calle Cesar Nicolas Penson, Santo Domingo)
Ambassador: Robert Anderson.

Of the Dominican Republic to the United Nations
Ambassador: Dr Eniquillo A. Del Rosario.

Books of Reference

Anuario estadístico de la República Dominicana, 1944–45. Ciudad Trujillo. 1949. This has been succeeded by separate annual reports covering foreign trade, vital statistics, banking, insurance, housing and communications.

Dirección General de Estadística. *21 años de estadísticas dominicanas 1936–1956.* Ciudad Trujillo, 1957.—*Republica Dominicana en Cifras 1978.* Ciudad Trujillo, 1979

Official Guide to the Dominican Republic, 79–80. Tourist Information Center, Santo Domingo, 1980

Atkins, G. P., *Arms and Politics in the Dominican Republic.* London, 1981

Bell, I., *The Dominican Republic.* London, 1980

Diederich, B., *Trujillo: The Death of the Goat.* London, 1978

Wiarda, H. J., and Kryzanek, M. J., *The Dominican Republic: A Caribbean Crucible.* Boulder, 1982

ECUADOR

Capital: Quito
Population: 8·6m. (1981)
GNP per capita: US$1,220 (1980)

República del Ecuador

HISTORY. The Spaniards under Francisco Pizarro founded a colony after their victory at Cajamarca (16 Nov. 1532). Their rule was first challenged by the rising of 10 Aug. 1809. Marshal Sucre defeated the Spaniards at Pichincha in 1821, and in 1822 Bolívar persuaded the new republic to join the federation of Gran Colombia. The Presidency of Quito became the Republic of Ecuador by amicable secession 13 May 1830.

AREA AND POPULATION. Ecuador is bounded on the north by Colombia, on the east and south by Peru, on the west by the Pacific ocean. The frontier with Peru has long been a source of dispute between the two countries. The latest delimitation of it was in the treaty of Rio, 29 Jan. 1942, when, after being invaded by Peru, Ecuador lost over half her Amazonian territories. Ecuador unilaterally denounced this treaty in Sept. 1961. *See* map in THE STATESMAN'S YEAR-BOOK, 1942. Fighting between Peru and Ecuador began again in Jan. 1981 over this border issue but a ceasefire was agreed in early Feb.

No definite figure of the area of the country can yet be given, as a portion of the frontier has not been delimited. One estimate of the area of Ecuador is 270,670 sq. km, excluding the litigation zone between Peru and Ecuador, which is 190,807 sq. km.

Ecuador has 3 distinct zones: the *Sierra* or uplands of the Andes, consisting of high mountain ridges with valleys, with 2·57m. of the population and high-priced farming land; the *Costa*, the coastal plain between the Andes and the Pacific, with 2·02m., whose permanent plantations furnish bananas, cacao, coffee, sugar-cane and many other crops; the *Oriente*, the upper Amazon basin on the east, consisting of tropical jungles threaded by large rivers.

The population is predominantly of Amerindians, with small proportions of people of European or African descent.

The official language is Spanish. The Amerindians of the highlands speak mainly the Quechua language; in the Oriental Region various tribes have languages of their own.

Census population in 1974, 6,521,710. Estimate (1981) 8·6m.

The population (census at 8 April 1974) was distributed by provinces (capitals in brackets):

Provinces	*Area (sq. km)*	*Population 1974*
Azuay (Cuenca)	7,799	367,324
Bolívar (Guaranda)	3,216	144,593
Cañar (Azogues)	2,677	146,570
Carchi (Tulcán)	3,582	120,857
Chimborazo (Riobamba)	6,161	304,316
Cotopaxi (Latacunga)	4,614	236,313
El Oro (Machala)	7,451	262,564
Esmeraldas (Esmeraldas)	15,866	203,151
Guayas (Guayaquil)	21,259	1,512,333
Imbabura (Ibarra)	4,903	216,027
Loja (Loja)	28,900	342,339
Los Ríos (Babahoyo)	5,937	383,432
Manabí (Portoviejo)	18,963	817,966
Pichincha (Quito)	16,438	988,306
Tungurahua (Ambato)	3,204	279,920

Provinces	*Area (sq. km)*	*Population 1974*
Napo (Tena)	296,390	62,186
Pastaza (Puyo)		23,465
Morona-Santiago (Macas)		53,325
Zamora-Chinchipe (Zamora)		34,493
Colon (Galápagos)	7,844	4,037
Total	455,454	6,521,710

There are 115 cantons, 212 urban parishes and 715 rural parishes. The chief towns (population census, 1974) are the capital, Quito (559,828), Guayaquil (823,219), Cuenca (104,470), Ambato (77,955), Machala (69,170), Esmeraldas (60,364), Portoviejo (59,550), Riobamba (58,087).

Vital statistics for calendar years: Births, (1964) 219,137, (1965) 226,436, (1966) 220,930; deaths, (1964) 58,989, (1965) 60,202, (1966) 59,618.

CONSTITUTION AND GOVERNMENT. On 22 June 1970 President José Maria Velasco Ibarra assumed dictatorial powers, following months of strife between student and security forces. For details of governments 1963–70, *see* THE STATESMAN'S YEAR-BOOK, 1974–75, pp. 875–76. On 15 Feb. 1972 President Velasco Ibarra was deposed. A National Military Government under Gen. Guillermo Rodriguez Lara was formed and the 1945 Constitution reintroduced. President Rodriguez Lara resigned in Jan. 1976 and a military Junta assumed power until the 1979 elections. A new Constitution came into force on 10 Aug. 1979.

National flag: Three horizontal stripes of yellow, blue, red, with the yellow of double width, and in the centre over all the national arms.

National anthem: Salve, oh patria! (words by J. L. Mera; tune by A. Neumann, 1866).

The following is a list of the presidents and provisional executives since 1940:

Carlos Alberto Arroyo del Rio, elected 12 Jan. 1940; resigned 30 May 1944.

Dr José María Velasco Ibarra, elected by Constituent Assembly, Aug. 1944; re-elected 11 Aug. 1946, but deposed 24 Aug. 1947.

Col. Carlos Mancheno, seized power 24 Aug. 1947; deposed 3 Sept. 1947.

Mariano Suárez Veintimilla (Vice-President), 3–15 Sept. 1947.

Carlos Julio Arosemena Tola (provisional), 15 Sept. 1947–31 Aug. 1948.

Galo Plaza Lasso, 1 Sept. 1948–31 Aug. 1952.

Dr José María Velasco Ibarra, 1 Sept. 1952–31 Aug. 1956.

Dr Camilo Ponce Enríquez, 1 Sept. 1956–31 Aug. 1960.

Dr José María Velasco Ibarra, 1 Sept. 1960–8 Nov. 1961 (withdrew).

Dr Carlos Julio Arosemena Monroy, 8 Nov. 1961–11 July 1963 (deposed).

Military Junta, 11 July 1963–31 March 1966.

Clemente Yerovi Indaburu, 31 March–16 Nov. 1966 (interim).

Dr Otto Arosemena Gómez, 17 Nov. 1966–1 Sept. 1968.

Dr José María Velasco Ibarra, 1 Sept. 1968–15 Feb. 1972 (deposed).

Gen. Guillermo Rodriguez Lara, 16 Feb. 1972–11 Jan. 1976 (resigned).

Adm. Alfredo Poveda Burbano, 11 Jan. 1976–10 Aug. 1979.

Jaime Roldós Aguilera, 10 Aug. 1979–24 May 1981.

President: Osvaldo Hurtado Larrea (sworn in on 24 May 1981).

The Cabinet in Nov. 1982 was as follows:

Foreign Affairs: Luis Valencia Rodríguez. *Interior:* Galo García Feraud. *Defence:* Gen. Jorge Maldonado Miño. *Finance:* Pedro Pinto. *National Resources and Energy:* Gustavo Galindo. *Health:* Francisco Huerta Montalvo. *Social Welfare:* Alfredo Mancero Samán. *Labour:* Vladimiro Alvarez. *Public Information:* Dr Ernesto Albán. *Industry, Trade and Integration:* Orlando Alcívar Santos. *Education and Sport:* Claudio Malo González. *Agriculture:* Carlos Vallejo. *Public Works and Communications:* Edwin Ripalda. *Central Bank President:* Abelardo Pachano. *Secretary-General of Administration:* Alfredo Negrete.

Local Government. The country is divided politically into 20 provinces; 4 of them comprise the 'Región Oriental' and one the Archipelago of Galápagos, officially called 'Colón', situated in the Pacific ocean about 600 miles to the west of Ecuador and comprising 15 islands. The provinces are administered by governors, appointed by the Government; their sub-divisions, or cantons, by political chiefs and elected cantonal councillors; and the parishes by political lieutenants. The Galápagos Archipelago is administered by the Ministry of National Defence.

DEFENCE. Military service is selective, with a 2-year period of conscription. The country is divided into 4 military zones, with headquarters at Quito, Guayaquil, Cuenca and Pastaza.

Army. The Army consists of 12 infantry brigades, 6 armoured brigades, 1 parachute battalion, 3 artillery battalions, 1 horsed regiment, 3 reconnaissance squadrons, 2 engineer battalions, 1 anti-aircraft battalion and 10 independent infantry companies. A military academy for cadets and a war academy for officers are maintained at Quito. Total strength (1983) 30,000.

Navy. The Navy consists of 2 Federal Republic of Germany-built diesel-electric powered patrol submarines; 1 old *ex*-US destroyer; 1 old frigate (*ex*-US destroyer escort transport), 3 Italian-built new corvettes, 3 fast missile boats, 3 fast torpedo boats, 2 gunboats, 5 patrol boats, 1 landing ship, 2 medium landing ships, 1 supply ship, 1 water carrier, 3 survey vessels, 2 coastguard service craft, 2 coastal patrol launches, 1 repair vessel, 2 training ships, 1 floating dock and 6 tugs. Three more corvettes are being completed in Italy. The two old *ex*-US PCE type escort vessels are now used one as a survey ship and the other as an harbour training ship. Naval personnel in 1983 totalled 3,800 officers and men.

Air Force. The Air Force, formed with Italian assistance in 1920, was reorganized and re-equipped with US aircraft after Ecuador signed the Rio Pact of Mutual Defence in 1947 but latest equipment acquired from Europe and Brazil. Current strength of about 4,800 personnel and 55 combat aircraft includes a strike squadron equipped with 10 single-seat and 2 two-seat Jaguars; an interceptor squadron of 15 single-seat and 2 two-seat Mirage F.1s; a squadron of 10 F-5E and 2 F-5F fighters; a bomber squadron with 3 Canberra B.6s; 2 counter-insurgency units equipped with 10 Cessna A-37B and 8 Strikemaster light jet attack and training aircraft, 1 squadron with 1 piston-engined DC-6 and 2 C-130, 2 Buffalo and 3 HS 748 turboprop transports; Alouette III, SA 330 Puma and SA 315B Lama helicopters; and Cessna 150, SIAI-Marchetti SF-260, T-28, T-33, T-34C and T-41A/D trainers; 14 EMB-326 Xavante light jet attack/trainers were acquired from Brazil in 1982. Many other transports are operated by the military airline TAME. Future equipment is expected to include Kfir-C2 fighters ordered from Israel.

INTERNATIONAL RELATIONS

Membership. Ecuador is a member of UN, OAS and LAIA (formerly LAFTA).

ECONOMY

Budget. Estimated revenue and expenditure for 1982 was 64,770m. sucres.

The division of the budget under main heads was, for 1982: Education and social development, 29·2%; defence, 9·1%; public works, 9·5%; agriculture, 6·4%.

Net international reserves, 31 Dec. 1980, were US$857m.

Currency. The monetary unit is the *sucre,* divided into 100 *centavos.* In circulation are a pure nickel 1-sucre and copper-nickel and copper-zinc 50-, 20-, 10- and 5-centavo pieces. The currency consists mainly of the notes of the Central Bank in denominations of 5, 10, 20, 50, 100, 500 and 1,000 sucres. In March 1983, US$1 = 35·15; £1 = 50·22.

Banking. The Central Bank of Ecuador, at Quito, with a capital of 20m. sucres, is modelled after the Federal Reserve Banks of US: through branches opened in 12 towns it now deals in mortgage bonds. On 31 July 1970 the Central Bank had gold and foreign-exchange reserves worth US$62m. Banks must hold cash equal to 21% of sight, short-term and savings deposits.

All commercial banks must be affiliated to the Central Bank; the commercial banks, 31 Oct. 1967, had capital and reserves of 463m. sucres and total assets of 4,536m. sucres. In circulation, Dec. 1972, 7,321m. sucres.

The Bank of London and Montreal, Ltd, had branches in Quito and Guayaquil.

Weights and Measures. By a law of 6 Dec. 1856 the metric system was made the legal standard but the Spanish measures are in general use. The quintal is equivalent to 101·4 lb.

The meridian of Quito has been adopted as the official time.

ENERGY AND NATURAL RESOURCES

Electricity. In 1982, total capacity of hydraulic and thermal plants was 990,000 kw. Estimated output was 2,000m. kwh.

Oil. Production of crude petroleum in 1981 was 77m. bbls; (1980) 75m. New drilling along the coast has had some success, but Ecuador has to import some crude oil. Proven oil reserves (1981, estimate) 1,100m. bbls.

Gas. In 1979, natural gas production was 14,834,061 cu. ft.

Minerals. A few firms are engaged in stoping mineralized vein material for copper, gold, silver, lead and zinc. Production is small: that of silver was 2 tonnes in 1972.

The country has some copper, iron and lead. There are coal deposits in the Biblián area, but their exploitation has so far proved uneconomic. Output of sea salt in 1970 was 40,000 tonnes.

Agriculture. Ecuador is divided into two agricultural zones: the coast and lower river valleys, where tropical farming is carried on in an average temperature of from 18° to 25° C.; and the Andean highlands with a temperate climate, adapted to grazing, dairying and the production of cereals, potatoes, pyrethrum and vegetables suitable to temperate climes. Some wheat has to be imported.

124,000 acres of rich virgin land in the Santo Domingo de los Colorados area has been set aside for settlement of smallholders.

Excepting the two agricultural zones and a few arid spots on the Pacific coast, Ecuador is a vast forest. Roughly estimated, 10,000 sq. miles on the Pacific slope extending from the sea to an altitude of 5,000 ft on the Andes, and the Amazon Basin below the same level containing 80,000 sq. miles, nearly all virgin forest, are rich in valuable timber, but much of it is still not commercially accessible.

The staple export products are bananas, cacao and coffee. Main crops, in 1,000 tonnes, in 1981: Rice, 402; wheat, 41; potatoes, 349; maize, 246; coffee, 88; barley, 27; cocoa, 96; bananas, 2,275.

Livestock (1981): Cattle, 3,032,000; sheep, 3,034,000; pigs, 3,721,000; poultry, 23·5m.

Forestry. In 1976, 4·03m. cu. metres of wood were cut.

Fisheries. Fisheries and fish product exports were valued at US$9·6m. in 1970; of these, shrimps comprised about half. In 1977, the total catch was 4,475,000 tonnes.

INDUSTRY AND TRADE

Industry. The Industrial Development of 1965 has stimulated the establishment of new industries, including textiles, refrigerators, pharmaceuticals, tinned food, batteries, etc. In 1971 there were 1,053 manufacturing units employing 50,000 people who earned 1·1m. sucres. Value of gross output, 11,172m. sucres. Cement output, 1976, from the country's 3 plants was 616,000 tonnes. Production in 1976: Sugar, 295,978 tonnes; beer, 1,370,406 hectolitres; tyres, 218,595; cigarettes, 3,704m.; cotton yarn (1975), 1,200 tonnes.

Commerce. Imports and exports for calendar years, in US$1m.:

	1977	*1978*	*1979*	*1980*	*1981*
Imports (c.i.f.)	1,288·7	1,630	1,997	2,170	1,946
Exports (f.o.b.)	1,189·4	1,494	2,192	2,590	2,542

Of the total exports (1980); petroleum, US$1,294·2; bananas, US$237·1m.; cocoa, US$211m.; coffee, US$144·1m.

USA furnished 35% of imports in 1970 and took 43% of the exports.

Total trade between Ecuador and UK (British Department of Trade returns, in £1,000 sterling):

	1978	*1979*	*1980*	*1981*	*1982*
Imports to UK	4,275	6,210	8,844	5,050	9,288
Exports and re-exports from UK	33,035	33,483	30,930	34,149	60,792

Tourism. There were 240,000 visitors in 1979, mainly from South American countries.

COMMUNICATIONS

Roads. In 1978, there were 28,000 km of roads of all types in this mountainous country, but most are narrow and subject to landslides. A trunk highway through the coastal plain is under construction which will link Machala in the extreme south-west with Esmeraldas in the north-west and with Quito and the northern section of the Pan-American Highway. In 1974, there were 43,600 cars and 68,400 trucks and buses.

Railways. A 1,067 mm gauge line runs from São Lorenzo through Quito to Guayaquil and Cuenca, total 971 km.

Aviation. The following international lines operate: Air France, Avianca, Braniff, British Caledonian, Ecuatoriana de Aviación, KLM, Lufthansa, Iberia, LAN Chile, and Aerovías Peruanas. They connect Quito with Panama, Bogotá (Colombia), Guayaquil, New York and Europe. All the leading towns are connected by an almost daily service, but landing fields are small.

Shipping. Ecuador has 7 seaports, of which Guayaquil is the chief. The merchant navy comprises 39,964 tons of seagoing and 21,232 tons of river craft. In 1970 ships totalling 8·88m. GRT entered Ecuadorean ports, unloading 1·52m. tons, and loading 1·77m. tons.

There is river communication, improved by dredging, throughout the principal agricultural districts on the low ground to the west of the Cordillera by the rivers Guayas, Daule and Vinces (navigable for 200 miles by river steamers in the rainy season).

Post and Broadcasting. Quito is connected by telegraph with Colombia and Peru, and by cable with the rest of the world. The main towns in the country are connected by radio-telephone. There are over 300 radio stations.

In 1980 there were 260,000 telephones in use, 103,200 in Quito and 97,267 in Guayaquil; most were operated by the Government; 96·2% were automatic. Television was inaugurated in 1960 in Guayaquil, in 1961 in Quito and in 1967 in Cuenca. In 1975 there were 1·7m. radio receivers and 252,000 television receivers.

Cinemas. (1974). Cinemas numbered about 185 with total seating capacity of 114,600.

Newspapers (1971). There were 22 daily newspapers with an aggregate daily circulation of 283,000; 7 papers in Quito and Guayaquil have the bulk of the circulation.

JUSTICE, RELIGION, EDUCATION AND WELFARE

Justice. The Supreme Court in Quito is the highest tribunal and consists of 5 justices and the Minister Fiscal. Of the 15 superior courts, 4 are composed of 6 judges and 11 of 3 judges each. There are numerous lower courts. The popular jury was abolished in 1928, and criminal cases are heard before a 'special jury' consisting of 1 judge and 3 members of the Ecuadorean bar, appointed annually by the superior courts. Capital punishment and all forms of torture are prohibited under the constitution, as are imprisonment for debt and contracts involving personal servitude or slavery. Substantial amendments expediting judicial procedure were introduced in 1936, and salaries for all judicial officials replaced remuneration by fees.

Religion. The state recognizes no religion and grants freedom of worship to all. Civil registration of births, deaths and marriages is obligatory. Divorce is permitted. Illegitimate children have the same rights as legitimate ones with respect to education and inheritance.

The Catholic Church has 1 cardinal, 3 archbishops and 18 bishops. A *modus vivendi* was concluded with the Holy See on 24 July 1937, governing the relations between the Catholic Church and the State. Protestants numbered 19,200 in 1966.

Education. Primary education is free and in principle obligatory. Private schools, both primary and secondary, are under some state supervision. There were (1976–77) pre-primary schools with 88,168 pupils, primary schools with 1,294,587 pupils; secondary schools with 425,765 pupils and universities with (1979–80) 230,637 students.

Social Welfare. From 1 May 1964 social benefits are extended to professional men, artisans and domestic workers; and to agricultural workers from 1 May 1965. The Ministry of Social Welfare and Labour was in 1967 divided into the Ministries of Social Welfare and of Public Health. In 1970 there were 199 hospitals with 14,024 beds.

DIPLOMATIC REPRESENTATIVES

Of Ecuador in Great Britain (3 Hans Crescent, London, SW1X 0LS)
Ambassador: Orlando Gabela (accredited 12 March 1980).

Of Great Britain in Ecuador (Calle Gonzalez Suarez 111, Quito)
Ambassador: A. C. Buxton, CMG.

Of Ecuador in the USA (2535–15th St., NW, Washington, D.C., 20009)
Ambassador: Dr Ricardo Crespo-Zaldumbide.

Of the USA in Ecuador (120 Avenida Patria, Quito)
Chargé d'Affaires: John J. Youle.

Of Ecuador to the United Nations
Ambassador: Dr Miguel A. Albornoz.

Books of Reference

Anuario de Legislación Ecuatoriana. Quito. Annual
Boletín del Banco Central. Quito
Boletín General de Estadística. Tri-monthly
Boletín Mensual del Ministerio de Obras Públicas. Monthly
Informes Ministeriales. Quito. Annual
Bibliografía Nacional, 1756–1941. Quito, 1942
Invest in Ecuador. Banco Central del Ecuador, Quito, 1980
Bromley, R. J., *Development Planning in Ecuador.* London, 1977
Buitrón, A., and Collier, Jr, J., *The Awakening Valley: Study of the Otavalo Indians.* New York, 1950
Cueva, A., *The Process of Political Domination in Ecuador.* London, 1982
Holdridge, L. R. and others, *The Forests of Western and Central Ecuador.* Washington, 1947
Martz, J. D., *Ecuador: Conflicting Political Culture and the Quest for Progress.* Boston, 1972

EGYPT

Jumhuriyat Misr al-Arabiya

Capital: Cairo
Population: 44m. (1982)
GNP per capita: US$580 (1980)

HISTORY. Part of the Ottoman Empire from 1517 until Dec. 1914 when it became a British protectorate, Egypt became an independent monarchy on 28 Feb. 1922. Following a military *coup* on 23 July 1952, a Republic was proclaimed on 18 June 1953. Egypt merged with Syria on 1 Feb. 1958 to form the United Arab Republic, retaining that name when Syria broke away from the union on 28 Sept. 1961, finally re-adopting the name of Egypt on 2 Sept. 1971.

AREA AND POPULATION. Egypt is bounded east by Israel, the Gulf of Aqaba and the Red Sea, south by Sudan, west by Libya and north by the Mediterranean. The total area is 997,667 sq. km (385,201 sq. miles), but the cultivated and settled area, that is, the Nile valley, delta and oases, covers only about 35,580 sq. km.

The area, population (1976 Census) and capitals of the governerates are:

Governorate	*Sq. km*	*1976 census*	*Capital*
Sinai	60,714	10,104	Al-Arish
Suez	17,840	194,001	Suez
Ismailia	1,442	351,889	Ismailia
Port Said	72	262,620	Port Said
Sharqîya	4,180	2,621,208	Zagazig
Daqahlîya	3,471	2,732,756	Mansûra
Damietta	589	557,115	Damietta
Kafr el Sheikh	3,437	1,403,468	Kafr el-Sheikh
Alexandria	2,679	2,318,655	Alexandria
Behera	4,589	2,517,292	Damanhur
Gharbîya	1,942	2,294,303	Tanta
Menûfîya	1,612	1,710,982	Shibin el-Kom
Qalyûbîya	971	1,674,006	Benha
Cairo	214	5,084,463	Cairo
Gîza	1,010	2,419,247	Gîza
Faiyûm	1,827	1,140,245	Faiyûm
Beni Suef	1,322	1,108,615	Beni-Suef
Minya	2,262	2,055,739	Minya
Asyût	1,530	1,695,378	Asyût
Sohag	1,547	1,924,960	Sohag
Qena	1,851	1,705,594	Qena
Aswân	679	619,932	Aswân
al-Bahr al-Ahmar	203,685	56,191	Al-Ghurdaqah
al-Wadi al-Jadid	376,505	84,645	Al-Kharijah
Mersa Matruh	298,735	112,772	Matruh
Total		36,656,180	

The principal towns, with their census 1976 populations, are:

Cairo	5,074,016	Mansûra	257,866	Minya	146,423
Alexandria	2,317,705	Asyût	213,983	Ismailia	145,978
Giza	1,246,713	Zagazig	202,637	Aswân	144,377
Shubra el-Khema	393,700	Suez	193,965	Beni-Suef	118,148
Mahalla el-Kubra	292,853	Damanhûr	188,927	Shibin el-Kom	102,840
Tanta	284,636	Faiyûm	167,081	Sohag	101,758
Port Said	262,760	Kafr el-Dwar	160,554		

Population (1982) 44m. and of Greater Cairo (1979) 8·54m. The 1976 census total excluded an estimated 1,572,000 nationals living abroad.

CONSTITUTION AND GOVERNMENT. The Constitution was

approved by referendum on 11 Sept. 1971. It defines Egypt as 'an Arab Republic with a democratic, socialist system' and the Eyptian people as 'part of the Arab nation' with Islam as the state religion and Arabic as the official language.

The President of the Republic is nominated by the People's Assembly and confirmed by plebiscite for a 6-year term. He is the supreme commander of the armed forces and presides over the defence council.

Presidents since the establishment of the Republic have been:

Gen. Mohamed Neguib, 18 June 1953–14 Nov. 1954 (deposed).
Col. Gamal Abdel Nasser, 14 Nov. 1954–28 Sept. 1970 (died).
Col. Mumammad Anwar Sadat, 28 Sept. 1970–6 Oct. 1981 (assassinated).
Lieut.-Gen. Muhammad Hosni Mubarak, 7 Oct. 1981–.

The People's Assembly is a unicameral legislature consisting of 382 members directly elected for a 5-year term; the President of the Republic may appoint up to 10 additional members. At the general elections held in June 1979, the National Democratic Party gained 330 seats, the Socialist Labour Party 29, the Liberal Socialist Party 3, and independents 10. By 1982, 13 of the SLP members had become independent or joined the NDP.

Following the abolition of the Arab Socialist Union in April 1980, a 210-member Consultative Council (*Shuwa*) was formed in Sept. 1980; all 140 of its elective seats were won by the NDP, and a further 70 members appointed by the President.

The President may appoint one or more Vice-Presidents, and appoints a Prime Minister and a Council of Ministers, whom he may remove as he wishes.

President of the Republic: Hosni Mubarak.

The Council of Ministers in March 1983 was composed as follows:

Prime Minister and Minister for Al-Azhar Mosque: Dr Fuad Mohieddin.

Deputy Prime Minister and Foreign Minister: Kamal Hassan Ali. *Deputy Prime Minister for Production and Oil Minister:* Ezzedin Hilal. *Deputy Prime Minister and Minister of Defence and Military Production:* Abdelhalim Abu-Ghazala. *Deputy Prime Minister for Services and Education and Minister of Scientific Research:* Mustafa Kamal Helmi. *Finance:* Mahmoud Salahadin Hamed. *Labour:* Saad Muhammad Ahmed. *Justice:* Ahmed Mamdouh Atteya. *Transport and Communications:* Suleiman Mutwally. *Irrigation:* Abdelhadi Samaha. *Electricity and Power:* Maher Abaza. *Planning:* Kamal Ahmed al-Ganzouri. *Interior:* Hassan Abu-Basha. *Investments and International Co-operation:* Wagih Shindi. *Economy and Foreign Trade:* Mustafa Kamal al-Said Ibrahim. *Tourism and Civil Aviation:* Tawfik Abon Ismial. *Local Administration:* Saad Maamoun. *Supply and Internal Trade:* Muhammad Nagui-Shatla. *Industry and Metals:* Muhammad Sayed al-Gharouri.

National flag: Three horizontal stripes of red, white, black, with the national emblem in the centre in gold.

Local Government. There are 25 governorates: 16 provinces, 5 cities and 4 frontier districts.

DEFENCE. The total strength of the defence forces was about 452,000 in 1983. There were also paramilitary forces of 139,000.

Army. Service in the Army is compulsory for all male citizens at the age of 18. The Army comprised (1981) 2 armoured divisions, 3 mechanized infantry divisions, 5 infantry divisions, 3 independent armoured and 8 independent infantry brigades, 1 parachute brigade, 2 airborne brigades, 7 artillery brigades and 6 commando groups. Its tank strength (1980) was about 1,680, mainly USSR. Total strength was (1983) about 320,000 men; conscripts, 180,000.

Navy. There are 12 elderly diesel-driven *ex*-Soviet submarines (nearing the end of their hull lives of which not more than 9 can be operational), 5 old destroyers, 3 very old frigates, 10 fleet minesweepers, 2 inshore minesweepers, 30 torpedo boats, 24 missile boats, 12 submarine chasers, 15 coastal patrol boats, 2 training ships, 3 medium landing ships, 14 landing craft, 2 survey vessels, 10 service craft, 2 tenders, 3 hovercraft, 7 auxiliaries and 2 tugs.

Naval bases are at Alexandria, Port Said, Mersa Matru, Port Tewfik, Hurghada and Safaqa. The Naval Academy is at Abu Qir.

Naval personnel in 1983 exceeded 20,000 officers and men, including the Coastguard, but not reserves of about 15,000.

Air Force. Until 1979, the Air Force was equipped largely with aircraft of USSR design, but current re-equipment involves aircraft bought in the West, as well as some supplied by China. Current strength is about 27,000 personnel and 400 combat aircraft, of which the interceptors are operated by an independent Air Defence Command, in conjunction with many 'Guideline', 'Goa' and 'Gainful' missile batteries. There are about 16 Tu-16 twin-jet strategic bombers, some equipped to carry 'Kelt' air-to-surface missiles. The strike force includes a few Il-28 twin-jet bombers, and about 50 Su-7B and 18 Su-20 supersonic fighter-bombers. Other interceptor/ground attack fighter divisions are equipped with 40 F-16 Fighting Falcons, 75 Mirage 5s, 35 F-4E Phantoms, 75 J-6s (Chinese-built MiG-19s), and more than 100 MiG-21s, with 60 to 80 J-7s (Chinese-built MiG-21s) reportedly on order, for assembly in Egypt. Transport units have 21 C-130H Hercules turboprop heavy freighters, 10 twin-turboprop Buffalos and up to 175 Gazelle, Mi-4, Mi-6, Mi-8, Sea King/Commando and Agusta-built CH-47C helicopters; 2 EC-130H Hercules are equipped for ECM duties. Training units are equipped with Gomhouria piston-engined trainers, Czech-built L-29 Delfin jet trainers, single-seat and two-seat versions of the MiG-15, MiG-17s, two-seat FT-6s, Mirage IIIs, MiG-21Us and Su-7Us, and Gazelle helicopters. Delivery has begun of 45 Alpha Jets, of which 15 will be equipped for close air support duties, to replace the MiG-15s and MiG-17s. On order for mid-80s delivery are 4 E-2C Hawkeye AWACS aircraft. Main aircrew training centre is the EAF Academy at Bilbeis.

INTERNATIONAL RELATIONS

Membership. Egypt is a member of UN, OAU, the Arab League and OAPEC.

ECONOMY

Planning. A 'permanent council of national production' was established in 1952.

A 5-year development plan runs 1980–84 and envisages and annual growth rate of 10%.

In 1961–62 a number of sweeping socialist measures were carried out, which contributed largely to the Syrian defection in Sept. 1961. In addition to the nationalization of banks, insurance companies, etc., about 1,000 private businessmen had their property confiscated by Jan. 1962. In 1963 complete nationalization was enforced of all cotton exporting and ginning firms, pharmaceutical factories and some 400 other companies in which the State had previously held a half-share. Share owners were compensated by government bonds redeemable over 15 years at 4% interest.

Budget. Ordinary revenue and expenditure for fiscal years ending 30 June, in £E1,000:

	1976 [1]	*1977* [1]	*1978* [1]	*1979* [1]
Revenue	5,976	5,503	6,516	10,249
Expenditure	5,976	5,503	6,516	12,929

[1]Estimates.

Currency. By decree of 18 Oct. 1916 (20 Zi-El-Higga 1934), the monetary unit of Egypt is the gold Egyptian pound of 100 *piastres* of 1,000 *millièmes*. Coins in circulation are 20, 10, 5, 2 piastres (silver); 2, 1 piastre, 5 millièmes, 1 millième (bronze). Gold coins are no longer in circulation. Silver coin is legal tender only up to £E1, and bronze coins up to 10 piastres. The Treasury issues 5- and 10-piastre currency notes. Bank-notes are issued by the National Bank in denominations of 5, 10, 25 and 50 piastres, £E1, 5, 10, 20, and 100.

In March 1983, £1 sterling = £E1·26; US$ = £E1·428.

Banking. On 18 Aug. 1960 a Central Bank of Egypt was established by decree. It manages the note issue, the Government's banking operations and the control of commercial banks. At the same date the National Bank founded in 1898 ceased to be the central bank and became a purely commercial bank. The position of the bank at 31 Dec. 1976 was (in £E): Capital and reserves, 28,778,550; investments, securities and other investments, 78,252,590; discounts, advances and sundry debit balances, 607,652,637; deposits, 525,853,275.

Weights and Measures. In 1951 the metric system was made official with the exception of the feddân and its subdivisions.

Capacity. Kadah = 1/96th ardeb = 3·36 pints. *Rob* = 4 kadahs = 1·815 gallons. *Keila* = 8 kadahs = 3·63 gallons. *Ardeb* = 96 kadahs = 43·555 gallons, or 5·44439 bu., or 198 cu. decimetres.

Weights. Rotl = 144 dirhems = 0·9905 lb. *Oke* = 400 dirhems = 2·75137 lb. *Qantâr* or 100 rotls or 36 okes = 99·0493 lb. 1 *Qantâr* of unginned cotton = 315 lb. 1 *Qantâr* of ginned cotton = 99·05 lb. The approximate weight of the ardeb is as follows: Wheat, 150 kg; beans, 155 kg; barley, 120 kg; maize, 140 kg; cotton seed, 121 kg.

Surface. Feddân, the unit of measure for land = 4,200·8 sq. metres = 7,468·148 sq. pics = 1·03805 acres. 1 sq. pic = 6·0547 sq. ft = 0·5625 sq. metre.

ENERGY AND NATURAL RESOURCES

Electricity. Electricity generated in 1980 was 18,500m. kwh.

Oil. The first commercial discovery of oil in the Middle East outside Iran was made in Egypt in 1909, but production long remained low and often insufficient to meet Egypt's domestic requirements. In 1979 production was rising again and with the newly-regained Sinai oilfields was 25·5m. tonnes. In 1976 a major exploration effort was being mounted and the Egyptian Government hoped that, as a result, production would reach 1m. bbls a day by 1981.

Policy is controlled by the Egyptian General Petroleum Corporation (EGPC) a wholly state-owned corporation answerable to the Minister of Petroleum. EGPC is whole or part-owner of the various production and refining companies and controls supplies to the domestic marketing companies.

In 1978, 24,299,000 tonnes of crude petroleum and 11,362,000 tonnes of refined products were produced.

Minerals. Production (1973 in tonnes): Phosphate rock, 553,000; iron ore, 656,000; marine salt, 454,000.

Agriculture. Rain seldom falls in Upper Egypt, and only at irregular intervals in Cairo, where the average for the year is no more than 1·2 in. At Alexandria the average is 8 in.

The cultivated area of Egypt proper was estimated in 1971 at 10·74m. feddâns (1 feddân = 1·038 acres) and of this 4,869,000 feddâns were under winter crops, 5,012,000 under summer crops and 613,000 under Nile crops.

The Agricultural Reform Decree of Sept. 1952 limits agricultural ownership to 200 feddâns, reduced to 100 feddâns in July 1961. Foreigners were debarred in 1963 from owning any land. Holdings in excess of this limit will be redistributed; compensation, equivalent to 10 times the rental value of the land, will take the form of 3% (from 1958: 1½%) bonds redeemable within 30 years (from 1958: 40 years). All national *waqfs* are to be dissolved.

Irrigation occupies a predominant place in the economic development of the country. The Aswân reservoir can now hold up to 5,500m. cu. metres of water, and the Gebel Aulia reservoir, completed in 1937, holds 2,000m. cu. metres. Barrages have been erected at Nag' Hammâdi, Asyût and Zifta, and at the bifurcation of the Nile below Cairo. Esna, Nag' Hammâdi barrage, completed in 1930, ensures full basin supplies even in low flood to Girga province, and will facilitate perennial irrigation when basin lands are converted. Asyût barrage, having been remodelled, will meet the greater demands of the area it now commands. The Esna barrage now secures basin irrigation to lands in Qena province. New barrages (Mohamed Ali barrages) have been completed at the bifurcation of the Nile below Cairo to replace the existing structures which, built in 1861, are now unable to meet the conditions following the increase in summer supplies, the reclamation of large areas of waste lands and the earlier watering of food crops.

On 8 Nov. 1959 the United Arab Republic and Sudan concluded agreements on the sharing of the Nile waters (after construction of the Aswân High Dam), and trade, payments and Customs dues. The agreement provides that from the time the High Dam started to store water (15 May 1964) Sudan will be entitled to 18,500m. cu. metres of the total annual flow and Egypt to 55,500m.

In 1979 the area (1,000 hectares) and production (1,000 tonnes) were: Wheat, 584(1,856); barley, 45(122); beans (dry), 7(13); lentils, 9(9); onions, 21(536); maize, 791(2,938); millet, 171(635); sugar-cane, 105(8,488).

The rice crop was 2·3m. tonnes in 1977.

Livestock (1981): 1·91m. cattle, 2·3m. buffaloes, 1·6m. sheep, 1·4m. goats, 84,000 camels and 15,000 pigs.

Fisheries. The catch of the Egyptian sea, Nile and lake fisheries in 1957 amounted to 102,600 tonnes. In 1952 there were 48,947 men and 16,347 boys engaged in fishing and 11,739 boats used for fishing.

INDUSTRY AND TRADE

Industry. In 1979 there were 1.5m. Egyptians employed in manufacturing. Production in 1978 included 600,000 tonnes of crude steel, 300,000 tonnes of pig-iron and 3m. tonnes of cement.

Electricity generated in 1969 was 7,316m. kw.

Trade Unions. Trade unions were first recognized in 1942. In 1952 the acts concerning trade unions, individual contracts, and conciliation and arbitration were recast. Employment exchanges and unemployment statistics were introduced in 1953. Social insurance was enacted in 1955.

Commerce. Imports and exports for 5 years (in £E1,000):

	1976	*1977*	*1978*	*1979*	*1980*
Imports	1,489,908	1,884,278	2,632,180	2,686,200	3,402,000
Exports	595,450	668,478	679,754	1,287,800	2,132,200

In 1979, raw cotton and cotton products represented 34% of total exports, crude oil 31% and petroleum products 11%; 27% of exports went to Italy, 8% to the USSR and 8% to the Netherlands; 18% of imports came from the USA, 11% from Federal Rep. of Germany.

Total trade between Egypt and UK (British Department of Trade returns, in £1,000 sterling):

	1978	*1979*	*1980*	*1981*	*1982*
Imports to UK	101,685	252,733	336,595	414,599	412,802
Exports and re-exports from UK	205,570	264,494	346,688	325,141	338,645

Tourism. In 1979, 1,064,000 foreigners visited Egypt.

COMMUNICATIONS

Roads. In 1980, the total length of roads was 21,637 km, of which 16,182 km were paved. Motor vehicles, in 1980, 325,500 private cars, 114,700 commercial vehicles (including buses).

Railways. In 1980 there were 4,446 km of state railways and 2,554 km of service tracks etc. The state railways have gauges of 1,435 mm and 740 mm.

In 1981–82 the railways carried 8·2m. tonnes of freight and 383m. passengers.

Aviation. There is an international airport at Cairo. A new airport at Cairo began operations in 1977. The national airline Egyptair has a fleet of 20 aircraft. Egyptair operates scheduled flights connecting Cairo with Athens, Rome, Frankfurt, Zürich, London, Khartoum, Tokyo, Bombay, Aden, Jeddah, Doha, Dharan, Kuwait, Beirut, Baghdad, Tripoli, Benghazi, Algiers, Entebbe, Nairobi, Dar-es-Salaam, Kano, Lagos, Accra, Abidjan, Damascus, Amman, Manilla, Paris, Munich, Copenhagen, Nicosia, Karachi, Aleppo, Bahrain, Abu Dhabi, Dubai, Sharjah, Sanaa and Vienna. In addition, Egyptair operates scheduled flights on a widespread domestic network connecting Cairo with Port Said, Mersa Matruh, Asyût, Luxor, Aswân.

Shipping. The Egyptian merchant navy in 1980 consisted of 75 steamers of 387,460 tons.

In 1977, 3,050 ships of 11,432,000 tons entered the port of Alexandria and 876 ships of 4,583,000 tons entered Port Said.

Suez Canal. The Suez Canal was opened for navigation on 17 Nov. 1869. By the convention of Constantinople of 29 Oct. 1888 the canal is open to vessels of all nations and is free from blockade, except in time of war, but the UAR Government did not allow Israeli ships to use the canal until May 1979, when the embargo was lifted. It is 173 km long (excluding 11 km of approach channels to the harbours), connecting the Mediterranean with the Red Sea. Its minimum width is 197 ft at a depth of 33 ft, and its depth permits the passage of vessels up to 38 ft draught.

In 1976 a 2-stage development project was started. The first stage which was completed in 1980 allowing vessels, of up to 150,000 tons, fully loaded, and up to 370,000 tons in ballast to pass through the canal and give a draught of 53 ft.

During the war with Israel in June 1967 Egypt blocked the Canal. The canal was cleared and re-opened to shipping on 5 June 1975. This is part of a programme to develop and rebuild the whole area of Suez to make it one of the largest tax-free industrial zones. Canal toll fees reached £E660m. in 1980, and in 1980 21,603 vessels (281·3m. tons) went through the canal.

On 1 Jan. 1981 charges were increased by 30%. The first tunnel below the canal, located 10 miles north of Suez City, was completed on 30 April 1980.

UNCTAD, *Economic Effects of the Closure of the Suez Canal.* Geneva, 1974
Baxter, R. R., *The Law of International Waterways.* Harvard Univ. Press, 1964
Lauterpacht, E. (ed.), *The Suez Canal Settlement, 1956–59.* London, 1960
Marlow, J., *The Making of the Suez Canal.* London, 1964

Post and Broadcasting. The telephone service was taken over by the Egyptian Government in April 1918. In 1958–59 the state telegraphs had a length of 15,381 km of wire, and telephones, 1,076,159 km. There were, in 1978, 1,590 postal agencies, 1,812 mobile offices, 1,579 government and 2,833 private post offices. Number of telephones in 1981, 534,021. Number of wireless licences in 1975, 5·12m. and 620,000 TV licences.

The internal telecommunications system is owned and operated by the Telecommunications Organization. Government landlines connect with those of the Gaza sector and the Sudan.

Cinemas (1971). There were 152 cinemas with a seating capacity of 140,900.

Newspapers. On 23 May 1960 all newspapers were nationalized.

JUSTICE, RELIGION, EDUCATION AND WELFARE

Justice. The National Courts in 1981 were as follows: Court of Cassation with a bench of 5 judges which constitutes the highest court of appeal in both criminal and civil cases; Courts of Appeal with 3 judges situated in Cairo and 4 other cities; Assize Courts with 3 judges which deal with all cases of serious crime; Central Tribunals with 3 judges which deal with ordinary civil and commercial cases; Summary Tribunals presided over by a single judge which hear civil disputes in matters up to the value of £E3,250, and criminal offences punishable by a fine or imprisonment of up to 3 years.

Religion. In 1947 the population (excluding Nomads) consisted of 17,397,946 Moslems (91·46%); 1,186,353 Orthodox Copts; 86,918 Protestant Copts; 72,764

Roman Catholic Copts; 89,062 other Orthodox; 50,200 other Roman Catholics; 16,338 other Protestants; 1,547 Jews, other and unknown.

There are in Egypt large numbers of native Christians connected with the various Oriental Churches; of these, the largest and most influential are the Copts, who adopted Christianity in the 1st century. Their head is the Coptic Patriarch. There are 25 metropolitans and bishops in Egypt; 4 metropolitans for Ethiopia, Jerusalem, Khartoum and Omdurman, and 12 bishops in Ethiopia. Priests must be married before ordination, but celibacy is imposed on monks and high dignitaries. The Copts use the Diocletian (or Martyrs') calendar, which begins in A.D. 284.

Education. Education was made compulsory for all children between the ages of 6 and 12 in 1933; primary education (6 years) was made free in 1944, secondary and technical education in 1950. Compulsory education is provided in primary schools (6 years).

In 1978–79 there were 4,287,124 primary school pupils and 127,021 teachers; 1,990,383 secondary school pupils and 67,567 teachers; and 492,664 technical school pupils with 29,353 teachers. Teacher-training colleges had 40,595 students and 3,373 teaching staff in 1978–79.

There are 12 universities in Egypt. Cairo University, founded in 1908 as a private institution and taken over by the Government in 1925; Alexandria University, founded by the Government in 1942; the Ein Shams University, founded by the Government in Cairo in 1950 and universities at Asyût Al-Azhar, Tanta, Mansûra, Zagazig, Helwan, Suez Canal, Minya and Menoufia. The number of students at universities was 476,537 in 1977–78.

Health. In 1966 there were about 6,000 doctors and (1970–71) 72,976 hospital beds.

DIPLOMATIC REPRESENTATIVES

Of Egypt in Great Britain (26 South St., London, W1Y 8EL)
Ambassador: Hassan Aly Abou-Seéda (accredited 27 Feb. 1980).

Of Great Britain in Egypt (Ahmed Ragheb St., Garden City, Cairo)
Ambassador: Sir Michael Weir, KCMG.

Of Egypt in the USA (2310 Decatur Pl., NW, Washington, D.C., 20008)
Ambassador: Dr Ashraf A. Ghorbal.

Of the USA in Egypt (5 Sharia Latin America, Cairo)
Ambassador: Alfred L. Atherton, Jr.

Of Egypt to the United Nations
Ambassador: Dr Ahmed Esmat Abdel Meguid.

Books of Reference

Statistical Information: The Department of Statistics and Census (15, Sharia Mansour, Cairo) was formed in 1905. *Chief:* Under-Secretary of State for Statistical Affairs, Dr Hasan M. Husein. Previously, various government departments had their own statistical sections. Estimates of population were made in 1800, 1821 and 1846; the first census took place in 1873. Among the publications of the Department are the following: *Annuaire Statistique* (Arabic and French). *Annual Return of Shipping* (Arabic and English). *Monthly Summary and Annual Statement of Foreign Trade* (Arabic and English). *Monthly Bulletin of Agriculture and Economic Statistics* (Arabic and English). *Vital Statistics* (Arabic and English). *Statistical Pocket Year-Book* (Arabic and English).

The Egyptian Almanac. Annual
Le Mondain Egyptien (Who's Who). Cairo. Annual
Cooper, M. N., *The Transformation of Egypt.* London, 1982
Dawisha, A. I., *Egypt in the Arab World.* London, 1976
Elias, E. A., *Modern Dictionary English–Arabic.* 5th ed. Cairo, 1946
Fedden, R., *Egypt: Land of the Valley.* London, 1977
Hirst, D., and Beeson, I., *Sadat.* London, 1981
Hopwood, D., *Egypt: Politics and Society 1945–1981.* London, 1982

Mabro, R., and Radwan, S., *The Industrialization of Egypt 1939–1973.* Oxford, 1976
Nelson, N., *Egypt.* London, 1976
Richmond, J. C. B., *Egypt 1798–1952.* London, 1977
Rubinstein, A. Z., *Red Star on the Nile: The Soviet–Egyptian Relationship Since the June War.* Princeton Univ. Press, 1977
Vatikiotis, P. J., *The History of Egypt: From Muhammad Ali to Sadat.* 2nd ed. London, 1980

EL SALVADOR

Capital: San Salvador
Population: 4·54m. (1980)
GNP per capita: US$590 (1980)

República de El Salvador

HISTORY. In 1839 the Central American Federation, which had comprised the states of Guatemala, El Salvador, Honduras, Nicaragua and Costa Rica, was dissolved, and El Salvador declared itself formally an independent republic in 1841.

AREA AND POPULATION. El Salvador is the smallest and most densely populated of the Central American states. Its area (including 247 sq. km of inland lakes) is estimated at 21,393 sq. km (8,236 sq. miles) with population (census 1980) of 4,539,500. The capital is San Salvador (1,902,500 inhabitants in 1980).

A Treaty was signed in Peru on 30 Oct. 1980 settling the border dispute between El Salvador and Honduras which caused 4 days of fighting in July 1979.

The republic is divided into 14 departments, each under an appointed governor. Their areas (in sq. km) and populations at census 1971 were:

Department	*Area*	*Population*	*Department*	*Area*	*Population*
San Salvador	892	681,656	La Paz	1,155	194,196
Santa Ana	1,829	375,186	Chalatenango	2,507	186,003
San Miguel	2,532	337,325	Ahuachapán	1,281	183,682
Usulután	1,780	304,369	Marazán	1,364	170,706
La Libertad	1,650	293,076	San Vicente	1,175	160,534
Sonsonate	1,133	239,688	Cuscatlán	766	158,458
La Unión	1,738	230,103	Cabañas	1,075	139,312

Important towns (with population census 1971) are: Santa Ana, 96,306; San Miguel, 59,304; Mejicanos, 54,916; Delgado, 44,367; Nueva San Salvador, 35,106; Sonsonate, 33,562.

There has been considerable emigration into nearby states. There are no tribal Indians. The language of the country is Spanish.

CONSTITUTION AND GOVERNMENT. The latest Constitution was enacted in Jan. 1962, slightly amending that of 1950. The Executive Power is vested in a President elected for a non-renewable term of 5 years, with Ministers and Under-Secretaries appointed by him. The Legislative power is an Assembly of 52 members elected by universal suffrage and proportional representation for a term of 2 years. The judicial power is vested in a Supreme Court, of a President and 9 magistrates elected by the Legislative Assembly for renewable terms of 3 years; and subordinate courts. For governments, 1961–79 *see* STATESMAN'S YEAR-BOOK 1982–83, p. 436.

The Constituent Assembly met on 22 April 1982 following the elections of 28 March. Dr Alvaro Magaña was elected interim President of the Constituent Assembly by 36 votes to 17, with 7 abstentions, on 29 April and was sworn in on 2 May.

On 4 May a 14-member cabinet took office including:

Interior: Manuel Isidro López Sermeno. *Foreign Affairs:* Dr Fidel Cháves Mena. *Economy:* Samuel Bicard.

In Sept. 1982 the President announced that general elections would be held in Sept. 1984 and a new Constitution would be drafted during 1983.

During 1982–3, there was continuing fighting between government forces and guerrillas and it was estimated that 13,000–16,000 people were killed in 1981 as a result of the violence.

The results of Constituent Assembly elections held on 28 March 1982 were: Christian Democratic Party, 24; Arena, 19; National Conciliation Party, 14; Democratic Action, 2; Salvadrean People's Party, 1.

National flag: Blue, white, blue (horizontal): the white stripe charged with the arms of the republic.

National anthem: Saludemos la patria orgullosos (words by J. J. Cañas; tune by J. Aberle).

DEFENCE

Army. The Army is organized in 3 territorial divisions of 3 infantry brigades, 1 artillery brigade, 1 air defence battalion, 1 engineer battalion, 1 parachute battalion, and 1 cavalry squadron. Total strength (1983), 15,900 men. There are also the National Guard, the National Police and the Treasury Police. Strength, 9,000.

Navy. The Navy includes 2 patrol boats, 1 new French-built tug, 2 cutters and 3 other small coastguard craft and 25 service launches. Personnel in 1983 totalled 140 officers and men.

Air Force. The Air Force underwent a major re-equipment programme in 1974–75, with most aircraft coming from Israel and US aid for transport units, but lost 18 aircraft in a guerilla attack in Jan. 1982. Combat squadron now has 6 A-37 and 5 Ouragan jet fighter-bombers, supported by 7 Israeli-built Magister jets and 6 piston-engined Rallyes for light attack duties, and 4 Cessna O-2s for reconnaissance. Transports include 1 C-47 and 4 Israeli-built light twin-engined Aravas, plus 1 Lama, 1 Alouette III and 14 UH-1H helicopters. Training types include about 20 piston-engined T-41Cs, T-6s and T-34s. Strength totalled about 1,000 personnel in 1982.

INTERNATIONAL RELATIONS

Membership. El Salvador is a member of UN and OAS.

ECONOMY

Budget. Revenue and expenditure for fiscal years ending 31 Dec., in 1,000 colónes (2·5 colónes = US$1):

	1975	*1976*	*1977*	*1978*	*1979*	*1980*
Revenue	729,700	1,069,000	1,252,000	1,252,000	1,452,000	1,676,000
Expenditure	729,700	1,069,000	1,252,000	1,252,000	1,452,000	1,676,000

External debt amounted to US$175·4m. on 30 June 1975.

Currency. The monetary unit is the *colón* (₡) of 100 *centavos*. The *colón* (₡) is issued in denominations of 1, 2, 5, 10, 25 and 100 *colónes*; 25 and 50 *centavos* (silver); 1, 2, 3, 5 and 10 *centavos* (copper–nickel and copper–zinc). In March 1983, £1 = ₡3·79; US$1 = ₡2·50.

Banking. There are 6 native commercial banks, including the Banco Salvadoreño (paid-up capital, 6m. colónes). The Bank of London and Montreal and the Citibank are the only foreign institutions. The Central Reserve Bank of El Salvador, constructed in 1934 out of the Banco Agricola Comercial, was nationalized on 20 April 1961. A stock exchange was officially inaugurated in Oct. 1962 with the declared intention of promoting investments in Central America; it began operations on 17 Aug. 1964 with a capital of 100,000 colónes subscribed by 360 shareholders. Its activities have been limited.

Weights and Measures. On 1 Jan. 1886 the metric system was made obligatory. But other units are still commonly in use, of which the principal are as follows: *Libra* = 1·014 lb. av.; *quintal* = 101·4 lb. av.; *arroba* = 25·35 lb. av.; *fanega* = 1·5745 bushels.

ENERGY AND NATURAL RESOURCES

Electricity. El Salvador's biggest national enterprise, begun in 1950, is the construction of a 200ft high dam across the (unnavigable) Lempa River, 35 miles north-east of San Salvador, designed to double the country's electric-power resources, from 31,000 to 78,000 kw. Production in 1979, 1,586m. kwh.; consumption (1975), 831·9m. kwh.

Oil. Production of petrol lubricants and petroleum derivatives during 1970 totalled ₡15·8m.

Minerals. The mineral output of the republic is now negligible, but the Ministry of Public Works has recently started to investigate 2 new silver mines in the department of Morazán.

Agriculture. El Salvador is predominantly agricultural; 32·5% of its total area is used for crops and 30·2% for pasture. Area devoted to coffee is about 308,000 acres, almost entirely owned by nationals. 50% of the working population is engaged in agriculture.

Production (1977, in 1m. quintales, 46 kg each): Coffee, 2·8; cotton, 1·6; maize, 8·2. A little rubber is exported.

Livestock (1981): 1·2m. cattle, 386,000 pigs, 4,000 sheep, 14,000 goats.

Forestry. In the national forests are found dye woods and such woods as mahogany, cedar and walnut. Balsam trees also abound: El Salvador is the world's principal source of this medicinal gum.

Fisheries. In 1978, shrimp exports were valued at US$10m. (1977, US$10·5m.).

INDUSTRY AND TRADE

Industry. Total production was valued at ₡550·2m. in 1972, which included: Footwear and clothing, ₡61·3m.; textiles, ₡70·2m.; food, ₡157·7m.; chemicals, ₡42.

Labour. A decree of Aug. 1950 permits the formation of trade unions except among agricultural workers and those engaged in seasonal work such as coffee-milling and sugar-refining; trade-union posts must be filled by natives, not foreigners.

Commerce. The imports (including parcels post) and exports have been as follows in calendar years in 1,000 colónes:

	1971	*1972*	*1973*	*1974*	*1975*	*1976*
Imports	619,500	691,400	934,423	1,408,548	1,495,734	1,794,700
Exports	569,500	694,000	895,745	1,156,188	1,281,387	1,801,800

Of total exports, coffee furnishes about 20% by weight and 51% by value. The coffee is of the 'mild' variety; it is sold in bags of 60 kg, but trade statistics use a bag of 69 kg.

In 1976 US took 587·9m. colónes of exports and furnished 512·3m. colónes of the imports. The chief imports are normally wheat, flour, fuel-oil, fertilizers, machinery, vehicles and iron and steel manufactures. The other Central American Republics, the Federal Republic of Germany, Japan, the Netherlands and the UK are also important trading partners.

Total trade between El Salvador and UK for 5 years (British Department of Trade returns, in £1,000 sterling):

	1978	*1979*	*1980*	*1981*	*1982*
Imports to UK	2,607	3,517	2,889	1,962	2,017
Exports and re-exports from UK	11,289	9,354	4,603	3,652	5,244

Tourism. There were 285,415 visitors in 1974 (236,137 in 1973).

COMMUNICATIONS

Roads. In 1974 there were 10,972 km of national roads in the republic, including 1,373 km of paved road; 4,868 km are usable all the year round and 4,622 only in the dry season. Motor vehicles registered, 1969, 63,949.

Railways. All railways (602 km) came under the control of National Railways of El Salvador *(Fenadesal)* in 1975. Lines run from Acajutla to San Salvador, Cutuco and Santa Ana; there is also a link to the Guatemalan system.

Aviation. International air traffic is expanding and in 1972 there were 80 flights a week. The airport at Ilopango, 5 miles from San Salvador, is equipped to handle jet aeroplanes and a new international airport at Cuscatlán opened in 1979.

Shipping. The principal ports are La Unión, La Libertad and Acajutla, all on the Pacific. Passengers (and some freight) use the Guatemalan port of Puerto Barrios on the Atlantic, reaching El Salvador by rail or road.

Post and Broadcasting. The telephone and telegraph systems are government-owned; the radio-telephone systems are partly private, partly government-owned. Telephone instruments, 1981, 75,920. Two radio transmitting and receiving stations at San Salvador maintain communications with Latin America. El Salvador has, 1965, over 500,000 wireless receiving sets. In 1973, there were 3 commercial television channels and 2 educational channels sponsored by the Ministry of Education.

Cinemas (1976). Cinemas numbered 65.

Newspapers (1970). There are 4 daily newspapers in San Salvador and 1 each in Santa Ana and San Miguel.

JUSTICE, RELIGION, EDUCATION AND WELFARE

Justice. Justice is administered by the Supreme Court of Justice, courts of first and second instance, besides minor tribunals. Magistrates of the Supreme Court and courts of second instance are elected by the Legislative Assembly for a renewable 3-year term.

An anti-Communist law, effective 29 Sept. 1962, has made the propagation of totalitarian or Communist doctrines an offence punishable by imprisonment; supplementary offences, contrary to democratic principles, are punished by prison terms of from 3 to 7 years.

Religion. The dominant religion is Roman Catholicism. Under the 1962 Constitution churches are exempted from the property tax; the Catholic Church is recognized as a legal person, and other churches are entitled to secure similar recognition. There is an archbishop in San Salvador and bishops at Santa Ana, San Miguel, San Vicente, Santiago de María and Usulután.

Education. Education is free and obligatory. In 1929 the State took over control of all schools, public and private, but the provision that the teaching in government schools must be wholly secular was removed in 1945.

In Dec. 1970 there were 2,892 (2,937 in 1972) primary schools (state, municipal and private), with 531,309 (869,065 in 1974) pupils and 14,193 teachers. Secondary education was given at 860 schools (86,853 pupils). The national university and the Catholic University had 186,500 students in 1974.

Social Welfare. The Social Security Institute now administers the sickness, old age and death insurance, covering industrial workers and employees earning up to ₡700 a month. Employees in other private institutions with salaries over this amount are included but are excluded from the medical and hospital benefits.

DIPLOMATIC REPRESENTATIVES

Of El Salvador in Great Britain (62 Welbeck St., London, W1)
Chargé d'Affaires: Gilberto Armando Cabrales.

Of Great Britain in El Salvador
Ambassador and Consul-General: C. J. Sharkey, MBE (resides in Tegucigalpa).

Of El Salvador in the USA (2308 California St., NW, Washington, DC., 20008)
Ambassador: Ernesto Rivas-Gallont.

Of the USA in El Salvador (25 Ave. Norte, Colnia Dueñas, San Salvador)
Ambassador: Deane R. Hinton.

Of El Salvador to the United Nations
Ambassador: Dr Mauricio Rosales-Rivera.

Books of Reference

Statistical Information: The Dirección General de Estadistica y Censos (Villa Fermina, Calle Arce, San Salvador) dates from 1937. *Director General:* Lieut.-Col. José Castro Meléndez. Its publications include *Anuario Estadistico.* Annual from 1911.—*Boletin Estadístico.* Quarterly.—*El Salvador en Gráficas.* Annual.—*Atlas Censal de El Salvador.* 1955 only.

Angel Gallardo, M., *Cuatro Constituciones Federales de Centro América y Las Constituciones Politicas de El Salvador.* San Salvador, 1945
Bevan, J., *El Salvador. Education and Repression.* London, 1981
Browning, D., *El Salvador: Landscape and Society.* OUP, 1971
Devire, F. J., *El Salvador: Embassy under Attack.* New York, 1981
Montgomery, T.S., *Revolution in El Salvador: Origins and Evolution.* Boulder, 1982
North, L., *Bitter Grounds: Roots of Revolt in El Salvador.* London, 1981
Vogt, W., *The Population of El Salvador and Its Natural Resources.* Washington, D.C., 1946
Wallich, H. C. (ed.), *Public Finance in a Developing Country: El Salvador.* Harvard Univ. Press, 1951
White, A., *El Salvador.* New York, 1973

EQUATORIAL GUINEA

Capital: Malabo
Population: 300,000 (1982)
GNP per capita: US$330 (1976)

República de Guinea Ecuatorial

HISTORY. The Republic of Equatorial Guinea became independent on 12 Oct. 1968 after having been a Spanish colony (Territorios Españoles del Golfo de Guinea) until 1959. From 1959 to 1963 the territory was made into two Spanish provinces with a status comparable to the metropolitan provinces. From 1964 to 1968 this Equatorial Region became an autonomous entity still retaining the status of two Spanish provinces, but with a certain amount of internal self-government. Serious political disturbances in Rio Muni occurred in March–April 1969. This led to the partial withdrawal of the Spanish community. Agreements for co-operation in education and economic development were signed with Spain in 1971, 1972 and 1979. While under the first President (1968–79) the republic depended heavily on the Soviet bloc including Cuba and the People's Republic of China, Spanish economic, technical and social co-operation has become essential since the overthrow of his régime in Aug. 1979.

AREA AND POPULATION. The total area is 28,051 sq. km (10,831 sq. miles). Total population, 245,989 (1960 census); 1982 estimate, 300,000.

The 6 provinces consist of 2 on the islands of Bioko (formerly Macias Nguema, formerly Fernando Poo) and Pagalu (formerly Annobon), and 4 on the mainland, with these separate areas having the following areas (in sq.km) and populations:

	Sq. km	*Census 1960*	*Chief town*
Bioko	2,034 [1]	62,612 [2]	Malabo
Rio Muni	26,017 [3]	183,377	Bata
	28,051	245,989	

[1] Including the island of Pagalu (17 sq. km). [2] Including Pagalu (1,415).
[3] Including the adjacent islets of Corisco, Elobey Grande and Elobey Chico (17 sq. km).

The majority of the Rio Munian population is Fang (Pámues in Spanish). Along the coast and in the islets are the Combes, the Bengas, the Bujebas, etc.

In Bioko the aborigines are called Bubis. These are now a minority (perhaps 15,000). Other ethnic groups are the Fernandinos (descendants of English-speaking Creoles), the Fangs, coast people from Rio Muni and formerly naturalized migrant workers from Nigeria, Cameroon and São Tomé. A fluctuating mass of plantation workers were about twice as numerous as the Equatorial Guineans. Pagalu is peopled by descendants of slaves brought by the Portuguese; they still speak a Portuguese patois. Pidgin English was the lingua franca in Bioko in spite of the official Spanish. Because of political and economic difficulties about 110,000 citizens are reported to live in neighbouring countries and Spain.

CONSTITUTION AND GOVERNMENT. Following the referendum of 11 Aug. and the elections of 22 and 29 Sept. 1968, Equatorial Guinea has become a sovereign state consisting of two provinces. The republic is administered by a President who is chief of the armed forces and head of government.

The first Assembly elected in 1968 was dissolved in 1971. The first President was appointed for life on 14 July 1972. A new Constitution was adopted in July 1973. All power rested with the Life President, Macías Nguema, and the nominal autonomy of the provinces did not exist. On 3 Aug. 1979 the President was overthrown by a 'revolutionary military council'. A 10-member cabinet was established and the country was placed under military rule and in Aug. 1982 the President's mandate was extended for 7 years.

President: Lieut.-Col. Teodoro Obiang Nguema Mbasogo.

National flag: Three horizontal stripes of green, white, red; a blue triangle based on the hoist; in the centre the national arms.

DEFENCE. Under President Macías the *Guardia Nacional* consisted mainly of Fang soldiers with Cuban and Chinese military advisers. Total strength about 1,000. Since the 1979 *coup*, Moroccan troops and Spanish military and police personnel have replaced Soviet bloc advisers.

INTERNATIONAL RELATIONS

Membership. Equatorial Guinea is a member of UN, OAU and is an ACP state of EEC.

ECONOMY

Budget. The 1981 budget envisaged income at 2,732m. Bikuele and expenditure at 2,673m. Bikuele.

Currency. In July 1973 the Guinean *peseta* was redesignated the *Ekuele* (plural, *Bikuele*).

Banking. The Banco Central de Guinea Ecuatorial in Malabo was established in 1969 with Spanish technical and financial assistance.

NATURAL RESOURCES

Agriculture. The chief products are cocoa (71,000 hectares in 1979), coffee (17,000 hectares) and wood; in 1981 production was about 7,000 tonnes of cocoa, most of it high-grade exported to Spain and the US. Production declined by 56%, 1965–76. Coffee, of mediocre quality, is chiefly a Fang product. Production (1981) 1,000–2,000 tonnes and is gradually decreasing. With the departure of Nigerian workers, Fang labourers from Rio Muni were recruited forcibly in 1976 and were still on the island of Bioko in late 1979.

Livestock (1981): Cattle, 4,000; sheep, 34,000; goats, 7,000; poultry, 134,000.

Forestry. Wood was almost entirely exported from Rio Muni to Spain and the Federal Republic of Germany (337,438 tonnes to Spain in 1967). Production: 1980, 25,000 tonnes (1969, 300,000 tonnes). Plantations in the hinterland have been abandoned by their Spanish owners and except for cocoa, commercial agriculture is under serious difficulties.

INDUSTRY AND TRADE

Industry. Bioko has very few industries. Electricity production in 1967: Bioko, 9·47m. kwh.; Rio Muni, 5·7m. kwh. Rio Muni has no industry except lumbering. Post-independence political conditions have not been conducive to private investment. Since 1979 the lumber industry has resumed activity but there was (1981) a shortage of labour.

Trade. In 1965 Equatorial Guinea exported 330,100 tonnes (value, 1,635·6m. pesetas; 1966, 1,817m.), of which 326,000 tonnes to Spain (value, 1,581·6m. pesetas). In 1970 total exports were 1,741m. EG pesetas, of which 91% went to Spain. Imports were 1,472m. EG pesetas, of which 80% came from Spain. In 1975 cocoa exports were US$13·4m. and coffee, US$7m. In 1978, cocoa accounted for 97% of exports.

Total trade between Equatorial Guinea and UK (British Department of Trade returns, in £1,000 sterling):

	1980	*1981*	*1982*
Imports to UK	—	19	156
Exports and re-exports from UK	54	142	633

COMMUNICATIONS

Roads. Bioko had a good tarmac road network, but Rio Muni had few surfaced roads; the main artery is Mbini–Bata–Micomeseng–Ebebiyin. Road reconstruction is envisaged.

Aviation. An international airfield exists in Malabo (28,029 passengers in 1967). Bata has more modest facilities (15,031 passengers in 1967). The line Madrid–Malabo–Bata is subsidized by Spain. Links with Douala (from Malabo) and Libreville (Gabon) exist.

Shipping. Malabo is the main port. The other ports are Luba, formerly San Carlos (bananas, cocoa) in Bioko and Bata, Kogo and Mbini (wood) in Rio Muni. A new harbour in Bata has been completed. In 1966 in the 5 ports 141,600 tonnes were unloaded and 429,000 loaded.

Post and Broadcasting. Estimated number of telephones (1969), 1,451. In 1977 there were 80,000 radio and 1,000 TV receivers.

JUSTICE, RELIGION, EDUCATION AND WELFARE

Justice. The Constitution guarantees an independent judiciary. The Supreme Tribunal is the highest court of appeal and is located at Malabo.

Religion. The population of Equatorial Guinea is nominally Roman Catholic (227,517 in 1966) with influential Protestant groups in Malabo and Rio Muni. By order of the President most churches were closed in 1975 and in June 1978 the Roman Catholic Church was banned. Since 1979, religious services have been restored.

Education. There were in 1981 about 45,000 pupils enrolled in primary schools and about 40,000 school-age children among the negroes abroad. In 1976 there were 3,984 pupils and 115 teachers in secondary schools, 370 students and 29 teachers at technical schools and 169 students and 21 teachers at teacher-training establishments.

Health. In 1967 there were 16 hospitals and dispensaries with 1,637 beds. In 1975 there were only 5 doctors, 2 midwives and 248 nursing personnel.

DIPLOMATIC REPRESENTATIVES

Of Equatorial Guinea in Great Britain
Ambassador: Julian Eshono Abaga Aga (resides in Paris).

Of Great Britain in Equatorial Guinea
Ambassador: Brian Sparrow (resides at Yaoundé).

Of Equatorial Guinea to the United Nations
Ambassador: Capt. Florencio Maye Ela.

Books of Reference

Atlas Historico y Geográfico de Africa Española. Madrid, 1955
Plan de Desarrollo Económico de la Guinea Ecuatorial. Presidencia del Gobierno. Madrid, 1963
Resumén estadistico del Africa española, 1965–66. Madrid, 1967
Berman, S., *Spanish Guinea: An Annotated Bibliography.* Microfilm Service, Catholic University. Washington, D.C. 1961
Liniger-Goumaz, M., *La Guinée équatoriale un pays méconnu.* Paris, 1980
Pélissier, R., *Les Territoires espagnols d'Afrique.* Paris, 1963.—*Los territorios españoles de Africa.* Madrid, 1964.–*Etudes Hispano-Guinéennes.* Orgeval, 1969

ETHIOPIA

Capital: Addis Ababa
Population: 32·4m. (1982)
GNP per capita: US$140 (1980)

Hebretesebawit Ityopia

HISTORY. The ancient empire of Ethiopia has its legendary origin in the meeting of King Solomon and the Queen of Sheba. Historically, the empire developed in the centuries before and after the birth of Christ, at Aksum in the north, as a result of Semetic immigration from South Arabia. The immigrants imposed their language and culture on a basic Hamitic stock. Ethiopia's subsequent history is one of sporadic expansion southwards and eastwards, checked from the 16th to early 19th centuries by devastating wars with Moslems and Gallas. Modern Ethiopia dates from the reign of the Emperor Theodore (1855–68).

Menelik II (1889–1913) defeated the Italians in 1896 and thereby safeguarded the empire's independence in the scramble for Africa. By successful campaigns in neighbouring kingdoms within Ethiopia (Jimma, Kaffa, Harar, etc.) he united the country under his rule and created the empire as it is today.

In 1936 Ethiopia was conquered by the Italians, who were in turn defeated by the Allied forces in 1941 when the Emperor returned.

The former Italian colony of Eritrea, from 1941 under British military administration, was in accordance with a resolution of the General Assembly of the UN, dated 2 Dec. 1950, handed over to Ethiopia on 15 Sept. 1952. Eritrea thereby became an autonomous unit within the federation of Ethiopia and Eritrea.

This federation became a unitary state on 14 Nov. 1962 when Eritrea was fully integrated with Ethiopia.

A provisional military government assumed power on 12 Sept. 1974 and deposed the Emperor. The deposed Emperor Hailé Selassié I, was born 23 July 1892; crowned King (Negus), on 7 Oct. 1928, proclaimed Emperor, after the death of the Empress Zauditu, on 2 April 1930, and crowned on 2 Nov. 1930. He married in 1911 Menen, who died on 15 Feb. 1962. The Emperor died on 27 Aug. 1975. Several members of the Royal Family are still imprisoned in Addis Ababa and others are living in exile in the West..

On 24 Nov. 1974 the Provisional Military Government announced that on 23 Nov. it had executed 60 former military and civilian leaders including Gen. Aman Andom who was Chairman of the Provisional Military Administrative Council.

On 3 Feb. 1977 it was announced that Brig.-Gen. Teferi Bante, the Chairman of PMAC and 6 other members of the ruling military council were executed.

In early 1978 a reversal of the position in the armed struggle in the Ogaden area of Ethiopia with Somali forces took place. After an offensive mounted with strong USSR and Cuban support the area was recaptured and in March Somalia withdrew all troops from the area. Control was re-established by Ethiopia later in 1978 and nationalist guerrillas were pushed back but sporadic fighting continued in 1982 in the Ogaden and along the border.

AREA AND POPULATION. Ethiopia is bounded north-east by the Red Sea, east by Djibouti and Somalia, south by Kenya and west by Sudan. It has a total area of 1,221,900 sq. km (471,800 sq. miles) and total population (1982) 32,395,000.

The dominant race of Ethiopia, the Amhara, inhabit the central Ethiopian highlands. To the north of them are the Tigréans, akin to the Amhara and belonging to the same Christian church, but speaking a different, though related, language. Both these races are of mixed Hamitic and Semitic origin, and further mixed by intermarriage with Galla and other races. The Gallas, some of whom are Christian, some Moslem and some pagan, comprise about 40% of the entire population, and are a pastoral and agricultural people of Hamitic origin. Somalis, another Hamitic race, inhabit the south-east of Ethiopia, in particular the Ogaden desert region. These like the closely related Afar people, are Moslem. The Afar stretch northwards from Wollo region into Eritrea.

Region	*Area (sq. km)*	*Population Jan. 1978*	*Chief town*	*Population Jan. 1978*
Addis Ababa	218	1,125,340	—	—
Arussi	23,500	1,084,700	Assela	30,694
Bale	124,600	830,000	Goba	6,116
Eritrea	117,600	2,295,800	Asmara	373,827
Gemu Goffa	39,500	946,300	Arba Minch	8,914
Gojjam	61,600	1,927,600	Debre Markos	35,818
Gondar (Begemdir)	74,200	1,942,400	Gondar	68,364
Hararge	259,700	2,955,400	Harar	59,122
Illubabor	47,400	764,000	Mattu	8,115
Kefa	54,600	1,527,500	Jimma	63,390
Shoa	85,200	4,929,900	—	—
Sidamo	117,300	2,654,900	Awassa	23,038
Tigre	65,900	2,044,400	Mekele	41,235
Wollega	71,200	1,910,400	Lekemti	21,694
Wollo	79,400	2,469,600	Dessie	65,571

Other large towns (population, Jan. 1978): Dire Dawa, in Hararge, 72,202; Nazret, in Shoa, 61,468.

Local Government. The country is divided into 15 administrative regions, each under a Chief Administrator, and under the administrative control of the Minister of the Interior. Each region is divided into about 7 districts under a district administrator. All revenues collected in the regions are under the control of the Minister of Finance.

CONSTITUTION AND GOVERNMENT. Pending the promulgation of a new constitution, Ethiopia is controlled by a Provisional Military Administration Council (the *Derg*) to whom the Council of Ministers is responsible. A Commission for Organizing the Party of the Working Peoples of Ethiopia (COPWE) was established in early 1980 and charged with the task of preparing the formation of a civilian party which will ultimately take over from the PMAC. The first congress of COPWE was held in June 1980 and elected a 93-member central committee and a 7-member central committee, both chaired by Mengistu. Two further congresses have taken place but the Party itself has not yet been formally created.

Chairman of the Derg, Head of State, Chairman of the Council of Ministers: Lieut.-Col. Mengistu Haile Mariam.

Vice-Chairman of the Council of Ministers: Lieut.-Col. Fisseha Desta.

Foreign Affairs: Dr Feleke Gedle-Ghiorgis.

National flag: Three horizontal stripes of green, yellow and red.

National anthem: Ityopya, Ityopia Kidemi (tune by Daniel Yohannes, 1975).

DEFENCE

Army. The Army, trained by British officers from 1947 to 1951 and by Swedish officers until 1964, comprises 14 infantry divisions, including 20 tank battalions, 1 light infantry division, 4 parachute commando brigades, 30 artillery and 2 engineering battalions. It is recruited by voluntary enlistment. Five artillery battalions, 5 anti-aircraft batteries, 2 combat engineer battalions, an airborne infantry battalion and ancillary service, make up the ground forces to a total of 244,500 in 1983. This includes a People's Militia of around 150,000.

A US military advisory and administrative group, established since 1954, working down to divisional level, was asked by the Ethiopian Government to disband in April 1977. Ethiopia's military rulers have moved away from US military assistance since they came to power and now rely on USSR for most of their military aid. Large amounts of USSR military equipment have been sent to help her in her conflict with Somalia over the Ogaden desert region. Ethiopian officers are trained at the National Military Academy, Harar, and at the National Military Training Centre, Holletta, near Addis Ababa.

Navy. The Navy, with headquarters at Addis Ababa, consists of 3 *ex*-Soviet fast missile boats, 2 *ex*-Soviet fast torpedo boats, 1 training ship (1,768 tons; *ex*-US seaplane tender), 1 *ex*-Netherlands coastal minesweeper, 4 patrol craft (*ex*-US coastguard motor gunboats), 4 patrol boats, 1 *ex*-Yugoslav submarine chaser, 4 harbour defence craft, 1 medium landing ship, 2 landing craft and 5 minor landing craft. The Naval Base and College is at Massawa.

Personnel, in 1983, totalled 1,500 officers and men. It is presumed that Soviet advisers remain embarked in the 5 attack craft recently acquired until Ethiopian naval officers and ratings have sufficient experience to operate independently the missiles and torpedoes.

Air Force. The Air Force, trained originally by Swedish and American personnel, but now operating many aircraft of Soviet origin, has its headquarters at Debre Zeit, near Addis Ababa. It includes a training school and a central workshop. Of 6 ground-attack fighter squadrons, 3 have MiG-21s, the others MiG-23s, F-5A/Es and MiG-17s respectively. There is a COIN squadron with 6 T-28Ds, a squadron of Mi-24 helicopter gunships, and a transport squadron equipped with An-12s, jet-augmented C-119Ks, C-54s, C-47s and Do 28D Skyservants. Training aircraft include two-seat F-5Bs, T-33 jet advanced trainers, L-39 jet basic trainers, and piston-engined Cessna 310s, T-28s and Saab-91s. More than 30 Agusta-Bell 204, Alouette III, UH-1H, Mi-6 and Mi-8 helicopters are in service. Personnel, 3,500 officers and men.

The frontier guard patrols the Somalia border, and commando police units are being employed to assist the Army and police in border patrols and anti-terrorist operations in Eritrea. Total paramilitary force, 20,000.

INTERNATIONAL RELATIONS

Membership. Ethiopia is a member of UN, OAU and is an ACP state of EEC.

ECONOMY

Planning. The third 5-year plan (1969–73, which was extended to 1974) involved a total expenditure of EB2,865m. (of which EB565m. for industry and EB624m. for transport and communications) and hoped to achieve a growth rate of 6% per annum. Actual growth rate was below 4% and the fourth 5-year plan was replaced in 1975 by a policy statement embodying a package approach to rural development. In 1978 a new development plan was launched envisaging growth of 6% in 1979–80 and 7% in 1980–81.

Budget. Revenue and expenditure estimates for financial years (ended 7 July) were as follows (in EB1m.):

	1975–76	*1976–77*	*1977–78*	*1978–79*	*1979–80*
Revenue	1,331	1,466	1,601	2,119	2,365
Expenditure	1,331	1,466	1,601	2,119	2,365

Of the estimated revenue in 1979–80, EB1,327m. is expected to come from taxes and EB417m. from external assistance. Of the 1979–80 expenditure, EB1,655m. is on current account and EB710m. for capital expenditure.

Currency. The Ethiopian *birr*, divided into 100 cents, is the unit of currency; it is based on 5·52 grains of fine gold. It consists of notes of EB1, 5, 10, 50 and 100 denominations, and bronze 1-, 5-, 10- and 25-cent coins. The former dollar notes were replaced by the new *birr* in Oct. 1976. Currency is issued by the National Bank, and, as at 30 Sept. 1975, was notes, EB673·7m.; coins, EB169·7m. The note issue, under the Banking Proclamation of 1963, must be backed by gold and foreign securities in the international reserve fund to at least 25% of its value. Foreign currency reserves stood at US$108·5m. in June 1979. *Birr* 4·44 = £1 sterling; *Birr* 2·01 = US$1 (in March 1981).

Banking. The State Bank was renamed the National Bank of Ethiopia in Oct.

1963, when its commercial activities were transferred to the newly established Commercial Bank of Ethiopia. At the same time another new bank, the Investment Bank of Ethiopia, was set up with a capital of EB10m., of which the Government held the majority of shares. In Sept. 1965 it became the Ethiopian Investment Corporation, which is a substantial shareholder in a number of industrial and other ventures.

The Investment Corporation has now been merged with the Development Bank of Ethiopia and the two are now known as the Agricultural and Industrial Development Bank, SC.

Two Italian banks have subsidiaries in Asmara, and one has a subsidiary in Addis Ababa. The Addis Ababa Bank Share Co. is connected with National & Grindlays Bank Ltd.

On 1 Jan. 1975 the Government nationalized all banks, mortgage and insurance companies.

Weights and Measures. The metric system of weights and measures is officially in use. Traditional weights and measures vary considerably in the various provinces: the principal ones are: *Frasilla* = approximately 37½ lb.; *gasha*, the principal unit of land measure, which is normally about 100 acres but can vary between 80 and 300 acres, depending on the quality of the land.

ENERGY AND NATURAL RESOURCES

Electricity. Installed electricity generating power of the Ethiopian Electric Light and Power Authority was 185 mw in 1972 and production in 1977 totalled 427m. kwh.

Oil. A Russian built state-owned oil refinery at Assab came on stream in 1967 with a capacity of 600,000 tonnes of crude.

Gas. A natural gas-strike was made offshore near Massawa in Dec. 1969, but it was not exploited. Traces of gas and oil have been found in south-east Ethiopia.

Minerals. Ethiopia has little proved mineral wealth. Salt (122,000 tonnes in 1974) is produced mainly in Eritrea, while a placer goldmine is worked by the Government of Adola in the south. Gold production, in 1974, was 15,754 troy oz. Small quantities of other minerals are produced including platinum. The potash deposits in the Dankali salt plains in the north-east part of the country were investigated by 2 US companies in 1966–70 but no exploitation has taken place. Japanese interests were engaged in the exploitation of significant copper deposits near Asmara, but the mine was closed down in March 1974 as a result of damage caused by ELF dissidents.

Agriculture. Coffee is by far the most important source of rural income. Harari coffee (long berry Mocha) is cultivated in the east; Abyssinian coffee is produced in Kaffa and the surrounding provinces, much of it growing wild.

Teff (*Eragrastis abyssinica*) is the principal food grain, followed by barley, wheat, maize and durra. Pulses and oilseeds are imported for local consumption and export. Cane sugar is an important crop.

Production (1979 in 1,000 tons): Maize, 1,000; sorghum, 760; barley, 730; pulses, 670.

Livestock (1981): 26m. cattle, 23·2m. sheep, 17·2m. goats; smaller numbers of donkeys, horses, mules and camels. Hides and skins and butter (ghee) are important for home consumption and export. Sheep, cattle and chickens (53m.) are the main providers of meat. All agricultural land was nationalized in March 1975, and a radical land reform was carried out. Tenants were given possessory rights to the land they tilled, absentee landlords were abolished, and a ceiling on landholding was instituted.

INDUSTRY AND TRADE

Industry. The most important products of the small but growing industries are cotton yarn (9,600 tons in 1978) and fabrics, cement (100,000 tons), sugar, salt, cigarettes, canned foodstuffs, beer, building materials, footwear, pharmaceuticals, tyres and paint. Most industry is centred around Addis Ababa and Asmara. Industry around Asmara has been severely hit by actions of Eritrean guerrillas.

Commerce. Coffee is by far the most important export, followed by pulses, oilseeds, hides and skins. Imports are textiles, foodstuffs, vehicles, machinery, manufactured goods and petroleum products.

Imports and exports (in US$1) for 4 years.

	1978	*1979*	*1980*	*1981*
Imports	440·1	521·3	649·6	629·8
Exports	308·3	429·1	419·3	374·1

In 1978 the main supplying countries were: Italy (14%), Japan (11%), Federal Republic of Germany (10%), Saudi Arabia (8%), UK (7%).

The chief items of import in 1978 were: Machinery and transport equipment (EB300·3m.), petroleum products (EB129·3m.). The main items of export were: Coffee (EB502·3m.), hides and skins (EB66·3m.), pulses (EB17·3m.).

Total trade between Ethiopia and UK (British Department of Trade returns, in £1,000 sterling):

	1977	*1978*	*1979*	*1980*	*1981*	*1982*
Imports to UK	4,689	4,471	12,947	10,281	8,079	10,833
Exports and re-exports from UK	19,111	17,091	16,039	20,962	19,569	27,584

COMMUNICATIONS

Roads. Loans totalling EB83·75m. have been made between 1951 and 1968 by the International Bank and the International Development Agency for 3 programmes for improving and extending the road system. A fourth programme began in 1968 and is being financed by EB190m. in foreign loans and was completed in 1972. A fifth programme is near completion with a projected cost of EB60m. A sixth programme, estimated to cost EB133m., is underway which will include about 400 km of gravel-surfaced feeder roads. The Highway Authority now maintains some 7,600 km of roads and is engaged in constructing another 850 km of all-weather roads. Chief motor roads: Massawa–Asmara–Sudan; Asmara–Dessie–Addis Ababa; Asmara–Gondar–Addis Ababa; Addis Ababa–Jimma; Addis Ababa–Lekemti; Addis Ababa–Nazareth; Dire-Dawa–Hargeisa; Dessie–Assab; Addis Ababa–Adola.

Estimated number of motor vehicles (1976): Cars, 63,100; lorries and trucks, 7,000; buses, 3,500; tractors, 3,000.

Railways. The former Franco-Ethiopian Railway Co. (782 km, metre-gauge) became the Ethiopian-Djibouti Railway Corp. in 1982, when the remaining France-owned shares were bought out.

Aviation. Ethiopian Air Lines, formed in 1946, provides services to Cairo, Athens, Frankfurt, London, Khartoum, Lagos, Accra, Rome, Nairobi, Entebbe, Kinshasa, Kigali, Dar es Salaam, Djibouti, Aden, Paris, Douala, Jedda, Peking, Seychelles, Bombay, San'a and Abu Dhabi, in addition to internal services. The following airlines operate through Asmara and Addis Ababa: Alitalia, Kenya Airways, Air India, Lufthansa, China Airline, Aeroflot, Air-France, British Airways and Air Djibouti.

Shipping. A state shipping line was established in 1964. In May 1973 it owned 4 cargo vessels and 2 tankers.

Post and Broadcasting. The postal system serves 301 offices, mainly by air-mail. All the main centres are connected with Addis Ababa by telephone or radio telegraph. International telephone services are available at certain hours to most countries in Europe, North America and India. Number of telephones (1981), 87,846 and 194 telex subscribers (1972).

The Ethiopian Broadcasting Service makes sound broadcasts on the medium and short waves in English, Amharic and in the vernacular languages spoken within the country. Radio Voice of the Gospel, owned by the Lutheran World Federation, was nationalized in March 1977 and renamed Radio Voice of Revolutionary Ethiopia.

It broadcasts from Addis Ababa in English, French, Amharic, Arabic, Somali and Afar. Television was introduced in 1964 and programmes broadcast from Addis Ababa for a radius of about 100 miles to the south and south-east of the capital and in Asmara from June 1977.

Cinemas (1974). There were 31 cinemas, with seating capacity of about 25,600.

Newspapers. In Addis Ababa there are 1 English, 1 French and 1 Amharic dailies, and in Asmara 2 Italian dailies, 1 part-Tigrinya, part-Arabic, and 1 Amharic weekly. All the papers are government-controlled and have small circulations, varying between 2,000 and 20,000.

JUSTICE, RELIGION, EDUCATION AND WELFARE

Justice. The legal system is said to be based on the Justinian Code. A new penal code came into force in 1958 and Special Penal Law in 1974. Codes of criminal procedure, civil, commercial and maritime codes have since been promulgated.

The extra-territorial rights formerly enjoyed by foreigners have been abolished, but any person accused in an Ethiopian court has the right to have his case transferred to the High Court, provided he asks for this before any evidence has been taken in the court of first instance.

Provincial and district courts have been established, and High Court judges visit the provincial courts on circuit. The Supreme Imperial Court at Addis Ababa is presided over by the Chief Justice.

Police. In 1948 the regular police force of the capital and some provincial cities was amalgamated with the irregular territorial forces under the provincial governors-general. The total force now numbers about 32,000 officers and other ranks.

Religion. Since the conversion of the Amharas to Christianity in the 4th century they have retained their connexion with the Alexandrian Church through the Abuna, or Metropolitan who was always an Egyptian Copt, and who was appointed and consecrated by the Coptic Patriarch of Alexandria. Both the Egyptian and Ethiopian Coptic Churches are monophysite, rejecting the decrees of the Council of Chalcedon (A.D. 451). After the restoration of the Emperor relations between the Ethiopian and Egyptian churches were strained until the summer of 1948, when an agreement was reached which envisaged the appointment of an Ethiopian Archbishop, and in Jan. 1951 Abuna Basilios (who died in 1970) was elected Archbishop of Ethiopia. A further agreement in 1959 made the Ethiopian Church autocephalous, and Basilios assumed the rank of Patriarch, with seniority immediately after the Patriarch of Alexandria. Abuna Theophilos was elected to the Patriarchate by an electoral college representing clergy, laity and Government and consecrated by the Ethiopian Archbishops in May 1971. In Aug. 1976 the third Patriarch, Abuna Tekle Haimanot, was invested. Christianity is predominant in the following provinces in the north: Tigré, Gondar, Gojjam, Shoa. Wollo province in the north-east is half Christian, half Moslem. In the southern half of the country the provinces of Hararge and Arussi have Moslem majorities, while all the other southern provinces have considerable Moslem minorities. In addition, the province of Gamu Gofa on the Kenya border and parts of Sidamo and Arussi have considerable pagan elements. Eritrea is half Moslem and half Christian. Each province now forms a diocese.

Islam is widely practised in the south and east of the Empire. Moslem minorities are found in Addis Ababa and in other commercial centres. The rite is mainly shafeitic. Harar is the most important Moslem centre. There are mosques and government schools for Moslems in most towns.

Education. In the academic year 1979–80 there were more than 1·8m. pupils in 5,246 primary schools with 30,597 teachers. In secondary schools there were 371,000 students and 8,982 teachers. Higher education is co-ordinated under the National University, chartered in 1961; in 1979–80, there were 14,562 students. The University College, the Engineering, Building and Theological Colleges are in Addis Ababa, the Agricultural College in Harar and the Public Health College in

Gondar. It is intended to develop these provincial colleges into universities in their own right.

Since the military takeover in 1974 education has been in a state of flux. A campaign, known as *zemetcha,* lasting from Dec. 1974 to July 1976, was launched, in which all higher academic institutions were closed and the students sent into the countryside to preach the revolution. Academic institutions are now in operation again, although it is not clear if numbers have recovered to a pre-1974 level.

The main language of instruction from the secondary level upwards is English.

A national adult literacy campaign was launched in 1979 with the aid of UNESCO. In Sept. 1980 it was claimed that 7m. adults, 70% of them women, had taken or were taking basic literacy or follow-up courses. Follow-up courses provide basic education in such fields as agriculture, health, home economics, handicrafts and co-operatives, as well as ideology.

Health. In 1977 there was one doctor for every 75,000 people and in 1981 it was found that Ethiopia has the shortest life expectancy in the world, at 40 years.

DIPLOMATIC REPRESENTATIVES

Of Ethiopia in Great Britain (17 Prince's Gate, London, SW7 1PZ)
Ambassador: Ato Ayalew Wolde-Giorgis.

Of Great Britain in Ethiopia (Fikre Mariam Abatechan St., Addis Ababa)
Ambassador: B. L. Barder.

Of Ethiopia in the USA (2134 Kalorama Rd., NW, Washington D.C., 20008)
Chargé d'Affaires: Tesfaye Demeke.

Of the USA in Ethiopia (Entoto St., Addis Ababa)
Chargé d'Affaires: David A. Korn.

Of Ethiopia to the United Nations
Ambassador: Mohamed Hamid Ibrahim.

Books of Reference

Area Handbook for Ethiopia. US Govt. Printing Office, Washington, 1971
Trade Directory and Guide Book of Ethiopia. Addis Ababa, 1971
Gilkes, P., *The Dying Lion: Feudalism and Modernisation in Ethiopia.* London, 1975
Halliday, F. and Molyneaux, M., *The Ethiopian Revolution.* London, 1981
Hess, R. L., *Ethiopia: The Modernization of Autocracy.* Cornell Univ. Press, 1970
Holmberg, J., *Grain Marketing and Land Reform in Ethiopia.* Uppsala, 1977
Mosley, L., *Haile Selassie.* London, 1964
Scholler, H. and Brictzke, P., *Ethiopia: Revolution, Law and Politics.* New York, 1976
Thompson, B., *Ethiopia: The Country That Cut Off Its Head.* London, 1975
Trevaskis, G. K. N., *Eritrea.* London, 1960
Ullendorff, E., *The Ethiopians.* New York, 1973
Wolde-Mariam, M., *An Atlas of Ethiopia.* Rev. ed. Addis Ababa, 1970

FALKLAND ISLANDS AND DEPENDENCIES

Capital: Stanley
Population: 1,813 (1980)

HISTORY. France established a settlement in 1764 and Britain a second settlement in 1765. In 1770 Spain bought out the French and drove off the British. In 1806 Spanish rule was overthrown in Argentina, and the Argentinians claimed to succeed Spain in the French and British settlements in 1820. The British objected and reclaimed their settlement in 1832 as a Crown Colony.

On 2 April 1982 Argentine forces invaded the Falkland Islands and the Governor was expelled. At a meeting of the UN Security Council, held on 3 April, the voting was 10 to 1 in favour of the resolution calling for Argentina to withdraw. Britain regained possession on 14–15 June after the Argentinians surrendered.

AREA AND POPULATION. The Crown Colony is situated in the South Atlantic Ocean about 480 miles north-east of Cape Horn. The numerous islands cover 4,700 sq. miles. The main East Falkland Island, 2,610 sq. miles; the West Falkland, 2,090 sq. miles, including the adjacent small islands. The Dependency of South Georgia lies 800 miles south-east of the Falklands, has an area of 1,450 sq. miles; the South Sandwich group, 470 miles south-east of South Georgia, has an area of 130 sq. miles.

The population of the Falkland Islands at census 1980 was 1,813. The only town is Stanley, in East Falkland, with a population of just over 1,000. A large garrison of British troops were stationed near Stanley in 1983. The population of South Georgia varies with the season, but the resident population in 1980 was 22 (males). The South Shetlands are uninhabited.

South Georgia, once a base for whaling and sealing operations, is now occupied by members of the British Antarctic Survey at the base at King Edward Point.

The population of the Falkland Islands is nearly all of British descent, with about 80% born in the islands.

CONSTITUTION AND GOVERNMENT. The Colony is administered by a Civil Commissioner, assisted by an Executive Council consisting of the Chief Secretary and Financial Secretary, both *ex-officio*; 2 members elected by the Legislature and 2 appointed members; and a Legislative Council composed of the Chief Secretary and Financial Secretary, both *ex-officio*; 3 elected members representing Stanley, 1 elected member from the East Falkland and 1 from the West Falkland and 1 representing the Camp as a whole.

Civil Commissioner: Sir Rex Hunt, CMG.
Chief Secretary: F. E. Baker, OBE.
Flag: British Blue Ensign with arms of Colony on a white disc in the fly.

ECONOMY

Budget. Revenue and expenditure (in £ sterling) for fiscal years ending 30 June:

	1976–77	*1977–78*	*1978–79*	*1979–80*	*1980–81*	*1981–82* [1]
Revenue	1,154,204	1,803,151	1,820,561	2,427,934	2,298,325	2,478,311
Expenditure	1,131,045	1,382,744	1,792,780	2,057,928	2,775,697	2,411,004

[1] Estimates.

Currency. The Falkland £ is at parity with the £ sterling.

Banking. On 30 June 1981 the government savings bank held a balance of £2,683,302. Some banking facilities are also offered by Lloyds Bank.

SHEEP FARMING. The whole acreage of the Colony is divided into large sheep runs. Wool is the principal product, but hides are exported. In 1980 there were 663,367 sheep, 8,056 cattle and 2,459 horses in the islands.

DEVELOPMENT. The economy is entirely dependent on the production of wool for export. A comprehensive economic survey, published in 1976, drew attention to the potential for exploitation of fish, kelp and possibly oil, and made recommendations for various areas of development. A further reappraisal was taking place in 1983 following the Argentinian invasion.

TRADE. Total imports, 1980, amounted to £2,590,321 and exports to £2,661,731.

COMMUNICATIONS

Roads. There are 13 miles of made-up roads in Stanley. Outside Stanley tracks link all the settlements which are passable in all but the worst weather. Work has continued on an all-weather road from Stanley to Darwin.

Aviation. Air communication was *via* Ascension Island in early 1983.

Shipping. A charter vessel calls 4 or 5 times a year to/from the UK. Communication with the Colony, the Dependencies and the British Antarctic Territory is kept up by the Royal research ships *John Biscoe* and *Bransfield* and by the ice-patrol vessel HMS *Endurance*.

Post and Broadcasting. Number of telephones (1980) 500. There is a government-operated broadcasting station at Stanley and the Government also operates a wired broadcasting service to subscribers.

EDUCATION AND WELFARE

Education. Education is compulsory between the ages of 5 and 15 years. In 1980 there were 312 children receiving education in the Colony. This includes Stanley schools, Darwin School and settlement schools, as well as pupils taught by itinerent teachers in rural areas. 9 children were being educated abroad.

Health. The Falkland Islands Medical Department, under the supervision of the senior medical officer, is responsible for the public health and sanitation of the Colony. The government medical department employs the following: 3 registered medical practitioners; 4 registered nurse/midwives; 8 partially trained nurses; 1 laboratory and X-ray technician and 1 dental surgeon. There is 1 general hospital situated in Stanley with 27 beds. There is also a routine/emergency flying doctor service operating to the outlying farm settlements.

WILD LIFE. The Falkland Islands and South Georgia are noted for their outstanding wild life, including penguin and seal. Four Nature Reserves have been declared and 18 Wild Animal and Bird Sanctuaries gazetted. The brown trout introduced between 1947 and 1952 can now be found in nearly all the rivers.

Books of Reference

Falkland Islands: The Facts. HMSO, London, 1982
Falkland Islands Journal. Stanley, from 1967
Falkland Islands Review [Franks Report] Cmnd. 8787. HMSO, London, 1983
Hanrahan, B., and Fox, R., *'I counted them all out and I counted them all back'.* London, 1982
Hastings, M., and Jenkins, S., *The Battle for the Falklands.* London, 1983
Phipps, C., *What Future for the Falklands?* London, 1977
Shackleton, E., *Falkland Islands Economic Study 1982.* HMSO, London, 1982
Strange, I. J., *The Falkland Islands.* Newton Abbot, 1972

FIJI

Capital: Suva
Population: 646,561 (1981)
GNP per capita: US$1,850 (1980)

HISTORY. The Fiji Islands were discovered by Tasman in 1643 and visited by Capt. Cook in 1774, but first recorded in detail by Capt. Bligh after the mutiny of the *Bounty* (1789). In the 19th century the search for sandalwood, in which enormous profits were made, brought many ships. Deserters and shipwrecked men stayed on; firearms salvaged from wrecks were used in native wars, new diseases swept the islands, and rum and muskets became regular articles of trade. Tribal wars became bloody and general until Fiji was ceded to Britain on 10 Oct. 1874, after a previous offer of cession had been refused. British administrators produced order out of chaos, and since then there has been steady political, social and economic progress. Fiji gained independent status on 10 Oct. 1970.

AREA AND POPULATION. Fiji comprises about 322 islands and islets (about 106 inhabited) lying between 15° and 22° S. lat. and 174° E. and 177° W. long. The largest is Viti Levu, area 10,429 sq. km (4,027 sq. miles), next is Vanua Levu, area 5,556 sq. km (2,145 sq. miles). The island of Rotuma (47 sq. km, 18 sq. miles), about 12° 30′ S. lat., 178° E. long., was added to the colony in 1881. Total area, 7,078 sq. miles (18,333 sq. km).

A population census is taken every 10 years. Total population (census, Dec. 1977), 601,485; 1981 (estimate) 646,561. The mid-1981 total population consisted of the following: 287,952 (44·5%) Fijians; 323,707 (50·7%) Indians; 11,145 (1·7%) Part Europeans; 4,048 (0·6%) Europeans; 8,073 (1·2%) Rotumans; 4,603 (0·7%) Chinese; 6,341 (0·9%) other Pacific Islanders; 692 (0·1%) others.

Suva, the capital, is on the south coast of Viti Levu; population (1981), 68,178. Suva was proclaimed a city on 2 Oct. 1953. Lautoka had 24,703 in 1981.

Vital statistics, 1978:

	Fijians	*Indians*	*Others* [1]	*Total*
Births	6,953	9,329	899	17,181
Deaths	1,037	1,329	190	2,556

[1] Includes Europeans, Part-Europeans, Rotumans, Other Pacific Islanders and Chinese.

CONSTITUTION AND GOVERNMENT. Fiji became an independent nation within the Commonwealth on 10 Oct. 1970. This had been agreed at a constitutional conference held in London in April 1970. There is a Lower House, the House of Representatives, which consists of 52 elected members and an Upper House, the Senate, of 22 members (8 nominations by the Council of Chiefs, 7 by the Prime Minister, 6 by the Leader of the Opposition and 1 by the Rotuma Council). Elections are held every five years.

At elections held in July 1982 for the 52 seats in the House of Representatives the Alliance Party won 28 seats, the National Federation Party won 22 seats and the Western United Front won 2 seats.

Local Government. The Fijian Administration, established in 1876, had jurisdiction over all Fijians.

Fiji is divided into 13 provinces, each with its own council. Elections to these councils in 90 constituencies were conducted for the first time in 1967 on a full adult franchise amongst Fijians.

The councils have wide powers to make by-laws and draw up their own budget subject to confirmation by the Fijian Affairs Board. Each council has its own treasury and levies rates to raise its revenue. These provincial rates vary from $F6 to $F9 per annum for every male adult, but those maintaining 5 or more children pay lower rates until their children become taxpayers. A start has been made, however, to change over to a system of land rating based upon the unimproved value of Fijian-owned land. This is considered to be more equitable and related to ability to pay.

These newly elected councils held their inaugural and 1968 budget meetings towards the end of 1967, when the chairman for each of these 13 councils was also elected from among its members. Members were elected for 2 years and new elections were held in 1969.

At the apex of the Fijian Administration is the Great Council of Chiefs presided over by the Minister for Fijian Affairs and Rural Development. The Council of Chiefs consists of 22 Fijian members elected to the House of Representatives, 30 representatives, elected by the Provincial Councils and 15 representatives nominated by the Minister for Fijian Affairs and Rural Development.

The Council of Chiefs advises the Government generally on Fijian affairs.

Governor-General: Ratu Sir Penaia Ganilau, KBE, CMG, CVO, DSO.
Prime Minister: Ratu Sir Kamisese Mara, KBE.
Flag: Light blue with the Union Flag in the canton and the shield of Fiji in the fly.

DEFENCE. The Fiji Military Forces Ordinance, 1949, provides for the maintenance of a small regular force, with territorial units and trained reserves. This force, comprising 2 infantry battalions, numbers (1983), 1,924.

Navy. A naval squadron was authorized in 1974 to perform fishery protection, surveillance, hydrographic surveying and coastguard duties. Present strength is 3 coastal minesweepers (*ex*-US MSC) and 1 survey craft. Naval personnel (trained in Australia) in 1983 numbered 20 officers and 140 ratings. The naval base is HMFS *Viti* in Suva.

INTERNATIONAL RELATIONS

Membership. Fiji is a member of the UN, the Commonwealth, the Colombo Plan and is an ACP state of the EEC.

ECONOMY

Budget. The financial year corresponds with the calendar year. All figures are in $1m. Fijian.

	1976	*1977*	*1978*	*1979*	*1980*
Revenue	128·7	151·7	161·6	198·7	227·1
Expenditure	129·6	155·0	170·2	245·9	278·0

Currency. Fiji changed to decimal currency on 13 Jan. 1969, with the major unit being $F1. In March 1983, £1 = $F1·47; US$ = $F0·997.

Banking. The Bank of New South Wales has 7 branches and 11 agencies; the Bank of New Zealand has 6 branches, 1 sub-branch and 17 agencies; the Australia and New Zealand Bank has 3 branches, 1 sub-branch and 1 agency and the Bank of Baroda has 7 branches and 5 agencies in Fiji. Barclays International has a branch in Suva.

The National Bank of Fiji had, at the end of 1978, deposits amounting to $F29,177,274 due to 190,621 accounts. The headquarters are at Suva, and there are 58 agencies, 4 branches and 3 sub-branches throughout Fiji.

NATURAL RESOURCES

Agriculture. Some 600,000 acres of land are in agricultural use. Sugar-cane is the principal cash crop (production, 1981, 469,972 tonnes), accounting for more than two-thirds of Fiji's export earnings; one quarter of the population depend on it directly for their livelihood. Copra, Fiji's second major cash crop (output, 1980, 22,000 tons), provides coconut oil and other products for export and employs nearly as many workers as the sugar industry. Ginger is the third major export crop replacing bananas which has declined through disease and hurricane. Other agricultural products include rice, cocoa, maize, tobacco and a variety of fruits and vegetables.

Fiji has a small but fast developing livestock industry.

Livestock (1981): Cattle, 155,000; horses, 39,000; goats, 55,000; pigs, 28,000; poultry, 957,000.

Forestry. Fiji supplies the bulk of its own timber requirements. A comprehensive pine scheme has been implemented with the aim of planting 186,000 acres by 1988.

INDUSTRY AND TRADE

Industry. Major industries include 4 large sugar-mills, the goldmines (92,300 grammes in 1979) and 3 mills which process copra into coconut oil and coconut meal. There is a great variety of light industries.

Trade Unions. In 1982 there were 45 trade unions operating with about 45,000 members.

Commerce. Exports in 1981, $F268,763,794 (including $F75m. of re-exports). Imports, $F540,071,695. Chief exports: Sugar, gold, molasses and canned fish.

Total trade between Fiji and UK (British Department of Trade returns, in $1,000 sterling):

	1977	*1978*	*1979*	*1980*	*1981*	*1982*
Imports to UK	45,948	47,521	45,694	36,759	51,144	39,826
Exports and re-exports from UK	12,584	14,717	14,154	12,786	11,401	9,088

Tourism. In 1980, there were 189,996 visitors.

COMMUNICATIONS

Roads. There is a principal highway round Viti Levu, the distance from Suva to Lautoka *via* Ra, Tavua and Ba (King's Road) being 265 km and *via* Navua and Sigatoka and Nadi (Queen's Road) being 221 km. Branch roads run for 52 km.

On Vanua Levu highways are in the neighbourhood of Labasa (Nasea) and Nasavusavu (Valeci). There are highways, 148 km south and 56 km west of Labasa. A highway extends to Buca Bay, 71 km east of Nasavusavu. Coastal roads connect villages and plantations on parts of the islands of Taveuni and Ovalau. Work is now complete on the reconstruction of the new bitumen surfaced highway between Suva and Nadi except for the section between Deuba and Sigatoka. The construction of a new gravel surfaced highway on Vanua Levu to link the towns of Nasavusavu and Labasa is complete.

Total road mileage is 2,019, of which 218 are sealed (paved), 1,663 are gravelled and 138 are unimproved. In 1980, there were 47,301 vehicles including 20,247 private cars, 14,483 goods vehicles, 1,058 buses, 3,655 tractors and 2,599 motor cycles.

Railway. There is a private 600mm-gauge railway (Fiji Sugar Corporation's Railway) of 644 km from Tavua to Sigatoka serving most of the sugar-cane producing area.

Aviation. Fiji provides an essential staging point for long-haul trunk-route aircraft operating between North America, Australia and New Zealand. Under the South Pacific Air Transport Council, which comprises the UK, Australia, New Zealand and Fiji, the international airport at Nadi has been developed and administered. Fourteen other airports are in use for domestic services.

Shipping. In 1981, 234 vessels of 19,479 net tons were registered. Suva has 4 slipways of 100, 200, 500 and 1,500 tons, and there are 3 shipbuilding and repair firms.

Post. There are 35 post offices and 158 agencies. Overseas telephone and telegram services are available through the Commonwealth cable to most countries except those in the South Pacific, which are served by direct radio circuits. The automatic telex network operates through New Zealand into the international telex system. There are ship-to-shore radio facilities. There were 45,323 telephones in 1981.

Cinemas. In 1979 there were 48 cinemas with a seating capacity of 28,100.

JUSTICE, RELIGION AND EDUCATION

Justice. Fijian courts have been abolished and merged into the magistrates' court.

Police. The Royal Fiji Police Force had (1981) a total strength of 1,404.

Religion. The 1976 census showed: Christians, 299,960; Hindus, 234,520; Muslims, 45,247; Confucians, 731.

Education (1981). School attendance is not compulsory in Fiji. There were 834 schools scattered over 56 islands, staffed by 6,500 teachers, of whom about 88·4% were trained. There were also 140 pre-schools. The primary and secondary schools had 162,034 pupils. The technical and vocational schools had (1978) 1,930 students and the teachers' colleges 613. There were 4 teacher-training colleges, 1 medical and 2 agricultural schools.

The University of the South Pacific opened in Feb. 1968 at Laucala Bay in Suva. It had about 1,500 full-time and 1,500 part-time students in 1983. The University has 3 schools, social and economic development, natural resources and education.

Total government expenditure on education in 1980 was over $F55·5m.

DIPLOMATIC REPRESENTATIVES

Of Fiji in Great Britain (34 Hyde Park Gate, London, SW7 5DN)
High Commissioner: Ratu Josua Brown Toganivalu, CBE (accredited 19 May 1981).

Of Great Britain in Fiji (Civic Centre, Stinson Parade, Suva)
High Commissioner: R. A. R. Barltrop.

Of Fiji in the USA (1140 19th St., NW, Washington, D.C., 20036)
Ambassador: Filipe N. Bole.

Of the USA in Fiji (31 Loftus St., Suva)
Ambassador: Fred J. Eckert.

Of Fiji to the United Nations
Ambassador: Filipe N. Bole.

Books of Reference

Statistical Information: A Bureau of Statistics was set up in 1950 (Government Buildings, Suva).
Trade Report. Annual (from 1887 [covering 1883–86]). Ministry of Information, Suva
Journal of the Fiji Legislative Council. Annual (from 1914 [under different title from 1885]). Suva
Fiji Today. Suva, Annual
Report of Commission of Inquiry Into Natural Resources and Population Trends in Fiji. Suva, Government Press, 1960
Ashford, J. E., *Social Security in Fiji.* Suva Government Press, 1964
Capell, A., *New Fijian Dictionary.* 2nd ed. Glasgow, 1957
France, P., *The Charter of the Land.* OUP, 1969
Nayacakalou, R. R., *Leadership in Fiji.* OUP, 1976
Roth, G. K., *The Fijian Way of Life.* 2nd ed. OUP, 1973
Sahlins, M. D., *Moala: Culture and Nature on a Fijian Island.* Univ. of Michigan Press, 1962

FINLAND

Capital: Helsinki
Population: 4·81m. (1981)
GNP per capita: US$10,030 (1981)

Suomen Tasavalta—Republiken Finland

HISTORY. Since the Middle Ages Finland was a part of the realm of Sweden. In the 18th century parts of south-eastern Finland were conquered by Russia, and the rest of the country was ceded to Russia by the peace treaty of Hamina in 1809. Finland became an autonomous grand-duchy which retained its previous laws and institutions under its Grand Duke, the Emperor of Russia. After the Russian revolution Finland declared itself independent on 6 Dec. 1917. The Civil War began in Jan. 1918 between the 'whites' and 'reds', the latter being supported by Russian bolshevik troops. The defeat of the red guards in May 1918 consequently meant freeing the country from Russian troops. A peace treaty with Soviet Russia was signed in 1920.

On 30 Nov. 1939 Soviet troops invaded Finland, after Finland had rejected territorial concessions demanded by the USSR. These, however, had to be made in the peace treaty of 12 March 1940, amounting to 32,806 sq. km and including the Carelian Isthmus, Viipuri and the shores of Lake Ladoga.

When the German attack on the USSR was launched in June 1941 Finland again became involved in the war against the USSR. On 19 Sept. 1944 an armistice was signed in Moscow. Finland agreed to cede to Russia the Petsamo area in addition to cessions made in 1940 (total 42,934 sq. km) and to lease to Russia for 50 years the Porkkala headland to be used as a military base. Further, Finland undertook to pay 300m. gold dollars in reparations within 6 years (later extended to 8 years). The peace treaty was signed in Paris on 10 Feb. 1947. The payment of reparations was completed on 19 Sept. 1952. The military base of Porkkala was returned to Finland on 26 Jan. 1956.

AREA AND POPULATION. The area and the population of Finland on 31 Dec. 1981 (Swedish names in brackets):

Province	*Area (sq. km)* [1]	*Population* [2]	*Population per sq. km* [2]
Uusimaa (Nyland)	9,893	1,138,664	115·1
Turku-Pori (Åbo-Björneborg)	22,163	704,995	31·8
Ahvenanmaa (Åland)	1,527	22,984	15·1
Häme (Tavastehus)	17,003	666,413	39·2
Kymi (Kymmene)	10,775	343,694	31·9
Mikkeli (St Michel)	16,343	208,524	12·8
Pohjois-Karjala (Norra Karelen)	17,772	176,806	9·9
Kuopio	16,511	252,709	15·3
Keski-Suomi (Mellersta Finland)	16,229	243,718	15·0
Vaasa (Vasa)	26,454	435,905	16·5
Oulu (Uleåborg)	56,907	421,450	7·4
Lappi (Lappland)	93,062	196,288	2·1
Total	304,643	4,812,150	15·8

[1] Excluding inland water area which totals 33,484 sq. km. [2] Resident population.

The growth of the population, which was 421,500 in 1750, has been:

End of year	*Urban*	*Rural*	*Total*	*Percentage urban*
1800	46,600	786,100	832,700	5·6
1900	333,300	2,322,600	2,655,900	12·5
1950	1,302,400	2,727,400	4,029,800	32·3
1960	1,707,000	2,739,200	4,446,200	38·4
1970	2,340,308	2,258,028	4,598,336	50·9
1980	2,865,063	1,922,715	4,787,778	59·8
1981	2,881,295	1,930,855	4,811,391	59·9

The population on 31 Dec. 1981 by language primarily spoken: Finnish, 4,500,986 (93·5%); Swedish, 300,150 (6·2%); other languages, 9,629; Lappish, 1,385.

The principal towns with resident census population, 31 Dec. 1981, are (Swedish names in brackets):

Helsinki (Helsingfors)—capital	483,051	Imatra	35,994
(metropolitan area)	910,414	Kajaani	35,018
Tampere (Tammerfors)	167,028	Kokkola (Gamlakarleby)	34,182
(metropolitan area)	245,893	Kouvola	31,322
Turku (Åbo)	163,526	Rauma (Raumo)	30,911
(metropolitan area)	242,362	Rovaniemi	30,759
Espoo (Esbo)	141,334	Mikkeli (St Michel)	28,623
Vantaa (Vanda)	134,040	Savonlinna (Nyslott)	28,451
Lahti	94,962	Kemi	26,732
Oulu (Uleåborg)	94,869	Seinäjoki	25,100
Pori (Björneborg)	79,223	Varkaus	24,770
Kuopio	75,255	Kerava	24,493
Jyväskylä	64,455	Riihimäki	24,005
Kotka	60,577	Järvenpää	23,788
Lappeenranta (Villmanstrand)	53,817	Nokia	23,764
Vaasa (Vasa)	53,903	Iisalmi	22,829
Joensuu	45,180	Valkeakoski	22,708
Hämeenlinna (Tavastehus)	41,992	Kuusankoski	22,381
Hyvinkää (Hyvinge)	37,559		

Vital statistics in calendar years:

	Living births	*Of which illegitimate*	*Still-born*	*Marriages*	*Deaths (exclusive of still-born)*	*Emigration*
1977	65,659	7,317	335	30,966	44,065	18,209
1978	63,983	7,263	314	29,760	43,692	16,327
1979	63,428	7,603	269	29,324	43,737	16,661
1980	63,064	8,247	266	29,325	44,398	14,824
1981	63,586	...	...	30,148	44,411	10,399

In 1981 the rate per 1,000 was: Births, 13·2; marriages, 6·3; deaths, 9·3, and infantile deaths (1980, per 1,000 live births), 7·6.

Population and Housing Census 1980. 19 vols. Helsinki, 1981–83
Population. Annual. Helsinki

CLIMATE. The climate is severe in winter, which lasts about 6 months, but mean temperatures in south and south-west are less harsh, 21°F (–6°C). In the north, mean temperatures may fall to 8·5°F (–13°C). Snow covers the ground for three months in the south and for over six months in the far north. Summers are short but quite warm, with occasional very hot days. Precipitation is light throughout the country, with one third falling as snow, the remainder mainly as convectional rain in summer and autumn.

Helsinki (Helsingfors), Jan. 21°F (–6°C), July 62°F (16·5°C). Annual rainfall 24·7″ (618 mm).

CONSTITUTION AND GOVERNMENT. Finland is a republic according to the Constitution of 17 July 1919.

Parliament consists of one chamber of 200 members chosen by direct and proportional election in which all Finnish citizens (men or women) who are 18 years have the vote (since 1969). The country is divided into 15 electoral districts with a representation proportional to their population. Every citizen over the age of 20 is eligible for Parliament, which is elected for 4 years, but can be dissolved sooner by the President.

The President is elected for 6 years by a college of 301 electors, elected by the votes of the citizens in the same way as the members of Parliament.

President of Finland: Dr Mauno Koivisto (elected 27 Jan. 1982).

State of Parties for Parliament elected on 18–19 March 1979: Conservative 47; Liberals, 4; Swedish Party, 10 (including 1 for Coalition of Åland); Centre, 36; Rural, 7; Social Democratic Party, 52; Communists, 35; Christian League, 9.

The Council of State (Cabinet), appointed by the President in Jan. 1983 was composed as follows:

Prime Minister: Kalevi Sorsa.

Agriculture and Forestry: Taisto Tähkämaa. *Foreign Affairs:* Pär Stenbäck. *Justice:* Cristoffer Taxell. *Interior:* Matti Ahde. *Interior (Deputy):* Mikko Jokela. *Defence:* Juhani Saukkonen. *Deputy Prime Minister and Finance:* Ahti Pekkala. *Economics and Finance:* Jermu Laine. *Education:* Kaarina Suonio. *Education (Deputy):* Arvo Salo. *Communications:* Jarmo Wahlström. *Trade and Industry:* Esko Ollila. *Social Affairs and Health:* Vappu Taipale. *Social Affairs and Health (Deputy):* Marjatta Väänänen. *Labour:* Viekko Helle. *Foreign Trade:* Arne Berner.

National flag: White with a blue Scandinavian cross.

National anthem: Maamme; Swedish: Vårt land (words by J. L. Runeberg, 1843; tune by F. Pacius, 1948).

Finnish and Swedish are the official languages of Finland.

Local Government. For administrative purposes Finland is divided into 12 provinces (*lääni*, Sw.: *län*). The administration of each province is entrusted to a governor (*maaherra*, Sw.: *landshövding*) appointed by the President. He directs the activities of the provincial office (*lääninhallitus*, Sw.: *länsstyrelse*) and of local sheriffs (*nimismies*, Sw.: *länsman*). In 1982 the number of sheriff districts was 223.

The unit of local government is the commune. Main fields of communal activities are local planning, roads and harbours, sanitary services, education, health services and social aid. The communes raise taxes independent from state taxation. Two different kinds of communes are distinguished: Urban communes (*kaupunki*, Sw.: *stad*) and rural communes. In 1982 there were altogether 461 communes of which 84 were urban and 377 rural. In all communes communal councils are elected for terms of 4 years; all inhabitants (men and women) of the commune who have reached their 18th year are entitled to vote and eligible. The executive power is in each commune vested in a board which consists of members elected by the council and one or a few chief officials of the commune. Several communes often form an association for the administration of some common institution, *e.g.*, a hospital or a vocational school.

The autonomous county *(landskap)* of Åland has a county council *(landsting)* of one chamber, elected according to rule corresponding to those for parliamentary elections. In addition to its provincial governor it has a county board with executive power in matters within the field of the autonomy of the county.

Constitution Act and Parliament Act of Finland. Helsinki, 1967
The Finnish Parliament. Porvoo, 1969
Local Self-Government in Finland and the Finnish Municipal Law. Helsinki, 1960
Report of the Second Parliamentary Defence Committee. Helsinki, 1976

DEFENCE. The period of military training is 240 to 330 days and refresher training 40 to 100 days. Total strength of trained and equipped reserves is about 700,000.

Army. The country is divided into 7 military regions. The Army consists of 1 armoured brigade, 7 infantry brigades, 7 independent infantry battalions, 3 field-artillery regiments, 2 independent field-artillery battalions, 2 coastal artillery regiments, 3 independent coastal artillery battalions, 1 anti-aircraft regiment, 1 surface-to-air missile battalion and 4 independent anti-aircraft battalions, making a total strength in 1983, of about 31,400.

Navy. The Fleet comprises 2 corvettes, 2 minelayers (including a modified *ex*-Soviet frigate), 1 coastal minelayer, 5 missile craft, 12 fast patrol boats, 6 inshore minesweepers, 5 patrol boats capable of minelaying, 6 support ships, 1 headquarters ship, 10 transport craft, 14 landing craft, 3 tugs, 1 supply ship and a cable ship. There is a naval academy. Personnel in 1983 totalled 2,500 (200 officers and 2,300 ratings).

The Frontier Guard comprises 4 large patrol vessels,9 coastal patrol craft and 34 coastal patrol boats.

Air Force. The Air Force has 2 fighter squadrons, 1 transport squadron, 1 training squadron, a military school of aviation, a technical school, a signal school and a depot. The fighter squadrons have MiG-21bis and Saab J35 Draken aircraft. Other equipment includes 30 Valmet Vinka piston-engined primary trainers of Finnish design, Magister jet basic trainers (being replaced by 50 Hawk trainers), MiG-21U and Saab J35C jet advanced trainers, C-47 and Fokker F.27 transport aircraft, Cessna 402 liaison aircraft, Learjet 35A target tugs, Piper Chieftain utility transports, and Mi-8 and Hughes 500 helicopters. Personnel total 3,000 officers and men.

INTERNATIONAL RELATIONS

Membership. Finland is a member of UN, the Nordic Council, OECD and an associate member of EFTA.

Treaties. A Treaty of friendship, co-operation and mutual assistance between Finland and the USSR was concluded in Moscow on 6 April 1948 for 10 years, extended on 19 Sept. 1955 to cover a period of 20 years and extended on 19 July 1970 for a further period of 20 years.

Treaty of Peace with Finland (10 Feb. 1947). Cmd. 7484

ECONOMY

Budget. Actual revenue and expenditure for the calendar years 1976–80, the ordinary budget for 1982 and the proposed budget for 1983 in 1m. marks:

	1976	*1977*	*1978*	*1979*	*1980*	*1981*	*1982*	*1983*
Revenue	32,132	35,168	40,393	43,319	48,916	58,795	64,917	72,107
Expenditure	31,094	35,064	38,938	45,036	50,812	57,797	64,916	72,106

Of the total revenue, 1981, 25% derived from sales tax, 27% from income and property tax, 18% from excise duties, 11% from other taxes and similar revenue, 10% from loans and 10% from miscellaneous sources. Of the total expenditure, 1981, 17% went to education and culture, 13% to social security, 10% to transport, 13% to agriculture and forestry, 9% to general administration, public order and safety, 9% to health, 5% to communities and housing policy, 6% to defence, 4% to promotion of industry and 14% to other expenditures.

At the end of Dec. 1981 the foreign loans totalled 13,331m. marks, of which 13,012m. were long-term loans, 319m. promissory notes to international organizations. The internal loans amounted to 8,771m. marks, of which, 8,724m. were consolidated debt. The cash surplus was 951m. marks. The total public debt was 22,102m. marks.

Currency. The unit of currency, starting 1 Jan. 1963, is the new *mark* of 100 *pennis*, equalling 100 old *marks*. The gold standard was suspended on 12 Oct. 1931. Aluminium bronze coins are 50, 20 and 10 *pennis*; copper coins, 5 and 1 *pennis*; aluminium coins, 5 and 1 *pennis*; silver, 1 *mark* pieces. Exchange rate in March 1983: 8·14 marks=£1; 5·38 marks=US$1.

Banking. The Bank of Finland (founded in 1811) is owned by the State and under the guarantee and supervision of Parliament. It is the only bank of issue, and the limit of its right to issue notes is fixed equal to the value of its assets of gold and foreign holdings plus 500m. marks. Notes of 500, 100, 50, 10, 5 and 1 marks are in circulation, and their total value at the end of 1981 was 5,153m. marks.

At the end of 1981 the deposits in banking institutions totalled 86,604m. marks and the loans granted by them 96,724m. marks. The most important groups of banking institutions were:

	Number of institutions	*Number of offices*	*Deposits (1m. marks)*	*Loans (1m. marks)*
Commercial banks	7	1,282	30,752	33,013
Savings banks	274	1,367	24,547	22,015
Post office savings bank	1	33 [1]	10,385	10,628
Co-operative banks	371	1,230	19,892	20,063

[1] In addition: 3,267 post offices.

Bank of Finland Monthly Bulletin. Helsinki, from 1926
Unitas. Quarterly Review, issued by Union Bank of Finland. Helsinki, from 1929
Economic Review (issued quarterly by Kansallis–Osake–Pankki). Helsinki, from 1948

Weights and Measures. The metric system of weights and measures was introduced in 1887 and is officially and universally employed.

Economic Survey of Finland. Annual

ENERGY AND NATURAL RESOURCES

Electricity. Electricity production was (in 1m. kwh.) 8,605 in 1960; 22,562 in 1970; 37,337 in 1979, 38,710 in 1980 and 39,075 in 1981, of which 34% was hydro-electric.

Minerals. The most important mines are Outokumpu (copper, discovered in 1910) and Otanmäki (iron, discovered in 1953). In 1981 the metal content (in tonnes) of the output of copper concentrates was 38,200, of zinc concentrates 52,200, of nickel concentrates 6,900, of iron concentrates and pellets 1·23m. and of lead concentrates 1,580.

Agriculture. The cultivated area covers only 9% of the land and of the economically active population 15% were employed in agriculture and forestry in 1975. The arable area was divided in 1980 into 224,721 farms, and the distribution of this area by the size of the farms was: Less than 5 hectares cultivated, 69,444 farms; 5–20 hectares, 125,978 farms; 20–50 hectares, 26,346 farms; 50–100 hectares, 2,566 farms; over 100 hectares, 387 farms.

The principal crops (area in 1,000 hectares, yield in tonnes) were in 1980:

Crop	*Area*	*Yield*	*Crop*	*Area*	*Yield*
Rye	45	63,900	Oats	444	1,007,500
Barley	602	1,080,100	Potatoes	39	477,800
Wheat	112	235,000	Hay	457	1,675,400

The total area under cultivation in 1981 was 2,539,900 hectares. Production of dairy butter in 1981 was 72,136 tonnes, and of cheese, 72,334 tonnes.

Livestock (1982): Horses, 34,200; cattle, 1,705,100; pigs (excluding piggeries of dairies), 1,475,300; poultry, 7,763,200; reindeer, 245,500.

Forestry. The total forest land amounts to 30–31m. hectares. The productive forest land covers 19·73m. hectares. The growing stock was valued at 1,520m. cu. metres in 1971–76 and the annual growth at 57·4m. cu. metres.

In 1981 there were exported: Round timber, 2,659,530 cu. metres; sawn wood, 5,409,187 cu. metres; plywood and veneers, 879,427 cu. metres.

Monthly Review of Agriculture. Board of Agriculture
Agriculture 1980: Annual Statistics of Agriculture. Helsinki

INDUSTRY AND TRADE

Industry. The following data cover establishments with a total personnel of 5 or more in 1981 [1]:

Industry	*Establishments*	*Personnel* [2]	*Value of production: Gross (1m. marks)*	*Value of production: Value added (1m. marks)*
Mining and quarrying	105	7,413	1,567	927
Metal ore mining	13	4,595	878	521
Other mining	92	2,808	692	416
Manufacturing	7,082	533,288	170,621	53,500
Manufacture of food, beverages and tobacco	1,148	61,800	30,792	7,383
Textile, wearing apparel and leather industries	938	67,346	9,919	4,895
Manufacture of textiles	307	23,734	4,036	1,944
Manufacture of wearing apparel, except footwear	437	32,218	4,079	2,136
Manufacture of wood and wood products, incl. furniture	1,079	57,246	12,413	4,632
Manufacture of paper and paper prod., printing, publishing	919	86,830	38,057	13,159
Manufacture of paper and paper products	192	50,517	29,707	8,478
Printing, publishing, etc.	727	36,366	8,363	4,723
Manufacture of chemicals and chemical, petroleum, coal, rubber and plastic products	449	39,922	28,186	7,076
Manufacture of industrial chemicals	150	54,077	7,983	2,128
Manufacture of other chemical products	116	10,850	3,608	1,771
Petroleum refineries	2	2,677	13,904	1,904
Manufacture of non-metallic mineral products	426	23,970	4,830	2,393
Basic metal industries	89	20,030	10,574	2,208
Iron and steel basic industries	58	14,855	7,096	1,673
Non-ferrous metal basic industries	31	1,773	3,477	534

[1] Preliminary. [2] Working proprietors, salaried employees and wage earners.

Industry	Establish-ments	Person-nel[1]	Value of production Gross (1m. marks)	Value added (1m. marks)
Manufacture of fabricated metal products, machinery, etc.	1,916	173,458	30,081	16,939
Manufacture of fabricated metal products, excl. machinery	654	31,846	6,300	3,256
Manufacture of machinery, except electrical	707	65,515	13,573	6,606
Manufacture of electrical machinery, apparatus, etc.	195	30,669	5,939	2,964
Manufacture of transport equipment	287	41,006	8,392	3,541
Other manufacturing industries	118	5,047	795	443
Electricity, gas and water	532	26,739	21,127	7,618
All industry	7,719	567,440	193,315	67,619

[1] Working proprietors, salaried employees and wage earners.

GDP (at market prices) *per capita* (1981) 44,163 marks.

Industrial Statistics of Finland. Annual

Commerce. Imports and exports for calendar years, in 1m. marks:

	1977	*1978*	*1979*	*1980*	*1981*
Imports	30,708	32,338	44,222	58,250	61,269
Exports	30,931	35,206	43,430	52,795	60,308

The trade with some principal import and export countries was (in 1,000 marks):

Country	*Imports 1980*	*Imports 1981*	*Exports 1980*	*Exports 1981*
Australia	62,382	52,342	517,201	558,509
Austria	692,772	717,527	391,035	369,846
Belgium–Luxembourg	976,248	1,050,913	764,954	910,487
Brazil	396,225	370,615	209,114	182,027
Canada	425,452	430,416	249,551	408,189
China	113,778	122,747	295,694	182,231
Colombia	440,978	293,465	63,031	83,585
Czechoslovakia	296,097	360,432	151,482	171,454
Denmark	1,393,609	1,335,918	1,840,758	1,999,591
France	1,776,878	1,931,561	2,389,103	2,379,890
German Dem. Rep.	328,139	378,672	331,221	404,945
Germany (Fed. Rep.)	7,331,646	7,442,233	5,606,220	5,510,085
Greece	62,681	66,732	306,775	443,251
Hungary	218,643	264,311	342,878	261,332
Iran	634,868	632,189	465,219	486,065
Iraq	973,625	1,499	582,468	561,082
Ireland	115,990	162,042	322,947	347,994
Israel	150,481	176,013	160,533	225,607
Italy	1,387,333	1,379,750	1,265,196	1,169,195
Japan	1,890,682	2,213,150	353,374	510,808
Netherlands	1,474,151	1,606,873	2,258,924	2,050,399
Norway	1,222,047	1,528,619	2,206,188	2,839,682
Poland	996,865	761,548	237,155	78,805
Portugal	279,751	279,502	177,020	181,029
Saudi Arabia	2,925,399	2,643,382	306,794	434,132
Spain	520,738	1,335,918	466,523	464,104
Sweden	7,022,617	6,920,340	8,717,462	8,058,531
Switzerland	923,714	1,024,476	843,371	816,175
USSR	12,232,926	14,378,000	9,301,990	14,923,625
UK	5,003,801	4,934,117	5,940,463	6,424,072
USA	3,372,468	4,577,509	1,667,268	2,229,888

Principal imports 1981 (in 1m. marks): Machinery, apparatus and appliances, 16,569; mineral fuels, lubricants, etc., 18,845; chemicals, 5,465; food and live animals, 3,555; road vehicles, 3,553; crude materials, inedible, except fuels, 3,196; textile yarn, fabrics, etc., 2,338; iron and steel, 1,880.

Principal exports in 1981 (in 1m. marks): Paper and paper-board, 13,219; machinery and transport equipment, 12,207; wood shaped or simply worked,

5,409; wood pulp, 3,558; ships, 3,147; clothing, 3,340; veneers, plywood, etc., and other wood manufactures, 879; food and live animals, 2,195; road vehicles, 982.

Total trade between Finland and UK (British Department of Trade returns, in £1,000 sterling):

	1978	*1979*	*1980*	*1981*	*1982*
Imports to UK	636,374	794,485	793,218	844,379	849,933
Exports and re-exports from UK	349,131	410,537	525,488	524,973	513,558

Foreign Trade. Annual.

Tourism. In 1981 tourism contributed 3,090m. marks to the economy.

COMMUNICATIONS

Roads. In Jan. 1981 there were 74,958 km of public roads, of which 35,656 km were paved. At the end of 1981 there were 1,279,192 registered cars, 52,698 lorries, 102,303 vans and 9,054 buses.

Railways. On 31 Dec. 1982 the total length of the line operated was 6,076 km (922 km electrified), of which all except 6 km was owned by the State. The gauge was 1,524 mm. In 1981 the number of passengers carried was 41m. and the amount of goods carried was 29·8m. tonnes. The total revenue in 1981 was 2,115m. marks and the total expenditure 2,806m. marks.

Aviation. The scheduled traffic of Finnish airlines covered 37m. km in 1981. The number of passengers was 2,751,100 and the number of passenger-km 2,513m. The air transport of freight and mail amounted to 57m. tonne-km.

Shipping. The total registered mercantile marine on 31 Dec. 1981 was 483 vessels of 2·48m. gross tons. In 1981 the total number of vessels arriving in Finland from abroad was 16,266 and the goods discharged amounted to 30·2m. tonnes. The goods loaded for export from Finland ports amounted to 18·4m. tonnes.

The lakes, rivers and canals are navigable for about 6,600 km. Timber floating is important, and there are about 41,500 km of floatable inland waterways. In 1981 bundle floating was about 5·7m. tonnes and river floating 1·6m. tonnes. In 1980, timber floated by vessels, 470,314 tonnes (rafts, 6·93m.).

On 27 Aug. 1963 the USSR leased to Finland the Russian part of the canal connecting Lake Saimaa with the Gulf of Finland. After extensive rebuilding the canal was opened for traffic in 1968. The Saimaa Canal and deepwater channels on Lake Saimaa (520 km) can be used by vessels with dimensions not larger than as follows: length 82 metres, width 11·8 metres, draught 4·4 metres and height of mast 24·5 metres.

Post and Broadcasting. In 1981 there were 3,847 post offices and 919 telegraph offices. The total length of telegraph wires was 565,101 km and that of domestic trunk and net group telephone wires 6·4m. km. The number of telephones was (1981), 2,511,306. All post and telegraph systems are administered by the State jointly with a large part of the telephone services. The total revenues from postal services were 1,779m. marks and from (wire and radio) telegraph services 1,900m. marks.

On 31 Dec. 1981 the number of television licences, 1,613,626, of which licences for colour television, 923,787. *Oy Yleisradio AB* broadcasts 2 programmes in Finnish and 1 in Swedish on long-, medium- and short-waves, and on FM. Two TV programmes (1 commercial) are broadcast.

Cinemas. In Dec. 1981 there were 362 cinemas with a seating capacity of 93,600.

Newspapers. In 1981 the number of newspapers published more often than once a week was 141, of which 130 in Finnish and 11 in Swedish.

JUSTICE, RELIGION, EDUCATION AND WELFARE

Justice. The lowest courts of justice are the municipal courts in towns and district courts in the country. Municipal courts are held by the burgomaster and at least 2 members of court, district court by judge and 5 jurors, the judge alone deciding, unless the jurors unanimously differ from him, when their decision prevails. From these courts an appeal lies to the courts of appeal *(Hovioikeus)* in Turku, Vaasa, Kuopio, Kouvola and Helsinki. The Supreme Court *(Korkein oikeus)* sits in Helsinki. Judges can be removed only by judicial sentence.

Two functionaries, the *Oikeuskansleri* or Chancellor of Justice, and the *Oikeusasiamies*, or Solicitor-General, exercise control over the administration of justice. The former acts also as counsel and public prosecutor for the Government; while the latter, who is appointed by the Parliament, exerts a general control over all courts of law and public administration.

At the end of 1981 the prison population numbered 4,692 men and 128 women; the number of convictions in 1980 was 320,477, of which 296,083 were for minor offences with maximum penalty of fines and 24,386 with penalty of imprisonment.

Religion. Liberty of conscience is guaranteed to members of all religions. National churches are the Lutheran National Church and the Greek Orthodox Church of Finland. The Lutheran Church is divided into 8 bishoprics (Turku being the archi-episcopal see), 78 provostships and 594 parishes. The Greek Orthodox Church is divided into 2 bishoprics (Kuopio being the archiepiscopal see) and 25 parishes, in addition to which there are a monastery and a convent.

Percentage of the total population at the end of 1980: Lutherans, 90·2; Greek Orthodox, 1·1; others, 0·9; not members of any religion, 7·8.

Education (1980–81). *Primary and Secondary Education:*

	Number of institu-tions	*Teachers*	*Students*
First-level Education	*4,245*	*25,959*	*373,347*
(Lower sections of the comprehensive schools, grades I–VI)			
Second-level Education	*1,603*	*33,958*	*444,165*
General education	1,062	19,822	341,054
(Upper sections of the comprehensive schools, grades VII–IX, and senior secondary schools)			
Vocational education	*541*	*14,136*	*103,111*

Higher Education. Education at the third level (including universities and third level education at vocational institutes) was provided for 103,111 students. Education at universities was provided at 21 institutions with 6,194 teachers and 84,176 students.

University Education. Universities and similar types of institutions and the number of teachers and students are:

	Founded	*Teachers*	*Students Total*	*Students Women*
Universities				
Helsinki	1640	1,654	23,920	13,285
Turku (Swedish)	1919	275	3,878	2,041
Turku (Finnish)	1922	721	8,566	4,816
Jyväskylä	1958	458	5,912	3,712
Oulu	1958	692	7,140	3,259
Tampere	1966	428	8,603	5,206
Joensuu	1969	232	2,760	1,789
Kuopio	1972	196	1,464	857
Lappi	1979	34	402	198
Polytechnic, Lappeenranta	1969	93	1,018	144
Polytechnic, Helsinki	1849	529	7,731	1,250
Polytechnic, Tampere	1972	178	2,620	284
College of Veterinary Medicine, Helsinki	1946	52	258	176
Schools for Economics				
Helsinki (Finnish)	1911	148	3,720	1,623
Helsinki (Swedish)	1927	79	1,516	599
Turku (Finnish)	1950	53	1,287	595
Vaasa	1968	62	1,265	679
Swedish school of social sciences and local administration	1964 [1]	21	371	262

[1] Previously Swedish Civic College since 1943.

			Students	
	Founded	*Teachers*	*Total*	*Women*
Educational Institutions for Art				
Sibelius Academy	1939	126	753	390
University of Industrial Arts	1949	121	907	545
Theatre Academy	1979	42	85	36
Teachers' training colleges [2]				

[2] Included in data for the universities above.

General adult education (at civic institutes, folk high schools and study centres) had 810,501 students.

General Education. Central Statistical Office, Helsinki (annual), *Higher Education.* Central Statistical Office, Helsinki (annual), *Vocational Education.* Helsinki (annual)

Health. In 1980 there were 9,016 physicians, 3,938 dentists and 74,280 hospital beds.

Social Security. The Social Insurance Institution administers general systems of old age pensions (to all persons over 65 years of age and disabled younger persons) and of health insurance. An additional system of compulsory old age pensions paid for by the employers is in force and works through the Central Pension Security Institute. Systems for child welfare, care of vagrants, alcoholics and drug addicts and other public aid are administered by the communes and supervised by the National Social Board and the Ministry of Social Affairs and Health.

The total cost of social security amounted to 42,419·3m. marks in 1980. Out of this 12,365m. (29·1%) was spent for health, 941m. (2·2%) for industrial accidents, 2,733m. (6·4%) for unemployment, 17,324m. (40·8%) old age and disability, 6,715m. (15·8%) for family allowances and child welfare, 522m. (1·2%) for general welfare purposes, 1,116m. (2·6%) for war-disabled, etc., 705m. (1·7%) as tax reductions for children. Out of the total expenditure 28% was financed by the State, 14% by local authorities, 47% by employers, 7% by the beneficiaries and 4% by users.

Labour Protection and Legislation. Helsinki, 1977
Social Welfare and Social Allowances. Helsinki, 1976
Social Security in the Nordic Countries 1978. Statistical Reports of the Nordic Countries, vol. 38. Stockholm, 1981
Arajarvi, E., *Social Expenditure in 1979 and Preliminary Data for 1980.* Official Statistics of Finland, Helsinki, 1981
Ellala, Esa, Suominen Risto, and Kotiranta, Maija-Liisa, *The Development of Social Security in Finland from 1950 to 1974.* Official statistics of Finland, special social studies XXXII : 48. Helsinki, 1976

DIPLOMATIC REPRESENTATIVES

Of Finland in Great Britain (38 Chesham Place, London, SW1X 8HW)
Ambassador: Ilkka Olavi Pastinen (accredited 24 Feb. 1983).

Of Great Britain in Finland (16–20 Uudenmaankatu, Helsinki 12)
Ambassador: Alan Brooke Turner.

Of Finland in the USA (3216 New Mexico Ave., NW, Washington, D.C., 20016)
Ambassador: Jaakko Iloniemi (accredited 10 Sept. 1977).

Of the USA in Finland (Itäinen Puistotie 14A, Helsinki 14)
Ambassador: Keith F. Nyborg.

Of Finland to the United Nations
Ambassador: Keijo Korhonen.

Books of Reference

Statistical Information: The Central Statistical Office (Tilastokeskus, Swedish: Statistikcentralen; address: PO Box 504, SF-00101 Helsinki 10) was founded in 1865 to replace earlier official statistical services dating from 1749 (in united Sweden–Finland). Statistics on foreign trade, agriculture, forestry, navigation, health and social welfare are produced by other state authorities. Its publications include: *Statistical Yearbook of Finland* (from 1879) and *Bulletin of Statistics* (monthly, from 1924). A bibliography of all official statistics of Finland was published in Finnish, Swedish and English in *Statistical publications 1856–1979.* Helsinki, 1980.

Constitution Act and Parliament Act of Finland. Helsinki, 1978
Suomen valtiokalenteri (*State Calendar of Finland;* a Swedish version *Finlands statskalender* is published separately). Helsinki. Annual
Facts About Finland. Helsinki. Annual (Union Bank of Finland)
Finland: Creation and Construction. London, 1968
Finland Facts and Figures. Helsinki, 1979
Finland in Figures. Helsinki, Annual
Statistical Yearbook of Finland. Helsinki, Annual
Yearbook of Finnish Foreign Policy. Helsinki, Annual
Finnish Foreign Policy: Studies in Foreign Politics. Political Science Association, Helsinki, 1963
The Finnish Banking System. Helsinki, 1980
Finnish Industry. Helsinki, 1981
Finnish Local Government. Helsinki, 1981
Health Services in Finland. Helsinki, 1980
Let's Have a Sauna. Helsinki, 1980
Alanne, V. S., *Finnish-English General Dictionary.* Helsinki, 1980
Hurme-Pesonen, *English–Finnish General Dictionary.* Helsinki, 1981
Jutikkala, E., and Pirinen, K., *A History of Finland.* 3rd ed. New York, 1979
Kekkonen, U., *Neutrality: The Finnish Position.* 2nd ed. London, 1973
Kirby, D. G., *Finland in the Twentieth Century.* London, 1979
Klinge, M., *A Brief History of Finland.* Helsinki, 1981
Korhonen, K., *Urho Kekkonen: A Statesman for Peace.* Helsinki, 1975
Layton, R., *Sibelius: The Master Musician.* London, 1978
Nousiainen, J., *The Finnish Political System.* Harvard Univ. Press, 1971
Paasivirta, J., *Finland and Europe. The Period of Autonomy and the International Crises 1808–1914.* London, 1981
Pearson, P., *Alvar Aalto and the International Style.* New York, 1978
Puntila, L. A., *The Political History of Finland, 1809–1966.* Helsinki, 1974
Pennia. *Finland in Maps.* (National Board of Survey). Helsinki, 1979
Suomi: Handbook of Finnish Geography. Finnish Geogr. Society, Helsinki, 1979
Törnudd, K., *The Electoral System of Finland.* London, 1968
Uotila, J., *The Finnish Legal System.* Helsinki, 1966
Wuolle, A., *Finnish–English School Dictionary.* Helsinki, 1976

FRANCE

Capital: Paris
Population: 54·09m. (1982)
GNP per capita: US$11,730 (1980)

République Française

HISTORY. The republic proclaimed on the fall of the Bourbon monarchy in 1792 lasted until the First Empire, under Napoleon I, was established in 1804. The Bourbon monarchy was restored in 1814 and (with an interval during 1815) lasted until the abdication of Louis Philippe in 1848. The Second Republic was established on 12 March 1848, the Second Empire (under Louis Napoleon) on 2 Dec. 1852. The Third Republic was established on 4 Sept. 1870 following the capture and imprisonment of Louis Napoleon in the Franco-Prussian war, and lasted until the German occupation of 1940. The Fourth Republic was established on 24 Dec. 1946 and lasted until 4 Oct. 1958.

AREA AND POPULATION. France is bounded north by the English Channel *(La Manche)*, north-east by Belgium and Luxembourg, east by Federal Republic of Germany, Switzerland and Italy, south by the Mediterranean (with Monaco as a coastal enclave), south-west by Spain and Andorra, and west by the Atlantic Ocean The total area is 543,965 sq. km (210,033 sq. miles).

The population (present in actual boundaries) at successive censuses has been:

1801	27,349,003	1881	37,672,048	Mar. 1946	40,506,639
1821	30,461,875	1891	38,342,948	May 1954	42,777,174
1841	34,230,178	1901	38,961,945	Mar. 1962	46,519,997
1861	37,386,313	1911	39,604,992	Mar. 1968	49,778,540
1866	38,067,064	1921	39,209,518	Feb. 1975	52,655,802
1872	36,102,921	1931	41,834,923		

The 1975 total included 3,442,415 foreigners, of whom 758,925 were Portuguese, 710,690 Algerian, 497,480 Spanish and 462,940 Italian.

The latest population estimate (at 1 Jan. 1982) is 54,085,000.

Vital statistics for calendar years:

	Marriages	*Divorces*	*Live births*	*Stillborn*	*Deaths*
1976	374,003	59,200	720,395	7,522	557,114
1977	368,000	72,000	745,830	8,600	535,900
1978	354,628	73,200	737,062	7,852	546,916
1979	339,770	86,900	756,960	7,570	541,050
1980	333,740	...	800,400	7,900	547,530
1981	314,600	...	805,680	7,735	555,360

Live birth rate in 1980 was 15 per 1,000 inhabitants; death rate, 10·3; marriage rate, 5·8; divorce rate, 1·6; infant mortality, 9·6 per 1,000 live births. Life expectation at birth; men, 70·2; women, 78·5.

The areas, populations and chief towns of the 22 Metropolitan regions were as follows:

Regions	*Area (sq. km)*	*Census April 1975*	*Estimate Jan. 1981*	*Chief town*
Alsace	8,280	1,517,330	1,570,500	Strasbourg
Aquitaine	41,308	2,550,340	2,584,400	Bordeaux
Auvergne	26,013	1,330,479	1,320,000	Clermont-Ferrand
Basse-Normandie	17,589	1,306,152	1,318,200	Caen
Bourgogne (Burgundy)	31,582	1,570,943	1,595,100	Dijon
Bretagne (Brittany)	27,208	2,595,431	2,665,200	Rennes
Centre	39,151	2,152,500	2,240,400	Orléans
Champagne-Ardenne	25,606	1,336,832	1,349,600	Reims
Corse (Corsica)	8,680	289,842	230,100[1]	Ajaccio
Franche-Comté	16,202	1,060,317	1,090,800	Besançon
Haute-Normandie	12,317	1,595,695	1,650,300	Rouen

Regions	Area (sq. km)	Census April 1975	Estimate Jan. 1981	Chief town
Île-de-France	12,012	9,878,524	10,117,200	Paris
Languedoc-Roussillon	27,376	1,789,474	1,844,700	Montpellier
Limousin	16,942	738,726	732,300	Limoges
Lorraine	23,547	2,330,821	2,311,500	Nancy
Midi-Pyrénées	45,348	2,268,245	2,272,900	Toulouse
Nord-Pas-de-Calais	12,414	3,913,773	3,926,300	Lille
Pays de la Loire	32,082	2,767,163	2,882,200	Nantes
Picardie	19,399	1,678,644	1,723,000	Amiens
Poitou-Charentes	25,810	1,528,118	1,541,700	Poitiers
Provence-Côte d'Azur	31,400	3,675,730	3,909,700	Marseille
Rhône-Alpes	43,698	4,780,723	4,967,400	Lyon

[1] Following special survey of Corsica.

Populations of the principal conurbations and towns at Census 1975:

	Conurbation	Town		Conurbation	Town
Paris	8,549,898	2,317,227	Limoges	167,664	147,406
Lyon	1,170,660	462,841	Avignon	162,562	93,024
Marseille	1,070,912	914,356	Mantes-la-Jolie	154,988	42,564
Lille	935,882	177,218	Amiens	152,997	135,992
Bordeaux	612,456	226,281	Béthune	145,155	28,279
Toulouse	509,939	383,176	Thionville	141,881	44,191
Nantes	453,500	263,689	Briey	133,853	—
Nice	437,566	346,620	Montbéliard	132,343	31,591
Grenoble	389,088	169,740	Nîmes	131,638	133,942
Rouen	388,711	118,332	Pau	126,859	85,860
Toulon	378,430	185,050	Troyes	126,611	75,500
Strasbourg	365,323	257,303	Besançon	126,349	126,187
Valenciennes	350,599	43,202	Bayonne	121,474	44,706
St-Étienne	334,846	221,775	Saint-Nazaire	119,418	69,769
Lens	328,741	40,281	Perpignan	117,689	107,971
Nancy	280,569	111,493	Bruay-en-Artois	116,340	25,951
Le Havre	264,422	219,583	Trappes	112,353	—
Cannes	258,479	71,080	Aix-en-Provence	110,659	114,014
Clermont-Ferrand	253,244	161,203	Lorient	105,797	71,923
Tours	245,631	145,441	Valence	104,330	70,307
Rennes	229,310	205,733	Annecy	103,543	54,954
Mulhouse	218,743	119,326	La Rochelle	100,649	77,494
Montpellier	211,430	195,603	Boulogne-sur-Mer	100,581	49,284
Douai	210,508	47,570	Angoulême	100,528	50,500
Orléans	209,234	109,956	Calais	100,327	79,369
Dijon	208,432	156,787	Poitiers	98,554	85,466
Reims	197,021	183,610	Forbach	97,970	25,385
Le Mans	192,057	155,245	Maubeuge	97,494	35,474
Brest	190,812	172,176	Béziers	88,619	85,677
Angers	188,695	142,966	Chambéry	88,081	56,788
Dunkerque	186,314	83,759	Bourges	86,041	80,379
Caen	181,390	122,794	Roanne	83,561	56,498
Metz	181,191	117,199	Colmar	83,435	67,410

Recensement de la population de 1975. Paris, Institut National de la Statistique et des Etudes Economiques, 1975

CLIMATE. The north-west has a moderate maritime climate, with small temperature range and abundant rainfall, but inland, rainfall becomes more seasonal, with a summer maximum, and the annual range of temperature increases. Southern France has a Mediterranean climate, with mild moist winters and hot dry summers. Eastern France has a continental climate and a rainfall maximum in summer, with thunderstorms prevalent.

Paris. Jan. 37°F (3°C), July 64°F (18°C). Annual rainfall 22·9″ (573 mm). Bordeaux. Jan. 41°F (5°C), July 68°F (20°C). Annual rainfall 31·4″ (786 mm). Lyon. Jan. 37°F (3°C), July 68°F (20°C). Annual rainfall 31·8″ (794 mm).

CONSTITUTION AND GOVERNMENT. The Constitution of the Fifth Republic, superseding that of 1946, came into force on 4 Oct. 1958. It consists of a preamble, dealing with the Rights of Man, and 92 articles.

France is a Republic, indivisible, secular, democratic and social; all citizens are equal before the law (Art. 2). National sovereignty resides with the people, who exercise it through their representatives and by referenda (Art. 3). Political parties carry out their activities freely, but must respect the principles of national sovereignty and democracy (Art. 4).

The President of the Republic sees that the Constitution is respected; he ensures the regular functioning of the public authorities, as well as the continuity of the state. He is the protector of national independence and territorial integrity (Art. 5). He is elected for 7 years by direct universal suffrage (Art. 6). He appoints a Prime Minister and, on the latter's advice, appoints and dismisses the other members of the Government (Art. 8). He presides over the Council of Ministers (Art. 9). He can dissolve the National Assembly, after consultation with the Prime Minister and the Presidents of the two Houses (Art. 12). He appoints to the civil and military offices of the state (Art. 13). In times of crisis, he may take such emergency powers as the circumstances demand; the National Assembly cannot be dissolved during such a period (Art. 16).

Previous Presidents of the Fifth Republic:

General Charles André Joseph de Gaulle, 8 Jan. 1959–28 April 1969 (resigned); Alain Poher (interim), 28 April 1969–20 June 1969; Georges Jean Raymond Pompidou, 20 June 1969–2 April 1974 (died); Alain Poher (interim), 2 April 1974–27 May 1974; Valéry Giscard d'Estaing, 27 May 1974–21 May 1981.

President of the Republic: François Mitterrand (elected 10 May 1981; took office 21 May 1981).

The government determines and conducts the policy of the nation (Art. 20). The Prime Minister directs the operation of the Government, is responsible for national defence and ensures the execution of laws (Art. 21). Members of the Government must not be members of Parliament (Art. 23).

In March 1983 a new French cabinet was appointed by President Mitterand consisting of 15 Ministers compared with 35 Ministers in the previous administration.

The Council of Ministers appointed in March 1983 was composed as follows:

Prime Minister: Pierre Mauroy (Soc.)

Finance and Budget: Jacques Delors (Soc.)

Social Affairs: Pierre Bérégovoy (Soc.)

Interior: Gaston Defferre (Soc.)

Transport: Charles Fiterman (Comm.)

Justice: Robert Badinter (Soc.)

Foreign Affairs: Claude Cheysson (Soc.)

Defence: Charles Hernu (Soc.)

Agriculture: Michel Rocard (Soc.)

Industry and Research: Laurent Fabius (Soc.)

Education: Alain Savary (Soc.)

Foreign Trade and Tourism: Mme Edith Cresson (Soc.)

Urbanism and Housing: Roger Quillot (Soc.)

Commerce: Michel Crépeau (MRG)
Professional Training: Marcel Rigout (Comm.)

Parliament consists of the National Assembly and the Senate; the National Assembly is elected by direct suffrage and the Senate by indirect suffrage (Art. 24). It convenes as of right in two ordinary sessions per year, the first on 2 October for 80 days and the second on 2 April for not more than 90 days (Art. 28).

The National Assembly comprises 491 Deputies, elected for a 5-year term from single-member constituencies – 474 in Metropolitan France, 11 in Overseas Departments, 1 for Mayotte (a 'special collectivity'), and 5 in Overseas Territories. The latest General Elections, held in June 1981, resulted in a new composition of 269 *Parti Socialiste,* 44 *Parti Communiste Française,* 14 *Mouvement des Radicaux de Gauche* and 6 others supporting the Government, together with 88 *Rassemblement Pour la République* (Gaullists), 63 *Union de la Démocratie Française* (Giscardians and Centrist Union), and 7 others forming the opposition.

The Senate comprises 305 Senators elected for 9-year terms (one third every 3 years) by an electoral college in each Department or Overseas Territory, made up of all members of the Departmental Council or Territorial Assembly together with all members of Municipal Councils within that area; 287 Senators represent Metropolitan France, 8 Overseas Departments, 1 Mayotte, 3 Overseas Territories and 6 Frenchmen residing outside France. Following the latest partial elections in Sept. 1980, the Senate is composed of 69 *Parti Socialiste*, 67 *Union Centrist,* 52 *Parti Républicaine* (Giscardians), 41 RPR (Gaullists), 26 *Gauche Démocratique,* 23 *Parti Communiste Française,* 13 MRG and 13 *non-inscrits* (unaffiliated). Its membership will be raised to 316 at the next elections (1983).

The Constitutional Council is composed of 9 members whose term of office is 9 years (non-renewable), one-third every 3 years; 3 are appointed by the President of the Republic, 3 by the President of the National Assembly, and 3 by the President of the Senate; in addition, former Presidents of the Republic are, by right, life members of the Constitutional Council (Art. 56). It oversees the fairness of the elections of the President (Art. 58) and Parliament (Art. 59) and of referenda (Art. 60), and acts as a guardian of the Constitution (Art. 61).

The Economic and Social Council advises on Government and Private Members' Bills (Art. 69). It comprises representatives of employers', workers' and farmers' organizations in each Department and Overseas Territory.

National flag: The Tricolour of three vertical stripes of blue, white, red.

National anthem: La Marseillaise (words and music by C. Rouget de Lisle, 1792).

Local Government. Under far-reaching legislation on decentralisation introduced from Jan. 1982, state-appointed Regional Prefects were abolished and their powers transferred to the Presidents of the Regional Councils, now directly elected. France is divided into 22 regions for national development work, for planning and for budgetary policy.

There are 96 *départements* within the 22 regions each governed by a directly-elected *Conseil Général.* From 1982 their Presidents' powers are greatly extended to take over local administration and expenditure from the former Departmental prefects, now called 'Commissioners of the Republic' with responsibility for public order. The *arrondissement* (324 in 1975) and the *canton* (3,509 in 1975), have little administrative significance.

The unit of local government is the *commune*, the size and population of which vary very much. There were, in 1975, in the 96 metropolitan departments, 36,394 communes. Most of them (31,593) had less than 1,500 inhabitants, and 16,550 had less than 300, while 229 communes had more than 30,000 inhabitants. The local affairs of the commune are under a Municipal Council, composed of from 9 to 36 members, elected by universal suffrage for 6 years by French citizens of 21 years or over after 6 months' residence.

Each Municipal Council elects a mayor, who is both the representative of the commune and the agent of the central government.

In Paris the *Conseil de Paris* is composed of 109 members elected from the 20 *arrondissements*. It combines the functions of departmental *Conseil Général* and Municipal Council.

d'Estaing, V. G., *French Democracy*. New York, 1977
Hayward, J., *The One and Invisible French Republic*. New York, 1973
Suleiman, E. N., *Politics, Power, and Bureaucracy in France*. Princeton Univ. Press, 1974
Wright, V., *The Government and Politics of France*. London, 1978

DEFENCE. The President of the Republic exercises command over the Armed Forces. He is assisted by the research organization of the High Council of Defence (*Conseil Supérieur de la Défense Nationale*) and two Committees (*Comité de Défense* and *Comité de Défense restreint*) which formulate directives. The Prime Minister is responsible for the national defence; he exercises his military responsibilities through the General Secretariat of National Defence (SGDN). Under the Prime Minister's authority, the *Comité d'Action Scientifique de Défense* co-ordinates research.

On 5 July 1969 the Army Ministry was replaced by the Ministry of State for National Defence which is responsible for the Army, Air Force and Navy. In addition to the powers of the Army Ministry, the Ministry of State prepares general directives for negotiations relating to defence. It has SGDN at its disposal for exercising these powers. It is assisted by the Departmental Assistant for Weapons, the Secretary-General for Administration, the Chief of Staff of the Armed Forces and the Chiefs of Staff of the 3 Armed Forces—Army, Navy and Air.

In 1962 the Armed Forces were reorganized in 3 groups: (1) nuclear strategic force; (2) operational forces; (3) home defence forces. Total strength (1982) 719,805 including 98,296 not included in totals for individual services.

French forces are not formally committed to NATO.

Army. The Army consists of regular officers and n.c.o.s, long-term n.c.o.s and soldiers, and conscripts serving 12 months.

The peace-time units comprise infantry, armoured troops and cavalry, artillery, engineering, signals, transport, matériel, naval infantry and artillery. In addition, there are the Foreign Legion, mountain and airborne troops and other specialized units.

In 1982 the effective strength of the Army was 356,843 all ranks (excluding *Gendarmerie)*.

Higher military instruction is provided in 3 stages: the staff school (*École d'État-major*) for officers of formation staffs; the *École Supérieure de Guerre* for officers earmarked for the higher command; the *Institut des Hautes Études de Défense Nationale* where high-ranking officers and civilians study together the problems of national defence.

Light Army Aircraft. Formed in 1952, the *Aviation Légère de l'Armée de Terre* (ALAT) is a well-equipped force, with 75 light aeroplanes and more than 550 helicopters for observation, reconnaissance, combat area transport, liaison and supply duties. Effective strength, 1981, 6,450.

The *Gendarmerie* is an integral part of the Army but also co-operates with the civil administration in maintaining public order. Effective strength, 1982, 81,898.

Navy. The Navy is under the supreme direction of the Minister of Defence, being administered by the Chief and Deputy Chiefs of Naval Staff.

All naval aircraft and coastal defences are under the control of the Navy, and have been reorganized in 3 coast 'naval frontier' districts (with headquarters in Cherbourg, Brest and Toulon), in relation to the aircraft attached to the active fleet.

The French Navy is manned partly by conscription but mainly by voluntary enlistment. In 1983 the active personnel was 69,130 officers and men, including 9,150 in the Naval Air Arm.

The following is a summary of the strength of the fleet at the periods shown:

	Completed at end of								
	1974	*1975*	*1976*	*1977*	*1978*	*1979*	*1980*	*1981*	*1982*
Aircraft carriers	3[3]	3[3]	3[3]	3[3]	3[3]	3[3]	3[3]	3[3]	3[3]
Submarines	23[2]	24[4]	24[4]	26[4]	27[4]	29[5]	28[5]	27[5]	28[5]
Cruisers	1	1	1	1	1	1	1	1	1
Destroyers	22	21	20	21	22	20	19	20	20
Frigates	28	28	27	29	27	24	22	22	25

[2] Including 3 nuclear-powered ballistic missile submarines.
[3] Including 1 helicopter-carrier.
[4] Including 4 nuclear-powered ballistic missile submarines.
[5] Including 5 nuclear-powered ballistic missile submarines.

The principal surface ships of the French Navy are as follows:

Completed	*Name*	*Standard displacement Tons*	*Aircraft*	*Principal armament*	*Shaft horse-power*	*Speed Knots*
			Aircraft Carriers			
1963 1961	Foch Clemenceau	27,300 (normal)	30 fixed wing, 4 helicopters	8 3·9 in.	126,000	32·0
			Helicopter Carrier			
1964	Jeanne d'Arc[1]	10,000	8 helicopters	4 3·9 in.	40,000	26·5
			Cruiser			
1959	Colbert	8,500	—	4 'Exocet' (singles) 1 twin 'Masurca' 2 3·9 in. AA	86,000	32·0

[1] Cruiser type forward, flat-topped midships to aft.

Capital (Strategic) Submarines

Class	*No.*	*Displacement (submerged) tons*	*Missile Tubes (vertical)*	*Nuclear Reactors*	*Shaft horse-power*	*Speed Knots*
'611'	6	8,940	16 M 20	1	16,000	25 dived 20 surface

In order of completion: *Le Redoutable* (1971), *Le Terrible* (1973), *Le Foudroyant (1974)*, *L'Indomptable* (1976), *Le Tonnant* (1980), *L'Inflexible* (1984)

The latter, completing, will be of intermediate type between her predecessors and a new class. Two more are reportedly planned and two or three more of an improved class envisaged.

All the named vessels above are also armed with four 21-inch torpedo tubes.

The sixth vessel will have M 4 missiles.

There are also 2 nuclear-powered fleet submarines of 2,670 tons (submerged), 21 diesel-powered submarines, 2 guided-missile destroyer leaders of 5,090 tons, 3 guided-missile leaders of 4,580 tons, 4 missile leaders of 3,830 tons, 1 missile leader of 3,500 tons, 10 old conventional destroyers of 2,750 tons, 22 escorts (frigates), of 950 to 1,750 tons, 5 fast attack missile craft, 2 offshore patrol vessels, and 4 as diving ships, 10 large minehunters (*ex*-ocean minesweepers), 8 coastal minehunters, 20 coastal minesweepers (4 used as patrol vessels and 4 as diving ships), 8 inshore minesweepers (used as diving craft), 8 surveying vessels, 1 coastal patrol craft, 2 dock landing ships, 8 tank landing ships, 14 landing craft, 30 minor landing craft, 7 maintenance, repair and depot ships, 8 oilers, 11 boom defence vessels, 6 support ships, 14 transports, 12 training vessels, 40 auxiliary ships and 90 tugs.

One more nuclear-powered ballistic missile submarine, 3 nuclear-powered fleet (torpedo-armed) submarines, 4 guided missile destroyers and 8 *avisos* (escorts) are under construction. Two nuclear-powered aircraft carriers, 4 more nuclear-powered fleet, torpedo-armed (hunter-killer) submarines, 6 fast missile craft and 14 mine-hunters are projected.

The naval air arm, known usually as *Aéronavale*, has 2 squadrons of nationally designed Etendard transonic fighter-bombers, 1 squadron of Etendard reconnaissance fighters, 2 squadrons of US-built Crusader all-weather fighters, 3 squadrons of Alizé turboprop anti-submarine aircraft, 5 maritime reconnaissance squadrons with Atlantic and Neptune aircraft and 3 anti-submarine and assault squadrons with Super Frelon and HSS-1 helicopters. Strength is 323 aircraft comprising 235 fixed-wing and 88 helicopters.

Air Force. Formed as the *Service Aéronautique* in April 1910, the *Armeé de l'Air* is organized in 7 major commands. Its bases and installations were regrouped and modernized in 1967. The *Commandement des Forces Aériennes Stratégiques* (CFAS) commands the nuclear deterrent force. The *Commandement de la Force Aérienne Tactique* (FATAC) directs the tactical air forces, commands the air force reserve and is responsible for support of the ground forces. Under FATAC the 1st *Commandement Aérien Tactique* (1° CATAC) controls tactical air units based in eastern France; the 2nd *Commandement Aérien Tactique* (2° CATAC) controls the reserve forces and the air component of the *Force d'Intervention.* The *Commandement du Transport Aérien Militaire (*COTAM) is responsible for air transport operations and for the training and transport of airborne forces. The *Commandement Air des Forces de Défense Aérienne* (CAFDA) controls air defence forces. The *Commandement des Écoles de l'Armée de l'Air* (CEAA) is responsible for training the personnel for all branches of the Air Force. The *Commandement des Transmissions* has responsibility for communications and electronic warfare. Finally, the *Commandement du Génie de l'Air,* made up mainly of Army personnel, undertakes airbase construction and maintenance under Air Force control.

The home-based French Air Force is divided territorially among 4 metropolitan air regions (Metz, Villacoublay, Bordeaux, Aix-en-Provence); overseas, small air units are integrated into the local joint-service commands. There are about 40 combat squadrons plus about 30 transport, helicopter and support squadrons, and the Air Force uses a total of 66 bases.

The strategic, tactical and air defence forces are equipped entirely with jet aircraft. The CFAS has 33 first-line Mirage IV supersonic nuclear bombers, and 10 reserves, deployed in 2 wings (each 3 squadrons) supported by 11 C-135F refuelling tanker transports. Twelve Mirage IVs are equipped for reconnaissance missions. The 1° CATAC deploys 7 wings (20 squadrons), consisting of about 180 Mirage III-E and 5F ground-attack and III-R reconnaissance fighters, and 120 Jaguar strike aircraft, plus 2 OCUs equipped with Mirage III-Bs and Jaguars. The 3 reconnaissance squadrons are re-equipping with Mirage F1-CRs in 1983–84. The air defence forces have 4 wings, with 8 squadrons of Mirage F1 multi-mission fighters and 1 squadron of Mirage III-Cs (to be replaced by Mirage 2000s). The COTAM is equipped with 3 wings of turboprop Transall C.160 transports, supplemented by 2 groups of DC-8, Caravelle, Nord 262, Mystère 20 and 50, Twin Otter and M.S. 760 Paris aircraft. Other units are equipped with Broussard observation and general-purpose monoplanes, and about 100 Alouette II/III and Puma helicopters. Training aircraft include CAP-10 piston-engined primary trainers, Epsilon piston-engined and Magister jet basic trainers, Alpha Jet and Mirage III-B advanced trainers, and two-seat Jaguars; 25 EMB-121 Xingus bought from Brazil and dual-purpose training/liaison aircraft.

Total personnel (1982), 100,400; 460 combat aircraft.

INTERNATIONAL RELATIONS

Membership. France is a member of UN, the Council of Europe, NATO and EEC.

ECONOMY

Planning. For the history of planning in France from 1947 to 1980, *see* THE STATESMAN'S YEAR-BOOK, 1982–83, p. 474. The eighth plan, covering the 1981–85 period, was set aside after the change of government in May 1981 and replaced by an interim plan for 1982–83, to be followed by a new ninth plan for 1984–88.

Budget. Budgets (in 1m. francs) for calendar years:

Receipts	*1980* [1]	%	*1981* [2]	%
Taxation				
Income tax	133,850	21·26	154,226	21·83
Corporation tax	62,338	9·90	65,309	9·25
Taxes on wealth	36,450	5·80	41,584	5·89
Taxes on consumption (VAT, etc.)	328,562	52·20	368,703	52·20
Other taxes (inc. payroll tax)	37,900	6·02	41,346	5·85
Non-fiscal receipts	30,360	4·82	35,143	4·98
Gross total	629,460		706,311	
Net budget receipts (gross total taxes minus various deductions)	529,995		592,104	
Expenditure				
Public authorities and general administration	59,064	10·80	68,332	10·75
Education and culture	133,682	24·45	154,857	24·35
Social affairs, health, employment	109,123	19·96	125,734	19·77
Agriculture and countryside	17,557	3·21	19,498	3·07
Housing and town planning	26,196	4·79	30,923	4·86
Transport and communications	28,113	5·14	30,147	4·74
Industry and services	26,063	4·77	27,414	4·31
External affairs	15,547	2·84	16,955	2·67
Defence	95,318	17·43	111,483	17·53
Miscellaneous expenditure	36,163	6·61	50,572	7·95
Total expenditure	546,831		635,915	

[1] Revised estimates. [2] Initial estimates.

The accounts of revenue and expenditure are examined by a special administrative tribunal (*Cour des Comptes*), instituted in 1807.

Currency. The unit of currency is the *franc*. Coins are issued for 5, 10, 20 and 50 centimes, 1, 2, 5 and 10 francs; and bank-notes for 10, 50, 100 and 500 francs. In March 1983, £1 sterling = 10.65 *francs*; US$1 = 7·26 *francs*.

Banking. The *Banque de France*, founded in 1800, and placed under the authority of a state-appointed Governor in 1806, has the monopoly (since 1848) of issuing bank-notes throughout France. Note circulation at 31 Dec. 1981 was 151,900m. francs.

On 2 Dec. 1945 a law was passed to nationalize the *Banque de France* and the principal deposit banks. It also established a new body, the National Credit

Council, formed to regulate banking activity and consulted in all political decisions on monetary policy. This new body comprises 45 members nominated by the Government; its president is the Minister for the Economy, its vice-president is the Governor of the *Banque de France* which as a Central Bank puts monetary policy into effect and supervises its application. On 11 Feb. 1982, a law was passed to nationalize the remaining deposit banks, the principal ones being: (*i*) those nationalized in 1945: Crédit Lyonnais (founded 1863), Banque Nationale de Paris (founded by amalgamation 1966) and the Société Générale (founded 1864), and (*ii*) among those nationalized in 1982: Crédit Industriel et Commercial, Crédit Commercial de France, the Banque de Paris et des Pays-Bas and the Crédit du Nord. Total deposits and short- and medium-term held bills by the banks at 31 Dec. 1981 was 1,302,800m. francs.

The rest of the banking system comprises the popular banks, the Crédit agricole, the Crédit mutuel, the Banque française du commerce exterieur and the various financial establishments.

The state savings organization (*Caisse nationale d'epargne*) is administered by the post office on a giro system. On 31 Dec. 1981 the private savings banks (*Caisses d'epargne et de prévoyance*), numbering about 500 had 434,000m. francs in deposits; the state savings banks had 206,300m. francs in deposits. Deposited funds are centralized by a non-banking body, the *Caisse de Dépôts et Consignations*, which finances a large number of local authorities and state aided housing projects, and carries an important portfolio of transferable securities.

Weights and Measures. The metric system is in general use.

ENERGY AND NATURAL RESOURCES

Electricity. Production of electrical power (in 1m. kwh.): 1978, 217,252; 1979, 230,700; 1980, 243,282. In 1978, 37% was hydro-electric and 9% nuclear.

Oil. In 1981 2·42m. tonnes of crude oil were produced. The greater part came from the Parentis oilfield in the Landes. France has an important oil-refining industry, utilizing imported crude oil. Total yearly capacity at the end of 1979 was about 166·84m. tonnes. The principal plants are situated in Basse Seine (capacity in tonnes, 1979), 56·1m.; Mediterranean, 45·5m.; Atlantic, 15·9m.; Nord, 14·8m.; Alsace, 13·9m.; Paris region, 11·6m.; Lyonnais, 9m.

There has been considerable development of the production of natural gas and sulphur in the region of Lacq in the foothills of the Pyrenees. Production of natural gas was 7,869m. cu. metres in 1978, 7,757 in 1979 and 7,529 in 1980.

Minerals. Principal minerals and metals produced, in 1,000 tonnes:

	1976	*1977*	*1978*	*1979*		*1976*	*1977*	*1978*	*1979*
Coal	21,879	21,293	19,690	18,612	Potash salts	1,738	1,719	1,928	2,075
Lignite	3,189	3,080	2,732	2,454	Pig-iron	19,024	18,257	18,497	19,415
Iron ore	45,181	36,630	33,454	31,627	Crude Steel	23,221	22,094	22,841	23,360
Bauxite	2,330	2,059	1,978	1,969	Aluminium	385	400	391	395

Agriculture. Of the total area of France (54·9m. hectares) 17·3m. were under cultivation, 12·9m. were pasture, 1·2m. were under vines, 14·3m. were forests and 8·3m. were uncultivated land in 1980.

The following table shows the area under the leading crops and the production for 4 years:

	Area (1,000 hectares)				*Produce (1,000 tonnes)*			
Crop	*1977*	*1978*	*1979*	*1980*	*1977*	*1978*	*1979*	*1980*
Wheat	4,126	4,167	4,063	4,580	17,546	21,057	19,411	23,668
Rye	129	138	116	128	389	432	353	405
Barley	2,909	2,814	2,816	2,648	10,319	11,414	11,238	11,758
Oats	625	611	539	534	1,938	2,194	1,865	1,927
Potatoes	279	269	252	227	8,190	7,459	6,698	6,722
Sugar-beet	585	556	547	541	24,500	24,488	26,444	26,206
Maize	1,639	1,802	2,003	1,754	8,316	9,473	10,293	9,254

Other crops in 1980 (figures for 1979 in brackets) include (in 1,000 tonnes): Rice, 27 (29); tobacco, 48 (53); flax, 293 (307).

France is the world's second largest producer of wine (after Italy); production in 1978 amounted to 5,882,000 tonnes.

The annual production of wine (in 1,000 hectolitres) appears as follows:

	Vineyards (1,000 hectares)	*Wine produced*		*Vineyards (1,000 hectares)*	*Wine produced*
1938	1,513	60,332	1977	1,180	53,137
1948	1,433	47,437	1978	1,141	58,599
1958	1,315	47,735	1979	1,219	80,319
1968	1,228	66,460	1980	1,174	71,546

The production of fruits (other than for cider making) and for 4 years was (in 1,000 tonnes) as follows:

	1977	*1978*	*1979*	*1980*		*1977*	*1978*	*1979*	*1980*
Apples	1,243	1,867	1,716	1,810	Cherries	53	99	112	106
Pears	273	366	418	422	Nuts	18	37	30	30
Plums	73	165	158	136	Grapes	211	234	213	192
Peaches	319	406	386	397	Strawberries	77	68	82	85
Apricots	72	81	59	71					

In 1981 the numbers of farm animals (in 1,000) were (figures for 1980 in brackets): Horses, 317 (364); cattle, 23,553 (23,919); sheep, 12,980 (11,911); goats, 1,241 (1,125); pigs, 11,629 (11,446); poultry, 185,965 (176,290).

Forestry. The total area of forested land (1980) was 148,633 sq. km. Timber sold (1981), 30,341m. cu. metres valued at 7,985m. francs.

Fisheries. (1980). There were 22,019 fishermen, and 11,090 sailing-boats, steamers and motor-boats. Catch (in 1,000 tonnes): Fish, fresh and frozen, 460·4; crustaceans, 29·8; shell fish, 11·3; oysters, 99·3.

INDUSTRY AND TRADE

Industry. Industrial production (in 1,000 tonnes) for 3 years was as follows:

	1979	*1980*	*1981*
Sulphuric acid	5,069	4,952	4,412
Caustic acid	1,449	1,333	1,314
Sulphur	1,940	1,839	1,700
Polystyrene	269	254	262
Polyvinyl	783	725	710
Polyethylene	1,173	1,074	883
Wool	62	64	63
Cotton	178	178	158
Linen	2·6	2·3	2
Silk	52	51	46
Man-made fibres, yarns	78	68	55
Jute	9	8	7
Cheese	1,040	1,067	...
Chocolate	111	116	118
Biscuits	334	368	379
Sugar	3,968	3,913	3,794
Fish preparations	99	85	...
Jams and jellies	107	116	120
Cement	28,825	29,104	28,229

Engineering production (in 1,000 units) for 3 years:

	1979	*1980*	*1981*
Motor vehicles	3,612	3,378	3,019
Television sets	1,854	1,928	1,960
Radio sets	2,773	2,141	2,266
Tyres	49,000	50,601	43,196

See map in THE STATESMAN'S YEAR-BOOK, 1968-69, Industrial Redeployment.

Employment (1975). Out of an economically active population of 21,061,215 persons, there are 2·01m. engaged in agriculture; 1,841,083 in building and public works; 6,327,818 in other manufacturing industries; 829,289 in transport; 3,632,478 in business, banking and insurance; 3,543,881 in services; 2,522,544 in commerce. In 1981, there were 23,044,900 employed (40·9% female), of whom 1,427,000 were foreign workers; in April 1982, there were 1,928,200 unemployed.

Trade Unions. The main unions considered as nationally representative are the CGT (Confédération Générale du Travail), which was founded in 1895 and has about 2·35m. members; the CGT-FO (Confédération Générale du Travail–Force Ouvrière) which broke away from the CGT in 1948 as a protest against Communist influence therein and has about 900,000 members; the CFTC (Confédération Française des Travailleurs Chrétiens), which was founded in 1919 and has about 225,000 members following its break-away in 1964 from the main body of the union which continues under the new name of CFDT (Confédération Française Démocratique du Travail) and has about 890,000 members; the CGC (Confédération Générale des Cadres) formed in 1944 which only represents managerial and supervisory staff and has about 300,000 members.

Membership is estimated because unions are not required to publish figures; some publish none, others define 'membership' in different terms.

Except for the CGC unions operate within the framework of industries and not of trades. Their main fields of influence are: CGT—steel, metallurgy, building, chemicals, mining, printing, ports and dockyards, electricity and gas, railways; CGT–FO—Civil service, Paris transport, agricultural and food trades, banking, insurance, electrical engineering, building and civil engineering, clothing, leather and hides; CFDT—metallurgy, rubber, oil, textiles, electrical engineering, banking, insurance; CFTC—mining, banking, insurance, air traffic control, oil, glass, pottery.

Commerce. Imports (c.i.f.) and exports (f.o.b.) in 1m. francs for 5 calendar years were (including gold):

	1978	*1979*	*1980*	*1981*	*1982*
Imports	368,401	457,100	569,900	653,100	758,339
Exports	344,594	414,700	470,400	548,700	606,967

The chief imports for home use and exports of home goods are to and from the following countries, in 1m. francs (including gold):

	Imports (c.i.f)			*Exports (f.o.b.)*		
Countries	*1980*	*1981*	*1982*	*1980*	*1981*	*1982*
Algeria	7,431	12,994	25,914	11,078	12,815	14,022
Belgium-Luxembourg	47,547	48,779	58,496	43,941	45,566	52,427
Germany (Fed. Rep.)	93,160	104,036	127,661	75,350	81,373	89,564
Italy	53,408	58,616	72,777	58,628	62,440	68,445
Netherlands	30,897	37,665	42,021	22,898	24,316	27,953
Saudi Arabia	37,053	65,783	48,105	6,167	10,193	12,896
Spain (excluding Canary Is.)	16,474	17,876	23,105	13,084	15,758	18,759
Sweden	8,739	9,476	11,175	6,116	5,953	6,949
Switzerland (and Liechtenstein)	12,810	13,841	15,262	22,088	23,651	24,168
USSR	15,062	18,406	18,782	10,352	9,991	10,225
UK	30,775	35,718	46,064	32,743	39,120	43,920
USA	45,350	53,305	59,733	20,783	30,372	34,333

Total trade between France and UK (British Department of Trade returns, in £1,000 sterling):

	1978	*1979*	*1980*	*1981*	*1982*
Imports to UK	3,211,837	4,064,233	3,899,174	3,978,646	4,269,103
Exports and re-exports from UK	2,530,837	3,070,498	3,651,470	3,625,923	4,486,458

Tourism. In 1982 foreign visitors contributed about 40,320m. francs to the French economy.

COMMUNICATIONS

Roads. At the end of 1978 the French road system consisted of 4,248 km of motorway, 29,068 km of national roads, 345,990 km of departmental roads and 424,950 km of local roads. Total, 804,256 km. In 1980, there were 19·13m. passenger cars and 2·46m. commercial vehicles in use.

Railways. As from 1 Jan. 1938 all the independent railway companies were merged with the existing state railway system in a Société Nationale des Chemins de Fer Français, in which the State holds 51% of the shares.

In 1981, the State railway totalled 34,596 km (10,477 km electrified) of 1,435 mm gauge, and carried 197m. tonnes of freight and 1,332m. passengers. A new railway for high-speed trains is under construction between Paris and Lyon, the first section of which was opened in 1981. In addition to the main network, there are some 2,000 km of independent or state-run minor railways.

The Paris transport network consisted in 1981 of 294 km of underground railway (métro) and regional express railways and 2,096 km of bus routes. In 1978 it carried 1,104m. passengers on the métro and 709m. by bus.

Aviation. Air France, UTA and Air Inter, the national airlines, had (31 Dec. 1979) a fleet of 166 aircraft, servicing Europe, North America, Central and South America, West and East Africa, Madagascar, the Near, Middle and Far East. There are local networks in the West Indies and Central America.

In 1980 Air France, UTA and Air Inter flew 2,093m. tonne-km (excluding mail, 120m. tonne-km) and 34,130m. passenger-km (18m. passengers).

Shipping. French merchant ships of more than 100 tons, with gross tonnage, on 1 Jan. 1978, 502 (11·86m.); 1979, 424 (11·63m.).

Shipping (excluding fishing vessels) in foreign trade in 1979: Entered, 85,026 vessels and disembarked 259·2m. tonnes of imports and loaded 71·6m. tonnes of exports. Total cargo traffic 330·8m. tonnes.

In 1981 there were 8,623 km of navigable rivers, waterways and canals, (of which 1,617 km accessible to vessels over 3,000 tons) with a total traffic of 83·6m. tonnes.

Post and Broadcasting. In 1977 the receipts on account of posts, telegraphs and telephones amounted to 56,275m. francs.

On 31 Dec. 1980 the telephone system (government-owned) had 24,686,319 subscribers; the Paris region (including the Paris and Seine-et-Marne, Yvelines, Essonne, Hauts-de-Seine, Seine-Saint-Denis, Val-de-Marne and Val-d'Oise departments) accounted for 4,153,586 in 1978.

Radio and television broadcasting was reorganized under the Act of 7 Aug. 1974 which replaced the Office de Radiodiffusion Télévision Française with 4 broadcasting companies, a production company and an audio-visual institute. Organization, development, operation and the maintenance of networks and installations became the responsibility of the Public Broadcasting Establishment. Radio programmes are broadcast from 298 transmitters (including 260 VHF) by 3 stations: *France Inter, France Musique* and *France Culture.* Television programmes are broadcast from 325 transmitters and 4,661 relay stations on 3 channels. There were about 19m. sets in use in 1981 (of which 8·9m. in colour).

Cinemas (1981). There were 4,532 cinemas with a seating capacity (1979) of 1,472,400; attendances totalled 187·6m.

Newspapers (1977). There were 69 daily papers published in the provinces with a circulation of 7·48m. copies, and 10 published in Paris with a national circulation of 3·05m. Among Paris dailies *France-Soir* sells 671,000; *Le Monde* 546,000; *Le Parisien Libéré* 474,000; *Le Figaro* 407,000, and *L'Aurore* 347,000. Among provincial dailies *Ouest-France* (Rennes) sells 749,000; *Le Progrés* (Lyon) 436,000; *La Voix du Nord* (Lille) 389,000; *Sud-Ouest* (Bordeaux) 383,000; *La Dauphine Libérée* (Grenoble) 362,000 and *Le Provençal* (Marseilles) 345,000.

JUSTICE, RELIGION, EDUCATION AND WELFARE

Justice. Since 1958, 469 *tribunaux d'instance* (10 in overseas departments), under a single judge each and with increased material and territorial jurisdiction, have replaced the former *juges de paix* (1 in each canton); and 181 *tribunaux de grande instance* (6 in overseas departments) have taken the place of the 357 *tribunaux de première instance* (1 in each *arrondissement*).

The *tribunaux de grande instance* usually have a collegiate composition, however a law dated 10 July 1970 has allowed them to administer justice under a single judge in some civil cases.

All petty offences (*contraventions*) are disposed of in the Police Courts (*Tribun-*

aux de Police) presided over by a Judge on duty in the *tribunal d'instance*. The Correctional Courts pronounce upon all graver offences (*délits*), including cases involving imprisonment up to 5 years. They have no jury, and consist of 3 judges who administer both criminal and civil justice. An Act of 29 Dec. 1972 established that there is only 1 judge; in some cases, the correctional courts may consist of a single judge each. In all cases of a *délit* or a *crime* the preliminary inquiry is made in secrecy by an examining magistrate (*juge d'instruction*), who either dismisses the case or sends it for trial before a court where a public prosecutor (*Procureur*) endeavours to prove the charge.

The Conciliation Boards (*Conseils des Prud'hommes*) composed of an equal number of employers and employees deal with small trade and industrial disputes. Commercial litigation goes to the Commercial Courts (*Tribunaux de Commerce*) composed of tradesmen and manufacturers elected for 2 years. The judges hold office for 2 years and they can be re-elected; 3 years for the President.

When the decisions of any of these Tribunals are susceptible of appeal, the case goes to one of the 35 Courts of Appeal (*Cours d'Appel*), (including 3 in overseas departments and 2 in overseas territories), composed each of a president and a variable number of members.

The Courts of Assizes (*Cours d'Assises*), composed each of a president, assisted by 2 other magistrates who are members of the Courts of Appeal, and by a jury of 9 people, sit in every *département*, when called upon to try very important criminal cases. The decisions of the Courts of Appeal and the Courts of Assizes are final; however, the Court of Cassation (*Cour de Cassation*) has discretion to verify if the law has been correctly interpreted and if the rules of procedure have been followed exactly. The Court of Cassation may annul any judgment, and the cases have to be tried again by a Court of Appeal or a Court of Assizes.

The State Security Court, established in 1963, was abolished by law on 4 Aug. 1981. Capital punishment was abolished in the same month.

On 24 Jan. 1973 the first Ombudsman (*médiateur*) was appointed for a 6-year period.

The French penal institutions consist of: (1) *maisons d'arfet* and *de correction*, where persons awaiting trial as well as those condemned to short periods of imprisonment are kept; (2) central prisons (*maisons centrales*) for those sentenced to long imprisonment; (3) special establishments, namely (*a*) schools for young adults, (*b*) hostels for old and disabled offenders, (*c*) hospitals for the sick and psychopaths, (*d*) institutions for recidivists. Special attention is being paid to classified treatment and the rehabilitation and vocational re-education of prisoners including work in open-air and semi-free establishments. There are 2 penal institutions for women.

Juvenile delinquents go before special judges and courts; they are sent to public or private institutions of supervision and re-education.

The population at 1 Aug. 1981 of all penal establishments was 29,448 men and 1,119 women.

Religion. No religion is officially recognized by the State. Under the law promulgated on 9 Dec. 1905, which separated Church and State, the adherents of all creeds are authorized to form associations for public worship (*associations culturelles*). The law of 2 Jan. 1907 provided that, failing *associations culturelles*, the buildings for public worship, together with their furniture, would continue at the disposition of the ministers of religion and the worshippers for the exercise of their religion; but in each case there was required an administrative act drawn up by the *préfet* as regards buildings belonging to the State or the departments and by the *maire* as regards buildings belonging to the communes.

There are 18 archbishops and 92 bishops of the Roman Catholic Church, with (1974) 43,557 clergy of various grades and 45·3m. church members. The Protestants of the Augsburg confession are, in their religious affairs, governed by a General Consistory, while the Reformed Church is under a Council of Administration, the seat of which is in Paris. In 1975 communicant Protestants numbered 750,000. There were (1978) about 2m. Moslems.

Education. The primary, secondary and higher state schools constitute the 'Université de France'. The Supreme Council of 84 members has deliberative, administrative and judiciary functions, and a Consultative Committee advise respecting the working of the school system, but the inspectors-general are in direct communication with the Minister. For local education administration France is divided into 25 academic areas, each of which has an Academic Council whose members include a certain number elected by the professors or teachers. The Academic Council deals with all grades of education. Each is under a Rector, and each is provided with academy inspectors, 1 for each department.

By decree of 6 Jan. 1959 the whole system of public instruction was reorganized and the structure of the Ministry of National Education has consequently been modified. A further Education Act was passed on 11 July 1975. Compulsory education is now provided for children of 6–16. The educational stages are as follows:

1. Non-compulsory pre-school instruction for children aged 2–5, to be given in infant schools or infant classes attached to primary schools.

2. Compulsory elementary instruction for children aged 6–11, to be given in primary schools and certain classes of the *lycées*. It consists of 3 courses: preparatory (1 year), elementary (2 years), intermediary (2 years). Physically or mentally handicapped children are cared for in special institutions or special classes of primary schools.

3. Lower secondary education (*Enseignement du premier cycle du Second Degré*) for pupils aged 11–15 consists of: 4 years of study in the *lycées* (grammar schools), *Collèges d'Enseignement Secondaire* or *Collèges d'Enseignement Général.*

4. Upper secondary education (*Enseignement du second cycle du Second Degré*) for pupils aged 15–18:

Long, général or *professionel* provided by the *lycées* and leading to the *baccalauréat* or to the *baccalauréat de technicien* after 3 years.

Court, professional courses of 3, 2 and 1 year are taught in the *lycées d'enseignement professionel*, or the specialized sections of the *lycées*, CES or CEG.

The following table shows the various types of schools in 1981 and the numbers of enrolled pupils:

Description	*Pupils* *State*	*Private*	*Total*
Pre-primary	2,070,060	313,386	2,383,446
Primary	3,940,782	668,660	4,609,442
Secondary:			
First and second cycle	3,983,623	1,030,043	5,013,666
Specialized	233,296	8,728	242,024
Total	10,227,761	2,020,817	12,248,578

The state schools in 1978 had 64,676 nursery, 172,969 primary, 18,908 special school, 143,572 secondary and 44,624 secondary technical school and 65,797 grammar school (*lycée*) teachers.

Higher Instruction is supplied by the State in the universities and in special schools, and by private individuals in the free faculties and schools. The law of 12 July 1875 provided for higher education free of charge. This law was modified by that of 18 March 1880, which granted the state faculties the exclusive right to confer degrees. A decree of 28 Dec. 1885 created a general council of the faculties, and the creation of universities, each consisting of several faculties, was accomplished in 1897, in virtue of the law of 10 July 1896.

The law of 12 Nov. 1968 laying down future guidelines for higher education redefined the activities and working of universities. Bringing several disciplines together, 780 units for teaching and research (UER–Unités d'Enseignement et de Récherche) were formed which decided their own teaching activities, research programmes and procedures for checking the level of knowledge gained. They and the other parts of each university must respect the rules designed to maintain the national standard of qualifications.

The UERs form the basic units of the 62 Universities, 6 Universities Centres and 3 National Polytechnic Institutes, all of which have university status. They are grouped geographically into 25 *académies* with student populations in 1978–79 as follows:

Academie	*1978–79*	*Academie*	*1978–79*	*Academie*	*1978–79*
Aix-Marseille	47,292	Lille	39,375	Paris	224,655
Amiens	10,661	Limoges	7,668	Poitiers	13,026
Besançon	11,149	Lyon	50,720	Reims	12,528
Bordeaux	42,985	Montpellier	36,604	Rennes	33,262
Caen	12,490	Nancy-Metz	28,223	Rouen	12,775
Clermont	15,191	Nantes	26,219	Strasbourg	27,495
Créteil	24,599	Nice	19,030	Toulouse	45,211
Dijon	13,297	Orléans-Tours	18,746	Versailles	44,901
Grenoble	31,896				
				Total	849,998

The following table shows the number of students by faculties, for 5 years:

Students of	*1974–75*	*1975–76*	*1976–77*	*1977–78*	*1978–79*
Law and economics	178,215	183,566	182,533	184,361	183,592
Medicine and dentistry	146,912	154,660	159,874	160,900	160,917
Science	117,389	121,028	122,205	125,945	129,441
Letters	233,954	251,421	252,134	253,364	260,090
Pharmacy	31,599	33,510	33,474	34,821	36,014
Technology	41,949	43,526	44,243	47,398	50,237
Multi-discipline courses	4,843	18,527	21,818	25,329	29,707
Total	754,861	806,238	816,281	838,118	849,998

In 1978–79 there were also 99,000 students in preparatory classes leading to the Grandes Écoles, the Sections de Techniciens Supérieurs and other bodies; there were also 21,000 students in Écoles normales d'instituteurs.

The other higher institutions under the Ministry of Public Instruction are the Collège de France (founded by Francis I in 1530), which has courses of study bearing on various subjects (literature and language, archaeology, mathematical, natural science, psychology and social science, political economy, etc.); the Museum of Natural History, giving instruction in science and natural history; the École Pratique de Hautes Études (history and philology, mathematical and physicochemical sciences, natural science, theology, economics and social science), having its seat at the Sorbonne; the École Normale Supérieure, which prepares teachers for secondary education and, since 1904, follows the curricula of the Sorbonne without special teachers of its own; the École des Chartes, which trains archivists and palaeographers; the École des Langues Orientales vivantes; the École du Louvre, devoted to art and archaeology; the Bureau des Longitudes, the central meteorological bureau; the Observatoire de Paris; and the French Schools at Athens, Rome, Cairo and South-East Asia.

Outside Paris there are 12 observatories (Meudon, Besançon, Bordeaux, etc.). The observatory at Nice belongs to the University of Paris.

There are free faculties in Paris (the Catholic Institute of Paris comprising theology and literary studies), Angers, Lille, Lyon and Toulouse.

Professional and Technical Instruction. The principal institutions of higher or technical instruction are: (*i*) The *Grandes Écoles* with 96,726 students in 1981, the Conservatoire des Arts et Métiers at Paris (with 20 evening courses on the applied sciences and social economy), the École Central des Arts et Manufactures (953 students in 1971–72), the École des Hautes Études Commerciales (803 students in 1972–73), 17 higher schools of commerce (4,461 pupils in 1969–70), under the Ministry of Public Instruction; (*ii*) the National Agronomic Institute at Paris, the veterinary school at Maisons-Alfort, Lyon and Toulouse, a school of forestry at Nancy, Écoles Nationales Supérieures Agronomiques at Grignon, Rennes, Montpellier, Nancy and Toulouse, 98 schools of agriculture, etc., under the Ministry of Agriculture; (*iii*) the École Supérieure de Guerre, the École Polytechnique, the military school at Coëtquidan (formerly St Cyr), the École d'Artillerie at Fontainebleau, the École de Cavalerie at Saumur and other schools under the Ministry of Defence; the Naval School at Brest under the Ministry of Marine; (*iv*) the School of Mines at Paris, the School of Civil Engineering at Paris, the School of Mines at St Etienne and the Schools of Miners at Alès and Douai with other schools under the Ministry of Public Works; (*v*) the École Nationale Supérieure des Beaux Arts, the École Nationale Supérieure des Arts Décoratifs and the Conservatoire de

Musique et de Déclamation under the Department of Fine Arts, which is attached to the Ministry of Cultural Affairs. In the provinces there are national schools of fine arts, and schools of music, and several municipal schools, as well as free subventional schools, etc.

Health. On 1 Jan 1980 there were 104,073 physicians, 36,491 pharmacists, 30,321 dentists, 245,994 nursing personnel and 9,382 midwives practising. On 1 Jan. 1981 there were 888 public hospitals (439,310 beds) excluding mental hospitals and 2,445 private hospitals (181,626 beds) including private mental homes.

Social Welfare. An order of 4 Oct. 1945 laid down the framework of a comprehensive plan of Social Security and created a single organization which superseded the various laws relating to social insurance, workmen's compensation, health insurance, family allowances, etc. All previous matters relating to Social Security are dealt with in the Social Security Code, 1956; this has been revised several times, and finally by orders laid down on 21 Aug. 1967, which were ratified on 31 July 1968. The Social Security general scheme covers all wage-earning workers in industry and commerce that are not covered by a special scheme of their own.

Contributions. All wage-earning workers or those of equivalent status are insured regardless of the amount or the nature of the salary or earnings. The funds for the general scheme are raised mainly from professional contributions, these being fixed within the limits of a ceiling (assessed at 68,760 francs per annum on 1 Jan. 1981) and calculated as a percentage of the salaries. The calculation of contributions payable for family allowances, old age and industrial injuries relates only to this amount; on the other hand, the amount payable for sickness, maternity expenses, disability and death is calculated partly within the limit of the 'ceiling' and partly on the whole salary. These contributions are the responsibility of both employer and employee, except in the case of family allowances or industrial injuries, where they are the sole responsibility of the employer.

Contributions and benefits paid in 1981 (in 1m. francs) were:

	Contributions	*Benefits*
Health service	173,800	146,798
Industrial injuries	26,078	18,700
Old age pensions	90,719	79,718
Family benefits	67,940	60,043

Self-employed Workers. From 17 Jan. 1948 allowances and old-age pensions were paid to self-employed workers by independent insurance funds set up within their own profession, trade or business. Schemes of compulsory insurance for sickness were instituted in 1961 for farmers and in 1966, with modifications in 1970, for other non-wage-earning workers.

Social Insurance. The orders laid down in Aug. 1967 ensure that the whole population can benefit from the Social Security Scheme; at present all elderly persons who have been engaged in the professions, as well as the surviving spouse, are entitled to claim an old-age benefit; 98% of the population, both working and retired, are covered by a compulsory scheme of insurance for sickness, the remaining 2% who are not covered by a compulsory insurance scheme have been able to participate in a voluntary scheme since 1967; the whole population benefit from the legislation regarding family allowances.

Sickness Insurance refunds the costs of treatment required by the insured, of the needs of his wife, of children under 16 and a half who are in his care and not earning, under 18 who are apprenticed, under 20 who are still studying or who cannot work on account of some chronic illness or infirmity, as well as relations older or younger or of similar age living under the same roof who are engaged exclusively in domestic duties and in the education of at least 2 children under 14. A decree of 12 Oct. 1976 laid down conditions on which students of 20 or over at public or private educational institutions, who do not benefit from a social security scheme in their own right, are guaranteed insurance benefits for sickness or maternity, holding their parents entitlement until the end of the academic year in which they attain their 21st birthday, provided they have proof that their studies have been interrupted by illness. The general principles relating to medical care consist of: a free choice by the patient of his doctor, his pharmaceutical chemist, his place of treatment, etc.; the medical practitioner is granted freedom of prescription. Reimbursement is not as a rule made in full; the insured person usually pays between 10% and 30% of the legal rate except in cases of exemption. The insured who is recognized as medically unfit for work receives daily allowances equal to half of the wage which has been used to calculate the contributions, or to two-thirds of this if the person has 3 or more children. These allowances may be paid for 3 years, plus 1 additional year if the insured undergoes re-adaptation treatment or takes up fresh vocational training.

Maternity Insurance covers the costs of medical treatment relating to the pregnancy, confinement and lying-in period; the beneficiaries being the insured person or the spouse. The daily allowances are equal to 90% of the salary on which contributions were calculated.

Insurance for Invalids is divided into 3 categories: (1) those who are capable of working; (2) those who cannot work; (3) those who, in addition, are in need of the help of another person. According to the category, the pension rate varies from 30 to 50% of the average salary for the last 10 years, with a minimum additional allowance for home help of 28,094·64 francs per year for the third category.

Old-age Pensions for workers were introduced in 1910 and are now fixed by the Social Security Code of 28 Jan. 1972. Since 1975 people who have paid insurance for at least 37½ years (150 quarters) receive at 60 a pension equal to 25% of basic annual salary, to be increased by 1·25% of the basic salary for every quarter that realization is deferred; thus at 65 the pension rate is equal to 50% of basic salary. People who have paid insurance for less than 37½ years but no less than 15 years can expect a pension equal to as many 1/150ths of the full pension as their quarterly payments justify. In the event of death of the insured person, the husband or wife of the deceased person receives half the pension received by the latter. Compulsory supplementary schemes ensure benefits additional to the old-age pensions.

Family Allowances. The system comprises: (*a*) Family allowances proper, equivalent to 25·5% of the basic monthly salary (1,246 francs) for 2 dependent children, 46% for the third child, 41% for the fourth child, and 39% for the fifth and each subsequent child; a supplement equivalent to 9% of the basic monthly salary for the second and each subsequent dependent child more than 10 years old and 16% for each dependent child over 15 years. (*b*) Family supplement (519 francs) for persons with at least 3 children or one child aged less than 3 years. (*c*) Antenatal grants. (*d*) Maternity grant equal to 260% of basic salary; increase for multiple births or adoptions, 198%; increase for birth or adoption of third or subsequent child, 457%. (*e*) Allowance for specialized education of handicapped children. (*f*) Allowance for orphans. (*g*) Single parent allowance. (*h*) Allowance for opening of school term. (*i*) Allowance for accommodation, under certain circumstances. (*j*) Minimum family income for those with at least 3 children. Allowances (*b*), (*g*), (*h*) and (*j*) only apply to those whose annual income falls below a specified level.

Workmen's Compensation. The law passed by the National Assembly on 30 Oct. 1946 forms part of the Social Security Code and is administered by the Social Security Organization. Employers are invited to take preventive measures. The application of these measures is supervised by consulting engineers (assessors) of the local funds dealing with sickness insurance, who may compel employers who do not respect these measures to make additional contributions; they may, in like manner, grant rebates to employers who have in operation suitable preventive measures. The injured person receives free treatment, the insurance fund reimburses the practitioners, hospitals and suppliers chosen freely by the injured. In cases of temporary disablement the daily payments are equal to half the total daily wage received by the injured. In case of permanent disablement the injured person receives a pension, the amount of which varies according to the degree of disablement and the salary received during the past 12 months.

A law promulgated on 11 Oct. 1946 has created a medical labour service of doctors who hold a diploma of 'industrial health specialists'. These doctors are entrusted with the control of hygiene and health matters in all industrial undertakings or groups of undertakings. In addition, it is the duty of this medical service to examine wage-earners when they are engaged, to carry out periodical medical examinations and to ensure the application of the existing rules relating to safety in work.

Unemployment Benefits vary according to circumstances (full or partial unemployment) which are means-tested. Since 1926 unemployment benefits have been paid from public funds. Full unemployment benefit amounts to 13·50 francs per day for the head of the family and 5·40 francs for the spouse or a dependent person. After 3 months the payment is reduced to 12·40 francs.

A collective agreement signed on 31 Dec. 1958 between the national council of employers and certain trade unions has established a system of special allowances for totally unemployed workers in industry and trade. The costs are shared by employers (2·76% of wages) and employees (0·84%) and the benefits vary according to circumstances. The system is now governed by the law of 16 Jan. 1979. A similar agreement of 21 Feb. 1968 extends the system to partial unemployment.

Social Security in France. I.N.S.E.E., 1970
Questions de Sécurité Sociale. Paris, 1970

DIPLOMATIC REPRESENTATIVES

Of France in Great Britain (58 Knightsbridge, London, SW1X 7JT)
Ambassador: Emmanuel de Margerie (accredited 27 March 1981)

Of Great Britain in France (35 rue du Faubourg St Honoré, Paris)
Ambassador: Sir John Fretwell, KCMG.

Of France in the USA (2535 Belmont Rd., NW, Washington, D.C., 20008)
Ambassador: Bernard Vernier-Palliez.

Of the USA in France (2 Ave. Gabriel, Paris)
Ambassador: Evan G. Galbraith.

Of France to the United Nations
Ambassador: Luc de la Barre de Nanteuil.

Books of Reference

Statistical Information: The Institut national de la Statistique et des Études économiques (18, Boulevard Adolphe Pinard, 75014 Paris) is the central office of statistics. It was established by a law of 27 April 1946, which amalgamated the Service National des Statistiques (created in 1941 by merging the Direction de la Statistique générale de la France and the Service de la Démographie) with the Institut de Conjoncture (set up in 1938) and some statistical services of the Ministry of National Economy. The Institut comprises the following departments: Metropolitan statistics, Overseas statistics, Market research and economic studies, Documentation, Research statistics and economics, Informatics, Foreign Economic Studies.

The main publications of the Institut include:

Annuaire statistique de la France (from 1878)
Annuaire statistique des Territoires d'Outre-Mer (from 1959)
Bulletin mensuel de statistique (monthly)
Documentation économique (bi-monthly)
Données statistiques africaines et Malgaches (quarterly)
Economie et Statisque (monthly)
Tableaux de l'Economie Française (biennially, from 1956)
Tendances de la Conjoncture (monthly)

Bonnefous, E., Duroselle, J. B., and Gerbet, P., *L'année politique, économique, sociale et diplomatique en France.* Paris, 1970
Caron, F., *An Economic History of Modern France.* London, 1979
Coffey, P., *The Social Economy of France.* London, 1973
Crozier, M., *A Strategy for Change: The Future of French Society.* MIT Press, 1982
Dyer, C., *Population and Society in Twentieth Century France.* London, 1978

Hoffman, S., *Decline or Renewal? France Since the 1930's.* New York, 1973
Ouston, P. A., *France in the Twentieth Century.* London, 1972
Peyrefitte, A., *The Trouble with France,* New York, 1981
Tint, H., *French Policy Since the Second World War.* New York, 1972
Tuppen, J. N., *France.* Folkstone, 1981

OVERSEAS DEPARTMENTS

GUADELOUPE

HISTORY. Discovered by Columbus in Nov. 1493, the two main islands were then known as *Karukera* (Isle of Beautiful Waters) to the Carib inhabitants, who resisted Spanish attempts to colonize. A French colony was established on 28 June 1635, and apart from short periods of occupancy by British forces, Guadeloupe has since remained a French possession. On 19 March 1946 the status of Guadeloupe was changed to that of an Overseas Department; in 1973 it additionally became an administrative region.

AREA AND POPULATION. Guadeloupe consists of a group of islands in the Lesser Antilles. The two main islands, Basse-Terre to the west and Grande-Terre to the east, are separated by a narrow channel, called Rivière Salée. Adjacent to these are the islands of Marie Galante *(Ceyre* to the Caribs) to the south-east, La Désirade to the east, and the Îles des Saintes to the south. The islands of St Martin and St Barthélemy lie 250 km to the north-west.

	Area in sq. km	*Census 1974*	*Estimate 1981*	*Chief town*
St Martin[1]	54	6,191	8,072	Marigot
St Barthélemy	21	2,491	3,059	Gustavia
Basse-Terre	848	135,746	309,009 (Basse-Terre and Grande-Terre)	Basse-Terre
Grande-Terre	587	159,424		Pointe-à-Pitre
Îles des Saintes	14	3,084	2,901	Terre-de-Bas
La Désirade	22	1,682	1,602	Grande Anse
Marie-Galante	158	15,912	13,757	Grand-Bourg
	1,780	324,530	338,400	

[1]Northern part only; the southern third belongs to the Netherlands.

Population (estimate, 1981) 338,400. The vast majority are black or mulatto, but the populations of St Barthélemy and Les Saintes are still mainly descended from 17th-century Breton and Norman settlers. French is the official language, but a Creole dialect is also widely used.

The seat of government is Basse-Terre (13,656 inhabitants) at the south-west end of that island but the largest towns are Pointe-à-Pitre (25,310 inhabitants), the economic centre with a large commercial harbour, and its suburb Abymes (53,605).

Vital statistics (1981): Births, 6,515; deaths, 2,161.

GOVERNMENT. Guadeloupe is under an appointed Commissioner, an elected general council of 36 members (assisted by an Economic and Social Committee of 40 members) and an elected regional council of 41 members. It is represented in the National Assembly by 3 deputies, in the Senate by 2 senators and on the Economic and Social Council by 2 councillors. There are 3 *arrondissements,* sub-divided into 34 communes, each administered by an elected municipal council.

Commissioner: Guy Maillard.

ECONOMY

Budget. The budget for 1981 balanced at 1,257m. francs.

Banking. The Banque des Antilles Françaises (founded 1853), with a capital of

22m. francs and reserve funds amounting to 1·44m. francs, advances loans chiefly for agricultural purposes. The Banque Populaire de la Guadeloupe has a capital of 5m. francs. The Banque Nationale de Paris has 7 branches in the department, the Crédit Agricole 25, the Banque Française Commerciale, Banque des Antilles Françaises and the Banque Populaire 2 each, and the Société Generale de Banque aux Antilles and the Chase Manhattan Bank 1 each. The Caisse Centrale de Co-opération économique is the official banking institution of the department, enjoying the privilege of issuing bank-notes. Silver coin has disappeared from circulation.

ENERGY AND NATURAL RESOURCES

Electricity. Production in 1981 totalled 311·7m. kwh.

Agriculture. Chief products (1981) are bananas (143,000 tonnes), sugar (838,000 tonnes), rum (91,640 hectolitres of pure alcohol), roots (22 tonnes), aubergines (4,300 tonnes).

Livestock (1981): Cattle, 82,120; goats, 17,500; sheep, 11,420; pigs, 36,000.

Fisheries. The catch in 1981 was 8,655 tonnes.

COMMERCE. Trade for 1981 (in 1m. francs) was imports 3,192 and exports 510. In 1981, 69% of imports were from France, while 64% of exports went to France and 18·7% to Martinique; bananas formed 43·7% of the exports and sugar 35%. St Martin and St Bartélemy are free ports.

There are Chambers of Commerce and Industry at Basse-Terre and Pointe-à-Pitre. There is a British consular agent at Point-à-Pitre.

Tourism. In 1981 there were 326,730 tourists.

COMMUNICATIONS

Roads. In 1981 there were 1,975 km of roads of which 323 km were national roads.

Aviation. Air France and 7 other airlines call at Guadeloupe. In 1981 there were 31,726 arrivals and departures of aircraft and 1,108,448 passengers at Pointe-à-Pitre airport making it the sixth most frequented French airport.

Shipping. Guadeloupe is in direct communication with France by means of 12 steam navigation companies. In 1981, 1,104 vessels arrived to disembark 28,046 passengers and 1,028,000 tonnes of freight and to embark 27,809 passengers and 516,000 tonnes of freight.

Post and Broadcasting. In 1981 there were 44 post offices and 50,207 telephones. ORTF broadcasts for 17 hours a day in French and television broadcasts for 5 hours a day. There were (1977) 13,979 radio and (1981) 32,886 TV receivers.

Newspapers. There was (1981) 1 daily newspaper with a circulation of 22,000.

JUSTICE, RELIGION, EDUCATION AND WELFARE

Justice. There are 4 *tribunaux d'instance* and 2 *tribunaux de grande instance* at Basse-Terre and Pointe-à-Pitre; there is also a court of appeal and a court of assizes at Basse-Terre.

Religion. The majority of the population are Roman Catholic.

Education. In 1981 there were 62,303 pupils at pre-primary schools and primary schools and 45,843 at secondary schools. The *University Antilles-Guyane* had 3,800 students in 1981–82, of which Guadeloupe itself had 1,661.

Health. The medical services in 1981 included 12 public hospitals (2,974 beds), 15 private clinics (1,261 beds) and 42 dispensaries. There were 515 physicians, 99 dentists, 135 pharmacists, 101 midwives and 770 nursing personnel.

Books of Reference

Information: Office du Tourisme du départemente, Point-à-Pitre. *Director:* Eric W. Rotin.
Lasserre, G., *La Guadeloupe, étude géographique.* 2 vols. Bordeaux, 1961.

GUIANA

Guyane Française

HISTORY. A French settlement on the island of Cayenne was established in 1604 and the territory between the Maroni and Oyapock rivers finally became a French possession in 1817. Convicts settlements were established from 1852, that on off-shore Devil's Island being most notorious; all were closed by 1945. On 19 March 1946 the status of Guiana was changed to that of an Overseas Department.

AREA AND POPULATION. French Guiana is situated on the north-east coast of South America, and has an area of about 91,000 sq. km (35,135 sq. miles) and a population at the 1982 Census of 73,022, of whom 4,500 are tribal Indians. Cayenne, the chief town, has a population of (1981) 38,901. These figures are exclusive of the floating population of miners, officials and troops.

Vital statistics (1981): Live births, 2,081; deaths, 417.

GOVERNMENT. French Guiana is administered by an appointed Commissioner and an elected council-general of 16 members. It is represented in the National Assembly by 1 deputy and in the Senate by 1 senator. There are 2 *arrondissements* (Cayenne and Saint-Laurent-du-Maroni) subdivided into 20 communes.

Commissioner: Claude Silberzahn.

ECONOMY

Budget. The budget for 1982 balanced at 578m. francs, excluding duplicated items and national expenditure.

Banking. The Bank of Guiana has a capital of 10m. francs and reserve fund of 2·39m. francs. Loans totalled 206m. francs in 1981.

AGRICULTURE. The country has immense forests (about 80,000 sq. km) rich in many kinds of timber. Only 9,695 hectares are under cultivation. The crops consist of rice (450 tonnes in 1980), maize (280 tonnes, 1981), manioc (7,650 tonnes), bananas (680 tonnes, 1981) and sugar-cane (7,500 tonnes) as well as a large variety of other fruits, vegetables and spices. The fishing of shrimps has been taken up by American companies and formed (1979) 21% of exports.

Livestock (1981): 9,290 cattle, 8,750 swine and 100,000 poultry.

COMMERCE. Trade in 1,000 tonnes and 1m. francs:

	1979		*1980*		*1981*	
	Quantity	*Value*	*Quantity*	*Value*	*Quantity*	*Value*
Imports	273·3	1,068	859·7	1,087	222·6	1,355
Exports	50·3	71	54·0	108	32·7	192

In 1981, 15% of imports came from Trinidad and Tobago, 53% from France and 10% from the USA, while 54% of exports went to the USA, 17% to Japan and 15% to France.

Total trade between Guiana and UK (British Department of Trade returns, in £1,000 sterling):

	1978	*1979*	*1980*	*1981*	*1982*
Imports to UK	10	24	117	844	1,956
Exports and re-exports from UK	933	1,213	1,264	7,117	6,840

COMMUNICATIONS

Roads. Three chief and some secondary roads connect the capital with most of the coastal area by motor-car services. There are (1981) 321 km of national and 269 km of departmental roads. Connexions with the interior are made by waterways which, despite rapids, are navigable by local craft.

Aviation. Air France calls at Cayenne (Rochambeau Airport) 4 times a week, Air Martinique twice a week and Cruseiro do Sul once a week; Air Guyane services interior connexions. In 1981, about 150,000 passengers and 3,600 tonnes of freight passed through the airport.

Shipping. The chief ports are: Cayenne, St-Laurent-du-Maroni and Kourou. Dégrad des Cannes, the port of Cayenne is visited regularly by ships of the Compagnie Général Maritime, the Compagnie Maritime des Chargeurs Réunis and Marseille Fret. There is also steamboat communication between the capital and the other towns of the department. In 1981, 594 arrivals and departures of vessels were registered in French Guiana (113,219 tonnes of petroleum products arrived and 165,140 tonnes of other freight arrived and departed).

Post and Broadcasting. An automatic telephone system connects Cayenne with 10 other communes as well as with Europe and most parts of North and South America. Number of telephones (1981), 18,134. There are wireless stations at Cayenne, Oyapoc, Régina, St-Laurent-du-Maroni and numerous other locations.

France-Régions 3 (Guiana Radio) broadcasts for 116 hours each week on medium- and short-waves and FM in French. Television is broadcast for 43 hours each week on 7 transmitters. In 1980 there were 35,000 radio and 9,063 TV receivers.

Newspapers. There was (1982) 1 daily newspaper *(Presse de la Guyane)* with a circulation of 1,000, a bi-weekly paper *(France-Guyane)* with a circulation of 3,200 and a weekly *(Debout Guyane)*.

JUSTICE, RELIGION, EDUCATION AND WELFARE

Justice. At Cayenne there is a *tribunal d'instance* and a *tribunal de grande instance*, from which appeal is to the regional *cour d'appel* in Martinique.

Religion. The majority of the population is Roman Catholic.

Education. Primary education has been free since 1889 in lay schools for the two sexes in the communes and many villages. In 1981 public primary schools had 580 teachers and 11,953 pupils, the *lycées* and *collèges d'enseignement secondaire*, 510 teachers and 7,277 pupils. Private schools had 119 teachers and 2,528 pupils. The *Institut Henri Visioz* forms part of the *Université des Antilles-Guyane.*

Health. There were (1981) 80 physicians, 14 dentists, 18 pharmacists, 16 midwives and 309 nursing personnel. In 1980 there were 5 hospitals with 907 beds and 3 private clinics.

Books of Reference

Abonnec, A., Hurrault, J., Saban, R., *Bibliographie de la Guyane Française.* 2 vols. Paris, 1957
Henry, *Guyane Française, son histoire 1604–1946*. Cayenne
Hurrault, J., *Guide du voyageur en Guyane*. Paris, 1949
Masse, D., *La Guyane Française: Histoire, Géographie, Possibilités*. Abbeville, 1978

MARTINIQUE

HISTORY. Discovered by Columbus in 1493, the island was known to its inhabitants as *Madinina*, from which its present name was corrupted. A French colony was established in 1635 and, apart from brief periods of British occupation, has since remained under French control. On 19 March 1946 its status was altered to that of an Overseas Department.

AREA AND POPULATION. The island, situated in the Lesser Antilles between Dominica and St Lucia, occupies an area of 1,079 sq. km (417 sq. miles). The total population, 1974 Census was 324,832 (1980, estimate, 308,169), of whom 98,807 lived in Fort-de-France, the capital and chief commercial town, which has a landlocked harbour nearly 40 sq. km in extent.

French is the official language, but the majority of the population use a Creole dialect.

Vital statistics (1979): Live births 2,571; deaths 1,057.

GOVERNMENT. The department is administered by an appointed Commissioner and an elected general council of 36 members; there are 3 *arrondissements*, sub-divided into 34 communes, each administered by an elected municipal council. Martinique is represented in the National Assembly by 3 deputies, in the Senate by 2 senators and on the Economic and Social Council by 1 councillor.

Commissioner: Marcel Julia.

ECONOMY

Budget. The budget, 1979, balanced at 925m. francs.

Banking. The Institut d'Émission des Départements d'Outre-mer is the official bank of the department. The Caisse Centrale de Coopération économique is used by the Government in assisting the economic development of the department.

The Banque des Antilles Françaises (with a capital of 10·8m. francs), the Crédit Martiniquais (11·4m. francs), branches of the Banque Nationale de Paris (22·6m. francs), Crédit Agricole, The Chase Manhattan Bank, Société Générale de Banque and Banque Française Commerciale are operating at Fort-de-France.

AGRICULTURE. Bananas, sugar and rum are the chief products, followed by pineapples, food and vegetables. In 1978 there were 7,000 hectares under sugar-cane, 10,300 hectares under bananas and 500 hectares under pineapples. There are 3 sugar works with distilleries attached, 28 agricultural distilleries producing rum and 3 factories for canning pineapples. In 1979 production of sugar was 9,375 tonnes; rum, 87,002 hectolitres.

Livestock (1981): 56,000 cattle, 53,000 sheep, 39,000 pigs, 23,000 goats and 2,000 horses.

COMMERCE. Trade in 1,000 tonnes and 1m. francs:

	1977		*1978*		*1979*	
	Quantity	*Value*	*Quantity*	*Value*	*Quantity*	*Value*
Imports	946	1,890	789	2,216	902	2,870
Exports	417	550	401	567	393	567

In 1979 the main items of import were foodstuffs; main items of export were bananas (44%), petroleum products (25%) and rum (12%); 63% of imports came from France and 52% of exports went to France and 30% to Guadeloupe.

Total trade of the French West Indian Islands with UK (British Department of Trade returns, in £1,000 sterling):

	1978	*1979*	*1980*	*1981*	*1982*
Imports to UK	336	21	578	295	34
Exports and re-exports from UK	2,043	2,539	2,588	2,268	2,400

The Chamber of Commerce and Industry administers the port, airport and industrial zones.

COMMUNICATIONS

Roads. There are 252 km of national roads, 618 km of district roads and 748 km of local roads. In 1974 there were 39,200 passenger cars and 2,200 commercial vehicles.

Aviation. In 1979, 729,000 passengers arrived and departed by air.

Shipping. The island is visited regularly by French and American steamers. In 1979, 1,354 vessels called at Martinique.

Post and Broadcasting. There were, in 1978, 44 post offices and, 1981, 64,154 telephones. Radio-telephone service to Europe is available. In 1978 there were 21,230 radio and 33,171 TV receivers.

Newspapers. In 1978 there was 1 daily newspaper with a circulation of 19,000.

JUSTICE, RELIGION, EDUCATION AND WELFARE

Justice. Justice is administered by 2 *tribunaux d'instance*, a *tribunal de grande instance*, a regional court of appeal, a commercial court, a court of assizes and an administrative court.

Religion. The majority of the population is Roman Catholic.

Education. Education is compulsory between the ages of 6 and 16 years. In 1979–80, there were 70,406 pupils and 3,345 teachers in primary schools, and 49,929 pupils and 2,993 teachers in secondary and technical schools. The *Institut Henri Visioz*, which forms part of the *Centre Universitaire Antilles-Guyane*, had (1978) 2,100 students of law, politics and economics.

Health. There were (1979) 14 hospitals with 4,200 beds and in 1978 there were 316 physicians, 124 pharmacists, 120 midwives and 98 dentists.

Books of Reference

Annuaire statistique de la Martinique. Paris. (Latest issue, 1959–60)
Monographie de la Martinique. Préfecture, Martinique, 1964
Hannau, H. W., *Martinique*. Munich, 1966
Nicolas, M., *Guide Touristique de la Martinique*. 2nd ed. Martinique, 1969

MAYOTTE

HISTORY. Mayotte was a French colony from 1843 until 1914, when it was attached, with the other Comoro islands, to the government-general of Madagascar. The Comoro group was granted administrative autonomy within the French Republic and became an Overseas Territory.

When the other 3 islands voted to become independent (as the Comoro state) in 1974, Mayotte voted against this and remained a French dependency. In 1976, it became (following a further referendum) a *collectivité territoriale*, being an intermediate status between Overseas Territory and Overseas Department.

AREA AND POPULATION. Mayotte, east of the Comoro Islands, has an area of 374 sq. km (144 sq. miles) and a 1978 Census population of 47,246 (1981, estimate, 53,000). The capital is Dzaoudzi (4,147 inhabitants) situated on a tiny offshore islet. The main languages are Mahorian (Swahili dialect) and French.

GOVERNMENT. The island is administered by an appointed Commissioner and an elected general council of 17 members. Mayotte is represented by 1 deputy in the National Assembly and by 1 member in the Senate.

Commissioner: Yves Bonnet.

ECONOMY

Budget. The budget for 1981 balanced at 106m. French francs.

Currency. In Feb. 1976 the currency was changed from the *franc CFA* to the (metropolitan) *French franc*.

NATURAL RESOURCES

Agriculture. The main products are vanilla, ylang-ylang, coffee and copra.

Fisheries. A lobster and shrimp industry has recently been created. Annual catch is about 2,000 tonnes.

COMMERCE. In 1981, exports totalled 9·2m. francs (50% to France) and imports 105·3m. francs (26% from Réunion and 33% from France). Total trade between Mayotte and UK (1978): Imports to UK, £10,000 and exports and re-exports from UK, £403,000.

COMMUNICATIONS

Roads. In 1980 there were 98 km of main roads (70 km bitumenized) and 126 km of local roads, with about 1,050 motor vehicles.

Aviation. In 1981, 7,458 passengers and 739 tonnes of freight arrived by air and 9,100 passengers (314 tonnes) departed.

JUSTICE, RELIGION AND EDUCATION

Justice. There is a *tribunal d'instance* and a *tribunal supérieur d'appel.*

Religion. The population is 99% Moslem, with a small Christian (mainly Roman Catholic) minority.

Education. In 1982 there were 11,338 pupils and 317 teachers in primary schools and 794 pupils and 40 teachers in secondary and technical schools.

RÉUNION

HISTORY. The island of Réunion became a French possession in 1642 and remained so until 19 March 1946, when its status was altered to that of an Overseas Department; in 1974 it additionally became part of an administrative region.

AREA AND POPULATION. Réunion (or Bourbon), about 569 miles east of Madagascar, has an area of 2,511·6 sq. km (968·5 sq. miles) and population of 515,814 (March 1982 census). The capital is Saint-Denis (1982 census) 109,072.

Vital statistics (1981): Live births, 11,800; deaths, 3,135.

The small islands of Juan de Nova, Europa, Bassas da India, Îles Glorieuses and Tromelin, with a combined area of less than 50 sq. km, are all uninhabited and lie at various points in the Indian Ocean adjacent to Madagascar. They remained integral parts of the French Republic after Madagascar's independence in 1960, and are now administered by Réunion. Both Mauritius and the Seychelles have laid claim to Tromelin (which had been transferred by the UK from the Seychelles to France in 1954), and Madagascar to all 5 islands.

GOVERNMENT. The region is under a Commissioner, an elected general council of 36 members and an elected regional council of 45 members. Réunion is represented in the National Assembly by 3 deputies, in the Senate by 2 senators, and in the Economic and Social Council by 1 councillor. There are 4 *arrondissements*, sub-divided into 24 communes each administered by an elected municipal council.

Commissioner: Michel Levallois.

ECONOMY

Budget. The budget for 1981 balanced at 5,341m. French francs.

Banking. The Institut d'émission des Départements d'Outre-mer has the right to issue bank-notes. Banks operating in Réunion are the Banque de la Réunion (Crédit Lyonnais), the Banque Nationale de Paris, the Caisse Régionale de Crédit Agricole Mutuel de la Réunion, the Banque Française Commerciale (BFC) and the Banque Populaire.

NATURAL RESOURCES

Agriculture (1981). The chief produce is sugar (251,000 tonnes), rum (74,100 hectolitres), maize (12,180 tonnes), potatoes (5,120 tonnes), onions (1,672 tonnes), vanilla, essences and tobacco. The forests occupy about 88,430 hectares.

Livestock (1981): 22,000 cattle, 73,500 swine, 3,000 sheep, 45,000 goats and 2·2m. poultry.

Fisheries. In 1981 the catch was 3,012 tonnes.

INDUSTRY AND TRADE

Industry (1978). Total number of workers (in 418 firms employing 10 or more) 20,173. The sugar industry employed (1981) 1,856.

Commerce. Trade in 1m. French francs:

	1976	*1977*	*1978*	*1979*	*1980*	*1981*
Imports	2,152	2,412	2,659	3,230	3,749	4,282
Exports	450	561	519	594	554	573

The chief export is sugar, forming (1979) 81% by value. In 1981 (by value) 62% of imports were from, and 76% of exports to, France.

Total trade between Réunion and UK (British Department of Trade returns, in £1,000 sterling):

	1978	*1979*	*1980*	*1981*	*1982*
Imports to UK	9,480	7,855	60	290	74
Exports and re-exports from UK	2,041	2,296	3,022	3,117	2,889

COMMUNICATIONS

Roads. There were, in 1981, 2,508 km of roads. There were 99,737 passenger cars and 46,000 other vehicles in 1981.

Aviation. Air France maintains an air service 6 times a week. In 1981, 163,393 passengers and 5,334 tonnes of freight arrived and 166,584 passengers and 2,374 tonnes of freight departed at Saint-Denis-Gillot airport.

Shipping. Four shipping lines serve the island. In 1981, 384 vessels visited the island to discharge 895,000 tonnes of freight and 426 passengers, and load 334,000 tonnes of freight and 337 passengers at Pointe-des-Galets.

Post and Broadcasting. There are telephone and telegraph connexions with Mauritius, Madagascar and metropolitan France. There are 50 post offices and a central telephone office; number of telephones (1981), 60,296.

France Régions 3 broadcast in French on medium- and short-waves for more than 18 hours a day. There is 1 television programme *via* 14 transmitters for 21 hours a week. In 1977 there were 53,380 radio and 59,210 TV receivers.

Newspapers. There were (1981) 3 daily newspapers with a combined circulation of 52,000 and 14 other periodicals with a circulation of 29,000.

JUSTICE, RELIGION, EDUCATION AND WELFARE

Justice. There are 3 *tribunaux d'instance,* 2 *tribunaux de grande instance,* 1 *Cour d'Appel,* 1 *tribunal administratif* and 2 *conseils de prud'homme.*

Religion. The vast majority of the population is Roman Catholic.

Education. Réunion had (1981) 6 *lycées,* 62 *collèges,* and 15 *lycées d'enseignement technique* with 61,995 pupils and 17 private secondary schools with 3,627 pupils. Primary education is given in 465 public schools with 4,325 teachers and 110,590 pupils; and in 48 private schools, with 301 teachers, and 9,990 pupils. The *Université Française de l'Océan Indien* (founded 1971) had 2,201 students in 1981.

Health. In 1982 there were 21 hospitals with 3,886 beds; in 1980 there were 508 physicians, 132 dentists, 141 pharmacists, 107 midwives and 1,568 nursing personnel.

Books of Reference

Bulletin de l'Académie de la Réunion. Biennial
Bulletin de la Chambre d'Agriculture de la Réunion
Statistiques et Indicateurs Economiques. 1983

ST PIERRE AND MIQUELON

HISTORY. The tiny remaining fragment of the once extensive French possessions in North America, the archipelago was settled from France in the 17th century and finally became a French territory from 1816 until July 1976, when its status was altered to that of an Overseas Department.

AREA AND POPULATION. The department consists of 8 small islands off the south coast of Newfoundland, with a total area of 242 sq. km, comprising the Saint-Pierre group (26 sq. km) and the Miquelon-Langlade group (216 sq. km). The population (census, 1982) was 6,041 of whom 5,415 were on Saint-Pierre and 626 on Miquelon. The chief town is St Pierre.

Vital statistics (1981): Births, 115; marriages, 40; deaths, 59.

GOVERNMENT. The department is administered by an appointed Commissioner and an elected General Council of 14 members; it is represented in the National Assembly by 1 deputy, in the Senate by 1 senator and in the Economic and Social Council by 1 councillor.

Commissioner: Claude Guyon.

BUDGET. The ordinary budget for 1981 balanced at 42·1m. francs.

INDUSTRY. The islands, being mostly barren rock, are unsuited for agriculture. The chief industry is fishing.

COMMERCE. Trade in 1,000 tonnes and 1,000 francs:

	1979		*1980*		*1981*	
	Quantity	*Value*	*Quantity*	*Value*	*Quantity*	*Value*
Imports	56·2	148,000	47·7	177,000	58·6	220,910
Exports	2·4	19,000	4·3	24,000	4·9	38,700

The imports comprise textiles, salt, wines, coal, petrol, foodstuffs, meat; and the exports (in 1981), dried and salted fish (25 tonnes); frozen and smoked fish (3,842 tonnes). In 1976, 64% of imports came from Canada and 27% from France, while 64% of exports were to Canada and 28% to the USA.

Total trade between St Pierre and Miquelon and UK (British Department of Trade returns in £1,000 sterling):

	1978	*1979*	*1980*	*1981*	*1982*
Imports to UK	—	224	3	1,352	254
Exports and re-exports from UK	382	435	884	481	363

COMMUNICATIONS

Roads. In 1974 there were 60 km of roads, of which 20 km were paved. In 1981 there were about 1,550 passenger cars and 491 commercial vehicles.

Aviation. Air Saint-Pierre connects the department with Halifax and Sydney (Nova Scotia), and there are occasional flights to and from St John's (Newfoundland), Gander and New York.

Shipping. St Pierre is in regular motor-vessel communication with North Sydney, Fortune (Newfoundland) and Halifax. In 1972, 89,000 tonnes of freight were loaded or unloaded.

Post and Broadcasting. There were 2,907 telephones in 1982. *France Régions 3* broadcasts in French on medium-waves. St Pierre is connected by radio-telecommunication with most countries of the world. Radio licences totalled 2,100 and TV 1,700 in 1975.

Cinemas. There were (1973) 2 cinemas with a seating capacity of 800.

JUSTICE, RELIGION, EDUCATION AND WELFARE

Justice. There is a *tribunal de premier instance* and a *tribunal supérieur d'appel* at St Pierre.

Religion. The population is chiefly Roman Catholic.

Education. Primary instruction is free. There were, in 1981–82, 7 nursery and primary schools with 1,053 pupils and 3 secondary schools (including 1 technical school) with 761 pupils.

Health. There was (1979) 1 hospital on St Pierre with 78 beds; 6 doctors, 2 dentists and 21 nurses.

Books of Reference

De Curton, E., *Saint-Pierre et Miquelon.* Paris, 1944
De La Rüe, E. A., *Saint-Pierre et Miquelon.* Paris, 1963
Ribault, J. Y., *Histoire de Saint-Pierre et Miquelon: Des Origines à 1814.* St Pierre, 1962

OVERSEAS TERRITORIES

SOUTHERN AND ANTARCTIC TERRITORIES

Terres Australes et Antarctiques Françaises

The Territory of the TAAF was created on 6 Aug. 1955. It comprises the islands of Saint Paul and Amsterdam (formerly Nouvelle Amsterdam), the Kerguelen and Crozet islands, and Terre Adélie.

The Administrator is assisted by a 7-member consultative council which meets twice yearly in Paris; its members are nominated by the Government for 5 years. The 12 members of the Scientific Council are appointed by the Senior Administrator after approval by the Minister in charge of scientific research. The administration has its seat in Paris.

Administrateur supérieur: Vice-Adm. Claude Piéri.

There are 4 postal agencies; the TAAF has its own postage stamps.

The scientific stations of the TAAF which took an important part in the International Geophysical Year, 1956–58, have been made permanent; the staff of the French bases (183 in 1975) is renewed annually and forms the only population.

Kerguelen islands, situated 48–50° S. lat., 68–70° E. long., consists of 1 large and 85 smaller islands and over 200 islets and rocks with a total area of 7,215 sq. km (2,786 sq. miles), of which Grande Terre occupies 6,675 sq. km (2,577 sq. miles). It was discovered in 1772 by Yves de Kerguelen, but was effectively occupied by France only in 1949. Port-aux-Français has several scientific research stations (92 members). Reindeer, trout and sheep have been acclimatized.

Crozet islands, situated 46° S. lat., 50–52° E. long., consists of 5 larger and 15 tiny islands, with a total area of 300 sq. km (116 sq. miles); the western group includes Apostles, Pigs and Penguins islands; the eastern group, Possession and Eastern islands. The archipelago was discovered in 1772 by Marion Dufresne, whose mate, Crozet, annexed it for Louis XV. A meteorological and scientific station (28 members) at Base Alfred-Faure on Possession Island was built in 1964.

Amsterdam Island and **Saint-Paul Island,** situated 38–39° S. lat., 77° E. long. Amsterdam, with an area of 100 sq. km (39 sq. miles) was discovered in 1522 by Magellan's companions; Saint-Paul, lying about 100 km to the south, with an area of 7 sq. km (2·7 sq. miles), was probably discovered in 1559 by Portuguese sailors. Both were first visited in 1633 by the Dutch explorer, Van Diemen, and were annexed by France in 1843. They are both extinct volcanoes, barren and uninhabited; but in 1949 an administrative office, research stations (37 members) and a hospital were established at Camp Heurtin on Amsterdam.

Terre Adélie comprises that section of the Antarctic continent between 136° and 142° E. long., south of 60° S. lat. The ice-covered plateau has an area of about 432,000 sq. km (166,800 sq. miles), and was discovered in 1840 by Dumont d'Urville. A research station (34 members) is situated at Base Dumont d'Urville, which is maintained by the French Polar Expeditions.

Books of Reference

T.A.A.F. Revue trimestrielle. Paris, 1957 ff
Expéditions Polaires Françaises. Études et Rapports. Paris, 1948–59

NEW CALEDONIA

Nouvelle Calédonie

HISTORY. New Caledonia was annexed by France in 1853 and, together with most of its former dependencies, became an Overseas Territory in 1958.

AREA AND POPULATION. The territory comprises the island of New Caledonia and various outlying islands, all situated in the south-west Pacific with a total land area of 19,103 sq. km (7,374 sq. miles). In 1976 the population (census) was 133,233, including 50,757 Europeans (majority French), 55,598 Melanesians, 7,054 Vietnamese and Indonesians, 6,391 Polynesians, 9,571 Wallisians, 3,862 others; 1982 (estimate) 142,800. The capital, Noumea had (1976) 74,335 inhabitants.

Vital statistics (1981): Live births, 3,861; deaths, 866.

The main islands are:

1. The island of New Caledonia with an area of 16,627 sq. km, has a total length of about 400 km, and an average breadth of 50 km, and a population (census, 1976) of 116,996.
2. The Loyalty Islands, 100 km (60 miles) east of New Caledonia, consisting of 3 large islands, Maré, Lifou and Uvéa, and many small islands with a total area of about 2,353 sq. km and a population (census, 1976) of 14,518, nearly all Melanesians except on Uvéa, which is partly Polynesian. The chief culture in the islands is that of coconuts: the chief export, copra.
3. The Isle of Pines, 50 km (30 miles) to the south-east of Nouméa, with an area of 153 sq. km and a population of 1,095 (census 1976), is a tourist and fishing centre.
4. The Bélep Archipelago, about 50 km north-west of New Caledonia, with an area of 70 sq. km and a population of 624 (census 1976).

The remaining islands are all very small and none have permanent inhabitants, although many were formerly exploited for their guano deposits. The largest are the Chesterfield Islands, a group of 11 well-wooded coral islets with a combined area of 10 sq. km, about 550 km west of the Bélep Archipelago. The Huon Islands, a group of 4 barren coral islets with a combined area of just 65 hectares, are 225 km north of the Bélep Archipelago. Walpole, a limstone coral island of 1 sq. km, lies 150 km east of the Isle of Pines; Matthew Island and Hunter Island, respectively 250 km and 330 km east of Walpole, are spasmodically active volcanic islands of similar size.

CONSTITUTION AND GOVERNMENT. From Jan. 1976 State affairs are administrated by the High Commissioner and Territorial affairs by a Council of Government of 7 elected members (until 1976 the Council was advisory). A Territorial Assembly of 36 elected members decides the more important territorial affairs including local revenue.

New Caledonia is represented in the National Assembly by 2 deputies, in the Senate by 1 senator and in the Economic and Social Council by 1 councillor.

At territorial elections held 1 July 1979, the *Rassemblement Pour la Calédonie dans la République* (Gaullists) gained 15 seats, *Front Indépendantiste* 14 seats, *Fédération pour une Nouvelle Société Cáledonienne* 7 seats.

The Territory is divided into 4 *circonscriptions* (of which the Loyalty Islands form one), and subdivided into 32 communes which are administered by locally elected councils and mayors.

High Commissioner: Christian Nucci.

ECONOMY

Budget. The budget for 1982 balanced at 22,860m. francs CFP. Revenues included special grants by France totalling 6,290m. francs CFP.

Currency. The unit of currency is the *franc* CFP, with a parity of CFP *francs* 18·18 to the French *franc*.

Banking. There are branches of the Banque de Indosuez, the Banque Nationale de Paris, the Banque de Paris et des Pays-Bas, and the Société Générale, in addition to the Banque de la Nouvelle-Calédonie (Crédit Lyonnais).

ENERGY AND NATURAL RESOURCES

Electricity. In 1981, production totalled 1,164m. kwh.

Minerals. The mineral resources are very great; nickel, chrome and iron abound; silver, gold, cobalt, lead, manganese, iron and copper have been mined at different times. The nickel deposits are of special value, being without arsenic. Production of nickel ore in 1981, 3·9m. tonnes. About 467,000 hectares of mining land are owned, and 97,000 hectares have been granted for exploitation. In 1981 the furnaces produced 15,330 tonnes of matte nickel and 27,989 tonnes of ferro-nickel.

Agriculture. Of the total area only about 6% is cultivable; about 416,000 hectares are pasture land; about 6,000 hectares are commercially cultivated and about 250,000 hectares contain forest; forest produce, 1976, 19,849 cu. metres. There are 4 forms of landownership: native reserves belonging to the local tribes, private estates, public land belonging to the New Caledonian territory and public land belonging to the metropolitan government. The chief agricultural products are beef, pork, poultry, coffee, maize, fruit and vegetables.

Livestock (1981): Cattle, 110,000; pigs, 18,000; goats, 8,000; poultry, 220,000.

INDUSTRY AND TRADE

Industry. Local industries include chlorine and oxygen plants, cement, soft drinks, barbed wire, nails, pleasure and fishing boats, clothing, pasta, household cleaners and confectionery.

Commerce. Imports and exports in 1m. francs CFP for 5 years:

	1977	*1978*	*1979*	*1980*	*1981*
Imports	26,032	23,926	27,791	35,041	40,434
Exports	27,809	17,484	28,549	29,652	33,435

In 1981, 32·5% of the imports came from, and 67% of the exports went to France.

Chief imports in 1981 were (in 1m. francs CFP): Food, 8,406; fuels and minerals, 11,777; machines and electrical equipment, 4,015. Chief exports: Nickel metal, 25,946; nickel ore, 5,037.

COMMUNICATIONS

Roads. There were, in 1979, 5,399 km of roads.

Aviation. New Caledonia is connected by air routes with France (by UTA), Australia (UTA, Air Pacific and Qantas), New Zealand (UTA and Air New Zealand), Fiji (by UTA and Air Pacific), Vanuatu, Wallis archipelago and Tahiti (by UTA), and Nauru (by Air Nauru). In 1979, 267,793 passengers landed or departed *via* Nouméa airport.

Shipping. In 1979, 447 vessels entered Nouméa unloading 801,500 tonnes of goods and loading 2·4m. tonnes. A new harbour for deep-water alongside discharge was completed in 1974.

Post and Broadcasting. There were 52 post offices and telex, telephone, radio and television services. There were (1981) 27,953 telephones. *Radio Nouméa* belongs to *Société Nationale des Programmes* and broadcasts in French on medium- and short-waves. *Télé Nouméa* broadcasts 1 television programme 28 hours a week. Number of receivers (1978): radio, 65,000; TV, 28,000.

Cinemas. In 1979 there were 10 cinemas.

Newspapers. In 1982 there was 1 daily newspaper with a circulation of 12,000 and 16 other periodicals.

JUSTICE, RELIGION, EDUCATION AND WELFARE

Justice. There is a *tribunal de grande instance* and a *cour d'appel* in Nouméa.

Religion. Over 60% of the population are Roman Catholic and 30% Protestant.

Education. In 1979, there were 33,939 pupils in 258 primary schools, 8,660 in 32 secondary schools, 3,038 in 21 technical and vocational schools and 396 students in higher education.

Health. In 1979 there were 158 physicians, 42 dentists, 42 pharmacists, 15 midwives and 436 nursing personnel. In 1978, 66 hospitals had a total of 1,541 beds.

Books of Reference

Journal Officiel de la Nouvelle Calédonie et Dépendances
Annuaire Statistique de la Nouvelle Calédonie et Dépendances

FRENCH POLYNESIA

Polynésie Française

HISTORY. French protectorates since 1843, these islands were annexed to France 1880–82 to form 'French Settlements in Oceania', which opted in Nov. 1958 for the status of an Overseas Territory within the French Community.

AREA AND POPULATION. The total area of these 5 archipelagoes, scattered over a wide area in the Eastern Pacific is 3,941 sq. km (1,522 sq. miles). The population, Census, 1977, was 137,382; 1982 estimate, 165,000. The islands are administratively divided into 5 *circonscriptions:*

1. The **Windward Islands** (Îles du Vent) (101,392 inhabitants in 1977) comprise Tahiti with an area of 1,042 sq. km and (1977) 95,604 inhabitants; Moorea with an area of 132 sq. km and 5,788 inhabitants; and the smaller Mehetia, Tetiaoro and Tubuai Manu. The capital is Papeete (62,735 inhabitants including suburbs).

2. The **Leeward Islands** (Îles sous le Vent) (16,311 inhabitants), comprising the volcanic islands of Huahine (3,140), Raiatéa (6,376), Tahaa (3,513), Bora-Bora (2,572), Maupiti (710) together with 4 small (uninhabited) atolls, the group having a total area of 507 sq. km. The chief town is Uturoa (2,517 inhabitants) on Raiatéa.

The Windward and Leeward Islands together are called the Society Archipelago (Archipel de la Société). Tahitian, a Polynesian language, is spoken throughout the archipelago.

3. The **Tuamotu Archipelago**, consisting of two parallel ranges of 78 atolls lying between 135° and 143° W. long. and 14° and 23° S. lat., east of the Society Archipelago, have a total area of 774 sq. km and a population of 8,537; its major

islands are Rangiroa, Hao and Turéia. The *circonscription* (total 9,052 inhabitants) also includes the **Gambier Islands** further east (of which Mangareva is the principal), an atoll having an area of 36 sq. km and a population of 515; the chief centre is Rikitea.

4. The **Austral or Tubuai Islands**, lying south of the Society Archipelago, comprise a 1,300 km chain of volcanic islands and reefs. They include Rimatara, Rurutu, Tubuai, Raivaevae and, 500 km to the south, Rapa-Iti, with a combined area of 174 sq. km and 5,208 inhabitants; the chief centre is Mataura on Tubuai.

5. The **Marquesas Islands**, lying north of the Tuamotu Archipelago, with a total area of 1,274 sq. km and 5,419 inhabitants, comprise Nuku-Hiva, Ua Pu, Ua Huka, Hiva-Oa, Tahuata, Fatu-Hiva and 5 smaller (uninhabited) islands; the chief centre is Taiohae on Hiva-Oa.

CONSTITUTION AND GOVERNMENT. Under the 1977 Constitution, the Territory is administered by a High Commissioner, a Council of Government (over which the High Comissioner presides) of 8 members, a Territorial Assembly of 30 members elected every 5 years by universal suffrage, and an advisory Economic and Social Committee. French Polynesia is represented in the National Assembly by 2 deputies, in the Senate by 1 senator, and in the Economic and Social Council by 1 councillor.

At the territorial elections held on 29 May 1977, the *Front Uni pour l'autonomie interne* and its supporters gained 16 seats in the Assembly, and the *Tahoeraa Huiraatira* (Gaullists) 10 seats, with 4 seats going to others.

High Commissioner: Paul Cousseran.

ECONOMY

Budget. The ordinary budget for 1978 balanced at 13,524·7m. francs CFP.

Currency. The unit of currency is the *franc* CFP, with a parity of CFP *francs* 18·18 to the French *franc.*

ENERGY AND NATURAL RESOURCES

Electricity. Production in 1979 amounted to 136·97m. kwh.

Agriculture. An important product is copra (coconut trees covering the coastal plains of the mountainous islands and the greater part of the low-lying islands), production (1979) 14,513 tonnes. Tropical fruits, such as bananas, pineapples, oranges, etc., are grown only for local consumption.

Livestock (1980): Cattle, 7,000; horses, 2,000; pigs, 22,000; sheep, 3,000; goats, 3,000; poultry, 477,000.

Fisheries. The catch in 1979 amounted to 4,217 tonnes of fish.

COMMERCE. Trade in 1,000 tonnes and 1m. francs CFP:

	1977		*1978*		*1979*	
	Quantity	*Value*	*Quantity*	*Value*	*Quantity*	*Value*
Imports	396	29,187	407	33,070	450	36,645
Exports	11	1,464	9	2,973	12	2,252

Total trade between the French possessions in the Pacific and UK (British Department of Trade returns, in £1,000 sterling):

	1978	*1979*	*1980*	*1981*	*1982*
Imports to UK	14	6	32	8	2
Exports and re-exports from UK	2,781	2,285	2,154	1,421	1,962

Chief imports (by value) include metalwork, textiles, petrol, sugar and flour. Chief exports are coconut oil, cultured pearls, vanilla and citrus fruits. Tourism is very important, earning almost half as much as the visible exports. There were 101,194 tourists in 1979.

COMMUNICATIONS

Aviation. Five international airlines connect Tahiti with Paris, Honolulu, USA, Mexico and New Zealand. There is also a regular air service between Faaa airport (on Tahiti) and the Leeward Isles with occasional connexions to the other groups. In 1976, 657,700 passengers arrived or departed *via* Faaa airport and 210,300 *via* Moorea airport.

Shipping. Several shipping companies connect France, San Francisco, New Zealand and Australia with Papeete.

Post and Broadcasting. Number of telephones (1981), 22,523. *Radio Tahiti* belongs to *Office de Radiodiffusion-Télévision Française* and broadcasts in French, Tahitian and English on medium- and short-waves and also broadcasts 1 television programme *via* 5 transmitters. Number of receivers (1978): radio, 75,000; TV, 15,000.

Cinemas. In 1975 there were 6 cinemas with a seating capacity of 3,200.

Newspapers. In 1975 there were 4 daily newspapers with a combined circulation of 11,000 and 2 other periodicals with 2,000.

JUSTICE, RELIGION, EDUCATION AND WELFARE

Justice. There is a *tribunal de grande instance* and a *cour d'appel* at Papeete.

Religion. In 1975 it was estimated that 50% of the inhabitants were Protestants, 34% Roman Catholic and 6% Mormon.

Education. Education at primary level was reorganized in 1974 and secondary education in 1975. There were, in 1979-80, 38,964 pupils and 1,687 teachers in primary schools, 9,613 pupils and 610 teachers in secondary schools, 2,757 pupils and 214 teachers in technical schools, and 225 students at teacher-training colleges.

Health. There were (1977) 117 physicians, 23 dentists, 10 pharmacists, 24 midwives and 286 nursing personnel. There was a main hospital at Mamao (on Tahiti), 6 secondary hospitals, 41 dispensaries and medical centres and 45 first aid posts.

DEPENDENCY. The uninhabited Clipperton Islands, 1,000 km off the coast of Mexico, are administered by the High Commissioner for French Polynesia but do not form part of the Territory; they comprise an atoll whose 2 islands cover 7 sq. km.

Books of Reference

Journal Officiel des Etablissements Françaises de l'Océanie, and *Supplement Containing Statistics of Commerce and Navigation*. Papeete
Andrews, E., *Comparative Dictionary of the Tahitian Language*. Chicago, 1944
Luke, Sir Harry, *The Islands of the South Pacific*. London, 1961
O'Reilly, P., and Reitman, E., *Bibliographie de Tahiti et de la Polynésie française*. Paris, 1967
O'Reilly, P., and Teissier, R., *Tahitiens. Répertoire bio-bibliographique de la Polynésie française*. Paris, 1963

WALLIS AND FUTUNA

HISTORY. French dependencies since 1842, the inhabitants of these islands voted on 22 Dec. 1959 by an overwhelming majority in favour of exchanging their status to that of an Overseas Territory, which took effect from 29 July 1961.

AREA AND POPULATION. The Territory comprises two groups of islands in the central Pacific, north-east of Fiji; the Wallis Archipelago (area 96 sq. km) and the Îles de Horn (159 sq. km). The capital of the Territory is Mata-Utu (558 inhabitants) on Uvea, the main island of the Wallis Archipelago.

The resident population (census 26 March 1976) was 9,192, comprising 6,019 on Uvea and 3,173 on Futuna in the Îles de Horn (whose other main island, Alofi, is uninhabited). About 11,000 Wallisians and Futunians live abroad, mainly in New Caledonia and Vanuatu. Uvean and Futunan are distinct Polynesian languages.

CONSTITUTION AND GOVERNMENT. The Senior Administrator carries out the duties of Head of the Territory, assisted by an elected 20-member Territorial Assembly. The territory is represented by 1 deputy in the National Assembly, by 1 senator in the Senate, and by 1 member on the Economic and Social Council.

Administrateur supérieur: Jacques de Agostini.
President of the Territorial Assembly: Manuele Lisiahi.

ECONOMY

Budget. The 1978 budget provided for expenditure of 148·45m. francs CFP.

Currency. The unit of currency is the *franc* CFP, with a parity of CFP *francs* 18·18 to the French *franc*.

AGRICULTURE. The chief products are copra, yams, taro roots and bananas.

Livestock: Cattle, 100 (1976); pigs, 4,000 (1980); horses, 400 (1978); goats, 7,000 (1980).

COMMERCE. Imports (1976) amounted to 217m. francs CFP.

COMMUNICATIONS

Roads. In 1977 there were 100 km of roads on Uvea.

Aviation. In 1977 there were 581 aircraft arrivals and departures at Hihifo airport, on Uvea. There is a weekly flight *via* Vila (Vanuatu) to Noumea (New Caledonia).

Post and Broadcasting. In 1979 a radio station was established on Uvea. In 1978 there were 148 telephones.

RELIGION, EDUCATION AND WELFARE

Religion. The majority of the population is Roman Catholic.

Education. In 1978, there were about 3,000 pupils in 9 primary and lower secondary schools.

Health. In 1974 there were 3 physicians and 26 nursing personnel (including 10 midwives). There were (1972) 5 small hospitals and dispensaries with 108 beds.

GABON

République Gabonaise

Capital: Libreville
Population: 1·23m. (1981)
GNP per capita: US$3,680 (1980)

HISTORY. First colonized by France in the mid-19th century, Gabon was annexed to French Congo in 1888 and became a separate colony in 1910 as one of the 4 territories of French Equatorial Africa. It became an autonomous republic within the French Community in 1958 and achieved independence on 17 Aug. 1960. The first President, Leon M'ba, died in 1967 and was succeeded on 2 Dec. by his Vice-President, Albert-Bernard (now Omar) Bongo.

AREA AND POPULATION. Gabon is bounded west by the Atlantic ocean, north by Equatorial Guinea and Cameroon and east and south by Congo. The area covers 267,667 sq. km; its population at the 1970 census was 950,007; estimate (1981) is 1,232,000. The capital is Libreville (251,400 inhabitants, 1974), other large towns being Port-Gentil (77,611) and Lambaréné (22,682).

Vital statistics (1975): Birth rate, 3·22%; death rate, 2·22%.

Provincial areas, populations (census 1970, in 1,000) and capitals are as follows:

Province	*sq. km*	*1970*	*Capital*	*Province*	*sq. km*	*1970*	*Capital*
Estuaire	20,740	195	Libreville	Nyanga	21,285	67	Tchibanga
Woleu-Ntem	38,465	148	Oyem	Ngounié	37,750	130	Mouila
Ogooué-Ivindo	46,075	60	Makokou	Ogooué-Lolo	25,380	52	Koulamoutou
Moyen-Ogooué	18,535	52	Lambaréné	Haut-Ogooué	36,547	127	Franceville
Ogooué-Maritime	22,890	120	Port-Gentil				

The largest ethnic groups are the Fang (30%) in the north, Eshira (25%) in the south-west, and the Adouma (17%) in the south-east. French is the official language.

CONSTITUTION AND GOVERNMENT. The 1967 Constitution (revised 1979) provides for an Executive President directly elected for a 7-year term, who appoints a Council of Ministers to assist him. The unicameral National Assembly consists of 84 members, directly elected for a 5-year term (latest elections, Feb. 1980) and a further 9 members nominated by the President.

The sole legal political party is the *Parti democratique gabonais* founded in 1968.

President: Omar Bongo (re-elected on 25 Feb. 1973 and 30 Dec. 1979).

Prime Minister: Léon Mébiame.

Foreign Minister: Martin Bongo.

Flag: Three horizontal stripes of green, yellow, blue.

Local government: There are 9 provinces, each administered by a prefect appointed by the President; they are sub-divided into 37 *départements*, each under a sub-prefect.

DEFENCE

Army. The Army consists of 1 all-arms battalion with support units, totalling (1983), 1,500 men.

Navy. The small naval flotilla in 1983 comprised 3 fast attack craft (3 more reportedly on order), 2 patrol craft and 1 landing craft with a base at Port-Gentil. Personnel, 170 officers and men. The Coastguard has 9 small patrol craft and 1 service tender.

Air Force. The Air Force has 5 single-seat and 2 two-seat Mirage 5 ground-attack aircraft, and 1 EMB-111 maritime patrol aircraft. Transport duties are performed primarily by 3 Hercules and 4 EMB-110 Bandeirante turboprop aircraft, supported by 3 C-47s and 3 Nord 262s. Single Mystère 20, YS-11 and DC-8 aircraft are used for VIP duties; 4 Broussards and a Cessna Skymaster for liaison. Four T-34C-1 armed turboprop aircraft are operated for *La Guard Présidential.* Also in service are 4 Puma and 3 Alouette III helicopters. Personnel number 500.

INTERNATIONAL RELATIONS

Membership. Gabon is a member of UN, OAU and OPEC; it is an ACP state of the EEC.

ECONOMY.

Planning. The 1982-84 Intermin Development Plan proposed public expenditure of 362,512m. francs CFA, of which 188,202m. were to develop the transport infrastructure.

Budget. The provisional budget for 1982 balanced at 453,500m. francs CFA.

Currency. The unit of currency is the franc CFA, divided into 100 centimes, with a parity value of 50 francs CFA to 1 French franc.

Banking. The *Banque des États de l'Afrique Centrale* is the bank of issue. There are 6 commercial banks situated in Gabon. The *Banque Gabonaise de Développement* and the *Union Gabonaise de Banque* are Gabonese controlled.

ENERGY AND NATURAL RESOURCES

Electricity. The semi-public *Société d'energie et d'eau du Gabon* produced 567m. kwh. in 1980, mainly from thermal plants but increasingly from hydro-electric schemes at Kinguélé, near Libreville, Tchimbélé and Poubara.

Oil. Extraction from offshore fields totalled 7·56m. tonnes in 1981. Gabon operates 2 refineries, at Port-Gentil and at nearby Pointe Clairette.

Gas. Natural gas production (1979) was 206m. cu. metres.

Minerals. Production (1981) of manganese ore (from deposits around Moanda in the south-east) amounted to 1·5m. tonnes. Uranium is mined nearby (1,062 tonnes in 1981). An estimated 1,000m. tonnes of iron ore deposits, discovered 1971 at Mékambo (near Bélinga in the north-east) await completion of the branch railway line to be exploited. Gold (50 kg in 1978), zinc and phosphates also occur.

Agriculture. Agriculture, forestry and fisheries occupy 85% of the working population. The major crops (production, 1981, in 1,000 tonnes) are: Sugar-cane, 140; cassava, 100; plantains, 63; maize, 10; bananas, 8; palm products, cocoa, coffee and rice.

Livestock (1981): 4,000 cattle, 100,000 sheep, 90,000 goats, 7,000 pigs.

Forestry. Gabon's equatorial forests covering 78% of the land area produced 1,225,000 cu. metres of *okoumé* in 1978. Hardwoods (mahogany, ebony and walnut) are also exported.

Fisheries. The total catch (1979) amounted to 13,200 tonnes in the Atlantic and 400 tonnes in inland waters.

TRADE. In 1978 imports totalled 139,174m. francs CFA and exports 249,849m. francs CFA. France, UK, USA, the Netherlands and the Federal Republic of Germany are Gabon's principal trading partners. Petroleum made up 72% of exports; metals, 18% and timber, 6%.

Total trade between Gabon and the UK (British Department of Trade returns, in £1,000 sterling):

	1977	*1978*	*1979*	*1980*	*1981*	*1982*
Imports to UK	3,216	4,401	12,893	10,657	36,726	27,634
Exports and re-exports from UK	5,626	7,725	8,507	9,155	12,099	14,179

COMMUNICATIONS

Roads. There were (1981) 7,276 km of roads and (1976) there were 30,100 (12,700 goods) vehicles.

Railways. A 1,435-mm gauge (Transgabonais) railway is under construction from Owendo *via* N'Djole and Booué to Moanda and Franceville with a projected branch from Booué to Bélinga. The first section, to N'Djole, was opened for traffic on 27 Dec. 1978 and the second, to Beoué, in 1982.

Aviation. There are 3 international airports at Port-Gentil, Franceville, and Libreville; internal services link these to 65 domestic airfields.

Shipping. Owendo (near Libreville), Mayumba and Port-Gentil are the main ports. In 1975, 5·58m. tonnes were loaded and 468,000 tonnes unloaded at the ports. In 1978 there were 15 merchant vessels of 98,645 gross tons.

Post and Broadcasting. Telephones (1981), 11,600. In 1980 there were 9,000 television and 96,000 radio licences.

Cinemas. In 1974 there were 6 cinemas with a seating capacity of 4,100.

Newspapers. There are 2 daily newspapers published in Libreville; *Gabon-Matin* has a circulation of 18,000 and *L'Union* 15,000.

JUSTICE, RELIGION, EDUCATION AND WELFARE

Justice. There are *tribunaux de grande instance* at Libreville, Port-Gentil, Lambaréné, Mouila, Oyem, Franceville and Koulamoutou, from which cases move progressively to a central Criminal Court, Court of Appeal and Supreme Court, all 3 located in Libreville.

Civil police number about 900.

Religion. It is estimated that 35% of the population is Christian (mainly Roman Catholic), the majority of the balance following animist beliefs. There are about 2,000 Moslems.

Education. Education is compulsory between 6–16 years. In 1978–79 there were 141,569 pupils with 3,088 teachers in primary schools; 20,344 pupils with 1,000 teachers in secondary schools; 3,405 students with 256 teachers in 9 technical schools; and 1,247 students with 235 teaching staff at 13 teacher-training schools.

The Université Omar Bongo, founded in 1970 in Libreville, had (1978) 1,284 students; about 750 Gabonese students study abroad.

Health (1977). There were 207 doctors, 20 dentists, 28 pharmacists (1971), 99 midwives and 823 nursing personnel. In 1981 there were 16 hospitals and 87 medical centres, with a total of 4,815 beds, as well as 258 local dispensaries.

DIPLOMATIC REPRESENTATIVES

Of Gabon in Great Britain (48 Kensington Ct., London, W8)
Ambassador: Léon N'Dong.

Of Great Britain in Gabon (Bâtiment Sogame, Blvd de l'Indépendance, Libreville)
Ambassador: Alan Grey.

Of Gabon in the USA (2034 20th St., NW, Washington, D.C., 20009)
Ambassador: Etienne Mezui Mendo.

Of the USA in Gabon (Blvd de la Mer, Libreville)
Ambassador: Francis McNamara.

Of Gabon to the United Nations
Ambassador: Jean Davin.

Books of Reference

Lasserre, G., *Libreville, la ville et sa région.* Paris, 1958
Remy, M., *Gabon Today.* Paris, 1977
Thiery, Y., and Delarozière, R., *Carte ethnique du Gabon.* Paris, 1945

THE GAMBIA

Capital: Banjul
Population: 592,000 (1980)
GNP per capita: US$250 (1980)

HISTORY. The Gambia was discovered by the early Portuguese navigators, but they made no settlement. During the 17th century various companies of merchants obtained trading charters and established a settlement on the river, which, from 1807, was controlled from Sierra Leone; in 1843 it was made an independent Crown Colony; in 1866 it formed part of the West African Settlements, but in Dec. 1888 it again became a separate Crown Colony. The boundaries were delimited only after 1890. The Gambia achieved full internal self-government on 4 Oct. 1963 and became an independent member of the Commonwealth on 18 Feb. 1965. The Gambia became a republic within the Commonwealth on 24 April 1970.

AREA AND POPULATION. The Gambia is bounded west by the Atlantic ocean and on all other sides by Senegal. Area of Banjul (formerly Bathurst) and environs, 87·8 sq. km. In the provinces (area, 10,601·5 sq. km) the settled population (1971) was 275,469, not including temporary immigrants. Total population (census, April 1973), 493,197. Estimate (1980) 592,000. The largest tribe is the Mandingo (186,241), followed by the Fulas (79,994), Woloffs (69,291), Jolas (41,988) and Sarahulis (38,478). The capital is Banjul (39,476), and the other chief town is Serekunda (16,833). There are 1,159 non-Africans.

CONSTITUTION AND GOVERNMENT. Parliament consists of the House of Representatives which consists of a Speaker, Deputy Speaker and 35 elected members; in addition, 4 Chiefs are elected by the Chiefs in Assembly; 3 nominated members are without votes and the Attorney-General is nominated and has a vote. *See* Senegal for details about Senegambia.

At the general election of 4–5 May 1982, the People's Progressive Party obtained 27, the National Convention Party 3, and Independents 5 seats.

The Government was in Jan. 1983 composed as follows:

President: Sir Dawda Kairaba Jawara.

Vice-President (Information and Tourism): Bakary B. Darbo. *External Affairs:* Alhaji Lamine Kiti Jabang. *Finance and Trade:* Sherif Sisay. *Agriculture (Finance and Trade):* Saikou Sabally. *Education, Youth and Sport:* Alhaji Abdoulie K. N'Jie. *Health, Labour and Social Welfare:* Momodou Cherno Jallow. *Works and Communications:* Lamine Bora M'Boge. *Economic Planning and Industrial Development:* Dr Momodou S. K. Manneh. *Justice and Attorney-General:* Fafa M'Bye. *Water Resources and Environment:* Omar A. Jallow. *Information and Tourism (Local Government):* Landing Jallow Sonko. *Interior:* Alhaji Maj. Abdoulie M'Boob. *Local Government:* Kebba Jawara.

National flag: Three horizontal stripes of red, blue, green, with the blue edged in white.

Local Administration. The Gambia is divided into 35 districts, each traditionally under a Chief, assisted by Village Heads and advisers. These districts are grouped into 6 Area Councils containing a majority of elected members, with the Chiefs of the district as *ex-officio* members. The city of Banjul is administered by a City Council.

INTERNATIONAL RELATIONS

Membership. The Gambia is a member of UN, OAU, the Commonwealth and is an ACP state of EEC.

ECONOMY

Budget. Revenue and expenditure for years ending 30 June are (in 1,000 dalasi):

	1975–76	*1976–77*	*1977–78*	*1978–79* [1]	*1979–80* [1]
Revenue	37,139	65,515	66,870	66,132	88,045
Expenditure	39,964	60,219	70,031	69,425	81,190

[1] Estimate.

Currency. The currency is the *dalasi* and is divided into 100 *butut.* 4 *dalasi* = £1 sterling; 2·65 *dalasi* = US$1 (March 1981).

Banking. There are 4 banks in the Gambia, the Standard Bank of Gambia Ltd, Central Bank of the Gambia, Commercial and Development Bank and la Banque Internationale pour le Commerce et l'Industrie (BICI). On 30 Nov. 1978 the government savings bank had about 36,000 depositors holding approximately 992,496 dalasi.

NATURAL RESOURCES

Minerals. Heavy minerals, including ilmenite, zircon and rutile, have been discovered (1m. tons up to 31 Dec. 1980) in Sanyang, Batakunku and Kartong areas.

Agriculture. Almost all commercial activity centres upon the marketing of groundnuts, which is the only export crop of financial significance. Cotton is also exported on a limited scale. Rice is of increasing importance for local consumption.

Livestock (1981): 333,000 cattle, 177,000 goats, 165,000 sheep, 11,000 pigs and 285,000 poultry.

Fisheries. Total catch (1975) 10,800 tonnes, of which 800 tonnes were from inland waters.

LABOUR. There are 4 large and 10 small trade unions.

TRADE. Chief items of imports are textiles and clothing, vehicles and machinery, metal goods and petroleum products.

Imports and exports, in 1,000 dalasi:

	1975–76	*1976–77*	*1977–78*	*1978–79*	*1979–80*
Imports	146,013	169,082	209,094	221,014	500,000
Exports	73,186	106,713	80,219	94,913	417,000

Chief items of exports are groundnuts, palm kernels, dried and smoked fish, hides and skins and groundnut oil.

Total trade between the Gambia and UK (British Department of Trade returns, in £1,000 sterling):

	1977	*1978*	*1979*	*1980*	*1981*	*1982*
Imports to UK	8,503	5,721	2,357	2,417	2,335	2,031
Exports and re-exports from UK	12,362	17,332	13,953	17,792	11,889	10,087

TOURISM. In 1980–81, 20,000 tourists visited the Gambia.

COMMUNICATIONS

Roads. There are 2,990 km of motorable roads, of which 1,718 km rank as all-weather roads including 306 km of bituminous surface and 531 km of laterite gravel. Number of licensed motor vehicles (1974–75): 11,765 private cars, 5,777 commercial vehicles, 240 buses and coaches, 410 tractors and 143 trailers.

Aviation. The Gambia is served by Air Guinea, Air Mali, British Caledonian Airways, Ghana Airways and Nigeria Airways. Air movements at Yundum Airport in 1975 numbered 2,756, including scheduled services.

Shipping. The chief port, Banjul, handled 303 ships of 686,300 DWT in 1975–76. The first phase of development of the port was completed in 1974; a new 400 ft berth will take one large vessel of up to 36 ft draught. Internal communication is maintained by steamers and launches.

The Gambia River Development Organization was founded in 1978 as a joint project with Senegal to develop the river and its basin.

Post and Broadcasting. There are several post offices and agencies; postal facilities are also afforded to all river towns by means of a travelling post office on the government river mail-steamers. Banjul is connected with St Vincent (Cape Verde islands) and with Sierra Leone by cable. Banjul is in wireless communication with London and the main centres up river. A trans-Gambia telephone system provides direct communications with Dakar and Ziguinchor. Telephones numbered 3,476 in Jan. 1980. A telex service was introduced in 1968.

Radio Gambia, a government station, broadcasts for about 12 hours a day; Radio Syd, a commercial station, broadcasts for 15 hours. Number of radio receivers (1976, estimate), 100,000.

Cinemas. In 1979 there were 10 cinemas.

Newspapers. There is an official (three times weekly) and several news-sheets.

JUSTICE, RELIGION, EDUCATION AND WELFARE

Justice. Justice is administered by a Supreme Court consisting of a chief justice and puisne judges. It has unlimited jurisdiction but there is a Court of Appeal. Two magistrates' courts and divisional courts are supplemented by a system of travelling magistrates. There are also Moslem courts, group tribunals dealing with cases concerned with customs and traditions, and one juvenile court.

Religion. About 70% of the population is Moslem. Banjul is the seat of an Anglican and a Roman Catholic bishop. There are some Methodist missions. Some sections of the population retain their original animist beliefs.

Education (1979–80). There were 133 primary schools (1,371 teachers, 37,644 pupils), 17 secondary technical schools (260 teachers, 5,274 pupils), 7 senior secondary schools (179 teachers, 3,040 pupils) and 1 post-secondary school; total number of teachers, 1,810. Gambia College, which is to replace Yundum College as a teacher-training and vocational centre, opened for agricultural students in 1979

Health. In 1980 there were 43 government doctors, 23 private doctors and about 635 hospital beds.

DIPLOMATIC REPRESENTATIVES

Of the Gambia in Great Britain (57 Kensington Ct., London, W8 5DG)
High Commissioner: Abdullah Mamadu Kalifa Bojang (accredited 4 Nov. 1980).

Of Great Britain in the Gambia (48 Atlantic Rd., Fajara, Banjul)
High Commissioner: D. F. B. Le Breton, CBE.

Of the Gambia in the USA and to UN (1785 Massachusetts Ave., NW, Washington, D.C., 20036)
Ambassador: Dr Lamin A. Mbye.

Of the USA in the Gambia (16 Buckle St., Banjul)
Ambassador: Larry G. Piper.

Books of Reference

The Gambia in Brief. Gambia Information Services, Banjul, 1979
The Gambia Independence Act, 1964
The Gambia Independence Order, 1965
The Gambia since Independence 1965–1980. Banjul, 1980

GERMANY

POST-WAR HISTORY. Since the unconditional surrender of the German armed forces on 8 May 1945 there has been no central authority whose writ runs in the whole of Germany. Consequently no peace treaty has been signed with a government representing the whole of Germany, and the country is virtually partitioned between the Federal Republic of Germany and the German Democratic Republic.

By the Berlin Declaration of 5 June 1945 the governments of the USA, the UK, the USSR and France assumed supreme authority over Germany. Each of the 4 signatories was given a zone of occupation, in which the supreme power was to be exercised by the C.-in-C. in that zone (*see* map in THE STATESMAN'S YEAR-BOOK, 1947). Jointly these 4 Cs.-in-C. constituted the Allied Control Council in Berlin, which was to be competent in all 'matters affecting Germany as a whole'. The territory of Greater Berlin, divided into 4 sectors, was to be governed as an entity by the 4 occupying powers.

At the Potsdam Conference (17 July–2 Aug. 1945) the northern part of the Province of East Prussia, including its capital Königsberg (renamed Kaliningrad), was transferred to the Soviet Union, pending final ratification by a peace treaty; and it was agreed that, pending the final peace settlement, Poland should administer those parts of Germany lying east of a line running from the Baltic Sea immediately west of Swinemünde along the river Oder to its confluence with the Western Neisse and thence along the Western Neisse to the Czechoslovak frontier.

The agreements between the war-time allies concerning the occupation zones (12 Sept. 1944) and control of Germany (1 May 1945) were repudiated by the USSR on 27 Nov. 1958.

A Treaty was signed in East Berlin between the German Democratic Republic and the Federal Republic of Germany on 21 Dec. 1972 agreeing the basis of relations between the two countries.

GERMAN DEMOCRATIC REPUBLIC

Capital: Berlin (East)
Population: 16·74m. (1981)
GNP per capita: US$7,180 (1980)

Deutsche Demokratische Republik

HISTORY. For the immediate post-war history *see* p. 509.

AREA AND POPULATION. Area and population, 30 June 1980 (in 1,000):

Districts	*Area in sq. km*	*Population Male*	*Female*	*Total*	*Per sq. km*
Berlin (East)	403	527·9	617·9	1,145·7	2,843
Cottbus	8,262	421·6	461·0	882·6	107
Dresden	6,738	834·1	975·0	1,809·0	268
Erfurt	7,349	582·9	654·3	1,237·2	168
Frankfurt	7,186	338·9	365·6	704·5	98
Gera	4,004	347·1	393·2	740·3	185
Halle	8,771	864·3	973·2	1,837·5	210
Karl-Marx-Stadt	6,009	890·5	1,042·8	1,933·3	322
Leipzig	4,966	653·0	762·1	1,415·1	285
Magdeburg	11,525	596·6	673·1	1,269·8	110
Neubrandenburg	10,794	299·9	322·8	622·7	57
Potsdam	12,568	527·1	589·3	1,116·4	89
Rostock	7,074	424·2	461·5	885·7	125
Schwerin	8,672	279·8	309·6	589·4	68
Suhl	3,856	259·0	289·1	548·1	142
German Democratic Republic	*108,177*	*7,846·8*	*8,890·4*	*16,737·2*	*154*

An agreement proclaiming the Oder–Neisse line the permanent frontier between Germany and Poland was concluded between the German Democratic Republic and Poland on 6 July 1950. A protocol on the delimitation of the frontier was signed on 27 Jan. 1951.

Resident population of the principal towns as at 30 June 1980:

Berlin (East), capital	1,145,743	Halle	232,217	Zwickau	122,592
Leipzig	563,388	Rostock	230,280	Schwerin	119,961
Dresden	516,284	Erfurt	210,687	Cottbus	111,502
Karl-Marx-Stadt	316,937	Potsdam	129,648	Jena	103,263
Magdeburg	288,725	Gera	124,146	Dessau	101,969

Vital statistics:

	Live births	*Marriages*	*Divorces*	*Deaths*
1977	223,152	147,402	43,137	226,233
1978	232,151	141,063	43,296	232,332
1979	235,233	136,884	44,735	232,805
1980 [1]	245,132	134,195	44,778	238,265

[1] Preliminary.

Crude birth rate per 1,000 population was 10·8 in 1975; 11·6 in 1976; 13·3 in 1977; 13·9 in 1978; 14 in 1979; 14·6 in 1980; marriage rate, 8·4 in 1975; 8·6 in 1976; 8·8 in 1977; 8·4 in 1978; 8·2 in 1979; 8 in 1980; death rate, 14·3 in 1975; 13·9 in 1976; 13·5 in 1977; 13·9 in 1978; 13·9 in 1979; 14·2 in 1980; infantile mortality per 100 live births, 1·6 in 1975; 1·4 in 1976; 1·3 in 1977, 1978 and 1979; 1·2 in 1980.

CLIMATE. The continental-type climate makes winters crisp and clear, but with cold easterly winds bringing very low temperatures and appreciable snowfall. Summers are hot, but with much convectional rainfall.

Berlin, Jan. 31°F (–0·5°C), July 66°F (19°C). Annual rainfall 22·5″ (563 mm). Dresden, Jan. 30°F (–1°C), July 65°F (18·5°C). Annual rainfall 27·2″ (680 mm).

CONSTITUTION AND GOVERNMENT. Upon the establishment of the Federal Republic of Germany, the People's Council of the Soviet-occupied zone, appointed in 1948, was converted into a provisional People's Chamber.

On 7 Oct. 1949 the provisional People's Chamber enacted a constitution of the 'German Democratic Republic'.

In July 1952 the 5 Länder of Mecklenburg, Saxony-Anhalt, Brandenburg, Saxony and Thuringia were replaced by 14 districts *(Bezirke)*.

A new 'socialist constitution' was approved by a referendum on 6 April 1968, when 94·54% of the electorate voted for the constitution; it came into force on 8 April 1968. The People's Chamber, of 500 deputies, is 'the supreme organ of state power'; it elects the Council of State, the Council of Ministers, the National Defence Council and the judges of the Supreme Court.

Council of State. After the death of President Wilhelm Pieck (7 Sept. 1960), the People's Chamber on 12 Sept. 1960 abolished the office of president and elected instead a council of state. This consists of a chairman, 6 deputy chairmen, 18 members and a secretary. The Council is authorized to issue decisions and to interpret existing laws. The Chairman of the Council of State represents the GDR in international law. *Chairman:* Erich Honecker.

On 13 Oct. 1978 the People's Chamber passed a 'law for the defence of the GDR'; the People's Chamber is authorized to declare a 'state of defence'.

At the elections held on 16 Oct. 1976, the list of the National Front parties and democratic organizations of the GDR received 99·86% of the valid votes.

The cabinet was, in March 1983, composed as follows:

Chairman: Willi Stoph.

First Deputy Chairmen: Alfred Neumann, Werner Krolikowski.

Deputy Chairmen: Günther Kleiber, Wolfgang Rauchfuss, Gerhard Schürer, Dr Gerhard Weiss, Dr Herbert Weiz, Manfred Flegel, Hans-Joachin Heusinger, Dr Hans Reichelt, Rudolph Schulze.

Members of the Presidium of the Council of Ministers: All members of the cabinet and Heinz Kuhrig, Walter Halbritter, Horst Sölle.

Considerable political power is exercised by the Politburo of the Socialist Unity Party (SUP).

National flag: Black, red, golden (horizontal); in the centre, on both sides, the coat of arms showing a hammer and compass with a wreath of grain entwined with a black, red and golden ribbon.

National hymn: Auferstanden aus Ruinen (words by Johannes R. Becher, tune by Hanns Eisler).

East Berlin ('Democratic Berlin') is the capital of the German Democratic Republic. *Head of the Administration (Magistrat):* Erhard Krack.

DEFENCE. On 18 Jan. 1956 the Diet passed laws for the establishment of a 'national people's army' and a defence ministry. A 12-member defence council, under the chairmanship of E. Honecker, General Secretary of the Central Committee, was set up on 10 Feb. 1960.

The 'law for the defence of the GDR', of 20 Sept. 1960, makes military service (in case of emergency) and civil defence compulsory for all citizens.

Conscription for men between 18 and 25 years was introduced on 24 Jan. 1962 (18 months' service in the army, 2 years in the navy and air force).

Twenty Soviet divisions of about 258,000 men with about 1,000 heavy tanks and 6,000 armoured vehicles are stationed in the German Democratic Republic, chiefly along the Polish border.

Army. The Army, set up on 1 March 1956, is organized in 2 army corps, including 2 armoured divisions and 4 motorized infantry divisions. Operationally these divisions are subordinate to the Soviet formations of the Warsaw Pact forces. They are armed with about 3,100 tanks (mostly Soviet T-54, T-55 and T-72), 216 self-propelled guns and ground-to-air 'Guideline' missiles. The Border Police was incorporated in the Army in Sept. 1961. Total army strength was (1983) 113,000 all ranks.

Police. The Police force *(Volkspolizei)* numbered 25,000 security and 46,500 border troops. There are also 450,000 militiamen organized in combat groups. The militia receive military instruction from the People's Police.

Navy. The 'People's Navy' includes 2 frigates, 5 corvettes, 15 missile boats, 50 torpedo boats, 8 patrol vessels, 50 coastal minesweepers, 3 intelligence ships, 16 coastguard boats, 12 tank landing ships, 10 oilers, 9 training ships, 4 supply ships, 5 survey vessels, 9 small survey craft, 13 buoy tenders, 3 diving vessels, 1 cable layer, 2 torpedo recovery craft, 3 icebreakers, 30 auxiliary ships and service craft and 13 tugs. Personnel in 1983 totalled 16,000 officers and men, including the GBK Coastal Frontier Guards *(Grenz Brigade Kuste).*

Air Force. The *ex*-'air-police', set up in Nov. 1950, had in 1982 a strength of about 38,000 officers and men and 300 combat aircraft. Two air defence divisions consist respectively of 2 and 4 regiments (each with 3 squadrons of 12 aircraft), plus a fighter training division, equipped with MiG-21 and a small number of MiG-23 supersonic day and all-weather interceptors. There is 1 squadron of MiG-21 reconnaissance fighters. Four ground attack squadrons have begun replacing MiG-17s with MiG-27s, and Mi-24 gunship helicopters have been delivered to Germany. Other units include a regiment of Mi-2, Mi-4 and Mi-8 helicopters, a regiment of An-2, Let L.410, Il-14, An-26 and Tu-134 transports and a Flight Training Division with Yak-18, Trener, L-29 Delfin, L-39 Albatros, MiG-15UTI and MiG-21U training aircraft. 'Guideline' and 'Goa' surface-to-air missile units are operational.

INTERNATIONAL RELATIONS

Membership. The German Democratic Republic is a member of UN and Comecon.

ECONOMY

Budget. The budget of the German Democratic Republic was as follows (in M 1m.) for calendar years:

	1975	*1976*	*1977*	*1978*	*1979*	*1980*
Revenue	114,662	117,588	124,543	132,612	140,633	160,652
Expenditure	114,160	117,128	124,103	132,103	140,223	160,283

Of the 1980 expenditures, 51,066m. was earmarked for health and social services, education and *Kultur*.

Currency. The circulating Reichsmark notes were in June 1948 exchanged for 'Deutsche Mark' (East), renamed 'Mark of the German Bank of Issue' (MDN) from 1 Aug. 1964 and further renamed 'the Mark of the GDR' (M) from 1967. The circulation of notes and coins at 31 Dec. 1980 was M 12,250m. Since 1 Nov. 1953 the M currency has been based on gold, the gold content of the M being fixed at 0·399902 gramme.

Banking. The most important banking institutions of the GDR are the Staatsbank der DDR Berlin, which is the bank of issue, and the Industrie- und Handelsbank der DDR. Savings, as at 31 Dec. 1980, totalled M 99,730m.

Weights and Measures. The metric system is in force.

ENERGY AND NATURAL RESOURCES

Electricity. Generation of electric power (in 1m. kwh.): 1950, 19,466; 1960,

40,305; 1970, 67,650; 1974, 80,286; 1975, 84,505; 1976, 89,150; 1977, 91,996; 1978, 95,963; 1979, 96,845; 1980, 98,808.

Minerals. In the production of lignite, the German Democratic Republic takes first place in world output. Rare metals, such as uranium, cobalt, bismuth, arsenic and antimony, are being exploited in the western Erzgebirge and eastern Thuringia.

The principal minerals raised are as follows (in 1,000 tonnes):

	1977	*1978*	*1979*	*1980*		*1977*	*1978*	*1979*	*1980*
Coal	349	85	256	258	Iron ore	63	70	...	...
Lignite	253,705	253,264	256,000	258,097	Potash	3,229	3,323	3,395	3,422

Agriculture. In 1980 the arable land was 4·76m. hectares; meadows and pastures, 1,235,300 hectares; forests, 2,954,700 hectares. Since 1945, the estates of Junkers, war criminals and leading Nazis have been sequestrated; 3·1m. hectares have been distributed among farmers. In 1980 there were 3,946 collective farms of 5m. hectares of land independently cultivated and 441,564 hectares of land given for co-operative cultivation and 469 state farms of 396,188 hectares.

The yield of the main crops in 1980 was as follows (in 1,000 tonnes): Potatoes, 9,214; sugar-beet, 7,034; barley, 3,979; wheat, 3,098; rye, 1,917; oats, 582.

Livestock (in 1,000) in 1981: Cattle, 5,722 (including 2,130 milch cows); pigs, 12,871; sheep, 2,038; goats, 24; horses, 70; poultry, 51,611.

Fisheries. Total catch (1980) 244,237 tonnes. Inland catch (1980) was 14,492 tonnes, of which 6,856 tonnes was carp.

INDUSTRY AND TRADE

Industry. Industry produced about 62% of the national income in 1980; the nationally owned and co-operative undertakings were responsible for 96·4% of the net product. The percentage of privately owned enterprises was 32·8 in 1950 and 2·4 in 1978.

There were, at 31 Dec. 1980, 5,031 industrial establishments with 3,153,359 employees.

Production of iron and steel (in 1,000 tonnes):

	1975	*1976*	*1977*	*1978*	*1979*	*1980*
Crude steel	6,472	6,732	6,850	6,976	7,023	7,308
Pig-iron	2,455	2,528	2,628	2,560	...	...
Rolled steel	4,281	4,593	4,802	5,002	5,100	5,128

Leading chemical products in 1980 were (in 1,000 tonnes): Sulphuric acid, 958; nitrogen fertilizers, 943; calcined soda, 866; caustic soda, 626; other industrial products: cement, 12,440; passenger cars (no.), 176,761; television receivers (no.), 578,000; shoes, 79m. pairs; plastics and synthetic resins, 861.

The 340-km pipeline from Schwedt on the Oder to Leuna near Halle was completed in Jan. 1967; it carried Soviet oil direct to the industrial centre of the GDR. Total pipeline length within GDR (1980) 1,301 km.

Commerce. Total trade was as follows (in 1m. Valuta-Mark):

	Total Imports	*Total Exports*		*Total Imports*	*Total Exports*
1970	39,597	15,485	1977	91,726	32,456
1975	74,394	26,539	1978	96,879	34,907
1976	85,457	27,785			

Total trade between the German Democratic Republic and UK (British Department of Trade returns, in £1,000 sterling):

	1977	*1978*	*1979*	*1980*	*1981*	*1982*
Imports to UK	95,446	88,392	111,705	88,127	93,507	133,921
Exports and re-exports from UK	54,440	47,466	58,162	94,124	82,975	63,665

COMMUNICATIONS

Roads. There were, in 1980, 45,475 km of classified roads. Road traffic amounted to 21,020m. ton-km of goods and 21,390m. passenger-km (by buses). Motor vehicles included, 2,677,703 passenger cars, 234,148 lorries and 1·3m. motor cycles.

Railways. There were, in 1980, 14,221 km of railway line, of which 1,680 km were electrified. Traffic amounted to 56,395m. ton-km of goods and 23,142m. passenger-km.

Aviation. Interflug operates services between Berlin and Prague, Warsaw, Budapest, Bucharest, Moscow, Sofia, Belgrade, Tirana, Cairo, Baghdad, Beirut and other capitals. Passengers carried (1980), 1,216,300; freight, 27,671 tonnes.

Shipping. The port of Rostock is being reconstructed and enlarged so as to absorb the sea-going traffic of the German Democratic Republic and the Czechoslovak hinterland. In 1980 navigable inland waterways had a length of 2,302 km; they handled 2,159m. ton-km of goods. The state-owned merchant fleet had, in 1980, 192 vessels of 1,305,084 BRT.

Post and Broadcasting. In 1978 there were 11,999 post offices and agencies and (1981) 3,156,661 telephone subscribers. *Staatliches Kommittee für Rundfunk*, the governmental broadcasting station, broadcasts 4 programmes on long-, medium- and short-waves, and on FM. The foreign service is broadcast in 11 languages on medium-and short-waves, using the name Radio Berlin International. The transmitters are located at Königswusterhausen, Leipzig and Nauen. Radio Volga transmits on long-waves from Burg and broadcasts in Russian for the Soviet Armed Forces in Germany. More than 80% of the programmes are relays from Radio Moscow. Radio Moscow is using relay transmitters on medium-waves at Leipzig for programmes in German. *Deutsche Freiheitssender 904* and *Deutsche Soldatensender* are clandestine stations claiming to be operating from the Federal Republic although they are located not far from Burg. *Fernsehen der DDR* broadcasts 2 TV programmes, of which the second broadcasts in colour, using SECAM-system. Number of wireless licences (1980), 6·41m.; TV licences, 5·73m.

Cinemas (1980). There were 826 cinemas with a seating capacity of 267,949.

Newspapers (1978). There were 39 daily newspapers with a combined circulation of 7·1m.

RELIGION, EDUCATION AND WELFARE

Religion. According to the census of 1950, 80·5% of the population were Protestants and 11% were Roman Catholics.

Education. There are 2 types of schools: *(a)* the General polytechnical secondary schools, with 10 grades (the former elementary and middle schools), numbering (1980) 5,106 with 2,203,991 pupils; *(b)* the Extended polytechnical secondary schools, with the 11th and 12th grades, numbering (1980) 282 with 46,927 pupils.

In addition there were (1980), 977 vocational schools *(Berufsschulen)* with (1979) 16,259 teachers and 459,500 pupils and 237 technical schools with 171,825 pupils. There were also 53 universities and other high schools with 129,970 students, including 63,266 women.

Health. In 1980, 559 (1978) hospitals had 171,895 beds. There were 561 polyclinics each with at least 6 special branches. There were 33,894 physicians and 9,709 dentists.

Social Welfare. Expenditure for social welfare in state budget, M 3,394m., and social insurance, M 29,410m. in 1980.

DIPLOMATIC REPRESENTATIVES

Of the German Democratic Republic in Great Britain (124 The Broadway, London, NW9 7BS)
Ambassador: Martin Bierbach.

Of Great Britain in the German Democratic Republic (108 Berlin, Unter den Linden 32/34)
Ambassador: P. M. Maxey, CMG.

Of the German Democratic Republic in the USA (1717 Massachusetts Ave., NW, Washington, D.C. 20036)
Ambassador: Dr Horst Grunert.

Of the USA in the German Democratic Republic (108 Berlin, Neustädtische Kirchstrasse 4-5)
Chargé d'Affaires: Walter B. Smith, II.

Of the German Democratic Republic to the United Nations
Ambassador: Harry Ott.

Books of Reference

Statistical Information: The central statistical agency is the Staatliche Zentralverwaltung für Statistik (Hans-Beimler-Str. 70–72, 102, Berlin).

The Zentralverwaltung publishes: *Statistisches Jahrbuch der Deutschen Demokratischen Republik* (from 1956).—*Statistisches Taschenbuch der DDR* (annual, from 1959; also Arabic, English, French, Russian, Spanish editions).—*Statistische Praxis* (from 1946).

Deutsche Demokratische Republik, Handbuch. Leipzig, 1979

Jahrbuch der Deutschen Demokratischen Republik, ed. Institut für Zeitgeschichte (latest issue, 1961).

Biermann, W., *Demokratisierung in der DDR?* Cologne, 1978
Childs, D., *East Germany.* London, 1969
Heitzer, H., *GDR: An Historical Outline.* Dresden, 1981
Jacobsen, H.-A., *Drei Jahrzehnte Aussenpolitik der DDR.* Munich, 1979
Krisch, H., *German Politics under Soviet Occupation.* New York and London, 1974
Legters, L. H., *The German Democratic Republic: A Developed Socialist Society.* Boulder, 1978

National Library: Deutsche Bücherei, Leipzig C.1. *Director:* Helmut Rötzsch.—Deutsche Staatsbibliothek, Berlin. *Director:* Professor H. Kunze.

FEDERAL REPUBLIC OF GERMANY

Capital: Bonn
Population: 61·7m. (1981)
GNP per capita: US$13,590 (1980)

Bundesrepublik Deutschland

HISTORY. The Federal Republic of Germany became a sovereign independent country on 5 May 1955 and is a member of EEC, the Council of Europe, Western European Union, NATO, the European Coal and Steel Community, Euratom, the European Monetary Agreement and the Agencies of the UN.

In June 1948 USA, UK and France agreed on a central government for the 3 western zones. An Occupation Statute, which came into force on 30 Sept. 1949, reduced the responsibilities of the occupation authorities. Formally, the Federal Republic of Germany came into existence on 21 Sept. 1949. The Petersberg Agreement of 22 Nov. 1949 freed the Federal Republic of numerous restrictions of the Occupation Statute. In 1951 USA, UK and France as well as other states terminated the state of war with Germany; the Soviet Union followed on 25 Jan. 1955. On 5 May 1955 the High Commissioners of USA, UK and France signed a proclamation revoking the Occupation Statute. On the same day, the Paris and London treaties, signed in Oct. 1954, came into force and established the sovereignty of the Federal Republic of Germany.

AREA AND POPULATION. In April 1949 some minor frontier rectifications were carried out in favour of the Netherlands (68 sq. km), Belgium (18 sq. km), Luxembourg (6 sq. km) and France (7 sq. km), subject to a final peace settlement. Belgium (1956) and the Netherlands (1963) returned most of this territory to Germany.

Area and estimated population as at 30 June 1981:

Länder	*Area in sq. km*	*Population* *Male*	*Female*	*Total*	*Per sq. km*
Schleswig-Holstein	15,720	1,260,800	1,355,000	2,615,700	166
Hamburg	755	765,900	874,100	1,640,000	2,143
Lower Saxony	47,424	3,483,300	3,777,400	7,260,700	153
Bremen	404	325,900	366,100	692,000	1,712
North Rhine-Westphalia	34,065	8,153,100	8,890,600	17,043,600	500
Hessen	21,114	2,694,500	2,908,400	5,602,900	265
Rhineland-Palatinate	19,848	1,740,800	1,900,500	3,641,300	183
Baden-Württemberg	35,752	4,472,500	4,802,600	9,275,000	259
Bavaria	70,546	5,235,900	5,703,900	10,939,800	155
Saarland	2,570	504,700	559,700	1,064,400	414
Berlin (West)	480	855,100	1,035,200	1,890,300	3,937
Federal Republic	*248,678* [1]	*29,492,300*	*32,173,500*	*61,665,800*	*248*

[1] 96,005 sq. miles.

Vital statistics for calendar years:

	Marriages	*Live births*	*Of these illegitimate*	*Deaths*	*Divorces*
1978	328,215	576,468	40,141	723,218	32,462 [1]
1979	344,823	581,984	41,504	711,732	...
1980	362,408	620,657	46,923	714,117	...
1981	359,360	624,557	49,363	722,192	...

[1] From 1 July 1977, pursuant to the First Law on the Reform of Marriage and Family 1976.

The annual rate of the population increase or decrease (including migration) was –0·2% in 1974; –0·6% in 1975; –0·3% in 1976; –0·2% in 1977; –0·1% in 1978; +0·2% in 1979.

Crude birth rate in 1980 was 10·1 per 1,000 population; marriage rate, 5·9; death rate, 11·6; infantile mortality (1979), 1·5 per 100 live births.

Migrants from Eastern Germany to the Federal Republic, including West Berlin, totalled about 2,022,000 between 1955 and 1961. The East German Government tried to stop the outflow by erecting a concrete wall which later became a heavily fortified barrier along the border in Berlin on 13 Aug. 1961; despite the Berlin wall, the figures registered for persons moving from Eastern Germany and East Berlin into the Federal Republic were 20,700 in 1970, 19,900 in 1971, 19,700 in 1972, 17,300 in 1973, 16,200 in 1974, 20,300 in 1975, 17,100 in 1976, 13,900 in 1977, 14,400 in 1978 and 15,400 in 1979; most of them are older people with permission to emigrate. Migrants from the Federal Republic to Eastern Germany totalled about 279,000 between 1955 and 1961, 2,500 in 1969, 2,100 in 1970, 1,900 in 1971, 1,800 in 1972, 1,700 in 1973, 1,500 in 1974, 1,400 in 1975, 1,300 in 1976, 1,200 in 1977, 1,200 in 1978 and 1,300 in 1979.

The resident population of the principal towns was estimated as follows on 30 June 1981:

Town	*Land*	*Population*
Berlin (West)	Berlin (West)	1,890,300
Hamburg	Hamburg	1,640,000
München	Bavaria	1,294,000
Köln	N. Rhine-Westph.	972,900
Essen	N. Rhine-Westph.	645,000
Frankfurt am Main	Hessen	625,700
Dortmund	N. Rhine-Westph.	606,200
Düsseldorf	N. Rhine-Westph.	588,800
Stuttgart	Baden-Württ.	582,400
Duisburg	N. Rhine-Westph.	556,400
Bremen	Bremen	553,500
Hanover	Lower Saxony	531,100
Nürnberg	Bavaria	483,700
Bochum	N. Rhine-Westph.	399,200
Wuppertal	N. Rhine-Westph.	392,000
Bielefeld	N. Rhine-Westph.	312,000
Mannheim	Baden-Württ.	304,100
Gelsenkirchen	N. Rhine-Westph.	303,000
Bonn	N. Rhine-Westph.	289,400
Wiesbaden	Hessen	274,200
Karlsruhe	Baden-Württ.	271,100
Münster (Westf.)	N. Rhine-Westph.	269,900
Braunschweig	Lower Saxony	260,700
Mönchengladbach	N. Rhine-Westph.	258,300
Kiel	Schleswig-Holstein	249,800
Augsburg	Bavaria	248,000
Aachen	N. Rhine-Westph.	243,600
Oberhausen	N. Rhine-Westph.	228,600
Krefeld	N. Rhine-Westph.	224,100
Lübeck	Schleswig-Holstein	219,700
Hagen	N. Rhine-Westph.	218,000
Kassel	Hessen	195,000
Saarbrücken	Saarland	193,000
Mainz	Rhinel.-Pal.	187,300
Herne	N. Rhine-Westph.	181,700
Mülheim a.d. Ruhr	N. Rhine-Westph.	179,900
Freiburg im Breisgau	Baden-Württ.	175,800
Hamm	N. Rhine-Westph.	171,700
Solingen	N. Rhine-Westph.	165,200
Leverkusen	N. Rhine-Westph.	160,400
Ludwigshafen am Rhein	Rhinel.-Pal.	158,900
Osnabrück	Lower Saxony	157,300
Neuss	N. Rhine-Westph.	149,100
Bremerhaven	Bremen	138,500
Darmstadt	Hessen	138,000
Oldenburg	Lower Saxony	137,000
Heidelberg	Baden-Württ.	133,600
Regensburg	Bavaria	132,200
Göttingen	Lower Saxony	130,200
Würzburg	Bavaria	128,700
Remscheid	N. Rhine-Westph.	128,400
Wolfsburg	Lower Saxony	125,600
Recklinghausen	N. Rhine-Westph.	119,400
Bottrop	N. Rhine-Westph.	114,200
Koblenz	Rhinel.-Pal.	113,300
Salzgitter	Lower Saxony	113,300
Heilbronn	Baden-Württ.	111,900
Siegen	N. Rhine-Westph.	111,700
Offenbach am Main	Hessen	110,800
Paderborn	N. Rhine-Westph.	109,600
Pforzheim	Baden-Württ.	106,100
Witten	N. Rhine-Westph.	105,500
Hildesheim	Lower Saxony	102,400
Erlangen	Bavaria	102,200
Bergisch Gladbach	N. Rhine-Westph.	101,600
Ulm	Baden-Württ..	100,700

CLIMATE. Oceanic influences are only found in the north-west where winters are quite mild but stormy. Eleswhere a continental climate is general. To the east and south, winter temperatures are lower, with bright frosty weather and considerable snowfall. Summer temperatures are fairly uniform throughout. Rainfall is well distributed over the year, varying from 20″ (500 mm) on low ground to 80″ (2,000 mm) in Alpine parts.

CONSTITUTION. The Constituent Assembly (known as the 'Parliamentary Council') met in Bonn on 1 Sept. 1948, and worked out a Basic Law which was approved by a two-thirds majority of the parliaments of the participating Länder and came into force on 23 May 1949.

The Basic Law *(Grundgesetz)* consists of a preamble and 146 articles. The first section deals with the basic rights which are legally binding for legislation, administration and jurisdiction.

The Federal Republic of Germany is a democratic and social federal state. For the time being the Basic Law applies to the Länder Baden-Württemberg, Bavaria, Bremen, Greater Berlin (temporarily suspended), Hamburg, Hessen, Lower Saxony, North Rhine-Westphalia, Rhineland-Palatinate, Saarland and Schleswig-Holstein. The Basic Law decrees that the general rules of international law form part of the federal law. The constitutions of the Länder must conform to the principles of a republican, democratic and social state based on the rule of law. Executive power is vested in the Länder, unless the Basic Law prescribes or permits otherwise. Federal law supersedes Land law.

The organs of the Federal Republic are:

The Federal Diet *(Bundestag)*, elected in universal, direct, free, equal and secret elections, for a term of 4 years.

The Federal Council *(Bundesrat)*, consisting of members of the governments of the Länder. Each Land has at least 3 votes. Länder with more than 2m. inhabitants have 4, Länder with more than 6m. inhabitants have 5 votes.

The Federal President *(Bundespräsident)* is elected by the Federal Assembly for a term of 5 years and represents the Federal Republic in international relations. Re-election is admissible only once. The Federal Assembly (which meets only for the election of the Federal President) consists of the members of the Federal Diet and an equal number of members elected by the popular representative bodies of the Länder according to a particular system of semi-proportional representation.

The Federal Government consists of the Federal Chancellor, elected by the Federal Diet on the proposal of the Federal President, and the Federal Ministers, who are appointed and dismissed by the Federal President upon the proposal of the Federal Chancellor.

The Federal Republic has exclusive legislation on: (1) foreign affairs (2) federal citizenship; (3) freedom of movement, passports, immigration and emigration, and extradition; (4) currency, money and coinage, weights and measures, and regulation of time and calendar; (5) customs, commercial and navigation agreements, traffic in goods and payments with foreign countries, including customs and frontier protection; (6) federal railways and air traffic; (7) post and telecommunications; (8) the legal status of persons in the employment of the Federation and of public law corporations under direct supervision of the Federal Government; (9) trade marks, copyright and publishing rights; (10) co-operation of the Federal Republic and the Länder in the criminal police and in matters concerning the protection of the constitution, the establishment of a Federal Office of Criminal Police, as well as the combating of international crime; (11) federal statistics.

For concurrent legislation in which the Länder have legislative rights if and as far as the Federal Republic does not exercise its legislative powers, *see* THE STATESMAN'S YEAR-BOOK, 1956, p. 1038.

Federal laws are passed by the Federal Diet and after their adoption submitted to the Federal Council, which has a limited veto. The Basic Law may be amended only upon the approval of two-thirds of the members of the Federal Diet and two-thirds of the votes of the Federal Council.

The foreign service, federal finance, railways, postal services, waterways and shipping are under direct federal administration.

In the field of finance the Federal Republic has exclusive legislation on customs and financial monopolies and concurrent legislation on: (1) excise taxes and taxes on transactions, in particular, taxes on real-estate acquisition, incremented value and on fire protection; (2) taxes on income, property, inheritance and donations; (3) real estate, industrial and trade taxes, with the exception of the determining of the tax rates.

Customs, the yield of monopolies, excise taxes with the exception of the beer tax, the transportation tax, the turnover tax and property dues serving non-recurrent purposes accrue to the Federal Republic. The Federal Republic can, by federal law, claim part of the income and corporation taxes to cover its expenditures not covered by other revenues. Financial jurisdiction is uniformly regulated by federal legislation.

National flag: Three horizontal stripes of black, red, gold.

National anthem: Einigkeit und Recht und Freiheit (words by H. Hoffmann, 1841; tune by J. Haydn, 1797).

GOVERNMENT. The *Federal Diet*, elected in March 1983 was composed of 498 members. In addition, there are 22 members for Berlin who, however, have no vote.

State of the parties: Social Democrats (SPD), 193 (1980: 218); Christian Democrats (CDU), 191 (174); Free Democrats (FDP), 34 (53); Christian Socialists (CSU), 53 (52); *Die Grünen* 27 (–).

Bonn on the Rhine is the capital of the Federal Republic.

Federal President: Karl Castens (elected 1 July 1979, re-elected 29 March 1983).

The Cabinet, a coalition of Christian Democrats, Christian Socialists and Free Democrats, in March 1983, was as follows:

Chancellor: Dr Helmut Kohl (CDU).
Deputy Chancellor, Minister of Foreign Affairs: Hans-Dietrich Genscher (FDP).
Interior: Dr Friedrich Zimmermann (CSU).
Justice: Hans A. Engelhard (FDP).
Finance: Dr Gerhard Stoltenberg (CDU).
Economics: Dr Otto Count Lambsdorff (FDP).
Food, Agriculture and Forestry: Ignaz Kiechle (CSU).
Intra-German Relations: Heinrich Windelen (CDU).
Labour and Social Affairs: Dr Norbert Blüm (CDU).
Defence: Dr Manfred Wörner (CDU).
Youth, Family Affairs and Health: Dr Heiner Geissler (CDU).
Transport: Dr Werner Dollinger (CSU).
Posts and Telecommunications: Dr Christian Schwarz-Schilling (CDU).
Regional Planning, Building and Urban Development: Dr Oscar Schneider (CSU).
Research and Technology: Dr Heinz Riesenhuber (CDU).
Education and Science: Dr Dorothee Wilms (CDU).
Economic Co-operation: Dr Jürgen Warnke (CSU).

DEFENCE. The Paris Treaties, which entered into force in May 1955, stipulated a contribution of the Federal Republic to western defence within the framework of NATO and the Western European Union. In 1977 the Federal Armed Forces *(Bundeswehr)* had a total strength of 495,000 all ranks (229,000 conscripts).

Army. In 1982 the Army consisted of 16 armoured brigades, 12 armoured infantry brigades, 3 Jäger brigades, 2 mountain brigades, 3 airborne brigades; total strength 335,500, of which conscripts, 180,000.

The principal combat unit is still the Brigade, however, under the 'Brigade 80' concept the number of battalions per brigade goes up, although the number of men per battalion comes down. The armoured brigade has 3,026 men and the armoured infantry 3,730. The main emphasis of the concept is to improve the anti-armour capability and the brigades will have to look to the divisional troops for reconnaissance, artillery and air-defence support in points of main effort. The Army is at present converting to the 'Brigade 80' concept. There are 3 corps and 12 divisions, each of 3 brigades. The Army has 1,342 M-48A2 Patton and 2,437 Leopard I and 150 Leopard II medium tanks with a further 1,550 Leopard II tanks on order; 1,400 artillery pieces; 65 *Honest John* and 26 *Lance* surface to surface missiles.

Territorial Army. The Territorial Army lies outside the Authority of Supreme

Commander NATO, but is tasked with securing the freedom of manoeuvre of NATO forces under national command as well as protecting points of military relevance. There are 3 Territorial Commands and 6 Home Defence Groups. Peacetime strength, 38,000.

Navy. The Federal Navy comprises 24 diesel-powered coastal submarines, 7 destroyers, 9 frigates, 6 corvettes, 33 fast missile boats (Exocet armed), 10 fast torpedo boats, a light cruiser type training ship, 11 frigate-type support ships, 18 coastal minesweepers and minehunters, 22 fast minesweepers, 20 inshore minesweepers, 22 landing craft, 13 supply and support ships, 2 fleet replenishment ships, 7 oilers, 8 coast patrol boats, 13 torpedo recovery vessels, 9 coastguard cutters, 3 repair ships, 24 tugs and 70 auxiliaries and service craft.

The construction programme includes 3 guided missile frigates and 7 large patrol (missile) vessels. Two more guided missile frigates and 10 minehunters are projected under the new development programme.

The Naval Air Arm has 2 wings (each 2 squadrons of 18 aircraft) of F-104G Starfighters and 1 wing of Breguet Atlantic maritime patrol bombers, supplemented by an anti-submarine helicopter wing (Lynx for new frigates). The air-sea rescue wing has re-equipped with Sea King helicopters.

Navy personnel in 1983 totalled 4,500 officers and 31,200 men, including the Naval Air Arm.

Air Force. Since Oct. 1970, the *Luftwaffe* has comprised the following commands: German Air Force Tactical Command, German Air Force Support Command (including two German Air Force Regional Support Commands—North and South) and General Air Force Office. Its strength in 1982 was approximately 105,900 officers and other ranks and about 560 first-line combat aircraft. Combat units, including 12 heavy fighter-bomber squadrons, 7 light ground attack/ reconnaissance squadrons, 4 reconnaissance squadrons, 8 surface-to-surface missile squadrons, and an air defence force of 4 interceptor squadrons, 24 batteries of *Nike-Hercules* and 36 batteries of *Improved Hawk* surface-to-air missiles, are assigned to NATO. There are 4 F-4F Phantom interceptor squadrons, 8 F-104G fighter-bomber squadrons (re-equipping with Tornados), 4 attack squadrons of F-4Fs, 4 RF-4E Phantom reconnaissance squadrons, and 7 light attack/ reconnaissance squadrons of Alpha Jets.Four transport squadrons (each 15 aircraft) with turboprop Transall C-160 aircraft and 1 wing of 5 helicopter squadrons with UH-1D Iroquois add to the air mobility of the *Bundeswehr*. There are also VIP, support and light transport aircraft, and Piaggio P.149D initial training aircraft. Guided weapons in service include 8 squadrons of *Pershing* surface-to-surface missiles and 6 battalions of *Nike-Hercules* and 9 battalions of *Improved Hawk* surface-to-air missiles.

Pilots undergo basic and advanced training in USA.

INTERNATIONAL RELATIONS

Membership. The Federal Republic of Germany is a member of UN, OECD, EEC, NATO and the Council of Europe.

ECONOMY

Budget. The budget of the Federal Government shows the following figures (in DM 1m.) for calendar years:

	1976	*1977*	*1978*	*1979*
Revenues				
Federal taxes and customs duties	35,647	37,130	39,343	40,656
Share of Federal Government in joint taxes and trade tax levy	95,253	106,874	114,744	125,480
Tax-like charges	0	4	2	0
Others	5,727	9,063	5,746	11,380
Total revenue	136,627	149,755	163,152	177,515

	1976	*1977*	*1978*	*1979*
Expenditures				
Defence	33,300	34,206	36,675	38,594
Social security	59,085	62,119	67,102	69,509
Agriculture and food	1,919	1,923	2,071	2,167
Transport and communications	11,491	11,853	12,932	14,511
Electricity, gas, water supply, industries and services	3,148	3,765	5,428	5,519
Education and science	8,450	8,569	9,632	10,934
Housing and settlements	2,046	2,077	1,779	2,265
All other expenditure	43,075	47,872	53,457	59,859
Total expenditure	162,514	171,952	189,508	203,358
Balance of transitory means	+ 31	− 10	+ 43	− 210
Net financing balance	−25,856	−22,206	−26,313	−26,053
Financed from:				
Loans	−46,316	−36,755	−46,505	−54,542
Coinage	− 74	− 494	− 373	− 443
Less:				
Redemption payments	+20,533	+15,043	+20,565	+28,931
Withdrawals from reserves	—	—	—	—

The total debt of the Federal Government, the Equalization of Burdens Fund, ERP-Special Fund and the Länder was DM 322,344m., as at 31 Dec. 1979 (excluding debt of communities/local authorities).

Currency. On 31 Aug. 1980 the circulation of coins in the Federal Republic amounted to DM 7,225m.; that of notes and coins to DM 87,981m. In March 1983, £1=3·56 DM; US$1=2·42.

Banking. On 14 Feb. 1948 the Bank of German Länder (Bank deutscher Länder) was established in Frankfurt as the central bank of issue for the Federal Republic and designated the exclusive agency for issuing notes and coins.

The Land Central Banks and the Berlin Central Bank were merged with the Bank deutscher Länder as from 1 Aug. 1957. The Bank deutscher Länder became the Deutsche Bundesbank.

The most important items of the balance sheets of the Deutsche Bundesbank in Frankfurt on 31 Aug. 1980 were as follows (in DM 1m.):

Assets	
Gold	13,688·0
Balances at foreign banks and money market investments abroad	42,886·3
Foreign notes, coins, bills and cheques	3,657·1
Loans to international institutions and consolidation loans	4,035·0
Domestic bills of exchange and advances against securities	37,233·1
Equalization claims [1]	8,136·4
Liabilities	
Bank-notes in circulation	80,755·4
Deposits	61,964·7

[1] From the monetary reform.

Weights and Measures. The metric system is in force.

ENERGY AND NATURAL RESOURCES

Electricity. In 1980, 368,770m. kwh. were produced.

Oil. In 1979, 67,445 tonnes of petroleum and 12,097,009 tonnes of diesel oil were produced.

Minerals. The great bulk of the minerals in Germany is produced in North Rhine-Westphalia (for coal, iron and metal smelting-works), Central Germany (for brown coal), Lower Saxony (Salzgitter for iron ore; the Harz for metal ore). The chief oil-fields are in Lower Saxony (Emsland).

The quantities of the principal minerals raised in the Federal Republic were as follows (in 1,000 tonnes):

Minerals	*1976*	*1977*	*1978*	*1979*	*1980*	*1981*
Coal	89,269	84,513	83,936	86,319	87,146	88,460
Lignite	134,535	122,920	123,559	130,579	129,833	130,619
Iron ore	3,034	2,868	1,608	1,655	1,945	1,594
Metal ore	1,034	1,031	762	...	...	...
Potash	21,178	23,799	25,260	27,674	29,317	28,192
Crude oil	5,524	5,401	5,059	4,774	4,631	4,459

The production of iron and steel in the Federal Republic was (in 1,000 tonnes):

	1976	*1977*	*1978*	*1979*	*1980*	*1981*
Pig-iron	31,849	28,959	30,148	35,167	33,873	31,876
Steel ingots and castings	42,415	38,985	41,253	46,040	43,838	41,610
Rolled products finished	30,398	29,411	31,102	33,616	...	...

Agriculture. In 1979 the agricultural holdings with a farm area of 1 hectare or more in the Federal Republic of Germany cultivated an agricultural area of 12·3m. hectares, of which the arable land was 7,290,400 hectares; meadows and pastures 4,796,700 hectares; vineyards, orchards, nurseries 226,400.

The total number of agricultural holdings in the Federal Republic, and their classification by size, according to the agricultural area, were as follows (1979):

	Total	*Under 1 hectare*	*1–5 hectares*	*5–20 hectares*	*20–100 hectares*	*Over 100 hectares*
Schleswig-Holstein	35,509	2,249	6,072	6,610	19,535	1,043
Hamburg	2,296	850	880	324	231	11
Lower Saxony	129,962	5,427	33,085	38,735	51,202	1,513
Bremen	610	114	163	115	215	3
North Rhine-Westphalia	107,151	4,918	32,290	38,030	31,383	530
Hessen	66,943	1,999	25,667	25,859	13,223	195
Rhineland-Palatinate	74,792	10,679	26,162	25,662	12,187	102
Baden-Württemberg	152,265	10,264	59,665	59,930	22,131	275
Bavaria	274,273	5,381	72,850	142,468	53,005	569
Saarland	5,690	375	2,382	1,611	1,294	28
Berlin (West)	283	136	88	31	28	—
Federal Republic	*849,774*	*42,392*	*259,304*	*339,375*	*204,434*	*4,269*

Area (in 1,000 hectares) and yield (in 1,000 tonnes) of the main crops in the Federal Republic, were as follows:

	Area				*Yield*			
	1978	*1979*	*1980*	*1981*	*1978*	*1979*	*1980*	*1981*
Wheat	1,619	1,627	1,668	1,631	8,118	8,061	8,156	8,313
Rye	651	564	546	484	2,457	2,114	2,098	1,729
Barley	1,951	1,989	2,001	2,044	8,608	8,184	8,826	8,687
Oats	749	728	691	682	3,202	2,994	2,658	2,678
Potatoes	355	276	258	246	10,510	8,716	6,694	7,585
Sugar-beet	402	393	395	444	18,777	18,340	19,122	24,380

Wine must production (in 1m. hectolitres): 7·4 in 1960; 9·9 in 1970; 10·7 in 1973; 6·8 in 1974; 9·2 in 1975; 8·7 in 1976; 10·4 in 1977; 7·3 in 1978; 8·2 in 1979; 4·6 in 1980; 7·2 in 1981.

Livestock on 3 Dec. 1981 were as follows: Cattle, 14,992,100 (including 5,437,900 milch cows); horses, 363,600; sheep, 1,108,000; pigs, 22,310,300; goats, 36,000; poultry, 77,743,200.

Forestry. Forestry is an industry of great importance, conducted under the care of the State on scientific methods. The forest area is 7·2m. hectares. In 1979 cuttings amounted to 27·3m. cu. metres in the Federal Republic.

Fisheries. In 1981 the yield of sea and coastal fishing in the Federal Republic was 300,345 tonnes live weight, valued at DM 343m.

At the end of 1981 the number of vessels of the fishing fleet was 32 trawlers (70,490 gross tons), 2 luggers and 646 cutters.

INDUSTRY AND TRADE

Industry. In 1979, 49,176 establishments (with 20 and more employees; production industries including handicrafts) in the Federal Republic employed 7,607,239 persons; of these 1,011,981 were employed in machine construction; 310,571 in textile industry; 969,444 in electrical engineering; 228,954 in mining; 559,729 in chemical industry (average of 12 months).

The production of important industrial products in the Federal Republic was as follows:

Products	*1977*	*1978*	*1979*	*1980*	*1981*
Aluminium (1,000 tonnes)	742	740	742	731	729
Potassium fertilizers, K_2O (1,000 tonnes)	2,341	2,470	2,616	2,737	2,592
Sulphuric acid, SO_3 (1,000 tonnes) [1]	3,819	3,813	4,136	3,900	3,945
Soda, Na_2CO_3 (1,000 tonnes) [1]	1,351	1,230	1,401	1,411	1,189
Cement (1,000 tonnes) [1]	32,163	34,000	35,659	34,551	31,498
Rayon:					
Staple fibre (1,000 tonnes)	68	73	76	73	149
Continuous rayon filament (1,000 tonnes) [1]	66	62	62	70	
Cotton yarn (1,000 tonnes) [1]	178	164	161	170	148
Woollen yarn (1,000 tonnes) [1]	54	53	56	60	52
Passenger cars (1,000) [2]	3,796	3,901	3,943	3,530	3,590
Commercial cars and buses (1,000)	294	282	297	...	...
Bicycles (1,000)	3,028	2,923	3,099	3,643	3,441

[1] Including the quantities processed in the same factories. [2] Including dual-purpose vehicles.

Labour. The economically active persons (excluding the armed forces) totalled 25·81m. at the 1%-sample survey of the microcensus of April 1979. Of the total, 2,339,000 were self-employed, 943,000 unpaid family workers and 22·53m. dependently employed persons. 1,441,000 were engaged in agriculture and forestry; 11,872,000 in production industries; 4,682,000 in commerce and transport; 7,817,000 in other industries; 852,000 were unemployed.

In June 1979 foreign workers numbered 1,933,651, including 540,471 Turks, 367,301 Yugoslavs, 300,442 Italians, 140,139 Greeks, 89,992 Spaniards and 495,306 others.

Trade Unions. The main trade union organization is the German Trade Union Federation *(Deutscher Gewerkschaftsbund)* with 7,751,523 members at 31 Dec. 1978 in 17 unions, the largest being *I.G.Metall* (with 2,680,798 members), *Gewerkschaft Öffentliche Dienste, Transport und Verkehr* (1,099,396 members), *I.G.Chemie-Papier-Keramik* (650,675 members), *I.G.Bau-Steine-Erden* (517,842 members), *Deutsche Postgewerkschaft* (428,878 members) and *Gewerkschaft der Eisenbahner Deutschlands* (414,195 members); they are organized in industrial branches such that only one union operates within each enterprise. Outside the DGB lie several smaller unions, the principal being the *Deutscher Beamtenbund* (DBB) or civil servants union with about 800,000 members and the *Deutsche Angestellten-Gewerkschaft* (DAG) or union of salaried staff with about 480,000 members. There is also a smaller Christian Trade Union movement with about 250,000 members.

Commerce. The distribution of the imports and exports of the Federal Republic according to principal countries was as follows (in DM 1m.):

	Imports			*Exports*		
Country	*1979*	*1980*	*1981*	*1979*	*1980*	*1981*
Argentina	1,442·4	1,289·5	1,125·8	1,623·4	2,285·3	2,360·6
Australia	1,288·7	1,298·1	1,405·6	1,987·3	2,092·5	2,703·9
Austria	8,403·9	9,825·4	10,279·3	16,461·2	19,257·4	20,009·7
Belgium–Luxembourg	23,402·2	24,461·6	24,674·8	26,753·7	27,481·7	28,907·0
Brazil	2,531·4	2,908·7	3,449·4	2,379·2	2,798·6	2,277·1
Canada	3,104·0	3,603·4	3,278·3	2,326·4	2,178·3	2,740·6
Denmark	4,641·4	5,735·2	5,926·9	6,837·1	6,668·4	7,525·8
Finland	2,476·1	2,953·9	3,363·8	2,514·3	3,309·4	3,697·1
France	33,195·2	36,591·0	40,123·8	39,992·1	46,614·8	51,909·9
Greece	2,396·8	2,754·2	2,946·5	3,765·2	3,774·2	4,653·0
India	1,002·0	1,134·8	1,278·6	1,284·8	1,372·2	2,249·4
Iran	4,225·3	3,381·9	1,527·0	2,349·2	2,734·4	3,639·5
Italy	25,803·9	27,083·4	27,562·0	24,534·1	29,935·9	31,306·5
Japan	7,912·1	10,434·3	12,910·0	4,150·8	3,960·0	4,758·7
Libya	5,540·5	7,865·8	7,417·1	2,159·6	2,282·5	3,379·9
Netherlands	35,841·8	39,147·5	44,322·9	31,297·7	33,273·3	33,884·0
Norway	5,332·0	7,737·8	9,418·1	3,305·0	4,016·4	4,950·3
Rep. of South Africa	3,641·5	3,262·5	3,184·0	3,136·2	4,595·0	6,160·5
Spain	3,840·0	4,410·8	4,662·4	4,457·5	5,068·2	6,283·9
Sweden	6,152·9	7,223·9	7,681·5	9,118·9	10,127·4	10,426·7
Switzerland	10,637·1	12,139·)	12,615·2	16,398·4	20,007·2	20,727·8
USSR	7,381·2	7,517·4	9,224·8	6,623·7	7,943·2	7,621·4
UK	17,215·9	22,859·7	27,502·2	21,033·6	22,917·3	26,162·9
USA	20,274·4	25,689·9	28,387·5	20,759·3	21,477·6	25,975·9

The main items of imports in 1979 were finished manufactures (US$61,963m.) and raw materials (US$23,383m.); exports, finished manufactures (US$112,875m.) and semi-finished manufactures (US$32,059m.).

Total trade between the Federal Republic of Germany and UK (British Department of Trade returns, in £1,000 sterling):

	1978	*1979*	*1980*	*1981*	*1982*
Imports to UK	4,512,838	5,799,403	5,700,861	5,941,130	7,414,073
Exports and re-exports from UK	3,104,901	4,243,975	5,113,032	5,515,965	5,414,733

Tourism. In 1979, 10·3m. arrivals and 24·7m. 'overnights' of foreign visitors were registered. Foreign exchange receipts from international tourism amounted to DM 10,524m.

COMMUNICATIONS

Roads. On 1 Jan. 1981 the total length of classified roads in the Federal Republic was 172,392 km, including 7,538 km autobahn, 32,558 km federal highways, 65,637 km first-class and 66,659 km second-class country roads. Motor vehicles licensed in the Federal Republic on 1 July 1979 numbered 26,109,079 (including 479,100 motor cycles, 22,535,469 passenger cars, 1,236,120 trucks, 68,360 buses and 1,624,713 tractors; not including 186,814 motor cycles and motor vehicles up to 50 cm^3 cylinder capacity and 2,014,129 mopeds).

Road casualties in 1979 totalled 486,441 injured and 13,222 killed.

Railways. Length of Federal Railway in 1981 was 28,335 km (1,435 mm gauge) of which 11,179 km was electrified. In 1980 it carried 69,895m. tonne-km and 47,690m. passenger-km. There are also some 3,000 km of privately-owned and other minor railways.

Aviation. The Deutsche Lufthansa AG (set up on 6 Jan. 1953, as AG für Luftverkehrsbedarf and renamed on 6 Aug. 1954), with headquarters at Cologne, has capital of DM 900m. The Federal Republic owns 74·3%, Land North Rhine-Westphalia 2·2%, the Federal Railways, 0·9%, Federal Post 1·8%, Kreditanstalt für Wiederaufbau 3% and private industry 17·8%.

Lufthansa operate internal, European, African, North and South Atlantic, Near and Far East routes. In 1979 the Lufthansa carried 13·7m. passengers, 399,327 tonnes of cargo and 47,730 tonnes of mail.

Shipping. On 31 Dec. 1979 the Federal German mercantile marine comprised 1,732 ocean-going vessels of 7,877,100 BRT.

The inland-waterways fleet in the Federal Republic on 31 Dec. 1979 comprised 3·79m. tons. The length of the navigable rivers and canals in use was 4,329 km.

Sea-going ships (foreign trade only) in 1979 loaded 36m. tonnes clearing and unloaded 121m. tonnes entering in the ports of the Federal Republic. Inland waterways carried 246m. tonnes in 1979.

Post and Broadcasting. The Federal Republic had, on 31 Dec. 1980, 18,688 post and telecommunications offices. Number of telephones, 28,554,000.

The postal bus services covered, in 1979, 187m. km and carried 331m. passengers.

The post office savings banks had, on 31 Dec. 1980, 18,966,000 depositors with DM 28,359m. to their credit.

In the financial year 1978 the postal revenues amounted to DM 35,501m. and the expenditure to DM 33,406m.

Arbeitsgemeinschaft der öffentlich-rechtlichen Rundfunkanstalten der Bundesrepublik Deutschland (ARD) is an organization for co-operation between the German broadcasting stations. ARD also broadcast a common TV programme under the name *Deutsches Fernsehen* throughout the Federal Republic. In addition regional programmes are broadcast. Number of wireless licences, 21,151,540; of television licences, 19,421,539 (1979).

Cinemas (31 Dec. 1977). There were 2,698 cinemas with a seating capacity of 800,000 and 12 drive-in cinemas for 9,978 cars.

Newspapers (1977). There were 372 daily newspapers with a combined circulation of 24m.

JUSTICE, RELIGION, EDUCATION AND WELFARE

Justice. Justice is administered by the federal courts and by the courts of the Länder. In criminal procedures, civil cases and procedures of non-contentious jurisdiction the courts on the Land level are the local courts *(Amtsgerichte)*, the regional courts *(Landgerichte)* and the courts of appeal *(Oberlandesgerichte)*. On the federal level decisions regarding these matters are taken by the Federal Court *(Bundesgerichtshof)* at Karlsruhe. In labour law disputes the courts of the first and second instance are the labour courts and the Land labour courts and in the third instance, the Federal Labour Court *(Bundesarbeitsgericht)* at Kassel. Disputes about public law in matters of social security, unemployment insurance, maintenance of war victims and similar cases are dealt with in the first and second instances by the social courts and the Land social courts and in the third instance by the Federal Social Court *(Bundessozialgericht)* at Kassel. In most tax matters the finance courts of the Länder are competent and in the second instance, the Federal Finance Court *(Bundesfinanzhof)* at Munich. Other controversies of public law in non-constitutional matters are decided in the first and second instance by the administrative and the higher administrative courts *(Observerwaltungsgerichte)* of the Länder, and in the third instance by the Federal Administrative Court *(Bundesverwaltungsgericht)* at Berlin.

For the inquiry into maritime accidents the admiralty courts *(Seeämter)* are competent on the Land level and in the second instance the Federal Admiralty Court *(Bundesoberseeamt)* at Hamburg.

The constitutional courts of the Länder decide on constitutional questions. The Federal Constitutional Court *(Bundesverfassungsgericht)* as the supreme German court decides such questions as loss of basic rights, unconstitutional character of political parties, validity of laws, charges against judges and complaints regarding violations of basic rights by the public force.

The death sentence is abolished.

Religion. Of the population 49% are Protestants, 44·6% Roman Catholics and 0·1% Jews (census, 1970).

The Evangelical Church in Germany consists of 18 member-churches in the Federal Republic of Germany and West Berlin (7 Lutheran Churches, 8 United-Lutheran-Reformed-Churches, 2 Reformed Churches and 1 Confederation of United member Churches: 'Church of the Union'). Its organs are the Synod, the Church Conference and the Council under the chairmanship of Bishop Dr Eduard Lohse (Hanover). The Protestants numbered about 26·5m. in 1978. There are also some 12 Evangelical Free Churches. The 8 territorial churches in German Democratic Republic established the Federation of Evangelical Churches in 1969.

There are 5 Catholic archbishops and 17 bishoprics. Chairman of the German Bishops' Conference is Cardinal Höffner, Archbishop of Cologne. A concordat between Germany and the Holy See was signed on 20 July and ratified on 10 Sept. 1933.

The 'Old Catholics', who are in full communion with the Anglican Churches, numbered about 30,000 in 1977; they have a bishop at Bonn.

Evangelische Kirche in Deutschland. Hanover, 1979
Taschenbuch der evangelischen Kirche in Deutschland. Frankfurt, 1980
Kirchliches Handbuch. Amtliches statistisches Jahrbuch der Katholischen Kirche Deutschlands. Vol. 28. Cologne, 1976
Pastoral der Kirche fremden—Eroffnungsreferat der Deutschen Bischofskonferenz 1979 in Fulda—von Kardinal Joseph Höffner. Bonn, 1979
Alt-Katholisches Jahrbuch. Bonn, 1978
Katholiken und ihre Kirche, Protestanten und ihre Kirche. Munich, 1977

Education. Schools providing general education are primary and post-primary schools *(Grund- und Hauptschulen)*, special schools *(Sonderschulen)*, secondary modern schools *(Realschulen)*, grammar schools *(Gymnasien)* and comprehensive schools. Primary schools: Attendance is compulsory for all children having completed their 6th year of age. Compulsory education extends 9 years. After the first 4 (or 6) years at primary school children may attend post-primary schools, secondary modern schools, grammar schools and other schools of general secondary education. The secondary modern school comprises 6, the grammar school 9 years. The final Grammar School Certificate (Abitur-Higher School Certificate) entitles the holder to enter any institution of higher education. There are also special schools for retarded, physically or mentally handicapped and socially maladjusted children.

In 1980 there were in the Federal Republic 18,411 primary and post-primary schools with 5,044,400 pupils; 2,856 special schools with 354,300 pupils, 2,623 secondary modern schools with 1,351,100 pupils; 2,477 grammar schools with 2,119,000 pupils; 255 comprehensive schools (primary and secondary stage) with 220,300 pupils.

Vocational education is provided in part-time, full-time and advanced vocational schools (*Berufs-*, *Berufsaufbau-*, *Berufsfach-* and *Fachschulen*, including *Fachschulen für Technik* and *Schulen des Gesundheitswesens*). Running parallel to the occupation, part-time vocational schools offer 6 to 12 hours per week of additional compulsory schooling. All young people who are apprentices, in some other employment or even unemployed have to attend them in general up to the age of 18 years or until the completion of the practical vocational training. Full-time vocational schools comprise courses of at least one year. They prepare for commercial and domestic occupations as well as specialized occupations in the field of handicrafts. Advanced full-time vocational schools are attended by pupils having completed their 18th year of age; courses vary from 6 months to 3 or more years.

In Nov. 1980 there were 6,981 full- and part-time vocational schools with 68,930 teachers and 2,477,084 pupils (1,074,967 female); 2,918 advanced vocational schools with 8,508 teachers and 191,631 pupils (124,892 female).

Higher Education. Universities and equivalent institutions; teacher-training colleges and equivalent institutions which train teachers for primary schools, special schools, intermediate schools and schools providing vocational education; colleges of music, fine arts and the college for physical education in Cologne.

Higher technical colleges offer highly qualified full-time vocational instruction. There were, in the winter term 1979–80, 111 higher technical colleges with 180,651 students (50,609 female).

During the winter term 1979–80 there were 228 academic institutions of higher education with 981,808 students (353,432 female; 56,601 foreigners); they comprise 64 universities with 728,334 students (258,422 female); 6 Roman Catholic theological colleges and 4 Protestant theological colleges with together 2,182 students (591 female).

In the winter term 1979–80 there were 17 teacher-training colleges and equivalent institutions with 53,665 students (36,133 female); 15 colleges of music, 10 colleges of fine arts and the college of film and television with together 16,976 students (7,677 female).

Health. There were in 1980, 3,234 hospitals with 707,710 beds in the Federal Republic. In 1978 public assistance (including aid to tuberculars) and aid to war victims amounted to DM 12,274m. or DM 200.14 per head of population.[1]

[1] All subsequent statistics relate to the end of 1978 or the calendar year 1978.

Social Welfare. *Social Health Insurance* (originally introduced in 1883). Compulsory insurants are in particular wage-earners and apprentices, salaried employees with an income below the limit of compulsory insurance and the social-insurance pensioners. Voluntary insurance is possible; insurants may voluntarily continue to insure when no longer liable to do so.

Benefits: Medical treatment, medicaments, hospital and nursing care, maternity benefits, death benefits for the insured and their families, sickness payments and out-patients' allowances.

Number of insurants, 34·4m., including compulsory insurants (19·8m.) and pensioners (10·2m.). Number of the cases of incapacity for work 23·4m. Total expenditure, DM 74,991m.

Accident Insurance (originally introduced in 1884). Insured are all persons in employment or service, apprentices and the greater part of the self-employed and the unpaid family workers.

Benefits in the case of industrial injuries and occupational diseases: Medical treatment and nursing care, sickness payments, pensions and other payments in cash and in kind, surviving dependants' pensions.

Number of insurants, 27m.; number of current pensions, 1m.; total expenditure, DM 8,916m.

Workers' and Employees' Old-age Insurance Funds (originally introduced in 1889). Compulsory insurants are all wage-earners and salaried employees, the members of certain liberal professions and—subject to certain conditions—self-employed craftsmen. Insurants may voluntarily continue to insure when no longer liable to do so or increase the insurance.

Benefits: Measures designed to maintain, improve and restore the earning capacity; pensions paid to persons incapable for work, old age and surviving dependants' pensions.

Number of pensions paid, 12m., of which pensions to insurants, 7·8m.; pensions to widows and widowers, 3·6m.; pensions to orphans, 0·5m. Total expenditure, DM 130,763m.

Miners' Pension Insurance Funds. Compulsory insurants are all persons employed in mining, excluding salaried employees functioning as employers. Insurants may voluntarily continue to insure when no longer liable to do so or increase the insurance.

Benefits: Measures designed to maintain, improve and restore the earning capacity; pensions paid to underground workers because of partial disability to work in mines, miners' pensions in the case of complete disability, miners' retirement benefits, surviving dependants' pensions.

Number of pensions paid, 0·7m., of which pensions to insurants, 0·4m.; pensions to widows and widowers, 0·3m.; pensions to orphans, 0·03m. Total expenditure, DM 12,401m.

Farmers' Old-age Pension Funds: Unemployment Insurance and *Unemployment Relief* granted to unemployed persons who are not entitled to unemployment pay. Number of insured, 0·7m.; number of current pensions, 0·3m. Total expenditure, DM 2,505m.

Assistance for War Victims (war-disabled and surviving dependants of war victims).

Benefits: Medical treatment and nursing care, aid to war victims, disablement pensions, basic and equalization pensions paid to widows and orphans, parents' pensions, allowances for nursing care, compensation for occupational detriment, funeral allowances, lump-sum indemnification and indemnification paid upon marriage.

Persons (including those with permanent residence abroad) qualifying for pensions, 2·1m., of which disabled persons, 1m.; widows and widowers, 1m.; orphans, 0·03m.; parents, 0·1m. Total expenditure, DM 12,693m.

Equalization of Burdens (public relief and compensation payments). Eligible are expellees and persons who suffered damage because of the war or in connexion with the currency reform.

Benefits: Basic compensation, war-damage pensions, compensation for household equipment, accommodation assistance, currency-conversion compensation, compensation for holders of 'old savings', training grants, loans and other promotive measures.

Number of recipients of war damage pensions, 0·3m.; payments made (1 Sept. 1952–31 Dec. 1978), DM 99,253m., including basic compensation, DM 24,235m.; war damage pension, DM 38,842m.; accommodation assistance, DM 5,611m.; compensation for household equipment, DM 9,127m.

Family Assistance. From 1 Jan. 1975, children's allowances are being paid, beginning with the first child, to all persons living in the area of application of the law, the income limit being abolished. The monthly allowance is for the first child DM 50. As from 1 Jan. 1978, the allowance has been raised for the second child from DM 70 to DM 80 and for the third and any further child from DM 120 to DM 150. Beginning with 1 Jan. 1979, the beneficiaries have been receiving for the third and any further child DM 200 each per month and as from 1 July 1979 for the second child DM 100. Before, the Federal Law on Children's Allowances *(Bundeskindergeldgesetz)* had provided that all persons living in the area of application of the law were to be paid children's allowances for the third and any further child, unless the beneficiaries were public service employees or recipients of social benefits and as such already entitled to children's allowances. For the second child allowances were paid only to persons who together with their husband/wife had a yearly income not exceeding DM 15,000 (as of 1 Jan. 1973 = DM 16,800, as of 1 Jan. 1974 = DM 18,360); this limitation did not apply in the case of persons with 3 or more children.

Accommodation Allowances for tenants, owners of a homestead, a freehold flat or a small-holder's cottage.

Public Welfare. Public assistance or welfare (the latter from 1 June 1962) for needy persons, namely livelihood aid and aid in special situations (including aid to tuberculars) provided outside and inside institutions, homes and similar establishments.

Aid provided outside institutions, DM 4,376m.; aid provided inside institutions, DM 6,973m.

Aid to War Victims. Benefits for disabled persons and members of their families as well as for surviving dependants, namely vocational assistance, education allowances, supplementary livelihood aid; recovery, accommodation and special assistance. Total expenditure, DM 925m.

Public Youth Welfare. In particular, supervision of foster children, official guardianship, assistance with adoptions and affiliations, social assistance in juvenile courts, educational assistance and correctional education under a court order. Total expenditure, DM 4,427m.

Übersicht über die soziale Sicherung. Bundesministerium für Arbeit und Sozialordnung. 9th ed. Bonn, 1977

Tietz, G., *Zahlenwerk zur Sozialversicherung in der Bundesrepublik Deutschland* (and supplements). Berlin, 1963

Arbeits- und Sozialstatistik. Bundesminister für Arbeit und Sozialordnung, Bonn (from 1950)

Fachserie 13 Sozialleistungen. Statistisches Bundesamt (from 1951)

Fachserie 12 Gesundheitswesen. Statistisches Bundesamt (from 1946)

DIPLOMATIC REPRESENTATIVES

Of the Federal Republic of Germany in Great Britain (21–23 Belgrave Sq., London, SW1X 8PZ)
Ambassador: Dr Jürgen Ruhfus, KBE.

Of Great Britain in the Federal Republic of Germany (Friedrich-Ebert-Allee 77, 5300, Bonn)
Ambassador: Sir Jock Taylor, KCMG.

Of the Federal Republic of Germany in the USA (4645 Reservoir Rd, NW, Washington, D.C. 20007)
Ambassador: Peter Hermes.

Of the USA in the Federal Republic of Germany (Deichmannsaue, 5300, Bonn)
Ambassador: Arthur F. Burns.

Federal Republic of Germany to the United Nations
Ambassador: Rüdiger von Wechmar.

Books of Reference

Statistical Information: The central statistical agency is the Statistisches Bundesamt, 62 Wiesbaden, Gustav Stresemann Ring 11. *President:* Franz Kroppenstedt. Its publications include:

Statistisches Jahrbuch für die Bundesrepublik Deutschland (latest issue, 1980); *Wirtschaft und Statistik* (monthly, from 1949); *Das Arbeitsgebiet der Bundesstatistik* (latest issue 1976; also in English: *Survey of German Federal Statistics*).

Documents on Germany under Occupation, 1945–54. Ed. B. Ruhm von Oppen. R. Inst. of Int. Affairs, 1955
Bluhm, G., *Die Oder-Neisse-Linie in der Deutschen Aussenpolitik.* Freiburg, 1963
Dickinson, R. E., *The Regions of Germany.* London, 1945
Grosser, A., *Germany in our Time: A Political History of the Postwar Years.* New York, 1971
Kohl, W. L., and Basevi, G., *West Germany: A European and Global Power.* London, 1982
Pounds, N. J. G., *The Economic Pattern of Modern Germany.* 2nd ed. London, 1966
Roberts, G. K., *West German Politics.* London, 1972
Ryder, A. J., *Twentieth-Century Germany: From Bismarck to Brandt.* London, 1973
Trene, W., *Germany Since 1884.* Bad Godesberg, 1969
Wiskemann, E., *Germany's Eastern Neighbours.* R. Inst. of Int. Affairs, 1956

National Library: Deutsche Bibliothek, Zeppelinallee 4–8; Frankfurt (Main). *Director:* Professor Dr Kurt Köster.

THE LÄNDER

BADEN–WÜRTTEMBERG

AREA AND POPULATION. Baden-Württemberg comprises 35,752 sq. km, with a population (at 31 July 1981) of 9,276,603 (4,473,120 males, 4,803,483 females).

The Land is administratively divided into 4 areas, 9 urban and 35 rural districts, and numbers 1,111 communes. The capital is Stuttgart.

Vital statistics for calendar years:

	Live births	*Marriages*	*Divorces*	*Deaths*
1978	89,924	46,943	4,089	93,987
1979	92,425	49,491	10,305	91,513
1980	99,721	52,646	12,899	92,418

CONSTITUTION. The Land Baden-Württemberg is a merger of the 3 Länder, Baden, Württemberg-Baden and Württemberg-Hohenzollern, which were formed in 1945. The merger was approved by a plebiscite held on 9 Dec. 1951, when 70% of the population voted in its favour.

The Diet, elected on 16 March 1980, consists of 68 Christian Democrats, 40 Social Democrats, 10 Free Democrats, 6 Ecologists.

The Government is formed by Christian Democrats, with Lothar Späth (CDU) as Prime Minister.

AGRICULTURE. Area and yield of the most important crops:

	Area (in 1,000 hectares)			*Yield (in 1,000 tonnes)*		
	1979	*1980*	*1981*[1]	*1979*	*1980*	*1981*[1]
Rye	18·9	19·6	17·5	68·9	72·7	63·6
Wheat	223·4	230·0	218·9	1,059·1	1,043·4	1,087·4
Barley	188·9	195·1	189·7	768·4	789·9	785·5
Oats	94·1	89·8	91·7	387·7	349·2	377·0
Potatoes	27·3	23·7	22·5	866·3	531·5	680·2
Sugar-beet	22·5	22·7	23·5	1,133·5	1,140·8	1,170·9

[1] Preliminary.

Livestock (1 Dec. 1980): Cattle, 1,855,524 (including 688,148 milch cows); horses, 47,794; pigs, 2,201,460; sheep, 205,184; poultry, 6,540,154.

INDUSTRY. In June 1981 10,285 establishments (with 20 and more employees) employed 1,462,530 persons; of these, 257,946 were employed in machine construction (excluding office machines, data processing equipment and facilities); 93,522 in textile industry; 239,268 in electrical engineering; 211,505 in car building.

LABOUR. The economically active persons totalled 4,251,100 at the 1%-sample survey of the microcensus of April 1980. Of the total 352,200 were self-employed, 142,100 unpaid family workers, 3,756,800 employees; 209,700 were engaged in agriculture and forestry; 2,203,700 in power supply, mining, manufacturing and building, 607,400 in commerce and transport, 1,230,300 in other industries and services.

ROADS. On 1 Jan. 1981 there were 27,708 km of 'classified' roads, including 912 km of autobahn, 4,835 km of federal roads, 12,692 km of first-class and 9,269 km of second-class highways. Motor vehicles, at 1 July 1981, numbered 4,348,633, including, 3,697,465 passenger cars, 8,684 buses, 178,943 lorries, 292,984 tractors and 124,120 motor cycles.

JUSTICE. There are a constitutional court *(Staatsgerichtshof)*, 2 courts of appeal, 17 regional courts, 108 local courts, a Land labour court, 9 labour courts, a Land social court, 8 social courts, a finance court, a higher administrative court *(Verwaltungsgerichtshof)*, 4 administrative courts.

RELIGION. On 1 Jan. 1981, 44% of the population were Protestants and 47·1% Roman Catholics.

EDUCATION. In 1981 there were 2,570 primary schools with 24,763 teachers and 715,795 pupils; 545 special schools with 6,669 teachers and 58,032 pupils; 430 intermediate schools with 9,007 teachers and 256,490 pupils; 413 high schools with 16,667 teachers and 339,696 pupils; 21 *Freie Waldorf* schools with 629 teachers and 10,847 pupils; 16 *Integrierte Gesamtschulen* (comprehensive schools) including stage of orientation, with 736 teachers and 14,380 pupils; 165 *Berufliche Gymnasien* (technical secondary schools) with 30,005 pupils; 382 part-time vocational schools with 284,119 pupils; 996 full-time vocational schools with 85,235 pupils; 204 advanced vocational schools with 10,360 pupils; 215 schools for public health occupations with 12,813 students; there were also 64 (full- and part-time) institutions for the training of technicians with 4,460 participants and 35 *Fachhochschulen* (colleges of engineering and others) with 29,185 students; in all vocational schools there were 14,367 teachers.

In the winter term 1980–81 there were 9 universities (Freiburg, 19,282 students; Heidelberg, 22,425; Konstanz, 3,631; Tübingen, 20,321; Karlsruhe, 11,556; Stuttgart, 13,243; Hohenheim, 3,846; Mannheim, 6,505; Ulm, 3,106); 10 teacher-training colleges with 13,127 students; 5 colleges of music and 2 colleges of fine arts, comprising together 3,332 students.

Statistical Information: Statistisches Landesamt Baden-Württemberg (P.O.B. 898, D7000 Stuttgart 1) (*President:* Prof. Max Wingen), publishes: Monatsschrift *'Baden-Wurttemberg in Wort und Zahl'; Jahrbücher für Statistik und Landeskunde von Baden-Württemberg; Statistik von Baden-Württemberg* (series); *Statistischer und prognostischer Jahres-bericht* (latest issue 1980–81); *Statistisches Taschenbuch* (latest issue 1981).

State Library: Württembergische Landesbibliothek, Konrad-Adenauer-Str. 8, 7000 Stuttgart 1. *Director:* Dr Hans-Peter Geh.

BAVARIA

Bayern

AREA AND POPULATION. Bavaria has an area of 70,546 sq. km. The capital is Munich. There are 7 areas, 96 urban and rural districts and 2,050 communes. The population (30 June 1981) numbered 10,939,834 (5,235,926 males, 5,703,908 females).

Vital statistics for calendar years:

	Live births	*Marriages*	*Divorces*	*Deaths*
1978	106,145	59,419	4,086	124,775
1979	107,667	63,146	11,340	122,271
1980	114,451	66,368	13,408	122,859

CONSTITUTION. The Constituent Assembly, elected on 30 June 1946, passed a constitution on the lines of the democratic constitution of 1919, but with greater emphasis on state rights; this was agreed upon by the Christian Social Union and the Social Democrats.

The elections for the Diet, held on 10 Oct. 1982, had the following results: 133 Christian Social Union, 71 Social Democrats. The cabinet of the Christian Social Union is headed by Minister President Dr Franz Josef Strauss (CSU).

AGRICULTURE. Area and yield of the most important products:

	Area (1,000 hectares)			*Yield (1,000 tonnes)*		
	1979	*1980*	*1981*	*1979*	*1980*	*1981*
Wheat	482·6	490·5	489·6	2,131·1	2,348·9	2,047·5
Rye	70·8	75·4	69·2	220·7	266·7	239·3
Barley	518·6	511·3	510·6	1,957·6	2,020·8	2,073·2
Oats	153·8	143·6	148·5	530·9	511·9	540·8
Potatoes	111·9	105·0	99·0	3,564·7	2,518·3	2,951·1
Sugar-beet	83·6	79·1	93·4 [1]	4,145·7	4,002·7	5,272·9 [1]

[1] Preliminary results.

Livestock (3 Dec. 1980): 4,942,500 cattle (including 1,986,300 milch cows); 57,400 horses; 291,900 sheep; 4,145,800 pigs; 15,618,600 poultry.

INDUSTRY. In July 1981, 10,005 establishments (with 20 and more employees) employed 1,356,762 persons; of these, 235,378 were employed in electrical engineering; 184,629 in mechanical engineering; 84,073 in clothing industry.

LABOUR. The economically active persons totalled 5,174,900 at the 1% sample survey of the microcensus of April 1980. Of the total, 538,500 were self-employed, 341,000 unpaid family workers, 4,295,200 employees; 2,331,500 in power supply, mining, manufacturing and building; 856,900 in commerce and transport; 1,464,100 in other industries and services.

ROADS. There were, on 1 Jan. 1980, 39,360 km of 'classified' roads, including 1,561 km of autobahn, 7,254 km of federal roads, 13,642 km of first-class and 16,903 km of second-class highways. Number of motor vehicles, at 1 July 1981, was 5,192,277, including 4,193,836 passenger cars, 225,404 lorries, 12,681 buses, 532,069 tractors, 187,136 motor cycles.

JUSTICE. There are a constitutional court *(Verfassungsgerichtshof)*, a supreme Land court *(Oberstes Landesgericht)*, 3 courts of appeal, 21 regional courts, 72 local courts, 2 Land labour courts, 11 labour courts, a Land social court, 7 social courts, 2 finance courts, a higher administrative court *(Verwaltungsgerichtshof)*, 6 administrative courts.

RELIGION. At the census of 27 May 1970 there were 69·9% Roman Catholics and 25·7% Protestants.

EDUCATION. In 1980–81 there were 2,832 primary schools with 42,328 teachers and 948,543 pupils; 402 special schools with 4,495 teachers and 48,502 pupils; 332 intermediate schools with 8,388 teachers and 178,770 pupils; 395 high schools with 18,173 teachers and 329,554 pupils; 273 part-time vocational schools with 6,581 teachers and 390,716 pupils; 555 full-time vocational schools with 3,202 teachers and 64,279 pupils including 215 schools for public health occupations with 595 teachers and 14,166 pupils; 267 advanced full-time vocational schools with 1,747 teachers and 24,243 pupils; 79 vocational high schools *(Berufsoberschulen, Fachoberschulen)* with 1,357 teachers and 27,549 pupils.

In the winter term 1980–81 there were 10 universities with 113,731 students (Augsburg, 4,549; Bamberg, 2,725; Bayreuth, 2,024; Eichstätt, 1,615; Erlangen-Nürnberg, 19,101; München, 41,989; Passau, 1,160; Regensburg, 10,473; Würzburg, 13,537; the Technical University of München, 16,558); 2 *Gesamthochschulen* with 2,856 students and the college of philosophy, München, 286. There were also 2 colleges of music, 2 colleges of fine arts and 1 college of television and film, with together 2,162 students; 13 vocational colleges *(Fachhochschulen)* with 33,822 students.

Statistical Information: Bayerisches Statistisches Landesamt, 51 Neuhauser Str. 8000 Munich, was founded in 1833. *President:* Dr Hans Helmut Scheidermaier. It publishes: *Statistisches Jahrbuch für Bayern.* 1894 ff.—*Bayern in Zahlen.* Monthly (from Jan. 1947).—*Zeitschrift des Bayerischen Statistischen Landesamts.* July 1869–1943; 1948 ff.—*Beiträge zur Statistik Bayerns.* 1850 ff.—*Statistische Berichte.* 1951 ff.—*Schaubilderhefte.* 1951 ff.—*Kreisdaten.* 1972 ff.—*Gemeindedaten.* 1973 ff.

Nawiasky, H., and Luesser, C., *Die Verfassung des Freistaates Bayern vom 2. Dez. 1946.* Munich, 1948; supplement, by H. Nawiasky and H. Lechner, Munich, 1953

State Library: Bayerische Staatsbibliothek, Munich 22. *Director:* Dr Franz G. Kaltwasser.

BERLIN

GOVERNMENT. Greater Berlin was under quadripartite Allied government (Kommandatura) until 1 July 1948, when the Soviet element withdrew. On 30 Nov. 1948, a separate Municipal Government was set up in the Soviet Sector (*see* p. 509).

AREA. The total area of Berlin is 883 sq. km, of which Western Berlin covers 480 sq. km and the Soviet Sector 403 sq. km. The *British Sector* includes the administrative districts of Tiergarten, Charlottenburg, Wilmersdorf and Spandau; the *American Sector* those of Kreuzberg, Neukölln, Tempelhof, Schöneberg, Zehlendorf and Steglitz; the *French Sector* covers the administrative districts of Wedding and Reinickendorf, and the *Soviet Sector,* those of Mitte, Friedrichshain, Prenzlauer Berg, Pankow, Weissensee, Lichtenberg, Treptow and Köpenick. The British, American and French sectors form an administrative unit, called Berlin (West).

On 13 Aug. 1961 the East German Government completely severed all communications between West and East Berlin.

BERLIN (WEST)

POPULATION. Population, 31 Dec. 1980, 1,896,230 (855,594 males, 1,040,636 females). According to the census of 27 May 1970, 70·2% were Protestants and 12·5% Roman Catholics.

Vital statistics for calendar years:

	Live births	*Marriages*	*Divorces*	*Deaths*
1978	16,678	10,804	5,600	36,060
1979	17,259	10,754	3,700	35,008
1980	19,000	12,000	5,600	35,000

CONSTITUTION AND GOVERNMENT. According to the constitution of 1 Sept. 1950, Berlin is simultaneously a Land of the Federal Republic (though not yet formally incorporated) and a city. It is governed by a House of Representatives (at least 200 members); the executive power is vested in a Senate, consisting of the Ruling Burgomaster, the deputy Burgomaster and not more than 16 senators.

In the municipal elections, held on 10 May 1981, the Christian Democrats obtained 65 seats; the Social Democrats, 51 seats; the Free Democrats, 7 seats.

Governing Mayor: Dr Richard v. Weizäcker (Christian Democrat).

ECONOMY

Currency. The legal tender of Berlin (West) is the German Mark (DM).

Banking. On 20 March 1949 when the DM (West) became the only legal tender of the Western Sectors, the Zentralbank of Berlin was established. Its functions were similar to those of the Zentralbanks of the Länder of the Federal Republic. The Berlin Central Bank was merged with the Bank deutscher Länder as from 1 Aug. 1957, when the latter became the Deutsche Bundesbank. The legal tender for the Western Sectors of Berlin is being issued by the Deutsche Bundesbank (formerly Bank deutscher Länder).

AGRICULTURE. Agricultural area (May 1980), 3,615 hectares, including 1,100 hectares arable land and 150 hectares gardens, orchards, nurseries.

Livestock (3 Dec. 1980): Cattle, 837; pigs, 4,469; horses, 3,086; sheep, 991.

INDUSTRY. In 1980 (monthly averages), 1,188 establishments (with 20 or more employees) employed 180,000 persons; of these, 64,000 were employed in electrical engineering, 19,000 in machine construction, 4,000 in cloth manufacture, 4,118 in steel construction.

LABOUR. The economically active persons totalled 841,900 at the 1%-sample survey of the microcensus of April 1979. Of the total, 71,900 were self-employed including unpaid family workers, 770,000 employees; 5,300 were engaged in agriculture and forestry; 274,400 in power supply, manufacturing and building; 167,600 in commerce and transport; 394,600 in other industries and services.

ROADS. There were, on 1 Jan. 1976, 117 km of 'classified' roads, including 25 km of autobahn and 92 km of federal roads. On 1 July 1981, 657,041 motor vehicles were registered, including 581,605 passenger cars, 38,050 lorries, 23,578 motor cycles, 2,220 buses and 3,031 tractors.

JUSTICE. There are a court of appeal *(Oberlandesgericht)*, a regional court, 7 local courts, a Land Labour court, a labour court, a Land social court, a social court, a higher administrative court, an administrative court and a finance court.

EDUCATION. In 1980 (preliminary figures) there were 448 schools providing general education (excluding special schools) with 14,784 teachers and 231,000 pupils; 64 special schools with 1,277 teachers and 10,300 pupils. There were a further 45 vocational schools with 1,068 teachers and 38,000 pupils; 24 full-time vocational schools with 432 teachers and 4,805 pupils; 13 *Fachoberschulen* (full-time vocational schools leading up to vocational colleges) with 125 teachers and 1,529 pupils; 34 advanced full-time vocational schools with 250 teachers and 4,754 pupils; 68 schools for public-health occupations with 340 teachers and 4,599 pupils. Moreover, there were 2 schools for technicians with 38 teachers and 543 participants.

In the winter term 1980–81 there was 1 university (142,929 students); 1 technical university (23,592); 1 theological (evangelical) college (354); 1 teacher-training college with 4,768 students; 1 college of fine arts with 3,194 students; 1 vocational college (for economics) (787); 2 colleges for social work (1,483); 1 technical college

(2,702), 1 college of the Federal postal administration (355) and 1 college for public administration (1,307).

Statistical Information: The Statistisches Landesamt Berlin, formerly Statistisches Amt der Stadt Berlin, was founded in 1862 (Fehrbelliner Platz 1, 1000 Berlin 31). *Director:* Günter Appel. It publishes: *Statistisches Jahrbuch* (from 1867): *Berliner Statistik* (monthly, from 1947).—*100 Jahre Berliner Statistik* (1962).

Childs, D. and Johnson, J., *West Berlin: Politics and Society.* London, 1981
Hillenbrand, M. J., *The Future of Berlin.* Monclair, 1981

State Library: Amerika-Gedenkbibliothek-Berliner Zentralbibliothek-, Blücherplatz 1, D1000 Berlin 61. *Director:* Dr Peter K. Liebenow.

BREMEN

Freie Hansestadt Bremen

AREA AND POPULATION. The area of the Land, consisting of the towns and ports of Bremen and Bremerhaven, is 404 sq. km. Estimated population, 31 Dec. 1980, 693,846 (326,865 males, 366,981 females).

Vital statistics for calendar years:

	Live births	*Marriages*	*Divorces*	*Deaths*
1978	5,817	3,713	287	8,972
1979	5,640	3,671	969	8,776
1980	5,945	3,778	1,461	8,762

CONSTITUTION. Political power is vested in the House of Burgesses *(Bürgerschaft)* which appoints the executive, called the Senate.

The elections of 7 Oct. 1979 had the following result: 52 Social Democratic Party, 33 Christian Democrats, 11 Free Democratic Party, 4 Bremer Grüne Liste. The Senate is only formed by Social Democrats; its president is Hans Koschnick (Social Democrat).

AGRICULTURE. Agricultural area comprised (1979), 14,440 hectares: yield of grain crops (1980), 8,471 tonnes; potatoes, 483 tonnes.

Livestock (3 Dec. 1980): 16,351 cattle (including 4,531 milch cows); 5,192 pigs; 389 sheep; 1,345 horses; 33,139 poultry.

INDUSTRY. In 1980, 408 establishments (20 and more employees) employed 89,564 persons; of these, 14,157 were employed in shipbuilding (except naval engineering); 7,405 in machine construction; 10,988 in electrical engineering; 5,123 in coffee and tea processing.

LABOUR. The economically active persons totalled 292,500 at the 1%-sample survey of the microcensus of April 1980. Of the total, 21,500 were self-employed, 267,800 employees; 100,600 in power supply, mining, manufacturing and building, 85,000 in commerce and transport, 105,100 in other industries and services.

ROADS. On 1 Jan. 1976 there were 139 km of 'classified' roads, including 45 km of autobahn, 82 km of federal roads, 7 km of first-class and 5 km of second-class highways. Registered motor vehicles on 1 July 1980 numbered 266,405, including 240,107 passenger cars, 15,944 trucks, 2,292 tractors, 660 buses and 5,152 motor cycles.

SHIPPING. Vessels entered in 1980, 10,366 of 44,957,165 net tons; cleared, 10,173 of 45,084,656 net tons. Sea traffic, 1980, incoming 16,856,680 tonnes; outgoing, 10,103,987 tonnes.

JUSTICE. There are a constitutional court *(Staatsgerichtshof)*, a court of appeal, a regional court, 3 local courts, a Land labour court, 2 labour courts, a Land social court, a social court, a finance court, a higher administrative court, an administrative court.

RELIGION. On 27 May 1970 (census) there were 82·4% Protestants and 10·2% Roman Catholics.

EDUCATION. In 1980 there were 331 new system schools with 6,637 teachers and 103,687 pupils; 26 special schools with 556 teachers and 4,164 pupils; 23 part-time vocational schools with 25,697 pupils; 22 full-time vocational schools with 1,646 pupils; 15 advanced vocational schools (including institutions for the training of technicians) with 1,881 pupils; 11 schools for public health occupations with 940 pupils.

In the winter term 1980–81 about 7,211 students were enrolled at the university. In addition to the university there were 7 other colleges in 1980 with about 4,732 students.

Statistical Information: Statistisches Landesamt Bremen (An der Weide 14–16 (P.B. 101309), D2800 Bremen 1), founded in 1850. *Director:* RD Volker Hannemann. Its current publications include: *Statistische Mitteilungen Freie Hansestadt Bremen* (from 1948).—*Monatliche Zwischenberichte* (1949–53); *Statistische Monatsberichte* (from 1954).—*Statistische Berichte* (from 1956).—*Statistisches Handbuch für das Land Freie Hansestadt Bremen (1950–60,* 1961; *1960–64,* 1967; *1965–69,* 1971; *1970–74,* 1975).—*Bremen im statistischen Zeitvergleich 1950–1976.* 1977.—*Bremen in Zahlen.* 1981.

Beutin, L., *Bremen und Amerika.* Bremen, 1953

University Library: Universitats Str., D2800 Bremen 33. *Director:* Gerhard Wenske.

HAMBURG

Freie und Hansestadt Hamburg

AREA AND POPULATION. In 1938 the territory of the town was re-organized by the amalgamation of the city and its 18 rural districts with 3 urban and 27 rural districts ceded by Prussia. Total area, 754·7 sq. km (1980), including the islands Neuwerk and Scharhörn (7 sq. km). Population (31 Dec. 1980), 1,645,095 (767,551 males, 877,544 females).

Vital statistics for calendar years:

	Live births	*Marriages*	*Divorces*	*Deaths*
1978	12,616	7,966	1,141	24,072
1979	12,722	8,296	3,183	23,760
1980	13,580	8,930	4,494	23,726

CONSTITUTION. The constitution of 6 June 1952 vests the supreme power in the House of Burgesses *(Bürgerschaft)* of 120 members. The executive is in the hands of the Senate, whose members are elected by the Bürgerschaft.

The elections of 6 June 1982 had the following results: Social Democrats, 55; Christian Democrats, 56; *Die Grünen* 9. The First Burgomaster is Dr Klaus von Dohnanyi (Social Democrat).

The territory has been divided into 7 administrative districts.

AGRICULTURE. The agricultural area comprised 24,100 hectares in 1980. Yield, in tonnes, of cereals, 21,800; potatoes, 1,100.

Livestock (3 Dec. 1980): Cattle, 13,105 (including 3,421 milch cows); pigs, 10,736; horses, 3,491; sheep, 1,699; poultry, 77,413.

FISHERIES. In 1979 the yield of sea and coastal fishing was 26,391 tonnes valued at DM 26·8m.

INDUSTRY. In June 1980, 993 establishments (with 20 and more employees) employed 167,799 persons; of these, 21,784 were employed in electrical engineering; 18,468 in machine construction; 13,945 in shipbuilding (except naval engineering); 15,355 in chemical industry.

LABOUR. The economically active persons totalled 748,900 at the 1%-sample survey of the microcensus of May 1980. Of the total, 63,800 were self-employed, 6,800 unpaid family workers, 678,300 employees; 9,400 were engaged in agriculture and forestry, 237,700 in power supply, mining, manufacturing and building, 213,700 in commerce and transport, 288,700 in other industries and services.

ROADS. On 1 Jan. 1980 there were 3,632 km of roads, including 60 km of autobahn, 157 km of federal roads. Number of motor vehicles (1 July 1981), 634,908, including 568,726 passenger cars, 36,968 lorries, 1,867 buses, 4,776 tractors, 15,982 motor cycles.

SHIPPING. Hamburg is the largest port in the Federal Republic.

Vessels		*1938*	*1958*	*1968*	*1978*	*1980*
Entered:	Number	18,149	19,033	18,802	16,636	15,551
	Tonnage	20,567,311	27,454,640	37,073,215	61,785,643	63,418,094
Cleared:	Number	19,316	20,363	19,320	17,414	16,326
	Tonnage	20,547,148	27,579,914	36,820,828	62,028,141	63,442,541

JUSTICE. There is a constitutional court *(Verfassungsgericht)*, a court of appeal *(Oberlandesgericht)*, a regional court *(Landgericht)*, 6 local courts *(Amtsgerichte)*, a Land labour court, a labour court, a Land social court, a social court, a finance court, a higher administrative court, an administrative court.

RELIGION. On 25 May 1970 (census) Evangelical Church and Free Churches 73·6%, Roman Catholic Church 8·1%.

EDUCATION. In 1980 there were 400 schools of general education (not including *Internationale Schule*) with 9,285 teachers and 209,662 pupils; 62 special schools with 1,029 teachers and 9,054 pupils; 47 part-time vocational schools with 49,635 pupils; 24 schools with 2,176 pupils in their vocational preparatory year; 21 schools with 1,594 pupils in manual instruction classes; 58 full-time vocational schools with 8,835 pupils; 9 economic secondary schools with 2,059 pupils; 25 advanced vocational schools with 3,591 pupils; 39 schools for public health occupations with 2,760 pupils; 11 vocational introducing schools with 483 pupils and 23 technical superior schools with 2,148 pupils; all these vocational and technical schools have a total number of 2,639 teachers.

In the winter term 1980–81 there was 1 university with 34,579 students; 1 college of music and 1 college of fine arts with together 1,825 students; 1 high school of the *Bundeswehr* with 2,009 students; 1 professional high school *(Fachhochschule)* with 8,104 students; 1 high school for economics and politics with 1,240 students; 1 high school of public administration with 646 students, as well as 1 private professional high school with 148 students.

Statistical Information: The Statistisches Landesamt der Freien und Hansestadt Hamburg (Steckelhörn 12, D2000 Hamburg 11) publishes: *Hamburg in Zahlen, Statistische Berichte, Statistisches Jahrbuch, Statistisches Taschenbuch, Statistik des Hamburgischen Staates.*

Klepsmann, E., *Geschichte der Stadt.* Hamburg, 1981
Meyer-Marwitz, B., *Großer Hamburg.* Hamburg, 1978
Studt, B., and Olsen, H., *Hamburg—eine kurzgefaßte Geschichte der Stadt.* Hamburg, 1964

State Library: Staats- und Universitätsbibliothek, Moorweidenstr. 40, D2000 Hamburg 13. *Director:* Dr Horst Gronemeyer.

HESSEN

AREA AND POPULATION. The state of Hessen comprehends the areas of the former Prussian provinces Kurhessen and Nassau (excluding the exclaves belonging to Hessen and the rural counties of Westerwaldkreis and Rhine-Lahn) and of the former Volksstaat Hessen, the provinces Starkenburg (including the parts of Rheinhessen east of the river Rhine) and Oberhessen. Hessen has an area of 21,114 sq. km. Its capital is Wiesbaden. Since 1 Jan. 1981 there have been 3 areas with 5 urban and 21 rural districts and 421 communes. Population, 30 June 1981, was 5,602,925 (2,694,529 males, 2,908,396 females).

Vital statistics for calendar years:

	Live births	*Marriages*	*Divorces*	*Deaths*
1978	51,139	28,085	2,630	64,047
1979	51,854	29,632	6,707	63,024
1980	54,535	30,199	8,396	63,625

CONSTITUTION. The constitution was put into force by popular referendum on 1 Dec. 1946. The Diet, elected on 26 Sept. 1982, consists of 52 Christian Democrats, 49 Social Democrats, 9 *Die Grünen*.

The Social Democrat and Free Democrat cabinet is headed by Minister President Holger Börner (SPD).

AGRICULTURE. Area and yield of the most important crops:

	Area (in 1,000 hectares)			*Yield (in 1,000 tonnes)*		
	1979	*1980*	*1981*	*1979*	*1980*	*1981*
Wheat	135·9	140·7	142·0	711·2	675·5	664·0
Rye	37·7	37·8	35·2	154·2	155·2	131·4
Barley	135·9	135·0	139·0	597·4	666·5	565·6
Oats	75·8	73·9	73·6	310·1	284·6	280·7
Potatoes	15·3	13·9	12·6	473·7	309·2	308·1
Sugar-beet	21·2	21·7	24·2	1,020·7	982·0	1,134·0

Livestock, 3 Dec. 1980: Cattle, 883,200 (including 296,600 milch cows); horses, 32,600; pigs, 1,353,100; sheep, 124,900; poultry, 4,430,400.

INDUSTRY. In Sept. 1981, 4,059 establishments (with 20 and more employees) employed 657,008 persons; of these, 95,889 were employed in chemical industry; 85,255 in electrical engineering; 84,688 in car building; 84,513 in machine construction; 31,757 in food industry.

LABOUR. The economically active persons totalled 2·45m. at the 1%-sample survey of the microcensus of April 1980. Of the total, 195,200 were self-employed, 64,600 unpaid family workers, 2,186,300 employees; 100,000 were engaged in agriculture and forestry, 1,110,400 in power supply, mining, manufacturing and building, 426,400 in commerce and transport, 809,300 in other services.

ROADS. On 1 Jan. 1981 there were 16,509 km of 'classified' roads, including 905 km of autobahn, 3,530 km of federal highways, 7,087 km of first-class highways and 4,987 km of second-class highways. Motor vehicles licensed on 1 July 1981 totalled 2,623,692, including 2,276,941 passenger cars, 5,675 buses, 118,362 trucks, 135,576 tractors and 67,749 motor cycles.

JUSTICE. There are a constitutional court *(Staatsgerichtshof)*, a court of appeal, 9 regional courts, 58 local courts, a Land labour court, 12 labour courts, a Land social court, 7 social courts, a finance court, a higher administrative court *(Verwaltungsgerichtshof)*, 4 administrative courts.

RELIGION. On 27 May 1970 (census) there were 60·5% Protestants and 32·8% Roman Catholics.

EDUCATION. In 1980 there were 1,293 primary schools with 14,641 teachers and 336,884 pupils; 258 special schools with 2,740 teachers and 27,403 pupils; 164 intermediate schools with 2,966 teachers and 67,658 pupils; 152 high schools with 7,772 teachers and 154,170 pupils; 173 *Gesamtschulen* (comprehensive schools) with 10,050 teachers and 206,844 pupils; 115 part-time vocational schools with 3,296 teachers and 164,225 pupils; 249 full-time vocational schools with 2,243 teachers and 36,762 pupils; 60 advanced vocational schools with 368 teachers and 5,242 pupils; 161 schools for public health occupations with 8,767 pupils; there were a further 35 full- and part-time institutions for the training of technicians with 2,754 participants.

In the winter term 1980–81 there were 3 universities (Frankfurt/Main, 24,874 students; Giessen, 14,822; Marburg, 12,806); 1 technical university in Darmstadt (12,004); 1 *Gesamthochschule* (7,511); 13 *Fachhochschulen* (19,327); 2 Roman Catholic theological colleges and 1 Protestant theological college with together 390 students; 1 college of music and 2 colleges of fine arts with together 1,034 students.

Statistical Information: The Hessisches Statistisches Landesamt (Rheinstr. 35–37, D6200 Wiesbaden). *President:* Götz Steppuhn. Main publications: *Statistisches Handbuch für das Land Hessen* (1978–79).—*Statistisches Taschenbuch für das Land Hessen* (1980–81).—*Staat und Wirtschaft in Hessen* (monthly).—*Beiträge zur Statistik Hessens.—Statistische Berichte.—Hessische Gemeindestatistik 1960–61* (5 vols., 1963 ff.).—*Hessische Gemeindestatistik 1970* (5 vols., 1972 ff.).—*Hessische Gemeindestatistik 1980* (1 vol.).—*Hessische Gemeindestatistik 1981.*

State Library: Hessische Landesbibliothek, Rheinstr. 55–57, D6200 Wiesbaden. *Director:* Dr Helmut Schwitzgebel.

LOWER SAXONY

Niedersachsen

AREA AND POPULATION. Lower Saxony (excluding the town of Bremerhaven, and the districts on the right bank of the Elbe in the Soviet Zone) comprises 47,423 sq. km, and is divided into 4 administrative districts, 39 rural districts, 9 towns and 1,017 communes; capital, Hanover.

Estimated population, on 31 Dec. 1980, was 7,256,386 (3,480,084 males, 3,776,302 females).

Vital statistics for calendar years:

	Live births	*Marriages*	*Divorces*	*Deaths*
1978	68,557	36,957	3,970	85,562
1979	67,637	38,569	8,524	84,169
1980	71,752	40,742	9,792	84,869

GOVERNMENT. The Land Niedersachsen was formed on 1 Nov. 1946 by merging the former Prussian province of Hanover and the *Länder* Brunswick, Oldenburg and Schaumburg-Lippe. The Diet, elected on 21 March 1982, consists of 87 Christian Democrats, 63 Social Democrats; Free Democrats, 10 and *Die Grünen,* 11.

The cabinet of the Christian Democratic Union is headed by Minister President Dr Ernst Albrecht (CDU).

AGRICULTURE. Area and yield of the most important crops:

	Area (in 1,000 hectares)			*Yield (in 1,000 tonnes)*		
	1978	*1979*	*1980*	*1978*	*1979*	*1980*
Wheat	263	281	293	1,357	1,467	1,475
Rye	255	230	217	946	817	841
Barley	468	494	498	2,152	2,007	2,226
Oats	189	183	175	823	802	691
Potatoes	85	76	72	2,618	2,502	2,210
Sugar-beet	145	144	148	2,212	5,977	6,334

Livestock, 3 Dec. 1980: Cattle, 3,114,897 (including 1,080,037 milch cows); horses, 85,973; pigs, 6,773,104; sheep, 156,171; poultry, 37,126,713.

FISHERIES. In 1979 the yield of sea and coastal fishing was 132,448 tonnes valued at DM 141m.

INDUSTRY. In Sept. 1980, 4,801 establishments (with 20 and more employees) employed 724,442 persons; of these 64,889 were employed in machine construction; 148,267 in car building; 67,872 in electrical engineering.

LABOUR. The economically active persons totalled 3,063,900 at the 1%-sample survey of the microcensus of April 1980. Of the total 266,700 were self-employed, 138,900 unpaid family workers, 2,658,300 employees; 235,300 were engaged in agriculture and forestry, 1,251,500 in power supply, mining, manufacturing and building, 575,300 in commerce and transport, 1,001,800 in other industries and services.

ROADS. At 1 Jan. 1980 there were 27,209 km of 'classified' roads, including 952 km of autobahn, 5,192 km of federal roads, 8,642 km of first-class and 12,423 km of second-class highways.

Number of motor vehicles, 1 Jan. 1981, was 3,219,154 including 2,718,267 passenger cars, 150,674 lorries, 8,729 buses, 241,757 tractors, 73,654 motor cycles.

JUSTICE. There are a constitutional court *(Staatsgerichtshof)*, 3 courts of appeal, 11 regional courts, 79 local courts, a Land labour court, 15 labour courts, a Land social court, 8 social courts, a finance court, a higher administrative court (together with Schleswig-Holstein), 3 administrative courts.

RELIGION. On 27 May 1970 (census) there were 74·6% Protestants and 19·6% Roman Catholics.

EDUCATION. In 1980 there were 2,307 primary schools with 28,092 teachers and 502,497 pupils; 293 special schools with 4,743 teachers and 43,450 pupils; 320 stages of orientation with 179,811 pupils; 270 intermediate schools with 7,157 teachers and 165,699 pupils; 241 grammar schools with 12,623 teachers and 207,542 pupils; 9 evening high schools with 138 teachers and 1,514 pupils; 20 integrated comprehensive schools with 1,684 teachers and 24,492 pupils; 17 co-operative comprehensive schools with 1,490 teachers and 26,186 pupils; 142 part-time vocational schools with 211,447 pupils; 114 year of basic vocational training with 21,071 pupils; 538 full-time vocational schools with 38,008 pupils; 89 *Fachgymnasien* with 8,696 pupils; 126 *Fachoberschulen* with 7,557 pupils (full-time vocational schools leading up to vocational colleges); 56 vocational extension schools with 1,544 pupils; 151 advanced full-time vocational schools (including schools for technicians) with 9,662 pupils; 219 public health schools with 11,527 pupils.

In the winter term 1980–81 there were 4 universities (Göttingen, 24,834 students; Hanover, 19,269; Oldenburg, 5,521; Osnabrück, 4,605); 2 technical universities (Braunschweig, 11,132; Clausthal, 2,904); the medical college of Hanover (2,887), the veterinary college in Hanover (1,538) and the colleges of Hildesheim (1,208) and Lüneburg (1,010).

Statistical Information: The Niedersächsisches Landesverwaltungsamt—Statistik' (Geibelstr. 65, D3000 Hanover 1) fulfils the function of the 'Statistisches Landesamt für Niedersachsen'. *Head of Division:* Abteilungsdirektor Dr Günter Koop. Main publications are: *Statistisches Jahrbuch Niedersachsen* (from 1950).—*Statistische Monatshefte Niedersachsen* (from 1947).—*Statistik Niedersachsen.*

State Library: Niedersächsische Staats- und Universitätsbibliothek, Prinzenstr. 1, 3400, Göttingen. *Director:* Helmut Vogt; Niedersächsische Landesbibliothek, Waterloostr. 8, D3000 Hannover 1. *Director:* Dr Wilhelm Totok.

NORTH RHINE-WESTPHALIA

Nordrhein-Westfalen

AREA AND POPULATION. The Land comprises 34,066 sq. km. It is divided into 5 areas, 23 urban and 31 rural districts. Capital Düsseldorf. Population, 31 Dec. 1980, 17,058,193 (8,160,022 males, 8,898,171 females).

Vital statistics for calendar years:

	Live births	*Marriages*	*Divorces*	*Deaths*
1978	158,478	93,067	11,434	197,249
1979	159,378	98,109	23,826	195,147
1980	169,828	103,547	28,397	195,205

GOVERNMENT. The Land Nordrhein-Westfalen is governed by Social Democrats; Minister President, Johannes Rau (SPD). The Diet, elected on 11 May 1980, consists of 106 Social Democrats and 95 Christian Democrats.

AGRICULTURE. Area and yield of the most important crops:

	Area (in 1,000 hectares)			*Yield (in 1,000 tonnes)*		
	1978	*1979*	*1980*	*1978*	*1979*	*1980*
Wheat	213·6	216·4	221·1	1,101·6	1,139·2	1,158·2
Rye	107·0	86·8	83·3	425·0	382·7	336·1
Barley	362·3	373·1	372·9	1,727·2	1,647·3	1,791·1
Oats	121·1	120·1	109·9	553·5	531·4	436·2
Potatoes	32·2	22·4	22·0	1,028·2	681·7	648·4
Sugar-beet	84·4	84·2	82·3	6,441·6	3,873·7	4,074·9

Livestock, 1 Dec. 1980: Cattle, 1,943,444 (including 629,199 milch cows); pigs, 5,506,457; sheep, 163,466; horses, 89,247; poultry, 14,989,246.

INDUSTRY. In June 1980, 11,376 establishments (with 20 and more employees) employed 2,142,282 persons; of these, 180,668 were employed in mining; 296,738 in machine construction; 192,179 in iron and steel production; 204,555 in chemical industry; 180,432 in electrical engineering; 75,422 in textile industry.

Output and/or production in 1,000 tonnes, 1980: Hard coal, 76,446; lignite, 117,652; pig-iron, 22,683; raw steel ingots, 26,539; rolled steel, 19,152; castings (iron, steel and malleable castings), 1,666; cement, 12,696; fireproof products, 1,201; sulphuric acid (including production of cokeries), 2,184; staple fibres and rayon, 304; metalworking machines, 147; equipment for smelting works and rolling mills, 130; machines for mining industry, 256; cranes and hoisting machinery, 68; installation implements, 81; cables and electric lines, 245; springs of all kinds, 226; chains of all kinds, 91; locks and fittings, 322; spun yarns, 168; electric power, 175,450m. kwh. Of the total population, 13% were engaged in industry.

LABOUR. The economically active persons totalled 6,948,400 at the 1%-sample survey of the microcensus of April 1980. Of the total, 538,800 were self-employed, 115,000 unpaid family workers, 6,294,600 employees; 171,200 were engaged in agriculture and forestry, 3,362,100 in power supply, mining, manufacturing and building, 1·26m. in commerce and transport, 2,158,500 in other industries and services.

ROADS. There were (1 Jan. 1981) 29,433 km of 'classified' roads, including 1,776 km of autobahn, 5,552 km of federal roads, 12,238 km of first-class and 9,867 km of second-class highways. Number of motor vehicles, 1 July 1981, 7,290,793, including 6,013,912 passenger cars, 462,178 lorries, 330,327 motor lorries/trucks, 17,217 buses, 206,134 tractors and 212,121 motor cycles.

JUSTICE. There are a constitutional court *(Verfassungsgerichtshof)*, 3 courts of appeal, 19 regional courts, 132 local courts, 2 Land labour courts, 29 labour courts, a Land social court, 8 social courts, 3 finance courts, a higher administrative court, 7 administrative courts.

RELIGION. On 27 May 1970 (census) there were 41·9% Protestants and 52·5% Roman Catholics.

EDUCATION. In 1980 there were 4,769 primary schools with 72,604 teachers and 1,416,185 pupils; 744 special schools with 12,429 teachers and 109,761 pupils; 559 intermediate schools with 16,626 teachers and 362,784 pupils; 46

Gesamtschulen (comprehensive schools) with 3,773 teachers and 53,808 pupils; 645 high schools with 35,606 teachers and 648,354 pupils; in 1980 there were 302 part-time vocational schools with 480,656 pupils; vocational preparatory year 265 with 29,914 pupils; 336 full-time vocational schools with 104,375 pupils; 239 full-time vocational schools leading up to vocational colleges with 27,946 pupils; 149 advanced full-time vocational schools with 13,819 pupils; 556 schools for public health occupations with 8,783 teachers and 28,481 pupils; 13 schools within the scope of a pilot system of courses with 26,428 pupils and 937 teachers.

In the winter term 1980–81 there were 7 universities (Bielefeld, 11,084 students; Bochum, 24,580; Bonn, 34,399; Dortmund, 14,312; Düsseldorf, 12,130; Cologne, 35,911; Münster, 38,351); the Technical University of Aachen (29,411); 1 Roman Catholic and 2 Protestant theological colleges with together 773 students. There were also 3 colleges of music, 1 college of fine arts and the college for physical education in Cologne with together 8,722 students; 17 *Fachhochschulen* (vocational colleges) with 61,846 students, and 6 *Gesamthochschulen* with together 59,052 students.

Statistical Information: The Landesamt für Datenverarbeitung und Statistik Nordrhein-Westfalen (Mauerstr. 51, D4000 Düsseldorf 1) was founded in 1946, by amalgamating the provincial statistical offices of Rhineland and Westphalia. *President:* A. Benker. The Landesamt publishes: *Statistisches Jahrbuch Nordrhein-Westfalen.* From 1949.—*Statistisches Taschenbuch Nordrhein-Westfalen.* From 1955 to 1971.

Müller-Wille, W., *Westfalen.* Münster, 1981.

Land Library: Universitätsbibliothek, Grabbeplatz 7, Düsseldorf. *Director:* Dr G. Gattermann.

RHINELAND-PALATINATE

Rheinland-Pfalz

AREA AND POPULATION. Rhineland-Pfalz comprises 19,848 sq. km. Capital Mainz. Population (at 31 Dec. 1980), 3,642,482 (1,741,137 males, 1,901,345 females).

Vital statistics for calendar years:

	Live births	*Marriages*	*Divorces*	*Deaths*
1978	34,346	21,613	2,137	44,029
1979	34,805	22,756	5,434	43,108
1980	37,253	23,268	5,579	43,576

CONSTITUTION. The constitution of the Land Rheinland-Pfalz was approved by the Consultative Assembly on 25 April 1947 and by referendum on 18 May 1947, when 579,002 voted for and 514,338 against its acceptance.

The elections of 18 March 1979 returned 51 Christian Democrats, 43 Social Democrats, 6 Free Democrats.

The cabinet is headed by Bernhard Vogel (Christian Democrat).

AGRICULTURE. Area and yield of the most important products:

	Area (1,000 hectares)			*Yield (1,000 tonnes)*		
	1978	*1979*	*1980*	*1978*	*1979*	*1980*
Wheat	122·3	117·5	115·7	588·8	567·6	506·0
Rye	41·3	35·1	35·2	165·0	140·1	129·8
Barley	142·5	135·7	138·3	580·3	577·5	546·0
Oats	52·5	49·3	49·2	219·7	191·8	189·5
Potatoes	28·4	16·2	15·4	707·5	440·9	318·4
Sugar-beet	24·5	22·6	22·8	1,247·4	1,168·6	1,168·1
Wine (1,000 hectolitres)	59·7	57·5	59·0	5,177·7	5,395·8	3,390·2
Tobacco	1·3	1·2	1·1	...	...	...

Livestock (3 Dec. 1980): Cattle, 672,900 (including 234,600 milch cows); horses, 21,300; sheep, 99,700; pigs, 695,200; poultry, 3,549,900.

INDUSTRY. In Sept. 1980, 2,893 establishments (with 20 and more employees) employed 400,814 persons; of these 72,968 were employed in chemical industry; 24,985 in production of leather goods and footwear; 50,639 in machine construction; 18,443 in processing stones and earthenware.

LABOUR. The economically active persons totalled 1,571,500 at the census of April 1980. Of the total, 143,900 were self-employed, 63,400 unpaid family workers, 1·36m. employees; 99,700 were engaged in agriculture and forestry, 690,600 in power supply, mining, manufacturing and building, 268,800 in commerce and transport, 512,400 in other industries and services.

ROADS. There were (1 Jan. 1981) 18,706 km of 'classified' roads, including 645 km of autobahn, 3,243 km of federal roads, 6,910 km of first-class and 7,853 km of second-class highways. Number of motor vehicles, 1 July 1981, was 1,763,217, including 1,467,615 passenger cars, 79,107 lorries, 4,805 buses, 142,119 tractors and 57,617 motor cycles.

JUSTICE. There are a constitutional court *(Verfassungsgerichtshof)*, 2 courts of appeal, 8 regional courts, 47 local courts, a Land labour court, 5 labour courts, a Land social court, 4 social courts, a finance court, a higher administrative court, 4 administrative courts.

RELIGION. On 27 May 1970 (census) there were 40·7% Protestants and 55·7% Roman Catholics.

EDUCATION. In 1980 there were 1,188 primary schools with 15,890 teachers and 309,022 pupils; 157 special schools with 2,460 teachers and 18,094 pupils; 104 intermediate schools with 3,176 teachers and 68,924 pupils; 139 high schools with 6,597 teachers and 126,845 pupils; 99 vocational schools with 129,427 pupils; 127 advanced vocational schools and institutions for the training of technicians (full-and part-time) with 6,775 pupils; 109 schools for public health occupations with 278 teachers and 6,344 pupils.

In the winter term 1980–81 there were the University of Mainz (22,282 students), the University of Kaiserslautern (3,695 students), the University of Trier (3,939 students), the *Hochschule für Verwaltungswissenschaften* in Speyer (307 students), the Roman Catholic Theological College in Trier (380 students) and the Roman Catholic College in Vallendar (49 students). There were also the Teacher-Training College of the Land Rheinland-Pfalz *(Erziehungswissenschaftliche Hochschule)* with 2,686 students and the *Fachhochschule des Landes Rheinland-Pfalz* (college of engineering) with 8,105 students; also 2 private colleges for social-pedagogy (777 students).

Statistical Information: The Statistisches Landesamt Rheinland-Pfalz (Mainzer Str., 15–16, D5427 Bad Ems) was established in 1948. *President:* Dr Weis. Its publications include: *Statistisches Jahrbuch für Rheinland-Pfalz* (from 1948); *Statistische Monatshefte Rheinland-Pfalz* (from 1958); *Statistik von Rheinland-Pfalz* (from 1949) 302 vols. to date; *Rheinland-Pfalz im Spiegel der Statistik* (1968); *Die kreisfreien Städte und Landkreise in Rheinland-Pfalz* (1977); *Rheinland-Pfalz heute* (from 1973); *Benutzerhandbuch des Landesinformations-systems* (1976); *Rheinland-Pfalz heute und morgen* (Mainz, 1974); *Raumordnungsbericht 1981 der Landesregierung Rheinland-Pfalz* (Mainz, 1981).

Klöpper, R., and Korber, J., *Rheinland-Pfalz in seiner Gliederung nach zentralörtlichen Bereichen.* Remagen, 1957

Süsterhenn, A., and Schäfer, H., *Verfassung von Rheinland-Pfalz: Kommentar.* Koblenz, 1950

SAARLAND

HISTORY. In 1919 the Saar territory was placed under the control of the League of Nations. Following a plebiscite, the territory reverted to Germany in 1935. In

1945 the territory became part of the French Zone of occupation, and was in 1947 accorded an international status inside an economic union with France. In pursuance of the German–French agreement signed in Luxembourg on 27 Oct. 1956 the territory returned to Germany on 1 Jan. 1957. Its re-integration with Germany was completed by 5 July 1959.

AREA AND POPULATION. Saarland has an area of 2,570 sq. km. Estimated population, 31 Dec. 1980, 1,066,299 (505,545 males, 560,754 females). The capital is Saarbrücken.

Vital statistics for calendar years:

	Live births	*Marriages*	*Divorces*	*Deaths*
1978	9,574	7,069	666	13,208
1979	9,787	7,331	2,259	13,106
1980	10,511	7,587	1,628	13.061

CONSTITUTION. Saarland now ranks as a *Land* of the Federal German Republic and is represented in the Federal Diet by 8 members. The constitution passed on 15 Dec. 1947 is being revised.

The Saar Diet, elected on 27 April 1980, is composed as follows: 24 Social Democrats, 23 Christian Democrats,4 Free Democrats.

Saarland is governed by Christian Democrats and Free Democrats in spite of deadlock in Parliament. Minister President: Werner Zeyer (Christian Democrat).

AGRICULTURE AND FORESTRY. The cultivated area occupies 126,500 hectares or slightly more than half the total area; the forest area comprises nearly 32% of the total.

Area and yield of the most important crops:

	Area (1,000 hectares)			*Yield (1,000 tonnes)*		
	1978	*1979*	*1980*	*1978*	*1979*	*1980*
Wheat	10·5	7·7	8·0	46·1	36·9	30·7
Rye	9·8	7·7	7·8	36·2	29·8	26·9
Barley	13·8	11·8	12·5	55·2	49·3	47·4
Oats	7·9	7·2	7·1	31·8	26·8	24·4
Potatoes	5·7	1·1	0·9	158·1	31·1	14·7
Sugar-beet	...	...	...	0·6	1·0	0·7

Livestock, 3 Dec. 1980: Cattle, 73,278 (including 25,461 milch cows); pigs, 49,559; sheep, 11,192; horses, 4,330; poultry, 445,709.

INDUSTRY. In June 1980, 597 establishments (with 20 and more employees) employed 153,664 persons; of these 23,513 were engaged in coalmining, 30,634 in iron and steel production, 12,290 in machine construction, 10,204 in steel construction. In 1980 the coalmines produced 10·1m. tonnes of coal. Four iron foundries had 13 blast furnaces working and produced 4·3m. tonnes of pig-iron and 4·9m. tonnes of crude steel.

LABOUR. The economically active persons totalled 406,800 at the 1%-sample survey of the microcensus of April 1980. Of the total, 27,800 were self-employed, 7,600 unpaid family workers, 371,400 employees; 6,500 were engaged in agriculture and forestry, 207,700 in power supply, mining, manufacturing and building, 66,000 in commerce and transport, 126,600 in other industries and services.

ROADS. At 1 Jan. 1981 there were 2,139 km of 'classified' roads, including 163 km of autobahn, 443 km of federal roads, 765 km of first-class and 767 km of second-class highways. Number of motor vehicles, 1 July 1981, 473,086, including 419,686 passenger cars, 21,286 lorries, 1,527 buses, 12,018 tractors and 15,041 motor cycles.

JUSTICE. There are a constitutional court *(Verfassungsgerichtshof)*, a court of appeal, a regional court, 11 local courts, a Land labour court, 3 labour courts, a Land social court, a social court, a finance court, a higher administrative court, an administrative court.

RELIGION. On 27 May 1970 (census) 73·8% of the population were Roman Catholics and 24·1% were Protestants.

EDUCATION. In 1981–82 there were 334 primary schools with 3,981 teachers and 76,598 pupils; 56 special schools with 643 teachers and 5,089 pupils; 37 intermediate schools with 1,032 teachers and 19,644 pupils; 37 high schools with 1,899 teachers and 31,853 pupils; 2 *Gesamtschule* (comprehensive high schools) with 105 teachers and 2,018 pupils; 1 *Freie Waldorfschule* with 23 teachers and 354 pupils; 42 part-time vocational schools with 34,435 pupils; year of commercial basic training: 80 institutions with 235 classes and 5,126 pupils; 20 advanced full-time vocational schools and schools for technicians with 2,352 pupils; 58 full-time vocational schools with 6,784 students; 22 vocational extension schools with 1,750 pupils; 12 *Fachoberschulen* (full-time vocational schools leading up to vocational colleges) with 3,309 students; 38 schools for public health occupations with 2,149 pupils; 2 evening high schools and 1 *Saarland-Kolleg* with together 409 pupils. The number of pupils visiting the vocational schools amounts to 56,314. They are instructed by 1,704 teachers.

In the winter term 1981–82[1] there was the University of the Saar with 14,567 students; 1 conservatory with 306 students (1980–81); 1 vocational college (economics, engineering and design) with 1,692 students; 1 *Fachhochschule* (vocational college) for social affairs with 162 students; 1 vocational college for public administration with 135 students.

[1] Preliminary.

Statistical Information: The Statistisches Amt des Saarlandes (Hardenbergstrasse 3, D6600 Saarbrücken 1) was established on 1 April 1938. As from 1 June 1935, it was an independent agency; its predecessor, 1920–35, was the Statistical Office of the Government Commission of the Saar. *Chief:* Direktor Dr Kunkel. The most important publications are: *Statistisches Handbuch für das Saarland,* from 1950.—*Statistisches Taschenbuch für das Saarland*, from 1959.—*Saarländische Bevölkerungsund Wirtschaftszahlen.* Quarterly, from 1949. —*Saarland in Zahlen* (special issues).—*Einzelschriften zur Statistik des Saarlandes,* from 1950.

Fischer, P., *Die Saar zwischen Deutschland und Frankreich.* Frankfurt, 1959
Freymond, J., *Le Conflit sarrois, 1945–55.* Brussels, 1959. [*The Saar Conflict.* New York, 1960]
Schmidt, R. H., *Saarpolitik 1945–57.* 3 vols. Berlin, 1959–62

SCHLESWIG-HOLSTEIN

AREA AND POPULATION. The area of Schleswig-Holstein is 15,720 sq. km; it is divided into 4 urban and 11 rural districts and 1,132 communes. The capital is Kiel. The population (estimate, 31 Dec. 1980) numbered 2,611,285 (1,258,079 males, 1,353,206 females).

Vital statistics for calendar years:

	Live births	*Marriages*	*Divorces*	*Deaths*
1978	23,185	12,579	...	31,257
1979	22,810	13,068	3,289	31,400
1980	24,545	13,460	4,609	31,278

GOVERNMENT. The elections of 29 April 1979 gave the Christian Democrats 37, the Social Democratic Party 31, the Free Democratic Party 4 and the South Schleswig Association 1 seat. Minister President, Dr Gerhard Stoltenberg (Christian Democrat).

AGRICULTURE. Area and yield of the most important crops:

	Area (1,000 hectares)			*Yield (1,000 tonnes)*		
	1978	*1979*	*1980*	*1978*	*1979*	*1980*
Wheat	140·3	161·0	166·8	932·3	936·5	906·0
Rye	82·9	75·1	67·6	321·7	293·5	263·1
Barley	136·2	128·4	136·1	706·6	571·4	730·0
Oats	53·4	44·0	41·7	238·2	208·2	166·8
Potatoes	6·4	5·6	5·3	172·8	153·0	142·0
Sugar-beet	18·6	18·3	18·7	712·8	686·5	719·9

Livestock, 3 Dec. 1980: 35,400 horses, 1,552,500 cattle (including 520,100 milch cows), 1,807,300 pigs, 123,200 sheep, 4,334,700 poultry.

FISHERIES. In 1979 the yield of small-scale deep-sea and inshore fisheries was 36,600 tonnes valued at DM47m.

INDUSTRY. In 1980 (average), 1,659 establishments (with 20 and more employees) employed 183,495 persons; of these, 15,116 were employed in shipbuilding (except naval engineering); 30,614 in machine construction; 25,628 in food and kindred industry; 19,618 in electrical engineering.

LABOUR. The economically active persons totalled 1·27m. at the 1%-sample survey of the microcensus of April 1980. Of the total, 107,000 were self-employed, 39,000 unpaid family workers, 1,128,000 employees; 73,000 were engaged in agriculture and forestry, 384,000 in power supply, mining, manufacturing and building, 220,000 in commerce and transport, 451,000 in other industries and services.

ROADS. There were (1 Jan. 1981) 9,681 km of 'classified' roads, including 321 km of autobahn, 1,983 km of federal roads, 3,511 km of first-class and 3,866 km of second-class highways. Number of motor vehicles, 1 Jan. 1981, was 1,130,609, including 968,560 passenger cars, 56,095 lorries, 2,732 buses, 73,400 tractors, 20,524 motor cycles.

SHIPPING. The Kiel Canal, 98·7 km (51 miles) long, is on Schleswig-Holstein territory. In 1938, 53,530 vessels of 22·6m. net tons passed through it; in 1978, 57,292 vessels of 48·3m. net tons; in 1979, 55,457 vessels of 49·3m. net tons; in 1980, 56,677 vessels of 53·9m. net tons.

JUSTICE. There are a court of appeal, 4 regional courts, 34 local courts, a Land labour court, 6 labour courts, a Land social court, 4 social courts, a finance court, an administrative court.

RELIGION. On 27 May 1970 (census) there were 86·5% Protestants and 6% Roman Catholics.

EDUCATION. In 1980–81 there were 730 primary schools with 6,775 teachers and 200,555 pupils; 168 special schools with 1,635 teachers and 19,612 pupils; 172 intermediate schools with 3,529 teachers and 88,526 pupils; 94 high schools with 4,292 teachers and 87,936 pupils; 5 *Integrierte Gesamtschulen* (comprehensive schools) with 221 teachers and 3,878 pupils; 69 part-time vocational schools with 1,422 teachers and 85,666 pupils; 135 full-time vocational schools with 450 teachers and 11,015 pupils; 65 advanced vocational schools with 303 teachers and 4,827 pupils; 54 schools for public health occupations with 3,225 pupils; 43 vocational grammar schools with 349 teachers and 5,353 pupils; 5 *Fachhochschulen* (vocational colleges) with 5,139 pupils in the summer term 1981.

In the summer term 1981 the University of Kiel had 13,599 students, 2 teacher-training colleges had 3,085 students, 1 music college had 343 students and 1 *Medizinische Hochschule* in Lübeck had 343 students.

Statistical Information: Statistisches Landesamt Schleswig-Holstein (Fröbel Str. 15–17, D2300 Kiel 1). *Director:* Dr Mohr. Publications: *Statistisches Taschenbuch Schleswig-Holstein,* since 1954.—*Statistisches Jahrbuch Schleswig-Holstein,* since 1951.—*Statistische Monatshefte Schleswig-Holstein,* since 1949.—*Statistische Berichte,* since 1947.—*Beitrage zur historischen Statistik Schleswig-Holstein,* since 1967.—*Lange Reihen,* since 1977.

Baxter, R. R., *The Law of International Waterways.* Harvard Univ. Press, 1964
Brandt, O., *Grundriss der Geschichte Schleswig-Holsteins.* 5th ed. Kiel, 1957
Handbuch für Schleswig-Holstein. 20th ed. Kiel, 1980

State Library: Schleswig-Holsteinische Landesbibliothek, Kiel, Schloss. *Director:* Prof. Dr Klaus Friedland.

GHANA

Capital: Accra
Population: 11·31m. (1980)
GNP per capita: US$420 (1980)

HISTORY. The State of Ghana came into existence on 6 March 1957 when the former Colony of the Gold Coast and the Trusteeship Territory of Togoland attained Dominion status. The name of the country recalls a powerful monarchy which from the 4th to the 13th century A.D. ruled the region of the middle Niger.

The Ghana Independence Act received the royal assent on 7 Feb. 1957. The General Assembly of the United Nations in Dec. 1956 approved the termination of British administration in Togoland and the union of Togoland with the Gold Coast on the latter's attainment of independence.

The country was declared a Republic within the Commonwealth on 1 July 1960 with Dr Kwame Nkrumah as the first President. On 24 Feb. 1966 the Nkrumah regime was overthrown in a military *coup* and ruled by the National Liberation Council until 1 Oct. 1969 when the military regime handed over power to a civilian regime under a new constitution. Dr K. A. Busia was the Prime Minister of the Second Republic. In Aug. 1975 the Government announced that they would commemorate the late Dr Nkrumah as 'a great Ghanaian responsible for taking the country to independence'.

On 13 Jan. 1972 the armed forces and police took over power again from the civilian regime in a *coup*.

In Oct. 1975 the National Redemption Council was subordinated to a Supreme Military Council (SMC). In 1979 the SMC was toppled in a *coup* led by Flight-Lieut. J. Rawlings. The new government permitted elections already scheduled and these resulted in a victory for Dr Hilla Limann and his People's National Party.

AREA AND POPULATION. The area of Ghana is 92,010 sq. miles (238,305 sq. km); census population 1970, 8,559,313. Estimate (1980) 11·31m.

The capital is Accra (population, 1970, 636,067).

Ghana is divided into 9 regions:

Regions	*Area (sq. km)*	*Population census 1970*	*Capital*	*Population census 1970*
Eastern	19,833	1,262,882	Koforidua	69,804
Western	24,214	770,089	Sekondi-Takoradi	254,543
Central	9,469	890,135	Cape Coast	71,594
Ashanti	25,123	1,505,049	Kumasi	351,629
Brong-Ahafo	39,709	766,509	Sunyani	61,772
Northern	70,338	728,572	Tamale	120,000
Volta	20,651	947,012	Ho	46,348
Upper	16,877	862,723	Bolgatanga	18,896
Greater Accra	2,023	903,445	Accra	636,067

Other chief towns (population, census, 1970); Asamankese, 101,144; Nsawam, 57,350; Oda, 40,740; Obuasi, 40,001; Winneba, 36,104; Keta, 27,461; Swedru (Agona), 23,843.

Estimated birth rate, between 47 and 52 per 1,000; death rate, about 23 per 1,000.

CONSTITUTION AND GOVERNMENT. Following a bloodless *coup* on 13 Jan. 1972 the armed forces of Ghana took over the government from Dr K. A. Busia. A National Redemption Council (NRC) was established to administer the affairs of the country.

The Constitution of the Second Republic of Ghana which came into force on 22 Aug. 1969 was suspended. The office of President was abolished and the National Assembly dissolved.

On 5 July 1978 officers of the Supreme Military Council ousted Gen. I. K.

Acheampong in a bloodless *coup*. They in turn were overthrown by a junior officers *coup* on 4 June 1979. An Armed Forces Revolutionary Council was formed but on 24 Sept. 1979 this made way in favour of a civilian government. Dr Hilla Limann became President of the Third Republic, but on 31 Dec. 1981 Rawlings led a second *coup* which dismissed the government and Parliament, suspended the Constitution, and established a Provisional National Defence Council to exercise all government powers.

For earlier political history of Ghana *see* THE STATESMAN'S YEAR-BOOK, 1971–72.

President: Dr Hilla Limann.

National flag: Red, gold, green (horizontal); a black star in the centre.

National anthem: Hail the name of Ghana.

DEFENCE. The Ministry of Defence is responsible for the armed services, the military academy and the border guards. The Military Academy provides a 2-year course for army officers, a 1-year course for later entrants in the flying-training school and a preliminary 6-month course for navy cadets.

Army. The Ghana Army consists of 6 infantry battalions, 1 reconnaissance battalion, 1 field engineer battalion, 1 mortar battalion, 5 with armoured cars,: and ancillary units. Total strength, (1983) 12,000. There are also 3 border battalions and a paramilitary militia of 5,000.

Navy. The Ghana Navy was formed in 1959. It comprises 2 British-built 500-ton corvettes, 4 fast attack craft, 2 patrol craft, 2 old seaward defence boats, 4 coastal patrol boats and 2 service craft. Naval personnel in 1983 numbered 1,360 officers and ratings.

Air Force. The Ghana Air Force was formed in 1959, when an Air Force Training School was established at Accra. Its first combat unit has 6 Italian-built Aermacchi M.B.326K light ground attack jets ordered in 1976. It has, for training, transport, search and rescue, and air survey operations, 5 Fokker Friendship twin-turboprop transports, and a twin-turbofan Fokker Fellowship for Presidential use, all built in the Netherlands; 6 Shorts Skyvan twin-engined STOL transports and 11 Bulldog primary trainers, all built in the UK; 2 Bell 212 helicopters built in the US; 2 French-built Alouette III helicopters, 8 Italian-built SF.260TP turboprop trainers, and 6 Aermacchi M.B.326F armed jet trainers. There are air bases at Takoradi and Tamale. Personnel strength (1983) about 1,400.

INTERNATIONAL RELATIONS

Membership. Ghana is a member of UN, the Commonwealth, OAU, ECOWAS and is an ACP state of EEC.

ECONOMY

Planning. In Jan. 1983 a 4-year economic reconstruction and development programme was announced.

Budget. Revenue and expenditure for fiscal years ending 30 June (excluding Ghana Railway and Takoradi Harbour accounts), in ₵ 1,000:

	1974–75	*1975–76*	*1976–77*	*1978–79*
Revenue [1]	804,800	814,800	1,171,300	3,206,430
Expenditure [2]	1,161,400	1,438,572	2,015,900	3,819,420

[1] Excludes redemption of loans.

[2] Excludes contribution to sinking funds, repayment of loans, loans and refunds of revenue.

Currency. The monetary unit is the *cedi* (₵), divided into 100 *pesewas* (P) and equivalent to £0·51 or US$0·87. Notes are issued of 1, 2, 5, 10 and 50 ₵; copper coins of ½ and 1 P, and cupro-nickel coins of 2½, 5, 10 and 20 P. In March 1983, £1 = ₵ 4·15; US$1 = 2·75.

Banking. The Bank of Ghana was established in Feb. 1957 as the central bank of the country. The Ghana Commercial Bank, also established in Feb. 1957, is the former Bank of the Gold Coast. It is a purely commercial institution and has 120 branches in the country, 1 in London and 1 in Lomé (Togo). Barclays Bank (Ghana) Ltd has 54 branches and agencies and the Standard Bank (Ghana) Ltd has 27 branches.

The Ghana National Investment Bank, opened in June 1963, is a finance-cum-development agency. The former post office savings bank has been transformed into the Ghana Savings Bank. The Bank for Housing and Construction opened in 1973.

ENERGY AND NATURAL RESOURCES

Oil. The Government announced in Jan. 1978 that oil had been found in commercial quantities with known reserves (1980) 7m. bbls.

Minerals. In 1979 gold production was 387,000 fine oz.; diamonds (1980), nearly 1m. carats; manganese (1977), 268,000 tons; bauxite (1977), 265,000 long tons. Old mines are being re-opened and exploration of mineral oil deposits, bauxite, limestone and iron ore is now extensive.

Agriculture. Cocoa is by far the most important crop and covers about 2m. acres. Production (1979–80) 300,000 tons. There has been considerable increase in cocoa yields as a result of the Capsid control and the introduction of improved varieties. A Cocoa Affairs Ministry has been established to formulate policy and provide technical supervision for developing cocoa, coffee, shea-nuts, copra and bananas. Coffee, improved types of oil-palm and coconut are being planted on an increased scale and production from these crops is increasing. Progress has been made in the planting of Clonal rubber in south-west Ghana. In the south-east coastal belt irrigation works have been constructed and black-clay farming is being successfully undertaken in the Accra plains.

Of the main foodstuffs in south and central Ghana, maize, rice, cassava, plantain, groundnuts, yam and cocoyam predominate. Tobacco is proving an attractive and very important cash crop in food-crop producing areas.

In northern Ghana the chief food crops are groundnuts, rice, maize, guinea corn, millet and yams, with tobacco and cotton as important cash crops.

Agricultural cash crops, *e.g.*, pepper, ginger, pineapple, avocado and citrus, etc., are being extensively cultivated for export. Active steps have also been taken to provide within the next few years industrial raw materials, *e.g.*, kenaf, cotton, tobacco, palm-oil, mango, pineapple, sugar-cane, etc., to feed the local factories. The trend is towards diversification of agriculture.

Production of main food crops (1977) was: Cassava, 2·3m. tons; plantain, 1,455,000 tons; coco yam, 905,000 tons; yam, 397,000 tons.

Livestock, 1981: Cattle, 950,000; sheep, 1·7m.; goats, 2·1m.; horses, 4,000; pigs, 415,000; poultry, 12m. The Central Veterinary Laboratory is located at Pong-Tamale under the Veterinary Research Officer. The efficient control of rinderpest and bovine pleuro-pneumonia, the two main killing diseases of cattle, has made it possible to quadruple the cattle in the past 20 years. The control of imported livestock is effected by 8 quarantine stations along the frontier, and new veterinary centres are being established.

Forestry. The total area of closed forest is 82,576 sq. km, of which 16,852·2 sq. km are reserved. Exports (1976) of logs, was 512,261 tons.

Fisheries. The fisheries sector of the economy is being developed, including fishing harbours and landing stages, workshops for repair and maintenance of outboard motors; development of fish culture and expansion of fish farms, establishment of fishing complexes, purchase of refrigerated vans for fish distribution and the establishment of more cold-stores.

COMMERCE. In 1981 exports were US$ 766·4m.; imports, US$ 748·7m. Principal exports: cocoa, timber and gold; imports were raw materials, capital equipment, petroleum and food.

Total trade between Ghana and UK (British Department of Trade returns, in £1,000 sterling):

	1978	*1979*	*1980*	*1981*	*1982*
Imports to UK	110,122	89,808	104,545	61,167	74,438
Exports and re-exports from UK	118,975	88,058	88,511	87,849	66,709

Tourism. In 1977 there were 60,000 tourists.

COMMUNICATIONS

Roads. The total mileage of roads maintained by the Public Works Department in 1974 was 21,762, of which 2,746 miles were bitumen surfaced and 5,016 miles gravel surfaced.

The number of vehicles in use (1977) was 121,700, of which private cars, 49,300.

Railways. Total length of railways open in 1980 was 953 km of 1,067 mm gauge. In 1976–77 railway income was ₵ 13·8m. from 6m. passenger-journeys and 1m. tonnes of freight carried.

Aviation. There are 4 major airports in Ghana, situated at Accra, Takoradi, Kumasi and Tamale; and 3 airstrips for domestic services. Accra airport is an international airport. The following airlines operate scheduled services: Ghana Airways, Air France, Nigerian Airways, Air Mali, United Arab Airlines, KLM, Swissair, PANAM, British Caledonian and several other companies. Total aircraft freight in 1975 was 3m. ton-km.

Shipping. The chief ports are Takoradi and Tema; the 'surf' ports at Accra, Winneba, Cape Coast and Keta ceased to operate when Tema harbour was opened in 1962, 18 miles east of Accra. In 1970, 4,164,329 tons of cargo were imported and 2,154,759 tons were exported by 3,116 ships.

Post and Broadcasting. There were (31 Dec. 1974) 2,190 miles of telegraph land wire, 20,948 miles of telephone trunks, 237 post offices and 710 postal agencies. There were 431 telephone exchanges and 742 call offices with (1980) 68,853 telephones in use. There are internal wireless stations at Accra, Kumasi, Bawku, Lawra, Kete-Krachi, Tamale, Yendi, Kpandu, Tumu and Sekondi-Takoradi.

Cinemas. In 1977 there were 8 cinemas with a seating capacity of 13,200.

Newspapers. There are 5 daily and 7 weekly papers, 8 fortnightly and 5 monthly magazines.

JUSTICE, RELIGION, EDUCATION AND WELFARE

Justice. The Courts are constituted as follows:

Supreme Court. The Supreme Court consists of the Chief Justice who is also the President and not less than 6 other Justices of the Supreme Court. The Chief Justice presides at the sittings of the Supreme Court and in his absence the most senior of the Justices of the Supreme Court as constituted presides. The Supreme Court is the final court of appeal in Ghana. The final interpretation of the provisions of the constitution has been entrusted to the Supreme Court.

Court of Appeal. The Court of Appeal consists of the Chief Justice together with not less than 5 other Justices of the Appeal court and such other Justices of Superior Courts as the Chief Justice may nominate. The Court of Appeal is duly constituted by 3 Justices. The Court of Appeal is bound by its own previous decisions and all courts inferior to the Court of Appeal are bound to follow the decisions of the Court of Appeal on questions of law. Divisions of the Appeal Court may be created, subject to the discretion of the Chief Justice.

High Court of Justice. The Court has jurisdiction in civil and criminal matters as well as those relating to industrial and labour disputes including administrative complaints. The High Court of Justice has supervisory jurisdiction over all inferior Courts and any adjudicating authority and in exercise of its supervisory jurisdiction has power to issue such directions, orders or writs including writs or orders in the nature of habeas corpus, certiorari, mandamus, prohibition and quo warrantto. The High Court of Justice has no power in a trial for the offence of treason to convict any person for any offence other than treason. The High Court consists of the Chief Justice and not less than twelve other judges and such other Justices of the Superior Court as the Chief Justice may appoint.

Police. The force was established in Oct. 1874. It is headed by an Inspector-General and consists of 7 divisions with a (1975) strength of 15,817.

Religion. Christians represent 43% of the population (Protestant, 29%; Roman Catholic, 14%), Moslem, 12%, animist, 38%.

Education. A complete re-organization of the system took place in 1974. There are kindergartens for the age-groups 4–6 years. Primary schools are free and attendance is compulsory. In 1978–79 there were 11,422 primary schools with 1,784,834 pupils. In 1979 there were 300 secondary schools with 1m. pupils. At the beginning of the 1979 academic year there were 41 training colleges with 12,350 students. In 1978–79 there were 8,455 students at the 3 universities (University of Ghana, the University of Science and Technology and the University of the Cape Coast). University education is free.

Health. Medical facilities include 50 government hospitals, 116 health centres and posts, 4 university hospitals, 3 mental hospitals, 4 leprosaria, 7 military hospitals, 1 prison hospital, 40 mission hospitals and 16 private hospitals. In addition, there are 30 nurses and midwives training schools.

There were 1,224 doctors, 7,608 nurses and 4,168 midwives at work in 1976.

DIPLOMATIC REPRESENTATIVES

Of Ghana in Great Britain (13 Belgrave Sq., London, SW1X 8PR)
High Commissioner: Kenneth Kweku Sinaman Dadzie (accredited 13 Oct. 1982).

Of Great Britain in Ghana (Barclays Bank Bldg., High St., Accra)
High Commissioner: J. Mellon, CMG.

Of Ghana in the USA (2460 16th St., NMW, Washington, D.C. 20009)
Ambassador: Ebenezer Amatei Akuete.

Of the USA in Ghana (Liberia and Kinbu Rds., Accra)
Ambassador: Thomas W. M. Smith.

Of Ghana to the United Nations
Ambassador: James Victor Gbeho.

Books of Reference

Digest of Statistics. Accra. Quarterly (from May 1953)
Ghana. Official Handbook. Annual
Trade Directory of the Republic of Ghana. 5th ed. London, 1967
The Volta River Project. 3 vols. HMSO, 1956
Afrifa, A. A., *The Ghana Coup 24th February 1966.* London, 1966
Austin, D., *Politics in Ghana, 1946–60.* OUP, 1964
Boateng, E. A., *A Geography of Ghana.* 2nd ed. CUP, 1966
Davidson, B., *Black Star.* London, 1973
James, C. L. R., *Nkrumah and the Ghana Revolution.* London, 1977
Jones, T., *Ghana's First Republic 1960–1966.* London, 1975
Killick, T., *Development Economics in Action: A Study of Economic Policies in Ghana.* London, 1978

GIBRALTAR

Population: 30,522 (1981)
GNP per capita: US$5,040 (1980)

HISTORY. The Rock of Gibraltar was settled by Moors in 711; they named it after their chief Jebel Tariq, 'the Mountain of Tarik'. In 1462 it was taken by the Spaniards, from Granada. It was captured by Admiral Sir George Rooke on 24 July 1704, and ceded to Great Britain by the Treaty of Utrecht, 1713. The cession was confirmed by the treaties of Paris (1763) and Versailles (1783).

On 10 Sept. 1967, in pursuance of a United Nations resolution on the decolonization of Gibraltar, a referendum was held in Gibraltar in order to ascertain whether the people of Gibraltar believed that their interests lay in retaining their link with Britain or in passing under Spanish sovereignty. Out of a total electorate of 12,762, 12,138 voted to retain the British connexion, while 44 voted for Spain.

On 15 Dec. 1982 the border between Gibraltar and Spain was re-opened for Spaniards and Gibraltarans pedestrians who are residents of Gibraltar. The border was closed by Spain in June 1969.

AREA AND POPULATION. Area, 2½ sq. miles (6·5 sq. km). Total population, including port and harbour (census, 6 Oct. 1970), 26,833 (13,501 males; 13,322 females). Estimate (1981) 30,522. The population is mostly of Genoese, Portuguese and Maltese as well as Spanish descent.

Vital statistics (1981): Births, 511; marriages, 429; deaths, 231.

CONSTITUTION AND GOVERNMENT. Following a Constitutional Conference held in July 1968, a new Constitution was introduced in 1969. The Legislative and City Councils were merged to produce an enlarged legislature known as the Gibraltar House of Assembly. Executive authority is exercised by the Governor, who is also Commander-in-Chief. The Governor, while retaining certain reserved powers, is normally required to act in accordance with the advice of the Gibraltar Council, which consists of 4 *ex-officio* members (the Deputy Governor, the Deputy Fortress Commander, the Attorney-General and the Financial and Development Secretary) together with 5 elected members of the House of Assembly appointed by the Governor after consultation with the Chief Minister. Matters of primarily domestic concern are devolved to elected Ministers, with Britain responsible for other matters, including external affairs, defence and internal security. There is a Council of Ministers presided over by the Chief Minister.

The House of Assembly consists of a Speaker appointed by the Governor, 15 elected and 2 *ex-officio* members (the Attorney-General and the Financial and Development Secretary).

A Mayor of Gibraltar is elected from among the members of the Assembly by the elected members of the Assembly.

Governor and C.-in-C.: Admiral Sir David Williams, GCB.

Chief Minister: Sir Joshua Hassan, CBE, MVO, QC.

Flag: White with a red strip along the bottom, a red triple-towered castle with a gold key depending from the gateway.

DEFENCE. The Gibraltar Regiment is a part-time infantry battalion with a small regular cadre. There is also a resident battalion from the British Army.

ECONOMY

Budget. Revenue and expenditure (in £ sterling):

	1977–78	*1978–79*	*1979–80*	*1980–81*	*1981–82*
Revenue	18,661,858	26,408,993	32,338,140	...	44,265,500
Expenditure	19,962,916	25,704,366	26,368,784	...	42,594,000

Currency. The legal currency consists of Gibraltar government notes and UK coins. The amount of local currency notes in circulation at 31 March 1979 was £5,651,410.

Banking. There are 5 banks, including a branch of Barclays Bank International. Government savings banks had 10,429 depositers and £1,890,333 savings at 31 March 1981.

INDUSTRY AND TRADE

Industry. There are a number of relatively small industrial concerns engaged in the bottling of beer and mineral waters, etc., mainly for consumption. There is a small but important commercial ship-repair yard.

Labour. The full-time labour force at 31 Dec. 1981, 12,633. The labour supply from the local population is insufficient to meet the demand and since the withdrawal of the Spanish frontier workers in June 1969, a substantial part of the labour has had to come from other places. A quota system is in existence which takes into account the demand from the various industries and seasonal variations and the issue of employment permits is based on this. Approximately 60% of the local labour force is employed by the UK departments or the Gibraltar government.

A considerable proportion of the workers are organized in one or other of the 13 registered employees' trade unions, of which the Transport and General Workers Union has the largest membership; 7 of these are local branches of parent associations in the UK.

Commerce. Imports and exports (in £ sterling):

	1978	*1979*	*1980*	*1981*
Imports	39,442,136	55,519,064	63,141,753	65,826,282
Exports [1]	3,248,546	4,695,339	4,182,217	5,701,416

[1] Exclusive of petroleum and petroleum products.

Britain and the Commonwealth provide the bulk of the imports, but fresh vegetables, fruit and fish come mainly from Morocco, Portugal and the Netherlands. Exports of local produce are negligible. Gibraltar depends largely on tourism, the entrepôt trade and the provision of supplies to visiting ships.

Tourism. The number of tourists in 1981 was 132,373 (1980, 153,756).

COMMUNICATIONS

Roads. There are 30 miles of roads including 4 miles of pedestrian way.

Aviation. There are 5 weekly flights between London and Gibraltar (3 operated by Gibraltar Airways and 2 by British Airways) during the winter; these are increased to daily flights during the summer.

The unilateral closure by Spain of their land frontier with Gibraltar makes overland travel from or to Spain impossible. However, there is a regular car ferry service and air services to Tangier and Morocco from where it is possible to cross over to the Spanish mainland.

Shipping. Gibraltar is a naval and air base of strategic importance. There is a deep Admiralty harbour of 440 acres. A total of 2,710 merchant ships, 17,689,240 NRT, entered the port during 1981. An additional 6,180 calls were made by yachts, 55,214 NRT.

Post and Broadcasting. An automatic telephone system exists in the town; number of telephones (1981), 9,388. There is also world-wide communication *via* the cable and/or wireless circuits of Cable & Wireless Ltd and international direct dialling facilities. Air-mails arrive by British Airways daily. A direct air-mail service between Gibraltar and Tangier is run by Gibraltar Airways, Ltd. Surface mails arrive direct and through France, Spain and Tangier. Radio Gibraltar broadcasts for 17 hours daily, in English and Spanish, and there are about 40 hours of television per week. Number of receivers (1981), radio, 83; TV, 6,500.

Cinemas. In 1981 there were 3 cinemas with a seating capacity of 2,400.

Newspapers. There were (1981) 1 daily and 5 weeklies.

JUSTICE, RELIGION, EDUCATION AND WELFARE

Justice. The judicial system is based on the English system. There is a Court of Appeal, a Supreme Court, presided over by the Chief Justice, a court of first instance and a magistrates' court.

Religion. Religion of civil population mostly Roman Catholic; 1 Anglican and 1 Roman Catholic cathedral and 2 Anglican and 6 Roman Catholic churches; 1 Presbyterian and 1 Methodist church and 4 synagogues; annual subsidy to each communion, £500.

Education. Free compulsory education is provided for children between ages 5 and 15 years. Scholarships are made available for universities, teacher-training and other higher education in Britain. The comprehensive system was introduced in Sept. 1972. There were (1981) 7 first, 4 middle, 1 primary school and 2 comprehensive schools. All first and middle schools are mixed but the comprehensives are single-sex. In addition, there are 2 Services primary schools and 1 private primary school. A new purpose-built Special School for Handicapped Children was opened in 1977. Technical education is available at the Gibraltar and Dockyard Technical College managed by the UK Ministry of Defence for which Government pays 50% of all recurrent costs and scholarships are made available in Britain for university, teacher training and other forms of higher education. In Sept. 1981, there were 2,619 pupils at government primary schools, 204 at private and 819 at services schools; 24 at the special school; 878 at the boys' comprehensive school and 916 at the girls' comprehensive. In addition there were 55 full-time and 249 part-time students in the Technical College. In 1980–81, government expenditure on education was £3,304,491

Health. In 1981 there was 1 hospital with 241 beds and 15 doctors. Total expenditure on medical and health services during year ended 31 March 1981 was £4,127,371.

Books of Reference.

Annual Report on Gibraltar, 1972. London, 1974
Gibraltar Year Book. Gibraltar, (Annual)
Dennis, P., *Gibraltar.* Newton Abbot, 1977
Ellicott, D., *Our Gibraltar.* Gibraltar, 1975
Garcia, S., *Gibraltar: An Analysis of How the Economy was Affected by the Spanish Restrictions 1963–72* (unpublished). Garrison Library, 1974
Green, M. M., *A Gibraltar Bibliography.* London, 1980.—*Supplement.* London, 1982
Hills, G., *Rock of Contention: A History of Gibraltar.* London, 1974
Howes, H. W., *The Story of Gibraltar.* London, 1946

GREECE

Capital: Athens
Population: 9·7m. (1981)
GNP per capita: US$4,520 (1980)

Elliniki Dimokratia

HISTORY. Greece gained her independence from Turkey in 1821–29, and by the Protocol of London, of 3 Feb. 1830, was declared a kingdom, under the guarantee of Great Britain, France and Russia. For details of the subsequent history to 1947 *see* THE STATESMAN'S YEAR-BOOK, 1957, pp. 1069–70 and for details of the monarchy *see* THE STATESMAN'S YEAR-BOOK, 1973–74, p. 1000.

AREA AND POPULATION. Greece is bounded north by Albania, Yugoslavia and Bulgaria, east by Turkey and the Aegean Sea, south by the Mediterranean and west by the Ionian Sea. The total area is 131,986 sq. km (50,960 sq. miles), of which the islands account for 24,761 sq. km (9,560 sq. miles).

The population was 9,706,687 according to the census of 5 April 1981.

Athens is the capital; population of Greater Athens, in 1981, 3,016,457.

The following table shows the prefectures *(Nomoi)* and their population:

Nomoi	*Area in sq. km*	*Population 1971*	*Capital*	*Population 1981*
Greater Athens [1]	*433*	*2,540,241*		
Central Greece and Euboea [2]	*24,475*	*992,077*		
Aetolia and Acarnania	5,447	228,989	Missolonghi	11,275
Attica [2]	2,496	201,948	Athens	885,136
Boeotia	3,211	114,675	Levadeia	17,697
Euboea	3,908	165,369	Chalcis	44,774
Evrytania	2,045	29,533	Karpenissi	5,243
Phthiotis	4,368	154,542	Lamia	42,019
Phokis	2,121	41,361	Amphissa	7,233
Piraeus [2]	879	55,660	Piraeus (1971)	187,458
Peloponnessos	*21,439*	*986,912*		
Argolis	2,214	88,698	Nauplion	10,554
Arcadia	4,419	111,263	Tripolis	21,140
Akhaïa	3,209	239,859	Patras	140,878
Elia	2,681	165,056	Pyrgos	21,992
Korinthia	2,289	113,115	Korinthos	22,495
Lakonia	3,636	95,844	Sparte	15,915
Messenia	2,991	173,077	Calamata	41,998
Ionian Islands	*2,307*	*184,443*		
Zakynthos	406	30,187	Zante	9,742
Kerkyra	641	92,933	Kerkyra	35,787
Kefallenia	935	36,742	Argostolion	7,294
Lefkas	325	24,581	Levkas	6,631
Epirus	*9,203*	*310,344*		
Arta	1,612	78,376	Arta	20,077
Thesprotia	1,515	40,684	Hegoumenitsa	6,190
Yannina	4,990	134,688	Yannina	44,362
Preveza	1,086	56,586	Preveza	13,555
Thessaly	*13,904*	*659,913*		
Karditsa	2,576	133,776	Karditsa	27,670
Larissa	5,354	232,226	Larisa	103,263
Magnessia	2,636	161,392	Volos	70,967
Trikkala	3,338	132,519	Trikkala	45,138

[1] Comprising parts of Attica and Piraeus prefectures.
[2] Excluding figures for the parts of Attica and Piraeus prefectures within Greater Athens.

Nomoi	Area in sq. km	Population 1971	Capital	Population 1981
Macedonia	*34,203*	*1,890,684*		
Grevena	2,338	35,275	Grevena	7,725
Drama	3,468	91,009	Drama	36,963
Imathia	1,699	118,103	Verria	37,528
Thessaloniki	3,560	710,352	Thessaloniki	402,443
Kavala	2,109	121,593	Kavala	56,260
Kastoria	1,685	45,711	Kastoria	20,532
Kilkis	2,597	84,375	Kilkis	11,694
Kozani	3,562	135,709	Kozani	31,247
Pella	2,506	126,085	Edessa	15,980
Pieria	1,548	91,728	Katerini	38,488
Serres	3,987	202,898	Serres	46,168
Florina	1,863	52,264	Florina	12,708
Khalkidiki	2,945	73,850	Polyghyros	5,228
Mount Athos	336	1,732	Karyai (1971)	301
Thrace	*8,578*	*329,582*		
Evros	4,242	138,988	Alexandroupolis	35,856
Xanthi	1,793	82,917	Xanthi	33,713
Rodopi	2,543	107,677	Komotini	37,633
Aegean Islands	*9,071*	*417,813*		
Cyclades	2,572	86,337	Hermoupolis	14,115
Lesvos	2,154	114,802	Mitylini	24,937
Samos	778	41,709	Limin Vatheos	5,892
Khios	904	53,948	Khios	24,115
Dodecanese	2,663	121,017	Rhodes	40,656
Crete	*8,331*	*456,642*		
Iraklion	2,641	209,670	Heraklion	101,668
Lassithi	1,818	66,226	Aghios Nikolaos	8,194
Rethymnon	1,496	60,949	Rethymnon	17,940
Canea	2,376	119,797	Canea	47,804

In 1971 cities (*i.e.*, communes of more than 10,000 inhabitants, including Greater Athens) had 4,667,489 inhabitants (53·2%), towns (*i.e.*, communes with between 2,000 and 9,999 inhabitants), 1,028,769 (11·7%), villages and rural communities (under 2,000 inhabitants), 3,072,383 (35·1%).

Mount Athos, the easternmost of the three prongs of the peninsula of Chalcidice, is a self-governing community composed of 20 monasteries. (*See* THE STATESMAN'S YEAR-BOOK, 1945, p. 983.) For centuries the peninsula has been administered by a Council of 4 members and an Assembly of 20 members, 1 deputy from each monastery. The Greek Government on 10 Sept. 1926 recognized this autonomous form of government; Articles 109–112 of the Constitution of 1927 gave legal sanction to the Charter of Mount Athos, drawn up by representatives of the 20 monasteries on 20 May 1924. Article 103 of the 1952 Constitution and Article 105 of the 1975 Constitution confirmed the special status of Mount Athos.

Vital statistics (1977): 143,739 live births; 1,566 still births; 1,918 illegitimate births; 76,228 marriages; 83,750 deaths; 16,510 emigrants (Jan.–Sept.); 12,572 immigrants (Jan.–Sept.).

CLIMATE. Coastal regions and the islands have typical Mediterranean conditions, with mild, rainy winters and hot, dry, sunny summers. Rainfall comes almost entirely in the winter months, though amounts vary widely according to position and relief. Continental conditions affect the northern mountainous areas, with severe winters, deep snow cover and heavy precipitation, but summers are hot.

Athens. Jan. 48°F (8·6°C), July 82·5°F (28·2°C). Annual rainfall 16·6″ (414·3 mm).

CONSTITUTION AND GOVERNMENT. A *coup d'état* took place on 21 April 1967, 'to avert the danger of a communist threat against the nation'. A Military Government was formed, which suspended the 1952 Constitution. Following the unsuccessful counter-*coup* in 1967, King Constantine went abroad.

Voting took place on 29 July 1973 in the referendum to change Greece from a Monarchy to a Republic and to elect a President. 77·2% of the valid votes were cast for a republican régime.

On 25 Nov. 1973, in a bloodless *coup*, President Papadopoulos was overthrown and Lieut.-Gen. Phaedon Ghizikis was sworn in. The military dictatorship collapsed on 23 July 1974 and the 1952 Constitution was reintroduced in a modified form. A new Constitution was introduced in June 1975. Parliamentary elections took place on 17 Nov. 1974.

A further referendum on the Monarchy took place on 8 Dec. 1974 and 69·2% of the valid votes were cast for an 'uncrowned democracy'.

Elections were again held on 18 Oct. 1981. The results were New Democracy, 115; Pan-Hellenic Socialist Movement, 172; Communists, 13.

President: Konstantinos Karamanlis (elected President in May 1980).

The Cabinet in Jan. 1983:

Prime Minister and Minister of Defence: Andreas Papandreou.

Minister to the Prime Minister: Agamemnon Koutsogiorgas. *Foreign Affairs:* Ioannis Charalambopoulos. *Defence:* Andreas Papandreou. *National Economy:* Gerasimos Arsenis. *Interior:* Giorgos Gennimatas. *Public Works:* Apostolos Tsochatzopoulos. *Justice:* Giorgos Mangakis. *Education and Religion:* Apostolos Kaklamanis. *Economy:* Dimitrios Koulourianos. *Agriculture:* Konstantinos Simitis. *Culture and Sciences:* Melina Mercouri. *Planning and Environment:* Antonis Tritsis. *Energy and Natural Resources:* Evangelos Kouloumbis. *Research and Technology:* Giorgos Lianis. *Commerce:* Giorgos Moraitis. *Labour:* Evangelos Giannopoulos. *Health and Social Welfare:* Paraskevas Avegerinos. *National Insurance:* Eleftherios Verivakos. *Communications:* Nikolaos Akritidis. *Public Order:* Ioannis Skoularikis. *Merchant Marine:* Georgios Katsifaras. *Northern Greece:* Vassilios Intzes. *Alternate Minister of National Economy:* Ioannis Pottakis.

National flag: Nine horizontal stripes of blue and white, with a canton of blue with a white cross.

National anthem: Hymn to Freedom, Imnos eis tin Eleftherian (words by Dionysios Solomos, 1824; tune by N. Mantzaros, 1828).

DEFENCE. In Aug. 1950 the Ministries of War, Marine and Military Aviation were fused into a single Ministry of National Defence. The General Staff of National Defence is directly responsible to the Minister on general defence questions, besides the special staffs for Army, Navy and Air Force. Defence expenditure in 1980 was 71,250m. drachmai.

Army. Military service is compulsory and universal. Liability begins in the 21st year and lasts up to the 50th. The normal term of service in the active Army is for 24–32 months for all arms, followed by 19 years in the first reserve of the active Army and 10 years in the second. The normal annual contingent of recruits in peace-time is about 50,000. Every 3 months a quarter of the current year's contingent is called up for service.

Since 1945, the organization and establishment of the Army units have been adapted to British models. In Feb. 1952 an American Mission took over from a British Military Mission the training of the Army.

The Army consists of 12 infantry and 1 armoured division, 1 infantry, 2 armoured and 1 para-commando brigade, and 12 artillery battalions, with a total strength of 163,000 men.

Navy. The Hellenic Navy includes 2 new Netherlands-built leader-size guided missile frigates, 10 submarines (8 modern German (Fed. Rep.)-built small and 2 old *ex*-US large), 14 old *ex*-US destroyers, 1 *ex*-German support frigate, 4 old *ex*-US frigates (small DE type), 2 coastal minelayers, 14 fast missile boats, 12 fast torpedo boats, 14 coastal minesweepers, 11 coastal patrol boats, 1 dock landing ship, 12 landing ships, 10 landing craft, 60 minor landing craft, 1 ammunition ship, 6 oilers, 2 transports, 1 depot ship, 4 surveying craft, 2 light-house tenders, 7 water carriers, 1 netlayer and 16 fleet tugs.

Personnel in 1983 exceeded 2,500 officers and 17,000 ratings (called up for 2 years, or enlisted).

Air Force. The Hellenic Air Force has a strength of about 24,500 officers and men and 275 combat aircraft, consisting of 3 squadrons of F-4E Phantom air-superiority fighters, 2 squadrons of F-104G Starfighters, 2 squadrons of Mirage F.1 fighters, 3 squadrons of A-7H Corsair II attack aircraft, 3 squadrons of F-5 fighters, 1 squadron of RF-4E and RF-5A reconnaissance fighters and 1 squadron of HU-16B Albatross ASW amphibians. There are also transport squadrons equipped with C-130H Hercules (12), Noratlas, NAMC YS-11 and C-47 aircraft, 7 Canadair CL-215 twin-engined amphibians, 36 T-2E Buckeye training/attack aircraft, other training and helicopter units, and anti-aircraft units equipped with Nike-Hercules and Hawk surface-to-air missiles.

The HAF is organized into Tactical, Training and Air Materiel Commands.

INTERNATIONAL RELATIONS

Membership. Greece is a member of UN, EEC, the Council of Europe and the political wing of NATO.

ECONOMY

Budget. The estimated revenue and expenditure for calendar years were as follows (in 1m. drachmai):

	1974	*1975*	*1976*	*1977*	*1978*	*1980*	*1981*
Revenue	129,380	138,320	174,362	210,234	249,202	359,100	438,900
Expenditure	129,380	170,496	210,231	252,094	300,950	460,500	650,500

Currency. On 11 Nov. 1944 the Greek currency was stabilized at 1 new *drachma* equalling 50,000m. old *drachmai*. Further readjustments took place in 1946, 1949 and 1953. A 'new issue' of notes and coins was put into circulation on 1 May 1954, 1 new drachma equalling 1,000 old drachmai (72 drachmai = £1; 30 drachmai = US$1). The 'new issue' comprises notes of 50, 100, 500 and 1,000 drachmai and metal coins of 1, 2, 5, 10 and 20 drachmai and 10, 20 and 50 *lepta*. Rate of exchange, March 1983, £1 = 126 drachmai; US$1 = 83·95.

Banking. The Bank of Greece *(Trapeza Tis Ellados)* is the bank of issue. On 31 Dec. 1978 bank-notes in circulation amounted to 228,771m. drachmai.

In 1953 the National Bank of Greece and the Bank of Athens were amalgamated; in 1957 its name was changed to National Bank of Greece *(Ethniki Trapeza tis Ellados)*.

The National Investment Bank for industrial development was set up in Dec. 1963; of its capital of 180m. drachmai, the National Bank provided 60%.

Other important banks are the Ionian and Popular Bank of Greece, the Commercial Bank of Greece, the National Mortgage Bank, the Hellenic Industrial Development Bank, the Investment Bank, the Commercial Credit Bank and the General Bank of Greece.

On 31 Dec. 1978, total private bank deposits were 410,718m. drachmai (107,941m. in 1970); total money supply was 316,738·8m. drachmai.

Weights and Measures. The metric system was made obligatory in 1959; the use of other systems is prohibited. The Gregorian calendar was adopted in Feb. 1923.

ENERGY AND NATURAL RESOURCES

Electricity. Total installed capacity of the Public Power Corporation was 5,410m. mw as at 31 Dec. 1980. Total net production in 1981 was 21,657m. kwh.

Minerals. Greece produces a variety of ores and minerals, including iron-pyrites (180,000 tonnes in 1976), bauxite (13·3m. tonnes, 1980), nickel (1·45m. tonnes, 1980), magnesite (1·6m. tonnes, 1980), dead burnt magnesite (342,000 tonnes, 1976), mixed sulphur ores (752,000 tonnes, 1976), barytes, chromite, marble (white and coloured) and various other earths, chiefly from the Laurium district, Thessaly, Euboea and the Aegean islands. There is little coal, and lignite of indifferent quality (22·2m. tonnes, 1976). Oil was struck in 1963 by British Petroleum at Kleisoura in west central Greece. Salt production (1970) 68,471 tonnes.

Agriculture. Of the total area only 33% is cultivable, but it supports about 45% of the whole population. The total area under cultivation in 1971 was 3,586,232 hectares, forest area (1965) was 2,512,418 hectares (445,715 of which were privately owned). The average holding was 3·42 hectares in 1975.

Yield (1,000 tonnes) of the chief crops (1979):

Wheat	2,394	Table grapes	235
Tobacco	132	Wine	471
Cotton	325	Citrus fruit	494
Sugar-beet	2,741	Other fruit	1,587
Currants and raisins	127	Milk	1,640
Olive oil	255	Meat and poultry	477

About 496,260 hectares of olives are under cultivation.

Rice is cultivated in Macedonia, the Peloponnese, Epirus and Central Greece. Successful experiments have been made in growing rice on alkaline land previously regarded as unfit for cultivation. The main kinds of cheese produced are sliced cheese in brine (commercially known as Fetta) and hard cheese, such as Kefalotyri.

Livestock (1981): 899,000 cattle, 2,000 buffaloes, 1m. pigs, 7·92m. sheep, 4·7m. goats, 120,000 horses, 120,000 mules, 250,000 asses, 30m. poultry.

Fisheries. In 1979, 9,697 fishermen were active and landed 95,939 tonnes of fish. 54,146 kg of sponges were produced in 1970.

INDUSTRY AND TRADE

Industry. The main products are canned vegetables and fruit, fruit juice, beer, wine, alcoholic beverages, cigarettes, textiles, yarn, leather, shoes, synthetic timber, paper, plastics, rubber products, chemical acids, pigments, pharmaceutical products, cosmetics, soap, disinfectants, fertilizers, glassware, porcelain sanitary items, wire and power coils and household instruments.

Production, 1976 (1,000 tonnes): Textile yarns, 137; cement, 8,714; fertilizers, 1,554; ammonia, 287; iron (concrete-reinforcing bars), 589; iron-nickel, 16; alumina, 450; aluminium, 133; electrical domestic goods (1,000 pieces), 325.

Labour. Of the economically active population in 1971, 1·96m. were engaged in agriculture. 677,451 in industry and 1,000,684 in other employment.

Pepelasis, A. A., and Yotopoulos, P. A., *Surplus Labor in Greek Agriculture, 1953–60.* Athens, 1962

Trade Unions. The status of trade unions in Greece is regulated by the Associations Act 1914. Trade-union liberties are guaranteed under the Constitution, and the right to strike is subject to the Settlement of Collective Labour Disputes Act of 21 Nov. 1935, which, while not making strikes illegal, introduced the principle of compulsory arbitration.

The national body of trade unions in Greece is the Greek General Confederation of Labour.

Commerce. Foreign trade (in US$1m.) for 2 calendar years was:

	1979	*1980*
Imports	10,110	10,903
Exports	3,932	4,094

Total trade between Greece and UK (British Department of Trade returns, in £1,000 sterling):

	1977	*1978*	*1979*	*1980*	*1981*	*1982*
Imports to UK	95,563	107,600	151,880	142,456	167,655	151,688
Exports and re-exports from UK	220,393	214,178	273,026	224,619	254,154	255,281

Tourism. Tourists visiting Greece in 1981 numbered 5,094,300. They spent the equivalent of US$1,878m.

COMMUNICATIONS

Roads. There were, in 1980, 37,000 km of roads, of which 8,680 were national and 27,253 provincial roads.

Number of motor vehicles in Dec. 1980: 1,418,993, of which 879,916 were passenger cars, 401,975 goods vehicles, 16,683 buses.

Railways. In 1980 the State network, Hellenic Railways (CH), totalled 2,548 km comprising 1,565 km of 1,435 mm gauge, 961 km of 1,000 mm gauge, and 22 km of 750 mm gauge, and carried 814m. tonne-km and 1,933m. passenger-km.

Aviation. Olympic Airways connects Athens with all important cities of the country, Europe, the Middle East and USA. Thirty-four foreign companies connect Athens with the principal cities of the world.

The principal airport is at Athens. In 1979, 90,700 aircraft arrived, carrying 7·7m. passengers.

Shipping. In March 1980 the merchant navy comprised 3,970 vessels of 39,327,594 GRT. Greek-owned ships under foreign flags totalled more than 11,192,683 GRT.

There is a canal (opened 9 Nov. 1893) across the Isthmus of Corinth (about 4 miles).

Post and Broadcasting. In 1973 there were 3,200 telephone exchanges, 1·8m. installed capacity of telephone exchanges, handling 8,000m. calls. There were (1981) 2,796,435 telephones.

Elliniki Radiophonia Tileorasis (ERT), the Hellenic National Radio and Television Institute, is the government broadcasting station. *Ypiressia Enimerosseos Enoplon Dhynameon Helladhos* (YENED), the Greek Armed Forces Information Service, broadcasts from a central station in Athens *via* medium- and short-waves and has regional stations in 11 towns. ERT and YENED each broadcasts 1 TV programme. AFRTS broadcasts 1 TV programme in Iraklion (Crete). Number of receivers: radio, 5m.; television, 1·4m.

Cinemas (1965). There were 1,400 cinemas.

Newspapers (1980). There were 14 daily newspapers published in Athens.

JUSTICE, RELIGION, EDUCATION AND WELFARE

Justice. There are administrative, civil and criminal courts and they are organized by special laws.

Religion. The Christian Eastern Orthodox faith is the established religion to which 98% of the population belong.

The Greek Orthodox Church is under an archbishop and 67 metropolitans, 1 archbishop and 7 metropolitans in Crete, and 4 metropolitans in the Dodecanese. The Roman Catholics have 3 archbishops (in Naxos and Corfu and, not recognized by the State, in Athens) and 1 bishop (for Syra and Santorin). The Exarchs of the Greek Catholics and the Armenians are not recognized by the State.

Complete religious freedom is recognized by the Constitution of 1968, but proselytizing from, and interference with, the Greek Orthodox Church is forbidden.

Education. Public education is provided in nursery, primary and secondary schools, starting at 6 years of age and since 1963 free at all levels.

In 1980–81 there were 4,752 nursery schools with 6,146 staff and 142,520 pupils; 9,541 public day primary schools with 36,168 staff and 902,558 pupils. There were 2,253 secondary schools with 31,057 staff and 648,742 pupils. There were 1,212 public and 644 private technical and vocational schools with a total of 155,750 students.

In 1980–81 there were 6 universities at Athens, Crete, Thessaloniki, Thrace, Patras and Ioannina with 119,000 students and 6,148 lecturers.

Illiteracy in the age groups of 10 years and over was 18% in 1961 (8% among men). 1972 estimate 12%.

The Greek language consists of 2 branches, *katharevousa*, a conscious revival of classical Greek, used for official purposes and in newspapers, and *demotiki*, the spoken language.

Health (1978). There were 701 hospitals and sanatoria with a total of 58,994 beds. There were 21,320 doctors and 6,825 dentists.

DIPLOMATIC REPRESENTATIVES

Of Greece in Great Britain (1A Holland Park, London, W11 3TP)
Ambassador: Nikolaos Kyriazides.

Of Great Britain in Greece (1 Ploutarchou St., Athens 139)
Ambassador: Peregrine Rhodes, CMG.

Of Greece in the USA (2221 Massachusetts Ave., NW, Washington, D.C. 20008)
Ambassador: Nicolas A. Karandreas.

Of the USA in Greece (91 Vasilissis Sophia Blvd., Athens)
Ambassador: Monteagle Stearns.

Of Greece to the United Nations
Ambassador: Mihalis Dountas.

Books of Reference

Clogg, R. and M. J., *Greece.* [Bibliography] Oxford and Santa Barbara, 1980
Holden, D., *Greece Without Columns: The Making of the Modern Greeks.* London, 1972
Katris, J. A., *Eyewitness in Greece: The Colonels Come to Power.* St Louis, 1971
Kayser, B., *Géographie humaine de la Grèce.* Paris, Presses Universitaires, 1964
Kolodny, E. Y., *La Population des Îles de la Grèce.* Aix-en-Provence, 1973
Kousoulas, D. G., *Revolution and Defeat: The Story of the Greek Communist Party.* OUP, 1965
Kykkotis, I., *English–Modern Greek and Modern Greek–English Dictionary.* 3rd ed. London, 1957
Mouzelis, N. P., *Modern Greece.* London, 1978
Munkman, C. A., *American Aid to Greece.* New York, 1958
Phillipson, A., *Die griechischen Landschaften: eine Landeskunde.* 4 vols. Frankfurt, 1951–59
Spring, J. T., *The Oxford Dictionary of Modern Greek.* 2 vols. OUP, 1966–67
Tsoukalis, L., *Greece and the European Community.* Farnborough, 1979
Woodhouse, C. M., *The Struggle for Greece, 1941–1949.* London, 1976
Xydis, S. G., *Greece and the Great Powers, 1944–47.* Thessaloniki, 1963
Young, K., *The Greek Passion.* London, 1967

GRENADA

Capital: St George's
Population: 110,394 (1978)
GNP per capita: US$690 (1980)

HISTORY. Grenada became an independent nation within the Commonwealth on 7 Feb. 1974. Grenada was formerly an Associated State under the West Indies Act, 1967.

AREA AND POPULATION. Grenada is the most southerly island of the Windward Islands with an area of 133 sq. miles (344 sq. km); population, census 1970, 92,775; estimated population 1978, 110,394. The borough of St George's, the capital, had population (1978) 30,813. The largest of the Grenadines attached to Grenada is Carriacou, area 32 sq. km; population 1970, 5,950 (including Petit Martinique).

Vital statistics (1978): Births, 2,521; deaths, 765; infant deaths, 73; marriages, 360.

CONSTITUTION AND GOVERNMENT. Grenada Constitution Order of 1973 was suspended on 13 March 1979 following a revolution. The People's Revolutionary Government now comprises 23 members with a Cabinet of 7 members.

Governor-General: Sir Paul Scoon.

Prime Minister: Maurice Bishop.

National flag: Divided into 4 triangles of yellow, top and bottom, and green, hoist and fly; in the centre a red disc bearing a gold star; along the top and bottom edged red stripes each bearing 3 gold stars; on the green triangle near the hoist a pod of nutmeg.

DEFENCE. A People's Revolutionary Army was created in 1979. Personnel about 1,000.

INTERNATIONAL RELATIONS

Membership. Grenada is a member of the UN, OAS, Caricom, the Commonwealth and is an ACP state of EEC.

ECONOMY

Budget. The 1981 estimates balanced at EC$169m. Public debt at 31 Dec. 1970 was EC$15,168,705.

Currency. The currency is the *Eastern Caribbean dollar.* In March 1983, £1 = EC$4·10; US$ = EC$2·70.

Banking. In 1981 there were 5 commercial banks in Grenada: The National Commercial Bank, Barclays Bank International, Royal Bank of Canada, Bank of Nova Scotia and the Grenada Co-operative Bank. The Grenada Agricultural Bank was established in 1965 to encourage agricultural development. In 1981, bank deposits were EC$164·7m.

AGRICULTURE (1981). The principal crops (production in lb.) are: Cocoa (6,409,227), nutmegs (6,767,199), bananas (25,609,408), and mace (506,950); coconuts, corn and pigeon peas, citrus, sugar-cane, root-crops and vegetables are also grown, in addition to small scattered cultivations of cotton, cloves, cinnamon, pimento, coffee and fruit trees The fish catch was about 3m. lb.

Livestock (1981): Cattle, 8,000; sheep, 16,000; goats, 13,000; pigs, 10,000; poultry, 250,000.

COMMERCE (1981). Total value of imports, EC$146,709,830; exports, EC$50,275,362. The main exports are cocoa, nutmegs and bananas.

Of exports in 1981, UK took 35·6%; Netherlands, 15·8%; Trinidad, 15·6%; Federal Republic of Germany, 9%; Canada, 2·8%; USA, 2·5%. Of 1981 imports, Trinidad furnished 19·2%; USA, 18·6%; UK, 16·6%; Canada, 5·5%; Netherlands, 1·6%; Federal Republic of Germany, 1·3%.

Total trade between Grenada and UK (British Department of Trade returns, in £1,000 sterling):

	1979	*1980*	*1981*	*1982*
Imports to UK	5,397	5,225	4,890	4,704
Exports and re-exports to UK	4,099	3,371	3,839	3,687

TOURISM. In 1981, there were 102,668 visitors; 131 cruise ships and 1,376 yachts visited the island.

COMMUNICATIONS

Roads. The scheduled road mileage is 577, of which 377 have an oiled surface and 210 are graded as third- and fourth-class roads. Vehicles registered (1979) 6,676.

Aviation. Pearls Airport has daily connections to London, New York and South America *via* nearby islands. There is a small airstrip on Carriacou.

Shipping. Total shipping for 1978 was 927 motor and steamships and 166 sailing and auxiliary vessels, with a total net tonnage of 2,210,532 and 7,479 respectively.

Post and Broadcasting. The telephone system is owned and operated by the Grenada Telephone Co. Ltd. The Government of Grenada is a shareholder. The system is completely automatic, and in 1981 served 5,648 subscribers. Cable & Wireless (W.I.) Ltd operates a VHF radio system (telephone and telegraph) to Trinidad and Barbados, from where connexion is made to all other parts of the world.

Radio Grenada is government owned and operated. There were (1978) 63,500 radios.

JUSTICE, RELIGION AND EDUCATION

Justice. The Grenada Supreme Court, situated in St George's, comprises a High Court of Justice, a Court of Magisterial Appeal (which hears appeals from the lower Magistrates' Courts exercising summary jurisdiction) and an Itinerant Court of Appeal (to hear appeals from the High Court).

Religion. The majority of the population are Roman Catholic; the Anglican and Methodist churches are also well represented.

Education. There are 20 primary schools, 4 junior schools and 16 secondary schools, as well as 46 schools taking the full age range. There is a Technical Centre in each district and a Technical Institute in St George's, where there is also a Teacher Training College and a branch of the University of the West Indies. There were 28,745 primary and 4,773 secondary school pupils in 1973.

DIPLOMATIC REPRESENTATIVES

Of Grenada in Great Britain (1 Collingham Gdns., London, SW5)
High Commissioner: Fennis Augustine.

Of Great Britain in Grenada
High Commissioner: Viscount Dunrossil, CMG (resides at Bridgetown).

Of Grenada in the USA (1704 R. St., NW, Washington, DC., 20009)
Ambassador: Bernard K. Radix.

Of the USA in Grenada
Ambassador: (Vacant).

Of Grenada to the United Nations
Ambassador: Caldwell Taylor.

Books of Reference

Hodge, M. and Searle, C. (eds), *Is Freedom We Making.* Govt. Information Service, 1981
Searle, C. and Rojas, D. (eds), *To Construct from Morning.* Grenada, 1982
Wheaton, P. and Sunshine, C. (eds), *Grenada: The Peaceful Revolution.* Washington, 1982

GUATEMALA

República de Guatemala

Capital: Guatemala City
Population: 7·25m. (1981)
GNP per capita: US$1,110 (1980)

HISTORY. From 1524 to 1821 Guatemala was a Spanish captaincy-general, comprising the whole of Central America. It became independent in 1821 and formed part of the Confederation of Central America from 1823 to 1839, when Rafael Carrera dissolved the Confederation.

AREA AND POPULATION. Guatemala is bounded on the north and west by Mexico, south by the Pacific ocean and east by El Salvador, Honduras and Belize, and the area is 108,889 sq. km (42,042 sq. miles). In March 1936 Guatemala, El Salvador and Honduras agreed to accept the peak of Mount Montecristo as the common boundary point.

The population was 7·05m. in 1979. About 45% are pure Indians, of 21 different groups descended from the Maya; most of the remainder are mixed Indian and Spanish and these supply the ruling classes. Density of population, 1978, 63 per sq. km.

Vital statistics, 1976: Births, 266,497; deaths, 81,677; marriages, 28,555; infant deaths, 20,576.

Guatemala is administratively divided into 22 departments, each with a governor appointed by the President. Population, 1976:

Departments	*Area (sq. km)*	*Population*	*Departments*	*Area (sq. km)*	*Population*
Alta Verapaz	8,686	372,572	Petén	35,854	71,463
Baja Verapaz	3,124	136,747	Quezaltenango	1,951	383,470
Chimaltenango	1,979	233,287	Quiché	8,378	363,579
Chiquimula	2,376	212,869	Retalhuleu	1,858	159,085
El Progreso	1,922	92,453	Sacatepéquez	465	116,259
Escuintla	4,384	353,302	San Marcos	3,791	473,341
Guatemala	2,126	1,239,749	Santa Rosa	2,955	225,597
Huehuetenango	7,403	422,717	Sololá	1,061	156,548
Izabal	9,038	205,305	Suchitepéquez	2,510	257,439
Jalapa	2,063	145,091	Totonicapán	1,061	207,954
Jutiapa	3,219	290,511	Zacapa	2,690	138,292

The capital is Guatemala City with about 1·5m. inhabitants (1979). Other towns are Quezaltenango (65,733), Puerto Barrios (38,956), Mazatenango (38,319), Antigua (26,631), Zacapa (35,769) and Cobán (43,538). An earthquake in central Guatemala in Feb. 1976 killed 24,103 people and destroyed 200,000 dwellings.

CONSTITUTION AND GOVERNMENT. On 23 March 1982 a junta, consisting of Brig.-Gen. Efrain Ríos Montt, Gen. Horacio Maldonado and Col. Francisco Gordillo, took power in a bloodless *coup*. Gen. Ríos Montt later became President. The Constitution and political activity was suspended, Congress abolished and government was to be by decree. Elections had been held on 7 March and Gen. Angel Anibal Guevara became President-elect having obtained 35% of the votes but there was great dissatisfaction with the conduct of the election.

National flag: Three vertical strips of blue, white, blue, with the national arms in the centre.

National anthem: ¡Guatemala! feliz (words by J. J. Palma; tune by R. Alvarez).

DEFENCE

Army. Military service is voluntary. The Army numbers 17,000, organized in 9 infantry, 1 parachute and 1 engineer battalions and some motorized units with some tanks. The Policía Nacional has 9,500 personnel.

Navy. A Naval force was formed in 1959. It comprises 15 small patrol craft, 2 landing craft, 2 small troop carriers, 6 motor launches, 2 utility cutters, 30 work boats, and 6 service craft. Since 1973 the base at Santo Tomas has had a 230-ton marine elevator (synchrolift), greatly improving naval repair facilities. Personnel in 1983 numbered 600 officers and men (including 210 marines).

Air Force. There is a small Air Force with 10 A-37B light attack aircraft, 1 DC-6, 11 C-47 and 10 Israeli-built Arava transports, 12 Pilatus PC-7 turboprop trainers, and a number of light aircraft and helicopters, including a few armed UH-1 Iroquois. Total strength is about 550 personnel and 70 aircraft.

INTERNATIONAL RELATIONS

Membership. Guatemala is a member of UN, OAS and CACM.

External Debt. In 1978 the external debt was Q.220m.

ECONOMY

Planning. In 1978 the Government announced its economic development programme and this included the continued development of agriculture, encouraging the development of agriculture-based industry and light engineering industry associated with agricultural development, promoting tourism, encouraging oil and mining development, improving roads and railway and airport facilities and continuing hydro-electric development. The 1979–82 National Economic Development Plan along these lines involves government investment of Q.1,937·5m.

Budget. The estimates of ordinary revenue and expenditure balanced as follows, in quetzales (1 quetzal = US$): 1980, 1,280m.; 1981, 1,467m.

Currency. The gold *quetzal* was established 7 May 1925 equal to 60 old Guatemala paper pesos, with a gold content equal to that of the US$. Coins of 25, 10, 5 and 1 *centavos* were issued by the Banco de Guatemala on 16 Sept. 1965; they are of a lower content value than the previous ones. There are also paper notes of 100, 50, 20, 10, 5, 1 and ½ *quetzales* (50 *centavos*). In March 1983, £1 = Q.1·52; US$1 = Q.1.

Banking. By an Act effective 4 Feb. 1946 the Central Bank of Guatemala (founded in 1926 as a mixed central and commercial bank) was superseded by a new institution, the Banco de Guatemala, to operate solely as a central bank. Savings and term deposits at commercial banks were Q.979·7m. at the end of 1980. Total currency circulation (backed by a gold reserve fixed by law at a minimum of 40%) on 31 Dec. 1980 was Q.923·9m.; total net international reserves amounted to Q.396·7m. on 31 Dec. 1980. In July 1965 the country's quota with the IMF was increased from US$15m. to 25m.

There are 17 banks, including the Banco de Guatemala, Banco Nacional de Desarollo, set up in 1971 to promote agricultural development, its counterpart for small industries (Banco de los Trabajadores) set up in Jan. 1966 with initial capital of US$1·3m., a branch of Lloyds Bank International Ltd and a branch of the Bank of America.

Weights and Measures. The metric system has been officially adopted, but is little used in local commerce.

Libra of 16 oz.	= 1·014 lb.	*League*	= 3 miles
Arroba of 25 libras	= 25·35 lb.	*Vara*	= 32 in.
Quintal of 4 arrobas	= 101·40 lb.	*Manzana*	= 100 varas sq.
Tonelada of 20 quintals	= 18·10 cwt	*Caballeria* of 64 manzanas	= 110 acres
Fanega	= 1½ Imp. bushels		

ENERGY AND NATURAL RESOURCES

Electricity. 1,045m. kwh. of electricity were generated in 1976. A large-scale hydro-electric development is now underway and others are planned.

Oil. Guatemala began exporting crude oil in 1980; exports, 1980, were valued at Q.23·7m. Production is from wells in Alta Verapaz department from where the oil is piped to Santo Tomas de Castilla. Further exploration is proceeding in the Petén.

Minerals. Mineral production includes zinc and lead concentrates, some antimony and tungsten, a small amount of cadmium and silver; some copper is also being mined. Exports (1980) Q.5·5m. In 1965 a subsidiary of International Nickel Company of Canada was granted a 40-year concession to extract and process nickel ore in northern Guatemala. Production and exports started in 1977 but production had ceased temporarily in 1982.

Agriculture. The Cordilleras divide Guatemala into two unequal drainage areas, of which the Atlantic is much the greater. The Pacific slope, though comparatively narrow, is exceptionally well watered and fertile between the altitudes of 1,000 and 5,000 ft, and is the most densely settled part of the republic. The Atlantic slope is sparsely populated, and has little of commercial importance beyond the chicle and timber-cutting of the Petén, coffee cultivation of Cobán region and banana-raising of the Motagua Valley and Lake Izabal district. Soil erosion is serious and a single week of heavy rains suffices to cause flooding of fields and much crop destruction.

On 17 June 1952 an 'Agrarian Reform Law' was enacted providing for the expropriation (with eventual compensation) of those parts of landed estates which were not under cultivation. The US Government in 1953 protested against the expropriation of 234,000 acres belonging to the United Fruit Company. Under the new government the expropriation was halted and the 'Agrarian Reform Law' was superseded by a 'Statute' early in 1956, which provided small holdings to several thousand peasant farmers. This distribution of land continues, now under the provisions of the 'Agrarian Transformation Law' of 1962.

The principal crop is coffee; there are about 12,000 coffee plantations with 138m. coffee trees on about 338,000 acres, but 80% of the crop comes from 1,500 large coffee farms employing 426,000 workers. Coffee exports in 1980 were valued at Q.463·9m. mainly to USA and Federal Republic of Germany.

Bananas are still an important export crop, but exports have at times been seriously reduced, partly by labour troubles and by hurricanes. Exports 1980 were worth Q.45·4m.

Cotton has become an important export and in 1980 was valued at Q.166·1m. Other important exports (1980) were sugar, Q.69·3m.; beef, Q.29·1m. Guatemala is, after Mexico, the largest producer of chicle gum (used for chewing-gum manufacture in USA). Rubber development schemes are under way, assisted by US funds. Guatemala is one of the largest sources of essential oils (citronella and lemon grass); exports in 1980 were valued at Q.2·7m. Cardamom, exported mainly to the Arab countries, is an increasingly important source of revenue; exports, 1980, Q.55·6m. Cattle-grounds (*potreros*) occupy about 758,000 acres. There were (1980) some 1·6m. head of cattle (mostly beef) in the country.

Forestry. The forest area has an extent of 17,784,000 acres. The department of Petén is rich in mahogany and other woods.

Fisheries. Exports were about Q.8m. in 1980.

INDUSTRY AND TRADE

Industry. The principal industries are food and beverages, tobacco, chemicals, hides and skins, textiles, garments and non-metallic minerals. New industries include electrical goods, plastic sheet and metal furniture.

Trade Unions. Trade unions are small. In 1954 the trade unions were ordered to reorganize and there are now two main federations.

Commerce. Values in Q.1,000 (1 quetzal = US$1) were:

	1975	1976	1977	1978	1979	1980
Imports (c.i.f.)	732,679	981,600	1,052,507	1,285,640	1,503,900	1,615,000
Exports (f.o.b.)	623,503	782,400	1,160,115	1,089,457	1,241,400	1,522,000

Value (in Q.1,000) of principal imports, 1977: Machinery and transport equipment, 355,191; chemicals, 191,952; petroleum products, 148,424; foodstuffs, 55,422. Chief exports are coffee, cotton, bananas, beef, essential oils, timber, chicle and shrimps. The main trading partners are USA, Japan and Federal Republic of Germany, and the partners of the Central American Common Market.

Total trade between Guatemala and UK for 6 years (British Department of Trade returns, in £1,000 sterling):

	1977	1978	1979	1980	1981	1982
Imports to UK	3,600	5,726	7,596	23,657	8,197	13,476
Exports and re-exports from UK	16,676	14,529	13,371	13,835	11,280	8,127

Tourism. There were 503,908 foreign visitors in 1979.

COMMUNICATIONS

Roads. In 1977 there were 17,139 km of roads,of which 2,765 are paved. There is a trunk highway from coast to coast *via* Guatemala City. There are 2 trunk highways from the Mexican to the Salvadorean frontier: the Pacific Highway serving the fertile coastal plain and the Pan-American Highway running through the highlands and Guatemala City. Motor vehicles number about 200,000.

Railways. The principal railway system is the government-owned (since 1968) *Ferrocarriles de Guatemala.* All railways are of 914 mm gauge. Total length of all lines is 820 km. Passengers carried, 1976, numbered 386,000, and freight carried (1976), 703,600 short tons. The bridge across the Suchiate River between Mexico and Guatemala in 1942 linked the railways of North and Central America, though differences in gauge make it necessary to change trains at Ayutla.

Aviation. The government-owned airline, Aviateca, furnishes both domestic and international services; 6 other airlines handle international traffic. In 1976 air cargo amounted to 16·1m. tons; number of passengers, 422,000.

Shipping. The chief ports on the Atlantic coast are Puerto Barrios and Santo Tomás de Castilla: on the Pacific coast, San José and Champerico. Total tonnage handled was, 1977, 2·6m. tons.

Post and Broadcasting. The Government own and operate the telegraph and telephone services; there were (1981) 81,622 telephone instruments. There are some 70 broadcasting stations. Radio receiving sets in use, 1976, numbered about 1m. There are 4 commercial TV stations, 1 government station and about 192,000 TV receivers.

Cinemas (1979). Cinemas numbered approximately 100.

Newspapers (1980). There are 8 daily newspapers.

JUSTICE, RELIGION, EDUCATION AND WELFARE

Justice. Justice is administered in a Supreme Court, 6 appeal courts and 28 courts of first instance. Supreme Court and appeal court judges are elected by Congress. Judges of first instance are appointed by the Supreme Court.

All holders of public office have to show on entering office, and again on leaving, a full account of their private property and income.

Religion. Roman Catholicism is the prevailing faith; but all other creeds have complete liberty of worship. Guatemala has an archbishopric.

Education. In 1976 there were 6,415 primary schools with 27,666 teachers and an attendance of 753,932 pupils; these figures include private schools. There are 357 secondary and other schools having 7,051 teachers and an attendance of 104,800 pupils; the autonomous University of San Carlos de Borromeo, founded in 1678, was reopened in 1910 with 7 faculties and schools and there are 4 new universities.

Students at state university (1977) approximately 25,925. All education is in theory free, but owing to a grave shortage of state schools private schools flourish. The 1964 census showed that 63% of those 10 years of age and older were illiterate.

Social Welfare. A comprehensive system of social security was outlined in a law of 30 Oct. 1946. Medical personnel include about 1,250 doctors and 275 dentists for the whole republic. There are about 60 public hospitals and about 100 dispensaries.

DIPLOMATIC REPRESENTATIVES

Of Guatemala in the USA (2220 R St., NW, Washington, D.C. 20008)
Ambassador: José Luis Zelaya Coronado.

Of the USA in Guatemala (7–01 Avenida de la Reforma, Zone 10, Guatemala City)
Ambassador: Jorge L. Zelaya.

Of Guatemala to the United Nations
Ambassador: Eduardo Castillo-Arriola.

Guatemala broke off diplomatic relations with UK on 31 July 1963 and consular relations were broken on 7 Sept. 1981.

Books of Reference

The official gazette is called *Diario de Centro America.*

Adler, J. H., and others, *Public Finance and Economic Development in Guatemala.* Stanford Univ. Press, 1952
Banco de Guatemala, *Memoria annual, Estudio económico* and *Boletín Estadístico*
Bloomfield, L. M., *The British Honduras–Guatemala Dispute.* Toronto, 1953
Franklin, W. B., *Guatemala.* [Bibliography] Oxford and Santa Barbara, 1981
Glassman, P., *Guatemala Guide.* Dallas, 1977
Holleran, M. P., *Church and State in Guatemala.* New York, 1949
Humphreys, R. A., *The Diplomatic History of British Honduras 1638–1901.* London, 1961
Immerman, R. H., *The CIA in Guatemala.* Univ. of Texas Press, 1982
Mendoza, J. L., *Britain and Her Treaties on Belize.* Guatemala, 1946
Morton, F., *Xeláhuh.* London, 1959
Plant, R., *Guatemala: Unnatural Disaster.* London, 1978
Schlesinger, S., and Kinzer, S., *Bitter Front: The Untold Story of the American Coup in Guatemala.* London and New York, 1982
Whetton, N. L., *Guatemala: The Land and the People.* Yale Univ. Press, 1961

National Library: Biblioteca Nacional, 5a Avenida y 8a Calle, Zona 1, Guatemala City.

GUINEA

Capital: Conakry
Population: 5·28m. (1982)
GNP per capita: US$290 (1980)

République populaire et révolutionnaire de Guinée

HISTORY. Guinea was proclaimed a French protectorate in 1888 and a colony in 1893. It became a constituent territory of French West Africa in 1904. The independent republic of Guinea was proclaimed on 2 Oct. 1958, after the territory of French Guinea had decided at the referendum of 28 Sept. to leave the French Community.

AREA AND POPULATION. Guinea, a coastal state of West Africa, is bounded north-west by Guinea-Bissau and Senegal, north-east by Mali, south-east by the Ivory Coast, south by Liberia and Sierra Leone, and west by the Atlantic Ocean.

The area is 245,857 sq. km (94,926 sq. miles), and the population, census, 1972, was 5,143,284, including an estimated 1·5m. living abroad (estimate, 1982, 5,277,000.). The largest towns (populations 1972 census) are Conakry, the capital (525,671), Kankan (85,310), Kindia, (79,861), Labé (79,670), and N'Zérékoré (about 23,000).

The ethnic composition is Fulani (40·3%, predominant in Moyenne-Guinée), Malinké (or Mandingo, 25·8%, prominent in Haut-Guinée), Susu (11%, prominent in Guinée-Maritime), Kissi (6·5%) and Kpelle (4·8%) in Guinée-Forestière, and Dialonka, Loma and others (11·6%).

CONSTITUTION AND GOVERNMENT. The provisional Constitution of 12 Nov. 1958 declared Guinea 'a democratic, secular and social republic'. The unicameral National Assembly consists of 210 deputies, elected by universal suffrage on a national list for a 7-year term (elections were held 27 Jan. 1980). The President is also directly elected for a 7-year term and can be re-elected; he is head of the Executive, and appoints a Council of Ministers to assist him.

All candidates are nominated by the National Council of the *Parti démocratique de Guinée*, the sole legal party. At the PDG's latest Congress in Nov. 1978 it elected a 25-member Central Committee (for 5 years; membership to be raised to 75) and a 15-member Political Bureau to administer the party until the election of a new National Council.

President: Ahmed Sékou Touré (elected Jan. 1961, re-elected Jan. 1968, Dec. 1974 and June 1980).
Prime Minister: Dr Louis Lansana Béavogui.
Foreign Affairs: Abdoulaye Touré.

The administrative division comprises 33 regions, grouped into 4 'supra-regions' which correspond to the 4 major geographical and ethnic areas: Guinée-Maritime (Lower Guinea, headquarters at Kindia); Moyenne-Guinée (Fouta Djallon, headquarters at Labé); Haute-Guinée (Upper Guinea, headquarters at Kankan) and Guinée-Forestière (Forest-Guinea, headquarters at N'Zérékoré).

The regional governer and PDG Party chief in each region are now popularly elected. The regions are divided into 175 *arrondissements,* each under a commandant.

National flag: Three vertical strips of red, gold, green.

Besides French, there are 8 official languages taught in schools: Fulani, Malinké, Susu, Kissi, Kpelle, Loma, Basari and Koniagi.

DEFENCE

Army. The Army of 8,500 men (1983), which comprises 1 armoured battalion, 4 infantry battalions, 1 commando and 1 engineering battalion, has been equipped with Soviet, Czech and Chinese weapons, armoured cars and artillery. There is also a people's militia of 9,200.

Navy. The Navy comprises an ocean minesweeper, 6 fast attack craft, 2 fast torpedo boats, 4 smaller torpedo boats, 6 coastal patrol craft, and 2 small landing craft. There are bases at Conakry and Kakanda. Personnel (1983) exceeded 600.

Air Force. The Air Force, formed with Soviet assistance, is reported to be equipped with 6 MiG-17 jet-fighters and 2 MiG-15UTI trainers, 2 Il-18 turboprop transports, 4 An-14 and 5 Il-14 piston-engined transports and a Yak-40 jet aircraft for VIP duties, all Russian built, plus a few helicopters, piston-engined Yak-18 and L-29 jet trainers. Personnel about 800.

INTERNATIONAL RELATIONS

Membership. Guinea is a member of UN, OAU and is an ACP state of EEC.

ECONOMY

Planning. The first 5-year development plan ran 1973–78 and the second, 1978–83. A10-year development plan runs 1981-90.

Budget. The budget for 1979 balanced at 11,250m. sylis.

Currency. The monetary unit is the *syli*, divided into 100 *cauris*, introduced in 1972. The issue consists of notes of 100, 50, 25 and 10 *sylis*, and coins of 50 *cauris*, 5, 2 and 1 *sylis*. In March 1983, £1 = 34·40 *sylis*; US$1 = 22·62 *sylis*.

Banking. In 1980 the Central Bank was replaced by a National Currency Institute, through which a governor with ministerial rank controls all banking and insurance, state monopolies since Jan. 1962.

ENERGY AND NATURAL RESOURCES

Electricity. Production of electrical energy was 500m. kwh. in 1977. The development of 2 new dams (1981) on the Konkouré river will expand capacity, primarily for the aluminium industry.

Minerals. Bauxite is mined at Fria, Boké and elsewhere in Guinée-Maritime; output 12,034,000 tonnes in 1980. Reserves (estimate,1982) 8,000m. tonnes. Production of iron ore from the Nimba and Simandou mountains commenced in 1981, following exhaustion of the Kaloum peninsula deposits. Diamond mining was suspended in 1978 but resumed in 1981.

Agriculture. There are experimental fruit gardens at Camayenne near Conakry, Kindia and Dalaba, 2 stations for rice selection (Kankan, Koba) and an experimental quinine station at Seredou. Coffee is grown in forest districts. Fouta Djallon contains cattle in abundance.

The chief crops (production, 1981, in 1,000 tonnes) are: Cassava, 600; rice, 330; plantains, 227; sugar-cane, 220; bananas, 100; groundnuts, 83; sweet potatoes, 75; maize, 63; palm-oil, 42; palm kernels, 35; pineapples, 17; coffee, 15; coconuts, 15.

Livestock (1981): Cattle, 1.8m.; sheep, 440,000; goats, 415,000; pigs,40,000.

Forestry: There were 5,756 sq. km of classified forests in 1977. Round-wood production amounted to 3·37m. cu. metres in 1978.

Fisheries: An estimated 10,000 tonnes are caught annually, 90% in coastal waters.

COMMERCE. In 1977 imports totalled 5,664m. sylis; exports, 6,629m. sylis. Alumina forms about 30% and bauxite 58% of the exports.

Total trade between Guinea and the UK (British Department of Trade returns, in £1,000 sterling):

	1978	*1979*	*1980*	*1981*	*1982*
Imports to UK	476	489	10,777	844	1,956
Exports and re-exports from UK	5,471	5,057	26,596	7,117	6,840

COMMUNICATIONS

Roads. There are 28,400 km of roads and tracks, of which 520 km are bitumenized. In 1978 there were 9,948 cars and 9,992 commercial vehicles.

Railways. A railway connects Conakry with Kankan (662 km) and may be extended to Bamako in Mali. A line 134 km long linking bauxite deposits at Sangaredi with Port Kamsar was opened in 1973 and a third line links Conakry and Fria (144 km).

Aviation. There are airports at Conakry and Kankan; in 1977, 66,000 passengers disembarked and embarked.

Shipping. There are ports at Conakry (facilities expanded 1976–80) and for bauxite exports at Kamsar (opened 1973). There were (1980) 15 vessels of 16,412 GRT registered in Guinea.

Post and Broadcasting. The territory is connected by cable with France and Pernambuco; also with Freetown, Monrovia and other places. There is a wireless station at Conakry affording communication with all territories of West Africa. Telephones, 1972, numbered about 7,488. There were 121,000 radio receivers in 1979; television broadcasting commenced 1977.

JUSTICE, RELIGION, EDUCATION AND WELFARE

Justice. There are *tribunaux du premier degré* at Conakry and Kankan, and a *juge de paix* at N'Zérékoré. The High Court, Court of Appeal and Superior Tribunal of Cassation are at Conakry, while the National Assembly serves as the 'supreme revolutionary tribunal'.

Religion. About 62% of the population is Moslem, 15% Christian and 35% follow tribal religions.

Education. There were, in 1977, 324,165 pupils in primary schools, 124,455 in secondary schools, 6,000 in technical schools and teacher-training colleges and 5,850 in higher education.

Health. In 1976 there were 314 hospitals and dispensaries with 7,650 beds; there were also 277 doctors, 21 dentists, 159 pharmacists, 394 midwives and 1,533 nursing personnel.

DIPLOMATIC REPRESENTATIVES

Of Guinea in Great Britain
Ambassador: Aboubacar Sompaŕe (resides in Paris).

Of Great Britain in Guinea
Ambassador: P. L. O'Keeffe, CVO. (resides in Dakar).

Of Guinea in the USA (2112 Leroy Pl., NW, Washington, D.C., 20008)
Ambassador: Mamady Lamine Conde.

Of the USA in Guinea (2nd Blvd. and 9th Ave., Conakry)
Ambassador: Allen C. Davis.

Of Guinea to the United Nations
Ambassador: Djebel Coumbassa.

Books of Reference

Bulletin Statistique et Economique de la Guinée. Monthly. Conakry
Adamolekun, L., *Sékou Touré's Guinea.* London, 1976
Camara, S. S., *La Guinée sans la France.* Paris, 1976
Rivière, C., *Guinea: The Mobilization of a People.* Cornell Univ. Press, 1977
Taylor, F. W., *A Fulani-English Dictionary.* Oxford, 1932

GUINEA-BISSAU

Capital: Bissau
Population: 810,000 (1982)
GNP per capita: US$160 (1980)

HISTORY. Guinea-Bissau, formerly Portuguese Guinea, on the coast of Guinea, was discovered in 1446 by Nuno Tristão. It became a separate colony in 1879. It is bounded by the limits fixed by the convention of 12 May 1886 with France. In 1951 Guinea-Bissau became an overseas province of Portugal. The armed struggle against colonial rule began in 1963. Independence was declared on 24 Sept. 1973. On 10 Sept. 1974 Portugal formally recognized the independence of Guinea-Bissau.

AREA AND POPULATION. Guinea-Bissau is bounded by Senegal in the north, the Atlantic ocean in the west and by Guinea in the east and south. It includes the adjacent archipelago of Bijagoz, with the island of Bolama. The capital and chief port is Bissau, estimated population (census 1979), 109,486. Other ports are Bolama and Cacheu. Area is 36,125 sq. km (13,948 sq. miles); population (census, 1979), 777,214 (estimate, 1982) 810,000.

The regional populations at the 1979 Census were as follows:

Bissau City	109,486	Bolama-Bijagos	25,713	Gabú	105,500
Bafatá	117,202	Buba	35,360	Oio	137,595
Biombo	57,724	Cacheu	134,108	Tombali	54,526

The main ethnic groups are the Balante (32%), Malinké (13%), Fulani (22%), Mandjako (14%) and Pepel (7%).

CONSTITUTION AND GOVERNMENT. A new Constitution was adopted on 10 Nov. 1980, 4 days before the *coup* which ousted President Luis Cabral. It retains the 150-member National People's Assembly as the legislature, and the *Partido Africano da Independencia da Guiné e Cabo Verde* (PAIGC) as the sole permitted Party, but provides for the President to become Head of government. Following the *coup*, the new Constitution remains in force, but the Assembly was suspended and a new 13-member Revolutionary Council proclaimed as the prime political institution, overseeing the work of the appointed Council of Ministers, which from 19 May 1982 was composed of the following:

President, Minister of Defence and the Interior: Maj. João Bernardo Vieira.
Prime Minister, Foreign Affairs: Vítor Saúde Maria.

Information and Culture: Filinto de Barros. *Agriculture:* Avito José da Silva. *Education:* Mário Cabral. *Natural Resources:* Samba Lamine Mane. *Finance:* Carlos Correia. *Transport and Tourism:* Maj. Manuel dos Santos. *Public Works:* Alberto Lima Gomez. *Fisheries, Trade and Handicrafts:* Joseph Turpin. *Economic Co-ordination and Planning:* Dr Vasco Cabral. *Justice:* Dr Fidelis Cabral d'Almada. *Health and Social Security:* Carmen Pereira. *Without Portfolio:* João Cruz Pinto. *Central Bank:* Dr Vítor Freire Monteiro. *Secretaries of State:* Maj. Brahima Bangura *(War Veterans)*, Adelino Nunes Correia *(Youth and Sport)*.

National flag: Horizontally yellow over green with red vertical strip in the hoist bearing a black star.

Local government: The administrative division is in 8 regions (each under an elected regional council), in turn subdivided into 37 sectors; and the city of Bissau, treated as a separate region.

DEFENCE

Army. The Army consisted in 1983 of 4 infantry battalions, 1 engineer unit and 1 tank squadron. Personnel, 6,000 men.

Navy. The naval force comprises 3 fast attack craft, 7 coastal patrol craft, 2 landing craft and 1 survey ship. Based at Bissau. Personnel (1983) 250.

Air Force. Formation of a small Air Force began in 1978 with the delivery of a French-built Cessna FTB-337 twin-engined counter-insurgency and general-purpose light transport. It has been followed by about 12–39 jet trainers, an Mi-8 and 2 Alouette III helicopters and 2 Dornier Do 27 utility aircraft.

INTERNATIONAL RELATIONS

Membership. Guinea-Bissau is a member of UN, OAU and is an ACP state of EEC.

ECONOMY

Budget. The revenue in 1979 was 890m. pesos; the expenditure, 1,474m. pesos.

Currency. The monetary unit is the *peso* divided into 100 *centavos*. In March 1983, £1 = 61·35 *pesos*; US$1 = 40·32 *pesos*.

NATURAL RESOURCES

Minerals. Mining is very little developed although bauxite (200m. tonnes) has been located in the Boé area. Exploration for oil is taking place but no reports of finds have been reported.

Agriculture. Chief crops (production, 1981, in 1,000 tonnes) are: Groundnuts, 30; sugar-cane, 25; plantains, 25; coconuts, 25; rice, 23; rubber, 23; palm kernels, 10; millet, 6; palm-oil, 5; sorghum, 5; maize, 4; timber, hides, seeds and wax.

Livestock (1981): Cattle, 210,000; sheep, 55,000; goats, 130,000; pigs, 120,000; chickens, 410,000.

COMMERCE. Imports in 1979, 2,070m. pesos; exports, 480m. of which 38% went to Portugal, 23% to Angola and 21% to Spain.

Total trade between Guinea-Bissau and UK (British Department of Trade returns, in £1,000 sterling):

	1979	*1980*	*1981*	*1982*
Imports to UK	835	1	–	–
Exports and re-exports from UK	600	483	595	431

COMMUNICATIONS

Roads. There were (1972) 3,570 km of roads.

Shipping. In 1972, 112 vessels of 232,912 net tons entered the ports.

Post. In 1972 there were 2,764 telephones and (1977) 15,000 radio receivers.

Cinemas. There were 7 cinemas (1972) with a seating capacity of 3,000.

RELIGION, EDUCATION AND WELFARE

Religion. About 40% of the population are Moslem and about 4% Christian.

Education. There were, in 1978, 93,256 pupils in primary schools with 2,620 teachers; 4,612 pupils in secondary schools and 284 students in teacher-training establishments.

Health. In 1976 there were 9 hospitals with 1,056 beds and 74 doctors, 2 dentists, 2 pharmacists, 70 midwives and 292 nursing personnel.

DIPLOMATIC REPRESENTATIVES

Of Great Britain in Guinea-Bissau
Ambassador: P. L. O'Keeffe, CVO (resides in Dakar).

Of Guinea-Bissau in the USA
Ambassador: Inacio Semedo.

Of the USA in Guinea-Bissau (Ave. Domingos Ramos, Bissau).
Ambassador: Peter Jon de Vos.

Of Guinea-Bissau to the United Nations
Ambassador: Dr Inacio Semedo, Jr.

Books of Reference

Relatório e Mapas do Movimento Comercial e Maritimo da Guiné. Bolama, Annual
Cabral, A., *Revolution in Guinea.* London, 1969.—*Return to the Source.* New York, 1973
Davidson, B., *Growing from the Grass Roots.* London, 1974
Gjerstad, O., and Sarrazin, C., *Sowing the First Harvest: National Reconstruction in Guinea-Bissau.* Oakland, 1978
Rudebeck, L., *Guinea-Bissau: A Study of Political Mobilization.* Uppsala, 1974

GUYANA

Capital: Georgetown
Population: 865,000 (1980)
GNP per capita: US$715 (1980)

HISTORY. The territory, including the counties of Demerara, Essequibo and Berbice, named from the 3 rivers, was first partially settled by the Dutch West Indian Company about 1620. The Dutch retained their hold until 1796, when it was captured by the English. It was finally ceded to Great Britain in 1814 and named British Guiana. On 26 May 1966 British Guiana became an independent member of the Commonwealth under the name of Guyana and the world's first Co-operative Republic on 23 Feb. 1970.

AREA AND POPULATION. Guyana is situated on the north-east coast of South America on the Atlantic ocean, with Suriname on the east, Venezuela on the west and Brazil on the south and west. Area, 83,000 sq. miles (216,000 sq. km). Estimated population (Dec. 1980), 865,000. Births (1972), 25,065; deaths (1974), 3,418. In 1976, the population comprised 362,700 Indians, 218,400 Africans, 2,100 Europeans, 3,400 Chinese, 800 others. The Greater Georgetown area had in 1978 an estimated population of 183,000.

In Nov. 1940 sites on the bank of the Demerara River, about 25 miles from the sea, and at Makouria about 40 miles up the Essequibo River, were leased to the USA as military bases. The site on the Demerara River is being operated by the Guyana Government as a civil airport. The US Government relinquished its claims to Atkinson on Guyana's attainment of independence. On 1 May 1969 the airport and surrounding area (formerly Atkinson) were renamed Timehri.

CONSTITUTION AND GOVERNMENT. A new Constitution was promulgated in Oct. 1980. The National Assembly consists of 53 elected members. Elections are held under the single-list system of proportional representation, with the whole of the country forming one electoral area and each voter casting his vote for a party list of candidates. The legislature is elected for 5 years unless earlier dissolved.

The elections held on 15 Dec. 1980 gave the People's National Congress 41 seats, the People's Progressive Party 10 seats, the Liberator Party 2 seats. The PNC with an overall majority formed a 25-member cabinet.

The Cabinet was in Dec. 1982 composed as follows:

President: L. F. S. Burnham.

Prime Minister and First Vice-President: Dr P. A. Reid.

Vice-President, Works Transport and Housing: S. S. Naraine. *Vice-President, Economic Planning and Finance:* H. D. Hoyte. *Vice-President and Agriculture:* H. Green. *Vice-President, Party and State Matters:* B. Ramsaroop. *Energy and Mines:* H. O. Jack. *Foreign Affairs:* R. E. Jackson. *Internal Trade and Consumer Protection:* F. E. Hope. *Attorney-General and Justice:* Dr M. Shahabudeen. *National and Regional Development:* R. H. O. Corbin. *Home Affairs:* J. E. Thomas. *Education, Social Development and Culture:* R. Chandisingh. *Health:* R. Van-West Charles. *Public Service and Information:* Y. Harewood-Benn. *Finance:* Sallahuddin. *Agriculture:* J. Maitland-Singh. *Internal Trade and Consumer Protection:* M. Corrica. *Youth and Sports:* R. Fredericks. *Labour, Manufacturing and Industrial Development:* K. Denny. *Co-operatives:* U. Johnson. *Office of the President:* H. Rashid.

There are 3 Ministers of State.

National flag: Green with a yellow triangle based on the hoist, edged in white, charged with a red triangle edged in black.

DEFENCE

Army. The Guyana Army has a strength of 7,000 (which includes all armed services), including a women's army corps. It comprises 2 infantry battalions.

Air Force. The Air Command is equipped with light aircraft and helicopters, including 2 Skyvan and 1 Super King Air 200 twin-turboprop transports, 6 Islander twin-engined STOL transports, a Cessna U206F utility lightplane, and 4 Bell 206/212 light helicopters.

INTERNATIONAL RELATIONS

Membership. Guyana is a member of UN, the Commonwealth, Caricom and is an ACP state of EEC.

ECONOMY

Budget. Revenue and expenditure for calendar years (in G$1,000):

	1976[1]	*1977*	*1978*	*1979*	*1980*	*1981*
Revenue	500,942	442,475	539,591	693,921	803,460	1,009,936
Expenditure	746,329	567,322	632,749	868,664	1,049,836	1,176,678

[1] Revised estimates.

These figures are exclusive of special receipts from the Colonial Development Fund, US grant and the related expenditure.

Chief items of revenue 1975 (in G$1,000): Customs and excise, 330,746; internal revenue, 124,071; fees, fines, etc., 4,082; posts, 3,841; rents, royalties, etc., 1,197; miscellaneous, 16,201. Expenditure: Public works, 91,522; agriculture, 60,443; education, 59,433; health, 29,248; post and telecommunications, 19,716.

Public debt, 31 Dec. 1975, was G$676·8m.

Currency. Accounts are kept in *dollars* and *cents* (£1 = G$5·80). The Bank of Guyana, established in 1965, issued Guyana dollar notes of $1, 5, 10 and 20 and coins of 1-, 5-, 10-, 25- and 50-cent pieces.

Banking. Barclays Bank International and the Royal Bank of Canada maintain branches in Berbice, Demerara and Essequibo while the Bank of Baroda (India) has branches in Demerara and Berbice. The Chase Manhattan Bank (USA) and the Bank of Nova Scotia each have a branch in Georgetown. The Guyana National Co-operative Bank opened in Feb. 1970 with headquarters in Georgetown and 12 branches throughout the country. In 1973 the Guyana Agricultural and Industrial Development Bank (Gaibank) and the Guyana Co-operative Mortgage Finance Bank were established.

NATURAL RESOURCES

Minerals. Placer gold mining commenced in 1884, and was followed by diamond mining in 1887. From 1884 to 1973 the output of gold was 431,413 bullion oz. (11,000 oz. in 1980). From 1901 to 1973 the production of diamonds was 4,008,211 metric carats (10,200 in 1980). There are large deposits of bauxite; 2,717,000 tons, 2,111,000 tons of alumina and 318,000 tonnes of alumina hydrate were produced in 1980. Full-scale production of manganese began in 1960 and 114,988 wet tons were produced in 1968. The North West Guyana Mining Co. Ltd, operating through the Manganese Mines Ltd, closed operation in Guyana by the end of 1968. Other minerals include uranium, oil, copper and molybdenum.

Agriculture. Production, 1980: Sugar-cane, 169,000 tons; rice, 274,000 tons. Other important products are coconuts, ground provisions and citrus fruit. Other tropical fruits and vegetables are grown mostly in scattered plantings; they include mangoes, papaws, avocado pears, melons, bananas and gooseberries. Other important crops are tomatoes, cabbages, black-eye peas, peanuts, carrots, onions, turmeric, ginger, pineapples, red kidney beans, soybeans, eschallot and tobacco. Large areas of unimproved land in the coastal region, which vary in width up to about 30 miles from the sea, are still available for agricultural and cattle-grazing projects.

Livestock estimate (1981): Cattle, 295,000; pigs, 140,000; sheep, 116,000; goats, 72,000; poultry, 13·3m.

Forestry. Guyana can be divided roughly into 3 regions: (1) A low coastal region varying in width up to about 30 miles and constituting the agricultural area; (2) an intermediate area about 100 miles wide, of slightly higher undulating land containing the chief mineral and forest resources of the country; and (3) a hinterland of several mountain ranges and extensive savannahs. 19,844,170 hectares of the land area is forested out of 21,497,000 hectares.

COMMERCE. Imports and exports (in G$) for calendar years:

	1977	*1978*	*1979*	*1980*	*1981*
Imports	804,265,086	711,056,000	811,000,000	1,009,664,425	1,236,488,611
Exports	652,451,438	739,589,440	732,900,000	992,608,557	974,327,562

Chief imports (1981): Wheat flour, 555,000 kg, $999,000; unmilled wheat, 42,569,000 kg, $30,311,000; milk, 4,748,000 gallons, $31,617,000; textile fabrics, 18,195,000 sq. metres, $25,221,000.

Chief domestic exports (1981): Sugar, 267,000 tonnes, $327·81m.; rice, 78,000 tonnes, $110m.; bauxite, dried, 1,011,000 tonnes, $78,123,000; bauxite, calcined, 496,000 tonnes, $259,464,000; alumina and alumina hydrate, 152,000 tonnes, $91,915,000; rum, 3,204,000 proof gallons, $24,046,000; timber, 36,000 cu. metres, $15,582,000; molasses, 85,344,000 kg, $12,902,000; shrimps, 477 kg, $7,849,000.

Imports (exclusive of transhipments), 1981, from CARICOM Territories, 35%; from USA, 25%; from UK, 16%; from Canada, 4%; exports (exclusive of transhipments) to UK, 26%; to CARICOM Territories, 17%; to Canada, 5%.

Total trade between Guyana and UK (British Department of Trade returns, in £1,000 sterling):

	1978	*1979*	*1980*	*1981*	*1982*
Imports to UK	50,623	43,009	47,143	50,841	50,495
Exports and re-exports from UK	27,292	27,607	30,191	28,969	13,145

COMMUNICATIONS

Roads. Roads and vehicular trails in the national, provincial and urban systems amount to 8,870 km. Motor vehicles, as of 31 Dec. 1976, totalled 64,272, including 26,599 passenger cars, 6,979 lorries and vans, 9,072 tractors and trailers, and 19,109 motor cycles. The main road on the Atlantic Coast, some 290 km (180 miles) long extends from Charity on the Pomeroon River to Crabwood Creek on the Corentyne, there are two unbridged gaps made by the Berbice and Essequibo Rivers, and the banks of the Demerara River are linked by a 1,853 metre (6,074 ft) floating bridge.

Railways. There is a government-owned railway in the North West District, while the Guyana Mining Enterprise operates a standard gauge railway of 133 km from Linden on the Demerara River to Ituni and Coomacka.

Aviation. Guyana Airways Corporation operates scheduled services within the state and also to Trinidad, Barbados, New York, Miami and Brazil. Other services in operation: British Airways 4 times weekly to the Caribbean, Europe and North America: PANAM 3 times weekly to North, Central and South America: Air France, to and from Guadeloupe, Paramaribo and Cayenne 4 times a week; British West Indian Airways, Ltd, to and from Trinidad 3 times a week, providing direct connexion with New York and London; Cubana Airlines once weekly. The International Airport at Timehri serves Guy-America Airways, BWIA, Cubana Airways, and ALM.

Shipping. In 1975, 1,273 vessels of 2,823,912 NRT entered and 1,225 of 2,266,220 NRT cleared the port of Georgetown.

Guyana is in direct sea-communication with the UK, France, Canada, USA, the West Indies, and Netherlands and French Guiana. There are 217 nautical miles of river navigation. There are ferry services across the mouths of the Demerara, Berbice and Essequibo rivers, the last providing a link between the islands of

Leguan and Wakenaam and the mainland at Adventure, and a number of coastal and river-boat services carrying both passengers and cargo. A number of launch services are operated in the more remote areas by private concerns.

Georgetown harbour, about ½ mile wide and 2½ miles long, has a minimum depth of 24 ft. New Amsterdam harbour is situated at the mouth of the Berbice River; there are wharves for coastal vessels only. Bauxite is loaded on ocean-going freighters at Mackenzie, 67 miles up the Demerara River, and at Everton on the Berbice River, about 10 miles from the mouth of the waterway. The Essequibo River has several timber-loading berths ranging from 20 to 40 ft. Springlands on the Corentyne River is the point of entry and departure of passengers travelling by launch services to and from Suriname. It is also a shipping point for rice and other produce from the Corentyne to Georgetown.

Post and Broadcasting. The inland public telegraph and radio communication services are operated and maintained by the Telecommunication Corporation, established on 1 March 1967. On 31 Dec. 1976 there were 57 post offices and 94 agencies (including travelling post offices and agencies).

The telephone exchanges had at the end of 1979 a total of 17,464 direct exchange lines with (1978), 27,064 telephone instruments. The number of route miles in the coastal and inland areas was 2,982 km. 39 land-line stations were maintained at post offices in the coastal area, and 8 telegraph stations in the interior provide communication with the coastal area through a central telegraph office in Georgetown.

Overseas radio-telephone and telegraphic communication were provided by Cable & Wireless (W.I.) Ltd, but were nationalized in 1977 and the service is now provided by the Guyana International Telecommunications Corporation Ltd (Guyintel). In Georgetown a central radio station provides facilities for radio communication with 5 branch offices operated in combination with the wireless telegraph stations mentioned above. 92 stations operated by other government departments, 31 stations operated by private concerns (including mining, ranching, timber and other commercial interests) and 12 coastal ships and launches. This system is linked with the telephone system and is available to the general public.

A Tropospheric Scatter System, operated by Guyintel, was opened on 26 March 1969. It provides for a maximum of 32 channels linking Guyana with the rest of the world *via* Trinidad, the nearest point for connexion in the company's broad band system. The Guyana Broadcasting Corporation, which came into operation on 1 July 1980, has 2 channels.

Cinemas (1981). There are 52 cinemas.

Newspapers (1982). There is 1 daily newspaper with a circulation of 42,000 and 4 weekly papers with a combined circulation of about 100,000.

JUSTICE, EDUCATION AND WELFARE

Justice. The law, both civil and criminal, is based on the common and statute law of England, save that the principles of the Roman–Dutch law have been retained in respect of the registration, conveyance and mortgaging of land.

The Supreme Court of Judicature consists of a Court of Appeal and a High Court.

Education. In Sept. 1976 the Government assumed total responsibility for education from nursery school to university. Private education was abolished. In Sept. 1981, the total number of schools was 886: Nursery, 375; primary, 424; community high, 30; secondary, 57.

There are now 5 technical and vocational schools and 2 schools for the teaching of home economics and domestic crafts. Training in co-operatives is provided by the Kuru-Kuru Co-operative College and agriculture by the Guyana School of Agriculture and the Burnham Agricultural Institute. Art training is provided by the Burrowes School of Art. The training of primary and secondary school teachers is undertaken by 3 institutions. Higher education is also provided by the University of Guyana which was established in 1963 with faculties of natural science, social science, art, technology and education as well as first year students in law. There were 1,889 students in July 1979.

Health. In 1981 there were 29 hospitals, 149 health centres and stations, 4 dispensaries and 11 medical outposts. There were (1977) 114 doctors and 11 dentists.

DIPLOMATIC REPRESENTATIVES

Of Guyana in Great Britain (3 Palace Court, London, W2 4LP)
High Commissioner: Cedric Joseph (accredited 17 Feb. 1982).

Of Great Britain in Guyana (44 Main St., Georgetown)
High Commissioner: W. K. Slatcher, CVO.

Of Guyana in the USA (2490 Tracey Place, NW, Washington, D.C., 20008)
Ambassador: Dr Cedric H. Grant.

Of the USA in Guyana (31 Main St., Georgetown)
Ambassador: Gerald E. Thomas.

Of Guyana to the United Nations
Ambassador: Noel G. Sinclair.

Books of Reference

Daly, P. H., *From Revolution to Republic.* Georgetown, 1970
Daly, Vere T., *A Short History of the Guyanese People.* Rev. ed. London, 1975
Hope, K. R., *Development Policy in Guyana: Planning, Finance and Administration.* London, 1979
Newman, P., *British Guiana—Problem of Cohesion in an Immigrant Society.* OUP, 1964
Report of the British Guiana Commission of Inquiry of the International Commission of Jurists on Racial Problems in the Public Service. Geneva, 1965
Smith, R. T., *British Guiana.* OUP, 1962
Swan, M., *British Guiana.* HMSO, 1957

HAITI

Capital: Port-au-Prince
Population: 6m. (1982)
GNP per capita: US$270 (1980)

République d'Haiti

HISTORY. Haiti occupies the western third of the large island of Hispaniola which was discovered by Christopher Columbus in 1492. The Spanish colony was ceded to France in 1697 and became her most prosperous colony. After the extirpation of the Indians by the Spaniards (by 1533) large numbers of African slaves were imported whose descendants now populate the country. The slaves obtained their liberation following the French Revolution, but subsequently Napoleon sent his brother-in-law, Gen. Leclerc, to restore French authority and re-impose slavery. Toussaint Louverture, the leader of the slaves who had been appointed a French general and governor, was kidnapped and sent to France, where he died in gaol. However, the reckless courage of the Negro troops and the ravages of yellow fever forced the French to evacuate the island and surrender to the blockading British squadron.

The country declared its independence on 1 Jan. 1804, and its successful leader, Gen. Jean-Jacques Dessalines, proclaimed himself Emperor of the newly-named Haiti. After the assassination of Dessalines (1806) a separate régime was set up in the north under Henri Christophe, a Negro general who in 1811 had himself proclaimed King Henry. In the south and west a republic was constituted, with the mulatto Alexander Pétion as its first President. Pétion died in 1818 and was succeeded by Jean-Pierre Boyer, under whom the country became re-united after Henry had committed suicide in 1820. From 1822 to 1844 Haiti and the eastern part of the island (later the Dominican Republic) were united. After one more monarchical interlude, under the Emperor Faustin (1847–59), Haiti has been a republic. From 1915 to 1934 Haiti was under United States occupation.

Following a military *coup* in 1950, and subsequent uprisings, Dr François Duvalier was elected President on 22 Oct. 1957 and subsequently became President for Life in 1964. He died on 21 April 1971 and was succeeded as president for life by his son, Jean-Claude Duvalier.

AREA AND POPULATION. The area is 27,750 sq. km (10,700 sq. miles), of which about three-quarters is mountainous. The population at the census in 1975 was 4,583,785, of which 85% are living in rural areas.

The areas and populations of the 5 *départements* are as follows:

Département	*Sq. km*	*1977*	*Chief town*	*1975*
Nord-Ouest	2,750	247,326	Port-de-Paix	21,733
Nord	4,100	747,360	Cap Haïtien	54,691
Artibonite	6,800	748,357	Gonaïves	36,736
Ouest	7,900	1,983,826	Port-au-Prince	458,675
Sud	6,200	1,041,232	Les Cayes	27,222
Totals	27,750	4,768,101		

The Île de la Gonave, some 40 miles long, lies in the gulf of the same name. Among other islands is La Tortue, off the north peninsula. The majority of the population are Negroes, with an important minority of mulattoes and only about 5,000 white residents, almost all foreign.

Haiti is the only French-speaking republic in the Americas. The standard French of government, parliament and the press is spoken by the small literate minority, but the great majority of the people habitually speak the dialect known as Créole.

CONSTITUTION AND GOVERNMENT. The 1957 Constitution, as subsequently amended, provides for an Executive President who is elected for life and may nominate his successor. He nominates a Cabinet to assist him and, in cases of national emergency, may dismiss both the Cabinet and the National Assembly and govern by decree.

The unicameral National Assembly comprises 58 deputies elected for 6-year terms (renewable) by universal suffrage at age 18. Of the deputies elected on 11 Feb. 1979, all but one belonged to the Parti de l'Unité Nationale of President Duvalier.

The Cabinet in Oct. 1982 was composed as follows:

President: Jean-Claude Duvalier.

Foreign Affairs and Worship: Jean-Robert Estimé. *Interior and Defence:* Dr R. Lafoutant. *Labour and Social Affairs:* Theodore Achille. *Co-ordination, Presidency and Information:* Jean-Marie Chanoine. *Agriculture and Natural Resources:* R. Leveillé. *Public Works, Transport and Communications:* Alix Cinéas. *Finance and National Economy:* Franz Merceron. *Public Health and Population:* Y. R. Joseph. *Commerce and Industry:* J. B. Siméon. *Justice:* B. Edouard. *Planning:* Claude Weil. *Mines and Energy:* Jean E. Pierre. *Education:* F. St Victor. *Youth and Sports:* H. Rémy.

National flag: Vertically black and red, with a small white panel in the centre bearing the national arms.

National anthem: 'La Dessalinienne': Pour le pays, pour les ancêtres (words by J. Lhérisson; tune by N. Geffrard, 1903).

DEFENCE. The Haitian Defence Force (*Forces Armées d'Haiti*) totalling about 7,500 men, is divided into Army, Navy, and Air Force. The President is Commander-in-Chief and appoints the officers.

Army. Total strength, about 7,000, organized into 9 Military Departments and the 'Leopards'. Three of the Departments are in Port-au-Prince and consist of the Presidential Guard (4 Companies); the Dessalines Barracks (7 Companies including the Dessalines Battalion and Headquarters troops); and the Port-au-Prince Police (6 Companies in blue uniforms). The other 6 Military Departments are located outside Port-au-Prince; their troops (21 Companies) operate as District Police. The Fire Brigade and the Prison Guard Company are also part of the Armed Forces. Only the Presidential Guard, the Dessalines Battalion and the Leopards (2 companies of 'Commandos' or Special Forces) with a third company of about 200 recruits, now in training, have any potential for tactical military operations. They are armed mainly with light infantry weapons but have a few elderly pieces of light artillery, 9 light tanks and 6 V-150 commando vehicles.

Navy. The Navy/coastguard of 40 officers and 260 men has 1 *ex*-US armed tug, and 5 coastal patrol boats. The base is at Port-au-Prince.

Air Force. Personnel strength is about 200, with about 28 aircraft of some 12 varieties. They include 8 Summit/Cessna O2-337 Sentry twin piston-engined counter-insurgency aircraft, 3 DC-3s, 5 light transports, 5 training/liaison aircraft, and 7 Hughes and Sikorsky helicopters.

Militia. There is in addition a volunteer civilian force, the *Volontaires de la Sécurité Nationale*, total strength is now estimated at about 14,900, about half of whom have access to antiquated rifles. This force, formerly of some importance as Dr François Duvalier's 'private army' of tough, devoted followers (sometimes called Tontons Macoute or Bogeymen) is much less prominent since his death, having been reduced in strength and reorganized under Defence Force Headquarters on lines roughly parallel to the regional Military Departments.

INTERNATIONAL RELATIONS

Membership. Haiti is a member of UN and OAS.

ECONOMY

Budget. Revenue and expenditure (fiscal year ending 30 Sept.) in US$1m. (5 gourdes = US$1), balanced as follows: 1971–72, 29·6; 1972–73, 31·3; 1973–74, 33·2; 1974–75, 38·9; 1975–76, 43·3.

Currency. The unit of currency is the *gourde* and its value fixed at 5 *gourdes* = US$1. In March 1983, £1 = 7·59 *gourdes.* There are copper–nickel coins for 50, 20, 10 and 5 *centimes* and copper–zinc–nickel coins of 10 and 5 centimes.

Banking. The Banque Nationale de la République d'Haiti, owned by the State, was established 21 Oct. 1910 with a capital of US$5m., and has a monopoly of the note issue. US dollars may be included in the minimum required reserves. The Royal Bank of Canada, the Citibank, the Bank of Nova Scotia, the Bank of Boston, the Banque de l'Union Haitienne (mainly local capital with participation from American, Canadian and Dominican Republic Banks), Banque Nationale de Paris and First National Bank of Chicago all have branches in Port-au-Prince.

Weights and Measures. The metric system is officially accepted.

ENERGY AND NATURAL RESOURCES

Electricity. The hydro-electric plant at Péligre, which was inaugurated in July 1971, provides some 45m. kw. to the capital. The thermal plant in Port-au-Prince, formerly US and now state-owned, is now on standby for emergencies. Generating capacity at Cap Haitien is 3·1m. kw.

Minerals. A US company is engaged in mining bauxite (792,600 tonnes in 1973–74). A Canadian firm mining copper (144,430 tonnes in 1970) had to suspend operations at the end of 1971, as uneconomical because of the world price of copper, but indications are that copper mining may start again. Haiti may possess undeveloped mineral resources of oil, gold, silver, antimony, sulphur, coal and lignite, nickel, gypsum and porphyry.

Agriculture. Only one-third of the country is arable and most people own the tiny plots they farm; the resulting pressure of population is the main cause of rural poverty. Number of farms is estimated at over 500,000.

The occupations of Haiti are nine-tenths agricultural, carried on in 7 large plains, from 200,000 to 25,000 acres, and in 15 smaller plains down to 2,000 acres. Irrigation is used in some areas. Haiti's most important product is coffee of good quality, classified as 'mild', and grown by peasants. Production in 1981 totalled about 33,000 tonnes. Second most important crop is sugar. Sisal is grown extensively. Much of the fibre is exported as or for cordage. New types of cotton are being tried with success. New varieties of rice should significantly boost future production, especially in the Artibonite Valley. Output of main crops in 1981 (in 1,000 tonnes) was: Sugar, 3,000; mangoes, 330; plantains; 300; sweet potatoes, 270; cassava, 255; bananas, 210; maize, 180; sorghum, 110; rice, 90; sisal, 10; cotton, 5; cocoa, 3.

Rum and other spirits are distilled. Essential oils from vetiver, neroli and amyris are important. Cattle and horse breeding are encouraged.

Livestock (1981); Cattle, 1·2m.; sheep, 90,000; pigs, 600,000; goats, 1m.; horses, 415,000; poultry, 4·9m.

INDUSTRY AND TRADE

Industry. Light manufacturing industries assembling or finishing goods for re-export constitute the fastest growing sector. There are 2 textile mills producing cheap denim with a total of 550 looms and 14,000 spindles. Soap factories produce laundry soap, toilet soap and detergent. A cement factory located near the capital produced 140,000 tons in 1973–74 and is extending to 300,000 tons per year. A steel plant making rods, beams and angles was opened in 1974. There are also a pharmaceutical plant, a tannery, a plastics plant, 2 paint works, 2 shoe factories, a large factory producing enamel cookingware, 2 pasta-making factories, a tomato cannery and a flour-mill, all located in or near Port-au-Prince.

Labour. Trade unions were recognized in Feb. 1946. Strong government influence is exercised over the insignificant portion of the labour force that is unionized and organized labour has virtually no strength in Haiti.

Commerce. Imports and exports for fiscal years ending 30 Sept. (in US$1m.):

	1972–73	*1973–74*[1]	*1974–75*[1]	*1975–76*[1]	*1976–77*[1]
Imports	76·7	119·9	142·5	201·0	225·4
Exports	51·3	100·8	81·1	117·5	143·3

[1] Provisional.

The leading imports are foodstuffs, textiles, machinery, mineral oils, raw materials for transformation industries and vehicles.

Total trade between Haiti and UK (British Department of Trade returns, in £1,000 sterling):

	1976	*1977*	*1978*	*1979*	*1980*	*1981*	*1982*
Imports to UK	882	1,063	635	1,118	915	1,439	2,615
Exports and re-exports from UK	2,697	3,394	4,155	3,162	2,818	2,541	3,704

Tourism. In 1976, 280,000 tourists visited Haiti.

COMMUNICATIONS

Roads. Total length of roads is some 4,000 km, little of which is practicable in ordinary motors in the rainy season. There were (1980) about 35,000 vehicles in Haiti.

Railways. The only railway is owned by the Haitian American Sugar Company.

Aviation. An airport capable of handling jets was opened at Port-au-Prince in 1965. US and French carriers provide daily direct services to New York, Miami, Jamaica, Puerto Rico and the French Antilles. There are also services to the Dominican Republic and the Netherlands Antilles. A Haitian company provides a cargo service to the US and Puerto Rico. Air services connecting Port-au-Prince with other Haitian towns are operated by Haiti Air Inter.

Shipping. US, French, Federal Republic of Germany, Dutch, British, Canadian and Japanese lines connect Haiti with the US, Latin America (except Cuba), Canada, Jamaica, Europe and the Far East.

Post and Broadcasting. Most principal towns are connected by the government telegraph system, telephones and wireless.

The telephone company, of which the Haitian Government is now the majority stockholder, is in process of being modernized. Telephone subscribers totalled 22,000 in 1980.

In 1980 there were 120,000 radio and 25,000 television receivers.

Cinemas (1980). There were 15 cinemas in Port-au-Prince.

Newspapers (1980). There were 4 daily newspapers in Port-au-Prince, also a monthly in English and 1 weekly newspaper in Cap Haitien.

JUSTICE, RELIGION, EDUCATION AND WELFARE

Justice. Judges, both of the lower courts and the court of appeal, are appointed by the President. The legal system is basically French. The divorce law has recently been amended to permit parties to obtain 'quick and painless' divorces at a moderate cost, in the hope of attracting the US trade, now that the Mexican 'divorce mills' have closed down. This has developed a useful flow of dollar revenue.

Police. The Police number about 750 in Port-au-Prince and are part of the armed forces.

Religion. Since the Concordat of 1860, the official religion is Roman Catholicism, under an archbishop with 5 suffragan bishops. There are still quite a number of foreigners, French and French Canadians mainly, among the clergy but the first Haitian archbishop took office in 1966. The Episcopal Church now has its first Haitian bishop who was consecrated in 1971. Other Christian churches number perhaps 10% of the population. The folk religion is Voodoo.

Education. Education is divided into primary (first 6 years), secondary (the next 7 years) and finally superior or university. The school system is modelled on that of France. The law calls for free and compulsory elementary education in the French language.

For the 1973–74 academic year, urban primary schools numbered 360 (221 lay and 139 religious) attended by 127,330 pupils with 3,532 teachers. There were, for the same period, at the secondary level, 21 public secondary *lycées* with 15,760 students (4,163 of them girls), 563 teachers (39 of them women). In the private secondary sector, 129 schools were reported with 35,414 students (16,398 girls), 1,172 teachers (107 women). Professional education is divided into 3 categories: (*a*) 41 pre-vocational schools; (*b*) 18 vocational schools which prepare trained workers, and (*c*) 5 vocational schools preparing technicians. There are also 10 licensed private commercial schools. The total number of students was 13,000, 2,000 of whom were in the private sector.

Higher education is offered at the following faculties of the University of Haiti: medicine and pharmacy, odontology (dentistry), science (engineering, architecture, natural sciences, physics, chemistry, biology) with a school of surveying, law and economic sciences, agronomy and veterinary medicine, ethnology, and the Institute of Administration and Management. A new Faculty Arts (Sciences and Humanities) was opened in Nov. 1974. The École Normal Supérieure has replaced the faculty of Letters and Pedagogy.

Health. There were, in 1972, 332 doctors and 104 dentists in practice, 44 hospitals, and 196 health centres and rural clinics. The hospitals had 3,329 beds, of which 776 were in private and charitable establishments.

DIPLOMATIC REPRESENTATIVES

Of Haiti in Great Britain (33 Abbots Hse., St Mary Abbots Terr., London, W14)
Chargé d'Affaires: Théo Duval.

Of Great Britain in Haiti
Ambassador: B. G. Smallman, CMG, CVO. (resides in Kingston).

Of Haiti in the USA (4400–17th St., NW, Washington, D.C., 20011)
Ambassador: Georges N. Leger.

Of the USA in Haiti (Harry Truman Blvd., Port-au-Prince)
Ambassador: Ernest H. Preeg.

Of Haiti to the United Nations
Ambassador: Fritz Cineas.

Books of Reference

The official gazette is *Le Moniteur.*

Revue Agricole d'Haïti. From 1946. Quarterly
Bellegarde, D., *Histoire du Peuple Haïtien.* Port-au-Prince, 1953
Chambers, F. J., *Haiti.* [Bibliography] Oxford and Santa Barbara, 1983
Diedrich, B., and Burt, D., *Papa Doc.* London, 1969
Laguerre, M. S., *The Complete Haitiana.* [Bibliography] London and New York, 1982
Nicholls, D., *From Dessalines to Duvalier: Race, Colour and National Independence in Haiti.* CUP, 1979
Rodman, S., *Haiti, the Black Republic.* New York, 1973

National Library: Bibliothèque Nationale, Rue du Centre, Port-au-Prince.

HONDURAS

República de Honduras

Capital: Tegucigalpa
Population: 3·69m. (1980)
GNP per capita: US$520 (1980)

HISTORY. On 5 Nov. 1838 Honduras declared itself an independent sovereign state, free from the Federation of Central America, of which it had formed a part.

EVENTS. A Treaty was signed in Peru on 30 Oct. 1980 settling the border dispute between El Salvador and Honduras.

AREA AND POPULATION. Honduras is bounded north by the Caribbean, east and north-east by Nicaragua, west by Guatemala, south-west by El Salvador and south by the Pacific ocean. Area is 112,088 sq. km (43,227 sq. miles), with a population, census (1974) of 2,656,948. Estimate (1980) 3,691,027.

The capital of Honduras is Tegucigalpa with (1980, estimate) a population of 472,700. The next most important town is San Pedro Sula, 342,800; other towns are: El Progreso, 94,600; Choluteca, 78,300; Danli, 71,000; Olanchito, 51,000; Juticalpa, 47,500; Comayagua, 44,300; Siguatepeque, 42,100; Santa Rosa de Copan, 26,100. The main ports are Henecan on the Pacific, and, on the Atlantic coast, La Ceiba (64,000), Puerto Cortés (58,100) and Tela (58,000). The port of entry for the Bay Islands is Roatán. A new port at Puerta Castilla, on the Atlantic coast, is under construction.

The republic is divided into 18 departments with their populations (1981, estimate): Atlántida (223,023); Choluteca (272,888); Colón (118,674); Comayagua (198,044); Copán (206,653); Cortés (566,937); El Paraíso (194,840); Francisco Morazán (683,138); Gracias a Dios (32,519); Intibucá (106,963); Islas de La Bahía (17,910); La Paz (84,308); Lempira (167,690); Ocotepeque (62,943); Olancho (213,525); Santa Barbara (269,054); Valle (120,498); and Yoro (281,344).

Aboriginal tribes number over 35,000, principally Miskito, Payas and Xicaques Indians and Sambos (the latter a mixture of Miskito and Negro), each speaking a different dialect. The Spanish-speaking inhabitants are chiefly *mestizos*, Indians with an admixture of Spanish blood. Gracias a Dios is still largely unexplored and is inhabited by pure native races who speak little or no Spanish.

In 1980 the birth rate was 49·3 per 1,000; death rate, 12·4 per 1,000 and infant mortality rate, 11·8 per 1,000 live births.

CONSTITUTION AND GOVERNMENT. Until a change of Government on 4 Dec. 1972, legislative power had been vested in a single chamber, the Congress of Deputies consisting of 64 members, chosen for 6 years by popular vote, in the ratio of 1 per 30,000 inhabitants. It used to meet for 180 days beginning 26 May and ending 26 Oct. A permanent commission of 5 members used to sit while Congress was not in session for the transaction of routine or emergency business. All men and women over 18 are entitled to vote.

In 1972 Congress was suspended. The Commander of the Armed Forces, Gen. Policarpo Paz García led a military *coup* in 1978 and a military junta was established.

A new Constitution was promulgated on 20 Jan. 1982. Elections were held on 29 Nov. 1981 for deputies to a Congress. The election results were Liberals, 44 deputies; Nationalists, 34 and Party of Innovation and Unity, 3; Christian Democratic Party, 1.

At the elections for President held on 29 Nov. 1981 Dr Roberto Suazo Córdova (Liberal) was elected for a 4-year term, with 53% of the votes.

President: Dr Roberto Suazo Córdova (sworn in 27 Jan. 1982).

National flag: Three horizontal stripes of blue, white, blue, with 5 blue stars in the centre.

National anthem: Tu bandera es un lampo de cielo (words by A. C. Coello; tune by C. Hartling).

DEFENCE

Army. Every male citizen is liable to serve in the Army from the age of 18 to 50. Service in the active Army is for approximately 1 year. Although there is no actual reserves programme, those men who have served on active duty for 1 year or more, are eligible for recall. The size of the regular Army is approximately 11,500 men; this does not include the National Police Force, which numbers 3,000. The Army is organized into 6 infantry battalions, 2 artillery battalions and minor units.

Air Force. Equipment, mostly of US origin, includes 12 J52-engined Super Mystère fighters acquired from Israel, 6 A-37B jet light attack aircraft, 1 or 2 F-86K jet fighters, 3 RT-33A reconnaissance aircraft, some Summit/Cessna O2-337 Sentry twin piston-engined COIN aircraft, 8 T-28S Fennec and 4 T-28E armed piston-engined trainers, 2 C-54, 5 C-47, 3 Israeli-built Arava and 1 Westwind transports, some helicopters, and T-37B, T-28, T-41A and T-6 trainers. Total strength is about 1,200 personnel, of whom many are civilian maintenance staff.

INTERNATIONAL RELATIONS

Membership. Honduras is a member of UN and OAS.

ECONOMY

Budget. The fiscal and calendar years have coincided since 1 Jan. 1957. Recent budgets (in 1m. lempiras) balance as follows: 1978, 831·9; 1979, 1,000; 1980, 1,136·7; 1981, 1,307; 1982 (estimate), 1,677m.

The largest sources of income (1981) were (in 1m. lempiras): Income tax, 179·3; production taxes, 177·8; import taxes, 198·5; export taxes, 113·6.

Total external debt (1981) was (in 1m. lempiras), 2,621·8 and net reserves of foreign currency, 34.

Currency. The unit of the monetary system is the *lempira* also known as a *peso*, comprising 100 *centavos*. Notes are issued by the Banco Central de Honduras which has the sole right to issue, in denominations of 100, 50, 20, 10, 5, 2 and 1 *lempiras*. Coins in circulation are 50 and 20 *centavos* in silver, 10 and 5 *centavos* in cupro-nickel and 2 and 1 *centavos* in copper.

Rate of exchange, March 1983: £1 = 3·05 *lempiras;* US$1 = 2 *lempiras*.

Banking. The central bank of issue is the Banco Central de Honduras. The Banco Atlántida has branches in Tegucigalpa, San Pedro Sula, Comayaguela, Puerto Cortés, La Ceiba, Tela, El Progreso, Choluteca and other towns. The Banco de Honduras which operates in many parts of the country is controlled by the Citibank. The Bank of America has branches in Tegucigalpa and San Pedro Sula. The Bank of London and Montreal has branches in Tegucigalpa, San Pedro Sula, Comayaguela and La Ceiba. The Central American Bank for Economic Integration has its head office in Tegucigalpa.

Weights and Measures. The metric system has been legal since 1 April 1897, but English pounds and yards and the old Spanish system are still in use: 1 *vara* = 32 in.; 1 *manzana* (10,000 sq. *varas*) = 700 sq. metres; 1 *arroba* = 25 lb.; 1 *quintal* = 100 lb.; 1 *tonelada* = 2,000 lb.

NATURAL RESOURCES

Minerals. Mineral resources include gold, silver, lead, tin, zinc and mercury, which are exported. There are probably reserves of other minerals which have not yet been exploited. The Rosario Resources Company, which owned and operated the famous Rosario mines near Tegucigalpa from 1882 to 1954, developed and now operates a mine at El Mochito (Department of Santa Barbara) while the Compañia Minera Los Angeles SA has a mine currently extracting lead, zinc and silver at Valle de Angeles (Department of Francisco Morazán).

Agriculture. Although Honduras is essentially an agricultural country, less than a quarter of the total land area is cultivated and by far the larger portion of this is on the Caribbean and Pacific coastal plains. Agriculture employs 58·9% of the working population and provides 80% of the exports. The main agricultural crops are: Bananas, coffee, sugar, tobacco and cotton. Exports of meat amounted to 92·6m. lempiras in 1982.

Livestock (1981): Cattle, 2·3m.; sheep, 5,000; pigs, 580,000; goats, 22,000; horses, 151,000; poultry, 4·9m.

Forestry. Forests cover nearly 45% of the total land area. Honduras has an abundance of hard- and soft-woods. Large stands of mahogany and other hardwoods—granadino, guayacán, walnut and rosewood—grow in the north-eastern part of the country, in the interior valleys, and near the southern coast. Stands of pine occur almost everywhere in the interior, but are severely damaged by bark beetle and fires. In 1982, total wood exports amounted to 86·3m. lempiras. The Olancho Forest Development Programme involving the construction of saw- and pulp-mills is in progress.

Fisheries. Commercial fishing in territorial waters is restricted to Honduran nationals and Honduran companies in which the controlling share of the capital is owned by a Honduran national. Shrimps and lobsters are important catches.

INDUSTRY AND TRADE

Industry. Small-scale local industries include beer and mineral waters, cement, flour, vegetable lard, coconut oil, sweets, cigarettes, cigars, textiles and clothing, panama hats, plastics, nails, matches, plywood, furniture, paper bags, soap, candles, fruit juices and household chemicals. An important hydro-electric scheme has been built at Rio Lindo to serve the Central and North Coast regions. The El Cajon hydro-electric project is now under construction and will come on stream in 1985 (290 mw). A small integrated steel-mill may be erected in Agalteca (Department of Francisco Morazán). The manufacturing industry employed 13% of the working population in 1979.

Labour. The organization of trade unions was begun in 1954 with the assistance of ORIT (Inter-American Regional Organization) sponsored by the USA trade unions. In 1972 there were 166 trade unions, of which only 119 were active, with about 67,956 members. A 'Charter of Labour' was granted in Feb. 1955 and an advanced Labour Code and Social Security Bill passed into law in May 1959. A Ministry of 'Labour, Social Assistance and the Middle Class' was created in 1955; the last four words of its title were expunged in 1957.

Commerce. Imports in 1981 were valued at 1,870·5m. lempiras and exports at 1,555·1 lempiras.

Imports (1981) in 1m. lempiras: Machinery and transport equipment, 509·4; mineral fuel and lubricants, 323·1; chemicals, 311·6; food products, 145; various products, 142.

Exports (1981) in 1m. lempiras: bananas, 431·6; coffee, 345·7; refrigerated meats, 92·6; timber, 86·3; silver, 46·6; shrimps and lobster, 50·7; soap, 26; lead and zinc, 38·7; tobacco, 25·9; cotton, 24·7.

Trade with main countries in 1m. lempiras (1981) was: USA, 1,604·5; Japan, 234·2; Federal Republic of Germany, 214·7; Venezuela, 99·9; Guatemala, 181·4; Netherlands, 102.

Total trade between Honduras and UK (British Department of Trade returns, in £1,000 sterling):

	1978	*1979*	*1980*	*1981*	*1982*
Imports to UK	2,219	4,000	3,687	4,065	4,695
Exports and re-exports from UK	8,443	9,013	11,835	8,617	4,659

Tourism. There were 97,581 tourists in 1980.

COMMUNICATIONS

Roads. Honduras is connected with Guatemala, El Salvador and Nicaragua by the Pan-American Highway. Out of a total of 14,001 km of road (1981), 1,756 are paved. There are good asphalted highways between Puerto Cortés in the north and Choluteca in the south passing through San Pedro Sula and Tegucigalpa with branches to Guatemala and El Salvador. In 1981 there were 95,997 motor vehicles.

Railways. Only 4 railways exist; they are confined to the north coastal region and are used mainly for transportation of bananas. Tegucigalpa, the capital, is not served by any railway, and there are no international railway connexions. The total railways operating in 1980 were 1,928 km of 1,067 mm and 914 mm gauge.

Aviation. Over a large part of the country the aeroplane is the normal means of transport for both passengers and freight. There are international airports at Tegucigalpa, San Pedro Sula, La Ceiba and over 30 smaller airstrips in various parts of the country.

Shipping. Sailings to the Atlantic coast port of Puerto Cortés from Europe are frequent, mainly operated by the Harrison Line, Cia Generale Transatlantique, the Royal Netherlands Steamships Co., Hapag Lloyd and vessels owned or chartered by the Tela Railroad Co., a subsidiary of United Brands, and the Standard Fruit Co.

Post and Broadcasting. The Government in April 1972 operated 18,845 km of telephone lines and 12,526 km of telegraph lines. Number of telephones in use, 1980, 29,951; telephone exchanges, 58; number of telegraph offices, 250; combined telephone and telegraph offices, 140. In 1980 there were 508 post offices and agencies, 148 commercial broadcasting stations. Commercial television began with a station in Tegucigalpa in Sept. 1959. There were (1979) 3 commercial channels and about 27,000 receivers in use. Transmission in colour commenced mid-1973.

Cinemas (1982). Cinemas numbered about 60 with seating capacity of some 60,000.

Newspapers (1982). The 4 most important daily papers are *El Heraldo* and *La Tribuna* in Tegucigalpa, *La Prensa* and *El Tiempo* in San Pedro Sula. Several others exist but their circulation is low and their influence is very limited.

JUSTICE, RELIGION, EDUCATION AND WELFARE

Justice. The judicial power resides in the Supreme Court, with 7 judges elected by the National Constituent Assembly in 1980 for 6 years; it appoints the judges of the courts of appeal, labour tribunals and the district attorneys who, in turn, name the justices of the peace.

Religion. Roman Catholicism is the prevailing religion, but the constitution guarantees freedom to all creeds, and the State does not contribute to the support of any.

Education. Instruction is free, compulsory (from 7 to 15 years of age) and secular. In 1981 the 5,682 primary schools had 636,528 children (17,378 teachers); the 300 secondary, normal and technical schools had 125,018 pupils (5,090 teachers); the teachers' college had 2,604 students (168 teachers); 6 university faculties had 27,109 students (1,419 teachers) at Tegucigalpa offering economics, engineering, law, medicine, dentistry, chemistry and pharmacy. Other courses offered are: Public administration, journalism, business administration, auditing and accounting, nursing, psychology, mechanical engineering, social service, agronomy (La Ceiba) and economics (San Pedro Sula). The José Cecilio del Volla University in Tegucigalpa and the Private University of San Pedro Sula opened in 1978; in 1981, the two universities had a total of 800 students and 125 teachers.

The illiteracy rate was 40% of those 10 years of age and older in 1978.

Health. In 1981 there were about 1,370 doctors, 530 health centres and 5,230 hospital beds.

DIPLOMATIC REPRESENTATIVES

Of Honduras in Great Britain (52 Manchester St., London, W1M 5PB)
Ambassador: Edgardo Dumas-Rodriguez (accredited 29 July 1982).

Of Great Britain in Honduras (Ave. República de Chile, Tegucigalpa)
Ambassador: C. J. Sharkey, MBE.

Of Honduras in the USA (4301 Connecticut Ave., NW, Washington, D.C., 20008)
Ambassador: Juan Agurcia Ewing.

Of the USA in Honduras (Ave. La Paz, Tegucigalpa)
Ambassador: J. D. Negroponte.

Of Honduras to the United Nations
Ambassador: Dr Mario Carias.

Books of Reference

The *Anuario Estadístico* (latest issue, *Comercio Exterior de Honduras*, 1980) is published by the Dirección de Estadísticas y Censos, Tegucigalpa. *Director:* Elizabeth Zavala de Turcios.

Monthly Bulletin.—Honduras en Cifras. Banco Central de Honduras, 1980
Checchi, V. (and others), *Honduras, a Problem in Economic Development.* New York, 1959
Rubio Melhado, A., *Geografía General de la Republica de Honduras.* Tegucigalpa, 1953
Stokes, W. S., *Honduras: An Area Study in Government.* Madison, Wisc., 1950

HONG KONG

Population: 5·23m. (1982)
GDP per capita: US$4,300 (1980)

HISTORY. The Crown Colony of Hong Kong was ceded by China to Great Britain in Jan. 1841; the cession was confirmed by the Treaty of Nanking in Aug. 1842, and the charter bears the date 5 April 1843. Since then Hong Kong has been under British administration, with the exception of the period from 25 Dec. 1941 to 30 Aug. 1945, when it was occupied by the Japanese.

AREA AND POPULATION. Hong Kong island is 32 km east of the mouth of the Pearl River and 130 km south-east of Canton. The area of the island is 78·12 sq. km. It is separated from the mainland by a fine natural harbour. On the opposite side is the peninsula of Kowloon (10·48 sq. km), which, with Stonecutters Island (0·75 sq. km), was added to the Colony by the Convention of Peking, 1860. By a further convention, signed at Peking on 9 June 1898, about 950 sq. km, consisting of all the immediately adjacent mainland and numerous islands in the vicinity, were leased to Great Britain by China for 99 years. This area is known as the New Territories. Total area of the territory is 1,064 sq. km (including recent reclamations), a large part of it being steep and unproductive hillside. Some 40% of the territory is conserved as country parks. Shortage of land suitable for development for housing and industry, is a serious problem. Since 1945, the Government has reclaimed about 11,500 hectares from the sea, principally from the seafronts of Hong Kong and Kowloon, facing the harbour. In the New Territories, the new town of Tsuen Wan, incorporating Tsuen Wan, Kwai Chung and Tsing Yi, already houses 680,000 of its planned ultimate population of 918,000. The construction of 5 further new towns at Sha Tin, Tuen Mun, Tai Po, Fanling and Yuen Long is now well underway, with designed population capacities of 756,000, 547,000, 220,000, 170,000 and 128,000 respectively. Planning has started for a new town at Junk Bay to house 300,000 people.

The climate is sub-tropical, the winter being cool and dry and the summer hot and humid. The average rainfall is 2,246 mm. (88 in.), May to Sept. being the wettest months.

The population was 5,021,066 at 1981 census. Estimate (mid-1982) 5·23m. During the war years the population of Hong Kong fluctuated sharply. In Sept. 1945, at the end of the Japanese occupation, it was about 600,000. In mid-1950 it was estimated at 2·24m. Since 1971 the average annual growth rate has been 2·4%. Of the present population about 36% are under 20 years of age. About 57% of the population was born in Hong Kong.

CONSTITUTION AND GOVERNMENT. The administration is in the hands of a Governor, aided by an Executive Council, composed of the Commander, British Forces, the Chief Secretary, the Attorney-General, the Secretary for Home Affairs, the Financial Secretary (who are members *ex officio*) and such other members, both official and unofficial, as may be appointed by the Queen upon the Governor's nomination. In 1982 there were, in addition to the 5 *ex-officio* members, 1 nominated official and 9 nominated unofficial members. There is also a Legislative Council, presided over by the Governor. In 1982 it consisted of 4 *ex-officio* members, namely the Chief Secretary, the Attorney-General, the Secretary for Home Affairs and the Financial Secretary, 27 nominated unofficial members and 22 nominated official members. Chinese and English are the official languages.

Governor and C.-in-C.: Sir Edward Youde, GCMG, MBE.
Commander British Forces: Maj.-Gen. Derek Boorman, CB.
Chief Secretary: Sir Philip Haddon-Cave, KBE, CMG.
Flag: British Blue Ensign with the arms of the Colony on a white disc in the fly.

DEFENCE. The Hong Kong Garrison, under the Commander British Forces, comprises units of all three services. Its principal rôle is to assist the Hong Kong Government in maintaining security and stability.

Army. The Army constitutes the bulk of the garrison. It comprises a UK battalion, based at Stanley Fort, and 4 Gurkha infantry battalions, one based at Lyemun, the other 3 in the New Territories; supporting units include the Queen's Gurkha Engineers, the Queen's Gurkha Signals, the Gurkha Transport Regiment, and 660 Squadron Army Air Corps.

Navy. The Naval Base is at HMS *Tamar*. The Hong Kong Squadron comprises five patrol craft, which are converted Ton-class minesweepers. In addition, 3 Raiding Squadron Royal Marines, equipped with fast 'Sea Rider' craft, are operating from HMS *Tamar*.

Air Force. The Royal Air Force is based at Sek Kong. No. 28 (Army Co-operation) Squadron operates 8 Wessex helicopters. In addition to its operational rôle in support of the army and navy, the RAF carries out search and rescue and medical evacuation tasks. It is also responsible for air traffic control services at Sek Kong, and provides a territory-wide air traffic advisory service.

Auxiliary Defence Units. The local Auxiliary Defence Units, consisting of the Royal Hong Kong Regiment and the Royal Hong Kong Auxiliary Air Force, are administered by the Hong Kong Government, but, if called out, would come under the command of the Commander British Forces. The Royal Hong Kong Regiment (The Volunteers) has a strength of about 700. It is fully mobile and its rôle is to operate in support of regular army battalions stationed in Hong Kong. The Royal Hong Kong Auxiliary Air Force is intended mainly for internal security and air-sea rescue duties. It has a strength of about 116, operating a fleet of seven aircraft – a twin-engined Britten-Norman Islander, a twin-engined Cessna 404 Titan Courier, two Scottish Aviation Bulldog Trainers and three Aérospatiale Dauphin 365C1 helicopters.

ECONOMY

Budget. The public revenue and expenditure for financial years ending 31 March were as follows (in HK$):

	1978–79	*1979–80*	*1980–81*	*1981–82*
Revenue	12,557,000,000	16,796,000,000	30,290,300,000	32,887,700,000
Expenditure	11,090,100,000	13,872,000,000	23,593,500,000	25,061,800,000

The revenue is derived chiefly from rates, licences, duties on liquor, tobacco and hydrocarbon oils, a tax on earnings and profits, land sales and stamp duties.

Currency. The unit of currency is the Hong Kong *dollar*. Banknotes (of denominations of $10 upwards) are issued by the Hongkong and Shanghai Banking Corporation, and the Chartered Bank. Their combined note issue was, in mid-1982, HK$11,346m. Subsidiary currency consisting of HK$5, HK$2, HK$1, 50-cent, 20-cent, 10-cent, 5-cent copper-nickel-alloy coins and 1-cent notes is issued by the Hong Kong Government and at 31 March 1981 totalled HK$1,001m.

Since 1975, the Hong Kong Government has issued annually a limited quantity of HK$1,000 gold coins. The first in the series was issued to commemorate the Queen's visit to Hong Kong in 1975. Gold coins have since been minted to mark the Chinese Lunar Years of the Dragon, the Snake, the Horse, the Goat, the Monkey, the Cockerel, and the Dog.

Banking. There are 123 licensed banks and 121 foreign banks maintaining representative offices in Hong Kong. Deposits in the first 8 months of 1982 totalled HK$177,528m.

Weights and Measures. Metric, British Imperial, Chinese and US units are all in current use in Hong Kong. However Government Departments have now effectively adopted metric units; all new legislation uses metric terminology and existing legislation is being progressively metricated. Metrication is also proceeding in the private sector.

The Chinese units in the table below are those which have statutory equivalents under Hong Kong's Weights and Measures Ordinance.

The statutory equivalent for the *chek* is 14 5/8 inches. The variation of the size of the *chek* with usage still persists in Hong Kong but the *chek* and derived units are now used much less than in the past. For the retail sale of cloth, a 'yard' of 24 Chinese inches (35.1 inches) is frequently used.

AGRICULTURE. In 1981, 176,000 tonnes of vegetables were produced. Livestock (1981): Cattle, 788; pigs, 432,000; poultry, 46m.

WATER. The provision of sufficient capacity to store the summer rainfall to meet water requirements, particularly during the dry winter months, has always been a serious problem. However, this has been alleviated to some extent by the raising of the Plover Cove Dams in 1973, giving the reservoir a capacity of 230m. cu. metres, and the completion in 1978 of the 273m. cu. metre High Island Reservoir which involved the conversion of another sea inlet to a fresh water lake, as was the case with Plover Cove.

Total available storage capacity now stands at 578m. cu. metres distributed in 18 impounding reservoirs. This is supplemented by water purchased from China for which the agreement is a supply of 182m. cu. metres in 1982 with provision for staged increases thereafter. These resources can be further supplemented when necessary by up to 181,000 cu. metres of fresh water a day from a desalting plant completed in 1976 and now considered as a 'reserve resource'.

INDUSTRY AND TRADE

Industry. An economic policy based on free enterprise and free trade; an industrious work force; an efficient and aggressive commercial infrastructure; modern and efficient sea-port (including container shipping terminals) and airport facilities: its geographical position relative to markets in North America and its traditional trading links with Britain have all contributed to Hong Kong's success as a modern industrial complex.

In June 1982, there were 47,926 factories employing 903,012 people out of a total population of approximately 5·2m. The type of factory involved ranges from the small cottage type to large highly complex modern establishments. Given the scarcity of land it is most common for light industry to operate in multi-storey buildings specially designed for this purpose. The main industry is textiles and clothing, which employs 18% of the labour force and accounts for 41% of total domestic exports. Other major light manufacturing industries include electronic products, clocks and watches, toys, plastic products, metalware, footwear, cameras and travel goods. Heavy industry includes ship-building, ship-repairing, aircraft engineering and iron and steel rolling. Agriculture, fishing and some mining are the main primary industries.

Commerce. Hong Kong's industries are mainly export oriented. The total value of domestic exports in 1981 was HK$80,423m. The major markets were USA (36%), Federal Republic of Germany (9%), UK (10%), Japan (4%), Australia (3%), and Singapore (2%). There is also a sizeable and flourishing entrepôt trade which accounted for another HK$41,739m. in 1981.

The total value of imports in 1981 was HK$138,375m., mainly from Japan (23%), China (21%), USA (10%), Taiwan (8%), Singapore (8%) and UK (5%).

The chief import items were machinery (30%), textiles (13%), foodstuffs (10%), chemicals (6%), petroleum products (7%), crude raw materials (4%).

Imports from the Commonwealth countries (HK$22,480m. in 1981) amounted to 16% of total imports, and exports to the Commonwealth countries (HK$17,565m.) accounted for 22% of Hong Kong's domestic exports.

Duties are levied only on tobacco, hydrocarbon oils, methyl alcohol and alcoholic liquors (including toilet preparations containing more than 1·2% of ethyl alcohol but excluding registered pharmaceutical products), whether imported into or manufactured in Hong Kong for local consumption.

All imports (apart from foodstuffs, which are subject to a flat charge of HK$2 per shipment) and exports are subject to a varying *ad valorem* charge.

The adverse balance on visible trade is offset by a favourable balance from exchange, shipping and insurance transactions, an inflow of capital, ship-repairing, a flourishing tourist industry, remittances from overseas Chinese, etc.

Hong Kong has a free exchange market. Foreign merchants may remit profits or repatriate capital. Import and export controls are kept to the minimum, consistent with strategic requirements.

Total trade between Hong Kong and UK (British Department of Trade returns, in £1,000 sterling) is given as follows:

	1977	*1978*	*1979*	*1980*	*1981*	*1982*
Imports to UK	454,056	531,368	689,252	850,340	898,634	872,545
Exports and re-exports from UK	271,194	362,444	442,452	559,420	618,525	732,489

Tourism. Tourists spent an estimated HK$8,900m. in Hong Kong in 1981. During the year tourists totalled over 2·5m.

COMMUNICATIONS

Roads. In 1982 there were 1,182 km of roads, distributed as follows: Hong Kong Island, 351; Kowloon and New Kowloon, 353, and New Territories, 478. A cross-harbour tunnel, 1·6 km in length, opened to traffic in Aug. 1972, now links Hong Kong Island with the Kowloon peninsula. The 1·4 km twin-tube Lion Rock Tunnel, which links Kowloon with Sha Tin New Town and other areas of the north-eastern New Territories, became fully operational in Oct. 1978.

Railways. There is an electric tramway 13·2 km, and a cable tramway connecting the Peak district with the lower levels in Victoria. The Government owns the section of the Kowloon-Canton Railway that runs for 34 km from the terminus at Hung Hom in Kowloon to the border point at Lo Wu. On 4 April 1979 a direct 'through' passenger train to Guangzhou (Canton) was re-introduced after a lapse of nearly 30 years. A second express train came into operation on 11 Feb. 1980. Both trains are invariably full and cater mainly for the business and tourist communities as well as Hong Kong residents visiting friends and relatives in China. There are also other passenger services to Lo Wu to allow for connexions to be made for onward trains at the Shenzhen border point (Chinese section). Mail and freight are conveyed across the border without transhipment.

The railway is undergoing a massive modernization and electrification programme. Stage I of the electrified inner suburban service between Kowloon and Sha Tin was opened on 6 May 1982. The remaining section of the line will be electrified in two stages—the first to Tai Po Market in Spring 1983 and the second to Lo Wu by late Summer 1983. The entire line will be electrified and fully double-tracked upon completion of the HK$3,500m. project. All existing stations are to be rebuilt and three new stations are planned for Tai Wai, Fo Tan and Kowloon Tong (already opened in May to cope with the electrified service). The Kowloon Tong Station is designed as an interchange with the underground Mass Transit Railway.

The status of the Kowloon-Canton Railway changed from a government department to a public corporation on 1 Jan. 1983. The decision was taken in view of the major development of the KCR into a much expanded and more sophisticated railway.

An underground Mass Transit Railway system, comprising 25 stations, is now in operation. The system consists of two lines, one linking the Central District of Hong Kong Island with Tsuen Wan in the west of Kowloon, and the other linking Kwun Tong in East Kowloon with Waterloo in Nathan Road. Cross platform interchange facilities are provided at Prince Edward and Argyle stations for passengers travelling between the two lines. The system is about 26 km in length.

Work began at the end of 1981 on the Island Line, which will serve the northern foreshore of Hong Kong Island. Scheduled to be fully operational in mid-1986, the new line will run for 12·5 km and incorporate 14 stations.

Aviation. Hong Kong International Airport is situated on the north shore of Kowloon Bay. It is regularly used by 31 airlines and many charter airlines which provide frequent services throughout the Far East to Europe, North America, Africa, the Middle East, Australia and New Zealand. British Airways operates 14 services per week, to UK, Africa and Japan. Cathay Pacific Airways, the Hong Kong-based airline, operates 182 passenger services to the UK, the Far and Middle East and Australia. During 1981, British Caledonian Airways also commenced scheduled services on the Hong Kong to London route. About 1,000 scheduled services are operated weekly to and from Hong Kong by various airlines. In 1982, 55,500 aircraft arrived and departed on international flights, carrying 8·6m. passengers and 305,000 tonnes of freight.

Shipping. The total vessels entering and clearing Hong Kong and engaged in foreign trade in the first 8 months of 1982 amounted to 14,798 ocean-going vessels of 83,032,000 net tons. Launches and junks engaging in local trade, totalled 55,077 vessels of 9,626,000 net tons. 697 vessels (3,680,750 gross tons) were registered in Hong Kong as British ships.

Telecommunications, Post and Broadcasting. There were 89 post offices in 1982; postal revenue totalled HK$488·5m.; expenditure, HK$369m. Telephone services are provided by the Hong Kong Telephone Co. Ltd. It operates through a network of 64 fully automatic main exchanges and served (1981) 1·8m. subscribers. Cable & Wireless Ltd is responsible for all external telecommunications and also provides for marine, meteorological and aeronautical communications. Telecommunication systems employed in Hong Kong include satellite, tropospheric scatter, HF, VHF, UHF, submarine and land coaxial cables. Services provided to the community include international telephone, telegram, telex, leased circuits, data transmission, facsimile and ship-shore communications.

There is a government broadcasting station, Radio Television Hong Kong, with daily transmissions in English and Chinese. Wireless licences were abolished as from 1 March 1967. A commercial station, the Commercial Broadcasting Co. Ltd, transmits daily in English and Cantonese. Two radio stations operate 8 channels.

Television Broadcasts Ltd and Asia Television Ltd transmit commercial television in English and Chinese on 4 channels, mainly in colour.

Cinemas. In 1982 there were 88 cinemas with a seating capacity of over 100,000. Attendance 61m. in 1981.

Newspapers. In 1982 there were 72 daily or weekly newspapers, registered and in circulation, including 5 daily English-language papers; the remainder are almost all in Chinese.

JUSTICE, EDUCATION AND WELFARE

Justice. There is a Supreme Court, having original, bankruptcy and companies winding-up, criminal, probate, divorce, admiralty and prize jurisdiction, and a court of appeal. There is also a District Court which, for administrative purposes, is divided into 3 geographical areas. It sits in several different buildings. There are 47 Magistrates sitting in 8 separate Magistracies. The District Court, apart from hearing civil cases where the claim does not amount to more than HK$20,000, also has jurisdiction over criminal matters. The labour tribunal provides speedy settlements to individual money claims arising from contracts of employment. The lands tribunal adjudicates on all statutory claims for compensation over land and certain landlord and tenant matters. The small claims tribunal deals with monetary claims involving amounts not exceeding HK$5,000.

Police. The Royal Hong Kong Police Force in 1982 totalled 27,380, composed of 373 gazetted, 2,003 inspectorate officers, 20,119 junior officers and 4,885 civilians. These figures include 2,057 women police officers, who are completely integrated throughout the force. There are also 5,435 part-time officers.

The maritime force operated by the Marine Division of the Royal Hong Kong Police comprises 107 vessels ranging from sea-going patrol launches and jet boats to inflatables and logistic support craft. Personnel in 1982 numbered 2,316 (137 officers, 553 n.c.o.s and 1,626 constables).

Education. The majority of schools have to be registered with the Education Department under the Education Ordinance. They are required to comply with regulations as to staff, building, fire and health requirements. From Sept. 1971, free and compulsory primary education was introduced in government and the majority of government-aided schools. Free junior secondary education of 3 years' duration was achieved in 1978 and it was made compulsory in stages beginning in Sept. 1979.

In March 1982 there were 213,480 pupils in kindergartens (all private), another 549,140 in primary schools and 472,225 in secondary schools.

There are 5 technical institutes with a total full-time and part-time enrolment of 32,048, 1 technical teachers' college and 3 colleges of education with a total enrolment of 3,118.

The University of Hong Kong had 5,089 undergraduates in 1982 and the Chinese University of Hong Kong, inaugurated in Oct. 1963, had 4,809 undergraduates. The Hong Kong Polytechnic, 1982, had a total of 7,625 full-time and 17,412 part-time students.

Health. In 1982 there were 4,000 doctors and about 21,500 hospital beds.

Social Security. The Government co-ordinates and implements expanding programmes in social welfare, which include social security, family services, child care, services for the elderly, youth and community work, probation and corrections and rehabilitation. More than 122 voluntary welfare agencies are subsidised by public funds.

The Government gives non-contributory cash assistance to needy families, unemployed able-bodied adults, the severely disabled and the elderly. Caseload at 31 Oct. 1982 totalled 263,756. Victims of natural disasters, crimes of violence and traffic accidents are financially assisted.

Books of Reference

Statistical Information: The Census and Statistics Department is responsible for the preparation and collation of Government statistics. These statistics are published mainly in the *Hong Kong Monthly Digest of Statistics* which is also available in a collected annual edition. The Department also publishes monthly trade statistics, economic indicators, annual review of overseas trade, etc. Statistical information is also published in the annual reports of Government departments. *Hong Kong 1982*, and other government publications are available from the Hong Kong Government Publications Centre, GPO Building, Connaught Place, Hong Kong, and the Hong Kong Government Office in London, 6 Grafton Street, London, W1X 3LB.

The Hong Kong Trade Development Council, Connaught Centre, Connaught Place, Hong Kong, issues a monthly *Hong Kong Enterprise* and other publications.

Hong Kong 1982. Hong Kong Government Press, 1982
Hong Kong Bibliography. Hong Kong Government Press, 1965
Beazer, W. F., *The Commercial Future of Hong Kong.* New York, 1978
Endacott, G. B., *A History of Hong Kong.* 2nd ed. OUP, 1973.–*Government and People in Hong Kong, 1841–1962. A Constitutional History.* OUP, 1965
Hopkins, K., *Hong Kong: The Industrial Colony.* OUP, 1971
Miners, N., *The Government and Politics of Hong Kong.* OUP, 1976
Rabushka, A., *The Changing Face of Hong Kong: New Departures in Public Policy.* Washington, 1973
Tregear, E. R., *Land Use in Hong Kong.* Hong Kong Univ. Press, 1958.—*Hong Kong Gazetteer.* Hong Kong Univ. Press, 1958.—*The Development of Hong Kong as Told in Maps.* Hong Kong Univ. Press, 1959

HUNGARY

Capital: Budapest
Population: 10·71m. (1981)
GNP per capita: US$4,180 (1980)

Magyar Népköztársaság

HISTORY. Hungary first became an independent kingdom in 1001. For events in Hungary since 1918 *see* THE STATESMAN'S YEAR-BOOK, 1945, pp. 1006–7, and 1957, p. 1096.

On 23 Oct. 1956 an anti-Stalinist revolution broke out, and the newly formed coalition government of Imre Nagy on 1 Nov. withdrew from the Warsaw Pact and asked the UN for protection. János Kádár, formed a counter-government on 3 Nov. and asked the USSR for support.

Russian troops suppressed the revolution and abducted Nagy and his Ministers, who were later secretly executed.

On 7 Sept. 1967 the Soviet-Hungarian treaty of friendship was renewed for 20 years.

In 1978 the crown of St Stephen, the symbol of Hungarian nationhood, which had been in US hands since 1945, was returned to Hungary.

AREA AND POPULATION. Hungary is bounded north by Czechoslovakia, north-east by the USSR, east by Romania, south by Yugoslavia and west by Austria. The peace treaty of 10 Feb. 1947 restored the frontiers as of 1 Jan. 1938. The area of Hungary is 93,032 sq. km (35,911 sq. miles).

The official language is Hungarian (Magyar), which is a member of the Finno-Ugrian group.

At the census of 1 Jan. 1980 the population was 10,710,000 (5,189,000 males). Population in 1981: 10·71m.

54% of the population is urban (20% in Budapest) 48·5% male. Population density, 115 per sq. km. Birth rate, 1980, 13·9 per 1,000; growth rate, 0·3% per annum; expectation of life (1979): males, 67; females, 74. In 1970 there were some 1·25m. Hungarian émigrés. There are Hungarian minorities in Romania, Yugoslavia and Czechoslovakia.

Vital statistics, 1980: Births, 148,810; marriages, 80,322; divorces, 27,800; deaths, 145,549; infant mortality, 23·1 per 1,000 live births.

Area (in sq. km) and population (in 1,000) of counties, county boroughs and county towns:

Counties	*Area*	*Population*	*Chief town (1980)*	*Population*
Baranya	4,487	434	Pécs	170
Bács-Kiskun	8,363	567	Kecskemét	93
Békés	5,632	435	Békéscsaba	66
Borsod-Abaúj-Zemplén	7,248	807	Miskolc	210
Csongrád	4,263	456	Hódmezovásárhely	54
Fejér	4,374	423	Székesfehérvár	102
Győ'r-Sopron	4,012	429	Győ'r	125
Hajdú-Bihar	6,212	553	Debrecen	195
Heves	3,638	350	Eger	60
Komárom	2,250	322	Tatabánya	75
Nógrád	2,543	239	Salgótarján	49
Pest	6,394	979	Budapest	2,060
Somogy	6,035	360	Kaposvár	73
Szabolcs-Szatmár	5,938	592	Nyíregyháza	107
Szolnok	5,608	445	Szolnok	77
Tolna	3,702	268	Szekszárd	34
Vas	3,337	285	Szombathely	82
Veszprém	4,689	388	Veszprém	55
Zala	3,786	317	Zalaegerszeg	55

County boroughs (1980)	*Area*	*Population*	*County boroughs (1980)*	*Area*	*Population*
Budapest (capital)	525	2,060	Szeged	145	175
Miskolc	224	210	Pécs	113	170
Debrecen	446	195	Győr	175	125

Ethnic minorities in 1980 (in 1,000): Germans, 200; Slovaks, 100; Croats and Serbs, 100; Romanians, 20–25.

CONSTITUTION AND GOVERNMENT. On 1 Feb. 1946 the National Assembly proclaimed a republic.

The present People's Republic was established by a constitution adopted on 18 Aug. 1949. Supreme power is vested in Parliament. Parliament elects a Presidential Council, which exercises the functions of Parliament between sessions. It can dissolve government bodies and annul legislation. The 1949 Constitution was amended in 1972. The distinction between 'working people' and 'citizens' disappears. Citizens are stated to have both indirect (through elected representatives) and direct (through local and enterprise councils) democratic rights. State and co-operative property are recognized as co-existing with equal status. Personal property is 'recognized and protected' up to the limit set by law (this includes for private artisans and, since 1 Jan. 1982, for various classes of small companies and 'economic working groups', places of business and machinery).

Ethnic minorities have equal rights and education in their own tongue.

National flag: Three horizontal stripes of red, white, green.

National anthem: God bless the Hungarians–Isten áldd meg a magyart (words by Ferenc Kölcsey, tune by Ferenc Erkel).

Chairman of the Presidential Council (Head of State): Pál Losonczi, appointed on 14 April 1967. *Deputy Chairmen:* Sándor Gáspar and Rezső Trautmann.

In 1949 the Hungarian Working People's Party (Communists), the Smallholders' Party, the National Peasant Party, the Trade Union Federation, the Association of Working Peasants, the Democratic Women's Association and the Federation of Working Youth were merged in the Hungarian People's Independence Front. In 1954 a new comprehensive organization was formed, the People's Patriotic Front. The Communist Youth Association (KISZ) had 870,000 members in 1981.

The Communist Party was reorganized after the 1956 revolution and changed its name to 'Hungarian Socialist Workers' Party'. It had 812,000 members in 1980 (32% women; 46% manual workers and peasants). Supreme *de facto* power is in the hands of the Party's Politburo, composed in March 1983 of: János Kádár, *First Secretary of the Central Committee*; György Aczél *(Secretary of the Central Committee)*; Valéria Benke; Sándor Gáspár; Ferenc Havasi; Mihály Korom; György Lázár; Pál Losonczi; László Márothy; Lajos Méhes; Károly Németh; Miklos Óvári; István Sárlos.

The Government was in March 1983 composed as follows:

Prime Minister: György Lázár.

Deputy Prime Ministers: János Borbándi, Lájos Faluvégi *(Chairman, State Planning Committee)*, Jozsef Marjai, István Sárlos. *Finance:* Dr István Hetényi. *Foreign Affairs:* Frigyes Puja. *Speaker, National Assembly:* Antal Apró. *Interior:* Dr István Horváth. *Culture and Education:* Dr Béla Köpeczi. *Defence:* Gen. Lájos Czinege. *Foreign Trade:* Péter Veress. *Justice:* Imre Markója.

Parliament consists of 352 deputies, elected for a 5-year term by all citizens over 18 years.

The right to select candidates is vested solely in pre-election nomination meetings open to all voters. More than one candidate is permitted to stand in each constituency. Such 'alternative' candidates must receive 30% of the votes at nomination meetings. All candidates must support the Patriotic People's Front (PPF). To be elected candidates must gain at least 50% of the votes cast.

Elections were held on 8 June 1980. Electorate, 7,661,361; votes cast, 7,577,401; votes for PPF candidates, 7,462,953; against, 54,070. Alternative candidates stood in 15 constituencies.

Local Government. Hungary is divided into the capital, Budapest, 19 counties *(megyék)* and 5 county boroughs (large towns with county status), which are subdivided into districts, towns and boroughs. All of these are administered by a hierarchy of local councils which in turn elect Executive Committees to carry on day-to-day administration. Members of county councils are elected by the lower councils. Elections are held every 5 years. The last local elections were held in June 1980.

DEFENCE. The 1947 Treaty authorized Hungary to have an army up to a strength of 65,000 personnel, and an air force of 90 aircraft, of which not more than 70 may be combat types with a personnel strength of 5,000.

By a law of 1976 the Presidential Council may establish a National Defence Council which in times of war would exercise supreme control over defence.

Men between the ages of 18 and 23 are liable for 18 months' conscription. Compulsory military service age-limits are 18 to 55 (18 to 45 women).

The security police (BKH) is controlled by the Ministry of the Interior.

The Workers' Militia is a para-military organization armed with automatic weapons. Strength (1983), 60,000.

Four Soviet divisions are stationed in Hungary.

Army. Hungary is divided into 4 army districts: Budapest, Debrecen, Kiskunfélegyháza, Pécs. The strength of the Army was (1983) 85,000 (including 50,000 conscripts). It is organized in 1 tank and 5 motorized divisions not all up to full strength, with about 1,250 T-54 and T-55 tanks.

Navy. The maritime wing of the Army in 1983 deployed over 500 officers and men operating 45 vessels, including 10 patrol craft of 100 tons, 5 utility landing craft and 30 river mine-warfare vessels, troop transports of up to 1,000 tonnes, river monitors, icebreakers, tugs and watch pickets, constituting the River Guard, and Army logistic and bridging vessels are active along the Danube.

Air Force. The Air Force is an integral part of the Army, with a strength of about 21,000 officers and men and 175 combat aircraft, in 2 fighter divisions. The interceptor division has 3 regiments of MiG-23 and MiG-21 fighters. Su-7 fighter-bombers equip the other division, supplemented by Mi-24 helicopter gunships. Transport units are equipped with An-2, An-24, An-26 and Il-14 aircraft. Other types in service include Ka-26, Mi-2, Mi-4 and Mi-8 helicopters and L-29 Delfin and MiG-15UTI trainers. 'Guideline' and 'Goa' surface-to-air missiles are also operational.

INTERNATIONAL RELATIONS

Membership. Hungary is a member of UN, the Warsaw Pact and Comecon and, since 1982, IMF and IBRD.

External Debt. Hungary settled its debt to the UK in 1967. By an agreement of 6 March 1973 Hungary is to meet US claims of US$189m. arising from war damage and nationalization in 20 yearly instalments.

ECONOMY

Planning. For details of past plans *see* THE STATESMAN'S YEAR-BOOK, 1975–76. A 'New Economic Mechanism' (NEM) came into effect on 1 Jan. 1968. It restricted central direction to overall policies, replaced direct by financial control and gave local managers more initiative. Reforms aimed ultimately at adapting the economy to world prices by reducing costs, bringing salaries into line with productivity, redeploying labour, cutting import subsidies and encouraging exports were set in train in 1980. Since 1976, enterprises have been required to repay state investment credits in full, usually over 10 years, and to cover unscheduled increases in costs. In 1982 it was decided to lease out to private enterprise small businesses that were previously state-run. Targets for the sixth 5-year plan (1976–80) were not met. The seventh 5-year plan (1981–85) is one of consolidation and envisages rises of only 6% in real incomes and 15% in the national income. In Aug. 1982 large increases in transport fares and the price of bread and other foodstuffs were announced.

Budget. The budget for calendar years was as follows (in 1,000 forints):

	1975	*1976*	*1977*	*1978*	*1979*	*1980*	*1981*
Revenue	313,264	320,384	361,272	382,900	411,600	423,500	477,900
Expenditure	316,224	322,874	364,808	386,400	415,200	428,000	482,400

1979 revenue included (in 1,000m. forints): 323·9 from enterprises, 12·2 from collective farms and 22·6 from personal taxation. Expenditure included: subsidies to enterprises, 135·4; investment, 81·9; welfare, 18·3; social security 62·2; culture, 31·3; defence, 15·4.

Currency. A decree of 26 July 1946 instituted a new monetary unit, the *forint* subdivided into 100 *fillér*. The rate of exchange (March 1983) 62 forints to the £1 sterling, 39·87 forints = US$1. A uniform exchange rate was established in Oct. 1981 as a final step before the introduction of external, central-bank convertibility for foreign trade in 1983. There was a 7% devaluation in July 1982.

Banking. All banking activities are controlled by the National Bank, including the National Savings Bank, which handles local government, as well as personal, accounts. (Deposits in 1980: 145,273m. forints.) The National Bank finances investment to individual enterprises and is the main authority over foreign-exchange transactions. There is also a Foreign Trade Bank for Hungarian enterprises trading abroad. The State Development Bank (formerly Investment Bank) finances large-scale investment projects and oversees national investment trends.

The National Credit Institute of Co-operatives handles all credit transactions for farmers, artisans and co-operatives. The Hungarian International Trade Bank opened in London in 1973. In 1980 the Central European International Bank was set up in Budapest with 7 Western banks holding 66% of the shares.

Weights and Measures. The metric system of weights and measures is in use. For land measure a cadastral yoke (1 acre = 0·7033 cadastral yoke) is used.

ENERGY AND NATURAL RESOURCES

Electricity. An 880-mw nuclear power station is being built with Soviet help at Paks to begin producing in 1982. A 750 kv power line linking Albertirsa in Hungary with the Soviet grid at Vinnitsa came into operation in 1978.

Oil. Oil and natural gas have been found in the Szeged basin and in Zala county. There are pipelines for crude oil ('Friendship' I and II from USSR) and natural gas totalling 4,262 km in 1978. The 2,700 km Orenburg–Hungary natural gas pipeline came on stream in 1980. Imports in 1980 (in 1,000 tonnes): Oil, 8,336; gas, 4,045. The Hungarian section of the Adria oil pipeline (from Rijeka to Czechoslovakia) came on stream 1978.

Minerals. Coal and bauxite are mined, and there is some iron ore.

Agriculture. The large private holdings which characterized pre-war agriculture were broken up by the Communist government and distributed as individual smallholdings. After 1950 this policy was superseded by collectivization. A land law of 1968 permits collectives to own land, and guarantees individuals' rights to private plots. Collectives meet in a National Council of Agricultural Co-operatives.

In 1980 the agricultural area was (in 1,000 hectares) 6,626, of which 4,735 were arable, 1,294 meadows and pastures, and 306 orchards and vineyards.

In 1980 there were 1,338 collective farms with 5·9m. hectares of land (including 441,000 hectares of household plots) and 131 state farms with 994,000 hectares of land. The irrigated area was 134,000 hectares; 55,000 tractors were in use.

Production statistics (in 1,000 tonnes):

Crops	*1978*	*1979*	*1980*	*Crops*	*1978*	*1979*	*1980*
Wheat	5,655	3,702	6,048	Maize	6,672	7,422	6,575
Rye	136	92	138	Potatoes	1,584	1,149	949
Barley	760	707	926	Sugar-beet	4,182	3,856	3,873
Oats	73	90	104	Sunflowers	222	416	453

Livestock in 1981 was (in 1,000 head) as follows: Cattle, 1,918; pigs, 8,330; poultry, 61,347; sheep, 3,090; horses, 120,000.

Livestock products (1980): Eggs, 4,382m.; milk, 2,461m. litres; wool, 12,012 tonnes; animals for slaughter, 2m. tonnes.

The north shore of Lake Balaton and the Tokaj area are important wine-producing districts. Tokaj viticulture was neglected before the 1970s, but now a Reconstruction Committee has reimposed rigorous standards. Wine production in 1980 was 551m. litres.

Forestry. The area under forest in 1980 was 1·61m. hectares. 26,000 hectares were afforested and 7·5m. cu. metres of timber were cut.

Fisheries. There are fisheries in the rivers Danube and Tisza and Lake Balaton, and in 1977 there were 24,000 hectares of commercial fishponds. Catch in 1980: 24,000 tonnes.

INDUSTRY AND TRADE

Industry. For a summary of the successive stages of nationalization from 1946 to 1952, *see* THE STATESMAN'S YEAR-BOOK, 1954, p. 1115.

Production statistics (in 1,000 tonnes):

	1976	*1977*	*1978*	*1979*	*1980*
Coal [1]	25,300	25,500	25,700	25,700	25,700
Iron ore	602	525	534	532	426
Pig-iron	2,221	2,286	2,330	2,369	2,214
Crude steel	3,652	3,723	3,877	3,907	3,763
Rolled steel	2,857	3,077	3,188	3,240	3,046
Bauxite	2,918	2,949	2,899	2,976	2,950
Aluminium	70	71	71	72	73
Alumina	732	786	785	793	811
Crude oil	2,142	2,191	2,200	2,027	2,031
Natural gas (1m. cu. metres)	6,082	6,598	7,333	6,506	6,127
Electricity (1m. kwh.)	22,049	23,390	25,542	24,519	23,876
Cement	4,298	4,620	4,764	4,857	4,660
Artificial fertilizers	783	805	887	1,043	1,045
Synthetic materials (PVC, etc.)	141	148	213	294	328
Sulphuric acid	617	632	644	588	590
Sugar	363	438	496	497	468
Cotton cloth (1m. sq. metres)	353	366	365	349	335
Woollen (1m. sq. metres)	41	43	43	41	43
Silk and rayon (1m. sq. metres)	57	57	62	57	56
Flax and hemp (1m. sq. metres)	23	21	20	19	19
Leather footwear (1m. pairs)	45	46	46	45	43

[1] Including lignite and brown coal.

Labour. In 1980 there were 5·07m. wage-earners (2·3m. female) in the following categories (females in brackets): Manual workers, 2·8m. (1·1m.); co-operative peasants, 648,900 (258,300); industrial managers, 100,800 (14,600); farm managers, 23,900 (1,500); professional workers, 1·3m. (808,500); self-employed tradesmen, 173,500 (88,200). In 1981 to simplify administration the Ministry of Labour was abolished and replaced by a National Office for Wages and Labour. A 42-hour 5-day week was introduced in 1982. Average monthly wages of employed persons in 1980: 4,500 forints. Retirement age: Men, 60; women, 55.

Trade Unions. Trade union membership was 4·3m. in 1980.

Commerce. Hungary is heavily dependent on foreign trade, which even under the 'New Economic Mechanism' remains basically under state control. Trade for calendar years (in 1m. forints):

	1975	*1976* [1]	*1977*	*1978*	*1979*	*1980*
Imports	61,500	230,056	267,300	300,900	308,900	299,900
Exports	52,200	204,834	238,600	240,700	282,100	281,000

[1] Official statistics for 1975 and before were expressed in exchange rate forints, but thereafter in commercial rate forints. The dramatic increase for 1976 is therefore only apparent. The index numbers are: 1975 = 100, 1976 = 96·9.

In 1980 Hungary's trade with communist countries totalled 306·7m. forints

(29% with USSR). Major exports to communist countries: Machinery, industrial consumer goods, raw materials; elsewhere, raw materials and industrial consumer goods.

All exports and imports require licensing by the Ministry of Foreign Trade, and may be handled by 29 specialized foreign-trade agencies. Enterprises may handle their own foreign trade relations, set up companies abroad and participate in foreign companies. Hard currency is available through the National Bank. Tax-free zones for foreign companies exporting their own products were established in 1983. The Marketexpo branch of the Hungarian National Market Research Institute will conduct research for foreign firms. The agency Interag acts for Western firms in Hungary. Main imports from the West are machinery, fuel and consumer goods. Hungarian indebtedness to the West was US$8,000m. in 1982. A US$260m. loan was granted by 15 Western banks.

Joint ventures with Western firms holding up to 49% of the capital have been permitted since 1972 on Hungarian soil. Foreign companies may set up offices in Hungary. In Nov. 1978 the US and Hungary signed a most-favoured-nation trade agreement. In May 1982 Hungary was granted membership of the IMF.

Total trade between Hungary and UK (British Department of Trade returns, in £1,000 sterling):

	1977	*1978*	*1979*	*1980*	*1981*	*1982*
Imports to UK	43,203	42,476	51,748	43,327	40,684	44,051
Exports and re-exports from UK	61,894	64,510	60,917	68,977	84,181	77,446

Tourism. In 1980, 13·99m. foreigners visited Hungary (1·94m. from the West), of whom 9·41m. were tourists (1·22m. from the West); and 4·69m. Hungarians travelled abroad (0·47m. to the West).

COMMUNICATIONS

Roads. In 1980 there were 29,805 km of roads. In 1978 passenger cars numbered 834,000 (788,000 private). 228m. tonnes of freight and 794m. passengers were transported by road in 1980 (excluding urban traffic).

Railways. Route length of public lines in 1981, 7,616 km, of which 1,550 km are electrified. 131m. tonnes of freight and 254m. passengers were carried.

Aviation. Hungarian Air Lines (Malév) operate from Ferihegy airport, 16 km from Budapest. 1980 arrivals, 724,786; departures, 725,561. Malév operates flights to Austria, Belgium, France, Federal Republic of Germany, Greece, Italy, Scandinavia, Egypt, UK and European communist capitals. British Airways, PANAM, Air France, SABENA, Swissair, OS, Lufthansa and KLM have services to Budapest.

Shipping. Permanently navigable waterways have a length of 1,302 km; 4·3m. tonnes of cargo were carried in 1980 and 4·6m. passengers were carried in 1975.

Post and Broadcasting. Number of post offices (1980), 2,518; number of telephones, 1,261,295 (1981). In 1979 there were 2·61m. radio licences issued. Radio licences were abolished in 1980;television licences, (1980) 2,766,000. *Magyar Rádio és Televízió* broadcasts 3 programmes on medium-waves and FM and also regional programmes, including transmissions in German and Serbo-Croat. Two TV programmes are broadcast. Colour broadcasts are only transmitted in Budapest, using the SECAM system.

Cinemas (1980). There were 3,624 cinemas; attendance totalled 61m. 30 full-length feature films were made.

Newspapers and Books. In 1980 there were 29 dailies and 529 other periodicals. The Party daily is *Népszabadság* ('People's Freedom') (average daily circulation, 800,000). 8,241 book titles were published in 1980.

JUSTICE, RELIGION, EDUCATION AND WELFARE

Justice. The administration of justice is the responsibility of the Procurator-General, who is elected by Parliament for a term of 6 years. Civil and criminal cases fall under the jurisdiction of the district courts, county courts and the Supreme Court in Budapest. Criminal proceedings are dealt with by district courts through 3-member councils and by county court and the Supreme Court in 5-member councils. A new Civil Code was adopted in 1978 and a new Criminal Code in 1979.

District Courts act only as courts of first instance; county courts as either courts of first instance or of appeal. The Supreme Court acts normally as an appeal court, but may act as a court of first instance in cases submitted to it by the Public Prosecutor. All courts, when acting as courts of first instance, consist of 1 professional judge and 2 lay assessors, and, as courts of appeal, of 3 professional judges. Local government Executive Committees may try petty offences.

District or county judges and assessors are elected by the district or county councils, all members of the Supreme Court by Parliament.

There are also military courts of the first instance. Military cases of the second instance go before the Supreme Court.

Judges are elected by the Presidential Council.

Religion. There are 20 authorized religious denominations which share proportionally an annual state subsidy of 70m. forints. 8·5m. of the population professed a religious faith in 1976; the number of active church members was put between 1m. and 1·5m.

Senior church appointments require the consent of the Presidential Council. Lower ones are ratified by the State Office for Church Affairs. Certain appointments become valid if the Office makes no comment within 15 days, and for the most minor church appointments neither state consent nor prior notification is required. Ecclesiastics are required to take an oath of allegiance to the state.

In 1976 there were 5·25m. Roman Catholics with 11 dioceses, 4,000 priests and 4,400 churches, and 500,000 uniates. In 1979 there were 3 seminaries and 1 uniate seminery, a theological academy, and 8 secondary schools. The Primate of Hungary is the Archbishop of Esztergom, Laszló Lekai, appointed Feb. 1976. There are also 2 archbishops, 8 bishops and an apostolic administrator. There is one Uniate bishopric.

In 1976 there were 2m. Calvinists with 4 dioceses, 1,300 ministers and 1,567 churches. There were 2 theological colleges (20% of students female) with 16 teachers, and 1 secondary school. There were 500,000 Lutherans with 16 dioceses, 374 ministers and 673 churches. There is a theological college with 6 teachers. The 10 denominations in the Association of Free Churches had 37,000 members, 230 ministers and 675 churches. There are 4 Orthodox denominations with 40,000 members in 1979. The Unitarian Church has 10,000 members, 11 ministers and 6 churches. In 1979 there were 80,000–100,000 Jews (825,000 in 1939) with 130 synagogues, 26 rabbis, a rabbinical college with 6 teachers and a secondary school.

Education. Education is free and compulsory from 6 to 14. Primary schooling ends at 14; thereafter education may be continued at secondary, secondary technical or secondary vocational schools, which offer diplomas entitling students to apply for higher education, or at vocational training schools which offer tradesmen's diplomas. Students at the latter may also take the secondary school diploma examinations after 2 years of evening or correspondence study.

In 1979–80 there were 4,690 kindergartens with 29,437 teachers and 478,000 pupils; 3,633 general schools with 75,422 teachers and 1·2m. pupils; 531 secondary schools with 15,460 teachers and 203,000 pupils. There are 4 universities proper (Budapest, Pécs, Szeged, Debrecen), and 14 specialized universities (6 technical, 4 medical, 3 arts, 1 economics). At these and at 37 other institutions of higher education there were, in 1979–80, 64,000 students and 13,890 teachers.

Libraries and Museums. In 1979 there were 4,986 public and 5,562 trade union libraries. Major national libraries (1980): National Széchenyi, 5·8m. volumes; Budapest University, 3·1m.; Academy of Sciences, 1·7m.; National Technical Library and Documentation Centre, 1·3m. In 1980 there were 487 museums with 16·27m. visitors.

Health. In 1980 there were 30,836 doctors and dentists and 95,539 hospital beds.

Social Security. Medical treatment is free. Patients bear 15% of the cost of medicines. Sickness benefit is 75% of wages, old age pensions (at 60 for men, 55 for women) 60–70%. In 1980, 83m. forints were paid out in social insurance benefits.

Pensions were raised in Jan. 1979 and Aug. 1982, and family allowances in July 1980.

DIPLOMATIC REPRESENTATIVES

Of Hungary in Great Britain (35 Eaton Place, London, SW1X 8BY)
Ambassador: Dr Rezső Bányász (accredited 21 July 1981).

Of Great Britain in Hungary (Harmincad Utca 6, Budapest V)
Ambassador: B. G. Cartledge, CMG.

Of Hungary in the USA (3910 Shoemaker St., NW, Washington, D.C., 20008)
Ambassador: János Petrán.

Of the USA in Hungary (Szabadság Tér 12, Budapest V)
Ambassador: Harry E. Bergold, Jr.

Of Hungary to the United Nations
Ambassador: Pál Rácz.

Books of Reference

Report of the Hungarian Statistical Office on the Economic Development and Plan Fulfilment. Budapest, annual from 1973
Statisztikai Évkönyv. Budapest, annual; since 1871, abridged English version, *Statistical Yearbook*
Statistical Pocket Book of Hungary (in English). Budapest, annual from 1959
Hungarian Digest. Budapest, 6 a year from 1980
The Hungarian Economy: a Quarterly Economic and Business Review. Budapest, since 1972
Hungary 66 (*67* etc.). Budapest, annual from 1966
Marketing in Hungary. Budapest, quarterly
Information Hungary. Budapest, 1980
The Constitution of the Hungarian People's Republic. Budapest, 1972
Bako, E., *Guide to Hungarian Studies.* 2 vols. Stanford Univ. Press, 1973
Berend, I. T., and Ranki, G., *Hungary: A Century of Economic Development.* New York and Newton Abbot, 1974; *Underdevelopment and Economic Growth: Studies in Hungarian Social and Economic History.* Budapest, 1979
Cave, M., *Alternative Approaches to Economic Planning.* London, 1981
Donath, F., *Reform and Revolution: Transformation of Hungary's Agriculture, 1945–1970.* Budapest, 1980
Enyedi, G., *Hungary: An Economic Geography.* Boulder, Colorado, 1976
Gadó, O., *The Economic Mechanism of Hungary.* Leiden and Budapest, 1976
Halász, Z., *Hungary: A Guide with a Difference.* 2nd ed. Budapest, 1979
Hare, P. G., and others (eds.), *Hungary: a Decade of Economic Reform.* London, 1981
Hegedüs, A., *The Structure of Socialist Society.* London, 1977
Ignotus, P., *Hungary.* London, 1972
Kabdebo, T., *Hungary.* [Bibliography] Oxford and Santa Barbara, 1980
Kádár, J., *For a Socialist Hungary.* Budapest, 1974
Kornai, J., *Economics of Shortage.* Oxford, 1980
Kourig, B., *Communism in Hungary.* Stanford, 1979
Macartney, C. A., *Hungary: A Short History.* London, 1962
Németh, G. (ed.), *Hungary: A Comprehensive Guide.* Budapest, 1980
Országh, L., *Hungarian-English Dictionary.* Budapest, 1977.—*English-Hungarian Dictionary.* Budapest, 1970
Pamlényi, E. (ed.), *A History of Hungary.* Budapest, 1975
Pécsi, M. and Sárfalvi, B., *Physical and Economic Geography of Hungary.* 2nd ed. Budapest, 1979
Toma, P. A., and Volgyes, I., *Politics in Hungary.* San Francisco, 1977

ICELAND

Lýðveldið Ísland

Capital: Reykjavík
Population: 234,980 (1982)
GNP per capita: US$11,330 (1980)

HISTORY. The first settlers came to Iceland in 874. Between 930 and 1264 Iceland was an independent republic, but by the 'Old Treaty' of 1263 the country recognized the rule of the King of Norway. In 1381 Iceland, together with Norway, came under the rule of the Danish kings, but when Norway was separated from Denmark in 1814, Iceland remained under the rule of Denmark. Since 1 Dec. 1918 it has been acknowledged as a sovereign state. It was united with Denmark only through the common sovereign until it was proclaimed an independent republic on 17 June 1944.

AREA AND POPULATION. Iceland is a large island in the North Atlantic, close to the Arctic Circle, and comprises an area of about 103,000 sq. km (39,758 sq. miles), with its extreme northern point (the Rifstangi) lying in 66° 32′ N. lat., and its most southerly point (Dyrhólaey, Portland) in 63° 24′ N. lat., not including the islands north and south of the land; if these are included, the country extends from 67° 10′ N. (the Kolbeinsey) to 63° 19′ N. (Geirfuglasker, one of the Westman Islands). It stretches from 13° 30′ (the Gerpir) to 24° 32′ W. long. (Látrabjarg). The skerry *Hvalbakur* (The Whaleback) lies 13° 16′ W. long.

The 25 constituencies of the country are now grouped in 7 districts.

District	*Inhabited land (sq. km)*	*Mountain pasture (sq. km)*	*Waste-land (sq. km)*	*Total area (sq. km)*	*Population (1 Dec. 1981)*
Reykjanes area	1,266	716	—	1,982	137,206
West	5,011	3,415	275	8,711	14,987
Western Peninsula	4,130	3,698	1,652	9,470	10,513
Northland West	4,867	5,278	2,948	13,093	10,723
Northland East	9,890	6,727	5,751	22,368	25,886
East } South }	16,921	17,929	12,555	21,991	12,953
				25,214	19,690
Iceland	42,085	37,553	23,181	102,819	231,958

In 1980, 26,828 were domiciled in rural districts and 205,130 in towns and villages (of over 200 inhabitants.) The population is almost entirely Icelandic.

In 1981 foreigners numbered 3,318; of these 966 were Danish, 667 US, 323 British, 282 Norwegian and 239 German (Fed. Rep.) nationals.

The capital, Reykjavík, had on 1 Dec. 1982, a population of 85,782; other towns (1981) were Akranes, 5,267; Akureyrí, 13,605; Bolungarvík, 1,273; Dalvík, 1,308; Eskifjörður, 1,090; Garðabaer, 5,140; Grindavík, 1,968; Hafnarfjörður, 12,312; Húsavík, 2,446; Ísafjörður, 3,399; Keflavík, 6,666; Kópavogur, 13,996; Neskaupstaður, 1,699; Njarðvík, 2,120; Ólafsfjörður, 1,141; Sauðárkrókur, 2,221; Selfoss, 3,453; Seltjarnarnes, 3,340; Seyðisfjörður, 992; Siglufjörður, 2,012; Vestmannaeyjar, 4,752.

Vital statistics for calendar years:

	Living births	*Still-born*	*Marriages*	*Divorces*	*Deaths*	*Infant deaths*
1977	3,996	25	1,568	407	1,435	*38*
1978	4,162	30	1,585	411	1,421	*47*
1979	4,475	17	1,451	394	1,482	*24*
1980	4,528	21	1,306	441	1,538	*35*
1981	4,345	21	1,357	463	1,655	*26*

CONSTITUTION AND GOVERNMENT. On 24 May 1944 the people of Iceland decided in a referendum to sever all ties with the Danish Crown. The voters were asked whether they were in favour of the abrogation of the Union Act, and whether they approved of the bill for a republican constitution: 70,725 voters were for severance of all political ties with Denmark and only 370 against it; 69,048 were in favour of the republican constitution, 1,042 against it and 2,505 votes were invalid. On 17 June 1944 the republic was formally proclaimed, and as the republic's first president the Alþingi elected Sveinn Björnsson for a 1-year term (re-elected 1945 and 1949; died 25 Jan. 1952). The President is now elected for a 4-year term.

President of the Republic of Iceland: Vigdís Finnbogadóttir (elected 29 June 1980, with 43,611 out of 129,049 valid votes, inaugurated 1 Aug. 1980).

National flag: Blue with a red white-bordered Scandinavian cross.

National anthem: Ó Guð vors lands (words by M. Jochumsson, 1874; tune by S. Sveinbjørnsson).

The official language is Icelandic (*íslenzka*).

The *Alþingi* (Parliament) is divided into two Houses, the Upper House and the Lower House. The former is composed of one-third of the members elected by the whole Alþingi in common sitting. The remaining two-thirds of the members form the Lower House. The members of the Alþingi receive payment for their services.

The budget bills must be laid before the two Houses in joint session, but all other bills can be introduced in either of the Houses. If the Houses do not agree, they assemble in a common sitting and the final decision is given by a majority of two-thirds of the voters, with the exception of budget bills, where a simple majority is sufficient. The ministers have free access to both Houses, but can vote only in the House of which they are members.

The electoral law enacted in 1959 provides for an Alþingi of 60 members. Of these, 49 are elected in 8 constituencies by proportional representation; the remaining 11 are apportioned to the parties according to their total vote.

At the elections held on 3 Dec. 1979 the following parties were returned: Independence Party, 21; Progressives, 17; People's Alliance, 10; Social Democrats, 10; Independents, 1.

The executive power is exercised under the President by the Cabinet. The coalition Cabinet, as constituted in Feb. 1980, was as follows:

Prime Minister: Gunnar Thoroddsen (Ind.).

Foreign Affairs: Ólafur Jóhannesson (Progress). *Justice:* Friðjón Thórðarson (Ind.). *Agriculture:* Pálmi Jónsson (Ind.). *Education:* Ingvar Gíslason (Progress). *Fisheries and Communications:* Steingrímur Hermannsson (Progress). *Trade and Commerce:* Tómas Arnason (Progress). *Health and Social Security:* Svavar Gestsson (P.A.). *Finance:* Ragnar Arnalds (P.A.). *Energy and Industry:* Hjörleifur Guttormsson (P.A.).

The ministers take responsibility for their acts. They can be impeached by the Alþingi, and in that case their cause will be decided by the *Landsdómur*, a special tribunal for parliamentary impeachments.

Local Administration. For administrative purposes Iceland is divided into 17 provinces (*sýslur*), each under a chief executive (*sýslumaður*). Each province forms one or two municipal districts with a council superintending the 202 rural municipalities. There are also 22 urban municipalities with a town council, independent of the provinces, and forming by themselves administrative districts co-ordinate with the provinces. The municipal councils are elected direct by universal suffrage (men and women over 20 years of age), in urban municipalities by proportional representation, but in rural municipalities by simple majority.

DEFENCE. Iceland possesses neither an army nor a navy. Under the North Atlantic Treaty, US forces are stationed in Iceland as the Iceland Defence Force. Four armed fishery protection vessels are maintained by the Coastguard, with 1 patrol aircraft and 2 helicopters. Coastguard Service personnel in 1982 totalled about 120 officers and men.

INTERNATIONAL RELATIONS

Membership. Iceland is a member of UN, EFTA, OECD, the Council of Europe, NATO and the Nordic Council.

ECONOMY

Budget. Current revenue and expenditure for calendar years (in 1,000 new kr.):

	1977	*1978*	*1979*	*1980*	*1981*	*1982*
Revenue	899,566	1,394,960	2,089,508	3,461,773	5,514,780	7,967,266
Expenditure	891,532	1,384,730	2,022,864	3,432,401	5,457,475	7,909,270

Main items of the Treasury accounts for 1980 (in 1,000 new kr.):

Revenue		*Expenditure*	
Direct taxes	983,122	Presidency	4,787
Indirect taxes	5,203,115	Alþingi	38,116
Profit from government enterprises	16,993	Cabinet	6,242
		Justice and ecclesiastical affairs	346,174
		Culture and education	945,168
		Social affairs	178,039
		Commerce	426,188
		Foreign affairs	69,967
		Fisheries and agriculture	373,600
		Finance	240,706
		Communications	621,668

The public debt of Iceland was on 31 Dec. 1981, 2,540m. new kr., of which the foreign debt amounted to 370m. new kr. and the internal debt to 2,170m. new kr.

Currency. The Icelandic monetary units are the *króna*, pl. *krónur* and the *eyrir*, pl. *aurar*. There are 100 *aurar* to the *króna*. On 1 Jan. 1981 a currency reform took place and 100 old krónur equal 1 new króna. In March 1983, US$1 = kr. 20·64; £1 = kr. 30·70. Note and coin circulation, 31 Dec. 1981, was 393m. new kr.

Banking. By Act of 29 March 1961 the Central Bank of Iceland was established, which took over the central bank function up to that date exercised by the *Landsbanki Íslands* (The National Bank of Iceland, owned entirely by the State). Other banks are: *Búnaðarbanki Íslands* (the Agricultural Bank of Iceland), a state bank, founded in 1930; *Útvegsbanki Íslands* (the Fisheries Bank of Iceland), founded in 1930 as a joint-stock bank, which in 1957 became a state bank; *Iðnaðarbanki Íslands* (Industrial Bank of Iceland Ltd), a joint-stock bank, established 1953, part of the shares being owned by the Government; *Verzlunarbanki Íslands* (Iceland Bank of Commerce Ltd), established in 1961; *Samvinnubanki Íslands* (The Icelandic Co-operative Bank), established in 1963; *Alþýðubankinn* (The People's Bank Ltd) established 1971. On 30 Oct. 1982 the accounts of the Central Bank balanced at 7,831·6m. new kr.

At the end of 1980 there were 42 savings banks with deposits amounting to 1,087m. new kr.

Weights and Measures. The metric system of weights and measures is obligatory.

ENERGY AND NATURAL RESOURCES

Electricity. The installed capacity of public power plants at the end of 1981 totalled 749,000 kw., of which 612,000 kw. comprised hydro-electric plants. Total energy production in public-owned plants in 1981 amounted to 3,258m. kwh.; in privately-owned plants, 14m. kwh.

Agriculture. Of the total area of Iceland, about six-sevenths is unproductive, but only about 0·5% is under cultivation, which is confined to hay, potatoes and turnips. In 1981 the total hay crop was 3,158,000 cu. metres; the crop of potatoes, 10,856 tonnes, and of turnips 362 tonnes. At the end of 1981 the livestock was as follows: Horses, 52,999; cattle, 60,366 (including 32,769 milch cows); sheep, 794,644; pigs, 12,473; poultry, 270,695.

Fisheries. Fishing vessels in Dec. 1981 numbered 841 with a gross tonnage of 108,571. Total catch in 1982, 766,000 tonnes; 1981, 1,431,550 tonnes.

The Icelandic Government announced that the fishery limits off Iceland were extended from 12 to 50 nautical miles from Sept. 1972. An interim agreement for 2 years signed by the UK and Iceland in Nov. 1973 expired in Nov. 1975.

On 15 July 1975 the Icelandic Government issued a decree that from 15 Oct. 1975 the fishery limits of Iceland were extended from 50 to 200 nautical miles. The Icelandic Government maintain that this extension is necessary to protect the fish stocks in Icelandic waters because the fishing industry is of vital importance to the national economy.

COMMERCE. Total value of imports and exports in 1,000 new kr.:

	1978	*1979*	*1980*	*1981*	*1982*
Imports	1,843,206	2,913,072	4,801,616	7,484,684	11,647,000
Exports	1,762,857	2,784,515	4,459,529	6,536,214	8,479,000

Leading exports (in 1,000 kg and 1,000 new kr.):

	1980		*1981*	
	Quantity	*Value*	*Quantity*	*Value*
Fish and whale products	548,157,500	3,339,284	493,449,900	5,115,457
Agricultural products	9,477,200	77,612	7,254,300	88,555

Leading imports (in 1,000 tonnes and 1,000 new kr.):

	1980		*1981*	
	Quantity	*Value*	*Quantity*	*Value*
Ships (number)	8	98,739	13	266,072
Fuel oil	465,316·1	576,161	434,309·4	845,571
Cereals	12,368,·3	28,718	12,935·3	45,465
Animal feed	62,010·7	65,335	60,401·5	114,255
Gasoline	88,665·7	151,418	93,587·2	234,751
Motor vehicles (number)	9,169	210,416	10,525	405,686
Fishing nets and other gear	2,145·6	62,103	1,910	87,165

Value of trade with principal countries for 3 years (in 1,000 new kr.):

	1979		*1980*		*1981*	
	Imports (c.i.f.)	*Exports (f.o.b.)*	*Imports (c.i.f.)*	*Exports (f.o.b.)*	*Imports (c.i.f.)*	*Exports (f.o.b.)*
Austria	13,034	2,215	23,300	4,139	45,625	4,483
Belgium	100,366	15,364	96,964	28,397	200,966	82,666
Brazil	37,025	7,098	56,430	6,752	66,220	6,907
Canada	17,056	15,208	67,778	26,656	83,704	44,026
Czechoslovakia	16,052	26,986	27,453	39,156	39,704	49,377
Denmark	257,960	51,243	391,990	94,429	777,031	111,857
Faroe Islands	306	13,576	900	23,172	33,105	55,917
Finland	70,159	55,854	131,786	136,316	168,610	92,480
France	66,918	80,608	118,774	111,294	169,689	124,718
German Dem. Rep.	7,589	2,149	11,768	2,220	20,653	1,118
Germany, Fed. Rep. of	312,135	233,327	478,857	438,262	858,315	420,804
Greece	421	34,295	426	57,758	993	73,318
Hungary	837	6,719	2,706	5,111	5,615	6,596
India	3,419	5,260	7,531	—	12,433	—
Ireland	5,257	7,748	8,746	3,386	12,862	12,341
Israel	3,406	70	5,110	355	8,289	833
Italy	60,150	101,007	117,264	212,864	174,219	209,162
Japan	90,769	84,883	193,377	65,230	336,976	108,871
Netherlands	223,623	51,024	437,674	45,406	555,675	75,634
Nigeria	7,118	25,072	41	317,928	188	858,367
Norway	246,107	54,126	359,990	75,086	734,040	78,694
Poland	16,634	58,279	23,207	108,465	27,338	56,464
Portugal	75,003	98,082	118,713	211,776	135,202	702,138
Spain	14,346	88,464	45,182	151,706	76,036	243,619
Sweden	219,997	71,395	343,017	94,460	623,417	110,218
Switzerland	37,950	98,596	45,020	154,009	85,050	165,371
USSR	326,216	108,046	467,720	238,824	600,047	403,047
UK	323,917	533,565	454,891	734,888	572,888	933,352
USA	190,165	779,103	450,456	962,133	581,713	1,361,073

Total trade between Iceland and UK (British Department of Trade returns, in £1,000 sterling):

	1978	*1979*	*1980*	*1981*	*1982*
Imports to UK	63,810	83,269	82,042	75,729	72,721
Exports and re-exports from UK	44,431	48,520	47,223	50,558	102,714

TOURISM. There were 72,194 visitors to Iceland in 1981.

COMMUNICATIONS

Roads. There are no railways in Iceland. Iceland possesses between 11,000–12,000 km of high roads and country roads. Motor vehicles registered at the end of 1981 numbered 100,936, of which 91,457 were passenger cars and 9,479 trucks; there were also 681 motor cycles. On 26 May 1968 Iceland changed from left-hand to right-hand traffic.

Aviation. One large and some small companies maintain regular services between Reykjavík and various places in Iceland (the large one 1981: 217,031 passengers; 812 tonnes of mail; 2,418 tonnes of freight). The large company maintains regular services between Iceland and the UK, the Scandinavian countries, some other European countries and USA. In 1981 the company carried in scheduled foreign flights 283,125 passengers, 1,210 tonnes of mail and 5,156 tonnes of freight.

Shipping. The mercantile marine of Iceland consisted in Dec. 1981 of 4 steam vessels (1,953 gross tons) and 946 motor vessels (192,529 gross tons).

Post and Broadcasting. At the end of 1981 the number of post offices was 160 and telephone and telegraph offices 129; number of telephones, 111,358. The government station, *Rikisútvarpid*, broadcasts 1 programme on long and medium-waves and on FM. *Rikisútvarpid-Sjónvarp* uses 150 transmitters and broadcasts 1 TV programme. Number of licenced receivers: radio, 69,700; television, 62,000.

Cinemas (1978). There were 29 cinemas with a seating capacity of 10,450.

Newspapers (1981). There are 5 daily newspapers, all in Reykjavík, with a combined circulation of about 125,000.

JUSTICE, RELIGION, EDUCATION AND WELFARE

Justice. The lower courts of justice are those of the provincial magistrates (*sýslumenn*) and town judges (*bæjarfógetar*). From these there is an appeal to the Supreme Court (*hæstiréttur*) in Reykjavík, which has 6 judges.

Religion. The national church, and the only one endowed by the State, is Evangelical Lutheran. But there is complete religious liberty, and no civil disabilities are attached to those not of the national religion. The affairs of the national church are under the superintendence of a bishop. In 1979, 4,099 persons (1·8%) were Dissenters and 2,710 persons (1·2%) did not belong to any religious community.

Education. Compulsory education for children began in 1907, and a university was founded in Reykjavík in 1911. There is in Reykjavík a teachers' training college and a technical high school; various specialized institutions of learning and a number of second-level schools are scattered throughout the country. There are many part-time schools of cultural activities, including music.

Compulsory education comprises 8 classes, 7-14 years of age. After completion of a facultative 9th class, attended by 92%-94% of the relevant age group, there is access to further schooling free of charge. Some 60% of the age groups 15-19 years old attend schools. Around 15%-20% of each age group go into handicraft apprenticeship. 25%-30% pass matriculation examination, generally at the age of 20. Approximately one third-level student out of every four goes abroad for studies, two-thirds of them to Scandinavia, the rest mainly to English- and German-speaking countries.

Immatriculation in Iceland in autumn 1980: Preceding the first level, 4,041. First-level (1st-6th class) 24,736. Second-level first stage (7th-9th class) 13,074.

Second-level second stage general programmes (4-year courses) 5,766. Second-level second stage vocational programmes (3 or 4 year courses) 7,428. Third-level first stage non-university 778. Third-level first and second stage university and equivalent 3,618.

Social Welfare. The main body of the Icelandic social welfare legislation is consolidated in six main acts:

(i) The social security legislation (a) health insurance, including sickness benefits; *(b)* social security pensions, mainly consisting of old age pension, disablement pension and widows' pension, and also children's pension; *(c)* employment injuries insurance.

(ii) The unemployment insurance legislation, where daily allowances are paid to those who have met certain conditions.

(iii) The subsistence legislation. This is controlled by municipal government, and social assistance is granted under special circumstances, when payments from other sources are not sufficient.

(iv) The tax legislation. In 1975 family allowances were abolished and children's support included in the tax legislation, according to which a certain amount is subtracted from levied taxes for each child in a family.

(v) The rehabilitation legislation.

(vi) Child and juvenile guidance.

Health insurance covers the entire population. Citizenship is not demanded and there is no waiting period. Most hospitals are both municipally and state run, a few solely state run and all offer free medical help. Medical treatment out of hospitals is partly paid by the patient, the same applies to medicines, except medicines of life-long necessary use, which are paid in full by the health insurance. Dental care is free for the age groups 6-15, but is paid 75% for those five years or younger and the age group 16 but 50% for old age and disabled pensioners. Sickness benefits are paid to those who lose income because of periodical illness. The daily amount is fixed and paid from the 11th day of illness. On 1 Jan. 1983 it was 104 new kr. a day.

Entitlement to old age and disablement pensions at the full rates is subject to the condition that the beneficiary has been resident in Iceland for 40 years at the age period of 16–67. For shorter period of residence, the benefits are reduced proportionally. Entitled to old age pension are all those who are 67 years old, and have been residents in Iceland for 3 years of the age period of 16–67. Entitled to disablement pension are those who have lost 75% of their working capacity and have been residents in Iceland for 3 years before application or have had full working capacity at the time when they became residents. Old age and disablement pension are of equally high amount, in the year 1982 the total sum was 23,989 new kr. for an individual. Married pensioners are paid 90% of two individuals' pensions. In addition to the basic amount, supplementary allowances are paid according to social circumstances and income possibilities. Widows' pensions are the same amount as old age and disablement pension, provided the applicant is over 60 when she becomes widowed. Women at the age 50–60 get reduced pension. Women under 50 are not entitled to widows' pensions.

The employment injuries insurance covers medical care, daily allowances, disablement pension and survivors' pension and is applicable to practically all employees.

All benefits within the above-mentioned laws shall go up in step with general wages within 6 months from their increase.

Social assistance is primarily municipal and granted in cases outside the social security legislation. Domestic assistance to old people and disabled is granted within this legislation, besides other services.

Child and juvenile guidance is performed by chosen committees according to special laws, such as home guidance and family assistance. In cases of parents' disablement the committees take over the guidance of the children involved.

DIPLOMATIC REPRESENTATIVES

Of Iceland in Great Britain (1 Eaton Terrace, London, SW1W 8EY)
Ambassador: Einar Benediktsson (accredited 11 Nov. 1982).

Of Great Britain in Iceland (Laufásvegur 49, 101 Reykjavík)
Ambassador and Consul-General: Richard Thomas.

Of Iceland in the USA (2022 Connecticut Ave., NW, Washington, D.C., 20008)
Ambassador: Hans G. Andersen.

Of the USA in Iceland (Laufasvegur 21, 101 Reykjavík)
Ambassador: Marshall Brement.

Of Iceland to the United Nations
Ambassador: Hörður Helgason.

Books of Reference

Statistical Information: The Icelandic Statistical Office, Hagstofa Íslands (Reykjavík) was founded in 1914. *Director:* Klemens Tryggvason. Its main publications are:

Hagskýrslur Íslands. Statistics of Iceland (from 1912)
Hagtíðindi (Statistical Journal) (from 1916)
Statistical Bulletin. Issued quarterly by the Statistical Bureau of Iceland and the Central Bank of Iceland (from 1931 to 1962, monthly). Ceased publication May 1980
Economic Statistics. Central Bank of Iceland (quarterly from 1980)
Icelandic Currency Reform January 1st 1981. Central Bank of Iceland, 1980
Heilbrigðisskýrslur. Public Health in Iceland (latest issue for 1977; published 1980)
Cleasby, R., *An Icelandic-English Dictionary.* 2nd ed. Oxford, 1957
Foss, H. (ed.), *Directory of Iceland.* Annual. Reykjavík, 1907–40, 1948 ff.
Hermannsson, Halldór, *Islandica.* An annual relating to Iceland and the Fiske Icelandic Collection in Cornell University Library. Ithaca (from 1908)
Hood, J. C. F., *Icelandic Church Saga.* London, 1946
Leaf, H., *Iceland Yesterday and Today.* London, 1949
Magnússon, S. A., *Northern Sphinx: Iceland and the Icelanders from the Settlement to the Present.* London, 1977
Nordal, J., and Kristinsson, V. (eds), *Iceland 874–1974.* Central Board of Iceland, Reykjavík, 1975
Þórðarson, Björn, *Iceland: Past and Present.* 2nd ed. Oxford, 1945
Þórðarson, Matthias, *The Althing, Iceland's Thousand-Year-Old Parliament, 930–1930.* Reykjavík, 1930
Þorsteinsson, Þorsteinn, *Iceland, 1946: A Handbook Published on the 60th Anniversary of the National Bank of Iceland.* 4th ed. Reykjavík, 1946
Trial, G. T., *History of Education in Iceland.* Cambridge, 1945
Zoëga, G. T., *Íslensk-ensk (and Ensk-íslensk) orðabók.* 3rd ed. 2 vols. Reykjavík, 1932–51

National Library: Landsbókasafnið, Reykjavík, *Librarian:* Dr Finnbogi Guðomundsson.

INDIA

Bharat

Capital: New Delhi
Population: 684m. (1981)
GDP per capita: US$240 (1980)

HISTORY. The Indus civilization was fully developed by *c.* 2500 B.C., and collapsed *c.* 1750 B.C. An Aryan civilization spread from the west as far as the Ganges valley by 500 B.C.; separate kingdoms were established and many of these were united under the Mauryan dynasty established by Chandragupta in *c.* 320 B.C. The Mauryan Empire was succeeded by numerous small kingdoms. The Gupta dynasty (A.D. 320–600) was followed by the first Arabic invasions of the north-west. Moslem, Hindu and Buddhist states developed together with frequent conflict until the establishment of the Mogul dynasty in 1526. The first settlements by the East India Company were made after 1600 and the company established a formal system of government for Bengal in 1700. During the decline of the Moguls frequent wars between the Company, the French and the native princes led to the Company's being brought under British Government control in 1784; the first Governor-General of India was appointed in 1786. The powers of the Company were abolished by the India Act, 1858, and its functions and forces transferred to the British Crown. Representative government was introduced in 1909, and the first parliament in 1919. The separate dominions of India and Pakistan became independent within the Commonwealth in 1947 and India became a republic in 1950.

AREA AND POPULATION. India is bounded north-west by Pakistan, north by China, Tibet, Nepál and Bhután, east by Burma, south-east, south and south west by the Indian ocean. The far eastern states and territories are almost separated from the rest by Bangladesh as it extends northwards from the Bay of Bengal. The area of the Indian Union (excluding the Pakistan and China-occupied parts of Jammu and Kashmir) is 3,166,828 sq. km. Its population according to the 1981 census (preliminary figures) was 683,810,051 (excluding the occupied area of Jammu and Kashmir); this represents an increase of 24·8% since 1971. Sex ratio was 940 females per 1,000 males (929 in 1971); density of population, 221 per sq. km. About 23·7% of the population was urban in 1981 (in Maharashtra, 35%; in Himachal Pradesh, 7·7%).

Many births and deaths go unregistered. Data from certain areas of better registration and field studies suggest that the average annual birth rate for the decade 1971–80 was about 36 per 1,000 population, the death rate 14·8 per 1,000. In 1980 (estimate) the age-group 0–14 years represented 39·7% of the population and only 5·5% were over 60. In 1981 expectation of life for men was 52 years, for women 50.

Marriages and divorces are not registered. The minimum age for a civil marriage is 18 for women and 21 for men; for a sacramental marriage, 14 for girls and 18 for youths.

The main details of the census of 1 March 1971 and of 1 March 1981 are:

Name of State	*Land area in sq. km (1971)*	*Population 1971*	*Population 1981*
States			
Andhra Pradesh	276,814	43,502,708	53,403,619
Assam	78,523	14,625,152	19,902,826
Bihar	173,876	56,353,369	69,823,154
Gujarat	195,984	26,697,475	33,960,905
Haryana	44,222	10,036,808	12,850,902
Himachal Pradesh	55,673	3,460,434	4,237,569
Jammu and Kashmir[1]	101,283	4,617,000	5,981,600

[1] Excludes the Pakistan-occupied area.

Name of State	Land area in sq. km (1971)	Population 1971	Population 1981
Karnataka	191,773	29,299,014	37,043,451
Kerala	38,864	21,347,375	25,403,217
Madhya Pradesh	442,841	41,654,119	52,131,717
Maharashtra	307,762	50,412,235	62,693,898
Manipur	22,356	1,072,753	1,433,691
Meghalaya	22,489	1,011,699	1,327,824
Nagaland	16,527	516,449	773,281
Orissa	155,782	21,944,615	26,272,054
Punjab	50,362	13,551,060	16,669,755
Rajasthan	342,214	25,765,806	34,102,912
Sikkim			315,682
Tamil Nadu	130,069	41,199,168	48,297,456
Tripura	10,477	1,556,342	2,060,189
Uttar Pradesh	294,413	88,341,144	110,858,019
West Bengal	87,853	44,312,011	54,485,560
Union Territories			
Andaman and Nicobar Islands	8,293	115,133	188,254
Arunachal Pradesh	83,578	467,511	628,050
Chandigarh	114	257,251	450,061
Dadra and Nagar Haveli	491	74,170	103,677
Delhi	1,485	4,065,698	6,196,414
Goa, Daman and Diu	3,813	857,771	1,082,117
Lakshadweep	32	31,810	40,237
Mizoram	21,087	332,390	487,774
Pondicherry	480	471,707	604,136
Grand total	3,159,530	547,949,809	683,810,051

Greatest density occurs in Delhi (4,178 per sq. km), Chandigarh (3,948), Lakshadweep (1,257) and Pondicherry (1,228). The lowest occurs in Arunachal Pradesh (7).

There were (1981) 353,347,249 males and 330,462,802 females.

In 1981, 502m. were rural (*c.* 76%) and 156m. were urban.

Cities and Urban Agglomerations (with states in brackets) having more than 250,000 population at the 1981 census were (1,000):

Agra (U.P.)	770
Ahmedabad (Guj.)	2,515
Ajmer (Raj.)	374
Aligarh (U.P.)	320
Allahabad (U.P.)	642
Amravati (Mah.)	261
Amritsar (Pun.)	589
Asansol (W.B.)	365
Aurangabad (Mah.)	316
Bangalore (Kar.)	2,914
Bareilly (U.P.)	438
Belgaum (Kar.)	300
Bhavnagar (Guj.)	308
Bhopal (M.P.)	672
Bikaner (Raj.)	280
Bokaro Steel City (Bih.)	261
Bombay[1] (Mah.)	8,227
Calcutta (W.B.)	9,166
Calicut (Ker.)	546
Chandigarh (Ch.)	421
Cochin (Ker.)	686
Coimbatore (T.N.)	917
Cuttack (Ori.)	326
Dehra Dun (U.P.)	294
Delhi	5,714
Dhanbad (Bih.)	677
Durgapur (W.B.)	306
Durg-Bhilainagar (M.P.)	490
Erode (T.N.)	275
Faridabad agglomeration	327
Ghaziabad (U.P.)	292
Gorakhpur (U.P.)	306
Guntur (A.P.)	367
Gwalior (M.P.)	560
Hubli-Dharwar (Kar.)	526
Hyderabad (A.P.)	2,528
Indore (M.P.)	827
Jabalpur (M.P.)	758
Jaipur (Raj.)	1,005
Jalandhar (Pun.)	406
Jamnagar (Guj.)	317
Jamshedpur (Bih.)	670
Jhansi (U.P.)	281
Jodhpur (Raj.)	494
Kanpur (U.P.)	1,688
Kolhapur (Mah.)	351
Kotah (Raj.)	347
Lucknow (U.P.)	1,007
Ludhiana (Pun.)	606
Madras (T.N.)	4,277
Madurai (T.N.)	904
Mangalore (Kar.)	306
Meerut (U.P.)	538
Moradabad (U.P.)	348
Mysore (Kar.)	476
Nagpur (Mah.)	1,298
Nasik (Mah.)	916
Patna (Bih.)	916
Pondicherry	251
Pune (Mah.)	1,685
Raipur (M.P.)	339
Rajahmundry (A.P.)	268
Rajkot (Guj.)	444
Ranchi (Bih.)	501
Rourkela (Ori.)	321
Saharanpur (U.P.)	294
Salem (T.N.)	515
Sangli (Mah.)	269
Sholapur (Mah.)	514
Srinagar (J. & K.)	520[2]
Surat (Guj.)	913
Thana (Mah.)	389
Tiruchirapalli (T.N.)	608
Tirunelveli (T.N.)	324
Trivandrum (Ker.)	520
Tuticorin (T.N.)	251
Ujjain (M.P.)	282
Ulhasnagar (Mah.)	648
Vadodara (Guj.)	744
Varanasi (U.P.)	794
Vijayawada (A.P.)	545
Visakhapatnam (A.P.)	594
Warangal (A.P.)	336

[1] Also called Mumbai. [2] Estimate

Report of the Officials of the Government of India and the People's Republic of China on the Boundary Question. New Delhi, Ministry of External Affairs, 1961
Census of India: Reports and Papers, Decennial Series. (Government of India.)
Annual Report on the Working of Indian Migration. Government of India, from 1956
Report of the Commissioner for Scheduled Castes and Scheduled Tribes. Government of India. Annual
Public Health. Report of the Public Health Commission with the Government of India. Annual
Agarwala, S. N., *India's Population Problems. New York,* 1973
Hutton, J. H., *Caste in India.* 4th ed. Bombay, 1963
Sovani, N. V., *Urbanization and Urban India.* London, 1966

CONSTITUTION AND GOVERNMENT. On 26 Jan. 1950 India became a sovereign democratic republic. India's relations with the British Commonwealth of Nations were defined at the London conference of Prime Ministers on 27 April 1949.

Unanimous agreement was reached to the effect that the Republic of India remains a full member of the Commonwealth and accepts the Queen as 'the symbol of the free association of its independent member nations and, as such, the head of the Commonwealth'. This agreement was ratified by the Constituent Assembly of India on 17 May 1949.

The constitution was passed by the Constituent Assembly on 26 Nov. 1949 and came into force on 26 Jan. 1950. It has since been amended 44 times.

India is a Union of States and comprises 22 States and 9 Union territories. Each State is administered by a Governor appointed by the President for a term of 5 years while each Union territory is administered by the President through an administrator appointed by him.

The capital is New Delhi.

Presidency. The head of the Union is the President in whom all executive power is vested, to be exercised on the advice of ministers responsible to Parliament. He is elected by an electoral college consisting of all the elected members of Parliament and of the various state legislative assemblies. He holds office for 5 years and is eligible for re-election. He must be an Indian citizen at least 35 years old and eligible for election to the Lower House. He can be removed from office by impeachment for violation of the constitution.

There is also a Vice-President who is *ex-officio* chairman of the Upper House of Parliament.

Central Legislature. The Parliament for the Union consists of the President, the Council of States *(Rajya Sabha)* and the House of the People *(Lok Sabha).* The Council of States, or the Upper House, consists of not more than 250 members; in 1980 there were 232 elected members and 12 members nominated by the President. The election to this house is indirect; the representatives of each State are elected by the elected members of the Legislative Assembly of that State. The Council of States is a permanent body not liable to dissolution, but one-third of the members retire every second year. The House of the People, or the Lower House, consists of 544 members, 525 directly elected on the basis of adult suffrage from territorial constituencies in the States, and 17 members to represent the Union territories, chosen in such manner as the Parliament may by law provide; in March 1982 there were 542 elected members and 2 members nominated by the President. The House of the People unless sooner dissolved continues for a period of 5 years from the date appointed for its first meeting; in emergency, Parliament can extend the term by 1 year.

State Legislatures. For every State there is a legislature which consists of the Governor, and *(a)* 2 Houses, a Legislative Assembly and a Legislative Council, in the States of Andhra Pradesh, Jammu and Kashmir, Karnataka, Madhya Pradesh, Maharashtra, Tamil Nadu and Uttar Pradesh, and *(b)* 1 House, a Legislative Assembly, in the other States. Every Legislative Assembly, unless sooner dissolved, continues for 5 years from the date appointed for its first meeting. In emergency the term can be extended by 1 year. Every State Legislative Council is a permanent body and is not subject to dissolution, but one-third of the members retire every year. Parliament can, however, abolish an existing Legislative Council or create a new one, if the proposal is supported by a resolution of the Legislative Assembly concerned.

Legislative Councils have one-third of the total membership of the Assemblies but not less than 40 members, of whom one-third are elected by local authorities, one-third by members of the Assembly, one-twelfth by state university graduates and one-twelfth by teachers of secondary school upwards; the rest are named by the Governor. Legislative Assemblies have between 60 and 500 directly elected members.

Legislation. The various subjects of legislation are enumerated in three lists in the seventh schedule to the constitution. List I, the Union List, consists of 97 subjects (including defence, foreign affairs, communications, currency and coinage, banking and customs) with respect to which the Union Parliament has exclusive power to make laws. The State legislature has exclusive power to make laws with respect to the 66 subjects in list II, the State List; these include police and public order, agriculture and irrigation, education, public health and local government. The powers to make laws with respect to the 47 subjects (including economic and social planning, legal questions and labour and price control) in list III, the Concurrent List, are held by both Union and State governments, though the former prevails. But Parliament may legislate with respect to any subject in the State List in circumstances when the subject assumes national importance or during emergencies.

Other provisions deal with the administrative relations between the Union and the States, interstate trade and commerce, distribution of revenues between the States and the Union, official language, etc.

Fundamental Rights. Two chapters of the constitution deal with fundamental rights and 'Directive Principles of State Policy'. 'Untouchability' is abolished, and its practice in any form is punishable. The fundamental rights can be enforced through the ordinary courts of law and through the Supreme Court of the Union. The directive principles cannot be enforced through the courts of law; they are nevertheless fundamental in the governance of the country.

Citizenship. Under the Constitution, every person who was on the 26 Jan. 1950, domiciled in India and *(a)* was born in India or *(b)* either of whose parents was born in India or *(c)* who has been ordinarily resident in the territory of India for not less than 5 years immediately preceding that date became a citizen of India. Special provision is made for migrants from Pakistan and for Indians resident abroad. Under the Citizenship Act, 1955, which supplemented the provisions of the Constitution, Indian citizenship is acquired by birth, by descent, by registration and by naturalization. The Act also provides for loss of citizenship by renunciation, termination and deprivation. The right to vote is granted to every person who is a citizen of India and who is not less than 21 years of age on a fixed date and is not otherwise disqualified.

Parliament. Parliament and the state legislatures are organized according to the following schedule (figures show distribution of seats in March 1982):

	Parliament		*State Legislatures*	
	House of the People (Lok Sabha)	*Council of States (Rajya Sabha)*	*Legislative Assemblies (Vidhan Sabhas)*	*Legislative Councils (Vidhan Parishads)*
States:				
Andhra Pradesh	42	18	294	90
Assam	14	7	126	–
Bihar	54	22	324	–
Gujarat	26	11	182	–
Haryana	10	5	90	–
Himachal Pradesh	4	3	68	–
Karnataka	28	12	224	63
Kerala	20	9	140	–
Madhya Pradesh	40	16	320	90
Maharashtra	48	19	288	78
Manipur	2	1	60	–

	Parliament: House of the People (Lok Sabha)	Parliament: Council of States (Rajya Sabha)	State Legislatures: Legislative Assemblies (Vidhan Sabhas)	State Legislatures: Legislative Councils (Vidhan Parishads)
Meghalaya	2	1	60	–
Nagaland	1	1	60	–
Orissa	21	10	147	–
Punjab	13	7	117	–
Rajasthan	25	10	200	–
Sikkim	1	1	32	–
Tamil Nadu	39	18	234	63
Tripura	2	1	60	–
Uttar Pradesh	85	34	425	108
West Bengal	42	16	294	–
Jammu and Kashmir	6	4	76[2]	36[4]
Union Territories:				
Andaman and Nicobar Islands	1	–	–	–
Arunachal Pradesh	2	1[3]	30	–
Chandigarh	1	–	–	–
Dadra and Nagar Haveli	1	–	–	–
Delhi	7	3	61	–
Goa, Daman and Diu	2	–	30	–
Lakshadweep	1	–	–	–
Mizoram	1	1	30	–
Pondicherry	1	1	30	–
Nominated by the President under Article 80 (1) (a) of the Constitution	–	12	–	–
Total	544[1]	244	4,034	528

[1] Includes 2 nominated members to represent Anglo-Indians.
[2] Excludes 25 seats for Pakistan-occupied areas of the State which are in abeyance.
[3] Nominated by the President. [4] Excludes seats for the Pakistan-occupied areas.

The number of seats allotted to scheduled castes and scheduled tribes in the House of the People is 77 and 42 respectively. Out of the 3,864 seats allotted to the Legislative Assemblies, 521 are reserved for scheduled castes and 329 for scheduled tribes.

Following the general election of Jan. 1980 the composition of the House of the People was: Indira Congress 352, Janata 31, Lok Dal 41, Communist Party (Marxist) 36, Dravida Munnetra Kazhagam 16, Congress 13, Communist Party of India 11; others 17; vacant, 16.

The Council of States (July 1980) was composed as follows: Indira Congress 121, Congress 21, Janata 17, Bhartiya Janata 14, Lok Dal 14, CPI (Marxist) 9, CPI 7, All-India Anna DMK 6, DMK 6, Akali Dal 3, National Conference 2, Muslim League 1, Kerala Congress 1, Forward Bloc 1, NNDP 1, RSP 1, RPI (Khobragade) 1, Socialist 1, Independent 6, Nominated 8, Vacant 3.

On 2 Jan. 1978 the Congress Party split into two: Congress and Indira Congress.

National flag: Three horizontal stripes of saffron (orange), white and green, with the wheel of Asoka in the centre in blue.

National anthem: Jana-gana-mana (words by Rabindranath Tagore).

Indian Independence Act, 1947. (Ch. 30.) London, 1947
The Constitution of India (Modified up to 15 April 1967). Delhi, 1967
Appadorai, A., *Indian Political Thinking in the Twentieth Century: From Naoroji to Nehru.* OUP, 1971.—*Documents on Political Thought in Modern India.* OUP, 1974
Austin, G., *The Indian Constitution.* OUP, 1972
Gandhi, I., *The Speeches and Reminiscences of Indira Gandhi.* London, 1975
Mansergh, N., ed. *The Transfer of Power 1942–47.* 5 vols. HMSO, 1970–75
Menon, V. P., *Transfer of Power in India.* Bombay, 1957
Pylee, M. V., *Constitutional Government in India.* 2nd ed. Bombay, 1965
Rao, K. V., *Parliamentary Democracy of India.* 2nd ed. Calcutta, 1965
Seervali, H. M., *Constitutional Law of India.* Bombay, 1967

Language. The Constitution provides that the official language of the Union shall be Hindi in the Devanagari script. It was originally provided that English should continue to be used for all official purposes until 1965. But the Official Languages Act 1963 provides that, after the expiry of this period of 15 years from the coming into force of the Constitution, English might continue to be used, in addition to Hindi, for all official purposes of the Union for which it was being used immediately before that day, and for the transaction of business in Parliament. According to the Official Languages (Use for official purposes of the Union) Rules 1976, an employee may record in Hindi or in English without being required to furnish a translation thereof in the other language and no employee possessing a working knowledge of Hindi may ask for an English translation of any document in Hindi except in the case of legal or technical documents.

The following 15 languages are included in the Eighth Schedule to the Constitution: Assamese, Bengali, Gujarati, Hindi, Kannada, Kashmiri, Malayalam, Marathi, Oriya, Punjabi, Sanskrit, Sindhi, Tamil, Telugu, Urdu.

There are numerous mother tongues grouped under each language. Hindi, Bengali, Telugu and Marathi languages (including mother tongues grouped under each) are spoken by 162·6m., 44.8m., 44·8m. and 42·3m. of the population respectively.

Ferozsons English–Urdu, Urdu–English Dictionary. 2 vols. 4th ed. Lahore, 1961
Fallon, S. W., *A New English–Hindustani Dictionary.* Lahore, 1941
Grierson, Sir G. A., *Linguistic Survey of India.* 11 vols. (in 19 parts). Delhi, 1903-28
Mitra, S. C., *Student's Bengali–English Dictionary.* 2nd ed. Calcutta, 1923
Scholberg, H. C., *Concise Grammar of the Hindi Language.* 3rd ed. London, 1955
University of Madras, *Tamil Lexicon.* 7 vols. Madras, 1924-39
Vyas, V. G., and Patel, S. G., *Standard English–Gujarati Dictionary.* 2 vols. Bombay, 1923

Government. *President of the Republic:* Zail Singh (sworn in July 1982).
Vice-President: Mohammad Hidayatullah.

There is a Council of Ministers to aid and advise the President of the Republic in the exercise of his functions; this comprises Ministers who are members of the Cabinet, Ministers of State who are not members of the Cabinet and Deputy Ministers. A Minister who for any period of 6 consecutive months is not a member of either House of Parliament ceases to be a Minister at the expiration of that period. The Prime Minister is appointed by the President; other Ministers are appointed by the President on the Prime Minister's advice.

The salary of each Minister is Rs 27,000 per annum, and that of each Deputy Minister is Rs 21,000 per annum. Each Minister is entitled to the free use of a furnished residence throughout his term of office. At the administrative head of each Ministry is a Secretary of the Government.

Following was the composition of the Cabinet in March 1983:

Prime Minister: Indira Gandhi.
Defence: R. Venkataraman.
Finance: P. Mukherjee
Home Affairs: P. C. Sethi
Industry, Steel and Mines: N. D. Tiwari
Agriculture and Rural Reconstruction: R. B. Singh.
Law and Justice, Company Affairs: J. Kaushal.
Health and Family Welfare: B. Shankaranand.
External Affairs: P. V. Narasimha Rao.
Parliamentary Affairs, Sports, Works and Housing: B. Narain Singh.
Energy, Petroleum and Coal: P. S. Shankar.
Shipping and Transport: V. B. Reddy.
Communications: (Vacant).
Planning: S. B. Chavan.
Irrigation: K. Pandey.
Railways: A. B. A. Ghani Khan Chaudhury.
Chemicals and Fertilizers: V. Sathe.
Labour and Rehabilitation: V. Patil.
Commerce: V. P. Singh.

Local Government. There were in 1980, 40 municipal corporations, 1,274 municipalities, 815 town area and notified area committees and 62 cantonment boards. The municipal bodies have the care of the roads, water supply, drainage, sanitation, medical relief, vaccination and education. Their main sources of revenue are taxes on the annual rental value of land and buildings, octroi and terminal, vehicle and other taxes. The municipal councils enact their own bye-laws and frame their budgets, which in the case of municipal bodies other than corporations generally require the sanction of the State government. All municipal councils are elected on the principle of adult franchise.

For rural areas there is a 3-tier system of *panchayati raj* at village, block and district level, although the 3-tier structure may undergo some changes in State legislation to suit local conditions. All *panchayati raj* bodies are organically linked, and representation is given to special interests. Elected directly by and from among villagers, the *panchayats* are responsible for agricultural production, rural industries, medical relief, maternity and child welfare, common grazing grounds, village roads, tanks and wells, and maintenance of sanitation. In some places they also look after primary education, maintenance of village records and collection of land revenue. They have their own powers of taxation. There are some judicial *panchayats* or village courts.

Panchayati raj now cover all the States with the exception of Nagaland and Meghalaya, although Nagaland has area, range and tribal councils. They exist in all the Union Territories except Mizoram and Lakshadweep. In Pondicherry they have been created by declaring existing Municipal Communes to be Commune Panchayat Councils; this is a transition arrangement. In Arunachal Pradesh and Chandigarh the 3-tier system of *panchayati raj* has been introduced. With most of the country covered by *panchayati raj*, the emphasis now is on consolidation and clarifying their role in rural development.

The powers and responsibilities of *panchayati raj* institutions are derived not only from State Legislatures, but also from the executive orders of State governments.

NAGARLOK (Municipal Affairs Quarterly). Quarterly. Institute of Public Administration. Delhi
Proceedings of the 13th Meeting of the Central Council of Local Self Government. Delhi, 1970
Report of the Committee on Budgetary Reforms in Municipal Administration. Delhi, 1974
State Machinery for Municipal Supervision. Institute of Public Administration. Delhi, 1970
Statistical Abstract of India. Annual. Delhi.

DEFENCE. The Supreme Command of the Armed Forces vests in the President of the Indian Republic. Policy is decided at different levels by a number of committees, including the Political Affairs Committee presided over by the Prime Minister and the Defence Minister's Committee. Administrative and operational control rests in the respective Service Headquarters, under the control of the Ministry of Defence.

The Ministry of Defence is the central agency for formulating defence policy and for co-ordinating the work of the three services. Among the organizations directly administered by the Ministry are the Research and Development Organization, the Production Organization, the National Defence College, the National Cadet Corps and the Directorate-General of Armed Forces Medical Services.

The Research and Development Organization (headed by the Scientific Adviser to the Minister) has under it about 30 research establishments. The Production Organization controls 8 public-sector undertakings and 28 ordnance and 2 departmental factories.

The National Defence College, New Delhi, was established in 1960 on the pattern of the Imperial Defence College (UK): the 1-year course is for officers of the rank of brigadier or equivalent and for senior civil servants. The Defence Services Staff College, Wellington, trains officers of the three Services for higher command for staff appointments. There is an Armed Forces Medical College at Pune.

The National Defence Academy, Khadakvasla, gives a 3-year basic training course to officer cadets of the three Services prior to advanced training at the respective Service establishments.

Army. The Army Headquarters functioning directly under the Chief of the Army Staff is divided into the following main branches: General Staff Branch; Adjutant General's Branch; Quartermaster-General's Branch; Master-General of Ordnance Branch; Engineer-in-Chief's Branch; Military Secretary's Branch.

The Army is organized into 4 commands–eastern, central, western and southern–each divided into areas, which in turn are subdivided into sub-areas.

Recruitment of permanent commissioned officers is through the Indian Military Academy, Dehra Dun. It conducts courses for ex-National Defence Academy, National Cadet Corps and direct-entry cadets, and for serving personnel and technical graduates.

The Territorial Army came into being in Sept. 1949, its role being to: (1) relieve the regular Army of static duties and, if required, support civil power; (2) provide anti-aircraft units, and (3) if and when called upon, provide units for the regular Army. The Territorial Army is composed of practically all arms of the Services.

The authorized strength of the Army is 944,000, that of the Territorial Army, 40,000. There are 2 armoured, 17 infantry and 10 mountain divisions, 5 independent armoured brigades, 1 independent infantry, 14 independent artillery brigades, 1 commando and 2 parachute brigades.

Navy. Since 26 Jan. 1950 the former Royal Indian Navy, which traced its history in an unbroken line from the foundation in 1613 of the East India Company's Marine, has been known as 'Indian Navy', and the ships referred to as 'INS' instead of 'HMIS'. There are 3 commands: Eastern, Western and Southern.

Principal ships of the Indian Navy:

Completed	*Name*	*Standard displacement Tons*	*Armour Belts in.*	*Armour Turrets in.*	*Principal armament*	*Shaft horse-power*	*Speed Knots*
		Aircraft Carrier					
1961	Vikrant (*ex*-Hercules)	16,000	–	–	15 40 mm. AA (22 aircraft)	40,000	24·5
		Cruisers [1]					
1940	Mysore (*ex*-Nigeria)	8,700	3-4½	2	9 6-in.; 8 4-in.	72,500	31·5

[1] The cruiser *Delhi* (ex-*Achilles*) completed in 1933, was scrapped in 1979.

The fleet also includes 8 *ex*-Soviet submarines, 3 new Soviet-built guided missile armed destroyers, 6 new broad beam 'Leander' class general purpose frigates (built in India), 2 anti-submarine frigates and 3 anti-aircraft frigates (built in Great Britain), 1 old *ex*-British frigate, 12 Soviet-built escorts, 3 *ex*-Soviet corvettes, 6 *ex*-Soviet ocean minesweepers, 4 *ex*-British coastal minesweepers, 4 inshore minesweepers 16 missile boats, 4 patrol craft, 7 landing ships, 4 landing craft, 5 survey ships, 1 repair ship, 1 submarine parent ship, 1 submarine rescue ship, 6 oilers, 13 service craft and 3 tugs.

New construction includes 2 West German-built patrol submarines, 3 enlarged and improved 'Leander' type frigates and 3 more scheduled to follow. Two indigenously built similar submarines, 3 more frigates and 4 corvettes are projected. Plans are reported for the purchase of a second carrier.

The major training establishments of the Navy include INS *Venduruthy* at Cochin (Basic and Divisional, Gunnery, Torpedo and Anti-Submarine, Navigation and Direction, Communication), INS *Vaisura* at Jamnagar (Electrical), INS *Shivaji* at Lonavla (Engineering), INS *Hansa* at Goa (Aviation), INS *Hamla* at Bombay (Supply and Secretariat) and INS *Circars* at Vishakhapatnam (Boys' Training).

The Fleet Requirement Unit of the Naval Aviation Station, INAS *Garuda*, is at Cochin. Over 100 aircraft include Sea Harriers, Sea Hawk fighters, Alize anti-submarine aircraft and Sea King anti-submarine helicopters acquired for the aircraft carrier.

Naval personnel in 1983 comprised 46,000 officers and ratings, including the Naval Air Arm.

The Coast Guard was constituted as an independent para-military service by

1978 Act of Parliament. It comprised the frigates *Kirpan* and *Kuthar* and five patrol craft all transferred from the Indian Navy and 2 larger patrol vessels custom-built. It has recently been augmented by new specifically built ships and aircraft, including three 1,040-ton offshore patrol vessels, three 205-ton inshore protection craft, 5 *ex*-Soviet cutters, 6 South Korean-built launches and 5 Defender aircraft. It is administered by a Director-General (Rear-Admiral) and a Deputy Director-General (Commodore). It functions under the Defence Ministry but is funded by the Revenue Department.

Air Force. The Indian Air Force Act was passed in 1932, and the first flight was formed in 1933.

The Air Headquarters, under the Chief of Air Staff, consists of 4 main branches, viz., Air Staff, Administration, Policy and Plans, and Maintenance. Units of the IAF are organized into 3 operational commands–Western at Delhi, Central at Allahabad, Eastern at Shillong–plus an operational group at Jodhpur administered directly by Air HQ. Training Command HQ is at Bangalore, Maintenance Command at Nagpur. Nominal strength in 1982 was about 113,000 personnel and 650 first-line combat aircraft in 31 squadrons, supported by 9 transport squadrons, 16 helicopter squadrons, training units and about 20 squadrons of 'Guideline' and 'Goa' surface-to-air missiles, supplemented by close-range missiles such as 'Gainful' and Tigercat.

Air defence units include 4 squadrons of Ajeet (Gnat Mk 2) fighters and 14 squadrons of MiG-21s. Initial delivery of MiG-21s from the Soviet Union was followed by large-scale licence production in India. There are 2 squadrons of Sukhoi Su-7s, 3 of Canberras, 1 of Jaguars, 3 of Hunter F56s, 3 of MiG-23 supersonic fighter-bombers and one of MiG-25 reconnaissance aircraft. Jaguars are being acquired to re-equip Canberra bomber and Hunter squadrons. Some of those flying MiG-21s and SU-7s are expected to re-equip with MiG-27s licence-built in India; also on order are 40 Mirage 2000s from France.

The large transport force includes An-12s, An-32s, jet-boosted C-119Gs, C-47s, HS 748s, Caribou, Otters, 2 Boeing 737s, and smaller aircraft and helicopters for VIP and other duties. Helicopter units have Mi-8s (4 squadrons), Chetaks (Aerospatiale Alouette IIIs) and licence-built Cheetahs (Aerospatiale Lamas); main training types are the Hindustan HPT-32 (being introduced in 1984) and Kiran, Polish built TS-11 Iskra, Hunter T.66 (to be replaced with 2-seat Ajeets), MiG-21UT1 and Su-7U.

Primary flying training is provided at the Elementary Flying School, Bidar, and advanced flying training at the Air Force Academy, Dundigal, Hyderabad. There is a Navigation and Signals School at Begumpet. The IAF Technical College, Jalahalli, imparts technical training, while the IAF Administrative College, Coimbatore, trains officers of the ground duty branch. There are also land-air warfare, flying instructors' and medical schools.

INTERNATIONAL RELATIONS

Membership. India is a member of the UN, the Commonwealth and the Colombo Plan.

External Debt. At the end of financial year 1980-81 India's external public debt was Rs 10,782 crores.

Treaties. India pursues a general policy of non-alignment; the exception is a Treaty of Peace, Friendship and Cooperation with the USSR, 1971; the parties agreed to mutual support short of force in the event of either being attacked by a third party.

ECONOMY

Planning. The sixth plan (1980-85) envisages total investment of Rs 1,587,100m., of which Rs 975,000m. is for the public sector. The amount of this financed from abroad would be Rs 90,630m. The aim is an annual 5·2% growth rate and the prime objective is to alleviate rural poverty. Intended investment in energy, Rs 265,350m.; in social services, Rs 140,350m.; transport and industry both get Rs 124,110m.

Ministry of Agriculture. *Serving the Small Farmer: Policy Choices in Indian Agricultural Development.* 1975
Dutt, A. K. (ed.), *India: Resources, Potentialities and Planning.* Rev. ed. Dubuque, India, 1973
Singh, T., *India's Development Experience.* London, 1975

Budget. Revenue and expenditure (on revenue account) of the central government[1] for years ending 31 March, in crores of rupees:

	1978-79[2]	*1979-80*[2]	*1980-81*[3]	*1981-82*	*1982-83*[3]
Revenue	11,019·85	11,177·0	12,894·0	15,373	17,601
Expenditure	11,148·31	12,048·0	13,682·0	948	18,227

[1] Excluding states' share of excise duties and other taxes.
[2] Revised. [3] Budget estimates.

Important items of revenue and expenditure on the revenue account of the central government for 1982-83 (estimates), in Rs 1m.:

Revenue		*Expenditure*	
Net tax revenue	133,680	General Services	56,060
Non-tax revenue	42,330	Defence	45,990
		Grants in aid to States, etc.	33,640

Total capital account receipts (1982-83), Rs 102,530m.; capital account disbursements, Rs 109,920m. Total (revenue and capital) receipts, Rs 278,540m.; disbursements, Rs 292,190m.

Under the Constitution (Part XII and 7th Schedule), the power to raise funds has been divided between the central government and the states. Generally, the sources of revenue are mutually exclusive. Certain taxes are levied by the Union for the sake of uniformity and distributed to the states. The Finance Commission (Art. 280 of the Constitution) advises the President on the distribution of the taxes which are distributable between the centre and the states, and on the principles on which grants should be made out of Union revenues to the states. The main sources of central revenue are: customs duties; those excise duties levied by the central government; corporation, income and wealth taxes; estate and succession duties on non-agricultural assets and property, and revenues from the railways and posts and telegraphs. The main heads of revenue in the states are: taxes and duties levied by the state governments (including land revenues and agricultural income tax); civil administration and civil works; state undertakings; taxes shared with the centre; and grants received from the centre.

Debt. At the end of the financial year 1980-81 the interest-bearing obligations of the Government of India were estimated to amount to Rs 40,325 crores, of which total obligations in India were Rs 29,008 crores.

Currency. A decimal system of coinage was introduced in 1957. The Indian *rupee* is divided into 100 *paise* (until 1964 officially described as *naye paise*), the decimal coins being 1, 2, 3, 5, 10, 20, 25 and 50 *paise.*

The rupee is valued in relation to a package of main currencies. The £ is the currency of intervention. On 18 Nov. 1982 the spot rate for buying was Rs 15.76 to £1; selling, Rs 15.84; dollar buying, Rs 9.50 to US$1.

The paper currency consists of: (1) Reserve Bank notes in denominations of Rs 2, 5, 10, 20, 50 and 100; and (2) Government of India currency notes of denominations of Re 1 deemed to be included in the expression 'rupee coin' for the purposes of the Reserve Bank of India Act, 1934.

According to the Reserve Bank of India, the total money supply with the public on the last Friday of June 1982 was Rs 26,423 crores.

100,000 rupees are called 1 lakh; 100 lakhs are called 1 crore.

Banking. The Reserve Bank, the central bank for India, was established in 1934 and started functioning on 1 April 1935 as a shareholder's bank; it became a nationalized institution on 1 Jan. 1949. It has the sole right of issuing currency-notes. The Bank acts as adviser to the Government on financial problems and is the banker for central and state governments, commercial banks and some other financial institutions. The Bank manages the rupee public debt of central and state governments. It is the custodian of the country's exchange reserve and supervises repatriation of export proceeds and payments for imports. The Bank gives short-term loans to state governments and scheduled banks and short and medium-term loans to state co-operative banks and industrial finance institutions. The Bank has extensive powers of regulation of the banking system, directly under the Banking Regulation Act, 1949, and indirectly by the use of variations in Bank rate, variation in reserve ratios, selective credit controls and open market operations. Bank rate was raised to 10% in July 1981. The statutory cash reserves were at 7% of net demand and time liabilities on 11 June 1982.

The statutory liquidity ratio was 35% in Oct. 1981. Except refinance for food credit and export credit, the Reserve Bank's refinance facility to commercial banks has been placed on a discretionary basis. The net profit of the Reserve Bank of India for the year ended June 1982, after making the usual or necessary provisions, amounted to Rs 210 crores.

The commercial banking system consisted of 201 scheduled banks (*i.e.*, banks which are included in the 2nd schedule to the Reserve Bank Act) and 4 non-scheduled banks on 30 June 1982; scheduled banks included 121 Regional Rural Banks. Total deposits in commercial banks, June 1982, stood at Rs 45,831 crores. The business of non-scheduled banks forms less than 0·1% of commercial bank business. Of the 201 scheduled banks, 18 are foreign banks which specialize in financing foreign trade but also compete for domestic business. The largest scheduled bank is the State Bank of India, constituted by nationalizing the Imperial Bank of India in 1955. The State Bank acts as the agent of the Reserve Bank and the subsidiaries of the State Bank act as the agents of the State Bank for transacting government business as well as undertaking commercial functions. Fourteen banks with aggregate deposits of not less than Rs 50 crores were nationalized on 19 July 1969. Six banks were nationalized in April 1980. The 28 public sector banks (which comprise the State Bank of India and its seven associate banks and 20 nationalised banks) account for over 90% of deposits and bank credit of all scheduled commercial banks.

Reserve Bank of India: Report on Currency and Finance.—Report on the Trend and Progress of Banking in India.—Report of the Central Board of Directors. Annual. Bombay

Weights and Measures. Uniform standards of weights and measures, based on the metric system, were established for the first time by the Standards of Weights and Measures Act, 1956, which provided for a transition period of 10 years. So far the system has been fully adopted in trade transactions but there are a few fields such as engineering, survey and land records and the building and construction industry where it has not; efforts are being made to complete the change as early as possible.

In order to align this legislation with the latest international trends an expert committee (Weights and Measures (Law Revision) Committee) was set up by the central government to suggest a revised Bill which was passed by Parliament in April 1976. The new Standards of Weights and Measures Act, 1976, has recognized the International System of Units and other units recommended by the General Conference on Weights and Measures and is in line with the recommendations of the International Organisation of Legal Metrology (OIML). The new Act also covers the system of numeration, the approval of models of weights and measures, regulation and control of inter-state trade in relation to weights and measures. The Act also protects consumers through proper indication of weight, quantity, identity, source, date and price on packaged goods. A draft Standards of Weights and Measures (Enforcement) Bill has also been prepared by the committee for adoption either by Parliament or State legislatures, as enforcement is now in the 'concurrent' list of legislation.

The provisions of the 1976 Act came into force in Sept. 1977, as did the accompanying Standards of Weights and Measures (Packaged Commodities) Rules, 1977.

While the Standards of Weights and Measures are laid down in the Central Act, enforcement of weights and measures laws is entrusted to the state governments; the central Directorate of Weights and Measures is responsible for co-ordinating activities so as to ensure national uniformity.

An Indian Institute of Legal Metrology trains officials of the Weights and

Measures departments of India and different developing countries. The Institute is being modernized with technical assistance from the Federal Republic of Germany.

There are 2 Regional Reference Standards laboratories at Ahmedabad and Bhubaneswar which (besides calibrating secondary standards of physical measurements) also provide testing facilities in metrological and industrial measurements. These laboratories are equipped with Standards next in line to the National Standards of physical measurements which are maintained at the National Physical Laboratory in New Delhi.

For weights previously in legal use under the Standards of Weight Act, 1956, *see* THE STATESMAN'S YEAR-BOOK, 1961, p. 171.

Calendar. The dates of the Saka era (named after the north Indian dynasty of the first century A.D.) are being used alongside Gregorian dates in issues of the *Gazette of India*, news broadcasts by All-India Radio and government-issued calendars, from 22 March 1957, a date which corresponds with the first day of the year 1879 in the Saka era.

ENERGY AND NATURAL RESOURCES

Electricity. In March 1981 about half of all villages had electricity. Total installed capacity (1981, provisional) was 33m. kw. Production of electricity was 111·6m. kwh. in 1981, of which 62m. kwh. came from thermal stations, 46·5m. kwh. from hydro-electric stations and 3m. kwh. from nuclear power stations.

Oil and Gas. The Oil and Natural Gas Commission, Oil India Ltd and the Assam Oil Co. are the only producers of crude oil. Total production, 1982, about 19m. tonnes; imports (1981) 16m. tonnes. The main fields are in Assam and offshore in the Gulf of Cambay (the Bombay High field). Natural gas production, 1979-80, 1,890m. cu. metres.

Water. The net area of 60m. hectares (1980) under irrigation exceeds that of any other country except China, and equals about 38% of the total area under cultivation. Irrigation projects have formed an important part of all three Five-Year Plans. The possibilities of diverting rivers into canals being nearly exhausted, the emphasis is now on damming the monsoon surplus flow and diverting that. Usable surface and groundwater resources were assessed (1972) at 870,000m. cu. metres. Utilization (1974) 337,000m. cu. metres. Irrigation plant in operation in 1976 could make use of 67m. hectare-metres of surface water and 26·5m. hectare-metres of ground water. Ultimate potential of irrigation is assessed at 107m. hectares, total cultivated land being 142m. hectares. In 1977 India and Bangladesh reached an agreement to share the water of the Ganges at the Farakka barrage: India needs this supply to supplement the Hooghly River in flushing silt from Calcutta port. A further agreement (1982) also includes the waters of the Brahmaputra.

Minerals. Bihar, West Bengal and Madhya Pradesh produce 42%, 25% and 19% of all coal, respectively. The coal industry was nationalized in 1973; planned state investment 1976-86, Rs 4·0 crores. Production, 1979-80, 104m. tonnes; reserves (including lignite) are estimated at 83,050m. tonnes. Production of other minerals, 1980 (in 1,000 tonnes): Iron ore, 39,000; bauxite, 1,532; chromite 305; copper ore, 1,997; manganese ore, 1,740; gold, 2,636 kg. Other important minerals are lead, zinc, limestone, apatite and phosphorite, dolomite, magnesite and silver. Value of mineral production, 1979, Rs 18,366m. of which mineral fuels produced Rs 14,134m., metallic minerals Rs 2,058m. and non-metallic Rs 2,174m.

Agriculture. The chief industry of India has always been agriculture. About 70% of the people are dependent on the land for their living. In 1981 it provided about two-fifths of GDP; growth rate, 1981-82, 5·4%.

Agricultural commodities account for about 20% by value of Indian exports, while agricultural commodities, machinery and fertilizers account for about 25-30% of imports. Tea accounts for about 40% of agricultural exports.

An increase in food production of at least 2% per annum is necessary to keep pace with the rising population. Foodgrain production, 78·4m. tons in 1962-63, was 135m. tonnes in 1981.

The Indian Council of Agricultural Research works through 22 Research Institutes, 2 Technological Research Laboratories and a Directorate of All India Soil and Land Use Survey, Universities (including Agricultural Universities) and other public and quasi-public research and educational bodies. It supports the establishment of at least 1 agricultural university in each of the states.

Agricultural production, 1980-81 (in 1,000 tonnes): rice, 56,000; wheat, 30,000; total foodgrains, 135,000; coffee, of which the main cash varieties are Arabica and Robusta (main growing areas Karnataka, Kerala and Tamil Nadu), 160 (1979-80); sugar cane (1979-80), 145,000; cotton, 7·8m. bales (of 170 kg); jute is grown in West Bengal (half total yield), Bihar and Assam, total yield, 8,300; oilseeds, 10,200; maize, 6,800; pulses, 11,500; milk (1979-80), 30,000.

The tea industry is important, with production concentrated in Assam, West Bengal, Tamil Nadu, Kerala and Karnataka. Total crop in 1980-81, about 580,000 tonnes from 370,000 hectares.

Production of natural rubber (1977) was 150,000 tonnes. Kerala produced about 93% of this.

Livestock (1979). Cattle, 181·8m.; sheep, 41m.; pigs, 9·9m.; horses, 760,000; asses, 1m.; goats, 71m.

Fertilizer consumption in 1980-81 was 5·58m. tonnes.

Land Tenure. There are three main traditional systems of land tenure: *ryotwari* tenure, where the individual holders, usually peasant proprietors, are responsible for the payment of land revenues; *zamindari* tenure, where one or more persons own large estates and are responsible for payment (in this system there may be a number of intermediary holders); and *mahalwari* tenure, where village communities jointly hold an estate and are jointly and severally responsible for payment.

Agrarian reform, initiated in the first Five-Year Plan, being undertaken by the state governments includes: (1) The abolition of intermediaries under *zamindari* tenure. (2) Tenancy legislation designed to scale down rents to ¼ – ⅕ of the value of the produce, to give permanent rights to tenants (subject to the landlord's right to resume a minimum holding for his personal cultivation), and to enable tenants to acquire ownership of their holdings (subject to the landlord's right of resumption for personal cultivation) on payment of compensation over a number of years. (3) Fixing of ceilings on existing holdings and on future acquisition; the holding of a family is between 4·05 and 7·28 hectares if it has assured irrigation to produce two crops a year; 10·93 hectares for land with irrigation facilities for only one crop a year; and 21·85 hectares for all other categories of land. Tea, coffee, cocoa and cardamom plantations have been exempted. (4) The consolidation of holdings in community project areas and the prevention of fragmentation of holdings by reform of inheritance laws. (5) Promotion of farming by co-operative village management (*see* p. 623).

The average size of holding for the whole of India is 2·63 hectares. Andhra Pradesh, 2·87; Assam, 1·46; Bihar, 1·53; Gujarat, 4·49; Jammu and Kashmir, 1·43; Karnataka, 4·11; Kerala, 0·75; Madhya Pradesh, 3·99; Maharashtra, 4·65; Orissa, 1·98; Punjab, 3·85; Rajasthan, 5·5; Tamil Nadu, 1·49; Uttar Pradesh, 1·78; West Bengal, 1·56.

Of the total 71m. rural households possessing operational holdings, 34% hold on the average less than 0·20 hectare of land each.

Opium. By international agreement the poppy is cultivated under licence, and all raw opium is sold to the central government. Opium, other than for wholly medical use, is available only to registered addicts.

Fisheries. Total catch (1980) was 2·5m. tonnes, of which Kerala, Tamil Nadu, and Maharashtra produced about half. Of the total catch, 1,612,140 tonnes were marine fish. There were about 13,000 mechanized fishing boats, including trawlers, operating at the beginning of 1976. Fishermen's co-operatives had 541,434 members in 1978; their total sales were worth Rs 257m.

Forestry. The lands under the control of the state forest departments are classified as 'reserved forests' (forests intended to be permanently maintained for the supply of timber, etc., or for the protection of water supply, etc.), 'protected forests' and 'unclassed' forest land.

In 1976 the total forest area was 74·6m. hectares, or 23% of the land area. Main types are teak (8·9m. hectares) and sal (11·6m.). Forests employed 13·6m. Forest revenue was Rs 1,322m. Production is low at 0·28 cu. metre per hectare per year (France, 3·9 cu. metres; Japan, 2·8 cu. metres; USA, 1·25 cu. metres). About 16% of the area is inaccessible, of which about 45% is potentially productive. Production, 1976, 22·8m. cu. metres, of which 13·7m. cu. metres are fuel wood. There are about 3,000 sawmills. In 1980 about 5% of forest was newly planted; this is considered insufficient to meet future demands for fuel and industrial wood. Some states have encouraged planting small areas around villages.

INDUSTRY AND TRADE

Industries. Railways, air transport, armaments and atomic energy are government monopolies. In a number of industries (including the manufacture of iron and steel and mineral oils, shipbuilding and the mining of coal, iron and manganese ores, gypsum, gold and diamonds) new units are set up only by the state. In a further group of industries (road transport, manufacture of chemicals such as drugs, dye-stuffs, plastics and fertilizers) the state established new undertakings, but private enterprise may develop either on its own or with state backing, which may take the form of loans or purchase of equity capital. Nationalized industries employed 4m. in 1981. Under the Industries (Development and Regulation) Act, 1951, as amended, industrial undertakings are required to be licensed; 162 industries are within the scope of the Act. The Government are authorized to examine the working of any undertaking, to issue directions to it and to take over its control if this be deemed necessary. A Central Advisory Council has been set up consisting of representatives of industry, labour, consumers and primary producers. There are Development Councils for individual industries and (1981) 4 national development banks.

Foreign investment is encouraged by a tax holiday on income up to 6% of capital employed for 5 years. There are special depreciation allowances, and customs and excise concessions for export industries.

Oil refinery installed capacity, 1981, was 35·3m. tonnes with the opening of Mathura refinery; production of refined oils (1980–81), 24·1m. tonnes. The Indian Oil Corporation was established in 1964 and had (1981) most of the market.

Industry, particularly steel, has suffered from a shortage of power and coal. There is expansion in petrochemicals, based on the oil and associated gas of the Bombay High field, and gas from Bassein field. Small industries (initial outlay on capital equipment of less than Rs 2m.) are important; they employ about 7m. and produced (1980) goods worth Rs 209,000m. The industrial growth rate, 1981-82 was 8·6%.

Industrial production, 1980–81 (in 1,000 tonnes): Pig-iron and ferro-alloys, 8,600; crude steel, 8,000 (estimate); finished steel, 6,800 (estimate); aluminium, 199; motor cycles (nos.), 317,000; commercial vehicles (nos.), 71,300; petroleum products, 24,100; sulphuric acid, 2,100; cement, 18,400; board and paper, 1,145; nitrogen fertilizer, 2,164; phosphate fertilizer, 840; jute goods, 1,400; rayon yarn, 132 (1979–80); cotton yarn, 1,281; cotton cloth, 9,700m. metres; diesel engines, 174,000 engines; electric motors, 4·1m. h.p.; refractories, 900; sugar, 5,100.

Labour. At the 1971 census there were 180·3m. workers, of whom 78m. were cultivators, 37·4m. agricultural labourers, 17m. in manufacturing, processing and servicing, 2·2m. in construction, 10m. in trade and commerce and 4·4m. in transport, communications and storage. There were 847 central unions registered and 19,865 state unions. The bond labour system was abolished in 1975. Man-days lost by industrial disputes, 1979, 37·10m., of which 6·66m. were in the public sector. An ordnance of July 1981 gave the government power to ban strikes in essential services; the ordnance was to remain in force for six months and would then be renewable.

Dasgupta, A. K., *A Theory of Wage Policy.* OUP, 1976

Companies. The total number of companies limited by shares at work in India, 31 March 1981, was 62,001; aggregate paid-up capital was Rs 14,676·5 crores. There were 9,101 public limited companies with an aggregate paid-up capital of Rs 3,952·1 crores, and 52,900 private limited companies (Rs 10,724·4 crores). There were also 176 companies with unlimited liability.

During 1980-81, 6,616 new limited companies were registered in the Indian Union under the Companies Act 1956 with a total authorized capital of Rs 968·3 crores; 594 were public limited companies (Rs 269·2 crores) and 6,022 were private limited companies (Rs 699·1 crores). There were 98 private companies with unlimited liability also registered in 1980–81, authorized capital Rs 0·27 crores. Of the new limited companies, 109 had an authorized capital of Rs 1 crore and above, and 149 of between Rs 50 lakhs and Rs 1 crore; 38 were government companies (i.e., companies in which Government owns at least 51% of share capital). During 1980-81, 167 companies with an aggregate paid-up capital of Rs 9,70 lakhs went into liquidation and 224 companies (Rs 60 lakhs) were struck off the register.

On 31 March 1981 there were 851 government companies at work with a total paid-up capital of Rs 10,853·1 crores; 352 were public limited companies and 499 were private limited companies.

On 31 March 1981, 300 companies incorporated elsewhere were reported to have a place of business in India; of these 133 were of UK and 57 of USA origin.

Department of Company Affairs, Govt. of India. *Joint Stock Companies in India.* New Delhi

Co-operative Movement. Agricultural primary credit societies (which constitute the base of the co-operative credit structure of the country) derive their funds from state co-operative banks which work with the central co-operative banks and the land development banks. The societies have been reorganised to ensure that each is big enough to be efficient. In 1981 there were about 110,000; short-term loans advanced had reached Rs 14,000m. in 1979, medium-term Rs, 1,130m. and long-term Rs 3,070m. To ensure that a fair proportion of this credit went to small farmers and labourers, Small and Marginal Farmers Development Agencies have been set up.

Following the recommendations (1954) of a committee appointed by the Reserve Bank of India, the co-operation movement was extended from its chief function of providing credit to include marketing, processing, warehousing, etc. In 1978 there were 156,817 non-credit societies including 3,592 primary marketing societies, 186 sugar factories, 848 other agricultural processing societies, 4,947 farming societies, 14,251 primary weavers' societies, 24,804 other industrial societies; there were 15,827 primary consumers' stores.

In 1978 non-credit societies marketed agricultural produce, agricultural requisites and consumer goods worth Rs 969 crores. Co-operative sugar factories crushed 29·7m. tonnes of cane and produced sugar worth Rs 6,018m.

Indian Labour Guide. Monthly. Delhi
Co-operative Movement in India, Statistical Statements Relating to. Annual. Reserve Bank of India, Bombay
Ghosh, A., *Indian Economy, its Nature and Problems.* 7th ed. Calcutta, 1963
Karnik, V. B., *Indian Trade Unions.* 2nd ed. Bombay, 1966
Kust, M. J., *Foreign Enterprise in India.* Bombay, 1964
Pant, S. C., *Indian Labour Problems.* Allahabad, 1965
Sharma, T. R., and Singh Chauhan, S. D., *Indian Industries.* 2nd ed. Agra, 1965
Sharma, V. S., *Sahayoga, or Indian Co-operation.* Hoshiarpur, 1964
Thorner, D., *Agricultural Co-operatives in India.* Bombay, 1964

Commerce. The external trade of India (excluding land-borne trade with Tibet and Bhutan) was as follows (in 1,000 rupees):

	Imports		*Exports and Re-exports*	
	Merchandise	*Treasure*	*Merchandise*	*Treasure*
1975–76	5,264,77,87	7,40	4,036,25,87	4,32
1976–77	5,073,79,13	9,04	5,142,24,84	3,88
1977–78	6,020,22,62	20,03	5,407,87,19	6,07
1978–79	6,810,63,93	65,82	5,726,07,00	7,82
1979–80	9,142,58,48	29,18	6,418,43,25	6,05
1980–81	12,560,28,75	8,36	6,710,70,55	2,53

The distribution of commerce by countries and areas was as follows in the year ended 31 March 1981 (in 1,000 rupees):

Countries	*Exports to*	*Imports from*	*Countries*	*Exports to*	*Imports from*
Afghánistán	19,22,96	8,47,16	Japan	596,88,55	748,78,15
Argentina	5,28,28	18,02,14	Kenya	33,30,08	12,42,08
Australia	91,60,91	170,07,65	Malaysia	52,24,86	266,07,45
Belgium	144,45,49	295,86,25	Nepál	77,97,96	23,61,02
Burma	3,31,08	7,47,86	Netherlands	150,62,03	214,50,07
Canada	62,20,72	332,34,10	New Zealand	18,57,05	12,80,49
Czechoslovakia	55,30,35	39,00,97	Poland	68,96,52	34,40,65
Denmark	26,38,40	20,50,45	Saudi Arabia	164,87,63	540,04,85
Egypt	85,81,32	29,60,35	Singapore	108,56,91	427,88,00
Federal Rep. of Germany	383,09,64	693,76,79	Sri Lanka	80,53,22	29,55,11
France	146,64,47	280,30,44	Sudan	38,62,56	1,53,01
German Dem. Republic	48,88,84	44,26,84	Switzerland	110,52,54	120,62,64
Hungary	15,81,37	31,37,04	USSR	1,225,71,75	1,013,70,88
Iran	123,18,34	1,338,90,29	UK	393,47,36	730,98,72
Italy	151,54,99	242,47,65	USA	739,39,99	1,518,61,04
			Yemen	26,22,23	23,91
			Yugoslavia	33,90,00	44,91,01

The value (in 1,000 rupees) of the leading articles of merchandise was as follows in the year ended 31 March 1981:

Exports	*Value*
Fish	212,88,83
Edible nuts and fresh fruits	161,27,25
Coffee	214,23,55
Tea and mate	425,50,39
Spices	111,35,78
Oilseed, oilnuts and oil kernels	60,49,14
Tobacco	140,67,92
Hides and skins, undressed	58,47
Wood (unworked)	2,96,66
Wool and other animal hair	97,76
Cotton, raw	177,10,29
Cottonwaste; shoddy	2,08,00
Stone, sand and gravel	29,45,13
Iron ore and concentrates	303,33,08
Iron and steel scrap	87,75
Ore and concentrates, non-ferrous base metals	41,02,50
Coal, coke and briquettes	2,93,21
Fixed vegetable oils	14,69,65
Leather	277,14,72
Textile yarn and thread	50,14,14
Textile fabrics (woven) except cotton and man-made fibre	203,71,00
Cotton fabrics, woven	276,48,73
Man-made fibre fabrics, woven	31,63,72
Floor coverings, tapestries, except cotton and jute	185,82,37
Manufactures of leather or artificial leather	59,14,08

Imports	
Milk and cream	41,09,70
Wheat, spelt and meslin	76,58,70
Rice	3,69,11
Edible nuts and fresh fruit	33,57,90
Pulp and waste paper	18,30,21
Wool and other animal hair	50,79,32
Cotton, raw	1,69
Jute	2,01,99
Vegetable fibres except cotton and jute	2,27,85
Crude fertilizers	79,05,59
Sulphur and unroasted iron pyrites	86,40,29
Petroleum, crude and partly refined	3,348,97,10
Petroleum products	1,914,50,10
Animal oils and fats	21,80,56

Imports	*Value*
Fixed vegetable oils	682,89,72
Organic chemicals	201,78,66
Medical and pharmaceutical products	84,58,11
Manufactured fertilizers	652,29,90
Plastic materials	121,37,21
Chemical materials and products, n.e.s.	72,10,53
Paper, paperboard and manufactures	186,51,31
Pearls, precious and semiprecious stones	416,74,88
Iron and steel bars, angles, shapes, sections	148,55,95
Iron and steel universals, plates and sheets	479,86,91
Iron and steel tubes, pipes, fittings	123,54,99
Copper	128,28,40
Zinc	44,51,09
Tin	30,99,16
Machinery other than electrical	1,038,61,73
Electrical machinery	259,70,88
Transport equipment	471,94,81

Total trade between India and UK (British Department of Trade returns, in £1,000 sterling):

	1978	*1979*	*1980*	*1981*	*1982*
Imports to UK	322,056	365,843	315,858	294,323	379,169
Exports and re-exports from UK	348,639	455,606	529,007	638,867	805,321

Annual Statement of the Foreign Trade of India. 2 vols. Calcutta
Monthly Statistics of the Foreign Trade of India. Calcutta
Review of the Trade of India. Annual. Delhi
India–Handbook of Commercial Information. 3 vols. Calcutta
Guide to Official Statistics of Trade, Shipping, Customs and Excise Revenue of India. Rev. ed. Calcutta

Tourism. There were 700,000 visitors to India in 1980.

COMMUNICATIONS

Roads. In 1980 there were about 1,534,000 km of roads, of which 658,000 km were metalled. Roads are divided into 5 main administrative classes, namely, national highways, state highways, major district roads, district roads and village roads. The national highways (31,358 km in 1982) connect capitals of states, major ports and foreign highways. The national highway system is linked with the ESCAP (Economic and Social Commission for Asia and the Pacific) international highway system. The state highways are the main trunk roads of the states, while the major district roads connect subsidiary areas of production and markets with distribution centres, and form the main link between headquarters and neighbouring districts.

There were (31 March 1980) about 4,106,000 motor vehicles in India, comprising 884,000 private cars and jeeps, 1,888,000 motor cycles, scooters and auto-rickshaws, 92,000 taxis, 133,000 buses and 436,000 goods vehicles.

Railways. The Indian railway system is government-owned and (under the control of the Railway Board) is divided into 9 zones, with route-km as follows at 31 March 1980:

Zone	*Headquarters*	*Route-km*
Central	Bombay (Mumbai)	5,892
Eastern	Calcutta	4,202
Northern	Delhi	10,688
North Eastern	Gorakhpur	5,113
North East Frontier	Gauhati	3,627
Southern	Madras	6,330
South Central	Secunderabad	6,479
South Eastern	Calcutta	6,990
Western	Bombay (Mumbai)	10,337

Passengers carried in 1979–80 were approximately 3,505m. Revenue-earning-goods traffic, 1980–81, 195m. tonnes.

Indian Railways pay to the central government a fixed dividend of 4·5% on capital-at-charge.

Financial years	Gross traffic receipts (Rs crores)	Working expenses (Rs crores)	Net revenues (Rs crores)	Net surplus or deficit (Rs crores)
1979–80	2,337·84	2,142·38	227·29	–66·24
1980–81[1]	2,707·22	2,468·61	272·09	–52·34
1981–82[2]	3,276·75	2,913·14	399·80	+49·89

[1] Revised estimate. [2] Budget.

Aviation. The air transport industry in India was nationalized in 1953 with the formation of two Air Corporations: Air India for operating long-distance international air services, and Indian Airlines for operating air services within India and to adjacent countries. A third airline, Vayudoot, was formed in 1981 to serve areas in the north-east. Air India has 11 Boeing 747s and 9 707s; it operates daily to New York *via* London with halts in the Middle East and Europe, 2 flights a week to London *via* Moscow and 11 flights a week to London with halts in the Middle East. Other scheduled flights are made to Perth and Sydney, Kuala Lumpur, Singapore, Tōkyō, Osaka, Bangkok and Hong Kong, Nairobi, Dar es Salaam, Aden and Addis Ababa, Lagos and Accra, Kuwait, Cairo, Baghdad, Mauritius, Seychelles, Dhahran, Jeddah, Bahrain, Doha, Abu Dhabi, Dubai and Muscat. A fleet of 49 aircraft consisting of Airbus A-300B2, Boeing 737, F-27 and HS-748 aircraft are flown by Indian Airlines on 220 flights covering 49,657 route-km.

In 1981-82 Indian Airlines aircraft flew about 220 flights, carrying about 6·2m. passengers and making a net profit of Rs11 crores. Air India (1980) carried 1·2m. passengers and (1978-79) 42,300 tonnes of freight.

The Civil Aviation Department maintains and operates 85 aerodromes. The management of the 4 international airports at Mumbai (Santa Cruz), Calcutta (Dum Dum), Delhi (Palam) and Madras is vested in the International Airports Authority of India.

Shipping. In March 1981, 389 ships totalling 5,740,000 GRT were on the Indian Register; of these, 58 ships of 250,000 GRT were engaged in coastal trade, and 331 ships of 5,490,000 GRT in overseas trade. Traffic of major ports, 1981-82, was as follows:

Port	Ships entered	Imports (1m. tonnes)	Exports (1m. tonnes)
Calcutta	811	5·02	2·0
Mumbai	2,530	9·5	3·8
Madras	962	5·1	3·6
Cochin	671	3·1	1·1
Marmagoa	339	0·8	8·1
Vishakhapatnam	401	2·9	4·8
Kandla	427	6·5	4·9
Paradip	80	0·2	1·2
New Mangalore	186	0·5	0·7
Tuticorin	276	1·7	0·2

The shipyard at Vishakhapatnam is capable of building vessels of a maximum of 21,500 DWT. Present capacity is about 64,500 DWT per year. The Cochin Shipyard can build Panamax type bulk carriers of 85,000 DWT each. On full development the capacity of the shipyard will be 2 such ships a year. Garden Reach Shipbuilders and Engineers are building bulk carriers of 26,000 DWT, ferry ships (6,000 DWT), hydrographic research ships, tugs and fast patrol craft. There are about 14,544 km navigable inland waterways, of which 10,241 km are rivers and 4,303 km canals.

Post and Broadcasting. On 31 March 1980 there were 137,000 post offices and 28,300 telegraph offices (including (1979) 2,570 licensed offices, 23,867 combined offices and 346 DTOs). Of the post offices, 117,260 were rural and 13,728 urban in 1979.

The telephone system is in the hands of the Indian Posts and Telegraphs Department. In 1981 there were 2,785,096 telephones. There were (1979) 117 telex exchanges and 16,449 subscribers.

There were (1978) 82 radio stations and 2 auxiliary centres; on 31 Dec. 1976, 17,359,710 receiver licences were in force and programmes were sent out from 155 transmitters. A communications satellite ('APPLE') went into operation in July 1981. 'Home Service' broadcasts reach 87·75% of the population. The television service was started at Delhi, 15 Sept. 1959. There were (1974) 275,424 television receiver licences. There were 7 television centres and a relay station at Pune. Entertainment films occupy 29·3% of broadcasting time, news and current affairs, 21·3%.

Cinemas. In 1976 there were 9,017 cinemas, including about 2,660 touring cinemas: about 500 feature films were produced.

Newspapers. In Dec. 1976 the total number of newspapers and periodicals was 13,320. Maharashtra published 1,948; 4,220 papers were published in Delhi, Mumbai, Calcutta and Madras. There were 875 daily and 3,801 weekly papers. Papers in 6 principal languages included 2,765 English papers with a circulation of 7,828,000; 3,289 Hindi, 7,738,000. About 115 papers claimed a circulation of over 50,000 copies; most had under 15,000. Total circulation, 34m.

Annual Report of the Register of Newspapers for India. New Delhi

JUSTICE, RELIGION, EDUCATION AND WELFARE

Justice. All courts form a single hierarchy, with the Supreme Court at the head, which constitutes the highest court of appeal. Immediately below it are the high courts and subordinate courts in each state. Every court in this chain, subject to the usual pecuniary and local limits, administers the whole law of the country, whether made by Parliament or by the state legislatures.

The states of Andhra Pradesh, Assam (in common with Nagaland, Meghalaya, Manipur and Tripura and the Union territories of Arunachal Pradesh and Mizoram), Bihar, Gujarat, Himachal Pradesh, Jammu and Kashmir, Karnataka, Kerala, Madhya Pradesh, Maharashtra, Orissa, Punjab (in common with the state of Haryana and the Union Territory of Chandigarh), Rajasthan, Tamil Nadu, Uttar Pradesh, West Bengal and Sikkim have each a High Court. The jurisdiction of Mumbai High Court extends to the Territory of Goa. There is a separate High Court for Delhi. For the Andaman and Nicobar Islands the Calcutta High Court, for Pondicherry the High Court of Madras, and for Lakshadweep the High Court of Kerala are the highest judicial authorities; in Dadra and Nagar Haveli the High Court of Mumbai is the relevant high court. The Allahabad High Court has a Bench at Lucknow, the Mumbai High Court has a Bench at Nagpur, the Madhya Pradesh High Court has Benches at Gwalior and Indore, the Patna High Court has a Bench at Ranchi and the Rajasthan High Court has a Bench at Jaipur. Judges and Division Courts of the Gauhati High Court also sit in Meghalaya, Manipur, Nagaland and Tripura. Below the High Court each state is divided into a number of districts under the jurisdiction of district judges who preside over civil courts and courts of sessions. There are a number of judicial authorities subordinate to the district civil courts. On the criminal side magistrates of various classes act under the overall supervision of the High Court.

The Code of Criminal Procedure, 1898, has been replaced by the Code of Criminal Procedure, 1973 (2 of 1974), which came into force with effect from 1 April 1974. The new Code provides for complete separation of the Judiciary from the Executive throughout India.

Police. The states control their own police force through the state Home Ministers. The Home Minister of the central government co-ordinates the work of the states and controls the Central Detective Training School, the Central Forensic Laboratory, the Central Fingerprint Laboratory as well as the National Police Academy at Mount Abu (Rajasthan) where the Indian Police Service is trained. This service is recruited by competitive examination of university graduates and provides all senior officers for the state police forces. The Central Bureau of Investigation functions under the control of the Cabinet Secretariat.

The cities of Pune, Ahmedabad, Nagpur, Bangalore, Calcutta, Madras, Mumbai and Hyderabad have separate police commissionerates.

Total sanctioned strength of police was 706,895 in 1971.

Sarkar, P. C., *Civil Laws of India and Pakistan.* 2 vols. Calcutta, 1953.—*Criminal Laws of India and Pakistan.* 2nd ed. 2 vols. Calcutta, 1956
Setalvad, M. C., *The Common Law of India.* London, 1960
Sharma, S. R., *Supreme Court in the Indian Constitution.* Delhi, 1959

Religion. The principal religions in 1971 (census) were: Hindus, 453·2m. (82·7%); Moslems, 61·4m. (11·21%); Christians, 14·2m. (2·6%); Sikhs, 10·3m. (1·89%); Buddhists, 3·8m. (0·7%); Jains, 2·6m. (0·47%).

In 1971 the Christian population consisted of 8·2m. Roman Catholics, 2·69m. Anglicans of the Church of South India, 1·37m. Anglicans of the Church of North India and about 2m. nonconformists.

Sundkler, B., *Church of South India.* London, 1954

Education. Literacy. According to the 1981 census the literacy percentage in the country (excluding age-group, 0-4) was 36 (34·45 in 1971): 46·74% among males, 24·88% among females. Of the states and territories, Chandigarh and Kerala have the highest rates.

Educational Organization. With some exceptions, education is the concurrent responsibility of state and Union governments. In the union territories it is the responsibility of the central government. The Union Government is directly responsible for the central universities and all institutions declared by parliament to be of national importance; the promotion of Hindi as the federal language; co-ordinating and maintaining standards in higher education, research, science and technology. Professional education rests with the Ministry or Department concerned, e.g., medical education, the Ministry or Department of Health. The Union Minister of Education is in overall charge of the separate Departments of Education and Culture, assisted by a Minister of State. There are several autonomous organizations attached to the Department of Education. The Central Advisory Board of Education meets periodically (in average intervals of 1 year) to recommend directions for educational policy. The University Grants Commission is a statutory body and is responsible for the funding of the central universities and some institutions deemed to be universities, besides providing developmental assistance to the state universities as well. The Commission also influences the policies and the course curricula of the universities. The National Council of Educational Research and Training provides advisory and consultancy services in respect of school education, and also produces standard school textbooks which can be used all over the country. The Union Ministry of Education is also concerned with non-formal education, youth activities, promotion of regional languages, sports, the institution of scholarships, the award of foreign scholarships, liaison with Unesco and its organizations and promoting book production.

School Education. The school system in India can be divided into four stages: pre-primary, primary, middle and high or higher secondary.

There are as yet not many pre-primary schools in India.

Primary education is imparted either at independent primary (or junior basic) schools or primary classes attached to middle or high schools. The period of instruction in this stage varies from 4 to 5 years and the medium of instruction is the mother tongue of the child or the regional language. Free education is available for all children. Legislation for compulsory education has been passed by 16 state governments and 3 Union Territories but it is not practicable to enforce compulsion and attendance is more often ensured by incentive.

The period for the middle stage varies from 2 to 3 years and instruction is given in middle classes of high schools or middle schools, the latter having, generally, primary classes attached to them.

The high-school extends from 2 to 4 years. Education is given in higher classes of high schools, which have middle or primary (or both) departments attached. English is generally taught as a compulsory subject. The medium of instruction is mostly the mother tongue or the regional language.

The eventual pattern is to be 10 years general school education and 2 years high secondary education with diversified courses.

There are, in addition, schools for professional subjects such as agriculture, commerce, fine arts, forestry, medicine, veterinary science, physical education, social service, teachers' training, technical, industrial and crafts subjects. There are also special schools for the physically and mentally handicapped and reformatory pupils. There are schools of oriental studies and adult education centres.

Higher Education. Higher education is given in arts, science or professional colleges, universities and all-India educational or research institutions. In 1979 there were 108 universities, 9 institutions of national importance and 10 institutions deemed as universities. Of the 108 universities, 7 are central: Aligarh Muslim University; Banaras Hindu University; University of Delhi; University of Hyderabad; Jawaharlal Nehru University; North Eastern Hill University; Visva Bharati. The rest are state universities.

Grants are paid through the University Grants Commission to the central universities and institutions deemed to be universities for their maintenance and development and to state universities for their development projects only; their maintenance is the concern of state governments. During 1978-79 the University Grants Commission sanctioned grants of Rs 68·95 crores.

Technical Education. The number of institutions awarding degrees in engineering and technology in 1979-80 was 149 (in 1947: 38), and those awarding diplomas in engineering and technology numbered 306 (in 1947: 53); the former admitted about 28,000, the latter about 47,500 students; enrolment in some has been less than capacity, following a period of unemployment in engineering. There were also 7 rural institutes and 30 Girls' Polytechnics with about 455 and 4,090 students respectively. For training high-level engineers and technologists 5 Institutes of Technology, the Indian Institute of Science, Bangalore, and 89 other institutions conduct postgraduate and research courses.

Adult Education. In spite of the improvement in the literacy rate, the number of adult illiterates over 14 was 210m. in 1971. Adult education is, therefore, being accorded a high priority. A National Adult Education Programme was launched on a massive scale throughout the country on 2 Oct. 1978. A provision of Rs 200 crores has been made for this programme in the Plan 1978-83. It is proposed to cover 100m. illiterate persons in the age-group 15-35. A National Board of Adult Education has been established for this purpose by the central government and similar boards have been established at the state level also. The Directorate of Adult Education, established in 1971, co-ordinates the programme with various states and is also responsible for producing teaching/learning materials, training and orientation, monitoring and evaluating the programme. Existing programmes include the rural functional literacy project, adult education programmes for urban workers, assistance to voluntary agencies working in the field of adult education. About 116,000 programmes were running in Jan. 1980.

Educational statistics for the year 1978-79:

Type of recognized institution	*No. of institutions*	*No. of students on rolls*	*No. of teachers*
Primary/junior basic schools	474,993	51,383,299	1,276,446
Middle/senior basic schools	110,902	26,671,872	821,600
High/higher secondary schools	46,859	19,552,903	759,663
Training schools and colleges	496	170,018[1]	–
Arts, Science and Commerce colleges	3,261	2,299,053[2]	–

[1] Enrolment by stages of teachers' training courses at school and college level.
[2] Enrolment by stages of all post-graduate and graduate courses.

Primary pupils represent 84·5% of the age-group 6-11; middle school pupils, 38·0% of 11s-14s; high school pupils, 18·8% of 14s-17s.

Expenditure (on recognized institutions) during the Sixth Plan (1980-85) is estimated at Rs 1,986 crores.

Health. Health programmes are primarily the responsibility of the state governments. The Union Government has sponsored and supported major schemes for disease prevention and control which are implemented nationally. These include the prevention and control of malaria, filaria, tuberculosis, leprosy, venereal diseases, smallpox, trachoma and cancer. There are also Union Government schemes in connexion with water supply and sanitation, and with nutrition. The Nutrition Advisory Committee of the Indian Council of Medical Research sponsors schemes for research and advises the Government. The National Nutrition Advisory Committee is to formulate a national nutrition policy and recommend measures for improving national standards.

Medical relief and service is primarily the responsibility of the states. In 1977 there were 5,372 primary health centres and 37,745 sub-centres. In 1975 there was 1 doctor to every 4,200 people. Medical education is also a state responsibility, but there is a co-ordinating Central Health Educational Bureau. In 1977 there were 106 medical colleges and 74 colleges for homeopathic medicine. There were 601 nursing schools. In 1977 there were 38 mental hospitals and 51 institutions for the mentally handicapped and retarded; there were 600 TB clinics.

Family planning is centrally sponsored and locally implemented. The goal is to reduce the birth-rate by means of education in family planning methods.

Health expenditure under the fifth development plan was Rs 681·66 crores, of which the greatest single item was the control of communicable diseases.

Social Security. Annual plan expenditure (estimate) 1977-78, Rs 1,286·65 lakhs: services for children in need of care, Rs 210 lakhs; assistance to voluntary organizations, Rs 375 lakhs; integrated child development services, Rs 107 lakhs; hostels for working women, Rs 161·5 lakhs; education for employment and vocational training for adult women, Rs 80 lakhs; national institute for the handicapped, Rs 65 lakhs; functional literacy, Rs 57·5 lakhs.

DIPLOMATIC REPRESENTATIVES

Of India in Great Britain (India House, Aldwych, London, WC2 4NA)
High Commissioner: Dr V. A. Seyid Mohammed.

Of Great Britain in India (Chanakyapuri, New Delhi 21, 1100-21)
High Commissioner: R. L. Wade-Gery, CMG.

Of India in the USA (2107 Massachusetts Ave., NW, Washington, D.C., 20008)
Ambassador: K. R. Narayanan.

Of the USA in India (Shanti Path, Chanakyapuri, New Delhi 21)
Chargé d'Affairs: Harry G. Barnes, Jr.

Of India to the United Nations
Ambassador: Natarajan Krishan.

Books of Reference

Special works relating to States are shown under their separate headings.

The Gazetteer of India. Central Gazetteers Unit. Delhi, 1965
India: A Reference Annual. Delhi Govt. Printer. Annual
Cambridge History of India. 6 vols. CUP, 1922-47. Supp., 1953
The Times of India Directory and Yearbook. Bombay and London. Annual
Bhatia, K., *Indira: A Biography of Prime Minister Gandhi.* New York, 1974
Cassen, R. H., *India: Population, Economy and Society.* London, 1978
Chatterjee, S. P., *Indian Climatology.* Calcutta, 1956.(ed.), *National Atlas of India (Preliminary* (Hindi) *edition*). Calcutta, 1957
Jones, W. M., *Politics Mainly Indian.* New Delhi, 1978
Kesavan, B. S., and Kulkarni, V. Y. (eds), *The National Bibliography of Indian Literature, 1901–53,* New Delhi, 1963 ff.
Hall, A., *The Emergence of Modern India.* Columbia Univ. Press, 1981
Majumdar, R. C., Raychandhuri, H. C., and Datta, K., *An Advanced History of India.* 2nd ed. London, 1950
Mitra, H. N., *The Indian Annual Register.* Calcutta, from 1953
Moraes, D., *Mrs. Gandhi.* London, 1980
Nanda, B. R. (ed.), *Socialism in India.* Delhi, Bombay, Bangalore, Kanpur, London, 1972
Pachauri, R. K., *Energy and Economic Development in India.* New York, 1977

Philips, C. H. (ed.), *The Evolution of India and Pakistan: Select Documents.* OUP, 1962 ff.– *Politics and Society in India.* London, 1963
Poplai, S. L. (ed.), *India, 1947–50* (select documents). 2 vols. Bombay and London, 1959
Smith, V. E., *Oxford History of India.* 3rd ed. OUP, 1958
Spear, P., *India: A Modern History.* 2nd ed. Univ. of Michigan Press, 1972
Sutton, S. C., *Guide to the India Office Library (founded in 1801).* HMSO, 1952
Yasdani, C. (ed.), *Early History of the Deccan.* 2 vols. London, 1960

STATES AND TERRITORIES

The Republic of India is composed of the following 22 States and 9 centrally administered Union Territories:

States	*Capital*	*States*	*Capital*
Andhra Pradesh	Hyderabad	Manipur	Imphal
Assam	Dispur	Meghalaya	Shillong
Bihar	Patna	Nagaland	Kohima
Gujarat	Ahmedabad	Orissa	Bhubaneswar
Haryana	Chandigarh	Punjab	Chandigarh
Himachal Pradesh	Simla	Rajasthan	Jaipur
Jammu and Kashmir	Srinagar	Sikkim	Gangtok
Karnataka	Bangalore	Tamil Nadu	Madras
Kerala	Trivandrum	Tripura	Agartala
Madhya Pradesh	Bhopal	Uttar Pradesh	Lucknow
Maharashtra	Bombay	West Bengal	Calcutta

Union Territories

Andaman and Nicobar Islands; Arunachal Pradesh; Chandigarh; Dadra and Nagar Haveli; Delhi; Goa, Daman and Diu; Lakshadweep; Mizoram; Pondicherry.

States Reorganization. The Constitution, which came into force on 26 Jan. 1950, provided for 9 Part A States (Assam, Bihar, Bombay, Madhya Pradesh, Madras, Orissa, Punjab, Uttar Pradesh and West Bengal) which corresponded to the previous governors' provinces; 8 Part B States (Hyderabad, Jammu and Kashmir, Madhya Bharat, Mysore, Patalia-East Punjab (PEPSU), Rajasthan, Saurashtra and Travancore-Cochin) which corresponded to Indian states or unions of states; 10 Part C States (Ajmer, Bhopal, Bilaspur, Coorg, Delhi, Himachal Pradesh, Kutch, Manipur, Tripura and Vindhya Pradesh) which corresponded to the chief commissioners' provinces; and Part D Territories and other areas (*e.g.*, Andaman and Nicobar Islands). Part A States (under governors) and Part B States (under rajpramukhs) had provincial autonomy with a ministry and elected assembly. Part C States (under chief commissioners) were the direct responsibility of the Union Government, although Kutch, Manipur and Tripura had legislatures with limited powers. Andhra was formed as a Part A State on its separation from Madras in 1953. Bilaspur was merged with Himachal Pradesh in 1954.

The States Reorganization Act, 1956, abolished the distinction between Parts A, B and C States and established two categories for the units of the Indian Union to be called States and Territories. The following were the main territorial changes: the Telugu districts of Hyderabad were merged with Andhra; Mysore absorbed the whole Kannada-speaking area (including Coorg, the greater part of 4 districts of Bombay, 3 districts of Hyderabad and 1 district of Madras); Bhopal, Vindhya Pradesh and Madhya Bharat were merged with Madhya Pradesh, which ceded 8 Marathi-speaking districts to Bombay; the new state of Kerala, comprising the majority of Malayalam-speaking peoples, was formed from Travancore-Cochin with a small area from Madras; Patalia-East Punjab was included in Punjab; Kutch and Saurashtra in Bombay; and Ajmer in Rajasthan; Hyderabad ceased to exist.

On 1 May 1960 Bombay State was divided into two parts: 17 districts (including Saurashtra and Kutch) in the north and west became the new state of Gujarat; the remainder was renamed the state of Maharashtra.

In Aug. 1961 the former Portuguese territories of Dadra and Nagar Haveli became a Union territory. The Portuguese territory of Goa and the smaller territories of Daman and Diu, occupied by India in Dec. 1961, were constituted a Union territory in March 1962. In Aug. 1962 the former French territories of Pondicherry, Karikal, Mahé and Yanaon were formally transferred to India and became a Union territory. In Sept. 1962 the Naga Hills Tuensang Area was constituted a separate state under the name of Nagaland. On 1 Nov. 1966, under the Punjab Reorganization Act 1966, a new state of Haryana and a new Union Territory of Chandigarh were created from parts of Punjab (India); for details, *see* pp. 638 and 670. On 26 Jan. 1971 Himachal Pradesh became a state. In 1972 the North East Frontier Agency and Mizo hill district were made Union territories (as Arunachal Pradesh and Mizoram) and Manipur, Meghalaya and Tripura full states. Sikkim became a state in 1975.

Report of the States Reorganization Commission. Government of India. Delhi, 1956

ANDHRA PRADESH

HISTORY. Andhra was constituted a separate state on 1 Oct. 1953, on its partition from Madras, and consisted of the undisputed Telugu-speaking area of that state. To this region was added, on 1 Nov. 1956, the Telangana area of the former Hyderabad State, comprising the districts of Hyderabad, Medak, Nizamabad, Karimnaga, Warangal, Khammam, Nalgonda and Mahbubnaga, parts of the Adilabad district and some taluks of the Raichur, Gulbarga and Bidar districts, and some revenue circles of the Nanded district. On 1 April 1960, 221·4 sq. miles in the Chingleput and Salem districts of Madras were transferred to Andhra Pradesh in exchange for 410 sq. miles from Chittoor district. The district of Prakasam was formed on 2 Feb. 1970. Hyderabad was split into 2 districts on 15 Aug. 1978. A new district, Vizianagaram, was formed in 1979.

AREA AND POPULATION. Andhra Pradesh is in south India and is bounded south by Tamil Nadu, west by Karnataka, north and northwest by Maharashtra, northeast by Madhya Pradesh and Orissa, east by the Bay of Bengal. The state has an area of 275,068 sq. km and a population (1981 preliminary) of 53·4m. Density, 194 per sq. km. Growth rate 1971-81, 22·76%. The principal language is Telugu. Cities with over 250,000 population (1981 census), see p. 610. Other large cities (1981): Nellore (236,879); Kakinada (225,151); Kurnool (190,888); Nizamabad (183,135); Eluru (168,074); Machilipatnam (138,525); Anantapur (119,536); Tenali (118,342); Tirupati (114,546); Vizianagaram (114,452); Adoni (108,849); Proddatur (106,869); Cuddapah (103,006); Bheemavaram (101,940).

CONSTITUTION AND GOVERNMENT. Andhra Pradesh has a bicameral legislature. Three regional committees composed of the elected members of Telangana, Rayalaseema and Coastal Regions are consulted by the Government on matters pertaining to those regions.

For administrative purposes there are 23 districts in the state. The capital is Hyderabad.

There are 295 seats in the Legislative Assembly and 90 in the Legislative Council. At the election of Jan. 1983, the Telegu Dasam party gained a two-thirds majority.

Governor: K. C. Abraham.
Chief Minister: N. T. Rama Rao.

BUDGET. The budget (revised) for 1981-82 showed total receipts of Rs 1,455·99 crores, and expenditure of Rs 1,377·75 crores. Budget estimates (1982–83) show receipts of Rs 1,626·27 crores and expenditure of Rs 1,544·65 crores.

ENERGY AND NATURAL RESOURCES

Electricity. There are hydro-electric plants at Machkund, Upper Sileru, Nizam

Sagar, Nellore and Kothagudam. Installed capacity, 1981, 2,298 mw., power generated 7,131m. kwh. In 1981 there were 17,509 electrified towns and villages.

Water. The irrigation potential of the state in 1980-81 was 10,300,000 hectares; actual area under irrigation, 3,460,000 hectares.

Minerals (1981).Production of principal minerals (in 1,000 tonnes): Coal, 9,800; limestone, 3,142; barytes, 340·7; iron ore (1980), 390. The state also has bauxite, asbestos, steatite, mica and chromite.

Agriculture. There were (1980-81) about 12·3m. hectares of cropped land, of which 33% is irrigated. Yield per hectare, in kg: Sugar-cane, 8,421; rice, 1,991; ground-nuts, 660; tobacco, 864; jowar, 527; cotton, 197; castor, 100.

Livestock (1979 census): Cattle, 12·03m.; Buffaloes, 7·16m.; goats, 4·4m.; sheep, 7·07m.

Forests. In 1982 it was estimated that forests occupy 23·3% of the total area of the state or 64,154 sq. km; main forest products are teak, eucalyuptus, cashew, casuarina, softwoods and bamboo.

Fisheries. Production 1980, 116,013 tonnes of marine fish and about 132,000 tonnes of inland water fish.

INDUSTRY. The main industries are textile manufacture, sugar-milling and paper-making. There is a coal-based fertilizer plant at Ramagundam. Other industries include cement, tanning and glass. There is an oil refinery at Vishakhapatnam, where India's only major shipbuilding yards are situated. There is an important fertilizer plant and a plant processing ferro-manganese. There were 8,836 registered factories in 1978-79 In 1982 a steel plant was under construction at Vishakhapatnam.

Cottage industry includes the manufacture of carpets, wooden and lacquer toys, brocades, bidriware, filigree and lace-work. The wooden toys of Nirmal and Kondapalli are particularly well known. Sericulture is developing rapidly.

Tourism is growing; the main centres are Hyderabad and Golconda.

COMMUNICATIONS

Roads. In 1980-81 there were 2,391 km of national highways, 5,996 km of state highways, 14,670 km of major district roads, 66,211 km of other roads. Number of vehicles, 1980–81: 147,969 motor cycles and scooters, 49,114 cabs and jeeps, 33,886 goods vehicles and 39,834 others.

Railways. In 1980–81 there were approximately 4,707 route-km of railway, of which 3,007 km were broad gauge.

Aviation. There are airports at Hyderabad, Tirupati, Vijayawada and Vishakapatnam, with regular scheduled services to Bombay, Delhi, Calcutta, Bangalore and Madras.

Shipping. The chief port is Vishakhapatnam. There are minor ports at Kakinada, Machilipatnam, Bheemunipatnam, Narsapur, Krishnapatnam, Vadarevu and Calingapatnam.

JUSTICE, RELIGION AND EDUCATION

Justice. The high court of Judicature at Hyderabad has a Chief Justice and 17 puisne judges.

Religion. At the 1971 census Hindus numbered 38,119,279; Moslems, 3,520,166; Christians, 1,823,436; Jains 16,103; Sikhs, 12,591; Buddhists, 10,035.

Education. In 1981, 29·94% of the population were literate (39·13% of men and 20·52% of women). There were, in 1980-81 40,408 primary schools (5,368,000 students); 4,577 upper primary (882,000); 3,706 secondary (811,000). Education is free for children up to 14.

There were 269 secondary schools attached to junior colleges, 246 junior colleges and 284 colleges. There were 53 oriental colleges and 9 universities: Osmania University, Hyderabad; Andhra University, Waltair; Sri Venkateswara University, Tirupati; Kakatiya University, Warangal; Nagarjuna University, Guntur; Sri Jawaharlal Nehru Technological University, Hyderabad; Central University, Hyderabad; A.P. Agricultural University, Hyderabad; Sri Krishnadevaraya University, Anantapur. An Open University was inaugurated at Nagarjunasagar in 1982.

ASSAM

HISTORY. Assam first became a British Protectorate at the close of the first Burmese War in 1826. In 1832 Cachar was annexed; in 1835 the Jaintia Hills were included in the East India Company's dominions, and in 1839 Assam was annexed to Bengal. In 1874 Assam was detached from Bengal and made a separate chief commissionership. On the partition of Bengal in 1905, it was united to the Eastern Districts of Bengal under a Lieut.-Governor. From 1912 the chief commissionership of Assam was revived, and in 1921 a governorship was created. On the partition of India almost the whole of the predominantly Moslem district of Sylhet was merged with East Bengal (Pakistan). Dewangiri in North Kamrup was ceded to Bhután in 1951. The Naga Hill district, administered by the Union Government since 1957, became part of Nagaland in 1962. The autonomous state of Meghalaya within Assam, comprising the districts of Garo Hills and Khasi and Jaintia Hills, came into existence on 2 April 1970, and achieved full independent statehood in Jan. 1972, when it was also decided to form a Union Territory, Mizoram, from the Mizo Hills district.

AREA AND POPULATION. Assam is in eastern India, almost separated from central India by Bangladesh. It is bounded west by West Bengal, north by Bhután and the Territory of Arunachal Pradesh, east by Nagaland, Manipur and Burma, south by Meghalaya, Bangladesh and Tripura. The area of the state is now approximately 78,523 sq km. Its population (1981 census) 19·9m. Density, 254 per sq. km. Growth rate since 1971, 36·09%. Principal towns with population (1971) are; Gauhati, 122,981; Dibrugarh, 80,344; Tinsukia, 55,392; Nowgong, 52,892; Silchar, 52,612. The principal language is Assamese.

CONSTITUTION AND GOVERNMENT. Assam has a unicameral legislature of 126 members. In Feb. 1983 elections were held despite unrest and an outbreak of communal violence against Bangladeshi immigrants. A congress (I) government was returned. The capital is Dispur.

Governor: P. Mehrotra.
Chief Minister: H. Saikia.

BUDGET. The budget estimates for 1979-80 showed total revenue receipts of Rs 271·13 crores and expenditure of Rs 277·49 crores. Outside the revenue account receipts are estimated at Rs 460·98 crores and expenditure at Rs 476·72 crores.

ENERGY AND NATURAL RESOURCES

Electricity. In 1978 there was an installed capacity of 141·5 mw and 2,260 villages (out of 21,995) with electricity. A further 583 mw capacity is to be installed by 1984. New power stations are under construction at Bongaigaon and Lakwa.

Oil. Assam contains important oilfields and produces about 50% of India's crude oil. There is also natural gas.

Water. In 1978, 88,300 hectares were irrigated and 228 projects were in hand. Intended Sixth Plan outlay, Rs 300 crores.

Minerals. Coal production (1973), 436,000 tonnes. The state also has limestone, refractory clay, dolomite, and corundum.

Agriculture. There are 756 tea plantations, and growing tea is the principal industry. Production in 1976, 276m. kg, over 50% of Indian tea. Over 72% of the cultivated area is under food crops, of which the most important is rice. Total foodgrains, 1976-77, 21·47m. tonnes. Main cash crops: jute, tea, cotton, oilseeds, sugar-cane, fruit and potatoes. Wheat has been introduced recently and yielded 71,045 tonnes in 1976-77. Cattle are important; milk production, 1976-77, 343m. litres.

Forestry. There are 1·62m. hectares of reserved forests under the administration of the Forest Department and 1,229,000 hectares of unclassed forests, altogether about 30% of the total area of the state. Revenue from forests, 1978-79, Rs 821 lakhs.

INDUSTRY. Sericulture and hand-loom weaving, both silk and cotton, are important home industries together with the manufacture of brass, cane and bamboo articles. Hand-loom weaving of silk is stimulated by state and central development schemes; outlay, Rs 18,34·5 lakhs. There is a silk-spinning mill and 2 cotton-mills. The main heavy industry is petro-chemicals; there are 3 oil refineries. Other industries include manufacturing paper, fertilizers, sugar, jute and plywood products, rice and oil milling.

COMMUNICATIONS

Roads. In 1972 there were 17,839 km of road maintained by the Public Works Department in Assam, including national highway. There were 63,616 motor vehicles in the state in 1976.

Railways. The open length of railways in 1974 was 2,193·65 km, of which 105·22 km are broad gauge.

Aviation. Daily scheduled flights connect the principal towns with the rest of India. There are airports at Gauhati, Tezpur, Jorhat, Dimapur, Silchar and Dibrugarh.

Shipping. Water transport is important in Lower Assam; the main waterway is the Brahmaputra River.

JUSTICE, RELIGION AND EDUCATION

Justice. The seat of the High Court is Gauhati. It has a Chief Justice and 6 puisne judges.

Religion. At the 1971 census Hindus numbered 10,604,618; Moslems, 3,592,124; Christians, 381,010; Buddhists, 22,565; Jains, 12,914; Sikhs, 11,920.

Education. The 1971 census showed 28·74% of the population to be literate.

In 1976 there were 26,000 primary schools; 2,504 middle schools; 1,657 high schools; 70 higher secondary schools; in 1977 there were 25,768 schools altogether, 126 general colleges and institutions for professional education, 507 vocational and technical schools, 31 teacher-training colleges and 3 universities.

Goswami, P. C., *Economic Development of Assam.* London, 1963
Reid, Sir Robert, *History of the Frontier Areas Bordering on Assam.* Shillong, 1942

BIHAR

The state contains the 2 ethnic areas of Bihar and Chota Nagpur. In 1956 certain areas of Purnea and Manbhum districts were transferred to West Bengal.

AREA AND POPULATION. Bihar is in north India and is bounded north by Nepal, east by West Bengal, south by Orissa, south-west by Madhya Pradesh and west by Uttar Pradesh. The area of Bihar is 173,876 sq. km and its population (1981 census), 69,823,154, a density of 402 per sq. km. Growth rate since 1971, 23·9%. Population of principal towns, *see* p. 610.

The official language is Hindi.

CONSTITUTION AND GOVERNMENT. Bihar has a unicameral legislature. The Legislative Assembly consists of 314 elected members. Following the elections of May 1980 (310 seats contested), Congress (I) hold 166 seats; Janata (Charan Singh), 42; CPI, 23; Bhartiya Janata, 21; Congress (U), 14; others, 68. For the purposes of administration it is divided into 5 divisions covering 23 districts. The capital is Patna; the hot-weather seat is Ranchi.

Governor: Dr A. R. Kidwai.
Chief Minister: Dr J. Mishra.

BUDGET. The budget estimates for 1981-82 show total receipts of Rs 15,221·3m and expenditure of Rs 14,443·5m.

ENERGY AND NATURAL RESOURCES

Electricity. Installed capacity (1976) 1,551 mw. There were 16,565 villages with electricity.

Minerals. Bihar is the foremost state for mineral deposits. Value of production, 1976, Rs 3,628·2m. Coal is the principal mineral; the Jharia and Bokaro fields are (with Raniganj across the West Bengal border) the most important in India. Jharia produces coking coal. Copper, of which Bihar is the only Indian producer, iron ore, ruby mica (61% of national output), chromite, manganese, kyanite and bauxite are important. The recently discovered large deposits of pyrites in the Shahabad district are being exploited.

Agriculture. About 26% of the cultivable area is irrigated. Main crops are rice, jute, sugar-cane, oilseeds, tobacco, wheat, jowar, bajra and maize; total foodgrains (1976), 9·3m. tonnes.

Livestock (1961 census): Buffaloes, 3,698,000; other cattle, 16,104,000; sheep, 1,156,000; goats, 8,671,000; horses and ponies, 133,000.

Forests cover 17% of the state.

INDUSTRY. Main plants are the Tata Iron and Steel Co., the Tata Engineering and Locomotive Co., the steel plant at Bokaro, oil refinery at Barauni and aluminium plant at Muri. Other important industries are machine tools, fertilizers, electrical engineering, sugar-milling, paper-milling, silk-spinning, manufacturing explosives and cement. There is a copper smelter at Ghatsila and a lead refining plant at Tundo. Industrial disputes lost 1·18m. man-days in 1979.

COMMUNICATIONS

Roads. In 1972 the state had 116,575 km of highway (including 88,040 km of unmetalled roads). Passenger transport has been nationalized in 7 districts. There were 123,461 motor vehicles in 1976.

Railways. The North Eastern and Eastern railways traverse the state.

Aviation. There are airports at Patna and Ranchi with regular scheduled services to Calcutta and Delhi.

Shipping. The length of waterways open for navigation is 900 miles.

JUSTICE, RELIGION AND EDUCATION

Justice. There is a High Court (constituted in 1916) at Patna with a Chief Justice, 17 puisne judges and 6 additional judges.

Police. The police force is under an inspector-general; there is 1 policeman to 1,211 of the population.

Religion. At the 1961 census Hindus numbered 39,347,050; Moslems, 5,785,631; Christians, 502,195; Sikhs, 44,413; Jains, 17,598; Buddhists, 2,885.

Education. At the census of 1981 the number of literates was 18·16m. There were, 1971, 2,581 high and higher secondary schools with 601,000 pupils, 8,025 middle schools with 965,000 pupils, 46,582 primary schools with 5,009,000 pupils. Primary schools had 144,559 teachers, higher secondary and high schools 25,740. Education is free for children aged 6-11.

There were 7 universities in academic year 1972-73; Patna University (founded 1917) with 12,577 full-time students (1970); Bihar University, Muzaffarpur (1952) with 4 constituent colleges, 35 affiliated colleges and 41,640 students (1970); Bhagalpur University (1960) with 40,746 students (1970); Ranchi University (1960) with 36,892 students (1968-69); Darbhanga Sanskrit University (1961); Magadha University, Gaya (1962) and Mithila University (1972), Darbhanga.

GUJARAT

HISTORY. On 1 May 1960, as a result of the Bombay Reorganization Act, 1960, the state of Gujarat was formed from the north and west (predominantly Gujarati-speaking) portion of Bombay State, the remainder being renamed the state of Maharashtra. Gujarat consists of the following districts of the former state of Bombay: Banas Kantha, Mehsana, Sabar Kantha, Ahmedabad, Kaira, Panch Mahals, Vadodara, Bharuch, Surat, Dangs, Amreli, Surendranagar, Rajkot, Jamnagar, Junagadh, Bhavnagar, Kutch, Gandhinagar and Bulsar.

AREA AND POPULATION. Gujarat is in western India and is bounded north by Pakistan and Rajasthan, east by Madhya Pradesh, south-east by Maharashtra, south and west by the Indian ocean and Arabian sea. The area of the state is 195,984 sq. km and the population at the 1981 census was 33,960,905; a density of 173 per sq. km. Growth rate 1971-81, 27·2%. The chief cities, *see* p. 610. Gujarati and Hindi in the Devanagari script are the official languages.

CONSTITUTION AND GOVERNMENT. Gujarat has a unicameral legislature, the Legislative Assembly, which has 181 elected members. Following the election of May 1980, Congress (I) held 140 seats; Janata, 22; Bhartiya Janata, 9; others, 10.

The capital is Gandhinagar. There are 19 districts.

Governor: Smt. S. Mukerjee
Chief Minister: M. Solanki

BUDGET. The budget estimates for 1981-82 showed a deficit of Rs 380m.

ENERGY AND NATURAL RESOURCES

Electricity. In 1979 the total generating capacity was 2,334 mw of electricity, serving 9,823 towns and villages and 185,306 wells and tube-wells. A thermal power station of 1,260 mw eventual capacity was commissioned at Vanakbori in 1981.

Oil and Gas. There were crude oil and gas reserves in 24 fields in 1978. Production: Crude oil, 4·2m. tonnes; gas, 7m. cu. metres.

Minerals. Chief minerals produced in 1978 (in tonnes) included chalk (76,030), lime stone (2·5m.), agate stone (2,897), calcite (1,428), quartz (45,689), bauxite (230,728), china clay (47,130), other clays (259,928), dolomite (195,789), crude fluorite (80,136), silica-glass sand (90,921) and lignite (134,674). Enormous reserves of coal were found under the Kalol and Mehsana oil and gas fields in May 1980. The deposit, mixed with crude petroleum, is estimated at 100,000m. tonnes, extending over 500 km.

Agriculture. Cropped area, 1973–74, was 10·5m. hectares. Area and production of principal crops, 1977-78 (in 1,000 hectares and 1,000 tonnes): Rice, 484, 669; groundnuts, 1,954, 1,723; cotton, 1,829, 1,942,000 bales of 170 kg.

Livestock (1972): Buffaloes, 3·46m.; other cattle, 6,457,284; sheep, 1,722,057; goats, 3,209,502; horses and ponies, 63,018.

Fisheries. There were (1977) about 49,227 active fishermen and (1978) 148 fishing co-operatives. There were (1978) 7,597 fishing vessels (2,545 motor vessels). The catch for 1977-78 (estimate) was 190,000 tonnes.

INDUSTRY. Gujarat is one of the 4 most industrialized states. In 1981 there were over 10,000 registered factories including over 2,000 textile factories. There were about 77 industrial estates. There were also about 35,000 small units. Principal industries are textiles, general and electrical engineering, vegetable oils, chemicals, soda ash and cement. Large fertilizer plants have been set up at Jawaharnagar, Kandla and Kalol. There is an oil refinery at Koyali near Vadodara, with a developing petro-chemical complex. Industrial production (1978) in tonnes: Cement, 2m.; soda ash, 223,400; caustic soda, 74,088; sugar, 297,288; sulphuric acid, 724,000; cotton yarn, 128,173; superphosphate, 93,370; paper and paper-board, 69,794; ceramics, 18,739; cotton cloth, 101·2m. metres; powered pumps, 77,000 (no.); diesel engines, 14,988 (no.); clocks, 151,909 (no.).

COMMUNICATIONS

Roads. In 1978 there were 42,359 km of roads. Gujarat State Transport Corporation operated 8,858 routes over 3·99 crore route-km.

Railways. In 1978 the state had 3,326 km metre gauge railway, 1,135 km narrow gauge and 1,155 km broad gauge.

Aviation. Ahmedabad is the main airport. There are 6 services daily between Bombay, Ahmedabad and Delhi. There are 8 other airports.

Shipping. The largest port is Kandla. There are 45 other ports, including Okha, Bedi, Bhavnagar, Verawal, Sikka and Porbandar.

Post. There were (1978) 7,423 post offices, 1,140 telegraph offices. Ahmedabad has direct dialling telephone connexion with Delhi, Bombay, Pune, Rajkot, Vadodara, Nadiad, Gandhinagar and Surat, and telex connexions with other cities.

JUSTICE, RELIGION, EDUCATION AND WELFARE

Justice. The High Court of Judicature at Ahmedabad has a Chief Justice and 10 puisne judges.

Religion. At the 1971 census Hindus numbered 23,835,471; Moslems, 2,249,055; Jains, 451,578; Christians, 109,341; Sikhs, 18,233; Buddhists, 5,469.

Education. In 1981 the number of literates was 14·85m. Primary and secondary education are free. In 1977-78 there were 22,806 primary schools; nearly all villages with more than 500 people have one. In 1977-78 there were 2,854 secondary schools with 956,000 pupils.

There are 6 universities in the state. Gujarat University, Ahmedabad, founded in 1949, is teaching and affiliating; it has 147 affiliated colleges. The Maharaja Sayajirao University of Vadodara (1949) is residential and teaching. The Sardar Vallabhnhai Vidyapeeth, Anand (1955) has 18 constituent and affiliated colleges. The 2 newer universities (1967) are Saurashtra University at Rajkot with 60 affiliated colleges, and South Gujarat at Surat with 35. Gujarat Vidyapeeth at Ahmedabad is of university status. In 1977-78 the total number of students was 250,000. There were also 1 agricultural and 1 Ayurvedic university.

There are 7 technical institutions for degree courses (student capacity 2,290) and 19 for diploma courses (3,950).

Health. In 1978 there were 251 primary health centres and 19,881 hospital beds. The annual intake at 5 medical colleges was 675.

Rushbrook Williams, L. F., *The Black Hills: Kutch in History and Legend.* London, 1958
Desai, I. F., *Untouchability in Rural Gujarat.* Bombay, 1977

HARYANA

HISTORY. The state of Haryana, created on 1 Nov. 1966 under the Punjab Reorganization Act, 1966, was formed from the Hindi-speaking parts of the state of Punjab (India). It comprises the districts of Hissar, Mohindergarh, Gurgaon, Rohtak and Karnal; parts of Sangrur and Ambala districts; and part of Kharar tehsil.

AREA AND POPULATION. Haryana is in north India and is bounded north by Himachal Pradesh, east by Uttar Pradesh, south and west by Rajasthan and north-west by Punjab. Delhi forms an enclave on its eastern boundary. The state has an area of 44,222 sq. km and a population (1981) of 12,850,902; density, 291 per sq. km. Growth rate, 1971-81, 28·04%. The principal language is Hindi.

CONSTITUTION AND GOVERNMENT. The state has a unicameral legislature with 90 members. After the elections of May 1982 when 89 seats were contested, Congress (I) held 36 seats; Lok Dal, 31; independents, 12 and others, 10. The state shares with Punjab (India) a High Court, a university and certain public services. The capital (shared with Punjab) is Chandigarh (*see* p. 670). There are 12 districts.

Governor: G. D. Tapase.
Chief Minister: Bhajan Lal.

BUDGET. Budget estimates for 1981-82 show income of Rs 872 crores and expenditure of Rs 921 crores.

ENERGY AND NATURAL RESOURCES

Electricity. Approximately 1,000 mw are supplied to Haryana, mainly from the Bhakra Nangar system. In 1976 installed capacity was 612 mw and all the 3,302 villages had electric power.

Minerals. Minerals include iron ore, limestone, china clay and marble. Value of production, 1976, Rs 8·6m.

Agriculture. Haryana has sandy soil and erratic rainfall, but the state shares the benefit of the Sutlej-Beas scheme. Agriculture employs over 82% of the working population; in 1981 there were about 900,000 holdings (average 3·7 hectares), and the gross irrigated area was 1·97m. hectares. Area under high-yielding varieties of foodgrains, 2·2m. hectares. During 1980-81 foodgrain production was 6·2m. tonnes; sugar (gur), oilseeds, and cotton, are important.

Forests cover 3·3% of the state.

INDUSTRY. Haryana has a large market for consumer goods in neighbouring Delhi. In 1981 there were 233 large and medium scale industries employing 100,000 and producing goods worth Rs 8,000m. There were 25,000 small units. The main industries are cotton textiles (11 mills in 1976), agricultural machinery, woollen textiles, scientific instruments, glass, cement, paper and sugar milling.

COMMUNICATIONS

Roads. There were (1971) about 13,259 km of metalled roads and 262 km unsurfaced. Road transport was nationalized by 1971; Haryana Roadways has a fleet of 725 vehicles running on 335 routes and daily carrying 125,255 passengers over 149,630 km.

Railways. The state is crossed by lines from Delhi to Agra, Ajmer, Ferozepur and Chandigarh. The main stations are at Ambala and Kurukshetra.

Aviation. There is no airport within the state but Delhi is on its eastern boundary.

JUSTICE AND EDUCATION

Justice. Haryana shares the High Court of Punjab and Haryana at Chandigarh which had (1968) a Chief Justice and 16 puisne judges.

Education. In 1981 the number of literates was 4·6m. In 1969-70 there were 5,967 schools and colleges with 1,250,590 attending. This includes 4,362 primary schools, 776 high and higher secondary schools, 777 middle schools and 47 colleges.

HIMACHAL PRADESH

HISTORY. The territory came into being on 15 April 1948 and comprised 30 former Hill States. The state of Bilaspur was merged with Himachal Pradesh in 1954. The 6 original districts were: Mahasu, Sirmur, Mandi, Chamba, Bilaspur and Kinnaur. On 1 Nov. 1966, under the Punjab Reorganization Act, 1966, certain parts of the state of Punjab (India) were transferred to Himachal Pradesh. These comprise the districts of Simla, Kulu, Kangra, and Lahaul and Spiti; and parts of Hoshiarpur and Ambala districts, with an estimated population (1967) of 1·5m.

AREA AND POPULATION. Himachal Pradesh is in north India and is bounded north by Kashmir, east by Tibet, south-east by Uttar Pradesh, south by Haryana, south-west and west by Punjab. The area of the state is 55,673 sq. km and it had a population at the 1981 census of 4,237,569. Density, 76 per sq. km. Growth rate, 1971-81, 22·46%. Principal language is Pahari.

CONSTITUTION AND GOVERNMENT. Full statehood was attained, as the 18th state of the Union, on 25 Jan. 1971.

On 1 Sept. 1972 districts were reorganized and 2 new districts created, Hamirpur and Una, making a total of 12. The capital is Simla.

There is a unicameral legislature. After the elections of May 1982 Congress (I) held 31 seats; Bhartiya Janata, 29; independents 6; Janata, 2.

Governor: A. N. Banerjee.
Chief Minister: R. Lal.

BUDGET. Budget estimates for 1980-81 showed revenue receipts of Rs 193 crores and expenditure on revenue account of Rs 161 crores. The capital account showed a deficit of Rs 73·57 crores.

ENERGY AND NATURAL RESOURCES

Electricity. In 1977 7,245 villages (out of 16,916) had electricity.

Water. An artificial confluence of the Sutlej and Beas rivers has been made, directing their united flow into Govind Sagar Lake.

Minerals. The state has rock salt, slate, gypsum, limestone, barytes, dolomite and pyrites.

Agriculture. Farming employs 76% of the people. Irrigated area is 16·7% of the area sown. Main crops are seed potatoes, wheat, maize, rice and fruits such as apples, peaches, apricots, nuts, pomegranates.

Production of foodgrains (1976) 1·13m. tonnes.

Livestock (1966 census): Buffaloes, 415,356; other cattle, 1,048,917; goats, 813,041.

Forestry. Himachal Pradesh forests cover 38·3% of the state and supply the largest quantities of coniferous timber in northern India. They are the main source of revenue of Pradesh. The forests also ensure the safety of the catchment areas of the Jumna, Sutlej, Beas, Ravi and Chenab rivers.

INDUSTRY. The main sources of employment are the forests and their related industries; there are factories making turpentine and rosin, fertilizers, cement and TV sets. There is a foundry and a brewery. Other industries include salt production and handicrafts, including weaving.

COMMUNICATIONS

Roads. The national highway from Chandigarh runs through Simla; other main highways from Simla serve Kulu, Manali, Kangra, Chemba and Pathankot. The rest are minor roads. Pathankot is also on national highways from Punjab to Kashmir. There were 9,400 motor vehicles in 1976.

Railways. There is a line from Chandigarh to Simla, and the Jammu-Delhi line runs through Pathankot.

Aviation. The state has no airport, but Chandigarh is on its southern boundary.

JUSTICE. The state has its own High Court at Simla.

EDUCATION. The number of literates in 1981 was 1·7m.

JAMMU AND KASHMIR

HISTORY. The state of Jammu and Kashmir, which had earlier been under Hindu rulers and Moslem sultans, became part of the Mogul Empire under Akbar from 1586. After a period of Afghan rule from 1756, it was annexed to the Sikh kingdom of the Punjab in 1819. In 1820 Ranjit Singh made over the territory of Jammu to Gulab Singh. After the decisive battle of Sobraon in 1846 Kashmir also was made over to Gulab Singh under the Treaty of Amritsar. British supremacy was recognized until the Indian Independence Act, 1947, when all states decided on accession to India or Pakistan. Kashmir asked for standstill agreements with both. Pakistan agreed, but India desired further discussion with the Government of Jammu and Kashmir State. In the meantime the state became subject to armed attack from the territory of Pakistan and the Maharajah acceded to India on 26 Oct. 1947, by signing the Instrument of Accession. India approached the UN in Jan. 1948; India-Pakistan conflict ended by ceasefire in Jan. 1949. Further conflict in 1965 was followed by the Tashkent Declaration on Jan. 1966. Following further hostilities between India and Pakistan a ceasefire came into effect on 17 Dec. 1971, followed by the Simla Agreement in July 1972, whereby a new line of control was delineated bilaterally through negotiations between India and Pakistan and came into force on 17 Dec. 1972.

AREA AND POPULATION. The state is in the extreme north and is bounded north by China, east by Tibet, south by Himachal Pradesh and Punjab and west by Pakistan. The area is 222,236 sq. km, of which about 78,932 sq. km is occupied by Pakistan and 42,735 sq. km by China; the population of the territory on the Indian side of the line, 1981 census, was 5,981,600. Growth rate, 1971-81, 29·57%. For the population of Srinagar, *see* p. 610. The official language is Urdu; other commonly spoken languages are Kashmiri, Dogri, Balti, Ladakhi and Punjabi.

CONSTITUTION AND GOVERNMENT. The Maharajah's son, Yuvraj Karan Singh, took over as Regent in 1950 and, on the ending of hereditary rule (17 Oct. 1952), was sworn in as Sadar-i-Riyasat. On his father's death (26 April 1961) Yuvraj Karan Singh was recognized as Maharajah by the Indian Government; he decided not to use the title while he was elected head of state.

The permanent Constitution of the state came into force in part on 17 Nov. 1956 and fully on 26 Jan. 1957. There is a bicameral legislature; the Legislative Council has 36 members and the Legislative Assembly has 76. The state of the parties in the Legislative Assembly in 1981 was: Congress, 10; National Conference, 48; Janata, 13; others, 5. Since the 1967 elections the 6 representatives of Jammu and Kashmir in the central House of the People are directly elected; there are 4 representatives in the Council of States. The Council of Ministers consists of 7 Ministers and 4 Junior Ministers.

Kashmir Province has 8 districts and Jammu Province has 6 districts. Srinagar is the summer and Jammu the winter capital.

Governor: B. K. Nehru
Chief Minister: Farooq Abdullah.

BUDGET. Budget estimates for 1980-81 show revenue of Rs 576·62 crores, and expenditure of Rs 578·37 crores.

Total planning expenditure for 1980-81 was Rs 147·48 crores., of which agriculture and allied sectors received Rs 26·38 crores; power Rs 21·25 crores; water supply Rs 16·50 crores and irrigation and flood control Rs 16·00 crores.

ENERGY AND NATURAL RESOURCES

Electricity. Installed capacity (1980) 208·78 mw.; 4,631 villages had electricity.

Minerals. Value of production, 1976, Rs 5·46m. Minerals include coal, bauxite and gypsum.

Agriculture. About 80% of the population are supported by agriculture. Rice, wheat and maize are the major cereals. The total area under food crops (1978-9) was estimated at 1,847,000 acres. Total foodgrains produced, 1980, 1·4m. quintals. Fruit is important; exports (1980-81 estimate), 360,000 tonnes.

The Agrarian Reforms Act came into force in July 1978; the Debtors Relief Act and the Restriction of Mortgage Properties Act also alleviate rural distress. The redistribution of land to cultivators is continuing.

Livestock (1977 census): Cattle, 2,138,000; buffaloes, 501,000; goats, 1,216,000; horses, 629,000, and poultry, 2,039,000.

Forestry. Forests cover about 21,080 sq. km., forming an important source of revenue, besides providing employment to a large section of the population. About 7,480 sq. km of forests yield valuable timber; state income in 1978-79 was Rs 231·1m.

INDUSTRY. The largest industrial complex is the Bari Brahmara estate in Jammu which covers 320 acres and accommodates diverse manufacturing, as does the Khanmuh estate. The Sopore industrial area in Kashmir Division is intended for industries based on horticulture. There are 6,386 small units (1980) with production valued at Rs 661·3m., employing 34,000. The main traditional handicraft industries are silk spinning and carpet-weaving.

COMMUNICATIONS

Roads. Kashmir is linked with the rest of India by the motorable Jammu-Pathankot road. The Jawahar Tunnel, through the Banihal mountain, connects Srinagar and Jammu, and maintains road communication with the Kashmir Valley during the winter months. In 1981 there were 7,866 km of roads; work on the Batote–Kishtwar road was in progress, up-grading to National Highway standard.

There were 33,361 motor vehicles in 1979-80.

Railways. Kashmir was linked with the Indian railway system on 3 Dec. 1972 when the line between Jammu and Pathankot was opened.

Aviation. Major airports, with daily service from Delhi, are at Srinagar and Jammu. Srinagar airport is being developed as an international airport.

Post. There were 1,290 post offices in 1980, 82 telephone exchanges and approximately 12,120 private telephones.

JUSTICE, RELIGION, EDUCATION AND WELFARE

Justice. The High Court, at Srinagar and Jammu, has a Chief Justice and 4 puisne judges.

Religion. The majority of the population, except in Jammu, are Moslems. At the 1971 census Moslems numbered 3,040,129; Hindus, 1,404,292; Sikhs, 105,873; Buddhists, 57,956; Christians, 7,182; Jains, 1,150.

Education. The proportion of literates was 18·59% in 1980. Education is free. There are (1981) 9,715 schools and about 953,000 children attend. Jammu and Srinagar Universities (founded 1948) have 37 teaching departments and 42 affiliated colleges. There are 2 medical colleges, an engineering college, 1 agricultural college, 2 polytechnics, 12 professional colleges, 8 oriental colleges and an Ayurvedic college.

Health. In 1979-80 there were 43 hospitals, 279 primary health units, 279 sub-centres, about 530 clinics and dispensaries, and 50 other units. There were 800 doctors. Expenditure on health was Rs 27·15 in 1980-81. There is a National Institute of Medical Sciences under construction.

Bamzai, P. N. K., *A History of Kashmir.* Delhi, 1962
Gupta, S., Kashmir: *A Study in IndiaPakistan Relations.* London, 1967

KARNATAKA

HISTORY. The state of Karnataka, constituted as Mysore under the States Reorganization Act, 1956, brought together the Kannada-speaking people distributed in 5 states, and consisted of the territories of the old states of Mysore and Coorg, the Bijapur, Kanara and Dharwar districts and the Belgaum district (except one taluk) in former Bombay, the major portions of the Gulbarga, Raichur and Bidar districts in former Hyderabad, and South Kanara district (apart from the Kasaragod taluk) and the Kollegal taluk of the Coimbatore district in Madras. The state was renamed Karnataka in 1973.

AREA AND POPULATION. The state is in south India and is bounded north by Maharashtra, east by Andhra Pradesh, south by Tamil Nadu and Kerala, west by the Indian ocean and north-east by Goa. The area of the state is 191,773 sq. km, and its population (1981 census), 37,043,451, an increase of 26·43% since 1971. Density, 193 per sq. km. Kannada is the language of administration and is spoken by about 60% of the people. Other languages include Telugu (8·7%), Urdu (8·6%), Marathi (4·5%), Tamil (3·6%), Tulu and Konkani. Principal cities, *see* p. 610.

CONSTITUTION AND GOVERNMENT. Karnataka has a bicameral legislature. The Legislative Council has 63 members. The Legislative Assembly consists of 223 elected members and 1 nominated member. After elections in Jan. 1983 the Janata party formed a government supported by Bharatiya Janata.

The state has 19 districts (of which Coorg is one) in 4 divisions: Bangalore, Mysore, Belgaum and Gulbarga. The capital is Bangalore.

Governor: Govind Narain.
Chief Minister: Ramakrishna Hegde.

BUDGET. Budget estimates for 1981-82 showed a deficit of Rs 461·1m.

ENERGY AND NATURAL RESOURCES

Electricity. In 1980 the state's installed capacity was to be revised (by the Kalinadi project) to 2,000 mw.

Water. About 2m. hectares were irrigated in 1980.

Minerals. Karnataka has India's only sources of gold and silver. The estimated reserves of high grade iron ore are 5,000m. tonnes. These reserves are found mainly in the Chitradurga belt. The National Mineral Development Corporation of India has indicated total reserves of nearly 1,000m. tonnes of magnesite and iron ore (with an iron content ranging from 25 to 40) which have been found in Kudremukh Ganga-Mula region in Chickmagalur District. The estimated reserves of manganese are over 100m. tonnes.

Limestone is found in many regions; deposits are about 1,500m. tonnes.

Karnataka is the largest producer of chromite. It is one of the only two states of

India producing magnesite. The other minerals of industrial importance are corundum and garnet.

Agriculture. Agriculture forms the main occupation of more than three-quarters of the population. Physically, Karnataka divides itself into four regions–the coastal region, the southern and northern 'maidan' or plain country, comprising roughly the districts of Bangalore, Tumkur, Chitaldrug, Kolar, Bellary, Mandya and Mysore, and the 'malnad' or hill country, comprising the districts of Chickmagalur, Hassan and Shimoga. Rainfall is heavy in the 'malnad' tracts, and in this area there is dense forest. The greater part of the 'maidan' country is cultivated. Coorg district is essentially agricultural.

The main food crops are rice and jowar, and ragi which is also about 30% of the national crop. Sugar, groundnut, castor-seed, safflower, mulberry silk and cotton are important cash crops. The state grows about 70% of the national coffee crop.

In 1975-76, 7·48m. hectares were under foodgrains (production, 5·53m. tonnes); other crops included oilseeds (950,000 tonnes), cotton (700,000 bales of 180 kg), arecanut (66,100 tonnes), chillies, tobacco, sugar-cane and rubber. Yield of raw rubber from 1,120 hectares, 2 tonnes per day. There were, in 1977, 730,241 hectares under cotton, 730,240 under groundnuts, 963,017 under rice, 1·8m. under jowar, 9·14m. under ragi and 362,713 under wheat.

Livestock (1977): Buffaloes, 3,215,873; other cattle, 10,018,714; sheep, 662,420; goats, 726,016.

Forestry. Total forest in the state (1979) is 18% of the land area, producing sandal wood, bamboo and other timbers, and ivory.

INDUSTRY. The Visvesvaraya Iron and Steel Works is situated at Bhadravati, while at Bangalore are national undertakings for the manufacture of aircraft, machine tools, light engineering and electronics goods. Other industries include textiles, vehicle manufacture, cement, chemicals, sugar, paper, porcelain and soap. In addition, much of the world's sandalwood is processed, the oil being one of the most valuable productions of the state. Sericulture is a more important cottage industry giving employment, directly or indirectly, to about 2·4m. persons; production is about 3,000 tonnes, over two-thirds of national production. Industrial production, 1972 (tonnes): Iron, 180,637; steel, 290,307; paper, 71,618; cement, 1·2m. and sugar, 254,000.

COMMUNICATIONS

Roads. In 1977 the state had 89,496 km of roads. There were 195,483 motor vehicles in 1976.

Railways. In 1976 there were 2,803 km of railway (including 154 km of narrow gauge) in the state.

Aviation. There are airports at Bangalore, Mangalore and Belgaum, with regular scheduled services to Bombay, Calcutta, Delhi and Madras.

Shipping. Mangalore is a deep-water port for the export of mineral ores. Karwar is being developed as an intermediate port.

JUSTICE, RELIGION AND EDUCATION

Justice. The seat of the High Court is at Bangalore. It has a Chief Justice and 11 puisne judges.

Religion. At the 1971 census Hindus numbered 25,332,388; Moslems, 3,113,298; Christians, 613,026; Jains, 218,862; Buddhists, 114,139; Sikhs, 6,830.

Education. The number of literates, according to the 1981 census, was 14·2m. In 1977 the state had 33,137 primary schools, 2,326 high schools, 314 schools for professional and technical education and 30 polytechnic and engineering schools. Education is free up to pre-university level.

The University of Mysore (founded in 1916) at Mysore has 3 university colleges at Mysore and 134 affiliated colleges. Karnatak University (1950) at Dharwar has 4 constituent colleges and 95 affiliated colleges. Bangalore University (1964) has 46 constituent colleges, the University of Agricultural Sciences, Hebbal, Bangalore, (1964) has 3 constituent colleges.

The Indian Institute of Science. Bangalore, is unaffiliated; it conducts diploma courses in engineering, metallurgy and technology. There are 415 other colleges, including medical, law and commercial.

Learmouth, A. T. A., and Bhat, L. T., *Mysore State*. 2 vols. London, 1961-62

KERALA

HISTORY. The state of Kerala, created under the States Reorganization Act, 1956, consists of the previous state of Travancore-Cochin, except for 4 taluks of the Trivandrum district and a part of the Shencottah taluk of Quilon district. It took over the Malabar district (apart from the Laccadive and Minicoy Islands) and the Kasa ragod taluk of South Kanara (apart from the Amindivi Islands) from Madras State.

AREA AND POPULATION. Kerala is in south India and is bounded north by Karnataka, east and south-east by Tamil Nadu, south-west and west by the Indian ocean. The state has an area of 38,855 sq. km. The 1981 census showed a population of 25,403,217; density of population was 654 per sq. km (highest of any state). Growth rate, 1971-81, 19%. Population of principal cities, *see* p. 610.

Languages spoken in the state are Malayalam, Tamil and Kannada.

The physical features of the land fall into three well-marked divisions: (1) the hilly tracts undulating from the Western Ghats in the east and marked by long spurs, extensive ravines and dense forests; (2) the cultivated plains intersected by numerous rivers and streams; and (3) the coastal belt with dense coconut plantations and rice fields.

CONSTITUTION AND GOVERNMENT. The state has a unicameral legislature of 140 members including the Speaker. After the elections of May 1982 the Indira Congress Party held 77 seats, the Democratic Front (CPI, CPI (M) and allies), 63.

The state has 12 districts. The capital is Trivandrum.

Governor: J. Vencatachellum.
Chief Minister: K. Karunakaran.

BUDGET. Budget estimates for 1980-81 showed revenue account receipts of Rs 591 crores, expenditure Rs 575 crores. Total receipts, Rs 1,491·79 crores; total expenditure, Rs 1,523·54 crores. Annual Plan expenditure, Rs 206·60 crores. The estimated budget deficit, 1981-82, was Rs 85m.

ENERGY AND NATURAL RESOURCES

Electricity. Installed capacity (1979), 1,011·5 mw.; energy generated in 1978-79 was 4,730·4m. kw. Stage I of the Idukki hydro-electric plant has a capacity of 390 mw, the Sabarigiri scheme 300mw.

Minerals. Next to Bihar, Kerala possesses the widest variety of economic mineral resources among the Indian States. The beach sands of Kerala contain monazite, ilmenite, rutile, zircon, sillimanite, etc. There are extensive whiteclay deposits; other minerals of commercial importance include mica, graphite, limestone, quartz sand and lignite. Iron ore has been found at Kozhikode (Calicut). Value of mineral production, 1976, Rs 11·5m.

Agriculture. The chief agricultural products of the state are rice, tapioca, coconut, arecanut, cashewnut, oilseeds, pepper, sugarcane, rubber, tea, coffee and cardamom. About 98% of Indian black pepper and about 95% of Indian rubber is produced in Kerala. Area and production of principal crops, 1978-79 (in 1,000 hectares and 1,000 tonnes): Rice, 799·2, 1,270; black pepper, 108·3, 25·1; ginger (dry), 11, 28; arecanut, 62·8, 10,576 (million nuts); bananas and other plantains, 50·9, 615·9; cashewnuts, 135·5, 89·7; coconuts, 678·6, 3,075 (million nuts); tea, 36·1, 47·2; coffee, 51·7, 21·7; rubber, 214·4, 123·6; tapioca, 289·8, 4,226; cardamom, 51·9, 2·9.

Livestock (1972, provisional); Buffaloes, 469,515; other cattle, 2,855,856; sheep, 10,390; goats, 1,450,587.

Forestry. About a third of the area is comprised of forests, including teak, sandal wood, ebony and blackwood and varieties of softwood. Forest revenue, 1978-79, Rs 26·2 crores, from timber, bamboos, reeds and ivory.

Fisheries. Fishing is a flourishing industry; the catch in 1979 was about 398,000 tonnes.

INDUSTRIES. Most of the major industrial concerns are either owned or sponsored by the Government. The Government owns 11 industrial concerns and has substantial shares in more than 40. Among the privately owned factories are the numerous cashew and coir factories. Other important factory industries are rubber, tea, tiles, oil, textiles, ceramics, fertilizers and chemicals, zinc-smelting, sugar, cement, rayon, glass, matches, pencils, monazite, ilmenite, titanium oxide, rare earths, aluminium, electrical goods, paper, shark-liver oil, etc.

The number of factories registered under the Factories Act 1948 on 31 Dec. 1978 was 7,784, with daily average employment of 272,392. Man-days lost by industrial disputes in 1979, 3·51m.

Among the cottage industries, coir-spinning and handloom-weaving are the most important, forming the means of livelihood of a large section of the people. Other industries are the village oil industry, ivory carving, furniture-making, bell metal, brass and copper ware, leather goods, screw-pines, mat-making, rattan work, bee-keeping, pottery, etc. These have been organized on a co-operative basis.

COMMUNICATIONS

Roads. In 1979 there were 90,440 km of roads in the state; national highways, 838 km. There were 154,595 motor vehicles in 1979.

Railways. There is a coastal line from Mangalore (Karnataka) which serves Mahe, Kozhikode (Calicut), Ernakulam (for Cochin) and Quilon, and connects them with main towns in Tamil Nadu. In 1980 there were 806 km broad gauge and 113 km metre gauge lines.

Aviation. There are airports at Cochin and Trivandrum with regular scheduled services to Bombay and Madras.

Shipping. Port Cochin, administered by the central government, is one of India's 6 major ports. There are 10 other ports and harbours.

JUSTICE, RELIGION AND EDUCATION

Justice. The High Court at Ernakulam has a Chief Justice and 11 puisne judges and 4 additional judges.

Religion. At the 1971 census Hindus numbered 12,683,277; Christians, 4,494,089; Moslems, 4,162,718; Jains, 3,336.

Education. Kerala is the most literate Indian State–with 17m. literates at the 1981 census. Education is free up to the age of 14.

In 1979–80 there was a total school enrolment of 5·59m. students. There were 7,013 lower primary schools 2,739 upper primary schools and 1,680 high schools. About 62% of schools are privately run.

Kerala University (established 1937) at Trivandrum, is affiliating and teaching; in 1979 it had 79 affiliated arts and science colleges and 25 affiliated professional colleges. The University of Cochin is federal, and for post-graduate studies only. The University of Calicut (established 1968) is teaching and affiliating and has 65 affiliated colleges. Kerala Agricultural University (established 1971) has 3 constituent colleges.

MADHYA PRADESH

HISTORY. Under the provisions of the States Reorganization Act, 1956, the State of Madhya Pradesh was formed on 1 Nov. 1956. It consists of the 17 Hindi districts of the previous state of that name, the former state of Madhya Bharat (except the Sunel enclave of Mandsaur district), the former state of Bhopal and Vindhya Pradesh and the Sironj subdivision of Kotah district, which was an enclave of Rajasthan in Madhya Pradesh.

For information on the former states, *see* THE STATESMAN'S YEAR-BOOK, 1958, pp. 180-84.

AREA AND POPULATION. The state is in central India and is bounded north by Rajasthan and Uttar Pradesh, east by Bihar and Orissa, south by Andhra Pradesh and Maharashtra, west by Gujarat. Madhya Pradesh is the largest Indian state in size, with an area of 442,841 sq. km. In respect of population it ranks sixth. Population (1981 census), 52,138,467, an increase of 25·15% since 1971. Density, 118 per sq. km.

Cities with over 250,000 population, *see* pp. 000–000. Other large cities (1981): Sagar, 207,401; Bilaspur, 186,885; Ratlam, 156,490; Burhanpur, 141,142; Mudwari-Katni, 125,096; Khandwa, 114,463; Rewa, 100,519.

The number of persons speaking each of the more prevalent languages (1971 census) were: Hindi, 32,873,079; Urdu, 988,275; Marathi, 1,385,952; Gujarati, 155,723.

CONSTITUTION AND GOVERNMENT. Madhya Pradesh is one of the 9 states for which the Constitution provides a bicameral legislature, but the Vidhan Parishad or Upper House (to consist of 90 members) has yet to be formed. The Vidhan Sabha or Lower House has 320 elected members. Following the election of May 1980 (318 seats contested), Congress (I) held 245; Bhartiya Janata, 59; others, 14.

For administrative purposes the state has been split into 11 divisions with a Commissioner at the head of each; the headquarters of these are located at Bhopal, Bilaspur, Gwalior (2), Hoshangabad, Indore, Jabalpur, Raipur, Rewa, Sagar and Ujjain. There are 45 districts.

The seat of government is at Bhopal.

Governor: B. D. Sharma.
Chief Minister: A. Singh.

BUDGET. Budget estimates for 1982–83 showed total revenue of Rs 14,26,51·83 lakhs, and expenditure of Rs 12,68,30 lakhs. Receipts included: Contributions and adjustments between central and state governments, Rs 4,84,55·97 lakhs; taxes on income, Rs 81,92 lakhs; state excise, Rs 68,63·70 lakhs; stamps and registration, Rs 26,45 lakhs; forests, Rs 1,95,00 lakhs; sales tax, Rs 2,40,96 lakhs; vehicles taxes, Rs 26,11 lakhs; debt services, Rs 77,49·27 lakhs; civil administration, Rs 22,39·68 lakhs; land revenue, Rs 12,98·00 lakhs. Expenditure included: Education, Rs 2,11,24·16 lakhs; public works and improvements, Rs 55,26·89 lakhs; irrigation, embankment, etc., Rs 40,24·01 lakhs; medical, and public health, Rs 1,34,46·65 lakhs; police, Rs 83,32·72 lakhs; agriculture, Rs 40,94·18 lakhs; general administration, Rs 20,13·25 lakhs; debt services, Rs 1,19,05·35 lakhs; community projects and local development, Rs 65,80·76 lakhs; industries, Rs 16,41·25 lakhs; forests, Rs 1,05,66·69 lakhs; social security and welfare, Rs 71,88·49 lakhs.

ENERGY AND NATURAL RESOURCES

Electricity. Madhya Pradesh is rich in low-grade coal suitable for power generation, and also has immense potential hydro-electric energy. The present installed capacity is 1,630·5 mw; of this 193 mw from hydro-electric power stations. The thermal power stations are at Korba in Bilaspur district, Amarkantak in Shahdol district and Satpura in Betul district; new stations are being built. The only hydro-electric power station is at Gandhi Sagar lake in Mandsaur district; this, with a maximum water surface of 165 sq. miles, is the biggest man-made lake in Asia.

Water. Major irrigation projects include the Chambal Valley scheme (started in 1952 with Rajasthan) which irrigates some 700,000 acres, the Tawa project in Hoshangabad district (750,000 acres), the Barna and Hasdeo schemes, the Mahanadi canal system (140,000) and schemes under construction (Bargi, Narmadasagar, and Bansagar). Up to the end of the planning year 1979–80 the state had an irrigation potential of 30·85 lakh hectares.

Minerals. The state has extensive mineral deposits including coal (35% of national deposits), iron ore (30%) and manganese (50%), bauxite (44%), ochre, sillimanite, limestone, dolomite, rock phosphate, copper, lead, tin, fluorite, barytes, china clay and fireclay, corundum, gold, diamonds, pyrophyllite and diaspore, lepidolite, asbestos, vermiculite, mica, glass sand, quartz, felspars, bentonite and building stone.

In 1980 the output of major minerals was (in tonnes): Coal, 25·1m.; limestone, 6·53m.; dolomite, 770,000; diamonds, 14,432 carats; bauxite, 470,000; iron ore, 9·7m.; manganese ore, 270,000. Value of production, 1980, Rs 3,626m.

Agriculture. Agriculture is the mainstay of the state's economy and 80% of the people are rural. Over 42% of the land area is cultivable, of which 11·5% is irrigated. The Malwa region abounds in rich black cotton soil, the low-lying areas of Gwalior, Bundelkhand and Baghelkhand and the Chhatisgarh plains have a lighter sandy soil, while the Narmada valley is formed of deep rich alluvial deposits. Production of principal crops, 1980–81 (in tonnes): Foodgrains, 12·4m.; sugar-cane (gur), 107,000; oilseeds, 608,000, and cotton, 268,000 bales (of 170 kg).

Livestock (1977 census): Buffaloes, 5,852,549; other cattle, 34,256,725; sheep, 968,595; goats, 6,573,467; horses and ponies, 121,908.

Forestry. In 1982 was 155,411 sq. km, or about 35% of the state's area is covered by forests. The forests are chiefly of sal, saja, bija, bamboo and teak. They are the chief source in India of best-quality teak; they also provide firewood for about 60% of domestic fuel needs, and form valuable watershed protection.

INDUSTRY. The major industries are the steel plant at Bhilai, Bharat Heavy Electricals at Bhopal, the aluminium plant at Korba, the security paper mills at Hoshangabad, the Bank Note Press at Dewas, the newsprint mill at Nepanagar and alkaloid factory at Neemuch, cement factories, vehicle factory, ordnance factory, and gun carriage factory. There are also 23 textile mills, 7 of them nationalized.

The Bhilai steel plant near Durg is one of the 6 major steel mills. A power station at Korba (Bilaspur) with a capacity of 420 mw serves Bhilai, the aluminium plant and the Korba coalfield.

The heavy electricals factory was set up by the Government of India at Bhopal during the second-plan period. This is India's first heavy electrical equipment factory and also one of the largest of its type in Asia. It makes a variety of highly complicated equipment required for generation, transmission, distribution and utilization of electric power.

Other industries include cement, sugar, straw board, paper, vegetable oil, refractories, potteries, textile machinery, steel casting and rerolling, industrial gases, synthetic fibres, drugs, biscuit manufacturing, engineering, tools, rayon and art silk. The number of heavy and medium industries in the state is 193, with 181 ancillary industries; the number of small-scale industries in production is 77,360. Thirty-nine out of 45 districts in the state are categorized as industrially backward districts.

The main industrial development agencies are Madhya Pradesh Financial Corporation, Madhya Pradesh Audyogik Vikas Nigam Ltd, Madhya Pradesh State Industries Corporation, Madhya Pradesh Laghu Udyog Nigam, Madhya Pradesh State Textile Corporation, Madhya Pradesh Handicrafts Board, Khadi and Village Industries Board and Madhya Pradesh State Mining Corporation.

The state is known for its traditional village and home crafts such as handloom weaving, best developed at Chanderi and Maheshwar, toys, pottery, lacework, woodwork, zari work, leather work and metal utensils. The ancillary industries of dyeing, calico printing and bleaching are centred in areas of textile production.

COMMUNICATIONS

Roads. Total length of roads in 1982 was 65,889 km, of which 50,934 km were surfaced. In 1977–78 there were 225,278 motor vehicles.

Railways. Bhopal, Bilaspur, Katni, Khandwar and Ratlam are important junctions for the central and northern networks.

Aviation. There are airports at Bhopal, Indore, Jabalpur, Khajuraho and Raipur with regular scheduled services to Bombay, Calcutta and Delhi.

JUSTICE, RELIGION AND EDUCATION

Justice. The High Court of Judicature at Jabalpur has a Chief Justice and 21 puisne judges.

Religion. At the 1971 census Hindus numbered 39,024,162; Moslems, 1,815,685; Christians, 286,072; Buddhists, 81,823; Sikhs, 98,973.

Education. The 1981 census showed 14·5m. people to be literate. Education is free for children aged up to 14.

In 1975–76 there were 355 higher educational institutions. Primary schools (1974–75) had 3·5m. pupils and higher secondary schools, 620,897 pupils.

There are 10 universities in Madhya Pradesh: the University of Sagar (established 1946), at Sagar, had 53 affiliated colleges and 26,516 students in 1975; Jabalpur University (1957) had 30 affiliated colleges and 12,962 students; Vikram University (1957), at Ujjain, had 46 affiliated colleges and 38,011 students; Indira Kala Sangeet Vishwavidyalaya (1956), at Khairagarh, had 9 affiliated colleges and 1,164 students on roll (this university teaches music and fine arts); Indore University (1964) had 21 affiliated colleges and 22,915 students; Jivagi University (1963), at Gwalior, had 43 affiliated colleges and 31,462 students; Jawaharlal Nehru Krishi University (1964), at Jabalpur, had 9 affiliated colleges and 2,274 students in 1964; Ravishankar University (1964), at Raipur, had 63 affiliated colleges and 41,607 students. In 1975-76 there were 256 degree-granting colleges, 19 teacher-training colleges, and 71 professional colleges including polytechnics.

MAHARASHTRA

HISTORY. Under the States Reorganization Act, 1956, Bombay State was formed by merging the states of Kutch and Saurashtra and the Marathi-speaking areas of Hyderabad (commonly known as Marathwada) and Madhya Pradesh (also called Vidarbha) in the old state of Bombay, after the transfer from that state of the Kannada-speaking areas of the Belgaum, Bijapur, Kanara and Dharwar districts which were added to the state of Mysore, and the Abu Road taluka of Banaskantha district, which went to the state of Rajasthan.

By the Bombay Reorganization Act, 1960, which came into force 1 May 1960, 17 districts (predominantly Gujarati-speaking) in the north and west of Bombay State became the new state of Gujarat, and the remainder was renamed Maharashtra.

The state of Maharashtra consists of the following districts of the former Bombay

State: Ahmednagar, Akola, Amravati, Aurangabad, Bhandara, Bhir, Buldana, Chanda, Dhulia (West Khandesh), Greater Bombay, Jalgaon (East Khandesh), Kolaba, Kolhapur, Nagpur, Nanded, Nasik, Osmanabad, Parbhani, Pune, Ratnagiri, Sangli, Satara, Sholapur, Thana, Wardha, Yeotmal; certain portions of Thana and Dhulia districts have become part of Gujarat.

AREA AND POPULATION. Maharashtra is in central India and is bounded north and east by Madhya Pradesh, south by Andhra Pradesh, Karnataka and Goa, west by the Indian ocean and north-west by Daman and Gujarat. The state has an area of 307,762 sq. km. The population at the 1981 census was 62,693,898 (an increase of 24·36% since 1971), of whom about 30m. were Marathi-speaking. Density, 204 per sq. km. The area of Greater Bombay (or Mumbai) was 603 sq. km. and its population 5,970,575. For other principal cities, *see* p. 610.

CONSTITUTION AND GOVERNMENT. Maharashtra has a bicameral legislature. The Legislative Council has 78 members. The Legislative Assembly has 287 elected members and 1 member nominated by the Governor to represent the Anglo-Indian community. Following the election of May 1980 Congress (I) held 186 seats; Congress (U), 47; Janata, 17; Bhartiya Janata, 14; others, 24.

The Council of Ministers consists of the Chief Minister, 13 other Ministers, 12 Ministers of State and 5 Deputy Ministers.

The capital is Bombay, also called Mumbai.

Governor: Sadiq Ali.
Chief Minister: Vasantrao Patil.

BUDGET. Budget estimates, 1980–81, show revenue receipts of Rs 1,921·97 crores, revenue account expenditure Rs 1,857·39 crores. Capital account receipts, Rs 799·03 crores; expenditure, Rs 873·33 crores. The estimates for 1981–82 showed a deficit of Rs 291m.

ENERGY AND NATURAL RESOURCES

Electricity. Installed capacity, 1981, 3,858 mw. (2,351 mw. thermal, 1,297 mw. hydro-electricity and 210 mw. nuclear).

Minerals. Value of production, 1976, Rs 26·7m. The state has coal, chromite, limestone, iron ore, manganese, bauxite.

Agriculture. About 10% of the cropped area is irrigated. Area (in 1,000 hectares) and production (in 1,000 tonnes) of principal crops in 1973–74: Rice, 1,351, 1,637; wheat, 965, 547; jowar, 6,088, 2,819; bajri, 2,215, 850; total cereals, 11,091, 6,177; total pulses, 2,762, 868; total foodgrains, 13,853, 7,045; sugar-cane, 215 (of gur, 1,544); groundnuts, 758, 566; cotton, 2,348 (1,058 bales of 180 kg). Total foodgrains, 1976, 9,119,000 tonnes. Cash crops, 1976: Sugarcane, 2m. tonnes; cotton, 781,000 bales (of 180 kg); groundnuts, 671,000 tonnes.

Livestock (1972 census): Buffaloes, 3,300,746; other cattle, 14,705,147; sheep, 2,128,036; goats, 5,910,554; horses and ponies, 58,287; poultry, 12,216,567.

Forestry. Forests occupy 17·4% of the state.

INDUSTRY. Industry is concentrated mainly in Mumbai, Pune and Thana. The main groups are chemicals and products, textiles, electrical and non-electrical machinery, petroleum and products, and food products. The state industrial development corporation had invested Rs 840m. in 57 industrial estates by 1980.

COMMUNICATIONS

Roads. On 31 March 1975 there were 89,007 km of roads, of which 41,484 km were surfaced. There were 432,901 motor vehicles in 1976. Passenger and freight transport has been nationalized.

Railways. The total length of railway is about 5,162 km. The main junctions and termini are Mumbai, Manmad, Akola, Nagpur, Pune and Sholapur.

Aviation. The main airport is Mumbai, which has national and international flights. Nagpur airport is on the route from Mumbai to Calcutta and there are also airports at Pune and Aurangabad.

Shipping. Maharashtra has a coastline of 720 km. Mumbai is the major port, and there are 42 minor ports.

JUSTICE, RELIGION AND EDUCATION

Justice. The High Court has a Chief Justice and 27 judges. There are 8 additional judges. The seat of the High Court is Mumbai, but it has a bench at Nagpur.

Religion. At the 1961 census Hindus numbered 32,530,901; Moslems, 3,034,332; Buddhists, 2,789,501; Christians, 560,594; Jains, 485,672; Sikhs, 57,617.

Education. The number of literates, according to the 1981 census, was 29·6m.

The total number of recognized institutions in 1975 was 56,656, with 10,528,258 students. Higher and secondary schools numbered 6,579 with 2,986,636 pupils; primary schools, 48,018, with 7,367,045 pupils; pre-primary schools, 827 with 62,781.

Mumbai University, founded in 1857, is mainly an affiliating university. It has 99 constituent colleges and 21 post-graduate departments in Mumbai with a total (1975-76) of 137,922 students. Colleges in Goa can affiliate to Mumbai University. Nagpur University (1923) is both teaching and affiliating. In addition to the 26 post-graduate departments there were (1975-76) 140 affiliated colleges and constituent colleges with 87,153 students. Pune University, founded in 1948, is teaching and affiliating; in 1975-76 it had 103 affiliated colleges and constituent colleges, 26 post-graduate departments and a total of 88,232 students. The SNDT Women's University had, in 1975-76, 16 constituent colleges and affiliated colleges with a total of 9,911 students. Marathwada University, Aurangabad, was founded in 1958 as a teaching and affiliating body to control colleges in the Marathwada or Marathi-speaking area, previously under Osmania University; in 1975-76 there were 82 affiliated and constituent colleges and 6 post-graduate departments and 71,419 students. Shiwaji University, Kolhapur, was established in 1963 to control affiliated colleges previously under Pune University. In 1975-76 it had 84 affiliated and constituent colleges and 14 post-graduate departments and 65,526 students. There are 4 agricultural universities with 16 affiliated colleges and 6,114 students in 1975-76. There were altogether 682 institutions for higher education in 1975-76, with 474,067 students.

Statistical Information: The Director of Publicity, Sachivalaya, Mumbai.

Annual Statistical Abstract (from 1951)

MANIPUR

HISTORY. Formerly a state under the political control of the Government of India, Manipur, on 15 Aug. 1947, entered into interim arrangements with the Indian Union and the political agency was abolished. The administration was taken over by the Government of India on 15 Oct. 1949 under a merger agreement, and it is centrally administered by the Government of India through a Chief Commissioner. In 1950-51 an Advisory form of Government was introduced. In 1957 this was replaced by a Territorial Council of 30 elected and 2 nominated members. Later in 1963 a Legislative Assembly of 30 elected and 3 nominated members was established under the Government of Union Territories Act 1963. Because of the unstable party position in the Assembly, it had to be dissolved on 16 Oct. 1969 and President's Rule introduced. The status of the administrator was raised from Chief Commissioner to Lieut.-Governor with effect from 19 Dec. 1969. On the 21 Jan. 1972 Manipur became a state and the status of the administrator was changed from Lieut.-Governor to Governor.

AREA AND POPULATION. The state is in north-east India and is bounded north by Nagaland, east by Burma, south by Burma and Mizoram, and west by Assam. Manipur has an area of 22,356 sq. km and a population (1981) of 1,433,691. Density, 64 per sq. km. Growth rate, 1971-81, 33·65%. The valley, which is about 1,813 sq. km, is 2,600 ft above sea-level. The hills rise in places to nearly 10,000 ft, but are mostly about 5,000–6,000 ft. The average annual rainfall is 65 in. The hill areas are inhabited by various hill tribes who constitute about one-third of the total population of the state. There are about 40 tribes and sub-tribes falling into two main groups of Nagas and Kukis. A large number of dialects are spoken, while Hindi is gradually becoming prevalent.

CONSTITUTION AND GOVERNMENT. With the attainment of statehood, Manipur has a Legislative Assembly of 60 members, of which 19 are from reserved tribal constituencies. There are 6 districts. Capital, Imphal (population, 1971, 100,366). Presidential rule was imposed in Feb. 1981.

Governor: L. P. Singh.

BUDGET. Revised estimates for 1977-78 show revenue of Rs 4,247·82 lakhs and expenditure on revenue account of Rs 4,774·24 lakhs.

ENERGY AND NATURAL RESOURCES

Electricity. Installed capacity, 1977-78, 104 mw. There were 212 villages with electricity.

Agriculture. Rice is the principal crop; production, 1977-78, 179,130 tonnes from 299,980 hectares. Total foodgrains, 1977-78, 193,670 tonnes.

INDUSTRY. Handloom weaving is a popular industry. Many development schemes are in progress under the 5-year plans.

COMMUNICATIONS. A national highway from Kazirangar (Assam) runs through Imphal to the Burmese frontier. There are no railways. There is an airport at Imphal with regular scheduled services to Gauhati and Calcutta.

EDUCATION AND HEALTH

Education. The 1981 census gave the number of literates as 600,000. In 1976-77 there were 3,467 primary schools, 337 middle schools, 235 high and higher schools and 20 colleges. There were 36 trade and vocational training colleges. The number enrolled at the schools and colleges was 333,868.

Health. In 1977-78 there were 33 hospitals (including primary health centres) and 125 dispensaries (including primary health centres).

MEGHALAYA

HISTORY. The state was created under the Assam Reorganization (Meghalaya) Act 1969 and inaugurated on 2 April 1970. Its status was that of a state within the State of Assam until 21 Jan. 1972 when it became a fully independent state of the Union. It consists of the former Garo Hills district and United Khasi and Jaintia Hills district of Assam.

AREA AND POPULATION. Meghalaya is bounded north and east by Assam, south and west by Bangladesh. In 1981 (census figure) the area was 22,489 sq. km and the population 1,327,824. Density 59 per sq. km. Growth rate, 1971-81, 31·25%. The people are mainly of the Khasi, Jaintia and Garo tribes.

CONSTITUTION AND GOVERNMENT. Meghalaya has a unicameral legislature. The Legislative Assembly has 60 seats.

There are 2 districts. The capital is Shillong.

Governor: L. P. Singh.
Chief Minister: D. D. Dohpugh.

BUDGET. Budget estimates for 1981-82 showed a deficit of Rs 6·6m. Annual Plan expenditure, Rs 464·5m.

ENERGY AND NATURAL RESOURCES

Electricity. Total installed capacity (1977) was 65·2 mw. 388 villages had electricity.

Minerals. The United Khasi and Jaintia Hills district produces coal, sillimanite (95% of India's total output), limestone, white clay and corundum. The state also has deposits of coal (estimated reserves 1,200m. tonnes), limestone (2,100m.), fire clay (100,000) and sandstone which are virtually untapped because of transport difficulties. Value of production, 1976, Rs 3·26m.

Agriculture. About 80% of the people depend on agriculture, and 27% of the cultivable area is irrigated. Principal crops are potatoes, fresh fruit and cotton. Production 1978 (in 1,000 tonnes): Foodgrains, 130; potatoes, 71; tapioca, 5; jute, 50,000 bales (of 180 kg). Annual production (in 1,000 tonnes, estimated) of pineapples, 70; oranges, 80; bananas, 35.

Forest products are the state's chief resources.

INDUSTRY. Apart from agriculture the main source of employment is the extraction and processing of minerals; there are also important timber processing mills.

COMMUNICATIONS. A national highway from Gauhati (Assam) runs through Dispur and Shillong. The state has no railways. There is no airport but Gauhati airport is on the northern boundary.

JUSTICE. There is a High Court at Shillong which is common to Assam, Meghalaya, Nagaland, Manipur, Tripura and the Union Territories of Mizoram and Arunachal Pradesh.

NAGALAND

HISTORY. The territory was constituted by the Union Government in Sept. 1962. It comprises the former Naga Hills district of Assam and the former Tuensang Frontier division of the North-East Frontier Agency; these had been made a Centrally Administered Area in 1957, administered by the President through the Governor of Assam. In Jan. 1961 the area was renamed and given the status of a state of the Indian Union, which was officially inaugurated on 1 Dec. 1963.

For some years a section of the Naga leaders sought independence. Military operations from 1960 and the prospect of self-government within the Indian Union led to a general reconciliation, but rebel activity continued. A 2-month amnesty in mid1963 had little effect. A 'ceasefire' in Sept. 1964 was followed by talks between a Government of India delegation and rebel leaders. The peace period was extended and the 'Revolutionary Government of Nagaland' (a breakaway group from the Naga Federal Government) was dissolved in 1973. Further talks with the Naga underground movement resulted in the Shillong Peace Agreement of Nov. 1975.

AREA AND POPULATION. The state is in the extreme north-east and is bounded west and north by Assam, east by Burma and south by Manipur. Nagaland has an area of 16,527 sq. km and a population (1981) census) of 773,281. Density 47 per sq. km. Growth rate, 1971-81, 49·73%. Towns include Kohima, Mokokchung, Tuensang and Dimapur. The chief tribes in numerical order are: Angami, Ao, Sema, Konyak, Chakhesang, Lotha, Phom, Khiamngan, Chang, Yimchunger, Zeliang-Kuki, Rengma and Sangtam.

CONSTITUTION AND GOVERNMENT. An Interim Body (Legislative Assembly) of 42 members elected by the Naga people and an Executive Council (Council of Ministers) of 5 members were formed in 1961, and continued until the State Assembly was elected in Jan. 1964. The initial strength of this Assembly was 46, with 8 cabinet ministers. Since 1974 there have been 60 members. The Governor has extraordinary powers, which include special responsibility for law and order. On 5 June 1980 a Naga National Democratic Party government took office.

The state has 7 districts (Kohima, Mon, Zunheboto, Wokha, Phek, Mokokchung and Tuensang). The capital is Kohima.

Governor: S. M. H. Burney.
Chief Minister: S. C. Jamir.

BUDGET. Budget estimates for 1974-75 show total revenue of Rs 47,43·32 lakhs and expenditure of Rs 47,53·19 lakhs. Receipts included: Statutory grant under the Finance Commission award, Rs 23,77 lakhs; share of central taxes and duties, Rs 1,17·18 lakhs; grants-in-aid for plan expenditure, Rs 6,40·80 lakhs; loans from the Government of India, Rs 71·20 lakhs; grant for roads, Rs 3,64·94 lakhs.

ENERGY AND NATURAL RESOURCES

Electricity. Installed capacity (1976) 2,126 kw; 273 towns and villages (out of 814) had electricity in 1981.

Agriculture. More than 80% of the people derive their livelihood from agriculture. The Angamis, in Kohima district, practise a fixed agriculture in the shape of terraced slopes, and wet paddy cultivation in the lowlands. In the other two districts there is a traditional form of shifting cultivation (*jhumming*). About 1,223,000 hectares were under cultivation in 1977. Production of rice (1977) was 94,530 tonnes.

Forests cover 17·56% of the state.

INDUSTRY. There is a forest products factory at Tijit; a paper-mill (100 tonnes daily capacity) and a distillery unit. There is also a sugar-mill (1,200 tonnes daily capacity). There are also over 600 small units.

COMMUNICATIONS. There is a national highway from Kaziranga (Assam) to Kohima and on to Manipur. There were 3,502 motor vehicles in 1976. There are no railways, and no airports.

RELIGION AND EDUCATION

Religion. At the 1971 census Christians numbered 344,798; Hindus, 59,031; Moslems, 2,966; others, 108. The Naga Baptist Christian Convention had, 1969, 632 churches and a total church membership of 73,500.

Education. The 1981 census records 300,000 literates, or 41·9%: 49·16% of men and 33·72% of women. In 1980 there were 3 government and 3 private colleges, 50 government and 47 private high schools, 201 government and 84 private middle schools and 1,109 primary schools, 1 polytechnic, 1 agricultural college, 2 law colleges. The North Eastern Hill University opened in 1978.

Aram, M., *Peace in Nagaland,* New Delhi, 1974

ORISSA

HISTORY. Orissa, ceded to the Mahrattas by Alivardi Khan in 1751, was conquered by the British in 1803. In 1803 a board of 2 commissioners was appointed to administer the province, but in 1805 it was designated the district of Cuttack and was placed in charge of a collector, judge and magistrate. In 1829 it was split up into 3 regulation districts of Cuttack, Balasore and Puri, and the non-regulation tributary states which were administered by their own chiefs under the ægis of the British Government. Angul, one of these tributary states, was annexed in 1847, and with the Khondmals, ceded in 1835 by the tributary chief of the Boudh state, constituted a separate non-regulation district. Sambalpur was transferred from the Central Provinces to Orissa in 1905. These districts formed an outlying tract of the Bengal Presidency till 1912, when they were transferred to Bihar, constituting one of its divisions under a commissioner. Orissa was constituted a separate province on 1 April 1936, some portions of the Central Provinces and Madras being transferred to the old Orissa division.

The rulers of 25 Orissa states surrendered all jurisdiction and authority to the Government of India on 1 Jan. 1948, on which date the Provincial Government took over the administration. The administration of 2 states, viz., Saraikella and Kharswan, was transferred to the Government of Bihar in May 1948. By an agreement with the Dominion Government, Mayurbhanj State was finally merged with the province on 1 Jan. 1949. By the States Merger (Governors' Provinces) Order, 1949, the states were completely merged with the state of Orissa on 19 Aug. 1949.

EVENTS. Serious flooding in Aug. 1982 caused the deaths of about 1,000 people.

AREA AND POPULATION. Orissa is in eastern India and is bounded north by Bihar, north-east by West Bengal, east by the Bay of Bengal, south by Andhra Pradesh and west by Madhya Pradesh. The area of the state is 155,707 sq. km, and its population (1981 census), 26,370,271, density 169 per sq. km. Growth rate, 1971-81, 20·17%. The second-largest city next to Cuttack (327,412) is Rourkela (322,610). The principal language is Oriya.

CONSTITUTION AND GOVERNMENT. The Legislative Assembly has 147 members. State of the parties in Sept. 1982: Congress (I), 118; Janata (Charan Singh), 13; others, 16.

The state consists of 13 districts.

The capital is Bhubaneswar (18 miles south of Cuttack).

Governor: C. M. Poonacha.
Chief Minister: J. B. Patnaik.

BUDGET. Budget estimates, 1980-81 showed total revenue of Rs 1,257·3 crores and expenditure of Rs 1,235·6 crores (capital and revenue accounts).

ENERGY AND NATURAL RESOURCES

Electricity. The Hirakud Dam Project on the river Mahanadi (started 1949) irrigates 628,000 acres and has a scheduled capacity of 270,000 kw. The dam (the largest earth dam in the world) was completed in 1957. Hydro-electric power totalling 85,000 kw. is now serving a large part of the state. The installed capacity of the Machkund hydro-electric project (financed jointly with Andhra Pradesh) is 114,750 kw. Total installed capacity, 1979, 923 mw.; there were 20,953 electrified villages in 1981.

Minerals. Orissa is India's leading producer of chromite (95% of national output), dolomite (50%), manganese ore (25%), graphite (80%), iron ore (16%), fire-clay (34%), limestone (20%), and quartz-quartzite (18%). Production in 1980 (1000 tonnes): iron ore, 7,019; manganese ore, 568; chromite, 261; coal, 3,042; limestone, 2,591; dolomite, 761; fire-clay, 100; china clay, 31; graphite, 32; quartz and quartzite, 53; lead ore, 40. About 56,000 workers are employed in the mines. Value of mineral production annually is about Rs 900m.

Agriculture. The cultivation of rice is the principal occupation of nearly 80% of the population. Production amounted to 4·44m. tonnes in 1978-79; only a very small amount of other cereals is grown. Production of foodgrains (1978-79) totalled 5·7m. tonnes from 6·7m. hectares. Jute (439,000 tonnes), wheat (110,000 tonnes), oilseeds (426,950 tonnes) and sugar-cane (281,000 tonnes) are also grown. Turmeric is cultivated in the uplands of the districts of Ganjam, Phulbani and Koraput, and is exported.

Livestock (1977 census): Buffaloes, 1,358,451; other cattle, 12·1m.; sheep, 1·5m.; goats, 3·4m.; horses and ponies, 3,675.

Forests. Forests occupy about 43% of the area of the state, the most important species being sal, teak, kendu, sandal, sisu, bija, kuruma, kongada and bamboo.

Fisheries. There were, in 1981, 484 fishery co-operative societies.

INDUSTRY. Fifty-five large industries have been set up (1978-79), mostly based on minerals, including the steel plant of Hindustan Steel Ltd at Rourkela, a pig-iron plant at Barbil, a ferrochrome plant, 2 ferromanganese plants at Joda and Rayagada, 1 ferrosilicon plant at Theruvelli and an aluminium smelter plant at Hirakud, 4 refractory plants and 2 cement plants. There are 3 large paper mills at Rayagada, Chowdwar and Brajrajnagar, two fertilizer plants, a caustic soda plant, a salt manufacturing unit and an industrial explosives plant. An aluminium-alumina plant at Damanjodi was begun in 1981.

Other industries of importance are sugar, glass, aluminium, heavy machine tools, a re-rolling mill and textile mills.

There are cottage and small-scale industries in the state, e.g., handloom weaving and the manufacture of baskets, wooden articles, hats and nets; silver filigree work and hand-woven fabrics are specially well known.

TOURISM. Tourist traffic is concentrated mainly on the 'Golden Triangle', Konark, Puri and Bhubaneswar, and its temples. Tourists also visit Gopalpur, the Similipal Forest and Chilka Lake.

COMMUNICATIONS

Roads. On 31 March 1980 length of roads was: State highway, 2,821 km; national highway, 1,631 km; major district roads, 4,974 km; other district roads, 2,748 km; village roads, about 5,796 km. There were 94,156 motor vehicles in 1979. A 144-km expressway, part national highway, connects the Daitari mining area with Paradip Port.

Railways. The total length of railway in 1979 was 1,948 km, of which 1,310 km was single line.

Aviation. There is an airport at Bhubaneswar with regular scheduled services to New Delhi, Calcutta, Vizag and Hyderabad.

Shipping. Paradip was declared a 'major' port in 1966 and has been developed to handle 4m. tons of traffic. Other minor ports at Chandbali and Gopalpur.

JUSTICE, RELIGION AND EDUCATION

Justice. The High Court of Judicature at Cuttack has a Chief Justice and 6 puisne judges.

Religion. There were in 1971: Hindus (including scheduled castes and scheduled tribes), 21,121,056; Christians, 378,888; Moslems, 326,507; Sikhs, 10,204; Buddhists, 8,462; Jains, 6,521.

Education. The percentage of literates in the population is 34·12% (males, 46·9%, females, 21·11%).

In 1981-82 there were 32,797 primary, 7,413 middle English and 2,466 high schools.

Utkal University was established in 1943 at Cuttack and moved to Bhubaneswar in 1962; it is both teaching and affiliating. It has 2 university colleges (law) and 113 affiliated colleges. Berhampur University has 20 affiliated colleges and Orissa University of Agriculture and Technology 4 constituent colleges. Sambalpur University has 42 affiliated colleges. Sri Jagannath Sanskrit Viswavidyalaya University was established in 1981 for oriental studies.

PUNJAB (INDIA)

HISTORY. The Punjab was constituted an autonomous province of India in 1937. In 1947, the province was partitioned between India and Pakistan into East and West Punjab respectively, under the Indian Independence Act, 1947, the boundaries being determined under the Radcliffe Award. The name of East Punjab was changed to Punjab (India) under the Constitution of India. On 1 Nov. 1956 the erstwhile states of Punjab and Patiala and East Punjab States Union (PEPSU) were integrated to form the state of Punjab. On 1 Nov. 1966, under the Punjab Reorganization Act, 1966, the state was reconstituted as a Punjabi-speaking state comprising the districts of Gurdaspur (excluding Dalhousie), Amritsar, Kapurthala, Jullundur, Ferozepore, Bhatinda, Patiala and Ludhiana; parts of Sangrur, Hoshiarpur and Ambala districts; and part of Kharar tehsil. The remaining area comprising an area of 18,000 sq. miles and an estimated (1967) population of 8·5m. was shared between the new state of Haryana and the Union Territory of Himachal Pradesh. The existing capital of Chandigarh was made the joint capital of Punjab and Haryana.

EVENTS. The Akali Dal party intensified a campaign for Sikh autonomy in autumn 1982; violent incidents took place in Amritsar, the Sikh holy city.

AREA AND POPULATION. The Punjab is in north India and is bounded at its northernmost point by Kashmir, north-east by Himachal Pradesh, south-east by Haryana, south by Rajasthan, west and north-west by Pakistan. The area of the state is 50,376 sq. km, with census (1981) population of 16,669,755. Density 331 per sq. km. Growth rate, 1971-81, 23·01%. The largest cities, *see* p. 610. The official language is Punjabi.

CONSTITUTION AND GOVERNMENT. Punjab (India) has a unicameral legislature of 117 members. The Legislative Council was abolished in Jan. 1970. The Legislative Assembly was composed as follows after the election of May 1980: Congress (I), 64; Akali Dal, 36; others, 17.

There are 12 districts. The capital is Chandigarh (*see* p. 670). There are 104 municipalities, 118 community development blocks and 9,331 elected village *panchayats.*

Governor: (Vacant).
Chief Minister: D. Singh.

BUDGET. Budget estimates, 1980-81, showed a deficit of Rs 70 crores. Annual Plan outlay, 1981-82, Rs 113·52 crores.

ENERGY AND NATURAL RESOURCES

Electricity. Installed capacity, 1979, was 1,541 mw; all villages had electricity.

Agriculture. About 75% of the population depends on agriculture. Agricultural prosperity is mainly due to irrigation. The irrigated area rose from 2·21m. hectares in 1950-51 to 5·5m. hectares in 1978-79: total production of foodgrains rose from 1·99m. tonnes to 11·9m. tonnes in 1980-81. Production in 1,000 tonnes (area in 1,000 hectares) in 1980-81: Wheat, 7,677 (2,812); maize, 605 (378); rice, 3,223 (1,178); oil-seeds, 167 (220); sugar-cane (gur), 397 (72); cotton, 605,000 bales (of 180 kg) from 1,178 hectares.

Livestock (1972 census): Buffaloes, 3,839,200; other cattle, 3·41m.; sheep and goats, 1,205,400; horses and ponies, 54,700; poultry, 3m.

Forestry. In 1981 there were 260,235 hectares of forest land, of which 130,008 hectares belonged to the Forest Department.

INDUSTRY. In Jan. 1981 the number of registered factories in the Punjab (India) was 7,397; 7,053 operational factories employed about 210,735 people. The chief manufactures are textiles (especially woollen hosiery), sewing machines, sports goods, sugar, starch, fertilizers, bicycles, scientific instruments, electrical goods, machine tools and pine oil. In 1981 there were 61,667 important small manufacturing units.

COMMUNICATIONS

Roads. The total length of metalled roads on 31 March 1980 was 33,288 km. State transport services cover 671,000 route km daily with a fleet of 2,776 buses carrying a daily average of 1m passengers. Coverage by private operators is estimated as 40%. In 1978 there were 276,748 motor vehicles.

Railways. The Punjab possesses an extensive system of railway communications, served by the Northern Railway. Total length, (1980) 3,511·4 km.

Aviation. There is an airport at Amritsar, and Chandigarh airport is on the north-eastern boundary; both have regular scheduled services to Delhi.

JUSTICE, RELIGION, EDUCATION AND WELFARE

Justice. The Punjab and Haryana High Court exercises jurisdiction over the states of Punjab and Haryana and the territory of Chandigarh. It is located in Chandigarh. It consists (1981) of a Chief Justice and 19 puisne judges.

Religion. At the 1971 census Hindus numbered 5,037,235; Sikhs, 8,159,172; Moslems, 114,447; Christians, 162,202; Jains, 21,383; Buddhists, 1,374.

Education. Compulsory education was introduced in April 1961; at the same time free education was introduced up to 8th class for boys and 9th class for girls as well as fee concessions. The aim is education for all children of 6-11.

In 1980 there were 17,784 primary schools, 1,432 middle schools and 2,313 higher secondary schools.

Punjab University was established in 1947 at Chandigarh as an examining, teaching and affiliating body. It is shared with Haryana and Himachal Pradesh. In 1962 Punjabi University was established at Patiala and an agricultural university at Ludhiana. Guru Nanak University has been established at Amritsar to mark the 500th anniversary celebrations for Guru Nanak Dev, first Guru of the Sikhs. Altogether there are 202 affiliated colleges, 160 for arts and science, 18 for teacher training, 8 medical, 2 dental, 2 engineering and 12 for other studies.

Health. Punjab claims the longest life expectancy (57·9 years for women, 58·5 for men) and lowest death rate (8·9 per 1,000). There were (1980) 254 hospitals, 467 Ayurvedic and Unani hospitals and dispensaries, 129 primary health centres and 1,485 dispensaries.

Singh, Khushwant, *A History of the Sikhs.* 2 vols. Princeton and OUP, 1964-67

RAJASTHAN

HISTORY. As a result of the implementation of the States Reorganization Act, 1956, the erstwhile state of Ajmer, Abu Taluka of Bombay State and the Sunel Tappa enclave of the former state of Madhya Bharat were transferred to the state of Rajasthan on 1 Nov. 1956, whereas the Sironj subdivision of Rajasthan was transferred to the state of Madhya Pradesh.

AREA AND POPULATION. Rajasthan is in north-west India and is bounded north by Punjab, north-east by Haryana and Uttar Pradesh, east by Madhya Pradesh, south by Gujarat and west by Pakistan. The area of the state is 342,214 sq. km and its population census (1981), 34,102,912, density 100 per sq. km. Growth rate, 1971-81, 32·36%. The chief cities, *see* p. 610.

CONSTITUTION AND GOVERNMENT. There is a unicameral legislature, the Legislative Assembly, having 200 members. The state of the parties in the Assembly after the election of May 1980, was: Congress (I), 137; Bhartiya Janata, 32; Janata, 8; Janata (Charan Singh), 7; others, 16.

The capital is Jaipur. There are 26 districts.

Governor: K. D. Sharma.

Chief Minister: S. Charan Mathur.

BUDGET. Budget estimates for 1979-80 show total revenue receipts of Rs 798·48 crores, and expenditure of Rs 854·92 crores. Receipts included: share in Central taxes, Rs 154·19 crores; state excise, Rs 21·54 crores, sales tax, Rs 133 crores; vehicles taxes, Rs 9·07 crores; non-tax revenue, Rs 245·46 crores. Expenditure included: Education, Rs 125·54 crores; water and power, Rs 184·43 crores; medical and public health, Rs 41·97 crores; agriculture, Rs 126·03 crores. Budget estimates 1980-81 showed a deficit of Rs 58·04 crores; gross Plan expenditure, Rs 348·36 crores (of which Rs 193·45 crores were for irrigation and power).

ENERGY AND NATURAL RESOURCES

Electricity. Installed capacity in 1979-80, 1,150 mw. By Aug. 1979, 12,651 villages and 160,366 wells had electric power.

Minerals. The state is rich in minerals. In 1976, 7m. tonnes of gypsum and 581,000 tonnes of rock phosphate were produced. Other minerals include silver, asbestos, felspar, copper, limestone and salt. Total value of principal mineral production in 1977 was about Rs 44 crores. Lead-zinc reserves have been found near Rampura-Agucha, estimated at 45m. tonnes.

Agriculture. The sown area is (1977-78) about 16·9m. hectares, of which 3·1m. is irrigated. Production of principal crops (in 1,000 tonnes), 1977-78: Rabi, 4,777; pulses (Kharif), 2,374; sugar-cane (gur), 2,825; total oilseeds, 224; cotton, 479,000 bales (of 180 kg). Total foodgrains, 1977, 7,480. Tractors numbered 36,250 in 1978-79.

Livestock (1977): Buffaloes, 4,592,489; other cattle, 12,469,509; sheep, 8,557,295; goats, 12,162,441; horses and ponies, 48,089; poultry, 1,235,036.

INDUSTRY. In 1979 there were 5,049 (1,949 in 1965) factories subject to the Factories Act, 1948. In Jan. 1979 there were 31,292 small industrial units employing 203,819; 121 industrial estates were developed. Total capital investment in small units, Rs 1,179m. Chief manufactures are cotton textiles, cement, glass and sugar. Production, 1977 estimate: Cloth, 69m. metres; yarn, 33m. kg; cement, 208,750 tonnes; sugar, 35,190 tonnes.

COMMUNICATIONS

Roads. In 1978-79 there were 39,194 km of roads including 10,893 km of unsurfaced roads in Rajasthan; there were 2,110 km of national highway. Motor vehicles numbered 238,114 in 1978.

Railways. Jodhpur, Marwar, Udaipur, Ajmer, Jaipur and Sawai Madhopur are important junctions of the north-western network.

Aviation. There are airports at Jaipur, Jodhpur and Udaipur with regular scheduled services to Mumbai and Delhi.

JUSTICE, RELIGION, EDUCATION AND WELFARE

Justice. The seat of the High Court is at Jodhpur. There is a Chief Justice and 11 puisne judges. There is also a bench of 5 judges at Jaipur.

Religion. At the 1971 census Hindus numbered 23,093,895; Moslems, 1,778,275; Jains, 513,548; Sikhs, 341,182; Christians, 30,202.

Education. The proportion of literates to the total population was 19·07% at the 1971 census.

In 1977-78 enrolment in 27,141 schools was 3,545,000; primary schools had 1·59m. students, 5,031 middle schools had 1m. students and 1,814 secondary and higher schools had 673,466. Elementary education is free but not compulsory. The percentage in 1977-78 of children attending schools in the age-group 6-11 was 57·29 (40·9 in 1961), in the 11-14 age-group 27·22 (14·4).

In 1980-81 there were 120 colleges. Enrolment at these and at the 3 universities was 135,543. Rajasthan University, established at Jaipur in 1947, is teaching and affiliating; Jodhpur University and Udaipur University were founded in 1962. There are also 2 agricultural colleges, 1 veterinary and animal science college, 2 engineering colleges, 3 Ayurvedic colleges and 7 polytechnics. There is 1 music college.

Health. In 1980 there were 1,169 hospitals and dispensaries, 232 primary health centres, 59 Unani, 63 homoepathic and 2 naturopathy hospitals. There were 104 maternity centres, and 2,425 Ayurvedic hospitals and dispensaries. There were 5 medical colleges and a nursing college.

SIKKIM

HISTORY. Sikkim became the twenty-second state of the Indian Union in May 1975. It is inhabited chiefly by the Lepchas, who are a tribe indigenous to Sikkim with their own dress and language, the Bhutias, who originally came from Tibet, and the Nepalis, who entered from Nepal in large numbers in the late 19th and early 20th century. The main languages spoken are Bhutia, Lepcha and Khaskura (Nepali). Being a small country Sikkim had frequently been involved in struggles over her territory, and as a result her boundaries have been very much reduced over the centuries. In particular the Darjeeling district was acquired from Sikkim by the British East India Company in 1839. The Namgyal dynasty had been ruling Sikkim since the 14th century; the first consecrated ruler was Phuntsog Namgya I who was consecrated in 1642 and given the title of 'Chogyal', meaning 'King ruling in accordance with religious laws', derived from Cho–religion and Gyalpo–king. The last Chogyal was deposed in 1975 and died in America in 1982.

Sikkim is a land of wide variation in altitude, climate and vegetation, and is known for the great number and variety of birds, butterflies, wild flowers and orchids to be found in the different regions. It is a fertile land and to the Sikkimese is known as Denjong, The Valley of Rice.

AREA AND POPULATION. Sikkim is in the Eastern Himalayas and is bounded north by Tibet, east by Tibet and Bhutan, south by West Bengal and west by Nepal. Area, 7,298 sq. km. Census population (1981), 314,999, of whom 36,768 lived in the capital, Gangtok. Density 43 per sq km. Growth rate, 1971-81, 50·01%.

CONSTITUTION AND GOVERNMENT. Sikkim was joined to the British Empire by a treaty in 1886 until 1947, but that relationship ceased when Britain withdrew from India in 1947. Thereafter there was a standstill agreement between India and Sikkim until a treaty was signed on 5 Dec. 1950 between India and Sikkim by which Sikkim became a protectorate of India and India undertook to be responsible for Sikkim's defence, external relations and strategic communications. The Chogyal had governed Sikkim with the help of the Sikkim Council, consisting of 18 elected members and 6 members nominated by the Chogyal. Sikkim parties represented were: National Party, Sikkim National Congress and, later, Sikkim Janta Congress.

Political reforms were demanded by the National Congress and the Janta Congress in March-April 1973 and Indian police took over control of law and order at the request of the Chogyal. On 13 April it was announced that the Chogyal had agreed to meet most of the political demands. Elections were held in April 1974 to a popularly-elected assembly. By the Government of Sikkim Act, June 1974, the Chogyal became a constitutional monarch with power of assent to the Assembly's legislation. By the Constitution (Thirty-Sixth Amendment) Act 1974 Sikkim became a state associated with the Indian Union. The office of Chogyal was abolished in April 1975. By the Constitution (Thirty-Eighth Amendment) Act 1975 Sikkim became the twenty-second state of the Indian Union. The Assembly has 32 members with a cabinet of 8 ministers including the Chief Minister. The Janata Parishad party, which merged with the Congress (I) party in July 1981, holds 23 seats, the Sikkim Revolutionary Congress party holds 7, Sikkim Prajatantra Congress holds 1, Independents, 1.

Governor: J. H. Taleyarkhan.
Chief Minister. N. Bahadur Bhandari.

The official language of the Government is English. Lepcha, Bhutia and Nepali have also been declared official languages.

Sikkim is divided into 4 districts for administration purposes, Gangtok, Mangan, Namchi and Gyalshing being the headquarters for the Eastern, Northern, Southern and Western districts respectively. Each district is administered by a District Collector. Within this framework are the Panchayats or Village Councils, representing the villages.

ECONOMY

Planning. The sixth Five-Year Plan began in 1980.

Budget. The annual budget for 1981-82 is Rs 23·13 crores.

ENERGY AND NATURAL RESOURCES

Electricity. There are 4 operational hydro-electric power stations; the Lagyap project is also being implemented by the Government of India as aid to meet the growing demand for electrical power for new industries. The first of its two 6 mv generators was commissioned 1 Sept. 1979.

Agriculture. The economy is mainly agricultural; main crops are rice, maize, millet, cardamom (a spice), mandarin oranges, apples, potatoes, ginger and soybean. A tea plantation has recently been started. Forests occupy about 1,000 sq. km. of the land area (excluding hill pastures) and the potential for a timber and wood-pulp industry is being explored. Some medicinal herbs are exported.

INDUSTRY AND TRADE

Industry. There is a state Industrial Development Investment Corporation and an Industrial Training Institute offering 7 trades. There is a distillery at Rangpo and a fruit preservation factory at Singtam. Copper, zinc and lead are mined by the Sikkim Mining Corporation. A recent survey by the Geological Survey of India and the Indian Bureau of Mines has confirmed further deposits of copper, zinc, silver and gold in Dikchu, North Sikkim. There is a jewel-bearing factory for the production of industrial jewels. A watch factory has been set up in collaboration with Hindustan Machine Tools (India). A number of small manufacturing units for leather, wire nails, storage cells batteries, candles, safety matches and carpets, are already producing in the private sector. Local crafts include carpet weaving, making handmade paper, wood carving and silverwork. To encourage trading in indigenous products, particularly agricultural produce, the State Trading Corporation of Sikkim has been established.

Tourism. There is great potential for the tourist industry; a 78-bed lodge at Gangtok and a 50-bed tourist lodge in West Sikkim have been opened. Tourism has been stimulated by the opening of new roads from Pemayangtse to Yuksam in West Sikkim and from Yuksam to the Dzongri Glacier.

COMMUNICATIONS

Roads. There are 1,355 miles of motorable roads, all on mountainous terrain, and 200 major bridges under the Public Works Department. Public transport and road haulage is nationalized.

Railways. The nearest railhead is at Siliguri (72 miles from Gangtok).

Aviation. The nearest airport is at Bagdogra (80 miles from Gangtok).

Post and Broadcasting. There are 790 telephones (1977) and 32 wireless stations. A radio broadcasting station, Akashvani Gangtok, was built in 1981.

RELIGION, EDUCATION AND WELFARE

Religion. The state religion is Mahayana Buddhism, but a large proportion of the population is Hindu. There are some Christians, Moslems and members of other religions.

Education. At the 1981 census there were 100,000 literates. Sikkim has 100 pre-primary schools, 321 primary schools, 44 junior high schools, 29 high schools, 8 higher secondary schools. Education is free up to class XII. There are 500 adult education centres. There is also a training institute for primary teachers, a law college and a degree college. Estimated spending on education, 1980-81, Rs 29·78m. (Rs 6·4m. in 1975).

Health. There are (1981) 4 district hospitals at Singtam, Gyalshing, Namchi and Mangan, and one central referral hospital at Gangtok, besides 15 primary health centres, 49 sub-centres and 8 dispensaries, a maternity ward, chest clinic and 2 blocks for tuberculosis patients. There is a blood bank at Gangtok. There are 86 doctors. Medical and hospital treatment is free; there is a health centre for every 20,000 of the population. Small-pox and Kala-azar have been completely eliminated and many schemes for the provision of safe drinking water to villages and bazaars have been implemented.

Coelho, V. H., *Sikkim and Bhutan.* New Delhi, 1970
Mele, F., *Sikkim.* Paris, 1974

TAMIL NADU

HISTORY. The first trading establishment made by the British in the Madras State was at Peddapali (now Nizampatnam) in 1611 and then at Masulipatnam. In 1639 the English were permitted to make a settlement at the place which is now Madras, and Fort St George was founded. By 1801 the whole of the country from the Northern Circars to Cape Comorin (with the exception of certain French and Danish settlements) had been brought under British rule.

Under the provisions of the States Reorganization Act, 1956, the Malabar district (excluding the islands of Laccadive and Minicoy) and the Kasaragod district taluk of South Kanara were transferred to the new state of Kerala; the South Kanara district (excluding Kasaragod taluk and the Amindivi Islands) and the Kollegal taluk of the Coimbatore district were transferred to the new state of Mysore; and the Laccadive, Amindivi and Minicoy Islands were constituted a separate Territory. Four taluks of the Trivandrum district and the Shencottah taluk of Quilon district were transferred from Travancore-Cochin to the new Madras State. On 1 April 1960, 405 sq. miles from the Chittoor district of Andhra Pradesh were transferred to Madras in exchange for 326 sq. miles from the Chingleput and Salem districts. In Aug. 1968 the state was renamed Tamil Nadu.

AREA AND POPULATION. Tamil Nadu is in south India and is bounded north by Karnataka and Andhra Pradesh, east and south by the Indian ocean and west by Kerala. Area, 130,357 sq. km. Population (1981 census), 48,297,456, density of 371 per sq. km. Growth rate, 1971-81, 17·23%. Tamil is the principal language and has been adopted as the state language with effect from 14 Jan. 1958. The principal towns, *see* p. 610.

CONSTITUTION AND GOVERNMENT. The Governor is aided by a Council of 16 ministers. There is a bicameral legislature; the Legislative Council has 63 members and the Legislative Assembly has 234 members. The Legislative Assembly was composed as follows after the election of May 1980: All-India Anna DMK, 129; DMK, 38; Congress (I), 30; CPM, 11; CPI, 10; others, 16.

There are 14 districts. The capital is Madras.

Governor: S. Ali.
Chief Minister: M. G. Ramachandran.

BUDGET. Budget estimates for 1981-82, revenue receipts, Rs 1,128·3 crores, revenue account expenditure, Rs 1,137·8 crores. Capital outlay, Rs 434·4 crores; capital account receipts, Rs 289·9.

ENERGY AND NATURAL RESOURCES

Electricity. Installed capacity 1977 amounted to 2,634 mw; 63,289 towns, hamlets and villages were supplied with electricity.

Minerals. Value of production, 1976, Rs 306·37m. The state has coal, chromite, bauxite, limestone, manganese, mica, quartz, salt, gypsum and feldspar.

Agriculture. Agriculture engages 29% of the population. The land is a fertile plain watered by rivers flowing east from the Western Ghats, particularly the Cauvery and the Tambaraparani. Temperature ranges between 18C. and 43C., rainfall between 25 in. and 75 in. Of the total land area (13·01m. hectares), 7,698,000 hectares were cultivable and 3m. hectares were irrigated in 1977. The staple food crops grown are paddy, maize, jawar, bajra, pulses and millets. Important commercial crops are sugar-cane, oilseeds, cashewnuts, cotton, tobacco, coffee, tea, rubber and pepper. The production of foodgrains was 7·39m. tonnes; sugar-cane and oilseeds, 1·35m., and 1,343,000 tonnes respectively.

Livestock (1966 census): Buffaloes, 2,753,049; other cattle, 11,009,368; sheep, 6,641,843; goats, 3,796,736; swine, 874,880; horses, ponies, mules, camels, etc., 185,336; poultry, 10,898,862.

Forestry. The revenue from forests in 1973-74 was Rs 7,35·40 lakhs: sandalwood, Rs 2,82·19 lakhs; timber, Rs 1,08·24 lakhs; firewood, Rs 1,07·91 lakhs. Area of forest land, 1977, 20,910 sq. km.

Fisheries. Landings, 1976, 510,000 tonnes.

INDUSTRY AND TRADE

Industry. The contribution of the industrial sector to the state income was Rs 373 crores in 1972-73. The number of registered factories was 6,713 in 1973. The consumption of power in the industrial sector was 49·5% of total state consumption in 1974. The biggest central sector project is Salem steel plant. Man-days lost in industrial disputes, 1979, 8·38m.

Cotton textiles is one of the major industries. There are nearly 180 cotton textile mills and most of the spinning mills supplying yarn to the decentralized handloom industry. Other important industries are tanning, manufacture of textile machinery, power-driven pumps, bicycles, electrical machinery, tractors, rubber tyres and tubes, bricks and tiles and silk. Tamil Nadu is the second largest producer of cement, while its sugar industry has been expanding rapidly.

Public sector undertakings include the Neyveli lignite complex, integral coach factory, high-pressure boiler plant, photographic film factory, surgical instruments factory, teleprinter factory, oil refinery, continuous casting plant and defence vehicles manufacture. Main exports: tanned hides and skins, leather and cotton goods, tea, coffee, spices, engineering goods, motor-car ancillaries.

Tourism. In 1973, 50,074 tourists visited the state, 35,929 of whom came by air and 14,145 by sea.

COMMUNICATIONS

Roads. At the end of 1973 the state had approximately 78,463 km of roads (about 50,000 km metalled). In 1976 there were 184,475 registered motor vehicles.

Railways. In 1970 there were 6,038 km of railway. Madras and Madurai are the main centres.

Aviation. There are airports at Madras, Tiruchirapalli and Madurai, with regular scheduled services to Bombay, Calcutta and Delhi. Madras is the main centre of airline routes in South India.

Shipping. Madras is the chief port. Important minor ports are Cuddalore and Nagapattinam. There are 9 intermediate ports. A harbour is under construction at Tuticorin.

JUSTICE, RELIGION AND EDUCATION

Justice. There is a High Court at Madras with a Chief Justice and 18 judges. *Police.* Strength of armed police battalions, 1973, 4,420; strength of the armed reserve (1972) in the state and in Madras, 356,461.

Religion. At the 1971 census Hindus numbered 36,674,150 (89·2%), Christians, 5·75%; Moslems, 5·11%.

Education. At the 1981 census 22·1m. people were literate.

Education is free up to pre-university level. In 1973-74 there were 2,823 high schools with a total enrolment of 1,627,030 students. The number of primary schools was 26,726, and their enrolment, 3,759,140; 5,773 upper primary schools had 2,113,981 pupils. Allotment of expenditure for education for 1974-75, Rs 1,08·52 crores.

There are 3 universities. Madras University (founded in 1857) is affiliating and teaching. It had (1968) 119 colleges for arts and sciences with 106,571 students. Annamalai University, Annamalainagar (founded 1928) is residential; Madurai University (founded 1966) is an affiliating and teaching university.

Statistical Information: The Department of Statistics (Fort St George, Madras) was established in 1948 and reorganized in 1953. *Director:* D. S. Rajabushanam, MA. Main publications: *Annual Statistical Abstract; Decennial Statistical Atlas; Season and Crop Report; Quinquennial Wages Census; Quarterly Abstract of Statistics.*

TRIPURA

HISTORY. A Hindu state of great antiquity having been ruled by the Maharajahs for 1,300 years before its accession to the Indian Union on 15 Oct. 1949. With the reorganization of states on 1 Sept. 1956 Tripura became a Union Territory. The Territory was made a State on 21 Jan. 1972.

AREA AND POPULATION. Tripura is bounded on the north, west and south by Bangladesh, and on the east by Mizoram. The major portion of the state is hilly and mainly jungle. It has an area of 10,477 sq. km and a population of 2,060,189 (1981 census); Density, 196 per sq. km. Growth rate, 1971-81, 32·37%.

The predominant language is Bengali.

GOVERNMENT. There is a Legislative Assembly of 60 members. The election of Jan. 1983 was won by the Communist Party of India (Marxist). The territory has 1 district, divided into 10 administrative sub-divisions, namely, Sadar, Khowai, Kailasahar, Dharmanagar, Sonamura, Udaipur, Belonia, Kamalpur, Sabroom and Amarpur.

The capital is Agartala.

Governor: L. P. Singh.
Chief Minister: N. Chakravarty.

BUDGET. Budget estimates 1980-81 show revenue receipts of Rs 107·1 crores, and expenditure on revenue account of Rs 108·8 crores. Annual plan expenditure, Rs 35 crores.

ENERGY AND NATURAL RESOURCES

Electricity. Installed capacity (1980), 14·72 mw; there were (1976) 245 electrified villages.

Agriculture. About 23% of the land area is cultivable. The tribes practise shifting cultivation, but this is being slowly replaced by modern methods. The main crops are rice, wheat, jute, mesta, potatoes, oilseeds and sugar-cane. Foodgrain production (1979-80), 310,000 tonnes. There are 56 registered tea gardens producing 4,500,000 kg. per year, and employing about 10,000.

Forestry. Forests cover about 65% of the land area. They have been much depleted by clearance for shifting cultivation and, recently, for refugee settlements of Bangladeshis. About 8% of the forest area still consists of dense natural forest; losses elsewhere are being replaced by plantation. Commercial rubber plantation has also been encouraged and covers over 65,000 hectares.

INDUSTRY. There is a jute mill, a steel re-rolling mill and a flour mill at Agartala; a second flour mill at Dharmanagar. Small scale industries produce diverse manufacture. The main village industries are hand-loom weaving, sericulture and cane-work. The Tripura Handloom and Handicrafts Development Corporation marketed goods worth Rs 6m. in 1979-80.

COMMUNICATIONS

Roads. Total length of motorable roads (1974) 3,692 km, of which 1,123 km were surfaced. Vehicles registered, 31 March 1980, 7,889.

Railways. There is a railway between Dharmanagar and Kalkalighat (Assam).

Aviation. There is 1 airport and 3 airstrips. The airport (Agartala) has regular scheduled services to Calcutta.

EDUCATION AND WELFARE

Education. In autumn 1978 there were 1,885 primary schools (209,836 pupils); 436 middle schools (51,418); 144 high schools (21,238), and 52 higher grade schools (6,202). There were 6 colleges of general education (7,772). 9 colleges of professional and technical education (1,346) and 859 social education centres.

Health. There were (1980) 12 hospitals, with 1,357 beds, 128 dispensaries, 297 doctors and 459 nurses. There were 26 primary health centres and about 35 other medical units.

UTTAR PRADESH

HISTORY. In 1833 the then Bengal Presidency was divided into two parts, one of which became the Presidency of Agra. In 1836 the Agra area was styled the North-West Province and placed under a Lieut.-Governor. The two provinces of Agra and Oudh were placed, in 1877, under one administrator, styled Lieut.-Governor of the North-West Province and Chief Commissioner of Oudh. In 1902 the name was changed to 'United Provinces of Agra and Oudh', under a Lieut.-Governor, and the Lieut.-Governorship was altered to a Governorship in 1921. In 1935 the name was shortened to 'United Provinces'. On Independence, the states of Rampur, Banaras and Tehri-Garwhal were merged with United Provinces. In 1950 the name of the United Provinces was changed to Uttar Pradesh.

AREA AND POPULATION. Uttar Pradesh is in north India and is bounded north by Himachal Pradesh, Tibet and Nepál, east by Bihar, south by Madhya Pradesh and west by Rajasthan, Haryana and Delhi. The area of the state is 294,413 sq. km. Population (1981 census), 110,885,874, a density of 377 per sq. km. Growth rate, 1971–81, 25·49%. Cities with more than 250,000 population, *see* p. 610. The official language is Hindi.

CONSTITUTION AND GOVERNMENT. Uttar Pradesh has had an autonomous system of government since 1937. There is a bicameral legislature. The Legislative Council has 108 members; the Legislative Assembly has 426, of which 424 are elective. Party strength in the Assembly, Oct. 1982: Congress (I) 320; Lok Dal, 54; Democratic Socialists, 11; Bhartiya Janata, 8; others, 29; vacant, 2.

There are 11 administrative divisions, each under a Commissioner, and 57 districts.

The capital is Lucknow.

Governor: C. P. N. Singh.
Chief Minister: Shripati Misra.

BUDGET. Budget estimates 1982–83 show revenue and capital receipts of Rs 3,088·00 crores; revenue and capital account expenditure, Rs 3,336·87 crores. An outlay of Rs 1,202 crores was approved for the 1982–83 annual plan.

ENERGY AND NATURAL RESOURCES

Electricity. The State Electricity Board had, 31 March 1982, an installed capacity of 3,494 mw. There were 46,162 villages with electricity.

Minerals. Value of production, 1976, Rs 31·769m. The state has magnesite, fire-clay, coal, copper, dolomite, limestone, soapstone, gypsum among others.

Agriculture. Agriculture occupies 78% of the work force. About 9·5m. hectares are irrigated. The state is India's largest producer of foodgrains; production (1980–81), 24·9m. tonnes; sugar-cane 64·2m.; oilseeds, 1·56m. The state is one of India's main producers of sugar. There were (1981) 1,199 veterinary centres for cattle.

Forests cover (1980) about 5·1m. sq. km.

INDUSTRY. Sugar production is important; other industries include textiles, distilleries, brewing, leather working, agricultural engineering, paper and chemicals. There is an aluminium smelter at Renukoot. An oil refinery at Mathura has capacity of 6m. tonnes per annum. Large public-sector enterprises have been set up in electrical engineering, pharmaceuticals, locomotive building, general engineering, electronics and aeronautics. Village and small-scale industries are important; there were 68,426 small units in 1982. About one-third of cloth output is from hand-looms. Total working population (1981) 30·8m., of whom 6·8m. were non-agricultural. Man days lost by industrial disputes, 1981, 2·39m

COMMUNICATIONS

Roads. There were, 31 March 1978, 184,263 km of motorable roads, of which 36,350 km were metalled. (This excludes forest roads.) In 1981 there were 533,836 motor vehicles of which 300,311 were motorcycles.

Railways. Lucknow is the main junction of the northern network; other important junctions are Agra, Kanpur, Allahabad and Varanasi.

Aviation. There are airports at Lucknow, Kanpur, Varanasi, Allahabad, Agra, Jhansi, Lalitpur and Gorakhpur.

JUSTICE, RELIGION AND EDUCATION

Justice. The High Court of Judicature at Allahabad (with a bench at Lucknow) has a Chief Justice and 46 puisne judges including additional judges. There are 56 sessions divisions in the state.

Religion. At the 1971 census Hindus numbered 73,997,597; Moslems, 13,676,533; Sikhs, 369,672; Christians, 131,810; Jains, 124,728; Buddhists, 39,639.

Education. At the 1981 census 30·3m. people were literate. In 1981–82 there were 125 nursery schools, 72,213 junior basic schools, 13,652 senior basic schools and 5,410 higher secondary schools.

Uttar Pradesh has 19 universities: Allahabad University (founded 1887); Agra University (1927); the Banaras Hindu University, Varanasi (1916); Lucknow University (1921); Aligarh Muslim University (1920); Roorkee University (1948), formerly Thomason College of Civil Engineering (established in 1847); Gorakhpur University (1957); Varanasaya Sanskrit Vishwavidyalaya, Varanasi (1958); Kashi Vidyapith, Varanasi (1963). Kanpur University and Meerut University were founded in 1966. Govind Ballabh Pant University, Pantnagar (1969); Garhwal University, Srinagar, (1973). Two universities of agriculture were founded in 1974–75 and Avadh, Kumaon, Rohilkhand and Jhansi Universities in 1975.

HEALTH. In 1982 there were 3,188 allopathic and 1,842 ayurvedic and unani hospitals. There were 8,569 doctors and 19,181 nurses and midwives in state service. There were TB hospitals and clinics with 3,437 beds.

WEST BENGAL

HISTORY. For the history of Bengal under British rule, from 1633 to 1947, *see* THE STATESMAN'S YEAR-BOOK, 1952, p. 183.

Under the terms of the Indian Independence Act, 1947, the Province of Bengal ceased to exist. The Moslem majority districts of East Bengal, consisting of the Chittagong and Dacca Divisions and portions of the Presidency and Rajshahi Divisions, became what was then East Pakistan.

AREA AND POPULATION. West Bengal is in north-east India and is bounded north by Sikkim and Bhután, east by Assam and Bangladesh, south by the Bay of Bengal and Orissa, west by Bihar and north-west by Nepál. The total area of West Bengal is 87,853 sq. km. At the 1981 census its population was 54,485,560, an increase of 23% since 1971, the density of population 614 per sq. km. Population of chief cities, *see* p. 610. The principal language is Bengali.

CONSTITUTION AND GOVERNMENT. The state of West Bengal came into existence as a result of the Indian Independence Act, 1947. The territory of Cooch-Behar State was merged with West Bengal on 1 Jan. 1950, and the former French possession of Chandernagore became part of the state on 2 Oct. 1954. Under the States Reorganization Act, 1956, certain portions of Bihar State (an area of 3,157 sq. miles with a population of 1,446,385) were transferred to West Bengal.

The Legislative Assembly has 294 seats. Distribution Sept. 1982: Communist Party of India (Marxist), 174; Forward Bloc, 28; Revolutionary Socialist Party, 19; Communist Party of India, 7; Revolutionary Communist Party of India, 2; Forward Bloc (Marxist), 2; Democratic Socialist Party, 3; Socialist Party, 3. Total "Left Front", 238. Opposition: Indian National Congress, 49; others, 7.

The capital is Calcutta.

For administrative purposes there are 3 divisions (Jalpaiguri, Burdwan and Presidency), under which there are 16 districts, including Calcutta. The Calcutta Metropolitan Development Authority has been set up to co-ordinate development in the metropolitan area (1,250 sq. km). For the purposes of local self-government there are 15 *zilla parishads* (district boards), 324 *panchayat samities* (regional boards), and 3,242 *gram* (village) *panchayats.* There are 112 municipalities. The Calcutta Corporation was reconstituted in 1969 with a mayor and deputy mayor, a commissioner, aldermen and standing committees.

Governor: B. D. Pande.
Chief Minister: J. Basu.

BUDGET. Budget estimates for 1982–83 showed a deficit of Rs 10m.

ENERGY AND NATURAL RESOURCES

Electricity. Installed capacity, 1979–80, 1,640 mw; 16,512 villages had electricity.

Water. The major irrigation and power scheme at present under construction is (1982) on the Teesta river. During 1979–80 government canals irrigated 851,582 hectares. At March 1982 there were 5,701 tubewells and 2,697 riverlift irrigation schemes.

Minerals. Value of production, 1980, over Rs 233·65m. The state has coal (the Raniganj field is one of the 3 biggest in India) including coking coal. Coal production (1980) 19·2m. tonnes.

Agriculture. About 71% of the cultivated area is rice-paddy, one-third of it irrigated. Total foodgrain production, 1980–81, 8·3m. tonnes; oilseeds (provisional), 132,500 tonnes; jute and other fibres, 4·7m. tonnes; wheat, 473,200 tonnes. The state produces about half the national output of jute.

Livestock (1971 census): 11,878,083 cattle, 824,161 buffaloes; 1981 census,

758,000 sheep and goats, and 15,052,000 poultry.

Forests cover 13·4% of the state.

Fisheries. Landings, 1981–82, about 337,000 tonnes. During 1980–81 Rs 5·57m. was invested in fishery schemes, including a new harbour near Diamondharbour.

INDUSTRY. The total number of registered factories, 1980, was 6,421, with average daily employment of 875,000. The coalmining industry had 109 units with average daily employment of 127,000. Man-days lost by industrial disputes, 1980, 6·05m.

There is a large automobile factory at Uttarpara, and there are aluminium rolling-mills at Belur and Asansol. At Durgapur a major steel plant was completed in 1962. Durgapur has other industries under the state sector—a thermal power plant, coke oven plant, fertilizer factory, alloy steel plant and ophthalmic glass plant. There are a locomotive factory and cable factory at Chittaranjan and Rupnarayanpur. A refinery and fertilizer factory are operating at Haldia.

COMMUNICATIONS

Roads. In 1980 the length of national highway was 1,401 km, of state highway 3,147 km and of other motorable roads 134,283 km. In 1976 the state had 225,889 motor vehicles.

Railways. The length of railways within the state (1980–81) is 4,922 km. The main centres are Howrah, Sealdah, Kharagpur, Asansol and New Jalpaiguri.

Aviation. The main airport is Calcutta which has national and international flights. The second airport is at Bagdogra in the extreme north, which has regular scheduled services to Calcutta and Delhi.

Shipping. Calcutta is the chief port: a barrage is being built at Farakka to control the flow of water and to provide a rail and road link between North and South Bengal. A second port is being developed at Haldia, halfway between the present port and the sea, which is intended mainly for bulk cargoes. West Bengal possesses 779 km of navigable canals.

JUSTICE, RELIGION AND EDUCATION

Justice. The High Court of Judicature at Calcutta has a Chief Justice and 38 puisne judges. The Andaman and Nicobar Islands *(see below)* come under its jurisdiction.

Police. In 1982 the police force numbered 48,128, under an inspector-general. Calcutta has a separate force under a commissioner directly responsible to the Government; its strength was 20,777.

Religion. At the 1971 census Hindus numbered 34,611,864; Moslems, 9,064,338; Christians, 251,752; Buddhists, 121,504; Sikhs, 35,084; Jains, 32,203.

Education. At the 1981 census 22·2m. people were literate. In 1981 there were 46,993 primary and junior basic schools, with about 6·8m. pupils and 5,129 secondary schools with about 2·3m. pupils. Primary education is free.

The University of Calcutta (founded 1857) is affiliating and teaching; in 1976–77 it had 234,661 students. Visva Bharati, Santiniketan, was originally established in 1951 and is residential and teaching; it had 2,911 students in 1977–78. The University of Jadavpur, Calcutta (1955), had 4,222 students in 1977–78. Burdwan University was established 15 June 1960 with 31 affiliated colleges previously under the supervision of the University of Calcutta; in 1977–78 there were 48,550 students. Kalyani University was established in 1960 (1,839 students in 1977). The University of North Bengal (1962) had 17,728 students in 1977–78. Rabindra Bharati University had 2,783 students in 1977–78. Bidhan Chandra Krishi Viswavidyalaya (1974) had 1,047 students in 1977–78.

UNION TERRITORIES

ANDAMAN AND NICOBAR ISLANDS. The Andaman and Nicobar Islands are administered by the President of the Republic of India acting through a Lieut.-Governor. There is a Pradesh Council, 5 members of which are selected by the Chief Commissioner as advisory counsellors. The seat of administration is at Port Blair, which is connected with Calcutta (1,255 km away) and Madras (1,190 km) by steamer service which calls about every 10 days; there is a bi-weekly air service from Calcutta and a weekly service from Madras. There are 2 districts.

The population (1981 census) was 188,254; density 23 per sq. km.; growth rate 1971–81, 63·5%.

Revised estimates for 1981–82 show total revenue receipts of Rs 6,61·19 lakhs, and total expenditure on revenue account of Rs 35,85·51 lakhs, and total capital expenditure of Rs 30,02·59 lakhs.

Lieut.-Governor: M. L. Kampani.

The **Andaman Islands** lie in the Bay of Bengal, 193 km from Cape Negrais in Burma, 1,255 from Calcutta and 1,190 from Madras. Five large islands grouped together are called the Great Andamans, and to the south is the island of Little Andaman. There are some 204 islets, the two principal groups being the Ritchie Archipelago and the Labyrinth Islands. The total area is about 6,475 sq. km. The Great Andaman group is about 467 km long and, at the widest, 51 km broad.

The original inhabitants live in the forests by hunting and fishing; they are of a small Negrito type and their civilization is about that of the Stone Age. Their exact numbers are not known, as they avoid all contact with civilization. The total population of the Andaman Islands (excluding the aboriginals) was in 1951, 18,962 (12,734 males and 6,228 females). Under a central government scheme started in 1953, some 4,000 displaced families, mostly from East Pakistan, had been settled in the islands by May 1967.

Japanese forces occupied the Andaman Islands on 23 March 1942. Civil administration of the islands was resumed on 8 Oct. 1945.

From 1857 to March 1942 the islands were used by the Government of India as a penal settlement for life and long-term convicts, but the penal settlement was abolished on re-occupation in Oct. 1945.

The Great Andaman group, densely wooded, contains many valuable trees, both hardwood and softwood. The best known of the hardwoods is the *padauk* or Andaman redwood; *gurjan* is in great demand for the manufacture of plywood. Large quantities of softwood are supplied to match factories. Annually the Forest Department export about 25,000 tons of timber to the mainland. Coconut, coffee and rubber are cultivated. The islands are slowly being made self-sufficient in paddy and rice, and now grow approximately half their annual requirements. The average yield of rice in 1966–67 was 1·24 tonnes per hectare. Total livestock (1961 census) was 38,617. There is a sawmill at Port Blair and a coconut-oil mill at Dunbar Point. There are about 338 km of black top road in the entire territory.

The islands possess a number of harbours and safe anchorages, notably Port Blair in the south, Port Cornwallis in the north and Elphinstone and Mayabandar in the middle.

The **Nicobar Islands** are situated to the south of the Andamans, 121 km from Little Andaman. The British formally took possession in 1869. There are 19 islands, 7 uninhabited; total area, 1,645 sq. km. The islands are usually divided into 3 subgroups (southern, central and northern), the chief islands in each being respectively, Great Nicobar, Camotra with Nancowrie and Car Nicobar. There is a fine landlocked harbour between the islands of Camotra and Nancowrie, known as Nancowrie Harbour.

The population numbered, in 1961, 14,563. The coconut and arecanut are the main items of trade, and coconuts are a major item in the people's diet.

The Nicobar Islands were occupied by the Japanese in July 1942; and Car Nicobar was developed as a big supply base. The Japanese built some roads in Car

Nicobar and small jetties at Malacca in Car Nicobar, and in the harbour at Nancowrie. The Allies reoccupied the islands on 9 Oct. 1945.

ARUNACHAL PRADESH. On 21 Jan. 1972 the former North East Frontier Agency of Assam was created a Union Territory. The territory includes the Kameng, Tirap, Subansiri, Siang and Lohit frontier divisions and has an area of 81,426 sq. km and a population (1981 census) of 628,050; density, 7 per sq. km.; growth rate, 1971–81, 34·34%.

There is a Legislative Assembly of 30 members and a Council of Ministers. The election of 1978 was won by the Janata party.

There are 5 districts. The centre of administration is at Itanagar.

Chief Commissioner: S. M. Krishnatry.
Chief Minister: Prem Khandu Thungon.

About 60% of the land area is forest. Agriculture employs 18·5% of the people. In 1970 there were 200,000 acres under cultivation, 32,600 acres of it irrigated. Crops include rice (13,000 tonnes, 1976), rubber, coffee, coconut, arecanut, fruits and spices. There were about 100 co-operatives. The budget estimates for 1980–81 provided Rs 81·7 crores, of which Rs 1·16 crores was allotted to agriculture.

CHANDIGARH. On 1 Nov. 1966 the city of Chandigarh and the area surrounding it was constituted a Union Territory. Population (1981), 450,061; density, 3,948 per sq. km.; growth rate, 1971–81, 74·9%. Area, 114 sq. km. It serves as the joint capital of both Punjab (India) and the state of Haryana, and is the seat of a High Court and of a university serving both states. The city will ultimately be the capital of just the Punjab; joint status is to last while a new capital is built for Haryana.

There is some cultivated land (foodgrain production, 1977, 8,000 tonnes) and some forest (27·5% of the territory).

Evenson, N., *Chandigarh.* Berkeley, Cal., 1966

DADRA AND NAGAR HAVELI. By the 10th amendment to the constitution the Portuguese territories of Dadra and Nagar Haveli became a centrally administered Union Territory with effect from 11 Aug. 1961, forming an enclave at the southernmost point of the border between Gujarat and Maharashtra. Area 491 sq. km.; population (1981), 103,677 (males 52,514, females 51,163); density 211 per sq. km; growth rate, 1971–81, 39·78%. Formerly for administrative purposes a part of Damão (on the south Gujarat coast), they were separated from it by a 26-km strip of Indian territory. In July 1954 'nationalist volunteers' occupied Dadra and Nagar Haveli and a pro-India administration was formed; this body made a request for incorporation into the Union, 1 June 1961, and has been recognized by the Indian Government as able to exercise an advisory role on the pattern of territorial councils. The Indian Government appointed an Administrator in Oct. 1960. Headquarters are at Silvassa. Dadra has 3 villages, Nagar Haveli 69. Languages used are Bhilli, Gujarat, Bhilodi (83%), Marathi and Hindi.

Administrator: Col. P. S. Gill.

Electricity. Electricity is supplied by Gujarat. A Silvassa sub-station is being built, and 44 villages had been electrified by 1977.

Agriculture. Farming is the chief occupation, and about 23,000 hectares were under crops in 1976–77. Much of the land is terraced and there is a 75% subsidy for soil conservation. The major food crops are rice and ragi; 9,600 hectares were under paddy cultivation and 11,285 under ragi and pulses in 1976–77. Some wheat is also grown. There is little irrigation (713 hectares). There are veterinary centres, an agricultural research centre and 2 breeding centres to improve strains of cattle and poultry. During 1977 the Administration distributed 43,000 kg of high yielding paddy seed, 16,000 kg of improved and high yielding wheat and 182 tonnes of fertilizer.

Forests. About 41·5% of the total area is forest, mainly of teak and khair. Timber production, 1977, 3,166 cu. metres including 1,151 cu. metres of teak.

Industry. An industrial estate has been set up at Piparia which had 49 operating factories in 1978 for chemical products, engineering, textiles, plastics, fertilizers and other manufactures. There were 15 units operating outside the estate. Concessions are available for small industries , and the whole Territory is included in the Rural Industrial Project. Estimated employment (total) in 1978, 1,380.

Communications. There are (1978) 167 km of motorable road. The railway line from Bombay to Ahmedabad runs through Silvassa. The nearest airport is Bombay.

Justice. The territory is under the jurisdiction of the Bombay (Maharashtra) High Court. There is a District and Sessions Court and one junior Division Civil Court at Silvassa.

Education. Literacy was 14·86% of the population at the 1971 census. In 1978 there were 11 pre-primary schools, 144 government primary schools, 12 mission schools, 1 higher secondary school and 4 high schools. Total primary enrolment was 11,357; high-school, 896.

Health. The territory has 1 hospital (27 beds), 2 primary health centres and 4 dispensaries.

DELHI. Delhi became a Union Territory on 1 Nov. 1956.

Area and Population. The territory forms an enclave inside the eastern frontier of Haryana in north India. Delhi has an area of 1,485 sq. km. At the 1981 census its population was 6,220,406 (density per sq. km, 4,194). Growth rate, 1971–81, 53%. In the rural area of Delhi there are 241 inhabited and 17 deserted villages in 5 community development blocks.

Government. Delhi is administered by an elected Metropolitan Council consisting of 61 members including 5 nominated by the President of India. The Lieut-Governor is the Administrator, assisted by 4 Executive Councillors (1 Chief Executive Councillor and 3 Executive Councillors) appointed by the President of India on the recommendation of the Union Home Ministry. The Territory is covered by 3 local bodies: Delhi Municipal Corporation, New Delhi Municipal Committee and Delhi Cantonment Board.

Lieut.-Governor: S. L. Khurana.

Budget. Budget estimates 1982–83 show total revenue of Rs 3,085·86m. and expenditure of Rs 4,220m. Biggest items of expenditure were social and community services, Rs 1,192·79m. Annual Plan outlay (1982–83) on transport and communication, Rs 170m.

Agriculture. The contribution to the economy is not significant. About 87,599 hectares are cultivated. Animal husbandry is increasing and mixed farms are common. Chief crops in 1980–81, production in 1,000 tonnes were: Wheat, 120; jowar and bajra, 14; gram, 1; sugar-cane (gur), 0·3; fruit, vegetables and flowers.

Industry. The modern city of Delhi and New Delhi is not only the largest commercial centre in northern India but is also an important industrial centre. Since 1947 a large number of industrial concerns have been established; these include factories for the manufacture of razor blades, sports goods and parts for radios, bicycles and station wagons, plastic and PVC goods including footwear. The number of industrial units functioning was about 45,000 in 1980–81; average number of workers employed was 450,000. Production was worth Rs 2,196 crores and investment was about Rs 867 crores.

Some traditional handicrafts, for which Delhi was formerly famous, still flourish; among them are ivory carving, miniature painting, gold and silver jewellery and papier mâché work. The handwoven textiles of Delhi were particularly fine; this craft is being successfully revived.

Roads. Five national highways pass through the city. There were (1981) 561,768 registered motor vehicles in Delhi including 6,583 taxis. The city transport service had 3,488 buses in 1981–82; this included the use of 304 private buses.

Railways. Delhi is an important rail junction with three main stations: Delhi, New Delhi, Hazart Nizamuddin.

Aviation. Palam airport operates internal and international flights.

Religion. At the 1971 census Hindus numbered 3,407,835; Sikhs, 291,123; Moslems, 263,019; Jains, 50,513; Christians, 43,720; Buddhists, 8,720.

Education. The proportion of literates to the total population was 61·54% at the 1981 census (68·4% of males and 53·07% of females).

The total number of educational institutions in 1980–81 was 4,421, with an enrolment of 1,411,869 students.

The University of Delhi was founded in 1922; it had 64 constituent colleges and institutions in 1981 with, a total of 74,875 students.

GOA, DAMAN AND DIU. The coast was captured for Portugal by Afonso de Albuquerque in 1510 and the inland area was added in the 18th century. Daman (Damão) on the Gujarat coast, 70 miles north of Bombay, was seized by the Portuguese in 1531 and ceded to them (1539) by the Shar of Gujarat. The island of Diu, captured in 1534, lies off the south-east coast of Kathiawar (Gujarat); there is a small coastal area. In Dec. 1961 the territories were occupied by India and incorporated into the Indian Union.

Area and Population. Goa, bounded on the north by Maharashtra and on the east and south by Karnataka, has a coastline of 105 km. The area of the territory is 3,813 sq. km, that of Goa itself being about 3,701 sq. km. Daman, 72 sq. km; Diu, 40 sq. km. Population (1981) 1,082,117. Density, 284 per sq. km. Growth rate, 1971–81, 26·15%. Panaji is the largest town, population (urban agglomeration, 1971) 59,258. The languages spoken are Gujarati and Konkani.

Government. The Indian Parliament passed legislation in March 1962 by which Goa, Daman and Diu became a Union Territory with retrospective effect from 20 Dec. 1961. Goa is represented by 2 elected members in the Indian House of the People. For judicial purposes the territory comes under the High Court of Bombay. The capital is Panaji. There are 194 village *panchayats*.

There is a Legislative Assembly of 30 members.

Administrator: Col. P. S. Gill.
Chief Minister: P. R. Rane.

Budget. Annual Plan expenditure, 1980–81, Rs 312·5m.: Agriculture, Rs 45·1m.; irrigation and power, Rs 89·5m.; social services, Rs 107·4m.

Electricity. Units sold, 176·53m. kwh. in 1978–79. Thirteen towns and 351 villages were supplied with electric power by March 1979. Power is generated in neighbouring states.

Minerals. Resources include manganese ore and iron ore, both of which are exported. There are also reserves of bauxite, limestone and clay.

Agriculture. Agriculture is the main occupation; important crops are rice, wheat, ragi, pulses, groundnuts, fruit and coconuts. The net area sown is 128,429 hectares in Goa, 4,353 in Daman and 793 in Diu. Area irrigated, 11,277 hectares. Area under paddy (1979–80), 29,539 hectares of high-yielding strain (producing 142,934 tonnes). Area under wheat, 55,000 hectares; pulses, 6,500; ragi, 7,000. Government poultry and dairy farming schemes yielded 497,634 eggs and 4·36m. litres of milk in 1979–80, with 7,298 kg of butter and 1,904 kg of ghee.

Fisheries. The fishing industry is important; fish is the territory's staple food. In 1979 the catch of seafish was 39,488 tonnes (value Rs 8,18·17 lakhs). The whole territory has a coastline of about 140 km. There are about 4,950 active fishing vessels.

Industry. At 19 Jan. 1980 there were 31 large and medium industrial projects and 1,711 small units registered, the largest being a fertilizer factory (investment, Rs 500m.). There were 7 government industrial estates. Small units were mainly occupied in rice- and flour-milling, boat repairs and forest products.

Employment. In 1979 there were 71 unions with 40,200 members.

Roads. In 1980 there were 2,642 km of motorable road (national highway, 223 km). A road bridge on national highway 17 is being built at Zuari. In 1980 there were 35,552 registered vehicles.

Railways. There is a metre gauge line from the Pune–Bangalore line into Goa. There are no railways on Diu or in Daman.

Aviation. There are regular services to Bombay and Bangalore.

Shipping. The main port is Marmagoa. There is a daily steamer service between Panaji and Bombay, and weekly service between Bombay and Cochin, calling at Marmagoa. The port handled 14·5m. tonnes of cargo, mainly iron ore, in 1979–80.

Post and Telegraphs. There are (1981) 219 post offices and 27 telephone exchanges with 7,220 lines. There are 3 telex exchanges.

Justice. The territory comes under the High Court of Bombay.

Religion. About 62% of the population is Hindu, 36% Christian, 2% Muslim and other communities.

Education. The 1971 census recorded 44·53% literacy. Education is free up to grade VIII. In 1979–80 primary schools numbered 1,202 with 124,840 pupils, middle schools 375 with 67,660 pupils and secondary schools 242 with 37,312 pupils. There were 17 higher secondary schools, with 6,465 pupils, and 9 arts, commercial and science colleges with 4,387 students. There were also 7 professional colleges and 5 non-degree colleges.

Health. There are (1980) 33 government hospitals (2,261 beds) including 3 tuberculosis hospital; also mobile and specialist clinics. There were also 55 private hospitals and nursing homes. Two health centres were opened in 1972; there are about 940 doctors. There is 1 medical college.

Richards, J. M., *Goa.* London, 1982
Soeiro de Brito, R., *Goa e as Praças do Norte.* Lisbon, 1966

LAKSHADWEEP. The territory consists of a group of 27 islands (10 inhabited), about 300 km off the west coat of Kerala. It was constituted a Union Territory in 1956 as the Laccadive, Minicoy and Amindivi Islands, and renamed in Nov. 1973. The total area of the islands is 32 sq. km. The northern portion is called the Amindivis. The remaining islands are called the Laccadives (including Minicoy Island). Androth is the largest island, 4·8 sq. km, and is nearest to Kerala. An Advisory Committee associated with the Union Home Minister and an Advisory Council to the Administrator assist in the administration of the islands; these are constituted annually. Population (1981 census), 40,237, nearly all Moslems. Density, 1,257 per sq. km.; growth rate, 1971–81. 26·49%. The language is Malayalam, but the language in Minicoy is Mahl. There were, in 1980, 8 high schools and 9 nursery schools, 18 junior basic schools, 4 senior basic schools and 1 junior college. There are 2 hospitals and 7 primary health centres. The staple products are coconut-husk fibre (coir), coconuts and fish. There is a tourist resort at Bangarem, an uninhabited island with an extensive lagoon. Headquarters of administration, Kavaratti Island.

Administrator: O. Saigal.

MIZORAM. On 21 Jan. 1972 the former Mizo Hills District of Assam was created a Union Territory. The area is approximately 21,090 sq. km and the population (1981 census), 487,774, of whom about 55% are literate and 90% are Christian. Density, 23 per sq. km.; growth rate, 1971–81, 46·75%.

There is a Council of Ministers responsible to a Legislative Assembly with 30 seats. The present ministry took office in June 1978. The nationalist Mizo National Front was banned in 1982. The main town is Aizawl, which is connected by a main road (not a national highway) to Silchar, Assam; Silchar is also the nearest airport. There are no railways.

The budget for 1980–81 estimated receipts of Rs 52·28 crores on revenue account and Rs 24·50 crores on capital account. Outlay for the sixth Five-Year Plan is Rs 24·50 crores.

Agriculture employs 46% of the people and 17% of cultivated land is irrigated; there are some terraced holdings, elsewhere shifting cultivation is practised in forest clearings. Industry is based on the forests. Total installed power capacity, 1975, 3·4 mw supplying 61 villages.

Lieut.-Governor: K. A. A. Raja.
Chief Minister: Brig. Sailo.

PONDICHERRY. Formerly the chief French settlement in India, was founded by the French in 1674, taken by the Dutch in 1693 and restored to the French in 1699. The English took it in 1761, restored it in 1765, re-took it in 1778, restored it a second time in 1785, retook it a third time in 1793 and finally restored it to the French in 1814. Administration was transferred to India on 1 Nov. 1954. A Treaty of Cession (together with Karikal, Mahé and Yanaon) was signed on 28 May 1956; instruments of ratification were signed on 16 Aug. 1962 from which date (by the 14th amendment to the Indian Constitution) Pondicherry, comprising the 4 territories, became a Union Territory.

Area and Population. The territory forms an enclave on the Coromandel Coast of Tamil Nadu, with Karikal forming a separate enclave further south. The total area of Pondicherry (with Karikal, Mahé and Yanaon) is 480 sq. km, divided into 4 Municipalities and 11 Communes. Population (1981 census), 604,136; density, 1,228 per sq. km.; growth rate, 1971–81, 28·07%. Pondicherry city had (1971) 90,637 inhabitants. The principal languages spoken are French, English, Tamil, Telegu and Malayalam.

Government. By the Government of Union Territories Act 1963 Pondicherry is governed by a Lieut.-Governor, appointed by the President, and a Council of Ministers (4) responsible to a Legislative Assembly of 30 members.

Lieut.-Governor: B. T. Kulkarni.
Chief Minister: D. Ramachandran.

Planning. Outlay for 1980–81 was Rs 135·1m. Of this, Rs 24·1m. was for agriculture, Rs 53·9m. for social and community services, Rs 19·7m. for irrigation, flood control and power development, Rs 13·2m. for transport and communications and Rs 7·5m. for industry.

Budget. Budget estimates for 1980–81 show revenue receipts of Rs 31,95·75.

Electricity. Power is bought from neighbouring states. All main villages have electricity. Consumption, 1979–80, 142·7m. units: 49% in industry, 28% in agriculture. Peak demand, 33·3 mw.

Agriculture. Nearly 45% of the population is engaged in agriculture and allied pursuits; 89% of the cultivated area is irrigated. The main food crop is rice. Estimated foodgrain production, 120,000 tonnes from 41,400 hectares in 1979–80, of which 99,000 tonnes was paddy; cash crops include groundnuts (10,900 tonnes), cotton (13,800 bales of 180 kg) and sugar-cane (145,000 tonnes).

Industry. There are no heavy industries or mines; manufacturing produces consumer goods such as textiles, sugar, electrical appliances, camphor, leather-goods, paper and bicycle parts. In 1980 there were about 30,000 people employed in 10 large and 13,000 small, industrial units engaged in varied manufacturing.

Railways. Pondicherry is on a branch from the main Madurai–Madras line.

Aviation. The nearest airport is Madras.

Education. There were, in 1980, 42 pre-primary schools (4,140 pupils and 78 teachers), 259 primary schools (73,047 and 1,043), 83 middle schools (31,669 and 1,071), 54 high schools (12,025 and 1,336) and 9 higher secondary schools (3,769 and 335). There were 9 general education colleges, a medical college, a law college and a polytechnic; these had a total of 6,636 students; there were 9 professional and vocational colleges.

Health. In 1980 there was one doctor to each 1,500 population, and one hospital bed to each 250. There were 251 nurses.

INDONESIA

Republik Indonesia

Capital: Jakarta
Population: 154m. (1981)
GNP per capita: US$420 (1980)

HISTORY. In the 16th century Portuguese traders in quest of spices settled in some of the islands, but were ejected by the British, who in turn were ousted by the Dutch (1595). From 1602 the Netherlands East India Company conquered the Netherlands East Indies, and ruled them until the dissolution of the company in 1798. Thereafter the Netherlands Government ruled the colony from 1816 to 1941, when it was occupied by the Japanese until 1945. An independent republic was proclaimed by Dr Sukarno and Dr Hatta on 17 Aug. 1945.

Complete and unconditional sovereignty was transferred to the Republic of the United States of Indonesia on 27 Dec. 1949, except for the western part of New Guinea, the status of which was to be determined through negotiations between Indonesia and the Netherlands within one year after the transfer of sovereignty. A union was created to regulate the relationship between the two countries. A settlement of the New Guinea (Irian Jaya) question was, however, delayed until 15 Aug. 1962, when, through the good offices of the United Nations, an agreement was concluded for the transfer of the territory to Indonesia on 1 May 1963. In Feb. 1956 Indonesia abrogated the union and in Aug. 1956 repudiated Indonesia's debt to the Netherlands.

During 1950 the federal system which had sprung up in 1946–48 (*see* THE STATESMAN'S YEAR-BOOK, 1950, p. 1233) was abolished, and Indonesia was again made a unitary state. The provisional constitution was passed by the Provisional House of Representatives on 14 and came into force on 17 Aug. 1950. On 5 July 1959 by Presidential decree, the Constitution of 1945 was reinstated and the Constituent Assembly dissolved. For history 1960–66 *see* THE STATESMAN'S YEAR-BOOK, 1982–83, p. 678.

On 11–12 March 1966 the military commanders under the leadership of Lieut.-Gen. Suharto took over the executive power while leaving President Sukarno as the head of State. The Communist Party was at once outlawed and the National Front was dissolved in Oct. 1966. On 22 Feb. 1967 Sukarno handed over all his powers to Gen. Suharto.

AREA AND POPULATION. Indonesia, covering a total land area of 741,097 sq. miles (1,919,443 sq. km), consists of the islands of Sumatra, Java and Madura, Sulawesi (Celebes), Kalimantan (Borneo), Nusa Tenggara (Lesser Sundas), Maluku (Moluccas), Irian Jaya (the western half of New Guinea) and some 3,000 smaller islands and islets. It extends about 3,200 miles east to west through three time-zones (East, Central and West Standard time) of 1 hour's difference. Indonesia has a tropical climate with two monsoons; the dry (June–Sept.) and the wet (Oct.–April).

The total population in 1980 (census) was 147,490,298, distributed as follows:

Province	*Sq. km*	*Census 1980*	*Chief town*	*Census 1971*
Aceh (D.I.)	59,904	2,611,271	Banda Aceh	53,668
Sumatera Utara	71,104	8,360,894	Medan	635,562
Sumatera Barat	49,333	3,406,816	Padang	196,339
Riau	124,084	2,168,535	Pakanbaru	145,030
Jambi	62,150	1,445,994	Telanaipura	158,559
Sumatera Selatan	104,363	4,629,801	Palembang	582,961
Bengkulu	20,760	768,064	Bengkulu	31,866
Lampung	33,866	4,624,785	Tanjungkarang	198,986
Sumatra	524,097	28,016,160		

Province	*Sq. km*	*Census 1980*	*Chief town*	*Census 1971*
Jakarta Raya (D.C.I.)	592	6,503,449	Jakarta	4,576,009
Jawa Barat	49,144	27,453,525	Bandung	1,201,730
Jawa Tengah	34,353	25,372,889	Semarang	646,590
Yogyakarta (D.I.)	3,090	2,750,813	Yogyakarta	342,267
Jawa Timur	46,865	29,188,852	Surabaya	1,556,255
Jawa and Madura	134,044	91,269,528		
Kalimantan Barat	157,066	2,486,068	Pontianak	217,555
Kalimantan Tengah	156,552	954,353	Palangkaraya	27,132
Kalimantan Selatan	33,966	2,064,649	Banjarmasin	281,673
Kalimantan Timur	202,619	1,218,016	Samarinda	137,521
Kalimantan	550,203	6,723,086		
Sulawesi Utara	24,200	2,115,384	Menado	169,684
Sulawesi Tengah	88,655	1,289,635	Palu	...
Sulawesi Selatan	83,799	6,062,212	Ujung Padang	434,766
Sulawesi Tenggara	32,454	942,302	Kendari	...
Sulawesi	229,108	10,409,533		
Bali	5,623	2,469,930	Denpasar	88,142
Nusu Tenggara Barat	21,740	2,724,664	Mataram	...
Nusu Tenggara Timur	48,889	2,737,166	Kupang	52,698
Loro Sae [1]	14,925	555,350	Dili	65,451
Maluku	83,675	1,411,006	Amboina	79,636
Irian Jaya	421,981	1,173,875	Jajapura	45,786
Palau–Palau Lain	596,833	11,071,991		
Totals	2,034,255	147,490,298		

[1] Formerly Portuguese East Timor.

Other major cities (1971): Malang, 422,428; Surakarta, 414,285; Bogor, 195,882; Kediri, 178,865; all on Java. Estimate (1981) 154m.

The principal ethnic groups are the Aceh, Bataks and Minangkabaus in Sumatra, the Javanese and Sundanese in Java, the Madurese in Madura, the Balinese in Bali, the Sasaks in Lombok, the Menadonese, Minahas, Torajas and Buginese in Sulawesi, the Dayaks in Kalimantan, Irianese in Irian Jaya, the Ambonese in the Moluccas and Timorese in Timor Timur.

Bahasa Indonesia is the official language of the Republic.

GOVERNMENT AND CONSTITUTION. Indonesia is a sovereign, independent republic.

The People's Consultative Assembly is the supreme power. It has 920 members and it sits at least once every 5 years. The House of People's Representatives has 460 members, 360 of them elected and 100 nominated by the President upon recommendation and sits for a 5-year term.

General elections to the 360 elected seats in the House of Representatives were held on 4 May 1982 and 242 seats were won by the Golkar Party

President, Prime Minister and Minister of Defence: Gen. Suharto, elected by the People's Consultative Assembly in 1968 and re-elected in 1973, 1978 and 1983.

Vice-President: H. Adam Malik. *Minister and Secretary of State:* Lieut.-Gen. S. H. Soedharmono. *Economics, Finance and Industry, and Chairman of the National Planning Board:* Dr Widjojo Nitisastro. *Public Welfare:* Gen. Surono. *Politics, Security and Defence:* Gen. Maraden Panggabean. *Development and Environment:* Dr Emil Salim. *Research and Technology:* Dr B. J. Habibie. *Administration Reform and Deputy Chairman of the National Planning Board:* Dr J. B. Soemarlin. *Agriculture:* Soedarsono Hadisapoetro. *Communications:*

Roesmin Nurjadin. *Defence, Security and Commander of the Armed Forces:* Gen. M. Yusuf. *Education and Culture:* Dr Daoed Joesoef. *Foreign Affairs:* Dr Mochtar Kusumaatmadja. *Health:* Dr Suwardjono Suryaningrat. *Home Affairs:* Amir Machmud. *Industry:* A. R. Soehoed. *Information:* Gen. Ali Moertopo. *Justice:* Ali Said. *Manpower and Transmigration:* Dr Harun Alrasjid Zain. *Mining and Energy:* Professor Dr Soebroto. *Public Works and Electric Power:* Dr Pernomosidi Hadjisaroso. *Religion:* Alamsjah Ratu Prawiranegara. *Social Affairs:* Sapardjo. *Trade and Co-operatives:* Dr Radius Prawiro.

There are 6 junior ministers.

National flag: Horizontally red over white.

National anthem: Indonesia Raya (tune by Wage Rudolf Supratman, 1928).

DEFENCE. The Indonesian Armed Forces were formally set up on 5 Oct. 1945. On 11 Oct. 1967 the Army, Navy, Air Force and Police were integrated under the Department of Defence and Security. Their commanders no longer hold cabinet rank. There is selective military service.

Army. There is 1 armoured cavalry brigade, 13 infantry brigades, 2 airborne infantry brigades, 1 artillery regiment, 1 engineer and 2 air defence regiments, 15 artillery battalions. Total strength in 1983 was 200,000.

Navy. The fleet comprises 4 diesel powered patrol submarines (2 new Fed. German built and 2 *ex*-Soviet), 10 small frigates, 8 fast missile boats, 2 fast torpedo boats, 15 patrol vessels, 4 fleet minesweepers, 8 small patrol craft, 14 landing ships, 2 landing craft, 2 training ships, 4 surveying vessels, 5 oilers, 2 command and support ships, 1 destroyer depot ship, 1 repair ship, 1 cable ship, 10 auxiliaries, 62 minor landing craft, 20 service craft and 9 tugs. The (*ex*-Soviet) cruiser was discarded in 1972; and only 2 of the 10 (originally 14) old submarines and none of the 8 old destroyers acquired from the USSR remain. The construction of 2 more small submarines is being undertaken in Germany (Fed. Rep.). The naval air arm has 43 aircraft, including 20 helicopters. There are 60 customs patrol cutters, 6 maritime security agency boats and 30 armed marine police craft.

Naval personnel in 1983 numbered 40,000 officers and men, including 5,000 of the Marine Commando Corps and 1,000 in the Naval Air Arm.

Air Force. Operational combat units comprise two squadrons of A-4E Skyhawk attack aircraft, and single squadrons of F-5E Tiger II fighters and OV-10F Bronco twin-turboprop counter-insurgency aircraft. There are 3 transport squadrons, equipped with turboprop C-130 Hercules, CASA Aviocar and F-27 Friendship, and piston-engined C-47 aircraft (3 specially-equipped Boeing 737 dual-purpose maritime surveillance/transports on order); and an assortment of other aircraft in transport, helicopter and training units including 12 Hawk attack/trainers, 16 T-34C-1 armed turboprop trainers, and 20 Swiss-built AS 202 Bravo piston-engined primary trainers. Personnel (1982) approximately 29,000.

INTERNATIONAL RELATIONS

Membership. Indonesia is a member of UN and ASEAN.

ECONOMY

Planning. The third Five-Year Development Plan (1979–84) provides funds from central government for food production and other programmes implemented by village, region, province and municipal authority. Village projects include building and credits to farmers; regions and municipalities implement schemes to create employment, often in road-making; provinces receive sums for specific projects. Aid is also provided for school building, health centres, irrigation and fertilizer plant. The largest single programme is that for increased production of paddy, secondary and horticultural crops (7·6% of plan budget). Other important programmes are those for stimulating fisheries and stock-farming, and for generally lessening dependence on rice by encouraging other food crops.

Budget. The ordinary budget, excluding the development budget, was as follows in 1982–83 (in Rp. 1m.): Gross revenue, 13,607,000m.; gross expenditure, 15,607,000m.

Currency. The monetary unit is the *rupiah* (abbreviated Rp.), divided into 100 *sen*. There are banknotes of 1, 2½, 5, 10, 25, 50 and 100 rupiahs and aluminium coins of 1, 5, 10, 25 and cupro-nickel coins of 50 sen.

In March 1983 there were 1,063 rupiahs = £1 sterling; 669 rupiahs = US$1.

Banking. The Bank Indonesia, formerly the Java Bank, established in 1828, was made the central bank of Indonesia on 1 July 1953. It had an original capital of Rp. 25m.; a reserve fund of Rp. 18m. and a special reserve of Rp. 84m.

Bank Negara Indonesia is a state bank and is designed to act as a source of credit for reconstruction purposes. The Bank Pembangunan Indonesia accords long-term credits for agricultural, industrial and mining projects. The Bank Koperasi Tani & Nelayan extends credits to co-operative societies and smaller business men.

There are 7 major commercial banks and 14 foreign banks; the latter include the Chartered Bank, the Hongkong and Shanghai Banking Corporation, the Bank of America, the Citibank, the Bank of Tōkyō, Chase Manhattan and the American Express International Banking Corporation.

In Aug. 1973, 18,377 co-operative societies, including 17,589 primary co-operatives with 2·8m. members and savings of Rp. 4,530m. (provisional), had a combined membership of 6·8m.

Weights and Measures. The metric system of weights and measures was officially introduced in Feb. 1923, and came into full operation on 1 Jan. 1938.

The following are the old weights and measures: *Pikol* = 136·16 lb. avoirdupois; *Katti* = 1·36 lb. avoirdupois; *Bau* = 1·7536 acres; *Square Pal* = 227 hectares = 561·16 acres; *Jengkal* = 4 yd; *Pal* (Java) = 1,506 metres; *Pal* (Sumatra) = 1,852 metres.

ENERGY AND NATURAL RESOURCES

Electricity. All gas and electricity undertakings were nationalized by presidential decree of 3 Oct. 1953, retroactive from 23 Dec. 1952. Three large-scale hydro-electric plants are operating on the Jatiluhur and Brantas rivers in Java and on the Asahan River in Sumatra. Electricity generated, 1978, 5·5m. mwh.

Oil. Indonesia is the principal producer of petroleum in the Far East, production coming from Sumatra, Kalimantan (Indonesian Borneo) and Java, where Anglo-Dutch and US interests operate. Indonesia is the tenth largest OPEC producer. The 1982 (preliminary) output of crude oil was 488m. bbls. Production rate, 1982, 77·5m. tonnes.

Gas. Pertamina, the state oil company, started to pump natural gas to Jakarta in 1979.

Minerals. The high cost of extraction means that little of the large mineral resources outside Java is exploited; however, there is copper mining in Irian Jaya, nickel mining and processing on Sulawesi, aluminium smelting in northern Sumatra. The tin mines of Bangka, Billiton and Riouw are worked by the Government. In 1981 their total yield was 33,600 tonnes. Output (in 1000 tonnes, 1981) of bauxite was 1,270; iron sand, 1,339; coal 329; copper, 180; silver, 2·4 (tons); gold, 233·9 kg.

Agriculture. Indonesian agriculture is divided between estate and smallholders cultivation.

Rice production (1979), 17·92m. tonnes. Other main crops are maize, rubber, cassava, sweet potatoes, copra, coffee, palms. In 1978 production on estates was (in 1,000 tonnes): Copra, 1,467; sugar 1,553; rubber, 844; palm oil, 519; tea, 85.

Livestock (1980): Cattle, 6,423,000; buffaloes, 2,353,000; horses, 618,000; sheep, 3,611,000; goats, 8,051,000; pigs, 2,755,000.

Forestry. The forest area is 122m. hectares. Production (1981): All timber, 27·38m. cu. metres.

Fisheries. In 1978 (provisional) the catch of sea fisheries was 1,655,000 tons.

INDUSTRY AND TRADE

Industry. There are shipyards at Jakarta Raya, Surabaya, Semarang and Amboina. There are many textile factories (total production in 1978–79, 1,400m. metres), large paper factories (83,496 tonnes, 1977–78), match factories, automobile and bicycle assembly works, large construction works, tyre factories, glass factories, a caustic soda and other chemical factories. Production (1977–78): Cement, 2,878,500 tonnes; fertilizers, 1·55m. tonnes; glass, 43,571,720 tons; 7·4m. cycle tyres; 2,339,100 motor vehicles; 6,806,000 cu. metres of oxygen; 305,000 cu. metres of acetylene.

There were (1978) 8 oil refineries with a combined capacity of 31·5m. bbls per day. Domestic consumption takes about 12% and the remainder is exported mainly to Japan and USA.

For details of nationalization *see* THE STATESMAN'S YEAR-BOOK, 1981–82, p. 677.

Trade Unions. The largest group of trade unions in Indonesia is the Serekat Organasasi Karyawan Seluruh Indonesia (SOKSI), the Central Council of All Indonesia Trade Unions, with a membership of 2·6m., to which 28 national unions and 832 local unions are affiliated. The second largest is the Kongres Buruh Seluruh Indonesia (KBSI), the All Indonesia Trades Union Congress, with a membership of nearly 400,000. To the KBSI 25 national unions and 54 local unions are affiliated. There are also the HISSBI (Federation of Indonesian Trade Unions) with a membership of 180,203, and the KBKI (Indonesian Democratic Labour Organization), with a membership of 94,477. In addition, there are also trade-union centres which are closely connected with the Islamic Parties, viz., Serikat Buruh Islam Indonesia, with a membership of 275,000; the Sarekat Buruh Muslimin Indonesia, with a membership of 11,950, and the Gerakan Organisasi Buruh Sjarekat Islam Indonesia, with a membership of 1,347.

Commerce. Imports and exports (including oil) in US$1m. for year April–March:

	1977	*1978*	*1979*	*1980*	*1981*
Imports	6,230·3	6,690·4	7,202·3	10,834·4	13,272·0
Exports	10,625·6	11,643·2	15,590·1	21,908·9	23,120·0

The main export items (in US$1m.) in 1979 were: Oil, 15,590·1; coffee, 614·5; rubber, 936·8; palm-oil and kernels, 186·9 (1977); tin ore, 404·4; tea, 834; tobacco, 56·6; copra, 36·2 (1977); wood, 1,796·7.

The main import items are non-crude oil, rice, consumer goods, fertilizer, chemicals, weaving yarn, iron and steel, industrial and business machinery.

Total trade between Indonesia and UK (British Department of Trade returns, in £1,000 sterling):

	1977	*1978*	*1979*	*1980*	*1981*	*1982*
Imports to UK	28,740	33,384	55,950	56,971	73,756	91,704
Exports and re-exports from UK	86,683	83,632	76,704	112,170	139,236	212,066

Tourism. In 1980 about 561,000 tourists visited Indonesia mainly from USA, Australia, Japan, Netherlands, Germany, France, UK and Singapore.

COMMUNICATIONS

Roads. The projected Trans-Sumatra trunk road will connect Aceh (north) and Lampung (south). The feeder-road between West Sumatra and Riau provinces was completed with the building of the bridge over the Kampar River at Pekanbaru in 1974. Motor vehicles, at 31 Dec. 1979, totalled 577,345 passenger cars, 383,648 vans and trucks, 69,545 buses and about 2,266,183 motor cycles.

Railways. In 1980 the State Railways totalled 6,877 km, comprising 4,922 km of 1,067 mm gauge on Java, and 1,458 km of 1,067 mm gauge and 497 km of 750 mm gauge on Sumatra. In 1978, 29·2m. passengers were carried.

Aviation. The Government and KLM in 1949 set up 'Garuda Indonesian Airways' as a mixed enterprise on a 50–50 capital basis under KLM management. The agreement was to last until 1960. In 1954, however, the Government bought up the shares held by KLM for 15m. guilders and nationalized GIA; and in Jan. 1958, the Government unilaterally terminated the contracts with the technical assistants provided by KLM. GIA maintains a direct service between Jakarta and Manila, Bangkok, Hong Kong, Tōkyō and Amsterdam. In 1978–79 the company flew 65,958 km and carried 3,970,557 passengers and 35,822 tons of goods on domestic flights, and on international flights flew 17m. flying hours, carried 269,746,000 passengers and 4,257 tons of goods.

Shipping. The national shipping company Pelajaran Nasional Indonesia (PELNI) had in 1973 a fleet of 312 vessels, and maintains interinsular communications. The Jakarta Lloyd maintains regular services between Jakarta, Amsterdam, Hamburg and London.

Post and Broadcasting. In 1979 the postal and telegraph services of Indonesia included 2,796 post offices. There were 660 telegraph offices which handled 3·9m. domestic and 488,000 international cables. Post offices handled 176m. letters and Rp. 250,000m. in money orders, Giro and postal cheques. Deposits with post office savings accounts, Rp. 31,210m. Number of telephones (1980), 392,563.

Radio Republik Indonesia, under the Department of Information, operates 26 stations. Television broadcasting covers 82m. people in an area of 72,100 sq. km. There were, in 1979, 82 transmission stations and 11 relay stations.

Newspapers (1973). There were 117 daily newspaper publishers with estimated daily circulation of 1·6m. There were 270 publishers of weekly papers and magazines with a circulation of 3·3m.

JUSTICE, RELIGION, EDUCATION AND WELFARE

Justice. There are courts of first instance, high courts of appeal in every provincial capital and a Supreme Court of Justice for the whole of Indonesia in Jakarta. Administrative matters on judicial organization are under the direction of the Department of Justice.

In civil law the population is divided into three main groups: Indonesians, Europeans and foreign Orientals, to whom different law systems are applicable. When, however, people from different groups are involved, a system of so-called 'inter-gentile' law is applied.

The present criminal law, which has been in force since 1918, is codified and is based on European penal law. This law is equally applicable to all groups of the population. For private and commercial law, however, there are various systems applicable for the various groups of the population. For the Indonesians, a system of private and agrarian law is applicable; this is called Adat Law, and is mainly uncodified. For the other groups the prevailing private and commercial law system is codified in the Private Law Act (1847) and the Commercial Law Act (1847). These Acts have their origins in the French *Code Civile* and *Code du Commerce* through the similar Dutch codifications. These Acts are entirely applicable to Indonesian citizens and to Europeans, whereas to foreign Orientals they are applicable with some exceptions, mainly in the fields of family law and inheritance. Penal law was in the process of being codified in 1981.

Religion. Religious liberty is granted to all denominations. The majority of the Indonesians are Moslems. There are nearly 6m. Christians; their main strength is in Central and East Java, North Sulawesi, East Nusa Tenggara, the Moluccas and Irian Jaya. There are also about 1m. Buddhists, probably for the greater part Chinese. Hinduism has 6m. members, of whom 2·5m. are on Bali.

In 1978–79 there were 423,570 Islamic houses of worship, 24,215 Christian (7,052 of them Catholic), 4,365 Hindu and 1,762 Buddhist.

Education. The following table shows the number of school and college students in 1978 (1,000):

Total population aged 7–13	23,000
Pupils in public and private elementary schools	97,948 [1]
Pupils in Islamic schools	3,032 [1]
Total population aged 13–18	16,196 [1]
Junior high school pupils	2,800 [1]
Senior high school pupils	1,472 [1]
Academy and university students	195,994

[1] 1979–80.

English is the first foreign language taught in schools.

There are 51 universities (23 are private).

In 1961 a separate Department of Higher Education and Science was set up. Five training centres for technical education were opened in May 1975 and these continue to expand.

Health. In 1978–79 there were 4,573 public health centres, 2,412 mother-and-child clinics, 4,180 polyclinics, 10,456 doctors and 31,061 nurses and midwives.

DIPLOMATIC REPRESENTATIVES

Of Indonesia in Great Britain (38 Grosvenor Sq., London W1X 9AD)
Ambassador: Sjahabuddin Arifin (accredited on 12 Nov. 1981).

Of Great Britain in Indonesia (Jalan, M.H. Thamrin, 75, Jakarta)
Ambassador: Robert Brash, CMG.

Of Indonesia in the USA (2020 Massachusetts Ave., NW, Washington, D.C., 20036)
Ambassador: A. Hasnan Habib.

Of the USA in Indonesia (Medan Merdeka Selatan 5, Jakarta)
Chargé d'Affaires: John C. Monjo.

Of Indonesia to the United Nations
Ambassador: Hadi Ahmad A. Wayarabi.

Books of Reference

Bemmelen, R. W. van, *Geology of Indonesia.* 2 vols. The Hague, 1949
Echols, J. M., and Shadily, H., *An Indonesian–English Dictionary.* 3rd ed. Cornell Univ. Press, 1975
Grant, B., *Indonesia.* Melbourne Univ. Press, 1964
Helsdingen, W. H. van, and Hoogenberk, H. (ed.), *Mission Interrupted; The Dutch in the East Indies . . . in the 20th century.* Amsterdam, 1946
Hindley, D., *The Communist Party of Indonesia, 1951–63.* California Univ. Press and CUP, 1965
Legge, J. D., *Sukarno: A Political Biography.* London, 1972
McDonald, H., *Suharto's Indonesia.* Univ. Press of Hawaii, 1981
Neill, W. T., *Twentieth-Century Indonesia.* Columbia Univ. Press, 1973
Polomka, P., *Indonesia Since Sukarno.* London, 1971
Taylor, A. M., *Indonesian Independence and the United Nations.* Cornell Univ. Press, 1960
Weinstein, F. B., *Indonesian Foreign Policy and the Dilemma of Dependence.* Cornell Univ. Press, 1977

IRAN

Jomhori-e-Islami-e-Irân

Capital: Tehrán
Population: 40·55m. (1982)
GNP per capita: US$2,160 (1977)

HISTORY. Persia was ruled by the Shahs as an absolute monarchy until 30 Dec. 1906 when the first Constitution was granted. Reza Khan took control after a *coup d'état* on 31 Oct. 1925 deposed the last Shah of the Qajar Dynasty, and became Reza Shah Pahlavi on 12 Dec. 1925. The country's name was changed to Iran on 21 March 1935. Reza Shah abdicated on 16 Sept. 1941 (and died 25 July 1944) in favour of his son, Mohammad Reza Pahlavi (born 26 Oct. 1919).

Following widespread civil unrest, the Shah left Iran with his family on 17 Jan. 1979 (and died in Egypt 27 July 1980). The Ayatollah Ruhollah Khomeini, spiritual leader of the Shi'a Moslem community, returned from 15 years exile on 1 Feb. 1979 and appointed a provisional government on 5 Feb. The Shah's government resigned and Parliament dissolvéd itself on 11 Feb. Following a referendum in March, an Islamic Republic was proclaimed on 1 Apr. 1979.

AREA AND POPULATION. Iran is bounded north by the USSR and the Caspian Sea, east by Afghánistán and Pakistan, south by the Gulf of Oman and the Persian Gulf, and west by Iraq and Turkey. It has an area of about 1,648,000 sq. km (636,000 sq. miles), but a vast portion is desert, and the average density is only (1982) 25 inhabitants to the sq. km.

The population at recent censuses was as follows: (1956) 18,944,821; (1966) 25,781,090; (1976) 33,591,875. Estimate (1982) 40,550,000.

The populations (census 1976) and capitals of the provinces *(ostán)* were:

Azarbáiján Bákhtari	1,407,970	Rezáyeh	Hamadán	1,093,079	Hamadán
Azarbáiján Khavari	3,204,761	Tabriz	Ilam	242,812	Abdanan
Bakhtiári va Chahár Mahál	398,807	Shahr Kord	Kermán	1,085,097	Kermán
Balúchestán va Sistán	662,677	Záhedán	Kermánsháhán	1,025,257	Kermánsháh
Boyer ahmadi va Kohkiluyeh	242,207	Yasoof	Khorásán	3,250,085	Mashhad
Bushehá	347,703	Bushehr	Khuzestán	2,187,198	Ahváz
Esfáhán	1,971,745	Esfáhán	Kordestán	783,740	Sánándáj
Fárs	2,020,942	Shiráz	Lorestan	932,297	Khorramábád
Gilán	1,579,317	Rasht	Markazi	6,954,729	Tehrán
			Mázándárán	2,386,956	Sári
			Semnán	487,531	Semnán
			Yazd	358,082	Yazd
			Zanjan	577,286	Zanjan

The principal cities at census 1976 were:

Tehrán	4,496,159	Qom	246,831	Karaj	138,774
Esfáhán	671,825	Rasht	187,203	Qazvin	138,527
Mashhad	670,180	Rezáyeh	163,991	Yazd	135,978
Tabriz	598,576	Hamadán	155,846	Arak	114,507
Shiráz	416,408	Ardabil	147,404	Desful	110,287
Ahváz	329,006	Khorramshahr	146,709	Khorramábád	104,928
Abadan	296,081	Kermán	140,309	Borujerd	100,103

The national language is Farsi or Persian, spoken by 45% of the population. 23% spoke related languages, including Kurdish and Luri in the west and Baluchi in the south-east, while 26% spoke Turkic languages, primarily the Azarbáijáni-speaking peoples of the north-west and the Turkomen of Khorásan in the north-east. 5% comprise Arabic-speakers, chiefly those of Khuzestan in the south-west.

CONSTITUTION AND GOVERNMENT. The Constitution of the Islamic Republic was approved by a national referendum in Dec. 1979. It gives supreme authority to a religious leader (*wali faqih*), which position will be held by Ayatollah

Khomeini for the rest of his natural life, and thereafter be elected by the Moslem clergy.

The President of the Republic is popularly-elected for a 4-year term and is head of the executive; he appoints a Prime Minister and other Ministers, subject to approval by the *Majlis*.

Presidents since the establishment of the Islamic Republic:

Abolhassan Bani-Sadr, 4 Feb. 1980–22 June 1981 (deposed)

Mohammad Ali Raja'i, 24 July 1981–30 Aug. 1981 (assassinated).

President: Hojatolislam Sayed Ali Khamenei (from 12 Oct. 1981).

Prime Minister: Mir Hussein Moussavi.

Foreign Affairs: Dr Ali Akbar Vellayati. *Interior:* Hojatolislam Ali Akbar Nateq Nouri. *Defence:* Col. Mohammed Salimi. *Labour and Social Affairs:* Ahmed Tavakolli. *Education and Training:* Ali Akbar Parvaresh. *Islamic Guidance:* (Vacant). *Commerce:* Habibollah Asgar-Owladi Mosalman. *Health:* Dr Hadi Manafi. *Posts and Telecommunications:* Morteza Nabavi. *Justice:* Sayyed Mohammed Asghari. *Roads and Transport:* Hadinezhad Hoseyniyan. *Industry:* Sayyed Mostafa Hashemi. *Higher Education and Culture:* Dr Mohammad Ali Najafi. *Mines and Metals:* Sayyed Hussein Musaviyani. *Agriculture:* Mohammed Salamati. *Housing and Urban Development:* Mohammed Shahab Gonabadi. *Energy:* Dr Hassan Ghafuri-Fard. *Oil:* Sayyed Mohammed Gharazi. *Heavy Industry:* Behzad Nabavi. *Economic Affairs and Finance:* Dr Hussein Namazi. *Ministers of State:* Dr Mohammad Taqi Banki *(Planning and Budget)*, Gholamreza Agazadeh *(Executive Affairs)*.

Legislative power is held by a 270-member Islamic Consultative Assembly *(Majlis)*, directly elected for a 4-year term on 9 May 1980; but all legislation is subject to approval by a 12-member Council of Guardians who ensure it is in accordance with the Islamic code and with the Constitution. Six members of this constitutional Council are appointed by the *wali faqih* and six by the judiciary.

National flag: Three horizontal stripes of green, white and red; on the borders of the green and red stripes the legend *Allah Akbar* in white Kufi script repeated 22 times in all; in the centre of the white stripe the national emblem in red.

Local Government. The country is divided into 21 provinces *(ostán)* and 2 governor-generalships; these are sub-divided into 172 *shahrestán* (counties), each under a *farmándár* (governor) and thence into 499 *bakhsh* (districts), each under a *bakhshdár*. The districts are sub-divided into *dehistán* (groups of villages) each under a *dehdár*, each village having its elected *kadkhodá* (headman).

DEFENCE

Army. The Army consists of about 150,000 men organized in 4 infantry divisions, 4 independent infantry brigades, 3 armoured divisions, and auxiliary units. Two years' military service is compulsory. *Gendarmerie* strength is about 75,000. Its function is internal security in rural areas.

Navy. The Navy, in a state of decline since the revolution, before the war comprised 3 very old destroyers, 4 frigates, 4 old corvettes, 3 old coastal minesweepers, 2 inshore minesweepers, 7 patrol boats, 14 hovercraft, 2 landing ships, 1 landing craft, 2 supply ships, 1 repair ship, 2 oilers, 4 survey vessels, 1 water carrier and 3 tugs. There were also 30 coastguard cutters and 2 customs craft.

The construction of 12 fast missile craft in France was to have been completed by mid-1979, but later boats did not receive their missiles and the last 3 boats were embargoed in France. They eventually sailed on 2 Aug. 1981 but one was seized by a Royalist group off Cadiz and after she surrended to the French all three were sent to Iran in a merchant ship to obviate further trouble. Two new landing ships had been projected.

The naval air arm comprised 14 assorted aircraft and 20 helicopters.

In 1983 personnel nominally totalled 20,000 officers and ratings including cadets, apprentices and marines, but few were on active service at sea.

With war following revolution and withdrawal of UK and US maintenance teams the fleet is suffering from lack of spares and the navy has run down, several ships being laid up. The situation is worsened by cessation of foreign help in training semi-illiterate conscripts and with poor morale following general instability and casualties the above ships do not represent an efficient maritime force.

Claims of sinkings during the Iran-Iraq war have not been officially confirmed. Figures for ship and personnel strengths should be interpreted with caution.

Air Force. In Aug. 1955 the Air Force became a separate and independent arm, and had a strength of about 23 first-line squadrons (each 15 aircraft, plus reserves), with 100,000 personnel before the 1979 revolution. There were 4 squadrons of F-14 Tomcat interceptors, with Phoenix missiles, 8 squadrons of F-5E Tiger II fighter-bombers, 10 squadrons of F-4D and F-4E Phantom interceptor/fighter bombers and 1 reconnaissance squadron of RF-4Es. Six P-3F Orions had been acquired for long-range anti-submarine duties. The transport wing was equipped with 54 C-130E/H Hercules and 18 F-27 Friendship turboprop transports and smaller types. Eleven Boeing 707-320C and 10 Boeing 747 transports included some adapted as tankers to support the tactical fighter and anti-submarine squadrons. The Air Force also operated some of the many hundreds of turbine-powered helicopters acquired for the Iranian services, including twin-engined CH-47C Chinooks, Super Frelons and Model 214 utility helicopters. Training aircraft included Bonanza basic trainers, T-33 advanced trainers and two-seat F-5B/Fs. Missiles in service included Rapier and Tigercat surface-to-air weapons. Strength in 1982 is uncertain, but has been estimated at 35,000 personnel and 90 serviceable combat aircraft, comprising 5 F-14s, 50 F-5Es, 30 F-4D/Es and 5 RF-4Es.

INTERNATIONAL RELATIONS

Membership. Iran is a member of UN, OPEC and the Colombo Plan.

ECONOMY

Planning. The sixth 5-year development plan, 1978–83 was abandoned following the revolution.

Budget. Budget estimate for year commencing 21 March 1981: Revenue 2,025,000m. *rials*; expenditure 3,300,000m. *rials*.

Currency. The Iranian unit of currency is the *rial* sub-divided into 100 *dinars*.

Notes in circulation are of denominations of 5–10,000 *rials*. Coins in circulation are bronze–aluminium and copper, 50 *dinar*; silver alloy, 1, 2, 5, 10 and 20 *rials*.

In March 1983, US$1 = 84·30 *rials*; £1 = 128 *rials*.

Banking. The *Bank Markazi Iran* was established in 1960 as the note-issuing authority and government bank of Iran. All other banks were nationalized in June 1979, and re-organized into 8 new state banking corporations.

All insurance companies were nationalized in June 1979.

Weights and Measures. By a law passed on 8 Jan. 1933, the official weights and measures are those of the metric system.

The Iranian year is a solar year running from 21 March to 20 March; the Hejira year 1362 corresponds to the Christian year 21 March 1983–20 March 1984.

ENERGY AND NATURAL RESOURCES

Electricity. Electric energy installed capacity, 1980, was 5·3m. kw., and 17,150m. kwh. was generated.

Oil. For a history of Iran's oil industry 1951–79, *see* STATESMAN'S YEAR-BOOK, 1982–83.

The petroleum industry was seriously disrupted by the 1979 revolution, and many facilities, including the vast refinery at Abadan, the new refinery at Bandar Khomeini and the tanker terminal at Kharg Island, have been destroyed or put out of action during the Gulf war with Iraq. All operating companies were nationalised in 1979 and operations are now run by the National Petrochemical Company.

Total production of petroleum, 73·7m. tonnes, 1980 (113·2m. tonnes, 1979).

Gas. Natural gas production (1979) was 44,300m. cu. metres.

Minerals. Iran has substantial mineral deposits relatively underdeveloped. Production figures for 1977 (in 1,000 tonnes): Iron ore, 670; coal, 900; zinc, 62; lead, 40; manganese, 15; chromite, 80; salt (1973), 500.

Agriculture. Reliable statistics of production are not available. It is estimated, however, that out of 164·8m. hectares of land area only 16,857,000 are crop land (including 10,300 hectares fallow), 27·8m. hectares are forests and ranges and 32·7m. hectares are potentially cultivable waste.

Crop returns for 1979 (in 1,000 tonnes): Wheat, 5,000; barley, 900; rice, 1,212; sugar-beet, 3,900; sugar-cane, 1,750; tobacco, 15.

Wool comes principally from Khorásán, Kermánsháh, Mázandarán and Azerbáiján. Production, 1972, 20,000 tonnes.

Rice is grown largely on the Caspian shores.

Tobacco is grown along the shores of the Caspian. It is purchased by the Tobacco Monopoly and manufactured in the government factory at Tehrán.

Opium, until 1955, was an important export commodity in Iran. On 7 Oct. 1955 an Act was approved by Parliament to prohibit the cultivation and usage of opium.

Livestock (1980): 32m. sheep, 13·6m. goats, 7·6m. cattle, 350,000 horses, 27,000 camels, 55,000 pigs and 1·8m. donkeys.

Fisheries. The Caspian Fisheries Co. (Shilát) is a government monopoly. Exports of caviar (1975) were valued at US$72m.

INDUSTRY AND TRADE

Industry. Iran's chief natural products are oil, wool, cotton, silk, fruit, nuts, cereals, vegetables, gum, timber, oil seeds, copper and other metalliferous ores, coal, cattle, sheep and goats. Its principal manufactured or processed products are textiles, carpets, skins, casings, vegetable oil, soap, metal products, plastic products, furniture, beet sugar, tea, tobacco and cigarettes, wine, vodka, soft drinks, caviar, footwear, petroleum products, glass products, tiles, bricks, cement, leather and leather goods, dairy products and manufactured foodstuffs, and printed matter.

In 1975 there were 215,087 manufacturing units employing about 2m. people. Apart from the oil industry, the industries employing most workers are textiles, sugar refining, flour-milling, fruit processing, tea, furniture, printing, leather, matches, glass, building materials and light metal goods. The most popular carpets are manufactured in the environs of Tabriz, Kermán, Arák, Káshán, Esfahán, Shiráz and Hamadán. Esfahán is the traditional textile manufacturing centre, but in recent years important textile mills, particularly cotton, have been built in other towns, including Tehrán. A number of automobile assembly plants have been set up in recent years employing several thousand workers. A steel-mill, a machine-tool factory, a tractor plant and a huge petrochemical complex are also going into production.

In March 1975 it was decreed that 99% of shares in all state-owned factories were to be sold to their workers and the public. This did not apply to the key industries—oil, steel, copper and transport. Production, 1972, in 1,000 tonnes: Cement, 3,600 (1975, 5,145); nitrogenous fertilizers, 108; hydrochloric acid, 15·6; sugar, 598 (1975, 558); wheat flour, 3,800; cotton yarn, 42; wool yarn, 29·2; ethyl alcohol, 33,000 hectolitres; woven silks, 7m. metres; cotton fabrics, 482m. metres, and woollen fabrics, 13m. metres.

Labour. Legislation regulating conditions of employment in certain industrial undertakings was first introduced in 1949. The subsequent adoption of certain international minimum standards led to the enactment of the Labour Act of 1959, which establishes basic provisions dealing with hours of work; holidays with pay; the payment of wages, salaries and overtime; the formation, registration and activities of employers' and workers' organizations; employment contracts and collective agreements; the settlement of disputes; industrial safety, health and welfare; and labour inspection. Regulations concerning safety, health and welfare in industrial premises, conciliation procedure and the settlement of disputes, the formation, registration and activities of trade unions, the duties and powers of labour inspectors have since been promulgated. The employment of foreigners is controlled by regulations promulgated in 1960. Responsibility for the enforcement of the Labour Act, 1959, and supporting legislation is entrusted to provincial and district departments of labour.

Commerce. Imports totalled 863,300m. rials and exports 963,500m. rials in 1980. Crude oil amounted to 73% of exports and refined products to 21%; 27% of exports went to Japan and 12% to Federal Republic of Germany while these two countries each provided 14% of imports.

Total trade between Iran and UK (British Department of Trade returns, in £1,000 sterling):

	1978	*1979*	*1980*	*1981*	*1982*
Imports to UK	534,388	243,589	107,176	154,385	225,971
Exports and re-exports from UK	751,265	231,798	393,335	402,753	333,715

COMMUNICATIONS

Roads. In 1980 there were 24,806 km of first-class roads and 26,484 km of second-class (graded, all weather) roads, and 11,825 km of third class (earth) roads.

In 1974 passenger cars and taxis numbered 119,851; commercial vehicles, 13,193; buses, 2,611, and motor cycles, 19,785.

Railways. The State Railways total 4,567 km, comprising 4,473 km of 1,435 mm gauge of which 145 km electrified and 94 km of 1,676 mm gauge. Revenue in 1978–79 was 9,119m. rials, and expenditure 13,513m. rials. In 1980–81 the railways ran 6,030m. passenger-km and 976m. tonne-km.

Aviation. The principal airlines which link Tehrán and Abadan with Europe and the Middle East are Air France, British Airways, Ariana, Iraqi Airways, Alitalia, PANAM, Swissair, LIA, KLM, PIA, SAS, Qantas, SABENA, El Al, Lufthansa, Aeroflot and Middle East Air Lines. British Airways, Qantas, Lufthansa, PANAM and Air France also connect Tehrán with the Far East. Aryana (Afghánistán) Airline connects Tehrán with Lebanon, Syria and Afghánistán. British Airways, KLM and SAS operate services to Abadán and Iran National Airlines Corporation, registered on 29 March 1962, has monopoly rights on all internal flights and also operates in the Persian Gulf; in 1965 it inaugurated European services. The Iranian Government owns 51% of its shares.

Shipping. In 1979, 80·22m. tonnes of goods were loaded at Iranian ports and 15m. tonnes were unloaded.

Navigation on the Lake of Rezáyeh, from Sharaf-Khaneh to Kolmankháneh, is served by some 5 tugs and 9 barges for the transport of goods and passengers. The service runs twice a week. On the river Karun likewise, from Khorramshahr to Ahwáz, an irregular service for cargo only both ways is run by the Iran Transport Co. and the Karun Navigation Co., and some local firms run daily trips by motor boat, for passengers and merchandise. By changing into lighter-draught boats at Ahwáz both can be taken up to Shallili near Shushtar.

Post and Broadcasting. Postal, telegraph and telephone services are administered by the Iranian Ministry of Posts, Telegraphs and Telephones.

There is wireless-telegraph communication between Tehrán and Tabriz, Meshed, Kermánshah, Kermán, Khorramshahr, Bushehr, Yezd, Shiráz and Lingeh and a wireless-telephone link between Tehrán and Tabriz. Tehrán is also in wireless communication with Europe and is linked by wireless telephone with Baghdad, London, Berne and New York. In 1981 the number of telephones was 1,227,293, of which some 419,025 were in Tehrán. Wireless sets numbered 10m. in 1980, and television sets 2·1m.

Cinemas (1975). There were 430 cinemas with 299,191 seats.

Newspapers. There were in 1982, 17 daily papers in Tehrán and other cities. Their circulation is relatively small, *Ettela'át* and *Kayhán* leading with about 220,000 and 350,000 respectively. Two English-language and a French-language daily ceased publication in March 1979.

JUSTICE, RELIGION, EDUCATION AND WELFARE

Justice. A new legal system based on Islamic law was introduced by the new constitution in 1979. The President of the Supreme Court and the public Prosecutor-General are appointed by the *wali faqih* (Ayatollah Khomeini).

Religion. The official religion is the Shia branch of Islam, known as the *Ithna-Ashariyya,* which recognizes 12 Imáms or spiritual successors of the Prophet Mohammad. Of the total population, 96% are *Shiá,* 3% are *Sunni* and 1% non-Moslem (mainly Armenian Christians).

The Shia Moslems reject the *Sunna* or tradition, as distinct from the actual text of the Koran, both of which are recognized by the Sunnî Moslems. The highest authority is the leading *ayatullah*, at present *ayatullah* Khomeini.

The Gregorian National Armenians form 3 dioceses. There are also a few thousand Roman Catholic Armenians, who have a bishop of their own rite at Esfahán, the bishop of the Latin rite residing at Rezayeh (Urmia). There is an Anglican bishop residing at Esfahán.

Education. A law providing for the gradual establishment of compulsory primary education was passed in July 1943. In 1972 schooling was available for 80% of the children of school age. The literate population is estimated at 36·9%.

The influence of the French educational system has been prominent. As in France, education is highly centralized.

The curricula for primary and secondary schools are drawn up by the Ministry of Education.

The great majority of primary and secondary schools are state schools. Grants are made to private schools. Elementary education in state schools and university education are free; small fees are charged for state-run secondary schools. Text-books are issued free of charge to pupils in the first 4 grades of elementary schools.

In 1978–79 there were 4,403,106 pupils in primary schools and 2,370,341 in secondary schools; there were 256,303 students in technical schools and 57,832 in teacher-training establishments. There were 17 universities and almost 200 other institutes of higher education, with 175,675 students in 1978–79.

Health. The Ministry of Health controls the health of the country through the Department of Public Health, which has achieved some remarkable results in the fight against malaria; large areas along the Caspian and the Persian Gulf and in Azerbáiján are now free from malaria. Opium addiction has been greatly reduced, and the cultivation of the poppy has been practically eradicated. Programmes to combat tuberculosis, smallpox, trachoma, venereal diseases, etc., have been introduced.

In 1975 about 45,604 hospital beds (half of them in Tehrán) were available in 498 hospitals. Medical personnel included 10,054 physicians and surgeons and 1,462 dentists.

Social Security. A system of social security benefits covering accident, sickness, retirement, death, marriage, maternity and childbirth and free medical attention and hospitalization for insured contributors and their families is embodied in the Workers' Social Insurance Law, 1960. This law provides for the insurance under the scheme of all workers in receipt of wages or salaries, but is at present being applied to some 683,496 workers employed mainly in industrial and mining establishments employing 10 or more workers. It also provides for the compulsory payment by employers of family allowances to workers with 2 or more children.

DIPLOMATIC REPRESENTATIVES

Of Iran in Great Britain (27 Prince's Gate, London, SW7 1PX)
Chargé d'Affaires: Alireza Farrokhrouz.

Of Great Britain in Iran (Ave. Ferdowsi, Tehrán)
Head of Interests Section: N. J. Barrington, CMG, CVO (at Swedish Embassy).

Of Iran in the USA (3005 Massachusetts Ave., NW, Washington, D.C., 20008)
Ambassador: (Vacant).

Of the USA in Iran (260 Takhte Jamshid Ave., Tehrán)
Ambassador: (Vacant).

Of Iran to the United Nations
Ambassador: Dr Said Rajaie-Khorassani.

Books of Reference

Statistical Information: The principal statistical agencies of the Government are: (1) Department of Census, Civil Registration, and Statistics (Ministry of the Interior). *Director-General:* Sayyed Mehdi Hesabi; Publications on demographical statistics, in Persian. (2) Publicity and Information Department of the Seven-year Plan Organization. *Director:* Dr Mohammed Ali Rashti; Publications on industry, labour, agriculture, in English and Persian. (3) Statistical and Economic Research Department of the Bank Melli Iran; Publishes *Monthly Bulletin*, in English and Persian. (4) Customs Department (Ministry of Finance), publishes monthly and annual reports, in French and Persian. (5) and (6) Ministry of Labour and Ministry of Industry and Mines, publish statistical year-books.

Adli, Abolfazi, *Aussenhandel und Aussenwirtschaftspolitik des Iran.* Berlin, 1960
Arberry, A. J. (ed.), *The Cambridge History of Iran.* 8 vols. CUP, 1968ff.
Bharier, J., *Economic Development in Iran, 1900–1970.* OUP, 1971
Forbis, W. H., *Fall of the Peacock Throne.* New York, 1979
Graham, R., *Iran: The Illusion of Power.* London, 1978
Haim, S., *Shorter Persian–English Dictionary.* Tehran, 1958
Heikal, M., *Iran: The Untold Story.* New York, 1982
Katouzian, H., *The Political Economy of Iran.* London, 1981
Keddie, N., *Roots of Revolution.* Yale Univ. Press, 1981
Lambton, A. K. S., *Landlord and Peasant in Persia.* OUP, 1953.—*Persian Vocabulary.* CUP, 1954
Looney, R. E., *The Economic Development of Iran: A Recent Survey with Projections to 1981.* New York, 1973
Rubin, B., *Paved with Good Intentions: The American Experience in Iran.* OUP, 1981
Steinglass, F. J., *A Comprehensive Persian–English Dictionary.* 2nd ed. London, 1930
Stempel, J. D., *Inside the Iranian Revolution.* Indiana Univ. Press, 1981
Sullivan, W. H., *Mission to Iran.* New York, 1981
Zabih, S., *Iran's Revolutionary Upheaval: An Interpretive Essay.* San Francisco, 1979.—*The Mosadegh Era: Roots of the Iranian Revolution.* Chicago, 1982
Zakhoder, B. N. (ed.), *Sovremennyi Iran.* Moscow, 1957

IRAQ

al Jumhouriya al 'Iraqia

Capital: Baghdad
Population: 14m. (1982)
GNP per capita: US$3,020 (1980)

HISTORY. Part of the Ottoman Empire from the 16th century, Iraq was captured by British forces in 1916 and became in 1921 a Kingdom under a League of Nations mandate, administered by Britain. It became independent on 3 Oct. 1932 under the Hashemite Dynasty, which was overthrown on 14 July 1958 by a military *coup* which established a Republic, controlled by a military-led Council of Sovereignty. The republican régime terminated the adherence of Iraq to the Arab Federation (*see* THE STATESMAN'S YEAR-BOOK, 1958, p. 806).

An attempt at succession by the Kurdish minority in the north-east of Iraq flared up in 1962, and fighting continued until the acceptance of a peace plan in June 1966. The Revolutionary Command Council formed after the 17 July 1968 *coup* announced in March 1970 a complete and constitutional settlement of the Kurdish issue.

In Sept. 1980 Iraq invaded Iran in a dispute over the Shatt-al-Arab waterway. Fighting continued during 1982.

AREA AND POPULATION. Iraq is bounded north by Turkey, east by Iran, south-east by the Gulf, south by Kuwait and Saudi Arabia, and west by Jordan and Syria. The country has an area of 434,924 sq. km (167,925 sq. miles) and its population census (1977) was 12,029,700 and (estimate) 1982, 14m.

The areas, populations (1976 estimate) and capitals of the governates were:

Governorate	*sq. km*	*1976*	*Capital*	*1970*
Al-Anbar	89,540	405,000	Ar-Ramadi	79,488
Al-Basrah	19,702	897,000	Al-Basrah	333,684
Al-Muthanna	49,206	184,000	As-Samawah	33,473 [2]
Al-Qadisayah	8,569	395,000	Ad-Diwaniyah	60,553 [2]
An-Najaf	26,834	354,000	An-Najaf	179,160
As-Sulaymaniyah [1]	16,482	656,000	As-Sulaymaniyah	98,063
Babil (Babylon)	5,503	565,000	Al-Hillah	128,811
Baghdad	5,023	3,036,000	Baghdad	2,183,760
Dahuk [1]	6,374	217,000	Dahuk	19,736
Dhi Qar	13,668	617,000	As-Nasiriyah	62,368
Diyala	19,047	663,000	Ba'qubah	39,186
Irbil [1]	14,428	492,000	Irbil	107,355
Karbala	52,856	243,000	Karbala	107,496
Maysan	16,774	419,000	Al-Amarah	80,078
Ninawa (Nineveh)	41,320	1,158,000	Mosul	293,079
Salah ad-Din	21,326	356,000	Samarra	62,008
Ta'min	9,426	439,000	Kirkuk	207,852
Wasit	17,922	386,000	Al-Kut	58,647

[1] Forming Kurdish Autonomous Region [2] Census 1965

The national language is Arabic, spoken by 81% of the population. There is a major minority group of Kurdish-speakers in the north-east (15·5%) and smaller groups speaking Turkic, Aramaic and Iranian languages.

CONSTITUTION AND GOVERNMENT. The Provisional Constitution was published on 22 Sept. 1968 and promulgated on 16 July 1970. The highest state authority remains the 9-member Revolutionary Command Council (RCC) but legislative power has now been given to the 250-member National Assembly, elected 20 June 1980 for a 4-year term.

The only legal political grouping is the National Progressive Front (founded July 1973) comprising the Arab Socialist Renaissance (Ba'ath) Party and various Kurdish parties; the Iraqi Communist Party left the Front in March 1979.

The President and Vice-President are elected by the RCC; the President appoints and leads a Council of Ministers responsible for administration.

President: Saddam Hussein at-Takriti (assumed office 17 July 1979).
Vice-President: Taha Moheddin Marouf.

The RCC was composed as follows in Jan. 1983:
Saddam Hussein at-Takriti *(Chairman)*, Taha Moheddin Marouf, Izzat Ibrahim *(Vice-Chairman)*, Na'im Hamid Haddad *(Secretary-General of the National Progressive Front)*, Taha Yasin Ramadan *(First Deputy Prime Minister)*, Gen. Adnan Khairallah *(Deputy Prime Minister, Defence)*, Tariq Aziz Isa *(Deputy Prime Minister, Foreign Affairs)*, Sa'doun Shakir Mahmud *(Interior)*, Hasan Ali Nasar al-Amiri *(Trade)*.

Besides those named above, the Council of Ministers comprises 5 Ministers of State, 21 other Ministers and 6 Presidential advisors with ministerial status.

National flag: Three horizontal stripes of red, white, black, with 3 green stars on the white stripe.

Local Government. Iraq is divided into 18 governorates *(liwa)*, each administered by an appointed Governor; three of the governorates form a (Kurdish) Autonomous Region, with an elected 20-member Kurdish Legislative Council. Each govornorate is divided into *qadhas* (under Qaimaqams) and *nahiyahs* (under Mudirs).

DEFENCE. Military training is compulsory for all men when they reach the age of 18. This consists of 2 years' service with the colours and 18 years on the reserve. However, a man may volunteer for service in the army or change his conscript service into voluntary service. In such circumstances voluntary service is for 2 years, and he may extend it by periods of 2 years until he reaches the age of 45. The 2-year compulsory service can be extended in a national emergency. Many technicians and technically qualified officers serve up to 4 or 5 years.

Army. The strength of the Iraqi Army in 1983 was 300,000, organized into 4 corps HQ, 6 armoured divisions, 3 mechanized divisions and 4 mountain infantry divisions.

Navy. The Navy comprises 1 new frigate/training ship, 12 *ex*-Soviet missile boats, 12 *ex*-Soviet torpedo boats, 4 *ex*-Soviet but Polish-built medium landing ships, 3 *ex*-Soviet submarine chasers, 2 fleet minesweepers, 3 inshore minesweepers, 1 training ship, 14 gunboats, 8 coastal patrol craft, 10 harbour patrol boats, 3 mine warfare boats, 1 presidential yacht, 1 harbour authority craft (former presidential yacht) and 1 diving tender.

In 1982 naval personnel totalled over 3,000 officers and ratings, to be increased on the acquisition of 4 frigates and 6 missile corvettes agreed to be built in Italy with a replenishment tanker, if this 1981 contract is fulfilled.

Under 1972 treaty the Soviet fleet gained access to the Iraqi base of Um Qasr in return for Soviet assistance to strengthen Iraq's defences. A further 1976 treaty reportedly provided for more permanent use of Um Qasr in return for the provision of missile ships, but this does not appear to have been implemented.

Air Force. Except for 1 squadron of Hunter jet fighter-bombers bought from Britain and 89 Mirage F.1E/B fighters, about 40 Alouette III, 10 Super Frelon, 20 Puma and 59 Gazelle helicopters acquired from France, the combat and transport squadrons are equipped primarily with aircraft of Soviet design, including 9 Tu-22 supersonic medium bombers, 80 Su-20 fighter-bombers, 70 MiG-23 and 80 MiG-21 interceptors, 41 Mi-24 gunship helicopters, Mi-4, Mi-6 and Mi-8 helicopters, and four turbofan Il-76, turboprop An-12 and An-24/26 transports. A few Il-14s and smaller types are used in a transport/communications role. Hunter, L-29 Delfin and L-39 Albatros aircraft are employed for training, with Swiss-built Bravo piston-engined primary trainers and Pilatus PC-7 turboprop basic trainers, Soviet MiG-15UTI trainers and other types in the Air Force College and operational conversion unit. Total strength is about 38,000 personnel and 350 combat aircraft. Soviet 'Guideline', 'Goa' and 'Gainful' surface-to-air missiles are operational.

INTERNATIONAL RELATIONS

Membership. Iraq is a member of UN and the Arab League.

ECONOMY

Planning. The 5-year plan 1976-80 envisaged expenditure of I.D. 10,000m.

Budget. Revenue and expenditure (in 1,000 Iraqi dinars) for 1981 balanced at I.D. 19,250m.

Oil revenues account for nearly 50%, customs and excise for about 26% of the total revenue.

The public debt was 260m. dinars on 31 Dec. 1972.

Currency. The monetary unit is the *Iraqi dinar* (I.D.) = 1,000 *fils* = 10 *riyals* = 20 *dirhams*. Silver alloy coins for 100 and 50 fils (*dirham*) and 25 fils are in circulation, and other coins for 10, 5 and 1 fils. Notes are for ¼, ½ and 1 dinar, and for 5 and 10 dinars. In March 1983, £1 = 0·47 *dinar*; US$1 = 0·311 *dinar*.

Banking. All banks were nationalized on 14 July 1964. The Central Bank of Iraq is the sole bank of issue. In 1941 the Rafidain Bank, financed by the Iraqi Government, was instituted to carry out normal banking transactions with head office in Baghdad and branches in the chief towns and abroad, including London. In addition, there are 4 government banks which are authorized to issue loans to companies and individuals: the Industrial Bank, the Agricultural Bank, the Estate Bank, and the Mortgage Bank.

In March 1972 post office savings amounted to 8,437,000 dinars held by 201,455 depositors.

Weights and Measures. The metric system is in general use.

ENERGY AND NATURAL RESOURCES

Electricity. Production in 1978 amounted to 6,950m. Kwh.

Oil. Following the nationalization of the Iraqi oil industry in June 1972, the Iraqi National Oil Company (INOC) is responsible for the exploration, production, transport and marketing of Iraqi crude oil and oil products. Other state establishments are responsible for the distribution and supply of oil products and gas, and for operating the refineries at Baghdad, Khanaqin, Kirkuk, Hadithah, Qayarah and Basrah.

The total crude petroleum production was (1980) 130·2m. tonnes. Revenue received by the Iraqi Government from oil amounted to US$11,000m. in 1978. Production of natural gas (1980) 1,760m. cu. ft.

Water. Iraq is a land of great potentialities. The soil of the country is rich, but there are vast areas which can be cultivated only if irrigated by canals or pumps. The Irrigation Ministry operates several canal systems, new dams have been completed and other irrigation works are under construction.

Agriculture. An Agrarian Reform Law, issued in Sept. 1958, limits land ownership to 1,000 *dunums* for flow-irrigated land and to 2,000 *dunums* for rain-irrigated land.

The chief winter crops (1980) are wheat, 1·3m. tonnes and barley, 575,000 tonnes. The chief summer crop is rice, 220,000 tonnes. The date crop is important (395,000 tonnes), the country furnishing about 80% of the world's trade in dates (exports, 1975, I.D.11,493,000); the chief producing area is the totally irrigated riverain belt of the Shatt-el-Arab. Wool is also an important export (1975: I.D.1,013,000). In 1975, I.D.20,000 of cotton were exported.

Livestock (1980): Cattle, 27m.; buffaloes, 220,000; sheep, 114m.; goats, 36m.; horses, 65,000; camels, 246,000; chickens, 17m.

Forestry. Up to 1969, 614,953 *dunums* have been demarcated and surveyed in Arbil, Mosul and Sulaimaniya Governorates.

INDUSTRY AND TRADE

Industry. Industrial and constructional establishments in 1974 numbered 26,332. Constructional establishments employed the largest number of workers. Other large employers were the brick industry, water and electricity services, date packing, the textile industry, cigarette factories, oil refining and the cement industry. Iraq is still relatively under-developed industrially but work has begun on 13 new industrial plants which are being established with Soviet equipment and technical assistance.

Commerce. Imports and exports for 4 calendar years were (in 1m. Iraqi dinars):

	1977	*1978*	*1979*	*1980*
Imports	1,151	1,244	2,225	4,440
Exports	2,854	3,251	6,350	7,782

In 1980, crude oil formed 99% of all exports, of which 18% went to France, 15% to Brazil and 14% to Japan. 18% of imports came from Japan, 15% from Federal Republic of Germany and 9% from France.

Total trade between Iraq and UK for 5 years (British Department of Trade returns, in £1,000 sterling):

	1978	*1979*	*1980*	*1981*	*1982*
Imports to UK	497,341	393,738	532,483	72,644	79,764
Exports and re-exports from UK	215,509	201,176	321,883	623,889	875,179

Tourism. About 600,000 tourists visited Iraq in 1977.

COMMUNICATIONS

Roads. About 9,291 km of roads and tracks had been developed for vehicular traffic. The main surfaced roads are: (1) the road north from Baghdad *via* Kirkuk, Arbil and Nineveh to a point near the Turkish frontier at Zakho, with branches from Kirkuk to the northern province of Sulaimaniya, from Arbil to the Iranian frontier, and from Nineveh to Sinjar; (2) about 350 miles of the main road west from Baghdad to the Jordan frontier; (3) the road east of Baghdad, which connects the road system of Iran near Khanaqin; and (4) the road south from Baghdad to Hilla and the holy city of Kerbela.

Vehicles registered in 1979 totalled 120,600 passenger cars and 129,400 commercial vehicles.

Railways. The Iraqi Republic Railways were originally largely metre gauge but now comprise a 1,435 mm gauge main line from Um Qasr through Basra to Baghdad, Mosul and Tel-Kotchek on the Syrian frontier, and the remaining metre gauge route from Baghdad to Khanaqin, Kirkuk and Erbil. A 1,435 mm gauge line is under construction from Baghdad to Husaiba (404 km) on the Syrian frontier, which will form part of a through route to the Mediterranean port of Latakia. A branch of 155 km has opened to serve phosphates deposits at Akashat. In 1981 the railways carried 5m. tonnes of freight and 3·8m. passengers.

Aviation. Baghdad and Basra airports are served by British Airways, Lufthansa, Alitalia, Swissair, KLM, Middle East Air Lines, PIA, Iraqi Airways, Iranian Airways, Air Liban, United Arab Airlines and Aeroflot. In 1977 there were 728,266 passengers using Iraqi airports and 10,000 tons of cargo handled.

Shipping. The merchant fleet in 1980 comprised 142 vessels (over 100 gross tons) with a total tonnage of 1,465,949. The ports of Basra and Um Qasr have been closed since Sept. 1980.

Post and Broadcasting. In 1973 there were 352 post and telegraph offices. Wireless telegraph services exist with UK, USA, UAR, Lebanon and Saudi Arabia, and wireless telephone services with UK, USA, Italy, UAR and USSR. Telephones, 1978, 319,591. In 1978 there were 2·1m. radio and 623,000 television receivers.

Cinemas (1979). There were 87 cinemas.

Newspapers (1976). In Baghdad there are 6 daily newspapers (one of which is in English with a circulation of 200,000).

JUSTICE, RELIGION, EDUCATION AND WELFARE

Justice. The courts are established throughout the country as follows: For civil matters: the court of cassation in Baghdad; 6 courts of appeal at Baghdad (2), Basra, Babylon, Mosul and Kirkuk; 18 courts of first instance with unlimited powers and 150 courts of first instance with limited powers, all being courts of single judges. In addition, 6 peace courts have peace court jurisdiction only. Tribal law was abolished in Aug. 1958.

For *Shara'* (religious) matters: the Shara' courts at all places where there are civil courts, constituted in some places of specially appointed Qadhis (religious judges) and in other places of the judges of the civil courts. For criminal matters: the court of cassation; 6 sessions courts (2 being presided over by the judge of the local court of first instance and 4 being identical with the courts of appeal). Magistrates' courts at all places where there are civil courts, constituted of civil judges exercising magisterial powers of the first and second class. There are also a number of third-class magistrates courts, powers for this purpose being granted to municipal councils and a number of administrative officials. Some administrative officials are granted the powers of a peace judge to deal with cases of debts due from cultivators.

Special religious courts for non-Catholic Christians at Baghdad, Basra and Nineveh which dealt with matters of personal status, such as divorce, separation and maintenance between husband and wife, have now been abolished, cases being dealt with by the civil courts.

Religion. In 1965 there were 7,711,712 Moslems, 232,406 Christians (1979), 2,500 Jews, 69,653 Yazidis and 14,262 Sabians.

Education. Primary and secondary education is free and primary education became compulsory in Sept. 1976. Primary school age is 6–12. Secondary education is for 6 years, of which the first 3 are termed intermediate. The medium of instruction is Arabic; Kurdish is used in primary schools in northern districts.

There were, in 1976–77, 8,156 primary schools with 1,947,182 pupils, and 1,320 secondary schools with 555,184 pupils. Eighty-two vocational schools had 28,365 students and 43 teacher-training colleges had 21,186 students.

There are 6 universities with (1977) 71,536 students and 15 other higher educational establishments with 9,962 students.

Health. In 1974 there were 4,734 doctors (including dentists); 162 hospitals with 21,582 beds.

DIPLOMATIC REPRESENTATIVES

Of Iraq in Great Britain (21–22 Queen's Gate, London, SW7 5JG)
Ambassador: Dr Wahbi Abdul-Razzaq Al Qaraghuli (accredited 19 Nov. 1982).

Of Great Britain in Iraq (Sharia Salah Ud-Din, Karkh, Baghdad)
Ambassador: John Moberly, CMG.

Of Iraq to the United Nations
Ambassador: Salah Omar Al-Ali.

Iraq broke off diplomatic relations with USA on 7 June 1967.

Books of Reference

Statistical Information: The Central Statistical Organization, Ministry of Planning, Baghdad (*President:* Dr Salah Al-Shaikhly) publishes an annual *Statistical Abstract* (latest issue 1973). Foreign Trade statistics are published annually by the Ministry of Planning.

Arfa, H., *The Kurds.* OUP, 1966
Ghareeb, E., *The Kurdish Question in Iraq.* Syracuse Univ. Press, 1981
Khadduri, M., *Independent Iraq.* OUP, 1960.—*Republican Iraq.* OUP, 1970.—*Socialist Iraq: A Study of Iraqi Politics since 1968.* OUP, 1978
Langley, K. M., *The Industrialization of Iraq.* Harvard Univ. Press, 1961

IRELAND

Capital: Dublin
Population: 3·44m. (1981)
GNP per capita: US$4,880 (1980)

Éire

HISTORY. In April 1916 an insurrection against British rule took place and a republic was proclaimed. The armed struggle was renewed in 1919 and continued until 1921. The independence of Ireland was reaffirmed in Jan. 1919 by the National Parliament (*Dáil Éireann*), elected in Dec. 1918.

In 1920 an Act was passed by the British Parliament, under which separate Parliaments were set up for 'Southern Ireland' (26 counties) and 'Northern Ireland' (6 counties). The Unionists of the 6 counties accepted this scheme, and a Northern Parliament was duly elected on 24 May 1921. The rest of Ireland, however, ignored the Act.

On 6 Dec. 1921 a treaty was signed between Great Britain and Ireland by which Ireland accepted dominion status subject to the right of Northern Ireland to opt out. This right was exercised, and the border between *Saorstát Éireann* (26 counties) and Northern Ireland (6 counties) was fixed in Dec. 1925 as the outcome of an agreement between Great Britain, the Irish Free State and Northern Ireland. The agreement was ratified by the three parliaments.

Subsequently the constitutional links between *Saorstát Éireann* and the UK were gradually removed by the *Dáil*. The remaining formal association with the British Commonwealth by virtue of the External Relations Act, 1936, was severed when the Republic of Ireland Act, 1948, came into operation on 18 April 1949.

AREA AND POPULATION. The Republic of Ireland lies in the Atlantic ocean, separated from Great Britain by the Irish Sea to the east, and bounded north-east by Northern Ireland.

Counties and county boroughs	*Area in hectares* [1]	*Population, 1981* *Males*	*Females*	*Total*
Province of Leinster				
Carlow	89,635	20,195	19,625	39,820
Dublin County Borough	11,499	248,016	277,866	525,882
Dublin [2]	78,937	209,533	213,253	422,786
Dun Laoghaire Borough	1,720	24,793	29,703	54,496
Kildare	169,425	53,967	50,155	104,122
Kilkenny	206,167	36,395	34,411	70,806
Laoighis	171,954	26,774	24,397	51,171
Longford	104,387	16,234	14,906	31,140
Louth	82,334	44,125	44,389	88,514
Meath	233,587	48,957	46,462	95,419
Offaly	199,774	30,290	28,022	58,312
Westmeath	176,290	31,388	30,135	61,523
Wexford	235,143	50,336	48,745	99,081
Wicklow	202,483	43,663	43,786	87,449
Total of Leinster	1,963,335	884,666	905,855	1,790,521
Province of Munster				
Clare	318,784	45,366	42,201	87,567
Cork County Borough	3,731	66,177	70,167	136,344
Cork	742,257	136,211	129,910	266,121
Kerry	470,142	63,492	59,278	122,770
Limerick County Borough	1,904	29,723	31,013	60,736
Limerick	266,676	51,872	49,053	100,925
Tipperary, N. R.	199,622	30,247	28,737	58,984
Tipperary, S. R.	225,836	39,256	37,021	76,277

[1] Exclusive of certain rivers, lakes and tideways.
[2] Excludes Dun Laoghaire borough.

Counties and county boroughs	*Area in hectares* [1]	*Males*	*Population, 1981 Females*	*Total*
Province of Munster—contd.				
Waterford County Borough	3,809	18,751	19,722	38,473
Waterford	179,977	25,762	24,356	50,118
Total of Munster	2,412,738	506,857	491,458	998,315
Province of Connacht				
Galway	593,966	88,330	83,688	172,018
Leitrim	152,476	14,699	12,910	27,609
Mayo	539,846	58,987	55,779	114,766
Roscommon	246,276	28,653	25,890	54,543
Sligo	179,608	28,183	27,291	55,474
Total of Connacht	1,712,172	218,852	205,558	424,410
Province of Ulster (part of)				
Cavan	189,060	28,338	25,517	53,855
Donegal	483,058	63,962	61,150	125,112
Monaghan	129,093	26,679	24,513	51,192
Total of Ulster (part of)	801,211	118,979	111,180	230,159
Total	6,889,456	1,729,354	1,714,051	3,443,405

[1] Exclusive of certain rivers, lakes and tideways.

The population has declined since 1841, when the 26 counties had 6,528,799 inhabitants; there were 3,221,823 in 1901; 3,139,688 in 1911; 2,971,992 in 1926; 2,968,420 in 1936; 2,955,107 in 1946; 2,898,264 in 1956; 2,884,002 in 1966; 2,978,248 in 1971, and 3,443,405 in 1981.

Vital statistics for 4 calendar years:

	Births	*Marriages*	*Deaths*		*Births*	*Marriages*	*Deaths*
1976	67,718	20,580	34,043	1979 [1]	72,352	20,864	32,790
1977	68,892	20,016	33,632	1980	74,388	21,723	32,980
1978	70,299	20,724	33,794	1981	72,355	20,550	32,410

[1] Provisional.

CLIMATE. Influenced by the Gulf Stream, there is an equable climate with mild south-west winds, making temperatures almost uniform over the whole country. The coldest months are Jan. and Feb. (39–45°F, 4–7°C) and the warmest July and Aug. (57–61°F, 14–16°C). May and June are the sunniest months, averaging 5·5 to 6·5 hours each day, but over 7 hours in the extreme S.E. Rainfall is lowest along the eastern coastal strip. Dublin has 30″ (750 mm). The central parts vary between 30–44″ (750–1,125 mm), and up to 60″ (1,500 mm) may be experienced in low-lying areas in the west.

CONSTITUTION AND GOVERNMENT. Ireland is a sovereign independent, democratic republic. Its parliament exercises jurisdiction in 26 of the 32 counties of Ireland.

The first Constitution of the Irish Free State came into operation on 6 Dec. 1922. Certain provisions which were regarded as contrary to the national sentiments were gradually removed by successive amendments, with the result that at the end of 1936 the text differed considerably from the original document. On 14 June 1937 a new Constitution was approved by Parliament (*Dáil Éireann*) and enacted by a plebiscite on 1 July 1937. This Constitution came into operation on 29 Dec. 1937. Under it the name Ireland (Éire) was restored.

The Constitution provides that, pending the reintegration of the national territory, the laws enacted by the Parliament established by the constitution shall have the same area and extent of application as those of the Irish Free State.

The *Oireachtas* or National Parliament consists of the President and two Houses, viz., a House of Representatives, called *Dáil Éireann*, and a Senate, called *Seanad Éireann*, consisting of 60 members. The *Dáil*, consisting of 166 members, is elected by adult suffrage. Of the 60 members of the Senate, 11 are nominated by the *Taoiseach* (Prime Minister), 6 are elected by the universities and the remaining 43 are elected from 5 panels of candidates established on a vocational basis, representing the following public services and interests: (1) national language and culture, literature, art, education and such professional interests as may be defined by law for the purpose of this panel; (2) agricultural and allied interests, and fisheries; (3) labour, whether organized or unorganized; (4) industry and commerce, including banking, finance, accountancy, engineering and architecture; (5) public administration and social services, including voluntary social activities. The electing body is a college of about 900 members, comprising members of the *Dáil*, Senate, county boroughs and county councils.

A maximum period of 90 days is afforded to the Senate for the consideration or amendment of Bills sent to that House by the *Dáil*, but the Senate has no power to veto legislative proposals.

No amendment of the Constitution can be effected except with the approval of the people given at a referendum.

Agreement on the establishment of a Council of Ireland was reached at a meeting held at Sunningdale on 6–9 Dec. 1973. Members of the Irish and UK governments attended together with the Northern Ireland Executive-designate.

Irish is the first official language; English is recognized as a second official language. For further details of the Constitution *see* THE STATESMAN'S YEAR-BOOK, 1952, pp. 1123–34.

President: Pádraig Óhlrighile (Patrick Hillery), installed on 3 Dec. 1976. The President holds office for 7 years.

Former Presidents: Dr Douglas Hyde (1938–45); Seán T. O. Ceallaigh (1945–59; 2 terms); Éamon de Valéra (1959–73; 2 terms); Erskine Childers (1973–74; died in office); Cearbhall Ó Dálaigh (1974–76; resigned).

A general election was held on 24 Nov. 1982: Fianna Fáil, 75 (Feb. 1982 election, 81); Fine Gael, 70 (66); Labour Party, 16 (15); Workers' Party, 2 (3); Independents, 3 (4).

There are no formal party divisions in the Senate.

The National Coalition Government consisted of the following members in Feb. 1983 (Fine Gael and Labour Parties):

Taoiseach (Prime Minister): Dr Garret Fitzgerald.

Tanaiste and Minister for Environment: Dick Spring. *Finance:* Alan Dukes. *Agriculture:* Austin Deasy. *Trade, Commerce and Tourism:* Frank Cluskey. *Foreign Affairs:* Peter Barry. *Industry and Energy:* John Bruton. *Education:* Gemma Hussey. *Justice:* Michael Noonan. *Transport, Posts and Telegraphs:* Jim Mitchell. *Gaeltacht, Fisheries and Forestry:* Paddy O'Toole. *Health and Social Welfare:* Barry Desmond. *Labour:* Liam Kavanagh. *Defence:* Paddy Cooney. *Public Service:* John Boland.

There were 14 Ministers of State.

National flag: Three vertical strips of green, white, orange.

National anthem: The Soldier's Song (words by P. Kearney; music by P. Heaney).

Local Government. The elected local authorities comprise 27 county councils, 4 county borough corporations, 7 borough corporations, 49 urban district councils and 23 Boards of Town Commissions. All the members of these authorities are elected under a system of proportional representation, normally every 5 years. All residents of an area who have reached the age of 18 are entitled to vote in the local election for their area. Women are eligible for election as members of local authorities in the same manner and on the same conditions as men. Elected members are not paid, but provision is made for the payment of travelling expenses and subsistence allowances.

The range of services for which local authorities are responsible is broken down into 8 main programme groups as follows: Housing and Building; Road Transportation and Safety; Water Supply and Sewerage; Development Incentives and Controls; Environmental Protection; Recreation and Amenity; Agriculture,

Education, Health and Welfare and Miscellaneous Services. Because of the small size of their administrative areas the functions carried out by town commissioners and some of the smaller urban district councils have tended to become increasingly limited, and the more important tasks of local government have tended to become the responsibility of the county councils.

The local authorities have a system of government which combines an elected council and a whole-time manager. The elected members have specific functions reserved to them which include the striking of rates (local tax), the borrowing of money, the adoption of development plans, the making, amending or revoking of bye-laws and the nomination of persons to other bodies. The managers, who are paid officers of their authorities, are responsible for the performance of all functions which are not reserved to the elected members, including the employment of staff, making of contracts, management of local authority property, collection of rates and rents and the day-to-day administration of local authority affairs. The manager for a county council is manager also for every borough corporation, urban district council and board of town commissioners whose functional area is wholly within the county. A central body called the Local Appointments Commission is charged with the duty of selecting suitable persons to be appointed by local authorities to chief executive offices, professional offices and other prescribed offices. Where a prescribed office becomes vacant, the local authority must request the Commissioners to recommend to them a suitable person. The Commissioners normally select persons for appointment by the machinery of selection boards.

The revenue expenditure of local authorities is financed by a local tax, called rates, on the occupation of immovable property, grants and subsidies from the central government and payments for certain services which they provide.

Since 1978 full rates relief has applied to houses, the domestic element of mixed property, *i.e.* property embodying a domestic as well as a non-domestic use, secondary schools, community halls and farm buildings not previously de-rated. Rates relief also applies to land subject to certain criteria. The central government recoups to local authorities in full the amount of rates foregone as a result of these rates reliefs.

DEFENCE. Under the direction of the President, and subject to the provisions of the Defence Act, 1954, the military command of the Defence Forces is exercisable by the Government through the Minister for Defence. To aid and counsel the Minister for Defence on all matters in relation to the business of the Department of Defence on which he may consult it, there is a Council of Defence consisting of the Minister for State at the Department of Defence, the Secretary of the Department of Defence, the Chief of Staff, the Adjutant-General and the Quartermaster-General. Establishments provide at present for a Permanent Defence Force of approximately 18,000 all ranks including the Air Corps and the Naval Service. The Reserve Defence Force caters for 23,000 all ranks. Recruitment is on a voluntary basis. Minimum term of enlistment is 3 years in the Permanent Defence Force and 6 years in the Reserve.

The Defence Estimates for the year ending 31 Dec. 1982 provide for an expenditure of £204m.

Since May 1978 an Irish contingent has formed part of the United Nations force in Lebanon. The contingent now comprises 654 men (all ranks). Irish officers are at present serving with the UN Truce Supervision Organization and the UN Disengagement Observer Force in the Middle East.

Army. There are at present 4 brigades in the Army. Each comprises 2 infantry battalions and an artillery regiment, and a squadron or company from each Corps (except Ordnance and Air). There are, in addition, 2 independent infantry battalions. Total strength, 14,554.

Navy. The Naval Service comprises 4 offshore patrol vessels completed at Cork in 1972, 1978, 1979 and 1980, 3 old coastal minesweepers acquired from Britain in 1971 for fishery protection, 1 supply and training ship, and 7 service craft. An order has been placed for a patrol vessel, carrying a helicopter, for service in 1984.

The naval base is at Haulbowline Island, Cork Harbour. Naval personnel in 1983 exceeded 1,200 officers and ratings.

Air Force. The Air Corps has a personnel establishment of approximately 1,172 all ranks and 35 aircraft. There are 7 Cessna FR-172H aircraft for border patrol, 6 Magister armed jet trainers and 9 SIAI-Marchetti SF.260W armed piston-engined trainers with dual combat responsibility; 8 Alouette III and 2 Gazelle helicopters; 1 Puma helicopter; 3 twin-turboprop Super King Airs for coastal fishery patrol and a BAe 125 twin-turbofan communications aircraft.

INTERNATIONAL RELATIONS

Membership. Ireland is a member of UN, OECD, the Council of Europe and EEC.

ECONOMY

Budget. Receipts and expenditures (in IR£1m.):

Receipts	*1980*	*1981*
Customs duties	47·3	58·5
Excise duties	850·9	1,060·4
Income tax	1,014·3	1,243·4
Corporation tax, etc.	139·8	200·0
Value-added tax	471·6	619·9
Stamp duties	48·0	67·4
Estate, etc., duties	3·0	2·2
Motor vehicle duties	25·5	38·9
Post Office	202·6	282·0
Capital taxes	14·4	16·4
Agricultural levies	4·6	6·8
Total (including other items)	3,155·3	3,596·5
Current expenditure		
Debt service	792·1	1,053·5
Agriculture, etc.	141·1	208·6
Education	461·4	606·6
Tourism and Transport	112·4	121·4
Post Office	181·1	206·0
Defence	142·1	166·3
Justice (including Police)	140·3	196·8
Social Welfare	485·9	695·5
Health	617·2	724·3
Superannuation	99·9	123·7
Industry and Energy	70·7	87·9
Total (including other items)	3,702·1	4,774·6

Capital expenditure amounted to £1,309m. in 1980, and £1,887m. in 1981.

On 31 Dec. 1980 the liabilities totalled £7,896m. The assets were: Electricity scheme, £42·6m.: local loans fund, £1,313·2m.; national transport organization, £33·3m.; industrial credit, £59·8m.; turf development, £29·6m.; reconstruction finance, £33m.; shares in companies established under state auspices, £240·7m.; exchequer balance, £613,000; other assets, £150·2m.; total, £1,903m.

Currency. The unit of currency is the Irish *pound* or *an punt Eirennach.* From 10 Sept. 1928 when the first Irish legal-tender notes were issued, the Irish currency was linked to Sterling on a one-for-one basis. This relationship was discontinued on 30 March 1979 when, following Ireland's adherence to the European Monetary System, market forces pushed sterling exchange rates beyond the upper intervention limit established for the Irish pound against the Belgian franc.

The Central Bank has the sole right of issuing legal tender notes; token coinage is issued by the Minister for Finance through the Bank. In March 1983, £1 = IR£1·12; US$ = IR£1·28.

The volume of legal-tender notes outstanding in June 1982 was £741,849,000. Total notes and coins outstanding amounted to £786·12m.

Banking. The Central Bank, which was established as from 1 Feb. 1943, in accordance with the Central Bank Act, 1942, replaced the Currency Commission, which was set up under the Currency Act, 1927, and had been responsible *inter alia* for the regulation of the note issue. In addition to the powers and functions of the Currency Commission the Central Bank has the power of receiving deposits from banks and public authorities, of rediscounting Exchequer bills and bills of exchange, of making advances to banks against such bills or against Government securities, of fixing and publishing rates of interest for rediscounting bills, or buying and selling certain Government securities and securities of any international bank or financial institution formed wholly or mainly by governments. The Bank also collects and publishes information relating to monetary and credit matters. The Central Bank Act, 1971, gives further powers to the Central Bank in the regulation of banking including licensing of banks, the supervision of their operations and control of liquidity and reserve ratios. The capital of the Bank is £40,000, of which £24,000 has been paid up and is held by the Minister for Finance.

The Board of Directors of the Central Bank consists of a Governor, appointed by the President on the advice of the Government, and 8 directors, all appointed by the Minister for Finance, 6 direct and 2 from among directors of the Associated Banks (the term applied to the 4 shareholding banks associated with the former Currency Commission).

There are 4 commercial banks associated with the Central Bank: The Bank of Ireland, Allied Irish Banks Ltd, the Ulster Bank and the Northern Bank.

At 19 May 1982 the Associated Banks had liabilities, within the State, of £5,608·8m. including current and deposit accounts amounting to £4,344m.; assets, within the State, amounted to £5,925·9m., of which the main components were liquid assets of £736·1m. and lending of £4,818·4m. At the same date liabilities, outside the State, stood at £4,667·1m. and assets at £4,349·4m., giving a net external liability of £317·1m. Total liabilities and assets balanced at £10,275·9m. The commercial banking system also includes 39 licensed banks not 'associated' with the Central Bank. At 19 May 1982 these non-associated banks had total liabilities and assets, within the State and elsewhere, balancing at £5,813·6m.

The post office savings bank has approximately 2·6m. (including 1·2m. dormant) accounts and the amount due at 31 Aug. 1982 was IR£278m. The trustee savings banks had deposits of IR£321m. at 31 Aug. 1982.

Weights and Measures. The Imperial system is in use but conversion to metric is in progress.

ENERGY AND NATURAL RESOURCES

Electricity. The generating and supplying of electricity and the construction and maintenance of the nationwide electricity distribution system is the function of the Electricity Supply Board, a State-sponsored body established in 1927. The total generating capacity is 3,287 mw. In the year ending 31 March 1982 the total sales of electricity amounted to 8,662m. units supplied to 1,096,950 consumers. Electricity generated by fuel source (1981–82): Oil, 40%; natural gas, 36%; peat, 14%; hydro, 10%. The nuclear option is being kept under review.

Oil and gas. About 551,500 sq. km of the Continental Shelf has been made an exploration area; at its furthest point the limit of jurisdiction is 520 nautical miles from the coast. Since 1970, 70 exploratory offshore oilwells have been drilled. There has been one discovery of natural gas, off the south-west coast at Kinsale Head. The total reserves of the field are 1,353,000m. cu. ft and the daily offtake is 180m. cu. ft. Distribution is controlled by the Irish Gas Board (BGE). By mid-1982 applications for exploration licences were received by 10 consortia involving 37 companies.

Peat. The country has very little indigenous coal, but possesses large reserves of peat, the development of which is handled by *Bord na Móna* (Peat Board). A total of 200,000 acres of bogland is being developed at present. In the year ending 31 March 1982, production totalled 4,885m. tonnes, of which 2,503,418 tonnes went to generate electricity and 857,676 tonnes for household and space heating.

Minerals. Lead and zinc concentrates are important. Metal content of production, 1981: zinc, 116,955 tonnes; lead, 28,849 tonnes. Barytes is also important, and there is some copper, pyrites, gypsum, dolomite, limestone, aggregates, coal, green and black marble. About 40 companies are prospecting.

Agriculture. General distribution of surface (in hectares) in 1976: Crops and pasture, 4,692,800; other land, including grazed mountain, 2,196,500; total, 6,889,200.

Estimated area (hectares) under certain crops calculated from sample returns:

	Area[1]			
Crops	*1979*	*1980*	*1981*	*1982*
Wheat	48,800	47,300	44,300	49,500
Oats	23,100	25,600	23,500	23,600
Barley	323,700	332,400	330,400	311,600
Potatoes	40,600	40,400	34,000	35,800
Sugar-beet	34,900	32,700	...	...

[1] Provisional.

Gross agricultural output (excluding value changes in livestock) for the year 1981 was valued at £1,906,761,000.

Livestock (1980): Cattle, 6·7m.; sheep, 3·5m.; pigs, 1·1m.; horses (1978), 75,500; poultry, 9·6m.

Forestry. The total area of state forests at 31 Dec. 1981 was 341,822 hectares.

Fisheries. The number of vessels and men engaged in fishing in 1979 were 1,539 boats propelled by outboard engines, sails and oars and 1,426 other fishing boats; men 8,711. The quantities and values of fish landed during 1979 were: Demersal fish, 21,092 tonnes, value £7,720,570; pelagic fish, 53,493 tonnes, value £9,783,479; shellfish, 11,113 tonnes, value £7,401,134. Total value, £22,905,183.

INDUSTRY AND TRADE

Industry. The census of industrial production for 1978 gives the following details of the values (in £1,000) of gross and net output for the principal manufacturing industries. The figures for net output are those of gross output minus cost of materials, including fuel, light and power, repairs to plant and machinery and amounts paid to others in connexion with products made.

	Gross output	*Net output*
Slaughtering, preparing and preserving meat	721,036	89,246
Dairy products	784,263	116,751
Bread, biscuit and flour confectionery	110,952	44,455
Sugar, cocoa, chocolate and sugar confectionery	196,668	58,898
Grain milling, animal and poultry foods	293,539	49,710
Brewing and malting	148,529	100,859
Tobacco products	153,526	34,732
Paper and paper products	111,932	44,751
Printing and publishing	132,608	88,808
Production and preliminary processing of metals	53,896	18,416
Manufacture of metal articles	205,276	92,584
Manufacture of non-metallic mineral products	314,905	141,684
Chemicals, including fertilizers and manmade fibres	619,268	400,604
Mechanical engineering	130,134	61,322
Manufacture of office machinery and data-processing machinery	137,620	52,992
Electrical engineering	203,199	91,912
Manufacture of motor vehicles, parts and accessories	167,003	44,910
Manufacture of other means of transport	82,389	44,040
Textiles (including knitting industry)	315,154	108,113
Footwear and clothing	158,956	75,012
Timber and wooden furniture	99,935	42,750
Processing rubber and plastics	133,231	55,705
Gas, water and electricity	291,901	146,424
All other industries [1]	611,649	197,720
Total (all industries)	6,117,569	2,202,398

[1] Including mining, fuel production, instrument engineering, various food and drink industries, etc.

Labour. The total labour force at mid-April 1980 was about 1,237,000, of which about 92,033 persons were out of work.

The number of trade unions holding negotiation licences in Sept. 1982 was 79, of which 63 were workers' trade unions and the remainder employers' trade unions. The total membership of these unions is estimated at 499,891, of whom 10,480 were in the employers' trade unions.

Commerce. Value of imports and exports of merchandise for calendar years (in £):

	1977	*1978*	*1979*	*1980*	*1981*
Imports	3,090,886,805	3,713,098,432	4,827,922,798	5,420,704,523	6,575,484,061
Exports	2,518,170,389	2,963,180,624	3,496,089,139	4,082,496,312	4,775,055,833

The values of the chief imports and total exports are shown in the following table (in £):

	Imports		*Exports*	
	1980	*1981*	*1980*	*1981*
Live animals and food	572,958,956	762,630,617	1,368,761,591	1,408,074,234
Raw materials	169,254,485	204,695,686	181,605,580	181,688,831
Mineral fuels and lubricants	803,203,980	966,278,264	26,723,188	31,637,412
Chemicals	560,212,920	691,184,268	519,954,961	642,555,102
Manufactured goods	991,045,677	1,126,628,291	520,492,459	592,347,782
Machinery and transport equipment	1,473,274,344	1,805,979,087	762,962,889	1,049,300,690
Manufactured articles [1]	633,911,669	767,341,152	446,867,327	539,412,367

[1] Not elsewhere specified.

Distribution of trade, by principal countries of origin in the case of imports and destination in the case of exports (in £):

	Imports		*Total exports*	
Country	*1980*	*1981*	*1980*	*1981*
Belgium and Luxembourg	108,067,039	135,733,710	207,751,245	199,026,006
Canada	73,558,115	95,387,299	52,908,630	87,029,804
Denmark	38,423,659	50,832,691	30,378,603	35,736,723
Finland	53,804,740	60,403,687	18,568,197	20,672,557
France	283,702,994	338,982,589	319,622,423	341,135,872
Germany, Fed. Rep. of	374,297,000	495,030,003	398,864,816	453,910,533
Hong Kong	19,692,102	25,286,779	3,461,059	7,314,323
India	18,167,538	19,696,536	5,031,564	8,536,599
Iran	39,941,774	217,372	12,535,649	6,036,583
Iraq	28,836,625	12,728	5,721,788	21,364,764
Israel	15,307,640	16,448,229	4,241,984	6,020,262
Italy	130,679,836	168,858,364	128,216,770	139,816,225
Japan	138,037,869	203,127,509	19,618,246	40,756,451
Kuwait	33,289,601	18,849,263	5,472,033	6,333,976
Malaysia	11,541,760	13,419,057	4,879,280	4,893,631
Netherlands	151,918,823	202,985,651	225,265,295	274,445,445
New Zealand	8,900,932	9,862,711	1,969,882	4,146,471
Norway	22,727,232	27,140,198	21,953,262	24,093,685
Poland	29,931,166	17,382,007	6,646,685	6,049,556
Portugal	16,301,868	18,099,588	10,139,117	17,988,058
Saudi Arabia	121,139,659	68,381,398	15,092,437	26,960,425
South Africa, Rep. of, and Namibia	11,682,197	10,881,369	11,040,041	21,766,846
Spain	43,074,287	64,592,074	35,765,092	47,885,639
Sweden	86,843,753	104,145,368	50,411,530	61,453,985
Switzerland	33,841,285	44,414,991	30,649,015	39,983,634
USSR	23,546,926	31,635,784	24,078,736	24,649,698
UK	2,754,729,838	3,267,394,497	1,763,781,467	1,919,450,856
USA	474,213,453	767,930,440	216,489,135	303,993,181

An Anglo-Irish free-trade agreement to remove progressively all duties between July 1966 and July 1975 was signed in London on 14 Dec. 1965.

Total trade between Ireland and UK (British Department of Trade returns, in £1,000 sterling):

	1978	*1979*	*1980*	*1981*	*1982*
Imports to UK	1,606,308	1,689,206	1,784,329	1,787,065	2,000,033
Exports and re-exports from UK	2,044,796	2,554,839	2,660,024	2,812,957	2,890,497

Tourism. Estimated number of visits by foreigners (including cross-border movement) in 1981 was 9,423,000; they spent £330m.

COMMUNICATIONS

Roads. At 31 Dec. 1979 there were 57,326 miles of public roads, consisting of 3,264 miles of national roads, 6,662 miles of main (trunk and link) roads other than national roads, 45,948 miles of county roads and 1,452 miles of county borough and urban roads; of the total mileage 54,300 (95%) was paved.

Number of licensed motor vehicles at 30 Sept. 1981: Private cars, 774,594; public-service vehicles, 5,210; goods vehicles, 67,014; agricultural tractors, 63,539; motor cycles, 28,140; other vehicles, 11,321.

The total number of km run by road motor passenger vehicles of the omnibus type during 1981 was 93,309,000. Passengers carried numbered 226,552,000 and the gross receipts from passengers were £66,572,000.

Railways. The total length of railway open for traffic at 31 Dec. 1981 was 1,791 km, all 1,600 mm gauge. Córas Iompair Éireann, the national transport undertaking, operates all rail services in the State.

Railway statistics for years ending 31 Dec.	*1980*	*1981*
Passengers (no.)	16,654,000	15,374,000
Miles run by coaching trains	5,405,000	5,300,000
Merchandise and mineral traffic conveyed (tons)	3,570,000	3,664,000
Miles run by freight trains	3,212,000	3,281,000
Receipts (£)	40,748,694	45,445,595
Expenditure (£)	85,938,695	105,663,970

Aviation. During the year ended 31 March 1982 Aer Lingus-Irish International Airlines carried 2,098,668 passengers, 37,489 short tons of cargo and 1,359 short tons of mail on its European services and 322,654 passengers, 14,836 short tons of cargo and 415 short tons of mail on its trans-Atlantic services.

Shipping. The total number of arrivals at ports in the country during 1981 was 14,990 of 18·96m. NRT; of these, 4,132 of 4,509,069 NRT, were Irish registered vessels. The Irish merchant fleet, of vessels of 100 gross tons or over, consisted of 73 vessels totalling 251,272 GRT at 31 Dec. 1981.

Inland Waterways. The principal inland waterways open to navigation are the Shannon Navigation (130 miles) and the Grand Canal and Barrow Navigation (156 miles). Merchandise traffic is not now transported on them and navigation is confined to pleasure craft operated either privately or commercially.

Post and Broadcasting (31 Dec. 1981). Number of post offices, 2,096; telegraph offices, 1,340; telephones, 536,000; public telephones, 3,925; telephone exchanges, 1,084.

Radio and television broadcasting is operated by Radio Telefis Éireann, a statutory public body appointed by the Minister for Posts and Telegraphs under the Broadcasting Authority Acts. On 31 Dec. 1981 there were 650,000 holders of current television licences.

Cinemas. There are 142 cinemas.

Newspapers (1982). There are 8 daily newspapers (all in English) with a combined circulation of 922,215; 6 of them are published in Dublin (circulation, 812,143).

JUSTICE, RELIGION, EDUCATION AND WELFARE

Justice. The Constitution provides that justice shall be administered in public in Courts established by law by Judges appointed by the President on the advice of the Government. The jurisdiction and organization of the Courts are dealt with in the Courts (Establishment and Constitution) Act, 1961, the Courts (Supplemental Provisions) Acts, 1961–81. These Courts consist of Courts of First Instance and a Court of Final Appeal, called the Supreme Court. The Courts of First Instance are the High Court with full original jurisdiction and the Circuit and the District Courts with local and limited jurisdiction. A judge may not be removed from office except for stated misbehaviour or incapacity and then only on resolutions passed by both Houses of the *Oireachtas*. Judges of the Supreme, High and Circuit Courts are appointed from among practising barristers. Judges of the District Court (called District Justices) may be appointed from among practising barristers or practising solicitors.

The Supreme Court, which consists of the Chief Justice (who is *ex officio* an additional judge of the High Court) and 5 ordinary judges, has appellate jurisdiction from all decisions of the High Court. The President may, after consultation with the Council of State, refer a Bill, which has been passed by both Houses of the *Oireachtas* (other than a money bill and certain other bills), to the Supreme Court for a decision on the question as to whether such Bill or any provision thereof is repugnant to the Constitution.

The High Court, which consists of a President (who is *ex officio* an additional Judge of the Supreme Court) and 15 ordinary judges, has full original jurisdiction in and power to determine all matters and questions, whether of law or fact, civil or criminal. In all cases in which questions arise concerning the validity of any law having regard to the provisions of the Constitution, the High Court alone exercises original jurisdiction. The High Court on Circuit acts as an appeal court from the Circuit Court.

The Court of Criminal Appeal consists of the Chief Justice or an ordinary Judge of the Supreme Court, together with either 2 ordinary judges of the High Court or the President and one ordinary judge of the High Court. It deals with appeals by persons convicted on indictment where the appellant obtains a certificate from the trial judge that the case is a fit one for appeal, or, in case such certificate is refused, where the court itself, on appeal from such refusal, grants leave to appeal. The decision of the Court of Criminal Appeal is final, unless that court or the Director of Public Prosecutions certifies that the decision involves a point of law of exceptional public importance, in which case an appeal is taken to the Supreme Court.

The High Court exercising criminal jurisdiction is known as the Central Criminal Court. It consists of a judge or judges of the High Court, nominated by the President of the High Court. The Court sits in Dublin and tries criminal cases which are outside the jurisdiction of the Circuit Court or which may be sent forward to it for trial from the Circuit Court on the application of the Director of Public Prosecution.

The country is divided into a number of circuits for the purposes of the Circuit Court. The President of the Circuit Court is *ex officio* an additional judge of the High Court. The jurisdiction of the court in civil proceedings is limited to £15,000 in contract and tort, £15,000 in actions founded on hire-purchase and credit-sale agreements, £5,000 in equity and £5,000 in probate and administration, save by consent of the parties, in which event the jurisdiction is unlimited. In criminal matters it has jurisdiction in all cases except murder, treason, piracy and allied offences. The Circuit Court acts as an appeal court from the District Court.

The District Court has summary jurisdiction in a large number of criminal cases where the offence is not of a serious nature. In civil matters the Court has jurisdiction in contract and tort (except slander, libel, seduction, slander of title and false imprisonment) where the claim does not exceed £2,500; in proceedings founded on hire-purchase and credit-sale agreements, the jurisdiction is £2,500.

All criminal cases, except those of a minor nature, are tried by a judge and a jury of 12. Juries are also used in many civil cases in the High Court. In a criminal case the jury must be unanimous in reaching a verdict, but in a civil case the agreement of 9 members is sufficient.

Religion. According to the census of population taken in 1971 the principal religious professions were as follows:

	Leinster	*Munster*	*Connacht*	*Ulster (part of)*	*Total*
Roman Catholics	1,387,644	849,382	378,613	180,027	2,795,666
Church of Ireland	60,115	17,807	6,084	13,733	97,739
Presbyterians	5,172	627	347	9,906	16,052
Methodists	3,187	1,321	248	890	5,646
Other religious denominations	6,914	1,269	272	426	8,881
Not stated or no religion	35,108	11,596	5,338	2,222	54,264

Education. *Elementary.* Elementary education is free and was given in about 3,405 national schools (including 113 special schools) in 1981. The average daily enrolment of pupils in 1981 was 555,656; the number of teachers of all classes (1981) about 19,932, including remedial teachers and teachers of special classes. Average daily pupil attendance is about 91%. There are 6 Colleges of Education for the training of primary school teachers, all co-educational. The estimated state expenditure on elementary education for 1982 (1 Jan.–31 Dec.) is £285,528,000, excluding the cost of administration.

Special provision is made for handicapped and deprived children in special schools which are recognized on the same basis as primary schools, in special classes attached to ordinary schools and in certain voluntary centres where educational services appropriate to the needs of the children are provided. Categories of handicapped children catered for include visually handicapped, hearing impaired, physically handicapped, mentally handicapped, emotionally disturbed, travelling children and other socially disadvantaged children. Provision is also being made on an increasing scale for children with dual or multiple handicaps. In each case a programme suited to the needs of the particular kind of handicap is provided. The number of children in each class in such schools is very much smaller than in ordinary classes in a primary school and because of the size of the catchment areas involved an extensive system of school transport has been developed. Many handicapped children who have spent some years in a special school or class are integrated into normal schools for part of their school career, if necessary with special additional facilities such as nursing services, special equipment, etc. For others who cannot progress within the ordinary school system the special schools or classes provide both the primary and secondary level of education. In addition to the services being provided on a full-time basis many children are being catered for by the provision of part-time teaching facilities in hospitals, child guidance clinics, rehabilitation workshops, special 'Saturday-morning' centres and home teaching schemes.

Special schools (1980–81) were numbered 113 with 8,324 pupils. There were 226 special classes attached to ordinary schools with 2,630 pupils. 574 remedial teachers were employed for backward pupils in ordinary schools. 30 peripatetic teachers were employed for children with hearing or visual impairments.

Secondary. Voluntary secondary schools are under private control and are conducted in most cases by religious orders; all schools receive grants from the State and are open to inspection by the Department of Education. The number of recognized secondary schools during the school year 1981–82 was 520, and the number of pupils in attendance was 204,392. Total estimated state expenditure for 1982 (1 Jan.–31 Dec.) is £167·64m.

Grants for the provision of a wide range of audio visual teaching aids are available to secondary schools. The schools television service, *Telefís Scoile*, provides programmes in Irish, English, history, geography, mathematics and science subjects for senior and junior pupils. The vast majority of secondary schools now have at least one television receiving set which was purchased with the aid of a state grant.

Vocational Education Committee schools provide courses of general and technical education. The number of vocational schools during the school year 1981–82 was 241, full-time students, 66,419. These schools are controlled by the local Vocational Education Committees, and are maintained partly from the rates and partly by state grants. The estimated state expenditure for 1982 (1 Jan.–31 Dec.) is £117m., and the estimated expenditure from the local rates, £2,301,000.

Comprehensive Schools which are financed by the State combine academic and technical subjects in one broad curriculum so that each pupil may be offered a range of educational options structured to his needs, abilities and interests. Pupils are prepared for the State examinations and for entrance to universities and institutes of further education. The number of comprehensive schools during the school year 1981–82 was 15 with 8,515 students.

Community Schools continue to be established through the amalgamation of existing voluntary secondary and Vocational Education Committee schools where this is found feasible and desirable and in new areas where a single larger school is considered preferable to 2 smaller schools under separate managements. These schools cater for all aspects of second-level education and provide adult education facilities in the areas in which they are situated. They also make facilities available to voluntary organizations and to the adult community generally. The number of community schools during the school year 1981–82 was 38 with 21,028 students. The estimated State expenditure on running costs for 1982 (1 Jan.–31 Dec.) is £27,175,000 for community and comprehensive schools.

Regional Technical Colleges and Colleges of Technology. Apprentice, technician and professional courses are provided in the colleges of technology of the City of Dublin Vocational Education Committee, the Limerick College of Technology and 9 regional technical colleges at Athlone, Carlow, Cork, Dundalk, Galway, Letterkenny, Sligo, Tralee and Waterford. Students (full-time) 1981–82, 12,393.

University Education is provided by the National University of Ireland, founded in Dublin in 1908, and by the University of Dublin (Trinity College), founded in 1592. The National University comprises 3 constituent colleges–University College, Dublin, University College, Cork, and University College, Galway. St Patrick's College, Maynooth, Co. Kildare, is a national seminary for Catholic priests and a pontifical university with the power to confer degrees up to doctoral level in philosophy, theology and canon law. It also admits lay students (men and women) to the courses in arts, celtic studies, science and education which it provides as a recognized college of the National University. Besides the University medical schools, the Royal College of Surgeons in Ireland, provides medical qualifications which are internationally recognized. There are six Colleges of Education for the training of primary school teachers. For degree awarding purposes, three of these colleges are associated with Trinity College, two with University College, Dublin and one with University College, Cork. Third-level courses with a technological bias, leading to degree, diploma and certificate qualifications are also provided by the National Institutes for Higher Education, Limerick and Dublin. The Thomond College of Education, Limerick, is a specialist teacher-training institution concerned with the training of post-primary teachers in the areas of physical education, rural and general science, metalwork and engineering science, woodwork and building science and commercial and secretarial subjects.

The National Council for Educational Awards, established on a statutory basis in 1979, is the validating and awarding authority for degree, diploma and certificate courses in the third-level non-university sector.

Agricultural. An Chomhairle Óiliuna Talmhaíochta (ACOT) is the agency responsible for providing agricultural advisory and training services. Full-time instruction in agriculture is provided for all sections of the farming community. There are 4 agricultural colleges for young people, administered by ACOT, and 7 private ACOT- aided agricultural colleges, at each of which a 1-year course in agriculture is given. Second-year courses in farm machinery and dairying are provided at a number of the colleges. Advanced courses in pig and poultry husbandry and management are also provided. Scholarships tenable at these colleges, all of which are residential, are awarded by ACOT which also provides a comprehensive agricultural advisory service and conducts winter classes in agriculture and horticulture at local centres. A more comprehensive course is provided in winter farm schools, which are intended, in general, for persons of not less than 17 years of age who are engaged in farming.

Horticultural. A 2-year course in commercial horticulture is provided at 3 residential colleges. There is also a 2-year course in amenity horticulture at the National Botanic Gardens in Dublin.

Poultry-keeping and Farm Home Management. An advanced 3-year residential course is provided at the Munster Institute, Cork, for young people who wish to qualify for teaching and advisory posts in farm home management. The farm home management course includes instruction in poultry-keeping, butter- and cheese-making, general farming and home management. A 1-year non-residential course of instruction for the training of young men and women as technicians in poultry husbandry is also provided at the Munster Institute (which is administered by the Department of Agriculture). In addition, if there are enough suitable applicants, a 6-month course in poultry husbandry and management is provided for young people at the Munster Institute.

Rural Home Economics and Rural Science. A 1-year course for young people in poultry-keeping, dairying and rural home economics is given at 5 private residential colleges of rural home economics and 1 private residential school of home economics. The County Committees of Agriculture award scholarships tenable at these institutions. Classes in poultry-keeping and farm home management are also conducted by the County Committees at local centres.

A scheme of farm apprenticeship and a trainee farmer scheme are operated by the Farm Apprenticeship Board, which represents various agricultural interests. The scheme provides for practical training on well-managed commercial farms.

Higher Education in Agriculture, Horticulture, Dairy Science and Veterinary Science. Higher education in general agriculture and horticulture is provided by University College, Dublin, and in dairy science by University College, Cork. Training in veterinary medicine and surgery is provided at the Veterinary College, Ballsbridge, Dublin.

Health Services. Persons in the lower income group (those who are unable to afford general practitioner services for themselves and their dependants) are entitled to a free comprehensive health service (family doctor, hospital and specialist services, maternity and infant-welfare services, dental, ophthalmic and aural services). Persons and dependants in the middle-income groups (less than £9,500 per annum income) are entitled to in-patient and out-patient hospital services including specialist services, free maternity care and help towards the cost of drugs and medicines. Such persons must pay a contribution of 1% of income, subject to a maximum of £95 per year, towards the cost of these services. All persons, irrespective of income, qualify for the benefit of assistance towards the cost of prescriptions, which limits the total outlay of a family to £16 per month. Hospital treatment for tuberculosis and certain other infectious diseases as well as for children suffering from certain long-term diseases and disabilities is provided free of charge to all classes of the community. Persons suffering from diabetes and other specified long-term conditions are eligible for a free supply of drugs and other necessary medicines, etc.

Pupils of national (elementary) schools are provided with a free school health-examination service and are also eligible for free dental, ophthalmic and aural services for defects discovered at school health examinations.

A free child-welfare clinic service for children under 6 years of age is available in many urban areas. A disabled persons maintenance allowance is payable in cases of need to chronically disabled persons over 16 who are not living in institutions. The disabled are also entitled to free travel and in certain circumstances to a free electricity allowance, a free television licence, free telephone rental and fuel vouchers. There is a mobility allowance of £250 per year for those unable to walk. The mother of a severely handicapped child maintained at home may qualify for a constant care allowance. There are also schemes which provide for the education of the blind, and for the training and placement in suitable employment of the blind and the disabled. Welfare services include day care services for children, families in stress and the old. Home helps, meals-on-wheels, home nursing etc, are provided where neccessary. All these services are provided by regional health boards under the direction and control of the Minister for Health.

Social Security. Social-welfare services concerned primarily with income maintenance are under the general control of the Minister for Social Welfare. The services administered by the Department of Social Welfare are divided into Insurance and Assistance schemes.

Insurance Services. All employees irrespective of their level of earnings are compulsorily insured from age 16 to 66 years and are liable for pay-related social insurance contributions. The majority of employees pay a contribution of 7·5% of their earnings while their employers pay a further 11·61% up to a prescribed ceiling of £9,500. (The insured population is approximately 1m.) Subject to appropriate statutory conditions (but without regard to the recipients' means) the following flat-rate insurance benefits are available: Disability benefit, invalidity pension, unemployment benefit, maternity benefit, widow's pension, deserted wife's benefit, orphan's allowance, treatment benefit, retirement pension payable at 65, old-age pension payable at 66 and a death grant. Pay-related benefit is payable with disability benefit, unemployment benefit, maternity allowance and injury benefit to persons whose employment is insurable at certain class rates of pay-related social insurance contribution. The cost of the flat-rate and pay-related benefits is met by pay-related social insurance contributions from employers and employees and by a state grant.

The insurance services also provide for payment of benefits in respect of injury, disablement or death, as well as medical care resulting from an occupational accident or disease. These benefits are available to employees, irrespective of age, and are paid from an Occupational Injuries Fund which is financed by employers' contributions and income from investments.

Assistance Services. Children's allowances are payable without a means test in respect of each child under 16 years of age and children between 16 and 18 who are at school, in apprenticeship or incapacitated for a prolonged period. The following Assistance services are subject to a means test: Non-contributory widows' and orphans' pensions to the survivors of persons whose lack of insurance (or inadequate insurance record) precludes payment of contributory pensions; deserted wife's allowance to women who have been deserted by their husbands and for whom the deserted wife's benefit is similarly precluded; allowances for unmarried mothers, prisoners' wives and single women between the ages of 58 and 66 years; old age pensions payable at age 66 to persons not entitled to insurance pensions; blind pensions (under the same general conditions as apply to old age pensions) payable at age 18; unemployment assistance payable during unemployment to persons not entitled to receive unemployment benefit; supplementary welfare allowance, payable when a person has no other resources or when such resources are insufficient to meet his needs.

DIPLOMATIC REPRESENTATIVES

Of Ireland in Great Britain (17 Grosvenor Place, London, SW1X 7HR)
Ambassador: Dr Eamon Kennedy.

Of Great Britain in Ireland (33 Merrion Rd., Dublin, 4)
Ambassador: Sir Leonard Figg, KCMG.

Of Ireland in the USA (2234 Massachusetts Ave., NW, Washington, D.C. 20008)
Ambassador: Tadhg F. O' Sullivan.

Of the USA in Ireland (42 Elgin Rd., Ballsbridge, Dublin)
Ambassador: Peter H. Dailey.

Of Ireland to the United Nations
Ambassador: Noel Dorr.

Books of Reference

Statistical Information: The Central Statistics Office (Earlsfort Terrace, Dublin, 2) was established in June 1949, and is attached to the Department of the Taoiseach. *Director:* T. P. Linehan, B.E., B.Sc.

The Central Statistics Office took over the work carried out since 1922 by the Statistics Branch, Department of Industry and Commerce, which in turn had continued the statistical work carried out by the Department of Agriculture and Technical Instruction (since 1900) and by the Irish Department of the Ministry of Labour, London (since 1919). Vital statistics from 1864, annual agricultural statistics prior to 1900 and decennial census of population were compiled by the Registrar-General for Ireland. The population censuses were carried out in 1926, 1936 and 1946 by the Statistics Branch of the Department of Industry and Commerce and are now the responsibility of the Central Statistics Office, which has also, as from July 1950, taken over from the Registrar-General the compilation of Vital Statistics. The Statistics Act 1926 confers wide powers for the collection, compilation and publication of statistics. Other Acts under which statistics are collected are Workmen's Compensation Act, Merchant Shipping Act, Customs Consolidation Act and Road Transport Act.

Principal publications of the Central Statistics Office are *National Income and Expenditure* (annually), *Statistical Abstract* (annually), *Census of Population Reports, Census of Industrial Production Reports, Trade and Shipping Statistics* (annually and monthly), *Trend of Employment and Unemployment* (annually), *Reports on Vital Statistics* (annually), *Irish Statistical Bulletin* (quarterly).

Aspects of Ireland. (Series). Dublin Department of Foreign Affairs.
Atlas of Ireland. Royal Irish Academy, Dublin, 1979
Facts About Ireland. Dublin Department of Foreign Affairs, 5th ed. 1981
The Gill History of Ireland. 11 vols. Dublin
Bartholomew, P. C., *The Irish Judiciary.* Dublin, Institute of Public Administration, 1974
Brown, T., *Ireland: A Social and Cultural History, 1922–1979.* London, 1981
Chubb, B., *The Constitution and Constitutional Change in Ireland.* Dublin, 1978
Delaney, V. T. H., *The Administration of Justice in Ireland.* 4th ed. Dublin, Institute of Public Administration, 1975
Eager, A. R., *A Guide to Irish Bibliographical Material.* 2nd ed. London, 1980
Encyclopaedia of Ireland. Dublin, 1968
Freeman, T. W., *Ireland: A General and Regional Geography.* 4th ed. London, 1972
Harbison, P., *Guide to the National Monuments of Ireland.* Dublin, 1975
Hickey, D. J. and Doherty, J. E., *A Dictionary of Irish History since 1800.* Dublin, 1980
Johnston, T. J., and others, *A History of the Church of Ireland.* Dublin, 1953
Keatinge, P., *Formulation of Irish Foreign Policy.* Dublin, 1973.—*A Place Among the Nations: Issues of Irish Foreign Policy.* Dublin, 1978
Kee, R., *The Green Flag.* London, 1972
Kelly, J. M., *Fundamental Rights in the Irish Law and Constitution.* 2nd ed. Dublin, 1967
Lehane, B., *The Companion Guide to Ireland.* London, 1973
Lyons, F. S. L., *Ireland Since the Famine.* London, 1971
McDunphy, Michael, *The President of Ireland: His Powers, Functions and Duties.* Dublin, 1945
Meenan, J., *The Irish Economy Since 1922.* Liverpool, 1970
Nevill, W. E., *Geology and Ireland.* Dublin, 1963
Thom's Directory of Ireland. 2 vols. (Dublin, Street Directory, Commercial). Dublin, 1979–80

ISRAEL

Capital: Jerusalem
Population: 3·92m. (1981)
GNP per capita: US$4,500 (1980)

Medinat Israel—State of Israel

HISTORY. In 1967, following some years of uneasy peace, local clashes on the Israeli-Syrian border were followed by Egyptian mass concentration of forces on the borders of Israel. The UN emergency force was expelled and a blockade of shipping to and from Israel was imposed by Egypt in the Red Sea. Israel struck out at Egypt on land and in the air on 5–9 June 1967. Jordan joined in the conflict which spread to the Syrian borders. By 11 June the Israelis had occupied the Gaza Strip and the Sinai peninsula as far as the Suez Canal in Egypt, West Jordan as far as the Jordan valley and the heights east of the Sea of Galilee, including Quneitra in Syria.

A further war broke out on 6 Oct. 1973 when an Egyptian offensive was launched across the Suez Canal and Syrian forces struck on the Golan Heights. Following UN Security Council resolutions a ceasefire finally came into being on 24 Oct. In Dec. agreement was reached by Egypt and Israel on disengagement and a disengagement agreement was signed with Syria on 31 May 1974. A further disengagement agreement was signed between Israel and Egypt in Sept. 1975.

Developments in 1977 included President Sadat of Egypt's visit to Israel and peace inititative and in March 1978 Israeli troops entered southern Lebanon but later withdrew after the arrival of a UN peace-keeping force.

In Sept. 1978 President Carter convened the Camp David conference at which Egypt and Israel agreed on frameworks for peace in the Middle East with treaties to be negotiated between Israel and her neighbours. Negotiations began in USA between Egypt and Israel in Oct. 1978 and a peace treaty was signed in Washington 26 March 1979.

Under the Israel-Egypt peace treaty signed in Washington on 26 March 1979, Israel withdrew from the Sinai Desert in two phases, part was achieved on 26 Jan. 1980 and the final withdrawal by 26 April 1982.

AREA AND POPULATION. The area of Israel, within the boundaries defined by the 1949 armistice agreements with Egypt, Jordan, the Lebanon and Syria, is 20,770 sq. km (8,017 sq. miles), with a population (May 1972 census) of 3·2m. (estimated, Jan. 1979, 3·83m.). Population of areas under Israeli administration as a result of the 6-day war was over 1m.; Judaea and Samaria (West Bank), 703,600, Gaza Strip and Northern Sinai, 441,300 and a few thousand on the Golan Heights.

Crude birth rate per 1,000 population of Jewish population (1981), 22; non-Jewish, 36·5; crude death rate, Jewish, 7·2; non-Jewish, 4·3; infant mortality rate per 1,000 live births, Jewish, 11·6; non-Jewish, 21·1.

Israel is administratively divided into 6 districts:

District	*Area (sq. km)*	*Population* [1]	*Chief town*
Northern	3,489	594,100	Nazareth
Haifa	855	557,400	Haifa
Central	1,243	766,400	Ramla
Tel Aviv	171	995,900	Tel Aviv
Jerusalem [2]	557	438,200	Jerusalem
Southern	14,387	464,600	Beersheba

[1] 1979. [2] Includes East Jerusalem, annexed from Jordan after 1967 War.

On 23 Jan. 1950 the Knesset proclaimed Jerusalem the capital of the State. On 14 Dec. 1981 the Knesset extended Israeli law into the Golan Heights. Population of the main towns (31 Dec. 1981): Tel-Aviv/Jaffa, 334,900; Jerusalem, 407,100; Haifa, 230,000; Ramat Gan, 120,400; Bat-Yam, 132,100; Holon, 130,900; Petach Tikva, 119,800; Beersheba, 109,600.

The official languages are Hebrew and Arabic.

Immigration. The following table shows the numbers of Jewish immigrants entering Palestine (Israel), including persons entering as travellers who subsequently registered as immigrants. For a year-by-year breakdown, *see* THE STATESMAN'S YEAR-BOOK, 1951, p. 1167.

1919–32	129,349	1940–47	101,173	1969–79	384,066
1933–39	235,170	1948–68	1,290,610	1979–80	34,406

During the period 1948–68, 45·5% of the immigrants came from Europe and America and 54·5% from Asia and Africa; during the period 1969–79, 79·5% came from Europe and America and 20·5% from Asia and Africa.

The Jewish Agency, which, in accordance with Article IV of the Palestine Mandate, played a leading role in laying the political, economic and social foundations on which the State of Israel was established, continues to be instrumental in organizing immigration.

CONSTITUTION AND GOVERNMENT. Israel is an independent sovereign republic, established by proclamation on 14 May 1948. For the history of the British Mandate, *see* THE STATESMAN'S YEAR-BOOK, 1920–49, under PALESTINE.

In 1950 the Knesset (*Parliament*), which in 1949 had passed the Transition Law dealing in general terms with the powers of the Knesset, President and Cabinet, resolved to enact from time to time fundamental laws, which eventually, taken together, would form the Constitution. The first of these fundamental laws, dealing with the Knesset, Israel Lands and the President, were passed in 1958, 1960 and 1964 respectively and with the Government in 1968.

National flag: White with 2 horizontal blue stripes, the blue Shield of David in the centre.

National anthem: Hatikvah (The Hope). Words by N. N. Imber (1878); adopted as the Jewish National Anthem by the first Zionist Congress (1897).

The Knesset, a one-chamber Parliament, consists of 120 members. It is elected for a 4-year term by secret ballot and universal direct suffrage. The system of election is by proportional representation. In June 1981 the Knesset was composed as follows: Likud, 48; Labour Party-Mapam Alignment, 47; National Religious Party, 6; Democratic Front for Peace and Equality, 4; Agudat Israel, 4; Citizens Rights Movement, 1. The President is elected by the Knesset by secret ballot by a simple majority; his term of office is 5 years. He may be re-elected once.

Former Presidents of the State: Chaim Weizmann (1949–52); Izhak Ben-Zvi (1952–63); Zalman Shazar (1963–68); Ephraim Katzir (1968–78); Yitzhak Navon (1978–83).

President: Chaim Herzog, elected 22 March 1983 by 61 votes to 56 against with 3 abstentions.

The Cabinet in Feb. 1983 was composed as follows:

Prime Minister: Menachem Begin.

Deputy Prime Minister and Minister of Agriculture: Simha Erlich. *Deputy Prime Minister and Minister of Construction and Housing:* David Levy. *Defence:* Moshe Arens. *Foreign Affairs:* Yitzhak Shamir. *Economic Affairs:* Yaacov Meridor. *Interior and Religious Affairs:* Dr Yosef Burg. *Finance:* Yoram Aridor. *Education and Culture:* Zevulun Hammer. *Commerce and Industry:* Gideon Patt. *Justice:* Moshe Nissim. *Labour and Social Welfare and Immigrant Absorption:* Aharon Uzzan. *Health:* Eliezer Shostak. *Transport:* Haim Corfu. *Energy and Infrastructure:* Yitzhak Moda'i. *Tourism:* Avraham Sharir. *Communications:* Mordechai Zipori. *Science and Technology:* Yuval Ne'eman. *Without Portfolio:* Ariel Sharon.

Local Government. Local authorities are of three kinds, namely, municipal corporations, local councils and regional councils. Their status, powers and duties are prescribed by statute. Regional councils are local authorities set up in agricultural areas and include all the agricultural settlements in the area under their jurisdiction. All local authorities exercise their authority mainly by means of bye-laws approved by the Minister of the Interior. Their revenue is derived from rates and a surcharge on income tax. Local authorities are elected for a 4-year term of office concurrently with general elections.

There are 36 municipalities (2 Arab), 115 local councils (46 Arab and 6 Druze) and 49 regional councils (1 Arab) comprising 700 villages.

DEFENCE. The Defence Service Law of 8 Sept. 1949, as amended, provides a compulsory 30-month conscription (extended to 39 months in 1980) for men between the ages of 18 and 26 and a 30-month conscription for men in the age-group of 27–29 years. Unmarried women aged 18–26 serve 24 months. After their term of military service, men are on the reserves until the age of 55 years. Until they are 40, men usually report for 31 days training annually and from then until they are 55, for 14 days. Commissioned and n.c.o.s usually serve 7 extra days a year.

The Israel Defence Force is a unified force, in which army, navy and air force are subordinate to a single chief-of-staff. The Minister of Defence is *de facto* commander-in-chief but from Oct. 1973 the cabinet formed a defence committee with authority to make decisions on military operations.

Army. The regular army had a strength in 1983 of 135,000 (25,000 regulars) including women, organized in 33 armoured, 10 mechanized, 12 infantry, 9 artillery and 5 parachute brigades. There is a reserve army of about 450,000 on mobilization.

The highest army rank is that of Lieut.-General (*Rav Alouf*), and the Chief-of-Staff, who is the C.-in-C., holds that rank. A divisional commander is a Brigadier (*Tat Alouf*), and a brigade commander a Colonel (*Alouf Mishne*).

Navy. The Navy includes 3 diesel-electric patrol submarines (built in Britain), 24 missile vessels (4 of 500 tons with helicopter and hangar, 8 of 415 tons and 12 of 220 tons), 2 fast attack craft of 47 tons (the smallest missile boats yet built), 2 missile-armed hydrofoils, 40 patrol craft, 2 transports, 3 medium landing ships, 6 landing craft, 1 ‘firefish’, 1 support ship, 1 training ship, 4 coastguard cutters, 3 hovercraft and 3 minor landing craft.

New construction includes 2 missile armed corvettes of 850 tons, and 10 improved guided-missile hydrofoils of 105 tons displacement, all being built in Israel.

The former Nautical School in Haifa has been reorganized as a Naval Officers’ School in Acre. Naval personnel in 1983 totalled 800 officers and 5,800 men, of whom 3,500 are conscripts, including a Naval Commando. There are also 5,000 naval reservists.

Air Force. The Air Force has a personnel strength of about 30,000, with about 600 first-line aircraft, all jets, of Israeli, US and French manufacture. They include a few Mirage III supersonic multi-mission fighters, 200 Israeli-built Kfirs based on the Mirage airframe, 50 F-15 Eagle fighters, the first 75 of a planned 150 F-16A/B fighters, about 135 F-4E Phantom fighter-bombers, 12 RF-4E reconnaissance fighters and about 170 A-4E/H/N Skyhawk light attack aircraft, supported by 4 E-2C Hawkeye airborne early warning and control aircraft and a few OV-1 Mohawk and RU-21 elint aircraft. There are transport squadrons of turboprop C-130/KC-130 Hercules, C-47, Arava, and Boeing 707 (some equipped for tanker or ECM duties) aircraft, helicopter squadrons of CH-53, Super Frelon, Huey-Cobra, Hughes 500M-D Defender, JetRanger, Agusta-Bell 205 and 212 aircraft, and training units with locally-built Magister jet trainers, which can be used also in a light ground attack role. Missiles in service include surface-to-air Hawks and surface-to-surface Lances.

INTERNATIONAL RELATIONS

Membership. Israel is a member of UN.

ECONOMY

Budget. The budget year runs from 1 April to 31 March (in shekel 1m.):

	1980–81	*1981–82*
Revenue	101,423	228,506
Revenue for development budget	20,156	44,804
Business enterprises	11,323	22,506
Expenditure	101,423	228,506

New economic measures were introduced in Sept. 1975; purchase tax was increased by 12·5% on luxury goods, and 5% on many basic consumer items. On 5 Jan. 1976, the Israeli pound was devalued from I£7.10 to the US$ to I£7.24.

In 1981–82 the main items of expenditure (in shekel 1m.) were: Defence, 63,816; education and culture, 15,202; health, 3,722; labour and social welfare, 8,070.

Income tax is levied progressively up to a maximum of 71·9%. A Defence Levy of 10% on income tax paid was introduced during the 6-Day War.

Currency. The unit of currency is the *shekel* equal to 10 Israeli £s. The new currency was announced in Feb. 1980. Currency in circulation on 31 Dec. 1978 was I£6,860m. (bank-notes and coins). In March 1983, £1 = 57·75 *shekel*; US$ = 38 *shekel*.

Banking. The Bank of Israel was established by law in 1954 as Israel's central bank. Its Governor is appointed by the President on the recommendation of the Cabinet for a 5-year term. He acts as economic adviser to the Government and has ministerial status. The assets of the Bank of Israel on 31 Dec. 1974 totalled I£20,551m., of which I£7,762m. was in foreign currencies and I£235m. in gold.

There are 21 commercial banks headed by Bank Leumi Le Israel, Bank Hapoalim and Israel Discount Bank.

Weights and Measures. The metric system is in general use. The (metrical) *dunam* = 1,000 sq. metres (about 0·25 acre).

Jewish Year. The Jewish year 5741 corresponds to 12 Sept. 1980–29 Sept. 1981; 5742 to 30 Sept. 1981–18 Sept. 1982; 5743 to 18 Sept. 1982–7 Sept. 1983.

ENERGY AND NATURAL RESOURCES

Electricity. Electric-power consumption amounted during 1979 to 10,636m. kwh.

Oil and Gas. Oil was first discovered in Sept. 1955 at Heletz in the Negev. Crude oil production in 1979 was 24m. litres and natural gas (1974) 66m. cu. metres.

Minerals. The most valuable natural resources of the country are the potash, bromine and other salt deposits of the Dead Sea, which are exploited by the Dead Sea Works, Ltd. Geological research and exploration of the natural resources in the Negev are undertaken by the Israel Mining Corporation. Potash production in 1979 was 1,194,000 tons.

A plant for the production of 46,000 tons of magnesium and 80,000 tons of hydrochloric acid per annum is being erected in the Arad area.

Agriculture. In the coastal plain (Sharon, Emek Hefer and the Shephelah) mixed farming, poultry raising, citriculture and vineyards are the main agricultural activities. The Emek (the Valley of Jezreel) is the main agricultural centre of Israel. Mixed farming is to be found throughout the valleys; the sub-tropical Beisan and Jordan plainlands are also centres of banana plantations and fish breeding. In Galilee mixed farming, olive and tobacco plantations prevail. The Hills of Ephraim are a vineyard centre; many parts of the hill country are under afforestation. In the northern Negev farming has been aided by the Yarkon–Negev water pipeline. This has become part of the overall project of the 'National Water Carrier', which is to take water from the Sea of Galilee (Lake Kinnereth) to the south. The plan includes a number of regional projects such as the Lake Kinnereth –Negev pipeline which came into operation in 1964; it has an annual capacity of 320m. cu. metres.

A land-utilization survey has graded the country as follows: 4·27m. dunams under dry farming and 2·89m. dunams under irrigation suitable for all types of cultivation, 697,000 dunams under dry farming and 1,339,000 dunams under irrigation suitable for plantations, 8·49m. dunams suitable for pasture, 882,000 dunams suitable for afforestation, 470,000 dunams unfit for any type of cultivation.

The area under cultivation (in 1,000 dunams) in 1976–77 was 4,300, of which 1,920 were under irrigation. Of the total cultivated area 2,662 dunams were under field crops, 367 under vegetables, potatoes, pumpkins and melons, 885 under citrus and orchards, 49 under fish ponds and 176 under miscellaneous crops, including auxiliary farms, nurseries, flowers, etc.

Industrial crops, such as cotton and sugar-beet, have successfully been introduced. In 1976–77 the area under cotton totalled 490,400 dunams and under sugar-beet 54,000.

Livestock (1981) included 265,000 cattle, 270,000 sheep, 119,000 goats, 24·6m. chickens.

Characteristic types of rural settlement are, among others, the following: (1) The *Kibbutz* and *Kvutza* (communal collective settlement), where all property and earnings are collectively owned and work is collectively organized. (2) The *Moshav Ovdim* (workers' co-operative smallholders' settlement) which is founded on the principles of mutual aid and equality of opportunity between the members, all farms being equal in size; hired labour is prohibited. (3) The *Moshav Shitufi* (co-operative settlement), which is based on collective ownership and economy as in the *Kibbutz,* but with each family having its own house and being responsible for its own domestic services. (4) The *Moshav* (smallholders' settlement), which resembles the *moshav ovdim* but lacks the latter's rigid ideological basis; hired labour, for instance, is permitted. (5) The *Moshava* (village), in which land and property are privately owned and every resident is responsible for his own well-being. In 1979, of the 808 rural settlements in Israel, 240 were kibbutzim (population, 101,600), 350 were moshavim (132,800), 27 moshavim shitufiim (6,800), 89 Arab villages (163,600, not including 53,000 Bedouin); the rest were temporary settlements and educational institutions.

INDUSTRY AND TRADE

Industry. A wide range of products is manufactured, processed or finished in the country, including chemicals, metal products, textiles, tyres, diamonds, paper, plastics, leather goods, glass and ceramics, building materials, precision instruments, tobacco, foodstuffs, electrical and electronic equipment.

Labour. The General Federation of Labour (Histadrut) founded in 1920, had, in 1973, 1,259,200 members (including 89,000 Arab and Druze members); including workers' families, this membership represents 56·1% of the population covering 85% of all wage-earners. Several trades unions of lesser importance also exist.

Histadrut participates in over 70% of Israeli agriculture and 23% of industrial production; it runs the Kuput Holim (workers' health service) and has large interests in banking, insurance, retail business, construction and building.

Commerce. External trade, in US$1,000, for calendar years:

	1975	*1976*	*1977*	*1978*	*1979*	*1980*
Imports	4,173	4,140	4,844	5,843	7,511	8,024
Exports	1,941	2,414	3,082	3,921	4,546	5,540

In 1977, of the imports 55·4% came from Europe (EEC, EFTA and COMECON countries), 21·6% from the US and Canada, 5·8% from Asia and Africa; of the exports 46·7% went to European countries, 18·3% to Africa and Asia, 9·6% to US and Canada.

The main exportable commodities are citrus fruit and by-products, fruit-juices, wines and liquor, sweets, polished diamonds, chemicals, tyres, textiles, metal products, machinery, electronic and transportation equipment, flowers. The main exports were, in 1979 (US$1m.): Diamonds, 1,418·8; chemical and oil products, 505; food, beverages and tobacco, 251; citrus fruit, 254·6.

Total trade between Israel and UK (British Department of Trade returns, in £1,000 sterling):

	1978	*1979*	*1980*	*1981*	*1982*
Imports to UK	189,200	227,600	236,599	256,000	275,139
Exports and re-exports from UK	243,570	270,733	231,658	212,000	224,362

Tourism. In 1981 there were about 1·2m. tourists. There are over 300 recommended hotels with over 25,000 rooms.

COMMUNICATIONS

Roads. There were 12,160 km of paved roads in 1979. Registered motor vehicles in 1979 totalled 524,950, including 6,771 buses, 80,772 trucks and 397,351 private cars.

Railways. Internal communications (1982) are provided by 552 km of standard gauge line. Construction is in progress (1982) of 215 km of new line linking Eilat on the Gulf of Aqaba with Sedom and the existing rail network by means of the 34 km line opened between Oron and Nahal Zin in Nov. 1977. In 1980–81, 3·2m. passengers and 5·4m. tonnes of freight were carried.

Aviation. Air communications are centred in the airport of Ben Gurion, near Tel-Aviv. In 1979, 11,586 planes landed at Israeli airports on international flights; 1·43m. passengers arrived, 1,396,000 departed; 80,266 tonnes of freight were loaded and 62,296 tonnes unloaded. The Israeli airline El Al maintains regular flights to London, Paris, Rome, Amsterdam, Brussels, Athens, Vienna, New York, Zurich, Munich, Nicosia, Istanbul, Johannesburg, Nairobi, Frankfurt and Copenhagen. In 1980–81 El Al carried 1·25m. passengers.

Shipping. Israel has 3 commercial ports, Haifa, Ashdod and Eilat. The deep-water port at Ashdod came into use at the end of 1965, when the ports of Tel-Aviv and Jaffa were closed for freight services. An Israel Ports Authority began to operate in 1962. In 1979, 3,157 ships anchored in Israeli ports; 12·4m. tons of freight (not including oil in bulk tankers) were handled. The Israeli merchant fleet consisted in 1974 of 106 vessels, totalling 2,304,253 GRT.

Post and Broadcasting. The Ministry of Posts controls the postal, telegraph and telephone service. In 1977 there were 615 post offices and postal agencies, 45 mobile post offices and (1981) 1,230,000 telephones.

The broadcasting station in Jerusalem, *Kol Israel*, is controlled by the Broadcasting Authority, established in 1965. Wireless licences in 1974 numbered approximately 460,000 and television licences 385,000.

Cinemas (1979). There were 214 cinemas with a seating capacity of approximately 152,300.

Newspapers (1974). There were 27 daily newspapers, including 13 in Hebrew, 4 in Arabic, 1 each in German, English, French, Hungarian, Yiddish, Russian, Romanian, Bulgarian, Spanish and Polish, with a total circulation of over 500,000.

JUSTICE, RELIGION, EDUCATION AND WELFARE

Justice. *Law.* Under the Law and Administration Ordinance, 5708/1948, the first law passed by the Provisional Council of State, the law of Israel is the law which was obtaining in Palestine on 14 May 1948 in so far as it is not in conflict with that Ordinance or any other law passed by the Israel legislature and with such modifications as result from the establishment of the State and its authorities.

Capital punishment was abolished in 1954, except for support given to the Nazis and for high treason.

The law of Palestine was derived from three main sources, namely, Ottoman law, English law (Common Law and Equity) and the law enacted by the Palestine legislature, which to a great extent was modelled on English law. The Ottoman law in its turn was derived from three main sources, namely, Moslem law which had survived in the Ottoman Empire, French law adapted by the Ottomans and the personal law of the non-Moslem communities.

Civil Courts. Municipal courts, established in certain municipal areas, have criminal jurisdiction over offences against municipal regulations and bye-laws and certain specified offences committed within a municipal area.

Magistrates courts, established in each district and sub-district, have limited jurisdiction in both civil and criminal matters.

District courts, sitting at Jerusalem, Tel-Aviv and Haifa, have jurisdiction, as courts of first instance, in all civil matters not within the jurisdiction of magistrates courts, and in all criminal matters, and as appellate courts from magistrates courts and municipal courts.

The Supreme Court has jurisdiction as a court of first instance (sitting as a High Court of Justice dealing mainly with administrative matters) and as an appellate court from the district courts (sitting as a Court of Civil or of Criminal Appeal).

In addition, there are various tribunals for special classes of cases, such as the Rents Tribunals and the Tribunals for the Prevention of Profiteering and Speculation. Settlement Officers deal with disputes with regard to the ownership or possession of land in settlement areas constituted under the Land (Settlement of Title) Ordinance.

Religious Courts. The rabbinical courts of the Jewish community have exclusive jurisdiction in matters of marriage and divorce, alimony and confirmation of wills of members of their community other than foreigners, concurrent jurisdiction with the civil courts in such matters of members of their community who are foreigners if they consent to the jurisdiction, and concurrent jurisdiction with the civil courts in all other matters of personal status of all members of their community, whether foreigners or not, with the consent of all parties to the action, save that such courts may not grant a decree of dissolution of marriage to a foreign subject.

The courts of the several recognized Christian communities have a similar jurisdiction over members of their respective communities.

The Moslem religious courts have exclusive jurisdiction in all matters of personal status over Moslems who are not foreigners, and over Moslems who are foreigners, if under the law of their nationality they are subject in such matters to the jurisdiction of Moslem religious courts.

Where any action of personal status involves persons of different religious communities, the President of the Supreme Court will decide which court shall have jurisdiction, and whenever a question arises as to whether or not a case is one of personal status within the exclusive jurisdiction of a religious court, the matter must be referred to a special tribunal composed of 2 judges of the Supreme Court and the president of the highest court of the religious community concerned in Israel.

Religion. Religious affairs are under the supervision of a special Ministry, with departments for the Christian and Moslem communities. The religious affairs of each community remain under the full control of the ecclesiastical authorities concerned: in the case of the Jews, the Sephardi and Ashkenazi Chief Rabbis, in the case of the Christians, the heads of the various communities, and in the case of the Moslems, the Qadis. The Druze were officially recognized in 1957 as an autonomous religious community.

In 1980 there were: Moslems, 479,000; Christians, 90,000; Druze and others, 50,000.

The Jewish Sabbath and Holy Days are observed as days of rest in the public services. Full provision is, however, made for the free exercise of other faiths, and for the observance by their adherents of their respective days of rest and Holy Days.

Education. The school system is under the direction of the Ministry of Education and Culture, and comprises kindergarten, primary, secondary and technical schools.

Laws passed by the Knesset in 1949 and 1978 provide for free and compulsory education from 5 to 16 years of age. There is free education until 18 years of age.

The State Education Law of 12 Aug. 1953 established a unified state-controlled elementary school system with a provision for special religious schools. The standard curriculum for all elementary schools is issued by the Ministry with a possibility of adding supplementary subjects comprising not more than 25% of the total syllabus. Many schools in towns are private, a number are maintained by municipalities and some are administered by teachers' co-operatives or trustees.

Statistics relating to schools under government supervision, 1979:

Type of School	*Schools*	*Teachers*	*Pupils*
Hebrew Education—Total	*2,743*	*64,175*	*739,240*
Primary schools	1,485	33,233	435,525
Schools for handicapped children	213	2,618	12,540
Schools of intermediate division	477	9,561	72,790
Secondary schools	231	18,763 (secondary, vocational and agricultural)	142,884
Vocational schools	310		70,361
Agricultural schools	27		5,140
Arab Education—Total	*477*	*8,362*	*163,711*
Primary schools	312	5,914	124,518
Schools for handicapped children	17	111	884
Schools of intermediate division	43	1,046	14,801
Secondary schools	71	1,291 (secondary, vocational and agricultural)	20,275
Vocational schools	32		2,460
Agricultural schools	2		773

There are also a number of private schools maintained by religious foundations—Jewish, Christian and Moslem—and also by private societies.

The Hebrew University of Jerusalem, founded in 1925, comprises faculties of the humanities, social sciences, law, science, medicine and agriculture. In 1978–79 it had a teaching staff of 2,184 and 14,000 students.

The Technion in Haifa had, in 1978–79, 21 faculties and departments with 1,500 teachers and 7,800 students. The Weizmann Institute of Science in Rehovoth is engaged in research in chemistry, mathematics, physics and biology; founded in 1949, it had a staff of 400 and 486 students in 1978–79.

In 1978–79 the Tel Aviv University had 16 faculties, some 2,388 teachers and 19,000 students. The religious Bar-Ilan University at Ramat Gan, opened in 1965 had, in 1978–79, 5 faculties (Jewish studies, humanities, natural sciences, social sciences, philology), 900 teachers and 7,600 students. The Haifa University had, in 1978–79, 29 faculties with 568 teachers and 7,522 students. The Ben Gurion University had, in 1978–79, 28 departments with 628 teachers and 4,300 students.

Social Welfare. In 1981 Israel had 148 hospitals with 26,754 beds. The 'Malben' organization cares for the aged. The Women's International Zionist Organization has a number of children's homes, crèches and kindergartens as well as vocational schools and training institutions for nurses. In addition, there are several other voluntary bodies providing specific services to the community.

The National Insurance Law, which took effect in April 1954, provides for old-age pensions, survivors' insurance, work-injury insurance, maternity insurance, family allowances and unemployment benefits.

DIPLOMATIC REPRESENTATIVES

Of Israel in Great Britain (2 Palace Green, London, W8 4QB)
Chargé d'Affaires: Yoav Biran.

Of Great Britain in Israel (192 Rehov Hayarkon, Tel Aviv 63405)
Ambassador: P. Moberly, CMG.

Of Israel in the USA (3514 International Drive, NW, Washington, D.C., 20008)
Ambassador: (Vacant).

Of the USA in Israel (71 Hayarkon St., Tel Aviv)
Ambassador: Samuel W. Lewis.

Of Israel to the United Nations
Ambassador: Dr Yehuda Z. Blum.

Books of Reference

Statistical Information: There is a Central Bureau of Statistics and Economic Research at the Prime Minister's Office, Jerusalem. It publishes monthly bulletins of economic statistics, social statistics, foreign trade statistics and an English summary.

Government Yearbook. Government Printer, Jerusalem. 1951 ff. (latest issue, 1971/72)
Facts about Israel. Government Printer, Jerusalem, 1979
Statistical Abstract of Israel. Government Printer, Jerusalem (from 1949/50)
Israel Yearbook. Tel-Aviv, 1948–49 ff.
Statistical Bulletin of Israel. 1949 ff.
Reshumoth (Official Gazette)
Middle East Record, ed. Y. Oron. London, 1960 ff.
Laws of the State of Israel. Authorized translation. Government Printer, Jerusalem, 1958 ff.
Alkalay, R., *The Complete English–Hebrew Dictionary.* 4 vols. Tel-Aviv, 1959–61
Atlas of Israel. Amsterdam, Jerusalem and London, 1970
Ben-Gurion, D., *Ben-Gurion Looks Back.* London, 1965.—*The Jews in Their Land.* London, 1966.—*Israel: A Personal History.* New York, 1971
Churchill, R. S. and W. S., *The Six-Day War.* London, 1967
Crossman, R., *Nation Reborn.* London, 1960
Dayan, M., *Breakthrough.* New York, 1981
Efrat, E. and Orni, E., *Geography of Israel.* Jerusalem, 1976
Eisenstadt, S. N., *Israel Society.* London, 1969
Frankel, W., *Israel Observed.* London, 1980
Gilbert, M., *The Arab-Israeli Conflict: Its History in Maps.* 3rd ed. London, 1981
Goldman, N., *The Jewish Paradox.* New York, 1978
Harris, W., *Taking Root: Israeli Settlement in the West Bank, The Golan and Gaza Sinai 1967–1980.* Chichester, 1981
Horowitz, D., *The Economics of Israel.* New York and Oxford, 1967.—*The Enigma of Economic Growth: A Case Study of Israel.* New York, 1972
Hyamson, A. M., *Palestine under Mandate, 1920–48.* London, 1951
Jiryis, S., *The Arabs in Israel.* New York, 1976
Karmon, Y., *Israel: A Regional Geography.* London, 1971
Laquer, W. (ed.), *The Israel–Arab Reader.* London, 1970.—*A History of Zionism.* New York, 1972
Likhovski, E. S., *Israel's Parliament: The Law of the Knesset.* Oxford, 1971
Lucas, N., *A Modern History of Israel.* London and New York, 1975
Luttwak, E., and Horowitz, D., *The Israeli Army.* London, 1975
Meir, G., *My Life.* New York, 1975
Peretz, D., *The Government and Politics of Israel.* Folkestone, 1979
Pryce-Jones, D., *The Face of Defeat: Palestinian Refugees and Guerrillas.* New York, 1973
Sachar, H., *A History of Israel.* London and New York, 1976
Safran, N., *Israel: The Embattled Ally.* Harvard Univ. Press, 1978
Segal, R., *Whose Jerusalem? The Conflicts of Israel.* London, 1973
Who's Who in Israel. Tel-Aviv, 1978

National Library: The Jewish National and University Library, Jerusalem.

ITALY

Capital: Rome
Population: 56m. (1981)
GNP per capita: US$6,480 (1980)

Repubblica Italiana

HISTORY. On 10 June 1946 Italy became a republic on the announcement by the Court of Cassation that a majority of the voters at the referendum held on 2 June had voted for a republic. The final figures, announced on 18 June, showed: For a republic, 12,718,641 (54·3% of the valid votes cast, which numbered 23,437,143); for the retention of the monarchy, 10,718,502 (45·7%); invalid and contested, 1,509,735. Total 24,946,878, or 89·1% of the registered electors, who numbered 28,005,449. For the results of the polling in the 13 leading cities, *see* THE STATESMAN'S YEAR-BOOK, 1951, p. 1175. Voting was compulsory, open to both men and women 21 years of age or older, including members of the Civil Service and the Armed Forces; former active Fascists and a few other categories were excluded.

On 18 June the then Provisional Government without specifically proclaiming the republic, issued an 'Order of the Day' decreeing that all court verdicts should in future be handed down 'in the name of the Italian people', that the *Gazzetta Ufficiale del Regno d'Italia* should be re-named *Gazzetta Ufficiale della Repubblica Italiana,* that all references to the monarchy should be deleted from legal and government statements and that the shield of the House of Savoy should be removed from the Italian flag.

Thus ended the reign of the House of Savoy, whose kings had ruled over Piedmont for 9 centuries and as Kings of Italy since 18 Feb. 1861. (For fuller account of the House of Savoy, *see* THE STATESMAN'S YEAR-BOOK, 1946, p. 1021.) The Crown Prince Umberto, son of King Victor Emmanuel III, became Lieut.-Gen. (*i.e.*, Regent) of the kingdom on 5 June 1944. Following the abdication and retirement to Egypt of his father on 9 May 1946, Umberto was declared King Umberto II; his reign lasted to 13 June, when he left the country. King Victor Emmanuel III died in Alexandria on 28 Dec. 1947.

AREA AND POPULATION. The population (present in actual boundaries) at successive censuses were as follows:

31 Dec. 1881	29,277,927	21 April 1936	42,302,680
10 Feb. 1901	33,370,138	4 Nov. 1951	47,158,738
10 June 1911	35,694,582	15 Oct. 1961	49,903,878
1 Dec. 1921	37,403,956	24 Oct. 1971	53,744,737
21 April 1931	40,582,043	25 Oct. 1981	56,243,935

The following table gives area and population of the Regions (census of 24 Oct. 1971 and census 1981):

Regions	*Area in sq. km (1971)*	*Resident pop. census, 1971*	*Resident pop. census, 1981* [1]	*Density per sq. km (1981)*
Piemonte	25,399	4,432,313	4,447,362	175
Valle d'Aosta	3,262	109,150	112,662	35
Lombardia	23,834	8,543,387	8,898,653	373
Trentino-Alto Adige	13,613	841,886	870,475	64
Bolzano-Bozen	*7,400*	*414,041*	*429,283*	*58*
Trento	*6,213*	*427,845*	*441,192*	*71*
Veneto	18,368	4,123,411	4,309,607	235
Friuli-Venezia Giulia	7,846	1,213,532	1,229,929	157
Liguria	5,413	1,853,578	1,799,055	332
Emilia Romagna	22,123	3,846,755	3,939,488	178
Toscana	22,992	3,473,097	3,570,926	155
Umbria	8,456	775,783	803,988	95
Marche	9,692	1,359,907	1,409,326	145
Lazio	17,203	4,689,482	4,970,681	289

[1] Provisional.

Regions	*Area in sq. km (1971)*	*Resident pop. census, 1971*	*Resident pop. census, 1981*[1]	*Density per sq. km (1981)*
Abruzzi	10,794	1,166,694	1,215,136	113
Molise	4,438	319,807	324,741	73
Campania	13,595	5,059,348	5,408,298	398
Puglia	19,347	3,582,787	3,849,598	199
Basilicata	9,992	603,064	603,959	60
Calabria	15,080	1,988,051	2,030,505	135
Sicilia	25,708	4,680,715	4,863,587	189
Sardegna	24,090	1,473,800	1,585,959	66
Total	301,245	54,136,547	56,243,935	187

[1] Provisional.

Vital statistics for calendar years:

	Marriages	*Living births* *Legitimate*	*Illegitimate*	*Total*	*Still-born*	*Deaths excl. of still-born*
1975	373,784	806,391	21,461	827,852	9,271	554,346
1976	354,202	757,187	24,451	781,638	8,345	550,565
1977	347,928	715,414	25,689	741,103	7,219	545,694
1978	331,416	681,350	27,693	709,043	6,564	540,671
1979	323,930	643,835	26,386	670,221	5,748	534,563
1980 [1]	323,362	617,878	26,123	644,001	5,193	551,408
1981 [1]	313,736	595,195	26,610	621,805	4,950	542,204

[1] Provisional.

Emigrants to non-European countries, by sea and air: 1977, 22,508; 1978, 23,589; 1979, 21,302; 1980, 20,360; 1981, 20,628. Since 1960 nearly nine-tenths of these emigrants have gone to Canada, USA and Australia.

Communes of more than 100,000 inhabitants, with population resident on 25 Oct. 1981 (census)[1]:

Roma (Rome)	2,830,569	Padova (Padua)	231,337	Bergamo	121,846
Milano (Milan)	1,634,638	Brescia	206,460	Sassari	118,158
Napoli (Naples)	1,210,503	Modena	179,933	Siracusa (Syracuse)	117,689
Torino (Turin)	1,103,520	Parma	176,750	La Spezia	115,215
Genova (Genoa)	760,300	Livorno (Leghorn)	175,371	Vicenza	113,931
Palermo	699,691	Reggio di C.	171,324	Terni	111,401
Bologna	455,853	Prato	158,797	Forli	109,815
Firenze (Florence)	453,293	Salerno	157,243	Piacenza	108,177
Catania	378,521	Foggia	157,126	Ancona	106,421
Bari	370,781	Ferrara	150,265	Cosenza	105,806
Venezia (Venice)	332,775	Perugia	142,522	Bolzano	104,606
Verona	261,208	Ravenna	137,597	Pisa	104,334
Messina	255,890	Pescara	131,345	Torre del Greco	102,890
Trieste	251,380	Reggio nell'E.	129,893	Novara	101,635
Taranto	242,774	Rimini	126,949	Udine	101,264
Cagliari	232,785	Monza	122,103	Alessandria	100,518

[1] Provisional.

CLIMATE. The climate varies considerably with latitude. In the south, it is warm temperate, with little rain in the summer months, but the north is cool temperate with rainfall more evenly distributed over the year.

Rome, Jan. 44·5°F (7°C), July 77°F (25°C). Annual rainfall 32·5″ (812 mm). Milan, Jan. 35°F (2°C), July 75°F (24°C). Annual rainfall 39″ (972 mm).

CONSTITUTION AND GOVERNMENT. The new Constitution was passed by the constituent assembly by 453 votes to 62 on 22 Dec. 1947; it came into force on 1 Jan. 1948. The Constitution consists of 139 articles and 18 transitional clauses. Its main dispositions are as follows:

Italy is described as 'a democratic republic founded on work'. Parliament consists of the Chamber of Deputies and the Senate. The Chamber is elected for 5 years by universal and direct suffrage and it consists of 630 deputies. The Senate is elected for 5 years on a regional basis; each Region having at least 7 senators, consisting of 315 elected senators; the Valle d'Aosta is represented by 1 senator only. The President of the Republic can nominate 5 senators for life from eminent men in the social, scientific, artistic and literary spheres. On the expiry of his term of office, the President of the Republic becomes a senator by right and for life, unless he declines.

The President of the Republic is elected in a joint session of Chamber and Senate, to which are added 3 delegates from each Regional Council (1 from the Valle d'Aosta). A two-thirds majority is required for the election, but after a third indecisive scrutiny the absolute majority of votes is sufficient. The President must be 50 years or over; his term lasts for 7 years. The President of the Senate acts as his deputy.

The President can dissolve the chambers of parliament, except during the last 6 months of his term of office.

The Cabinet can be forced to resign only on a motivated motion of censure; the defeat of a government bill does not involve the resignation of the Government.

A Constitutional Court, consisting of 15 judges who are appointed, 5 each, by the President of the Republic, Parliament (in joint session) and the highest law and administrative courts, has rights similar to those of the Supreme Court of the USA. It can decide on the constitutionality of laws and decrees, define the powers of the State and Regions, judge conflicts between the State and Regions and between the Regions, and try the President of the Republic and the Ministers. The court was set up in Dec. 1955.

The reorganization of the Fascist Party is forbidden. Direct male descendants of King Victor Emmanuel are excluded from all public offices, have no right to vote or to be elected, and are banned from Italian territory; their estates are forfeit to the State. Titles of nobility are no longer recognized, but those existing before 28 Oct. 1922 are retained as part of the name.

National flag: Three vertical strips of green, white, red.

National anthem: Fratelli d'Italia (words by G. Mameli; tune by M. Novaro, 1847).

The peace treaty was signed in Paris on 10 Feb. 1947, and ratified on 15 Sept. 1947. Italy ceded to France 4 frontier districts on the Little St Bernard Pass, the Mont-Cenis Plateau, the Mont-Thabor and Chaberton areas, and the upper valleys of the Tinée, Vésubie and Roya (*see* map in THE STATESMAN'S YEAR-BOOK, 1948); to Yugoslavia, nearly the whole of the provinces of Venezia Giulia, the commune of Zara and the island of Pelagosa; to Greece, the Dodecanese; to Albania, the island of Saseno; to China the Italian concession at Tientsin. Italy also gave up her former colonies.

Under the peace treaty Italy was to pay reparations to the following states: Greece, US$105m.; Yugoslavia, US$125m.; USSR, US$100m.; Ethiopia, US$25m.; Albania, US$5m. By 30 Nov. 1967 the whole debt had been paid.

Head of State: On 8 July 1978 Chamber and Senate in joint session elected by an absolute majority (832 votes out of 1,008 votes cast) Alessandro Pertini (Socialist; born 1896), President of the Republic.

Former Presidents of the Republic: Luigi Einaudi (1948-55); Giovanni Gronchi (1955-62); Antonio Segni (1962-64); Giuseppe Saragat (1964-71); Giovanni Leone (1971-78).

General elections for the Senate and Chamber of Deputies took place on 3-4 June 1979.

Senate. Christian Democrats, 138; Communists, 109; Socialists, 32; Italian Social Movement, 13; Social Democrats, 9; Republicans, 6; other groups, 8. Total: 315.

Chamber. Christian Democrats, 262; Communists, 201; Socialists, 62; Italian Social Movement, 30; Republicans, 16; Social Democrats, 20; Radical Party, 18; other groups, 21. Total: 630.

The coalition government was composed as follows in Jan. 1983.

Prime Minister: Amintore Fanfani (CD).
Foreign Affairs: Emilio Colombo (CD).
Interior Affairs: Virginio Rognoni (CD).
Justice: Clelio Darida (CD).
Defence: Lelio Lagorio (Soc.).
Finance: Francesco Forte (Soc.).
Treasury: Giovanni Goria (CD).
Industry: Filippo Pandolfi (CD).
Agriculture and Forestry: Calogero Manino (CD).
Health: Renato Altissimo (Lib.).

European Affairs: Alfredo Biondi (Lib.).
Budget: Guido Bodrato (CD).
Civil Service: Loris Fortuna (Soc.).
Regional Affairs: Fabio Fabri (Soc.).
Southern Region: Claudio Signorile (Soc.).
Education: Franca Fulcucci (CD).
Scientific Research: Pier Luigi Romita (Soc. D.).
Public Works: Franco Nicolazzi (Soc. D.).
Labour: Vincenzo Scotti (CD).
Trade: Capria Nicola (Soc.).
Transport: Mario Casalinuovo (Soc.).
Post and Telecommunications: Remo Gaspari (CD).
Merchant Marine: Michele di Giesi (Soc. D.).
State Participation: Gianni De Michelis (Soc.).
Tourism: Nicola Signorello (CD).
Culture: Nicole Vernola (CD).
Parliamentary Relations: Luigi Abis (CD).
Organization of Public Administration: Dante Schietroma (Soc. D.).

Adams, J. C., and Barile, P., *The Government of Republican Italy.* Boston, Mass., 1961
Allum, P. A., *Italy: Republic Without Government.* New York, 1974
Cross, E. (ed.), *La Constitution Italienne de 1948.* Paris, 1950
Ruini, M., and others, *La Nuova Costituzione Italiana.* Rome, 1947
Vedovato, G., *Il Trattato di Pace con l'Italia.* Rome, 1947

Regional Administration. Italy is administratively divided into regions (*regioni*), provinces (*province*) and municipalities (*comuni*).

Art. 116 of the 1948 constitution provided for the establishment of 5 autonomous regions with special statute (*regioni autonome con statuto speciale*) and 15 autonomous regions with ordinary statute (*regioni autonome con statuto normale*). The regions have their own parliaments (*consiglio regionale*) and governments (*giunta regionale e presidente*) with certain legislative and administrative functions adapted to the circumstances of each region.

A government commissioner co-ordinates regional and national activities. The results of the last regional elections were as follows:

Regions	*Election date*	*Christian Democrats*	*Communists*	*Socialists*	*Social Movement*	*Social Democrats*	*Republicans*	*Liberals*	*Others*	*Total*
Piemonte	8 June 1980	20	20	9	2	3	2	3	1	60
Valle d'Aosta [1]	25 June 1978	7	7	1	–	1	1	–	18[2]	35
Lombardia	8 June 1980	34	23	11	3	3	2	2	2	80
Trentino-Alto Adige [1]	19 Nov. 1978	22	7	4	2	2	1	1	31[3]	70
Veneto	8 June 1980	32	13	7	2	2	1	1	2	60
Friuli-Venezia Giulia [1]	25 June 1978	26	14	5	2	3	1	1	9[4]	61
Liguria	8 June 1980	13	15	5	2	2	1	2	–	40
Emilia-Romagna	8 June 1980	13	26	4	1	2	2	1	1	50
Toscana	8 June 1980	15	25	5	1	1	1	1	1	50
Umbria	8 June 1980	9	14	4	1	1	1	–	–	30
Marche	8 June 1980	16	15	4	1	1	1	1	1	40
Lazio	8 June 1980	22	19	6	6	3	2	1	1	60
Abruzzi	8 June 1980	20	12	4	2	1	1	–	–	40
Molise	8 June 1980	17	5	3	1	2	1	1	–	30
Campania	8 June 1980	25	15	7	7	3	1	1	1	60
Puglia	8 June 1980	22	13	6	4	2	1	1	1	50
Basilicata	8 June 1980	14	8	4	2	2	–	–	–	30
Calabria	8 June 1980	18	10	7	2	2	1	–	–	40
Sicilia [1]	21 June 1981	38	20	14	6	2	5	3	2	90
Sardegna [1]	17 June 1979	32	22	9	4	4	3	1	5[5]	80

[1] Autonomous regions with special statute.
[2] Including 4 Democrates Populaires, 9 Union Valdôtaine, 1 Union Valdôtaine Progressiste.
[3] Including 21 Südtiroler Volkspartie.
[4] Including 1 Slovenian Union, 2 Movimento Friuli.
[5] Including 3 Sardinian Action Party.

DEFENCE. Most of the restrictions imposed upon Italy in Part IV of the peace treaty signed on 10 Feb. 1947 were repudiated by the signatories on 21 Dec. 1951, only the USSR objecting.

Head of the armed forces is the Defence Chief of Staff. In 1947 the ministries of war, navy and air were merged into the ministry of defence. The technical and scientific council for defence directs all research activities.

National service lasts 12 months in the Army and Air Force, and 18 months in the Navy.

Army. The Army is divided into the expeditionary force and the national defence force. It is composed of 3 mechanized divisions, 1 armoured division (with M-47, M-60 and Leopard tanks), 5 Alpini brigades, 1 airborne brigade, 6 independent brigades, 1 rocket brigade, 2 amphibious battalions and various special and support units. Total strength (1983), 257,000.

Navy. Particulars of the principal surface ships in the Italian Navy:

Completed	*Name*	*Standard displacement Tons*	*Aircraft*	*Principal armament*	*Torpedo tubes*	*Shaft horsepower*	*Speed Knots*
			Cruisers				
1969	Vittorio Veneto	7,500	9 helicopters	8 3-in.; twin 'Terrier';	6	73,000	32
1964 1964	Andrea Doria [1] Caio Duilio [1]	6,000	4 helicopters	8 3-in.; twin 'Terrier';	6	60,000	31

[1] Rated as guided-missile escort cruisers.

There are also 10 diesel-powered submarines, 4 guided-missile destroyers, 2 anti-submarine destroyers, 14 frigates, 8 corvettes, 4 ocean minesweepers, 12 minehunters, 16 coastal minesweepers, 5 inshore minesweepers, 6 hydrofoil missile boats, 4 fast torpedo-boats, 2 fast gunboats, 2 landing ships, 4 surveying vessels, 2 salvage ships, 1 transport, 1 support ship, 4 training ships, 2 replenishment oilers, 16 water carriers, 1 netlayer, 7 repair craft, 18 auxiliaries, 8 coastal transports (landing craft), 50 motor transports (minor landing craft), and 60 tugs.

Giuseppe Garibaldi of 10,000 tons standard displacement, a flat-topped ship designed as an improved helicopter cruiser with 18 helicopters, but latterly regarded as a light aircraft carrier, is under construction. Six frigates, 4 minehunters and 1 missile hydrofoil are also under construction. Six corvettes and 4 minehunters are projected.

The coastline of the peninsula is divided into zones, with headquarters at Spezia, Naples, Taranto and Ancona; all are under the jurisdiction of flag officers with the status of C.-in-C. The admirals commanding on the coasts of Sardinia and Sicily do not rank as C.-in-C.

Other localities of strategic importance under naval administration are Brindisi, where there is an admiral commanding, and Genoa, Leghorn, Augusta and Venice, each of which is under a senior naval officer.

The personnel of the Navy in 1983 numbered 41,900 officers and ratings, including the naval air arm and the marine battalion.

Air Force. Control is exercised through 2 regional HQ near Taranto and Milan. Units assigned to NATO comprise the 1st air brigade of Nike-Hercules surface-to-air missiles, 6 fighter-bomber, 3 light attack, 6 interceptor and 2 tactical reconnaissance squadrons, with supporting transport, search and rescue, and training units. One of the fighter-bomber squadrons has F-104G Starfighters, 3 have F-104S Starfighters, and 2 have Aeritalia G91Ys. (Starfighter squadrons are re-equipping with Tornados). The light attack squadrons operate G91Rs. F-104S Starfighters have been standardized throughout the interceptor squadrons. The reconnaissance force operates RF-104G Starfighters.

One transport squadron has turboprop C-130H Hercules aircraft; 2 others have turboprop Aeritalia G222s. There is a VIP and personnel transport squadron, equipped with DC-9, DC-6B, PD-808 and P.166M aircraft.

ECM duties are performed by specially equipped G222s and PD-808s. Two land-based anti-submarine squadrons operate Breguet Atlantics. ASW helicopters, including Italian-built SH-3D Sea Kings, operate from ships of the Italian Navy. Search and rescue are performed by 12 Agusta-Sikorsky HH-3F helicopters and smaller types. There are also strong support and training elements; some MB 339 jet trainers have armament provisions for secondary close air support and anti-helicopter roles.

Air Force strength in mid-1982 was about 69,000 officers and men, about 300 combat aircraft, 500 fixed-wing second-line aircraft and over 100 helicopters.

INTERNATIONAL RELATIONS

Membership. Italy is a member of UN, NATO and EEC.

ECONOMY

Budget. Total revenue and expenditure for fiscal years, in 1m. lire:

	Revenue	*Expenditure*		*Revenue*	*Expenditure*
1974	22,930,800	29,557,700	1978	51,696,512	78,844,114
1975	32,312,962	40,201,458	1979	62,431,447	92,127,557
1976	37,882,716	50,036,796	1980	88,303,000	128,994,000
1977	43,666,361	59,548,331	1981	105,343,000	149,246,000

In the revenue for 1981 turnover and other business taxes accounted for 26,989,000m. lire, customs duties and indirect taxes for 11,476,000m. lire.

The public debt at 31 Dec. 1981 totalled 219,369,000m. lire, including consolidated debt of 42,200m. lire and the floating debt 153,479,400m. lire.

Currency. The standard coin is the *lira.* From 30 March 1960 the gold standard was formally established as equal to 0·00142187 gramme of gold per lira.

State metal coins are of 5, 10, 20, 50, 100, 200, and 500 lire. There are also in circulation State notes of 500 and bank-notes of 1,000, 2,000, 5,000, 10,000, 20,000, 50,000 and 100,000 lire; they are neither convertible into gold as foreign moneys nor exportable abroad, nor importable from abroad into Italy (except for certain specified small amounts).

Circulation of money at 28 Feb. 1982: State coins and notes, 757,000m. lire; bank-notes, 28,152,500m. lire.

In March 1983 the rate of exchange was 1,418 lire per US$1 and 2,145 lire per £1 sterling.

Banking. According to the law of 6 May 1926 there is only one bank of issue, the Banca d'Italia. Its gold reserve amounted to 34,791,500m. lire in Dec. 1981; the foreign credit reserves of the Exchange Bureau (*Ufficio Italiano Cambi*) amounted to 15,258,300m. lire at the same date.

Since 1936, all credit institutions have been under the control of a State organ, named 'Inspectorate of Credit'; the Bank of Italy has been converted into a 'public institution', whose capital is held exclusively by corporate bodies of a public nature. Other credit institutions, totalling 1,079, are classified as: (1) 6 chartered banks (Banco di Napoli, Banco di Sicilia, Banca Nazionale del Lavoro, Monte dei Paschi di Siena, Istituto di S. Paolo di Torino, Banca di Sardegna); (2) 3 banks of national interest (Banca Commerciale Italiana in Milan, Credito Italiano in Genoa and Banco di Roma); (3) banks and credit concerns in general, including 158 joint-stock banks and 155 co-operative banks; (4) 90 savings banks and Monti di pegno (institutions granting loans against personal chattels as security); (5) 665 *Casse rurali e agrarie* (agricultural banks, established as co-operative institutions with unlimited liability of associates); (6) 5 Istituti di Categoria.

At 31 Dec. 1981 there were 303 credit institutes handling 95% of all deposits and current accounts, with capital and reserves of 16,761,855m. lire.

On 31 March 1982 the post office savings banks had deposits and current accounts of 44,270,000m. lire; credit institutions, 269,743,000m. lire.

Insurance. By a decree of 29 April 1923 life-assurance business is carried on only by the National Insurance Institute and by other institutions, national and foreign, authorized by the Government. At 31 Dec. 1978 the insurances vested in the *Istituto Nazionale delle Assicurazioni* amounted to 4,877,000m. lire, including the decuple of life annuities.

Weights and Measures. The metric system is in general use.

ENERGY AND NATURAL RESOURCES

Electricity. Italy has greatly developed her water-power resources. In 1980 the total power generated was 186,089m. kwh., of which 47,521m. kwh. were generated by hydro-electric plants.

Oil. The Sicilian district of Ragusa, Gela and Fontanarossa is rapidly developing into one of the largest European oilfields. Production in 1980 amounted to 1,800,130 tonnes, of which 828,153 came from Sicily.

Minerals. The Italian mining industry is most developed in Sicily (Caltanissetta), in Tuscany (Arezzo, Florence and Grosseto), in Sardinia (Cagliari, Sassari and Iglesias), in Lombardy (particularly near Bergamo and Brescia) and in Piedmont.

Italy's fuel and mineral resources are wholly inadequate. Only sulphur and mercury outputs yield a substantial surplus for exports. In 1980 outputs, in tonnes, of raw steel was 26,501,381; rolled iron, 21,518,742; cast-iron ingots, 12,149,242; coal and similar fuels, 1,932,571.

Production of metals and minerals (in tonnes) was as follows:

	1975	*1976*	*1977*	*1978*	*1979*	*1980*
Iron pyrites	808,731	854,477	863,785	786,666	804,469	858,992
Iron ore	631,542	514,172	478,198	352,611	218,762	184,624
Manganese	...	4,461	9,314	9,741	9,782	9,165
Zinc	234,052	274,725	169,717	120,492	100,825	79,190
Crude sulphur	499,246	349,132	627,690	523,355	108,309	100,852
Bauxite	32,265	24,200	34,525	24,410	26,095	23,260
Mercury	1,094	757	14	5	–	–
Lead	33,197	42,601	33,152	31,110	27,237	40,477
Aluminium	190,070	205,723	255,397	270,770	266,814	265,803

Agriculture. The area of Italy in 1981 comprised 301,266 sq. km, of which 269,655 sq. km was agricultural and forest land and 31,611 sq. km was unproductive; the former was mainly distributed as follows (in 1,000 hectares): Forage and pasture, 9,108; woods, 6,355; cereals, 5,017; vines, 1,297; olive trees, 1,050; olive trees grown among other crops, 1,082; garden produce, 518; vines grown among other crops, 418; leguminous plants, 326.

At the second general census of agriculture (25 Oct. 1970) agricultural holdings numbered 3,620,799 and covered 25,091,267 hectares. 3,142,608 owners (86·8%) farmed directly 14,706,204 hectares (58·6%); 278,157 owners (7·7%) worked with hired labour on 8,523,107 hectares (34%); 130,648 share-croppers (3·6%) tilled 1,271,485 hectares (5·1%); the remaining 69,408 holdings (1·9%) of 590,471 hectares (2·3%) were operated in other ways.

According to the labour force survey in July 1978 persons engaged in agriculture numbered 3·17m. (2·02m. males and 1·15m. females).

In 1976, 909,580 farm tractors were being used.

The production of the principal crops (in 1,000 metric quintals) in 1981: Sugar beet, 178,320; wheat, 89,565; maize, 72,641; tomatoes, 45,279; potatoes, 29,314; oranges, 18,015; rice, 8,446; barley, 9,927; lemons, 8,042; oats, 4,290; olive oil, 5,850; tangerines, 3,880; other citrus fruit, 584; rye, 310.

Production of wine, 1981, 70·5m. hectolitres; of tobacco, 130,971 tonnes.

In 1981 consumption of chemical fertilizers in Italy was as follows (in 1,000 tons): Perphosphate, 713·2; nitrate of ammonia, 728·1; sulphate of ammonium, 440·6; potash salts, 134·6; nitrate of calcium$^{15}/_{16}$, 92; deposed slags, 51·7.

Livestock estimated in 1981: Cattle, 8,903,000; pigs, 9,015,000; sheep and goats, 10·62m.; horses, 272,300; donkeys, 124,200; mules, 83,700.

Fisheries. The Italian fishing fleet comprised in 1981, 22,981 motor boats (316,788 gross tons) and 12,276 sailing vessels (15,109 gross tons). The catch in 1981 was 392,261 tonnes.

INDUSTRY AND TRADE

Industry. The textile industry is the largest and most important. Silk culture, while flourishing most extensively in Lombardy, Piedmont and Venezia, is carried on all over Italy. The production of artificial and synthetic fibre (including staple fibre and waste) in 1980 was 480,771 tonnes in 16 factories. Output, 1980 (in tonnes): Pure cotton yarns, 170,187; jute yarns, 5,640; pure wool yarns, 65,709.

The food industry produced 1,815,783 tonnes of sugar in 1980.

The chemical industry produced, in 1980 (in tonnes): Sulphuric acid (at 50 Be), 4,523,997; mineral phosphate, 1,402,355.

Production of motor vehicles was 1,632,289 in 1980.

Labour. The census of industry and commerce, of 25 Oct. 1971, recorded 2,425,204 establishments employing 11,077,533 workers. Mining employed 71,460 workers; food and tobacco manufacture, 400,699; textile industries, 541,030; clothing, shoes, skins and leather industries, 645,310; engineering, 1,905,316; metallurgy, 245,648; chemical, rubber and paper industries, 427,586; building, 997,534; transport and communications, 894,567; commerce, 2,796,897; banking and insurance, 293,005; electricity, gas and water works, 155,156.

As at April 1982, 20·1m. persons were employed, 1·9m. unemployed (figures from a new series of statistics on the labour force, 1977, which is not comparable with previous series).

Trade Unions. Membership of the 4 main groups: Confederazione Generale Italiana del Lavoro (Communist-dominated), 4,485,930 (1977); Confederazione Italiana Sindacati Lavoratori (Catholic), 3,059,800 (1980); Unione Italiana del Lavoro, 1,151,370 (1977); Confederazione Italiana Sindacati Nazionali Lavoratori, 1,015,988 (1961).

Commerce. The territory covered by foreign trade statistics includes Italy, the Republic of San Marino, but excludes the municipalities of Livigno and Campione.

The following table shows the value of Italy's foreign trade (in 1m. lire):

	1976	*1977*	*1978*	*1979*	*1980*	*1981*
Imports	36,730,621	42,429,110	47,867,899	64,597,204	85,564,303	103,675,361
Exports	31,166,722	39,967,593	47,505,301	59,926,272	66,719,410	86,071,400

The following table shows trade by countries in 1m. lire:

	Imports into Italy from			*Exports from Italy to*		
Countries	*1979*	*1980*	*1981*	*1979*	*1980*	*1981*
Argentina	594,210	426,463	476,809	395,098	543,517	491,175
Australia	459,949	493,688	579,799	361,109	392,551	575,115
Austria	1,261,545	1,614,537	1,876,706	1,506,529	1,788,047	1,914,913
Belgium-Luxembourg	2,303,261	3,042,358	3,205,825	2,046,812	2,219,349	2,370,595
France	9,031,839	11,857,740	12,935,373	8,873,195	10,094,105	11,690,676
Germany, Fed. Rep. of	11,106,912	14,180,383	16,186,170	11,336,093	12,210,666	13,356,364
Japan	735,313	1,110,781	1,435,879	650,115	605,763	762,717
Netherlands	2,713,836	3,632,428	4,287,944	2,746,676	2,461,582	2,623,194
Switzerland	1,772,883	2,175,340	3,292,673	2,561,807	2,951,636	3,458,503
USSR	1,714,965	2,695,919	3,536,909	1,014,631	1,090,618	1,467.879
UK	2,613,185	3,783,634	4,010,774	3,916,101	4,064,060	4,998,563
USA	4,380,571	5,920,974	7,024,081	3,876,841	3,554,502	5,843,361
Yugoslavia	660,286	773,152	837,292	1,037,690	1,045,999	1,237,968

In 1981 the main imports were maize, wood, greasy wool, metal scrap, pit-coal, petroleum, raw oils, meat, paper, rolled iron and steel, copper and alloys, mechanical and electric equipment, motor vehicles. The main exports were fruit and vegetables, fabrics, footwear and other clothing articles, rolled iron and steel, machinery, motor vehicles, plastic materials and petroleum by-products.

Italy's balance of trade (in 1,000m. lire) has been estimated as follows:

	Goods and services			*Income from investments and work, balance*	*Net balance*
	Export	*Import*	*Balance*		
1976	38,160	40,320	−2,160	−437	−2,597
1977	49,412	47,277	+2,135	−142	+1,993
1978	58,866	53,465	+5,401	+184	+5,585
1979	74,377	71,123	+3,254	+702	+3,956
1980	83,710	93,967	−10,257	+927	−9,330
1981	106,002	113,879	−7,877	−2,003	−9,880

Remittances from Italians abroad (in US$1m. until 1969 and then 1,000m. lire): 1950, 72; 1960, 214; 1970, 289; 1973, 360; 1974, 351; 1975, 338; 1976, 385; 1977, 626; 1978, 785; 1979, 956; 1980, 1,059.; 1981, 1,325.

Total trade between Italy and UK (British Department of Trade returns, in £1,000 sterling):

	1978	*1979*	*1980*	*1981*	*1982*
Imports to UK	1,934,964	2,491,013	2,311,071	2,330,349	2,745,094
Exports and re-exports from UK	1,123,777	1,469,048	1,899,181	1,742,514	2,022,711

Tourism. In 1980, 47·7m. foreigners visited Italy; they included 10·5m. German, 8·8m. Swiss, 7·4m. French, 4·3m. Austrian, 3·1m. Yugoslav, 2m. British, 1·8m. Dutch and 1·7m. US citizens. They spent about 7,034,600m. lire.

COMMUNICATIONS

Roads. Italy's roads totalled (31 Dec. 1981) 297,232 km, of which 45,447 km were state roads, 104,919 km provincial roads, 141,666 km communal roads. Motor vehicles, Dec. 1980: Cars, 17·69m.; buses, 58,149; lorries, 1,370,628; motor cycles, light vans, etc., 4,551,877.

The Mont Blanc tunnel road (11·6 km) from Entreves to Les Pelerins (France) was opened on 16 July 1965.

Railways. Railway history in Italy begins in 1839, with a line between Naples and Portici (8 km). Length of railways (31 Dec. 1981), 19,833 km, including 16,162 km of state railways, of which 7,404 had not yet been electrified. The first section of a new high-speed direct railway linking Rome and Florence opened in Feb. 1977. In 1981 the state railways carried 377m. passengers and 50,961,000 tonnes of goods. The Rome Underground opened in Feb. 1980.

Aviation. The Italian airline Alitalia (with a capital of 120,000m. lire, of which 98·7% is owned by the State) operates flights to every part of the world. Airports include 21 international, 32 national and 75 club airports. Domestic and international traffic in 1981 registered 13,306,664 passengers arrived and 13,345,414 departed, while freight and mail (excluding luggage) amounted to 143,110 tonnes unloaded and 179,246 tonnes loaded.

Shipping. The mercantile marine at 31 Dec. 1981 consisted of 2,446 vessels of 10,358,639 gross tons, not including pleasure boats (yachts, etc.), sailing and motor vessels. There were 1,425 motor vessels of 100 gross tons and over.

In 1981, 264,147,274 tonnes of cargo were unloaded, and 91,180,853 tonnes of cargo were loaded in Italian ports.

In 1972 navigable waterways had a length of 2,237 km (849 km of which were canals).

Post and Broadcasting. On 31 Dec. 1977 there were 13,963 post offices and 13,064 telegraph offices. The maritime radio-telegraph service had 22 coast stations. On 1 Jan. 1981 the telephone service had 19,269,340 apparatus. *Radiotelevisione Italiana* broadcasts 3 programmes and additional regional programmes, including transmissions in English, French, German and Slovenian on medium- and short-waves and on FM. It also broadcasts 2 TV programmes. Radio licences numbered 532,800; television and radio licences, 13,400,609.

Cinemas. There were 7,475 cinemas in 1980.

Newspapers. There were 74 daily newspapers with a combined circulation of 6·71m. copies; of the papers 15 are published in Rome and 8 in Milan. One daily each is published in German and Slovene, and 2 in English.

JUSTICE, RELIGION, EDUCATION AND WELFARE

Justice. Italy has 1 court of cassation, in Rome, and is divided for the administration of justice into 23 appeal court districts (and 3 detached sections), subdivided into 159 tribunal districts, and these again into *mandamenti* each with its own magistracy (*Pretura*), 899 in all. There are also 89 first degree assize courts and 26 assize courts of appeal. For civil business, besides the magistracy above mentioned, *Conciliatori* have jurisdiction in petty plaints.

On 31 Dec. 1980 there were 21,988 male and 1,364 female prisoners in establishments for preventive custody, 6,215 males and 115 females in penal establishments and 1,991 males and 92 females in establishments for the execution of safety measures.

Religion. The treaty between the Holy See and Italy, of 11 Feb. 1929, confirmed by article 7 of the Constitution of the republic, lays down that the Catholic Apostolic Roman Religion is the only religion of the State. Other creeds are permitted, provided they do not profess principles, or follow rites, contrary to public order or moral behaviour.

The appointment of archbishops and of bishops is made by the Holy See; but the Holy See submits to the Italian Government the name of the person to be appointed in order to obtain an assurance that the latter will not raise objections of a political nature.

Catholic religious teaching is given in elementary and intermediate schools. Marriages celebrated before a Catholic priest are automatically transferred to the civil register. Marriages celebrated by clergy of other denominations must be made valid before a registrar. In 1972 there were 279 dioceses with 28,154 parishes and 43,714 priests. There were 187,153 members (154,796 women) of about 20,000 religious houses.

In 1962 there were about 100,000 Protestants and about 50,000 Jews.

Annuario Cattolico d'Italia, a cura del CNEC. 14th ed. 1969-70, Rome, 1970
Annuario di Pastorale. Rome, 1970
Burgalassi, S., *La Sociologia della Religione in Italia dalle originial 1967.* Rome, 1967

Education. Education is compulsory from 6 to 14 years of age. An optional preschool education is given to the children between 3 and 5 years in the preparatory schools (kindergarten schools). Illiteracy of males over 6 years was 4% in 1971, of females 6·3%.

Compulsory education can be classified as primary education (5-year course) and junior secondary education (3-year course).

Senior secondary education is subdivided in classical (*ginnasio* and classical *liceo*), scientific (scientific *liceo*), language lyceum, professional institutes and technical education: agricultural, industrial, commercial, technical, nautical institutes, institutes for surveyors, institutes for girls (5-year course) and teacher-training institutes (4-year course).

University education is given in Universities and in University Higher Institutes (4, 5, 6 years, according to degree course).

Statistics for the academic year 1981–82:

Elementary schools	*No.*	*Pupils*
Kindergarten	29,612	1,783,140
Public elementary schools	27,359	4,003,732
Private elementary schools Private elementary recognized schools (*parificate*)	2,426	332,179
Government secondary schools		*Total students*
Junior secondary schools	10,056	2,865,757
Classical lyceum	756	205,843
Lyceum for science	973	344,983
Language lyceum	253	44,832
Teachers' schools	206	31,457
Teachers' institutes	670	209,693
Professional institutes	1,674	458,494
Technical institutes, of which:		
Industrial institutes	639	276,919
Commercial institutes	1,126	532,790
Surveyors' institutes	498	139,740
Agricultural institutes Nautical institutes Technical institutes for tourism Managerial institutes Girls technical schools	370	131,373
Artistic studies	245	57,581

Universities and higher institutes	*Date of foundation*	*Students*	*Teachers*	*Universities and higher institutes*	*Date of foundation*	*Students*	*Teachers*
Ancona	1965	6,729	243	Padova	1222	42,510	2,067
Arezzo	1971	1,118	75	Palermo	1805	43,706	2,033
Bari	1924	47,434	1,841	Parma	1502	16,597	1,012
Bergamo	1970	2,369	118	Pavia	1390	18,038	1,097
Bologna	1200	57,101	2,850	Perugia	1276	19,112	995
Brescia	1970	2,576	74	Pescara	1965	8,425	148
Cagliari	1626	18,074	879	Piacenza	1924	656	48
Camerino	1727	2,667	219	Pisa	1338	26,614	1,663
Cassino	1968	1,683	41	Reggio di C.	1968	8,083	72
Catania	1434	33,354	1,257	Roma	1303	149,267	5,817
Chieti	1965	5,330	121	Salerno	1944	20,739	521
Cosenza	1972	5,046	422	Sassari	1677	8,367	521
Feltre (Belluno)	1969	372	30	Siena	1300	9,904	584
Ferrara	1391	6,278	457	Teramo	1965	3,861	87
Firenze	1924	42,719	2,066	Torino	1404	56,227	2,368
Genova	1243	31,933	1,812	Trento	1965	2,742	159
L'Aquila	1956	6,293	444	Trieste	1924	12,611	997
Lecce	1959	6,703	321	Udine	1969	2,060	108
Macerata	1290	4,007	192	Urbino	1564	10,974	390
Messina	1549	24,846	1,188	Venezia	1868	18,828	665
Milano	1924	108,270	2,998	Vercelli	1981	409	...
Modena	1678	8,174	593	Verona	1969	8,223	86
Napoli	1224	112,397	3,582	Viterbo	1980	595	9
Novara	1981	660	...				

Health. In 1976 there were 130,846 doctors and 588,103 hospital beds.

Social Security. Social expenditure is made up of transfers which the central public departments, local departments and social security departments, make to families. Payment is principally for pensions, family allowances and health services. Expenditure on subsidies, public assistance to various classes of people and people injured by political events or national disasters are also included.

In 1975 government expenditure on social welfare amounted to 27,291,000m. lire.

DIPLOMATIC REPRESENTATIVES

Of Italy in Great Britain (14 Three Kings Yard, London, W1Y 2EH)
Ambassador: Andrea Cagiati, GCVO (accredited 20 Feb. 1980).

Of Great Britain in Italy (Via XX Settembre 80A, 00187, Rome)
Ambassador: Lord Bridges.

Of Italy in the USA (1601 Fuller St., NW, Washington, D.C., 20009)
Ambassador: Rinaldo Petrignani.

Of the USA in Italy (Via Veneto 119/A, Rome)
Ambassador: Maxwell M. Rabb.

Of Italy to the United Nations
Ambassador: Umberto La Rocca.

Books of Reference

Statistical Information: The Istituto Centrale di Statistica (16 Via Cesare Balbo 00100 Rome) was set up by law of 9 July 1926 as the central institute in charge of census and all statistical information. *President:* Prof. Guido Mario Rey. *Directors-General:* Dr Carlo Viterbo and Dr Luigi Pinto. Its publications include:

Annuario statistico italiano. 1982
Compendio statistico italiano. 1982
Bollettino mensile di statistica. Monthly, from 1950
Annuario di statistiche industriali. 1979-80
Annuario di statistiche demografiche. 1980
Popolazione e movimento anagrafico dei Comuni. Vol. XXIV, 1981

Annuario di statistica agraria. 1980
Annuario statistico della navigazione marittima. 1981
Annuario statistico del commercio interno e del turisimo. 1979
Statistica annuale del commercio con l'estero. 1980
Statistica mensile del commercio con l'estero. Monthly
Annuario di statistiche del lavoro. 1981
Censimento generale dell'agricoltura, 1970. 7 vols.
Censimento generale della popolazione, 1981. 1 vol.
Censimento generale dell'industria e del commercio, 1971. 9 vols.
Sintesi Statistica di un Ventennio di Vita Economica Italiana, 1952-71
Cinquanta anni di attivita, 1926-1976. 1978

Italy. Documents and Notes. Servizi delle Informazioni, Rome. 1952 ff.
Italian Books and Periodicals. Bimonthly from 1958
Banco di Roma, *Review of the Economic Condition in Italy* (in English). Bimonthly, 1947 ff.
Credito Italiano, *The Italian Economic Situation.* Bimonthly. Milan, from June 1961 (in Italian), from June 1962 (in English)
Compendio Economico Italiano. Rome, Unione Italiana delle Camere di Commercio. Annually from 1954
Allum, P. A., *Italy; Republic Without Government.* London, 1973
Carone, G., *Il Turismo nell'economia internazionale.* Milan, 1959
Clough, S. B., *The Economic History of Modern Italy.* Columbia Univ. Press, 1964
Di Vittorio, G. (ed.), *I sindacati in Italia.* Bari, 1955
Grindrod, M., *The Rebuilding of Italy, 1945-55.* R. Inst. of Int. Affairs, 1955
Large, P. and Tarrow, S. (eds.), *Italy in Transition – Conflict and Consensus.* London, 1980
Nichols, P., *Italia, Italia.* London, 1974
Wiskemann, E., *Italy Since 1945.* London, 1971
Woolfe, S. J. (ed.), *The Rebirth of Italy, 1943-50.* New York, 1972

National Library: Biblioteca Nazionale Centrale Vittorio Emanuele II Viale Castro Pretorio, Rome. *Director:* Dr L. M. Crisari.

IVORY COAST

République de la Côte d'Ivoire

Capital: Abidjan
Population: 8·92m. (1982)
GNP per capita: US$1,150 (1980)

HISTORY. France obtained rights on the coast in 1842, but did not actively and continuously occupy the territory till 1882. On 10 Jan. 1889 Ivory Coast was declared a French protectorate, and it became a colony on 10 March 1893; in 1904 it became a territory of French West Africa. On 1 Jan. 1933 most of the territory of Upper Volta was added to the Ivory Coast, but on 1 Jan. 1948 this area was returned to the re-constituted Upper Volta. The Ivory Coast became an autonomous republic within the French Community on 4 Dec. 1958 and acheived full independence on 7 Aug. 1960.

AREA AND POPULATION. Ivory Coast is bounded West by Liberia and Guinea, north by Mali and Upper Volta, east by Ghana, and south by the Gulf of Guinea. It has an area of 322,463 sq km and a population at the 1975 census of 6,671,827 (of whom 31·8% were urban). Estimate (1982) 8,918,000.

The areas and populations of the 26 departments at the 1975 census were:

Department	*Sq. km*	*Population*	*Department*	*Sq. km*	*Population*
Abengourou	6,713	175,891	Danané	4,650	169,589
Abidjan	14,819	1,388,321	Dimbokro	13,822	478,054
Aboisso	6,135	146,876	Divo	9,869	275,171
Adzopé	5,151	159,502	Ferkéssédougou	19,292	90,901
Agboville	3,900	140,250	Gagnoa	6,873	256,006
Biankouma	2,897	74,408	Guiglo	14,232	135,252
Bondoukou	16,465	293,838	Katiola	8,469	75,909
Bouaflé	8,362	265,875	Korhogo	12,164	276,846
Bouaké	23,405	805,359	Man	7,004	277,648
Bouna	21,470	77,232	Odienné	21,336	124,196
Boundiali	10,273	132,160	Sassandra	26,263	195,620
Dabakala	8,694	55,356	Séguéla	22,861	157,644
Daloa	13,918	367,414	Touba	8,767	77,696

The principal cities (populations, census 1975) are the capital, Abidjan (685,828), Bouaké (173,248), Daloa (59,500), Man (48,521), Korhogo (45,146) and Gagnoa (42,000). The new capital is to be at Yamoussoukro.

The principal ethnical groups are the Agnis-Ashantis, Kroumen, Mandé, Baoulé, Dan-Gouro and Koua.

CONSTITUTION AND GOVERNMENT. Under the constituton, the sole legal Party is the *Parti Démocratique de la Côte d'Ivoire.* There is a 147-member National Assembly elected by universal suffrage (latest elections, Nov. 1980) for a 5-year term. The President is also directly elected for a 5-year term (renewable).

The Government was in Nov. 1981 composed as follows:

President: Félix Houphouet-Boigny. (Re-elected for a fifth 5-year term in 1980).

Minister of State: Auguste Denise. *Minister of State responsible for Reform of State-owned Companies:* Mathieu Ekra. *Public Health and Population:* Lazeni N. P. Coulibaly. *Minister of State:* Alexis Thierry-Lebre. *Justice:* Camille Alliali. *Defence and Civic Service:* Jean Konan Banny. *Interior:* Leon Konan Koffi. *Foreign Affairs:* Siméon Ake. *Economy and Finance:* Abdoulaye Koné. *Planning and Industry:* Maurice Seri Gnoleba. *Agriculture:* Denis Bra Kanon. *Scientific Research:* Balia Keita. *Technical Education and Vocational Training:* Ange Francois Barry-Battesti. *National Education:* Paul Akoto Yao. *Social Affairs:* Yaya Ouattara. *Cultural Affairs:* Bernard Dadié. *Commerce:* Amoakon Edjampan

Thiemele. *Public Works and Transport:* Désiré Boni. *Construction and Town Planning:* Eugene Niagne Lasme. *Animal Production:* Dicoh Garba. *Labour and 'Ivorization' of Personnel:* Albert Vanié-Bi-Tra. *Youth, Popular Education and Sport:* Laurent Dona-Fologo. *Information:* Amadou Thiam. *Mines:* Paul Gui Dibo. *Water and Forests:* Christian Lohourigno Zagote. *Primary Education and Educational Television:* Pascal N'Guessan Dikébié. *Internal Security:* Gaston Ouanessan Koné. *Posts and Telecommunications:* Kouassi Apete. *Navy:* Lamine Fadika. *Public Service:* Emile Kei Boguinard. *Women's Affairs:* Jeanne Gervais. *Tourism:* Duon Sadia. *Relations with the National Assembly:* Emile Brou.

National flag: Three vertical strips of orange, white, green.

Local government: Since the 1975 census, 8 further *départements* have been created (Bongouanou, Issia, Lakota, Mankono, Oumé, Soubré, Tengréla and Zuénoula) bringing the total to 34 *départements*, sub-divided into 163 sub-prefectures.

DEFENCE

Army. The Army consisted of 3 infantry battalions and support units in 1983; total strength, 4,000.

Navy. The Navy operates 4 large patrol craft, 4 coastal patrol craft, 1 training vessel and 3 landing craft. Personnel (1983) 550.

Air Force. The Air Force, formed in 1962, has 6 Alpha Jet advanced trainers, with combat potential, 2 turboprop C-130H Hercules, 2 turbofan F-28 Fellowship and 1 turbofan Gulfstream II transports, 1 Falcon light jet transport, 2 Reims-Cessna 150s, 6 Beech F-33Cs and 2 Reims-Cessna 337s for liaison and training, and 3 SA330 Puma, 4 Dauphin 2 and 3 Alouette II/III helicopters. Other transport aircraft are leased to the national airline. Personnel total 570.

INTERNATIONAL RELATIONS

Membership. Ivory Coast is a member of UN, OAU and is an ACP state of EEC.

ECONOMY

Budget. The budget for 1982 balanced at 712,200m. francs CFA. Reserves (Dec. 1977) 546·9m. francs CFA.

Currency. The currency is the *franc CFA* with a parity rate of 50 *francs CFA* to 1 French *franc.* In March 1983, £ sterling = 518 francs CFA; US$1 = 340 francs CFA.

ENERGY AND NATURAL RESOURCES

Electricity. Production in 1980 amounted to 1,830m. kwh.

Oil. Petroleum has been produced (offshore) since Oct. 1977. Production (1978) 1·55m. tonnes.

Minerals. Diamond fields are being exploited; 299,708 carats in 1973. Manganese deposits yielded 123,060 tonnes in 1970.

Agriculture. Coffee is the largest export commodity (1980–81), 361,000 tons. Production (1981) cocoa, 400,000 tonnes; palm oil, 848,000 tonnes. Other crops include maize, yams, sweet potatoes, cassava and plantains. The cultivation of cotton has been developed. Production (1980) 115,000 tonnes. Coconuts and a small quantity of rubber are collected. The mahogany forests inland are worked.

Several factories produce palm-oil, fruit preserves and fruit juice.

Livestock, 1981: 720,000 cattle, 1·25m. sheep, 1·3m. goats, 360,000 pigs, 1,000 horses and 1,000 donkeys.

Fisheries. The catch in 1979 amounted to 92,000 tonnes.

Forestry. Production in 1979 was 11·7m. cu. metres.

TRADE. Trade for calendar years in 1m. francs CFA:

	1976	*1977*	*1978*	*1979*	*1980*
Imports	311,608	429,566	522,515	528,850	539,600
Exports	392,501	529,212	524,380	534,850	628,000

In 1979 exports of coffee furnished 31% of exports, cocoa 28% and timber 16%; 24% went to France, 17% to the Netherlands, 10% to the USA, 8% to Italy and 6% to Federal Republic of Germany. Of the imports, France supplied 37%, the USA 7% and Japan 6%.

Total trade between the Ivory Coast and UK (British Department of Trade returns, in £1,000 sterling):

	1978	*1979*	*1980*	*1981*	*1982*
Imports to UK	57,983	73,622	53,563	63,055	56,097
Exports and re-exports from UK	24,572	24,001	27,916	30,128	28,238

Tourism. In 1976 there were122,246 foreign tourists.

COMMUNICATIONS

Roads. In 1978 roads totalled 3,000 km bitumenized and 44,000 km secondary. In 1978 there were 181,801 vehicles.

Railways. From Abidjan a metre-gauge railway runs to Léraba and thence through Upper Volta to Ouagadougou (1,140 km). An extension to Tambao is proposed and a new network for the export of iron ore from the port of San Pedro is under study. In 1978 the railways carried 3,364m. passenger-km and 1,069m. tonne-km of freight.

Aviation. The main airport is at Abidjan-Port-Buet. In 1978 it handled 564,830 passengers and 25,396 tonnes of freight and 1,216 tonnes of mail.

Shipping. The main ports are Abidjan, San Pedro and Tabou. In 1972 Abidjan port handled 5,925,000 tonnes.

Post and Broadcasting. There were 78,370 telephones in 1980 and (1978), 939 telex machines. In 1977 there were 300,000 television and 800,000 radio receivers.

Cinemas. There were 80 cinemas in 1972 with a seating capacity of 80,000.

Newspapers. In 1976 there were 3 daily newspapers with a combined circulation of 63,000.

JUSTICE, RELIGION, EDUCATION AND WELFARE

Justice. There are a court of first instance, 2 courts of second instance and a court of appeal.

Religion. Of the total population, 23·5% are Moslems, 12·5% Christians and 65% animists.

Education. There were, in 1978, 894,184 pupils in primary schools, 144,605 in secondary schools and 22,437 in technical schools. The *Université Nationale de Côte d'Ivoire,* at Abidjan (founded 1964), had 12,765 students in 1980.

Health. In 1978 there were 9,962 hospital beds, 429 doctors, 36 dentists, 615 midwives, 3,052 nurses and 76 pharmacists.

DIPLOMATIC REPRESENTATIVES

Of the Ivory Coast in Great Britain (2 Upper Belgrave St., London, SW1X 8BJ)
Ambassador: Dieudonné Essienne (accredited 4 Oct. 1978).

Of Great Britain in the Ivory Coast (Immeuble 'Les Harmonies', Blvd. Corde, Abidjan)
Ambassador: Michael Francis Daly.

Of the Ivory Coast in the USA (2424 Massachusetts Ave., NW, Washington, D.C., 20008)
Ambassador: Amani Rene.

Of the USA in the Ivory Coast (5 Rue Jesse Owens, Abidjan)
Ambassador: Nancy V. Rawls.

Of the Ivory Coast to the United Nations
Ambassador: Amara Essy.

Books of Reference

Statistical Information: Şervice de la Statistique, Abidjan. It publishes *Bulletin Statistique Mensuel and Inventoire Économique de la Côte d'Ivoire.*

La Côte d'Ivoire en Chiffee. Abidjan, 1979
Panorama de la Côte d'Ivoire, 1978, ed. Direction de l'Information, Abidjan
Holas, B., *Industries et cultures en Côte d'Ivoire.* Abidjan, 1979
Zolberg, A. R., *One-Party Government in the Ivory Coast.* Rev. ed. Princeton Univ. Press, 1974

JAMAICA

Capital: Kingston
Population: 2·19m. (1980)
GNP per capita: US$1,030 (1980)

HISTORY. Jamaica was discovered by Columbus in 1494, and was occupied by the Spaniards between 1509 and 1655, when the island was captured by the English; their possession was confirmed by the Treaty of Madrid, 1670. Self-government was introduced in 1944 and gradually extended until Jamaica achieved complete independence within the Commonwealth on 6 Aug. 1962.

AREA AND POPULATION. The area of Jamaica is 4,411 sq. miles (11,425 sq. km). The population at the census of 7 April 1970 was 1,861,300, distributed on the basis of the 14 parishes of the island as follows: Kingston and St Andrew, 550,100 (estimate 1977, 643,800); St Thomas, 71,400 (78,800); Portland, 68,500 (74,300); St Mary, 100,000 (108,900); St Ann, 121,300 (134,300); Trelawny, 61,300 (67,600); St James, 103,700 (122,800); Hanover, 59,000 (64,200); Westmoreland, 113,200 (121,600); St Elizabeth, 126,000 (139,000); Manchester, 123,500 (142,600); St Catherine, 186,000 (217,900); Clarendon, 176,600 (193,900).

Estimated population, in 1980, was 2·19m.

Vital statistics (1979): Births, 58,257; deaths, 13,311; infant deaths, (1978) 869; emigrants (1978) to USA, 19,265; to Canada, 3,858, and to UK, 599.

CONSTITUTION AND GOVERNMENT. A new Constitution was enacted with independence in Aug. 1962. The Crown is represented by a Governor-General appointed by the Crown on the advice of the Prime Minister. The Governor-General is assisted by a Privy Council.

The Legislature comprises two chambers, an elected House and a nominated Senate. The executive is chosen from both chambers.

The Executive comprises the Prime Minister, who is the leader of the majority party, and Ministers appointed by the Prime Minister. Together they form the Cabinet, which is the highest executive power. An Attorney-General is a member of the House and is legal adviser to the Cabinet.

The Senate consists of 21 senators appointed by the Governor-General, 13 on the advice of the Prime Minister, 8 on the advice of the Leader of the Opposition. The House of Representatives (60 members, Dec. 1976) is elected by universal adult suffrage for a 5-year period. Electors and elected must be Jamaican or Commonwealth citizens resident in Jamaica for at least 12 months before registration. The powers and procedure of Parliament correspond to those of the British Parliament.

The Privy Council consists of 6 members appointed by the Governor-General in consultation with the Prime Minister.

Governor-General: Florizel Augustus Glasspole.

National flag: A yellow diagonal cross dividing triangles of green, top and bottom, and black, hoist and fly.

The elections to House of Representatives, held on 30 Oct. 1980, returned 51 members of the Jamaica Labour Party and 9 members of the People's National Party.

The Cabinet in Nov. 1981 was comprised as follows:

Prime Minister, Minister of Finance and Planning and Mining and Energy: Edward Seaga.

Deputy Prime Minister, Minister of Foreign Affairs and Foreign Trade: Hugh Shearer. *Without Portfolio:* Dr Ronald Irvine. *Construction:* Bruce Golding. *Agriculture:* Dr Percival Broderick. *National Security and Justice and Attorney-General:* Winston Spaulding. *Local Government:* Pearnel Charles. *Labour and*

Public Service: J. A. G. Smith. *Public Utilities and Transport:* Alva Ross. *Industry and Commerce:* Douglas Vaz. *Education:* Dr Mavis Gilmour. *Social Security:* Neville Lewis. *Youth and Community Development:* Errol Anderson. *Tourism:* Anthony Abrahams. *Health:* Dr Kenneth Baugh.

DEFENCE

Army. The Jamaica Defence Force consists of a Regular and a Reserve Force. The Regular Force is comprised of the 1st battalion, Jamaica Regiment and Support Services which include the Air Wing and Coast Guard. The Reserve Force consists of the 3rd battalion, Jamaica Regiment. Total strength (all services, 1983), 1,700.

Air Force. The Air Wing of the Jamaica Defence Force was formed in July 1963 and has since been expanded and trained successively by the British Army Air Corps and Canadian air force personnel. Equipment for army liaison, search and rescue, police co-operation, survey and transport duties includes a Twin Otter; 2 Defender armed STOL transports; 1 Beech King Air, 1 Cessna 210 and 1 Cessna 337 light transports; 4 JetRanger and 3 Bell 212 light helicopters.

INTERNATIONAL RELATIONS

Membership. Jamaica is a member of UN, the Commonwealth, OAS and is an ACP state of EEC.

ECONOMY

Budget. Revenue and expenditure for fiscal years ending 31 March (in J$):

	1977–78	*1978–79*	*1979–80*	*1980–81*
Revenue	661,400,000	1,045,200,000	1,112,000,000	2,202,000,000
Expenditure	1,238,700,000	1,826,400,000	1,860,000,000	2,415,000,000

The chief heads of recurrent revenue are customs and excise duties, income tax, motor vehicle licences and post office receipts. Capital revenue is derived mainly from royalties.

Public debt at 31 Dec. 1980, J$4,037·6m.

Remittances from overseas amounted to approximately J$98·5m. in the year ending 31 Dec. 1979.

Currency. The currency, is the *dollar*, divided into 100 cents. Currency circulation in Dec. 1980 was J$302·1m., comprising notes of J$283·6m. and J$18·5m. coin. In March 1983, £1 = J$2·71; US$1 = J$1·78.

Banking. On 1 May 1961 the Bank of Jamaica opened for business as Jamaica's Central Bank. It has the sole right to issue notes and coins in Jamaica, acts as Banker to the Government and to the commercial banks, and administers the island's external reserves and exchange control.

There are 8 commercial banks with about 170 branches and agencies in operation, with main offices in Kingston. Six of these banks are subsidiaries of major British and North American banks, of which 4 are incorporated locally. The Workers' Savings and Loan Bank is owned by the Government, Trade Unions and the private sector. The National Commercial Bank (Jamaica) Ltd, formally Barclays Bank Jamaica Ltd, is 100% government-owned. The other 6 banks which operate are: The Bank of Nova Scotia (Jamaica) Ltd, City Bank of North America, Royal Bank (Jamaica) Ltd, Bank of Commerce, Jamaica Citizens Bank Ltd and First National Bank of Chicago (Jamaica) Ltd.

ENERGY AND NATURAL RESOURCES

Electricity. The Jamaica Public Service Co. is the public supplier of electricity. The bauxite companies, sugar estates and the Caribbean Cement Co. generate their own electricity.

Minerals. Bauxite, ceramic clays, marble, silica and gypsum are commercially valuable. Jamaica has become the world's third largest producer of bauxite and alumina. The bauxite deposits are worked by a Canadian and 4 American companies.

Three companies process bauxite into alumina. In 1980, 6,135m. tons of bauxite ore was mined and 2,478m. tons of alumina were produced.

Agriculture (1980). Production: Sugar-cane, 2,736,000 tons; sugar (commercial), 247,000 tons; rum, 5,532,000 proof gallons; molasses, 101 tons; bananas, 33,000 tons; citrus fruit, 1,112,000 boxes; pimento, 928 tons; cocoa, 1,368 tons; coffee, 250,000 boxes; ginger, 438 short tons; copra, 1,738 short tons; meat, 109m. lb.; fish, 36m. lb.; eggs, 102m.; root crops, 481m. lb; vegetables, 290m. lb.

Livestock (1980): Cattle, 300,000; goats, 380,000; pigs, 255,000; poultry, 4·2m.

INDUSTRY AND TRADE

Industry. In 1976 there were 1,280 registered factories employing 52,633. From processing only a few agricultural products—sugar, rum, condensed milk, oils and fats, cigars and cigarettes—the island is now producing a wide range of manufactures using both local and imported raw materials. Among the manufactured goods are clothing, footwear, textiles, paints, building materials, including cement, agricultural machinery and toilet articles. An oil refinery in Kingston meets local fuel demand. In 1980 manufacturing contributed J$721·2m. to the total GDP at current prices.

Commerce. Value of imports and domestic exports for calendar years (in J$1m.):

	1976	*1977*	*1978*	*1979*	*1980*
Imports	829·8	781·6	1,260·0	1,002·0	1,173·0
Domestic exports	575·0	686·4	1,057·1	814·7	959·3

Principal imports in 1978 (in J$1,000): Raw materials, 537·1; capital goods, 171·6; consumer goods, 184·8.

Principal exports, 1978 (in J$1m.): Alumina, 554·9; bauxite, 202·2; sugar, 92·5.

In 1978 total balance of visible trade with USA, UK and Canada amounted to J$86m.

Total trade between Jamaica and UK (British Department of Trade returns, in £1,000 sterling):

	1977	*1978*	*1979*	*1980*	*1981*	*1982*
Imports to UK	78,229	96,081	82,145	95,578	114,219	92,760
Exports and re-exports from UK	39,650	48,751	44,554	33,122	42,650	56,025

Tourism. In 1982, 530,000 tourists arrived in Jamaica, spending about J$340m.

COMMUNICATIONS

Roads (1978). The island has 2,944 miles of main roads, and over 7,264 miles of parochial and subsidiary roads. Main roads in the corporate area of Kingston and St Andrew are constructed and maintained by that corporation, those elsewhere by the Public Works Department of the Ministry of Public Utilities. Parochial or subsidiary roads are constructed and maintained by parish councils.

Railways. There are 303 km of railway open of 1,435 mm gauge, operated by the Jamaica Railway Corporation, which also operates 31 km (Alcoa Mineral Railway) on behalf of one of the bauxite companies. In 1980 total revenue was J$9m. and expenditure J$15·6m.

Aviation. In 1978, 11 scheduled commercial international airlines served Jamaica, operating through the Norman Manley and Sangster international airports at Palisadoes and Montego Bay. Trans-Jamaica Airlines Ltd operates internal flights. Air Jamaica, originally set up in conjunction with BOAC and BWIA in 1966, became a new company, Air Jamaica (1968) Ltd, and is affiliated to Air Canada. In 1969 it began operations as Jamaica's national airline. In 1978 Air Jamaica had a revenue of J$131,628,000 and operating expenses of J$122,033,000.

Shipping. Jamaica has 19 specified ports. In 1980 the port of Kingston unloaded 1·1m. tons of cargo.

Post and Broadcasting. Post and telecommunications are the responsibility of the

Ministry of Public Utilities. In the financial year 1980 there were 318 post offices and 471 postal agencies.

The Jamaica Telephone Co. operates the telephone system. In Dec. 1980 there were 119,402 telephones in use. All telephone exchanges are automatic. Jamaica is linked to USA by a submarine telephone cable. Jamaica International Telecommunications Ltd (JAMINTEL) established in 1971, provides a wide range of international telecommunications services for Jamaica. There are 1 commercial and 1 publicly owned broadcasting stations; the latter also operates a television service.

Cinemas. In 1981 there were 25 cinemas and 3 drive-in cinemas.

JUSTICE, RELIGION, EDUCATION AND WELFARE

Justice. The Judicature comprises a Supreme Court, a court of appeal, a revenue court, resident magistrates' courts, petty sessional courts, coroners' courts, a traffic court and a family court which was instituted in 1975. The Chief Justice is head of the judiciary. All prosecutions are initiated by the Director of Public Prosecutions.

Police. The Constabulary Force in 1980 stood at approximately 6,000 officers, sub-officers and constables (men and women). There are, in addition, district constables and special constables.

Religion. Freedom of worship is guaranteed under the Constitution. The main Christian denominations are Anglican, Baptist, Roman Catholic, Methodist, Church of God, United Church of Jamaica, and Grand Cayman (Presbyterian–Congregational) Moravian, Seventh-day Adventists, Pentecostal, Salvation Army, Quaker, and Disciples of Christ. Pocomania is a mixture of Christianity and African survivals. Non-Christians include Hindus, Jews, Moslems and Bahai followers. There is also a growing number of Rastafarians who believe in the deity of the late Emperor, Hailé Selassié of Ethiopia.

Education. In Sept. 1973 education became free for all government grant-aided schools (the majority of all schools) and for all Jamaicans entering the University of the West Indies, the College of Arts, Science and Technology and the Jamaica School of Agriculture. In 1979–80 there were 283 primary schools (2,168,103 pupils); 504 all-age schools (256,411 pupils).

In 1980 there were 2 vocational schools, 7 technical high schools, 11 teacher-training colleges, 4 special education schools, 4 community colleges, the College of Arts, Science and Technology, C. G. Foster Sports College, the Cultural Training Centre and the Mona campus of the University of the West Indies.

Health. In 1980 there were about 700 doctors and 29 government hospitals with 6,229 beds. There are several private hospitals and nursing homes.

DIPLOMATIC REPRESENTATIVES

Of Jamaica in Great Britain (50 St James's St., London, SW1A 1JS)
High Commissioner: H. S. Walker.

Of Great Britain in Jamaica (Trafalgar Rd., Kingston 10)
High Commissioner: B. G. Smallman, CMG, CVO.

Of Jamaica in the USA (1850 K. St., NW, Washington, D.C., 20006)
Ambassador: Keith Johnson.

Of the USA in Jamaica (2 Oxford Rd., Kingston)
Chargé d'Affaires: W. Robert Warne.

Of Jamaica to the United Nations
Ambassador: Sir Egerton Richardson, CMG.

Books of Reference

Statistical Information: The Department of Statistics (93 Hanover St., Kingston) was set up in

1945—the nucleus being the Census Office, which undertook the operations of the 1943 Census of Jamaica and its Dependencies. *Director:* Mrs C. P. McFarlane. Publications of the Bureau include the *Bulletin of Statistics on External Trade* and the *Annual Abstract of Statistics.*

Economic and Social Survey, Jamaica 1976. National Planning Agency. Yearly
Social and Economic Studies. Institute of Social and Economic Research, Univ. of the West Indies. Quarterly
Beckford, G. and Witter, M., *Small Garden ... Bitter Weed. The Political Struggle and Change in Jamaica.* 2nd ed. London, 1982
Black, C. V., *History of Jamaica.* London, 1965
Cassidy, F. G., and Le Page, R. B., *Dictionary of Jamaican English.* CUP, 1966
Clarke, C. G., *Jamaica in Maps.* London, 1974
Delattre, R., *A Guide to Jamaica Reference Material.* Kingston, 1965
Floyd, B., *Jamaica: An Island Microcosm.* London, 1979
Hurwitz, S. J. and E. F., *Jamaica: A Historical Portrait.* New York, 1971 and London, 1972
Jefferson, O., *The Post-War Economic Development of Jamaica.* Kingston, 1972
Kuper, A., *Changing Jamaica.* London and Boston, 1976
Lacey, T., *Violence and Politics in Jamaica, 1960–70.* Manchester Univ. Press, 1977
Manley, M., *A Voice at the Work Place.* London, 1975
Stone, C., *Class, Race and Political Behaviour in Urban Jamaica.* Kingston, 1973.
—*Democracy and Clientalism in Jamaica.* London and New Brunswick, N.J., 1981
Bibliography of Jamaica, 1900–1963. Jamaica Library Service, 1963

Libraries: Institute of Jamaica, Kingston. Jamaica Library Service, Kingston.

JAPAN

Nippon (*or* Nihon)

Capital: Tōkyō
Population: 117·8m. (1981)
GNP per capita: US$9,890 (1980)

HISTORY. The house of Yamato, from about 500 B.C. the rulers of one of several kingdoms, in about A.D. 200 united the nation; the present imperial family are their direct descendants. From 1186 until 1867 successive families of Shoguns exercised the temporal power. In 1867 the Emperor Meiji recovered the imperial power after the abdication on 14 Oct. 1867 of the fifteenth and last Tokugawa Shogun Keiki (in different pronunciation: Yoshinobu). In 1871 the feudal system (Hōken Seido) was abolished; this was the beginning of the rapid westernization.

At San Francisco on 8 Sept. 1951 a Treaty of Peace was signed by Japan and representatives of 48 countries. For details *see* THE STATESMAN'S YEAR-BOOK, 1953, p. 1169. On 26 Oct. 1951 the Japanese Diet ratified the Treaty by 307 votes to 47 votes with 112 abstentions. On the same day the Diet ratified a Security Treaty with the US by 289 votes to 71 votes with 106 abstentions. The treaty provided for the stationing of American troops in Japan until she was able to undertake her own defence. The peace treaty came into force on 28 April 1952, when Japan regained her sovereignty. In 1960 Japan signed the Japan–US Mutual Security Treaty, valid for 10 years, which was renewed in 1970. In June 1971 the Okinawa Reversion Agreement providing for the return from the US to Japan of Okinawa on 15 May 1972 was signed.

AREA AND POPULATION. Census population, 1 Oct. 1981, was 117,881,000 with density of 316·3 per sq. km (58m. males, 60m. females). Foreigners registered 31 Dec. 1981 were 792,946, of whom 667,325 were Koreans, 55,616 Chinese, 23,266 Americans, 5,321 British, 6,729 Philippines, 2,931 Germans, 2,842 Vietnamese, 2,137 Indians, 1,722 Canadians, 2,535 stateless persons.

Japanese overseas, Oct. 1981, 450,873; of these 131,363 lived in Brazil, 125,432 in USA, 15,984 in Argentina, 13,942 in Federal Republic of Germany, 13,508 in Canada, 8,408 in Peru.

The leading cities, with census population, 1 Oct. 1980 (in 1,000), are:

Akita	285	Kitakyushu	1,065	Otaru	181
Amagasaki	524	Kōbe	1,367	Sagamihara	439
Aomori	288	Kōchi	301	Sakai	810
Asahikawa	353	Koriyama	286	Sapporo	1,402
Chiba	746	Kumamoto	526	Sasebo	251
Fujisawa	300	Kurashiki	404	Sendai	665
Fukuoka	1,089	Kure	235	Shimonoseki	269
Fukushima	263	Kyōto	1,473	Shizuoka	458
Fukuyama	346	Machida	295	Suita	332
Funabashi	479	Maebashi	265	Takamatsu	317
Gifu	410	Matsudo	401	Takatsuki	341
Hachioji	387	Matsuyama	402	Tokushima	249
Hakodate	320	Miyazaki	264	Tōkyō	8,349
Hamamatsu	491	Nagano	324	Toyama	305
Higashiosaka	522	Nagasaki	447	Toyohashi	304
Himeji	446	Nagoya	2,088	Toyonaka	403
Hirakata	353	Naha	296	Toyota	282
Hiroshima	899	Nara	298	Urawa	358
Ichinomiya	253	Neyagawa	256	Utsunomiya	378
Ichikawa	364	Niigata	458	Wakayama	401
Iwaki	342	Nishinomiya	410	Yao	273
Kagoshima	505	Oita	360	Yokkaichi	255
Kanazawa	418	Okayama	546	Yokohama	2,774
Kawaguchi	379	Omiya	354	Yokosuka	421
Kawasaki	1,041	Osaka	2,648		

Vital statistics (in 1,000) for calendar years:

	1973	*1974*	*1975*	*1976*	*1977*	*1978*	*1979*	*1980*	*1981*
Births	2,101	2,030	1,901	1,833	1,755	1,709	1,643	1,616	1,546
Deaths	706	710	702	703	690	696	690	722	725

Crude birth rate of Japanese nationals in present area, 1981, was 13 per 1,000 population (1947: 3·43); crude death rate, 6·1; crude marriage rate, 6·6; infant mortality rate per 1,000 live births, 7·1.

EMPEROR. The Emperor bears the title of Nihon-koku Tennō ('Emperor of Japan'). **Hirohito,** born in Tōkyō, 29 April 1901; succeeded his father, Yoshihito, 25 Dec. 1926; married 26 Jan. 1924, to Princess Nagako, born 6 March 1903. Living sons: (1) Prince Akihito (Tsugunomiya), born 23 Dec. 1933; formally installed as Crown Prince on 10 Nov. 1952; married to Michiko Shoda (born 20 Oct. 1934), 10 April 1959. *Offspring:* Prince Naruhito (Hironomiya), born 23 Feb. 1960; Prince Fumihito (Ayanomiya), born 30 Nov. 1965; Princess Sayako (Norinomiya), born 18 April 1969. (2) Prince Masahito (Hitachinomiya), born 28 Nov. 1935; married to Hanako Tsugaru, 30 Sept. 1964.

By the Imperial House Law of 11 Feb. 1889, revised on 16 Jan. 1947, the succession to the throne was fixed upon the male descendants.

CONSTITUTION AND GOVERNMENT. Japan's Government is based upon the Constitution of 1947 which superseded the Meiji Constitution of 1889. In it the Japanese people pledge themselves to uphold the ideas of democracy and peace. The Emperor is the symbol of the States and of the unity of the people. Sovereign power rests with the people. The Emperor has no powers related to government. Japan renounces war as a sovereign right and the threat or the use of force as a means of settling disputes with other nations. Fundamental human rights are guaranteed.

National flag: White, with a red disc.

National anthem: Kimi ga yo wa (words 9th century, tune by Hiromori Hayashi, 1881).

Legislative power rests with the Diet, which consists of the House of Representatives (of 511 members), elected by men and women over 20 years of age for a 4-year term, and the House of Councillors of 252 members (100 elected at large and 152 from prefectural districts), one-half of its members being elected every 3 years. The Lower House controls the budget and approves treaties with foreign powers.

The former House of Peers is replaced by the House of Councillors, whose members, like those of the House of Representatives, are elected as representatives of all the people. The House of Representatives has pre-eminence over the House of Councillors.

In Jan. 1983 the House of Representatives consisted of 284 Liberal-Democrats, 104 Socialists, 34 Komeito, 31 Democratic Socialists, 29 Japan Communist Party, 13 New Liberal Club and Social Democratic Federation, 7 Independents and 9 vacancies.

The Cabinet, as constituted in Nov. 1982, was as follows:

Prime Minister: Yasuhiro Nakasone.
Justice: Akira Hatano.
Foreign Affairs: Shintaro Abe.
Finance: Noboru Takeshita.
Education: Mitsuo Setoyama.
Health and Welfare: Yoshiro Hayashi.
Agriculture, Forestry and Fishery: Iwazo Kaneko.
Trade and Industry: Sadanori Yamanaka.
Transport: Takashi Hasegawa.
Postal Service: Tokutaro Higaki.

Labour: Akira Ono.
Construction: Hideo Utsumi.
Home Affairs: Sachio Yamamoto.

Local Government. The country is divided into 47 prefectures (*Todōfuken*), including Tōkyō-to (the capital), Ōsaka-fu and Kyōto-fu, Hokkai-dō, and 43 *Ken.* Each *Todōfuken* has its governor (*Chiji*) elected by the voters in the area. The prefectural government of Tōkyō-to is also responsible for the urban part (formerly Tōkyō-shi) of the prefecture. Each prefecture, city, town and village has a representative assembly elected by the same franchise as in parliamentary elections.

New legislation, which came into effect on 1 July 1954, has given the central government complete control of the police throughout the country.

DEFENCE

Army. The 'Ground Self-Defence Force' had in 1982 an authorized strength of 180,000 uniformed personnel, plus a reserve of 41,000 men. The Army is organized in 12 infantry divisions, 1 armoured division, 1 airborne brigade, 2 air defence brigades, 1 artillery, 5 engineer, 1 signal, 2 composite and 1 helicopter brigades in addition to 4 anti-aircraft artillery groups. Equipment includes 890 tanks.

The Northern Army, stationed in Hokkaido, consists of 4 divisions (1 of which is armoured), an artillery brigade, an anti-aircraft artillery brigade, a tank group and an engineering brigade. The Western Army, stationed in Kyushu, consists of 2 divisions and 1 composite brigade. The North-Eastern Army (2 divisions), the Eastern Army (2 divisions) and 1 airborne brigade, the Middle Army (3 divisions and 1 composite brigade). The infantry division establishment is approximately 9,000 with 4 infantry regiments or 7,000 (lower establishment) with 3 infantry regiments. Each infantry division has an artillery unit, an anti-tank unit, a tank battalion and an engineering battalion in addition to administrative units.

Navy. The 'Maritime Self-Defence Force' comprises 14 submarines, 2 large destroyers of 5,200 tons each and 2 destroyers of 4,700 tons each carrying 3 helicopters, 3 guided-missile destroyers, 26 other destroyers, 16 frigates, 1 minelayer/support ship, 11 large patrol vessels, 2 modern purpose-built training ships (destroyer and frigate types, with hangars), 37 coastal minesweepers, 2 minesweeper support ships, 2 submarine rescue vessels, 6 minesweeping boats, 5 fast torpedo-boats, 9 patrol boats, 8 landing ships, 1 new fleet support ship, 1 experimental ship, 7 surveying vessels, 2 icebreakers (antarctic support ship), 1 cable layer (ocean survey), 1 cable layer (*ex*-minelayer), 2 oilers, 24 harbour tankers, 34 tugs, 12 tenders, 20 auxiliaries and 60 minor craft.

The Fleet Air Arm, numbering 13 squadrons, comprises 90 patrol aircraft and 19 flying boats for anti-submarine patrol, 85 trainers and 104 helicopters.

Personnel in 1982 numbered 44,000 officers and ratings including the Naval Air Arm. There are also 5,000 in civil maritime defence.

Air Force. An 'Air Self-Defence Force' was inaugurated on 1 July 1954. In 1982 its equipment included 1 interceptor squadron of F-15J/DJ Eagles (total of 138 aircraft to be acquired by 1987); 3 squadrons of F-104J Starfighters, and 6 of F-4EJ Phantoms; 3 squadrons of Mitsubishi F-1 close-support fighters; 1 squadron of RF-4E reconnaissance fighters; ECM flight with 2 YS-11Es; 3 squadrons of turbofan Kawasaki C-1 and turboprop NAMC YS-11 transports. About 35 helicopters, including S-62s and KV-107s, and MU-2 twin-turboprop aircraft perform search, rescue and general duties. Training units use piston-engined Fuji T-3 basic trainers, Fuji T-1 jet intermediate trainers, T-33 jet trainers and supersonic Mitsubishi T-2 jet advanced trainers. Six surface-to-air missile groups (19 squadrons) are in service. Total strength is about 310 combat aircraft and 46,000 officers and men.

INTERNATIONAL RELATIONS

Membership. Japan is a member of UN, the Colombo Plan and OECD.

ECONOMY

Planning. The 1981–85 Plan envisages an onward growth rate of 5·5%. The real growth rate for 1983 is envisaged at 3·4% and the nominal 5·6%.

Budget. Ordinary revenue and expenditure for fiscal year ending 31 March 1983 balanced at 46,680,800m. yen.

Of the proposed revenue in 1982 (in 1m. yen), 366·24m. was to come from taxes and stamps, 10·44m. from public bonds. Main items of expenditure: Social security, 9,084,800; public works, 6,655,400; local government, 9,230,900; education, 4,863.700; defence, 2,586,100.

The outstanding national debt incurred by public bonds was estimated in March 1982 to be 83,641,100m. yen, including 11,200m. yen of Japan's foreign currency bonds.

The estimated 1982 budgets of the prefectures and other local authorities forecast a total revenue of 47,054,200m. yen, to be made up partly by local taxes and partly by government grants and local loans.

Currency. Coins of 1, 5, 10, 50, 100 and 500 *yen* are in circulation as well as notes of the Bank of Japan, of 100, 500, 1,000, 5,000 and 10,000 *yen*. Bank-notes for 100 *yen* are still in circulation in country districts but are gradually being replaced by coins. In March 1983, £1 = 359 *yen*; US$1 = 238 *yen*.

In Dec. 1981 the currency in circulation consisted of 20,237,700m. yen Bank of Japan notes and 1,020,300m. yen subsidiary coins.

Banking. The modern banking system dates from 1872. The Nippon Ginko (Bank of Japan) was founded in 1882. The Bank of Japan has undertaken to finance the Government and the banks; its function is similar to that of a Central Bank in other countries. The Bank undertakes the actual management of Treasury funds and foreign exchange control.

Gold bullion and cash holdings of the Bank of Japan at 31 Dec. 1981 stood at 245,800m. yen.

The Yokohama Specie Bank (specializing in foreign exchange) became the Bank of Tōkyō in Aug. 1954. Total assets of all banks at 31 Dec. 1981 was 249,887,200m. yen.

The post office savings bank is modelled upon the British; deposits amounted to 70,418,400m. yen in July 1982.

Many foreign banks operate branches in Japan including: Bank of Indo-China, Hongkong & Shanghai Banking Corporation, Chartered Bank of India, Australia and China, Bank of India, Mercantile Bank of India, Bank of Korea, Bank of China, Algemene Bank Nederland NV, National Handelsbank NV, Bank of America, National City Bank of New York, Chase Manhattan Bank, Bangkok Bank and American Express Co.

Weights and Measures. The metric system was made obligatory by a law passed in March 1921, and the period of grace for its compulsory use ended on 1 April 1966.

ENERGY AND NATURAL RESOURCES

Electricity. In 1980 generating facilities were capable of an output of 143,698,000 kw.; electricity produced was 577,521,000 kwh.

Oil and Gas. Output of crude petroleum, 1980, was 503,000 kl, almost entirely from oilfields on the island of Honshu, but 256,833,000 kl crude oil had to be imported. Output of natural gas, 1980, 21,594,973m. kilocalories.

Minerals. Ore production in tonnes, 1980, of chromite, 13,610; coal, 18·05m.; iron, 476,658; zinc, 238·1m.; molybdenum, 100; manganese, 79,579; copper, 52,553; lead, 44,746; tungsten, 1,894; silver, 267,592 kg.; gold, 3,183 kg.

Agriculture. Agricultural workers in 1981 were 6,685,220, including 919,370 subsidiary and seasonal workers; 9% of the labour force as opposed to 24·7% in 1962. The arable land area in 1981 was 5,442,000 hectares (5,796,000 in 1970). Division of ordinary fields to non-agricultural use accounted largely for this decrease. Rice cultivation accounted for 2,278,000 hectares in 1980. The area planted with industrial crops such as rapeseed, tobacco, tea, rush, etc., was 262,000 hectares in 1980.

In 1981 there were 4,224,700 power cultivators and tractors in use together with 336,439 power sprayers and power dusters.

Output of rice was 12·6m. tonnes in 1978, 12m. in 1979, 9·6m. in 1980 and 10,259,000 in 1981.

Production in 1980 (in 1,000 tonnes) of barley was 332; wheat, 582·8; soybeans, 173·9. Sweet potatoes, which in the past mitigated the effects of rice famines, have, in view of rice over-production, decreased from 4,955,000 tons in 1965 to 1,317,000 tons in 1980. Domestic sugar-beet and sugar-cane production accounted for only 25·7% of requirement in 1980. In 1980, 2,266,000 tonnes were imported, 33·9% of this being imported from Australia, 6·8% from Thailand, 20·7% from South Africa, 6·8% from Formosa, 17·8% from Philippines, 12·8% from Cuba.

Fruit production, 1980 (in 1,000 tonnes): Mandarins, 2,892; apples, 960; pears, 496; grapes, 323; peaches, 245; and persimmons, 265.

Livestock (1981): 4·4m. cattle (including about 2·1m. milch cows), 23,500 horses, 10,065,000 pigs, 15,900 sheep, 61,700 goats, 295m. chickens. Milk (1980), 6·5m. tonnes.

Forestry. Forests and grasslands cover about 25m. hectares (nearly 70% of the whole land area), with an estimated timber stand of 2,484m. cu. metres in 1981. In 1980, 43m. cu. metres were felled.

Fisheries. Before the War, Japanese catch represented one-half to two-thirds of the world's total fishing, in 1979 it was 14·2%. The catch in 1980 was 11·1m. tonnes, excluding whaling. Japan now ranks second to the USSR in whaling.

INDUSTRY AND TRADE

Industry. Japan's industrial equipment, 1979, numbered 739,304 plants of all sizes, employing 10·86m. production workers.

Since 1920 there has been a shift from light to heavy industries. The production of electrical appliances and electronic machinery has made great strides: television sets (1980: 16·3m.), radio sets (1980: 17m.), cameras (1980: 14m.), computing machines and automation equipment are produced in increasing quantities. The chemical industry ranks third in production value after machinery and metals (1980). Production, 1980, included (in tonnes): Sulphuric acid, 6·8m.; caustic soda, 3·1m.; ammonium sulphate, 1·9m.; calcium superphosphate, 591,000.

Output (1980), in 1,000 tonnes, of pig iron was 87,041; crude steel, 111,395; ordinary rolled steel, 88,888.

In 1980 paper production was 10·54m. tonnes; paperboard, 7·6m. tonnes.

Japan's textile industry before the War had 13m. cotton-yarn spindles. After the War she resumed with 2·78m. spindles; in 1964, 8·42m. spindles were operating. Output of cotton yarn, 1980, 503,800 tonnes, and of cotton cloth, 20,202m. sq. metres.

In wool, Japan aims at wool exports sufficient to pay for the imports of raw wool. Output, 1980, 119,200 tonnes of woollen yarns and 294·2m. sq. metres of woollen fabrics.

Output, 1980, of rayon woven fabrics, 800m. sq. metres; synthetic woven fabrics, 3,158m. sq. metres; silk fabrics, 152m. sq. metres.

Shipbuilding has been decreasing and in 1980, 6·2m. gross tons were launched, of which 3,132,000 GRT were tankers.

Labour. Total labour force, Oct. 1981, was 55·8m., of which 5·1m. were in agriculture and forestry, 470,000 in fishing, 100,000 in mining, 5·4m. in construction,

13·9m. in manufacturing, 14·7m. in commerce and finance, 3·76m. in transport and other public utilities, 10·3m. in services (including the professions) and 1·94m. in government work.

In 1981 there were 12,471,000 workers organized in 73,694 unions. The largest federation is the 'General Council of Japanese Trade Unions' (Sōhyō) with 4,569,000 members. The 'Japanese Confederation of Labour' (Dōmei Kaigi) had 2,182,000 members. The 'Federation of Independent Unions' (Chūritsu Rōren) founded in 1956 had 1,391,000 members.

In Aug. 1981, 1·15m. (2%) were unemployed. In 1981, 1,553,726 working days were lost in industrial stoppages.

Commerce. Trade, excluding bullion and specie (in US$1m.; US$1 = 360 yen, 1,000 yen = US$2.77; from 1 Jan. 1972, US$1 = 308 yen, 1,000 yen = US$3.24):

	1975	*1976*	*1977*	*1978*	*1979*	*1980*	*1981*
Imports	57,863	64,799	70,808	79,343	110,672	140,528	152,030
Exports	55,753	67,225	80,494	97,543	103,031	129,807	143,289

Distribution of trade by countries (customs clearance basis) (US$1m.):

	Exports		*Imports*	
	1980	*1981*	*1980*	*1981*
Africa	4,886	5,760	2,139	2,397
Australia	3,389	4,779	6,982	7,419
Canada	2,437	3,399	4,724	4,464
China	5,078	5,095	4,323	5,292
Fed. Rep. of Germany	5,756	5,968	2,501	2,429
Hong Kong	4,761	5,311	569	669
Latin America	8,917	10,487	5,700	6,649
Philippines	1,683	1,928	1,951	1,731
South-east Asia	30,970	34,321	31,751	31,784
Thailand	1,917	2,251	1,119	1,061
USSR	2,778	3,259	1,860	2,021
UK	3,782	4,789	1,954	2,694
USA	31,367	38,609	24,408	25,297

Principal items in 1981, with value in 1m. yen were:

Imports, c.i.f.		*Exports, f.o.b.*	
Mineral fuels	15,920,535	Machinery and transport equipment	22,043,294
Foodstuffs	3,498,970	Metals and metal products	4,949,063
Metal ores and scrap	1,600,268	Textile products	1,583,290
Machinery and transport equipment	2,248,420	Chemicals	1,502,500
Textile fibres	525,444		

Total trade between Japan and UK (British Department of Trade returns, in £1,000 sterling):

	1978	*1979*	*1980*	*1981*	*1982*
Imports to UK	1,283,181	1,490,288	1,712,108	2,236,170	2,657,977
Exports and re-exports from UK	542,310	606,011	597,147	620,273	681,483

Tourism. In 1980, 1,316,600 foreigners visited Japan, 319,000 of whom came from USA, 90,900 from UK. Japanese travelling abroad totalled 4,006,388m. in 1981.

COMMUNICATIONS

Roads. The total length of roads (including urban and other local roads) was 1,113,388 km at 1 April 1980; the 'national' roads extended 40,212 km, of which 38,408 km were paved. Motor vehicles, at 31 Dec. 1981, numbered 39m., including 21·5m. passenger cars and 1·4m. commercial vehicles.

Railways. The first railway was completed in 1872, between Tōkyō and Yokohama (29 km). Total length of railways, in 1980, was 26,937 km, of which the national railways had 21,322 km (8,279 km electrified) and private railways, 5,615 km

(4,934 km electrified). In 1981 the national railways carried 6,825m. passengers and 122m. tons of freight (private, 45m.).

Aviation. The principal airlines are Japan Airlines and All Nippon Airways. Japan Airlines, founded in 1953, operate international services from Tōkyō to the USA, Europe, the Middle East and Southeast Asia, including flights to London over the North Pole and to Moscow by way of Siberia. In 1979 Japanese companies carried 40,909,839 passengers in domestic services and 4,953,417 passengers in international services.

Shipping. On 30 June 1981 the merchant fleet consisted of 8,817 vessels (over 100 gross tons); there were 708 ships for passenger transport (1·12m. gross tons), 2,931 cargo ships (3,245,000 gross tons) and 1,708 oil tankers (16·9m. gross tons).

Coastguard. The 'Maritime Safety Agency' (Coastguard) consists of 11 regional MS headquarters, 65 MS offices, 51 MS bases, 14 air bases, 6 Control Communications Centres, 1 Traffic Advisory Service Centre, 4 hydrographic observatories and 137 navigation aids offices (with 4,895 navigation aids facilities) and controls 42 large patrol vessels, 47 medium patrol vessels, 19 small patrol vessels, 230 patrol craft, 22 hydrographic service vessels, 5 firefighting vessels, 10 firefighting boats, 63 guard and rescue boats and 83 navigation aids service supply vessels. Personnel in 1982 numbered 12,027 officers and men.

The Coastguard aviation service includes 21 fixed-wing aircraft and 32 helicopters.

Post and Broadcasting. The telephone services, operated by a public corporation, at 31 Dec. 1981 had 58,677,000 instruments.

On 31 Dec. 1980, 98·5% of all households owned colour television sets, 20% black and white television sets.

Cinemas (1981). Cinemas numbered 2,298 with an annual attendance of 149m. (1960: 1,014m.).

Newspapers (1981). Daily newspapers numbered 125 with aggregate circulation of 67,292,563, including 4 major English-language newspapers.

JUSTICE, RELIGION, EDUCATION AND WELFARE

Justice. The Supreme Court is composed of the Chief Justice and 14 other judges. The Chief Justice is appointed by the Emperor, the other judges by the Cabinet. Every 10 years a justice must submit himself to the electorate. All justices and judges of the lower courts serve until they are 70 years of age.

Below the Supreme Court are 8 regional higher courts, district courts (*Chihōsaibansho*) in each prefecture (4 in Hokkaidō) and the local courts.

The Supreme Court is authorized to declare unconstitutional any act of the Legislature or the Executive which violates the Constitution.

Religion. There has normally been religious freedom, but Shintō (literally, The Way of the Gods) was given the status of *quasi*-state-religion in the 1930s; in 1945 the Allied Supreme Command ordered the Government to discontinue state support of Shintō. State subsidies have ceased for all religions, and all religious teachings are forbidden in public schools.

In Dec. 1980 Shintoism claimed 95,848,103 adherents, Buddhism 87,745,179; these figures obviously overlap. Christians numbered 1,018,634, of whom 643,563 are Protestants and 375,071 Catholics.

Education. Education is compulsory and free between the ages of 6 and 15. All institutions are co-educational. On 1 May 1981 there were 15,059 kindergartens with 100,231 teachers and 2,292,811 pupils; 25,004 elementary schools with 473,957 teachers and 11,924,706 pupils; 10,810 junior high schools with 258,479 teachers and 5,299,281 pupils; 5,219 senior high schools with 247,719 teachers and 4,682,829 pupils; 523 junior colleges with 16,696 teachers and 372,406 pupils.

There were also 877 special schools for handicapped children (35,200 teachers, 94,100 pupils).

Japan has 7 main state universities, formerly known as the Imperial Universities: Tōkyō University (1877); Kyōto University (1897); Tōhoku University, Sendai (1907); Kyūshū University, Fukuoka (1910); Hokkaidō University, Sapporo (1918); Osaka University (1931), and Nagoya University (1939). In addition, there are various other state and municipal as well as private universities of high standing, such as Keio (founded in 1859), Waseda, Rikkyo, Hosei, Meiji universities, and several women's universities, among which Tōkyō and Ochanomizu are most notable. There are 451 colleges and universities with (1 May 1980) 1,822,117 students and 105,117 teachers.

Social Welfare. Hospitals at the end of 1980 numbered 9,055 with 1,319,406 beds. Physicians at the end of 1980 numbered 156,235; dentists, 53,602.

There are in force various types of social security schemes, such as health insurance, unemployment insurance and old-age pensions. The total population come under one or more of these schemes.

In 1981 11,270,712 persons and 9,080,712 households received some form of regular public assistance.

DIPLOMATIC REPRESENTATIVES

Of Japan in Great Britain (43 Grosvenor St., London, W1X 0BA)
Ambassador: Tsuyoshi Hirahara (accredited 24 Feb. 1982.)

Of Great Britain in Japan (1 Ichiban-cho, Chiyoda-ku, Tōkyō 102)
Ambassador: Sir Hugh Cortazzi, KCMG.

Of Japan in the USA (2520 Massachusetts Ave., NW, Washington, D.C. 20008)
Ambassador: Yoshio Ōkawara

Of the USA in Japan (10–5, Akasaka 1-chome, Minato-Ku, Tōkyō)
Ambassador: Michael J. Mansfield.

Of Japan to the United Nations
Ambassadors: Masahiro Nishibori and Wataru Miyakawa.

Books of Reference

Statistics Bureau of the Prime Minister's Office: *Statistical Year-Book* (from 1949).—*Statistical Abstract* (from 1950)).—*Statistical Handbook of Japan 1977.*—*Monthly Bulletin* (from April 1950)

Economic Planning Agency: *Economic Survey* (annual), *Economic Statistics* (monthly), *Economic Indicators* (monthly)

Ministry of International Trade: *Foreign Trade of Japan* (annual)

The Bank of Japan Research Department. *Money and Banking in Japan.* London, 1973

Japan Times Year Book. (I. Year Book of Japan. II. Who's Who in Japan. III. Business Directory of Japan.) Tōkyō, first issue 1933

Treaty of Peace with Japan. (Cmd. 8392). HMSO, 1951; (Cmd. 8601). HMSO, 1952

Ackerman, E. A., *Japan's National Resources.* Univ. of Chicago Press, 1953

Allen, G. C., *Short Economic History of Modern Japan.* London, 1946.—*The Japanese Economy.* London, 1981

Asahi Newsprinting Co., *This is Japan.* Tōkyō, annual from 1954

Baerwald, H. H., *Japan's Parliament.* CUP, 1974

Boltho, A., *Japan: An Economic Survey, 1953–1973.* OUP, 1976

Hirschmeier, J., and Tsunehiko, Y., *The Development of Japanese Business, 1600–1973.* London, 1976

Kahn, H., and Pepper, T., *The Japanese Challenge.* New York, 1979

Kenkyusha's *New Japanese–English [and English–Japanese] Dictionary.* 2 vols. New ed. Cambridge, Mass., and Berkeley, Cal., 1960

Kennedy, M. D., *A History of Japan,* London, 1963

Kitamura, H., *Choices for the Japanese Economy.* London, 1976
Langdon, F. C., *Japan's Foreign Policy.* Univ. of British Columbia Press, 1973
McNelly, T., *Politics and Government in Japan.* 2nd ed. London, 1972
Miyazaki, S., *The Japanese Dictionary Explained in English.* Tōkyō, 1950
Murata, K., *An Industrial Geography of Japan.* London, 1980
Nippon: A Chartered Survey of Japan. Tsuneta Yano Memorial Society. Tōkyō, annual
Ohkawa, K., and Rosovsky, H., *Japanese Economic Growth: Trend Acceleration in the Twentieth Century.* Stanford Univ. Press, 1973
Richardson, B. M., *The Political Culture of Japan.* Univ. of California Press, 1974
Sansom, G. B., *The Western World and Japan.* New York, 1950.—*A History of Japan.* 3 vols. London, 1958–64
Simonis, H. and U. E. (ed.), *Japan: Economic and Social Studies in Development.* Wiesbaden, 1974
Tanaka, K., *Building a New Japan: A Plan for Remodelling the Japanese Archipelago.* Tōkyō, 1973
Vogel, E. F., *Japan as Number One.* Harvard Univ. Press, 1979
Yabuki, K. (ed.), *Japan Bibliographic Annual.* 2 vols. Tōkyō, annual

THE HASHEMITE KINGDOM OF JORDAN

Capital: Amman
Population: 2·23m. (1980) E. Bank
0·8m. (1976) W. Bank
GNP per capita: US$1,420 (1980)

Al Mamlaka al Urduniya al Hashemiyah

HISTORY. By a Treaty, signed in London on 22 March 1946, Britain recognized Transjordan as a sovereign independent state. A new Anglo-Transjordan treaty was signed in Amman on 15 March 1948. The treaty was to remain in force for 20 years, but by mutual consent was terminated on 13 March 1957.

The Arab Federation between the Kingdoms of Iraq and Jordan, which was concluded on 14 Feb. 1958, lapsed after the revolution in Iraq of 14 July 1958, and was officially terminated by royal decree on 1 Aug. 1958.

On 25 May 1946 the Amir Abdullah assumed the title of King, and when the treaty was ratified on 17 June 1946 the name of the territory was changed to that of 'The Hashemite Kingdom of Jordan'. The legislature consists of a lower house of 60 members elected by universal suffrage (30 from East Jordan and 30 from West Jordan), and a senate of 30 members nominated by the King.

AREA AND POPULATION. The part of Palestine remaining to the Arabs under the armistice with Israel 3 April 1949, with the exception of the Gaza strip, was in Dec. 1949 placed under Jordan rule and formally incorporated in Jordan on 24 April 1950. For the frontier lines *see* map in THE STATESMAN'S YEAR-BOOK, 1951. On 10 Aug. 1965 a treaty with Saudi Arabia provided for an exchange of about 6,000–7,000 sq. km in order to facilitate the development of the port of Aqaba.

Total East Bank area, 91,000 sq. km. West Bank enclaves 5,000 sq. km: census population (18 Nov. 1961), 1,706,226; estimate, 1976, 2,751,968 (1,951,968 in East Bank, 800,000 in West Bank). In 1961, 805,450 lived in West Jordan and 834,589 in East Jordan, including some 550,000 refugees from Palestine but excluding some 53,000 nomads. About 63,000 Jordanians live abroad. Density of population per sq. km, 51 in East Jordan, 143 in West Jordan.

The country is divided into 8 districts (*muhafaza*), viz., Amman, Irbid, Balqa, Karak, Ma'an, Jerusalem, Hebron and Nablus. The last 3 named districts are known collectively as the West Bank, which, since the hostilities of June 1967, has been occupied by Israel.

The largest towns, with estimated population, 1980: Amman, the capital, 1,232,600; Zarka, 269,780 (1977); Irbid, 634,200.

In 1979 registered births numbered 91,622; deaths, 6,547; marriages, 15,491; divorces, 3,295.

KING. The Kingdom is a constitutional monarchy headed by HM King **Hussein**, GCVO, eldest son of King Talal, who, being incapacitated by mental illness, was deposed by Parliament on 11 Aug. 1952 and died 8 July 1972. The King was born 14 Nov. 1935, and married Princess Dina Abdul Hamid on 19 April 1955 (divorced 1957), Toni Avril Gardiner (Muna al Hussein) on 25 May 1961 (divorced 1972), Alia Toukan on 26 Dec. 1972 (died in air crash 1977) and Elizabeth Halaby on 15 June 1978. *Offspring:* Princess Alia, born 13 Feb. 1956; Prince Abdulla, born 30 Jan. 1962; Prince Faisal, born 11 Oct. 1963; Princesses Zein and Aisha, born 23 April 1968; Princess Haya, born 3 May 1974; Prince Ali, born 23 Dec. 1975; Prince Hamzah, born 1 April 1980; Prince Hashem, born 10 June

1981. *Crown Prince* (appointed 1 April 1965): Prince Hassan, younger brother of the King.

CONSTITUTION AND GOVERNMENT. The Constitution passed on 7 Nov. 1951 provides that the Cabinet is responsible to Parliament.

On 9 Nov. 1974 both Houses of Parliament approved amendments to the Constitution by which the King was empowered to dissolve Parliament and delay calling elections for 12 months.

On 5 Feb. 1976 both Houses of Parliament approved amendments to the Constitution by which the King was empowered to postpone calling elections until further notice. The lower house was dissolved. This step was taken because no elections could be held in the West Bank which has been under Israeli occupation since June 1967.

The Cabinet, in Jan. 1982, was composed as follows:

Prime Minister and Minister of Defence: Modar Badran.

Information: Adnan Abo Odeh. *Finance:* Salem Musadeh. *Culture, Youth, Tourism and Antiquities:* Maan Abu Nowwar. *Justice:* Ahmad Abdul Karim Tarawneh. *Agriculture:* Marwan Dodeen. *Communications:* Mohammad Adoub Al-Zaber. *Occupied Territories:* Hasan Ibrahim. *Awqaf and Religious Affairs:* Kamel Sharif. *Foreign Affairs:* Marwan Al-Kasim. *Interior:* Suleiman Arar. *Supplies:* Ibrahim Ayoub. *Transport, and Minister of State for Prime Minister's Affairs:* Ali Suheimat, Hikmat Alsaket. *Education:* Said El-Tall. *Health:* Zuhair Malhas. *Social Development:* Inam Mufti. *Labour:* Jawad Anani. *Industry and Commerce:* Waleed Asfour. *Public Works:* Awni Al-Masri. *Municipal and Rural Affairs:* Hasan Al-Momani.

There is also a National Consultative Council; the present 60-member council took office in April 1980 under the presidency of Ahmed Mahhud al-Tarawinah.

National flag: Three horizontal stripes of black, white, green, with a red triangle based on the hoist, bearing a white 7-pointed star.

The official language of the country is Arabic.

DEFENCE

Army. The Army is organized in 5 armoured, 2 infantry and 6 mechanized brigades, 1 independant Royal Guards brigade and 16 artillery battalions. In addition there are 3 special forces battalions. Total strength (1983) 65,000 men.

Navy. The Coastal Guard or Jordan Sea Force has 1 command boat and 14 patrol launches based at Aqaba. Personnel (1983) totalled 300 officers and ratings.

Air Force. The Air Force has 1 ground attack and 3 interceptor squadrons equipped with Mirage F1 and F-5E Tiger II fighters and 2-seat F-5Fs, plus an OCU equipped with F-5A fighters and 2-seat F-5Bs. There are 5 C-130B/H Hercules and 3 CASA Aviocar turboprop transports, S-76, Alouette III and Hughes 500D helicopters, piston-engined Bulldog basic trainers and T37B jet trainers. Aircraft on order include 24 AH-1S HueyCobra anti-tank helicopters for 1985 delivery. Hawk surface-to-air missiles equip 14 batteries. Strength is about 7,500 officers and men.

INTERNATIONAL RELATIONS

Membership. Jordan is a member of the UN and the Arab League.

ECONOMY

Planning. A 5-year plan (1981–85) aims at achieving a growth rate of 10·4% per annum.

Budget. The budget estimates for the year 1980 provide for revenue of JD.504,233,000 and expenditure of JD.529,233,000. Of revenue, JD.203,333,000 was from foreign grants and aid.

Currency. The Jordan *dinar,* divided into 1,000 *fils.* The following bank-notes and coins are in circulation: 10, 5 dinars, 1 dinar, 500 fils (notes), 250, 100, 50, 25, 20 fils (cupronickel), 10, 5, 1 fils (bronze). In March 1983, £1 = JD.0·536; US$ = JD.0·36.

Banking. The Central Bank of Jordan started operations on 1 Oct. 1964, taking over the sterling assets and the commitments of the Jordan Currency Board. Commercial bank deposits in March 1979 were JD.508·5m.

NATURAL RESOURCES

Minerals. Phosphates production in 1980 was 3,911,166 tons. Potash is found in the Dead Sea. Reserves, over 800m. tonnes. A potash plant is being built on the southeast shore to extract compounds by solar evaporation. Cement production (1980), 912,707 tons.

Agriculture. The country east of the Hejaz Railway line is largely desert; north-western Jordan is potentially of agricultural value and an integrated Jordan Valley project began in 1973; 21,000 hectares had been irrigated by 1980. The main crops are tomatoes and other vegetables, fruit, wheat (badly affected by drought 1975-80).

Production in 1980 included (in tonnes): Tomatoes, 162,900; citrus fruit, 48,500; grapes, 18,200; wheat, 133,600.

Livestock (1981): 1m. sheep; 490,000 goats; 37,000 cattle; 13,000 camels. 2,923 tractors and 189 cultivators were in use in 1975.

COMMERCE. Imports in 1981 were valued at JD.935,250,000 and exports and re-exports at JD.269,740,000.

Total trade between Jordan and UK (British Department of Trade returns, in £1,000 sterling):

	1978	*1979*	*1980*	*1981*	*1982*
Imports to UK	6,153	7,855	8,152	10,300	17,487
Exports and re-exports from UK	67,450	86,894	100,318	203,651	295,274

INDUSTRY. The most important activity is processing potash and other minerals. There is a large chemical fertilizer plant at Aqaba, an oil refinery at Zarka and a cement plant at Fuhers.

TOURISM. In 1980, 1·6m. foreigners visited Jordan.

COMMUNICATIONS

Roads. Asphalt roads connect Amman with all the chief towns in the country. Unmetalled roads have been constructed, making motor traffic possible from Amman to most other areas. The road from Amman to Ma'an and Aqaba (394 km) has branches to Karak, Tafileh, Shobak and Wadi Musa (Petra). The town of Jerash is joined by a good road to Amman. The normal asphalted route from Amman to Deraa (in Syria) and thence to Damascus is through Jerash. The oasis of Azraq may be reached by motor car from Mafraq, Zarka or Amman. Total length of public highways, 4,095 km. Motor vehicles in 1980 included 73,078 private passenger cars, 11,207 taxis, 1,415 buses, 29,517 goods vehicles, 4,888 motor cycles.

Railways. The 1,050 mm gauge Hejaz Railway runs from the Syrian border at Nassib to Ma'an and Naqb Ishtar and Aqaba Port (total, 618 km). The railway linking Damascus with Ma'an passes through Amman. In 1981 the railways carried 57,753 passengers and 10,000 tons of freight.

Aviation (1975). The Royal Jordanian Airlines (ALIA) maintains services from Amman to Amsterdam, Athens, Abu Dhabi, Aleppo, Aqaba, Baghdad, Bahrain, Bangkok, Beirut, Brussels, Cairo, Casablanca, Colombo, Copenhagen, Damascus, Deir ez Zor, Dhahran, Doha, Dubai, Frankfurt, Geneva, Istanbul, Jidda, Kuala Lumpur, Kuwait, London, Madrid, Oman, Paris, Rome, Singapore, Tehrán and Vienna. Alitalia, KLM, Middle East Airways, Egyptian Airlines, Saudi Arabian, Iraqi, Kuwaiti, British Airways, Swissair, Syrian Arab Airlines, and Aeroflot also operate in Jordan.

Shipping (1980). The port of Aqaba handled 6,598,591 tons of cargo.

Post. In 1982 there were 791 post offices and 60,533 telephones in 1980 (39,207 in Amman, 1979).

Cinemas (1975). Cinemas numbered 40 with a total attendance of 4,341,900.

Newspapers (1980). There were 4 daily (including 1 in English) and 5 weekly papers.

RELIGION, EDUCATION AND WELFARE

Religion. About 80% of the population are Sunni Moslems.

Education (1980, East Bank only). There were 189 pre-primary schools with 639 teachers and 17,160 pupils; 1,095 primary schools with 13,898 teachers and 448,411 pupils; 341 secondary schools had 3,648 teachers and 80,173 pupils and 16 teacher-training institutes had 362 teachers and 8,621 students. The University of Jordan, inaugurated on 15 Dec. 1962 had in 1980-81, 10,767 students and 431 teachers. The Yarmouk University (Irbid) was inaugurated in 1976 with (1980-81) 5,677 students and 225 teachers.

In 1976 3 agricultural schools had 40 teachers and 591 students; 10 industrial schools had 157 teachers and 1,911 pupils, and 3 nursing, midwifery and child-care schools had 25 teachers and 323 students. One social service institute had 6 teachers and 52 students. Six vocational centres had 32 teachers and 424 pupils.

Health (1980). There were 1,715 physicians, 351 dentists and 35 hospitals with 2,743 beds.

DIPLOMATIC REPRESENTATIVES

Of Jordan in Great Britain (6 Upper Phillimore Gdns., London, W8 7HB)
Ambassador: Ibrahim Izziddin.

Of Great Britain in Jordan (Third Circle, Jebel Amman)
Ambassador: A. B. Urwick, CMG.

Of Jordan in the USA (2319 Wyoming Ave., NW, Washington, D.C., 20008)
Ambassador: Abd-El Hadi Majali

Of the USA in Jordan (Jebel Amman, Amman)
Ambassador: Richard N. Viets.

Of Jordan to the United Nations
Ambassador: Dr Hazem Nuseibeh.

Books of Reference

The Department of Statistics, Ministry of National Economy, publishes a *Statistical Yearbook* (in Arabic and English), latest issue 1968, and a *Statistical Guide,* latest issue 1965.–*External Trade Statistics*, 1968.–*National Accounts and Input-Output Analysis, 1959-65,* 1967

The Constitution of the Hashemite Kingdom of Jordan. Amman, 1952

Aruri, N. H., *Jordan: A Study in Political Development (1921-1965).* The Hague, 1972

Glubb, J. B., *The Story of the Arab Legion.* London, 1948.–*A Soldier with the Arabs.* London, 1957

Gubser, P., *Jordan.* Boulder, 1982

Haas, J., *Husseins Königreich: Jordaniens Stellung in Nahen Osten.* Munich, 1975

Morris, J., *The Hashemite Kings.* London, 1959

Seton, C. R. W., *Legislation of Transjordan, 1918-30.* London, 1931. [Continued by the Government of Jordan as an annual publication: *Jordan Legislation.* Amman, 1932 ff.]

Toni, Y. T., and Mousa, S., *Jordan: Land and People.* Amman, 1973

KENYA

Capital: Nairobi
Population: 15·8m. (1980)
GNP per capita: US$420 (1980)

Jamhuri ya Kenya

HISTORY. Until Kenya became independent on 12 Dec. 1963, it consisted of the colony and the protectorate. The protectorate comprised the mainland dominions of the Sultan of Zanzibar, viz., a coastal strip of territory 10 miles wide, to the northern branch of the Tana River; also Mau, Kipini and the Island of Lamu, and all adjacent islands between the rivers Umba and Tana. The Sultan on 8 Oct. 1963 ceded the coastal strip to Kenya with effect from 12 Dec. 1963.

The colony and protectorate, formerly known as the East African Protectorate were, on 1 April 1905, transferred from the Foreign Office to the Colonial Office and in Nov. 1906 the protectorate was placed under the control of a governor and C.-in-C. and (except the Sultan of Zanzibar's dominions) was annexed to the Crown as from 23 July 1920 under the name of the Colony of Kenya, thus becoming a Crown Colony.

The territories on the coast became the Kenya Protectorate.

A treaty was signed (15 July 1924) with Italy under which Great Britain ceded to Italy the Juba River and a strip from 50 to 100 miles wide on the British side of the river. Cession took place on 29 June 1925. The northern boundary is defined by an agreement with Ethiopia in 1947.

AREA AND POPULATION. Kenya is bounded by Ethiopia in the north, Uganda in the west, Tanzania in the south and the Somali Republic and the Indian ocean in the east. The total area is 224,960 sq. miles (582,600 sq. km), of which 219,790 sq. miles is land area. In the 1969 census, the population was 10,942,708, of which 10,735,192 were Africans, 139,037 Asians, 40,593 Europeans, 27,886 Arabs. Census (1979) 15,322,000; estimate (1980) 15·8m.

On the coast the Arabs and Swahili predominate, farther inland the races speaking Bantu languages, and non-Bantu tribes, such as the Luo, the Nandi and Kipsigis, the Masai, the Somali and the Gallas. There are more than forty tribes.

Population of the provinces (1979): Rift Valley, 3·24m.; Eastern, 2,717,000; Nyanza, 2,634,000; Central, 2,348,000; Coast, 1,339,000; Western, 1,033,000; Nairobi district, 835,000; North-Eastern, 373,000.

Nairobi, the capital, was given a Royal charter on 30 March 1950; the 1969 census showed a population of 509,286, including 19,195 Europeans and 67,189 Asians. Estimate (1975) 700,000.

Population of the largest towns: Mombasa, 342,000; Kisumu, 150,000; Nakuru, 93,000; Meru, 73,000; Eldoret, 50,000; Thika, 41,000; Nyeri, 35,000. A new town is being developed (in 1981) at Bura, which will be the centre of a production area using irrigated water from the Tana river.

GOVERNMENT. A Constitution conferring internal self-government was brought into force on 1 June 1963, and full independence was achieved on 12 Dec. 1963. On 12 Dec. 1964 Kenya became a republic.

President of the Republic: Daniel Arap Moi.
Vice-President and Home Affairs: Mwai Kibaki.
Foreign Affairs: Robert Ouko.

The House of Representatives and the Senate were in Dec. 1966 amalgamated into one National Assembly.

On 10 Nov. 1964 Kenya became a one-party state of the Kenya African National Union (KANU) when the voluntary dissolution of the Kenya African Democratic Union (KADU) was declared. Later a second party, the Kenya People's Union (KPU) was formed but on 30 Oct. 1969 was proscribed.

At general elections held in Oct. 1979 there were over 800 candidates for 157 seats.

National flag: Three horizontal stripes of black, red, green, with the red edged in white; bearing in the centre an African shield in black and white with 2 crossed spears behind.

Administration. The country is divided into the Nairobi Area and 7 provinces over which there are local councils with administrative functions. The provinces are: Coast, Central, Eastern, Rift Valley, Western, Nyanza and North Eastern.

Swahili became the official language in 1974 but English is in general use.

DEFENCE

Army. The Army consists of 5 infantry battalions, 2 artillery, 1 armoured car, 1 transport and 2 engineering battalions and a support group which includes a para-troop company; total strength (1983), 13,000.

Navy. The Navy in 1983 consists of 7 British built patrol craft and 350 officers and ratings. The base is at Mombasa which has a dry dock.

Air Force. An air force, formed 1 June 1964, was built up with RAF assistance but was disbanded following a *coup d'état* in 1982. It is expected to be re-established as a component of the Army. Equipment prior to the *coup* included 12 F-5E/F-5F supersonic combat aircraft/trainers, 12 Hawk and 5 BAC 167 Strikemaster light jet attack/trainers, 6 twin-turboprop Buffaloes and 5 twin-engined Caribou for transport, air ambulance, anti-locust spraying and security duties, 6 Skyservant and 1 VIP Navajo Chieftain light twin, 14 Bulldog piston-engined primary trainers and Alouette II, Puma, Gazelle and Bell 47 helicopters. In process of delivery to the Kenyan Army are 32 Hughes Defender helicopters, of which 15 are to be armed with TOW missiles. Personnel about 3,000 in 1982.

INTERNATIONAL RELATIONS

Membership. Kenya is a member of UN, the Commonwealth, OAU and is an ACP state of EEC.

ECONOMY

Budget. Ordinary revenue and expenditure (in K£1,000) for 1981–82: Revenue, 833,000; expenditure, 826,000.

Funded public debt at 31 March 1977 was Sh.3,569·76m.

Currency. The monetary unit is the Kenya *Shilling* divided into 100 *cents*. In March 1983, £1 = 19·40 *Shilling*; US$1 = 12·88 *Shilling*.

Banking. Banks operating in Kenya: the National & Grindlays Bank International, Ltd; the Standard Bank, Ltd; Barclays Bank International; Algemene Bank Nederland NV; Bank of India, Ltd; Bank of Baroda, Ltd; Habib Bank (Overseas), Ltd; Commercial Bank of Africa, Ltd; Citibank; The Co-operative Bank of Kenya, Ltd; National Bank of Kenya, Ltd; The Kenya Commercial Bank; The Central Bank of Kenya.

NATURAL RESOURCES

Minerals. By mid-1970 over 75% of the area of Kenya had been geologically mapped. A special and 2 ordinary oil-prospecting licences were extant at the end of 1969, together covering 22,250 sq. miles. A joint UN–Kenya Government project is investigating the mineral resources in western Kenya and the exploration and development of mineral deposits is proceeding.

Mineral production in 1975 (provisional) was: Soda ash, 91,733 tons; gold (refined), 3,062 grammes; limestone and products, 197,414 tons; diatomite, 1,799 tons; salt, 5,553 tons. Other minerals comprised barytes, magnesite, felspar, sapphires, guano, fluorspar ore, garnets, sand and raw soda.

Agriculture. As agriculture is possible from sea-level to altitudes of over 9,000 ft, tropical, sub-tropical and temperate crops can be grown and mixed farming can be advocated. Four-fifths of the country is range-land which produces mainly livestock products and wild game which constitutes the major attraction of the country's tourist industry.

The main areas of crop production are the Central, Rift Valley, Western and Nyanza Provinces and parts of Eastern and Coastal Provinces. Coffee, tea, sisal, pyrethrum, maize and wheat are crops of major importance in the Highlands, while coconuts, cashew nuts, cotton, sugar, sisal and maize are the principal crops grown at the lower altitudes. Principal crops with production for sale (in 1,000 tonnes, 1980): Wheat, 142; maize, 1,942; rice paddy, 23; pyrethrum extract (1979), 113·7; sugar-cane (1979), 3,148; clean coffee, 75; sisal, 36·5; tea, 99·3.

Livestock (1981): Cattle, 11·5m.; sheep, 4·7m.; goats, 4·58m.; pigs, 77,000; poultry, 17·25m.

Forestry. The total area of gazetted forest reserves in Kenya amounts to 16,800 sq. km, of which the greater part is situated between 6,000 and 11,000 ft above sea-level, mostly on Mount Kenya, the Aberdares, Mount Elgon, Tinderet, Londiani, Mau watershed, Elgeyo and Charangani ranges. These forests may be divided into coniferous, broad-leaved or hardwood and bamboo forests. The upper parts of these forests are mainly bamboo, which occurs mostly between altitudes of 8,000 and 10,000 ft and occupies some 10% of the high-altitude forests. Plantations established by 31 Dec. 1975 (provisional) total 142,500 hectares, of which 121,600 are exotic softwood. In addition 3,100 hectares of pines have been planted for pulpwood. The Forest Department employs about 11,000 men and primary forest industries about 8,000. Water catchment is no longer considered to be the primary role of forests. Revenue from timber royalties, fuel royalties and from exports of forest-based products continues to increase.

COMMERCE. Total domestic exports (1981) K£532·4m.; imports K£955·9m.

Chief imports (1980): Mineral fuels, K£325m.; machinery and transport equipment, K£274m. Chief exports (1980): Petroleum products, K£163m.; unroasted coffee, K£108m.; tea, K£58m.

Total trade between Kenya and UK (British Department of Trade returns, in £1,000 sterling):

	1977	*1978*	*1979*	*1980*	*1981*	*1982*
Imports to UK	155,067	114,604	115,624	105,443	95,238	104,312
Exports and re-exports from UK	118,464	195,679	170,278	259,103	173,663	153,858

TOURISM. In 1979, about 350,000 overseas visitors travelled to Kenya.

COMMUNICATIONS

Roads. In 1976 there were 4,045 km of bitumen surfaced roads and 46,046 km of gravel-surfaced roads.

Railways. On 11 Feb. 1977 the independent Kenya Railways Corporation was formed following break-up of the East African Railways administration. The network totals 2,654 km of metre-gauge and extensive upgrading and re-equipment was in progress in 1980. In 1980, the railways carried 2·4m. passengers and ran 2,285m. tonne-km.

Aviation. Total number of passengers handled at the 4 airports (1976) was 2,188,000. Jomo Kenyatta Airport, Nairobi, handles nearly 30 international airlines as well as Kenya Airways.

Shipping. A national shipping service is planned (1981) to be based in Mombasa, the Kenyan main port at Kilindini on the Indian Ocean. The port handles cargo freight both for Kenya as well as for the neighbouring East African states. The Port Authority also runs a modern harbour college.

Post and Broadcasting. The Voice of Kenya operates 2 national services (Swahili–English) from Nairobi and regional services in Kisumu, Nairobi and Mombasa.

The television service provides programmes mainly in English and Swahili. A new television station opened in Mombasa in 1970. Telephones (1981) 198,294.

Cinemas (1971). Cinemas numbered 32, with seating capacity of 18,800.

JUSTICE, RELIGION, EDUCATION AND WELFARE

Justice. The courts of justice comprise the High Court, established in 1921, with full jurisdiction both civil and criminal over all persons and all matters in Kenya, including Admiralty jurisdiction arising on the high seas and elsewhere, and Subordinate Courts. The High Court has its headquarters at Nairobi and consists of the Chief Justice and 11 puisne judges; it sits continuously at Nairobi, Mombasa, Nakuru and Kisumu; civil and criminal sessions are held regularly at Eldoret, Nyeri, Meru, Kitale, Kisii and Kericho.

The Subordinate Courts are presided over by Senior Resident, Resident or District Magistrates and are established in the main centres of all districts. They sit throughout the year. There are also Moslem Subordinate Courts established in areas where the local population is predominantly Moslem; they are presided over by Kadhis and exercise limited jurisdiction in matters governed by Moslem law.

Religion. The indigenous African background is largely influenced by belief in God in Judaic forms, but Christianity is making an important contribution to the life of the whole territory, not only through the educational and medical services of Christian missions, but by the growth of churches under African leadership, and by its impact on the thought and policy of the country. The Roman Catholic Church (about 1·5m. adherents) has been developed mainly by Irish, British, Dutch and Italian missionary bodies and is now organized in 12 dioceses under the archbishop of Nairobi.

The Protestant Churches (about 950,000 adherents) were started mainly by British and American mission societies; most of them are now linked together by the National Christian Council of Kenya. The Church of the Province of Kenya, formerly the Anglican Church Province of East Africa, was inaugurated on 3 Aug. 1970; at the same time the first Archbishop of Kenya was enthroned. The East African Yearly Meeting of Friends (Religious Society of Friends) has 90,000 adherents.

The Arabs on the coast are Moslems, and Islam has spread among some of the African coastal tribes and the cities. The Asians are Hindus and Moslems, with the exception of the Goans, who are Roman Catholics.

Education. *Primary* (1975). 8,161 primary schools (7,989 maintained, 142 assisted and 30 unaided), with together 2,881,155 children, of whom 1,319,654 were girls and 1,561,501 boys.

Secondary (1975). There were 1,160 secondary schools (379 maintained, 43 assisted and 738 unaided), with a total enrolment of 226,835, of whom 81,529 are girls and 145,306 are boys.

Technical (1976). The Kenya Polytechnic in Nairobi, with an enrolment of 1,860 students, and Mombasa Technical Institute, with an enrolment of 805 students, are the most advanced institutions.

Teacher training (1975). 8,630 students were training as primary teachers, 488 as secondary teachers (recruitment from university graduates only) and 36 teachers for the deaf.

Higher Education. The University of East Africa, which had 3 constituent Colleges, Makerere University College in Kampala, Uganda, the University College in Nairobi, Kenya, and University College in Dar es Salaam, Tanzania, was disbanded in 1970. The University of Nairobi was inaugurated on 10 Dec. 1970. The University of Nairobi is now wholly supported by Kenya Government, and provides courses in arts, science, education, agriculture, medicine, art, architecture, engineering, veterinary, law and domestic science. In 1975–76 there were some 5,950 Kenya students at college in East Africa, 4,060 of them at University of Nairobi. In 1976, 5,813 Kenya students were enrolled in diploma and degree courses in education at the universities.

Health. In 1974 beds in hospitals (including mission hospitals) totalled 16,934. 603 health centres, including sub-centres and dispensaries, were in operation. Free medical service for all children and adult out-patients was launched in 1965.

DIPLOMATIC REPRESENTATIVES

Of Kenya in Great Britain (45 Portland Pl., London, W1N 4AS)
High Commissioner: Bethuel A. Kiplagat (accredited 31 July 1981).

Of Great Britain in Kenya (Moi/Haile Salassie Avc., Nairobi)
High Commissioner: Sir Leonard Allison KCVO, CMG.

Of Kenya in the USA (2249 R. St., NW, Washington, D.C., 20008)
Ambassador: John P. Mbogua.

Of the USA in Kenya (Cotts Hse., Wabera St., Nairobi)
Ambassador: William C. Harrop.

Of Kenya to the United Nations
Ambassador: Charles Gatere Maina.

Books of Reference

Kenya Economic Survey, 1981. Nairobi, 1982
Statistical Abstract. Government Printer, Nairobi, 1969
Standard English–Swahili Dictionary. Ed. Inter-territorial Language Committee of East Africa. 2 vols. London, 1939
Who's Who in Kenya 1982-1983. London, 1983
Arnold, G., *Kenyatta and the Politics of Kenya.* London, 1974.—*Modern Kenya.* London, 1982
Bienen, H., *Kenya: The Politics of Participation and Control.* Princeton Univ. Press, 1974
Bolton, K., *Haramble Country: A Guide to Kenya.* London, 1970
Collison, R. L., *Kenya.* [Bibliography] London and Santa Barbara, 1982
Harbeson, J. W., *Nation-Building in Kenya: The Role of Land Reform.* Northwestern Univ. Press, 1973
Hazlewood, A., *The Economy of Kenya: The Kenyatta Era.* OUP, 1980
Huxley, E., and Perham, M., *Race and Politics in Kenya.* Rev. ed. London, 1956
Langdon, S. W., *Multinational Corporations in the Political Economy of Kenya.* London, 1981
Leys, C., *Underdevelopment in Kenya.* London, 1975
Mutalik-Desai, P., *Economic and Political Development in Kenya.* Bombay, 1979
Rothchild, D., *Racial Bargaining in Independent Kenya.* OUP, 1973
Werlin, H. W., *Governing an African City: A Study in Nairobi.* New York, 1974

KIRIBATI

Capital: Tarawa
Population: 58,518 (1980)
GNP per capita: US$770 (1980)

HISTORY. The Gilbert and Ellice Islands were proclaimed a protectorate in 1892 and annexed (at the request of the native governments) as the Gilbert and Ellice Islands Colony on 10 Nov. 1915 (effective on 12 Jan. 1916). On 1 Oct. 1975 the former Ellice Islands severed its constitutional links with the Gilbert Islands and took a new name Tuvalu.

Internal self-government was obtained on 1 Nov. 1976 and independence achieved on 12 July 1979 as the Republic of Kiribati.

AREA AND POPULATION. Kiribati consists of 3 groups of coral atolls and one isolated volcanic island, spread over a large expanse of the Central Pacific with a total land area of 684 sq. km (264 sq. miles). It comprises Banaba or Ocean Island (5 sq. km), the 16 Gilbert Islands (295 sq. km), the 8 Phœnix Islands (55 sq. km), and 8 of the 11 Line Islands (329 sq.km), the other 3 Line Islands (Jarvis, Palmyra and Kingman Reef) being uninhabited dependencies of the US. Banaba, all 16 Gilbert Islands, and 3 atolls in the Line Islands (Teraina, Tabuaeran and Kiritimati—formerly Washington, Fanning and Christmas Islands respectively) are inhabited; their populations in 1980 were as follows:

Banaba (Ocean Is.)	300	Kuria	803	Arorae	1,527
Makin	1,419	Aranuki	850	Teraina	416
Butaritari	3,149	Nonouti	2,284	Tabuaeran	434
Marakei	2,335	Tabiteuea	4,157	Kiritimati	1,265
Abaiang	3,447	Beru	2,212	Aboard ships	255
Tarawa	22,148	Nikunau	1,829	In Nauru and Overseas	2,299
Maiana	1,688	Onotoa	2,034		
Abemama	411	Tamana	1,349		
				Total	58,518

The remaining 13 atolls have no permanent population; the 8 Phœnix Islands comprise Birnie, Rawaki (formerly Phœnix), Enderbury, Kanton (or Abariringa), Manra (formerly Sydney), Orona (formerly Hull), McKean and Nikumaroro (formerly Gardner), while the others are Malden and Starbuck in the Central Line Islands and Caroline, Flint and Vostok in the Southern Line Islands. The population is almost entirely Micronesian.

GOVERNMENT. Under the independence Constitution the republic has a unicameral legislature, comprising 36 members elected from 20 constituencies for a 4-year term. The *Beretitenti* (President) is both Head of State and of Government.

In Dec. 1982 the government was composed as follows:

President and Foreign Affairs: Ieremia Tabai, KCMG.

Vice-President, Home Affairs and Decentralisation: Teatao Teannaki. *Trade, Industry and Labour:* Boanareke Boanareke. *Finance:* Tiwau Awira. *Health and Family Planning:* Ataraoti Bwebwenibure. *Natural Resource Development:* Babera Kirata. *Education, Training and Culture:* Teewe Arobati. *Communications:* Taomati Iuta, OBE. *Minister for the Line and Phoenix Group of Islands:* Ieremia Tata. *Works and Energy:* Batika Toun. *Attorney-General:* R. L. Davey.

Flag: Red, with blue and white wavy lines in base, and in the centre a gold rising sun and a flying frigate bird.

INTERNATIONAL RELATIONS

Membership. Kiribati is a member of the Commonwealth and is an ACP state of the EEC.

ECONOMY

Budget. Revenue for the calendar year 1980 amounted to $A13,099,320; principal items: customs duties, $A2·9m.; direct taxation, $A700,000; taxation on phosphate, $A6,642,000. Expenditure in 1975 amounted to $A30,405,012.

Currency. The currency in use is the Australian *dollar.*

AGRICULTURE. The land is basically coral reefs upon which coral sand has built up, and then been enriched by humus from rotting vegetation and flotsam which has drifted ashore. The principal tree is the coconut, which grows prolifically on all the islands except some of the Phœnix Islands. Other food-bearing trees are the pandanus palm and the breadfruit. As the amount of soil is negligible, the only vegetable which grows in any quantity is a coarse calladium (alocasia) with the local name 'babai', which is cultivated most laboriously in deep pits. Pigs and fowls are kept throughout the Colony, and there is an abundance of fish.

Copra production is mainly in the hands of the individual landowner, who collects the coconut products from the trees on his own land.

Livestock (1979): Pigs, 10,000; poultry, 163,000.

TRADE. The principal imports are rice, flour, cotton piece-goods, tobacco and manufactured articles such as bicycles. The value of imports for 1977 amounted to $A11,565,685; exports, $A18,211,996. Exports are almost exclusively copra. The British Phosphate Commissioners withdrew from Banaba in Dec. 1979 and the Co-operative Federation is responsible for the export of copra.

Total trade between Kiribati and UK (British Department of Trade returns, in £1,000 sterling):

	1980	*1981*	*1982*
Imports to UK	47	8	79
Exports and re-exports from UK	413	573	321

COMMUNICATIONS

Shipping. The main ports are at Banaba and at Betio (Tarawa). In 1977, 256 vessels were handled at Betio.

Aviation. Air Tungaru is the national carrier. It operates services from Tarawa to the other 15 outer Islands in the Gilbertese Group, services varying between one and four flights each week. It also operates a weekly service to Christmas Island, in the Line Islands, which continues to Honolulu. A weekly service operates externally to Apia, Funafuti, Majuro, Nandi and Pago Pago. There are five flights per week to Nauru, while Air Nauru also has five flights from Nauru to Tarawa. There are air fields at Maiana and Christmas Island from which local services link to Tarawa.

Post and Broadcasting. There were 724 telephones in 1981. Radio Tarawa transmits daily in English and Gilbertese.

Cinemas. In 1974 there were 5 cinemas with a seating capacity of 2,000.

Newspapers. There was (1980) 1 weekly newspaper and 1 monthly.

JUSTICE, RELIGION, EDUCATION AND WELFARE

Justice. In 1978 Kiribati had a police force of 188 under the command of a Commissioner of Police. The Commissioner of Police is also responsible for prisons, immigration, fire service (both domestic and airport) and firearms licensing.

Religion. The majority of the population belong to the Roman Catholic or Protestant (Congregational) church; there are small numbers of Seventh-day Adventist and Baha'i.

Education (1979). The Government maintains a co-educational boarding school, the King George V and Elaine Bernacchi School at Tarawa, with (1977) 211 boys and 178 girls, 87 primary schools, with a total of 13,092 pupils, 1 government secondary school with 385 pupils, and 4 community high schools with 562 pupils attending the first year of a new rurally oriented 3-year post-primary course. The

Government also maintains a teachers' training college with 100 students and a marine training school with 180 full-time students. The Tarawa Technical Institute at Betio offers a variety of part-time and evening technical and commercial courses to about 500 students each year in addition to providing full-time courses for 34 students. The Marine Training School, also at Betio, offers training for 150 merchant seamen every year. There are in addition 4 Mission secondary schools with a total enrolment of 213 boys and 230 girls.

In 1978, 120 islanders were in overseas countries for secondary and further education or training.

Welfare. Government maintains free medical and other services. There are few towns, and the people are almost without exception landed proprietors, thus eliminating child vagrancy and housing problems to a large extent, except in the Tarawa urban area. Destitution is almost unknown.

DIPLOMATIC REPRESENTATIVES

Of Kiribati to Great Britain
High Commissioner: Atenroi Ba'teke, OBE (resides in Tarawa).

Of Great Britain in Kiribati (Tarawa)
High Commissioner: D. H. G. Rose.

Books of Reference

Kiribati, Aspects of History. Univ. of South Pacific, 1979
Bailey, E., *The Christmas Island Story.* London, 1977
Cowell, R., *Structure of Gilbertese.* Suva, 1950
Grimble, Sir Arthur, *A Pattern of Islands.* London, 1953.—*Return to the Islands.* London, 1957
Maude, H. E., *Of Islands and Men.* London, 1968.—*Evolution of the Gilbertese Boti.* Suva, 1977
Sabatier, E., *Astride the Equator.* Melbourne, 1978
Whincup, T., *Nareau's Nation.* London, 1979

KOREA

Han Kook

Capital: Seoul
Population: 38·72m. (1981)
GNP per capita: US$1,506 (1980)

HISTORY. Korea was united in a single kingdom under the Silla dynasty from 668. China, which claimed a vague suzerainty over Korea, recognized Korea's independence in 1895. Korea concluded trade agreements with the USA (1882), Great Britain, Germany (1883). After the Russo-Japanese war of 1904–5 Korea was virtually a Japanese protectorate until it was formally annexed by Japan on 22 Aug. 1910 thus ending the rule of the Yi dynasty which had begun in 1392.

Following the collapse of Japan in 1945, American and Russian forces entered Korea to enforce the surrender of the Japanese troops there, dividing the country for mutual military convenience into two portions separated by the 38th parallel of latitude. Negotiations between the Americans and Russians regarding the future of Korea broke down in May 1946.

On 25 June 1950 the North Korean forces crossed the 38th parallel and invaded South Korea. The same day, the Security Council of the United Nations asked all member states to render assistance to the Republic of Korea. When the UN forces had reached the Manchurian border Chinese troops entered the war on the side of the North Koreans on 26 Nov. 1950 and penetrated deep into the south. By the beginning of April 1951, however, the UN forces had regained the 38th parallel.

On 23 June 1951 Y. A. Malik, President of the Security Council, suggested a cease-fire, and on 10 July representatives of Gen. Ridgway met representatives of the North Koreans and of the Chinese Volunteer Army. An agreement was signed on 27 July 1953.

For the contributions of member-nations of the United Nations to the war, *see* THE STATESMAN'S YEAR-BOOK, 1954, p. 1195, and 1956, p. 1180.

On 16 Aug. 1953 the USA and Korea signed a mutual defence pact and on 28 Nov. 1956 a treaty of friendship, commerce and navigation.

On 4 July 1972 it was announced in Seoul and Pyongyang (North Korea) that talks had taken place aimed at 'the peaceful unification of the fatherland as early as possible'. By late 1975 no progress had been made.

A North Korean–UN agreement of 6 Sept. 1976 established a joint security area 850 metres in diameter, divided into 2 equal parts to ensure the separation of the two sides.

AREA AND POPULATION. South Korea is bounded north by the demilitarized zone (separating it from North Korea), east by the Sea of Japan, south by the Korea Strait (separating it from Japan) and west by the Yellow Sea. After a transfer of some frontier districts by the United Nations command on 12 Aug. 1954, the area of South Korea is now 98,992 sq. km (38,221 sq. miles). The population (census, 1 Nov. 1980) was 37,449,000 (male, 18,764,000).

The areas (in sq. km) and 1980 census populations of the provinces are as follows:

Province	*sq. km*	*1980*	*Province*	*sq. km*	*1980*
Seoul (city)	613	8,367,000	Chollapuk	8,051	2,288,000
Kyonggi	10,958	4,935,000	Chollanam	12,060	3,779,000
Kangwon	16,712	1,792,000	Kyongsangpuk	19,798	4,962,000
Chungchongpuk	7,437	1,424,000	Kyongsangnam	11,948	3,323,000
Chungchongnam	8,699	2,956,000	Pusan (city)	373	3,160,000
Cheju	1,830	463,000			

The chief cities (populations in 1980) are:

Seoul	8,366,756	Kwangchu	727,627	Seongnam	376,447
Pusan	3,160,276	Taejon	651,642	Chonchu	366,997
Taegu	1,607,458	Ulsan	418,415	Suweon	310,757
Incho'n	1,084,730	Masan	386,773		

CONSTITUTION AND GOVERNMENT. A new constitution was approved by national referendum on 22 Oct. 1980 and came into force on 27 Oct. It provides for a President with reduced executive powers, to be indirectly elected for a single 7-year term (by an electoral college of 5,271 directly-elected members), a State Council of ministers whom he appoints and leads, and a National Assembly (276 members) directly elected for 4 years (184 from 2-member constituencies and 92 by proportional representation).

The National Assembly elected on 25 March 1981 comprised 151 members of the Democratic Justice Party, 81 Democratic Korea Party, 25 Korean National Party, 8 from other parties and 11 independents.

President of the Republic: Gen. Chun Doo-Hwan (inaugurated March 1981).
Prime Minister: Kim Sang-Hyup
Deputy Prime Minister and Minister of Economic Planning Board: Kim Joon-Sung. *Foreign Affairs:* Lee Bum-Suk. *Home Affairs:* Rho Tae-Woo. *Finance:* Kang Kyung-Shik. *Justice:* Pae Myung-In. *National Defence:* Yun Sung-Min. *Agriculture and Fisheries:* Park Chong-Mun. *Education:* Lee Kyu-Ho. *Commerce and Industry:* Kim Dong-Whie. *Energy and Resources:* Suh Sang-Chul. *Construction:* Kim Chong-Ho. *Health and Social Affairs:* Kim Chung-Rye. *Labour:* Chung Han-Soo. *Transportation:* Lee Hui-Sung. *Communication:* Choi Soon-Dal. *Culture and Information:* Lee Chin-Ui. *Government Administration:* Park Chan-Keung. *Science and Technology:* Lee Chong-Oh. *National Unification Board:* Sohn Jae-Shik. *Sports:* Lee Won-Kyung. *First Minister of State:* Oh Se-Ung.

National flag: White charged in the centre with the *yang-um* in red and blue and with 4 black *pal-kwar* trigrams.

Local government: South Korea is divided into 9 provinces (Do) and 4 cities with provincial status (Seoul, Pusan, Taegu and Inchon); the provinces are sub-divided into 138 districts (Gun) and 46 cities (Si).

DEFENCE

Army. The Army, in 1983, had 520,000 men in 20 infantry divisions, 1 mechanized division, 2 armoured brigades equipped with 860 M-47, M-48 and M-60 tanks, 2 independent infantry brigades, 7 special forces brigades, 2 AA Atry brigades, 7 tank battalions, 36 artillery battalions, 2 SSM battalions, 2 SAM brigades. Reserves, 1·1m. and Popular Militia, 2·8m.

Navy. The Navy comprises 1 indigenously built new fast frigate, 12 aged (1943–46) *ex*-US destroyers, 7 equally old *ex*-US frigates (1 of destroyer-escort type and 6 former fast transports, *ex*-destroyer escorts), 9 fast missile patrol craft, 3 corvettes (*ex*-US fleet minesweepers), 8 fast attack craft, 10 new patrol vessels, 22 new patrol boats, 8 coastal minesweepers, 1 minesweeping boat, 20 landing ships, 4 landing craft, 1 repair ship, 6 surveying vessels, 2 salvage ships, 4 supply ships, 4 oilers, 13 auxiliary ships, 35 service craft, and 2 tugs. Nearly all South Korea's naval vessels are *ex*-US ships.

New construction projected includes submarines and frigates reportedly to be built in South Korean yards where light corvettes and fast attack craft are planned.

The South Korean Coastguard operates 25 vessels including rescue craft and tugs.

Personnel in 1983 exceeded 20,000 (2,400 officers and 17,600 ratings) in Navy; plus nearly 20,000 (2,300 officers and 17,700 men) in Marine Corps.

Air Force. With a 1982 strength of about 32,600 men, the Air Force is undergoing rapid expansion with US assistance. Its combat aircraft include about 55 F-4D/E Phantoms, 36 F-16 Fighting Falcons, 65 F-5A/B tactical fighters, more than 200

F-5E/F tactical fighters (being delivered from local production), 10 RF-5A reconnaissance fighters, 12 O-2A forward air control aircraft, 20 Tracker anti-submarine aircraft and 10 Hughes 500-D Defender ASW helicopters. There are also 6 C-130H turboprop transports, 25 C-123 piston-engined transports, 2 VIP HS 748s; UH-19, UH-1D and Bell 212 helicopters, and T-41, T-28, T-33 and T-37C trainers.

ECONOMY

Planning. The fifth 5-year social and economic plan (1982–86) aims at an annual growth rate of 7–8%.

Budget. The 1982 budget balanced at 9,578,100m. won.

Currency. Notes are issued by the Bank of Korea in denominations of 10,000, 5,000 and 500 *won* and coin in denominations of 500, 100, 50, 10, 5 and 1 *won*. The exchange rate is determined daily by the Bank of Korea. In March 1983, 751 *won* = US$1; 1,338 *won* = £1 sterling.

Banking. State-run banks include the Bank of Korea, the Korean Development Bank, the Medium & Small Industry Bank, the Citizen's National Bank, the Korea Exchange Bank, the National Agricultural Co-operatives Federation, the Federation of Fisheries Co-operatives serving as banking and credit institutions for farmers and fishermen, the Korea Housing Bank, the Export and Import Bank of Korea.

There are 5 commercial banks: the Bank of Seoul & Trust Co. Ltd, the Cho Heung Bank Ltd, the Commercial Bank of Korea, the Korea First Bank, the Hanil Bank, Ltd, the Taegu Bank Ltd. The Bank of Korea is the central bank and the only note-issuing bank, the authorized purchaser of domestically produced gold.

In addition, there are non-bank financial institutions consisting of 19 insurance companies, the Land Bank of Korea, the Credit Guarantee Fund, 10 short-term financial companies, 211 mutual credit companies, and the Merchant Banking Corporation.

ENERGY AND NATURAL RESOURCES

Electricity. Electricity generated (1981) was 40,207m. kwh.

Minerals. In 1979, 1,779 mining companies employed 79,229 people. Mineral deposits are mostly small, with the exception of tungsten; the Sangdong mine is one of the world's largest deposits of tungsten. Korea's output, 1981, included (in 1,000 tonnes): Anthracite coal, 19,994; iron ore, 494; tungsten concentrate, 4,761 short tons; kaolin, 225; copper ore, 7·6; lead ore, 23; gold refined, 1,264 kg; silver refined, 97,926 kg.

Agriculture. The arable land in South Korea comprises 24·4m. acres, of which over 5·5m. acres are cultivated.

The chief crops are rice (1981: 5·1m. tonnes), barley, wheat, beans, grain of all kinds and tobacco.

Output of tobacco manufactures, a government monopoly, was 144,000 tonnes in 1977.

Raising of livestock has recently become a flourishing industry. In 1981 cattle numbered 1,477,500.; pigs, 1,831,500.; poultry, 43m.

Fisheries. Deep-sea fishing fleets increased from 5 ships (600 gross tons) in 1962 to 455 ships (160,000 gross tons) in 1972 and 833 ships (316,000 gross tons) in 1975. In 1976, 849 Korean deep-sea fishing vessels were engaged based on 25 overseas fishing bases, 345 in the Atlantic, 143 in the Indian and 361 in the Pacific oceans.

INDUSTRY AND TRADE

Industry. Manufacturing industry, which (Dec. 1981) employed 2·9m. persons, was concentrated primarily in the production of light consumer goods for domestic consumption and export. This is now shifting towards heavy and petro-chemical industries rapidly.

Output of principal products in 1981 (in tonnes): Cotton yarn, 245,057; Portland cement, 23·5m.; fertilizers, 1·1m.

Trade Unions. Membership of trade unions at 31 Dec. 1977 was 954,682.

Commerce. In 1981 the total exports were equal to US$20,886m., while imports (including 'aid goods') were US$23,871m. Japan provided 24·1% and USA 23·1% of imports; USA received 26·7% of exports, Japan 16·5%.

Total trade between Korea and UK (British Department of Trade returns, in £1,000 sterling):

	1978	*1979*	*1980*	*1981*	*1982*
Imports to UK	214,358	269,706	244,583	325,650	321,691
Exports and re-exports from UK	129,141	145,319	101,103	158,811	167,752

Tourism. In 1981 there were 1,093,214 tourists. They spent the equivalent of US$447·64m.

COMMUNICATIONS

Roads. In 1979 there were 46,951 km of roads. Motor vehicles (1980) totalled 744,227 including 226,940 trucks, 42,463 buses, 249,102 passenger cars.

Railways. In 1981, 3,135 km of railways existed, including 428 km electrified, and in 1980 carried 431m. passengers and 49m. tonnes.

Shipping. In 1981, there were registered 81,484 vessels of 5,234,880 GRT, excluding state-owned fishing vessels and lease-purchased vessels.

Aviation. There are regular international services by Korean Air Lines, Japan Air Lines, Northwest Airlines, China Air Lines, Cathay Pacific Airways, Thai International, Singapore Airlines and Malaysian Airlines. In 1978, 2·7m. passengers and nearly 78m. tons of cargo were carried.

Post. Post offices total 2,082; telephones (all government-owned) were 4,007,000 in 1980; a direct distance dialling telephone system was completed in 1976.

Cinemas. In 1980 there were 447 with a seating capacity of 300,000.

Newspapers (1977). There were 28 daily papers, including 6 national dailies and 2 in English appearing in Seoul.

RELIGION, EDUCATION AND WELFARE

Religion. Basically the religions of Korea have been Animism, Buddhism (introduced A.D. 372) and Confucianism, which was the official faith from 1392 to 1910. Catholic converts from China introduced Christianity in the 18th century, but the ban on Roman Catholics was not lifted until 1882. Estimated Christian population in 1980 was 8·5m. (1,321,293 Catholics, 7,180,627 Protestants).

Education. In 1980 Korea had 5,658,002 pupils enrolled in 6,487 elementary schools, 2,471,997 pupils in 2,103 middle schools and 1,696,792 pupils in 1,355 high schools (including 605 vocational schools).

For higher education, 563,997 students who attended 224 universities, colleges and junior colleges. There are 121 graduate schools granting master's degrees in 2 years and doctor's degrees in 4 years, where 33,939 students attend. An Open University was inaugurated in March 1982.

The Korean language belongs to the Ural–Altaic group, is polysyllabic, agglutinative and highly developed syntactically. The modern Korean alphabet of 10 vowels and 14 consonants forms a script known as Hangul.

Health. In Dec. 1980 there were 25,979 physicians (including herb doctors), 3,620 dentists, 4,222 midwives, 101,445 nurses (including assistant nurses), 4,712 technicians and 21,392 pharmacists. There were 11,181 hospitals and clinics.

DIPLOMATIC REPRESENTATIVES

Of Korea in Great Britain (4 Palace Gate, London, W8 5NF)
Ambassador: Dr Young Hoon Kang (accredited 25 Feb. 1981).

Of Great Britain in Korea (4 Chung-Dong, Chung-Ku, Seoul)
Ambassador and Consul-General: John A. L. Morgan, CMG.

Of Korea in the USA (2320 Massachusetts Ave., NW, Washington, D.C., 20008)
Ambassador: Byong Hyon Lew.

Of the USA in Korea (Sejong-Ro, Seoul)
Ambassador: Richard L. Walker.

Books of Reference

A Handbook of Korea. 4th ed. Seoul, 1982
Economic Planning Board. *Guide to Investment in Korea.* Seoul, 1980
Korea Annual 1982. 19th ed. Seoul, 1982
Korea: Its Land, People and Culture of All Ages. Seoul, 1960
Korea: Past and Present. Seoul, 1972
Korea Statistical Year Book. Seoul, 1981
UNESCO Korean Survey. Seoul, 1960
Guide to Geographical Names in Korea (Chosen). United States Board of Geographical Names. Washington, 1945
Major Economic Indicators, 1979–80. Seoul, 1980
Monthly Statistics of Korea. Seoul, 1980
Bartz, P. M., *South Korea.* OUP, 1972
Lew, H. J., *New Life Korean–English, English–Korean Dictionary.* 2 vols. Seoul, 1947–50
Martin, S. F. (ed.), *A Korean–English Dictionary.* Yale Univ. Press, 1968
Wright, E. R., *Korean Politics in Transition.* Univ. of Washington Press, 1976

NORTH KOREA

Capital: Pyongyang
Population: 16m. (1975)
GNP per capita: US$730 (1978)

Chosun Minchu-chui Inmin Konghwa-guk

HISTORY. In northern Korea the Russians, arriving on 8 Aug. 1945, one month ahead of the Americans, established a Communist-led 'Provisional Government'. The newly created Korean Communist Party merged in 1946 with the New National Party into the Korean Workers' Party. In July 1946 the KWP, with the remaining pro-Communist groups and non-party people, formed the United Democratic Patriotic Front. On 25 Aug. 1948 the Communists organized elections for a Supreme People's Assembly, both in Soviet-occupied North Korea (212 deputies) and in US-occupied South Korea (360 deputies, of whom a certain number went to the North and took their seats). A People's Democratic Republic was proclaimed on 9 Sept. 1948. In 1973 North Korea was admitted to WHO, and in 1973 granted observer status at the UN. Talks between North and South Korea on reunification began in Feb. 1980, but were broken off by the North in Sept. 1980. In 1981 North Korea announced a new reunification plan, but plans put forward by South Korea were rejected in Jan. 1982.

AREA AND POPULATION. The area of North Korea is 47,225 sq. miles (122,370 sq. km). Population in 1975, 16m. Rate of population increase, 2·8% per annum. Death rate, 1979: 4·4 per mille. Marriage is discouraged before the age of 32 for men and 29 for women. Expectation of life 1980, 70 (men), 76 (women). The capital is Pyongyang, with 1·5m. inhabitants.

The country is divided into 13 administrative units: 4 cities (Pyongyang, Chongjin, Hamheung and Kaesong) and 9 provinces (capitals in brackets): South Pyongan (Nampo), North Pyongan (Sinuiji), Jagang (Kanggye), South Hwanghai (Haeju), North Hwanghai (Sariwon), North Kangwon (Wonsan), South Hamgyong (Hamheung), North Hamgyong (Chongjin), Yanggang (Hyesan).

CONSTITUTION AND GOVERNMENT. The political structure is based upon the Constitution of 27 Dec. 1972, which supersedes that of 1948 as amended in 1954 and 1955. The Constitution provides for a Supreme People's Assembly elected every 4 years by universal suffrage. Citizens of 17 years and over can vote and be elected. Elections were held in 1948, 1957, 1962, 1972, 1977 and 1 March 1982. At the latter it was claimed that 100% of the electorate voted for the candidates presented. There are 615 deputies.

In practice the country is ruled by the Korean Workers' (*i.e.*, Communist) Party which elects a Central Committee which in turn appoints a Politburo, the first 5 members of which constitute its Standing Committee. In March 1983 this was composed of: Marshal Kim Il Sung, *General Secretary of the Party, President of the Republic, Supreme Commander of the Armed Forces*; Kim Il *(Vice-President of the Republic)*; O Jin U *(Defence Minister)*; Kim Jong Il (Kim Il Sung's son and designated successor); Li Jong Ok *(Prime Minister)*; Pak Sung Chul *(Vice-President of the Republic);* Rim Chun Chu; So Chol; O Baek Ryong; Kim Jung Rin; Kim Yong Nam; Chon Mun Sop; Kim Hwan; Yon Hyong Muk; O Guk Ryol; Kang Song San *(First Deputy Prime Minister)*; Paek Hak Rim Choe Yong Rim; So Yun Sok. There are also 16 'alternate members'.

Ministers not full members of the Politburo include Ho Dam *(Deputy Prime Minister, Foreign Minister)*; Kye Ung Tae *(Deputy Prime Minister)*; Yun Gi Jong *(Finance)*; Choe Jong Gun *(Trade)*; Chong Song Nam *(Foreign Economic Affairs)*; Hong Song Ryong *(Deputy Prime Minister, Chairman, State Planning Commission)*; Lee Jin Su *(Public Security)*.

In 1981 the Party had some 2m. members.

There are also the puppet religious Chongu and Korean Social Democratic Parties and various organizations combined in a Fatherland Front.

National flag: Blue, red and blue horizontal stripes separated by narrow white bands. The red stripe bears a white circle within which is a red 5-pointed star.

National anthem: The Song of General Kim Il Sung.

Local government is administered by People's Assemblies at city (or province), county (or district) and *ri* (town, workers' or rural commune) level. The latest elections were on 6 March 1983. There are 27,846 local deputies.

DEFENCE. Military service is compulsory at the age of 17 and lasts 3–4 years.

Army. In 1983 the Army was believed to number about 700,000 men, organized in 2 armoured and 38 infantry divisions, with 2,500 Soviet tanks and support units; it has about 300 'Guideline' surface-to-air missiles, and Soviet Sam-2 rockets and Frog-5 missiles.

Navy. The Navy comprises 18 diesel-powered patrol submarines (14 *ex*-Chinese and 4 *ex*-Soviet), 4 small frigates, 18 missile boats, 175 fast torpedo boats, 150 fast gunboats, 28 patrol vessels, 30 coastal patrol craft, 20 light gunboats, 9 utility landing craft, 100 minor landing craft, 30 trawlers and auxiliaries and 100 service craft. Up to 5 small submarines are reported as built locally. Personnel in 1983 totalled 31,000 officers and men, plus 40,000 reservists.

Air Force. With Chinese and Soviet assistance, the Air Force has been increased to a total of about 930 aircraft and 51,000 personnel. Equipment is believed to include about 120 supersonic MiG-21 interceptors, 250 MiG-17s for ground attack and reconnaissance, 30 Su-7 fighter-bombers, 70 Il-28 twin-jet light bombers, and a variety of transport and training aircraft and helicopters.

ECONOMY

Planning. Past plans: 3-year plan, 1954–56, rehabilitated the country after the Korean War (1950–53); 5-year plan, 1957–61; 7-year plan, extended in 1966 to 1970; 6-year plan, 1971–76, during which an average annual industrial growth rate of 16·3% was claimed. 1977 was a year of planning hiatus ('readjustment'), but it was finally announced in that year that all the 1971–76 plan targets had been reached, and a 7-year plan for 1978–84 was adopted which gives priority to the fuel and mining industries, foreign trade development and transport, and expects an annual industrial growth rate of 12·1%.

Budget (in 1m. won) for calendar years:

	1976	*1977*	*1978*	*1979*	*1980*	*1981*	*1982*
Revenue	12,626	13,789	15,923	17,478	19,139	20,479	22,546
Expenditure	12,326	13,349	15,923	16,972	18,837	20,479	22,546

In 1978, 15·1% of budget expenditure was on defence. Average monthly income was 70 won in 1970. Personal taxation was abolished in 1974.

Currency. The monetary unit is the *won*, divided into 100 *jun*. In March 1983, US$1 = 0·94 *won*; £1 = 1·49 *won*.

Weights and Measures. While the metric system is in force traditional measures are in frequent use. The *jungbo* = 1 hectare; the *ri* = 3,927 metres.

ENERGY AND NATURAL RESOURCES

Electricity. There are thermal power stations at Pyongyang, Unggi and Chongchongang. There are hydro-electric plants at Kanggye, Unbong and Sodusu, and another is under construction at Taedonggang. Output in 1975, was 28,000m. kwh. Hydroelectric potential exceeds 8m. kw. In 1972 thermal power generation accounted for 38% of total output. An oil pipeline from China was opened in Jan. 1976.

Minerals. North Korea is rich in minerals (coal, iron, lead, zinc, copper, tungsten, nickel, manganese and graphite) and has important metallurgical works. Oilwells went into production in 1957. Coalmines are being enlarged and modernized.

There are large opencast workings at Yonghung. 50m. tonnes of coal were mined in 1975. 7·4m. tonnes of iron ore and 12,000 tonnes of copper ore were extracted in 1969.

Agriculture. Only 2m. hectares of the land area are cultivable. Intensive water and soil conservancy is practised and land reclamation from the sea has a high priority. In 1946 all Japanese-owned and landowners' property above 5 *jungbo* was distributed among some 724,500 landless peasants and smallholders.

Collectivization took place between 1954 and 1958, when there were 13,309 'co-operatives' averaging 130 *jungbo*. In 1958 these were merged into 3,843 larger units *(ri)*, averaging 500 *jungbo*, modelled on the Chinese communes. 90% of the cultivated land is farmed by co-operatives. A law of 1977 proclaims that there is no private property in land; land belongs either to the State or to co-operatives, and it is intended gradually to transform the latter into the former. Livestock farming is mainly carried on by large state farms.

Some 3m. *jungbo* are under cultivation, of which 1m. *jungbo* have regular irrigation. There were 37,600 km of irrigation canals in 1976. The 6-year plan (1971–76) extended irrigation so as to make possible 2 rice harvests a year. In 1974 the number of tractors (15 h.p. units) was between 70,000 and 80,000. The technical revolution in agriculture (nearly 95% of ploughing, etc., is mechanized) considerably increased the yield of grain (sown on 2·3m. *jungbo* of land); this was 9m. tonnes in 1979 (mainly rice). Maize is being fostered to replace millet as the major dry-field crop.

Livestock (FAO estimates for 1980): 950,000 cattle, 2·1m. pigs.

Forestry. Between 1961 and 1970, 800,000 hectares were afforested, 500,000 hectares of oil-bearing trees are scheduled for planting.

Fishery. The annual catch is about 1·6m. tonnes. There is a fishing fleet of about 3,400 modern motor and sailing fishing craft, equipped with factory and refrigerator ships.

INDUSTRY AND TRADE

Industry. Industries were intensively developed by the Japanese, notably cotton spinning, hydro-electric power, cotton, silk and rayon weaving, and chemical fertilizers. Production (in tonnes) in 1975: Chemical fertilizers, 3m.; cement, 8m.; steel, 4m.; textiles, 600m. sq. metres. Industrial workers make up some 40% of the total work force. There is a steel complex at Kangson with an annual productive capacity of 4m. tonnes. Average wage 1977: Workers, 70 won per month; managers, 200 won per month. Workers have 2 weeks, managers 4 weeks, annual holiday.

Commerce. Exports in 1979: US$1,553m.; imports, US$1,337m. 51·5% of trade was with Communist countries (85% in 1971). In 1978 North Korea's indebtedness was estimated at US$2,000m. An agreement regulating the repayment of North Korea's US$390m. debt to Japan over 10 years was signed in Sept. 1979. The chief exports are metal ores and products, the chief imports machinery and petroleum products.

Exports to the USSR in 1980 (and 1979) were worth 284·2m. (256·2m.) roubles; imports from the USSR, 287·9m. (235·4m.) roubles.

Total trade between North Korea and UK (British Department of Trade returns, in £1,000 sterling):

	1977	*1978*	*1979*	*1980*	*1981*	*1982*
Imports to UK	3,262	1,494	961	391	701	235
Exports and re-exports from UK	1,288	851	808	981	727	3,857

COMMUNICATIONS

Roads. Motor transport is very important, as about one-third of the inhabited places are without railway communications. Roads are bad and mostly unpaved; statistics about their length, etc., are lacking. In 1961 lorries and coaches transported 17·7m. tons of freight.

Railways. Extensive railway construction was carried out under the Japanese occupation. Because these lines served strategic purposes, however, and because of the separation of North and South Korea, not all of them were suitable for inclusion in the present railway network. The two trunk-lines Pyongyang–Sinuiji and Pyongyang–Myongchon are both electrified, and the Pyongyang–Sariwon trunk is in course of electrification. The 'Wonra' line runs from Wonsan to Rajin and is electrified from Myongchon to Rajin. The Chagangsamgang–Unbong line was opened in 1980. Lines are under construction from Pukchong to Toksong, from Palwon to Kujang and Kanggye *via* Hyesan to Musan. The Hyesan–Samsok section of the latter opened to traffic in 1971. In 1979 there were some 4,400 km of track, about 35% electrified. In 1980, 87% of trains were hauled by electricity and 30·6m. tonnes were transported in 1969. Electrification of the 100 km Chongjin–Puryong–Musan line has been completed.

Aviation. There are weekly flights to Moscow and Peking. Domestic lines: Pyongyang–Hamheung–Chongjin.

Shipping. The leading ports are Chongjin and Heungnam (near Hamheung). Nampo, the port of Pyongyang, has been dredged and expanded. Pyongyang is connected to Nampo by railway and river.

The biggest navigable river is the Yalu, 698 km up to the Hyesan district.

Broadcasting. In 1961 there were 600,000 radio receivers. The Pyongyang central broadcasting station was rebuilt about 1955.

Newspapers. The party newspaper is *Nodong* (or *Rodong*) *Sinmun* (Labour Party News. Circulation about 1m.).

JUSTICE, EDUCATION AND WELFARE

Justice. The judiciary consists of the Supreme Court, whose judges are elected by the Assembly for 3 years; provincial courts; and city or county people's courts. The procurator-general, appointed by the Assembly, has supervisory powers over the judiciary and the administration; the Supreme Court controls the judicial administration.

Education. In 1975–76 the 10-year system of free compulsory universal technical education was extended to 11 years (1 pre-school year, 4 years primary education starting at the age of 6, followed by 6 years secondary).

In 1970–71, 9,260 schools of all grades were attended by 3·2m. pupils, including 214,000 students in institutes of higher education, two-thirds of whom were studying technical and engineering subjects. There were some 100,000 teachers. In 1975–76 there were 5–6m. children in the 11-year system and nearly 1m. students in higher education. In 1980 there were 170 institutes of higher education, including 3 universities—Kim Il Sung University (founded 1946), Kim Chaek Technical University, Pyongyang Medical School—and an Academy of Sciences (founded 1952).

In 1977–78 Kim Il Sung University had some 17,000 students.

Health. Medical treatment is free. In 1980 there were 23·3 doctors and 120 hospital beds per 10,000 population.

Books of Reference

Baik Bong, *Kim Il Sung: Biography.* 3 vols. New York, 1969–70
Brun, E., and Hersh, J., *Socialist Korea: A Case Study in the Strategy of Economic Development.* New York, 1976
Chung, C.-S., (ed.), *North Korean Communism: A Comparative Analysis.* Seoul, 1980
Chung, J. S.H., *The North Korean Economy: Structure and Development.* Stanford, 1974
Kim Han Gil, *Modern History of Korea.* Pyongyang, 1979
Kim, I. J., *Communist Policies in North Korea.* New York, 1975
Kim Il Sung, *Selected Works.* Pyongyang, 1965 in progress
Kim, Y. S., (ed.), *The Economy of the Korean Democratic People's Republic, 1945–1977.* Kiel, 1979
Kiyosaki, W. S., *North Korea's Foreign Relations.* New York, 1976
Lee, C.-S., *The Korean Workers' Party: A Short History.* Stanford, 1978
McCormack, G., and Selden, M. (eds.), *Korea North and South: The Deepening Crisis.* New York, 1978
Scalapino, R. A., and Lee, C.-S., *Communism in Korea. Part I: The Movement. Part II: The Society.* Univ. of Calif. Press, 1972

KUWAIT

Capital: Kuwait
Population: 1·46m. (1981)
GNP per capita: US$22,840 (1980)

Dowlat al Kuwait

HISTORY. The independent and sovereign State of Kuwait is situated on the north-western coast of the Arabian Gulf. The ruling dynasty was founded by Shaikh Sabah al-Owel, who ruled from 1756 to 1772. In 1899 the then ruler Shaikh Mubarak concluded a treaty with Great Britain wherein, in return for the assurance of British protection, he undertook not to alienate any of his territory without the agreement of Her Majesty's Government. In 1914 the British Government recognized Kuwait as an independent government under British protection. On 19 June 1961 an agreement reaffirmed the independence and sovereignty of Kuwait and recognized the Government of Kuwait's responsibility for the conduct of internal and external affairs; the agreement of 1899 was terminated and Her Majesty's Government expressed their readiness to assist the Government of Kuwait should they request such assistance.

AREA AND POPULATION. Area, about 9,375 sq. miles (24,280 sq. km); the total population at the census of 1980 was 1,355,827, of which about 59% were non-Kuwaitis.

The country is divided into 3 governorates, Kuwait (the capital, 80,405 population 1970; metropolitan area, 217,749), Ahmadi and Hawali (106,542).

The Neutral Zone (3,560 sq. miles, 5,700 sq. km), jointly owned and administered by Kuwait and Saudi Arabia from 1922 to 1966, was partitioned between the two countries in May 1966, but the exploitation of the oil and other natural resources will continue to be shared.

RULER. HH Shaikh Jabir al-Ahmad al-Jabir al-Sabah the 13th Amir of Kuwait, succeeded on 31 Dec. 1977.

CONSTITUTION AND GOVERNMENT. Elections for a National Assembly of 50 members were held on 27 Jan. 1975 but in Aug. 1976 the Amir dissolved the Assembly and at the same time parts of the Constitution were suspended. Elections were held on 24 Feb. 1981 for the National Assembly.

The official language is Arabic; English is used as the second language.

The Cabinet in March 1981 was composed as follows:

Prime Minister: Shaikh Saad al-Abdullah al-Salem al-Sabah.

Deputy Prime Minister, Foreign Affairs and Information: Shaikh Sabah al-Ahmad al-Jaber al-Sabah. *Interior:* Shaikh Nawwaf al-Ahmad al-Jaber al-Sabah. *Defence:* Shaikh Salem al-Sabah al-Salem al-Sabah. *Oil:* Shaikh Ali al-Khalifah al-Sabah. *Public Health:* Abdel-Rahman Abdullah al-Awadi. *Social Affairs, Labour and Housing:* Hamad Isa al-Rajib. *Public Works:* Abdullah al-Rashid. *Electricity and Water:* Khalaf Ahmad al-Khalaf. *Justice, Legal Affairs and Administrative Affairs:* Shaikh Salman al-Duaij al-Sabah. *Finance and Planning:* Abdel-Latif Yousef al-Hamad. *Education:* Yacoub Yousef al-Ghunaim. *Commerce and Industry:* Jassem al-Marzouk. *Communications:* Isa al-Mazidi. *Awqaf and Islamic Affairs:* Ahmad Saad al-Jasser. *Minister of State (Cabinet Affairs):* Abdel-Aziz Hussain.

Flag: Three horizontal stripes of green, white, red, with a black trapezium based on the hoist.

DEFENCE

Army. Kuwait maintains a small, well-equipped and mobile army of 2 brigades and 3 mechanical infantry battalions (10,000 men in 1983).

Air Force. From a small initial combat force the Air Force has grown rapidly. It has 1 squadron with 17 Mirage F1-C fighters and 2 Mirage F1-B 2-seat trainers; and 2 squadrons with 36 A-4KU/TA-4KU Skyhawk attack aircraft. Other equipment includes 2 DC-9 jet transports, 2 L-100-20 and 4 L-100-3D Hercules turboprop transports, 9 BAC 167 Strikemaster armed jet trainers, 10 Puma and 23 missile-armed Gazelle helicopters. Hawk surface-to-air missiles are in service. Personnel strength (1983) about 1,900.

INTERNATIONAL RELATIONS

Membership. Kuwait is a member of UN, the Arab League, OPEC and OAPEC.

ECONOMY

Budget. The financial year runs 1 April–31 March. In 1981–82 revenue, KD 5,279m.; expenditure, KD 5,279m.

Currency. The Kuwait *dinar* of 1,000 *fils* replaced the Indian external rupee on 1 April 1961. In March 1983, £1 sterling = KD 0·444; US$1 = KD 0·293. Coins in circulation are, 1, 5, 10, 20, 50 and 100 fils.

Banking. Seven banks operate in Kuwait: the Bank of Kuwait and Middle East, the Kuwait National Bank, the Commercial Bank of Kuwait Ltd, the Gulf Bank of Kuwait, the Alahli Bank, The Burgan Bank, Savings and Credit Bank.

Weights and Measures. The metric system was adopted in 1962.

ENERGY AND NATURAL RESOURCES

Oil. Kuwait oil comes mainly from the Burgan oilfields, the residential and administrative centre for oil operations being at Ahmadi. Oil reserves in Kuwait and its share of the neutral zone was estimated at 77,000m. bbls in 1975. The Kuwait Petroleum Gas and Energy Co. (KPGEC) formed in 1974 as a result of the Government's take-over of 60% of oil production, is controlling all oil exploration and the processing and marketing of oil and gas. Production of crude oil (in 1m. tonnes); 1979, 113·2; 1980, 71·2.

Gas. Production (1980) 310,066m. cu. ft.

Agriculture. Major crops (production, 1981, in tonnes) are melons (5,000), tomatoes (12,000), onions (3,000), dates (1,000), radishes, clover.

Livestock (1981): Cattle, 11,000; sheep, 158,000; goats, 110,000; poultry, 6·2m.

Fisheries. Shrimp fishing is becoming one of the important non-oil industries.

INDUSTRY AND TRADE

Industry. Industries, apart from oil, include boat building, fishing, food production, petrochemicals, gases and construction. The manufacture or import of alcoholic drinks is prohibited.

Labour. Of the working population 75% are foreigners.

Commerce. The port of Kuwait formerly served mainly as an entrepôt for goods for the interior, for the export of skins and wool, and for pearl fishing. Entrepôt trade continues but, with the development of the oil industry, is declining in importance. Pearl fishing is now on a small scale. Dhows and launches of traditional construction are still built.

In 1979 total imports were US$4,600m.; exports, US$17,564m.

Total trade between Kuwait and UK (British Department of Trade returns, in £1,000 sterling):

	1978	*1979*	*1980*	*1981*	*1982*
Imports to UK [1]	621,530	743,149	655,024	477,262	104,793
Exports and re-exports from UK	332,278	233,438	258,696	281,203	333,247

[1] Including oil.

COMMUNICATIONS

Roads. Number of private cars (1977) 379,100.

Aviation. Kuwait Airways flew over 9,000 flights in 1980, carrying 1·76m. passengers and 25,000 tonnes of freight. British Airways, Kuwait Airways, Iraqi Airways, Iranian Airways, United Arab Airlines, Middle East Airlines, Saudi Arabian Airways, Lebanese International Airways, Air Liban, Air India, Lufthansa, Japanese Airlines, TWA, PIA, Aden Air Lines, Air France, Alitalia, SAS, Swiss Air, SABENA, KLM and Gulf Aviation operate scheduled air services.

Shipping. Ships of 27 lines make regular calls at Kuwait.

Post and Broadcasting. Wireless communication was taken over by the Kuwait Government in 1956, internal postal services in Feb. 1958 and external postal services in 1959. There were (1981), 214,763 telephones in Kuwait. There are a broadcasting and a television station.

Cinemas. In 1976 there were 10 cinemas with a seating capacity of 13,000.

EDUCATION AND WELFARE

Education. In 1976 there were 201,907 pupils at 326 government schools. In 1969–70 there were 2,200 students at teacher-training institutes (354 teachers) and teacher-training colleges had 100 students (28 teachers). A technical college was opened in 1954 and in 1970 had 931 students (212 teachers). The University of Kuwait had 6,500 students in 1976.

Health. Medical services are free to all residents. There were (1976) 20 hospitals with over 4,764 beds in the State and 481 clinics and health centres. The Ministry of Health employs 1,219 physicians and 122 dentists. Expenditure on health services 1975–76, KD 45m.

DIPLOMATIC REPRESENTATIVES

Of Kuwait in Great Britain (45 Queen's Gate, London, SW7)
Ambassador: Ghazi Mohammed Amin Al-Rayes (accredited 12 Feb. 1981).

Of Great Britain in Kuwait (Arabian Gulf St., Kuwait)
Ambassador: M. R. Melhuish, CMG.

Of Kuwait in the USA (2940 Tilden St., NW, Washington, D.C., 20008)
Ambassador: Shaikh Saud. Naser Al-Sabah.

Of the USA in Kuwait (PO Box 77, Kuwait)
Ambassador: François M. Dickman.

Of Kuwait to the United Nations
Ambassador: Abdalla Abou Al-Hassan.

Books of Reference

Arabian Year Book. Kuwait, 1978
Annual Statistical Abstract of Kuwait. Kuwait
Education in Kuwait, 1969–70. Kuwait Government Press, 1971
Kuwait Economy 1968–69. Kuwait Government Press, 1970
The Oil of Kuwait: Facts and Figures. 3rd ed. Kuwait Government Press, 1970
Khouja, M. W., and Sadler, P. G., *The Economy of Kuwait.* London, 1979
Sabah, Y. S. F., *The Oil Economy of Kuwait.* London, 1980
Shiber, S. G., *The Kuwait Urbanization.* Kuwait Government Press, 1964
Winstone, H. V. F., and Freeth, Z., *Kuwait: Prospect and Reality.* London, 1972

LAOS

Capital: Vientiane
Population: 3·52m. (1979)
GNP per capita: US$90 (1978)

HISTORY. The Lao People's Democratic Republic was founded on 2 Dec. 1975. Until that date Laos was a Kingdom, once called Lanxang (the land of a million elephants).

In 1893 Laos became a French protectorate and in 1907 acquired its present frontiers. In 1941 French authority was suppressed by the Japanese. When the Japanese withdrew in 1945 an independence movement known as Lao Issara (Free Laos) set up a government under Prince Phetsarath, the Viceroy of Luang Prabang. This government collapsed with the return of the French in 1946 and the leaders of the movement fled to Thailand.

Under a new Constitution of 1947 Laos became a constitutional monarchy under the Luang Prabang dynasty, and in 1949 became an independent sovereign state within the French Union. Most of the Lao Issara leaders returned to Laos but a few remained in dissidence under Prince Souphanouvong, who allied himself with the Vietminh and subsequently formed the 'Pathet Lao' (Lao State) rebel movement.

The war in Laos from 1953 to 1973 between the Royal Lao Government (supported by American bombing and Thai mercenaries) and the Patriotic Front *Pathet Lao* (supported by large numbers of North Vietnamese troops) ended in 1973 when an agreement and a protocol were signed. A provisional coalition government was formed by the two sides in 1974. However, after the communist victories in neighbouring Vietnam and Cambodia in April 1975, the *Pathet Lao* took over the running of the whole country, although maintaining the façade of a coalition. On 29 Nov. 1975 HM King Savang Vatthana signed a letter of abdication and the People's Congress proclaimed a People's Democratic Republic of Laos. For the history of *Pathet Lao* and the military intervention of the Vietminh, *see* THE STATESMAN'S YEAR-BOOK, 1971–72, pp. 1126–28 and 1975–76 ed., pp. 1115–16.

AREA AND POPULATION. Laos is a landlocked country of about 91,400 sq. miles (236,800 sq. km) bordered on the north by China, the east by Vietnam, the south by the People's Republic of Democratic Kampuchea (Cambodia) and the west by Thailand and Burma. Apart from the Mekong River plains along the border of Thailand, the country is mountainous, particularly in the north, and in places densely forested. The climate is of a tropical monsoon type with a wet season from May to Oct. and a dry one from Nov. to April. Most of northern Laos receives about 40–80 in. of rainfall annually, while parts of the Bolovens Plateau in southern Laos have over 150 in.

There has been no complete census in Laos, but estimates place the population at about 3·5m. The most heavily populated areas are the Mekong River plains by the Thailand border. Otherwise, the population is sparse and scattered, particularly in the northern provinces, and the eastern part of the country has been depopulated by war. The majority of the population is officially divided into 4 groups: about 56% Lao-Lum (Valley-Lao), 34% Lao-Theung (Lao of the mountain sides); and 9% Lao-Soung (Lao of the mountain tops), who comprise the Meo and Yaoe. Other minorities include Vietnamese, Chinese, Europeans, Indians and Pakistanis.

The Lao-Lum and Lao-Tai belong to the Lao branch of the Tai peoples, who migrated into South-East Asia at the time of the Mongol invasion of South China. The valley Lao are Buddhists, following the Hinayana (Theravada) form. The majority of the Lao-Theungma diverse group consisting of many tribes but mostly belonging to the Mon-Khmer group—are animists.

The Meo and Yaoe live in northern Laos. Far greater numbers live in both North Vietnam and China, having migrated over the last century. Their religions have strong Confucian and animistic features but some are Christians.

There are 13 provinces. Compared with other parts of Asia, Laos has few towns. The administrative capital and largest town is Vientiane, with a population of (census, 1973) 176,637; estimate (1979) 90,000. Other important towns are Luang Prabang, the royal capital, 44,244; Pakse, 44,860, in the extreme south, and Savannakhet, 50,690.

Language: Lao is the official language of the country. The liturgical language of Theravada Buddhism is Pali.

GOVERNMENT. On 1–2 Dec. 1975 a national congress of 264 people's representatives met and declared Laos a People's Democratic Republic. A People's Supreme Council was appointed to draw up a new Constitution.

President: Prince Souphanouvong.

Prime Minister, Secretary General of the Central Committee of the Lao People's Revolutionary Party: Kaysone Phomvihane.

There are 4 deputy prime ministers.

National flag: Three horizontal stripes of red, blue, red, with blue of double width with in the centre a large white disc.

National anthem: Peng Sat Lao (Hymn of the Lao People).

Provincial Administration: All provincial administration is in the hands of the Lao People's Revolutionary Party. Orders come from the Central Committee through a series of 'People's Revolutionary Committees' at the province, town and village level.

DEFENCE

Army. The 'Lao People's Army' is about 46,000 strong. It is organized in 1 armoured, 64 infantry, 4 artillery and 4 anti-aircraft battalions. There are about 46,000 active North Vietnamese troops in Laos.

Navy. In 1983 there were nominally 4 river squadrons comprising 42 small craft of 6 different types, of which 14 were in commission and 28 in reserve. Naval personnel totalled 500 officers and ratings.

Air Force. Since 1975, the Air Force has received aircraft from the USSR, including about 20 MiG-21 fighters, 6 An-24 and 3 An-26 turboprop transports and 10 Mi-8 helicopters. They may be supplemented by a few of the T-28D piston-engined light strike aircraft, AC-47 gunships, C-47 transports, T-41D trainers and UH-34 helicopters supplied by the USA to the former régime. Personnel strength, about 1,000.

INTERNATIONAL RELATIONS

Membership. Laos is a member of UN.

Aid. Foreign aid in 1981 (estimate), was US$72·1m.; 1980, 78·2m.; 1979, 75m.

ECONOMY

Planning. Following the completion of the original 3-year Development Plan 1978–80, a 5-year plan (1981–85), which is basically a list of investment projects, has been drawn up by the government.

Budget. Total revenue 1981, K.1,190m.; total expenditure, K.2,152m.

Currency. The currency is the *kip*. 1 *kip* = 100 *att*. Coinage, 1, 2 and 5 *att*; banknotes, 1, 5, 10, 20 and 50 *kip*. The official rate of exchange was (March 1983) K.10 = US$1; £1 = K15·18, but the black market rate in 1982 was at least 300% higher.

ENERGY AND NATURAL RESOURCES

Electricity. Only a few towns in Laos have an electricity service. A power plant with a capacity of 8,000 kw. is installed at Vientiane, but there are only small thermo-electric plants in other towns. The Nam Ngum Dam situated about 45 miles north of Vientiane was inaugurated in Dec. 1971 with an initial installed capacity of 30,000 kw. and a planned ultimate capacity of 130,000 kw. The generators of Phase II of the scheme were brought into operation in 1978, giving an installed capacity of 110,000 kw. Transmission lines to Vientiane and to Thailand have been constructed. Other sources of electric power are the dams on the Sedone River about 20 miles north of Pakse and on the Nam Dong about 5 miles south of Luang Prabang, with installed capacities of 2,400 and 1,200 kw. respectively. Production (1979) 840m. kwh.

Minerals. Various minerals are found, but only tin is mined to any significant extent at present, and only at 2 mines (Tin exports (1980) US$500,000). There are extremely rich deposits of high-quality iron in Xieng Khouang province and potash near Vientiane.

Agriculture. The chief products are rice (production in 1980, 1m. tonnes; 1978, estimate, 420,000 tonnes), maize (production 27,200 tonnes), tobacco (4,200 tonnes), cotton (2,100 tonnes), citrus fruits, sticklack, benjohn tea and in the Boloven plateau coffee (2,070 tonnes), potatoes, cardamom and cinchara. Opium is produced but is the subject of legislation designed to control its manufacture.

Livestock (1981): Cattle, 445,000; buffaloes, 879,000; horses, 34,000; pigs, 1,176,000; goats, 54,000; poultry, 5·6m.

Forestry. The forests, which cover nearly 50% of the country, produce valuable woods such as teak. Their potential is being exploited with Swedish and Soviet aid.

INDUSTRY AND TRADE

Industry. Industry is limited to beer, rubber sandals, cigarettes, matches, soft drinks, plastic bags, saw-mills, rice-mills, weaving, pottery, distilleries, ice, plywood, bricks, etc. but most factories have been working at limited capacity in recent years. Plans for increased production are limited by lack of funds and skilled machine operators.

Commerce. In 1981 imports amounted to US$119·7m. and exports to US$21·2m. The main imports were food and beverages, petroleum products and agricultural and other machinery. The chief supplying countries were Thailand, Japan, USA and Indonesia. The main exports were timber, coffee and electricity.

Total trade between Laos and UK (British Department of Trade returns, in £1,000 sterling):

	1977	*1978*	*1979*	*1980*	*1981*	*1982*
Imports to UK	4	17	49	32	65	355
Exports and re-exports from UK	340	1,527	264	720	542	880

COMMUNICATIONS

Roads. In 1981 the national road network, which was nearing completion, consisted of 1,300 km paved, 5,300 km gravel and 3,600 km earth roads.

Railways. There is no railway in Laos, but the Thai railway system extends to Nongkhai, on the Thai bank of the Mekong, which is connected by ferry with Thadeua about 12 miles east of Vientiane and to Udon Ratchathani which is close to the southern border of Thailand/Laos.

Aviation. Lao Aviation provides scheduled domestic air services linking major towns in Laos and international services to Bangkok, Phnom Penh and Hanoi. Thai Airways, Aeroflot and Air Vietnam provide direct flights from Bangkok, Hanoi, Rangoon, Ho Chi Min City and Moscow.

Shipping. The river Mekong and its tributaries are an important means of transport, but rapids, waterfalls and narrow channels often impede navigation and make trans-shipments neccessary.

Telecommunications. There is a radio network in Laos as well as an experimental TV service with the main station at Vientiane. A ground station constructed near Vientiane under the Soviet aid programme enables USSR television programmes to be received in the capital. It also provides a telephone service to Hanoi and Eastern Europe.

In 1974 there were 5,506 telephones in Laos.

RELIGION, EDUCATION AND WELFARE

Religion. The majority of the population is Buddhist (Hinayana).

Education. At the end of the 1978–79 school year there were 5,900 elementary schools (451,000 pupils); 260 secondary schools (60,400 pupils); 86 senior high schools (7,800 pupils); 72 nursery schools (3,400 pupils); 24 teacher training schools (8,300 students) and 7 technical schools (2,000 students).

Literacy has improved from 40% in 1975, 65% in 1978 to 85% in 1981 according to official reports.

There is 1 teachers' training college, 1 college of education, 1 school of medicine, 1 agricultural college and an advanced school of Pali.

Health. In 1981 there were about 30 qualified doctors and 8,729 hospital beds.

DIPLOMATIC REPRESENTATIVES

Of Laos in Great Britain (5 Palace Green, London, W8 4QA)
Chargé d'Affaires: Thongkhoun Sengphachanh.

Of Great Britain in Laos (Rue Pandit J. Nehru, Vientiane)
Ambassador: W. B. J. Dobbs.

Of Laos in USA (2222 S St., NW, Washington, D.C., 20008)
Chargé d'Affaires: Bounkeun Sangsomsak.

Of USA in Laos (Rue Bartholonie, Vientiane)
Chargé d'Affaires: William W. Thomas, Jr.

Of Laos to the United Nations
Ambassador: (Vacant).

Books of Reference

La Constitution du Laos. Notes et Etudes. 1957

International Conference on the Settlement of the Laotian Question. Geneva, 12th May 1961–23rd July 1962 (Cmnd. 1828). HMSO, 1962

Declaration and Protocol on the Neutrality of Laos. Geneva, 23rd July 1962 (Cmnd. 2025). HMSO, 1963

White Book on the Violations of the Geneva Accords of 1962 by the Government of North Vietnam. Ministry of Foreign Affairs, Vientiane, 1968

Halpern, Joel M., *Economy and Society of Laos: Brief Survey.* Yale Univ. Press, 1964.—*Government, Politics and Social Structure in Laos.* Yale Univ. Press, 1964

Zasloff, J. J., *The Pathet Lao: Leadership and Organization.* Lexington, Toronto and London, 1973

LEBANON

al-Jumhouriya al-Lubnaniya

Capital: Beirut
Population: 2·6m. (1980)
GNP per capita: US$1,070(1974)

HISTORY. After 20 years' French mandatory regime, Lebanon was proclaimed independent at Beirut on 26 Nov. 1941. On 27 Dec. 1943 an agreement was signed between representatives of the French National Committee of Liberation and of Lebanon, by which most of the powers and capacities exercised hitherto by France were transferred as from 1 Jan. 1944 to the Lebanese Government. The evacuation of foreign troops was completed in Dec. 1946.

In early May 1958 the opposition to President Chamoun, consisting principally (though not entirely) of Moslem pro-Nasserist elements, rose in insurrection; and for 5 months the Moslem quarters of Beirut, Tripoli, Sidon and the northern Bekaa were in insurgent hands. On 15 July the US Government acceded to President Chamoun's request and landed a considerable force of army and marines who re-established the authority of the Government.

In the subsequent presidential elections, Gen. Fouad Chehab replaced President Chamoun and a return to normality enabled US forces to be withdrawn.

In 1970 Suleiman Frangié succeeded President Helou for a 6-year term.

Israeli attacks on Lebanon resulted from the presence and activities of armed Palestinian resistance units. Internal problems, which had long been latent in Lebanese society, were exacerbated by the politically active Palestinian population and by the deeply divisive question of the Palestine problem itself. An attempt to regulate the activities of Palestinian fighters through the secret Cairo agreement of 1969 was frustrated both by the inability of the Government to enforce its provisions and by an influx of battle-hardened fighters expelled from Jordan in Sept. 1970. A further attempt to control the guerrillas in 1973 also failed. From March 1975, Lebanon was beset by civil disorder causing considerable loss of life and economic life was brought to a virtual standstill.

By Nov. 1976 it was estimated that 40,000 people has been killed and up to 100,000 injured. By the end of the year, however, large scale fighting had been brought to an end by the intervention of the Syrian-dominated Arab Deterrent Force which ensured sufficient security to permit Lebanon to establish quasi-normal conditions under President Sarkis. Large areas of the country, however, remained outside Governmental control, including West Beirut which was the scene of frequent conflict between opposing militia groups. The South, where the Arab Deterrent Force could not deploy, remained unsettled and subject to frequent Israeli attacks. In March 1978 there was an Israeli invasion following a Palestinian attack inside Israel. Israeli troops eventually withdrew in June, but instead of handing over all their positions to UN Peacekeeping Forces they installed Israeli-controlled Lebanese militia forces under Maj. Sa'ad Haddad in border areas. Severe disruption continued in the South. In June 1982, following on the attempted assassination of the Israeli ambassador in London, Israeli forces once again invaded, this time in massive strength, and swept through the country, eventually laying siege to and devastatingly bombing Beirut. In Sept. Palestinian forces, together with the PLO leadership, evacuated Beirut. On 23 Aug. Bashir Gemayel was elected President of Lebanon in succession to Sarkis. On 14 Sept. he was assassinated. His brother, Amin Gemayel, was elected in his place on 21 Sept.

AREA AND POPULATION. Lebanon is a mountainous country about 135 miles long and varying between 20 and 35 miles wide, bounded on the north and east by Syria, on the west by the Mediterranean and on the south by Israel. Between the two parellel mountain ranges of Lebanon and Anti-Lebanon lies the fertile Bekaa Valley. About one-half of the country lies at an altitude of over 3,000 ft.

The area of Lebanon is estimated at 10,400 sq. km (3,400 sq. miles) and the population at 2·6m. (1980, estimate). The principal towns, with estimated population, are: Beirut (the capital), 702,000; Tripoli 175,000; Zahlé, 46,800; Saida (Sidon), 24,740; Tyre, 14,000.

Vital statistics. 1971: Births. 76,099; deaths, 12,799; marriages, 16,516; divorces, 1,382.

The official language is Arabic. French and, increasingly, English are widely spoken in official and commercial circles.

CONSTITUTION AND GOVERNMENT. Lebanon is an independent republic. The first Constitution was established under the French Mandate on 23 May 1926. It has since been amended in 1927, 1929, 1943 (twice) and 1947. It is a written constitution based on the classical separation of powers, with a President, a single chamber elected by universal adult suffrage, and an independent judiciary. The Executive consists of the President and a Prime Minister and Cabinet appointed by him. The system is, however, adapted to the peculiar communal balance on which Lebanese political life depends. This is done by the electoral law which allocates deputies according to the confessional distribution of the population, and by a series of constitutional conventions whereby, *e.g.*, the President is always a Maronite Christian, the Prime Minister a Sunni Moslem and the Speaker of the Chamber a Shia Moslem. There is no highly developed party system other than on religious confessional lines.

President of the Republic: Amin Gemayel (elected on 21 Sept. and took office on 23 Sept. 1982).

Cabinet appointed 7 Oct. 1982:

Prime Minister: Chafik Al Wazzan.
Foreign Minister: Elie Salem.

National flag: Three horizontal stripes of red, white, red, with the white of double width and bearing in the centre a green cedar of Lebanon.

National anthem: Kulluna lil watan lil 'ula lil' alam (words by Rashid Nachleh, tune by Mitri El-Murr).

DEFENCE

Army. The Army strength was officially estimated in 1983 at 22,250. The Army comprises 2 armoured reconaissance, 12 infantry and 1 artillery battalions. The *gendarmerie* was about 5,000 and the police force about 600. Army and *gendarmerie* use mainly British, American and French equipment.

Navy. The Navy consisted in 1983 of 4 patrol boats and 6 coastal patrol craft. Personnel totalled 400 officers and men.

Air Force. The Air Force has about 1,250 men and 50 aircraft. In addition to a single combat squadron of Hunter jet fighter-bombers, it has (in storage) 9 Mirage III supersonic fighters and 1 Mirage 2-seat trainer. Other aircraft include 1 Dove light transport, 12 Alouette II and III and 10 Agusta-Bell 212 helicopters, and Fouga Magister jet and piston-engined Bulldog trainers.

INTERNATIONAL RELATIONS

Membership. Lebanon is a member of UN and the Arab League.

ECONOMY

Planning. Since the civil war a Development and Reconstruction Council has been responsible for co-ordinating all efforts.

Budget. The budget for 1979 provides for a total expenditure of £Leb.3,103·91m.

(2,583·66m. in 1978). A draft budget for 1980 envisages a total expenditure of £Leb4,109·5m.

Currency. The Lebanese *pound*, divided into 100 *piastres*, is issued by the Banque du Liban, which commenced operations on 1 April 1964. There is a fluctuating official rate of exchange, fixed monthly (March 1983: £Leb.6·21 = £1 sterling; £Leb.4·16 = US$1), this in practice is used only for the calculation of *ad-valorem* customs duties on Lebanese imports and for import statistics. For other purposes the free market is used.

On 15 Oct. 1979 the note circulation was £Leb.3,664·5m.

Banking. Beirut was an important international financial centre, and there were about 80 banks registered with the central bank in 1979, including 2 British banks, the British Bank of the Middle East and the Chartered Bank. As a result of the civil war in 1975–76, Beirut lost much of its status as an international and regional banking centre; in general only local offices for banks remain.

Weights and Measures. The use of the metric system is legal and obligatory throughout the whole of the country. In outlying districts the former weights and measures may still be in use. They are: 1 *okiya* = 0·47 lb.; 6 *okiyas* = 1 *oke* = 2·82 lb.; 2 *okes* = 1 *rottol* = 5·64 lb.; 200 *okes* = 1 *kantar*.

ENERGY AND NATURAL RESOURCES

Oil. There are 2 oil refineries in Lebanon, one at Tripoli, which refines oil brought by ship from Iraq, and the other at Sidon, which refines oil brought from Saudi Arabia by a pipeline owned by the Trans-Arabian Pipeline Co. These refineries received 2m. tonnes of crude oil in 1977 and their production is normally sufficient to meet the country's requirements of refined fuel.

Minerals. Iron ore exists but is difficult to work. Other minerals known to exist are iron pyrites, copper, bituminous shales, asphalt, phosphates, ceramic clays and glass sand; but the available information is of doubtful value.

Agriculture. Lebanon is essentially an agricultural country, although owing to its physical character only about 38% of the total area of the country is at present cultivated. The forests of the past have been denuded by exploitation and the unrestricted grazing of goats, and only about 80,000 hectares of indifferent timber remain, and soil erosion is considerable.

The estimated yield (in 1,000 tonnes) of the main crops in 1979 was as follows: Citrus fruits, 320; apples, 135; grapes, 135; potatoes, 112; sugar-beet, 108; wheat, 40; bananas, 18; olives, 15.

Livestock (estimated, 1981): Goats, 445,000; sheep, 148,000; cattle, 60,000; camels, 1,000; pigs, 20,000; horses, 2,000; donkeys, 10,000; mules, 4,000.

INDUSTRY AND TRADE

Industry. Industry suffered badly during the civil war. The manufacturing industry was small but had doubled in size in the 10 years before the war. As a result of the war some industrial concerns have closed but a few light industries had been established in 1977–79.

Commerce. Foreign as well as local wholesale and retail trade is the principal source of income in Lebanon and provides about 31% of the total. Because of the protectionist policies followed in some neighbouring countries, this sector has been declining, the sectors to gain being those of banking, real estate, government and services.

In 1978 imports were estimated at £Leb.5,220m.; exports were valued at £Leb.1,639m. Imports came mainly from USA, Federal Republic of Germany, France, Italy and UK. Exports went mainly to Saudi Arabia, Kuwait, Syria, Libya and Iraq.

Total trade between Lebanon and UK (British Department of Trade returns, in £1,000 sterling):

	1978	*1979*	*1980*	*1981*	*1982*
Imports to UK	8,058	9,892	9,076	7,470	24,237
Exports and re-exports from UK	58,893	65,793	70,692	61,945	67,640

Customs duties are usually imposed on an *ad-valorem* basis: the receipts are the Lebanese Government's main source of income; actual yield in 1978, £Leb.509m. The considerable adverse balance of trade is offset by invisible receipts, including foreign capital investment in Lebanese real estate, remittances from émigrés and receipts from tourism and international arbitrage operations.

Tourism. Receipts from tourism were £Leb.573m. in 1973; since 1975 they have been negligible, this sector having suffered badly as a result of the war.

COMMUNICATIONS

Roads. The main roads in Lebanon are good. The surface is normally of asphalt and they are well maintained in normal times. In Dec. 1971 there were 570 km of international roads, 1,420 km of main roads and 4,310 km of secondary and local roads, all asphalted. The main arterial routes are the north–south coastal road and the west–east trunk road (Beirut to Damascus).

At 31 Dec. 1978 there were 282,404 cars and taxis, 2,592 buses and 28,553 commercial vehicles.

Railways. There are 3 railway lines in Lebanon, all operated by the *Office des Chemins de Fer de l'Etat Libanais* (CFL): (1) Nakoura–Beirut–Tripoli (standard gauge); the Nakoura–Sidon section has been idle since the establishment of Israel: (2) a narrow-gauge line running from Beirut to Riyak in the Bekaa Valley (now closed) and thence to Damascus, Syria; (3) a standard-gauge line from Tripoli to Homs and Aleppo in Syria, providing access to Ankara and Istanbul. From Homs a branch of the CFL line extends south and re-enters Lebanon, terminating at Riyak. Total length 417 km.

Aviation. Beirut International Airport is used by many international airlines which connect Lebanon with most countries in the world. Extensive local services cover the Middle East, Persian Gulf and Europe. There are 2 national airlines, Middle East Airlines/Air Liban and Trans-Mediterranean Airways. In 1978, 24,500 flights passed through Beirut international airport (1974: 44,406), carrying a total of 1,405,600 passengers (1974: 2,806,632).

Shipping. Beirut is by far the largest and busiest port. In 1978, 1,786 vessels and 1,753,000 tonnes of goods were handled. Activity in the port of Tripoli is growing due to increased movements in goods and petroleum. The small port of Sidon in the south, near to the closed Lebanese-Israeli frontier, is at present of little importance. General activity since the civil war has been reduced to about 60%, but was increasing in late 1977. However, sporadic fighting in Beirut closed the port at times in 1978 and 1979.

Post and Broadcasting. There is an automatic telephone system in Beirut, Tripoli, Sidon, Zahlé and several other towns and villages, which is being extended to all parts of the country. There are no telegraph, postal or telephone communications with Israel. Number of telephones (1978), 231,000.

The state radio transmits in Arabic, French, English and Armenian. Before 1978 there were 2 commercial television stations, transmitting in Arabic, French and English. In 1978 they were amalgamated into a new company in which the Government has a 50% shareholding. There were 325,000 sets in 1975.

Cinemas (1973). There were 161 cinemas with a seating capacity of about 77,400.

Newspapers (1977). There were about 30 daily newspapers in Arabic, 2 in French, 1 in English and 4 in Armenian, with a total circulation of 215,000.

RELIGION, EDUCATION AND WELFARE

Religion. Probably less than half the population are Christians, some of whom have been indigenous since the earliest time of Christianity. There were in 1958,

792,000 Christians, of whom 424,000 were Maronites, 150,000 Greek Orthodox, 69,000 Armenians, 91,000 Greek and Roman Catholics, 14,500 Armenian Catholics, 14,000 Protestants. Moslems numbered 536,000, of whom 286,000 were Sunnis and 250,000 Shiites. There were also 88,000 Druzes and 6,600 Jews.

Education. Government schools in 1970 comprised 1,290 primary and secondary schools. There were also 1,484 private primary and secondary schools. There are also 5 teachers' training colleges and 5 universities, namely the Lebanese (State) University, the American University of Beirut, the French University of St Joseph (founded in 1875), the Arab University, a branch of Alexandria University and Beirut University College. The French Government runs the École Supérieure de Lettres and the Centre d'Études Mathématiques. The Maronite monks run the University of the Holy Spirit at Kaslik.

The Lebanese Academy of Fine Arts includes schools of architecture, art, music, political and social science.

Health. In 1973 there were 2,300 physicians and 8,000 hospital beds.

DIPLOMATIC REPRESENTATIVES

Of Lebanon in Great Britain (21 Kensington Palace Gdns., London, W8 4QM)
Ambassador: Ahmad al-Hajj.

Of Great Britain in Lebanon (Ave. de Paris, Ras Beirut)
Ambassador: D. A. Roberts, CMG, CVO.

Of Lebanon in the USA (2560–28th St., Washington, D.C., 20008)
Ambassador: Khalil Itani.

Of the USA in Lebanon (Corniche at Rue Ain Mreisseh, Beirut)
Ambassador: Robert S. Dillon.

Of Lebanon to the United Nations
Ambassador: Kesrewan Lebaki.

Books of Reference

Statistical Information: Import and export figures are produced by the Conseil Supérieur des Douanes. The Service de Statistique Généralé (M. A. G. Ayad, *Chef du Service*) publishes a quarterly bulletin (in French and Arabic) covering a wide range of subjects, including foreign trade, production statistics and estimates of the national income.

Cowan, J. M., *Dictionary of Modern Arabic.* Wiesbaden, 1961
Deeb, M., *The Lebanese Civil War.* New York, 1980
Hitti, P. K., *A Short History of Lebanon.* London, 1965
Khairallah, S., *Lebanon.* [Bibliography] Oxford and Santa Barbara, 1979
Murray, G., *Lebanon: The New Future.* London, 1974
Salem, E. A., *Modernization Without Revolution: Lebanon's Experience.* Indiana Univ. Press, 1973
Salibi, K. S., *Modern History of Lebanon.* London, 1965.—*Crossroads to Civil War: Lebanon 1958–76.* New York, 1976

National Library: Dar el Kutub, Parliament Sq., Beirut.

LESOTHO

Capital: Maseru
Population: 1·3m. (1980)
GNP per capita: US$390 (1980)

HISTORY. Basutoland first received the protection of Britain in 1868 at the request of Moshesh, the first paramount chief. In 1871 the territory was annexed to the Cape Colony, but in 1884 it was restored to the direct control of the British Government through the High Commissioner for South Africa.

On 4 Oct. 1966 Basutoland became an independent and sovereign member of the Commonwealth under the name of the Kingdom of Lesotho.

AREA AND POPULATION. Lesotho is bounded on the west by the Orange Free State, on the north by the Orange Free State and Natal, on the east by Natal and East Griqualand, and on the south by the Cape Province. The altitude varies from 5,000 to 11,000 ft. The climate is dry and rigorous, with extremes of heat and cold both seasonal and diurnal. The temperature varies between 93° F (34° C) and 3° F (– 16° C). The rainfall is variable, the average being about 29 in. per annum.

The area is 11,716 sq. miles (30,340 sq. km). Lesotho is a purely African territory, and the few European residents are government officials, traders, missionaries and artisans.

The census taken on 12 April 1976 showed a total population of 1,246,815 persons. Estimate (1980) 1·3m.

The capital is Maseru (population, 1976, 45,000).

The official languages are Sesotho and English.

CONSTITUTION AND GOVERNMENT. On 4 Oct. 1966 the country became the Kingdom of Lesotho, with the Paramount Chief as King.

Parliament consists of the National Assembly (60 members elected by adult suffrage) and a Senate (22 principal chiefs and 11 members nominated by the King). The general election held on 30 April 1965 returned 31 members of the National Party, 25 members of the Congress Party and 4 members of the Marematlou Freedom Party. The elections of 27 Jan. 1970 were declared invalid on 31 Jan. Parliamentary rule, with a National Assembly of nominated members, was reintroduced in April 1973.

A Constitution is being drafted.

King of Lesotho: Moshoeshoe II.

Prime Minister: Chief Leabua Jonathan. *Minister of the Interior:* Chief Sekhonyana 'Maseribane.

The College of Chiefs settles the recognition and succession of Chiefs and adjudicates cases of inefficiency, criminality and absenteeism among them.

National flag: Blue with a white Basuto hat; in the hoist 2 vertical strips of green and red.

Local Government. The country is divided into 10 districts as follows: Maseru, Qacha's Nek, Mokhotlong, Leribe, Butha–Buthe, Teyateyaneng, Mafeteng, Mohale's Hoek, Quthing, Thaba–Tseka. Each district is subdivided into wards, most of which are presided over by hereditary chiefs allied to the Moshoeshoe family.

District councils, established in 1944, were abolished on 17 Jan. 1966; their functions are now exercised by officials appointed by the Ministry of Local Government.

INTERNATIONAL RELATIONS

Membership. Lesotho is a member of UN, OAU, the Commonwealth and is an ACP state of the EEC.

ECONOMY

Planning. A third 5-year plan (1981–84), to exploit natural resources and promote investment was being prepared in 1981.

Budget. The financial year ends on 31 March.

	1970–71 [1]	*1971–72*	*1972–73*	*1973–74*	*1974–75*	*1977–78* [1]
Revenue	11,704,510	12,409,839	16,052,000	26,516,000	33,320,000	48,906,000
Expenditure	11,041,480	12,440,471	17,187,000	20,900,800	24,203,000	34,465,000

[1] Estimates.

The major items of expenditure in 1977–78 were education (R8·8m.), agriculture (R4·6m.), internal security and justice (R4·1m.) and health (R2·8m.). The revenue situation was greatly improved by the re-negotiation of the Republic of South Africa's customs agreement in 1970. Of the 1977–78 revenue R32m. was generated from domestic sources including the customs union.

Currency. The currency is the *Loti* (plural *Maloti*) divided into 100 *Lisente* which is at par with the South African *Rand*. In March 1983, £1 = 1·65 *Maloti*; US$1 = 1·09 *Maloti.*

Banking. The Standard Bank of South Africa and Barclays Bank International have branches at Maseru, Mohale's Hoek and Leribe. The Lesotho Bank has branches throughout the country.

ENERGY AND NATURAL RESOURCES

Electricity. A feasibility study was announced (1982) to be undertaken by the Republic of South Africa and Lesotho to divert river waters from Lesotho to South Africa and to provide hydro-electricity for Lesotho.

Agriculture. The chief crops are wheat, maize and sorghum; barley, oats, beans, peas and other vegetables are also grown. The land is held in trust for the nation by the King and may not be alienated.

Soil conservation and the improvement of crops and pasture are matters of vital importance. A total area of 1,006,817 acres has been protected against soil erosion by means of terracing, training banks, tree planting and grass strips. Efforts are being made to secure the general introduction of rotational grazing in the mountain area.

Livestock (1981): Cattle, 600,000; horses, 102,000; donkeys, 105,000; sheep, 1·2m.; goats, 780,000; mules, 1,000.

INDUSTRY AND TRADE

Industry. Industrial development is progressing under the National Development Corporation. Diamond exports, 1978, were valued at R16,695,446.

Commerce. Lesotho, Botswana and Swaziland are members of the South African customs union, by agreement dated 29 June 1910.

Total values of imports and exports into and from Lesotho (in R1,000):

	1974	*1975*	*1976*	*1977*
Imports	79,120	117,300	179,600	199,374
Exports	9,809	9,200	14,600	12,180

Principal imports in 1977 were food, livestock, drink and tobacco (R43m.), machinery and transport equipment (R24m.), mineral fuels and lubricants (R18m.); principal exports were wool and mohair (R4·5m.) and diamonds.

The majority of international trade is with the Republic of South Africa.

Total trade between Lesotho and UK (British Department of Trade returns, in £1,000 sterling):

	1979	*1980*	*1981*	*1982*
Imports to UK	105	340	489	682
Exports and re-exports from UK	2,233	394	1,483	1,260

Tourism. In 1974 there were 75,000 visitors. The Lesotho National Development

Corporation is helping the development of tourism and more hotels and resorts are planned.

COMMUNICATIONS

Roads. There were (1975) 125 miles of tarred roads and 529 miles of gravel-surfaced roads along the western border of Lesotho, with outlets to the border ports of exit. Regular motor services of the South African Railways operate between Zastron (OFS) and Quthing, Zastron (OFS) and Mohale's Hoek, and between Fouriesburg (OFS) and Butha Buthe. In addition to the main roads there were (1975) 1,029 miles of tracks leading to trading stations and missions. Communications into the mountainous interior are by means of bridlepaths suitable only for riding and pack animals, but a mountain road of 80 miles has been constructed, and some parts are accessible by air transport, which is being used increasingly. In 1977 there were 11,509 motor vehicles.

Railways. A railway built by the South African Railways, 1 mile long, connects Maseru with the Bloemfontein–Natal line at Marseilles.

Aviation. There is a scheduled passenger service between Maseru and Jan Smuts Airport, Johannesburg operated jointly by Lesotho National Airways and SAA. There are also 30 airstrips for light aircraft.

Post and Broadcasting. There were 3,726 telephones on 1 Jan. 1975. Radio Lesotho transmits daily in English and Sesotho. Radio receivers (1976), about 20,000.

Cinemas. In 1971 there were 2 cinemas with a seating capacity of 800.

JUSTICE, RELIGION, EDUCATION AND WELFARE

Justice. An appeal court for Lesotho was established at Maseru on 4 Oct. 1966.

The police force on 31 Dec. 1972 had an establishment of 111 officers and subordinate officers and 1,194 other ranks.

Religion. About 70% of the population are Christians, 40% being Roman Catholics.

Education. Education is largely in the hands of the 3 main missions (Paris Evangelical, Roman Catholic and English Church), under the direction of the Ministry of Education. In 1974 the total enrolment in 1,087 primary schools was 218,038; in 84 secondary schools, 14,908; in 7 teacher-training schools enrolment was 510 in 1972. University education was provided at the University of Botswana, Lesotho, Swaziland, which now has a campus in each of the 3 countries. Total enrolment in 1974–75 was 538, of which 322 were Basotho students. In 1975 a National University was established. Recurrent government expenditure on education was estimated at R3,948,700 in 1973–74. Bursaries are provided at all stages for secondary, teacher-training and university work. In 1972, 106 Basotho were studying at universities and places of higher education, outside Lesotho.

Health. The government medical staff of the territory consists of 1 Permanent Secretary for Health and chief medical officer, 1 medical superintendent, 26 medical officers, 1 medical officer of health and 6 specialist physicians and surgeons.

There are 10 government hospitals staffed by 333 matrons, sisters and nurses. There is accommodation for 2,106 patients in government hospitals. The 316-bed Queen Elizabeth II hospital in Maseru was completed in 1957. There are 9 mission hospitals subsidized by the Government with 729 beds. Health centres and mountain dispensaries provide outpatient medical facilities and maternity services to people living in remote areas. The leper settlement 5 miles out of Maseru had 189 patients at the end of 1972.

Typhus and plague occur.

DIPLOMATIC REPRESENTATIVES

Of Lesotho in Great Britain (10 Collingham Rd., London, SW5)
High Commissioner: Joseph Molelekoa Kaibe Mollo (accredited 13 May 1982).

Of Great Britain in Lesotho
High Commissioner: C. C. Clemens, MC.

Of Lesotho in the USA (1601 Connecticut Ave., NW, Washington, D.C., 20009)
Ambassador: N. Tau.

Of the USA in Lesotho (P.O. Box MS 333, Maseru, 100)
Ambassador: Keith L. Brown.

Of Lesotho to the United Nations
Ambassador: Molefi Ntlhoki.

Books of Reference

Statistical Information: Bureau of Statistics, PO Box 455, Maseru, Lesotho.
Lesotho: Report for 1968. Maseru, 1969
Ambrose, A., *The Guide to Lesotho.* Johannesburg and Maseru, 1976
Ashton, H., *The Basuto.* 2nd ed. OUP, 1967
Hailey, Lord, *The Republic of South Africa and the High Commission Territories.* OUP, 1963
Jones, D., *Aid and Development in Southern Africa.* London, 1977
Khaketla, B. M., *Lesotho 1970.* London, 1971
Spence, J. E., *Lesotho.* OUP, 1968
Stevens, C., *Food, Aid and the Developing World.* London, 1979

LIBERIA

Capital: Monrovia
Population: 1·9m. (1981)
GNP per capita: US$520 (1980)

HISTORY. The Republic of Liberia had its origin in the efforts of several American philanthropic societies to establish freed American slaves in a colony on the West African coast. In 1822 a settlement was formed near the spot where Monrovia now stands. On 26 July 1847 the State was constituted as the Free and Independent Republic of Liberia. The new State was first recognized by Great Britain and France, and ultimately by other powers.

AREA AND POPULATION. Liberia has about 350 miles of coastline, extending from Sierra Leone, on the west, to the Ivory Coast, on the east, and it stretches inland to a distance, in some places, of about 250 miles. The boundaries were determined by the Anglo-Liberian agreement of 1885 and the Franco-Liberian agreements of 1882 and 1907–10. In 1911 the territory of Kailahun was transferred to Sierra Leone in exchange for a strip on the south side of Mano River, which now is the boundary.

The total area is about 43,000 sq. miles (112,600 sq. km). A census taken in 1978 gave the total population as 1,715,973 (872,105 males). Estimate (1981) 1·9m. The indigenous natives belong in the main to 4 principal stocks: Mendetan, West Atlantic, Mande-fu, and Kru. These are in turn subdivided into 16 major tribes, namely: Bassa, Belle, Gbandi, Mende, Gio, Dey, Mano, Gola, Kpelle, Kissi, Krahn, Kru, Loma, Mandingo, Vai and Grebo.

Monrovia, the capital, had (1981) a population of 306,460 and is administered as a city corporation by a mayor to be elected by popular vote. It is one of the 4 ports of entry along the 350 miles of coast, the others being Buchanan (Grand Bassa), River Cess, Greenville (Sinoe), Harper (Maryland). Other towns are Kolba City, Voinjama, Tubmanburg, Bensonville, Zorzor, Kakata, Suakoko, Gbarnga, Ganta, Sanniquellie, Saclape, Tappita, Robertsport, Bendja, Yekepa and Zwedru.

The country is divided into 9 counties and 6 territories and the federal district of Monrovia.

CONSTITUTION AND GOVERNMENT. The Constitution of the Republic is modelled on that of the US. The executive power is vested in a President and the legislative power in a legislature of 2 Houses, the Senate (27 members) and the House of Representatives (71 members). The President is elected for 8 years in the first instance, the House of Representatives for 4 and the Senate for 6 years. A Legislative Act was approved on 22 July 1974, setting up a National Commission to give consideration to possible changes in the Constitution in preparation for a return to civilian rule in 1985.

On 12 April 1980, President Tolbert was assassinated; his government was overthrown and the Constitution suspended. President Tolbert's party, the True Whig Party, was formed in 1860 and had been in power since 1870. Recent economic decline and pressure for change had undermined the Government. In March 1980, the newly formed People's Progressive Party was banned and its leaders arrested. The *coup* was led by Master-Sergeant Doe who was later installed as Head of State and Commander-in-Chief of the army.

Executive power is vested in the Head of State and a Cabinet of 17 which is supervised by a People's Redemption Council.

Head of State and Commander-in-Chief: Samuel Kanyon Doe.
Foreign Minister: Dr Henry Boima Fahnbulleh, Jr.

The official language is English.

National flag: Six red and 5 white horizontal stripes alternating. In the upper corner, nearest the staff, is a square of blue covering a depth of 5 stripes. In the centre of this blue field is a 5-pointed white star.

National anthem: All hail, Liberia, hail! (words by President Warner; tune by O. Lucas, 1860).

On 22 Dec. 1950 an agreement of assistance and co-operation was signed in Washington whereby a development programme was implemented under control of a joint American-Liberian Commission.

DEFENCE. For defence every citizen from 16 to 45 years of age capable of bearing arms is liable to serve. On 31 March 1942 an agreement was signed between the USA and Liberia by which the US were given the right to construct, control, operate and defend airports in Liberia for the duration of the war. On 8 June 1943 a further mutual aid agreement was concluded with the US, which extended lend-lease aid to Liberia for the purpose of defence and enabled it to increase its Armed Forces.

Army. The establishment organized on a militia basis numbers 4,900 (1983), divided into 5 infantry battalions with support units. There is in addition an enlisted frontier force, the Liberian National Guard, of 93 officers and 2,200 men.

Navy. The small naval service or coastguard comprises 3 small patrol boats and 3 new coastguard cutters. Personnel in 1983 totalled 425 officers and men.

Air Force. The nucleus of an Air Force has been formed, as the Air Reconnaissance Unit, to support the Liberian Army. Equipment includes 2 C-47 transports and a small number of Cessna 172, 185, 207 and 337G light aircraft. HAL Chetak (licence-built Alouette III) helicopters are expected to follow from India. Personnel about 250.

INTERNATIONAL RELATIONS

Membership. Liberia is a member of UN, OAU, ECOWAS and is an ACP state of EEC.

ECONOMY

Budget. The budgets for calendar years were as follows (in US$1,000):

	1977	*1978*	*1979*	*1980*	*1981*
Revenue	166,500	185,500	204,100	222,400	223,000
Expenditure	194,000	227,600	286,300	279,300	303,000

Currency. The legal currency of Liberia is the *dollar* which is equivalent to US$1 which itself has been in circulation since 3 Nov. 1942, but there is a Liberian coinage in silver and copper. Official accounts are kept in dollars and cents. The Liberian coins are as follows: Silver,$5, $1, 50-, 25-, 10- and 5-cent pieces; alloy, 2-and 1-cent pieces. The Government has not yet issued paper money. In March 1983, £1 = 1·52 Liberian $; US$1 = 1 Liberian $.

Banking. The First National City Bank (Liberia) was founded in 1935. The Bank of Liberia, Inc., was founded on 28 July 1955 but closed in 1981. An Italian bank, Tradevco, started business in 1955. The International Trust Co. of Liberia opened a commercial banking department at the end of 1960. The Commercial Bank of Liberia opened in 1961 but closed in 1981. A branch of the Chase Manhattan Bank opened in 1961. The Union National Bank (Liberia) Inc., opened in 1962 but closed in 1981. The Liberian Bank for Development and Investment (LBDI) was founded in 1964 and began operations in 1965. The National Bank of Liberia opened on 22 July 1974, to act as a central bank. The National Housing and Savings Bank opened on 20 Jan. 1972. The Liberian Finance & Trust Corporation was incorporated Oct. 1976 and began operations in May 1977. The Liberian Agricultural and Co-operative Development Bank started operations in 1978. The Bank of Credit & Commerce International opened in Sept. 1978.

Weights and Measures. Weights and measures are the same as in UK and USA.

NATURAL RESOURCES

Minerals. The National Iron Ore Co. near the Mano River, the Liberian Swedish Mineral Co. in the Nimba Mountains and the Bong Mining Co. (DELIMCO) at Bong

Mountain Range are exploiting their iron-ore concession areas. Iron ore production amounted to 20·6m. tonnes in 1981. Total employment in iron ore mining was 8,815 in 1981. Gold and diamonds are found on a small scale.

Agriculture. The soil is productive, but due to excessive rainfall (from 160 to 180 in. per year), there are large swamp areas. Rice, cassava, coffee, citrus and sugarcane are cultivated. The Government is negotiating the financing of large-scale investment in rice production aimed at making the country self-sufficient in rice production. Coffee, cocoa and palm-kernels are produced mainly by the traditional agricultural sector. In 1981, the total volume of coffee and cocoa exports alone were 18·3m. lb. (US$19·4m.), and 14·8m. lb. (US$13·8m.), respectively.

The Liberia Produce Marketing Corporation (LPMC) operates an oil-mill in Monrovia, processing most of the palm-kernels. There were 2 large commercial oil-palm plantations in the country. The Liberia Industrial Co-operative (LBINC) has 6,000 acres of oil-palm (of which 5,000 acres are in production) in Grand Bassa County,and West Africa Agricultural Co. (WAAC) has 4,020 acres in production in Grand Cape Mount County.

Livestock (1981): Cattle, 40,000; pigs, 107,000; sheep, 210,000; poultry, 2·6m.

Forestry. The Firestone Plantation Co. have large rubber plantations, employing over 40,000 men. Their concession comprises about 1m. acres and expires in the year 2025. About 100,000 acres have been planted. Independent producers have a further 65,000 acres planted. In 1976 the total area under rubber cultivation was 294,400 acres, of which 195,800 acres were under actual production.

Other rubber producing companies include Goodrich Rubber Plantation, Allen L. Grant, L. A. C. and Salala Rubber Co. Together, the foreign concessions produced 131·6m. lb. in 1981 while independent Liberian farmers produced 148·7m. lb. in 1981.

The production of logs in 1981 was 451m. cu. metres; 1980, 745m.

INDUSTRY AND TRADE

Industry. There are a number of small factories (brick and tile, soap, nails, mattresses, shoes, plastics, paint, oxygen, acetylene, tyre retreading, a brewery, soft drinks, cement, matches, candy and biscuits).

Commerce. Foreign trade for 6 calendar years was as follows (in US$1m.):

	1976	*1977*	*1978*	*1979*	*1980*	*1981*
Imports	399·2	463·5	486	537	533·8	477·4
Exports	457·0	447·4	481	505	600·4	529·2

The principal exports in 1981 were: Iron ore, and concentrates, US$325·4m.; rubber, US$86·7m.; logs and lumber, US$36·8m. The principal imports in 1981 were machinery and transport equipment (US$118·9m.) and manufactured goods (US$61·3m.). Main suppliers in 1981 were: Asia and European countries (US$200m.), USA (US$142·1m.), other countries (US$136·3m.).

Total trade between Liberia and UK (British Department of Trade returns, in £1,000 sterling):

	1978	*1979*	*1980*	*1981*	*1982*
Imports to UK	12,511	14,359	8,671	6,014	8,213
Exports and re-exports from UK	32,992	78,408	46,412	24,262	14,069

The figures for exports from the UK include the value of shipping transferred to the Liberian flag; the genuine exports are considerably lower.

Liberia was placed in the American account area in 1952.

Tourism. The National Bureau of Culture and Tourism was created in July 1981 to promote tourism.

COMMUNICATIONS

Roads. In 1981, there were 4,794 miles of public roads (1,165 primary, 366 paved, 799 all-weather, 3,629 secondary and feeder) and 1,474 miles of private roads (93 paved, 1,381 laterite and earth). The principal highway connects Monrovia with the road system of Guinea, with branches leading into the Eastern and Western areas of Liberia. The latter branch reaches the Sierra Leone border and joins the Sierra Leone road system. A bridge over the St Paul River carries road and rail traffic to the iron-ore mines at Bomi Hills.

In the interior, communication is maintained by telecommunication and road transport, all goods being carried by motor transport from farms on secondary roads being constructed by local communities with state assistance.

Railway. A railway (for freight only) was built in 1951, connecting Monrovia with the Bomi Hills iron-ore mines about 69 km distant; this has been extended to the National Iron Ore Co. area by 79 km. A line from Nimba to Lower Buchanan (267 km) was completed in 1963 and another line from Bong to Monrovia (78 km) was completed in 1965.

Aviation. The airport for Liberia is Roberts Airport (30 miles from Monrovia). The James Spriggs Payne Airfield, 5 miles from Monrovia, can be used by light aircraft and mini jumbo jets. Air services are maintained by PANAM, Ghana Airways, Nigeria Airways, UTA, Middle East Airlines, Air Mali, Air Afrique, SAS, KLM, Swissair, British Caledonian, Air Guinée, SABENA, Iberia Airlines, Romanian Airlines and Air Liberia.

Shipping. In 1981, 2,277 vessels entered Monrovia.

The Liberian merchant navy, in 1976, consisted of 2,666 ships of 76,412,842 GRT. The Liberian Government requires only a modest registration fee and an almost nominal annual charge and maintains no control over the operation of ships flying the Liberian flag.

Constructed under the auspices of the US Government under lend-lease terms, the port of Monrovia, a free port, was opened on 26 July 1948.

A modern port for the shipment of iron-ore from the mines at Nimba has been built at Lower Buchanan, capable of accommodating vessels up to 75,000 tons.

The river St Paul is navigable for a distance of 8 miles from its mouth for small craft of shallow draught. The Cavalla River is navigable for 8 miles.

Post and Broadcasting. There is cable communication (French) with Europe and America *via* Dakar, and a wireless station is maintained by the Government at Monrovia. There is a telephone service (7,079 telephones, 1980), in Monrovia, which is gradually being extended over the whole country. An earth station constructed by Itacable in 1976 is equipped for 24 telephone type channels and its traffic can be increased to 60 telephone type channels. With the aid of the satellite, automatic telephone and telegraph services to and from many countries are transmitted on a 24-hour basis.

There are wireless stations at Monrovia, Bassa, Harper, Kolahun, Cape Mount and Sinoe. The wireless stations at Harbel, Montserrado County, Maryland County, and Gedetarbo, have since 1928 been operated as a public utility by the US–Liberia Radio Corporation, a subsidiary of Firestone Plantation Co.

A commercial broadcasting station, ELBC, opened in Dec. 1959 and a television service on 1 Jan. 1964. ELWA opened in 1959, station of the Sudan Interior Mission; ELCM opened in 1981, FM Station of the Roman Catholic Mission in Liberia.

JUSTICE, RELIGION, EDUCATION AND WELFARE

Justice. Justice is administered by a Supreme Court of 5 judges, circuit courts and lower courts. A new Liberian code of laws has been published (5 vols. to 1956).

Religion. The main denominations represented in Liberia are Methodist, Baptist, Episcopalian, African Methodist, Pentecostal, Seventh-day Adventist, Lutheran and Roman Catholic, working through missionaries and mission schools. There is also a fairly large Moslem community.

Education. Schools are classified as: (1) Public schools, maintained and run by the Government; (2) Mission schools, supported by foreign Missions and subsidized by the Government, and operated by qualified Missionaries and Liberian teachers; (3)

Private schools, maintained by endowments and sometimes subsidized by the Government.

By the end of 1981 there were estimated to be 1,651 schools with 8,804 teachers and 303,268 pupils. In 1975, 800 US Peace Corps Volunteers were teaching in schools throughout the country.

Health. There were 236 doctors in 1981 and about 3,000 hospital beds.

DIPLOMATIC REPRESENTATIVES

Of Liberia in Great Britain (21 Prince's Gate, London, SW7 1QB)
Ambassador: Dr Harry Moniba (accredited 13 May 1981).

Of Great Britain in Liberia (Mamba Point, Monrovia)
Ambassador and Consul-General: D. G. Reid.

Of Liberia in the USA (5201–16th St., NW, Washington, D.C., 20011)
Ambassador: Joseph S. Guannu.

Of the USA in Liberia (United Nations Drive, Monrovia)
Ambassador: William L. Swing.

Of Liberia to the United Nations
Ambassador: Dr Abeodu B. Jones.

Books of Reference

Presidential Papers, July 1971–July 1972. Monrovia, 1973
Economic Survey of Liberia, 1981. Ministry of Planning and Economic Affairs
Clower, R. W. (ed.), *Growth Without Development: An Economic Survey of Liberia.* Evanston, North-western Univ. Press, 1966
Dunn, D. E., *The Foreign Policy of Liberia during the Tubman Era, 1944–71.* London, 1979
Fraenkel, M., *Tribe and Class in Monrovia.* OUP, 1964
McLaughlin, R. U., *Foreign Investment and Development in Liberia.* New York, 1966
Wilson, C. M., *Liberia: Black Africa in Microcosm.* New York, 1971

LIBYA

Al-Jamahiriyah Al-Arabiya Al-Libya Al-Shabiya Al-Ishtirakiya

Capital: Tripoli
Population: 3·5m. (1982)
GNP per capita: US$8,640 (1980)

HISTORY. Tripoli fell under Turkish domination in the 16th century, and though in 1711 the Arab population secured some measure of independence, the country was in 1835 proclaimed a Turkish vilayet. In Sept. 1911 Italy occupied Tripoli and on 19 Oct. 1912, by the Treaty of Ouchy, Turkey recognized the sovereignty of Italy in Tripoli.

After the expulsion of the Germans and Italians in 1942 and 1943, Tripolitania and Cyrenaica were placed under British, and the Fezzan under French, military administration. Britain recognized the Amir Mohammed Idris Al-Senussi as Amir of Cyrenaica in June 1949.

Libya became an independent, sovereign, federal kingdom under the Amir of Cyrenaica, Mohammed Idris Al-Senussi, as King of the United Kingdom of Libya, on 24 Dec. 1951, when the British Residents in Tripolitania and Cyrenaica and the French Resident in the Fezzan transferred their remaining powers to the federal government of Libya, in pursuance of decisions passed by the United Nations in 1949 and 1950.

On 1 Sept. 1969 King Idris was deposed by a group of army officers. Twelve of the group of officers formed the Revolutionary Command Council chaired by Col. Muammar Qadhafi and proclaimed a republic. The RCC ruled the country through an appointed Council of Ministers until 2 March 1977, when both were abolished as constitutional government was resumed.

AREA AND POPULATION. The area is estimated at 1,759,540 sq. km (679,358 sq. miles). The population, according to the census of 1973, was 2,249,237. Estimate (1982) 3·5m.

According to an arrangement with France (12 Sept. 1919) the western frontier extends in a curve from west of Ghadames to south of Tummo, including Ghat. According to the agreement with France of 7 Jan. 1935, the southern frontier runs along a line between Tummo and a cross-point indicated by 24° E. long. from Greenwich and 18° 45′ N. lat. Further frontier agreements with France were signed on 10 Aug. 1955 and 26 Dec. 1956. In 1926 Egypt ceded the oasis of Jarabub to Italy, in exchange for a rectification of the frontier near Sollum. The eastern boundary follows in general the 25° parallel E. long. (*See* map in THE STATESMAN'S YEAR-BOOK, 1952.)

The country is administratively divided into the following 10 provinces (with population, 1973, census): Tripoli (735,083), Benghazi (337,423), Sebha (113,006), Zawia (247,628), Kalig (106,647), Khoms (162,126), Misurata (177,939), Derna (122,984), Jebel Akhdar (131,940), Gharian (155,958).

The 3 most important towns are Tripoli (551,477 inhabitants), Misurata (103,302), Benghazi (282,192).

CONSTITUTION AND GOVERNMENT. Under the new 1977 Constitution, Libya is now divided into 46 municipalities and 186 'Basic People's Congresses', which form the primary level of government. The General People's Congress, created in Jan. 1976 as the national legislature, comprises 3 delegates from each of the 186 Basic People's Congresses. The General People's Committee, which replaced the Council of Ministers, is assisted by the 5-member General People's Secretariat, which replaced the Revolutionary Command Council. It was ruled by the Revolutionary Command Council (RCC) under the leadership of Col. Muammar Qadhafi.

In March 1977 a new form of direct democracy, the 'Jamahiriya' (state of the masses) was promulgated and the official name of the country was changed to Socialist Peoples Libyan Arab Jamahiriya. At local level authority is now vested in 186 Basic and 46 Municipal People's Congresses which appoint Popular Committees to execute policy. Officials of these Congresses and Committees form at national level the General People's Congress, a body of some 1,000 delegates which normally meets for about a week twice a year. This is the highest policy-making body in the country. The General People's Congress appoints its own General Secretariat and the General People's Committee, whose members head the 20 government departments which execute policy at national level. The Secretary of the General People's Committee has functions similar to those of a Prime Minister.

Following the re-organization of March 1979 Col. Qadhafi retained his position as leader of the Revolution. But neither he nor his former RCC colleagues have any formal posts in the new administration.

Arabic is the official language. Tripoli is the capital.

Secretary-General of the General Secretariat of the General People's Congress: Abdul Iati Ai-Ubaidi.

National flag: Plain green.

DEFENCE

Army. The Army, of 55,000 men (1983), is organized in 20 tank, 1 National Guard, 30 mechanized and 10 artillery battalions.

Navy. The fleet comprises 5 *ex*-Soviet diesel-driven submarines, 1 missile-armed frigate, 5 missile-armed corvettes, 1 gun corvette, 2 ocean minesweepers, 25 fast missile craft, 9 patrol boats, 1 medium (dock type) logistic support ship, 2 landing ships, 5 landing craft, 1 maintenance repair craft, 1 diving ship, 1 transport and 5 tugs. Under construction or projection are 1 submarine, 3 missile-armed corvettes and 7 landing craft.

Libya has procured naval equipment and weapons from both the East (particularly the USSR) and the West; and the increasing and up-to-date fleet constitutes a force of critical importance in the Mediterranean.

Personnel in 1983 was upwards of 3,000 officers and ratings, including coastguard. A large proportion of naval personnel have been trained in the Soviet Union since 1975.

Air Force. The creation of an Air Force began in 1959. In 1974, delivery was completed of a total of 110 Mirage 5 combat aircraft and trainers, of which about 50 remain. They have been followed by 20 Tu-22 supersonic reconnaissance bombers, 58 MiG-25 interceptors and reconnaissance aircraft, 102 Su-22 ground attack fighters, 94 MiG-21s, and about 160 MiG-23 variable-geometry fighters and fighter-bombers from the USSR. Other equipment includes 30 Mirage F1 fighters from France, 6 Mirage F1-B two-seat trainers, Mi-24 gunship helicopters, 7 C-130H Hercules, 20 Aeritalia G222T and 9 C-47 transports, 7 Super Frelon and 20 Agusta-built CH-47C Chinook heavy-lift helicopters, and a total of about 23 Bell 212, Bell 47, Alouette III and Mi-8 helicopters. Training is performed on piston-engined SF-260Ms (some of which are armed for light attack duties) from Italy, and L-39 Albatros, Galeb and Magister jet aircraft. Personnel total about 5,000, with many of the combat aircraft operated by foreign aircrew. Aircraft on order include Mirage F1 fighters from France.

INTERNATIONAL RELATIONS

Membership. Libya is a member of UN, OAU and the Arab League.

ECONOMY

Planning. The 5-year development plan (1981–85) aims to assist in the transformation of Libya into a welfare state, largely independent of oil, by the year 2000. It envisages an investment of LD18,500m.

Budget. The administrative budget for 1982 allows for expenditure of LD1,250m.; development budget, LD2,640m.

Currency. The currency is the Libyan *dinar* which is divided into 1,000 *millemes.* Rate of exchange, March 1983: LD0·45 = £1; LD0·30 = US$1.

Banking. A National Bank of Libya was established in 1955; it was renamed the Central Bank of Libya in 1972. On 31 Dec. 1976, its assets amounted to LD1,793·9m. All foreign banks were nationalized by Dec. 1970. In 1972 the Libyan Government set up the Libyan Arab Foreign Bank whose function is overseas investment and to participate in multinational banking corporations. The National Agricultural Bank, which has been set up to give loans and subsidies to farmers to develop their land and to assist them in marketing their crops, has offices in Tripoli, Benghazi, Sebha and other agricultural centres. The National Industrial and Real Estate Bank, which has been established to give loans to house buyers and to give short and medium loans to private sector industrial ventures, also has offices in Tripoli and Benghazi.

Weights and Measures. Although the metric system has been officially adopted and is obligatory for all contracts, the following weights and measures are still used: *oke* = 1·282 kg; *kantar* = 51·28 kg; *draa* = 46 cm; *handaza* = 68 cm.

ENERGY AND NATURAL RESOURCES

Electricity. Electricity output capacity in 1972 was 190 mw and was increased to 581 mw by the end of 1975.

Oil. In 1968, 41 companies were working concession areas; the most important discoveries so far made are: (i) Zelten, about 200 miles south from Benghazi and 100 miles from the nearest point on the coast; discovered by Esso (the local subsidiary of the Standard Oil Co. of New Jersey) in April 1959. Exports from this field began at the end of 1961, the oil being piped to the port of Marsa Bregha. (ii) Dahra, roughly midway between Tripoli and Benghazi and about 90 miles from the coast, discovered in 1958–59; a pipeline to Ras El Sidr was completed in 1962. (iii) Beida, about 140 miles from the coast and just east of the Tripolitanian/Cyrenaican border, discovered by Caltex in 1959. (iv) Other discoveries, either non-commercial or not yet evaluated, have been made by Mobiloil of Canada, Shell, Gulf, CPTL. British Petroleum has also discovered oil in commercial quantities in southern Cyrenaica some 400 miles from the coast, connected to the Tobruk terminal by pipeline. Occidental Oil Co. have made 2 high-yield strikes and are planning the construction of a pipeline and terminal at Zueitina.

Production (1981) 420m. bbls. On 7 Dec. 1971 the British Petroleum Exploration (Libya) Co. was nationalized and on 11 June 1973 its partner Nelson Bunker Hunt. The rights and concessions were listed in the Arabian Gulf Exploration Co. The Oasis and Occidental companies agreed in Aug. 1973 to 51% participation by the Libyan National Oil Co. in their rights and operations. A decree of 1 Sept. 1973 nationalized 51% of the rights and assets of the following companies: Mobil, Exxon, Amoco, Amoseas and Shell. On 11 Feb. 1974 Amoco and Amoseas were totally nationalized. Compensation has been paid to Shell, BP and Nelson Bunker Hunt.

Gas. Reserves (1982) 670,000m. cu. metres. Production (1982) 29,000m. cu. metres.

Minerals. The production of cement was 1,065,000 tonnes in 1977, though the existing 2 cement plants are being expanded to give a future combined production of 850,000 tonnes per annum. A third cement factory has been built in eastern Libya with a capacity of 1m. tonnes per year, and another one of the same capacity has also been opened. A limestone factory is also to be built shortly in Benghazi. Gypsum output (1975) 15,000 tonnes.

Agriculture. Tripolitania has 3 zones from the coast inland—the Mediterranean, the sub-desert and the desert. The first, which covers an area of about 17,231 sq. miles, is the only one properly suited for agriculture, and may be further sub-divided into: (1) the oases along the coast, the richest in North Africa, in which thrive the date palm, the olive, the orange, the peanut and the potato; (2) the steppe district, suitable for cereals (barley and wheat) and pasture; it has olive, almond, vine, orange and mulberry trees and ricinus plants; (3) the dunes, which are being gradually afforested with acacia, robinia, poplar and pine; (4) the Jebel (the mountain district, Tarhuna, Garian, Nalut-Yefren), in which thrive the olive, the fig, the vine and other fruit trees, and which on the east slopes down to the sea with the fertile hills of Msellata. Of some 25m. acres of productive land in Tripolitania, nearly 20m. are used for grazing and about 1m. for static farming. The sub-desert zone produces the alfa plant. The desert zone and the Fezzan contain some fertile oases, such as those of Ghadames, Ghat, Socna, Sebha, Brak.

Cyrenaica has about 10m. acres of potentially productive land, most of which, however, is suitable only for grazing. Certain areas, chief of which is the plateau known as the Barce Plain (about 1,000 ft above sea-level), are suitable for dry farming; in addition, grapes, olives and dates are grown. With improved irrigation, production, particularly of vegetables, could be increased, but stock raising and dry farming will remain of primary importance. About 143,000 acres are used for settled farming; about 272,000 acres are covered by natural forests. The Agricultural Development Authority plans to reclaim 6,000 hectares each year for agriculture.

In the Fezzan there are about 6,700 acres of irrigated gardens and about 297,000 acres are planted with date palms.

Production (1980, in tonnes): Wheat, 141,000; barley, 71,000; milk, 85,000; meat, 119,000. Olive trees number about 3·4m. and productive date-palm trees about 3m.

Livestock (1981): 6·26m. sheep, 1·5m. goats, 185,000 cattle, 5·9m. poultry.

INDUSTRY AND TRADE

Industry. Among the traditional industries of Tripolitania and Cyrenaica are sponge fishing, tunny fishing, tobacco growing and processing, dyeing and weaving of local wool and imported cotton yarn, and olive oil. Tripolitania also produces bricks, salt, leather and esparto grass for paper-making. Home industries of both territories include the making of matting, carpets, leather articles and fabrics embroidered with gold and silver. The Government has embarked on an ambitious programme of industrial development aimed at the local manufacture of building materials (steel and aluminium pipes and fittings, electric cables, cement, bricks, glass, etc.), foodstuffs (dairy products, flour, tinned fruits and vegetables, dates, fish processing and canning, etc.), textiles and footwear (ready-made clothing, woollen and cotton cloth, blankets, leather footwear, etc.) and development of mineral deposits (iron ore, phosphates, mineral salts). Private sector industrialization is encouraged by government loans and subsidies.

Production (1975): Footwear, 680,000 pairs; hides, 70,000 sq. ft. On 21 Sept. 1969 a decree laid down that all business concerns should be 100% Libyan-owned, but oil companies and banks were excluded.

Commerce. Total imports in 1980 were valued at US$8,951 (f.o.b.) and exports of US$22,574 (f.o.b.), mostly crude oil.

Total trade between Libya and UK (British Department of Trade returns, in £1,000 sterling):

	1978	*1979*	*1980*	*1981*	*1982*
Imports to UK	98,230	62,167	46,528	74,810	342,476
Exports and re-exports from UK	214,697	253,153	288,358	550,416	260,937

COMMUNICATIONS

Roads. Good motor roads connect Tripoli through Zuara with Tunis, and through Homs and Misurata with Benghazi and thence with Tobruk and Alexandria. Other roads go south and south-west from Tripoli to Tiagura, Garian, Yefren, Nalut and Ghadames. A road connects Sebha in the south with the main coastal road. An ambitious road building programme is being implemented and a road will eventually link Libya with Chad and Niger through Sebha. A further main road is being built to link Kufra, a major agricultural centre in the south-eastern part of Libya with the coastal road.

Surface communication between Benghazi and Tripoli is by frequent bus service, and there are also bus services between Benghazi and Alexandria, and between Tripoli, Tunis and Algiers.

Railways. There were in 1982 no railways, but contracts were made in 1982 for the first stage of a 364 km coastal line from Ras Jedir to Tripoli and Misurata.

Aviation. Benghazi and Tripoli are both served by international airlines, linking them with each other and Athens, Cairo, Rome, Malta, Tunis, Frankfurt, Paris, Amsterdam, Algiers, Khartoum, Lagos and London. British Caledonian has 3 flights weekly between Tripoli and London.

A national airline, the Libyan Arab Airlines (LAA), was inaugurated on 30 Sept. 1965. Apart from internal flights LAA operate to Athens, London, Rome, Beirut, Cairo, Paris, Malta, Algiers, Khartoum, Moscow, Cotonou and Tunis.

Post and Broadcasting. Tripoli is connected by telegraph cable with Malta and by microwave link with Bengardane (Tunis). There are overseas wireless-telegraph stations at Benghazi and Tripoli, and radio-telephone services connect Libya with most countries of western Europe. In 1971 some 41,495 telephones were in use and in 1978 there were 130,000 radio sets and 155,000 television receivers.

JUSTICE, RELIGION, EDUCATION AND WELFARE

Justice. The Civil, Commercial and Criminal codes are based mainly on the Egyptian model. Matters of personal status of family or succession matters affecting Moslems are dealt with in special courts according to the Moslem law. All other matters, civil, commercial and criminal, are tried in the ordinary courts, which have jurisdiction over everyone. In 1971 the Revolutionary Command Council set up a Commission with the task of revising Libyan laws.

There are civil and penal courts in Tripoli and Benghazi, with subsidiary courts at Misurata and Derna; courts of assize in Tripoli and Benghazi, and courts of appeal in Tripoli and Benghazi.

Religion. Islam is declared the State religion, but the right of others to practise their religions is provided for.

Education. There were (1975–76) 534,209 pupils (282,451 boys and 251,758 girls) in primary schools, 116,630 in elementary schools and 16,839 in secondary schools. There were 13,517 students at the 2 universities of Al Fatah (in Tripoli) and Garyounes (in Benghazi).

There are several schools, mainly in Tripoli, providing British, French, Italian, American and Dutch curricula, mainly on elementary and intermediate levels and chiefly for the non-Libyan communities.

Social Welfare. In 1975 there were 12,241 hospital beds and 42 hospitals with surgical facilities.

DIPLOMATIC REPRESENTATIVES

Of Libya in Great Britain (5 St James's Sq., London, SW1)
Secretary-General of the People's Committee: Adem Saleh Kuwiri.

Of Great Britain in Libya (30 Sharia Gamal Abdul Nasser, Tripoli)
Ambassador: J. M. Edes, CMG.

USA suspended all embassy activities in Tripoli on 2 May 1980.

Of Libya to the United Nations
Ambassador: Vacant.

Books of Reference

The Economic Development of Libya. International Bank, 1960

Allen, J. A., *Libya: The Experience of Oil.* London and Boulder, 1981
Ansell, M. O., and al-Arif, I. M., *The Libyan Revolution.* London, 1972
Bianco, M., *Gadafi: Voice from the Desert.* London, 1975
Waddhams, F. C., *The Libyan Oil Industry.* London, 1980
Wright, J., *Libya: A Modern History.* London, 1982

LIECHTENSTEIN

Capital: Vaduz
Population: 26,130 (1981)
GNP per capita: US$8,000 (1974)

HISTORY. The Principality of Liechtenstein, situated between the Austrian province of Vorarlberg and the Swiss cantons of St Gallen and Graubünden, is a sovereign state whose history dates back to 3 May 1342, when Count Hartmann III became ruler of the county of Vaduz. Additions were later made to the count's domains, and by 1434 the territory reached its present boundaries. It consists of the two former counties of Schellenberg and Vaduz (until 1806 immediate fiefs of the Roman Empire). The former in 1699 and the latter in 1712 came into the possession of the house of Liechtenstein and, by diploma of 23 Jan. 1719, granted by the Emperor Charles VI, the two counties were constituted as the Principality of Liechtenstein.

AREA AND POPULATION. Liechtenstein is bounded on the east by Austria and the west by Switzerland. Area, 160 sq. km (61·8 sq. miles); population, of Alemannic race (census 1981), 26,130. In 1981 there were 369 births and 161 deaths. Population of Vaduz (census 1981), 4,980.

REIGNING PRINCE. Francis Joseph II, born 16 Aug. 1906; succeeded his great uncle, 26 July 1938; married on 7 March 1943 to Countess Gina von Wilczek; there are 4 sons, Princes Hans Adam (*heir apparent*, born 14 Feb. 1945; married on 30 July 1967 to Countess Marie Kinsky), Philip Erasmus (married on 11 Sept. 1971 to Isabelle de l'Arbre de Malander), Nikolaus Ferdinand and Franz Josef Wenzel, and one daughter, Princess Nora Elisabeth. The monarchy is hereditary in the male line.

National flag: Horizontally blue over red, with a gold coronet in the first quarter.
National anthem: Oben am jungen Rhein (words by H. H. Jauch, 1850; tune, 'God save the Queen').

CONSTITUTION AND GOVERNMENT. Liechtenstein is a constitutional monarchy ruled by the hereditary princes of the House of Liechtenstein. The present constitution of 5 Oct. 1921 provides for a unicameral parliament (Diet) of 15 members elected for 4 years. Election is by universal adult male suffrage and is on the basis of proportional representation. In 2 communes (Vaduz and Gamprin) women are allowed to vote and hold office on communal basis. The prince can call and dismiss the parliament. On parliamentary recommendation, he appoints the prime minister and the 4 councillors for a 4-year term. Any group of 600 persons or any 3 communes may propose legislation (initiative). Bills passed by the parliament may be submitted to popular referendum. A law is valid when it receives a majority approval by the parliament and the prince's signed concurrence. The capital and seat of government is Vaduz and there are 10 more communes all connected by modern roads. The 11 communes are fully independent administrative bodies within the laws of the principality. They levy additional taxes to the state taxes. Since Feb. 1921 Liechtenstein has had the Swiss currency, and since 29 March 1923 has been united with Switzerland in a customs union. Switzerland has also since 1919 represented the Principality diplomatically.

At the elections for the Diet, on 7 Feb. 1982, the Fatherland Union obtained 8 seats, the opposition Progressive Citizens' Party, 7 seats.

Head of Government: Hans Brunhart.

INTERNATIONAL RELATIONS

Membership. Liechtenstein is a member of EFTA, the Council of Europe and the International Court of Justice.

ECONOMY

Budget. Budget estimates for 1982: Revenue, 243,579,000 Swiss francs; expenditure, 240,056,000 Swiss francs. There is no public debt.

Currency. The Swiss *franc*.

Banking. There were (1982) 3 banks: Liechtensteinische Landesbank, Bank in Liechtenstein Ltd, Verwaltungs-und Privatbank Ltd.

Weights and Measures. The metric system is in force.

ENERGY AND NATURAL RESOURCES

Electricity. Electricity produced in 1981 was 61,587,000 kwh.

Agriculture. The rearing of cattle, for which the fine alpine pastures are well suited, is highly developed. In July 1982 there were 5,869 cattle (including 2,531 milch cows), 106 horses, 1,740 sheep, 135 goats, 3,207 pigs. Total production of dairy produce, 1981, 9,280,183 kg.

INDUSTRY AND TRADE

Industry. The country has a great variety of light industries (textiles, ceramics, steel screws, precision instruments, canned food, pharmaceutical products, heating appliances, etc.).

Liechtenstein has during the past 30 years changed from a predominantly agricultural country to a highly industrialized country. The farming population has gone down from 70% in 1930 to only 3·35% in 1981. The rapid change-over has led to the immigration of foreign workers (Austrians, Germans, Italians, Spaniards). Industrial undertakings in 1981 employed 6,414 workers earning 251m. Swiss francs.

Commerce. Exports of home produce in 1981 amounted to 882m. Swiss francs. 32·2% went to EFTA countries, of which Switzerland took 210·1m. (23·8%) and 40·5% went to EEC countries.

Total trade with UK is included with Switzerland from 1968.

Tourism. In 1981, 85,282 foreign visitors stayed in Liechtenstein.

COMMUNICATIONS

Roads. There are 250 km of roads. Postal buses are the chief means of public transportation within the country and to Austria and Switzerland.

Railways. The 18·5 km of main railway passing through the country is operated by Austrian Federal Railways.

Post and Broadcasting. In 1981 there were 10,600 telephones, 392 telex, 7,758 wireless sets and 7,296 television sets. The post and telegraphs are administered by Switzerland.

Cinemas. There were 3 cinemas in 1982.

Newspapers. In 1982 there were 2 daily newspapers with a total circulation of 14,500.

JUSTICE, RELIGION, EDUCATION AND WELFARE

Justice. The principality has its own civil and penal codes. The lowest court is the county court, *Landgericht*, presided over by one judge, which decides minor civil cases and summary criminal offences. The criminal court, *Kriminalgericht*, with a bench of 5 judges is for major crimes. Another court of mixed jurisdiction is the court of assizes (with 3 judges) for misdemeanours. The superior court, *Obergericht*, and Supreme Court, *Oberster Gerichtshof*, are courts of appeal for civil and criminal cases (both with benches of 5 judges). An administrative court of appeal from government actions and the State Court determines the constitutionality of laws.

Police. The principality has no army. Police force, 37; auxiliary police, 22 (1981).

Religion. In 1981, 84·7% of the population was Roman Catholic and 8·8% was Protestant.

Education (1982). In 14 primary, 3 upper, 4 secondary and 1 grammar school there were 3,815 pupils and 290 teachers. There is also an evening technical school, a music school, 3 schools for backward children and a children's pedagogic-welfare day school.

Health. In 1982 there was 1 hospital, but Liechtenstein has an agreement with the Swiss cantons of St Gallen and Graubünden that her citizens may use certain hospitals.

DIPLOMATIC REPRESENTATIVES

British Consul-General: G. N. Smith (resident in Zürich).
USA Consul-General: Dr Alfred P. Brainard (resident in Zürich).

Books of Reference

Statistical Information: Press and Information Service, Vaduz.

Rechenschaftsbericht der Fürstlichen Liechtensteinischen Regierung. Vaduz. Annual, from 1922

Jahrbücher der Historischen Vereins. Vaduz. Annual since 1901

Kranz, W., *The Principality of Liechtenstein.* Press and Information Service. 5th ed. Vaduz, 1981

The Liechtenstein Economy. Press and Information Service, Vaduz, 1978

Batliner, E. H., *Das Geld- und Kreditwesen des Fürstentums of Peace.* Vaduz, 1967

Malin, G., *Kunstführer Liechtenstein.* Berne, 1977

Steger, B., *Fürst und Landtag nach Liechtensteinischem Recht.* Vaduz, 1950.—*A Survey of Liechtenstein History.* Vaduz, 1970

LUXEMBOURG

Grand-Duché de Luxembourg

Capital: Luxembourg
Population: 364,600 (1981)
GNP per capita: US$14,510 (1980)

HISTORY. The country formed part of the Holy Roman Empire until it was conquered by the French in 1795. In 1815 the Grand Duchy of Luxembourg was formed under the house of Orange-Nassau, also sovereigns of the Netherlands. In 1839 the Walloon-speaking area was joined to Belgium. In 1890 the personal union with the Netherlands ended with the accession of a member of another branch of the house of Nassau, Grand Duke Adolphe of Nassau-Weilburg.

AREA AND POPULATION. Luxembourg has an area of 2,586 sq. km (998 sq. miles) and is bounded on the west by Belgium, south by France, east by the Federal Republic of Germany. The population (1981) was 364,600. The capital, Luxembourg, had 79,000 inhabitants; Esch-Alzette, the centre of the mining district, 25,142; Differdange, 8,588; Dudelange, 14,074, and Petange, 6,416. In 1981 the foreign population was about 95,800.

Vital statistics (1981): 4,414 births, 4,105 deaths, 2,023 marriages.

REIGNING GRAND DUKE. Jean, born 5 Jan. 1921, son of Grand Duchess Charlotte and the late Prince Felix of Bourbon-Parma; succeeded 12 Nov. 1964 on the abdication of his mother; married to Princess Joséphine-Charlotte of Belgium, 9 April 1953. *Offspring:* Princess Marie Astrid, born 17 Feb. 1954, married Christian of Habsbourg-Lorraine 6 Feb. 1982; Prince Henri, *heir apparent*, born 16 April 1955, married Maria Teresa Mestre 14 Feb. 1981; *Offspring:* Prince Guillaume Jean Joseph Marie, born 11 Nov. 1981; Prince Jean and Princess Margaretha, born 15 May 1957; Prince Guillaume, born 1 May 1963.

The civil list is fixed at 300,000 gold francs per annum, to be reconsidered at the beginning of each reign.

On 28 Sept. 1919 a referendum was taken in Luxembourg to decide on the political and economic future of the country. The voting resulted as follows: For the reigning Grand Duchess, 66,811; for the continuance of the Nassau-Braganza dynasty under another Grand Duchess, 1,286; for another dynasty, 889; for a republic, 16,885; for an economic union with France, 60,133; for an economic union with Belgium, 22,242. But France refused in favour of Belgium, and on 22 Dec. 1921 the Chamber of the Grand Duchy passed a Bill for the economic union between Belgium and Luxembourg. The agreement, which is for 60 years, provides for the disappearance of the customs barrier between the two countries and the use of Belgian, in addition to Luxembourg, currency as legal tender in the Grand Duchy. It came into force on 1 May 1922.

The Grand Duchy was under German occupation from 10 May 1940 to 10 Sept. 1944. The Grand Duchess Charlotte and the Government carried on an independent administration in London. Civil government was restored in Oct. 1944.

National flag: Three horizontal stripes of red, white, blue.

National anthem: Ons Hemecht (words by M. Lentz, 1859; tune by J. A. Zinnen).

CONSTITUTION AND GOVERNMENT. The Grand Duchy of Luxembourg is a constitutional monarchy, the hereditary sovereignty being in the Nassau family. The constitution of 17 Oct. 1868 was revised in 1919, 1948, 1956 and 1972.

The revision of 1948 has abolished the 'perpetually neutral' status of the country and introduced the concepts of right to work, social security, health services, freedom of trade and industry, and recognition of trade unions. The revision of 1956 provides for the devolution of executive, legislative and judicial powers to international institutions.

The national language is Luxemburgish; French, German and English are widely used.

The country forms 4 electoral districts. An elector must be a citizen (male or female) of Luxembourg and have completed 18 years of age; to be eligible for election the citizen must have completed 21 years of age.

The Chamber of Deputies consists of 24 Christian Social, 14 Socialists, 15 Democrats, 2 Social Democrats, 2 Communists, 1 Independent Socialist and 1 co-opted deputy (elections of 10 June 1979). Members are elected for 5 years; they receive a salary and a travelling allowance.

The head of the state takes part in the legislative power, exercises the executive power and has a certain part in the judicial power. The constitution leaves to the sovereign the right to organize the Government, which consists of a Minister of State, who is President of the Government, and of at least 3 Ministers.

The Cabinet was, in Feb. 1983, composed as follows:

President of the Government, Minister of State, Treasury, Culture, General Affairs, National Protection, Information and Press: Pierre Werner.

Vice-President, Foreign Affairs, External Commerce and Co-operation, Economy and Middle Classes, Justice: Colette Flesch. *Health, Public Forces, Physical Education and Sport:* Emile Krieps. *Agriculture, Viticulture, Water and Forests:* Ernest Mühlen. *Environment, Transport, Communications and Information, Energy:* Josy Barthel. *Finance:* Jacques Santer. *Public Works and Functions:* René Konen. *Interior, Family, Social Living and Social Solidarity:* Jean Spautz. *National Education and Tourism:* Fernand Boden. *Secretary of State for Foreign Affairs, External Commerce and Co-operation, Economy and Middle Classes, Justice:* Paul Helminger. *Labour and Social Security:* Jean-Claude Juncker.

Besides the Cabinet there is a Council of State. It deliberates on proposed laws and Bills, and on amendments; it also gives administrative decisions and expresses its opinion regarding any other question referred to it by the Grand Duke or the Government. The Council of State is composed of 21 members chosen for life by the sovereign, who also chooses a president from among them each year.

DEFENCE. A law passed by Parliament on 29 June 1967 abolished compulsory service and instituted a battalion-size army of volunteers enlisted for 3 years. Strength (1983) 690. The defence estimates for 1982 amounted to 1,308m. francs. Luxembourg is an original member of NATO and the battalion is committed to NATO ACE mobile force.

INTERNATIONAL RELATIONS

Membership. Luxembourg is a member of the UN, Benelux, the EEC, OECD, the Council of Europe, NATO and WEU.

ECONOMY

Budget. Revenue and expenditure (including extraordinary) for years ending 30 April (in 1m. francs):

	1978	*1979*	*1980* [1]	*1981* [1]	*1982* [2]	*1983*
Revenue	42,603·6	42,579·0	48,244·0	53,412·3	54,791·2	60,100·5
Expenditure	41,582·3	43,665·2	48,918·4	54,975·0	56,074·2	60,603·4

[1] Provisional. [2] Budget.

Consolidated debt at 31 Dec. 1982 amounted to 31,719·8m. francs (long-term) and 2,250·4m. francs (short-term).

Currency. On 14 Oct. 1944 the Luxembourg *franc* was fixed at par value with the Belgian franc. Notes of the Belgian National Bank are legal tender in Luxembourg.

Banking. On 31 Dec. 1981 there were 301,680 depositors in the State Savings Bank with a total of 29,067m. francs to their credit. There are 115 banks established in Luxembourg which has become an international financial centre.

Weights and Measures. The metric system is in force.

ENERGY AND NATURAL RESOURCES

Electricity. Power production was 1,210m. kwh. in 1981.

Minerals. The mining and metallurgical industries are the most important. In 1982 production (in tonnes) of pig-iron, 2,586,820; of steel, 3,509,850.

Agriculture. Agriculture is carried on by about 8,900 of the population; 128,227 hectares were under cultivation in 1981. The principal crops are potatoes, barley, beet, oats and wheat.

Livestock (1982): 1,386 horses, 222,061 cattle, 67,867 pigs, 3,459 sheep.

INDUSTRY AND TRADE

Commerce. By treaty of 5 Sept. 1944, signed in London, and the treaty of 14 March 1947, signed in The Hague, the Grand Duchy, together with Belgium and the Netherlands, became a party to the Benelux Customs Union, which came into force on 1 Jan. 1948. For further particulars *see* p. 201.

Total trade between Luxembourg and UK included with Belgium from 1974.

Tourism. In 1981 there were 434,300 tourists.

COMMUNICATIONS

Roads. In 1982 the network had a total of 5,108 km. Motor vehicles registered in Luxembourg on 1 Jan. 1982 included 137,900 passenger cars, 8,954 trucks, 696 buses, 17,197 tractors and special vehicles.

Railways. In 1981 there were 270 km of railway (standard gauge).

Aviation. Findel is the airport for Luxembourg.

Post and Broadcasting. In 1981 the telephone system had 5,224 km of telegraph and telephone line, 214,964 telephones, 104 post offices and 395 telegraph offices. *Compagnie Luxembourgeoise de Télédiffusion* broadcasts 1 programme in Luxembourgian on FM. Powerful transmitters on long-, medium- and short-waves are used for commercial and religious programmes in French, Dutch, German, English and Italian. Five TV programmes are broadcast. Colour transmission by SECAM system. Number of receivers (estimate): radio, more than 200,000; TV, 140,000.

Cinemas (1977). There were 20 cinemas.

Newspapers (1982). There were 6 daily newspapers with an aggregate circulation of 130,000.

RELIGION, EDUCATION AND WELFARE

Religion. The population is Catholic, save (31 Dec. 1970) 3,900 Protestants, 700 Jews, 2,100 belonging to other denominations and 3,700 without religion (or having given no indication on this subject). The Protestant Church is organized on an interdenominational basis.

Education (1981–82). Education is compulsory for all children between the ages of 6 and 15. The nursery schools had 7,551 pupils; primary schools had 27,927 pupils; technical secondary schools, 15,950 pupils; secondary schools, 9,100 pupils; the Superior Institute of Technology, 600 pupils; pedagogic education, 152 pupils; university studies, 232 pupils.

Health. In 1981 there were 563 doctors and 4,778 hospital beds.

DIPLOMATIC REPRESENTATIVES

Of Luxembourg in Great Britain (27 Wilton Crescent, London, SWIX 8SD)
Ambassador: Roger Hastert, CMG.

Of Great Britain in Luxembourg (28 Boulevard Royal, Luxembourg)
Ambassador and Consul-General: The Hon. Humphrey Maud, CMG.

Of Luxembourg in the USA (2200 Massachusetts Ave. NW, Washington, D.C., 20008)
Ambassador: Adrien Meisch.

Of the USA in Luxembourg (22 Blvd. Emmanuel Servais, Luxembourg)
Ambassador: John E. Dolibois.

Of Luxembourg to the United Nations
Ambassador: Paul Peters.

Books of Reference

Statistical Information: The Service Central de la Statistique et des Études Économiques was founded in 1900 and reorganized in 1962 (19–21 boulevard Royal, C.P. 304 Luxembourg-City). *Director:* Georges Als. Main publications: *Bulletin du Statec.—Annuaire statistique.—Cahiers économiques.*

Bulletin de Documentation. Government Information Service. From 1945 (monthly)
The Institutions of the Grand Duchy of Luxembourg. Press and Information Service, Luxembourg, 1976
Als, G., *Le Luxembourg, situation politique, économique et sociale.* Luxembourg, 1982
Calmes, C., *Au Fil de l'Histoire.* Luxembourg, 1977
Cooper-Pritchard, A. H., *History of the Grand-Duchy of Luxembourg.* Luxembourg, 1950
Heiderscheid, A., *Aspects de Sociologie Religieuse du Diocèse de Luxembourg.* 2 vols. Luxembourg, 1961
Hury, C. and Christophory, J., *Luxembourg.* [Bibliography] Oxford and Santa Barbara, 1981
Majerus, P., *Le Luxembourg independant.* Luxembourg, 1948.—*L'État Luxembourgeois.* Luxembourg, 1948
Trausch, G., *Le Luxembourg à l'Époque Contemporaine.* Luxembourg, 1975

Archives of the State: Luxembourg-City. *Director:* Paul Spang.
National Library: Luxembourg-City, 14a Boulevard Royal. *Director:* Gilbert Trausch.

MADAGASCAR

Capital: Antananarivo
Population: 9·21m. (1982)
GNP per capita: US$350 (1980)

Repoblika Demokratika n'i Madagaskar

HISTORY. Madagascar was discovered by the Portuguese, Diego Diaz, in 1500. The island was unified under the Imérina monarchy between 1797 and 1861, but French claims to a protectorate led to hostilities culminating in the establishment of a protectorate on 30 Sept. 1895. The monarchy was abolished and Madagascar became a French Colony on 6 Aug. 1896.

Madagascar became an Overseas Territory in 1946, and on 14 Oct. 1958, following a referendum, was proclaimed the autonomous Malagasy Republic within the French Community, achieving full independence on 26 June 1960.

The government of Philibert Tsirana, President from independence, resigned on 18 May 1972 and executive powers were given to Maj.-Gen. Gabriel Ramanantsoa, who replaced Tsirana as President on 11 Oct. 1972. On 5 Feb. 1975, Col. Richard Ratsimandrava became Head of State, but was assassinated 6 days later. A National Military Directorate under Brig.-Gen. Gilles Andriamahazo was established on 12 Feb. On 15 June it handed over power to a Supreme Revolutionary Council (SRC) under Didier Ratsiraka.

AREA AND POPULATION. Madagascar is situated off the south-east coast of Africa, from which it is separated by the Mozambique channel, the least distance between island and continent being 250 miles; its length is 980 miles; greatest breadth, 360 miles.

The area is 587,041 sq. km (226,658 sq. miles). In 1975 (census) the population was 7,603,790 (more than 50% under 18 years). Estimate (1982) 9·21m.

Province	*Area in sq. km*	*Population 1978*	*Chief town*	*Population 1978*
Antseranana	42,725	620,228	Antseranana	48,000
Mahajanga	152,165	857,610	Mahajanga	57,500
Toamasina	72,212	1,254,639	Toamasina	59,100
Antananarivo	57,775	2,322,019	Antananarivo	400,000
Fianarantsoa	100,326	1,908,465	Fianarantsoa	55,500
Toliary	162,283	1,084,083	Toliary	34,000

Vital statistics, 1972: Births, 280,131; deaths, 81,760.

The indigenous population are of Malayo-Polynesian stock, divided into 18 linguistic groups of which the principal are Merina (30%) of the central plateau, the Betsimisaraka (15%) of the east coast, and the Betsileo (14%) of the southern plateau. Foreign communities include Europeans, mainly French (40,000), Indians (16,000), Chinese (9,000), Comorians and Arabs.

CONSTITUTION AND GOVERNMENT. The new Constitution of the Democratic Republic of Madagascar was approved by referendum on 21 Dec. 1975 and came into force on 30 Dec. It provides for a bicameral Parliament, comprising a Senate of 50 members and a National People's Assembly of 137 members elected by universal suffrage for a 5-year term from the single list of the *Front National pour la Défense de la Révolution Malgache;* following the general elections held on 30 June 1977, this comprised 112 members of the *Avant-garde de la Révolution Malgache,* 16 of the *Parti du Congrès de l'Indépendence* and 9 others.

Executive power is vested in the President, elected for 7 years, who appoints a Council of Ministers to assist him, with the guidance of the 20-member Supreme Revolutionary Council.

President: Lieut.-Cdr. Didier Ratsiraka.

The Council of Ministers in Oct. 1982 was composed as follows:

Prime Minister: Lieut.-Col. Désiré Rakotoarijaona.

Foreign Affairs: Richard Christian Rémi. *Defence:* Capt de Vaisseau Guy Sibon. *Interior:* Portos Ampy. *Civil Service and Labour:* Georges Ruphin. *Finance:* Pascal Rakotomavo. *Health:* Jean-Jacques Séraphin. *Industry and Commerce:* Georges Solofoson. *Rural Development and Agrarian Reform:* Nirina Andriamanerasoa. *Posts and Telecommunications:* Rakotavao Andriantiana. *Secondary and Basic Education:* Théophile Andrianoelisoa. *Higher Education and Scientific Research:* Ignace Rakoto. *Information and Ideological Guidance:* Bruno Rakotomavo. *Revolutionary Art and Culture:* Gisêle Rabesahala. *Youth and Sports:* Ali Koussay Said. *Transport, Supply and Tourism:* Joseph Bedo. *Public Works:* Cmdt Victor Ramahatra. *Population and Social Welfare:* Dr Remi Tiandraza. *Justice:* Gilbert Sambson.

National flag: Horizontally red over green, in the hoist a vertical white strip.

National anthem: Ry tanindrazanay malala ô!

Malagasy, which is a language of Malayo-Polynesian origin, is the official language. French and English are understood and taught in Malagasy schools.

Local Government: The six provinces are sub-divided into 18 prefectures, which in turn are divided in 92 sub-prefectures and finally into 11,000 *fokontany* (the traditional communal divisions).

DEFENCE

Army. The Army in 1983 had a strength of 20,000 organized in 2 infantry battalions, and 1 engineer, 1 signals and 1 service regiment.

Navy. The Navy in 1983 had a strength of 600 (including a company of marines), equipped with 1 large patrol craft, 5 patrol boats, 1 landing ship, 7 small landing craft and a training ship.

Air Force. Created in 1961, the Malagasy Air Force received its first combat equipment in 1978, with the arrival of 8 MiG-21 and 4 MiG-17 fighters, plus flying and ground staff instructors, from North Korea. Other equipment includes 4 An-26 turboprop transports, 6 L-39 jet trainers, 1 Britten-Norman Defender armed transport, 5 C-47s, 2 Yak-40s for VIP use, 1 Aztec, 3 Cessna Skymasters, 4 Cessna 172Ms and 6 helicopters, comprising 2 Mi-8s, 1 Bell 47, 1 Alouette II and 2 Alouette IIIs. Personnel about 500.

INTERNATIONAL RELATIONS

Membership. Madagascar is a member of UN, OAU and is an ACP state of EEC.

ECONOMY

Planning. A development plan, 1978–80, envisaged an annual growth rate of 5%. The main aim was to increase agricultural production through the rural reform plan based on the *fokonolona* communes and distributive co-operatives.

Budget. The local revenue is derived chiefly from income tax, from customs and other indirect taxes, from territorial lands, from posts and telegraphs, markets and miscellaneous sources. The chief branches of expenditure are general administration, public works, health services, education, the post office and the public debt. The general budget for 1982 provided for an expenditure of 256,050m. FMG.

Currency. The Malagasy *franc* (FMG) = 0·02 French franc.

Banking. A Central Bank was formed in July 1973, replacing the former *Institut d'Emission Malgache* as the central bank of issue. All commercial banking and insurance was nationalised in June 1975. Industrial development is financed through the *Bankin'ny Indostria,* and other commercial banking undertaken by the *Bankin'ny Tantsaha Mpamokatra* and the *Banky Fampandrosoana ny Varotra.*

Weights and Measures. The metric system is in use.

ENERGY AND NATURAL RESOURCES

Oil. The oil refinery at Toamasina has a capacity of 12,000 bbls a day.

Minerals. Mining production (in tonnes) included: Mica (1977), 1,498; graphite (1977), 15,726; chrome (1979), 200,000; ilmenite, 1,857; zircon, 209; beryl, 1971 (industrial), 52; gold (1971), 17 kg; garnet, 1971 (industrial), 40.

Agriculture. In 1978, 83% of the working population was employed in agriculture. The principal agricultural products in 1979 were (in 1,000 tonnes): Rice, 2,327; cassava, 1,348; mangoes, 278; bananas, 450; potatoes, 134; sugar, 115; corn, 100; sweet potatoes, 340; coffee, 90; oranges, 83; pineapples, 53; groundnuts, 30; sisal, 25; cotton, 12; tobacco, 5.

Cattle breeding and agriculture are the chief occupations. There were, in 1980, 8·8m. cattle, 570,000 pigs, 630,000 sheep, 1·6m. goats and 14·8m. poultry.

Forestry. The forests contain many valuable woods, while gum, resins and plants for tanning, dyeing and medicinal purposes abound.

Fisheries. The fish catch in 1979 was 54,000 tonnes.

INDUSTRY AND TRADE

Industry. Industry, hitherto confined mainly to the processing of agricultural products, is now extending to cover other fields.

Commerce. Trade in 1m. FMG:

	1977	*1978*	*1979*	*1980*
Imports (c.i.f)	85,217	99,632	135,319	126,775
Exports (f.o.b)	82,634	87,214	83,826	84,781

The chief exports in 1980 were coffee (53%) and cloves (8%); France took 20% of exports, the USA 20% and Japan 10%, while France provided 41% of imports, Federal Republic of Germany 10% and Japan 5%.

Total trade between Madagascar and UK (British Department of Trade returns, in £1,000 sterling):

	1978	*1979*	*1980*	*1981*	*1982*
Imports to UK	4,162	2,963	4,148	2,937	3,355
Exports and re-exports from UK	3,592	4,152	11,817	5,322	3,548

COMMUNICATIONS

Roads. In 1979 there were 27,556 km of roads of which 4,526 km bitumenized, with 57,000 passenger cars and 50,000 commercial vehicles (including buses).

Railways. In 1980 there were 883 km of railways, all metre gauge. In 1980, 3·5m. passengers and 698,000m. tonnes of cargo were transported.

Aviation. Air France and Air Madagascar connect Antananarivo with Paris, Alitalia connects with Rome. Several weekly services operated by Air Madagascar connect the capital with the ports and the chief inland towns. The main airfields are at Ivato, Toamasina, Toliary and Mahajanga. In 1979, 326,275 passengers arrived and 8,684 tonnes of cargo departed on international flights.

Shipping. Toamasina, Mahajanga, Antseranana, Toliary, Nossi-Bé and Manakara are the principal ports. In 1980, registered merchant marine was 56 vessels (of more than 100 GRT) with a total of 91,211 GRT.

Post and Broadcasting. There were in 1971, 547 post offices and agencies and 55 wireless telegraph stations. The telegraph line has a length of 17,400 km. There were 66,000 km of telephone line and, in 1978, 28,686 telephone subscribers. In Dec. 1977, there were more than 1m. radio receivers and 12,000 television receivers.

Cinemas. There were, in 1974, 31 cinemas with a seating capacity of 12,500.

JUSTICE, RELIGION, EDUCATION AND WELFARE

Justice. The Supreme Court and the Court of Appeal are in Antananarivo. In each provincial capital there is a Court of First Instance (for civil and commercial cases) and a *juge de paix* (for criminal cases).

Religion. Since 1818 a large portion of the Merina and other ethnic groups in the central districts have been Christianized. Many of the missionary societies which worked in Madagascar have now established churches. The 2 largest religious bodies are Roman Catholics with 1·8m. members (5,000 churches) and Fiangonan'i Jesosy Kristy eto Madagascar (FJKM) with 1·3m. members and 5,161 churches. There are also other smaller Christian churches and 75 mosques.

Education. Education is compulsory from 6 to 14 years of age in the primary schools. In 1978 there were 1,311,000 pupils and 23,937 teachers in public primary schools, while in 1976 there were 114,468 pupils in secondary schools and about 7,000 in technical schools. The University of Madagascar has a main campus at Antananarivo and 5 university centres in the other provincial capitals, with about 21,000 students in 1979.

There are also 4 agricultural schools at Nanisana, Ambatondrazaka, Marovoay and Ivoloina.

Health. In 1976 there were 886 hospitals and dispensaries with 19,781 beds; there were also 767 doctors, 93 dentists, 141 pharmacists, 1,010 midwives and 2,252 nursing personnel.

DIPLOMATIC REPRESENTATIVES

Of Madagascar in Great Britain
Ambassador: Henri Raharijaona (resides in Paris).

Of Great Britain in Madagascar (Immeuble Ny Havana, Cite de 67 Ha, Antananarivo)
Ambassador: R. J. Langridge.

Of Madagascar in the USA (2374 Massachusetts Ave., NW, Washington, D.C., 20008)
Ambassador: Benjamin Razafintseheno.

Of USA in Madagascar (14 rue Rainitovo, Antsohavola, Antananarivo)
Ambassador: Fernando E. Rondon.

Of Madagascar to the United Nations
Ambassador: Blaise Rabetafika.

Books of Reference

Statistical Information: The Service de Statistique Générale in Antananarivo published the *Bulletin mensuel de Madagascar* (from 1971); continuation of the trimestrial *Bulletin de statistique générale* (1949–71), the *Revue de Madagascar,* the *Madagascar à travers ses provinces* (latest issue, 1953), the *Annuaire Statistique de Madagascar* (vol. 1, 1938–51, published 1953, the *Situation Economique au Janvier 1968, Population de Madagascar au 1er Jan. 1971,* and the *Statistiques du Commerce Extérieur de Madagascar).*
Bulletin de l'Académie Malgache (from 1902)
Brown, M., *Madagascar Rediscovered.* London, 1978
Deschamps, H., *Histoire de Madagascar.* Paris, 4th ed. 1972
Heseltine, N., *Madagascar.* London and New York, 1971

MALAWI

Capital: Lilongwe
Population: 5·9m. (1980)
GNP per capita: US$230 (1980)

HISTORY. Malawi was formerly the Nyasaland (until 1907 British Central Africa) Protectorate, constituted on 15 May 1891.

Nyasaland became a self-governing country on 1 Feb. 1963, and on 6 July 1964 an independent member of the Commonwealth under the name of Malawi. It became a republic on 6 July 1966.

AREA AND POPULATION. Malawi lies along the southern and western shores of Lake Malawi (the third largest lake in Africa), and is otherwise bounded north by Tanzania, south by Mozambique and west by Zambia. Land area (excluding inland water of Lakes Palombe, Chilwa and Chiuta) 36,325 sq. miles, divided into 3 regions and 24 districts, each administered by a District Commissioner.

Lake Malawi waters belonging to Malawi are 9,250 sq. miles and the whole Lake Malawi (including the waters under Mozambique by an agreement made between the two countries in 1950) is 11,650 sq. miles.

The results of the census held in Aug. 1966: 4,020,724 Africans, 11,299 Asians, 7,395 Europeans, 165 undetermined; total 4,039,583 (1,913,262 males, 2,126,321 females). Estimate (1980), 5·9m. Over 90% of the population live in rural areas.

Population of main towns (census 1977) was as follows: Blantyre, 219,011; Lilongwe, 98,718; Zomba, 24,234; Mzuzu, 16,108. The capital was Zomba, and on 1 Jan. 1975 Lilongwe, in the Central Region, was officially declared the capital. All ministries were to be located there by 1977–78. A new Constitution was introduced in 1966.

Population of the regions, 1966 (and census 1977): Northern, 497,491 (648,853); Central, 1,474,952 (2,143,716); Southern, 2,067,140 (2,754,891).

CONSTITUTION AND GOVERNMENT. The President of the republic is also head of Government and of the Malawi Congress Party. Malawi is a one-party state. Parliament is composed of 87 elected members elected for up to 5 years, and any number of nominated members. Elections were held in June 1978.

Life President, External Affairs, Agriculture, Justice, Works and Supplies: Ngwazi Dr H. Kamuzu Banda. (Took office 6 July 1966 and became Life President on 6 July 1971).

Finance: L. C. Chaziya Phiri. *Transport and Communications:* Henry Harawa. *Education and Culture:* Dick Tennyson Matenje. *Local Government:* Louis Chimango. *Trade and Industry:* S. Zondwayo Jere. *Health:* John Twaibu Sangala. *Youth and Sports:* D. D. Chimphwanya. *Labour and Social Welfare:* Wadson Bini Deleza. *OAU and UN Affairs:* M. M. Lungu. *Without Portfolio, Secretary-General of Malawi Congress Party:* Elson Bakili Muluzi. *Regional Ministers:* Edward Chitsulo Isaac Bwanali (*Southern Region*), Robson Watayachanga Chirwa (*Northern Region*), Aaron E. Gadama (*Central Region*).

National flag: Three equal horizontal stripes of black, red, green, with a red rising sun on the centre of the black stripe.

DEFENCE

Army. The army consists of a headquarters—a large infantry battalion complete with its own supporting arms and services—and a depot back-up of an engineering workshop and an ordnance depot in Zomba, Lilongwe and at Mzuzu. The total strength is 4,650 (all services, 1983). The army is organized into 5 infantry battalions and 4 support battalions.

Navy. There are 3 small lake patrol boats and 1 gunboat. Uniformed personnel in 1983 totalled 30.

Air wing. To support the infantry battalion, the Air Wing has 4 C-47 Transport aircraft, 1 Defender armed light transport, 12 Do28D Skyservant light transports, 6 Do 27 training aircraft, and 6 Puma and 1 Alouette III helicopters. An HS 125 jet is used for VIP transport.

INTERNATIONAL RELATIONS

Membership. Malawi is a member of UN, the Commonwealth, OAU, and is an ACP state of EEC.

ECONOMY

Planning. The Government of Malawi operates a 3-year 'rolling' public-sector investment programme, revised annually to take into account changing needs and the expected level of resources available. The greatest part of the development programme is annually financed from external aid, and priority in the use of resources has always been given to providing the counterpart contributions to funds received from external sources. The balance of these local resources is used for financing projects commanding high national priority for which no external funds can be secured.

The two tables below give a summary of the Government's Development Programme for the 3 years 1977–80 and the sources of finance (in K.1m.).

Government Development Expenditure	*1977-78*	*1978-79*	*1979-80*	*Total 3 Years*	*%*
Agriculture and natural resources	22·1	19·1	18·7	59·9	17·2
Transportation	50·3	58·9	51·8	161·0	46·4
Posts and telecommunications	4·2	4·4	1·4	10·0	2·9
Power	10·5	14·8	15·0	40·3	11·6
Education	5·9	6·4	5·2	17·5	5·0
Health	1·9	2·8	2·2	6·9	2·0
Water supplies and sanitation	6·4	5·5	3·1	15·0	4·3
New capital–Lilongwe	2·7	1·2	0·8	4·7	1·4
Housing	3·0	2·5	1·7	7·2	2·1
Other	8·5	11·3	4·9	24·7	7·1
Total	115·5	126·9	104·8	347·2	100·0
Finance					
British government loan	11·5	10·6	11·2	33·3	9·5
Other externally financed	2·8	1·5	—	4·3	1·2
External financed	88·1	101·2	80·4	269·7	77·7
Counterpart to external aid	8·9	9·0	8·3	26·2	7·6
Wholly locally financed projects	4·2	4·6	4·9	13·7	3·9
Total	115·5	126·9	104·8	347·2	100·0

Budget. Revenue Account receipts and expenditure (in K.1,000) for years ending 31 March:

	1974–75	*1975–76*	*1976–77*[1]	*1977–78*	*1978–79*
Revenue	78,687	89,701	89,860	132,340	173,820
Expenditure	73,831	84,422	90,827	184,850	254,520

[1]Provisional.

Main revenue items (in K.1,000) in 1976–77 are: Direct taxes, 34,902; indirect taxes, 34,805.

Main expenditure items (in K.1,000) in 1975–76 were: Public debt charges, 12,714; education, 11,867; general administration, 9,152.

Currency. In 1971 a new decimalized currency was introduced, the *kwacha* (dawn), which is subdivided into 100 *tambala* (cockerels). From 9 June 1975 the kwacha has been pegged to Special Drawing Rights. In March 1983: £1 sterling = K.1·67, US$1 = K.1·1126.

Banking. In July 1964 the Reserve Bank of Malawi was set up with a capital of K.1m. to be responsible for the issue of currency and the holding of external reserves and to issue treasury bills and local registered stock on behalf of the Government. Since then, the Reserve Bank has fully assumed the responsibilities of a Central Bank.

The National Bank of Malawi has a total of 10 branches in major urban areas and 19 static and 35 mobile agencies in rural areas. The Commercial Bank of Malawi Ltd opened in 1970 and has branches at Limbe, Lilongwe and Zomba and an agency in Dedza and headquarters at Blantyre.

In 1972 The Investment Development Bank of Malawi was established in Blantyre. Its resources are derived from domestic and foreign official sources and its objective is to provide medium and long-term credits to private entities considered of importance to the economy.

The post office savings bank has 223 offices conducting savings business throughout the country, and the New Building Society has agencies in Limbe, Zomba and Lilongwe with its head office in Blantyre. Two finance houses now operate in Malawi, providing longer-term industrial and consumer finance.

Weights and Measures. British measures are in use; the metric system is being introduced gradually.

ENERGY AND NATURAL RESOURCES

Electricity. The first stage of the Tedzani Project, two 8 mw sets, was commissioned in July 1973 which, together with the 24 mw Nkula hydro-electric station, will meet the power demands of the interconnected systems of the Southern Region and Lilongwe. With the completion of a barrage at Tedzani these machines will be uprated to 10 mw each and, with the addition of thermal plant to the system sufficient power will be available to meet forecast demands prior to the commissioning in 1977 of the second stage of the Tedzani Project, a further two 10 mw sets. The Electricity Supply Commission also operates stations at Mangochi, Mzuzu, Kasungu, Liwonde, Chikwawa and Salima. A total of 252·96m. kwh. were sold by the Electricity Supply Commission in 1976.

Minerals. The main product in 1976 was marble (149,254 tonnes) for the manufacture of cement.

Agriculture. Malawi is predominantly an agricultural country. Up to March 1977 519,300 of the rural population had been reached by self-help piped water projects, of which 427,700 were in the Southern region. In 1976 agriculture contributed 46·1% to the GDP, and agricultural produce accounted for over 79% of total exports. Of the total area of 23·3m. acres, 13·1m. could be cultivated and, in 1969, 3·36m. were being cultivated, of which 2·64m. were under maize. Maize is the main subsistence crop and is grown by over 95% of all smallholders. Almost all the surplus crops produced by smallholders are sold to the Agricultural Development and Marketing Corporation. In 1976 the corporation purchased: Tobacco, K.6·03m.; groundnuts, K.5·38m.; maize, K.3·54m.; cotton, K.3·02m.; rice, K.2·42m.; pulses, K.1·9m.

Livestock in 1980: Cattle, 823,000; sheep, 75,000; goats, 630,000; pigs, 180,000.

Forestry. In 1976 (estimate) 535,510 cu. ft of sawn timber were produced, valued at K.1·3m. The value of other forest products was K.536,986.

Fisheries. Landings in 1977 (provisional) were 66,000 short tons valued at K.6·6m.

INDUSTRY AND TRADE

Industry. Index of manufacturing output (1970 = 100): manufacturing for domestic consumption 177·7 (229·5 in 1980); of this consumer goods were at 191·9 (252·5) and intermediate goods mainly for building and construction were at 128·6 (150·4). Manufacturing for export, 172·3 (201·6).

Labour:

	1978		
	Private	*Government*	*Total*
Agriculture, forestry, fishing	147,962	21,371	169,333
Mining and quarrying	564	–	564
Manufacturing	34,862	1,093	35,955
Electricity and water	2,459	463	2,922
Building and construction	27,418	4,052	31,470
Trade, hotels, restaurants	26,829	382	27,211
Transport storage, communications	13,809	3,808	17,617
Financial services	6,194	623	6,817
Community, social, personal services	10,794	36,601	47,395
Total	270,891	68,393	339,284

Commerce. The main items of export in 1979 were (in K.1m.): Tobacco, 98·6; tea, 30·6; sugar, 16·1; groundnuts, 8·7. Malawi's imports in the same year (in K.1m.) included capital equipment, 44·6; means of transport, 46·1; consumer goods, 46·7; building materials, 25·2.

Trade statistics for calendar years are (in K.1m.):

	1977	*1978*	*1979*	*1980*
Imports	209·8	284·7	324·8	356·2
Exports	180·3	155·7	181·7	238·2

Total trade between Malawi and UK (British Department of Trade returns, in £1,000 sterling):

	1979	*1980*	*1981*	*1982*
Imports to UK	46,464	45,651	34,744	42,478
Exports and re-exports from UK	27,088	25,749	21,503	20,893

Tourism. There were 47,220 visitors to Malawi in 1980.

COMMUNICATIONS

Roads. In 1976 there were 1,877 miles of main road, of which 772 were bitumen-surfaced and 206 gravel; 1,520 miles of secondary roads, of which 215 were surfaced; 3,426 miles of district and other roads, of which 148 were surfaced. Motor vehicles licensed, 29,085, of which 10,222 were cars and 10,642 goods vehicles.

Railways. Malawi Railways (789 km–1,067 mm gauge) operates a main line from Salima to the Mozambique border near Nsanje, from which running powers over the Trans-Zambesia Railway allow access to the port of Beira; a branch opened in 1970 runs eastwards from a point 16 km south of Balaka to the Mozambique border to give a direct route to the deep-water port of Nacala. The 26-km section from Nsanje to the border is operated by the Central Africa Railway Co. Ltd. An extension of 111 km from Salima to the new state capital of Lilongwe was opened in Feb. 1979, and a further extension to Mchinji on the Zambian border (120 km) was completed in 1981. In 1981, 1·2m. tonnes hauled, 77·9m. passenger-km run.

Aviation. In 1980 Chileka airport handled 188,514 passengers and 12,472 tonnes of freight. Lilongwe airport handled 50,223 and 538 tonnes.

Shipping. In 1976 lake ships carried 131,000 passengers and 33,000 short tons of freight.

Post. Number of telephones (1981) 15,130.

Newspapers (1980). *The Daily Times* (English, Monday to Friday); 5,700–6,300 copies daily (1977). *Malawi News* (English and Chichewa, Saturdays); 16,000 copies weekly. *The African* (English and Chichewa, fortnightly).

JUSTICE, RELIGION, EDUCATION AND WELFARE

Justice. Justice is administered in the High Court, the magistrates' courts and traditional courts. There are 23 magistrates' courts, 176 traditional courts and 23 local appeal courts.

Appeals from traditional courts are dealt with in the traditional appeal courts and in the national traditional appeal court. Appeals from magistrates' courts lie to the High Court, and appeals from the High Court to Malawi's Supreme Court of Appeal.

Religion. In 1972 the Roman Catholic Church claimed 1,073,000 members; the Presbyterian Church of Central Africa, 846,000; the Diocese of Malawi (part of the Province of Central Africa of the Anglican Communion), 79,000; Seventh-day Adventist Church, 93,000; Zambezi Evangelical Church (formerly Nyasa Mission), 36,000; Assemblies of God, 7,000; Seventh-day Baptists (Central Africa conference), 11,000; Churches of Christ, 21,000; African Evangelical Church, 7,000; Evangelical Church of Malawi, 18,000. Moslems are estimated to number between 500,000 and 1m.

Education (1978–79). The Ministry of Education and Culture controls all aspects of education.

The number of pupils in the 2,250 primary schools was 705,956; in the 62 secondary schools, 15,500. There were 11,425 teachers in primary schools and 739 in secondary schools. The primary school course is of 8 years duration, followed by a 4-year secondary course. English is taught from the 1st year and becomes the general medium of instruction from the 4th year.

Teacher-training is undertaken in 8 residential colleges, 3 of which are directly controlled by the Ministry; the others receive grants in aid as assisted institutions. Courses last 3 years. Enrolment 1,100. Technical and trade courses are offered in commerce, building, woodwork and mechanical engineering, as well as home craft for girls; 1,904 trainees undertook courses at government and voluntary schools in 1966.

The University of Malawi was inaugurated on 6 Oct. 1965. In 1975–76 there were 1,148 students taking degree and diploma courses.

Health. In 1979 there were 482 medical institutions and 8,991 hospital beds.

DIPLOMATIC REPRESENTATIVES

Of Malawi in Great Britain (33 Grosvenor St., London, W1)
High Commissioner: C. Mkona.

Of Great Britain in Malawi (Lingadzi Hse., Lilongwe, 3)
High Commissioner: A. H. Brind.

Of Malawi in the USA (1400 20th St., NW, Washington, D.C., 20036)
Ambassador: N. T. Mizere.

Of the USA in Malawi (PO Box 30016, Lilongwe)
Ambassador: John A. Burroughs, Jr.

Of Malawi to the United Nations
Ambassador: N. T. Mizere.

Books of Reference

General Information: The Chief Information Officer, PO Box 494, Blantyre.
Boeder, R. B. *Malawi.* [Bibliography] Oxford and Santa Barbara, 1981
McMaster, C., *Malawi: Foreign Policy and Development.* London, 1974
Read, F. E., *Malawi, Land of Promise.* Govt. Dept. of Information, 1967.—*Malawi, Land of Progress.* Govt. Dept.of Information, 1969
Williams, T. D., *Malawi: The Politics of Despair.* Cornell Univ. Press, 1979

MALAYSIA

Capital: Kuala Lumpur
Population: 14·42m. (1982)
GNP per capita: US$1,670 (1980)

HISTORY. On 16 Sept. 1963 Malaysia came into being, consisting of the Federation of Malaya, the State of Singapore and the colonies of North Borneo (renamed Sabah) and Sarawak. The agreement between the UK and the 4 territories was signed on 9 July (Cmnd. 2094); by it, the UK relinquished sovereignty over Singapore, North Borneo and Sarawak from independence day and extended the 1957 defence agreement with Malaya to apply to Malaysia. Malaysia became automatically a member of the Commonwealth of Nations. *See* map in THE STATESMAN'S YEAR-BOOK, 1964–65.

On 9 Aug. 1965, by a mutual agreement dated 7 Aug. 1965 between Malaysia and Singapore, Singapore seceded from Malaysia to become an independent Sovereign nation.

POPULATION. 1981 census gave 11,428,000 in Peninsular Malaysia, 1,034,000 in Sabah, and 1,323,000 in Sarawak. Total population 13,785,000.

CONSTITUTION AND GOVERNMENT. The Constitution of Malaysia is based on the Constitution of the former Federation of Malaya, but includes safeguards for the special interests of Sabah and Sarawak.

The federal capital is Kuala Lumpur, established on 1 Feb. 1974 with an area of approximately 94 sq. miles. The official language is Malay.

The Constitution provides for one of the 9 Rulers of the Malay States to be elected from among themselves to be the *Yang di-Pertuan Agong* (Supreme Head of the Federation). He holds office for a period of 5 years. The Rulers also elect from among themselves a Deputy Supreme Head of State, also for a period of 5 years.

Supreme Head of State (Yang di-Pertuan Agong): HM Sultan Haji Ahmad Shah Al-Musta'in Billah Ibni Al-Marhum Sultan Abu Bakar Ri'Ayatuddin Al-Mu'Adzam Shah, DKM, DKP, DK, SSAP, SPCM, SPMJ, elected as 7th *Yang di-Pertuan Agong* from 26 April 1979.

Raja of Perlis: HRH Tuanku Syed Putra ibni Al-Marhum Syed Hassan Jamalullail, DK, DKM, DMN, SMN, SPMP, SPDK, acceded 12 March 1949.

Sultan of Kedah: HRH Tuanku Haji Abdul Halim Mu'adzam Shah ibni Al-Marhum Sultan Badlishah, DK, DKH, DKM, DMN, DUK, SPMK, SSDK, acceded 20 Feb. 1959.

Sultan of Johore: HRH Almutawakkil Alallah Sultan Iskandar Al-Haj, acceded 11 May 1981.

Sultan of Selangor: HRH Sultan Salahuddin Abdul Aziz Shah ibni Al-Marhum Sultan Hisamuddin 'Alam Shah Al-Haj, DK, DMN, SPMS, SPDK, acceded 28 June 1961.

Sultan of Perak: HRH Sultan Idris Al-Mutawakkil Alallahi Shah ibni Al-Marhum Sultan Iskandar Shah Kadasallah, DK, DMN, SPMP, SPCM, SPTS, CMG, PJK, acceded 26 Oct. 1963.

Yang di-Pertuan Besar of Negeri Sembilan: HRH Tuanku Ja'afar ibni Al-Marhum Tuanku Abdul Rahman, DMN, DK, acceded 8 April 1968.

Sultan of Kelantan: HRH Sultan Ismail Petra ibni Al-Marhum Sultan Yahya Petra, DK, SPMK, SJMK, SPSM, appointed 29 March 1979.

Sultan of Trengganu: HRH Sultan Mahmud Al Muktafi ibni Al-Marhum Tuanku Al-Sultan Ismail Nasiruddin Shah, DK, SPMT, SPCM, appointed 20 Sept. 1979.

Acting Sultan of Pehang: HRH Tengku Abdullah Ibni Sultan Haji Ahmad Shah Al-Musta'in Billah, DK, SSAP, SIMP, appointed 28 June 1980.

Yang di-Pertua Negeri Pulau Pinang: HE Dato' Dr Awang bin Hassan, DUPN, SPMJ, appointed 1 May 1981.

Governor of Malacca: HE Tun Haji Syed Zahiruddin bin Syed Hassan, DUNM, PSM, SMN, SPMP, JMN, PJK, appointed 23 May 1975; re-appointed 23 May 1979.

Yang di-Pertua Negeri Sarawak: HE Tan Sri Dr Haji Abdul Rahman bin Ya'kub, DP, PMN, SPMJ, SIMP, SPMK, SSDK, SPMP, SPMS, SPDK, appointed 2 April 1981.

Yang di-Pertua Sabah: HE Datuk Mohamad Adnan Roberts, SMN, SPDK, appointed 26 June 1978.

Parliament consists of the *Yang di-Pertuan Agong* and two *Majlis* (Houses of Parliament) known as the *Dewan Negara* (Senate) of 68 members and *Dewan Rakyat* (House of Representatives) of 154 members. There are 149 members from the states in Malaysia and 5 from the Federal Territory. Appointment to the Senate is for 3 years. The maximum life of the House of Representatives is 5 years, subject to its dissolution at any time by the *Yang di-Pertuan Agong* on the advice of his Ministers.

National flag: Fourteen horizontal stripes of red and white, with a blue quarter bearing a crescent and a star of 14 points, all in gold.

The elections to the House of Representatives held on 22 April 1982, returned the following members: National Front, 139; Democratic Action Party, 9; PAS, 5; Independent, 8.

The Cabinet was in March 1983 composed as follows:

Prime Minister and Minister of Defence: Datuk Seri Dr Mahathir bin Mohamad, SSDK, SPMJ, SPMS, SSAP, DP.

Deputy Prime Minister and Home Affairs: Dato Musa Hitam, SPMJ, SSIJ. *Transport:* (Vacant). *Science, Technology and Environment:* Datuk Amar Stephen Yong. *Foreign Affairs:* Tan Sri Haji Muhammad Ghazali bin Shafie, PMN, SSAP, SIMP, SDPK. *Welfare Services:* Datin Paduka Hajjah Aishah binti Haji Abdul Ghani, DPMS, JMN. *Trade and Industry:* Tengku Ahmad Rithauddeen bin Tengku Ismail. *Finance:* Tengku Tan Sri Razaleigh Hamzah, DK, SPMK, PSM. *Health:* Tan Sri Chong Hon Nyan, PSM, JMN. *Land and Federal Development:* Dato Rais bin Yatim. *Information:* Encik Adib bin Adam. *Labour and Manpower:* Dato Mak Hon Kam. *Primary Industries:* Dato Paul Leong Khee Seong, DPCM. *Agriculture:* Dato Abdul Manan bin Othman, DPMT, PPT. *Energy, Telecommunications and Posts:* Datuk Leo Moggie Anak Irok, PNBS. *Housing and Local Government:* Dato Dr Neo Yee Pan, SPMJ, DPMJ. *Works and Public Utilities:* Datuk Samy Vellu, DPMS, PCM, AMN. *Culture, Youth and Sports:* Dato Mokhtar bin Hashim, DSNS. *Public Enterprises:* Datin Paduka Rafidah Aziz, DPMS, AMN. *Education:* Dato Dr Sulaiman bin Haji Daud. *Federal Territory:* Datuk Pengiran Othman bin Haji Pengiran Rauf, PGDK, ADK. *National and Rural Development:* Datuk Sanusi bin Junid. *Without Portfolio:* Dato Abdullah Ahmad.

DEFENCE. The Malaysian Armed Forces are made up of the Malaysian Army, the Royal Malaysian Navy and the Royal Malaysian Air Force. Each Service has its own component of reserves.

The Malaysian Constitution provides for the *Yang di-Pertuan Agong* (Supreme Head of State) to be the Supreme Commander of the Armed Forces who exercises his powers and authority in accordance with the advice of the Cabinet. Under the general authority of the Yang di-Pertuan Agong and the Cabinet, there is the Armed Forces Council which is responsible for the command, discipline and administration of all other matters relating to the Armed Forces, other than those relating to its operational use.

The Armed Forces Council is chaired by the Minister of Defence and its membership consists of the chief of the Defence Forces, the 3 Service Chiefs and 2 other senior military officers, the Secretary-General of the Ministry of Defence, a representative of State Rulers and an appointed member.

The chief of the Armed Forces Staff is the professional head of the Armed Forces and the senior military member in the Armed Forces Council. He is the principal adviser to the Minister of Defence on the military aspects of all defence matters. The chief of the Armed Forces Staff's committee, established under the authority of the Armed Forces Council, is the highest level at which joint planning and co-ordination with the Armed Forces are carried out. The Committee is chaired by the chief of the Armed Forces Staff and its membership consists of the chief of the Army, Navy and Air Force, the chief of Personnel Staff, the chief of logistic Staff and the chief of Staff of the Ministry of Defence.

Army. The Malaysian Army is made up of both regular and volunteer Force. The regular force comprises 11 Infantry brigade groups in 3 Divisions and 1 semi-independent regional security command. Each brigade consists of Infantry, reconnaissance, artillery, signals, engineers and is supported by adequate logistics units. The Malaysian army is still in the process of implementing its expansion programme. The regular force has a total strength of approximately 80,000.

The Volunteer Force has one division made up of combatant reserve units and manpower reserve pool with an approximately total strength of 30,000. Reserve Officer Training Units (ROTU) are also being set up in all Institutions of higher learning to act as officers reserve pool in time of emergency.

The Royal Military College (RMC) at Sungei Besi near Kuala Lumpur and Officer Cadet School (OCS) at Port Dickson train regular and short service commissioned officers respectively. The RMC has a Boys' Wing (Academic Wing) which shapes-up young Malaysians to be officers in the Armed Forces, Officers in the higher divisions of the public service and as leaders in the professional, commercial and industrial life of the country.

Navy. The Royal Malaysian Navy is commanded by the Chief of the Naval Staff from the integrated Ministry of Defence in Kuala Lumpur. The main naval bases are KD Malaya situated on Singapore Island, KD Sri Labuan on Labuan Island and KD Pelandok in Lumut, Perak. These establishments are responsible for the operation and administration of the ships, and KD Pelandok for the training of personnel.

The ships include 2 British (Yarrow)-built frigates (including the former HMS *Mermaid*), 1 logistic support ship, 2 coastal minesweepers, 8 fast missile craft, 6 fast gunboats, 22 patrol craft, 3 landing ships, 1 diving tender, 1 survey vessel and 6 tugs. The peace-time tasks include fishery protection and anti-piracy patrols. There are also 50 armed patrol launches, 46 operated by the Royal Malaysian Police and 2 by the Government of Sabah (North Borneo) which also operates 3 patrol boats, 1 landing craft and a yacht.

Future plans include the provision of 4 corvettes, 4 mine countermeasures vessels, 6 coastguard patrol craft and 12 marine police patrol boats.

Naval personnel in 1983 exceeded 6,000 officers and ratings, plus 1,000 reservists and 800 volunteer reserve.

Air Force. Formed on 1 June 1958, the Royal Malaysian Air Force is equipped primarily to provide air defence and air support for the Army, Navy and Police. Its secondary rôle is to render assistance to Government departments and civilian organizations, especially during periods of national disasters. There were in early 1983 11 squadrons, of which 6 operated transport aircraft and helicopters. Up to 68 *ex*-US Navy A-4L/C Skyhawks are being refurbished progressively as the primary attack force. Other equipment includes 13 F-5E Tiger II jet fighter-bombers, 2 RF-5E reconnaissance-fighters, and 4 F-5F trainers, 11 Canadair CL-41G Tebuan dual-purpose light jet strike and training aircraft (being supplemented with Aermacchi MB 339s), 9 C-130H/H-MP Hercules four-turboprop heavy transports and maritime reconnaissance aircraft, 2 F.28 Fellowship VIP transports, 15 Caribou twin-engined STOL transports, 35 Sikorsky S-61A-4 Nuri heavy troop and cargo transport helicopters, 20 Alouette III, 3 Agusta-Bell 212, 9 Bell 47 and 5 Bell 206B JetRanger helicopters, 12 Cessna 402Bs for twin-engine training and liaison, 44 PC-7 Turbo-Trainers and 2 H.S. 125 Merpati twin-jet executive transports. Personnel (1982) totalled about 11,000.

Volunteer Forces. The Army Volunteer Force (Territorial Army) consists of first-line infantry, signals, engineer and logistics units able to take the field with the active army, and a second-line organization to provide local defence. There is also a small Naval Volunteer Reserve with Headquarters in Penang and Kuala Lumpur. The Royal Malaysian Air Force Volunteer Reserve has both air and ground elements.

INTERNATIONAL RELATIONS

Membership. Malaysia is a member of UN, the Commonwealth, the Colombo Plan and ASEAN.

ECONOMY

Planning. The fourth 5-year plan, 1981–85 envisaged an expenditure of M$42,830m. and aimed at national unity through the two-pronged objectives of eradicating poverty irrespective of race and of restructuring society to eliminate the identification of race with economic functions, are achieved.

Budget. Revenue and expenditure for calendar years, in M$1m.:

	1977	*1978*	*1979*[1]	*1980*[1]	*1981*[2]
Revenue	7,760	8,841	10,505	13,926	14,972
Operating expenditure[3]	7,398	8,041	10,040	13,617	14,600
Development expenditure	3,782	3,782	4,282	5,140	6,190

[1] Latest Estimate. [2] Budget Estimate.
[3] Including contribution to sinking fund from 1975.

Currency. Bank Negara Malaysia (Central Bank of Malaysia) assumed sole currency issuing authority in Malaysia on 12 June 1967. The unit of currency issued by Bank Negara Malaysia is the Malaysian *ringgit* ($) which is divided into 100 *sen*. Currency notes are of denominations of $1, 5, 10, 50, 100 and $1,000. Coins are of denominations of 1 *sen*, 5, 10, 20, 50 *sen* and $1, $5, $10, $15, $25, $100, $200, $250 and $500. The circulation of currency on 31 Dec. 1980 was M$5,104·61m.

Rate of exchange, March 1983: 2·30 *ringgit*=US$1; 3·34 *ringgit*=£1.

Banking. Thirty-eight banks were operating in Dec. 1980; of these 21 were domestic banks with a total of 398 banking offices. Five were banks incorporated in Singapore with 63 banking offices and the remaining 12 banks were foreign incorporated with 85 banking offices. Total deposits amounted to M$23,326·3m. on 31 Dec. 1980 and loans and advances amounted to M$20,872m.

The National Savings Bank (formerly known as the post office savings bank) held M$973·8m. due to 3,600,948 depositors at 31 Dec. 1978.

TRADE. Total trade of Malaysia with UK (British Department of Trade returns, in £1,000 sterling):

	1979	*1980*	*1981*	*1982*
Imports to UK	221,488	187,050	188,327	185,239
Exports and re-exports from UK	187,425	223,516	196,213	210,805

COMMUNICATIONS

Post. The Postal Services in Malaysia are under the Ministry of Power, Telecommunications and Post and are headed by the Director-General of Post, Malaysia.

Cinemas. In 1974 there were 500 cinemas with a seating capacity of 345,400.

JUSTICE. By virtue of Art. 121(1) of the Federal Constitution judicial power in the Federation is vested on 2 High Courts of co-ordinate jurisdiction and status namely the High Court of Malaya and the High Court of Borneo, and the inferior courts. The Federal Court with its principal registry in Kuala Lumpur is the Supreme Court in the country.

The Lord President as the supreme head of the Judiciary, the 2 Chief Justices of the High Courts and 6 other Judges form the constitution of the Federal Court. Apart from having exclusive jurisdiction to determine appeals from the High Court the Federal Court is also conferred with such original and consultative jurisdiction as is laid out in Articles 128 and 130 of the Constitution.

A panel of 3 Judges or such greater uneven number as may be determined by the Lord President preside in every proceeding in the Federal Court.

The right of appeal to the Yang di-Pertuan Agong (who in turn refers the appeal to the Judicial Committee of the British Privy Council) from a decision of the Federal Court in respect of criminal and constitutional matters was abolished on 1 July 1978.

DIPLOMATIC REPRESENTATIVES

Of Malaysia in Great Britain (45 Belgrave Sq., London, SW1X 8QT)
High Commissioner: M. H. Kassim (accredited 16 March 1983).

Of Great Britain in Malaysia (Wisma Damansara, Jalan Semantan, Kuala Lumpur)
High Commissioner: William Bentley, CMG.

Of Malaysia in the USA (2401 Massachusetts Ave., NW, Washington, D.C., 20008)
Ambassador: Datuk Zain Azraai bin Zainal Abidin.

Of the USA in Malaysia (A.I.A. Bldg., Jalan Ampang, Kuala Lumpur)
Ambassador: Ronald D. Palmer.

Of Malaysia to the United Nations
Ambassador: Dato Zainal Abidin bin Sulong.

Books of Reference

Statistical Information: The Department of Statistics, Malaysia, Kuala Lumpur, was set up in 1963, taking over from the Department of Statistics, States of Malaya. *Chief Statistician:* Khoo Teik Huat. Main publications: *Peninsular Malaysia Monthly* and *Annual Statistics of External Trade; Malaysia External Trade* (quarterly); *Peninsular Malaysia Statistical Bulletin* (monthly); *Rubber Statistics* (monthly); *Rubber Statistics Handbook* (annual); *Oil Palm Statistics* (monthly); *Oil Palm, Coconut and Tea Statistics* (annual); *Survey of Manufacturing Industries, 1974; National Accounts Statistics, 1973–1977; Malaysia Industrial Classification, 1972; Monthly Industrial Statistics, Malaysia; Census of Selected Service Trades, 1973.*

Huk Tee, L., and Sook Jean, W., Malaysia. [Bibliography] Oxford and Santa Barbara, 1983
Snodgrass, D. R., *Inequality and Economic Development in Malaysia.* OUP, 1982

PENINSULAR MALAYSIA

AREA AND POPULATION. The total area of Peninsular Malaysia is about 50,806 sq. miles (131,870 sq. km). The federal capital is Kuala Lumpur (94 sq. miles).

State	*Area (sq. miles)*	*Population (1980 Census)*	*Capital*	*Population (1980 Census)*
Johore	7,330	1,601,504	Johore Bharu	249,880
Kedah	3,639	1,102,200	Alor Star	71,682
Kelantan	5,765	877,575	Kota Bharu	170,559
Malacca	637	453,153	Malacca	88,073
Negeri Sembilan	2,565	563,955	Seremban	136,252
Pahang	13,886	770,644	Kuantan	136,625
Penang	399	911,586	Georgetown	250,578
Perak	8,110	1,762,288	Ipoh	300,727
Perlis	307	147,726	Kangar	12,956
Selangor	3,074	1,467,441	Shah Alam	24,138
Trengganu	5,002	542,280	Kuala Trengganu	186,608
Federal Territory	94	937,875	Kuala Lumpur	937,875
Peninsular Malaysia	50,806	11,128,227		

Population by races (1981 Census): 11,428,000 Malays; 6,168,000 Chinese; 3,995,000 Indians; 1,183,000 others. In 1974 Kuala Lumpur became a Federal District. Shah Alam became capital of Selangor. Vital statistics (1979): Births, 336,848; deaths, 64,345.

CONSTITUTION AND GOVERNMENT. The States of the Federation of Malaya, now known as Peninsular Malaysia, comprises the 11 States of Johore, Pahang, Negeri Sembilan, Selangor, Perak, Kedah, Perlis, Kelantan, Trengganu, Penang and Malacca. On 31 Aug. 1957 the Federation became the 11th sovereign member-state of the Commonwealth of Nations.

For earlier history of the States and Settlements *see* THE STATESMAN'S YEAR-BOOK, 1957, p. 241.

The Constitution is based on the agreements reached at the London conference of Jan.-Feb. 1956, between HM Government in the UK, the Rulers of the Malay states and the Alliance Party (which at the first federal elections on 27 July 1955 obtained 51 of the 52 elected members), and subsequently worked out by the Constitutional Commission appointed after that conference.

ECONOMY

Budget. Revenue and expenditure for calendar years, in M$1m.:

	1977	*1978*	*1979* [2]	*1980* [2]	*1981* [3]
Revenue	7,760	8,841	10,505	13,926	14,972
Current expenditure [1]	7,398	8,041	10,040	13,617	14,600
Development expenditure	3,782	3,782	4,282	5,140	6,190

[1] Excluding contribution to development and water supply funds but including recurrent expenditure from water supply fund, loan repayments and interest.

[2] Estimates. [3] Budget estimate.

Weights and Measures. The standard measures are the imperial yard, pound and gallon. The Weights and Measures Act of 1972 provides for a 10-year transition to the metric system, and was completed by 31 Dec. 1981.

ENERGY AND NATURAL RESOURCES

Electricity. In 1980, 8,974·1m. kwh. were generated; commerce and industry are the main consumers.

Minerals. Production (in tonnes): Tin-in-concentrates: 1980, 61,404; 1979, 62,995. Iron ore: 1980, 371,186; 1979, 350,498. Bauxite: 1980, 920,356; 1979, 386,520. Ilmenite (exports): 1980, 189,121; 1979, 199,819. Gold: 1980, 4,621 troy oz.; 1979, 5,273.

Agriculture. Total area under agricultural crops, 1978, 8m. acres. This included 254,830 acres of second season rice crops.

Rice: Production in 1982, 1,365,900 tons from 771,080 hectares.

Rubber: Production in 1982, 1·41m. tonnes; Oil-palms: Production in 1982 (estimate), 3·2m. tonnes of palm oil; 50,500 tonnes of cocoa; 257,000 tonnes of coconut oil.

Tea: Production in 1980, 3,202,000 kg.

Livestock: (1980) Cattle, 430,000; buffaloes, 293,000; sheep, 46,000; swine, 1,188,000; goats, 375,000.

Forestry (1982). Reserved forests, 4·9m. hectares. Production of logs (estimate), 6·4m.cu. metres; sawn timber, 5,488,000 cu. metres; plywood, 88,168,000 sq. metres (5mm thickness). Exports of veneer, 31·9m. sq. metres (5mm thickness).

Fisheries. Landings in 1982 (estimate), 861,000 tons; 1981, 827,700 tons. Number of vessels in 1979, 21,439 powered, 5,955 non-powered.

INDUSTRY AND TRADE

Trade Unions. There were, on 31 Dec. 1979, 385 registered trade unions with 568,419 members in Malaysia.

Commerce. Imports and exports for calendar years in M$1m.:

	1975	*1976*	*1977*	*1978*	*1979*	*1980*
Imports	7,516·1	8,513·5	9,880·7	12,156·7	17,161	23,539
Exports	7,695·8	10,042·7	11,230·9	13,680·3	24,219	28,201

Chief imports (1981); Machinery and transport equipment, M$9,864m.; manufactured goods, M$5,404m.; food, M$2,941m.

Chief exports (1981): Rubber, 1,485,000 tonnes (M$3,712m.); crude petroleum (M$2,904m.); sawn timber, 15,816,000 cu. metres (M$2,473m.); other exports (1980) palm oil, 871,349 tonnes (M$1,103m.); palm oil, crude, 619,705 tonnes (M$745·3m.); saw logs, 227,297 cu. metres (M$22·9m.); bauxite, 718,300 tonnes (M$20·8m.).

In 1980 imports came chiefly from Japan (M$4,245·6m.), USA (M$3,154·9m.), Singapore (M$2,155·9m.), Saudi Arabia (M$1,446·4m.), Australia (M$1,222m.), Federal Republic of Germany (M$1,135·5m.), Thailand (M$600·2m.), China (M$421·5m.), Indonesia (M$141·1m.). Exports went mainly to Singapore (M$4,519·9m.), USA (M$3,267·3m.), Japan (M$2,997m.), Netherlands (M$1,569·9m.), Federal Republic of Germany (M$924m.), UK (M$662·3m.), USSR (M$629·6m.), France (M$489·8m.), Italy (M$436·3m.).

Tourism. In 1978, 3,017,864 foreigners visited Peninsular Malaysia.

COMMUNICATIONS

Roads. In 1980 the Public Works Department maintained 21,834·5 km of public roads, of which 15,983·44 km was of bituminous metalled surface, 81·44 km waterbound metalled surface, 1,799 km hard surface bitumen sealed, 2,931·99 km hard surface waterbound and 1,038·67 km earth surface.

In 1980, 374,939 motor vehicles were registered, including 124,428 private cars, 854 buses, 23,436 lorries and vans, 210,682 motor cycles.

Railways. The Malayan Railway main line runs from Singapore to Butterworth opposite Penang Island. From Bukit Mertajam 8 miles south of Butterworth a branch line connects Peninsular Malaysia with the State Railways of Thailand at the frontier station of Padang Besar. Other branch lines connect the main line with Port of Klang, Teluk Anson, Port Dickson and Ampang. The east-coast line, branching off the main line at Gemas, runs for over 300 miles to Tumpat, Kelantan's northernmost coastal town; a 13-mile branch line linking Pasir Mas with Sungei Golok makes a second connexion with Thailand.

The route mileage in 1980 was 1,337 (metre gauge) and the annual budget is about M$147m.

Aviation (1980). There are 9 airports used by scheduled air services and international air services are operated into Kuala Lumpur and Penang airports. The national carrier, Malaysian Airlines System (MAS), began operation on 1 Oct. 1972 to provide both domestic and international services. The Malaysian Airlines System (MAS) operate international services to Amsterdam, Bandar Seri Begawan, Bangkok, Dubai, Frankfurt, Haadyai, Hong Kong, Jakarta, Jeddah, Kuwait, London, Madras, Manila, Medan, Melbourne, Paris, Perth, Seoul, Singapore, Sydney, Taipei and Tōkyō. The number of domestic points served by the airline is 37. Charter services are provided within Peninsular Malaysia by Malaysia Air Charter Co., Pan Malaysia Air Charter, Wira Kris, Genting Helicopter Service and Kris Udara Malaysia. The following airlines operate scheduled services through Kuala Lumpur besides MAS: Air Lanka, Cargoluse Airways, Bangladesh Beiman, Iraqi Airways, Philippine Airlines, PIA, Aeroflot Soviet Airlines, Air India, British Airways, Cathay Pacific Airways, Czechoslovakia Airlines, Garuda Indonesian Airways, Japan Airlines, KLM, PANAM, SAS, SABENA, Singapore Airlines,

Thai International Airways and Trans Mediterranean Airways. The airlines operating scheduled services through Penang besides MAS are Garuda Indonesian Airways, Cathay Pacific Airways, Thai Airways Co. and Thai Airways International.

Civil aviation statistics for airports in Peninsular Malaysia (1980): Aircraft movements, 90,530; terminal passengers, 3,940,078; freight, 37,511 tonnes; mail, 3,473 tonnes.

Shipping. The major ports of Peninsular Malaysia are Penang, Malacca, Port Klang, Pasir Gudang, Port Dickson and Kuantan. The volume of shipping (vessels of over 75 NRT only) handled at these ports, exclusive of coasting trade, was as follows (in 1,000 NRT):

Ports		*Arrivals*		*Departures*	
		Number	*Tonnage*	*Number*	*Tonnage*
Penang	1979	1,711	7,236	1,720	7,244
	1980	1,805	7,627	1,796	7,610
Port Klang	1979	2,794	16,463	2,799	16,434
	1980	2,785	15,891	2,796	15,996
Total (all ports)	1979	5,399	34,103	5,408	34,090
	1980	5,611	34,132	5,558	34,072

The total cargo handled in all ports during 1979 was 25·37m. tonnes; 1980, 27·25m. tonnes.

Post and Broadcasting. As at 31 Dec. 1979, 445 post offices, 1,381 postal agencies, 177 mobile post offices and 1 riverine postal office were operating in Malaysia, and the cash turnover for the year amounted to M$4,688,113,241.

There were 598,944 telephones on 1 Jan. 1980 serviced by 398 exchanges. In 1979, 208,731 wireless licences and 911,749 television licences were issued.

JUSTICE, RELIGION, EDUCATION AND WELFARE

Justice. Unlike the Federal Court and the High Court which were established under the Constitution, the subordinate courts in Peninsular Malaysia comprising the sessions court, the Magistrate's court and the Penghulu's court were established under a Federal Law (the subordinate Courts Act, 1948 (Revised 1972)).

All offences other than those punishable with death are tried before a Sessions Court President who is empowered to pass any sentence allowed by law other than the sentence of death. In civil matters, the sessions court has jurisdiction to hear all actions and suits where the amount in dispute does not exceed M$25,000.

A First Class Magistrate's criminal jurisdiction is limited to offences for which the maximum term provided by law does not exceed 10 years imprisonment and to certain specified offences where the term of imprisonment provided for may be extended to 14 years imprisonment or which are punishable with fine only.

Juvenile courts established under the Juvenile Courts Act, 1947 for juvenile offenders below the age of 18 are presided over by a First Class Magistrate assisted by 2 advisers.

There are 30 penal institutions, including Borstal establishments and an open prison camp. The average prison population (1979) was 9,254.

Religion. More than half the population are Muslims, and Islam is the official religion. In 1970 there were 4,673,670 Muslims, 765,250 Hindus, 220,897 Christians and 2,495,739 Buddhists.

Education. In 1981 there were 4,357 state assisted primary schools with 1,675,340 pupils and 4,357 teachers and in 1980, 208 private primary schools with 5,130 pupils and 224 teachers.

In 1980 there were 2,855 secondary schools with 1,040,762 pupils and 46,960 teachers.

There were (1980): 10 special schools with 1,312 pupils and 104 teachers; 401 classes for further education with 10,281 students and 997 teachers; 25 teacher training colleges with over 12,000 students.

In the academic year 1980–81 there were 9 institutions of higher learning:

	Staff	*Students*
Ungku Omar Polytechnic, Ipoh	112	2,449
Kuantan Polytechnic, Kuantan	49	575
MARA Institute of Technology, Shah Alam	665	8,997
Tunku Ab. Rahman College, Kuala Lumpur	156	6,272
University of Malaya, Kuala Lumpur	1,085	8,851
University of Kebangsaan, Bangi	864	5,307
University of Science, Penang	417	3,983
University of Agriculture, Serdang	502	3,496
University of Technology, Kuala Lumpur	431	4,150

Health. In 1981 Government maintained 65 general, district hospitals with 29,712 beds, 2 institutions with 2,688 beds for the treatment of Hensens' disease, 2 mental institutions with 6,577 beds and 1 institution (293 beds) for tuberculosis treatment. For the care of the rural population there were 3,131 medical and health facilities comprising 65 main health centres, 254 health sub-centres, 1,375 midwives' clinics, 414 static, 284 travelling dispensaries, 739 dental clinics, 41 maternal and child health clinics. The Government also maintains an Institute for Medical Research with 2 branch laboratories at Ipoh and Penang.

Books of Reference

Morris, M. W., *Local Government in Peninsular Malaysia.* London, 1980
Wilkinson, R. J., *Malay-English Dictionary.* 2 vols. New ed. London, 1956
Winstedt, Sir R., *Malaya and Its History.* 3rd ed. London, 1953.—*An English–Malay Dictionary.* 3rd ed. Singapore, 1949.—*The Malays: A Cultural History.* London, 1959

SABAH

HISTORY. The territory now named Sabah, but until Sept. 1963 known as North Borneo, was in 1877-78 ceded by the Sultans of Brunei and Sulu and various other rulers to a British syndicate, which in 1881 was chartered as the British North Borneo (Chartered) Company. The Company's sovereign rights and assets were transferred to the Crown with effect from 15 July 1946. On that date, the island of Labuan (ceded to Britain in 1846 by the Sultan of Brunei) became part of the new Colony of North Borneo. On 16 Sept. 1963 North Borneo joined the new Federation of Malaysia and became the State of Sabah.

AREA AND POPULATION. Area, about 29,388 sq. miles (80,520 sq. km), with a coastline of about 900 miles. The interior is mountainous, Mount Kinabalu being 13,455 ft (4,175 metres) high. Population, 1970 census 655,295, (1978 estimate, 981,544), of whom, 421,962 (613,150) were natives, 140,969 (178,469) Chinese, 2,489 Europeans 97,717 (189,925) others. The native population comprises Kadazans (largest and mainly agricultural), Bajaus and Bruneis (agriculture and fishing), Muruts (hill tribes), Suluks (mainly seafaring) and several smaller tribes.

The island of Labuan, 35 sq. miles (75 sq. km) in area, lying 6 miles off the north-west coast of Borneo is a free port. It has a fine port, Victoria Harbour.

The principal towns are situated on or near the coast. They include Kota Kinabalu, the capital (formerly Jesselton), 1980 census population (preliminary), 59,500, Sandakan (73,815), Tawau (45,249), Kudat (10,938); and Keningau in the hinterland (4,279).

CONSTITUTION AND GOVERNMENT. The Constitution of the State of Sabah provides for a Head of State, called the *Yang Dipertua Negeri Sabah.* Executive authority is vested in the State Cabinet headed by the Chief Minister.

Head of State: Tun Mohamed Adam Robert, SMN, SPDK.

Flag: Four horizontal stripes of red, white, yellow and blue, with a green quarter bearing an outline of Mount Kinabalu in brown.

The Cabinet was composed as follows in March 1982:

Chief Minister and Minister of Natural Resources: Datuk Harris bin Mohd. Salleh, SPDK.

Deputy Chief Minister and Industrial Development: Datuk James Peter Ongkili, DIMP. *Financial Planning and Development:* Datuk Hj. Mohd. Noor Mansoor, PGDK. *Agriculture and Fisheries:* Datuk Lim Guan Sing, DPMK. *Work and Utilities:* Datuk Suffian Koroh, PGDK. *Community Services:* Toh Puan Hajjah Rahimah Stephens, PGDK. *Local Government and Housing:* Datuk Joseph Pairin Kitingan, PGDK. *Manpower and Environmental Development:* Datuk Yap Pak Leong, PGDK. *Culture, Youth and Sports:* Datu Abdul Hamid bin Tun Datu Haji Mustapha.

The Legislative Assembly consists of the Speaker, 48 elected members and not more than 6 nominated members.

The official language was English for a period of 10 years from Sept. 1963 but in Aug. 1973 Bahasa Malaysia was introduced and in 1974 was declared the official language.

ECONOMY

Budget. Budgets for calendar years, in M$:

Ordinary Budget	*1975*	*1976*	*1977*	*1978*	*1979*
Revenue	265,757,626	557,496,990	716,291,841	777,282,219	1,439,748,354
Expenditure	414,619,046	342,008,618	556,660,409	637,510,015	926,035,864
Development Budget					
Revenue	133,855,491	122,458,589	184,895,412	198,347,347	201,937,626
Expenditure	160,517,426	120,620,884	165,749,561	186,816,759	264,620,018

Banking. There are branches of The Chartered Bank at Kota Kinabalu, Sandakan, Tawau, Labuan, Kudat, Tenom and Lahad Datu. The Hongkong and Shanghai Bank has branches at Kota Kinabalu, Sandakan, Labuan, Beaufort, Papar and Tawau. The Hock Hua Bank (S) has branches at Kota Kinabalu, Sandakan and Tawau. The Chung Khiaw Bank has branches at Kota Kinabalu, Tuaran and Sandakan. Malayan Banking Ltd has branches at Kota Kinabalu, Tawau, Semporna and Sandakan. United Overseas Bank and the Overseas Chinese Banking Corporation have each a branch at Kota Kinabalu. Bank Bumiputra Malaysia has branches at Kota Kinabalu. Lahad Datu, Sandakan and Keningau. Overseas Union Bank and the Development and Commercial Bank have each a branch at Sandakan. The Sabah Bank Berhad and Sabah Development Bank were established in Kota Kinabalu in 1979.

The National Savings Bank has taken over the functions of the post office savings bank as from 1 Dec. 1974 and had (1981) M$29·4m. due to 118,436 depositors. It also provides additional services to depositors including the granting of loans for housing.

COMMERCE. The main imports are machinery, tobacco, provisions, petroleum products, metals, rice, textiles and apparel, vehicles, sugar, building material. Statistics for calendar years, in M$:

	1977	*1978*	*1979*	*1980*	*1981*[1]
Imports	1,233,017,652	1,527,640,000	2,035,061,720	3,060,819,153	3,644,335,488
Exports	2,704,317,201	2,709,779,873	4,132,247,959	4,455,982,812	4,357,069,197

The main imports and exports were (in M$1m.):

Imports	*1960*	*1970*	*1978*	*1979*	*1980*	*1981*[1]
Rice	8·4	15·4	63·8	57·8	47·9	88·0
Provisions	22·3	45·7	124·3	158·1	218·8	254·8
Textiles and apparel	9·2	20·5	61·0	77·3	87·9	109·1
Tobacco, cigars and cigarettes	12·8	32·9	67·6	76·4	92·2	96·0
Sugar	3·5	6·7	22·2	21·9	34·0	38·5
Vehicles	8·1	47·6	223·4	217·9	389·1	389·7

[1] Provisional

Imports	*1960*	*1970*	*1978*	*1979*	*1980*	*1981*[1]
Machinery	30·0	109·0	69·6	86·0	138·3	175·1
Petroleum products	16·1	28·6	139·1	180·2	332·9	437·0
Metals	12·1	36·8	151·0	202·7	296·8	408·6
Building materials	2·8	13·0	47·2	57·6	89·7	128·3
Exports						
Rubber	49·5	36·5	73·5	79·8	82·3	55·9
Timber	90·7	396·8	1,339·7	2,077·0	1,855·1	1,776·4
Hemp	5·2	0·3	–	–	–	–
Fish, fresh, dried and salted	0·9	8·0	34·1	44·4	34·3	40·7
Copra (including re-exports)	40·2	6·8	31·2	34·5	33·3	22·5
Cocoa beans	15·8	4·4	62·8	64·8	67·6	83·1
Veneer sheets	0·5	2·5	1·4	10·0	10·4	18·1
Palm oil	–	18·1	156·0	183·4	159·6	159·6
Copper concentrates	–	–	97·5	134·3	177·3	167·3

[1] Provisional.

Tourism. In 1981 some 162,413 tourists visited Sabah.

COMMUNICATIONS

Roads (1981). There were 2,950 miles of roads, of which 1,170 miles were bitumen surfaced, 1,730 miles gravel surfaced and 50 miles of earth road. Work is in progress on a network of roads, notably the Kota Kinabalu-Sandakan and Sandakan-Lahad Datu road links.

Railways. A metre-gauge railway, 140 km, runs from Kota Kinabalu on Gaya Bay to Tenom in the interior.

Aviation. External communications are provided from the international airport at Kota Kinabalu by Cathay Pacific Airways Ltd to Hong Kong; Malaysian Airways to Hong Kong, Manila, Brunei, Kuching, Singapore and Kuala Lumpur; Brunei Airways to Brunei and Kuching and Philippine Airlines to Manila.

The total air traffic handled at Sabah airports during 1981 was 2,145,707 passengers, 13,927,363 kg freight and 2,545,199 kg mail.

Shipping (1981). Merchant shipping totalling 11,845,711 NRT used the ports, handling 11,638,120 tonnes of cargo.

Post. As at 31 Dec. 1976 there were 32 post offices, 13 mobile post offices and 84 postal agencies. There were 46,826 telephones on 31 Dec. 1981. As at 31 Dec. 1981, there were 62,335 wireless and 66,312 television licences issued.

JUSTICE, EDUCATION AND WELFARE

Justice. Pursuant to the Subordinate Courts Ordinance (Cap. 20) (1951) Courts of a Magistrate of the First Class, Second Class and Third Class were established to adjudicate upon the administration of civil and criminal law. The civil jurisdiction of a First Class Magistrate is limited to cases where the amount in dispute does not exceed M$1,000. but provision is made for the Chief Justice to enlarge that jurisdiction to M$3,000. This has been established so as to confer this jurisdiction on all stipendiary magistrates. A Second Class Magistrate can only try suits where the amount involved does not exceed M$500 and a Third Class Magistrate where it does not exceed M$100.

The criminal jurisdiction of these Magistrates' Courts is limited to offences of a less serious nature although stipendiary magistrates have enhanced jurisdiction. There are no Juvenile Courts.

There are also Native Courts with jurisdiction to try cases arising from breach of native law and custom (including Moslem Law and custom) where all parties are natives or one of the party is a native (if the matter is a religious, matrimonial or sexual one). Appeals from Native Courts lie to a District Judge or a Native Court of Appeal presided over by a Judge.

In 1981, 4,102 convictions were obtained in 1,169 cases taken to court.

Education. In 1981, there were 149,969 primary and 67,550 secondary pupils. There are 832 primary schools (650 government, 171 grant-aided and 11 private), and 106 general secondary schools (55 government, 37 grant-aided and 14 private) throughout the State. There are 3 teacher-training colleges, with (1980) 1,020 students.

The Government also runs 4 vocational schools in Kota Kinabalu and Sandakan offering carpentry, motor mechanics, electrical installation, fitting/turning, radio and television and heavy plant fitting.

The Department of Education also runs further education classes in most towns and districts. The main medium of instruction in primary schools is Bahasa Malaysia although there are some Chinese medium primary schools. Secondary education is principally English but this is progressively being replaced by Bahasa Malaysia.

Health. The principal diseases are malaria, pulmonary tuberculosis and intestinal infestations. Specific control programmes for malaria and tuberculosis have drastically reduced the incidence of these two diseases.

As at 31 Dec. 1981 there were 16 hospitals (2,381 beds).Seventy-eight fixed dispensaries in outlying districts providing in-patient and out-patient care are staffed by hospital assistants under the supervision of district medical officers. There are mental hospitals at Sandakan and Kota Kinabalu. There are 17 district health centres and 45 travelling clinics throughout the State providing maternal and child health care.

Book of Reference

Statistical Information: Director, Federal Department of Information, Kota Kinabalu.

Tregonning, K. G., *North Borneo.* HMSO, 1960

SARAWAK

HISTORY. The Government of part of the present territory was obtained on 24 Sept. 1841 by Sir James Brooke from the Sultan of Brunei. Various accessions were made between 1861 and 1905. In 1888 Sarawak was placed under British protection. On 16 Dec. 1941 Sarawak was occupied by the Japanese. After the liberation the Rajah took over his administration from the British military authorities on 15 April 1946. The Council Negri, on 17 May 1946, authorized the Act of Cession to the British Crown by 19 to 16 votes, and the Rajah ceded Sarawak to the British Crown on 1 July 1946.

On 16 Sept. 1963 Sarawak joined the Federation of Malaysia.

AREA AND POPULATION. The area is about 48,250 sq. miles (121,449 sq. km), with a coastline of 450 miles and many navigable rivers.

The population at 1980 census was 1,294,753 (1978 estimate, 1,173,906, including 386,260 Dayaks; 182,700 Malays; 103,194 other natives; 294,020 Chinese; 9,735 others). The annual rate of increase is 3% (estimate). Working population (1980), 480,000.

The chief towns are the capital, Kuching, about 21 miles inland, on the Sarawak River (1980 population: 120,000), Sibu, 80 miles up the Rejang River, which is navigable by large steamers (1980 population: 76,000), and Miri, the headquarters of the Sarawak Shell Ltd (1980 population: 45,000).

CONSTITUTION AND GOVERNMENT. On 24 Sept. 1941 the Rajah began to rule through a constitution. Since 1855 two bodies, known as Majlis Mesyuarat Kerajaan Negeri (Supreme Council) and the Dewan Undangan Negeri (State Legislature), had been in existence. By the constitution of 1941 they were given, by the Rajah, powers roughly corresponding to those of a colonial executive council and legislative council respectively. Sarawak has retained a considerable measure of local autonomy in state affairs. The State or Legislature consists of 48 elected members and sits for 5 years unless sooner dissolved.

A ministerial system of government was introduced in 1963. The Chief Minister presides over the Supreme Council, which contains no more than 8 other Council Negri members, all of whom are Ministers.

Elections to the State Legislature on 22 Sept. 1979 returned 3 Independents and 45 members of the Sarawak Barisan Nasional comprising the Party Pesaka Bumiputra Bersatu, the Sarawak United Peoples' Party, and Sarawak National Party.

Sarawak has 24 seats in the Malaysia House of Representatives (154 members) and 5 seats in the Senate (58 members).

Sarawak has 7 divisions each under a Resident.

Head of State: Tun Datuk Patinggi Tan Sri Haji Abdul Rahman Ya'kub, SMN, DP, PMN, SPMJ, SPMK, SIMP, SPMS, SSDK, SPMP, SPDK, PNBS.

Chief Minister: Datuk Patinggi Haji Abdul Taib Mahmud, DP, SPMJ, PGDK.

Deputy Chief Ministers: Tan Sri Datuk Amar Sim Kheng Hong, PSM, DA, PGDK (*Finance and Development*), Daniel Tajem anak Miri, JMN (*Agriculture and Community Development*), Datuk Alfred Jabu anak Numpang, PNBS, KMN (*Housing*). *Communications and Works:* Datuk Dr Wong Soon Kai, PNBS. *Local Government:* Joseph Balan Seling. *Forestry:* Datuk Haji Noor Tahir, PNBS, AMN. *Culture, Youth and Sports:* Hafsah Harun, JMN.

State Secretary: Datuk Amar Abang Haji Yusuf Puteh, DA, PNBS, PGDK, JSM. *State Attorney-General:* Datuk Jemuri Serjan, PNBS, JBS. *State Financial Secretary:* Datuk Haji Bujang mohd Nor, PNBS, JBS, JSM.

The official languages are Malay and English. The continuing use of English as official language in Sarawak will be reviewed in 1985.

Flag: Horizontally red over white with a blue triangle on the hoist.

ECONOMY

Budget. In 1980 State revenue was M$398·6m.; expenditure, M$439·1m. The revenue is mainly derived from royalties on oil and timber.

The fourth Malaysian 5-year development plan (1981-85) provides for Sarawak an expenditure of M$2,608m.; of this sum M$2,491m. is to be spent on roads and bridges, land development, port development, education, electricity and water supply and agriculture.

Currency. The Malaysian *dollar* is on a par of £0·24 or US$0·42.

Banking. The post office savings bank had 57,514 depositors at the beginning of 1980; the amount to their credit was M$30·4m. There is a branch of Bank Negara Malaysia in Kuching, and branches of the Chartered Bank, the Hongkong & Shanghai Bank, the Overseas Chinese Banking Corporation, the Malayan Bank and 9 other banks.

PRODUCTION. The State produces rubber (exports, 1980, 35,209 net tons, M$88m.; 1981, 27,958 net tons, M$27·9m.), timber logs (exports, 1980, 6·7m. tons, M$816m.; 1981, 6·9m. tons, M$812m.), sawn timber (exports, 1980, 173,352m. tons, M$104m.; 1981, 162,963m. tons, M$84·8m.), palm oil (exports, 1980, 25,562 tons, M$32·5m.; 1981, 18,660 tons, M$21·9m.), pepper (exports, 1980, 30,709 tons, M$103·7m.; 1981, 28,606 tons, M$81·3m.), and other jungle produce. There are also gold (1978, 971 troy oz.;) and antimony ore (1978, 432 tons).

COMMERCE. Export of crude oil in 1981 was 4·07m. tons (M$2,686m.), about 62% of total exports. The bulk of crude production was exported to Japan, USA, Philippines and Thailand.

Total import value, 1980, M$2,299m.; 1981, M$3,001m. Export, 1980, M$4,049m.; 1981, M$4,514m.

COMMUNICATIONS

Roads. There are no railways. In 1978 there were 2,823 miles of roads, consisting of

886 miles of bitumen surfaced, 1,250 miles of gravel or stone surfaced and 687 miles of earth roads.

Aviation. There are daily Malaysian Airline System (MAS) B737 flights between Kuching and Kuala Lumpur *via* Singapore, and also scheduled flights between Kuching, Brunei and Hong Kong. Major towns in Sarawak are linked up by internal air routes.

Shipping. In 1978 Sarawak ports loaded 9·92m. tons (1977: 7·25m. tons) and discharged 710,000 tons (1977: 1·13m. tons). New Kuching wharf, operational since Dec. 1974, can accommodate vessels up to 15,000 tons.

Post and Broadcasting. There are 53 post offices, 19 mobile offices, wireless-telegraph stations and 53 agencies. A telephone system with 57 exchanges (41,356 telephones) covers the country. There is communication by wireless with Singapore and other Commonwealth countries. The government radio and television service had, at the end of 1978, 32,596 registered receivers.

Newspapers (1980). There are 1 Malay, 2 English and 7 Chinese daily; 1 English weekly; 1 Malay and 1 Iban (Sea Dayak) monthly newspapers as well as a weekly news review in Malay and Iban published by Government.

JUSTICE, RELIGION, EDUCATION AND WELFARE

Justice (1980). In Sarawak subordinate courts were established pursuant to the Subordinate Courts Ordinance (Cap. 42) (1952). The limits of civil and criminal jurisdiction of a First Class, Second Class and Third Class Magistrate are the same as in Sabah. As in Sabah, here too there is provision for the Chief Justice to enhance the jurisdiction of a First Class Magistrate in civil and criminal matters, the reason being that there are no Sessions Courts in both Sabah and Sarawak.

Native Courts were set up under the Native Courts Ordinance (Cap. 43) (1955) with the same limited jurisdiction as Native Courts in Sabah. In addition these courts have jurisdiction to try civil cases where the amount in dispute does not exceed M$50. Appeals from Native Courts lie to a Resident's Native Court and, subject to some limitations, to the Native Court of Appeal which is presided over by a High Court Judge. There are no Juvenile Courts. There are 6 prisons. There were 2,498 admissions, of whom 1,376 were sentenced to penal imprisonment and 883 committed on remand or awaiting trial, and 47 paid fines. Daily average prison population was 322.

Police. There is a Royal Malaysia Police, Sarawak Component, with a total establishment of about 8,000 regular officers and men.

Religion. There are Church of England, Roman Catholic, American Methodist, Seventh-day Adventist and Borneo Evangelical missions. There is a large Moslem population and many Buddhists. Islam is the national religion.

Education (1980). All schools (government, missions, private) numbered about 1,500 with 480,000 pupils, of whom about 90,000 were in secondary classes. There are 3 teacher-training centres and an agricultural university campus conducting pre-university courses.

Health. At the end of 1980 there were 15 government and private hospitals (2,576 beds), 119 static and 53 travelling dispensaries, 1 urban health centre, 88 public dental and school dental clinics and 180 maternal and child health centres. There were 151 registered doctors.

Books of Reference

Population and Housing Census of Malaysia, 1970. Dept. of Statistics, Kuala Lumpur
Sarawak Annual of Statistics. Dept. of Statistics, Kuching, 1979
Sarawak Annual External Trade Statistics. Dept. of Statistics, Kuching, 1980
1981 Sarawak Budget. Information Dept., Sarawak
MacDonald, M., *Borneo People.* London, 1956
Milne, R. S., and Ratnam, K. J., *Malaysia, New States in a New Nation: Political Development of Sarawak and Sabah in Malaysia.* London, 1974
Runciman, S., *The White Rajahs.* CUP, 1960
Scott, N. C., *Sea Dyak Dictionary.* Govt. Printing Office, Kuching, 1956

National Library: The Sarawak Central Library, Kuching.

MALDIVES

Capital: Malé
Population: 143,046 (1978)
GNP per capita: US$260 (1980)

Divehi Jumhuriya

HISTORY. The islands were under British protection from 1887 to mid–1965. They now enjoy complete independence under the agreement signed in Colombo on 26 July 1965. Maldives became a republic on 11 Nov. 1968.

AREA AND POPULATION. The Republic of Maldives, 400 miles to the south-west of Sri Lanka, consists of some 2,000 low-lying coral islands (only 220 inhabited), grouped into 12 clearly defined clusters of atolls but divided into 19 districts for administrative purposes. Area 115 sq. miles (298 sq. km). Population (census 1978), 143,046. Capital Malé (29,555 inhabitants).

CONSTITUTION AND GOVERNMENT. The President is elected every 5 years by universal adult suffrage. He is assisted by the Ministers' *Majlis*, a cabinet of ministers of his own choice whom he may dismiss at will. There is also a Citizens' *Majlis* (House of Representatives) which consists of 48 members, 8 nominated by the President, 2 elected from Malé and 2 elected from each of the 19 atolls. The life of the Citizens' *Majlis* is 5 years. There are no political parties.

President and Prime Minister: Maumoon Abdul Gayoom.

The official language is Divehi, which is akin to Elu or old Sinhalese.

National flag: Red with a green panel bearing a white crescent.

INTERNATIONAL RELATIONS.

Membership. The Republic of the Maldives is a member of UN and a special member of the Commonwealth.

ECONOMY

Budget. There is no direct taxation.

Currency. The *rufiyaa* (Maldivian rupee) is divided into 100 *laaris*; there are notes of 1, 2, 5, 10, 50 and 100 rufiyaa.

NATURAL RESOURCES

Agriculture. The islands are covered with coconut palms and yield millet and fruit as well as coconut produce.
Production in 1981 included (in 1,000 tonnes): Coconuts, 9; copra, 2.

Fisheries. The Maldivian economy is based on the fishing industry.

INDUSTRY AND TRADE

Commerce. Bonito ('Maldive fish') is the main export commodity and Japan the main buyer. Exports (1978) US$4·1m.: imports, US$13·1m.
Total trade between the Republic of Maldives and UK (British Department of Trade returns, in £1,000 sterling):

	1979	*1980*	*1981*	*1982*
Imports to UK	57	294	254	57
Exports and re-exports from UK	196	1,121	2,403	615

Tourism. Tourism, introduced in 1972, is expanding and there were 35,000 visitors in 1978–79.

COMMUNICATIONS

Aviation. The Maldives' national airline, Maldives International Airline, was established in 1977, and is a joint venture between the Maldives' government and Indian Airlines. It replaced an earlier airline, Air Maldives which was wound up in 1977. The airline operates one Boeing 737, leased from Indian Airlines, from Hulule airport on Malé atoll. Hulule airport is being extended. The Maldives' government hopes to reactivate the former RAF staging post on Gan in order to attract additional tourist traffic.

Shipping. The merchant fleet consists of about 50 vessels of 200,000 GRT.

Post and Broadcasting. There were (1981) 2,100 telephones. An external telephone service links Tortola with Bermuda and the rest of the world, and cable communications also exist to all parts of the world. Radio ZBVI transmits 10,000 watts and has stand-by transmitting facilities of 1,000 watts. Cable and Wireless operate a commercial cable television service to provide subscribers with good quality reception of approximately 7 television channels plus a number of FM stereo broadcasting stations.

JUSTICE, RELIGION EDUCATION AND WELFARE

Justice. Justice is based on the Islamic Shari'ah.

Religion. The State religion is Moslem of the Sunni sect.

Education. In 1978 there were 8,749 pupils in primary and 3,652 in secondary schools.

Health. In 1977 there was a 40-bed hospital in Malé, and 9 doctors, 1 dentist, 177 midwives and 34 nursing personnel.

DIPLOMATIC REPRESENTATIVES

Of Great Britain in the Republic of Maldives
Ambassador: Sir John Nicholas, KCVO, CMG (resides in Colombo).

Of the Republic of Maldives to the United Nations
Ambassador: Ahmed Zaki.

Books of Reference

Bell, H. C. P., *History, Archaeology and Epigraphy of the Maldive Islands.* Ceylon Govt. Press, Colombo, 1940

Bernini, F. and Corbin, G., *Maldive.* Turin, 1973

MALI

Capital: Bamako
Population: 7·02m. (1982)
GNP per capita: US$190 (1980)

République du Mali

HISTORY. Annexed by France between 1881 and 1895, the region became the territory of French Sudan as a part of French West Africa. It became an autonomous state within the French Community on 24 Nov. 1958, and on 4 April 1959 joined with Sénégal to form the Federation of Mali. The Federation achieved independence on 20 June 1960, but Sénégal seceded on 22 Aug. and Mali proclaimed itself an independent republic on 22 Sept. The National Assembly was dissolved on 17 Jan. 1968 by President Modibo Keita, whose government was then overthrown by an Army *coup* on 19 Nov. 1968; power was assumed by a Military Committee for National Liberation led by Lieut. (now General) Moussa Traoré, who became President on 19 Sept. 1969.

AREA AND POPULATION. Mali is a landlocked state, consisting of the Middle and Upper Niger basin in the south, the Upper Sénégal basin in the south-west, and the Sahara in the north. It is bounded west by Sénégal, north-west by Mauritania, north-east by Algeria, east by Niger and south by Upper Volta, the Ivory Coast and Guinea. The republic covers an area of 1,240,142 sq. km (478,832 sq. miles) and had a population of 6,398,914 at the 1976 Census; the latest estimate (1982) is 7·02m. The chief cities (with populations in 1976) are Bamako, the capital (404,022), Ségou (64,890), Mopti (53,885), Sikasso (47,030) and Kayes (44,736).

The population of the regions (census 1976): Kayes, 871,871; Kaulikoro, 916,148; Capital district, 404,022; Sikasso, 1,044,664; Ségou, 1,111,810; Mopti, 1,104,708; Tombouctou, 487,278; Gao, 367,819.

The various indigenous languages belong chiefly to the Mande group; of these the principal are Bambara (spoken by 60% of the population), Soninké, Malinké and Dogon; non-Mande languages include Fulani, Songhai, Senufo and Minianka. The official language is French.

CONSTITUTION AND GOVERNMENT. A new constitution was announced on 26 April 1974 and approved by a national referendum on 2 June; it was amended by the National Assembly on 2 Sept. 1981. The sole legal party is the *Union démocratique du peuple malien* (UDPM), formally constituted on 30 March 1979 and governed by a 19-member Central Executive Bureau responsible to a 137-member National Council who nominate all candidates for election.

The President is directly elected and his term of office is now 6 years; Gen. Moussa Traoré was elected unopposed on 19 June 1979. The 82-member National Assembly is also directly elected (latest elections, 13 June 1982); its term of office is now 3 years.

The Council of Ministers, as re-organized in July 1982, comprised:

President, Head of Government, Defence and Security: Gen. Moussa Traoré.

Ministers of State: Brig.-Gen. Amadou Baba Diarra *(Equipment),* Oumar Coulibaly *(Economy and Plan).*

Foreign Affairs and Co-operation: Alioune Blondin Béye. *Planning:* Ahmed Mohamed Ag Hamani. *Agriculture:* Nfagnanama Kone. *Education:* Lieut.-Col. Sékou Ly. *Labour and Civil Service:* Modibo Keita. *Energy and Mines:* Robert Tieble N'daw. *Rural Development:* Mady Diallo. *Justice:* Lieut.-Col. Issa Ongoiba. *Public Works and Transport:* Mamadou Haidara. *Health and Social Affairs:* Dr Ngolo Traoré. *Finance and Commerce:* Ydrissa Keita. *State Enterprises:* Bandiougou Bidia Doucoure. *Interior:* Lieut.-Col. Abdourahmane Maiga. *Information and*

Telecommunications: Gakou Nee Fatou Niang. *Sports, Arts and Culture:* N'tji Idriss Mariko.

National flag: Three vertical stripes of green, yellow, red.

Local Government: Mali is divided into the Capital District of Bamako and 7 regions, sub-divided into 46 *cercles* and then into 279 *arrondissements*.

DEFENCE

Army. The Army consists of 5 infantry battalions and 1 artillery battalion with support units; strength, 4,600 (1983).

Air Force. The Air Force has 5 MiG-17 jet fighters, 1 MiG-15UTI jet trainer, some Yak-18 piston-engined trainers, 2 An-24 and 3 An-2 transports, and 3 Mi-8 and Mi-4 helicopters from USSR. A twin-turbofan Corvette is used for VIP transport. Personnel total about 300.

INTERNATIONAL RELATIONS

Membership. Mali is a member of UN, OAU and is an ACP state of EEC.

ECONOMY

Planning. The 1981–85 Four Year Plan provides for expenditure of MF 937,000m., comprising 30·1% for the rural sector (114 projects), 26·9% for town planning, housing and communications (111 projects), 30·4% for the industrial, water supply, energy and mining sectors (127 projects), 8·3% in the social sector (163 projects) and 4·3% for greenfields developments.

Budget. The budget for 1982 balanced at MF 88,800m.

Currency. The unit of currency is the *Mali franc* (MF), introduced in July 1962. It has a parity value of MF 100 to 1 French franc. In March 1983, £1 = MF 1,065; US$1 = MF 726·25.

Banking. The *Banque Centrale du Mali* (founded in 1968) is the bank of issue.

ENERGY AND NATURAL RESOURCES

Electricity. Production (1980) totalled 110m. kwh. Hydro-electric dams have been built at Selingué (near Bamako) on the Upper Niger and at Manantali (near Kayes) on the Sénégal river.

Minerals. Mineral resources are limited, but marble (at Bafoulabé) and limestone (at Diamou) are being extracted in the Upper Sénégal valley; iron ore deposits in this area await development. Salt is mined at Taoudenni in the far north (5,000 tonnes in 1979).

Agriculture. Production in 1981 included (in 1,000 tonnes): Millet, 930; sugar-cane, 225; groundnuts, 190; rice, 142; maize, 80; cottonseed, 70; cotton lint, 40; cassava, 7.

Livestock, 1981: Cattle, 5,134,000; horses, 139,000; asses, 420,000; sheep, 6·35m.; goats, 7m.; camels, 173,000; chickens, 12·5m.

Important irrigation schemes have been carried out in the Ségou and Mopti districts on the Niger River, of which the Sansanding Barrage and the Sahel Canal are the most important; 50,000 hectares of cotton and rice lands are being irrigated.

Fisheries. About 100,000 tonnes of fish per annum are caught in the rivers.

TRADE. Imports in 1980 totalled MF 176,300m., exports, 74,200m. Chief imports are foodstuffs, automobiles, petrol, building material, sugar, salt, beer; in 1977, 38% were from France, 19% from Ivory Coast, 8% from Sénégal, 7% from Federal Republic of Germany and 5% from China. Chief exports (1977) were cotton (57% of total), livestock, peanuts, dried fish and skins; 29% went to France, 14% to Ivory Coast, 14% to the UK, 12% to China.

Total trade between Mali and UK (British Department of Trade returns, in £1,000 sterling):

	1978	*1979*	*1980*	*1981*	*1982*
Imports to UK	3,257	12,108	11,318	4,534	3,385
Exports and re-exports from UK	3,245	6,120	7,878	2,761	4,403

Tourism. There were 19,583 foreign tourists in 1976.

COMMUNICATIONS

Roads. There were (1980) 13,360 km of roads, of which 6,869 km are usable in all seasons; they include 2,606 km of metalled road Dakar–Niger (of which 1,693 km are in Mali). There were 19,500 road vehicles in 1974.

Railways. Mali has a railway from Kayes to Koulikoro by way of Bamako, a continuation of the Dakar–Kayes line in Sénégal. An agreement was signed in May 1968 between Mali, Guinea and China to extend the railway from Kourousa–Kankan in Guinea to Bamako, though no work had been done by early 1983. Total length 645 km and in 1979 the railways ran 129m. passenger-km and 149m. tonne-km.

Aviation. Air services connect the republic with Paris, Dakar and Abidjan. There are international airports at Bamako and Mopti, and Air Mali operates domestic services to 10 other airports.

Shipping. For about 7 months in the year small steamboats perform the service from Koulikoro to Tombouctou and Gao, and from Bamako to Kouroussa.

Post and Broadcasting. There were, in 1976, 8,000 telephones and (1981) 90,000 radio receivers.

JUSTICE, RELIGION, EDUCATION AND WELFARE

Justice. The Supreme Court was established at Bamako in 1969 with both judicial and administrative powers. The Court of Appeal is also at Bamako, at the apex of a system of regional tribunals and local *juges de paix*.

Religion. In 1979, 65% of the population were Sunni Moslems, 30% animists and 5% Christians.

Education. In 1979 there were 293,227 pupils and 6,877 teachers in primary schools, 64,491 pupils (1978) in secondary schools, (1977) 2,609 in technical schools, 2,261 in teacher-training colleges and 4,216 students in higher educational establishments. A further 30,000 students were at 1,321 adult literacy centres.

Health. In 1980 there were 12 hospitals, 327 health centres and 445 dispensaries, with a total of 3,200 beds; there were 319 doctors, 18 surgeons, 12 dentists (1976), 18 pharmacists (1976), 250 midwives and 1,312 nursing personnel.

DIPLOMATIC REPRESENTATIVES

Of Mali in Great Britain
Ambassador: Yaya Diarra (resides in Brussels).

Of Great Britain in Mali
Ambassador: L. O'Keeffe, CMG (resides in Dakar).

Of Mali in the USA (2130 R. St., NW, Washington, D.C., 20008)
Ambassador: Maki Koreissi Aguibou Tall.

Of the USA in Mali (Rue Testard and Rue Mohamed V, Bamako)
Ambassador: Parker W. Borg.

Of Mali to the United Nations
Ambassador: Seydou Traoré.

Books of Reference

Hopkins, N. S., *Popular Government in an African Town.* Univ. of Chicago Press, 1972
Jones, W., *Planning and Economic Policy: Socialist Mali and Her Neighbors.* New York, 1974

MALTA

Capital: Valletta
Population: 319,936 (1981)
GNP per capita: US$3,470 (1980)

Repubblika Ta' Malta

HISTORY. Malta was held in turn by Phoenicians, Carthaginians and Romans, and was conquered by Arabs in 870. From 1090 it was joined to Sicily until 1530, when it was handed over to the Knights of St John, who ruled until dispersed by Napoleon in 1798. The Maltese rose in rebellion against the French and the island was subsequently blockaded by the British aided by the Maltese from 1798 to 1800. The Maltese people freely requested the protection of the British Crown in 1802 on condition that their rights and privileges be preserved. The islands were finally annexed to the British Crown by the Treaty of Paris in 1814.

On 15 April 1942, in recognition of the steadfastness and fortitude of the people of Malta during the Second World War, King George VI awarded the George Cross to the island.

AREA AND POPULATION. The area of Malta is 246 sq. km (94·9 sq. miles); Gozo, 67 sq. km (25·9 sq. miles); Comino, 3 sq. km (1·1 sq. miles); total area, 316 sq. km (121·9 sq. miles). Population, census 27 Nov. 1967, 314,216; estimate (31 Dec. 1981) 319,936. Malta, 296,529; Gozo and Comino, 23,407. Chief town and port, Valletta, population 14,249 (1981).

Vital statistics, 1981, estimate: Births, 5,292; deaths, 3,062; marriages, 2,997; emigrants, 1,966; returned emigrants, 1,644.

CLIMATE. The climate is warm, with little fog, frost or snow. Average temperature from Nov. to April is 57°F (14°C) and from May to Oct. 73°F (23°C). Average daily sunshine in winter is 6·5 hours and in summer over 10 hours. The hottest period is mid-July to mid-Sept., when temperatures vary between 86–91°F (30–33°C). Rain falls for only short periods, mainly between Nov. and March, and the annual total is 22" (560 mm).

CONSTITUTION AND GOVERNMENT. Malta became independent on 21 Sept. 1964 and became a republic within the Commonwealth on 13 Dec. 1974. For earlier constitutional and government history *see* THE STATESMAN'S YEAR-BOOK, 1980–81, p. 837.

In 1971 Malta began to follow a policy of strict non-alignment and closed the NATO base. In March 1972 agreement was reached on the phasing out of the British Military base which was closed down completely on 31 March 1979.

Malta is a democratic republic and the Constitution, which was amended in 1965, 1966, 1970, 1972 and 1974, provides for a parliament consisting of a House of Representatives of elected members and a Cabinet consisting of the Prime Minister and such number of Ministers as may be appointed. The 1974 Constitution which is founded on work, makes provision for the protection of fundamental rights and freedom of the individual, and ensures that all persons in Malta shall have full freedom of conscience and religious worship.

Maltese and English, and such other language as may be prescribed by Parliament, are the official languages.

Elections were held on 12 Dec. 1981. State of parties in Feb. 1983: Malta Labour Party, 34; Nationalist Party, 31.

President: A. Barbara.

The Cabinet (Malta Labour Party) was as at Nov. 1982:

Prime Minister: Dom Mintoff.

Senior Deputy Prime Minister and Minister of Justice and Parliamentary Affairs: Dr Joseph Cassar. *Deputy Prime Minister and Minister of Economic Development, Acting Minister of Labour and Social Services:* Wistin Abela. *Interior:* Lorry Sant. *Parastatal and People's Investments:* Dr Patrick Holland. *Agriculture and Fisheries:* Freddie Micallef. *Health:* Dr Vincent Moran. *Education:* Dr Philip Muscat. *Tourism:* Reno Calleja. *Industry:* Joseph Grima. *Works:* Karmenu Vella. *Foreign Affairs:* Dr Alex Sceberras Trigona. *Finance:* Lino Spiteri.

National flag: Vertically white and red, with a representation of the George Cross medal in the canton.

DEFENCE. The Maltese armed forces include 800 personnel, organized into 1 regiment and 3 Pioneer Corps battalions, and supported by a Helicopter Flight equipped with 4 Bell 47G-2 and 1 JetRanger light helicopters received in 1972–73, and 1 Agusta-Bell 204 received subsequently. Duties of the Flight include patrol, search and rescue. There is also a para-military force of 1,100.

A coastal patrol force of small craft has been formed. It is manned by the Maltese Regiment and primarily employed as a coastguard. In 1983 it comprised 13 patrol craft and customs launches manned by 120 officers and men.

All UK forces were withdrawn in March 1979.

INTERNATIONAL RELATIONS

Membership. Malta is a member of UN, the Commonwealth and the Council of Europe.

ECONOMY

Planning. The Development Plan for Malta (1981–85) aims to bolster the economy through the development of intensive agriculture and fisheries, industry, ship-repair and ship-building, and the tertiary sector, where industry and tourism are considered to be the prime movers with agriculture and fisheries having a supportive role. It is further envisaged that Malta will continue with its efforts to exploit the Island's strategic position by establishing a major transhipment centre for the Middle East and the North African hinterland.

Budget. Revenue and expenditure (in £M) for financial years ending 31 March:

	1977–78	*1978–79*	*1979* [1]	*1980* [2]	*1981* [2]
Revenue	97,349,476	110,268,917	98,708,773	170,152,444	204,661,944
Expenditure	92,966,747	107,780,619	105,603,164	161,490,920	192,435,435

[1] Nine months. April–Dec. [2] Calendar year.

The most important sources of revenue are customs duties, income tax, receipts from the Central Bank of Malta and until 1979, rent from defence facilities.

Currency. Central Bank of Malta notes of £M1, £M5 and £M10 denominations are in circulation. On 16 May 1972 a new decimal system was introduced and UK coinage previously in circulation ceased to be legal tender in Malta after 4 Oct. 1972. Malta coins are issued in the following denominations: 50, 25, 10, 5, 2 and 1 cents; 5, 3 and 2 *mils*. Total notes in circulation on 31 Dec. 1981 was £M240m.; coins, £M4·9m. In March 1983, £1 sterling = £M0·63; US$1 = £M2·33.

Banking. The Central Bank of Malta was founded in 1968. Commercial banking facilities are provided by Bank of Valletta Ltd, Lombard Bank Ltd and Mid-Med Bank Ltd. The other domestic banking institutions are the Government Savings Bank, the Investment Finance Bank, the Apostleship of Prayer Savings Bank Ltd, Lohombus Corporation Ltd, Singer and Friedlander (Malta) Ltd and Melita Bank International Ltd (Offshore Bank).

ENERGY AND NATURAL RESOURCES

Electricity. All towns and villages in Malta and Gozo are provided with electric current. Up to Sept. 1978 the islands obtained their electricity power supplies from 2 interconnected power stations located at Marsa (Malta) having a total installed capacity of 115 mw. The bigger power station with a generating capacity of 85 mw is also equipped with distillation plant capable of also producing fresh water for public consumption at the rate of 4m. gallons per day. An expansion programme is currently under way for the erection of two 30 mw turbo-generating sets and boiler plant which will increase the installed capacity to 175 mw.

In Oct. 1978 another power station, which was formerly used to supply foreign military installations on the Island, was handed over to the Government of Malta and has been integrated in the national electricity supply system. The station has a generating capacity of 12 mw.

The gross electricity generated in 1981 was 557·9m. kwh.

Agriculture. In 1980 agriculture contributed £M13·2m. to the Gross Domestic Product as against £M11·1m. in 1979. (The 1980 figure represents a share of 3·8% in the GDP.) In 1980 there was a slight decrease in the cultivable area, which totalled 12,299 hectares as against 12,353 hectares in 1979. In 1980 agriculture employed 5,085 full-time farmers, 438 full-time wage earners and 10,480 part-time farmers against, 5,643, 411 and 10,432 respectively in 1979. (The 1980 figure for full-time farmers and full-time wage earners represents 4·6% of the gainfully occupied population.)

In 1981 the value of Malta's main agricultural exports reached £M1·5m. The 1981 exports consisted mainly of: Potatoes, £M451,200; seeds, cut-flowers and plants, £M577,579; wine, £M144,880; onions, £M66,980; hides and skins, £M104,894; live animals, £M3,156; capers, £M73,100.

Livestock (1981): Cattle, 15,000; pigs, 25,000; sheep, 5,000; goats 7,000; poultry, 1·3m.

Fisheries. In 1980 the fishing industry occupied 964 power propelled and 105 other fishing boats, engaging 360 full-time and 582 part-time fishermen. The catch in 1981 was 921 tonnes valued at £M991,217 at first sale.

INDUSTRY AND TRADE

Industry. Investors in industry in Malta are offered the following advantages: political stability, excellent industrial relations, a strategic geographic location, a special association agreement with the EEC, a fully developed and highly functional infrastructure, free repatriation of profits and capital, easily trainable and highly adaptable labour force, financing facilities at favourable rates of interest, ready-built factories at attractive rents. About 260 aided firms are in operation in various industrial sectors, of which the majority are foreign-owned or have foreign interests. The Malta Development Corporation is the Government agency responsible for promoting and implementing new industrial projects, including joint ventures. The Corporation may also participate by way of equity capital, in certain projects jointly with Maltese or foreign industrialists.

Labour. The total work force in Dec. 1981 was 122,867; males, 91,708; females, 31,159, distributed as follows: Agriculture and fisheries, 6,641; manufacturing, 32,923; building, construction and quarrying, 6,216; services, 38,020; electricity, gas and drydocks, 6,059; government, 24,091; armed forces, 739; Dejma and auxiliary workers, 1,534. The number of registered unemployed under Part I of the Employment Register was 5,680, and under Part II, 964.

There were 20 trade unions registered as at 30 June 1982, with a total membership of 49,457 and 22 employers' associations with a total membership of 6,123.

Commerce. Imports and exports including bullion and specie (in £M1,000):

	1975	*1976*	*1977*	*1978*	*1979*	*1980*	*1981*
Imports	144,448	179,923	217,681	221,505	271,960	323,737	332,269
Exports	63,899	97,409	121,791	131,949	152,169	166,722	173,725

In 1981 the principal items of imports were: Semi-manufactures, £M105·5m.; machinery and transport, £M63·7m.; food, £M47·9m.; fuels, £M44·5m.; manufactures, £M26·9m.; chemicals, £M20·8m.; others, £M23m. Of domestic exports: Manufactures, £M103·4m.; machinery and transport, £M22·2m.; semi-manufactures, £M17·4m.; beverages and tobacco, £M5·1m.; food, £M4·1m.; others, £M2m.

In 1981, £M88·3m. of the imports came from Italy, £M60·3m. from UK, £M48·6m. from Federal Republic of Germany, £M27·9m. from Asia, £M23·7m. from USA, £M14·3m. from the EFTA, £M4·3m. from Africa, £M3·8m. from Oceania, £M55m. from other European countries; of domestic exports, £M48·2m. to Federal Republic of Germany, £M31·4m. to UK, £M14·9m. to Africa, £M10·5m. to Italy, £M7·6m. to Asia, £M6·1m. to EFTA, £M3·5m. to USA, and £M30·5m. to other European countries.

Total trade between Malta and UK (British Department of Trade returns, in £1,000 sterling):

	1979	*1980*	*1981*	*1982*
Imports to UK	53,569	46,609	40,713	42,792
Exports and re-exports from UK	79,083	87,527	78,286	71,823

Tourism. In 1981, 705,710 tourists visited Malta, 514,062 from UK, 29,953 from Italy, 25,290 from Scandinavia, 20,035 from Federal Republic of Germany, 14,538 from Libya, 13,500 from France and 7,084 from USA. In 1980, gross tourist expenditure was £M111·9m. (estimate).

COMMUNICATIONS

Roads. Every town and village is served by motor omnibuses. There are ferry services running between Malta and Gozo; cars can be transported on the ferries. Motor vehicles registered at 31 Dec. 1981 totalled 104,530, of which 69,973 were private cars, 4,800 hire cars, 17,288 commercial vehicles, 297 buses, 10,988 motor cycles and 1,184 other motor vehicles.

Aviation. In 1981 the principal airlines, Air Malta, Alitalia, British Airways, Libyan Arab Airlines, Union de Transports Aeriens, Yugoslav Air Transport, Austrian Airlines, Arab International Airlines, Balkan Airlines and Tunisavia, operated scheduled services between Malta and UK, Austria, Belgium, Bulgaria, Egypt, Federal Republic of Germany, France, Italy, Libya, Netherlands, Nigeria, Switzerland, Tunisia and Yugoslavia. In 1981 there were 15,775 civil aircraft movements at Luqa Airport. 1,456,636 passengers, 5,756 tonnes of freight and 502 tonnes of mail were handled.

Shipping. The number of ships registered in Malta on 31 Dec. 1981 was 306, 305,363 GRT. Ships entering harbour during 1980, 2,356.

Post and Telecommunications. Telegraph and telephone services are administered by Telemalta Corporation with exchanges at Malta and Gozo. On 31 Dec. 1981 there were 90,997 telephones. A world-wide cable and telex service is also operated.

Cinemas (1981). There were 29 cinemas with a seating capacity of 20,179.

Newspapers. There were (1982) 1 English, 3 Maltese daily newspapers and 5 weekly papers.

JUSTICE, RELIGION, EDUCATION AND WELFARE

Justice. The number of persons convicted of crimes in 1980 was 1,301; those convicted for contraventions against various laws and regulations numbered 5,337. Sixty-six were committed to prison and 2,749 were awarded fines.

Police. On 31 Dec. 1980 police numbered 41 officers and 1,243 other ranks, including 21 women police.

Religion. The majority of the population belong to the Roman Catholic Church.

Education. Education in Malta is compulsory between the ages of 6 and 16 and free in government schools. In 1981 there were 204 kindergarten groups, with nearly 3,774 children in 62 centres throughout Malta and Gozo. The primary level enrols children between 5 and 11 years in a 6-year course. There were 24,334 children (12,634 boys and 11,766 girls) in 80 government schools. Four new Junior Lyceums (2 on Malta and 2 on Gozo) were opened in Sept. 1981 with a total of 2,450 students

(855 boys, 1,595 girls). There were 31 other government secondary schools with a total of 11,766 (5,111 boys, 6,655 girls). Secondary schools run 5-year courses leading to GCE 'O' level. Two-year courses leading to GCE 'A' level on a worker/pupil system which alternates work with study periods are provided for in the New Lyceum, *i.e.*, upper secondary schools (1,117 students). Enrolment in craft and technician courses in 3 technical institutes amounted to 1,073, while 3,796 (2,658 boys and 1,138 girls) were enrolled in the 12 trade schools for boys and 6 trade schools for girls. Another 153 students are enrolled in specialized vocational schools. Trade schools offer 2- to 4-year courses in specialized trades and are open to students who finish their third year of secondary education. The number of children in special education amounted to 765.

There were 80 private schools with a population of 4,074 at the nursery level, 9,071 at the primary level and 6,429 at the secondary level.

4,074 students attended evening courses in academic, commercial, technical and practical subjects established in 82 centres. The School of Art had an enrolment of 253 students while another 2,138 students enrolled in courses organized by the School of Music.

The University of Malta consists of 6 faculties: Law, Medicine and Surgery, Engineering and Architecture, Dental Surgery, Education and Management Studies (1,244 students in 1981–82). Degrees in Law, Mechanical Engineering, Electrical Engineering, Architecture and Civil Engineering, Accountancy, Business Management, Public Administration, Education, Medicine and Surgery, Pharmacy and Dental Surgery are conferred by the University.

Welfare. The National Insurance Act, 1956, provides cash benefits for marriage (women only), sickness, unemployment, widowhood, orphanhood, invalidity, old age, children's allowances and industrial injury. An agreement, signed on 26 Oct. 1956, established reciprocity in matters of social insurance between Malta and the UK.

The total number of persons in receipt of benefits on 31 Dec. 1981 was 78,931, viz., 1,095 in receipt of sickness benefit, 870 unemployment benefit, 340 injury benefit, 221 disablement benefit, 104 death benefit, 19,290 retirement pensions, 5,281 widows' pensions, 27 widows' special allowance, 13 guardian's allowance, 4,512 invalidity pensions, 45,763 children's allowances and 1,415 maternity benefit.

The National Assistance Act, 1956, provides for the payment of social assistance and medical assistance, while the Old Age Pensions Act of 1948 provides for the payment of non-contributory old-age pensions to persons over 60 years of age and to blind persons over the age of 14 years.

The number of households in receipt of social assistance and of medical assistance on 31 Dec. 1981 was 4,284 and 4,521 respectively, and the number of old-age pensioners under the Old Age Pensions Act, 1948, was 8,016.

DIPLOMATIC REPRESENTATIVES

Of Malta in Great Britain (24 Haymarket, London, SW1Y 4DJ)
Deputy High Commissioner: Francis Cassar.

Of Great Britain in Malta (7 St Anne St., Floriana)
High Commissioner: Charles L. Booth, CMG., MVO.

Of Malta in the USA (2017 Connecticut Ave., NW, Washington, D.C., 20008)
Ambassador: Leslie Agius.

Of the USA in Malta (Development Hse., St Anne St., Floriana)
Ambassador: James Malone Rentschler.

Of Malta to the United Nations
Ambassador: Victor J. Gauci.

Books of Reference

Statistical Information: The Central Office of Statistics (Auberge de Castille, Valletta) was set up in 1947. It publishes *Statistical Abstracts of the Maltese Islands*, a quarterly digest of statistics, quarterly and annual trade returns, annual vital statistics and annual publications on shipping and aviation, education, agriculture and industry and National Accounts and Balance of Payments.

Government publications: Information Division (Kastilja, Malta), set up in 1955, publishes *The Malta Government Gazette* (twice weekly), *Il Gzejjer* (quarterly), *Malta Today* (bimonthly), *Malta Handbook, Economic Survey, Malta: Guidelines for Progress, Development Plan for Malta 1981–85* and *Supplement Paper Currency in Malta, Heritage of an Island, Reports on the Working of Government Departments.* Malta, 1981.

Malta Independence Constitution (Cmnd 2406). HMSO, 1964
Constitution of the Republic of Malta. Information Division, 1975
Malta Manufacturers and Exporters. Department of Industry, 1980
Malta Who's Who. Malta, 1969–70
Economic Survey 1981. Malta, 1981
Malta Handbook 1981. Information Division
Blouet, Brian, *The Story of Malta.* London, 1967
Busuttil, E. D., *Kalepin Dizzjunarju Malti-Ingliz.* Valletta, 1971.—*Kalepin Dizzjunarju Ingliz-Malti.* 1976
Cassar, P., *Medical History of Malta.* London, 1966
Cremona, J. J., *The Malta Constitution of 1835 and its Historical Background.* Malta, 1959.—*The Constitutional Developments of Malta under British Rule.* Malta Univ. Press, 1963.—*Human Rights Documentation in Malta.* Malta Univ. Press, 1966
Dobie, E., *Malta's Road to Independence.* Univ. of Oklahoma, Norman, USA, 1967
Gerada, E. and Zuber, C., *Malta: An Island Republic.* Paris, 1979
Luke, Sir Harry, *Malta.* 2nd ed. London, 1962
Price, G. A., *Malta and the Maltese: A Study in 19th-century Migration.* Melbourne, 1954
Smith, Harrison, *Britain in Malta.* 2 vols. Malta, 1954

MAURITANIA

Capital: Nouakchott
Population: 1·73m. (1982)
GNP per capita: US$320 (1980)

République Islamique de Mauritanie

HISTORY. Mauritania became a French protectorate in 1903 and a colony in 1920. It became an autonomous republic within the French Community on 28 Nov. 1958 and achieved full independence on 28 Nov. 1960. Under its first President, Moktar Ould Daddah, Mauritania became a one-party state in 1964, but following his deposition by a military *coup* on 10 July 1978, the ruling *Parti du peuple mauritanien* was dissolved.

Following the Spanish withdrawal from Western Sahara on 28 Feb. 1976, Mauritania occupied the southern part (88,667 sq. km) of this territory and incorporated it under the name of Tiris el Gharbia; on 8 Aug. seven additional members of the National Assembly were nominated to represent this territory. However in Aug. 1979 Mauritania renounced sovereignty and withdrew from Tiris el Gharbia.

Following the *coup* of 10 July 1978, power was placed in the hands of a Military Committee for National Recovery (CMRN); the constitution was suspended and the 70-member National Assembly dissolved. Col. Mustafa Ould Salek, Head of the CMRN, assumed the Presidency on 20 March 1979, and on 6 April the CMRN was replaced by a Military Committee for National Salvation (CMSN). On 3 June Col. Salek was replaced as President by Lieut.-Col. Mohamed Mahmoud Ould Ahmed Louly, who was in turn replaced on 4 Jan. 1980 by his Prime Minister, Lieut.-Col. Mohamed Khouna Ould Haydalla. A draft Constitution was published in Dec. 1980.

AREA AND POPULATION. Mauritania is bounded west by the Atlantic ocean, north by Western Sahara, north-east by Algeria, east and south-east by Mali, and south by Sénégal. The total area is 1,030,700 sq. km (398,000 sq. miles), and the population at the Census of 1976 was 1,419,939 including 12,897 in Tiris el Gharbia; latest estimate (1982) 1·73m. The main towns (with 1976 populations) are the capital Nouakchott (134,986), Nouâdhibou (21,961), Kaédi (20,848), Zouérate (17,474), Rosso (16,466) and Atâr (16,326).

In 1976, 22% of the population were urban and 36% were nomadic. 68% of the inhabitants are Moorish, speaking the Hassaniyah dialect of Arabic, while the other 32% consist of Negro peoples, speaking mainly Fulani (20%) and Wolof (12%), and inhabiting the Sénégal valley in the extreme south.

The official languages are French and Arabic.

CONSTITUTION AND GOVERNMENT. A draft Constitution was published on 19 Dec. 1980, providing for a multi-Party democracy (although the PPM would remain banned), with a non-executive President to be directly-elected for a 6-year term, a National Assembly directly elected for 4 years, and a Prime Minister designated by the President and approved by the National Assembly from among the Parliamentary majority.

The Cabinet in Aug. 1982 was composed as follows:

President: Lieut.-Col. Mohamed Khouna Ould Haydalla.

Prime Minister, Minister of Defence: Lieut.-Col. Moaouia Ould Sidi Mohamed Taya.

Foreign Affairs and Co-operation: Cdr Ahmed Ould Minneh. *Interior:* Lieut.-Col. Ahmedou Ould Abdallah. *Justice and Islamic Affairs:* Abdel Aziz Ould Ahmed. *Planning and Territories:* Lieut.-Col. Aane Amadou Baba Ly. *Finance:* Sidi Ould Ahmed Deya. *Industry and Commerce:* Lieut. Diop Moustapha. *Mines and Energy:* Dieng Boubou Farba. *Rural Development:* Mohamed Ould Amar. *Equipment and Transport:* Cdr Gabriel Cimper. *Housing and Water:* Mahjoub Ould Bayyeh. *National Education:* Hassiny Ould Didi. *Employment and Training:* Yahya Ould Menkouss. *Health and Social Affairs:* Cdr Mohamed Mahmoud Ould Deh. *Culture, Youth and Sports:* Dr Diagana Youssouf. *Telecommunications and Information:* Mohamed El Mokhtar Ould Zamel. *Under-Ministers:* Mohamed Fadel Ould Dah *(Foreign Affairs and Co-operation),* N'Sgam Lirwane *(Interior). Secretary-General of the Government:* Ba Mahmout.

National flag: Green, with a crescent beneath a star in yellow in the centre.

Local government: Mauritania is divided into the District of Nouakchott and 12 regions—Hodh ech Chargui, Hodh el Gharbi, Assaba, Gorgol, Brakna, Trarza, Adrar, Dakhlet Nouâdhibou, Tagent, Guidimaka, Tiris Zemmour and Inchiri. The regions are sub-divided into 44 *départements.*

DEFENCE

Army. The Army consists of 1 infantry and 1 artillery battalion, 2 armoured car squadrons and support units; total strength, 8,000 in 1983.

Navy. The Navy consists of 4 patrol vessels and 5 small patrol craft. Personnel (1983) 320.

Air Force. The Air Force has 7 Britten-Norman Defender armed light transports, 2 Surveillance Cheyennes for coastal patrol, 2 DC-4, 1 Caravelle (VIP), 2 Buffalo and 2 Skyvan transports, 2 Broussard liaison aircraft, and 4 Reims-Cessna 337 Milirole twin-engined counter-insurgency, forward air control and training aircraft. Personnel 150.

INTERNATIONAL RELATIONS

Membership. Mauritania is a member of UN, OAU, the Arab League and is an ACP state of EEC.

ECONOMY

Planning. The 1981–85 development plan stresses the development of agriculture and light industry.

Budget. The ordinary budget for 1979 balanced at 10,726m. ouguiyas.

Currency. The monetary unit is *ouguiya* which is divided into 5 *khoums.* Banknotes of 1,000, 200 and 100 *ouguiya* and coins of 20, 10, 5 and 1 *ouguiya* and 1 *khoum* are in circulation. In March 1983, £1 = 79·25 *ouguiya;* US$1 = 53·55 *ouguiya.*

Banking. *The Banque Centrale de Mauritanie* (created 1973) is the bank of issue, and there are 5 commercial banks situated in Nouakchott.

ENERGY AND NATURAL RESOURCES

Electricity. Production (1977) 96m. kwh.

Minerals. Iron ore deposits of (estimate) 200m. tonnes are found at Zouérate. Production (1977) 9m. tonnes.

Agriculture. Agriculture is mainly confined to the south, in the Sénégal river valley.

Production (tonnes) (1981) of millet, 67,000; dates, 14,000; potatoes, 4,000; maize, 6,000; sweet potatoes, 2,000; rice, 6,000. Rubber production (1970–71) 5,464 tonnes.

In 1981 there were 742,000 camels, 1·2m. cattle, 140,000 asses, 13,000 horses, 7·8m. sheep and goats.

Fisheries. About 300,000 tonnes of fish are caught in Mauritanian coastal waters each year, but only 34,200 tonnes (1978) are landed in the country (mainly at Nouâdhibou).

Forestry. There are 151,340 sq. km of forests, chiefly in the southern regions, where wild acacias yield the main product, gum arabic.

TRADE. In 1980 imports totalled 13,119m. ouguiya, and exports, 8,916 ouguiya.

In 1980, iron ore comprised 78% of exports and salted and dried fish 22%; 29% of exports went to France, and 19% to Italy, while France provided 34% of imports.

Total trade between Mauritania and UK (British Department of Trade returns, in £1,000 sterling):

	1978	*1979*	*1980*	*1981*	*1982*
Imports to UK	7,595	7,450	9,438	9,679	5,462
Exports and re-exports from UK	3,258	2,845	5,647	3,517	1,943

Tourism. In 1975 there were 20,700 tourists.

COMMUNICATIONS

Roads. There were 8,900 km of roads in 1978. In 1976 there were 6,600 passenger cars and 4,250 commercial vehicles.

Railways. A 652-km railway links Zouérate with the port of Point-Central, 10 km south of Nouâdhibou, and is used primarily for iron ore exports.

Aviation. There are international airports at Nouakchott, Nouâdhibou and Néma.

Shipping. The major ports are at Point-Central (for mineral exports), Nouakchott and Nouâdhibou.

Post and Broadcasting. There were, in 1977, over 2,000 telephones and 82,000 radio receivers.

Cinemas. In 1977 there were 12 cinemas with a seating capacity of 8,800.

JUSTICE, RELIGION, EDUCATION AND WELFARE

Justice. There are *tribunaux de première instance* at Nouakchott, Atar, Kaédi, Aïoun el Atrouss and Kiffa. The Appeal Court and Supreme Court are situated in Nouakchott. Islamic jurisprudence was adopted in Feb. 1980.

Religion. Over 99% of Mauritanians are Moslem, mainly of the Qadiriyah sect.

Education. In 1979 there were 82,408 pupils in primary schools, 11,957 in secondary schools, and (in 1975) 1,591 in technical schools.

Health. In 1976 there were 9 hospitals with 567 beds; there were 71 doctors, 4 dentists, 5 pharmacists, 20 midwives and 560 nursing personnel.

DIPLOMATIC REPRESENTATIVES

Of Mauritania in Great Britain
Ambassador: Abdel Khader Kamara (accredited 24 Nov. 1981).

Of Great Britain in Mauritania
Ambassador: P. L. O'Keeffe, CVO. (resides in Dakar).

Of Mauritania in the USA (2129 Leroy Pl., NW, Washington, D.C., 20008)
Ambassador: Abdellah Ould Daddah.

Of the USA in Mauritania (PO Box 222, Nouakchott)
Chargé d'Affaires: Edward Brynn.

Of Mauritania to the United Nations
Ambassador: Mohamed Said Ould Hamody.

Books of Reference

Stewart, C. C., and Stewart, E. K., *Islam and Social Order in Mauritania.* New York, 1970
Westebbe, R. M., *The Economy of Mauritania.* New York, 1971

MAURITIUS

Capital: Port Louis
Population: 983,692 (1981)
GNP per capita: US$1,060 (1980)

HISTORY. Mauritius was known to Arab navigators probably not later than the 10th century. It was probably visited by Malays in the 15th century, and was discovered by the Portuguese between 1507 and 1512, but the Dutch were the first settlers (1598). In 1710 they abandoned the island, which was occupied by the French under the name of Ile de France (1715). The British occupied the island in 1810, and it was formally ceded to Great Britain by the Treaty of Paris, 1814. Mauritius attained independence on 12 March 1968.

AREA AND POPULATION. The island, situated 20° S. lat., 57½° E. long., is of volcanic origin. The climate is free from extremes of weather, except for tropical cyclones at times. Yearly rainfall varies from 30 in. on the north-west coast to 200 in. in the uplands.

Mauritius has an area of about 720 sq. miles (1,865 sq. km). According to the census of 30 June 1972, the population of the island was 826,199 (413,580 males, 412,619 females); that of the dependencies was 25,135 (30 June 1972). The estimated population of the island at the end of 1981 was 983,692, and the population of Port Louis, the capital with its suburbs, numbered 148,389. Port Louis was granted city status on 25 Aug. 1966. Other towns: Beau Bassin-Rose Hill, 87,682; Curepipe, 57,505; Quatre Bornes, 56,491; Vascoas-Phoenix, 55,512.

Rodrigues (formerly a dependency but now a part of Mauritius) is about 350 miles east of Mauritius, 9½ miles long, 4½ miles broad. Area, 40 sq. miles (103·6 sq. km). Population (31 Dec. 1981, estimate), 32,977. Imports, 1980, Rs 75·11m.; 1978, Rs 54,605,564. Exports, 1980, Rs 1·9m.; 1978, Rs 2,872,012. There are 5 government, 5 aided primary, 1 private and 1 state secondary school.

Vital statistics, June 1980: Births, 24,983 (27 per 1,000); marriages, 8,629; deaths, 6,685 (7·2 per 1,000).

The official language is English.

Dependencies. Agalega and St Brandon Group. St Brandon is 250 miles from Mauritius. Area, 71 sq. km. Total population of the dependencies, census 1972, 366; estimated population on 31 Dec. 1981, 350. The main exports (to Mauritius) in 1974 were 227 tonnes of salted fish.

In 1965 the Chagos Archipelago was transferred to the newly created colony of British Indian Ocean Territory *see* p. 238.

CONSTITUTION AND GOVERNMENT. Mauritius became an independent state and a monarchial member of the British Commonwealth on 12 March 1968 after 7 months of internal self-government. The Governor-General is the local representative of HM the Queen, who remains the Head of the State.

In accordance with the Mauritius Independence Order 1968 the Cabinet is presided over by the Prime Minister. Each of the other 18 members of the Cabinet is responsible for the administration of specified departments or subjects and is bound by the rule of collective responsibility. 10 Parliamentary Secretaries may also be appointed by the Governor-General on the advice of the Prime Minister but in 1981 there were only 8.

The Legislative Assembly consists of a Speaker, elected from its own members, and 62 elected members (3 each for the 20 constituencies of Mauritius and 2 for Rodrigues) and 8 additional seats in order to ensure a fair and adequate representation of each community within the Assembly. General Elections are held every 5 years on the basis of universal adult suffrage.

The Constitution also provides for the Public Service Commission and the Judicial and Legal Service Commission, which have both assumed executive powers for appointments to the Public Service. An Ombudsman assumed office on

2 March 1970. Adequate provision is also made for the protection of fundamental rights and freedoms of the individual.

Elections are to be held on 11 June 1982.

Governor-General: Sir Dayendranath Burrenchobay, KBE, CMG, CVO.
Prime Minister: Hon. Anerood Jugnauth, QC.
National flag: Horizontally 4 stripes of red, blue, yellow and green.

DEFENCE. The Mauritius Police, which is responsible for defence, is equipped with arms; its strength at 30 June 1982 was 4,082 officers and men.

INTERNATIONAL RELATIONS

Membership. Mauritius is a member of UN, the Commonwealth, OAU and is an ACP state of EEC.

ECONOMY

Budget. Revenue and expenditure (in Rs) for years ending 30 June:

	1978–79	*1979–80*	*1980–81*	*1981–82*	*1982–83*[1]
Revenue	1,486,394,583	1,863,872,536	2,163,055,708	2,398,000,000	2,846,000,000
Expenditure	1,769,964,582	2,016,144,439	2,525,190,433	3,075,000,000	3,716,048,000

[1] Estimate.

Principal sources of revenue, 1982–83 (estimate): Direct taxes, Rs 499·3m.; indirect taxes, Rs 1,822·4m.; receipts from public utilities, Rs 125·1m.; receipts from public services Rs 111·2m.; interest and royalties, Rs 207·9m., reimburse ment, RS 71·2m. Capital expenditure, June 1982, was Rs 1,275. Capital revenue, Rs 853·9m.

On 30 June 1981 the public debt of Mauritius was Rs 4,232,068,803 after deducting the value of accumulated sinking funds.

Currency. The unit of currency is the Mauritius *Rupee*, divided into 100 *cents*.

The currency consists of: (i) Bank of Mauritius notes of Rs 50, 25, 10 and 5; (ii) Cupro-nickel coins of 1 rupee, ½ rupee, ¼ rupee and 10 cents; (iii) Bronze coins of 5 cents, 2 cents and 1 cent. In March 1983, £1 = 16·52 *rupees*; US$1 = 10·44.

Notes and coins in circulation as at 31 Dec. 1979 amounted to Rs 803·5m. and Rs 28·3m. respectively.

Banking. The Bank of Mauritius was established in 1966, with an authorized capital of Rs 10m., to exercise the function of a central bank. There are 12 commercial banks, the Mauritius Commercial Bank Ltd (established 1838), Barclays Bank International, the Bank of Baroda Ltd, The Mercantile Bank Ltd, the Mauritius Co-operative Central Bank Ltd, Banque Nationale de Paris (Intercontinentale), the Habib Bank (Overseas) Ltd, Citibank, the State Commercial Bank, the Bank of Credit and Commerce International SA, Indian Ocean International Bank Ltd and Habib Bank (Zurich). Other financial institutions include the Mauritius Housing Corporation, the Development Bank of Mauritius and the post office savings bank.

On 30 June 1982 the post office savings bank held deposits amounting to Rs 113·5m., belonging to 187,098 depositors.

NATURAL RESOURCES

Agriculture (1981). The area planted with sugar-cane was 209,010 acres. There were 21 factories in operation and the amount of sugar produced was: Raw sugar, 537,000 tonnes; white sugar, 38,000 tonnes; molasses, 159,000 tonnes.

The main secondary crops are tea (9,370 acres, yielding 4,666,000 kg of tea), tobacco (1,759 acres, yielding 1,259·5 tonnes of tobacco), potatoes (15,999 tonnes) and onions (2,295 tonnes).

Livestock (1981): Cattle, 26,887; goats, 14,737; poultry, 306,526.

Forestry. The total forest area is estimated at 21,027 hectares including some

11,600 hectares of plantations; if scrub and grazing are included the total area is approximately 56,110 hectares.

In 1981 sales of forest produce from Crown land totalled 29,806 cu. metres, round wood.

INDUSTRY AND TRADE

Labour. There were on 31 Dec. 1981, 330 registered trade unions with a total membership of 68,666 (on roll).

Commerce. Total trade (in Rs) for calendar years:

	1977	*1978*	*1979*	*1980*	*1981*
Imports [1]	2,950,800,000	3,076,400,000	3,634,400,000	4,721,400,000	4,976,800,000
Exports [2]	2,041,200,000	1,987,100,000	2,432,700,000	3,341,300,000	2,999,200,000

[1] Excluding bullion and specie.
[2] Including value of sugar quota certificates.

In 1981, Rs 535·2m. of the imports came from France, Rs 480·5m. from South Africa, Rs 423·5m. from UK and Rs 275·8m. from Australia; 1,651·4m. of the exports went to UK, Rs 587·3m. to France, Rs 161·1m. to Federal Republic of Germany and Rs 150·1m. to USA.

Sugar exports in 1980, 617,400 tonnes (Rs 2,168·3m.); 1981, 432,800 tonnes (Rs 1,625m.).

Total trade between Mauritius and UK (British Department of Trade returns, in £1,000 sterling):

	1977	*1978*	*1979*	*1980*	*1981*	*1982*
Imports to UK	102,906	122,892	116,004	145,227	97,435	119,450
Exports and re-exports from UK	34,403	31,705	30,370	24,688	21,612	20,857

Tourism. In 1981, 121,740 tourists visited Mauritius.

COMMUNICATIONS

Roads. There are 25·5 miles of motorway, 523 miles of main roads, 361 miles of urban roads and 216 miles of rural roads. All the main urban and rural roads have a bitumen surface. At 31 Dec. 1981 there were 25,180 cars, including 3,151 for public hire, 1,469 buses, 8,087 motor cycles and 17,703 auto cycles. Commercial vehicles comprised 12,762 lorries and vans.

Aviation. Mauritius is linked by air with Europe, Africa, Asia and Australia by the following airlines: Air France, Air India, Air Malawi, Air Mauritius, Alitalia, British Airways, Lufthansa, South African Airways and Zambia Airways. In addition to passenger services a weekly cargo flight is operated by Air France on the Mauritius–Paris route.

Air Mauritius operates a Boeing 707 service to London *via* Nairobi and Rome and to Bombay *via* the Seychelles, and Twin Otter services to Réunion and Rodrigues. The company has commercial arrangements with Air France, Lufthansa, Alitalia, Zambia Airways and Air Malawi for the operation of services to Paris, Frankfurt, Rome, Lusaka and Blantyre.

Shipping. In 1981 1,075 vessels entered Port Louis; total tonnage of cargo, about 1·7m. tonnes.

Post and Broadcasting. In Dec. 1981 there were 31 telephone exchanges and 37,812 individual telephone installations in Mauritius and Rodrigues. Communication with other parts of the world is established *via* radio links. A radio-telephone service operates with countries all over the world.

Television was introduced in Feb. 1965. At 31 Dec. 1981 there were 84,184 television sets and 114,580 radio sets.

Cinemas (1981). There were 46 cinemas, with a seating capacity of about 45,000.

Newspapers. There are 5 French daily papers (with occasional articles in English) and 2 Chinese daily papers with a combined circulation of about 75,000.

RELIGION, EDUCATION AND WELFARE

Religion. At the 1972 census there were 245,570 Roman Catholics, 7,050 Protestants (Church of England and Church of Scotland). The Hindus numbered 421,707 and the Moslems. 136,997. State aid is granted to the churches and Rs 4·9m. is budgeted for 1982–83.

Education. Primary education is free but not compulsory, though under the Education Ordinance of 1957 compulsion may be introduced as circumstances permit. In 1981 there were 222 government and 50 state-aided primary schools, 2 Hindu and 48 Roman Catholic. Enrolment at government schools was 99,762 and at state-aided primary schools 27,680. There were 8 special schools (blind, deaf, educationally sub-normal and industrial).

For secondary education there were in 1981, 5 government boys' schools (one of which has technical and commercial streams), 16 junior secondary schools (including one in Rodrigues) and 3 government girls' schools and 125 private secondary schools (including Mahatma Gandhi Institute) with 78,332 pupils.

There is also a teachers' training college, known as the Mauritius College of Education, and 9 private vocational and technical training centres, 1,040 on roll including students following part-time courses.

Government recurrent expenditure on education in 1982–83 is estimated at Rs 497m.

Health. In 1981 there were 562 doctors, including 114 specialists, and 2,776 hospital beds.

DIPLOMATIC REPRESENTATIVES

Of Mauritius in Great Britain (32–33 Elvaston Pl., London, SW7)
High Commissioner: L. Claude Obeegadoo (accredited 9 Feb. 1983).

Of Great Britain in Mauritius (Cerné Hse., Chausée, Port Louis)
High Commissioner: James Nicholas Allan, CBE.

Of Mauritius in the USA (4301 Connecticut Ave., NW, Washington, D.C., 20008)
Ambassador: Chitmansing Jesseramsing.

Of the USA in Mauritius (Rogers Bldg., John Kennedy St., Port Louis)
Ambassador: Roger C. F. Gordon.

Of Mauritius to the United Nations
Ambassador: Armand Maudave.

Books of Reference

Statistical Information: The Central Statistical Information Office (Rose Hill, Mauritius) was founded in July 1945. Its main publication is the *Bi-annual Digest of Statistics.*

Barnwell, P. J., and Toussaint, A., *A Short History of Mauritius.* London, 1949
Brouard, N. R., *A History of Woods and Forests in Mauritius.* Government Printer, 1964
Buckory, S., *Our Constitution.* Port Louis, 1971.—*An Outline of Local Government.* Port Louis, 1970
Central Statistical Office, *Population Census of Mauritius and its Dependencies.* 2 vols. 1962
Chelin, A., *Une île et son passé (1507–1947).* Mauritius Printing, 1973
Meade, J. E., *The Economic and Social Structure of Mauritius.* Government Printer, 1960
Ministry of Industry. *Handbook of Commerce and Industry.* Port Louis, 1970
Ministry of Information and Broadcasting, *Mauritius at a Glance.* Mauritius Printing, 1972.—*Fruits of Political and Social Democracy.*—*Mauritius Facts and Figures 1980*
Napal, D., *Les constitutions de l'île Maurice.* Port Louis, 1962
Société de l'Histoire de l'Ile Maurice. *Dictionnaire de biographie mauricienne.* Port Louis, 1967
Toussaint A., *History of Mauritius.* London, 1978
The Census of Industrial Production, 1964. Government Printer, 1965
10 années de réalisations. Ministry of Information and Broadcasting, 1967
Bi-annual Survey of Employment and Earnings in Large Establishments, 30 March 1972. Government Printer, 1972

Development Strategy (1971–1980), Ministry of Economic Planning and Development, Port Louis, 1970
4-Year Plan for Social and Economic Development 1971–75. Government Printer, 1971
5-Year Plan for Social and Economic Development 1975–80. Government Printer, 1975
2-Year Plan for Social and Economic Development 1980–82. Government Printer, 1980

Library: The Mauritius Institute Public Library, Port Louis.

MEXICO

Capital: Mexico City
Population: 72·1m. (1982)
GNP per capita: US$2,130 (1980)

Estados Unidos Mexicanos

HISTORY. Mexico's history falls into four epochs: the era of the Indian empires (before 1521), the Spanish colonial phase (1521–1810), the period of national formation (1810–1910), which includes the war of independence (1810–21) and the long presidency of Porfirio Díaz (1876–80, 1884–1911), and the present period which began with the social revolution of 1910–21 and is regarded by Mexicans as the period of social and national consolidation.

AREA AND POPULATION. Mexico is at the southern extremity of North America and is bounded in the north by USA, west and south-west by the Pacific, south by Guatemala and Belize and east by the Gulf of Mexico and comprises 1,967,183 sq. km (761,530 sq. miles), excluding inland waters and uninhabited islands (5,363 sq. km) offshore.

Census results for 1970 and 1980 are shown in the following table (capital of states in brackets):

States	*Area (sq. km)*	*Census 1970*	*Census 1980*	*Approx. density per sq. km in 1970*
Aguascalientes (Aguascalientes)	5,589	338,142	503,410	60·50
Baja California (Mexicali)	70,113	870,421	1,225,436	12·41
Baja California Sur (La Paz)	73,677	128,019	221,389	1·74
Campeche (Campeche)	51,833	251,556	372,277	4·85
Chiapas (Tuxtla Gutiérrez)	73,887	1,569,053	2,096,812	21·24
Chihuahua (Chihuahua)	247,087	1,612,525	1,933,856	6·53
Coahuila (Saltillo)	151,571	1,114,956	1,558,401	7·36
Colima (Colima)	5,455	241,153	339,202	44·21
Distrito Federal (México City)	1,499	6,874,165	9,373,353	4,585·83
Durango (Durango)	119,648	939,208	1,160,196	7·85
Guanajuato (Guanajuato)	30,589	2,270,370	3,044,402	74·22
Guerrero (Chilpancingo)	63,794	1,597,360	2,174,162	25·04
Hidalgo (Pachuca)	20,987	1,193,845	1,516,511	56·88
Jalisco (Guadalajara)	80,137	3,296,586	4,293,549	41·14
México (Toluca)	21,461	3,833,185	7,545,692	178·61
Michoacán (Morelia)	59,864	2,324,226	3,048,704	38·83
Morelos (Cuernavaca)	4,941	616,119	931,675	124·70
Nayarit (Tepic)	27,621	544,031	730,024	19·70
Nuevo León (Monterrey)	64,555	1,694,689	2,463,298	26·25
Oaxaca (Oaxaca)	95,364	2,015,424	2,518,157	21·13
Puebla (Puebla)	33,919	2,508,226	3,279,960	73·95
Querétaro (Querétaro)	11,769	485,523	726,054	41·25
Quintana Roo (Chetumal)	50,350	88,150	209,858	1·75
San Luis Potosi (San Luis Potosi)	62,848	1,281,996	1,670,637	20·40
Sinaloa (Culiacán)	58,092	1,266,528	1,880,098	21·80
Sonora (Hermosillo)	184,934	1,098,720	1,498,931	5·94
Tabasco (Villa Hermosa)	24,661	768,387	1,149,756	31·16
Tamaulipas (Ciudad Victoria)	79,829	1,456,858	1,924,934	18·25
Tlaxcala (Tlaxcala)	3,914	420,638	547,261	107·47
Veracruz (Jalapa)	72,815	3,815,422	5,264,611	52·40
Yucatán (Mérida)	39,340	758,355	1,034,648	19·28
Zacatecas (Zacatecas)	75,040	951,462	1,145,327	12·68
Total	1,967,183 [1]	48,225,238	67,382,581	24·51

[1] Excludes islands (5,363 sq. km).

At the 1980 census the total population was 67,382,581 of which, 33,295,260 were males, 34,087,321 females. Urban population, 1978, was 65·2% and rural population was 34·8%. The official language is Spanish, the mother tongue of over 90% of the population, but there are 5 indigenous language groups (Náhuatl, Maya, Zapotec, Otomi and Mixtec) from which are derived a total of 59 dialects spoken by 3,111,415 inhabitants (1970 census). In 1980, about 16% of the population were of European ethnic origin, 55% mestizo and 29% Amerindian.

Estimates (1978) of the largest cities (proper) were:

Mexico [1]	8,988,230	Aguascalientes	247,764	Uruapan	138,264
Netzahuacóyotl [2]	2,067,992	Saltillo	245,738	Ciudad Madero	135,059
Guadalajara [3]	1,813,131	Tampico	239,970	Tepic	133,353
Monterrey [4]	1,054,029	Morelia	239,377	Oaxaca de Juárez	131,193
Puebla de Zaragoza	677,959	Cuernavaca	226,649	Monclova	130,918
Ciudad Juárez	597,096	Toluca de Lerdo	222,885	Ciudad Victoria	121,379
Léon de los Aldamas	589,950	Reynosa	218,683	Coatzacoalcos	120,059
Tijuana	534,993	Victoria de Durango	218,629	Orizaba	118,354
Acapulco de Juárez	421,088	Nuevo Laredo	214,161	Cordoba	116,148
Chihuahua	369,545	Jalapa Enríquez	191,096	Celaya	114,365
Mexicali	338,423	Poza Rica de Hidalgo	188,928	Minatitlán	112,577
San Luis Potosí	315,228	Matamoros	186,480	Los Mochís	111,779
Culiacán Rosales	302,229	Mazatlán	177,673	Pachuca	105,225
Hermosillo	299,687	Querétaro	176,200	Campeche	103,613
Veracruz Llave	295,297	Ciudad Obregón	172,974	Tuxtla Gutiérrez	101,668
Torreón	268,664	Villa Hermosa	165,468	Gómez Palacio	100,215
Mérida	263,186	Irapuato	155,601		

[1] Greater Mexico City, 13,993,866.
[2] Suburb of Mexico City.
[3] Greater Guadalajara, 2,343,034.
[4] Greater Monterrey, 1,923,402.

Vital statistics for calendar years:

	Marriages	*Births*	*Deaths*
1976	427,335	2,156,430	406,033
1977	419,047	2,278,233	404,880
1978	444,700	2,277,708	402,322

Crude birth rate in 1978 was 34 per 1,000 population; crude death rate (1978), 6 (26·1 in 1932); infant mortality rate, 77 per 1,000 live births (375 in 1933); crude marriage rate (1978) 6·6 per 1,000 population; divorces (1976), 0·29 per 1,000 population.

CONSTITUTION AND GOVERNMENT. A new Constitution was promulgated on 5 Feb. 1917 and has been amended from time to time. Mexico is a representative, democratic and federal republic, comprising 31 states and a federal district, each state being free and sovereign in all internal affairs, but united in a federation established according to the principals of the Fundamental Law. Citizenship, including the right of suffrage, is vested in all nationals of 18 years of age and older who have 'an honourable means of livelihood'.

There is complete separation of legislative, executive and judicial powers (Art. 49). Legislative power is vested in a General Congress of 2 chambers, a Chamber of Deputies and a Senate (Art.50). The Chamber of Deputies consists of 400 members directly elected for 3 years, 300 of them from single-member constituencies and 100 chosen under a system of proportional representation (Arts.51–55). At the general elections held on 4 July 1982, 299 of the single-member seats were won by the *Partido Revolucionario Institucional* (PRI) and 1 by the *Partido de Acción Nacional* (PAN); of the extra 100 seats, 54 were won by PAN, 17 by the *Partido Socialista Unido Mexicana,* 11 by the *Partido Popular Socialista,* 10 by the *Partido Socialista de los Trabajadores* and 8 by the *Partido Demócrata Mexicano.* The Senate comprises 64 members, 2 from each state and 2 from the federal district, directly elected for 6 years (Arts.56–58). At the elections of 4 July 1982, the PRI won all 64 seats. Members of both chambers are not immediately re-eligible for election (Art.59). Congress sits from 1 Sept. to 31 Dec. each year; during the recess there is a permanent committee of 15 deputies and 14 senators appointed by the respective chambers.

The President is the supreme executive authority. He appoints the members of the Council of Ministers and the senior military and civilian officers of the state. He is directly elected for a single 6-year term.

The names of the presidents from 1920 are as follows:

Gen. Alvaro Obregón, 1 Dec. 1920–30 Nov. 1924.
Gen. Plutarco Elias Calles, 1 Dec. 1924–30 Nov. 1928.
Emilio Portes Gil (Provisional).[1] 1 Dec. 1928–4 Feb. 1930.
Pascual Oritz Rubio, 5 Feb. 1930–3 Sept. 1932 (resigned).
Gen. Abelardo L. Rodriguez, 4 Sept. 1932–30 Nov. 1934.
Gen. Lázaro Cárdenas, 1 Dec. 1934–30 Nov. 1940.
Gen. Manuel Avila Camacho, 1 Dec. 1940–30 Nov. 1946.
Miguel Alemán Valdés, 1 Dec. 1946–30 Nov. 1952.
Adolfo Ruiz Cortines, 1 Dec 1952–30 Nov. 1958.
Adolfo Lopez Mateos, 1 Dec. 1958–30 Nov. 1964.
Gustavo Diaz Ordaz, 1 Dec. 1964–30 Nov. 1970.
Luis Echeverría Alvarez, 1 Dec. 1970–30 Nov. 1976.
José Lopez Portilloy Pacheco, 1 Dec. 1976–30 Nov. 1982.

[1] Took office after the assassination on 17 July 1928, of Gen. Obregón, the President-elect.

President: Miguel de la Madrid Hurtado (born in 1934), formerly Minister of Planning, elected 4 July 1982 to serve for 6 years. He assumed office on 1 Dec. 1982.

In Dec. 1982 the Council of Ministers was composed as follows:

Agrarian Reform: Luis Martinez Villicana. *Agriculture and Water Resources:* Horacio Garcia Aguilar. *Commerce:* Hector Hernandez Cervantes. *Communication and Transport:* Rodolfo Felix Valdes. *Finance and Public Credit:* Jesus Silva Herzog Flores. *Foreign Relations:* Bernardo Sepulveda Amor. *Interior:* Manuel Bartlett Diaz. *Health and Assistance:* Dr Guillermo Soberon Acevedo. *Human Settlements and Public Works:* Marcelo Javeli Girard. *Labour and Social Welfare:* Arsenio Farell. *National Defence:* Gen. Juan Arevalo Gardogui. *Navy:* Adm. Miguel Angel Gomez Ortega. *Patrimony and Industrial Development:* Francisco Labastida Ochoa. *Planning and Budget:* Carlos Salinas de Gortari. *Public Education:* Jesus Reyes Heroles. *Tourism:* Antonio Enriquez Savignac.

National flag: Three vertical strips of green, white, red, with the national arms in the centre.

National anthem: Mexicanos, al grito de guerra (words by F. González Bocanegra; tune by Jaime Nunó, 1854).

Local Government. Mexico is divided into 31 states and a Federal District. The latter is co-extensive with Mexico City and is administered by a Governor appointed by the President. Each state has its own constitution, with the right to legislate and to levy taxes (but not inter-state customs duties); its Governor is directly elected for 6 years and its unicameral legislature for 3 years; judicial officers are appointed by the Federal government.

DEFENCE. Supreme command is vested in the President, exercised through the Ministries of Defence (for Army and Air Force) and Marine.

Army. The country is divided into 35 zones in which both the regular army and volunteer corps are trained. The Army, in 1981, had 1 mechanized, 2 infantry and 1 parachute brigade, 64 independent garrison battalions and 23 independent cavalry regiments. Peace-time strength is 95,000. Military education is provided for officers, at the National Military School, the Application Centre for Army Officers and the Staff College, as well as in other specialized schools. To combat illiteracy in the Army, schools have been established in every regular and volunteer group.

Navy. The Navy consists of 2 old *ex*-US destroyers, 5 old *ex*-US frigates (including 4 former destroyer escort transports), 1 armed transport and 4 old *ex*-US armed tugs used as patrol ships, 18 old *ex*-US fleet minesweepers, 16 old *ex*-US escort minesweepers, 21 fishery protection cutters of 130 tons built in Britain in 1974–76 and 10 built in Mexico in 1978–80, 14 patrol boats, 4 survey ships, 1 transport, 3 landing ships (2 used for rescue and 1 for light forces repair), 2 oilers, 11 auxiliary vessels and 8 tugs. There are 6 naval zones on the Gulf and 8 on the Pacific coast and 6 naval air bases holding 54 aircraft. Naval personnel in 1983 totalled 19,420 officers and men including naval air force and coastguard. There were also 3,810 marines, with 1 regiment in reserve.

Air Force. The Air Force has a strength of nearly 5,000 officers and men, and has nine operational groups, each with one or two squadrons. No. 1 Group comprises No. 208 Squadron with 10 IAI Aravas for transport, search and rescue and counter-insurgency duties; and No. 209 Squadron with Bell 205A, 206B Jet-Ranger, 47G, Alouette III and Puma helicopters. No. 2 Group has two Squadrons (Nos. 206 and 207) of Swiss-built Pilatus PC-7 Turbo-Trainers for light attack duty. No. 3 Group (203 and 204 Squadrons) also operates PC-7s; No. 4 Group (201 and 205 Squadrons) is in process of conversion. No. 5 Group consists of No. 101 communications Squadron and a photo-reconnaissance unit, both equipped with Aero Commander 500S piston-engined light twins. Nos. 301 and 302 Squadrons, in No. 6 Group, operate a total of 5 C-54, 2 C-118A and 1 DC-7 piston-engined transports. The main combat Group, No. 7, comprises No. 401 Squadron with 13 F-5E Tiger II and F-5F 2-seat fighters; and No. 202 Squadron with AT-33A jet trainer/fighter-bombers. No. 8 Group has 7 C-47s in a VIP transport squadron. No. 9 Group operates the Air Force's remaining 12 or more C-47s in Nos. 311 and 312 transport Squadrons. There is a Presidential Squadron with 2 Boeing 727-100s, 1 737-247, 1 HS.125, 1 JetStar and 1 Bell 212. The Military Academy continues to fly 14 veteran Stearman PT-17 biplanes. Other training aircraft include 20 Mudry CAP-10Bs, 20 Beech Musketeers, 20 Bonanzas, and PC-7 Turbo-Trainers.

INTERNATIONAL RELATIONS

Membership. Mexico is a member of UN, OAS and ALIDE (formerly LAFTA).

External Debt. The public sector external debt (June 1980) was US$27,939m.

ECONOMY

Budget. The 1982 budget provides for expenditure of 3,286,000m. pesos.

Currency. The monetary unit is the *peso* divided into 100 *centavos.*

There are coins for 1, 5 and 10 pesos and 50, 20, 10 and 5 centavos; notes for 10,000, 5,000, 500, 100, 50, 20, 10 and 5 pesos.

Rate of exchange, March 1983: 107 pesos = US$1; 118 pesos = £1.

Banking. The Bank of Mexico, established 1 Sept. 1925, is the central bank of issue; it is modelled on the Federal Reserve system, with large powers to 'manage' the currency. The Government holds 51% of the capital stock.

On 1 Sept. 1982 the private banking sector was nationalized.

In 1983 the total outstanding public external debt was US$80,000m.

Weights and Measures. The metric system was introduced in 1896, and its sole use is enjoined by law of 14 Dec. 1928.

ENERGY AND NATURAL RESOURCES

Electricity. In 1979 the 3,928 electric generating plants had installed capacity of 16·9m. kw. Production (in 1m. kwh): 1977, 50,632; 1978, 55,203; 1979, 59,412.

Oil. The chief Mexican oilfields had proven reserves of oil and gas, in 1981, of 67,800m. bbls (potential, 250,000m. bbls). In 1980 the oil industry generated 6% of the GDP and supplied about 85% of the energy consumed in the country. Since the nationalization of the industry in 1938, Petróleos Mexicanos, a government-owned enterprise, has exclusive rights to the exploitation, refining and sale of oil and its by-products. PEMEX is exploiting mainly the rich Poza Rica and Faja de Oro fields in the state of Veracruz (discovered in 1938), which extend into the Gulf of Mexico shelf and the nearby fields in Escolín and Mecatepec. New discoveries in Reforma, state of Chiapas, and Samaria, state of Tabasco, however, increased oil production in 1974 over the previous year by 25%. 43% of the current national yield is obtained from these two states. Exploration has been intensified in various states throughout Mexico leading to important discoveries in Cotaxtla, state of Veracruz, and Chac, state of Campeche. Crude petroleum output was 2·3m. bbls per day in 1981. Mexico exports crude oil but still imports petrol, gasoil (diesel), fuel oil and some petroleum gas.

Gas. Natural gas production came to 32,350m. cu. metres in 1980.

Minerals. Mining is an important industry and, of the 48 principal non-metallic minerals in the world, Mexico produces at least 23. However, in view of the international price of mineral-metallurgical products, mining production, lacking incentives, has been both sluggish and fluctuating. Mining policy is aimed at the rational exploitation and increased industrialization of its mineral resources, procuring, at the same time, to completely Mexicanize the firms dedicated to this activity. This policy is implemented by the law regulating Article 27 of the Constitution regarding the exploitation and use of mineral resources. Based on this legislation, 769 mining companies had been Mexicanized by the end of Aug. 1972. The contribution, in monetary terms, of the Mexican mining companies to total national mining output soared from 26% in 1964 to 98% in Aug. 1972. In addition to the uranium deposits discovered in the states of Chihuahua, Durango, Sonora and Queretaro announced in 1959, rich deposits have been located at General Bravo, state of Nuevo León, with up to 450 tonnes of uranium oxide. Total reserves (estimate 1976) 2,860 tonnes of uranium 308.

Silver output (in tonnes) was 1,537 in 1979; 1,473 in 1980. About half the production is minted, including a 'token' coin (1949) weighing 1 troy oz. Gold output: 1980, 6,096 kg.

Mexico has large coal resources, calculated at 675m. tonnes, including high-grade coking coal at Sabinas in Coahuila. There are large underdeveloped reserves of iron ore with known reserves of 300m. tonnes; the new Peña Colorado field in Colima State seems to be promising. Output, 1980 (in tonnes): Iron ore, 5,087,361; lead, 145,549; copper, 175,399; zinc, 238,231; fluorite, 916,455; crude steel, 7·6m.; cement, 16,263,000; pig iron, 5·15m.; sulphur, 2,102,000.

Agriculture. About 80% of Mexico's territory is made up of arid and semi-arid lands. Irrigation is needed, 43% of the land having less than 500 mm of rain a year. In 1977 Mexico had 21·7m. hectares of arable land. In 1980, the government launched the *Sistema Alimentaria Mexicana* to raise food production and rationalize land tenure, with the aim of achieving self-sufficiency in basic crops. Grains occupy 68% of the cultivated land, with about 53% given to maize and about 9% to wheat. In the 1970 census there were 91,354 tractors. It is estimated that Mexico should be self-supporting with at least 17m. hectares of land under irrigation and 20·3m. hectares under cultivation. Government agricultural programmes are being carried out by the National Basic Commodities Company (CONASUPO) and the National Deposit Warehouses (ANDSA) which regulate the market, intervening in the marketing process and protecting the low-income producers as well as the low-income consumer by assuring him access to basic commodities. ANDSA has undertaken the construction of silos, warehouses, storage, machinery and equipment.

The volume of credit channelled towards agriculture is dealt with by the National Ejidal Credit Bank. In addition, the Fund for Technical Assistance and Agricultural Credit Guarantees was set up in recent years to assist government and private banks in projects to finance and provide technical assistance, organizational counselling, primary industrialization and marketing to small farm producers.

Livestock (1981): Cattle, 31·8m.; sheep, 7·9m.; pigs, 12·9m.; horses, 6·5m.; goats, 7·2m.; mules, 3·3m.; donkeys, 3·2m.; poultry, 153·2m.

Production of hides reached 9·5m. in 1976; production of meat, 909,733 tonnes.

Mexico's basic food crop is maize, and a rapid expansion of this crop is one of the chief aims of Mexican agricultural policy, balanced by the demand for 'cash crops' for export, such as cotton, sugar, garbanzos (chick peas), bananas, winter vegetables and coffee.

Production of crops for 1981 was as follows (in 1,000 tonnes):

Crop	*1981*	*Crop*	*1981*	*Crop*	*1981*
Maize	14,766	Sugar-cane	35,975	Oranges	1,894
Sorghum	6,296	Tomatoes	1,093	Bananas	1,163
Wheat	3,189	Potatoes	...	Lemons	562
Barley	559	Dry beans	1,469	Pineapples	655
Rice	644	Soybeans	712	Apples	296
Cottonseed	530	Coconuts	113	Grapes	578
Cotton lint	344	Coffee	217	Mangoes	914

Sugar-cane is linked closely with the export markets, although not to the same degree as coffee, in view of the fact that despite the large crop, the national consumption of sugar, at approximately 35 kg a year per person, is one of the highest in the world. Exports have however remained more or less stable: 1972 exports represented 25% of total output.

Forestry. Timber lands represent 22% of the Mexican territory and are estimated to extend over 43m. hectares (about 43% of commercial importance), containing pine, spruce, cedar, mahogany, logwood and rosewood. Despite the existence of forests that would support a higher production, output for 20 years up to 1973, averaged an annual growth of only 1·1%. In 1973 only 15·7% of the productive capacity of the country's forests was being exploited. Reckless lumbering had destroyed the timber stands on many watersheds, resulting in spring floods and lowered water supplies in summer. In 1951 federal edicts had halted all timber-cutting in 22 states, regardless of concessions; but they have been resumed under strict supervision. There are 14 forest reserves (nearly 800,000 hectares) and 47 national park forests of 750,000 hectares. In 1977 total roundwood production amounted to 11·7m. cu. metres.

Fisheries. Fishing is important because of Mexico's 9,903 km of coastline. Catch (1979, tonnes): Anchoveta, 200,430; pilchards, 164,436; shrimp and prawns, 44,979; oysters, 29,395; tuna, 26,261; sea perch *(mojarras)*, 19,371; sea bass, 10,216.

Total catch in 1979 was 850,525 tonnes.

INDUSTRY AND TRADE

Industry. In 1980, the primary sector (agriculture, mining etc.) provided 9·3% of GDP, the oil and petrochemical industry 7%, manufacturing and construction 29·1% and the service sector (commerce, transport and communications, power supply and other services) 54·6%.

Labour. In 1980, the economically active population was 23·7m., of whom 35% were engaged in agriculture and 18% in manufacturing. Approximately 5m. people belong to trade unions, of whom 85% are affiliated to the *Congreso del Trabajo.*

Commerce. Trade for calendar years in 1m. pesos:

	1977	*1978*	*1979*	*1980*
Imports	126,352	177,278	273,775	448,290
Exports	94,452	131,403	199,973	351,479

Export figures for metals and for certain foreign-owned agricultural products are heavily undervalued to reduce export taxes.

Of total imports in 1980, 66% came from USA, 5% from Japan, 5% from Federal Republic of Germany and 3% from France. Leading imports were machinery, transport equipment, iron and steel, chemicals, machine tools, parts and spares.

Of total exports in 1980, 63% went to USA, 7% to Spain, 4% to Japan and 3% to Israel. The main visible exports (1980) were crude oil (60%), machinery and industrial goods, coffee, chemicals and cotton.

Total trade between Mexico and UK (British Department of Trade returns, in £1,000 sterling):

	1978	*1979*	*1980*	*1981*	*1982*
Imports to UK	41,593	36,336	111,636	108,749	106,067
Exports and re-exports from UK	108,585	134,816	188,133	209,596	162,946

Tourism. Tourism is the largest single source of dollar income and, in 1979, 4·9m. tourists visited Mexico. Tourist net revenue in 1979, including border visitors, amounted to US$1,422m.

COMMUNICATIONS

Roads. Total length, (1980) 213,192 km, of which 978 km were motorways. Motor vehicles registered in 1980 comprised 4,031,970 passenger cars, and 1,534,100 commercial vehicles.

Railways. In 1937 the main railway lines were nationalized. The principal group is the *Ferrocarriles Nacionales de México*, with 20,288 km of track. Three lines (215 km) remain privately owned. In 1979, FNM carried 55m. tonnes of freight and 18·6m. passengers.

Aviation. Mexico has an excellent air service. There are 28 international and 20 national airports. Each of the larger states has a local airline which links them with main airports, which, in turn, furnish services to US, Central and South America and Europe. Thirty companies in 1976 maintained international services, of these 2 were Mexican. Domestic flights are handled by 77 companies. In 1975 commercial aircraft carried 9·63m. national and international passengers with 127,025 tonnes of baggage and some 97,923 tonnes of mail and freight.

Shipping. Mexico has 49 ocean ports, of which, on the Gulf coast, the most important include Tampico, Veracruz, Coatzacoalcos, Progreso and Yucalpletón. On the Pacific are Ensenada, La Paz, Santa Rosalía, Guaymas, Mazatlán, Manzanillo, Acapulco and Salina Cruz.

Merchant shipping loaded 39·8m. tonnes and unloaded 30·7m. tonnes in 1976. Passengers (1976), embarked, 375,042; landed, 373,320. In 1980, the merchant marine comprised 361 vessels (of over 100 GRT) with a total tonnage of 1,006,417 GRT.

Post and Broadcasting. On 31 Dec. 1975 the federal, state and private telegraph and telephone system had 5,938 offices and 220,442 km of telegraph lines and 16·2m. km of telephone line. *Teléfonos de México*, a state-controlled company, controls about 98% of all the telephone service. Telephones in use, Jan. 1980, 4,532,557; 98·7% were automatic.

In 1980 there were 810 commercial broadcasting stations and 46 cultural government radio stations while 8,761,920 homes had receiving sets. In 1981 commercial stations numbered 124 and cultural stations 4; there were 4,873,560 homes with receiving sets.

Cinemas (1979). Cinemas numbered 1,833 with annual attendance of 271m.

Newspapers (1974). There were 178 dailies and 21 weeklies, with an aggregate circulation in excess of 5m.; 23 in México City have about half of the total circulation.

JUSTICE, RELIGION, EDUCATION AND WELFARE

Justice. Magistrates of the Supreme Court are appointed for 6 years by the President and confirmed by the Senate; they can be removed only on impeachment. The courts include the Supreme Court with 21 magistrates, 12 collegiate circuit courts with 3 judges each and 9 unitary circuit courts with 1 judge each, and 68 district courts with 1 judge each.

The penal code of 1 Jan. 1930 abolished the death penalty, except for the Army, and set up a commission of alienists and other specialists, in place of courts, to deal with criminal cases (for federal offences); each state also appoints its own local magistrates.

The Mexican Constitution provides a guarantee of individual rights by means of a judicial procedure known as *amparo*, which gives any injured person whose constitutional rights have, in his opinion, been infringed, right to immediate access to the courts and full remedy, combining the swiftness of the Anglo-Saxon writ of *habeas corpus* and the breadth of remedy available through the injunction.

Religion. The prevailing religion is the Roman Catholic (51m. members in 1976); with (1976) 2 cardinals, 9 archbishops and 84 bishops, but by the constitution of 1857, the Church was separated from the State, and the constitution of 1917 provided strict regulation of this and all other religions. No ecclesiastical body may acquire landed property, and since 1917 the property of the Church has been held to belong to the State. In the 1920s the Government suppressed the political influence of the priesthood and temporarily (1929–31) closed the churches. An understanding between State and Church was, however, reached, and all churches eschewing public affairs flourish freely. At the 1970 census 876,879 Protestants, 49,181 Jews and 150,329 members of other religions were also numbered.

Education. Primary and secondary education is free and compulsory, and secular. Clergy are forbidden to establish primary schools. All private schools must conform to government standards. Military drill is compulsory for boys of 18 years. In the Federal District education is controlled by the national government; elsewhere by the state authorities.

In 1980–81 there were:

	Schools	*Teachers*	*Students*
Nursery	13,021	32,368	1,071,619
Primary	76,179	375,220	14,666,257
Secondary	11,010	226,532	4,042,188
Preparatory/Vocational	3,218	28,658	491,665
Teacher-training	485	12,988	207,997
Higher education	291	77,653	897,726

The most important university is the Universidad Nacional Autónoma de México (UNAM) in México City which, with its associated institutions, had, in 1979, 271,266 students (excluding post-graduates). UNAM was founded in 1551, re-organized in 1910, and granted full autonomy in 1920. Other universities of particular importance in México City are the Instituto Politécnico Nacional, specializing in technology and applied science, with over 110,000 students, and the Universidad Autónoma Metropolitana with 20,170 students, opened in 1973. Outside México City the principal universities are, in Monterrey, the Universidad de Nuevo León with 80,000 students and the Instituto Tecnólogico y de Estudios Superiores de Monterrey with 17,000 students; in Guadalajara, the Universidad de Guadalajara (156,621 students) and the Universidad Autónoma de Guadalajara (19,002 students); in Xalapa, the Universidad Veracruzana (40,414 students); and at Morelia, the Universidad Michoacana (29,167 students).

Health. In 1974 Mexico had 45,322 physicians; there were 5,469 state and private hospitals and clinics with 76,413 beds.

Social Welfare. The social welfare system administered by the Mexican Social Security Institute covered 38m. on 31 Dec. 1979.

DIPLOMATIC REPRESENTATIVES

Of Mexico in Great Britain (8 Halkin St., London, SW1X 7DW)
Ambassador: Francisco Cuevas-Cancino (accredited 11 Feb. 1983)

Of Great Britain in Mexico (Lerma 71, Col. Cuauhtémoc, México City 06500, D.F.) *Ambassador:* C. C. C. Tickell, MVO.

Of Mexico in the USA (2829–16th St., NW, Washington, D.C., 20009)
Ambassador: Bernardo Sepulveda.

Of the USA in Mexico (Paseo de la Reforma 305, México City 5, D.F.)
Ambassador: John A. Gavin.

Of Mexico to the United Nations
Ambassador: Porfirio Muñoz Ledo.

Books of Reference

Anuario Estadístico de los Estados Unidos Mexicanos. Annual (latest issue 1965)
México A Vuelo de Pajaro. Secretaria de la Presidencia, 1976
México Statistical Data. Banco National de México, 1975
Petroleos Mexicanos: Anuario Estadistico, 1975. Mexico City
Revista de Estadística (Monthly); *Revista de Economia* (Monthly)
Alba, V., *A Concise History of Mexico.* London, 1973
Banco de México S.A., Annual report
Banco Nacional de Comercio Exterior. *Comercio Exterior,* monthly.—*Mexico.* Annual (in Spanish or English)
Bazant, J., *A Concise History of Mexico.* CUP, 1977
Calvert, P., *Mexico.* London, 1973
Carrada-Bravo, F., *Oil, Money, and the Mexican Economy.* Boulder, 1982
Cheetham, N., *New Spain, the Birth of Modern Mexico.* London, 1974
Davies, N., *The Aztecs.* London, 1973
Dominguez, J. I., (ed.) *Mexico's Political Economy: Challenges at Home and Abroad.* London, 1982
Johnson, K. F., *Mexican Democracy: A Critical View.* Rev. ed. New York, 1978
Kaufman, S., (ed.) *The Politics of Mexican Oil.* Univ. of Pittsburgh Press, 1981
Ker, A. M., *Mexican Government Publications: A Guide, 1821–1936.* Washington, 1940
López-Portillo, J., *Mexico in Facts and Figures.* México City, 1976
Parkes, H. B., *A History of Mexico.* Rev. ed. Boston, 1950
Peña, M. T. de la, *El Pueblo y su Tierra.* México City, 1964
Ross, J. B., *The Economic System of Mexico.* Stanford, 1971

MONACO

Capital: Monaco
Population: 28,000 (1980)

HISTORY. Monaco is a small Principality on the Mediterranean, surrounded by the French Department of Alpes Maritimes except on the side towards the sea. From 1297 it belonged to the house of Grimaldi. In 1731 it passed into the female line, Louise Hippolyte, daughter of Antoine I, heiress of Monaco, marrying Jacques de Goyon Matignon, Count of Torigni, who took the name and arms of Grimaldi. The Principality was placed under the protection of the Kingdom of Sardinia by the Treaty of Vienna, 1815, and under that of France in 1861. Prince Albert I (reigned 1889–1922) acquired fame as an oceanographer; and his son Louis II (1922–49) was instrumental in establishing the International Hydrographic Bureau.

AREA AND POPULATION. The area is 190 hectares or 467 acres. The Principality is divided into 4 districts: Monaco-Ville, la Condamine, Monte-Carlo and Fontvieille. Population (1980), 28,000. The official language is French.

REIGNING PRINCE. Rainier III, born 31 May 1923, son of Princess Charlotte, Duchess of Valentinois, daughter of Prince Louis II, 1898–1977 (married 19 March 1920 to Prince Pierre, Comte de Polignac, who had taken the name Grimaldi, from whom she was divorced 18 Feb. 1933). Prince Rainier succeeded his grandfather Louis II, who died on 9 May 1949. He married on 19 April 1956 Miss Grace Kelly, a citizen of the USA (died 14 Sept. 1982). *Issue:* Princess Caroline Louise Marguerite, born 23 Jan. 1957; married Philippe Junot on 28 June 1978, divorced, 9 Oct. 1980. Prince Albert Alexandre Louis Pierre, born 14 March 1958 *(heir apparent)*; Princess Stephanie Marie Elisabeth, born 1 Feb. 1965.

CONSTITUTION AND GOVERNMENT. Prince Rainier III on 28 Jan. 1959 suspended the Constitution of 5 Jan. 1911, thereby dissolving the National Council and the Communal Council. On 28 March 1962 the National Council (18 members elected every 5 years, last elections 1978) and the Communal Council (16 members elected every 4 years, last elections 1979) were re-established as elected bodies.

On 17 Dec. 1962 a new constitution was promulgated. It maintains the hereditary monarchy, though Prince Rainier renounces the principle of divine right. The supreme tribunal becomes the custodian of fundamental liberties, and guarantees are given for the right of association, trade union freedom and the right to strike. It provides for votes for women and the abolition of the death penalty.

The constitution can be modified only with the approval of the elected National Council. Women were given the vote in 1945.

Monegasque relations with France were based on a convention of neighbourhood and administrative assistance of 1951. This was terminated by France on 11 Oct. 1962, but has been replaced by several new conventions signed on 18 May 1963.

National flag: Horizontally red over white.

ECONOMY

Planning. A 55-acre site has been reclaimed from the sea at Fontvieille. This land has been earmarked for office and residential development. The present industrial zone is to be reorganized and developed with a view to attracting new light industry to the Principality.

Budget. The budget (in 1,000 francs) was as follows:

	1976	*1977*	*1978*	*1979*	*1980*
Revenue	528,246	595,874	671,035	784,319	987,158
Expenditure	464,421	515,207	518,129	551,632	629,449

Currency. The monetary unit is the French *franc* divided into 100 *centimes*.

Weights and Measures. The metric system is in use.

INDUSTRY AND TRADE

Tourism. There were 218,000 tourists in 1979; 214,000 in 1980.

Trade Unions. Membership of trade unions is estimated at 2,500 out of a work force of 22,822 (1980).

Commerce. International trade is included with France.

COMMUNICATIONS

Roads. There were 46 km of roads in 1982.

Railways. The 1·6m. km of main line passing through the country is operated by the French National Railways (SNCF).

Aviation. The nearest airport is at Nice, France.

Shipping. The harbour has an area of 47 acres, depth at the entrance 90 ft, and alongside the quay 24 ft at least. In 1980 there was 1 registered ship of 12,573 GRT.

Post and Broadcasting. Telephone subscribers numbered about 15,000 in 1980 and telex subscribers, 446. Monaco issues its own postage stamps.

Radio Monte Carlo broadcasts 2 commercial programmes in French (long- and medium-waves). Radio Monte Carlo owns 55% of Radio Monte Carlo Relay Station on Cyprus. The foreign service is dedicated exclusively to religious broadcasts and is maintained by free-will contributions. It operates in 36 languages under the name 'Trans World Radio' and has relay facilities on Bonaire, West Indies, and is planning to build relay facilities in the southern parts of Africa. *Télé Monte-Carlo* broadcasts TV programmes in French, Italian and English.

Cinemas. In 1981 there were 3 cinemas (one open air) with seating capacity of 800.

JUSTICE, RELIGION, EDUCATION AND WELFARE

Justice. The Code Louis, adopted in 1919, is based upon the French codes. There is a Court of First Instance as well as a Juge de Paix's Court. A semi-military police force has taken the place of the 'guard of honour' and troops formerly maintained.

Religion. There has been since 1887 a Roman Catholic bishop, directly dependent on the Holy See.

Education. In 1980 there were 3,412 pupils with over 400 teachers.

Health. In 1980 there were 357 hospital beds and 61 physicians.

DIPLOMATIC REPRESENTATIVES

British Consul-General (resident in Marseille): (Vacant).
Consul-General for Monaco in London: I. S. Ivanovic.

Books of Reference

Journal de Monaco. Bulletin Officiel. 1858 ff.
Handley-Taylor, G., *Bibliography of Monaco.* London, 1968
La Gorce, P. M. de, *Monaco.* Lausanne, 1969

MONGOLIAN PEOPLE'S REPUBLIC

Capital: Ulan Bator
Population: 1·73m. (1981)
GNP per capita: US$940 (1978)

Bügd Nayramdakh Mongol Ard Uls

HISTORY. Outer Mongolia was a Chinese province from 1691 to 1911, an autonomous state under Russian protection from 1912 to 1919 and again a Chinese province from 1919 to 1921. On 13 March 1921 a Provisional People's Government was established which declared the independence of Mongolia and on 5 Nov. 1921 signed a treaty with Soviet Russia annulling all previous unequal treaties and establishing friendly relations. On 26 Nov. 1924 the Government proclaimed the country the Mongolian People's Republic.

On 5 Jan. 1946 China recognized the independence of Outer Mongolia after a plebiscite in Mongolia (20 Oct. 1945) had resulted in an overwhelming vote for independence. A Sino-Soviet treaty of 14 Feb. 1950 guaranteed this independence.

AREA AND POPULATION. Mongolia is bounded north by the USSR, east and south and west by China. Area, 1,565,000 sq. km (604,250 sq. miles); population (1981) 1,732,000 (in 1977 719,000 urban; 51% male). Density, 1·07 per sq. km. Birth rate (1981), 37·9 per 1,000; death rate, 10·4 per 1,000. Rate of increase, 1982, 3%. The population is predominantly made up of Mongolian peoples (75% Khalkha). There is a Turkic Kazakh minority (5·2% of the population) and 8 Mongol minorities. The official language is Mongol.

The republic is administratively divided into 3 cities (Ulan Bator, the capital, population 400,000 (1978), Darkhan, 52,000 (1981) and Erdenet 35,000 (1978)), and 18 provinces *(aimag)*. Local government is administered by People's Deputies' Khurals. The provinces are sub-divided into districts *(somon)*.

CONSTITUTION AND GOVERNMENT. According to the fourth Constitution (1960) power is vested in the *Great People's Khural* of deputies elected for 5 years by universal suffrage of voters over 18 years of age on a basis of 1 deputy per 2,500 inhabitants. It elects from its number 9 members of the Presidium, which carries on current state affairs. *De facto* power is in the hands of the only political party, the Mongolian People's Revolutionary (*i.e.*, Communist) Party, which had 76,240 members and candidates in 1981 (workers 33%; peasants, 18%; women, 27%). The youth organization had over 180,000 members in 1982.

The last general election took place on 21 June 1981; 99·99% of an electorate of 792,896 were said to have voted for the 370 deputies (344 Party members; 100 industrial workers; 90 women).

The Chairman of the Presidium of the Khural and head of state is Yumjagiin Tsedenbal, who is also *Secretary-General of the People's Revolutionary Party*. The *Prime Minister* is Dr Jambyn Batmunkh. The other members of the Politburo of the Party are: D. Maydar, *First Deputy Prime Minister and Chairman, State Committee for Science and Technology*; T. Ragchaa, *First Deputy Prime Minister*; D. Molomjamts, S. Jalanaajav, D. Gombojav, B.-O. Altangerel. *Candidate members:* B. Dejid, N. Jagvaral. Ministers not in the Politburo include: *Chairman, State Planning Commission:* D. Sodnom; *Minister of Defence:* Col.-Gen. J. Avkhia; *Minister of Public Security:* O. Choijilsuren; *Foreign Minister:* Mangalyn

Dügesüren; *Minister of Foreign Trade:* Yë Ochir. *Minister of Agriculture:* S. Sodnomdorj.

National flag: Red–sky-blue–red (vertical), with a golden 5-pointed star and under it the golden *soyonbo* emblem on the red stripe nearest to the flagpole.

DEFENCE. Military service is 2 years. The Army was estimated to number some 31,500 in 1983. It is equipped with Soviet weapons and includes mechanized units, 1 construction and 2 infantry brigades. The Air Force has about 3,100 personnel and more than 60 aircraft, including 12 MiG-21 fighters; a total of about 30 An-2, An-24, An-26 and Il-14 transports used mainly on civil air services; 3 Wilga utility aircraft; 10 Mi-4 and 3 Mi-8 helicopters; and Yakovlev trainers. There is a para-military security force of about 10,000 men. A civil defence force was set up in 1970. There are some 25,000 Soviet service personnel in the country.

INTERNATIONAL RELATIONS

Membership. Mongolia is a member of UN and Comecon.

Aid. Mongolia receives economic aid from the USSR and other communist countries. There is also a UN development aid programme running at US$2m. per annum.

Treaties. Relations with the USSR were based on treaties of friendship and mutual aid (27 Feb. 1946), trade (17 Dec. 1957), economic and technical assistance (9 Sept. 1960), now replaced by a 20-year treaty of friendship, co-operation and mutual assistance (15 Jan. 1966).

Relations with China were based on treaties of economic and cultural co-operation (4 Oct. 1952), economic and technical aid (29 Aug. 1956), friendship and mutual aid (31 May 1960), commerce (26 April 1961 and 18 March 1963) and a border agreement (26 Dec. 1962). Sino-Mongolian relations have deteriorated since the estrangement between China and USSR.

On 28 Oct. 1961 Mongolia was admitted to the United Nations.

ECONOMY

Planning. Mongolia has had for centuries a traditional nomadic pastoral economy, which the Government aims to transform into an 'agricultural–industrial economy'. For earlier plans *see* THE STATESMAN'S YEAR-BOOK, 1976–77, p. 1156. The 5-year plan (1976–80) increased national income by 30·9%, industrial production by 50% and agricultural production by 6·3% (Targets were 42%, 63% and 30%). The seventh 5-year plan is running from 1981 to 1985. Industrial output is scheduled to rise by 58%, agricultural by 25%. There is also a long-term plan to 1990 which emphasizes energy production, mining, metallurgy, chemicals, food processing and building.

Budget (in 1m. tugriks):

	1973	*1974*	*1975*	*1976*	*1977*	*1978*	*1980*
Revenue	2,678	2,716	2,696	2,988	3,312	3,660	4,070
Expenditure	2,530	2,670	2,686	2,973	3,300	3,650	4,058

In the 1971–75 planning period 7,010m. tugriks were invested in the national economy. During the 1976–80 plan period overall investment was doubled.

Currency. 100 *möngö* = 1 *tugrik*. Official exchange rates: £1 = 4·96 *tugriks*; 1 rouble = 4·44 *tugriks*; US$1 = 3·36 *tugriks*.

Weights and Measures. The metric system is in use.

ENERGY AND NATURAL RESOURCES

Electricity. There are 6 thermal electric power stations. Production of electricity, 1980, 1,400m. kwh.

Minerals. There are large deposits of copper, nickel, zinc, molybdenum, phosphorites, tin, wolfram and fluorspar; annual production of the latter is 300,000 tonnes, entirely exported to the USSR. The ore-dressing plant at Erdenet was completed in 1981. There are major coalmines near Ulan Bator and Darkhan. Coal (mainly lignite) production in 1981 was 4·1m. tonnes. Oil was produced in the eastern Gobi desert at Dzüünbayan (production was 45,000 tonnes in 1969), but is no longer being extracted. There are reports of uranium and gold deposits.

Agriculture. The economy remains predominantly agricultural (70% of agricultural production derives from cattle-raising). In 1980 there were 2m. horses, 620,000 camels, 2·4m. cattle, 14m. sheep and 4·7m. goats. Pastures occupy 84% of the total area, forests 10·5%. In 1981 there were 255 collective farms, 30 inter-farm associations and 57 state farms. All cultivated land and 75% of livestock belong to collective or state farms. Farms cover vast areas. In 1978 collective farms averaged 64,000 head of cattle and state farms about 36,000.

The sown area 1978 was some 680,000 hectares, 500,000 hectares of which were sown to grain. The 1980 crop was 207,000 tonnes of wheat; 1,700 tonnes of rye; 31,800 tonnes of barley. Production of hay fodder was 10·4m tonnes in 1977. In 1981 there were 7,500 tractors (15 h.p. units) and 2,000 combine harvesters.

Forestry. Forests, chiefly larch, cedar, fir and birch, occupy 150,000 sq. km. Production, 1976: 1,067,000 cu. metres of timber.

INDUSTRY AND TRADE

Industry. Industry though still small in scale and local in character, is being vigorously developed and now accounts for a greater share of GNP than agriculture. The main industrial centre is Ulan Bator; others are being built at Darkhan, Erdenet and Choybalsan. Production figures (1980): textiles, 1·4m. cu metres; leather, 1·4m. tonnes; cement, 178,000 tonnes; leather footwear, 2·1m. pairs; meat, 56,700 tonnes; animal fat, 3,800 tonnes; beer 98,000 hectolitres.

Employment. The labour force was 370,000 in 1980, including 130,000 shepherds. Average wage was 500 tugriks per month in 1981. Trade union membership was 400,000 in 1982.

There is a serious labour shortage necessitating the employment of military personnel, and workers from the USSR and Eastern Europe.

Commerce. Foreign trade is a state monopoly. Trade figures for 1976 (in 1m. tugriks): exports, 775; imports, 1,007, Mongolia has been a member of Comecon since 1962. The main exports are live cattle and horses, wool and hair, meat, grain, hides, furs, ores, and butter. 92% of foreign trade is with communist countries (80% with USSR). There is a chronic trade deficit. Just over 25% of imports are consumer goods and the remainder are machinery and industrial raw materials. In 1976 trade with China was 28m. tugriks. Trade with Japan, previously valued at US$1m. per annum, increased slightly after the establishment of diplomatic relations in 1972.

Mongolia exported goods to the UK valued at £3,861,000 in 1982 and imported from the UK goods valued at £64,000 (British Department of Trade and Industry returns). In 1972 contracts were placed for UK agricultural and textile machinery and exports of furs to UK increased. Exports to USSR in 1976 (and 1975): 139·8m. (125·3m.) roubles; imports: 474·7m. (355·1m.) roubles.

COMMUNICATIONS

Roads. There are surfaced roads in and around Ulan Bator, from Ulan Bator to Darkhan and at points on the frontier with USSR. Truck services run throughout the country where there are no surfaced roads. 120m. passengers were carried in 1981.

Railways. The Trans-Mongolian Railway (1,425 km in 1973) connects Ulan Bator with the Soviet Union and China. The Moscow–Ulan Bator–Peking express runs each way once a week. There are spur lines to Erdenet and to the coalmines at Nalaykha and Sharin Gol. A separate line connects Choybalsan in the east with

Borzya on the Trans-Siberian railway. 1·1m. passengers and 8·1m. tonnes of freight were carried in 1976.

Aviation. Mongolair operates internal services and a flight to Irkutsk which links with the Moscow service. 7,000 tons of freight were carried in 1976 and 370,000 passengers. Soviet airlines (Aeroflot) and Mongolair jointly operate an approximately twice-weekly service to Moscow.

Shipping. There is a steamer service on the Selenge River and a tug and barge service on Hobsgol Lake. 3,000 tonnes of freight were carried in 1976.

Post and Broadcasting. There were, in 1976, 382 post offices and 218 telephone exchanges. Number of telephones (1977), 37,792.

There are wireless stations at Ulan Bator, Gobi Altai and Olgiy. In 1978 there were 128,000 radio and 3,800 television receivers. Television services began in 1967. A Mongolian television station opened in 1970.

Cinemas. In 1976 there were 23 cinemas, 439 mobile cinemas and, in 1981, 10 theatres.

Newspapers and books. In 1982, 13 newspapers and 32 journals were published. The Party daily paper *Ünen* ('Truth') had a circulation of 112,000 in 1978. 400 book titles were published in 1982 in 70m. copies

JUSTICE, RELIGION, EDUCATION AND WELFARE

Justice. The Procurator-General is appointed, and the Supreme Court elected, by the *Khural* for 4 years. There are also courts at province, town and district level. Lay assessors sit with professional judges.

Religion. Tibetan Buddhist Lamaism was the prevalent form of religion. The Church was suppressed in the 1930s, and only one functioning monastery exists today, at Ulan Bator.

Education. Schooling begins at the age of 8. There are 8- and 10-year schools. In 1982-83 there were 885 'general' schools with 385,000 pupils, and 37 technical schools with 21,100 pupils. There is a state university (founded 1942) at Ulan Bator (40 professors, 240 lecturers and 10,000 students in 1982), and 7 other institutes of higher learning (teacher training, medicine, agriculture, economics, etc.) with 14,000 students in 1982 under the supervision of an Academy of Sciences (founded 1953) which has 15 institutes and 190 research workers. In 1977 there were 23,550 students in institutes of higher learning, and some 6,000 students a year are sent to study abroad, principally in the USSR. In 1982–83 there were 885 'general' schools with 385,000 pupils and 37 technical schools with 21,100 pupils.

In 1946 the Mongolian alphabet was replaced by a modern Cyrillic alphabet.

Health. In 1982 there were 22 doctors and 107 hospital beds per 10,000 inhabitants.

DIPLOMATIC REPRESENTATIVES

Of Mongolia in Great Britain (7 Kensington Ct., London, W8 5DL)
Ambassador: Oyuny Hosbayar.

Of Great Britain in Mongolia (30 Enkh Taivny Gudamzh, Ulan Bator)
Ambassador and Consul General: J. R. Paterson.

Of Mongolia to the United Nations
Ambassador: Buyantiyn Dashtseren.

Books of Reference

The Central Statistical Office: *Economic Statistics of the MPR for 40 Years.* 1961.—*40 Years of the MPR Revolution.* 1961.—*National Economy MPR 1973.* 1974
Bawden, C. R., *The Modern History of Mongolia.* London, 1968
Boberg, F., *Mongolian–English, English–Mongolian Dictionary.* 3 vols. Stockholm, 1954–55
Haltod, M. (ed.), *Mongolian–English Dictionary.* Berkeley, Cal., 1961

Jagchid, S., and Hyer, P. *Mongolia's Culture and Society.* Folkestone, 1979
Lattimore, O., *Nationalism and Revolution in Mongolia.* Leiden, 1955.—*Nomads and Commissars.* OUP, 1963
News from Mongolia. Ulan Bator, fortnightly, Jan. 1980
Petrov. V. P., *Mongolia: A Profile.* London, 1971
Rupen, R. A., *How Mongolia is Really Ruled: A Political History of the Mongolian People's Republic, 1900–1978.* Stanford, 1979
Sanders, A. J. K., *The People's Republic of Mongolia: A General Reference Guide.* OUP, 1968
Shirendev, B., and Sanjdorj, M. (eds.), *History of the Mongolian People's Republic.* Vol. 3 (vols. 1 and 2 not translated). Harvard Univ. Press, 1976
Socialist Mongolia. Ulan Bator, 1981

MONTSERRAT

Capital: Plymouth
Population: 12,073 (1980)
GNP per capita: US$1,370 (1980)

HISTORY. Montserrat was discovered by Columbus in 1493 and colonized by Irish settlers in 1632.

AREA AND POPULATION. Montserrat is situated in the Caribbean Sea 25 miles south-west of Antigua. The area is 39·5 sq. miles (106 sq. km). Population, 1980, 12,073. Chief town, Plymouth, 3,200 inhabitants.

CONSTITUTION AND GOVERNMENT. Montserrat is a crown colony. The Executive Council is composed of 4 unofficial members (the Chief Minister and 3 other Ministers) and 2 official members (Attorney-General and Financial Secretary). The Legislative Council consists of 7 elected and 2 official members (the Attorney-General and Financial Secretary) and 2 nominated members. The Executive Council is presided over by the Governor and the Legislative Council by the Speaker.

Governor: D. K. H. Dale, CBE.
Chief Minister: Dr J. A. Osborne.
Flag: The British Blue Ensign with the shield of Montserrat in the fly.

FINANCE. In 1981 the budget estimates balanced at EC$19m. (US$7m.). In 1981 the territorial budget ceased to be grant-aided by the British Government.

AGRICULTURE. Agriculture has been in decline for several years, but is likely to recover with the progress of the Integrated Sea Island Cotton Project and revised land tenure and settlement arrangements associated with the government's acquisition of a number of estates.

Livestock (1981); Cattle, 9,000; pigs, 3,000; sheep, 3,000; goats, 3,000; poultry, 31,000.

INDUSTRY AND TRADE

Industry. Considerable light industry was attracted to the territory from abroad during 1979–81 and there is 75,000 sq. ft of modern factory space available.

Commerce. Imports in 1981 totalled EC$51m. (US$19m.); domestic exports, EC$6m. Chief imports were manufactured goods, food and beverages, machinery and transport equipment and fuel. Chief exports in 1981 were hot peppers, live plants, cattle and manufactured articles.

Total trade between Montserrat and UK (British Department of Trade returns, in £1,000 sterling):

	1980	*1981*	*1982*
Imports to UK	125	397	193
Exports and re-exports from UK	1,351	935	1,786

Tourism. In 1981, 21,400 tourists arrived in Montserrat.

COMMUNICATIONS

Aviation. At the modernized Blackburne airport 3,200 aircraft landed in 1981, disembarking 26,882 passengers and 2,000 tons of cargo.

Shipping. In 1981, 349 vessels arrived, landing 35,366 and loading 772 tons of cargo.

Post. Number of telephones (1981), 2,602.

JUSTICE, RELIGION, EDUCATION AND WELFARE

Justice. There are 2 magistrates' courts, at Plymouth and Cudjoe Head. Strength of the police force (1980), 2 gazetted officers, 4 inspectors and 100 other ranks.

Religion. In 1981 there were 1,329 Roman Catholics, 4,332 Anglicans, 3,249 Methodists, 804 Seventh Day Adventists, 1,091 Pentecostals and 254 members of the Church of God. There is also a Christian Council of Churches.

Education. There are 12 government elementary, 1 government secondary, 2 grant-aided denominational elementary schools, 2 junior secondary schools, 2 preparatory private schools for children between the ages of 5 and 12 and 11 nursery schools. In 1981, 1,943 children were enrolled in the primary schools, with 84 teachers; 872 in the secondary schools, with 61 teachers. There was 1 technical college with 50 students and 9 teachers.

Health. In 1981 there were 8 doctors and 67 hospital beds.

Books of Reference

Overseas Trade 1977. Montserrat Government
Statistical Digest 1979. Montserrat Government

Library: Public Library, Plymouth. *Librarian:* Miss J. Grell.

MOROCCO

Capital: Rabat
Population: 21 m. (1983)
GNP per capita: US$860 (1980)

al-Mamlaka al-Maghrebia

HISTORY. From 1912 to 1956 Morocco was divided into a French protectorate (established by the treaty of Fez concluded between France and the Sultan on 30 March 1912), a Spanish protectorate (established by the Franco-Spanish convention of 27 Nov. 1912) and the international zone of Tangier (set up by France, Spain and Great Britain on 18 Dec. 1923).

On 2 March 1956 France and the Sultan terminated the treaty of Fez; on 7 April 1956 Spain relinquished her protectorate, and on 29 Oct. 1956 France, Spain, Great Britain, Italy, USA, Belgium, the Netherlands, Sweden and Portugal abolished the international status of the Tangier Zone.

A tripartite agreement was announced on 14 Nov. 1975 providing for the transfer of power from Spanish Sahara (Western Sahara) to the Moroccan and Mauritanean governments on 28 Feb. 1976. Spanish troops left El Aaiún on 20 Dec. 1975. On 14 April 1976 a Convention was signed by Mauritania and Morocco in which the 2 countries agreed on their borders in Western Sahara. On 14 Aug. 1979 the Wad Ed-Dahab province was added to the Kingdom when Mauritania renounced its claim to Tiris El-Gharbia.

AREA AND POPULATION. Morocco is bounded by Algeria to the east and south-east, Western Sahara to the south-west, the Atlantic ocean to the north-west and the Mediterranean to the north. Excluding the Western Saharan territory claimed and occupied since 1976 by Morocco, the total area is 458,730 sq. km and its total population at the June 1971 Census was 15,379,259; the latest estimate (1983) is 21m. The Western Sahara (252,120 sq. km) had an estimated 165,000 population in 1979.

The areas (in sq. km) and populations of the provinces are:

Province	*sq. km*	*1981*	*Province*	*sq. km*	*1981*
Agadir	17,460	985,000	Ouarzazate	46,460	612,200
Al-Hoceima	3,550	323,100	Oujda	20,700	822,000
Azizal	10,050	415,000	Rabat-Salé[1]	1,275	941,200
Beni-Mellal	7,075	610,900	Safi	7,285	678,300
Ben Slimane	2,760	191,300	Settat	9,750	727,300
Boulemane	14,395	133,600	Tangier	1,195	404,800
Casablanca[1]	1,615	2,553,300	Tan-Tan	17,295	27,900
Chaouèn	4,350	314,400	Taounate	5,585	591,700
El Jadida	6,000	734,400	Tata	25,925	111,000
El-Kelâa-Srarhna	10,070	587,100	Taza	15,020	652,000
Er-Rachidia	59,585	424,900	Tétouan	6,025	723,100
Essaouira	6,335	489,400	Tiznit	6,960	353,000
Fès	5,400	788,100			
Figuig	55,990	113,700	Morocco	458,730	20,646,000
Guelmin	28,750	97,500			
Kénitra	8,805	1,264,900			
Khémisset	8,305	449,300	Boujdour (Bojador)		
Khénifra	11,115	313,900	Es-semara (Smara)		
Khouribga	4,250	453,100	Laâyoune (El Aaiún)		
Marrakesh	14,755	1,288,400	Wad El-Dahab		
Meknès	8,510	823,500			
Nador	6,130	646,700	Sahara	252,120	165,000[2]

[1] Urban prefectures [2] 1979.

The population of the largest municipalities (census) June 1971: Casablanca, 1,506,373; Rabat (capital), 367,620; Marrakesh, 332,741; Fez, 325,327; Meknès,

248,369; Tangier, 187,894; Oujda, 175,532; Salè, 155,557; Kenitra, 139,206; Tétuan, 139,105; Safi, 129,113; Khouribga, 73,667; Mohammedia, 70,392; Agadir, 61,192; El Jadida, 55,501.

The official language is Arabic; French, Spanish and English are considered subsidiary languages.

REIGNING KING. Hassan II, born on 9 July 1929, succeeded on 3 March 1961, on the death of his father Mohammed V, who reigned 1927–61. The royal style was changed from 'His Sherifian Majesty the Sultan' to 'His Majesty the King' on 18 Aug. 1957. *Heir apparent:* Crown Prince Sidi Mohammed, born 21 Aug. 1963.

The King holds supreme civil and religious authority; the latter in his capacity of Emir-el-Muminin or Commander of the Faithful. He resides usually at Rabat, but occasionally in one of the other traditional capitals, Fez (founded in 808), Marrakesh (founded in 1062), or at Skhirat.

CONSTITUTION AND GOVERNMENT. A new Constitution was approved by referendum in March 1972 and amendments were approved by referendum in May 1980. The Kingdom of Morocco is a constitutional monarchy with a legislature of a single chamber composed of 267 deputies. Deputies for 89 seats are elected by indirect vote through an electoral college representing the town councils, the regional assemblies, the chambers of commerce, industry and agriculture, and the trade unions. Deputies for the remaining 178 seats are by general election. The King, as sovereign head of State, appoints the Prime Minister and other Ministers, has the right to dissolve Parliament and approves legislation.

National flag: Red, with a green pentacle star in the centre.

Cabinet in March 1983:

Prime Minister and Minister of Justice: Maati Bouabid.

Foreign Affairs: Mohamed Boucetta. *Co-operation:* Mahjoubi Abardane. *Without portfolio:* Mohamed Bahnini, Moulay Ahmed Alaoui. *Planning, Executive and Professional Training:* Mhamed Douiri. *Interior:* Driss Basri. *National Education:* Azzedine Laraki. *Labour and National Promotion:* Arsalane El-Jadidi. *Handicrafts and Social Affairs:* Abbes El-Fassi. *Transport:* Mansouri Ben Ali. *Public Health:* Rahal Rahhali. *Energy:* Moussa Saadi. *Commerce, Industry and Tourism:* Azzedine Guessous. *Information, Youth and Sports:* Abdelwahab Belakziz. *Finance:* Abdellatif Jouahri. *Fisheries and Merchant Navy:* Bensalem Smili. *Cultural Affairs:* Said Belbachir. *Justice:* Mustapha Benlarbi Alaoui. *Parliamentary Relations:* Amhem Belhadj. *Housing, Urban Affairs and Environment:* M'Fadel Lahlou. *Waqfs and Islamic Affairs:* Hachmi Filali. *Equipment:* Mohamed Kabbaj. *Posts and Telecommunications:* Mohamed El-Anssar. *Agriculture:* Othmane Demnati. *Prime Minister's Office:* Abdelkrim Ghallab. *Secretary-General of the Government:* Abbes Kaisi. There are 5 Secretaries of State.

Local Government: The country is administratively divided into 39 provinces and 2 urban prefectures.

DEFENCE

Army. The Army numbered (1983) 125,000 officers and men, organized in 9 motorized infantry battalions, 5 armoured battalions, 1 light security brigade, 2 engineer battalions, 1 paratroop brigade, 18 infantry battalions and desert troops.

Navy. Navy includes 2 new large patrol vessels or small corvettes, 4 new fast attack ships, 1 coastal minesweeper, 1 patrol vessel, 1 gunboat, 1 seaward patrol craft, 9 coastal patrol boats, 4 landing craft acquired from France and 1 yacht training vessel. A frigate, 2 more small corvettes and 6 coastal patrol boats are under construction. Personnel in 1983 totalled 1,800 officers and ratings including 500 marines. There are also 12 small customs cutters and a coastguard picket.

Air Force. The Air Force was formed in Nov. 1956. Equipment in current use is mainly of US and West European origin. It includes 43 Mirage F1, 20 F-5E Tiger II, 4 two-seat F-5F and 12 F-5A supersonic fighter-bombers, 2 RF-5A reconnaissance-fighters and 3 two-seat F-5Bs, 6 OV-10 Bronco counter-insurgency aircraft and 24 Hughes 500MD Defender armed helicopters, 24 Alpha Jet advanced trainers, 22 Magister armed jet basic trainers, 12 T-34C-1 turboprop armed basic trainers, 10 Swiss-built Bravo primary trainers, 7 Broussard liaison aircraft, 80 Agusta-Bell 205 and 212, Puma and JetRanger helicopters, 10 Do 28D Skyservants for coastal patrol, 12 CH-47C heavy-lift helicopters, 19 C-130H turboprop transport aircraft, 3 KC-130H tanker/transports and 6 turboprop King Air light transports. Personnel strength is about 10,000.

INTERNATIONAL RELATIONS

Membership. Morocco is a member of UN, OAU and the Arab League.

ECONOMY

Planning. A 5-year plan (1973–77) envisaged a total investment of 11,751,874m. DH. A new 3-year plan (1978–80) was approved in Dec. 1978. The 5-year plan (1981–85) was approved in June 1981.

Budget. The budget for 1981 envisaged revenue of 31,800m. DH and expenditure of 34,800m. DH.

Currency. In Oct. 1959, a national currency was introduced. Its unit is the *dirham* (abbreviated DH), equalling 100 *centimes* (1 French franc = 1·025 DH; US$1 = 5·01 DH; £1 = 10·135 DH. Notes: 5, 10, 50, 100 DH; coins: 0·02, 0·05, 0·10, 0·20, 0·50, 1 DH. The exchange rate in March 1983 was £1 sterling = 9·30 DH; US$1 = 6·41 DH.

Banking. The bank of issue is the Banque du Maroc in Rabat. Other important institutions are the Banque Marocaine du Commerce Extérieur (Casablanca), the Banque Nationale pour le Développement Economique (Rabat), Crédit Populaire and the Crédit Immobilier et Hotelier (Casablanca). There are 23 other banks in Casablanca, 3 in Tangier and 1 each in Tetouan, Fez, Kenitra, Meknès, Oujda and Rabat.

Weights and Measures. The metric system of weights and measures is the sole legal system.

ENERGY AND NATURAL RESOURCES

Electricity. Electric power-plants produced 4,785·3m. kwh. in 1981.

Oil. Crude oil production, 48,000 tonnes 1980.

Minerals. The principal mineral exploited is phosphate, the output of which (under a state monopoly) was 18·56m. tonnes in 1981. Other important minerals (in 1,000 tonnes) are: Iron ore (49·9), lead (168·4), cobalt (6), zinc (14·7), manganese (109·6), silver (21·2). Production of minerals (1978) 2,829,284m. dirhams.

Agriculture. Agriculture is by far the most important industry, on which 70% of the population exists. The principal crops are cereals, especially wheat and barley; beans, chickpeas, fenugreek and other legumens; canary seed; cumin and coriander; linseed; olives; almonds and other fruits, especially citrus. The almost universal wild palmetto is put to various uses, including the manufacture of *crin végétal*. The trees include cork, cedar, arar, argon, oak and various conifers. Wine production, 1975, 830,000 hectolitres. Tizra wood is exported for tanning purposes. Stock-raising is an important industry.

Production (in 1,000 tonnes) in 1978–79: Barley, 18,862; wheat, 17,964; maize, 4,116; sugar-cane, 2,887; vegetables 2,626; citrus fruit, 917.

Livestock (in 1,000 heads), 1981: Camels, 230; horses, 310; cattle, 3,240; pigs, 11; sheep, 14,840; goats, 6,200; poultry, 25m.

Fishing. The chief fishing centres are Agadir, Safi, Essaouira and Casablanca.

There are over 5,000 fishing vessels and about 100 freezing and processing plants. The industry employs 50,000 workers. Total catch in 1980 was 300,000 tons.

COMMERCE. Imports and exports were (in 1m. DH):

	1977	*1978*	*1979*	*1980*	*1981*
Imports	14,401	12,361	14,327	16,792	22,455
Exports	5,860	6,262	7,622	9,645	12,002

Main imports, 1981, consumer goods and industrial products. Main exports, (1980), phosphates (31%), fruit and vegetables (21%), phosphoric acid (8%) and metal ores (6%).

Main trading partners (1981): Exports, France (22%), Federal Republic of Germany (7%), Spain (7%). Imports, France (25%), Saudi Arabia (15%) Spain (7%), USA (7%).

A royal proclamation of 30 Aug. 1959 abrogated the former economic status of Tangier and integrated the zone in the Kingdom. However, Tangier was declared a free port from 1 Jan. 1962; and commercial transactions within the free zone were further liberalized by decree of 8 Nov. 1965.

Total trade between Morocco and UK (British Department of Trade returns, in £1,000 sterling):

	1977	*1978*	*1979*	*1980*	*1981*	*1982*
Imports to UK	46,268	44,079	50,392	62,582	67,697	60,219
Exports and re-exports from UK	67,971	76,535	67,604	69,223	55,939	95,487

TOURISM. In 1982, 1·9m. foreign visitors came to Morocco.

COMMUNICATIONS

Roads. In 1980 there were 57,634 km of classified roads, of which (1978) 27,671 km were surfaced. At the end of 1980 there were in use 200,559 lorries, 447,992 private cars and (1978) 17,820 motor cycles.

Railways. In 1981 there were 1,756 km of railways, of which 708 km were electrified. The principal standard-gauge lines are from Casablanca eastward to the Algerian border, forming part of the continuous rail line to Tunis; Casablanca to Marrakesh with 2 important branches, one eastward to Oued Zem tapping the Khouribga phosphate mines, the other westward to the port of Safi. Another branch serves the manganese mines at Bou Arfa. Two new double-track electrified lines are to serve a new deep-water port at Jorf Lasfar, and a 650 km south-east extension from Marrakesh to Laayoun in the south Sahara is planned.

In 1981 the railways ran 1,040m. passenger-km and 5,156m. tonne-km of goods.

Aviation. There are 19 airfields, of which Casablanca–Arfa and Casablanca–Nouaceur are the most important. Total international air services in 1981 comprised 3,205,314 passengers arrived and departed and 32,893 tonnes of freight including mail.

Shipping. In 1980, 17,752 vessels of 46m. net tons entered and cleared the ports of Morocco. In 1980 the merchant marine consisted of 145 vessels (of over 100 gross tons) with a total tonnage of 359,552 GRT.

Post and Broadcasting. Communication with Europe is maintained by cables between Casablanca and Brest, Tangier–Casablanca–Le Havre, Tangier–Gibraltar, Tangier–Cádiz, Larache–Cádiz *via* Algeciras.

Telephone subscribers totalled 227,000 in 1980.

Broadcasting is done in Arabic, Berber, French, Spanish and English from Rabat and Tangier; television in Arabic and French began in 1962. In 1977 there were 1·6m. radio and 597,000 television receivers.

Cinemas. There were about 235 cinemas in 1971.

JUSTICE, RELIGION, EDUCATION AND WELFARE

Justice. A uniform legal system is being organized, based mainly on French and

Islamic law codes and French legal procedure. The judiciary consists of a Supreme Court, courts of appeal, regional tribunals and magistrates' courts.

Religion. Islam is the established state religion. The majority of the Moroccans are Sunni Moslems of the Malekite school. The French and Spanish settlers are Roman Catholics under the Archbishop of Rabat. The once large Jewish population is diminishing.

Education. In 1959 a standardization of the various school systems (French, Spanish, Israeli, Moslem, etc.) was begun. Education has been made compulsory from the age of 7 to 13.

In 1981 there were 2,331,000 pupils and 55,303 teachers in state primary schools; 826,500 pupils and (1980) 31,794 teachers in secondary schools; 10,020 students in technical schools and (1980) 10,746 students in teacher-training establishments.

The language of instruction in primary schools is Arabic during the first 2 years, and half-Arabic and half-French during the following 3 years; in secondary schools lessons are in French and Arabic. A third language of the choice of the student is learnt during the last 3 years of secondary education.

There are six universities, Mohamed V at Rabat, Hassan II at Casablanca, Mohamed Ben Abdallah at Fez, Quaraouyine at Fez, Oujda and Marrakesh with a total enrolment of 80,345 students and 2,558 teaching staff in 1981.

Health. In 1981 there were 1,153 doctors and (1979) 24,453 hospital beds.

DIPLOMATIC REPRESENTATIVES

Of Morocco in Great Britain (49 Queen's Gate Gdns., London, SW7 5NE)
Ambassador: Medhi Benabdeljalil (accredited 11 Feb. 1982).

Of Great Britain in Morocco (17 Blvd de la Tour Hassan, Rabat)
Ambassador: S. J. G. Cambridge, CMG, CVO.

Of Morocco in the USA (1601 21st St., NW, Washington, D.C., 20009)
Ambassador: Ali Benjelloun.

Of the USA in Morocco (2 Ave. de Marrakech, Rabat)
Ambassador: Joseph V. Reed, Jr.

Of Morocco to the United Nations
Ambassador: Mehdi Mrani Zentar.

Books of Reference

Statistical Information: The Service Central des Statistiques (BP 178, Rabat) was set up in 1942. Its publications include: *Annuaire de Statistique Générale.—La Conjoncture Économique Marocaine* (monthly; with annual synthesis).—*Résultats du Recensement général de la population de 1971.—Bulletin économique et social du Maroc* (trimestral).—*La situation Economique du Maroc, 1975*

Bulletin Official (in Arabic and French). Rabat. Weekly
Barber, N., *Survey of North Africa,* 2nd ed. OUP, 1962.—*Morocco.* London, 1965
Decroux, P., *Les sociétés au Maroc.* Paris, 1950
Drague, G., *Esquisse d'histoire religieuse du Maroc.* Paris, 1951
Kinross, Lord, and Hales-Gary, D., *Morocco.* London, 1971
Mercier, H., *Dictionnaire arabic–français.* Rabat, 1951
Miège, J. L., *Morocco.* New York, 1953
Rivière, P. L., *Précis de Législation marocaine.* New ed. in collaboration with G. Catteriz. 2 vols. Caen, 1942–46

National Library: Bibliothèque Générale et Archives, Rabat.

MOZAMBIQUE

República Popular de Moçambique

Capital: Maputo
Population: 13·25m. (1982)
GNP per capita: US$270 (1980)

HISTORY. Trading settlements were established by Arab merchants at Sofala (Beira), Quelimane, Angoche and Mozambique Island in the fifteenth century. Mozambique Island was visited by Vasco da Gamba's fleet on 2 March 1498, and Sofala was occupied by Portuguese in 1506. At first ruled as part of Portuguese India, a separate administration was created in 1752, and on 11 June 1951 Mozambique became an Overseas Province of Portugal. Following a decade of guerrilla activity, Portugal and the nationalists jointly established a transitional government on 20 Sept. 1974. Complete independence was achieved on 25 June 1975.

AREA AND POPULATION. Mozambique is bounded east by the Indian ocean, south by South Africa, south-west by Swaziland, west by South Africa and Zimbabwe and north by Zambia, Malawi and Tanzania. It has an area of 799,380 sq. km (308,642 sq. miles) and a population, according to the census of 1980, of 12·13m. Estimate (1982) 13·25m. The country is divided into 10 provinces. The capital is Maputo with population (1970 census) 354,684; other large towns are Nampula (126,126) and Beira (113,770). The official language is Portuguese. The climate is mainly tropical.

CONSTITUTION AND GOVERNMENT. Under the Constitution adopted at independence on 25 June 1975, the directing power of the state is vested in the *Frente de Libertação de Moçambique* (FRELIMO), the liberation movement, which in Feb. 1977 was reconstituted as sole political Party. The legislative organ is the People's Assembly of 210 members, elected in Dec. 1977.

The Council of Ministers in April 1982 consisted of:

President: Samora Moïses Machel (assumed office 25 June 1975).

Foreign Affairs: Joaquim Chissano. *National Defence:* Lieut-Gen. Alberto Joaquim Chipande. *Sofala Province:* Armando Emilio Guebuza. *Interior:* Mariano de Araujo Matsinhe. *Chief of the General Staff of the Mozambique Armed Forces, Deputy Minister of Defence:* Lieut-Gen. Sebastiao Marcos Mabote. *Security:* Jacinto Soares Veloso. *Planning:* Mario de Graça Muchungo. *Minister in the Presidency:* Jose Oscar Monteiro. *Finance:* Rui Baltazar dos Santos Alves. *Education and Culture:* Graça Machel. *Information:* Jose Luis Cabaço. *Public Works and Housing:* Julio Zamith Carrilho. *Foreign Trade:* Solomao Munguambe. *Agriculture:* Sergio Vieira. *Justice:* Teodato Hunguana. *Industry and Energy:* Antonio Lima Rodrigues Branco. *Health:* Pascoal Manuel Mocumbi. *Ports and Surface Transport:* Luis Maria Alcantara Santos. *Posts, Telecommunications and Civil Aviation:* Rui Lousa. *Internal Trade:* Manuel Jorge Aranda da Silva. *Governor of the Bank of Mozambique:* Prakash Ratilal.

Deputy Ministers: Salesio Teodoro Malyambipano (Security); Fernando Everard do Rosario Vaz *(Health)*; Carlos Raposo Pereira *(Interior)*.

Flag: Four rays coloured green, red, black and yellow, with white fimbriations, radiating from the upper hoist corner, in which is placed over all the national emblem in colour.

DEFENCE

Army. The Army consists of (1983) 20,000 men, armed with Chinese and Soviet light weapons, medium armour and some SAM missiles.

Navy. The small flotilla comprises 6 former Portuguese coastal patrol boats, 4 *ex-*

Soviet gunboats, 1 *ex*-Portuguese survey ship (former British fleet minesweeper) and 1 *ex*-Portuguese landing craft (used as a transport). Naval personnel in 1983 totalled 700 officers and men.

Air Force. The Air Force is reported to have about 40 MiG-17 and 20 MiG-21 fighters, probably flown by Cuban pilots, An-26 turboprop transports, a Tu-134A for VIP use. Mi-8 helicopters, about 28 L-39 jet trainers, Zlin 326 primary trainers and a few *ex*-Portuguese Air Force transport/liaison aircraft.

INTERNATIONAL RELATIONS

Membership. Mozambique is a member of UN and OAU.

ECONOMY

Budget. In 1982 the revenue was 18·5m. contos; expenditure, 21,370,372 contos (deficit 2·6m. contos).

Currency. In June 1980 the currency became the *metical* (pl. *meticais*) divided into 100 *centavos.* The *metical* was established at par with the former *escudo.* In March 1983, £1 = 45·98 *meticais*; US$1 = 31·38 *meticais.*

Banking. Most banks had been nationalized by 1979.

Weights and Measures. The metric system is in force.

ENERGY AND NATURAL RESOURCES

Electricity. Production (1978) 7,800 kwh.

Minerals. Coal mining is the main mineral being exploited. Output reached 565,000 tonnes in 1975 but has since fallen. Coal reserves (estimate) 400m. tonnes. Small quantities of bauxite, gold, titanium, fluorite and colombo-tantalite are produced. Iron ore deposits and natural gas are known to exist.

Agriculture. Production in tonnes (1979): cereals, 573,000; tea, 16,000; tobacco, 3,000; cotton fibre, 15,000; rice, 35,000; maize, 350,000; bananas, 36,000; sisal, 18,000.

Livestock 1981: 1·42m. cattle, 340,000 goats, 108,000 sheep, 125,000 pigs, 20,000 asses.

Fisheries. In 1975, 4,801 tonnes of sea products were exported.

INDUSTRY AND TRADE

Industry. Although the country is overwhelmingly rural, there is some substantial industry in and around Maputo (steel, engineering, textiles, processing, docks and railways).

Commerce. Imports in 1979 totalled 23,000m. meticals and exports 12,700m. meticals. 15·3% of imports came from the Republic of South Africa and 12·7% from the Federal Republic of Germany. Exports (1976 in tonnes): Coal, 204,843; petroleum, 93,986; molasses, 76,059; sugar, 71,945; copra 41,104. Portugal took 25% of exports and USA 23·7%.

Total trade between Mozambique and UK (British Department of Trade returns, in £1,000 sterling):

	1979	*1980*	*1981*	*1982*
Imports to UK	11,039	11,416	5,716	10,611
Exports and re-exports from UK	15,730	11,345	21,763	14,473

COMMUNICATIONS

Roads. There were, in 1982, 26,000 km of roads, of which 4,600 km were tarred. Motor vehicles, in 1979, included 102,400 passenger cars and 24,600 lorries and buses and 4,081 motor cycles. The Government is devoting effort to constructing a new North/South road link, and to improving provincial rural feeder road systems.

Railways. The Mozambique State Railways consist of 5 independent networks known as the Maputo, Mozambique, Sofala (Beira), Inhambane and Gaza, and Quelimane systems. The Maputo system has links with the Republic of South Africa, Swaziland and Zimbabwe railways; the Sofala system links with Zimbabwe at Machipanda and by way of the Trans–Zambesia Railway with Malawi at Dona Ana; and the Mozambique system links with Malawi at Entre Lagos. The Inhambane and Quelimane systems have no international connections. Total route-km (1980), 3,696 km (1,067 mm gauge), and 147 km (762 mm gauge). Trans–Zambesia Railway, 318 km (1,067 mm gauge). In 1981, 12m. passengers and 5,166m. tonne-km of goods were carried. Rail links with Zimbabwe reopened in 1979.

Aviation. Regular air services exist between Maputo and Berlin, Brazzaville, Johannesburg, Luanda, Mbabane, Lusaka, Paris, Rome, Tananarive, Manzini, Dar es Salaam and Lisbon; and between Beira and Blantyre.

Shipping. The total tonnage handled by Mozambique ports (1977) was 10,554,660. The principal ports are: Maputo (1,880 vessels of 9,522,105 net tons handled in 1972), Beira (1,043 vessels of 4,254,728 net tons), Mozambique (71 vessels of 263,841 net tons) and Nacala (345 vessels of 1,261,379 net tons).

Post and Broadcasting. Maputo is connected by telegraph with the Transvaal system. Quelimane has telegraphic communication with Chiromo. In 1971 there were 103,533 km of telegraph line, 37 wireless stations, 125 telephone stations and 217 telegraph stations; length of telephone lines, 103,533 km, including 86,018 km of conductor wires in cable; number of telephones (1980), 51,600.

Radio Moçambique broadcasts 5 programmes in Portuguese, English, Afrikaans, Ronga and Shangane as well as 4 regional programmes in 8 languages. Number of receivers (1977): radio, 230,000; TV, 1,200.

Cinemas. There were, in 1971, 31 cinemas with a seating capacity of 20,195.

Newspapers. There are 2 daily newspapers in Mozambique: *Noticias,* published in Maputo, and *Diario de Mozambique.* There is also a weekly magazine, *Tempo.* The Mozambique Information Agency *(AIM)* was established in 1976.

RELIGION, EDUCATION AND WELFARE

Religion. Two-thirds of the population follow traditional animist religions, while some 21% are Christian (mainly Roman Catholic) and 10% Moslem.

Education. In 1979 there were 1,494,729 pupils in primary schools and 105,263 in secondary schools. The *Universidade Eduardo Mondlane* had 906 students in 1977. About 500,000 attend adult literacy classes.

Health. There were (1972) about 500 doctors and 12,500 hospital beds. Most Portuguese doctors left at independence and by 1975 there were only 80 doctors.

DIPLOMATIC REPRESENTATIVES

Of Great Britain in Mozambique (Ave. Vladimir 1 Lenine, 310, Maputo)
Ambassador: J. A. B. Stewart, CMG, OBE.

Of USA in Mozambique (35 Rua Da Mesquita, Maputo)
Chargé d'Affaires: William H. Twaddell.

Of Mozambique to the United Nations
Ambassador: José Carlos Lobo.

Books of Reference

Boletim da Republica (Government Gazette). Maputo, 1975
Boletim Mensal de Estatistica. Maputo, 1976
Henriksen, T. H., *Mozambique: A History.* London and Cape Town, 1978
Houser, G., and Shore, H., *Mozambique: Dream the Size of Freedom.* New York, 1975
Isaacman, A., *A Luta Continua: Building a New Society in Mozambique.* New York, 1978

NAURU

Population: 7,254 (1977)

HISTORY. The island was discovered by Capt. Fearn in 1798, annexed by Germany in Oct. 1888, and surrendered to the Australian forces in 1914. It was administered under a mandate, effective from 17 Dec. 1920, conferred on the British Empire and approved by the League of Nations until 1 Nov. 1947, when the United Nations General Assembly approved a trusteeship agreement with the governments of Australia, New Zealand and UK as joint administering authority. Independence was gained in 1968.

AREA AND POPULATION. The island is situated 0° 32′ S. lat. and 166° 56′ E. long. Area, 5,263 acres (2,130 hectares). It is an oval-shaped upheaval coral island of approximately 12 miles in circumference, surrounded by a reef which is exposed at low tide. There is no deep water harbour but offshore moorings, reputedly the deepest in the world, are capable of holding medium-sized vessels, including 30,000 tonne capacity bulk carriers. On the seaward side the reef dips abruptly into the deep waters of the Pacific at an angle of 45°. On the landward side of the reef there is a sandy beach interspersed with coral pinnacles. From the sandy beach the ground rises gradually, forming a fertile section ranging in width from 150 to 300 yd and completely encircling the island. On the inner side of the fertile section there is a coral cliff which rises to a height of 200 ft. Above the cliff there is an extensive plateau bearing phosphate of a high grade, the mining rights of which were vested in the British Phosphate Commissioners until 1 July 1970, subject to the rights of the Nauruan landowners. In July 1970 the Nauru Phosphate Corporation assumed control and management of the enterprise. It is chiefly on the fertile section of land between the sandy beach and the plateau that the Nauruans have established themselves. With the exception of a small fringe round a shallow lagoon, about 1 mile inland, the plateau, which contains the phosphate deposits, has few foodbearing trees and is not settled by the Nauruans.

At the census held on 22 Jan. 1977 the population totalled 7,254, of whom 4,174 were Nauruans.

Vital statistics, 1977: Births, 226 (137 Nauruan); deaths, 47 (33 Nauruan).

CONSTITUTION AND GOVERNMENT. A Legislative Council was established by the Nauru Act, passed by the Australian Parliament in Dec. 1965 and was inaugurated on 31 Jan. 1966. The trusteeship agreement terminated on 31 Jan. 1968, on which day Nauru became an independent republic but having special relationship with the Commonwealth. An 18-member Parliament is elected on a 3-yearly basis.

President and Minister for Foreign Affairs: Hammer DeRoburt, OBE.

National flag: Blue with a narrow horizontal gold stripe across the centre, beneath this near the hoist a white star of 12 points.

FINANCE. Revenue and expenditure (in $A) for financial year ending 30 June 1977: revenue, 22,643,375; expenditure, 28,052,000 (health, 715,110; education, 1,179,581).

The interests in the phosphate deposits were purchased in 1919 from the Pacific Phosphate Company by the governments of the UK, the Commonwealth of Australia and New Zealand at a cost of £Stg3·5m., and a Board of Commissioners representing the 3 governments was appointed to manage and control the working of the deposits. In May 1967, in Canberra, the British Phosphate Corporation agreed to hand over the phosphate industry to Nauru and on 15 June 1967 agreement was reached that the Nauruans could buy the assets of the B.P.C. for approximately $A20m. over 3 years. Final payment was made on 23 April 1969 and control was handed over on 1 July 1970.

It is estimated that the deposits will be exhausted by 1993.

COMMERCE. The export trade consists almost entirely of phosphate shipped to Australia, New Zealand and Japan. Phosphate exported, 1976–77, 1m. tonnes. The imports consist almost entirely of food supplies, building construction materials and machinery for the phosphate industry. Value of imports, 1973–74, $A10m.

Total trade between Nauru and UK (British Department of Trade returns, in £1,000 sterling):

	1978	*1979*	*1980*	*1981*	*1982*
Imports to UK	135	160	70	83	32
Exports from UK	351	619	821	326	1,843

COMMUNICATIONS

Aviation. There is an airfield on the island capable of accepting medium size jet aircraft. Air Nauru, a wholly owned government subsidiary, operates services with Boeing 727 and 737 aircraft to Melbourne, Hong Kong, Apia, Honiara, Guam, Tarawa, Majuro, Kagoshima, Noumea, Port Vila, Fiji, Ponape, Manila and Taipei.

Shipping. The Nauru Local Government Council, through its agency the Nauru Pacific Shipping Line, owns 5 ships and has 3 on charter. These ships ply between Australia, Pacific Islands, west coast of USA, and Japan. Other shipping coming to the island consists of those under charter to the phosphate industry.

Telecommunications. An earth satellite station became operational in 1976, offering 24 hour telephone, telegram and telex services world-wide. Number of telephones (1978) 1,500. Direct daily high frequency service is maintained with Tarawa and both long- and short-wave transmissions with merchant shipping. A separate tele-radio service exists between Nauru and Ocean Island.

Cinemas. In 1978 there were 7 cinemas with an approximate seating capacity of 1,500.

EDUCATION. Attendance at school is compulsory for all children between the ages of 6 and 15 (if European) and 6 and 16 (if Nauruan). In June 1978 there were 8 infant and primary schools and 2 secondary schools. There were 129 teachers and 2,139 pupils in infant, primary and secondary schools. In addition, there is a trade school with 4 instructors and an enrolment of 61 trainees. Scholarships are available for Nauruan children to receive secondary and higher education and vocational training in Australia and New Zealand. In June 1978, 75 Nauruans were receiving secondary education abroad in Australia and New Zealand and 12 were enrolled in university and vocational training courses in Australia, New Zealand and Fiji.

DIPLOMATIC REPRESENTATIVE

Of Great Britain in Nauru
High Commisioner: R. A. R. Barltrop (resides in Suva).

Books of Reference

Report to the General Assembly of the United Nations on the Administration of the Territory of Nauru. 1949–1968
Text of Trusteeship Agreement. (Cmd. 7290; Treaty Series No. 89, 1947)
Territory of Nauru—Annual Report. Dept. of Territories. Canberra, 1920–40 and from 1947–48
Packett, C. N., *Guide to the Republic of Nauru.* Bradford, 1970
Pittman, G. A., *Nauru, the Phosphate Island.* London, 1959
Viviani, N., *Phosphate and Political Progress.* Canberra, 1970

NEPÁL

Capital: Káthmándu
Population: 15·02m. (1981)
GNP per capita: US$140 (1980)

HISTORY. From 1846 to 1951 Nepál was virtually ruled by the Ráná family, a member of which always held the office of prime minister, the succession being determined by special rules. The last Ráná prime minister (and, until 18 Feb. 1951, Supreme C.-in-C.) was HH Máháraja Mohan Shumsher Jung Bahádur Ráná, who resigned in Nov. 1951.

AREA AND POPULATION. Nepál, situated between 26° 20′ and 30° 10′ N. lat. and between 80° 15′ and 88° 15′ E. long., is bounded on the north by Tibet, on the east by Sikkim and West Bengal, on the south and west by Bihar and Uttar Pradesh. On 5 Oct. 1961 a treaty was signed in Peking, according to which the Chinese–Nepalese boundary line 'runs generally south-eastwards along the mountain ridge, passing through Cho Oyu mountain, Pumoli mountain, Mount Chomo Lungma (the Chinese name for Everest) and Lhotse Too Makalu mountain'. Nepál gained about 300 sq. miles of territory. Area about 54,600 sq. miles (141,400 sq. km); population (estimate, 1981), 15·02m.

Capital, Káthmándu, 75 miles from the Indian frontier; population about 195,260. Other towns (1971) include Pátan (also called Lalitpur), 48,577; Moráng (Biratnagar), 44,938; Bhádgáon (Bhaktapur), 40,112.

The aboriginal stock is Mongolian with a considerable admixture of Hindu blood from India. They were originally divided into numerous hill clans and petty principalities, one of which, Gorkha or Gurkha, became predominant in 1559 and has since given its name to men from all parts of Nepál. The 15 feudal chieftainships were integrated into the kingdom on 10 April 1961.

The country is administratively divided into 14 zones and 75 development districts.

RULING KING. The sovereign is HM Mahárájádhirája **Birendra Bir Bikram Sháh Dev**, who succeeded his father Mahendra Bir Bikram Sháh Dev on 31 Jan. 1972.

CONSTITUTION AND GOVERNMENT. On 18 Feb. 1951 the King proclaimed a constitutional monarchy, and on 16 Dec. 1962 a new Constitution of the 'Constitutional Monarchical Hindu State'. The village and town *panchayat*, recognized as the basic units of democracy, elect the district *panchayat*, these elect the zonal *panchayat*, and these finally the 112 members of the national *panchayat*. The Constitution was amended in 1975. In addition, 28 representatives of professional organizations and royal nominees not exceeding 15% of the elected members, will be included in the national *panchayat*. The executive power is vested in the King, who appoints a council of ministers from the national *panchayat*. A state council will advise the King and proclaim the successor or, if the heir is a minor, a regency council. Art. 81 empowers the King to declare a state of emergency and to suspend the Constitution.

On 25 Aug. 1963 the King formed a National Guidance Council and in Jan. 1973 appointed a new cabinet which was reshuffled Nov. 1974.

Relations with the UK are regulated by the treaty of peace and friendship signed on 29 Oct. 1950, which supersedes the treaties of 1792, 1815 and 1923. Diplomatic relations with the USA were established in 1947.

The Cabinet appointed in June 1981 was as follows:

Prime Minister, Royal Palace Affairs and Foreign Affairs: Surya Bahadur Thapa.
Home Affairs: Nain Bahadur Swanr. *Panchayat Affairs and Local Development:* Navaraj Subedi. *Industry, Commerce and Supplies:* Balaram Gharti Magar. *Finance:* Yadav Prasad Pant. *Law and Justice, and Land Reform:* Bakhan Singh

Gurung. *Foreign Affairs and Water Resources:* Padam Bahadur Khatri.
There are also 9 Ministers of State and 19 Assistant Ministers.

National flag: Two triangular parts of red, with a blue border all round, bearing symbols of the moon and the sun in white.
National anthem: 'May glory crown our illustrious sovereign' (1952).

DEFENCE

Army. The Army consists of about 25,000 men, mainly infantry, all of whom are regulars. There are 5 infantry brigades, 1 paratroop battalion and support units. It is being modernized with the aid of Britain and USA.

Air Force. Independent of the army since 1979, the Air Force has 2 Skyvan and 1 Turbo-Porter transport aircraft, 1 Puma helicopter and 5 Alouette III helicopters. An H.S. 748 turboprop transport and a Puma helicopter are operated by the Royal Flight.

INTERNATIONAL RELATIONS

Membership. Nepál is a member of UN and the Colombo Plan.

ECONOMY

Planning. The fifth plan runs from 1975 to 1980. Its cost is estimated at NRs 10,110m. Priority is being given to transport, communications, power, agriculture, irrigation, training of technicians and schools.

Budget. The general budget for the fiscal year 1982–83 envisages total expenditure of NRs 9,200m. Revenues are estimated at NRs 4,000m.

Currency. The Nepalese *rupee* is 171 grains in weight, as compared with the Indian rupee, which weighs 180 grains. The rate of exchange is 135 Nepalese rupees for 100 Indian rupees. 100 Nepalese *pice* = 1 Nepalese rupee. Coins of all denominations are minted. The Rástra Bank also issues notes of 1, 5, 10, 100 and 1,000 rupees. In March 1983, US$1 = 13·20 *rupees*; £1 = 20 *rupees*.

AGRICULTURE. Nepál has valuable forests in the southern part of the country. In the northern part, on the slopes of the Himálayas, there grow large quantities of medicinal herbs which find a world-wide market. Of the total area, nearly one-third (11·2m. acres) is under forest; 5·4m. acres is covered by perpetual snow; 9·6m. acres is under paddy, 2·9m. maize and millet, 800,000 wheat. Production (1978–79 in tonnes): Rice, 2·33m.; maize, 743,000; wheat, 454,000.
Livestock (1981); Cattle, 6·9m., including about 441,000 cows; 4·2m. buffaloes; sheep and goats, 4·9m.; pigs, 355,000; poultry, 22m.

INDUSTRY AND TRADE

Industry. New industries, such as jute- and sugar-mills, match, leather, cigarette, and shoe factories, and chemical works have been established, including two industrial estates at Pátan and Balaju. The third economic plan envisages a 60,000-kw. capacity from hydro-electric plants.

Commerce. The principal articles of export are food grains, jute, timber, oilseeds, ghee (clarified butter), potatoes, medicinal herbs, hides and skins, cattle. The chief imports are textiles, cigarettes, salt, petrol and kerosene, sugar, machinery, medicines, boots and shoes, paper, cement, iron and steel, tea. The trade is mostly financed by the Nepál Bank, Ltd (established in 1937) and the Rástra Bank of Nepál (established in 1956). A large proportion of international trade is with India.
Imports and exports in NRs 1,000:

	1979	*1980*	*1981*
Imports	3,509,600	3,911,700	4,332,400
Exports	1,136,900	964,200	1,797,500

Total trade between Nepál and UK (British Department of Trade returns, in £1,000 sterling):

	1977	*1978*	*1979*	*1980*	*1981*	*1982*
Imports to UK	680	642	1,591	2,253	2,324	3,844
Exports and re-exports from UK	2,747	1,572	5,096	2,956	2,980	4,650

Tourism. There were 148,789 Tourists in 1980.

COMMUNICATIONS

Roads. With the co-operation of India and the USA 900 miles of motorable roads are being constructed, including the East-West Highway through southern Nepál. A road from the Tibetan border to Káthmándu was recently completed with Chinese aid.

There are about 1,300 miles motorable roads. A ropeway for the carriage of goods covers the 14 miles from Dhursing above Bhimphedi into the Káthmándu valley.

A road connects Káthmándu with Birgung.

Railways. Railways (762 mm gauge) connect Jayanagar on the North Eastern Indian Railway with Janakpur and thence with Bijulpura (54 km).

Aviation. The Royal Nepál Airline Corporation has linked Káthmándu, the capital, with 11 districts of Nepál; and 23 more airfields are under construction. The Royal Nepalese Airline Corporation has services between Káthmándu and Calcutta, Patna, New Delhi, Bangkok, Rangoon and Dacca, employing Boeing 727 jet aircraft.

Post and Broadcasting. Káthmándu is connected by telephone with Birganj and Raxaul (North Eastern Indian Railway) on the southern frontier with Bihar; and with the eastern part of the Terai foothills; an extension to the western districts is being completed. Number of telephones (1978) 9,425, of which 5,431 were in Káthmándu. Under an agreement with India and the USA, a network of 91 wireless stations exists in Nepál, with further stations in Calcutta and New Delhi. Radio Nepál at Káthmándu broadcasts in Nepáli and English. Wireless telecommunication was inaugurated on 1 Oct. 1964.

All post, telephone and telegraph services have been taken over from India. The Indian, originally English, post office, established 1816, closed on 13 April 1965.

JUSTICE, RELIGION, EDUCATION AND WELFARE

Justice. The Supreme Court Act, established a uniform judicial system, culminating in a supreme court of a Chief Justice and no more than 6 judges. Special courts to deal with minor offences may be established at the discretion of the Government.

Religion. Sánáton of Pauranic, *i.e.*, traditional or ancient Hinduism, and Buddhism are the religions of the bulk of the people. Christian missions are admitted, but conversion is forbidden.

The royal family is Hindu.

Education. In 1979 there were 9,886 primary schools, 3,705 secondary schools, 98 colleges and the Tribhuvan University (founded 1960).

About 20% of the population are literate. The national language is Nepáli.

Health. There were about 420 doctors and 2,586 hospital beds in 1979.

DIPLOMATIC REPRESENTATIVES

Of Nepál in Great Britain (12a Kensington Palace Gdns., London, W8 4QU)
Ambassador: (Vacant).

Of Great Britain in Nepál (Láincháur, Káthmándu)
Ambassador: J. B. Denson, CMG, OBE.

Of Nepál in the USA (2131 Leroy Pl. NW, Washington, D.C., 20008)
Ambassador: Bhekh Bahadar Thapa.

Of the USA in Nepál (PaniPokhari, Káthmándu)
Ambassador: Carlton S. Coon.

Of Nepál to the United Nations
Ambassador: Uddhav Deo Bhatt.

Books of Reference

Statistical Information: A Department of Statistics was set up in Káthmándu in 1950.

Baral, L. S., *Political Development in Nepal.* London, 1980
Bezruchka, S., *A Guide to Trekking in Nepal.* Leicester, 1981
Karan, P. P., and Jenkins, W. M., *Nepal: A Cultural and Physical Geography.* Univ of Kentucky Press, 1960
Muni, S. D., *Foreign Policy of Nepal.* New Delhi, 1973
Shaha, R., *Nepali Politics: Retrospect and Prospect.* OUP, 1975
Turner, R. L., *Nepali Dictionary.* 1980.
Wadhwa, D. N., *Nepal.* [Bibliography] Oxford and Santa Barbara, 1982

THE NETHERLANDS

Koninkrijk der Nederlanden

Capital: Amsterdam
Seat of Government: The Hague
Population: 14·25m. (1981)
GNP per capita: US$11,470 (1980)

HISTORY. William of Orange (1533–84), as the German count of Nassau, inherited vast possessions in the Netherlands and the Princedom of Orange in France. He was the initiator of the struggle for independence from Spain (1568–1648); in the Republic of the United Netherlands he and his successors became the 'first servants of the Republic' with the title of 'Stadhouder' (governor). In 1689 William III acceded to the throne of England, becoming joint sovereign with Mary II, his wife. William III died in 1702 without issue, and after a stadhouderless period a member of the Frisian branch of Orange–Nassau was nominated hereditary stadhouder in 1747; but his successor, Willem V, had to take refuge in England, in 1795, at the invasion of the French Army. In Nov. 1813 the United Provinces were freed from French domination.

The Congress of Vienna joined the Belgian provinces, the 'Austrian Netherlands' before the French Revolution, to the Northern Netherlands. The son of the former stadhouder Willem V was proclaimed King of the Netherlands at The Hague on 16 March 1815 as Willem I. The union was dissolved by the Belgian revolution of 1830, and the treaty of London, 19 April 1839, constituted Belgium an independent kingdom.

Netherlands Sovereigns

Willem I	1815–1840 (died 1843)	Wilhelmina	1890–1948 (died 1962)
Willem II	1840–1849	Juliana	1948–1980
Willem III	1849–1890	Beatrix	1980–

AREA AND POPULATION. The Netherlands is bounded north and west by the North Sea, south by Belgium and east by the Federal Republic of Germany. Growth of census population:

1829	2,613,298	1909	5,858,175	1960	11,461,964
1849	3,056,879	1920	6,865,314	1971	13,060,115
1869	3,579,529	1930	7,935,565		
1889	4,511,415	1947	9,625,499		

Area, density and estimated population on 1 Jan. 1972 and 1982:

Province	*Land area (in sq. km) 1982*	*Population 1972*	*Population 1982*	*Density per sq. km 1982*
Groningen	2,336·58	526,555	559,135	239
Friesland	3,353·00	532,524	592,374	177
Drenthe	2,654·07	379,595	423,627	160
Overijssel	3,812·52	945,882	1,033,789	271
Gelderland	5,009·02	1,558,334	1,719,111	343
Utrecht	1,331·87	827,343	916,694	688
Noord-Holland	2,668·26	2,273,594	2,312,266	867
Zuid-Holland	2,904·83	3,013,439	3,121,471	1,075
Zeeland	1,786·80	316,124	353,697	198
Noord-Brabant	4,965·08	1,850,495	2,085,420	420
Limburg	2,171·50	1,022,354	1,077,193	496
Dronten [1]	329·97	13,314	20,879	63
Lelystad [1]	220·38	—	48,177	219

[1] Dronten and Lelystad are municipalities and have not been incorporated into any province.

Province	Land area (in sq. km) 1982	Population 1972	Population 1982	Density per sq. km 1982
Zuideijke Ijsselmeerpolders [1]	404·47	6,665	20,699	51
Central Register of population [2]	—	3,345	1,297	—
Total	33,948·35	13,269,563	14,285,829	421

[1] The Zuidelijke Ijsselmeerpolders (drained in 1957) are part of the former Zuiderzee, now called Ijsselmeer; they have not been incorporated into any province.

[2] The Central population register includes persons who are residents of the Netherlands but who have no fixed residence in any particular municipality (living in caravans and houseboats, population on inland vessels, etc.).

Of the total population on 1 Jan. 1982, 7,081,566 were males, 7,204,263 females.

The total area of the Netherlands up to the low water line (*i.e.*, sea-level at low tide) is 41,160 sq. km (15,892 sq. miles), of which 33,948·35 sq. km (13,107·47 sq. miles) is land area.

On 14 June 1918 a law was passed concerning the reclamation of the Zuiderzee. The work was begun in 1920; the following sections have been completed: 1. The Noordholland–Wieringen Barrage (2·5 km), 1924; 2. The Wieringermeer Polder (210 sq. km), 1930 (inundated by the Germans in 1945, but drained again in the same year); 3. The Wieringen–Friesland Barrage (30 km), 1932; 4. The Noordoost Polder (501 sq. km), 1942; 5. Oost Flevoland (651 sq. km), 1957; 6. Zuidelijk Flevoland (428 sq. km), 1967.

The polder Markerwaard (400 sq. km) is being reclaimed. A portion of what used to be the Zuiderzee behind the barrage will remain a fresh-water lake: Ijsselmeer (1,250 sq. km). The 'Delta-project', scheduled to be completed in the 1980s, comprises the building of enclosure dams in the estuaries between the islands in the south-western part of the country, excluding the sea-entrances to the ports of Rotterdam and Antwerp; it will also create fresh-water reservoirs. *See* map in THE STATESMAN'S YEAR-BOOK, 1959.

Vital statistics for calendar years:

	Live births Total	Live births Illegitimate	Still births	Marriages	Divorces	Deaths	Net migration
1979	174,979	6,003	1,240	85,648	23,748	112,565	+44,774
1980	181,294	7,454	1,205	90,182	25,735	114,279	+53,034
1981	178,569	8,609	1,222	85,574	28,509	115,515	+16,988

Population of principal municipalities on 1 Jan. 1982:

Achtkarspelen	26,934	Dordrecht	108,576	Den Helder	63,364
Alkmaar	77,761	Ede (Gld.)	85,025	Hellendoorn	33,242
Almelo	63,313	Eindhoven	195,599	Hellevoetsluis	26,000
Alphen a/d Rijn	53,182	Emmen	90,662	Helmond	58,787
Amersfoort	88,024	Enschede	144,590	Hengelo (O.)	76,399
Amstelveen	69,745	Epe	33,409	's-Hertogenbosch	89,601
Amsterdam	700,759	Etten-Leur	29,696	Hilversum	90,883
Apeldoorn	142,367	Geldrop	26,572	Hoogeveen	44,389
Arnhem	129,160	Geleen	35,803	Hoogezand-Sappemeer	35,591
Assen	45,517	Goes	31,038	Hoorn	44,003
Barneveld	37,536	Gorinchem	28,484	Huizen	31,975
Bergen op Zoom	45,052	Gouda	59,212	Kampen	30,989
Beverwijk	35,534	's-Gravenhage	454,300	Katwijk	38,494
de Bilt	32,106	Groningen	165,146	Kerkrade	53,177
Breda	117,754	Haarlem	156,025	Krimpen a/d Ijssel	28,115
Brunssum	29,971	Haarlemmermeer	80,785	Landgraaf	39,134
Bussum	34,252	Hardenberg	31,643	Leeuwarden	84,689
Capelle a/d Ijssel	46,204	Harderwijk	31,485	Leiden	103,457
Delft	85,268	Heemskerk	31,917	Leidschendam	30,140
Delfzijl	25,379	Heemstede	26,044	Lelystad	48,177
Deurne	28,079	Heerenveen	37,353	Maarssen	31,006
Deventer	64,505	Heerhugowaard	33,415	Maassluis	33,241
Doetinchem	37,855	Heerlen	91,291		

Maastricht	111,487	Rijswijk (Z.-H.)	51,378	Velsen	59,779
Middelburg	38,655	Schiedam	72,903	Venlo	62,495
Naaldwijk	25,584	Sittard	43,856	Venray	33,605
Nieuwegein	46,944	Smallingerland	49,395	Vlaardingen	78,124
Noordoostpolder	37,545	Sneek	28,431	Vlissingen	46,348
Nijmegen	147,172	Soest	40,670	Voorburg	43,371
Oldenzaal	28,626	Spijkenisse	47,552	Waalwijk	29,059
Oosterhout	44,994	Stadskanaal	34,334	Wageningen	31,212
Opsterland	26,017	Stein	26,308	Wassenaar	27,031
Oss	48,830	Terneuzen	35,606	Weert	38,982
Papendrecht	25,058	Tiel	29,614	Winterswijk	27,554
Purmerend	38,166	Tietjerksteradeel	29,757	Zaanstad	129,864
Raalte	25,101	Tilburg	153,957	Zeist	62,055
Renkum	34,009	Uden	33,415	Zevenaar	27,236
Rheden	48,755	Utrecht	234,543	Zoetermeer	71,742
Ridderkerk	47,136	Valkenswaard	27,446	Zutphen	31,919
Roermond	38,192	Veendam	28,499	Zwolle	85,135
Roosendaal	55,754	Veenendaal	41,401	Zwijndrecht	39,382
Rotterdam	568,167	Veldhoven	34,526		

Urban agglomerations as at 1 Jan. 1982: Rotterdam, 1,025,580; Amsterdam, 945,062; The Hague, 677,962; Utrecht, 494,898; Eindhoven, 373,233; Arnhem, 290,506; Heerlen-Kerkrade, 264,107; Enschede-Hengelo, 247,266; Nijmegen, 227,840; Haarlem, 221,551; Tilburg, 220,511; Groningen, 204,010; Dordrecht-Zwijndrecht, 197,543; 's-Hertogenbosch, 186,627; Geleen-Sittard, 178,011; Leiden, 174,501; Maastricht, 155,312; Breda, 152,449; Zaanstad, 141,991; Velsen-Beverwijk, 127,230; Hilversum, 108,227.

CLIMATE. A cool temperate maritime climate, marked by mild winters and cool summers, but with occasional continental influences. Coastal temperatures vary from 37°F (3°C) in winter to 61°F (16°C) in summer, but inland the winters are slightly colder and the summers slightly warmer, Rainfall is least in the months Feb. to May, but inland there is a well-defined summer maximum in July and Aug.

The Hague, Jan. 37°F (2·7°C), July 61°F (16·3°C). Annual rainfall 32·8″ (820 mm). Amsterdam, Jan. 36°F (2·3°C), July 62°F (16·5°C). Annual rainfall 34″ (850 mm). Rotterdam, Jan. 36·5°F (2·6°C), July 62°F (16·6°C). Annual rainfall 32″ (800 mm).

REIGNING QUEEN. Beatrix Wilhelmina Armgard, born 31 Jan. 1938 daughter of Queen Juliana and Prince Bernhard; married to Claus von Amsberg on 10 March 1966; succeeded to the crown on 1 May 1980, on the abdication of her mother. *Offspring:* Prince Willem-Alexander, born 27 April 1967; Prince Johan Friso, born 25 Sept. 1968; Prince Constantijn, born 11 Oct. 1969.

Mother of the Queen: Queen Juliana Louise Emma Marie Wilhelmina, born 30 April 1909, daughter of Queen Wilhelmina (born 31 Aug. 1880, died 28 Nov. 1962) and Prince Henry of Mecklenburg-Schwerin (born 19 April 1876, died 3 July 1934); married to Prince Bernhard Leopold Frederick Everhard Julius Coert Karel Godfried Pieter of Lippe-Biesterfeld (born 29 June 1911) on 7 Jan. 1937. Abdicated in favour of her daughter, the Reigning Queen, on 30 April 1980.

Sisters of the Queen: Princess Irene Emma Elisabeth, born 5 Aug. 1939, married to Prince Charles Hugues de Bourbon-Parma on 29 April 1964, divorced 1981 (*sons:* Prince Carlos Javier Bernardo, born 27 Jan. 1970; Prince Jaime Bernardo, born 13 Oct. 1972; *daughters:* Princess Margarita Maria Beatriz, born 13 Oct. 1972; Princess Maria Carolina Christina, born 23 June 1974); Princess Margriet Francisca, born in Ottawa, 19 Jan. 1943, married to Pieter van Vollenhoven on 10 Jan. 1967 (*sons:* Prince Maurits, born 17 April 1968; Prince Bernhard, born 25 Dec. 1969; Prince Pieter-Christiaan, born 22 March 1972; Prince Floris, born 10 April 1975); Princess Maria Christina, born 18 Feb. 1947, married to Jorge Guillermo on 28 June 1975 (*sons:* Bernardo, born 17 June 1977; Nicolas Daniel Mauricio, born 6 July 1979; *daughter:* Juliana, born 8 Oct. 1981).

CONSTITUTION AND GOVERNMENT. According to the Constitution of the Kingdom of the Netherlands, the Kingdom consists of the Netherlands and the Netherlands Antilles. Their relations are regulated by the 'Statute' for the Kingdom, which came into force on 29 Dec. 1954. Each part enjoys full autonomy; they are united, on a footing of equality, for mutual assistance and the protection of their common interests.

The first Constitution of the Netherlands after its restoration as a Sovereign State was promulgated in 1814. It was revised in 1815 (after the addition of the Belgian provinces, and the assumption by the Sovereign of the title of King), 1840 (after the secession of the Belgian provinces), 1848, 1884, 1887, 1917, 1922, 1938, 1946, 1948, 1953, 1956, 1963 and 1972.

The Netherlands is a constitutional and hereditary monarchy. The royal successsion is in the direct male line in the order of primogeniture; in default of male heirs, the female line ascends the throne. The Sovereign comes of age on reaching his 18th year. During his minority the royal power is vested in a Regent—designated by law—and in some cases in the Council of State.

The central executive power of the State rests with the Crown, while the central legislative power is vested in the Crown and Parliament (the *Staten-Generaal*), consisting of 2 Chambers. After the 1956 revision of the Constitution the Upper or First Chamber is composed of 75 members, elected by the members of the Provincial States, and the Second Chamber consists of 150 deputies, who are elected directly. Members of the States-General must be Netherlanders or recognized as Netherlands subjects and 25 years of age or over; they may be men or women. They receive an allowance.

First Chamber (as constituted in 1981): Labour Party, 28; Christian Democrats, 28; Party for Freedom and Democracy, 12; Democrats 1966, 4; Radical Political Party, 1; Communists, 1; Political Calvinist Party, 1.

Second Chamber (elected on 8 Sept. 1982): Labour Party, 47; Christian Democrats, 45; Party for Freedom and Democracy, 36; Democrats 1966, 6; Pacifist Socialists, 3; Political Calvinist Party, 3; Communists, 3; Radical Political Party, 2; Evangelical Political Federation, 2; Calvinist Political Association, 1; Evangelical People's Party, 1; Party of the Centre, 1.

The revised Constitution of 1917 has introduced an electoral system based on universal suffrage and proportional representation. Under its provisions, members of the Second Chamber are directly elected by citizens of both sexes who are Netherlands subjects not under 18 years (since 1972). Criminals, lunatics and certain others are disqualified; for certain crimes and misdemeanours there may be temporary disqualification.

The members of the Second Chamber are elected for 4 years, and retire in a body, whereas the First Chamber is elected for 6 years, and every 3 years one-half retires by rotation. The Sovereign has the power to dissolve both Chambers of Parliament, or one of them, subject to the condition that new elections take place within 40 days, and the new House or Houses be convoked within 3 months.

The Sovereign and the Second Chamber may propose Bills; the First Chamber can only approve or reject them without inserting amendments. The meetings of both Chambers are public, though each of them may by a majority vote decide on a secret session. It is a fixed custom, that Ministers and Secretaries of State, on their own initiative or upon invitation of the Parliament, attend the sessions to defend their policy, their budget, their proposals of Bills, etc., when these are in discussion. A Minister or Secretary of State, however, cannot be a member of Parliament at the same time.

The Constitution can be revised only by a Bill declaring that there is reason for introducing such revision and containing the proposed alterations. The passing of this Bill is followed by a dissolution of both Chambers and a second confirmation by the new States-General by two-thirds of the votes. Unless it is expressly stated, all laws concern only the realm in Europe, and not the overseas parts of the kingdom.

Every act of the Sovereign has to be covered by a responsible Minister.

The Ministry, a coalition of Christian Democrats and Liberals, was composed as follows in Nov. 1982:

Prime Minister: Ruud Lubbers (CDA).

Deputy Prime Minister and Economic Affairs: Gijs van Ardenne (VVD). *Foreign Affairs:* Hans van den Broek (CDA). *Finance:* Dr Herman Ruding (CDA). *Defence:* Jacob de Ruiter (CDA). *Development Aid Co-operation:* Eegje Schoo (VVD). *Social Affairs and Employment:* Jan de Koning (CDA). *Home Affairs:* Koos Rietkerk (VVD). *Justice:* Frits Korthals Altes (VVD). *Agriculture and Fisheries:* Gerrit Braks (CDA). *Welfare, Public Health and Culture:* Elco Brinkman (CDA). *Education and Science:* Wim Deetman (CDA). *Transport and Public Works:* Neelie Smit Kroes (VVD). *Housing, Physical Planning and Environment:* Pieter Winsemius (VVD).

There are also 16 state secretaries.

The Council of State *(Raad van State)*, appointed and presided over by the Sovereign, is composed of a vice-president and not more than 28 members. It can be consulted on all legislative matters. Decisions of the Crown in administrative disputes are prepared by a special committee of the Council.

The Hague is the seat of the Court, Government and Parliament.

National flag: Three horizontal stripes of red, white, blue.

National anthem: Wilhelmus van Nassouen (words by Philip Marnix van St Aldegonde, *c.* 1570).

Local Government. The kingdom is divided in 11 provinces and about 820 municipalities. The creation of more provinces by splitting up the most densely populated provinces is in preparation. Each province has its own representative body, the Provincial States. The members are elected for 4 years, directly from the Netherlands inhabitants of the province who are 18 years of age. The electoral register is the same as for the Second Chamber. The members retire in a body and are subject to re-election. The number of members varies according to the population of the province, from 83 for South Holland to 43 for Zeeland. The Provincial States are entitled to issue ordinances concerning the welfare of the province, and to raise taxes pursuant to legal provisions. The provincial budgets and the provincial ordinances and resolutions relating to provincial property, loans, taxes, etc., must be approved by the Crown. The members of the Provincial States elect the First Chamber of the States-General. They meet twice a year, as a rule in public. A permanent commission composed of 6 of their members, called the 'Deputy States', is charged with the executive power and, if required, with the enforcement of the law in the province. Deputy as well as Provincial States are presided over by a Commissioner of the Sovereign, who in the former assembly has a deciding vote, but attends the latter in only a deliberative capacity. He is the chief magistrate in the province. The Commissioner and the members of the Deputy States receive an allowance.

Each municipality forms a Corporation with its own interests and rights, subject to the general law, and is governed by a Municipal Council, directly elected for 4 years, by the electorate registered for the Provincial States, provided they are residents of the municipality. All Netherlands inhabitants 23 years of age are eligible, the number of members varying from 7 to 45, according to the population. The Municipal Council has the right to issue bye-laws concerning the communal welfare. The Council may levy taxes pursuant to legal provisions; these ordinances must be approved by the Crown. All bye-laws may be vetoed by the Crown. The Municipal Budget and resolutions to alienate municipal property require the approbation of the Deputy States of the province. The Council meets in public as often as may be necessary, and is presided over by a Burgomaster, appointed by the Sovereign. The day-to-day administration is carried out by the Burgomaster and 2–7 Aldermen *(wethouders)*, elected by and from the Council; this body is also charged with the enforcement of the law. The Burgomaster may suspend the execution of a resolution of the council for 30 days, but is bound to notify the Deputy States of the province. In maintaining public order, the Burgomaster acts as the chief of police. The Burgomaster and Aldermen receive allowances.

DEFENCE. The Netherlands are bordered on the south by Belgium, on the east by the Federal Republic of Germany. On both sides the country is quite level and has no natural defences, except the barriers of some large rivers, running east to west and south to north. The country has an excellent roadnet and a vast railway system, enabling rapid movement. The west part of the country is densely populated.

Army. Service is partly voluntary and partly compulsory; the voluntary enlistments bear a small proportion to the compulsory. The total peacetime strength amounts to 72,000, including Military Police. The number of regulars is 24,000. The Army also employs 13,000 civilians. The legal period of active service for national servicemen is 22–24 months; the actual service period is 14 months for other ranks and 16 months for reserve-officers and n.c.o.s. The balance may be spent at will as 'short leave'. After their period of actual service or short leave, conscript personnel are granted long leave. However, they will be liable to being called up for refresher training or in case of mobilization until they have reached the age of 35 (n.c.o.s 40, reserve officers 45).

The 1st Netherlands Army Corps is assigned to NATO. It consists of 10 brigades and Corps troops. The active part of the Corps comprises 2 armoured brigades and 4 armoured infantry brigades, grouped in two divisions and 40% of the Corps troops. Part of this force is stationed in the Federal Republic of Germany. The peacetime strength of the active brigades is 80% of the war-authorized strength.

The mobilizable part of the Corps comprises 1 armoured brigade, 2 armoured infantry brigades, 1 infantry brigade and the remaining Corps troops.

The mechanized brigades comprise tank battalions (Centurion and Leopard I), armoured infantry battalions (YP-408 and YPR-765), medium artillery battalions (155 mm self-propelled), armoured engineer units, armoured reconnaissance units and armoured anti armoured units. The Corps troops comprise headquarters units, combat-support units, including Engineer and Corps artillery (203 mm, 155 mm and Lance) and service-support units. Helicopter squadrons are also available.

The National Territorial Command forces consist of territorial brigades, security forces, some logistical units and staffs. The major part of these units is mobilizable. Some units in the Netherlands are earmarked for assignment to the United Nations as peace-keeping forces. Since early 1979 an armoured infantry battalion, composed of regulars and conscripts, has been involved in the UN peace-keeping operations in Lebanon. For civil defence purposes there are a number of mobilizable fire-fighting, rescue and medical battalions. The army is responsible for the training of these units which in time of war are placed under the command of the National Commander of the Civil Defence.

Navy. The Royal Netherlands Navy has its main base in the Netherlands at Den Helder and minor bases at Flushing and Curaçao (Netherlands Antilles). The Ministry of Defence is located in The Hague.

Principal surface ships of the Royal Netherlands Navy:

Completed	*Name*	*Standard displacement (tons)*	*Guided Missile launchers*	*Guns*	*Shaft horse-power*	*Max. speed (knots)*
1975 1976	Tromp De Ruyter	4,300	8 single Harpoon 1 single Tartar 1 octuple Sea Sparrow	2 4·7 in. (1 twin)	50,000	30

There are also 6 diesel-electric patrol submarines, 9 standard frigates, 6 general-purpose frigates, 2 fast combat support ships, 6 corvettes, 3 mine countermeasures support ships (*ex*-ocean minesweepers), 11 coastal minesweepers, 4 coastal mine-hunters, 3 diving vessels, 16 inshore minesweepers, 1 torpedo maintenance vessel (*ex*-ocean minesweeper), 5 patrol vessels, 3 hydrographic survey ships, 10 landing craft, 2 training ships, 12 tugs and 39 small auxiliary ships.

Three missile armed general purpose (standard) frigates and 2 diesel-electric patrol submarines are under construction. The future construction programme includes 5 frigates and 15 mine countermeasure vessels, the latter in close co-operation with Belgium and France.

On 1 Jan. 1983 naval personnel provided for totalled 16,800 officers and other ranks, including the Naval Air Service (1,700) and the Royal Netherlands Marine Corps. There are also 6,400 civilians in service.

The naval air service maintains 15 Orion P3C, 6 Breguet Atlantics (SP-13A), 18 Westland Lynx SH14B/C embarked and 6 Lynx UH 14A for SAR, utility and transport.

Naval estimates (in 1m. guilders): 1975, 1,618; 1976, 1,683; 1977, 1,883; 1978, 2,069; 1979, 2,075; 1980, 2,006; 1981, 2,218; 1982, 2,352; 1983, 2,446.

Air Force. The Royal Netherlands Air Force was established 1 July 1913. Its current strength is approximately 19,000 personnel and it has a first-line combat force of 9 squadrons of aircraft and 12 squadrons of surface-to-air missiles. All squadrons are operated by Tactical Air Command. Aircraft operated are F-16 (3 squadrons for air defence and ground attack, 1 for tactical reconnaissance), F-104G, Starfighter (1 ground attack squadron, to re-equip with F-16s), and NF-5A/B fighter-bombers (4 squadrons, to complete re-equipment with F-16s by 1989). Also under control of Tactical Air Command is 1 squadron of the USAF, flying F-15C Eagles in the air defence role. 3 squadrons of Alouette III and Bölkow BO 105C helicopters are under control of the Royal Netherlands Army, but flown and maintained by the RNethAF for use in the communications and observation roles. Also operated is 1 squadron of F.27 Friendship/Troopship transport aircraft, and another (based in Curaçao) with 2 F.27 maritime patrol aircraft.

Training of RNethAF pilots is undertaken in Canada and the USA. The 12 squadrons of surface-to-air missiles consist of 4 squadrons of Nike Hercules (high altitude) and 8 squadrons of Hawk (low and medium altitude).

INTERNATIONAL RELATIONS

Membership. The Netherlands is a member of UN, EEC, OECD, the Council of Europe and NATO.

ECONOMY

Budget. The revenue and expenditure of the central government (ordinary and extraordinary) were, in 1m. guilders, for calendar years:

	1976 [2]	*1977* [3]	*1978* [3]	*1979* [3]	*1980* [3]	*1981* [4]	*1982* [6]
Revenue [1]	73,722	83,902	92,230	98,742	107,090	116,593	122,211
Expenditure [5]	82,468	90,324	101,067	110,770	121,077	129,095	140,176

[1] Without the revenue of loans. [2] Accounts. [3] Preliminary accounts.
[4] Revised budget figures. [5] Without redemption of loans. [6] Budget figures.

The revenue and expenditure of the Agriculture Equalization Fund, the Fund for Central Government roads, the Property Acquisition Fund (established in 1971), the Fund for the Development of a fast Breeder Reactor (established in 1972) and of the Investment Account Fund (established in 1978) have been incorporated in the general budget.

The national debt, in 1m. guilders, was on 31 Dec.:

	1977	*1978*	*1979*	*1980*	*1981*
Internal funded debt	47,029	55,180	64,086	78,090	96,830
„ floating „	14,683	17,356	20,314	21,433	21,629
Total	61,712	72,537	84,400	99,523	118,459

Currency. The monetary unit is the *gulden* (guilder, florin) of 100 *cents*. In March 1983 the rate of exchange was US$1 = 2·72 guilders; £1 = 3·96 guilders.

Legal tender are bank-notes, silver 10-guilder pieces, nickel 2½- and 1-guilder pieces, 25-cent, 10-cent pieces, bronze 5-cent and 1-cent pieces. Note circulation, 31 Dec. 1980, 21,709m. guilders and 31 Dec. 1981, 21,895m.

Banking. The Netherlands Bank, founded as a private institution, was nationalized on 1 Aug. 1948, the shareholders receiving, for a share of 1,000 guilders, a security of 2,000 guilders on the 2½% National Debt. Since 1863 the bank has the sole right of issuing bank-notes. The bank does the same business as other banks, but with more guarantees. The capital amounts to 20m. guilders.

In the year 1981 the state post office savings bank had deposits of 5,935m. guilders and withdrawals of 5,919m. guilders. Private savings banks: Deposits, 17,777m. guilders; withdrawals, 17,322m. guilders.

Weights and Measures. The metric system of weights and measures was adopted in the Netherlands in 1820.

ENERGY AND NATURAL RESOURCES

Electricity. The total production of electrical energy (in 1m. kwh.) amounted in 1938 to 3,688; 1958, 13,854; 1970, 40,859; 1978, 61,596; 1979, 64,464; 1980, 64,806; 1981, 64,053.

Gas. Production of manufactured gas (milliard k joule): 1978, 181,033; 1979, 233,553; 1980, 210,011; 1981, 197,586. Production of natural gas in 1950, 8m. cu. metres; 1955, 139; 1960, 384; 1970, 31,688; 1978, 88,730; 1979, 96,488; 1980, 91,153; 1981, 84,617.

Minerals. On 1 Jan. 1975 all coalmines were closed.

The production of crude petroleum (in 1,000 tonnes) amounted in 1943 (first year) to 0·2; 1953, 820; 1970, 1,919; 1976, 1,371; 1977, 1,382; 1978, 1,402; 1979, 1,316; 1980, 1,280; 1981, 1,316.

There are saltmines at Hengelo and Delfzijl; production (in 1,000 tonnes), 1950, 412·6; 1960, 1,096; 1970, 2,871; 1976, 3,026; 1977, 3,111; 1978, 2,939; 1979, 3,951; 1980, 3,464; 1981, 3,578.

Agriculture. The net area of all holdings was divided as follows (in hectares):

	1978 [1]	*1979* [1]	*1980* [1]	*1981*	*1982*
Field crops	698,518	700,126	704,710	702,510	702,287
Grass	1,221,458	1,212,634	1,197,592	1,187,719	1,178,098
Market gardening	96,218	89,706	87,121	89,600	94,210
Land for flower bulbs	13,498	13,949	14,307	14,390	14,189
Flower cultivation	4,548	4,829	5,180	5,267	5,472
Nurseries	5,924	6,049	6,228	6,413	6,386
Fallow land	5,255	6,190	5,099	4,769	4,577
Total	2,045,419	2,033,483	2,020,237	2,010,668	2,005,219

[1] Excluding holdings of less than 10 SFU (SFU = standard farm unit). 10 SFU is equal to a computed net value added at factor cost of about 4,000 guilders, in 1975.

The net areas [1] under special crops were as follows (in hectares):

Products	*1981*	*1982*	*Products*	*1981*	*1982*
Autumn wheat	119,233	112,760	Colza	10,955	10,753
Spring wheat	12,393	18,123	Flax	2,903	3,178
Rye	7,484	5,938	Agricultural seeds	20,561	17,734
Autumn barley	13,872	6,590	Potatoes, edible [2]	98,067	100,856
Spring barley	38,949	37,088	Potatoes, industrial [3]	66,887	65,089
Oats	21,165	23,685	Sugar-beet	130,362	133,973
Peas	3,996	6,006	Fodder-beet	1,866	2,314

[1] Excluding non-agrarian holdings of less than 10 SFU.
[2] Including early and seed potatoes.
[3] Including seed potatoes.

The yield of the more important products, in tonnes, was as follows:

Crop	*Average 1940–49*	*Average 1950–58*	*1979*	*1980* [1]	*1981*
Wheat	322,003	348,464	835,593	882,174	882,055
Rye	439,055	454,992	49,288	38,640	28,616
Barley	145,892	258,049	287,832	257,791	248,531
Oats	315,642	464,041	109,030	94,054	114,655
Field beans	15,799	5,693	...	...	1,184
Peas	65,460	93,664	14,407	14,776	15,297
Colza	24,763	18,358	18,093	28,503	37,205
Flax, unrippled	82,906	138,165	28,575	31,069	23,771
Potatoes, edible [2]	2,861,793	2,745,505	3,504,128	3,950,120	3,913,288
Potatoes, industrial	1,242,326	1,003,994	2,772,710	2,316,521	2,531,435
Sugar-beet	1,667,711	2,935,881	5,491,283	5,930,991	7,060,677
Fodder-beet	...	...	135,811	135,375	166,451

[1] Excluding holdings of less than 10 SFU. [2] Including early potatoes.

Livestock, May 1982: 5,240,687 cattle, 10,253,907 pigs; 42,354 horses, 3 years old and over, 776,404 sheep, 87·1m. poultry.

In 1981 the production of butter, under state control, amounted to 183,441 tonnes; that of cheese, under state control, to 457,372 tonnes. Export value of arable crops amounted to 14,851m. guilders; animal produce, 17,211m. guilders and horticultural produce, 7,518m. guilders.

Fisheries. The total produce of fish landed from the sea and inshore fisheries in 1981 was valued at 595m. guilders; the total weight amounted to 399,438 tonnes. In 1981 the herring fishery had a value of 26m. guilders and a weight of 16,710 tonnes. The quantity of oysters produced in 1981 amounted to 573 tonnes (10m. guilders).

INDUSTRY AND TRADE

Industry. Numbers employed (in 1,000) and turnover (in 1m. guilders) in manufacturing enterprises with 10 employees and more, excluding building:

	Numbers employed		*Turnover*	
Class in industry	*1980*	*1981*[1]	*1980*	*1981*[1]
Mining and quarrying	7·5	7·8	21,870	29,500
Manufacturing industry	893·0	856·3	204,200	223,600
Foodstuffs and tobacco products	144·7	141·0	54,700	60,900
Textile industry	32·5	28·9	4,420	4,300
Clothing	17·4	14·0	1,810	1,600
Leather and footwear	7·9	7·1	810	800
Wood and furniture industry	34·5	30·7	4,320	4,000
Paper industry	25·9	23·9	4,910	5,300
Graphic industry, publishers	64·0	62·5	9,460	9,600
Petroleum industry	10·4	10·8	27,240	32,600
Chemical industry, artificial yarns and fibre industry	85·2	84·9	28,680	33,700
Rubber and synthetic materials processing industry	24·7	23·9	4,000	4,100
Building materials, earthenware and glass	37·6	35·0	5,660	5,500
Basic metal industry	36·5	35·9	7,850	8,600
Metals products (excl. machinery and means of transport)	83·8	79·1	10,560	10,400
Machinery	84·4	80·3	10,690	11,300
Electrical industry	117·1	112·8	17,410	17,900
Means of transport	72·0	71·7	10,180	11,400
Instrument making and optical industry	8·9	8·9	910	1,100
Other industries	5·6	5·3	610	600
Public utilities	46·4	47·0	15,780	19,200

[1] Preliminary.

Commerce. On 5 Sept. 1944 and 14 March 1947 the Netherlands signed agreements with Belgium and Luxembourg for the establishment of a customs union. On 1 Jan. 1948 this union came into force and the existing customs tariffs of the Belgium–Luxembourg Economic Union and of the Netherlands were superseded by the joint Benelux Customs Union Tariff. It applies to imports into the 3 countries from outside sources, and exempts from customs duties all imports into each of the 3 countries from the other two. The Benelux tariff has 991 items and 2,400 separate specifications.

Returns of special imports and special exports (including parcel post and diamond trade, excluding unrefined and partly-worked gold, gold coins and coins in current circulation made of other metal) for calendar years (in 1,000 guilders):

	Imports	*Exports*		*Imports*	*Exports*
1949	5,331,569	3,851,126	1978[1]	114,371,926	108,205,427
1959	14,968,454	13,702,927	1979[1]	134,828,391	127,630,182
1969	39,955,406	36,205,110	1980[1]	152,279,265	146,859,848
1977[1]	111,973,874	107,195,386	1981[1]	163,998,929	170,772,393

[1] Including unrefined and partly-worked gold and gold coins.

Value of the trade (including parcel post and diamond trade, excluding unrefined and partly-worked gold, gold coins and coins in current circulation made of other metal) with leading countries (in 1,000 guilders):

Country	Imports 1979	Imports 1980	Imports 1981	Exports 1979	Exports 1980	Exports 1981
Belgium–Luxembourg	16,445,112	17,736,654	18,627,846	19,773,617	22,059,745	24,486,748
France	9,836,507	10,232,238	10,535,248	13,598,728	15,503,378	17,860,028
Germany (Fed. Rep.)	32,664,727	33,943,703	35,202,710	38,922,380	43,971,158	50,272,569
Indonesia	527,885	544,226	582,710	408,810	929,156	678,251
Italy	4,910,921	4,819,585	4,892,484	6,721,876	8,477,227	9,543,802
Kuwait	2,852,928	2,785,330	2,506,535	169,820	204,096	344,519
Sweden	2,600,676	2,824,146	2,956,972	2,346,703	2,579,750	2,541,386
UK	10,343,796	12,465,829	14,003,953	10,735,460	11,575,763	14,112,136
USA	11,351,673	13,433,621	15,567,121	3,578,672	3,685,728	5,495,426
Venezuela	170,088	346,677	424,431	267,075	268,149	352,819

Total trade between the Netherlands and UK (British Department of Trade returns, in £1,000 sterling):

	1978	1979	1980	1981	1982
Imports to UK	2,524,634	3,446,271	3,406,928	3,895,486	4,474,663
Exports and re-exports from UK	2,255,980	3,062,642	3,845,412	4,019,435	4,653,416

Tourism. There were 2,846,000 foreign visitors in 1981 (hotels and boarding houses only). 605,000 came from the Federal Republic of Germany, 537,200 from UK and 311,600 from USA. Total income from tourism (1980) US$1,640m.

COMMUNICATIONS

Roads. In 1981 the length of the Netherlands network of surfaced inter-urban roads was 53,222 km, of which 1,749 km were motor highways. Number of private cars (1981), 4·6m.

Railways. All railways are run by the mixed company 'N.V. Nederlandsche Spoorwegen'. Length of line in 1981 was 2,956 km, of which 1,799 km were electrified. Passengers carried (1981), 205m.; goods transported, 21·1m. tonnes.

Aviation. The Royal Dutch Airlines (KLM) was founded on 7 Oct. 1919. The company has a paid-up capital of 799m. guilders (1981–82). Revenue traffic, 1981–82: Passengers, 4·5m.; freight, 244m. kg; mail, 12m. kg.

Sea-going Shipping. Survey of the Netherlands mercantile marine as at 1 Jan. (capacity in 1,000 GRT):

Ships under Netherlands flag (including Netherlands Antilles)	*1981 Number*	*1981 Capacity*	*1982 Number*	*1982 Capacity*
Passenger ships [1]	6	94	9	144
Freighters (500 GRT and over)	453	2,633	457	2,524
Freighters (under 500 GRT)	83	37	64	27
Tankers	85	2,566	87	2,331
	627	5,330	617	5,026

[1] With accommodation for 13 or more cabin passengers.

In 1981, 42,132 sea-going ships of 330·9m. gross tons entered Netherlands ports (1980, 42,980 ships of 352m. gross tons).

Total goods traffic by sea-going ships in 1981 (with 1980 figures in brackets), in 1m. tonnes, amounted to 245·3 (268·6) unloaded, of which 116·7 (136·5) tankshipping, and 74·9 (78) loaded, of which 28·9 (35·8) tankshipping. The total seaborne freight traffic at Rotterdam was 250·3m. (276·4m.) and at Amsterdam 21·3m. (22·4m.) tonnes.

The number of containers at Rotterdam in 1981 was: unloaded from ships, 703,055, of which 194,568 from North America, and 743,885 loaded into ships, of which 127,529 to North America.

Inland Shipping. The total length of navigable rivers and canals is 4,387 km, of which about 1,974 km is for ships with a capacity of 1,000 and more tonnes. On 1

Jan. 1982 the Netherlands inland fleet actually used for transport (with carrying capacity in 1,000 tonnes) was composed as follows:

	Number	*Capacity*
Self-propelled barges	5,521	3,740
Dumb barges	469	461
Pushed barges	451	894
	6,441	5,095

In 1981, 254m. (1980: 269m.) tonnes of goods were transported on rivers and canals, of which 172m. (181m.) was international traffic. Goods transport on the Rhine across the Dutch–German frontier near Lobith amounted to 123m. (129m.) tonnes.

Post and Broadcasting. On 1 Jan. 1982 there were 5·1m. telephone connexions (36 per 100 inhabitants). Number of telex lines, 34,000; teleprinters, 37,000. *Nederlandse Omroep Stichting* (NOS) provides 4 programmes on medium-waves and FM in co-operation with broadcasting organizations. Regional programmes are also broadcast.

Advertisements are transmitted. NOS broadcasts 2 TV programmes. Advertisements, in the last quarter of 1980, were restricted to 4% of the transmission time in the evening. Television sets (1 Aug. 1981) totalled 4·3m.; holders of television licences may, in addition, have wireless receiving sets.

Cinemas (end 1981). There were 553 cinemas with a seating capacity of 155,000.

Newspapers (31 Dec. 1981). There were 84 daily newspapers with a total circulation of over 4·6m.

JUSTICE, RELIGION, EDUCATION AND WELFARE

Justice. Justice is administered by the High Court of the Netherlands (Court of Cassation), by 5 courts of justice (Courts of Appeal), by 19 district courts and by 62 cantonal courts; trial by jury is unknown. The Cantonal Court, which deals with minor offences, is formed by a single judge; the more serious cases are tried by the district courts, formed as a rule by 3 judges (in some cases one judge is sufficient); the courts of appeal are constituted of 3 and the High Court of 5 judges. All judges are appointed for life by the Sovereign (the judges of the High Court from a list prepared by the Second Chamber of the States-General). They can be removed only by a decision of the High Court.

At the district court the juvenile judge is specially appointed to try children's civil cases and at the same time charged with administration of justice for criminal actions committed by young persons between 12 and 18 years old, unless imprisonment of 6 months or more ought to be inflicted; such cases are tried by 3 judges.

Number of persons convicted including those who paid a fine to the public prosecutor to evade prosecution (tax offenders excluded):

Major offences	*1978*	*1979*	*1980*	*Minor offences*	*1979*	*1980*	*1981*
Males	56,608	58,299	62,750	Males	1,298,410	1,295,067	1,246,192
Females	4,226	4,345	4,809	Females	201,720	216,811	228,875

In addition, prosecution was evaded by paying a fine to the police in 1,206,142 cases in 1978, 1,159,025 in 1979, 55,406 in 1980 and 1,045,000 in 1981.

Police. There are both State and Municipal Police. The State Police, about 8,200 men strong, serves 640, and the Municipal Police, about 19,300 men strong, serves 140 municipalities. The State Police includes ordinary as well as water, mounted and motor police. The State Police Corps is under the jurisdiction of the Police Department of the Ministry of Justice, which also includes the Central Criminal Investigation Office, which deals with serious crimes throughout the country, and the International Criminal Investigation Office, which informs foreign countries of international crimes.

Religion. Entire liberty of conscience is granted to the members of all denominations. The royal family belong to the Dutch Reformed Church.

The number of adherents of the Churches according to the census of 1971 was: Dutch Reformed Church, 3,075,565; Reformed Churches (excluding other reformed denominations), 937,840; Roman Catholics, 5,273,665; other creeds (including other reformed denominations), 694,405; no religion, 3,078,640; total, 13,060,115.

The government of the Reformed Church is Presbyterian. On 1 July 1972 the Dutch Reformed Church had 1 synod, 11 provincial districts, 54 classes, 147 districts and 1,905 parishes.

Their clergy numbered 2,000. The Roman Catholic Church had, Jan. 1973, 1 archbishop (of Utrecht), 6 bishops and 1,815 parishes and rectorships. The Old Catholics had (1 July 1972) 1 archbishop (Utrecht), 2 bishops and 29 parishes. The Jews had, in 1970, 46 communities.

Education. Statistics for the scholastic year 1980–81:

	Full-time			*Part-time* [1]		
		Pupils			Pupils	
	Schools	*Total*	*Female*	*Schools*	*Total*	*Female*
Nursery schools	8,050	409,576	198,795	—	—	—
Primary Schools	8,727	1,333,342	658,509	—	—	—
Special schools	963	92,428	29,281	—	—	—
Secondary general schools	1,511	823,730	428,252	77	107,290	78,836
Secondary vocational schools:						
Junior—						
Technical, nautical	388	203,196	9,884	507	129,924	39,110
Agricultural	130	27,963	6,392	224	4,574	1,120
Domestic science	568	122,648	119,484	...	487	485
Other	207	48,915	27,748	14	819	9
Senior—						
Technical, nautical	122	58,557	3,538	54	5,646	182
Agricultural	48	13,174	1,906	25	2,031	39
Domestic science	196	40,267	38,458	18	3,045	2,975
Teachers' training (nursery schools)	50	7,190	7,119	50	3,493	3,476
Other	161	49,294	22,443	87	22,536	12,455
Third level non-university training:						
Technical, nautical	61	33,320	3,595	41	4,964	460
Agricultural	11	4,750	688	—	—	—
Arts	37	11,460	5,481	19	3,707	1,360
Teachers' training:						
Primary schools	91	15,091	9,266	127	18,271 [2]	16,038
Secondary general schools	32	22,076	10,511	96	29,792	15,808
Secondary vocational schools	3	74	10	20	5,124	153
Other	118	45,000	25,135	60	16,880	8,351

[1] Including apprenticeship schemes, young workers' educational institutes.
[2] Including 300 sex unknown.

Full-time: 1981–82 [1]

		Pupils	
	Schools	*Total*	*Female*
University education:			
Humanities	14	27,661	13,837
Social sciences		65,986	23,434
Natural sciences		15,029	3,006
Technical sciences		18,237	1,004
Medical sciences		17,814	5,562
Agricultural sciences		5,632	1,569

[1] Provisional figures.

Health. On 1 Jan. 1982 there were 28,037 doctors and about 69,600 licensed hospital beds.

DIPLOMATIC REPRESENTATIVES

Of the Netherlands in Great Britain (38 Hyde Park Gate, London, SW7 5DP)

Ambassador: Jan Louis Reinier Huydecoper van Nigtevecht, GCVO (accredited 3 March 1982).

Of Great Britain in the Netherlands (Lange Voorhout, 10, The Hague)
Ambassador: Philip Robert Aked Mansfield, CMG.

Of the Netherlands in the USA (4200 Linnean Ave., NW, Washington, D.C., 20008–3896)
Ambassador: Dr J. H. Lubbers.
Of the USA in the Netherlands (Lange Voorhout, 102, The Hague)
Ambassador: William J. Dyess.

Of the Netherlands to the United Nations
Ambassador: Hugo Scheltema.

Books of Reference

Statistical Information: The 'Centraal Bureau voor de Statistiek' at Voorburg, near The Hague, is the official Netherlands statistical service. *Director-General of Statistics:* Prof. Dr W. Begeer.

The Bureau was founded in 1899. Prior to that year, statistical publications were compiled by the 'Centrale commissie voor de statistiek', the 'Vereniging voor staathuishoudkunde en statistiek' and various government departments. These activities have gradually been taken over and co-ordinated by the Central Bureau, which now compiles practically all government statistics.

Its current publications include:

Statistical Yearbook of the Netherlands. From 1923/24 (preceded by *Jaarciifers voor het Koninkrijk der Nederlanden, 1898–1922);* latest issue, 1981
Statistisch zakboek (Pocket Year Book). From 1899/1924 (1 vol.); latest issue, 1981
CBS Select 1 (Statistical Essays), 1980
Maandstatistiek van de buitenlandse handel (monthly statistical bulletin of foreign trade). From 1917
Monografieën Volkstelling 1971. Nr. 1–18. From 1978
Nationale Rekeningen (National Accounts). From 1948–50; latest issue, 1981
Statistisch Magazine. From 1981
Statistische onderzoekingen. From 1977
Statistical Studies. From 1953

Other Official Publications

Central Economic Plan. Centraal Plan-bureau, The Hague (Dutch text), annually, from 1946
Netherlands. Organization for Economic Co-operation and Development. Paris, annual from 1964
Staatsalmanak voor het Koninkrijk der Nederlanden. Annual. The Hague, from 1814
Staatsblad van het Koninkrijk der Nederlanden. The Hague, from 1814
Staatscourant (State Gazette). The Hague, from 1813
Atlas van Nederland. Government Printing Office, The Hague, 1970 and supplements up to and including 1973
De Nederlandse Economie in 1980. Centraal Planbureau, The Hague, 1976
Memoranda on the Condition of the Netherlands State Finances. Ministry of Finance, The Hague, from 1906
Basic Guide to the Establishing of Industrial Operations in the Netherlands 1976. Ministry of Economic Affairs, The Hague, 1976
The Kingdom of the Netherlands. Ministry of Foreign Affairs, The Hague, Occasional
Huggett, F. E., *The Dutch Today.* Ministry of Foreign Affairs, The Hague, 1973.–*The Dutch Connection.* Ministry of Foreign Affairs, The Hague, 1982
Aspects of Dutch Agriculture. Ministry of Agriculture and Fisheries, The Hague, 1976

Non-Official Publications

Jansonius, H., *Groot Nederlands—Engels Woordenboek Voor Studie en Praktijk.* 3 vols. Leiden, 1972 (Vols. 1 and 2)
Newton, G., *The Netherlands: An Historical and Cultural Survey, 1795–1977.* Boulder, 1978
Pinder, D., *The Netherlands.* Folkestone, 1976
Veldman, J., *Agriculture in the Netherlands.* Utrecht, 1974
Pyttersen's Nederlandse Almanak. Zaltbommel, annual, from 1899
Commerce and Industry in the Netherlands. Amsterdam–Rotterdam Bank. Amsterdam, 1977
Foreign Investment in the Netherlands. The Hague, 1975

The Information You Need When Planning a Business in the Netherlands. Algemene Bank Nederland. Amsterdam, 1975
A Compact Geography of the Netherlands. Utrecht, 1980
De Economische Geschiedenis van Nederland. Groningen, 1977

National Library: De Koninklijke Bibliotheek, Prinz Willem Alexanderhof 5, The Hague. *Director:* Dr C. Reedijk.

THE NETHERLANDS ANTILLES
De Nederlandse Antillen

AREA AND POPULATION. The Netherlands Antilles are an integral part of the Netherlands and comprise two groups of islands, viz., the Leeward Islands, Curaçao, Aruba and Bonaire, and the Windward Islands, St Maarten, St Eustatius and Saba. The Leeward Islands are situated 40–70 miles north of the Venezuelan coast between 12° and 13° N. lat. and 68° and 71° W. long. The Windward group lies east of Puerto Rico. For the constitutional position of the Netherlands Antilles *see* p. 882. The total area is 993 sq. km (383 sq. miles) and the population was 265,000 in 1980.

Leeward group	*Sq. km*	*Population*	*Windward group*	*Sq. km*	*Population*
Curaçao	444	170,000	St Maarten (St Martin)[1]	34	17,000
Aruba	193	65,000	St Eustatius	21	1,500
Bonaire	288	9,500	Saba	13	1,000

[1] The southern part belongs to the Netherlands Antilles, the northern to France.

The capital is Willemstad on Curaçao, population (1970) 50,000.

In 1972, 4,941 births, 1,138 deaths, 1,471 marriages and 350 divorces were registered.

GOVERNMENT. Since Dec. 1954, the Netherlands Antilles have been fully autonomous in internal affairs, and constitutionally equal with the Netherlands and Surinam. The Sovereign of the Kingdom of the Netherlands is Head of the Government of the Netherlands Antilles and is represented by a Governor.

The executive power in internal affairs rests with the Governor and the Council of Ministers, who together form the Government. The Ministers are responsible to the unicameral legislature (*Staten*). This consists of 22 members (12 from Curaçao, 8 from Aruba, 1 from Bonaire, 1 from the Windward Islands) and is elected by general suffrage. It was agreed in 1977 that the 2 smallest islands, Saba and St Eustatius would each have a representative (non-voting) in the *Staten*.

The executive power in external affairs is vested in the Council of Ministers of the Kingdom, in which the Antilles is represented by a Minister Plenipotentiary with full voting powers.

In 1951 the Netherlands Antilles Islands Regulation provided for self-government of each of the 4 insular communities Aruba, Bonaire, Curaçao and the Windward Islands. The autonomous powers of the insular communities are divided between the Island Council (elected by general suffrage), the Executive Council and the Lieut.-Governor (*Gezaghebber*), who is responsible for maintaining public peace and order.

At the general election held on 25 June 1982, 6 of the 12 *Staten* seats in Curaçao were won by the *Movimiento Antijas Nobo,* 3 by the Democratic Party and 3 by the *Nationale Volkspartij-Unie;* of the 8 seats in Aruba, 5 were won by the *Movimiento Electoral di Puebla,* 2 by the *Arubaanse Volkspartij* and 1 by the *Partido Patriotico Arubano;* the 1 seat in Bonaire was won by the *Unión Patriotico Bonairiano* and the 1 seat in the Windward Islands by the Democratic Party. Following an earlier referendum, the government of the Netherlands announced on 28 Oct. 1981 that it had agreed that Aruba should at an early date proceed to independence separately from the other islands.

Governor: Dr B. M. Leito.

Prime Minister: Dominico F. Martina.
Deputy Prime Minister: Gualberto Hernández.

Flag: White, with a red vertical strip crossed by a blue horizontal strip bearing 6 white stars.

Dutch is the official language. Spanish and English are also spoken. In addition a 'lingua franca', *Papiamento* has evolved out of Spanish, Dutch and some other languages.

FINANCE. The central budget for 1972 envisaged 121,796,700 guilders revenue and 121,231,500 guilders expenditure.

The public debt was 252m. guilders as at 31 Dec. 1971.

The official rate of exchange was £1 = 2·63 *Antillian guilder*; US$1 = 1·80 *Antillian guilder* in March 1983.

ENERGY AND NATURAL RESOURCES

Oil. The economy of the Netherlands Antilles is almost entirely based on the refining of oil imported from Venezuela to Curaçao and Aruba. About 25% (Curaçao) and 30% (Aruba) of the gainfully occupied are working at the refineries or their shipping establishments. On account of the activities of the oil companies (affiliated to the Royal Dutch/Shell and the Standard Oil of New Jersey), the prosperity on Curaçao and Aruba is good in comparison with the other islands.

Minerals. About 100,000 tons of calcium phosphate are annually mined in Curaçao.

Agriculture. Livestock (1981): Cattle, 9,000; goats, 21,000; poultry, 122,000.

INDUSTRY AND TRADE

Industry. In Aruba there are some petrochemical factories; Curaçao has a paint factory, 2 cigarette factories, a textile factory, a brewery and some smaller industries. The Texas Instruments Co. and Electronic Fabriek have established electronic factories. Almost all products needed for consumption and production are imported, as the rocky soil permits little agriculture and local fishing is insufficient for home consumption. Bonaire has a textile factory and a modern-equipped salt plant. St Maarten has a rum factory and fishing is important. St Eustatius and Saba are of less economic importance.

Trade (1978). Total imports amounted to US$3,537m., total exports to US$3,035m.

Total trade between the Netherlands Antilles and UK (British Department of Trade returns, in £1,000 sterling):

	1978	*1979*	*1980*	*1981*	*1982*
Imports to UK	25,646	44,841	36,243	29,761	62,946
Exports and re-exports from UK	107,784	59,070	33,375	135,017	47,396

The Free-Zones Ordinance of 1956 has established free zones in the ports of Curaçao and Aruba.

Tourism. In 1981, 764,000 foreign tourists visited the Netherlands Antilles.

COMMUNICATIONS

Roads. In 1972, the Netherlands Antilles had 1,150 km of surfaced highway distributed as follows: Curaçao, 929; Aruba, 389; Bonaire, 125; St Maarten, 60. Number of motor vehicles (31 Dec. 1975): 41,955 in Curaçao, 15,393 in Aruba.

Shipping (1971). There entered the port of Curaçao, 5,333 vessels of 42m. gross tons; Aruba, 2,394 vessels of 34·8m. gross tons. Curaçao has a dry dock of 120,000 tons.

Post and Broadcasting. Number of telephones, 1 Jan. 1978, 49,633. Eight radio stations are operating on medium-waves from Curaçao, Aruba, Bonaire, and St Maarten. These stations broadcast in *Papiamento*, Dutch, English and Spanish and are mainly financed by income from advertisements. In addition, Radio Nederland and Trans World Radio have powerful relay stations operating on medium- and short-waves from Bonaire. There were (1975) 132,000 radio and 35,000 TV receivers.

Cinemas (1973). Curaçao and Aruba had 13 cinemas with a seating capacity of 11,000. There is a drive-in for 500 cars in Curaçao, for 200 cars in St Maarten and for 350 cars in Aruba.

RELIGION, EDUCATION AND WELFARE

Religion. In 1980, 82% of the population were Roman Catholics, 8% were Protestants.

Education (1972). Schools numbered 280, with 66,409 pupils and 2,516 teachers.

Health. In June 1973 there were 155 physicians, 55 specialists, 33 dentists and 18 pharmacists. In 1973, 11 hospitals had 2,037 beds.

DIPLOMATIC REPRESENTATIVE

USA Consul-General: Alta F. Fowler.

The British consulate closed on 1 Sept. 1976.

Books of Reference

Statistical Information: Statistical publications (on population, trade, cost of living, etc., are obtainable on request from the Statistical Office, Willemstad, Curaçao. *Statistical Jaarboek 1970* (text in Dutch, English and Spanish).

De West Indische Gids. The Hague. Monthly from 1919

Braam, H. L., *Hoe ons land geregeerd wordt.* Willemstad, 4th ed. 1972

Hartog, J., *Aruba.* Oranjestad, 1953.—*Bonaire.* Oranjestad, 1958.—*Curaçao.* Oranjestad, 1961

Nordlohne, E., *De Economisch-geographische Structuur der Benedenwindse Eilanden.* Rotterdam, 1951

Poll, W. van de, *De Nederlandse Antillen.* The Hague, 1950

Walle, J. van de, *De Nederlandse Antillen.* Willemstad, 1954

Westerman, J. H., *Overzicht van de geologische en mijnbouwkundige kennis der Nederlandse Antillen.* Amsterdam, 1949

NEW ZEALAND

Capital: Wellington
Population: 3·2m. (1982)
GNP per capita: US$7,090 (1980)

HISTORY. The first European to discover New Zealand was Tasman in 1642. The coast was explored by Capt. Cook in 1769. From about 1800 onwards, New Zealand became a resort for whalers and traders, chiefly from Australia. By the Treaty of Waitangi, in 1840, between Governor William Hobson and the representatives of the Maori race, the Maori chiefs ceded the sovereignty to the British Crown and the islands became a British colony. Then followed a steady stream of British settlers.

The Maoris are a branch of the Polynesian race, having emigrated from the eastern Pacific before and during the 14th century. Between 1845 and 1848, and between 1860 and 1870, misunderstandings over land led to war, but peace was permanently established in 1871, and the development of New Zealand has been marked by racial harmony and integration.

AREA AND POPULATION. New Zealand lies south-east of Australia in the south Pacific, Wellington being 1,233 miles from Sydney by sea. There are two principal islands, the North and South Islands, besides Stewart Island, Chatham Islands and small outlying islands, as well as the territories overseas (*see* pp. 911–13).

New Zealand (*i.e.*, North, South and Stewart Islands) extends over 1,750 km from north to south. Area, excluding territories overseas, 268,704 sq. km.; North Island, 11,469,000 hectares; South Island, 15,046,000 hectares; Stewart Island, 174,000 hectares; Chatham Islands, 96,000 hectares; minor islands, 82,900 hectares. Census population, exclusive of territories overseas:

	Total population	*Average annual increase %*		*Total population*	*Average annual increase %*
1858	115,462	—	1921	1,271,644	2·27
1874	344,984	—	1926	1,408,139	2·06
1878	458,007	7·33	1936	1,573,810	1·13
1881	534,030	5·10	1945[1]	1,702,298	0·83
1886	620,451	3·05	1951[1]	1,939,472	2·37
1891	668,632	1·50	1956[1]	2,174,062	2·31
1896	743,207	2·13	1961[1]	2,414,984	2·12
1901[1]	815,853	1·89	1966[1]	2,676,919	2·10
1906	936,304	2·75	1971[1]	2,862,631	1·34
1911	1,058,308	2·52	1976[1]	3,129,383	1·71
1916[1]	1,149,225	1·50	1981[1]	3,175,737	0·20

The census of New Zealand is quinquennial, but the census falling in 1931 was abandoned as an act of national economy, and owing to war conditions the census due in 1941 was not taken until 25 Sept. 1945.

[1] Excluding members of the Armed Forces overseas.

The areas and populations of statistical areas (with principal centres) at the Population Census, 24 March 1981 were as follows [1]:

Statistical area [2]	*Sq. km*	*Total population*
Northland (Whangarei)	12,649	114,295
Central Auckland (Auckland)	5,600	829,519
South Auckland—Bay of Plenty (Hamilton)	36,775	491,304
East Coast (Gisborne)	10,885	48,573
Hawke's Bay (Napier, Hastings)	11,303	147,222
Taranaki (New Plymouth)	9,720	105,153
Wellington (Wellington)	27,715	586,423
Total, North Island	*114,647*	*2,322,989*

[1] For statistical purposes, the 9 provincial districts have now been replaced by 13 statistical areas.
[2] Listed from north to south.

Statistical area [1]	*Sq. km*	*Total population*
Marlborough (Blenheim)	10,859	36,027
Nelson (Nelson)	18,046	77,223
Westland (Greymouth)	15,415	23,489
Canterbury (Christchurch)	43,371	424,280
Otago (Dunedin)	37,100	183,559
Southland (Invercargill)	29,624	108,170
Total, South Island	*155,415*	*852,748*
Total, New Zealand	269,062	3,175,737

[1] Listed from north to south.

New Zealand-born residents made up 85·4% of the population at the 1981 census. Foreign-born (provisional): UK, 253,810; Australia, 44,500; Netherlands, 21,630; Samoa, 26,180; Cook Islands, 14,370; USA, 5,430; Ireland, 6,970; others, 97,070.

Maori population: 1896, 42,113; 1936, 82,326; 1945, 98,744; 1951, 115,676; 1961, 171,553; 1971, 227,414; 1976, 270,035; 1981 (provisional), 280,380.

Populations of statistical divisions and main urban areas at the 1981 Census were as follows:

Auckland	829,519	Invercargill	53,868
Christchurch	321,720	Nelson	43,121
Dunedin	114,033	New Plymouth	44,095
Hamilton	160,215	Rotorua	48,314
Napier–Hastings	112,045	Tauranga	53,097
Palmerston North	91,821	Timaru	29,225
Wellington	343,982	Wanganui	39,595
Urban areas:		Whangarei	40,212
Gisborne	32,062		

Vital statistics for calendar years:

	Total live births	*Ex-nuptial births*	*Deaths*	*Marriages*	*Divorces (decrees absolute)*
1979	52,279	10,942	25,340	22,326	6,101
1980	50,542	10,857	26,676	22,981	6,493
1981	50,794	11,441	25,150	23,660	8,590

Birth rate, 1981, 16·09 per 1,000; death rate, 7·97 per 1,000; marriage rate, 7·5 per 1,000; infant mortality, 11·65 per 1,000 live births.

External migration (exclusive of crews and through passengers) for years ended 31 March:

	Arrivals	*Departures*		*Arrivals*	*Departures*
1977	667,224	683,494	1980	925,939	947,253
1978	715,780	737,936	1981	970,427	986,636
1979	805,876	832,420	1982	946,287	951,030

Population and Migration: Part B—External Migration. Dept. of Statistics, Wellington, Annually

CONSTITUTION AND GOVERNMENT. Definition was given the status of New Zealand by the (Imperial) Statute of Westminster of Dec. 1931, which had received the antecedent approval of the New Zealand Parliament in July 1931. The Governor-General's assent was given to the Statute of Westminster Adoption Bill on 25 Nov. 1947.

The powers, duties and responsibilities of the Governor-General and the Executive Council under the present system of responsible government are set out in Royal Letters Patent and Instructions thereunder of 11 May 1917, published in the *New Zealand Gazette* of 24 April 1919. In the execution of the powers vested in him the Governor-General must be guided by the advice of the Executive Council.

The following is a list of Governors-General, the title prior to June 1917 being Governor:

Earl of Liverpool	1917–20	Lord Norrie	1952–57
Viscount Jellicoe	1920–24	Viscount Cobham	1957–62
Sir Charles Fergusson, Bt	1924–30	Sir Bernard Fergusson	1962–67
Lord Bledisloe	1930–35	Sir Arthur Porrit, Bt	1967–72
Viscount Galway	1935–41	Sir Denis Blundell	1972–77
Sir Cyril Newall	1941–46	Sir Keith Holyoake	1977–80
Lord Freyberg, VC	1946–52	Sir David Beattie	1980–

National flag: The British Blue Ensign with 4 stars of the Southern Cross in red, edged in white, in the fly.

National anthems: God Save the Queen; God Defend New Zealand (words by Thomas Bracken, music by John J. Woods).

Since Nov. 1977 both 'God Save the Queen' and 'God Defend New Zealand' have equal status as national anthems.

Parliament consists of the House of Representatives, the former Legislative Council having been abolished since 1 Jan. 1951.

The statute law on elections and the life of Parliament is contained in the Electoral Act, 1956. In 1974 the voting age was reduced from 20 to 18 years.

The House of Representatives from Nov. 1978 consists of 92 members, including 4 members representing Maori electorates, elected by the people for 3 years. The 4 Maori electoral districts cover the whole country and adult Maoris of half or more Maori descent are the electors. From 1976 a descendant of a Maori is entitled to register either for a general or a Maori electoral district. Women's suffrage was instituted in 1893: women became eligible as members of the House of Representatives in 1919. The House in 1982 included 8 women members.

During Parliamentary sittings the proceedings of the House are broadcast regularly on sound radio.

House of Representatives as composed following the General Election in Nov. 1981: National Party, 47; Labour, 43; Social Credit, 2.

The Executive Council was composed as follows in Jan. 1983:

Governor-General and C.-in-C.: The Hon. Sir David Beattie, GCMG, GCVO (from Oct. 1980).

Prime Minister, Finance, Legislative Department, Audit Department, Security Intelligence Service: Robert Muldoon.

Deputy Prime Minister, Agriculture and Fisheries, Rural Bank: Duncan MacIntyre.

Minister of State, Leader of the House of Representatives, Defence, State Services, War Pensions, Rehabilitation: David Thomson.

Energy, National Development, Regional Development: William Birch.

Labour: James Bolger.

Transport, Railways, Civil Aviation and Meteorological Services: George Gair.

Trade and Industry: Hugh Templeton.

Foreign Affairs, Overseas Trade: Warren Cooper.

Attorney-General and Justice: James McLay.

Housing, Works and Development: Anthony Friedlander.

Social Welfare, Public Trust Office, Government Printing Office: Venn Young.

Internal Affairs, Local Government, Arts, Recreation and Sport, Civil Defence: Allan Highet.

Education: Mervyn Wellington.

Maori Affairs and Police: Benjamin Couch.

Health and Immigration: Anthony Malcolm.

Environment, Science and Technology, Broadcasting: Dr Ian Shearer.

Postmaster-General, Tourism and Publicity: Rob Talbot.

Lands, Forests, Valuation: Jonathan Elworthy.

Inland Revenue, Friendly Societies, Statistics, Associate Minister of Finance: John Falloon.

Customs, Government Life Insurance, State Insurance Office, Earthquake and War Damage Commission, Associate Minister of Trade and Industry: Kenneth Allen.

The Prime Minister (provided with residence) had in 1982 a salary of NZ$79,717 plus a tax-free expense allowance of $14,000 per annum; Ministers with portfolio, $55,115 plus a tax-free expense allowance of $5,750 (Minister of Foreign Affairs $10,750) per annum; Minister without portfolio, $44,572 plus a tax-free expense allowance of $4,500 per annum; Parliamentary Under-Secretaries, $42,814 plus an expense allowance of $4,500 per annum. In addition, Ministers and Parliamentary Under-Secretaries not provided with residence at the seat of Government receive $600 per annum house allowance. An allowance of $58 per day while travelling within New Zealand on public service is payable to Ministers.

The Speaker of the House of Representatives receives $51,161 plus an expense allowance of $7,100 per annum in addition to his electorate allowance, and residential quarters in Parliament House, and the Leader of the Opposition $55,115 plus expense allowance of $5,750 per annum, and allowances for travelling and housing.

Members were paid $32,271 per annum, plus an expense allowance varying from $4,500 to $9,250 according to the area of electorate represented.

There is a compulsory contributory superannuation scheme for members; retiring allowances are payable to a member after 9 years' service and the attainment of 50 years of age.

Dollimore, H. N., *The Parliament of New Zealand and Parliament House.* 3rd ed. Wellington, 1973
Milne, R. S., *Political Parties in New Zealand.* OUP, 1966
Scott, K. J., *The New Zealand Constitution.* OUP, 1962

Local Government. For purposes of local government New Zealand is divided into counties, district councils, boroughs and town districts. Some counties are subdivided into ridings. There are also numerous other local authorities created for specific functions, such as electric-power districts, river (*i.e.*, river protection) districts, pest destruction districts, etc.

DEFENCE. The control and co-ordination of defence activities is obtained through the Ministry of Defence. This is a unitary department combining not only all joint-Service functions but also the former Departments of Army, Navy and Air.

Army. The Chief of the General Staff commands the Army, assisted by the General Staff and the staffs of Defence Headquarters. A regular force battalion is stationed in Singapore.

Regular personnel, in 1983, totalled 5,675 all ranks; territorial personnel totalled 5,934; the cadet corps totalled (1981) 3,399 Army School cadets.

Navy. The Royal New Zealand Navy is administered by the Chief of Naval Staff and the Deputy Chief of Naval Staff at Defence Headquarters.

The RNZN ships include 6 frigates (including *Bacchante* and *Dido* transferred from the Royal Navy in 1982 and 1983 respectively), 1 surveying vessel, 4 patrol craft, 5 old harbour defence motor launches, 2 survey boats, 1 oceanographic research ship, 1 tug and 1 tender.

Personnel, in 1983, totalled 3,000 officers and ratings and 450 in the naval reserve.

Air Force. The Chief of Air Staff and Air Officer Commanding the RNZAF exercises command and administration of the RNZAF. Operational units of the RNZAF comprise a utility helicopter support unit (UH-1H Iroquois) based in Singapore as part of the NZ force, South-east Asia; maritime (P-3B Orion), long and medium-range transport (Boeing 727, C-130H Hercules, Andover, F.27 Friendship) and helicopter (Sioux, Iroquois, Wasp) squadrons based at RNZAF Base Auckland; and offensive support (A-4K Skyhawk) and medium-range transport/communications squadrons (Andover, F.27 Friendship), Cessna 421 at RNZAF Base Ohakea. Flying training units (Airtrainer, Strikemaster, TA-4K Skyhawks, Sioux) are located at RNZAF Bases Wigram and Ohakea; ground training is carried out at RNZAF Bases Auckland, Woodbourne and Wigram.

The strength in 1982 was 4,395 regular personnel, 1,197 reserves.

INTERNATIONAL RELATIONS

Membership. New Zealand is a member of UN, the Commonwealth, OECD and the Colombo Plan.

ECONOMY

Budget. The following tables of revenue and expenditure relate to the Consolidated Account, which covers the ordinary revenue and expenditure of the general government—*i.e.*, apart from capital items, commercial and special undertakings, advances, etc. Revenue in the Account (in NZ$1m.) was as follows:

Year ended 31 March	*Customs and excise*	*Sales tax*	*Income tax*	*Other taxes*	*Trading profits and departmental receipts*	*Interest*	*Total*
1979	345·0	449·7	3,655·2	380·2	371·6[1]	450·3	5,652·2
1980	389·8	624·1	4,465·6	401·0	418·8	539·0	6,838·3
1981	413·6	775·6	5,298·9	373·4	493·1	597·8	7,952·4
1982	549·4	1,084·1	6,514·7	438·3	592·5	664·4	9,843·4

[1] Includes amounts previously recorded in the Works Trading Account.

Expenditure from Consolidated Account, year ended 31 March, was as follows (in NZ$1m.):

	Debt services	*Social services* [1]	*Industrial development*	*Defence*	*Total (including other)*
1979	670·2	3,809·4 [2]	779·8 [2]	299·5	6,512·8
1980	825·6	4,353·8	814·2	346·1	7,529·1
1981	999·9	5,296·7	999·7	455·9	8,992·5
1982	1,327·2	6,205·9	1,337·4	593·6	11,124·9

[1] Includes education, health and social welfare.
[2] Includes amounts previously recorded in the Works Trading Account.

Taxation receipts in 1981–82 for all purposes amounted to $8,798m., giving an average of $2,782 per head of mean population. Included in the total taxation is $211·6m. National Roads Fund taxation. The estimate for 1982–83 is $10,230m., the total being inclusive of an estimated $230m. of National Roads Fund taxation.

The gross public debt at 31 March 1982 was $14,381m., of which $8,832m. was held in New Zealand, $4,503m. in London, Europe and Asia, $1,029m. in USA and $16m. with the World Bank. The gross annual interest charge on the public debt at 31 March 1982 was $1,202,928.

New Zealand System of National Accounts. This replaces the National Income and Expenditure Accounts which have been produced since 1948. National Accounts aggregates for 4 years are given in the following table (in NZ$1m.):

Year ended 31 March	*Gross domestic product*	*Gross national product*	*National income*
1978	15,217	14,880	13,682
1979	17,541	17,121	15,791
1980	20,966	20,513	19,034
1981	24,127	23,615	21,965

Currency. The monetary unit is the New Zealand *dollar*, divided into 100 *cents*. In March 1983, £1 = 2·258NZ$; US$1 = 1·534NZ$.

Banking. The Reserve Bank is the sole note-issuing authority. Six denominations of Reserve Bank notes are issued: NZ$1, 2, 5, 10, 20, 100.

The New Zealand banking system comprises a central bank, the Reserve Bank of New Zealand, and 5 commercial or trading banks. There are also 12 trustee savings banks and the Post Office Savings Bank, while each trading bank has a private savings bank subsidiary. In addition, a number of trading companies, investment societies, etc., perform quasi-banking functions, accepting deposits and granting credits to clients.

The primary functions of the Reserve Bank are to act as the central bank, to advise the Government on matters relating to monetary policy, banking and overseas exchange, and to give effect to the monetary policy of the Government.

Of the 5 trading banks 3 are primarily Australian concerns, 1 until recently had its head office in London and the Bank of New Zealand has been state owned since 1 Nov. 1945.

At the end of March 1982 the amount on deposit at trading banks was NZ$7,279·8m., while advances amounted to NZ$5,987·2m. The weekly average of bank debits for 1981 was $4,185m. excluding government.

The number of accounts with the post office savings bank at 31 March 1982 was 3·11m.; amount deposited during year ended March 1982, $4,066m.; withdrawn, $4,025m., total amount to credit of depositors at end of year, $1,955m. At 31 March 1982, $2,267m. was on deposit in Trustee Savings Banks to the credit of 2·8m. depositors. The amount to the credit of depositors with savings accounts in the trading banks was $1,057m. at 31 March 1982.

Weights and Measures. Conversion to the metric system of weights and measures has been completed.

ENERGY AND NATURAL RESOURCES

Electricity. The general policy of the Government in regard to electric power is to supply power in bulk, leaving the reticulation and retail supply in the hands of local authorities; some of these are cities and boroughs but most are electric power boards. Hydro energy provides over 87% of the national electricity supply, the balance coming from coal, oil, natural gas and geothermal energy. The last is obtained from Wairakei in the thermal region; natural steam is used to drive the turbines.

The transmission systems of the North and South Islands are linked by a high-voltage direct-current transmission and 40 km of submarine cable in Cook Strait.

Principal statistics for 4 years ended 31 March are:

	1978	*1979*	*1980*	*1981*
Number of establishments	80	81	79	81
Generators (capacity) AC (1,000 kw.)	5,633	5,623	5,860	6,018
Units generated (1m. kwh.)	21,268	21,693	21,607	22,111
Revenue ($1,000)	743,509	804,974	1,154,206	1,276,853
Expenditure:				
Operating ($1,000)	432,189	446,435	580,000	666,419
Management, etc. ($1,000)	70,027	82,519	96,933	118,898
Capital charges ($1,000)	183,155	226,277	266,611	299,756
Capital outlay:				
During year ($1,000)	355,600	382,000	350,500	370,700
To date ($1,000)	2,733,900	3,087,000	3,414,200	3,359,100

Natural Gas. Resources discovered in the Taranaki area of the North Island in 1961 are now supplying gas for household use to North Island cities including Auckland and Wellington. The much larger Maui offshore gasfield was discovered in 1969 and is at present being developed.

Minerals. New Zealand's production of minerals in 1980 included 200 kg of gold, 3,000 tonnes of bentonite, 130,700 tonnes of clay for bricks, tiles, etc., 46,100 tonnes of potters' clays, 3,389,500 tonnes of iron sand, 1,581,400 tonnes of limestone for agriculture and 172,500 tonnes of limestone for industry, 1,388,600 tonnes of limestone, marl, etc., for cement, 13,500 tonnes of pumice, 80,900 tonnes of serpentine, 135,900 tonnes of silica sand. Mineral fuel production amounted to 2,128,700 tonnes of coal, 418,941 cu. metres of petroleum condensate and 1,069·05m. cu. metres of natural gas. Salt produced by the solar evaporation of sea water amounted to 5,500 tonnes. Mineral production for the year was valued at $153·7m.

Agriculture. Two-thirds of the surface of New Zealand is suitable for agriculture and grazing. The total area under cultivation at 30 June 1979 was 10,584,463 hectares (including residential area and domestic orchards). There were 9,778,103 hectares of sown pasture, including areas sown with crops, and 806,360 hectares of timber plantations. The area of Crown lands (other than reserves) leased under various tenures at 31 March 1981 was 5,589,606 hectares.

The largest freehold estates are held in the South Island. The extent of occupied holdings as at 30 June 1979 (exclusive of holdings within borough boundaries) was as follows:

Size of holdings (hectares)	*Number*	*Aggregate area (hectares)*	*Size of holdings (hectares)*	*Number*	*Aggregate area (hectares)*
Under 5	6,903	20,927	400–799	4,370	2,392,742
5–19	10,481	105,091	800–999	816	723,685
20–39	6,673	192,012	1,000–1,199	478	524,104
40–79	12,885	739,143	1,200–1,999	943	1,440,523
80–99	4,491	396,640	2,000–3,999	595	1,633,744
100–149	7,001	856,640	4,000 and over	592	8,766,813
150–199	4,792	830,318			
200–299	6,299	1,529,365	Total	70,452	21,231,289
300–399	3,133	1,079,542			

The area and yield for each of the principal crops are given as follows (area and yield for threshing only, not including that grown for chaff, hay, silage, etc.):

	Wheat		*Maize*		*Barley*	
Crop years	*Area (1,000 hectares)*	*Yield (1,000 tonnes)*	*Area (1,000 hectares)*	*Yield (1,000 tonnes)*	*Area (1,000 hectares)*	*Yield (1,000 tonnes)*
1979	87·2	295·0	22·3	179·0	77·5	263·6
1980	86·0	305·8	19·4	156·5	66·5	228·3

Private air companies are carrying out such aerial work as top-dressing, spraying and crop-dusting, seed-sowing, rabbit poisoning, aerial photography and surveying, and dropping supplies to deer cullers and dropping fencing materials in remote areas. In 1980 a total area of 6,485,500 hectares was top-dressed with fertilizer and lime; 2,336,400 tonnes by ground spread and 1,260,200 by air.

Livestock at 30 June 1981: 8,112,000 cattle, 70m. sheep and (1980) 434,000 pigs. Total meat produced in the year ended 30 Sept. 1981 was estimated at 1·2m. tonnes (including 480,800 tonnes of beef and 425,700 tonnes of lamb). Total liquid milk produced in the year ended 31 May 1981 was 6,356m. litres.

Production of wool for 1980–81, 381,000 tonnes (greasy basis).

Agricultural Statistics. Dept. of Statistics, Wellington. Annual.
New Zealand Agriculture. Ministry of Agriculture and Fisheries, Wellington, 1974
Allsop, F., *The First Fifty Years of New Zealand's Forest Service.* Wellington, 1973
Evans, B. L., *A History of Agricultural Production and Marketing.* Palmerston North, 1969
Levy, E. B., *Grasslands of New Zealand.* Wellington, 1970

Forestry. Of the 6·2m. hectares of indigenous forest only about 1m. hectares are merchantable; they are being depleted at the rate of 5,000 hectares a year (although the rate of cutting is diminishing) and mainly for sawn timber. There are about 740,000 hectares of productive exotic forest, and this produces far more timber than the indigenous forests. Introduced conifer pines form the bulk of the large exotic forest estate and among these radiata pine is the best multi-purpose tree, reaching saw-log size in 25–30 years. Other major species are Douglas fir, Corsican pine and ponderosa pine. The table below shows production of rough sawn timber in cu. metres for years ending 31 March:

	Indigenous			*Exotic*			*All Species*
	Rimu and Miro	*Beech*	*Total*	*Exotic Pines*	*Douglas Fir*	*Total*	*Total*
1978–79	152,481	18,716	207,899	1,478,838	131,562	1,657,582	1,865,481
1979–80	137,036	23,061	195,073	1,608,894	163,454	1,815,420	2,010,493
1980–81	121,971	19,280	175,101	1,798,060	168,025	2,007,245	2,182,346

Forest industries consist of 377 saw-mills, 9 plywood and veneer plants, 3 particle board mills, 7 pulp and paper mills and 2 fibreboard mills.

The basic products of the pulp and paper mills are mechanical and chemical pulp which are converted into newsprint, kraft and other papers, paperboard and fibreboard. Production of woodpulp, 31 March 1981, amounted to 1·2m. tonnes and of paper (including newsprint paper and paperboard) to 724,000 tonnes.

Fisheries. The total value of New Zealand Fisheries exports during the year ended 30 June 1981 was $168·1m., an increase of $43·5m. (34·9%) over the previous year.

	Exports, 1980		*Exports, 1981*	
	Quantity kg (1,000)	*Value $ (1,000)*	*Quantity kg (1,000)*	*Value $ (1,000)*
Finfish or wetfish	58,263	62,854	86,590	101,552
Rock lobster	2,259	28,351	2,527	31,879
Shellfish (squid, mussels, oysters, etc)	24,792	33,392	30,858	34,683
Total	85,314	124,597	119,974	168,113

INDUSTRY AND TRADE

Industry. Major industrial developments in recent years have included the establishment of an oil refinery, an iron and steel industry using New Zealand iron sands and an aluminium smelter using hydro-electric power.

Statistics of manufacturing industries for 3 years:

Production year	*Persons engaged*	*Salaries and wages paid (NZ$1,000)*	*Cost of materials (NZ$1,000)*	*Value of production (NZ$1,000)*	*Net output (net value added) (NZ$1,000)*
1976–77	306,177	1,801,717	6,381,347	8,987,242	2,865,278
1978–79	298,331	2,293,756	7,595,457	10,925,685	3,478,002

The following is a statement of the provisional value of the products (including repairs) of the principal industries for the year 1976–77 (in NZ$1,000):

Industry group	*Value of production*
Food manufacturing	2,366,961
Beverages	185,706
Tobacco manufactures	66,305
Textiles	439,285
Wearing apparel	259,994
Fur and leather	82,818
Footwear (except rubber, plastic or wooden)	74,245
Wood and cork products	457,358
Furniture	144,236
Paper and paper products	594,180
Printing and publishing	318,112
Industrial chemicals	316,758
Other chemical products	256,321
Petroleum refineries	53,105
Petroleum and coal products	14,917
Rubber products	140,846
Plastic products not elsewhere specified	150,470
Pottery, china and earthenware	15,433
Glass and products	69,345
Other non-metallic mineral products	270,370
Iron and steel	201,258
Non-ferrous metal	157,076
Metal products (except machinery and equipment)	704,584
Machinery (except electrical)	386,108
Electrical machinery, apparatus, appliances and supplies	458,009
Transport equipment	569,415
Measuring and controlling equipment, etc.	21,488
Other manufacturing industries	81,762
Total	8,856,465

Census of Manufacturing. Dept. of Statistics, Wellington. Annual

Labour. In Dec. 1981 there were 258 industrial unions of workers with a total of 519,705 members.

The industrial distribution of the labour force as estimated in Sept. 1981 was: Primary industries, 146,700; manufacturing, 303,800; construction, 87,300; commerce, 320,000; transport and communication, 109,900; services, 297,600; armed forces, 10,700; unemployed, 49,400; total labour force, 1,325,400.

By the Accident Compensation Act 1972 immediate compensation without proof of fault is provided for every injured person and wherever the accident occurred. Compensation is paid both for permanent physical disability and also—in the case of earners—for income losses on an income related basis. Regular adjustment in the level of payment is provided for in accordance with variations in the value of money. Non-earners such as tourists, housewives, children, students, retired people do not normally qualify for earnings related compensation but are eligible for all other benefits. These are not taxable. Housewives—including visiting women from overseas—who are non-earners are eligible for the benefits available to non-earners and home help can be paid for or the husband compensated for loss of earnings while he is looking after the home until the injured wife can resume her duties.

After the first week's incapacity and for the ensuing 4 weeks the earner can be paid 80% of his average earnings for the 28 days preceding the accident; after that the 80% is related to average earnings over the 12 preceding months. In addition—for earners—lump sums are payable for impairment, pain and disfigurement and for funeral expenses and weekly sums and lump payments to their widows and dependent children. All employees are covered by the Accident Compensation Act 1972.

Commerce. Trade (excluding specie and bullion) in NZ$1,000 for 12 months ended 30 June:

	Total merchandise imported (v.f.d.)[1]	*Exports of domestic produce*	*Re-exports*	*Total merchandise exported (f.o.b.)*
1978–79	3,574,139	3,945,961	121,417	4,067,378
1979–80	4,809,625	5,012,453	139,759	5,152,212
1980–81	5,587,323	5,830,031	235,245	6,065,277
1981–82	6,907,719	6,594,275	313,127	6,907,402

[1] Value for duty.

The principal imports for the 12 months ended 30 June 1982 (provisional):

Commodity	*Value (NZ$1,000) (c.i.f.)*
Cereals and cereal preparations	27,232
Fruit and vegetables	100,558
Sugar and sugar preparations	63,285
Coffee, tea, cocoa, spices, etc.	56,028
Beverages	48,649
Tobacco and manufactures	24,694
Crude rubber	35,791
Textile fibres	25,529
Crude fertilizers and minerals other than coal	152,214
Petroleum and petroleum products	1,356,329
Organic chemicals	148,944
Inorganic chemicals	108,716
Dyeing, tanning, etc. materials	45,322
Medicinal and pharmaceutical products	121,665
Fertilizers, manufactured	80,939
Plastic materials, etc.	241,425
Miscellaneous chemical materials and products	80,069
Rubber manufactures [1]	55,972
Paper and paperboard manufactures	100,819
Textile yarn and fabrics, etc.	460,943
Non-metallic mineral manufactures [1]	101,837
Iron and steel	426,676
Non-ferrous metals	125,984
Manufactures of metals	180,848
General industrial machinery	321,711
Electric machinery	261,778
Road vehicles	746,874
Professional scientific instruments	122,600
Miscellaneous manufactured articles [1]	266,196
Total merchandise imported [2]	7,463,243

[1] Not elsewhere specified. [2] Including commodities not listed.

The principal exports of New Zealand produce for the 12 months ended 30 June 1982 (provisional) were:

Commodity	*Value (NZ$1,000)*	*Commodity*	*Value (NZ$1,000)*
Meat		Dairy products	
Beef and veal	619,067	Fresh milk and cream	12,659
Lamb	707,104	Butter	557,068
Mutton	146,363	Cheese	175,707
Edible offals	65,221	Fish	229,957
		Cereals and cereal preparations	18,447

Commodity	*Value (NZ$1,000)*	*Commodity*	*Value (NZ$1,000)*
Apples	50,741	Newsprint	110,642
Animal feeding stuff	57,923	Textile yarn	46,315
Wood and cork	107,546	Carpets	53,377
Pulp and waste paper	155,274	Aluminium	205,825
Wool	918,832	Metal manufactures	89,994
Sausage casings (hanks)	48,574	General industrial machinery	54,392
Tallow	52,989	Electric machinery, etc.	83,280
Casein	176,172	Total produce exported	6,594,275

The following table shows the trade with different countries for the year ended 30 June (in NZ$1,000):

Countries	*Imports v.f.d. from* 1981[1]	1982[1]	*Exports and re-exports f.o.b. to* 1981[1]	1982[1]
Australia	1,043,634	1,365,584	798,687	1,028,962
Bahrain	61,787	92,781	8,093	9,753
Belgium	22,559	40,562	45,369	53,452
Canada	125,386	149,099	132,209	128,204
China	34,981	47,930	172,804	122,704
Fiji	22,009	22,539	86,533	91,763
France	48,380	72,771	94,756	106,960
Germany (Fed. Rep. of)	160,522	280,640	133,826	122,268
Greece	1,248	2,551	50,099	49,378
Hong Kong	59,902	90,149	80,492	94,963
India	24,870	33,853	29,673	60,781
Iran	136	166	243,073	103,506
Italy	60,462	86,799	83,270	112,130
Japan	827,839	1,199,587	784,336	873,340
Korea, Republic of	37,084	52,974	57,488	102,217
Kuwait	69,451	31,437	6,581	13,464
Malaysia	24,580	36,510	85,106	101,818
Netherlands	57,916	76,739	94,171	89,616
Philippines	4,859	8,351	80,506	98,938
Saudi Arabia	286,710	273,622	49,157	50,754
Singapore	311,580	278,809	98,478	97,277
Sweden	41,782	58,857	4,450	5,495
UK	585,087	634,464	760,028	960,608
USSR	11,595	9,018	222,416	347,651
USA	979,271	1,094,153	767,061	850,049

[1] Provisional.

Total trade between New Zealand and UK was as follows (British Department of Trade returns, in £1,000 sterling):

	1979	*1980*	*1981*	*1982*
Imports to UK	415,432	414,630	427,174	539,137
Exports and re-exports from UK	314,354	250,413	253,373	323,201

Tourism. The country has a growing tourist industry. In the year ended 31 March 1982, 472,581 travellers visited New Zealand (including 357,138 tourists), compared with 463,456 (including 348,960 tourists) in 1981.

COMMUNICATIONS

Roads. Total length of formed roads and streets in New Zealand at 31 March 1978 was 96,525 km. There were 13,297 bridges of over 3 metres in length with a total length of 300,497 metres at 31 March 1978. The network of state highways comprised, at 31 March 1978, 10,677 km, including the principal arterial traffic routes.

Total expenditure on roads, streets and bridges by the central government and local authorities combined for the financial year 1981–82 amounted to $247·53m.

In the main, roads are financed from the National Roads Fund which is administered by the National Roads Board. This fund which is derived largely from petrol tax is used for the maintenance and improvement of existing roads. The board's income is currently of the order of $251m. per annum, and is apportioned according to fixed percentages, with 50% allocated to state highways, 23% to counties and 16% to municipalities. These sector percentages have been varied twice in the last 10 years in the light of changing needs.

At 31 March 1981 motor vehicles licensed numbered 2,220,990, of which 1,232,963 were cars, 4,810 omnibuses and contract vehicles, 264,548 goods service vehicles. Included in the remaining numbers were 137,063 motor cycles, 1,748 power cycles and 89,435 farm tractors, road graders, etc.

Railways. On 31 March 1982 there were 4,418 km of 1,067 mm gauge railway open for traffic. Operating earnings from government railways, 1981–82, $399,334,928; operating expenses, $459,299,850. In 1981–82 the tonnage of goods (including livestock) carried was 11,520,401 tonnes, and passengers numbered 14,339,907. In addition, the railways road motor services carried 17·9m. passengers. Four rail/road ferries maintain a regular service between the North and South Islands.

The total revenue (including road motor and other subsidiary services) amounted to $507,347,328, and total expenditure $563,977,581 in 1981–82.

Aviation. International services are operated to and from New Zealand by a state-owned company, Air New Zealand Ltd, and by a number of overseas companies. Air New Zealand Ltd also operates most domestic scheduled passenger services. Non-scheduled services are run by the main companies and also by a number of small operators and aero clubs.

Domestic scheduled services during the 12 months ended Dec. 1981: Passengers carried, 2,356,000. International services: Passengers carried, 1,776,000; mail, 3,016 tonnes; freight, 64,042 tonnes.

Shipping. Container ships operate from Auckland, Wellington, Lyttelton and Port Chalmers to the UK, Europe, North America and Japan. The government-owned New Zealand Shipping Corporation has begun to increase its activity into New Zealand—UK and Pacific trades.

Entrances and clearances of vessels from overseas:

	Entrances		*Clearances*	
	No.	*Tons*	*No.*	*Tons*
1977	3,400	22,317,000	3,409	22,296,000
1978	3,251	23,134,000	3,261	23,186,000
1979	3,438	25,199,000	3,433	25,313,000

Post and Broadcasting. Receipts of the Post Office for year ended 31 March 1982 were $816·5m.; total expenditure was $740·4m. Personnel numbered 39,279.

The telegraph and telephone systems are operated by the Post Office. At 31 March 1982 there were 1,875,538 telephones. The telecommunications receipts for the year 1981–82 were $609·7m.

An earth satellite station has been built north of Auckland to link with the Pacific satellite Intelsat III to augment the Compac and Seacon telecommunications systems which link New Zealand with overseas countries.

There are 2 TV channels both operated by the state-owned New Zealand Broadcasting Corporation, which also operates most of the broadcasting stations. Over 85% of New Zealand households have TV sets. There are 65 medium-wave broadcasting stations and 2 short-wave transmitters. Some commercial material is broadcast by both sound and TV services. Number of TV receiving licences at 31 March 1982 was 913,837.

Cinemas. There were in 1975, 203 cinemas with a seating capacity of 119,000.

Newspapers. There were (1979), 32 daily newspapers (8 morning and 24 evening) with a combined circulation of 1,043,000. Seven of these newspapers (2 each in Auckland, Wellington and Christchurch and 1 in Dunedin) had a circulation of 718,000.

JUSTICE, RELIGION, EDUCATION AND WELFARE

Justice. The judiciary consists of the Court of Appeal, the High Court and District Courts. All exercise both civil and criminal jurisdiction. Other special courts include the Maori Land Court, Family Courts and Young Persons' Courts. At the end of Dec. 1981 the gaols and Borstal institutions contained 2,464 prisoners, 2,374 males and 90 females. The death penalty for murder was replaced by life imprisonment in 1961.

The Criminal Injuries Act, 1963, which came into force on 1 Jan. 1964, provided for compensation of persons injured by certain criminal acts and the dependants of persons killed by such acts. However, this has now been phased out in favour of the Accident Compensation Act, 1972, except in the residual area of property damage caused by escapers. Since 1970 legal aid in civil proceedings (except divorce) has been available for persons of small or moderate means. For the year ended 31 March 1982 expenditure amounted to $3,452,615 and 7,441 applications for aid were granted.

Police. The police in New Zealand are a national body maintained wholly by the central government. The total strength at 31 March 1981 was 4,946, the proportion of police to population being 1 to 699. The total cost of police services for the year 1979–80 was NZ$111m., equivalent to $36 per head of population. In New Zealand the police do not control traffic.

Ombudsmen. The office of Ombudsman was created in 1962. From 1975 additional Ombudsmen have been authorized. There are currently three. Ombudsmen's functions are to investigate complaints from members of the public relating to administrative decisions of government departments, local authorities and statutory organizations.

During the year ended 31 March 1982, 1,986 complaints were received, 94 of which were sustained.

Religion. No direct state aid is given to any form of religion. For the Church of England the country is divided into 7 dioceses, with a separate bishopric (Aotearoa) for the Maoris. The Presbyterian Church is divided into 23 presbyteries and the Maori Synod. The Moderator is elected annually. The Methodist Church is divided into 10 districts; the President is elected annually. The Roman Catholic Church is divided into 4 dioceses, with the Archbishop of Wellington as Metropolitan Archbishop.

Religious denomination	*Number of clergy (April 1977)*	*Number of adherents 1976 census*	*1981 census*[1]
Church of England	780	915,202	817,110
Presbyterian	686	566,569	531,440
Roman Catholic (including 'Catholic' undefined)	931	478,530	453,440
Methodist	349	173,526	150,480
Baptist	254	49,442	50,860
Brethren	187	24,414	...
Ratana	142	35,082	34,370
Protestant (undefined)	—	33,309	...
Salvation Army	241	22,019	...
Church of Christ	54	8,087	...
Latter-day Saints (Mormon)	162	36,130	37,750
Congregationalist	10	6,600	...
Seventh-day Adventist	55	11,958	...
Ringatu	88	6,230	...
Christian (undefined)	—	52,478	...
Christian Scientist	—	583	...
Jehovah's Witnesses	125	13,392	...
Hebrew	7	3,921	...
Lutheran	15	6,297	...
All other religious professions	—	106,512	357,080
Object to state	—	438,511	470,610
No religion (so returned) and not specified	—	140,591	277,060
Total	4,712	3,129,383	3,180,190

[1] Provisional.

Education. New Zealand has 6 universities, the University of Auckland, University of Waikato (at Hamilton), Victoria University of Wellington, Massey University (at Palmerston North), the University of Canterbury (at Christchurch) and the University of Otago (at Dunedin). There is, in addition, Lincoln College near Christchurch, a university college of agriculture, which is a constituent college of the University of Canterbury. The number of students in 1981 was 52,988. There were 8 teachers' training colleges with 5,901 students in 1981.

At 1 July 1981 there were 271 state secondary schools with 12,217 full-time teachers and 192,788 pupils. There were also 34 district high schools with 2,639 scholars in the secondary division. At 1 July 1981, 103,700 part-time pupils attended technical classes, and 30,091 received part-time instruction from the technical correspondence institute. At 1 July 1981, 989 pupils received tuition from the secondary department of the correspondence school. There were 66 registered private secondary schools with 1,705 teachers and 27,980 pupils.

At 1 July 1981, there were 2,517 state primary schools (including intermediate schools and departments), with 454,414 pupils; the number of teachers was 19,350. A correspondence school for children in remote areas and those otherwise unable to attend school had 1,353 primary pupils. There were 279 registered private primary schools with 1,588 teachers and 38,997 pupils.

Education is compulsory between the ages of 6 and 15. Children aged 3 and 4 years may enrol at the 528 free kindergartens maintained by Free Kindergarten Associations, which receive government assistance. There are also 680 play centres which also receive government subsidy. In July 1981 there were 38,768 and 16,198 children on the rolls respectively.

Total expenditure out of government funds in 1981–82 upon education was NZ$1,493m.

The universities and the affiliated agricultural colleges are autonomous bodies. Most secondary schools are controlled by their own boards. Virtually all state primary schools are controlled by the district education boards: there are 10 education districts. The Department of Education exercises certain defined functions in connexion with the general supervision of the education provided in state primary and secondary schools and disburses the government grants payable to controlling authorities for the running of those schools. Education in state schools is free for children under 19 years of age. Private schools are regularly visited by state school inspectors.

Report of the Minister of Education ('E.1. Report'). Annually. Wellington, Government Printer

NZ Committee on Secondary Education. *Towards Partnership.* Dept. of Education, 1976

Social Welfare. New Zealand's record for progressive legislation reaches back to 1898, when it was second only to Denmark in introducing non-contributory old-age pensions.

The present system came into operation from 1 April 1972. It provides for retirement, unemployment, widowhood, invalidity and sickness, as well as hospital and other medical care. Since 1 April 1969 the scheme has been financed from general taxation. Previously there was a special social security tax on virtually all income of individuals and companies in excess of $4 a week which met approximately three-quarters of the cost of the scheme, the balance being met from general taxation.

At 31 March 1981 the current weekly rates of widows', invalids', sickness, domestic purposes, unemployment and miners' benefits were $127·28 for a married couple, $76·37 for an unmarried person aged 20 years or over, and $58·10 for those under 20 years.

There are additional payments for dependent children.

All benefits except superannuation and family allowances are subject to an income test.

Family Benefit. A family benefit of $6 a week is payable for each dependent child.

Unemployment Benefit. The payment is subject to the condition that the applicant is capable and willing to undertake suitable employment.

Sickness Benefit. Payment is subject to medical evidence of incapacity of a person who has suffered a loss of weekly earnings as a result.

Other benefits include emergency benefits and additional benefits for those in need but who either do not qualify for one of the standard benefits or who have special needs or commitments for which a benefit at the standard rate is insufficient.

Medical, Hospital and Related Benefits. Medical, hospital and other related benefits are also provided under the Social Welfare scheme. These consist mainly of the payment of certain fees for medical attention by private practitioners, free treatment in public and mental hospitals, certain fees for treatment in private hospitals, maternity benefits (including ante-natal and post-natal treatment and services of doctors and nurses at confinements), pharmaceutical benefits (medicines, drugs, etc., prescribed by medical practitioners), etc. There are also benefits in connexion with dental services up to the age of 16, X-ray diagnosis, massage, home-nursing, artificial aids, etc.

Pensions. Provision is made for the payment of pensions and allowances to members or dependants of disabled, deceased or missing members, of the New Zealand Forces who served in the South African War, the two World Wars, the Korean War and the Vietnam War, to members of the New Zealand Mercantile Marine during the Second World War, or in connexion with any emergency whether arising out of the obligations undertaken by New Zealand in the Charter of the United Nations or otherwise. Principal rates are: War pensions are payable to widows at a rate of $37·59 a week, together with a mother's allowance of $44·91 a week, increased by $5 a week for each additional child, in addition to the normal child allowances of $6 per week for each child. These rates may be increased by an amount not exceeding $30·58 per week if the pensioner is suffering from total blindness, two or more serious disabilities or one extremely severe disability.

An 'economic pension' is defined as a supplementary pension granted on economic grounds and is additional to any pension payable as of right in respect of death or disablement. The maximum weekly rates are $63·64 to a married person (if unmarried, $76·37); to the widow or dependent widowed mother of a member, $76·37.

War veterans' allowances are $76·37 weekly for a single person and $63·64 for a married person, plus an equal amount to a wife, increased by $1.50 a week each at age 65, subject to income qualifications.

Domestic Purposes Benefit. A domestic purposes benefit is payable to unsupported male and female solo parents including divorced, separated and unmarried persons, prisoners' spouses and also to those who are required to give full-time care to a person (other than their spouse) who would otherwise have to be admitted to hospital.

Death Benefit. A death benefit of $1,000 is payable to a widow or widower if totally dependent on the deceased plus $500 for each dependent child but not exceeding $1,500.

Social Welfare Benefits and War Pensions:

Benefits	*Number in force at 31 March 1982*	*Total payments 1981–82 (NZ$1,000)*
SOCIAL WELFARE:		
Monetary—		
Superannuation	430,175	1,895,845
Widows	14,737	62,164
Orphans	365	943
Family	459,994	297,705
Invalids	17,891	60,453
Miners	16	72
Unemployment	32,596	156,429
Sickness	7,177	43,529
Domestic purposes	43,447	252,654
Total	1,006,398	2,769,795

Benefits	Number in force at 31 March 1981	Total payments 1980–81 (NZ$1,000)
SOCIAL WELFARE (*contd.*):		
Health, etc.—		
Medical		49,581
Hospital		31,879
Maternity		8,326
Pharmaceutical		147,278
Supplementary		35,020
Total		272,084
WAR PENSION, ETC.:		
First World War	3,171	10,365
Second World War	22,069	48,414
Korean War	304	318
Vietnam War	263	...
War veterans' allowances	3,187	16,037
Mercantile Marine	20	44
Other	47	...
Total	29,061	75,178

Reciprocity with Other Countries. There are reciprocal arrangements between New Zealand and Australia in respect of age, invalids', widows', family, unemployment and sickness benefits, and between New Zealand and the UK in respect of family, age, superannuation, widows', orphans', invalids', sickness and unemployment benefits.

Superannuation. Following the change of Government in Dec. 1975 the earnings-related superannuation scheme described in THE STATESMAN'S YEAR-BOOK, 1977–78, was abolished. Under the new system (operative from Feb. 1977) superannuation is payable to all New Zealanders on reaching the age of 60. It is taxable but not subject to an income test. The rates are based on the national average wage, of which married couples now receive 80% and single persons 60% of the married rate.

Health. At 30 June 1981 there were 8,327 doctors on the medical register. At 31 March 1981 there were 26,716 public hospital beds, of which 2,431 were for maternity cases.

MINOR ISLANDS

The minor islands (total area, 320 sq. miles, 775 sq. km) included within the geographical boundaries of New Zealand are the following: Kermadec Islands, Three Kings Islands, Auckland Islands, Campbell Island, Antipodes Islands, Bounty Islands, Snares Islands, Solander Island. With the exception of Raoul Island in the Kermadec Group (population, 5, 1981 census) and Campbell Island (population, 10, 1981 census) none of these islands is inhabited.

The **Kermadec Islands,** which were annexed to New Zealand in 1887, have no separate administration and all New Zealand laws apply to them. Situation, 29° 10′ to 131° 30′ S. lat., 177° 45′ to 179° W. long., 600 miles NNE of New Zealand. Area, 13 sq. miles (33·5 sq. km). The largest of the group is Raoul or Sunday Island, 20 miles in circuit, while Macaulay Island is 3 miles in circuit.

A meteorological station and an aeradio station have been established on Raoul Island, the official staff being the only inhabitants.

TERRITORIES OVERSEAS

Territories Overseas coming within the jurisdiction of New Zealand consist of Tokelau and the Ross Dependency.

Tokelau. Situated some 480 km to the north of Western Samoa between 8° and 10° S. lat., and between 171° and 173° W. long., are the 3 atoll islands of Atafu, Nukunonu and Fakaofo of the Tokelau (Union) group. Formerly part of the Gilbert and Ellice Islands Colony, the group was transferred to the jurisdiction of New Zealand on 11 Feb. 1926. By legislation enacted in 1948, the Tokelau Islands were declared part of New Zealand as from 1 Jan. 1949. The area of the group is 1,011 hectares; the population at census 25 Oct. 1976 was 1,575; estimate, 31 Dec. 1981, 1,572.

By the Tokelau Islands Act 1948 the Tokelau Group was included within the territorial boundaries of New Zealand; legislative powers are now invested in the Governor-General in Council. The inhabitants are British subjects and New Zealand citizens. In Dec. 1976 the territory was officially renamed 'Tokelau', the name by which it has customarily been known to its inhabitants.

From 8 Nov. 1974 the office of Administrator was invested in the Secretary of Foreign Affairs. Certain powers are delegated to the district officer in Apia, Western Samoa.

Because of the very restricted economic and social future in the atolls, the islanders agreed to a proposal put to them by the Minister of Island Territories in 1965 that over a period of years most of the population be resettled in New Zealand. Up to March 1975, 528 migrants entered New Zealand as permanent residents under Government sponsorship. At the request of the people the scheme has now been suspended.

New Zealand Government aid to Tokelau totalled $1·82m. for the year ended 31 March 1982.

Ross Dependency. By Imperial Order in Council, dated 30 July 1923, the territories between 160° E. long. and 150° W. long. and south of 60° S. lat. were brought within the jurisdiction of the New Zealand Government. The region was named the Ross Dependency. From time to time laws for the Dependency have been made by regulations promulgated by the Governor-General of New Zealand.

The mainland area is estimated at 400,000–450,000 sq. km and is mostly ice-covered. In Jan. 1957 a New Zealand expedition under Sir Edmund Hillary established a base in the Dependency. In Jan. 1958 Sir Edmund Hillary and 4 other New Zealanders reached the South Pole.

The main base—Scott Base—at Pram Point, Ross Island—is manned throughout the year, about 12 people being present during winter. Vanda Station in the dry ice-free Wright Valley is manned every summer.

Quartermain, L. B., *New Zealand and the Antarctic.* Wellington, 1971

SELF-GOVERNING TERRITORIES OVERSEAS

THE COOK ISLANDS

HISTORY. The Cook Islands, which lie between 8° and 23° S. lat., and 156° and 167° W. long., were proclaimed a British protectorate in 1888, and on 11 June 1901 were annexed and proclaimed part of New Zealand.

AREA AND POPULATION. The islands within the territory fall roughly into two groups—the scattered islands towards the north (Northern group) and the islands towards the south known as the Lower group. The names of the islands with their populations as at the census of 1 Dec. 1981[1] were as follows:

Lower Group—	Area sq. km	Population	Northern Group—	Area sq. km	Population
Rarotonga	67·2	9,530	Nassau	1·2	134
Mangaia	51·8	1,364	Palmerston (Avarau)	2·0	51
Atiu	26·9	1,225	Penrhyn (Tongareva)	9·8	608
Aitutaki	18·0	2,335	Manihiki (Humphrey)	5·4	405
Mauke (Parry Is.)	18·4	681	Rakahanga (Reirson)	4·1	272
Mitiaro	22·3	256	Pukapuka (Danger)	5·1	796
Manuae and Te au-o-tu	6·2	12	Suwarrow (Anchorage)	0·4	—
			Total		17,754

[1] Provisional.

In 1980, 461 live births and 101 deaths were registered.

CONSTITUTION AND GOVERNMENT. The Cook Islands Constitution Act 1964, which provides for the establishment of internal self-government in the Cook Islands, came into force on 4 Aug. 1965.

The Act establishes the Cook Islands as fully self-governing but linked to New Zealand by a common Head of State, the Queen, and a common citizenship, that of New Zealand. It provides for a ministerial system of government with a Cabinet consisting of a Premier and 6 other Ministers. The New Zealand Government is represented by a New Zealand Representative and the position of a Queen's Representative has recently been created by changes in the Constitution. The Resident Commissioner became the High Commissioner of the Cook Islands, who exercises the dual functions of representative of the Queen and of the New Zealand Government. New Zealand continues to be responsible for the external affairs and defence of the Cook Islands, subject to consultation between the New Zealand Prime Minister and the Premier. The changed status of the Islands does not affect the consideration of subsidies or the right of free entry into New Zealand for exports from the group.

Prime Minister: Sir Thomas Davis, KBE.

ECONOMY AND TRADE

Budget. Revenue is derived chiefly from customs duties which follow the New Zealand customs tariff, income tax and stamp sales.

Grants from New Zealand, mainly for medical, educational and general administrative purposes totalled $5·7m. in 1980–81.

Agriculture. Livestock (1980): Pigs, 17,000; goats, 3,000; poultry, 66,000.

Commerce. Exports, mainly to New Zealand, were valued at $5m. in 1981. Main items of export were fresh fruit and vegetables, fruit juice, canned pineapple, copra and clothing. Imports totalled $23·6m. in 1980; 61·2% of the total were imports (including re-exports from New Zealand). The main items were foodstuffs, manufactured goods (including transport equipment), petrol and oil.

COMMUNICATIONS

Aviation. New Zealand has financed the construction of an international airport at Rarotonga which became operational for jet services in Sept. 1973.

Shipping. A fortnightly cargo shipping service is provided between New Zealand, Niue and Rarotonga.

Telecommunications. Wireless stations are maintained at all the permanently inhabited islands. In 1982 there were 1,583 telephones.

EDUCATION AND HEALTH

Education. Twenty-eight primary schools are established in the various islands. Of these two are Roman Catholic missionary schools and two are Seventh-Day Adventist missionary schools. Five primary schools have secondary school attachments, and there are also ten secondary schools. Two of these secondary schools are run by missions; one by the Roman Catholic Mission and the other by the Seventh-Day Adventist Mission. The number of students enrolled at school on 31 March 1982, was 6,424.

The instruction given at school is based on the New Zealand School syllabus and students can sit for the New Zealand School Certificate and University Entrance examinations. Most schools teach in both the English and Cook Island Maori languages, but the use of Cook Islands Maori is restricted to the primary school level.

There were 94 Government-funded students studying at overseas tertiary or technical institutes in 1982.

Health. All Cook Islanders receive free medical and surgical treatment in their villages, the hospital and the tuberculosis sanatorium. Cook Island Maori patients in the hospital and the sanatorium and all schoolchildren receive free dental treatment.

NIUE ISLAND

History. Niue Island achieved internal self-government in Oct. 1974.

Area and Population. Distance from Auckland, New Zealand, 1,343 miles; from Rarotonga, 580 miles. Area, 100 sq. miles; circumference, 40 miles; height above sea-level, 220 ft. Population at 28 Sept. 1981 was 3,296; 1982, estimate, 3,267. During 1982 births registered numbered 100, deaths 21. Migration to New Zealand is the main factor in population change.

Constitution and Government. There is a Legislative Assembly of 20 members, and legislative measures apply as in the case of the Cook Islands.

Premier: Robert R. Rex, CMG, OBE.

Budget. Financial aid from New Zealand, 1981–82, totalled $4,666,730.

Agriculture. The most important products of the island in 1982 were passion fruit, honey, limes and root crops.

Trade. Exports, 1981, $590,440; imports, $3,837,575.

Communications. There is a wireless station at Alofi, the port of the island. Two weekly commercial air services link Niue with Western Samoa, Cook Islands, American Samoa and New Zealand.

Education. There were 8 government schools with 938 pupils in 1982.

Health. There is a 30-bed hospital in Alofi and clinics in some villages.

Quarterly Statistical Bulletin. Statistics Office, Rarotonga

Buck, P. H., *Vikings of the Sunrise.* New York, 1938.—*The Coming of the Maori.* Wellington, 1950

Ross, A. (ed.), *New Zealand's Record in the Pacific Islands in the Twentieth Century.* Auckland, 1969

DIPLOMATIC REPRESENTATIVES

Of New Zealand in Great Britain (New Zealand Hse, Haymarket, London, SW1Y 4TQ)
High Commissioner: William Young (accredited 5 Nov. 1982).

Of Great Britain in New Zealand (Reserve Bank of New Zealand Bldg., 2 The Terrace, Wellington, 1)
High Commissioner: Sir Richard Stratton, KCMG.

Of New Zealand in the USA (37 Observatory Cir., NW, Washington, D.C., 20008)
Ambassador: L. R. Adams-Schneider.

Of the USA in New Zealand (29 Fitzherbert Terrace, Wellington)
Ambassador: H. Monroe Brown.

Of New Zealand to the United Nations
Ambassador: Harold H. Francis.

Books of Reference

Statistical Information: The central statistical office for New Zealand is the Department of Statistics (Wellington, 1).

The beginning of a statistical service may be seen in the early 'Blue books' prepared annually from 1840 onwards under the direction of the Colonial Secretary, and designed primarily for the information of the Colonial Office in England. A permanent statistical authority was created in 1858. The Department of Statistics functions under the Statistics Act 1975 and reports to Parliament through the Minister of Statistics. A comprehensive statistical service has been developed to meet national requirements, and close contact is maintained with the United Nations Statistical Office and other international statistical organizations; through the Conference of Asian Statisticians assistance is being given with the development of statistics in the region.

The oldest publications consist of *(a)* census results from 1858 onwards and *(b)* annual volumes of statistics (first published 1858 but covering years back to 1853). Main current publications:

New Zealand Official Yearbook. Annual, from 1893
Catalogue of New Zealand Statistics. 1972
Statistical Reports of New Zealand. Annual
Monthly Abstract of Statistics. From 1914
Pocket Digest of Statistics. Annual, 1927–31, 1938 ff.

Parliamentary Reports of Government Departments. Annual
Pacific Islands Yearbook. Sydney, 1977
Dictionary of New Zealand Biography. 2 vols. Wellington, 1940
Encyclopaedia of New Zealand. 3 vols. Wellington, 1966
National Bibliography. Wellington, 1968
New Zealand Financial System. Wellington, 1966
Oxford New Zealand Encyclopaedia. London, 1965
Bedggood, D., *Rich and Poor in New Zealand.* Sydney, 1980
Bright, T. N., *Banking Law and Practice in New Zealand.* 2nd ed. Wellington, 1969
Bush, G., *Local Government and Politics in New Zealand.* Sydney, 1980
Easton, B., *Social Policy and the Welfare State in New Zealand.* Auckland, 1980
Grover, R. F., *New Zealand.* [Bibliography] Oxford and Santa Barbara, 1981
Holcroft, M. H., *The Shaping of New Zealand.* Auckland, 1975
Kennaway, R., Jackson, K., Henderson, J. (eds.) *Beyond New Zealand: The Foreign Policy of a Small State.* Auckland, 1980
Levine, S. (ed.), *Politics in New Zealand.* London, 1978.—*The New Zealand Political System.* London, 1979
Morrell, W. P., and Hall, D. O. W., *A History of New Zealand Life.* Christchurch and London, 1957
Oliver, W. H. (ed.), *The Oxford History of New Zealand.* OUP, 1981
Robson, J. L. (ed.), *New Zealand: The Development of its Laws and Constitution.* 2nd ed. London, 1967
Roth, B., *Trade Unions in New Zealand.* Wellington, 1974
Shadbolt, M. F. R., *The Shell Guide to New Zealand.* Christchurch, 1976
Sinclair, K., *A History of New Zealand.* Rev. ed. London, 1980
Traue, J. E., *Who's Who in New Zealand.* 11th ed. Wellington, 1978
Wards, I., *A Descriptive Atlas of New Zealand.* Wellington, Government Printer, 1976
Watters, R. F. (ed.), *Land and Society in New Zealand.* Wellington, 1965
Wise's New Zealand Guide. 7th ed. Auckland, 1979

NICARAGUA

Capital: Managua
Population: 2·5m. (1980)
GNP per capita: US$720 (1980)

República de Nicaragua

HISTORY. Active colonization of the Pacific coast was undertaken by Spaniards from Panama, beginning in 1523. After links with other Central American territories, and Mexico, Nicaragua became completely independent in 1838, but subject to a prolonged feud between the 'Liberals' of León and the 'Conservatives' of Granada. Mosquitia remained an autonomous kingdom on the Atlantic coast, under British protection until 1860.

On 5 Aug. 1914 the Bryan–Chamarro treaty between Nicaragua and the US was signed, under which the US in return for US$3m. acquired a permanent option for a canal route through Nicaragua and a 99-year option for a naval base in the Bay of Fonseca on the Pacific coast and Corn Island on the Atlantic coast. It was ratified by Nicaragua on 7 April 1916 and by the US on 22 June 1916. US Marines finally left in 1933.

The Bryan–Chamarro treaty was abrogated on 14 July 1970.

AREA AND POPULATION. Area estimated at 148,000 sq. km (57,143 sq. miles) or 139,000 sq. km (54,296 sq. miles) if the lakes are excluded. The coastline runs 336 miles on the Atlantic and 219 miles on the Pacific. Population at the census of April 1971 was 1,911,543 (922,433 males, 989,110 females). Estimate (1980) 2,568,000.

Nicaragua is the largest in area and most thinly populated of the Central American republics. Crude birth rate, 1977, 42·31 per 1,000 population; crude death rate, 5·54; infantile mortality rate, 36·98 per 1,000 live births; crude marriage rate, 5·48 per 1,000 population.

In 1977 about 52% of the inhabitants lived in urban areas and 48% in rural areas.

The people of the western half of the republic are principally of mixed Spanish and Indian extraction, some of pure Spanish descent and many Indians. The population of the eastern half is composed mainly of Mosquito and other Indians and Zambos, and Negroes from Jamaica and other islands of the Caribbean. The main ethnic groups in 1974 were: Mestizo, 69%; white, 19%; Negro, 9%; Indio, 5%.

Nicaragua is administratively divided into the following 16 departments with population as on 31 Dec. 1978:

Boaco	79,641	Jinotega	112,591	Matagalpa	199,433
Carazo	97,388	Leon	220,878	Nueva Segovia	85,025
Chinandega	199,156	Madriz	64,491	Río San Juan	25,481
Chontales	81,416	Managua	677,963	Rivas	96,546
Esteli	96,119	Masaya	131,518	Zelaya	176,921
Granada	99,537				

Of the 134 *municipios*, 98 have from 2,000 to 50,000 inhabitants. The capital is Managua, situated on the lake of the same name, 180 ft above sea level, with (1978) 552,900 inhabitants. Other cities: León, 81,647; Granada, 56,232; Masaya, 47,276; Chinandega, 44,435; Matagalpa, 26,986; Estelí, 26,892; Bluefields, 18,252; Jinotega, 14,088; Juigalpa, 13,468; Boaco, 8,684.

CONSTITUTION AND GOVERNMENT. On 31 Aug. 1971 the Congress voted in favour of dissolution and the abrogation of the Constitution.

On 14 March 1974 a new Constitution came into force and provided for a national congress consisting of a Chamber of Deputies of 70 members and a Senate of 30 members but on 20 July 1979, following the fall of Gen. Somoza, a

Government Junta abrogated the Constitution; members of the Junta are Violeta B. de Chamorro, Sergio Ramirez Mercado, Moisés Hassan M, Alfonso Robelo Callejas and Daniel Ortega Saavedra.

In Aug. 1980 it was announced that elections had been postponed until 1985 and in March 1982 a state of emergency was declared.

The republic is divided into 16 departments, each of which is under a political head (appointed by the President), who has supervision of finance, education and other matters. The departments have 134 *municipios*, headed by a mayor (*alcalde*). The Mosquito Reserve now forms part of the departments of Zelaya and Río San Juan.

National flag: Three horizontal stripes of blue, white, blue, with the national arms in the centre.

National anthem: Salve a ti Nicaragua (words by S. Ibarra Mayorga, 1937).

DEFENCE

Army. The Army numbered (1983) 20,000 with the addition of a border guard organized in 2 armed battalions and 10 infantry battalions with additional supporting units.

Navy. Four coastguard cutters, 11 coastal patrol craft and 1 landing craft operated by the marine section of the National Guard picket the east and west coasts. Personnel in 1983 totalled 200 officers and men.

Air Force. Formed in June 1938 as the Nicaraguan Army Air Force, the Air Force has been semi-independent since 1947. Its combat units have 5 Summit 02-337 Sentry counter-insurgency aircraft, 4 T-33 armed jet trainers, and 6 T-28 armed piston-engined trainers. Other equipment includes some C-47s, 5 Spanish-built Aviocar and 2 Israeli-built Arava STOL transports and smaller communications aircraft and helicopters. Approximate strength is 1,500 personnel and 45 aircraft.

INTERNATIONAL RELATIONS

Membership. Nicaragua is a member of the UN, OAS and the Central American Common Market.

ECONOMY

Planning. The objects of the National Reconstruction Plan 1975–79 included the reconstruction of Managua which took one-third of the US$6,000m. envisaged for the plan.

Budget. Revenue and expenditure for fiscal years, ending 31 Dec., in 1m. córdobas:

	1974	*1975*	*1976*	*1977*	*1978*	*1979*
Revenue	2,093·2	1,820·3	2,052·3	2,774·3	3,255·3	3,760·1
Expenditure	1,710·3	1,881·9	2,223·1	2,427·6	3,433·8	3,409·0

The 1979 budget included 371·1m. for defence, 358·2m. for education, 120·8m. for the Ministry of Finance and Public Credit, 111·2m. for health and 60·6m. córdobas for commerce and public works.

The external debt at the end of 1978 was 556·8m. córdobas; the internal debt was 17·6m. córdobas.

Currency. The monetary unit is the *córdoba* (C$), divided into 100 *centavos*. On 31 Dec. 1978 total money supply was 1,887·8m. córdobas. Bills form the greater part of the currency, in denominations from 1,000 córdobas to 1 córdoba. Silver coins struck, but now out of circulation, are 50, 25 and 10 centavos; copper–nickel and copper–zinc coins, 1 córdoba, 50, 25, 10 and 5 centavos. March 1983, US$1 = 10 *córdobas*; £1 = 14·72 *córdobas*.

Banking. The National Bank of Nicaragua at Managua founded in 1912, owned by the Government since 1924 was reorganized in July 1979, becoming the National

Development Bank and including the National Development Institute (INFONAC) and Special Fund for Development (FED). This new law gave it increased responsibilities as a development bank. The Central Bank of Nicaragua came into operation on 1 Jan. 1961 as an autonomous bank of issue, absorbing the issue department of the National Bank.

In July 1979 private financial banking was nationalized and branches of foreign banks were prohibited from receiving deposits.

Weights and Measures. Since 1893 the metric system of weights and measures has been recommended.

ENERGY AND NATURAL RESOURCES

Electricity. Installed capacity for electric energy was 357,700 kw. in 1977 and 1,180·3 kwh. was produced.

Minerals. Production of gold in 1980 was 67,000 troy oz.; of silver, 167,000 troy oz.; of copper, 3,000 tonnes. There is no iron or coalmining. Large deposits of tungsten in Nueva Segovia were announced in 1961. Exploration for petroleum began off the Pacific and Atlantic coasts in 1965. A petroleum refinery of 650,000 tonnes capacity is functioning at Managua.

Agriculture. Agriculture is the principal source of national wealth, finding work for 65% of the labour force, and furnishing, 1975, 22% of the GNP.

Of the total land area (about 36·5m. acres), about 17·5m. acres are under timber 0·9m. acres are used for grazing and 2·1m. acres are arable. The unit of area used locally is the *manzana* (= 1·73 acres). Of the arable only 1·2m. acres are actively cultivated, 780,000 in annual crops such as cotton and rice and the remainder in perennial crops such as coffee and sugar-cane, or in two harvests a year in the cases of maize, sorghum and beans.

The products of the western half are varied, the most important being cotton, coffee, now under the aegis of the new *Instituto del Café*, sugar-cane, cocoa, maize, sesame and beans. Production (1979–80.): Coffee (in bags of 60 kg) 860,000; sugar (tonnes) 200,000; cotton (bales of 478lb.) 100,000.

There were about 2·3m. head of cattle in 1981. There are now 4 modern meat-packing plants; slaughterings were 481,700 heads in 1978. There were 510,000 pigs (1981). Beef exports in 1978 were valued at US$67·7m.

Forestry. Timber production has been declining, though the forests, which cover 10m. acres and 4 distinct zones, contain mahogany and cedar, which were formerly largely exported, three varieties of rosewoods, guayacán (*lignum vitae*) and dye-woods. In 1968–69 exploitation of these vast areas of timber with a potential production of 300,000 tonnes per annum was begun. Production of sawn wood in 1978, 270,000 tonnes.

Fishery. On the Atlantic coast fisheries are an important subsistence activity. Over 6·4m. lb. of shrimps were exported in 1978 and were processed in 3 plants at Schooner Cay, El Bluff and Corn Island. The fishing limit off the coast has been defined as 200 nautical miles. Within that limit, fishing is subject to the provisions of the National Resources Exploration Law.

INDUSTRY AND TRADE

Industry. Chief local industries are cane sugar, cooking oil, cigarettes, beer, leather products, plastics, textiles, chemical products, metal products, cement (210,600 tonnes in 1977), strong and soft drinks, soluble coffee, dairy products, meat, plywood. Production of oil products, in 1978, was valued at 526m. córdobas; food products, 3,338·4m.; beverages, 565·8m.; textiles, 328·7m.; chemical substances and products, 1,054m.

Labour. In 1975 there were some 654,683 persons gainfully employed; of these: agriculture, 47·9%; manufacturing, construction, mining and power, 15·4%; services, transport and commerce, 35%.

Commerce. The foreign trade of Nicaragua, in US$1m., was as follows in calendar years:

	1977	*1978*	*1979*	*1980*	*1981*
Imports	761·9	553·0	388·0	870·0	807·6
Exports	636·8	645·9	598·0	469·7	520·0

The main imports in 1977 (in US$1m.) Machinery and vehicles, 239·9; chemicals, 161·4; crude oil, 77·9; foodstuffs, 33·2. These were supplied mainly by USA, Venezuela, Federal Republic of Germany, Japan, Costa Rica and Guatemala.

In 1978 the main exports (in US$1m.) were: Coffee, 199·6; cotton, 140·9; meat, 67·7; chemical products, 52·2; sugar, 19·6.

Total trade between Nicaragua and UK (British Department of Trade returns, in £1,000 sterling):

	1977	*1978*	*1979*	*1980*	*1981*	*1982*
Imports to UK	1,393	1,414	895	1,510	1,030	3,282
Exports and re-exports from UK	8,841	7,560	3,229	2,478	4,269	4,940

COMMUNICATIONS

Roads. In 1978, 1,570 km were paved, out of a total of 18,197 km. The whole 368·5 km of the Nicaraguan section of the Pan-American Highway is now paved. The all-weather Roosevelt Highway linking Managua with the river port Rama was completed in 1968, to provide the first overland link with the Atlantic coast. There are paved roads to San Juan del Sur, Puerto Somoza and Corinto. In 1977 there were 46,381 passenger cars and vans in use.

Railways. The Pacific Railroad of Nicaragua, owned and operated by the Government, has a total length of 373 km, all single-track, and connects Corinto, Chinandega, León, Managua, Masaya and Granada. Passengers carried (1978) 448,932; freight, 66,452 tonnes.

Aviation. LANICA, the Nicaraguan airline has daily flights to Miami and 6 flights a week to Guatemala and to the inner cities of Bluefields, Puerto Cabezas and the mining towns of Siuna and Bonanza. PANAM and TACA (Transportes Aéreos Centroamericanos), COPA (Compañía Panameña de Aviacíon), have daily services to Panama, Mexico, the other Central American countries and USA. SAM (Servicio Aéreo de Medellín) has 3 flights a week to Nicaragua and Colombia. In 1977, 223,420 passengers and 24·2m. tonnes of cargo were carried.

Shipping. The Pacific ports are Corinto (the largest), San Juan del Sur and Puerto Saudino through which pass most of the external trade. The chief eastern ports are El Bluff (for Bluefields) and Puerto Cabezas. The merchant marine consists solely of the Mamenic Line with 8 vessels. In 1977, 724,966 short tons of goods were loaded and 1·42m. tonnes unloaded at Nicaraguan ports.

Post and Broadcasting. There are (1977) 16,000 km of (government-owned) telegraph line and 328 offices and (1978) there were 55,803 telephones.

The Tropical Radio Telegraph Company maintains a powerful station at Managua, and branch stations at Bluefields and Puerto Cabezas. The Government operates the National Radio with 47 broadcasting stations: there are 31 commercial stations and some 70 others. Number of wireless sets in 1972 was 115,000 and television sets 60,000. There are 2 television stations at Managua.

Cinemas. Cinemas numbered over 100 in 1977 and seated over 60,000.

Newspapers. There are 3 daily newspapers (2 in Managua and 1 in León), with a total circulation of about 105,000.

JUSTICE, RELIGION, EDUCATION AND WELFARE

Justice. The judicial power is vested in a Supreme Court of Justice at Managua, 5 chambers of second instance (León, Masaya, Granada, Matagalpa and Bluefields) and 153 judges of inferior tribunals.

Religion. The prevailing form of religion is Roman Catholic, but religious liberty is guaranteed by the Constitution. The republic constitutes 1 archbishopric (seat at Managua) and 7 bishoprics (León, Granada, Estelí, Matagalpa, Juigalpa, Masaya and Puerto Cabezas). Protestants, established principally on the Atlantic coast, numbered 54,100 in 1966.

Education. There were, in 1977, 2,334 elementary schools, with a total of 368,895 pupils and 9,729 teachers; and 275 secondary schools, with 105,429 pupils and 2,954 teachers. Illiterate persons, of all ages, number 63·7% of the population. In 1977 there were 6 universities and technical colleges with 1,204 professors and 23,171 students.

Social Welfare. In 1977 the minimum wage ranged from 6·58 to 21·60 córdobas daily according to different zones and workers' classifications. In 1977 there were 41 hospitals with 4,670 beds.

DIPLOMATIC REPRESENTATIVES

Of Nicaragua in Great Britain (8 Gloucester Rd., London, SW7 4PP)
Ambassador: Francisco d'Escoto.

Of Great Britain in Nicaragua
Ambassador and Consul-General: J. Michael Brown (resides in San José).

Of Nicaragua in the USA (1627 New Hampshire Ave., NW, Washington, D.C., 20009)
Ambassador: Francisco Fiallos Navarro.

Of the USA in Nicaragua (Km. 4½ Carretera Sur., Managua)
Ambassador: Anthony C. Quainton.

Of Nicaragua to the United Nations
Ambassador: Javier Chamorto Mora.

Books of Reference

Dirección General Estadística y Censos, *Boletín de Estadística* (irregular intervals); and *Indicadores Economicos.*
Boletín de la Superintendencia de Bancos. Banco Central, Managua
Nicaragua Comercio Exterior, 1978. Managua, 1979
Walker, T. W., *Nicaragua: The Land of Sandino.* Boulder, 1982
Weber, H., *Nicaragua: The Sandinista Revolution.* London and New York, 1981

National Library: Biblioteca Nacional, Managua, D.N.

NIGER

République du Niger

Capital: Niamey
Population: 5·62m. (1982)
GNP per capita: US$330 (1980)
Inflation rate: 12% (1981)

HISTORY. Niger was occupied by France between 1883 and 1899, and became a territory of French West Africa in 1904. It became an autonomous republic within the French Community on 18 Dec. 1958 and achieved full independence on 3 Aug. 1960.

On 15 April 1974 the first President, Hamani Diori, was overthrown in a military *coup* led by Lieut.-Col. Seyni Kountché, who suspended the constitution, dissolved the National Assembly and banned political groups.

AREA AND POPULATION. Niger is bounded north by Algeria and Libya, east by Chad, south by Nigeria, south-west by Benin and Upper Volta and west by Mali. Area, 1,186,408 sq. km (458,075 sq. miles), with a population (1982), 5·62m. The major towns (populations 1977) are: Niamey, the capital (225,314 inhabitants), Zinder (58,436), Maradi (45,852), Tahoua (31,265), Agadez (20,475). The population is composed chiefly of Hausa (54%), Songhai and Djerma (23%), Fulani (10%), Beriberi-Manga (9%) and Tuareg (3%).

Precipitation determines the geographical division into a southern zone of agriculture, a central zone of pasturage and a desert-like northern zone. The country lacks water, with the exception of the south-western districts, which are watered by the Niger and its tributaries, and the southern zone, where there are a number of wells.

The official language is French.

CONSTITUTION AND GOVERNMENT. The country is administered by a Supreme Military Council of 12 officers led by the President, who appoints a Council of Ministers to assist him.

The Council of Ministers, as re-organized in Jan. 1983, comprised:

Head of State, President of SMC, Defence and Interior: Maj.-Gen. Seyni Kountché.

Prime Minister: Oumarou Mamane.

Ministers of State: Lieut.-Col. Moussa Tondi *(Finance),* Annou Mahamane *(Planning, Commerce and Transport).*

Ministers: Daouda Diallo *(Foreign Affairs and Co-operation),* Capt. Sidi Koutoubi *(Information),* Capt. Mamane Ousseini *(National Education),* Brah Mamane *(Posts and Telecommunications),* Yahaya Tounkara *(Hydrology and Environment),* Issoufou Mayaki *(Civil Service and Labour),* Oumar Diallo *(Mines and Industry),* Dr Ari Toubo Ibrahim *(Rural Development),* Illa Maikassoua *(Higher Education and Research),* Amadou Djibo *(Youth, Sports and Culture),* Moumouni Yacouba *(Public Works and Town Planning),* Dr Abdou Moudi *(Public Health and Social Affairs),* Allele Ehhadj Habibou *(Justice).*

Ministers-Delegate: Hamid Algabit *(Finance),* Amadou Fity Maiga *(Interior).*

Secretaries of State: Modieli Amadou *(National Education),* Al-Housseini Mouloul *(Planning),* Almoustapha Soumeila *(Commerce and Transport).*

National flag: Three horizontal strips of orange, white and green, with an orange disc in the middle of the white strip.

Local government: Niger is divided into 7 *départements* (Agodez, Diffa, Dosso, Maradi, Niamey, Tahoua and Zindar), each under a prefect; they are sub-divided into 38 *arrondissements*, each under a sub-prefect.

DEFENCE

Army. The Army consists of 1 paratroop, 1 engineer and 4 infantry companies and 2 armoured-car squadrons; total strength (1983) 2,150.

Air Force. The Air Force has 70 officers and men, 5 ex-*Luftwaffe* Noratlas transports, 4 C-130H, 1 C-54, and 1 C-47 transport, 1 Boeing 737 VIP transport, 2 Cessna Skymasters, 3 Do 28D Skyservants and 1 Aero Commander 500 for communications duties.

INTERNATIONAL RELATIONS

Membership. Niger is a member of UN, OAU and is an ACP state of the EEC.

ECONOMY

Planning. An economic development plan, covering the period 1965–68 was followed by a 3-year preparatory plan and was part of a 10-year economic programme (1965–74). This was followed by a further 10-year plan (1973–82).

Budget. The ordinary budget for 1980 balanced at 80,600m. francs CFA.

Currency. The unit of currency is the *franc CFA*, with a parity rate of 50 francs CFA to 1 French franc.

Banking. The *Banque Centrale des États de l'Afrique de l'Ouest* is the bank of issue, and there are 7 commercial banks in Niamey.

ENERGY AND NATURAL RESOURCES

Electricity. Production (1977) amounted to 70,000 kwh.

Oil. Deposits in the Lake Chad area, located in 1978, are to be exploited.

Minerals. Large uranium deposits are mined at Arlit and Akouta, in the Aïr mountains of northern Niger, with French and Japanese assistance. Concentrate production (1979) 3,600 tonnes. Phosphates are mined in the Niger valley, and coal reserves are to be exploited by open-cast mining. Salt and natron are produced at Manga and Agadez, tin ore in Aïr.

Agriculture. The chief agricultural products in 1981 (in 1,000 tonnes) were: Millet, 1,117; pulses, 280; sorghum, 273; cassava, 225; sugar-cane, 190; in the river districts, cotton and rice (38,000 tonnes). Gum arabic is produced at Gouré, nearly all of which is exported to Nigeria.

Livestock (1981): Cattle, 3·3m.; horses, 435,000; asses, 460,000; sheep and goats, 10m.; camels, 365,000; chickens, 7·8m.

INDUSTRY AND TRADE

Industry. Some small manufacturing industries, mainly in Niamey, produce textiles, food products, furniture and chemicals.

Trade Unions. The sole national body is the *Union Nationale des Travailleurs du Niger,* which has 15,000 members in 31 unions.

Commerce. Imports in 1980 were valued at 111,000m. francs CFA and exports at 97,000m. francs CFA.

Total trade between Niger and UK (British Department of Trade returns, in £1,000 sterling):

	1978	*1979*	*1980*	*1981*	*1982*
Imports to UK	235	297	184	5,762	574
Exports and re-exports from UK	11,930	16,576	7,885	5,201	17,346

In 1980, France provided 45% of imports and took 74% of the exports. Main exports were uranium, livestock and peanut oil.

COMMUNICATIONS

Roads. In 1980 there were 8,219 km of roads. Niamey and Zinder are the termini of two trans-Sahara motor routes; the Hoggar–Aïr–Zinder road extends to Kano and the Tanezrouft-Gao-Niamey road to Benin. There were (1980), 25,800 private cars and 4,400 commercial vehicles.

Aviation. There are international airports at Niamey, Zinder and Maradi. Air Niger operates domestic services to over 20 other public airports.

Post and Broadcasting. There were (1977) 8,147 telephones. In 1975 there were 100,000 radio receivers.

Cinemas. In 1970 there were 4 cinemas with a seating capacity of 3,800.

Newspapers. In 1977 there was 1 daily newspaper with a circulation of 3,000.

JUSTICE, RELIGION, EDUCATION AND WELFARE

Justice. There are Magistrates' and Assize Courts at Niamey, Zinder and Maradi, and justices of the peace in smaller centres. The Court of Appeal is at Niamey.

Religion. In 1979, 85% of the population was Moslem and the remainder mainly followed animist beliefs. There were about 20,000 Christians.

Education. There were, in 1978, 177,620 pupils in 1,401 primary schools, 21,944 in 53 secondary schools, 333 in the technical school in Maradi and 782 at the University of Niamey.

Health. In 1974 there were 56 hospitals with 3,734 beds. In 1976 there were 110 doctors, 6 dentists, 8 pharmacists, 70 midwives and 575 nursing personnel.

DIPLOMATIC REPRESENTATIVES

Of Niger in Great Britain
Ambassador: Arouna Mounkeila (accredited 24 March 1982, resides in Paris).

Of Great Britain in Niger
Ambassador and Consul-General: M. F. Daly (resides in Abidjan).

Of Niger in the USA (2204 R. St., NW, Washington, D.C. 20008)
Ambassador: André Wright.

Of the USA in Niger (PO Box 11201, Niamey)
Ambassador: William R. Casey, Jr.

Of Niger to the United Nations
Ambassador: Idé Oumarou.

Books of Reference

Bonardi, P., *La République du Niger.* Paris, 1960
Séré de Rivières, E., *Histoire du Niger.* Paris, 1965

NIGERIA

Capital: Lagos
Population: 90m. (1982)
GNP per capita: US$1,010 (1980)

Federal Republic of Nigeria

HISTORY. The Federal Republic comprises a number of areas formerly under separate administrations. Lagos, ceded in Aug. 1861 by King Dosunmu, was placed under the Governor of Sierra Leone in 1866. In 1874 it was detached, together with Gold Coast Colony, and formed part of the latter until Jan. 1886, when a separate 'colony and protectorate of Lagos' was constituted. Meanwhile the United African Company had established British interests in the Niger valley, and in July 1886 the company obtained a charter under the name of the Royal Niger Company. This company surrendered its charter to the Crown on 31 Dec. 1899, and on 1 Jan. 1900 the greater part of its territories was formed into the protectorate of Northern Nigeria. Along the coast the Oil Rivers protectorate had been declared in June 1885. This was enlarged and renamed the Niger Coast protectorate in 1893; and on 1 Jan. 1900, on its absorbing the remainder of the territories of the Royal Niger Company, it became the protectorate of Southern Nigeria. In Feb. 1906 Lagos and Southern Nigeria were united into the 'colony and protectorate of Southern Nigeria', and on 1 Jan. 1914 the latter was amalgamated with the protectorate of Northern Nigeria to form the 'colony and protectorate of Nigeria', under a Governor. On 1 Oct. 1954 Nigeria became a federation under a Governor-General.

On 1 Oct. 1960 Nigeria became sovereign and independent and a member of the Commonwealth and on 1 Oct. 1963 Nigeria became a republic.

For the history of Nigeria from 1961 to 1978, see THE STATESMAN'S YEAR-BOOK, 1979–80, pp. 923-924.

AREA AND POPULATION. Area approximately 356,669 sq. miles (923,773 sq. km). Census population, Nov. 1963, 55,670,052.

There are 19 states:

States	*Area (in sq. km)*	*Population*	*States*	*Area (in sq. km)*	*Population*
Anambra	17,675	3,596,618	Kwara	66,869	1,714,485
Bauchi	64,605	2,431,296	Lagos	3,345	1,443,568
Bendel	35,500	2,460,962	Niger	65,037	1,194,508
Benue	45,174	2,427,017	Ogun	16,762	1,550,966
Borno	116,400	2,997,498	Ondo	20,959	2,729,690
Cross River	27,237	3,478,131	Oyo	37,705	5,208,884
Gongola	91,390	2,605,263	Plateau	58,030	2,026,657
Imo	11,850	3,672,654	Rivers	21,850	1,719,925
Kaduna	70,245	4,098,306	Sokoto	102,535	4,538,787
Kano	43,285	5,774,840			

See map in THE STATESMAN'S YEAR-BOOK, 1977–78.

The results of the 1973 census were abandoned in Aug. 1975 because they 'will not command general acceptance throughout the country'. There is considerable uncertainty over the total population, but one estimate based on electoral registration in 1978 is 95m. and the World Bank give an estimate of 81,039,000.

The populations of the largest towns were (1975 estimate) as follows: Lagos, 1,060,848; and (in 1,000) Ibadan, 847; Ogbomosho, 432; Kano, 399; Oshogbo, 282; Ilorin, 282; Abeokuta, 253; Port Harcourt, 242; Zaria, 224; Ilesha, 224; Onitsha, 220; Iwo, 214; Ado-Ekiti, 213; Kaduna, 202; Mushin, 197; Maiduguri, 189; Enugu, 187; Ede, 182; Aba, 177; Ife, 176; Ila, 155; Oyo, 152; Ikere-Ekiti, 145; Benin, 136; Iseyin, 129.

It was announced in Feb. 1976 that the federal capital would be moved inland from Lagos to Abuja area (federal district, 8,094 sq. km) north of river Niger, and in Sept. 1982, Abuja was established as the capital.

CLIMATE. The climate varies with the types of country, but Nigeria lies wholly within the tropics, and temperatures are high. Temperatures of over 100°C are common in the north; coast temperatures are seldom over 90°C, but the humidity at the coast is much higher than in the north. Most of the rain falls between April and Sept. in the north and between March and Nov. in the south; rainfall varies from under 25 in. a year to 150 in. During the dry-season the 'harmattan' wind, laden with fine particles of dust, blows from the north-east.

CONSTITUTION AND GOVERNMENT. Under the Constitution drafted and ratified in 1977–78 by the Constitution Drafting Committee (CDC) and the Constituent Assembly respectively, Nigeria is a sovereign, federal republic comprising 19 states and a federal capital district. The Head of State is the President, in whom all executive power is vested; the President and Vice-President are directly elected. Presidential elections are due on 6 Aug. 1983.

President: Alhaji Shehu Shagari (elected 11 Aug. 1979, taking office 1 Oct.).
Vice-President: Dr Alex Ifeanyichukwu Ekwueme.

The two central legislative bodies are collectively referred to as the National Assembly which consists of a Senate of 96 members (5 from each of the 19 states) and the House of Representatives of 449 members. In the general elections of 1979, the election for the Senate took place on 7 July, for the States House of Assemblies and the House of Representatives on 14 July, for the Gubernatorial on 28 July, and the Presidential election on 10 Aug.

The official language is English but Hausa, Igbo and Yoruba languages are also used in the National Assembly, *i.e.* the Senate and the House of Representatives as well as in each of the State Houses of Assembly.

National flag: Three vertical strips of green, white, green.

Local Government: Elections were held on 21 July 1979 for the House of Assembly in each State. Beneath the State is a third tier of government.

DEFENCE

Army. The Army consists of 4 infantry divisions, 4 reconnaissance regiments, 4 artillery and 4 engineer brigades. Total strength (1983) 125,000.

Navy. The Nigerian Navy was established in 1958. It includes the new large guided missile frigate *Aradu* (built in FR Germany in 1978–81) and the frigate *Obuma* (*ex*-Nigeria) acting as a training ship (built in the Netherlands in 1964–65), 4 corvettes built in Britain in 1970–72 (*Dorina* and *Otobo*), and 1975–80 (*Erinmi* and *Enyimiri*), 6 fast missile-armed attack vedettes (3 built in France and 3 in FR Germany), 12 patrol craft, 50 coastal patrol boats, 2 tank landing ships, 1 survey ship, 1 training ship, 50 launches and 3 tugs. There are also 14 small patrol launches operated by the Nigerian Police. Naval personnel in 1983 totalled 500 officers and 3,550 ratings, and there were 2,000 reservists.

Air Force. The Nigerian Air Force was established in Jan. 1964. Pilots were trained initially in Canada, India and Ethiopia. The Air Force was built up subsequently with the aid of a Federal Republic of Germany mission; much first-line equipment has since been received from the Soviet Union. It includes 18 MiG-21 supersonic jet-fighters, a few MiG-15UTI and MiG-21U fighter-trainers, and 12 Alpha Jet armed jet trainers. About 20 BO 105 twin-turbine helicopters have been acquired from the Federal Republic of Germany for search and rescue. Transport units operate 8 C-130H Hercules 4-turboprop heavy transports, 5 twin-turboprop F.27s, the Presidential Boeing 707, a Gulfstream II and a Fokker F.28 Fellowship twin-turbofan airliner for VIP use, 2 Navajos and a Navajo Chieftain. Training types include 30 Bulldog primary trainers and some L.29 Dolphin jets, plus 20 Dornier Skyservants for instrument training, transport and ambulance duties. Thirteen medium-lift Aérospatiale Pumas and a few light helicopters are also in service. Personnel (1982) total about 9,000.

INTERNATIONAL RELATIONS

Membership. Nigeria is a member of UN, the Commonwealth, ECOWAS, OAU, OPEC and is an ACP state of EEC.

ECONOMY

Planning. The fourth plan (1981–85) was launched in 1981 but was rescheduled because of lower oil prices.

Budget. Expenditure 1979–80 totalled ₦9,510m. Education (10%) and defence (14%). Budgets are to run for calendar years from 1981.

In July 1980 external reserves were ₦5,200m.

Currency. Since 1 Jan. 1973 a decimal currency has been issued by the Central Bank of Nigeria, consisting of *Naira* (₦) and divided into 100 *kobo* (k). Notes in circulation ₦20, ₦10, ₦5, ₦1, 50k. Coins, 25k, 10k, 5k, 1k, ½k.

In March 1983, £1 = ₦1·07; US$1 = ₦0·68.

Banking. In Aug. 1967 statutory foreign-exchange cover of the Central Bank was reduced from 40 to 25%, and the percentage of government securities the Bank is permitted to hold was raised to 50% of its total liabilities.

There are 20 commercial banks including the First Bank of Nigeria (formerly Standard), Union Bank of Nigeria (formerly Barclays) and the United Bank of Africa. Eleven of the banks are indigenous. There are 3 merchant banks and 3 government-owned development banks in addition to the Post Office Savings Bank. In 1976 the Government took a 60% shareholding in all foreign banks.

Weights and Measures. The metric system is in force and the transitional period from the imperial system ended in 1977.

ENERGY AND NATURAL RESOURCES

Electricity. The National Electric Power Authority generated 4,712m. kwh. in 1977–78. The Niger dams at Kainji were completed in early 1969 (investment of £87m.) and provide cheap hydro-electricity for rapid industrialization.

Oil. There are refineries at Port Harcourt, Warri and at Kaduna. Oil represents 93% of exports. Production, 1981, 73·3m. tonnes.

Gas. Natural gas is being used at electric power stations at Afam and Ughelli. Production, 1972, 601,237,000 cu. ft. Reserves: 1,422,000m. cu.metres.

Minerals. Production (1977): Tin, 4,400 tonnes; columbite (the world's largest producer), 800 tonnes; coal (1981) 114,875 tonnes. There are large deposits of iron ore, coal (reserves estimate 245m. tonnes), lead and zinc. There are small quantities of gold and uranium.

Agriculture. Groundnuts, cotton and soybean come mainly or wholly from the north, palm produce, cocoa, timber and rubber from the south. Tobacco is grown in commercial quantities. Production (estimates) 1981 were (in tonnes): Groundnuts (unshelled), 580,000; cocoa, 160,000; cereals, 9·9m. In 1981, the National Rice Production Scheme was launched; production (1981), about 75,000 tons from 66,000 hectares.

Livestock (1981). There were 12·5m. cattle, 12m. sheep, 25m. goats, 1·1m. pigs and 130m. poultry.

Forestries. There are plywood factories at Epe, Sapele and Calabar, and numerous saw-mills. The most important timber species include mahogany, iroko, obeche, abwa, ebony and camwood.

INDUSTRY AND TRADE

Industry. There were more than 2,000 industrial establishments in 1982. Timber and hides and skins are major export commodities. Industrial products include soap, cigarettes, beer, margarine, groundnut oil, meat and cake, concentrated fruit juices, soft drinks, canned food, metal containers, ply-wood, textiles, ceramic products and cement. Of growing importance is the local assembly of motor vehicles, bicycles, radio equipment, electrical goods and sewing machines. In 1982, the Delta Steel Plant opened at Ovwian—Aladja in Bendel State.

Under a decree on indigenization Nigerians must have a minimum of 40% shareholding in all foreign enterprises.

Trade Unions. All trade unions were dissolved in 1976 and 42 new unions, each organized around a particular occupation, have since been created.

Commerce. There is a great deal of internal commerce in local foodstuffs and imported goods moving by rail, lorry and pack animals overland, and by launches, rafts and canoes along an extensive and complex network of inland waterways. Kano is still, as it has been for centuries, the focus of caravan routes linking a territory which stretches from the Sudan in the east to Senegal in the west, with branches northwards across the Sahara.

Total trade in N̶m. for 4 years:

	1979	*1980*	*1981*	*1982*
Imports (c.i.f.)	7,139·4	8,716·4	11,876·5	7,800·0
Exports and re-exports (f.o.b.)	10,106·8	12,800·9	10,529·6	7,215·9

Total trade between Nigeria and UK (according to British Department of Trade returns, in £1,000 sterling):

	1978	*1979*	*1980*	*1981*	*1982*
Imports to UK	286,212	186,046	151,563	95,069	356,802
Exports and re-exports from UK	1,133,373	638,239	1,204,358	1,428,018	1,225,164

COMMUNICATIONS

Roads (1977). There were 105,000 km of maintained roads, of which 43,360 km are paved.

In 1976, 410,315 vehicles were registered. Bus services, by private owners, operate in the larger towns and between the main towns in southern Nigeria, but the bulk of passenger and goods traffic by road is carried in lorries (mammy wagons). Taxis are available in the large towns.

Railways. There are 3,505 route-km of line 1,067 mm gauge, which in 1979 carried 988,000 tonnes of freight and 6·7m. passengers.

Aviation. There is an extensive system of internal and international air routes, serving Europe, USA, Middle East and South and West Africa. Regular services are operated by Nigerian Airways (WAAC), British Caledonian, UTA, KLM, SABENA, Swissair, PANAM and other lines. In 1981, 2·3m. passengers were carried on domestic and international transport.

Shipping. The principal ports are Lagos, Port Harcourt, Warri and Calabar.

Post and Broadcasting. Postal facilities are provided at 1,667 offices and agencies; telegraph, money order and savings bank services are provided at 280 of these. Most internal letter mail is carried by air at normal postage rates. External telegraph services are owned and operated by Nigerian External Telecommunications, Ltd, at Lagos, from which telegraphic communication is maintained with all parts of the world. There were 128,352 telephones in use in 1978, of which 45,433 were in Lagos and 9,949 in Ibadan. There is also a telex service.

Federal and some state governments have established commercial corporations for sound and television broadcasting, which are widely used in schools.

Cinemas (1974). There were 120 cinemas, with a seating capacity of 60,000. Mobile cinemas are used by the Federal and States Information Services.

Newspapers. There are over 119 newspapers, magazines and periodicals; the highest circulation of a daily is about 125,000. Most of the papers are published in English but some in the vernaculars.

JUSTICE, RELIGION, EDUCATION AND WELFARE

Justice. The highest court is the Federal Supreme Court, which consists of the Chief Justice of the Republic, not less than 2 Federal Judges and the Chief Justice of each State. It has original jurisdiction in any dispute between the Federal Republic and any State or between States; and to hear and determine appeals from any of the High Courts and from any court or tribunal established by Parliament. It may be given powers of advisory jurisdiction by Parliament in respect of the exercise of the prerogative of mercy by the Heads of State of the Republic or the States.

High Courts, presided over by a Chief Justice, are established in most of the states. Magistrates' courts are established throughout the Republic, and customary law courts in southern Nigeria. In northern States of Nigeria there are the Sharia Court of Appeal and the Court of Resolution. Moslem Law has been codified in a Penal Code and is applied through Alkali courts.

The Advisory Judicial committee has powers of appointment and discipline.

Religion. The 1963 census figures were: Moslems, 26·2m.; Christians, 19·2m.; others, 10·1m. Northern Nigeria is mainly Moslem; Southern Nigeria is predominantly Christian. The Protestant and Roman Catholic Churches have 2·5m. each.

Education. Free education for all primary school children within the 6–12-year age group was implemented in the Western State in Jan. 1955 and in Lagos and the Eastern State in Jan. 1957 and in Sept. 1976 primary education became free throughout the country. Literacy rate (1973) 25%

In 1973 there were 14,525 primary schools with 4·7m. pupils and (1971) 116,640 teachers. The demand for secondary education continues to exceed the number of places available, particularly in southern States and in Lagos. In 1973 there were 1,499 secondary schools, including some secondary modern schools, with 448,904 pupils and (1971) 18,351 teachers. All external examinations of the Universities of London and Cambridge have been taken over by the West African Examination Council.

Teacher-training institutions totalled 157 in 1973. There were also 67 trade centres and vocational training institutes for sub-professional technicians and tradesmen.

There are 13 universities in Nigeria, providing 3–5-year courses leading to the award of a first degree in various disciplines. Three technical universities at Benue, Imo and Bauchi opened in 1980–81. There are also opportunities for taking higher degrees. Free tuition was provided from 1977. The total number of students (1978) was 43,551.

University	*Students*	*University*	*Students*
Ahmadu Bello Zaria (1962)	7,366	Jos (1975)	2,555
Bayero, Kano (1975)	2,128	Lagos (1962)	5,586
Benin (1970)	3,942	Maiduguri (1975)	1,013
Calabar (1975)	1,559	Nigeria, Nsukka and Enugu (1960)	6,790
Ibadan (1948)	7,348	Port Harcourt (1975)	707
Ife (1961)	7,726	Sokoto (1975)	389
Ilorin (1975)	442		

Health. Most tropical diseases are endemic to Nigeria. Blindness, yaws, leprosy, sleeping sickness, worm infections, malaria are major health problems which, however, are yielding to remedial and preventative measures. In co-operation with the World Health Organization river blindness and malaria are being tackled on a large scale, while annual campaigns are undertaken against the danger of smallpox epidemics. Dispensaries and travelling dispensaries are found in most parts of the country.

The teaching hospital at Lagos University has 350 beds; there is also a nursing school and a teaching hospital at Ibadan University. There are medical courses at Ahmadu Bello University, University of Ife, Benin University and at Nsukka.

DIPLOMATIC REPRESENTATIVES

Of Nigeria in Great Britain (9 Northumberland Ave., London, WC2N 5BX)
High Commissioner: Alhaji Shehu Awak.

Of Great Britain in Nigeria (11 Eleke Cres., Victoria Island, Lagos)
High Commissioner: Sir Mervyn Brown, KCMG, OBE.

Of Nigeria in the USA (2201 M. St., NW, Washington, D.C., 20037)
Ambassador: Chief Abundu Yesufu Eke.

Of the USA in Nigeria (2 Eleke Cres., Lagos)
Ambassador: Thomas R. Pickering.

Of Nigeria to the United Nations
Ambassador: Alhaji Yusuff Maitama-Sule.

Books of Reference

National Development Plan 1962–68. Ministry of Economic Development, 1962
Nigeria Digest of Statistics. Lagos, 1951 ff. (quarterly)
Annual Abstract of Statistics. Federal Office of Statistics. Lagos, 1960 ff.
Nigeria Trade Journal. Federal Ministry of Commerce and Industries (quarterly)
Nigeria Handbook 1975–76. Ministry of Information, Lagos, 1975
Afolabi Ojo, G. J., *Yoruba Culture.* Univ. of London Press, 1967
Arnold, G., *Modern Nigeria.* London, 1977
Barbour, K. M. (ed.), *Nigeria in Maps.* London, 1982
Blitz, F. (ed.), *The Politics and Administration of Nigerian Government.* Lagos and London, 1965
Burns, Sir Alan, *History of Nigeria.* 8th ed. London, 1972
Comhaire, J., *Le Nigeria et ses populations.* Brussels, 1981.
Kirk-Greene, A., and Rimmer, D., *Nigeria since 1970.* London, 1981
Luckham, R., *The Nigerian Military: A Sociological Analysis of Authority and Revolt, 1960–67.* CUP, 1971
Nnoli, O., *Path to Nigerian Development.* Dakar, 1981
Olaloku, F. A., (ed.) *Structure of the Nigerian Economy.* London, 1980
Oyediran, O., *Nigerian Government and Politics under Military Rule, 1966–1979.* New York, 1980
Panter-Brick, S. K., *Nigerian Politics and Military Rule: Prelude to Civil War.* London, 1970.—*Soldiers and Oil.* London, 1978
Peil, M., *Nigerian Politics: The People's View.* London, 1976
Simmons, M., and Obe, O. A., *Nigerian Handbook 1982–83.* London, 1982
Tijjani, A. and Williams, D., (eds.) *Shehu Shagari: My Vision of Nigeria.* London, 1981
Williams, D., *President and Power in Nigeria.* London, 1982
Williams, G., *Nigeria: Economy and Society.* London, 1977

NORWAY

Capital: Oslo
Population: 4·1m. (1981)
GNP per capita: US$13,497 (1981)

Kongeriket Norge

HISTORY. By the Treaty of 14 Jan. 1814 Norway was ceded to the King of Sweden by the King of Denmark, but the Norwegian people declared themselves independent and elected Prince Christian Frederik of Denmark as their king. The foreign Powers refused to recognize this election, and on 14 Aug. a convention proclaimed the independence of Norway in a personal union with Sweden. This was followed on 4 Nov. by the election of Karl XIII (II) as King of Norway. Norway declared this union dissolved, 7 June 1905, and Sweden agreed to the repeal of the union on 26 Oct. 1905. The throne was offered to a prince of the reigning house of Sweden, who declined. After a plebiscite, Prince Carl of Denmark was formally elected King on 18 Nov. 1905, and took the name of Haakon VII.

Norwegian Sovereigns

Inge Baardssøn	1204	Erik of Pomerania	1389
Haakon Haakonssøn	1217	Kristofer af Bavaria	1442
Magnus Lagabøter	1263	Karl Knutssøn	1449
Eirik Magnussøn	1280	Same Sovereigns as in Denmark	1450–1814
Haakon V Magnussøn	1299	Christian Frederik	1814
Magnus Erikssøn	1319	Same Sovereigns as in Sweden	1814–1905
Haakon VI Magnussøn	1355	Haakon VII	1905
Olav Haakonssøn	1381	Olav V	1957
Margreta	1388		

AREA AND POPULATION. Norway is bounded north by the Arctic ocean, east by the USSR, Finland and Sweden, south by the Skagerrak Straits and west by the North Sea.

Fylker (counties)	*Area (sq. km)*	*Census population 1 Nov. 1970*	*Population 1 Jan. 1982*	*Pop. per sq. km (total area) 1982*
Oslo (City)	453·97	477,898	450,386	992·1
Akershus	4,916·44	322,321	372,347	75·7
Østfold	4,183·43	220,892	233,957	55·9
Hedmark	27,388·31	178,923	187,541	6·8
Oppland	25,259·59	172,163	181,265	7·2
Buskerud	14,933·22	198,225	215,983	14·5
Vestfold	2,215·77	174,640	187,649	84·7
Telemark	15,315·28	156,405	162,047	10·6
Aust-Agder	9,211·77	80,575	91,563	9·9
Vest-Agder	7,280·33	124,013	137,835	18·9
Rogaland	9,140·57	268,171	308,706	33·8
Hordaland	15,633·73	372,172	392,752	25·1
Sogn og Fjordane	18,633·50	100,761	106,185	5·7
Møre og Romsdal	15,104·20	223,360	236,416	15·7
Sør-Trøndelag	18,831·38	233,420	245,406	13·0
Nord-Trøndelag	22,463·25	117,718	126,339	5·6
Nordland	38,327·01	240,461	245,156	6·4
Troms	25,953·88	136,224	147,568	5·7
Finnmark	48,648·96	75,791	77,962	1·6
Total	323,894·59 [1]	3,874,133	4,107,063	12·7

[1] 125,056 sq. miles.

On 1 Nov. 1980, 2,870,975 persons lived in densely populated areas and 1,220,167 in sparsely populated areas.

Population of the principal towns at 1 Jan. 1982:

Oslo	450,386	Sandnes	37,413	Halden	26,361
Bergen	207,419	Sandefjord	35,010	Gjøvik	26,026
Trondheim	134,690	Ålesund	34,743	Moss	25,088
Stavanger	91,021	Bodø	33,498	Lillehammer	21,843
Kristiansand	61,476	Porsgrunn	31,102	Harstad	21,727
Drammen	50,098	Fredrikstad	27,719	Molde	20,932
Skien	47,167	Haugesund	26,982	Kongsberg	20,703
Tromsø	47,148	Ringerike	26,870	Steinkjer	20,667

Vital statistics for calendar years:

	Marriages	*Divorces*	*Births*	*Still-born*	*Illegitimate* [2]	*Deaths*
1979	23,055	6,608	51,580	382	6,729	41,632
1980	22,230	6,634	51,039	363	7,392	41,340
1981	22,271	7,136	50,708	299	8,169	41,844 [1]

[1] Provisional figures. [2] Excluding still-born.

CLIMATE. There is considerable variation in the climate because of the extent of latitude, the topography and the varying effectiveness of prevailing westerly winds and the Gulf Stream. Winters along the whole west coast are exceptionally mild but precipitation is considerable. Oslo. Jan. 41°F (5°C), July 63°F (17°C). Annual rainfall 29·6″ (740 mm). Bergen. Jan. 35°F (1·5°C), July 59°F (15°C). Annual rainfall 78·3″ (1,958 mm). Trondheim. Jan. 26°F (–3·5°C), July 57°F (14°C). Annual rainfall 32·1″ (870 mm).

REIGNING KING. Olav V, born 2 July 1903, married on 21 March 1929 to Princess Märtha of Sweden (born 28 March 1901, died 5 April 1954), daughter of the late Prince Carl (son of King Oscar II). He succeeded on the death of his father, King Haakon VII, on 21 Sept. 1957. *Offspring:* Princess Ragnhild Alexandra, born 9 June 1930 (married, 1953, Hr. Erling Lorentzen); Princess Astrid Maud Ingeborg, born 12 Feb. 1932 (married, 12 Jan. 1961, Hr. Johan Martin Ferner); Crown Prince Harald, born 21 Feb. 1937, married, 29 Aug. 1968, Sonja Haraldsen. *Offspring:* Princess Märtha Louise, born 22 Sept. 1971; Prince Haakon Magnus, born 20 July 1973.

CONSTITUTION AND GOVERNMENT. Norway is a constitutional and hereditary monarchy. The royal succession is in direct male line in the order of primogeniture. In default of male heirs the King may propose a successor to the Storting, but this assembly has the right to nominate another, if it does not agree with the proposal.

The Constitution, voted by the constituent assembly at Eidsvoll on 17 May 1814 and modified at various times, vests the legislative power of the realm in the Storting (Parliament). The royal veto may be exercised twice; but if the same Bill passes three Stortings formed by separate and subsequent elections it becomes the law of the land without the assent of the sovereign. The King has the command of the land, sea and air forces, and makes all appointments.

Since June 1938 all branches of the Government service, including the state church, are open to women.

National flag: Red with a blue white-bordered Scandinavian cross.

National anthem: Ja, vi elsker dette landet (words by B. Bjørnson, 1865; tune by R. Nordraak, 1865).

The Storting assembles every year. The meetings take place *suo jure*, and not by any writ from the King or the executive. They begin on the first weekday in Oct. each year, until June the following year. Every Norwegian subject of 18 years of age is entitled to vote, unless he is disqualified for a special cause. Women are, since 1913, entitled to vote under the same conditions as men. The mode of election is direct and the method of election is proportional. The country is divided into 19 districts, each electing from 4 to 15 representatives.

At the elections for the Storting held in 1981 the following parties were elected: Labour, 66; Conservative, 53; Centre Party, 11; Christian Democratic Party, 15; Socialist Left Party, 4; Party of Progress, 4, and Liberal, 2.

The Storting, when assembled, divides itself by election into the *Lagting* and the *Odelsting*. The former is composed of one-fourth of the members of the Storting, and the other of the remaining three-fourths. Each Ting (the Storting, the Odelsting and the Lagting) nominates its own president. Most questions are decided by the Storting, but questions relating to legislation must be considered and decided by the Odelsting and the Lagting separately. Only when the Odelsting and the Lagting disagree, the Bill has to be considered by the Storting in plenary sitting, and a new law can then only be decided by a majority of two-thirds of the voters. The same majority is required for alterations of the Constitution, which can only be decided by the Storting in plenary sitting. The Storting elects 5 delegates, whose duty it is to revise the public accounts. The Lagting and the ordinary members of the Supreme Court of Justice (the *Høyesterett*) form a High Court of the Realm (the *Riksrett*) for the trial of ministers, members of the *Høyesterett* and members of the Storting. The impeachment before the *Riksrett* can only be decided by the Odelsting.

The executive is represented by the King, who exercises his authority through the Cabinet or Council of State *(Statsråd)*, composed of a Prime Minister (*Statsminster*) and (at present) 16 ministers *(Statsråder)*. The ministers are entitled to be present in the Storting and to take part in the discussions, but without a vote.

A Conservative Government was formed and took office on 14 Oct. 1981; the members of the Government were:

Prime Minister: Kåre Willoch.

Foreign Affairs: Svenn Stray. *Finance:* Rolf Presthus. *Defence:* Anders C. Sjaastad. *Agriculture:* Johan C. Løken. *Commerce and Shipping:* Arne Skauge. *Justice:* Mona Røkke. *Ecclesiastical Affairs and Education:* Tore Austad. *Culture:* Lars Roar Langslet. *Local Government and Labour:* Arne Rettedal. *Industry:* Jens Halvard Bratz. *Communications:* Inger Koppernæs. *Environment:* Wenche Frogn Sellæg. *Social Affairs:* Leif Arne Heløe. *Consumer Affairs and Government Administration:* Astrid Gjertsen. *Fisheries:* Thor Listau. *Oil and Energy:* Vidkunn Hveding.

The official languages are Bokmål (or Riksmål) and Nynorsk (or Landsmål).

Local Government. For the purposes of administration the country is divided into 19 counties *(fylker)*, in each of which the central government is represented by a county governor *(fylkesmannen)*. In addition, there are 47 urban districts *(bykommuner)* and 407 rural districts *(herredskommuner)*, each of which usually corresponds in size to a parish *(prestegjeld)*. The districts are administered by district councils *(kommunestyrer)*, whose membership may vary between 13 and 85 councillors, and by a committee *(formannskap)* which is elected by and from the members of the council. The council is four times the size of the committee. The council elects a chairman and a vice-chairman from among its members. Councillors are elected in accordance with rules which are in most cases identical with the rules governing election to Parliament.

Each of the 18 counties forms a county district *(fylkeskommune)*, while the remaining one, Oslo, comprises an urban district. The supreme authority in a county district is the county council *(fylkesting)*. Every district council has until now elected its district representatives in the proportion of one to every 6,000 inhabitants, though no one district may elect more than one-third of the total number of representatives in the county council. From 1 Jan. 1976, members of the county council are elected directly by the electors of the county and the number of representatives varies between 25 and 85. In a county district the county committee *(fylkesutvalg)* occupies a position corresponding to that of the committee *(formannskap)* in the primary districts. The county committee is elected by and from among the members of the county council. The number of county committee members is one-fourth of the membership of the county council, but must be not more than 15. The county council elects from among the members of the county committee a county sheriff *(fylkesordfører)* and a deputy sheriff.

DEFENCE. Service is universal and compulsory, liability in peace-time commencing at the age of 19 and continuing till the age of 44. The training period in the Army is 12 months, in the Navy and Air Force, 15 months. The Norwegian Defence forces are organized into 2 integrated regional commands.

Army. Major units are organized mainly in Regimental Combat Teams. Peace establishment includes 1 RCT, a number of independent units and supporting elements as well as training units. Tanks include Leopard, M-48 med and NM-116 tanks (M-24/90). Total strength (1983), 24,400 (17,800 conscripts).

Navy. The Navy consists of the coastal batteries and other static defence systems and the following naval units: 15 coastal submarines, 5 frigates, 2 minelayers, 2 corvettes, 40 fast missile craft, 8 fast torpedo boats, 1 patrol vessel, 9 coastal minesweepers, 1 minehunter, 1 coastal minehunter, 1 controlled minelayer, 2 coastal patrol boats, 1 research ship, 2 diving tenders, 7 coastal transports, 1 torpedo recovery vessel, 2 training craft, 7 landing craft, 1 depot ship, 2 tugs and the royal yacht.

Personnel in 1983 totalled 8,500 officers and ratings including 1,600 in the Coast Artillery.

Coastguard. The Coastguard was established in 1977 within the framework of the Naval and Defence Command. Main tasks are Fishery Protection and Oil Rig Patrol. The Coastguard assists other government agencies in rescue service, environment, surveillance and police duties. It comprises 3 frigate-size monitors each equipped with a Lynx helicopter, 3 corvette type cutters, 7 armed trawlers (chartered until completion of new construction patrol vessels), 1 survey vessel and 20 inspection vessels.

Air Force. The Royal Norwegian Air Force consists of 2 squadrons of F-16 Fighting Falcons, 3 squadrons of F-5 supersonic fighter-bombers (to be replaced in part by F-16s), 1 unit equipped with RF-5A reconnaissance fighters, 1 maritime patrol squadron of P-3B Orions, 1 squadron of 6 C-130H Hercules transports and 3 Mystère 20s equipped for ECM duties, 1 squadron with 4 Twin Otter light transports, and a number of UH-1B Iroquois helicopters, communications and training units, as well as 4 Nike surface-to-air missile batteries and several light anti-aircraft artillery units. Ten Westland Sea King helicopters are used for search and rescue duties; 6 Lynx helicopters are shipborne for fishing protection, search and rescue and oilrig surveillance duties.

Total strength is approximately 8,300 (5,000 conscripts).

Home Guard. The Home Guard is organized in small units equipped and trained for special tasks in their home area. Compulsory service after basic training is 50 hours a year. The total strength is approximately 85,000.

INTERNATIONAL RELATIONS

Membership. Norway is a member of UN, NATO, EFTA, OECD, the Council of Europe and the Nordic Council.

ECONOMY

Budget. Current revenue and expenditure for years ending 31 Dec. (in 1,000 kroner):

	1977	*1978*	*1979*	*1980*	*1981*	*1982*[1]
Revenue	48,600,912	54,299,000	61,112,000	82,938,000	100,924,000	148,072,000
Expenditure	64,299,932	72,280,000	78,360,000	95,767,000	107,593,000	161,084,000

[1] Voted budget.

National debt[1] for years ending 31 Dec. (in 1,000 kroner):

1973	29,521,000	1976	50,290,300	1979	103,605,000
1974	33,943,000	1977	66,786,000	1980	106,908,000
1975	41,082,800	1978	86,556,000	1981	107,662,000

[1] At the rate of par on foreign loans: including treasury bills (in 1m. kroner) which amounted to 3,592 in 1976; 8,690 in 1977; 6,000 in 1978; 9,600 in 1979; 14,600 in 1980 and 17,200 in 1981.

Currency. The Norwegian *krone*, of 100 øre, is of the value of about 11 *kroner* to £1 sterling. National bank-notes of 10, 50, 100, 500 and 1,000 *kroner* are legal means of payment. March 1983, US$1 = 7·222 *kroner*; £1 = 10·675 *kroner*.

On 31 Aug. 1982 the nominal value of the coin in circulation was 867m. kroner; notes in circulation, 19,363m. kroner.

Banking. The Bank of Norway is a joint-stock bank; in 1949 the state acquired all the shares hitherto privately owned. The bank is governed by laws enacted by the State, and its directors are elected by the Storting, except the president and vice-president of the head office, who are nominated by the King. It is the only bank of issue.

At the end of 1981 there were 22 private joint-stock banks. Their total amount of capital and funds was 4,434m. kroner (capital 2,273m., funds 2,161m.). Deposits amounted to 96,770m. kroner, of which 22,348m. kroner were at call and notice, and 74,422m. kroner on time.

The number of savings banks at the end of 1981 was 308. The total amount of funds of the savings banks amounted to 3,923m. kroner, and total deposits 71,339m. kroner, of which 12,368m. kroner were at call and notice and 58,971m. kroner on time.

Weights and Measures. The metric system of weights and measures has been obligatory since 1875.

ENERGY AND NATURAL RESOURCES

Electricity. Norway is a large producer of hydro-electric energy. The potential total hydro-electric power, for a whole year at regulated minimum water flow and by 82% efficiency, is estimated at 15m. kw. or about 131,000m. kwh. annually. About 60% of the water power suitable for development consists of waterfalls with a height of at least 900 ft.

By the end of 1980 the capacity of the installations for production of thermo-electric energy amounted to only 239,927 kw. On 31 Dec. 1980, the total capacity of generators (of hydro-electric plants) was 23·21m. kva.

In 1980 the total production of electricity amounted to 84,099m. kwh. of which 99·8% was produced by hydro-electric plants.

Most of the electricity is used for industrial purposes, especially by the chemical and basic metal industries for production of nitrate of calcium and other nitrogen products, carbide, ferrosilicon and other ferro-alloys, aluminium and zinc. The paper and pulp industries are also big consumers of electricity.

Bjerve, P. J., *Planning in Norway 1947–1956.* Amsterdam, 1959
Bourneuf, A., *Norway, the Planned Revival.* Cambridge, Mass., 1958
Galenson, W., *Labor in Norway.* Cambridge, Mass., and London, 1949
Leiserson, M. W., *Wages and Economic Control in Norway, 1945–57.* Harvard Univ. Press, 1959

Minerals. Production and value of the chief concentrates, metals and alloys were:

	1979		*1980*	
Concentrates and minerals	*Tonnes*	*1,000 kroner*	*Tonnes*	*1,000 kroner*
Copper concentrates	113,492	189,685	113,857	211,993
Pyrites	240,553	...	421,367	...
Iron ore and titaniferous concentrates	4,885,504	...	4,711,427	...
Zinc and lead concentrates	58,984	69,326	56,422	62,427
Metals and alloys				
Copper	27,339	...	33,690	...
Nickel	30,686	...	37,123	...
Aluminium	663,916	4,408,136	653,377	5,240,115
Ferro-alloys	901,210	2,369,038	814,703	2,204,338
Pig-iron	650,235	...	611,660	...
Zinc	77,763	...	79,416	...
Lead and tin	452	...	328	...

Agriculture. Norway, including Svalbard and Jan Mayen, is a barren and mountainous country. The arable soil is found in comparatively narrow strips, gathered in deep and narrow valleys and around fiords and lakes. Large, continuous tracts fit for cultivation do not exist. Of the total area, 79·3% is unproductive, 18% productive forest and 2·7% under cultivation.

Principal crops	Area[1] (hectares) 1979	1980	1981	Produce[1] (tonnes) 1979	1980	1981
Wheat	17,002	15,560	13,010	67,000	65,000	58,200
Rye	1,686	1,410	880	5,300	4,700	2,900
Barley	200,084	186,910	176,190	649,200	651,000	607,600
Oats	100,672	112,690	125,860	381,500	427,800	463,100
Mixed corn	453	630	480	1,400	2,400	2,000
Potatoes	21,401	20,500	20,610	433,900	488,900	452,400
Hay	409,717	405,470	411,320	2,733,600	2,852,600	2,862,700

Livestock, 1981[1]: 17,700 horses, 1,016,700 cattle (380,700 milch cows), 2,155,400 sheep, 90,500 goats, 690,000 pigs, 3,462,000 hens.

Fur production in 1981–82 was as follows (1980–81 in brackets): Silver fox, 31,000 (12,000); blue fox, 350,000 (406,000); mink, 761,000 (850,000).

[1] Holdings with at least 5 decares agricultural area in use.

Forestry. The forests are one of the chief natural sources of wealth. The area covered with productive forests is 66,600 sq. km. 81% of the productive forest area consisted of conifers and 19% of broadleaves. Forests in public ownership cover 8,470 sq. km of productive forests. Besides the home consumption of timber and fuel wood, the essential part of the cut is consumed as raw material in sawmills and the pulp and paper industry. The annual natural increase (estimate, 1979) is about 16m. cu. metres. In 1980–81, 9·2m. cu. metres were cut for production of pulp, sawn timber and other industrial wood products.

Fisheries. The total number of persons engaged in fisheries in 1981 was 35,311, of whom 10,022 had another chief occupation. The number of fishing vessels with motor was 26,684 in 1981, and of these, 18,149 were open boats.

The value of sea fisheries in 1m. kroner in 1981 was: Cod, 1,273; capelin, 688; mackerel, 107; coal-fish (saithe), 502; deep-water prawn, 340; haddock, 197; herring, 48; dogfish, 12. The catch totalled in 1981, 2·7m. tons, valued at 3,820m. kroner.

From 1 Jan. 1977 Norway established an economic zone of 200 nautical miles, and from 3 June 1977 a fishery protection zone of 200 nautical miles around Svalbard.

INDUSTRY AND TRADE

Industry. Industry is chiefly based on raw materials produced within the country (wood, fish, etc.) and on water power, of which the country possesses a large amount. Crude petroleum and natural gas production, the manufacture of paper and paper products, industrial chemicals and basic metals are the most important export manufactures. In the following table are given figures for industrial establishments in 1980, excluding one-man units. Electrical plants, construction and building industry are not included. The values are given in 1m. kroner.

Industries	Establishments	Number of Salaried staff	Number of Wage earners	Gross value of production	Value added
Coalmining	1	172	647	116	36
Crude petroleum and natural gas	6	3,053	1,981	44,344	41,677
Metal-mining	14	802	3,201	1,229	411
Other-mining	543	489	2,738	1,184	598
Food manufacturing	2,479	9,421	40,855	29,498	1,918
Beverages	65	1,398	3,756	2,276	1,416
Tobacco	6	487	632	1,058	826
Textiles	468	2,091	9,960	3,034	1,065
Clothing, etc.	371	1,135	5,825	1,247	520
Footwear	47	164	1,233	271	116
Leather	78	174	972	271	100
Wood	1,601	4,424	18,371	8,934	2,922
Furniture and fixtures	580	1,715	7,972	2,741	1,017
Pulp and paper	173	4,055	13,419	9,071	2,204
Printing and publishing	1,610	12,444	22,927	8,055	3,312
Chemical, industrial	60	4,252	5,611	7,698	2,184
Chemical, other	173	3,225	4,497	3,147	1,097

Industries	*Establishments*	*Number of Salaried staff*	*Number of Wage earners*	*Gross value of production*	*Value added*
Petroleum, refined	3	336	458	11,469	511
Petroleum and coal	56	612	1,264	1,229	272
Rubber	90	447	1,679	578	250
Plastics	308	1,471	5,441	2,552	845
Ceramics	39	229	958	222	131
Glass	60	615	1,901	732	270
Other mineral products	499	1,897	6,561	3,796	1,401
Iron, steel and ferro-alloys	52	3,135	10,315	5,822	1,897
Non-ferrous metals	72	3,642	10,065	10,914	3,698
Metal products, except machinery	1,539	5,369	20,543	7,158	3,071
Machinery and equipment	1,073	10,211	22,592	16,286	4,758
Electrical apparatus and supplies	400	8,157	13,280	6,309	2,668
Transport equipment	1,021	8,729	36,735	14,238	5,005
Professional and scientific instruments, photographic and optical goods	55	322	1,004	311	160
Other manufacturing industries	295	699	2,624	778	313
Total (all included)	13,837	95,372	280,017	206,568	86,669

The following table sets forth the estimated value of net production, at factor cost by industries, in 1m. kroner:

	1976	*1977*	*1978*	*1979*	*1980* [1]	*1981* [1]
Agriculture	5,159	6,703	7,283	7,273	7,844	9,259
Forestry	1,397	1,349	1,410	1,535	1,735	2,114
Fishing	1,338	1,381	1,043	1,162	1,405	1,633
Mining and quarrying	728	779	767	809	818	1,185
Manufacturing	32,376	34,008	35,309	41,484	42,299	47,059
Crude petroleum and gas production	3,692	4,116	8,458	15,346	32,623	38,320
Electricity, gas and water	2,895	2,912	3,975	4,020	4,141	5,803
Construction [2]	10,213	11,927	13,476	13,326	14,721	17,028
Wholesale and retail trade	15,012	16,489	18,256	18,336	23,094	26,978
Restaurants and hotels	1,824	2,190	2,490	2,682	3,068	3,726
Water transport	3,080	2,230	3,235	4,708	6,323	6,012
Other transport [3]	6,665	7,303	8,386	9,192	10,460	12,576
Financial institutions	5,322	5,977	7,217	8,164	10,241	12,886
Real estate	5,281	6,113	6,731	7,407	8,466	9,923
Business services	3,128	3,843	4,278	5,665	6,305	7,720
Government services, social and personal services	31,890	36,567	40,825	43,596	49,069	56,609
Imputed bank service charge	-4,959	-5,629	-6,158	-7,278	-8,727	-11,540
Net production at factor cost	125,041	138,258	156,981	177,427	213,885	247,291
+ Indirect taxes	31,012	36,327	37,946	41,106	48,105	54,998
- Subsidies	11,624	14,111	16,446	16,743	19,504	21,112
Net domestic product (market price)	144,429	160,474	178,481	201,790	242,486	281,177

[1] Provisional figures.
[2] Including drilling of crude oil and natural gas wells.
[3] Including pipeline transport of oil and gas.

Labour. The distribution of the population according to professions in 1980, showed 142,025 (7%) economically active[1] in agriculture, forestry and gardening; 598,567 (29·6%) in mining, manufacturing, building, etc.; 308,408 (15·3%) in commerce; 176,605 (8·7%) in transport; 21,694 (1·1%) in fishery, sealing and whaling; 773,772 (38·3%) in public administration, liberal professions and services; total, 2,021,071.

[1] Persons aged 16 or more with at least 100 hours paid work in one year.

Commerce. Total imports and exports in calendar years (in 1,000 kroner):

	1976	*1977*	*1978*	*1979*	*1980*	*1981*
Imports	60,532,915	68,579,245	60,168,613	69,338,924	83,601,605	89,687,802
Exports	43,330,277	46,438,663	57,083,799	68,527,167	91,672,433	104,265,370

Trading according to countries was as follows (in 1,000 kroner):

	1980		1981	
Countries	*Imports*	*Exports*	*Imports*	*Exports*
Argentina	123,838	92,457	97,472	124,707
Australia and New Zealand	636,283	270,541	789,888	260,620
Belgium and Luxembourg	2,829,350	943,643	2,482,085	1,037,904
Brazil	873,487	481,546	825,975	386,017
Canada	2,011,024	374,139	1,747,167	389,810
Czechoslovakia	203,598	137,779	213,957	139,546
Denmark	5,157,762	3,815,751	5,451,703	4,156,264
Fed. Republic of Germany	11,598,335	15,480,248	13,179,236	18,698,078
Finland	3,122,841	1,479,796	3,914,027	1,883,965
France	3,027,134	2,096,651	3,135,168	2,221,306
India	104,322	204,603	113,948	284,214
Italy	1,934,885	1,342,769	1,890,708	1,287,315
Netherlands	2,827,405	3,361,591	2,870,960	3,833,542
Poland	713,174	338,985	378,711	307,670
Portugal	487,993	189,637	519,537	354,894
Spain	626,081	444,565	738,602	490,603
Sweden	13,999,270	8,505,791	14,737,658	9,377,609
Switzerland	1,366,119	670,465	1,344,503	790,756
UK	12,265,840	37,897,118	12,195,035	41,658,718
USA	6,790,588	2,729,115	8,271,973	3,872,343
USSR	457,496	554,160	1,019,231	715,252

Principal items of import in 1981 (in 1,000 kroner): Machinery, transport equipment, etc., 30,702,053; fuel oil, etc., 12,977,783; base metals and manufactures thereof, 8,044,125; chemicals and related products, 5,676,914; textiles, 2,511,056.

Principal items of export in 1981 (in 1,000 kroner): Machinery and transport equipment, 13,147,440; base metals and manufactures thereof, 12,796,095; crude oil, 31,047,335; edible animal products, 5,079,893; pulp and paper, 4,690,638.

Total trade between Norway and UK (British Department of Trade returns, in £1,000 sterling):

	1978	*1979*	*1980*	*1981*	*1982*
Imports to UK	1,444,752	1,327,212	1,441,418	1,943,206	2,023,441
Exports and re-exports from UK	650,106	768,815	791,530	876,937	924,651

COMMUNICATIONS

Roads. On 31 Dec. 1981 the length of the public roads (including roads in towns) was 82,482 km. Of these, 57,020 km were main roads; 48,375 km had some kind of paving, mostly bituminous and oil-gravel treatment, the rest being gravel-surfaced.

Number of registered motor vehicles (31 Dec. 1981) was 1,753,508, including 1,278,817 passenger cars (including taxis), 158,740 lorries and vans, 12,936 buses, 152,575 motor cycles and mopeds. The scheduled bus and lorry services in 1980 drove 4,257m. passenger-km and 645m. net ton-km.

Railways. The length of state railways on 31 Dec. 1981 was 4,242 km; of private companies, 16 km. On 2,443 km of state and 16 km of private railways electric traction is installed. Total receipts of the state railways and road traffic in 1981 were 2,171m. kroner; total expenses (excluding depreciation and interest on capital), 2,848m. kroner. The state railways carried 26·3m. tonnes of freight (of which 15·7m. was iron ore on the Ofoten railway) and 38·9m. passengers.

Aviation. Det Norske Luftfartselskap (DNL) started its post-war activities on 1 April 1946. On 1 Aug. 1946 DNL, together with DDL (Danish Airlines) and ABA/SILA (Swedish Airlines), formed the 'Scandinavian Airlines System'—SAS. The 3 companies remained independent units, but all services were co-ordinated. In 1951 a new agreement was signed (retroactive from 1 Oct. 1950) according to which the 3 national companies became holding partners in a new organization which took over the entire operational system. Denmark and Norway hold each two-sevenths and Sweden three-sevenths of the capital, but they have joint responsibility towards third parties.

In the autumn of 1982 SAS had a fleet of 86 jet planes. Length of route network, about 252,000 km. Scheduled air services are run by SAS, Braathens South-American and Far East Air transport service (SAFE) and Wideroes Flyveselskap service. The Norwegian share of the scheduled air service run by SAS is two-sevenths of the SAS service on international routes and the total SAS service in Norway.

	1,000 km flown	*Passengers carried*	*1,000 passenger-km*	*Post, luggage, freight and passengers (1,000 ton-km) Total*	*Of which post*
1978	56,525	4,487,440	3,789,000	476,000	16,000
1979	58,950	4,866,926	4,070,000	497,000	16,000
1980	57,885	4,809,612	4,068,000	493,000	18,000
1981	55,091	4,967,880	4,062,000	498,000	19,000

Shipping. The total registered mercantile marine on 1 Jan. 1982 was 1,682 vessels, 21·7m. gross tons (steam and motor vessels above 100 gross tons). These figures do not include fishing and catching boats, tugs, salvage vessels, icebreakers and similar special types of vessels, totalling 793 vessels of 360,000 gross tons.

Vessels entering Norway from foreign countries 1980	*Total No.*	*Net tons*
Norwegian	7,720	13,635
Foreign	8,545	23,635
Total entered	16,265	37,270

Goods (in 1,000 tonnes) in 1981 discharged, 18,327; loaded, 35,659, of which 14,062 was Swedish iron ore shipped from Narvik.

Post and Broadcasting. Number of telephones on 31 Dec. 1981 was 1,992,000 (49 per 100 of population). Receipts, 5,201·7m. kroner; expenses, 5,074·3m. kroner (interest on capital included) for State Telecommunications. *Norsk Rikskringkasting* is a non-commercial enterprise operated by an independent state organization and broadcasts 1 programme (P1) on long-, medium-, and short-waves and on FM and 1 programme (P2) on FM. Local programmes are also broadcast. It broadcasts 1 TV programme from 1,300 transmitters. Colour programmes are broadcast by PAL system. Number of television licences, 1,232,854.

Cinemas. There were 445 cinemas with a seating capacity of 137,437 in 1980.

Newspapers. There were 71 daily newspapers with a combined circulation of 1,803,000 in 1981.

JUSTICE, RELIGION, EDUCATION AND WELFARE

Justice. The judicature in Norway is common to both civil and criminal cases. The same judges, who are state officials, preside over both kinds of cases. The participation of lay assessors and jurors, summoned for each case, varies according to the civil or criminal nature of the case.

The ordinary Court of First Instance *(Herreds- og byrett)* is presided over by a judge who in criminal cases is, and in civil cases may be, assisted by 2 lay assessors, chosen by ballot from a panel elected by the district council. In criminal matters the Court of First Instance is generally competent in cases where the maximum penalty incurred is 5 years imprisonment. Altogether there are 100 Courts of First Instance. There is a Conciliation Council *(Forliksråd)* for each community, consisting of 3 men or women, elected by the district council, before which, as a general rule, civil cases must first be brought for mediation.

The Court of Second Instance *(Lagmannsrett)* is presided over by a judge, together with 2 other judges. In civil matters they may be assisted by lay assessors, ordinarily 4 but in some cases 2, chosen and elected in the same way as mentioned above. In criminal cases the lay element is a jury composed of 10 jurors deciding the question of guilt. This court is an ordinary court of appeal in civil cases. In criminal cases competence of the court is limited to appeals directed against alleged mistakes by the lower court in its adjudication of the question of guilt and in such cases a renewed trial will take place. (If the complaint is only based on other alleged mistakes by the lower court the appeal goes to the Supreme Court, see below.) In addition, as a court of first instance, this court takes cognizance of all criminal cases (other than those coming under the *Riksrett*—the court for impeachments) which do not come under the competence of the Court of First Instance. The kingdom is divided into 5 districts *(Lagdømmer)* for the purpose of the Courts of Second Instance.

The Supreme Court *(Høyesterett)* is the ultimate court of appeal. In criminal cases competence of the court, however, is limited to complaints against the application of laws, measuring out of the penalty and trial of the case of the subordinate courts. The Supreme Court consists of a president and 17 judges. In each single case the court consists of 5 judges. A new Act on Criminal Procedure has been adopted by Parliament, but has not yet been implemented. The new act does not, in any major way, change the procedure in criminal cases.

All serious offences are prosecuted by the State. The public prosecution is led by a general prosecutor *(riksadvokat)* and there are 19 district prosecutors *(statsadvokater)*. Counsel for the defence is, generally, paid by the State.

There are 3 central penal and correctional institutions for delinquents in which were detained (3 Oct. 1982), 322 persons. There are also 35 local prisons in which were detained (3 Oct. 1982) 1,598 persons.

Religion. There is complete freedom of religion, the Evangelical Lutheran Church, however, being the national church, endowed by the State. Its clergy are nominated by the King. Ecclesiastically Norway is divided into 10 *Bispedømmer* (bishoprics), 89 *Prostier* (provostships or archdeaconries) and 614 *Prestegjeld* (clerical districts). There were 133,028 members of registered religious communities outside the Evangelical Lutheran Church, subsidized by central government and local authorities in 1981. The Roman Catholics are under a Bishop at Oslo, a Vicar Apostolic at Trondheim and a Vicar Apostolic at Tromsø.

Education. In Norway the children normally start their school attendance the year they complete 7 and finish compulsory school the year they complete 16.

On 1 Oct. 1981 the number of primary schools and pupils were as follows: 3,526 primary schools, 586,141 pupils; 92 special schools for the handicapped, 3,340 pupils.

On 1 Oct. 1980 the number of pupils in upper secondary schools, *i.e.*, folk high schools, secondary general schools and vocational schools, was 183,664.

There are in Norway 4 universities and 8 institutions equivalent to universities. In autumn 1980 the total number of students was 40,620. The University of Oslo, founded in 1811, had 18,863 students. The University of Bergen, founded in 1948, had 7,588 students. The University of Trondheim consists of the Norwegian Institute of Technology, founded in 1910, and the College of Arts and Science, founded in 1925. At each of them the number of students was in autumn 1980, 4,802 and 3,263 respectively. The University of Tromsø was established in 1968; 1,680 students were registered in autumn 1980. The other university institutions had 4,424 students.

In addition there were at other schools of higher education, 33,236 students. These included 13,696 at colleges for teachers, 6,249 at colleges for engineers and 4,902 at district colleges.

In 1980 there were 4,724 Norwegian students and pupils attending foreign universities and schools.

Health. In 1980 there were 8,981 doctors and 64,909 hospital beds.

Social Security. In 1981, 48·53m. kroner were paid under different social insurance schemes, amounting to 17·3% of the net national income.

The National Insurance Act of 17 June 1966, which came into force on 1 Jan. 1967, replaced the schemes relating to old age pensions, disability benefits, widows' and mothers' pensions, benefits to unmarried women, 'survivors' benefit for children and rehabilitation aid. Schemes relating to health insurance, unemployment insurance and occupational injury insurance were revised and incorporated in National Insurance Scheme on 1 Jan. 1971. As from 1 Jan. 1981, benefits to divorced and separated supporters also are covered by the National Insurance Scheme.

The following conspectus gives a survey of schemes established by law. Many municipalities grant additional benefits to old-age, disablement and survivor's pensions.

Type of scheme	*Intro-duced*[1]	*Scope*	*Principal benefits as from 1 May 1982*
National insurance	1967 (1982)		
Sickness benefits[2]	1911	All residents	Medical benefits: hospital expenses; about ⅔ of doctors' fees, important medicines, etc., daily sickness allowances: kr. 13 to 634 per day cash. The new sickness allowance scheme (1 July 1978) entitles employees to a daily allowance equal to 100% of their gross earned income (within certain limits) from and including the first day of absence; self-employed persons, ordinary 65% of gross earned income as from the 15th day. Supplementary insurance available. The allowances are taxable
Unemployment benefits[2]	1939	Nearly all wage-earners	Daily allowance during unemployment kr. 36 to 396 per day, taxable as from 1 Jan. 1980. Contributions to training and retraining, removal expenses, wage subsidies in the case of relief work
Rehabilitation benefits[3]	1961	Persons unfit for work because of disablement and persons who have a substantially limited general functional capacity	Training; treatment; rehabilitation allowance grants and loans Full rehabilitation allowance equals old age pension
Disability benefits[3]	1961	All residents disabled before the age of 67	*A basic grant* (ordinary rate kr. 2,928 per annum) and *an assistance grant* (ordinary rate kr. 4,872 per annum) to persons with special needs. In certain cases the benefits may be increased. The rates are fixed by the Storting, independent of the basic amount. *Disability pension* to persons between 16 and 67 years of age, occupationally disabled by at least 50%, unfit for rehabilitation Full disability pension equals old age pension
Occupational injury benefits[2] (industrial workers 1895; fishermen 1909; seamen 1913; military personnel 1953, combined in the act of occupational injury insurance *1960*)	1960	All employed persons, school children and students; self-employed on a voluntary basis	The ordinary benefits of the National Insurance, *e.g.*, sickness and rehabilitation benefits, basic grants, assistance grants, disability pensions, and benefits to survivors granted according to special rules which in almost all cases are more favourable for the insured person —or his survivors than the ordinary rules *An occupational injury compensation,* alone or in addition to a disability pension
Old age pensions[3]	1937	All persons above 67 years of age	Basic pensions: Single, kr. 21,200; couples, kr. 31,800 per annum; supplementary pensions based on previous pensionable income; basic grant; assistance grant; various allowances
Death grants	1967	All residents	A certain amount fixed by the Storting, for the time being kr. 4,000

For notes *see* bottom of table overleaf.

Type of scheme	*Introduced* [1]	*Scope*	*Principal benefits as from 1 May 1982*
Survivors' benefits [3]	1965	All residents	Full pension = kr. 21,200 per annum + 55% of the supplementary pension due to the deceased, *transitional benefits,* child care allowance and educational allowances
Children's pension [3]	1958	Under 18 (20) years of age, after loss of one or both parents	40% of basic amount (kr. 8,480) for first child, 25% (kr. 5,300) for each additional child. If both parents are dead, full survivors' pension for first, 40% of basic amount for second, 25% third, etc., child
Benefits to unmarried supporters [3]	1965	Unmarried mothers or fathers	Maternity grant kr. 6,438, transitional benefit, full amount kr. 21,200 per annum, child care allowance and educational allowances
Benefits to divorced and separated supporters [4]	1972	Divorced and separated supporters	Same kind of benefits as unmarried supporters above
Benefits to unmarried persons forced to live at home [3]	1965	Unmarried persons under 67 years of age having stayed at home for at least 5 years to give necessary care and attention to parents or other near relatives	Transitional benefit or a pension that equals the basic amount, educational allowances
Special supplement to National Insurance pensions or transitional benefits	1969 (1982)	Pensioners and persons with transitional allowance on basic rates	Full special supplement to married pensioner 46% of basic amount, others 49% of basic amount
Compensation supplement to National Insurance pensions or transitional benefits	1970	Pensioners, persons with transitional benefits (except unmarried, divorced and separated supporters) or rehabilitation allowances	Full compensation supplement kr. 500 for single persons and kr. 750 for married couples
Family allowances	1946 (1982)	All families with children under 16 years of age	Kr. 3,252, for the first child, kr. 4,008 for the second, kr. 5,028 for the third, kr. 5,412 for the fourth and kr. 5,700 for the fifth and each additional child. Single supporters receive benefit for one more child than the actual number of children
War pensions	1946 (1981)	War victims, 1939–45	Pensions up to kr. 89,700 per annum; widows' and children's pensions
Special pension schemes:		Persons with at least: [5]	Maximum old-age pension for couples:
Seamen	1948 (1982)	150 months service (360 „ „)	Kr. 69,480 [6] per annum (officers) Kr. 49,632 [6] „ „ (others)
Forestry workers	1952 (1980)	750 premium weeks (1,500 „ „)	Kr. 18,000 per annum
Fishermen	1958 (1981)	750 premium weeks (1,500 „ „)	Kr. 22,500 „ „

[1] Date of latest revision in brackets.
[2] Transferred to national insurance scheme and revised in 1971.
[3] Transferred to national insurance scheme and revised in 1967.
[4] Transferred to national insurance scheme and revised in 1981.
[5] Requirements for maximum pensions in brackets.
[6] Supplements for service during war not included.

Provisions have been laid down for the integration of more than one benefit, pension, etc., so as to limit the total amount.

SVALBARD

An archipelago situated between 10° and 35° E. long. and between 74° and 81° N. lat. Total area, 62,000 sq. km (24,000 sq. miles).

The main islands of the archipelago are Spitsbergen (formerly called Vestspitsbergen), Nordaustlandet, Edgeøya, Barentsøya, Prins Karls Forland, Bjørnøya, Hopen, Kong Karls Land, Kvitøya, and many small islands. The arctic climate is tempered by mild winds from the Atlantic.

The archipelago was probably discovered by Norsemen in 1194 and rediscovered by the Dutch navigator Barents in 1596. In the 17th century the very lucrative whale-hunting caused rival Dutch, British and Danish–Norwegian claims to sovereignty and quarrels about the hunting-places. But when in the 18th century the whale-hunting ended, the question of the sovereignty of Svalbard lost its significance; it was again raised in the 20th century, owing to the discovery and exploitation of coalfields. By a treaty, signed on 9 Feb. 1920 in Paris, Norway's sovereignty over the archipelago was recognized. On 14 Aug. 1925 the archipelago was officially incorporated in Norway.

Coal is the principal product. Of the 3 Norwegian and 3 Soviet mining camps, 2 Norwegian and 2 Soviet camps are operating. Total population on 31 Dec. 1981 was 3,910, of which 1,400 Norwegians, 2,498 Soviet citizens, and 12 Poles. In 1981, 397,652 tonnes of coal were exported from the Norwegian and 477,915 tonnes from the Soviet mines.

Norwegian and foreign companies have been prospecting for oil. So far 5 deep drillings have been made, but oil and gas finds have not been reported.

There are Norwegian meteorological and/or radio stations at the following places: Bjørnøya (since 1920), Hopen (1945), Isfjord Radio (1934), Longyearbyen (1930), Svalbard Lufthavn (1975) and Ny-Ålesund (1961). A research station, administered by Norsk Polarinstitutt, was erected at Ny-Ålesund in 1968 for various observations and investigations. An airport near Longyearbyen (Svalbard Lufthavn) opened in 1975.

Norsk Polarinstitutt, Skrifter, Oslo, from 1948 (under different titles from 1922)
Greve, T., *Svalbard: Norway in the Arctic.* Oslo, 1975
Hisdal, V., *Geography of Svalbard.* Norsk Polarinstitutt, Oslo, 1976
Orvin, A. K., 'Twenty-five Years of Norwegian Sovereignty in Svalbard 1925–1950' (in *The Polar Record,* 1951)

JAN MAYEN

This bleak, desolate and mountainous island of volcanic origin and partly covered by glaciers, is situated 71° N. lat. and 8° 30′ W. long., 300 miles NNE of Iceland. The total area is 380 sq. km (147 sq. miles). Beerenberg, its highest peak, reaches a height of 2,277 metres. Volcanic activity, which had been dormant, was reactivated in Sept. 1970.

The island was possibly discovered by Henry Hudson in 1608, and it was first named Hudson's Tutches (Touches). It was again and again rediscovered and renamed. Its present name derives from the Dutch whaling captain Jan Jacobsz May, who indisputably discovered the island in 1614. It was uninhabited, but occasionally visited by seal hunters and trappers, until 1921 when Norway established a radio and meteorological station. On 8 May 1929 Jan Mayen was officially proclaimed as incorporated in the Kingdom of Norway. Its relation to Norway was finally settled by law of 27 Feb. 1930. A LORAN station (1959) and a CONSOL station (1968) have been established.

BOUVET ISLAND
Bouvetøya

This uninhabited volcanic island, mostly covered by glaciers and situated 54° 25′ S. lat. and 3° 21′ E. long., was discovered in 1739 by a French naval officer, Jean Baptiste Loziert Bouvet, but no flag was hoisted till, in 1825, Capt. Norris raised the Union Jack. In 1928 Great Britain waived its claim to the island in favour of Norway, which in Dec. 1927 had occupied it. A law of 27 Feb. 1930 declared Bouvetøya a Norwegian dependency. The area is 50 sq. km (19 sq. miles). From 1977 Norway has had an automatic meteorological station on the island, and 5 men operated a meteorological station there during the 1978–79 season.

PETER I ISLAND
Peter I Øy

This uninhabited island, situated 68° 48′ S. lat. and 90° 35′ W. long., was sighted in 1821 by the Russian explorer, Admiral von Bellingshausen. The first landing was made in 1929 by a Norwegian expedition which hoisted the Norwegian flag. On 1 May 1931 Peter I Island was placed under Norwegian sovereignty, and on 24 March 1933 it was incorporated in Norway as a dependency. The area is 180 sq. km (69 sq. miles).

QUEEN MAUD LAND
Dronning Maud Land

On 14 Jan. 1939 the Norwegian Cabinet placed that part of the Antarctic Continent from the border of Falkland Islands dependencies in the west to the border of the Australian Antarctic Dependency in the east (between 20° W. and 45° E.) under Norwegian sovereignty. The territory had been explored only by Norwegians and hitherto been ownerless. Since 1949 expeditions from various countries have explored the area. In 1957 Dronning Maud Land was given the status of a Norwegian dependency.

DIPLOMATIC REPRESENTATIVES

Of Norway in Great Britain (25 Belgrave Sq., London, SW1X 8QD)
Ambassador: Rolf Busch.

Of Great Britain in Norway (Thomas Heftyesgate 8, Oslo, 2)
Ambassador: Dame Gillian Brown, DCVO, CMG.

Of Norway in the USA (2720 34th Street, NW, Washington, D.C., 20008)
Ambassador: Knut Hedemann.

Of the USA in Norway (Drammensveien 18, Oslo, 2)
Ambassador: Mark E. Austad.

Of Norway to the United Nations
Ambassador: Tom Vraalsen.

Books of Reference

Statistical Information: The Central Bureau of Statistics, Statistisk Sentralbyrå (Dronningensgate 16, Oslo 1), was founded in 1876 as an independent state institution. *Director:* Arne Øien. The earliest census of population was taken in 1769. The Sentralbyrå publishes the series *Norges Offisielle Statistikk,* Norway's official statistics (from 1828), and *Social Economic Studies* (from 1954). The main publications are:

Statistisk Årbok for Norge (annual, from 1880; from 1952 bilingual Norwegian–English)
Økonomisk Utsyn (annual, from 1935; with English summary from 1952)
Historisk Statistikk 1978 (historical statistics; bilingual Norwegian–English)
Statistisk Månedshefte (monthly, from 1880; with English index)
Sosialt Utsyn 1980 (social survey). Irregular

Norges Statskalender. From 1816; annual from 1877
Facts about Norway. Ed. by Aftenposten. 17th ed. Oslo, 1982
Derry, T. K., *A History of Modern Norway, 1814–1972.* OUP, 1973.—*A History of Scandinavia.* London, 1979
Ekeland, S., *Norway in the Modern World.* Oslo, 1976
Glässer, E., *Norwegen* [bibliography] Darmstadt, 1978

Gleditsch, Th., *Engelsk–norsk ordbok*, 2nd ed. Oslo, 1948
Grønland, E., *Norway in English, Books on Norway . . . 1742–1959*. Oslo, 1961
Haugen, E., *Norwegian–English Dictionary*, Oslo, 1965
Helvig, M., *Norway: Land, People, Industries, a Brief Geography*. 3rd ed. Oslo, 1970
Holtedahl, O. (ed.), *Geology of Norway*. Oslo, 1960
Hove, O., *The System of Education*. Oslo, 1968
Imber, W., *Norway*. Oslo, 1980
Knudsen, O., *Norway at Work*. Oslo, 1972
Larsen, K., *A History of Norway*. New York, 1948
Midgaard, J., *A Brief History of Norway*. Oslo, 1969
Nielsen, K., and Nesheim, A., *Lapp Dictionary: Lapp–English–Norwegian*. 5 vols., Oslo 1963
Orvik, N. (ed.), *Fears and Expectations: Norwegian Attitudes Toward European Integration*. Oslo, 1972
Paine, R., *Coast Lapp Society*. 2 vols. Tromsø, 1957–65
Popperwell, R. G., *Norway*. London, 1972
Udgaard, N. M., *Great Power Politics and Norwegian Foreign Policy*. Oslo, 1973
Vorren, Ø. (ed.), *Norway North of 65*. Oslo, 1960

National Library: The University Library, Drammensvein 42b, Oslo. *Director:* Ben Rugaas.

OMAN

Capital: Muscat
Population: 1·5m. (1982)
GNP per capita: US$4,380 (1980)

Sultanate of Oman

AREA AND POPULATION. The Sultanate of Oman, known as the Sultanate of Muscat and Oman until 1970, is an independent sovereign state, situated in south-east Arabia. Its coastline is over 1,000 miles long and extends from the Ras al Khaimah Shaikdom near Bukha on the west side of the Musandum Peninsula to Ras Dharbat Ali, which marks the boundary between Oman and the territory of the People's Democratic Republic of Yemen. The Sultanate extends inland to the borders of the Rub' al Khali ('Empty Quarter') across three geographical divisions—a coastal plain, a range of hills and a plateau. The coastal plain varies in width from 10 miles near Suwaiq to practically nothing in the vicinity of Mutrah and Muscat towns, where the hills descend abruptly into the sea. These hills are for the most part barren except at the highest part of the mountainous region of the Jebel Akhdar (summit 9,998 ft) where there is some cultivation. The plateau has an average height of 1,000 ft. With the exception of oases there is little or no cultivation. North-west of Muscat the coastal plain, known as the Batinah, is fertile and prosperous. The date gardens extend for over 150 miles. Whereas the coastline between the capital, Muscat, and the southern province of Dhofar is barren, Dhofar itself is highly fertile. Its principal town is Salalah on the coast which is served by the port of Rasut.

In the valleys of the interior, as well as on the Batinah, date cultivation has reached a high level, and there are possibilities of agricultural development subject to present water resources and soil surveys. The average annual crop of dates is estimated at 50,000 tons, most of which is exported to India. Camels are bred in large numbers by the inland tribes. There are no industries of any importance, although a copper industry was being established in 1980, and fishing, water resources, soil and agricultural surveys are being undertaken.

The area has been estimated at about 105,000 sq. miles and the population at 1·5m., chiefly Arabs; of these, some 40,000 live in Dhofar. The town of Muscat is the capital which, while formerly of some commercial importance, has now lost most of its trade to the adjacent port of Mutrah (combined populations, 25,000), the starting point for the trade routes into the interior. The population of both towns consists of pure Arabs, Indians, Pakistanis and Negroes; numerous merchants are Khojas (from Sind and Kutch) and Hindus (mostly from Gujarat and Bombay). Other ports are Sohar, Khaburah and Sur, Rasut in the south; none, however, affords shelter from bad weather.

The port of Gwadur and a small tract of country on the Balúchistán coast of the Gulf of Oman were handed over to Pakistan on 8 Sept. 1958.

The **Kuria Muria** islands were ceded to the UK in 1854 by the Sultan of Muscat and Oman for the purpose of a cable station. On 30 Nov. 1967 the islands were retroceded to the Sultan of Muscat and Oman, in accordance with the wishes of the population.

RULER. The present Sultan is Qaboos bin Said (born Nov. 1940). He took over from his father Said bin Taimur, on 23 July 1970 in a Palace *coup*.

In Oct. 1981 the Sultan issued three decrees establishing a 45-member State advisory council.

CONSTITUTION AND GOVERNMENT. Oman is an absolute monarchy and there is no formal constitution. The Sultan legislates by decree and appoints a Cabinet to assist him; he holds the posts of Prime Minister and Minister of Foreign

Affairs, Defence and Finance. Besides 17 departmental Ministers, the Cabinet also includes:

Deputy Prime Minister for Security and Defence: Sayyid Fahar Bin-Taimur al-Said.

Deputy Prime Minister for Legal Affairs: Sayyid Fahad Bin-Mahmoud al-Said.

Special Advisor to Sultan, Governor of Muscat: Sayyid Thuwaini Bin-Shihab al-Said.

Special Advisor to Sultan on Religious and Historical Affairs: Mohammad Bin-Ahmad.

Minister of State for Foreign Affairs: Qais Abdel-Moneim al-Zawawi.

Minister of State, Governor of Dhofar: Hilal Bin-Saud Bin-Hareb al-Busaidi.

National flag: Red, with a white panel in the upper fly and a green one in the lower fly, and in the canton the national emblem in white.

Local government: Oman is divided into 10 provinces *(liwas)* and sub-divided into 41 governates *(wilayats)* each under a governor *(wali).*

DEFENCE

Army. The Army is of 8 infantry battalions with personnel of (1983) 15,000 with 3 artillery regiments, a signals regiment, a sapper company, a paratrooper squadron and an armoured-car regiment. There is also a Royal Guard brigade.

Navy. The Navy comprises 1 very fast missile-armed corvette, 2 fast missile-armed patrol boats, 4 fast gunboats, 4 inshore patrol craft, a logistic support ship, 1 supply ship, 6 landing craft, 1 survey craft, 1 training ship and 1 royal yacht (corvette type). Under construction are 2 more missile-armed very fast corvettes. All the warships are British-built. The marine police operate 10 coastal patrol boats, 7 launches, 1 logistics support craft and 6 harbour patrol boats. Naval personnel in 1983 totalled 1,500 officers and ratings.

Air Force. The Air Force, formed in 1959, had in 1983 a strike/interceptor squadron of Jaguars, a ground attack/interceptor squadron of Hunters, a squadron of Strikemaster light jet training/attack aircraft, 3 BAC One-Eleven twin-turbofan transports, 1 Falcon VIP transport, 3 C-130H Hercules, 1 twin-turboprop Buffalo, 7 Defender and 15 Skyvan light transports, 27 Agusta-Bell 205, 212, 214B and JetRanger helicopters for security duties and 2 Bravo piston-engined trainers. Further Jaguars are on order. Air defence force has batteries of Rapier low-level surface-to-air missiles. Personnel (1983) about 2,100.

INTERNATIONAL RELATIONS

Membership. Oman is a member of UN and the Arab League.

Treaties. The Treaty of Friendship, Commerce and Navigation between Britain and the Sultan signed on 20 Dec. 1951, reaffirmed the close ties which have existed between the British Government and the Sultanate of Oman for over a century and a half. A Memorandum of Understanding signed in June 1982 provided for regular consultations on international and bilateral issues.

ECONOMY

Planning. The 5-year development plan (1976–80) had an expenditure of R.O. 2,556m. Expenditure for the second 5-year plan (1981–85) is (estimate) R.O. 7,368m.

Budget. Revenue (1981) R.O. 1,399m. (1,204m. from oil); expenditure, 1,410m. (defence, 582m.).

Currency. The *Rial Omani* was introduced in Nov. 1972 replacing the *Rial Saidi.* It is divided into 1,000 *baiza.* There are notes of 100, 250 and 500 *baiza* and 1, 5 and 10 *Rial Omani* and coins of 2, 5, 10, 20, 50 and 100 *baiza.* The exchange rate in March 1983 was £1 = 512 *baiza*; US$1 = 346 *baiza.*

Weights and Measures. The metric system of measurement is in operation. Transactions in the former measurements are now illegal.

OIL. The economy of Oman is dominated by the oil industry, which provides nearly all Government revenue. In 1937 Petroleum Concessions (Oman) Ltd, a subsidiary of the Iraq Petroleum Co., was granted a 75-year oil concession extending over the whole of Oman, although it relinquished Dhofar in 1950. In 1951 the company's name was changed to Petroleum Development (Oman) Ltd. The company (PDO) regained the Dhofar concession area in 1969. When some of the IPC partners withdrew from Oman in 1960, Shell took over the management of PDO with an 85% interest (minority interests were held by Compagnie Française des Pétroles, 10% and Gulbenkian, 5%). At the beginning of 1974 the Oman Government bought a 25% share in PDO, increasing this retroactively to 60% in July. A Joint Management Committee was established. Other companies active in exploration activities in Oman, with mixed success, include Amoco, Elf-Acquitaine and a consortium of Deminex, Agip and Hispanoil with BP as operator.

Oil in commercial quantities was discovered in 1964 and production began at a rate of 200,000 bbls per day in 1967. Production has fluctuated from year to year, peaking in 1976 at 366,000 bbls per day. Due to conditions on the international oil market, production fell to a low of 282,000 bbls per day in 1980 but was restored to about 330,000 bbls per day in 1981. Production in 1982 remained close to this level. Total reserves were estimated in 1981 to be 2,482m. bbls, or sufficient for 20 years at the current rate of production.

Oman is not a member of OPEC or OAPEC but tends to follow OPEC pricing policy.

COMMERCE. Trade is mainly with UK, India, Australia, Japan and the neighbouring Gulf States. Total imports for 1980 were valued at R.O. 713·3m., mainly rice, wheat, flour, milk and milk products, machinery, cement, vehicles and accessories, electrical goods, petroleum products and building materials. The main countries exporting to Oman in 1981 were UK, USA, UAE, Japan, India, Australia, Netherlands and the Federal Republic of Germany.

Exports, which, excluding oil, consisted of dates, limes, dried fish, tobacco leaf, fruits and vegetables, were valued at R.O. 1,294·6m. in 1980 (non-oil, R.O. 50m.).

Total trade between Oman and UK (Brtish Department of Trade returns, in £1,000 sterling):

	1977	*1978*	*1979*	*1980*	*1981*	*1982*
Imports to UK	15,147	41,942	31,844	28,728	40,460	46,425
Exports and re-exports from UK	172,856	125,721	129,729	131,094	170,835	265,283

COMMUNICATIONS

Roads. A network of adequate graded roads links all the main sectors of population, and only a few mountain villages are not accessible by Land-Rover. A rapid road construction programme began in 1976, and by the end of the year there were 1,272 km of paved roads and 8,500 km of graded roads. There are good waterproof roads in the north of Oman, between Muscat and Sohar, Sohar and Buraimi, Nizwa and Buraimi and Nizwa and Seeb. In Dhofar tarmac roads have been completed from Raysut through Salalah to Taqa and also Bid Bid to Sur.

Aviation. Gulf Air run regional services in and out of Seeb international airport (20 miles from Muscat) to Bahrain, Doha, Abu Dhabi, Dubai, Karachi and Bombay. They and British Airways each operate daily flights to and from London. Other airlines serving Muscat are MEA, Kuwait Airlines, PIA, Air India, Iran Air, TMA (cargo) and Trade Winds (cargo).

Shipping. In Mutrah a deep-water port (named Mina Qaboos) was completed in 1974 at a cost of R.O. 18·2m. It provides 12 berths, 9 of which are deep-water berths, warehousing facilities and a harbour for dhows and coastal vessels. The annual handling capacity has been raised to 1·5m. tons.

Post and Broadcasting. There are Sultanate post offices in Muscat and Mutrah, relying solely upon a Post Office Box system for delivery. Omantel maintain a telegraph office at Muscat and an automatic telephone exchange (13,068 lines, 1978) which includes Mutrah, Bait-al-Falaj and Mina al-Fahal, the oil company terminal. A high-frequency radio link with Bahrain was opened in Aug. 1972 providing communications with other parts of the world. Internally, there are radio telephone, telex and telegraph services direct between Salalah and Muscat, and a VHF radio link between Seeb international airport and Muscat. The airport is also served by a SITA telex system.

A colour television service covering Muscat and the surrounding area started transmission in Nov. 1974. A television service for Dhofar opened in 1975.

EDUCATION AND WELFARE

Education. Until 1970 there were only 3 schools in Oman, and it has been estimated that as many as 80% of Omanis are still illiterate. In 1978 there were 257 primary schools with about 78,000 pupils. Secondary education is still extremely limited with only 9 secondary schools, total number of students, 685. All Omanis desiring further education must obtain it abroad, but plans are being implemented for the development of technical and agricultural training and craft training at intermediate and secondary level. Oman's first university, in Nizwa, was under construction in 1981. There are also programmes to combat adult illiteracy.

Health. Health services in 1980 were widely spread with 13 hospitals in use and 2 more planned, 12 health centres and 47 dispensaries. There are also Save the Children Fund Welfare Clinics at Sohar and Sur.

DIPLOMATIC REPRESENTATIVES

Of Oman in Great Britain (44A Montpelier Sq., London, SW7 1JJ)
Ambassador: Ahmed Mohamed Nasser Al-Lamki (accredited 29 Oct. 1982).

Of Great Britain in Oman (PO Box 300, Muscat)
Ambassador: Duncan Slater, CMG.

Of Oman in the USA (2342 Massachusetts Ave., NW, Washington, DC., 20008)
Ambassador: Sadek Jawad Sulaiman.

Of the USA in Oman (PO Box 966, Muscat)
Ambassador: John R. Countryman.

Of Oman to the United Nations
Ambassador: Mahoud Aboul-Nasr.

Books of Reference

Achievements. Ministry of Health. Oman, 1975
Hints to Exporters: UAE and the Sultanate of Oman 1981–82. British Overseas Board
Oman in 10 years. Ministry of Information. Oman, 1980
Oman: A MEED Practical Guide. London, 1981
Clements, F. A., *Oman: The Reborn Land.* London and New York, 1980.—*Oman.* [Bibliography] Oxford and Santa Barbara, 1981
Hawley, D., *Oman and its Rennaissance.* London, 1977
Morris, J., *Sultan in Oman.* London, 1966
Peterson, J. E., *Oman in the Twentieth Century.* London and New York, 1978
Phillips, W., *Unknown Oman.* London, 1967.—*Oman: A History.* London, 1968
Shannon, M. O., *Oman and South-eastern Arabia: A Bibliographic Survey.* Boston, 1978
Skeet, I., *Muscat and Oman: The End of an Era.* London and New York, 1974
Thesiger, W., *Arabian Sands.* London, 1959
Townsend, J., *Oman: The Making of the Modern State.* New York and London, 1977
Wikan, U., *Behind the Veil in Arabia: Women in Oman.* John Hopkins Univ. Press, 1982

PAKISTAN

Capital: Islamabad
Population: 85·6m. (1982)
GNP per capita: US$300 (1980)

Islamic Republic of Pakistan

HISTORY. Pakistan was constituted as a Dominion on 14 Aug. 1947, under the provisions of the Indian Independence Act, 1947, which received the royal assent on 18 July 1947. The Dominion consisted of the following former territories of British India: Balúchistán, East Bengal (including almost the whole of Sylhet, a former district of Assam), North-West Frontier, West Punjab and Sind; and those States which had acceded to Pakistan.

On 23 March 1956 an Islamic republic was proclaimed after the Constituent Assembly had adopted the draft constitution on 29 Feb.

On 7 Oct. 1958 President Mirza declared martial law in Pakistan, dismissed the central and provincial Governments, abolished all political parties and abrogated the constitution of 23 March 1956. Field Marshal Mohammad Ayub Khan, the Army Commander-in-Chief, was appointed as chief martial law administrator and assumed office on 28 Oct. 1958, after Maj.-Gen. Iskander Mirza had handed all powers to him. His authority was confirmed by a ballot in Feb. 1960. He proclaimed a new constitution on 1 March 1962.

On 25 March 1969 President Ayub Khan resigned and handed over power to the army under the leadership of Maj.-Gen. Agha Muhammad Yahya Khan who immediately proclaimed martial law throughout the country, appointing himself chief martial law administrator on the same day. On 29 March 1970 the Legal Framework Order was published, defining a new constitution: Pakistan to be a federal republic with a Moslem Head of State; the National Assembly and Provincial Assemblies to be elected in free and periodical elections, the first of which was held on 7 Dec. 1970.

At the general election the Awami League based in East Pakistan and led by Sheikh Mujibur Rahman gained 167 seats and the Peoples' Party 90. Martial law continued pending the settlement of differences between East and West, which developed into civil war in March 1971. The war ended in Dec. 1971 and the Eastern province declared itself an independent state, Bangladesh. On 20 Dec. 1971 President Yahya Khan resigned and Mr Z. A. Bhutto became President and chief martial law administrator. On 30 Jan. 1972, Pakistan withdrew from the Commonwealth.

A new Constitution was adopted by the National Assembly on 10 April 1973 and enforced on 14 Aug. 1973. It provided for a federal parliamentary system with the President as constitutional head and the Prime Minister as chief executive. President Bhutto stepped down to become Prime Minister and Fazal Elahi Chaudhry was elected President.

The Chief of the Army Staff, Gen. M. Zia-ul-Haq, proclaimed martial law on 5 July 1977 and the armed forces took control of the administration; scheduled elections were postponed. Mr Bhutto was hanged (for conspiracy to murder) on 4 April 1979. Gen. M. Zia-ul-Haq succeeded Fazai Elahi Chaudhry as President in Sept. 1978.

Governors-General of Pakistan: Quaid-I-Azam Mohammed Ali Jinnah (14 Aug. 1947–11 Sept. 1948); Khawaja Nazimuddin (14 Sept. 1948–18 Oct. 1951; took over the premiership after the assassination of Liaquat Ali Khan); Ghulam Mohammad (19 Oct. 1951–6 Oct. 1955); Maj.-Gen. Iskander Mirza (assumed office of President on 6 Oct. 1955, elected President on 5 March 1956).

AREA AND POPULATION. Pakistan is bounded north-west by Afghánistán, north by the USSR and China, east by India and south by the Arabian Sea. The total area of Pakistan is 310,400 sq. miles (803,943 sq. km); population (1981 census), 83·78m.; male to female ratio, 111 to 100. Density, 105 per sq. km. Urban population, 28·2%. Annual average growth rate, 1978–81, 3%.

The population of the principal cities is:

Census of 1981		*Census of 1972*			
Islamabad	201,000	Bahawalpur	133,956	Peshawar	268,368
Karachi	5,103,000	Gujranwala	360,419	Quetta	156,000
Lahore	2,922,000	Gujrat	100,581	Sahiwal	106,213
Faisalabad	1,092,000	Jhang	137,722	Sargoda	201,407
Rawalpindi	928,000	Kasur	102,531	Sialkot	203,779
Hyderabad	795,000	Mardan	115,218	Sukkur	158,876
		Multan	542,195		

Population of the provinces (census of 1972) was:

	Area (sq. miles)	*Total population (1,000)*	*Male (1,000)*	*Female (1,000)*	*Density per sq. mile*
North-west Frontier Province	28,773	8,402	4,376	4,026	296
Federally administered Tribal Areas	10,510	2,507	1,291	1,216	237
Federal Capital Territory Islamabad	350	235	130	105	671
Punjab	79,284	37,374	19,871	17,503	475
Sind	54,407	13,965	7,474	6,491	260
Balúchistán	134,050	2,409	1,275	1,134	18

Language. The commonest languages are Urdu and Punjabi. Urdu is the national language while English is used in business and in central government. Provincial languages are Punjabi, Sindhi, Pushtu (North-West Frontier Province), Baluchi and Brahvi.

CONSTITUTION AND GOVERNMENT. Under the Constitution of 1973 Parliament is bi-cameral, comprising the National Assembly and the Senate. The strength of the National Assembly is 210 including 10 women. The Senate consists of 63 members, 14 from each province, 5 from Federally Administered Tribal Areas and 2 from the federal capital area, elected by the members of the Provincial Assemblies. A constitutional amendment of 29 March 1976 provided 6 National Assembly seats reserved for non-Moslem minority representatives.

With the proclamation of martial law the Constitution has been kept in abeyance, but not abrogated: The Provisional Constitution Order, 1981, promulgated on 24 March 1981, retains 119 Articles in whole or in part. Articles not included in the Order are 34 comprising Part II of the Constitution, a further 56 relating to the President's office, Parliament and Legislative procedure, articles relating to the Judiciary, the six Schedules and Part XI.

The Constitution obliges the Government to use such ways and means as may enable the people to order their lives collectively and individually in accordance with the principles of Islam. The Council of Islamic Ideology was set up to this end under article 228 of the Constitution.

An Ombudsman was appointed in Jan. 1983.

In Jan. 1982 a Federal Council of 288 members was inaugurated, under the chairmanship of K. M. Safdar. The Council, which may have up to 350 members, is to act as an interim body until an elected Parliament can be set up. Members are nominated by the President. Members of the Cabinet and Ministers of State are *ex-officio* members. The Council's role is advisory.

President and Chief Martial Law Administrator, Chairman of the Planning Commission, Science and Technology, States and Frontier Regions, Establishment: Gen. M. Zia-ul-Haq.

Federal Cabinet in Jan. 1983:

Finance and Economic Affairs: G. Ishaq Khan. *Foreign Affairs:* S. Y. Khan. *Attorney-General:* S. Pirzada. *Interior:* M. A. Haroon. *Defence:* A. A. Talpur. *Housing and Works:* Air Marshal I. Haq Khan. *Water and Power:* R. Sikandar

Zaman. *Industry:* E. Bux Soomro. *Culture, Sports and Tourism:* A. Niaz Mohammad. *Local Government and Rural Development:* F. Imam. *Labour, Manpower and Overseas Pakistanis:* G. Dastegir Khan. *Kashmir and Northern Affairs:* Maj.-Gen. J. Dar. *Education:* M. Ali Khan. *Food, Agriculture and Co-operatives:* Vice-Adm. M. F. Janjua. *Communications:* M. Baluch. *Health and Social Welfare:* N. ud-Din Jogezai. *Petroleum and Natural Resources:* Maj.-Gen. R. F. Ali Khan. *Railways:* Lieut.-Gen. S. Qadir. *Information and Broadcasting:* Maj.-Gen. M. R. Khan. *Without portfolio;* A. M. A. Khan Abbas.

National flag: Green, charged at the centre, with a white crescent and white 5-pointed star, a white vertical stripe at the mast to one-quarter of the flag.

Local Government. Pakistan comprises the provinces of the Punjab, the North-West Frontier, Sind and Balúchistán, the states of Bahawalpur and Khairpur, the Balúchistán States Union, the frontier states and the tribal areas of Balúchistán and the north-west. These were merged into a single unit on 14 Oct. 1955. In July 1970 the single unit was dissolved into the original 4 provinces. The provincial capitals are Peshawar (NW Frontier Province), Lahore (Punjab), Karachi (Sind) and Quetta (Balúchistán). Provincial governors are appointed by the President and are assisted by provincial councils.

Within the provinces there are divisions administered by Commissioners appointed by the President; the divisions are divided into districts and agencies administered by Deputy Commissioners or Political Agents who are responsible to the Provincial Governments.

Kashmir. Between one-third and one-half of Kashmir is controlled by Pakistan. This area is known as Azad (Free) Kashmir, and is the northern and western portion of the country. It has an area of 83,806 sq. km. and a population of about 1·3m. Under a United Nations resolution of 1949 its future was to be decided by plebiscite; it is still a disputed territory. The people of Azad Kashmir have their own Assembly (42 members including 2 women), their own Council (of 14 members), High Court and Supreme Court. There is a Parliamentary form of Government with a Prime Minister as the executive head and the President as the Constitutional head.

The Pakistan Government is directly responsible for Gilgit and Baltistan.

Elections to the Legislative's 40 general seats are to be held within 10 days of the general elections in Pakistan, according to a presidential proclamation of 8 Oct. 1977. The seat of government is Muzaffarabad.

DEFENCE

Army. The Pakistan Army consists of 16 infantry divisions and 2 armoured divisions, 4 independent armoured brigades, 4 independent infantry brigades, 6 artillery and 2 air defence brigades. Total strength (1983), 420,000. General headquarters is at Rawalpindi. The entire officers cadre receives its precommission training in the Military Academy at Kakul.

Navy. The fleet comprises 6 diesel-powered patrol submarines (completed in France in 1969–80), 6 midget submarines, 1 "County" class destroyer, *Babur* (*ex*-HMS *London*) transferred from the Royal Navy in 1982 to replace (and take the name of) the ex-British very old light cruiser (cadet training ship), 10 old destroyers (6 *ex*-US and 4 *ex*-British), 4 corvette-type patrol vessels, 12 fast gunboats, 4 fast (hydrofoil) torpedo boats, 4 fast attack craft, 1 seaward defence boat, 19 coastal patrol launches, 1 survey ship (*ex*-frigate), 6 coastal minesweepers, 1 destroyer parent ship, 1 fleet replenishment ship, 1 degaussing vessel, 1 rescue ship, 2 oilers, 1 water carrier and 4 tugs.

The principal naval base and dockyard are at Karachi. Naval personnel in 1983 totalled 1,000 officers and 10,000 ratings.

The naval air arm comprises 5 fixed-wing aircraft and 10 helicopters.

Air Force. The Pakistan Air Force came into being on 14 Aug. 1947.It has its headquarters at Peshawar and is organized within 3 air defence sectors, in the northern, central and southern areas of the country. Tactical units include 1 squadron of B-57B (Canberra) bombers, at least 4 squadrons of Mirage III-EP/50 supersonic fighters, 7 or 8 squadrons of MiG-19 (F-6) supersonic fighter-bombers acquired from China, 1 squadron equipped with Mirage III-RP reconnaissance aircraft, and C-130 Hercules turboprop transports. Delivery of 32 F-16A and 8 F-16B Fighting Falcons began in late 1982, for operational service from 1984. Also being delivered are 42 Chinese-built Q-5 ('Fantan') attack aircraft, developed from the F-6. Flying training schools are equipped with Masshaq (Saab Supporter) armed piston-engined primary trainers, T-37B/C jet trainers supplied by the USA, Mirage III-DPs and Chinese-built FT-5s (two-seat MiG-17s). Three Breguet Atlantics and 4 Super Frelon helicopters, plus a small number of Alouette III helicopters, are available to perform maritime reconnaissance, search and rescue duties in co-operation with Sea King helicopters of the Pakistan Navy Air Arm. A VIP transport squadron operates the Presidential F27 turboprop aircraft, a twin-jet Falcon 20 and smaller types. There is a flying college at Risalpur and an aeronautical engineering college at Korangi Creek. Total strength in 1982 was about 250 combat aircraft and 18,000 all ranks.

INTERNATIONAL RELATIONS

External Debt (June 1981), about US$11,344m., of which US$1,914m. to the World Bank and the rest to USA (US$2,529), OPEC, individual countries and consortia.

Membership. Pakistan is a member of the UN, the Colombo Plan, and Regional Co-operation for Development.

Treaties. A mutual defence assistance agreement between Pakistan and the USA was signed in Karachi on 19 May 1954.

ECONOMY

Planning. The fifth 5-year plan (1978–83) envisages a total fixed investment of Rs 204,000m. including Rs 61,670m. in the private sector. Real growth in GDP is planned at 7·2% annually (agriculture 6%; industry 10%). Expenditure will be met mainly (75%) from internal resources. Allocations for new industrial capacity (Rs 31,841m.), industrial improvement (Rs 7,467m.), and public sector development in health (Rs 6,600m.), education, (Rs 10,280m.), transport and communications (Rs 27,400m.) and water and power (Rs 45,050m.) have been made.

Budget. The following table shows the budget for the years 1981–82 and 1982–83 in Rs 1m.:

	1981–82 Revised	*1982–83 Budget*
Current account		
Tax revenue	39,934	44,352
Non-tax revenue	10,958	12,834
Transfers to provinces	9,232	9,980
Expenditure	38,089	46,907
Capital:		
Receipts	21,553	23,324
Development outlay	27,000	31,465

Currency. The monetary unit is the Pakistan *rupee.* The official rate (March 1983) is Rs 18·76 = £1; Rs 12·88 = US$1. Decimal coinage was introduced on 1 Jan. 1961. The rupee, which previously consisted of 64 *pice*, now consists of 100 *paisas*. The notes are of Rs 100, 50, 10 and 5 denominations issued by the State Bank in the name of the Government, and Rs 1 issued by the State Bank incurring no liability; the coinage in the decimal series is 0·5, 0·25, 0·1, 0·05 and 0·01 rupee.

Total monetary assets (including currency in circulation and deposits) in March 1980 amounted to Rs 93,087m. Currency in circulation, Oct. 1980, Rs 30,812·4m.

Banking. The State Bank of Pakistan is the central bank; it came into operation as the Central Bank on 1 July 1948 with an authorized capital of Rs 30m. and was nationalized in Jan. 1974. As on 28 June 1979 total assets or liabilities of the issue department amounted to Rs 25,250m. and those of the banking department Rs 24,297m.; reserve fund, Rs 2,120m. and total deposits, Rs 12,989m. It is the sole bank of issue for Pakistan, custodian of foreign exchange reserves and banker for the federal and provincial governments and for scheduled banks. It also manages the rupee public debt of federal and provincial governments. It provides short-term loans to the Government and commercial banks and short- and medium-term loans to specialized banks. The State Bank raised the bank rate from 9 to 10% with effect from 7 June 1977, but it provides finance for export sales of locally manufactured machinery at 2% per annum and for other export sales at 3% per annum. The Bank's subsidiary Federal Bank for Co-operatives makes loans to provincial co-operative banks. Loans made 1979–80, Rs 601·2m.

There were 24 scheduled banks (banks with capital and reserves of an aggregate value of not less than Rs 500,000) in Pakistan on 30 June 1979. Of these 9 were Pakistani including 5 commercial banks (National Bank of Pakistan, Habib Bank Ltd, United Bank Ltd, Muslim Commercial Bank Ltd and Allied Bank Ltd), 2 specialized banks (Agricultural Development Bank of Pakistan and Industrial Development Bank of Pakistan) and 2 co-operative banks (Punjab Provincial Co-operative Bank and Federal Bank for Co-operatives). Pakistani scheduled banks were nationalized in Jan. 1974. In addition, there were 15 foreign banks operating in Pakistan on 30 June 1979. In 1980 foreign banks were given the option of meeting part or all of their reserve requirements with the State Bank in specified foreign currencies. The total number of offices of scheduled banks in 1982 was 7,000, of foreign banks 58. Total deposits of all the scheduled banks stood at Rs 77,000m. in 1982.The National Bank of Pakistan acts as an agent of the State Bank for transacting Government business and managing currency chests at places where the State Bank has no offices of its own.

Weights and Measures. The metric system is in general use.

ENERGY AND NATURAL RESOURCES

Electricity. Installed capacity (1981) by type of generation: Thermal 1,648,830 kw.; hydro-electric, 1,767,200 kw.; nuclear, 137,000 kw. Total generated electrical energy in 1980, 13,000m. kwh; 60% of this was hydro-electricity, the main source being the Tarbela Dam.

Oil. Oil comes mainly from the Potowar Plain, from fields at Meyal, Tut, Balkassar, Joya Mair and Dhullian. Production in 1981 was 11m. tonnes. Oil reserves were also found at Dhodak in Dec. 1976. Exploitation is mainly through government incentives and concessions to foreign private sector companies. The Pak-Arab refinery pipeline runs 865 km. from Karachi to Multan; capacity, 4·5m. tonnes of oil annually.

Gas. Gas pipelines from Sui to Karachi (345 miles) and Multan (200) supply natural gas to industry and domestic consumers. A pipeline between Quetta and Shikarpur was approved in 1980, to be constructed in 1982. There are 4 other productive fields. Reserves (1982), 452,000m. cu. metres; production in Feb. 1983 was about 42% of energy needs.

Water. The Indus water treaty of 1960, concluded between India and Pakistan, has created the basis for a large-scale development programme. The Indus Basin Development Fund Agreement has been subscribed by Australia, Canada, Federal Republic of Germany, New Zealand, UK and USA and is administered by the International Bank; the works to be constructed call for expenditure of US$1,000m. The main purpose of the treaty is the division of the water power of the Indus and its 5 tributaries between India and Pakistan. After the construction of some 460 miles of canals, the Indus and the 2 western tributaries will serve Pakistan and the entire flow of the 3 eastern tributaries will be released for use in India.

The largest project is the construction of the Tarbela Dam, an earth-and-rock filled dam on the river Indus, 485 ft high, which has a gross storage capacity of 11·1m. acre feet of water for irrigation.

The Lloyd Barrage and Canal Construction Scheme, consists of a barrage across the river Indus at Sukkur and 7 canals—4 on the left and 3 on the right bank. Another barrage across the Indus, 4½ miles north of Kotri, called the Ghulam Muhammad Barrage, was completed in 1955. The Taunsa barrage on the Indus, 80 miles downstream of Kalabagh, was completed in 1958. The Gudu barrage, 10 miles from Kashmore, was completed in 1962.

The province of the Punjab set up in 1949 the Thal Development Authority to colonize the Thal desert between the Indus and Jhelum rivers.

The Chashma canal will carry water 172 miles across Dera Ismail Khan from the Chashma barrage on the Indus. The Mangla Dam on the Jhelum was inaugurated in Nov. 1967.

Minerals. The main agencies are the Pakistan Mineral Development Corporation, the Resource Development Corporation and the Gemstone Corporation of Pakistan. Coal is mined at Sharigh and Harnai on the Sind–Pishin railway and in the Bolan pass, also in Sor Range and Degari in the Quetta–Pishin district and in the Punjab; total recoverable reserves, about 480m. tonnes, mainly low-grade. A further 55m. tonnes was found at Lakhra in 1980 and reserves of over 500m. tonnes were found in the 300 sq. mile Thatta Sadha field in 1981. Chromite is extracted in and near Muslimbagh. Limestone is quarried generally. Gypsum is mined in the Sibi district and elsewhere; reserves, about 350m. tonnes. Iron ore is being worked in Kalabagh and elsewhere; reserves, about 400m. tonnes, low-grade. A further 18m. tonnes, high-grade, has been found in Balúchistán. Uranium has been found in Dera Ghazi Khan. At Saindak a foreign consortium proposes to mine and process copper (1·69m. tonnes recoverable metal), gold (2·24m. oz.), silver (2·49m. oz.), and magnetite (128m. tonnes). Other minerals of which useful deposits have been found are magnesite, sulphur, barites, china clay, marble, bauxite, antimony ore, bentonite, celestite, dolomite, fireclay, fluorite, fuller's earth, phosphate rock, silica sand and soapstone.

Agriculture. The entire area in the north and west is covered by great mountain ranges. The rest of the country consists of a fertile plain watered by 5 big rivers and their tributaries. Agriculture is dependent almost entirely on the irrigation system based on these rivers. It employs 52% of labour and provides about 30% of GNP and 36% of foreign exchange earnings. Growth rate, 1981–82, 4%. The main crops are wheat, cotton, maize, sugar-cane and rice, while the Quetta and Kalat divisions (Balúchistán) are known for their fruits and dates.

By 31 March 1977, 3·34m. acres of land had been taken away from landlords, and 1·48m. acres had been distributed to 137,005 tenants. An ordinance of Jan. 1977 reduced the upper limit of land holding to 100 irrigated or 200 non-irrigated acres; it also replaced the former land revenue system with a new agricultural income tax, from which holders of up to 25 irrigated or 50 unirrigated acres are exempt. Land resumed by the Government, unless required for public purposes, is granted free to tenants who were in possession and cultivating during certain seasons of 1975 and 1976. About 9·5m. of the 10m. landowners held less than 25 acres; about 35,000 landowners would have had to surrender land. Of the surveyed area of 156m. acres, cultivated land accounts for 63m. acres, of which 11m. acres consist of fallow land, so that the net area sown is 52m. acres.

Production, 1981–82 (in 1,000 tonnes): Rice (cleaned), 3,338; wheat, 11,750; sugar-cane (gur), 34,540; cotton (lint, 1,000 bales), 4,400.

Livestock (FAO estimate, 1979): Cattle, 15m.; buffaloes, 11·31m.; sheep, 24·2m.; goats, 27·8m.; poultry, 48·9m.

Forestry. There were (1976) 7·3m. acres of reserved and protected forests and 10·6m. acres managed as pasture ranges by the Forest Department. Of the forests 1·5m. acres are in Punjab, 1·66m. in Balúchistán, 1·46m. in Sind and 2·65m. in the North-West Frontier Province. Forests produce an annual average of over 20m. cu. ft of timber and 16m. cu. ft of fuel. Annual value of this and other produce, about Rs. 60m. Forest lands are also used as national parks, wildlife and game reserves.

Fisheries. Landings of inland water and marine fish, about 200,000 tonnes annually.

INDUSTRY AND TRADE

Industry. Industry employs about 10% of the population. The growth rate in manufacturing, 1981–82, was 12·1%. Woollen and other cottage industries especially cotton weaving (with 220,000 workers) and carpet weaving, have made great strides. The population engaged in the fishing industry is about 39,000. In 1972 public sector companies were re-organized under a Board of Industrial Management. In 1976 all cotton-ginning, rice-husking and flour-milling plants were nationalized (except small flour-mills of less than 6 rollers outside Balúchistán). Pakistan is self-sufficient in cotton cloth and sugar. A public sector steel-mill has been built at Port Qasim near Karachi, capacity 1·1m. tonnes; production of coke and pig-iron began in autumn 1981. Also recently completed are a heavy mechanical complex and a heavy forge and foundry plant at Taxila. There are plants processing barites and china clay. A private sector ferrous alloys plant has been approved near Peshawar, capacity 40 tonnes of ferrous silicon and manganese per day. There is an Export Processing Zone at Karachi, covering 500 acres; at 30 June 1981 investment here stood at US$58·8m. The largest project (approved Aug. 1981) is a Pakistan-Saudi aluminium extrusion plant. At Machi Goth there is a fertilizer plant under construction, capacity 1,800 tonnes per day.

Production 1980–81: Cotton cloth, 308m. sq. metres; cotton yarn, 375m. kg.; cement, 3·5m. tonnes; fertilizers (urea), 645,000 tonnes.

Labour. The Labour Force Survey of 1974–75 gave the total work force as 20·42m., of whom 54·8% (11·22m.) were engaged in agriculture, forestry and fishing, 13·6% (2·8m.) in manufacturing; the textile industry was the largest single manufacturing employer. Estimates (1979–80) gave a labour force of 22·97m., 5·6m. of them urban.

Commerce. Total value of exports during 1980–81 amounted to Rs 29,279m., and the total value of imports to Rs 53,544m. The value of the chief articles imported into and exported from Pakistan in 1980–81 was (in Rs 1m.):

Imports		*Exports*	
Petroleum and products	15,199	Cotton, raw	5,203
Non-electrical machinery	5,684	Cotton manufactures	4,440
Transport equipment	4,686	Rice	5,602
Oil vegetables	2,625	Synthetic textiles	1,272
Chemical fertilizers	3,537	Petroleum and products	1,675
		Carpets and rugs	2,243

Total trade between Pakistan and UK (British Department of Trade returns, in £1,000 sterling):

	1977	*1978*	*1979*	*1980*	*1981*	*1982*
Imports to UK	48,790	54,387	68,021	58,289	63,249	81,531
Exports and re-exports from UK	121,051	92,723	139,759	139,692	149,370	199,178

Tourism. Earnings in 1980, US$154m. There were 292,000 tourists.

COMMUNICATIONS

Roads. At the end of financial year 1975–76 Pakistan had 31,029 miles of roads, of which 16,875 miles were all-weather roads. The Karakoram highway to the Chinese border, through Kohistan and the Hunza valley, was opened in 1978. An all-weather road linking Skardu and the remote NE Indus valley to the highway was built in 1980.

In 1979 there were about 1m. vehicles registered, including 421,000 motor-cycles and 279,000 cars.

Railways. Pakistan Railways had (1980) a route of 8,815 km mainly on 1,676 mm.

gauge, with some metre gauge and narrow gauge line. Railway budget, 1980–81: revenue account receipts Rs 3,300m.; expenditure, Rs 3,254m.

Aviation. Karachi is served by British Airways, KLM, PANAM, Lufthansa, Swissair, SAS, Iran National Airlines, Air France, Garuda, Gulf Air and by Philippine, Japanese, Chinese, East African, Syrian, Iraqui, Kuwait, Jordanian, Saudi Arabian, Romanian, Egyptian and Russian airlines.

Pakistan International Airlines (founded 1955; the majority of shares is held by the Government) had 4 DC-10s, 7 Boeing 707Cs, 5 720Bs, 2 747Bs and 8 Fokker F27s in 1977; 2 other Boeing 720Bs were on lease to Air Malta. Services operate to 20 home airports, New York, Paris, Amsterdam, Copenhagen, Istanbul, Athens, Rome, Cairo, Tripoli, Nairobi, Dhahran, Damascus, Amman, Baghdad, Persian Gulf points, Tōkyō, Peking (Beijing), Zahedan, Singapore, Manila, Kuala Lumpur, Bangkok, Colombo, London, Frankfurt, Bombay, Delhi, Dacca, Kábul, Tehrán and Jeddah.

Shipping. There is a seaport at Karachi. A second port is being built at Phitti Creek on the Makram coast, 26 miles east of Karachi, to be called Port Muhammad Bin Qasim; this port will have iron and coal berths for Pakistan Steel Mills, multi-purpose berths, bulk-cargo handling, oil and container-traffic terminals; the first phase (handling bulk and bagged cargo) will be operational it is hoped in 1983. The Pakistan National Shipping Corporation had 51 vessels in 1982, of 700,000 DWT, carrying 38% of dry cargo handled. National flag carriers now operate between Pakistan and UK; USA and Canada; the Far East; the (Persian) Gulf, Arabian Gulf, Red Sea, Black Sea and Mekran Coast; Continental Europe and the Middle East. The Karachi Shipyard and Engineering Works Ltd construct all types of vessels up to 27,000 DWT and repairs all types; dry-dock and under-water repairs can be done on vessels up to 29,000 DWT, above-water repairs on vessels and drilling rigs of all sizes.

Post and Broadcasting. The telegraph and telephone system is government-owned. Telephones, on 1 Jan. 1981, numbered 367,080; a nationwide dialling system is in operation between 46 cities. In 1979 there were 10,488 post offices (8,193 rural) and 93 main telegraph offices; emphasis was laid on improving rural communications and 28 public call offices and 47 small exchanges were opened. Pakistan has international telephone connections by 102 satellite, 7 HF, 4 microwave and 10 carrier circuits. An international direct-dialling exchange with 25,000 connections was opened in July 1980. The Pakistan Broadcasting Corporation had 16 radio stations in Dec. 1982. Television stations operate in Lahore, Karachi, Peshawar, Quetta and Rawalpindi–Islamabad.

Cinemas (1972). There are 578 cinemas seating 300,000.

Newspapers. Dailies and periodicals numbered 1,200 in 1973: 19 were English language dailies, 83 were vernacular dailies and the rest were periodicals in English and regional languages.

JUSTICE, RELIGION, EDUCATION AND WELFARE

Justice. The Central Judiciary consists of the Supreme Court of Pakistan, which is a court of record and has three-fold jurisdiction, namely, original, appellate and advisory. There are 4 High Courts in Lahore, Peshawar, Quetta and Karachi. Under the Constitution, each has power to issue directions of writs of *Habeas Corpus, Mandamus, Certiorari* and others. Under them are district and sessions courts of first instance in each division; they have also some appellate jurisdiction. Criminal cases not being sessions cases are tried by district magistrates and subordinate magistrates. There are subordinate civil courts also.

Jurisdiction of the Judicial Committee of the Privy Council ceased on 30 April 1950.

The Constitution provides for an independent judiciary, as the greatest safeguard of citizens' rights. The Laws (Continuance in Force) (Eleventh Amendment) Order, 1980, prescribed the date of 14 Aug. 1981 by which the judiciary shall be separated from the executive. There is an Attorney-General, appointed by the President, who has right of audience in all courts.

A Federal Shariat Court at the Supreme Court level has been established to decide whether any law is wholly or partially un-Islamic. Islamic law is to be enforced as the law of the state; penalties for offences involving intoxicating liquor, offences against property and sexual offences have been specified. Imprisonment remains as a penalty in general use, but some offences in all the above categories are liable to whipping and some property offences, to amputation.

Religion. Religious groups (1972 census): Moslems, 63·28m.; Christians, 907,861; Scheduled Castes, 603,369; Caste Hindus, 296,837; Parsees, 9,589; Buddhists, 4,318; others, 205,250. There is a Ministry to safeguard the constitutional rights of religious minorities.

Education. At the census of 1972, there were about 9·3m. people in Pakistan who were able to read and write, representing 21·7% of the population over 10 years old.

The principle of free and compulsory primary education has been accepted as the responsibility of the state. The duration of primary education has been fixed provisionally at 5 years. It is hoped that all boys aged 5 will be enrolled in schools by 1982 and girls by 1987. Adult literacy programmes have been established. Present policy stresses vocational and technical education, disseminating a common culture based on Islamic ideology.

Number of schools, enrolments and teachers, 1978–79 (estimate): Primary schools, 55,173 (6·17m. enrolments; 150,000 teachers); secondary schools, 8,376 (1·86m.; 109,400); vocational secondary schools, 167 (30,000; 2,100).

There were also 445 general colleges (241,000 enrolments; 12,684 teachers); 91 professional colleges (57,500; 3,200); 89 teacher-training colleges (10,100; 1,080); 15 universities, including the open university at Islamabad (26,000; 2,600).

Health. In 1980 there were 536 hospitals (42,469 beds) and about 23,000 doctors.

Social Security. In 1981–82 expenditure on cash benefits under the employees' social security scheme was Rs15·3m., on medical care, Rs.93·2m.

DIPLOMATIC REPRESENTATIVES

Of Pakistan in Great Britain (35–36 Lowndes Sq., London, SW1X 9JN)
Ambassador: Ali Arshad (accredited 13 Feb. 1981).

Of Great Britain in Pakistan (Diplomatic Enclave, Ramna 5, Islamabad)
Ambassador: O. G. Forster, CMG, MVO.

Of Pakistan in the USA (2315 Massachusetts Ave., NW, Washington, D.C., 20008)
Ambassador: Ajaz Azim.

Of the USA in Pakistan (AID/UN Bldg., Islamabad)
Ambassador: Ronald I. Spiers.

Of Pakistan to the United Nations
Ambassador: Niaz A. Naik.

Books of Reference

Pakistan Year-Book, Annual
Burke, S. M., *Pakistan's Foreign Policy.* OUP, 1973
Burki, S. J., *Pakistan Under Bhutto.* London, 1980
Griffin, K., and Khan, A. R. (ed.), *Growth and Inequality in Pakistan.* London and New York 1972
Hasan, M., (ed.) *Pakistan in a Changing World.* Karachi, 1978
Jennings, Sir Ivor, *Constitutional Problems in Pakistan.* CUP, 1957
Siddiqui, K., *Conflict, Crisis and War in Pakistan.* London, 1972

PANAMA

Capital: Panama City
Population: 1·83m. (1980)
GNP per capita: US$1,730 (1980)

República de Panamá

HISTORY. A revolution, inspired by the USA, led to the separation of Panama from the United States of Colombia and the declaration of its independence on 3 Nov. 1903. The *de facto* Government was on 13 Nov. recognized by the USA, and soon afterwards by the other Powers. In 1914 Colombia agreed to recognize the independence of Panama. This treaty was ratified by the USA and Colombia in 1921, and on 8 May 1924 diplomatic relations between Colombia and Panama were established. On 10 Oct. 1979 Panama assumed sovereignty over what was previously known as the Panama Canal Zone and now called the Canal Area.

For the treaties regulating the relations between Panama and the USA *see* pp. 960–61.

AREA AND POPULATION. Panama is bounded north by the Caribbean, east by Colombia, south by the Pacific and west by Costa Rica. Extreme length is about 480 miles (772 km); breadth between 37 (60) and 110 miles (177 km); coastline, 426 miles (685 km) on the Atlantic and 767 (1,234 km) on the Pacific; total area (excluding the Canal Zone) is 29,761 sq. miles (77,082 sq. km); population according to the census of 11 May 1980 was 1,830,175. Over 75% are of mixed blood and the remainder Indians, negroid, white and Asiatic.

There are approximately 2,500 British Commonwealth citizens from the Caribbean area.

The capital is Panama City, on the Pacific coast; estimated population, 1980, 467,000. There are 9 provinces (with populations, 1980) as follows (the capitals in brackets): Bocas del Toro (Bocas del Toro), 53,579; Chiriquí (David), 287,801; Coclé (Penonomé), 140,320; Colón (Colón), 166,439; Los Santos (Las Tablas), 70,200; Herrera (Chitré), 81,866; Darién (La Palma), 26,497 ; Panama (Panama City), 830,278; Veraguas (Santiago), 173,195. The port of Colón on the Atlantic coast had 95,300 (78,000). Smaller ports on the Pacific are Aguadulce, Pedregal, Montijo, Puerto Mutis and Puerto Armuelles; in the Atlantic, Bocas del Toro, Almirante, Portobello, Mandinga and Permé. A new fishing port came into operation at Vacamonte in Aug. 1979.

Birth rate, 1981, was 29 per 1,000 population.

CONSTITUTION AND GOVERNMENT. The constitution of 1946 contained provisions for a National Assembly of 42 members with a mandate for 4 years. The term of the President of the Republic, elected by direct vote, was 4 years, he was not eligible for the two succeeding terms. Women had equal rights with men.

There were normally 2 vice-presidents, elected every 4 years by direct popular vote, and a cabinet of 7 ministers nominated by the President, who might attend and address the legislature but could not vote. The Comptroller-General was elected by the National Assembly for 4 years.

On 11 Oct. 1968, however, the newly elected President, Dr Arnulfo Arias, was deposed after only 11 days in office, in a *coup* conducted by the National Guard. The National Assembly was suspended and a provisional government set up consisting of a two-man military Junta and a civilian cabinet. In Dec. 1969 the military members of the Junta resigned and were replaced by civilians after an abortive attempt to depose the Commander of the National Guard, Brig.-Gen. Omar Torrijos.

A new Constitution which came into force in 1972, as amended in 1978, provides for an Assembly of 505 representatives of municipal districts elected on a community rather than a party basis, a Legislative Council of 56 members, 37 of whom are elected by the Assembly (the other 19 are to be elected by direct vote (2 from each Province and 1 from the Territory of San Blas) elections due to be held in 1980) and a directly-elected President and Vice-President; The formation of political parties is now permitted, subject to statutory regulations, and 5 such parties had achieved full legal recognition by Sept. 1981.

Elections, the first to be held in Panama for 12 years, for the National Legislative Council were held in Sept. 1980. The Democratic Revolutionary Party (PRD) gained 10 of the 19 seats; Liberals, 5; Christian Democrats, 2; Independents, 2.

President of the Republic: Ricardo de la Espriella.
Vice-President of the Republic: Jorge Illueca.
Minister for Foreign Affairs: Juan José Amanda.
Commander-in-Chief of the National Guard: Gen. Rubén Dario Paredes.

The official language is Spanish.

National flag: Quarterly: first a white panel with a blue star, second red, third blue, fourth white with a red star.

National anthem: Alcanzamos por fin la victoria (words by J. de la Ossa; tune by Santos Jorge, 1903).

Local government: The 9 provinces are sub-divided into 64 municipal districts and 2 *comarcas* (special districts) and are further sub-divided into 505 *corregimientos* (electoral districts).

DEFENCE

Army. The *Guardia Nacional* is the only military type force with police as well as military and para-military functions. It has a strength of about 11,000 and includes a coastguard section.

Navy. Divided between both coasts, the flotilla comprises 4 patrol craft, 2 utility cutters, 3 medium landing ships, 3 utility landing craft and 3 logistic support vessels. In 1983 personnel totalled 500 officers and men.

Air Force. The air force has 1 Lockheed Electra, 3 C-47, 3 CASA 212, 2 Islander and 2 Twin Otter transports, 3 Cessna and 2 DHC-3 Otter liaison aircraft, a Shorts Skyvan, a Falcon VIP jet transport, and 17 UH-1B/D/H Iroquois and twin-engined UH-1N helicopters.

INTERNATIONAL RELATIONS

Membership. Panama is a member of UN and OAS.

ECONOMY

Budget. The 1981 budget provided for expenditure of 966,686,670 balboas and revenue of 752·9m. balboas.

Public sector debt was 2,355·5m. balboas in Dec. 1980.

Currency. The monetary unit is the *balboa*, which is of the same size and fineness as the US silver dollar but is maintained equivalent to the gold dollar. Other coins whose metallic content is required by law to correspond exactly to that of similar US coins are the half-balboa (equal to 50 cents US); the quarter and tenth of a balboa piece; a cupro-nickel coin of 5 cents, and a copper coin of 1 cent. US coinage is also legal tender. Volume of the currency has not been disclosed since 31 Dec. 1950, when it stood at 1·5m. balboas. The only paper currency used is that of the USA.

In March 1983, US$1 = 1 *balboa*; £1 = 1·47 *balboas.*

Banking. There is no statutory central bank. The Government accounts are handled through the *Banco Nacional de Panama.* The number of commercial banks rose from 9 in 1964 to 116 by Sept. 1981; 62 have a general licence, 42 an international licence and 12 a representational licence. Leading banks are the Citibank, Lloyds Bank International (Bahamas) Ltd., and the Chase Manhattan Bank of New

York. Other foreign-owned banks include the Bank of America, as well as Canadian, Columbian, Swiss, Federal German, French, Spanish, Dutch, Taiwan, Japanese and Brazilian banks.

Weights and Measures. English weights and measures are in general use; those of the metric system are also used.

ENERGY AND NATURAL RESOURCES

Electricity. Production of electric energy, 1981, amounted to 1,792·38m. kwh.

Minerals. There are known to be copper deposits in the provinces of Chiriquí, Colón and Darien. The most important, containing possibly the largest undeveloped reserves in the world, is Cerro Colorado (Chiriquí) on which a feasibility study is being undertaken by the Rio Tinto Zinc Coporation Ltd. If it is eventually decided to develop the mine, it is expected that the annual production of copper will reach 260,000 to 280,000 tonnes within a few years. The cost of construction is estimated at about US$1,800m. The deposit has estimated reserves of 1,300m. tonnes, with an average grade of 0·76% copper.

Agriculture. Of the whole area (1975) 18·5% is cultivated, 57·1% is natural or artificial pasture land and 9·5% is fallow. Of the remainder only a small part is cultivated, though the land is rich in resources. About 60% of the country's food requirements are imported. The Ministry of Agricultural Development (MIDA) buys leading crops at field prices. Of the land under cultivation, 26·4% is owned and 44·7% is usufructuary. The most important export products are bananas, grown by an affiliate of the United Brands Company and sugar from 4 state-owned and 2 private mills. Value of exports of these commodities in 1980 was 24·7m. balboas and 31·6m. balboas respectively. Most important food crop, for home consumption, is rice, grown on 80% of the farms; Panama's *per capita* consumption is very high. Output of rough rice from 99,110 hectares, was 3·6m. quintals in 1978–79. Other products are maize (68,600 hectares, yielding 1·4m. quintals in 1978–79), cocoa, coffee and coconuts. Beer, whisky, rum, 'seco', anise and gin are produced. Coffee is mainly grown in the province of Chiriquí, near the Costa Rican frontier; total production in 1978–79 was 135,500 quintals, and small amounts were exported. The country has great timber resources, notably mahogany. According to the livestock estimate of 1981 there were 1·6m. cattle, 202,000 pigs and 5·2m. poultry. Hides are among minor articles of export.

INDUSTRY AND TRADE

Industry. Local industries include cigarettes, clothing, food processing, shoes, soap, cement factories; foreign firms are being encouraged to establish industries, and a petrol refinery is operating in Colón.

Commerce. The imports and exports (including re-exports) for the Republic of Panama, for 6 calendar years are as follows (in 1,000 balboas; 1 balboa = US$1):

	Imports	*Exports*		*Imports*	*Exports*
1975	789,700	262,000	1978	862,000	381,700
1976	783,500	378,200	1979	1,185,000	291,506
1977	777,761	243,051	1980	1,277,000	407,000

The huge adverse visible trade balance is mainly with the USA and is due to the heavy import of consumer goods, most of it covered by a large invisible surplus. In 1977 the USA furnished 29·7% of Panama's imports and took 43·2% of her exports. The UK was the eighth largest supplier.

A Free Zone exists at Colón for the storage, processing, repacking and re-exporting or sale of goods in transit. The imports and exports (including re-exports) for the Colón Free Zone, for 6 calendar years are as follows (in 1,000 balboas):

	Imports	*Exports*		*Imports*	*Exports*
1974	475,900	510,800	1977	786,804	905,451
1975	415,700	543,100	1978	1,095,000	1,230,000
1976	558,033	651,020	1979	1,328,576	1,529,921

Chief exports (45·9% to the USA) in 1979 (in 1m. balboas) were: Petroleum products, bananas, sugar, shrimps.

Chief imports, 1979, were valued (in 1m. balboas f.o.b.): Machinery and transport material, 214·7; manufactured goods, 308·9; fuel, minerals and similar, 319·4; chemicals, 116·7; food, 77·1. USA provided 32% of imports in 1979.

Total trade between Panama (including Colón Free Zone) and UK (British Department of Trade returns, in £1,000 sterling):

	1978	*1979*	*1980*	*1981*	*1982*
Imports to UK	982	4,131	3,941	7,815	9,521
Exports and re-exports from UK [1]	19,758	26,384	24,032	35,855	83,250

[1] Including new ships built for foreign owners and registered in Panama.

Tourism. In 1980, 392,062 people visited Panama.

COMMUNICATIONS

Roads. Panama had on 1 Jan. 1980, 8,606 km of roads. The road from Panama City westward to the cities of David and Concepción and to the Costa Rican frontier, with several branches, is part of the Pan-American Highway. A concrete highway connects Panama City and Colón.

On 1 Jan. 1980 registered motor vehicles, private and commercial, numbered 111,052, this excludes vehicles owned by government departments.

Railways. The *Ferrocarril de Panama* (Panama Railroad) (1,524 mm gauge) (through the Canal area), which connects Ancón on the Pacific with Cristóbal on the Atlantic, is the principal railway. It is 76 km long and runs along the banks of the Canal. As most vessels unload their cargo at Cristóbal (Colón), on the Atlantic side, the greater portion of the merchandise destined for Panama City is brought overland by the *Ferrocarril de Panama.* The United Brands owned railway runs from Almirante to Guabito on the Costa Rica border and on to Fields in Costa Rica (82 km).

The Chiriquí National Railroad (914 mm gauge) operates 169 km between David and Puerto Armuelles (United Brands) and about 35 km around Concepción.

Aviation. Commercial aviation has developed rapidly. PANAM, Braniff Airways, British Airways, KLM, Iberia Airlines and other international companies operate at Tocumen Airport, 17 miles from Panama City. Air Panama provides services between Panama City and New York, Los Angeles, Miami, Central America and some countries in South America. The *Compañía Panameña de Aviación* (COPA) and *Aerolineas Las Perlas* provide a local service between Panama City and the provincial towns. COPA also provides an international service to Central America.

Shipping. Ships under Panamanian registry on 25 Sept. 1981 numbered 10,859 of 27·2m. gross tons; most of these ships elect Panamanian registry because fees are low and labour laws lenient. All the international maritime traffic for Colón and Panama runs through the Canal ports of Cristóbal, Balboa and Bahia Las Minas (Colón); Almirante is used for both the provincial and international trade. There is an oil transfer terminal at Puerto Armuelles on the Pacific coast.

Panama Canal. On 18 Nov. 1903 a treaty between the USA and the Republic of Panama was signed making it possible for the US to build and operate a canal connecting the Atlantic and Pacific oceans through the Isthmus of Panama. The treaty granted the US in perpetuity the use, occupation and control of a Canal Zone, approximately 10 miles wide, in which the US would possess full sovereign rights 'to the entire exclusion of the exercise by the Republic of Panama of any such sovereign rights, power or authority'. In return the US guaranteed the independence of the republic and agreed to pay the republic $10m. and an annuity of $250,000. The US purchased the French rights and properties—the French had been labouring from 1879 to 1899 in an effort to build the Canal—for $40m. and in addition, paid private landholders within what would be the Canal Zone a mutually agreeable price for their properites.

Two new treaties between Panama and USA were agreed on 10 Aug. and signed on 7 Sept. 1977. One deals with the operation and defence of the canal until the end of 1999 and the other guarantees permanent neutrality.

The USA maintains control over all lands, waters and installations, including military bases, necessary to manage, operate and defend the canal until 31 Dec. 1999. A new agency of the US Government, the Panama Canal Commission, operates the canal, replacing the Panama Canal Co., and assuring US control of the canal to the end of the century. A policy-making board of 5 US citizens and 4 Panamanians serves on the board of directors. Until 1990 the canal administrator will be a US citizen and the deputy will be Panamanian. After that date the position will be reversed.

Six months after the exchange of instruments of ratification Panama assumed general territorial jurisdiction over the former Canal Zone and became able to use portions of the area not needed for the operation and defence of the canal. Panamanian penal and civil codes became applicable. Within 30 months of the treaty entering into force responsibility for the police courts, postal service, ship repairs and supplies, railway and pier operations and passengers were among other areas formerly administered by the Canal Co. and the Canal Zone Government for which Panama assumed responsibility.

66% of the electorate of Panama agreed to the ratification of the treaties when a referendum was held on 23 Oct. 1977 and on 18 April 1978 the treaty was ratified by the US Congress. The treaty went into effect on 1 Oct. 1979.

The treaty of 1936 increased the annuity to US$430,000 and, as desired by Panama, withdrew the guarantee of independence. In 1955 the annuity was increased to US$1·93m., and the Panama Canal Co. turned over to the Republic the Panama City railroad yards and other properties valued at US$22m. At the end of 1962 the US completed the construction of a high-level bridge over the Pacific entrance to the Canal, and the flags of Panama and the US were flown jointly over areas of the Canal Zone under civilian authority. Following the devaluation of the dollar in 1972 and 1973, the annuity was adjusted proportionally to US$2·1m. and US$2·33m. respectively.

The Panama Canal Commission, a US Government Agency, is concerned primarily with the actual operation of the Canal. On 8 July 1974 and 18 Nov. 1976 tolls were increased. These were the first increases of toll rates in the history of the Canal. Tolls were raised again on 1 Oct. 1979. The new rates are US$1.67 a Panama Canal ton for vessels carrying passengers or cargo. A Panama Canal ton is equivalent to 100 cu. ft of actual earning capacity. The new toll rate for warships, colliers, hospital ships and supply ships, which pay on a displacement basis, is 93 US cents a ton.

The changes were designed to continue the approximately break-even financial operating results after paying its own expenses and reimbursing the US Treasury for the net cost of the Canal Zone Government and paying interest on the net direct investment of the US in the Canal.

Administrator of the Panama Canal Commission: Dennis P. McAuliffe.
Deputy Administrator: Fernando Manfredo (Panama).

The total civilian and military population of the Canal area is 34,700 (estimate), of whom about 30,750 are US citizens. The total force employed by the Panama Canal Commission is 7,856, comprising 1,705 US citizens, 5,896 Panamanians and 255 others.

There are 144·4 miles of improved streets and highways in the Canal area, exclusive of those within Armed Forces reservations. Motor vehicles number over 25,000.

The Canal was opened to commerce on 15 Aug. 1914. It is 85 ft above sea-level. It is 51·2 statute miles in length from deep water in the Caribbean Sea to deep water in the Pacific ocean, and 36 statute miles from shore to shore. The channel ranges in bottom-width from 500 to 1,000 ft; the widening of Gaillard Cut to a minimum width of 500 ft was completed in 1969. Normally, the average time of a vessel in Canal waters is 18·5 hours, 8 of which are in transit through the Canal proper. The Canal is expected to reach the limits of its capacity in 2010 and proposals have been advanced by USA and Japan for a new sea-level canal. A map showing the Panama, Suez and Kiel canals on the same scale will be found in THE STATESMAN'S YEAR-BOOK, 1959 and a new map in the 1978–79 edition.

Particulars of the ocean-going commercial traffic through the canal are given as follows (vessels of 300 tons Panama Canal net and 500 displacement tons and over; cargo in long tons):

Fiscal year ending 30 Sept.	*North-bound (Pacific to Atlantic)*		*South-bound (Atlantic to Pacific)*		*Total*		*Tolls levied (in US$)*
	Vessels	*Cargo*	*Vessels*	*Cargo*	*Vessels*	*Cargo*	
1978	6,283	74,413,939	6,394	68,104,349	12,677	142,518,288	194,773,111
1979	6,209	75,142,979	6,726	78,967,887	12,935	154,110,866	208,376,741
1980	6,390	82,473,041	7,117	84,741,894	13,507	167,214,935	291,838,590
1981	...	...	...	...	13,884	171,221,762	301,828,204
1982	6,618	...	7,391	...	14,009	185,452,332	324,031,594

In the fiscal year ending 30 Sept. 1982, of the 14,009 ships which passed through the Canal, 2,473 were US; 1,805 Panamanian; 1,673 Liberian; 1,155 Greek; 1,145 Japanese; 718 British; 531 Russian; 410 Norwegian; 315 Peruvian; 285 Danish; 273 Ecuadorian.

Statistical Information: The Panama Canal Commission Office of Public Affairs.

Annual Reports on the Panama Canal, by the Administrator of the Panama Canal Commission.
Rules and Regulations Governing Navigation of the Panama Canal. The Panama Canal Commission, Miama, Florida *or* Washington, DC
Cameron, I., *The Impossible Dream.* London, 1972
Le Feber, W., *The Panama Canal: The Crisis in Historical Perspective.* OUP, 1978
McCullough, D., *The Path Between the Seas.* New York and London, 1978

Post and Broadcasting. There are telegraph cables from Panama to North America and Central and South American ports, and from Colón to the USA and Europe. There is also inter-continental communication by satellite. There are 93 licensed commercial broadcasting stations, nearly all operated by private companies, one of which functions in the canal. There are 5 television stations, one of them run by the US Army at Fort Clayton. On 1 Jan. 1981 there were 191,913 telephones.

Cinemas. In 1977 there were 52 cinemas in the district of Panama. All films must have Spanish subtitles.

Newspapers. There are 1 English language and 4 Spanish language daily morning newspapers and 1 English/Spanish evening newspaper.

JUSTICE, RELIGION, EDUCATION AND WELFARE

Justice. The Supreme Court consists of 9 justices appointed by the executive. There is no death penalty.

Religion. 95% of the population is Roman Catholic and 5% Protestant. There is freedom of religious worship and separation of Church and State. Clergymen may teach in the schools but may not hold public office.

Education. Elementary education is compulsory for all children from 7 to 15 years of age, with an estimated 545,800 students in schools in 1977. The University of Panama at Panama City, inaugurated on 7 Oct. 1935, had a total enrolment (1978) of 32,868 students. The Catholic university Sta. Maria La Antigua, inaugurated on 27 May 1965, had 1,916 students in Sept. 1978.

In 1978, 16% of the population over 10 years old were illiterate, excluding the tribal Indians.

DIPLOMATIC REPRESENTATIVES

Of Panama in Great Britain (109 Jermyn St., London, SW1)
Ambassador: Dr Calixto Arias (accredited 21 Feb. 1983).

Of Great Britain in Panama (Apartado 889, Panama City 1)
Ambassador: T. H. Steggle.

Of Panama in the USA (2862 McGill Terr., NW, Washington, D.C., 20008)
Ambassador: Aquilino E. Boyd.

Of the USA in Panama (Ave. Balboa y Calle 38, Panama City)
Chargé de Affaires: Melville E. Blake, Jr.

Of Panama to the United Nations
Ambassador: Carlos Ozores.

Books of Reference

Statistical Information: The Comptroller-General of the Republic (Contraloria General de la República, Calle 35 y Avenida 6, Panama City) publishes an annual report and other statistical publications.

Castillero, Ernesto J., *Historia de Panamá.* 5th ed. Panama City, 1965
Langstaff, E. DeS., *Panama.* [Bibliography] Oxford and Santa Barbara 1982
Larsen, H. and M., *The Forests of Panama.* London, 1964
Ropp, S. C., *Panamanian Politics.* New York, 1982

National Library: Biblioteca Nacional, Departamento de Información. Calle 22, Panama.

PAPUA NEW GUINEA

Capital: Port Moresby
Population: 3·08m. (1981)
GNP per capita: US$780 (1980)

HISTORY. To prevent that portion of the island of New Guinea not claimed by the Netherlands or Germany from passing into the hands of a foreign power, the Government of Queensland annexed Papua in 1883. This step was not sanctioned by the Imperial Government, but on 6 Nov. 1884 a British Protectorate was proclaimed over the southern portion of the eastern half of New Guinea, and in 1887 Queensland, New South Wales and Victoria undertook to defray the cost of administration, and the territory was annexed to the Crown the following year. The federal government took over the control in 1901; the political transfer was completed by the Papua Act of the federal parliament in Nov. 1905, and on 1 Sept. 1906 a proclamation was issued by the Governor-General of Australia declaring that British New Guinea was to be known henceforth as the Territory of Papua. The northern portion of New Guinea was a German colony until the First World War. It became a League of Nations mandated territory in 1921, administered by Australia, and later a UN Trust Territory (of New Guinea).

The Papua New Guinea Act 1949–1972 provides for the administration of the UN Australian Trust Territory of New Guinea in an administrative union with the Territory of Papua, in accordance with Art. 5 of the New Guinea Trusteeship Agreement, under the title of Papua New Guinea.

Australia granted Papua New Guinea self-government on 1 Dec. 1973 and, on 16 Sept. 1975, Papua New Guinea became a fully independent state.

AREA AND POPULATION. Papua New Guinea extends from the equator to Cape Baganowa in the Louisiade Archipelago to 11° 40′ S. lat. and from the border of West Irian to 160° E. long. with a total area of 462,840 sq. km. According to the census the 1980 population was 3,010,727. Port Moresby, (1980) 123,624; Lae, 61,617; Rabaul, 14,954; Madang, 21,335; Mount Hagen, 13,441. Area and population of the provinces:

Provinces	*Sq.km*	*Census 1971*	*Census 1980*	*Capital*
Milne Bay	14,000	109,460	127,975	Alotau
Northern	22,800	66,514	77,442	Popondetta
Central	29,500	117,330	116,964	Port Moresby
National Capital District	240	76,507	123,624	—
Gulf	34,500	58,564	64,120	Kerema
Western	99,300	70,898	78,575	Daru
Southern Highlands	23,800	192,854	236,052	Mendi
Enga	12,800	346,032	164,534	Wabag
Western Highlands	8,500		265,656	Mount Hagen
Chimbu	6,100	160,245	178,290	Kundiawa
Eastern Highlands	11,200	239,640	276,726	Goroka
Morobe	34,500	249,032	310,622	Lae
Madang	29,000	170,953	211,206	Madang
East Sepik	42,800	181,893	221,069	Wewak
West Sepik	36,300	93,978	114,192	Vanimo
Manus	2,100	24,866	26,036	Lorengau
West New Britain	21,000	61,515	88,941	Kimbe
East New Britain	15,500	113,750	133,197	Rabaul
New Ireland	9,600	59,543	66,028	Kavieng
North Solomons	9,300	96,363	128,794	Arawa

Vital statistics (1979): Crude birth rate, 45 per 1,000; crude death rate, 14·9.

CONSTITUTION AND GOVERNMENT. Papua New Guinea has a Westminster type of government. A single legislative house, known as the National

Parliament, is made up of 109 members from all parts of the country. The members are elected under universal suffrage and general elections are held every 5 years. All persons over the age of 18 who are Papua New Guinea citizens are eligible to vote and stand for election. Voting is by secret ballot and follows the preferential system.

The first Legislative Council was established in 1951. It was abolished in 1964 and replaced with the House of Assembly. In 1950 the first village council was formed which established the basis of the now extensive local government system. A system of provincial government was introduced in 1976.

The elections in 1972 saw the formation of the first indigenous controlled central government in the history of the country. It also saw the emergence of four major political parties—the Pangu Pati, United Party, People's Progress Party and the New Guinea National Party. A number of other parties had also been formed before these elections. A coalition group was formed and the group was able to place its members in the ministerial positions, and with its combined majority in the House of Assembly, also formed a working government.

Also in 1972, the coalition government appointed a constitutional planning committee to make recommendations for a Constitution specifically suited to conditions in the country. The committee's final report was presented to the House of Assembly in 1974 and provided the basis for the Constitution of the Independent State of Papua New Guinea introduced in 1975. In 1977, following the first general election since independence, the Pangu Pati, the People's Progress Party and independent members formed a coalition with support from 69 members of Parliament.

The administrative centre and capital is located at Port Moresby. National administration is carried out by a public service of 28 departments. In accordance with the decentralization provisions of the Constitution, the country has been divided into the National Capital District and 19 provinces: Western, Gulf, Central, Milne Bay, Northern, Southern Highlands, Enga, Western Highlands, Chimbu, Eastern Highlands, Morobe, Madang, East Sepik, West Sepik, Manus, New Ireland, East New Britain, West New Britain, and North Solomons. Each of the provincial governments has a secretariat headed by an Administrative Secretary. In many provinces the system of local governments still operates, although the provinces may make changes to this if they wish.

Governor-General: Sir Tore Lokoloko, GCMG, OBE.

The Cabinet in Nov. 1982 was as follows:

Prime Minister: Michael Thomas Somare.

Deputy Prime Minister, Minister for National Planning and Development, and Primary Industry: Paias Wingti. *Commerce and Industry:* Karl Stack. *Correctional Services and Liquor Licensing:* Pundia Kange. *Culture and Tourism:* McKenzie Javopa. *Decentralisation:* John Nilkare. *Defence:* Epel Tito. *Education:* Barry Holloway. *Environment and Conservation:* Halalu Mai. *Finance:* Phillip Bouraga. *Foreign Affairs and Trade:* Rabie Namaliu. *Forests:* Lucas Waka. *Health:* Martine Tovadek. *Home Affairs:* Roy Evara. *Justice:* Tony Bais. *Labour and Employment:* Caspar Anggua. *Lands:* Bebes Korowaro. *Media:* Boyamo Sali. *Minerals and Energy:* Francis Pusal. *Parliamentary Services:* Pital Lus. *Police:* John Giheno. *Public Service:* Tony Siaguru. *Religion, Youth and Recreation:* Tom Awasa. *Transport and Civil Aviation:* Mathew Bendumb. *Urban Development:* Kala Swokin. *Works and Supply:* Pato Kakarya.

The seat of the Government is at Port Moresby.

National flag: Diagonally ochre-red over black, on the red a bird of paradise in gold, and on the black 5 stars of the Southern Cross in white.

DEFENCE. The Papua New Guinea Defence Force has a total strength of 3,400 (1983) consisting of land, maritime and air elements. The Army is organized in 2 infantry battalions, 1 engineer and 1 signals battalion with logistic units. The nucleus of an Air Force was formed by 4 DC-3 piston-engined transports delivered from Australia in 1975; two more were delivered later. They have been followed by

7 Australian-built Missionmaster twin-turboprop support transports. Personnel total 100.

INTERNATIONAL RELATIONS

Membership. Papua New Guinea is a member of UN, the Commonwealth, the Colombo Plan and is an ACP state of EEC.

ECONOMY

Budget. Revenue (in K1,000) for calendar years was:

Source	*1979*	*1980*
Customs and excise	97,512	111,866
Other taxes	108,698	131,015
Foreign government grants [1]	174,835	174,598
Loans	91,395	72,689
Other revenue	77,615	93,469
Total	550,055	583,637

[1] Mainly from Australia.

Expenditure (in K1,000) for the same periods:

Source	*1979*	*1980*
Consumption	275,504	292,641
Capital	57,420	86,777
Other expenditure [1]	209,161	208,203
Total	542,085	587,621

[1] Includes transfers to provincial governments.

Currency. The unit of currency is the *kina* divided into 100 *toea* and is the sole legal tender. In March 1983, £1 = K1·23; US$1 = K0·84.

Banking. The Bank of Papua New Guinea assumed the central banking functions formerly undertaken by the Reserve Bank of Australia on 1 Nov. 1973.

A national banking institution which has been named the Papua New Guinea Banking Corporation, has been established. This bank has assumed the Papua New Guinea business of the Commonwealth Trading Bank of Australia except where certain accounts give rise to special financial or contractual problems.

The subsidiaries of 3 Australian commercial banks also operate in Papua New Guinea. These are the Australia and New Zealand Banking Group (PNG) Ltd, the Bank of New South Wales (PNG) Ltd, and the Bank of South Pacific Ltd, all of which offer trading and savings facilities. As from 1 Nov. 1973 these banks operated under Papua New Guinea banking legislation.

In addition to the subsidiaries of Australian banks operating in Papua New Guinea, the Papua New Guinea Development Bank has provided long-term development finance with particular attention to the needs of small-scale enterprises since 1967 and during its first 10 years has lent K71·7m.

Weights and Measures. The metric system is in force.

ENERGY AND NATURAL RESOURCES

Electricity. In 1981 installed capacity was 168,016 mw, production 1,236·7m. kwh.

Minerals. Copper is the main mineral product. Oil companies have been searching for oil, but by 1983 no commercial deposits have yet been found. Gold, copper and silver are the only minerals produced in quantity. Major copper deposits in the Kieta district of Bougainville have proved reserves of about 800m. tonnes and are worked by Bougainville Copper Ltd and production of copper concentrates for export began in 1972 from this source. Copper and gold deposits which were found in the Star Mountains of the Western Province are being developed by Ok Tedi Mining Ltd at the Mt. Fubilan mine and production is expected to commence in 1984. In 1981, B.C.L. exported 605,862 tonnes of copper concentrate containing approximately 173,758 tonnes of copper. 17·55 kg of gold and 44·55 kg of silver were exported yielding a sales revenue of K295m.

Agriculture. At 31 Dec. 1980, the total area of larger holdings was 396,000 hectares, of which 231,000 hectares were for agricultural purposes, the principal crops being coffee, copra and cocoa. Production of palm oil is of growing importance. Minor commercial crops include pyrethrum, tea, peanuts and spices. Locally consumed food crops include sweet potatoes, taro, bananas, rice and sago. Tropical fruits grow abundantly. There is extensive grassland and a sugar industry and a beef-cattle industry are being developed.

Livestock (1981): Cattle, 132,000; pigs, 1·41m.; goats, 16,000; poultry, 1·4m.

Forestry. Timber production is of growing importance for both local consumption and export. In 1979, about 1,118,000 cu. metres of logs were harvested; logs exported, 473,000 cu. metres.

Production of sawn timber, 1980, 136,000 cu. metres; exports of woodchips, 123,908 tonnes.

Fisheries. Tuna, both skipjack and yellowfin species, is the major fisheries resource; in 1979 the catch was 27,000 tonnes. Exports of various crustacea, 1979, 1,116 tonnes, value K6·2m.

INDUSTRY AND TRADE

Industry. Secondary and service industries are expanding for the local market. Industries include the manufacture of paint, gases, concrete, twist tobacco and cigarettes, matches, soap, brewing, boat-building, furniture and the assembly of electrical appliances. In 1980 there were 776 factories employing 25,580 persons. Value of output K482m.

Labour. In 1976 about 352,000 indigenous wage-earners were in regular employment.

Trade. Imports (in K1,000) for year 1976 ended 30 June and calender years 1980 and 1981.

	1976	*1980*	*1981*
Food and live animals	73,098	133,176	136,339
Beverages and tobacco	5,810	8,690	8,362
Crude materials, inedible, except fuels	1,109	2,117	3,569
Mineral fuels, lubricants and related materials	47,220	117,863	158,369
Oils and fats (animal and vegetable)	846	1,870	1,877
Chemicals	18,945	36,584	45,055
Manufactured goods, chiefly by material	48,051	91,607	108,510
Machinery and transport equipment	109,192	206,329	224,595
Miscellaneous manufactured articles	27,992	52,891	54,593
Commodities and transactions of merchandise trade, not elsewhere specified	10,748	33,044	10,149
Total, excluding outside packages	343,000	...	...
Outside packages	3,397	...	...
Total imports	346,397	684,172	751,419

Exports (in K1,000) for calendar years:

	1979	*1980*	*1981*
Coconut and copra products—			
Copra	38,162	24,594	19,476
Copra (coconut) oil	20,599	16,610	12,508
Copra cake and pellets	1,951	1,484	689
Total	60,712	42,688	32,673
Coffee beans	124,996	118,643	74,218
Cocoa beans	60,872	46,493	34,135
Crude rubber	3,497	3,751	3,403
Tea	7,982	8,507	7,131
Pyrethrum extract	202	19	890

	1979	1980	1981
Forest and timber products			
Logs	20,883	29,979	31,517
Sawn timber	7,683	6,155	3,897
Veneers	259	281	272
Plywood	3,819	2,520	3,000
Other	4,951	7,748	6,982
Total	37,595	46,684	45,667
Crocodile skins	1,610	1,620	1,320
Crayfish and prawns	6,210	6,560	6,851
Gold	4,141	7,811	7,132
Other domestic produce	322,153 [1]	354,972 [2]	332,170 [3]
Total domestic produce	629,970	637,748	545,589
Re-exports	56,914	53,972	19,334
Total exports	686,884	691,720	564,923

[1] Includes K288,065,000 for copper ore concentrate.
[2] Includes K313,264,000 for copper ore and concentrate.
[3] Includes K292,336,000 for copper ore and concentrate.

Of exports in 1980, Japan took 37%, West Germany, 27% and Australia, 9%; of imports, Australia furnished about 50%.

Total trade between Papua New Guinea and UK (British Department of Trade returns, in £1,000 sterling):

	1977	1978	1979	1980	1981	1982
Imports to UK	30,577	24,469	30,148	22,861	18,506	28,031
Exports and re-exports from UK	10,038	10,185	10,409	10,978	11,316	15,911

Tourism. In 1977, there were 15,084 visitors.

COMMUNICATIONS

Roads. In Sept. 1976 there were approximately 19,538 km of roads including approximately 1,016 km of urban roads. Motor vehicles numbered (1979) 47,436 including 12,980 cars.

Aviation. Frequent air services operate to and from Australia (Sydney, Brisbane and Cairns), and there are regular flights to Djayapura (Indonesia), Manila, Hong Kong, Kagoshima (Japan), Djakarta and Honolulu. A service is also maintained to Honiara in the Solomon Islands. In addition to Air Niugini, the national flag carrier, Qantas, Philippine Airlines and Cathay Pacific operate in and out of Papua New Guinea.

Shipping. There are regular shipping services between Australia and Papua New Guinea ports, and also services to New Zealand, Japan, Hong Kong, US west coast, Singapore, Solomon Islands, Taiwan, Philippines and Europe. Small coastal vessels run between the various ports. In 1979 cargo discharged from overseas was 1·7m. tonnes; cargo loaded for overseas was 1·8m. tonnes.

Post and Broadcasting. Telephones numbered 45,274 on 1 Jan. 1981. The National Broadcasting Commission broadcasts on short-wave and medium-wave from Port Moresby, Rabaul, Wewak, Goroka, Lae, Daru, Alotau, Vanimo and Madang. There are 11 other stations broadcasting on short-wave only, at a number of centres, broadcasting programmes in several local languages.

Cinemas (1972): 28 with a total seating capacity of 18,800.

JUSTICE, EDUCATION AND WELFARE

Justice. In 1978, 893 cases were heard in the National Court and (1977) 45,289 cases in the district courts.

Police. Total strength (1979) 4,268.

Education. At 31 Dec. 1981 about 277,200 children attended 2,118 primary schools and 43,800 enrolled in 192 secondary, technical and vocational schools. The University of Papua New Guinea and the Papua New Guinea University of Technology had 2,621 students in 1979.

Health. In 1978, there were 20 hospitals, 384 health centres and 235 doctors.

DIPLOMATIC REPRESENTATIVES

Of Papua New Guinea in Great Britain (14 Waterloo Pl., London, SW1R 4AR)
High Commissioner: Dr Alexis Sarei, CBE.

Of Great Britain in Papua New Guinea (Douglas St., Port Moresby)
High Commissioner: A. J. Collins, OBE.

Of Papua New Guinea in the USA (1140, 19th St., NW, Washington D.C., 20036)
Ambassador: Kubulan Los.

Of the USA in Papua New Guinea (Armit St., Port Moresby)
Ambassador: M. Virginia Schafer.

Of Papua New Guinea to the United Nations
Ambassador: (Vacant).

Books of Reference

The Territory of Papua. Annual Report. Commonwealth of Australia. 1906–1940–41 and from 1945–46
The Territory of New Guinea. Annual Report. Commonwealth of Australia. 1914–1940–41 and from 1946–47
Papua New Guinea, Annual Report. From 1970–71
Report on New Guinea. UN visiting missions to . . . Nauru and New Guinea. New York, 1962
Bettison, D. G., and others, *Independence of Papua–New Guinea.* Sydney, 1962.—*The Papua–New Guinea Elections 1964.* Canberra, 1966
Essal, B., *Papua and New Guinea.* Melbourne, 1961
Hasluck, P., *A Time for Building.* Melbourne Univ. Press, 1976
Hastings, P. (ed.), *Papua New Guinea: Prospero's Other Island.* London, 1971
Ross, A. C., and Langmore, J., *Alternative Strategies for Papua New Guinea.* OUP, 1974
Ryan, J., *The Hot Land.* London, 1970
Ryan, P. (ed.), *Encyclopaedia of Papua and New Guinea.* Melbourne Univ. Press, 1972
Skeldon, R., (ed.) *The Demography of Papua New Guinea.* Institute of Applied Social and Economic Research, 1979

PARAGUAY

República del Paraguay

Capital: Asunción
Population: 3·02m. (1982)
GNP per capita: US$1,340 (1980)

HISTORY. The Republic of Paraguay gained its independence from Spain on 14 May 1811. In 1814 Dr José Gaspar Rodríguez de Francia was elected dictator, and in 1816 perpetual dictator by the National Assembly. He died 20 Sept. 1840. In 1844 a new constitution was adopted, under which Carlos Antonio López (first elected in 1842, died 10 Sept. 1862) and his son, Francisco Solano López, ruled until 1870. During the devastating war against Brazil, Argentina and Uruguay (1865–70) Paraguay's population was reduced from about 600,000 to 232,000. Argentina, in Aug. 1942, and Brazil, in May 1943, voided the reparations which Paraguay had never paid. Further severe losses were incurred during the war with Bolivia (1932–35) over territorial claims in the Chaco. A peace treaty by which Paraguay obtained most of the area her troops had conquered was signed in July 1938.

AREA AND POPULATION. The area of the Oriental province is officially estimated at 159,827 sq. km (61,705 sq. miles) and the Occidental province at 246,925 sq. km (95,337 sq. miles), making the total area of the republic 406,752 sq. km (157,042 sq. miles).

The population according to the official census in 1982 was 3,023,092. The capital, Asunción, had 455,517 inhabitants; other towns: Caaguazú (299,227), Itapúa (263,021), Paraguarí (202,152) and Concepcíon (135,068).

The 19 departments had the following populations in 1982:

Central	494,575	Misiones	79,278
Caaguazú	299,227	Neembucu	70,689
Itapua	263,021	Amambay	68,422
Paraguari	202,152	Canendiyú	65,807
Cordillera	194,826	Presidente Hayes	43,787
San Pedro	189,751	Boquerón	14,685
Alto Paraná	188,351	Alto Paraguay	4,535
Guairá	143,374	Chaco	286
Concepción	135,068	Nueva Asunción	231
Caazapá	109,510		

Number of births, 1976, was 88,371; deaths, 13,754.

The population is overwhelmingly *mestizo* (mixed Spanish and Guaraní Indian) forming a homogeneous stock. There are some 46,700 unassimilated Indians of other tribal origin, in the Chaco and the forests of eastern Paraguay. There are some small traces of Negro descent. About half the population speak only Guaraní; some 4% speak only Spanish; the rest are bilingual.

Mennonites who arrived in 3 groups (1927, 1930 and 1947) are settled in the Chaco and Oriental Paraguay and were estimated in 1969 to number 13,000, of whom 2,000 came from Canada and 11,000 from Germany. The Japanese colonists in the Oriental section, who first came in 1935, were reckoned to number 7,000 in 1969. Under an agreement signed with Japan in 1959 up to 85,000 Japanese were to be admitted over 30 years. An agreement with Korea was signed in 1966 and there were (1978) about 3,000 Korean families living in Paraguay.

CONSTITUTION AND GOVERNMENT. A new constitution replacing that of 1940 was drawn up by a Constituent Convention in which all legally recognized political parties were represented and was signed into law on 25 Aug. 1967. It provides for a two-chamber parliament consisting of a 30-seat Senate and a 60-seat Chamber of Deputies, each elected for a 5-year term. Two-thirds of the seats in each Chamber are allocated to the majority party and the remaining one-third shared among the minority parties in proportion to the votes cast. Voting is compulsory for all citizens over 18. The President is directly elected for a 5-year (renewable) term; he appoints the Cabinet and during parliamentary recess can govern by decree through the Council of State, the members of which are representatives of the Government, the armed forces and other bodies.

On 6 Feb. 1977 elections were held for a 60-member Constitutional Assembly to revise the 1967 Constitution.

President: Gen. Alfredo Stroessner, Commander-in-Chief, elected 11 July 1954 to complete the presidential period of his predecessor. He was re-elected as 'Colorado' candidate in 1958, 1963, 1968, 1973, 1978 and 1983.

The following is a list of past presidents since 1940, with the date on which each took office:

Gen. Higinio Morínigo, 7 Sept. 1940 (resigned).
Dr Juan Manuel Frutos, 3 June 1948.[1]
Dr J. Natalicio González, 15 Aug. 1948 (deposed).
Gen. Raimundo Rolón, 30 Jan. 1949.
Dr Felipe Molas López, 26 Feb. 1949[1] (resigned).
Dr Federico Chávez, 16 July 1950 (resigned).
Tomás Romero Pereira, 4 May 1954.

[1] Provisional, *i.e.*, following a *coup d'état.*

The President has a cabinet of 11 ministers.

Interior: Dr Sabino A. Montanaro. *Foreign Affairs:* Dr Alberto Nogués. *Finance:* César Barrientos. *Education and Worship:* Dr Raúl Peña. *Public Works and Communications:* Juan A. Cáceres. *Agriculture and Livestock:* Hernando Bertoni. *National Defence:* Marcial Samaniego. *Public Health and Social Welfare:* Dr Adan Godoy Giménez. *Justice and Labour:* Dr Saúl González. *Industry and Commerce:* Dr Delfín Ugarte Centuríon. *Without Portfolio:* Vacant.

National flag: Red, white, blue (horizontal); the white stripe charged with the arms of the republic on the obverse, and, on the reverse, with a lion and the inscription *Paz y Justicia*—the only flag in the world with different obverse and reverse.

National anthem: ¡ Paraguayos, república o muerte! (words by F. Acuña de Figueroa; tune by F. Dupey).

The country is divided into 2 provinces: the 'Oriental', east of Paraguay River, and the 'Occidental', west of the same river. The Oriental section is divided into 13 departments and the capital. The more important departments are supervised by a *Delegado* appointed by and directly responsible to the central government. The Occidental province, or Chaco, is divided into 3 departments.

DEFENCE. The army, navy and air forces are separate services under a single command. The President of the Republic is the active Commander-in-Chief. The armed forces total about 15,500 officers and men. Of these, the Army account for about 12,500 (75% conscripts), the Navy about 2,000 (25% conscripts) and the Air Force about 1,000 (25% conscripts). There are also about 4,000 armed police (75% conscripts). Military service is compulsory between the ages of 18 and 20 but there are many exemptions.

Army. The main units of the Army are: a Presidential escort battalion, 6 infantry battalions, a cavalry brigade with 2 regiments and a battalion, 1 artillery regiment and an engineer command with 5 battalions. Strength (1983), 12,500.

Navy. The Navy consists of 5 armoured river defence gunboats (2 ancient monitors of 636 tons built in Italy and 3 old *ex*-Argentinian minesweepers of 620 tons), 1 helicopter lighter, 1 river patrol boat, 2 patrol launches, 6 coastal patrol craft, 2 landing craft, 1 survey craft, 1 transport training ship, 12 service craft and 2 tugs. Personnel in 1983 totalled 2,000 officers and men including coastguard and 500 marines.

Air Force. The Air Force came into being in the early thirties. After operating only transport and training aircraft for a number of years, it received 6 A-37B light jet attack aircraft from USA in 1978, followed by 10 Xavante light jet strike/training aircraft from Brazil. Other types in service include 5 DC-6B and 2 C-54 four-engined transports more than 20 C-47 and 4 Banderante twin-engined transports, 1 Convair C-131A, a Twin Otter, an Otter, 8 Brazilian-built Uirapuru primary trainers, 22 T-6 Texan armed basic trainers and a number of light aircraft and helicopters. HQ and flying school are at Campo Grande, Asunción. Personnel total about 1,000.

INTERNATIONAL RELATIONS

Membership. Paraguay is a member of UN, OAS and LAIA (formerly LAFTA).

ECONOMY

Budget. In 1981 revenue was Gs.64,626m. and expenditure Gs.70,908m.

The 1982 budget provided Gs.13,307m. for national defence, Gs.13,412m. for education and worship and Gs.6,002m. for public health and social welfare. Total external debt outstanding at the end of Dec. 1981 was US$948·6m.

Currency. The *guaraní* was established on 5 Oct. 1943 equal to 100 old paper pesos. Total monetary circulation was Gs.71,871m. in Dec. 1981.

Rate of exchange, March 1983: 126 *guaranies* = US$1; 185 *guaranies* = £1.

Banking. The Banco Central del Paraguay opened 1 July 1952 to take over the central banking functions previously assigned to the National Bank of Paraguay, which had opened in March 1943 and been reorganized as the Banco del Paraguay in Sept. 1944 with a monetary, a banking and a mortgage department. The Banco del Paraguay closed in Nov. 1961 and has been replaced, with the aid of a US loan of US$3m., by the Banco Nacional de Fomento; the latter's assets in Jan. 1979 were Gs.27,546m.

The Banco Central in Dec. 1981 had gold and exchange reserves amounting to US$733·5m.; contribution to the IMF was Gs.47·7m.

The Banco Nacional de Fomento, Bank of London and South America, Ltd, Banco Exterior do Brasil, Citibank, Banco de Asunción, Banco Exterior SA, Banco Unión SA, Banco Paraguayo de Comercio, Banco Real del Paraguay SA, Banco Aleman Transatlantico, Banco Holandés Unido, Banco Nacional del Estado de São Paulo, Yegros y Azara, Bank of America, Chase Manhattan Bank, Bank of Boston and Interbanco all have agencies in Asunción and branches in some main towns.

Weights and Measures. The metric system was officially adopted on 1 Jan. 1901.

ENERGY AND NATURAL RESOURCES

Electricity. Electricity from a 90,000 kw. hydro-electric plant at Acaray, with an output of 180,000 kw. (1979), supplies Asunción and 70 small towns and villages. Electricity is exported to Argentina and Brazil. Paraguay has signed agreements with Brazil to build jointly a 10m. kw. scheme on the river Paraná which will be in operation in 1982, and with Argentina another which will yield approximately 3m. kw.

Oil. The oil refinery at Villa Elisa, which has been in operation since 1966, has a production of about 3,500 bbls a day. Exploration for petroleum in the Chaco yielded negative results but prospecting was continuing in 1979.

Minerals. Iron, manganese and other minerals have been reported but have not been shown to be commercially exploitable. There are large deposits of limestone, and also salt, kaolin and apatite. *Pennzoil Paraguay* and other national and international firms have acquired licences to prospect for oil and natural gas in the Chaco. A uranium survey was being carried out in 1978 in the Oriental region.

Agriculture. In 1981 it was estimated that agriculture absorbs some 51·4m. hectares. Area (in hectares) and yield (in tonnes per hectare) of the main agricultural products in 1981:

	Area	Yield		Area	Yield
Cotton	243,782	265,000	Soybeans	393,890	850,000
Maize [1]	420,000	680,000	Mandioca [1]	135,000	2,049,807
Tobacco	7,597	10,332	Rice (Paddy) [1]	38,300	72,779
Wheat	49,032	80,000			

[1] 1979–80 figures.

Wheat, soybean (850,000 tons, 1981), cotton, sugar, tobacco, coffee are increasing in importance, as are also essential oils and oilseeds. *Yerba maté*, or strongly flavoured Paraguayan tea, continues to be produced but is declining in importance; 712 tons were exported in 1981.

Livestock (1981). Paraguay had about 6·3m. cattle, 329,000 horses, 1·02m. pigs, 423,000 sheep. Exports of meat products in 1981 amounted to US$3,000.

Forestry. In the Oriental section there are huge reserves of hardwoods and cedars that have scarcely been exploited. Palms, tung and other trees are exploited for their oils. The Japanese are experimenting with mulberries for silk growing. Pines and firs have been introduced under a United Nations project. In the Chaco the accessible Quebracho forests have nearly been worked out but plans are being made to open up new areas. In 1979, 5,206 tons of timber were exported and 393 tons of quebracho.

INDUSTRY AND TRADE

Industry. Production, 1981 (tons): Hides, 9,519; preserved meat, 257; frozen meat, 311; cotton fibre, 105,869 (1,000 metres); tannin, 17 (1978); petit grain, 220; tung oil, 12 (1978); cement, 161,419; sugar, 76,518; cigarettes (1,000 packets), 37,826; matches (1,000 boxes), 14,901. There are 3 meat-packing plants and other factories producing vegetable oils. A textile industry in Pilar and Asunción meets a large part of local needs. A cement works at Valle-mi, with a capacity of 7,000 bags a day, was inaugurated in Jan. 1970. Foreign investment is encouraged by industries being exempted from 30–50% of their tax bill for 5 years. In development areas this may be increased up to 100% for 10 years. Various degrees of duty exemption are permitted on capital equipment and raw materials.

Labour. Trade unionists number about 30,000 (*Confederación Paraguaya de Trabajadores* and *Confederación Cristiana de Trabajadores*).

Commerce. Imports and exports (in US$1m.):

	1975	1976	1977	1978	1979	1980	1981
Imports	212·7	180·2	250·4	375	402	517·1	506
Exports	176·2	181·8	278·9	285	276	310·2	295

Chief exports in 1981 included (in US$1m.): Fruit, 152; cotton, 129·2; sugar, 72; soybeans, 47·5; timber, 36·9; yerba maté, 34·9; palm shoots, 30; vegetable oils, 22·4; tung oil, 11·6; tobacco, 6.4.

Chief imports 1981 in (US$1m.): Machinery and apparatus, 107·7; fuels and lubricants, 94·5; foodstuffs, 89·2; vehicles and accessories, 65·4; iron and manufactures, 22·6; drinks and tobacco, 12·7.

Imports and exports (in US$), by country, 1981:

Country	Imports	Exports
Algeria	27,458	...
Argentina	100,090	68,542
Belgium	2,392	3,027
Brazil	131,257	54,156
Federal Republic of Germany	41,038	32,902
France	9,098	4,603
Italy	6,005	...
Japan	41,990	24,940
Netherlands	2,599	13,257
Spain	6,014	3,791
Sweden	4,283	...
Switzerland	3,078	14,651
UK	24,898	2,894
Uruguay	15,475	9,124
USA	49,156	15,308

Total trade between Paraguay and UK (British Department of Trade returns, in £1,000 sterling):

	1977	*1978*	*1979*	*1980*	*1981*	*1982*
Imports to UK	8,183	7,418	2,107	1,279	2,241	2,790
Exports and re-exports from UK	8,318	11,772	12,746	13,384	13,105	16,915

Tourism. Visitors numbered 93,023 in 1972; 95,086 in 1973.

COMMUNICATIONS

Roads. In 1978 there were 12,000 km of roads, of which 1,200 were paved, 582 of gravel and 6,990 of earth. The principal paved roads are Route No. 2/7 running from Asunción to the bridge over the Paraná at Puerto Presidente Stroessner, and thence down to the ocean at Paranaguá; and Route No. 1 to Encarnación in the south. The other main arteries are Coronel Oviedo-Pedro Juan Caballero road (unpaved from Coronel Oviedo) in the north and the Trans-Chaco road which starts from the bridge across the river Paraguay north of Asunción and ends at Nueva Asunción on the Bolivian border, 200 km of this are paved and work is continuing. Unpaved roads are closed when it rains. In the Argentine, a paved road starts from Pilcomayo, opposite Asunción, and provides good communication with Buenos Aires. Motor cars, 1976, numbered 17,600; commercial vehicles, 15,200, and passenger vehicles, 7,580.

Railways. The President Carlos Antonio López (formerly Paraguay Central) Railway runs from Asunción to Encarnación, on the Río Alto Paraná, with a length of 441 km (1,435 mm gauge). In 1980, traffic amounted to 191,724 tonnes and 287,318 passengers.

Aviation. International services are operated by 9 airlines (domestic and foreign) and internal routes by military airlines and some small private lines.

Shipping. In flood the Paraguay River, which divides the country into two distinct parts, is navigable for 12ft-draught vessels as far as Concepción, 180 miles north of Asunción, and for smaller vessels for a further distance of 600 miles northward. Drought conditions often restrict navigation to lighter traffic. The Paraná River is navigable by large boats from Corrientes up to Puerto Aguirre, at the mouth of the Yguazú River. Boats of a few hundred tons capacity navigate the tributary rivers.

Asunción, the chief port, is 950 miles from the sea. In June 1945 the Government formed—after a break of 80 years—a national merchant marine which operates in the river Plate basin, connecting with Argentine, Uruguayan and Brazilian ports. The cargo fleet includes 25 vessels of 300–1,000 tons, 3 tankers of 1,100–1,700 tons, 2 passenger river boats and 1 ocean-going freighter of 713 tons.

Post and Broadcasting. The national telegraph (137 offices) connects Asunción with Corrientes and Posadas in the Argentine Republic, and thus with the outside world; new direct links have been opened with the Federal Republic of Germany, USA, Bolivia and Chile. In addition, 34 stations are operated by the President Carlos Antonio López Railway; total, 2,070 miles. Three companies (12 stations) offer radio-telegraph and telex services to several countries. The telephone system has been under government control since 5 Oct. 1945; a new government agency, the National Telephone Administration, took over the telecommunication services in July 1947. Telephones, 1981, 58,713, of which 45,818 were in Asunción and were automatic. There are 1 state and 9 commercial radio stations in Asunción, 22 in provincial towns, 2 commercial television stations in Asunción and 1 in Encarnación in the south.

Cinemas (1974). Cinemas numbered 65 in Asunción. The larger country towns usually have an outdoor cinema.

Newspapers (1980). There are 5 daily newspapers in Asunción with an aggregate circulation of about 200,000.

JUSTICE, RELIGION AND EDUCATION

Justice. The highest court is the Supreme Court with 5 members. There are special

Chambers of Appeal for civil and commercial cases, and criminal cases. Judges of first instance deal with civil, commercial and criminal cases in 6 departments. Minor cases are dealt with by Justices of the Peace.

The Attorney-General represents the State in all jurisdictions, with representatives in each judicial department and in every jurisdiction. In matters of revenue, taxes, etc., the State is represented by the *Abogado del Tesoro.*

Religion. Religious liberty is guaranteed by the 1967 constitution. Article 6 thereof recognizes Roman Catholicism as the official religion of the country. The same article disposes that relations between Paraguay and the Holy See shall be regulated by concordats or other bilateral agreements, but no such agreements have yet been negotiated.

The Roman Catholic Church is organized into the Archdiocese of Asunción, 3 other dioceses (San Juan Bautista de las Misiones, Concepción and Villarrica); 4 Prelatures (Coronel Oviedo, Encarnación, Alto Paraná and Caacupé); and 2 Vicariates Apostolic (Chaco and Pilcomayo). The bishops meet in a Conference of Paraguayan Bishops. Only civil marriages are legally valid. There are numerous non-catholic communities, the largest of whom are the Mennonites. There is a small Anglican church in Asunción, with missions in the Chaco, which comes under the jurisdiction of an Anglican Bishop resident in Asunción.

Education. Education is free and nominally compulsory, but schools are not everywhere available, and the system has been extensively revised to provide, *inter alia,* primary education for adults. Illiteracy is estimated at 22% (urban) and 30% (rural). In 1973 there were 2,288 government primary schools and 421 private schools, with 459,393 pupils and 15,871 teachers; 652 secondary schools had 66,746 students and 6,729 teachers. In 1978 there was an intensive school building programme in progress. The National University in Asunción had, in 1973, 7,919 students and 1,209 professors. In 1973 the Catholic University and associated colleges had 4,546 students and 355 professors.

DIPLOMATIC REPRESENTATIVES

Of Paraguay in Great Britain (51 Cornwall Gdns, London, SW7 4AQ)
Ambassador: Antonio R. Zuccolillo.

Of Great Britain in Paraguay (Calle Presidente Franco, 706, Asunción)
Ambassador and Consul-General: Derrick Mellor.

Of Paraguay in the USA (2400 Massachusetts Ave., NW, Washington, D.C., 20008)
Ambassador: Dr Mario López Escobar.

Of the USA in Paraguay (1776 Mariscal López Ave., Asunción)
Ambassador: Arthur H. Davis, Jnr.

Of Paraguay to the United Nations
Ambassador: Dr Luis Gonzalez Arias.

Books of Reference

Gaceta Official, published by Imprenta Nacional, Estrella y Estero Bellaco, Asunción
Anuario Daumas. Asunción
Anuario Estadístico de la República del Paraguay. Asunción. Annual
Lewis, P. H., *Paraguay under Stroessner.* Univ. of North Carolina Press, 1980
Maybury-Lewis, D. and Howe, J., *The Indian Peoples of Paraguay: Their Plight and Their Prospects.* Cambridge, Mass., 1980
Pendle, G., *Paraguay, A Riverside Nation.* R. Inst. of Int. Affairs, 3rd ed., 1967
Raine, P., *Paraguay.* New Brunswick, N.J., 1956

National Library: Biblioteca Nacional, De la Rosidenta, Asunción.

PERU

Capital: Lima
Population: 18·3m. (1982)
GNP per capita: US$980 (1980)

República del Perú

HISTORY. The Republic of Peru, formerly the most important of the Spanish vice-royalties in South America, declared its independence on 28 July 1821; but it was not till after a war, protracted till 1824, that the country gained its actual freedom.

AREA AND POPULATION. The total area of Peru is estimated to be 1,285,215 sq. km (496,093 sq. miles).

The long-standing dispute with Chile over the provinces of Tacna and Arica (*see* THE STATESMAN'S YEAR-Book, 1928, p. 1198) reached an amicable settlement on 3 June 1929 at Lima, Tacna going to Peru and Arica to Chile. In response to demands by Bolivia for permanent access to the Pacific Coast, proposals for a Bolivian corridor to the sea and a new Bolivian port to be built in the disputed area have been put forward by Chile and Peru. To date, little progress has been made. One result has been increased tension along the Chilean–Peruvian border, there is no sign of a settlement of the border dispute, and the armed forces of both countries remain on the alert in the disputed border area. Fighting broke out between Peruvian and Ecuadorean Forces, in early 1981, along part of the disputed border (the Cordillera del Condor) which has to date not been adequately mapped. A number of proposals for settling the issue permanently have been put forward but a final settlement is unlikely to be reached in the near future. For an account of the settlement of other boundary disputes, *see* THE STATESMAN'S YEAR-Book, 1948, p. 1173.

A map of the boundary with Ecuador is to be found in THE STATESMAN'S YEAR-BOOK, 1942.

The census taken in 1979 gave the population as 17,293,100. Children under 15 years, 7·2m. (45% of total population). Birth rate, 4·2%; death rate, 1·3%. Lima, the capital, had 3,158,417 population. Other major cities (with census population 1972), are Callao (296,220), Arequipa (304,653), Trujillo (241,882), Chiclayo (189,685), Chimbote (159,045), Piura (126,702), Cuzco (120,881), Huancayo (115,693), Iquitos (111,327). The language is Spanish, but the Indian population speak either Quechua (the second official language) or Aymará.

The area of the 23 departments and the constitutional province of Callao are given below with the population, according to the official census of 1961 and 1972. The area of the department of Puno includes the Peruvian zone of Lake Titicaca, 4,996·28 sq. km. The chief towns are shown in brackets:

Departments	*Area (sq. km) 1959*	*Population 2 July 1961 (census)*	*Population 2 June 1972 census (provisional)*	*Pop. per sq. km 1961*
Amazonas (Chachapoyas)	41,297·1	129,003	196,469	2·85
Ancash (Huaraz)	36,308·3	605,548	726,665	16·20
Apurímac (Abancay)	20,654·6	303,648	307,805	16·36
Arequipa (Arequipa)	63,527·6	407,163	530,528	6·47
Ayacucho (Ayacucho)	45,503·1	430,289	459,747	9·85
Cajamarca (Cajamarca)	35,417·8	786,599	916,331	21·15
Callao (Callao)[1]	73·8	219,420	315,605	2,901·46
Cuzco (Cuzco)	84,140·9	648,168	708,719	7·30
Huancavelica (Huancavelica)	22,870·9	315,730	331,155	13·07
Huánuco (Huánuco)	35,314·6	355,003	420,764	10·24
Ica (Ica)	21,251·4	261,126	357,973	11·48
Junín (Huancayo)	32,354·4	548,662	691,216	15·64
La Libertad (Trujillo)	23,241·3	609,105	806,368	25·29
Lambayeque (Chiclayo)	16,585·9	353,657	515,363	20·93
Lima (Lima)	33,894·9	2,093,435	3,485,411	68·42
Loreto (Iquitos)	478,336·2	411,340	494,895	0·69

[1] With province.

Departments	Area (sq. km.) 1959	Population 2 July 1961 (census)	2 June 1972 census (provisional)	Pop. per sq. km 1961
Madre de Dios (Maldonado)	78,402·7	25,269	21,968	0·19
Moquegua (Moquegua)	16,174·7	53,260	74,573	3·60
Pasco (Cerro de Pasco)	21,854·1	150,575	176,750	5·79
Piura (Piura)	33,067·1	692,414	854,668	21·68
Puno (Puno)	72,382·4	727,309	799,594	10·20
San Martín (Moyobamba)	53,063·6	170,456	224,310	3·06
Tacna (Tacna)	14,766·6	67,800	95,623	4·68
Tumbes (Tumbes)	4,731·5	57,378	75,399	21·10
Total	1,285,215·6	10,420,357	13,567,939	8·06

A new department of Ucayali is to be created in the central Amazon area, to include the provinces of Coronel Portillo and Ucayali, which were previously part of the department of Loreto. Pucallpa will be the capital of the new department.

CONSTITUTION AND GOVERNMENT. On 3 Oct. 1968 a military junta overthrew the government of President Fernando Belaúnde Terry and installed Gen. Juan Velasco Alvarado as President of a 'Revolutionary Government' with a cabinet composed entirely of officers of the armed services. Gen. Velasco was ousted in bloodless *coup* in Aug. 1975 and was replaced by Gen. Francisco Morales Bermudez. The new democratic government, under President Fernando Belaúnde Terry, took office on 28 July 1980.

The new Constitution, which became effective when a civilian government was installed in July 1980, provides for a Legislature consisting of a Senate (60 members) and a Chamber of Deputies (180 members) and an Executive formed of the President of the Republic and a Council of Ministers appointed by him. Elections were held in May 1980. They will be held every 5 years with the President and Congress elected, at the same time, by separate ballots. All Peruvians over the age of 18 are eligible to vote; in May 1980 the number of registered voters was over 6m., including 1m. in Lima province. Voting is compulsory; women were fully enfranchised in 1955.

Augusto Bernardino Leguia, 4 July 1919–24 Aug. 1930.[1]
Gen. Manuel Ponce (Acting), 24 Aug. 1930–28 Aug. 1930.[2]
Col. Louis M. Sánchez Cerro (Acting), 28 Aug. 1930–1 March 1931.[2]
Richardo Leoncio Elias (Acting), 1 March 1931–5 March 1931.[2]
Col. Gustavo A. Jiménez (Acting), 5 March 1931–10 March 1931.[2]
David Samanez Ocampo (Acting), 10 March 1931–8 Dec. 1931.
Gen. Luis M. Sánchez Cerro (Constitutional), 8 Dec. 1931–30 April 1933.[3]
Gen. Oscar Raimundo Benavides, 30 April 1933–8 Dec. 1939.
Dr Manuel Prado Ugarteche, 8 Dec. 1939–28 July 1945.
Dr José Luis Bustamante y Rivero, 28 July 1945–27 Oct. 1948.[1]
Gen. Manuel A. Odría (Acting), 27 Oct. 1948–1 June 1950.[2]
Gen. Zenón Noriega, 1 June 1950–28 July 1950.
Gen. Manuel A. Odría, 28 July 1950–28 July 1956.
Dr Manuel Prado y Ugarteche, 28 July 1956–July 1962.
Gen. Ricardo Pérez Godoy, 18 July 1962–3 March 1963.[1]
Gen. Nicolás Lindley López, 3 March–28 July 1963.
Fernando Belaúnde Terry, 28 July 1963–3 Oct. 1968.[1]
Gen. Juan Velasco Alvarado, 3 Oct. 1968–29 Aug. 1975.[1]
Gen. Francisco Morales Bermudez, 29 Aug. 1975–28 July 1980.

[1] Deposed. [2] Resigned. [3] Assassinated.

President: Fernando Belaúnde Terry.

The Cabinet was in Jan. 1983 composed as follows:
Prime Minister and Foreign Minister: Fernando Schwalb.
Agriculture: Mirko Cuculiza. *Education:* José Benavides Muñoz. *Transport and Communications:* Carlos Pestana. *Health:* Juan Franco Ponce. *Labour:* Alfonso

Grados Bertorini. *Justice:* Amando Buendia Gutierrez. *Housing and Construction:* Javier Velarde. *Industry, Integration and Tourism:* Gonzalo de la Puente Lavalle. *Fisheries:* Luis Percovitch. *Interior:* Pernando Rincon. *Energy and Mines:* Fernando Montero Aramburu. *War:* Gen. Oscar Brush Noel. *Air Force:* Lieut.-Gen. Hernan Boluarte. *Navy:* Vice-Adm. Jorge du Bois. *Economy and Trade:* Carlos Rodriguez Pastor.

As of 30 June 1965 the 23 departments are divided into 148 provinces (plus the constitutional province of Callao) and 1,662 districts; the province of Callao has some of the functions of a department.

National flag: Three vertical strips of red, white, red, with the national arms in the centre.

National anthem: Somos Libres, seámoslo siempre (words by J. de la Torre Ugarte; tune by J. B. Alcedo, 1821).

DEFENCE.

Army. While military service is compulsory youths are only conscripted to fill the annual quota. The term of service is 2 years and all males of 20–25 years of age are liable. The country is divided into 5 military regions.

The Army comprises (1983) approximately 75,000 all ranks, of which some 6,000 are regular officers. There are 8 infantry and mechanized brigades, 1 para-commando and 2 armoured brigades, 1 jungle brigade, 3 armoured reconaissance squadrons and 10 artillery and 4 engineer battalions. There is an air element of 4 Helio Courier 395 communications aircraft. Equipment consists of approximately 420 tanks (T-54/-55, M-4 and AMX-13), over 100 light armoured fighting vehicles and 105-mm./155-mm. field artillery.

The section of the national police force with a para-military role is known as the *Guardia Civil* and comprises approximately 25,000 personnel.

Navy. The principal surface ships of the Peruvian Navy are the cruisers:–

Completed	*Name*	*Standard Displacement (tons)*	*Main Guns*	*Aircraft*	*Shaft horsepower*	*Max. Speed (knots)*
1953	*Aguirre* (ex-*De Zeven Provincien*)	9,850	4 6in.	3	85,000	32
1953	*Almirante Grau* [1] (ex-*De Ruyter*)	9,530	8 6in.	–	85,000	32
1943	*Colonel Bolognesi* (ex-HMS *Ceylon*)	8,780	9 6in.	–	72,500	31·5

[1] When the Dutch cruiser *De Ruyter* was purchased in 1973 she was re-named *Almirante Grau* after Peru's principal naval hero. In consequence the cruiser whose name had been changed from *Newfoundland* to *Almirante Grau* when she was purchased from Britain in 1959 was again re-named *Capitan Quinones*, after an air force hero; but this ship has since been retired (latterly used as harbour training ship). *Aquirre* was bought from the Netherlands in 1976.

There are also 12 submarines comprising 6 completed in Federal Germany in 1974–82, 4 completed in USA in 1954–57 and 2 old *ex*-USN; 2 reconstructed 'Daring' class destroyers delivered from Britain during 1973; 2 old destroyers acquired from USA during 1960–61; 5 old destroyers purchased from the Netherlands in 1978–81, 2 new Italian-built frigates, 6 new French-built fast missile-armed corvettes, 1 training ship and 1 submarine accommodation ship (both old *ex*-US destroyer escorts); 3 landing ships; 2 medium landing ships; 5 river gunboats; 3 river patrol boats, 6 coastal patrol launches, 6 small patrol craft; 2 transports; 3 hospital craft; 1 research craft; 7 oilers; 4 survey vessels; 1 repair ship; 4 floating docks; 4 water carriers, and 5 tugs.

All naval training takes place in the Callao area at various schools. The main naval base and dockyard are also in Callao. Smaller bases are at Iquitos on the Amazon, and at San Lorenzo.

Naval personnel in 1983 totalled 2,000 officers and 18,500 men including the Naval Air Arm. There was also a brigade of 1,400 marines.

The new construction programme includes 2 frigates being built in Peru (sister ships of 2 completed in Italy in 1978–80)

The Coast Guard includes 1 new patrol vessel built in Peru, 6 fast patrol craft built in Britain in 1964–65, 2 former US gunboats, 4 coastal patrol boats and 11 minor patrol craft.

Air Force. The Air Force is under the direction of the Air Minister, who is also C.-inC.

The operational force consists of 3 combat groups. No 13 Group has 2 squadrons of Mirage 5 jet fighters and 1 squadron of A-37B light attack aircraft; No. 21 Group has 2 squadrons of Canberra light jet bombers and 1 squadron of A-37Bs; No. 12 Group has about 50 Soviet-built Su-22 variable-geometry fighter bombers in 3 operational squadrons. Other aircraft in service include medium transports (1 F.28 Fellowship, 16 An-26, 8 C-130), light transports (13 Twin Otter, 15 Buffalo and 12 Turbo-Porter), helicopters (6 Mi-6 and a total of 54 Mi-8, Bell 212, BO 105, Alouette III and Bell 47G), 70 training aircraft (including Aermacchi MB 339, T-33, T-34, T-37 and T-41D) and a small number of miscellaneous types for photographic and communications duties. The T-33 and T-37 trainers, and A-37B attack aircraft, will be replaced from 1985 by further MB 339s, built in Peru. Two DC-9s and some of the C-54 and C-130 aircraft are used by the Air Force to run a commercial airline network (SATCO(. There are military airfields at Talara, Chiclayo, Piura, Pisco, Lima (2), Iquitos and La Joya, and a sea-plane base at Iquitos. All officers and pilots are trained at the Air Academy at Lima (Las Palmas). The approximate strength of the Peruvian Air Force is 40,000 personnel and 120 combat aircraft.

INTERNATIONAL RELATIONS

Membership. Peru is a member of UN, OAS, Andean Group and LAIA (formerly LAFTA).

ECONOMY

Planning. A Public Investment Programme for 1981–85 envisages expenditure of US$11,500m.

Budget. The authorized budget for 1981 envisaged expenditure of S/.1,859,000m. and income of S/.1,634,000m.

The external debt was US$6,925m. in 1981.

Currency. The monetary unit is the *sol.* In March 1983, £1=1,729·46; US$1=1164·48.

Coins include 50,000 soles (gold) and 10,000 soles (silver) coins as well as 10- and 5-sole pieces (copper 75%; nickel 25%), the sol and half sol (copper 30%; zinc 70%); the 20, 10 and 5 centavos (copper–zinc) and the 2- and 1-centavo pieces (zinc) have been discontinued. Peru has a paper currency issued by the Banco Central de la Reserva in denominations of 5,000, 1,000, 500, 200, 100 and 50. The 10 and 5 soles notes have been discontinued.

Banking. The government bank of issue is the Banco Central de la Reserva del Perú, which was established in 1922. A new charter for the bank was promulgated in Aug. 1968; this, *inter alia,* extended the bank's authority with regard to the organization of the commercial banking system. This bank also regulates the certificate exchange market through which import, export and foreign currency loan operations are channelled. As at March 1971 its paid-up capital and reserves stood at S/.311m. Net foreign currency reserves at June 1980 were US$1,794·6m.

The Government's fiscal agent is the Banco de la Nación which, since May 1970, has control of the 'giro' market through which most non-trade foreign currency transactions are channelled.

Banks, domestic and foreign, are supervised by the Superintendent of Banks and Insurance. There were in March 1971, 7 state banks, 11 commercial banks (of which 3 were controlled by the Banco de la Nación), 6 regional banks (with head office outside Lima or Callao) and 4 foreign banks (1 British, 2 American and 1 Japanese).

Weights and Measures. The metric system of weights and measures was established by law in 1869, and since 1916 has come into general use.

ENERGY AND NATURAL RESOURCES

Electricity. In 1972 control of electricity production and distribution passed to ELECTROPERU, a state company. In 1979 the production of electric energy was 8,261 gwh. An electrification programme to construct a series of large hydro-electric power stations, was started in 1980.

Oil. Proven oil reserves in the jungle region amount to about 500m. bbls. A further 75m. tonnes have been found in the north-west, some of it offshore. The new 850 km pipeline, linking the new jungle oilfields to coastal terminals, was opened in 1977. Output amounted to 192,000 bbls per day by 1979 and Peru became an oil exporter in that same year. The total value of exports in 1980 of petroleum and derivative was US$809m. In 1981, 26 oil wells were drilled.

Minerals. Mineral exports are expected to account for about 50% of value of exports in 1979. Lead, copper, iron, silver, zinc and petroleum are the chief minerals exploited. Mineral exports in 1978: Copper, US$423m.; lead, US$162m.; zinc, US$131m.; silver, US$118m.; iron ore, US$74m. Crude petroleum output in 1978 was 69·35m. bbls. Mineral production (in tonnes, 1978) of iron, 3,275,325; zinc, 386,453; copper, 336,254; lead, 160,708; antimony, 745; silver, 634·3 (refined); bismuth, 610·7; molybdenum, 586·9; cadmium, 514·1; tungsten, 396·9; tin, 458; tellurium, 15·4; selenium, 12·9; gold, 3·5; indium, 106,000 oz.

Agriculture. There are 4 natural zones: the coast strip, with an average width of 80 km; the Sierra or Uplands, formed by the coast range of mountains and the Andes proper; the Montaña or high wooded region which lies on the eastern slopes of the Andes, and the jungle in the Amazon Basin, known as the Selva. Land under cultivation, 1967, was about 2·75m. hectares. There are 4 fertilizer factories, near Callao and in Cuzco.

Nearly half of the population is dependent on agriculture, which accounted for 13% of the GDP in 1981–82. Peru's third land reform law, that of June 1969, is one of the most comprehensive. It provides for the large sugar estates in the north of Peru to be turned into co-operatives. Maximum permitted sizes for other types of land holding are stipulated for the various regions of the country. These range from 150 hectares for irrigated land on the coast to an area capable of supporting 5,000 sheep for pasture land in the Sierra. These sizes may be increased if certain efficiency criteria are met. Holdings too small to be economically viable are to be consolidated into co-operative units. The chief agricultural productions of Peru are, in the order named: Sugar, cotton, coffee and wool. The cotton industry was nationalized on 1 Oct. 1974.

Production in 1981 (in 1,000 tonnes): Sugar-cane, 4,160; sugar, 493; cotton, 87; coffee, 95; wool, 13.

Output of cattle and buffalo hides (in tonnes), 1981, 13,220; sheepskins, 7,350; goatskins, 2,100. Output of sheep wool in 1976 was 9,000 tonnes. Exports, 1970, were sheep wool, unwashed, 606 tonnes; llama, alpaca and vicuña wool, 1,537 tonnes.

Livestock (1981): 653,000 horses, 3·9m. cattle, 1·9m. goats, 14·7m. sheep, 2·1m. swine, 38m. poultry.

Fisheries. Until the early 1970s Peru was the world's foremost fishing nation in terms of value of catch, due mainly to anchoveta which was converted into fish-meal for export as animal feed. Peru produced almost 45% of the world's fishmeal supplies, or nearly 2m. tonnes a year. However, abnormal marine conditions and over-fishing combined had, by 1977, reduced the anchoveta catch to 792,000 tonnes compared to 12·28m. tonnes in 1970.

Since then the industry has been partly denationalized and the number of fishing vessels reduced by approximately 50%, to some 700. Increased attention has been paid to fishing for human consumption.

Fish production 1978 (1,000 tonnes): Anchoveta, 1,156; other species, 1,589. Fresh, 151·3; frozen, 186·7; dried salted, 15·4; conserves, 226·2. Fish caught include (1978, tonnes): Anchoveta, 1,156,628; sardine, 1,074,519; jurel, 462,250; hake, 420,903; horse mackerel, 97,165; dogfish, 10,155.

INDUSTRY AND TRADE

Industry. About 70% of Peru's manufacturing industries are located in or around the Lima/Callao metropolitan area.

Peru's first iron and steel mill came into production at Chimbote in April 1958. Products include pig-iron, blooms, billets, largets, round and round-deformed bars, wire rod, black and galvanized sheets and galvanized roofing sheets. Refractories are manufactured at Lima.

The Government has a monopoly of the import and/or local manufacture and sale of guano, salt, alcohol and explosives. The monopoly of matches was abandoned in 1954 and that of tobacco in June 1955.

Peru's manufacturing industry stagnated since 1972 but by 1980 had recovered substantially, mainly due to exports of non-traditional goods. Output fell in 1977 by 6%. In 1977 production in the following industries was (in tonnes):

Cement	1,964,000	Refined lead	169,000
Tyres (units)	700,000	TV receivers (units)	100,000
Refined zinc	389,000	Sulphuric acid	60,000
Refined copper	350,000	Vehicle assembly	11,300
Crude steel	347,000		

Labour. In 1976 the total labour was considered to number 5m. persons, of which 40% was either under-employed or unemployed. This was 52% of the urban population of the country or about 30% of the country's population. The population was distributed roughly as follows in 1972: Agriculture, stock-raising and fishing, 2m.; manufacturing industry, 611,000; construction, 183,000; mining, 98,000; government, 317,000; commerce, 475,000; services, 477,000.

Trade Unions. Trade unions have about 2m. members (approximately 1·5m. in peasant organizations and 500,000 in industrial). The major trade union organization is the *Confederación de Trabajadores del Perú*, which was reconstituted in 1959 after being in abeyance for some years. The other labour organizations recognized by the Government are the *Confederación General de Trabajadores del Perú*, the *Confederación Nacional de Trabajadores* and the *Central de Trabajadores de la Revolución Peruana*.

Commerce. The value of trade has been as follows (in US$1m.):

	1975	*1976*	*1977*	*1978*	*1979*	*1980*
Imports	1,380	1,360	1,726	1,601	2,090	3,100
Exports	2,480	2,100	2,095	1,941	3,474	3,850

In 1980 the principal imports were: Machinery and appliances (40·6%); fuel, lubricants and other non-metallic minerals (21·2%).

Total trade between Peru and UK (British Department of Trade returns, in £1,000 sterling):

	1978	*1979*	*1980*	*1981*	*1982*
Imports to UK	29,022	61,518	77,487	66,726	92,120
Exports and re-exports from UK	25,183	23,949	46,541	50,280	39,370

COMMUNICATIONS

Roads. There were at 30 June 1966, 45,549 km, of which 17,114 km were made up and 4,547 km asphalted. Work on the Carretera Marginal de la Selva (South American Marginal Forest Highway) started in 1965; the 5,600 km road between the Colombian–Venezuelan border and Sta. Cruz, Bolivia, of which the Peruvian portion consists of 394 km already existing, 503 km now under construction and 1,565 km outstanding, to make a sectional total of some 2,460 km.

In 1974 there were 266,910 private cars and 139,950 commercial vehicles.

Railways. Since 1972 all public railways have been nationalized and run by Peruvian National Railways (ENAFER). Total length (1980), 1,628 km on 1,435- and 914-mm gauges. In 1980 railways carried 2·3m. tons and 3·5m. passengers.

Aviation. Air services connect Lima and the capitals of every South American republic.

Shipping. In 1966, 6,900 vessels of 26,602,270 tons entered, and 6,871 of 26,610,772 tons cleared the ports. Since 1928 the coasting trade has been largely reserved for Peruvian-owned vessels with Peruvian crews; in 1960 it handled 2,246,000 tonnes, valued at S/.1,665m.

Post and Broadcasting. An earth satellite ground communication station at Lurin connects Peru through Intelsat. III to the US and Europe. In 1981 there were 487,123 telephones, 359,869 in Lima. Length of telegraph lines was 26,121 km. In 1970 the Lima Telephone Co. was nationalized and the Government have announced their intention to nationalize progressively the entire telephone and communications network. Radio-telephone circuits connect Lima with distant towns. Three submarine telegraph cables connect Peru and Chile, and one connects Peru and the republics to the north. There are 153 broadcasting stations, of which 29 are in Lima. Wireless receiving sets, about 2m. There are 7 television stations in Lima, 16 in the provinces and 45 relay stations. All radio and television stations are supervised by the Government.

Cinemas. In 1972 there were 276 cinemas.

Newspapers. The main Lima newspapers are *La Prensa, El Comercio, Expreso, Correo* and *La Crónica.*

JUSTICE, RELIGION, EDUCATION AND WELFARE

Justice. The Peruvian judicial system is a pyramid at the base of which are the justices of the peace who decide minor criminal cases and civil cases involving small sums of money. The apex is the Supreme Court with 17 members; in between are the judges of first instance, who usually sit in the provincial capitals, and the superior courts of which there are 18.

The Revolutionary Government decreed in Dec. 1969 that all judges, except justices of the peace, would in future be elected by the National Council of Justice, composed of representatives of the Executive, the Legislature, the Judiciary, the National Federation of the College of Lawyers and 2 of the university law faculties. Justices of the peace are appointed, by the superior courts.

Religion. Religious liberty exists, but the Roman Catholic religion is protected by the State, and since 1929 only Roman Catholic religious instruction is permitted in schools, state or private. In 1972 there were 1 Roman Catholic cardinal, 7 archbishops, 14 bishops, 3 vicars-general, 8 vicars apostolic, 2,672 priests, 506 cloistered monks and 4,558 members of religious orders.

Protestants numbered 128,000 in 1966.

All marriages must be civil, regardless of religion and preceded by medical examination; there are liberal divorce regulations, including divorce for 'absence without just cause for more than 2 years', and by mutual consent. Divorcees may remarry immediately. A law of 1936 emphasizes that the religious obligations of marriage are fully recognized.

Education. A new law for education was promulgated in March 1972. Elementary education is compulsory and free for both sexes between the ages of 7 and 16; secondary education is also free. But schools, despite substantial increases, are still too few. The system is highly centralized; all teaching appointments are made by the Minister of Education for the public schools; for the private schools he supervises plant and equipment and limits fees but does not appoint teachers.

In 1970 there were 20,034 public, private and primary schools, with 64,004 teachers and 2·75m. pupils; 1,452 secondary schools, with 21,863 teachers and 674,000 students. Training in 414 public technical schools is also free; in 1970 they had 6,333 teachers and 223,300 pupils. The 90 teacher-training schools had 1,075 teachers and 18,000 pupils. Total literacy (1975) was 68% of total population. Because of the increase in the number of pupils state schools have divided their teaching timetable into three divisions, morning, afternoon and evening. Those pupils in the last shift have to spend an extra year at school to make up for the difference in the length of the daily timetable.

In 1970 the total number of university students was 105,600.

Social Welfare. Contributory social security schemes exist for employees and workers. These are administered by the Ministry of Labour. There were in 1975, 182 hospitals (33,350 beds). In addition in 1969 there were 63 health centres, 307 medical posts and 842 sanitary posts, all administered by the authorities. In 1975 there were 9,445 doctors, 2,119 obstetricians, 115 chemists and 8,920 trained nurses.

DIPLOMATIC REPRESENTATIVES

Of Peru in Great Britain (52 Sloane St., London, SW1X 9SP)
Chargé d'Affaires: Armando Lecaros de Cossio.

Of Great Britain in Peru (Edificio El Pacifico Washington, Ave. Arequipa, Lima)
Ambassador: C. W. Wallace, CVO.

Of Peru in the USA (1700 Massachusetts Ave., NW, Washington, D.C., 20036)
Ambassador: Fernando Schwalb.

Of the USA in Peru (PO Box 1995, Lima)
Ambassador: Frank V. Ortiz, Jr.

Of Peru to the United Nations
Ambassador: Juan José Calle y Calle.

Books of Reference

The official gazette is *El Peruano*, Lima.

Anario Estadistico del Perú. Annual.—*Boletin de Estadistica Peruana.* Quarterly.—*Demarcación Política del Perú.* (Dirección Nacional de Estadística), Lima
Censo Nacional Población, 4 June 1972. Lima, 1972
Estadística del Comercio Exterior (*Superintendencia de Aduanas*). Lima
Banco Central de Reserva. Monthly Bulletin.—*Renta Nacional del Perú.* Annual, Lima

Ministerio de Fomento Lima publishes separate annual statistics on the mining and petroleum industries and on general industry; the wool textile and cotton textile industries, the Peruvian Chamber of Commerce furnish annual studies.

Alba, V., *Peru.* Boulder, 1977
Bourricaud, F., *Pouvoir et Société dans le Pérou contemporain.* Paris, 1965
Fitzgerald, E. V. K., *The State and Economic Development: Peru Since 1968.* CUP, 1976.—*The Political Economy of Peru 1958–78.* CUP, 1979
Hemming, J., *The Conquest of the Incas.* London, 1970
Lowenthal, A. F., *The Peruvian Experiment.* Princeton Univ. Press, 1975
Marrett, Sir R., *Peru.* London, 1969
Mejía Baca, J., and Tauro, A., *Diccionário Enciclopédico del Perú.* 3 vols. 1966
Philip, G. D. E., *The Rise and Fall of the Peruvian Military Radicals, 1968–1976.* London, 1978
Pike, *A Modern History of Peru.* London, 1967
Sharp, D. A. (ed.), *US Foreign Policy and Peru.* Univ. of Texas Press, 1972
Stepan, A., *The State and Society. Peru in Comparative Perspective.* Princeton Univ. Press, 1978
Thorp, R., and Bertram, G., *Peru 1890–1977.* London, 1978
Vargas, Padre, *Historia General del Perú.* Lima, 1967
Webb, R. C., *Government Policy and the Distribution of Income in Peru, 1963–1973.* Harvard Univ. Press, 1977

National Library: Avenida Abancay, Lima.

REPUBLIC OF THE PHILIPPINES

Capital: Manila
Population: 50·74m. (1982)
GNP per capita: US$720 (1980)

República de Filipinas—Republika ñg Pilipinas

HISTORY. Before the Spanish discovery of the Philippines, the native Filipinos came in contact with India, China and Arabia. According to the early records of China, 'some Filipinos from the country of Ma-i arrived in Canton and sold their merchandise' as early as 982. The Philippine islands were discovered by Magellan in 1521 and conquered by Spain in 1565. Following the Spanish–American war, the islands were ceded to the USA on 10 Dec. 1898, after the Filipinos had tried in vain to establish an independent republic in 1896.

The Republic of the Philippines came into existence on 4 July 1946, by agreement with the US Government embodied in an Act of Congress signed by President Roosevelt on 24 March 1934, accepted by the Philippine Legislature on 1 May 1934 and ratified at a plebiscite on 14 May 1935. This Act established a 10-year transitional period, designated as that of the Philippine Commonwealth, at the end of which complete independence was automatically effective.

AREA AND POPULATION. The Philippines is situated between 21° 25′ and 4° 23′ N. lat. and between 116° and 127° E. long. It is composed of 7,100 islands and islets, 2,773 of which are named. Approximate land area, 115,830 sq. miles (300,000 sq. km). The 16 most important islands with their areas (in sq. miles) are: Luzon, 40,420; Mindanao, 36,537; Samar, 5,050; Negros, 4,906; Palawan, 4,550; Panay, 4,446; Mindoro, 3,759; Leyte, 2,786; Cebu, 1,707; Bohol, 1,492; Masbate, 1,262; Sulu group, 379; Tawi-tawi, 229; Romblon, 32; Marinduque, 347, and Siquijor, 129.

Census population 1980 was 48,098,460. Estimate (1982) 50·74m.

The population of Manila, the present capital, in 1980 was 1,630,485 (metropolitan Manila, 5,925,884). The old capital, Quezon City, just north-east of Manila, had a population of 1,165,865. Other cities, with their population in May 1980 are: Iloilo on Panay, 244,827; Cebu on Cebu, 490,281; Zamboanga on Mindanao, 343,722; Davao on Mindanao, 610,375; Bacolod on Negros, 262,415; San Carlos on Negros Occidental, 91,627; San Carlos on Pangasinan, 101,243; Pasay on Rizal, 287,770.

On 7 June 1946 the President of the Philippines approved a law, effective 4 July 1946, making a new language (Pilipino) based on Tagalog (a Malayan dialect) the official national language of the republic. In 1970 about 16,409,133 people spoke English and about 1,335,945 Spanish; for government and commercial purposes these two languages are commonly used. Some 77 native languages are spoken in the Philippines, of which 9 are of major importance; they belong to the Malayo-Polynesian family.

CONSTITUTION AND GOVERNMENT. The republic was governed by a constitution adopted on 14 May 1935 and amended in 1939, 1940 and 1947. On 17 Jan. 1973 a new constitution was ratified naming President Marcos President and Prime Minister without a fixed term of office. The President is assisted by 26 ministers in charge of Foreign Affairs, Finance, Justice, Agriculture, Public Works and Highways, Transportation and Communications, Education and Culture, Labour and Employment, National Defence, Energy, Trade and Industry, Health, Social Services and Development, Agrarian Reform, Media Affairs, Local Government, Tourism, Natural Resources, Human Settlements, National Economic and Development Authority, Budget, National Science and Technology Authority, the Presidential Executive Assistant, Muslim Affairs, Presidential Assistant on National Minorities and the Solicitor-General.

President: Ferdinand E. Marcos (re-elected for a third 6-year term in June 1981).
Prime Minister and Minister of Finance: Cesar Virata.

Martial law was introduced on 21 Sept. 1972. A referendum held in Dec. 1977 decreed that President Marcos should remain in power. On 12 June 1978 a limited experiment in parliamentary democracy began and the President also became Prime Minister. Limited power to legislate was given to the new Assembly but the right to legislate by decree was retained by the President and no date was given for lifting the martial law. On 17 Jan. 1981 martial law was lifted but the President retained wide powers under a National Security Code and Public Safety Act.

The 1973 Constitution provides that all male and female citizens 15 years of age or older who can read or write Spanish, English or a native dialect and who meet certain residential qualifications are entitled to vote.

The constitution vests in the republic all ownership of the country's natural resources, which, apart from public agricultural land, may not be alienated.

National flag: Horizontally blue over red, with a white triangle based on the hoist bearing a gold sun of 8 rays and 3 gold stars.

National hymn: 'Tierra Adorada', 'Land of the morning', lyric in English by M. A. Sane and C. Osias, in Spanish by José Palma (1899), tune by Julian Felipe (1898); 'Pambansang Awit ñg Pilipinas', Tagalog lyric by the Institute of National Language, music by Julian Felipe.

Local Government. The country is administratively divided into 13 regions, 73 provinces, 60 cities, 1,493 municipalities, 21 municipal districts, 40,207 *barangays* with 241,242 councilmen. On 14 Nov. 1975 the name of provincial boards and city or municipal boards or councils was changed into *Sangguniang Bayan.* The latter assumes all the powers and responsibilities on matters of legislation of the defunct provincial, city or municipal boards.

The *Sangguniang Pambayan* is the direct successor of the old municipal council; *Sangguniang Panglunsod* for the old city council; *Sangguniang Panlalawigan* for the old provincial council and *Batasang Pambansa* for the defunct Congress.

DEFENCE. On 14 March 1947 the Philippine and US Governments signed a 99-year military-base arrangement since reduced to 25 years and will end in 1991. The USA was granted the use of a series of army, navy and air bases, with the right to use a number of others on mutual agreement. On 21 March a second agreement provided for a US Military Advisory Group as well as military assistance. A treaty of mutual assistance was signed in Washington on 30 Aug. 1951; the instruments of ratification were exchanged in Manila on 27 Aug. 1952. The Philippines is also a signatory of the S.E. Asia Collective Defence Treaty.

The Chief of Staff of the Armed Forces has overall command over the Army, Air Force, Navy and Constabulary.

Army. The Army consists of 70,000 officers and men in the active force. It is organized in 4 light infantry divisions and 1 independent, 1 Special Services and 2 engineer brigades.

Navy. The Navy includes 7 old frigates (3 former US destroyer escorts and 4 *ex*-USCG cutters, *ex*-USN seaplane tenders); 10 corvettes (3 *ex*-US fleet minesweepers and 7 *ex*-US escorts), 2 *ex*-US PC-type patrol vessels, 7 other patrol craft, 6 gunboats, 59 coastal patrol craft, 1 training ship, 24 landing ships, 4 medium landing ships, 6 landing craft (3 LSSL and 3 LCU), 3 repair ships, 2 oilers, 3 water carriers, 1 supply ship, 4 survey ships, 5 tenders, 68 minor landing craft, 2 yachts (command ships), 6 tugs, 16 auxiliaries and 30 coastguard utility cutters.

Naval personnel in 1983 totalled 1,605 officers and 13,070 men. There are also 330 officers and 6,500 enlisted men in the marine corps, and 300 officers and 1,700 men in the Coastguard.

The Philippine Navy was considerably increased in 1976 by taking over many vessels (nearly all former US warships) from the Vietnamese Navy which escaped from Indo-China when the Saigon government collapsed in 1975. But some 60 of the larger ships are aged (40 years). Three missile-armed fast attack craft are being built.

Air Force. The Air Force has a strength of 16,800 officers and men, with 390 aircraft, and was built up with US assistance. Its fighter-bomber wing is equipped with 1 squadron of supersonic F-5A/Bs and 1 squadron of F-8H Crusaders. There are transport, observation, air/sea rescue, helicopter and training units, for which recently acquired equipment has included 3 Fokker F27 Maritime patrol aircraft, a squadron of OV-1 Mohawk observation aircraft, 12 Australian-built Mission-master twin-turboprop STOL light transports, 8 HU-16 Albatross amphibians and a total of 48 Italian-built SF.260WP (armed) and SF.260MP piston-engined trainers. Many of the Air Force's other trainers are armed for counter-insurgency duties. No. 16 and 18 squadrons of the 15th Strike Wing each operate 16 T-28Ds. No. 17 has 16 SF.260WPs.

Police. Public order is maintained partly through the Philippine constabulary and partly through the local police forces. The constabulary now forms part of the Armed Forces and has 27,000 personnel.

INTERNATIONAL RELATIONS

Membership. The Republic of the Philippines is a member of UN and the Colombo Plan.

External Debt. At 31 March 1982 the external debt amounted to US$11,933·2m.

ECONOMY

Budget. The revenues and expenditures of the central government for calendar years were, in 1m. Philippine pesos, as follows:

	1980	*1981*	*1982*[1]	*1983*[1]
Revenue	34,716	35,152	38,634	44,300
Expenditure	41,955	52,945	59,749	65,000

[1] Estimate.

Expenditure (1981) included (in 1m. pesos): National defence, 5,616; education, health and social services, 12,010; economic development, 22,887; public debt, 3,950.

At 30 June 1982 the total internal public debt outstanding of the national and local governments, including those of the government corporations, stood at P.53,868m.

Currency. Total money supply, Aug. 1982, was P.21,133·8m., of which P.9,865·8m. was currency in circulation and P.11,268m. were demand deposits. The coins used are: 5 *peso*, 1 *peso*, one-half *peso*, quarter *peso*, media *peseta* (10 *centavos*), all contain 70 grammes copper, 18 grammes zinc and 12 grammes nickel; 5 *centavo* in copper and zinc, and 1 *centavo* in aluminium and magnesium zinc. Central Bank notes are issued in 2, 5, 10, 20, 50, 100 *pesos* denominations.

In March 1983, £1 = 13·83 *pesos*; US$1 = 9·65 *pesos*.

Banking. On 31 July 1982 there were 1,815 branches of commercial banks operating under 34 head offices, with 4 overseas, 1 each in New York, Hong Kong, Taipei and London. Agencies exist in Honolulu, San Francisco and Los Angeles. Total deposits of the commercial banks in July 1982 were P.82,288·2m.

Under the law passed 15 June 1948 the Central Bank of the Philippines was created to have sole control of the credit and monetary supply, independent of the Treasury. It has a capital of P.10m. furnished solely by the Government. Its total assets, at 31 July 1982 were P.84,420·6m.

Weights and Measures. The metric system of weights and measures was established by law in 1869, and since 1916 has come into general use.

ENERGY AND NATURAL RESOURCES

Electricity. Government and private electric systems furnish the Philippines with electric power, with total generating capacity of 2,794,279 mw (1979). The Manila Electric Co., was bought by the Government in July 1978. MECO plants generated a total of 2,207,964 mwh. in 1979 while the Government's National Power Corporation produced 10,282,411 mwh.; others, 303,073 mwh.

Minerals. Mineral production in 1981 (in tonnes): Lead concentrate, 1,992; nickel metal, 21,485; nickel direct shipping ore, 345,310; zinc concentrate, 100,479; copper concentrate, 1,120,382; cobalt metal, 997; coal, 318,170; salt, 355,289; gold, 23,435 kg; silver, 62,565 kg. Other minerals include cement, rock asphalt, sand and gravel.

Agriculture. Of the total area of 30m. hectares, 7·04m. hectares are commercial forests; 5·4m. hectares non-commercial forests; 794,000 hectares open grassland; 115,000 hectares mangrove and marshes; 14,794,000 hectares cultivated.

About 98·4% of the total cultivated area is owned by Filipinos; the average size of the farm is 3·21 hectares. The principal products are unhusked rice (palay), Manila hemp (abaca), copra, sugar-cane, maize and tobacco. On 31 Dec. 1981, 9,548,305 persons were employed in agriculture (50·24% of the working population).

The products (in tonnes) are (1981, provisional): Rough rice, 7·7m.; copra, 3·1m.; coconut, 4·6m.; sugar (centrifugal muscovado and molasses), 3·2m.; shelled corn, 3·2m.; tobacco, 38,868; abaca fibre, 148,577.

Minor crops are fruits, nuts, root crops, vegetables, onions, beans, coffee, cacao, peanuts, ramie, rubber, maguey and kapok.

Livestock, estimated in 1981: 2·8m. carabaos (water buffaloes), 1·9m. cattle, 7·6m. pigs, 1·4m. goats and 60·8m. poultry.

Forestry. The forests covered some 12,457,000 hectares in 1981. Log production, 5,399,000 cu. metres, of which 706,399 cu. metres were exported in 1981.

Fisheries. Fish production from all sources was 1,772,897 tonnes and was valued at P.13,953,798 in 1981.

INDUSTRY AND TRADE

Industry. Manufacturing is a major source of economic development contributing 24·9% to GNP in 1981. Leading growth sectors were textile, footwear and wearing apparel, chemical and chemical products, beverage industries and food manufacture. In 1978 (census), there were 9,976 large manufacturing establishments (employing 20 or more workers), of which 2,282 were engaged in food; 1,018 wearing apparel; 237 footwear; 440 industrial chemicals and other chemical products; 96 beverages; 5 petroleum refineries; 388 transport equipment, and 1,368 wood and wood and cork products including furniture. The non-agricultural labour force during the last quarter of 1981 was 8,467,365 out of a total of 18,015,670 employed.

Commerce. The values of imports and exports (f.o.b.) for calendar years are stated as follows in US$1m.:

	1978	*1979*	*1980*	*1981*
Imports	4,732	6,142	7,727	7,946
Exports	3,425	4,601	5,788	5,722

The principal exports in 1981 were (in US$1m.): Coconut oil (crude), 533·5; copper concentrates, 429·4; sugar, 566·6; lumber, 125·7; logs, 76·3; iron ore agglomerates, 56·8; plywood, 110·7; desiccated coconut, 101·9; gold from copper ore and concentrates, 215·2; copra, 33·6.

Main imports in 1981 (in US$1m.): Mineral fuels, lubricants and related materials, 2,458; machinery other than electric, 945; base metals, 408; transport equipment, 460; materials for the manufacture of electrical and electronic machinery, 119; chemical elements and compounds, 298; electrical machinery, apparatus and appliances, 392; explosives and miscellaneous chemical materials and products, 214; cereals and cereal preparations, 230; metal manufactures, 148.

For over a half-century the foreign trade has been chiefly with the USA. The trade relationship of the two countries is governed by the Philippine Trade Act of 1946 as amended.

Philippine products entering the USA paid 10% of the US tariff in 1959–61, 20% in 1962–64, 40% in 1965–67, 60% in 1968–70, 80% in 1971–73 and 100% from 1 Jan. 1974.

Total trade between the Philippines and UK (British Department of Trade returns, in £1,000 sterling):

	1977	*1978*	*1979*	*1980*	*1981*	*1982*
Imports to UK	44,696	63,447	81,122	99,018	105,535	127,061
Exports and re-exports from UK	92,721	115,038	105,709	88,998	85,650	97,908

Tourism. In 1981, 938,953 tourists visited the Philippines spending US$344m.

COMMUNICATIONS

Roads. In 1981 highways totalled 153,528·08 km; of this, 10,260·23 km were concrete; 17,475·51, asphalt; 55,210·82, earth; 70,581·52, macadam. In 1981 there were registered 1,006,130 motor vehicles of all types.

Railways. The National Railways totals 1,027 km of 1,067 mm gauge on Luzon, and Phividec Railways operates 116 km on Panay Island. In 1981, 7,807,721 passengers and 115,980 tonnes of freight were carried by rail.

Aviation. The Philippine Air Lines, Inc., with a working capital of P.292m., in 1981 carried 3,523,000 passengers, 55,234,396 kg of cargo and 928,676 kg of mail.

Shipping. In 1981, 71,787 vessels of 24,608,624 net tons entered and 71,796 vessels of 23,834,150 net tons cleared all ports.

Post and Broadcasting. In 1981 there were in operation 2,038 post offices and 1,439 telecommunication stations. The Philippine Long Distance Telephone Co. had 537,795 telephones in service in 1981 while the Government Telephone System which operates 13 automatic exchanges within the Greater Manila Area had 33,042 subscribers.

Licensed radio stations in 1981 numbered 23,530, including 1,930 ship stations and 590 aircraft stations.

Newspapers (1979). There were 300 registered publications (210 published in Manila), 15 of which were dailies.

JUSTICE, RELIGION, EDUCATION AND WELFARE

Justice. There is a Supreme Court which is composed of a chief justice and 14 associate justices; it can declare a law or treaty unconstitutional by the concurrent votes of the majority sitting. There is a court of appeal, headed by a presiding justice, with 35 associate justices. There are 16 judicial districts sub-divided into 357 branches, each with a presiding judge of first instance. Every city has a city court and every municipality has 1 municipal judge. In addition, the juvenile and domestic relations court in Manila has exclusive jurisdiction to try all cases involving minors and matrimonial disputes.

Religion. In 1970 there were 31,169,488 Roman Catholics, 1,434,688 Aglipayans, 1,584,963 Moslems, 1,122,999 Protestants, 475,407 members of the Iglesia ni Kristo, 33,639 Buddhists and 863,302 others.

The Roman Catholics are organized in 12 archbishoprics, 30 bishoprics, 12 prelatures nullius, 4 apostolic vicariates, 4 apostolic prefectures and some 1,633 parishes. The Philippine Independent Church, founded in 1902, and comprising about 3·9% of the population, denies the spiritual authority of the Roman Pontiff. It is divided into two groups, one of which has accepted ordinations by the Episcopalian Church.

Education. Formal education consists of 3 levels: elementary, secondary and further education. Public elementary education is free and public elementary schools are established in almost every *barangay* or *barrio*. The majority of the secondary and post-secondary schools are private, sectarian or non-sectarian. The number of years required to complete the elementary and secondary levels are 6 and 4 years respectively, while the tertiary level requires at least 4 years for an academic degree. Pre-school education is also offered mostly in private schools to children from ages 3–6.

Non-formal education consists of adult literacy classes, agricultural and farming training programmes, occupation skills training, youth clubs, and community programmes of instructions in health, nutrition, family planning and co-operatives.

Public and private schools in 1980–81 enrolled 8·3m. pupils in primary schools, 3m. in secondary schools and 1·3m. students in further education. The University of the Philippines (founded in 1908) had 34,531 students in 1982–83.

Health. In 1981 there were 43,736 registered physicians and 88,070 hospital beds.

Social Welfare. The Government programme includes the construction of urban and rural housing units for lease or sale to middle and low-income families to ease the housing problem, the settlement of landless families, the opening of rural farm-to-market roads, the setting up of rural schools and rural health units, the granting of loans to farmers, fishermen and small cottage industries, self-employment assistance to the most disadvantaged persons and practical skills development and job placement services to out-of-school youths, jobless family heads and disabled persons, and the extension of emergency services like rescue and relief operations in times of typhoons, earthquakes, fires and other calamities.

DIPLOMATIC REPRESENTATIVES

Of the Philippines in Great Britain (9A Palace Green, London, W8 4QE)
Ambassador: José V. Cruz (accredited 17 Dec. 1982).

Of Great Britain in the Philippines (115 Esteban St., Manila)
Ambassador: M. H. Morgan, CMG.

Of the Philippines in the USA (1617 Massachusetts Ave., NW, Washington, D.C., 20036)
Ambassador: Benjamin T. Romualdez.

Of the USA in the Philippines (1201 Roxas Blvd., Manila)
Ambassador: Michael H. Armacost.

Of the Philippines to the United Nations
Ambassador: Luis Moreno-Salcedo.

Books of Reference

Philippine Yearbook 1983. National Census and Statistics Office, Manila, 1983
Gazetteer of the Philippine Islands. United States Department of Commerce. Washington, 1945
Foreign Trade Statistics of the Philippines, 1981. National Census and Statistics Office, Manila, 1981
Burley, T. M., *The Philippines. An Economic and Social Geography.* London, 1973
Chapman, A., *Philippine Nationalism.* New York, 1950
Golay, F. H., *The Philippines: Public Policy and National Economic Development.* Cornell Univ. Press, 1961
Hainsworth, R. G., and Moyser, R. T., *Agricultural Geography of the Philippine Islands.* Washington, 1945
Lightfort, K., *The Philippines.* London, 1973
Meyer, M. W., *A Diplomatic History of the Philippine Republic.* Univ. of Hawaii Press, 1965

PITCAIRN ISLAND

HISTORY. It was discovered by Carteret in 1767, but remained uninhabited until 1790, when it was occupied by 9 mutineers of HMS *Bounty*, with 12 women and 6 men from Tahiti. Nothing was known of their existence until the island was visited in 1808. In 1856 the population having become too large for the island's resources, the inhabitants (194 in number) were, at their own request, removed to Norfolk Island; but 43 of them returned in 1859–64.

AREA AND POPULATION. Pitcairn Island (1·75 sq. miles; 4·6 sq. km) is situated in the Pacific Ocean, nearly equidistant from New Zealand and Panama (25° 04′S. lat., 130° 06′ W. long). The population has been declining and on 30 June 1982 it was 54.

The uninhabited islands of Henderson (12 sq. miles), Ducie (1½ sq. miles) and Oeno (2 sq. miles) were annexed in 1902 and are included in the Pitcairn group.

CONSTITUTION. Pitcairn was brought within the jurisdiction of the High Commissioner for the Western Pacific in 1898 and transferred to the Governor of Fiji in 1952. When Fiji became independent in Oct. 1970, the British High Commissioner in New Zealand was appointed Governor.

The Local Government Ordinance of 1964 constitutes a Council of 10 members, of whom 4 are elected, 5 are nominated (3 by the 4 elected members and 2 by the Governor) and the Island Secretary is an *ex-officio* member. The Island Magistrate, who is elected triennially, presides over the Council; other members hold office for only 1 year. Liaison between Governor and Council is through a Commissioner in the Auckland, New Zealand, office of the British Consulate-General.

TRADE. Fruit, vegetables and curios are sold to passing ships; fuel oil, machinery, building materials, flour, sugar and other foodstuffs are imported.

Governor: Sir Richard Stratton, KCMG (resides in Wellington).
Island Magistrate: Ivan Christian (re-elected Dec. 1981).

Books of Reference

A Guide to Pitcairn. Pitcairn Island Administration, Auckland, revised ed. 1976
Ball, I., *Pitcairn: Children of the Bounty.* London, 1973
Ross, A. S. C., and Moverly, A. W., *The Pitcairnese Language.* London, 1964

POLAND

Capital: Warsaw
Population: 35·9m. (1982)
GNP per capita: US$3,900 (1980)

Polska Rzeczpospolita Ludowa

HISTORY. In 1966 Poland celebrated its millennium, but modern Polish history begins with the partitions of the once-powerful kingdom between Russia, Austria and Prussia in 1772, 1793 and 1795. For 19th cent. events *see* THE STATESMAN'S YEAR-BOOK 1980–81.

On 10 Nov. 1918 independence was proclaimed by Józef Piłsudski, the founder of the Polish Legions during the war. On 28 June 1919 the Treaty of Versailles recognized the independence of Poland.

On 1 Sept. 1939 Germany invaded Poland, on 17 Sept. 1939 Russian troops entered eastern Poland, and on 29 Sept. 1939 the fourth partition of Poland took place. After the German attack on Russia, the Germans occupied the whole of Poland. By March 1945 the country had been liberated by the Russians.

In July 1944 the USSR recognized the Polish Committee of National Liberation *(Polski Komitet Wyzwolenia Narodowego)* established in Lublin as an executive organ of the National Council of the Homeland *(Krajowa Rada Narodowa).* The Committee was transformed into the Provisional Government in Dec. 1944, and on 28 June 1945, supplemented by members of the Polish Government in London (which had been recognized by the UK and USA), it was re-established—in Moscow—as the Polish Provisional Government of National Unity and on 6 July recognized as such by the UK and USA.

Elections were held on 19 Jan. 1947. Of the 12·7m. votes cast, 11·24m. were recognized as valid and 9m. were given for the Communist-dominated 'Democratic Bloc'. After riots in Poznań in June 1956 nationalist anti-Stalinist elements gained control of the Communist Party, under the leadership of Wladyslaw Gomułka.

In 1970 the Federal Republic of Germany recognized Poland's western boundary as laid down by the Potsdam Conference of 1945 (the 'Oder–Neisse line').

In Dec. 1970 strikes and riots in Gdańsk, Szczecin and Gdynia led to the resignation of a number of leaders including Gomułka. He was replaced by Edward Gierek.

The introduction of price rises in June 1976 was again followed by strikes and riots. The rises were withdrawn and some demonstrators were imprisoned. In the campaign of protest which followed a Committee for the Defence of the Workers (KOR) was formed.

The raising of meat prices on 1 July 1980 resulted in a wave of strikes which broadened into generalized wage demands and eventually by mid-Aug. acquired a political character. Workers in Gdańsk, Gdynia and Sopot elected a joint strike committee, led by Lech Wałęsa demanding the right to strike and form independent Trade Unions, the abolition of censorship, access to the media and the release of political prisoners.

Gierek offered pay rises, but no political concessions at first.

However, on 24 Aug. Gierek reshuffled the Party and Government leadership, and Józef Pińkowski replaced Edward Babiuch as Prime Minister. On 31 Aug. the Government and Wałęsa signed the 'Gdańsk Agreements' permitting the formation of independent Trade Unions.

On 5 Sept. Gierek suffered a heart attack and was replaced as First Secretary by Stanislaw Kania (Gierek was expelled from the Party in July 1981). On 17 Sept. various Trade Unions decided to form a national confederation ('Solidarity') and applied for legal status, which was granted on 24 Oct. after some Government resistance. A reference inserted into its charter to the supremacy of the party was removed by the Supreme Court on 10 Nov.

On 9 Feb. Pińkowski was replaced as Prime Minister by the Defence Minister, Gen. Wojciech Jaruzelski, and resigned from the Party Politburo in Apr. On 12 June Jaruzelski dismissed five cabinet ministers and proposed a reconstruction of the Government to tackle the severe economic crisis. The crisis led to pressure for an extraordinary Communist Party congress in July at which a new leadership was elected by democratic vote. Four more cabinet ministers were dismissed on 30 July. At Solidarity's first national congress (4–10 Sept. and 2–8 Oct. 1981) Wałęsa was re-elected chairman and a radical programme of action was adopted. KÓR dissolved itself on the grounds that its activities were now being fulfilled by Solidarity. On 18 Oct. Kania resigned from the Party leadership and was replaced by Jaruzelski. On 13 Dec. 1981 the Government imposed martial law (*stan wojenny*), banning a wide range of civil liberties, and establishing the rule of a 20-member Military Council of National Salvation (WRON). Solidarity was proscribed and its leaders detained. Government control was consolidated only after mass arrests and some bloodshed. The proclamation of martial law was retroactively approved by the Sejm on 26 Jan. 1982 with only one dissident vote and 5 abstentions. The Party Central Committee similarly approved the measure on 25 Feb. Jaruzelski announced on 21 July 1982 that 1,227 of those arrested had been released, leaving 637 still detained. Wałęsa was released in Nov. 1982. On 8 Oct. the Sejm voted (with 12 dissident votes and 9 abstentions) a law dissolving all registered trade unions including Solidarity. These will be replaced by workplace unions which must register in court and pledge support for the Communist Party and the Constitution. After a year, industrial unions can be set up on a national scale. In Dec. 1982 martial law was suspended as what Jaruzelski called a substantial step towards the complete lifting of military rule: internment has been ended, the Army withdrawn from many sectors of public life and a restricted amnesty has been granted for some sentenced by martial law courts.

AREA AND POPULATION. Poland is bounded north by the Baltic and the RSFSR, east by Lithuania, White Russia and the Ukraine, south by Czechoslovakia and west by the German Democratic Republic. Poland comprises an area of 312,683 sq. km (120,628 sq. miles). In 1975 the administrative structure was reorganized. (For previous administrative divisions see THE STATESMAN'S YEAR-BOOK, 1975–76.) The country is divided into 49 voivodships (*wojewodztwo*) (including 3 urban: Warsaw, Kraków and Łódź) and these in turn are divided into 803 towns and 2,070 wards (*gmina*). The capital is Warsaw (Warszawa).

Area (in sq. km) and population (in 1,000, with percentage urban in brackets) in 1979.

Voivodship	*Area*	*Population*	*Voivodship*	*Area*	*Population*
Biała Podlaska	5,348	285 (29)	Opole	8,535	968 (49)
Białystok	10,055	636 (53)	Ostrołęka	6,498	368 (28)
Bielsko–Biała	3,703	819 (48)	Piła	8,205	432 (52)
Bydgoszcz	10,349	1,027 (62)	Piotrków	6,266	600 (41)
Chełm	3,865	230 (36)	Płock	5,117	492 (42)
Ciechanów	6,362	403 (30)	Poznań	8,151	1,222 (69)
Częstochowa	6,182	746 (49)	Przemyśl	4,436	378 (34)
Elbląg	6,103	436 (57)	Radom	7,295	698 (41)
Gdańsk	7,394	1,313 (76)	Rzeszów	4,398	641 (34)
Gorzów	8,484	450 (58)	Siedlce	8,499	613 (25)
Jelenia Góra	4,378	490 (64)	Sieradz	4,869	392 (30)
Kalisz	6,512	662 (43)	Skierniewice	3,959	395 (39)
Katowice	6,650	3,677 (87)	Słupsk	7,453	365 (52)
Kielce	9,211	1,062 (42)	Suwałki	10,490	419 (46)
Konin	5,139	5,139 (36)	Szczecin	9,981	887 (74)
Koszalin	8,470	456 (60)	Tarnobrzeg	6,283	551 (30)
Kraków (Cracow)	3,255	1,154 (68)	Tarnów	4,151	602 (32)
Krosno	5,702	443 (31)	Toruń	5,348	604 (59)
Legnica	4,037	449 (62)	Wałbrzych	4,168	715 (72)
Leszno	4,154	355 (44)	Warsaw	3,788	2,288 (88)
Łódź	1,525	1,122 (91)	Włocławek	4,402	414 (43)
Łomża	6,684	324 (31)	Wrocław	6,287	1,065 (72)
Lublin	6,793	925 (53)	Zamość	6,980	472 (22)
Nowy Sącz	5,577	622 (35)	Zielona Góra	8,868	603 (57)
Olsztyn	12,320	675 (54)			

Population (in 1,000) of the largest towns (1979):

Warsaw	1,572	Bydgoszcz	344	Zabrze	196
Łódź	832	Lublin	298	Radom	188
Kraków (Cracow)	705	Sosnowiec	241	Kielce	184
Wrocław (Breslau)	608	Częstochowa	233	Toruń	170
Poznań	544	Bytom	232	Tychy	160
Gdańsk (Danzig)	448	Gdynia	231	Bielsko-Biala	160
Szczecin (Stettin)	388	Białystok	218	Ruda Słaska	158
Katowice	353	Gliwice	196	Chorzów	150

At the census of 7 Dec. 1978 the population was 35,032,000 (17m. males; 58% urban). Population on 1 Jan. 1982, 35,902,000 (18·5m. females; 21m. urban), density, 112 per sq. km. Vital statistics, 1980 (per 1,000): Marriages, 9; divorces, 1·1; live births, 18·8; deaths, 9·1; infant mortality (per 1,000 live births), 20·5.

The rate of natural growth, 1981, 9·7 per 1,000. Expectation of life in 1980 was 66 years for males, 74·4 years for females. In 1979, 50% of the population was under 30.

Ethnic minorities in 1963: 180,000 Ukrainians, 165,000 Byelorussians, 21,000 Slovaks, 10,000 Lithuanians. There were 10,000 Jews in 1977. By a treaty of March 1976, Poland agreed to repatriate 125,000 ethnic Germans by 1980 and thereafter to issue exit permits to the remaining 155,000.

In 1969, 10·33m. Poles lived abroad (6·5m. in USA, 1·4m. in USSR, 150,000 (1976) in UK). In 1981 there were 1,400 immigrants and 23,800 emigrants.

CLIMATE. Climate is continental, marked by long and severe winters. Rainfall amounts are moderate, with a marked summer maximum. Warsaw. Jan. 26°F (–3·5°C), July 66°F (19°C). Annual rainfall 22·1″ (553 mm).

CONSTITUTION AND GOVERNMENT. The present Constitution was adopted on 22 July 1952. Constitutional amendments were adopted in Feb. 1976. Two amendments referring to the leading role of the Communist Party and the special relationship with the USSR provoked a wave of protest when circulated in draft form and were adopted in a modified form.

The titular head of state is the Chairman of the Council of State, Henryk Jabłoński.

The Constitution defines the position of political parties as follows: 'The leading political force in Polish society is the Polish United Workers' (*i.e.* Communist) Party. Co-operation between the Polish United Workers' Party, the United Peasants' Party and the Democratic Party constitutes the basis for the National Unity Front.' A new civic body, the Patriotic Movement for National Renaissance (PRON), was set up on 24 Nov. 1982.

At the 9th, extraordinary, congress of the Communist Party on 19 July 1981 a new Politburo was elected by democratic vote. Only four of the 16 former members were re-elected. Changes were made in the Party and Government leadership in July and Oct. 1982. In March 1983 the Politburo consisted of: Wojciech Jaruzelski *(First Secretary, Prime Minister and Minister of Defence)*; Kazimerz Barcikowski; Tadeusz Czechowicz; Józef Czyrek; Zofia Grzyb; Stanisław Kalkus; Hieronim Kubiak; Zbigniew Messner; Mirosław Milewski; Stefan Olszowski *(Foreign Minister)*; Stanisław Opalko; Tadeusz Porebski; Jerzy Romanik; Albin Siwak; Marian Wozniak. Candidate members: Stanisław Bejger Jan Główczyk; Czesław Kiszczak *(Minister of the Interior)*; Włodzimierz Mokrzyszczak; Gen. Florian Siwicki. Ministers not in the Politburo include: *(Deputy Prime Ministers)* Zenon Komender *(Catholic representative),* Edward Kowalczyk; Zbigniew Madej; Roman Malinowski; Janusz Obodowski *(Chairman, State Planning Commission)*;Mieczysław Rakowski; Zbigniew Szalajda; Mieczysław Moczar *(Chairman, Supreme Chamber of Control)*; Zdzisław Krasiński *(Minister responsible for prices)*; Władysław Baka *(Plenipotentiary for the economic reform)*; Gen. Tadeusz Kupalowski *(Administration and Environment)*; Jerzy Wojtecki *(Agriculture and Food)*; Stanisław Niekarz *(Finance)*; Tadeusz Nesterowicz *(Foreign Trade)*; Zygmunt Łakomiec *(Home Trade)*; Sylwester Zawadzki *(Justice)*; Stefan Ciosek *(Trade union affairs)*.

The 9th Party congress approved a new statute granting elected bodies more control, limiting Party officials' terms of office and separating Government and Party posts. This was never ratified by the Central Committee.

In 1981 the Polish United Workers' Party had 2,690,600 (3,091,900 in 1980) members, the United Peasants' Party 463,100, and the Democratic Party, 112,000.

The authority of the republic is vested in the Sejm, elected for 4 years by all citizens over 18. The Sejm elects a Council of State, composed of a Chairman, the Secretary and 14 members, including 4 vice-chairmen; and a Council of Ministers. Local government is carried out by People's Councils elected every 4 years at voivodship and community level. Alongside these are the offices of state administration. The chairman of the People's Council is the Secretary of the regional organization for the area.

The last local elections were held on 23 March 1980.

The last elections for the Sejm were held on 23 March 1980. 646 candidates stood on the single list of the National Unity Front and obtained 99·52% of the vote. 98·87% of the electorate voted. The 460 seats are distributed as follows: 261 United Workers' Party, 113 United Peasants' Party, 37 Democratic Party, 49 independents, including 5 Catholic representatives nominated by the Government but repudiated by the Church. There are 106 women deputies.

National flag: Horizontally white over red.

National anthem: Jeszcze Polska nie zginęła (words by J. Wybicki, 1797; tune by M. Ogiński, 1796).

DEFENCE. Poland is divided into 3 military districts: Warsaw (the eastern part of Poland); Pomerania (Baltic coast, part of central Poland; headquarters at Bydgoszcz); Silesia (Silesia and southern Poland; headquarters at Wrocław).

Armed forces are on Soviet lines and divided into army and air force (2 years' service), navy (3 years), anti-aircraft, rocket and radio-technological units (3 years) and internal security forces (2 years). In 1965 the security forces were taken away from the Ministry of Internal Affairs and placed under the Defence Ministry. The military age extends from the 19th to the 50th year. The strength of the armed forces was (1983) 207,000, plus 85,000 security and frontier forces. Security forces include armoured brigades.

Army. The Army consists of 5 armoured, 8 motorized, 1 airborne and 1 amphibious assault divisions (not all at full strength) with support units. Total strength (1983), 207,000. Tanks (mostly T-54, T-55) number 3,190.

Navy. The Navy comprises 4 submarines, 1 destroyer, 24 fleet minesweepers, 13 missile craft, 23 patrol boats, 10 torpedo boats, 42 coastal patrol boats, 1 inshore minesweeper, 23 medium landing ships, 3 intelligence vessels, 8 training ships, 3 degaussing vessels, 2 salvage ships, 2 torpedo recovery vessels, 20 minor landing craft, 25 minesweeping boats, 3 surveying vessels, 7 oilers, 20 tugs and 40 auxiliaries and tenders. The Fleet Air Arm has 40 fixed-wing aircraft (MiG-17) and 20 helicopters. Personnel in 1983 totalled 22,500 comprising 7,500 afloat, 2,000 under training 5,000 of coastal defence, 2,000 in naval aviation and 6,000 on shore support.

Air Force. The Air Force has a strength of some 88,000 officers and men and 700 first-line jet aircraft of Soviet design, forming 4 air divisions. There are 10 air defence regimenta (33 squadrons) with more than 400 MiG-21 supersonic interceptors, and 6 regiments (18 squadrons) operating variable-geometry MiG-23BM and Su-20, Su-7B and MiG-17 close-support fighters. Another fighter division supports the Navy. There are also reconnaissance, ECM, transport, helicopter (including Mi-24 gunship) and training units. Soviet 'Guideline' 'Goa', 'Gainful' and 'Gaskin' surface-to-air missiles are operational.

Two Soviet armoured divisions are stationed on Polish territory.

INTERNATIONAL RELATIONS

Membership. Poland is a member of UN, Comecon and the Warsaw Pact.

Planning. For planning history until 1980 *see* THE STATESMAN'S YEAR-BOOK 1981–82, p.1002. Industrialization without sufficient expenditure on infrastructure; neglect of agriculture and the inefficiency of the planning mechanism, exacerbated by higher prices and declining Western demand for exports, and the social unrest since 1980, have brought the economy to a state of paralysis. Basic foodstuffs are rationed, and massive price increases were introduced in Feb. 1982. In Apr. 1982 a Consultative Economic Council was set up as an advisory body to the Government. A socio-economic plan for 1983–85 has the task of overcoming the economic crisis.

Budget. Budget in 1m. złotys, for calendar years:

	1976	*1977*	*1978*	*1979*	*1980*	*1981*
Revenue	881,401	993,948	1,103,457	1,154,800	1,222,700	1,284,300
Expenditure	799,494	887,599	994,158	1,107,700	1,139,200	1,397,900

Main items of 1981 revenue (in 1m. złotys): Sales tax and profits tax from state enterprises, 848,000; finance and insurance, 263,100; income tax, 18,800.

Main items of 1981 expenditure (in 1m. złotys): State enterprises, 935,500; welfare, 118,000; defence, 69,600; administration, 54,900; education, 102,300.

Debts to the UK at the time of the Communist takeover have been repaid. Poland does not accept liability for the £495,000 debts of Danzig (Gdańsk). Gold seized by the Nazis from Danzig was returned to Poland by the USA in 1976.

Currency. The currency unit is the *złoty*, divided into 100 *groszy*. The currency consists of notes of 50, 100, 500, 1,000 and 2,000 złotys; and of coins of 10, 20 and 50 groszy and 1, 2, 5, 10 and 20 złotys. In Jan. 1982 the złoty was substantially devalued against Western currencies. In Apr. 1983, £1 sterling = 129·29 złotys, US$1 = 87 złotys.

Banking. The National Bank of Poland (established 1945) is the central bank, has exclusive authority to issue currency, is charged with control of money and credit, and has responsibility for financial implementation of the national economic plan. Since its merger with the former Investment Bank on 1 Jan. 1970 it exercises centralized control over investment financing. The Agricultural Bank (Bank Rolny) has exclusive responsibility for direct financing of rural areas through both short-term and investment loans. It operates banks. The General Savings Bank (Powszechna Kasa Oszczedności) exercises central control over savings activities, transfers and checking transactions, including activities of workers' co-operative banks.

In addition to the National Bank of Poland other authorized foreign-exchange banks are: Bank for the National Economy, the Polish Welfare Bank (Bank Polska Kasa Opieki SA) and the Commercial Bank of Warsaw (Bank Handlowy w Warszawie SA).

Deposits in savings institutions amounted to 664,578m. złotys on 31 Dec. 1981.

Weights and Measures. The metric system is in general use.

ENERGY AND NATURAL RESOURCES

Energy. Power sources in 1979: Coal, 76%; lignite, 22%; hydroelectric, 2%. A nuclear power station is being built at Zarnowiec.

Minerals. Poland is a major producer of coal (reserves of some 71,000m. tonnes) and sulphur. Copper reserves are estimated at 10m. tonnes. There is also iron ore, lead and zinc. Production in 1981 (in 1,000 tonnes): Coal, 163,000 (190,000 in 1982); brown coal, 35·5; copper ore, 22,819; zinc-lead ores, 5,035; iron ore, 105.

Agriculture. In 1981 there were 18·9m. hectares of agricultural land, of which 14·2m. hectares were in private hands, 3·8m. in state farms, 0·78m. in co-operatives and 0·17m. in agricultural circles. There were 2·9m. private farms in 1981. Private holdings average 5·3 hectares, and may not exceed 100 hectares. 11m. hectares were arable, 238,000 orchards, 1·9m. meadows, 1m. pasture lands.

Collectivization has been largely abandoned but remains a long-term aim and the number of co-operatives has been increasing: 1975, 1,092; 1980, 2,286; 1981, 2,350. A new agricultural policy of 1981 gave more autonomy to co-operatives, linked wages to productivity and equalized resources between the state and private sectors. The peasants' organization 'Rural Solidarity' was accorded the status of trade union in May 1981 but dissolved by the trade union law of Oct. 1982. A compulsory contributory pension scheme was introduced in 1978 for farmers who turn over their farms to their successors or the State. 250,000 such pensions had been paid by June 1980. 'Agricultural circles' numbered 30,000 with 2·2m. members in 1981. In 1981 there were 4,233 state agricultural holdings.

	Area (1,000 hectares)			*Yield (1,000 tonnes)*		
Crops	*1979*	*1980*	*1981*	*1979*	*1980*	*1981*
Wheat	1,549	1,609	1,418	4,187	4,175	4,203
Rye	2,868	3,039	3,002	5,201	6,566	6,731
Barley	1,470	1,322	1,294	3,731	3,420	3,540
Oats	1,094	997	1,156	2,186	2,245	2,730
Potatoes	2,441	2,344	2,258	49,572	26,391	42,562
Sugar-beet	455	460	470	14,154	10,139	15,867

Livestock (1981): 11·8m. cattle (5·8m. cows), 18·5m. pigs, 3·9m. sheep, 1·7m. horses, 71m. poultry. Milk production in 1981 was 14,847m. litres.

Tractors in use in 1981: 903,000 (in 15-h.p. units).

Forestry. In 1981, 8·6m. hectares were forests (predominantly coniferous). 70,000 hectares were afforested in 1981, and 21·9m. cu. metres of timber gained.

Fisheries. In 1981 the fishing fleet had 103 deep-sea vessels totalling 315,900 GRT. In 1981 the catch was 644,400 tonnes.

In 1966 Poland joined the Fisheries Convention of 1964, extending the fishing limits from 3 to 12 miles.

INDUSTRY AND TRADE

Industry. Production in 1981 (and 1980) (in 1,000 tonnes): Coke, 17,900 (19,800); pig-iron, 9,351 (11,953); crude steel, 15,719 (19,485); rolled steel, 11,064 (13,551); cement, 14,200 (18,400); sulphuric acid (100%), 2,776 (3,019); fertilizers, 2,242 (2,237); aluminium, 66 (95); electrolytic copper, 327 (357); lead, 69 (82); zinc, 167 (217); crude oil, 315 (329); salt, 4,271 (4,533); sugar, 1,685 (1,067); electricity, 115,000m. kwh. (122,000m.); natural gas, 6,172m. cu. metres (6,329m.). In 1981, 38 ships over 100 DWT were built (322,000 DWT), 240,000 cars, 42,200 lorries and 11,200 buses were built in 1981.

Output of light industry in 1981 (and 1980): Cotton fabrics, 738m. metres (884); woollen fabrics, 106m. metres (121); silk and synthetic fibres. 142m. metres (163); shoes, 145m. pairs (162); household glass, 71,500 tonnes (89,200); paper, 909,000 tonnes (1,033,000); 713,000 washing machines, 555,000 refrigerators and 760,000 TV sets were produced in 1981.

Labour. In 1981 the total number in employment was 16·5m. (including 7·9m. women), of whom 12·7m. worked in the state-controlled sector and 3·8m. in the private sector, and including in agriculture 4·3m., industry 5·2m., building 1·3m., trade 1·4m. and transport and communications 1·1m. Founded in Aug. 1980 the 'independent self-governing union' organization Solidarity held its first national congress 4–10 Sept. and 2–8 Oct. 1981. Lech Wałęsa was re-elected chairman by 462 votes (total number of delegates, 892). An action programme of economic and political reform was adopted. Solidarity was proscribed in Dec. 1981 and dissolved by law in Oct. 1982 along with all other trade unions. Some 2,500 new unions, organized at workplace level, began operating in Jan. 1983. The initial rate of recruitment was low. Membership of Solidarity was 9,447,000 in Sept. 1981. Average wage in 1980, 7,306 złotys per month. A law of Oct. 1982 makes voluntary unemployment an offence; offenders are liable for compulsory labour for the state.

Commerce. Trade statistics for calendar years (in 1m. złotys):

	1975	*1976*	*1977*	*1978*	*1979*	*1980*	*1981*
Imports	41,645	46,100	48,600	50,938	54,015	58,299	52,013
Exports	34,161	36,600	40,800	44,685	50,141	51,908	44,529

Main imports in 1981 (in tonnes): Petroleum, 13·5m.; iron ore, 15·9m.; fertilizers, 5·7m.; wheat, 3·4m.; coal, 1m.; passenger cars, 42,469 units.

Main exports in 1981 (in tonnes): Coal, 15m.; coke, 1·4m.; sawn softwood, 564,000 cu. m.; ships, 329,000 DWT.

58% of Poland's trade is with Comecon countries.

Foreign trade deals should be made directly with the appropriate foreign trade enterprise. Information may be obtained from the Polish Chamber of Foreign Trade, Trebacka 4, 00–950 Warsaw. Joint ventures with Western firms are encouraged both at home and abroad. The Western partner may own up to 49% of the shares of ventures on Polish soil, and is guaranteed a share of profits and interest.

An over-ambitious programme of imports coinciding with the world recession and rise in oil prices was followed by a decline in output caused by the social and economic unrest of 1980–2. This left Poland with a US$27,000m. debt to the West, of which some US$16,000m. are owed to private banks. An agreement to reschedule repayment of the latter was signed in Vienna in Nov. 1982. In 1982 Poland also owed 3,800m. roubles to Comecon countries, mainly the USSR. The USSR has agreed to defer until 1985 repayment of Polish credits granted 1976–80. 1982 saw a 23% drop in Western imports and a trade surplus of £250m.

Soviet exports include plant and equipment and raw materials; Polish exports, machinery, ships, coal, chemicals and consumer goods.

Total trade between Poland and UK for 5 years (British Department of Trade returns £1,000 sterling):

	1978	*1979*	*1980*	*1981*	*1982*
Imports to UK	212,239	229,318	194,523	133,605	151,737
Exports and re-exports from UK	265,911	260,606	296,254	175,728	133,340

An Anglo-Polish 10-year agreement on the development of economic, industrial, scientific and technical co-operation was signed on 20 March 1973, and a 10-year programme implementing this was signed on 4 Sept. 1975. Some Polish imports are subject to quota restrictions.

Economic sanctions have been applied by the USA and other Western countries as a mark of disapproval of the imposition of martial law in Dec. 1981. In Oct. 1982 the US suspended Poland's most-favoured-nation status in retaliation to the proscription of Solidarity.

Tourism. In 1981, 2,172,000 tourists visited Poland (578,000 from the West) and 4,232,000 Polish citizens made visits abroad (1,248,000 to the West).

COMMUNICATIONS

Roads. In 1981 Poland had 148,907m. of hard-surfaced roads. A road-improvement programme is bringing 75% of all roads up to suitability for heavy traffic. Number of motor vehicles: Passenger cars, 2,534,000 (of which, 2,483,000 private); lorries, 639,000 (167,000 private); motor cycles, 1,779,000.

In 1981 road transport carried 2,340m. passengers and 1,553m. tonnes of freight.

Railways. The length of the standard gauge railway system was (1981) 24,356 km (7,091 km electrified). In 1981 the railways carried 402m. tons of freight and 1,114m. passengers.

Aviation. In 1976 the state airline 'Lot' had 35 aircraft including Il-62s, operated 11 internal routes and in 1981 flew services to 33 countries. 1,711,000 passengers were flown and 15,476 tonnes of freight. There are British Airways, SABENA, KLM, PANAM, Alitalia, Swissair, Air France, Austrian Airlines and Lufthansa services to Okęcie (Warsaw) airport.

Shipping. The principal ports are Gdynia, Gdańsk (Danzig) and Szczecin (Stettin). A new port (Port Pólnocny) to take ships of 100,000 DWT is under construction near Gdańsk. The merchant marine is grouped into Polish Ocean Lines (179 vessels totalling 1·04m. DWT in 1975) based on Gdynia and operating regular liner services, and the Polish Shipping Company based on Szczecin and operating cargo services. Poland also has a share in the Gdynia America Line. There are

4,040 km of inland navigable waterways. 16·6m. tonnes of freight were carried in 1981.

In 1981 the merchant marine had 322 vessels totalling 2,993,000 GRT (including 34 vessels over 20,000 tons). There are regular lines to London, Hull, China, Indonesia, Australia, Vietnam and some African and Latin-American countries.

Total shipping entering Polish ports in 1981 was 8,677 vessels of 21·7m. NRT. Freight traffic in 1981 was 21·8m.

Pipeline. In 1981 there were 1,975 km of oil pipeline.

Post and Broadcasting. In 1981 there were 8,181 post offices and 3,387,396 telephones.

Polskie Radio i Telewizja broadcasts 3 programmes in Polish on long-, medium- and short-waves and on FM. There are 2 TV programmes. Colour programmes are transmitted by SECAM system. Wireless licences in 1981 numbered 8·74m.; television licences, 8·19m.

Cinemas and Theatres. In 1981 there were 2,159 cinemas, 96 theatres and 46 concert halls. Cinema attendance was 99m.; theatres, 7·8m.

Newspapers (1981). There were 88 papers with an overall circulation (in 1980) of 2,627m. 2,662 periodicals were published. The Party newspaper is *Trybuna Ludu* (People's Tribune), weekend circulation 1·1m.

JUSTICE, RELIGION, EDUCATION AND WELFARE

Justice. The penal code was adopted in 1969. Espionage and treason carry the severest penalties For minor crimes there is provision for probation sentences and fines. A more liberal law of censorship came into force on 1 Oct. 1981. Trade union publications are freed from censorship, but restrictions remain on matters concerning national security, foreign policy, foreign allies and morals. The Censor's office has been placed under the Council of State, and its rulings are subject to appeal.

There exist the following courts: The Supreme Court; voivodship, district and special courts. Judges and lay assessors are elected. The State Council elects the judges of the Supreme Court for a term of 5 years, and appoints the Prosecutor-General. The office of the Prosecutor-General is separate from the judiciary.

Family courts were established (1977) for cases involving divorce and domestic relations.

Religion. In 1978, 93% of the population was baptized into the Catholic Church, and 78% of the population attended church regularly. Church–State relations are regulated by agreements of 1950, 1956 and 1972. A joint government-episcopal commission was reactivated in Sept. 1980, and religious broadcasting began. The Church has a university (Lublin), an Academy of Catholic Theology and a seminary in every diocese. Religious education of children is conducted in 'catechism centres' of which there were 18,254 in 1973–74.

The archbishop of Warsaw and Gniezno is the primate of Poland (since 1981, Cardinal Józef Glemp). The Vatican considers the archbishoprics of Lwów and Vilnius (incorporated in the USSR in 1940) as still being under Polish jurisdiction. In 1977 there were 5 archbishoprics, 27 dioceses and 6,716 parishes, 75 bishops, 19,642 priests, 30,162 monks and nuns and 14,162 churches and chapels. In 1983 there were 2 cardinals. In 1975 some 4,000 students were studying for the priesthood. In Oct. 1978 Cardinal Karol Wojtyla, archbishop of Cracow, was elected Pope as John Paul II.

On 28 June 1972 the Vatican adjusted the Church boundaries, to coincide with the State's western frontier ('Oder–Neisse line') and the 4 apostolic administrators in the former German territories became bishops.

Figures for other churches in 1977: Polish Autocephalous Orthodox, 4 dioceses, 233 parishes, 301 churches, 221 priests, 2 monasteries (460,000 adherents in 1975). Lutheran, 6 dioceses, 122 parishes, 310 churches, 100 parsons (100,000 adherents in 1975). Uniate, 3 dioceses, 84 parishes, 89 churches, 90 priests

(200,000 adherents in 1975). Old-Catholic Mariavite, 3 dioceses, 42 parishes, 56 churches, 33 priests (30,000 adherents in 1975). Methodist, 5 districts, 66 parishes, 65 chapels, 39 parsons (4,133 adherents in 1975). United Evangelical, 222 congregations, 68 chapels, 215 parsons. Seventh-day Adventist, 124 communities, 122 churches, 66 parsons. Baptist, 127 congregations, 53 chapels, 60 parsons (2,300 adherents in 1975). Moslems, 6 communities, 2 mosques, 6 imams. Jews, 16 congregations, 24 synagogues (12,000 adherents in 1978). Epiphany World Mission, 80 communities, 157 churches, 427 priests.

Education. Basic education from 7 to 15 is free and compulsory. Free secondary education is then optional in general or vocational schools. Primary schools are organized in complexes based on wards under one director ('gmina collective schools'). In 1980–81 there were: Kindergartens, 27,135 with 1·21m. pupils and 75,000 teachers; primary schools, 13,926 (of which 1,755 gmina collective schools) with 4,342,000 pupils and 225,000 teachers; secondary schools, 1,201 with 393,000 pupils and 22,000 teachers; vocational schools, 10,441 with 1,692,000 pupils and 82,000 teachers, and 91 institutions of higher education (including 10 universities, 18 polytechnics, 9 agricultural schools, 6 schools of economics, 11 teachers' training colleges and 10 medical schools) with 423,500 students and 55,450 teaching staff.

Beginning in 1978–79 the 8-year primary school is being progressively replaced by a 10-year general secondary school.

Health. In 1981 there were 683 hospitals (including 40 mental hospitals) with 239,000 beds, 5,875 dispensaries and 3,229 health centres. There were 65,012 doctors and 16,962 dentists.

Social Security. In 1981, 160,774m. złotys were paid out in 4·78m. retirement pensions, 18·13m. zlotys in family allowances and 41·53m. złotys in sick pay.

DIPLOMATIC REPRESENTATIVES

Of Poland in Great Britain (47 Portland Place, London, W1N 3AG)
Ambassador: Stefan Staniszewski (accredited 12 Feb. 1982).

Of Great Britain in Poland (Aleje Roz No. 1, Warsaw)
Ambassador: C. M. James, CMG.

Of Poland in the USA (2640–16th St., NW, Washington, D.C., 20009)
Ambassador: Zdzislaw Ludwiczak.

Of the USA in Poland (Aleje Ujazdowskie 29/31, Warsaw)
Ambassador: Francis J. Meeham.

Of Poland to the United Nations
Ambassador: Eugeniusz Wyzher.

Books of Reference

Statistical Information: The Central Statistical Office, Warsaw (Wawelska 1–3), publishes *Rocznik statystyczny* (annual, 1930–39; 1947–); *Concise Statistical Yearbook of Poland* (1959–); *Statystyka Polski* (irreg., 1947–); *Biuletyn statystyczny* (monthly, 1957–).

Constitution of the Polish People's Republic. Warsaw, 1964
Ascherson, N., *The Polish August: The Self-Limiting Revolution.* London, 1981
Beneš, V. L., and Pounds, N. G. J., *Poland.* London, 1970
Blazynski, G., *Flashpoint Poland.* Oxford and New York, 1979
Budrewicz, O., *Poland for Beginners.* 3rd ed. Warsaw, 1980
Bulas, K., and others, *English–Polish and Polish–English Dictionary.* 2 vols. The Hague, 1959
Burda, A., *Parliament of the Polish People's Republic.* Wrocław, 1978
Davies, N., *Poland, Past and Present: A Select Bibliography of Works in English.* Newtonville, 1977.—*God's Playground: A History of Poland.* OUP, 1981
Dobbs, M., *Poland, Solidarity, Wałęsa.* New York, 1981
Dziewanowski, M. K., *Poland in the Twentieth Century.* Columbia Univ. Press, 1977
Gieysztory, A., and others, *History of Poland. 2nd ed. Warsaw, 1979*
Halecki, O., *A History of Poland.* 3rd ed. London, 1978.–(ed)., *Poland.* New York, 1957
Kieniewicz, S. (ed.) *History of Poland.* 2nd ed. Warsaw, 1979
Lane, D., and Kolankiewicz, G. (ed.) *Social Groups in Polish Society.* London, 1973
Leslie, R. F., (ed.) *The History of Poland since 1863.* CUP, 1980
Letowski, J. (ed.) *Administration in People's Poland.* Wrocław, 1980

Lewanski, R. C., *Poland.* [Bibliography] Oxford and Santa Barbara, 1983
MacShane, D., *Solidarity: Poland's Independent Trade Union.* Nottingham, 1981
Polonsky, A. and Drukier, B., *The Beginnings of Communist Rule in Poland.* London, 1980
Pomian-Srzednicki, M. *Religious Change in Contemporary Poland: Secularization and Politics.* London, 1982
Portes, R., *The Polish Crisis: Western Economic Policy Options.* London, 1981
Potel, J.-I., *The Summer Before the Frost: Solidarity in Poland.* London, 1982
Raina P., *Political Opposition in Poland, 1954–1977.* London, 1978.—*Independent Social Movements in Poland.* London, 1981
Robinson, W.F. (ed.) *August 1980: the Strikes in Poland.* Munich, 1980
Roos, H., *A History of Modern Poland.* London, 1966
Ruane, K., *The Polish Challenge.* London, 1982
Simon, M. D. and Kanet, R. E. (eds.) *Background to Crisis: Policy and Politics in Gierek's Poland.* Boulder, 1980
Singer, D., *The Road to Gdańsk: Poland and the USSR.* New York and London, 1981
Szczypiorski, A., *The Polish Ordeal: The View from Within.* London, 1982
Wielka Encyklopedia Powszechna. 13 vols. Warsaw, 1962–70
Woodall, J., (ed.) *Policy and Politics in Contemporary Poland: Reform, Failure and Crisis.* London, 1982

National Library: Biblioteka Narodowa, Rakowiecka 6, Warsaw.

PORTUGAL

República Portuguesa

Capital: Lisbon
Population: 9·8m. (1981)
GNP per capita: US$2,350 (1980)

HISTORY. Portugal has been an independent state since the 12th century. The Portuguese Republic was proclaimed on 5 Oct. 1910 after the deposition of King Manuel II. A military dictatorship set up in 1926 was replaced in 1932 by a civil dictatorship under Antonio Salazar.

AREA AND POPULATION.

	Area (sq. km)	*Population 1970 (census)*	*Population 1981 (estimate)*
Continent	88,500	8,108,214	9,294,200
Islands	3,131	540,155	509,200
Portugal (total)	91,631 [1]	8,648,369	9,803,400
Districts:			
Aveiro	2,708	548,039	623,800
Beja	10,240	204,816	186,300
Braga	2,730	612,710	700,700
Bragança	6,545	179,763	181,400
Castelo Branco	6,704	255,575	232,400
Coimbra	3,956	401,160	442,900
Évora	7,393	178,538	179,200
Faro	5,072	268,440	322,900
Guarda	5,496	213,538	205,100
Leiria	3,516	379,429	422,800
Lisboa	2,762	1,577,390	2,061,600
Portalegre	5,882	145,929	140,600
Porto	2,282	1,312,392	1,550,800
Santarém	6,689	430,885	455,400
Setúbal	5,152	467,946	649,100
Viana do Castelo	2,108	251,219	253,500
Vila Real	4,239	267,079	264,900
Viseu	5,019	413,366	420,800
Islands:			
Angra do Heroismo	703	86,458	77,400 [2]
Funchal	796	251,059	265,100 [2]
Horta	780	41,422	35,800 [2]
Ponta Delgada	852	161,216	146,600 [2]

[1] 34,861 sq. miles. [2] 1979.

In 1970 (based on 20% of 1970 census figures) the population consisted of 4,109,360 males and 4,553,892 females, or 109 females to every 100 males.

The Azores islands are divided into 3 widely separated groups, with clear channels between São Miguel together with Santa Maria being in the most easterly. About 100 miles north-west of them lies the central cluster of Terceira, Graciosa, São Jorge, Pico and Faial. Still another 150 miles to the north-west are Flores and Corvo, the latter being the most isolated and primitive of the islands. São Miguel, Terceira and Pico are the largest, the first measuring 41 miles in length and 9 in breadth, and containing over half the total population of the archipelago. For political and administrative purposes they are divided into 3 districts, each sending its representatives to the Chamber at Lisbon. The capitals of the 3 districts are the chief seaports, Ponta Delgada on São Miguel Island; Horta on Faial Island and Angra do Heroísmo on Terceira Island.

Vital statistics for calendar years:

	Births	*Still-births*	*Marriages*	*Divorces*	*Deaths*	*Emigrants*
1977	181,064	2,682	91,403	7,781	96,111	19,543
1978	167,467	2,319	81,111	6,997	96,194	22,112
1979	160,311	2,156	77,993	5,866	92,732	26,318

In 1979 the births included 87,124 (1978: 82,726) boys and 80,343 (1979: 77,585) girls; deaths, 49,628 (1979: 47,896) males and 46,566 (1979: 44,836) females.

At the census of 15 Dec. 1970 the population of Lisbon (capital) was 769,044 (metropolitan 1,034,141); Porto, 306,176 (metropolitan area, 693,170). According to 1970 census: Amadora, 66,189; Coimbra, 56,568; Barreiro, 53,200; Setúbal, 50,730; Vila Nova de Gaia, 50,219; Braga, 49,693; Almada, 38,714; Covilhã, 27,018; Guimarães, 25,113; Evora, 24,003; Matosinhos, 22,475; Moscavide, 21,647; Faro, 20,687.

In 1977, 557 emigrants went to Brazil and 6,822 to USA.

CLIMATE. Because of westerly winds and the effect of the Gulf Stream, the climate ranges from the cool, damp Atlantic type in the north to a warmer and drier Mediterranean type in the south. July and Aug. are virtually rainless everywhere. Inland areas in the north have greater temperature variation, with continental winds blowing from the interior. Lisbon. Jan. 52°F (11°C), July 72°F (22°C). Annual rainfall 27·4" (686 mm).

CONSTITUTION AND GOVERNMENT. Portugal has been an independent state since the 12th century; until 1910 it was a monarchy. The last King was Manuel II of the house of Braganza-Coburg, born 15 Nov. 1889, died 2 July 1932. On 5 Oct. 1910 the republic was proclaimed with Dr Teófilo Braga as the provisional president (5 Oct. 1910 to 24 Aug. 1911). Thereafter there were duly elected presidents, as follows:

Dr Manuel de Arriaga, 24 Aug. 1911–29 May 1915.[1]
Dr Joaquim Teófilo Braga, 29 May 1915–5 Oct. 1915.
Dr Bernardino Luis Machado Guimarães, 5 Oct. 1915–11 Dec. 1917.[2]
Dr Sidonio Bernardino Cardoso da Silva Pais, 11 Dec. 1917–14 Dec. 1918.[3]
Adm. João de Canto e Castro Silva Antunes, 16 Dec. 1918–5 Oct. 1919.
Dr António José de Almeida, 5 Oct. 1919–5 Oct. 1923.
Manuel Teixeira Gomes, 5 Oct. 1923–11 Dec. 1925.[1]
Dr Bernardino Luís Machado Guimarães, 11 Dec. 1925–1 June 1926.[1]
Provisional government, 1 June–29 Nov. 1926.
Marshal António Oscar Fragoso Carmona, 29 Nov. 1926–18 April 1951.
Marshal Francisco Higino Craveiro Lopes, 22 July 1951–9 Aug. 1958.
Rear-Adm. Américo de Deus Rodrigues Tomás, 9 Aug. 1958–25 April 1974.[2]
Gen. Antonio de Spinola, 25 April 1974–30 Sept. 1974.[4]
Gen. Francisco da Costa Gomes, 30 Sept. 1974–27 June 1976.[4]
Gen. Antonio Ramalho Eanes, 14 July 1976–

[1] Resigned. [2] Deposed. [3] Assassinated. [4] Not elected.

National flag: Vertical green and red, with the red of double width, and over all on the dividing line the national arms.

National anthem: A Portuguesa (words by Lopes de Mendonça, 1890; tune by Alfredo Keil).

In 1933 a constitution declared that the Portuguese state was a unitary and corporative republic, and the Constitution was adopted by plebiscite. The president was to be elected for 7 years by an electoral college, constituted of members of the National Assembly and the Corporative Chamber, with representatives of municipalities and oversea legislative councils.

On 25 April 1974 a military *coup* led by Gen. Antonio de Spinola overthrew the government of Dr Caetano. Gen. Spinola announced on 26 April that there would be elections within 12 months, that political prisoners would be released and that there would be freedom of expression and the Press. The deposed President, Rear-Adm. Tomás and deposed Prime Minister, Dr Caetano, were taken to Madeira.

General Spinola resigned as President on 30 Sept. 1974.

Several military officers attempted to overthrow the Portuguese Government on 11 March 1975. Gen. Spinola went into exile but denied taking part in the *coup*.

At the legislative elections held in 1979 the Democratic Alliance gained 45% of the votes and 125 seats in the Assembly; Socialists, 27%; 73 seats; Communist Party, 19%, 47 seats; Democratic Popular Union, 2%, 1 seat.

At the presidential elections held on 7 Dec. 1980 Gen. Ramalho Eanes gained 56·43% of the votes cast.

President: Gen. Antonio Ramalho Eanes.

In Feb. 1983 President Eanes announced the dissolution of Parliament. General elections are to be held on 25 April.

Prime Minister: Francisco Pinto Balsemão (resigned 19 Dec. 1982).

Assistant Prime Minister and Defence: Dr Pinto Diogo Freitas do Amaral. *Minister of State and for Quality of Life:* Gonçalo Ribeiro Teles. *Minister of State for the Prime Minister's Office:* Dr Fernando do Amaral. *Interior:* Dr José Angelo Correia. *Justice:* Dr José Meneses Sampaio Pimentel. *Foreign Affairs:* Dr André Gonçalves Pereira. *Finance and Planning:* Dr João Maurício Fernandes Salgueiro. *Education:* Dr Vítor Pereira Crespo. *Labour:* Dr António José Barros Queirós Martins. *Social Affairs:* Dr Luís Eduardo da Silva Barbosa. *Agriculture, Fishing and Commerce:* Dr Basílio Adolfo de Mendonça Horta da França. *Industry, Energy and Exports:* Ricardo Manuel Simões Baião Horta. *Housing, Public Works and Transport:* José Carlos Viana Batista. *Culture and Science:* Dr Francisco Lucas Pires.

DEFENCE. Every Portuguese citizen in good physical condition is subject to compulsory military service from the age of 20 to 45 years for a period of 15 months.

Pre-military training is entrusted to the *Colégio Militar* and the *Instituto Técnico e Profissional dos Pupilos do Exército*, with particular emphasis on physical and moral training of youths aged from 9 to 19 years.

Army. The Army consists of 1 infantry brigade, 1 tank, 3 cavalry and 15 infantry regiments, 4 artillery, 1 commando, 2 engineer and 1 signals regiments. Effective strength (1983), 41,000 all ranks. In 1983 the Republican Guard *(Guarda Nacional Republicana)* consisted of 14,600 all ranks, the Police *(Policia de Legurança Pública)* of 16,124 all ranks and the Fiscal Guard *(Guarda Fiscal)* of 7,519 all ranks.

Navy. The Navy comprises 3 small French-built diesel-powered patrol submarines, 17 frigates, 10 patrol vessels, 4 coastal minesweepers, 17 patrol launches, 1 sail training ship, 4 surveying vessels, 1 fleet oiler, 2 landing craft, 12 minor landing craft, 6 tugs and 1 harbour tanker. The navy personnel in 1983 totalled 14,000 officers and men including 2,000 marines.

Following the withdrawal from Africa there was a considerable disposal list of over 80 warships (some 30 were transferred to Angola and Mozambique) and the Portuguese Navy became comparatively small.

Air Force. Formed in 1912, the Air Force has been independent since 1952, when it was combined with the naval air service and given equal status with the Army and Navy. In 1982, it had a strength of about 9,500 officers and men, excluding paratroops.

Equipment comprises a strike squadron of 20 A-7P Corsair IIs; 2 squadrons of G.91Rs for dual attack and air defence (with Sidewinder missiles); 1 squadron of 5 C-130H Hercules for transport and secondary maritime surveillance duties; 2 transport squadrons, a survey squadron, a search and rescue unit and an OCU equipped with 22 Spanish-built CASA 212 Aviocars, of which 4 are equipped for photographic duties; 32 Cessna 337 Skymasters for counter-insurgency and liaison duties; and a force of Puma and Alouette III helicopters. Other aircraft in service include Chipmunk piston-engined trainers, T-37C jet basic trainers, T-33, T-38A Talon and G.91T jet advanced trainers.

INTERNATIONAL RELATIONS

Membership. Portugal is a member of UN, EFTA, OECD and NATO.

ECONOMY

Planning. The aim of 1981–84 plan is to modernize existing industry and pave the way for entry into the European Community.

Budget. Revenue and expenditure for calendar years (in 1,000 contos):

	1975	*1976*	*1977*	*1978*	*1979*	*1980*	*1981*
Revenue	79,683	125,373	159,173	219,571	283,395	391,727	490,017
Expenditure	86,620	124,688	159,173	219,571	283,395	391,727	490,017

Currency. The unit of currency is the *escudo* of 100 *centavos*, which contains 0·66567 gramme of fine gold. It was stabilized on 9 June 1931, and the paper currency re-linked to gold when the notes of the Bank of Portugal became payable in gold or its equivalent in foreign currency. 1,000 escudos is called a *conto*.

At present there are silver coins of 50, 25, 20, 10 and 5 escudos; 10, 5 and 2½ escudos (nickel and copper); alpaca coins of 1 and ½ escudo (50 centavos), bronze coins of 1 and ½ escudo and 20 and 10 centavos and aluminium coins of 10 centavos.

In March 1983, £1 = 141·00 *escudos*; US$1 = 94·00 *escudos*.

Banking. The one bank of issue for the mainland of the country and adjacent islands is the Bank of Portugal, founded 19 Nov. 1846. It was nationalized on 13 Sept. 1974 and its organic law came into force on 15 Nov. The capital of the bank was fixed at 200m. escudos and it is the central bank of the republic. The bank issues notes of 1,000, 500, 100, 50 and 20 escudos. All other Portuguese banks and insurance companies were nationalized on 14 March 1975.

The National Development Bank began operations on 4 Jan. 1960. Its total capital is 1,500m. escudos.

There are 11 commercial banks registered on the mainland and 1 in the islands, with cash in hand on 31 Dec. 1979, 9,913m. escudos; bills, loans and other credits, 551,644m. escudos; deposits, 656,965m. escudos. The deposits in the savings banks including the general deposit bank (state) amounted to 253,236m. escudos.

There are also 3 foreign banks, the Bank of Brazil, Bank of London and South America and Crédit Franco-Portugais.

Weights and Measures. The metric system of weights and measures is the legal standard.

ENERGY AND NATURAL RESOURCES

Electricity. Total production of electrical power in 1977 was 13,818m. kwh. (1978: 14,653,006); the installed capacity totalled 4,475,150 kva. (1978: 4,660,034), of which 2,683,604 kva. (1976: 2,523,604) were hydro-electric. New power plants were inaugurated in 1951 (Castelo do Bode, Venda Nova, Belver), 1953 (Salamonde), 1954 (Cabrill), 1955 (Caniçada and Bouçã), 1958 (Picote), 1960 (Miranda), 1964 (Bemposta), 1965 (Tàvora), 1970 (Drives and Bugalheira), 1971 (Carrapatelo) and 1975 (France, Fratel, Valeira).

Minerals. Portugal possesses considerable mineral wealth. Production in tonnes:

	1977	*1978*	*1979*		*1977*	*1978*	*1979*
Coal	195,265	180,101	179,118	Gold (refined)	0·275	0·284	0·320
Cupriferous pyrites	359,687	313,845	349,172	Wolframite	1,703	1,873	2,348
Tin ores	379	403	346	Hematite	21,669	19,761	22,198
Kaolin	72,860	73,555	80,039				

Uranium mining commenced in Aug. 1979. Annual production, 115 tonnes; reserves, 7,000 tonnes.

Agriculture. The following figures show the area (in hectares) and yield (in tonnes) of the chief crops:

Crop	1978 Area	1978 Yield	1979 Area	1979 Yield	1980 Area	1980 Yield
Wheat	354,873	249,922	285,600	252,200	345,900	432,800
Maize	369,226	449,437	394,100	506,000	393,600	532,000
Oats	176,981	63,994	159,100	69,500	174,700	96,000
Barley	85,556	43,877	72,000	41,200	79,200	53,700
Rye	213,289	122,617	208,800	120,200	205,800	138,400
Rice	32,933	134,906	34,700	145,300	34,700	154,800
Dried beans	281,526	41,856	260,000	43,500	272,700	46,000
Potatoes	119,358	1,127,823	117,100	1,109,600	122,800	1,270,100

Wine production (in hectolitres), 1980, 10,290,400; 1979, 14,414,900; olive oil (hectolitres), 1980, 348,200; 1979, 624,800. In 1955, 228,996 hectolitres of port wine were exported; 1970, 352,090; 1972, 445,741; 1973 (tonnes), 48,244; 1974, 43,063; 1975, 37,713; 1976, 41,209; 1977, 48,622; 1978, 51,937.

Livestock (1981). Portugal (continental only) possessed 29,000 horses, 92,000 mules, 182,000 asses, 1m. cattle, 750,000 goats, 5·2m. sheep and 3·4m. pigs.

Forestry. Forest area covers 3m. hectares, of which 1·33m. are pine, 652,580 cork oak, 576,070 other oak, 213,960 eucalyptus, 29,730 chestnut and 366,660 other species.

Portugal surpasses the rest of the world in the production of cork (in tonnes): 1977, 177,759; 1978, 145,206; 1979, 115,355; 1980, 91,154. Most of it is exported crude; exports of cork and cork products totalled (in tonnes) 162,227 in 1972; 153,702 in 1973; 138,421 in 1974; 103,967 in 1975. Production of resin (in tonnes) was 100,319 in 1976; 123,968 in 1977; 96,279 in 1978; 105,763 in 1979; 134,339 in 1980; more than two-thirds are exported. Exports of turpentine (in tonnes) were 14,229 in 1972; 12,953 in 1973; 14,012 in 1974; 6,816 in 1975.

Fisheries. The fishing industry for the continent and adjacent isles is of importance. At 31 July 1979 there were 37,422 men and boys employed, with 10,936 boats. The sardine catch, 1980, was 106,537 tonnes valued at 1,173,566 contos; 1979, 90,523 tonnes valued at 1,480,113 contos. Exports of tinned sardines (in tonnes) amounted to 22,001 in 1974, 23,293 in 1975 and 28,577 in 1976. The most important centres of the sardine industry are at Matosinhos, Peniche, Setúbal, Portimão and Olhão.

TRADE

Commerce. Imports for consumption and exports (exclusive of coin and bullion and re-exports) for calendar years, in 1,000 escudos:

	1975	1976	1977	1978	1979	1980
Imports	99,474,040	130,858,582	190,684,496	230,128,372	331,926,551	475,486,000
Exports	49,328,112	55,088,512	77,685,327	106,450,574	176,050,692	231,623,000

The principal exports were wine, cork, pulp wood, sardines and resin; imports included petroleum, motor vehicles, oil seeds, cotton, iron ingots, sugar, coffee and wheat.

The distribution of the imports and exports (in 1,000 escudos):

From or to	Imports from 1978	Imports from 1979	Imports from 1980	Exports to 1978	Exports to 1979	Exports to 1980
Angola	321,823	777,993	768,800	2,899,357	5,872,874	8,904,300
Belgium	7,325,535	9,164,821	14,644,600	3,442,644	5,631,832	7,200,700
France	20,724,091	28,389,285	34,534,500	9,598,629	17,079,442	24,530,700
Germany, Fed. Rep. of	31,905,410	41,822,440	55,810,800	14,044,798	21,575,018	31,373,000
Italy	12,626,116	17,054,902	24,936,000	6,124,198	10,361,450	13,233,800
Mozambique	893,300	2,029,206	1,100,700	1,527,000	1,128,784	1,860,200
Netherlands	8,147,004	11,113,963	13,561,500	4,391,544	8,242,548	10,945,500
Spain	12,513,460	19,258,798	26,144,700	2,255,396	5,068,528	8,348,600
UK	23,197,417	30,747,430	41,616,700	19,430,507	31,421,884	34,325,400
USA	27,151,118	38,958,800	52,325,200	7,512,813	10,783,354	13,219,700

Total trade between Portugal (excluding the Azores and Madeira) and UK (British Department of Trade returns, in £1,000 sterling):

	1977	*1978*	*1979*	*1980*	*1981*	*1982*
Imports to UK	229,889	256,222	338,337	335,112	333,355	379,949
Exports and re-exports from UK	299,321	286,488	307,670	389,849	368,080	430,684

Trade Unions. 331 unions had in 1976 a membership of 1,436,142.

Tourism. Tourism is of increasing importance for the invisible balance of payments. In 1981 there were 7,277,000 visitors and income from tourism represented 5–6% of GNP.

COMMUNICATIONS

Roads (1980). There were 33,984 km of road. There were registered in continental Portugal in 1980, 1,624,980 motor vehicles, including 93,959 motor cycles and 109,064 tractors; not counting vehicles used by the armed forces.

Railways. In 1980 total railway length was 3,588 km (1,668 mm and metre gauges), of which 430 km of broad-gauge was electrified. In 1980, 224,191,000 passengers were carried and 3·74m. tons of merchandise transported.

Aviation. Regular services connect Lisbon with Caracas, Rio de Janeiro, São Paulo, San Salvador, Recife, Montreal, Boston, New York, Sal Island, Bissau, Luanda, Maputo, Johannesburg, Kinshasa, Brazzaville, Madrid, Paris, London, Barcelona, Brussels, Luxembourg, Amsterdam, Copenhagen, Frankfurt, Dusseldorf, Milan, Rome, Lyon and Zürich. These lines in 1979 carried 2·1m. passengers and 40,307 tonnes of freight. The national airline changed its name to Air Portugal in 1979.

Shipping. In 1980, 14,437 vessels of 63,692,101 tons entered the ports (continental and islands). Of those entering in 1979 5,522 (14,598,113 tons) were Portuguese, 627 (5,796,988 tons) British and 612 (2,083,121 tons) Spanish. On 31 Dec. 1978 the merchant marine consisted of 99 transport vessels of 1,075,224 tons.

Post and Broadcasting (1978). The number of telegraph offices was 1,735. The State owned (1979) 5,526,742 km of telephone line and the *Telefones de Lisboa e Porto* (nationalized in 1977) owned 2,521,718 km of lines. Number of telephones was 1,371,731 (1981).

Radio Difusão Portuguesa broadcasts 3 programmes on medium-waves and on FM as well as 3 regional services. *Radiotelevisão Portuguesa SARL* broadcasts 2 commercial TV programmes. *Radio Clube Português* is a commercial, nationwide network. In addition there are 6 local, commercial stations, operating on medium-waves. Radio Trans Europe is a high-powered short-wave station, retransmitting programmes of different broadcasting organizations, *e.g.*, IBRA, Radio Canada and Deutsche Welle. Radio Free Europe also has relay facilities on short-waves in Portugal. Number of receivers (1975): Radio, 1,510,703; TV, 722,315.

Cinemas (1978). There were 448 cinemas with a seating capacity of 249,348.

Newspapers (1978). There were 34 daily newspapers with a combined circulation of 196,002; 15 of these, with a combined circulation of 120,641, appeared in Lisbon.

JUSTICE, RELIGION AND EDUCATION

Justice. Portuguese law distinguishes civil (including commercial) and penal, labour, administrative and fiscal law, each branch having its lower courts, courts of appeal and the Supreme Court.

The republic is divided for civil and penal cases into 214 *comarcas*; in every comarca there is a lower court. In the comarca of Lisbon there are 38 lower courts (22 for criminal procedure and 16 for civil or commercial cases); in the comarca of Oporto there are 21 lower courts (12 for criminal and 9 for civil or commercial cases); at Coimbra, Setúbal, Sintra and Vila Nova de Gaia there are 4 courts; at

Almada, Braga, Cascais, Funchal, Guimarães, Leiria, Loures, Matosinhos, Oeiras, Santarém and Viseu there are 3 courts; 19 comarcas have 2 courts each. There are 4 courts of appeal *(Tribunal de Relação)* at Lisbon, Coimbra, Evora and Oporto, and a Supreme Court in Lisbon *(Supremo Tribunal de Justiça)*.

Capital punishment was abolished completely after the new constitution of 1976.

The prison population as at 31 Dec. 1980 was 6,759.

Religion. The predominant faith is the Roman Catholic, but there is freedom of worship, both in public and private, with the exception of creeds incompatible with morals and the life and physical integrity of the people.

Education. According to the latest statistics, 70% of the population over 7 years could read and write. Compulsory education has been in force since 1911. In 1978–79 there were 9,290 public primary schools with 970,712 pupils and 36,568 teachers. In 1977–78 private elementary schools numbered 627 with 57,635 pupils and 2,366 teachers. Basic preparatory schools numbered 1,765 with (1978–79) 307,156 pupils. Secondary instruction is supplied in two types of schools: in the *liceus* and other grammar schools, and in schools of technical instruction. In 1977–78 there were 422 *liceus* and 185 institutions of *liceu* standard, with 146,634 pupils, and 164 professional and technical secondary schools, with 77,335 pupils. There were also (1978–79) 19 schools which taught art activities (cinema, music and theatre) with 5,049 students. For higher education there are 6 universities; at Aveiro (founded in 1973), Lisbon (founded in 1911), Coimbra (founded 1290), Porto (founded 1911), Minho (founded 1974) and a new university at Lisbon (founded 1974). In 1978–79 the number of students at the universities was 50,579; and the Technical University at Lisbon (founded in 1930) had 11,837 students. There are also a military and a naval school, art schools in Lisbon and Porto (3,013 students) and 1 college of music (257 students). At upper level there are other colleges, public and private, which were attended by 15,309 and 2,477 students respectively.

DIPLOMATIC REPRESENTATIVES

Of Portugal in Great Britain (11 Belgrave Sq., London, SW1X 8PP)
Ambassador: João C. L. C. de Freitas-Cruz (accredited 6 March 1980).

Of Great Britain in Portugal (35-39 Rua S. Domingos à Lapa, Lisbon)
Ambassador: H. C. Byatt, CMG.

Of Portugal in the USA (2125 Kalorama Rd., NW, Washington, D.C., 20008)
Ambassador: Leonardo Mathias.

Of the USA in Portugal (Ave. Duque de Loule 39, Lisbon)
Chargé d'Affaires: Edward M. Rowell

Of Portugal to the United Nations
Ambassador: Rui E. Barbosa de Medina.

Books of Reference

Statistical Information: The Instituto Nacional de Estatistica (Avenida Dr António José de Almeida, Lisbon) was set up in 1935 in succession to the Direcção-Geral de Estatistica. The Centro de Estudos Económicos and the Centro de Estudos Demográficos were affiliated to the Instituto in 1944. The main publications are:

Anuário Estatistíco. Annuaire statistique. Annual, from 1875

Estatísticas do Comércio Externo. 2 vols. Annual from 1967 (replacing *Comércio Externo,* 1936–66, and *Estatística Comercial,* 1865–1935)

Censo da População de Portugal. 1864 ff. Decennial (latest ed. 1972)

Estatística da Organização Corporativa. 1938–49. Estatísticas da Organização Corporativa e Previdência Social. 1950 ff.

Estatísticas das Finanças, Publicas and *Estatísticas Nometárias.* 1969 ff. (replacing *Estatísticas Financeiras.* 1947–68 and *Situação Bancária,* 1919–46)

Estatísticas Agrícolas. Statistique Agricole. 1943–64; replaced by *Estatísticas Agrícolas e Alimentares.* From 1965. Annual
Estatísticas Industrials. 1967 ff. (replacing *Estatística Industrial. Statistique Industrielle.* 1943–66)
Estatísticas Demográficas. From 1967 (replacing *Anuário Demográfico*, 1929–66)
Boletim Mensal do Instituto Nacional de Estatística. Monthly since 1929
Centro de Estudos Económicos. Revista. 1945 ff.
Centro de Estudos Demográficos. Revista. 1945 ff.
Estatísticas das Contribuições e Impostos. Annual from 1967 (replacing *Anuário Estatístico das Contribuições e Impostos*, 1936–66)
Estatísticas da Educação. 1940 ff.
Estatísticas da Justica. 1968 ff. (replacing *Estatísticas Judiciária.* 1936–66)
Estatísticas das Sociedades. 1939 ff.
Estatísticas do Turismo. 1969 ff.
Estatísticas do Energia. 1969 ff.

Azevedo, Gonzaga de, *Historia de Portugal.* 6 vols. Lisbon, 1935–44
Bradford, S., *Portugal.* London, 1973
Brazão, E., *The Anglo-Portuguese Alliance.* London, 1957
Bruce, N., *Portugal: The Last Empire.* Newton Abbot, 1975
Ferreira, J. A., *Dictionario inglês-portugês.* 2 vols. Porto, 1948
Figueiredo, A. de, *Fifty Years of Dictatorship.* Harmondsworth, 1975
Guerreiro, A. D. (ed.), *Bibliografia sobre a economia portuguesa, 1948–69.* 21 vols. Lisbon, 1958–72
Harvey R., *Portugal: Birth of a Democracy.* London, 1978
Livermore, H. V., *Portugal: A Short History.* Edinburgh, 1973
Marques, A. H. de O., *History of Portugal.* 2 vols. Columbia Univ. Press, 1973
Mota, J. G., *A Resistência.* Lisbon, 1976
Pereira, A. M., *Organização politica e administrativa de Portugal.* Oporto, 1949
Robertson, I., *Blue Guide: Portugal.* London, 1982
Robinson, R., *Contemporary Portugal.* London, 1979
Rodrigues, A., Borga, C. and Cardosa, M., *Portugal depois de Abril.* Lisbon, 1976
Rogers, F. M., *Atlantic Islanders of the Azores and Madeiras.* North Quincy, 1979
Salazar, A. de O., *Doctrine and Action: Integral and Foreign Policy of the New Portugal, 1928–39.* London, 1939.—*Discursos, 1928–58.* 5 vols. 5th ed. Coimbra, 1958.—*Política Portuguesa.* Santiago de Chile, 1952
Soares, M., *Le Portugal Bâillonné: Une Témoignage.* Paris, 1972
Sobel, L. A. (ed.), *Portuguese Revolution 1974–76.* New York, 1976
Spinola, A. de, *Portugal e o Futoro.* Lisbon, 1974
Stanislawski, D., *The Individuality of Portugal: A Study in Historical-Political Geography.* Univ. of Texas Press, 1959
Taylor, J. L., *Portuguese-English Dictionary.* London, 1959

National Library: Biblioteca Nacional, Campo Grande, Lisbon. *Director:* A. H. C. Marques.

OVERSEAS TERRITORIES

On 11 June 1951 the status of the Portuguese overseas possessions was changed from 'colonies' to 'overseas territories'. In 1972 greater autonomy was granted to the overseas territories. Angola and Mozambique became States instead of overseas provinces and had their own legislative assemblies. A Governor-General from each State would continue to be appointed by Lisbon but he would have the rank of Minister of State. In Sept. 1961 all Africans were given full Portuguese citizenship, thereby achieving the same status as the inhabitants of Portuguese India and the other provinces. On 27 July 1974 Gen. Spinola announced that Portugal was prepared to offer independence to her African overseas territories of Angola, Mozambique and Portuguese Guinea (Guinea-Bissau) and to 'recognize the right of the populations of our overseas territories to take their destinies into their own hands'. A new constitutional law on decolonization, published on 24 July, formally repealed the section of 1933 Constitution which forbade the surrender of Portugal's overseas territories.

During 1974–76 independence was achieved by Angola (11 Nov. 1975); Cape Verde (5 July 1975); Guinea-Bissau (10 Sept. 1974); Mozambique (25 July 1975); São Tomé e Principe (12 July 1975).

East Timor was invaded by Indonesian forces on 7 Dec. 1975 after civil war had raged since August. On 17 July 1976 East Timor became a province of Indonesia and was renamed Loro Sae.

Approval has also been given for greater autonomy in Madeira and the Azores.

Books of Reference

Atlas de Portugal Ultramarino. Lisbon: Ministério das Colónais. 1948
Anuàrio Estatistico, II: Ultramar. Annuaire statistique, II: Outre-mer. Lisbon, 1961 ff. (1950–60 under the title *Anuário Estatístico do Ultramar)*
Boletin da Agência Geral do Ultramar. Lisbon. Monthly
Documentacão ultramarina portuguesa. Centro de Estudos Históricos Ultramarinos. Lisbon, 1960
Andrade, A. A., *O Tradicional Anti-Racismo da Acção Civilizadora Portuguesa* (in Portuguese and English). Lisbon, 1953
Bahia dos Santos, F., *Unidade e cooperação entre a metrópole e o ultramar.* Lisbon, 1953
Boxer, C. R., *Race Relations in the Portuguese Empire.* OUP, 1963
Caetano, M., *Tradições, Princípios e Métodos Colonização Portuguesa* (in Portuguese, French and English). Lisbon, 1951
Cunha, S., *O Sistema Português de Politica Indigena.* Lisbon, 1953
Duffy, J., *Portuguese Africa.* Harvard Univ. Press, 1959.—*Portugal in Africa.* Harmondsworth, 1962
Freyer, G., *The Portuguese and the Tropics.* Lisbon, 1961
Galvão, H., and Selvagem, C., *Império Ultramarino Português.* 4 vols. Lisbon, 1950–53
Oliveira, J. da Costa, *Aplicação de capitais nas províncias ultramarinas.* Lisbon, 1961
Pattee, R., *Portugal na Africa contemporânea.* Coimbra, 1959

MACAO

HISTORY. Macao was visited by Portuguese traders from 1513 and became a Portuguese colony in 1557; it remains a Portuguese-administered territory by virtue of a Sino-Portuguese treaty of 1 Dec. 1887.

AREA AND POPULATION. The territory, which lies at the mouth of the Canton (Pearl) River, comprises a peninsula (5 sq. km) on which is built the city of Macao, and the island of Taipa (4 sq. km), linked to Macao by a 2-km bridge, and Coloane (7 sq. km) linked to Taipa by a 2-km causeway (total area, 16 sq. km (6 sq. miles). The population (Census, 1981) is 276,673, of which 90% live in the city of Macao. The official language is Portuguese, but Cantonese is used by virtually the entire population.

CONSTITUTION AND GOVERNMENT. By agreement with Beijing in 1974, Macao is a Chinese territory under Portuguese administration. An 'organic statute' was published on 17 Feb. 1976. It defined the territory as a collective entity, *pessoa colectiva,* with internal legislative authority which, while remaining subject to Portuguese constitutional laws, would otherwise enjoy administrative, economic and financial autonomy.

Governor: Adm. Vasco Almeida e Costa.

ECONOMY

Budget. The budget for 1980 balanced at 303m. *patacas.*

Currency. The unit of currency is the *pataca,* of 100 *avos,* which is tied to the Hong Kong dollar at a rate of 104 *patacas*=HK$100.

COMMERCE. The trade, mostly transit, is handled by Chinese merchants. Imports, in 1979, were 1,817·9m. patacas and exports, 2,014·3m. patacas.

COMMUNICATIONS. The province is served by a Portuguese and various

British and Dutch steamship lines. In 1977, 24,815 vessels of 7,151,287 gross tons entered the port. Regular services connect Macao with Hong Kong, 65 km to the north-east.

The province has 1,577 km of telephone line (14,364 instruments in 1981). One government and 1 private commercial radio station are in operation on medium-waves broadcasting in Portuguese and Chinese. Number of receivers (1974), 65,000.

EDUCATION. In 1980 there were 33,334 pupils and 732 teachers in elementary schools, 13,034 pupils and 619 teachers in secondary schools, and 2,261 students and 67 teachers in technical schools. A university has been established in Macao.

Books of Reference

Anuário Estatístico de Macau. Macao
Brazáo, E., *Macau.* Lisbon, 1957

STATE OF QATAR

Capital: Doha
Population: over 260,000 (1982)
GNP per capita: US$26,080 (1980)

HISTORY. The State of Qatar declared its independence from Britain on 3 Sept. 1971, ending the Treaty of 3 Nov. 1916 which was replaced by a Treaty of friendship between the 2 countries.

AREA AND POPULATION. The State of Qatar, which includes the whole of the Qatar peninsula, extends on the landward side from Khor al Odeid to the boundaries of the Saudi Arabian province of Hasa. Area, 11,437 sq. km; population estimate in 1982 over 260,000, including a number of migrant labourers from neighbouring states.

The capital is Doha (population, 190,000), which is the main port. Other towns are Dukhan, the centre of oil production, Umm Said, oil-terminal of Qatar and Ruwais, Wakra, Al-Khour and Umm-Bab.

RULER. *The Amir:* HH Shaikh Khalifa bin Hamad Al-Thani, assumed power on 22 Feb. 1972. On 31 May 1977, HH Shaikh Hamed bin Khalifa Al-Thani, was appointed Heir Apparent of the State of Qatar, the portfolio of Minister of Defence was added to his existing responsibility of Commander-in-Chief of the Armed Forces.

Foreign Minister: Shaikh Ahmed bin Saif Al-Thani.
Flag: Maroon, with white serrated border on hoist.

DEFENCE

Army. The Army consists of 2 armoured car regiments, 1 Guards' infantry battalion, 1 tank, 3 infantry and 1 artillery battalions. Personnel (1983) 5,000.

Air Force. The Air Force has 12 single-seat and 2 two-seat Mirage F1 fighters, 2 Hunter jet fighter-bombers, 1 Hunter 2-seat trainer, 2 Boeing 707, 1 Boeing 727 (VIP) and 1 Islander transport aircraft, 4 Commando, 2 Whirlwind, 3 Lynx and some Puma helicopters, 6 Alpha Jet armed trainers and Tigercat surface-to-air missile systems. Personnel (1982) 300.

INTERNATIONAL RELATIONS

Membership. Qatar is a member of UN and the Arab League.

ECONOMY

Budget. Revenue (1981) 19,243m. riyals; expenditure 14,743m. riyals.

Currency. On 13 May 1973 the Qata *Riyal* (of 100 *dirhams*) was introduced. In March 1983, £1 = 5·39 *riyals*, US$1 = 3·64 *riyals*.

Banking. Banks operating in Qatar include: Qatar National Bank, the Commercial Bank of Qatar (also Qatari-owned), the Arab Bank, Bank Al Mashrek, Bank Saderat Iran, Doha Bank, Banque de Paris et des Pays Bas, British Bank of the Middle East, the Chartered Bank, the First National City Bank, Grindlays Bank, the Bank of Oman and United Bank.

ENERGY AND NATURAL RESOURCES

Electricity. Production (1980) 1,450m. kwh.

Oil. On 9 Feb. 1977 Qatar gained national control over its 2 natural resources, oil and gas, with the signing of an agreement with Shell Qatar over the procedure for the transfer to the State of the company's remaining 40% share. A similar agreement had been reached with the Qatar Petroleum Co. on 16 Sept. 1976.

The Qatar General Petroleum Corporation (QGPC) had been established by decree in July 1974 to assume overall responsibility for the State's domestic and foreign oil interests and operations. On 16 Oct. 1976 the Qatar Petroleum Producing Authority (QPPA) was established to serve as the executive arm of the QGPC—but in 1980 it was merged into the QGPC, which now directly oversees oil production through two operational divisions, Onshore and Offshore. A new 50,000 bbls a day refinery has been constructed at Umm Said to supplement the existing 10,000 bbls a day refinery.

Production, 1981, 147,800,000m. bbls. Proven reserves (1982) 3,434,000m. bbls.

Gas. The North West Dome oilfield is being developed which contains 12% of the known world gas reserves. Production (1981) 220,000m. cu. feet (47,000 offshore).

Agriculture. 10% of the working population is engaged in agriculture and between Jan.–May Qatar is self-sufficient in fruit and vegetables.

Livestock (1980): Cattle, 7,000; camels, 9,000; sheep, 42,000; goats, 48,000; poultry, 58,000.

INDUSTRY AND TRADE

Industry. Several major projects have been established including the production of ammonia, urea and cement. The Qatar Iron and Steel Co. factory was opened in April 1978 and the Qator Petro-chemical Company polyethylene plant in Feb. 1981, both in the Umm Said industrial zone.

Commerce. In 1981 exports totalled 21,272m. riyals, and imports, 5,224m. riyals. Japan provided 18% of imports, the UK 18% and the USA 11%, while 12% of exports went to the Netherlands, 11% to Japan and 11% to France; crude oil was 95% of exports.

Total trade between Qatar and UK (British Department of Trade returns, in £1,000 sterling):

	1978	*1979*	*1980*	*1981*	*1982*
Imports to UK	30,437	40,503	44,654	10,675	33,984
Exports and re-exports from UK	90,781	101,486	101,898	135,722	245,390

Tourism. Tourism was being developed in 1978.

COMMUNICATIONS

Roads. In 1981 there were about 800 miles of road.

Aviation. The Gulf Aviation Co., Ltd (owned equally by Qatar, Bahrain, Oman and the UAE), operates daily services from Bahrain; British Airways, Middle East and about 15 other airlines operate regular international flights from Doha airport.

Shipping. Ships of several lines used to call at Umm Said; with the completion in 1969 of the new Doha port, it has become the main port of Qatar.

Post and Telecommunications. Telephone and radio-telephone services connect Qatar with Europe and America; there were 53,324 telephones in Jan. 1981. An earth satellite station was inaugurated in March 1976.

Cinemas. In 1981 there were 5 cinemas with a seating capacity of 7,000.

RELIGION, EDUCATION AND WELFARE

Religion. The population is almost entirely Moslem.

Education. There were, in 1979–80, 24,248 pupils (12,452 boys, 11,796 girls) at 85 elementary schools with 1,072 teachers in boys' and 1,836 teachers in girls' schools. In addition, 6,902 boys and 6,498 girls were attending 54 secondary schools. In 1980–81 the total number of pupils was 39,944. Students in higher institutions and universities numbered 2,700 in 1980, many of whom attended the 2 colleges of education in Doha, the nucleus of the University of the Lower Gulf.

941 university students graduated from 1976–80. Post-graduate students abroad numbered 1,305. In 1980, 7,458 men and 2,541 women attended evening classes.

Health. There are 5 hospitals (including 1 for women and 1 for gynaecology and obstetrics) with a total of 682 beds. The 660-bed hospital at Doha is nearing completion and clinics are being built throughout the State. In 1974 there were 96 doctors, 7 dentists, 3 pharmacists and 247 midwives and nursing personnel.

DIPLOMATIC REPRESENTATIVES

Of Qatar in Great Britain (27 Chesham Pl., London, SWIX 8HG)
Ambassador: Sharida Sa'ad Jubran Al Ka'abi (accredited 26 March 1981).

Of Great Britain in Qatar (Doha, Qatar)
Ambassador: S. P. Day.

Of Qatar in the USA (600 New Hampshire Ave., NW, Washington, D.C., 20037)
Ambassador: Abdelkader Braik Al-Ameri.

Of the USA in Qatar (Farig Bin Omran, Doha, Qatar)
Ambassador: Charles E. Marthinsen.

Of Qatar to the United Nations
Ambassador: Jasim Yousif Jamal.

Books of Reference

Qatar into the Seventies. Information Ministry, Doha, 1973
El Mallakh, R., *Qatar: The Development of an Oil Economy.* New York, 1979
Unwin, P. T. H., *Qatar.* [Bibliography] Oxford and Santa Barbara, 1982

ROMANIA

Republica Socialistă România

Capital: Bucharest
Population: 22·2m. (1980)
GNP per capita: US$2,340 (1980)

HISTORY. 1918 is celebrated as the year of foundation of the 'unitary national Romanian state'. For the history and constitution of Romania from 1859 to 1947, *see* THE STATESMAN'S YEAR-BOOK, 1947, pp. 1187–89. On 30 Dec. 1947 King Michael abdicated under Communist pressure and parliament proclaimed the 'People's Republic'.

AREA AND POPULATION. The area of Romania is 237,500 sq. km (91,699 sq. miles). Pre-war Romania had an area of 113,918 sq. miles. Population at censuses: 1930, 18,057,208 (14,280,729 within present-day Romania); 1948, 15,872,624 (48·3% male); 1966, 19,103,163 (49% male, 38·2% urban); 1975, 21,559,910 (49·3% male, 47·5% urban).

On 1 July 1980 the population was 22·2m., density per sq. km, 93·5. Vital statistics, 1980 (per 1,000 population): Live births, 18; deaths, 10·4; marriages, 8·2; divorces, 1·54; stillborn (per 1,000 live births), 8·7; infant mortality (per 1,000 live births), 29·3; population growth rate, 7·6 per 1,000.

Administratively, Romania is divided into 40 counties (*judeţ*), 236 towns (*oraş*) (of which 56 are municipalities) and 2,705 local authorities (*comune*). The capital is Bucharest (Bucureşti) a municipality with county status.

District	*Area in sq. km*	*Population 1980*	*Capital*	*Population 1980*
Alba	6,231	416,697	Alba Iulia	50,943
Arad	7,654	509,953	Arad	178,248
Argeş	6,801	654,247	Piteşti	139,029
Bacău	6,603	691,322	Bacău	149,033
Bihor	7,535	644,846	Oradea	184,871
Bistriţa-Năsăud	5,305	300,710	Bistriţa	55,505
Botoşani	4,965	463,981	Botoşani	78,636
Braşov	5,351	635,766	Braşov	304,670
Brăila	4,724	391,491	Brăila	214,940
Buzău	6,072	519,780	Buzău	112,760
Caraş-Severin	8,514	392,401	Reşiţa	94,040
Călăraşi	4,754	340,462	Călăraşi	60,200
Cluj	6,650	733,504	Cluj-Napoca	283,647
Constanţa	7,055	649,716	Constanţa	283,629
Covasna	3,705	215,202	Sf. Gheorghe	55,162
Dîmboviţa	4,026	549,056	Tîrgovişte	75,550
Dolj	7,413	761,559	Craiova	227,444
Galaţi	4,425	607,893	Galaţi	260,898
Giurgiu	3,810	383,301	Giurgiu	55,987
Gorj	5,641	356,554	Tîrgu Jiu	72,743
Harghita	6,610	344,546	Miercurea-Ciuc	39,521
Hunedoara	7,016	533,792	Deva	70,349
Ialomiţa	4,912	319,404	Slobozia	37,043
Iaşi	5,469	754,997	Iaşi	271,441
Maramures	6,215	516,748	Baia Mare	117,763
Mehedinţi	4,900	326,872	Drobeta-Turnu Severin	83,170
Mureş	6,696	607,551	Tîrgu Mureş	134,287
Neamţ	5,890	552,635	Piatra-Neamţ	88,145
Olt	5,507	531,972	Slatina	60,041
Prahova	4,694	841,862	Ploieşti	211,505
Satu Mare	4,405	402,482	Satu Mare	111,358
Sălaj	3,850	265,422	Zalău	40,296
Sibiu	5,422	495,530	Sibiu	161,049
Suceava	8,555	655,054	Suceava	74,513

District	Area in sq. km	Population 1980	Capital	Population 1980
Teleorman	5,870	520,987	Alexandria	40,778
Timiş	8,678	709,822	Timişoara	287,543
Tulcea	8,430	261,396	Tulcea	70,660
Vaslui	5,300	450,987	Vaslui	46,181
Vîlcea	5,705	420,670	Rîmnicu Vîlcea	78,097
Vrancea	4,863	379,809	Focşani	65,341
Bucharest [1]		2,090,408	Bucharest [2]	1,861,007

[1] Total conurbation. [2] Central area.

Ethnic groups: In 1978 there were 1·7m. Hungarians, mainly in Transylvania, and some 400,000 Germans. The official language is Romanian.

Severe financial penalties were imposed on emigrants in Nov. 1982.

CLIMATE. A continental climate with a large annual range of temperature and rainfall showing a slight summer maximum.

Bucharest. Jan. 27°F (–2·7°C), July 74°F (23·5°C). Annual rainfall 23·1″ (579 mm).

CONSTITUTION AND GOVERNMENT. The present Constitution was adopted on 21 Aug. 1965 and supersedes those of 13 April 1948 and 24 Sept. 1952. Under it Romania becomes a 'Socialist' (as opposed to 'People's') Republic. The leading role of the Communist Party is reaffirmed. The Grand National Assembly of 369 is elected for 5 years (before 1972 for 4 years). It holds short sessions twice a year, and between sessions delegates its legislative rights to the State Council (the President, head of state; 3 Vice-presidents, 1 secretary and 20 members).

All citizens of 18 and over have the right to vote and electoral law provides for the nomination of 'one or more' candidates in each constituency.

Local government is carried out by people's councils at all admistrative levels. In the municipal elections of Nov. 1982 117,316 candidates stood for 45,893 seats.

The National Council of the Socialist Democracy and Unity Front functions as a consultative body on home and foreign affairs. It has central and local councils in which workers, peasants, professional bodies, ethnic minorities and the Communist Party are represented. It replaced the Popular Democratic Front (*see* STATESMAN'S YEAR-BOOK, 1979–80).

Elections were held on 30 Nov. 1952, 3 Feb. 1957, 5 March 1961, 7 March 1965, 2 March 1969, 9 March 1975 and 9 March 1980.

At the 1980 elections 99·9% of the 15·6m. electorate voted, 98·52% of these for the Socialist Democracy and Unity Front. 2 candidates stood in 151, and 3 in 39, constituencies.

In 1965 the Romanian Workers' Party was renamed the Romanian Communist Party. The Party Congress elects the General Secretary, and its Central Committee elects the Executive Political Committee, the Permanent Bureau and the Secretariat (General Secretary and 8 secretaries). The Party had 2,960,917 members in 1980 (of whom 53% workers, 28% women). During 1982 extensive purges of Government and Party leaders took place, including the Prime Minister, Ilie Verdeţ, and other members of President Ceauşescu's family.

President of the Republic and Chairman of the State Council: Nicolae Ceauşescu, succeeded Chivu Stoica in Dec. 1967. *Vice-Chairmen:* Stefan Voitec, Gheorghe Radulescu, Iosif Kovacs, Maria Ciocan, Petru Enache.

In April 1983 the Permanent Bureau of the Party consisted of: Nicolae Ceauşescu (*General Secretary*); Ştefan Andrei; Iosif Banc; Emil Bobu; Cornel Burtică; Virgil Cazacu; Elena Ceauşescu; Nicolae Constantin; Constantin Dăscălescu; Paul Niculescu; Gheorghe Oprea; Ion Păţan; Dumitru Popescu; Gheorghe Rădulescu; Ilie Verdeţ.

Council of Ministers (April 1983). *Chairman* (*Prime Minister*): Constantin Dăscălescu. *First Deputy Prime Ministers:* Elena Ceauşescu, Gheorghe Oprea, Ion

Dinca; *Deputy Prime Ministers:* Alexandra Găinuşe; Gheorghe Petrescu; Ludovic Fazekaş; Ion Nicolae; Ioan Totu. Other ministers include: Stefan Bîrlea (*Chairman, State Planning Committee)* Ion Tesu (*Agriculture and Food*); Petre Gigea (*Finance*); Ştefan Andrei (*Foreign*); Maj.-Gen. Constantin Olteanu (*Defence*); Gheorghe Homoştean (*Interior*); Maxim Berghianu (*Labour*). Vasile Pungan (*Foreign Trade*); Gheorghe Chivulescu (*Justice*).

In July 1970 Romania signed a treaty of friendship, co-operation and mutual assistance with the USSR. A previous such treaty had expired in 1968. Since the mid-1960s Romania has been taking an increasingly independent stand in foreign affairs, and in Nov. 1978 publicized its refusal of a Soviet request to integrate its armed forces into a more unified Warsaw Pact command structure and step up its financial contributions.

National flag: Three vertical strips of blue, yellow, red, with the national arms in the centre.

National anthem: Trei culori (Three colours). Introduced, 1977. Music by Ciprian Porumbescu.

DEFENCE. Defence is the responsibility of the Defence Council, which is controlled by the Council of State and headed by President Ceauşescu.

Army. Service is 16 months. Strength in 1983 was 140,000 men plus 37,000 in paramilitary forces (frontier troops, internal-security troops, militia, military firemen).

Units of the Ministry of the National Defence are under one of the 3 military regions of Iaşi, Bucharest and Cluj. There are 2 tank and 8 motorized divisions (not all at full strength), 3 mountain brigades, 2 artillery brigades, 2 SSM brigades and 1 airborne regiment. The AA artillery consists of 2 regiments. There are 1,700 T-34, T-54, T-55 and T-72 tanks. A Territorial Defence Force was set up in 1970.

Navy. The fleet comprises 3 small escorts, 5 fast missile boats, 25 fast torpedo boats, 20 fast gunboats, 3 old patrol vessels, 4 old minesweepers, 20 inshore minesweepers, 2 training ships, 8 minesweeping boats, 42 river patrol craft, 12 landing craft, 2 survey vessels, 10 transports, 3 oilers and 4 tugs. Headquarters of the Navy is at Mangalia, and of the Danube flotilla at the main river port of Brăila. The naval school is in Constanţa. Personnel in 1983 totalled 10,500 officers and ratings including 2,000 Coastal Defence. National service is 2 years.

Air Force. Service is 2 years. The Air Force numbers some 34,000 men, with 290 combat aircraft in 2 air divisions (4 regiments). These are organized into 12 interceptor squadrons with MiG-21 fighters, 6 ground-attack and close-support squadrons with MiG-17 fighters, and 1 reconnaissance squadron of Il-28s. There are also more than 300 training aircraft, An-24/26/30 transports and helicopters. Under delivery are 185 IAR-93 close-support/interceptors, and Puma helicopters. 'Guideline' and 'Gaskin' surface-to-air missiles are operational, and short-range surface-to-surface missiles have been displayed.

INTERNATIONAL RELATIONS

Membership. Romania is a member of UN, IMF, Comecon and the Warsaw Pact.

ECONOMY

Planning. In Oct. 1982 the Supreme Council of Economic and Social Development, presided over by Nicolae Ceauşescu, was raised to the level of an economic legislative chamber. Annual growth targets of the sixth 5-year plan (1981–85): GNP, 9%; national income, 10%; industrial production, 10%; agricultural production, 24·5–27·5%. Romania is committed to intensive industrialization and President Ceauşescu admitted in Feb. 1981 that agriculture had been neglected. Bread rationing was introduced in Oct. 1981 and food prices were raised by 35% in Feb. 1982. Virtual rationing was introduced in 1982 in the form of limitations of calorie intake. Industries scheduled for particular development: machine-building, iron and steel, non-ferrous metals, chemicals and electric power. A 10-year programme introduced in 1980 is designed to make Romania self-sufficient in energy. For previous plans *see* THE STATESMAN'S YEAR-BOOK, 1976–77.)

There is no move towards any fundamental decentralization of planning authority but limited devolutions of reponsibility in an attempt to improve efficiency were introduced in 1967 and 1979. There are 102 economic units intermediate between ministeries and enterprises.

Budget. Revenue and expenditure (in 1m. lei) for calendar years:

	1974	*1975*	*1976*	*1977*	*1978*	*1979*	*1980*
Revenue	210,111	238,553	254,528	281,980	300,836	339,309	298,004
Expenditure	207,322	236,169	250,148	280,423	299,314	337,629	296,787

In 1980 sources of revenue (in 1m. lei) included: Profit payments of state enterprises, 151,995; turnover tax, 39,420; personal taxes, 38,136; insurance contributions, 32,324. Expenditure: National economy, 185,081; social and cultural, 70,978; defence, 10,394.

Revenues of local councils yielded 53,140m. lei in 1980; expenditure, 51,988m.

In 1974 a Court of Preventive Financial control was set up to oversee most official transactions and combat waste and corruption.

By an agreement signed 12 Jan. 1976 Romania paid £3·5m. as 'full and final settlement' of defaulted Romanian bonds held by UK citizens in 4 annual instalments of £875,000 starting at the end of 1976. Payments of £1·25m. in settlement of UK claims arising out of the peace treaty were completed by 31 Jan. 1967.

Currency. The monetary unit is the *leu*, pl.*lei* (of 100 *bani*). On 1 Feb. 1954 the gold content of the leu was to 0·148112 gramme of fine gold. Exchange rates (March 1983): £1 = 6·80 lei; US$1 = 4·47 lei; 1 rouble = 6·67 lei. Tourist rates: £1 = 20·40 lei; US$1 = 11 lei; 1 rouble = 8·30 lei.

Bank-notes of 1, 5, 10, 25, 50 and 100 *lei* are issued by the National Bank, and there are coins of 5, 10, 15 and 25 *bani* and 1, 3 and 5 *lei*.

Banking. The National Bank of Romania (founded 1880, nationalized 1946) is the State Bank under the Minister of Finance. Half its profits are allotted to the State budget. There are also a Bank of Investments, a Foreign Trade Bank, an Agriculture and Food Industry Bank and a Savings Bank. In 1972 Romania joined IMF. The US Export-Import Bank has granted Romania borrowing rights. In 1974 the American bank Manufactures Hanover Trust Co. opened a branch in Bucharest, the first Western bank to do so in a Communist country.

Weights and measures. The Gregorian calendar was adopted in 1919. The metric system is in use. Tubes and pipes are measured in *tol* (= 1 inch).

ENERGY AND NATURAL RESOURCES

Electricity. Installed electric power 1980: 16,109,000 kw.; output (1980), 67,958m. kwh. A joint Romanian–Yugoslav hydro-electric power plant on the Danube at the 'Iron Gates' was opened in 1972; yearly output is 11,000m. kwh. A nuclear power programme has been subject to cut-backs and delays. A nuclear power station (capacity 660,000 kw.) is due to open in 1985.

Oil. The oilfields are in the Prahova, Băcau, Gorj, Crişana and Argeş districts. Petrol prices were raised by 60% and restrictions placed on official and private car use in 1979. Oil imports are approximately equivalent to domestic production. Oil reserves are expected to be exhausted by the mid-1990s.

Minerals. The principal minerals are oil and natural gas, salt, brown coal, lignite, iron and copper ores, bauxite, chromium, manganese and uranium. Salt is mined in the lower Carpathians and in Transylvania; production in 1980 was 5·1m. tonnes.

Output, 1980 (and 1979) (in 1,000 tonnes): Iron ore, 2,511 (2,333); crude oil, 11,511 (12,323); coal, 37,814 (34,888); methane gas (cu. metres), 28,156m.

(27,189m.). The share of coal in the overall production of energy rose from 28% in 1975 to 40% in 1980 and is expected to reach 60% by 1990.

Agriculture. There were 14·96m. hectares of agricultural land in 1980, including (in 1,000 hectares): Arable, 9,834; meadows and pasture, 4,467; vineyards and fruit trees, 662.

Production in 1980 (in 1,000 tonnes): Wheat and rye, 6,467; barley, 2,466; maize, 11,153; potatoes, 4,135; sunflower seeds, 817; sugar-beet, 5,562.

Livestock (1981): 6·5m. cattle, 11·5m. pigs, 15·9m. sheep and 97·8m. poultry.

In 1980 there were 4,643 collective farms, with 9m. hectares of land (7·3m. arable; 921,200 in private plots). State farms numbered 407, with 2m. hectares of land, of which 1·64m. hectares were arable. A further 2·4m. hectares of land were in the hands of other state agricultural organizations. There were 714 agriculture mechanization stations with 140,074 tractors. Individual holdings totalled 1·41m. hectares. In Aug. 1981 the Government allocated more land to individuals to encourage production. The National Union of Agricultural Co-operatives promotes self-management in collective farms, and gives guidance on planning and marketing. A minimum income is guaranteed to peasants. In 1982 there were 2·3m. hectares of irrigated land.

Forestry. Total forest area was 6·34m. hectares in 1980. In 1980, 62,241 hectares were afforested.

INDUSTRY AND TRADE

Industry. Output of main products in 1980 (and 1979) (in tonnes): Pig-iron, 9,012 (8,879); steel, 13,157 (12,909); steel tubes, 1,464 (1,500); blast furnace coke, 3,033 (3,066); rolled steel, 9,319 (9,482); chemical fertilizers, 2,451 (2,522); washing soda, 937 (893); caustic soda, 723 (704); paper, 822 (819); cement, 15,611 (14,656); sugar, 509 (525); edible oils, 369 (375); butter, 35 (40). Fabrics (in 1m. sq. metres): Cotton, 748 (707); woollens, 128 (125); man-made fibres, 205,753 (196,200). In 1,000 units: Radio sets, 863 (757); TV sets, 541 (574); bicycles, 214 (205); washing machines, 344 (294); refrigerators, 376 (446); motor cars, 88,232 (75,020); footwear, 113m. pairs (104m.).

Labour. The employed population in 1980 was 10·35m., of whom 3·05m. worked in agriculture and 4·52m. industry and building. Wage differentials are in accordance with the 'social evaluation' of the work and a range of incentives for productivity. The average monthly wage was 2,256 lei in 1980. Minimum monthly wage 1,425 lei in 1980. The working week is of 44 hours with alternate Saturdays free. Men retire at 62, women at 57. The chairman of the trade union organization ceased to exercise the functions of Minister of Labour in 1981. An independent trade union movement which emerged in Feb. 1979 was subject to police prosecution.

Commerce. Some 60% of external trade is with Communist countries (15% with the USSR).

In 1980 exports totalled 53,890m. lei and imports 59,006m. lei.

Principal exports in 1980 were (in 1,000 tonnes): Petroleum products, 9,175; cement, 2,791; cereals, 1,720; tractors, 52,744 units; oilfield equipment, 1,852m. lei; equipment for cement mills, 80m. lei; equipment for chemical factories, 483m lei; shipbuilding, 852m. lei. Principal imports (in 1,000 tonnes): Iron ore, 15,984; industrial coke, 3,133; rolled ferrous metals, 1,040; electrical equipment, 1,239m. lei; motor cars, 19,329 units, and industrial and agricultural equipment.

In 1980 Romania's main trading partners (trade in 1m. lei) were: USSR (19,286), Federal Republic of Germany (8,299), USA (6,453), German Democratic Republic (5,647), Iraq (5,528), China (5,361).

Total trade between Romania and UK for calendar years (British Department of Trade returns, in £1,000 sterling):

	1978	*1979*	*1980*	*1981*	*1982*
Imports to UK	51,724	65,914	64,795	46,518	51,515
Exports and re-exports from UK	74,965	70,372	98,914	150,256	115,244

On 18 Sept. 1975 Romania and the UK signed a 10-year economic co-

operation agreement. In Nov. 1976 Romania and the USA signed a 10-year commercial agreement. Both the UK and the USA have joint economic commissions with Romania.

Romania owed some US$10,000m. to Western banks in 1982, and unilaterally suspended principal payments in Jan. 1973 pending a rescheduling of the loans. The IMF suspended credit from Nov. 1981 until certain economic conditions were accepted by Romania in June 1982.

Joint companies with Western firms have been set up; at least 51% of the capital must be in Romanian hands. The 'Romconsult' and 'Publicom' agencies will carry out respectively market research and publicity campaigns on behalf of foreign firms.

Romania has a trade link with EEC under the generalized preference system.

Agreements with the EEC on industrial products and establishing a joint economic commission were reached in March 1980.

On 1 Jan. 1975 a 2-tier tariff system was introduced, graded according to the grant of most favoured nation status to Romania.

COMMUNICATIONS

Roads. There were in 1980, 14,676 km of national roads of which 11,453 km were modernized. Freight carried, 451m. tons; passengers, 1,034m.

Railways. Length of route (1,435 mm gauge) in 1980 was 11,110 km and (narrow-gauge), 559 km. A total of 2,367 km is electrified. Freight carried, 275m. tons; passengers, 348m.

Aviation. TAROM (*Transporturi Aeriene Române*), the state airline, operates all internal services, and also services to Amsterdam, Athens, Beirut, Belgrade, Berlin, Brussels, Budapest, Cairo, Cologne, Copenhagen, Düsseldorf, Frankfurt, Istanbul, London, Moscow, Paris, Prague, Rome, Sofia, Tel-Aviv, Vienna, Warsaw and Zürich. Bucharest is also served by British Airways, PANAM, SABENA, Aeroflot, Air France, Interflug, ČSA, MALEV, Austrian Air Lines, SAS, Lot, TABSO, El Al, Alitalia, Lufthansa and Swissair. An air agreement with China was signed in 1973.

Bucharest's airports are at Băneasa (internal flights) and Otopeni (international flights; 12 miles from Bucharest). Air transport in 1980 carried 1,871,000 passengers and 33,000 tons of freight.

Shipping. The main ports are Constanţa on the Black Sea and Galaţi and Brăila on the Danube. A new port is under construction at Mangalia on the Black Sea. The largest shipyard is at Galaţi.

In 1975 the mercantile marine (NAVROM) had 94 ships totalling 1,365,000 DWT. In 1980 sea-going transport carried 16·21m. tons of freight; river transport, 12·34m. tons.

Post and Broadcasting. *Radio-televiziunea Româna* broadcasts 3 programmes on medium-waves and FM. There are also 6 regional programmes, including transmission in Hungarian, German and Serbo-Croat. Two TV programmes are broadcast. Number of telephone subscribers, in 1980, 1,617,707. Radio receiving sets, in 1980 3·2m.; TV sets, 3·7m.

Cinemas and Theatres. There were, in 1980, 5,801 cinemas and 148 theatres and concert halls. 32 full-length feature films were made in 1980.

Newspapers. There were, in 1980, 59 newspapers and 432 periodicals. These figures include 38 in minority languages. The party newspaper is *Scînteia* ('The Spark').

JUSTICE, RELIGION, EDUCATION AND WELFARE

Justice. Justice is administered by the Supreme Court, the 40 district courts, and lower courts. Lay assessors (elected for 4 years) participate in most court trials, collaborating with the judges. The Procurator-General exercises 'supreme supervisory power to ensure the observance of the law' by all authorities, central and local, and all citizens. The Procurator's Office and its organs are independent of any organs of justice or administration, and only responsible to the Grand National Assembly (which appoints the Procurator-General for 4 years) and between its sessions, to the State Council. The Ministry of the Interior is responsible for ordinary police work. State security is the responsibility of the State Security Council. A new penal code came into force on 1 Jan. 1969. It is based on 'the rule of law' and is aimed at preventing illegal trials. The death penalty is retained for 'specially serious offences' (treason, some classes of murder, theft of property having serious consequences).

Religion. Churches are organized and function in accordance with art. 30 of the Constitution. Churches administer their own affairs and run seminaries for the training of priests. Expenses and salaries are paid by the State. There are 14 Churches, all under the control of the 'Department of Cults'. The largest is the Romanian Orthodox Church, which claimed 13·67m. members in 1950. It is autocephalous, but retains dogmatic unity with the Eastern Orthodox Church. It is administered by the consultative Holy Synod and National Ecclesiastical Assembly and the executive National Ecclesiastical Council and Patriarchal Administration. It is organized into 12 dioceses grouped into 5 metropolitan bishoprics (Hungaro-Wallachia; Moldavia-Suceava; Transylvania; Olt; Banat), and headed by Patriarch Justin Moisescu (since May 1948). There are some 11,800 churches, 2 theological colleges and 6 'schools of cantors', as well as seminaries.

The Uniate (Greek Catholic) Church (which severed its connexion with the Vatican in 1698) was suppressed in 1948. It had 1·6m. adherents and 1,818 priests. Estimates for 1973: 700,000 adherents and 600 priests.

Other churches: Serbs have a Serbian Orthodox Vicariate at Timişoara. In 1979 there were 1·4m. Roman Catholics, mainly among the Hungarian and German minorities. There is a bishop of Alba Iulia. There were 820 priests and 254 monks in 1958. The Church has not secured approval for a Statute and has no hierarchical ties with the Vatican.

Calvinists (780,000; mainly Hungarian) have bishoprics at Cluj and Oradea; Lutherans (250,000, mainly Germans) a bishopric at Sibiu and Unitarians bishoprics at Cluj and Timişoara. These sects share a seminary at Cluj.

In 1973 there were 70 Jewish communities comprising some 90,000 persons under a Chief Rabbi (Moses Rosen). There were 130 synagogues.

Moslems have a Muftiate at Constanţa.

Education. Education is free and compulsory for 10 years (6 to 16), consisting of 8 years of primary school and 2 years of secondary (gymnasium). Further secondary education is available at *lycées*, professional schools or advanced technical schools.

In 1980–81[1] there were 13,467 kindergartens with 38,512 teachers and 935,711 children; 14,381 primary and secondary schools with 156,817 teachers and 3,308,462 pupils; 971 *lycées* with 46,500 teachers and 979,741 pupils; 603 professional schools with 1,954 teachers and 139,758 pupils; and 300 advanced technical schools with 257 teachers and 28,380 pupils. There are general and secondary schools for minorities, with over 250,000 pupils.

There are universities at Iaşi (founded 1860), Bucharest (1864), Cluj (1919), Timişoara (1962), Craiova (1965) and Braşov (1971). In 1980–81 there were in all 134 faculties of higher education, with a student population of 192,769.

The Academy, with seat at Bucharest, has 2 branches at Iaşi and Cluj. The National Council for Scientific Research co-ordinates research.

[1] Figures include evening classes.

Health. In 1980 there were 208,213 hospital beds and 39,791 doctors.

DIPLOMATIC REPRESENTATIVES

Of Romania in Great Britain (4 Palace Green, London, W8 4QD)
Ambassador: Vasile Gliga.

Of Great Britain in Romania (24 Strada Jules Michelet, Bucharest)
Ambassador: P. C. H. Holmer, CMG.

Of Romania in the USA (1607–23rd St., NW, Washington, D.C., 20008)
Ambassador: Mircea Malitza.

Of the USA in Romania (7–9 Strada Tudor Arghezi, Bucharest)
Ambassador: David B. Funderburk.

Of Romania to the United Nations
Ambassador: Teodor Marinescu.

Books of Reference

Anuarul Statistic al R.S.R. Bucharest, annual
Atlas Geografic Republica Socialistă Romania. Bucharest, 1965
Dicţionar Enciclopedic Român. Bucharest, 1962–66
Economic and Commercial Guide to Romania. Bucharest, annual since 1969
Mic Dicţionar Enciclopedic. Bucharest, 1973
Revista de Statistică. Bucharest, monthly
Romania: An Encyclopaedic Survey. Bucharest, 1980
Romania Facts and Figures. Bucharest, 1980
Academia Republicii Socialiste România. *Dicţionar Englez-Român.* Bucharest, 1974
Ceauçescu, N.,. *Romania on the Way of Completing Socialist Construction.* 3 vols. Bucharest, 1968–69.—*Romania on the Way of Completing the Many-sided Developed Socialist Society.* Bucharest, 1970 *ff.*
Fischer-Galati, S. A., *Rumania: A Bibliographical Guide.* Library of Congress, 1963.—*The New Rumania.* Mass. Inst. of Technology, 1968.—*The Socialist Republic of Rumania.* Baltimore, 1969.—*Twentieth Century Rumania.* New York, 1970
Gilberg, T., *Modernization in Romania Since World War II.* New York, 1975
Giurescu, C. C. (ed.), *Chronological History of Romania.* 2nd ed. Bucharest, 1974
Graham, L. S., *Romania, a Developing Socialist State.* Boulder, 1982
Hemy, G. W., *Romania: Business Opportunities.* London, 1977
Ionescu, A. (ed.), *The Grand National Assembly of the Socialist Republic of Romania: A Brief Outline.* Bucharest, 1974
King, R. R., *History of the Romanian Communist Party.* Stanford, 1980
Leviţchi, L., *Dicţionar Român-Englez.* 2nd ed. Bucharest, 1965
Morariu, T., and others, *The Geography of Rumania.* 2nd ed. Bucharest, 1969
Nelson, D. N. (ed.), *Romania in the 1980's.* Boulder, 1981
Turnock, D., *An Economic Geography of Romania.* London, 1974

RWANDA

Capital: Kigali
Population: 5·11m. (1981)
GNP per capita: US$200 (1980)

HISTORY. From the 16th century to 1959 the Tutsi kingdom of Rwanda shared the history of Burundi (*see* p. 255). In 1959 an uprising of the Hutu destroyed the Tutsi feudal hierarchy and led to the departure of the Mwami Kigeri V. Elections and a referendum under the auspices of the United Nations in Sept. 1961 resulted in an overwhelming majority for the republican party, the Parmehutu (*Parti du Mouvement de l'Emancipation du Bahutu*), and the rejection of the institution of the Mwami. The republic proclaimed by the Parmehutu on 28 Jan. 1961 was recognized by the Belgian administration (but not by the United Nations) in Oct. 1961. Internal self-government was granted on 1 Jan. 1962, and by decision of the General Assembly of the UN the Republic of Rwanda became independent on 1 July 1962. An agreement, signed with Burundi under United Nations auspices at Addis Ababa in April 1962, provided for a monetary and customs union. These and other common organizations came to an end by 1 Oct. 1964.

AREA AND POPULATION. Rwanda lies between lat. 1° and 3° S. and long. 29° and 31° E., with an area of 26,330 sq. km (10,166 sq. miles). The Nile–Congo mountain divide (about 9,000 ft) and the Kirunga volcanoes (Mt. Karisimbi, 14,825 ft), rising steeply from Lake Kivu in the west, slope down first to a hilly central plateau (7,000–5,000 ft) and farther eastwards to a complex of marshy lakes in the upper reaches of the Kagera River. Rwanda is bounded in the south by Burundi, in the west by Lake Kivu and the Congo, in the north by Uganda and in the east by Tanzania.

The population, the densest in Africa outside the Nile delta (182 inhabitants per sq. km) was 4,819,317 (Census 1978); estimate (1981) 5·11m. There are 3 ethnic groups, the Tutsi (Nilotic), the Hutu (Bantu) and a few Twa (pygmoid). The Tutsi, traditionally the ruling caste and about 15% of the population have greatly diminished in number since the troubles of 1959–61, as a result of which over 140,000 took refuge in neighbouring territories. In Jan. 1964 several thousand Tutsi were massacred by the Hutu, and an exodus of 12,000 more Tutsi followed. The Tutsi now form only 9% of the population. There are some 1,200 Europeans and 750 Asians.

Kigali, the capital, had a census population of 117,749 in 1978. Nyanza (between Kigali and Butare) is the seat of the High Court. Other centres are Gisenyi (12,436) and Cyangugu on Lake Kivu, Butare (21,691) and Ruhengeri (16,025).

Vital statistics (1975): Live births, 113,154; deaths, 41,385; marriages, 13,899.

GOVERNMENT. Rwanda is a republic with an executive President as Head of State, assisted by a Council of 12 Ministers. The National Assembly consists of 47 members elected by universal suffrage for 4 years. The administrative divisions are 10 prefectures (Kigali, Kibungo, Byumba, Ruhengeri, Gisenyi, Kibuye, Gitarama, Gikongoro, Butare, Cyangugu) and 144 communes.

On 5 July 1973 President Gégoire Kayibanda who had been in office since 1961 was deposed in a bloodless *coup*. A new Constitution was introduced in Dec. 1978.

President: Maj.-Gen Juvénal Habyarimana (confirmed in office for 5-year term in Dec. 1978).

Foreign Affairs: François Ngarukiyintwari.

Flag: Three equal vertical panels of red, yellow and green (left to right), the letter 'R' in black superimposed on the centre panel.

DEFENCE

Army. The national army had a strength of 5,000 (1983) all ranks, including a Belgian cadre.

Air Force. Initial equipment ordered for the Air Force in 1972 comprised 3 Italian-built Aeritalia/Aermacchi AM.3C liaison aircraft, now supplemented by 3 armed Magister jet trainers, 1 twin-engined Defender, 2 C-47s, 2 Islander light transports and 2 Alouette III helicopters. A Caravelle is operated on VIP duties. Personnel, about 150.

INTERNATIONAL RELATIONS

Membership. Rwanda is a member of UN, OAU and is an ACP state of EEC. With Burundi and Zaïre it forms part of the Economic Community of Countries of the Great Lakes.

ECONOMY

Planning. The 1981–90 Development Plan gave priority to rural development.

Budget. The budget for 1982 envisaged expenditure of US$174·5m.

Currency. The currency is the *Rwanda franc*. The official rate of Rwanda francs 140·10 = £1; 92·84 = US$1 (March 1983).

Banking. On 5 April 1967 the Development Bank of Rwanda *(Banque Rwandaise de Développement—BRD)* was created with a capital of 50m. Rwanda francs. On 1 Sept. 1978 the share capital was expanded to 416m. Rwanda francs with ownership distributed as follows: Public sector 62·5%, domestic private sector 15·8%, foreign shareholders 21·7%. Other banks are the Central Bank *(Banque Nationale du Rwanda)*; 2 commercial banks which are majority foreign owned—the *Banque Commerciale du Rwanda* and the *Banque de Kigali*; the People's Bank, the Savings Association and the *Caisse Hypothécaire.*

AGRICULTURE. Subsistence agriculture accounts for most of the gross national product. Staple food crops are beans, cassava, maize, sweet potatoes, peas, groundnuts and sorghum. The annual rainfall varies from under 40 in. in the north-east to 60 in. in the west and over 70 in. in the extreme north-west.

The main cash crop is *aravica* coffee in Burundi; the 1980 crop was about 430,000 sacks (60 kg). Tea and pyrethrum are also produced. There is a pilot rice-growing project.

On 30 July 1964 the Rwanda Industrial Produce Bureau was established, which is responsible for organizing and controlling the quality of Rwandese agricultural exports, notably coffee. Coffee exports (1978) 23,700 tons earning 4,200m. Rwanda francs.

Tea plantations are being developed and projects are being financed by the World Bank and the African Development Bank. Fresh vegetables are produced for export (600 tonnes, 1975).

Long-horned Ankole cattle, 639,000 head in 1980, play an important traditional role. Efforts are being made to improve their present negligible economic value. There were (1981) 920,000 goats and some 300,000 sheep.

INDUSTRY. There are about 100 small-sized modern manufacturing enterprises in the country. Food manufacturing is the dominant industrial activity (64%) followed by construction (15·3%) and mining (9%). There are 4 hydro-electric installations and a large modern brewery. The industrial sector's contribution to GDP in 1976 was 23%.

COMMERCE. Imports (1980) US$195·8m. and exports US$133·6m.

Total trade between Rwanda and UK (British Department of Trade returns, in £1,000 sterling):

	1978	*1979*	*1980*	*1981*	*1982*
Imports to UK	3,576	4,145	4,666	2,058	510
Exports and re-exports from UK	1,220	1,508	1,245	1,446	2,079

COMMUNICATIONS

Roads. There are about (1975) 8,000 miles of main and 3,500 miles of secondary roads. There are road links with Burundi, Uganda, Tanzania and Zaïre. There were in 1976 3,352 cars and 4,456 trucks. Most imports and exports travel to and from Mombasa *via* Uganda.

Shipping. Shipping on Lake Kivu in 1967 amounted to 70,000 tonnes. Kigali has an international airport, with services to Bujumbura, Bukavu *via* Kamembe, Entebbe, Goma, Lubumbashi, Athens and Brussels.

Post. Telephones (1978) 4,543.

Cinemas. In 1975 there were 3 cinemas with a seating capacity of 1,000.

RELIGION, EDUCATION AND WELFARE

Religion. The population is predominantly Roman Catholic (45%); there is an archbishop (Kabgayi) and 3 bishops. 45% of the population follow traditional religions, 9% are Protestants and 1% Moslems. The Ruanda Mission of the Church Missionary Society have 4 stations.

Education. In 1979 there were 515,712 pupils attending primary schools with (1977) 8,161 teachers. There were secondary schools of various types with a total of 13,799 pupils and (1977) 820 teachers. The National University, opened at Butare in 1963, had 975 students in 1979.

The local language is Kinyarwanda, a Bantu language. French is also an official language, and Kiswahili is spoken in the commercial centres.

Health. In 1976 there were 272 hospitals and health centres with 8,383 beds; there were also 109 doctors, 3 dentists, 10 pharmacists, 527 midwives and 268 nursing personnel.

DIPLOMATIC REPRESENTATIVES

Of Rwanda in Great Britain
Ambassador: Callixte Hatungimana (resides in Brussels).

Of Great Britain in Rwanda
Ambassador: J. M. O. Snodgrass, CMG (resides in Kinshasa).

Of Rwanda in the USA (1714 New Hampshire Ave, NW, Washington, D.C., 20009)
Ambassador: Simon Insonere.

Of the USA in Rwanda (Blvd. de la Revolution, Kigali)
Chargé d'Affaires: Donald V. Hester.

Of Rwanda to the United Nations
Ambassador: Juvénal Renzaho.

Books of Reference

Hance, W. A., *African Economic Development.* London, 1967
Lacroix, B., *Le Rwanda.* Montreal, 1966
Northumb, D., *Un Humanisme Africain.* Brussels, 1965

ST CHRISTOPHER (ST KITTS)—NEVIS

Capital: Basseterre
Population: 44,404 (1980)
GNP capita: US$ 920 (1980)

HISTORY. St Christopher (known to its Carib inhabitants as *Liamuiga*) and Nevis were discovered and named by Columbus in 1493. They were settled by Britain in 1623 and 1628 respectively, but ownership was disputed with France until 1713. Forming part of the Leeward Islands Federation from 1871 to 1956, and part of the Federation of the West Indies from 1958 to 1962, the colony achieved self-government as an Associated State of the UK on 27 Feb. 1967.

AREA AND POPULATION. The islands form part of the Lesser Antilles in Eastern Caribbean. The area is 261 sq. km: St Kitts, 168; Nevis, 93. Population, 1980: St Kitts, 35,104; Nevis, 9,300. Chief town of St Kitts, Basseterre (14,725); of Nevis, Charlestown (1,771).

CONSTITUTION AND GOVERNMENT. In Feb. 1967 the colonial status was replaced by an 'association' with Britain, giving the islands full internal self-government, while Britain remains responsible for defence and foreign affairs. There is an elected House of Assembly and a cabinet system of Government. The Premier is the head of the Government and presides at cabinet meetings.

Discussions on independence were taking place in 1983.

Governor: Sir Clement Athelston Arrindell.

Prime Minister: Dr Kennedy Alphonse Simmonds.

Flag: Three vertical stripes of green (for agriculture), yellow (for sunshine), blue (for the sky), with a black palm tree in the centre of the flag.

ECONOMY

Budget. The 1982 budget envisaged revenue of EC$105,044,598 and expenditure of EC$104,591,599.

Banking. The National Bank operates 4 branches in St. Kitts and Nevis. The main office is located in Basseterre. Other banks include Barclay's Bank International, with a sub-branch in Nevis, Royal Bank of Canada, Bank of Commerce, and the Nevis Co-operative Bank in Charlestown. A branch of the Bank of Nova Scotia is located in Basseterre.

AGRICULTURE. The main crops are sugar and cotton. There are 30 sugar estates and 202 acres of cotton. Most of the farms are small-holdings and there are a number of coconut estates amounting to some 1,000 acres under private ownership. Sugar production (1982) 35,955 tons and 48 bales of cotton were produced in 1980.

INDUSTRY AND TRADE

Industry. The main employer of labour is the sugar industry.

Commerce. Imports, (1981) EC$128·77m.; exports, EC$65·5m. Chief exports (1981) were sugar (29,131 tons) and molasses (1·3m. gallons).

Tourism. In 1981, there were 35,484 tourists.

COMMUNICATIONS

Roads. There are about 200 km of roads.

Railways. There are 36 miles of railway operated by the sugar industry.

Shipping. A deep water port was opened in 1981 at Bird Rock with accommodation for cargo, tourist, roll-on-roll-off ships and bulk sugar and molasses loading.

Aviation. There is an airport at Golden Rock (St Kitts) which is served by BWIA, LIAT, WINAIR, PRINAIR, AIR BVI, CARICARGO. 35,296 passengers arrived by air in 1981.

Post and Telecommunications. There is a general post office in Basseterre. Five branches are on the island. Charlestown has a general post office, and there are two branches in Nevis. There were 3,290 telephones on 1 Oct. 1982.

JUSTICE AND EDUCATION

Justice. Justice is administered by the Supreme Court and by Magistrates' Courts. They have both civil and criminal jurisdiction.

Education. There were (1982) 34 government, 14 private and 6 denominational schools in St Kitts and Nevis. Primary education is compulsory for all children between the ages of 5 and 14, but no pupil is required to leave school before the age of 16 years. There is an Extra-Mural Department of the University of the West Indies, a Technical College and a Teachers' Training College which prepares approximately 30 teachers annually in a two-year course.

Library: Public Library, Basseterre. *Librarian:* Miss V. Archibald.

ST HELENA

Capital: Jamestown
Population: 5,268 (1981)

HISTORY. The island was administered by the East India Company from 1659 and became a British colony in 1834.

AREA AND POPULATION. St Helena, of volcanic origin, is 1,200 miles from the west coast of Africa. Area, 47 sq. miles (121·7 sq. km), with a cultivable area of about 600 acres (243 hectares). The port of the island is Jamestown, population (1976) 1,516.

Population (1981), 5,268. Births, 129; deaths, 47; marriages, 44.

GOVERNMENT. The Government of St Helena is administered by a Governor, with the aid of a Legislative Council consisting of the Governor, 2 *ex-officio* members (the Government Secretary and the Treasurer) and 12 elected members. Committees of the Legislative Council are responsible for the general oversight of the activities of government departments and have, in addition, statutory and administrative functions.

The Governor is also assisted by an Executive Council consisting of the 2 *ex-officio* members and the chairmen of the five Council committees.

Governor and C.-in-C.: J. D. Massingham.
Government Secretary: P. Dale, OBE.

Flag: The British Blue Ensign with the shield of the colony in the fly.

FINANCE AND TRADE, for years from 1 April-31 March, in £ sterling:

	1975-76	*1976-77*	*1977-78*	*1978-79*	*1979-80*	*1980-81*
Revenue [1]	1,481,539	2,014,981	2,244,550	2,683,681	4,226,899	4,488,257
Expenditure [1]	1,544,027	1,952,642	2,200,299	2,764,150	4,325,910	4,551,657
Imports [2]	1,192,418	1,430,168	1,758,337	1,164,437	1,835,000	2,117,126

[1] Including imperial grants (1975-76, £1,060,342; 1976-77, £1,461,739; 1977-78, £1,657,231; 1978-79, £1,771,618; 1979-80, £3,347,631; 1980-81, £3,232,093).
[2] Including government stores.

The revenue from customs was, in 1975-76, £93,039; 1976-77, £122,029; 1977-78, £150,438; 1978-79, £193,576; 1979-80, £215,995; 1980-81, £283,068.

The colony's liabilities at 31 March 1981 exceeded the assets by £151,644.

Total trade between Ascension and St Helena and UK (British Department of Trade returns, in £1,000 sterling):

	1977	*1978*	*1979*	*1980*	*1981*	*1982*
Imports to UK	156	192	207	476	224	754
Exports and re-exports from UK	2,387	2,031	2,570	3,016	3,471	7,049

BANKING. Savings-bank deposits on 31 March 1981, £1,238,766, belonging to 3,447 depositors.

COMMUNICATIONS

Roads. There were 85 km of all-weather motor roads.

Shipping. The number of merchant vessels that called in 1980-81 was 28; total tonnage entered and cleared was 453,468.

Post and Broadcasting. The Cable & Wireless Ltd cable connects St Helena with Cape Town and Ascension Island. There is a telephone service with 85 miles of wire and (1981), 310 telephones.

St Helena Government Broadcasting Station broadcasts in English on medium-waves. Number of radio receivers (1981), 1,500.

JUSTICE, RELIGION, EDUCATION AND WELFARE

Justice. Police force, 31; cases dealt with by police magistrate, 205 in 1981.

Religion. There are 10 Anglican churches and 4 Baptist chapels.

Education. Three pre-school playgroups, 8 primary, 3 senior and 1 secondary schools controlled by the Government had 1,251 pupils in Sept. 1981.

Health. There were 3 doctors, 1 dentist and 54 hospital beds in 1981.

Ascension is a small island of volcanic origin, of 34 sq. miles (88 sq. km), 700 miles north-west of St Helena. In Nov. 1922 the administration was transferred from the Admiralty to the Colonial Office and annexed to the colony of St Helena. There are 120 hectares providing fresh meat, vegetables and fruit. Population, 31 Dec. 1981, was 971; St Helenians 617, others 354.

The island is the resort of sea turtles, which come to lay their eggs in the sand annually between Jan. and May. Rabbits, wild goats and partridges are more or less numerous on the island, which is, besides, the breeding ground of the sooty tern or 'wideawake', these birds coming in vast numbers to lay their eggs every eighth month.

Cable & Wireless Ltd own and operate a cable station, connecting the island with St Helena, Sierra Leone, St Vincent, Rio de Janeiro and Buenos Aires. There is an airstrip (Miracle Mile) near the settlement of Georgetown.

Administrator: B. E. Pauncefort.

Tristan da Cunha, a small group of islands in the Atlantic, halfway between the Cape and South America, in 37° 6′ S. lat., 12° 1′ W. long. Besides Tristan da Cunha and Gough Island, there are Inaccessible and Nightingale Islands, the former 2 and the latter 1 mile long, and a number of rocks. As from 12 Jan. 1938 the 4 islands have become dependencies of St Helena.

Tristan consists of a volcano rising to a height of 6,760 ft, with a circumference at its base of 21 miles. The volcano, believed to be extinct, erupted unexpectedly early in Oct. 1961. The whole population was evacuated without loss and settled temporarily in the UK. In 1963 they returned to Tristan where they all dwell in the settlement of Edinburgh.

Before the disaster occurred the habitable area was a small plateau on the north west side of about 12 sq. miles, 100 ft above sea-level. Only about 30 acres was under cultivation, three-quarters of it for potatoes. There were apple and peach trees. Potatoes remain the chief crop, cattle, sheep and pigs are now reared, and fish are plentiful.

The island is extremely lonely, but the community is growing. In 1880 it numbered 109, in 1982, 325. The original inhabitants were shipwrecked sailors and soldiers who remained behind when the garrison from St Helena was withdrawn in 1817.

At the end of April 1942 Tristan da Cunha was commissioned as HMS *Atlantic Isle*, and became an important meteorological and radio station. In Jan. 1949 a South African company commenced crawfishing operations. An Administrator was appointed at the end of 1948 and a body of basic law brought into operation. The Island Council, which was set up in 1932, in 1982 consisted of a Chief Islander, 3 nominated and 7 elected members under the chairmanship of the Administrator. Women's affairs are discussed by the Island Women's Council, which presents them for consideration to the general council.

Administrator: C. F. Redston.

Books of Reference

Booy, D. M., *Rock of Exile: A Narrative of Tristan da Cunha.* London, 1957
Crawford, A., *Tristan da Cunha and the Roaring Forties.* Edinburgh, 1982
Cross, A., *Saint Helena.* Newton Abbot, 1981
Holdgate, M., *Mountains in the Sea.* London, 1958
Munch, P. A., *Sociology of Tristan da Cunha.* Oslo, 1945.—*Crisis in Utopia.* New York, 1971
Stonehouse, B., *Wideawake Island* (Ascension). London, 1960

ST LUCIA

Capital: Castries
Population: 115,783 (1980)
GNP per capita: US$850 (1980)

HISTORY. St Lucia was discovered about 1500 A.D. Attempts to colonize the island by the English took place in 1605 and 1638. The French settled in 1650 and St Lucia was ceded to Britain in 1814. Self-government was achieved in 1967 and independence on 22 Feb. 1979.

AREA AND POPULATION. St Lucia is a small island of the Lesser Antilles situated in the Eastern Caribbean, 238 sq. miles (616 sq. km); population (1979) 113,000. The capital is Castries (population, 45,000). Vital statistics (1974): Births, 3,909; deaths, 829.

CONSTITUTION AND GOVERNMENT. There is a 17-seat House of Assembly elected for 5 years; an 11-seat Senate appointed by the Governor-General, 6 on the advice of the Prime Minister, 3 on the advice of the Leader of the Opposition, and 2 'after consultation with appropriate religious, economic or social bodies or associations'.

At the elections in May 1982, the United Workers' Party gained 14 seats, the St Lucia Labour Party, 2 and the Progressive Labour Party, 1.

Governor-General: Boswell Williams.

Prime Minister: John George Melvin Compton.

Flag: Blue with a design of a black triangle edged in white, bearing a smaller yellow triangle, in the centre.

INTERNATIONAL RELATIONS

Membership. St Lucia is a member of UN, OAS, Caricom, the Commonwealth and is an ACP state of the EEC.

ECONOMY

Budget. The budget in 1978–79 amounted to EC$93·9m. expenditure, of which EC$49·8m. was recurrent expenditure and EC$44·1m. capital expenditure.

Banking. There are Barclays Bank International with 2 branches and 4 agencies, the Royal Bank of Canada, the Bank of Nova Scotia and the Canadian Imperial Bank of Commerce (all of which have 1 branch each), the Chase Manhattan Bank, the St Lucia Co-operative bank and the Government Savings Bank. The Government Savings Bank (end of 1974), 8,400 depositors, $359,086 deposits.

INDUSTRY AND TRADE

Agriculture. Bananas, cocoa, copra and coconut oil are the chief products.

Livestock (1981): Cattle, 11,000; pigs, 10,000; sheep, 13,000; goats, 10,000; poultry, 199,000.

Commerce. Value of imports (1979), EC$273·2m.; of exports, EC$75·6m., including coconut oil, cocoa beans, copra and bananas. Main items of imports were artificial silk and cotton piece-goods, cement, plastic goods, iron and steel products, hardware, motor vehicles, agricultural machinery, fertilizers, wheat flour, codfish and rice, meat and meat preparations.

Tourism. The total number of visitors during 1978 was 107,000.

COMMUNICATIONS

Roads. The island has 500 miles of main and secondary roads.

Aviation. The island is served on a scheduled basis by Leeward Islands Air

Transport, British West Indian Airways and Eastern Airline. There are 2 airfields—Hewanorra International Airport, with 9,000 ft runway, and Vigie.

Shipping. Registered fleet (31 Dec. 1974): 3 motor vessels (94 gross tons). In 1974, 2,798 vessels of 3·5m. gross tons entered Castries and Vieux Fort.

Post and Broadcasting. There are 104 miles of telephone trunk lines, plus 300 miles of local lines. There were (1978) 7,157 telephone instruments coupled to some (1982) 4,881 exchange lines. They operate through 10 automatic exchanges. There were 1,700 TV and 82,000 radio receivers in 1975.

Cinemas. There were 9 cinemas in 1970 with a seating capacity of 9,500.

JUSTICE, EDUCATION AND WELFARE

Justice. The island is divided into 2 judicial districts, and there are 9 magistrates' courts. Appeals lie with the Court of Appeal of the Windward and Leeward Islands, subject to exceptions and conditions as may be enacted by the St Lucia legislature.

Police establishment in 1974 was 11 officers, 11 inspectors and 267 others.

Education (31 Dec. 1974). 74 primary schools (51 Roman Catholic, 3 Anglican, 3 Methodist, 17 government), with 30,000 pupils on roll; government expenditure, 1974, $5,526,945. Primary education is free and compulsory by law, but the legislation is not enforced. There are 12 secondary schools (2 Roman Catholic, 1 Seventh-day Adventist, 9 government) with 4,600 pupils. There is 1 technical college with 250 students.

Health. Victoria Hospital (in Castries) has 409 beds; there is also a 126-bed mental hospital and 24 health centres. In 1975 there were 26 doctors, 4 dentists, 12 pharmacists and 64 nursing personnel.

Library: The Central Library, Castries. *Acting Librarian:* Frances Niles.

DIPLOMATIC REPRESENTATIVES

Of St Lucia in Great Britain (10 Kensington Ct., London, W8)
High Commissioner: Dr Claudius C. Thomas, CMG.

Of Great Britain in St Lucia (Colombus Sq., Castries)
High Commissioner: Viscount Dunrossil, CMG. (resides in Bridgetown).

Of St Lucia in USA and to the United Nations
Ambassador: Donatus St Aimee.

ST VINCENT AND THE GRENADINES

Capital: Kingstown
Population: 119,942 (1979)
GNP per capita: US$520 (1980)

HISTORY. The date of discovery of St Vincent is not known. In 1969 St Vincent became a self-governing Associated State of UK and acquired full independence on 27 Oct. 1979.

AREA AND POPULATION. The total area of 389 sq. km (150·3 sq. miles) comprises the island of St Vincent itself (345 sq. km) and the Northern Grenadines (44 sq. km) of which the largest are Bequia, Mustique, Canouan, Mayreau and Union. Population, estimate, 1979, 119,942. Capital, Kingstown, population (1978), 22,782. Vital statistics (1980): Live births, 3,075; still births, 42; deaths, 724; marriages, 414.

CONSTITUTION AND GOVERNMENT. Independence from the UK was achieved on 27 Oct. 1979. The House of Assembly consists of 13 elected members, directly elected for a 5-year term from single-member constituencies, the Attorney-General (elected) and 6 Senators appointed by the Governor-General (4 on the advice of the Prime Minister and 2 on the advice of the Leader of the Opposition).

Governor-General: Sir Sydney Gun-Munro, MBE.
Prime Minister: Robert Milton Cato, PC.

National Flag: Three vertical stripes of blue, yellow, green, with white fimbriations, charged in the centre with a green leaf of bread-fruit bearing the arms of St Vincent.

INTERNATIONAL RELATIONS

Membership. St Vincent is a member of UN, OAS, Caricom, the Commonwealth and is an ACP state of the EEC.

ECONOMY

Budget. Revenue (estimate), 1982–83, $79,826,671; development aid, $9,960,280, and other sources, $48,170,833; expenditure, $72,935,261; $9,960,280 on British development projects and $48,170,833 on other projects. Public debt at the end of the financial year 1981–82 was $10,249,900.

Currency. The currency is the Eastern Caribbean *dollar*. In March 1983, £1 = EC$4; US$1 =EC$2·70.

Banking. There are branches of Barclays Bank International, the Royal Bank of Canada, the Canadian Imperial Bank of Commerce, the National Commercial Bank, the Bank of Nova Scotia, St Vincent Co-operative Bank and the St Vincent Agricultural Credit and Loan Bank at Kingstown.

ENERGY AND NATURAL RESOURCES

Electricity. The electricity system is owned jointly by the Government (49%) and the Commonwealth Development Corporation (51%) and operated by the St Vincent Electricity Services (CDC). The system consists of 4 power stations: South Rivers Hydro (800 kw.); Cane Hall Diesel (3,650 kw.); Kingstown Diesel (115 kw.) and Richmond Hydro (1,040 kw.), which are linked by 11,000-volt transmission lines covering the island from Richmond through Kingstown to Georgetown. In Bequia there is one diesel station (800 kw.) with transmission at 11,000, 3,300 and 400 volts to Hamilton and Port Elizabeth. Current is supplied at 400 volts 3-phase,

50 cycles for industrial purposes and 230 volts single phase for domestic purposes. At 31 Dec. 1979 there were 10,800 consumers in St Vincent, 900 in Bequia and 300 in Union Island.

Agriculture. The estimated alienated area is about 47,000 of the total acreage of 85,120. 34,000 acres are under forest and woodland; of these about 5,000 acres are used for grazing; 3,000 are considered potentially productive for agriculture and 5,000 for forestry. About 14,000 acres are considered unsuitable for either agriculture or forestry. Of the total alienated area, 34,000 acres are considered arable land, of which 20,000 acres are under temporary crops, 4,000 acres under temporary meadows, 300 acres devoted to market-garden crops with temporary fallow and all other arable land making up a further 9,700 acres. About 11,000 acres are devoted to permanent crops, of which approximately 6,000 acres are under coconuts; the remainder produce cocoa, nutmegs, mangoes, avocado pears, guavas and miscellaneous crops. About 2,000 acres are under permanent meadow, of which 750 are cultivated.

Land ownership: Crown, 38,000 acres; planters, 17,000 acres; small farmers, 25,500 acres; settlements, 6,000 acres.

Livestock (1981): Cattle, 6,300; pigs, 5,000; sheep, 12,500; goats, 4,300; chickens, 50,000.

INDUSTRY AND TRADE

Trade (1981). Imports, EC$157,465,738; exports, EC$65,735,767. Value of imports from the UK (1982), £10,891,000; of exports to the UK (1982), £3,265,000.

Principal exports, 1981:

		EC$			*EC$*
Arrowroot starch	1,402,564 lb.	2,815,089	Sweet potatoes	2,143,547 lb.	804,902
Eddoes	4,823,918 lb.	3,352,100	Coconuts	1,828,750 nuts	747,687
Bananas	65,429,355 lb.	27,147,878	Coconut oil	260,028 litres	592,666

Labour (1980). The Department of Labour serves both worker's and employers' organizations as a conciliatory body in case of dispute. Conciliatory meetings are held on dispute matters such as delay in the recognition of a union as collective bargaining agent for the workers, dismissals, overtime pay, delay in finalizing collective agreement and other conditions of work. There are 8 registered trade unions: the St Vincent Union of Teachers, the Public Service Union, the Commercial, Technical and Allied Workers' Union, the St Vincent Workers' Union, the National Workers' Movement, the Farmers' and National General Workers' Union, the Workers' and Peasants' Union and the National Progressive Workers' Union. The St Vincent Employers Federation continued to render services on behalf of the employers.

Tourism. There were 83,283 visitors in 1981.

COMMUNICATIONS

Roads. There are 313 km of all-weather roads, 160 km of rough motorable roads and 161 km of tracks.

Aviation. Scheduled services are operated daily by LIAT and Air Martinique. Passengers are able to travel daily through the chain of islands stretching as far north as San Juan, Puerto Rico and south to Trinidad. Connexions to the USA, Canada, South America and Europe are possible *via* Barbados, Antigua and Trinidad.

Shipping (1980): (*a*) 21 auxiliary sailing vessels of 994 NRT entered and cleared. (*b*) 37 steamships of 234,847 NRT entered and cleared. (*c*) 617 motor vessels of 593,098 NRT entered and cleared. (*d*) 51 tankers of 41,639 NRT bringing 7,840 tons of fuel entered. A deep-water harbour at Kingstown was completed in 1964.

Post and Broadcasting. There is a General Post Office at Kingstown and 47 district post offices. There is a telephone system with 2,000 miles of line and (1981), 3,687 subscribers; 5,745 stations and a radio telephone service to Bequia, Mustique,

Union Island, Petit St Vincent and Palm Island. In 1974 there were 600 TV and 30,000 radio receivers.

Cinemas. There were 3 cinemas in 1979 with a seating capacity of 2,400.

JUSTICE, EDUCATION AND WELFARE

Justice (1981). There were 3,552 criminal matters disposed of in the 3 magisterial districts which comprise 11 courts. Strength of police force (1981), 489 (including 12 officers).

Education (1981). Sixty-two primary schools; pupils on roll, 24,158, average attendance, 20,146. Expenditure on primary education, $6,595,040. There is also a secondary school for girls (669 pupils), a co-educational school (525 pupils), as well as 11 assisted secondary schools (2,724 pupils) and 6 junior secondary schools with 1,411 pupils. Expenditure on secondary education, $1,848,480.

Health. There is a General Hospital in Kingstown (204 beds), 3 rural hospitals at Chateaubelair, Georgetown and Bequia, 3 specialist hospitals and 34 medical clinics. In 1982 there were 30 doctors, 3 dentists, 6 midwives, 208 nursing personnel and 30 community health aides.

Library: St Vincent Public Library, Kingstown. *Librarian:* Mrs Lorna Small.

DIPLOMATIC REPRESENTATIVES

Of St Vincent and the Grenadines in Great Britain (10 Kensington Ct, London, W8)
High Commissioner: Dr Claudius C. Thomas, CMG.

Of Great Britain in St Vincent and the Grenadines
High Commissioner: Viscount Dunrossil, CMG (resides in Bridgetown).

Of St Vincent and the Grenadines in the USA and to the United Nations
Ambassador: Vacant.

SAN MARINO

Capital: San Marino
Population: 21,622 (1981)

Repubblica di San Marino

HISTORY. On 22 March 1862 San Marino concluded a treaty of friendship and co-operation, including a *de facto* customs union with the kingdom of Italy, preserving the independence of the ancient republic, although completely surrounded by Italian territory. The treaty was renewed on 27 March 1872, 28 June 1897 and 31 March 1939, with 7 amendments in 1942–71.

The republic has extradition treaties with Belgium, France, the Netherlands, UK and USA.

AREA AND POPULATION. San Marino is a land-locked state in central Italy, 20 km from the Adriatic, The frontier line is 38·6 km in length, area is 61·19 sq. km (24·1 sq. miles) and the population (30 June 1981), 21,622; some 20,000 citizens live abroad.

CONSTITUTION AND GOVERNMENT. The legislative power is vested in the Great and General Council of 60 members elected every 5 years by popular vote, 2 of whom are appointed every 6 months to act as regents *(Capitani reggenti).*

The elections held on 28 May 1978 gave 26 seats to the Christian Democrats, 16 to the Communists, 15 to Socialist parties, 3 to others. A political crisis arose following the election and a 'Government of Democratic Collaboration' was established finally on 17 July 1978.

The regents exercise executive power together with the Congress of State *(Congresso di Stato)*, which comprises 11 departments, and through Commissions on social welfare, public works, etc.

National flag: Horizontally white over light blue, with the national arms over all in the centre.

DEFENCE. The militia consists, in case of necessity, of all able-bodied citizens between the ages of 16 and 55, with certain exceptions (teachers and students, etc.).

ECONOMY. The budget (ordinary and extraordinary) for the financial year ending 31 Dec. 1981 balanced at 144,103,052,187 lire.

The chief exports are wood machinery, chemicals, wine, textiles, tiles, varnishes and ceramics.

Italian and Vatican City currency is in general use, but the republic issues its own postage stamps and coins.

In 1980, 3·5m. tourists visited San Marino.

COMMUNICATIONS

Roads. A bus service connects San Marino with Rimini.

Aviation. There is a helicopter service to Rimini in summer.

Post. In 1981 there were 7,685 telephones.

Cinemas. In 1974 there were 8 cinemas with a seating capacity of 2,300.

JUSTICE AND EDUCATION

Justice. Law is administered by a Commissioner for civil and commercial cases and a Commissioner for criminal cases (acting with a penal judge), from whom appeals can be made to a civil appeals judge and a criminal appeals judge respectively. The highest legal authority is, in certain cases, the *Consiglio dei XII*.

Education. There are 19 infant schools, 16 elementary schools, a secondary school and a grammar school, the diplomas of which are recognized by Italian universities. Civil marriage was instituted in Sept. 1953.

DIPLOMATIC REPRESENTATIVES

British Consul-General (resides at Florence): R. A. Eilbeck.
USA Consul-General (resides at Florence): Donald A. Johnston.
Consul-General in London: Charles Forte.

Books of Reference

Information: Segreteria di Stato per gli Affari Esteri; Ente Governativo per il Turismo.

Garbeletto, A., *Evoluzione storica della costituzione di S. Marino.* Milan, 1956
Packett, C. N., *Guide to the Republic of San Marino.* Bradford, 1970
Rossi, G., *San Marino.* San Marino, 1954

SÃO TOMÉ E PRINCIPE

Capital: São Tomé
Population: 95,000 (1981)
GNP per capita: US$490 (1980)

HISTORY. The islands of São Tomé and Príncipe, were discovered in 1471 by Pedro Escobar and João Gomes, and from 1522 until independence had constituted a province of Portugal.

On 26 Nov. 1974 the Government of Portugal and the liberation movement of São Tomé e Príncipe signed an agreement granting independence to the archipelago on 12 July 1975 to become the Democratic Republic of São Tomé e Príncipe.

AREA AND POPULATION. The republic, which lies about 200 km off the west coast of Gabon, in the Gulf of Guinea, comprises the main islands of São Tomé (845 sq. km) and Príncipe and several smaller islets including Pedras Tinhosas and Rolas. It has a total area of 964 sq. km (372 sq. miles). Total population (census, 1970) 73,631 (São Tomé, 69,032; Príncipe, 4,599). Estimate (1981) 95,000. Capital, São Tomé (20,000).

Vital statistics (1978): Births, 3,479; deaths, 800.

CONSTITUTION AND GOVERNMENT. A new constitution was approved by the Constitutional Assembly (elected 6 July 1975) on 12 Dec. 1975. Under it, the sole legal party is the *Movimento de Libertação de São Tomé e Príncipe*, who nominate candidates for the Presidency and People's Assembly. The President is elected by the People's Assembly for a 4-year term; he is also head of government and appoints a Cabinet of Ministers to assist him. The 33-member People's Assembly is also elected for 4 years.

The Cabinet was composed as follows in Jan. 1982:

President, Prime Minister, National Security and Defence: Dr Manuel Pinto da Costa.

Foreign Affairs: Maria do Nascimento da Graça Amorim. *Education and Culture:* Joaquim Rafael Branco. *Information:* Maria de Rosário Lima Barros. *Health:* Carlos Alberto Tini. *Planning:* Enrique Pinto da Costa. *Labour and Social Security:* Dionisio Dias. *Industry, Works and Housing:* Lieut. Oscar de Sousa Aguiar. *Commerce:* Fausto Vera Cruz. *Justice:* Celestino Rocha da Costa. *Secretaries of State:* Arlindo Gomes *(Agriculture and Fishing)*, Fernando Paquete da Costa *(Transport and Communications)*.

Flag: Three horizontal stripes of green, yellow, green, with the yellow of double width and bearing 2 black stars; in the hoist a red triangle over all.

INTERNATIONAL RELATIONS

Membership. São Tomé e Príncipe is a member of UN, OAU and is an ACP state of EEC.

DEFENCE. Armed forces strength (estimate, 1976) 160.

ECONOMY

Budget. In 1977 the budget envisaged revenue of 179·6m. dobra and expenditure of 454·2m. dobra.

Currency. The currency is the *dobra*, introduced in 1977, divided into 100 *centavos*. In March 1983, £1 = 61·36 *dobra*; US$1 = 41·96 *dobra*.

Banking. *Banco Nacional de São Tomé e Príncipe* (established, 1975) is the central bank.

AGRICULTURE. The chief commercial products are cacao, copra, coconut, coffee, palm-oil and cinchona. In 1981 there were 4,000 goats, 2,000 sheep, 3,000 pigs and 3,000 cattle.

COMMERCE. Imports in 1975 amounted to 288,469,000 dobras and exports to 180,432,000 dobras, the main exports being cocoa (87%), copra (8%), coffee, bananas and palm-oil. In 1975 Portugal provided 61% of imports and Angola 13%, while the Netherlands took 52% of exports and Portugal 33%.

Total trade between São Tomé e Príncipe and UK (British Department of Trade returns, in £1,000 sterling):

	1979	*1980*	*1981*	*1982*
Imports to UK	525	99	207	494
Exports and re-exports from UK	1,036	2,103	625	1,510

COMMUNICATIONS

Roads. There were 288 km of roads in 1973.

Shipping. In 1973, 220 vessels of 435,971 net tons entered the ports.

Post. There were, in 1973, 3 wireless stations with (1977) 21,000 radio receivers, 352 km of telephone lines and a telephone exchange (with 850 instruments in 1980).

Cinemas. In 1972 there was 1 cinema with a seating capacity of 1,000.

RELIGION, EDUCATION AND WELFARE.

Religion. The vast majority of the population are Roman Catholic.

Education. In 1977 there were 14,162 pupils and 527 teachers in primary schools, 3,012 pupils and 81 teachers in secondary schools, and 155 students and 30 teachers in technical schools.

Health. In 1976 there were 11 hospitals and dispensaries with 530 beds. In 1973 there were 12 doctors, 6 midwives and 63 nursing personnel.

DIPLOMATIC REPRESENTATIVES

Of Great Britain in São Tomé and Príncipe
Ambassador: Francis Kennedy, CBE (resides in Luanda).

Of São Tomé and Príncipe to the United Nations
Ambassador: Vacant.

Book of Reference

S. Tomé e Príncipe. Agência-Geral do Ultramar, 1964

SAUDI ARABIA

al-Mamlaka al-ʻArabiya as-Saʻudiya

Capital: Riyadh
Population: 8·63m. (1981)
GNP per capita: US$11,260 (1980)

HISTORY. Saudi Arabia was founded by Abdul-Aziz ibn Abdur-Rahman al-Faisal Al Saʻud, GCB, GCIE (born about 1880; died 9 Nov. 1953), who had been proclaimed King of the Hejaz on 8 Jan. 1926 and had in 1927 changed his title of Sultan of Nejd and its dependencies to that of king, thus becoming 'King of the Hejaz and of Nejd and its Dependencies'. On 20 May 1927 a treaty was signed at Jiddah between Great Britain and Ibn Saʻud, by which the former recognized the complete independence of the dominions of the latter. The name of the State was changed to 'The Saudi Arabian Kingdom' by decree of 23 Sept. 1932.

In Nov. 1937 a general agreement between Saudi Arabia and the Yemen concerning the settlement of disputes was ratified, and an agreement regarding the delimitation of the frontiers was negotiated.

In March 1953 the treaty of Taif, first signed with the Yemen in May 1934, was extended for 20 lunar years.

In 1942 Saudi Arabia and the British Government, acting on behalf of the Shaikh of Kuwait, signed agreements for friendship and neighbourly relations, for the extradition of offenders and for the regulation of trade between Saudi Arabia and Kuwait.

In Aug. 1962 Saudi Arabia and Jordan agreed on measures of co-operation in the military, political and economic fields.

King Faisal ibn Abdul-Aziz was assassinated on 25 March 1975 by his nephew. There appeared to be no political motive.

AREA AND POPULATION. The total area of Saudi Arabia is estimated to be 927,000 sq. miles (2·4m. sq. km).

The principal cities of the Western Province (formerly *Hejaz*) are Jiddah (561,104 inhabitants at the 1974 Census), Mecca (366,801), Taif (204, 857) and Medina (198,196); of the Central Province (formerly *Nejd*) are Riyadh, the national capital (666,840), Buraidah (69,940), Ha'il (40,502), Anaiza and Al-Kharj; of the Northern Province are Tabouk (74,825), Al-Jawf and Sakaka; of the Eastern Province (formerly *Al-Hasa*) are Dammam (127,844), Hofuf (101,271), Haradh (100,000), Al-Mobarraz (54,325), Al-Khabar (48,817) and Qatif; and of the Southern Province (formerly *Asir*) are Khamis-Mushait (49,581), Najran (47,501), Qizan (32,814) and Abha (30,150). New industrial cities are being built at Jubail (future pop. 300,000) and Yanbu (150,000).

Taif, about 3,800ft above sea-level and some 50 miles from Mecca,is a summer resort.

The total population was (1974 census) 7,012,642, of which 5,128,655 were categorized as settled and 1,883,987 as nomadic. Estimate (1981) 8·63m.

Slavery was declared illegal in Nov. 1962.

KING. Fahd bin Abdulaziz; succeeded in May 1982, after King Khalid's death. *Crown Prince:* Prince Abdullah ibn Abdul-Aziz, First Deputy Prime Minister, brother of the King.

National flag: Green, with the text 'There is no God but Allah and Mohammed is his prophet' in white Arabic script, and beneath this a white sabre.

GOVERNMENT AND CONSTITUTION. The Kingdom has been welded together from Hejaz, Nejd, Asir and Al-Hasa. Riyadh is the political capital and Mecca the religious capital. There is no formal Constitution.

In May 1958 a 'Cabinet system' was instituted under which, from 1962, effective power devolved upon the President of the Council of Ministers.

The King has the post of Prime Minister.

First Deputy Prime Minister and Commander of the National Guards: Prince Abdullah ibn Abdulaziz.
Second Deputy Prime Minister and Defence and Aviation: Prince Sultan ibn Abdul-Aziz.
Foreign Minister: Prince Saud al Faisal
Interior: Prince Nayef ibn Abdul-Aziz.
Petroleum and Natural Resources: Sheikh Ahmed Zaki Yamani.
Finance and Economy: Sheikh Muhammad Ali Aba al Khail.

The religious law of Islam is the common law of the land, and is administered by religious courts, at the head of which is a chief judge, who is responsible for the Department of Sharia (legal) Affairs. There are provisions for the setting up of certain advisory councils, comprising a consultative Legislative Assembly in Mecca, municipal councils in each of the towns of Mecca, Medina and Jidda, and village and tribal councils throughout the provinces. The country is divided for administrative purposes into 6 major and 12 minor provinces.

DEFENCE. In 1937 a Ministry of Defence and a training school for officers were established. British Military and Civil Air Missions helped in training the Army and civil aviation from 1947 to 1951. The US now maintains a Military Mission (with an Air Force element) as do France and Pakistan. UK provides small army and air force teams. Personnel are trained in Saudi Arabia, France, Pakistan, UK and the USA.

Army. The Army comprises 3 infantry, 1 mechanized and 1 armoured brigade, and 2 parachute, 1 Royal Guard and 3 artillery battalions, 18 AA batteries and 10 Hawk missile batteries. Service is voluntary and the strength (1982) 35,000.

National Guard. The National Guard comprises 1 mechanized brigade (trained by the US), 1 Special Security Unit. An additional mechanized brigade is planned. Additionally there are a number of regular and irregular units, the total strength of the National Guard amounting to approximately 30,000. National Guard's primary role is the protection of the Royal Family and vital points in the Kingdom. It does not come under command of the Ministry of Defence and Aviation.

Navy. The Navy, with recent impetus under the aegis of USA and France, comprises 4 new US-built missile-armed fast corvettes, 9 fast missile craft (all completed in 1980–82 in USA), 3 *ex*-German torpedo boats, 4 US-built MSC-type coastal minesweepers, 1 *ex*-US coastguard cutter, 8 new French-built patrol craft, 30 coastal patrol boats, 6 custom launches, 8 hovercraft, 2 air-sea rescue launches, 1 training ship, 4 landing craft, 8 minor landing craft, 1 salvage vessel, 2 tugs and the royal yacht. New construction includes 4 frigates in France and 2 replenishment tankers. There are 24 helicopters. An intensive training programme is under-way in USA and Saudi Arabia. $70m. is being spent on three naval bases.

Naval personnel in 1983 exceeded 3,500 officers and men plus instructors and trainees.

The Coast Guard operates 130 coastal patrol craft, 300 inshore patrol cutters, 3 small oilers and 12 service crafts.

Air Force. Formed as a small army support unit in 1932, the Air Force has been built up considerably with British and US assistance since 1946. Complete re-equipment began in 1966 and delivery of 62 F-15 Eagles to equip 3 air superiority squadrons began in 1982; they will operate in conjunction with 5 E-3A Sentry AWACS aircraft and 6 KC-707 flight refuelling tankers. Current combat units include 1 squadron of Lightning F.53 supersonic interceptors, supported by 2-seat fighter-trainers. There are 3 squadrons of F-5E Tiger II supersonic fighter-bombers, supported by a conversion unit with F-5B/F combat trainers. Two squadrons of Strikemaster light jet attack/trainers are based at the King Faisal Air Academy, Riyadh, together with 12 Reims/Cessna FR172 piston-engined primary trainers. Other types in current service include 34 C-130E/H and 8 KC-130H Hercules transports and tankers, 2 C-130H hospital aircraft, 1 Boeing 747 SP, 1 Boeing 707, and 2 JetStar VIP jet transports, more than 30 Agusta-Bell 205, 212 and JetRanger helicopters, 2 Agusta AS-61A-4 VIP transport helicopters, 6 Kawasaki-Boeing Vertol KV-107 helicopters, and communications aircraft. On order are 40 Indonesian-built CASA Aviocar twin-turboprop transports.Personnel, about 14,500.

INTERNATIONAL RELATIONS

Membership. Saudi Arabia is a member of UN, the Arab League and OPEC.

ECONOMY

Planning. Growth rate of GDP was 16·3% during the first plan and 8% during the second plan (4·8% in the oil sector and 15·1% in the non-oil economy).

The third development plan runs 1980–85, and emphasizes industrial development and the training of an indigenous work force. GDP is expected to grow at 6·2% in the non-oil economy: industrial growth will be much higher than this, but an anticipated decline in the construction sector depresses the figure. Government expenditure during the third plan is expected to total 783,000m. rials, of which 262,000m. for the development of economic resources, 130,000m. for education and training, 61,000m. for social welfare and 249,000m. for physical infrastructure.

Budget. The fiscal year runs from 1 Rajab to 30 Jumad II in the lunar calendar, and consequently starts approximately 10 days earlier each year. Main expenditure allocations in 1982–83 budget were 92,889m. rials for defence, 32,533m. for physical communications and telecommunications, 26,224m. for public works, 31,864m. for education and training, 17,010m. for social welfare and 45,427m. for development of economic resources (agriculture, industry, petroleum and minerals: equally divided between direct finance and loans funds available to private investors.)

Currency. The paper *rial* is divided into 100 *halalas*. In March 1983, £1 = 5·06 *rials*; US$1 = 3·44 *rials*.

Banking. There are 2 commercial banks of Saudi Arabian origin: the National Commercial Bank and the Riyadh Bank. It is government policy to encourage foreign banks operating in the kingdom to become Saudized. By 1982 there were 7 banks in which foreign capital represents only 40%: al Jazira Bank (National Bank of Pakistan), Saudi Dutch Bank (Algemene Bank Nederland), Saudi French Bank (Banque de l'Indochine et de Suez), Saudi British Bank (British Bank of the Middle East), Saudi Cairo Bank (Banque du Caire), the Saudi-American Bank (Citibank) and the Arab National Bank (Arab Bank of Jordan). All these banks are entitled to open branches nationwide.

In addition the Banque du Liban et d'Outremer and the Bank Melli in Jiddah and the United Bank (of Pakistan) in Dammam have invited subscription to an eighth bank that will operate by 1983.

ENERGY AND NATURAL RESOURCES

Electricity. 7,010m. kwh. was generated by the main electricity companies in 1977, 9,435m. kwh. in 1978 and 17,597m. kwh in 1980.

Oil. The first general geologic–geographical survey of Saudi Arabia was completed in 1961 under the joint sponsorship of the Saudi Arabian and US governments but surveying continues.

The original oil concession agreement was signed in 1933 with Standard Oil Co. of California. The name Aramco appeared in 1944, and by 1948 Exxon, Texaco and Mobil held shares in the company. In 1973 the Saudi Arabian Government acquired a 25% interest in Aramco: this became 60% in 1974, and in 1979 it was announced that the Government had taken full control of Aramco equity retroactively from Jan. 1976. By 1979 Aramco retained only 189,000 sq. km or 15·4% of the original concession areas.

Two other companies have concessions of Saudi Arabia's oil rights in the Kuwait/Saudi Arabian Neutral Zone. Getty Oil's concession dates from 1953 and that of the Arabian Oil Co. (Japanese) from 1958.

Crude oil production in 1980 was 3,623·8m. bbls. Crude oil exports in 1980 were 3,374m. bbls, of which Aramco provided 97·4%, Arabian Oil 1·94% and Getty Oil 0·6%. 1980 oil exports earned US$101,421m. (95m. for crude) and Aramco earned 98% of this total.

The agency responsible for co-ordination of national oil policy is Petromin (General Petroleum and Minerals Organization). Petromin manages exploration and concession agreements, oil refineries (except that of Aramco at Ras Tanura) and the distribution and marketing of oil and oil products.

In 1980, when Aramco produced 3,525m. bbls of crude oil, 96m. (2·7%) were sent by pipeline to Bahrain and by Tapline to the Mediterranean port of Saida, and 3,192m. (92·9%) were shipped out *via* Gulf terminals. The volume of crude exported will decline as the national refining capacity increases. In 1981 total refining capacity was 674,000 bbls per day including Ras Tanura (Aramco) 450,000 bbls per day, 120,000 bbls per day at Riyadh and 104,000 bbls per day at Jiddah (both Petromin). Work was underway to expand Jiddah to 265,000 bbls per day and to build 4 new refineries of an initial capacity of 250,000 bbls per day each at Jubail and Yanbu for export, 170,000 (domestic) at Yanbu and 325,000 (export) at Rabigh. In 1980, 302m. bbls of refined products were produced by Saudi Arabian refineries, of which fuel oil accounted for 89m., gasoline, 72m., LPG, 75m. and diesel oil, 44m.

The gas collection programme under Aramco management was initiated in 1975. The first phase (Shedgum and Juaymah, 75% of the project) came on stream in 1980, and the entire system is planned to be completed by 1985. It will provide fuel gas for local industry, feedstock for petrochemical plants, and a surplus for export. The programme includes a pipeline to carry gas to the industrial zone at Yanbu. In 1980 Aramco produced 135m. bbls of natural gas liquids, obtained in association with crude production.

Water Resources. Intensive efforts are underway to provide adequate supplies of water for urban, industrial, rural and agricultural use. There is an important programme to tap non-renewable (3,450m. cu. metres per annum) and renewable (1,145m. cu. metres) water reserves by wells and small dams, and there are plans to reclaim urban waste water. Most investment however has gone into seawater desalination. By early 1982 14 plants in 10 towns had the capacity to produce 373,000 cu. metres per day and 5 more, totalling 1,143,000 cu. metres per day were under construction. Another 12, amounting to 554,000 cu. metres per day, were at various stages of planning.

Minerals. Surveys were launched during the second development plan to investigate potential mineral wealth other than oil. Deposits of several minerals including viable quantities of iron and gold have been found. There are also reports of uranium deposits.

Agriculture. Since 1970 the Government has devoted huge resources to raise the Kingdom's agricultural potential, and spent substantially on desert reclamation, irrigation schemes, drainage and control of surface water and control of moving sands. Undeveloped land has been distributed to farmers and there are research and extension programmes. Large scale private investment has concentrated on meat, poultry and dairy production. Support finance from the Saudi Arabian Agricultural Bank in 1980 totalled 1,129m. rials, chiefly for equipment 223m., well drilling 196m. and purchases of poultry stock 121m.

In 1978 the most productive provinces were Jizan, the West, Asir, Riyadh and Qasim. The principal crops (in 1,000 tonnes) were: Alfalfa, 605; dates, 411; tomatoes, 166; sorghum, 152; water melons, 140; wheat, 120; dry onions, 95; grapes, 56. The use of greenhouses and hydroponics is increasing.

Livestock estimates for 1981 include 410,000 cattle, 118,000 asses, 162,000 camels, 4·2m. sheep and 2m. goats.

INDUSTRY AND TRADE

Industry. The Government actively encourages the establishment of manufacturing industries in the country. The policy includes the provision of industrial estates and loans covering 50% of capital investment. By the end of 1980, 1,170 private industrial plants were in operation, with authorized capital investment of 17,000m. rials. The Government has also established two industrial poles at Jubail and Yanbu, to be the focus of heavy industrial development. Linked by gas and oil pipelines both are to have petrochemical complexes producing, initially, ethylene and methanol, for which agreements have been signed with American and Japanese companies. Six plants are under construction, to come on stream in 1985. In addition an integrated steel complex (German partners) and a urea fertilizer factory (Taiwanese), both in Jubail will start production in 1983.

Commerce. Exports amounted to 405,481m. rials in 1981 and imports 119,298m. rials. In 1981 the USA was the main supplier, accounting for 21·4% of the total. Other major supplying countries were Japan (18·3%), Federal Republic of Germany (9·5%), Italy (6·2%) and the UK (6·2%). The main imports were machinery and electrical equipment (25·4%), metal articles (14·6%), transport equipment (14·4%) and foodstuffs (14·4%).

Total trade between Saudi Arabia and UK (British Department of Trade returns, in £1,000 sterling):

	1978	*1979*	*1980*	*1981*	*1982*
Imports to UK	870,537	1,108,644	1,927,583	1,892,605	1,447,775
Exports and re-exports from UK	786,265	893,600	1,050,145	1,133,921	1,361,665

COMMUNICATIONS

Roads. All the main regions and population centres of the Kingdom are linked by asphalted roads, of which there were 22,501 km in 1981 and 28,586 km of graded, unpaved agricultural roads. An additional 12,492 km of roads were under construction including the Trans-Peninsula Expressway. There are road links with Yemen, Jordan, Kuwait and Qatar, and a causeway link to Bahrain is being built. In 1980 there were nearly 200,000 cars, over 142,000 commercial vehicles and about 4,500 buses.

Railways. A railway from Riyadh to Dammam on the Gulf (571 km, 1,435 mm gauge) *via* Dhahran and the oilfields Abqaiq, Ithmaniya (near Hofuf) and Haradh was completed in Oct. 1951. A 'dry port' at Riyadh station opened in 1981, and a new 465 km Dammam-Riyadh direct line should operate in 1985. There are plans to extend the line *via* Medina to Jiddah. That section of the Hejaz Railway which is in Saudi Arabian territory is not now in working order, but studies have been initiated to restore the whole line from Damascus to Medina.

Aviation. Saudi Arabian Air Lines, a government-owned company operates regular internal air services, and international routes to Africa, the Middle East, Europe and the Far East, as well as special flights for pilgrims. The pilots are mainly Saudi-Arabians. There are 3 major international airports at Jiddah, Dhahran and Riyadh and 19 domestic airports. In 1981, 9·4m. passengers and 100,000 tonnes of cargo were carried.

Shipping. The ports of Dammam and Jubail on the Gulf and Jiddah, Yanbu and Jizan on the Red Sea had 101 deep-water piers at 31 Dec. 1981 and discharged 53·3m. freight tonnes.

Post and Broadcasting. Jiddah, Mecca, Taif, Riyadh and Dammam are linked by telephone, Jiddah and Cairo by radio-telephone. An international radio-telephone station at Riyadh was opened in 1956. Number of telephones (1981), 442,514. Number of post offices (1981) 437. In 1982 there were (estimate) 2·7m. radio receivers and 1·7m. television receivers.

Newspapers. There are 8 daily newspapers in Arabic and 2 in English and 9 weekly or monthly magazines.

EDUCATION AND WELFARE

Education. Administration is in educational districts. Schooling is in three stages, primary, intermediate and secondary which is to prepare older pupils for university; pre-primary schools are being introduced. Education is free in all these stages; monthly scholarships are paid to students in higher education. Girls' education is separate. In 1981 there were 184 pre-primary schools with 27,843 pupils, 5,744 primary schools with 930,436 pupils and 50,010 teachers, and 2,181 intermediate/secondary schools with 377,681 students and 24,866 teachers. There were also adult literacy classes (136,103 students, 35% women), and special schools for 1,971 handicapped children.

There were 107 teacher-training schools in 1980.

During the third plan the Government has laid special emphasis on vocational and technical training, including a large construction programme. In 1981 there were 18 vocational centres, where 3,684 primary school graduates were instructed in basic trades. There were also 5 technical and 8 commercial secondary schools, taking 5,418 intermediate school graduates, and 4 industrial, one agricultural and 2 commercial higher institutes (1,466 students).

University courses concentrating on science, engineering, agriculture and medicine, but also covering education, commerce and arts, are available at the Riyadh University, King Abdulaziz University, Jiddah, and King Faisal University, Dammam and Hofuf. New general universities are to be created in Abha and Mecca. Specialized engineering studies are available at the University of Petroleum and Minerals, Dhahran, and Arabic and Sharia law studies at the Islamic University, Medina and the Imam Muhammad bin Saud University, Riyadh. There were 54,397 university students (about 19% women) in 1981.

Welfare. The Ministry of Health is responsible for medical services, serving both Saudi citizens, foreign residents and pilgrims. In 1979 there were 65 hospitals with 10,978 beds, 824 clinics and health centres, 2,883 doctors, 5,159 nurses and midwives, 1,247 pharmacists and assistants and 1,161 X-ray and laboratory technicians. There were also 25 private hospitals (2,019 beds) and 22 private clinics employing 666 doctors. Five new hospitals with 2,275 beds opened in 1980 and a further five with 900 beds in 1981. In 1982 33 hospitals (7,112 beds) were under construction and another 11 (4,150 beds) were projected. The Jiddah Quarantine Centre, designed by WHO and primarily for pilgrims, can take 2,400 patients. In 1980 there were 7 schools for female nurses and 4 institutes for male trainees. There is a strict system of health controls for visiting pilgrims and strict supervision of sanitation and water supply.

DIPLOMATIC REPRESENTATIVES

Of Saudi Arabia in Great Britain (30 Belgrave Sq., London, SW1X 8QB)
Ambassador; Sheikh Nasser H. Almanaour, GCVO.

Of Great Britain in Saudi Arabia (PO Box 393, Jiddah)
Ambassador: Sir James Craig, KCMG.

Of Saudi Arabia in the USA (1520–18th Street, NW, Washington, D.C. 20036)
Ambassador: Sheikh Faisal al Hegelan.

Of the USA in Saudi Arabia (Palestine Rd., Ruwais, Jiddah)
Ambassador: Richard W. Murphy.

Of Saudi Arabia to the United Nations
Ambassador: (Vacant).

Books of Reference

The Gulf Handbook. Bath (annual)
Anderson, N., *The Kingdom of Saudi Arabia.* (Rev. ed.). London, 1982
Clements, F. A., *Saudi Arabia.* [Bibliography] Oxford and Santa Barbara, 1979
Doughty, C. M., *Travels in Arabia Deserta.* 2 vols. London, 1936
Helms, C. M., *The Cohesion of Saudi Arabia.* Baltimore, 1981
Hobday, P., *Saudi Arabia Today: An Introduction to the Richest Oil Power.* London, 1978

Holden, D. and Johns, R., *The House of Saud.* London and New York, 1981
Lewis, B., *Handbook of Diplomatic and Political Arabic.* London, 1947
Looney, R. E., *Saudi Arabia's Development Potential.* Lexington, 1982
McMaster, B., *The Definitive Guide to Living in Saudi Arabia.* London, 1980
Niblock, T., *State, Society and Economy in Saudi Arabia.* New York, 1981
Pesce, A., *Jiddah: Portrait of an Arabian City.* 3rd ed. Cambridge, 1978
Philby, H. St. J. B., *Arabian Jubilee.* London, 1952.—*Sa'udi Arabia.* London, 1955
Quandt, W. B., *Saudi Arabia in the 1980's: Foreign Policy, Security and Oil.* Washington, 1981
Stacey International (ed.) *The Kingdom of Saudi Arabia.* (4th ed.) London, 1979
Troeller, G., *The Birth of Saudi Arabia: Britain and the Rise of the House of Sa'ud.* London, 1976

SENEGAL

Capital: Dakar
Population: 5·97m. (1982)
GNP per capita: US$450 (1980)

République du Sénégal

HISTORY. France established a fort at Saint-Louis in 1659 and later acquired other coastal settlements from the Dutch; the interior was occupied in 1854–65. Senegal became a territory of French West Africa in 1902 and an autonomous state within the French Community on 25 Nov. 1958. On 4 April 1959 Senegal joined with French Sudan to form the Federation of Mali, which achieved independence on 20 June 1960, but on 22 Aug. Senegal withdrew from the Federation and became a separate independent republic. Senegal was a one-Party state from 1966 until 1974, when a pluralist system was re-established. Léopold Sédar Senghor, President since independence, resigned on 31 Dec. 1980 and was succeeded by his Prime Minister, Abdou Diouf. From 1 Feb. 1982 Senegal joined with Gambia to form a Confederation of Senegambia.

AREA AND POPULATION. Senegal is bounded by Mauritania to the north and north-east, Mali to the east, Guinea and Guinea-Bissau to the south and the Atlantic to the west with The Gambia forming an enclave along that shore. The republic has a total area of 196,722 sq. km; the population (census, 1976) 5,085,388 (estimate, 1982) 5·97m. The capital is Dakar (population 1979, 978,553), Thiès (126,886), Kaolack (115,679), Saint-Louis (96,594), Ziguinchor (79,464) and Diourbel (55,307) are other important towns.

The principal ethnic groups are the Wolof (29% of the population), Serer (17%), Fulani (17%), Tukulor (10%), Diola (8%), Malinké (6%), Bambara (6%) and Sarakole (2%).

CONSTITUTION AND GOVERNMENT. Under the Constitution promulgated on 7 Mar. 1963 (as subsequently amended) there are simultaneous elections by universal adult suffrage for 5-year terms for both the Presidency and for the unicameral 120-member National Assembly; for the latter 60 members are elected in single-member constituencies and 60 by a form of proportional representation.

In the general election of Feb. 1978 the *Parti socialiste* gained 82 and the *Parti démocratique sénégalais* 18 of the, then, 100 seats.

On 14 Nov. 1981, President Diouf of Senegal and President Jawara of The Gambia issued a joint communiqué proposing the establishment of a confederation, to be known as Senegambia. Both parliaments ratified the agreement at the end of the year. The instruments of ratification were exchanged in Banjul on 11 Jan. 1982 and the Confederation formally came into existence on 1 Feb.

The agreement stated that each confederal state shall maintain its independence and sovereignty and calls for the integration of the armed security forces, economic and monetary union, co-operation in the fields of communications and external relations, and the establishment of joint institutions (*i.e.* President, Vice President, Council of Ministers, Confederal Parliament). The President of the Confederation would be President Diouf, and the Vice President President Jawara, The Confederal Parliament would have one third Gambian representation and two thirds Senegalese.

President Jawara said in Nov. 1981 that 'the Confederation would not compromise any of the agreements which link The Gambia direct to Britain and the rest of the Commonwealth'.

President of the Republic: Abdou Diouf (took office on 1 Jan. 1981).
Prime Minister: Habib Thiam.
Foreign Minister: Mustapha Niasse.

National flag: Three vertical strips of green, yellow, red, with a green star in the centre.

The official language is French.

Local Government. Senegal is divided into 8 *régions,* each with an appointed governor and an elected regional assembly. They are divided into 28 *départements,* each under an appointed *Préfet,* and thence into 99 *arrondissements.*

DEFENCE

Army. The Army had a strength of 8,500 (1983), organized in 5 infantry battalions, 1 engineer battalion and minor units.

Navy. The Navy has 1 patrol vessel, 3 patrol craft, 3 fast gunboats, 12 small patrol craft, 1 fishery protection trawler, 4 coastal patrol launches, 1 landing craft, 2 minor amphibious craft and 1 training tender. Personnel (1983) 360.

Air Force. The Senegal Air Force, formed with French assistance, has 1 Summit O2-337 Sentry counter-insurgency aircraft, 2 Magister jet trainers, 1 Boeing 727 VIP transport, 5 DC-3/C-47 transports, 6 F.27 twin-turboprop transports, 2 Broussard liaison aircraft, 6 Puma and 1 Gazelle helicopter. Personnel total about 500.

INTERNATIONAL RELATIONS

Membership. Senegal is a member of UN, OAU and is an ACP state of EEC.

ECONOMY

Planning. The 1977-81, 4-year plan includes investment in mineral exploration, tourism, cotton, fishing, livestock, seed selection, rice growing and fertilizers.

Budget. The budget for 1980-81 balanced at 143,000m. francs CFA.

Currency. The currency is the *franc* CFA, with a parity value of 50 *francs* CFA to 1 French *franc.*

Banking. The bank of issue is the *Banque Centrale des États de l'Afrique de l'Ouest.* The principal commercial bank is the *Union Sénégalaise de la Banque pour le Commerce et l'Industrie* (established 1961 with assistance from Crédit Lyonnais) in which the Senegalese government has the majority share-holding; also state controlled is the *Banque Nationale de Développement du Sénégal.* There are 3 private banks.

At 31 Dec. 1979 the savings banks had deposits of 122,378m. francs CFA.

NATURAL RESOURCES

Minerals. Extraction of phosphate rock in 1979 amounted to 1,845,042 tonnes. Titanium ores and zirconium are extracted from coastal (sand) deposits. Iron ore deposits amounting to an estimated 980m. tonnes have been located at La Faleme.

Agriculture. 80% of the labour force is engaged in agriculture. The main food crops (1979 production in 1,000 tonnes) are millet (805), rice (146), maize (53), cassava and sorghum, while the primary cash crop is groundnuts (1,051).

Livestock (1981): 3·2m. sheep and goats, 2·3m. cattle, 202,000 pigs, 270,000 asses, 7,000 camels and 255,000 horses.

Fisheries. Annual catch 200,000 tonnes.

INDUSTRY AND TRADE

Industry. Dakar has numerous industrial works. A major ship-repairing complex has been constructed there for vessels of up to 28,000 tonnes. Cement production (1979) 311,507 tonnes.

Trade Unions. There are two major unions, the *Union Nationale des Travailleurs Sénégalais* (government-controlled) and the *Conféderation Nationale des Travailleurs Sénégalais* (independent) which broke away from the former in 1969.

Commerce. The chief imports (1978) (in tonnes): Rice (238,996), sugar (55,647), petroleum products (921,771), textiles and machinery.

Imports in 1977 totalled 187,500m. francs CFA; exports, 152,900m.

Total trade between Senegal and UK (British Department of Trade returns, in £1,000 sterling):

	1978	*1979*	*1980*	*1981*	*1982*
Imports to UK	15,334	18,088	15,440	17,430	14,196
Exports and re-exports from UK	10,109	11,000	16,030	26,276	22,349

Tourism. In 1979, 198,433 tourists visited Senegal.

COMMUNICATIONS

Roads. The length of roads (1979) was 13,869 km of which 2,960 km was bitumenized.

Railways. There are 5 railway lines: Dakar-Kidira (continuing in Mali), Thiès-Saint-Louis (193 km), Guinguinéo-Kaolack (22 km), Louga-Linguère (129 km), and Diourbel-Touba (46 km). Total length (1979), 1,186 km (metre gauge). In 1979-80 railways carried 732,000 passengers and 1·7m. tonnes of freight.

Aviation. In 1979 aircraft disembarked 297,170 and embarked 322,921 passengers and disembarked 7,676 tonnes and embarked 5,605 tonnes of freight at Yoff (Dakar).

Shipping. In 1978, 4,870 vessels entered the port of Dakar. There is a river service on the Senegal from Saint-Louis to Podor (363 km) open throughout the year, and to Kayes (924 km) open from July to Oct. The Senegal River is closed to foreign flags. The Saloum River is navigable as far as Kaolack, the Casamance River as far as Ziguinchor.

Post and Broadcasting. There were, in 1972, 74 post offices. Telephones in 1978 numbered 42,105, of which 33,863 were in Dakar. In 1975 there were 287,000 radio receivers and 1,800 television sets.

Cinemas. In 1975 there were 77 with a seating capacity of 33,500.

JUSTICE, RELIGION, EDUCATION AND WELFARE

Justice. There are *juges de paix* in each *département* and a court of first instance in each region. Assize courts are situated in Dakar, Kaolack, Saint-Louis and Ziguinchor, while the Court of Appeal resides in Dakar.

Religion. The population is 86% Moslem, 5% Christian (mainly Roman Catholic) and 9% animist.

Education. Secondary education is provided at 11 *lycées, 66 collèges d'enseignement secondaire, 2 lycées techniques, 2 écoles normales* and 3 *cours normaux.* Total pupils in the elementary schools in 1979 was 370,412, including 44,262 attending private schools; in the secondary schools, 82,631 (of whom 15,969 attend private colleges). The University in Dakar was established on 24 Feb. 1957, with faculties of law, science, the arts and a school of medicine and pharmacy; it had 10,309 students in 1979.

Health. In 1976 there were 43 hospitals with 6,025 beds; also 311 doctors, 37 dentists, 90 pharmacists, 380 midwives and 3,080 nursing personnel.

DIPLOMATIC REPRESENTATIVES

Of Senegal in Great Britain (11 Phillimore Gdns., London, W8 7QG)
Ambassador: Ousmane Camara (accredited 20 May 1981)

Of Great Britain in Senegal (20 Rue du Docteur Guillet, Dakar)
Ambassador: Laurence O'Keeffe, CVO.

Of Senegal in the USA (2112 Wyoming Ave., NW, Washington, D.C., 20008)
Ambassador: Abdourahmane Dia.

Of the USA in Senegal (Ave. Jean XXIII, Dakar)
Ambassador: Charles W. Bray, III.

Of Senegal to the United Nations
Ambassador: Massamba Sarré

Books of Reference

Crowder, M., *Senegal: A Study in French Assimilation.* OUP, 1962
Gellar, S., *Senegal.* Boulder, 1982
Samb, M. (ed.), *Spotlight on Senegal.* Dakar, 1972

SEYCHELLES

Capital: Victoria
Population: 64,035 (1981)
GNP per capita: US$1,770 (1980)

HISTORY. The islands were first colonized by the French in 1768, in order to establish plantations of spices to compete with the Dutch monopoly. They were captured by the English in 1794 and incorporated as a dependency of Mauritius in 1814. In Nov. 1903 the Seychelles archipelago became a separate colony. Internal self-government was achieved on 1 Oct. 1975 and independence as a republic within the Commonwealth on 29 June 1976. The first President, James Mancham, was deposed in a *coup* on 5 June 1977 and replaced by his Prime Minister.

AREA AND POPULATION. The Seychelles consists of 112 islands and islets in the Indian ocean, north of Madagascar, with a combined area of 156 sq. miles (404 sq. km) within two distinct groups. The Mahé or Granitic group of 32 islands cover 87 sq. miles (234 sq. km); the principal island is Mahé, with 56 sq. miles (144 sq. km) and 45,204 inhabitants at the 1971 census, the other inhabited islands of the group being Praslin, La Digue, Silhouette, Frigate and North, which together have 6,660 inhabitants.

The Outer or Coralline group comprises 60 islands spread over a wide area of ocean between the Mahé group and Madagascar, with a total land area of 69 sq. miles and a population of less than 1,000. The main islands are the Amirante Isles (including Desroches, Poivre, Daros and Alphonse), Coetivy Island and Platte Island, all lying south of the Mahé group; the Farquhar, St Pierre and Providence Islands, north of Madagascar; and Aldabra, Astove, Assumption and the Cosmoledo Islands, about 1,000 km south-west of the Mahé group. Aldabra (whose lagoon covers 55 sq. miles), Farquhar and Desroches were transferred to the new British Indian Ocean Territory in 1965, but were returned by Britain to the Seychelles on the latter's independence in 1976. Population (1981, estimate) 64,035.

Vital statistics (1981): Births, 1,802; deaths, 442.

CONSTITUTION AND GOVERNMENT. A new Constitution came into force on 5 June 1979, under which the Seychelles People's Progressive Front is the sole legal Party and nominates all candidates for election. There is a unicameral People's Assembly comprising 23 members elected for 4 years with 2 further nominated members. There is an Executive President directly elected for a 5-year term, who nominates and leads a Council of Ministers.

The official languages are Creole, English and French but 95% of the population speak Creole.

President: Hon. F. Albert René.

National flag: Divided horizontally red over green by a wavy white stripe, with red of double width.

DEFENCE. A People's Liberation Army was created in 1977. Personnel (1983) 750.

INTERNATIONAL RELATIONS

Membership. Seychelles is a member of UN, the Commonwealth, OAU and is an ACP state of EEC.

ECONOMY

Budget, in 1m. rupees, for calender years:

	1978	*1979*	*1980* [1]	*1981* [1]
Recurrent revenue	207·8	315·5	394·7	383·9
Recurrent expenditure	206·0	327·4	395·7	380·9

[1] Provisional.

Currency. The currency is the Seychelles *rupee.* In March 1983, £1 = 9·83 *rupees;* US$1 = 6·71 *rupees.*

Banking. Barclays Bank International, Standard Bank, Bank of Credit and Commerce, Banque Francaise Commerciale, Habib Bank, Bank of Baroda and Seychelles Development Bank, have branches in Victoria, Mahé.

ENERGY AND NATURAL RESOURCES

Electricity. Production (1981) 50·7m. kwh.

Agriculture. Chief crops (production 1981, in tonnes) are copra (3,136), cinnamon bark (419) and tea (171). Food crop production is being increased for home consumption and fishing is actively pursued mainly for home consumption but also for export as frozen fish.

Livestock (1981): Cattle, 2,000; pigs, 11,000; goats, 4,000; poultry, 130,000.

INDUSTRY AND TRADE

Industry. Local industry is expanding, the largest development in recent years being the brewery, (output, 1981, 4,553,000 litres), but steel fabricated goods, furniture, plastics, soap manufacturing form a growing element. In 1981, 3,049,000 litres of soft drinks and 44·7m. cigarettes were produced.

Commerce. Total trade, in rupees, for calendar years:

	1978	*1979*	*1980*	*1981*
Imports (less re-exports)	402,100,000	534,800,000	631,400,000	589,000,000
Domestic exports	24,700,000	30,900,000	32,900,000	27,500,000

Principal imports (1981): Manufactured goods, Rs 162·7m.; food, Rs 116·3m.; petroleum products, Rs 129·2m., machinery and transport equipment, Rs 122·2m. Principal exports (1981): Copra, Rs 17m.; frozen fish, Rs 4·3m.; cinnamon bark, Rs 1·8m., guano, Rs 0·4m.

Imports (1977) from: UK, Rs 94·59m.; Kenya, Rs 40·79m.; Republic of South Africa, Rs 31·85m.; Singapore, Rs 21·22m.; Australia, Rs 18·44m.

Exports (1977) to: Pakistan, Rs 14·04m.; Mauritius, Rs 2·6m.; USA, Rs 671,292.

Tourism. Tourism has now established itself as an important sector of the economy. The number of visitors has grown very rapidly since the opening of the international airport in 1978 and in 1979 there were 78,852, but the rapid growth has been reversed in 1980 (71,762) and 1981 (60,425).

COMMUNICATIONS

Roads. There is a good system of tarmac (84 miles) and earth roads (21 miles) in Mahé; Praslin and La Digue have 28 miles (9 miles tarmac); extensive roadmaking is being undertaken. At 31 Dec. 1981, there was a total of 139 km surfaced, and 83 km unsurfaced.

Aviation. British Airways operates 3 services a week between London and Seychelles, twice weekly from Colombo, Hong Kong and Tōkyō, and once a week from Mauritius and Johannesburg. Air France operates 2 services a week, Air India, Air Tanzania, Air Madagascar, Ethiopian Airlines, Somalia Airlines and Condor Airlines operate a weekly service. Kenya Airways operates a service 3 times a week. In 1981 aircraft movements were 1,954; passenger movements, 206,000 (including domestic flights); freight loaded, 343 tonnes, unloaded, 1,059 tonnes.

Shipping. Shipping (1981), goods unloaded, 166,000 tonnes, goods loaded, 13,000 tonnes. There are regular cargo vessels from Australia and the Far East, South Africa and Europe. The vessel *Nordvaer* travels to and from Mombasa and visits the outlying islands.

Post and Broadcasting. Services operated by Cable & Wireless Ltd provide telegraphic communications with all parts of the world by satellite, the company's radio-telephone service also extends to all principal countries in the world. In 1978, an automatic dialling telex system was introduced. Telephones in Jan. 1981 numbered 7,105.

Cinemas. In 1978 there was 1 cinema with seating capacity of 500.

JUSTICE, EDUCATION AND WELFARE

Justice. In 1977, 6,337 criminal and other cases were recorded by the police. The police force numbered 492 all ranks and 69 special constabulary.

Education. Equality of educational opportunity exists for all children for a minimum of 9 years. In Jan. 1977 there were 35 primary schools, 14 junior secondary schools, 3 secondary grammar schools, 4 vocational and technical schools and 1 teacher-training college.

In Jan. 1982 there were 14,597 pupils in primary schools, 2,362 pupils in junior secondary and secondary grammar schools, 639 pupils in vocational and technical schools and (1977) 141 in the teacher-training college. In 1977, a total of 122 students were undergoing training overseas, mainly in the UK; 68 were in university, 35 were undergoing professional/technical training, 12 teacher-training and 7 nursing.

Health. In 1981 there were 45 doctors and dental officers in government service, 336 nurses and 315 hospital beds.

DIPLOMATIC REPRESENTATIVES

Of Great Britain in Seychelles (Victoria Hse., Victoria)
High Commissioner: Eric Young, OBE.

Of Seychelles in USA
Ambassador: Giovinella Gonthier.

Of the USA in Seychelles (resides in Nairobi)
Ambassador: William C. Harrop.

Books of Reference

Statistical Information: Information Office, 52 Kingsgate House, Victoria, Mahé.
Report of Seychelles Constitutional Conference. HMSO, 1970
Population Census 1960.–Agricultural Census 1960. Government Printer, 1961
Seychelles Handbook. Government Printer, 1976
Benedict, B., *People of the Seychelles.* HMSO, 1966
Franda, M., *The Seychelles: Unquiet Islands.* Boulder, 1982
Lionnet, G., *The Seychelles.* Newton Abbot, 1972
Webb, A. W. T., *Story of Seychelles.* Government Printer, 1965

SIERRA LEONE

Capital: Freetown
Population: 3·47m. (1980)
GNP per capita: US$270 (1980)

HISTORY. The Colony of Sierra Leone originated in the sale and cession, in 1787, by native chiefs to English settlers, of a piece of land intended as a home for natives of Africa who were waifs in London, and later it was used as a settlement for Africans rescued from slave-ships. The hinterland was declared a British protectorate on 21 Aug. 1896. Sierra Leone became independent as a member state of the Commonwealth on 27 April 1961, and a republic on 19 April 1971.

AREA AND POPULATION. Sierra Leone is bounded on the north-west, north and north-east by the Republic of Guinea, on the south-east by Liberia and on the south-west by the Atlantic ocean. The coastline extends from the boundary of the Republic of Guinea to the north of the mouth of the Great Scarcies River to the boundary of Liberia at the mouth of the Mano River, a distance of about 212 miles (341 km). The area of Sierra Leone is 27,925 sq. miles (73,326 sq. km). Population (census Dec. 1974, provisional), 3,002,426, of whom about 2,000 are Europeans, 3,500 Asiatics and 30,000 non-native Africans. Estimate (1980) 3·47m. The capital is Freetown, with 274,000 inhabitants.

Vital statistics (1981); Live births, 43,140; deaths, 17,908.

Sierra Leone is divided into 3 provinces and the Western Area:

	Sq. km	*Estimate 1976*	*Capital*	*Census 1974*
Western Area	663	400,000	Freetown	274,000
Southern Province	20,378	744,000	Bo	42,000
Eastern Province	15,219	970,000	Kenema	34,000
Northern Province	36,066	1,126,000	Makeni	28,500

The principal peoples are the Temnes, Limbas, Lokos and Korankos in the north, the Temnes in the centre, the Mendis in the south, and the Kissis and Konos in the east.

CONSTITUTION AND GOVERNMENT. For earlier Constitutional history *see* THE STATESMAN'S YEAR-BOOK 1978–79, p. 1046. Following a referendum in June 1978, a new Constitution was instituted under which the ruling All People's Congress (APC) became the sole legal Party. The 100-member Parliament elected in May–June 1982 comprised 85 members all belonging to the APC.

President: Dr Siaka Probyn Stevens.
Vice-Presidents: Sorie Ibrahim Koroma, Christian Alusine Camara-Taylor.
Foreign Affairs: Dr Abdulai Conteh.

National flag: Three horizontal stripes of green, white, blue.

Local Government. The provinces are administered through the Ministry of the Interior and divided into 148 Chiefdoms, each under the control of a Paramount Chief and Council of Elders known as the Tribal Authorities, who are responsible for the maintenance of law and order and for the administration of justice (except for serious crimes). All of these Chiefdoms have been organized into local government units, empowered to raise and disburse funds for the development of the Chiefdom concerned.

DEFENCE

Army. The Army consists of 2 infantry battalions with supporting services including an engineer squadron. Strength (1983), 3,000 officers and men.

Navy. There are 2 fast attack craft based at Freetown, 1 coastal patrol craft and 3 landing craft. Personnel (1983), over 150.

Air Force. The nucleus of an air arm for the defence forces came into existence in 1973. It operates currently a single MBB BO 105 helicopter. Personnel, about 30.

INTERNATIONAL RELATIONS

Membership. Sierra Leone is a member of UN, OAU, the Commonwealth and is an ACP state of EEC.

ECONOMY

Planning. A 5-year plan (1974–79) was launched to develop industry and plantation agriculture but failed its main objectives.

Budget. Revenue and expenditure (in leone) for years ending 30 June:

	1970–71	*1971–72*	*1972–73*	*1973–74*	*1974–75*
Revenue	51,000,000	54,000,000	59,100,000	82,500,000	86,700,000
Expenditure	41,300,000	55,000,000	58,200,000	82,500,000	86,700,000

Currency. The Bank of Sierra Leone, which was established on 4 Aug. 1964, is responsible for providing the currency in the country. It introduced on 4 Aug. 1964 a decimal currency, the *leone* and the *cent*. The paper currency consists of 1, 2, 5 *leone* and 50-*cent* notes; the coinage of 1, 5, 10, 20 and 50 *cents*.

At 30 June 1976 total Sierra Leone notes and coins in circulation was Le. 39·19m. In March 1983, £1 = 3·80 *leone*; US$1 = 1·87 *leone*.

Banking. The Standard Bank Sierra Leone, the National Commercial Bank, International Bank of Credit and Commerce, International Bank of Trade and Industry and Barclays Bank Sierra Leone have their headquarters at Freetown; the Standard Bank has 13 and Barclays Bank 12 branches and agencies.

NATURAL RESOURCES

Minerals. The chief minerals mined are diamonds (850,000 carats, 1978) and bauxite (750,000 tonnes, 1978). Molybdenite and gold are being prospected. Rutile production started in 1979 with expected production of 54,000 tonnes per annum and a potential of 100,000 tonnes per annum.

Agriculture. In the western area farming is largely confined to the production of cassava and garden crops, such as maize and vegetables, for local consumption. In the provincial areas the principal products include rice, which is the staple food of the country, and export crops such as palm-kernels, cocoa beans, coffee and ginger. Cattle production is important in the northern part of the country, and most of the poultry, eggs and pork are produced in the Western Area.

Livestock (1981): Cattle, 348,000; goats, 150,000; sheep, 268,000; chickens, 3·85m.

Fisheries. There has been a gradual expansion of the industry due to the introduction of new fishing techniques and gear. The estimated tonnage of catch of all species of fish during 1973–74 was over 50,000 tonnes. The FAO has carried out a 5-year survey of pelagic fish resources along the coastline and continental shelf.

Total catch of fish is still below the demand of the country. In 1975, 94,601 cwt of fish were imported. Total catch for 1975 was 206,000 tons.

INDUSTRY AND TRADE

Industry. Four pioneer oil-mills for the expressing of palm-oil are operated by the Sierra Leone Produce Marketing Board. Government also operates 4 rice-mills, and there are a number of privately owned mills. At Kenema the Government Corporation Forest Industries produces sawn timber, joinery products (including prefabricated buildings) and high-class furniture. In addition, there is a smaller privately owned saw-mill at Panguma and several small furniture workshops throughout the country. All these products are used internally. Village industries include fishing, fish curing and smoking, weaving and hand methods of expressing palm-oil and cracking palm kernels.

Labour. A large proportion of the population was engaged in agriculture and about 125,000 workers were in wage-earning employment. The number of workers in establishments employing 6 or more persons was 72,314 in 1975, distributed as follows: Services, 33·2%; mining and quarrying, 15%; transport, storage and communications, 14·9%; construction, 12·4%; commerce, 8·7%; manufacturing, 8·1%; agriculture, forestry and fishing, 5·1%; electricity and water services, 2·6%.

There are 27 registered trade unions (22 workers and 5 employers). The number of persons registered for employment at the end of 1971 was 7,210, excluding maritime, articled and the dock workers who are registered in the Port Labour (Maritime, Articled and Harbour) Pools; registrations in these Pools numbered 8,471.

Commerce. Total trade (in leone) for calendar years:

	1975	*1976*	*1977*	*1978*
Imports	152,760,000	171,258,000	206,228,000	290,844,000
Exports	116,470,000	109,312,000	156,734,000	194,000,000

Of the imports (1971) 28·8% came from UK, 10·2% from Japan, 7·1% from Federal Republic of Germany. Of the exports (1971) 62·8% went to UK, 9·4% to Netherlands, 6·8% to Japan and 6·5% to the USA.

Total trade between Sierra Leone and UK (British Department of Trade returns, in £1,000 sterling):

	1977	*1978*	*1979*	*1980*	*1981*	*1982*
Imports to UK	40,053	39,093	75,744	65,697	43,303	14,438
Exports and re-exports from UK	19,669	31,702	32,753	36,785	24,591	19,110

Tourism. Tourism is being developed and was a major growth industry in 1981.

COMMUNICATIONS

Roads. There were (1977) about 4,406 miles of main roads, of which 665 miles are surfaced with bitumen.

Motor vehicles licensed in 1975 totalled 21,135; passenger cars, 14,267; buses and trucks, 3,384, and motor cycles, 3,484.

Railways (1977). The government railway closed in 1974, and an 84-km mineral line of 1,067-mm gauge connecting Marampa with the port of Pepel is now used only occasionally.

Aviation. Freetown Airport (Lungi), situated north of Freetown in the Port Loko District, is the only international airport in Sierra Leone and all aircraft entering and leaving the country must land at Lungi.

The airport is served by Sierra Leone Airlines, Ghana/Nigeria Airways, British Caledonian, Union de Transport Aériens, KLM, Air Afrique and Aeroflot. A once weekly non-stop flight from London (Gatwick) to Freetown and *vice versa* is also provided.

Sierra Leone Airlines provide domestic flights daily (except Sundays) from Hastings (14 miles from Freetown) to Gbangbatoke, Bo, Kenema, Yengema, twice weekly to Bonthe and occasional flights to Marampa and Port Loko on charter basis.

Shipping. During 1981 the total imports handled by the port of Freetown amounted to 423,447 freight-tons and exports 166,994 freight-tons; a total of 576 vessels called at Freetown; 564 were cargo vessels and 12 were tourist ships with a total of 718 passengers.

Bonthe-Sherbro, 80 miles south of Freetown, is used for the shipment of piassave, palm kernels, rutile and bauxite. Pepel lies some 12 miles from Freetown but is no longer in use.

Post and Broadcasting. The Posts and Telecommunications Department maintains a trunk network of radio and overhead telephone and telegraph routes of approximately 3,000 miles linking the Western Area with the other provinces. Automatic telephone exchanges have been introduced at the provincial centres of Bo, Kenema and Makeni; microwave radio relay link now replaces overhead open wire on main trunk routes. An extension programme to link important mining areas at Koidu and Mokanji to the national network by microwave links is well on the way.

The wired broadcasting relay service was replaced in Jan. 1964 by a transistor radio service. Approximately 20,000 transistor radios purchased under this scheme are now in service.

Number of telephones (1981) 220,000. Telegraphic facilities are provided at 58 offices.

There are 137 post offices and postal agencies.

The number of private wireless-licence holders (1981, estimate) was 500,000 and 20,000 television sets were in operation.

JUSTICE, RELIGION, EDUCATION AND WELFARE

Justice. The High Court has jurisdiction in civil and criminal matters. Subordinate courts are held by magistrates in the various districts. Native Courts, headed by court Chairmen, apply native law and custom under a criminal and civil jurisdiction. Appeals from the decisions of magistrates' courts are heard by the High Court. Appeals from the decisions of the High Court are heard by the Sierra Leone Court of Appeal. Appeal lies from the Sierra Leone Court of Appeal to the Supreme Court which is the highest court.

Police. The police force at 31 Dec. 1975 had an authorized strength of 82 superior police officers, 211 junior police officers and 3,833 other ranks including 382 women. In the provinces each Chiefdom keeps an additional force known as Chiefdom Police.

A non-pensionable force, known as the Auxiliary Force and consisting of 2 Junior police officers and 272 other ranks, are helping the regular force in maintaining law and order in the diamond protected area in the Eastern Province.

Religion. The majority of the population follow traditional tribal religions. Islam was brought to the region by the nomadic cattle-rearing Fula people from the north around 1600. The Temne people in the north-west form the main part of the Moslem community who were estimated in 1977 to comprise about 20% of the population.

Christianity came to West Africa in the 16th century from Portugal and Spain. The Roman Catholics have 2 dioceses in Sierra Leone and number about 25,000 (1977).

The Evangelical group who led the anti-slavery movement in England founded the Sierra Leone Company in 1791 to settle freed slaves in and around Freetown. In 1966 there were 16 Protestant denominations with a total community of 77,000. Members of the Sierra Leone Church (Anglican) were 25,000 in 1977.

Education (1975–76). There were over 1,974 registered primary schools with a total enrolment of over 205,910. Primary education is partially free but not compulsory though parents and guardians are urged to send their children and wards to school. School attendance varies considerably in different parts of the country. There were 132 secondary schools with a total enrolment of 48,609 pupils; 71 of these schools are fully assisted by the Government. Technical education was provided in 2 technical institutes, 2 trade centres and in the technical training establishments of the mining companies. There is also a rural institute.

Non-graduate teacher-training is offered at two levels: the teachers certificate trains teachers for primary schools and the higher teachers certificate trains teachers for the lower forms of secondary schools.

Fourah Bay College (1,016 students) and Njala University College (586 students) are the 2 constituent colleges of the University of Sierra Leone. The Institute of Education, which is part of the University, is now responsible for teacher education, educational research and curriculum development in the country.

Health (1977). In the Western Area there are 12 government hospitals (1,108 beds and 217 cots), including a maternity hospital, a children's hospital and an infectious diseases hospital near Freetown. There are 6 government health centres in the Western Area. Three private hospitals are located in Freetown with 108 beds. A mental hospital at Kissy has accommodation for 224 patients. In the provinces there are 14 government hospitals, 4 hospitals associated with mining companies and 7 mission hospitals. There is a school of nursing in Freetown. There are 156 government dispensaries and health treatment centres and two military hospitals with 124 beds.

DIPLOMATIC REPRESENTATIVES

Of Sierra Leone in Great Britain (33 Portland Pl., London, W1N 3AG)
High Commissioner: Victor E. Sumner.

Of Great Britain in Sierra Leone (Standard Bank of Sierra Leone Ltd Bldg., Lightfoot Boston St., Freetown)
High Commissioner: T.D.O'Leary, CMG.

Of Sierra Leone in the USA (1701 19th St., NW, Washington, D.C., 20009)
Ambassador: Dauda S. Kamara.

Of the USA in Sierra Leone (Corner Walpole and Siaka Stevens St., Freetown)
Ambassador: Theresa A. Healy.

Of Sierra Leone to the United Nations
Ambassador: Abdul G. Koroma.

Books of Reference

Atlas of Sierra Leone. Ed. Survey and Lands Dept. Freetown, 1953
Sierra Leone Studies. Ed. J. D. Hargreaves, Freetown, 1953 ff.
Fyfe, C., *A History of Sierra Leone*. OUP, 1962.—Fyfe, C., and Jones, E. (ed.), *Freetown*. Sierra Leone Univ. Press and OUP, 1968
Fyfe, C. N. and Jones, E. D., *A Krio–English Dictionary*. OUP and Sierra Leone Univ. Press, 1980
Kup, A. P., *Sierra Leone*. Newton Abbot, 1975
Porter, A. T., *Creoledom: A Study in the Development of Freetown Society*. OUP, 1963
Saylor, R. G., *The Economic System of Sierra Leone*. Duke Univ. Press, 1968

REPUBLIC OF SINGAPORE

Population: 2·47m. (1982)
GNP per capita: US$6,515 (1980)

HISTORY. For the early history of the settlement (1819) and colony (1867) *see* THE STATESMAN'S YEAR-BOOK, 1959, pp. 246 f.

By an agreement entered into between the Governments of Malaysia and of the State of Singapore on 7 Aug. 1965, effective on 9 Aug. 1965, Singapore ceased to be one of the 14 states of the Federation of Malaysia and became an independent sovereign state. The separation was ratified by the Constitution and Malaysia (Singapore Amendment) Act of the Malaysian Parliament on 9 Aug. The 2 governments agreed to enter into a treaty on external defence and mutual assistance. The Singapore Government retains its executive authority and legislative powers under its State Constitution and took over the powers of the Malaysian Government under the Malaysian Constitution in Singapore. The sovereignty and jurisdiction of the head of the Malaysian State was transferred to the Singapore Government. Civil servants working in Singapore for the Federal Departments became Singapore civil servants. Singapore citizens ceased to be Malaysian citizens.

Singapore accepted responsibility for international agreements entered into by the Malaysian Government on its behalf.

AREA AND POPULATION. The Republic of Singapore consists of Singapore Island itself, and some 54 islets.

Singapore Island is situated off the southern extremity of the Malay peninsula, to which it is joined by a causeway carrying a road, railway and water pipeline. The Straits of Johore between the island and the mainland are about three-quarters of a mile wide. The island is some 26 miles (41·8 km) in length and 14 miles (22·5 km) in breadth, and about 241·4 sq. miles (617·9 sq. km) in area, including the adjacent islets.

Census of population (1980): 1,856,237 Chinese, 351,508 Malays, 154,632 Indians and 51,568 others; total 2,413,945. Estimate (mid-1982), 2,471,800.

Report on the Census of Population 1980. Dept. of Statistics, Singapore, 1980

CONSTITUTION AND GOVERNMENT. By a constitutional amendment the name of the state was changed to 'Republic of Singapore', the head of state was named 'President of Singapore' and the legislative assembly was renamed 'Parliament'.

Malay, Chinese, Tamil and English are the official languages; English is the language of administration.

Parliament consists of 75 members, elected by secret ballot from single-member constituencies, and is presided over by a Speaker, chosen by Parliament from its own members or from outside the Assembly. In the latter case, the Speaker has no vote. With the customary exception of those serving criminal sentences, all citizens over 21 are eligible to vote irrespective of sex, race, education or property qualification. There is a common roll without communal electorates. Citizenship is automatic by birth; it can also be acquired by registration or by naturalization.

A Presidential Council was established under Part IVA of the Constitution enacted on 9 Jan. 1970. The general function of the Council is to consider and report on matters affecting persons of any racial or religious community in Singapore as referred to it by Parliament or the Government. The Council will draw attention to any bill or subsidiary legislation which in the opinion of the Council is a differentiating measure.

Parliament, as from Nov. 1981, is composed of 74 People's Action Party members and one member from the Workers' Party.

President of Singapore: Devan Nair (sworn in 24 Oct. 1981).

The People's Action Party Cabinet at Jan. 1982 was composed as follows:
Prime Minister: Lee Kuan Yew.

First Deputy Prime Minister and Education: Dr Goh Keng Swee. *Second Deputy Prime Minister and Foreign Affairs:* S. Rajaratnam. *Labour and Communications:* Ong Teng Cheong. *Culture and Foreign Affairs:* S. Dhanabalan. *National Development:* Teh Cheang Wan. *Law and Leader of the House:* E. W. Barker. *Defence and Second Minister for Health:* Goh Chok Tong. *Home Affairs:* Chua Sian Chin. *Social Affairs:* Dr Ahmad Mattar. *Finance:* Hon Sui Sen. *Health:* Howe Yoon Chong. *Environment:* Ong Pang Boon. *Trade and Industry:* Tony Tan Keng Yam.

National flag: Horizontally red over white, charged in the canton with a crescent and a circle of 5 stars, all in white.

DEFENCE. The Ministry of Defence exercises command and control over all armed forces in the republic. It comprises 5 major divisions, *i.e.*, the general staff, manpower, logistic, security and intelligence and finance divisions. Compulsory military service in peace-time was introduced in 1967.

The governments of Australia, Britain, Malaysia, New Zealand and Singapore continue to co-operate closely in defence arrangements and have agreed on a new 5-nation defence set-up in SE Asia designed to protect Malaysia and Singapore against outside attack. The new defence arrangement came into force on 1 Nov. 1971.

Army. There are 9 full-time infantry battalions and 1 commando battalion organized in 3 brigades and commanded directly by a divisional headquarters. These are complemented by artillery, engineers, signals, armour and service units. The personnel of these units are mainly national servicemen who, on completion of national service, are posted to reserve battalions and the People's Defence Force. Regular strength, 35,000, and reserves, 120,000.

Navy. Naval vessels comprise 9 large and fast attack craft, missile armed, of German design, 6 fast patrol craft built by Vosper Thornycroft (2 at Portsmouth, Britain, and 4 in Singapore), 2 *ex*-US coastal minesweepers, 1 seaward defence boat, 1 training vessel, 6 landing ships (*ex*-USN LST) and 6 small landing craft (2 *ex*-Australian). Personnel in 1983 numbered 3,000 officers and men. There are 22 coastal patrol craft operated by the marine police and 3 small survey craft operated by the Singapore Port Authority.

Air Defence Command. The formation of an Air Defence Command began in 1968. The Republic of Singapore Air Force now has 1 squadron of F-5E supersonic fighters supported by 2-seat F-5Fs; 2 fighter-bomber squadrons equipped with A-4S Skyhawks, supported by TA-4S two-seat trainers; 2 squadrons of Hunter jet fighters and reconnaissance-fighters, supported by Hunter 2-seat trainers, a radar unit and a Bloodhound surface-to-air missile squadron; a transport squadron of C-130s and Skyvans equipped for search and rescue; a squadron of Bell UH-1H Iroquois and Bell 212 helicopters; and training units equipped with SF.260MS piston-engined basic trainers, T-33A jets, and AS 350 Ecureuil helicopters. Personnel strength about 4,000.

INTERNATIONAL RELATIONS

Membership. Singapore is a member of UN, the Commonwealth, the Colombo Plan and ASEAN.

ECONOMY

Planning. The GDP in 1981, at current factor cost was $25,200m., an increase of 15·8% over 1980.

Budget. Public revenue and expenditure for financial years (in S$1m.):

	1977	*1978*	*1979*	*1980*	*1981*[1]
Revenue	3,555	3,739	4,603	5,904	6,335
Expenditure	5,442	5,879	6,839	9,363	12,552

[1] Estimate.

Currency. The *Singapore dollar* (S$) is divided in 100 *cents*. Gross circulation on 31 Dec. 1981 was S$3,689·6m. In March 1983, £1 = 3·09 *dollars*; US$1 = 2·09 dollars.

Banking. The functions of the Commissioner of Banking have been assumed by the Monetary Authority of Singapore from 1 Jan. 1971.

The Development Bank of Singapore was established in 1968, primarily to provide long-term financing of manufacturing and other industries. In Dec. 1981 it had a paid up capital of S$228·5m. and shareholders' funds amounted to S$725·6m.

There were 116 commercial banks with 347 banking offices operating in Singapore as at July 1982. The total assets/liabilities amounted to S$45,607·5m. as at July 1982. Total deposits of non-bank customers amounted to S$19,828·1m. while loans and advances including bills financing, totalled S$26,641·7m.

In 1982, the total balance of the Singapore Post Office Savings Bank was S$4,105·6m.

Weights and Measures. The metric system or the International System of Units (SI) was introduced in 1971 in Singapore.

ENERGY AND NATURAL RESOURCES

Electricity. The Public Utilities Board is responsible for the provision of electricity, gas and water. Electrical power is generated by 5 power stations, with a total generating capacity of 2,010 mw at the end of 1981.

Fisheries. As the prospect of increasing fish production from inshore waters is poor, in 1967 various projects were introduced, with the aim of making Singapore self-sufficient in fish as well as a major fishing base in the region.

The Jurong fishing port and fish market began operating 26 Feb. 1969. A Fishery Training Institute was established at Changi with the assistance of the United Nations Development Programme (Special Fund) to train youths and fishermen in modern fishing techniques. At Changi, too, a Marine Fisheries Research Department was set up under the sponsorship of the South-East Asian Fisheries Development Centre. Research on fish culture and ornamental fish was carried out at the Freshwater Fisheries Laboratory at Sembawang. Ornamental fish industry is fast becoming a valuable foreign exchange earner. Export of aquarium fish in 1981, S$35·4m. The local catch of fresh fish in 1981 was 16,111 tonnes.

INDUSTRY AND TRADE

Industry. The largest industrial area is the Jurong Industrial Estate with 1,259 factories employing 105,500 workers as at March 1981.

Industries in Jurong include shipbuilding and those manufacturing steel rods, steel pipes, tyres, chemicals, pharmaceuticals, plywood and veneer, plastics, cement, bricks, cables, textiles and wiremesh. Smaller industrial estates have light industry factories producing food, paper and miscellaneous consumer goods.

Labour. In June 1981, 1,112,819 persons were employed, of whom 947,016 were employees, 43,839 were employers, 96,507 were self-employed and 25,457 were unpaid family workers. The majority were working in manufacturing, 338,100; commerce, 242,000; transport and communications, 127,000.

There were 134 registered trade unions comprising 86 employee unions, 47 employer unions and 1 federation of trade unions in 1981. The total membership of employee unions numbered 224,362, of whom 214,679 of the unionized workers belonged to 61 employee unions affiliated to the National Trades Union Congress. Members of employer unions numbered 6,798.

The Employment Act and the Industrial Relations Act provide principal terms and conditions of employment such as hours of work, sick leave and other fringe benefits. A new labour legislation was introduced allowing youths of 14-16 years to work in industrial establishments, and also children from 12-14 years to be employed in approved apprenticeship schemes. A trade dispute may be referred to the Industrial Arbitration Court which was established in 1960.

The Ministry of Labour operates 3 employment exchanges to assist job seekers to obtain suitable employment and employers to recruit suitable workers. The Central Provident Fund was established in 1955 to make provision for employees in their old age. In 1981 there were 1,649,700 members with S$12,149·8m. standing to their credit in the fund. The total number of active employers registered with the board in 1981 was 71,612 comprising 58,609 business employers and 13,003 domestic employers.

Commerce. The major trading countries for 1981 were Japan (15%), Malaysia (14%), US (13·5%), Saudi Arabia (11·5%) and the EEC (10%). In 1981, imports (S$58,248m.) rose by 13%, mainly due to more imports of raw materials and semi-manufactured goods. Exports rose from S$41,452m. in 1980 to S$44,291m. in 1981, mainly due to increases in petroleum products, electronic products, crude rubber, machinery and transport equipment and furniture.

In the following table (British Department of Trade returns, in £1,000 sterling) the imports include produce from Borneo, Sarawak and other eastern places, transhipped at Singapore, which is thus entered as the place of export:

	1978	*1979*	*1980*	*1981*	*1982*
Imports to UK	116,747	185,290	214,698	245,209	245,453
Exports and re-exports from UK	255,908	270,718	355,662	406,791	406,172

COMMUNICATIONS

Roads. Singapore has 2,478 km of public roads, of which 2,183 km are asphalt-paved. In 1981 motor vehicles registered in Singapore numbered 401,805, of which 161,692 were private cars, 6,950 buses, 9,862 taxis and 127,722 motor cycles and scooters.

Railways. A 16-mile (25·8-km) main line runs through Singapore, connecting with the States of Malaysia and as far as Bangkok. Branch lines serve the port of Singapore and the industrial estate at Jurong.

Aviation. The new international airport at Changi was completed and operational from 1 July 1981. Thirty-four international airlines operated 1,306 scheduled services a week, totalling 73,500 aircraft movements at Singapore International Airport in Paya Lebar and Changi in 1981. Freight handled (1981) 193,143 tonnes and there were 8·1m. passengers.

Shipping. A total of 52,231 vessels of 345·2m. NRT entered into and cleared from Singapore during 1981.

Post. In Sept. 1982, 72 post offices and 63 postal agencies were in operation. Telephones numbered 775,000 in 1981.

Cinemas (1981). There were 73 cinemas and 1 drive-in cinema, with a total seating capacity of 74,000.

Newspapers (1981). There were 11 daily newspapers, in 4 languages, with a total daily circulation of 644,310.

JUSTICE, EDUCATION AND WELFARE

Justice. There is a Supreme Court in Singapore which consists of the High Court, the Court of Appeal and the Court of Criminal Appeal. The Supreme Court is composed of a Chief Justice and 6 Judges. An appeal from the High Court lies to the Court of Appeal in civil matters and to the Court of Criminal Appeal in criminal matters. Further appeal can in certain cases be made to the Judicial Committee of the Privy Council. The High Court has original civil and criminal jurisdiction as well as appellate civil and criminal jurisdiction in respect of appeals from the Subordinate Courts. There are 9 district courts, 11 magistrates' courts, 1 juvenile and 1 coroner's court.

Education. Statistics of schools in 1981:

	Schools	Pupils	Teachers
Primary			
Government schools	200	214,763	8,386
Government-aided schools	125	74,756	2,711
Private schools	2	178	11
Secondary			
Government schools	90	128,127 [1]	7,249
Government-aided schools	51	47,333 [1]	1,493
Private schools	4	1,778 [1]	65

[1] Includes pre-university classes.

The National University of Singapore was established on 8 Aug. 1980 following the merger of the University of Singapore and the Nanyang University. The National University of Singapore has 8 faculties: Arts and social sciences, law, science, medicine, dentistry, engineering, architecture and building, accountancy and business administration and 3 schools, post-graduate medical studies, post-graduate dental studies, and school of management.

The Department of Extramural Studies and the English Language Proficiency Unit are non-faculty departments. Total student enrolment for 1981 was 10,386. The Nanyang Technological Institute, situated in the former Nanyang University, was established on 8 Aug. 1981. The institute admitted about 650 second-year students of the University's Faculty of Engineering in July 1982. It will be developed into a University of Technology by 1992. The Singapore Polytechnic had 8,850 students and the Ngee Ann Technical College, re-named Ngee Ann Polytechnic on 16 April 1982, had 3,137 students in 1981–82. The Institute of Education, established on 1 April 1973, is now the only institution responsible for teacher education in Singapore and for promoting research in education. There were 1,783 students in 1981.

The Adult Education Board and the Industrial Training Board were merged to form the Vocational and Industrial Training Board, on 1 April 1979. The VITB has taken over all the functions and responsibilities in vocational training and continuing education. The VITB runs 17 training institutes and centres offering full-time and part-time courses. The total student enrolment for 1981 was 11,187.

Health. There were 13 government hospitals with a total of 8,365 beds in 1981. There were 2,091 doctors registered.

DIPLOMATIC REPRESENTATIVES

Of Singapore in Great Britain (2 Wilton Cres., London, SW1X 8RW)
High Commissioner: Jek Yeun Thong (accredited 1 Dec. 1977).

Of Great Britain in Singapore (Tanglin Rd, Singapore, 1024)
High Commissioner: Sir Peter Moon, KCVO, CMG.

Of Singapore in the USA(1824 R St., NW, Washington, D.C., 20009)
Ambassador: P. Coomaraswamy.

Of the USA in Singapore (30 Hill St., Singapore, 0617)
Ambassador: Harry E. T. Thayer.

Of Singapore to the United Nations
Ambassador: T. T. B. Koh.

Books of Reference

Statistical Information: The Department of Statistics (PO Box 3010, Singapore) was established 1 Jan. 1922. Its publications include: *Singapore External Trade Statistics* (quarterly), *Monthly Digest of Statistics, Yearbook of Statistics, Population Estimates of Singapore* (bi-annual). *Census of Population 1980. Singapore Yearbook of Labour Statistics. Chief Statistician:* Khoo Chian Kim.

National Library. *Books About Singapore.* Singapore. Biennial
National Trades Union Congress, *Singapore. Towards Tomorrow.* Singapore, 1973

Singapore. Constitution. The Constitution of Singapore. Singapore, 1966
The Budget for the Financial Year 1982–83.
Singapore. Singapore, Publicity Division, Ministry of Culture (formerly *Annual Report*)
Singapore. Government Gazette (published weekly with supplement)
Economic Survey of Singapore, 1981. Ministry of Trade and Industry, Singapore, 1981
Singapore. Facts and Pictures. Singapore, Publicity Division, Ministry of Culture (annual)
Singapore Government Directory. Singapore, Publicity Division, Ministry of Culture
The Statutes of the Republic of Singapore. 8 vols., 1970 (with annual supplements)
George, T. J. S., *Lee Kuan Yew's Singapore.* London, 1973
Goh, K. S., *The Economics of Modernisation.* Singapore, 1972
Gramer, R. E., *The Politics of Urban Development in Singapore.* OUP, 1972
Josey, A., *Lee Kuan Yew, The Struggle for Singapore.* London, 1980.—*Singapore: Its Past, Present and Future.* Singapore, 1979
Lee, S. Y., *Public Finance and Public Investment in Singapore.* Singapore, 1978
Ooi, J. B. (ed.), *Modern Singapore.* Singapore, 1969
Saw, S.-H., *Population Control for Zero Growth in Singapore.* Singapore, 1980
Tan, C. H., *Financial Institutions in Singapore.* Singapore, 1978
Turnbull, C. M., *A History of Singapore, 1819–1975.* OUP, 1977
Wee, T.B. (ed.), *The Future of Singapore; The Global City.* Singapore, 1977
Wilson, R., *The Future Role of Singapore.* OUP, 1972
Yeo, K. W., *Political Development in Singapore, 1945–1955.* Singapore Univ. Press, 1973

National Library: National Library, Stamford Rd, Singapore. *Director:* Mrs Hedwig Anuar.

SOLOMON ISLANDS

Capital: Honiara
Population: 234,000 (1981)
GNP per capita: US$430 (1981)

HISTORY. The Solomon Islands were discovered in 1568 by Alvaro de Mendana, on a voyage of discovery from Peru; 200 years passed before European contact was again made with the Solomons. The Solomon Islands lie within the area 5° to 12° 30′ S. lat. and 155° 30′ to 169° 45′ E. long. The group includes the main islands of Guadalcanal, Malaita, San Cristobal, New Georgia, Santa Isabel and Choiseul; the smaller Florida and Russell groups; the Shortland, Mono (or Treasury), Vella La Vella, Kolombangara, Ranongga, Gizo and Rendova Islands; to the east, Santa Cruz, Tikopia, the Reef and Duff groups; Rennell and Bellona in the south; Ontong Java or Lord Howe to the north; and innumerable smaller islands.

The 4 first-named were placed under British protection in 1893; the other islands were added in 1898 and 1899.

AREA AND POPULATION. The land area of the Solomons is estimated at 11,500 sq. miles (29,785 sq. km). The larger islands are mountainous and forest clad, with flood-prone rivers of considerable energy potential. Guadalcanal has the largest land area and the greatest amount of flat coastal plain.

The population of Guadalcanal (including Honiara the main town) was 46,619 at census date (Feb. 1976); Malaita (58,721).

Population of the Solomon Islands was (1978) 215,000. Census (1976) 196,823, over 50% being under 20 years (183,665 Melanesians, 7,821 Polynesians, 452 Chinese, 1,359 Europeans, 2,753 Gilbertese and 773 others).

The islands are administratively divided into 5 provinces replacing the former districts. These provinces are (with 1976 Census population): Western Province (40,329), Guadalcanal (46,619), Central Islands and Santa Isabel (23,996), Malaita (60,043) and Makula and Temotu (formerly Eastern District, 25,836). The government has announced plans to create a federal system.

The capital, Honiara, on Guadalcanal, is the largest urban area, with census population in 1979 of 18,346. Rainfall at Honiara (which lies in a rain shadow) is 90 in. per annum; elsewhere as high as 300 in.; the average is 120-140 in.

CONSTITUTION AND GOVERNMENT. A Constitutional Conference was held in London during Sept. 1977, where it was agreed that there should be full independence for the Solomon Islands and this was granted on 7 July 1978.

The main provisions of the 1978 Constitution are that Solomon Islands is a constitutional monarchy with the British Sovereign (represented locally by a Governor-General, who must be a Solomon Island citizen) as Head of State, while legislative power is vested in the unicameral National Parliament composed of 38 members, elected by universal adult suffrage for four years (subject to dissolution), and executive authority is effectively held by the Cabinet, led by the Prime Minister.

The Governor-General is appointed for up to five years, on the advice of Parliament, and acts in almost all matters on the advice of the Cabinet. The Prime Minister is elected by and from members of Parliament. Other Ministers are appointed by the Governor-General on the Prime Minister's recommendation, from members of Parliament. The Cabinet is responsible to Parliament. Emphasis is laid on the devolution of power to provincial governments, and traditional chiefs and leaders have a special role within the arrangement.

The Constitution contains comprehensive guarantees of fundamental human rights and freedom, and provides for the introduction of a leadership code and the appointment of an Ombudsman and a Public Solicitor. It also provides for the establishment of the underlying law, based on customary law and concepts of the Solomon Islands people.

Solomon Islands citizenship was automatically conferred on the indigenous people of the islands and on other residents with close ties with the islands upon independence. The acquisition of land is reserved for indigenous inhabitants or their descendants.

Governor General: Sir Baddeley Devisi, GCMG.
Prime Minister: Solomon Mamaloni.
National flag: Divided blue over green by a diagonal yellow band, and in the canton 5 white stars.

INTERNATIONAL RELATIONS

Membership. The Solomon Islands is a member of UN and is an ACP state of EEC.

ECONOMY

Planning. The overall objective of the $A60m. first National Development Plan covering the years 1975-79 was to provide guidelines for the development of the country. A review of the first 2 years of operation of the plan has shown that many of the targets have been met, while the prospects for the rest of the Plan period appear cautiously optimistic, with increased production and export earnings, a likely favourable balance of trade and improved revenue.

Budget. The budget for 1980 envisaged revenue of SI$27·5m. and expenditure SI$27·4m.

Currency. The medium of exchange is Australian decimal currency introduced in Feb. 1966, but the *Solomon Island dollar* (SI$) was introduced in 1977. In March 1983, US$1 = 1·12 *dollars*; £1 = 1·66 *dollars*.

NATURAL RESOURCES

Agriculture. Coconuts, cocoa, rice and other minor crops are grown. Oil-palm is being developed successfully with a total of 3,355 hectares having been planted by Dec. 1979. Production of copra (1980), 29,169 tonnes.

An oil-mill became operational in 1976. 3,500 tons of palm-oil out of 300 tons of palm-kernels were exported in 1976.

Rice-cropping in 1980 yielded 5,670 tonnes of milled rice.

Timber extraction is an important development in the Solomons. Timber (logs, sawn timber and veneer sheets) exports for 1980 were 258,000 cu. metres ($A149m.).

Livestock (1980): Cattle, 27,000; pigs, 37,000; poultry, 140,000.

Fisheries. A total catch of 20,700 tonnes of skipjack was made in 1978. Exports of fish totalled 21,578 tonnes ($A19·8m.) in 1980.

INDUSTRY AND TRADE

Commerce. The main imports (1980) were food, fuels and capital goods and totalled $A61·5m. Exports comprised copra (316,821 tonnes, $A10·5m.), frozen fish (21,578 tonnes, $A19·8m.), rough timber (258,000 cu. metres, $A149m.), palm-oil (15,619 tonnes), marine shell, cocoa and manufactured tobacco; total exports, $A60·8m. In 1976, Australia supplied 38% of the imports; Japan, 13%; Singapore, 10%, and of the exports, 36% went to Japan, 13% to UK, 11% to Puerto Rico and 11% to American Samoa.

Tourism. In 1980, there were 7,100 tourists.

COMMUNICATIONS

Roads. These were 455 km of main roads in 1976.

Aviation. Regular flights from Fiji and Australia (*via* Papua New Guinea) provide the main communication link. Solair, the internal airline, and innumerable small ships, provide inter-island transport.

Shipping. Shipping services are maintained with Australia, New Zealand, UK and the Far East.

Post. Number of telephones (Jan. 1981), 2,474. A VHF radio telephone service operates internally as well as overseas.

Newspapers. There are 4 weekly newspapers, 1 with a circulation of 4,000 and the other 3 with 3,000.

RELIGION, EDUCATION AND WELFARE

Religion. At the 1976 census, 34% of the population were Anglican, 19% Roman Catholic, 17% South Sea Evangelical and 25% other Protestant.

Education. In 1981 there were 28,831 primary school pupils. There were five aided national secondary schools, one private national secondary school and eight new secondary schools. Total enrolment secondary schools, 3,547 (1980).

Training of teachers is carried out at Solomon Islands Teachers' College and trade and vocational training is carried out at Honiara Technical Institute. There were 160 students on pre-service scholarships overseas and 73 students on overseas professional course.

Health. In 1980 there were 8 hospitals, 183 clinics and health centres and 30 doctors.

DIPLOMATIC REPRESENTATIVES

Of the Solomon Islands in Great Britain
High Commissioner: (Vacant).

Of Great Britain in the Solomon Islands (Soltel House, Mendana Ave., Honiara)
High Commissioner: George Stansfield, OBE.

Books of Reference

B.S.I.P. Annual Report, 1969. Honiara, 1970
Pacific Islands Year Book and Who's Who. Sydney, 1968
Building the Nation. Honiara, 1975
Amhurst, Lord, and Thompson, B., *The Discovery of the Solomon Islands in 1568.* London, 1967
Fox, C. E., *The Threshold of the Pacific.* London, 1924
Kent, J., *The Solomon Islands.* Newton Abbot, 1972
Miller, J., *Guadalcanal: The First Offensive.* Washington, 1949

SOMALIA

Capital: Mogadiscio
Population: 3·86m. (1982)
GNP per capita: US$130 (1978)

Jamhuriyadda Dimugradiga Somaliya

HISTORY. The Somali Republic came into being on 1 July 1960 as a result of the merger of the British Somaliland Protectorate, which became independent on 26 June 1960, and the Italian Trusteeship Territory of Somalia.

For the previous history of these territories *see* THE STATESMAN'S YEAR-BOOK, 1960, pp. 337 and 1367.

On 21 Oct. 1969 the Somali armed forces led by Maj.-Gen. Mohammed Siyad Barre took power in a *coup*, suspended the Constitution and formed a Supreme Revolutionary Council to administer the country, which was renamed the Somali Democratic Republic. Constitutional government was re-established on 23 Sept. 1979.

AREA AND POPULATION. Somalia is bounded north by the Gulf of Aden, east and south by the Indian ocean, and west by Kenya, Ethiopia and Djibouti. Total area of 637,657 sq. km (246,201 sq. miles). Census population (1975) 3,253,024 of whom 15% urban. Estimate (1982) 3,862,000 excluding an estimated 750,000 Somali-speaking refugees from the disputed Ogaden area of Ethiopia, now living in camps in Somalia.

The capital is Mogadiscio (377,000), other large towns being Hargeisa (70,000), Kisimayu (70,000), Merca (60,000) and Berbera (55,000).

There are long-standing territorial disputes with Kenya and Ethiopia.

CONSTITUTION AND GOVERNMENT. A new Constitution was approved by referendum on 23 Aug. 1979 and came into force on 23 Sept. The sole legal Party (since 1 July 1976) is the Somali Revolutionary Socialist Party, administered by a 73-member Central Committee. There is an Executive President nominated by the Central Committee and elected for a 6-year term by the People's Assembly; the latter consists of 121 members elected by universal suffrage for a 5-year term and a further 6 members appointed by the President. *President:* Maj.-Gen. Mohammed Siyad Barre.

The Council of Ministers, appointed and led by the President, also includes:

Presidential Advisors: Maj.-Gen. Hussein Kulmia Afrah (*Government Affairs*), Brig.-Gen. Ahmed Suleyman Abdulle (*National Security*). *Minister of Defence:* Brig.-Gen. Mohamed Ali Samater. (These 3, together with the President and the Chairman of the People's Assembly, Gen. Ismael Ali Aboker, constitute the Political Bureau of the SRSP.) *Foreign Affairs:* Dr. Abderrahman Jama Barreh.

National flag: Light blue with a white star in the centre.

The national language is Somali. Arabic is also an official language and English and Italian are extensively spoken.

Local Government. There were (1982) 17 regions, sub-divided into 78 districts.

DEFENCE

Army. The Army of 60,000, plus 20,000 militia, includes 3 tank brigades, 16 infantry brigades, 13 field artillery, 10 AA artillery battalions and 3 commando brigades. Border guards number 1,500.

Navy. The Navy has 4 submarine chasers (fast-attack/torpedo/patrol craft), 2 fast missile craft, 4 fast torpedo boats, 5 patrol craft, 1 medium landing ship and 4 minor landing craft. All are former Soviet naval units. Personnel (1983) 350.

Air Force. Formed with a nucleus of aircraft taken over from the former Italian Air Corps of Somalia, in 1960, the Air Corps was built up with Soviet aid. Current equipment includes 7 MiG-21 supersonic fighters, about 9 MiG-17 jet-fighters and 2 MiG-15UTI two-seat advanced trainers, a few Il-28 light jet bombers, and small transport, helicopter and training units. Latest equipment includes 4 Aeritalia G222 twin-turboprop transports and 4 Agusta-Bell 212 helicopters from Italy, and at least 10 J-6 (Chinese-built MiG-19) fighters. Personnel total about 2,000.

INTERNATIONAL RELATIONS

Membership. Somalia is a member of UN, OAU, the Arab League and is an ACP state of EEC.

ECONOMY

Planning. The 1979-81 development plan envisages expenditure of Som.Sh. 7,104m., of which 37% is allocated to livestock, agriculture and mineral development, 7% to health and education.

Budget. The budget for 1982 envisaged Som.Sh.3,130m. expenditure.

Currency. The currency is the *Somali shilling,* divided into 100 cents. The money is issued in notes of 1, 5, 10, 20 and 100 shillings and coins of 1, 5, 10, 50 cents and 1 shilling. Currency in circulation (1979) Som.Sh.1,152·6m. In March 1983 £1 = 22·38 Som.Sh.; US$1 = 13·30 Som.Sh.

Banking. The Banco di Roma, Napoli, National & Grindlays Bank and Banco di Portsaid have all more than one branch each in the country. The Somali National Bank and the Somali Development Bank are both state-owned.

Weights and Measures. The metric system is in use.

ENERGY AND NATURAL RESOURCES

Electricity. Electricity production (1980) was 75m. kwh.

Minerals. Deposits of iron ore in the south and gypsum in the north are known to exist. Beryl and columbite are also found in the north. None are commercially exploited. Several firms hold exploration and drilling licences for oil. Uranium is found in Juiba region.

Agriculture. Somalia is essentially a pastoral country, and about 80% of the inhabitants depend on livestock-rearing (cattle, sheep, goats and camels). In Southern Somalia, especially along the Shebeli and Giuba rivers, there are Somali and Italian plantations with a cultivated area of some 90,000 hectares. Estimated production, 1978 (in 1,000 tons): Sugar, 200; bananas, 150; maize, 100; sorghum, 130; grapefruit, 6; cotton, 1. Fresh fruit and oil seeds are grown in increasing quantities.

Livestock (1981): 16·5m. goats; 10·1m. sheep; 5·5m. camels; 3·9m. cattle; 1,000 horses, 24,000 asses and 22,000 mules.

INDUSTRY AND TRADE

Industry. In 1975, 275 industrial establishments employed 10,383 workers and produced a gross output of Som.Sh.405m., of which Som.Sh.157m. was in food manufacturing. In 1971 a sugar refinery at Jowhar had 5,300 workers; a textile factory at Balad employed 750; and a meat canning plant at Kisimayu employed 500; there is also a fish processing plant at Las Korey, and a milk bottling plant at Mogadiscio.

Trade. In 1980 imports were Som.Sh.1,734m. and exports Som.Sh.880m. The chief exports are fresh fruit, livestock, hides and skins.

In 1978, 30% of imports came from Italy, 11% from Federal Republic of Germany and 10% from the UK, while 86% of exports went to Saudi Arabia.

Total trade between the Somali Republic and UK (British Department of Trade returns, in £1,000 sterling):

	1977	*1978*	*1979*	*1980*	*1981*	*1982*
Imports to UK	257	274	96	303	856	883
Exports and re-exports from UK	14,198	19,980	20,959	6,682	12,606	12,095

COMMUNICATIONS

Roads. Somalia has no developed transport system. Internal freight and passenger transport is almost entirely by means of road haulage. In 1978 there were 19,380 km of roads (2,153 km were paved). In 1977 there were 4,200 passenger cars and 5,700 commercial vehicles, including buses.

Aviation. There is a commercial national airline, Somali Airlines. Mogadiscio airport is used by Alitalia, Alyemda, Aeroflot and Kenya Airways.

Shipping. There are 3 deep-water harbours at Kisimayu, Berbera and Mogadiscio. Because of the shape of the country, coastal shipping is an important form of internal transport. The merchant fleet (1980) amounted to 22 vessels of 45·55m. gross tons. In 1973, 900,000 tonnes of international seaborne goods were handled in the main ports.

Post and Broadcasting. There is a manual telephone system in several towns, but Mogadiscio has an automatic system; number of telephones (1971), about 4,740. The state radio stations transmit in Somali, Arabic, English and Italian from Mogadiscio, Hargeisa, Anhazic, Koti. Receivers (1977) 75,000.

Cinemas. In 1970 there were 26 cinemas with a seating capacity of 23,000.

JUSTICE, RELIGION, EDUCATION AND WELFARE

Justice. There are 84 district courts, each with a civil and a criminal section. There are 8 regional courts and 2 Courts of Appeal (at Mogadiscio and Hargeisa), each with a general section and an assize section. The Supreme Court is in Mogadiscio.

Religion. The population is almost entirely Sunni Moslems. There are very few Roman Catholics, mainly in the capital.

Education. The nomadic life of a large percentage of the population inhibits education progress. In 1977-78 there were 165,694 pupils at 767 primary schools and 14,178 at 48 secondary schools. In 1972 the Somali script was introduced and in 1975 a mass literacy campaign was launched. Teachers in training (1978) 2,281.

The National University of Somalia in Mogadiscio (founded 1959) had 3,607 students in 1978.

Health. In 1976 there were 179 doctors, 21 pharmacists (1972), 586 medical assistants, 480 nurses (1972), 193 midwives (1972), 75 hospitals and 187 dispensaries (1972). There was a total of 5,691 beds.

DIPLOMATIC REPRESENTATIVES

Of Somalia in Great Britain (60 Portland Place, London, W1N 3DG)
Ambassador: Mohamed Jama Elmi.

Of Great Britain in Somalia (Waddada Xasan Geeddi Abtoow 7/8, Mogadiscio)
Ambassador: R. M. Purcell.

Of Somalia in USA (600 New Hampshire Ave., NW, Washington, D.C., 20037)
Ambassador: Mohamud Haji Nur.

Of USA in Somalia (Corso Primo Luglio, Mogadiscio)
Ambassador: Donald K. Petterson.

Of Somalia to the United Nations
Ambassador: Ahmed Mohamed Adan.

Books of Reference

Background to the Liberation Struggle of the Western Somalis. Ministry of Foreign Affairs, Mogadiscio, 1978
The Agricultural Economy of Somalia. US Dept. of Agriculture, Washington, 1971
Legum, C. and Lee, B., *Conflict in the Horn of Africa.* London, 1977
Lewis, I. M., *A Pastoral Democracy.* London, 1962–*The Modern History of Somaliland.* London, 1965
Lytton, The Earl of, *The Stolen Desert.* London, 1966
Touval, S., *Somali Nationalism.* Harvard Univ. Press and OUP, 1963

REPUBLIC OF SOUTH AFRICA

Capital: Pretoria
Population: 25·59m. (1982)
GNP per capita: US$2,290 (1980)

Republiek van Suid-Afrika

HISTORY. The Union of South Africa was formed in 1910 and comprised the former self-governing British colonies of the Cape of Good Hope, Natal, the Transvaal and the Orange Free State.

The Union remained a member of the British Commonwealth until it became a republic on 31 May 1961.

AREA AND POPULATION. South Africa is bounded north by South West Africa, Botswana and Zimbabwe, north-east by Mozambique and Swaziland, east by the Indian ocean, south and west by the South Atlantic. Lesotho forms an enclave between the Orange Free State and Natal. The total area of the republic is 440,355[1] sq. miles (1,140,519 sq. km), divided between the provinces as follows: Cape Province, 253,529 (656,641); Natal, 33,578 (86,967); Transvaal, 103,829 (268,918); Orange Free State, 49,418 (127,993).

On 25 Dec. 1947 the Union formally took possession of Prince Edward Island and, on 30 Dec., of Marion Island, about 1,200 miles south-east of Cape Town.

[1] Excludes Walvis Bay (434 sq. miles), which is an integral part of the Cape Province but is administered under Act No. 24 of 1922 by South West Africa, and Transkei (16,675 miles, 43,188 km).

The census taken in 1904 in each of the 4 colonies was the first simultaneous census taken in South Africa. In 1911 the first Union census was taken.

	All races			Whites		Non-whites	
	Total	*Whites*	*Non-Whites*	*Males*	*Females*	*Males*	*Females*
1904	5,174,827	1,117,234	4,057,593	635,317	481,917	2,046,370	2,011,223
1911	5,972,757	1,276,319	4,696,438	685,206	591,113	2,383,879	2,312,559
1921	6,927,403	1,521,343	5,406,060	783,006	738,337	2,753,188	2,652,872
1936	9,587,863	2,003,334	7,584,529	1,017,557	985,777	3,818,211	3,766,318
1946	11,415,925	2,372,044	9,043,881	1,194,201	1,177,843	4,610,862	4,433,019
1951	12,671,452	2,641,689	10,029,763	1,322,754	1,318,935	5,109,331	4,920,432
1960	15,994,181	3,080,159	12,914,022	1,534,923	1,545,236	6,504,317	6,409,705
1970	21,402,470	3,726,540	17,675,930	1,856,180	1,870,360	8,689,920	8,986,010
1980	24,885,960	4,528,100	20,357,860	2,265,400	2,262,700	10,393,780	9,964,080

Of the non-White population in 1980, 16,923,760 were Bantu, 2,612,780 Coloured and 821,320 Asiatic. The numerically leading Bantu nations are the Zulu (5,682,520), Xhosa (2,987,340), Sepedi (North Sotho) (2,347,600), Seshoeshoe (South Sotho) (1,742,060), Tswana (1,357,360). White population, 1982, 4,603,000.

In 1980 (estimate) Afrikaans was the home language of 2,360,000 Whites, English of 1,652,000 Whites. Of the 15,970,019 Bantu about 50% could read and write, and 3·5m. (75%) of Bantu children of school-going age were attending school in 1981.

Vital statistics for calendar years:

	Whites					Asians and Coloureds		
	Births	*Deaths*	*Marriages*	*Immigrants*	*Emigrants*	*Births*	*Deaths*	*Marriages*
1977	74,037	35,280	38,537	24,822	26,000	83,995	30,217	26,442
1978	73,216	35,877	41,048	18,669	20,686	85,843	27,097	26,796
1979	73,090	35,814	41,813	18,680	15,694	91,360	28,618	26,746
1980	74,777	37,664	45,165	29,365	11,363	92,741	28,850	28,511

The registration of Bantu essential data was introduced on a compulsory basis many years ago. However, despite serious efforts on the part of the registering authorities, the Bantu are still largely reluctant to have their essential data registered. Consequently no complete vital statistics are available for this population group.

Principal cities (excluding suburbs) according to the latest statistics (1980) are:

Town	*Whites*	*Africans*	*Coloureds*	*Asians*	*Total*
Alberton (Trans.)	45,902	177,123	7,410	232	230,667
Benoni (Trans.)	56,508	135,752	997	13,553	206,810
Bloemfontein (O.F.S.)	90,625	124,768	15,295	...	230,688
Boksburg (Trans.)	61,337	73,385	15,408	157	150,287
Brakpan (Trans.)	31,902	46,135	1,674	21	79,732
Cape Town (C. Prov.)	124,876	5,608	80,748	2,598	213,830
Durban (Natal)	232,616	73,701	44,020	155,626	505,963
East London (C. Prov.)	62,735	77,372	18,150	2,325	160,582
Germiston (Trans.)	117,492	33,740	1,616	2,587	155,435
Johannesburg (Trans.)	435,586	947,290	101,769	51,812	1,536,457
Kempton Park (Trans.)	71,505	217,998	295	17	289,815
Kimberley (C. Prov.)	33,440	66,162	44,125	1,196	144,923
Krugersdorp (Trans.)	46,280	53,752	277	2,631	102,940
Pietermaritzburg (Natal)	53,780	62,330	11,424	51,438	178,972
Port Elizabeth (C. Prov.)	128,605	241,844	115,383	6,308	492,140
Pretoria (Trans.)	351,590	146,766	14,746	15,305	528,407
Roodepoort Maraisburg (Trans.)	83,217	77,511	3,620	967	165,315
Springs (Trans.)	49,752	101,691	1,254	1,277	153,974
Vereeniging (Trans.)	65,500	72,432	7,930	3,548	149,410
Welkom (O.F.S.)	38,027	133,679	4,902	...	176,608

Millin, S. G., *The People of South Africa.* London, 1951
Patterson, S., *Colour and Culture in South Africa.* London, 1953
Ritter, E. A., *Shaka Zulu.* London, 1955
Saron, G., and Hotz, L., *The Jews in South Africa.* London, 1955
Schapera, I., *The Bantu-speaking Tribes of South Africa.* Cape Town, 1953

CONSTITUTION AND GOVERNMENT. The Republic of South Africa Constitution Act 1961 established with effect from 31 May 1961, the republic, consisting of the 4 provinces–the Cape of Good Hope, Natal, the Transvaal and the Orange Free State–which until then comprised the Union of South Africa.

On 5 Oct. 1960 a referendum was held among the white voters (1,800,426 on roll) to decide whether the Union should become a republic. Of the 1,634,240 votes polled, 850,458 were in favour of a republican constitution, 775,878 against it; 7,904 votes were invalid. The voting was as follows: Transvaal, 406,632 for, 325,041 against; Cape Province, 271,418 for, 269,784 against; Orange Free State, 110,171 for, 33,438 against; Natal, 42,299 for, 135,598 against; South West Africa, 19,938 for, 12,017 against.

The head of the republic is the State President; he is elected for a 7-year term (at a meeting specially convened for the purpose) by an electoral college consisting of the members of the House of Assembly and presided over by the Chief Justice or a judge of appeal designated by him.

On 29 May 1980 the Republic of South Africa Constitution Fifth Amendment Bill was passed and became operative on 1 Jan. 1981. The Senate was abolished from 1 Jan. 1981 and a 60-member President's Council was formed. It consists of White, Coloured, Indian and Chinese representatives nominated by the President for a 5-year term. It was envisaged that a separate advisory council would represent Black views, but this proposal was rejected by Black leaders. Black representation is still being negotiated.

A session of Parliament must be held once at least in every year.

The House of Assembly consists of 165 members chosen in electoral divisions as follows: Transvaal, 76; Cape of Good Hope, 55; Natal, 20; Orange Free State, 14. There are also 4 members (one for each province) nominated by the President.

A member of the House of Assembly must be a white South African citizen, qualified as a voter and resident for 5 years within the republic. Every House of Assembly continues for 5 years unless sooner dissolved.

Only the House of Assembly can originate money bills, but may not pass a bill for taxation or appropriation unless it has been recommended by the State President during the session. Restrictions are placed on the amendment of money bills by the Senate. Provision is made respecting disagreements between the Houses and the State President's assent to bills.

To hold an office of profit under the State (with certain exceptions) is a disqualification for membership of either House, as are also insolvency, crime and insanity. Pretoria is the seat of government, and Cape Town is the seat of legislature.

The state of the parties in the House of Assembly after the general election of April 1981 was as follows: National Party, 131; Progressive Federal Party, 26; New Republic Party, 8; South African Party, 3. In March 1982 a group of MPs was expelled from the National Party after their refusal to support party policy on power-sharing with Coloureds and Asians. They formed the Conservative Party of South Africa (17 members in June 1982) led by Dr A. P. Treurnicht.

State President: Marais Viljoen.

The Executive Council (National Party) was, Oct. 1982, composed as follows:

Prime Minister, Minister of National Security: P. W. Botha.

Manpower: S. P. Botha. *Co-operation and Development:* Dr P. G. J. Koornhof. *Transport:* H. Schoeman. *Industrial Affairs and Trade and Tourism:* D. J. de Villiers. *Finance:* O. P. F. Horwood. *Internal Affairs:* F. W. de Klerk. *Justice:* H. J. Coetzee. *Health and Welfare:* Dr C. V. van der Merwe. *Posts and Telecommunications:* L. A. P. A. Munnik. *Foreign Affairs and Information:* R. F. Botha. *Mines and Energy:* P. T. C. du Plessis. *Law and Order:* L. le Grange. *National Education:* Dr G. V. N. Viljoen. *Education and Training:* D. Steyn. *Constitutional Development:* J. C. Hennis. *Defence:* Gen. M. Malan. *Community Development and State Auxiliary Services:* S. F. Kotzé. *Agriculture:* J. J. G. Wentzel.

The Prime Minister receives an annual salary of R43,000 and a reimbursive allowance of R20,000; a member of the Cabinet an annual salary of R23,500 and a reimbursive allowance of R6,500; and a Deputy Minister an annual salary of R19,000 and a reimbursive allowance of R6,500.

The English and Afrikaans languages are both official, subject to amendments carried by a two-thirds majority in joint session of both Houses of Parliament.

National flag: Three horizontal stripes of orange, white, blue, with the flags of the Orange Free State and the Transvaal, and the Union Jack side by side in the centre.

National anthem: The Call of South Africa/Die Stem van Suid-Afrika (words by C. J. Langenhoven, 1918; tune by M. L. de Villiers, 1921).

Provincial Administration. In each province there is an Administrator appointed by the State President-in-Council for 5 years, and a provincial council elected for 5 years, each council electing an executive committee of 4 (either members or not of the council), the Administrator acting as chairman. Members of the provincial council are elected on the same system as members of Parliament. The provincial committees and councils have authority to deal with local matters, of which provincial finance, education (primary and secondary, other than higher education and technical education), hospitals, roads and bridges, townships, horse and other racing, and game and fish preservation are the most important. In 1953 the administration and control of Black education was transferred from the provincial councils to the central government. All ordinances passed by a provincial council are subject to the veto of the State President-in-Council.

Bantu Administration. In 1951 the Bantu Authorities Act was enacted to provide a system of Bantu tribal, regional and territorial authorities. These were given limited administrative, executive and judicial functions and limited legislative powers. In 1959 the main ethnic groups received legislative recognition by the passing of the Promotion of Bantu Self-Government Act, which provided *inter alia* for the various ethnic groups to develop into self-governing national units, each with a Commissioner-General representing the Government of the Republic.

As the territorial authorities became experienced an executive body in the form of a government service was set up for each authority to increase their administrative power.

As the Act envisages eventual political autonomy for each of the various national units and as representation in the highest White governing bodies is regarded as a retarding factor, the representation of Bantu by Whites in Parliament and the Cape Provincial Administration was abolished with effect from 30 June 1960.

In 1968 the Ciskei (whose people are also Xhosa-speaking) and the Tswana Territorial Authorities were established, followed by the Lebowa (North Sotho), Machangana (Tsonga-Shangaan), Venda and South Sotho Territorial Authorities in 1969 and the Zulu Territorial Authority in 1970.

During 1971 these authorities, with the exception of the Zulu, were granted increased powers in terms of the Bantu Homelands Constitution Act 1971. In terms of the provisions of part I of this Act, 6 of the existing 7 territorial authorities in the Republic of South Africa (the Transkei became a self-governing territory in 1963 by virtue of the provisions of the Transkei Constitution Act of 1963) have been converted to Legislative Assemblies with extended legislative and administrative powers.

Part II of the Bantu Homelands Constitution Act makes provision for the areas of these legislative assemblies to be proclaimed self-governing territories with *inter alia* the power to repeal or amend, with minor exceptions, acts of the Republican Parliament. Executive power is vested in an Executive Council. These Councils, each headed by a Chief Councillor, consist of 6 members, except in the case of the South Sotho, where there are only 4. Each of these Councillors is responsible for the administration of a Department. A civil service has been established in each instance, staffed by citizens of the respective homelands. White officials will serve the homeland governments on secondment, until trained Bantu citizens are able to take over all duties.

In 1961 the ex-chief of the Umvoti Mission reserve, Albert Luthuli, was awarded the Nobel Peace Prize for his advocacy of peaceful means in the achievement of Black aspirations.

The Coloured Peoples Representative Council consists of 40 elected and 20 nominated members. Elections took place in Sept. 1969 and Tom Swartz, leader of the Federal Party, was appointed Chairman of the Council by the State President. On his death in 1975 he was succeeded by Dr W. Bergins. The Council has legislative powers and its Executive, consisting of 5 members, is responsible on behalf of the Coloured community for the management of finance, education, community welfare and pensions, local government and rural areas and settlements. The Administration of Coloured Affairs has approximately 20,000 administrative and professional posts for Coloureds.

The South African Indian Council is a statutory body consisting of 25 nominated representatives of Indian communities in the Transvaal, Natal and the Cape Province. It advises the Government on the economic, social, cultural and political interests of the Indian population. The S.A. Indian Council Amendment Bill of 1972 enlarges the Council to 30 representatives, the additional 5 to be elected. Voters rolls are being compiled. The number of elected representatives can be amended in the future.

In 1971 the Zulus established a Legislative Assembly. Their seat of government is Ulundi.

The Transkei, territory of the Xhosa nation, became independent on 25 Oct. 1976 (*see* p. 1095), Bophuthatswana on 6 Dec. 1977 (*see* p. 1093), Venda on 13 Sept. 1979 (*see* p. 1096) and Ciskei on 4 Dec. 1981 (*see* p. 1098).

Rhoodie, N. J., and Venter, H. J., *Apartheid: A Socio-Historical Exposition of the Origin and Development of the Apartheid Idea.* Cape Town, 1959

DEFENCE. The South African Defence Force comprises a Permanent Force, a Citizen Force and a Commando organization. The Permanent Force consists of professional soldiers, airmen and seamen who are responsible for the administration and training of the whole Defence Force in peace-time, but who are gradually absorbed into the Citizen Force in time of war. The Permanent Force and the Citizen Force consist of Army, Air Force and Naval components; the Commando organization is an army and air organization.

Every white male citizen between 18 and 65 is liable to undergo training and to render personal service in time of war. Those between the ages of 16 and 25 are liable to undergo a compulsory course of peace training. Peace-time training in Commando organizations extends over a period of 16 years' intermittent training. Training in the Citizen Force takes the form of 2 years of continuous training, followed by 9 years during which training takes place at regular intervals.

Aliens have become liable for military service after 5 years' residence by Act of Parliament, 1967.

The S.A. Defence Force is administered by the Chief of the Defence Force, his advisers being the Chief of the Army, Chief of the Air Force and Chief of the Navy, Chief of Staff Operations, Chief of Staff Personnel, the Chief of Staff Management Services and the Surgeon-General.

Army. South Africa is divided into 9 territorial Commands: Western Province, Eastern Province, Natal, Orange Free State, North Western, Northern Transvaal, Witwatersrand, South West Africa and Southern Cape Commands. Within the various Commands are training units, of which members of the Permanent Force form the permanent staff. Courses of various types are held also at the S.A. Military College. The Army includes 1 armoured, 1 mechanized, 4 motorized and 1 parachute brigade. Equipment includes 250 Centurion/Olifant tanks. Total strength (1983), 67,400 and 130,000 Citizen Force.

Navy. The South African Navy has its headquarters at Pretoria.

A custom-built submarine complex incorporating an operations centre alongside a Syncholift marine elevator capable of docking all South African warships except the large tanker, was opened at Simonstown in July 1972. A new maritime headquarters was opened at Silvermine in March 1973.

The Navy includes 3 French-built diesel-powered patrol submarines, 2 British-built anti-submarine frigates, 7 fast missile armed patrol vessels (4 built in Durban and 3 in Israel), 10 coastal minesweepers, 5 seaward defence boats (1 used for surveying), 1 modern British-built survey ship, 1 fleet replenishment ship, 1 boom defence vessel, 1 small training vessel, 1 torpedo recovery vessel, 4 rescue launches, 16 harbour patrol boats and 3 tugs.

New construction included 2 small frigates of the French 'A 69' class built in Lorient and 2 diesel-electric patrol submarines of the French 'Agosta' class built in Nantes, but delivery was stayed by UN resolution. Five missile-armed fast attack craft and 8 patrol launches are being built in South Africa.

Naval personnel in 1983 totalled 700 officers and 4,500 ratings, plus some 1,600 national service men.

Air Force. There is 1 light bomber squadron with 6 Canberra B.12 and 2 Canberra T.4; 1 light bomber squadron with 6 Buccaneer Mk.50; 1 maritime reconnaissance squadron equipped with 5 Shackletons (to be withdrawn from service in 1984); 1 coastal patrol squadron with 18 Piaggio P.166S; 1 fighter-bomber squadron with 32 Mirage F1-AZ ground attack aircraft; 1 general-purpose fighter squadron with Mirage IIICZ interceptors and Mirage IIIRZ reconnaissance fighters; and 1 squadron with Mirage F1-CZ interceptors. Transport squadrons have 9 Transall C-160s, 7 C-130B/E Hercules, more than 50 C-47s, 5 C-54s, 1 Viscount, 4 twin-jet HS.125s and 5 twin-turboprop Merlin IVA light transports. Four helicopter squadrons and No. 22 Flight have more than 50 Alouette IIIs, 11 Wasps, 60 Pumas and 14 Super

Frelons. T-6Gs are used for primary training, followed by advanced training on Impalas and Mirage IIIEZ/DZ, weapons training on Impalas, and multi-engine/crew training on C-47s. Built under licence in the Republic of South Africa, about 150 two-seat Impala Mk. 1s have been followed by 75 single-seat Impala Mk. 2s, based on the Aermacchi MB.326M and 326K respectively. Three squadrons operate C4M Kudu and AM.3C Bosbok liaison aircraft.

The Citizen Force has 5 squadrons of Impalas and 1 of Harvards for counter-insurgency duties and 1 squadron of C4M Kudu and AM.3C Bosbok liaison aircraft. CF personnel have additional functions in regular SAAF squadrons, notably those equipped with C-47 transports and P.166 light transport/coastal patrol aircraft. Total strength (1982) was about 9,000 regular officers and men and 4,000 Citizen Force.

INTERNATIONAL RELATIONS

Membership. The Republic of South Africa is a member of UN.

ECONOMY

Budget. A new basis of subsidy has, with effect from the 1971–72 financial year, been brought into operation by the Government following the investigation of the commission of enquiry into the financial relations between the central government and the provinces. The formula on which this subsidy is based is mainly derived from the calculation of: (1) The needs of the various provinces in respect of the services which they have to provide in the fields of education, health, roads and miscellaneous services; (2) the capacity to pay of the various provinces in respect of the different sources from which their 'own' revenue has to be derived; (3) the deficit which arises when the available revenue of each province, as reflected in its capacity to pay, is subtracted from its expenditure, as adjusted in accordance with its needs.

Ordinary revenue and expenditure of the central government (excluding Railways and Harbours Administration) in R1m.:

	1977–78	*1978–79*	*1979–80*	*1980–81* [2]
Revenue	7,451·2	8,590·0	10,202·4	12,188·2
Expenditure [1]	8,960·5	9,955·3	11,480·0	12,823·5

[1] Excluding subsidies. [2] Estimate.

Details of ordinary revenue and expenditure (1978-79) of the central government for years ended 31 March (in R1,000):

Revenue	
Customs	330,000
Excise	891,700
Income tax	4,205,200
General sales tax	395,000
Interest	640,014

Expenditure	
Plural relations and development	578,023
Foreign affairs	183,766
Defence	1,554,375
Education	326,354
Social welfare and pensions	449,710
Public health	148,858
Police	220,450
Indian affairs	98,994
Coloured relations—Rehoboth affairs	283,646

Public debt on 31 March 1981, R19,986m., of which R606m. was foreign debt; internal debt, R19,380m.

Currency. Decimal coinage was introduced in 1959, the units being the *rand* (abbreviated as R) and the *cent* (abbreviated as c). The rand/cent coinage system came into operation on 14 Feb. 1961. The decimal coins are: *Gold coins*. 2 rand; 1 rand. *Silver coins*. 50 cents; 20 cents; 10 cents; 5 cents. *Bronze coins*. 2 cents; 1 cent. In March 1983, £1 = R1·60; US$1 = R1·09.

Banking. In Dec. 1920, under the South African Currency and Banking Act, 1920, a Central Reserve Bank was established at Pretoria. It commenced operations in

June 1921, and began to issue notes in April 1922. The bank has branches in Pretoria (Head Office), Johannesburg, Cape Town, Durban, Port Elizabeth, East London, Bloemfontein, Pietermaritzburg and Windhoek.

In Jan. 1981 there were 9 commercial banks (total liabilities R14,214m.), 25 general banks (R8,000m.), 10 merchant banks (R1,560m.) and 3 discount houses (R1,090m.). The powers of the South African Reserve Bank to control banking and credit were extended by the Banks Act, 1965.

Weights and Measures. Prior to 1969 the imperial system of weights and measures was generally used in the country. However, during 1969 the Weights and Measures Act was amended to provide for the gradual change-over to the metric system of weights and measures.

ENERGY AND NATURAL RESOURCES

Oil. Small amounts of oil and gas were found off-shore (south west of Mossel Bay) in Oct. 1982.

Electricity. The total capacity of the power plants controlled by the Electricity Supply Commission was 18,000 mw at the end of 1980. There were 20 coal-fired stations, 2 hydro-electric stations (540 mw) and 2 gas-turbine stations (342 mw).

Water. The government activities in respect of the control and utilization of water are governed by the Water Act, 1956 (as amended), which is administered by the Directorate of Water Affairs. A Water Research Commission was established in 1971 to co-ordinate and promote research; it is responsible for hydrological research, major water resource development, water pollution control. The combined average flow of South Africa's rivers is about 52,000m. cu. metres annually, most of it lost by evaporation and spillage. About 3,100m. cu. metres annually is available from storage dams, and 1,100m. cu. metres from ground water. Water demand (now mainly urban-industrial) grows at 7% annually.

The Orange River Project, launched in 1966, is near completion of its first phase. The estimated cost (at April 1981) was R490m. It is to embrace 3 major dams on the Orange River, 9 smaller dams or weirs, a 51½-mile tunnel, 20 hydro-electric power stations and a system of canals. The first of the major dams–the Hendrik Verwoerd Dam–was built 5 miles upstream from Norvalspont.

Minerals. Value of the main mineral production sales (in R1,000):

	1978	*1979*	*1980*	*1981*
Antimony	10,881	21,636	13,734	15,359
Asbestos	121,682	106,421	102,148	117,335
Chrome ore	88,444	88,752	90,276	86,304
Coal	875,748	1,145,878	1,495,016	2,112,532
Copper	210,296	270,989	299,605	277,604
Diamonds	452,670	524,678	553,043	339,915
Fluorspar	23,312	30,131	36,673	48,042
Gold	3,666,425	5,844,041	10,369,611	8,556,613
Iron ore	219,735	293,829	296,141	361,162
Lime and limestone	79,297	92,508	119,052	142,222
Manganese	117,136	175,522	145,486	165,645
Nickel	32,056	...	65,295	...
Phosphate	51,067	62,714	69,135	64,153
Silver	14,693	29,608	81,693	70,143
Tin	29,973	29,362	38,424	30,575
Vermiculite	7,487	6,458	7,998	12,816
Zinc	14,920	...	17,304	...

Total value of all minerals sold (1981), R13,747·9m.

Mineral production 1981: Coal, 130,267,000 tonnes; iron ore, 28,319,000 tonnes; phosphates, 17,712,400 tonnes; manganese ore, 5·04m. tonnes; chrome, 2·87m. tonnes; asbestos, 235,900 tonnes; copper, 199,400 tonnes; vermiculite, 190,600 tonnes; zinc concentrates (1980), 158,137 tonnes; gold, 655,728 kg; silver, 235,393 kg; diamonds, 9,526,000 carats.

In 1979 the number of persons engaged in mining was 692,209. Of these, 457,792 were engaged in goldmining. Total salaries R1,830,632,000.

The Mineral Resources of the Union of South Africa, With a Summary of the Mineral Resources of South West Africa. Geological Survey, Department of Mines. 5th ed. Pretoria, 1976

Minerals. A Quarterly Report of Production and Sales. Department of Mines. Pretoria, from 1936

Agriculture. Much of the land suitable for mechanical farming has unreliable rainfall. Of the total area natural pasture occupies 58% (71·3m. hectares); about 14m. hectares are suitable for dry-land farming, of which 10·6m. are actually cultivated.

South African farmers produced mainly the following crops for the years indicated:

Product (1,000 tonnes)	*1977–78*	*1978–79*	*1979–80*
Maize	10,081	8,271	10,234
Sorghum	612	366	577
Wheat	1,860	1,690	2,086
Lucerne hay	1,294	1,279	1,254
Groundnuts	226	139	214
Sunflower seed	454	321	330
Sugar-cane	19,009	18,821	18,425
Grapes	1,059	1,128	1,153
Citrus fruit	733	702	730
Apples	350	351	387
Potatoes	701	696	686
Tomatoes	270	293	276

Livestock, in 1,000 (1981): 12,200 cattle, 31,650 sheep, 5,330 goats, 1,320 pigs. In 1979–80, 2·7m. cattle and 7·1m. sheep and goats were slaughtered.

The 1981 production of butter was 16,584 tonnes; condensed milk, 41,367 tonnes; milk powder, 12,873 tonnes; cheese, 32,309 tonnes.

Wool sold in 1981 was 101,764 tonnes.

Cotton-growing is now undertaken by many farmers, the plant being found a better drought resistant than either tobacco or maize. Value of production (1979–80), R77m.

Viticulture produced grapes and products valued at R116m. (1979–80).

In 1979-80 the gross value of agricultural production was R5,712m. (field crops, R2,772m.; livestock products, R2,015m.; horticultural products, R925m.).

Forestry. The commercial forests occupy about 1·62m. hectares, of which 148,000 hectares are indigenous trees and the rest exotic trees (pine, gum, wattle). The annual output of forest products is about 85m. cu. metres. Production now meets about 90% of domestic need. Capital invested is about R1,100m., and the number of employees about 100,000.

Fisheries. South Africa is no longer engaged in whaling.

In 1980 sea fisheries caught 629,000 tonnes, including 380,500 tonnes of pelagic shoal fish, mainly anchovy. Trawl fisheries (hake and sole) are the most important economically; they landed 145,000 tonnes.

INDUSTRY AND TRADE

Industry. Net value of sales of the principal groups of industries (in R1,000) in 1979: Food, beverages and tobacco, 10,508,954; motor vehicles, 1,686,117; basic metals, 4,885,571; chemicals and products, 6,842,261; non-electrical machinery, 2,126,420; non-metallic mineral products, 2,276,153; electrical machinery, 1,558,267; clothing, 1,079,566; paper and products, 1,456,414; textiles, 1,615,003; total net value including other groups, 46,495,383. Manufacturing industry contributed 24·8% to gross domestic product in 1976.

Industrial employment (except mining) in 1981: Manufacturing employed 1,468,400 workers (earning R8,348,978,000); construction, 440,600 (R1,868,346,000); transport, communications, 349,317 (R2,395,787,000); trade and accommodation services, 764,722 (R3,590,420,000); government and services, 976,135 (R5,283,077,000).

Of the above figures the following proportion of jobs and salaries were held by white South Africans: Total jobs in manufacturing, 322,500 (earning

R4,386,540,000); construction, 57,800 (R758,721,000); transport, communications, 160,895 (R1,832,601,000); trade and accommodation services, 278,909 (R2,378,377,000); government and services, 342,725 (R3,373,738,000).

In 1981 in private manufacturing 174,600 workers were employed in the food industry (earning R696,092,000); textiles employed 118,400 (R437,742,000); clothing, 115,900 (R307,998,000); transport equipment, 115,800 (R831,572,000); non-metallic mineral products, 94,300 (R449,853,000).

Communications comprises the Department of Posts and Telegraphs. Transport comprises South African Railways and Harbours.

Trade Unions. In 1979 there were 176 trade unions with an estimated total membership of 777,067: 74,183 Blacks, 459,679 Whites and 243,205 Coloureds and Asians.

The Industrial Conciliation Amendment Act (1979) provides for freedom of association to all workers irrespective of race; it is now possible for a Black trade union (as opposed to a union with some Black members) to register. Unions are barred from political activity.

Commerce. South Africa, Botswana, Lesotho, Swaziland and Transkei are members of a customs union and the foreign trade statistics shown below represent the combined imports and exports of these countries. The total value of the imports and exports, exclusive of specie and gold bullion, was as follows (in R1m.):

Imports		*Exports*	
1976	5,867	1976	4,542
1977	5,141	1977	5,683
1978	6,274	1978	7,270
1979	7,034	1979	9,459
1980	10,267	1980	10,647

The principal commodity groups of imports and exports (in R1m.) in 1980 were:

Imports		*Exports*	
Chemicals	1,024	Food, beverages and tobacco	692
Base metals and metal manufactures	703	Pearls, precious stones and precious metals	2,888
Machinery and parts	3,536	Base metals and metal manufactures	1,569
Textiles	536	Mineral products	1,549
Artificial resins, plastics and products	477	Vegetables and products	808
Vehicles, aircraft and other transport equipment	1,857		

In 1981 total imports were R18,171m.; total exports R17,666m.

The geographical origin of South Africa's imports and the direction of its export trade were mainly as follows (in R1m.) in 1980:

	Imports	*Exports*
Africa	280·6	1,102·4
Europe	5,723·0	5,176·1
America	2,227·6	2,129·3
Asia	1,808·3	1,985·0
Oceania	108·4	95·5

Total trade between South Africa and UK (British Department of Trade returns, in £1,000 sterling):

	1978	*1979*	*1980*	*1981*	*1982*
Imports to UK	767,770	533,659	756,397	649,166	745,803
Exports and re-exports from UK	667,052	713,466	1,002,073	1,219,949	1,192,891

Tourism. In 1980, 702,794 tourists visited the Republic of South Africa, spending approximately R476m.

COMMUNICATIONS

Roads. The railway administration operates the long-distance road motor services, together with private operators.

There were at 31 March 1981, 181,389 km of roads, of which some 1,742 km of national roads and 45,589 km of provincial roads were tarred.

Motor vehicles in operation in 1980 included 2,333,172 passenger cars, 870,894 commercial vehicles, 95,430 buses and mini-buses and 192,134 motor cycles. Motor vehicles licensed in 1980, 3,793,481.

Railways. Railway history in South Africa begins in 1860 with the line Durban–Point. With the formation of the Union in 1910, the state-owned lines in the 4 provinces (12,194 km) were amalgamated into one state undertaking, which also took over the control of the harbours–the South African Railways and Harbours Administration.

Government-owned lines operated by the administration (1982) totalled 23,546 km, of which 7,060 km were electrified. Two important lines were completed during 1976: a privately owned railway linking Sishen with the port of Saldanha Bay (860 km) for the export of iron ore; and a 509 km link comprising new construction and upgraded lines between Broodsnyersplaas and the new deep-water port of Richards Bay, for the export of coal. Passenger journeys, 1980–81, 725m.; goods traffic, 184·5m. tonnes.

Aviation. Civil aviation in South Africa is controlled by the Department of Transport, which administers the following state-owned airports: Jan Smuts Airport, Johannesburg; D. F. Malan Airport, Cape Town; Louis Botha Airport, Durban; J. B. M. Hertzog Airport, Bloemfontein; Ben Schoeman Airport, East London; H. F. Verwoerd Airport, Port Elizabeth; B. J. Vorster Airport, Kimberley; P. W. Botha Airport, George; Upington Airport. At 13 other airports the Department provides air navigation services.

South African Airways, as the national air carrier, operate scheduled international air services within Africa and to Europe, South America, the USA, the Far East and Australia. Twenty-three other lines also operate scheduled international air services; they include British Airways, PANAM, KLM, SAS, TAP, Swissair, Olympic Air, El-Al, Alitalia, SABENA, Lufthansa, DETA, Air Zimbabwe, Iberia, DJA, UTA, LUXAIR, Lesotho Airways, Swazi Air, Air Malawi, Air Madagascar. Luxavia operate international non-scheduled flights.

Eighteen independent operators provide internal flights.

During 1979–80 South African Airways carried 3,796,977 passengers and 69,678 tons of freight and mail.

Shipping. The main ports are Durban, Cape Town, Saldanha, Richards Bay, Port Elizabeth and East London. Smaller ports are Mossel Bay, Port Nolloth, Walvis Bay and Lüderitz. During 1979–80 these ports handled 77·2m. tons of cargo, of which Richards Bay handled 25·7m. tons and Durban handled 19·8m. tons.

Post and Broadcasting. On 31 March 1981 there were in South Africa 2,227 post offices and 773 telegraph offices.

In 1981 the international telex switchboard enabled 20,085 telex subscribers in South Africa to communicate with telex subscribers in 184 countries. There were 520 automatic telephone exchanges. There were 26,389 public call offices and 2,662,399 telephones in 1980.

The South African Broadcasting Corporation had, in Sept. 1980, 2·3m. listeners' licences.

On 5 Jan. 1976 the South African Television Service began official transmissions. There were 1·45m. licences in 1980.

Cinemas (1980). There were 620 including 140 drive-ins.

Newspapers (1981). There are 8 Afrikaans and 14 English daily newspapers.

JUSTICE, RELIGION, EDUCATION AND WELFARE

Justice. The common law of the republic is the Roman–Dutch law–that is, the uncodified law of Holland as it was at the date of the cession of the Cape in 1806. The law of England as such is not recognized as authoritative, though by statute the principles of English law relating to evidence and to mercantile matters, *e.g.*, companies, patents, trademarks, insolvency and the like, have been introduced. In shipping and insurance, English law is followed in the Cape Province, and it has also largely influenced civil and criminal procedure throughout the republic. In all other matters, family relations, property, succession, contract, etc., Roman–Dutch law rules, English decisions being valued only so far as they agree therewith.

The Supreme Court of South Africa is constituted as follows: (i) The Appellate Division, consisting of the Chief Justice and as many Judges of Appeal as the State President may stipulate, is the highest court and its decisions are binding on all courts. It has no original jurisdiction, but is purely a Court of Appeal. (ii) The Provincial Divisions: In each province there is a provincial division of the Supreme Court, while in the Cape there are three such divisions possessing both original and appellate jurisdiction. (iii) The Local Divisions: There is a local division each in the Transvaal and Natal exercising the same original jurisdiction within limited areas as the provincial divisions. The judges hold office till they attain the age of 70 years. No judge can be removed from office except by the State President upon an address from both Houses of Parliament on the ground of misbehaviour or incapacity. The circuit system is fully developed.

The Bantu appeal courts and 3 Bantu divorce courts have jurisdiction to some extent concurrent with and in certain respects exclusive of that of the Supreme Court in cases in which the parties are Bantu.

Each province is further divided into districts with a magistrate's court having a prescribed civil and criminal jurisdiction. From this court there is an appeal to the provincial divisions of the Supreme Court, and thence to the appellate division. Magistrates' convictions carrying sentences above a prescribed limit are subject to automatic review by a judge. In addition, several regional divisions consisting of a number of districts have been constituted. Convictions of such courts are not subject to automatic review by a judge.

Courts of Bantu affairs commissioners have been constituted in defined areas to hear all civil cases and matters between Bantu and Bantu only. An appeal lies to the Bantu appeal court, whose decision is final, unless the court consents to an appeal to the appellate division of the Supreme Court on a point stated by the court itself. Bantu affairs commissioners have concurrent criminal jurisdiction with magistrates' courts in respect of certain offences committed by Bantu, while a limited civil and criminal jurisdiction is conferred upon the Bantu chief or headman over his own tribe.

Police. In 1980 the staff of the Police department numbered 34,271 (18,370 White). There were 46 police stations manned exclusively by Blacks, 16 by Coloureds and 1 by Indians.

Religion. A sample tabulation of the 1980 census results as regards religious denominations shows the following: *Whites:* Nederduits Gereformeerde Kerk, 1,693,640; Anglicans, 218,960; Methodists, 414,080; Roman Catholics, 393,640; Nederduits Hervormde Kerk, 246,340; Presbyterians, 128,920; Jews, 119,220; Gereformeerde Kerk, 128,360; Apostolics, 271,080; Congregationalists, 23,780; other Christians, 283,220; others, 255,320. *Non-Whites:* Bantu Churches (1970), 2,758,001; Methodists, 1,698,720; Roman Catholics, 1,962,660; Afrikaans Churches (1970), 1,571,114; Anglicans, 626,460; Lutherans, 795,180; Presbyterians, 370,160; Hindus, 517,940; Congregationalists, 383,220; Mohammedans (1970), 268,970; Apostolics, 659,480; other Christians (1970), 1,825,104; others and unspecified, 4,461,760.

Education. *Higher Education.* There are 17 universities in the republic: (1) The University of Cape Town. (2) The University of Natal, Durban and Pietermaritzburg. (3) The University of the Orange Free State at Bloemfontein. (4) Potchefstroom University for Christian Higher Education, Potchefstroom. (5) The University of Pretoria. (6) Rhodes University, Grahamstown, C.P. (7) The University of Stellenbosch. (8) The University of the Witwatersrand, Johannesburg. (9) The University of South Africa, with its seat in Pretoria, which conducts a Division of External Studies by means of correspondence and vacation courses; it is also an examining body. (10) The University of Port Elizabeth. (11) Rand Afrikaans University, Johannesburg.

The University of Fort Hare (12), the University of the North (13) near Pietersburg and the University of Zululand (14) near Empangeni, Natal, are operated by the Department of Education and Training and provide education at university level for Blacks, the University of the Western Cape (15), Bellville (Cape), offers university facilities to the Coloured population and is administered by the Department of Coloured Affairs; while the University for Indians (16), the University of Durban-Westville, at Durban falls under the Department of Indian Affairs. The Medical University of South Africa (17) is for Black students.

The following statistics refer to 1980:

University	*Students*	*University*	*Students*
Cape Town	10,202	Pretoria	16,317
Durban-Westville	5,003	Rand Afrikaans	5,017
Fort Hare	3,062	Rhodes	2,903
Medunsa	334	South Africa	56,144
Natal	8,191	Stellenbosch	11,581
North	2,752	West Cape	4,153
Orange Free State	8,167	Witwatersrand	13,093
Port Elizabeth	2,985	Zululand	2,072
Potchefstroom	6,682		

Technical and Vocational Education. Technical, vocational and special education for persons other than those for whom specific provision is made (*e.g.,* Black): The Department of National Education is responsible for the maintenance, management and control of or the payment of subsidies to colleges for advanced technical education, technical colleges, technical institutes, special schools, schools of industries and reform schools. Colleges for advanced technical education provide education on an advanced level for a variety of technical, commercial and general courses of study as well as secondary education on a part-time basis. Technical colleges and technical institutes are mainly responsible for the training of apprentices and the education, on a part-time basis, of persons not subject to compulsory school attendance. Special schools for handicapped children cater for the educational needs of those who are blind, partially sighted, deaf, hard of hearing, epileptic, cerebral palsied and physically handicapped. Children found to be in need of care by a children's court, are admitted to schools of industries and reform schools.

The Department of Coloured Affairs has taken over all schools of this nature for Coloureds.

In 1982, 77 technical and training colleges for Whites had 95,184 students; 12 for Coloureds had about 9,160 students; 1 for Asians had 3,911 students. Provision is made for technical education for Black students at 4 institutions for advanced technical education and 33 industrial or trade schools; total enrolment at these institutions was 15,519 in 1982.

State and State-aided Education other than Higher Education. Primary and secondary public education, other than that specifically provided elsewhere, falls under the Provincial Administration. In terms of the National Education Policy Act, 1967, the Minister of Education, Arts and Science may, after consultation with the Provincial Administrators and the National Advisory Education Council, determine general educational policy within the framework of the Act. Black education is the responsibility of the Department of Black Education and Training, while education for Coloureds and Indians is controlled by the Departments of Coloured Affairs and Indian Affairs respectively.

Public schools in 1982: 2,373 for Whites with 50,387 teachers and 931,429 pupils; 1,990 for Coloureds with 27,924 teachers and 764,804 pupils; 410 for Asians with 9,186 teachers and 224,229 pupils; 12,014 for Blacks (in the republic) with 91,994 teachers and 3,603,039 pupils.

Private Schools. To a certain extent the activities of private schools are controlled by government regulations. Their pupils generally sit for the state schools' examinations. These schools make provision for kindergarten, elementary and preparatory, general primary, secondary and commercial education.

In 1982, 134 private or aided schools for Whites had 3,024 teachers and 43,985 students. In 1982, 13 schools for Coloureds had 160 teachers and 2,536 students; 1 for Asians had 13 teachers and 93 students; in 1975 416 for Bantu had 1,878 teachers and 80,904 students.

Teacher-training colleges in 1982: 20 for Whites had 1,248 teachers and 13,196 students;16 for Coloureds and Asians had 234 teachers and 2,909 students; 35 for Bantu had 12,900 students.

Health. In 1980 there were 15,663 medical practitioners, 4,026 specialists, 2,077 hospital interns, 2,654 dental specialists and dentists; in 1980 there were 139,011 hospital beds. More tuberculosis patients were treated as outpatients than in hospital.

Social Welfare. *Social Security.* Pensions paid in 1981:

	Beneficiaries	*Amount (R1,000)*
Old age	457,987	335,519
War veterans	22,389	25,868
Blind	7,232	3,907
Disability grants	185,209	117,025
Maintenance	95,271	114,320

Welfare Services. South Africa is not a welfare state, yet provides many services for the community. Welfare work on behalf of the Government is done by the Departments of Social Welfare and Pensions, Coloured Affairs, Indian Affairs, and Plural Relations and Development.

There are also a great number of voluntary welfare societies which undertake a variety of welfare services. Social assistance is not based on compulsory insurance but is financed from taxation.

The Department of Social Welfare and Pensions formulates the broad policy and takes care of the co-ordination of the various welfare services. The National Council for Welfare, a statutory body set up under the National Welfare Act of 1965, among others, is used by the Government for the execution of this policy. Four specialized commissions serve under the National Council. These are: the Social Work Commission, the Commission for Family Life, the Commission for Welfare Planning and the Commission for Welfare Organizations. The Department also provides such personal services as pensions and allowances, and practical assistance to individuals or families who may have social problems, neglected and uncared-for children, juvenile delinquents, adults needing special guidance and alcoholics. There is assistance for mental or physical disability, death or absence of the breadwinner. There are professional field services and institutions available as well as financial help.

Voluntary Welfare Societies. These organizations supply supplementary services to those provided by the Government. Voluntary welfare organizations must register at the Department of Social Welfare and Pensions under the National Welfare Act of 1965. There are more than 2,000 registered welfare organizations; they have organized themselves into national and provincial councils so as to co-ordinate their activities.

Funds for these voluntary services are raised from Government subsidies and by public subscription.

In the past the State, with the assistance of local authorities, voluntary welfare agencies and church organizations, provided welfare services for the Blacks, the voluntary agencies being controlled by White committees. However, this situation is gradually changing as more Blacks are taking an interest in welfare work. The various Black nations are being encouraged and assisted to form their own voluntary agencies and so to provide, as far as possible, welfare services for their own people. As far as is practicable, the institutions required for the care of the aged and the disabled and for needy children are sited in the homelands, and are staffed by Blacks.

Child and Family Welfare. Welfare or professional officers employed by the State are responsible for the implementation and administration of the Children's Act (amended and consolidated in 1960). This Act makes provision for the prevention and treatment of neglected and maladjusted children, with the full integration of the services of voluntary child and family welfare organizations. Children's institutions, mainly established and controlled by private organizations, are subsidized by the State, as are crèches, community centres and other projects in aid of child and family welfare.

DIPLOMATIC REPRESENTATIVES

Of South Africa in Great Britain (South Africa Hse., Trafalgar Sq., London, WC2N 5DP)
Ambassador: Marais Steyn (accredited 27 Nov. 1980).

Of Great Britain in South Africa (6 Hill St., Arcadia, Pretoria, 0002)
Ambassador: Ewen Fergusson.

Of South Africa in the USA (3051 Massachusetts Ave., NW, Washington, D.C., 20008)
Ambassador: Bernardus G. Fourie.

Of the USA in South Africa (225 Pretorius St., Pretoria)
Ambassador: Herman W. Nickel.

Of South Africa to The United Nations
Ambassador: David W. Steward.

Books of Reference

Statistical Information: The Bureau (formerly Office) of Census and Statistics (Schoeman St., Pretoria), established on 1 April 1917 as a division of the Department of the Interior and now directly under the Minister of Economic Affairs, is based mainly on the Consolidated Census Act, No. 76, of 1957, and the Consolidated Statistics Act, No. 73, of 1957. Main publications:

Official Year Book of the Union of South Africa and of Basutoland, Bechuanaland Protectorate and Swaziland. From 1918 (preceded by the *Statistical Year Book, 1913–17)*
Union Statistics for 50 Years: Jubilee Issue, 1910–1960 (1960)
Statistical Year Book. From 1964
Statistics of Production: Industrial. Annual, from 1915/16 (but suspended from 1929/30 to 1931/32 and from 1938 to 1942)
Statistics of Production: Agricultural. Annual, from 1917/18 (but suspended from 1920/30 to 1931/32 and from 1939 to 1946)
Monthly Bulletin of Statistics (from 1922)
Population Census, 1970. (Various special reports in course of publication)
South African Reserve Bank, *Quarterly Bulletin of Statistics*
South Africa 1979. Official Yearbook of the Republic of South Africa
Official South African Municipal Year Book 1977
Homelands: The Role of the Corporations in the Republic of South Africa, Johannesburg, 1976

The Customs and Excise Office, Pretoria, publishes *Monthly Abstract of Trade Statistics* (from 1946) and *Trade and Shipping of the Union of South Africa* (annually, 1910–55); *Foreign Trade Statistics* (annually, from 1956)

Barber, J., *South Africa's Foreign Policy.* OUP, 1973
Bissell, R. E., and Crocker, C. A., *South Africa in the 1980s.* Boulder, 1979
Böhning, W. R., *Black Migration to South Africa.* Geneva, 1981
Bosman, D. B., *Tweetalige Woordeboek.* 2 vols. Cape Town, 1946–49
Branford, J., *A Dictionary of South African English.* Rev. ed. OUP, 1980
Brotz, H., *The Politics of South Africa: Democracy and Racial Diversity.* OUP, 1977
Davenport, T. R. H., *South Africa: A Modern History.* London, 1977
de Villiers, L., *South Africa: A Skunk Among Nations.* London, 1975
Friedman, B., *Smuts: A Reappraisal.* London, 1975
Gann, L. H. and Duignan, P., *Why South Africa will Survive.* London, 1981
Heard, K. A., *General Elections in South Africa, 1943–70.* OUP, 1974
Hellmann, E. and Lever, H., *Race Relations in Africa, 1929–1979.* London, 1980
Hepple, A., *Verwoerd.* Harmondsworth, 1967
Kruger, D. W., *The Making of a Nation.* Johannesburg, 1969
Lacour-Gayet, R., *A History of South Africa.* London, 1977
Metrowich, F. R., *Africa in the Sixties.* Pretoria, 1970
Muller, C. F. J., *500 Years of South African History.* Pretoria, 1969
Musiker, R., *South Africa,* [Bibliography] Oxford and Santa Barbara, 1980
Talbot, A. M. and W. J., *Atlas of South African History.* Pretoria, 1969
Troup, F., *South Africa: An Historical Introduction.* London, 1972
Walker, E. A., *History of Southern Africa.* London, 1957
The Oxford History of South Africa. OUP, Vol. 1, 1969; Vol. 2, 1971

PROVINCE OF THE CAPE OF GOOD HOPE

Kaapprovinsie

HISTORY. The colony of the Cape of Good Hope was founded by the Dutch in the year 1652. Britain took possession of it from 1795 to 1803 and again in 1806, and it was formally ceded to Great Britain by the Convention of London, 13 Aug. 1814. Letters patent issued in 1850 declared that in the colony there should be a Parliament which should consist of the Governor, a Legislative Council and a House of Assembly. On 31 May 1910 the colony was merged in the Union of South Africa, thereafter forming an original province of the Union.

AREA AND POPULATION. The following table gives the population of the Cape of Good Hope[1] (area (1980) 646,332 sq. km) at the last census:

		All races		*Whites*		*Non-Whites*	
	Total	*Males*	*Females*	*Males*	*Females*	*Males*	*Females*
1936	3,527,865	1,663,169	1,864,796	396,058	394,993	1,267,011	1,469,803
1946	4,051,424	1,924,334	2,127,090	433,849	436,300	1,490,485	1,690,790
1951	4,426,726	2,110,674	2,316,052	463,917	471,168	1,646,757	1,844,884
1960	5,360,234	2,553,245	2,806,989	493,370	507,398	2,059,875	2,299,591
1970[2]	4,293,726	2,151,629	2,142,097	546,761	567,448	1,604,868	1,579,649
1980[2]	5,091,360	2,575,460	2,515,900	624,680	639,360	1,950,780	1,876,540

[1] Including Walvis Bay (699 sq. km). [2] Excluding Republic of Transkei.

Present area (excluding Griqualand East, Mafigerg and the Republic of Bophuthatswana), 646,332 sq. km (400,762 sq. miles).

Of the non-White population in 1980, 32,120 were Asians, 1,569,040 were Blacks and 2,226,160 Coloureds.

Vital statistics for calendar years:

		Whites			*Asians and Coloureds*	
	Births	*Deaths*	*Marriages*	*Births*	*Deaths*	*Marriages*
1966	21,818	10,290	10,055	72,771	24,110	9,758
1978	17,993	11,859	11,129	58,421	19,274	16,711
1979	17,755	11,594	11,081	63,145	20,591	16,488

ADMINISTRATION. The division of parties in the Provincial Council (Feb. 1982) was: National Party, 44; Progressive Federal Party, 10; New Republic Party, 1; 1 vacancy.

Cape Town is the seat of the provincial administration.

Administrator: Eugene Louw.

The province is divided into 119 magisterial districts and 38 divisional council divisions. Each division has a council of at least 6 members (15 in the Cape Division) elected quinquennially by the owners or occupiers of immovable property. The duties devolving upon divisional councils include the construction and maintenance of roads and bridges, local rating, vehicle taxation (except motor vehicle taxation) and preservation of public health. There are 218 municipalities, each governed by a mayor and councillors. Municipal elections are held biennially.

FINANCE. In 1982–83 revenue amounted to R1,309,064,000 and expenditure to R1,313,064,000.

MINING. For mineral production, *see* p. 1076.

AGRICULTURE. Viticulture in the republic is almost exclusively confined to the Cape Province, but practically all other forms of agricultural and pastoral activity are pursued.

INDUSTRY. The province has brick, tile and pottery works, saw-mills, engineering works, foundries, grain-mills, distilleries and wineries, clothing factories, furniture, boot and shoe factories, etc.

RELIGION. Sample tabulation, 1970 census. *Whites:* Nederduits Gereformeerde Kerk, 553,548; Gereformeerde Kerk, 11,771; Nederduits Hervormde Kerk, 7,102; Anglicans, 141,858; Presbyterians, 34,243; Congregationalists, 11,590; Methodists, 98,717; Lutherans, 12,433; Roman Catholics, 77,608; Apostolics, 33,044; other Christians, 67,149; Jews, 32,076; others, 28,070. *Non-Whites:* Afrikaans Churches, 585,570; Anglicans, 397,668; Presbyterians, 50,863; Congregationalists, 189,823; Methodists, 393,843; Lutherans, 101,881; Roman Catholics, 198,692; Apostolics, 149,801; Black Christian Churches, 253,055; other Christians, 185,096; Islam, 127,523; Hindus, 5,722; others, 551,422.

EDUCATION. *Training.* Higher education is under the control of the Department of National Education, Pretoria. Primary and secondary education (including vocational education and the training of primary teachers) are controlled by the Provincial Administration in respect of White pupils, by the Department of Education and Training in respect of Black pupils and by the Department of Internal Affairs in respect of Coloured pupils. Education is compulsory for all White children. Primary and secondary education is free to the end of the calendar year in which the age of 19 years is attained.

Whites (1982). There were 837 government and aided schools with 14,730 teachers and 240,183 pupils; 8 teacher-training colleges with 337 lecturers and 2,351 students; 39 private schools with 11,428 pupils.

Coloureds (1982). There were 1,810 state and aided schools with 24,499 teachers and 664,286 pupils; 12 teacher-training colleges with 3,748 students; 14 private schools with 2,687 pupils (1981).

Black (1981). There were 1,137 state schools with 5,703 teachers and 248,553 pupils and 17 private schools with 118 teachers and 5,063 pupils.

Asians (1982). There were 7 state schools with 191 teachers and 4,068 pupils.

PROVINCE OF NATAL

HISTORY. Natal was annexed to Cape Colony in 1844, placed under separate government in 1845, and on 15 July 1856 established as a separate colony. By this charter partially representative institutions were established, and in 1893 the colony obtained responsible government. The province of Zululand was annexed to Natal on 30 Dec. 1897. The districts of Vryheid, Utrecht and part of Wakkerstroom, formerly belonging to the Transvaal, were annexed in Jan. 1903. On 31 May 1910 the colony was merged in the Union of South Africa as an original province of the Union.

AREA AND POPULATION. The province (including Zululand, 10,375 sq. miles) has an area of 33,578 sq. miles, with a seaboard of about 360 miles. The climate is sub-tropical on the coast and somewhat colder inland. The province is divided into 45 magisterial districts.

The returns of the total population at the census were:

	All races			*Whites*		*Non-Whites*	
	Total	*Males*	*Females*	*Males*	*Females*	*Males*	*Females*
1936	1,946,468	944,220	1,002,248	95,157	95,392	849,063	906,856
1946	2,202,392	1,073,510	1,128,882	117,425	119,272	956,085	1,009,600
1951	2,406,318	1,182,931	1,223,387	136,300	137,940	1,046,631	1,094,447
1960	2,979,034	1,443,561	1,535,473	166,404	222,750	1,227,157	1,362,468
1970	4,236,770	2,009,410	2,227,360	171,005	214,960	1,794,430	2,004,610
1980	2,676,340	1,360,600	1,315,740	276,240	285,620	1,084,360	1,030,120

Of the non-White population in 1980, 665,340 were Asians, 91,020 Coloureds and 1,358,120 Blacks.

Vital statistics for calendar years:

	Whites			*Asians and Coloureds*		
	Births	*Deaths*	*Marriages*	*Births*	*Deaths*	*Marriages*
1961	7,301[1]	3,412	2,803	19,234[1]	3,509	3,617
1962	7,622[1]	3,561[1]	...	18,575[1]	3,728	...
1966	...	3,901	3,612	...	4,008	4,446

[1] Preliminary.

ADMINISTRATION. At the provincial council elections in 1981 there were returned: New Republic Party, 5; National Party, 14; Progressive Federal Party, 1.

The seat of provincial government in Natal is Pietermaritzburg. In April 1978 the area of East Griqualand was transferred to Natal from Cape Province.

Administrator: The Hon. Jan Christoffel Greyling Botha.

FINANCE. In 1981–82 revenue amounted to R524·48m. and expenditure to R512·63m.

MINING. The province is rich in mineral wealth, particularly coal. For figures of mineral production, *see* p. 1076.

AGRICULTURE. Sugar and citrus growing are of major importance. On the coast and in Zululand there are vast plantations of sugar-cane (about 800,000 acres), producing, in 1967, 15,547,000 tons. Cereals of all kinds (especially maize), fruits, vegetables, the *Acacia molissima* (the bark of which is much used for tanning purposes) and other crops are produced. Large areas are being afforested.

INDUSTRY. Natal is highly industrialized. There are metallurgical, chemical, paper, rayon and food-processing plants, iron and steel foundries, petrol refineries, pulp-mills, explosives and fertilizer plants, milk- and meat-canning factories.

RELIGION. Sample tabulation, 1960 census. *Whites:* Nederduits Gereformeerde Kerk, 64,052; Gereformeerde Kerk, 2,895; Nederduits Hervormde Kerk, 5,319; Anglicans, 94,349; Presbyterians, 25,852; Congregationalists, 4,652; Methodists, 53,283; Lutherans, 7,226; Roman Catholics, 35,747; Apostolics, 9,827; other Christians, 18,973; Jews, 6,266; others, 11,794. *Non-Whites:* Afrikaans Churches, 25,411; Anglicans, 128,400; Presbyterians, 35,013; Congregationalists, 16,267; Methodists, 173,088; Lutherans, 122,052; Roman Catholics, 270,744; Apostolics, 25,229; Bantu Churches, 495,747; other Christians, 95,828; Mohammedans, 59,957; Hindus, 282,797; others, 909,152.

EDUCATION. The Natal Provincial Administration controls primary and secondary technical and vocational education for Whites. Higher technical and vocational education for all races is provided by the central government. *See also* pp. 1080–81.

Whites (1982). There were 309 government and aided schools with 114,424 pupils; 3 teacher-training colleges with 1,185 students; 11 private schools with 960 pupils.

Coloureds (1982). There were 61 government and aided schools with 1,201 teachers and 30,589 pupils; 8 pre-primary schools with 27 teachers and 569 pupils (1981); 1 teacher-training college with 230 students and 29 lecturers; 1 technical college with 311 students and 31 lecturers (1981).

Blacks (1982). There were 1,000 schools with 4,584 teachers and 184,911 pupils. These schools are situated in the white area of Natal and the south-eastern Transvaal.

Asians (1982). There were 333 state and state-aided schools with 7,749 teachers and 191,296 pupils.

PROVINCE OF THE TRANSVAAL

HISTORY. The Transvaal was one of the territories colonized by the Boers who left the Cape Colony during the Great Trek in 1831 and following years. In 1852, by the Sand River Treaty, Great Britain recognized the independence of the Transvaal, which, in 1853, took the name of the South African Republic. In 1877 the republic was annexed by Great Britain, but the Boers took up arms towards the end of 1880. In 1881 peace was made and self-government, subject to British suzerainty and certain stipulated restrictions, was restored to the Boers. The London Convention of 1884 removed the suzerainty and a number of these restrictions but reserved to Great Britain the right of approval of the Transvaal's foreign relations, excepting with regard to the Orange Free State. In 1886 gold was discovered on the Witwatersrand, and this discovery, together with the great influx of foreigners which it occasioned, gave rise to many grave problems. Eventually, in 1899, war broke out between Great Britain and the Transvaal. Peace was concluded on 31 May 1902, the Transvaal and the Orange Free State both losing their independence. The Transvaal was governed as a crown colony until 12 Jan. 1907, when responsible government came into force. On 31 May 1910 the Transvaal became one of the four provinces of the Union.

AREA AND POPULATION. The area of the province is 103,829 sq. miles, divided into 53 districts. The following table shows the population at each of the last censuses:

	All races			*Whites*		*Non-Whites*	
	Total	*Males*	*Females*	*Males*	*Females*	*Males*	*Females*
1936	3,341,470	1,846,576	1,494,894	424,470	396,286	1,422,108	1,098,608
1946	4,283,038	2,374,323	1,908,715	541,053	522,068	1,833,270	1,386,647
1951	4,812,838	2,619,314	2,193,524	737,194	731,111	2,575,119	2,230,053
1960	6,270,711	3,310,948	2,959,763	735,845	729,730	2,575,103	2,230,034
1970	8,717,530	4,460,130	4,257,400	946,430	938,210	3,513,700	3,319,190
1980	8,350,500	4,567,500	3,783,000	1,190,740	1,171,320	3,376,760	2,611,680

Of the non-White population in 1980, 5,644,660 were Black, 115,560 Asians and 228,220 Coloureds.

Important towns of the province are listed on p. 0000.

Vital statistics for calendar years:

	Whites			*Asians and Coloureds*		
	Births	*Deaths*	*Marriages*	*Births*	*Deaths*	*Marriages*
1951	39,725[1]	11,658	14,555	6,194[1]	1,900	941
1962	40,199[1]	12,600[1]	...	6,330[1]	2,242[1]	...
1966	...	13,440	...	...	2,322	1,290

[1] Preliminary.

ADMINISTRATION. At the provincial council election in 1981 there were returned: National Party, 67; Progressive Federal Party, 9.

The seat of provincial government is at Pretoria, which is also the administrative capital of the Republic of South Africa.

Administrator: Willem Cruywagen.

FINANCE. In 1976–77 revenue amounted to R560,953,000 and expenditure to R667,523,000.

MINING. For mineral production, *see* p. 1076. Gold output in 1967 was 19,591,000 oz. worth R492,978,000.

AGRICULTURE. The province is in the main a stock-raising country, though there are considerable areas well adapted for agriculture, including the growing of tropical crops.

INDUSTRY. The province has iron and brass foundries and engineering works, grain-mills, breweries, brick, tile and pottery works, tobacco, soap, and candle factories, coach and wagon works, clothing factories, etc.

RELIGION. Sample tabulation, 1960 census. *Whites:* Nederduits Gereformeerde Kerk, 539,491; Gereformeerde Kerk, 72,404; Nederduits Hervormde Kerk, 167,693; Anglicans, 137,207; Presbyterians, 50,196; Congregationalists, 3,071; Methodists, 123,218; Lutherans, 13,880; Roman Catholics, 91,235; Apostolics, 67,550; other Christians, 90,504; Jews, 74,221; others, 37,635. *Non-Whites:* Afrikaans Churches, 278,006; Anglicans, 309,047; Presbyterians, 50,924; Congregationalists, 29,839; Methodists, 318,424; Lutherans, 365,836; Roman Catholics, 270,493; Apostolics, 179,739; Bantu Churches, 1,030,853; other Christians, 310,162; Mohammedans, 42,707; Hindus, 23,190; others, 1,595,952.

EDUCATION. All education for Whites except that of universities is under the provincial authority. The province has been divided for the purposes of local control and management into 21 school districts. Instruction in government schools, both primary and secondary, is free. The medium of instruction is the home language of the pupil. The teaching of the other language begins at the earliest stage at which it is appropriate on educational grounds. Both languages are taught as examination subjects to every pupil.

Whites (1982). There were 1,153 public schools with 27,797 teachers and 547,452 pupils; 5 teacher-training colleges with 5,904 students; 84 private schools with 2,009 teachers and 31,597 pupils.

Coloureds (1982). There were 92 state and state-aided schools with 1,898 teachers and 59,547 pupils; 1 teacher-training college with 272 students.

Asians (1982). There were 71 public schools with 1,259 teachers and 28,958 pupils; 1 teacher-training college with 30 teachers and 377 students.

Blacks (1977). There were 2,170 public and private school sections with 15,450 teachers and 735,325 pupils (Homelands excluded).

PROVINCE OF THE ORANGE FREE STATE

Oranje-Vrystaat

HISTORY. The Orange River was first crossed by Europeans in the middle of the 18th century. Between 1810 and 1820, settlements were made in the southern parts of the Orange Free State, and the Great Trek greatly increased the number of settlers during and after 1836. In 1848, Sir Harry Smith proclaimed the whole territory between the Orange and Vaal rivers as a British possession called the 'Orange River sovereignty'. However, in 1854, by the Convention of Bloemfontein, British sovereignty was withdrawn and the independence of the country was recognized.

During the first 5 years of its existence the Orange Free State was much harassed by incessant raids by the Basutos. These were at length conquered, but, owing to the intervention of the British Government, the treaty of Aliwal North incorporated only part of the territory of the Basutos in the Orange Free State.

On account of the treaty with the South African Republic, the Orange Free State took a prominent part in the South African War (1899–1902) and was annexed on 28 May 1900 as the Orange River Colony. Crown colony government continued until 1907, when responsible government was introduced. On 31 March 1910 the Orange River Colony was merged in the Union of South Africa as the province of the Orange Free State.

AREA AND POPULATION. The area of the province is 49,418 sq. miles; it is divided into 34 administrative and 57 magisterial districts. The census population has varied as follows:

		All races		*Whites*		*Non-Whites*	
	Total	*Males*	*Females*	*Males*	*Females*	*Males*	*Females*
1936	772,060	381,903	390,157	101,872	99,106	280,031	291,051
1946	879,071	432,896	446,175	101,874	100,203	331,022	345,972
1951	1,016,570	519,166	497,404	115,637	112,015	403,529	385,389
1960	1,386,202	731,486	654,716	139,304	137,103	601,182	553,613
1970	1,716,350	899,140	817,210	148,110	148,030	751,030	669,180
1980	1,931,860	1,039,220	892,640	166,380	159,840	872,840	732,800

Of the non-White population in 1980, 1,549,600 were Black and 56,040 Coloureds.

Vital statistics for calendar years:

		Whites			*Asians and Coloureds*	
	Births	*Deaths*	*Marriages*	*Births*	*Deaths*	*Marriages*
1961	7,136[1]	2,297	2,314	781[1]	467	126
1962	7,088[1]	2,441[1]	...	858[1]	567[1]	...
1966	...	2,450[1]	2,855[1]	...	...	...

[1] Preliminary.

ADMINISTRATION. At the provincial council election in 1981 there were returned 28 National Party.

The seat of provincial government is at Bloemfontein. There are 68 municipalities and 8 village management boards.

Administrator: A. C. van Wyk.

FINANCE. In 1976–77 revenue amounted to R134,288,000 and expenditure to R159,883,000.

MINING. For mineral statistics, *see* p. 1076. The production of the gold-fields in the province has increased tremendously since 1951, when the output was 18,545 oz. valued at R230,186. The output in 1961 was 7,235,647 oz. valued at R181,320,401.

AGRICULTURE. The province consists of undulating plains, affording excellent grazing and wide tracts for agricultural purposes. The rainfall is moderate. The country was mainly devoted to stock-farming, but now a rapidly increasing quantity of grain is being raised, especially in the eastern districts.

INDUSTRY. The more important manufacturing industries in the province are the oil-from-coal factory (as well as industries based on its by-products) at Sasolburg; fertilizer, agricultural implements, blanket and woollen products, clothing, hosiery, cement and pharmaceutical factories, grain-mills and brick, tile and pottery works.

RELIGION. Sample tabulation, 1960 census. *Whites:* Nederduits Gereformeerde Kerk, 190,458; Gereformeerde Kerk, 14,018; Nederduits Hervormde Kerk, 9,297; Anglicans, 11,433; Presbyterians, 3,926; Congregationalists, 109; Methodists, 14,226; Lutherans, 1,281; Roman Catholics, 7,303; Apostolics, 8,344; other Christians, 10,480; Jews, 3,190; others, 2,680. *Non-Whites:* Afrikaans Churches, 210,379; Anglicans, 80,554; Presbyterians, 21,414; Congregationalists, 8,309; Methodists, 193,439; Lutherans, 16,504; Roman Catholics, 119,629; Apostolics, 78,001; Bantu Churches, 183,109; other Christians, 52,083; others, 146,374.

EDUCATION. *Whites.* Primary, secondary and vocational education and the training of primary teachers are controlled and financed by the Provincial Administration. The province is divided into 11 school board areas.

Education is free in all public schools up to the university matriculation standard. Attendance is compulsory between the ages of 7 and 16, but exemption may be granted in special cases. The home language of the pupil is the medium of instruction.

Whites (1982). There were 208 government and aided schools with 4,232 teachers and 73,355 pupils.

Coloureds (1982). There were 40 government and aided schools with 452 teachers and 12,918 pupils.

Blacks (1977). There were 2,026 school sections with 5,880 teachers and 302,286 pupils (Homelands excluded).

SOUTH WEST AFRICA

Suidwes-Afrika—Namibia

HISTORY. The territory (excluding Walvis Bay and certain islands) was proclaimed a German protectorate in 1884, but was surrendered to the Forces of the Union of South Africa on 9 July 1915 at Khorab. The administration was vested in the Government of the Union of South Africa by mandate of the League of Nations dated 17 Dec. 1920. In 1921 the Governor-General delegated certain of his functions to the Administrator of the Territory, who was assisted by an Advisory Council and, from 1925, by an Executive Committee and the Legislative Assembly. On 18 July 1966 the International Court of Justice decided, by the President's casting vote, that Ethiopia and Liberia had no legal right in applying for a decision on the international status of South West Africa. In 1971 the International Court of Justice ruled in an advisory opinion that the Republic of South Africa's presence in South West Africa was illegal. In Dec. 1973 the UN appointed Sean McBride as UN Commissioner for Namibia. The Republic of South Africa was given until May 1975 to declare its intentions on the future of Namibia, by the UN.

Independence was envisaged for 31 Dec. 1978. However in Dec. 1978 an election for a Constituent Assembly was held without UN supervision. The Democratic Turnhalle Alliance Party gained 41 of the 50 seats. The South West Africa People's Organisation (SWAPO) boycotted the election. The Constituent Assembly was not recognized by the UN, the Western Powers or SWAPO. UN plans for a ceasefire and UN-supervised elections were rejected by the Constituent Assembly on 20 April 1979. Discussions continued during 1980 aiming at solutions to the Namibia problem and in Jan. 1981 a UN Conference was held in Geneva but this also ended in failure as did various discussions held in 1982.

AREA AND POPULATION. The total area of the Territory, including the Caprivi-Zipfel, is 318,261 sq. miles (824,269 sq. km); this figure includes that of Walvis Bay, administered by South West Africa, 434 sq. miles (1,124 sq. km).

The country is bounded on the north by Angola and Zambia, on the west by the Atlantic ocean, on the south and southern portion of the eastern boundary by the Cape Province, and on the remainder of the eastern boundary by Botswana and Zambia. There are 3 main regions: the Namib, an extremely arid and desolate region stretching along the entire coastline to a width of between 80 to 130 km. The major portion of the Namib receives an annual rainfall of less than 50 mm. the Central Plateau is the region lying to the east of the Namib. It varies in altitude between 1,000 and 2,000 metres and offers a diversified landscape of rugged mountains, rocky outcrops, sand-filled valleys and plains. It covers approximately 50% of the total area; the Kalahari covers the eastern, north-eastern and northern areas of South West Africa.

The rainfall increases steadily from less than 50 mm. in the west and south-west up to 600 mm. in the Caprivi Strip.

The Kunene River and the Okavango, which form portions of the northern border of the country, the Zambesi, which forms the eastern boundary of the

Caprivi-Zipfel, the Kwando or Mashi, which flows through the Caprivi-Zipfel from the north between the Okavango and the Zambesi, and the Orange River in the south, are the only permanently running streams. But there is a system of great, sandy, dry river-beds throughout the country, in which water can generally be obtained by sinking shallow wells. In the Grootfontein area there are large supplies of underground water, but except for a few springs, mostly hot, there is no surface water in the country.

On 13 Oct. 1964 and 29 Jan. 1969 the Republic of South Africa and Portugal signed agreements on the common use of the Kunene River.

Owing to the difficulty of satisfactorily controlling that part of the Caprivi-Zipfel, east of the line running due south from Beacon 22, situated west of the Kwando (or Mashi) River, the control of this area was in Aug. 1939 transferred to the Union Department of Native Affairs.

The population at the census 1960 and 1970 and estimate 1982 was:

	1960	*1970*	*1982*
Ovambos	239,363	342,455	516,600
Whites	73,464	90,658	75,600
Damaras	44,353	64,973	76,800
Hereros	44,588	55,670	77,600
Namas	34,806	32,853	49,700
Kavangos	27,871	49,577	98,000
Caprivians	15,840	25,009	39,500
Coloureds	12,708	28,275	43,500
Basters	11,257	16,474	23,800
Bushmen	11,762	21,909	29,900
Tswana	...	4,407	6,800
	516,012	732,260	1,039,800

The population grew at a rate of 3·7% per annum between 1960 and 1970.

The Ovambos are a Bantu race and are both agriculturists and owners of stock. They still possess tribal organization to its full extent.

The Hereros are a pastoral people who formerly owned enormous herds of cattle. Wars with Namas and Germans destroyed their tribal organization. Under the Union and Republic administration, reserves have been set apart and they have considerably increased in numbers and in animal wealth.

The ethnic origin of the Bergdamaras or Damara is still not certain. They were alternatively the slaves of the Hereros and the Namas, whose language they now speak, in pre-European days.

The Namas consist of 2 distinct sections: one, the Hamitic, whose remnants are found in the central portions of the country, being of pure native extraction, is thought to have migrated from the region of the Central African lakes in prehistoric times; the other, the Khoisan, is composed of tribes whose members are descended from persons born in the Cape a couple of centuries ago with an admixture of European and Nama blood.

The Bushmen are among the oldest inhabitants of southern Africa.

In the centre of the country just south of the Windhoek district is the Rehoboth Gebiet, occupied by a race known as the Basters, who are of mixed Nama–European descent and whose ordinary language is Afrikaans.

ADMINISTRATION. The South West Africa Affairs Amendment Act, 1949, abolished the Advisory Council and the nominated members of the Legislative Assembly. All 18 members of the Assembly are now elected by the registered voters of the Territory.

The election held on 24 April 1974 returned 18 Nationalists.

Until 1977 the Territory was represented in the South African House of Assembly by 6 members elected by the registered voters of the Territory, and in the Senate by 4 Senators, of which number 2 were elected by the members of the Legislative Assembly and the representatives of the Territory in the House of Assembly, and 2 nominated by the President of the Republic. Under the South West Africa Constitution Amendment Act 1977 this representation was abolished.

A commission of inquiry, appointed by the South African Government, in 1964 recommended the establishment of 'homeland areas' for the non-White groups. All these areas should be governed by legislative councils, headed by executive committees; franchise should be granted to males and females over 18 years who qualify for citizenship in their respective homelands.

On 17 Oct. 1968, 22 Oct. 1970 and 15 March 1973 respectively the first sessions of the Legislative Councils of Ovambo (77 members), Kavango (30 members) and Eastern Caprivi (28 members) were opened.

On 1 May 1973 and 9 May 1973 respectively Ovambo and Kavango obtained self-government.

On 13 Oct. 1966 the security and apartheid laws of the Republic of South Africa were extended to South West Africa, retrospective to 1950. The Legislative Assembly adopted a resolution on 22 Nov. 1974 inviting the representatives of the various population groups to deliberate with the representatives of the Whites on the manner in which they should exercise their right of self-determination in view of the South African government's desire that the inhabitants of South West Africa should themselves decide upon their future.

The seat of the administration is Windhoek. The country is divided into 22 districts controlled by magistrates and commissioners.

Administrator-General: Dr Willem van Niekerk.

ECONOMY

Budget. The revenue and expenditure (in R1,000) were:

	1977–78	*1978–79*	*1979–80*	*1980–81*	*1982–83*
Revenue	189,500	293,800	460,600	888,267	839,591
Expenditure	218,300	320,100	519,900	837,442	840,111

Banking. Barclays Bank International, Volkskas Bank, Standard Bank, French Bank, Netherlands Bank, Trust Bank, South African Reserve Bank and Boland Bank have branches in the Territory. The only indigenous bank, The Bank of South West Africa, was established in 1973.

NATURAL RESOURCES

Minerals. Mineral export/sales amounted to R545·05m. in 1979. Diamonds, which constitute the principal production, are mainly recovered from alluvial terraces on a 60-mile stretch along the coastline from the Orange River mouth northward.

Agriculture. South West Africa is essentially a stock-raising country, the scarcity of water and poor rainfall rendering agriculture, except in the northern and north-eastern portions, almost impossible. Generally speaking, the southern half is suited for the raising of small stock, while the central and northern portions are better fitted for cattle.

Livestock (1982): 2m. cattle, 2·8m. sheep, 1·2m. goats. In 1981, 330,642 head of cattle and 48,889 beef carcasses and 583,182 head of small stock were exported.

In 1977–78, 188,402 kg of butter and 115,197 kg of factory cheese were manufactured. Other products produced are maize, 9,239 tons (1978); millet, 25,000 tons (1978); sunflower, 2,000 tons (1977); peanuts, 500 tons (1977).

The production of karakul pelts is of increasing importance. In 1982, 1,956,946 pelts, worth R20,097,835 were produced.

Fisheries. The total catch in 1979 was 324,000 tonnes. The sales value of fish products (1977) was R67m.

COMMERCE. The statistics concerning the external trade of South West Africa are included in those of the Republic of South Africa (*see* p. 1075).

The bulk of the direct imports into the country is landed at Walvis Bay.

Total trade between South West Africa and UK (British Department of Trade returns, in £1,000 sterling):

	1978	*1979*	*1980*	*1981*	*1982*
Imports to UK	14,844	20,446	18,898	45,301	45,413
Exports and re-exports from UK	2,215	1,593	2,726	2,028	3,973

COMMUNICATIONS

Roads. In 1981 there were 3,892 km of trunk roads, 19,579 km of district roads, of which 3,743 km are bitumen surfaced. In 1974 there were 71,272 registered motor vehicles.

Railways. The South West Africa system connects with the main system of the South African Railways at De Aar. The total length of the line inside South West Africa is 2,340 km of 1,065 mm gauge.

Aviation. In 1977 the Territory's 4 major airports handled 177,901 passengers.

Shipping. In 1979–80 Walvis Bay harbour handled 1,899 vessels, of which 570 were freighters, and Luderitz, 233 vessels.

Post and Broadcasting. At 31 March 1982 there were 81 post offices and postal agencies, and 629 private bag services distributed by rail or road transport.

There were 25,563 circuit km of trunk lines, 449,162 circuit km of microwave channels, 432,763 km of carrier circuits, 334,266 km of telegraph circuits and 49,204 km of farm telephone lines; 78 telegraph offices, 146 telephone exchanges, and 54,891 telephones. There were 7,679 licensed radio stations in operation.

In 1981–82, 47,208 wireless licences and 9,857 television licences were issued. There were 18,270 km of broadcast circuits.

A post office savings bank was established in 1916. The number of accounts opened in 1981–82 was 3,487. The balance due to holders as at 31 March 1982 amounted to R1,339,904.

EDUCATION AND WELFARE

Education (1981). There were 1,045 schools for all races, 249,019 pupils and 8,016 teachers. This included 29 academic high schools, a centre for handicapped children and 4 agricultural colleges.

Health (1982). There were 54 hospitals and 104 clinics. The ratio of beds per population was 7·50 per 1,000. There were 180 general practitioners, 17 specialists and 25 dentists. Nursing staff numbered 3,069.

Books of Reference

The Territory of South West Africa. (In *Official Year Book of the Republic of South Africa*)
Department of Mines: *Quarterly Information Circulars: Industrial Minerals*
Cockram, G.-M., *South West African Mandate.* Cape Town, 1976
Green, R. H., Kiljunen, K. and Kiljunen, M.-L. (eds.) *Namibia: The Last Colony.* London, 1982
Serfontein, J. H. P., *Namibia?* London, 1977
Thomas, W. H., *Economic Development in Namibia.* Munich, 1978
Tötemeyer, G. *Namibia Old and New.* New York, 1979
Vigne, R., *A Dwelling Place of Our Own: The Story of the Namibian Nation.* London, 1973

BOPHUTHATSWANA

HISTORY. Bophuthatswana was first to obtain self-government under the Bantu Homelands Constitution Act of 1971 and was the second black homeland to ask the Republic of South Africa for full independence, which was granted on 6 Dec. 1977.

AREA AND POPULATION. The total area is 40,000 sq. km.

In 1976 Bophuthatswana had a *de jure* population of 2,103,000, of which 65%

lived in the White areas. The remaining 35% (736,000) lived in the homeland. In addition, the homeland has a further population of about 300,000 non-Tswanas, giving the homeland a *de facto* population of about 1,036,000.

CONSTITUTION AND GOVERNMENT. The Bophuthatswana Government is a compromise between the traditional chief-in-council system and a democratic electoral system. There are 48 nominated and 48 elected members in the Legislative Assembly. Self-government was granted in 1972. Each regional authority (coinciding with the 12 districts of the homeland) nominates 4 members, and each district elects the same number to the Legislative Assembly.

Executive power vests in the President, who is elected by the Assembly, and he elects his Cabinet.

The first general election was held in Oct. 1972, 2 political parties taking part. Chief Lucas Mangope's Bophuthatswana National Party (BNP) won 20 of the 24 contested seats, but in 1974 he formed the Bophuthatswana Democratic Party which in 1979 held two-thirds of the seats in the Assembly.

Members of regional authorities are elected from among the tribal and community authorities in their area.

The Cabinet in Oct. 1980 consisted of:

President and Minister of Economic Affairs: Chief L. L. M. Mangope.

Education: H. L. Setlalentoa. *Foreign Affairs:* T. M. Molatlhwa. *Works:* Chief B. L. M. I. Motsatsi. *Agriculture and Community Development:* Chief E. M. Mokgoko. *Urban Affairs, Land Tenure and Housing:* D. C. M. Mokale. *Law and Order:* A. T. Gaelejwe. *Communications:* M. A. Kgomongwe. *Internal Affairs:* G. J. Makodi. *Finance:* Sir C. Hatty. *Defence:* Brig. H. F. Riekert. *Health and Social Welfare:* Dr K. P. Mokhobo.

Flag: Blue, crossed by a diagonal orange stripe, and in the canton a white disc charged with a leopard's face in black and white.

INTERNATIONAL RELATIONS

Aid. The Republic of South Africa granted aid of R22m. in 1980–81.

ECONOMY

Budget. The 1981–82 budget balanced at R421m.

Currency. South African Rand.

NATURAL RESOURCES

Water. The Department of Agriculture inherited the following improvements from South Africa: 2,833 reservoirs; 6,845 boreholes, of which more than 4,000 have been equipped; 648 earth dams.

Minerals. The territory is particularly rich in minerals. In 1976 there were 34 mines employing 53,000 people. Minerals include platinum, asbestos, iron ore, manganese, chrome, vanadium, limestone, diamonds and fluorspar.

Exploration for more platinum, chrome and coal is currently being carried out both by the private sector and by the Mining and Geological Survey Division of the Department of Economic Affairs. The platinum mines around Rustenburg produce about 66% of the free world's total production. The major chrome mines are near Rustenburg and Marico, while vanadium is mined in the Odi district near Brits.

The Rustenburg, Western and Impala Platinum mines which Bophuthatswana shares with the Republic of South Africa produce about 1·9m. oz. a year.

AGRICULTURE. Bophuthatswana is a semi-arid area of bushveld and grass veld suitable for stock farming. The annual rainfall is 300 mm in the west and 700 mm in the east and there are 3 river catchment areas—those of the Molopo, Limpopo and Vaal rivers.

Although the land tenure system militates against establishing large farms, some land which is unsuitable for building on is leased by the Government to successful farmers.

Livestock (1980): Cattle, 601,711.

Only 6·6% of the territory is suited to dryland cropping, but crop yields have shown a steady improvement in recent years. Plant production in 1972 yielded R2·4m. In Ditsobotla district, 3,500 hectares of fertile land has been developed by 3 primary co-operatives comprising 190 Tswana farmers. Silkworm farming was being tried in 1983.

INDUSTRY. The first industries were started on an agency basis at Babelegi; the fastest growing industrial area in the homeland, in 1977 it covered 183 hectares and by March 1976 more than R56m. had been invested in the project. Other industries include 2 breweries at Tlhabane and Garankuwa. There is also a furniture factory near Heystekrand, and a tannery at Montshiwa. Border industries are also promoted by the central government, notably Rosslyn where 128 industries had been established by Dec. 1975.

COMMUNICATIONS

Roads. Total length (1977) 6,300 km, of which 63 km are tarred. 1976–77, 32 km were covered by bus, and 116m. passengers transported.

EDUCATION AND WELFARE

Education. In 1980 the territory's total school attendance was 439,599 at 1,025 educational institutions which include special schools and technical schools. Primary school attendance grew from 252,000 (1970) to 343,482 (1980) and secondary school enrolment increased from 15,000 (1970) to 91,372 (1980). The number of pupils to one teacher was 50 in 1980, and the situation has improved since then.

Education is free apart from a nominal contribution to school funds, and hostel fees at post-primary schools.

Instruction from Grade I to Standard 2 is in Setswana, while Standard 4 to senior standards are taught in English. The education is controlled by the Department of Education.

Health. In 1979 Bophuthatswana had 11 hospitals, 140 clinics, 6,000 hospital beds, 127 doctors and 2,805 nurses. The health budget in 1979–80 was R30m.

Book of Reference

The Independence of Bophuthatswana. Dept. of Information, South African Embassy, London

TRANSKEI

HISTORY. Transkei is the homeland of the Xhosa nation and was granted self-government by the Republic of South Africa in 1963. Over 1·5m. Transkeians live permanently in the Republic of South Africa but were deprived of their South African citizenship on independence.

AREA AND POPULATION. The total area is 16,910 sq. miles (43,798 sq. km). Population (1976 estimate) 1·9m., of which Coloured 7,650 and Whites 10,000.The capital is Umtata (population (1976) 24,805; 20,196 Blacks, 1,067 Coloured and 3,542 Whites). Other towns include Gcuwa, Kwabhaca, Umzimvubu and Lusikisiki.

CONSTITUTION AND GOVERNMENT. The Status of Transkei Bill passed its third reading in the South African House of Assembly on 11 June 1976

and received its second reading in the Senate on 17 June. The Bill gave Transkei a unicameral National Assembly instead of the then existing Legislative Assembly.

General elections were held on 29 Sept. 1976 and the Transkei National Independence Party gained 69 of the 75 elective seats in the National Assembly. Members were elected for a 5-year period. In addition there are 75 traditional (co-opted) members (70 chiefs and 5 paramount chiefs).

President: Paramount Chief Dr K. D. Matanzima.

Prime Minister: Chief George Matanzima.

Defence, Police, Foreign Affairs and Information: G. T. Vika. *Finance and Auditor-General:* R. Madikizela. *Local Government and Local Tenure:* G. S. Ndabankulu. *Interior:* S. N. Sigcau. *Education:* H. H. Bubu. *Works and Energy, Commerce and Industry:* W. S. Mbanga. *Posts, Telecommunications and Transport:* A. N. Jonas. *Health:* D. D. P. Ndamase. *Prisons and Justice:* T. T. Letlaka. *Agriculture and Forestry:* E. Z. Booi.

Flag: Three horizontal stripes of ochre, white, green.

FINANCE. The budget (1981–82) balanced at R374,560,800.

AGRICULTURE. Livestock (1976): Cattle, 1·3m.; sheep, 2·5m.; goats, 1·25m.

COMMUNICATIONS

Roads. There are above 8,800 km of roads.

Railways. There is a 209 km railway line linking Umtata with the port of East London in the Republic of South Africa.

Aviation. An international airport exists at Umtata.

Shipping. A start was made in 1978 on a 'free port' at Mnganzana. It will be completed in 5–6 years at a cost of R125m. by a French consortium.

Post. There were 11,498 telephones in 1978.

DIPLOMATIC REPRESENTATIVES

No country, other than the Republic of South Africa, has recognized Transkei as an independent state.

VENDA

HISTORY. Traditionally the territory of the Vhavenda, the country was granted self-government in 1973, and became the third black homeland to be granted independence by the Republic of South Africa on 13 Sept. 1979.

AREA AND POPULATION. The total area is 6,500 sq. km. Of the 381,000 Vhavenda living in the Republic of South Africa in 1970, nearly 70% lived in Venda. In 1980 the *de jure* population of Venda was estimated at 513,890, the *de facto* population at 343,480.

CONSTITUTION AND GOVERNMENT. Executive power is vested in the President, who is elected for the duration of each Parliament, which consists of the President and the National Assembly; legislative power is vested in Parliament. In addition to the National Assembly there is an Executive Council, or Cabinet, and a judiciary independent of the Executive. The National Assembly comprises the 28 chiefs, 15 members designated by 4 regional councils, 42 members elected by popular vote and 3 members nominated by the President. A new Assembly must be elected after every 5 years, but it may be dissolved at any time by the President. All existing tribal, community and regional councils were retained with their status and powers unchanged, like those of the tribal leaders.

The first general election was held in Aug. 1973; the sole political party, the Venda Independence People's Party (VIPP) won 10 of the 18 contested seats. Shortly after, the Chief Minister, Chief Mphephu, formed the Venda National Party (VNP); in the second general election of July 1978 the VIPP won 31 of the 42 contested seats, VNP the remaining 11. Chief Mphephu was re-elected Chief Minister.

President: Paramount Chief P. R. Mphephu.

Foreign Affairs: Chief A. M. Madzivhandila. *Economic Affairs:* Headman F. N. Ravele. *Education:* Headman E. R. B. Nesengani. *Urban Affairs and Land Tenure:* Chief C. A. Nelwamondo. *Justice:* Chief J. R. Rambuda. *Health and Welfare:* Chief C. N. Makuya. *Agriculture and Forestry:* G. M. Ramabulana. *Internal Affairs:* Chief M. M. Mphaphuli. *Transport, Works and Communications:* A. A. Tshivhase. *Deputy for Posts and Telecommunications:* Headman B. R. Nemulodi. *Deputy for Information and Broadcasting and of Public Service Commission:* W. R. Rabuma.

Flag: Three horizontal stripes of green, yellow, and brown, with a brown V on the yellow stripe, and a blue vertical strip in the hoist.

INTERNATIONAL RELATIONS

Aid. The Republic of South Africa granted aid of R45m. in 1981–82.

ECONOMY

Budget. The 1982–83 budget balanced at R115·07m.

Currency. South African Rand.

NATURAL RESOURCES

Water. In Oct. 1982 there were 118 hectares of canals, 250 dams and 520 boreholes.

Minerals. Venda is relatively poor in mineral resources, although there are large supplies of stone for construction. Coal is the most important mineral; there are large deposits in the west near Makhado and in the north-east, bordering on the Kruger National Park, which it is hoped will soon be exploited. In addition there are deposits of graphite, copper sulphides, phosphates and magnesite; in 1978 the 2 graphite and 2 magnesite mines provided employment for 233 people, and the value of their output was R963,900.

Agriculture. About 85% of Venda is suitable only for the raising of livestock because of insufficient rainfall and poor soils, while some 10% is suited to dry-land crop production. Over 10,965 hectares have been given over to forest, mainly pine and eucalyptus. Eighteen irrigation schemes are being developed and there is extensive reclamation and conservation of eroded or overgrazed land; nearly R2m. were spent on these projects in 1980–81. Only maize is grown on a comparatively large scale, but tea, sisal, groundnuts, coffee and sub-tropical fruits are increasing in importance. A fish-breeding project produced 3 tonnes in 1980–81.

Over 80% of the working population are engaged in agriculture. The Venda Agricultural Corporation (Agriven) was established on 1 April 1982 to promote agricultural development.

INDUSTRY. Industrial development is still in its early stages, and since Venda's location is unfavourable, the Government is concentrating on the promotion of agro-industries utilizing local produce, and small-scale industries. A chutney factory has recently been established, in addition to a tea processing plant, a furniture factory and several saw-mills. A copper-chrome arsenate preservation plant has been established at Phiphidi. At Shayandima a 20-hectare industrial area has been prepared. The construction industry is particularly important owing to the substantial increase in the demand for buildings caused by the recent expansion of government, educational and health services.

In Dec. 1982 total investment in industry was estimated at R18·9m. The Venda Development Corporation was established in 1975 to promote and finance economic developments.

COMMUNICATIONS

Roads. There were (1982) 1,226 km of roads, of which 50 km had a permanent surface.

Aviation. An airline, inaugurated in 1981, operates between Nwangundu in Thohoyandu and Johannesburg *via* Pietersburg and Pretoria.

Post and Broadcasting. In 1982 there were 28 post offices and postal agencies. Telephones (1982) numbered, 1,547. In 1982 the government-owned Radio Thohoyandu broadcast 15 hours daily.

EDUCATION AND WELFARE

Education. The Department of Education assumed responsibility for education on independence. Education is free up to Standard 2, and pupils are taught in the native tongue, Luvenda, for the first 4 years (up to Standard 2), after which English is gradually introduced. Secondary education comprises Standards 6 to 10.

The number of primary schools increased from 233 (1970) to 472 (1982), the number of pupils from 65,500 (1970) to 157,014 (1982) and the number of teachers from 956 (1970) to 4,586 (1982).

In 1970 there were 12 secondary schools, which had increased to 112 by 1982. Pupils numbered 2,465 in 1970, 33,432 in 1982, while the number of teachers increased from 100 (1970) to 1,062 (1982).

In addition there is a technical school at Sibasa with about 320 pupils, an agricultural school at Dimani with 476 pupils, and a school for the handicapped at Shayandima. There are 2 teacher-training colleges; enrolment was 270 in 1970, and 704 in 1982. The University of Venda was established in 1981.

Health. In 1982 there were 5 hospitals/homes with 1,506 beds and 43 clinics. White doctors numbered 10 and coloured, 3; there were 712 nurses.

Welfare. In 1981–82 the Government spent R7·3m. on grants and pensions to 22,249 recipients. There is one welfare home.

CISKEI

HISTORY. On 4 Dec. 1981 the Republic of South Africa gave independence to Ciskei the fourth of the tribal homelands.

AREA AND POPULATION. Ciskei lies between latitudes 32° and 33°35′ and longitudes 26°20′ and 27°48′, and has a coastal boundary between East London and Port Alfred. The total area is about 7,700 sq. km. The population was (1981) 2·1m. but only 660,000 live in Ciskei. The remainder work in the Republic of South Africa and as a result can be deported as aliens.

Populations of towns (1980): Mdantsane, 158,864; Zwelitsha, 30,773; Sada, 28,966; Dimbaza, 18,715.

CONSTITUTION AND GOVERNMENT. In 1981 Ciskei became an independent democratic republic with an Executive Council consisting of the President, Vice-President and 11 ministers appointed by the President. The legislature is a National Assembly consisting of about 87 members of which a maximum of 37 are traditional leaders, the others being elected on the basis of adult suffrage every five years.

President: Dr Lennox Sebe.

Flag: Blue, a broad diagonal band from lower hoist to upper fly, charged with a black crane.

National Anthem: Nkosi Sikelel' i Afrika, composed by Enoch Sontonga.

ECONOMY

Budget. In 1980–81, revenue was R119·09m. and expenditure R137·71m.

Currency. South African Rand.

ENERGY AND NATURAL RESOURCES

Electricity. Ciskei is totally dependent on power supply lines maintained by the Republic of South Africa.

Minerals. Mineral resources are mainly undeveloped and in 1981 no mines existed in Ciskei.

Agriculture. In 1977–78, total agricultural production was valued at R8·26m.

In 1979–80, the dryland products included (in tons): Maize, 4,458; wheat, 481; dry beans, 148; dry peas, 141; grain sorghum, 69. The main crops produced under irrigation were (in tons): Potatoes, 385; lucerne, 364; maize, 333; beans, 77; wheat, 64.

Livestock (1980): 187,000 cattle, 215,000 sheep, 187,000 goats, 15,525 pigs.

Forestry. In 1976–77, 1,434 hectares were planted with conifers. The indigenous forest covered some 18,700 hectares. In 1977–78, production of timber was valued at R960,000.

INDUSTRY AND TRADE

Industry. In 1977 industry was valued at R5·6m. and construction at R11·2m. The chief manufactures include wood and leather goods, metal products, crafts and light industrial articles.

Commerce. International trade is mainly with the Republic of South Africa and no separate figures are available. The main exports are pineapples, timber and manufactured goods.

Tourism. Tourism is an important and developing industry.

COMMUNICATIONS

Roads. In 1980 there were 407 km of tarred roads and 1,397 km of gravel roads.

Railways. There are two main railway lines serving the southern part of Ciskei only.

Aviation. Ciskei depends mainly on East London's airport though there is a small airfield at King William's Town and minor landing strips elsewhere.

Shipping. Ciskei has no harbour of its own but has full access to the facilities of East London in the Republic of South Africa.

Post and Broadcasting. All major centres have post offices and manual telephone exchanges; automatic exchanges and telex are gradually being provided. Radio Xhosa broadcasts daily.

Newspapers (1981). There were two Ciskeian newspapers, one of which, *Imvo,* was first published in 1884.

JUSTICE, RELIGION, EDUCATION AND WELFARE

Justice. The Supreme Court acts as Court of Appeal for the seven Magistrates' Courts, which in turn act as Courts of Appeal for the chiefs' courts. Appeals from the Supreme Court are heard by the Appellate Division of the Republic of South Africa's Supreme Court in Bloemfontein.

Religion. In 1980 (estimate) the population was 24% Methodists, 21% Independent, 8% Presbyterian Congregationalists, 7% Anglicans, 6% Roman Catholics, 2%

Dutch Reformed Church, 2% other Christians, 28% ancestor worship and 2% other religions.

Education. In 1981 there were 498 primary schools with 180,214 pupils and 4,058 teachers; 123 secondary and teacher-training schools with 46,913 pupils and 1,463 teachers; and 2 vocational schools with 304 pupils and 32 teachers. The University of Fort Hare had a total of 2,304 students in 1981.

Health. In 1979–80, there were 5 hospitals with 1,491 beds, and a total of 2,643 nursing staff.

Social Welfare. Pensions paid in 1980:

	Beneficiaries	*Amount (R1,000)*
Old age	32,319	9,365
Blind	598	188
Disability	4,773	1,474
War veterans	49	13

Books of Reference

Mayer, P., *Townsmen or Tribesmen.* OUP, 1961
Pauw, B. A., *Christianity and the Xhosa Tradition.* OUP, 1975
Van der Kooy, R, (ed.) *The Republic of Ciskei: A Nation in Transition.* Pretoria, 1981

SPAIN

Capital: Madrid
Population: 37·75m. (1981)
GNP per capita: US$5,350 (1980)

España

HISTORY. Although Spain has traditionally been a monarchy there have been two Republics, the first in 1873, which lasted for 11 months, and the second 1931–39; both were democratically and peacefully proclaimed. Part of the army rebelled against the republican government on 18 July 1936, thus beginning the Spanish Civil War, *see* THE STATESMAN'S YEAR-BOOK, 1939, pp. 1325–26. The new regime was led by Gen. Franco, who had been proclaimed Head of State and Government in 1936, and its institutions were based on single party rule, with the *Falange* as the only legal political organization.

In July 1969, Prince Don Juan Carlos de Borbón y Borbón, grandson of Alfonso XIII, was sworn in as successor to the Head of State and he had the title of HRH Prince of Spain until he became King.

Gen. Francisco Franco y Bahamonde died on 20 Nov. 1975 and on 22 Nov. Prince Juan Carlos de Borbón y Borbón took the oath as Juan Carlos I, King of Spain.

On 23 Feb. 1981 there was an attempted military *coup.* During 18 hours the deputies of the lower house of Parliament and the Cabinet were held hostage. The King, the only high authority who kept his liberty, obtained the surrender of the rebels without bloodshed.

AREA AND POPULATION. Spain is bounded north by the Bay of Biscay and the Pyrenees (which form the frontier with France and Andorra), east and south by the Mediterranean and the Straits of Gibraltar, south-west by the Atlantic and west by Portugal and the Atlantic. Continental Spain has an area of 492,592 sq. km, and including the Balearic and Canary Islands and the towns of Ceuta and Melilla 504,750 sq. km (194,884 sq. miles).

The growth of the population has been as follows:

Census year	*Population*	*Rate of annual increase*	*Census year*	*Population*	*Rate of annual increase*
1860	15,655,467	0·34	1950	27,976,755	0·81
1910	19,927,150	0·72	1960	30,903,137	0·88
1920	21,303,162	0·69	1970	33,823,918	0·94
1930	23,563,867	1·06	1981	37,746,260	1·15
1940	25,877,971	0·98			

Area and population of the autonomous communities and provinces, census of 1 March 1981:

Autonomous community / *Province*	*Area (sq. km)*	*Population*	*Per sq. km*
Andalusia	*87,268*	*6,441,755*	*73*
Almería	8,774	405,513	47
Cádiz	7,385	1,001,716	135
Córdoba	13,718	717,213	52
Granada	12,531	761,734	60
Huelva	10,085	414,492	41
Jaén	13,498	627,598	46
Málaga	7,276	1,036,261	142
Sevilla	14,001	1,477,428	105
Aragón	*47,669*	*1,213,099*	*25*
Huesca	15,671	219,813	14
Teruel	14,804	150,900	10
Zaragoza	17,194	842,386	48
Asturias	*10,565*	*1,127,007*	*106*
Baleares	*5,014*	*685,088*	*136*
Basque Country, The	*7,261*	*2,134,967*	*296*
Álava	3,047	260,580	85
Guipúzcoa	1,997	692,986	347
Vizcaya	2,217	1,181,401	532
Canary Islands	*7,273*	*1,444,626*	*200*
Palmas, Las	4,065	756,353	185
Santa Cruz de Tenerife	3,208	688,273	217

Autonomous community Province	Area (sq. km)	Population	Per sq. km
Cantabria	*5,289*	*510,816*	*96*
Castilla-La Mancha	*79,226*	*1,628,005*	*20*
Albacete	14,858	334,468	22
Ciudad Real	19,749	468,327	23
Cuenca	17,061	210,280	12
Guadalajara	12,190	143,124	11
Toledo	15,368	471,806	30
Castilla-León	*94,147*	*2,577,105*	*27*
Ávila	8,048	178,997	22
Burgos	14,269	363,474	25
León	15,468	517,973	33
Palencia	8,029	186,512	23
Salamanca	12,336	368,055	29
Segovia	6,949	149,286	21
Soria	10,287	98,803	9
Valladolid	8,202	489,636	59
Zamora	10,559	224,369	21
Catalonia	*31,930*	*5,958,208*	*186*
Barcelona	7,773	4,618,734	598
Gerona	5,886	467,945	80
Lérida	12,028	355,451	29
Tarragona	6,283	516,078	82
Extremadura	*41,602*	*1,050,119*	*25*
Badajoz	21,657	635,375	29
Cáceres	19,945	414,744	20
Galicia	*29,434*	*2,753,836*	*93*
Coruña, La	7,876	1,083,415	137
Lugo	9,803	399,185	40
Orense	7,278	411,339	56
Pontevedra	4,477	859,897	192
Madrid	*7,995*	*4,726,986*	*591*
Murcia	*11,317*	*957,903*	*84*
Navarra	*10,421*	*507,367*	*48*
Rioja, La	*5,034*	*253,295*	*50*
Valencian Community	*23,305*	*3,646,765*	*156*
Alicante	5,863	1,148,597	195
Castellón	6,679	431,755	64
Valencia	10,763	2,066,413	192
Ceuta [1]	*18*	*70,864*	...
Melilla [1]	*14*	*58,449*	...
Total	*504,750*	*37,746,260*	*74*

[1] Ceuta and Melilla are municipalities located in the northern coast of Morocco.

The capitals of the provinces are in the towns from which they take the name, except in Álava (capital Vitoria), Asturias (Oviedo), Baleares (Palma de Mallorca), Cantabria (Santander), Guipúzcoa (San Sebastián), La Rioja (Logroño), Navarra (Pamplona) and Vizcaya (Bilbao).

In 1981 there were 19,216,496 females and 18,529,764 males.

By decree of 21 Sept. 1927 the islands which form the Canary Archipelago were divided into 2 provinces, under the name of their respective capitals: Santa Cruz de Tenerife and Las Palmas de Gran Canaria. The province of Santa Cruz de Tenerife is constituted by the islands of Tenerife, La Palma, Gomera and Hierro, and that of Las Palmas by Gran Canaria, Lanzarote and Fuerteventura, with the small barren islands of Alegranza, Roque del Este, Roque del Oeste, Graciosa, Montaña Clara and Lobos. The area of the islands is 7,273 sq. km; population (census 1981), 1,444,626. Places under Spanish sovereignty in Morocco are: Alhucemas, Ceuta, Chafarinas, Melilla and Peñón de Vélez.

The following were the registered populations of principal towns at census 1981:

Town	Population	Town	Population	Town	Population
Albacete	117,126	Getafe	127,060	Reus	80,710
Alcalá de Henares	142,862	Gijón	255,969	Sabadell	184,943
Alcorcón	140,657	Granada	262,182	Salamanca	167,131
Algeciras	86,042	Hospitalet	294,033	San Baudilio del Llobregat	74,550
Alicante	251,387	Huelva	127,806	San Fernando	71,846
Almería	140,946	Jerez de la Frontera	176,238	San Sebastián	175,576
Avila	86,584	Jaén	96,424	Santa Coloma de Gramanet	140,588
Badajoz	114,361	Laguna, La	112,635	Santa Cruz de Tenerife	190,784
Badalona	227,744	Leganés	163,426	Santander	180,328
Baracaldo	117,422	León	131,134	Santiago de Compostela	93,695
Barcelona	1,754,900	Lérida	109,573	Sevilla	653,833
Bilbao	433,030	Logroño	110,980	Tarragona	111,689
Burgos	156,449	Lugo	73,986	Tarrasa	155,360
Cáceres	71,852	Madrid	3,188,297	Torrejón de Ardoz	75,398
Cádiz	157,766	Málaga	503,251	Valencia	751,734
Cartagena	172,751	Mataró	96,467	Valladolid	330,242
Castellón	126,464	Móstoles	149,649	Vigo	258,724
Córdoba	284,737	Murcia	288,631	Vitoria	192,773
Cornellá	90,956	Orense	96,085	Zaragoza	590,750
Coruña, La	232,356	Oviedo	190,123		
Elche	162,873	Palencia	74,080		
Ferrol, El	91,764	Palma de Mallorca	304,422		
Fuenlabrada	77,626	Palmas, Las	366,454		
Gerona	87,648	Pamplona	183,126		

Vital statistics for calendar years:

	Marriages	*Births*	*Deaths*
1976	260,974	677,456	299,007
1977	262,015	656,357	294,324
1978[1]	258,070	636,892	296,781
1979[1]	245,856	597,252	289,864
1980[1]	213,363	565,401	287,621
1981[1]	199,057	532,255	286,400

[1] Provisional figures.

CLIMATE. Most of Spain has a form of Mediterranean climate with mild, moist winters and hot, dry summers, but the northern coastal region has a moist, equable climate, with rainfall well-distributed throughout the year, mild winters and warm summers, though having less sunshine than the rest of Spain.

Madrid. Jan. 41°F (5°C), July 77°F (25°C). Annual rainfall 16·8″ (419 mm). Barcelona. Jan. 46°F (8°C), July 74°F (23·5°C). Annual rainfall 21″ (525 mm). Cartagena. Jan. 51°F (10·5°C), July 75°F (24°C). Annual rainfall 14·9″ (373 mm). La Coruña. Jan. 51°F (10·5°C), July 66°F (19°C). Annual rainfall 32″ (800 mm). Sevilla. Jan. 51°F (10·5°C), July 85°F (29·5°C. Annual rainfall 19·5″ (486 mm).

KING. Juan Carlos I, born 5 Jan. 1938. The eldest son of Don Juan, Conde de Barcelona. Juan Carlos was given precedence over his father as pretender to the Spanish throne in an agreement in 1954 between Don Juan and Gen. Franco. Don Juan resigned his claims to the throne in May 1977. King (then Prince) Juan Carlos married, in 1962, Princess Sophia of Greece, daughter of the late King Paul of the Hellenes and Queen Frederika. *Offspring:* Elena, born 20 Dec. 1963; Cristina, 13 June 1965; Felipe, Prince of Asturias, Heir to the throne, 30 Jan. 1968.

CONSTITUTION AND GOVERNMENT. The *Cortes* (Parliament) was freely elected on 15 June 1977. The text of the new Constitution was approved by referendum on 6 Dec. 1978, and came into force 29 Dec. 1978. It established a parliamentary monarchy, with King Juan Carlos I as head of state. Legislative power is vested in the *Cortes,* a bicameral parliament composed of the Congress of Deputies (lower house) and the Senate (upper house). The Congress of Deputies has not less than 300 nor more than 400 members (350 in the general elections of 1977, 1979 and 1982), all elected in a proportional system regarding the population of every province. The members of the Senate are elected in a majority system: the 47 peninsular provinces elect 4 senators each, regardless of population; the insular provinces electing 5 (Baleares, Las Palmas) or 6 (Santa Cruz de Tenerife); and Ceuta and Melilla, 2 senators each. There are 208 senators, to whom are added some other members of the upper house elected by the parliaments of the autonomous communities. Deputies and senators are elected in universal (but not compulsory), direct, free, equal and secret suffrage, for a term of 4 years. Executive power is vested in the President of the Government (prime minister), with his Cabinet; he is elected by the Congress of Deputies.

A general election took place on 28 Oct. 1982.

Congress of Deputies (350 members): Spanish Workers Socialist Party (PSOE), 202; Popular Alliance (AP, conservative), 106; Centre Democratic Union (UCD), 12; Convergence and Union (CiU, Catalan nationalists), 12; Basque Nationalist Party (PNV), 8; Spanish Communist Party (PCE), 4; Social and Democratic Centre (CDS), 2; Herri Batasuna (Basque independentists), 2; Euskadido Eskerra (non-radical Basque independentists), 1; Esquerra Republicana de Catalunya (Catalan republican nationalists), 1.

Senate (208 members, excluding those elected by regional parliaments): PSOE, 134; AP, 54; CiU, 7; PNV , 7; UCD, 4; Asamblea Majorera (from Canary island of Fuerteventura). 1; independent from Soria province, 1.

The *Council of Ministers* appointed 2 Dec. 1982 was composed as follows:

President of the Government (Prime Minister): Felipe González Márquez (Secretary-General of PSOE).

Vice-President of the Government (Deputy Premier): Alfonso Guerra González. *Foreign Affairs:* Fernando Morán López. *Economy, Finance and Commerce:* Miguel Boyer Salvador. *Industry and Energy:* Carlos Solchaga Catalán. *Interior:* José Barrionuevo. *Defence:* Narcís Serra i Serra. *Public Administration:* Javier Moscoso del Prado. *Education and Science:* José María Maravall. *Public Works:* Julián Campo. *Justice:* Fernando Ledesma Bartret. *Culture:* Javier Solana Madariaga. *Territorial Administration (relations with Autonomous Communities):* Tomás de la Quadra Salcedo. *Agriculture, Fisheries and Food:* Carlos Romero Herrero. *Health and Consumers Affairs:* Ernest Lluch i Martín. *Labour and Social Security:* Joaquín Almunia Amann. *Transport, Tourism and Communications:* Enrique Barón Crespo.

All ministers are members of PSOE, excepting the Minister of Justice, who is a non-party magistrate.

National flag: Three horizontal stripes of red, yellow, red, with the yellow of double width, and charged near the hoist with the national arms.

National anthem: Marcha real.

Regional and local government. The Constitution of 1978 establishes a semi-federal system of regional administration, with the autonomous community *(Comunidad Autónoma)* as its basic element. There are 17 autonomous communities, each of them having a Parliament, elected by universal vote, and a regional government; all possess exclusive legislative and executive power in many matters, as listed in the national Constitution and in their own fundamental law *(estatuto de autonomía).* The Basque Country and Catalonia elected their parliaments in March 1980, Galicia in Oct. 1981 and Andalusia in May 1982. All others are due in May 1983.

There are 7 autonomous communities composed of one only province, i.e., Asturias (*ex*-Oviedo province), Cantabria (*ex*-Santander province), La Rioja (*ex*-Logroño province), Navarra, Baleares, Murcia and Madrid. The other 10 are formed by 2 or more provinces. In all, there are in Spain 50 provinces, since the administrative division established in 1833; Ceuta and Melilla, municipalities in the northern coast of Morocco, are not part of any province. The provincial council *(Diputación Provincial)* is the administrative organ of the province, except in the 7 autonomous communities composed of one only province, where there are only the regional legislative and executive powers. Each of the 7 main islands of the Canaries (provinces of Las Palmas and Santa Cruz de Tenerife) has a corporation, the *Cabildo Insular,* to rule its special interests.

The provinces are constituted by the association of municipalities (8,022 in 1981 census). Municipalities are autonomous in their own sphere. At their head stands the municipal council *(Ayuntamiento),* members of which are elected in a universal ballot every 4 years, and they, in turn, elect one of them as Mayor *(Alcalde).*

DEFENCE. On 26 Sept. 1953 the US and Spain signed three agreements covering the construction and use of military facilities in Spain by the US, economic assistance, and military end-item assistance. These agreements were renewed several times, the last in July 1982. The American naval and air base at Rota (near Cádiz) is connected by pipelines with the American bomber bases at Morón de la Frontera (near Seville), Torrejón (near Madrid) and Zaragoza.

Length of service is 16 months in the army, 24 months in the navy and 18 months in the air force.

Army. The Army consists of 1 armoured division with AMX-30, M-47 and M-48 tanks, 2 mechanized infantry divisions, 2 mountain divisions, 10 independent infantry brigades, 1 armoured cavalry brigade, 1 high mountain brigade, 1 parachute brigade, 1 airportable brigade and 1 battalion with surface-to-air missiles.

Army personnel consisted (1982) of 255,000 officers and other ranks. Total strength in Ceuta and Melilla, about 35,000 men, including 3 regiments of the Foreign Legion.

Navy. Particulars of the principal ship:

Com-pleted	*Name*	*Standard displace-ment Tons*	*Guns*	*Aircraft*	*Shaft horse-power*	*Speed Knots*
			Helicopter Carrier			
1943	Dedalo[1]	13,000	26 40-mm. A.A.	7 VSTOL aircraft and 20 helicopters	100,000	32 (original) now reduced

[1] The former US fixed-wing aircraft carrier *Cabot*, converted in 1966 and transferred to Spain on loan in 1967 and purchased in 1973.

There are also 8 diesel-powered patrol submarines (2 new French-built, 4 modern French-built and 2 old *ex*-US), 12 destroyers, 13 frigates, 4 old corvettes, 12 new fast attack craft, 10 new patrol vessels, 4 ocean minesweepers, 6 coastal minesweepers, 6 patrol ships (*ex*-coastal minesweepers), 44 coastal patrol craft, 30 inshore patrol launches, 1 dock landing ship, 6 survey ships, 3 landing ships, 9 landing craft, 90 minor landing craft, 1 replenishment ship, 15 oilers, 2 attack vehicle and troop transports, 2 tenders, 2 training ships, 1 boom defence vessel, 30 tugs, 1 royal yacht, 10 water carriers, 40 auxiliary craft and 40 service barges.

The Spanish Navy is being renewed and modernized. Ships under construction include 1 small aircraft carrier scheduled to be completed in 1986 and 2 more patrol submarines of French design. Ships projected include 3 missile armed frigates and 8 corvettes, although a modified new construction programme is being considered including 2 large destroyers, 5 frigates and 2 minehunters.

Shipbuilding is mainly carried on at the dockyards at El Ferrol and Cartagena, Cádiz having a smaller share in it. Barcelona, Bilbao, Seville and Cádiz are the chief naval yards.

There are naval radio telegraphic stations at Cádiz, Barcelona, Mahón, Pontevedra, Cartagena and El Ferrol.

In 1983 naval personnel totalled 63,250, comprising 4,200 naval officers, 37,900 ratings, 8,950 civil branch, 700 marine officers and 11,500 marine other ranks.

The Naval Air Service operates 40 fixed-wing aircraft and 30 helicopters.

Air Force. The Air Force is organized as an independent service, dating from 1939. It is administered through 4 operational commands. These comprise Air Defence Command which controls interceptor squadrons (including USAF elements) and the control and warning radar network, Tactical and Transport Commands, and Air Command of the Canaries. Strength is about 38,000 and 160 combat aircraft.

The Tactical Air Command has 1 fighter-bomber squadron of Spanish-built Northrop SF-5s, 1 squadron of HA-220 Super Saeta light attack jet aircraft of Spanish design and manufacture, 1 reconnaissance squadron of HA-220s, 1 aeronaval co-operation squadron with 6 P-3A Orion anti-submarine aircraft, and a liaison flight at Tablada with CASA 127s and Bird Dogs. Defence Command has 2 squadrons of Mirage III-Es, 2 squadrons of F-4C/RF-4C Phantom IIs and 2 squadrons of Mirage F1-Cs, plus a flight of CASA 127 liaison aircraft. Four KC-130H tankers support the F-4C squadrons. Three wings of Air Transport Command operate C-130 Hercules, Caribou and Spanish-built CASA Aviocars. Air Command of the Canaries has 3 squadrons, equipped with Aviocar transports; SF-5 fighter-bombers; F27 Maritime aircraft and Super Puma helicopters for search and rescue. Other equipment includes 2 DC-8s, 4 Falcons, a Cheyenne and helicopters for VIP transport; and aircraft for photographic, firefighting, target towing and research duties. Air-sea rescue units have Aviocars and Super Puma helicopters. Replacement of F-4s and SF-5s with a total of 84 F-18 Hornets will begin in 1986.

American-built Bonanza, T-34A and T-6 piston-engined aircraft are used for basic training, after which pupil pilots progress to CASA C-101 and T-33A jet aircraft. Two-seat versions of operational types are used as advanced trainers. Other training types include Beechcraft King Air C90s for instrument flying and liaison duties.

INTERNATIONAL RELATIONS

Membership. Spain is a member of UN, the Council of Europe, NATO and OECD.

ECONOMY

Budget. Revenue and expenditure in 1m. pesetas:

	1977	*1978*	*1979*	*1980*	*1981*	*1982*
Revenue	967,250	1,433,000	1,747,500	2,284,456	2,823,000	3,533,820
Expenditure	967,250	1,433,000	1,747,500	2,284,456	2,823,000	3,533,820

The budget is made up as follows (in 1m. pesetas):

Revenue (1982)	
Direct taxes	1,195,912
Indirect taxes	1,100,022
Levies and taxes	209,910
Current transactions	158,204
Investment income	169,846

Expenditure (1982)	
H.M. House	254
Cortes (Parliament)	3,895
Court of Accounts	239
Constitutional Court	444
Council of State	212
Public Debt	132,495
Civil Service Pensions	273,535
Council of the Judicial Power	366
Presidency of the Government	71,400
Ministry of Foreign Affairs	17,698
,, Justice	59,249
,, Defence	409,284
,, Finance	38,111
,, Interior	166,682
,, Public Works	169,873
,, Education	485,365
,, Labour, Health and Social Security	659,030
,, Industry and Energy	142,309
,, Agriculture	129,830
,, Commerce and Tourism	17,731
,, Transport and Communications	228,013
,, Culture	30,306
Regional governments	194,097
Regional Compensation Fund	180,000

Currency. The *pesetas* is divided into 100 *céntimos*.

Bank-notes of 5,000, 1,000, 500 and 100 *pesetas* and coins of 1 *peseta* (copper and aluminium), 2, 5, 25, 50, 100 *pesetas* (nickel and copper) are in circulation. In Jan. 1982 the circulation of bank-notes was 1,371,192m. *pesetas* and of coins, 53,095m. *pesetas.*

In March 1983, £1 = 200 *pesetas*; US$1 = 135·90.

Banking. On 1 Jan. 1922 the Bank of Spain came under the Bank Ordinance Law, according to which the Government participate in its net profits.

The 10 largest banks are: Banco Español de Crédito; Banco Central; Banco Hispano Americano; Banco de Bilbao; Banco de Vizcaya; Banco de Santander; Banco Exterior de España; Banco Popular Español; Banco Urquijo; Banco Pastor.

Savings bank deposits (Popular Savings Banks) in Spain, 31 Dec. 1980, amounted to 3,298,412m. pesetas. Post office savings banks opened on 12 March 1916. Deposits, 31 Dec. 1980, amounted to 160,304m. pesetas; private banks saving deposits, 7,468,000m. pesetas.

Weights and Measures. On 1 Jan. 1859 the metric system of weights and measures was introduced.

ENERGY AND NATURAL RESOURCES

Electricity. Electric power-stations in 1980 had a total installed capacity of 30·8m. kw., of which 13·3m. was hydro-electric. The total output 1981, amounted to 111,180m. kwh of which 23,270m. hydro-electric and 9,568m. nuclear.

Gas. Production in 1977 was 783m. cu. metres.

Oil. Crude oil production (1980) 1,596,000 tonnes.

Minerals. Spain is relatively rich in minerals. The production of the more important minerals in 1980 were as follows (in 1,000 tonnes):

Anthracite	4,047	Iron ore	9,227	Tin ore	0·7
Coal	9,070	Lead ore	134	Zinc ore	329·4
Lignite	15,390	Copper	199	Wolfram ore	0·7
Uranium ore	501	Mercury	95·2		

Agriculture. Spain is mainly an agricultural country. In 1981 the total value of agricultural produce was 805·2m. pesetas; of livestock, 651·3m.; of forestry, 49·9m. Land under cultivation in 1980 (in 1,000 hectares) included: Cereals, 7,470; vegetables, 549; potatoes, 355. In 1980, 523,907 tractors and in 1979, 44,669 harvesters were in use.

Principal crops	*Area (in 1,000 hectares)* 1977[1]	1978[1]	1979[1]	1980	*Yield (in 1,000 tonnes)* 1977[1]	1978[1]	1979[1]	1980
Wheat	2,715	2,752	2,551	2,698	4,064	4,806	4,082	6,039
Barley	3,348	3,519	3,477	3,575	6,766	8,068	6,251	8,705
Oats	406	442	436	458	418	553	456	680
Rye	236	228	220	217	228	251	221	283
Rice	68	68	69	68	379	401	427	433
Maize	442	443	467	454	1,892	1,969	2,212	2,313
Potatoes	403	371	355	355	5,881	5,364	5,637	5,737
Sugar-beet	253	235	166	183	8,307	8,292	5,124	6,908
Tomatoes	73	72	64	61	2,358	2,223	2,204	2,147

[1]Provisional.

In 1980, 1,657,000 hectares were under vines; production of wine was 42·4m. hectolitres. The area of onions was 32,000 hectares, yielding 905,900 tons. Production of oranges and mandarines was 2,604,000 tons. Other products are esparto, flax, hemp and pulse. Spain has important industries connected with the preparation of wine and fruits. Silk culture is carried on in Murcia, Alicante and other South-eastern provinces; 3,000 tons were produced in 1978. Spain produced in 1980, 12,513 tonnes of honey and 680 tonnes of beeswax. Alcoholic beverages produced totalled 102·2m. litres in 1977.

Tobacco crop in 1980 was 36,800 tonnes; sugar-cane, 297,200 tonnes.

Livestock (1981): Horses, 242,000; mules, 190,000; cattle, 4,531,000; sheep, 14,887,000; goats, 2,170,000; pigs, 10,692,000; poultry (1980), 53·5m.

Forestry. Total forests (1980) 26m. hectares; production value, 45,810m. pesetas.

Fisheries. The most important catches are those of sardines, tunny fish and cod. The total catch amounted in 1981 to 1·22m. tons, representing a value of 139,896·3m. pesetas. In the tinned fish industry there were, in 1978, 405 factories, producing 129,265 tons. The Spanish fishing fleet in 1980 consisted of 17,390 vessels of 759,421 tons.

INDUSTRY AND TRADE

Industry. The manufacture of cotton and woollen goods is important, principally in Catalonia. In 1978 there were 3,756 textile factories in operation. Production, in 1,000 tonnes (1978): Wool yarn, 29; cotton (yarn, 61; fabrics, 62); rayon fabrics, 6. 245 paper-mills produced in 1977, 2m. tonnes of writing, printing, packing and other paper. The production of cement reached 28,044,000 tonnes in 1980. Steel production (1980) 12·6m. tonnes; the three great blast-furnaces concentrations are in Bilbao area, Avilés (Asturias) and Sagunto (Valencia). The chemical industry is located in the areas of Madrid, Barcelona and Bilbao; sulphuric acid production (1980), 3m. tonnes; nitrogenous fertilizers, 834,000 tonnes. The 9 oil refineries refined 49,416,000 tonnes of crude oil. In 1979 930,000 TV sets (570,000 colour sets), 1·1m. refrigerators, 970,000 washing machines and 687,000 bicycles were manufactured. Spain has important toys and shoe industries, toys especially in

Alicante and Barcelona provinces and shoe in Alicante province and the Balearic islands.

Spanish shipyards launched 630,000 BRT in 1981. In 1980, 1,389,813 vehicles were built, including (1981) 855,325 passenger cars.

Labour. The daily minimum wage for workers is 1,072 pesetas (Jan. 1983).

The economically active population numbered 13,101,900 in Jan. 1982. Of these, 2·08m. were occupied in agriculture and fishing, 3·23m. in manufactures, 1·31m. in construction industry, 5·73m. in trade and other public and personal services.

Commerce. Foreign trade of Spain (Peninsula, Baleares, Canaries, Ceuta, Melilla) (in 1m. pesetas):

	1976	*1977*	*1978*	*1979*	*1980*	*1981*
Imports	1,169,412	1,350,352	1,431,538	1,704,022	2,450,652	2,970,435
Exports	583,222	775,150	1,001,599	1,221,441	1,493,187	1,888,422

In 1980 the most important items of import were (in 1m. pesetas): Crude petroleum, 807,425; chemical products, 106,241; oleaginous seeds and fruits, 67,780; natural gases, 58,409; maize, 47,803; refined petroleum products, 37,753; fish (fresh and canned), 37,716; metallic minerals, 35,010; car parts, 34,907. The most important items of export were: Cars and other vehicles, 110,352; citric fruits, 56,955; footwear, 46,761; refined petroleum products, 37,184; vegetables, 33,566; iron and steel bars, 32,559; books, 31,722; tyres, 30,088; car parts, 29,608.

Sherry wine exported in 1980, 138,696 tonnes with a value of 14,230m. pesetas; other wines, 414,883 tonnes (10,547m. pesetas).

Total trade between Spain and UK (British Department of Trade returns, in £1,000 sterling):

	1977	*1978*	*1979*	*1980*	*1981*	*1982*
Imports to UK	435,176	505,894	710,901	804,232	804,781	956,935
Exports and re-exports from UK	464,829	472,035	573,015	708,998	707,767	870,416

Total trade of the Spanish territories and UK (British Department of Trade returns, in £1,000 sterling):

	Imports to UK			*Exports from UK*		
	1980	*1981*	*1982*	*1980*	*1981*	*1982*
Canary Islands	61,565	61,450	44,574	46,108	42,124	83,508
North Africa	7	6	...	6,860	6,859	4,679

Tourism. In 1981, 40,129,323 tourists visited Spain (from France, 10·66m.; Portugal, 9·38m.; Federal Germany, 4·56m.; UK, 4·06m.). Receipts of foreign currency (1980) US$6·97m.

COMMUNICATIONS

Roads. In 1980 the total length of highways and roads in Spain was 147,963 km, of which 124,923 km were macadamized or had other good surface. Motorways, 1,923 km. Number of cars was 7,943,325, lorries, 1,396,809 and buses, 43,303 in 1981.

Railways. The total length of the state railways in 1980 was 13,533 km, mostly 1,676-mm gauge. There are 5,612 km of lines electrified. On 1 Feb. 1941 the Spanish railways, of broad gauge only, passed into state ownership; they are under a board known as the *Red Nacional de Ferrocarriles Españoles* (RENFE). The gauge of the principal Spanish railways has, for strategic reasons, been kept different from that of France; passengers therefore must change trains at the French frontier stations except by certain trains having variable gauge axles. In 1980 freight carried was 10,887m. tonne-km and 13,527m. passenger-km.

Aviation. The most important Spanish airline is 'Iberia': it maintains a regular service with Europe, America, Africa and the Middle East. 'Aviaco' operates mainly internal flights. There are 43 airports open to civil traffic; those of Madrid, Palma de Mallorca and Barcelona are the most active. A small airport in Seo de Urgel, in the Pyrenees, used especially for the air service of Andorra was opened in 1982.

Aircraft movements in 1981 (provisional), 295,551 internal and 224,127 international, carrying 46m. passengers and 362,594 tonnes of merchandise.

Shipping. The merchant navy in 1981 contained 1,115 vessels of a gross tonnage of 7,688,000.

In 1981 (provisional), 102,402 ships entered Spanish ports, carrying 6,871,000 passengers and discharging 449,367,000 tonnes of cargo.

Post and Broadcasting. The receipts of the post office in 1981 were 53,277m. pesetas; expenses, 57,921m. pesetas. There were in 1981, 13,694 post offices and 12,310,230 telephones, all privately operated.

Radio Nacional de España broadcasts 4 programmes on medium-waves and FM, as well as many regional programmes; it does not broadcast advertising. There is another state broadcasting network, *Radio-Cadena Española,* this self-financing with advertising. The greatest radio audience is that of a private network, *Sociedad Española de Radiodifusión* (SER); *Cadena de Ondas Populares Españolas* (COPE) belongs to the Roman Catholic church. Two private broadcasting networks were established in 1982 covering the whole of Spain, *Antena 3* and *Radio 80. Televisión Española* broadcasts 2 programmes. Colour transmissions are carried by PAL system. Number of receivers (1979): radio, 9·6m.; television, 9·4m. (about 50% colour sets).

Cinemas (1980). There were 4,096 cinemas with an estimated seating capacity of 4m.

Newspapers (1981). There were about 100 daily newspapers with a total daily circulation of about 5m. copies.

JUSTICE, RELIGION, EDUCATION AND WELFARE

Justice. Justice is administered by *Tribunales* and *Juzgados* (Tribunals and Courts), which conjointly form the *Poder Judicial* (Judicial Power). Judges and magistrates cannot be removed, suspended or transferred except as set forth by law. The Constitution of 1978 has established a new organ, the *Consejo General del Poder Judicial* (General Council of the Judicial Power), formed by magistrates, judges, attorneys and lawyers, governing the Judicial Power in full independence from the other two powers of the State, the Legislative (Cortes) and the Executive (President of the Government and his Cabinet). The territorial organization of justice is being gradually changed, adapting it to the new map of the country in Autonomous Communities.

The Judicature is composed of the *Tribunal Supremo* (Supreme High Court); 15 *Audiencias Territoriales* (Division High Courts); 50 *Audiencias Provinciales* (Provincial High Courts); 579 *Juzgados de Primera Instancia* (Courts of First Instance), and 9,203 *Juzgados Municipales, Comarcales y de paz* (District Court, or Court of Lowest Jurisdiction held by Justices of the Peace).

The *Tribunal Supremo* consists of a President (appointed by the King, on proposal from the *Consejo General del Poder Judicial*) and various judges distributed among 6 chambers: 1 for trying civil matters, 3 for administrative purposes, 1 for criminal trials and 1 for social matters. The *Tribunal Supremo* has disciplinary faculties; is court of cassation in all criminal trials; for administrative purposes decides in first and second instance disputes arising between private individuals and the State, and in social matters resolves in the last instance all cases involving over 100,000 pesetas.

The *Audiencias Territoriales* have power to try in second instance sentences passed by judges in civil matters.

The *Audiencias Provinciales* try and pass sentence in first instance on all cases filed for delinquency. The jury system, re-established by the art. 125 of the Constitution, had not been applied by Jan. 1983, pending its parliamentary regulation.

The *Juzgados Municipales* try small civil cases and petty offences. The *Juzgados Comarcales* deal with the same charges, but their jurisdiction embraces larger districts.

Military cases are tried by the *Tribunal Supremo de Justicia Militar* but its sentences can now pass to the (civil) *Tribunal Supremo,* as final cassation instance.

The *Tribunal Constitucional* (Constitutional Court) has power to solve conflicts between the State and the Autonomous Communities, to determine if legislation passed by the Cortes is contrary to the Constitution and to protect constitutional rights of the individuals violated by any authority. Its 12 members are appointed by the King in the following way: 4, on proposal of the Congress of Deputies; 4, on proposal of the Senate; 2 on proposal of the *Consejo General del Poder Judicial;* and 2 on proposal of the Cabinet.

The death penalty was abolished in 1978 by the Constitution (art. 15). Divorce is again in force since July 1981.

The prison population was, on 31 Dec. 1981, 21,185.

Religion. Roman Catholicism is the religion of the majority. There are 11 metropolitan sees and 52 suffragan sees, the chief being Toledo, where the Primate resides.

The archdioceses of Madrid-Alcalá and Barcelona depend directly from the Vatican.

The Constitution guarantees full religious freedom and states that no religion has an established legal condition (art. 16); so, since 29 Dec. 1978 there has been no official religion in Spain. A report issued in 1982 by the Episcopal Conference of the Roman Catholic Church claims that 82·76% of all children born in 1981 were baptized in that church.

There are about 100,000 other Christians, including several Protestant denominations, Jehovah Witnesses and Mormons. The British and Foreign Bible Society was, on 10 March 1963, allowed to resume its activities.

The first synagogue since the expulsion of the Jews in 1492 was opened in Madrid on 2 Oct. 1959. The number of Jews is estimated at about 12,000.

Education. Primary education is compulsory and free between 6 and 14 years of age.

In 1980–81 pre-primary education (under 6 years) was conducted by 35,610 schools, with 35,588 teachers and 1,182,425 pupils. Primary or basic education (6 to 14 years): 176,424 schools, 211,074 teachers and 5,606,452 pupils. Secondary education (14-17 years) is conducted on two branches: 2,445 middle schools *(Institutos),* with 66,160 teachers and 1,091,197 pupils, and 2,142 vocational and technical centres *(Formación Profesional),* with 36,556 teachers and 558,808 pupils. For higher education there were (in 1979–80) 559 centres, with 20,445 teachers and 544,834 pupils.

In 1982 there were in all 33 universities: 22 State Universities, in Madrid, Barcelona, Valencia, Granada, Sevilla, Santiago de Compostela, Zaragoza, Bilbao (University of the Basque Country), Oviedo, Valladolid, Salamanca (founded in 1215), La Laguna (Canaries), Murcia, Málaga, Córdoba, Badajoz-Cáceres (University of Extremadura), Cádiz, León, Santander, Alicante, Palma de Mallorca and Alcalá de Henares; 4 Polytechnic Universities, in Madrid, Barcelona, Valencia and Las Palmas (Canaries); 2 Autonomous Universities, in Madrid and Barcelona; 4 private (catholic) universities, in Deusto (Bilbao), Pamplona, Salamanca and Madrid (University of Comillas); and the *Universidad Nacional de Educación a Distancia* (National University for Education at Home), which teaches by mail, radio and TV, with its central seat at Madrid. The number of university students was 460,458 (1979–80), and teachers 26,533.

DIPLOMATIC REPRESENTATIVES

Of Spain in Great Britain (24 Belgrave Sq., London SW1X 8QA)
Ambassador: José Joaquín Puig de la Bellacasa.

Of Great Britain in Spain (Calle de Fernando el Santo, 16, Madrid, 4)
Ambassador: Sir Richard Parsons, KCMG.

Of Spain in the USA (2700–15th St., NW, Washington, D.C., 20009)
Ambassador: Nuno Aguirre de Carcer.

Of the USA in Spain (Serrano 75, Madrid)
Ambassador: Terence A. Todman.

Of Spain to the United Nations
Ambassador: Jaime de Piniés.

Books of Reference

Statistical Information: The Instituto Nacional de Estadistica (Paseo de la Castellana, 183, Madrid) combines the administrative work of a government department attached to the Presidency of the Government with a centre of statistical studies. *Director-General:* José Montes. Its publications include: *Anuario Estadístico de España.* Annual. *Edición manual* (latest vol., 1981).—*Reseñas estadísticos provinciales.*—*Nomenclátor de las ciudades, villas lugares, aldeas, y demás entidades de población de España.* 52 vols. Madrid, 1963.—*Poblaciones de Derecho y de Hecho de los Municipios Españoles: Censo de Poblacion de 1981.* Madrid, 1982.—*Diccionario Corográfico de España.* 4 vols. Madrid, 1948.—*Boletín de Estadística.* Madrid. (No. 1, Jan.–March 1939: monthly from 1948).—*Estadística española. Revista trimestral* (from 1959).

Spain at a Glance, 1972. Servicio Informativo Español, Madrid, 1972

Aguilar (ed.), *Nuevo Atlas de España.* Madrid, 1961
Altamira y Crevea, R., *A History of Spain.* New York and London, 1950
Anuario del Mercado Español. Madrid, 1965
Bell, D., (ed.), *Democratic Politics in Spain.* London, 1983
Carr, R., *Modern Spain, 1875–1980.* OUP, 1980
Enciclopedia Universal Ilustrada. 70 vols., 10 appendices, 10 supplements. Madrid
Garcia Venero, M., *Historia del Nacionalismo Vasco, 1793–1936.* Madrid, 1945
Lafuente, M., and Valera, J., *Historia General de España.* New ed. 25 vols. Barcelona, 1925
Lieberman, S., *The Contemporary Spanish Economy: A Historical Perspective.* London, 1982
López Oliván, J., *Repertorio Diplomático Español. [Collection of treaties, 1125–1935.]* Madrid, 1944
Maravall, J., *The Transition to Democracy in Spain.* London, 1982
Morris, J., *Spain.* London, 1979
Russell, P. E. (ed.), *Spain: A Companion to Spanish Studies.* 6th ed. London, 1973
Vicens Vives, J., *Historia Económica de España.* 5 vols. Barcelona, 1959
Wright, A., *The Spanish Economy 1959–1976.* London, 1977

National Library: Biblioteca Nacional, Madrid. *Director:* Guillermo Cuastavino Callent.

FORMER PROVINCE IN AFRICA (WESTERN SAHARA)

It was announced in Madrid on 14 Nov. 1975 that Spain, Morocco and Mauritania had reached agreement on the transfer of power over Western Sahara to Morocco and Mauritania on 28 Feb. 1976. Morocco occupied El Aiaún in late Nov. and on 12 Jan. 1976 the Spanish army withdrew from Western Sahara which had ceased to be a Spanish province on 31 Dec. 1975. The country was partitioned by Morocco and Mauritania. In Aug. 1979 Mauritania withdrew from the territory it took over in 1976. The area was taken over by Morocco and reorganized into provinces.

Algeria stated that the former province should be handed over to the people of the territory, objected to the partition and is (1982) backing the claims of *Frente Polisario* for an independent state. In spite of occupation of all western centres by Moroccan troops, Saharan guerrillas based in Algeria continue to attempt to liberate their country. They have renamed it the Democratic Saharan Arab Republic and hold most of the desert beyond a defensive line built by Moroccan troops encompassing Smara, Bu Craa and Laayoune.

In 1982 the Democratic Saharwi Arab Republic became a member of the Organization of African Unity (OAU).

The area was 266,769 sq. km (102,680 sq. miles). The population at the census (1970) was 76,425; Saharans, 59,777 and 16,648 Europeans. The capital was El Aaiún (Laayoune) (population, 24,048).

Rich phosphate deposits were discovered in 1963 at Bu Craa. Morocco holds 65% of the shares of the former Spanish state-controlled company. While production reached 5·6m. tonnes in 1975, exploitation has been severely reduced by guerrilla activity in 1976 and 1977. After a nearly complete collapse, production and transportation of phosphate resumed in 1978, ceased again, and then resumed in 1982.

Books of Reference

Atlas Histórico y Geográfico de Africa Española. Madrid, 1955
Resumén estadistico del Africa española. 1965–66. Madrid, 1967
Caro Baroja, J., *Estudios saharianos.* Madrid, 1955
Hernández-Pacheco, E., and others, *El Sahara español.* Madrid, 1949
Mercer, J., *Spanish Sahara.* London, 1976
Pélissier, R., *Les Territoires Espagnols d'Afrique.* Paris, 1963.—*Los Territorios Españoles de Africa.* Madrid, 1964
Rumeu de Armas, A., *España en el Africa Atlántica.* 2 vols. Madrid, 1956–57
Thompson, V. and Adloff, R., *The Western Saharans: Background to Conflict.* London, 1980

SRI LANKA

Capital: Colombo
Population: 14·9m. (1981)
GNP per capita: US$270 (1980)

Ceylon

HISTORY. According to the Mahawansa chronicle, an Indian prince from the valley of the Ganges, named Vijaya, arrived in the 6th century B.C. and became the first king of the Sinhalese. The monarchical form of government continued until the beginning of the 19th century when the British subjugated the Kandyan Kingdom in the central highlands.

In 1505 the Portuguese formed settlements on the west and south, which were taken from them about the middle of the next century by the Dutch. In 1796 the British Government annexed the foreign settlements to the presidency of Madras. In 1802 Ceylon was constituted a separate colony.

Ceylon reached fully responsible status within the British Commonwealth when the Ceylon Independence Act, 1947, came into force on 4 Feb. 1948. Sri Lanka became a republic in 1972.

AREA AND POPULATION. Sri Lanka lies off the south-east coast of the Indian State of Tamil Nadu, separated from it by the Indian ocean but almost joined to it by the chain of islands called Adam's Bridge. On 28 June 1974 the frontier between India and Sri Lanka in the Palk Strait was re-defined, giving to Sri Lanka the island of Kachchativu. Area (in sq. km.) and census population on 17 March 1981.

Provinces	*Area*	*Population*	*Provinces*	*Area*	*Population*
Western	3,708·87	3,915,001	North-Central	10,723·21	850,575
Central	5,590·17	2,005,956	Uva	8,481·90	922,636
Southern	5,558·77	1,882,912	Sabaragamuwa	4,901·56	1,478,879
Northern	8,882·05	1,111,468			
Eastern	9,951·34	976,475	Total	65,609·63	14,850,001
North-Western	7,811·73	1,706,099			

Population (1981 census), 14,850,001, an increase of 17·1% since 1971. Population (in 1,000) according to race and nationality at the 1981 census: 10,986 Sinhalese, 1,872 Ceylon Tamils, 1,057 Ceylon Moors, 38 Burghers, 43 Malays, 825 Indian Tamils, 29 others. Non- nationals of Sri Lanka totalled 1,202,000. By agreement with the Government of India in 1964 and 1974, Indian nationals who have not been granted Sri Lanka citizenship were to be repatriated. The 1964 agreement covered 525,000 people; the 1974 agreement, 150,000.

Vital statistics, 1981: birth-rate (per 1,000 population), 28·0; death-rate, 6·0; infant death-rate (per 1,000 live births), 43·7 in 1980.

The urban population was 21·5% of the total in 1981. The principal towns and their population according to the census of 1981 are: Colombo, 585,776; Dehiwela-Mt. Lavinia, 174,385; Moratuwa, 135,610; Jaffna, 118,215; Kotte, 101,563; Kandy, 101,281; Galle, 77,183; Negombo, 61,376; Trincomalee, 44,913; Batticaloa, 42,934; Matara, 39,162; Ratnapura, 37,354; Anuradhapura, 36,248; Badulla, 32,954; Kalutara, 31,495. Population of the Greater Colombo area, 1980, about 1m.

The national languages are Sinhala, English and Tamil; Sinhala is the official language and Tamil is used in the northern and eastern provinces.

CONSTITUTION AND GOVERNMENT. A new constitution for the Democratic Socialist Republic of Sri Lanka was promulgated in Sept. 1978.

The Executive President is directly elected by the people and has to receive more than one-half of the valid votes cast. His term of office is six years and he shall not hold the office for more than two consecutive terms. He is the Head of the State, the Head of the Executive and of the Government and the Commander-in-chief of the Armed Forces. He does not have any veto power over legislation; even in a time of public emergency, he must act with Parliamentary control and approval.

Parliament consists of one chamber, composed of 168 members elected by universal suffrage, and proportional representation. The Senate was abolished by constitutional amendment in Sept. 1971.

The term of Parliament is six years. In Nov. 1982 Parliament voted to extend its present term (expiring Aug. 1983) for a further six years. The vote was subject to national referendum on 20 Dec. 1982; 71% of the electorate voted and 55% approved the extension.

The Prime Minister is appointed by the President and both in consultation appoint the Cabinet. The President is head of the Cabinet.

The electorate consists of all who are 18 years of age and over.

National flag: A yellow field bearing 2 panels: in the hoist 2 vertical strips of green and orange; in the fly, dark red with a gold lion holding a sword and in each corner a gold 'bo' leaf.

The Cabinet was in March 1983 as follows:

President, Defence, Higher Education, Janata Estates, State Plantations, Power and Energy, and Plan Implementation: J. R. Jayawardene.

Prime Minister, Leader of the House, Local Government, Highways, Housing and Construction: Ranasinghe Premadasa.

Land, Land Development and Mahaweli Development: Gamini Dissanayake. *Foreign Affairs:* A. C. S. Hameed. *Home Affairs:* K. W. Devanayagam. *Trade and Shipping:* Lalith Athulathmudali. *Rural Development:* Wimala Kannangara. *Justice:* N. P. Wijeyeratne. *Finance and Planning:* Ronnie de Mel. *Labour:* Capt.C. P. J. Seneviratne. *Industries and Scientific Affairs:* Cyril Mathew. *Cultural Affairs:* E. L. B. Hurulle. *Fisheries:* F. Perera. *Health:* R. Atapattu. *Post and Telecommunications:* D. B. Wijetunge. *Parliamentary Affairs and Sports:* M. Vincent Perera. *Transport:* H. M. Mohamed. *Agricultural Development and Research:* G. Jayasuriya. *Public Administration and Plantation Industries:* M. Jayawickreme. *Textile Industry:* W. Mendis. *Social Services:* Asoka Karunaratne. *Food and Co-operatives:* S. B. Herat. *Rural Industrial Development:* R. S. Thondaman. *Youth Affairs, Education and Employment:* R. Wickremasinghe. *State:* A. de Alwis. *Regional Development:* C. Rajadurai.

For purposes of general administration, the island is divided into 24 districts, administered by government agents. There are 12 Municipal Councils and 24 Development Councils.

The capital is Colombo.

DEFENCE

Army. The Army was constituted on 10 Oct. 1949 and consists of the Regular Force, the Regular Reserve, the Volunteer Force and the Volunteer Reserve. Strength (1983), 11,000, organized into 5 infantry brigades, 2 reconnaissance, 1 engineer, 1 signals and 1 artillery regiment. Reserves, 15,000.

Navy. The Navy was constituted on 9 Dec. 1950. It comprises 8 (1 *ex*-Soviet and 7 *ex*-Chinese) fast gunboats, 25 small patrol boats and 1 service craft. *Gemunu* and *Rangalla* are commissioned as shore establishments. The naval base is established at Trincomalee. Personnel in 1983 numbered 220 officers and 2,740 ratings. Naval personnel are sent to the UK for training. There is also a Volunteer Naval Reserve of 43 officers and 540 ratings, and a Naval Reserve of 130.

Air Force. The Air Force was formed on 10 Oct. 1950. Its flying bases are at Katunayake and China Bay, Trincomalee. Equipment includes 6 Chipmunk and 6 Cessna 150 trainers, 3 Heron and 3 Dove light transports, 1 HS748, 1 Convair 440, 2 DC-3s, 4 Cessna Skymasters for coastal reconnaissance and transport, and 2

Dauphin, 7 JetRanger and 2 Bell 47G helicopters for internal security operations. In storage are 3 MiG-17F jet fighter-bombers, 1 MiG-15UTI jet trainer, 2 Jet Provosts (armed). Total strength about 2,600 officers and airmen. There is also an Air Force Reserve.

INTERNATIONAL RELATIONS

Membership. Sri Lanka is a member of UN, the Commonwealth, the Non-Aligned Movement and the Colombo Plan.

External debt. External debt in Dec. 1981 was Rs29,172m.

ECONOMY

Planning. The 1982-86 plan aims at 6% annual growth rate. Investment allocated is mainly for agriculture, including the Mahaweli energy and irrigation scheme. Total investment, about Rs 112,585m.

Budget. Revenue and expenditure of central government in Rs 1m. for financial years ending 31 Dec.:

		Expenditure		
Year	*Revenue*	*Recurrent*	*Capital*	*Total*
1978-79	12,730	12,530	7,809	20,339
1979-80	14,068	16,488	12,044	28,532
1980-81	16,228	17,728	11,765	29,493
1981-82 [1]	19,319	20,564	17,109	37,673

[1] Estimate.

The principal sources of revenue in 1981–82 were (in Rs 1m.): Income tax, 2,953; import duties, 3,600; export duties, 2,907; other indirect taxes, 7,761.

The principal items of recurrent expenditure in 1981-82 (in Rs 1m.): Administration including defence, 3,878; food subsidies, 100; education, social services and health, 3,171; interest on public debt, 5,612. Capital expenditure on agriculture, 921; communications, 1,242.

Currency. The Monetary Law (Amendment) Act No. 16 of 1967 provides that the standard monetary unit is the Ceylon *rupee*.

The Central Bank is the sole authority for the issue of currency and all currency notes and coins issued by the Central Bank are legal tender for the payment of any amount, except notes of Rs 50 and Rs 100 dated before 25 Oct. 1970. Currency notes are issued in the denominations of Rs 2, 5, 10, 20, 50, 100, 500 and 1,000. Coins are issued in the denominations of 1, 2, 5, 10, 25 and 50 cents; Rs 1, 2 and 5. The total circulation was Rs 6,042m. on 30 June 1982. In March 1983, £1 = Rs 33·56; US$1 = Rs 22·97.

Banking. The narrow money supply (M1)at 30 June 1982 stood at Rs 10,815m.

The main commercial banks in Sri Lanka are: The Bank of Ceylon and the People's Bank (state-managed), the State Bank of India, Grindlays Bank, the Hongkong and Shanghai Banking Corporation, the Chartered Bank, the Commercial Bank of Ceylon, the Hatton National Bank, the Habib Bank (Overseas) Ltd., Citibank, American Express and the Indian Overseas Bank Ltd. Total assets of 25 commercial banks at 30 June 1982, Rs 32,102·8m.

The state-owned Ceylon Insurance Corporation and the National Insurance Corporation have a monopoly of all insurance business.

Sri Lanka National Savings Bank at 30 June 1982 had a balance to depositors' credit of Rs 5,802·3m. Sri Lanka State Mortgage and Investment Bank, National Development Bank, Development Finance Corporation and the National Housing Department are the main long-term credit institutions.

Weights and Measures. The metric system has been established by the Weights and Measures (Amendment) Law No. 24 of 1974.

ENERGY AND NATURAL RESOURCES

Electricity. Installed capacity of electric energy (1981), 481,000 kw. Energy produced, 1,872m. kwh; the main source is hydro-electricity. The Mahaweli power scheme is planned to begin production in 1984; installed capacity, 507mw.

Water. The Mahaweli Ganga irrigation scheme has entered phase 2 and will benefit 896,000 acres. Two major river diversions, at Polgolla near Kandy and at Bowatenna on the Amban Ganga River, will benefit 120,000 acres of land already cultivated and irrigate an extra 104,000 acres of new land. There is a Water Resources Board (set up in 1966) and a National Water Supply and Drainage Board (1974). Water supply to the city and area of Colombo comes from the Labugama and Kalatuwawa reservoirs. Consumption within Colombo city limits is estimated at 10,000m. gallons a year.

All domestic consumers receive a free water allowance; commercial consumers do not.

Minerals. Gems are among the chief minerals mined and exported. Precious and semi-precious stones are found among the layers of older alluvium and river gravels of quaternary age in the valleys of the Ratnapura district in the south-west. The most important are sapphire, ruby, crysoberyl, beryl, topaz, spinel, garnet, ziran and tourmaline. Value of gemstones exported in 1981, Rs 304m.

Graphite is also important. The State Graphite Corporation was set up in 1971. There were 3 large mines (Bogala, Kahatagaha and Kalangaha), and several smaller mines working at the end of 1976. Graphite produced (1980), 7,794 tonnes, 1981 7,453.

The Ceylon Mineral Sands Corporation was established in 1957, mainly to extract ilmenite. Production of ilmenite, 1981, 80,000 tonnes. Some rutile is also produced (13,301 tonnes in 1981).

Salt extraction is the oldest industry in Sri Lanka and is now controlled by the National Salt Corporation. The method is solar evaporation of sea-water. Production, 1981, 104,388 tonnes.

Agriculture. The area of the island is approximately 6,560,962·6 hectares, of which 2,155,132·5 hectares are under cultivation. Agriculture engages about 44% of the labour force. The main crops in 1981 were as follows: Paddy (2·2m. tonnes from 842,473 hectares), rubber, tea and coconuts (2,258·6m. nuts).

In March 1976 the Sri Lanka State Plantation Corporation took over management of all private tea and rubber estates. Compensation was paid on condition that it be re-invested in Sri Lanka. The Sri Lanka Tea Corporation was formed in March 1972. Tea production (1981) 210,148 tonnes; rubber, 123,946 tonnes.

Livestock in 1981(estimate): 1·7m. cattle, 898,100 buffaloes, 93,700 swine, 512,200 goats, 29,500 sheep, 6·3m. poultry.

Fisheries. The Government is implementing a programme (1979-83) for the development of fisheries. Production for 1981 was 203,586 tons including 172,318 tons of coastal water fish, 29,124 tons of fresh water fish and 2,144 tons from deep-sea fisheries. In 1981 there were 28,584 fishing craft, of which 6 were trawlers and 15,715 were not motorized.

INDUSTRY AND TRADE

Industry. The Business Undertakings (Acquisition) Act was passed in May 1971 empowering the Government to acquire any business for the state. The British Ceylon Corporation Ltd and its subsidiaries were nationalized in Feb. 1972. The nationalization of the oil industry was completed in Dec. 1971. The first objective was the development of heavy industry through state investment in small companies and the setting up of public corporations. Three such corporations have been established for the mining and processing of graphite; the importing, manufacture and distribution of pharmaceuticals; the importing and distribution of materials for textile manufacture. Other important manufactures are ceramics, vegetable oils, fertilizers, cement, wood and paper products, leather, rubber products and sugar. The government has set up Investment Promotion Zones; by Aug. 1980 these had 119 projects employing over 7,600; the main industry was clothing manufacture. Foreign investment is encouraged by a tax holiday of up to 10 years for approved industries. Export profits may have a 3-year tax holiday.

Trade unions. The registration and control of trade unions are regulated by the Trade Unions Ordinance (Ch. 138 of the Legislative Enactments). In 1979 there were 105 registered trade unions with a membership of 1,440,720.

Commerce. The values of total imports and exports (imports excluding bullion, specie and postal articles; exports, including re-exports and ship's stores) for calendar years (in Rs 1,000):

	1978	*1979*	*1980*	*1981* [1]
Imports	14,687,000	22,560,000	33,637,000	35,530,358
Exports	13,206,000	15,273,000	17,273,000	19,733,255

[1] Provisional

Principal exports (domestic) in 1981 (in Rs 1m.): Tea, 6,444; rubber, 2,895; copra, coconut oil and desiccated coconut, 1,011; other crops, 1,301; textiles and garments, 3,000; precious and semi-precious stones, 304.

Principal imports (Rs 1m.) in 1981 were petroleum, 8,627m.; machinery and equipment, 3,876m.; vehicles and transport equipment, 2,229; food and beverages, 4,888.

In 1981 the principal sources of imports were (in Rs 1m.): Saudi Arabia, 6,193; Japan, 4,970; UK, 2,139; USA, 2,489; India, 1,460; Iran, 2,349; Singapore, 1,904; FRG. 1,741; South Korea, 1,556.

Principal export destinations 1981 were (in Rs 1m.): UK, 1,290; China, 861; USA, 2,806; Japan, 685; Pakistan, 1,073; FRG, 1,115; Saudi Arabia, 632.

Total trade between Sri Lanka and UK (British Department of Trade returns, in £1,000 sterling):

	1978	*1979*	*1980*	*1981*	*1982*
Imports to UK	39,659	40,826	53,681	36,569	42,000
Exports and re-exports from UK	49,110	55,260	76,831	59,236	60,211

Tourism. About 370,742 tourists visited the country in 1981.

COMMUNICATIONS

Roads. There are about 25,330 km. of motorable roads, of which 75% are black-topped.

Number of motor vehicles, 31 Dec. 1981, 374,110, including 126,256 private cars and cabs, 68,427 lorries, 40,681 tractors, 96,851 motor cycles, 23,092 buses.

Railways. In 1982 there were about 1,435 km of railway open, of which 1,394 km were broad gauge and 59 narrow gauge. In 1980 railways ran 3,798m.passenger-km and 206m. tonne-km.

Aviation. Air Lanka operates international services. Foreign airlines which operate scheduled services to Sri Lanka are British Airways, UTA, India Airlines Corporation, Swissair, Aeroflot, Garuda, KLM, Singapore Airlines, Thai Airways International, Pakistan International Airlines, Korean Airlines, Gulf Air, Royal Nepal Airlines, Balkan Bulgarian Airlines, Kuwait Airlines and Maldivian International Airlines; various others operate charter services.

Shipping. In 1981, merchant vessels totalling 14·1 GRT entered the ports of Sri Lanka. The Sri Lanka Shipping Corporation began functioning as ship-owners, charterers, brokers and shipping agents in 1979. The Sri Lanka Port Authority was also established in 1979.

Post and Broadcasting. In 1981 there were 422 post offices, 3,093 sub-post offices and 1,766 telegraph offices. There were 63,500 telephones. Throughout the Greater Colombo Area inter-dialling facilities are now available between 48 stations.

The Overseas Telecommunication Service operates telegraph and telephone services to most parts of the world. Broadcasting is provided by the Sri Lanka Broadcasting Corporation, which assumed the functions of Radio Ceylon on 5 Jan. 1967.

Cinemas. In 1981 there were 358 cinemas with a seating capacity of about 189,000. The National Film Corporation established in 1971 has exclusive rights to import films and arranges distribution of foreign and local films. Films released, 1981, 174.

Newspapers. There are 4 main newspaper groups: Associated Newspapers of Ceylon Ltd (5 daily and 3 weekly papers and other periodicals); Times of Ceylon Ltd (2 daily, 2 weekly and other periodicals); Express Newspapers (Ceylon) Ltd (2 daily and 2 weekly papers); Independent Newspapers Ltd. (3 daily and 3 weekly papers and other periodicals).

There are 4 daily and 3 weekly papers in Sinhala; 3 daily and 3 weekly in Tamil; 3 daily and 3 weekly in English.

JUSTICE, RELIGION, EDUCATION AND WELFARE

Justice. The systems of law which obtain in Sri Lanka are the Roman-Dutch law, the English law, the Tesawalamai, the Moslem law and the Kandyan law.

The Kandyan law applies to the Kandyan Sinhalese in the Central, North-Central, Uva and Sabaragamuwa provinces in respect of all matters relating to inheritance, matrimonial rights and donations. The law of England is observed in most commercial matters. The law of Tesawalamai is applied to all Tamil inhabitants of Jaffna, in all matters relating to inheritance, marriages, gifts, donations, purchases and sales of land. The Moslem law is applied to all Moslems in respect of succession, donations not involving Fidei Commissa, marriage, divorce and maintenance. These customary and religious laws have been modified in many respects by local enactments.

The courts of original jurisdiction are the High Courts, district courts, magistrates' courts and primary courts. The High Courts try major crimes and also exercise admiralty jurisdiction. The district court has unlimited civil jurisdiction in civil, revenue, trust, insolvency and testamentary matters, over persons and estates of persons of unsound mind, and wards. Family Courts were estabished in 1978; District Courts can act as Family Courts. The magistrates' courts exercise criminal jurisdiction carrying the power to impose terms of imprisonment not exceeding 2 years and fines not exceeding Rs 1,500. The Primary Courts which were established in 1978 exercise civil jurisdiction where the value of the subject matter does not exceed Rs 1,500 and also have jurisdiction in respect of by-laws of local authorities and matters relating to the recovery of revenue of such local authorities. Primary Courts exercise exclusive criminal jurisdiction in respect of offences which may be prescribed by regulation by the Minister. A Judge of a Primary Court has a duty to make every effort to settle such matter whether civil or criminal, by conciliation. The Primary Courts have the power to impose sentences of imprisonment not exceeding three months and fines not exceeding Rs 250.

The Constitution of 1978 provided for the establishment of two superior courts, the Supreme Court and the Court of Appeal.

The Supreme Court is the highest and final superior court of record and exercises jurisdiction in respect of constitutional matters, jurisdiction for the protection of fundamental rights, final appellate jurisdiction, consultative jurisdiction, jurisdiction in election petitions, jurisdiction in respect of any breach of the privileges of Parliament. The Court of Appeal exercises appellate jurisdiction for the correction of all errors in fact or in law committed by any court, tribunal or institution, the power to grant and issue orders in the nature of writs of certiorari, prohibition, procedendo, mandamus, quo warrants and Habeas corpus, the power to grant injunctions and jurisdiction to try election petitions in respect of election of Members of Parliament.

Police. The strength of the police service on 31 Aug. 1982 was 15,941.

Religion. Buddhism was introduced from India in the 3rd century B.C. and is the religion of 69·3% of the inhabitants. There were (1981) 10,292,586 Buddhists, 2,292,858 Hindus, 1,111,736 Christians, 1,134,556 Moslems and 15,265 others.

Education. Education is free from the kindergarten to the university and is imparted in the medium of the mother tongue. In 1981 about 86% of the population (10 years old and older) was literate.

In 1981 there were 9,879 schools including 9,521 government schools; the rest were private and estate schools. The government schools had 138,770 teachers and 3·4m. students from grades I to XII. Department of Education expenditure (1981), Rs 1,947·4m. Education is now administered under 31 regional directors.

The overall control of the education regions is vested in the Ministry of Education.

There are 6 Universities: Peradeniya, Colombo, Jaffna, Sri Jayawardenepura, Moratuwa and Kelaniya, and two University Colleges: Ruhuna and Batticaloa. Dumbara Campus comes under Peradeniya University.

In 1981 there were 17,636 students and 1,871 teachers. There were 15 institutions for technical education, 7 of which were polytechnics.

Health. In 1981 there were 488 hospitals, 102 maternity homes and 340 central dispensaries. Hospitals had 44,029 beds and there were 2,889 Department of Health doctors (one to every 5,188 population). Total state budget expenditure on health, 1981, Rs 931·4m.

Social Security. The activities of the Department of Social Services fall into five main divisions:

Public assistance (monthly allowances); casual relief; relief to leprosy and tuberculosis patients and their dependants.

Relief of widespread distress due to failure of crops, floods, storms, etc., including relief to individual cases of distress among fishermen due to acts of God such as fire, storms and accidents; rehabilitation and resettlement of flood victims.

Provision of custodial care and welfare services to the elderly and infirm.

Provision of vocational training facilities, rehabilitation measures and aids and appliances for the physically handicapped.

Provision of custodial care, vocational training and rehabilitation for socially handicapped persons.

Financial assistance to voluntary institutions that provide welfare services.

Special study of social problems affecting the community.

The payment of compensation to workmen meeting with accidents in the course of their work is provided for under the Workmen's Compensation Ordinance No. 19 of 1934, as amended in 1957, 1959 and 1966. It was brought into operation in 1935, and has been administered by the Ministry of Justice since 1980.

DIPLOMATIC REPRESENTATIVES

Of Sri Lanka in Great Britain (13 Hyde Park Gdns., London, W2 2LX)
High Commissioner: Arambamoorthy T. Moorthy (accredited 18 Feb. 1981).

Of Great Britain in Sri Lanka (Galle Rd., Kollupitiya, Colombo 3)
High Commissioner: Sir John Nicholas, KCMG.

Of Sri Lanka in the USA (2148 Wyoming Ave., NW, Washington, D.C., 20008)
Ambassador: Ernest Corea

Of the USA in Sri Lanka (44 Galle Rd., Kollupitiya, Colombo 3)
Ambassador: John H. Reed.

Of Sri Lanka to the United Nations
Ambassador: Ignatius Benedict Fonseka

Books of Reference

The Sri Lanka Year Book
Census Publications from 1871
Performance 1980. Ministry of Plan Implementation, Colombo. 1981
Review of the Economy. Central Bank of Ceylon. Annual
Statistical Pocket-Book. Department of Census and Statistics. Colombo, 1980

de Silva, K. M. (ed.), *Sri Lanka: A Survey.* London, 1977.–*A History of Sri Lanka.* 1980

Ferguson's *Ceylon Directory*. Annual (from 1858)
Jennings, Sir I., *The Constitution of Ceylon*. 3rd ed. London, 1953
Johnson, B. L. C., and Scrivenor, M. le M., *Sri Lanka: Land, People and Economy*. London, 1981.
Kearney, R. N., *The Politics of Ceylon (Sri Lanka)*. Cornell Univ. Press, 1973
Ponnambalam, S., *Dependent Capitalism in Crisis: The Sri Lankan Economy 1948–80*. London, 1980.
Pyatt, G. and Roe, A., *Social Accounting for Development Planning with Special Reference to Sri Lanka*. CUP, 1977
Ratnasuriya, M. D., and Wijeratne, P. B. F., *Shorter Sinhalese-English Dictionary*. Colombo, 1949
Richards, P., and Gooneratne, W., *Basic Needs, Poverty and Government Policies in Sri Lanka*. Geneva, 1981.
Robinson, M. S., *Political Structure in a Changing Sinhalese Village*. CUP, 1975
Wilson, A. J., *Politics in Sri Lanka 1947-73*. London, 1974.—*The Gaullist System in Asia: the Constitution of Sri Lanka*. London, 1980

THE DEMOCRATIC REPUBLIC OF THE SUDAN

Jamhuryat es-Sudan Al Democratia

Capital: Khartoum
Population: 18·9m. (1981)
GNP per capita: US$470 (1980)

HISTORY. Sudan was proclaimed a sovereign independent republic on 1 Jan. 1956. On 19 Dec. 1955 the Sudanese parliament passed unanimously a declaration that a fully independent state should be set up forthwith, and that a Council of State of 5 should temporarily assume the duties of Head of State. The Codomini, the UK and Egypt, gave their assent on 31 Dec. 1955.

For the history of the Condominium and the steps leading to independence, *see* THE STATESMAN'S YEAR-BOOK, 1955, pp. 340–341.

On 8 July 1965 the Constituent Assembly elected Ismail El-Azhari as President of the Supreme Council. Following a crisis in the coalition Cabinet the Prime Minister, Mohammed Ahmed Mahgoub resigned on 23 April 1969. For political history *see* THE STATESMAN'S YEAR-BOOK, 1973–74, p. 1333. The Government was taken over by a 10-man Revolutionary Council on 25 May 1969 under the Chairmanship of Col. Jaafar M. al Nemery. This Council was dissolved in 1972.

AREA AND POPULATION. Sudan is bounded north by Egypt, north-east by the Red Sea, east by Eritrea and Ethiopia, south by Kenya, Uganda and Zaïre, west by the Central African Republic and Chad, north-west by Libya. Sudan covers an area of 967,500 sq. miles (2·5m. sq. km). The Eritrea-Sudan frontier and the frontier with the Chad and Central African Republic have been delimited and demarcated, as also has the greater part of the frontier with Ethiopia.

The population according to the 1973 census was 14,171,732 (estimate (1981) 18·9m.), and consists mainly (two-thirds to four-fifths) of Moslem Arabs, and Nubians in the north and Nilotic and Negro tribes in the south.

The capital is Khartoum (census, 1973, 333,921; estimate, 1980, 1m.). Other important cities are: Omdurman (299,401), Khartoum North (150,991), Port Sudan (132,631), Wadi Medani (106,776), Kassala (98,751), El Obeid (90,060), Al-Qadarif (66,465), Atbara (66,116), Kosti (65,257).

In 1982 there were 18 provinces.

CONSTITUTION AND GOVERNMENT. A new Constitution was introduced in 1973 (amended in 1975). Legislative power lies with a National Assembly of 151 members. Executive power lies with the President.

A measure of autonomy has been given to southern Sudan and a People's Assembly of 60 was elected in May 1980. The Assembly is situated at Juba.

The government in Jan. 1983 was composed as follows:

President and Prime Minister and Minister of Defence: Jaafar Mohammed Nemery (re-elected for a second term in April 1977).

First Vice-President, Director of State Security: Maj.-Gen. Umar Mohammed al Tayib. *Second Vice-President:* Lieut.-Gen. Joseph Lagu. *Transport and Communications:* Maj.-Gen. Khalid Hassan Abbas. *Attorney General:* Dr Hassan Abdalla al Turabi. *Finance and Economic Planning:* Ibrahim Munim Mansur. *Education:* Dr Uthman Said Ahmed Ismail. *Prime Minister's Office:* Abu Bakr Mohammed Osman Salih. *Presidential Affairs:* Dr Baha el Din Mohammed Idris. *Energy and*

Mining: Dr Muhammad Sharif el Tuhami. *Guidance and National Information:* Dr Mohammed Uthman Abu Saq. *Co-operation, Trade and Supply:* Faroug Ibrahim al Magboul. *Internal Affairs:* Ahmed Abdel Rahman Muhammad. *Foreign Affairs:* Mohammed Mirghani Mubarak. *Adviser to Prime Minister, Minister for Manpower Affairs:* Hayder Muhammad Khabsoun. *President's Office:* Khalid al-Khayr Umar. *Minister and Legal Adviser in President's Office:* Dr Yusuf Mikael Bakhit. *Minister and Adviser in President's Office for Decentralization:* Shaykh Bashir ash-Shaykh. *Minister and Press Adviser to President:* Muhammad Mahjub Sulayman. *Construction and Public Works:* Babkir Ali at-Tawm. *Health:* Dr Ali Muhammad Fadl. *Industry:* Muhammad al-Bashir al-Waqi. *Chairman of the High Council for Religious Affairs:* Dafalla el Haj Yusuf. *Chairman of the National Council for Mass Sports and Youth Welfare:* Ali Muhammad Shummu. There were 5 Ministers of State.

On 9 Dec. 1965 the Constituent Assembly proscribed the Communist Party.

National flag: Three horizontal stripes of red, white, black, with a green triangle based on the hoist.

DEFENCE

Army. The Army is organized in 2 armoured, 1 parachute and 7 infantry brigades, with 6 artillery and 1 engineer regiment. There are about 190 Russian tanks. Total strength (1983), 53,000.

Navy. The Navy was established in 1962 with 4 patrol boats built in Yugoslavia and a training mission from the Yugoslav Navy until 1972. Since 1969 another 2 patrol boats, 6 fast gun (*ex*-torpedo) boats, 5 landing craft (3 in service), an oiler, a water carrier and a survey ship have been acquired from Yugoslavia and 3 coast-guard cutters from Iran. Personnel in 1983 totalled 600 officers and men.

Air Force. The Air Force was built up with Soviet and Chinese assistance, and is now receiving equipment from the USA. Three combat squadrons are equipped with 10 F-5E Tiger II and 2 F-5F fighters, about 8 MiG-21 fighters and 18 J-5 (Chinese-built MiG-17) and J-6 (MiG-19) fighter-bombers. There is 1 transport squadron, with 6 C-130H Hercules and 4 DHC-5D Buffalo turboprop transports; 8 Turbo-Porter light transports; 1 helicopter squadron with 10 BO 105s; and 5 armed Jet Provost trainers. Ten Puma helicopters have been ordered. Personnel total about 3,000.

INTERNATIONAL RELATIONS

Membership. Sudan is a member of UN, OAU, the Arab League and is an ACP state of EEC.

ECONOMY

Planning. The 1978–83 6-year development plan was published in 1977 and envisaged a total investment of £S2,670m.

Budget. The 1982-83 budget envisages revenue of £S1,300m. and expenditure of £S1,900m.

Currency. The monetary unit is the Sudanese *pound* (£S) divided into 100 *piastres* and 1,000 *milliemes*. Sudanese bank-notes of £S10, £S5, £S1, 50 and 25 *piastres* and Sudanese coins of P. 10, 5, 2; m/ms 10, 5, 2, 1 are in circulation. In March 1983, £1 = £S0·99; US$1 = £S0·76.

Banking. The Bank of Sudan opened in Feb. 1960 with an authorized capital of £S1·5m. as the central bank of the country; it has the sole right to issue currency. Its foreign reserves stood at £S12,631,000m. as at 31 Dec. 1978. All foreign banks were nationalized in 1970.

Weights and Measures. The metric system is in use.

ENERGY AND NATURAL RESOURCES

Oil. Two oil wells in the south-west produce 15,000 bbls per day of high quality oil.

An oil refinery is being constructed and 2 oil companies are prospecting for oil and natural gas in the Red Sea area.

Minerals. The following minerals are known to exist in Sudan: gold, graphite, sulphur, chromium-ore (estimate, 13,000m. tonnes in 1977), iron-ore, manganese-ore, copper-ore, zinc-ore, fluorspar, natron, gypsum and anhydrite, magnesite, asbestos, talc, halite, kaolin, white mica, coal, diatomite (kieselguhr), limestone and dolomite, pumice, lead-ore, wollastonite, black sands, vermiculite pyrites.

Gold is being exploited on a small scale at Gabeit and at Abirkateib (in Kassala Province); alluvial gold is occasionally exploited in Southern Fung and Equatoria. Total production of good ores was 9 kg in 1977. Iron-ore was discovered in Red Sea area in 1976 with estimated reserves of 250m. tonnes.

About 10m. tons of copper ore were proved at Hofrat-en-Nahas, an ancient copper working. Manganese mining activities started in the 1950s but this industry did not develop well and in 1977 only 400 tonnes was produced. Processed and scrap white mica have been mined since the late fifties; it went out of production for almost a decade, but started again in 1970 when 170 tonnes were produced; 1977, 400 tonnes. A big deposit of vermiculite and a medium-sized deposit of pyrophyllite are known to occur in the Sinkat District. Reserves of metallurgical grade chromite occur in the Ingessana Hills, Blue Nile Province, but only 47,060 tonnes of this mineral were exported in 1970. Huge reserves of chrysotile asbestos are proved in this vicinity and also in Qala El Nahal area, Kassala Province. Deposits of magnesite, with or without talc, are known to occur in the Ingessana Hills and Qala El Nahal areas in addition to other occurrences in the Halaib area, Red Sea Province, but only 400 tonnes of magnesite were shipped in 1970.

Reserves of high grade gypsum and anhydrite are known to occur in the Red Sea Province 40 miles north of Port Sudan. Salt pans at Port Sudan supply the whole needs of the country and a surplus of about 70,000 tonnes was shipped in 1970; production, 1977 (estimate), 92,000 tonnes. High grade quartz for the glass industry occurs in the Sinkat area and reserves of limestone occur in the Atbara and Rabak areas supplying the needs of cement factories in these areas. Wolfram and tin occur in the Halaib area and nickel, with or without platinum, occurs in the Halaib and Ingessana Hills areas.

Agriculture. The Sudan is a predominantly agricultural country; in 1974–75 agriculture contributed 40·6% of GDP (manufacturing, 9·6%). Cotton is by far the most important cash crop on which the Sudan depends for earning foreign currency. The two types of cotton grown in the Sudan are: (*a*) long staple sakellaridis and sakel types (derivatives of sakellaridis), grown in Gezira, White Nile, Abdel Magid and private pump schemes; (*b*) short staple, mainly American types, in Equatoria and Nuba Mountains, generally by rain cultivation.

Production (1979) in 1,000 tonnes: Sorghum, 1,970; sugar-cane, 1,700 (estimate); groundnuts, (1978–79) 1,050; cotton, 131 (estimate); millet, 370; wheat, 266; sesame, 210 (estimate); cotton seed, 320.

One of the largest sugar complexes in the world was opened at Kenana in March 1981. It is capable of processing 330,000 tonnes a year.

Livestock (1979): Cattle, 17·3m.; sheep, 17·2m.; goats, 12·2m.; poultry, 26m.

Forestry. Gum arabic, mainly hashab gum from *Acacia senegal*, is the sole forest produce exported from the Sudan on a major scale. 26,508 tons (80% of the total world supply) was exported in 1978–79. Production is declining as trees are cut down for higher priority agriculture. It ranks as the fourth cash crop after cotton, groundnuts and sesame. The bulk of gum production originates from the central provinces.

A forest research and education institute has been established by the Sudan Government in co-operation with the United Nations Special Fund.

COMMERCE. Total trade for calendar years, in US$1m.:

	1978	*1979*	*1980*	*1981*
Imports[1]	624	736	1,127	1,643
Exports	563	514	689	796

[1] Including government imports.

Total trade between Sudan and UK (British Department of Trade returns, in £1,000 sterling):

	1978	*1979*	*1980*	*1981*	*1982*
Imports to UK	19,470	19,747	13,362	10,889	9,929
Exports and re-exports from UK	114,079	106,403	124,697	118,647	136,636

COMMUNICATIONS

Roads. In the Northern Sudan there are about 550 km of asphalted roads, other than town roads. The remaining roads are only cleared tracks mostly impassable directly after rain. The El Gedaref to Kassala road (1,190 km) opened in 1980, and the section from Khartoum to Port Sudan was almost complete in 1980. In Upper Nile Province motor traffic is limited mostly to the months Jan.–May. In the other 5 southern provinces there are a number of good gravelled roads with permanent bridges which can be used all the year round, though minor roads become impassable after rain. Private cars (1972) 29,000; commercial vehicles, 21,500.

Railways. The main railway lines run from Khartoum to El Obeid *via* Wad Medani, Sennar Junction, Kosti and El Rahad (701 km); El Rahad to Nyala *via* Abu Zabad, Babanousa and Ed-Daein (698 km); Sennar Junction to Kassala *via* Gedaref (455 km) and to Roseires *via* Singa (220 km); Kassala to Port Sudan *via* Haiya Junction and Sinkat (550 km); Khartoum to Wadi Halfa *via* Shendi, El Dammer, Atbara, Berber and Abu Hamad Junction (924 km); Abu Hamad to Karima (248 km); Atbara to Haiya Junction (271 km); Babanousa to Wau (444 km). The main flow of exports and imports is to and from Port Sudan *via* Atbara and Kassala. The total length of line open for traffic (1980) was 1,786 km. The gauge is 1,067 mm. Several new lines are planned, including a link from Wadi Halfa across the Egyptian border. In 1979–80, the railways carried 1,167m. passenger-km and 2,620m. tonne-km.

Aviation. Sudan Airways is a government-owned airline, with its headquarters in Khartoum, operating domestic and international services. The latter include services to Asmara, Addis Ababa, Aden, Jiddah, Cairo, Athens, Rome, London, Beirut, Nairobi, N'djamena, Tripoli and Entebbe. In 1977 Sudan Airways carried 379,000 passengers and 10·3m. kg of mail and freight.

Shipping. Supplementing the railways are regular river steamer services of the Sudan Railways, between Karima and Dongola, 319 km; from Khartoum to Kosti, 319 km; from Kosti to Juba, 1,436 km, and from Kosti to Gambeila, 1,069 km. Port Sudan is the country's only seaport; it is equipped with 13 berths. A modernization programme began in Feb. 1980.

Post and Broadcasting (1975). There are 213 permanent post and telegraph offices, 24 travelling post and telegraph offices and 372 agencies. There are 27 wireless telegraph and 99 radio-telephone stations, 36 automatic telephone exchanges and 340 telephone call boxes; number of telephones in 1981 was 65,038 (42,266 in Greater Khartoum). Radio receivers (1977) 1·4m. The television service broadcasts for 35 hours per week. There were (1978) 95,000 TV receivers and 4 colour transmitters.

Cinemas. In 1975 there were 58, seating capacity 112,000 and also 43 mobile units.

JUSTICE, RELIGION, EDUCATION AND WELFARE

Justice. The judiciary is a separate and independent department of state directly and solely responsible to the President of the Republic. The general administrative supervision and control of the judiciary is vested in the High Judicial Council.

Civil Justice is administered by the courts constituted under the Civil Justice Ordinance, namely the High Court of Justice—consisting of the Court of Appeal and Judges of the High Court, sitting as courts of original jurisdiction—and Province Courts—consisting of the Courts of Province and District Judges. The law administered is 'justice, equity and good conscience' in all cases where there is no special enactment. Procedure is governed by the Civil Justice Ordinance.

Justice in personal matters for the Moslem population is administered by the Mohammedan law courts, which form the Sharia Divisions of the Court of Appeal, High Courts and Kadis Courts; President of the Sharia Division is the Grand Kadi. The religious law of Islam is administered by these courts in the matters of inheritance, marriage, divorce, family relationship and charitable trusts.

Criminal Justice is administered by the courts constituted under the Code of Criminal Procedure, namely major courts, minor courts and magistrates' courts. Serious crimes are tried by major courts, which are composed of a President and 2 members and have the power to pass the death sentence. Major Courts are, as a rule, presided over by a Judge of the High Court appointed to a Provincial Circuit or a Province Judge. There is a right of appeal to the Chief Justice against any decision or order of a Major Court, and all its findings and sentences are subject to confirmation by him.

The President of the Supreme Council of the Armed Forces has power to commute a capital sentence. The Chief Justice has power to remit any case subject to confirmation by him to the Court of Criminal Appeal composed of the Chief Justice and 2 Magistrates of the first class, one of whom has to be a Judge of the High Court.

Lesser crimes are tried by Minor Courts consisting of 3 Magistrates and presided over by a Second Class Magistrate, and by Magistrates' Courts consisting of a single Magistrate or a bench of lay magistrates. In provinces in which circuits of the High Court exist the High Court Judge, in other cases the Province Judge, exercises an appellate jurisdiction and a general supervision over these courts. The greater part of the criminal law is codified in the Sudan Penal Code.

Religion. The population of the 12 northern provinces is almost entirely Moslem (Sunni), the majority of the 6 southern provinces is pagan. There are small Christian communities, with 2 Coptic Bishops, a Greek Orthodox metropolitan, 4 Anglican bishops, 4 Roman Catholic bishops and Greek Evangelical, Evangelical and Maronite congregations.

Education (1977). 4,945 elementary schools had 1,302,040 pupils (41% female); there were 326,250 pupils in secondary schools and 24,109 in tertiary education. In 1979 Khartoum University with 10 faculties had 8,777 students. The Khartoum branch of Cairo University with 4 faculties had about 5,000 students and the Islamic University of Omdurman with 3 faculties had 1,472 students. Juba University, founded in 1975 with 5 faculties had 425 students.

Health. In 1976 the Ministry of Health maintained 151 hospitals, 1,500 dispensaries and dressing stations, 139 health centres and 620 clinics (with together 17,324 beds) and 1,652 doctors.

DIPLOMATIC REPRESENTATIVES

Of Sudan in Great Britain (3 Cleveland Row, London, SW1A 1DD)
Ambassador: Nasr el Din Mustafa Ahmed (accredited 7 May 1982).

Of Great Britain in Sudan (New Aboulela Bldg, Barlaman Ave., Khartoum)
Ambassador: R. A. Fyjis-Walker, CMG, CVO.

Of Sudan in the USA (2210 Massachusetts Ave., NW, Washington, D.C., 20008)
Ambassador: Omer Salih Eissa.

Of the USA in Sudan (Gamhouria Ave., Khartoum)
Ambassador: C. William Kontos.

Of Sudan to the United Nations
Ambassador: Abdel-Rahman Abdalla.

Books of Reference

Sudan Almanac. Khartoum (annual)
al Rahim, M. Abd, *Changing Patterns of Civilian-Military Relations in the Sudan.* Uppsala, 1978

Barnett, T., *The Gezira Scheme: An Illusion of Development.* London, 1977
Daly, M. W., *Sudan.* [Bibliography] Oxford and Santa Barbara, 1983
El Bushra, El.-S., *An Atlas of Khartoum Conurbation.* Khartoum Univ Press, 1976
Fabunni, L. A., *The Sudan in Anglo-Egyptian Relations.* London and New York, 1960
Gaitskell, A., *Gezira: A Story of Development in the Sudan.* London and New York, 1959
Holt, P. M., *A Modern History of the Sudan.* New York, 3rd ed. 1979
Lees, F. A., *The Economic and Political Development of the Sudan.* London, 1977
Nimeiri, S., *Evaluation of the Six Year Development Plan 1977–78—1982–83.* Khartoum, 1978
Wai, D. M. (ed.), *The Southern Sudan: The Problem of National Integration.* London, 1973
Wickens, G. E., *The Flora of Jebel Marra.* London, 1977
Woodward, P., *Condominium and Sudanese Nationalism.* London, 1979

SURINAME

Capital: Paramaribo
Population: 385,000 (1982)
GNP per capita: US$2,840 (1980)

HISTORY. At the peace of Breda (1667) between Great Britain and the United Netherlands, Suriname was assigned to the Netherlands in exchange for the colony of New Netherland in North America, and this was confirmed by the treaty of Westminster of Feb. 1674. Since then Suriname has been twice in British possession, 1799–1802 (when it was restored to the Batavian Republic at the peace of Amiens) and 1804–16, when it was returned to the Kingdom of the Netherlands according to the convention of London of 13 Aug. 1814, confirmed at the peace of Paris of 20 Nov. 1815. On 25 Nov. 1975, Suriname gained full independence and was admitted to the UN on 4 Dec. 1975.

AREA AND POPULATION. Suriname is situated on the north coast of South America and bounded on the north by the Atlantic ocean, on the east by the Marowijne River, which separates it from French Guiana, on the west by the Corantijn River, which separates it from Guyana, and on the south by forests and savannas, which separate it from Brazil.

Area, 163,820 sq. km. Census population (1980), 352,041. Estimate (1982) 385,000. The capital, Paramaribo, had (1971 census) 151,500 inhabitants. Annual rate of growth decreased from 4·34% during 1950–64 to 2·3% during 1964–71, mainly through severe migration primarily to the Netherlands. It is estimated that Suriname lost a total of 150,000 persons by migration (1975–80).

Suriname is divided into 9 districts (populations census 1980): Paramaribo (urban district), 67,718; Commewijne, 14,082; Coronie, 2,756; Marowijne, 22,583; Nickerie, 34,598; Saramacca, 10,333; Suriname, 164,879; Brokopondo, 20,448 and Para, 14,644.

The official languages are Dutch and English. English is widely spoken next to Hindi, Javanese and Chinese as inter-group communication. A vernacular, called 'Sranan Tongo' or 'Surinamese', is used as a lingua franca. In 1976 the Government announced that Spanish would become the nation's principal working language.

CONSTITUTION AND GOVERNMENT. On 25 Feb. 1980 the Prime Minister, Henck Arron, was ousted in a *coup*. A National Military Council was established. In Feb. 1982 the civilian Prime Minister, Dr Henk Chin-a-Sen, was dismissed by the Military Council. In March there was an attempted *coup* by a right-wing military group but this failed. A 4-man military committee administered government departments from Feb. to April 1982 under the chairmanship of Lieut-Col. Deysi Bonterse, the army commander and chairman of the National Military Council. In March 1983 Errol Alibux became Prime Minister.

Before the 1982 *coup* there was a council of 13 ministers who were responsible to the Legislative Council (*Staten van Suriname*). The Legislative Council (39 members) was elected for a 4-year period by universal adult suffrage. Seven political parties were represented in the Legislative Council.

Flag: Horizontally green, red, green with the red of double width with yellow 5-pointed star in centre of red bar.

DEFENCE. Armed forces of the Republic of Suriname consist of regular local officers and conscripted personnel with a strength of about 600 at the time of independence.

INTERNATIONAL RELATIONS

Membership. Suriname is a member of UN, OAS and is an ACP state of the EEC.

ECONOMY

Planning. For 15 years from independence approximately 3,500m. guilders is available from the Netherlands to carry out an extensive social and economic development programme devised by a joint Dutch and Surinamese team of experts. This programme envisaged, the creation of greater employment and the improvement of the living conditions of the people, but by 1980 only a third of the aid had been spent.

Budget. The expenditures and local revenues (derived from import, export and excise duties, taxes on houses and estates, personal imports and some indirect taxes) are as follows (in 1,000 Suriname guilders):

	1973	*1974*[1]	*1975*	*1976*	*1977*	*1978*
Revenues	185,000	204,579	234,600	354,600	541,100	623,100
Expenditures	219,000	249,700	363,900	404,900	581,500	650,500

[1] Provisional figures.

Outstanding loans in 1974: Local, 31·7m.; foreign, 184·9m. Suriname guilders. Public debt as at 30 March 1974, 216·6m. Suriname guilders.

Currency. Notes ranging from 5 to 1,000 *Suriname guilders* are legal tender. Currency notes of 1·00 and 2·50 guilders are issued by the Government. In March 1983, US$1 = 1·79 Suriname guilders; £1 sterling = 2·63 Suriname guilders.

Banking. The Central Bank of Suriname is a bankers' bank and also a bank of issue; the Surinaamsche Bank, the Algemene Bank Nederland and the O.R.G. Vervuurt's Banking Corporation Ltd, are commercial banks; the Suriname People's Credit Bank operates under the auspices of the Government; Surinaamse Postspaarbank (postal savings bank); Surinaamse Hypotheekbank NV (mortgage bank); Surinaamse Investerings Mij. NV (investment bank); Agentschap van de Maatschappij tot financiering van het Nationaal Herstel NV (long-term investments); National Development Bank; The Agrarian Bank.

Weights and Measures. The metric system is in force.

NATURAL RESOURCES

Minerals. Bauxite is the most important mineral; it is being mined in the Suriname and Marowijne districts. Fresh deposits have been found in the western areas. The ore is exported mainly to USA, but partly processed locally into alumina and aluminium. Exports (1981 in 1,000 tonnes): Bauxite, 1,281; alumina, 1,185; aluminium, 32.

Agriculture. Agriculture is restricted to the alluvial coastal zone; cultivated area in 1973, 54,656 hectares. The staple food crop is rice; 46,471 hectares of paddy were planted in 1973, chiefly in the Nickerie, Commewijne, Saramacca and Coronie districts. Principal products (in 1,000 units) in 1975:

Sugar-cane (kg)	159,543	Maize on cob (kg)	365	Orange (pieces)	15,036
Cocoa (kg)	55	Bananas (kg)	43,095	Grapefruit (pieces)	5,530
Coffee (kg)	88	Rum 50% (litres)	2,422	Coconuts (pieces)	5,525
Paddy (kg)	174,845	Molasses (kg)	5,727		

Livestock (1979): 27,000 head of cattle, 10,000 sheep and goats, 19,000 pigs, 1m. poultry.

Forestry. Suriname has great timber resources. Production 1975 included 29 tonnes of balata, 12,775 cu. metres of sleepers, 1,397 cu. metres of fuel wood, 14,225 cu. metres of plywood and 9,054 cu. metres of particle board, chiefly from the Suriname and Marowijne districts.

Fishery. The catch in 1975 amounted to 2,634 tonnes.

INDUSTRY AND TRADE

Industry. There are 3 large bauxite plants, 1 alumina and 1 aluminium smelting plants, sugar- and rice-mills, 2 paint factories, a fruit-juice plant, 2 shrimp freezing plants, a plywood factory, timber-mills, a milk pasteurization plant, a butter and margarine factory and a number of various medium and small industries. Shortage of skilled personnel inhibits expansion.

Commerce. Imports and exports in calendar years (in US$1m.):

	1978	*1979*	*1980*	*1981*
Imports	344	370	454	511
Exports	411	444	514	474

Total trade between Suriname and UK (British Department of Trade returns, in £1,000 sterling):

	1978	*1979*	*1980*	*1981*	*1982*
Imports to UK	14,992	16,825	20,181	11,416	7,593
Exports and re-exports from UK	7,719	7,707	8,112	8,074	10,586

COMMUNICATIONS

Roads. There are 1,335 km of main roads. Two of them lead from Paramaribo to the bauxite centres of Smalkalden (29 km) and Paranam (30 km) and to the airport of Zanderij (49 km). Another main road runs across the districts of Saramacca (71 km) and Coronie (68 km), a fourth across the Commewijne district (41 km) and a fifth in the Marowijne district, from the bauxite centre Moengo to Albina (45 km).

The 'East–West connexion' is almost completed, linking the Corantijn and the Marowijne rivers (375 km).

In 1974 there were 23,227 passenger cars, 5,369 trucks, 1,898 buses, 34,799 powered bicycles and 4,354 motor cycles and scooters.

Railway. There is one single-track railway, running from Onverwacht to Bronsweg (86 km); part of the track, from Paramaribo to Onverwacht (34 km) has been removed.

Aviation. Regular air services are maintained by KLM, SLM, Air France and Cruzeiro do Sul. The international airfield at Zanderij is capable of handling all types of planes.

Suriname Airways Ltd provides daily services between all major districts and maintains also a charter service.

In 1975, 1,205 aircraft landed at Zanderij airport with 40,416 passengers and 1,225 tons of incoming mail and freight.

Shipping. The Royal Netherlands Steamship Co. plies between Amsterdam, Rotterdam, Antwerp, Hamburg and Paramaribo, and New York, Baltimore, New Orleans and Paramaribo. Regular sailings are made to Georgetown, Ciudad Bolivar and most Caribbean ports. The Suriname Navigation Co. maintains services from Paramaribo to Georgetown and Cayenne, and once a month to the Caribbean area. A French and an Italian company maintain passenger services to Europe. The Alcoa Steamship Co. has a fortnightly service to New York, Baltimore, Mobile and New Orleans; a Japanese line sails once a month from Hong Kong and Yokohama to Paramaribo; the Boomerang Line maintains a monthly freight and passenger service between Suriname and Australia. In 1974, 615 vessels totalling 3·58m. GRT entered and in 1975 1,172 of 6·5m. GRT cleared Paramaribo.

Post and Broadcasting. Automatic telephone service links most of the districts in the interior. In 1978 there were 20,787 telephones. Wireless telephone connects Suriname with the Netherlands, USA, Curaçao, Guyana, French Guiana and Trinidad. There are 6 broadcasting and 1 television stations. In 1974 there were 170,000 radios and 36,000 TV sets. Automatic telex was established in 1972.

Cinemas (1973). There are 31 cinemas with a seating capacity of 19,000, and 1 drive-in cinema.

Newspapers (1974). There are 5 daily newspapers and 5 weeklies with a combined circulation of over 24,000.

JUSTICE, RELIGION, EDUCATION AND WELFARE

Justice. There is a court of justice, whose members are nominated by the President. There are 3 cantonal courts.

Religion. There is entire religious liberty. At the end of 1971 the various religious bodies were: Hindus, 112,047; Moslems, 74,078; Roman Catholics, 70,175; Moravian Brethren, 51,868; Reformed and Lutheran, 3,911; Confucians, 80; others, 27,228.

Education. During school-year 1975–76 there were 413 schools with a total of 134,656 pupils and 4,813 teachers. There are also a University with faculties of medicine and law, social and economic studies, 3 technical schools and 5 teachers' training colleges.

Schooling is compulsory from 6 to 12 years of age. Primary education is free and is undertaken by the Government in public schools and by the Roman Catholic and Protestant Missions in denominational schools.

Social Security. The Government subsidizes orphanages and other religious or philanthropical institutions, and maintains an almshouse and institutions for delinquent boys and girls. There are 13 modern hospitals in the country, 4 of which are operated by missions, 2 by a private company, 1 by the military forces and 6 by the Government.

DIPLOMATIC REPRESENTATIVES

Of Great Britain in Suriname
Ambassador: W. K. Slatcher, CVO (resides in Georgetown).

Of Suriname in the USA (2600 Virginia Ave., NW, Washington, D.C. 20037)
Ambassador: Henricus A. F. Heidweiller.

Of the USA in Suriname (Dr Sophie Redmondstraat 129, Paramaribo)
Ambassador: Robert W. Duemling.

Of Suriname to the United Nations
Ambassador: Inderdew Sewrajsing.

Books of Reference

Statistical Information: The General Bureau of Statistics in Paramaribo was established on 1 Jan. 1947. Its publications comprise trade statistics, *Suriname in Figures* (including, from 1953, the former *Handelsstatistiek*) and *Statistische Berichten.*

Economische Voorlichting Suriname. Ministry of Economic Affairs, Paramaribo
Annual Report of the Central Bank of Suriname

SWAZILAND

Capital: Mbabane
Population: 580,000 (1981)
GNP per capita: US$680 (1980)

HISTORY. The Swazi migrated into the country to which they have given their name, in the last half of the 18th century. They settled first in what is now southern Swaziland, but moved northwards under their chief, Sobhuza–known also to the Swazi as Somhlolo. Sobhuza died in 1838 and was succeeded by Mswati. The further order of succession has been Mbandzeni and Bhunu, whose son, Sobhuza II, was installed as King of the Swazi nation in 1921 after a long minority.

The independence of the Swazis was guaranteed in the conventions of 1881 and 1884 between the British Government and the Government of the South African Republic. In 1890, soon after the death of Mbandzeni, a provisional government was established representative of the Swazis, the British and the South African Republic Governments. In 1894 the South African Republic was given powers of protection and administration. In 1902, after the conclusion of the Boer War, a special commissioner took charge, and under an order-in-council in 1903 the Governor of the Transvaal administered the territory, through the Special Commissioner. Swaziland became independent on 6 Sept. 1968.

On 25 April 1967 the British Government gave the country internal self-government. It changed the country's status to that of a protected state with the Ngwenyama, Sobhuza II, recognized as King of Swaziland and head of state. King Sobhuza died on 21 Aug. 1982.

AREA AND POPULATION. Swaziland is bounded on the north, west and south by the Transvaal Province, and on the east by Mozambique and Zululand. The area is 6,705 sq. miles (17,400 sq. km).

The country is divided geographically into 4 longitudinal regions running from north to south; 3 of roughly equal width–Highveld (westernmost), Middleveld, Lowveld–and the Lubombo plateau in the east. The mountainous region on the west rises to an altitude of over 6,000 ft (1,800 metres). The Middleveld is mostly between 1,700 and 3,000 ft, while the Lowveld has an average height of not more than 1,000 ft (300 metres). The whole country is now virtually free from malaria. The Highveld and the Middleveld are well watered. Innumerable small streams unite with the large rivers, notably the Usutu and Komati, which traverse the country from west to east. Except for these the Lowveld is not very well watered. The climate is good except for a few months in summer, when the heat is somewhat excessive in low-lying parts.

Population (census 1976), 527,791. Estimate (1981) 580,000. Mbabane, the administrative capital (22,262). The main urban areas with 1971 populations are: Manzini (16,000); Havelock Mine (4,500); Siteki (3,600); Big Bend (2,900); Mhlume (2,200); Nhlangano (1,700) and Pigg's Peak (1,400).

CONSTITUTION AND GOVERNMENT. Britain's protection ended at independence, when a Constitution similar to the 1967 Constitution was brought into force. The general elections (by universal adult franchise) in April 1967 gave the royalist and traditional Imbokodvo National Movement all 24 seats. The Parliament consists of a House of Assembly, with 24 elected and 6 nominated members and the Attorney-General, who has no vote, and a Senate comprising 12 members, 6 of whom are elected by the House of Assembly and 6 appointed by the King. The executive authority is vested in the King and exercised through a Cabinet presided over by the Prime Minister, and consisting of the Prime Minister, the Deputy Prime Minister and up to 8 other ministers. In April 1973 the King assumed supreme power and the Constitution was suspended and in 1976 it was abolished. On 27 Oct. 1978 a general election took place to elect an electoral college of 80 members. This college elected 40 members for the National Assembly. The King nominated 10 additional members.

Regent: Queen Dzewile.

In March 1983, the Cabinet was composed as follows:

Prime Minister: Prince Bhekimpi Dlamini.

Deputy Prime Minister: B. Sibandze. *Home Affairs:* Prince Gabheni Dlamini. *Agriculture and Cooperatives:* A. K. Hlophe. *Health:* Dr S. Hynd. *Education:* S. D. Dlamini. *Finance:* J. L. F. Simelane. *Justice:* P. L. Dlamini. *Power and Telecommunications:* Dr V. S. Leibrandt. *Commerce, Industry, Mines and Tourism:* Prince Nqaba Dlamini. *Foreign Affairs:* R. V. Dlamini. *Establishments and Training:* E. B. Simelane.

National flag. Horizontally 5 unequal stripes of blue, yellow, red, yellow, blue; in the centre of the red strip an African shield of black and white, behind which are 2 assegais and a staff, all laid horizontally.

Local Government. In Dec. 1963 the former 6 districts were replaced by the 4 districts of Shiselweni, Lubombo, Manzini and Hhohho. They are administered by District Commissioners.

DEFENCE

Army Air Wing. First military aircraft acquired by Swaziland, in mid-1979, were 2 Israeli-built Arava light twin-turboprop transports with underwing weapon attachments for light attack duties.

INTERNATIONAL RELATIONS

Membership. Swaziland is a member of UN, OAU, the Commonwealth and is an ACP state of EEC.

ECONOMY

Budget. Revenue and expenditure (in 1,000 emalangeni) for financial years ending 31 March:

	1978–79	*1979–80*	*1981–82*
Revenue	87,000	115,000	139,000
Expenditure	169,000	169,000	199,000

Chief items of estimated revenue, 1975-76: Customs and excise, E18m.; income tax, E20·2m.

The external public debt expenditure was estimated at E71m. in 1977.

Currency. The currency in circulation in Swaziland, from 1974, is the *emalangeni,* but remains in the rand monetary area. In March 1983, £1=1·60 *emalangeni;* US$1=1·09 *emalangeni.*

Banking. Barclays Bank International and the Standard Bank Ltd maintain branches at Mbabane and Manzini; sub-branches and agencies are operated in 17 other places. Bank rates are those in force throughout South Africa and are prescribed by the main South African offices of the 2 banks. The Swaziland Credit and Savings Bank, now known as The Swazi Bank, a statutory body, was opened in 1965. It specializes in credit for agriculture and low-cost housing. Its head office is in Mbabane and it has branches or agencies at 3 other places. A fourth bank, The Bank of Credit and Commerce International opened in Sept. 1978; its head office is in Manzini and it has a branch in Mbabane.

ENERGY AND NATURAL RESOURCES

Minerals. Swaziland produced a large tonnage of iron ore from the Ngwenya mine near Mbabane (but mining has now ceased) and asbestos from the Havelock Mine (38,046 tons in 1977). Coal is mined at Mpaka (150,000 tons in 1980). Small quantities of quarry stone, kaolin, barytes and pyrophyllite are also mined. Total mineral production was valued in 1968, R18,277,300.

A railway has been built from the Ngwenya hæmatite deposits to Goba, in Mozambique, chiefly for the transportation of iron ore. The extensive deposits of low-volatile bituminous coal in the Lowveld are being worked to provide coal for the railway, sugar-mills and export.

Agriculture. Some 60% of the country, which covers 4,290,944 acres, is reserved for occupation by the Swazi. The main crops are sugar (employing 13,000 people), citrus and rice, all of which are grown under irrigation, and cotton, maize (the staple product), sorghum, tobacco and pineapples. It is usually necessary to import maize from South Africa. Sugar, first produced in 1958, and woodpulp and other forest products are the two main agricultural exports (worth E80m. and E12·5m respectively in 1975).

Livestock (1979): Cattle, 650,000; goats, 265,000; sheep, 33,000; poultry, 600,000.

COMMERCE. By agreement with the Republic of South Africa, Swaziland is united in a customs union with the republic and receives a *pro rata* share of the customs dues collected.

Total exports in 1979 amounted to E202·5m. The chief items were: Sugar, wood-pulp and other forest products, asbestos, iron ore, citrus fruit, meat and meat products. Imports in 1979 were E298·8m.

Total trade between Swaziland and UK (British Department of Trade returns, in £1,000 sterling):

	1977	*1978*	*1979*	*1980*	*1981*	*1982*
Imports to UK	13,340	34,021	37,361	30,438	23,884	40,049
Exports and re-exports from UK	559	1,580	1,333	691	7,132	7,654

Tourism. There were 115,000 visitors in 1975.

COMMUNICATIONS

Roads. There is daily (except Sundays) communication by railway motor-buses between Manzini, Mbabane and Breyten; Manzini, Mankayana and Piet Retief. There are 241 km of tarred trunk roads. Total length of roads 2,750 km.

Railways. The 389 km railway of 1,067 mm gauge built in 1962-64 to haul iron ore from Kadake to Maputo in Mozambique for export was (1982) largely out of use as the iron ore is worked out. Part of the route is being used for a new direct line from Koomatipoort to Richards Bay in the Republic of South Africa, while a southern link to the Republic of South Africa was opened in 1978. In 1981 the railway carried 1·2m. tonnes.

Aviation. The country's chief airport is at Matsapa. It is served by Royal Swazi National Airways connecting with Johannesburg, Durban, Lusaka, Nairobi, Mauritius and Salisbury and South African Airways, connecting with Johannesburg and Durban. Lesotho National Airways flies from Matsapa to Maseru.

Post. There were (1980) 55 post offices, 2 telephone-telegraph agencies and 10 telephone agencies. There were, in Jan. 1981, 12,028 telephones in the country.

Cinemas. There were 5 cinemas in 1980 with a total seating capacity of 1,625.

Newspapers. There were in 1983 one daily, one weekly and one monthly newspaper.

JUSTICE, RELIGION, EDUCATION AND WELFARE

Justice. The judiciary is headed by the Chief Justice. A High Court having full jurisdiction and subordinate courts presided over by Magistrates and District Officers are in existence. During 1969 there were 6,624 convictions in subordinate courts and 36 convictions in the High Court.

There is a Court of Appeal with a President and 3 Judges. It deals with appeals from the High Court. There are 16 Swazi courts of first instance, 2 Swazi courts of appeal and a Higher Swazi Court of Appeal. The channel of appeal lies from Swazi Court of first instance to Swazi Court of Appeal, to Higher Swazi Court of Appeal, to the Judicial Commissioner and thence to the High Court of Swaziland.

Police. The police force in 1969 had a strength of 30 senior and 188 subordinate officers and 448 other ranks.

Religion. In 1975 there were about 95,000 Christians and about 50,000 adults holding traditional beliefs. A large number of churches and missionary societies are established throughout the country and, in addition to evangelism, are doing important work in the fields of education and medicine. In the larger centres there are churches of several denominations—Protestant, Roman Catholics and others.

Education. In 1982 there were 556 schools with 119,913 pupils in primary classes and 24,826 in secondary classes. The Swaziland Agricultural College and University Centre at Luyengo was opened in Oct. 1966. Technical and vocational training classes are run at the Government's Industrial Training Institute and its Staff Training Institute. The Government also operates a police college. There are 2 teacher training colleges. In 1975 Botswana and Swaziland formed a joint university with campuses in each territory.

Health. In 1980 there were 80 doctors and about 1,560 hospital beds.

DIPLOMATIC REPRESENTATIVES

Of Swaziland in Great Britain (58 Pont St., London SW1X 0AE)
High Commissioner: George Mbikwakhe Mamba (accredited 16 Feb. 1978).

Of Great Britain in Swaziland (Allister Miller St., Mbabane)
High Commissioner: Desmond M. Kerr, OBE.

Of Swaziland in the USA (4301 Connecticut Ave., NW, Washington, D.C., 20008)
Ambassador: Lawrence Mfana Mncina.

Of the USA in Swaziland (PO Box 199, Mbabane)
Ambassador: Robert H. Phinny.

Of Swaziland to the United Nations
Ambassador: N. M. Malinga.

Books of Reference

The Kingdom of Swaziland. Swaziland Government Information Services, 1968
Post Independence Development Plan. Mbabane, 1969
Barker, D., *Swaziland.* HMSO, 1965
Grotpeter, J. J., *Historical Dictionary of Swaziland.* Metuchen, 1975
Holleman, J. F. (ed.), *Experiment in Swaziland: Sample Survey 1960.* OUP, 1964
Jones, D., *Aid and Development in Southern Africa.* London, 1977
Kuper, H., *An African Aristocracy.* New ed. London, 1961.—*The Uniform of Colour.* Johannesburg, 1947.—*The Swazi: An Ethnographical Survey.* London, 1952
Matsebula, J. S. M., *A History of Swaziland.* London, 1972
Nyeko, B., *Swaziland.* [Bibliography] Oxford and Santa Barbara, 1982
Potholm, C. P., *Swaziland: The Dynamics of Political Modernization.* Univ. of California Press, 1972

SWEDEN

Konungariket Sverige

Capital: Stockholm
Population: 8·3m. (1981)
GNP per capita: US$13,520 (1980)

HISTORY. Organized as an independent unified state in the 10th century, Sweden became a constitutional monarchy in 1809. In 1809 she also ceded Finland to Russia. In 1815 German possessions were ceded to Prussia and Sweden was united with Norway, which union lasted until 1905.

AREA AND POPULATION. The first census took place in 1749, and it was repeated at first every third year, and, after 1775, every fifth year. Since 1860 a general census has been taken every 10 years and, in addition, in 1935, 1945, 1965 and 1975.

Latest census figures: 1940, 6,371,432 (annual increase since 1935: 0·38%); 1945, 6,673,749 (0·94% since 1940); 1950, 7,041,829 (1·1% since 1945); 1960, 7,495,316 (0·64% since 1950); 1965, 7,766,424 (1·04% since 1960); 1970, 8,076,903 (1·04% since 1965); 1975, 8,208,544 (1·02% since 1970).

Counties (Län)	*Land area: sq. km*	*Census population 1 Nov. 1975*	*Estimated population 31 Dec. 1981*	*Pop. per sq. km 1 Jan. 1981*
Stockholm (city)[1] / Stockholm (county)[1]	6,488	1,493,546	1,535,539	236
Uppsala	6,989	230,028	245,398	35
Södermanland	6,060	251,913	252,191	42
Östergötland	10,569	387,088	392,694	37
Jönköping	9,944	301,986	302,531	30
Kronoberg	8,453	169,438	174,169	21
Kalmar	11,168	240,724	241,098	22
Gotland	3,140	54,400	55,623	18
Blekinge	2,919	155,336	152,628	53
Kristianstad	6,054	272,014	280,652	46
Malmöhus	4,929	740,069	742,978	151
Halland	5,454	219,780	232,715	42
Göteborg and Bohus	5,112	715,012	710,122	139
Älvsborg	11,394	418,026	425,538	37
Skaraborg	7,938	263,218	270,127	34
Värmland	17,609	284,249	283,175	16
Örebro	8,515	273,923	273,712	32
Västmanland	6,302	259,921	258,566	41
Kopparberg	28,344	281,109	286,482	10
Gävleborg	18,191	294,412	293,657	16
Västernorrland	21,786	268,034	267,115	12
Jämtland	49,917	133,433	134,945	3
Västerbotten	55,432	236,397	244,789	4
Norrbotten	98,906	264,386	266,589	3
Total	411,615[2]	8,208,442	8,323,033	20

[1] From Jan. 1968 Stockholm city and Stockholm county have been united in Stockholm county. [2] Total area of Sweden, 449,964 sq. km.

On 31 Dec. 1981 there were 4,118,622 males and 4,204,411 females.

On 31 Dec. 1981 aliens in Sweden numbered 414,001. Of these, 171,994 were Finns, 38,771 Yugoslavs, 28,305 Danes, 13,820 Greeks, 25,352 Norwegians, 13,337 Germans, 4,524 Italians and 3,243 Austrians.

Vital statistics for calendar years:

	Total living births	Of which illegitimate [1]	Stillborn	Marriages	Divorces	Deaths exclusive of still-born
1979	96,255	36,123	445	37,273	20,314	91,074
1980	97,064	38,558	436	37,569	19,887	91,800
1981	94,065	38,742	380	37,793	20,198	92,034

[1] From 1977 children born to women who were single, divorced or widowed.

Immigration: 1979, 37,025; 1980, 39,426; 1981, 32,272. Emigration: 1979, 23,467; 1980, 29,389; 1981, 29,440.

In 1860 the urban population numbered 435,000 (11% of the total population) and on 31 Dec. 1965, 4,177,212 (54%); including other densely populated areas, the urbanized population in 1965 was 77·4%.

On 1 Nov. 1975, population in densely populated areas was 6,789,432 (82·7%).

Population of largest communities, 31 Dec. 1981:

Stockholm	647,421	Botkyrka	78,290	Falun	50,867
Göteborg	428,181	Halmstad	76,208	Solna	49,905
Malmö	231,609	Skellefteå	74,281	Trollhätten	49,212
Uppsala	147,732	Karlstad	74,037	Hässleholm	49,020
Norrköping	118,664	Kristianstad	68,940	Mölndal	48,073
Västerås	117,392	Huddinge	67,809	Täby	47,855
Örebvo	116,872	Luleå	66,847	Borlänge	46,689
Linköping	113,346	Växjö	65,066	Sollentuna	46,084
Jönköping	107,464	Nyköping	64,248	Uddevalla	46,066
Helsingborg	102,164	Örnsköldsvik	60,354	Skövde	46,013
Borås	101,701	Karlskrona	59,678	Varberg	44,623
Sundsvall	94,779	Haninge	59,283	Kungsbacka	44,322
Eskilstuna	90,104	Nacka	58,105	Sandviken	42,495
Gävle	87,556	Östersund	56,014	Motala	41,845
Umeå	82,096	Gotland	55,625	Norrtälje	41,140
Södertälje	80,302	Järfälla	54,171	Västervik	40,992
Lund	79,060	Kalmar	53,101		

Befolkningsförändringar (Population Changes). Annual. 3 vols. National Central Bureau of Statistics, Stockholm

Folkmängd 31 Dec. (Population). Annual. 3 vols. National Central Bureau of Statistics, Stockholm

Historisk statistik för Sverige. I: Befolkning (Population), 1720–1967. 2nd ed. National Central Bureau of Statistics, Stockholm, 1969

CLIMATE. North Sweden suffers from severe winters, with snow lying for 4–7 months. Summers are fine but cool, with long daylight hours. Further south, winters are less cold, summers are warm and rainfall generally well-distributed over the year, though with a slight summer maximum. Stockholm. Jan. 27°F (-2·7°C), July 62°F (16·5°C). Annual rainfall 21·5″ (536 mm).

REIGNING KING. Carl XVI Gustaf, born 30 April 1946, succeeded on the death of his grandfather Gustaf VI Adolf, 15 Sept. 1973, married 19 June 1976 to *Silvia* Renate Sommerlath, born 23 Dec. 1943 (Queen of Sweden). *Daughter* and *Heir Apparent:* Crown Princess Victoria Ingrid Alice Désirée, Duchess of Västergötland, born 14 July 1977; *son:* Prince Carl Philip Edmund Bertil, Duke of Värmland, born 13 May 1979; *daughter:* Princess Madeleine Thérèse Amelie Josephine, Duchess of Hälsingland and Gästrikland, born 10 June 1982.

Sisters of the King. Princess Margaretha, born 31 Oct. 1934, married 30 June 1964 to Mr John Ambler; Princess Birgitta (Princess of Sweden), born 19 Jan. 1937, married 25 May 1961 (civil marriage) and 30 May 1961 (religious ceremony) to Johann Georg, Prince of Hohenzollern; Princess Désirée, born 2 June 1938, married 5 June 1964 to Baron Niclas Silfverschiöld; Princess Christina, born 3 Aug. 1943, married 15 June 1974 to Tord Magnuson.

Uncles of the King. Sigvard, Count of Wisborg, born on 7 June 1907; Prince Bertil, Duke of Halland, born on 28 Feb. 1912, married 7 Dec. 1976 to Lilian May Davies, born 30 Aug. 1915 (Princess of Sweden, Duchess of Halland); Carl Johan, Count of Wisborg, born on 31 Oct. 1916.

Aunt of the King. Princess Ingrid (Princess of Sweden), born 28 March 1910, married 24 May 1935 to Frederik, Crown Prince of Denmark (King Frederik IX), died 14 Jan. 1972.

The following is a list of the kings and queens of Sweden, with the dates of their accession from the accession of the House of Vasa:

House of Vasa	
Gustaf I	1521
Eric XIV	1560
Johan III	1568
Sigismund	1592
Carl IX	1599
Gustaf II Adolf	1611
Christina	1632

House of Pfalz-Zweibrücken	
Carl X Gustaf	1654
Carl XI	1660

House of Pfalz-Zweibrücken (contd.)	
Carl XII	1697
Ulrica Eleonora	1719

House of Hesse	
Fredrik I	1720

House of Holstein-Gottorp	
Adolf Fredrik	1751
Gustaf III	1771
Gustaf IV Adolf	1792
Carl XIII	1809

House of Bernadotte	
Carl XIV Johan	1818
Oscar I	1844
Carl XV	1859
Oscar II	1872
Gustaf V	1907
Gustaf VI Adolf	1950
Carl XVI Gustaf	1973

The royal family of Sweden have a civil list of 9·7m. kronor; this does not include the maintenance of the royal palaces.

CONSTITUTION AND GOVERNMENT. Sweden's present Constitution came into force in 1975 and replaced the 1809 Constitution. Under the present Constitution Sweden is a representative and parliamentary democracy. Parliament (*Riksdag*) is declared to be the central organ of government. The executive power of the country is vested in the Government, which is responsible to Parliament. The King is Head of State, but he does not participate in the government of the country. Since 1971 Parliament has consisted of one chamber. It has 349 members, who are elected for a period of 3 years in direct, general elections.

Every man and woman who has reached the age of 18 years on election-day itself, and who is not under wardship has the right to vote and to stand for election.

The manner of election to the *Riksdag* is proportional. The country is divided into 28 constituencies. In these constituencies 310 members are elected. The remaining 39 seats constitute a nation-wide pool intended to give absolute proportionality to parties that receive at least 4% of the votes. A party receiving less than 4% of the votes in the country is, however, entitled to participate in the distribution of seats in a constituency, if it has obtained at least 12% of the votes cast there.

The *Riksdag*, elected 1982, has 166 Social Democrats, 86 Conservatives, 56 Centre Party, 21 Liberals and 20 Communists.

The Social Democratic Cabinet was composed as follows in Feb. 1983:

Prime Minister: Olof Palme.

Deputy Prime Minister and Minister with special responsibility for Research: Ingvar Carlsson. *Agriculture:* Svante Lundkvist. *Finance:* Kjell-Olof Feldt. *Health and Social Affairs, with special responsibility for the Social and Health Services:* Gertrud Sigurdsen. *Housing:* Hans Gustafsson. *Labour:* Anna-Greta Leijon. *Education and Cultural Affairs:* Lena Hjelm-Wallen. *Industry:* Thage Peterson. *Health and Social Affairs:* Sten Andersson. *Justice:* Ove Rainer. *Transport and Communications:* Curt Boström. *Foreign Affairs:* Lennart Bodström. *Defence:* Anders Thunborg. *Education, with special responsibility for cultural affairs, the mass media and comprehensive schools:* Bengt Göransson. *Labour, with special responsibility for immigrant and equality affairs:* Anita Gradin. *Industry, with special responsibility for energy questions:* Birgitta Dahl. *Industry, with special responsibility for state enterprises:* Roine Carlsson. *Public Administration:* Bo Holmberg.

All the members of the Cabinet are responsible for the acts of the Government.

Public administration in Sweden is characterized by a unique degree of functional decentralization. The Ministries are not really administrative agencies. They prepare bills for the *Riksdag*, issue general directives and make higher appointments, but, as a rule, do not take individual administrative decisions. The routine administrative work is attended to by the central boards (*centrala ämbetsverk*). Each board's sphere of activity depends partly on its organization which is decided by the appropriations granted by the Riksdag. The Government often asks the boards' opinion on proposed measures.

National flag: Blue with a yellow Scandinavian cross.

National anthem: Du gamla, du fria, du fjällhöga nord (words by R. Dybeck, 1844; folk-tune).

The official language is Swedish. The capital is Stockholm.

Local Government. For administrative purposes Sweden is divided into 24 counties (*län*), in each of which the central government is represented by a county administrative board (*länsstyrelse*). The governor (*landshövding*), appointed by the government, is chairman of the board, which in addition to the governor has 14 members elected by the county council.

Local government and the levying of local taxes are based on the fundamental law and are regulated by the local government act and special acts. According to the local government act Sweden is divided into municipalities in which all men and women who have reached the age of 18 on election-day itself, and not under wardship, are entitled to elect the municipal council. These councils are named *kommunfullmäktige*. The number of municipalities has, since 1951, been reduced from about 2,500 to 284. The municipalities deal with a great variety of different tasks such as social welfare, education and culture, public health, town planning, housing etc. Each county, except Gotland, which consists of only one municipality, has a county council (*landsting*) elected by men and women who enjoy local suffrage. The county councils chiefly administer the health services and medical care. The municipalities of Gothenburg and Malmö do not belong to county councils. Ecclesiastical affairs in all parishes with more than 1,000 inhabitants are dealt with by church councils (*kyrkofullmäktige*); smaller parishes may make the same arrangement. All elections are conducted on a proportional basis.

Elder, N. C. M., *Government in Sweden: The Executive at Work.* Oxford, 1970
Lewin, L., Jansson, B., and Sörbom, D., *The Swedish Electorate 1887–1968.* Stockholm, 1972
Ministry of Local Government, *Local Government in Sweden.* Stockholm, 1978
Vinde, P., *Swedish Government Administration.* 2nd rev. ed. Stockholm, 1978

DEFENCE. A Supreme Commander is, under the Government, in command of the three services. He is assisted by the Defence Staff under a chief of staff.

The military forces are recruited on the principle of national service, supplemented by voluntarily enlisted personnel who form the permanent cadres for training purposes, staff duties, etc.

Liability to service commences at the age of 18, and lasts till the end of the 47th year. The period of training for the Army and Navy is 7½-15 months and for the Airforce 8-15 months.

The territorial organization consists of 6 military commands each one under a general officer commanding.

Army. The C.-in-C. of the Royal Swedish Army has at his disposal the Army Staff under a chief of staff. The peace-time Army consists for training purposes of 16 infantry, 6 armour, 7 artillery, 6 AA, 3 engineer, 3 signal and 4 Army Service Corps units, most of which are called 'regiments' (*regementen*).

The Army is organized and equipped with regard to the varying geographical and climatic conditions of the country. The voluntary Home Guard (*Hemvärnet*) with a total strength of more than 100,000 men ready for action within 2 hours, raised during the War continues to be in force.

Sweden's ground forces, total 700,000 men, can be said to consist of an Army which for the most part is on indefinite leave, but which on short notice can be ready for action. One of the basic principles of the Swedish system of mobilization is the local recruitment of as many units as possible. The storage of equipment and supplies is decentralized on more than 1,500 places.

The active personnel of the Army comprises (1982) about 44,500, including 36,000 conscripts doing basic training.

Navy. The C.-in-C. of the Royal Swedish Navy is assisted by the Chief of Naval Staff, the Chief of Naval Materiel Department and the C.-in-C. of Coastal Fleet. The Navy is divided into two branches, the Royal Swedish Navy and the Royal Coast Artillery. There are 3 Naval Base Areas: those of the southern, eastern and western coasts.

There are 12 submarines, 2 destroyers, 16 fast missile boats, 18 fast torpedo craft, 2 patrol craft 3 minelayers, 9 coastal minelayers, 10 coastal minesweepers, 4 patrol vessels (*ex*-minesweepers), 18 inshore minesweepers, 27 coastal patrol craft, 2 mine transports, 16 minelaying boats, 3 torpedo recovery vessels, 15 tenders, 4 surveying vessels, 8 icebreakers, 2 oilers, 1 salvage vessel, 9 artillery landing craft, 81 utility landing craft, 54 minor landing craft, 2 sail training ships, 1 supply ship, 2 water carriers and 12 tugs.

Four submarines, 2 missile armed fast attack craft, 5 coastal minelayers and 6 coastal minesweepers are under construction.

The Naval Air Arm comprises 10 Boeing Vertol 107 helicopters, 10 JetRanger helicopters and 5 Alouette II training helicopters.

The coast artillery defence areas are those of the Stockholm archipelago, Blekinge, Gothenburg, Gotland and Norrland. There are 5 coastal artillery regiments.

The Swedish Fleet has been progressively reduced over the last few years, the cruiser, 6 destroyers, 8 frigates, and 16 submarines having been disposed of, and with the imminent disposal of the remaining destroyers, the largest remaining surface ships being minelayers, will constitute only a coastal defence navy.

The personnel of the navy and coast artillery in 1983 totalled 14,200 officers and men, comprising 3,700 regulars, 3,500 reservists and 7,000 national servicemen (additionally 8,000 conscripts train annually).

The Coast Guard operates 130 cutters, patrol boats and service craft and lists 5 aircraft. Personnel in 1983 numbered 570.

Air Force. The C-in-C. of the Royal Swedish Air Force has at his disposal the Air Staff under a chief of staff. Directly subordinate to the C.-in-C. of the Air Force are also the Inspectors of Air Base Control and Reporting Services, and of Flying Safety.

The combat force consists of 6 fighter-interceptor, 3 ground-attack and one mixed interceptor/attack wings (*flottiljer*), each with 2-3 squadrons of 12-15 aircraft, including 3 reconnaissance squadrons (*divisioner*). Total peace-time strength of the combat units is 21 squadrons with nearly 400 first-line aircraft.

Night and all-weather fighters are the Swedish-built Saab J35 Draken, equipping 9 squadrons, and JA37 Viggen, equipping 3 squadrons (5 more Draken squadrons are to convert to JA37s). The ground-attack wings have 5 squadrons of Saab AJ37 Viggens, and there is provision for 5 light ground-attack squadrons of twin-jet Saab-105s (Sk60s), most of which could be withdrawn in wartime from training units. One Sk60 squadron is designated as part of the primary ground attack force. The 3 reconnaissance squadrons have SF37 (overland) and SH37 (maritime) Viggen reconnaissance aircraft; and there are transport, helicopter and other support units. The Sk60A is the Air Force's standard advanced trainer, to which pupils progress after initial training on piston-engined Bulldogs. Other trainers in service include the Sk35C Draken and Sk37 Viggen.

Active strength consists of about 9,500 personnel, including 4,500 conscripts.

INTERNATIONAL RELATIONS

Membership. Sweden is a member of UN and EFTA.

ECONOMY

Budget. Revenue and expenditure of the ordinary budget for fiscal years ending 30 June (in 1,000 kr.):

	Revenue	Expenditure		Revenue	Expenditure
1976–77	101,974,916	106,705,827	1979–80	128,592,812	170,694,993
1977–78	109,286,130	125,936,282	1980–81[2]	155,287,000	215,238,000
1978–79	116,263,786	148,375,628	1981–82[1 2]	167,124,000	236,469,000

[1] Preliminary.
[2] By the introduction of a reformed budget system, the current budget and the capital budget have been consolidated.

The preliminary revenue and expenditure (current accounts) for the fiscal year 1 July 1981 to 30 June 1982 was as follows (in 1m. kr.):

Revenue		*Expenditure*	
Taxes:		Royal Household	25
Taxes on income, capital gains and profits	36,251	Justice	7,721
Statutory social security fees	31,250	Foreign Affairs	5,797
Taxes on property	2,741	Defence	19,135
Value-added tax	40,665	Health and Social Affairs	62,195
Other taxes on goods and services	29,564	Communications	12,211
Total revenue from taxes	140,471	Economic Affairs	444
Non-tax revenue	17,757	Budget	12,653
Capital revenue	47	Education	31,547
Loan repayment	2,644	Agriculture	6,410
Computed revenue	6,205	Commerce	1,743
Total revenue	167,124	Labour	12,760
		Housing and Physical Planning	17,544
		Industry	15,114
		Local Government	2,960
		Parliament and agencies	477
		Interest on National Debt, etc.	27,724
		Unforeseen expenditure	9
		Total expenditure	236,469

Revenue and expenditure of state business enterprises (in 1m. kr.):

	Revenue	*Expenditure*		*Revenue*	*Expenditure*
Forest Service, 1980	1,484·5	1,193·1[1]	Post Office, 1978–79	5,282·1	5,243·5
Power Administration, 1979–80	6,088·3	4,740·4	Telecommunications, 1979–80	7,579·7	5,322·3
Railways, 1979–80	5,703·0	5,951·9			

[1] Operating costs.

On 31 Dec. 1981 the national debt amounted to 295,590m. kr.

Riksgäldskontoret (National Debt Office), *årsbok*. Annual. Stockholm, from 1920
Riksskatteverket (National Tax Board), *årsbok*. Annual. Stockholm, from 1971
The Swedish Budget. Ministry of Economic Affairs and Ministry of the Budget, from 1962/63

Currency. The monetary unit is the Swedish *krona,* of 100 *öre*. In March 1983, £1 = 11·08 *krona*; US$1 = 7·54 *krona.*

Gold coins do not exist as a currency. Central banknotes for 5, 10, 50, 100, 1,000 and 10,000 kr. are legal means of payment.

Banking. The Riksbank, or Central Bank of Sweden, belongs entirely to the State and is managed by directors elected for 3 years by the Parliament, except the chairman, who is designated by the Government. The bank is under the guarantee of the Parliament, its capital and reserve capital are fixed by its constitution. Since 1904, only the Riksbank has the right to issue notes. On 31 Dec. 1981 its note circulation amounted to 37,055m. kr.; its gold and foreign-exchange reserves totalled 20,464m. kr.

There are 14 commercial banks. On 31 Dec. 1981 their total deposits amounted to 195,618m. kr.; advances to the public amounted to 171,743m. kr.

On 31 Dec. 1981 there were 162 savings banks; their total deposits amounted to 95,719m. kr.; advances to the public were 66,023m. kr. Co-operative banks had total deposits of 22,518m. kr.; advances to the public were 15,415m. kr.

Sveriges Riksbank, årsbok. Annual. Stockholm, from 1908
Skandinaviska Enskilda Banken, Kvartalskrift. Quarterly Review (in English). Stockholm, from 1920

Weights and Measures. The metric system is obligatory.

ENERGY AND NATURAL RESOURCES

Electricity. Sweden is rich in hydro-power resources. The total electric energy production in 1980 was 96,695m. kwh. About 61% of this energy was produced in hydro-electric plants. Additional electric energy consumption will in the future mainly by covered by nuclear power and conventional thermal power.

Minerals. Sweden is one of the leading exporters of iron ore. The largest deposits are found north of the polar circle in the area of Kiruna and Gällivare-Malmberget. The ore is exported *via* the Norwegian port of Narvik and the Swedish port of Luleå. There are also important resources of iron ore in southern Sweden (Bergslagen). The most important fields are Grängesberg and Stråssa and the ores are shipped *via* the port of Oxelösund. Some of the southern deposits have, in contrast to the fields in North Sweden, a low phosphorus content.

There are also some deposits of copper, lead and zinc ores especially in the Boliden area in the north of Sweden. These ores are often found together with pyrites. Non-ferrous ores, except zinc ores, are used in the Swedish metal industry and barely satisfy domestic needs.

The total production of iron ores amounted to 27·2m. tons in 1980 and exports to 17·4m. tons. The production of copper ore was 180,910 tons, of lead ore 101,770 tons, of zinc ore 306,166 tons.

There are also deposits of raw materials for aluminium not worked at present. In southern Sweden there are big resources of alum shale, containing oil and uranium.

Agriculture. According to the farm register which is revised annually the following data was provided for 1981. The number of farms in cultivation of more than 2 hectares of arable land, was 115,136; of these there were 70,261 of 2-20 hectares; 41,591 of 20-100 hectares; 3,284 of above 100 hectares. Of the total land area of Sweden (41,161,500 hectares), 2,937,878[1] hectares were arable land, 356,285[1] hectares cultivated pastures and (1976) 22,598,565 hectares forests.

	Area (1,000 hectares)[1]			*Production (1,000 tonnes)*		
Chief crops	*1979*	*1980*	*1981*	*1979*	*1980*	*1981*
Wheat	251·0	297·2	230·8	1,030	1,193	1,066
Rye	60·4	68·5	52·4	195	225	180
Barley	754·1	694·4	729·3	2,346	2,172	2,452
Oats	489·5	484·1	507·8	1,524	1,567	1,816
Mixed grain	59·1	59·5	64·1	148	157	...
Peas and vetches	12·7	12·0	14·2	26	24	30
Potatoes	41·2	40·0	40·2	1,284	1,084	1,213
Sugarbeet	51·9	52·1	52·5	2,206	2,257	2,484
Tame hay	701·6	707·5	706·8	4,183	4,132	4,326
Oil seed	160·6	177·5	171·1	302	326	323

Area of rotation meadows for pasture was (in 1,000 hectares[1]): 1979, 192; 1980, 191; 1981, 192.

Total production of milk (in 1,000 tonnes): 1979, 3,408; 1980, 3,481; 1981, 3,514. Butter production in the same years was (in 1,000 tonnes): 65, 66, 64; and cheese, 96, 101, 108.

Livestock (1981): Cattle, 1·9m.; sheep, 403,000; pigs, 2·6m.; poultry, 8·3m.

Number of farm tractors in 1981, 189,654; combines in 1981, 48,990.

The number of pelts produced in 1980–81 was as follows: Fox, 41,440; mink, 1·2m.; others, 10,000.

[1] Figures refer to holdings of more than 2 hectares of arable land.

Forestry. Nearly 23·5m. hectares or 57% of the total land area are covered with forests. The total amount of standing timber, excluding dead trees, is estimated at 2,475m. cu. metres with bark; 84% of this volume consists of coniferous wood (pine and spruce). Half of the forest area is privately owned, the other half is equally divided between public authorities (Crown, Church, communities, etc.) and joint-stock companies. The total removals in 1980 were 47m. cu. metres solid volume (without bark); of these, 22m. were coniferous saw timber, 22m. pulpwood, 2m. fuel wood and 1m. other wood. In 1979 the total removals were 46m. cu. metres.

In 1979 there were about 2,600 saw-mills with a total production of 11·3m. cu. metres sawn wood; 615 saw-mills had a production of more than 1,000 cu. metres per annum. The production of the 72 pulp-mills in Sweden in 1981 amounted to 8·5m. tonnes pulp (dry weight). In 1981, there was a net import of roundwood and chips corresponding to 5·5m. cu. metres solid volume. In 1981, exports of sawn softwood amounted to 5·6m. cu. metres, of plywood (including blockboards) to 24,000 cu. metres, of pulp 2·9m. tonnes, of fibre building board 174,000 tonnes and of particle board 348,000 tonnes.

Fisheries. In 1981 the total catch of the sea fisheries was 253,000 tons, live weight, value 507m. kr.

INDUSTRY AND TRADE

Manufacturing. The most important sector of Swedish manufacturing is the production of metals, metal products, machinery and transport equipment, covering almost half of the total value added by manufacturing. Production of high-quality steel is an old Swedish speciality. A large part of this production is exported. The production of ordinary steel is slightly decreasing and is still short of domestic demand. The total production of steel amounted to 4·2m. tons in 1980. There is also a large production of other metals (aluminium, lead, copper) and rolled semi-manufactured goods of these metals.

These basic metal industries are an important basis for the production of more developed metal products, machinery and equipment, which are to a large extent sold on the world market, *i.e.*, hand tools, mining drills, ball-bearings, turbines, pneumatic machinery, refrigerating equipment, machinery for pulp and paper industries, etc., sewing machines, machine tools, office machinery, high-voltage electric machinery, telephone equipment, cars and trucks, ships and aeroplanes.

Another important manufacturing sector is based on Sweden's forest resources. This sector includes saw-mills, plywood factories, joinery industries, pulp- and paper-mills, wallboard and particle board factories, accounting for about 15% of the total value of manufacturing. A fast increasing sector is the chemical industry, especially the petro-chemical branch. Minerals industries include production of building materials, decorative arts products of glass and china.

	No. of establishments		*Average no. of wage-earners*		*Sales value of production (gross) in 1m. kr.*	
Industry groups	*1979*	*1980*	*1979*	*1980*	*1979*	*1980*
Mining and quarrying	*141*	*121*	*10,854*	*10,447*	*3,221*	*3,834*
Metal-ore mining	41	34	9,587	9,151	2,747	3,324
Other mining	100	87	1,267	1,296	474	510
Manufacturing	*10,393*	*10,152*	*607,666*	*601,941*	*275,732*	*309,619*
Manufacture of food, beverages and tobacco	993	956	54,081	54,209	37,250	41,229
Textile, wearing apparel and leather industries	864	826	33,212	31,595	7,788	7,896
Manufacture of wood products including furniture	1,792	1,734	58,639	56,820	22,152	24,961
Manufacture of paper and paper products, printing and publishing	1,102	1,110	72,012	72,310	36,593	41,742
Manufacture of chemicals and chemical, petroleum, coal, rubber and plastic products	714	709	42,784	44,444	36,429	47,372
Manufacture of non-metallic mineral products, except products of petroleum and coal	546	483	21,359	20,730	7,313	7,999
Basic metal industries	176	179	47,334	47,042	23,936	26,292

Industry groups	No. of establishments 1979	1980	Average no. of wage-earners 1979	1980	Sales value of production (gross) in 1m. kr. 1979	1980
Manufacture of fabricated metal products, machinery and equipment	4,085	4,037	274,009	270,799	103,123	110,869
Other manufacturing industries	121	118	4,236	3,992	1,148	1,259
Electricity, gas and water	*881*	*872*	*11,493*	*11,507*	*32,892*	*38,706*
Electricity, gas and steam	762	741	10,571	10,839	31,726	37,606
Water works and supply	140	131	922	668	1,166	1,100

Arbetsmarknadsstatistik (Labour Market Statistics). Monthly. National Labour Market Board, Stockholm, from 1963
Arbetsmarknadsstatistisk Årsbok (Year Book of Labour Statistics). National Central Bureau of Statistics, Stockholm, from 1973
Carlson, B., *Trade Unions in Sweden.* Stockholm, 1969
Historisk statistik för Sverige, II (Climate, land surveying, agriculture, forestry, fisheries). National Central Bureau of Statistics, Stockholm, 1959
Johansson, Ö., *The Gross Domestic Product of Sweden and its Composition 1861–1955.* Stockholm, 1967
Jörberg, L., *A History of Prices in Sweden 1732–1914.* 2 vols. Stockholm, 1972
Jordbruksekonomiska meddelanden (Journal of Agricultural Economics, published monthly by the National Agricultural Market Board). Stockholm, from 1939
Jordbruksstatistisk årsbok (Yearbook of Agricultural Statistics). National Central Bureau of Statistics, Stockholm, from 1965
The Swedish Economy. Ministry of Economic Affairs and National Institute of Economic Research. Stockholm, from 1960

Trade Unions. The Swedish Confederation of Trade Unions (LO) had a total membership of 2,140,800 in 1981, including the Municipal Workers' Union with 540,200 members and the Metal Workers' Union with 448,100.

Commerce. The imports and exports of Sweden, unwrought gold and coin not included, have been as follows (in 1m. kr.):

	1975	*1976*	*1977*	*1978*	*1979*	*1980*	*1981*
Imports	74,000	84,000	90,246	92,717	122,952	141,641	146,069
Exports	72,012	80,195	85,678	98,205	118,147	131,002	144,523

On 1 Jan. 1974 a new Customs procedure for the imports was introduced. This means that during 1974, 1975 and 1976, a great part of the imports were recorded in the statistics with an extra delay of up to 2 weeks as compared to the registration before 1974.

Corrected import values for 1974, 1975 and 1976, adjusted for the effects of the new time-lags, have been calculated in order to facilitate comparisons with earlier years and to show the development of the trade balance.

The adjustments have not been made by commodity and country. Beginning Jan. 1977 the statistics cover the goods which were actually imported to and exported from Sweden during the period to which the statistics refer.

Imports and exports by products (in 1m. kr.):

	Imports *1980*	*1981*	*Exports* *1980*	*1981*
Food and live animals chiefly for food	8,572	8,758	2,597	3,124
Cereals and cereal preparations	485	620	874	1,000
Vegetables and fruit	2,593	2,839	173	244
Coffee, tea, cocoa, spices and manufactures thereof	2,230	2,018	217	275
Feeding stuff for animals (not including unmilled cereals)	884	984	44	46
Beverages and tobacco	953	1,037	99	117
Crude materials, inedible, except fuels	6,062	6,642	15,553	16,335
Hides, skins and furskins, raw	247	244	401	403
Crude rubber (including synthetic and reclaimed)	365	314	56	66
Cork and wood	1,396	2,040	5,680	5,469
Pulp and waste paper	218	283	6,074	6,798
Textile fibres (other than wool tops) and their wastes (not manufactured into yarn or fabric)	217	202	228	235

	Imports		Exports	
	1980	*1981*	*1980*	*1981*
Crude fertilizers and crude minerals (excluding coal, petroleum and precious stones)	834	885	249	270
Metalliferous ores and metal scrap	1,805	1,675	2,591	2,798
Mineral fuels, lubricants and related materials	34,148	36,302	5,848	6,579
Coal, coke and briquettes	931	1,040	89	162
Petroleum, petroleum products and related materials	32,679	34,888	5,301	5,655
Chemicals and related products, n.e.s.	11,438	11,913	6,990	7,894
Artificial resins and plastic materials, and cellulose esters and ethers	3,465	3,447	2,335	2,402
Manufactured goods classified chiefly by material	24,240	22,850	36,363	38,524
Paper, paperboard, and articles of paper pulp, of paper or of paperboard	1,342	1,448	12,746	14,548
Textile yarn, fabrics, made-up articles, n.e.s., and related products	4,140	3,916	1,787	1,913
Non-metallic mineral manufactures, n.e.s.	2,016	2,012	1,443	1,580
Iron and steel	6,012	5,253	9,641	9,097
Non-ferrous metals	3,860	3,422	3,057	3,017
Manufactures of metal, n.e.s.	4,070	4,057	5,066	5,564
Machinery and transport equipment	38,033	39,566	52,062	59,734
Power generating machinery and equipment	2,930	2,865	3,274	3,915
Machinery specialized for particular industries	4,319	4,106	6,669	7,362
Metal working machinery	1,412	1,516	1,550	1,701
General industrial machinery and equipment, n.e.s. and machine parts, n.e.s.	6,925	7,077	9,929	10,949
Office machines and automatic data processing equipment	3,607	3,912	3,069	2,922
Telecommunications and sound recording and reproducing apparatus and equipment	2,415	2,927	4,738	5,207
Electrical machinery apparatus and appliances, n.e.s., and electrical parts thereof (including non-electrical counterparts, n.e.s., of electrical household type equipment)	6,800	6,773	4,993	5,463
Road vehicles (including air cushion vehicles)	8,399	8,996	15,397	18,177
Other transport equipment	1,225	1,393	2,443	4,040
Miscellaneous manufactured articles	17,123	17,626	9,052	9,884

Principal import and export countries (in 1m. kr.):

	Imports from		Exports to	
	1980	*1981*	*1980*	*1981*
Belgium-Luxembourg	4,646	4,665	4,270	4,538
Denmark	8,650	8,990	11,061	11,240
Federal Republic of Germany	23,779	23,603	16,103	16,374
Finland	9,648	9,674	8,229	9,369
France	6,140	5,637	7,652	7,722
Italy	3,969	4,378	4,984	4,750
Netherlands	5,253	5,560	6,262	6,549
Norway	7,375	9,004	12,828	13,885
Switzerland	2,649	2,809	2,982	2,919
USSR	3,177	2,655	1,781	2,107
UK	16,730	17,440	13,035	14,387
USA	10,334	12,013	7,022	8,824

Total trade between Sweden and UK (British Department of Trade returns, in £1,000 sterling):

	1978	*1979*	*1980*	*1981*	*1982*
Imports to UK	1,343,864	1,605,942	1,475,506	1,533,580	1,673,165
Exports and re-exports from UK	1,170,893	1,542,197	1,623,511	1,601,166	1,935,264

Historisk Statistik för Sverige, 3: Utrikeshandel (Foreign Trade), *1732–1970*. National Central Bureau of Statistics, Stockholm, 1972
Utrikeshandel (Foreign Trade). National Central Bureau of Statistics, Stockholm. Annually, 2 vols, from 1911
Utrikeshandel, kvartalsstatistik (Foreign Trade, Quarterly Bulletin). National Central Bureau of Statistics, Stockholm, from 1961. From 1976 published in *Statistical Reports*, Series H
Utrikeshandel, månadsstatistik (Foreign Trade, Monthly Bulletin). National Central Bureau of Statistics, Stockholm, from 1913. From 1976 published in *Statistical Reports*, Series H

COMMUNICATIONS

Roads. On 1 Jan. 1982 there were 184,177 km of public roads comprising State-administered roads, 97,871 km, municipal, 17,598 km, private roads with subsidies, 68,708 km, of which 87,136 km were surfaced. Motor vehicles on 31 Dec. 1981 included 2,893,242 passenger cars, 199,325 buses and lorries and 15,683 heavy motor cycles (all in use).

Railways. At the end of 1981 the total length of railways was 11,951 km, of which 11,335 km belonged to the State; 7,601 km were electrified. In 1981 the number of passengers on the railways was 92m.; weight of goods, including Lapland ore, 49m. tonnes.

Aviation. Commercial air traffic is maintained in (1) Sweden and other parts of the world by Scandinavian Airlines System (SAS), of which AB Aerotransport (ABA = Swedish Air Lines) is the Swedish partner (DDL = Danish Air Lines and DNL = Norwegian Air Lines being the other two); (2) only within Sweden by Linjeflyg AB. Scandinavian Airlines System have a joint paid-up capital of about Sw. kronor 733m. Capitalization of ABA, Sw. kronor 346m., of which 50% is owned by the Government and 50% by private enterprises. Capitalization of Linjeflyg, Sw. kronor 130m., of which 50% is owned by SAS and 50% by ABA.

In scheduled air traffic during 1981 the total number of km flown was 66·5m.; passenger-km, 5,450·6m.; goods, 180·2m. ton-km; mail, 21·6m. ton-km. These figures represent the Swedish share of the SAS traffic (Swedish domestic and three-sevenths of international traffic) and the Linjeflyg traffic.

Shipping. The Swedish mercantile marine consisted on 30 June 1982 of 484 vessels of 3·48m. gross tons (only vessels of at least 100 gross tons, and excluding fishing vessels and tugs). Stockholm and Göteborg, with together 228 vessels of 2·88m. gross tons in June 1982 are the two largest ports.

Vessels entered from and cleared for foreign countries, exclusive of passenger liners and ferries, with cargoes and in ballast, in 1981, are as follows (only vessels of at least 40 net tons included): With cargoes, 25,718 of 47·2m. net tons; in ballast, 13,177 of 28·2m. net tons.

Post and Broadcasting. The length of telegraph circuits in Dec. 1979 was 1,591,000 km. The circuits of the telephone had a length of 28·2m. km at 31 Dec. 1980. On 1 Jan. 1981 there were 6·41m. instruments employed in the telephone service.

Number of combined radio and television reception fees paid at the end of 1980 was 3,165,000, of which 2·55m. included extra fees for colour television. As from 1 April 1978, special sound broadcasting licences were discontinued.

Sveriges Radio AB is a non-commercial semi-governmental corporation, transmitting 3 programmes on long-, medium-, and short-waves and on FM. There are also regional programmes. It also broadcasts 2 TV programmes. Colour programmes are broadcast by PAL system.

The overseas radio-telegraph and radio-telephone services are conducted by the Swedish Telecommunications Administration.

The number of post offices at the end of 1979 was 1,873. For receipts of the post and telecommunication services *see* the section on Economy.

Cinemas (1981). There were 1,239 cinemas.

Newspapers (1980). There were 161 daily newspapers with a total circulation of 4·9m.

JUSTICE, RELIGION, EDUCATION AND WELFARE

Justice. The administration of justice is entirely independent of the Government. The *Justitiekansler*, or Chancellor of Justice (a royal appointment) and the *Justitieombudsmän* (Judicial Commissioners appointed by the Diet), exercise a control over the administration. In 1968 a reform was carried through which meant that the offices of the former *Justitieombudsman* (Ombudsman for civil affairs) and the *Militieombudsman* (Ombudsman for military affairs) were turned into one sole institution with 3 Ombudsmen, each styled *Justitieombudsman*. They exert a general supervision over all courts of law, the civil service, military laws and the military services. In 1981–82 they received altogether 3,516 cases; of these, 95 were instituted on their own initiative and 3,399 on complaints.

Bruzelius, A., and Ginsburg, R. B., *The Swedish Code of Judicial Procedure.* South Hackensack, 1968
Justitieombudsmännens ämbetsberättelse avgiven till Riksdagen. Annual. Stockholm
The Penal Code of Sweden: As Amended 1 Jan. 1972. South Hackensack, 1972
Rowat, D. C., *The Ombudsman: Citizen's Defender.* London, 1965
Rättsstatistisk årsbok (Year Book of Legal Statistics). National Central Bureau of Statistics, Stockholm, from 1975

The *Riksåklagaren* (a royal appointment) is the chief public prosecutor.

The kingdom has a Supreme Court of Judicature and is divided into 6 Courts of Appeal districts and 100 district-court divisions (*tingsrätter*). Regarding rent and tribunal cases the kingdom has an Apartment Appeal Court and 12 rent and tenancy tribunals.

Of the district courts 27 also serve as real estate courts and 6 as water rights courts.

These district courts (or courts of first instance) deal with both civil and criminal cases. More serious criminal cases are generally tried by a judge and a jury (*nämnd*) of 4-5 members (lay judges); petty cases are tried by the judge alone. Civil cases are tried as a rule by 3 to 4 judges or in minor cases by 1 judge. Disputes of greater consequence relating to the Marriage Code and the Code relating to Parenthood and Guardianship are tried by a judge and a *nämnd*. When cases concerning real estate are being tried the court consists of 2 qualified lawyers, 1 specialist on technical matters and 2 lay assessors.

In trials by *nämnd* the judge decides the case except when the majority of the *nämnd* (at least 4 members of 5 or 3 members of 4) differs from him, in which case the decision of the *namnd* prevails. The cases in Courts of Appeal are generally tried by 4 or 5 judges, but the same cases, which are tried with a judge and a *nämnd* in the first instance, are tried by 3 or 4 judges and a *nämnd* of 2-3 members (lay judges). The court consists in cases concerning real estate of a specialist on technical matters instead of one of the judges and in water-right cases of 3 or 4 judges and 1 or 2 specialists on technical water matters.

Those with low incomes can receive free legal aid out of public funds. In criminal cases a suspected person has the right to a defence counsel, paid out of public funds.

The Attorney-General (*Justitiekanslern*) and the Parliamentary Commissioner (*Justitieombudsmannen*) for the Judiciary and Civil Administration supervises the application in the public sector of acts of parliament and regulations. The Attorney-General is the Government's legal adviser and also the Public Prosecutor.

The holders of the office of Parliamentary Commissioner, 4 in number, are appointed by Parliament.

There were 74 penal and correctional institutions for delinquents, with 3,591 male and 157 female inmates on 1 Jan. 1982 (including delinquents in remand prison). Besides, there were 18 institutions with 497 places for children and juveniles in need of care owing to viciousness, maladjustment or delinquency on 31 Dec. 1981; on 31 Dec. 1981, 413 youths were committed to these institutions.

Religion. The overwhelming majority of the population belong to the Evangelical Lutheran Church, which is the established national church. There were 13 bishoprics (Uppsala being the metropolitan see) and 2,575 parishes at the beginning of 1979. The clergy are chiefly supported from the parishes and the proceeds of the church lands. The nonconformists mostly still adhere to the national church. The largest denominations, on 1 Jan. 1981, were: Pentecost Movement, 99,047; The

Mission Covenant Church of Sweden, 80,351; Salvation Army, 34,589; Swedish Evangelical Mission, 24,417; Swedish Baptist Church, 20,913; Orebro Missionary Society, 19,621; Swedish Alliance Missionary Society, 13,117; Holiness Mission, 5,956; Methodists (1979), 5,924.

There were also 105,590 Roman Catholics (under a Bishop resident at Stockholm), about 35,000 Orthodox Catholics (1978) and about 15,000 Jews (1978).

Parliament and Convocation (*Kyrkomötet*) decided in 1958 to admit women to ordination as priests.

Murray, R., *L'église Suédoise. Son Histoire et Son Organisation.* Stockholm, 1970

Education. By the Swedish Higher Educational Act of 1977 a unified educational system was created by integrating institutions which had previously been administered separately. This new *högskola* includes not only traditional university studies but also those of various professional colleges as well as a number of study programmes offered by the secondary school system. One of the goals of the 1977 university reform was to introduce an increased element of professional training into Swedish higher education. A Certificate of Education is awarded on completion of a general study programme. This certificate states the number of courses taken as well as the points and grades obtained on each course in the study programme.

In Dec. 1980 there were, in these new integrated institutions for higher education, *högskola*, 92,000 registered for undergraduate studies at general study programmes, and 70,900 registered at (*a*) separate courses, (*b*) specialized continuation courses, (*c*) local or individual study programmes. The number of registered students at the general study programmes distributed by sector is as follows: Education for technical professions, 22,600; education for social work and economic and administrative professions, 23,900; education for medical and paramedical professions, 20,000; education for the teaching professions, 21,400; and education for information, communication and cultural professions, 4,100. The number of students enrolled for post-graduate studies was 12,300.

In autumn term in the school year 1980–81 there were 666,700 pupils in primary education (grades 1–6 in compulsory comprehensive schools). Secondary education at the lower stage (grades 7–9 in compulsory comprehensive schools) comprised 365,300 pupils. In secondary education at the higher stage (the integrated upper secondary school), there were 241,500 pupils (excluding about 31,000 pupils in the 4-year technical group regarded as third-level education). The folk high schools, 'people's colleges', had 14,000 pupils in courses of more than 15 weeks.

In municipal adult education there were in the school year 1979–80, 152,000 pupils (corresponding to a gross number of 322,000 participants) and in state adult education there were about 23,000 pupils (of which 19,000 taking correspondence courses).

There are also special schools for pupils with visual and hearing handicaps and those who are mentally retarded (about 13,700 pupils in 1980–81).

Goals for Educational Policy in Sweden. OECD, Paris, 1980
Higher Education for Visiting Students.—Series Studying in Sweden.—National Board of Universities and Colleges. Stockholm, 1978
Götberg, B., and Svärd, S., *The Swedish 'Folk High School': Its Background and its Present Situation.*
Marklund, S., *The Democratization of Education in Sweden.* Univ. of Stockholm, 1980
Marklund, S. and Bergendal, G., *Trends in Swedish Educational Policy.* Stockholm, 1979
Stenholm, B., *Education in Sweden.* Stockholm, 1970
Sundgvist, A., *New Rules for Swedish Study Circles.* Stockholm, 1982

Social Welfare. The social security schemes are greatly expanding. Supported by a referendum, the Diet in 1958 and 1959 decided that the national pensions should be increased successively until 1968 and supplementary pensions paid from 1963. These pensions are of invariable value. In 1969 the Diet decided that as from 1 July 1969 an increment to the basic pension was to be paid to persons without supplementary pensions, and this amount is to be successively increased in a 10-year period. The basic and supplementary pensions consist of old-age and family pensions, as well as pensions paid to the disabled. The financing of the supplementary system is based on the current-cost method.

The most important social welfare schemes are described in the conspectus below.

Type of scheme	*Introduced*	*Scope*	*Principal benefits*
Sickness insurance (compulsory–current law, 1962)	1955	All residents	Hospital fees, most private doctors charge the insured person normally 35 kr., district physicians and doctors in hospitals charge the insured person only 30 kr. for full medical treatment, some reimbursement of cost of transportation as well as costs of physiotherapy, convalescent care, etc., medicines at reduced prices or free of charge. During sickness daily allowance 90% of the yearly income in between 6,000 and 133,500 kr. There is generally no maximum benefit period. Dental care is available to all residents from 17 years of age, the maximum payable by the patient being 60% up to 2,500 kr. and 25% thereafter.
Employment injury insurance (compulsory–current law, 1976)	1901	All employed persons	Medical treatment, medicine and medical appliances, hospital care, sickness benefit 100% of the yearly income in between 6,000 and 133,500 kr. (first 90 days covered by sickness insurance), disability annuities, funeral benefit and survivor's pensions.
Unemployment insurance (current law, 1973)	1935	Members of recognized unemployment insurance societies (about 70% of all employees)	90-230 kr. per day subject to tax.
Basic pensions (current law, 1962)			
Old-age	1914	All citizens	Payable from the age of 65 or, at a reduced rate, from the age of 60. 44,322 kr. per annum for married couples, 25,276 kr. for others (including the special increment of 16,732 kr. and 8,366 kr. respectively for those without supplementary pension); about half of them receive municipal housing supplement.
Disability	1914	All citizens	Payable before the age of 65. Full pension 33,286 kr. per annum (including the special increment of 16,732 kr.).
Survivors	1948	All citizens	Widow's pension is payable before the age of 65. The pension is 25,276 kr. (including the special increment of 8,366 kr.) but less for those who have become widows before the age of 50 and have no child below 16. Many of them receive municipal housing supplements.

Type of scheme	*Introduced*	*Scope*	*Principal benefits*
Survivors (cont.)			Child pension is payable before the age of 18. The pension amounts to 7,298 kr. (fatherless or motherless) and 11,036 kr. (orphans).
Supplementary pensions (current law, 1962)			
Old-age	1960	All gainfully occupied persons	Payable from the same age as the basic pension (*see above*). The pension is in principle 60% of the insured person's average annual earnings during the best 15 years except an amount corresponding to the basic pension and subject to a ceiling.
Disability	1960	All gainfully occupied persons	Payable before the age of 65. Full pension corresponds in principle to supplementary old-age pension.
Survivors	1960	All gainfully occupied persons	Payable to widow and children, before the age of 19, of a deceased person as a certain percentage of the deceased's supplementary pension.
Partial pensions (current law, 1979)	1976	All employees between 60–65 years of age	The pension is payable between 60-65 years of age. The insured must have reduced his working time by 5 hours on an average a week and the part-time work must thereafter comprise at least 17 hours per week. Furthermore the insured must have worked during at least 5 of the last 12 months and achieved a right to supplementary pension for 10 years after the age of 45. The partial pension is paid out by 50% of the loss of income in connection with the change-over to part-time work.
Parents benefit	1974	All resident parents in connection with confinement	Parents cash benefit of 37 kr. a day during 180 days. Employed parents entitled to daily parents cash benefit of 90% of the daily income (in between 6,000–133,500 kr. yearly) for 180 days. Maximum daily parents cash benefit 329 kr.
Special parents benefit	1978	All resident parents	Special parents cash benefit with the same amount as for parents cash benefit for care of each child during 180 days for the parents together until the child reaches 8 years of age or until the end of the child's first school year if that is later.

Type of scheme	Introduced	Scope	Principal benefits
Children's allowances	1948	All children below 16	3,000 kr. per annum. From 1 Jan. 1982, an additional allowance will be paid out for the third child with one-quarter of a full allowance and one-half an allowance for each additional child.
		Children at school 16–18	250 kr. per month during school-courses. Children at school (16–19 years) living more than 6 km from school may receive supplementary allowance of 150–405 kr. per month; other allowance income-tested up to 180 kr. per month and means-tested up to 230 kr. per month.

Total social expenditure, including also hygiene, care of the sick and social assistance, amounted to 160,441m. kr. in 1980, representing 30·9% of the GDP.

The Cost and Financing of the Social Services in Sweden, 1974. Stockholm, 1976
Modern Trends in Swedish Pension Systems. Stockholm, 1968
Socialnytt (Official Journal of the National Board of Health and Welfare). Stockholm, from 1968
Social Benefits in Sweden. Stockholm, 1974
Faramond, G. de, *La Suède et la qualité de la Vie.* Paris, 1975
Fors, Å., *Social Policy and How it Works,* Stockholm, 1972
Heclo, H., *Modern Social Politics in Britain and Sweden: From Relief to Income Maintenance.* New Haven, 1974
Michanek, E., *For and Against the Welfare State: Swedish Experiences.* Stockholm, 1964
Mollstedt, B., *Public Health in Sweden. Health Services, Environmental Hygiene and Health Education.* Stockholm, 1972
Rosenthal, A.-H., *The Social Programs of Sweden, A Search for Security in a Free Society.* Minneapolis, 1967

DIPLOMATIC REPRESENTATIVES

Of Sweden in Great Britain (23 North Row, London, W1R 2DN)
Ambassador: Leif Leifland (accredited on 1[redacted]982).

Of Great Britain in Sweden (Skarpögatan 6-8, 115 27 Stockholm)
Ambassador: Donald Frederick Murray, CMG.

Of Sweden in the USA (600 New Hampshire Avenue., NW, Suite 1200, Washington, D.C., 20037)
Ambassador: Count Wilhelm H. F. Wachtmeister.

Of the USA in Sweden (Strandvägen 101, 115 27 Stockholm)
Ambassador: Franklin S. Forsberg.

Of Sweden to the United Nations
Ambassador: Anders I. Thunborg.

Books of Reference

Statistical Information: The National Central Bureau of Statistics (Statistiska, Centralbyrån, S-11581 Stockholm) was founded in 1858, in succession to the Kungl. Tabellkommissionen, which had been set up in 1756. *Director-General:* Lennart Nilsson. Its Publications include:

Levnadsförhållanden, årsbok (Living Conditions). Annual. From 1975.—*Rapport.* from 1976
Samhällsguiden. Ministry of Local Government, Stockholm, 1981
Statistisk årsbok för Sverige (Statistical Abstract of Sweden). From 1914
Siffror om Sverige (Sweden). From 1971. Also in English as *Sweden*
Historisk statistik för Sverige (Historical Statistics of Sweden). 1955 ff. (4 vols. to date)
Sveriges officiella statistik (Official Statistics of Sweden). From 1911. (With summary in French; from 1952 in English)

Allmän månadsstatistik (Monthly Digest of Swedish Statistics). From 1963
Statistiska meddelanden (Statistical Reports). From 1963
Ahlmann, H. W. (ed.), *Sverige, Land och Folk.* 3 vols. Stockholm, 1967
Andersson, L., *A History of Sweden.* Stockholm, 1962
Atlas över Sverige. Stockholm, 1953–71. [Publ. in separate parts dealing with population, economics, etc.]
Britten Austin, P., *The Swedes: How They Live and Work.* Newton Abbot, 1970
Courtier, E., *En Suède.* Montreal, 1970
Documentation on Sweden. Stockholm, 1976
Documents on Swedish Foreign Policy, 1973. Stockholm, 1976
Faramond, G. de, *Un Politique du Bien-Être.* Paris, 1972
Fullerton, B., and Williams, A. F., *Scandinavia.* London, 1972
Furer, H. B. (ed.), *The Scandinavians in America 986–1970. A Chronology and Fact Book.* Dobbs Ferry, 1972
Gullberg, I. E., *Swedish–English Dictionary of Technical Terms.—Svensk-Engelsk Fackordbok.* Stockholm, 2nd ed. 1977
Hancock, M. D., *Sweden. The Politics of Post-Industrial Change.* Hinsdale, Ill., 1972
Heilborn, A., *Travel, Study and Research in Sweden.* 6th ed. Stockholm, 1965
Mead, W. R., and Hall, W., *Scandinavia.* London, 1972
Nobel, The Man and His Prizes. Published by the Nobel Foundation. Stockholm, 1950
Nordic Council, *Yearbook of Nordic Statistics.* From 1962 (in English and one Nordic Language)
Nording, R., *Suède Socialiste et Libre Entreprise.* Paris, 1970
Parent, J., *Le Modèle Suédois.* Paris, 1970
Paul, W. W., *The Story of Scandinavia.* Cincinnati, 1971
Scobbie, I., *Sweden.* London, 1972
Stomberg, A. A., *A History of Sweden.* New York, 1970
Scott, F. D., *Sweden: The Nation's History.* Univ. of Minnesota Press, 1977
Tomason, R. F., *Sweden: Prototype of Modern Society.* New York, 1970
Toyne, S. M., *The Scandinavians in History.* Freeport, 1970
Turner, B., *Sweden.* London, 1976
Sveriges statskalender. Published by Vetenskapsakademien. Annual, from 1813

National Library: Kungliga Biblioteket, Stockholm. *Director:* Lars Tynell.

SWITZERLAND

Schweiz—Suisse—Svizzera

Capital: Bern
Population: 6·4m. (1980)
GNP per capita: US$16,440 (1980)

HISTORY. On 1 Aug. 1291 the men of Uri, Schwyz and Unterwalden entered into a defensive league. In 1353 the league included 8 members and in 1513, 13. Various territories were acquired either by single cantons or by several in common, and in 1648 the league became formally independent of the Holy Roman Empire, but no addition was made to the number of cantons till 1798. In that year, under the influence of France, the unified Helvetic Republic was formed. This failed to satisfy the Swiss, and in 1803 Napoleon Bonaparte, in the Act of Mediation, gave a new Constitution, and out of the lands formerly allied or subject increased the number of cantons to 19. In 1815 the perpetual neutrality of Switzerland and the inviolability of her territory were guaranteed by Austria, France, Great Britain, Portugal, Prussia, Russia, Spain and Sweden, and the Federal Pact, which included 3 new cantons, was accepted by the Congress of Vienna. In 1848 a new Constitution was passed. The 22 cantons set up a Federal Government (consisting of a Federal Parliament and a Federal Council) and a Federal Tribunal. This Constitution, in turn, was on 29 May 1874 superseded by the present Constitution. In a national referendum held in Sept. 1978, 69·9% voted in favour of the establishment of a new canton, Jura, which was established on 1 Jan. 1979.

AREA AND POPULATION. Area and population, according to the census held on 1 Dec. 1970 and the census held on 1 Dec. 1980.

Canton	*Area (sq. km)*	*Census population* 1 Dec. 1970	*Census population* 1 Dec. 1980	*Pop. per sq. km, 1980*
Zürich (Zurich) (1351)	1,729	1,107,788	1,122,839	650
Bern (Berne) (1553)	6,887	983,296	912,022	151
Luzern (Lucerne) (1332)	1,494	289,641	296,159	198
Uri (1291)	1,075	34,091	33,883	31
Schwyz (1291)	908	92,072	97,354	107
Obwalden (Obwald) (1291)	492	24,509	25,865	53
Nidwalden (Nidwald) (1291)	274	25,634	28,617	104
Glarus (Glaris) (1352)	684	38,155	36,718	54
Zug (Zoug) (1352)	239	67,996	75,930	318
Fribourg (Freiburg) (1481)	1,670	180,309	185,246	111
Solothurn (Soleure) (1481)	791	224,133	218,102	276
Basel-Stadt (Bâle-V.) (1501)	37	234,945	203,915	5,485
Basel-Land (Bâle-C.) (1501)	428	204,889	219,822	513
Schaffhausen (Schaffhouse) (1501)	298	72,854	69,413	233
Appenzell A.-Rh. (Rh.-Ext.) (1513)	243	49,023	47,611	196
Appenzell I.-Rh. (Rh.-Int.) (1513)	172	13,124	12,844	75
St Gallen (St Gall) (1803)	2,016	384,475	391,995	195
Graubünden (Grisons) (1803)	7,109	162,086	164,641	23
Aargau (Argovie) (1803)	1,404	433,284	453,442	323
Thurgau (Thurgovie) (1803)	1,006	182,835	183,795	181
Ticino (Tessin) (1803)	2,811	245,458	265,899	95
Vaud (Waadt) (1803)	3,211	511,851	528,747	164
Valais (Wallis) (1815)	5,231	206,563	218,707	42
Neuchâtel (Neuenburg) (1815)	797	169,173	158,368	199
Genève (Genf) (1815)	282	331,599	349,040	1,237
Jura (1979)	...	...	64,986	78
Total	41,288[1]	6,269,783	6,365,960	154

[1] 15,941 sq. miles.

Population (1980 census) 6,365,960.

The German language is spoken by the majority of inhabitants in 19 of the 25 cantons above (French names given in brackets), the French in 6 (Fribourg, Vaud, Valais, Neuchâtel, Jura and Genève, for which the German names are given in brackets), the Italian in 1 (Ticino). In 1970, 64·9% spoke German, 18·1% French, 11·9% Italian, 0·8% Romansch and 1·4% other languages; counting only Swiss nationals, the percentages were 74·5, 20·1, 4, 1 and 0·4. On 8 July 1937 Romansch was made the fourth national language; it is spoken mostly in Graubünden.

At the end of 1980 the population figures of the principal towns (and their '*agglomérations*' or conurbations, 1980) were as follows: Zürich, 369,522 (706,220); Basel, 182,143 (364,813); Geneva, 156,505 (335,401); Bern, 145,254 (286,903); Lausanne, 127,349 (226,145); Winterthur, 86,758 (107,752); St Gallen, 75,847 (88,361); Luzern, 63,278 (156,867); Biel, 53,793 (84,056); La Chaux-de-Fonds, 37,234.

The number of foreigners resident in Switzerland at 31 Dec. 1981 was 909,906. Of these, 185,686 were in Zürich canton, 101,120 in Vaud and 98,668 in Geneva.

Vital statistics for calendar years:

	Live births					
	Total	*Illegitimate*	*Marriages*	*Divorces*	*Still births*	*Deaths*
1978	71,375	2,921	32,120	10,497	435	57,718
1979	71,986	3,190	33,987	10,394	412	57,454
1980	73,661	3,496	35,721	10,910	361	59,097

The excess of emigrants over remigrants was: 1974, 2,087; 1975, 2,967; 1976, 3,873; 1977, 3,510; 1978, 3,209; 1979, 3,129; 1980, 3,339.

CLIMATE. The climate is largely dictated by relief and altitude and includes continental and mountain types. Summers are generally warm, with quite considerable rainfall; winters are fine, with clear, cold air and cloudless skies. Bern. Jan. 32°F (0°C), July, 65°F (18·5°C). Annual rainfall 39·4″ (986 mm).

CONSTITUTION AND GOVERNMENT. Switzerland is a republic. The highest authority is vested in the electorate, *i.e.*, all Swiss citizens of over 20. This electorate—besides electing its representatives to the Parliament—has the voting power on amendments to, or on the revision of, the Constitution. It also takes decisions on laws and international treaties if requested by 30,000 voters or 8 cantons (facultative referendum), and it has the right of initiating constitutional amendments, the support required for such demands being 50,000 voters (popular initiative).

The Federal Government is supreme in matters of peace, war and treaties; it regulates the army, the railway, telecommunication systems, the coining of money, the issue and repayment of bank-notes and the weights and measures of the republic. It also legislates on matters of copyright, bankruptcy, patents, sanitary policy in dangerous epidemics, and it may create and subsidize, besides the Polytechnic School at Zürich and at Lausanne, 2 federal universities and other educational institutions. There has also been entrusted to it the authority to decide concerning public works for the whole or great part of Switzerland, such as those relating to rivers, forests and the construction of national highways and railways. By referendum of 13 Nov. 1898 it is also the authority in the entire spheres of common law. In 1957 the Federation was empowered to legislate on atomic energy matters and in 1961 on the construction of pipelines of petroleum and gas.

National flag: Red with a white couped cross.

National anthem: Trittst im Morgenrot daher (words by Leonard Widmer, 1808–68; tune by Alberik Zwyssig, 1808–54); adopted by the Federal Council in 1962.

The legislative authority is vested in a parliament of 2 chambers, a *Ständerat*, or Council of States, and a *Nationalrat*, or National Council.

The *Ständerat* is composed of 46 members, chosen and paid by the 23 cantons of the Confederation, 2 for each canton. The mode of their election and the term of membership depend entirely on the canton. Three of the cantons are politically divided—Basel into Stadt and Land, Appenzell into Ausser-Rhoden and Inner-Rhoden, and Unterwalden into Obwalden and Nidwalden. Each of these 'half-cantons' sends 1 member to the State Council.

The *Nationalrat*—after the referendum taken on 4 Nov. 1962—consists of 200 National Councillors, directly elected for 4 years, in proportion to the population of the cantons, with the proviso that each canton or half-canton is represented by at least 1 member. The members are paid from federal funds at the rate of 150 francs for each day during the session and a nominal sum of 10,000 francs per annum.

In 1980 the 200 members were distributed among the cantons[1] as follows:

Zürich (Zurich)	35	Appenzell—Outer- and Inner-Rhoden	3
Bern (Berne)	29	St Gallen (St Gall)	12
Luzern (Lucerne)	9	Graubünden (Grisons)	5
Uri	1	Aargau (Argovie)	14
Schwyz	3	Thurgau (Thurgovie)	6
Unterwalden–Upper and Lower	2	Ticino (Tessin)	8
Glarus (Glaris)	1	Vaud (Waadt)	16
Zug (Zoug)	2	Valais (Wallis)	7
Fribourg (Freiburg)	6	Neuçhâtel (Neuenburg)	5
Solothurn (Soleure)	7	Geneve (Genf)	11
Basel (Bâle)—town and country	14	Jura	2
Schaffhausen (Schaffhouse)	2		

[1] The name of the canton is given in German, French or Italian, according to the language most spoken in it, and alternative names are given in brackets.

At the elections held on 21 Oct. 1981 the following parties were returned to the National Council: Social Democrats, 51; Radicals, 51; Christian-Democratic People's Party, 44; Central Democrats, 23; Independents, 11; Protestant Party, 3; Liberal Democrats, 8; Communists, 3; Action Party, 3; Independent Socialists, 6.

Council of States (1983): Catholic Democrats, 18; Radicals, 11; Socialists, 9; Central Democrats, 5; Liberals, 3.

A general election takes place by ballot every 4 years. Every citizen of the republic who has entered on his 20th year is entitled to a vote, and any voter, not a clergyman, may be elected a deputy. Laws passed by both chambers may be submitted to direct popular vote, when 50,000 citizens or 8 cantons demand it; the vote can be only 'Yes' or 'No'. This principle, called the *referendum*, is frequently acted on.

Women's suffrage, although advocated by the Federal Council and the Federal Assembly, was on 1 Feb. 1959 rejected, but in a subsequent referendum, held on 7 Feb. 1971, women's suffrage was carried.

The chief executive authority is deputed to the *Bundesrat*, or Federal Council, consisting of 7 members, elected from 7 different cantons for 4 years by the *Vereinigte Bundesversammlung*, *i.e.*, joint sessions of both chambers. The members of this council must not hold any other office in the Confederation or cantons, nor engage in any calling or business. In the Federal Parliament legislation may be introduced either by a member, or by either House, or by the Federal Council (but not by the people). Every citizen who has a vote for the National Council is eligible for becoming a member of the executive.

The President of the Federal Council (called President of the Confederation) and the Vice-President are the first magistrates of the Confederation. Both are elected by the Federal Assembly for 1 calendar year and are not immediately re-eligible to the same offices. The Vice-President, however, may be, and usually is, elected to succeed the outgoing President.

President of the Confederation for 1983: Pierre Aubert.

The 7 members of the Federal Council—each of whom has a salary of 203,000 francs per annum, while the President has 215,000 francs—act as ministers, or chiefs of the 7 administrative departments of the republic. The city of Berne is the seat of the Federal Council and the central administrative authorities.

The Federal Council is composed as follows (elected Dec. 1979):

Foreign Affairs: Pierre Aubert.
Interior: Alphons Egli.

Justice and Police: Rudolf Friedrich.
Military: Georges-André Chevallaz.
Finance: Willi Ritschard.
Public Economy: Kurt Furgler.
Transport, Communications and Energy: Léon Schlumpf.

Local Government. Each of the cantons and demi-cantons is sovereign, so far as its independence and legislative powers are not restricted by the federal constitution; all cantonal governments, though different in organization (membership varies from 5 to 11, and terms of office from 1 to 5 years), are based on the principle of sovereignty of the people.

In all cantons a body chosen by universal suffrage, usually called *der Grosse Rat*, or *Kantonsrat*, exercises the functions of a parliament. In all the cantonal constitutions, however, except those of the cantons which have a *Landsgemeinde*, the referendum has a place. By this principle, where it is most fully developed, as in Zürich, all laws and concordats, or agreements with other cantons, and the chief matters of finance, as well as all revisions of the Constitution, must be submitted to the popular vote. In Appenzell, Glarus and Unterwalden the people exercise their powers direct in the *Landsgemeinde*, *i.e.*, the assembly in the open air of all male citizens of full age. In all the cantons the *popular initiative* for constitutional affairs, as well as for legislation, has been introduced, except in Lucerne, where the *initiative* exists only for constitutional affairs. In most cantons there are districts (*Amtsbezirke*) consisting of a number of communes grouped together, each district having a Prefect (*Regierungsstatthalter*) representing the cantonal government. In the larger communes, for local affairs, there is an Assembly (legislative) and a Council (executive) with a president, maire or syndic, and not less than 4 other members. In the smaller communes there is a council only, with its proper officials.

Basler Handelskammer, *La neutralité suisse*, 1962
Bonjour, E., *Swiss Neutrality*. London, 1946
Huber, H., *How Switzerland is Governed*. Zürich, 1947
Hughes, C., *The Federal Constitution of Switzerland. Translation and Commentary*. Oxford, 1954
Hughes, C. J., *The Parliament of Switzerland*. Hansard Society, 1962
Marx, Dr Paul, *Systematisches Register zu den geltenden Staatsverträgen der schweizerischen Eidgenossenschaft und der Kantone mit dem Auslande*. Zürich, 1918. *Appendix*, 1934
Rappard, W. E., *La Constitution fédérale de la Suisse*. Zürich, 1948.—*Collective Security in Swiss Experience*. London, 1948
Ruck, Erwin, *Schweizerisches Staatsrecht*. Zürich, 1933
Silbernagel-Caloyanni, Alfred, *Suisse: Organisation Politique, Administrative et Judiciaire de la Confédération Helvétique et de Chaque Canton*. Paris, 1936

DEFENCE. There are fortifications in all entrances to the Alps and on the important passes crossing the Alps and the Jura. Large-scale destructions of bridges, tunnels and defiles are prepared for an emergency.

Army. Switzerland depends for defence upon a *national militia*. Service in this force is compulsory and universal, with few exemptions except for physical disability. Those excused or rejected pay certain taxes in lieu. Liability extends from the 20th to the end of the 50th year for soldiers and of the 55th year for officers. The first 12 years are spent in the first line, called the *Auszug*, or *Élite*, the next 10 in the *Landwehr* and 8 in the *Landsturm*. The unarmed *Hilfsdienst* comprises all other males between 20 and 50 whose services can be made available for non-combatant duties of any description.

The initial training of the Swiss militia soldier is carried out in recruits' schools, and the periods are 118 days for infantry, engineers, artillery, etc. The subsequent trainings, called 'repetition courses', are 20 days annually; but after going through 8 courses further attendance is excused for all under the rank of sergeant. The *Landwehr* men are called up for training courses of 13 days every 2 years, and the *Landsturm* men have to undergo a refresher course of 13 days.

The Army is divided into 3 field corps each of 1 armoured and 2 infantry divisions, 11 independent frontier brigades, 3 mountain divisions, and independent redoubt-, fortress- and territorial-brigades, organized in 4 army corps. Strength on mobilization: 580,000, and 400,000 reserves.

The administration of the Swiss Army is partly in the hands of the Cantonal authorities, who can promote officers up to the rank of captain. But the Federal Government is concerned with all general questions and makes all the higher appointments.

In peace-time the Swiss Army has no general; only in time of war the Federal Assembly in joint session of both Houses appoints a general.

The Swiss infantry are armed with the Swiss automatic rifle and with machine-guns, bazookas and mortars. The field artillery is armed with a Q.F. shielded 10·5 Bofors and field howitzers of 10·5 cm calibre. The heavy artillery is armed with guns of 10·5 cm and howitzers of 15 cm calibre. The armoured troops are equipped with the light French AMX, the British Centurion and a modern Swiss tank.

Air Force. The Air Force has 3 flying regiments, with about 334 combat aircraft. The fighter squadrons are equipped with Swiss-built F-5E Tiger IIs (4 squadrons), Mirage IIIS supersonic interceptor/ground-attack (2 squadrons), Mirage IIIRS fighter/reconnaissance (1 squadron), Venom ground-attack (3 squadrons) and Hunter interceptor/ground-attack (9 squadrons) aircraft. Bloodhound surface-to-air missile batteries are operational.

Training aircraft are Pilatus P-2 and PC-7 Turbo-Trainer and Vampire; there are also communications and transport aircraft and helicopters. Personnel numbers, 45,000 on mobilization.

INTERNATIONAL RELATIONS

Membership. Switzerland is a member of OECD, EFTA and the Council of Europe.

ECONOMY

Budget. Revenue and expenditure of the Confederation, in 1m. francs, for calendar years:

	1975	*1976*	*1977*	*1978*	*1979*	*1980*
Revenue	13,541	14,287	14,026	15,106	15,050	16,460
Expenditure	12,232	15,863	15,493	15,824	16,764	17,532

The public debt, comprising consolidated debt and flowing debt, of the Confederation in 1980 amounted to 14,126m. francs. The floating debt in 1980 was 4,255m. francs.

Schweizerisches Finanz-Jahrbuch. Bern. Annual. From 1899
Staatstechnung der Schweizerischen Eidgenossenschaft. Bern, 1976

Currency. The *franc* of 100 *Rappen* or *centimes* is the monetary unit. On 10 May 1971 there was a revaluation to 0·21759 gramme of fine gold.

The legal gold coins are 20- and 10-franc pieces; cupro-nickel coins are 5, 2, 1 and ½ franc, 20, 10 and 5 centimes; bronze, 2 and 1 centime. Notes are of 1,000, 500, 100, 50, 20, 10 and 5 francs.

On 10 July 1981 the notes in circulation (of francs of nominal value) was as follows: In 1,000 franc notes, 8,685·1m. francs; in 500, 4,201·9m. francs; in 100, 6,687·3m. francs; in 50, 1,058·3m. francs, and in lower denominations 1,195·8m.

In March 1983, £1 = 3·06 *francs*; US$1 = 2·08 *francs*.

Banking. The National Bank, with headquarters divided between Bern and Zürich, opened on 20 June 1907. It has the exclusive right to issue bank-notes. In 1981 the condition of the bank was as follows (in 1m. francs): Gold, 11,903·9, foreign exchange (currency), 25,495; currency in circulation, 23,336·7.

In 1976 there were 1,740 banking institutions with total assets of 347,710·5m. Swiss francs. They included 28 cantonal banks (79,376m. francs), 5 big banks (161,382m.), 225 regional banks (38,138m.), 185 other banks (43,267m.).

On 31 Dec. 1976 the total amount of savings deposits in Swiss banks was 73,903m. francs, with 11·2m. depositors.

National Bank: Bulletin mensuel.—Das schweizerische Bankwesen. Yearly. From 1920

Weights and Measures. The metric system of weights and measures was made compulsory by the federal law on 3 July 1875 and since 1 Jan. 1887 only metric units have been legal. By the federal law of 24 June 1909 the international electric units were also adopted.

ENERGY AND NATURAL RESOURCES

Electricity. The total production of energy amounted to 51,515m. kwh. in 1981; 36,097m. kwh. were generated by hydro-electric plants.

Gas. The production of gas in 1981 was 39,063,000 cu. metres.

Minerals. There are 2 salt-mining districts; that in Bex (Vaud) belongs to the canton, but is worked by a private company, and those at Schweizerhalle, Rheinfelden and Ryburg are worked by a joint-stock company formed by the cantons interested. The output of salt of all kinds in 1981 was 430,807 tonnes.

Agriculture. Of the total area of the country of 4,129,315 hectares, about 1,057,794 hectares (25·6%) are unproductive. Of the productive area of 3,071,521 hectares, 1,051,991 hectares are wooded. The agricultural area, in 1980, consisted of 287,283 hectares arable land (including vineyards), 106,406 hectares artificial meadows and 561,311 hectares permanent meadow. In 1980 there were 125,274 farms with a total area of 1,086,060 hectares. The gross value of agricultural products was estimated at 6,409·7m. francs in 1975 and 7,243·1m. francs in 1980.

In 1980, 176,942 hectares were planted with cereals, of which 85,301 hectares were wheat; barley, 46,111; rye, 8,058; potatoes, 23,664; sugar-beet, 13,075; vegetables, 8,196; tobacco, 769. Production, 1980 (in 1,000 tonnes): Potatoes, 853; sugar-beet, 674; wheat, 372; barley, 211; rye, 35; tobacco, 1·3. Milk production (in 1,000 tonnes): 1960, 3,112; 1970, 3,204; 1978, 3,542; 1979, 3,671; 1980, 3,679; 1981, 3,680.

The fruit production (in 1,000 tonnes) in 1980 was: Apples, 320; pears, 119; plums, 54; cherries, 46; nuts, 6.

Wine is produced in 18 of the cantons. In 1980 Swiss vineyards (13,736 hectares) yielded 854,804 hectolitres of wine, valued at 349,725 francs.

Livestock (1981): 44,800 horses, 335,500 sheep, 1,954,300 cattle (including about 870,000 milch cows), 2,071,000 pigs, 5,955,600 poultry.

Forestry. Of the forest area of 993,499 hectares, 56,153 were owned by the Federation or the cantons, 636,018 by communes and 301,328 by private persons or companies in 1981. The utilization of timber, in 1980, was 4,383,664 cu. metres, of which 331,513 in state-owned, 2,816,164 in communal and 1,235,987 in private forests.

INDUSTRY AND TRADE

Industry. The chief food producing industries, based on Swiss agriculture, are the manufacture of cheese, butter, sugar and meat. The production in 1980 was (in tonnes): Cheese, 119,900; butter, 34,700; sugar (1981), 120,811. There are 46 breweries, producing in 1978, 4·05m. hectolitres of beer. Tobacco products in 1981: Cigars, 394·44m.; cigarettes, 27,569m.

Among the other industries, the manufacture of textiles, wearing apparel and footwear, chemicals and pharmaceutical products, bricks, glass and cement, the manufacture of basic iron and steel and of other metal products, the production of machinery (including electrical machinery and scientific and optical instruments) and watch and clock making are the most important. In 1981 there were 8,738 factories with 693,243 workers. Of these, 35,286 were working in textile industries, 34,089 in the manufacture of textile goods and clothing, 62,772 in chemical works, 19,786 in the manufacture of stone and clay products, 95,198 in manufacture of metal products, 237,273 in the manufacture of machinery and 43,410 in watch and clock making and in the manufacture of jewellery.

Production in 1981 was: Woollen and blended yarn, 16,600 tonnes; woollen and blended cloth, 9,152 metres; footwear, 5·87m. pairs; cement, 4,348,214 tonnes;

raw aluminium, 82,221 tonnes; chocolate, 77,780 tonnes, 25·38m. watches and clocks were exported.

Labour. According to the census of industries, 1975, the total working population was reduced to about 2·7m., of which 6·3% were active in agriculture and forestry, 44·7% in manufacture and construction and 48·9% in services. In all non-agricultural sectors there were 288,470 establishments (including 594 being shut down) with 2,537,738 occupied persons, divided in 159,289 occupants and 2,378,449 employees.

The main groups show the following numbers of gainfully occupied persons: Engineering, 254,185; retail trade, 228,751; construction 225,533; metalwork, 175,983; agriculture and forestry, 172,649; transport and postal services, 171,081; catering, 158,500; wholesale trade, 113,197; banking and insurance, 105,106; food processing, 103,306; textiles, 89,660; chemical industry, 68,975; watchmaking, 61,058.

The foreign labour force with permit of temporary residence was 706,309 in Aug. 1980. Of the number recorded 300,974 were Italians, 85,703 Spaniards, 68,558 Frenchmen, 63,790 Germans and 27,056 Austrians. 90,566 were construction workers, 45,385 metalworkers and mechanics and 47,535 housekeepers, hotel and restaurant workers.

The Swiss Federal Union of Administrative and Public Service Workers had, in 1981, a membership of 125,151. The Federation of Trade Unions had about 459,150 members.

Commerce. The special commerce, excluding gold (bullion and coins) and silver (coins), was (in 1m. Swiss francs) as follows:

	1975	*1976*	*1977*	*1978*	*1979*	*1980*	*1981*
Imports	34,268	36,871	43,026	42,299	48,730	60,859	60,034
Exports	33,430	37,045	42,159	41,779	44,024	49,607	52,821

The following table, in 1m. francs, shows the distribution of the special trade of Switzerland among the principal countries:

	Imports from				*Exports to*			
Countries	*1978*	*1979*	*1980*	*1981*	*1978*	*1979*	*1980*	*1981*
Federal Rep. of Germany	12,233·5	13,946·5	16,766·3	16,908·4	7,537·2	8,642·6	9,749·8	9,687·4
France	5,285·6	6,273·3	7,461·8	7,428·5	3,612·5	3,845·2	4,547·6	4,751·3
Italy	4,147·7	5,054·9	5,844·6	5,849·3	2,633·7	3,127·2	3,898·8	4,069·9
Netherlands	1,544·9	2,089·3	2,469·6	2,445·2	1,210·2	1,240·9	1,383·7	1,316·5
Belgium–Luxembourg	1,629·9	2,003·2	2,502·5	2,543·2	1,185·8	1,255·5	1,565·2	1,396·9
UK	3,377·6	3,754·9	5,072·6	3,457·6	2,869·3	3,090·9	3,134·4	3,428·6
Denmark	383·7	417·6	508·8	549·4	583·5	532·1	548·4	576·9
Ireland	100·0	114·7	150·9	176·1	104·7	113·5	91·1	134·7
Greece	...	...	...	90·9	...	...	...	370·4
EEC Total	28,702·9	33,654·4	40,777·2	39,448·6	19,736·9	21,847·9	24,919·0	25,732·6
Austria	1,649·4	1,830·0	2,184·4	2,262·7	1,938·8	2,010·9	2,271·0	2,263·0
Norway	151·9	178·9	229·1	186·3	395·8	373·1	428·9	444·7
Sweden	875·4	1,041·1	1,229·4	1,215·2	889·4	933·1	1,024·5	1,052·7
Portugal	104·7	127·6	179·4	190·0	324·8	339·7	400·7	476·5
Finland	230·5	274·0	343·5	338·3	288·4	326·3	397·2	454·4
Iceland	40·1	44·3	47·9	37·2	12·3	13·9	15·2	19·9
EFTA	3,052·0	3,495·9	4,213·7	4,229·7	3,849·5	3,997·0	4,537·5	4,711·2
Spain	440·0	490·9	578·8	617·2	763·3	840·8	903·1	1,020·4
Gibraltar, Malta	3·9	3·2	2·9	2·6	14·0	23·1	21·9	27·1
German Dem. Republic	55·9	56·4	68·5	79·9	196·0	242·7	220·3	232·9
Poland	142·5	137·7	240·1	103·5	334·3	320·5	287·5	181·4
Czechoslovakia	122·5	165·9	194·0	168·2	217·2	207·5	234·2	227·4

Countries	Imports from 1978	1979	1980	1981	Exports to 1978	1979	1980	1981
Hungary	159·9	150·7	166·5	236·3	325·4	285·3	285·5	339·5
Yugoslavia	124·8	154·1	173·5	145·8	540·1	587·9	552·7	567·5
Greece	56·5	77·0	66·3	...	252·5	294·2	300·4	...
Bulgaria	25·3	24·9	40·9	40·4	98·9	100·5	119·7	171·1
Romania	75·5	53·9	60·7	53·6	248·5	178·0	133·6	110·4
USSR	917·5	1,296·7	1,607·9	1,728·3	475·6	441·2	499·1	402·5
Turkey	92·3	94·4	113·4	141·4	239·4	175·7	265·5	423·5
Other European countries	4·0	4·2	8·4	8·0	17·7	24·3	45·0	25·0
Europe Total	33,975·5	39,860·3	48,312·8	47,003·5	27,309·3	29,566·6	33,325·0	34,172·5
Egypt	42·7	33·5	71·5	70·9	221·2	280·0	306·4	368·8
Sudan	11·2	4·1	4·4	2·2	40·2	49·8	42·2	53·7
Libya	190·5	258·6	516·5	368·2	188·6	89·7	143·6	195·2
Tunisia	7·6	56·0	11·9	13·3	33·3	35·8	46·8	57·7
Algeria	34·8	151·4	67·4	366·6	197·1	231·4	276·2	204·4
Morocco	27·7	28·3	46·1	21·2	85·0	73·7	66·4	78·6
Ivory Coast	54·6	37·9	35·8	48·1	52·1	44·4	41·4	31·0
Guinea	0·2	1·5	0·3	1·0	12·8	9·3	9·4	9·3
Ghana	55·8	42·8	48·9	33·5	137·8	23·5	23·1	31·5
Nigeria	118·1	137·0	356·5	195·3	421·4	263·2	530·5	683·2
Zaïre	23·0	21·7	20·9	6·7	32·2	23·6	25·2	29·9
SW Africa	18·9	7·9	11·6	10·8	35·6	19·0	52·6	46·1
S Africa, Rep. of	109·1	142·8	212·2	153·4	362·4	382·7	499·3	669·6
Zambia	23·2	32·4	21·9	43·5	10·8	16·9	14·3	14·7
Zimbabwe	19·5	11·4	8·7	29·6	3·3	3·6	17·4	40·4
Tanzania	6·0	7·6	3·8	6·4	19·9	20·3	29·8	16·5
Kenya	23·2	19·6	33·7	27·1	31·7	38·3	48·1	45·0
Other African countries	83·5	84·5	89·3	91·9	254·0	171·0	237·7	193·5
Africa Total	849·6	1,079·0	1,561·4	1,489·7	2,139·4	1,776·2	2,410·4	2,769·1
Syria	8·8	11·4	36·6	18·5	76·8	98·5	85·1	101·5
Lebanon	5·1	34·9	86·8	53·6	76·6	124·3	238·5	330·2
Israel	175·2	196·7	209·5	205·4	963·4	973·0	871·7	452·3
Iraq	0·2	0·3	0·4	0·8	220·3	229·6	354·9	527·2
Kuwait	14·3	24·8	44·6	2·7	164·4	132·5	128·3	200·8
Iran	145·9	79·3	136·8	81·6	686·2	368·0	463·7	464·4
Saudi Arabia	72·0	186·5	257·3	413·0	928·9	951·6	1,042·4	1,181·8
UAE	276·0	374·4	673·2	665·9	172·9	154·3	173·1	236·1
Pakistan	23·9	23·2	40·8	51·4	55·1	67·9	64·8	110·1
India	157·1	139·0	127·8	153·1	195·7	214·9	220·8	288·8
Thailand	52·4	107·3	191·9	104·8	71·1	87·2	103·6	144·0
Malaysia	25·7	41·1	52·1	51·1	40·3	52·4	58·1	67·0
Singapore	49·1	47·9	99·9	81·7	194·1	219·1	267·5	315·4
China	88·8	90·7	128·6	153·7	167·3	197·3	233·4	241·7
Hong Kong	323·6	378·9	572·4	610·0	766·1	800·7	934·6	999·0
Korea, Rep. of	86·0	86·0	113·7	170·0	173·2	267·4	122·9	200·6
Taiwan	103·6	107·5	164·1	143·5	111·2	172·1	184·2	110·7
Japan	1,220·2	1,338·6	1,989·8	2,297·8	1,185·0	1,300·4	1,273·5	1,435·8
Philippines	24·2	22·0	30·3	34·7	78·0	75·9	84·4	94·9
Indonesia	62·1	62·6	61·8	65·2	84·3	89·4	103·2	159·5
Other Asian countries	55·0	87·7	154·5	85·0	223·1	236·0	236·5	350·1
Asia Total	2,969·2	3,440·8	5,172·9	5,443·5	6,634·0	6,812·5	7,245·2	8,011·9
Canada	202·9	220·0	339·2	364·2	381·3	384·3	420·4	536·6
USA	3,170·8	3,048·8	4,104·9	4,475·5	2,974·2	2,992·8	3,552·0	4,129·1
Mexico	68·4	65·2	84·6	31·6	229·7	281·2	371·9	526·1
Guatemala	64·0	53·4	58·2	45·9	48·4	57·1	45·7	47·6
Honduras	28·6	29·9	42·4	43·9	13·0	9·7	11·2	10·6
Costa Rica	56·4	44·1	51·9	49·1	12·6	17·0	13·8	10·8

Countries	Imports from 1978	1979	1980	1981	Exports to 1978	1979	1980	1981
Panama	267·5	215·9	302·6	273·1	222·8	224·3	226·9	342·5
Cuba	10·6	12·7	21·1	12·4	57·5	43·5	45·9	61·6
Colombia	50·3	56·7	116·2	77·2	112·1	112·1	130·5	137·1
Venezuela	18·7	12·1	15·0	10·6	242·4	200·4	179·6	227·4
Brazil	143·9	210·4	263·6	287·6	446·7	483·8	497·6	451·9
Uruguay	17·2	14·4	20·6	30·9	16·9	30·6	29·1	33·0
Argentina	148·3	115·4	116·4	137·4	229·8	309·0	318·2	323·2
Chile	17·8	13·5	11·1	11·7	73·2	57·6	72·7	76·7
Bolivia	1·2	2·5	2·5	2·3	23·9	28·8	13·5	39·6
Peru	44·6	31·9	44·9	48·4	62·1	74·3	96·0	141·3
Ecuador	21·6	21·8	14·6	15·4	59·7	70·9	66·4	55·0
Other American countries	79·7	93·0	100·6	113·5	133·2	130·5	173·0	205·1
Australia and Oceania	93·1	88·4	110·7	126·7	357·3	361·3	362·6	513·2

Custom receipts (in 1,000 francs): 1977, 2,920,800; 1978, 2,989,707; 1979, 3,002,117; 1980, 3,170,700; 1981, 3,243,631.

Total trade between Switzerland (including Liechtenstein) and UK for calendar years (British Department of Trade, in £1,000 sterling):

	1978	*1979*	*1980*	*1981*	*1982*
Imports to UK	2,156,014	2,564,773	2,614,690	1,708,058	1,669,922
Exports and re-exports from UK	1,913,744	2,407,328	3,076,337	1,601,164	1,196,203

Federal Customs Office, *Statistique mensuelle du commerce extérieur de la Suisse.* From 1925.—*Statistique annuelle du commerce extérieur de la Suisse.* 2 vols. From 1840.—*Rapport annuel de la statistique du commerce Suisse.* From 1889

Tourism. Tourism is an important industry. In 1981, overnight stays in hotels and sanatoria were 37,133,312 (21·56m. by foreign visitors) and in other accommodation 39,566,000.

COMMUNICATIONS

Roads. There are (1980) 66,544 km of main roads, including 1,170 km of 'national roads' for motor cars only. There is a postal autobus service, which, in 1976, carried 53·7m. passengers. Motor vehicles, as at 30 Sept. 1981, numbered 2,877,169, including 2,394,455 private cars, 42,946 trucks, 152,508 motor cycles, 11,122 buses and 104,148 agricultural tractors and special cars.

Railways. Railway history in Switzerland begins in 1847. In 1980 the length of the general traffic railways was 4,999 km, and of special lines (funiculars etc.), 840 km. The operating receipts of general traffic lines amounted to (1980) 3,373,416,000 francs; operating expenses, 4,101,371,000 francs. Traffic was 59·66m. tonnes and 314·15m. passengers.

There are many privately-owned lines, the most important of which are the Bern–Lotschberg–Simplon (115 km) and Rhaetian (363 km) networks.

Aviation. In 1981 civil aviation on domestic and international routes carried 12,166,842 passengers, 331,391 tonnes of mail, freight and luggage.

The air transport organization Swissair (founded in 1931) in 1982 carried 189,139 tonnes of freight and 7,168,567 passengers. Swissair had a capital of 422m. francs on 15 May 1977. Its fleet consisted of 53 aircraft in Jan. 1983.

Shipping. A merchant marine was created by a decree of the Swiss Government dated 9 April 1941, the place of registry of its vessels being Basel. In 1981 it consisted of 31 vessels with a total of 313,662 GRT. In 1981, 8,277,359 tonnes of goods were handled in the port of Basel.

Post and Broadcasting. In 1981 there were 3,906 post offices. On 1 Jan. 1981 there were 4,780,760 telephones, all integrated in one dial system.

Wireless communication is furnished by 3 main medium-wave stations and 1 short-wave station. There are 3 television studios and more than 100 transmitters. TV programmes are financed by licence fees and advertisements. Advertisements are limited to 15 minutes each day. All stations are operated by the Federal Post, Telephone and Telegraph (PTT) services. Radio-telegraph circuits are operated by Radio Suisse SA, radio-telephone circuits by the PTT. Radio licences, 1981, 2,291,247; television licences, 2,012,930.

The total expenditure of the PTT in 1981 was 6,413·3m. francs, the total gross receipts 6,745·8m. francs.

Cinemas (1981). There were 477 cinemas with a seating capacity of 159,867.

Newspapers (1980). The number of daily newspapers was estimated to be 126.

JUSTICE, RELIGION, EDUCATION AND WELFARE

Justice. The Federal Tribunal (*Bundes-Gericht*), which sits at Lausanne, consists of 26-28 members, with 11-13 supplementary judges, appointed by the Federal Assembly for 6 years and eligible for re-election; the President and Vice-President serve for 2 years and cannot be re-elected.The President has a salary of 170,000 francs a year, and the other members 158,000 francs. The Tribunal has original and final jurisdiction in suits between the Confederation and cantons; between cantons and cantons; between the Confederation or cantons and corporations or individuals, the value in dispute being not less than 8,000 francs; between parties who refer their case to it, the value in dispute being at least 20,000 francs; in such suits as the constitution or legislation of cantons places within its authority; and in many classes of railway suits. It is a court of appeal against decisions of other federal authorities, and of cantonal authorities applying federal laws. The Tribunal also tries persons accused of treason or other offences against the Confederation. For this purpose it is divided into 4 chambers: Chamber of Accusation, Criminal Chamber (*Cour d'Assises*), Federal Penal Court and Court of Cassation. The jurors who serve in the Assize Courts are elected by the people, and are paid 100 francs a day when serving.

On 3 July 1938 the Swiss electorate accepted a new federal penal code, to take the place of the separate cantonal penal codes. The new code, which abolished capital punishment, came into force on 1 Jan. 1942.

By federal law of 5 Oct. 1950 several articles of the penal code concerning crime against the independence of the state have been amended with a view to reinforcing the security of the State.

Thormann, P., and Overbeck, A. (ed.), *Das Schweizerische Strafgesetzbuch.* Zürich, 1939

Religion. There is complete and absolute liberty of conscience and of creed. No one is bound to pay taxes specially appropriated to defraying the expenses of a creed to which he does not belong. No bishoprics can be created on Swiss territory without the approbation of the Confederation.

According to the census of 1 Dec. 1970 Roman Catholics numbered 3,097,000 (49·4%) of the population; Protestants, 2,992,000 (47·7%) and others, 181,000 (2·9%). In 1960 Protestants were in a majority in 10 of the cantons and Catholics in 12. Of the more populous cantons, Zürich, Bern, Vaud, Neuchâtel and Basel (town and land) were mainly Protestant, while Luzern, Fribourg, Ticino, Valais and the Forest Cantons are mainly Catholic. The Roman Catholics are under 6 Bishops, viz., of Basel (resident at Solothurn), Chur, St Gallen, Lugano, Lausanne–Geneva–Fribourg (resident at Fribourg) and Sitten (Sion), all of them immediately subject to the Holy See. The Old Catholics have a theological faculty at the university of Bern.

Education. Education is administered by the cantons. Before the year 1848 most of the cantons had organized a system of primary schools, and since that year elementary education has steadily advanced. In 1874 it was made obligatory for the whole country (the school age varying in the different cantons) and placed under the civil authority. In some cantons the cost falls almost entirely on the communes, in others it is divided between the canton and communes. In all the cantons primary instruction is free.

In most cantons there are also secondary schools for youths of from 12 to 15, gymnasia, higher schools for girls, teachers' seminaries, commercial and administrative schools, trade schools, art schools, technical schools, schools for the instruction of girls in domestic economy and other subjects, agricultural schools, schools for horticulture, for viticulture, for arboriculture and for dairy management. There are also institutions for the blind, the deaf and dumb and feeble-minded.

There are 7 universities in Switzerland. These universities are organized on the model of those of Germany, governed by a rector and a senate, and divided into 4 faculties of theology, jurisprudence, philosophy and medicine. In 1980–81 the Federal Institute of Technology at Zürich (founded in 1855) had 658 teachers and (1981–82) 7,556 matriculated students; the Federal Institute of Technology at Lausanne, independent of the university since 1946, had 217 teachers and (1981–82) 2,316 students; the St Gall School of Economics and Social Sciences, founded in 1899, had 148 teachers and (1981–82) 2,008 matriculated students.

University statistics in the winter of 1981–82:

	Theology	*Law*	*Economics*	*Medicine*	*Science*	*Others*	*Total*	*Teaching staff (1980–81)*
Basel (1460)	191	905	537	1,676	1,167	1,554	6,030	506
Zürich (1523 & 1833)	222	2,529	1,044	3,122	2,071	6,464	15,452	1,618
Bern (1528 & 1834)	224	1,556	488	1,823	1,405	2,312	7,808	810
Genève (1559[1] & 1873[1])	126	986	870	1,498	1,382	5,454	10,316	831
Lausanne (1537[1] & 1890[2])	93	818	717	1,491	780	1,809	5,708	433
Fribourg (1889)	432	635	593	375	471	2,012	4,518	465
Neuchâtel (1866 & 1909)	52	215	237	91	463	926	1,984	215

[1] Founded as an academy. [2] Reorganized as a university.

These numbers are exclusive of 'visitors', but inclusive of women students.

Social Security. The Federal Insurance Law against illness and accident, of 13 June 1911, entitles all Swiss citizens to insurance against illness; foreigners may be admitted to the benefits. Compulsory insurance against illness does not exist as yet, but cantons and communities are entitled to declare insurance obligatory for certain classes or to establish public benefit (sick fund) associations, and to make employers responsible for the payment of the premiums of their employees. In 1980 the 469 societies insuring against illness had 6,811,581 members.

Unemployment insurance is based since 13 June 1976 upon a Constitution amendment which stipulates unemployment insurance as compulsory for all wage-earners.

A federal law was in preparation in 1976. At 30 Sept. 1975 there existed 123 public and private unemployment insurance organizations with a total membership (31 March 1977) of 1,435,577 (53·5% of working population).

Insurance against accident is compulsory for all officials, employees and workmen of all the factories, trades, etc., which are under the federal liability law. The Swiss Accident Insurance Institution commenced operations on 1 April 1918.

On 6 July 1947 a federal law was accepted by a referendum, providing compulsory old age and widows and widowers insurance for the whole population, as from 1 Jan. 1948. In March 1981 the number of normal pensioners was 983,063, the number of interim pensioners, 34,379. On 1 Jan. 1960 the old-age insurance scheme was extended to cover invalidity. In March 1981, 184,174 invalids received a regular annuity and 20,731 invalids an interim annuity.

DIPLOMATIC REPRESENTATIVES

Of Switzerland in Great Britain (16–18 Montagu Place, London, W1H 2BQ)
Ambassador: Claude Caillat.

Of Great Britain in Switzerland (Thunstrasse 50, 30005 Bern)
Ambassador: John Powell-Jones, CMG.

Of Switzerland in the USA (2900 Cathedral Ave., NW, Washington, D.C., 20008)
Ambassador: Anton Hegner.

Of the USA in Switzerland (Jubilaeumstrasse 93, 3005, Bern)
Ambassador; Faith Ryan Whittlesey.

Books of Reference

Statistical Information: The Bureau fédéral de statistique (15 Hallwyl St, Bern) was established in 1860. *Director:* J.-J. Senglet. Its principal publications are:

Annuaire statistique de la Suisse. Bâle. From 1891
Statistique de la Suisse. From 1930
Contributions à la Statistique Suisse. From 1930
Bibliographie Suisse de statistique et d'économie politique. Annual, from 1937

Swiss Confederation
Annuaire; Budget; Message du Budget; Compte d'Etat (annual) *Feuille Fédérale; Recueil des Lois fédérales* (weekly)
Recueil systématique des lois et ordonnances, 1848–1947 (in German, French and Italian). Bern, 1951
Sammlung der Bundes- und Kantonsverfassungen (in German, French and Italian). Bern, 1937

Federal Department of Economics
La vie économique (and supplements). Monthly. From 1928
Législation sociale de la Suisse. Annual, from 1928

Behrendt, R. F. (ed.), *Strukturwandlugen der schweizerischen Wirtschaft und Gesellschaft.* Bern, 1962
Bonjour, E., Offler, H. S., and Potter, G. R., *A Short History of Switzerland.* Oxford, 1952
Dürrenmatt, P., *Schweizer Geschichte.* Zürich, 1963.—*Schweiz.* Zürich, 1962.—*Wir Schweizer und der totale Krieg.* Zürich, 1960
Imhof, E. (ed.), *Atlas der Schweiz.* Bern, 1965 ff.
Riklin, A., *et al, Handbuch der schweizerischen Aussenpolitik.* Bern, 1975
Schwarz, U., *The Eye of the Hurricane: Switzerland in World War Two.* Boulder, 1980
Sorell, W., *The Swiss: A Cultural Panorama of Switzerland.* Indianapolis, 1972. London, 1973
Unser Schweizer Standpunkt 1914, 1939, 1964. Bern, 1964

National Library: Bibliothèque Nationale Suisse, 15 Hallwyl St, Bern. *Director:* F. G. Maier.

SYRIA

Capital: Damascus
Population: 9·31m. (1981)
GNP per capita: US$1,340 (1980)

al-Jamhouriya al Arabia as-Souriya

HISTORY. For the history of Syria from 1920 to 1946 *see* THE STATESMAN'S YEAR-BOOK, 1957, pp. 1408 f. Complete independence was achieved on 12 Apr. 1946. Syria merged with Egypt to form the United Arab Republic from 2 Feb. until 29 Sept. 1961, when independence was resumed following a *coup* the previous day. Lieut.-Gen. Hafez al-Assad became Prime Minister following the fifth *coup* of that decade on 13 Nov. 1970, and assumed the Presidency on 22 Feb. 1971.

AREA AND POPULATION. Syria is bounded by the Mediterranean and the Lebanese Republic on the west, by Israel and Jordan on the south, by Iraq on the east and by Turkey on the north. The frontier between Syria and Turkey (Nisibim-Jeziret ibn Omar) was settled by the Franco-Turkish agreement of 22 June 1929.

The area of Syria is 185,680 sq. km (71,772 sq. miles), of which 35,000 sq. km have been surveyed. The census of 17 Sept. 1970 gave a total population of 6,304,685, showing about 10% less than the estimates. Estimate (1980) 8·98m. The 14 *mohafaza* (administrative districts) with population, 1975, are: City of Damascus, 1,042,000; Damascus, excluding city, 732,000; Aleppo, 1,523,000; Homs, 629,000; Hama, 514,748; Lattakia, 389,552; Deir-el-Zor, 332,000; Idlib, 428,000; Hassakeh, 532,000; Raqqa, 281,000; Sweida, 162,000; Derá, 282,000; Tartous, 348,000; Kunaitra, 19,000.

Principal towns (census 1970), Damascus, 836,668; Aleppo, 639,428; Homs, 215,423; Hama, 137,421; Lattakia, 125,716; Deir-el-Zor, 66,143.

Arabic is the official language.

CONSTITUTION AND GOVERNMENT. A new Constitution was approved by plebiscite on 12 March 1973 and promulgated on 14 March. It confirmed the Arab Socialist Renaissance *(Ba'ath)* Party, in power since 1963, as the 'leading party in the State and society'. Legislative power is held by a 195-member People's Council, elected for a 4-year term. At the latest elections on 10 Nov. 1981, all seats were won by the National Progressive Front, a coalition of the Ba'ath Party and 4 smaller ones.

President: Lieut.-Gen. Hafez al Assad (re-elected for further 7-year term in 1978).

Prime Minister: Dr Abdul Rauf al-Kasm.

Deputy Prime Ministers: Abdul Halim Khaddam *(Foreign Affairs)*, Brig. Walid Hamdoun *(Service Affairs)*, Abdul Qadir Qaddoura *(Economic Affairs)*.

National flag: Three horizontal stripes of red, white, black, with 2 green stars on the white stripe.

DEFENCE

Army. The Army in 1983 was composed of about 170,000 trained men. The USSR supplies technical advisers and equipment, which include over 3,990 tanks (1,000 T-62). The Army was organized (1983) into 4 armoured and 2 mechanized infantry divisions, 2 armoured, 4 mechanized, 2 artillery brigades, 5 commando and 1 parachute regiment and 32 surface-to-air missile batteries.

Navy. The Navy includes 2 small frigates, 18 missile boats, 8 torpedo boats, 1 minesweeper, 2 coastal minesweepers, 1 inshore minesweeper and 1 diving ship (all *ex*-Soviet) and the 3 patrol vessels (*ex*-French) transferred in 1962 to form the nucleus of the Syrian Navy. Personnel in 1983 totalled 2,500 officers and men.

Air Force. The Air Force, including Air Defence Command, is believed to have about 50,000 personnel and about 450 first-line jet combat aircraft, made up of about 200 MiG-21, 20 MiG-23 and 24 MiG-25 supersonic interceptors, 60 MiG-23, 16 Su-7, 40 Ju-22 and 80 MiG-17 fighter-bombers. Many additional aircraft are being purchased from the USSR with Saudi Arabian aid. Training units have Spanish-built Flamingo piston-engined primary trainers and Czechoslovakian L-29 Delfin jet basic trainers. There are also transport units with An-12, An-24/26, C-47, Il-14 and other types, and helicopter units with Soviet-built Ka-25s, Mi-8s and Mi-24 gunships, and French-built Gazelles. 'Guideline', 'Goa', 'Gainful' and 'Gaskin' surface-to-air missiles are widely deployed in Syria by Air Defence Command.

INTERNATIONAL RELATIONS

Membership. Syria is a member of UN and the Arab League.

ECONOMY

Budget. The ordinary budget for the calendar year 1980 gave revenue at £Syr.29,000m. and ordinary and development expenditure at £Syr.29,000m.

Currency. The monetary unit is the Syrian *pound*, divided into 100 *piastres*. In March 1983, £1 = £Syr.10; US$1 = £Syr.3·95.

Banking. The Central Bank has the sole right of issuing currency. Other banks were nationalized in March 1963, namely, the Omaya Bank and its subsidiary, the Popular Mortgage Bank; the Orient Arab Bank; the Bank of Syria and Overseas; the Agricultural Bank; the Arab World Bank. Number of branches, 1973: Central Bank of Syria, 9; Commercial Bank of Syria, 22; Industrial Bank, 3; Agricultural Co-operative Bank, 50; Real Estate Bank, 3; Bank of Popular Discount, 27.

Weights and Measures. A decree dated 22 Aug. 1935 makes the use of the metric system legal and obligatory throughout the whole of the country. In outlying districts the former weights and measures may still be in use. They are: 1 *okiya* = 0·47 lb.; 6 *okiyas* = 1 *oke* = 2·82 lb.; 2 *okes* = 1 *rottol* = 5·64 lb.; 200 *okes* = 1 *kantar*.

ENERGY AND NATURAL RESOURCES

Oil. A branch of the Iraq Petroleum Co.'s oil pipeline from Kirkuk crosses Syria between Makaleb in the east and Nahr el Kebir valley in the west. The Iraq Petroleum Co. has constructed a new pipeline from Kirkuk to the small fishing port of Banias (south of Lattakia), which came into use in April 1952; the Trans-Arabian Pipeline Co.'s line to Sidon crosses southern Syria. Another pipeline is being constructed from the Karachouk oilfield *via* Homs to the port of Tartous. Crude oil production (1981) 9m. tonnes.

Gas. Gas reserves (1982) 700,000m. cubic ft.

Minerals. Phosphate deposits have been discovered at two places near al-Shargiya and at Khneifis. Production, 1975, 857,000 tonnes; other minerals were salt, 34,000; natural asphalt, 31,000. There are indications of lead, copper, antimony, nickel, chrome and other minerals widely distributed. Manganese ore was mined before 1914. Sodium chloride and bitumen deposits are being worked. There is abundance of good calcareous building stone and basalt.

Agriculture. Syria is an agricultural country but is moving towards greater industrialization, the bulk of the population being engaged in the cultivation of the soil and in cattle breeding. In 1977 the irrigated area was 531,000 hectares; in 1980, 139,000 hectares under cotton and 1,449,000 hectares were under wheat, 1,587,000 hectares under barley. The total cultivable area was 14·47m. hectares, including 455,000 hectares of forest and 8,631,000 hectares of steppe and pasture.

Yield of principal crops, 1980 (in 1,000 tonnes): Wheat, 2,226; barley, 1,587;

cotton, 323; olives, 392; lentils, 83; millet, 19; sugar-beet, 505.

Livestock (1979): Cattle, 705,000; asses, 270,000; sheep, 7·6m.; goats, 1m.; poultry, 12·7m.

INDUSTRY AND TRADE

Industry. The most important industries are flour, oils, soap, cement, tanning, tobacco, textiles, knitwear, glassware, spinning, sugar, margarine, hosiery, footwear and brassware.

Industrial production in 1975 included (in 1,000 tonnes): Woollen fabrics, 1,254; cement, 994; sugar, 117; cottoncake, 103; salt, 34; cotton yarn, 31·6; vegetable oil, 22·1; manufactured tobacco, 6·7. In addition, 3·7m. pairs of shoes were manufactured and 50,040 refrigerators assembled.

Commerce. Trade in calendar years in £Syr. 1m. was as follows:

	1977	*1978*	*1979*	*1980*
Imports	9,719	8,935	13,067	16,188
Exports	4,199	4,160	6,453	8,273

Cotton is one of the chief exports. Others include oil, cereals, live animals and phosphates. Imports include industrial raw materials, machinery, chemicals and electrical equipment.

Total trade between Syria and UK (British Department of Trade returns, in £1,000 sterling):

	1978	*1978*	*1980*	*1981*	*1982*
Imports to UK	4,285	7,001	12,241	4,555	25,644
Exports and re-exports from UK	57,977	66,667	81,584	85,244	89,535

Tourism. In 1979, 1,270,944 tourists visited Syria.

COMMUNICATIONS

Roads. In 1975 there were 10,740 km of asphalted roads, 1,500 km of paved non-asphalted road and 2,364 km of levelled roads. The first-class roads are capable of carrying all types of modern motor transport and are usable all the year round, while the second-class roads are usable during the dry season only, *i.e.*, for about 9 months. The Nairn Transport Company operate a trans-desert pullman motor coach service between Damascus and Baghdad. There are also two pullman transport companies (Elkarnak, Syrian, and Jett, Jordanian) operating a joint service between Damascus and Amman. The motor vehicles registered in 1979 were 28,542 motor cycles, 7,420 buses, 66,243 cars and 85,978 goods vehicles.

Railways. In Syria the following railways are open (in addition to those listed under LEBANON (p. 785): Standard gauge from Aleppo to Meidan-Ekbes (Turkish frontier), 116 km; Aleppo to Tel-Kotchek (Iraq frontier), 523 km; narrow gauge from Damascus to El Hammé, 195 km; Damascus to Dera'a (Jordan frontier), 130 km. Two lines have recently been constructed: a standard gauge from Akari to Tartous, 42 km, and the 755-km Latakia-Aleppo-Kamechli, opened to traffic in 1976 while the standard gauge Homs to Damascus line is open as far as Mhine, with a branch to Palmyra. Total network 1,533 km, traffic carried (1980) 1·3m. passengers, 2·4m. tonnes.

Aviation. In 1975, 7,582 aircraft arrived at Damascus and Aleppo airports, disembarking 346,552 passengers and embarking 359,711. Syrian Air carried 480,000 passengers in 1976.

Shipping. The amount of cargo discharged in 1980 was 2·6m. tons and the amount loaded 430,000 tons.

Post and Broadcasting. An automatic telephone system has been installed in Damascus, and most other towns. Number of telephones (1978), 193,044; of these, 76,035 were in Damascus and 37,797 in Aleppo. There are 1·6m. radio sets.

Newspapers. There were (1977) 3 national daily newspapers in Damascus; other dailies and periodicals appear in Hama, Homs, Aleppo and Latakia.

RELIGION, EDUCATION AND WELFARE

Religion. The population is composed mainly of Sunni Moslems and there are also Shiites and Ismailis. There are also Druzes and Alawites. Christians include Greek Orthodox, Greek Catholics, Armenian Orthodox, Syrian Orthodox, Armenian Catholics, Protestants, Maronites, Syrian Catholics, Latins, Nestorians and Assyrians. There are also Jews and Yezides.

Education. The Syrian University was founded in 1924, although the faculties of law and of medicine had existed previously. In 1975 there were 3 universities comprised of 25 faculties with 61,156 students. In 1974–75 there were 42,204 students at the University of Damascus; 15,805 at the University of Aleppo; 3,147 at the University of Teshreen.

In 1975, 6,760 primary schools had 34,995 teachers and 1,211,570 pupils; 1,050 secondary and intermediate schools, 20,479 teachers and 314,272 pupils; 58 vocational schools, 2,304 teachers and 21,211 pupils; 23 teacher-training colleges, 506 teachers and 5,913 students; 95 various schools and mining institutes, 4,449 teachers and 15,719 students.

Health. In 1977 there were 7,479 hospital beds (1 per 983 persons) in 31 state hospitals, 69 private hospitals and 4 sanatoria.

DIPLOMATIC REPRESENTATIVES

Of Syria in Great Britain (8 Belgrave Sq., London, SW1X 8PH)
Ambassador: Loutof Allah Haydar (accredited 9 Dec. 1982).

Of Great Britain in Syria (Quarter Malki, 11 Mohammed Kurd Ali St., Damascus)
Ambassador: The Hon. Ivor Lucas, CMG.

Of Syria in the USA (2215 Wyoming Ave., NW, Washington, D.C., 20008)
Ambassador: Dr Rafic Jouejati.

Of the USA in Syria (Abu Rumaneh, Al Monsur St., Damascus)
Ambassador: Robert P. Paganelli.

Of Syria to the United Nations
Chargé d'Affaires: Dia-Allah El-Fattal.

Books of Reference

Statistical Information: There is a Central Statistics Bureau affiliated to the Council of Ministers, Damascus. It publishes a monthly summary and an annual Statistical Abstract (in Arabic and English).

Census of Population 1960. 15 vols. Ministry of Planning, Damascus, 1961–65
The Economic Development of Syria. International Bank Report. Baltimore, 1955
Asfour, E. Y., *Syria: Development and Monetary Policy.* Harvard Univ. Press, 1959
Barthélemy, A., *Dictionnaire arabe-français. Dialectes de Syrie.* 4 vols. Paris, 1935–50
Hourani, A. H., *Syria and Lebanon.* 2nd ed. R. Inst. of Int. Affairs, 1954
Petran, T., *Syria.* London, 1972

UNITED REPUBLIC OF TANZANIA

Capital: Dodoma
Population: 18·5m. (1981)
GNP per capita: US$260 (1980)

HISTORY. German East Africa was occupied by German colonialists from 1884 and placed under the protection of the German Empire in 1891. It was conquered in the First World War and subsequently divided between the British and Belgians. The latter received the territories of Ruanda and Urundi and the British the remainder, except for the Kionga triangle, which went to Portugal. The country was administered as a League of Nations mandate until 1946 and then as a UN trusteeship territory until 9 Dec. 1961.

Tanganyika achieved responsible government in Sept. 1960 and full self-government on 1 May 1961. On 9 Dec. 1961 Tanganyika became a sovereign independent member state of the Commonwealth of Nations. It adopted a republican form of government on 9 Dec. 1962. For history from the end of the 17th century until 1884 *see* THE STATESMAN'S YEAR-BOOK 1982–83, p. 1170.

On 24 June 1963 Zanzibar became an internal self-governing state and on 9 Dec. 1963 she became independent. On 24 June 1963 the Legislative Council was replaced by a National Assembly.

On 12 Jan. 1964 the sultanate was overthrown and the sultan sent into exile by a revolt of the Afro-Shirazi Party leaders who established the People's Republic of Zanzibar.

On 26 April 1964 Tanganyika, Zanzibar and Pemba combined to form the United Republic of Tanganyika and Zanzibar (named Tanzania on 29 Oct.).

AREA AND POPULATION. Tanzania is bounded north-east by Kenya, north by Lake Victoria and Uganda, north-west by Rwanda and Burundi, west by Lake Tanganyika, south-west by Zambia and Malawi and south by Mozambique. The census of Aug. 1978 gave 17,551,925 for the United Republic, of which 17,076,270 were counted in mainland Tanzania and 475,655 in Zanzibar. Estimate (1981) 18·5m.

The chief towns (1978 census populations) are Dar es Salaam, the chief port and former capital (851,522), Musoma (219,127), Mwanza (169,660), Dodoma (158,577), Tanga (143,878), Arusha (86,845), Mbeya (78,111), Bukoba (77,022), Morogoro (74,114), Shinyanga (68,746), Wete (58,923), Kigoma (58,788), Sumbawanga (57,802), Singida (55,892), Songea (49,303), Mtwara (48,575), Chake Chake (47,759), and Lindi (27,308). A Ministry of Capital development was established in 1975 to supervise gradual transfer of the government secretariat to Dodoma, to be completed in 1983.

The populations of the 22 regions were as follows at the 1978 Census:

Arusha	928,478	Mara	723,295	Rukwa	451,897
Dar es Salaam	851,522	Mbeya	1,080,241	Ruvuma	564,113
Dodoma	971,921	Morogoro	939,190	Shinyanga	1,323,482
Iringa	922,801	Mtwara	771,726	Singida	614,030
Kagera	1,009,379	Mwanza	1,443,418	Tabora	818,049
Kigoma	648,950	Pemba	205,850	Tanga	1,088,592
Kilimanjaro	902,394	Pwani	516,949	Zanzibar	273,365
Lindi	527,902				

Kiswahili is the national language.

CONSTITUTION AND GOVERNMENT. An 'interim constitution' was approved by parliament on 5 July 1965 and assented to by the President on 8 July 1965. A new permanent Constitution was approved in April 1977.

The country is a one-party state. The Tanganyika African National Union and the Afro-Shirazi Party in Zanzibar merged into one revolutionary party, *Chama cha Mapinduzi*, in Jan. 1977.

The President of the United Republic is head of state, chairman of the party and commander-in-chief of the armed forces. The vice-president is head of the executive in Zanzibar and vice-chairman of the party; the Prime Minister is also the leader of the National Assembly.

The National Assembly is composed of 111 elected members, 32 Parliament Members from the Zanzibar Revolutionary Council, 20 Nominated Members from Zanzibar, 25 National Members representing regions, 15 National Members representing mass organizations affiliated to the party, 10 Nominated Members from the mainland and 25 regional secretaries who are *ex-officio* members.

In Dec. 1979 a separate Constitution for Zanzibar was approved. Although at present (1981) under the same Constitution as Tanzania, Zanzibar has, in fact, been ruled by decree since 1964.

The Government was in Dec. 1982 composed as follows:

President of the United Republic: Dr Julius K. Nyerere (re-elected for a further 5-year term in Oct. 1980).

Vice-President: Aboud Jumbe. *Prime Minister:* Cleopa Msuya.

Foreign Affairs: Salim Ahmed Salim. *Defence and National Service:* Abdallah Twalipo. *Home Affairs:* Brig. Muhiddin Kimaryo. *Finance:* Amir Jamal. *Agriculture:* John B. Machunda. *Justice:* Julie Manning. *Industry:* Basil Mramba. *Land, Housing and Urban Development:* Mustafa Nyang'anyi. *Labour and Social Welfare:* Alfred Tandau. *National Education:* Tabitha Siwale. *Trade:* Lt.-Col. Ali S. Mchumo. *Water and Energy:* Al Noor Kassimu. *Mines:* Jackson Makweta. *Communication and Transport:* John W. Malecela. *Information and Culture:* Daudi Mwakawago. *Animal Husbandry:* Herman Kirigini. *Works:* Samuel Sitta. *Health:* Aaron D. Chiduo. *Natural Resources and Tourism:* Ali H. Mwinyi. *Ministers of State:* George Kahama *(President's Office);* Aboud Aboud, Kighoma Malima *(Vice-President's Office);* Pius Ng'wandu, Paul Kimiti, Getrude Mongella *(Prime Minister's Office). Without Portfolio:* Rashid Kawawa, Abdallah Natepe.

National flag: Divided diagonally green, black, blue, with the black strip edged in yellow.

DEFENCE

Army. The Army consists of 1 tank and 1 engineer regiment, 9 infantry battalions and 9 artillery battalions. Strength, (1983) 38,500.

Air Force. The Tanzanian People's Defence Force Air Wing was built up initially with the help of Canada, but combat equipment is now being acquired from China. Personnel totalled about 1,000 in 1982, with about 11 J-7 (MiG-21), 10 J-6 (MiG-19) and 3 J-5 (MiG-17) jet fighters; 1 F28 Fellowship VIP transport; 4 Buffalo twin-engined STOL transports; 3 HS 748 turboprop transports; 1 An-2 light transport; 2 Cessna 404 liaison aircraft; 2 Agusta-built Chinook helicopters; 6 Agusta-Bell JetRanger and 2 Bell 47G light helicopters; and Piper Cherokee, Cessna 310, L-39 Albatros and MiG-15UTI trainers.

INTERNATIONAL RELATIONS

Membership. Tanzania is a member of UN, OAU, the Commonwealth and is an ACP state of EEC.

ECONOMY

Planning. The third 5-year plan starting 1977 envisaged small but actively growing industrial factories to manufacture small parts with the object of improving foreign exchange earnings.

Budget. Revenue and expenditure (in Tanzanian Sh. 1m.) for financial years ending 30 June:

	1977–78	1978–79	1979–80	1980–81	1981–82	1982–83[1]
Revenue	9,556·2	9,523·0	7,270·0	12,296·1	10,460	10,700
Expenditure	9,556·0	12,267·2	9,100·0	14,802·4	13,687	14,144

[1]Estimate.

Import duties in 1978–79 amounted to Sh. 950m. and income tax to Sh. 1,574m. The main items of expenditure for the year 1969–70 were communications, transport and labour (Sh. 278·5m.), education (Sh. 56·2m.) and agriculture, food and co-operatives (Sh. 109·9m.).

Development expenditure, 1982–83 (estimate), was Sh. 4,816m.

Currency. The monetary unit is the *Tanzanian shilling* divided into 100 *cents*. The Tanzanian coinage has denominations of 5, 10, 20, 50 cents, 1 Sh., 5 Sh., 20 Sh. and 1,500 Sh.; notes, 10 Sh., 20 Sh. and 100 Sh. Notes and coins in circulation at the end of Dec. 1978 were Sh. 3,143m. In 1966 the country left the East African Currency Board, establishing its own national currency, the Tanzanian shilling. In March 1983, £1 = Sh. 14·37; US$ = Sh. 9·70.

Banking. On 14 June 1966 the central bank called the Bank of Tanzania, with a government-owned capital of Sh. 20m., began operations.

On 6 Feb. 1967 all commercial banks with the exception of National Co-operative Banks were nationalized and their interests vested in the National Bank of Commerce on the mainland and the Peoples' Bank in Zanzibar.

Weights. Tanzania has adopted the International System of Weights and Measures (SI), which has been introduced progressively since 1969. An important local unit of weight is the frasla (or frasila) = 35 lb. av.

ENERGY AND NATURAL RESOURCES

Electricity. A hydro-electric station on the Pangani River near Tanga has been built; £3m. of its estimated cost of £5·25m. is being provided by the Commonwealth Development Corporation. The second phase of the Kidatu power-station in Morogoro region is nearing completion; total power generated, 200 mw. Kiwira River power project, estimated to cost Sh.55m., has been completed, total capacity 24 mw. The Musoma power-station has also been completed with a capacity of 6 mw. The Mbeya-Iyunga power-station, capacity 12·5 mw, was completed in 1981.

Minerals. The value of mineral exports in 1976 was Sh. 550m. Principal exports, 1977, were (in Sh. 1m.): Diamonds, 181·3; gold, 50·9; salt, 12; gemstones, 1·8. New discoveries of coal and iron ore were made in the south while copper, cobalt, nickel and tin deposits have been found in Western Tanganyika. Gas, at shallow depths, has been found off the coast.

Agriculture. Production of main agricultural crops in 1981 (in 1,000 tons) was: Maize, 750; sisal, 81; cotton, 167; sugar, 1,287; coffee, 68; wheat, 70; tobacco, 21. Production of sisal has been declining since 1967. The Tanganyika Sisal Corporation has embarked on a diversification programme by introducing various new crops. Crops already planned are cardamon, beans, cashew nuts, citrus, cocoa, coconuts, cotton, maize and timber. Cattle ranching, dairying and twine spinning have also been introduced.

Zanzibar provides the greater part of the world's supply of cloves. There are about 40,000 hectares under cloves with about 1·5m. trees; five-sixths of the clove output is produced on Pemba. Cloves and clove oil (distilled from the stems) form more than half Zanzibar's exports. In recent years cloves production has decreased from an average annual figure of 12,000 tons to 4,000 in 1974 but reached 10,000 tons in 1976.

The coconut industry ranks next in importance. There are about 5·5m. bearing trees in both islands. Chillies, cocoa, limes, other tropical fruits and coil tobacco are also cultivated. The chief food crops are rice, bananas, cassava, pulses, maize and sorghum.

Livestock (1981, including Zanzibar): 12·7m. cattle, 3·8m. sheep, 5·7m. goats, 24m. poultry.

Forestry. Total production (1979) 67,000 cu. metres (coniferous 20,000).

Fisheries. A Fisheries Development Co. is catching sardines and tuna for export. In 1976, 400 tons were exported valued at Sh. 3·5m.

INDUSTRY AND TRADE

Industry. Industry is limited and is mainly textiles, food processing, tobacco and brewing.

Commerce. Total trade (in Sh. 1m.):

	1976	*1977*	*1978*	*1979*	*1980*	*1981*
Imports	5,350	6,200	8,582	8,941	10,047	10,065
Exports	4,108	4,537	3,514	4,296	4,165	5,248

In 1977 imports (in Sh. 1m.) were: UK, 933; Federal Republic of Germany, 700; Japan, 700; USA, 287. Exports: Federal Republic of Germany, 795; UK, 675; USA, 600.

Major export items 1981 (in Sh. 1m.): Coffee, 1,456; cotton, 689; sisal, 291; cloves, 417; tea, 182; tobacco, 165.

Total trade between Tanzania and UK (British Department of Trade returns, in £1,000 sterling):

	1979	*1980*	*1981*	*1982*
Imports to UK	43,655	36,501	25,290	19,521
Exports and re-exports from UK	121,504	110,910	83,643	71,985

Tourism. In 1981 about 91,600 tourists visited Tanzania.

COMMUNICATIONS

Roads. Motor traffic is possible over 25,000 miles of road during dry season and at almost all times over 21,500 miles. In Zanzibar there are 279 miles of tarmac roads and 70 miles of all-weather unsealed roads; in Pemba there are 86 miles of tarmac roads and 184 miles of dry-weather earth roads.

Railways. On 23 Sept. 1977 the independent Tanzanian Railway Corporation was formed following the break-up of the East African Railways administration. The network totals 2,600 km (metre-gauge), excluding the Tan-Zam Railway 969 km in Tanzania (1,067 mm gauge) operated by a separate administration. In 1980, the state railway carried 2.6m. passengers and 1.2m. tonnes of freight.

Aviation. There are 53 aerodromes and landing strips maintained or licensed by Government; of these, 2 are of international standards category and 18 are suitable for Dakotas. Air Tanzania Corporation provide regular and frequent services to all the more important towns within the territory and to Mozambique, Zambia, Seychelles, Comoro, Rwanda, Burundi and Madagascar.

There is an all-weather landing-ground in Zanzibar and a smaller all-weather landing-ground in Pemba.

Shipping. In 1980 there were 1,296 ships of 3,176,000 NRT.

Post and Broadcasting. In 1981 there were 93,238 telephones. There are 2 broadcasting stations and colour television operates in Zanzibar.

Newspapers (1976). There were 2 dailies, 1 Sunday newspaper, 2 fortnightlies and several monthly magazines.

EDUCATION AND WELFARE

Education. The educational system has been integrated on non-racial lines. Schools are maintained by the Government, private and agencies, including missions.

In 1981 there were 9,980 primary schools with 3,538,183 pupils.

Technical and vocational education is provided at several secondary and technical schools and at the Dar es Salaam Technical College.

There were, in 1981, 35 colleges of national education, including the college at Chang'ombe for secondary-school teachers, with 14,785 students and (1980) 170 secondary schools with 9,178 pupils. Five technical secondary schools had 3,129 students in 1981.

In 1981, the Dar es Salaam University had a total of 3,650 students. In the 4 years (1972–76) illiteracy was reduced to about 31%. The University of Dar es Salaam, independent since 1970, has faculties of science, law, arts, social sciences, medicine, agriculture, engineering, commerce and management, veterinary science and forestry.

Health. In 1981 there were 599 doctors and 149 hospitals with 21,352 beds.

DIPLOMATIC REPRESENTATIVES

Of Tanzania in Great Britain (43 Hertford St., London, W1)
High Commissioner: Anthony Balthazar Nyakyi (accredited 15 Dec. 1982).

Of Great Britain in Tanzania (Hifadhi Hse., Samora Ave., Dar es Salaam)
High Commissioner: John Sankey.

Of Tanzania in the USA (2139 R St., NW, Washington, D.C., 20008)
Ambassador: Benjamin Mkapa.

Of the USA in Tanzania (36 Laibon Rd., Dar es Salaam)
Ambassador: David C. Miller, Jr.

Of Tanzania to the United Nations
Ambassador: Paul Rupia.

Books of Reference

Atlas of Tanganyika. 3rd ed. Dar es Salaam, 1956
Tanganyika Notes and Records. Tanganyika Society, Dar es Salaam. (Twice yearly, from 1936) *The Economic Development of Tanganyika. Report . . . by the International Bank.* John Hopkins Univ. Press and OUP, 1961
Ayany, S. G., *A History of Zanzibar.* Nairobi, 1970
Coulson, A., *Tanzania: A Political Economy.* OUP, 1982
Ingle, C. R., *From Village to State in Tanzania.* London, 1973
Lofchie, M. F., *Zanzibar: Background to Revolution.* Princeton Univ. Press, 1965
Mwansasu, B., *Towards Socialism in Tanzania.* Univ. of Toronto Press, 1979
Nellis, J. R., *A Theory of Ideology: The Tanzanian Example.* New York, OUP, 1972
Nyerere, J., *Freedom and Development.* New York, 1976
Samoff, J., *Tanzania: Local Politics and the Structure of Power.* Univ. of Wisconsin Press, 1975
Yu, G. T., *China's African Policy: A Study of Tanzania.* New York, 1975

THAILAND

Capital: Bangkok
Population: 48·4m. (1982)
GNP per capita: US$670 (1980)

Prathes Thai, or Muang-Thai

HISTORY. Until 24 June 1932 Siam was an absolute monarchy. On that date a *coup d'état* was effected and a Provisional Constitution Act was promulgated on 27 June. This was replaced by the constitution of 10 Dec. 1932, which in turn was superseded by new constitutions.

AREA AND POPULATION. The area of Thailand is 514,000 sq. km (198,250 sq. miles) and is bounded west by Burma and the Indian Ocean, east by the Gulf of Thailand, Cambodia and east and north by Laos.

At the census taken in 1979 the registration gave a population of 45,221,625 (22,775,852 males, 22,445,773 females), of whom 30·4% lived in the Central region, 35·2% in the North-East region, 12·5% in the South region, 21·9% in the North region. Estimate (1982) 48,399,993 (24,337,808 females).

Vital statistics, 1979: Birth rate, 25 per 1,000 population; infant mortality, 56; death rate, 5 per thousand live births.

Bangkok Metropolis is the capital (population 1979, 4,870,509). Other towns (1979 estimate) are Chiang Mai (105,230), Nakhon Ratchasima (87,371), Khon Kaen, (80,286), Udon Thani (76,173), Pitsanulok (73,175), Hat Yai (67,117), Songkhla (65,523), Nakhon Si Thammarat (61,049), Nakhon Sawan (55,741).

REIGNING KING. Bhumibol Adulyadej, born 5 Dec. 1927, younger brother of King Ananda Mahidol, who died on 9 June 1946. King Bhumibol married on 28 April 1950 Princess Sirikit, and was crowned 5 May 1950. Children: Princess Ubol Ratana (born 5 April 1951), Crown-Prince Vajiralongkorn (born 28 July 1952, married 3 Jan. 1977 Soamsawali Kitiyakra), Princess Maha Chakri Sirindhorn (born 2 April 1955), Princess Chulabhorn (born 4 July 1957, married 27 Jan. 1982 Virayudth Didyasarin).

CONSTITUTION AND GOVERNMENT. The military government resigned on 14 Oct. 1973 and a new government was formed. New Constitutions were enacted on 7 Oct. 1974 and on 9 Nov. 1977. However on 20 Oct. 1977 a further military *coup* took place in order to return more swiftly to democracy. A new Constitution designed to restore democracy was promulgated in Dec. 1978 and elections took place on 22 April 1979. Elections are due in April 1983.

Prime Minister: Gen. Prem Tinsulanonda.

Agriculture: Chuan Leekpai. *Commerce:* Dr Punnamee Punsri. *Communications:* Adm. Amorn Sirikaya. *Defence:* Gen. Prem Tinsulanonda. *Education:* Dr Kasem Sirisumpundh. *Finance:* Sommai Hoontrakul. *Foreign Minister:* Air Chief Marshall Siddhi Savetsila. *Industry:* Maj.-Gen. Chatchai Choonhavan. *Interior:* Gen. Sitthi Jirarote. *Justice:* Marut Bunnag. *Public Health:* Dr Sem Pringpuangkaew. *Science, Technology, Energy:* Wing Cdr Thinnakorn Bhandhugravi. *State Universities Bureau:* Dr Kasem Suwanagul.

National flag: Five horizontal stripes of red, white, blue, white, red, with the blue of double width.

Local Government. For purposes of administration Thailand is divided into 72 provinces *(changwads)*, each under the control of a *changwad* governor. The *changwads* are subdivided into 576 districts *(amphurs)* and 80 sub-districts *(king amphurs)*, 5,317 communes *(tambons)* and 49,841 villages *(moobans)*. Local legislative and executive bodies with limited powers are being established with functions, procedure and method of election modelled on those of central Assembly.

DEFENCE. Under the Ministry of Defence Organization Act of 1960 the Ministry of Defence has assumed the Supreme Command and the control of the Army, Navy and Air Force with the advice of the Defence Council headed by the Ministry of Defence. The National Defence College, the Armed Forces Staff College and the Military Preparatory School serve the education of officers. Each service has its own C.-in-C., service council, schools of arms and Command and General Staff College.

Under the Military Service Act of 1954 every able-bodied man between the ages of 21 and 30 is liable to serve 2 years with the colours; 7 years in the first reserve; 10 years in the second reserve; 6 years in the third reserve.

Army. The Army is organized in 6 infantry divisions (including 4 tank battalions), 1 cavalry division and 3 independent regimental combat teams with support units. Equipment includes light American armoured vehicles. Peacetime strength is 160,000.

Navy. The Fleet includes 4 frigates (1 modern built in Britain, 2 very old *ex*-US, and 1 very old *ex*-US destroyer escort), 2 corvettes (small frigates), 3 fast large attack gunboats, 4 coastal minesweepers, 6 fast missile craft, 7 patrol vessels, 1 mine counter-measures support ship, 18 gunboats, 23 coastal patrol boats, 8 landing ships, 7 landing craft, 40 minor landing craft, 5 minesweeping boats, 3 surveying ships, 3 surveying boats, 40 river patrol craft, 2 transports, 2 oilers, 3 training ships (old frigate, old corvette, old escort minesweeper), 18 coastguard vessels, 2 water carriers and 5 tugs.

This is an aged fleet, only 1 frigate, 2 corvettes, 6 missile craft and a few coastal patrol craft being under 10 years old. Replacement of most other vessels is overdue.

Naval personnel in 1983 totalled 30,000, including the Marine Corps of 20,000. There is a Royal Naval Academy at Paknam.

At the mouth of the Chao Praya River are the Paknam forts. The naval dockyard was reconstructed.

Air Force. The Royal Thai Air Force was reorganized with the assistance of a US Military Air Advisory Group. It has a strength of about 43,100 personnel, and is made up of a headquarters and Combat, Logistics Support, Training and Special Services Groups. The 3 squadrons of 1st Wing form the primary combat element, equipped with 40 F-5A/E supersonic fighter-bombers, some of the 40 OV-10C Bronco light reconnaissance/attack aircraft, and 24 T-33A/RT-33A and 4 RF-5A armed reconnaissance aircraft acquired from the USA. Six light attack squadrons in 2nd Wing operate the remaining OV-10Cs, about 40 T-28 armed piston-engined trainers, 16 A-37B light jet attack aircraft and 25 AU-23A Peacemakers, for security duties. There are transport units equipped with about 70 C-130H/H-30 Hercules, HS 748, C-123 Provider, C-47 and smaller aircraft, including 20 Australian-built Missionmasters; training units with Airtrainer CT/4 primary trainers built in New Zealand, Italian-built SF.260MTs, T-37 intermediate and T-33A advanced trainers; and large numbers of helicopters for assault and rescue duties. In 1984, delivery will begin of 16 Model 400 and 31 Model 600 Fantrainers, of which the first 6 will be built in Germany, the remainder partially manufactured and assembled in Thailand.

INTERNATIONAL RELATIONS

Planning. The Fifth National Development Plan, 1982–86 envisages a more equal distribution of income between the urban and rural population.

Membership. Thailand is a member of UN, ASEAN and the Colombo Plan.

ECONOMY

Budget. Ordinary expenditures in 1982 (in 1m. baht): Defence, 31,395; agriculture,

13,587; communications, 10,312; education, 32,630; public health, 6,234.

Revenue in 1980 derived from taxes and duties, sales and charges and government enterprises, 114,835m. baht.

In 1980 the national internal debt was 109,780·6m. baht and the external debt totalled 80,508·7m. baht.

Currency. The unit of currency is the *baht*, formerly called in English the *tical*, which is divided into 100 *satang*. Silver coins have gone out of circulation. Only nickel, copper, tin and bronze coins are now minted, in denominations of 1, 5 *baht*, 50, 25, 10 and 5 *satang*. Currency notes, first issued in 1902, now comprise, 5, 10, 20, 100, 500 *baht* notes.

On 31 March 1976 the total amount of notes and coins in circulation was 30,280m. baht.

In March 1983, £1 = 33·70 *baht*; US$1 = 23 *baht*.

Banking. In 1942 the Bank of Thailand was established under the Bank of Thailand Act, B.E. 2485 (1942) and began operations on 10 Dec. 1942, with the functions of a central bank. The Bank was organized on similar lines to the Bank of England, having its banking activities entirely separate from the management of the note issue. The Bank also took over the note issue previously performed by the Treasury Department of the Ministry of Finance. Although the entire capital is owned by the Government, the Bank is an independent body. Its gold and foreign-exchange reserves, at the end of Dec. 1973, amounted to US$1,082m.

In Jan. 1966 the Agricultural Bank and the Provincial Bank merged in the Krung Thai Bank (capital 105m. baht, of which 80% is owned by the Government).

Banks incorporated under Thai law include the Bangkok Bank Ltd, the Bangkok Bank of Commerce Ltd, the Bank of Asia for Industry & Commerce Ltd, the Bank of Ayudhya Ltd, Bangkok Metropolitan Bank Ltd, the Laem Thong Bank Ltd, the Siam City Bank Ltd, the Siam Commercial Bank Ltd, First Bangkok City Bank Ltd, Union Bank of Bangkok Ltd and the Wang Lee Chan Bank Ltd. Foreign banks include the Chartered Bank, the Hongkong and Shanghai Banking Corporation, the Mercantile Bank Ltd, Banque de l'Indochine, Bank of Canton Ltd, Bank of China Ltd, Bank of America, N.T. & S.A., the Mitsui Bank Ltd, The Asia Trust Bank Ltd, Bharat Overseas Bank Ltd, The Chase Manhattan Bank, United Malayan Banking Corporation and the Bank of Tokyo Ltd.

The commercial Thai banks had, in 1981, 1,484 branches in Thailand and 12 abroad; only Mae Hongson province has no commercial bank services. The deposits held by commercial banks in June 1981 amounted to 334,884m. baht.

The Government Savings Bank, which was established as an independent organization in 1947, originated in 1913 when the Government Savings Office was established.

Weights and Measures. The metric system was made compulsory by a law promulgated on 17 Dec. 1923. The actual weights and measures prescribed by law are: Units of weight: 1 *standard picul* = 60 kg; 1 *standard catty* (1/100 picul) = 600 grammes; 1 *standard carat* = 20 centigrammes. Units of length: 1 *sen* = 40 metres; 1 *wah* (1/20 sen) = 2 metres; 1 *sauk* (½ wah) = 0·50 metre; 1 *keup* (½ sauk) = 0·25 metre. Units of square measure: 1 *rai* (1 sq. sen) = 1,600 sq. metres: 1 *ngan* (¼ rai) = 400 sq. metres; 1 *sq. wah* (1/100 ngan) = 4 sq. metres. Units of capacity: 1 *standard kwien* = 2,000 litres; 1 *standard ban* (½ kwien) = 1,000 litres; 1 *standard sat* (1/50 ban) = 20 litres; 1 *standard tannan* (1/20 sat) = 1 litre.

Legislation passed in 1940 provided that the calendar year shall coincide with the Christian Year, and that the year of the Buddhist era 2484 shall begin on 1 Jan. 1941. (The New Year's Day was previously 1 April.) The years B.E. 2514–2518 therefore correspond to A.D. 1974 and 1975.

ENERGY AND NATURAL RESOURCES

Electricity. In 1981, steam power accounted for 52% of production (81% of the fuel being imported) and 34% hydro-electric. Only 20% of the population had access to electricity on 31 Dec. 1976.

Oil. Extensive oil and gas exploration in the Gulf of Thailand were producing commercial quantities in Sept. 1981.

Minerals. The mineral resources are extensive and varied, including cassiterite (tin ore), wolfram, scheelite, antimony, coal, copper, gold, iron, lead, manganese, molybdenum, rubies, sapphires, silver, zinc and zircons. By far the most important are tin and wolfram. Ore output in 1978 (in tonnes): Iron, 88,121; manganese, 72,211; tin (1980), 46,526; lead, 39,121; antimony, 6,759; wolfram, 5,815; lignite, 638,942; gypsum, 280,905.

Agriculture. The chief produce of the country is rice, which forms the national food and the staple article of export. The area under paddy is about 18m. acres. With the completion of the Chao Phya dam located near Chainat in 1957 the irrigable area in the Central Plain had by 1962 been extended to about 8,409,000 rai (3,363,600 acres). Additional projects now under construction will bring the irrigable lands to the total of about 11,605,900 rai (4,642,360 acres). Tank irrigation projects which were designed to ensure water supply for upland crop cultivation, especially in the north-eastern part, irrigate 325,418 rai (130,167 acres).

Output of the major crops in 1981 was (in tonnes): Paddy, 19m.; cassava, 17·9m.; maize, 3·7m.; sugar-cane, 18·6m.; kenaf, 260,000 (1980); tobacco, 87,000; tapioca-root, 7·2m. (1980); soybeans, 120,000.

Livestock, 1981 (in 1,000): Elephants (1967), 11,500; horses, 167; buffaloes, 6,299; cattle, 5,062; pigs, 5,386; poultry, 71,015.

Forestry. About 60% of the land area of Thailand is under forest. In the north, mixed deciduous forests with teak *(Tectona grandis, Linn.)*, growing in mixture with several other species, predominate. In the north-eastern section hardwood of the *Dipterocarpus* species, especially *Shorea obtusa* and *Pentacme Siamensis, Kurz* exist in most parts. In all other regions of the country tropical evergreen forests are found, with the well-known timber of commerce, Yang (*Dipterocarpus alatus, Roxb* and *Dipterocarpus* spp.) as the outstanding crops. Most of the teak timber exploited in northern Thailand is floated down to Bangkok. Some of them, however, are exported through the Salween into Burma.

About one-third of the teak-forest area is being exploited by the Forest Industry Organization, and the remaining two-thirds is to be worked by timber company lessees and other private enterprises.

Output of main forestry products in 1978 was (in 1,000 cu. metres): Teak, 112; yang, 476; other woods, 2,019; firewood, 855; charcoal, 284.

Rubber production (in 1,000 tonnes), 1955, 133·3; 1960, 170·8; 1968, 259; 1969, 281·8; 1973, 384; 1976, 393; 1977, 440; 1978, 470.

Fisheries. In 1976 the catch of sea fish was 1·5m. tonnes; of freshwater fish, 147,294 tonnes, and of marine prawns, shrimps and crabs, 160,000 tonnes.

INDUSTRY AND TRADE

Industry. Production of manufactured goods in 1978 included 5,004,490 tonnes of cement, 46,818 tonnes of white cement, 1,584,453 tonnes of sugar, 149·8m. gunny bags, 39,721 tonnes of paper, 23,905 tonnes of cigarettes, 95,363 tonnes of sweetened condensed milk, 15,830 tonnes of evaporated milk, 108·3m. litres of beer, 875m. sq. yd of cotton textiles, 887·2m. sq. yd of man-made textiles, 4,673,432 sheets of plywood and 1,166,614 sq. metres of vinyl tiles.

Trade Unions. The Thai National Trade Union Congress is a member of the International Confederation of Free Trade Unions.

Commerce. The foreign trade (in 1m. baht) was as follows:

	1975	*1976*	*1977*	*1978*	*1979*	*1980*
Imports (c.i.f.)	66,835	72,877	96,062	108,899	146,161	188,238
Exports (f.o.b.)	45,007	60,797	70,463	83,065	108,179	133,252

In 1980 the main imports (in 1m. baht): Fuels and lubricants, 58,667; machinery, 43,113; manufactured goods, 28,505; chemicals, 22,385.

In 1980 the main items of export (in 1m. baht): Rice, 19,505; tapioca products, 14,838; rubber, 12,400; tin, 11,347; maize, 7,296; sugar, 2,975; prawns, 1,959; tobacco leaves, 1,376; kenaf and jute, 155; teak and woods, 3.

Total trade between Thailand and UK (British Department of Trade returns, in £1,000 sterling):

	1978	*1979*	*1980*	*1981*	*1982*
Imports to UK	37,289	52,188	52,004	56,343	76,529
Exports and re-exports from UK	86,428	94,115	96,926	91,473	104,825

Tourism. In 1980 about 1,858,801 foreigners visited Thailand, including 509,882 neighbouring visitors and 1,348,919 overseas visitors.

COMMUNICATIONS

Roads. In 1981 the length of highways and provincial roads open to traffic was 43,840 km, of which about 13,226 km (1978) were concrete or asphalt-surfaced. Motor vehicles registered in 1975 included 248,561 passenger cars, 22,079 buses, 178,425 lorries and 456,651 motor cycles.

Railways. In 1981 there were 3,800 km of state railways (metre gauge) open to traffic.

The northern line runs from Bangkok to Chiang Mai (741 km), the extreme northern terminus. The southern line (990 km) runs from Bangkok down the Peninsula to the frontier station of Padang Besar, where it connects with the Malayan railway from Penang, and to Singapore. Another line (214 km) branching off from Haad Yai on the southern line runs along the east coast of the peninsula to Su-gnai Kolok, where it connects with the Malayan railway line. There are branch lines (totalling 190 km) to Song Khla, Nakhon-Si Thammarat, Kan Tang and Tha-Kanon. The extensions of the north-eastern line (264 km) from Nakhon Ratsima (Korat) to Nong Khai (360 km) and from Kaeng Koi to Buayai (250 km) have been completed. The Nakhon Ratsima–Ubol line (311 km) has been completed as far as Ubol Rat Thani. The eastern line (255 km) runs from Makkasan to Aran Pradet on the Kampuchea frontier. The northern and southern railway systems are linked by a railway bridge over the Menam Chao Phya, and both systems terminate in Bangkok. All state railways are under one management and in 1981 carried 78·8m. passengers and 6m. tons of freight.

Aviation. Thai Airways Co. Ltd (TAC), established in 1947, is the sole Thai air transport enterprise, with authorized capital of 300m. baht. The Company operates 11 domestic routes and 3 international routes. On 24 Aug. 1959 Thai Airways and the Scandinavian Airlines System set up a new company, Thai International Airways, to operate the international air services from Thailand. In 1981–82, more than 2m. passengers were carried.

Shipping. In 1978, 2,736 vessels of 11,731,083 NRT entered and 2,521 of 9,888,190 NRT cleared the port of Bangkok.

The port of Bangkok, about 30 km from the mouth of the Chao Phya River, is capable of berthing ocean-going vessels of 10,000 gross tons and 28 ft draught. Bangkok is now a port of entry for Laos, and goods arriving in transit are sent up by rail to Nong Khai and ferried across the river Mekhong to Vientiane.

Post and Broadcasting. In 1974 there were 555 post offices proper, 341 licensed and Amphur post offices and 545 railway-station post offices. In 1967, the length of telegraph lines was 21,203 km. In 1981 there were 496,558 telephones, of which 368,128 were in Bangkok.

In 1981, there were 265 radio stations and 9 television stations.

Cinemas (1978). There were 366 cinemas with a seating capacity of 263,738.

Newspapers (1979). There are 20 daily newspapers in Bangkok, including 3 in English and 7 in Chinese, with a combined circulation of more than 800,000.

JUSTICE, RELIGION, EDUCATION AND WELFARE

Justice. The judicial power is exercised in the name of the King, by *(a)* courts of first instance, *(b)* the court of appeal *(Uthorn)* and *(c)* the Supreme Court *(Dika)*. The King appoints, transfers and dismisses judges, who are independent in conducting trials and giving judgment in accordance with the law.

Courts of first instance are subdivided into 20 magistrates' courts *(Kwaeng)* with limited civil and minor criminal jurisdiction; 85 provincial courts *(Changwad)* with unlimited civil and criminal jurisdiction; the criminal and civil courts with exclusive jurisdiction in Bangkok; the central juvenile courts for persons under 18 years of age in Bangkok.

The court of appeal exercises appellate jurisdiction in civil and criminal cases from all courts of first instance. From it appeals lie to Dika Court on any point of law and, in certain cases, on questions of fact.

The Supreme Court is the supreme tribunal of the land. Besides its normal appellate jurisdiction in civil and criminal matters, it has semi-original jurisdiction over general election petitions. The decisions of Dika Court are final. Every person has the right to present a petition to the Government who will deal with all matters of grievance.

Religion. About 95% of the population are Buddhists, 4% Moslems, 1% Christians, Hindus and others.

Education. Primary education is compulsory for children between the ages of 7–14 and free in local municipal schools. In 1978 there were 7,612,534 students enrolled in 31,966 government schools and 1,119,528 in 2,327 private schools. In 1977 there were 45 teachers' training schools with 4,986 teachers and 115,117 students and 180 government vocational schools with 8,100 teachers and 147,997 students. In 1978 there were 12 universities: Chulalongkorn University (1917), Thammasat University (1934), Universities of Medical Science, Agriculture and Fine Arts; Ramkamhaeng University (1971)—all in Bangkok; Chiengmai University (1964), the Khon Kaen University (1966) in the north-east and Prince of Songkhla University (1968) in the south.

Health. In 1977 there were 1,149 hospitals and health centres throughout the country. In 1977 there were 5,789 physicians, 816 dentists and 2,236 pharmacists.

DIPLOMATIC REPRESENTATIVES

Of Thailand in Great Britain (30 Queen's Gate, London, SW7 5JB)
Ambassador: Phan Wannamethee (accredited 19 Dec. 1977).

Of Great Britain in Thailand (Wireless Rd., Bangkok)
Ambassador: Justin Staples, CMG.

Of Thailand in the USA (2300 Kalorama Rd., NW., Washington, D.C., 20008)
Ambassador: M. R. Kasem S. Kasemsri.

Of the USA in Thailand (95 Wireless Rd., Bangkok)
Ambassador: John Gunther Dean.

Of Thailand to the United Nations
Ambassador: M. L. Birabhongse Kasemsri.

Books of Reference

Thailand into the 80's. Office of the Prime Minister, Bangkok, 1979
Thailand Statistical Yearbook 1978. National Statistical Office, Bangkok
Thailand 1982: Plans, Problems and Prospects. Government's Public Relations Department, Bangkok, 1982
Thailand in Brief. Government's Public Relations Department, Bangkok, 1977
Thailand Official Yearbook 1968. Government Printer, Bangkok
Bibliography of Materials About Thailand in Western Languages. Chulalongkorn University, Bangkok, 1960
Douner, W., *The Five Faces of Thailand.* Hamburg and London, 1978
Exell, F. K., *The Land and People of Thailand.* London, 1960
Haas, M. R., *Thai–English Student's Dictionary.* OUP, 1966
Kirkup, J., *Bangkok.* London, 1968
Morrell, D. and Samudavanija, C., *Political Conflict in Thailand.* Cambridge, Mass., 1981

TOGO

Capital: Lomé
Population: 2·85m. (1982)
GNP per capita: US$410 (1980)

République Togolaise

HISTORY. The Republic of Togo became independent on 27 April 1960, after having been a German protectorate (1894–1914, subsequently divided between the French and the British), a mandate of the League of Nations (20 July 1922) and a trusteeship territory of the United Nations (14 Dec. 1946).

On 28 Oct. 1956 a plebiscite was held to determine the status of the territory. Out of 438,175 registered voters, 313,458 voted for an autonomous republic within the French Union and the end of the trusteeship system. The trusteeship was abolished on the achievement of independence on 27 April 1960.

On 13 Jan. 1963 the President Sylvanus Olympio was murdered by n.c.o.s. of the army. Nicolas Grunitzky, a former prime minister and Olympio's brother-in-law, was appointed President of the Republic and head of government. On 13 Jan. 1967 in a bloodless *coup* the army under Col. Etienne Eyadéma made President Grunitzky 'voluntarily withdraw'. On 14 April 1967 Col. Eyadéma assumed the offices of President and Defence. There was a return to constitutional government in Jan. 1980.

AREA AND POPULATION. Togo is bounded west by Ghana, north by Upper Volta, east by Benin and south by the Bight of Benin. Area, about 56,785 sq. km. The population of Togo in 1970 (census) was 1,953,778; 1982 (estimate) 2·85m. The capital is Lomé (population, 1979, 247,000), other towns (1977, population) being Sokodé (33,500), Kpalimé (25,500), Atakpamé (21,800), Bassar (17,500), Tsévié (15,900) and Anécho (13,300).

The southern part of Togo is peopled by tribes using several different languages, of which the principal, Ewe and Mina, are languages of the Kwa group. The northern half contains, ethnologically, a totally different population descended largely from Hamitic tribes and speaking a fairly large number of different languages of the Voltaic (Gur) group, of which Dagomba, Tem and Kabre are the most important. French is the official language.

CONSTITUTION AND GOVERNMENT. Following approval in a referendum on 30 Dec. 1979, a new Constitution came into force on 13 Jan. 1980, when the Third Togolese Republic was proclaimed. It provides for an Executive President, directly elected for a 7-year term, and for a National Assembly of 67 deputies, elected on a regional list system for a 5-year term. Elections were held on 30 Dec. 1979.

All candidates are nominated by the *Rassemblement du peuple togolais*, the sole legal Party since 1969; it is administered by a 33-member Central Committee and a 9-member Political Bureau appointed by the President.

The government in Oct. 1982 was composed as follows:

President, Minister of Defence: Gen. Gnassingbe Eyadéma.

Foreign Affairs and Co-operation: Dr Anani Kuma Akakpo-Ahianyo. *Planning and Administrative Reform:* Koffi Walla. *Interior:* Kpotivi Têvi′ Djidjogbe Lacle. *Economy and Finance:* Têtê Têvi Bénissan. *Public Works, Mines, Energy and Water Resources:* Barry Moussa Barque. *Health and Social Affairs:* Hodabalo Bodjona. *Rural Development:* Anani Gassou. *Labour and Civil Service:* Nyandi Seibou Napo. *Parliamentary Affairs:* Mme. Massa Dagadzi. *Rural Supplies:* Samon Korto. *Information, Posts and Telecommunications:* Gbegnon Amegboh. *Youth, Sports and Culture:* Koffi Sama. *First and Second Cycle Education:* Komlan Agbetiafa. *Third and Fourth Cycle Education:* Ayssa Agbetra. *Justice:* Ayite Mawuko Ajavon. *Commerce and Transport:* Poli Djalla. *Secretaries of State:*

Mme. Sophie Meatchi *(Health and Women's Affairs),* Yao Agbo *(Industry and State Enterprises).*

National flag: Five horizontal stripes of green and yellow, a red quarter with a white star.

Local Government: There are 5 regions (Maritime, Des Plateaux, Du Centre, De La Kara and Des Savanes), each under an inspector appointed by the President; they are divided into 21 *prefectures,* each administered by a district chief assisted by an elected district council.

DEFENCE

Army. The Army consists of 3 infantry, 2 parachute and 1 commando battalion of 3,400 men. There is also a para-military force of about 1,500.

Navy. In 1983 there were 2 British-built coastal patrol craft, 2 defence launches and a naval base at Lomé. Naval personnel exceeded 100 officers and men.

Air Force. An Air Force, established with French assistance, has 6 Brazilian-built EMB-326 Xavante (Aermacchi MB.326) armed jet trainers; 5 Alpha Jet advanced trainers, with strike capability, 1 four-turboprop Hercules, 1 twin-turbofan F28 Fellowship, 2 turboprop Buffalo and 2 C-47 transports; 2 Broussard communications aircraft; 5 Magister jet trainers; 1 Puma and 1 Lama helicopter.

INTERNATIONAL RELATIONS

Membership. Togo is a member of UN, OAU and is an ACP state of EEC.

ECONOMY

Planning. The fourth 5-year development plan (1981–85) provides for investment of 368,490m. francs CFA, of which 116,397m. are for rural development, 98,625m. for industrial development and 100,690m. for infrastructure.

Budget. The ordinary budget for 1982 balanced at 72,300m. francs CFA.

Currency. The unit of currency is the *franc* CFA with a parity rate of 50 *francs* CFA to 1 French *franc.* The rate of exchange (March 1983) was 532·3 francs CFA to £1; US$1 = 383.1.

Banking. The bank of issue is the *Banque Centrale des Etats de l'Afrique de l'Ouest.* Seven commercial and 3 development banks are based in Lomé.

ENERGY AND NATURAL RESOURCES

Electricity. Production (1980) 75m. kwh.

Minerals. A Mines Department was set up in 1953 after the discovery of very rich deposits of phosphate and bauxite; mining began in 1961. Output of phosphate rock (1980) 2,895,000 tonnes. Other mineral deposits are limestone, estimated at 200m. tons; iron ore, estimated at 550m. tons with iron content varying between 40% and 55%, and marble estimated at 20m. tonnes.

Agriculture. Inland the country is hilly, rising to 3,600 ft, with streams and waterfalls. There are long stretches of forest and brushwood, while dry plains alternate with arable land. Maize, yams, cassava, plantains, groundnuts, etc., are cultivated; oil palms and dye-woods grow in the forests; but the main commerce is based on coffee, cocoa, palm-oil, palm-kernels, copra, groundnuts, cotton, manioc. There are considerable plantations of oil and cocoa palms, coffee, cacao, kola, cassava and cotton. Production, 1981 (in 1,000 tonnes): Cassava, 470; maize, 137; millet, 107.

Livestock (1981): Cattle, 240,000; sheep, 820,000; swine, 348,000; horses, 3,000; asses, 1,000; goats, 750,000.

INDUSTRY AND TRADE

Industry. There is a cement works (production, 1978; 327,000 tonnes); a second is being built in co-operation with Ghana and Ivory Coast with a capacity of 1·2m. tonnes per annum. An oil refinery of 1m. tonne capacity opened in Lomé in 1978 and a steel mill (20,000 tonne capacity) in 1979. Industry, though small, is developing and there are about 40 medium sized enterprises in the public and private sectors, including textile and food processing plants.

Trade (in 1m. francs CFA):

	1976	*1977*	*1978*	*1979*	*1980*
Imports	44,420	69,834	85,887	110,208	116,357
Exports	24,914	39,115	53,035	46,432	71,285

In 1978, of the exports, phosphates amounted to 39%, cocoa beans 29% and coffee 9% by value; 31% of exports went to the Netherlands and 14% to France. Of the imports, France supplied 34%, Switzerland 10% and the UK 10%.

Total trade between Togo and UK (British Department of Trade returns, in £1,000 sterling):

	1978	*1979*	*1980*	*1981*	*1982*
Imports to UK	5,175	3,991	7,395	4,981	1,827
Exports and re-exports from UK	18,156	18,773	28,967	21,423	21,881

Tourism. There were 59,615 tourists in 1977.

COMMUNICATIONS

Roads. There were, in 1980, 7,450 km of roads, of which 2,513 km were paved. In Dec. 1978 there were 21,733 passenger cars and 11,818 commercial vehicles.

Railways. There are 4 metre-gauge railways connecting Lomé with Anécho (continuing to Cotonou in Benin), Kpalimé, Tabligbo and (*via* Atakpamé) Blitta; total length 565 km.

Aviation: Air services connect Lomé with Paris, Dakar, Abidjan, Douala, Accra, Lagos, Cotonou and Niamey and by internal services with Sokodé, Mango and Dapaong.

Shipping. In 1978, 808 vessels landed 1,119,000 tonnes and cleared 326,000 tonnes at Lomé. The merchant marine comprises 7 vessels of 25,714 gross tons. In addition 2·9m. tonnes of phosphate were loaded at the port of Kpémé.

Post and Broadcasting. There were (1972) 39 post offices and 16 postal agencies and (1981), 7,870 telephones. Togo is connected by telegraph and telephone with Ghana, Benin, Abidjan and Dakar, and by wireless telegraphy with Europe and America. There were 5,000 television receivers and 125,000 radio receivers in 1981.

Newspapers. There is 1 daily newspaper (circulation 10,000).

JUSTICE, RELIGION, EDUCATION AND WELFARE

Justice. The Supreme Court and two Appeal Courts are in Lomé, one for criminal cases and one for civil and commercial cases. Each receives appeal from a series of local tribunals.

Religion. In 1975, 18% of the population were Catholics, 10% Moslem and 5% Protestant; two-thirds of the population follow animist religions.

Education. In 1978 there were 421,436 pupils and 7,251 teachers in primary schools, 88,409 pupils and 2,030 teachers in secondary schools, 6,618 students and 326 teachers in technical schools and 388 students and 21 teachers at the teacher-training college. The University of Benin at Lomé (founded in 1970) had 3,700 students in 1980.

Health. In 1977 there were 61 hospitals with 3,438 beds; there were also 128 doctors, 5 dentists, 26 pharmacists, 554 midwives and 880 nursing staff.

DIPLOMATIC REPRESENTATIVES

Of Togo in Great Britain (116 Knightsbridge, London SW1)
Chargé d'Affaires: Abou Yacoubai.

Of Great Britain in Togo
Ambassador: James Mellon, CMG (resides in Accra).

Of Togo in the USA (2208 Massachusetts Ave., NW, Washington, D.C., 20008)
Ambassador: Yao Grunitzky.

Of the USA in Togo (Rue Pelletier Caventou, Lomé)
Ambassador: Howard K. Walker.

Of Togo to the United Nations
Ambassador: Biyemi Kekch.

Books of Reference

Cornevin, R., *Histoire du Togo.* 3rd ed., Paris, 1969
Feuillet, C., *Le Togo en general.* Paris, 1976
Piraux, M., *Le Togo aujourd'hui.* Paris, 1977

TONGA

Capital: Nuku'alofa
Population: 100,143 (1982)
GNP per capita: US$520 (1980)

Friendly Islands

HISTORY. The Kingdom of Tonga attained unity under Taufa'ahau Tupou (George I) who became ruler of his native Ha'apai in 1820, of Vava'u in 1833 and of Tongatapu in 1845. By 1860 the kingdom had become converted to Christianity (George himself having been baptized in 1831). In 1862 the king granted freedom to the people from arbitrary rule of minor chiefs and gave them the right to the allocation of land for their own needs. These institutional changes, together with the establishment of a parliament of chiefs, paved the way towards the democratic constitution under which the kingdom is now governed, and provided a background of stability against which Tonga was able to develop her agricultural economy.

The kingdom continued up to 1899 to be a neutral region in accordance with the Declaration of Berlin, 6 April 1886. By the Anglo-German Agreement of 14 Nov. 1899 subsequently accepted by the USA, the Tonga Islands were left under the Protectorate of Great Britain.

A protectorate was proclaimed on 18 May 1900, and a British Agent and Consul appointed.

AREA AND POPULATION. The kingdom consists of some 169 islands and islets with a total area of 289 sq. miles (748 sq. km; including inland waters), and lies between 15° and 23° 30′ S. lat and 173° and 177° W. long., its western boundary being the eastern boundary of Fiji. The islands are split up into the following groups reading from north to south: The Niuas, Vava'u, Ha'apai, Kotu, Nomuka, Otu Tolu and Tongatapu. The 3 main groups, both from historical and administrative significance, are Tongatapu in the south, Ha'apai in the centre and Vava'u in the north. The Tongatapu group was discovered by Tasman in 1643.

The capital is Nuku'alofa on Tongatapu (18,312).

The islands to the east, being mostly of limestone formation, are low lying and with but a few exceptions seldom exceed 100 ft above sea-level. The islands to the west are of a volcanic nature, approximately 11, average between 350 and 3,433 ft in height. After a violent volcanic eruption in Sept. 1946 on the island of Niuafo'ou (Tin Can Island to philatelists, so named because of the method that was used of collecting and delivering mail) the 1,300 inhabitants were evacuated, most of them to Tongatapu and 'Eua, but more than 600 have returned since 1958. It was thought that a new island had been born when an eruption took place on the Metis Shoal on 12 Dec. 1967; during the volcanic activity a small rocky mass reached a maximum elevation of about 50 ft, but by Feb. 1968 the area was once more awash.

The climate is mild and healthy, malaria being unknown. The temperature from May to Nov. rarely exceeds 84° F. in the shade, with a minimum temperature of 52°F. Census population (1976) 90,128 (males, 46,029); estimate, 1982, 100,143.

CONSTITUTION AND GOVERNMENT. Relations between the UK and Tonga have been governed by the 1900 Treaty of Friendship and Protection and several subsequent revisions. For earlier history of this relationship *see* THE STATESMAN'S YEAR-BOOK, 1970–71. By exchange of letters on 19 May 1970 it was agreed that the UK Government should, as from 4 June 1970, cease to have any responsibility for the external relations of the Kingdom of Tonga.

King: HM King Taufa'ahau Tupou IV, GCVO, GCMG, KBE, born 4 July 1918, succeeded on 16 Dec. 1965 on the death of his mother, Queen Salote Tupou III; his coronation took place on 4 July 1967.

Prime Minister: HRH Prince Tu'ipelehake, KCMG, KBE, younger brother of the King.

National flag: Red with a white quarter bearing a red couped cross.

The present Constitution is almost identical with that granted in 1875 by King George Tupou I. There is a Privy Council, Cabinet, Legislative Assembly and Judiciary. The legislative assembly, which meets annually, is composed of 7 nobles elected by their peers, 7 elected representatives of the people and the Privy Councillors (numbering 8); the King appoints one of the 7 nobles to be the Speaker. The elections are held triennially. In 1960, women voted for the first time.

INTERNATIONAL RELATIONS

Membership. Tonga is a member of the Commonwealth and is an ACP state of EEC.

ECONOMY

Planning. The Third Plan 1975–80 was the kingdom's first attempt at formal, comprehensive indicative planning covering both the public and private sectors. Estimated expenditure for the public sector during the plan period amounted to T$31m. A Fourth Plan, 1980–85, is being implemented.

Budget. Revenue and expenditure in T$1,000:

	1977–78	*1978–79*	*1979–80*	*1980–81*[1]	*1981–82*[1]
Revenue	8,628	8,722	10,596	12,147	14,744
Expenditure	8,515	8,932	10,538	11,899	14,736

[1] Estimate.

The principal sources of revenue are import dues, income tax, port and service tax, wharfage, philatelic revenue and telephone rentals.

The public debt at 30 June 1980 was T$16,428,909.

Currency. There is a government note issue of *pa'anga* (T$)10, 5, 2, 1 and ½ and coin issue of T$2, T$1 and *seniti* 50, 20, 10, 5, 2 and 1. In Sept. 1974, following devaluation by Australia, the Australian dollar equalled 88 *seniti.* In April 1963 gold coins were issued in denominations of 1, ½ and ¼ *koula* (1 *koula* = T$20) and in July 1967, Coronation Palladium coins of 1, ½ and ¼ *hau* (1 *hau* = T$100). In Nov. 1975, gold coins (T$100, 75, 50 and 25) and silver coins (T$20, 10 and 5) were issued to commemorate the centenary of the Constitution. In July 1978, 2 silver coins (T$2 and T$1) were issued to commemorate the sixtieth birthday of the King. In March 1983, £1 = 1·70 *pa'anga*; US$1 = 1·15 *pa'anga.*

AGRICULTURE. Tongan produce (exports 1977) consists of copra (T$3,931,390); packaged desiccated coconut (T$866,942); bananas (T$401,519); swamp taros (T$246,485).

Livestock (1981): Cattle, 10,000; horses, 15,000; pigs, 78,000; goats, 18,000; poultry, 170,000.

COMMERCE. Imports in 1981 were valued at T$19,828,703; exports (1971), T$2·2m. In 1981, the main imports were: Petrol, etc (T$5,525,903); meat, (T$1,670,152); vehicles (T$1,625,822); flour (T$1,399,224); canned meat (T$1,386,468) and timber (T$1,273,866). Of exports (in T$) in 1981, New Zealand took 1,795,206; Australia, 1,471,793; Sweden, 882,349; Singapore, 773,655; UK, 725,767; Fiji, 457,054. Of 1981 imports, Australia furnished 14,337,242; New Zealand, 12,496,094; Japan, 1,884,018; Fiji, 1,673,684; USA, 1,622,703; UK, 705,479; Hong Kong, 479,491; China, 426,404; Singapore, 319,363.

Total trade between Tonga and UK (British Department of Trade returns, in £1,000 sterling):

	1979	*1980*	*1981*	*1982*
Imports to UK	145	9	56	38
Exports and re-exports from UK	710	821	286	764

COMMUNICATIONS

Roads. In 1980 there were 2,849 registered motor vehicles.

Aviation. International air service connexions to Tongatapu are now provided by Air Pacific and Polynesian Airlines with 5 flights per week to Auckland, 3 to Fiji, 5 to Western Samoa and 2 to Niue. South Pacific Island Airways provide a service 3 times per week from Pago Pago, American Samoa, TonVava'u in the Northern Group and through to Tongatapu. Internal air service flights are operated daily, except Sundays to 'Eua, Ha'apai and Vava'u island groups.

Shipping. The Union Steamship Co. of New Zealand maintains a fortnightly service New Zealand–Fiji–Samoa–Tonga, and cargo steamers visit the group from time to time for shipments of copra. Shipping cleared at all ports in 1977, 102 cargo vessels, 30 cruise vessels, 3 gas vessels and 12 tankers.

Cruise ships from the following lines call at Vava'u and Nuku'alofa: P & O, Chandris, Sitmar, Royal Viking, Shaw Savill, Pacific Far East Line. The Pacific Navigation Co. Ltd maintains a regular inter-island shipping service between 'Eua, Ha'apai and Vava'u.

Post. The kingdom has its own issue of postage stamps. Telephones numbered 2,196 in 1981.

JUSTICE, RELIGION AND EDUCATION

Justice. Now that British extra-territorial jurisdiction has lapsed British and foreign nationals charged with an offence against the laws of Tonga (the enforcement of which is a responsibility of the Minister of Police) are fully subject to the jurisdiction of the Tongan courts to which they are already subject in all civil matters.

Religion. The Tongans are Christian, the vast majority being adherents of the Wesleyan Church.

Education. The Tongans enjoy free education, free medical attendance and dental treatment. In 1980 there were 97 government and 13 denominational primary schools, with a total of 19,012 pupils. There were 7 government and 65 mission schools and 1 private school at which post-primary education was provided for both boys and girls, with a total roll of 14,881. There was one government teacher-training college with 123 students; 4 government technical and vocational schools with 266 pupils and 6 denominational technical and vocational schools with 367 students. 175 students were undergoing training overseas.

DIPLOMATIC REPRESENTATIVES

Of Tonga in Great Britain (New Zealand Hse., Haymarket, London, SW1Y 4TE)
High Commissioner: Sonatane Tuá Taumoepeau-Tupou (accredited 18 Feb. 1983).

Of Great Britain in Tonga (Nuku'alofa)
High Commissioner: B. Coleman.

Of the USA in Tonga
Ambassador: F. Eckert, Jr (resides in Suva).

Books of Reference

Bain, K. R., *Royal Visit to Tonga: Tonga Government Official Record.* London, 1954.–*The Friendly Islanders.* London, 1967
Churchward, C. M., *Tongan Dictionary.* London, 1959
Luke, Sir Harry, *Queen Salote and Her Kingdom.* London, 1954
Wood, A. H., *A History and Geography of Tonga.* Rev. ed. Nuku'alofa, 1963

TRINIDAD AND TOBAGO

Capital: Port-of-Spain
Population: 1·2m. (1980)
GNP per capita: US$4,370 (1980)

HISTORY. Trinidad was discovered by Columbus in 1498 and colonized by the Spaniards in the 16th century. During the French Revolution a large number of French families settled in the island. In 1797, Great Britain being at war with Spain, Trinidad was occupied by the British and ceded to Great Britain by the Treaty of Amiens in 1802. Trinidad and Tobago were joined in 1889.

Under the Bases Agreement concluded between the governments of the UK and the USA on 27 March 1941, and the concomitant Trinidad–US Bases Lease of 22 April 1941, defence bases were leased to the US Government for 99 years. On 8 Dec. 1960 the US agreed to abandon 21,000 acres of leased land and the US has since given up the remaining territory, except for a small tracking station.

AREA AND POPULATION. Area: Trinidad, 1,864 sq. miles (4,828 sq. km); Tobago, 116 sq. miles (300 sq. km). Population (census 7 April 1970): 931,071 (459,512 males and 471,559 females) (Trinidad, 892,317; Tobago, 38,754). Capital, Port-of-Spain, 62,680; other important towns, San Fernando (36,879) and Arima (11,636). The majority are of African descent (42·83%), the balance being made up of Indians (40·11%), mixed races (14·17%), Chinese (0·86%) and Syrian Lebanese (0·11%). English is spoken generally.

Estimated population in 1980, 1·2m.

Vital statistics (rate per 1,000), 1979: Births, 23·8; deaths, 6·6; infant deaths, 23·9. Proportion of population under 15 years (1979) 36·5%.

Tobago is situated about 21 miles north-east of Trinidad. Main town is Scarborough.

Principal goods shipped from Tobago to Trinidad are copra, cocoa, livestock and poultry, fresh vegetables, coconut oil and coconut fibre.

CONSTITUTION AND GOVERNMENT. On 31 Aug. 1962 Trinidad and Tobago became an independent member state of the British Commonwealth. A Republican Constitution was adopted on 26 Oct. 1976.

The Constitution provides for a bicameral legislature of a Senate and a House of Representatives. The Senate consists of 31 members, 16 being appointed by the President on the advice of the Prime Minister, 6 on the advice of the Leader of the Opposition and 9 at the discretion of the President.

The voting age in the 1976 election was reduced from 21 to 18 years and ballot boxes were re-introduced in place of the voting machines used in previous elections.

Tobago has a 15-man House of Assembly (with limited powers).

The House of Representatives consists of 36 (34 for Trinidad and 2 for Tobago) elected members and a Speaker elected from outside the House.

The Cabinet consists of the Prime Minister, appointed by the President, and other Ministers, including the Attorney-General.

In Nov. 1981 the People's National Movement held the 27 seats.

President: Ellis Clarke.
Prime Minister and Minister of Finance and Planning: George Chambers.
National flag: Red with a diagonal black strip edged in white.

DEFENCE. The Defence Force has a small air element, equipped with a Cessna Skymaster light transport, a JetRanger helicopter, and 2 S-76 helicopters for surveillance, liaison and casualty evacuation. Personnel in 1983 totalled 1,950.

INTERNATIONAL RELATIONS

Membership. Trinidad and Tobago is a member of UN, the Commonwealth, Caricom and is an ACP state of EEC.

ECONOMY

Budget. Statistics of 5 calendar years (in TT$1,000):

	1975	*1976*	*1977*	*1978*	*1979*	*1980*
Revenue	1,769,000	...	3,212,000	3,226,000	3,592,000	3,801,300
Expenditure	1,768,800	...	2,066,500	3,140,100	3,592,000	3,970,000
Public debt	634,800	613,600	1,057,220	1,355,600	1,448,600	1,533,000

The principal item of revenue during 1978 was direct taxes, $1,982·9m.
Public debt at 31 Dec. 1978, TT$1,341·8m.

Currency. The currency is the *Trinidad and Tobago dollar* of 100 *cents.* £1 = TT$3·53; US$1 = TT$2·40 (March 1983).

Banking. Banks operating: Barclays Bank of Trinidad and Tobago Ltd; Royal Bank of Trinidad and Tobago Ltd; Bank of Commerce, Trinidad and Tobago Ltd; Bank of Nova Scotia; Chase Manhattan Bank; Citibank; National Commercial Bank of Trinidad and Tobago; Workers' Bank of Trinidad and Tobago. A Central Bank began operations in Dec. 1964.

Government savings banks are established in 62 offices, with a head office in Port-of-Spain, the amount of deposits at the end of 1973 being $8,316,739, and the total number of depositors, 137,349.

ENERGY AND NATURAL RESOURCES

Oil. Oil production is one of Trinidad's leading industries and an important source of revenue. Commercial production began in 1909; production of crude oil in 1982 was 100,000 bbls per day. Trinidad also possesses 3 refineries, with throughput capacity of 144·2m. bbls annually; crude oil is imported from Venezuela, Indonesia, Ecuador, Nigeria, Brazil, and Saudi Arabia and refined in Trinidad. The 'Pitch Lake' is an important source of asphalt.

Agriculture. Of the total area of 1,267,236 acres (Trinidad, 1,192,844 acres, and Tobago, 74,392 acres), about half has been alienated. Acres under cultivation and care include (1973): Forest, 685,604; cocoa, 119,703; sugar, 118,703; coconuts, 35,797; citrus, 13,667; tonca beans, 1,735. Sugar production in 1980 was 110,000 (1976: 200,000) tons. The territory is still largely dependent on imported food supplies, especially flour, dairy products, meat and rice. Areas have been irrigated for rice, and soil and forest conservation is practised.

Livestock (1981): Cattle, 78,000; sheep, 11,000; goats, 47,000; pigs, 60,000; poultry, 7·5m.

INDUSTRY AND TRADE

Labour. The working population in 1979 was 446,250 (134,800 women) and unemployment was 49,150 (11%), 23,400 women.

Commerce. Chief imports, 1979:

	TT$1,000
Machinery and transport equipment	1,458,600
Mineral fuels, lubricants, etc.	1,444,600

The principal domestic exports during 1979 were (in TT$1,000): Petroleum products, 5,743,800; chemicals, 196,100.

The chief country of origin of imports (1978) was USA ($968·7m.). Exports were shipped chiefly to USA ($3,228·3m.).

Total trade of Trinidad and Tobago with UK (British Department of Trade returns, in £1,000 sterling):

	1978	*1979*	*1980*	*1981*	*1982*
Imports to UK	31,630	41,243	35,088	37,153	65,154
Exports and re-exports from UK	110,788	104,562	120,270	121,465	158,436

Tourism. In 1979, 196,060 foreigners visited Trinidad and Tobago spending TT$298·2m.

COMMUNICATIONS

Roads. There are 2,630 miles of main and local roads. Motor vehicles registered in 1978 totalled 176,895, including 112,572 private cars, 18,895 hired and rented cars, and 27,399 goods vehicles.

Aviation. The following airlines operate scheduled passenger, mail and freight services. British West Indian Airways, Ltd, Air Canada, PANAM, KLM, Linea Aeropostal Venezolana, Aerolinas Argentinas, Leeward Islands Air Transport, Air France, ASPA, Air India, Caribair, British Airways, American Airlines and Guyana Airways.

Shipping. In 1977 48m. tons of cargo were handled.

Post and Broadcasting. International communications to all parts of the world are provided by Trinidad and Tobago External Telecommunications Co. Ltd (TEXTEL) by means of a satellite earth station and various high quality radio circuits. The marine radio service is also maintained by TEXTEL. Number of post offices (1979), 63; postal agencies offering limited services, 175; number of telephones (1979), 77,799.

Four wireless stations are maintained by the Trinidad Government and 3 by airline companies. A meteorological station is maintained at Piarco airport.

Cinemas (1973). There are 72 cinemas and 4 drive-in cinemas.

Newspapers (1979). There are 2 daily newspapers with a total daily circulation of 179,400, 3 Sunday newspapers with a total circulation of 186,200, 2 evening papers and 5 weekly newspapers.

JUSTICE, RELIGION, EDUCATION AND WELFARE

Justice. The High Court consists of the Chief Justice and not fewer than 10 puisne judges. In criminal cases a judge of the High Court sits with a jury of 12 in cases of treason and murder, and with 9 jurors in other cases. The Court of Appeal consists of the Chief Justice and 3 Justices of Appeal; there is a limited right of appeal from it to the Privy Council. There are 10 High Courts and 28 magistrates' courts.

Religion. In 1970, 18·1% of the population were Anglicans (under the Bishop of Trinidad and Tobago), 35·6% Roman Catholics (under the Archbishop of Port-of-Spain), 4·2% Presbyterians, 24·7% Hindus and 6·3% Moslems.

Education. In 1972–73 there were 476 primary and intermediate schools (government assisted) and (1971–72) 116 secondary schools (47 government and assisted and 69 private).

There were 222,928 pupils on roll in the primary and intermediate schools and 35,302 in the secondary schools (government and assisted). Education in government and assisted secondary schools was made free in 1960. There are also 5 training colleges. Technical and commercial education is provided by 4 government sponsored technical schools.

Health. State medical services are free and in 1972 a National Insurance Scheme was established.

DIPLOMATIC REPRESENTATIVES

Of Trinidad and Tobago in Great Britain (42 Belgrave Sq., London, SW1X 8NT)
High Commissioner: Frank O. Abdullah (accredited 9 March 1983).

Of Great Britain in Trinidad and Tobago (Furness Hse., 90 Independence Sq., Port-of-Spain)
High Commissioner: D. N. Lane.

Of Trinidad and Tobago in the USA (1708 Massachusetts Ave., NW, Washington, D.C., 20036)
Ambassador: Victor C. McIntyre.

Of the USA in Trinidad and Tobago (15 Queen's Park West, Port-of-Spain)
Ambassador: Melvin H. Evans.

Of Trinidad and Tobago to the United Nations
Ambassador: Frank Owen Abdulah.

Books of Reference

Statistical Information: The Central Statistical Office, Government of Trinidad and Tobago, 2 Edward St., Port-of-Spain. *Director:* J. Harewood. Publications include *Annual Statistical Digest, Quarterly Economic Report, Annual Overseas Trade Report, Population and Vital Statistics Annual Report.*

Report of the Trinidad and Tobago Independence Conference, 1962. (Cmnd. 1757.) HMSO, 1962

Facts on Trinidad and Tobago. Public Relations Division, Prime Minister's Office, Port-of-Spain, 1978

Immigration Guidelines. Government Printer, Port-of-Spain, 1980

Oil and Energy, Trinidad and Tobago. Government Printer, Port-of-Spain, 1980

Trinidad and Tobago Year Book. Port-of-Spain. Annual (from 1865)

Cooper, St G. C. and Bacon, P. R. (eds.), *The Natural Resources of Trinidad and Tobago.* London, 1981

Central Library: The Central Library of Trinidad and Tobago, Queen's Park East, Port-of-Spain. *Acting Librarian:* Mrs L. Hutchinson.

TUNISIA

Al-Djoumhouria Attunusia

Capital: Tunis
Population: 6·75m. (1982)
GNP per capita: US$1,310 (1980)

HISTORY. Tunisia was a French protectorate from 1881 and achieved independence on 20 March 1956. The Constituent Assembly, elected on 25 March 1956, abolished the monarchy (of the Bey of Tunis) on 25 July 1957 and proclaimed a republic.

AREA AND POPULATION. The boundaries are on the north and east the Mediterranean Sea, on the west Algeria and on the south Libya. The area is about 164,150 sq. km (63,362 sq. miles), including that portion of the Sahara which is to the east of the Djerid, extending towards Ghadamès.

At the census of 8 May 1975 there were 5,588,209 inhabitants (2,840,913 males and 2,747,209 females). Estimate (1982) 6,747,000.

The census populations of the *gouvernorats* were as follows as at 8 May 1975:

Béja	248,770	Kassérine	238,499	Sfax	474,879
Bizerta	343,708	Le Kef	233,155	Sidi Bouzid	218,511
Gabès	255,717	Mahdia	218,217	Siliana	192,668
Gafsa	237,844	Médénine	292,970	Sousse	254,601
Jendouba	299,702	Monastir	223,150	Tunis Nord	944,130
Kairouan	338,477	Nabeul	368,114	Tunis Sud	205,097

Tunis, the capital, had (census, 1975) 550,404 inhabitants: Sfax, 171,297; Sousse, 69,530; Bizerta, 62,856; Djerba, 70,217; Kairouan, a holy city of the Moslems, 54,546; Gafsa, 42,225; Gabès, 40,585; Béja, 39,226.

Vital statistics (1976). Births, 208,728; deaths, 36,912; marriages, 47,940.

CONSTITUTION AND GOVERNMENT. The Constitution of the republic was promulgated on 1 June 1959. The President and the National Assembly are elected simultaneously by direct universal suffrage for a period of 5 years. The President cannot be re-elected more than 3 times consecutively, however on 18 March 1975 the National Assembly proclaimed Bourguiba 'President for Life'. An amendment to the Constitution in 1969 gives the Prime Minister power to act as President in case of a sudden vacancy of the Presidency.

Elections were held on 1 Nov. 1981, when all 136 seats in the National Assembly were won by the *Front National*, an alliance of the ruling *Parti Socialiste Destourien* (109 seats) and the *Union générale des travailleurs tunisiens* (27 seats).

President of the Republic and Head of Government: Habib Ben Ali Bourguiba (elected 25 July 1957, re-elected 8 Nov. 1959, 8 Nov. 1964, 2 Nov. 1969 and elected President for life in Nov. 1974).

The Cabinet in Dec. 1981 was composed as follows:

Prime Minister: Mohammed M'Zali.

Special Adviser to the President: Habib Bourguiba, Jr. *Justice:* M'hamed Chaker. *Foreign Affairs:* Beji Caied Essebsi. *Interior:* Idris Guiga. *Defence:* Salaheddine Bali. *Planning and Finance:* Mansour Moalla. *National Economy:* Abdelaziz Lasram. *Housing:* Moncef Belhaj Amor. *Equipment:* Mohamed Sayah. *Information:* Tahar Belkhodja. *National Education:* Mohamed Frej Chedli. *Higher Education and Scientific Research:* Abdelaziz Ben Dhia. *Agriculture:* Lassaad Ben Osman. *Public Health:* Rashid Sfar. *Transport and Communications:* Sadok Ben Jamaa. *Social Affairs:* Mohamed Ennaceur. *Youth and Sports:* Mohamed Kraiem. *Minister-Delegate responsible for Prime Minister's Office:* Mongi Kooli. *Minister-*

Delegate attached to Prime Minister responsible for Civil Service and Administrative Reform: Mezri Chekir. *Secretary of State for Posts and Telecommunications:* Brahim Khouaja. *Secretary of State for Foreign Affairs:* Mahmoud Mestiri.

Local Government. The country is divided into 18 *gouvernorats*, each subdivided into *délégations, communes and imadas*. The official language is Arabic.

Flag: Red with a white circle in the middle, on which is a 5-pointed red star encircled by a red crescent.

DEFENCE. A Tunisian National Army consisted in 1983 of about 24,000 officers and men. Selective military service is 1 year. Officer-cadets are being trained in France.

Army. The Army consists of 2 combined arms and 3 armoured regiments, 2 para-commando, 1 desert, 2 artillery and 1 engineer battalion.

Navy. The Navy consists of 1 frigate (*ex*-US old destroyer-escort), 2 fast gunboats (*ex*-Chinese), 2 fast attack craft (British-built in 1977), 2 coastal minesweepers, 4 patrol vessels (French built), 10 patrol boats, 2 protection launches and 1 large tug. Three light corvette type, missile armed fast attack craft are being built in France. In 1983 naval personnel totalled 2,600 officers and ratings.

Air Force. Equipment of the Air Force, acquired from various Western sources, includes 1 squadron of Aermacchi M.B.326K/L jet light attack aircraft (re-equipping with 6 F-5E Tiger II fighers and 2 F-5Fs); 12 SF.260W piston-engined light trainer/attack aircraft; 3 Flament light transports, 4 S.208 liaison aircraft, 6 SF.260M trainers, 12 T6 Texan advanced trainers, 8 M.B.326B and 4 F-5F jet trainers, 1 Puma, 6 UH-1H, 18 AB.205 and about 12 Alouette II and III helicopters. Personnel, about 2,000.

INTERNATIONAL RELATIONS

Membership. Tunisia is a member of UN, OAU and the Arab League.

ECONOMY

Planning. A sixth development plan (1982-86) envisaged investment of 8,000m. dinars.

Budget (in 1,000 dinars). Budget estimates, 1981, revenue, 1,028,979; expenditure, 632,400.

Currency. On 1 Nov. 1958 a new currency, the *dinar*, divided into 1,000 *millimes*, was established. The Central Bank of Tunisia is the note-issuing agency. Note circulation, Aug. 1980, was 910m. *dinars*.

Currency consists of coins of 1, 2, 5, 10, 20, 50, 100 and 500 *millimes*, and notes of 500 *millimes*, 1 *dinar*, 5 and 10 *dinars*. £1 = 0·89 *dinar*; US$1 = 0·65 *dinar* (March 1983).

Banking. In 1981 there were 21 banks operating in Tunisia, including 3 French and 1 British banks. Bank deposits amounted to 1,715m. dinars at 31 Dec. 1981.

Weights and Measures. The metric system of weights and measures has almost entirely taken the place of those of Tunisia, but corn is still sold in *kaffis* and *wibas*. The *kfiz* (of 16 *wiba*, each of 12 *sa'*) = 16 bushels. The *ounce* = 31·487 grammes.

The principal measure of length is the metre.

ENERGY AND NATURAL RESOURCES

Electricity. The electricity, gas and water services, formerly run by a French company, were nationalized on 26 Nov. 1959 and are now run respectively by the Société Tunisienne d'Electricité et du Gaz (STEG) and the Société Nationale d'Exploitation et de Distribution du Eaux (SONEDE).

Electrical energy generated was 2,800m. kwh. in 1980, of which 2,432m. was produced by STEG.

Oil. Crude oil production (1980) 5,627,300 tonnes.

Gas. National gas production (1980) 360m. cu. metres.

Minerals. Mineral production (in 1,000 tonnes) in 1980 (and 1981): Phosphate, 4,500 (4,978); iron ore, 389·5 (400); lead ore, 14·2 (14); zinc ore, 16·3 (15). Processed minerals (in 1,000 tonnes) in 1980: Pig iron, 152; crude steel, 177.

Agriculture. Tunisia may be divided into 5 districts—the north, characterized by its mountainous formation, having large and fertile valleys (*e.g.*, the valley of the Medjerdah and the plains of Mornag, Mateur and Béja); the north-east, with the peninsula of Cap Bon, the soil being specially suited for the cultivation of oranges, lemons and tangerines; the Sahel, where olive trees abound; the centre, the region of high table lands and pastures, and the desert of the south, famous for its oases and gardens, where dates grow in profusion.

Agriculture is the chief industry, and large estates predominate. Of the total area of 15,583,000 hectares, about 9m. hectares are productive, including 2m. under cereals, 3·6m. used as pasturage, 900,000 forests and 1·3m. uncultivated.

Products		*1979–80*	*1980–81*	*1981–82*
Hard wheat	(in 1,000 tonnes)	740	800	900
Soft wheat		130	160	180
Barley		300	270	300
Olive oil		85	145	90
Oranges and lemons		160	220	170
Dates		47	46	...
Wine (in 1,000 hectolitres)		619	619	555

Other products are apricots, pears, apples, peaches, plums, figs, pomegranates, almonds, shaddocks, pistachios, esparto grass, henna and cork. Agricultural tractors numbered 35,000 in 1977.

Livestock (1981): Horses, 50,000; asses, 210,000; mules, 71,000; cattle, 950,000; sheep, 4,967,000; goats, 987,000; camels, 170,000; pigs, 4,000.

Fisheries. In 1980, 6,209 boats with 22,555 men were engaged in fishing. In 1980 the catch amounted to 60,500 tonnes; 1981, 57,500.

INDUSTRY AND TRADE

Industry. Major modern plants include a sugar refinery in Béja (57,700 tonnes in 1975), a cellulose plant in Kassérine (22,000 tonnes in 1976), a petroleum refinery in Bizerta and a steel plant at Menzel Bourguiba. There is a marble work plant and a tyre factory at Mégrine.

In 1972 a phosphoric acid plant opened at Ghannouche with an annual capacity of 120,000 tonnes.

Production, 1977 (in 1,000 tonnes): Refined oil, 1,130; cement, 680; metal castings, 200; steel, 200; rounded bars, 145; paper pulp, 22.

Trade Unions. The Union Générale des Travailleurs Tunisiens won 27 seats in the parliamentary elections (1 Nov. 1981). There are also the Union Tunisienne de l'Industrie, du Commerce et de l'Artisanat (UTICA, the employers' union) and the Union National des Agriculteurs (UNA, farmers' union).

Commerce. The imports and exports for calendar years (in 1,000 dinars) were as follows:

	1975	*1976*	*1977*	*1978*	*1979*	*1980*	*1981*
Imports	572,800	656,700	735,000	834,000	1,156,800	1,483,170	1,649,000
Exports	345,600	338,300	390,000	440,000	726,700	891,410	1,042,200

Exports to France in 1980 totalled 139·5m. dinars, and imports from France, 358·7m. dinars and exports to USA were valued at 63·3m. dinars and imports from USA were valued at 69·1m. dinars.

In 1977 exports of iron ore totalled 55,000 tonnes; lime phosphates, and hyper-phosphates, 2,087,400; crude petroleum, 4,144,900.

Total trade between Tunisia and UK (British Department of Trade returns, in £1,000 sterling):

	1978	*1979*	*1980*	*1981*	*1982*
Imports to UK	11,964	9,084	17,566	22,070	12,628
Exports and re-exports from UK	21,365	24,660	29,872	35,157	38,632

Tourism. In 1981, 2·2m. tourists visited Tunisia, not counting ships' passengers in transit.

COMMUNICATIONS

Roads. In 1975 there were 16,695 km of roads, of which 10,645 km were main roads.

Number of motor vehicles, 1977, included 110,002 private cars, 81,370 commercial cars, 10,764 motor cycles and 35,598 tractors.

Railways. In 1980 there were 2,013 km of railways, owned by the state Société Nationale des Chemins de Fer Tunisiens. Traffic in 1979 was 25m. passengers and 7·6m. tonnes of freight.

Aviation. The national airline is 'Tunis-Air'. The main airport is at Tunis-Carthage. In 1981, 3,515,675 passengers were carried.

Shipping. The main port is Tunis, and its outer port is Tunis-Goulette. These two ports and Sfax, Sousse and Bizerta are directly accessible to ocean going vessels. The port of La Skhirra, in the south, is used for the shipping of Algerian and Tunisian oil.

In 1981, 5,055 ships of 20,422,000 tons entered Tunisian ports.

Post and Broadcasting. There were, in 1981, 188,476 telephones. There were, in 1978, 403 post offices, and 6 wireless transmitting stations. Wireless sets in use in 1976 were 1,124,000. Television began in 1966 and in 1979 there were 255,700 sets.

Cinemas (1976). There were 175 cinemas with a seating capacity of 44,000.

Newspapers. There are 2 Arabic and 3 French daily newspapers.

JUSTICE, RELIGION, EDUCATION AND WELFARE

Justice. The Government has abolished the multiple jurisdictions of religious (shara'ic and rabbinic) tribunals. These have been integrated into the civil courts so as to form a single three-level jurisdiction (courts of primary jurisdiction, courts of appeal and the High Court).

A Personal Status Code was promulgated on 13 Aug. 1956 and applied to Tunisians from 1 Jan. 1957. This raised the status of women, made divorce subject to a court decision, abolished polygamy and decreed a minimum marriage age.

Religion. The constitution recognizes Islam as the state religion. There are about 14,000 Roman Catholics, under the Prelate of Tunis. The Greek Church, the French Protestants and the English Church are also represented.

Education. All education was in 1956 made dependent on the Ministry of National Education. The 208 independent koranic schools have been nationalized and the distinction between religious and public schools has been abolished. All education is free from primary schools to university. A teachers' training college (*école normale supérieure*) was established in 1955. There are also a high school of law, 2 centres of economic studies, 2 schools of engineering, 2 medical schools, a faculty of agriculture and 2 institutes of business administration.

In 1979–80 primary schools had 1,038,800 pupils; secondary, technical and vocational schools had 259,100 pupils; higher education mainly at the University of Tunis had 30,500 students.

Health. In 1976 there were 268 hospitals (13,145 beds). The registered medical personnel in Tunisia comprised 1,210 doctors (843 Tunisians and 367 foreigners), 313 pharmacists, 176 dentists and 60 veterinaries.

Social Security. A system of social security was set up in 1950 (amended 1963, 1964 and 1970).

DIPLOMATIC REPRESENTATIVES

Of Tunisia in Great Britain (29 Prince's Gate, London, SW7 1QG)
Ambassador: Sadok Bouzayen (accredited 26 Nov. 1981).

Of Great Britain in Tunisia (5 Place de la Victoire, Tunis)
Ambassador and Consul-General: Sir Alexander Stirling, KBE, CMG.

Of Tunisia in the USA (2408 Massachusetts Ave., NW, Washington, D.C., 20008)
Ambassador: Habib Ben Yahia.

Of the USA in Tunisia (144 Ave. de la Liberté, Tunis)
Ambassador: Walter L. Cutler.

Of Tunisia to the United Nations
Ambassador: Taieb Slim.

Books of Reference

Statistical Information: Institut National de la Statistique (27 Rue de Liban, Tunis) was set up on 13 March 1947. Its main publications are: *Annuaire statistique de la Tunisie* (latest issue, 1975).

Journal Officiel de la République Tunisienne (in Arabic and French)
Tunisie, 1953. (L'Encyclopédie d'outre-mer.) Paris, 1953
Bannour, A. (ed.), *Economic Yearbook of Tunisia.* 2nd ed. Tunis, 1966
Findlay, Allan M., Findlay, Anne M., and Lawless, R. I., *Tunisia.* [Bibliography] Oxford and Santa Barbara, 1982
Garas, F., *Bourguiba et la Naissance d'une Nation.* Paris, 1956
Knapp, W., *Tunisia.* London, 1970
Ling, D. L., *Tunisia: From Protectorate to Republic.* Indiana Univ. Press, 1967
Rossi, P., *Bourguiba's Tunisia.* Tunis, 1967
Rudebeck, L., *The Tunisian Experience: Party and People.* London, 1970
Sylvester, A., *Tunisia.* London, 1969

TURKEY

Türkiye Cumhuriyeti

Capital: Ankara
Population: 45·7m. (1981)
GNP per capita: US$1,114 (1980)

HISTORY. The Turkish War of Independence (1919–22), following the disintegration of the Ottoman Empire, was led and won by Mustafa Kemal (Atatürk) on behalf of the Grand National Assembly which first met in Ankara on 23 April 1920. On 20 Jan. 1921 the Grand National Assembly voted a constitution which declared that all sovereignty belonged to the people and vested all power, both executive and legislative, in the Grand National Assembly. The name 'Ottoman Empire' was later replaced by 'Turkey'. On 1 Nov. 1922 the Grand National Assembly abolished the office of Sultan and Turkey became a republic on 29 Oct. 1923.

On 27 May 1960 the Turkish Army, directed by a National Unity Committee under the leadership of Gen. Cemal Gürsel, overthrew the government of the Democratic Party. The Grand National Assembly was dissolved and party activities were suspended. Party activities were legally resumed on 12 Jan. 1961. A new constitution was approved in a referendum held on 9 July 1961 and general elections were held the same year.

On 12 Sept. 1980, the Turkish armed forces overthrew the Demirel Government (Justice Party). Parliament was dissolved and all activities of political parties were suspended. The Constituent Assembly was convened in Oct. 1981, and prepared a new Constitution which was enforced after a national referendum on 7 Nov. 1982. New legislation regarding political parties and elections are being prepared in 1983.

AREA AND POPULATION. The Treaty of Peace between the Allied Powers and Turkey, which was signed at Lausanne on 24 July 1923, defined the European frontier of the new Turkey and to some extent her Asiatic frontiers. This treaty was ratified by the Grand National Assembly in Ankara on 23 Aug. 1923 and entered into force 6 Aug. 1924.

The Treaty of Lausanne and the conventions attached to it provided for the demilitarization of zones adjoining the European frontier, the Dardanelles and the Bosphorus, subject to the right to maintain a garrison at Istanbul, for the demilitarization of İmroz, Bozcaada (Tenedos) and Tavşan Islands, as well as the islands in the Sea of Marmara with one exception and for a special administrative regime in İmroz and Bozcaada.

On 10 July 1936 a new Straits Convention was signed at Montreux (ratified on 9 Nov. 1936) to take the place of the 1923 Convention, whereby Turkey obtained the right of re-militarizing the zone of the Straits, and this area was re-occupied by Turkish troops on 21 July 1936. The International Commission of the Straits ceased to function on 30 Sept. 1936.

By an agreement between the Turkish and French Governments concluded at Ankara on 23 June 1939, the Sanjak of Alexandretta (the Hatay) was incorporated in the Turkish Republic.

The area of Turkey (including lakes) is 779,452 sq. km (300,947 sq. miles). Area in Europe (Trakya), 23,764 sq. km. Area in Asia (Anadolu), 755,855 sq. km; population, 1975, 40,197,670; 1981, 45,747,000.

The census population of Turkey is given as follows:

	Males	*Females*	*Total*	*Increase* %
1935	7,936,770	8,221,248	16,158,018	21·2
1940	8,898,912	8,922,038	17,820,950	17·3
1945	9,446,580	9,343,594	18,790,174	10·5
1950	10,527,085	10,420,103	20,947,188	22·9
1955	12,233,421	11,831,342	24,064,763	29·7
1960	14,163,888	13,590,932	27,754,820	28·9
1965	15,996,964	15,394,457	31,391,421	24·9
1970	18,006,986	17,598,190	35,605,176	25·1
1975	20,744,730	19,602,989	40,347,719	25·4

The population of the provinces, at the census of Oct. 1980, was as follows:

Adana	1,485,743	Erzincan	282,022	Maraş	738,032
Adıyaman	367,595	Erzurum	801,809	Mardin	564,967
Afyonkarahisar	597,516	Eskişehir	543,802	Muğla	438,145
Ağrı	368,009	Gaziantep	808,697	Muş	302,406
Amasya	341,287	Gireşun	480,083	Nevşehir	256,933
Ankara	2,854,689	Gümüşane	275,191	Niğde	512,071
Antalya	748,706	Hakkari	155,463	Ordu	713,535
Artvin	228,997	Hatay	856,271	Rize	361,258
Aydin	652,488	İsparta	350,116	Sakarya	548,747
Balıkesir	853,177	İçel	843,931	Samsun	1,008,113
Bilecik	147,001	İstanbul	4,741,890	Siirt	445,483
Bingöl	228,702	İzmir	1,976,763	Sinop	276,242
Bitlis	257,908	Kars	700,238	Sivas	750,144
Bolu	471,751	Kastamonu	450,946	Tekirdağ	360,742
Burdur	235,009	Kayseri	778,383	Tokat	624,508
Bursa	1,148,492	Kırklareli	283,408	Trabzon	731,045
Çanakkale	391,568	Kırşehir	240,497	Tunceli	157,974
Çankırı	258,436	Kocaeli	596,899	Urfa	602,736
Çorum	571,831	Konya	1,562,139	Uşak	247,224
Denizli	603,338	Kütahya	497,089	Van	468,646
Diyarbakir	778,150	Malatya	606,996	Yozgat	504,433
Edirne	363,286	Manisa	941,941	Zonguldak	954,512
Elâziğ	440,808				

The population of towns of over 100,000 inhabitants, at the census of Oct. 1980, was as follows:

İstanbul	2,772,708	Samsun	198,749	Elaziğ	142,983
Ankara	1,877,755	İzmit	190,423	Denizli	135,373
İzmir	757,854	Erzurum	190,241	Adapazari	130,977
Adana	574,515	Malatya	179,074	İskenderun	124,824
Bursa	445,113	K. Maraş	178,557	Balikesir	124,051
Gaziantep	374,290	Kirikkale	178,401	Tarsus	121,074
Konya	329,139	Kağithane	175,540	Zonguldak	109,044
Eskişehir	309,431	Antalya	173,501	Trabzon	108,403
Kayseri	281,320	Sivas	172,864	Buca	103,105
Diyarbakir	235,617	Bayrampaşa	165,723	Küçükköy	100,406
Mersin	216,308	Urfa	147,488		

The population of Turkey according to 'mother tongue' (1965 census) comprises 28,289,680 Turks, 2,219,502 Kurds, 365,340 Arabs, 57,337 Circassians, 48,143 Greeks, 48,096 Armenians, 33,094 Georgians, 23,715 Lazes and 9,124 Spanish-speaking Jews.

CONSTITUTION AND GOVERNMENT. The Turkish Grand National Assembly was dissolved on 12 Sept. 1980. The National Security Council took over its functions and powers. On 23 Oct. 1981 a Consultative Assembly was inaugurated. In early 1983 the National Security Council was acting as the upper house and the Consultative Assembly as the lower house.

Religious courts were abolished in 1924, Islam ceased to be the official state religion in 1928, women were given the franchise and western-style surnames were adopted in 1934.

The task of the Consultative Assembly was to prepare a new Constitution to replace that of 1961. The Assembly began its work in Oct. 1981 under the presidency of Sadi Irmak and on 7 Nov. 1982 a national referendum established that 98% of the electorate were in favour of the new Constitution.

Turkish men and women are entitled to vote at the age of 21 and to become deputies at the age of 30 and second members of Senate at the age of 40. Secret ballot was introduced by law on 10 July 1948.

National flag: A white crescent and star on red.

National anthem: Korkma! Sönmez bu şafaklarda yüzen al sancak (words by Mehmed Akif Ersoy; tune by Zeki Güngör; adopted 12 March 1921).

Past Presidents of the Republic: Mustafa Kemal Atatürk (29 Oct. 1923–10 Nov. 1938), İsmet İnönü (11 Nov. 1938–21 May 1950), Celâl Bayar (22 May 1950–27 May 1960), Cemal Gürsel (26 Oct. 1961–27 March 1966), Cevdet Sunay (29 March 1966–28 March 1973), Fahri S. Korutürk (6 April 1973–6 April 1980).

Head of State, Head of National Security Council and Chief of General Staff: Gen. Kenan Evren.

Members of the Council: Gen. Nurettin Ersin; Gen. Tahsin Sahinkaya; Adm. Neja t Tümer; Gen Sedat Celasun. *Secretary-General:* Gen. Necdet Üruğ.

Prime Minister: Adm. Bülend Ulusu.

Local Government. The Constitution of 1921 provided for the administrative division of the country into *İl*, (province, now 67 in number), divided into *İlçe* (district), subdivided in their turn into *Bucak* (township or commune). At the head of each İl is a Vali representing the Government. Each İl has its own elective council.

The İlçe is regarded as a mere grouping of Bucaks for certain purposes of general administration. The Bucak or commune is an autonomous entity and possesses an elective council charged with the administration of such matters as are not reserved to the State.

According to the municipal law passed in 1930, Turkish women have the right to be electors and to be elected at municipal elections.

DEFENCE. Several bills for the reorganization of the armed forces were passed in June 1961 by the Grand National Assembly. One of these placed all organizations connected with national defence under the authority of the Minister of National Defence. Another created a Supreme Council of National Security, under the chairmanship of the Prime Minister, with the object of co-ordinating the resources of the country in case of war. Besides the Minister of National Defence and the Chief of the General Staff, the heads of economic Ministries are members of this council.

Military service in Army, Air Force and Navy is 18 months for officers and 20 months for other ranks. Men are called up when they reach the age of 20. The average number of men liable to be called up is 175,000 every year. The strength of the forces is about 567,000 officers and men. The total number that could be mobilized is estimated at over 2m.

Army. The land forces contain 16 infantry divisions (2 mechanized), 1 armoured division and 6 armoured brigades (M-48 tanks), 1 commando and 7 infantry brigades, 4 mechanized infantry brigades, 1 parachute brigade. The units are largely equipped with 10·5 cm, 15·5 cm and 20·3 cm howitzer guns. Ground forces have been assigned to the South-Eastern Command of NATO, of which Izmir is the headquarters. Total strength (1983), 470,000; conscripts, 420,000.

Navy. The Navy includes 15 diesel-powered submarines (5 new designed in Federal Republic of Germany and 10 old *ex*-US patrol submarines), 13 old *ex*-US destroyers, 2 modern Turkish-built frigates, 1 minelayer, 6 coastal minelayers, 1 fast attack gunboat (light corvette type), 13 fast missile craft, 7 fast torpedo boats, 22 coastal minesweepers, 8 patrol vessels, 4 inshore minesweepers, 9 minehunting boats, 44 patrol craft, 3 repair ships, 2 submarine support ships, 1 large training ship, 1 training ship (*ex*-German support frigate), 5 landing ships, 50 landing craft, 20 minor landing craft, 3 submarine rescue ships, 9 oilers, 10 transports, 2 survey ships, 3 survey boats, 4 boom defence vessels, 3 depot ships, 4 training craft, 3 gate vessels, 25 auxiliary vessels, 14 tugs, 2 tenders, 9 water carriers, and 7 floating docks.

Ships under construction include a sixth diesel-electric patrol submarine designed in the Federal Republic of Germany, but being built in Turkey (and 6 more are planned); 1 more fast missile craft and 5 fast attack craft.

The naval bases are at Gölcük in the Gulf of İzmit, at İskenderun, at Taskizak (İstanbul) and at İzmir.

Personnel strength in 1983 totalled 45,000 officers and ratings.

Air Force. The Air Force is under the control of the General Staff and, operationally, under 6 ATAF. It is organized as 2 tactical air forces, with F-5s equipping 6 fighter-bomber/interceptor and 1 reconnaissance squadrons: F-100 Super Sabres in 4 fighter-bomber squadrons; F-104G and F-104S Starfighters in 6 squadrons; F-4E and RF-4E Phantoms in 4 squadrons; plus Nike-Hercules surface-to-air missile batteries. The 6 transport squadrons are equipped with Transall C-160, C-130 Hercules, Viscount and C-47 aircraft, and UH-IH helicopters. Training types include T-33A, T-37 and T-38 advanced trainers, T-34 basic and T-41 primary trainers. Personnel strength is about 53,000, with over 320 combat aircraft.

INTERNATIONAL RELATIONS

Membership. Turkey is a member of UN, OECD, NATO and Council of Europe and an Associate of EEC.

ECONOMY

Planning. The first 5-year development plan, 1963–67, provided for investments of TL68,000m. (at 1965 prices); TL64,000m. were invested, the gross national product increasing at the rate of 6·7% per annum. The second 5-year plan (1968–72) aimed at achieving an annual growth of 7%; external financing amounting to US$1,716m. The third 5-year plan (1973–78) set out to achieve an annual growth of 7·4%. The fourth 5-year plan (1979–83) sets out to achieve an annual growth of 8%.

Budget. Estimates of revenue and expenditure (in TL1,000) for financial years 1 March–28/29 Feb.:

	1976–77	*1977–78*	*1978–79*	*1979–80*
Revenue	139,719,980	203,449,003	308,350,000	395,871,000
Expenditure	153,637,351	222,949,003	341,173,000	406,876,000

Currency. The Turkish *Lira* (TL) is divided into 100 *kuruş (piastres).* Coins in general circulation are of the following values: 25 and 50 *kurus,;* 1, 2½ and 5 *Lira.* Bank-notes in circulation are as follows: 5, 10, 20, 50, 100, 500, 1,000 and 5,000 *Lira.* In March 1983, US$1 = 202 *Lira*; £1 = 294.

Banking. The Turkish banking system is composed of the Central Bank of the Republic of Turkey (Merkez Bankası) and 44 other banks. Thirteen (including the Central Bank) are established by special laws.

The 13 banks established by special laws carry out specialized banking activities beside their general banking transactions. Five of them are state economic enterprises whose capital is owned wholly by the State. They include: Ziraat Bankası (rural credits, capital: TL1,500m.), Sümerbank (textiles, etc., capital: TL2,250m.), Etibank (mining, energy, capital: TL3,250m.), İller Bankası (urban works, capital: TL2,000m.), İstanbul Emniyet Sandığı (savings bank). Six of them are joint-stock companies; the majority of their share capital is owned by the public sector. They include: the Emlâk Kredi Bankası (housing, capital: TL1,000m.), Denizcilik Bankası (shipping, capital: TL2,000m.), Türkiye Vakıflar Bankası (investments of pious foundations, funds, capital: TL200m.), Türkiye Halk Bankası (small business, capital: TL1,000m.); Türkiye Öğretmenler Bankası (teachers' housing, capital: TL30m.), T. C. Turizm Bankası (tourism, capital: TL1,000m.).

The development banks are: Devlet Yatırım Bankası (investment credits to state economic enterprises, capital: TL1,000m.), Türkiye Sınaî Kalkınma Bankası (investment credit to the private sector, capital: TL328·66m.), Sınaî Yatırım ve Kredi Bankası (industrial medium-term credit, capital: TL40m.).

Of the 31 commercial banks, 5 are foreign banks established in Turkey, and one is a bank whose capital is shared by a foreign bank.

The total credit volume of banks at 31 Dec. 1978 amounted to TL463,310m.

Weights and Measures. The metric system came into force on 1 Jan. 1934. On 24 May 1928 the Grand National Assembly made European numerals obligatory as from 1 June 1929.

On 1 March 1917 the Gregorian calendar was introduced into Turkey, to be used side by side with the Hegira calendar, while as from 26 Dec. 1925 it was decided finally to adopt the Gregorian calendar alone.

ENERGY AND NATURAL RESOURCES

Electricity. The potential hydro-electric power in Turkey is estimated at 56,000m. kwh. In 1981 the electrical power plants (hydro-electric or thermal) produced 24,900m. kwh.

Oil. Oil is being produced in Garzan and Raman by the Turkish Petroleum Co. Under the oil law of 14 Oct. 1954 private companies can explore and produce oil. Turkish companies produced 940,000 tons in 1980 and foreign companies 1,376,000 tons. The 3 refineries refined 12m. tons of crude oil in 1975. With a fourth refinery, introduced in 1973, total refining capacity now reaches 24m. tons a year. The oil pipeline Batman–Iskenderun (494 km) was opened on 4 Jan. 1967. Imports (refined locally) in 1980 were 11·5m. tonnes.

Minerals. The Turkish provinces, especially those in Asia, are reported rich in minerals. Turkey is one of the four principal producers of chrome in the world.

Production of principal minerals (in 1,000 tonnes) was:

	1979	*1980*	*1981*
Coal	4,051	3,602	3,973
Lignite	11,051	13,639	15,057
Chromite	176	170	208
Copper concentrate	127	101	159
Sulphur	21	23	29
Wolfram concentrates (tonnes)	258	294	293
Phosphate	27	21	43
Alumina	75	137	131

Of the Government organizations producing these ores, Zonguldak coal mines operate under the Turkish State Coal Exploitation; while the copper mines at Murgul and Ergani, the Eastern chromite mines, Keçiborlu sulphur, Emet colemanite, Küre pyrite and cupriferous pyrite, Keban argentiferous lead mines operate under the Etibank.

Agriculture. The number of people aged 15 and over engaged in agriculture in 1975 was 9,463,310.

In 1980, 27,895,000 hectares were cultivated land, 20,145,000 hectares of its own and 7·75m. hectares fallow; vineyards, fruit orchards and olive groves occupied 3·5m. hectares; forest occupied 20·17m. hectares.

The soil for the most part is very fertile; the principal products are cotton, tobacco, cereals (especially wheat), figs, silk, olives and olive oil, dried fruits, liquorice root, nuts, almonds, mohair, skins and hides, furs, wool, gums, canary seed, linseed and sesame. The principal tobacco districts are Samsun, Bafra, Çarsamba, İzmit and İzmir. Two-thirds of the exports of leaf tobacco goes to the USA. The principal centre for silk production is Bursa. The production of olive oil, mainly confined to the Ils of Aydın and Balıkesir, is very important (107,000 tonnes in 1981). Sugar production (refined) in 1981 was 1·3m. tonnes. Agricultural production (in tonnes) in 1981 included 3·6m. grapes, 1·02m. oranges and lemons, 350,000 hazelnuts, 1·2m. apples, 600,000 olives, 1·05m. onions, 3m. potatoes. Tea production (fresh leaves) was 210,000 tonnes.

Turkey produced 2,000 tonnes of flax fibre and 14,000 tonnes of hemp fibre in 1981. Cotton production was 542,000 tonnes in 1981. Agricultural tractors numbered 436,367 in 1980.

Yield (in 1,000 tonnes) of principal crops:

	1977	*1978*	*1979*	*1980*	*1981*
Wheat	16,650	16,700	17,500	16,500	17,000
Barley	4,750	4,750	5,240	5,300	5,900
Maize	1,265	1,300	1,350	1,240	1,110
Rye	690	620	620	525	500
Tobacco	248	293	217	234	200
Oats	370	370	370	355	350
Rice	165	190	225	143	...

On 7 June 1945 the Grand National Assembly passed the Land Reform Bill under which large tracts of agricultural land are being distributed to peasants without land or with insufficient for their subsistence.

Livestock (1981): 48·63m. sheep, 19,043,000 goats, 15,894,000 cattle, 1,345,000 asses, 794,000 horses, 1·03m. buffaloes.

In 1981 Turkey produced 33·6m. tonnes of wool, 547,000 tonnes of cattle and sheep meat and 256,000 tonnes of poultry.

Forestry. On 8 Feb. 1937 a new forest law was voted, providing for state control of all forests, including those under private ownership. It contains measures for planting, protection against fire, marauders and insects, and lays down penalties for infringements of its clauses. The most wooded Ils are Kastamonu, Aydın, Bursa, Bolu, Trabzon, Konya and Balıkesir. Of the forest land, 10,417,560 hectares belonged to the State in 1951. In 1980 total forest land was 20·17m. hectares.

Fisheries. On 25 Aug. 1964 Turkey extended her waters in which she has exclusive fishing rights to 12 nautical miles. In 1980, 424,451 tons of sea and fresh water food was produced.

INDUSTRY AND TRADE

Industry. Production in 1981 included 15,043,000 tonnes of cement and 365,000 tonnes of paper. Industrial plants number about 30,000.

In 1981 Turkey produced (in tonnes) 4,203,000 of iron and steel, 10,449,000 of petroleum products, 2,364,000 of crude oil, 2,346,000 of iron ore (1978), 15,057,000 of lignite (clean), 3,973,000 of coal (clean), 208,000 of chrome, 27,300 of copper, 828,000 of boron (1978). There are steel works at Karabük, Ereğli and Iskenderun.

Labour. On 27 June 1945 a Ministry of Labour was set up, superseding the Department of Labour under the control of the Ministry of Economic Affairs. According to the strikes and lock-outs law, which came into effect on 24 Aug. 1963, strikes and lock-outs may be declared only after due effort has been made to negotiate and after the local authorities as well as the Ministry of Labour have been informed.

Conditions of work are regulated by the Labour Act of 12 Aug. 1967, which covers all places of work, employing more than 3 persons, outside agriculture. Children under 16 must not be employed for more than 8 hours a day, and employment should not impede school attendance. The Act provides for annual paid holidays of 12–24 working days and regulates overtime payment.

The trade-union movement began in 1947. There are 4 national confederations (including Türk-İş and Disk) and 6 federations. There are 35 unions affiliated to Türk-İş and 17 employers' federations affiliated to Disk, whose activities were banned on 12 Sept. 1980. In 1979, labour unions totalled 802 and employers' unions, 108.

Employment, 1975: Manufacturing, 1,243,567; construction, 447,342; transport, communications and warehousing, 512,327; mining, 108,506; services, 176,207. There were 157,466 manufacturing firms, 236,995 trading establishments and 580,635 service establishments.

Commerce. Imports and exports (in US$1m.) for calendar years:

	1978	*1979*	*1980*	*1981*
Imports	4,599	5,069	7,909	8,933
Exports	2,288	2,261	2,910	4,703

Exports (1980) in US$1m.: Cotton, 323·6; hazelnuts, 395·8; tobacco, 233·7; textiles, 424·3; raisins, 130·3; citrus fruit, 86·6; wheat, 80·4.

Imports (1980) in US$1m.: Crude oil, 2,710·1; machinery, 842·4; chemicals, 1,121·7; motor vehicles, 222·4; iron and steel, 462·5; petroleum products, 723·5; electrical appliances, 270·4; rubber and plastics, 181·4.

Total trade between Turkey and UK (British Department of Trade returns, in £1,000 sterling):

	1978	*1979*	*1980*	*1981*	*1982*
Imports to UK	64,574	67,060	49,243	128,226	207,763
Exports and re-exports from UK	110,571	135,734	147,118	159,849	218,116

Tourism. A tourist industry is developing. The number of foreign tourists was over 1·4m. in 1981.

COMMUNICATIONS

Roads. Turkey had, in 1980, 60,761 km of national highways, of which 54,318 were hard surfaced. In 1980 there were registered 1,134,803 motor vehicles, including 710,915 passenger cars and 96,707 buses.

Railways. The total length of railway lines in 1980 was 8,141 km, all state-owned; 202 km are electrified.

In 1980 Turkish railways carried 2·6m. passengers and 1·2m. tonnes of freight.

Aviation. The State Airways Administration, formed in 1938, has been converted into the mixed company Turkish Airlines (Türk Havayollari Anonim Ortaklığı); British Airways became a partner in July 1957. It conducts foreign services to Athens, Beirut, Brussels, Amsterdam, Munich, Rome, Frankfurt, Vienna, London, Paris, Belgrade, Nicosia, Tel-Aviv and Baghdad.

In 1977 Turkish Airlines carried 6,545,000 passengers, 1·39m. kg of mail (1972) and 144·5m. kg of freight (1972). İstanbul or Ankara are connected with all the principal countries by 27 national airlines.

Shipping. In 1977 Turkish Maritime Lines and private companies had a gross tonnage of 1,699,910, with a total of 347 ships. The main ports in order of tonnage capacity are: İstanbul, İzmir, Samsun, Mersin, İskenderun and Trabzon.

Ports built or extended since 1950 are İskenderun, Ereğli, Trabzon, Samsun, Mersin, Zonguldak, Giresun, Hopa, Antalya and Bandirma. New facilities have been provided at Haydarpaşa, Salıpazari, Hopa, Yarımca and İzmir.

Post and Broadcasting. Number of telephones in 1980 was 1,747,854; İstanbul, 553,603; Ankara, 343,192.

In 1980 there were 4,283,753 licensed wireless sets. There were 3,348,138 television receivers.

Newspapers. In 1975 there were 2,362 daily newspapers and periodicals in the Turkish language, 2 in Greek, 1 in French, 1 in Armenian and 1 in English. In 1976, 27 dailies were published in Ankara, 40 dailies in İstanbul, 6 dailies in İzmir, 5 dailies in Bursa and 4 dailies in Konya.

JUSTICE, RELIGION, EDUCATION AND WELFARE

Justice. The unified legal system consists of: (1) justices of the peace (single judges with limited but summary penal and civil jurisdiction); (2) courts of first instance (single judges, dealing with cases outside the jurisdiction of (3) and (4)); (3) central criminal courts (a president and 2 judges, dealing with cases where the crime is punishable by imprisonment over 5 years); (4) commercial courts (3 judges); (5) state security courts, to prosecute offences against the integrity of the state (a president and 4 judges, 2 of the latter being military).

The civil and military Courts of Cassation sit at Ankara.

The Council of State is the highest administration tribunal; it consists of 5 chambers. Its 31 judges are nominated from among high-ranking personalities in politics, economy, law, the army, etc.

The Military Court of Cassation in Ankara is the highest military tribunal. The Military Administrative Court deals with the judicial control of administrative acts and deeds concerning military personnel.

The Constitutional Court, set up under the Constitution, can review and annul legislation and try the President of the Republic, Ministers and senior judges. It consists of 15 regular and 5 alternate members.

The Civil Code and the Code of Obligations have been adapted from the corresponding Swiss codes. The Penal Code is largely based upon the Italian Penal

Code, and the Code of Civil Procedure closely resembles that of the Canton of Neuchâtel. The Commercial Code is based on the German.

Religion. Freedom of religion is guaranteed by the Constitution. Although Islam is not the official state religion of Turkey, Moslems form 98·2% of the population. The administration of the Moslem religious organizations is in charge of the Presidency of Religious Affairs, attached to the Prime Minister's office. The Turkish Republic is a secular state.

İstanbul is the seat of the Œcumenical Patriarch, who is the head of the Orthodox Church in Turkey. The Armenian Church (Gregorian) is ruled by a Patriarch in İstanbul who is subordinate to the Katholikos of Etchmiadzin, the spiritual head of all Armenians. The Armenian Apostolic Church is ruled by the Patriarch of Cilicia. The Chaldeans (Nestorian Uniats) have a Bishop at Mardin. The Syrian Uniats have a See of Mardin and Amida, but it is united with their Patriarchate of Antioch (residence, Damascus). Greek Uniats (Byzantine Rite) have as their Ordinary in İstanbul, the Titular Bishop of Gratianopolis. The Latins have an Apostolic Delegate in İstanbul and an Archbishop in İzmir, but their Patriarch of İstanbul is titular and non-resident. There is a Grand Rabbi (Hahambaşı) in İstanbul for the Jews, who are nearly all Sephardim.

At the 1965 census there were in Turkey 31,391,421 Moslems, 73,725 Orthodox, 69,526 Gregorians, 25,833 Roman Catholics, 22,883 Protestants, 14,758 other Christians (unspecified), 38,267 Jews, 14,661 adherents of other religions, 1,212 without religion, 602 undeclared or unknown.

A law passed in Dec. 1934 forbids the wearing of clerical garb for those other than religious leaders except in places of worship and during divine service. The constitution forbids the political exploitation of religion or any impairment of the secular character of the republic.

In lieu of religious formulae, all citizens take oaths on their honour.

Education. Elementary education is compulsory and co-educational and, in state schools, free. All children from 7 to 12 are to receive primary instruction, which may be given in state schools, schools maintained by communities, or private schools, or, subject to certain tests, at home. The state schools are under the direct control of the Ministry of Education. They include primary schools, secondary or middle schools, and *lycées* or secondary schools of a superior kind. There are also training schools for male and female teachers, and technical schools. In 1979 there were 18 universities and 102 other institutes of higher education; in 1982, a further 8 universities were founded. The important non-Moslem communities in İstanbul maintain their own schools, which, like all 'private' schools, are subject to the supervision of the Ministry of Education.

Literacy of the population of 6 years and over was 10·6% in 1927, 19·2% in 1935, 29% in 1945, 40·9% in 1955, 48·7% in 1965, 49% in 1970, 61·7% in 1975.

Religious instruction in schools, hitherto prohibited, was made optional in elementary and middle schools in May 1948. There are many training schools for Moslem clergy as well as a Faculty of Theology in Ankara.

Statistics for 1979–80	*Number*	*Teachers*	*Students*
Primary schools (state and private)	44,303	199,245	5,622,000
Middle schools (state and private)	4,100	30,959	1,179,000
Lycées (state and private)	1,104	36,266	532,000
Professional and technical schools	1,719	28,644	515,000
Faculties (university and higher education)	347	20,643	270,000

On 1 Nov. 1928 the Grand National Assembly voted a law for the adoption of Latin characters as from 1 Dec. 1928. The publication of books in Arabic characters was forbidden after 1 Jan. 1929.

Health. Public health is the responsibility of the Ministry of Health and Social Welfare, established in 1920; social insurance for workers comes under the Workers' Insurance Institution attached to the Ministry of Labour. A law promulgated in 1961 and being implemented from 1963 provides for the nationalization of the health services within 15 years. In 1980, 2·2m. workers and employees were covered by social insurance, including free medical care.

In 1980 there were 27,241 doctors and 99,117 beds in some 827 hospitals.

The counterpart of the Red Cross in Turkey is the Red Crescent Society founded in 1877.

DIPLOMATIC REPRESENTATIVES

Of Turkey in Great Britain (43 Belgrave Sq., London, SW1X 8PA)
Ambassador: Rahmi Gümrükçüoğlu (accredited 4 Aug. 1981).

Of Great Britain in Turkey (Sehit Ersan Caddesi 46/A, Cankaya, Ankara)
Ambassador: R. M. Russel.

Of Turkey in the USA (1606–23rd St., NW, Washington, D.C., 20008)
Ambassador: Şükrü Elekdağ.

Of the USA in Turkey (110 Ataturk Blvd., Ankara)
Ambassador: Robert Strausz-Hupe.

Of Turkey to the United Nations
Ambassador: Coşkun Kirca.

Books of Reference

Statistical Information: The State Institute of Statistics in Ankara consists of a research bureau and 10 sections dealing with agriculture, education, foreign trade, etc. It published an *Annuaire Statistique/Istatistik Yılığı* (1928–53) and *Aylık Istatistik Bülteni*, Monthly Bulletin of Statistics.

Almanac: Turkey 1981. 1981
The Turkish Constitution, 1971. Ankara, 1972
Resmî Gazete, Official Gazette. Ankara
Konjonktür. Ministry of Commerce (three times a year, from 1940)
Banque Centrale de la République de Turquie. *Bulletin Mensuel* (from Jan. 1953)
Bulletins of the Chambers of Commerce of Istanbul and Izmir
Ahmad, F., *The Turkish Experiment in Democracy.* London, 1977
Goodwin, G., *A History of Ottoman Architecture.* London, 1971
Guclu, M., *Turkey.* [Bibliography] Oxford and Santa Barbara, 1981
Hale, W., *The Political and Economic Development of Modern Turkey.* London, 1981
Kazancigil, A. and Ozbudun, E., (eds.) *Atatürk: Founder of a Modern State.* London, 1981
Kinross, Lord, *Atatürk.* London, 1964
Koray, Enver, *Türkiye Tarih Yayınları Bibliografyası 1729–1950 (Bibliography of Historical Works on Turkey).* Ankara, 1952
Kortepeter, C. M., *Ottoman Imperialism During Reformation: Europe and the Caucasus.* London, 1972
Landau, J. M., *Radical Politics in Modern Turkey.* Leiden, 1974
Sezer, D. B., *Turkey's Security Policies.* London, 1981
Tamkoc, M., *The Warrior Diplomats.* Univ. of Utah Press, 1976
Weiker W., *Political Tutelage and Democracy in Turkey.* Leiden, 1972.—*The Modernization of Turkey.* New York, 1981

State Library: MilliKütüphane Müdürlüğü, Ankara. *Director-General:* Müjgân Cunbur.

THE TURKS AND CAICOS ISLANDS

Capital: Grand Turk
Population: 7,436 (1980)

HISTORY. After a long period of rival French and Spanish claims the islands were eventually secured to the British Crown by the appointment in 1766 of a Resident British Agent, and became a separate colony in 1973 after association at various times with the colonies of the Bahamas and Jamaica.

AREA AND POPULATION. The Turks and Caicos Islands are geographically part of the Bahamas extremity, of which they form the south-eastern archipelago. There are upwards of 30 small cays; area 192 sq. miles (430 sq. km). Only 6 are inhabited; the largest, Grand Caicos, is 30 miles long by 2 to 3 miles broad. The seat of government is at Grand Turk, 7 miles long by 1·25 broad; 3,146 inhabitants. Population, 1980 census, 7,436; South Caicos, 1,392; Middle Caicos, 371; North Caicos, 1,266; Providenciales, 979; Salt Cay, 282.

Vital statistics (1980): Births, 247; marriages, 32; deaths, 13.

CONSTITUTION AND GOVERNMENT. A new Constitution was introduced in Aug. 1976, providing for an Executive Council and a Legislative Council. The Governor retains responsibility for external affairs, internal security, defence and certain other matters. The Executive Council comprises 3 official members: the Chief Secretary, the Financial Secretary and the Attorney-General; a Chief Minister and 3 other ministers from among the elected members of the Legislative Council; and is presided over by the Governor. The Legislative Council consists of a Speaker, the 3 official members of the Executive Council, 11 elected members and 2 appointed members.

Governor: C. J. Turner, OBE.

Flag: British Blue Ensign with the shield of the Colony in the fly.

ECONOMY

Budget. 1981–82 revenue US$5,338,000; budgetary aid, US$1,346,000; expenditure, US$6,684,000.

Currency. The currency in circulation is US$.

Banking. In 1980 there were 6 commercial banks operating in the Islands. The Government Savings Bank has 3 branches. Barclays Bank International and the Oxford International Bank and Trust Co. Ltd have offices in Grand Turk with branches in South Caicos, North Caicos and Providenciales.

COMMERCE (1981–82). Exports, US$2,668,080, and imports, US$15,233,973. Principal imports, food, drink, tobacco and clothing. The main exports are crawfish, dried and fresh conch, and conch shells. The catch is processed in three plants operating in South Caicos.

Total trade between Turks and Caicos Islands and UK (British Department of Trade returns, in £1,000 sterling):

	1979	*1980*	*1981*	*1982*
Imports to UK	257	8	5	5
Exports and re-exports from UK	276	295	973	405

TOURISM. Number of hotels and guest houses, 19 (beds 432). Number of visitors, 1981, 11,509.

COMMUNICATIONS

Aviation. There is a 6,335 ft paved airfield on Grand Turk. On South Caicos there is a 6,000 ft paved airstrip under construction and on Providenciales a 7,000 ft paved airstrip. There are small paved and unpaved airstrips on the other 3 inhabited islands. Air Florida Airlines operate a thrice weekly passenger service to Miami. Bahamas Air operate a twice weekly scheduled passenger service to the Bahamas. Air Turks and Caicos operate a twice daily service to the islands and 2 flights a week to Cap Haitien (Haiti). Turks Air Ltd operates a regular weekly cargo service to Miami.

Shipping. Registered shipping (1981), 165 sailing vessels of 2,366 tons and 34 motor vessels of 5,015 tons.

Post and Broadcasting. Air-mail is received and dispatched by Miami twice or thrice weekly. Surface mail from all parts of the world is routed *via* the US arriving at 3 weekly intervals from Miami, Florida. There is no regular outgoing surface mail. Cable & Wireless (West Indies) provide internal and international cable, telephone, telex and telegraph services. There were (1981) 932 telephones. North Caicos and Salt Cay are linked with the Providenciales and Grand Turk exchanges respectively. The Government operates a radio broadcasting service from the Islands to Grand Turk, call sign VSI radio Turks and Caicos, for a total of 106 hours a week on 1,460 KHZ medium wave. Number of receivers, approximately 6,000.

EDUCATION AND WELFARE

Education. Education is free and compulsory up to 15 years of age in the 14 government primary and 3 government secondary schools. There are also 3 private primary schools. Number on rolls, 1 Jan. 1982, 2,124; Turks and Caicos High School, 375; South Caicos and Providenciales, 110; North Caicos Junior High, 121. Expenditure on education 1981–82 was US$1,000,278.

Health. In 1981 there were 3 doctors and 30 hospital beds.

TUVALU

Capital: Funafuti
Population: 7,349 (1979)
GNP per capita: US$570 (1980)

HISTORY. Formerly the Ellice Islands, a British Protectorate since 1892. On the recommendation of a Commissioner, appointed by the British Government, to consider requests that the island group be separated from the Gilbert Islands, a referendum was held in 1974. There was a large majority in favour of separation and this took place in Oct. 1975. Independence was achieved on 1 Oct. 1978.

AREA AND POPULATION. Tuvalu (formerly the Ellice Islands) lie between 5° 30′ and 11° S. lat. and 176° and 180° E. long. and comprise Nanumea, Nanumanga, Niutao, Nui, Vaitupu, Nukufetau, Funafuti (administrative centre), Nukulaelae and Niulakita. Population (census 1979) 7,349. Area approximately 9½ sq. miles (24 sq. km). The population is of a Polynesian race.

CONSTITUTION AND GOVERNMENT. The Constitution provides for a Prime Minister and 4 other Ministers to be elected from among the 12 elected members of the House of Parliament, for which general elections took place on 8 Sept. 1981. The Cabinet, chaired by the Prime Minister, consists of the 4 ministers and 2 *ex officio* members, the Attorney-General and the Secretary for Finance, who are also *ex officio* members of the House of Assembly. Local Government services are provided by an elected Island Council on each of the 8 atolls.

Governor-General: Fiatau Penitala Teo, GCMG, MBE.
Prime Minister: Dr Tomasi Puapua.
Finance: Henry F. Naisali. *Social Services:* Falaile Pilitati. *Commerce and Natural Resources:* Lale Seluka. *Works and Communications:* Metia Tealoi.

National flag: Light blue with the Union Jack in the canton, and 9 gold stars in the fly arranged in the same pattern as the 9 islands.

Local Government. There is a town council on Funafuti and island councils on the 7 other main islands, each consisting of 6 elected members including a president.

INTERNATIONAL RELATIONS

Membership. Tuvalu is a member of the Commonwealth and is an ACP state of EEC.

ECONOMY

Budget. In 1983 the budget envisaged expenditure of $A3·5m.

Currency. The unit of currency is the Australian *dollar* although Tuvaluan coins up to $A1 are in local circulation.

Banking. The Tuvalu National Bank was established at Funafuti in 1980.

NATURAL RESOURCES

Agriculture. Coconut palms are the main crop. Fruit and vegetables are grown for local consumption.

Fisheries. Sea fishing is excellent but is largely unexploited.

INDUSTRY AND TRADE

Industry. The main sources of income are from overseas remittances from Tuvaluans working abroad, philatelic and copra sales, and handicrafts.

Employment. A significant number of the population are employed in the phosphate industry on Nauru. The remainder are engaged in harvesting coconuts and fishing.

Commerce. Commerce is dominated by co-operative societies, the Tuvalu Co-operative Wholesale Society being the main importer. Imports (1981) $124,480.

Total trade between Tuvalu and UK (British Department of Trade returns, in £1,000 sterling):

	1979	*1980*	*1981*	*1982*
Imports to UK	174	34	6	7
Exports and re-exports from UK	67	362	132	48

COMMUNICATIONS

Aviation. Tuvalu is linked to the outside world by Fiji Air which operates twice a week, on Monday and Thursday, and Air Tungaru once a week on Tuesdays.

Shipping. Funafuti is the only port and a deep-water wharf was opened in 1980. Inter-island communication is by ship; a limited service using an amphibious plane came into operation in 1980.

Post and Broadcasting. The Tuvalu Broadcasting Service transmits daily in Tuvaluan and English and all islands have daily radio communication with Funafuti.

JUSTICE, RELIGION, EDUCATION AND WELFARE

Justice. There is a High Court presided over by the Chief Justice of Fiji. Appeals lie to the Fiji Court of Appeal.

Religion. The majority of the population are Christians mainly Protestant but with small groups of Roman Catholics, Seventh Day Adventists, Jehovah's Witnesses and Bahai's.

Education. In 1980 there was 1 secondary school jointly administered by the Government and the Church. In addition there were 8 primary schools with (1982, inclusive of 300 pupils in community training centres) 1,290 pupils run by Island Councils and subsidized by the central government. In 1979, a maritime school was opened on Amatuku islet. Tuvaluans requiring further education must seek it abroad.

Health. In 1978 there was 1 central hospital with 36 beds situated at Funafuti. There were 3 doctors.

DIPLOMATIC REPRESENTATIVES

Of Great Britain in Tuvalu
High Commissioner: Roger Barltrop (resides in Suva).

Of Tuvalu in the USA
Ambassador: Ionatana Ionatana (resides in Tuvalu).

UGANDA

Capital: Kampala
Population: 13·22m. (1979)
GNP per capita: US$280 1980)

HISTORY. Uganda became a British Protectorate in 1894, the province of Buganda being recognized as a native kingdom under its Kabaka. In 1961 Uganda was granted internal self-government with federal status for Buganda. The country became independent in 1962.

AREA AND POPULATION. Uganda is bounded on the north by Sudan, on east by Kenya, on south by Tanzania and west by Zaïre. Total area 91,343 sq. miles (236,860 sq. km), including 15,217 sq. miles (39,459 sq. km) of swamp and water.

The population of Uganda was 13·22m. (1979 estimate). On 4 Aug. 1972 President Amin announced that he would ask the UK to take responsibility for Asians in Uganda holding British passports. Later that year 27,200 Asians had left Uganda for Britain. The majority of the Africans (1,044,000) are Baganda, the tribe from which the country takes its name.

About 3m. Africans speak Bantu languages; there are a few Congo pygmies living near the Semliki River; the rest of the Africans belong to the Hamitic, Nilotic and Sudanese groups. Ki-Swahili is generally understood in trading centres. The capital is Kampala; the population of greater Kampala (1975), 332,000.

The official language is English.

CONSTITUTION AND GOVERNMENT. Uganda became a fully independent member of the Commonwealth on 9 Oct. 1962 after nearly 70 years of British rule. Full sovereign status was granted by the Uganda Independence Act, 1962, and the Constitution is embodied in the Uganda (Independence) Order in Council, 1962. The post of Governor-General was on 9 Oct. 1963 replaced by that of President as head of state, elected by the National Assembly for a 5-year term.

Uganda became a republic on 8 Sept. 1967. Under the 1967 Constitution, the executive authority is vested in the President.

In 1971, Dr A. Milton Obote was overthrown by troops led by Gen. Idi Amin.

In April 1979 a force of the Tanzanian Army and Ugandan exiles advanced into Uganda taking Kampala on 11 April. On 14 April Dr Yusuf Lule was sworn in as President and the country is to be administered, initially, by the Uganda National Liberation Front.

The former Attorney-General, Godfrey Lukongwa Binaisa, QC, was appointed President by the National Consultative Council on 20 June 1979. Dr Lule subsequently left the country. Dr Binaisa was subsequently overthrown in May 1980 by the army. At the elections held on 10–11 Dec. 1980, the Uganda People's Congress was declared to have held 72 of the 124 elective seats in the new Parliament, the Democratic Party 51 seats, and the Uganda Patriotic Movement 1 seat.

President, Minister of Foreign Affairs and Finance: Dr Milton Obote.
Vice-President, Minister of Defence: Paulo Muwanga.
Prime Minister: Otema Alimadi.

National flag: Six horizontal stripes of black, yellow, red, black, yellow, red, in the centre a small white disc bearing a representation of a Balearic Crested Crane.

For administrative purposes Uganda is divided into 10 provinces, subdivided into 38 districts. The provinces are: Busoga, Central, Eastern, Karamoja, Nile, North Buganda, Northern, South Buganda, Southern, Western.

DEFENCE

Army. The Army had a strength of 5,000 in 1982 and was organized into 9 infantry, 2 reconnaissance, 1 mechanized, 1 commando and 1 training battalion.

Navy. A small lake patrol was initiated in 1977.

Air Force. The Air Force was formed in 1964 and later underwent rapid expansion with the assistance of Israeli and Czechoslovakian training missions. Prior to the events of 1979 equipment included about 10 MiG-21 and 12 MiG-17 jet fighter-bombers, 2 MiG-15 UTI two-seat trainers, about 5 L-29 Delfin and 8 Israeli-built Magister armed jet trainers, 11 Super Cub liaison aircraft, 5 Piaggio P 149 piston-engined trainers, 6 Swiss-built Bravo primary trainers, 6 Agusta-Bell 205, 2 Agusta-Bell 206 JetRanger and some Mi-8 helicopters. Personnel numbered about 1,000. In addition the Police Air Wing had 1 Twin Otter and 1 Caribou twin-engined STOL transports, 1 Turbo-Beaver and 1 Piper Aztec light transports, and about 7 Bell 205, JetRanger, Bell 212 and Scout helicopters. The status of these aircraft was unknown in early 1983.

INTERNATIONAL RELATIONS

Membership. Uganda is a member of UN, OAU, the Commonwealth and is an ACP state of EEC.

ECONOMY

Budget. The revenue and expenditure (exclusive of loan disbursements) for fiscal years (1 July–30 June) were (in Uganda Sh. 1m.):

	1976–77	*1977–78*	*1978–79*	*1979–80*
Revenue	4,305	5,856	3,197	4,871
Expenditure	5,201	6,287	5,441	6,805

Currency. East African Currency Board notes ceased to be legal tender from 14 Sept. 1967. The monetary unit is the *Uganda shilling* divided into 100 *cents*. In March 1983, £1 = 117 Uganda shillings; US$1 = 116 Uganda shillings.

Banking. The Bank of Uganda was set up on 16 May 1966; its external assets as at 31 Aug. 1967 were £9m. The Uganda Credit and Savings Bank, set up in 1950, was on 9 Oct. 1965 reconstituted as the Uganda Commercial Bank, with its capital fully owned by the Government.

Barclays Bank International has 11 branches and 7 agencies; National & Grindlays Bank Ltd has 12 branches and 12 agencies; the Standard Bank Ltd has 6 branches and 2 agencies; the Bank of Baroda Ltd has 3 branches; the Bank of India Ltd has 2 branches. Other banks operating in Uganda are the Algemene Bank Nederland NV and the Commercial Bank of Africa.

ENERGY AND NATURAL RESOURCES

Electricity. Industrial expansion is based on hydro-electric power provided by the Owen Falls scheme, which has a capacity of 150,000 kwh. Production (1976) 696m. kwh.

Minerals. With the opening of the Kilembe mine in 1956, copper has become Uganda's most valuable mineral export. Production (1978) in tonnes: Blister copper, 600; tin, 120; phosphate rock (1977) 5,000.

Agriculture. In 1980, agriculture was still recovering from the administration of 1971–79. Cotton and coffee are the principal exports, the former being grown entirely and the latter very largely by African farmers. Production (1980) in 1,000 tonnes: Tobacco, 3; coffee, 135·2; cotton lint, 13·3; tea, 1·5; sugar, 1·5.

Livestock (1981): Cattle, 5m.; asses, 16,000; sheep, 1m.; goats, 2·2m.; pigs, 250,000; poultry, 13·3m.

Forestry. Exploitable forests consist almost entirely of hardwoods. Internal consumption is rising. During 1964–65 approximately 28,000 tonnes of sawn timber were produced. About half of the timber exported goes to the UK and another quarter to Kenya and Tanganyika, from which the bulk of the softwood imports are obtained.

Fishery. With its 13,600 sq. miles of lakes and many rivers, Uganda possesses one of the largest fresh-water fisheries in the world. In 1966 fish production was 80,000 tonnes with a retail value of £6·5m. Fish farming (especially carp and tilapia) is a growing industry.

COMMERCE. Trade (in US$1m.):

	1979	*1980*	*1981*[1]
Imports	322·1	503·7	400·0
Exports	397·2	319·1	220·0

[1] Estimate.

Total trade between Uganda and UK (British Department of Trade returns, in £1,000 sterling):

	1978	*1979*	*1980*	*1981*	*1982*
Imports to UK	47,651	19,189	30,735	18,186	23,107
Exports and re-exports from UK	39,358	18,881	33,526	24,650	31,272

COMMUNICATIONS

Roads. There are 3,876 miles of all-weather roads maintained by the Ministry of Works, of which 796 miles are two-lane bitumenized highways, and some 11,230 miles of other roads, maintained by district governments.

Railways. On 26 Aug. 1977 Uganda Railways was formed following break-up of the East African Railways administration. The network totals 1,120 km (metre gauge). In 1980 railways carried 1·3m. passengers and 168,365 tonnes of freight.

Aviation. Entebbe had a first-class international airport which had direct flights to Europe, Rhodesia, Sudan, Kenya, Burundi, Ghana, Ethiopia, Zaïre, Nigeria, USSR, and Rwanda by Sudan Airways, Air Congo, SABENA, Air France, Ethiopian Airlines, Air Zaïre and Aeroflot. The airport was damaged during the 1979 invasion. Eleven other government airfields are used for internal communications.

Posts. There were 48,884 telephones in use at 1 Jan. 1978.

Cinemas. In 1971 there were 16 cinemas with a seating capacity of 8,000.

JUSTICE, EDUCATION AND WELFARE

Justice. The High Court of Uganda, presided over by the Chief Justice and 12 puisne judges, exercises original and appellate jurisdiction throughout Uganda. Subordinate courts, presided over by Chief Magistrates and Magistrates of the first, second and third grade, are established in all areas: jurisdiction varies with the grade of Magistrate. Chief and first-grade Magistrates are professionally qualified; second-and third-grade Magistrates are trained to diploma level at the Law School, Entebbe.

Chief Magistrates exercise supervision over and hear appeals from second- and third-grade courts.

The Court of Appeal for Eastern Africa was re-established on 9 Dec. 1962 as the Court of Appeal for Uganda; it hears appeals from the High Court.

A law school has been established at Entebbe to train magistrates in civil and criminal law.

The African courts have been integrated with the Central Government Courts so that a unified courts system has been established.

Education. Education is a joint undertaking by the Government, local authorities and, to some extent, voluntary agencies. The education system is divided into 3 sectors, primary, secondary and post-secondary. The primary course covers 7 years. There were 786,899 pupils in grant-aided primary schools in 1972. Education at secondary level falls into 4 categories, namely, secondary schools, which are the grammar type of schools with a course extending over 6 years to High School Certificate; technical schools; farm schools; and primary teacher-training colleges. Further education is provided at the Uganda Technical College, the National Teachers' College, the Uganda College of Commerce and Agricultural Colleges.

There are also several Departmental Training Schools for training staff for different departments.

The medical department has 8 such schools for training nurses, midwives, medical assistants, health inspectors, and other medical staff.

University level education is available at Makerere University College and the 2 other constituent Colleges of the University of East Africa; the University College, Nairobi, in Kenya, and the University College, Dar es Salaam, in Tanzania. Uganda students also go to universities and colleges outside East Africa for higher education.

Health. In 1973 there were 300 doctors and over 15,000 hospital beds.

DIPLOMATIC REPRESENTATIVES

Of Uganda in Great Britain (Uganda Hse., Trafalgar Sq., London, WC2N 5DX)
High Commissioner: Shafiq Arain (also Minister of Portfolio in Ugandan cabinet).

Of Great Britain in Uganda (10/12 Obote Ave., Kampala)
High Comissioner: W. N. Hillier-Fry, CMG.

Of Uganda in the USA (5909, 16th St., NW, Washington, D.C., 20011)
Ambassador: John Wycliffe Lwamafa.

Of USA in Uganda
Ambassador: Gordon R. Beyer.

Of Uganda to the United Nations
Ambassador: Olara Otunnu.

Books of Reference

Atlas of Uganda. Dept. of Lands and Surveys. Kampala, 1962
Collison, R. L., *Uganda.* [Bibliography] Oxford and Santa Barbara, 1981
Faller, L. A. (ed.), *The King's Men.* OUP, 1964
Gukiina, P. M., *Uganda: A Case Study in African Political Development.* Univ. of Notre Dame Press, 1972
Hills, D., *The White Pumpkin.* New York, 1976
Jørgensen, J. J., *Uganda: A Modern History.* London, 1981
Kitching, A. L., and Blackledge, G. R., *A Luganda–English and English–Luganda Dictionary.* Kampala, 1925
Larimore, A. E., *The Alien Town: Patterns of Settlement in Uganda.* Chicago, 1959
Listowel, J., *Amin.* Irish Univ. Press, 1973

UNION OF SOVIET SOCIALIST REPUBLICS

Capital: Moscow
Population: 271·2m. (1983)
GNP per capita: US$4,550 (1980)

Soyuz Sovyetskikh Sotsialisticheskikh Respublik

POST-REVOLUTION HISTORY. Up to 12 March 1917 the territory now forming the USSR, together with that of Finland, Poland and certain tracts ceded in 1918 to Turkey, but less the territories then forming part of the German, Austro-Hungarian and Japanese empires–East Prussia, Eastern Galicia, Transcarpathia, Bukovina, South Sakhalin and Kurile Islands–which were acquired during and after the Second World War, was constituted as the Russian Empire. It was governed as an autocracy under the Tsar, with the aid of Ministers responsible to himself and a State Duma with limited legislative powers, elected by provincial assemblies chosen by indirect elections on a restricted franchise.

On 8 March 1917 a revolution broke out. The Duma parties, on 12 Dec. set up a Provisional Committee of the State Duma, while the factory workmen and the insurgent garrison of Petrograd elected a Council (Soviet) of Workers' and Soldiers' Deputies. Soviets were also elected by the workmen in other towns, in the Army and Navy and, as time went on, by the peasantry. On 15 March 1917 the Tsar abdicated, and the Provisional Committee, by agreement with the Petrograd Soviet, appointed a Provisional Government and, on 14 Sept., proclaimed a republic. However, a political struggle went on between the supporters of the Provisional Government–the Mensheviks and the Socialist-Revolutionaries–and the Bolsheviks, who advocated the assumption of power by the Soviets. When they had won majorities in the Soviets of the principal cities and of the armed forces on several fronts, the Bolsheviks organized an insurrection through a Military-Revolutionary Committee of the Petrograd Soviet. On 7 Nov. 1917 the Committee arrested the Provisional Government and transferred power to the second All-Russian Congress of Soviets. This elected a new government, the Council of People's Commissars, headed by Lenin.

On 25 Jan. 1918 the third All-Russian Congress of Soviets issued a Declaration of Rights of the Toiling and Exploited People, which proclaimed Russia a Republic of Soviets of Workers', Soldiers' and Peasants' Deputies; and on 10 July 1918 the fifth Congress adopted a Constitution for the Russian Soviet Federal Socialist Republic. In the course of the civil war other Soviet Republics were set up in the Ukraine, Belorussia and Transcaucasia. These first entered into treaty relations with the RSFSR and then, in 1922, joined with it in a closely integrated Union.

AREA AND POPULATION. The total area of the Soviet Union in April 1983 was 22·4m. sq. km (8·65m. sq. miles). The census population on 15 Jan. 1970 was 241·7m. (111·4m. males, 130·3m. females; 136m. urban, 105·7m. rural). The census population on 17 Jan. 1979 was 262·4m. (122·3m. males, 140·1m. females, 163·6m. urban, 98·9m. rural). The increase of 27·6m. in urban population between 1970 and 1979 was due to natural increase and 15·6m. rural dwellers becoming part of the urban population resulting from migration because of the development of industry and transport, and increased farm mechanization, and from the urbanization of large rural centres. Consequently, despite a natural increase of 8·7m. in rural areas, there was a net decrease of 6·9m. over this period. Population at 1 Jan. 1982, 268·8m. (125·7m. males, 143·1m. females; 171·7m. urban; 97·1m. rural).

Regions, towns, streets, factories, schools, etc., named after Stalin were renamed in Nov. 1961 when Stalin's body was removed from the Lenin-Stalin tomb in Red

Square in Moscow. Similarly, in Jan. 1962 towns bearing the names of Molotov, Kaganovich and Malenkov were renamed.

The areas (in 1,000 sq. km) and population (in 1m., in Jan. 1982) of the constituent republics are as follows (capitals in brackets):

Constituent Republics	*Area*	*Population*	*Constituent Republics*	*Area*	*Population*
RSFSR (Moscow)	17,075	140·0	Tadzhikistan (Dushanbe)	143	4·1
Ukraine (Kiev)	604	50·3	Kirgizia (Frunze)	199	3·7
Uzbekistan (Tashkent)	447	16·6	Lithuania (Vilnius)	65	3·5
Kazakhstan (Alma-Ata)	2,717	15·3	Armenia (Yerevan)	30	3·1
Belorussia (Minsk)	208	9·7	Turkmenistan (Ashkhabad)	488	3·0
Azerbaijan (Baku)	87	6·3	Latvia (Riga)	64	2·6
Georgia (Tbilisi)	70	5·1	Estonia (Tallinn)	45	1·5
Moldavia (Kishinev)	34	4·0			

Nationalities. The most numerous nationalities at the 1979 census were: 137·4m. Russians, 42·3m. Ukrainians, 12·5m. Uzbeks, 9·5m. Belorussians, 6·6m. Kazakhs, 6·3m. Tatars, 5·5m. Azerbaijanians, 4·1m. Armenians, 3·6m. Georgians, 3m. Moldavians, 2·9m. Tadzhiks, 2·9m. Lithuanians, 2m. Turkmenians, 1·9m. Germans, 1·9m. Kirgiz, 1·8m. Jews, 1·8m. Chuvashes, 1·4m. Latvians, 1·4m. Bashkirs, 1·2m. Mordovians, 1·2m. Poles, 1m. Estonians. The great majority (in each case 73-99%) indicated the language of their nationality as their native tongue; exceptions were the Bashkirs (67%), Germans (57%), Poles (29%) and Jews (14%).

Estimated losses of population in the Second World War, 20m., of which 7m. were military losses.

The following tables show the growth of the population in Russia:

1897 (Russian Empire)	126,900,000	1959 (census)	208,826,650
1913 (Russian Empire)	170,900,000	1970 (census)	241,720,134
1913 (present frontiers)	159,153,000	1979 (census)	262,436,227
1939 (census)	170,557,093		

The following was the population on 1 Jan. 1981 of the larger towns (in 1,000):

Aktyubinsk	205	Engels	168	Kramatorsk	183
Alma-Ata	975	Ferghana	180	Krasnodar	581
Andizhan	238	Frunze	552	Krasnoyarsk	820
Angarsk	245	Gomel	405	Kremenchug	215
Arkhangelsk	391	Gorlovka	338	Krivoi Rog	663
Armavir	165	Gorky	1,367	Kuibyshev	1,238
Ashkhabad	325	Grodno	212	Kurgan	322
Astrakhan	470	Grozny	379	Kursk	390
Baku	1,046	Irkutsk	568	Kustanai	174
Barnaul	549	Ivano-Frankovsk	169	Kutaisi	200
Belaya Tserkov	162	Ivanovo	470	Kzyl-Orda	163
Belgorod	255	Izhevsk	574	Leninakan	213
Berezniki	188	Kalinin	422	Leningrad	4,676
Biisk	215	Kaliningrad	366	Lipetsk	415
Blagoveshchensk	179	Kaluga	276	Lvov	688
Bobruisk	203	Kamensk-Uralski	191	Lyubertsy	163
Bratsk	222	Karaganda	583	Magnitogorsk	413
Brest	194	Kaunas	383	Makeyevka	442
Bryansk	407	Kazan	1,011	Makhachkala	269
Bukhara	192	Kemerovo	486	Melitopol	165
Cheboksary	340	Kerch	159	Minsk	1,333
Chelyabinsk	1,055	Khabarovsk	545	Mogilev	308
Cherepovetz	279	Kharkov	1,485	Moscow	8,203
Cherkassy	242	Kherson	329	Murmansk	394
Chernigov	252	Kiev	2,248	Naberezhnye Chelny	346
Chernovtzy	224	Kirov	396	Nalchik	213
Chimkent	334	Kirovabad (Azerbaijan)	243	Namangan	241
Chita	315	Kirovograd	246	Nikolayev	458
Djambul	277	Kishinev	539	Nizhni Tagil	404
Dneprodzerzhinsk	257	Klaipeda	181	Norilsk	184
Dnepropetrovsk	1,100	Komsomolsk-on-Amur	274	Novgorod	198
Donetsk	1,040	Kostroma	259	Novocherkassk	186
Dushanbe	510			Novokuznetsk	551
Dzerzhinsk (Gorky region)	263				

Novorossiisk	165	Ryazan	470	Tomsk	439
Novosibirsk	1,343	Rybinsk	243	Tselinograd	241
Odessa	1,072	Samarkand	489	Tula	521
Omsk	1,044	Saransk	280	Tyumen	378
Ordzhonikidze		Saratov	873	Ufa	1,009
(Vladikavkaz)	287	Semipalatinsk	291	Ulan-Ude	310
Orel	315	Sevastopol	315	Ulyanovsk	485
Orenburg	482	Severodvinsk	208	Uralsk	176
Orsk	254	Shakhty	214	Ust-Kamenogorsk	286
Osh	178	Simferopol	314	Vilnius	503
Pavlodar	288	Smolensk	311	Vinnitsa	332
Penza	500	Sochi	295	Vitebsk	310
Perm	1,018	Stavropol	271	Vladimir	307
Petropavlovsk-		Sterlitamak	228	Vladivostok	565
Kamchatski	223	Sumgait	201	Volgograd	948
Petropavlovsk (North		Sumy	240	Vologda	247
Kazakhstan)	212	Sverdlovsk	1,239	Volzhsky	220
Petrozavodsk	241	Syktyvkar	180	Voronezh	809
Podolsk	205	Syzran	169	Voroshilovgrad	474
Poltava	284	Taganrog	281	Yaroslavl	608
Prokopyevsk	267	Tallinn	442	Yerevan	1,050
Pskov	179	Tambov	277	Yoshkar-Ola	213
Riga	850	Tashkent	1,858	Zaporozhye	812
Rostov-on-Don	957	Tbilisi	1,095	Zhdanov	511
Rovno	192	Temirtau	217	Zhitomir	254
Rubtsovsk	158	Togliatti	533	Zlatoust	201

Narodnoe khozyaistvo SSSR, Moscow, annual
Ezhegodnik Bol'shoi Sovetskoi Entsiklopedii, Moscow, annual
Itogi Vsesoyuznoi perepisi naseleniya 1959 goda. SSSR (svodnyi tom), Moscow, 1962
Itogi Vsesoyuznoi perepisi naseleniya 1970 goda, 7 vols. Moscow, 1972–74
Naselenie SSSR: spravochnik, Moscow, 1974
Naselenie SSSR po dannym Vsesoyuznoi perepisi naseleniya 1979 goda, Moscow, 1980
Desfosses, H., *Soviet Population Policy: Conflicts and Restraints.* Oxford, 1981
Kish, G., (ed.), *An Economic Atlas of the Soviet Union.* (2nd ed.), Ann Arbor, 1971
Lorrimer, F., *The Population of the Soviet Union.* Geneva, 1946
Mathieson, R. S., *The Soviet Union: An Economic Geography.* London, 1975
Mellor, R. H., *The Soviet Union and its Geographical Problems.* London, 1982
Sovetskii Soyuz. Geograficheskoe opisanie, 22 vols. Moscow, 1966–72

CLIMATE. The USSR comprises several different climatic regions, ranging from polar conditions in the north, through sub-arctic and humid continental, to sub-tropical and semi-arid conditions in the south. Rainfall amounts are greatest in areas bordering the Baltic, Black Sea, Caspian Sea and eastern coasts of Asiatic Russia. In most cases, there is a summer maximum.

Moscow, Jan. 15°F (–9·4°C), July 65°F (18·3°C). Annual rainfall 25·2″ (630 mm). Arkhangelsk, Jan. 5°F (–15°C), July 57°F (13·9°C). Annual rainfall 20·1″ (503 mm). Leningrad, Jan. 17°F (–8·3°C), July 64°F (17·8°C). Annual rainfall 19·5″ (488 mm). Vladivostok, Jan. 6°F (–14·4°C), July 65°F (18·3°C). Annual rainfall 24″ (599 mm).

CONSTITUTION

Constituent Republics. The Union of Soviet Socialist Republics was formed by the union of the RSFSR, the Ukrainian Soviet Socialist Republic, the Belorussian Soviet Socialist Republic and the Transcaucasian Soviet Socialist Republic; the Treaty of Union was adopted by the first Soviet Congress of the USSR on 30 Dec. 1922. In Oct. 1924 the Uzbek and Turkmen Autonomous Soviet Socialist Republics and in Dec. 1929 the Tadzhik Autonomous Soviet Socialist Republic were declared constituent members of the USSR, becoming Union Republics.

At the 8th Congress of the Soviets, on 5 Dec. 1936, a new constitution of the USSR was adopted. The Transcaucasian Republic was split up into the Armenian Soviet Socialist Republic, the Azerbaijan Soviet Socialist Republic and the Georgian Soviet Socialist Republic, each of which became constituent republics of the Union. At the same time the Kazakh Soviet Socialist Republic and the Kirghiz

Soviet Socialist Republic, previously autonomous republics within the RSFSR, were proclaimed constituent republics of the USSR.

In Sept. 1939 Soviet troops occupied eastern Poland as far as the 'Curzon line', which in 1919 had been drawn on ethnographical grounds as the eastern frontier of Poland, and incorporated it into the Ukrainian and Belorussian Soviet Socialist Republics. In Feb. 1951 some districts of the Drogobych Region of the Ukraine and the Lublin Voivodship of Poland were exchanged.

On 31 March 1940 territory ceded by Finland was joined to that of the Autonomous Soviet Socialist Republic of Karelia to form the Karelo-Finnish Soviet Socialist Republic, which was admitted into the Union as the 12th Union Republic. On 16 July 1956 the Supreme Soviet of the USSR adopted a law altering the status of the Karelo-Finnish Republic from that of a Union (constituent) Republic of the USSR to that of an Autonomous (Karelian) Republic within the RSFSR.

On 2 Aug. 1940 the Moldavian Soviet Socialist Republic was constituted as the 13th Union Republic. It comprised the former Moldavian Autonomous Soviet Socialist Republic and Bessarabia (44,290 sq. km, ceded by Romania on 28 June 1940), except for the districts of Khotin, Akerman and Ismail, which, together with Northern Bukovina (10,440 sq. km), were incorporated in the Ukrainian Soviet Republic. The Soviet-Romanian frontier thus constituted was confirmed by the peace treaty with Romania, signed on 10 Feb. 1947. On 29 June 1945 Ruthenia (Sub-Carpathian Russia, 12,742 sq. km) was by treaty with Czechoslovakia incorporated into the Ukrainian Soviet Socialist Republic.

On 3, 5 and 6 Aug. 1940 Lithuania, Latvia and Estonia were incorporated in the Soviet Union as the 14th, 15th and 16th Union Republics respectively. The change in the status of the Karelo-Finnish Republic reduced the number of Union Republics to 15.

After the defeat of Germany it was agreed by the governments of the UK, the USA and the USSR (by the Potsdam declaration) that part of East Prussia should be embodied in the USSR. The area (11,655 sq. km), which includes the towns of Konigsberg (renamed Kaliningrad), Tilsit (renamed Sovietsk) and Insterburg (renamed Chernyakhovsk), was joined to the RSFSR by decree of 7 April 1946.

By the peace treaty with Finland, signed on 10 Feb. 1947, the province of Petsamo (Pechenga), ceded to Finland on 14 Oct. 1920 and 12 March 1946, was returned to the Soviet Union. On 19 Sept. 1955 the Soviet Union renounced its treaty rights to the naval base of Porkkala-Udd and on 26 Jan. 1956 completed the withdrawal of the forces from Finnish territory.

In 1945, after the defeat of Japan, the southern half of Sakhalin (36,000 sq. km) and the Kurile Islands (10,200 sq. km) were, by agreement with the Allies, incorporated in the USSR. [1]

[1] However, Japan asks for the return of the Etorofu and Kunashiri Islands as not belonging to the Kurile Islands proper. The Soviet Government informed Japan on 27 Jan. 1960 that the Habomai Islands and Shikotan would be handed back to Japan on the withdrawal of the American troops from Japan.

GOVERNMENT. The Soviet Union is a socialist state of the whole people (1977 constitution), the political units of which are the Soviets of People's Deputies. All central and local authority is vested in these Soviets.

The economic foundation of the USSR is the socialist system of economy and the socialist ownership of the means of production. There are two forms of socialist property: (1) state property (property of the whole people); (2) co-operative and collective farm (*Kolkhoz*) property (property of individual collective farms and property of co-operative associations). The land, mineral deposits, waters, forests, mills, factories, mines, railways, water and air transport, banks, means of communication, large state-organized agricultural enterprises, such as state farms (*Sovkhozy*), machine-repair stations and the like, as well as municipal enterprises and the principal dwelling-house properties in the cities and industrial localities, are state property, but the land occupied by collective farmers is secured to them in perpetuity so long as they use it in accordance with the laws of the country. The members of the *Kolkhozy* may have small plots of land attached to their dwellings for their own use. Peasants unwilling to enter a Kolkoz may retain their individual farms, but they are not allowed to employ hired labour. The right of personal property of citizens in their income from work and in their savings, in their dwelling houses and auxiliary household economy, their domestic furniture and utensils and objects of personal use and comfort, as well as the right of inheritance of personal property of citizens, are protected by law. The constitution recognizes the right of all citizens to work, rest, leisure, education, health protection, housing, maintenance in old age, sickness or incapacity, without distinction of sex, race or nationality, and lays down that any direct or indirect restriction of the rights of, or conversely, the establishment of direct or indirect privileges for, citizens on account of their race, or nationality, as well as the advocacy of racial or national exclusiveness, or hatred or contempt, is punishable by law. The franchise is enjoyed by all citizens of the USSR, including members of the Armed Forces, who have reached the age of 18, irrespective of sex, with the exception of the legally certified insane. Candidates for election to the Supreme Soviet of the USSR must be 21 years of age; for all other authorities the minimum age for candidates is 18. A member of any Soviet may be recalled by a decision of a majority of his or her electors if he or she fails to give satisfaction (law on procedure for this, 30 Oct. 1959).

The USSR consists of 15 Union Republics, each inhabited by a major nationality which gives its name to the republic. These are divided into 128 territories and regions, and these again into 3,196 districts and 2,089 towns and 3,863 urban settlements (1 Jan. 1981). Within the villages there are 41,511 rural districts (usually each including a number of villages). The territories and regions also include a number of smaller nationalities, forming their own self-governing units–20 Autonomous Soviet Socialist Republics, 8 Autonomous Regions and 10 Autonomous Areas.

The highest legislative organ is the Supreme Soviet of the USSR. It consists of two chambers with equal legislative rights, elected for a term of 5 years: the Council of the Union and the Council of Nationalities. Each has 750 members. The present Supreme Soviet, the 'Tenth Convocation', was elected on 4 March 1979.

The Council of the Union is elected by the citizens of the USSR on the basis of constituencies with equal populations (approximately 1 deputy for every 300,000 population). Its Chairman since 1970 has been A. P. Shitikov. The Council of Nationalities is elected by the citizens of the USSR on the basis of national-territorial areas (32 deputies from each Union Republic, 11 from each Autonomous Republic, 5 from each Autonomous Region and 1 from each Autonomous Area). Its Chairman since 1974 has been V. P. Ruben. Plenary sessions of the Supreme Soviet are normally held twice a year for two or three days at a time.

Each chamber elects 17 standing commissions: mandates; legislative proposals; foreign affairs; planning and budget; industry; transport and communications; building and the building materials industry; agriculture; science and technology; consumer goods and trade; utilities and services; health and social security; education and culture; women's work and social conditions and the protection of motherhood and childhood; youth affairs; energy; and conservation and the rational use of natural resources. Membership of the commissions presently embraces 1,210 deputies (80·7% of the total).

Deputies are elected by the voters on the basis of universal, equal and direct suffrage by secret ballot. The only legal political party is the Communist Party of the Soviet Union; non-members are classed as non-party citizens. Candidates are selected at preliminary 'constituency electoral consultation' meetings (selection conferences), to which organizations which have put forward nominations send delegates, who discuss the various nominees. As a consequence, to date, a single candidate has been agreed upon in each consitituency, whose name appears on the ballot paper to be endorsed (by non-deletion) or struck out as the voter desires. These procedures are governed by the Law on Elections to the Supreme Soviet of the USSR, adopted in April 1978. At the election on 4 March 1979, 174,920,221 electors voted (99·99% of the total). The Supreme Soviet elected on that day consists of 1,075 Communist and 425 non-party deputies; 487 are women, 522 manual workers in industry and state farms, and 244 collective farmers.

The highest executive and administrative body of state authority in the USSR is the Council of Ministers of the USSR, which is appointed by the USSR Supreme Soviet at a joint sitting of the two chambers. It consists of a Chairman (in effect the Soviet Prime Minister), First Vice-Chairmen and Vice-Chairmen, Ministers of the USSR, and Chairmen of State Committees of the USSR. Chairmen of the Councils of Ministers of the Union Republics are *ex officio* members of the USSR Council of Ministers. The Council of Ministers of the USSR had more than 100 members in 1983, and day-to-day co-ordination of governmental matters is accordingly delegated to a smaller body, the Presidium of the Council of Ministers, which meets approximately every week. The Council of Ministers is responsible and accountable to the Supreme Soviet and is required to report regularly to the Supreme Soviet upon its work. Between sessions of the Supreme Soviet the Council of Ministers is responsible to the Presidium of the USSR Supreme Soviet.

The Presidium of the Supreme Soviet of the USSR is elected from among the deputies at a joint session of both chambers of the Supreme Soviet. It consists of a chairman (in effect the President of the USSR), a first vice-chairman, 15 vice-chairmen (1 from each Union Republic), 21 members and a secretary (39 members in all). The Presidium acts as the supreme state authority between sessions of the Supreme Soviet and is accountable to it for all its actions. The Presidium convenes sessions of the Supreme Soviet and co-ordinates the work of its standing commissions; it interprets the law of the USSR and ratifies and denounces international treaties; it confers medals, orders and other distinctions; it decides matters such as citizenship, amnesties, pardons, martial law and states of emergency; and it appoints the high command of the Soviet Armed forces and Soviet diplomatic representatives. It is empowered to adopt decrees *(ukazy)* and resolutions *(postanovleniya)*.

Soon after the adoption of the 1936 Constitution all the constituent republics of the Union held their Soviet congresses, at which they adopted their own constitutions based in all essentials upon the Constitution of the Union but adapted where necessary to local requirements. In April 1978 the Supreme Soviets of the Union Republics similarly adopted new republican constitutions based upon the new Constitution of the USSR approved by the Supreme Soviet in Oct. 1977. Article 73 of the 1977 Constitution of the USSR reserves to the central government the spheres of war and peace, diplomatic relations, defence, foreign trade, state security, economic planning, education, the basic principles of legislation, and other matters of 'all-Union significance'. The right of the constituent republics to withdraw from the Union is, however, recognized in Article 72. Union Republics have their own Supreme Soviets, Presidiums and Councils of Ministers, and exercise a wide range of devolved powers in local matters.

There are 20 Autonomous Republics in the USSR, which are similarly governed by their own Supreme Soviets, Presidiums and Councils of Ministers exercising devolved powers over local matters. Most (16) are in the RSFSR; 2 are in Georgia and 1 each in Azerbaijan and Uzbekistan. Five Autonomous Regions are in the RSFSR, 1 each in Azerbaijan, Georgia, and Tadzhikistan. All 10 Autonomous Areas are in the RSFSR. Elections are held every five years to the Supreme Soviets of Union and Autonomous Republics. At the most recent elections (Feb. 1980), 10,188 deputies were elected; 3,799 (37·3%) were women, 3,476 (34·1%) were non-Party, 3,531 (43·7%) were industrial workers and 1,622 (15·9%) were collective farmers.

Regions and territories, districts, towns and rural areas are similarly governed by their own Soviets, elected for a term of 2½ years. At the most recent elections (June 1982), 2,288,885 deputies were elected to these Soviets; 1,145,591 (50·1%) were women, 1,308,239 (57·2%) were non-Party, 1,013,101 (44·3%) were industrial workers and 570,001 (24·9%) were collective farmers. On 1 Jan. 1981 there were 47,412 rural and urban Soviets in the USSR with 2·3m. deputies and 2·6m. voluntary co-opted members participating in the work of their standing committees.

State flag: Red, with sickle and hammer in gold in the upper corner near the staff, and above them a 5-pointed star bordered in gold.

National anthem: Soyuz nerushimy respublik svobodnykh (words by S. Mikhalkov and G. El-Registan; music by A. V. Alexandrov; 1944, revised 1977).

Chairman of the Presidium of the Supreme Soviet of the USSR: (Vacant).
First Vice-Chairman: Viktor Vasilievich Kuznetsov (Oct. 1977).
Secretary of the Presidium: Tengiz Menteshashvili.
Chairman of the Council of Ministers of the USSR: Nikolai Alexandrovich Tikhonov (Oct. 1980).
First Vice-Chairman: I. V. Arkhipov (Dec. 1980).
Minister of Defence: Marshal D. F. Ustinov. *Minister of Foreign Trade:* N. S. Patolichev. *Minister for Foreign Affairs:* A. A. Gromyko.

Constitution (Fundamental Law) of the USSR. Moscow, 1977
Konstitutsiya SSSR. Konstitutsii Soyuznykh Sovetskikh Respublik. Moscow, 1978
Unger, A. L., *Constitutional Development in the USSR.* London, 1981
Ezhegodnik Bol'shoi Sovetskoi Entsiklopedii. Moscow, annual
F. J. M. Feldbrugge, (ed.), *The Constitution of the USSR and the Union Republics.* Alphen aan den Rijn, 1979
Hough, J. and Fainsod, M., *How the Soviet Union is Governed.* Camb. Mass., 1979

Communist Party of the Soviet Union. According to the rules adopted by the 22nd Congress of the Party on 31 Oct. 1961, the Communist Party of the Soviet Union 'unites, on a voluntary basis, the more advanced, politically more conscious section of the working class, collective-farm peasantry and intelligentsia of the USSR', whose principal objects are to build a Communist society by means of gradual transition from Socialism to Communism, to raise the material and cultural level of the people, to organize the defence of the country and to strengthen ties with the workers of other countries.

The Party is built on the territorial-industrial principle. The supreme organ is the Party Congress. Ordinary congresses are convened not less than every 5 years. The Congress elects a Central Committee which meets at least every 6 months, carries on the work of the Party between congresses, and guides the work of central Soviet and public organizations through Party groups within them.

The Central Committee forms a Political Bureau *(Politburo)* to direct the work of the Central Committee between plenary meetings, a Secretariat to direct current work and a Party Control Committee to deal with disciplinary matters; it also elects the General Secretary. Similar rules hold for the regional, territorial and republican levels of the party organization. The 'basis of the Party', the primary Party organization, exists in factories, state and collective farms, units of the Soviet Army and Navy, in villages, offices, educational establishments etc. where there are at least 3 Party members. There were over 414,000 primary Party organizations in 1981.

The Central Committee elected by the 26th Congress in March 1981 consisted of 319 members and 151 candidate (non-voting) members. Of these 39·6% were drawn from the central and regional party apparatus, and 5·7% were workers or peasants.

In March 1983 the Politburo of the Central Committee consisted of the following members: Yu. V. Andropov, G. A. Aliev, M. S. Gorbachev, V. V. Grishin, A. A. Gromyko, D. A. Kunaev, A. Ya. Pelshe, G. V. Romanov, N. A. Tikhonov, D. F. Ustinov, K. U. Chernenko, V. V. Shcherbitsky, and the following candidate (non-voting) members: P. N. Demichev, V. I. Dolgikh, V. V. Kuznetsov, B. N. Ponomarev, Sh. R. Rashidov, E. A. Shevardnadze and M. S. Solomentsev.

Secretariat: Yu. V. Andropov *(General Secretary);* K. U. Chernenko; V. I. Dolgikh; I. V. Kapitonov; B. N. Ponomarev; M. S. Gorbachev; K. V. Rusakov; N. I. Ryzhkov and M. V. Zimyanin.
Chairman of the Party Control Committee: A. Ya. Pelshe.
Chairman of the Central Auditing Commission: G. F. Sizov.

In Jan. 1982 the Communist Party had 17,769,668 members (about 9·3% of the adult population). Of these, 43·7% were classified as workers, 12·6% as collective farmers and 43·7% as office workers; 27% were women, and 59·8% were Russians. The party's youth wing, the Komsomol (All-Union Leninist Communist Union of

Youth), had 41·7m. members in 1982. In Dec. 1982, V. M. Mishin was elected First Secretary of its Central Committee.

Istoriya Kommunisticheskoi partii Sovetskogo Soyuza, 6 vols. Moscow, 1964ff.
Istoriya Kommunisticheskoi partii Sovetskogo Soyuza, 6th ed. Moscow, 1982
Rules of the Communist Party of the Soviet Union. Moscow, 1977
KPSS v rezolyutsiyakh i resheniyakh s"ezdov, konferentsii i plenumov TsK, 8th ed., 13 vols. Moscow, 1970–1981
Resolutions and Decisions of the Communist Party of the Soviet Union, ed. R. H. McNeal, 4 vols. Toronto, 1974
Spravochnik partiinogo rabotnika. Moscow, annual
Hill, R. and Frank, P., *The Soviet Communist Party*. London, 1981
Schapiro, L. B., *The Communist Party of the Soviet Union*. 2nd ed., London, 1970

DEFENCE. On 25 Feb. 1946 the control of the Soviet Armed Forces was unified under a single Ministry of the Armed Forces. On 25 Feb. 1950 the Defence Ministry was divided into a War Ministry and a Navy Ministry; on 15 March 1953 a single Ministry of Defence was reconstituted.

In 1955 the Air Defence Command and in 1960 the Strategic Rocket Forces were established as the 4th and 5th 'branches' of the armed forces beside the army, navy and air force.

The direction of Party and political work in the Armed Forces is exercised by the Central Committee of the Communist Party of the Soviet Union through the chief political directorate of the Ministry of Defence. The chiefs of the political departments of military commands, fleets and armies must be Party members of 5 years' standing and the chiefs of political departments of divisions and regiments Party members of 3 years' standing. About 90% of the officers are members of the Communist Party or Young Communist League, and 50% have had an engineering and technical education.

Military service begins at the age of 19 (or 18 for graduates of secondary schools). Active service lasts 2 years for privates in the Army and M.V.D. troops, 3 years for n.c.o.s in the Army and M.V.D. troops and for privates and n.c.o.s in the Air Force, 4 years for privates and n.c.o.s in the Coastal Defence, 5 years for ratings in the Navy. Reserve service lasts up to the ages of 35, 45 or 50 years according to fitness, family status and other considerations. Conscientious objection is treated as a criminal offence. Students in places of higher education are freed from military service, but receive military instruction. About half the service personnel have had higher, or 10-year, education and over 80% are members of the Communist Party.

In Jan. 1960 Prime Minister Khrushchev quoted the following figures of the armed forces of the Soviet Union: 1927, 586,000; 1937, 1,433,000; 1941, 4,207,000; May 1945, 11,365,000; 1948, 2,874,000; 1955, 5,763,000; 1959, 3,623,000; 1960, 2,423,000. The reduction, according to Khrushchov, was mainly due to the switch-over to rocket and nuclear weapons.

The estimated expenditure on defence (in 1m. roubles) for 1961 was 9,255; 1970, 17,900; 1980, 17,100; 1983, 17,050.

Army. The Army was, in 1982, thought to consist of about 188 divisions, of which some 100 are of combat readiness, numbering about 1,825,000 men.

The mechanized and tank divisions are equipped with the T54 medium tank, mounting an 85-mm gun, and with the Stalin III heavy tank, mounting a 122-mm gun. The T54 is being replaced by the T62 medium tank mounting a 115-mm gun. Rocket units are stated to be 'the main force' of the Army.

In addition to the Soviet Army, there are some 560,000 security and border troops.

Navy. The Soviet Fleet is steadily expanding and progressively modernizing under a continuity of policy and technology given by the quarter century in office of Admiral of the Fleet of the Soviet Union Sergei Georgiyevich Gorshkov, C.-in-C. of the Soviet Navy and Deputy Minister of Defence. The overall picture is of an unprecedentedly powerful and well-balanced navy, the capacity of which is increasing annually by scientific application and numerical strength.

The principal surface ships of the Soviet Navy are as follows:

Completed	*Name*	*Standard displacement Tons*	*Aircraft*	*Principal armament*	*Shaft horse-power*	*Speed Knots*
			Aircraft Carriers [1]			
1982	Novorossiisk	39,000	13 fixed wing aircraft 22 helicopters	4 twin SS missile launchers; 4 twin SA missile launchers; 1 twin AS missile launcher; 4 76-mm AA guns	180,000	32
1978	Minsk					
1976	Kiev					

[1] *See* Aircraft carriers under construction, successors of *Kiev* and *Minsk*, next page. Projected fourth name was *Kharkov*.

Completed	*Name*	*Standard displacement Tons*	*Aircraft*	*Principal armament*	*Shaft horse-power*	*Speed Knots*
			Battle Cruisers [1]			
1980	Kirov [2]	22,000	3 helicopters	4 SS missile launchers; 10 SA missile launchers; 4 AS missile launchers; 2 100-mm guns	120,000	35

[1] The first battle cruisers, and the largest combatant warships, apart from aircraft carriers, to be built for any navy since the Second World War.
[2] A sister ship is under construction.

Completed	*Name*	*Standard displacement Tons*	*Aircraft*	*Principal armament*	*Shaft horse-power*	*Speed Knots*
			Helicopter Carriers			
1968	Leningrad	16,500	18 helicopters	2 twin SA missile launchers; 1 twin AS missile launcher; 2 twin 57-mm AA guns	100,000	30
1967	Moskva					
			Cruisers			
1982	Kulakor	8,500	2 helicopters	2 quadruple SS missile launchers; SA missile launchers; 2 single 100-mm guns	120,000	33
1982	Udaloy					
1982	Sovremenny	8,000	1 helicopter	SS missile launchers; New SA systems; 4 130-mm guns	100,000	32
1982	Sovietsky Soyuz	13,000	2 helicopters	SS, SA and AS missile launchers; 100-mm guns	100,000	32
1979	Tallin	8,200	1 helicopter	2 quadruple SS missile launchers; 8 twin SA missile launchers; 4 76-mm AA guns	120,000	34
1978	Tashkent					
1977	Petropavlovsk					
1976	Azov [3]					
1975	Kerch					
1974	Ochakov					
1973	Nikolaiev					
1958	Admiral Senyavin [1]	15,450		12 6-in.; 12 3·9-in.	110,000	30
1957	Mikhail Kutuzov					
1956	Dimitri Pojarski					
1956	Oktyabrskaya Revolutsiya (*ex*-Molotovsk)					
1956	Admiral Lazarev					
1955	Alexandr Suvorov					
1954	Admiral Ushakov					
1954	Dzerzhinski [2]					
1953	Alexandr Nevski					
1953	Murmansk					
1953	Zhdanov [1]					
1953	Sverdlov [4]					

[1] *Admiral Senyavin* now has a helicopter pad and hangar ('X' and 'Y' turrets removed) while *Zhdanov* has high deckhouse ('X' turret removed). Each carries twin surface-air missile launchers. Both latterly employed as command and communications ships.
[2] *Dzerzhinski* has only nine 6-in. guns in 3 triple turrets, 'X' turret having been replaced by a twin surface-air missile launcher.
[3] *Azov* of this class is reported to be of a modified design.
[4] Of the older cruisers, *Kirov* and *Slava* (ex-*Molotov*) were deleted from the effective list in 1976-77 and *Zheleznyakov* in 1978. *Komsomolets* is used as a training ship.

Capital Support Ship

1977 Berezina [1]	40,000	2 helicopters	Twin SA missile launcher; 4 57-mm guns	54,000	22

[1] Very impressive militarised replenishment ship designed to support the new Soviet aircraft carriers.

Submarines

70(8)[3]	SSBN	Nuclear powered	Ballistic missile armed [1]*q.v.*
16	SSB	Diesel-electric powered	Ballistic missile armed
50	SSGN	Nuclear powered	Cruise (guided) missile armed
20	SSG	Diesel-electric powered	Cruise missile armed
60	SSN	Nuclear powered	Torpedo (only) armed
255[2]	SS	Conventionally (diesel) powered	Conventionally (torpedo) armed

[1] See table. All missile-carrying submarines are also armed with torpedoes.
[2] Including some 100 patrol submarines in reserve or used for training only.
[3] Eight reportedly had missile tubes removed for conversion to fleet submarines, SSN (nuclear propelled).

Capital (Strategic) Submarines (SSBN)

Class	*No.*	*Displacement Tons*	*Missile Tubes (vertical)*	*Nuclear Reactors*	*Shaft horse-power*	*Speed Knots*
New [1]	1	30,000	20 SS–NX–20	2	120,000	24
D3	14	13,350	16 SS–N–18	1	60,000	24
D2	4	11,400	16 SS–N–8	1	60,000	25
D1	18	10,000	12 SS–N–8	1	60,000	25
Y	34	9,300	16 SS–N–6	1	40,000	30
H3	1	5,750	3 SS–N–8	1	25,000	26
H2	6	5,600	3 SS–N–5	1	25,000	26

[1] 'Typhoon' is the largest submarine ever built. Launched in Sept. 1980. The vertical missile cylinders are mounted forward of the fin.
Note: All these classes also carry six 21-inch torpedo tubes.

There are also 15 other missile-armed light-cruise size leaders, 40 missile-armed destroyers, 40 gun-armed destroyers, (including 14 in reserve), 32 missile-armed frigates, 50 gun-armed frigates, 3 ocean minelayers, 75 missile-armed corvettes, 145 gun-armed corvettes, 150 fleet minesweepers, 100 coastal minesweepers, 40 minehunters, 70 inshore minesweepers, 40 minesweeping boats, 130 fast missile craft, 30 fast torpedo boats, 90 fast anti-submarine boats, 55 patrol craft, 18 hydrofoil missile boats, 30 hydrofoil torpodo boats, 15 hydrofoil gunboats, 30 coastal patrol launches, 80 river patrol boats, 70 major amphibious and auxiliary roll-on roll-off ships, 2 dock landing ships, 30 tank landing ships, 60 medium landing ships, 35 utility landing craft, 70 minor landing craft, 60 intelligence collecting ships, 70 major support ships, 13 space associated ships, 130 survey ships, 56 oceanographic research ships, 6 missile range ships, 3 nuclear powered icebreakers, 46 icebreakers, 20 training ships, 200 fishery protection ships, 15 fleet replenishment ships, 55 oilers, 13 special tankers, 25 salvage vessels, 65 transports, 25 submarine rescue ships, 135 tenders, 10 lifting ships, 15 cable ships, 35 degaussing ships, 110 fleet tugs, 50 hovercraft and thousands of auxiliaries, para-military ships and service craft.

The new construction programme includes another medium-sized aircraft carrier, 1 considerably larger and reportedly nuclear-powered aircraft carrier, 1 battle cruiser, 3 very large nuclear powered ballistic missile submarines, 2 nuclear powered cruise missile submarines, 6 nuclear powered torpedo-armed submarines and 10 guided missile cruisers.

In the revised forward procurement programme more aircraft carriers of improved 'Kiev' class are envisaged, together with nuclear powered surface ships and specialized support ships, to fit into the Soviet global and strategic maritime pattern.

There are 5 shipyards in and near Leningrad; Black Sea yards are at Nikolaiev and Sevastopol, new shipyards are at Molotovsk in the White Sea region and at Komsomolsk on the Amur.

The completion of a through canal system between the Baltic and White Seas, allowing regular traffic *via* the North-East Passage (during the ice-free season), facilitates the navigation of suitable ships between the Baltic and Far East.

Estimated number of personnel in 1983 totalled 448,000, including naval aviation, naval infantry, coastal defence, cadets and apprentices (but excluding 75,000 civilians in administration and new construction). Only 18% of naval personnel are volunteers, *i.e.*, officers and petty officers, the remainder comprising national service men serving 3 years at sea and 2 if ashore.

Air Force. The Soviet Air Force (excluding the strategic bomber force and PVO air defence force) was believed to have a personnel strength, in 1982, of over 470,000 officers and men. To supplement long-range rocket missiles (estimated at 1,398 emplaced ICBM, 600 MRBM/IRBM), the DA strategic bomber force has still about 105 Tupolev Tu-95 ('Bear')[1] 4-turboprop bombers, 80 Myasishchev M-4 4-jet bombers and flight-refuelling tankers ('Bison'), 400 twin-jet Tupolev Tu-16 ('Badger'), and 120 supersonic Tupolev Tu-22 ('Blinder') bombers, ECM and reconnaissance aircraft, and at least 150 Tupolev ('Backfire') swing-wing bombers. All types are used also by the Naval Air Force for long-range maritime reconnaissance; the Tu-16, Tu-95, Tu-22 and 'Backfire' can carry air-to-surface guided self-propelled missiles and all 5 types have provision for flight refuelling. A new swing-wing strategic bomber ('Blackjack'), larger than the American B-1, is being flight tested, together with new fighters designated MiG-29 ('Fulcrum') and Su-27.

The FA tactical air forces, under local army command in the field, have an estimated total of 4,500 ground attack, ECM and reconnaissance aircraft, including 1,800 MiG-23/27 ('Flogger') and 600 two-seat Sukhoi Su-24 ('Fencer') supersonic swing-wing aircraft, 200 twin-jet Yakovlev Yak-28 ('Brewer') multi-purpose combat aircraft, 125 single-jet Sukhoi Su-7B ('Fitter-A'), 900 swing-wing Su-17 ('Fitter-C/D/G/H/J'), and 700 MiG-21 ('Fishbed') fighter-bombers, and an increasing number of new Su-25 ('Frogfoot') twin-engined ground attack aircraft supported by 125 MiG-21 and 170 MiG-25 ('Foxbat') reconnaissance aircraft, and 3,500 helicopters, including up to 1,000 heavily-armed Mi-24 ('Hind') assault helicopters, in transport and gunship versions. The PVO defence forces, organized as a separate service, have an estimated total of 2,200 jet interceptors. A high proportion of the squadrons are equipped with MiG-23 ('Flogger'), Su-15 ('Flagon'), MiG-25 ('Foxbat') and improved MiG-25 ('Foxhound') all-weather interceptors, armed with air-to-air missiles. The twin-jet Yak-28P ('Firebar') and Tu-28P ('Fiddler') make up the balance of the force. Early warning and fighter-control duties are performed by radar-carrying adaptations of the Tu-114 turboprop transport, redesignated Tu-126 ('Moss'); these will be replaced by a more effective radar-equipped AWACS version of the Il-76 ('Candid') transport. Very large numbers of surface-to-air guided missiles are operational, on some 10,000 launchers, including the 'Guild', 'Guideline', 'Goa', 'Gainful' and 'Ganef', the long-range 'Gammon' and the 'Galosh' which is deployed around Moscow on 32 launchers and has anti-missile capability.

Soviet Air Force transport squadrons have an estimated total of 1,700 aircraft, including 500 An-12 ('Cub') 4-turboprop transports and 50 An-24s ('Coke') and An-26s ('Curl'), with 50 very large An-22s ('Cock'), 140 Il-76 ('Candid') heavy four-jet freighters, a variety of older and smaller types. Training aircraft include the piston-engined Yak-18 primary trainer, the Czech-built L-29 Delfin and L-39 jet basic trainers and versions of operational types such as MiG-21, MiG-23, MiG-25, MiG-15, Su-7, Su-17, Yak-28 and Tu-22.

[1] For convenience Soviet aircraft and missiles are usually referred to by invented English names in non-Soviet military writings.

Naval Air Force. Operating 1,440 fixed-wing aircraft and helicopters, the Soviet Navy has the world's second largest naval air arm. Under the control of the various naval commands, *i.e.*, Baltic, Black Sea and Pacific, the Naval Air Arm has an estimated 270 Tu-16 ('Badger') twin-jet bombers, and 100 'Backfire' swing-wing bombers, able to carry air-to-surface missiles, 40 supersonic twin-jet Tu-22 ('Blinder') bombers, a small number of Su-17 ('Fitter') shore-based fighters, and 80 Beriev M-12 ('Mail') maritime patrol amphibians. For reconnaissance and electronic warfare there are about 140 Tu-142 ('Bear') 4-engined bombers, Tu-16s, and Tu-22s, plus a small number of Il-18s ('Coot-A') and 55 Il-38s ('May'). The Tu-142 also has an important targeting rôle for ships fitted with anti-shipping missile launchers. Over 250 anti-submarine helicopters, notably the Ka-32 ('Helix') and Ka-25 ('Hormone'), are carried in naval vessels, including 3 aircraft carriers (which also operate Yak-36 ('Forger') VTOL attack/reconnaissance aircraft) and 2 helicopter carriers. Several hundred transport, flight refuelling tanker ('Badger'), utility and training fixed-wing aircraft and Mi-14 ('Haze') shore-based ASW helicopters are also under Navy control.

Berman, H. J., and Kerner, M. (ed.), *Soviet Military Law and Administration.* 2 vols. Harvard Univ. Press, 1955
Scott, H. F., and Scott, W. F., *The Armed Forces of the USSR.* 2nd ed. Boulder, 1981
Smith, M. J., *The Soviet Navy, 1941–1978: A Guide to Sources in English.* Oxford and Santa Barbara, 1981
Suvorov, V., *The Liberators: The Soviet Army.* London, 1981
Watson, B. W., *Red Navy at Sea.* Boulder, 1982

INTERNATIONAL RELATIONS

Membership. USSR is a member of UN, Comecon and the Warsaw Pact.

ECONOMY

Planning. Planning is based on public ownership in industry and trade, and on mixed public and collective (co-operative) ownership in agriculture. The first plan drawn up by Gosplan (the State Planning Commission) was the 'Goelro' drawn up in 1920. This was to be the basis for the economic development of the country and for the construction of a system of electrical power plants with an aggregate capacity of 1·75m. kw., in the course of 15 years.

For details of Planning 1925–1942 *see* THE STATESMAN'S YEAR-BOOK, 1981–82 p. 1226.

For details of the fourth 5-year plan, 1946–50, *see* THE STATESMAN'S YEAR-BOOK, 1952, pp. 1424 f. The 1950 target of the gross output of industry was exceeded by 2%.

On 10 Oct. 1952 the 19th Congress of the Communist Party issued directives for the fifth 5-year plan, 1951–55; for details, *see* THE STATESMAN'S YEAR-BOOK, 1953, pp. 1435-36. During Sept. and Oct. 1953 the Government issued a number of decrees to stimulate the development of agriculture, the output of consumer goods and the expansion of the home trade. For details of these decrees, *see* THE STATESMAN'S YEAR-BOOK, 1955, pp. 1448-50.

The directive for the sixth 5-year plan, 1956-60, was adopted by the 20th Congress of the Communist Party on 25 Feb. 1956; for details *see* THE STATESMAN'S YEAR-BOOK, 1958, p. 1472.

In May 1955 Gosplan was reorganized to consist of 2 state commissions for long-term planning (Gosplan) and for current planning (Gosekonomkomissiya); at the same time a committee was set up to improve the application to industry of advanced science and technology (Gostekhnika).

Between 1954 and 1956 considerable changes were made in planning methods. In March 1954 collective farms were given greater authority over planning their own output, only the quantities required by the State in fixed deliveries being determined beforehand, and voluntary sales by contract. In 1955 they were authorized to make changes in their statutes, which had followed a fixed model since 1935. In 1955-57 over 15,000 industrial establishments in various basic industries, previously controlled by the Union Government, and later a number of entire light industries were turned over to the constituent (Union) Republics. By 1962 they controlled from 95 to 100% of all industrial output.

In 1957 a comprehensive plan for decentralization of management of industry was initiated. Industrial establishments responsible for about 71% of all Soviet industrial output were turned over to Economic Councils set up in 104 (in 1963: 47) economic administrative areas. These in 1962 controlled 73% of all industrial production. The Ministries previously responsible for the industries concerned were either abolished or transformed into purely planning and supervisory bodies. The State Committee for current planning was abolished, and Gosplan was given wider powers.

In consequence of this change a 7-year plan for 1959-65 was adopted by the 21st Congress of the Communist Party in Feb. 1959. Industrial output was to increase by 80%; it was in fact, in 1965, 84% above that of 1959. Capital investments would roughly equal the total for 1917-58: special attention was to be given to mechanization of agriculture and arduous industrial labour, automation and new technological processes, and housing. Diesel or electric traction of railway freight was to rise to 85%. Real incomes were to rise 40%, the 7-hour day (6 hours for miners) became general in 1960 and the 40-hour week in 1961, and introduction of the 35-hour week (30 hours for miners) began in 1964.

In Oct. 1965 the regional and Republic Economic Councils were abolished and also 28 Ministries for various branches of industry (17 Union-Republican, *i.e.*, corresponding to similar Ministries in the Union Republics, and 11 all-Union).

A 20-year plan was adopted by the 22nd Congress of the Communist Party on 31 Oct. 1961, which envisaged a ninefold growth in electricity output and big increases in production of steel, oil, coal, machinery and cement, and also in grain, milk and meat. Two new iron and steel centres were to be developed in Kazakhstan and in Kursk region. A single deepwater system was to link the main inland waterways in the European USSR. Some rivers in northern Asia were to be diverted south for irrigation purposes. A 6-hour day for a 6-day week or 35 hours for a 5-day week were to be achieved by 1970. Housing, water, gas, heating, public urban transport and school meals were to be free by 1980. These and cognate measures were to provide 'the material and technical basis of communism'.

The 23rd Congress of the Communist Party in April 1966 adopted 'directives' for a 5-year plan for 1966-70. Under these, power output was to reach 830,000-850,000m. kwh.; oil, 345-355m. tons; coal, 665-675m. tons; steel, 124-129m. tons; mineral fertilizers, 62-65m. tons; machine-tools, 220,000-230,000; cars, 700,000-800,000; tractors, 600,000-625,000; paper, 5-5·3m. tons; cement, 100-105m. tons; fabrics, 9·5-9·8m. sq. metres; leather footwear, 610-630m. pairs; meat, 5·9-6·2m. tons; butter, 1·2m. tons; sugar, 9·8-10m. tons. The average annual output of grain was to increase 30% over 1964-65. 7,000 km of new railway line, 63,000 km of new motor roads and 35-40 new airports were to be built; marine tonnage was to be increased by 50%.

The 9th Five-Year Plan adopted in 1971 provided for an increase in electric power output to 1,065,000m. kwh.; oil to 496m. tons; gas, 320,000m. cu. metres; steel, 146m. tons; coal, 695m. tons; mineral fertilizers, 90m. tons; tractors, 575,000; passenger cars, 1·26m., and lorries, 750,000. Grain output was to rise to 195m. tons in 1975; meat, approximately 16m. tons; milk, 100m. tons; textiles, 11,000m. sq. metres; leather footwear, 830m. pairs. Average wages were to increase by 22%, incomes of collective farmers 30-35%, and the average of real incomes by 31%. 3,400 miles of new railway tracks were to be built and 3,700 miles electrified, with 17,000 miles of new oil pipelines, and 40% more cargo carried by sea. Over 16m. flats and houses were to be built.

By July 1972, 43,000 industrial plants had been transferred to the new system of decentralized cost-accounting; they produced 94% of total output of Soviet industry and 95% of its total profit. All public establishments in trade and catering and all the state farms have gone over to the new system.

On 29 Oct. 1976, the Supreme Soviet adopted the 10th Five-Year Plan (1976–80). This provided for an increase of industrial output from 104·3% of the 1975 level to 136%, an average annual increase of agricultural output by 16%, freight traffic (all forms) from 105·7% to 132%, state capital investments from 105·1% of the 1975 level in 1976 to 114·6% in 1980, real income per head from 103·7% to 121%, retail commodity turnover from 103·6% to 128·7%. 550m. sq. metres of new housing were to be built. Children in pre-school establishments would increase by 104·4% in 1976 and 125·5% in 1980, pupils in day schools from 108·9% to 148·8%, and students in higher education from 100·4% to 105·4%. Hospital beds were to increase from 102·2% in the first year to 109·7% in the final year.

A far-reaching plan for land improvement, increasing of agricultural, housing and road facilities and expansion of village amenities, from 1976 to 1980, in the 'Non-Black-Earth Zone' (northern and central European Russia), was begun in 1975-76, at a total cost of 35,000m. roubles.

In 1979 it was decided that from 1981 detailed plans would be drawn up at the outset for each year of a 5-year plan, so that enterprises could spread their potential more rationally over the whole period.

The 11th Five-Year Plan adopted in 1981, aims to raise living standards. The focus is Siberia and the Soviet Far East, with their large resources of energy and raw materials, and also Central Asia, with its favourable combination of labour resources and raw materials. Virtually no industries will be developed in the European part of the USSR and the plan envisages speeding up the development of labour-intensive branches of agriculture, consumer goods and engineering industries in Central Asia. National income (in the Soviet definition) is to increase by 18% between 1980 and 1985; industrial production is to increase by 26%, capital investment by 5·4%, freight traffic by 19·4%, real incomes by 16·5%, agricultural production by 13%, and retail trade in the state and co-operative sectors by 23% over the same period. Pensions are to be raised and the minimum wage is to be increased to 80 roubles a month, and efforts are to be made to increase state assistance to families with young children and to improve the food and care given to them in schools and pre-school institutions.

In May 1982 the CPSU Central Committee adopted a series of resolutions intended to bring about an improvement in agricultural production more particularly. The resolutions, described as the party's 'food programme', are designed to achieve an expansion in all sectors of production and a reduction in imports from the West by means of a simplified and more decentralised system of management, increased procurement prices for many products, and enhanced bonuses and other incentives.

Narodnoe khozyaistvo SSSR za 60 let (1917–1977). Moscow, 1977
Narodnoe khozyaistvo SSSR. Moscow, annual
Resheniya partii i pravitel'stva po khozyaistvennym voprosam. Vol. 1ff. Moscow, 1967ff
Ekonomicheskaya entsiklopediya: Politicheskaya ekonomiya. Vol. 1ff. Moscow, 1972ff
Istoriya sotsialisticheskoi ekonomiki SSSR. 7 vols. Moscow, 1976–80
Nove, A., *An Economic History of the USSR.* Rev. ed., Harmondsworth, 1982.—*The Soviet Economic System.* 2nd ed., London, 1980
US Congress, Joint Economic Committee, *The Soviet Economy in a Time of Change,* 2 vols. Washington D.C., 1979
Gregory, P. R. and Stuart, R. C., *Soviet Economic Structure and Performance.* 2nd ed., New York, 1981
Tikhonov, N. A., *Guidelines for the Economic and Social Development of the USSR for 1981–1985 and for the period ending in 1990.* Moscow, 1981

Budget. Revenue and expenditure in 1,000m. roubles for calendar years:

	1976	*1977*	*1978*	*1979*	*1980*	*1983*
Revenue	232,200	247,800	265,800	275,600	302,700	354,106
Expenditure	226,700	242,800	260,200	275,100	294,600	353,905

The 1983 budget allotted 198,256m. roubles to the national economy, 17,054m. to defence and 114,206m. to social and cultural services.

The social insurance budget, which is controlled by the Central Council for

Trade Unions and its affiliated bodies, was 27,992m. roubles in 1976, 29,476m. in 1977, 31,179m. in 1978, 33,089m. in 1979 and 35,296 in 1980.

The national income was assessed (in 1,000m. roubles) at 152·9 in 1961, 261·9 in 1969, 289·9 in 1970, 305 in 1971, 313·6 in 1972, 337·8 in 1973, 353·7 in 1974, 440·6 in 1979, 458·5 in 1980 and 474 in 1981.

Income tax was abolished on 1 Oct. 1961 for earnings up to 60 roubles per month and reduced for earnings between 61 and 70 roubles; in Dec. 1967 further cuts of 25% were made for earnings from 61 to 80 roubles; in 1972 earnings up to 70 roubles were freed of income tax, and taxes on incomes up to 90 roubles were cut by about 33⅓%. Capital investment (1980) was 133,500m. roubles, including 120,000m. by State and co-operative enterprises, 11,900m. by collective farms and 1,600m. by individuals (on housing).

Currency. As from 1 Jan. 1961 the gold content of the *rouble* was raised from 0·222 168 to 0·987 412 gramme. The official exchange rates (March 1983) 1·089 *roubles* = £1; 0·778 *roubles* = US$1.

The gold holdings of the USSR were, in Dec. 1955, estimated at about 200m. fine oz. (US$7,000m.), or about 20% of the world total of monetary gold.

The currency in circulation is: (1) State Bank notes in denominations of 10, 25, 50 and 100 *roubles;* (2) Treasury notes in denominations of 1, 3 and 5 *roubles;* (3) cupro-nickel coins in denominations of 10, 15, 20 and 50 *kopeks* and 1 *rouble*; (4) cupro-zinc coins in denominations of 1, 2, 3 and 5 *kopeks.*

Banking. The State Bank began operations on 16 Nov. 1921. By an edict of 7 April 1959 a number of specialized banks for planned long-term investments, which had existed since 1932, were abolished. The State Bank, in addition to short-term credits, effects long-term investments in agriculture and in individual rural house building. The Bank for Financing Capital Investments (*Stroibank*) covers industry, transport, urban housing schemes and public utilities and individual house-building in towns.

Deposits in 79,905 savings banks were over 156,500m. roubles to the credit of 142,100m. depositors at 1 Jan. 1980.

Weights and Measures. The metric system has been in use since 1 Jan. 1927.

The Gregorian Calendar was adopted as from 14 Feb. 1918.

ENERGY AND NATURAL RESOURCES

Electricity. There were (1982) 57 fuel-burning power stations of over 1m. kw. capacity, and these account for nearly 80% of the country's electricity.

Hydro-electric stations have been constructed on major rivers. Among them are the Bratsk (4.5m. kw.), completed in 1967 — until recently the world's largest, Ust-Ilimsk, Central Siberia (3.6m. kw.), Krasnoyarsk (6m. kw.) and a 1·26m. kw. station on the River Pechora (Far North). The Sayano-Shushenskaya hydro-power station, part of the Yenisei chain, and already in part operation, will have a 6·4m. kw. capacity when completed in 1983. A 245m. high dam has to be built before completion, in a gorge in the Sayan Range. Another large hydro-electric station is under construction on the River Kureika, Siberia, to provide energy for the mining and metallurgical centre at Norilsk in the Arctic.

Total installed capacity of power stations in 1938 was 8·7m. kw. and 266·7m. kw. in 1980. Industry consumes about 70% of the total electricity. Over 35,000 small rural power stations have been closed in recent years owing to supply from State stations becoming available, but there are still many operating in the countryside. 800 towns and urban settlements were heated by central thermal plants.

The world's first commercial nuclear power station in Obninsk, built in 1954, was followed by the Beloyarsk, Novo-Voronezh, Leningrad, Kursk, Chernobyl, Armenian and Shevchenko nuclear stations. Soviet nuclear power plants so far have standard slow 1m. kw. reactors, but a 1·5m. kw. reactor has now been designed. A fast reactor is functioning at Shevchenko.

The general design for a nuclear thermal station has been developed, and practical experience in this field has been obtained at the Bilibino nuclear power station in the Arctic, which supplies electricity and heat to the inhabitants on the Chukchi Peninsula.

In 1979 a 500,000 kw. MHD pilot project was started in Ryazan. This first-generation MHD station will have an efficiency of 50% as against 40% in the best thermal power stations and will consume about 20% less fuel. An experimental tidal energy station is working at Kislaya Guba (Murman coast).

Total electricity output in 1980 was 1,295,000 kwh.

The country's integrated power grid is now in operation, covering over 900 power stations, which are handled by a central control panel in Moscow.

A unified power grid ('Mir') with all the Socialist countries of eastern Europe was built up between 1962 and 1967. Total capacity (1972) was 58m. kw.

Oil. In the 1930s practically all Soviet oil came from the Caucasian fields, of which the Baku fields yielded 75-80% and the Grozny and Maikop fields between them 15%. Since then, the distribution has considerably changed. The Ural-Volga area, the 'Second Baku', has 4 large centres in operation, at Samarska Luka (Kuibyshev), Tuimazy (Bashkiria), Ishimbaev (Bashkiria) and Perm, producing nearly 100m. tonnes annually.

A large new oilfield has been developed in the Trans-Volga area of the Saratov region. The Tyumen (West Siberian) complex, now accounts for over 50% of the USSR's oil output. In 1980 the USSR extracted over 600m. tonnes of oil.

The total length of pipeline on 1 Jan. 1939 was 4,212 km, divided as follows: Baku-Batumi, 1,717 km; Grozny-Makhachkala, 150 km; Grozny-Armavir-Tuapse, 618 km; Armavir-Trudovaya, 488 km; Guriev-Orsk, 845 km, and other, 394 km. One pipeline (1,700 km) was completed in 1955, connecting Tuimazy in Bashkiria with the refineries of Omsk. In 1957 the Almetyevsk-Gorky pipeline (580 km) and 479 km of the Stavropol-Moscow pipeline were completed. At the end of 1979 there were 67,400 km of pipeline, through which (in 1979) were conveyed over 600m. tonnes of oil.

The construction of the 'Druzhba' pipeline of about 5,327 km from the oilfields near Kuibyshev to Poland and the German Democratic Republic (northern branch) and to Czechoslovakia and Hungary (southern branch)–separating in Belorussia–begun in 1960, was completed in 1965. Now a double line, it has an annual throughput of 50m. tonnes.

In 1976 the USSR exported 111m. tonnes of crude oil and oil products.

Meyerhoff, A. A., *The Oil and Gas Potential of the Soviet Far East.* Beaconsfield, 1981

Gas. A natural-gas pipeline from Gazli, near Khiva, to Voskresensk, near Moscow (2,750 km), with a planned capacity of 100m. cu. metres per day, began operating in Oct. 1967. Since then it has been extended to Czechoslovakia, where a 1,000 km extension, for transmission of Soviet gas to Austria, Italy and German Democratic Republic and Federal Republic of Germany, is under construction and another to Bulgaria. Another natural-gas pipeline, over 3,000 km from Medvezhye (Tyumen Region) to Moscow, began operating in Oct. 1974. A second pipeline from this region, linking the Urengoi deposit with Petrovsky in the Central European area of the USSR, became operational in 1980, and is to be continued to the southern Ukraine, to a total length of 3,000 km. A gas pipeline starting from Orenburg (Urals), passing across the Volga at Kamyshin, and continuing across the Ukraine *via* Kremenchug and Vinnitsa to Czechoslovakia (2,750 km), reached the Soviet frontier in Jan. 1979. When completed, it is to supply Czechoslovakia, Poland, Bulgaria and Hungary with 14,000m. cu. metres annually and Romania with 1,500m. A unified gas-grid exceeding 124,000 km now exists.

By Dec. 1981 construction work had begun on the 5,000 km Urengoi (West Siberia)-Uzhgorod-West Europe gas pipeline.

Over 50,000 km of long-distance trunk gas pipelines were built and put into service in the 10th Five-Year Plan period, bringing the total to 130,000 km.

Minerals. Mining experts are trained in 6 mining, 3 oil and 1 peat institutes, the mining faculties of 17 higher educational establishments, oil faculties of 2 industrial institutes and a peat faculty at the Belorussian Polytechnical Institute.

The Soviet Union is rich in minerals. Soviet scientists claim that it contains 58%

of the world's coal deposits, 58·7% of its oil, 41% of its iron ore, 76·7% of its apatite, 25% of all timber land, 88% of its manganese, 54% of its potassium salts and nearly one-third of its phosphates.

Estimated output (in tonnes) in 1962: Copper, 634,900; zinc, 399,000; lead, 363,000; tungsten, 10,500; antimony, 5,980; silver, 27m. fine oz. Output in 1963: Baryte, 199,500; magnesium, 31,745; aluminium, 961,400; manganese ore (1977), 8·6m.; graphite, 54,000; bauxite, 4·3m.; asbestos, 1·3m.; phosphate rock, 3·7m. (plus 7·4m. apatite); chromite, 1·23m.; gold, 12·5m. fine oz.; molybdenum, 12·5m. lb.; cadmium (1956), 160.

Output of iron and steel in the USSR (in 1m. tonnes):

	Pig-iron	*Ingot steel*	*Rolled steel*		*Pig-iron*	*Ingot steel*	*Rolled steel*
1913	4·2	4·2	3·5	1960	46·8	65·3	50·9
1928–29	4·0	4·8	3·9	1965	66·2	91·0	61·7
1932	6·2	5·9	4·4	1970	85·9	115·9	80·6
1940	14·9	18·3	13·1	1978	110·7	151·5	122·0
1946	10·0	13·4	9·6	1979	109·0	149·1	119·0
1950	19·2	27·3	20·9	1980	107·3	147·9	118·3

Coal production (in 1m. tonnes) was 29·1 in 1913, 64·4 in 1932, 165·9 in 1940, 261·1 in 1950, 513 in 1960, 624 in 1970, 668 in 1973, 685 in 1974, 701 in 1975, 711 in 1976, 722 in 1977, 724 in 1978, 719 in 1979, 718 in 1982.

The main centre of the atomic ore industry is at Ust-Kamenogorsk in the Altai Mountains. Uranium deposits are being worked near Taboshar (south-east of Tashkent), Andizhan (in the Tynya-Muyan Mountains), Slyudianka (near Lake Baikal), on the Kolyma River and in Southern Armenia.

Output of natural gas reached 501,000m. cu. metres in 1982; oil (including gas condensate), 613m. tonnes.

Agriculture. The Soviet Union, up to about 1928 predominantly agricultural in character, has become an industrial-agricultural country. Of the gross social product, industry and transport accounted for 42·1% in 1913 and 78·8% in 1977; agriculture for 57·9% in 1913 and 14·6% in 1977. Of the total state land fund of 2,227·5m. hectares, agricultural land in use in 1979 amounted to 1,050·3m., state forests and state reserves to 1,114·4m. hectares. 21% of all gainfully employed in 1979 were engaged in agriculture (1913, 75%).

The total area under cultivation (including single-owner peasant farms, state farms and collective farms) was (in the same territory) 118·2m. hectares in 1913, 129·7m. in 1933, 146·3m. in 1950, 203m. in 1960, 206·7m. in 1970, 217·9 in 1976, 217·6m. in 1977, 226·9m. in 1978, 226·4m. in 1980.

Collective farms on 1 Nov. 1980 possessed 248·3m. hectares, of which 102·8m. were under crops of various kinds; state farms and other state agricultural undertakings possessed 794·9m. hectares, of which 120·2m. were under crops; manual and clerical workers held 4m. hectares as allotments.

In Nov. 1969 the Third Congress of collective farmers adopted a new model constitution, considerably enlarging the planning powers of collective farms and making payments to their members a priority.

Since 1969 conferences of collective farms have elected 2,417 district collective farm councils with 85,000 members, to study and co-ordinate local experience in methods and finance. Processing and other joint agricultural productive establishments in 1980 numbered 9,638.

Produce marketed (after consumption by collective farmers) was, in 1m. tonnes, for the present area of the USSR:

	1950	*1960*	*1970*	*1980*		*1950*	*1960*	*1970*	*1980*
Grain	38·2	54·1	80·8	81·3	Meat[2] and fats	2·5	6·0	9·4	11·8
Raw Cotton[1]	3·5	4·3	6·9	10·0	Milk and milk products	11·4	29·1	48·0	59·4
Sugar-beet	19·7	52·2	71·4	64·4					
Potatoes	14·0	13·7	18·1	16·6	Wool	138·0	319·0	395·0	453·0
Other vegetables	4·3	8·0	13·8	20·6	Eggs (1,000m.)	3·5	10·5	22·1	46·5

[1] Seed-cotton unginned. [2] Slaughter weight.

Since 1954 grain crops have been measured in 'barn crop' (*i.e.*, net quantities delivered to barns) and not in 'gross harvest' or 'biological yield' (*i.e.*, calculated as growing crops) as previously. Average annual crops (in 1m. tonnes): 1909–13, 72·5; 1946–50, 64·8; 1951–55, 88·5; 1956–60, 121·5; 1961–65, 130·3; 1966–70, 167·5; 1971–75, 181·6; 1978–79, 179; 1979–80, 189·1.

Other produce (in 1m. tonnes) in 1980: Milk, 90·7; sugar-beet, 79·6; potatoes, 66·9; vegetables, 25·9; meat (slaughter weight), 15·1; raw cotton, 9·96; sunflower, 4·6; 67,700m. eggs.

In Dec. 1963 collective farms comprised 99·7% of all peasant holdings. In 1978 they produced 90% of all sugar-beet, cotton 70%, milk 52%, marketed grain 45%, meat 41%, potatoes 30%, other vegetables 31%, eggs 11%.

Between 1953 and 1 Jan. 1980 the number of collective farms was reduced, mainly by amalgamation and partly by transformation into state farms, from 93,300 to 26,000, their cultivated area falling from 132m. hectares to 95·5m. The number of state farms rose in the same period from 4,857 to 20,800, their cultivated area from 15·2m. hectares to 119·9m.

State purchases in 1980 (in 1m. tonnes; 1979 figures in brackets): Grain, 69·4 (62·8); sugar-beet, 64·4 (69·3); milk, 57·2 (59); meat (live weight), 15·9; cotton, 9·96 (9·2); eggs (1,000m.), 43·1 (41).

By 1978 the main field work on state and collective farms and joint inter-farm enterprises (ploughing, sowing of grain, cotton and sugar-beet, and the harvesting of grain and silage crops) was fully mechanized; 83% of sugar-beet pulling and 65% of cotton-picking were mechanized, as was 87% of the milking.

Rural power stations in 1940 had a capacity of 265,000 kw.; in 1976, 2·9m. kw. 99·9% of collective farms and 99·9% of state farms were using electric power in 1973. In 1979 agriculture consumed 102,300m. kwh. of electric power.

Investments in agriculture in 1979 were 21,600m. roubles by the state and 10,200m. by collective farms. Total agricultural output in 1979 was valued at 123,500m. roubles.

In 1913 the total of irrigated land was 4m. hectares; in 1953, 11m.; in 1980, 17·5m. The total of land drained was 8·4m. hectares in 1956 and 16·8m. in 1980. In 1975 nearly 85m. hectares were treated from the air against weed, pest and disease.

In 1913, 188,000 tonnes of mineral fertilizers were used; in 1950, 5·3m. tonnes, and in 1980, 82m. On 1 Jan. 1980 there were 2·5m. tractors, 706,300 grain combine harvesters and 1·6m. lorries in the countryside.

An All-Union Academy of Agricultural Sciences, founded in 1929, has regional branches in Siberia and Central Asia and 310 research institutes.

Livestock (1 Jan. 1981), in 1m. head: Cattle, 115 (including 43 milch cows); pigs, 73·4; sheep, 141. Since 1957 the enumeration of livestock has been made on 1 Jan. instead of 1 Oct., *i.e.*, after the winter sales and slaughter for the market. Percentage of farm production in 1978:

	All grain	*Cotton*	*Sugar-beet*	*Potatoes*	*Other vegetables*	*Meat*	*Milk*	*Eggs*	*Wool*
State	60	33	10	29	56	46	43	83	48
Collective	40	67	90	30	30	40	51	10	33
Private [1]	0	0	0	41	14	14	6	7	19

[1] *i.e.*, household plots of collective farmers.

Forestry. On the 791·6m. hectares of forest land of the USSR, 772·2m. hectares is administered and worked by the State; the remainder, 19·4m. hectares in extent, is granted for use to the peasantry free of charge.

The largest forest areas are 515m. hectares in the Asiatic part of USSR, 51·4m. along the northern seaboard, 25·4m. in the Urals and 17·95m. in the north-west.

On 24 Oct. 1948 a plan was published for planting crop-protecting forest belts, introducing crop rotation with grasses and building of ponds and water reservoirs in the steppe and forest-steppe areas of the European part of the USSR. By the middle of 1952 some 2·6m. hectares had been planted with shelter-belt trees and 13,500 ponds and reservoirs had been built. The planting of the shelter belts in the Kamyshin-Volgograd and Byelgorod-Don areas has in the main been completed. A

Volga forest belt has been planted along 1,200 km of railway. Re-afforestation was carried out on 2·5m. hectares of land in 1980.

Fisheries. The fishing catch including whaling (in 1,000 tons): 1913, 1,051; 1940, 1,422; 1960, 3,541; 1980, 9,526.

Belov, F., *The History of a Soviet Collective Farm.* New York, 1956
Shaffer, H. G., *Soviet Agriculture.* New York, 1977
Simush, P., *The Soviet Collective Farm* (in English). Moscow, 1971
Symons, L., *Russian Agriculture: A Geographic Survey.* London, 1972
Vasiliev, P., and Kozlovsky, V., *Forest Wealth of the USSR* (in Russian). Moscow, 1959

INDUSTRY AND TRADE

Industry. The organization of industry in the USSR is based on state ownership and control, administered by a separate Ministry for each large industry.

Under the successive 5-year plans, large-scale modern industrial works have been constructed, namely: 1st, over 1,500; 2nd, 4,500; 3rd (up to June 1941), 3,000; wartime, 3,500 (apart from reconstruction of destroyed plants); 4th, 6,200; 5th, 3,200; 6th, 2,700; 7th (1959–65), 5,470; 8th (1966–70), 1,870; 9th (1971–75), 2,000; 10th (1976–80), 1,200.

Output of some heavy industries was as follows:

Industry	*1913*	*1950*	*1960*	*1970*	*1980*	*1982*
Iron ore (1m. tonnes)	9·2	39·7	106·2	197·3	244·7	244·0
Oil (1m. tonnes)	9·2	37·9	148·0	353·0	603·2	613·0
Electric power (1,000m. kwh.)	1·9	91·2	292·0	740·9	1,295·0	1,366·0
Mineral fertilizers (1m. tonnes)	0·07	5·5	13·8	55·4	103·9	111·9
Machine tools (1,000)	1·5	70·6	154·0	202·0	216·0	–
Steam and gas turbines (1,000 kw.)	5·9	2,381·0	9,200·0	16,191·0	20,300·0	17,300·0
Oil industry equipment (1,000 tonnes)	–	47·9	92·8	118·0	184·0	–
Diesel locomotives (1,000 h.p.)	–	125·0	1,303·0	3,794·0	3,836·0	3,600·0
Electric locomotives (1,000 h.p.)	–	2,428·0	2,972·0	2,428·0	3,395·0	3,700·0
Lorries and buses (1,000)	–	294·4	384·8	571·9	872·3	865·7
Automobiles (1,000)	–	64·6	138·8	344·2	1,327·0	1,307·0
Tractors (1m. h.p.)	–	5·5	11·4	29·4	47·0	47·9
Looms (1,000)	4·6	8·7	16·4	19·8	21·8	–
Excavators (no.)	–	3,540·0	12,290·0	30,800·0	42,000·0	42,000·0
Timber (commercial, 1m. cu. metres)[1]	27·2	161·0	261·5	298·5	277·7	270·0
Cement (1m. tonnes)	1·8	10·2	45·5	95·2	125·0	124·0

[1] Excluding collective farm production.

The process of industrial mechanization and the installation of automatic remote control is being pushed ahead. About 90% of Soviet pig-iron and 87% of the steel is produced in fully automatic furnaces. All hydro-electric plants (in terms of capacity) are fully automatic. Coal production in open-cast mines has been completely mechanized; hydraulic mining is coming into general use. Coal-cutting and underground haulage was over 99% mechanized by the end of 1962 (loading on inclined seams 56%); peat-cutting, 100%, and loading, nearly 80%; timber-cutting, 98%; haulage to loading centres, 93%, and despatch, 97%.

Output in some consumer industries was as follows:

Industry	*1913*	*1950*	*1960*	*1970*	*1980*	*1982*
Cotton fabrics (1m. linear metres)	2,672	3,899	6,387	7,482	8,063	
Woollen fabrics (1m. linear metres)	108	156	342	496	564	11,100
Silk fabrics (1m. linear metres)	43	130	810	1,241	1,632	
Leather footwear (1m. pairs)	60	203	419	679	744	730
Clocks and watches (1m.)	1	8	26	40	67	70
Radio receivers (1m.)	–	1	4	8	9	9
Television sets (1m.)	–	–	2	7	8	8
Refrigerators (1,000)	–	1	530	4,140	5,925	5,800
Paper (1,000 tonnes)	269	1,193	2,334	4,185	5,288	5,400
Meat (slaughter weight, 1m. tonnes)	5	5	9	12	15	15
Butter (1,000 tonnes)[1]	104	336	737	963	1,278	1,300
Granulated sugar (1,000 tonnes)	1,363	2,523	6,360	10,221	10,127	12,100
Canned foods (1m. tins)	116	1,113	4,864	10,678	15,268	16,600

Since 1945 the cotton industry has expanded, especially in the Urals, Central

Asia and Siberia. Large mills have been built at Kamyshin, Kherson, Barnaul, Engels, Alma-Ata, Chernigov and Frunze.

Trade Unions and Labour. Trade unions are organized on an industrial basis, all workers, whether manual or brain, in every branch of a given industry being eligible for membership of the same union. Collective farmers may join trade unions.

Since 1933 the trade unions have carried out the functions of the former Labour Commissariat; they control and supervise the application of labour laws, introduce new labour laws for approval by the Government and administer social insurance and factory inspection. Social insurance is non-contributory. The All-Union Congress has met at irregular intervals; the 14th Congress met in 1968, the 15th in 1972 and the 18th in 1982.

In 1944 there were 176 unions. This number was reduced by amalgamation of unions to 22 in 1958, but increased to 30 in 1977. Contributions range from 0·5 to 6% of wages. There are 167 regional and Republican Trades Councils. Membership (1982) 130m.

Chairman, Central Council of Trade Unions: S. Shalayev.

Industrial and clerical workers engaged (1982) in the whole national economy were 115·2m., 51% of them women; a further 13m. were engaged in collective-farm agriculture. The 7-hour day (6 hours for miners underground and other heavy trades) was generally in operation by the end of 1960. The average working week since 1970 has been 39·4 hours and the working day in industry 6·93 hours. The 5-day week (without reduction of total working hours) was introduced in 1967.

New 'Fundamentals of Labour Legislation', intended to codify and extend labour laws adopted in the last 40 years, were adopted by the Supreme Soviet in July 1970. They lay down, *inter alia,* the right to receive wages irrespective of the income of the enterprise concerned, the right to free vocational and advanced technical training; the right to form trade unions without state registration; the right of trade unions to participate in and supervise management and planning, labour legislation, safety regulation and housing, fixing of working conditions and wages, etc. Pensioners in Jan. 1980 numbered 48·7m., including 33·1m. old age. Average monthly wages in the state sector were 177·3 roubles in 1982.

Profsoyuzy SSSR. Dokumenty i materialy. 5 vols., Moscow, 1963–74
Sbornik postanovlenii VTsSPS. Moscow, 1960ff, quarterly
Ruble, B. A., *Soviet Trade Unions. Their Development in the 1970s.* CUP, 1981

Commerce. Retail home trade takes three forms–state, co-operative and the free market, *i.e.,* sales by individual collective-farm members and by the collective farms of their surplus products, after having fulfilled their statutory deliveries and made their regular allocations to their members.

In 1979 the consumer co-operative societies had 63m. members and did over 23% of the retail trade of the USSR. They were organized in 5,100 societies, employing about 3m. workers, with 369,000 retail shops, 90,000 catering establishments, 12,700 bakeries and 324 canneries. Their central union is affiliated to the International Co-operative Alliance. Retail trade by the State and co-operatives totalled 270,547m. roubles in 1980; by collective farm markets (agricultural produce), 6,200m. roubles. Total state and co-operative retail trade turnover represented (in comparable prices) an increase of 70% on 1970.

Foreign trade is organized as a state monopoly. Importation and exportation of goods are effected under licences issued by the Ministry for Foreign Trade and its respective departments in pursuance of a plan annually sanctioned by the Government. The right of purchasing goods for importation, and that of selling Soviet exports abroad, is vested in Trade Delegations and representatives of the appropriate state corporations in foreign countries.

There are 29 state import and export organizations, including chartering and tourist corporations (one, Vostokintorg, dealing with Mongolia, Sinkiang and Afghanistan). The Central Union of Consumers' Societies (Tsentrosoyuz) is also authorized to conduct foreign trade operations.

For foreign trade up to 1938 *see* THE STATESMAN'S YEAR-BOOK, 1951, p. 1465. The Central Statistical Department of the USSR estimates that, in comparable prices, the volume of foreign trade in 1938 was less than one-third that of 1913, but was in 1978, 31 times as large as in 1913. Exports in 1980 were valued at 42,400m. roubles (26,900m. to the Socialist countries), and imports at 44,500m. roubles (23,700m. from the Socialist countries).

Russia's imports of fuel and raw materials, between 1940 and 1977, declined from 33·1 to 21·7%, of machinery and equipment increased from 32·4 to 38·1%; imports of foodstuffs and manufactured consumer goods increased from 16·3% in 1940 to 33·7% in 1977.

Main items of exports in 1974:

Oil (1m. tonnes)	116·2	Cotton (1,000 tonnes)	739·10
Coal (1m. tonnes)	26·2	Vegetable oil (1,000 tonnes)	513·0
Iron ore (1m. tonnes)	43·3	Tractors (1,000)	40·1
Iron and rolled metal (1m. tonnes)	11·3	Motor cars and lorries (1,000)	327·4
Manganese ore (1,000 tonnes)	1,500·0	Clocks and watches (1,000)	15,700·0
Paper (1,000 tonnes)	650·0	Grain (1m. tonnes)	4·9

Total trade between the USSR and UK for calendar years (British Department of Trade returns, in £1,000 sterling):

	1979	*1980*	*1981*	*1982*
Imports to UK	491,600	422,000	426,717	645,135
Exports and re-exports from UK	416,200	449,200	408,254	355,678

Tourism. Pre-revolutionary Russia was never a country for any but the most hardy and better-off tourists, as the introductory pages of Baedeker's guide made clear. For her subjects, too, touring was no more inviting. Acute shortage of hotels and boarding-houses, poor roads, lack of ordinary services for visitors were among the least of their difficulties. These have not by any means been fully overcome: but very great efforts to meet them have been made.

	1972	*1973*	*1974*	*1975*
Foreign visitors to the USSR	2,316,974	2,909,158	3,446,933	3,690,751
Of whom, from non-Socialist countries	875,395	1,309,979	1,558,522	1,582,741
Soviet visitors abroad	1,973,333	2,082,385	2,224,601	2,450,087
Of whom, to non-Socialist countries	854,792	868,725	893,059	932,119

Within the USSR, tourism by Soviet citizens has been much encouraged by the trade unions, which are developing an extensive network of facilities, particularly for hikers, campers and climbers. These facilities number more than 10,000 tourist camps, 650 tourist 'bases' (supply depots for hiring equipment), and over 4,000 cabins for anglers, hunters and mountaineers. The Central Council of Trade Unions also owns or controls 137 river or seagoing ships, 120 trains and 8,000 motor coaches exclusively for tourist use.

Soviet tourists recorded by this network numbered 40,000 in 1950; 1,997,000 in 1965; 5,041,000 in 1970 and about 19m. in 1978.

COMMUNICATIONS

Roads. By 1940 there were over 1·5m. km of constructed roads, of which 143,000 km were suitable for motor traffic. The total length of motor roads in 1979 was 770,000 km. Road freights by lorry amounted to 859m. tonnes in 1940 and 23,175m. tonnes in 1979. Passengers carried were 590m. in 1940 and 41,300m. in 1979. In 1979, 21,800 inter-urban bus routes had a total length of 3,205,000 km.

Railways. The length of railways in Jan. 1982 was 142,800 km (1913: 58,500 km), of which 44,800 km was electrified. Diesel and electric traction now account for almost 100% of all movements, with the electrified network handling 56% of the traffic. In 1979 60% of all freight traffic and 40% of passengers went by rail (1913: 57% and 91% respectively), and railways ran 3,465,000m. tonne-km in 1982.

Operations are centred on 32 regions with headquarters at: Baku, Alma-Ata, Tyndin, Minsk, Irkutsk, Gorki, Khabarovsk, Donetsk, Chita, Tbilisi, Aktyubinsk, Novosibirsk, Kemerovo, Krasnoyarsk, Kuibyshev, Lvov, Kishinev, Moscow,

Odessa, Leningrad, Riga, Saratov, Dnepropetrovsk, Sverdlovsk, Yaroslavl, Rostov-on-Don, Tashkent, Tselinograd, Voronezh, Kharkov and Chelyabinsk.

Extensive railway construction is in progress, including routes northwards from Surgut to Urengoi and Nizhe-Vartovskoye, and the great Baikal-Amur Magistral (BAM) project. This is a new main line to the east, sited well to the north of the existing Trans-Siberian route to the Pacific ports of Nakhodka and Vladivostok. It runs from Lena, on the Lena river, to Komsomolsk-on-Amur, 3,145 km distant, and will be double-track and electrified. When open throughout in 1983–84, BAM will become the principal route for export traffic to the eastern ports, easing the very heavy pressure on the Trans-Siberian line, which is only partially electrified and not double-track throughout.

BAM is the most arduous railway building project ever tackled by Soviet engineers, and the greatest drawback to development of the region has been its severe geological and climatic conditions. There is permafrost throughout the area, and winter temperatures fall to –60°C. Construction work has occupied nearly a decade, and has required over 3,200 bridges, tunnels and culverts.

Underground railways have been built in Moscow, Leningrad, Kiev, Tbilisi, Kharkov, Tashkent, Baku, Gorky and Yerevan. Others are under construction at Minsk, Novosibirsk, Omsk, Dnepropetrovsk, Kuibyshev and Sverdlovsk.

Aviation. In 1982 total length of internal airlines in the USSR was approximately 780,000 km; 108m. passengers were carried internally and externally. The Central Asian Airways in some instances provide the only means of communication across the desert and mountainous regions of the local republics. An 8,500-km air service was opened in Feb. 1941 between Moscow and Anadyr (Eastern Siberia), through Archangel, Igarka, Khatanga, Tiksi Bay and Cape Schmidt, *i.e.*, along the entire course of the Northern Sea Route. There are also other Arctic airlines, *e.g.*, Igarka-Gulf of Kozhevnikov; Igarka-Dickson Island; Yakutsk-Tiksi Bay; Yakutsk-Viluisk; Yakutsk-Verkhoiansk.

Direct air services are maintained throughout the year between Moscow and the capitals of all Soviet republics as well as London, New York, Montreal, Tōkyō, Delhi, Rangoon, Belgrade, Peking, Pyongyang, Ulan Bator, Kábul, Tirana, Paris, Warsaw, Prague, Budapest, Bucharest, Sofia, Vienna, Berlin, Helsinki, Stockholm, Copenhagen, Jakarta, Dakar and Gander. Soviet air services reached 87 countries in 1981, and 20 foreign lines have regular services to the USSR, including British Airways, KLM, SAS, Air France, SABENA, Air India, PANAM. The first Soviet airbus, the 350-seater IL-86, began flights on civil aviation routes in 1981. The 120-seater YAK-42 will gradually replace the TU-134 and AN-24 on major shorter routes.

MacDonald, H., *Aeroflot: Soviet Air Transport Since 1923.* London, 1975

Shipping. In 1977 the Soviet mercantile marine comprised 7,000 self-propelled vessels, of which 80% were built between 1957 and 1966. By May 1977 the gross cargo capacity was (including fishing vessels) 20·8m. registered tonnes (16m. tonnes dead-weight).

Freights carried were: In 1913 (present frontiers), 35·1m. tonnes; in 1940, 73·9m. tonnes; and in 1982, 604m. tonnes; 138m. passengers were carried. The Soviet share in world marine tonnage was 2% in 1960 and 6% in 1977. Deep-sea ports are under construction at Vostochny (Far East) and Grigorevsky (Black Sea) with new deep-sea wharves at Ventspils (Latvia), Murmansk and Archangel (for Arctic traffic). Archangel is kept open by icebreakers all the year round from 1979. Foreign freights in 1977 totalled 14% of all Soviet seaborne trade.

The North Sea route affords convenient communication between the European USSR and the Far East along the Soviet coast, for the produce of the basins of the Ob, Yenissei, Lena and Kolyma rivers.

The length of navigable rivers and canals in exploitation was (1980) 142,000 km, of which the length of floatable rivers is 88,500 km. There are several thousand miles of canals and other artificial waterways; among them the Baltic and White Sea Canal (235 km), the Moscow-Volga Canal (130 km). Goods turnover on inland waterways was 28,900m. tonne-km in 1913, 35,900m. in 1940, 45,900m. in 1950 and 263,000m. in 1982; freight carried rose from 35·1m. tonnes in 1913 to 521m. tonnes in 1977.

The Volga-Don Shipping Canal was opened for traffic in 1952. The Volga-Don waterway from Volgograd to Rostov is 540 km long, of which the Volga-Don canal comprises 101 km. The canal has transformed the section of the river from Kalach, where the Don is joined by the Volga-Don canal, to Rostov into a deep-water highway suitable for big Volga shipping. The canal links the White, Baltic, Caspian, Azov and Black Seas into a single water transport system. In Oct. 1964 the 2,430-km Baltic-Volga waterway, linking Klaipeda on the Baltic to Kakhovka at the mouth of the Dnieper and suitable for 5,000-tonne vessels, was begun. Reconstruction of the 18th-century Mariinsky canal system in north-west Russia was completed, providing a through waterway from Leningrad to Rybinsk (on the Upper Volga) and cutting the passage of freight from 18 to 2½ days.

At the end of 1977 the longest train ferry route in the world was opened between the Soviet Union and Bulgaria (Ilyichovsk-Varna).

The first section of Vostochny port, in Wrangel Bay on the Pacific coast, is completed. It will be the country's largest deep-sea port.

In 1962 a canal was completed across the Kara-Kum desert in southern Turkmenistan (replacing an earlier project for a more costly scheme across the north of the republic). The canal, from Bussag on the river Amu-Darya to Archnan, northwest of Ashkhabad, through the Murgab oasis, 900 km long, supplies water to an area exceeding 200,000 hectares, suitable for cotton, fruit, vineyards and livestock. An extension to the Caspian (500 km) is under construction: the complete system will irrigate 1m. hectares.

An irrigation canal system (250 miles), bringing water from Kakhovka on the Dnieper to the North Crimea, is nearing completion. Work to divert water from the Pechora and Vychegda rivers (flowing into the White Sea) south to the Volga is in progress. Work has begun on a 300-mile canal which will supply water from the Irtysh to Karaganda in Central Kazakhstan, irrigating over 150,000 acres; the first 37 miles were opened in 1965 and another 45 miles in Dec. 1967. Most of the 11 reservoirs required had been completed by 1 Jan. 1972. Other irrigation canals under construction are Kuibyshev (279 km long, to supply over 100,000 hectares) and Stavropol (481 km, irrigating 200,000 hectares); the second section of the latter went into commission in Nov. 1974, 14 months ahead of schedule. In Sept. 1972 the Saratov Canal (irrigating 1m. hectares) went into commission.

Post and Broadcasting. In Dec. 1981 the number of post, telegraph and telephone offices was 90,723 and of general telephones 25·1m.

The international radio-telecommunications services are operated by the Ministry of Communications of the USSR. The Great Northern Telegraph Co., Ltd, of Denmark, operates cables connecting Denmark with Leningrad, whence connexion is made by means of a trans-Siberian landline with Vladivostok. From the latter place the Great Northern Telegraph Co. owns cables connecting with Japan, China and Hong Kong. Direct radio and telephone communication with India is provided for in an agreement concluded in 1955.

The State Committee for Broadcasting and Television produces 3 programmes in Moscow, broadcasting throughout the Union. In addition the regional radio stations produce 1, 2 or 3 programmes for the republics as well as local programmes for a town or region. The foreign service from Moscow is beamed to all parts of the world, in 64 languages. Chinese has 28½ hours programme time a day. Several republics have their own foreign services. English is broadcast from Moscow, Kiev, Tashkent, Vilnius and Yerevan. There are 116 TV centres in the USSR, several of them producing more than 1 programme. In Moscow there are 4 programmes. Colour programmes are broadcast by the SECAM system. A nationwide system of space telecommunications, consisting of satellites and ground stations, takes TV broadcasts to distant parts of the country.

Number of receivers, Jan. 1980: radio, 66m.; television, 64·3m.

Cinemas and theatres (Jan. 1981). There were 143,400 permanent and 9,200 mobile cinemas. In Jan. 1981 there were 604 theatres, to which 120m. visits were made.

Newspapers. In 1981, 8,172 newspapers with a total daily circulation of 178m. copies were published in 57 languages of the USSR.

JUSTICE, RELIGION, EDUCATION AND WELFARE

Justice. The basis of the judicial system is the same throughout the Soviet Union, but the constituent republics have the right to introduce modifications and to make their own rules for the application of the codes of laws. The Supreme Court of the USSR is the chief court and supervising organ for all constituent republics and is elected by the Supreme Soviet of the USSR for 5 years. Supreme Courts of the Union and Autonomous Republics are elected by the Supreme Soviets of these republics, and Territorial, Regional and Area Courts by the respective Soviets, each for a term of 5 years. At the lowest level are the People's Courts, which are elected directly by the population.

Court proceedings are conducted in the local language with full interpreting facilities as required. All cases are heard in public, unless otherwise provided for by law, and the accused is guaranteed the right of defence.

Laws establishing common principles of legislation in various fields are adopted by the Supreme Soviet and are then enacted in more specific form and implemented by subordinate levels of state and judicial authority.

The Law Courts are divided into People's Courts and higher courts. The People's Courts consist of the People's Judge and 2 Assessors, and their function is to examine, as the first instance, most of the civil and criminal cases, except the more important ones, some of which are tried at the Regional Court, and those of the highest importance at the Supreme Court. The Regional Courts supervise the activities of the People's Courts and also act as Courts of Appeal from the decisions of the People's Court. Special chambers of the higher courts deal with offences committed in the Army and the public transport services.

People's Judges and Assessors, who serve on a rota basis, are elected directly by the citizens of each constituency: judges for 5 years, assessors for 2½. Should a judge be found not to perform his duties conscientiously and in accordance with the mandate of the people, he may be recalled by his electors.

The People's Assessors are called upon for duty for 2 weeks in a year. The People's Assessors for the Regional Court must have had at least 2 years' experience in public or trade-union work. The list of Assessors for the Supreme Court is drawn up by the Supreme Soviet of the republic.

The Labour Session of the People's Court supervises the regulations relating to the working conditions and the protection of labour and gives decisions on conflicts arising between managements and employees, or the violation of regulations.

Disputes between State institutions must be referred to an arbitration commission. Disputes between Soviet State institutions and foreign business firms may be referred by agreement to a Foreign Trade Arbitration Commission of the All-Union Chamber of Commerce.

The Procurator-General of the USSR is appointed for 5 years by the Supreme Soviet. All procurators of the republics, autonomous republics and autonomous regions are appointed by the Procurator-General of the USSR for a term of 5 years. The procurators supervise the correct application of the law by all state organs, and have special responsibility for the observance of the law in places of detention. The procurators of the Union republics are subordinate to the Procurator-General of the USSR, whose duty it is to see that acts of all institutions of the USSR are legal, that the law is correctly interpreted and uniformly applied; he has to participate in important cases in the capacity of State Prosecutor.

Capital punishment was abolished on 26 May 1947, but was restored on 12 Jan. 1950 for treason, espionage and sabotage, on 7 May 1954 for certain categories of murder, in Dec. 1958 for terrorism and banditry, on 7 May 1961 for embezzlement of public property, counterfeiting and attack on prison warders and, in particular circumstances, for attacks on the police and public order volunteers and for rape (15 Feb. 1962) and for accepting bribes (20 Feb. 1962).

In view of criminal abuses, extending over many years, discovered in the security system, the powers of administrative trial and exile previously vested in the security authorities (MVD) were abolished in 1953; accelerated procedures for trial on charges of high treason, espionage, wrecking, etc., by the Supreme Court were abolished in 1955; and extensive powers of protection of persons under arrest or serving prison terms were vested in the Procurator-General's Office (1955). Supervisory commissions, composed of representatives of trade unions, youth organizations and local authorities, were set up in 1956 to inspect places of detention.

Further reforms of the civil and criminal codes were decreed on 25 Dec. 1958. Thereby the age of criminal responsibility has been raised from 14 to 16 years; deportation and banishment have been abolished; a presumption of innocence is not accepted, but the burden of proof of guilt has been placed upon the prosecutor. Secret trials and the charge of 'enemy of the people' have been abolished. Articles 70 and 190 of the Criminal Code, which deal with 'anti-Soviet agitation and propaganda' and 'crimes against the system of administration' respectively, have however been widely used against political dissidents in more recent years.

Barry, D. D. et al., (eds.), *Soviet Law since Stalin.* 3 vols., Leyden, 1977–79
Butler, W. E., *The Soviet Legal System. Selected Contemporary Legislation and Documents.* New York, 1978
Hazard, J., Butler, W. E. and Maggs, P., *The Soviet Legal System.* 3rd ed., New York, 1977
Simons, W. B., (ed.), *The Soviet Codes of Law.* Alphen aan den Rijn, 1980

Religion. With the Revolution the Orthodox Church lost its position as the dominant religion and all religions were placed on an equal footing. Article 52 of the 1977 Soviet Constitution reads as follows: 'Citizens of the USSR are guaranteed freedom of conscience, that is, the right to profess or not to profess any religion, and to conduct religious worship or atheistic propaganda. Incitement of hostility or hatred on religious grounds is prohibited. In the USSR the church is separated from the state, and school from the church.'

By decree of 2 Feb. 1918 the Orthodox Church was disestablished; its property, together with that of all other denominations, was nationalized. The congregations themselves have to maintain their churches and clergy, regardless of confession or denomination. A minimum of 20 persons may request and receive the use of a church building, free of charge, except for maintenance, insurance, land taxes, etc. About two-thirds of all the churches have been closed since 1917, but about 20,000 churches and 18 religious seminaries were reported to be in operation in 1980. Religious instruction may be given in private, but otherwise only in church classes. The income of religious communities is not subject to taxation. Religious instruction in classes for persons under 18 is forbidden. The state supplies paper and printing facilities to all denominations for producing the Bible, the Koran, prayer books, missals, etc.

Relations between the religious communities of all creeds and the Government are maintained through a Council for Religious Affairs which is attached to the Council of Ministers of the USSR. (*Chairman*, V. A. Kuroyedov).

The Russian Orthodox Church, represented by the Patriarchate of Moscow, had, in 1980, about 50m. regular worshippers. There are still many Old Believers, whose schism from the Orthodox Church dates from the 17th century. The Russian Church is headed by the Patriarch of Moscow and All Russia, assisted by the Holy Synod, which has 6 members–the Patriarch himself and the Metropolitans of Krutitsy and Kolomna (Moscow), Leningrad and Kiev *ex officio*, and 3 bishops alternating for 6 months in order of seniority from the 3 regions forming the Moscow Patriarchate. The Patriarchate of Moscow maintains jurisdiction over a few parishes of Russian Orthodox abroad, at Tehrán, Jerusalem, German Democratic Republic, France (1 archbishop), England, North and South America (2 bishops). There are 20 monasteries and nunneries, and 6 Orthodox academies and seminaries with 6 journals.

After the Russian Orthodox Church the next Christian community in importance are the Armenians; their Catholicos (Patriarch), whose seat is at Etchmiadzin, is head of all the Armenian (Gregorian) communities throughout the world. There is an Armenian Orthodox academy and a seminary.

The Georgian Orthodox Church has its own organization under a Catholicos (Patriarch) who is resident in Tbilisi and who directs the church's seminary in Mtskheta.

Protestantism is represented chiefly by the Evangelical Christian Baptists, with over 512,000 baptized adult members and some 5,000 churches; the Lutherans are concentrated mainly in the Baltic States (350,000 in Estonia, 600,000 in Latvia), the Reformed in the Transcarpathian Region of the Ukraine (70,000). Both Baptists and Lutherans conduct theological courses. The Methodist Church functions in Estonia.

The Roman Catholics are most numerous in Lithuania and the western Ukraine. There are 2 Roman Catholic arch-episcopates and 4 episcopates in Lithuania with 630 churches and a seminary at Kaunas providing a 5-year course. In 1946 some 3·5m. Uniates in the USSR were compelled to withdraw their allegiance to Rome and came under the jurisdiction of the Orthodox Patriarchate in Moscow. In Latvia there are an arch-episcopate and 1 episcopate (Riga and Liepaja) of the Roman Catholic Church.

The Moslems (estimate 30m. members, mainly Sunnis), are divided into 4 administrative regions, 3 of them (Central Asia, European Russia and Siberia, Northern Caucasus) headed by a Mufti; the largest (Transcaucasia, with its centre at Baku) by a Shaikh-ul-Islam.

There is a Moslem academy and a madrasah in Central Asia. Several editions of the Koran have appeared in recent years.

There are various Jewish communities, the chief being in Moscow and Kiev. Large synagogues maintain bakeries for producing unleavened bread. There is a Jewish Yeshiva in Moscow (established 1956) and about 60 synagogues (over 50% in Georgia). The Central Buddhist Council of the USSR is headed by a Lama with communities in Buryatia, Tuva, Kalmykia and in the national (minority) areas of the Chita and Irkutsk regions.

O religii i tserkvi: sbornik vazhneishikh vyskazivanii klassikov Marksizma-Leninizma, dokumentov KPSS i sovetskogo gosudarstva 2nd ed., Moscow, 1981
Bordeaux, M., *Opium of the People. The Christian Religion in the USSR.* London, 1965.– *Religious Ferment in Russia.* London, 1968
Curtiss, J. S., *The Russian Church and the Soviet State, 1917–50.* New York, 1953
Kochan, L., (ed.), *Jews in Soviet Russia since 1917.* 3rd ed., Oxford, 1977
Kolarz, W., *Religion in the Soviet Union.* London, 1961
Kuroedov, V. A., *Religiya i tserkov' v sovetskom gosudarstve.* Moscow, 1981
Lane, C., *Christian Religion in the Soviet Union.* London, 1978

Education. Education is free and compulsory from 7 to 16/17. Co-education was reintroduced in all schools on 1 Sept. 1954. There are 2 types of general schools–with an 8-year or a 10-year curriculum; the minimum school-leaving age is now 17. Pupils who leave an 8-year school continue their education at either a 10-year school or a vocational training school. A 10-year school pupil may also transfer to vocational school after the 8th year. Vocational school pupils must reach the same standard of general education as those at 10-year general schools, and so stay on at school longer. Instruction is given in more than 100 languages.

In 1980–81 there were 145,000 primary and secondary schools. Pupils in general educational schools numbered 44·3m. (9·9m. of them in the ninth and tenth forms) and the teachers 2·6m. Those at vocational and specialized technical secondary schools numbered 8·5m.

At the end of 1940 labour reserve schools (both vocational and industrial) were organized, admitting applicants from 14 to 17 years of age. From 1959 onwards these and other technical schools were reorganized as town and rural vocational and technical schools, at which pupils stay for a year longer than at general schools, combining completion of general secondary education with vocational training. From 1940 to 1977 inclusive they trained 35m. skilled workers. In 1978, 2·3m. graduated from such schools, including 628,000 for agriculture; 600,000 agricultural mechanics were trained in state and collective farms. Over 4,300 vocational training schools existed in 1981, training 2·17m. boys and girls, all of whom receive a full secondary education. In 1982, over 15m. children of from 3 to 7 years of age attended kindergartens. Children in boarding schools numbered over 800,000 in 1972–73.

In 1980–81 there were 4,383 technical colleges with 4·6m. students, and 883 universities, institutes and other places of higher education, with 5·2m. students (including 1·6m. taking correspondence or evening courses). Among the 65 university towns are: Moscow, Leningrad, Kharkov, Odessa, Tartu, Kazan, Saratov, Tomsk, Kiev, Sverdlovsk, Tbilisi, Alma-Ata, Tashkent, Minsk, Gorky and Vladivostok.

On 1 Jan. 1981 there were 1·37m. scientific workers in places of higher education, research institutes and Academies of Sciences. There are 33,000 foreign students from 130 countries.

The Academy of Sciences of the USSR had 732 members and corresponding members. Total learned institutions under the USSR Academy of Sciences number 244, with 46,000 scientific staff. Fourteen of the Union Republics have their own Academies of Sciences, with scientific staff numbering 49,079. There are also Siberian, Far Eastern and other branches of the USSR Academy. On 1 Jan. 1981 there were 96,820 post-graduate students in Academy and other higher educational institutions, 59% studying on a part-time basis.

The Academy of Pedagogical Sciences had 14 research institutes with 1,712 staff.

In 1982 over 103m. people were studying at schools, colleges and training or correspondence courses. 182 per 1,000 of the employed population had a higher education (1939, 13; 1959, 33).

Grant, N., *Soviet Education.* 4th ed., Harmondsworth, 1979
Matthews, M., *Education in the Soviet Union.* London, 1982

Health and Social Security. All health services are free of charge although payment is required for medicines; but private practice exists. The health service is administered by the Ministry of Health of the USSR, which supervises the work of the Health Ministries of the Union Republics and the Autonomous Republics.

In 1944 an Academy of Medical Sciences was formed; it has under its direct control 42 research institutes. In all, there were, in 1976, 393 medical research institutions with 70,000 research staff. Smallpox, trachoma and malaria have been virtually eliminated.

In 1979–80, 98 institutes and medical faculties had a total of 374,400 students taking a 6-year course.

In Dec. 1980 there were 23,100 civil hospitals with 3·3m. beds. There were 873,000 infants in day nurseries. 960,000 doctors (including dentists) were in the health service. All confinements in towns and 75% in the country were in hospital.

There were 36,123 outpatients' clinics, apart from the 24,000 women's consultation centres and children's clinics.

The death-rate in the USSR in 1980 was 10·3 per 1,000, and the birth rate 18·3 per 1,000. Infant death rate was 27·9 (per 1,000 live births) in 1974, compared with 273 in 1913, 184 in 1940 and 81 in 1950. Average expectation of life, 70 (1913, 32).

Social insurance is administered by the trade unions, through social insurance councils elected in places of work and social insurance sub-committees of factory committees: about 5m. volunteers are engaged in this work. 37·7m. people went to holiday sanatoria or rest homes in 1980. 50·2m. people, including 11·1m. collective farmers, were receiving state pensions in Jan. 1980; of these, 9·8m. were old-age pensioners.

Total number of holiday sanatoria providing toning-up treatment at resorts in 1980 was 2,333, with accommodation for 542,000; in addition, there were 2,576 overnight sanatoria at large plants for treatment of mild disorders without absence from work, accommodating 121,200. There were also 1,204 trade union-managed holiday hotels with a capacity of 380,000, holidays being partly or wholly at trade unions' expense.

State expenditure (in 1m. new roubles) on health services proper, 1960, 4,800; 1970, 9,300; 1978, 13,500; 1979, 14,100; 1980, 14,800.

Between 1950 and 1977 56,748,000 apartments (in towns) and houses (in rural areas) were built. In 1980, 1·7m. apartments and houses were built. Rents in the USSR have not been increased since 1928 and in 1982 account for about 3% of the expenditure of an average worker's family. By the end of 1980, 71% of all housing in urban settlements and 65% in villages had had a gas supply installed, and 80% of the urban population lived in individual rather than communal apartments.

DIPLOMATIC REPRESENTATIVES

Of the USSR in Great Britain (13 Kensington Palace Gdns., London, W8 4QX)
Ambassador: Viktor I. Popov.

Of Great Britain in the USSR (Naberezhnaya Morisa Toreza 14, Moscow 72)
Ambassador: Sir Iain Sutherland, KCMG.

Of the USSR in the USA (1125-16th St., NW, Washington, D.C., 20036)
Ambassador: Anatoly F. Dobrynin.

Of the USA in the USSR (Ulitsa Chaikovskogo 19, Moscow)
Ambassador: Arthur A. Hartman.

Of the USSR to the United Nations
Ambassador: Oleg Aleksandrovich Troyanovsky.

Books of Reference

Narodnoye Khozyaistvo SSSR 1922–1982 (National Economy of the USSR). Statistical Summary. 1982
SSSR v Tsifrakh. Central Statistical Department, 1975
Pravda (Truth). Daily organ of the Central Committee of the Communist Party
Izvestia (News). Daily organ of the Presidium of the Supreme Soviet of the USSR
Viedomosti Verkhovnovo Sovieta. Bulletin of the Supreme Soviet of the USSR, in the languages of the 15 republics
Sovietskaia Torgovlia. Thrice-weekly publication of the Ministry of Trade of the USSR
Planovoye Khoziaistvo. Monthly. Moscow
Voprosy Torgovli. A monthly journal published by the Ministry of Trade of the USSR
Vneshnaya Torgovlya. Published by the Ministry for Foreign Trade. Monthly. Moscow
Trud. The daily organ of the All-Union Central Council of Trade Unions
Professionalnye Soyuzy. A trade union fortnightly. Moscow
Kommunist. A fortnightly organ of the Communist Party of the Soviet Union
Finansy i Khoziaitstov. A weekly publication of the Ministry for Finance
Soviet Foreign Policy During the Patriotic War; Documents and Materials. 2 vols. (translated by A. Rothstein). London, 1946–47
History of the USSR. Published by the Soviet Academy of Sciences. 3 vols. Moscow, 1948–57. (In Russian.) German edition, *Geschichte der Völker der Sowjetunion.* Basle, 1945
Bolshaya Sovietskaya Entsiklopedia. 65 vols. Moscow, 1926–47; 2nd ed., 51 vols. Moscow, 1949–58; 3rd ed., Moscow, 1959–78; annual supplement (*Yezhegodnik*)
Soviet Union. A monthly pictorial. Moscow. (In English)
Soviet Import-Export Dictionary (in Russian, with English, etc., terms). Moscow, 1952
Velikaia Otechestvennaya Voina Sovetskogo Soyuza. Moscow, 1965
Soviet Studies; A Quarterly Review. Ed. J. Miller and R. J. A. Schlesinger. Glasgow, 1949 ff.
The Current Digest of the Soviet Press. Published by Joint Committee on Slavic Studies. Weekly. Washington, D.C.
Baylis, J., and Segal, G., (eds.) *Soviet Strategy.* London, 1981
Beloff, M., *The Foreign Policy of Soviet Russia, 1929–41.* 2 vols. 1947–49.–*Soviet Policy in the Far East.* Oxford, 1953.–*Soviet Policy in Asia, 1944–52.* Oxford, 1953
Brown, A., and Kaser, M., *The Soviet Union Since the Fall of Krushchev.* London, 2nd ed. 1978.—*Soviet Policy for the 1980s.* London, 1982
Carr, E. H., *A History of Soviet Russia.* 14 vols. London, 1951–78
Clarke, R. A., and Matko, D. J. I., (eds.), *Soviet Economic Facts 1917–80.* London, 1983
Degras, J. (compiler), *Soviet Documents on Foreign Policy, 1917–41.* 3 vols. London, 1948–52
Deutscher, I., *Trotsky.* 3 vols. OUP, 1954 ff.
Fitzsimmons, T., and others, *USSR; Its People, Its Society, Its Culture.* New Haven, 1960
Galperin, I. R., *New English-Russian Dictionary.* 2 vols. Moscow, 1972
Gruzinov, V. F., *The USSR's Management of Foreign Trade.* London, 1980
Hammond, T. T. (ed.), *Soviet Foreign Relations and World Communism: A Selected Bibliography.* Princeton, 1965
Hough, J. F. and Fainsod, M., *How the Soviet Union is Governed.* Rev. ed. Harvard Univ. Press, 1979
Jones, D. L., *Books in English in the Soviet Union 1917–73: A Bibliography.* London and New York, 1975
Kaiser, R. G., *Russia: The People and the Power.* London, 1976
Kelly, D. R., (ed.), *Soviet Politics in the Brezhnev Era.* London, 1980
Lenin, V. I., *Collected Works.* 45 vols. London, 1960–70
McCauley, M., *The Soviet Union since 1917.* London, 1981
Nove, A., *The Soviet Economic System.* London, 1977
Pares, Sir B., *A History of Russia.* London, 1962

Preobrazhensky, A. G., *Etymological Dictionary of the Russian Language.* Columbia Univ. Press, 1951
Riasanovsky, N. V., *A History of Russia.* 3rd ed. OUP, 1977
Shabad, T., and Mote, V.L., *Gateway to Siberian Resources (The BAM).* New York and London, 1977
Schapiro, L., and Godson, J., *The Soviet Worker.* London, 1981
Shinkarev, L., *The Land Beyond the Mountains: Siberia and its People Today.* London, 1973
Slusser, R. M., and Triska, J. F., *A Calendar of Soviet Treaties, 1917–57.* Stanford Univ. Press, 1959
Smirnitzky, A. I. (ed.), *Russko-angliiskii slovar.* 4th ed. Moscow 1959
Stalin, J. V., *Collected Works.* 13 vols. London, 1952–55
Thompson, A., *Russia/USSR: A Selective Annotated Bibliography of Books in English.* Oxford and Santa Barbara, 1979
Treadgold, D. W., *Twentieth Century Russia.* 5th ed. Boston, 1981
Utechin, S. V. (ed.), *Everyman's Concise Encyclopaedia of Russia.* London, 1961
Vernadsky, G., *A History of Russia.* 4th ed. Yale Univ. Press, 1954
Wheeler, M., *The Oxford Russian-English Dictionary.* OUP, 1972

RUSSIAN SOVIET FEDERAL SOCIALIST REPUBLIC (RSFSR)

Rossiiskaya Sovietskaya Federativnaya Sotsialisticheskaya Respublika

AREA AND POPULATION. The RSFSR occupies over 76% of the total area of the USSR stretching from the Far North to the Black Sea in the south and from the Far East to Kaliningrad in the west. 82·6% of its population in Jan. 1979 were Russians, the rest being 38 national minorities such as the Tatars, Ukrainians, Jews, Mordovians, Chuvashis, Bashkirs, Poles, Germans, Udmurts, Buryats, Mari, Yakuts and Ossetians. The 2 principal cities are Moscow, the capital, with a population (Jan. 1981) of 8·2m. (without suburbs, 8,015,000) and Leningrad, the second capital, 4,676,000 (without suburbs, 4,156,000). Among other important large towns are Gorki, Rostov-on-Don, Volgograd, Sverdlovsk, Novosibirsk, Chelyabinsk, Kazan, Omsk and Kuibyshev.

The RSFSR has a variety of climates (ranging from arctic to sub-tropical) and of geographical conditions (tundra, forest lands, steppes and rich agricultural soil). It also contains great mineral resources: iron ore in the Urals, the Kerch Peninsula and Siberia; coal in the Kuznetz Basin, Eastern Siberia, Urals and the sub-Moscow Basin; oil in the Urals, Azov-Black Sea area, Bashkiria, and West Siberia. It also has abundant deposits of gold, platinum, copper, zinc, lead, tin and rare metals.

The RSFSR produces about 70% of the total industrial and agricultural output of the Soviet Union. Industrial and office workers averaged 64·7m. in 1979.

CONSTITUTION AND GOVERNMENT. The RSFSR adopted its present constitution at a meeting of the Supreme Soviet in April 1978, following 330,000 town and country meetings in which 25m. citizens took part.

Chairman, Presidium of the Supreme Soviet: M. A. Yasnov.
Chairman, Council of Ministers: M. S. Solomentsev.
Foreign Minister: F. E. Titov.

The RSFSR consists of:

(1) *Territories:* Altai, Khabarovsk, Krasnodar, Krasnoyarsk, Primorye, Stavropol.

(2) *Regions:* Amur, Archangel, Astrakhan, Belgorod, Briansk, Chelyabinsk, Chita, Gorki, Irkutsk, Ivanovo, Kaluga, Kalinin, Kaliningrad, Kamchatka, Kemerovo, Kirov, Kostroma, Kuibyshev, Kurgan, Kursk, Leningrad, Lipetsk, Magadan, Moscow, Murmansk, Novgorod, Novosibirsk, Omsk, Orel, Orenburg, Penza, Perm, Pskov, Rostov, Ryazan, Sakhalin, Saratov, Smolensk, Sverdlovsk, Tambov, Tomsk, Tula, Tyumen, Ulyanovsk, Vladimir, Volgograd, Vologda, Voronezh, Yaroslavl.

(3) *Autonomous Soviet Republics:* Bashkir, Buryat, Checheno-Ingush, Chuvash, Daghestan, Kabardino-Balkar, Kalmyk, Karelian, Komi, Mari, Mordovian, North Ossetia, Karachayevo-Cherkess, Tartar, Tuva, Udmurt, Yakut.

(4) *Autonomous Regions:* Adygei, Karachai-Circassian, Gorno-Altai, Jewish, Khakass.

(5) *Autonomous Areas:* Aginsky-Buryat, Chukot, Evenki, Khanty-Mansi, Komi-Permyak, Koryak, Nenetz, Taimyr (Dolgano-Nenetz), Ust-Ordynsky-Buryat, Yamalo-Nenetz.

The Supreme Soviet, elected in Feb. 1980, consisted of 975 deputies (1 per 150,000 population); 650 were Communists, 341 women, 591 workers and collective farmers.

On 20 June 1982, 1,139,925 deputies were elected to local authorities; 578,461 (50·7%) were women, 658,241 (57·7%) non-Party and 773,073 (67·8%) industrial workers and collective farmers.

FINANCE. Revenue and expenditure balanced as follows (in 1m. roubles): 1982, 67,205; 1983 (estimate), 74,319. These figures, and those for the other 14 Union Republics, include grants from the Union Budget.

COMMUNICATIONS. Length of railways on 1 Jan. 1980 was 82,030 km, inland waterways, 126,000 km, hard-surface motor roads, 418,900 km.

Newspapers. In 1980 there were 4,413 newspapers, 4,109 of them in Russian. Daily circulation of Russian-language newspapers, 116·6m., other languages, 3m.

EDUCATION. In 1980–81 there were 20·2m. pupils in primary and secondary schools; 3,045,800 students in 494 higher educational establishments (including correspondence students) and 2,641,600 students in 2,505 technical colleges of all kinds (including correspondence students). There were 8·1m. children attending pre-school institutions. There were, on 1 Jan. 1981, 937,000 scientific staff in over 3,000 learned and scientific institutions.

In 1957 a Siberian branch of the Academy of Sciences was organized, in charge of all scientific research institutions from the Urals to the Pacific.

There is an Academy of Municipal Economy (with 5 research institutions and a staff of 437).

HEALTH. Doctors at the end of 1981 numbered 559,200, and hospital beds 1·8m. (133,400 in 1913 and 482,000 in 1940).

BASHKIR AUTONOMOUS SOVIET SOCIALIST REPUBLIC

Area 143,600 sq. km (55,430 sq. miles), population (Jan. 1981) 3·86m. Capital, Ufa. Bashkiria was annexed to Russia in 1557. It was constituted as an Autonomous Soviet Republic on 23 March 1919. Population, census 1979, included 24·3% Bashkirians, 40·3% Russians, 24·5% Tatars, and 3·2% Chuvashes.

280 deputies were elected on 24 Feb. 1980, 109 of them women.

In 1979–80 there were over 5,000 schools with 746,000 pupils. There is a state university and a branch of the USSR Academy of Sciences with 8 learned institutions (511 research workers). There were 126,000 students in technical colleges and higher schools.

In Jan. 1979 there were 11,400 doctors and 46,205 hospital beds.

There are expanding chemical, coal, steel, electrical engineering, timber and paper industries. There were 631 collective farms and 160 state farms in 1977. Crop area was 4,573,000 hectares. Bashkiria is a major oil producer in USSR.

BURIAT AUTONOMOUS SOVIET SOCIALIST REPUBLIC

Area is 351,300 sq. km (135,650 sq. miles). The Buriat Republic, situated to the south of the Yakut Republic, adopted the Soviet system 1 March 1920. This area was penetrated by the Russians in the 17th century and finally annexed from China by the treaties of Nerchinsk (1689) and Kyakhta (1727). The population (Jan. 1981) was 929,000. Capital, Ulan-Udé. The name of the republic was changed from 'Buriat-Mongol' on 7 July 1958. The population (1979 census) includes 23% Buriats and 72% Russians.

170 deputies were elected on 24 Feb. 1980, 59 of them women.

The main industries are coal, timber, building materials, fisheries, sheep and cattle farming. In 1977 there were 100 state and 59 collective farms. Crop area was 888,700 hectares. Gold, molybdenum and wolfram are mined.

In 1979–80 there were over 700 schools with 157,000 pupils, 16 technical colleges with 219,000 students and 2 higher educational institutions with 22,400 students. A branch of the Siberian Department of the Academy of Sciences had 4 learned institutions with 281 research workers.

At the end of 1979 there were 2,700 doctors and (1978) 11,102 hospital beds.

CHECHENO-INGUSH AUTONOMOUS SOVIET SOCIALIST REPUBLIC

Area, 19,300 sq. km (7,350 sq. miles); population (Jan. 1981), 1·17m. Capital, Grozny. After 70 years of almost continuous fighting, the Chechens and Ingushes were conquered by Russia in the late 1850s. In 1918 each nationality separately established its 'National Soviet' within the Terek Autonomous Republic, and in 1920 (after the Civil War) were constituted areas within the Mountain Republic. The Chechens separated out as an Autonomous Region on 30 Nov. 1922 and the Ingushes on 7 July 1924. In Jan. 1934 the two regions were united, and on 5 Dec. 1936 constituted as an Autonomous Republic. This was dissolved in 1944, but reconstituted on 9 Jan. 1957: 232,000 Chechens and Ingushes returned to their homes in the next 2 years. The population (1979 census) includes 52·9% Chechens, 11·7% Ingushes, and 29·1% Russians.

175 deputies were elected on 24 Feb. 1980, 95 of them women.

The republic has one of the major Soviet oilfields: also a number of large engineering works, chemical factories, building materials works and food canneries. There is an expanding timber, woodworking and furniture industry. In 1977–78 there were 100 state and 45 collective farms. Crop area was 460,400 hectares.

There were, in 1979–80, 534 schools with 259,000 pupils, 12 technical colleges with 14,400 students and 2 places of higher education with 12,100 students.

In 1977 there were 75 hospitals, 2,900 (1980) doctors and 11,210 hospital beds.

CHUVASH AUTONOMOUS SOVIET SOCIALIST REPUBLIC

Area, 18,300 sq. km (7,064 sq. miles); population (Jan. 1981), 1,311,000. Capital, Cheboksary. The territory was annexed by Russia in the middle of the 16th century. On 24 June 1920 it was constituted as an Autonomous Region, and on 21 April 1925 as an Autonomous Republic. The population (1979 census) includes Chuvashes (68·4%), Russians (26%), Tatars (2·9%) and Mordovians (1·6%).

200 deputies were elected on 24 Feb. 1980, 79 of them women.

Like most of the Autonomous Republics, Chuvashia before 1914 was a region of primitive agriculture with a certain development of the timber industry. Today it has several big railway repair works, an expanding electrical and other engineering industries, building materials, chemicals, textiles and food industries; timber felling and haulage are largely mechanized. In 1977 there were 210 collective farms and 96 state farms. Grain crops account for nearly two-thirds of all sowings and fodder crops for nearly a quarter. Fruit and wine-growing are a developing branch of agriculture. Crop area was 829,300 hectares.

In 1979–80 there were 254,200 pupils at school, 24,500 students at technical colleges and 14,300 students undertaking higher education.

There were 2,901 doctors and 13,950 hospital beds.

DAGESTAN AUTONOMOUS SOVIET SOCIALIST REPUBLIC

Area, 50,300 sq. km (19,416 sq. miles); population (Jan. 1981), 1·7m. Capital, Makhachkala. Over 30 nationalities inhabit this republic apart from Russians (11·6% at 1979 census); the most numerous are the Avartsy (25·7%), Dargintsy (15·2%), Lezginy (11·6%), Kumyki (12·4%), Laki (5·1%), Tabasarany (4·4%) and Azerbaidjanis (4%). Annexed from Persia in 1723, Dagestan was constituted an Autonomous Republic on 20 Jan. 1921.

210 deputies were elected on 24 Feb. 1980, 82 of them women.

There are large engineering, oil, chemical, woodworking, textile, food and other light industries. Agriculture is very varied, ranging from wheat to grapes, with sheep farming and cattle breeding; in 1977 there were 311 collective farms and 233 state farms. Crop area was 413,900 hectares. A chain of power stations is under construction in the Sulak River (total capacity 2·5m. kw.).

In 1977–78 there were 1,576 schools with 475,900 pupils, 33,800 technical students (1979–80) and 4 higher education establishments with 23,400 students; and a branch of the USSR Academy of Sciences with 4 learned institutions (373 research workers). Doctors numbered 5,300 and hospital beds 17,300.

KABARDINO-BALKAR AUTONOMOUS SOVIET SOCIALIST REPUBLIC

Area, 12,500 sq. km (4,825 sq. miles); population (Jan. 1981) 688,000. Capital, Nalchik. Kabarda was annexed to Russia in 1557. The republic was constituted on 5 Dec. 1936. Population (1979 census) includes Kabardinians (45·6%), Balkars (9%), Russians (35·1%).

160 deputies were elected on 24 Feb. 1980, 70 of them women.

Main industries are ore-mining, timber, engineering, coal, food processing, timber and light industries, building materials. Grain, livestock breeding, dairy farming and wine-growing are the principal branches of agriculture. There were, in 1977, 54 state and 74 collective farms.

In 1979–80 there were 250 schools with 144,000 pupils, 11,600 students in 11 technical colleges and 8,600 students receiving higher education; 2,500 doctors and 7,530 hospital beds.

KALMYK AUTONOMOUS SOVIET SOCIALIST REPUBLIC

Area, 75,900 sq. km (29,300 sq. miles); population (Jan. 1981), 301,000. Capital, Elista (64,000). The population (1979 census) includes 41·5% Kalmyks, 42·6% Russians, 6·6% Kazakhs, Chechens and Dagestanis.

The Kalmyks migrated from western China to Russia (Nogai Steppe) in the early 17th century. The territory was constituted an Autonomous Region on 4 Nov. 1920, and an Autonomous Republic on 22 Oct. 1935; this was dissolved in 1943. On 9 Jan. 1957 it was reconstituted as an Autonomous Region and on 29 July 1958 as an Autonomous Republic once more.

130 deputies were elected on 24 Feb. 1980, 54 of them women.

Main industries are fishing, canning and building materials. Cattle breeding and irrigated farming (mainly fodder crops) are the principal branches of agriculture. In 1977 there were 90 state and 23 collective farms. Crop area was 831,400 hectares.

In 1979–80 there were 60,500 pupils in 242 schools, 7,902 students in technical colleges and 4,800 in higher education; 858 doctors and 4,355 hospital beds.

KARELIAN AUTONOMOUS SOVIET SOCIALIST REPUBLIC

HISTORY. Before 1917, Karelia (then known as the Olonetz Province) was noted chiefly as a place of exile for political and other prisoners.

After the November Revolution of 1917, Karelia formed part of the RSFSR. In June 1920 a Karelian Labour Commune was formed and in July 1923 this was transformed into the Karelian Autonomous Soviet Socialist Republic (one of the autonomous republics of the RSFSR). On 31 March 1940, after the Soviet–Finnish war, practically all the territory (with the exception of a small section in the neighbourhood of the Leningrad area) which had been ceded by Finland to the USSR was added to Karelia and the Karelian Autonomous Republic was transformed into the Karelo-Finnish Soviet Socialist Republic as the 12th republic of the USSR. In 1946, however, the southern part of the republic, including its whole seaboard and the town of Viipuri (Vyborg) and Keksholm, was attached to the RSFSR and in 1956 the republic reverted to ASSR status with the RSFSR.

AREA AND POPULATION. The Karelian Autonomous Republic, capital Petrozavodsk, covers an area of 172,400 sq. km, with a population of 746,000 (Jan. 1981). Karelians represent 11·1% of the population, Russians, 71·3%, Belorussians 8·1%, Ukrainians 3·2%, Finns 2·7% (1979 census).

150 deputies were elected on 24 Feb. 1980, 53 of them women.

NATURAL RESOURCES. Karelia is chiefly noted for its wealth of timber, some 70% of its territory being forest land. It is also rich in other natural resources, having large deposits of diabase, spar, quartz, marble, granite, zinc, lead, silver, copper, molybdenum, tin, baryta, iron ore, etc. Karelia takes first place in the USSR for the production of mica. It has 43,643 lakes, which, as well as its rivers, are rich in fish.

Agriculture. There were 10 collective fisheries and 60 state farms in 1976. Livestock on 1 Jan. 1980 included 93,400 cattle, 40,000 pigs, 100,000 sheep and goats.

INDUSTRY. The republic has 25 large-scale enterprises, such as timber-mills, paper-cellulose works, mica, chemical plants, power stations and furniture factories. Output, 1977: Timber, 12·3m. cu. metres; paper and cellulose, 1,733,700 tonnes; power, 2,796m. kwh.; canned fish, 12·3m. tins.

The construction of the White Sea–Baltic Canal had a powerful influence on the economic development of Karelia. New refrigerating plants, cellulose factories and timber industry equipment began working in 1970.

COMMUNICATIONS. A railway between Petrozavodsk and Suoyarvi connects the capital and the Murmansk Railway with the main railway line Sortavala–Vyborg. A railway line was also laid between Kandalaksha and Kuolayarvi. Length of track, 1,600 km.

EDUCATION. In 1979–80 there were 115,600 pupils in 747 schools. There were 10,200 students in 3 places of higher education and 10,200 in 10 technical colleges.

There are in Petrozavodsk a university (4,028 full-time students, 2,036 taking correspondence courses and 622 evening students in 1971), 2 other higher institutes and a teachers' training college. A branch of the Academy of Sciences was set up in 1949 with 8 learned institutions (349 research workers).

HEALTH. There were over 3,000 doctors in 1980, and 11,600 hospital beds.

KOMI AUTONOMOUS SOVIET SOCIALIST REPUBLIC

Area, 415,900 sq. km (160,540 sq. miles); population (Jan. 1981), 1,147,000. Capital, Syktyvkar (176,500). Annexed by the princes of Moscow in the 14th century and occupied by British and American forces in 1918–19, the territory was constituted as an Autonomous Region on 22 Aug. 1921 and as an Autonomous Republic on 5 Dec. 1936. The population (1979 census) includes Komi (25·3%), Russians (56·7%), Ukrainians and Belorussians (10·7%).

180 deputies were elected on 24 Feb. 1980, 59 of them women.

There are large coal, oil, timber, gas, asphalt and building materials industries; light industry is expanding. Livestock breeding (including dairy farming) is the main branch of agriculture. There were 51 state farms in 1977. Crop area, 92,000 hectares.

In 1979–80 there were 189,000 pupils in 789 schools, 12,000 students receiving higher education, 18,400 students in 13 technical colleges; and a branch of the Academy of Sciences with 4 learned institutions (297 research workers).

There were 3,900 doctors and 16,200 hospital beds.

MARI AUTONOMOUS SOVIET SOCIALIST REPUBLIC

Area, 23,200 sq. km (8,955 sq. miles); population (Jan. 1981), 711,000 Capital, Yoshkar-Ola. The Mari people were annexed to Russia, with other peoples of the Kazan Tatar Khanate, when the latter was overthrown in 1552. On 4 Nov. 1920 the territory was constituted as an Autonomous Region, and on 5 Dec. 1936 as an Autonomous Republic. The population (1979 census) includes Mari (43·5%), Tatars (5·8%), Chuvashes (1·1%), Russians (47·5%).

150 deputies were elected on 24 Feb. 1980, 57 of them women.

There are over 300 modern factories. The main industries are metalworking, timber, paper, woodworking and food processing. In 1977 there were 105 collective farms and 72 state farms. Over 69% of cultivated land is grain, but flax, potatoes, fruit and vegetables are also expanding branches of agriculture, as is also livestock farming. 625,300 hectares were under crops.

Estimated reserves of the Pechora coalfield are 262,000m. tons.

In 1979–80 there were 714 schools with 130,100 pupils. Technical colleges and higher education establishments had a total of 33,300 students.

There were 3,000 doctors and 8,500 hospital beds.

MORDOVIAN AUTONOMOUS SOVIET SOCIALIST REPUBLIC

Area, 26,200 sq. km (10,110 sq. miles); population (Jan. 1981), 984,000. Capital, Saransk. By the 13th century the Mordovian tribes had been subjugated by the Russian princes of Ryazan and Nizhni-Novgorod. In 1928 the territory was constituted as a Mordovian Area within the Middle-Volga Territory, on 10 Jan. 1930 as an Autonomous Region and on 20 Dec. 1934 as an Autonomous Republic. The population (1979 census) includes Mordovians (34·2%), Russians (59·7%), Tatars (4·6%)

175 deputies were elected on 24 Feb. 1980, 74 of them women.

The Republic has a wide range of industries: Electrical, timber, cable, building materials, furniture, textile, leather and other light industries. Agriculture is devoted chiefly to grain, sugar-beet, sheep and dairy farming. In 1977 there were 76 state and 275 collective farms.

There were 173,800 children at school, 38,100 students in technical colleges and at the state university and institutes, in 1979–80. There were 2,835 doctors and 12,400 hospital beds.

NORTH OSSETIAN AUTONOMOUS SOVIET SOCIALIST REPUBLIC

Area, 8,000 sq. km (3,088 sq. miles); population (Jan. 1981), 601,000. Capital, Ordzhonikidze (formerly Vladikavkaz). The Ossetians, known to antiquity as Alani (who were also called by their immediate neighbours 'Ossi' or 'Yassi'), were annexed to Russia after the latter's treaty of Kuchuk-Kainardji with Turkey, and in 1784 the key fortress of Vladikavkaz was founded on their territory (given the name of Terek region in 1861). On 4 March 1918 the latter was proclaimed an Autonomous Soviet Republic, and after the Civil War this territory with others was set up as the Mountain Autonomous Republic (20 Jan. 1921), with North Ossetia as the Ossetian (Vladikavkaz) Area within it. On 7 July 1924 the latter was constituted as an Autonomous Region and on 5 Dec. 1936 as an Autonomous Republic. The population (1979 census) comprises chiefly Ossetians (50·5%), Russians (33·9%), Ingushi and other Caucasian nationalities (8·1%).

150 deputies were elected on 24 Feb. 1980, 68 of them women.

The main industries are non-ferrous metals (mining and metallurgy), maize-processing (at the Beslan Works, the largest in Europe) timber and woodworking, textiles, building materials, distilleries and food processing. There is also a prosperous and varied agriculture. In 1977 there were 36 state and 44 collective farms.

There were in 1979–80, 106,700 children in 205 schools, 15,100 students in technical colleges and 18,800 students in 4 higher educational establishments (pedagogical, agriculture, medical and mining-metallurgical institutes). There were over 3,000 doctors and over 7,000 hospital beds.

TATAR AUTONOMOUS SOVIET SOCIALIST REPUBLIC

Area, 68,000 sq. km (26,250 sq. miles); population (Jan. 1981), 3,453,000. Capital, Kazan. From the 10th to the 13th centuries this was the territory of the flourishing Volga-Kama Bulgar State; conquered by the Mongols, it became the seat of the Kazan (Tatar) Khans when the Mongol Empire broke up in the 15th century, and in 1552 was conquered again by Russia. On 27 May 1920 it was constituted as an Autonomous Republic. The population (1979 census) includes Tatars (47·7%), Chuvashes, Mordovians and Udmurts (5·9%), Russians (44%).

250 deputies were elected on 24 Feb. 1980, 97 of them women.

The Republic has highly developed engineering, oil and chemical industries, while timber, building materials, textiles, clothing and food industries are also expanding. The Kama works at Naberezhnye Chelny plan to produce 400,000 vehicles annually. In 1977, 552 collective and 238 state farms served a total area under crops of 3·8m. hectares.

In 1979–80 there were 3,492 schools with 638,000 pupils, 39 technical colleges with 62,000 students and 12 higher educational establishments with 71,000 students (including a state university). There is a branch of the USSR Academy of Sciences with 5 learned institutions (512 research workers).

Doctors at the end of 1979 numbered 11,000 and hospital beds 40,000.

TUVA AUTONOMOUS SOVIET SOCIALIST REPUBLIC

Area, 170,500 sq. km (65,810 sq. miles); population (Jan. 1981), 269,000. Capital, Kyzyl (59,000). Tuva was incorporated in the USSR as an autonomous region on 13 Oct. 1944 and elevated to an Autonomous Republic on 10 Oct. 1961. It is situated to the north-west of Mongolia, between 50° and 53°N. lat. and between 90°

and 100°E. long. It is bounded to the east, west and north by Siberia, and to the south by Mongolia. The Tuvans are a Turkic people, formerly ruled by hereditary or elective tribal chiefs. (For the earlier history of the former Tannu-Tuva Republic, *see* THE STATESMAN'S YEAR-BOOK, 1946, p. 798.) The population (1979 census) includes Tuvans (60·5%) and Russians (36·2%).

130 deputies were elected to its Supreme Soviet on 24 Feb. 1980, 53 of them women.

Tuva is well-watered and has much good pastoral land; 47 hydro-electric stations have been set into operation. The Tuvans are mainly herdsmen and cattle farmers, but, in 1977, 376,000 hectares were under crops. There are deposits of gold, cobalt and asbestos. The main exports are hair, hides and wool, and the imports manufactured goods and iron. There are 60 state farms. Mining, wood-working, garment, leather, food and other industries are rapidly developing.

In 1979–80 there were 194 schools with 71,500 pupils; 5 technical colleges with 4,200 students, and an Institute of Linguistics, Literature and History with 2,700 students; 11 newspapers (2 in Russian). There were 860 doctors and 4,530 hospital beds.

A Soviet steamer-service along the river Yenisei maintains communication with Minussinsk, in Central Siberia. Internal transport is chiefly by lorry and motor coach. There is an air service from Kyzyl to Krasnoyarsk.

UDMURT AUTONOMOUS SOVIET SOCIALIST REPUBLIC

Area, 42,100 sq. km (16,250 sq. miles); population (Jan. 1981), 1,516,000. Capital, Izhevsk. The Udmurts (formerly known as 'Votyaks') were annexed by the Russians in the 15th and 16th centuries. On 4 Nov. 1920 the Votyak Autonomous Region was constituted (the name was changed to Udmurt—used by the people themselves—in 1932), and on 28 Dec. 1934 was raised to the status of an Autonomous Republic. The population (1979 census) includes Udmurts (32·2%), Tatars (6·6%), Russians (58·3%).

200 deputies were elected on 24 Feb. 1980, 78 of them women.

Heavy industry includes the manufacture of locomotives, machine tools and other engineering products, timber and building materials. There are also light industries—clothing, leather, furniture, food, etc.

There were 95 state and 261 collective farms in 1977; crop area 1·4m. hectares.

In 1979–80 there were 513 schools with 252,000 pupils; 5,800 finished technical colleges and 3,800 schools of higher education.

There were over 5,000 doctors and over 16,000 hospital beds.

YAKUT AUTONOMOUS SOVIET SOCIALIST REPUBLIC

The area is 3,103,000 sq. km (1,197,760 sq. miles); population (Jan. 1981), 883,000. Capital, Yakutsk (149,000). The Yakuts were subjugated by the Russians in the 17th century. The territory was constituted an Autonomous Republic on 27 April 1922. The population (1979 census) includes Yakuts (36·9%), other northern peoples (2·2%), Russians (50·4%).

205 deputies were elected on 24 Feb. 1980, 92 of them women.

The principal industries are mining (gold, tin, mica, coal) and livestock-breeding. The Soviet Soyuz-Zoloto Trust and a number of individual prospectors are working the fields. Silver- and lead-bearing ores and coal are worked; large diamond fields have been opened up. Timber and food industries are developing. There was 1 collective farm in 1975 with 82 state farms, with an area under crops of 95,000 hectares. Trapping and breeding of fur-bearing animals (sable, squirrel, silver fox, etc.) are an important source of income. A severe climate and lack of railways are serious obstacles to the economic development of the republic. There are, however, 10,000 km of roads and internal air lines totalling 10,000 km including an air service between Irkutsk and Yakutsk.

In 1979–80 there were 179,800 secondary school pupils, 10,200 technical college students and 6,600 at university and teacher training colleges.

There were 3,094 doctors and 12,700 hospital beds.

ADYGEI AUTONOMOUS REGION

Part of Krasnodar Territory. Area, 7,600 sq. km (2,934 sq. miles); population (Jan. 1980), 405,300. Capital, Maikop (128,000). Established 27 July 1922.

Chief industries are timber, woodworking, food processing; but engineering is rapidly expanding. Cattle breeding predominates in agriculture. There were 39 collective and 26 state farms in 1976.

In 1977–78 there were 267 schools with (1980) 68,900 pupils, 6 technical colleges with (1980) 13,100 students and a pedagogical institute with 4,000 students. Regional newspapers are in Adygei and Russian. There were 1,089 doctors and 5,240 hospital beds.

GORNO-ALTAI AUTONOMOUS REGION

Part of Altai Territory. Area, 92,600 sq. km (35,740 sq. miles); population (Jan. 1980), 173,000. Capital, Gorno-Altaisk (39,000). Established 1 June 1922 as Oirot Autonomous Region; renamed 7 Jan. 1948.

Chief industries are gold, mercury and brown-coal mining, timber, chemicals and dairying. Cattle breeding predominates; pasturages and hay meadows cover over 1m. hectares, but 142,000 hectares are under crops. There were 20 collective and 33 state farms in 1977.

In 1979–80 there were 29,500 school pupils; technical colleges had 4,540 students and 3,539 students were receiving higher education. There were 410 doctors and 2,470 hospital beds.

JEWISH AUTONOMOUS REGION

Part of Khabarovsk Territory. Area, 36,000 sq. km (13,895 sq. miles); population (Jan. 1980), 193,400 (Russians, 84·1%; Ukrainians, 6·3%; Jews, 5·4%). Capital, Birobidjan (67,000). Established as Jewish National District in 1928, became an Autonomous Region 7 May 1934.

Chief industries are non-ferrous metallurgy, building materials, timber, engineering, textiles, paper and food processing. There were in 1977, 50 factories, 156,000 hectares under crops, 88,500 cattle and 39,000 pigs. There were 35 state farms and 2 collective farms in 1976.

In 1979–80 there were 31,900 schoolchildren; students in technical colleges numbered 5,500. There are a Yiddish national theatre, a Yiddish newspaper and a Yiddish broadcasting service. Doctors numbered 488 and hospital beds 2,860.

KARACHAYEVO-CHERKESS AUTONOMOUS REGION

Part of Stavropol Territory. Area, 14,300 sq. km (5,442 sq. miles); population (Jan. 1980), 370,000. Capital, Cherkessk (89,000). A Karachai Autonomous Region was established on 26 April 1926 (out of a previously united Karachayevo-Cherkess Autonomous Region created in 1922), and dissolved in 1943. A Cherkess Autonomous Region was established on 30 April 1928. The present Autonomous Region was re-established on 9 Jan. 1957.

Ore-mining, engineering, chemical and woodworking industries have been built up since 1917. There are 70 large factories, and a copper works and sugar factory are under construction. A large irrigation scheme, Kuban-Kalaussi, is being developed, to irrigate 200,000 hectares. Livestock breeding and grain growing predominate in agriculture; crop area in 1977 was 197,900 hectares. There were 14 collective farms and 40 state farms in 1976.

In 1979–80 there were 73,000 pupils in (1977–78) 220 schools, 6 technical colleges (1977–78) with 6,500 students and 2 institutes with 3,300 students; 935 doctors and (1977–78) 3,720 hospital beds.

KHAKASS AUTONOMOUS REGION

Part of Krasnoyarsk Territory. Area, 61,900 sq. km (23,855 sq. miles); population (Jan. 1980), 503,000. Capital, Abakan (123,000). Established 20 Oct. 1930.

Coal- and ore-mining, timber and woodworking industries have been highly developed since 1917. The region is linked by rail with the Trans-Siberian line. Large textile and sugar factories are being built.

In 1979, 619,200 hectares were under crops. Livestock breeding, dairy and vegetable farming are developed. There are 58 state farms.

In 1979–80 there were 70,900 pupils in (1977–78) 363 schools, 7 (1977–78) technical colleges with 9,300 students and 5,800 students in higher educational establishments; 1,170 doctors and 6,800 hospital beds. A Khakass alphabet was created after the Revolution.

Books of Reference

Armstrong, T., *Russian Settlement in the North.* CUP, 1965
Conolly, V., *Beyond the Urals. Economic Developments in Soviet Asia.* London, 1967
Dallin, D. J., *The Rise of Russia in Asia.* New York, 1949.—*Soviet Russia and the Far East.* London, 1949
Kolarz, W., *The Peoples of the Soviet Far East.* London, 1954
Istoriya Sibiri s drevneishikh vremen do nashikh dnei. 5 vols., Leningrad, 1968–69

UKRAINE

Ukrainska Radyanska Sotsialistichna Respublika

HISTORY. The Ukrainian Soviet Socialist Republic was proclaimed on 25 Dec. 1917 and was finally established in Dec. 1919. In Dec. 1920 it concluded a military and economic alliance with the RSFSR and on 30 Dec. 1922 formed, together with the other Soviet Socialist Republics, the Union of Soviet Socialist Republics. On 1 Nov. 1939 Western Ukraine (about 88,000 sq. km) was incorporated in the Ukrainian SSR. On 2 Aug. 1940 Northern Bukovina (about 6,000 sq. km) ceded to the USSR by Romania 28 June 1940, and the Khotin, Akkerman and Izmail provinces of Bessarabia were included in the Ukrainian SSR, and on 29 June 1945 Ruthenia (Sub-Carpathian Russia), about 7,000 sq. km, was also incorporated. From the new territories 2 new regions (provinces) were formed, Chernovitz and Izmail.

AREA AND POPULATION. The Ukraine is in south-west USSR; it has a Black Sea coast and western frontiers with Romania, Hungary, Poland and Czechoslovakia. It is bounded north by Belorussia and otherwise by the RSFSR. In 1938 the Ukrainian SSR covered an area of 445,000 sq. km (171,770 sq. miles); it now covers 603,700 sq. km (231,990 sq. miles).

Population, Jan. 1981, 50,135,000 (in 1979, 73·6% Ukrainians, 21·1% Russians, 1·3% Jews, 0·8% Belorussians).

The principal towns are the capital Kiev, Kharkov, Donetsk, Odessa, Dnepropetrovsk, Lvov, Zaporozhye and Krivoi Rog.

The Ukrainian Soviet Socialist Republic consists of the following regions: Cherkassy, Chernigov, Chernovtzy, Crimea (transferred from the RSFSR on 19 Feb 1954), Dnepropetrovsk, Donetsk, Ivan Franko, Khmelnitsky (formerly

Kamenetz-Podolsk), Kharkov, Kherson, Kiev, Kirovograd, Lvov, Nikolayev, Odessa, Poltava, Rovno, Sumy, Ternopol, Vinnitza, Volhynia, Voroshilovgrad, Zakarpatskaya (Transcarpathia), Zaporozhye, Zhitomir.

CONSTITUTION AND GOVERNMENT. The Supreme Soviet, elected on 24 Feb. 1980, consists of 650 deputies (1 per 90,000 population); 447 are Communists and 234 women. A new Constitution, based on that of the USSR, was adopted in April 1978.

At elections to regional district, urban and rural Soviets (19 June 1982), out of 525,500 deputies returned, 258,808 (49·2%) were women, 295,174 (56·2%) non-Party and 378,018 (72·4%) industrial workers and collective farmers.

Chairman, Presidium of the Supreme Soviet: A. F. Vatchenko.
Chairman, Council of Ministers: A. P. Lyashko.
Foreign Minister: G. G. Shevel.
First Secretary, Communist Party: V. V. Shcherbitsky.

FINANCE. Budget estimates (in 1m. roubles), 1980, 20,832; 1982, 24,102.

AGRICULTURE. The Ukraine contains some of the richest land in the USSR. It raises wheat, buckwheat, beet, sunflower, cotton, flax, tobacco, soya, hops, the rubber plant kok-sagyz, fruit and vegetables, and in 1976 provided nearly 20% of the grain production in the USSR and over 62% of the sugar-beet. Nine-tenths of the grain exported from USSR came from the Ukraine. The area under cultivation was 27·9m. hectares in 1913, 27m. in 1939 before the new territories were added, and 34·2m. in 1978.

Output (in 1m. tonnes) in 1979 (1913 figures in tons in brackets): Sugar-beet, 47·1 (9·3); sunflower seed, 2·4 (0·07); flax, 0·014 (0·004); potatoes, 23·9 (8·5); meat and fats, 3·6 (1·1); milk, 22·5 (4·7); wool, 0·028 (0·015); 13,747m. eggs (3,005m.); grain, 50·6m.

On 1 Jan. 1979 there were 25·4m. cattle, 20·7m. pigs, 9·2m. sheep and goats. In 1949 silver-fox breeding farms were started.

On 1 Jan. 1980 there were 2,104 state farms and 6,963 collective farms.

Irrigation networks supplied 1·82m. hectares of land; 2·2m. hectares were drained.

Tractors numbered 408,800 at 1 Jan. 1981 and combine harvesters, 89,900.

INDUSTRY. Coal in the Donetz field (25,900 sq. km stretching from Donetsk to Rostov), estimated to contain 60% of the bituminous and anthracite-coal reserves of the USSR, yielded, in 1961, 186·1m. tonnes—about 36% of the USSR production. Large new seams have been found near Novo-Moskovsk (Dnepropetrovsk region), Kharkov, Lugansk (beyond the Don) and on the left bank of the Dnieper. Within the present frontiers of the Ukraine, coal output was 22·8m. tons in 1913, 83·8m. tons in 1940, 78m. tons in 1950 and 217m. tons in 1977.

Combining coal from the Donetz field with the iron-ore from the mines in Krivoi Rog has made possible the development of a large ferrous metallurgical industry in the Ukraine. Output of iron ore was 6·9m. tons in 1913, 18·9m. tons in 1940 and 126m. tons in 1977.

Manganese is also available at Nikopol; output in 1976, 6·7m. tons.

Pig-iron output was 2·9m. tons in 1913, 9·6m. tons in 1940, 9·2m. tons in 1950 and 46·4m. tons in 1975. Steel output (within present frontiers) was 2·4m. tons in 1913, 8·9m. in 1940, 8·4m. in 1950 and 53·7m. in 1977.

The Ukraine also contains oil, rich deposits of salt and various important chemicals. Oil output was 1m. tons in 1913 (in present frontiers), 353,000 tons in 1940 and 10·5m. tons in 1977; with 68·7m. cu. metres of natural gas.

The Ukraine has highly developed chemical and machine-construction industries producing one-fifth of the total output of machinery and chemicals in the USSR. 142,000 tractors and 3,500 main-line diesel locomotives were produced in 1979.

In Northern Bukovina there are deposits of gypsum, oil, alabaster, brown coal and timber. Output of mineral fertilizers was 36,000 tons in 1913 and 19·5m. tons in 1979; cement output increased in the same years from 269,000 to 22·5m. tons (in present frontiers in both cases). Paper output in 1977 was 250,000 tons (1913: 26,900).

Consumer goods and food industries are important. Output of cotton fabrics was (in present frontiers) 4·7m. linear metres in 1913, 13·8m. in 1940, 20·6m. in 1950 and 429·4m. in 1975. Granulated sugar output was 1913, 1·1m. tons; 1940, 1·6m. tons; 1950, 1·8m. tons, and 1977, 6·8m. tons. Leather footwear manufactured in 1940 totalled 40·8m. pairs; 1979, 176m.

The number of industrial and office workers at the end of 1950 was 6·9m., and the average in 1980, 20m. There were 1,816,000 specialists with a higher education.

During the first 5-year plan (1929–32) the Dnieper power-station was built; destroyed during the War, it was restored during the fourth plan (1946–50). Another large hydro-electric station at Kakhovka began operations during the fifth plan (1951–55). Power output (in 1,000m. kwh.) increased as follows: 1913, 0·5; 1940, 12·4; 1950, 14·7; 1980, 236.

COMMUNICATIONS. The total length of railways of the Ukrainian SSR in 1978 was 22,440 km, the navigable rivers, 3,900 km. Length of hard-surface motor roads was 127,900 km.

Airlines connect Kiev, Lvov, Chernovtsy and Odessa with Crimean and Caucasian spas, Kiev with Tbilisi, Odessa with Riga and Donetsk.

Newspapers (1980). Out of 1,737 newspapers, 1,278 were in Ukrainian. Daily circulation of Ukrainian-language newspapers, 16m., other languages, 8m.

RELIGION. Several Christian Churches have their adherents in the Ukraine, the chief being the Orthodox Greek Church and the Catholic Church. The Western Ukraine Uniate Church, which in 1596 had been forced by the Poles to establish unity with the Roman Church, severed this connexion in March 1946 and joined the Orthodox Church. There are also some Protestants as well as Jews and others.

EDUCATION. In 1980–81 the number of pupils in 23,400 primary and secondary schools was 7·5m.; 146 higher educational establishments had 880,400 students, and 725 technical colleges 803,100 students; 2·4m. children were attending 17,400 pre-school institutions.

The Ukrainian Academy of Sciences was established in 1919; in 1980 it had 70 institutions with 13,369 scientific staff. There is an academy of building and architecture. Total scientific staff in 814 learned institutions numbered 185,100.

HEALTH. Doctors numbered 182,500 in 1980, and hospital beds, 627,100.

Books of Reference

Allen, W. E. D., *The Ukraine: A History.* London, 1940
Andrusyshen, C. H. (ed.), *Ukrainian-English Dictionary.* Toronto, 1955
Chamberlin, W. H., *The Ukraine.* New York, 1945
Chirovsky, N. L., *The Ukrainian Economy.* New York, Paris, Toronto, 1965
Hrushevsky, M., *A History of the Ukraine.* New Haven, 1941
Manning, C. A., *Twentieth-century Ukraine.* New York, 1951
Mirchuk, L. (ed.), *Ukraine and its People.* London, 1949
Istoriya Ukrainskoi SSR. 2 vols. Kiev, 1969
Soviet Ukraine. (English ed.) Ukrainian Soviet Encyclopaedia, 1970
Ukraine: A Concise Encyclopaedia. 2 vols. Toronto, 1963–71

BELORUSSIA

Belaruskaya Sovietskaya Sotsialistychnaya Respublika

HISTORY. The Belorussian Soviet Socialist Republic was set up on 1 Jan. 1919. It forms one of the constituent republics of the USSR.

AREA AND POPULATION. Belorussia is situated along the Western Dvina and Dnieper. It is bounded west by Poland, north by Latvia and Lithuania, east by the RSFSR and south by the Ukraine. The area is 207,600 sq. km (80,134 sq. miles). The capital is Minsk. Other important towns are Gomel, Vitebsk, Mogilev, Bobruisk, Grodno and Brest. On 2 Nov. 1939 western Belorussia was incorporated with an area of over 108,000 sq. km and a population of 4·8m. The population (Jan. 1981) was 9·7m. 79·4% of this population in 1979 (census) were Belorussians, 4·2% Poles, 11·9% Russians, 2·4% Ukrainians and 1·4% Jews.

Belorussia now comprises the following regions: Brest, Gomel, Grodno, Mogilev, Minsk, Vitebsk.

CONSTITUTION AND GOVERNMENT. The Supreme Soviet, elected in 1980, consists of 485 deputies (1 per 20,000 population); 328 are Communists and 180 women. A new Constitution was adopted in April 1978.

At elections to regional, district, urban and rural Soviets (20 June 1982), of 85,394 deputies returned, 42,326 (49·6%) were women, 48,743 (57·1%) non-Party and 58,839 (68·9%) industrial workers and collective farmers.

Chairman, Presidium of the Supreme Soviet: I. E. Poliakov.
Chairman, Council of Ministers: A. N. Aksyonov.
Foreign Minister: A. E. Gurinovich
First Secretary, Communist Party: N. Slyunkov.

FINANCE. Budget estimates (in 1m. roubles), 1980, 5,277; 1983, 5,737.

NATURAL RESOURCES. Belorussia is hilly, with a general slope towards the south. It contains large tracts of marsh land, particularly to the south-west, and valuable forest land wooded with oak, elm, maple and white beech: there are over 6,500 peat deposits.

AGRICULTURE. Agriculturally, Belorussia may be divided into three main sections—Northern: growing flax, fodder, grasses and breeding cattle for meat and dairy produce; Central: potato growing and pig breeding; Southern: good natural pasture land, hemp cultivation and cattle breeding for meat and dairy produce. The area under cultivation (in hectares) was 4·5m. in 1913, 5·2m. in 1940 and 6·3m. in 1979. There were 6·8m. cattle, 4·6m. pigs and 540,000 sheep and goats on 1 Jan. 1980.

Output of main agricultural products (in 1,000 tonnes) in 1979 (1913 figures in brackets): Flax, 78 (33); sugar-beet, 1,383 (0); potatoes, 15,253 (4,024); meat, 915 (219); milk, 6·3 (1·4); wool, 1·1 (2·3); grain, 4·6 (2·6); 2,894m. eggs (413m.).

At the end of 1977 there were 1,887 collective farms and 894 state farms. About 2·5m. hectares of marsh land had been drained for agricultural use, 828,200 of these for crops. This land has been found to be as rich as the soil of the Black Earth Zone, and yields good harvests of grain, fodder, potatoes, koksagyz and other crops. In Jan. 1980, 2·6m. hectares were drained and 36,300 hectares of land irrigated.

In Jan. 1981 there were 117,200 tractors and 27,400 grain combine harvesters.

INDUSTRY. Industry in this republic was almost completely destroyed during the years 1941–45. By 1956, aggregate industrial output was three times what it had been in 1940. Plants producing tip-lorries, machine-tools and agricultural machinery are prominent.

The republic also contains timber works; a match factory in Borisov; building materials, machine, prefabricated house construction, glass-blowing and other factories; canneries, creameries and other food industries; chemical, textiles, artificial-silk, flax-spinning and leather works.

The automobile and tractor industry produced 89,100 tractors and 32,500 lorries in 1979. Cement output, 33,000 tons in 1913, was 2·17m. tons in 1975. Leather footwear output 9·8m. pairs in 1940, was 41·6m. pairs in 1979. Linen fabrics, 13,000 linear metres in 1913, 68·4m. in 1975; woollens, 37,000 linear metres in 1913, 29m. in 1975.

Particular attention has been paid to the development of the peat industry with a view to making Belorussia as far as possible self-supporting in fuel, and in 1939 local peat provided 67·5% of her total requirements of fuel. The average annual output is about 18m. tonnes.

There are also rich deposits of rock salt. In 1951 the first sugar refinery in Belorussia was opened in Grodno; sugar output in 1979 was 313,900 tonnes.

Output of electricity in 1980, 34,100m. kwh. (508m. in 1940). New power-plants have been built in Baranovichi, Grodno, Molodechno and Lida.

The number of industrial and office workers at the end of 1980 was 4m.

COMMUNICATIONS. In 1978 there were 5,520 km of railways, 71,700 km of motor roads (39,000 km hard-surface) and 3,900 km of navigable waterways.

Newspapers (1980). Of 198 newspapers published 128 were in Belorussian. Daily circulation of Belorussian-language newspapers, 1·6m., other languages, 1·3m.

EDUCATION. In 1980–81 there were 177,000 students in 32 places of higher education and 162,800 students in 135 technical colleges. There were 36,500 scientific personnel in 178 institutions, and 340,000 specialists with a higher education employed in the national economy. The Belorussian Academy of Sciences controlled 32 learned institutions with 5,378 scientific staff. The number of children in primary and secondary schools was 489,000 in 1914–15, and 1·5m. in 1980–81. 488,000 children were attending pre-school institutions in 1980–81.

HEALTH. In 1980–81 there were 33,000 doctors (900 in 1913, within present frontiers), and 120,800 hospital beds (6,400 in 1913).

Books of Reference

Vakar, N. P., *Belorussia.* Harvard Univ. Press, 1956.—*A Bibliographical Guide to Belorussia.* Harvard Univ. Press, 1956

Istoriya Belorusskoi SSR. 2nd ed. 2 vols. Minsk, 1961

AZERBAIJAN

Azarbaijchan Soviet Sotsialistik Respublikasy

HISTORY. The 'Mussavat' (Nationalist) party, which dominated the National Council or Constituent Assembly of the Tatars, declared the independence of Azerbaijan on 28 May 1918, with a capital, first at Ganja (Elizavetpol) and later at Baku. On 28 April 1920 Azerbaijan was proclaimed a Soviet Socialist Republic. From 1922, with Georgia and Armenia it formed the Transcaucasian Soviet Federal Socialist Republic. In 1936 it assumed the status of one of the Union Republics of the USSR.

AREA AND POPULATION. Azerbaijan covers an area of 86,600 sq. km (33,430 sq. miles) and has a population (Jan. 1981) of 6,262,000. Its capital is Baku. Other important towns are Kirovabad and Sumgait. Nakhichevan is the capital of the Autonomous Republic of the same name.

Azerbaijan includes the Nakhichevan Autonomous Republic and the Nagorno-Karabagh Autonomous Region. Situated in the eastern area of Transcaucasia, it is protected by mountains in the west and north, washed by the Caspian Sea in the east and bounded by Iran in the south. Its climate is inclined to drought.

In 1979 (census) 78·1% of the population were Azerbaijanis. Other nationalities were Russians (7·9%), Armenians (7·9%) and Daghestanis (3·4%).

CONSTITUTION AND GOVERNMENT. The Supreme Soviet, elected in 1980, consists of 450 deputies (1 per 10,000 population); 312 are Communists and 179 women. A new Constitution was adopted in April 1978.

At elections to the Nagorno-Karabagh regional Soviet and the district, urban and rural Soviets (20 June 1982), of 50,799 deputies returned, 24,432 (48·1%) were women, 28,775 (56·6%) non-Party and 34,059 (67%) industrial workers and collective farmers.

Chairman, Presidium of the Supreme Soviet: K. A. Khalilov.
Chairman, Council of Ministers: G. Seidov.
First Secretary, Communist Party: K. M. Bagirov.

FINANCE (in 1m. roubles). Budget estimates, 1980, 1,953; 1983, 2,428.

AGRICULTURE. The chief agricultural products are grain, cotton, rice, grapes, fruit, vegetables, tobacco and silk. The Mexican rubber plant *grayule* has been acclimatized. A new kind of high-yielding winter wheat has been produced for use in mountainous parts of the republic.

Livestock on 1 Jan. 1979: Cattle, 1·7m.; pigs, 167,000; sheep and goats, 5·3m.

Output of main agricultural products (in 1,000 tonnes) in 1978 (1913 figures in brackets): Cotton, 742 (4); potatoes, 131 (38); tea, 20 (0); meat, 136 (40); milk, 768 (203); wool, 10·2 (4·1); grapes, 1,045; fruit, 217; 691m. eggs (97m.).

Azerbaijan has become an important cotton-growing and sub-tropical base. About 70% of cultivated land is irrigated. On the irrigated land crops of Egyptian and Sea-Island cotton are obtained. Here, too, rice and lucerne are cultivated, and in the mountain valleys there are also orchards, vineyards and silk cultures.

In the south along the coast of the Caspian, where the climate is more moist, there are tea plantations, and citrus fruits and other sub-tropical plants are grown.

In 1941 a scientific research institute for sub-tropical research was opened to develop the culture of sub-tropical plants in Azerbaijan and other parts of Transcaucasia. A forestry research institute was opened in 1949.

There were on 1 Jan. 1981, 625 collective farms, 676 state farms, 35,300 tractors and 4,300 grain combine harvesters.

INDUSTRY. The republic is rich in natural resources: oil, iron, aluminium, copper, lead, zinc, precious metals, sulphur pyrites, limestone and salt. Iron and steel and aluminium works have been built at Sumgait.

The most important industry is the oil industry, especially in the Baku region. The output of oil was 7·7m. tonnes in 1913, 22·2m. tonnes in 1940 and 16·5m. tonnes in 1976. The largest producing area lies along the western shore of the Caspian Sea, north and south of Baku, where the largest refineries are located. Other wells lie west of Baku, and some have been drilled in the Caspian itself, off the Apsheron Peninsula. Baku is connected by a double pipeline with Batum on the Black Sea. All the oilfields have been electrified and are connected with Baku.

Azerbaijan has also copper, chemical, cement and building material, food, timber, salt, textiles and fishing industries. 788,000 tonnes of steel were produced in 1976, 1·4m. tons of cement, 130·4m. linear metres of cotton fabrics, 15·8m. pairs leather footwear, 32·3m. linear metres of silk fabrics, 1·3m. tons of iron ore.

In addition to Baku, other important industrial centres are Kirovabad, Nukha, Stepanakert, Nakhichevan, Lenkoran.

In 1980 electric power output was 15,000m. kwh. Output of gas, which began in 1928 with 176m. cu. metres, was 10,989m. in 1976. Pipelines from Karadag to Baku and Sumgait supply gas fuel for all oil-cracking factories and most engineering works.

Synthetic rubber works (Sumgait), tyre works and a worsted combine (Baku) and a large textile combine (Mingechaur) have been built.

The number of industrial and office workers in 1980 (average for year) was 1·8m.

COMMUNICATIONS. Railway lines, apart from narrow gauge, 1,880 km. The first electrical railway (42 km) in the USSR was constructed in Azerbaijan in 1924; in 1949, 27 km was added, and the line now runs Baku-Surakhany-Sabunchi-Buzovny-Baku. The capital is also linked by rail with Tbilisi, Yerevan, Derbent, Julfa and Astara. There were, in 1978, 23,800 km of motor roads (17,100 km hard-surface) and 500 km of inland waterways.

Newspapers (1980). There were 117 newspapers, 92 in the Azerbaijani language (circulation 2·18m.), other languages, 491,000.

EDUCATION. In 1980–81 there were 1·6m. pupils in 4,200 elementary and secondary schools and 147,000 children attending pre-school institutions. There were 75 technical colleges with 79,800 students, 17 higher educational institutions, including a state university at Baku, with 105,200 students (including correspondence students).

The Azerbaijan Academy of Sciences has 28 research institutions with 4,314 research workers. There are 142 learned and scientific institutions, with 21,500 research workers in all.

HEALTH. In 1980 there were 20,700 doctors and 60,900 hospital beds. There were also 619 maternity and infant welfare centres.

NAKHICHEVAN AUTONOMOUS SOVIET SOCIALIST REPUBLIC

Area, 5,500 sq. km (2,120 sq. miles), population (Jan. 1981), 247,000. Capital, Nakhichevan (37,000). This territory, on the borders of Turkey and Iran, forms part of the Azerbaijan SSR although separated from it by the territory of Soviet Armenia. Its population, mainly Azerbaijanis, had a chequered history for 1,500 years under the ancient Persians, Arabs, Seljuk Turks, Mongols, Ottoman Turks and modern Persians before being annexed by Russia in 1828. On 9 Feb. 1924 it was constituted as an Autonomous Republic within Azerbaijan. Its Supreme Soviet, elected 24 Feb. 1980, has 110 members including 52 women.

The republic has silk, clothing, cotton, canning, meat-packing and other factories. Nearly 70% of the people are engaged in agriculture, of which the main branches are cotton and tobacco growing. Fruit and grapes are also produced in increasing quantity. There are 47 collective and 26 state farms. Crop area 37,400 hectares.

In 1977–78 there were 225 (218, 1979–80) primary, 8-year and 11-year schools with 70,800 pupils. There were 1,700 pupils in 4 technical colleges and a pedagogical institute with 2,400 students.

Doctors numbered 503, and hospital beds, 2,378.

NAGORNO-KARABAKH AUTONOMOUS REGION

Area, 4,400 sq. km (1,700 sq. miles); population (Jan. 1981),164,000. Capital, Stepanakert (33,000). Populated by Armenians (75·9%) and Azerbaijanis (23%), a separate khanate in the 18th century, it was established on 7 July 1923 as an Autonomous Region within Azerbaijan.

Main industries are silk, wine, dairying and building materials. Crop area is 67,200 hectares; cotton, grapes and winter wheat are grown. There are 53 collective and 21 state farms.

In 1979–80 there were 188 schools, 5 technical colleges, a teacher training college and a higher educational institution with 42,000 students; 402 doctors and 1,720 hospital beds.

Books of Reference

Baddeley, J. F., *The Rugged Flanks of Caucasus.* 2 vols. Oxford, 1941
Tutaeff, D., *The Soviet Caucasus.* London, 1942

GEORGIA

Sakartvelos Sabchota Sotsialisturi Respublica

HISTORY. The independence of the Georgian Social Democratic Republic was declared at Tiflis on 26 May 1918 by the National Council, elected by the National

Assembly of Georgia on 22 Nov. 1917. The independence of Georgia was recognized by the USSR on 7 May 1920. On 12 Feb. 1921 a rising broke out in Mingrelia, Abkhazia and Adjaria, and Soviet troops invaded the country, which, on 25 Feb. 1921, was proclaimed the Georgian Soviet Socialist Republic. At the first Transcaucasian Soviet Congress, 15 Dec. 1922, Georgia, together with Armenia and Azerbaijan, united to form the Transcaucasian Soviet Federal Socialist Republic, and a federal constitution was adopted and published 10 Jan. 1923. In 1936 the Georgian Soviet Socialist Republic became one of the constituent republics of the USSR and, like other republics of USSR, adopted a new Constitution.

AREA AND POPULATION. Georgia is bounded west by the Black Sea and south by Turkey, Armenia and Azerbaijan. It occupies the whole of the western part of Transcaucasia and covers an area of 69,700 sq. km (26,900 sq. miles). Its population on 1 Jan. 1981 was 5·1m. The capital is Tbilisi (Tiflis). Other important towns are Kutaisi (194,000), Rustavi (129,000), Batumi (124,000), Sukhumi (114,000), Poti (54,000), Gori (54,000).

Protected from the north by the Caucasian mountains and receiving in the west the warm, moist winds from the Black Sea into which most of its rivers flow, Georgia is outstanding for its fine, warm climate and its natural wealth, variety and beauty. It has the highest snow-capped peaks of the Caucasian mountains. Georgia contains valuable sulphur and other medicinal springs. Georgians, an ancient people, were (1979 census) 68·8% of the population; Armenians 9%; Russians, 7·4%; Azerbaijanis, 5·1%; Ossetians, 3·2%; Abkhazians, 1·7%.

CONSTITUTION AND GOVERNMENT. The Georgian Soviet Socialist Republic includes the Abkhazian ASSR, the Adjarian ASSR and the South Ossetian Autonomous Region.

The Supreme Soviet, elected in 1980, consists of 440 deputies (1 per 10,000 population); 158 are women, 290 Communists. A new Constitution was adopted in April 1978.

At elections to the district, rural and urban Soviets, and that of the South Ossetian region (20 June 1982), of 50,643 deputies returned 25,403 (50·2%) were women, 29,083 (57·4%) non-Party and 34,780 (68·7%) industrial workers and collective farmers.

Chairman, Presidium of the Supreme Soviet: P. G. Gilashvili.
Chairman, Council of Ministers: D. L. Kartvelishvili.
First Secretary, Communist Party: E. A. Shevardnadze.

FINANCE (in 1m. roubles). Budget estimates, 1980, 1,953; 1983, 2,387.

AGRICULTURE. There are 3 main agricultural areas: (1) The moist subtropical area along the Black Sea Coast, where are cultivated tea, citrus fruits (lemons, oranges, mandarins, etc.), the tung tree (which yields special industrial oils), eucalyptus, bamboo, high-quality tobacco; (2) Imeretia (the Kutais region) where the chief cultures are grapes and silk, and (3) Kakhetia, along the Alazani (a tributary of the Kura river), famed for its orchards and wines. Land (in hectares) under cultivation was 748,000 in 1913, 896,000 in 1940, 778,000 in 1961, 800,000 in 1979.

Output of main agricultural products (in 1,000 tonnes) in 1978 (1913 figures in brackets): Sugar-beet, 115 (0); fruit, 811; grapes, 784; tea in leaf, 454; meat, 133 (49); wool, 5·5 (3·4); milk, 631 (222); wine, 19·9m. decalitres; 629m. eggs (119m.).

On 1 Jan. 1980 there were 686 collective farms working over 66% of all agricultural land, 471 state farms working nearly 34% of such land. In the Colchis area 115,000 hectares of extremely rich land have been reclaimed. There are 389,000 hectares of irrigated land. 151,400 hectares of marsh land have been drained. Tractors numbered 24,900 on 1 Jan. 1981; grain combines, 1,500.

Livestock on 1 Jan. 1980: Cattle, 1·5m.; pigs, 940,400; sheep and goats, 2m.

Georgia is rich in forest lands where fine varieties of timber are grown. Area covered by forests, 2·4m. hectares.

INDUSTRY. The most important mining industry of Georgia is the exploitation of the manganese deposits, the richest of which lie in the Chiatura region, where 1·6m. tonnes of ore were produced in 1971. Manganese deposits in Georgia are calculated at 250m. tonnes, distributed over an area of 140 sq. km. The most important coal seams are at Tkvarcheli (deposits estimated at 250m. tonnes) and Tkibuli (deposits of 80m. tonnes). Other important minerals are baryta, the best in the USSR, fire-resisting and other clays, diatomite shale, oil, agate, marble, cement, alabaster, iron and other ores, building stone, arsenic, molybdenum, tungsten and mercury. In 1941 a goldfield was discovered. Output of coal in 1976 was 1·9m. tonnes (625,000 in 1940).

Since the Second World War the Transcaucasian Metallurgical Plant has been built at Rustavi (near Tbilisi) and a motor works at Kutaisi. There are modern factories for processing green tea-leaves, creameries and breweries; Georgia has also textile and silk industries.

In 1977, 784,000 tonnes of pig-iron, 1·5m. tonnes of steel, 1,334,000 tonnes of rolled metal were produced; also 1·7m. tonnes of cement, 748,000 tonnes of mineral fertilizer, 56·7m. linear metres of cotton fabrics, 43·8m. linear metres of silk fabrics, 14·8m. pairs of leather footwear and 46,200 tons of granulated sugar.

Georgia's fast flowing rivers form an abundant source of energy. One of the most powerful stations completed in recent years is Tbilisi (1m. kw.). Power output in 1980 was 14,700m. kwh. (742m. in 1940).

There were 1·9m. industrial and office workers in 1979.

COMMUNICATIONS. Length of railways in 1978 was 1,420 km. The trunk line leading from Batumi through Tbilisi to Baku on the Caspian Sea has several narrow-gauge branches on Georgian territory to the coalmines of Tkibuli, to the port of Poti, to the manganese mines of Chiatura, to the mineral springs of Borjom and the health resort Bakuriani, to the towns Signakh and Telavi, in Kakhetia, and to the Armenian frontier, across the coalmine district of Alaverdi. The last branch divides in Armenia, going on the one side to Tabriz in Iran, and on the other to Erzerum in Anatolia. A railway line from Akhal-Senaki along the Black Sea coast, through Sukhumi to Tuapse, was completed in 1946. All lines are electrified or work on diesel traction. In 1978 there were 22,000 km of motor roads, 18,500 km of them hard-surfaced.

Newspapers (1980). Out of 141 newspapers, 123 were in Georgian. Daily circulation in Georgian language newspapers, 3m., other languages, 500,000.

EDUCATION. In 1980–81 there were 900,000 pupils in 3,900 primary and secondary schools, 53,400 in 91 technical colleges and 88,500 students in 19 higher educational institutions. Tbilisi University has 16,300 students. In towns, 11 years' education is usual. In Abastuman there is an astro-physical observatory. In 1936 a branch of the Academy of Sciences of the USSR was formed in Tbilisi, and in Feb. 1941 a Georgian Academy of Sciences was opened, which in 1980 had 43 institutions with scientific staff totalling 5,617. There were in all 194 research institutions with 25,500 scientific staff.

In 1980, 169,000 children were attending pre-school institutions.

HEALTH. There were 23,600 doctors and 54,100 hospital beds in 1980.

ABKHAZIAN AUTONOMOUS SOVIET SOCIALIST REPUBLIC

Area, 8,600 sq. km (3,320 sq. miles); population (Jan. 1981), 509,000. Capital Sukhumi. This area, the ancient Colchis, included Greek colonies from the 6th century B.C. onwards. From the 2nd century B.C. onwards, it was a prey to many invaders—Romans, Byzantines, Arabs, Ottoman Turks—before accepting a Russian protectorate in 1810. However, from the 4th century A.D. a West Georgian kingdom was established by the Lazi princes in the territory (known to the Romans as 'Lazica') and by the 8th century the prevailing language was Georgian and the name

Abkhazia. On March 1921 a congress of local Soviets proclaimed it a Soviet Republic, and its status as an Autonomous Republic, within Georgia, was confirmed on 17 April 1930.

Population (1979 census) Abkhazians, 17·1%, Georgians, 43·9% and Russians, 16·4%.

140 Deputies were elected on 24 Feb. 1980, 57 of them women.

The Abkhazian coast (along the Black Sea) possesses a famous chain of health resorts—Gagra, Sukhumi, Akhali-Antoni, Gulripsha and Gudauta—sheltered by thickly forested mountains.

The republic has coal, electric power, building materials and light industries. In 1976 there were 93 collective farms and 48 state farms; main crops are tobacco, tea, grapes, oranges, tangerines and lemons. Crop area 41,400 hectares.

Livestock, 1 Jan. 1980: 32,500 cattle, 16,200 pigs, 9,200 sheep and goats.

101,500 pupils were attending 460 schools in 1976–77. There were 7 technical colleges with 3,100 students; 6,100 students were receiving higher education (including correspondence courses). A university has been opened in Sukhumi.

There were 152,700 industrial and office workers, and 13,200 specialists with a higher education in the national economy in 1978. Doctors, 1,883; hospital beds, 5,800.

ADJARIAN AUTONOMOUS SOVIET SOCIALIST REPUBLIC

Area, 3,000 sq. km (1,160 sq. miles); population (Jan. 1981), 362,000. Capital, Batumi. After a history similar to that of Abkhazia, it fell under Turkish rule in the 17th century, and was annexed to Russia (rejoining Georgia) after the Berlin Treaty of 1878. On 16 July 1921 the territory was constituted as an Autonomous Republic within the Georgian SSR.

Population (1979 census) Georgians, 80·1%, Russians, 9·8% and Armenians 4·6%.

110 deputies were elected on 24 Feb. 1980, 43 of them women.

The republic specializes in sub-tropical agricultural products. These include tea, mandarines and lemons, grapes, bamboo, eucalyptus, etc. Livestock: 116,000 cattle, 10,000 sheep and goats. In 1976 there were 77 collective farms and 21 state farms.

There are shipyards at Batumi, modern oil-refining plant (the pipeline from the Baku oilfields ends at Batumi), food-processing and canning factories, clothing, building materials, drug factories, etc.

Health resorts are Kobuleti, Tsikhisdziri, Batumi on the coast and Beshumi in the hills. The sub-tropical climate and flora, and the combination of mountains and sea, make this republic (like Abkhazia) a favourite holiday area.

In 1979 there were 76,400 pupils at school, several technical colleges with 3,500 students, a pedagogical institute and several research institutions. 2,000 students were receiving a higher education.

There were (1978) 92,700 industrial and office workers, and 10,500 specialists with a higher education in the national economy. Doctors, 1,097; hospital beds, 3,695.

SOUTH OSSETIAN AUTONOMOUS REGION

This area was populated by Ossetians from across the Caucasus (North Ossetia), driven out by the Mongols in the 13th century. The region was set up within the Georgian SSR on 20 April 1922. Area, 3,900 sq. km (1,505 sq. miles); population (Jan. 1981), 97,000 (1979 census, Ossetians, 66·4% and Georgians, 28·8%). Capital, Tskhinvali (34,000).

Main industries are mining, timber, electrical engineering and building materials. Crop area, chiefly grains, was 21,700 hectares in 1979; other pursuits are sheep-farming (103,500 sheep and goats) and vine-growing. There were 14 collective farms and 13 state farms.

There are a pedagogical institute (2,345 students) and several technical colleges (700 students). In 1976 there were 24,000 pupils in elementary and secondary schools.

There were (1978) 34,900 industrial and office workers, and 3,800 specialists with a higher education in the national economy. Doctors, 401; hospital beds, 1,350.

Books of Reference

Lang, D. M., *A Modern History of Georgia.* London, 1962.— *The Georgians.* London, 1966
Tutaeff, D., *The Soviet Caucasus.* London, 1942
Istoriya Gruzii. 3 vols. Tbilisi, 1962–73

ARMENIA

Haikakan Sovetakan Sotsialistakan Respublika

HISTORY. On 29 Nov. 1920 Armenia was proclaimed a Soviet Socialist Republic. The Armenian Soviet Government, with the Russian Soviet Government, was a party to the Treaty of Kars (March 1921), which confirmed the Turkish possession of the former Government of Kars and of the Surmali District of the Government of Yerevan. From 1922 to 1936 it formed part of the Transcaucasian Soviet Federal Socialist Republic. In 1936 Armenia was proclaimed a constituent republic of the USSR.

AREA AND POPULATION. Armenia covers an area of 29,800 sq. km (11,490 sq. miles). It is bounded in the north by Georgia, in the east by Azerbaijan and in the south and west by Turkey and Iran. It is a very mountainous country with but little forest land, has many turbulent rivers and a highly fertile soil, but subject to drought. In Jan. 1981 the population was 3·12m. Census (1979) 89·7% of the population were Armenians, the rest are Russians (2·3%), Kurds (1·7%), Azerbaijanians (5·3%). The capital is Yerevan. Other large towns are Leninakan (210,000) and Kirovakan (149,000).

CONSTITUTION AND GOVERNMENT. The Supreme Soviet, elected in 1980, consists of 340 deputies (1 per 5,000 population); 121 are women, 218 Communists. A new Constitution was adopted in April 1978.

At elections to the district, urban and rural Soviets (20 June 1982), of 27,165 deputies returned 13,513 (49·7%) were women, 15,376 (56·6%) non-Party and 18,975 (69·9%) industrial workers and collective farmers.

Chairman, Presidium of the Supreme Soviet: B. E. Sarkisov.
Chairman, Council of Ministers: F. T. Sarkisian.
First Secretary, Communist Party: K. S. Demirchian.

FINANCE. Budget estimates (in 1m. roubles), 1980, 1,337; 1983, 1,625.

AGRICULTURE. The chief agricultural area is the valley of the Arax and the area round Yerevan. Here there are considerable cotton plantations as well as orchards and vineyards. Sub-tropical plants, such as almonds and figs, are also grown. Olive groves and pomegranate plantations occupy large areas; experiments are being made to naturalize cork oak. In the mountainous areas the chief pursuit is livestock raising. In 1913 the total cultivated area of Armenia amounted to 346,000 hectares; in 1940, 434,000; in 1965, 400,000; in 1970, 409,000; in 1978, 500,000.

Output of main agricultural products (in 1,000 tonnes) in 1978 (1913 figures in brackets): Wheat, 318 (110); sugar-beet, 162 (0); potatoes, 223 (47); fruit, 157; grapes, 244; meat, 83·5 (19); milk, 495 (129); wool, 5 (2·3); and 440m. eggs (54m.).

Area of irrigated land in Armenia in 1979 was 270,000 hectares.

There were, in Dec. 1979, 314 collective farms, and these together with the 434 state farms tilled 99·9% of the total cultivated area. Livestock included 233,000 pigs, 772,100 cattle and 2·3m. sheep and goats. All the state farms and collective farms had been electrified by the end of 1960. There were 13,000 tractors and 1,500 grain and cotton combines in Jan. 1980.

INDUSTRY. Armenia contains large deposits of copper, zinc, aluminium, molybdenum and other metals. It is also rich in marble, granite, cement and other building materials. The mining of these minerals is becoming more and more important. Among other industries are the chemical, producing chiefly synthetic rubber and fertilizers, and the extraction and processing of building materials such as cement, pumice-stone, tuffs, marble, volcanic basalt and fire-proof clay, ginning- and textile-mills, carpet weaving, food, including wine-making, fruit, meat-canning and creameries. Machine-tool and electrical engineering works have also been established. Among the industrial centres are Yerevan, Leninakan, Alaverdi, Kafan, Kirovakan, Daval, Megri and Oktemberyan. Output of electricity in 1980 was 13,500m. kwh. A chain ('cascade') of 8 hydro-electric stations on the river Razdan, as it falls about 3,300 ft from the mountain lake Sevan to its junction with the Arax, has been completed.

In 1977 there were produced 1,828,000 tons of cement, 416,000 tons of mineral fertilizers, 95·6m. linear metres of cotton fabrics, 18·5m. linear metres of silk fabrics, 11·8m. pairs of leather footwear, 13,900 tons of granulated sugar and 8·9m. decalitres of wine (excluding collective farm output).

There were 1,192,000 industrial and office workers employed in the national economy in 1980.

COMMUNICATIONS. Length of railways in 1978, 710 km; motor roads, 8,700 km (hard surface, 6,300); airlines,570 km.

Newspapers (1980). Out of 86 newspapers 76 appeared in Armenian. Daily circulation of Armenian-language newspapers, 1·4m., other languages, 114,000.

EDUCATION. In 1980–81 there were 600,000 pupils in 1,535 primary and secondary schools; 65 technical colleges with 54,800 students; 13 higher educational institutions with 58,100 students (including correspondence students). Yerevan houses the Armenian Academy of Sciences, 43 scientific institutes, a medical institute and other technical colleges, and a state university. 31 learned institutions with 2,992 scientific staff are under the Academy of Sciences. Scientific workers totalled 17,700 in 101 institutions in 1978.

In 1980 there were 135,000 children in pre-school institutions.

HEALTH. In 1980 there were 11,100 doctors and 26,000 hospital beds.

Books of Reference

Aslanyan, A., Bagdasarian, A. *et al., L'Arménie Sovietique.* Moscow, 1972
Kurkjian, V., *A History of Armenia.* New York, 1958
Lang, D.M., *Armenia: Cradle of Civilization.* London, 1978
Missakian, J., *A Searchlight on the Armenian Question, 1878–1950.* Boston, Mass., 1950
Shaginyan, M., *A Journey Through Soviet Armenia.* Moscow (English ed., 1954)

MOLDAVIAN SOVIET SOCIALIST REPUBLIC

Respublika Sovietike Sochialiste Moldovenyaske

HISTORY. The Moldavian Soviet Socialist Republic, capital Kishinev, was formed by the union of part of the former Moldavian Autonomous Soviet Socialist Republic (organized 12 Oct. 1924), formerly included in the Ukrainian Soviet Socialist Republic, and the areas of Bessarabia (ceded by Romania to the USSR, 28

June 1940) with a mainly Moldavian population. As from 2 Aug. 1940 the MSSR includes the following regions of the former Moldavian Autonomous Soviet Socialist Republic: Grigoriopol, Dubossarsk, Kamensk, Rybnitz, Slobodzeisk and Tiraspol, and the following districts of Bessarabia: Beltsk, Bendery, Kagulsk, Kishinev, Orgeev and Sorok. The republic, however, is divided not into regions but into 36 rural districts, 21 towns and 40 urban settlements.

AREA AND POPULATION. Moldavia is bounded in the east and south by the Ukraine and on the west by Romania. The area is 33,700 sq. km (13,000 sq. miles). In Jan. 1981 the population was 4m., of whom (1979 census) 63·9% are Moldavians. Others include Ukrainians (14·2%), Russians (12·8%), Gagauzi (3·5%), Jews (2%). Apart from Kishinev, larger towns are Tiraspol (142,000), Beltsk (128,000) and Bendery (104,000).

CONSTITUTION AND GOVERNMENT. The Supreme Soviet, elected in 1980, consists of 380 deputies (1 per 10,000 population); 138 are women, 253 Communists. A new Constitution was adopted in April 1978.

At elections to the district, urban and rural Soviets (20 June 1982), of 37,626 deputies returned, 18,865 (50·1%) were women, 21,286 (56·6%) non-Party and 26,519 (70·5%) industrial workers and collective farmers.

Chairman, Presidium of the Supreme Soviet: I. P. Kalin.
Chairman, Council of Ministers: I. G. Ustiyan.
First Secretary, Communist Party: S. K. Grossu.

FINANCE. Budget estimates (in 1m. roubles), 1980, 1,639; 1983, 1,952.

AGRICULTURE. On 1 Jan. 1979 there were 422 collective farms and 291 state farms. All ploughing and sowing is mechanized. Livestock included (1 Jan. 1979) 1·1m. cattle, 2m. pigs and 1·2m. sheep and goats. There were 50,300 tractors and 3,800 combine harvesters.

Output of main agricultural products (in 1,000 tonnes) in 1978 (1913 figures in tons in brackets): Wheat, 1,288 (526); maize, 1,165 (639); sugar-beet, 2,807 (15), sunflower seeds, 350 (9); potatoes, 335 (119); other vegetables, 1,227; fruit, 929; grapes, 1,377; meat, 253 (53); milk, 1,200 (210); wool, 2·5 (3); 880m. eggs (275m.).

Bessarabia has an equable climate and very fertile soil. It contains nearly one quarter of the vineyards of the USSR. Bessarabia is also rich in fish in the south: sturgeon, mackerel, brill.

INDUSTRY. There are canning plants, wine-making plants, woodworking and metallurgical factories, a factory of ferro-concrete building materials, and footwear and textile plants. Moldavia takes third place in the USSR in the production of wine, tobacco and food-canning. Power output in 1978 was 13,600m. kwh. Production in 1977 included 28·9m. linear metres of silk fabrics, 16·3m. pairs of leather footwear, 424,100 tons of granulated sugar, 1,525m. tins of preserves and 24·7m. decalitres of wine. Meat and dairy produce are rapidly expanding food industries.

There are lignite, phosphorites, gypsum and valuable building materials.

In 1980 there were 1·5m. industrial and office workers working in the national economy. Electricity generated (1980) 15,600m. kwh.

COMMUNICATIONS. Length of railways, 1,110 km. There is direct air communication with Leningrad, Moscow, Kiev, Lvov and across the Black Sea. There are 10,500 km of motor roads (8,700 hard surface), and 1,100 km of inland waterways.

Newspapers (1980). There were 175 newspapers, 75 were in Moldavian. Daily circulation of Moldavian-language newspapers, 1·2m., other languages, 807,000.

EDUCATION. In 1980–81 there were 700,000 pupils in 1,800 primary, secondary and special schools, 58,900 students in 51 technical colleges and 51,300 students in 8 higher educational institutions including the state university. A Moldavian Academy of Sciences was established in 1961: it had 17 research institutions and a scientific staff of 962 in 1979. In all, there are 68 learned institutions with 8,100 scientific staff. In 1980 there were 266,000 children attending pre-school institutions.

HEALTH. Moldavia has 800 medical centres, many district hospitals, a state medical institute and 9 medical schools with over 2,500 students. Doctors in 1980 numbered 12,600; hospital beds, 48,000.

Books of Reference

Zlatova, Y., and Kotelnikov, V., *Across Moldavia* (English ed.). Moscow, 1959
Istoriya Moldavskoi SSR. 2nd ed. 2 vols. Kishinev, 1965–68

ESTONIA
Eesti Nōukogude Sotsialistlik Vabariik

HISTORY. The workers' and soldiers' Soviets in Estonia took over power on 8 Nov. 1917, were overthrown by the German occupying forces in March 1918, and were restored to power as the Germans withdrew in Nov. 1918, establishing the 'Estland Labour Commune'. It was overthrown with the assistance of British naval forces in May 1919, and a democratic republic proclaimed. In March 1934 this regime was, in turn, overthrown by a fascist *coup*.

The secret protocol of the Soviet-German agreement of 23 Aug. 1939 assigned Estonia to the Soviet sphere of interest. An ultimatum (16 June 1940) led to the formation of a government acceptable to the USSR; on 21 July the State Duma proclaimed the establishment of an Estonian Soviet Socialist Republic and applied to join the USSR: on 6 Aug. the Supreme Soviet accepted the application. The incorporation has been accorded *de facto* recognition by the British Government, but not by the US Government, which continues to recognize an Estonian consul-general in New York.

AREA AND POPULATION. Estonia is bounded west and north by the Baltic, east by the RSFSR and south by Latvia. Area, 45,100 sq. km (17,410 sq. miles); population, 1·49m. (Jan. 1981). Census (1979) 64·7% were Estonians, 27·9% Russians, 2·5% Ukrainians and 1·6% Belorussians. The capital is Tallinn. Other large towns are Tartu (106,000), Pärnu, Narva (74,000). There are 15 districts, 33 towns and 26 urban settlements.

CONSTITUTION AND GOVERNMENT. The Supreme Soviet, elected in 1980, consists of 285 deputies (1 per 10,000 population); 101 are women, 193 Communists. A new Constitution was adopted in April 1978.

At elections to district, urban and rural Soviets (20 June 1982), out of 11,010 deputies returned 5,459 (49·6%) were women, 6,090 (55·3%) non-Party and 7,438 (67·6%) industrial workers and collective farmers.

Chairman, Presidium of the Supreme Soviet: I. G. Kebin.
Chairman, Council of Ministers: V. I. Klauson.
First Secretary, Communist Party: K. G. Vaino.

FINANCE. Budget estimates (in 1m. roubles), 1980, 1,028; 1983, 1,259.

AGRICULTURE. Agriculture and dairy farming are the chief occupations. Area under cultivation was 697,000 hectares in 1913, 918,000 hectares in 1940 and 954,000 hectares in 1978. There were 143 agricultural and 8 fishery collectives and 158 state farms in 1980 using 19,400 tractors and 3,500 grain combines. 97% of state farms and 70% of collective farms were receiving electric power.

On 1 Jan. 1980 there were 822,000 head of cattle, 150,000 sheep and goats, 1,052,000 pigs and 5·8m. poultry.

Output of main agricultural products (in 1,000 tonnes) in 1979 (1913 figures in brackets): Potatoes, 1,243 (689); grains, 1,052 (428); other vegetables, 109; meat (slaughter weight), 188 (60); milk, 1,138 (415); wool, 0·3 (0·7); 493m. eggs (67m.).

INDUSTRY. Some 22% of the territory is covered by forests which provide good material for its sawmills, furniture, match and pulp industries, as well as wood fuel. Since the end of the war, 80,000 hectares have been afforested. 966,700 hectares of marsh land had been reclaimed by 1977.

Estonia has rich high-quality shale deposits (particularly in the north-east) which are estimated at 3,700m. tons. Shale output was 1·9m. tons in 1940 and 30m. in 1977. A factory for the production of gas from shale and a pipeline (208 km long) from Kohtla-Järve supplies shale gas to Leningrad and Tallinn. Estonian factories are now turning out agricultural and peat-digging machines, complex control and measuring instruments. The 'Volta' factory in Tallinn produces electric motors.

In the neighbourhood of Tallinn, phosphorites have been found, and in 1947 a plant for refining and for the production of super-phosphates was started. Estonia also contains valuable peat deposits, and some of her electrical stations work on peat. There are 350 rural electric stations. Electricity generated (1980) 18,900m. kwh. Output of mineral fertilizers in 1977 was 1·4m. tons; cement, 1·26m. tons; paper, 106,000 tons; cotton fabrics, 196m. linear metres; linen fabrics, 6·1m. linear metres; sawn timber, 733,000 cu. metres; leather footwear, 6·1m. pairs.

In 1980 there were 700,000 industrial and office workers and 62,000 specialists with a higher education engaged in the national economy.

COMMUNICATIONS. Length of main railways 970 km, of secondary lines 730 km. Estonia has 20 ports, but Tallinn handles four-fifths of the total sea-going transport. Inland waterways total 500 km; motor roads, 29,700 km (hard surface, 23,500 km). Airlines link Tallinn with Moscow, Leningrad, Riga and the Estonian islands.

Newspapers (1980). There were 43 newspapers, 31 of them in Estonian. Daily circulation of Estonian-language newspapers, 1,005,000, other languages, 185,000.

EDUCATION. Estonia has retained an 11-year school curriculum, when it was reduced to 10 years elsewhere in the USSR. In 1980–81 pupils in 600 primary, secondary and special schools numbered 216,000. There were 25,500 students in 6 higher educational establishments, including Tartu (Dorpat) University, founded in 1632, and 23,900 students in 37 technical colleges.

The Estonian Academy of Sciences, founded in 1946, has 24 institutions with 985 scientific staff; in all, 6,000 scientists are working in 72 institutions.

In 1980 there were 86,000 children attending pre-school institutions.

HEALTH. In 1980 there were 6,200 doctors and 18,400 hospital beds.

Books of Reference

Istoriya Estonskoi SSR. 3 vols. Tallin, 1961–74
Kareda, E., *Estonia in the Soviet Grip.* London, 1949
Küng, A., *A Dream of Freedom.* Cardiff, 1980
Parming, T., and Jarvesro, E., (eds.) *A Case Study of a Soviet Republic.* Boulder, 1978
Silvet, J., *Inglise—eestisõnaraamat.* Vadstena, 1949
Varetz, E. F., and Tarmisto, V. Y., *Estoniya.* Moscow, 1967 (in Russian)

LATVIA

Latvijas Padomju Socialistiska Republika

HISTORY. In the part of Latvia unoccupied by the Germans, the Bolsheviks won 72% of the votes in the Constituent Assembly elections (Nov. 1917). Soviet power was proclaimed in Dec. 1917, but was overthrown when the Germans occupied all Latvia (Feb. 1918). Restored when they withdrew (Dec. 1918), it was overthrown once more by combined British naval and German military forces (May–Dec. 1919), and a democratic government set up. This régime was in turn replaced when a fascist *coup* took place in May 1934.

The secret protocol of the Soviet–German agreement of 23 Aug. 1939 assigned Latvia to the Soviet sphere of interest. An ultimatum (16 June 1940) led to the formation of a government acceptable to the USSR; on 21 July a People's Diet proclaimed the establishment of the Latvian Soviet Socialist Republic and applied to join the USSR: whose Supreme Soviet accepted the application on 5 Aug. The incorporation has been accorded *de facto* recognition by the British Government, but not by the US Government, which continues to recognize the *Chargé d'Affaires* in Washington, D.C.

AREA AND POPULATION. Latvia is bounded north by Estonia and the Baltic Sea, west by the Baltic, south by Lithuania and Belorussia and east by the RSFSR. Latvia has a total area of 63,700 sq. km (25,590 sq. miles). Population, Jan. 1981, 2·5m., of whom (1979 census) 53·7% are Latvians and 32·8% Russians. There are 26 districts, 56 towns and 36 urban settlements.

The chief town is Riga (the capital); other principal towns are Daugavpils (Dvinsk) (117,000), Liepāja (108,000), Jelgava (Mitau) (69,000) and Ventspils (Windau).

CONSTITUTION AND GOVERNMENT. The Supreme Soviet, elected in 1980, consists of 325 deputies (1 per 10,000 population); 113 are women, 218 Communists. A new Constitution was adopted in April 1978.

At elections to district, urban and rural Soviets (20 June 1982), of 23,369 deputies returned, 11,490 (49·2%) were women, 12,389 (53%) non-Party and 15,609 (66·8%) industrial workers and collective farmers.

Chairman, Presidium of the Supreme Soviet: P. Y. Strautmanis.
Chairman, Council of Ministers: Y. Y. Ruben.
First Secretary, Communist Party: A. E. Voss.

FINANCE. Budget estimates (in 1m. roubles), 1980, 1,568; 1983, 1,862.

AGRICULTURE. Latvia is now no longer mainly an agricultural country. The urban population, 35% of the total in 1939, was 67% in Jan. 1978.

Latvian forest lands, state and private (2·4m. hectares), produced in 1937–38, 3·4m. cu. metres of timber; 1977 output, 3·9m. cu. metres.

Area under cultivation was 1·4m. hectares in 1913, 2m. in 1940, 1·7m. in 1978. 1·8m. hectares of marsh land have been drained (1979).

Cattle breeding and dairy farming are the chief agricultural occupations. Oats, barley, rye, potatoes and flax are the main crops.

After the establishment of the Soviet regime about 960,000 hectares were distributed among the landless peasants or those with very small holdings. On 1 Jan. 1979 there were 243 state farms and 347 collective farms. There were 32,900 tractors and 6,800 grain combine harvesters. By 1 Jan. 1964, all state farms and collective farms were using electric power.

Livestock (1 Jan. 1980): Cattle, 1·4m. (1939: 1·3m.); sheep, 211,000 (1939: 1·5m.); pigs, 1·4m. (1939: 891,500).

Output of main agricultural products (in 1,000 tonnes) in 1979 (1913 figures in brackets): Sugar-beet, 195 (0); potatoes, 1,626 (645); all grains, 1,171 (880); other vegetables, 147; fruit, 35; meat and fats, 25 (122); milk, 1,664 (673); wool, 0·5 (1·4); flax, 4·1 (21); 720m. eggs (136m.).

INDUSTRY. Latvia is the main producer of electric railway passenger cars and long-distance telephone exchanges in the USSR, fourth in output of paper and woollen goods, fifth of sawn timber, sixth of mineral fertilizers.

Industrial output in 1977 (in 1,000 tons) included: Steel, 502; rolled metal, 630; cement, 903; granulated sugar, 271; paper, 169; fish catch, 550; cotton fabrics, 62·8m. linear metres; linen fabrics, 21·3m. linear metres; woollens, 14m. linear metres; silks, 19·9m. linear metres; leather footwear, 10·2m. pairs; radio sets, 2·4m. (no.). Electricity generated (1980) 4,700m. kwh.

Peat deposits extend over 645,000 hectares or about 10% of the total area, and it is estimated that total deposits are 3,000–4,000m. tons; output, 1971, 2·3m. tons. There are also gypsum deposits; amber is frequently found in the coastal districts.

In 1980 industrial and office workers numbered 1·2m.

COMMUNICATIONS. In 1978 the length of railways was 2,450 km, and motor roads, 24,300 km (hard surface, 14,900 km). Riga is the largest port in the Baltic after Leningrad.

Newspapers (1980). There were 103 newspapers (62 in Lettish). Daily circulation of Lettish-language newspapers, 1·2m., other languages 457,000.

RELIGION. The Latvian Lutheran Church numbered 600,000 members in 1956.

EDUCATION. In 1980–81 there were 900 primary and secondary schools, with a total of 400,000 pupils: 114,000 children attended pre-school institutions. Ten places of higher education had 47,200 students, 55 technical colleges had 42,200 students; there were also 21 music and art schools, 3 teachers' training colleges and an agricultural academy. In 1946 an Academy of Sciences was opened which in 1979 had 16 research institutes with a staff of 1,700 scientific workers; there were over 12,000 scientific workers in 101 research institutions.

HEALTH. There were 11,100 doctors and 34,500 hospital beds in 1980.

Books of Reference

Latvian Academy of Sciences, *Istoriya Latviiskoi SSR.* Riga. 3 vols. 1952–58
Bilmanis, A., *A History of Latvia.* Princeton Univ. Press, 1951
Roze, B. and K., *Latviska–Angliska Vārdnıcā. Göppingen, 1948*
Spekke, A., History of Latvia. Stockholm, 1951
Turkina, E., *Angliski–Latviska Vārdnīca.*Riga, 1948.—*Latviešu-Angļu Vārdnīca.* Riga, 962

LITHUANIA

Lietuvos Tarybu Socialistine Respublika

HISTORY. In 1914–15 the German army occupied the whole of Lithuania. On its withdrawal (Dec. 1918) Soviets were elected in all towns and a Soviet republic was proclaimed. In the summer of 1919 it was overthrown by Polish, German and nationalist Lithuanian forces, and a democratic republic established. In Dec. 1926 this regime was in turn overthrown by a fascist *coup*.

The secret protocol of the Soviet–German frontier treaty of 28 Sept. 1939 assigned the greater part of Lithuania to the Soviet sphere of influence. In Oct. 1939 the province and city of Vilnius (in Polish occupation 1920–39) were ceded by the USSR. An ultimatum (16 June 1940) led to the formation of a government acceptable to the USSR. A people's Diet, elected on 14–15 July, proclaimed the establishment of the Lithuanian Soviet Socialist Republic on 21 July and applied for admission to the USSR, which was effected by decree of the USSR Supreme Soviet on 3 Aug. and included also those parts of Lithuania which had been reserved for inclusion in Germany. This incorporation has been accorded *de facto* recognition by the British Government, but not by the US Government, which continues to recognize a Lithuanian *Chargé d'Affaires* in Washington, D.C.

AREA AND POPULATION. Lithuania is bounded north by Latvia, east and south by Belorussia, west by Poland, the Kaliningrad area of the RSFSR and the Baltic Sea. The total area of Lithuania is 65,200 sq. km (25,170 sq. miles) and the population (Jan. 1980) 3·4m., of whom 80% were Lithuanians, 8·6% Russians and 7·7% Poles (1979 census).

The capital is Vilnius (Vilna). Other large towns are Kaunas (Kovno), Klaipeda (Memel), Šiauliai (121,000) and Panėvežys (104,000). There are 44 rural districts, 92 towns and 21 urban settlements.

CONSTITUTION AND GOVERNMENT. The Supreme Soviet, elected in 1980, consists of 350 deputies (1 per 15,000 population); 125 are women, 235 Communists. A new Constitution was adopted in April 1978.

At elections to district, urban and rural Soviets (20 June 1982), of 28,410 deputies returned, 14,140 (49·8%) were women, 16,139 (56·8%) non-Party and 19,291 (67·9%) industrial workers and collective farmers.

Chairman, Presidium of the Supreme Soviet: A. S. Barkauskas.
Chairman, Council of Ministers: R.-B. I. Songeila.
First Secretary, Communist Party: P. P. Griškevičius.

FINANCE. Budget estimates (in 1m. roubles), 1980, 2,330; 1983, 2,704.

AGRICULTURE. Lithuania before 1940 was a mainly agricultural country, but has since been considerably industrialized. The urban population was 23% of the total in 1937 and 59% in Jan. 1978. The resources of the country consist of timber and agricultural produce. Of the total area, 49·1% is arable land, 22·2% meadow and pasture land, 16·3% forests and 12·4% unproductive lands.

Area under cultivation in 1913 was 1·9m.; in 1938, 2·7m.; in 1977, 2·4m. hectares. By 1978 over 2·5m. hectares of swamps had been drained.

Output of main agricultural products (in 1,000 tonnes) in 1978 (1913 figures in brackets): All grains, 2,225 (1,449); sugar-beet, 803 (0); flax, 12 (17); potatoes, 2,313 (1,375); other vegetables, 365; fruit, 153; meat and fats, 463 (159); milk, 2,681 (832); wool, 0·2 (1·5); 943m. eggs (264m.).

On 1 Jan. 1980 there were 2·2m. cattle, 2·6m. pigs, 60,000 sheep and goats.

Forests cover 1,554,000 hectares; 70% of the forests consist of conifers, mostly pines. Peat reserves total 4,000m. cu. metres.

Between 1940 and 1947 about 575,500 hectares (about 1·4m. acres) were distributed among the landless and poor peasant farmers. In 1979 there were 45,900 tractors and 10,300 grain combines serving 787 collective farms and 327 state farms.

INDUSTRY. Heavy engineering, shipbuilding and building material industries are developing. Industrial output included, in 1977: Cement, 2·99m. tons; granulated sugar, 207,100 tons; paper, 124,000 tons; cotton fabrics, 86·3m. linear metres; linens, 19m. linear metres; woollens, 12·4m. linear metres; sawn timber, 1m. cu. metres; leather footwear, 9·4m. pairs; electric power, 11·700m. kwh.

In 1980 there were 1·5m. industrial and office workers employed in the national economy.

COMMUNICATIONS. Length of railways, 2,030 km. Vilnius has one of the largest airports of the USSR. There are 32,100 km of motor roads (19,900 km hard surface) and 600 km of inland waterways. Klaipeda, as a non-freezing harbour and fishery base, is of national importance.

Newspapers (1980). Of 124 newspapers, 98 were in Lithuanian. Daily circulation of Lithuanian-language newspapers, 1·9m., other languages, 260,000.

RELIGION. In 1956, the Lithuanian Lutheran Church had 215,000 members; Roman Catholics, including those in Estonia and Latvia, numbered 2·5m.

EDUCATION. In 1980–81 there were 600,000 pupils in 2,400 primary, secondary and special schools. The University of Vytautas the Great, at Kaunas, was opened on 16 Feb. 1922. On 15 Jan. 1940 certain faculties were transferred to Vilnius to join the ancient University of Vilnius (founded 1570). In 1980–81 there were 12 higher educational institutions with 71,000 students: in 70 technical colleges of all kinds there were 68,400 students. The Lithuanian Academy of Sciences, founded in 1941, had 11 institutions with a total scientific staff of 1,727; there were 88 scientific institutions with 13,500 research personnel. 152,000 children in 1980 were attending pre-school institutions.

HEALTH. In 1980 there were 13,800 doctors and 41,200 hospital beds.

Books of Reference

Griškevičius, P. P., *Land on the Nemunas*. Moscow, 1977
Jurgėla, C. R., *History of the Lithuanian Nation*. New York, 1948
Kantantas, F., *A Lithuanian Bibliography*. Univ. of Alberta Press, 1975
Peteraitis, V., *Lithuanian–English Dictionary*. 2 vols. Chicago, 1960
Vardys, S., (ed.) *Lithuania under the Soviets: Portrait of a Nation, 1940–45*. New York, 1965

SOVIET CENTRAL ASIA

Soviet Central Asia embraces the Kazakh Soviet Socialist Republic, the Uzbek Soviet Socialist Republic, the Turkmen Soviet Socialist Republic, the Tadzhik Soviet Socialist Republic and the Kirghiz Soviet Socialist Republic.

Turkestan (by which name part of this territory was then known) was conquered by the Russians in the 1860s. In 1866 Tashkent was occupied and in 1868 Samarkand, and subsequently further territory was conquered and united with Russian Turkestan. In the 1870s Bokhara was subjugated, the emir, by the agreement of 1873, recognizing the suzerainty of Russia. In the same year Khiva became a vassal state to Russia. Until 1917 Russian Central Asia was divided politically into the Khanate of Khiva, the Emirate of Bokhara and the Governor-Generalship of Turkestan.

In the summer of 1919 the authority of the Soviet Government became definitely established in these regions. The Khan of Khiva was deposed in Feb. 1920, and a People's Soviet Republic was set up, the medieval name of Khorezm being revived. In Aug. 1920 the Emir of Bokhara suffered the same fate, and a similar regime was set up in Bokhara. The former Governor-Generalship of Turkestan was constituted an Autonomous Soviet Socialist Republic within the RSFSR on 11 April 1921.

In the autumn of 1924 the Soviets of the Turkestan, Bokhara and Khiva Republics decided to redistribute the territories of these republics on a nationality basis; at the same time Bokhara and Khiva became Socialist Republics. The redistribution was completed in May 1925, when the new states of Uzbekistan, Turkmenistan and Tadzhikistan were accepted into the USSR as Union Republics. The remaining districts of Turkestan populated by Kazakhs were united with Kazakhstan which was established as an ASSR in 1925 and became a Union Republic in 1936. Kirghizia, until then part of the RSFSR, was established as a Union Republic in 1936.

Books of Reference

Nove, A. and Newth, J. A., *The Soviet Middle East*. London, 1967
Rwykin, M., *Moscow's Muslim Challenge*. New York, 1982
Wheeler, G., *The Modern History of Soviet Central Asia*. London, 1964.—*The Peoples of Soviet Central Asia*. London, 1966
Yuldashev, M. (ed.), *Oktiabrskaya Sotsialisticheskaya Revolutsya i Grakhdanskaya Voina v Turkestane*. Tashkent, 1957
Zevelyov, A. (ed.), *Za Sovetskii Turkestan*. Tashkent, 1963

KAZAKHSTAN

Kazak Soviettik Sotzialistik Respublikasy

HISTORY. On 26 Aug. 1920 Uralsk, Turgai, Akmolinsk and Semipalatinsk provinces formed the Kirgiz (in 1925 renamed Kazakh) Autonomous Soviet Socialist Republic within the RSFSR. It was made a constituent republic of the USSR on 5 Dec. 1936. To this republic were added the parts of the former Governorship of Turkestan inhabited by a majority of Kazakhs. It consists of the following regions: Aktyubinsk, Alma-Ata, Chimkent, Dzhambul, Dzhezkazgan, East Kazakhstan, Guryev, Karaganda, Kokchetav, Kustanai, Kzyl-Orda, Mangyshlak, North Kazakhstan, Pavlodar, Semipalatinsk, Taldy-Kurgan, Tselinograd, Turgai, Uralsk.

AREA AND POPULATION. Kazakhstan is bounded on the west by the Caspian Sea and the RSFSR, on the east by China, on the north by the RSFSR and on the south by Uzbekistan and Kirghizia. The area of the republic is 2,717,300 sq. km (1,049,155 sq. miles). It is the next in size to the RSFSR, is far larger than all the other Central Asian Soviet Republics combined and stretches nearly 3,000 km from west to east and over 1,500 km from north to south. Population (Jan. 1981) 15·01m., of whom 55% live in urban areas. The Kazakhs form 36%, Russians 40·8% and Ukrainians 6·1% of the population, as a result of the industrialization of the country since 1941 and the opening of virgin lands since 1945. The population includes over 100 nationalities.

The capital is Alma-Ata, formerly Verny; other large towns are Karaganda, Semipalatinsk, Chimkent and Petropavlovsk. In all there are 82 towns, 189 urban settlements and 218 rural districts.

CONSTITUTION AND GOVERNMENT. The Supreme Soviet, elected in 1980, consists of 510 deputies (1 per 20,000 population); 182 are women, 336 Communists. A new Constitution was adopted in April 1978.

At elections to the regional, district, urban and rural Soviets (20 June 1982), out of 128,365 deputies returned, 63,006 (49·1%) were women, 74,480 (58%) non-Party and 87,991 (68·6%) industrial workers and collective farmers.

President, Presidium of the Supreme Soviet: S. N. Imashav.
Chairman, Council of Ministers: B. A. Ashimov.
First Secretary, Communist Party: D. A. Kunayev.

FINANCE. The budget (in 1m. roubles) balanced as follows: 1980, 8,400; 1983, 9,351.

AGRICULTURE. Kazakh agriculture has changed from primarily nomad cattle breeding to production of grain, cotton and other industrial crops. In 1978 the crop area was 35·3m. hectares—over 16% of the total cultivated area of the USSR (1913, 4·2m.; 1940, 6·8m.).

1,827,000 hectares of land have an irrigation network.

The 'Ukrainka' winter wheat has been transformed into a spring wheat suitable for cultivation in Kazakhstan. Tobacco, rubber plants and mustard are also cultivated. Kazakhstan has rich orchards and vineyards; 25,000 hectares were under vines and 101,000 under orchards in 1978. Between 1954 and 1959, over 23m. hectares of virgin and long fallow land were opened up, 544 new state grain farms being organized for the purpose. Grain deliveries to the state were 10·5m. tons in 1960; 2·4m. in 1965; 13·4m. in 1970; 5·1m. in 1975; 8·2m. in 1977; 16,784 in 1978.

Kazakhstan is noted for its livestock, particularly its sheep, from which excellent quality wool is obtained. The Akharomerino is a newly developed crossbreed of merino sheep and the wild Akhar mountain ram. Livestock on 1 Jan. 1979 included 8·01m. cattle, 34·2m. sheep and goats and 2·6m. pigs.

There were, on 1 Jan. 1979, 418 collective farms and 2,035 state farms with 237,400 tractors and 109,700 grain combine harvesters. There were 5,293 rural power stations of 307,800 kwh. capacity.

Output of main agricultural products (in 1m. tonnes) in 1978 (1913 figures in brackets): All grains, 34·5 (2·2); cotton, 0·3 (0·015); sugar-beet, 2·5 (0); potatoes, 1·83 (0·18); other vegetables, 2·29; meat, 1 (0·44); milk, 4·4 (0·85); 3,352m. eggs (233m.); wool, 0·1 (0·04).

INDUSTRY. Kazakhstan is extremely rich in mineral resources. Coal and tungsten in Karaganda (in the centre), oil along the river Emba (in the west), copper, lead and zinc—Kazakhstan contains about one-half of the total deposits of these three metals contained in the USSR—Iceland spar (in the south), nickel and chromium in the Kustanai and Semipalatinsk regions, molybdenum and other minerals.

In 1943 big deposits of manganese were found in Eastern Kazakhstan; new coal seams were also discovered there. In South Kazakhstan new copper and bauxite deposits have been found.

Coal, oil, non-ferrous metallurgy, heavy engineering and chemical industries have brought Kazakhstan to the third place among the industrial republics of the USSR.

Coal output in 1977 was 93·7m. tons; oil, 23·3m. tons; steel, 5·6m. tons; rolled metal, 4·4m. tons; cement, 6·8m. tons; mineral fertilizers, 6·5m. tons; cotton fabrics, 101·2m. linear metres; leather footwear, 31·2m. pairs; woollen fabrics, 16·7m. linear metres; granulated sugar, 120,100 tons. The Leninogorsk and Chimkent lead plants, the Balkhash, Irtysh and Karaskpai copper-smelting works and others supply the country with non-ferrous metals. A meat-packing plant has been built in Semipalatinsk, a fish cannery in Guryev, a chemical plant in Aktyubinsk, a tractor works at Pavlodar, and a superphosphate plant in Dzhambul. The oil industry in Emba and Aktyubinsk yields high-quality aviation oil. Iron ore output in 1977 was 23·4m. tons.

Aviation plays an important part in agriculture. About 14m. hectares were in 1970 treated from the air (destruction of pests, surface feeding of sugar-beet plantations, pollination of orchards, etc.).

Among recent enterprises are a large textile combine at Kustanai, hosiery factories at Djezkazgan, Leninogorsk and Aktyubinsk, a sugar factory at Aksu, meat canneries at Djetygar and Kzyl-Orda.

Electric power output in 1980 was 61,500m. kwh.

There were, in 1980, 6m. (average for year) industrial and office workers in the national economy.

COMMUNICATIONS

Roads. In 1978 there were 97,400 km of motor roads (66,900 km hard surface).

Railways. A 430-km railway line between the settlements of Mointi and Chu in Kazakhstan to complete the Transkazakh trunk line, connecting Petropavlovsk, Akmolinsk, Karaganda and Balkhash, was opened in 1953. The new line links the Transkazakh trunk line with the Turkestan–Siberian railway carrying Karaganda coal to South Kazakhstan. The Akmolinsk–Pavlodar railway (438 km), a section of the South Siberian line, was opened in Dec. 1953. Other lines in operation are Dzhambul–Chalaktan, Akmolinsk–Kartaly, Uralsk–Iletsk, Guriev–Kandagach. In 1977 the total length of railways in operation was 14,160 km. Over 600 km of narrow-gauge line and 700 km of broad-gauge line were built in the virgin lands area in 1951-57.

Inland waterways. Total length 5,500 km.

Newspapers (1980). Of 430 newspapers, 161 were in the Kazakh language. Daily circulation of Kazakh-language newspapers, 1·8m., other languages, 3·5m.

EDUCATION. Nearly the whole population is literate. In 1980–81 there were 3·3m. pupils at 8,700 elementary and secondary schools; 231 technical colleges with 265,400 students, 55 higher educational institutions with 260,000 students, and 207 research institutes with 34,700 scientific personnel. The Kazakh Academy of Sciences, founded in 1945, had, in 1980, 31 institutions, the scientific staff of which numbered 4,139. 877,000 children were attending pre-school institutions.

HEALTH. In 1980 there were 47,800 doctors and 195,800 hospital beds.

Books of Reference

Istoriya Kazakhskoi SSR. 2 vols. Alma-Ata, 1957–59

Alampiev, P., *Soviet Kazakhstan.* Moscow, 1958.—*Where Economic Inequality is No More.* Moscow, 1959

TURKMENISTAN

Tiurkmenostan Soviet Sotsialistik Respublikasy

HISTORY. The Turkmen Soviet Socialist Republic was formed on 27 Oct. 1924 and covers the territory of the former Trans-Caspian Region of Turkestan, the Charjiui vilayet of Bokhara and a part of Khiva situated on the right bank of the Oxus. In May 1925 the Turkmen Republic entered the Soviet Union as one of its constituent republics.

AREA AND POPULATION. Turkmenistan is bounded on the north by the Autonomous Kara-Kalpak Republic, a constituent of Uzbekistan, by Iran and Afghánistán on the south, by the Uzbek Republic on the east and the Caspian Sea on the west. The principal Turkmen tribes are the Tekkés of Merv and the Tekkés of the Attok, the Ersaris, Yomuds and Goklans. All speak closely related varieties of a Turkic language (of the south-western group); many are Sunni Mohammedans.

The country passed under Russian control in 1881, after the fall of the Turkoman stronghold of GökTépé. Census (1979) 68·4% of the population were Turkmenians, most of whom were nomads before the First World War. 12·6% are Russians living mostly in urban areas, and 8·5% Uzbeks. There are also Kazakhs (2·9%), Tatars, Ukrainians, Armenians and others.

The area of Turkmenistan is 488,100 sq. km (186,400 sq. miles), and its population in Jan. 1981 was 2·9m.

There are 5 regions: Chardzhou, Maruy, Ashkhabad, Tashauz and Krasnovodsk, comprising 42 rural districts, 15 towns and 74 urban settlements.

The capital is Ashkhabad (Poltoratsk); other large towns are Chardzhou (140,000), Maruy (Merv) (72,000), Nebit-Dag (67,000) and Krasnovodsk (55,000).

CONSTITUTION AND GOVERNMENT. The Supreme Soviet, elected in 1980, consists of 330 deputies (1 per 5,000 population); 107 are women, 224 Communists. A new Constitution was adopted in April 1978.

At elections to regional, district, urban and rural Soviets (20 June 1982), of 23,478 deputies returned, 11,623 (49·5%) were women, 13,317 (56·7%) non-party and 16,312 (69·5%) industrial workers and collective farmers.

Chairman, Presidium of the Supreme Soviet: B. Yazkuliev.
Chairman, Council of Ministers: C. S. Karryev.
First Secretary, Communist Party: M. G. Gapurov.

FINANCE. Budget estimates (in 1m. roubles), 1980, 982; 1983, 1,193.

AGRICULTURE. The main occupation of the people is agriculture, based on irrigation. Turkmenistan produces cotton, wool, Astrakhan fur, etc. It is also famous for its carpets, and produces a special breed of Turkoman horses and the famous Karakul sheep.

There were 318 collective farms and 78 state farms in 1979, with 37,100 tractors and 1,100 grain combines. There were 608 rural power stations.

A considerable area is under Egyptian cotton, and from it has been evolved an original Soviet long-fibred cotton.

The main grain grown is maize. Sericulture, fruit and vegetable growing are also important; dates, olives, figs, sesame and other southern plants are grown. There is fishing in the Caspian. 900,000 hectares were under cultivation in 1978 (1913, 318,000; 1940, 411,000).

Between 1958 and 1970 the Kara-Kum Canal was extended to 860 km. In 1971 the fourth section, to reach the Caspian, was begun to reach 1,000 km. By 1978 over 892,000 hectares had been irrigated.

Livestock on 1 Jan. 1980: Cattle, 602,000; pigs, 158,000; sheep and goats, 4·5m.

Output of main agricultural products (in 1,000 tonnes) in 1978 (1913 figures in brackets): Wheat, 281 (113); cotton, 1,215 (69); vegetables, 284; grapes, 63; fruit, 39; meat, 67 (58); milk, 307 (63); wool, 15·3 (9·7); 243m. eggs (18m.).

INDUSTRY. Turkmenistan is rich in minerals, such as ozocerite, oil, coal, sulphur and salt. Industry is being developed, and there are now chemical, tailoring, textile, light, food, agricultural implements, cement and other factories, oil refineries, as well as ore-mining.

In the Kara-Kum Desert deposits of magnesium, minerals and coal have been discovered, as well as some 50 new saltmines. Here a new oil town, Nebit-Dag, has sprung up. On the Kara-Bogaz bay a sulphate industry has been developed. Industrial output in 1977 included 14·8m. tons of oil, 564,000 tons of cement, 23·1m. linear metres of cotton fabrics, 3·5m. pairs of leather footwear. Electric power output was 6,700m. kwh. (in 1980); 62,581m. cu. metres of natural gas were produced.

In 1980 there were 711,000 industrial and office workers in the national economy.

COMMUNICATIONS. Length of motor roads 9,900 km (7,800 km hard surface). Motor communication exists between Ashkhabad and Meshed (Iran).

Length of railways, 2,120 km. The line Chardzhou–Kungrad crosses the Chardzhou and Tashauz regions of Turkmenia and runs across Uzbekistan. Another line connects Chardzhou and Urgench. Inland waterways, 1,300 km.

Airlines connect Leninsk and Tashauz, and Ashkhabad and remote areas in the west, north and east.

Newspapers (1980). Of 58 newspapers, 45 were in the Turkmen language. Daily circulation of Turkmenian-language newspapers, 775,000, other languages, 210,000.

EDUCATION. In 1980–81 there were 1,900 primary and secondary schools with 700,000 pupils, 7 higher educational institutions with 35,800 students, 35 technical colleges with 34,000 students, and 11 music and art schools. The Turkmen Academy of Sciences directs the work of 14 learned institutions with a staff of 972 scientists; there were 58 research institutions in all, with 5,000 research workers, in 1978. A Turkmenian State University was opened in 1951: in 1973 it had 10,124 students.

In 1980, 138,000 children were attending pre-school institutions.

HEALTH. In 1980 there were 8,100 doctors and 30,300 hospital beds.

Book of Reference

Istoriya Turkmenskoi SSR. 2 vols. Ashkanbad, 1957

UZBEKISTAN

Ozbekiston Soviet Sotsialistik Respublikasy

HISTORY. In Oct. 1917 the Tashkent Soviet assumed authority, and in the following years established its power throughout Turkestan. The semi-independent Khanates of Khiva and Bokhara were first (1920) transformed into People's Republics, then (1923–24) into Soviet Socialist Republics and finally merged in the Uzbek SSR and other republics.

The Uzbek Soviet Socialist Republic was formed on 27 Oct. 1924 from lands formerly included in Turkestan. It includes a large part of the Samarkand region, the southern part of the Syr Darya, Western Ferghana, the western plains of Bukhara, the Kara-Kalpak ASSR and the Uzbek regions of Khorezm. In May 1925 Uzbekistan, by the decision of the Congress of Soviets of the USSR, was accepted as one of the constituent republics of the Soviet Union.

AREA AND POPULATION. Uzbekistan is bordered on the north by the Kazakh Soviet Socialist Republic, on the east by the Kirghiz Soviet Socialist Republic and the Tadzhik Soviet Socialist Republic, on the south by Afghánistán and on the west by the Turkmen Soviet Socialist Republic. The Uzbeks, who form 68·7% (1979 census) of the population, were the ruling race in Central Asia until the arrival of the Russians during the third quarter of the 19th century. The several native states over which Uzbek dynasties formerly ruled were founded in the 15th century upon the ruins of Tamerlane's empire. The Uzbek speak Jagatai Turkish, which is related to Osmanli and Azerbaijan Turkish; many are Sunni Moslems. Russians numbered (census 1979) 10·8%, Tadzhiks, 3·9%, Tatars 4·2%.

The area of Uzbekistan is 447,400 sq. km (172,741 sq. miles). The population in Jan. 1981 was 16,158,000 (40% urban). The country comprises the following regions: Andizhan, Bukhara, Dzhizak, Ferghana, Kashkadar, Khorezm, Namangan, Navoi, Samarkand, Surkhan-Darya, Syr-Darya, Tashkent and the Autonomous Soviet Socialist Republic of Kara Kalpakia. The capital of the Republic is Tashkent; other large towns are Samarkand, Andizhan, Namangan. There are 87 towns, 84 urban settlements and 138 rural districts.

On 19 Sept. 1963 the Supreme Soviet of the USSR confirmed decisions of the Supreme Soviets of Kazakhstan and Uzbekistan, transferring over 40,000 sq. km from the former to the latter to ensure more efficient use of the 'Hungry Steppe'.

CONSTITUTION AND GOVERNMENT. The Supreme Soviet, elected in 1980, consists of 510 deputies (1 per 15,000 population); 178 are women, 346 Communists. A new Constitution was adopted in April 1978.

At elections to the regional, district, urban and rural Soviets (20 June 1982), of 102,699 deputies returned, 50,883 (49·5%) were women, 58,248 (56·7%) non-Party and 71,026 (69·2%) industrial workers and collective farmers.

President, Presidium of the Supreme Soviet: I. B. Usmankhodjayev.
Chairman, Council of Ministers: N. D. Khudaiberdyev.
First Secretary, Communist Party: S. R. Rashidov.

FINANCE. Budget estimates (in 1m. roubles), 1980, 5,225; 1983, 6,551.

AGRICULTURE. Uzbekistan is a land of intensive farming, based on artificial irrigation. It is the chief cotton-growing area in the USSR and the third in the world. About 3·3m. hectares of collective and state farmland have irrigation networks, totalling 150,000 km in length, and all are in full use.

In 1939 the Ferghana Canal (270 km) was built. During 1940, among the irrigation canals completed were: the North Ferghana Canal (165 km), and Andreyev South Ferghana Canal (108 km) and the first section of the Tashkent Canal (63 km). A canal from the Amu-Darya to Bokhara across the Kzyl-Kum and Ust-Urt deserts (180 km) was completed in 1965. A 200-km canal joining the river Zeravshan with the Kashka Darya at the village of Paruz was completed in Aug. 1955; it is part of the Iski–Angara Canal. The first section (93 km) of a canal irrigating the southern 'Hungry Steppe' was opened in 1960; 500,000 hectares of this desert were under cultivation in 1967.

Agriculture flourishes, particularly in the well-watered, warm, rich oases areas, such as the Ferghana valley, Zeravshan, Tashkent and Khorezm, where cotton, fruit, silk and rice are cultivated. In the higher-lying plains grain is grown; the wide desert and semi-desert area of Western Uzbekistan is mainly given to pasture land and the breeding of the Karakul sheep; there is a Karakul institute at Samarkand.

Orchards occupied 195,000 hectares and the vineyards 70,000 hectares in 1977. The Central Asian Branch of the Scientific Research Institute of Viticulture in Tashkent has produced new frost resistant grapes by crossing the wild Amur grape with Central Asian and European types. In 1979 there were 927 collective farms and 744 state farms, with 157,300 tractors and 8,500 cotton picking and grain combines. Ploughing, cotton-sowing and cultivation are completely mechanized; cotton picking over 46%.

Uzbekistan provides 67% of the total cotton, 50% of the total rice and 60% of the total lucerne grown in the USSR. The area under crops was 2,189,000 hectares in 1913, 3,036,000 hectares in 1940 and 3·9m. hectares in 1978.

Livestock on 1 Jan. 1979: 3·23m. cattle, 8·1m. sheep and goats and 368,000 pigs.

Output of main agricultural products (in 1,000 tonnes) in 1978 (1913 figures in tons in brackets): Wheat, 757 (513); maize, 1,052 (39); cotton, 5,763 (517); potatoes, 227 (46); fruit, 124; grapes, 103; meat, 302 (89); milk, 2,073 (231); wool, 28·4 (5·3); 1,397m. eggs (87m.)

Afforestation over an area of 50,000 hectares has been carried out to protect the Bokhara and Karakul oases from the advancing Kzyl-Kum sands and to stop the sand-drifts in a number of districts of Central Ferghana.

INDUSTRY. Of its mineral resources, in addition to oil and coal, copper and building materials and ozocerite deposits are now also exploited. New very rich coal deposits were discovered in 1944 and 1947 near Tashkent.

There are nearly 1,600 factories and mills. They include a factory of agricultural machinery (in Tashkent), a cement factory, a sulphur-mine, an oxygen factory, a paper-mill, a leather factory, textile-mills, clothing factories, iron and steel works, the Chirchik electro-chemical plant, a superphosphate plant in Kokand and oil refineries, coalmines, etc. Output in 1977 included 5·4m. tons of coal, 411,000 tons of steel, 1·4m. tons of oil, 3·54m. tons of cement, 5·9m. tons of mineral fertilizers, 223·1m. linear metres of cotton fabrics, 107m. linear metres of silk fabrics, 27·1m. pairs of leather footwear, 784,000 hectolitres of wine (apart from collective farm output). Gold is being worked at Muruntau, Chadak and Kochbulak.

The Tashkent power station (2m. kw.) was completed in 1971. Power output in 1980 was 34,900m. kwh. (481m. kwh. in 1940). Two natural-gas pipelines (Djaikak–Tashkent, Ferghana–Kokand) and a third from Bokhara to the Urals are operating. Natural gas output (1976) was 36,100m. cu. metres.

In 1980 there were 4·2m. industrial and office workers in the national economy.

COMMUNICATIONS. The total length of railway in 1978 was 3,390 km. Branches lead to Karshe-Kitab, Kerki-Termez, Jalal-Abad, Namangan, Andijan and other centres. In 1947–55 a new line was built from Chardzhou to Kungrad.

The Great Uzbek Highway was completed in April 1941. Total length of motor roads in 1978 was 51,900 km (hard surface, 31,800 km). Inland waterways, 1,100 km.

An airline, serving all of Central Asia, is most developed in Uzbekistan.

Newspapers (1980). There were 190 newspapers in the Uzbek and Kara-Kalpak languages out of a total of 281. Daily circulation of Uzbek-language newspapers, 3·7m., other languages, 1·2m.

EDUCATION. In 1980–81 there were 9,500 elementary and secondary schools with 4·1m. pupils, 43 higher educational establishments with 278,100 students and 222 technical colleges with 237,700 students. Uzbekistan has an Academy of Sciences and 188 research institutes with 33,600 scientific staff, 3,878 of them in 30 institutions of the Uzbek Academy of Sciences. There are universities and medical schools in Tashkent and Samarkand In 1980, 915,000 children were attending pre-school institutions.

The Uzbek Arabic script was in 1929 replaced by the Latin alphabet which in 1940 was superseded by one based on the Cyrillic alphabet.

HEALTH. In 1980 there were 46,200 doctors and 182,800 hospital beds.

Book of Reference

Istoriya Uzbekskoi SSR. 4 vols. Tashkent, 1967–68

KARA-KALPAK AUTONOMOUS SOVIET SOCIALIST REPUBLIC

Area, 165,600 sq. km (63,920 sq. miles); population (Jan. 1981), 957,000. Capital, Nukus (113,400). The Karakalpaks are first mentioned in written records in the 16th century as tributary to Bokhara, and later to the Kazakh Khanate. In the second half of the 19th century, as a result of the Russian conquest of Central Asia, they came under Russian rule. On 11 May 1925 the territory was constituted within the then Kazakh Autonomous Republic (of the Russian Federation) as an Autonomous Region. On 20 March 1932 it became an Autonomous Republic within the Russian Federation, and on 5 Dec. 1936 it became part of the Uzbek SSR. Census (1979) Karakalpaks were 31·1% of population, Uzbeks, 31·5% and Kazakhs, 26·9%.

185 deputies were elected to its Supreme Soviet on 20 Feb. 1980, of whom 68 were women and 118 Communists.

Its manufactures are in the field of light industry—bricks, leather goods, furniture, canning, wine. Output of cotton in 1977 was 371,000 tons (in 1913, 8,000 tons). There were 4,217 tractors. Cattle numbered 308,000 and sheep and goats 621,000. There were 43 collective and 84 state farms. 218,300 industrial and office workers, and 14,800 specialists with a higher education, were employed in the national economy.

In 1979–80 there were 256,400 pupils at schools, 24,718 at technical colleges, and 5,543 at university. There is a branch of the Uzbek Academy of Sciences with 190 scientific staff.

There were 1,878 doctors and 8,920 hospital beds.

TADZHIKISTAN
Respublikai Sovieth Sotsialistii Tojikiston

HISTORY. The Tadzhik Soviet Socialist Republic was formed from those regions of Bokhara and Turkestan where the population consisted mainly of Tadzhiks. It was admitted as a constituent republic of the Soviet Union on 5 Dec. 1929.

AREA AND POPULATION. Tadzhikistan is situated between 39° 40′ and 36° 40′ N. lat. and 67° 20′ and 75° E. long., north of the Oxus (Amu-Darya). On the west and north it is bordered by Uzbekistan and by the Kirghiz Soviet Socialist Republic; on the east by Chinese Turkestan and on the south by Afghánistán. It includes three regions (Leninabad, Kurgan-Tyube and Kulyab) and 41 rural districts, 18 towns and 49 urban settlements, together with the Gorno-Badakhshan Autonomous Region. Its highest mountains are Communism Peak (7,495 metres) and Lenin Peak (7,127 metres). Even the lowest valleys in the Pamirs are not below 3,500 metres above sea-level. The huge mountain glaciers are the source of many rapid rivers—the tributaries of the Amu-Darya, which flows from east to west along the southern border of Tadzhikistan. About 58·8% of the population are Tadzhiks. They speak an Iranian dialect, little different from Persian, and they are considered to be the descendants of the original Aryan population of Turkestan. Unlike the Persians, the Tadzhiks are mostly Sunnis. Of the rest, 22·9% are Uzbeks living in the north-west of the republic. Russians and Ukrainians number 10·4% (1979 census).

The area of the territory is 143,100 sq. km (55,240 sq. miles). Population (Jan. 1981), 3·4m. The capital is Dushanbe. Other large towns are Leninabad (130,000), Kurgan-Tyube, Kulyab.

CONSTITUTION AND GOVERNMENT. The Supreme Soviet, elected in 1980, consists of 349 deputies (1 per 5,000 population); 123 are women and 238 Communists. A new Constitution was adopted in April 1978.

At elections to the district, urban and rural Soviets and the regional Soviet of Gorno-Badakhshan (20 June 1982), out of 26,627 deputies returned 13,216 (49·6%) were women, 15,227 (57·2%) non-Party and 18,677 (70·1%) industrial workers and collective farmers.

Chairman, Presidium of the Supreme Soviet: M. Kholov.
Chairman, Council of Ministers: K. N. Makhkamov.
First Secretary, Communist Party: R. Nabiyev.

FINANCE. Budget estimates (in 1m. roubles), 1980, 1,256; 1983, 1,370.

AGRICULTURE. The occupations of the population are mainly farming, horticulture and cattle breeding. Area under crops in 1978 was 800,000 hectares (1913, 494,000; 1940, 807,000). Wine production, 1976 was 450,000 hectolitres.

There are 43,000 km of irrigation canals: the irrigation networks cover about 602,000 hectares of land.

Tadzhikistan grows many varieties of fruit, including apricots, figs, olives, pomegranates, a local variety of lemons and oranges, and in the south sugar-cane has been grown. Even on the highest mountain plateaux of the Pamirs, 'the roof of the world', the biological station of Tadzhikistan (3,860 metres above sea-level) has succeeded in raising crops of 60 varieties of barley, 10 varieties of oats, 4 of wheat, as well as vegetables. Eucalyptus and geranium are grown for the perfumery industry. Jute, rice and millet are also grown.

Tadzhikistan contains rich pasture lands, and cattle breeding is a very important branch of its agriculture. Livestock on 1 Jan. 1979: 1·1m. cattle, 2·9m. sheep and goats and 123,000 pigs.

The Gissar sheep is famous in the south for its meat and fat; the Karakul sheep is widely bred for its wool.

There were 179 collective farms (all with electric power) and 198 state farms in 1980, with 31,700 tractors and 1,400 cotton and grain combine harvesters.

Output of main agricultural products (in 1,000 tonnes) in 1978 (1913 figures in tons in brackets): Wheat, 183 (133); maize, 48 (2); cotton, 903 (32); potatoes, 142 (10); other vegetables, 340; fruit, 287; grapes, 175; meat, 92·4 (48); milk, 461 (102); wool, 5·6 (2·1); 337m. eggs (20m.).

INDUSTRY. The original small-scale handicraft industries have been replaced by big industrial enterprises, including mining, engineering, food, textile, clothing and silk factories.

There are rich deposits of brown coal, lead, zinc and oil (in the north of the republic), rare elements, such as uranium, radium, arsenic and bismuth. Asbestos, mica, corundum and emery, lapis lazuli, potassium salts, sulphur and other minerals have been found in other parts of the republic.

Industrial output in 1977 included: 800,000 tons of coal, 274,000 tons of oil, 1·01m. tons of cement, 116m. linear metres of cotton fabrics, 58m. linear metres of silk fabrics; leather footwear, 7·3m. pairs; refrigerators, 134,400.

There are 80 big electrical stations. The hydro-electric Varzob station began to operate in 1954, that at Kairak-Kum on the Syr Darya River was completed in 1957 and 2 more at Murgab in 1964. Output in 1980 was 13,600m. kwh. (in 1940, 62m. kwh.).

Construction of an electro-chemical combine, the largest in the USSR, has begun in the Yavan steppe in south Tadzhikistan, and the 3·2m. kw. power station in the upper reaches of the Vakhsh River was near completion in 1979.

In 1980 there were 927,000 industrial and office workers in the national economy.

COMMUNICATIONS

Roads. There are 13,200 km of motor roads. Of these, 10,500 km are hard surface, including the Osh–Khorog (700 km), Yasui–Bazar–Charm (107 km) and Dushanbe–Khorog in the Pamirs (557 km) roads.

Railways. A railway line between Termez and Dushanbe (258 km) connects the republic with the railway system of the USSR. The mountainous nature of the republic makes ordinary railway construction difficult; accordingly 345 km of narrow gauge railways have been constructed (Kurgan–Tyube–Piandzh and Dushanbe–Kurgan–Tyube, connecting Dushanbe with the cotton-growing Vakhsh valley are particularly important).

Aviation. Dushanbe is connected by air with Moscow, Tashkent, Baku and the regional and district centres of the republic.

Shipping. A steamship line on the Amu-Darya runs between Termez, Sarava and Jilikulam on the river Vakhsh (200 km).

Newspapers. (1980). 60 newspapers had a total daily circulation of 1·29m. Of these, 52 with 946,000 circulation, were in Tadzhik.

EDUCATION. In 1980–81 there were 3,100 primary and secondary schools with 1·1m. pupils, 10 higher educational institutions with 56,800 students and 38 technical colleges with 40,100 students; the Tadzhik state university had 12,467 students. In 1980, 109,000 children were attending pre-school institutions. In 1951 an Academy of Sciences was established; it has 17 institutions, the scientific staff of which numbers 1,324; there are 61 research institutions in all, with 6,900 scientific personnel. The Pamir research station is the highest altitude meteorological observatory in the world.

In 1940 a new alphabet based on Cyrillic was introduced.

HEALTH. There are 277 hospitals as well as maternity homes, clinics and special institutes to combat tropical diseases. There were 9,400 doctors in 1980 and 39,600 hospital beds.

GORNO-BADAKHSHAN AUTONOMOUS REGION

Comprising the Pamir massif along the borders of Afghánistán and China, the region was set up on 2 Jan. 1925. Area, 63,700 sq. km (24,590 sq. miles); population (Jan. 1979), 127,000 (83% Tadjiks, 11% Kirghiz). Capital, Khorog (14,800).

There were 36,800 pupils in 268 schools in 1977–78 and 170 students in technical colleges, 151 doctors and 1,005 hospital beds.

Mining industries are developed (gold, rock-crystal, mica, coal, salt). Wheat, fruit and fodder crops are grown and cattle and sheep are bred in the western parts. In 1978 there were 65,500 cattle, 347,000 sheep and goats.

In 1976 there were 17 collective farms and 15 state (livestock) farms.

Books of Reference

Academy of Science of Tadzhikistan, *Istoriya Tadzhikskogo Naroda.* 3 vols. Moscow, 1963–65

Chumichev, D. A., *Tadzhikskaya SSR.* Moscow, 1954

Luknitsky, P., *Soviet Taikistan* [In English]. Moscow, 1954

KIRGHIZIA

Kyrgyz Sovietik Sotsialistik Respublikasy

HISTORY. After the establishment of the Soviet regime in Russia, Kirghizia became part of Soviet Turkestan, which itself became an Autonomous Soviet Socialist Republic within the RSFSR in April 1921. In 1924, when Central Asia was reorganized territorially on a national basis, Kirghizia was separated from Turkestan and formed into an autonomous region within the RSFSR. On 1 Feb. 1926 the Government of the RSFSR transformed Kirghizia into an Autonomous Soviet Socialist Republic within the RSFSR, and finally in Dec. 1936 Kirghizia was proclaimed one of the constituent Soviet Socialist Republics of the USSR.

AREA AND POPULATION. The territory of Kirghizia covers 198,500 sq. km (76,460 sq. miles), and its population in Jan. 1981 was 3·7m. The republic comprises 3 regions: Issyk-Kul, Naryn and Osh. There are 18 towns, 31 urban settlements and 37 rural districts. Its capital is Frunze (formerly Pishpek). Other large towns are Osh (173,000), Przhevalsk (52,000), Kyzyl-Kia, Tokmak.

Kirghizia is situated on the Tian-Shan mountains and bordered on the east by China, on the west by Kazakhstan and Uzbekistan, on the north by Kazakhstan and in the south by Tadzhikistan. The Kirghizians are of Turkic origin and form 47·9% (1979 census) of the population; the rest are Russians (25·9%), Ukrainians (3·1%), Uzbeks (12·1%) and Tatars (2%).

CONSTITUTION AND GOVERNMENT. The Supreme Soviet, elected in 1980, consists of 350 deputies (1 per 5,000 population); 126 are women, 235 Communists. A new Constitution was adopted in April 1978.

At elections to the regional, district, urban and rural Soviets (20 June 1982), of the 27,875 deputies returned, 13,966 (50·1%) were women, 15,671 non-Party and 19,314 (69·3%) industrial workers and collective farmers.

Chairman, Presidium of the Supreme Soviet: T. Kh. Koshoev.
Chairman, Council of Ministers: A. Duisheev.
First Secretary, Communist Party: T. U. Usubaliev.

FINANCE. Budget estimates (in 1m. roubles), 1980, 1,440; 1983, 1,647.

AGRICULTURE. Kirghizia is famed for its livestock breeding. On 1 Jan. 1979 there were 957,000 cattle, 298,000 pigs, 10m. sheep and goats. Yaks are bred as meat and dairy cattle, and graze on high altitudes unsuitable for other cattle. Crossed with domestic cattle, hybrids are produced much heavier than ordinary Kirghiz cattle and giving twice the yield of milk. The Kirghizian horse is famed for its endurance, but it is of small stature; it has in recent years been crossed with Don, Arab and other breeds.

On 1 Jan. 1979 there were 182 collective and 214 state farms. Area under crops (1978), 1·3m. hectares (1913, 640,000; 1940, 1,056,000). There were 26,300 tractors and 4,400 grain combine harvesters and 1,600 cotton combines in 1980; nearly all collective and state farms received electric power.

Kirghizia raises wheat sufficient for its own use and other grains and fodder, particularly lucerne; also sugar-beet, hemp, kenaf, kendyr, tobacco, medicinal plants and rice. Sericulture, fruit, grapes and vegetables and bee-keeping are major branches of Kirghiz agriculture. Agriculture is highly mechanized; nearly all the area under crops is worked by tractors. In 1977 irrigation networks in collective and state farms covered 933,000 hectares; practically all were in use. A canal in the western Tien-Shan ranges and a reservoir in the Urto-Tokoi mountains are being constructed.

The health resorts of Jety-Oguz (7,200 ft) and Jalal-Abad are famous for their mild alpine climate and mineral springs.

Output of main agricultural products (in 1,000 tonnes) in 1979 (1913 figures in tons in brackets): Wheat, 767 (250); maize, 193 (37); cotton, 28 (28); sugar-beet, 1,418 (0); potatoes, 227 (19); other vegetables, 361; fruit, 177; grapes, 70; meat, 154 (39); milk, 662 (91); wool, 33 (4·7); 416m. eggs (19m.).

INDUSTRY. Kirghizia contains 500 large modern industrial enterprises including sugar refineries, tanneries, cotton and wool-cleansing works, flour-mills, a tobacco factory, food, timber, textile, engineering, metallurgical, oil and mining enterprises.

The output of coal in 1976 was 4·3m. tons; oil, 230,000 tons; silk fabrics, 9·7m. linear metres; cotton fabrics, 64m. linear metres.

Granulated sugar, (1977) 270,000 tons; leather footwear, 10·1m. pairs.

Hydro-electric power stations are being built in the Central Tien-Shans and the cotton-growing districts in the Osh Region, the Chui valley and on the shore of Lake Issyk-Kul. Power output (1980) was 9,200m. kwh.

There were, in 1979, 1,076,000 industrial and office workers in the national economy.

COMMUNICATIONS. In the north a railway runs from Lugovaya through Frunze to Rybachi on Lake Issyk-Kul. Towns in the southern valleys are linked by short lines with the Ursatyevskaya–Andizhan railway in Uzbekistan. Total length of railway is 370 km. Most of the traffic is by road; there were 22,300 km of motor roads (15,200 hard surface) in 1978. A road tunnel through the Tien Shan mountains at an altitude of 9,600 ft, connecting Frunze and Osh, is being constructed. Inland waterways, 600 km. Airlines link Frunze with Moscow and Tashkent.

Newspapers (1980). Of 107 newspapers with a daily 1.21m. circulation (1980), 60 with 766,000 circulation are in the Kirghiz language.

EDUCATION. Kirghizia had 1,700 primary, continuation (8-year) and secondary schools with 900,000 pupils in 1980–81; 151,000 children attended 853 preschool institutions. There were also 10 higher educational institutions with 55,400 students, 39 technical and teachers' training colleges with 48,300 students, as well as music and art schools. The Kirghizian Academy of Sciences was established in

1954. In 1980 there were 65 research institutes, 18 of them, with 1,509 scientific staff, operating under its auspices; the others have scientist staffs of 6,225. A university was opened in 1951. It has 13,370 students, 6,268 full-time, 1,054 evening and 6,048 correspondence students taking a full degree course. In Sept. 1940 a new alphabet, based on Cyrillic, was introduced.

HEALTH. In 1980 there were 10,600 doctors and 43,700 hospital beds.

Books of Reference

Istoriya Kirgizskoi SSR. 2 vols. Frunze, 1967–68
Ryazantsev, S. N., *Kirghizia.* Moscow, 1951

UNITED ARAB EMIRATES

Population: 1·04m. (1980)
GNP per capita: US$30,070 (1980)

HISTORY. From Sha'am, 35 miles south-west of Ras Musam dam, for nearly 400 miles to Khor al Odeid at the south-eastern end of the peninsula of Qatar, the coast, formerly known as the Trucial Coast, of the Gulf (together with 50 miles of the coast of the Gulf of Oman) belongs to the rulers of the 7 Trucial States. In 1820 these rulers signed a treaty prescribing peace with the British Government. This treaty was followed by further agreements providing for the suppression of the slave trade and by a series of other engagements, of which the most important are the Perpetual Maritime Truce (May 1853) and the Exclusive Agreement (March 1892). Under the latter, the sheikhs, on behalf of themselves, their heirs and successors, undertook that they would on no account enter into any agreement or correspondence with any power other than the British Government, receive foreign agents, cede, sell or give for occupation any part of their territory save to the British Government.

British forces withdrew from the Gulf at the end of 1971 and the treaties whereby Britain had been responsible for the defence and foreign relations of the Trucial States were terminated, being replaced on 2 Dec. 1971 by a treaty of friendship between Britain and the United Arab Emirates. The United Arab Emirates (formed 2 Dec. 1971) consists of the former Trucial States: Abu Dhabi, Dubai, Sharjah, Ajman, Umm al Qawain, Ras al Khaimah (joined in Feb. 1972) and Fujairah. The small state of Kalba was merged with Sharjah in 1952. *See* map in THE STATESMAN'S YEAR-BOOK, 1972-73, The Gulf States of the Middle East.

AREA AND POPULATION. The Emirates are bounded north by the Persian Gulf, east by Oman, south and west by Saudi Arabia, north-west by Qatar. The area of these states is approximately 32,300 sq. miles (92,100 sq. km). The total population at census (1980), 1,040,275 (717,475 male). About one-tenth are nomads.

Population (1980 census): Abu Dhabi, 449,000; Ajman, 36,100; Dubai, 278,000; Fujairah, 32,200; Ras al Khaimah, 73,700; Sharjah, 159,000; Umm al Qawain, 12,300.

GOVERNMENT. The Emirates are a federation, headed by a Supreme Council which is composed of the 7 rulers and which in turn appoints a Council of Ministers. The Council of Ministers drafts legislation and a federal budget; its proposals are submitted to a federal National Council of 40 elected members which may propose amendments but has no executive power.

President: HH Sheikh Zayed bin Sultan al Nahyan, Ruler of Abu Dhabi.

Members of the Supreme Council of Rulers:

HH Sheikh Rashid bin Saeed al-Maktoum, Vice-President and Ruler of Dubai.
HH Sheikh Sultan bin Mohammed al-Qasimi, Ruler of Sharjah.
HH Sheikh Saqr bin Mohammed al-Qasimi, Ruler of Ras al Khaimah.
HH Sheikh Rashid bin Ahmed al-Mualla, Ruler of Umm al Qaiwain.
HH Sheikh Hamad bin Mohammed al Sharqi, Ruler of Fujairah.
HH Sheikh Humaid Rashid bin al-Nuaimi, Ruler of Ajman.

The Council of Ministers formed in July 1979 was:

Prime Minister: H.H. Sheikh Rashid bin Saeed al-Maktoum.
Deputy Prime Ministers: Sheikh Maktoum bin Rashid al-Maktoum; Sheikh Hamdan bin Mohammed al-Nahyan.
Interior: Sheikh Mubarak bin Mohammed al-Nayhan. *Finance and Industry:* Sheikh Hamdan bin Rashid al-Maktoum. *Defence:* Sheikh Mohammed bin Rashid

al-Maktoum. *Petroleum and Mineral Resources:* Dr Mana Said al-Otaiba. *Economy and Commerce:* Vacant. *Information and Culture:* Sheikh Ahmed bin Hamed. *Communications:* Mohammed Said al-Mualla. *Internal Affairs:* Vacant. *Public Works and Housing:* Mohammed Khalifa al-Kindi. *Education and Youth:* Said Salman. *Planning:* Vacant. *Cabinet Affairs:* Said al-Ghaith. *Minister of State for Supreme Council Affairs:* Sheikh Abdul Aziz al-Qasimi. *Justice, Islamic Affairs and AWQAF:* Mohammed Abdul Rahman al-Bakr. *Agriculture and Fisheries:* Said al-Ragbani. *Minister of State for Foreign Affairs:* Rashid Abdullah. *Water and Electricity:* Humaid Nasser al-Owais. *Labour and Social Affairs:* Seif al-Jarwan. *Health:* Hamad Abdul Rahman al-Midfa.

National flag: Three horizontal stripes of green, white, black, with a vertical red strip in the hoist.

DEFENCE

Army. The Army consists of 1 Royal Guard brigade, 4 armoured, 9 infantry, 3 artillery and 3 air defence battalions. The strength was (1983) 46,000.

Navy. The Navy has 6 new German-built missile armed fast attack craft, 9 British-built patrol craft and 2 tenders and 40 light launches are operated by the Coast Guard. Personnel in 1983 numbered 1,200 officers and ratings.

Air Force. Formation of an air wing in Abu Dhabi, to support land forces, began in 1968 with the purchase of 2 Britten-Norman Islander light STOL transports and some light helicopters. Expansion has been rapid. Current equipment includes 25 Mirage 5 supersonic fighter-bombers, 3 Mirage 5R tactical reconnaissance aircraft and 2 Mirage 5D 2-seat trainers; 7 Hunter fighters and reconnaissance fighters and 2 Hunter 2-seat trainers (to be replaced with 6 Alpha Jets); 4 C-130 Hercules and 4 Buffalo turboprop transports; 3 Caribou piston-engined transports; 4 CASA C-212 Aviocar ECM/elint aircraft; about 40 Gazelle, Alouette III, Puma and Agusta-Bell 205 helicopters; and 14 PC-7 Turbo-Trainers. Initial personnel were mostly British but considerable assistance is now being received from Arab countries and from Pakistan. The air wing became the Air Force of Abu Dhabi in 1972, in which year 3 JetRanger helicopters were transferred to the air wing of the Union Defence Force, since combined with the Dubai Police Air Wing to form a single component of the United Emirates Air Force. Current equipment of the Dubai Air Wing of the UEAF, bought mainly in Italy, comprises 6 Aermacchi MB 326K jet light attack aircraft, 1 Aeritalia G222 twin-turboprop transport, 1 piston-engined SF.260W armed basic trainer, 6 SF.260TP turboprop trainers, and 2MB 326L jet trainers, 4 Bell 205A-1, 3 Bell 212 and 6 JetRanger helicopters and 1 Cessna 182 liaison aircraft, plus an L-100-30 Hercules transport and a Boeing 720B and a variety of other types for VIP use.

INTERNATIONAL RELATIONS

Membership. The UAE is a member of UN and of the Arab League.

External Debt. The UAE (mainly the government of Dubai) borrowed about $205m. on Eurocurrency markets in 1976 and about $850m. in 1977.

ECONOMY

Planning. The first 5-year plan (1981-85) envisages expenditure of UD 13,000m.

Budget. Revenue is principally derived from oil-concession payments. The federal budget (1982) DH 22,955m.

Currency. The UAE issued its own currency in 1972 based on the *dirham.* 1 UAE *dirham* = 10 *dinar* = 1,000 *fils.* There are notes of 1, 5, 10, 50, 100 and 1,000 *dirham* and coins of 1, 5, 10, 25, 50 and 100 *fils.* Rate of exchange, March 1983: £1 = 5·45 *dirham;* US$1 = 3·673 *dirham.*

Banking. The British Bank of the Middle East has branches in Dubai, Abu Dhabi, Sharjah, Fujairah, Ajman and Ras al Khaimah; the Chartered Bank has branches in Dubai, Sharjah, Abu Dhabi and Al Ain; the National & Grindlays Bank (Ottoman Branch) has branches in Abu Dhabi and Sharjah. The Arab Bank has branches in Ajman, Ras al Khaimah, Sharjah, Abu Dhabi and Dubai; the Citibank has branches in Dubai, Sharjah and Abu Dhabi; the Habib Bank of Pakistan has branches in Abu Dhabi, Dubai and Sharjah and the United Bank Ltd of Pakistan branches in Dubai, Sharjah, Abu Dhabi and Al Ain. Barclays Bank International has branches in Abu Dhabi, Dubai, Ras Al Khaimah and Sharjah. There is also the National Bank of Dubai, formed in 1963 which has a branch in Abu Dhabi and Umm al Qaiwain, and the Bank of Oman Ltd, formed in 1967, which has branches in Ajman, Abu Dhabi and Dubai. The Commercial Bank opened in Dubai in 1969. The Bank Sadarat of Iran has branches in Abu Dhabi, Dubai and Sharjah. The National Bank of Abu Dhabi, formed in 1967, has its head office in Abu Dhabi and a branch office in Dubai.

ENERGY AND NATURAL RESOURCES

Oil. *Abu Dhabi.* Until the end of 1972 production was in the hands of 2 major companies, the Abu Dhabi Petroleum Co. and the Abu Dhabi Marine Area. The Government has acquired a 60% interest in both companies. Ownership in 1976 was as follows: *ADPC*, 60% Government; 9·5% BP; 9·5% Shell; 9·5% CFP; 4·75% Mobil; 2% Partex. *ADMA*, 60% Government; 26·7% BP/Japan Oil Development Co.; 13·3% CFP. A Japanese company, Abu Dhabi Oil Co. (ADOCO) began production from its Mubarraz field in 1973. There are other companies which have concessions in the State: Japan's Middle East Oil; a US consortium led by Pan Ocean Oil and Sunningdale Oils of Canada. A State Petroleum Co., the Abu Dhabi National Oil Co. (ADNOC), was formed in 1971 and began to set up its own tanker fleet known as the Abu Dhabi National Tankers Co. (ADNATCO). At the end of 1972 Abu Dhabi signed a participation agreement which would have given it an immediate 25% interest in the companies, rising to 51% by 1982. Oil production, 1981, 660·2m. bbls.

Dubai. In July 1975 Dubai decided to take full control of all foreign oil and gas operations in the State. The companies were to remain however. A Dubai producing group was set up to comprise the foreign interests–US and continental companies. Dubai Petroleum Co. (DPC–a subsidiary of Continental Oil) has a 30% interest in this group; the other members are Dubai Marine Areas (*Compagnie Française des Pétroles*) with 50%; Deutsche Texaco with 10%; Dubai Sun Oil 5%; and Delfzee Dubai Petroleum (Wintershall) 5%. Oil production, 1980, 127·8m. bbls.

Sharjah. In Sharjah the concession is given to Crescent Oil, its shareholders are: Ashland Oil, Skelly Oil, Kerr-McGee, Cities Services and Juniper. Other oil concessions have recently been given to the Crystal Oil Co. of USA and the Reserves Oil and Gas Co. Oil production, 1980, 3·7m. bbls.

Ajman. An oil concession was awarded to United Refining in 1974.

Umm al Qawain. The concession here was given to US Occidental Petroleum; another was awarded to a consortium led by the US company United Refinery.

Ras al Khaimah. The Dutch oil firm Vitol took over Union's concession in 1973. Shell began prospecting in 1969 but pulled out in 1971. A concession in the same area was awarded to Peninsula Petroleum, a subsidiary of the US California Time Group, in 1973.

Gas. Abu Dhabi has reserves of natural gas, nationalized in 1976. The Abu Dhabi Gas Liquefaction Plant at Das Island (51% ADNOC) has a capacity of 2m. tons LNG, 1m. tons LPG, 220,000 tons of light distillate and 230,000 tons of pelletized sulphur. Gas exports (1980) US$350m.

Agriculture. The fertile Buraimi Oasis, known as Al Ain, is largely in Abu Dhabi territory, but owing to lack of water and good soil there is little agriculture in the rest of UAE. There are 15,000 hectares of cultivated land. However, since the establishment of an agricultural trials station and an agricultural school in Ras al

Khaimah the number of gardens under cultivation has more than doubled and there have been remarkable increases in the variety of crops and the length of the agricultural season. An experimental agricultural farm exists in Al Ain which produces vegetables for Abu Dhabi.

Livestock (1981): Cattle, 26,000; camels, 59,000; sheep, 139,000; goats, 361,000.

Fisheries. The industry is still a major employer. Sharjah exports shrimps and prawns; a fishmeal plant is operating in Ras al Khaimah and plants are planned for Ajman and Sharjah.

INDUSTRY. Main industries in Abu Dhabi relate to the construction industry and to oil and gas extraction; there is also a steel rolling mill. Dubai has a cement factory of 500,000 tons annual capacity, and a dry dock. Twenty companies are now fully operational at the complex in Jebel Ali consisting of a liquefied petroleum gas plant. An aluminium smelter with power station and desalination plant was opened in Feb. 1979. Sharjah has a cement factory and various manufacturing estates. Ras al Khaimah also produces cement and crushed rock.

COMMERCE. Imports in 1980 for UAE were DH32,425m. Exports and re-exports totalled DH76,884m. Oil exports accounted for 95% of the total.

Total trade between the UAE (excluding Abu Dhabi) and UK (British Department of Trade returns, in £1,000 sterling):

	1978	*1979*	*1980*	*1981*	*1982*
Imports to UK	146,435	143,071	239,519	118,697	82,706
Exports and re-exports from UK	273,160	328,773	287,615	245,388	286,079

Total trade between Abu Dhabi and UK (British Department of Trade returns, in £1,000 sterling):

	1978	*1979*	*1980*	*1981*	*1982*
Imports to UK	123,376	93,990	246,422	274,651	184,253
Exports and re-exports from UK	125,150	159,426	214,309	246,672	272,889

COMMUNICATIONS

Aviation. International airports at Dubai and Abu Dhabi are served by a large number of major airlines, as well as by Gulf Air partially owned by the Government of the UAE. Abu Dhabi's new airport opened and commenced operations in Jan. 1982. A new international airport was inaugurated at Sharjah in 1979. A Ras al Khaimah international airport was opened early in 1976 although it initially had only one scheduled service by Kuwait Airways. An airstrip exists at Al Ain, in the Buraimi Oasis, and in the oilfields, both onshore and offshore, on Das Island, while construction of a strip at Khor Fakkan is planned.

Abu Dhabi and Dubai are served by Alia, Air France, Air India, British Airways, Egyptair, Iran Air, Kuwait Airways, Middle East Airlines, PIA, KLM, Gulf Air, Iraqi Airways, Olympic, SABENA, Saudia, Syrian Arab Airlines and TMA. Lufthansa and Singapore Airlines initiated scheduled flights to Dubai in mid-1976, while Sharjah is served by Gulf Air and TMA. A number of cargo airlines also fly regularly to the country's major airports. An air-taxi service, Emirates Air Services, flying between Abu Dhabi and Dubai, began in June 1976.

Shipping. In 1980 Port Rashid was enlarged to 37 berths. Abu Dhabi has dry docks and there are smaller ports at Sharjah and Ras al Khaimah. Jebel Ali is a port and industrial estate 35 km south-west of Dubai city and had (1982) 66 berths.

In 1976, the Government of the UAE joined with Qatar, Bahrain, Saudi Arabia, Kuwait and Iraq in forming the United Arab Shipping Co.

Post and Broadcasting. In 1980 there were 155,565 telephones, of which 43,016 were in Abu Dhabi and 65,037 in Dubai. In Sharjah a new telephone company has been formed and the other Northern States are now linked by telephone. The new Cable and Wireless Station at Jebel Ali in the State of Dubai links the system with the international communication network.

Television stations are at Abu Dhabi and Dubai, with extension of the service well advanced to the rest of the Emirates. Stations for The Voice of the United Arab Emirates began broadcasting in 1972 at Abu Dhabi, Dubai, Ras al Khaimah and Sharjah. Estimated radios (1976) 50,000 and television sets over 16,000.

Newspapers (1982). There are a number of daily and weekly publications mostly in Arabic, but some in English, notably *The Emirates News* of Abu Dhabi, *The Gulf News,* a daily, published in Dubai and the *Khaleed Times* (daily), also published in Dubai.

JUSTICE, RELIGION, EDUCATION AND WELFARE

Justice. UAE subjects and citizens of all Arab and Moslem states are subject to the jurisdiction of the local courts. In the local courts the rules of Islamic law prevail. A new code of law is being produced for Abu Dhabi. In Dubai there is a court run by a *qadi*, while in some of the other States all legal cases are referred immediately to the Ruler or a member of his family, who will refer to a *qadi* only if he cannot settle the matter himself. In Abu Dhabi a professional Jordanian judge presides over the Ruler's Court. The 95th article of the provisional Constitution of 1971 provided for the setting up of a Union Supreme Court and Union Primary Tribunals.

Religion. Nearly all the inhabitants are Moslem of the Sunni and Shi'ite sects.

Education (1982). Primary and secondary education for boys and girls is available in the UAE, and there are now 383 schools with over 113,000 pupils, with a further 379 planned. There are 4 junior colleges and 112 adult education centres, established to eliminate illiteracy. The education system is the same as that followed in Kuwait, and many of the teachers are supplied by the Kuwait, Qatar, Egypt, Jordan and Bahrain education departments. The oil companies in Abu Dhabi operate apprentice training schools and there is also a vocational training institute. A vocational training centre is under construction.

There are trade schools in Sharjah, Dubai and Ras al Khaimah. The UAE university had 3,500 students with 406 lecturers in 1981.

Health. A tuberculosis sanatorium is to be constructed by the State of Kuwait in Sharjah. In 1980 there were more than 20 hospitals (2,972 beds) and over 47 clinics. There were 1,202 doctors.

DIPLOMATIC REPRESENTATIVES

Of the UAE in Great Britain (30 Prince's Gate, London, SW7 1PT)
Chargé d'Affaires: Mirza Husain Hasan Al-Sayegh.

Of Great Britain in the UAE
Ambassador: H. B. Walker, CMG (at the British Embassy, Abu Dhabi).

Of the UAE in the USA (600 New Hampshire Ave., NW, Washington, D.C., 20037)
Ambassador: Ahmed S. Al-Mokarrab.

Of the USA in the UAE (Sheikh Khalid Bldg., Corniche Rd., Abu Dhabi)
Ambassador: George Quincy Lumden, Jr.

Of the UAE to the United Nations
Ambassador: Fahim Sultan Al-Qasimi.

Books of Reference

Middle East Annual Review. London
United Arab Emirates: A Record of Achievement, 1979–1981. Ministry of Information and Culture. Abu Dhabi, 1981
Abdullah, M.M. *The UAE: A Modern History.* London and New York, 1978
Al-Baharna, H. M., *The Legal Status of the Arabian Gulf States.* Manchester, 1969
Bey, F.H., *From Trucial States to United Arab Emirates.* London, 1982
Busch, B. C., *Britain and the Persian Gulf 1894–1914.* California, 1967
Daniel, John, *Abu Dhabi: A Portrait.* London, 1974
Fenelon, K. G., *The United Arab Emirates: An Economic and Social Survey.* 2nd ed. London, 1973

Hawley, D. F., *Courtesies in the Trucial States.* 1965.—*The Trucial States.* London, 1971
Hopwood, D., *The Arabian Peninsula.* London, 1972
Izzard, M., *The Gulf,* 1980
Khalifa, A. M., *The U.A.E.: Energy Development.* London, 1980
Mann, C., *Abu Dhabi: Birth of an Oil Sheikhdom.* Beirut, 1964
Mallakh, R.S., *The Economic Development of the United Arab Emirates,* London, 1981
Marlowe, J., *The Persian Gulf in the 20th Century.* London, 1962
Miles, S. B., *The Countries and Tribes of the Persian Gulf.* 3rd ed. London, 1966
Mostyn, T., *UAE-A MEED Practical Guide.* London, 1982
Sadiq, M. T. *with* W. P. Snavely, *Bahrain, Qatar and the UAE: Colonial Past, Present Problems and Future Prospects.* Lexington, Mass., 1972
Soffan, L. U., *Women of the United Arab Emirates.* London, 1980
Wilson, Sir A. T., *The Persian Gulf.* 1928
Zahlan, R. S., *The Origins of the United Arab Emirates.* London, 1978

UNITED KINGDOM OF GREAT BRITAIN AND NORTHERN IRELAND

Capital: London
Population: 55·93m. (1976)
GNP per capita: US$7,920 (1980)

'Great Britain' is a geographical term describing the main island of the British Isles which comprises England, Scotland and Wales (so called to distinguish it from 'Little Britain' or Brittany). By the Act of Union, 1801, Great Britain and Ireland formed a legislative union as the United Kingdom of Great Britain and Ireland. Since the separation of Great Britain and Ireland in 1921 Northern Ireland remained within the Union which is now the United Kingdom of Great Britain and Northern Ireland. The United Kingdom does not include the Channel Islands or the Isle of Man which are direct dependencies of the Crown with their own legislative and taxation systems.

GREAT BRITAIN

AREA AND POPULATION. Area (in sq. km) and population at the census taken 5 April 1981:

Divisions	*Area*	*Males*	*Females*	*Total*
England	130,357	22,471,000	23,750,000	46,221,000
Wales (incl. Monmouthshire)	20,761	1,354,000	1,436,000	2,790,000
Scotland	78,762	2,461,000	2,655,000	5,116,000
Isle of Man	572	29,000	32,000	61,000 [1]
Channel Islands	194	64,000	69,000	133,000
	230,646	26,379,000	27,942,000	54,321,000

[1] 1976 census.

Population at the 4 previous decennial censuses:

Divisions	*1931*	*1951*	*1961*	*1971*
England	37,359,045	41,159,213	43,460,525	46,019,000
Wales	2,158,374	2,598,675	2,644,023	2,731,000
Scotland	4,842,980	5,096,415	5,178,490	5,228,963
Isle of Man	49,308	55,253	48,151	56,289
Channel Islands	93,205	102,806	104,378	123,063
Army, Navy and Merchant Seamen abroad	434,532	—	—	—
Total	44,937,444	50,383,283	52,867,716	54,158,315

In 1971 in Wales and Monmouthshire 32,725 persons 3 years of age and upwards were able to speak Welsh only, and 509,700 able to speak Welsh and English: these totals represent 20% of the total population. In Scotland in 1971, 338 persons could speak Gaelic only, and 88,415 could speak Gaelic and English, totalling 1·8% of the population.

At the census of 1971, in England and Wales, there were 16,509,905 private households; in Great Britain, 18,195,965.

The age distribution in 1971 of the population of England and Wales and Scotland was as follows (in 1,000):

Age-group	*England and Wales*	*Scotland*	*Great Britain*
Under 5	3,904	444	4,349
5 and under 10	4,044	468	4,512
10 ,, 15	3,627	442	4,069
15 ,, 20	3,313	392	3,705
20 ,, 25	3,731	390	4,121
25 ,, 35	6,062	616	6,676
35 ,, 45	5,721	611	6,333
45 ,, 55	6,022	617	6,651
55 ,, 65	5,815	598	6,414
65 ,, 70	2,399	247	2,647
70 ,, 75	1,778	179	1,957
75 ,, 85	1,892	180	2,072
85 and upwards	424	36	461
Total	48,749	5,228	53,978

At 30 June 1981 the estimated sex distribution of the population of England and Wales was: between 0 and 15, 5,166,300 males, 4,902,300 females; 15 and under 65, 15,976,700 males; 15 and under 60, 14,569,300 females; aged 65 and over, 2·97m. males; 60 and over, 6m. females.

England and Wales: The census population of England and Wales 1801 to 1981:

Date of enumeration	*Population*	*Pop. per sq. mile*	*Date of enumeration*	*Population*	*Pop. per sq. mile*[1]
1801	8,892,536	152	1891	29,002,525	497
1811	10,164,256	174	1901	32,527,843	558
1821	12,000,236	206	1911	36,070,492	618
1831	13,896,797	238	1921	37,886,699	649
1841	15,914,148	273	1931	39,952,377	685
1851	17,927,609	307	1951	43,757,888	750
1861	20,066,224	344	1961	46,104,548	791
1871	22,712,266	389	1971	48,749,575	323
1881	25,974,439	445	1981	49,011,417	325

[1] Per sq. km from 1971

There is only one other major country in Europe, Netherlands (population density 415 persons per sq. km), more crowded than England and Wales.

Local authority areas in being from April 1974. Area in sq. km and population census 1981:

ENGLAND	*Area sq. km*	*Population*
Metropolitan counties		
Greater London	1,580	6,696,008
Greater Manchester	1,286	2,594,778
Merseyside	652	1,513,070
South Yorkshire	1,560	1,301,813
Tyne and Wear	540	1,143,245
West Midlands	899	2,644,634
West Yorkshire	2,039	2,037,510
Non-metropolitan counties		
Avon	1,338	909,408
Bedfordshire	1,235	504,986
Berkshire	1,256	675,153
Buckinghamshire	1,883	565,992
Cambridgeshire	3,409	575,177
Cheshire	2,322	926,293
Cleveland	583	565,775
Cornwall and Isles of Scilly	3,546	430,506
Cumbria	6,809	483,427

Non-Metropolitan counties—contd.	*Area sq. km*	*Population*
Derbyshire	2,631	906,929
Devon	6,715	952,000
Dorset	2,654	591,990
Durham	2,436	604,728
East Sussex	1,795	652,568
Essex	3,674	1,469,065
Gloucestershire	2,638	499,351
Hampshire	3,772	1,456,367
Hereford and Worcester	3,927	630,218
Hertfordshire	1,634	954,535
Humberside	3,512	847,666
Isle of Wight	381	118,192
Kent	3,732	1,463,055
Lancashire	3,043	1,372,118
Leicestershire	2,553	842,577
Lincolnshire	5,885	547,560
Norfolk	5,355	693,490
Northamptonshire	2,367	527,532
Northumberland	5,033	299,905
North Yorkshire	8,317	666,610

Non-Metropolitan counties—contd.	*Area sq. km*	*Population*
Nottinghamshire	2,164	982,631
Oxfordshire	2,611	515,079
Shropshire	3,490	375,610
Somerset	3,458	424,988
Staffordshire	2,716	1,012,320
Suffolk	3,800	596,354
Surrey	1,655	999,393
Warwickshire	1,981	473,620
West Sussex	2,016	658,562
Wiltshire	3,481	518,167
Total		46,220,955

WALES	*Area sq. km*	*Population*
Clwyd	2,425	390,173
Dyfed	5,765	329,977
Gwent	1,376	439,684
Gwynedd	3,868	230,468
Mid-Glamorgan	1,019	537,866
Powys	5,077	110,467
South Glamorgan	416	384,633
West Glamorgan	815	367,194
Total Wales		2,790,462
Total—England and Wales		49,011,417

County districts with populations of over 90,000 (census 1981):

ENGLAND	
Allerdale	95,664
Amber Valley	109,379
Arun	119,206
Ashfield	106,521
Aylesbury Vale	132,709
Barnsley	224,906
Basildon	152,301
Basingstoke and Deane	129,899
Bassetlaw	101,970
Beverley	105,698
Birmingham	1,006,908
Blackburn	141,758
Blackpool	147,854
Bolton	260,830
Bournemouth	144,803
Bradford	457,677
Braintree	111,818
Breckland	96,444
Brighton	146,134
Bristol	387,977
Broadland	98,323
Broxtowe	102,801
Burnley	93,779
Bury	176,568
Calderdale	191,292
Cambridge	90,440
Canterbury	116,829
Carlisle	100,692
Charnwood	134,204
Chelmsford	138,318
Cherwell	106,947
Chester	116,157
Chesterfield	96,710
Chichester	97,617
Chiltern	91,728
Chorley	90,986
Colchester	133,681
Coventry	314,124
Crewe and Nantwich	98,217
Dacorum	128,801
Darlington	97,788
Derby	215,736
Doncaster	288,801
Dover	100,751
Dudley	299,351
East Devon	106,320
East Hertfordshire	106,994
Eastleigh	92,491
East Lindsey	104,546
East Staffordshire	94,862
Elmbridge	110,683
Epping Forest	116,204
Erewash	101,838
Exeter	95,621
Gateshead	211,658
Gedling	104,184
Gillingham	93,741
Gloucester	92,133
Gravesham	95,841
Grimsby	92,147
Guildford	120,072
Halton	121,972
Harrogate	139,736
Hartlepool	94,359
Havant	116,649
Horsham	100,647
Huntingdon	123,450
Ipswich	120,447
Kingston upon Hull	268,302
Kirklees	371,780
Knowsley	173,356
Lancaster	120,914
Langbaurgh	149,508
Leeds	704,974
Leicester	279,791
Liverpool	510,306
Luton	164,049
Macclesfield	149,003
Maidstone	130,053
Manchester	449,168
Mansfield	99,349
Mid-Bedfordshire	102,063
Middlesbrough	149,770
Mid-Sussex	118,311
Milton Keynes	123,782
Newark	104,139
Newbury	120,231
Newcastle under Lyme	117,922
Newcastle upon Tyne	277,674
New Forest	145,123
Northampton	156,848
Northavon	118,804
North Bedfordshire	132,084
North-East Derbyshire	96,547
North Hertfordshire	106,986
North Tyneside	198,266
North Wiltshire	102,492
Norwich	122,270
Nottingham	271,080

ENGLAND—*contd.*	
Nuneaton and Bedworth	113,521
Oldham	219,817
Oxford	98,521
Peterborough	132,464
Plymouth	243,895
Poole	118,922
Portsmouth	179,419
Preston	125,886
Reading	132,037
Reigate and Banstead	116,191
Rochdale	207,255
Rochester upon Medway	143,384
Rotherham	251,336
Rushcliffe	92,587
St Albans	124,867
St Helens	189,909
Salford	243,736
Salisbury	100,929
Sandwell	307,389
Scarborough	101,425
Sedgefield	92,887
Sefton	300,011
Sevenoaks	109,402
Sheffield	536,770
Slough	97,008
Solihull	198,287
Southampton	204,406
South Bedfordshire	106,790
South Cambridgeshire	107,979
Southend on Sea	156,683
South Kesteven	97,600
South Lakeland	97,664
South Norfolk	92,842
South Oxfordshire	128,596
South Ribble	97,164
South Staffordshire	96,493
South Tyneside	160,551
Spelthorne	92,898
Stafford	117,555
Staffordshire Moorlands	95,842
Stockport	289,730
Stockton on Tees	172,138
Stoke on Trent	252,351
Stratford on Avon	100,431
Stroud	101,356
Suffolk Coastal	95,223
Sunderland	295,096
Swale	109,506

ENGLAND—*contd.*	
Tameside	217,341
Teignbridge	95,665
Tendring	113,819
Test Valley	90,853
Thamesdown	152,112
Thanet	121,150
Thurrock	126,870
Tonbridge and Malling	96,205
Torbay	115,582
Trafford	221,406
Tunbridge Wells	96,051
Vale of White Horse	100,749
Vale Royal	111,521
Wakefield	311,787
Walsall	266,128
Warrington	168,846
Warwick	113,740
Waveney	99,239
Waverley	108,901
Wealden	116,498
Welwyn Hatfield	93,000
West Lancashire	106,735
West Norfolk	120,754
West Wiltshire	99,301
Wigan	308,927
Windsor and Maidenhead	130,054
Wirral	339,488
Wokingham	113,938
Wolverhampton	252,447
Woodspring	162,295
Worthing	91,668
Wrekin	123,525
Wychavon	95,123
Wycombe	155,591
Wyre	97,721
Wyre Forest	91,474
Yeovil	130,583
York	99,787
WALES	
Cardiff	273,856
Newport	133,698
Ogwr	129,773
Rhymney Valley	105,525
Swansea	186,199
Taff Ely	93,127
Torfaen	90,133
Vale of Glamorgan	110,777
Wrexham Maelor	111,724

The following table shows the distribution of the urban and rural population of England and Wales in 1951, 1961, 1971, and 1981.

		Population		*Percentage*	
	England and Wales	*Urban districts* [1]	*Rural districts* [1]	*Urban* [1]	*Rural*
1951	43,757,888	35,335,721	8,422,167	80·8	19·2
1961	46,071,604	36,838,442	9,233,162	80·0	20·0
1971	48,755,000	38,151,000	10,598,000	78·2	21·5
1981	49,011,417	37,686,863	11,324,554	76·9	23·1

[1] As existing at each census.

Conurbations. These are aggregates of local-authority areas with high population densities. In April 1981 there were 6 in England and Wales, with a population of 14·7m. (30% of total population). Their populations were: Greater London, 6·7m.; Tyneside, 0·7m.; W. Yorks., 1·67m.; S.E. Lancs., 2·24m.; Merseyside, 1·13m.; W. Midlands, 2·24m.

Greater London Boroughs. Census population in April 1981.

Barking and Dagenham	150,175	Hammersmith and Fulham	148,054	Lambeth	245,739
Barnet	292,331	Haringey	203,175	Lewisham	233,225
Bexley	214,818	Harrow	195,999	Merton	164,912
Brent	251,257	Havering	240,318	Newham	209,290
Bromley	294,451	Hillingdon	229,183	Redbridge	225,019
Camden	171,563	Hounslow	199,782	Richmond-on-Thames	157,867
Croydon	316,557	Islington	159,754	Southwark	211,708
Ealing	280,042	Kensington and Chelsea	138,759	Sutton	168,407
Enfield	258,825	Kingston upon Thames	132,411	Tower Hamlets	142,975
Greenwich	211,806			Waltham Forest	215,092
Hackney	180,237			Wandsworth	255,723
				Westminster	190,661

The City of London (677 acres) is part of the County of Greater London but retains some independent powers. Resident population (1981 census) 5,893.

Census of England and Wales, 1961. HMSO. 1961–65
Royal Commission on Local Government in Greater London, Report. HMSO, 1960 (Cmnd. 1164)
Census 1971, England and Wales, Preliminary Report. HMSO, 1971
Census 1971, Great Britain; Advance Analysis. HMSO, 1972

Scotland: Area 78,762 sq. km, including its islands, 186 in number, and inland water 1,580 sq. km.

Population (including military in the barracks and seamen on board vessels in the harbours) at the dates of each census:

Date of enumeration	*Population*	*Pop. per sq. mile*	*Date of enumeration*	*Population*	*Pop. per sq. mile*
1811	1,805,864	60	1891	4,025,647	135
1821	2,091,521	70	1901	4,472,103	150
1831	2,364,386	79	1911	4,760,904	160
1841	2,620,184	88	1921	4,882,497	164
1851	2,888,742	97	1931	4,842,980	163
1861	3,062,294	100	1951	5,096,415	171
1871	3,360,018	113	1961	5,179,344	174
1881	3,735,573	125	1971	5,229,963	175
			1981	5,117,146	...

The 1981 population included 2,461,519 males, 2,655,627 females.

Population of the local authority areas:

Regions	*Districts*	*Area sq.km*	*Census population 1981*
Borders		4,662	99,248
	Berwickshire		18,092
	Ettrick and Lauderdale		31,594
	Roxburgh		35,180
	Tweeddale		14,382
Central		2,590	273,078
	Clackmannan		47,806
	Falkirk		144,437
	Stirling		80,835
Dumfries and Galloway		6,475	145,078
	Annandale and Eskdale		35,338
	Nithsdale		56,493
	Stewartry		23,138
	Wigtown		30,109
Fife		1,308	326,480
	Dunfermline		122,232
	Kirkcaldy		141,861
	N.E. Fife		62,387

Regions	*Districts*	*Area sq. km*	*Census population 1981*
Grampian		8,550	470,596
	Aberdeen City		203,612
	Banff and Buchan		81,446
	Gordon		62,151
	Kincardine and Deeside		42,112
	Moray		81,269
Highland		26,136	200,030
	Badenoch and Strathspey		12,355
	Caithness		27,383
	Inverness		56,557
	Lochaber		20,539
	Nairn		10,139
	Ross and Cromarty		47,305
	Skye and Lochalsh		11,327
	Sutherland		14,425
Lothian		1,756	735,892
	E. Lothian		80,187
	Edinburgh City		436,271
	Midlothian		81,661
	W. Lothian		137,773
Strathclyde		13,856	2,397,827
	Argyll and Bute		68,786
	Bearsden and Milngavie		39,322
	Clydebank		51,825
	Clydesdale		57,361
	Cumbernauld and Kilsyth		61,707
	Cumnock and Doon Valley		45,509
	Cunninghame		138,265
	Dumbarton		78,041
	E. Kilbride		82,499
	Eastwood		53,547
	Glasgow City		763,162
	Hamilton		107,987
	Inverclyde		99,966
	Kilmarnock and Loudoun		82,149
	Kyle and Carrick		114,463
	Monklands		110,455
	Motherwell		150,015
	Renfrew		205,884
	Strathkelvin		86,884
Tayside		7,668	391,529
	Angus		92,841
	Dundee		180,064
	Perth and Kinross		118,624
Island Authority Areas			
Orkney Islands		974	18,906
Shetland Islands		1,427	26,716
Western Isles		2,901	31,766

Population of cities and large towns:

	Census population 1961	*1971*	*1981*
Glasgow	1,055,017	893,790	762,288
Edinburgh	468,361	453,025	419,187
Dundee	182,978	182,930	174,746
Aberdeen	185,390	181,785	190,200
Paisley	95,750	95,067	84,789
Greenock	74,560	69,171	57,324
Kilmarnock	47,509	48,992	52,080
Dunfermline	47,151	51,738	52,057
Clydebank	49,651	48,170	51,656
Hamilton	41,928	46,376	51,529
Coatbridge	53,825	51,985	50,866

Larger New Towns: East Kilbride, 71,316; Irvine, 55,278.

The birthplaces of the 1971 population were Scotland, 4,759,475; England, 279,340; Wales, 11,905; Northern Ireland, 32,790; Ireland 31,260; Commonwealth, 43,600; foreign countries, 51,345 (including 7,470 aliens).

The population of the Central Clydeside conurbation in 1981 was 1,713,287.

At 30 June 1981 the estimated sex distribution of the population in Scotland was: between 0 and 15, 564,600 males, 536,700 females; 15 and 65, 1,641,300 males, 15 and 60, 1,540,600 females; 65 and over, 278,900 males, 60 and over, 587,500 females.

Isle of Man and Channel Islands:

Islands	*Area in sq. km*	*Census population 1961*	*1971*	*1981*
Isle of Man	572	48,151	56,289	62,000[1]
Jersey	116	57,200	69,329	77,000
Guernsey, Herm and Jethou	64			
Alderney	8	47,178	53,734	56,000
Sark, Brechou and Lihou	6			

[1] 1976 census.

Vital statistics for England and Wales:

	Estimated home population at 30 June[1]	*Total live births*	*Illegitimate live births*	*Deaths*	*Marriages*	*Divorces, annulments and dissolutions*
1975	49,157,100	603,445	54,891	582,841	380,620	120,522
1976	49,142,400	584,270	53,766	598,516	358,567	126,694
1977	49,119,500	569,259	55,379	575,928	356,954	129,053
1978	49,117,300	596,418	60,637	585,901	368,258	143,667
1979	49,170,800	638,028	69,467	593,019	368,853	138,706
1980	49,244,300	656,234	77,372	581,385	370,022	148,301
1981[2]	49,592,900	634,492	80,983	578,171[3]	351,973	145,713

[1] The population actually in England and Wales.
[2] New census base and change in definition of population: residents absent outside England and Wales are included, and overseas visitors are excluded; previously the reverse was the case.
[3] Provisional.

In 1981 the proportion of male to female births was 1,055 male to 1,000 female; the live birth rate was 12·8 and the death rate (provisional) 11·7 per 1,000 of the population; infant mortality rate (provisional), 11·1 per 1,000 of live births. The average age at marriage (1980) was 29·4 years for males and 26·7 years for females.

Vital statistics for Scotland:

	Estimated home population at 30 June[1]	*Total births*	*Illegitimate births*	*Deaths*	*Marriages*	*Divorces, annulments and dissolutions*
1975	5,206,200	67,943	6,314	63,125	39,191	8,319
1976	5,205,100	64,895	6,025	65,253	37,543	8,692
1977	5,195,000	62,342	5,968	62,294	37,288	8,823
1978	5,179,400	64,295	6,304	65,123	37,814	8,458
1979	5,167,000	68,366	6,960	65,747	37,860	8,837
1980	5,153,000	68,892	7,678	63,299	38,501	10,530
1981	5,149,500	69,054	8,447	63,828	36,237	9,895

[1] Includes merchant navy at home and forces stationed in Scotland.

In 1981 the proportion of male to female births was 1,045 male to 1,000 female; the live birth rate was 13·4 and the death rate 12·4 per 1,000 of the population; infant mortality rate, 11 per 1,000 live births. The average age of marriage was 28 years for males and 25 years for females.

Emigration and Immigration. During the last hundred years the UK has most often been an exporter of population. Throughout the period 1881–1931 there was a consistent net loss from migration, though the fifteen years 1931–46 brought a reversal of the trend as a result of immigration from Europe. Since the Second

World War the loss has largely continued. However, during the five years 1956–1961, increased immigration particularly from the new Commonwealth and Pakistan, resulted in a net gain. Decreased emigration in 1979 also produced a small net gain.

Since 1964 migration figures have been available from the International Passenger Survey. This is a sample survey conducted by the Office of Population, Censuses and Surveys, covering all the principal air and sea routes between the UK and overseas, except those to and from the Republic of Ireland. For the years 1964–71 the survey shows an average annual net loss for the UK of 69,000. During the decade 1972–1981 the annual net outflow has been reduced to an average of 39,000. Both immigration and emigration have decreased.

The table below, derived from the International Passenger survey, summarizes migration statistics for 1981 (in 1,000):

UK migration 1980 (in 1,000):

By country of last or future intended residence		*Into UK*	*Out from UK*	*Balance*
All Countries		153·3	232·8	−79·4
Australia, New Zealand, Canada		20·4	78·6	−58·2
India, Bangladesh, Sri Lanka		18·0	2·4	+15·6
Other Commonwealth		29·2	25·9	+ 3·3
EEC		22·8	28·5	− 5·6
USA		16·6	24·7	− 8·1
South Africa		2·9	23·3	−20·3
Rest of World		43·4	49·5	− 6·1
	By sex/age			
Males	0–14	16·0	25·2	− 9·1
	15–24	24·1	28·9	− 4·9
	25–44	33·7	64·5	−30·8
	45 and over	8·8	14·2	− 5·4
	All ages	82·6	132·8	−50·2
Females	0–14	14·2	23·7	− 9·6
	15–24	24·1	21·6	+ 2·5
	25–44	25·9	43·6	−17·7
	45 and over	6·6	11·0	− 4·4
	All ages	70·8	99·9	−29·2

CLIMATE. The climate is cool temperate oceanic, with mild conditions and rainfall evenly distributed over the year, though the weather is very changeable because of cyclonic influences. In general, temperatures are higher in the west and lower in the east in winter and rather the reverse in summer. Rainfall amounts are greatest in the west, where most of the high ground occurs.

London. Jan. 40°F (4·5°C), July 64°F (18°C). Annual rainfall 24″ (600 mm). Aberdeen. Jan. 39°F (4°C), July 57°F (14°C). Annual rainfall 31·3″ (783 mm). Belfast. Jan. 40°F (4·5°C), July 61°F (16°C). Annual rainfall 34·6″ (865 mm). Birmingham. Jan. 35°F (1·5°C), July 58°F (14·5°C). Annual rainfall 26·5″ (663 mm). Cardiff. Jan. 40°F (4·4°C), July 61°F (16·3°C). Annual rainfall 42·6″ (1,065 mm). Edinburgh. Jan. 38°F (3·5°C), July 58°F (14·5°C). Annual rainfall 26·7″ (668 mm). Glasgow. Jan. 39°F (4°C), July 60°F (15·5°C). Annual rainfall 37·2″ (930 mm). Manchester. Jan. 41°F (5°C), July 62°F (16·5°C). Annual rainfall 34·1″ (853 mm).

QUEEN, HEAD OF THE COMMONWEALTH. Elizabeth II Alexandra Mary, born 21 April 1926 daughter of King George VI and Queen Elizabeth; married on 20 Nov. 1947 Lieut. Philip Mountbatten (formerly Prince Philip of Greece), created Duke of Edinburgh, Earl of Merioneth and Baron Greenwich on the same day and created Prince Philip, Duke of Edinburgh, 22 Feb. 1957; succeeded to the crown on the death of her father, on 6 Feb. 1952. Offspring: *Charles* Philip Arthur George, Prince of Wales (Heir Apparent), born 14 Nov. 1948, married Lady Diana Spencer on 29 July 1981. Offspring: *William* Arthur Philip Louis, born 21 June 1982; Princess *Anne* Elizabeth Alice Louise, born 15 Aug. 1950, married Mark Anthony Peter Phillips on 14 Nov. 1973. Offspring:

Peter Mark Andrew, born 15 Nov. 1977; *Zara* Anne Elizabeth, born 15 May 1981. Prince *Andrew* Albert Christian Edward, born 19 Feb. 1960; Prince *Edward* Antony Richard Louis, born 10 March 1964.

The Queen Mother: Queen Elizabeth, born 4 Aug. 1900, daughter of the 14th Earl of Strathmore and Kinghorne; married the Duke of York, afterwards King George VI, on 26 April 1923.

Sister of the Queen: Princess Margaret Rose, born 12 Aug. 1930; married Antony Armstrong-Jones (created Earl of Snowdon, 3 Oct. 1961) on 6 May 1960; divorced, 1978. Offspring: *David* Albert Charles (Viscount Linley), born 3 Nov. 1961; Lady *Sarah* Frances Elizabeth Armstrong-Jones, born 1964.

Children of the late Duke of Gloucester (died 10 June 1974): William Henry Andrew Frederick, born 18 Dec. 1941, died 28 Aug. 1972; Richard Alexander Walter George, Duke of Gloucester, born 26 Aug. 1944, married Birgitte van Deurs on 8 July 1972 (offspring: Alexander Patrick Gregers Richard Windsor, Earl of Ulster, born 24 Oct. 1974; Davina Elizabeth Alice Benedikte Windsor, born 19 Nov. 1977; Rose Victoria Birgitte Louise Windsor, born 1 March 1980).

Children of the late Duke of Kent (died 25 Aug. 1942): Edward George Nicholas Patrick, Duke of Kent, born 9 Oct. 1935; married Katharine Worsley on 8 June 1961 (offspring: George Philip Nicholas, Earl of St Andrews, born 26 June 1962; Lady Helen Windsor, born 28 April 1964; Lord Nicholas Charles Edward Jonathan Windsor, born 25 July 1970). Alexandra Helen Elizabeth Olga Christabel, born 25 Dec. 1936; married 24 April 1963, Angus Ogilvy (offspring: James Robert Bruce, born 29 Feb. 1964; Marina Victoria Alexandra, born 31 July 1966). Michael George Charles Franklin, born 4 July 1942; married Marie-Christine von Reibnitz on 30 June 1978 (offspring: Lord *Frederick* Michael George David Louis Windsor, born 6 April 1979; Lady *Gabriela* Marina Alexander Ophelia Windsor, born 23 April 1981).

The Queen's legal title rests on the statute of 12 and 13 Will. III, c. 3, by which the succession to the Crown of Great Britain and Ireland was settled on the Princess Sophia of Hanover and the 'heirs of her body being Protestants'. By proclamation of 17 July 1917 the royal family became known as the House and Family of Windsor. On 8 Feb. 1960 the Queen issued a declaration varying her confirmatory declaration of 9 April 1952 to the effect that while the Queen and her children should continue to be known as the House of Windsor, her descendants, other than descendants entitled to the style of Royal Highness and the title of Prince or Princess, and female descendants who marry and their descendants should bear the name of Mountbatten-Windsor. For the Royal Style and Titles of Queen Elizabeth *see* Commonwealth section.

By letters patent of 30 Nov. 1917 the titles of Royal Highness and Prince or Princess are restricted to the Sovereign's children, the children of the Sovereign's sons and the eldest living son of the eldest son of the Prince of Wales.

Provision is made for the support of the royal household by the settlement of the Civil List soon after the beginning of each reign. (For historical details, *see* THE STATESMAN'S YEAR-BOOK, 1908, p. 5, and 1935, p. 4). According to the Civil List Act of 1 Jan. 1972 and the Civil List (Increase of Financial Provision) Order 1975, the Civil List of the Queen, after the usual surrender of hereditary revenues, was (1983) £3,710,400.

The Civil List Acts of 1983 provide for an annuity of £111,700 to the Princess Anne; £179,300 to Prince Philip; £321,500 to Queen Elizabeth (the Queen Mother); £108,700 to the Princess Margaret.

Sovereigns of Great Britain, from the Restoration (with dates of accession):

House of Stewart	
Charles II	29 May 1660
James II	6 Feb. 1685
House of Stewart-Orange	
William and Mary	13 Feb. 1689
William III	28 Dec. 1694
House of Stewart	
Anne	19 March 1702
House of Hanover	
George I	1 Aug. 1714
George II	11 June 1727
George III	25 Oct. 1760
George IV	29 Jan. 1820
William IV	26 June 1830
Victoria	20 June 1837
House of Saxe-Coburg and Gotha	
Edward VII	22 Jan. 1901
House of Windsor	
George V	6 May 1910
Edward VIII	20 Jan. 1936
George VI	11 Dec. 1936
Elizabeth II	6 Feb. 1952

CONSTITUTION AND GOVERNMENT. The supreme legislative power is vested in Parliament, which in its present form, as divided into two Houses of Legislature, the Lords and the Commons, dates from the middle of the 14th century.

Parliament is summoned by the writ of the sovereign issued out of Chancery, by advice of the Privy Council, at least 20 days previous to its assembling. Every session ends with a prorogation, and all Bills which have not been passed during the session then lapse.

A dissolution may occur by the will of the sovereign, or, as is most usual, during the recess, by proclamation, or finally by lapse of time, the statutory limit of the duration of any Parliament being 5 years.

Under the Parliament Acts 1911 (1 and 2 Geo. V, ch. 13) and 1949 (12, 13 and 14 Geo. VI, ch. 103), all Money Bills (so certified by the Speaker of the House of Commons), if not passed by the House of Lords without amendment, may become law without their concurrence on the royal assent being signified within 1 month. Public Bills, other than Money Bills or a Bill extending the maximum duration of Parliament, if passed by the House of Commons in 2 successive sessions, whether of the same Parliament or not, and rejected each time, or not passed, by the House of Lords, may become law without their concurrence on the royal assent being signified, provided that 1 year has elapsed between the second reading in the first session of the House of Commons and the third reading in the second session. All Bills coming under this Act must reach the House of Lords at least 1 month before the end of the session.

The House of Lords consists of: (1) 799 hereditary peers and peeresses sitting by virtue of creation or descent, other than those who have disclaimed their titles for life under the provisions of the Peerage Act, 1963; (2) life peers being *(a)* 21 Lords of Appeal (active and retired), under the Appellate Jurisdiction Act, 1876, as amended; *(b)* (25 Dec. 1982) 327 life peers (including 44 women peers) under the Life Peerages Act, 1958: (3) 2 archbishops and 24 bishops of the Church of England (as long as they hold their sees).

The full House thus consists of 1,173, and the average attendance is about 300; at the end of Dec. 1982 153 peers were on leave of absence and 94 peers (including 7 minors) were without writs of summons.

The House of Commons consists of members representing county and borough constituencies. Persons under 21 years of age, Clergy of the Church of England and of the Scottish Episcopal Church, Ministers of the Church of Scotland, Roman Catholic clergymen, civil servants, members of the regular armed forces, policemen and most judicial officers are disqualified from sitting in the House of Commons. No English or Scottish peer can be elected to the House of Commons unless he has disclaimed his title for life under the Peerage Act, 1963, but Irish peers and holders of courtesy titles, who are not members of the House of Lords, are eligible. Under the Parliament (Qualification of Women) Act, 1918, women are also eligible.

In Aug. 1911 provision was first made for the payment of a salary of £400 per annum to members, other than those already in receipt of salaries as officers of the House, as Ministers or as officers of Her Majesty's household. As from June 1982 the salaries of members are £14,510 per annum, with income-tax relief on expenses incurred in the course of parliamentary duties. There is a secretarial allowance of up to £8,820 per annum and a living allowance, for an additional home, of up to £5,674 per annum. Members of the House of Lords are entitled to recover expenses incurred for the purpose of attendance at sittings of the House within a maximum of £12·10 for each day's attendance. For those Lords who incur the additional expense of overnight accommodation away from their main residence the limit is £25·40 for each day of such attendance and for general office expenses or on secretarial and research assistance, £11 for each day's attendance. Members of the House may also recover travelling expenses incurred between permanent places of residence and London.

The Representation of the People Act 1948, abolished the business premises and University franchises, and the only persons entitled to vote at Parliamentary elections are those registered as residents or as service voters. No person may vote in more than one constituency at a general election. Persons may apply on certain grounds to vote by post or by proxy.

All persons over 18 years old and not subject to any legal incapacity to vote and who are either British subjects or citizens of Ireland are entitled to be included in the register of electors for the constituency containing the address at which they were residing on the qualifying date for the register and are entitled to vote at elections held during the period for which the register remains in force. The current register was published in Feb. 1983.

Members of the armed forces, Crown servants employed abroad, and the wives accompanying their husbands, are entitled, if otherwise qualified, to be registered as 'service voters' provided they make a 'service declaration'. To be effective for a particular register, the declaration must be made on or before the qualifying date for that register.

The Representation of the People Act 1969, abolished the occupier's qualification for voting in Local Government elections.

The House of Commons (Redistribution of Seats) Acts 1944, 1949 and 1958, provided for the setting up of Boundary Commissions for England, Wales, Scotland and Northern Ireland. The Commissions are required to make general reports at intervals of not less than 10 and not more than 15 years and to submit reports from time to time with respect to the area comprised in any particular constituency or constituencies where some change appears necessary. Any changes giving effect to reports of the Commissions are to be made by Orders in Council laid before Parliament for approval by resolution of each House. The electorate of the United Kingdom and Northern Ireland in the register used at the election of 3 May 1979 numbered 41,569,787, of whom 34,608,491 were in England, 2,083,771 in Wales, 3,837,019 in Scotland and 1,040,506 in Northern Ireland.

At the general election held in May 1979, 635 members were returned, 516 from England, 71 from Scotland, 36 from Wales and 12 from Northern Ireland. Every constituency returns a single member.

Devolution in Wales and Scotland was decided by referendum on 1 March 1979. In Wales the result was 956,330 against a regional Assembly and 243,048 for. In Scotland 1,230,937 (32·85% of those entitled to vote) voted for an Assembly and 1,153,502 against. However, the Scotland and Wales Acts stated that the relevant Secretary of State must lay order for the repeal of legislation if less than 40% of those entitled to vote voted 'Yes' and the Acts were repealed in June 1979.

The following is a table of the duration of Parliaments called since the accession of King Edward VII.

Reign	*When met*	*When dissolved*	*Duration (years and days)*	
Edward VII	13 Feb. 1906	10 Jan. 1910	3	328
Edward VII and George V	15 Feb. 1910	28 Nov. 1910	0	287
George V	31 Jan. 1911	25 Nov. 1918	7	301
,,	4 Feb. 1919	26 Oct. 1922	3	269
,,	20 Nov. 1922	16 Nov. 1923	0	362
,,	8 Jan. 1924	9 Oct. 1924	0	276
,,	2 Dec. 1924	10 May 1929	4	161
,,	25 June 1929	7 Oct. 1931	2	75
,,	3 Nov. 1931	25 Oct. 1935	3	358
George V, Edward VIII and George VI	26 Nov. 1935	15 June 1945	9	205
George VI	1 Aug. 1945	3 Feb. 1950	4	188
,,	1 Mar. 1950	5 Oct. 1951	1	219
George VI and Elizabeth II	31 Oct. 1951	6 May 1955	3	188
Elizabeth II	7 June 1955	18 Sept. 1959	4	105
,,	20 Oct. 1959	25 Sept. 1964	4	341
,,	27 Oct. 1964	10 Mar. 1966	1	134
,,	18 Apr. 1966	29 May 1970	4	81
,,	29 June 1970	8 Feb. 1974	3	225
,,	12 Mar. 1974	20 Sept. 1974	0	224
,,	22 Oct. 1974	7 April 1979	4	167
,,	15 May 1979	—		—

The executive government is vested nominally in the Crown, but practically in a committee of Ministers, called the Cabinet, which is dependent on the support of a majority in the House of Commons.

The head of the Ministry is the Prime Minister, a position first constitutionally recognized, and special precedence accorded to the holder, in 1905. His colleagues in the Ministry are appointed on his recommendation, and he dispenses the greater portion of the patronage of the Crown.

Heads of the Administrations since 1908 (C. = Conservative, L. = Liberal, Lab. = Labour, Nat. = National, Coal. = Coalition, Care. = Caretaker):

H. H. Asquith (L.)	8 Apr. 1908	W. S. Churchill (Care.)	23 May 1945
H. H. Asquith (Coal.)	25 May 1915	C. R. Attlee (Lab.)	26 July 1945
D. Lloyd George (Coal.)	7 Dec. 1916	W. S. Churchill (C.)	26 Oct. 1951
A. Bonar Law (C.)	23 Oct. 1922	Sir Anthony Eden (C.)	6 Apr. 1955
S. Baldwin (C.)	22 May 1923	H. Macmillan (C.)	10 Jan. 1957
J. R. MacDonald (Lab.)	22 Jan. 1924	Sir Alec Douglas-Home (C.)	18 Oct. 1963
S. Baldwin (C.)	4 Nov. 1924	H. Wilson (Lab.)	16 Oct. 1964
J. R. MacDonald (Lab.)	5 June 1929	E. Heath (C.)	19 June 1970
J. R. MacDonald (Nat.)	25 Aug. 1931	H. Wilson (Lab.)	12 Mar. 1974
S. Baldwin (Nat.)	7 June 1935	J. Callaghan (Lab.)	5 Apr. 1976
N. Chamberlain (Nat.)	28 May 1937	M. Thatcher (C.)	4 May 1979
W. S. Churchill (Coal.)	10 May 1940		

In March 1983 the Government consisted of the following members:

(a) Members of the Cabinet

1. *Prime Minister and First Lord of the Treasury and Minister for Civil Service:* Rt Hon. Margaret Thatcher, MP, born 1925. (Salary £28,950 per annum.)

2. *Secretary of State for the Home Department:* Rt Hon. William Whitelaw, CH, MC, MP, born 1918. (£28,950.)

3. *Lord High Chancellor of Great Britain:* Rt Hon. The Lord Hailsham, CH, born 1907. (£28,950.)

4. *Chancellor of the Exchequer:* Rt Hon. Sir Geoffrey Howe, QC, MP, born 1926. (£28,950.)

5. *Secretary of State for Foreign and Commonwealth Affairs:* Rt Hon. Francis Pym, MC, MP, born 1922. (£28,950.)

6. *Secretary of State for Education and Science:* Rt Hon. Sir Keith Joseph, Bt, MP, born 1918. (£28,950.)

7. *Secretary of State for Northern Ireland:* Rt Hon. James Prior, MP, born 1927. (£28,950.)

8. *Minister of Agriculture, Fisheries and Food:* Rt Hon. Peter Walker, MBE, MP, born 1932. (£28,950.)

9. *Secretary of State for Defence:* Rt Hon. Michael Heseltine, MP, born 1933. (£28,950.)

10. *Secretary of State for Scotland:* Rt Hon. George Younger, MP, born 1931. (£28,950.)

11. *Secretary of State for Wales:* Rt Hon. Nicholas Edwards, MP born 1934. (£28,950.)

12. *Secretary of State for Industry:* Rt Hon. Patrick Jenkin, MP, born 1926. (£28,950.)

13. *Lord President of the Council and Leader of the House of Commons:* Rt Hon. John Biffen, MP, born 1930. (£28,950.)

14. *Secretary of State for Transport:* Rt Hon. David Howell, MP, born 1936. (£28,950.)

15. *Secretary of State for the Social Services:* Rt Hon. Norman Fowler, MP, born 1938. (£28,950.)

16. *Chief Secretary to the Treasury:* Rt Hon. Leon Brittan, QC, MP, born 1939. (£28,950.)

17. *Lord Privy Seal:* Rt Hon. Baroness Young, born 1926. (£28,950.)

18. *Secretary of State for Energy:* Rt Hon. Nigel Lawson, MP, born 1932. (£28,950.)

19. *Secretary of State for Employment:* Rt Hon. Norman Tebbit, MP, born 1931. (£28,950.)

20. *Chancellor of the Duchy of Lancaster and Paymaster General:* Rt Hon. Cecil Parkinson, MP, born 1931. (Unpaid.)

21. *Secretary of State for Trade:* Rt Hon. Lord Cockfield, born 1916. (£28,950.)

22. *Secretary of State for the Environment:* Rt Hon. Tom King, MP, born 1933. (£28,950.)

(b) Law Officers

23. *Attorney-General:* Rt Hon. Sir Michael Havers, QC, MP, born 1923. (£30,700.)

24. *Lord Advocate:* Baron MacKay of Clashfern, of Eddachillis, born 1927. (£29,000.)

25. *Solicitor-General:* Sir Ian Percival, QC, MP, born 1921. (£23,350.)

26. *Solicitor-General for Scotland:* Peter Fraser, QC, MP, born 1945. (£21,750.)

(c) Ministers not in the Cabinet

27. *Parliamentary Secretary, Treasury:* Rt Hon. Michael Jopling, MP, born 1930. (£24,150.)

28. *Minister of State, Home Office:* Patrick Mayhew, QC, MP, born 1929. (£20,575.)

29. *Minister of State, Home Office:* David Waddington, QC, MP, born 1929. (£20,575.)

30. *Financial Secretary, Treasury:* Rt Hon. Nicholas Ridley, MP, born 1929. (£20,575.)

31. *Minister of State, Treasury:* Barney Hayhoe, MP, born 1925. (£20,575.)

32. *Economic Secretary, Treasury:* John Bruce-Gardyne, MP, born 1930. (£20,575.)

33. *Minister of State, Treasury:* John Wakeham, MP, born 1932. (£20,575.)

34. *Minister of State, Foreign and Commonwealth Office:* Rt Hon. Douglas Hurd, CBE, MP, born 1930. (£20,575.)

35. *Minister of State, Foreign and Commonwealth Office and Minister for Overseas Development:* Rt Hon. Timothy Raison, MP, born 1929. (£20,575.)

36. *Minister of State, Foreign and Commonwealth Office:* Rt Hon. Lord Belstead, born 1932. (£20,575.)

37. *Minister of State, Foreign and Commonwealth Office:* Cranley Onslow, MP, born 1926. (£20,575).

38. *Minister of State, Department of Education and Science, Minister for the Arts:* Rt Hon. Paul Channon, MP, born 1935. (£20,575.)

39. *Minister of State, Northern Ireland Office:* The Earl of Gowrie, born 1939. (£24,200.)

40. *Minister of State, Northern Ireland Office:* Hon. Adam Butler, MP, born 1931. (£20,575.)

41. *Minister of State, Ministry of Agriculture, Fisheries and Food:* The Earl Ferrers, born 1929. (£24,200.)

42. *Minister of State, Ministry of Agriculture, Fisheries and Food:* Rt Hon. Alick Buchanan-Smith, MP, born 1932. (£20,575.)

43. *Minister of State, Ministry of Defence, Armed Forces:* Peter Blaker, MP, born 1922. (£20,575.)

44. *Minister of State, Ministry of Defence, Defence Procurement:* Geoffrey Pattie, MP, born 1936. (£20,575.)

45. *Minister of State, Scottish Office:* The Earl of Mansfield, born 1930. (£24,200.)

46. *Minister of State, Department of Industry, Minister for Information Technology:* Kenneth Baker, MP, born 1934. (£20,575.)

47. *Minister of State, Department of Industry:* Norman Lamont, MP, born 1942. (£20,575.)

48. *Minister of State, Department of Health and Social Security, Minister for Health:* Kenneth Clarke, QC, MP, born 1940. (£20,575.)

49. *Minister of State, Department of Health and Social Security, Minister for Social Security:* Hugh Rossi, MP, born 1927. (£20,575.)

50. *Minister of State, Department of Energy:* Hamish Gray, MP, born 1927. (£20,575.)

51. *Minister of State, Department of Employment:* Rt Hon. Michael Alison, MP, born 1926. (£20,575.)

52. *Minister of State, Department of Trade, Minister for Trade:* Peter Rees, QC, MP, born 1926. (£20,575.)

53. *Minister of State, Department of Trade, Minister for Consumer Affairs:* Dr Gerard Vaughan, MP, born 1923. (£20,575.)

54. *Minister of State, Department of the Environment, Minister for Housing and Construction:* John Stanley, MP, born 1942. (£20,575.)

55. *Minister of State, Department of the Environment, Minister of Local Government and Environmental Services:* The Lord Bellwin, born 1923. (£24,200.)

Leader of the Opposition in the House of Commons: The Rt Hon. Michael Foot, MP, born 1913. (£26,575.)

Leader of the Opposition in the House of Lords: The Rt Hon. The Lord Cledwyn of Penrhos, born 1916. (£19,350.)

Craig, F. W. S., *British Electoral Facts 1885–1975.* London, 1976.—*The Most Gracious Speeches to Parliament 1900–1974.* London, 1975
Ford, P. and G., *A Guide to Parliamentary Papers.* New ed. OUP, 1956
Herman, V., and Att, J. E., *Cabinet Studies.* London, 1976
Jennings, Sir I., *Cabinet Government.* 3rd. ed. CUP, 1959.—*The British Constitution.* 5th ed. CUP, 1966.—*Parliament.* 2nd ed. CUP, 1957.—*Party Politics.* 3 vols. CUP, 1960–62
Jones, J. M., *British Nationality Law.* Rev. ed. London, 1955
King, A. (ed.), *The British Prime Minister.* London, 1969.—*British Members of Parliament.* London, 1974
Laundy, P., *The Office of Speaker.* London, 1964
Lindsay, T. F., *The Conservative Party 1918–1970.* London, 1976
Mackintosh, J. P., *The British Cabinet.* 3rd ed. London, 1977.—*The Government and Politics of Britain.* 4th ed. London, 1977
May, Sir T. E., *Treatise on the Law, Privileges, Proceedings and Usage of Parliament.* 19th ed., London, 1976
Mellors, C., *The British MP.* London, 1982
Pelling, H., *A Short History of the Labour Party.* London, 1976
Rush, M., and Shaw, M., *House of Commons.* London, 1974
Stacey, F., *British Government 1966–1975.* London, 1975
Taylor, E., *The House of Commons at Work.* 7th ed. London, 1967

Wilding, N., and Laundy, P., *An Encyclopaedia of Parliament.* 4th ed. London, 1972
Young, R., *The British Parliament.* London, 1962

European Parliament: On 7 June 1979 Great Britain elected 81 representatives to the European Parliament, of which 66 came from England, 8 from Scotland and 4 from Wales, each constituency returning a single member by a first past the post system. Northern Ireland returned 3 members by single transferable vote. 13,446,076 votes were cast, on a 33% poll. The seats were won as follows: Conservative 60, Labour 17, Scottish Nationalists 1, Ulster Unionists 1, Democratic Unionists 1, Social, Democratic and Labour Party 1.

Local Government. Local Administration is carried out by four different types of bodies, namely: (i) local branches of some central ministries, such as the Department of Health and Social Security; (ii) local sub-managements of nationalized industries (coal, electricity, gas, public transport and the post office); (iii) specialist authorities such as water authorities; and (iv) the system of *local government* described below. The phrase 'local government' has come to mean that part of the local administration conducted by elected councils.

There are two separate systems: one for England and Wales and one for Scotland, but both systems are financed by a species of tax on property, levied locally, combined with government grants which, in the aggregate, amount to more than the yield of the local tax. This local tax is called 'the rate'. The system of financing local government was the subject of a major review in 1975.

Local Government: England and Wales—*Outside London.* England and Wales have slightly differing systems. Each country has three types of councils namely, county, district and English parish or Welsh Community Councils. In addition, England has some metropolitan county and district councils.

Councillors are elected by their local electors for 4 years. The chairman of the council is one of the councillors elected by the rest. In a district with the status of city or borough his title is mayor, or in a few famous places Lord Mayor. Any parish or community council can by simple resolution adopt the style 'town council' and the status of town for the parish or community. The chairman of the council will be known as the town mayor.

Counties and Districts: There are 47 non-metropolitan counties (of which 8 are in Wales) and 6 metropolitan counties (Greater Manchester, Merseyside, South Yorkshire, Tyne and Wear, West Yorkshire and West Midlands). Within the counties there are 369 districts (36 metropolitan and 333 non-metropolitan, of which 37 are in Wales).

Parishes and Communities: There are some 10,000 parishes within the English districts, of which 7,000 or so have councils. About 300 are former small boroughs or urban districts which became successor parishes. Parishes generally, however, remain comparatively unaffected by reorganization.

In Wales, parishes have been replaced by communities. Unlike England, where many areas are not in any parish, communities have been established for the whole of Wales. There is one for each former parish, county borough, borough or urban district (or part thereof where the former area is divided by a new boundary). There are 1,004 communities altogether, of which 800 or so have councils.

The Local Government Act 1972 laid down the boundaries for all the counties and districts in England and Wales except the English non-metropolitan districts.

Permanent Local Government Boundary Commissions for England and for Wales advise the Secretaries of State on boundaries and electoral arrangements.

A council has only those powers which have been conferred upon it expressly by Act of Parliament, and no more. The relationship between the different types of council is one of specialization, not of hierarchy. The larger do not supervise the smaller; each being, within its own sphere, entitled to make its own decisions. Government sanction, however, is required to borrow money and to sell land below its market value, and certain types of land use are subject to planning control.

Councils are kept within the law by a system of publicly regulated audit, and in the last resort they can be restrained from exceeding their powers by the courts.

Local government functions may be classified into county, district and parish or community functions, but whereas county and district functions are distinct, the parish and community functions are mostly concurrent with those of the districts. Arrangements may, however, be made so that any council may discharge functions of any other as its agent.

The following is the classification of powers given above: *Parish and Community Functions.* Allotments, burial and cremation, halls, meeting places and entertainments, facilities for exercise and recreation, public lavatories, street lighting, off-street vehicle parking, footpaths, the support of local arts and crafts, the encouragement of tourism and the right to be consulted by the district council on planning applications and certain byelaws. *District Functions.* In addition to the Parish and Community functions, aerodromes, civic restaurants, housing, markets, refuse collection, the administration of planning control, the formulation of local plans, sewerage, on behalf of the water authority, museums, the licensing of places of entertainment and refreshment, and the constitutional oversight of parishes and communities. *County Functions.* The formulation of structure plans, traffic, transportation and roads, education, public libraries and museums, youth employment and social services.

There are, in addition, a number of special arrangements. Four district councils in Wales have been designated as library authorities and Welsh district councils have powers in relation to allotments currently with community councils. The county councils in England and Wales separately or jointly appoint the fire and police authorities, and the bodies responsible for national parks. In Metropolitan counties the district not the county councils are responsible for education, social services and libraries.

The total number of local government electors in England and Wales was 37,492,810 in 1982.

Greater London. Since 1965 London has been governed by the Greater London Council covering the whole metropolitan area, and by 32 London Boroughs and the City of London, each with responsibilities in its own area. In the City and the 12 boroughs covering the inner part of Greater London education is the responsibility of the Inner London Education Authority, a special Committee of the GLC but independent of it, while in the 20 outer boroughs the London Borough Council is the education authority. Other functions are divided between the GLC and the boroughs. The main responsibilities of the GLC are strategic planning, major roads, public transport (through the London Transport Executive, which is responsible to it), housing, major parks and open spaces, the fire service, refuse disposal and Thames flood prevention. The boroughs are the primary housing authorities in their own areas, while the GLC is concerned with matters affecting the whole of London. The City has preserved a large measure of independence and has its own powers regarding police, justice, bridges, sanitation, etc. Except in the City the police authority covering the whole of Greater London is the Metropolitan Police, which is responsible direct to the Central Government.

Estimated population of Greater London in June 1981 was 6,851,500, and rateable value at 1 April 1982 was £1,988,458,546. Estimated gross revenue expenditure of the GLC in 1982–83 was £2,828·9m. (including £913·6m. for the ILEA and £799m. for London Transport). Estimated gross capital expenditure, 1982–83 was £530m., including ILEA £21m., London Transport £134m. and £15m. for housing loans. The GLC outstanding debt at 1 April 1982 was £2,220,279,000; ILEA, £188·72m.

Scotland. Under the system, which came into effect in 1975, the Scots mainland is divided into 9 regions, and in addition there are the 3 islands areas of Orkney, Shetland and the Western Isles. There is no equivalent to the English metropolitan county. The regions are divided into districts which total 53. All these units have a council consisting of councillors elected for 4 years and a chairman elected by the councillors for 4 years. Community councils have been established under schemes submitted by district and islands councils. These community councils cannot claim public funds as of right, nor do they have powers directly conferred by Statute: consequently they are not local authorities in the sense that Welsh Community Councils are.

As in England and Wales a permanent Local Government Boundary Commission advises the Secretary of State on Local Authority Boundaries and electoral arrangements.

On the mainland, functions are allocated between regional and district authorities, in the same way (with minor exceptions) as they are allocated between English counties on the one hand and English districts and parishes on the other, but the councils of the islands areas, which have no districts, perform both sets of functions.

Despite differences of nomenclature the effect of the reforms of 1972 (England) and 1973 (Scotland) is to assimilate the systems of mainland Scotland and of England and Wales more closely than has been the case in the past.

The total number of local government electors in Scotland was 3,885,462 in 1981.

Complaints. Under both systems, complaints, by members of the public, of maladministration may be investigated by a Commissioner for Local Administration. Initially a complaint must be referred to him through a councillor, but a direct approach to him is possible if this fails. He can deal only with matters for which there is no other remedy; he reports to the council concerned and may publish his report.

For map of regions *see* THE STATESMAN'S YEAR-BOOK, 1974–75.

Our Changing Democracy: Devolution to Scotland and Wales. HMSO, 1975
Arnold-Baker, C., *The Local Government Act 1972.* London, 1973

DEFENCE. The Defence Council was established on 1 April 1964 under the chairmanship of the Secretary of State for Defence, who is responsible to the Sovereign and Parliament for the defence of the realm. Vested in the Defence Council are the functions of commanding and administering the Armed Forces. The Secretary of State heads the Ministry of Defence as a Department of State. There are 4 subordinate Ministers; 2 Ministers of State and 2 Parliamentary Under Secretaries of State.

Defence Council membership comprises the Secretary of State, 2 Ministers of State, the 2 Parliamentary Under-Secretaries, the Chief of the Defence Staff, the 3 single Service Chiefs of Staff, the Vice Chief of Defence Staff (Personnel and Logistics), the Chief of Defence Procurement, the Chief Scientific Adviser and the Permanent Under-Secretary of State.

There are 3 Service Boards, each of which enjoys delegated powers for the administration of matters relating to the naval, military and air forces respectively.

Defence policy decision making is a collective Governmental responsibility. Important matters of policy are considered by the full Cabinet or, more frequently, by the Defence and Oversea Policy Committee under the chairmanship of the Prime Minister. Other members of this Committee include the Secretary of State for Defence, the Foreign and Commonwealth Secretary and the Home Secretary.

Logistics Services. Since the inception of a unified Ministry of Defence in 1964, progress has been made in the rationalization of the logistics services of the Royal Navy, the Army and the Royal Air Force. Airfield construction for all Services is now the responsibility of the Army's Royal Engineers; the Air Force Department is responsible for accommodation stores for maintenance and for the initial furnishing of new buildings; the Army Department is the single management authority for the design, development, procurement and inspection of clothing other than certain specialized clothing; the Navy Department has for some time been responsible for ration policy provisioning, procurement, storing and distribution of food to main depots and to Army forward supply depots in BAOR and is responsible for water transport to its tri-service responsibilities. The supply of Naval air stores has been integrated with those of the RAF. Considerable savings in money and in Service and civilian manpower have already been realized and are expected to continue.

The Procurement Executive. An important development in 1971 was the creation of a Procurement Executive to combine the Defence Procurement responsibilities of the Ministry of Defence and the former Ministry of Aviation Supply.

Service Strengths at 1 Jan. 1982, all ranks, males and females, UK personnel only: Royal Navy and Royal Marines, 74,041; Army, 165,682; Royal Air Force, 91,850; Total, 331,573.

Defence Budget Estimates: 1982–83, £14,091m.; 1981–82, £12,274m.

Army. Control of the British Army is vested in the Defence Council and is exercised through the Army Board, which consists of 7 civilian and 5 military members. The Secretary of State for Defence is Chairman of the Army Board. The other civilian members are the Minister of State for the Armed Forces and the Secretaries of State for the Armed Forces and Defence Procurement, the Chief Scientist (Army) and the Deputy Under-Secretary of State (Army) and the Second Permanent Under-Secretary of State who attend meetings as appropriate.

The Military members of the Army Board are the Chief of the General Staff, the Adjutant-General, the Quartermaster-General, the Master-General of the Ordnance and the Vice-Chief of the General Staff. The Chief of the General Staff is the professional head of his Service and the professional adviser to Ministers on the Army aspects of military problems. He is responsible for the fighting efficiency of his Service; for the consideration of all Army aspects of policy planning; for Army advice on the conduct of operations; and for the issuing of such single Service operational orders as may be appropriate resulting from defence policy decisions. He is also responsible for the Territorial Army. The Chief of the General Staff is a member of the Chiefs of Staff Committee which is collectively responsible to HM Government for professional advice on strategy and military operations and on the military implication of defence policy. This advice is tendered to the Secretary of State for Defence by the Chairman of the Chiefs of Staff Committee, the Chief of the Defence Staff. In exercise of his General Staff responsibilities the Chief of the General Staff is assisted by the Vice-Chief of the General Staff. The Adjutant-General is responsible for Army manpower within the policy set up by the General Staff; for recruiting and selection; for the administration and individual training of military personnel; for the discipline of the Army; for pay and allowances and pensions; for Army medical services; for dental and nursing services; for legal services; for the veterinary and remount services; for the Army Cadet Forces; for questions of Army welfare and education including school children overseas; and for resettlement and sports. The Quartermaster-General is responsible for logistic planning for the Army; for the storage, distribution, maintenance, repair and inspection of equipment, stores and ammunition; for development of stores; for supply, transport and accommodation; for the development, production and inspection of clothing; for military movements and transportation; for the Army postal, catering, salvage and fire services; and for questions connected with canteens, institutes and military labour. The Master General of the Ordnance is a member of both the Army Board and of the Procurement Executive Management Board. He is responsible to the Chief of Defence Procurement for the financial and technical management of the approved programme for the procurement of land service equipment for the Armed Services, and to the Army Board for the co-ordination of the Army's total equipment programme. The Chief Scientist (Army) is responsible for providing scientific advice to the Army Board and its members and for ensuring that the Defence Research Programme properly reflects their needs. He is also a member of the Procurement Executive as Deputy Controller, Research and Development Establishments, and Research (B). The Deputy Under-Secretary of State (Army) is responsible for the general co-ordination of Army Board business and, under the Permanent Under-Secretary of State and the Second Permanent Under-Secretary of State, for providing the Board with financial and administrative guidance.

Headquarters United Kingdom Land Forces at Wilton commands all Army units in UK except Ministry of Defence controlled units. The Ministry of Defence retains direct operational control of units in Northern Ireland. Command by HQ

United Kingdom Land Forces is exercised through 9 district headquarters. There are 3 major overseas Commands: Land Forces Cyprus, Hong Kong and the British Army of the Rhine. There are also garrisons in Berlin, Gibraltar, Falkland Islands and Belize.

The strength of the Regular Army (less the Brigade of Gurkhas and locally enlisted personnel) on 1 Jan. 1982 was 159,551 men and 6,131 women. The citizen force is the Territorial Army.

The Territorial Army has an establishment of about 75,000. Its role is to provide a national reserve for employment on specific tasks at home and overseas and to meet the unexpected when required; and, in particular, to complete the Army Order of Battle of NATO committed forces and to provide certain units for the support of NATO Headquarters, to assist in maintaining a secure UK base in support of forces deployed on the Continent of Europe and to provide a framework for any future expansion of the Reserves. In addition, men who have completed service in the Regular Army normally have some liability to serve in the Regular Reserve. All members of the TA and Regular Reserve may be called out by a Queen's Order in time of emergency or imminent national danger and most of the TA and a large proportion of the Regular Reserve may be called out by a Queen's Order when warlike operations are in preparation or in progress. There is a special reserve force in Northern Ireland, the Ulster Defence Regiment, 7,100 strong, which gives support to the regular army.

Men, women and juniors enlist in the Army for 22 years' active and reserve service. However, under a scheme introduced in May 1981 they are entitled to give 12 months' notice to leave active service provided they serve for a minimum of 3 years. Alternatively, they can agree to serve for 6 or 9 years to receive the benefit of higher rates of pay. Those enlisting in certain technical trades must agree to serve for a minimum of 6 years. Recruits under the age of 17½ on reaching the age of 18 are entitled either to confirm their original engagement or to reduce their period of service to 3 years.

Women serve in both the Regular Army and the TA in the Queen Alexandra's Royal Army Nursing Corps, the Ulster Defence Regiment and the Women's Royal Army Corps, the latter's employments including communications, motor transport, clerical and catering duties. Some officers of the Women's Royal Army Corps are employed on the staffs of military headquarters.

Barnett, C., *Britain and her Army 1509–1970.* London, 1970
Blaxford, G., *The Regiments Depart: A History of the British Army 1945–70.* London, 1971
Haswell, J., *The British Army.* London, 1975
Johnson, F. A., *Defence by Ministry: The British Ministry of Defence 1944–1974.* London, 1980
Stanhope, H., *The Soldiers: An Anatomy of the British Army.* London, 1979

Navy. The Royal Navy is a permanent establishment, governed by the Admiralty Board of the Defence Council. The Secretary of State for Defence is Chairman of the Admiralty Board. The naval members and their responsibilities are as follows: The Chief of the Naval Staff and First Sea Lord (professional head of the Royal Navy), assisted by the Vice-Chief of the Naval Staff, responsible for fighting efficiency, policy planning and operations advice; The Chief of Naval Personnel and Second Sea Lord, responsible for the manning of the Fleet, service conditions, training, discipline and welfare; The Controller of the Navy (formerly also Third Sea Lord), responsible for research and development, design, production, inspection, repair and maintenance of ships, their weapons and equipment; The Chief of Fleet Support, known until 1968 as Chief of Naval Supplies and Transport and Vice-Controller (formerly also Fourth Sea Lord), responsible for the provision of naval armament, victualling and medical stores and fuels, and for the movement of transport of persons and material, and superintending Dockyard organization and maintenance of the Fleet. The post of Second Permanent Under-Secretary of State (Royal Navy) (formerly Permanent Secretary) lapsed in 1968 (he was Civil Service head, responsible for general co-ordination of the Admiralty Board business, the interior economy of the Navy department, Navy contracts and the administration of civil staff, and accounting officer for Navy Votes responsible for the control of expenditure and adviser to the Admiralty Board on financial questions). Thus the office of Samuel Pepys, of which the last holder was the 33rd, passed into history.

The following is a summary of the more important units:

Category	*1974*	*1975*	*1976*	*1977*	*1978*	*1979*	*1980*	*1981*	*1982*
	Completed by the end of								
Aircraft carriers	3[1]	3[1]	3[2]	3[2]	3[2]	3[3]	3	3	3
Submarines	32	30	31	31	30	31	31	32	33
Destroyers	10	10	10	10	11	14	14	15	13
Frigates	60	58	56	56	54	56	55	47	47

[1] Included 2 commando carriers.
[2] Included 1 helicopter/V/STOL carrier and 1 commando carrier in reserve.
[3] Included the new ASW/carrier of Sea Harrier V/STOL aircraft and Sea King helicopters.

There are also 2 assault ships, 2 maintenance ships, 1 ice patrol ship, 3 fast training boats, 2 seaward defence boats, 12 surveying vessels, 5 coastal patrol vessels (*ex*-coastal minesweepers), 18 minehunters, 16 coastal minesweepers, 2 trawler minesweepers, 3 inshore minesweepers, 1 mine countermeasures support ship, 4 trials ships, 1 helicopter support ship, 1 submarine tender (ocean-going tug type), 9 offshore patrol vessels (fishery protection), 4 inshore patrol boats, 10 mooring, salvage and boom vessels, 10 fleet support and supply ships, 14 fleet oilers, 40 other auxiliaries, 4 logistic landing ships, 60 minor landing craft, 9 fleet tugs, 55 other tugs, and 67 tenders. In the following table the principal surface warships are grouped in classes, in descending order of modernity.

Completed	*Name*	*Standard displacement Tons*	*Aircraft*	*Armament*	*Shaft horse-power*	*Speed knots*
		Anti-Submarine Warfare/Commando Carriers[1]				
1959	Hermes[2]	24,000	5 Sea Harriers; 9 Sea King helicopters	2 quadruple 'Seacat' missile launchers	78,000	28·0

[1] *Bulwark*, converted from fixed wing aircraft carrier to commando carrier 1959–60 and reduced to care and maintenance reserve in April 1976: brought forward in Jan. 1978 for unwrapping, refit, re-storing and docking before re-commissioning for operational service in Feb. 1979 as an anti-submarine helicopter carrier with V/STOL aircraft capability, was finally decommissioned in Aug. 1981. Her sister ship *Albion*, converted in 1961–62, was decommissioned in May 1973 and towed away for disposal in Dec. 1973.

[2] Converted from fixed wing aircraft carrier to commando carrier 1971–73. Converted to anti-submarine helicopter and V/STOL aircraft role in 1976–77. Fitted with 'Ski-jump' launching ramp during 1980–81 refit.

The large fixed-wing aircraft carrier *Ark Royal*, 43,060 tons, returned to Devonport from her last active service mission on 4 Dec. 1978 and was decommissioned in 1979 for disposal. She was towed to Scotland in Sept. 1980 for breaking up.

Her sister ship *Eagle*, reconstructed Dec. 1959 to May 1964, was de-stored in 1972 and laid up at Devonport (providing spares for *Ark Royal*) until Oct. 1978 when she was towed to Scotland for breaking up.

The aircraft carrier *Victorious*, scheduled for disposal in Nov. 1967, decommisioned on 13 March 1968 and left Portsmouth for breaking up at Faslane on 11 July 1969. The aircraft carrier *Centaur* used 1965–1970 as accommodation ship for aircraft carriers and commando carriers refitting, was officially declared for disposal in Feb. 1971 and broken up in 1973.

Completed	*Name*	*Standard displacement Tons*	*Aircraft*	*Armament*	*Shaft horse-power*	*Speed knots*
		Anti-Submarine Warfare/Carriers				
1982 1980	Illustrious[1] Invincible	16,000	5 Sea Harriers; 9 Sea King helicopters	Twin 'Sea Dart' surface-to-air missile launchers	112,000	28·0

[1] Originally designed as 'Command Cruiser', subsequently re-rated as 'Through-deck Cruiser' (meaning long underdeck hangar with flat-top or near full-length flight deck) and later designated 'Anti-Submarine Cruiser'. Officially listed as ASW carrier in 1980.

Cruisers[1]

[1] Britain's last cruiser, *Blake*, was partially converted (aft) into a helicopter carrier 1965–69.

Standby Reserve 1980. Officially listed for disposal in April 1981, thus bringing to an end the 'cruiser' era which started in the Royal Navy a century ago.

Sister ship *Tiger*, partially converted (aft) into a helicopter carrier 1968–72. Reduced to Reserve in 1979. Approved for disposal in 1980. But both she and *Blake* were still extant in 1983 (laid up). Sister ship *Lion*, not converted into a helicopter carrier (reconstruction rescinded in Oct. 1970), was scheduled for disposal in 1972, and broken up in 1975.

The cruiser *Belfast*, reclassified as harbour accommodation ship in June 1966, ceased in this capacity in Feb. 1971, and on 21 Oct. 1971 became museum ship on the Thames.

The cruisers *Ceylon* and *Newfoundland* were sold to Peru in 1959. *Birmingham* scrapped in 1960; *Jamaica* and *Superb* in 1961; *Kenya* and *Swiftsure* in 1962; *Bermuda* and *Mauritius* in 1965. *Sheffield* towed to the shipbreakers in 1967; *Gambia* in 1968.

Capital (Strategic) Submarines

Class	*No.*	*Displacement (submerged) tons*	*Missile Tubes (vertical)*	*Nuclear Reactors*	*Shaft horse-power*	*Speed Knots*
"R"	4[1]	8,400	16 Polaris A3	1	15,000	25 dived 20 surface

[1] *Renown, Repulse, Resolution* and *Revenge* (former battleship names) completed in 1967–69. All also have six 21-in. torpedo tubes.

Other submarines are of the following classes: 'Trafalgar' (nuclear powered), 1; 'Swiftsure' (nuclear powered), 6; 'Churchill' (nuclear powered), 3; 'Valiant' (nuclear powered), 2; 'Dreadnought' (nuclear powered), 1; 'Oberon', 13; 'Porpoise', 3. Surface displacements range from 2,030 to 7,500 tons.

The first nuclear-powered fleet submarine, *Dreadnought*, was commissioned on 17 April 1963 (de-commissioned in 1982); and the first nuclear powered ballistic missile submarine, *Resolution*, was accepted in Oct. 1967.

The destroyers of the Royal Navy are of the following classes: 'Sheffield' (Type 42), 9; 'Bristol' (Type 82), 1; County', 3. Standard displacements range from 3,500 to 6,100 tons.

Frigates are of the following classes; 'Broadsword' (Type 22), 4; 'Amazon' (Type 21), 6; 'Leander', 24; 'Tribal' (Type 81) from reserve, 3; 'Rothesay', 9; 'Whitby' (Type 12), 1. Displacements range from 2,150 to 3,500 tons.

Two Type 42 destroyers, *Coventry* and *Sheffield*, and two Type 21 frigates, *Antelope* and *Ardent*, were lost during the South Atlantic operations in May 1982. Four frigates were brought forward from the Stand-By-Squadron or Reserve to compensate.

Ships under construction or on order include 4 nuclear powered submarines, 3 guided missile armed destroyers, 9 frigates, and 6 mine counter-measures vessels.

The 'through-deck' (flat-top) 'anti-submarine cruiser' (small vertical aircraft/helicopter carrier) *Invincible*, ordered in April 1973, laid down in July 1973 and launched in May 1977 was commissioned on 11 July 1980; and a sister ship, *Illustrious*, ordered in 1976, was launched on 1 Dec. 1978, when the third ship of the class, to be named *Ark Royal*, was ordered, perpetuating the name of the large aircraft carrier broken up in 1980–81.

The Navy Estimates are now included in a total Defence Budget (*q.v.*)

The total number of officers and ratings provided for was (in 1,000) 1979–80, 74·5; 1980–81, 74·4; 1981–82, 74·3; 1982–83, 70·4.

Blackman, R. V. B., *The World's Warships.* London, 1969
Blackman, R. V. B., *Ships of the Royal Navy.* London, 1975
Moore, J. E. (ed.), *Jane's Fighting Ships.* London, annual

Air Force. In May 1912 the Royal Flying Corps first came into existence with military and naval wings, of which the latter became the independent Royal Naval Air Service in July 1914. On 2 Jan. 1918 an Air Ministry was formed, and on 1 April 1918 the Royal Flying Corps and the Royal Naval Air Service were amalgamated, under the Air Ministry, as the Royal Air Force.

In 1937 the units based on aircraft carriers and naval shore stations again passed to the operational and administrative control of the Admiralty, as the Fleet Air Arm. In 1964 control of the Royal Air Force became a responsibility of the unified Ministry of Defence.

The Royal Air Force is administered by the Air Force Board, of which the Secretary of State for Defence is Chairman. The Minister of State for the Armed Forces is Vice-Chairman, and normally acts as Chairman on behalf of the Secretary of State. Other members of the Board are the Under-Secretary of State for the Armed Forces, the Under-Secretary of State for Defence Procurement, the Chief of the Air Staff, Vice-Chief of the Air Staff, Air Member for Personnel, Air Member for Supply and Organization, Controller of Aircraft, Chief Scientist (Royal Air Force), Deputy Under-Secretary of State (Air) and Second Permanent Under-Secretary of State for Administration. The Royal Air Force is organized into commands:

Home Commands. Strike and Support Commands. The Air Training Corps and the Air Sections of the Combined Cadet Force are under the administrative control of Support Command and functionally controlled by the Ministry of Defence.

Overseas Commands. Royal Air Force Germany. Small units in Gibraltar, the Falkland Islands, Belize, Cyprus and Hong Kong.

The RAF College, which trains general-duties, engineering, and supply and secretarial graduates for permanent commissions, is at Cranwell. The RAF Staff College is at Bracknell. The Department of Air Warfare is at Cranwell. The RAF Central Flying School is at Leeming. Estimated strength in April 1982, including WRAF and boys, was 91,700.

There is a single multi-rôle operational command in the UK, known as Strike Command, made up of 4 Groups, of which 2 were to be merged during 1983. No. 1 Group is responsible for the strike/attack, air-to-air refuelling and reconnaissance forces. The Tornado is entering service to replace the now-retired Vulcan and will eventually replace the Buccaneer which continues in the overland and maritime strike/attack rôle for the time being. Victor, Vulcan and Hercules tanker aircraft are being supplemented by *ex*-civil VC10s and TriStars, converted to the tanker rôle. No. 11 Group controls the defence forces, consisting of Lightning and Phantom supersonic all-weather interceptors, Bloodhound surface-to-air missiles, ground environment radars and associated communications systems, including the Ballistic Missile Early Warning System at Fylingdales. The Nimrod airborne early warning aircraft is shortly to enter service, and will replace the Shackleton in this rôle. No. 11 Group also controls the Hunters and Hawks of the Tactical Weapons training units which, in war, supplement the air defence fighters at bases throughout the UK. No. 18 Group is mainly responsible for the Nimrod maritime patrol force, most of which are now modified to Mk. 2 standard, but will also operate Canberra survey and photographic aircraft, Nimrod special-purpose aircraft, and Buccaneers transferred from No. 1 Group. This Group also runs the search and rescue units which are equipped with Sea King and Wessex helicopters. No. 38 Group, which is being merged into No. 1 Group, contains the army support and transport elements of the front line, consisting of Jaguar and Harrier ground attack aircraft, reconnaissance Jaguars, VC10 and Hercules transports, Wessex, Puma and Chinook support helicopters, and some short-range communications aircraft, to be supplemented by 2 BAe 146 transports. The RAF Regiment short-range air defence squadrons, armed with Rapier, and the field squadrons also form part of No. 38 Group, as does the Tactical Communications Wing. The Queen's Flight, with 3 Andovers and 2 Wessex helicopters, is also in No. 38 Group. The Military Air Traffic Operations organization also has the status of a Group. Strike Command has NATO commitments, but is available for overseas reinforcement. The training element of RAF Support Command utilizes Bulldog and Chipmunk primary trainers, Jet Provost basic trainers, Hawk advanced trainers, Jetstreams for multi-engine pilot training, twin-jet Dominies for training navigators and other non-pilot aircrew, and Gazelle and Wessex helicopters.

Squadrons of RAF Germany, which form part of NATO's 2nd Allied Tactical Air Force under SACEUR, have Harrier and Jaguar attack and reconnaissance aircraft, Phantom fighters, Buccaneer strike aircraft, Chinook and Puma helicopters, Pembroke communications aircraft and Rapier surface-to-air missiles. A squadron of Phantom fighters is based in the Falkland Islands; a squadron of Wessex helicopters is based in Hong Kong, and other helicopters are based in Cyprus to support the UN Force there. New types of aircraft under development include the air defence variant of the Tornado and an improved GR Mk. 5 version of the Harrier being developed jointly with the US Marine Corps.

The Royal Air Force, 1939–45. Vols. I, II, III. HMSO, 1953–54
Taylor J. W. R. (ed.), *Jane's All the World's Aircraft.* London. Annual from 1909

INTERNATIONAL RELATIONS

Membership. The UK is a member of UN Commonwealth, EEC, OECD, the Council of Europe, NATO and the Colombo Plan.

ECONOMY

Budget. Revenue and expenditure for years ending 31 March, in £ sterling:

Revenue	*Estimated in the Budgets*	*Actual receipts into the Exchequer*	*More than estimates*
1979	42,746,000,000	43,088,000,000	342,000,000
1980	51,013,000,000	53,369,000,000	2,256,000,000
1981	65,415,000,000	66,814,000,000	1,399,000,000
1982	75,524,000,000	76,288,000,000	764,000,000
1983	82,895,000,000	83,350,000,000	455,000,000

The Budget estimate of ordinary revenue for 1983–84 is £87,822m.

Expenditure	*Budget and supplementary estimates*	*Actual payments out of the Exchequer*	*More than estimates*
1979	51,378,000,000	51,469,000,000	91,000,000
1980	59,371,000,000	60,753,000,000	1,382,000,000
1981	73,175,000,000	76,728,000,000	3,553,000,000
1982	83,697,000,000	85,425,000,000	1,728,000,000
1983	90,891,000,000	89,041,000,000	-850,000,000

The Budget estimate of ordinary expenditure for 1983–84 is £95,557m.

The imperial revenue in detail for 1982–83 and the expenditure, are given below, as is the budget estimate for 1983–84 (in £1m.):

Sources of revenue	*Net receipts 1982–83*	*Budget estimate 1983–84*
Inland Revenue:		
Income	30,222	31,400
Corporation tax	5,480	6,200
Petroleum revenue tax	3,280	5,250
Supplementary petroleum duty	2,400	—
Capital Gains tax	630	600
Development land tax	65	55
Estate duties	13	10
Capital transfer tax	500	540
Stamp duties	850	975
Total Inland Revenue	43,440	45,030
Customs and Excise:		
Value Added Tax	13,900	15,500
Oil	5,250	5,675
Tobacco	3,500	3,700
Spirits, beer, wine, cider and perry	3,025	3,900
Betting and gaming	580	610
Car tax	575	615
Other excise duties	20	20
Customs duties	1,000	1,130
Agricultural levies	250	250
Total Customs and Excise	28,100	31,400

	Net receipts 1982–83	Budget estimate 1983–84
Customs and Exercise (contd.):		
Vehicle Excise duties	1,792	1,944
National insurance surcharge	2,830	1,697
Total taxation	76,162	80,071
Miscellaneous receipts:		
Broadcasting receiving licences	736	766
Interest and dividends	382	370
Gas levy	470	555
Other	5,600	6,060
Total	83,350	87,822

The following are the branches of expenditure for year ended 31 March 1983 and the estimates for the year 1983–84 (in £1m.):

	Estimates 1982–83	*Estimates 1983–84*
Social Security	32,500	34,400
Defence	14,400	16,000
Health and Social Services	13,900	14,600
Education and Science	12,600	12,600
Scotland	6,300	6,400
Industry, Energy, Trade and Employment	5,900	5,600
Transport	4,300	4,300
Order and Protective Services	4,300	4,600
Other Environmental Services	3,400	3,600
Northern Ireland	3,600	3,800
Housing	2,600	2,800
Wales	2,400	2,500
Overseas Services	2,200	2,200
Other Public Services	1,700	1,700
Common Services	1,600	1,000
Agriculture, Fisheries, Ford and Forestry	1,800	1,700
Government Lending to Nationalized Industries	1,400	1,100
Arts and Libraries	600	600
	112,500	119,300
Gross Debt Interest	15,000	14,800
Total	127,500	134,100

A single graduated income tax came into operation on 6 April 1973, replacing the existing income tax and surtax.

Rates of Personal Tax from 6 April 1983	%
Income between	
£0–£14,600	30
£14,601–£17,200	40
£17,201–£21,800	45
£21,801–£28,900	50
£28,901–£36,000	55
Over £36,000	60

Surcharge on investment income from 1982–83 is at the single rate of 15% on income in excess of £7,100. There is no separate exemption level for taxpayers who are 65 or over.

Under the tax system, the amounts of the personal allowances are adjusted so that they retain their equivalent in relation to earned income.

Personal Allowances	*1983–84* £
Single person / Wife's earned income	1,785
Married man	2,795
Additional allowance	1,010
Dependent relative:	
Single women claimant	145
Others	100
Housekeeper	100
Relative taking charge of younger brother or sister	100
Daughter's services	55
Blind person	360

Deductions of tax under PAYE extend over the full range of unified tax rates and not merely the basic rate. Similarly, assessment on business profits and on other income which was directly assessed to tax, such as rents and interest on bank deposits, are made by reference to the full scale of rates, including where appropriate the investment income surcharge.

The standard rate of 30% is the rate at which tax is deducted from payments of interest, etc., and corresponds under the new corporation tax system, to the tax credit on dividends. Where an individual's total income is such that he is liable on this taxed investment income at rates exceeding 30%, or if his investment income is high enough to make him liable to the surcharge, the higher rate or surcharge liability on this taxed investment income will in general be assessed separately after the end of the tax year.

Corporation Tax. Corporation Tax applies, with certain exceptions, to trades or businesses carried on by bodies corporate or by unincorporated societies or other bodies and this tax came into force from April 1966 replacing Profits Tax. The rate of this tax for 1969–71, 45%; but in Oct. 1970 this was reduced to 42·5% for financial year 1969–70 and reduced again to 40% in 1970–71. There are reduced rates of Corporation Tax for small companies and for 1983–84 the rate is 38% and the limit for that rate £100,000, limit for marginal relief £500,000.

Capital Gains Tax. Gains resulting from the disposal of capital assets (other than British Government and Government guaranteed securities and certain exempted forms of property such as a private car and personal residences) are taxed under the Finance Act 1965. In 1983–84 exemption was granted for all gains made in a financial year which in total did not exceed £5,300 and a lower rate of 15% and most trusts on the first £2,650.

Value Added Tax. Value Added Tax was introduced from 1 April 1973 at the rate of 10% on the supply of goods (with certain exceptions) and services. From 18 June 1979 the rate of tax was fixed at 15%.

Kay, J. A. and King, M. A., *The British Tax System.* OUP, 1980

Local Taxation. The rateable value on which rates were leviable in England and Wales on 1 April 1980 was £7,318m. In England and Wales, the average amount of the rates collected per £ of rateable value was £0·34 in 1913–14; and estimated to be 109·16p for 1980–81. In Scotland the rateable value on which rates are leviable on 1 April 1982 was £1,298m. and the average amount per £ of rateable value of the rates was 122·7p. The average water rate was 10p in the £.

Under the Local Government Planning and Land Act 1980, the Government gives general financial assistance to local authorities by means of rate support grants. The Rate Support Grant Supplementary Report (England) (No. 2) 1982 deals with the distribution of these grants to local authorities in England only. The grants for 1981–82 contain (i) Block Grant £8,289m., the object of which is to give authorities sufficient grant to put them in a position where they can provide similar standards of service for a similar rate in the £, and (ii) Domestic Grant £663m., which will provide a relief of 18½p for domestic ratepayers except for those in the Cities of London and Westminster where the relief provided is 34·3p and 25·6p respectively. There is also provision in the 1980 Act for payment of National Parks Supplementary Grant (£4·5m.) to county councils with all or part of a national park in their area, and Transport Supplementary Grant (£416·5m.) payable to county councils and the Greater London Council. Grants are also payable on revenue expenditure for specific services, including police and housing, and capital expenditure on certain services also attracts grant.

In Scotland, rate support grants are paid under the Local Government (Scotland) Act 1966, as amended by the Local Government (Scotland) Act 1975. The total rate support grant and the amounts of the component parts for the local authority financial year 1983–84, as prescribed in the Rate Support Grant (Scotland) (No. 2) Order 1982 are as follows: total £1,744·25m. comprising needs element £1,513·75m.; resources element £216·2m.; domestic element £14·3m. The domestic element is paid to rating authorities to offset the cost of reducing by 3p in the £ rates payable on domestic properties. A small part of the needs element, £15m. in 1983–84, is apportioned among those local authorities incurring extraordinary expenses in connection with developments relating to exploration for or exploitation of offshore petroleum. As in England and Wales capital and revenue grants are also payable on expenditure for certain specified services.

The rateable value of Greater London was £1,988,458,546 on 1 April 1982. The outstanding debt of the Greater London Council on 1 April 1982 was £2,220,279,000 and the Inner London Education Authority, £188,720,000.

Rates and Rateable Values, 1974–75. HMSO
Rates and Rateable Values in Scotland, 1977–78. HMSO
Estimates, 1982–83. GLC
Analysis of Rateable Values List. GLC, 1977
Report on Rate Support Grant Order 1979. HMSO

Gross National Product:	*1946*	*1960*	*1970*	*1980*	*1981*
Expenditure (£*1m.*)					
Consumers' expenditure	7,273	16,939	31,773	135,738	151,042
Central government final consumption	2,282	4,206	8,961	48,424	55,151
Gross domestic fixed capital for mation	925	4,190	9,462	39,411	39,377
Value of physical increase in stocks and work in progress	–126	562	425	–2,706	–4,160
Total domestic expenditure at market prices	10,354	25,897	50,581	220,867	241,410
Exports of goods and services	1,775	5,153	11,533	63,158	67,854
Less Imports of goods and services	–2,083	–5,549	–11,122	–57,913	–60,866
Less Taxes on expenditure	–1,573	–3,378	–8,416	–36,882	–43,471
Subsidies	384	493	884	5,308	5,861
Gross domestic product at factor cost	8,855	22,616	43,460	194,538	210,788
Factor incomes (£*1m.*)					
Income from employment	5,758	15,174	30,404	*136,050*	*147,197*
Income from self-employment[1]	1,126	2,008	3,735	*17,581*	*18,569*
Gross trading profits of companies[1]	1,476	3,730	5,935	*27,708*	*27,101*
Gross trading surplus of public corporations[1]	20	534	1,447	*6,222*	*7,551*
Gross trading surplus of other public enterprises[1]	86	189	151	*242*	*242*
Rent[2]	429	1,086	2,833	*13,390*	*15,282*

[1] Before providing for depreciation and stock appreciation.
[2] Before providing for depreciation.

	1946	*1960*	*1970*	*1980*	*1981*
Total domestic income before providing for depreciation and stock appreciation	8,895	22,863	44,837	203,304	218,260
Less Stock appreciation	–125	–122	–1,090	–6,456	–5,692
Residual error	...	–125	–287	–2,310	–1,780
Gross domestic product at factor cost	8,770	22,616	43,460	194,538	210,788
Net property income from abroad	85	233	559	273	1,004
Gross national product	8,855	22,849	44,019	194,265	211,792
Less Capital consumption	...	–2,047	–4,420	–27,223	–30,613
National income	...	20,802	39,599	167,042	181,179

National Economic Development Council. The NEDC (Neddy), which first met in 1962, is the national forum for economic consultation between government, management and unions. It includes leading representatives of the Government, CBI and TUC and also chairmen of nationalized industries and independent members. It meets usually under the chairmanship of the Chancellor of the Exchequer although the Prime Minister takes the chair from time to time. Discussions at the monthly council meetings are normally based on papers, presented by the participating parties, which deal primarily with questions of medium-term national economic performance and prospects, besides seeking to agree on ways of improving industrial efficiency. Council meetings are held in private to encourage the frank exchange of views between members, and discussions are summarized at a press conference taken by the Director-General of the National Economic Development Office (NEDO) following each meeting. The Economic Development Committees (Little Neddies), and the Sector Working Parties, like the NEDC, bring together representatives of management and unions and officials from Government, who use this neutral meeting place to study the efficiency and prospects of individual industries and sectors and to suggest ways in which these could be improved. The National Economic Development Office (NEDO) provides the professional staff for the NEDC, the EDCs and the Sector Working Parties.

Currency. The monetary unit of Great Britain is the *pound sterling.* A gold standard was adopted in 1816, the sovereign or twenty-shilling piece weighing 7·98805 grammes 0·916⅔ fine. Currency notes for £1 and 10*s.* were first issued by the Treasury in 1914, replacing the circulation of sovereigns. The issue of £1 and 10*s.* notes was taken over by the Bank of England in 1928. The issue of 10*s.* notes ceased on the issue of the 50p coin in 1969.

Following the post-war fluctuations in the value of the pound, Great Britain returned to the Gold Standard in 1925 with the pound fixed at the pre-war parity of US$4.8665. But the world financial crisis of 1931 forced the country off the Gold Standard again, and in the following year the Exchange Equalization Account was set up for the purpose of checking undue fluctuations in the exchange value of the pound. With the relative stability of the pound which followed, a 'Sterling Bloc' emerged consisting of most Empire countries and those others who voluntarily pegged their currencies to the pound.

The Bloc was superseded at the outbreak of the Second World War by the 'Sterling Area'. The pound was then fixed at $4.03 and remained at that rate until Sept. 1949, when it was devalued to $2.80. On 18 Nov. 1967 it was further devalued to $2.40. Following the general international currency re-alignment of Dec. 1971, the rate for the pound, in terms of the US$, was fixed at £1 = $2.6057 but in June 1972 the pound was allowed to float. March 1983, £1 = US$ 1·46.

When the pound was floated in June 1972 measures were also introduced to control payments between the 'Scheduled Territories' (*i.e.*, the UK including the Channel Islands, the Isle of Man and Ireland), and the rest of the

Sterling Area as well as the rest of the world. Exchange control restrictions were lifted in Oct. 1979 except for Rhodesia (Zimbabwe) and these were lifted in Dec. 1979.

Coinage. The sovereign (£1) weighs 123·27447 grains, or 7·98805 grammes, 0·916⅔ (or eleven-twelfths) fine, and consequently it contains 113·00159 grains or 7·32238 grammes of fine gold. On 15 Feb. 1971 (Decimalization Day) a decimal currency system was introduced retaining the *pound sterling* as the major unit but now divided into 100 *new pence* instead of 240 old pence. The decimal coins are the 50p (equilateral curve heptagon, 30 mm diameter, 13·5 grammes weight); 20p (equilateral curved heptagon 21·4 mm diameter, 5 grammes); 10p (28·5 mm, 11·31 grammes); 5p (23·6 mm, 5·65 grammes); 2p (25·9 mm, 7·12 grammes); 1p (20·3 mm, 3·56 grammes) and ½p (17·1 mm, 1·18 grammes). The Decimal Currency Act, 1967 and the Proclamation of 27 Dec. 1968 required that the 50p, 10p and 5p be made of cupro-nickel and the 2p, 1p and ½p of mixed metal; copper, tin and zinc (bronze). The Decimal Currency Act, 1969, provided that the coins of the Queen's Maundy Money should continue to be made in silver to a millesimal fineness of 925.

By Proclamation dated 28 July 1971, which came into force on 30 Aug. 1971, the crown, double-florin, the florin, the shilling and the sixpence are to be treated as coins of the new currency and as being of the denominations respectively of 25, 20, 10, 5 and 2½ new pence. The sixpence was demonetised on 30 June 1980.

The Coinage Act, 1971, specified that the legal tender limits for coins were: Gold coins, for payment of any amount; coins of cupro-nickel and silver of denominations of more than 10p, for payment of any amount not exceeding £10; coins of cupro-nickel and silver of not more than 10p, for payment of any amount not exceeding £5; coins of bronze, for payment of any amount not exceeding 20p.

The value of money issued in the 12 months up to March 1982 was £49m.

A £1 coin will be released in April 1983.

UK coins produced in 1980 totalled 1,439·8m., as follows, in millions: 50p 94·035, 25p 11, 10p 93·95, 5p 203, 2p 462·1, 1p 485·4, ½ 184·332.

It is estimated that the following coins were in circulation in the UK at 31 March 1982, in millions: 50p 710, 10p 2,124, 5p 1,972, 2p 2,324, 1p 3,518, ½p 3,536 making a total of 13,184m. coins with a face value of £760m.

Bank-notes. The Bank of England issues notes in denominations of £1, £5, £10, £20 and £50 for the amount of the fiduciary note issue. Under the provisions of the Currency and Bank Notes Act, 1954, which came into force on 22 Feb. 1954, the amount of the fiduciary note issue was fixed at £1,575m., but this figure might be altered by direction of HM Treasury after representations made by the Bank of England.

All Bank of England notes are legal tender in England and Wales, and notes of denominations less than £5 are legal tender in Scotland and Northern Ireland. The banks in Scotland and Northern Ireland have certain note-issuing powers.

The total amount of notes issued at 31 Dec. 1982 was £11,800m., of which £11,786m. were in the hands of other banks and the public and £14m. in the Banking Department of the Bank of England.

Banking. The Bank of England, Threadneedle Street, London, is the Government's banker and the 'banker's bank'. It has the sole right of note issue in England and Wales and manages the National Debt. The Bank operates under royal charters of 1694 and 1946 and the Bank of England Act, 1946. The capital stock has, since 1 March 1946, been held by the Treasury.

The statutory return is published weekly. End-Dec. figures for the past 6 years are as follows (in £1m.):

	Notes in circulation	*Notes and coin in Banking Department*	*Public deposits (government)*	*Other deposits*[1]
1977	8,302	23	30	2,219
1978	9,551	24	28	2,135
1979	10,750	25	26	1,948
1980	10,819	6	36	1,292
1981	11,577	23	45	2,260
1982	12,014	11	109	2,668

[1] Including Special Deposits.

The fiduciary note issue was £11,800m. at 31 Dec. 1982. All the profits of the note issue are passed on to the National Loans Fund.

Official reserves of gold and convertible currencies, SDR and reserve position in the IMF at 31 Dec. 1982 were US$16,997m.

The value of paper debit bank clearings for 1982, £5,771m. Paper credit clearings for 1982, £63m. Automatic direct debits, 1982, £39m.; automatic credit transfers, 1982, £91m.

The following statistics relate to the 6 London clearing banks at mid-Dec. 1982. Total deposits (sterling and currency), £83,481m.; sterling market loans £10,801m.; advances (sterling and currency), £50,291m.; sterling investments (other than reserve assets), £4,831m.

Total net profits from the operations of the 4 clearing bank groups in 1982 amounted to £1,115m., of which £235m. in gross dividends, £880m. transferred to reserves.

The clearing banks cover all aspects of banking business in UK including corporate business, and are also actively involved in international banking.

Trustee Savings Banks. Trustee Savings Banks started in Scotland in 1810. They are managed by Boards of Trustees, under the terms of the Trustee Savings Bank Act 1981. There are 16 banks with a network of 1,650 branches throughout the UK and the Channel Islands. The banks are supervised by the TSB Central Board, a statutory body established by the TSB Act 1976.

On 20 Nov. 1982 the funds of all Trustee Savings Banks totalled £6,400m., the total number of accounts exceeded 13m.

National Savings Bank. Statistics for 1980 and 1981:

	Ordinary accounts		*Investment accounts*	
	1980	*1981*	*1980*	*1981*
Accounts open at 31 Dec.	20,087,115[1]	20,038,438[1]	1,519,057	1,939,304
Amounts—	*£1,000*	*£1,000*	*£1,000*	*£1,000*
Received	601,600	565,693	448,777	1,264,228
Interest credited	83,951	81,790	229,488	324,083
Paid	779,047	694,864	337,486	587,719
Due to depositors at 31 Dec.	1,739,847	1,692,465	1,870,756	2,871,348
Average amount due to each depositor in active accounts	£86·34	£84·18	£1,231·52	£1,480·61

[1] Excluding accounts with balances of less than £1 which have been inactive for 3 years or more.

The amount due to depositors in Ordinary Accounts on 1 Jan. 1983 was approximately £1,662,471,169 and in Investment Accounts £3,688,539,775.

The National Girobank (founded 1968) has 1m. customers with balances of £500m.

Bank of England Quarterly Bulletin. Bank of England
Bank of England Annual Report. Bank of England
British Banking and other Financial Institutions. HMSO, 1977
Central Statistical Office, Financial Statistics. HMSO (monthly)
Report of the Committee on the Working of the Monetary System. HMSO, 1959
Report of the Select Committee on Nationalised Industries—The Bank of England. HMSO, 1970

The Royal Mint. 6th ed. HMSO, 1977
Clapham, Sir J. H., *The Bank of England: A History*. 2 vols. CUP, 1944
Craig, J., *The Mint*. Cambridge, 1953
Horne, H. O., *History of Savings Banks*. London, 1947
Sayers, R. H., *The Bank of England 1891–1944*. CUP, 1976

Weights and Measures. Conversion to the metric system was in progress (1978) which will replace the imperial system at present in force.

ENERGY AND NATURAL RESOURCES

Electricity. The electricity industry was vested in the British Electricity Authority on 1 April 1948. Following the re-organization of the electricity supply industry after the passing of the Electricity Act, 1957, the statutory bodies comprising the electricity service in England and Wales are the Electricity Council, the Central Electricity Generating Board and the 12 Area Electricity Boards.

The Electricity Council has functioned from Jan. 1958 as the central council for the supply industry in England and Wales for consultation on, and formulation of, general policy; its main functions are to advise the Secretary of State for Energy on all matters affecting the supply industry, and to promote and assist the maintenance and development by the Central Electricity Generating Board and the Area Boards (known collectively as Electricity Boards) of an efficient, co-ordinated and economical system of electricity supply. The Council can also perform services for the Boards, and, in addition, has certain specific functions, particularly in matters of finance, research and industrial relations.

The Central Electricity Generating Board is responsible for the generation and bulk supply of electricity to the 12 Area Boards in England and Wales. It therefore plans the provision of new generating and transmission capacity, including the siting and construction of new generating stations, both conventional and nuclear, and is responsible for the operation and maintenance of generating stations and the main transmission system.

Area Electricity Boards. Each of the 12 Area Electricity Boards acquires bulk supplies of electricity from the Generating Board and is responsible for distribution networks and sales of electricity to its Area consumers. Thus distribution and utilization of electricity, and also the contracting and sale of appliances side of the industry, are their responsibilities.

The number of power stations owned by the Generating Board in England and Wales on 31 March 1982 was 108 with a total output capacity, of 55,185 mw. Total number of customers in England and Wales on 31 March 1981 was 20,519,748 (on 31 March 1982, 20,663,882).

Electricity sold in England and Wales in 1981–82 amounted to 196,163m. units. Revenue from sales of electricity in 1981–82 was £7,980·8m. Coal used for electricity generation in 1981–82 amounted to 77m. tonnes (79·7m. tonnes in 1980–81). Total fuel (coal equivalent) used in 1981–82 amounted to 94·9m. tonnes and in 1980–81 to 97·6m. tonnes. Nine nuclear stations of total output capacity 4,467 mw provided 11·1% of total units supplied in 1981–82. Eight of these are gas cooled graphite-moderated stations using natural uranium fuel canned in magnesium alloy (Magnox) and 1 is an advanced gas-cooled station (AGR). With 4 AGR stations under construction, output capacity will reach 10,350 mw by Dec. 1988.

The number of persons employed by the Generating Board, the Electricity Council and Area Boards at the end of March 1982 was 146,655.

The North of Scotland Hydro-Electric Board, established under the Hydro-Electric Development (Scotland) Act 1943, is the nationalized authority responsible not only for generating and transmitting electricity but also for distributing and selling it to over 500,000 consumers.

The Board's district covers a quarter of the land mass of Great Britain and lies generally north and west of a line joining the firths of Clyde and Tay as well as all the island groups extending to the Outer Hebrides, Orkney and Shetland. About 99% of potential consumers have now been provided with supply. On the mainland the Board operates generating stations with a total installed generating capacity of 2,551 mw consisting of 1,752 mw of hydro power and pumped storage, together with 660 mw of steam. Diesel stations with a total installed capacity of 126 mw supply the principal island groups together with 13 mw gas turbine, while a further 1,320 mw of oil/gas fired thermal plant is nearing completion at Peterhead.

The main transmission system consists of 5,097 circuit km of 275 kv and 132 kv lines linking the power stations and the bulk supply points serving the distribution networks. The system control centre at Pitlochry co-ordinates the operation of the transmission system and power stations together with the continuous interchange of power with the South of Scotland Electricity Board. The number of staff at the end of the year was 4,005.

The South of Scotland Electricity Board was established in April 1955 by the Electricity Reorganisation (Scotland) Act 1954, replacing in South Scotland 2 Electricity Boards and 2 Divisions of the British Electricity Authority. The area of Scotland served by the Board lies south of a line from the Firth of Clyde to the Firth of Tay and extends to about 8,000 sq. miles, including the industrial belt of Scotland, with a population of 4m. By special arrangement a small part of North-East England is also supplied. The remainder of Scotland is served by the North of Scotland Hydro-Electric Board.

The Board differs from those established in England and Wales in that its responsibilities cover not only the distribution of electricity and retail sale of electrical appliances but also the generation and transmission of bulk power within South Scotland.

At 31 March 1982 the Board operated 17 generating stations (including 2 nuclear and 7 hydro-electric stations) with a total output capacity of 7,826 mw (total effective capacity however, has been reduced by placing 1,510 mw of plant at 2 stations in storage for an indefinite period). In 1981–82 the Board sold 17,806m. units to more than 1·6m. consumers and had a total revenue of £716m. The number of staff employed at the end of the year was 13,005.

Oil. Production 1981, in 1,000 tons (1980 in brackets): Throughput of crude and process oils, 78,336 (86,393); refinery use, 5,494 (6,317); gases, 1,466 (1,458); naphtha, 3,406 (3,541); motor spirits, 17,140 (16,609); kerosene, 6,463 (7,232); diesel oil, 20,411 (22,153); fuel oil, 19,069 (23,700); lubricating oils, 1,063 (1,250); bitumen, 1,735 (1,928). Total output of refined products, 72,006 (79,227). 1979 investment in North Sea oil and gas production: £2,062m. (£2,168m.).

Gas. The British gas industry, nationalized in 1949, was reorganized as the British Gas Corporation on 1 Jan. 1973. Under the terms of the Gas Act 1972, the Corporation has the general duty 'to develop and maintain an efficient, co-ordinated and economical system of gas supply'. The chairman and members of the Corporation are appointed by the Secretary of State for Energy. British Gas explores for and produces natural gas, manufactures substitute natural gas, transmits, distributes and sells gas, and sells, installs and maintains gas appliances.

Gas Council (Exploration) Ltd and Hydrocarbons Great Britain Ltd, wholly owned subsidiaries of British Gas, have been involved in exploration for oil and gas in the Irish Sea, the English Channel and Celtic Sea and, in partnership with oil companies, in the North Sea and onshore. British Gas is a partner in gasfields in the southern North Sea, and the Beryl, Hutton and Montrose oilfields in the northern North Sea and discovered the Morecambe gasfield in the Irish Sea and the Wytch Farm oilfield in Dorset.

In 1981–82, British Gas sold 16,876m. therms of gas. Conversion to natural gas was completed in 1977. There were 15·13m. domestic customers, who used 8,922m. therms; 81,000 industrial customers, who used 5,698m. therms; and

496,000 commercial customers, who used 2,256m. therms.

The turnover of British Gas in 1981–82 was £5,235m. and the average net assets employed at current cost was £10,513m. The surplus for the year was £311m. before tax. In March 1982, there were 105,000 employees.

Minerals. The number of National Coal Board mines producing coal on 31 March 1981 was 211. Statistics of the coalmining industry (including licensed mines) for recent years are as follows:

	1977–78[1]	*1978–79*	*1979–80*	*1980–81*
Saleable output of coal:				
Total deep-mined (1m. tonnes)	107·3	106·4	110·3	111·4
Opencast (1m. tonnes)	13·6	13·5	13·0	15·3
Average weekly number of wage-earners on colliery books:				
All workers (NCB only)	240,500	234,900	232,500	229,808
Underground workers (NCB only)	190,744	186,390	184,367	183,631
Coal exports:				
Total (1m. tonnes)	1·84	2·07	2·52	4·84

[1] 12-month period ending March.

Total stocks of coal on 31 March 1981 amounted to 38·4m. tonnes (17·5m. tonnes distributed, 20·9m. tonnes undistributed). Trading profit made by the NCB for the year ended 31 March 1981 amounted to £69·5m. Interest payable was £256·2m., of which to the Secretary of State for Energy, £166·3m. There was a Deficit grant of £149m. from the Government for the year ended 31 March 1981.

Production of coke (including coke breeze) amounted in 1980–81 to 3·9m. tonnes.

In 1980–81 inland consumption (in 1,000 tonnes) of coal is estimated to have been 120,269, some of the principal users being: Power stations, 87,756; coke ovens, 11,295; domestic, 8,534; other conversion industries, 2,869; collieries, 634; industry, 7,434.

Ezra, D., *Coal and Energy*. London, 1980

The UK is among the 10 largest steel producing countries in the world. Output in recent years was as follows (in 1,000 tonnes):

	Pig-iron	*Crude steel*	*Home consumption*[1]
1977	12,232	20,411	20,520
1978	11,434	20,311	20,530
1979	12,898	21,464	20,160
1980[2]	6,316	11,277	15,990
1981	9,554	15,573	14,893

[1] Finished steel (ingot equivalent).
[2] 1980 figures affected by 3-month industrial dispute.

Exports of finished steel products were 2·6m. tonnes in 1980 and imports, 4·6m. tonnes.

Iron Castings. Production of iron castings was 1·6m. tonnes in 1981 (1·8m. tonnes in 1980).

The industry is divided between the 'public sector' and the 'private sector'.

The British Steel Corporation, which was established by the Iron and Steel Act 1967, took over the 14 largest UK iron and steel making concerns (and their subsidiaries) in July 1967 and merged them into a single publicly owned business. With a turnover of more than £3,443m. and a crude steel output of 13·6m. tonnes in 1981–82, the British Steel Corporation ranks as one of Britain's major manufacturing industries and is one of the world's largest steel makers. The number of employees at the end of 1982 was 89,900. A substantial part of the British steel industry remains in private ownership and there were in 1983 a number of significant producers in mixed public/private ownership. Although responsible for only 15% of UK crude steel production, companies other than the British Steel Corporation produce much higher proportions of steel in finished form. For some products such as wire rod, reinforcement steel, bright bars, wire, open-die forgings and high speed and tool steels, they cover nearly all UK production. Because of the involvement of these companies in higher value steels it accounts for over a third of the total turnover of the British steel industry but employs a smaller proportion of the total labour force.

Production of non-ferrous metals in 1981 (in 1,000 tonnes): Refined copper, 136·1 (161·3 in 1980); refined lead, 198 (211·4 in 1980); tin metal, 11·4 (1980); virgin aluminium, 339·2 (374·4 in 1980); slab zinc, 81·7 (86·7 in 1980).

Agriculture. The total land area of the UK is 24m. hectares, of which 18·72m. (1982) is agricultural.

Distribution of the culitvated area in the UK (in 1,000 hectares):

	1980	*1981*
Corn crops[1]	3,919	3,979
Green crops[2]	982	1,014
Hops	6	6
Fruit	65	66
Bare fallow	59	76
Rotation grasses including lucerne	1,965	1,911
Permanent pasture	5,140	5,103

[1] Includes wheat, barley, rye and oats.
[2] Green crops include beans, potatoes, turnips and swedes, mangolds, sugar-beet, cabbage, etc., for fodder, vegetables, and all other crops.

The number of workers employed in agriculture, forestry and fishing in the UK was, in June 1981, 352,000; 333,700 were solely engaged in agriculture; there were also (Dec. 1982) 186,400 farmers, partners and directors.

In Dec. 1980 there were 419,000 tractors and 47,600 combine harvesters in use.

Principal crops in the UK as at June in each year:

	Wheat	*Barley*	*Oats*	*Beans*	*Potatoes*	*Fodder crops*[1]	*Man-gold*	*Sugar-beet*
			Acreage (1,000 hectares)					
1977	1,076	2,400	195	55	233	97	7	202
1978	1,257	2,348	180	55	214	223	—	209
1979	1,371	2,343	136	60	204	204	—	214
1980	1,441	2,330	148	61	206	200	—	213
1981	1,491	2,327	144	58	191	222	—	210
			Total product (1,000 tonnes)					
1977	5,244	10,738	778	269	6,632	5,869	457	6,382
1978	6,610	9,850	705	285	7,330	9,835	—	7,080
1979	7,140	9,550	535	286	6,485	9,049	—	7,660
1980	8,470	10,320	600	251	7,105	8,335	—	7,380
1981	8,580	10,150	620	238	6,215	—	—	7,395

[1] Includes mangolds from 1978.

Livestock in the UK as at June in each year (in 1,000):

	1978	*1979*	*1980*	*1981*	*1982*
Cattle	13,625	13,543	13,426	13,137	13,275
Sheep	29,686	29,860	31,446	32,091	33,049
Pigs	7,708	7,844	7,815	7,828	8,082
Poultry	137,329	134,700	135,105	132,286	...

Forestry. On 31 March 1980 the area of productive woodland in Britain was 1,769,000 hectares of which the Forestry Commission managed 896,000 hectares and the private sector 873,000 hectares.

The Forestry Commission employed 2,167 non-industrial staff at 31 March 1980 (2,255 in 1979), and 5,785 industrial staff (6,068 in 1979). In addition a further 10,650 were employed in private forestry with an estimated 12,400 engaged in the wood processing industry.

James, N. D. G., *A History of English Forestry*. London, 1981

Fisheries. Quantity (in 1,000 tonnes) and value (in £1,000) of fish of British taking landed in Great Britain (excluding salmon and sea-trout):

Quantity	*1977*	*1978*	*1979*	*1980*	*1981*
Wet fish	830·4	880·6	764·1	679·0	664·6
Shell fish	73·9	64·4	62·5	68·6	62·9
	904·3	945·0	826·6	747·6	727·5
Value					
Wet fish	222,130	219,412	211,892	184,847	188,152
Shell fish	25,189	30,492	35,545	32,245	34,405
	247,319	249,904	247,437	217,092	222,557

The fishing fleet of England and Wales comprised (1981) 4,637 vessels including 1,750 trawlers and 794 line fishing vessels; the Scottish fleet (1981) 2,370 vessels including 769 trawlers and 929 creel fishing vessels.

INDUSTRY AND TRADE

Industry. Statistics of a cross-section of industrial production are as follows (in 1,000 tonnes):

	1979	*1980*	*1981*
Sulphuric acid	3,498	3,381	2,889
Synthetic resins	2,647	2,259	. . .
Tractors (no.)	116,000	104,000	779,002
Commercial motor vehicles (no. 1,000)	408	389	230
Cotton single yarn	79	61	43
Wool tops	79	66	67
Woollen yarn	105	81	72
Man-made fibres (rayon, nylon, etc.)	596	450	395
Newsprint	364	363	113
Other paper and board	3,889	3,454	3,295
Fertilizers, phosphate, super phosphate, basic slag and compounds (1,000 tons)	2,858	3,350	. . .
Cement	16,140	14,805	12,729
Fabricated aluminium (to consumers)	574	521	444

Engineering. In 1981 the number (in 1,000) of passenger cars produced amounted to 955 (1980: 923); computers sold, value £977m. (1980: £1,022m.).

Electrical Goods. Manufacturers' sales (in £1m.) for 1981 (1980 in brackets): Radio and electronic components, 1,352 (1,456); broadcasting receiving and sound reproducing equipment, 522 (533); gramophone records and tape recordings, 131 (135); television sets, 2·34m. (1980) units (2·48, 1979); domestic electrical appliances, 920 (944).

Textile Manufacturers. Production of woven cloth for 1981 (1980 in brackets): cotton (1m. metres), 278 (314); man-made fibres (1m. metres), 230 (299); woven woollen and worsted fabrics (1m. sq. metres), deliveries, 97 (118).

Construction. Total value (in £1m.) of constructional work by all agencies in 1981 was 21,251 (22,036 in 1980), including new housing, 3,786. Value of industrial buildings for private developers completed in 1981 was £2,417m.; commercial buildings,£2,999m. New work (other than housing) for public authorities was valued at £3,789m.

Annual Abstract of Statistics. HMSO
Chester, Sir N., *The Nationalisation of British Industry, 1945–51.* HMSO, 1976
Kelf-Cohen, R., *British Nationalization: 1945–1973.* New York, 1973
Statistical Summary of the Mineral Industry. HMSO, annual

Labour. The distribution of total manpower in Great Britain was in June 1981 (in 1,000): Total working population, 25,435 (15,598 males, 9,837 females). Total employed in armed forces and women's services, 334. Total in civil employment, 20,729, including agriculture, 332; mining and quarrying, 331; metal manufacture, 326; national and local government service, 1,526; transport and communications,

1,420; construction, 1,105; distributive trades, 2,583; insurance, banking, business, professional and scientific services, 4,799; self-employed, 1,795.

The average monthly numbers (in 1,000) of registered unemployed in Great Britain were: 1976, 1,304 (11 months total; males, 988; females, 315); 1977, 1,423 (males, 1,027; females, 395); 1978, 1,410 (males, 995; females, 414); 1979, 1,326 (males, 920; females, 406); 1980, 1,716 (males, 1,180; females 536); 1981, 2,628 (males, 1,870; females, 758).

Trade Unions. In Dec. 1982 there were 105 unions affiliated to the Trades Union Congress with a total membership of 11,005,984 (including about 3·5m. women). The unions affiliated to the TUC in 1982 ranged in size from the Transport and General Workers' Union, with 1,695,818 members, to the Cloth Pressers' Society with 18 members. Non-manual workers accounted for nearly a third of the total TUC membership.

The TUC's executive body, the General Council, is elected at the annual Congress. It is composed of 44 members elected from 18 industrial groupings of unions (railways, mining and quarrying, etc.), to ensure that the Council is broadly representative of the whole trade union movement. Five members are elected to represent women workers.

The General Secretary is elected by the Congress but is not subject to annual re-election.

The TUC General Council appoints committees, which draw upon the services of specialist departments in preparing policies on economic, education, international, employment, industrial organization, and social questions.

The TUC is affiliated to the International Confederation of Free Trade Unions, the Trade Union Advisory Committee of OECD, the Commonwealth Trade Union Council and the European Trade Union Confederation. The TUC provides a service of trade union education. It provides members to serve, with representatives of employers, on joint committees advising the Government on issues of national importance (e.g., National Economic Development Council and various Royal Commissions) and on the managing boards of such bodies as the Health and Safety Commission; Advisory, Conciliation and Arbitration Service; and Manpower Services Commission.

The following table is a statistical summary relating to trade disputes for recent years:

	No. of workers involved	*Working days lost through stoppages*
1979	4,583,000	29,474,000
1980	830,000	11,964,000
1981	1,499,000	4,266,000

Lovell, J., and Robert, B. C., *A Short History of the T.U.C.* London, 1968
Pelling, H., *A History of British Trade Unionism.* 2nd ed. London, 1972

Commerce. Value of the imports and exports of merchandise (excluding bullion and specie and foreign merchandise transhipped under bond) of the UK for 6 recent years (in £1,000):

	Total imports	*Total exports*		*Total imports*	*Total exports*
1977	36,493,152	32,951,476	1980	51,650,267	49,510,791
1978	40,969,066	37,362,739	1981	51,163,579	50,995,080
1979	48,467,400	42,803,609	1982	56,940,267	55,538,408

The value of goods imported is generally taken to be that at the port and time of entry, including all incidental expenses (cost, insurance and freight) up to the landing on the quay. For goods consigned for sale, the market value in this country is required and recorded in the returns. For exports, the value at the port of shipment (including the charges of delivering the goods on board) is taken. Imports are entered as from the country whence the goods were consigned to the UK, which may, or may not, be the country whence they were last shipped. Exports are credited to the country of ultimate destination as declared by the exporters.

For details of imports and exports for 1980 and 1982, *see* pp. 1322–24.

Trade according to countries for 1980 and 1982 (in £1,000):

Countries	Imports of merchandise from 1980[1]	Imports of merchandise from 1982[1]	Exports of merchandise to 1980[1]	Exports of merchandise to 1982[1]
Foreign countries				
Europe and Overseas Possessions—				
Albania	107	45	1,478	4,453
Austria	307,267	404,318	279,681	251,032
Belgium and Luxembourg	2,596,962	2,861,809	2,624,108	2,298,118
Bulgaria	14,425	21,009	35,242	46,104
Czechoslovakia	87,812	82,007	81,026	70,105
Denmark and Faroe Islands	1,114,149	1,344,565	1,034,959	1,099,039
Finland	793,218	849,933	525,488	513,558
France	3,899,174	4,269,103	3,651,470	4,486,458
German Dem. Rep.	88,127	133,921	94,124	63,665
Germany (Fed. Rep. of)	5,700,861	7,414,073	5,113,032	5,414,733
Greece	142,456	151,688	224,619	255,281
Hungary	43,327	44,051	68,977	77,446
Iceland	82,042	72,721	47,223	102,714
Italy	2,311,071	2,745,094	1,899,181	2,022,711
Netherlands	3,406,928	4,474,663	3,845,412	4,653,416
Netherlands Antilles	36,243	76,421	33,375	59,359
Norway	1,441,418	2,023,441	791,530	924,651
Poland	194,523	151,737	296,254	133,340
Portugal, Azores and Madeira	335,112	379,949	389,849	430,684
Romania	64,795	51,515	98,914	115,244
Spain	804,232	956,935	708,998	870,416
Canary Islands	61,565	44,574	46,108	83,508
Sweden	1,475,506	1,673,165	1,623,511	1,935,264
Switzerland and Liechtenstein	2,614,690	1,669,922	3,076,337	1,196,203
Turkey	49,243	207,763	147,118	218,116
USSR	786,176	645,135	455,310	355,678
EEC	20,802,915	25,252,103	20,825,802	23,117,856
EFTA	7,049,252	7,073,449	6,733,619	5,354,105
Yugoslavia	56,802	52,115	190,503	158,881
Africa—				
Algeria	114,054	176,304	142,552	199,234
Angola	83,125	7,368	27,811	25,781
Burundi	1,881	8,737	583	1,522
Cameroon	9,798	9,108	17,470	22,462
Egypt	336,595	412,802	346,688	338,645
Ethiopia	10,281	10,833	20,962	27,584
Ivory Coast	53,563	56,097	27,916	28,238
Liberia	8,671	8,213	46,412	14,069
Libya	46,528	342,476	288,385	260,937
Mali	11,318	3,385	7,878	4,403
Mauritania	9,438	5,462	5,647	1,943
Morocco	62,582	60,219	69,223	95,487
Mozambique	11,416	10,611	11,345	14,473
Rwanda	4,666	510	1,245	2,079
Senegal	15,440	14,196	16,030	22,349
South Africa, Republic of	756,397	745,803	1,002,073	1,192,891
S.W. Africa/Namibia	18,898	45,413	2,726	3,973
Sudan	13,362	9,929	124,697	136,636
Tunisia	17,566	12,628	29,872	38,632
Zaïre	52,585	15,801	27,629	20,557
Asia—				
Afghánistán	20,174	20,855	6,818	9,344
Bahrain	25,063	35,459	115,569	152,272
Burma	5,379	5,342	20,494	44,242
China	153,433	193,231	169,500	103,051
Indonesia	56,971	91,704	112,170	212,066
Iran	107,176	225,971	393,335	333,715
Iraq	532,483	79,764	321,883	875,179
Israel	236,599	275,139	231,658	224,362
Japan	1,712,108	2,657,977	597,147	681,463
Jordan	8,152	17,487	100,318	295,274
Korea (South)	244,583	321,691	101,103	167,752
Kuwait	655,024	104,793	258,696	333,247

[1] Provisional figures.

Countries	Imports of merchandise from 1980[1]	1982[1]	Exports of merchandise to 1980[1]	1982[1]
Asia—(contd.)				
Lebanon	9,076	24,237	70,692	67,640
Pakistan	58,289	81,531	139,692	199,178
Philippines	99,018	127,061	88,998	97,908
Qatar	44,654	33,984	101,898	245,390
Saudi Arabia	1,927,583	1,447,775	1,050,145	1,361,665
Syria	12,241	25,644	81,584	89,535
Thailand	52,004	76,529	96,920	104,825
America—				
Argentina	114,286	58,728	172,830	37,349
Bolivia	33,179	20,899	8,684	4,943
Brazil	296,430	443,956	218,159	158,837
Chile	126,273	111,206	55,741	56,897
Colombia	34,289	34,502	41,920	50,328
Costa Rica	5,424	15,068	8,302	5,455
Cuba	26,208	17,688	35,272	64,835
Dominican Republic	4,788	5,752	11,514	10,161
Ecuador	8,844	9,288	30,930	60,792
El Salvador	2,889	2,017	4,603	5,244
Guatemala	23,657	13,476	13,835	8,127
Haiti	915	2,615	2,818	3,704
Honduras (not British)	3,687	4,693	11,835	4,659
Mexico	111,636	106,067	188,133	162,946
Nicaragua	1,510	3,282	2,478	4,940
Panama	3,941	9,521	24,032	83,250
Paraguay	1,279	2,790	13,384	16,915
Peru	77,487	92,120	46,541	39,370
Puerto Rico	33,002	33,445	16,970	25,735
Uruguay	16,884	23,107	26,619	13,926
USA	6,043,774	6,638,250	4,668,342	7,457,114
Venezuela	117,614	141,892	131,684	148,666
Total (including those not specified above)	44,145,486	49,263,388	40,547,007	45,697,731
Commonwealth countries:				
In Europe—				
Cyprus	128,386	89,908	153,754	111,882
Gibraltar	3,285	4,229	26,672	29,712
Malta	46,609	42,792	87,527	71,823
In Africa				
West Africa:				
Gambia	2,417	2,031	17,792	10,087
Ghana	104,545	78,438	88,511	66,709
Nigeria, Federation of	151,563	356,802	1,204,358	1,225,164
Sierra Leone	65,697	14,438	36,785	19,110
South Africa:				
Botswana	4,044	19,140	2,644	5,163
Lesotho	340	682	394	1,260
Malawi	45,651	42,478	25,749	20,893
Swaziland	30,438	40,049	691	7,654
Zambia	94,610	39,957	103,941	61,248
Zimbabwe	28,632	62,584	16,209	95,019
East Africa:				
Kenya	105,443	104,312	259,103	153,858
Mauritius	145,227	119,450	24,688	20,857
Tanzania	36,501	19,521	110,910	71,985
Uganda	30,735	23,107	33,526	31,272
Seychelles	601	696	9,772	10,086
St Helena	476	754	3,016	7,049
In Asia—				
Bangladesh	73,084	25,558	110,408	58,179
Hong Kong	850,340	872,545	559,420	732,489
India	315,858	379,169	529,007	805,321
Malaysia	187,050	185,239	223,516	210,805
Singapore	535,915	245,453	328,112	406,172
Sri Lanka	53,681	42,000	76,831	60,211

[1] Provisional figures.

Countries	Imports of merchandise from 1980[1]	1982[1]	Exports of merchandise to 1980[1]	1982[1]
In Oceania—				
Australia	484,112	493,196	815,652	1,043,615
Fiji Islands	36,759	39,826	12,786	9,088
Nauru	70	32	821	1,843
New Zealand	414,630	539,137	250,413	323,201
Papua New Guinea	22,861	28,031	10,978	15,911
Western Samoa	572	107	710	285
In America—				
Bahamas	59,123	18,273	77,366	26,364
Barbados	7,630	14,887	29,860	26,886
Belize	13,168	13,326	11,824	10,455
Bermuda	2,900	5,128	24,499	18,222
Canada	1,412,156	1,439,619	758,367	851,703
Falkland Islands	2,846	2,568	2,083	4,150
Guyana	47,143	50,495	30,191	13,145
Jamaica	95,578	92,760	33,122	56,025
Leeward Islands	4,533	12,094	14,915	18,388
Trinidad and Tobago	35,088	65,154	120,270	158,436
Windward Islands	25,704	37,797	21,344	16,961
Total, Commonwealth countries (including those not specified above)	5,720,452	5,676,846	6,303,710	6,950,180
Ireland	1,784,329	2,000,033	2,660,074	2,890,497
Grand Total	51,650,267	56,940,267	49,510,791	55,538,408

[1] Provisional figures.

Imports and exports for 1980 and 1982 (Great Britain and Northern Ireland) (in £1,000):

Import values c.i.f. Export values f.o.b.	Total imports 1980[1]	1982[1]	Domestic exports 1980[1]	1982[1]
0. *Food and Live Animals*				
Live animals (excluding zoo animals, dogs and cats)	105,324	133,113	139,971	179,076
Meat and meat preparations	1,225,862	1,370,861	327,180	346,028
Dairy products and eggs	500,211	567,914	298,477	318,557
Fish and fish preparations	349,253	404,249	154,519	162,303
Cereals and cereal preparations	604,031	549,897	456,213	773,863
Fruit and vegetables	1,240,114	1,608,300	153,195	153,757
Sugar, sugar preparations, honey	403,012	429,548	112,220	121,059
Coffee, tea, cocoa, spices	677,035	722,413	262,576	249,880
Feeding stuff for animals	249,231	446,507	63,655	68,244
Miscellaneous food preparations	148,775	181,130	94,608	123,798
Total of Section 0	5,502,849	6,413,933	2,062,613	2,496,565
1. *Beverages and Tobacco*				
Beverages	439,929	517,531	898,035	1,059,266
Tobacco and tobacco manufactures	235,198	319,226	307,966	391,426
Total of Section 1	675,127	836,757	1,206,001	1,450,692
2. *Crude Materials, Inedible, except Fuels*				
Hides, skins and furskins, undressed	226,970	189,451	189,920	180,479
Oil seeds, oil nuts and oil kernels	265,149	259,586	2,888	7,938
Crude rubber (including synthetic and reclaimed)	182,699	182,907	75,645	122,786
Wood and cork	684,077	673,469	16,236	28,590
Pulp and waste paper	398,944	412,465	122,796	11,602
Textile fibres and their waste	376,199	410,704	313,077	315,042
Crude fertilizers and crude minerals (excluding fuels)	302,892	263,478	235,288	224,582

[1] Provisional figures.

Import values c.i.f. *Export values f.o.b.*	*Total imports* 1980[1]	1982[1]	*Domestic exports* 1980[1]	1982[1]
2. *Crude Materials, Inedible, except Fuels*—Contd.				
Metalliferous ores and metal scrap	968,082	977,530	471,702	346,594
Crude animal and vegetable materials, not elsewhere specified	184,789	243,320	48,613	57,341
Total of Section 2	3,589,801	3,612,910	1,376,165	1,294,953
3. *Mineral Fuels, Lubricants and Related Materials*				
Coal, coke and briquettes	238,944	224,382	180,024	330,339
Petroleum and petroleum products	6,101,877	6,274,079	6,121,316	10,641,634
Gas, natural and manufactured; electric energy	566,943	902,722	115,920	221,213
Total of Section 3	6,907,764	7,401,183	6,417,260	11,193,187
4. *Animal and Vegetable Oils and Fats*	260,418	316,958	71,073	46,467
5. *Chemicals*				
Chemical elements and compounds	1,330,953	1,711,635	1,918,565	2,287,128
Dyeing, tanning and colouring materials	145,883	197,962	433,062	464,121
Medicinal and pharmaceutical products	222,488	374,592	745,415	977,966
Essential oils and perfume; toilet and cleansing preparations	174,580	242,219	464,703	523,999
Fertilizers, manufactured	90,048	127,027	52,267	48,766
Plastic materials	763,883	1,017,735	874,939	875,332
Total[2] of Section 5	3,148,323	4,181,221	5,290,010	6,119,360
6. *Manufactured Goods Classified Chiefly by Material*				
Leather and dressed furs	137,257	154,552	212,275	202,149
Rubber	264,490	326,180	447,293	417,855
Wood and cork (excluding furniture)	369,125	436,614	84,221	83,235
Paper, paperboard	1,287,926	1,678,457	475,033	502,867
Textile yarn, fabrics	1,544,866	1,929,693	1,363,425	1,190,783
Non-metallic mineral manufactures	3,422,410	1,520,408	3,550,426	1,611,113
Iron and steel	1,448,892	1,369,214	984,234	1,293,521
Non-ferrous metals	2,487,368	1,495,679	1,759,757	1,244,721
Manufactures of metal, not elsewhere specified	866,360	950,357	1,309,570	1,394,900
Total of Section 6	11,828,693	9,861,155	10,186,233	7,941,146
7. *Machinery and Transport Equipment*				
Boilers, engines, motors and power-units	962,701	1,482,724	2,233,023	2,809,218
Agricultural and Industrial machinery	3,029,493	3,499,368	5,379,910	5,537,489
Office machinery	1,396,221	2,122,756	1,347,247	1,599,470
Electrical machinery, apparatus, not elsewhere specified	2,344,353	3,766,589	2,512,833	3,010,643
Transport equipment	5,317,982	5,486,084	5,535,909	5,141,026
Total of Section 7	12,763,538	16,357,521	17,008,922	18,097,846

[1] Provisional figures. [2] Includes items not specified here.

Import values c.i.f. Export values f.o.b.	Total imports 1980[1]	1982[1]	Domestic exports 1980[1]	1982[1]
8. *Miscellaneous Manufactured Articles*				
Sanitary, plumbing, heating and lighting fixtures	78,432	103,578	109,071	106,934
Furniture	283,436	400,065	239,197	240,898
Travel goods, handbags and similar articles	95,049	108,580	19,488	19,099
Clothing	1,231,122	1,500,755	807,558	840,351
Footwear	354,653	468,490	130,389	115,259
Scientific instruments; watches and clocks	1,400,834	1,815,226	1,468,193	1,812,333
Miscellaneous manufactured articles, not elsewhere specified	1,733,441	2,286,557	1,730,549	2,022,945
Total of Section 8	5,176,967	6,683,253	4,504,446	5,157,818
9. *Commodities and Transactions not Classified According to Kind*				
Post parcels	171,117	207,668	550,460	612,854
Special transactions	275,569	530,844	251,946	336,031
Total[2] of Section 9	1,509,664	1,275,376	1,388,069	1,740,375
Total[2] of all classes	51,650,267	56,940,267	49,510,791	55,538,408

[1] Provisional figures. [2] Includes items not specified here.

Tourism. There were an estimated 11·5m. overseas visitors in 1981. Foreign exchange from tourism was £3,850m. including £850m. from fares to British air and shipping lines.

COMMUNICATIONS

Roads. Central government responsibility for highways in England rests with the Secretary of State for Transport. His responsibilities are administered by the Department of Transport through a number of Directorates at Headquarters together with 9 Regional Offices. For Welsh and Scottish roads central government responsibility rests with the Secretaries of State for Wales and Scotland respectively.

The Secretary of State is responsible for all trunk roads. Under the local government system introduced in 1974, the responsible authorities for principal roads are the County Councils. District Councils may claim maintenance powers for urban roads which are neither trunk roads nor classified roads. In London responsibility is shared between the Greater London Council and the London Boroughs.

The Secretary of State has powers to provide roads designed for limited classes of motor traffic, and to confirm schemes for the provision of such special roads by local authorities. The former have the status of trunk roads; the latter principal roads. They are generally referred to as motorways. About 1,520 miles of motorways in England were open to traffic by Sept. 1981 and some 150 miles are under construction or in preparation.

The design and supervision of the construction of major trunk roads is carried out by firms of consulting engineers and by local authorities which act as the Secretary of State's agents. The Regional Offices ensure that schemes progress in accordance with the Secretary of State's statutory and financial responsibilities.Regional Controllers (Roads and Transportation) are responsible for smaller trunk road schemes and for the maintenance of all trunk roads, including motorways. Local authorities can act as the Secretary of State's agents for construction and maintenance. The work is carried out by them or by contractors on their behalf and the cost borne by Central Government.

Aid to local authorities' transport expenditure is now given through Rate Support Grant and through Transport Supplementary Grant which is paid to County Councils whose expenditure for the year, as accepted by the Secretary of State, exceeds the level determined by a formula prescribed in the Rate Support Grant

Report.

Public highways in Great Britain at 1 April 1981, excluding mileages of unsurfaced roads (green lanes), had a total length of 341,987 miles (England, 260,149 miles; Wales, 31,870; Scotland, 49,969). There were 15,154 miles of all-purpose trunk roads, 2,833 of motorways (both trunk and principal), 34,544 were principal roads and 292,289 were other roads.

At 1 April 1974 there were about 6,000 miles of unsurfaced roads (green lanes) in England and 2,000 in Wales.

Motor vehicles for which licences were current under the Vehicles (Excise) Act, 1971, numbered, at 31 Dec. 1981, 19·35m., including 15·56m. private cars and private vans, 1·37m. mopeds, scooters and motor cycles, 110,000 public transport vehicles (including taxis) and 1·73m. goods vehicles.

New vehicle registrations in 1981 numbered 2·03m.

Road casualties in Great Britain numbered in 1981, 325,000 including 5,846 killed; in 1980, 329,000 including 6,010 killed.

Railways. The nationalized railway system, known as 'British Rail', together with British Transport Hotels Ltd, Travellers-Fare, British Rail Engineering Ltd, British Rail Investments Ltd, Freightliners Ltd, Transportation Systems and Market Research Ltd (Transmark), Sealink UK Ltd and the British Rail Property Board are owned and managed by a public authority, the British Railways Board. The Board is required to direct its affairs in such a way as to ensure that standards of public service and safety are maintained while at the same time keeping within specified financial constraints.

The role of the British Railways Board is to determine policies and objectives, establish the organization to carry them out, monitor performance and take major decisions.

The management of the railways, which forms the bulk of the Board's activity, is the responsibility of the Chief Executive (Railways). In this role he establishes plans and budgets for the achievement of objectives set by the Board, monitors and achieves results against those plans and budgets and directs the organization and deployment of manpower resources. He is assisted by other Board Members with responsibility for Engineering and Research, Finance and Planning, Marketing, Operating and Productivity, and Personnel.

He also directs the General Managers of the 5 operating Regions of the railways. The responsibilities of these managers are for the day-to-day operation of the passenger and freight railway systems throughout the country.

The management of each subsidiary activity is the responsibility of each Managing Director, directed by a Subsidiary Board.

The Transport Act, 1968, reduced the railways commencing debt from £1,562m. to £300m. The Act also enabled the Secretary of State for the Environment to make grants for the maintenance of unremunerative passenger services and, additionally, to make grants, until 1973, towards the cost of surplus track and signalling equipment. The Railways Act, 1974, introduced a new system of financial support in accordance with EEC Regulations 1191/69 and 1192/69. On 1 Jan. 1975, the Board's capital debt was reduced to £250m. and their borrowing limit, including commencing debt, was increased to £600m. extendable to £900m. The power to make grants for unremunerative passenger services was withdrawn. The Secretary of State is authorized to impose general obligations on the Board in respect of passenger services and is empowered to compensate the Board for providing adequate transport services. Aggregate compensation is limited to £900m., extendable to £1,500m. subject to Parliamentary approval.

In 1981 the total freight traffic amounted to 155·1m. tonnes, comprising coal and coke 95·2m. tonnes, iron and steel 18·2m. tonnes and other freight, excluding carryings for National Carriers Ltd, for which tonnage figures are not available, 41·8m. tonnes. Passenger journeys amounted to 718·5m. Rolling stock (standard gauge) at the end of 1980 included 3,131 locomotives (including 181 high speed power units), 15,472 passenger-carrying vehicles (including Pullman carriages), 2,796 luggage and parcel vans and 87,955 freight vehicles. At the end of the year 10,831 (standard gauge) route-miles were open to traffic.

The London Transport Executive is the authority responsible for the operation of the capital's Underground and bus services. Overall policy and financial control is exercised by the Greater London Council. In Jan. 1982, London Transport had 241 route miles of railway open for traffic and also operated over 19 miles of track owned by British Rail. Rolling stock owned: Underground, 4,267 (2,835 motor cars, 1,432 trailer cars); buses, 6,378. Total number of miles run in passenger service (1981) was 383m. miles. The number of passengers carried in 1981 was: Underground 541m.; buses 1,080m. Average takings per passenger journey (1981) were: Underground 46·4p; buses 19·1p.

Gross receipts in 1980 for these Boards were: British Railways Board, from 1975 the Railways Act 1974 introduced, *inter alia*, new arrangements for the financial support of the railway passenger system and provided for the reconstruction of the finances of the Board, (1981), £1,664·8m.[1]; London Transport Executive, (1981), £463·3m.[1]; British Transport Docks Board, £131·2m.; National Bus Company, £4,603m.[1]; National Freight Corporation, £417m., and British Waterways Board, £13·1m.[1].

[1] Excludes support grants.

Railway Finances. [Serpell Report] HMSO, London, 1983

Aviation. The British Airways Board was set up by the Civil Aviation Act 1971, part of which was later consolidated within The British Airways Board Act 1977, to incorporate the 2 state-owned airlines (BOAC and BEA) as the British Airways divisions of a larger group to be known as the British Airways Group.

The British Overseas Airways Corporation (BOAC) was set up under the British Overseas Airways Act 1939 and British European Airways (BEA) was established under the Civil Aviation Act 1946. In addition to the nationalized corporation, there are about 20 independent air transport operators.

British Airways is engaged on long-haul operations. Its scheduled services link Britain with Europe, the Middle East, the Far East, Australasia, Africa and North America. It co-operates closely with airlines of several other Commonwealth countries.British Airways also operates a network of short-haul services to places in Britain, Europe, North Africa and the Middle East.

The 2 State Corporations had a statutory monopoly up to 1961, although there was an arrangement by which independent operators could provide services as private companies associated with the Corporations. There has been a significant expansion by independent operators who have carried increasing numbers of passengers and volumes of freight on a network of scheduled and non-scheduled domestic and international services, in particular British Caledonian Airways has emerged as the principal independent scheduled airline.

British Airways carried 15·2m. passengers in 1981–82. In March 1982 it had a fleet of 198 aircraft (including 36 helicopters) and 43,221 personnel were employed.

Following the Civil Aviation Act 1971, the Civil Aviation Authority was established as an independent public body responsible for the economic and safety regulation of British civil aviation. It took over the resposibilities of the former Air Transport Licensing Board and Air Registration Board, and also runs the National Air Traffic Services in conjunction with the Ministry of Defence.

In addition to the public transport operators there are a number of companies engaged in miscellaneous aviation activities such as crop-spraying, aerial survey and photography, and flying instruction.

The operating and traffic statistics of the UK airlines on scheduled services during the calendar year 1981 (and 1980) are as follows: Aircraft km flown, 360m. (384m.); revenue passengers carried, 21·4m. (22.2m.); cargo (freight and mail) carried 294,866 (294,692) tonnes.

Traffic between the UK airports and places abroad in 1981 (and 1980) on all services included 495,759 (506,861) air transport aircraft movements.

There were 7,265 civil aircraft registered in the UK at 15 Oct. 1982.

Shipping. The UK flag merchant fleet in July 1982 totalled 35·2m. DWT (dry cargo, 14·3m. DWT; tankers 20·9m. DWT) representing 5·1% of the world fleet. The total number of UK flag ships was 1,425. The number of UK nationality seafarers was about 54,000 as at 30 Nov. 1982.

Capital investment in new tonnage and facilities by British shipping companies 1970–81 (inclusive) was over £5,300m. In 1981 capital expenditure was an estimated £354m. The average age of UK owned and registered tonnage in mid-1980 was 8 years.

Total gross earnings by UK owned and registered ships in 1981 amounted to £2,778m. The net contribution to UK balance of payments was £1,123m. and, in addition, there were gross import savings of £449m.

On 30 Nov. 1982, 72 UK flag ships (4·6m. DWT) were laid up out of a world total of 1,489 ships (81·5m. DWT).

GCBS Facts and Figures 1980. 1980
Committee of Inquiry into Shipping. Cmnd 4337. HMSO, 1970
Bird, J., *The Major Seaports of the United Kingdom.* London, 1963
Sturmey, S. G., *British Shipping and World Competition.* London, 1962

Inland Waterways. There are approximately 2,500 miles of navigable canals and locked river navigations in Great Britain. Of these, the British Waterways Board is responsible for some 300 miles of commercial waterways (maintained for freight traffic) and some 1,100 miles of cruising waterways (maintained for pleasure cruising, fishing and amenity). The Board is also responsible for a further 600 miles of canals, some of which are no longer navigable and whose future is being considered in conjunction with local authorities; a number of these lengths have been restored for cruising or as local amenities. The Board's gross receipts for the year 1981 were £15·8m. The total traffic on their waterways was 4.6m. tonnes.

The most important of the river navigations and canals under other authorities include the rivers Thames, Great Ouse, Nene and Yorkshire Ouse, the Norfolk Broads and the Manchester Ship Canal.

Manchester, one of the leading ports in the UK, was opened to maritime traffic in 1894 by the construction of the Manchester Ship Canal, which is 35¼ miles in length and owned and operated by the Manchester Ship Canal Company. The entrance lock is 80 ft (24·38 metres) wide and the maximum width of other locks within the canal is 65 ft (19·81 metres). Ships up to 28 ft 10 in. (8·78 metres) fresh-water draught can navigate to Ince Oil Berth; ships up to 24 ft (7·31 metres) draught can navigate to Manchester docks but within these docks draught is limited to 22 ft (6·70 metres).

The Port of Manchester includes the Queen Elizabeth II Oil Dock at Eastham (separate entrance lock 100 ft wide), the oil docks at Stanlow and a considerable number of public and private wharves and installations along the canal, as well as the container terminals at Manchester and Ellesmere Port. Total sea-borne and barge traffic in 1982 amounted to 12·3m. tonnes; operating revenue, £23·9m.; operating deficit, £146,000. The total issued capital at 31 Dec. 1980 was £19·4m.

Edwards, L. A., *Inland Waterways of Great Britain and Northern Ireland.* 5th ed. St. Ives, 1972
Farnie, D. A., *The Manchester Ship Canal and the Rise of the Port of Manchester.* Manchester Univ. Press, 1980
Hadfield, C., *British Canals.* 6th ed. Newton Abbot, 1979
McKnight, H., *The Shell Book of Inland Waterways.* Newton Abbot, 1975
Paget-Tomlinson, E. W., *Complete Book of Canal and River Navigations.* Albrighton, 1978

Posts and Telecommunications. In Oct. 1981 the Post Office ceased to control telecommunications services, which became the responsibility of a separate corporation, British Telecom. The Post Office provides: Royal Mail general collection and delivery services, handling more than 37m. letters and parcels a day; Royal Mail Special Services including guaranteed delivery to any UK address overnight (Datapost), locally and to other major towns and cities on the same day (Expresspost) and by facsimile transmission to many UK and overseas centres; International Datapost offers guaranteed swift delivery to 28 countries; postal, National Girobank and many agency services on behalf of government departments at 22,000 post office counters; full banking facilities through National Girobank, a separately managed business within the Corporation. Number of post offices at 31 March 1982 was 22,405; number of posting boxes including those at post offices, over 100,000; staff employed, 178,000 (including 20,800 sub-postmasters employed on an agency basis).

	1978–79 (1m.)	*1979–80 (1m.)*	*1980–81 (1m.)*	*1981–82 (1m.)*
Correspondence (incl. registered items) posted	9,965	10,208	9,969	9,883
Parcels handled	172	180	172	183

Income (1981-82) 2,438m. Profit, £92m.

On 31 March 1982 there were 6,319 local exchanges, 281 automanual centres, 120 main network switching centres, 76,884 call offices, 18,963,000 exchange connections and 28,454,000 telephone stations. There were 92,378 telex exchange connections and 93,252 datel modems. During the year 17,360m. local telephone calls, 3,446m. trunk calls and 287m. international calls were made.

2,276m. inland telegrams and 9,245m. international telegrams were sent.

95,545m. inland telex calls were made and 447,400m. international telex minutes recorded.

Broadcasting. Radio and television services are provided by the BBC and by the Independent Broadcasting Authority and its programme contractors. The BBC, constituted by Royal Charter until 31 Dec. 1996, has responsibility for providing domestic and external broadcast services, the former financed from the television licence revenue, the latter by Government grant. The domestic services include 2 national television services, 4 national radio network services and an expanding local radio service.

The IBA constituted until 31 Dec. 1996 by the Broadcasting Act 1981 provides an independent television service on a regional basis, with programmes provided by its programme contractors. The 1981 Act provided for the establishment of the fourth television channel and of the Welsh Fourth Channel Authority (WFCA) which provides a Welsh service on that channel in Wales; they started broadcasting in Nov. 1982. The IBA also provides independent local radio services. All these services are financed by the sale of broadcast advertising time.

The BBC's domestic radio services are available on LF, MF and VHF; those of the IBA on MF and VHF. The television services of the 2 authorities BBC1, BBC2, ITV, and Channel 4 are broadcast at UHF in 625-line definition and in colour.

The broadcasting authorities, whose governing bodies are appointed (by HM the Queen in the case of the BBC and by the Home Secretary in the case of the IBA and WFCA) as trustees for the public interest in broadcasting, are independent of government in matters of programme content and are publicly accountable to Parliament for the discharge of their responsibilities.

In 1981 the Broadcasting Complaints Commission was set up to consider and adjudicate upon complaints of unfair or unjust treatment in broadcast programmes or of unwarranted infringement of privacy in or in the making of programmes. The number of broadcast receiving licences in force on 30 Nov. 1982 was 18·41m., including 14·41m. for colour.

25 Years of ITV. London, 1980

Cinemas. In 1983 there were 1,500 cinemas and in 1979 there were 112m. admissions with box office takings of £127m.

Newspapers. In 1978 there were 9 national dailies with a circulation of over 13m.

Benn's Press Directory. Tunbridge Wells, Annual

JUSTICE RELIGION, EDUCATION AND WELFARE

Justice. *England and Wales.* The legal system of England and Wales, divided into civil and criminal courts has at the head of the superior courts, as the ultimate court of appeal, the House of Lords, which hears each year a number of appeals in civil matters, including a certain number from Scotland and Northern Ireland, as well as some appeals in criminal cases. In order that civil cases may go from the Court of Appeal to the House of Lords, it is necessary to obtain the leave of either the Court of Appeal or the House itself, although in certain cases an appeal may lie direct to the House of Lords from the decision of the High Court. An appeal can be brought from a decision of the Court of Appeal or the Divisional Court of the Queen's Bench Division of the High Court in a criminal case provided that the Court is satisfied that a point of law 'of general public importance' is involved, and either the Court or the House of Lords is of the opinion that it is desirable in the public interest that a further appeal should be brought. As a judicial body, the House of Lords consists of the Lord Chancellor, the Lords of Appeal in Ordinary, commonly called Law Lords, and such other members of the House as hold or have held high judicial office. The final court of appeal for certain of the Commonwealth countries is the Judicial Committee of the Privy Council which, in addition to Privy Counsellors who are or have held high judicial office in the UK, includes others who are or have been Chief Justices or Judges of the Superior Courts of Commonwealth countries.

Civil Law. The main courts of original civil jurisdiction are the county courts for less important cases, and the High Court for the more important ones.

There are about 300 county courts located throughout the country, grouped in districts, and each presided over by a circuit judge. They have a general jurisdiction to determine all actions founded on contract or tort involving sums of not more than £5,000 and can also deal with other classes of use, such as landlord and tenant, probate, equity and admiralty, up to certain limits. Certain matters, such as actions of libel and slander, are entirely reserved for the High Court. In addition, certain designated county courts have jurisdiction in matrimonial proceedings. Divorce proceedings must now commence in these courts and, subject to being transferred to the High Court upon becoming defended, are determined in the County Court.

The High Court has both appellate and original jurisdiction, covering virtually all civil causes not determined in the county court. The judges of the High Court are attached to one of its 3 divisions: Chancery; Queen's Bench; and Family; each with its separate field of jurisdiction. There are 76 such judges, called puisne judges. For the hearing of cases at first instance, the High Court judges sit singly. Appellate jurisdiction is usually exercised by Divisional Courts consisting of 2 (sometimes 3) judges, though in certain circumstances a judge sitting alone may hear the appeal.

The Restrictive Practices Court was set up in 1956 under the Restrictive Trade Practices Act, and is responsible for deciding whether a restrictive trade agreement is in the public interest. It is presided over by a High Court judge, but laymen sit on the bench also. Another specialist court is the Employment Appeal Tribunal, with similar composition, which hears appeals in employment cases from lower tribunals.

The Court of Appeal (Civil Division) hears appeals in civil actions from the High Court and County Courts and certain special courts such as the Restrictive Practices Court and the Employment Appeal Tribunal. Its President is the Master of the Rolls, aided by 18 Lords Justices of Appeal sitting in 6 or 7 divisions of 2 or 3 judges each.

Civil proceedings are instituted by the aggrieved person, but, as they are a private matter, they are frequently settled by the parties to a dispute through their lawyers before the matter actually comes to court. In some cases, at the instance of either party, a jury may sit to decide questions of fact and award of damages.

Criminal Law. At the base of the system of criminal courts are the lay justices who try the great proportion of minor offenders (over 98% of all criminal cases) as well as undertaking a small proportion of civil work. Magistrates' courts are comprised of 3 lay justices who are unpaid and need not possess legal qualifications (though they undergo a course of training), though they do have the assistance on points of law of a professional clerk to justices. In central London and large cities there exist stipendiary magistrates, paid for their duties. These are professional lawyers and usually sit alone. Exercising summary jurisdiction in petty sessions, justices have power to pass sentences of imprisonment up to, in general, 6 months, and to impose fines up to, in general, £1,000. One of their functions is to examine persons charged with indictable offences and to determine whether they should be committed for trial at the Crown Court. Justices deal each year with about 2m. cases, including thefts, assaults, road traffic infringements, drug abuse, breaches of licensing laws, etc. There are some 22,286 justices who are appointed to the Commission of the Peace by the Lord Chancellor, and some 3,648 justices appointed by the Chancellor of the Duchy of Lancaster; each assisted by advisory committees. Women are eligible to be appointed justices, and the number on the Commission of the Peace is 10,328.

Specially qualified justices sit in juvenile courts to deal with cases involving persons under 17 years of age charged with criminal offences (other than homicide and other grave offences) or brought before the court as being in need of care or control. These courts normally sit with 3 justices, including 1 woman, and are accommodated separately from other courts.

Specially qualified justices also sit in the domestic courts to deal with matrimonial proceedings, custody, guardianship and maintenance of children, affiliation and adoption. These courts normally sit with 3 justices including 1 woman.

Above the magistrates' courts is the Crown Court. This was set up by the Courts Act 1971 to replace quarter sessions and assizes. Unlike quarter sessions and assizes, which were individual courts, the Crown Court is a single court which is capable of sitting anywhere in England and Wales. It has power to deal with all trials on indictment and has inherited the jurisdiction of quarter sessions to hear appeals, proceedings on committal of persons for sentence, and certain original proceedings on civil matters under individual statutes.

The jurisdiction of the Crown Court is exercisable by a High Court judge, a Circuit judge or a Recorder (who is a part-time judge) sitting alone, or, in specified circumstances, with justices of the peace. The Lord Chief Justice has given directions as to the types of case to be allocated to High Court judges (the more serious cases) and to Circuit judges or Recorders respectively.

Appeals from magistrates' courts go either to a Divisional Court of the High Court (when a point of law alone is involved) or to the Crown Court where there is a complete re-hearing.Appeals from the Crown Court in cases tried on indictment lie to the Court of Appeal (Criminal Division). Appeals on questions of law go by right, and appeals on other matters by leave. The Lord Chief Justice or a Lord Justice sits with judges of the High Court to constitute this court.

There remains as a last resort the invocation of the royal prerogative exercised on the advice of the Home Secretary. In 1965 the death penalty was abolished for murder.

All contested criminal trials, except those which come before the magistrates' courts, are tried by a judge and a jury consisting of 12 members. The defence may object, without showing cause, to up to 3 jurors. The prosecution may ask that any number may 'stand by' until the jury panel is exhausted, and only then need to show cause. When these peremptory challenges have been exhausted further challenges may only be made for cause and this rarely happens. The jury decides whether the accused is guilty or not. The judge is responsible for summing up on the facts and explaining the law; he sentences convicted offenders. If, after at least 2 hours of deliberation, a jury is unable to reach a unanimous verdict it may, provided that in a full jury of 12 at least 10 of its members are agreed, bring in a majority verdict. The failure of a jury to agree on a unanimous verdict or to bring in a majority verdict involves the retrial of the case before a new jury.

The Employment Appeal Tribunal. The Employment Appeal Tribunal which is a superior Court of Record with the like powers, rights, privileges and authority of the High Court, was set up in 1976 to hear appeals on questions of fact and law against decisions of industrial tribunals and of the Certification Officer. The appeals are heard by a High Court Judge sitting with 2 members (in exceptional cases 4) appointed for their special knowledge or experience of industrial relations either on the employer or the trade union side, with always an equal number on each side. Industrial tribunals are responsible for deciding questions under Employment Protection (Consolidation) Act, 1978, Equal Pay Act, 1970, Sex Discrimination Act 1975, Employment Protection Act 1975, Employment Act 1980,

Race Relations Act, 1976, and Employment Acts 1980 and 1982. The great bulk of their work is concerned with the problems which can arise between employees and their employers. The Certification Officer is responsible for deciding questions under the Trade Union Act 1913, the Trade Union (Amalgamations, etc.) Act 1964, the Trade Union and Labour Relations Act 1974 and the Employment Protection Act 1975.

Military Courts. Offences by persons subject to service law against the system of military law created under the powers of the Army Act, Air Force Act or Naval Discipline Act are dealt with either summarily or by courts-martial. Petitions may be made to the Defence Council. Subsequent appeals lie to a Courts-Martial Appeals Court, and from that court an appeal may lie to the House of Lords.

The Personnel of the Law. All judicial officers except the Lord Chancellor (who is a member of the Cabinet) are independent of Parliament and the Executive. They are all appointed by the Crown on the advice of the Prime Minister or the Lord Chancellor and hold office until retiring age. The legal profession is divided; barristers, who advise on legal problems and conduct cases in court, usually act for the public only through solicitors, who deal directly with the legal business brought to them by the public. Most judicial appointments are made from barristers of long standing, though solicitors are eligible for appointment as Recorders, who may, after 3 years, be appointed Circuit Judges.

There are 2 kinds of civil legal aid. Firstly there is legal advice and assistance, otherwise known as the 'Green Form' scheme. This includes advice and help on anything that is normally regarded as being within a solicitor's practice but except in rare circumstances it does not cover representation. However, since May 1980, assistance by way of representation has been available for many civil proceedings in magistrates' courts. Secondly, there is legal aid for civil court proceedings which covers all the work up to and including the court proceedings and representation. Under the provisions of the Legal Aid Act 1974, aid is available to those of low or moderate means either free or subject to a contribution, depending on means. In 1981–82 there were over 649,000 applications for advice and assistance under the Legal Advice and Assistance Scheme over 168,000 legal aid certificates were issued. The cost of legal aid in civil cases is met from (*a*) contributions from assisted persons; (*b*) the operation of the statutory charge which gives the Law Society a first charge on money or property recovered or preserved for an assisted person to the extent of that person's liability for his own costs; (*c*) costs recovered from opposing parties and (*d*) a grant from the Exchequer. The net cost of civil legal aid to the state in the year 1981–82 amounted to £55·8m. and the cost of the legal advice and assistance scheme was £31·6m. of which £7·1m. was accounted for by assistance by way of representation.

Under Part II of the Legal Aid Act 1974 a court dealing with criminal proceedings may order legal aid to be given if it considers it is desirable in the interests of justice and if it also considers that the defendant (or appellant) requires financial assistance in meeting the costs he may incur. The interests of justice are not statutorily defined but may include, for example, situations where the defendant is in real danger of going to prison or losing his job, where substantial questions of law are to be argued or where the defendant is unable to follow the proceedings and explain his case due to inadequate knowledge of English, mental illness or other mental or physical disability. Legal aid must be granted, subject to means, in the following circumstances: where a person is committed for trial on a charge of murder, where the prosecutor appeals or applies for leave to appeal from the criminal division of the Court of Appeal or the Courts-Martial Appeal Court to the House of Lords, and in certain circumstances where the court is considering depriving a defendant of his liberty.

The costs of legal aid in criminal proceedings are paid by the central government, but courts have power to require legally aided persons to contribute towards the cost of legal aid given to them. The net cost of legal aid in criminal proceedings in the year 1981–82 was £95m., £48·1m. of this was for legal aid in the higher courts which is paid for out of the Lord Chancellor's vote and £46·8 for legal aid in the magistrates' courts which is paid from the legal aid fund.

Under the Parliamentary Commissioner Act, passed 22 March 1967, M.P.s may refer to the Parliamentary Commissioner complaints received from the public regarding improper or inequitable administration in most spheres of central government affairs. Generally, other available remedies (such as legal action) must be exhausted before a complaint can be investigated. If a complaint is found to require a remedy the Parliamentary Commissioner makes a report to Parliament.

Commissions for Local Administration in England and Wales were set up under the Local Government Act 1974. The Commissioners carry out similar functions in relation to local government bodies to those the Parliamentary Commissioner discharges with regard to maladministration in central government.

Police. The authorized establishment of the police force in England and Wales in Dec. 1982 was 121,480: the actual strength was 109,936 men and 11,015 women. In addition there were 15,160 special constables (including 3,228 women). Total police net expenditure (estimated) in England and Wales for 1980–81 was £1,805·4m.

Blom-Cooper, L., and Drewry, G., *Final Appeal: A Study of the House of Lords in its Judicial Capacity.* OUP, 1972

Critchley, T. A., *A History of Police in England and Wales.* Rev. ed. London, 1978

SCOTLAND. The High Court of Justiciary is the supreme criminal court in Scotland and has jurisdiction in all cases of crime committed in any part of Scotland, unless expressly excluded by statute. It consists of the Lord Justice-General, the Lord Justice-Clerk and 19 other judges, who are the same judges as of the Court of Session, the Scottish supreme civil court. The Court, which is presided over by the Lord Justice-General, whom failing, the Lord Justice-Clerk, exercises an appellate jurisdiction as well as one of first instance, sits as business requires in Edinburgh both as a Court of Appeal (the *quorum* being 3 judges) and as a court of first instance and on circuit as a court of first instance. The decisions of the Court in either case are not subject to review by the House of Lords. One judge sitting with a jury of 15 persons can, and usually does, try cases, but 2 or more (with a jury) may do so in important or complex cases. It has a privative jurisdiction over cases of treason, murder, rape, deforcement of messengers and breach of duty by magistrates. It also, in practice, is the only court which tries cases of incest, sodomy and other serious or aggravated crimes against person or property and generally those cases in which a sentence greater than imprisonment for 2 years may be imposed either under statute or common law. Moreover, the Court has inherent power to try and to punish all acts which are plainly criminal though previously unknown and not dealt with by any statute.

The appellate jurisdiction of the High Court of Justiciary extends to all cases tried on indictment, whether in the High Court or the Sheriff Court, and persons so convicted may appeal to the Court against conviction or sentence or both except that there is no appeal against any sentence fixed by law. By such an appeal, a person may bring under review of the High Court of Justiciary any alleged miscarriage of justice including any alleged miscarriage of justice on the basis of the existence and significance of additional evidence which was not heard at the trial and which was not available and could not reasonably have been made available at the trial. It is also a court of review from courts of summary criminal jurisdiction, and on the final determination of any summary prosecution either party may appeal to the Court by way of stated case on questions of law, procedure, etc., but not on questions of fact, except in relation to a miscarriage of justice alleged by the person accused on the basis of the existence and significance of additional evidence which was not heard at the trial and which was not available and could not reasonably have been made available at the trial. A further or complementary form of process of review which can be resorted to by convicted persons in these courts is by Bill of Suspension (and Liberation), but it is of strictly limited application. A prosecutor in cases tried on indictment or under summary criminal procedure may also bring under review a decision in law, prior to final judgment of the case, by way of Bill of Advocation. The Court also hears appeals under the Courts-Martial (Appeals) Act 1951.

The Sheriff Court has an inherent universal criminal jurisdiction (as well as an extensive civil one) limited in general to crimes and offences committed within a sheriffdom (a specifically defined region), which has, however, been curtailed by statute or practice under which the High Court of Justiciary has exclusive jurisdiction in relation to the crimes above-mentioned. This Court is presided over by a Sheriff-Principal or Sheriff, and when trying cases on indictment sits with a jury of 15 persons. His power of awarding punishment involving imprisonment is restricted to 2 years in the maximum, but he may under certain statutory powers remit the prisoner to the High Court for sentence. The Sheriff also exercises a wide summary criminal jurisdiction and when doing so sits without a jury; and he has concurrent jurisdiction with every other court within his sheriffdom in regard to all offences competent for trial in summary courts. The great majority of offences which come before the courts are of a minor nature and, as such, are disposed of in the Sheriff Courts. In cases to be tried on indictment either in the High Court of Justiciary or in the Sherriff Court, the judge may, and in some cases must, before the trial, hold a Preliminary Diet to decide questions of a preliminary nature, whether to the competency or relevancy or otherwise. Any decision at a preliminary diet can be the subject of an appeal to the High Court of Justiciary prior to the trial.

New procedures have been introduced during 1981 by the introduction of the Criminal Justice (Scotland) Act 1980.

District Courts in each local authority district have jurisdiction in minor offences occurring within the district. These courts are presided over by lay magistrates, known as justices, and have limited powers of fine and imprisonment.

The Court of Session, presided over by the Lord President (the Lord Justice-General in criminal cases), is divided into an Inner House comprising 2 divisions of 4 judges each with mainly appellate function, and an Outer House comprising 13 single judges, sitting individually at first instance; it exercises the highest civil jurisdiction in Scotland, with the House of Lords as a court of appeal.

Police. The police forces in Scotland at the end of 1981 had an authorized establishment of 13,262; the strength was 12,445 men and 749 women. Whole-time 'additional' policemen numbered 66, and there were 2,814 part-time special constables. The total police net expenditure in Scotland was £179·6m. for 1980–81.

Civil Judicial Statistics

England and Wales	*1979*	*1980*	*1981*
Appellate Courts			
Judicial Committee of the Privy Council	46	61	54
House of Lords	76	85	65
Court of Appeal	1,419	1,488	. . .
High Court of Justice (appeals and special cases from inferior courts)	916	1,360	1,282
Courts of First Instance			
High Court of Justice:			
Chancery Division[1]	13,848	16,328	15,650
Queen's Bench Division	149,244	200,989	182,620
Family Division	1,041	1,100	1,000
County courts: Divorce	167,511	177,415	176,162
Other	1,478,965	1,766,029	1,916,095
Other courts[2]	6,321	6,328	6,345
Scotland			
House of Lords (Appeals from Court of Sessions)	5	4	12
Court of Session—General Department	27,497	29,459	30,043
Sheriff's Ordinary Court	26,563	35,757	37,364
Summary Cause	137,734	151,941	131,855

[1] Including contentious probate, 3rd Patents Court.

[2] From Jan. 1972 certain 'other' courts, namely, the Palatine Chancery Court of Lancaster and Durham were merged with the High Court; the Mayor's and City of London Court became a County Court; Borough Courts of Record were abolished. The figure 6,345 for 1981 represents: Court of Protection, 4,266; Lands Tribunal, 1,262; Employment Appeal Tribunal, 793; Transport Tribunal, 24.

Criminal Statistics

England and Wales

	Total number of offenders 1979	Total number of offenders 1980	Indictable offences[1] 1980	Indictable offences[1] 1981
Aged 10 and over				
Proceeded against in magistrates' courts[2]	2,048,878	2,377,953	506,669	522,597
Found guilty at magistrates' courts	1,847,480	2,152,699	396,417	401,585
Found guilty at the Crown Court	50,672	59,008	59,008	62,977
Cautioned[3]	136,599	145,881	100,925	103,896
Aged 10 and under 17				
Proceeded against in magistrates' courts[2]	125,764	139,465	98,082	94,706
Found guilty at magistrates' courts	115,519	126,979	89,192	85,322
Found guilty at the Crown Court	957	1,108	1,108	1,288
Cautioned[3]	98,226	104,423	85,511	87,602

Scotland	1978	1980	1981
Crimes and Offences—			
Number of persons proceeded against in all courts	228,141	264,845	...
Number of persons proceeded against summarily	224,451	260,726	...
Miscellaneous offences—			
Proceedings taken	183,923	210,471	...
Children[4]—			
Proceeded against in court	1,639	1,202	...
Police warnings and referred to reporter	23,403	22,401	...

[1] Includes offences which can be tried either at the Crown Court or at magistrates' courts.
[2] Almost all defendants are initially proceeded against in magistrates' courts.
[3] Offenders who, on admission of guilt, are given an oral caution by or on the instruction of a senior police officer as an alternative to court proceedings. Such cautions are not given for motoring offences.
[4] Young persons under 16 years of age.

Average population in prisons, borstals and detention centres (1981) in England and Wales was 43,311 (convicted 38,123; untried 4,804, and 384 non-criminal prisoners); in Scotland (1981), 4,518 (sentenced, 3,769; remanded, 746 and 3 others).

Prison Statistics, England and Wales. HMSO, 1981
Paterson, A., *The Law Lords.* London, 1982

Religion. The Anglican Communion has originated from the Church of England and parallels in its fellowship of autonomous churches the evolution of British influence beyond the seas from colonies to dominions and independent nations. There is no terrestrial head of the Anglican Communion; the Archbishop of Canterbury presides as *primus inter pares* at the decennial meetings of the bishops of the Anglican Communion at the Lambeth Conference.

The Anglican churches, in addition to the Church of England, comprise the churches, councils, and provinces in communion with the see of Canterbury; which are situated in Wales; Ireland; Scotland; United States of America; Canada; Australia; New Zealand; West Indies; Brazil; South Africa; Central Africa; West and East Africa; Jerusalem and the Middle East; South East Asia; Burma; Sri Lanka; Japan; South America; China.

In addition to the dioceses included within the Provinces of Canterbury and York, there are several dioceses overseas over which the Archbishop of Canterbury exercises metropolitical jurisdiction, while Church of England chaplaincies in North and Central Europe formerly under the jurisdiction of the Bishop of London now form the diocese of Europe.

England and Wales. The established Church of England, which baptizes about 40% of the children born in England (*i.e.* excluding Wales but including the Isle of Man and the Channel Islands), is Protestant Episcopal. Civil disabilities on account of religion do not attach to any class of British subject. Under the Welsh Church Acts, 1914 and 1919, the Church in Wales and Monmouthshire was disestablished as from 1 April 1920, and Wales was formed into a separate Province.

The Queen is, under God, the supreme governor of the Church of England, with the right, regulated by statute, to nominate to the vacant archbishoprics and bishoprics. The Queen, on the advice of the First Lord of the Treasury, also appoints to such deaneries, prebendaries and canonries as are in the gift of the Crown, while a large number of livings and also some canonries are in the gift of the Lord Chancellor.

There are 2 archbishops (at the head of the 2 Provinces of Canterbury and York), and 42 diocesan bishops including the bishop of the diocese of Europe, which is part of the Province of Canterbury. Each archbishop has also his own particular diocese, wherein he exercises episcopal, as in his Province he exercises metropolitan, jurisdiction. In Dec. 1982 there were 69 suffragan and assistant bishops, 38 deans and provosts of cathedrals and 102 archdeacons. The General Synod, in England, consists of a House of Bishops, a House of Clergy and a House of Laity, and has power to frame legislation regarding Church matters. The first two Houses consist of the members of the Convocations of Canterbury and York, each of which consists of the diocesan bishops and elected representatives of the suffragan bishops, 6 for Canterbury province and 3 for York (forming an Upper House), deans, provosts, and archdeacons, and a certain number of proctors elected as the representatives of the inferior clergy, together with, in the case of Canterbury Convocation, representatives of the Universities of Oxford, Cambridge and London and in the case of York a representative for the Universities of Durham and Newcastle; the chaplains in the Forces (forming the Lower House). They are elected by their fellow suffragans. The House of Laity is elected by the lay members of the Deanery Synods. Parochial affairs are managed by annual parochial church meetings and parochial church councils. Every Measure passed by the General Synod must be submitted to the Ecclesiastical Committee, consisting of 15 members of the House of Lords nominated by the Lord Chancellor and 15 members of the House of Commons nominated by the Speaker. This committee reports on each Measure to Parliament, and the Measure receives the Royal Assent and becomes law if each House of Parliament resolves that the Measure be presented to the Queen.

At 31 Dec. 1981 there were 13,660 ecclesiastical parishes, inclusive of the Isle of Man and the Channel Islands. These parishes do not, in many cases, coincide with civil parishes. Owing to the pastoral re-organization, although most parishes have their own churches, not every parish nowadays can have its own incumbent or minister; so that in some areas one or more parishes may be served by a clergyman, who must be in priest's orders, and in these cases he holds the parishes in plurality. In Dec. 1980 there were 10,639 parochial incumbencies in which 1,961 benefices were under suspension of presentation. In Dec. 1982 there were 7,065 beneficed clergymen excluding dignitaries, 1,322 other clergymen of incumbent status and 1,730 assistant curates working in the parishes.

Private persons possess the right of presentation to over 2,000 benefices; the patronage of the others belongs mainly to the Queen, the bishops and cathedrals, the Lord Chancellor, and the universities of Oxford and Cambridge. In addition to the 10,117 parochial incumbents and assistant curates, there were (1981) 361 dignitaries, 363 non-parochial clergymen working within the diocesan framework and approximately 2,000 non-parochial clergymen outside the framework.

In 1980 there were estimated to be 1·8m. Easter and 1·8m. Christmas Communicants.

Of the 40,459 churches and chapels registered for the solemnization of marriages at 30 June 1982, 16,660 belonged to the Established Church and the Church in Wales and 23,799 to other religious denominations. Of the 351,973 marriages celebrated in 1981 (370,022 in 1980), 34% were in the Established Church and the Church in Wales, 17% in churches or chapels of other denominations and 49% were civil marriages in a Register Office.

Roman Catholics in England and Wales were 4,269,019 in 1982. There were 5 archdioceses and 16 dioceses, 6,995 clergy and 2,671 parish churches and 1,222 other churches open to the public. Convents, 1,311.

The Unitarians have about 250 places of worship, the Catholic Apostolic Church over 80, the New Jerusalem Church about 75. The Salvation Army, a religious body with a quasi-military organization, carries on both spiritual and social work at home and abroad, and had, in British Territory, 1981, 2,175 officers, 1,120 corps. There were also 38 eventide homes, 13 maternity homes, 2 maternity hospitals, 46 hostels for men, 14 hostels for women and girls, and 9 approved and training schools.

The following is a summary of statistics of certain churches in England and Wales, Channel Islands and Isle of Man:

Denomination	*Full members*	*Ministers in charge*	*Local and lay preachers*
Methodist	487,972	3,506	14,847
Independent Methodist	4,600	150	—
Wesleyan Reform Union	3,590	24	174
United Reform	150,000	1,700	—
Baptist	223,086	1,757	—
Calvinistic Methodist Church of Wales	85,041	230	—
Moravian	4,600	30	—
Society of Friends	18,549	—	—

There are about 400,000 Jews in the UK with about 240 synagogues.

Scotland. The Church of Scotland (established in 1560 at the Reformation and re-established in 1688 as part of the Revolution Settlement) is Presbyterian, the ministers all being of equal rank. There is in each parish a kirk session consisting of the minister and a number of laymen called elders. There are presbyteries (formed by groups of parishes), meeting frequently throughout the year, and these are again grouped in synods, which meet half-yearly and can be appealed to against the decisions of the presbyteries.

The supreme court is the General Assembly, which now consists of some 1,250 members, half clerical and half lay, chosen by the different presbyteries. It meets annually in May (under the presidency of a Moderator appointed by the Assembly, the Sovereign being present or represented by a Lord High Commissioner, appointed by the Queen on the nomination of the Government of the day), and sits for 7 days. Any matters not decided during this period may be left to a Commission which will sit if required.

On 2 Oct. 1929 the Church of Scotland and the United Free Church of Scotland were reunited under the name of The Church of Scotland, and the two bodies met in General Assembly in Edinburgh as one. The united Church had, in Scotland, on 31 Dec. 1981, 1,846 congregations, 953,933 members; 20,138 teachers and 120,138 scholars in attendance in Sunday schools. The Church courts are the General Assembly, 12 synods, 46 presbyteries in Scotland, 1 in England and 2 on the Continent. Income in 1981 was £30,665,558. There are divinity faculties in 4 Scottish universities of Edinburgh, Glasgow, Aberdeen and St Andrews, with 60 professors and lecturers who are mostly ministers of the Church of Scotland.

The Episcopal Church of Scotland is a province of the Anglican Church and is one of the historic Scottish churches. It consists of 7 dioceses. As at 31 Dec. 1982 it had 286 churches and missions, 231 clergy and 70,787 members, of whom 40,477 were communicants.

There are in Scotland some small outstanding Presbyterian bodies and also Baptists, Congregationalists, Methodists and Unitarians.

The Roman Catholic Church which celebrated the centenary of the restoration of the hierarchy in 1978, had in Scotland (1982) 1 cardinal, 1 archbishop and 9 bishops, 1,127 clergy, 476 parishes, and 824,400 adherents.

The proportion of marriages in Scotland according to the rites of the various Churches in 1981 was: Church of Scotland, 40·1%; Roman Catholic, 14·5%; Episcopal, 1·4%; United Free, 0·4%; others, 4·2%; civil, 39·1%.

Bossy, J., *The English Catholic Community, 1570–1850.* London, 1975
Moorman, J. R. H., *A History of the Church in England.* London, 1973

Education. *The Publicly Maintained System of Education England and Wales:* Compulsory schooling begins at the age of 5 and the minimum leaving age for all pupils is 16.[1] No tuition fees are payable in any publicly maintained school (but it is open to parents, if they choose, to pay for their children to attend other schools). The post-school stage, which is voluntary, includes universities, polytechnics and other further education establishments (including those which provide courses for the training of teachers), as well as adult education and the youth service. Financial assistance is generally available to students on higher education courses in the university and non-university sectors and to some students on other courses in further education.

Nursery Education. Children under 5 may be provided for in nursery schools and nursery classes in primary schools. In the public sector no fees are payable. There were (1982) 582 nursery schools accommodating 48,989 children while some 3,662 primary schools contained nursery classes accommodating 186,412 children. Over 80% of all these children attend on a part-time basis. There are also 201,279 children under 5 attending maintained primary schools.

Primary Schools. Children normally begin primary school when they are 5. Nearly half of the 20,482 primary schools take the complete age-range from 5 upwards. About 3,900 take infants only, up to about 7 years; the rest take juniors only, from 7 or 8 on. The great majority of primary schools take both boys and girls. Nearly 13,000 of these schools had between 100 and 300 pupils each; of the remainder, over half had 100 pupils or less.

There are 1,930 primary schools in Wales. In those primary schools (and some secondary schools) which are in the predominantly Welsh-speaking areas, the main language of instruction is Welsh. There are also 'Welsh', or, more accurately, bilingual schools in mainly English-speaking parts of Wales. Generally children transfer from primary to secondary schools at 11.

[1] As a result of the Education (School Leaving Dates) Act 1976, one of the two former leaving dates was amended. This means that pupils whose dates of birth fall between 1 Feb. and 31 Aug. (inclusive) cease to be of compulsory school age on the Friday before the last Monday in May. Some of these pupils will leave school before their 16th birthdays. Pupils whose dates of birth fall between 1 Sept. and 31 Jan. (inclusive) remain of compulsory school age until the end of the Easter term following their 16th birthdays.

Middle Schools. In some areas middle schools have been developed. These cover the age-ranges 8 to 12, 9 to 12, 9 to 13, 10 to 13 or 10 to 14. In Jan. 1982 there were 1,413 middle schools, just one more than in 1981; this stabilizing of numbers comes after a decade of rapid growth (there were only 15 middle schools in 1969).

Secondary Education. In some areas, pupils are still selected at 11 for grammar schools on the basis of ability. The grammar schools, of which there were 185 at Jan. 1982, provide a mainly academic course from age 11 to 18. There were also a small number of technical schools which are the academic equals of grammar schools but can specialize to a greater or lesser extent in technical studies. Modern schools provide a general education up to the minimum school leaving age, though some pupils can, and increasingly do, stay on beyond that age. At Jan. 1982 there were 357 of these schools. There are also a small number of other schools which are various combinations of grammar, technical and modern schools.

Many authorities now operate comprehensive schools to which pupils are admitted without reference to ability or aptitude. In Jan. 1982 there were 3,358 fully comprehensive schools with over 3·15m. pupils, in comparison with 221 such schools with about 210,000 pupils in 1965. With the development of comprehensive education various patterns of secondary school organization have come into operation, of which the main ones are: all through schools with an age-range of 11–18 or 11–16 (with possible transfer to an 11–18 school or to a sixth form college (*i.e.*, 16–19) for further studies); 3-tier systems, which incorporate middle schools with a transfer age of 12, 13 or 14, and corresponding 12–18, 13–18 or 14–18 schools; or a system of junior and senior comprehensive schools, catering for the 11–18 age group with a transfer age of 13 or 14.

Direct Grant Grammar Schools. These schools receive grants direct from the Department of Education and Science for their secondary departments (or 'upper schools') and are independent of local education authorities. In 1975 the Government decided to phase out direct grant and invited the schools to join the maintained sector as comprehensive schools. Out of a total of 170 direct grant schools in England and Wales, 4 have been closed, 44 have become maintained or are about to do so and 122 have opted for independent status.

Pupils who were admitted before Sept. 1976, to those schools which are becoming independent will continue to attract grant aid (thereby paying lower fees), and will also be eligible for fee remission related to their parents' income until they leave.

Assisted Places Scheme. In order to give able children a wider range of educational opportunity the government set up, in 1981, the assisted places scheme to give help with tuition fees at independent schools to parents who could not otherwise afford them. In the school year 1982–83, the 220 participating schools offered a total of 5,613 assisted places, 4,617 for entry at age 11, 12 or 13, and 996 for entry at sixth form level.

Special Education. Since 1971, when the education of severely mentally handicapped children became the responsibility of the education service, the right of all handicapped children to education, however severe their disability has been recognized. Although most handicapped children are currently educated in special schools, it has long been the Government's policy that no child should be placed in a special school if his needs can be met in an ordinary school.

Whilst, under the existing system, special educational treatment is provided on the basis of defined categories of bodily or mental handicap the Education Act 1981, which is due to be fully implemented by the academic year 1982–83, provides for handicapped children to be educated in accordance with their special educational needs.

The majority of handicapped children attend special schools of which there are nearly 1,600 at present catering for about 123,000 pupils. Approximately 4,400 of these children are in schools in hospitals where they are receiving medical treatment as in-patients. In addition nearly 7,400 pupils attend independent schools catering wholly or mainly for handicapped pupils, the majority placed by LEAs.

Increasingly, however, handicapped children are being integrated into ordinary schools either in designated classes or on an individual basis. At present there are about 16,000 handicapped children receiving their education alongside non-handicapped children. Over three-quarters of the maintained special schools are day schools. For some children with severe handicaps, for whom day special schools are not suitable, and for children who live out of reach of a suitable day school, free boarding education is provided. Attendance is compulsory from 5 to 16. In addition, local authorities can provide special educational treatment below the age of 5 for those ascertained as being in need of it and until the age of 18 for those who want it (education from 16–18 may be provided either in a school or a college of further education). In addition to the provision in ordinary and special schools, authorities make special arrangements for educating children at home, in small groups or in hospitals when there is no special school. In Jan. 1980 about 4,800 pupils were being educated otherwise than at school. There are also some establishments which provide further education, pre-vocational training and for assessment for employment purely for handicapped school leavers.

Ancillary Services. Local education authorities may provide registered pupils at any school maintained by them with milk, meals and refreshment and they may make such charges as they think fit for anything they provide. For pupils whose parents are in receipt of supplementary benefit or family income supplement, however, authorities are required to ensure that such provision is made for the pupil at mid-day as appears to them to be requisite and anything which is provided must be free of charge. Authorities are also required to remit the charge for anything they provide for other pupils if having regard to their circumstances, they consider it appropriate to do so. Facilities must also be provided, free of charge, for consuming any meals or other refreshments which pupils bring to school themselves.

Local education authorities also have power to provide milk, meals and refreshment for pupils in non-maintained schools, if they wish to do so, under such terms as may be agreed with the proprietors as long as the cost does not exceed what it would have been if the pupils had been at a school maintained by an authority.

Further Education. In Nov. 1981 there were about 522 institutions in England and Wales providing courses of further education, ranging from shorthand instruction to degree-level, postgraduate work and courses of teacher-training. Course enrolments numbered 531,542 full-time (including 59,000 sandwich students) and 1·31m. part-time and evening; students released by their employers numbered 452,757. There were in addition 4,318 adult education centres (formerly known as evening institutes), and youth clubs which provided mainly part-time courses of non-advanced general education and were attended by 1·61m. students. At the top end of this range are the 30 polytechnics, these are engaged almost entirely in higher education, offering degrees of a standard comparable to those of universities, professional qualifications and courses in a wide range of disciplines leading to Higher National Diplomas and Certificates and to awards of the Technician Education Council and Business Education Council. Many other colleges of further education are however involved to a greater or lesser extent in the higher education sector of further education; and all polytechnics and most further education colleges cater for full-time, part-time and sandwich students, whose periods of study at college alternate with periods of practical training in industry.

Courses were also provided by the Workers' Educational Association (7,375), the University extramural departments (7,460) and the Welsh National Council of YMCAs (60). The total number of students registered at these courses was 332,376.

Education at institutions of further education is not free, but fees are generally low, and are remitted for most students under the age of 18 by the local authority.

The Youth Service. A wide range of facilities for the leisure-time recreation and informal special education of young people primarily of post-school age is provided by local education authorities and voluntary youth organizations. A duty is laid upon local education authorities by the provisions of the 1944 Education Act to secure the adequacy of such facilities for young people in their area; to this end they either provide, maintain and staff youth clubs, centres and other facilities from their own resources or assist voluntary agencies to do so.

Grants to voluntary agencies to help meet the cost of capital projects and to national voluntary bodies towards their headquarters and training expenses are made by the Government.

Awards to Students. Local education authorities are responsible for making mandatory awards to suitably qualified students taking first-degree and comparable courses, courses of initial teacher-training and certain other advanced level courses. These awards cover fees and maintenance but the maintenance grants are subject to the income of the student and his parents or spouse. In addition scholarships may be available both from universities and other sources. The authorities may also give discretionary awards to students who do not qualify for mandatory awards including those taking non-degree level courses.

In 1980–81 there were 379,407 full value awards current in all, 52% at university and 36,259 were for teacher-training courses. These include awards to students at university departments of education for which responsibility was transferred to local authorities in 1975–76. Lesser value awards, for which the maximum rate of grant payable is below the full cost of the student's fees and maintenance, were also made by the authorities. There were 64,975 awards taken up in the academic year 1980–81.

The Research Councils (generally in science and social science subjects) and the Department of Education and Science (generally in the arts and the humanities) make awards to students at postgraduate level. The Research Councils gave 5,851 new awards in 1981–82 and there were 11,780 current awards in that academic year. The Department gave 1,774 new awards (state studentships and state bursaries) in 1982–83 and current awards totalled about 3,450.

Teachers. In order to qualify for work in maintained schools, most teachers take a course of professional training. Graduates and holders of some specialist qualifications obtained before 1 Jan. 1970 are regarded as qualified to teach without training, but anyone obtaining these qualifications after that date is obliged to take a training course before being appointed for the first time to a primary school, and since 1 Jan. 1974 before first appointment to a secondary school. For the time being, however, this requirement has been waived for graduates in science and mathematics because of the acute shortage of teachers in these subjects.

In 1982 there were some 75 non-university institutions (including 23 polytechnics) and 32 university departments of education providing courses of initial teaching in England and Wales.

In Oct. 1981 there were about 32,000 students on initial teacher-training courses.

On 30 Sept. 1982, 421,000 full-time teachers (175,000 men and 246,000 women) were employed by local education authorities in maintained nursery, primary and secondary schools in England and Wales.

Finance. Total current and capital expenditure on education in England from public funds (excluding university education) is estimated at £9,335m. for 1981–82 as compared with £8,617m. for 1980–81.

Scotland. The statistics on schools relate to education authority and grant-aided schools. From 1974–75 all teachers employed in these schools require to be qualified; figures given are full-time equivalents.

Nursery Education. In Sept. 1980 there were 519 nursery schools and departments, with a total enrolment of 32,644 pupils.

Primary Education. In Sept. 1980 there were 2,543 primary schools and departments and the number on the registers was 524,889.

In Sept. 1980, 25,846 teachers were employed in primary schools and departments.

Secondary Education. In Sept. 1980 there were 467 secondary schools with 419,373 pupils. Of these schools, 374 were all-through comprehensive establishments providing the full range of Scottish Certificate of Education courses and also non-certificate courses. A further 64 schools were comprehensive in intake and provided both non-certificate and certificate courses, the latter however only up to Ordinary grade. Of the remaining 29 schools, these were selective in intake, 20 provided certificate courses only (Ordinary grade and Higher grade) and 9 non-certificate and certificate courses, the latter again not extending beyond Ordinary grade. Pupils who start their secondary education in schools which do not cater for courses beyond Ordinary grade may in the light of their performance, or for other reasons, be transferred at the end of their second or fourth year to schools providing Higher grade courses.

There were 29,290 teachers in secondary schools at Sept. 1980.

Special Schools. In Sept. 1980 there were 319 special schools and departments. The total number of handicapped children under instruction was 11,816, of which 8,826 were mentally handicapped, 939 were physically handicapped, 329 were blind or partially blind and 632 were deaf or partially deaf, and 1,090 were otherwise handicapped.

At Sept. 1980 there were 25 'List D' schools (these establishments correspond to Community Homes in England and Wales) with a total enrolment of 1,242.

Further Education. Centres and colleges for formal further education numbered 192 in 1980–81.

The student population was 208,836, of whom 45,155 attended full-time (advanced courses, 23,113; non-advanced, 22,042) and 163,681 part-time (advanced courses, 33,379; non-advanced, 130,302).

Teacher-Training. In Nov. 1980 there were 4,871 students in 10 colleges of education on pre-service courses of teacher-training.

Finance. Total expenditure on education met from revenue in 1980–81 was £1,164·8m. (excluding university education and loan charges).

Independent Schools. Outside the state system of education there were in England and Wales nearly 2,350 independent schools in Jan. 1983, ranging from large 'public' schools to small local ones. There were (Jan. 1982) 510,074 full-time and 10,914 part-time pupils in these schools. Fees are charged by all these schools, which receive no grant from central government sources. Recognized as efficient status has been discontinued but the requirement for the registration of all independent schools by the Department and their inspection by HM Inspectors, remains unchanged. The term 'public schools' refers to independent schools in membership of the Headmasters' Conference, Governing Bodies Association or the Governing Bodies of Girls' Schools Association. Qualifications under which a school may be represented at the Headmasters' Conference include the measure of independence enjoyed by the governing body and the amount of advanced courses undertaken. Some of these schools are for boarders only, but the majority include non-resident 'day-pupils'. In Scotland there were 95 independent schools, with a total of 16,652 pupils in Sept. 1978. A small number of the Scottish independent schools are of the 'public school' type but they are not known as 'public schools' since in Scotland this term is used to denote education authority (*i.e.*, state) schools.

The earliest of the schools were founded by, and attached to, the medieval churches. Many were founded as 'grammar' (classical) schools in the 16th century, receiving charters from the reigning sovereign. Reformed mainly in the middle of the 19th century, these schools now provide the highest form of English pre-university education. Among the most well-known independent schools are Eton College, founded in 1440 by Henry VI, with 1,250 boys; Winchester College, 1394, founded by William of Wykeham, Bishop of Winchester, 600 boys; Harrow School, founded in 1560 as a grammar school by John Lyon, a yeoman, 740 boys; Charterhouse, 1611, 670 boys. Among the earliest foundations are King's School, Canterbury, founded 600; King's School, Rochester, 604; St Peter's, York, 627.

Universities. In *England* there are 33 traditional degree-giving universities. In addition there are the University of Manchester Institute of Science and Technology; the London and Manchester Business Schools and the Open University. Eight new universities have been established since 1961.

In *Wales* there is 1 university, the University of Wales, with colleges at Aberystwyth, Bangor, Cardiff, Lampeter and Swansea. The Welsh National School of Medicine is a school of the University, and the University of Wales Institute of Science and Technology became a constituent college in Nov. 1967.

In *Scotland* there are 8 universities, Aberdeen, Dundee, Edinburgh, Stirling, Strathclyde, Heriot-Watt, Glasgow and St Andrews. The Carnegie Trust for Scottish Universities (founded, 1901) has a capital (1980) of £7m. and an annual income of £490,000; 50% of the income is devoted to the improvement and expansion of Scottish Universities and 50% to assist students with their fees.

All these universities and colleges are independent, self-governing institutions, although they receive substantial aid from the State (in the case of the Open University by direct grant from the Department of Education and Science, and the traditional universities through the University Grants Committee). The UGC is a committee appointed by the Secretary of State for Education and Science designed to advise the Government on the needs of the universities, and to prepare plans for future development. The members are drawn from education and industry. The Government receives advice on the universities' requirements for central computing facilities from the Computer Board for the Universities and Research Councils whose members are also drawn from the universities and industry.

The Royal College of Art and the Cranfield Institute of Technology are post-graduate institutions which award higher degrees under charters granted in 1967 and 1969 respectively. They receive grants direct from the Department of Education and Science.

The local education authorities have no responsibility for universities.

The Open University received its charter on 1 June 1969 and is an independent, self-governing institution, awarding its own degrees. It is financed by the Government through the Department of Education and Science and by the receipt of students' fees.

Tuition is by means of correspondence textbooks, radio and television broadcasts and summer schools. Students can also attend one of 269 local study centres. No formal qualifications are required for entry to undergraduate or associate student courses.

Anyone resident in the UK aged 21 or over may apply. There are 131 undergraduate courses; many are available on a one-off basis to associate students.

Since it began teaching, in 1971, 180,000 people have finally registered as undergraduates. 63,000 courses have been taken by associate students, and a similar number of short community eduction, teaching and technical up-dating courses.

At the university's headquarters in Milton Keynes there are 420 full-time academic staff; another 232 full-time academics are based in 13 regional offices. There are 5,000 part-time tutors and counsellors.

The University College at Buckingham, an independent institution of higher education, took its first students in Feb. 1976 and in Feb. 1983 it was granted a Royal Charter. It offers a first degree (licence) in 2 academic years of 40 weeks each (the academic year Jan.–Dec. has 4 terms). There are 6 schools of study: Accounting, Business and Economics; European Studies; History, Politics, and English Literature; Law; Life Sciences; Politics, Economics, and Law. The Licence in European Studies takes three years and includes an intercalated year abroad. The College also offers a number of post-graduate courses. In 1982 there were 474 full-time students.

All universities charge fees, but financial help is available to students from several sources.

The universities themselves provide scholarships of various kinds and all local education authorities have a system of awards to help suitable students to attend university.

The amount of aid given generally depends upon the parents' means. The majority of the students at the English and Welsh universities are in receipt of some form of financial assistance.

Awards known as state studentships are offered on a competitive basis by the Department from among candidates considered by the universities to be qualified for post-graduate studies in the humanities; similar awards, tenable at universities or technical colleges, are offered by the Research Councils to students studying science, mathematics and technology at the post-graduate level.

The following table gives the approximate number of professors, lecturers, etc., and students (full-time and sandwich courses) for 1980–81:

University or college	Students	Staff
Aston	5,306	644
Bath	3,581	453
Birmingham	8,884	1,505
Bradford	5,060	590
Bristol	7,010	1,127
Brunel	2,826	366
Cambridge	11,479	1,200
City	2,825	355
Durham	4,770	580
East Anglia	4,206	461
Essex	2,970	340
Exeter	4,064	603
Hull	5,498	582
Keele	2,801	348
Kent	3,956	475
Lancaster	4,627	557
Leeds	10,885	1,395
Leicester	4,789	622
Liverpool	7,859	1,148
London Business School	229	66
London	40,538	7,891
Loughborough	5,399	590
Manchester Business School	162	49
Manchester	11,327	1,655
Univ. of Manchester Inst. of Science and Technology	4,137	622
Newcastle	7,805	1,140
Nottingham	7,053	948
Oxford	11,802	1,994
Reading	5,819	753
Salford	4,549	508
Sheffield	8,369	1,088
Southampton	6,168	1,020
Surrey	3,255	498
Sussex	4,463	660
Warwick	5,002	637
York	3,357	407
Wales—		
Aberystwyth U.C.	3,224	451
Bangor U.C.	2,962	414
Cardiff U.C.	5,724	707
St David's, Lampeter	767	71
Swansea U.C.	4,022	508
Welsh Nat. School of Medicine	742	255
Univ. of Wales Institute of Science and Technology	2,961	329
Scotland—		
Aberdeen	5,590	887
Dundee	3,060	533
Edinburgh	9,783	1,529
Glasgow	9,830	1,501
Heriot-Watt	3,205	372
St Andrews	3,348	381
Stirling	2,925	302
Strathclyde	6,707	900

Women students are admitted on equal terms with men. Number of women students: England, 86,344; Wales, 7,998; Scotland, 18,041. There are, however, colleges exclusively for female students at Oxford and Cambridge. Total number of full-time or sandwich students at universities listed above: England, 233,830; Wales, 20,402; Scotland, 44,448; total, 298,680.

McIntosh, N. E., Calder, J.A. and Swift, B., *A Degree of Difference.* London, 1976
Perry, W., *Open University: A Personal Account.* Open Univ. Press, 1976
Tunstall, J., *The Open University.* London, 1974

The British Council. The British Council was established in Nov. 1934 and incorporated by Royal Charter in 1940. Its aims are the promotion of an enduring understanding and appreciation of Britain in other countries through cultural, educational and technical co-operation.

The Council's expenditure in 1981–82 amounted to £147·1m. Funds were provided by a grant-in-aid of £34·1m. from the Overseas Information (Foreign and Commonwealth Office) vote and a contribution of £19·4m. from the Overseas Aid Vote. A further £57·4m. was provided by the Overseas Development Administration to cover the cost of administration of, and the reimbursement of sums expended on technical co-operation schemes. The balance of £36·2m. was derived from Council earnings and from international agencies, overseas governments, etc. for educational services.

The Council is governed by a board consisting of up to 30 members, 2 of whom are nominated by Ministers. There are advisory committees for Scotland and Wales and also advisory committees for the main branches of the Council's work. In Jan. 1983 the Council had staff in 81 countries.

The Council is designated by the British Government to carry out over 30 bilateral cultural agreements, including that with the Soviet Union. The Council's work broadly divides into English language teaching; education and training; the development of university links and interchange; the promotion of wider use and availability of British books and periodicals; the development of personal contacts and the provision of information abroad on British experience and resources in the fields of education, medicine, science, technology and the arts.

The general policy in the field of English language teaching is to advise and assist education authorities overseas, particularly in curriculum and materials development and the training of local teachers of English; courses are provided in Britain and abroad for the further training of English language teaching experts from overseas. In many countries the Council runs its own English teaching centres. The Council acts as a centre for the dissemination of information about British educational thought and practice at all levels and, through its complement of education specialists working overseas, it has become closely involved with the administration of aid on behalf of the Overseas Development Administration. It assists in producing English teaching and other educational television and radio programmes overseas and arranges overseas consultancies and training in TV, radio and the application of media to development both in Britain and overseas. A prominent aspect of its education work is the assistance given in developing countries to the adoption of modern and locally relevant methods of science and mathematics teaching in schools. Following the merger with TETOC in 1982, the Council is responsible for advising ODA on its policies in the fields of technical education, industrial training, agricultural education, public administration and management development. Over 850 lecturers etc., mainly in the field of English language, are working overseas, having been recruited by the British Council on behalf of universities, schools, etc. in over 100 different countries. The Council is concerned to promote closer international academic collaboration through a variety of interchange and linking schemes, and through the provision of information and advice on educational institutions; it also administers the British Government's Technical Co-operation Training Programme and scholarship programmes on behalf of a large number of international organizations, notably UN and EEC. It administers examinations on behalf of a number of British examining boards.

During recent years the Council has collaborated with British educational institutions and firms in designing and implementing a wide range of education projects, for which overseas authorities or multilateral agencies pay the full cost.

The sciences, including medicine, technology and agriculture, form an increasingly important part of Council work. Contacts are built up and information collected and distributed through the specialist departments in London and the qualified scientists serving overseas, who also advise on training in Britain and the provision of experts abroad.

The importance of the arts as a medium for fostering cultural relations is reflected in the Council's encouragement of the appreciation of British achievements in the performing and the visual arts, both by supporting local activity and by sending theatre and ballet companies, orchestras and chamber groups, and exhibitions both of fine arts, crafts and photographs, from Britain on tours overseas. The Council also produces booklets, records and tapes on a wide range of literary and artistic subjects and in addition makes extensive use of films and video cassettes in support of its arts and educational work.

The Council runs, or is associated with, over 100 libraries in the countries in which it is represented. It arranges touring exhibitions of new British books and periodicals (some 77,000 books were exhibited in 270 exhibitions 1981–82). Additional publicity for British books is provided by the publication *British Book News*, and the distribution of specialized book lists. The Council also administers ODA funds (approximately £2·5m. in 1981–82) for library development, the presentation of books and periodicals to educational institutions in developing countries and the subsidized publication of low-priced books for students under the imprint of the English Language Book Society.

The Council arranges short advisory tours overseas by British experts. In a number of countries it is also the overseas administrative arm of the British Volunteer Programme. It awards scholarships and bursaries and arranges study programmes for some 30,000 visitors a year in Britain. It administers central government funds for youth exchanges with other countries.

In Britain the Council administers the programmes of award schemes for overseas students, meets many students on arrival from overseas, and provides an accommodation service for students from overseas for whom it has a special responsibility. The Council runs offices in Britain, mainly in university cities, for these purposes.

The Council is increasingly called on to administer training schemes and educational services financed by overseas authorities, or by multilateral agencies, on a contractual basis. The Council's specialist courses and summer schools provide advanced study in a number of fields, notably medicine, science, literature and the arts, English language and education. Payment is made by the student, or his parent organization, or by some other sponsor.

The Council publishes the following periodicals: *British Medical Bulletin, Media in Education and Development* and *British Book News*. Other publications produced include the series *Writers and their Work, Notes on Literature, British Education, British Books and Libraries;* a number of booklets including *Higher Education in the United Kingdom, Introducing Wales, How to Live in Britain* and *Statistics of Overseas Students in Britain*. The Council has sponsored two major series of literature recordings, *The Complete Works of Shakespeare* and *The English Poets from Chaucer to Yeats*.

Chairman: Sir Charles Troughton, CBE, MC, TD.
Director-General: Sir John Burgh, KCMG, CB.
Headquarters: 10 Spring Gdns., London, SW1A 2BN.

Arts Council of Great Britain. The Arts Council is an independent organization established by Royal Charter in 1946, and is the principal channel for British Government aid to the arts. The Council's objects are to develop and improve the knowledge, understanding and practice of the arts, to increase their accessibility to the public, and to advise and co-operate with government departments, local authorities and other organizations.

The Council consists of a Chairman and not more than 19 other members who are appointed by the Secretary of State for Education and Science, after consultation with the Secretaries of State for Scotland and Wales. The Council is advised by panels and committees concerned with different aspects of the arts. With the approval of the appropriate Minister, the Council appoints committees for Scotland and Wales known respectively as the Scottish Arts Council and the Welsh Arts Council.

The Council receives a grant-in-aid from the Government voted annually by Parliament. The grant-in-aid for 1983–84 is £92m., including £1·1m. for the Housing the Arts Fund.

As well as giving financial help and advice to several hundred artistic organizations from the major opera, dance, drama companies, orchestras and festivals, to the smallest touring theatre and experimental group, the Council encourages such diverse interests as contemporary dance, photography, art films, and helps professional creative writers, dramatists, poets, musicians, composers, artists and photographers by means of bursary and award schemes. The Council provides funds for specialist training courses in the arts, and assists projects for the construction of new buildings, or improvements to existing ones under its 'Housing the Arts' scheme.

A growing proportion of the Council's funds is channelled to the network of regional arts associations which practically covers the whole of England and Wales. The regional arts associations are not branches of the Arts Council, but are autonomous bodies, financed by a combination of Arts Council, local authority and private funds.

The Council mounts art exhibitions at the Hayward and Serpentine and other galleries in London and also in the regions. Other direct promotions include tours of opera and drama companies, of the Council's own films on the arts and of music groups under the Contemporary Music Network scheme. The Council has a library of contemporary British poetry at its headquarters.

Chairman: Sir William Rees-Mogg.
Secretary-General: Luke Rittner.
Headquarters: 105 Piccadilly, London W1V 0AU. *The Scottish Arts Council:* 19–20 Charlotte Sq., Edinburgh, EH2 4DF. *The Welsh Arts Council:* 9 Museum Place, Cardiff, CF1 3NX.

National Insurance. The National Insurance Act, 1946, came into operation on 5 July 1948, repealing the existing schemes of health, pensions and unemployment insurance. This Act, along with later legislation, was consolidated as the National Insurance Act, 1965.

The Social Security Act 1975 introduced, from 6 April 1975, a new system of national insurance contributions to replace the previous system of flat-rate and graduated contributions. Since 6 April 1975, Class 1 contributions have been related to the employee's earnings and are collected with PAYE income tax, instead of by affixing stamps to a card. Class 2 and Class 3 contributions remain flat-rate, but, in addition to Class 2 contributions, those who are self-employed may be liable to pay Class 4 contributions, which for the year 1983–84 will be at the rate of 6·3% on profits or gains between £3,800 and £12,000, which are assessable for income tax under Schedule D. The non-employed and others whose contribution record is not sufficient to give entitlement to benefits are able to pay a Class 3 contribution voluntarily to qualify for a limited range of benefits. Class 2 contributions for 1983–84 are £4·40 a week for men and women. Class 3 contributions are £4·30 a week.

From 6 April 1978 the Social Security Pensions Act 1975 introduced earnings-related retirement, invalidity and widows' pensions. Employee's national insurance contribution liability depends on whether he is in contracted out or not contracted out employment. The not-contracted out employee pays 9% on all earnings up to £235 a week. The employer's rate is 10·45% and a 1·45% surcharge of all earnings. An employee's contracted-out contribution is 9% of the first £32·50 a week of earnings and 6·85% of earnings between £32·50 and £235 a week. The employer's contribution is 10·45% (and the 1·5% surcharge) of the first £32·50 of weekly earnings and 6·35 (and the 1·5% surcharge) of earnings up to £235 a week.

The State supplements the contributions paid by contributors and employers, from general taxation. Contributions (other than the surcharge) and supplement together with interest on investments form the income of the National Insurance Fund from which benefits are paid.

Statutory Sick Pay (SSP). The Social Security and Housing Benefits Act 1982 provides that, from 6 April 1983, employers will be responsible for paying statutory sick pay (SSP) to their employees for up to 8 weeks of sickness absence in a tax year. SSP will replace the employee's entitlement to State sickness benefit which will not be payable as long as any employer's responsibility for SSP remains.

Benefits. The range of benefits are unaffected by the new arrangements from 5 April 1975. The benefits are: (1) Unemployment benefit; (2) Sickness benefit; (3) Invalidity benefit; (4) Maternity benefit; (5) Widow's benefit; (6) Guardian's allowance; (7) Child's special allowance; (8) Retirement pension; (9) Death grant.

Qualification for any benefit depends upon fulfilment of the appropriate contribution conditions employed persons may qualify for or the benefits self-employed may qualify for all except unemployment benefit. Employed persons may qualify for all the benefits; self-employed may qualify for all except unemployment.

Sickness and Unemployment Benefit. From 25 Nov. 1982 the rate is £25 a week plus £15·45 a week for an adult dependant, plus £0·30 for each child for whom child benefit is in payment.

Unemployment benefit is paid through the local unemployment benefit offices of the Department of Employment.

Invalidity Benefit replaces sickness benefit after 168 days of entitlement. It comprises a basic invalidity pension of £31·45 weekly and an invalidity allowance of £6·90 if incapacity began before age 40: £4·40 if incapacity began between 40 and 50 or £2·20 if it began between 50 and 60 (55 for women). Increases are: £18·85 for an adult dependant plus £7·95 for each child for whom child benefit is payable.

Maternity Benefit. For a confinement a woman may receive a maternity grant of £25 and, where 2 or more children are born at the confinement, a further grant of £25 for each additional child who is alive 12 hours after its birth. There are no contribution conditions. The grant is paid on the satisfaction of a simple 'presence in Great Britain' test by the mother. If the woman has been gainfully employed or self-employed, and has paid sufficient full-rate national insurance contributions in the relevant income tax year, she may receive a maternity allowance of £25 a week normally payable for 18 weeks commencing 11 weeks before the expected week of confinement, provided she does not work during this period. Maternity allowance may be increased in certain circumstances in respect of dependants in the same way as sickness and unemployment benefits.

Widow's Benefit. On her husband's death a widow normally qualifies for 26 weeks for an allowance of £45·95 a week for herself plus an increase of £7·95 a week for each child for whom child benefit is payable. At the end of the 26 weeks she may qualify for a widowed mother's allowance of £32·85 for herself, and the increases for the children for whom child benefit is payable continue at the same rate as for the first 26 weeks of widowhood. She may also receive her allowance at the personal rate of £32·85 a week if she has living with her a son or daughter who is under 19. The child increase for widow's allowance and widowed mother's allowance is, generally speaking, payable only in respect of a child for whom child benefit is payable.

A widow's pension may be paid to: (i) A widow after the termination of her widow's allowance, if she does not qualify for widowed mother's allowance and was aged 40 or more when her husband died; (ii) A widow after she ceases to be entitled to a widowed mother's allowance if she is then aged 40 or more. The standard rate of this pension is £32·85 a week if the widow was 50 or more when her husband died or when her entitlement to widowed mother's allowance ended. If she was between 40 and 50, however, the standard rates of total pension range in 7% steps from 93% of the full age-50 rate (*i.e.*, £30·55 a week) for the widow who was 49 at that time to 30% (*i.e.*, £9·86 a week) for the widow who was then 40.

Child's Special Allowance. An allowance may be payable for the children of divorced parents where the father has died. It is payable to the mother if she has not remarried and her former husband was contributing, or legally liable to contribute, at least 25p a week towards the children's support in cash or kind or if she took reasonable steps to enforce maintenance and she was entitled to child benefit for the child(ren) when her former husband died or it is her child by her former husband and he was entitled to child benefit for the child(ren) when he died. It is similar to the increases for widow's children and is payable at the same rates.

Guardian's Allowance. A person who is responsible for an orphan child may be entitled to a guardian's allowance of £7·95 a week in addition to the amount of child benefit payable in respect of that child. Normally both the child's parents must be dead but when the child is illegitimate, or the parents were divorced, or one parent is missing, or serving a long sentence of imprisonment, the allowance may, in certain circumstances, be paid on the death of one parent only.

Retirement Pension. In order to receive a retirement pension, men between 65 and 70, and women between 60 and 65 must have retired from regular employment. From 6 April 1979 a woman divorced over the age of 60 must satisfy the retired conditions before a pension is payable. The standard rates of basic pensions are £32·85 a week for a man or woman on his or her own contributions and £19·70 for a married woman through her husband's contributions. Proportionately reduced pensions are payable where contribution records are deficient. For a person who reaches pension age on or after 6 April 1979, additional pension may also be payable. This is based on the earnings on which he or she has paid Class 1 contributions in each complete tax year between April 1978 and pension age. If the person has been a member of a contracted-out occupational pension scheme, that scheme will be responsible for paying the whole or part of the additional pension. An increase of £19·70 a week may be payable for a dependent wife. If she resides with the beneficiary the increase is gradually reduced for earnings over £45 a week. If she does not reside with the beneficiary an increase is not payable if she earns more than £19·70 a week. In addition £7·95 a week may be payable for each child for whom child benefit is payable. In certain circumstances an increase of £19·70 a week may be payable for a woman having care of the pensioner's children. In addition, a man who had paid graduated contributions receives 4·28p per week for every £7·50 of graduated contributions paid, and a woman 4·28p per week for every £9 paid. Although no further graduated contributions have been paid after April 1975, pension already earned will be paid along with the basic pension in the normal way. If, after being awarded a retirement pension, a man under 70 or a woman under 65 earns more than £57 in a calendar week the pension for the next pension week, including any increase for dependants, will be reduced by 5p for every 10p earned between £57 and £61 and by 5p for every 5p earned over £61. If retirement is postponed after minimum pension age increments of basic pension can be earned for periods of deferred retirement. Between 6 April 1975 and 5 April 1979 increments were earned at the rate of one-eighth penny per £1 of the pension rate for every 6 days (excluding Sundays) for which the pension had been foregone. From 6 April 1979 increments are earned at the rate of one-seventh penny per £1 of basic pension for every 6 days (excluding Sundays) for which pension has been foregone. Any days for which another benefit has been paid will not count. These increments must be at least 1% of the pension rate unless the minimum was earned under the arrangements which applied before 6 April 1979. For periods between 6 April 1975 and that date, the rate was one-eighth penny per £1 of the basic pension rate for every 6 days and for periods of deferred retirement before 6 April 1975 increments were based on the number of contributions paid as an employed or self-employed person. At age 70 for a man (65 for a woman) the pension for which a person has qualified may be paid in full whether a person continues in work or not irrespective of the amount of earnings. At the age of 80 an age addition of £0·25 a week is payable. In addition non-contributory pensions are now payable, subject to residence conditions, to persons aged 80 and over who do not qualify for a retirement pension or qualify for one at a low rate. The rates of these pensions, which are financed by Exchequer funds, are £19·70 a week for a single person and £11·80 for a married woman. These amounts do not include the £0·25 age addition.

Death Grant. This is a lump sum paid on the death of an insured person or his close relative. The normal amount of the payment is: For an adult, £30; for a child aged 6 but under 18, £22·50; for a child aged 3 but under 6, £15; for a child under 3, £9. For the death of a person who was within 10 years of pensionable age on 5 July 1948 (*i.e.*, a man over 55 and a woman over 50 on that date) only half the standard amount is payable. No grant is payable for the death of a person who was over the pensionable age on 5 July 1948.

The Industrial Injuries Provisions of the Social Security Act, 1975. The Industrial Injuries Act, which also came into operation on 5 July 1948, with its later amending Acts, was consolidated as the National Insurance (Industrial Injuries) Act, 1965. This legislation was incorporated in the Social Security Act, 1975. The scheme provides a system of insurance against 'personal injury by accident arising out of and in the course of employment' and against certain prescribed diseases and injuries due to the nature of the employment. It takes the place of the Workmen's Compensation Acts and covers persons who are employed earners under the Social Security Act. There are no contribution conditions for the payment of benefit. Three types of benefit are provided:

(1) Injury benefit, payable for incapacity for work due to an industrial accident or certain of the prescribed diseases for a maximum of 26 weeks from the date of the accident or the development of the disease. The rate of this benefit is £27·75 a week, with increases of £15·45 for 1 adult dependant and £0·30 for each child for whom child benefit is payable. If the employed earner is under 18 years of age and is not entitled to a dependant's increase, benefit will be payable at a reduced rate—£25. For children under 16 years of age in part-time employment, the rate is £8·30. Injury benefit was abolished from 6 April 1983.

(2) Disablement benefit. This is payable where, as the result of an industrial accident or prescribed disease, there is a loss of faculty. The loss of faculty will be assessed as a percentage by comparison with a person of the same age and sex

whose condition is normal. If the assessment is 20%, or more, benefit will be a pension varying according to the assessment, from £10·72 a week to £53·60 a week. If the assessment is under 20% benefit will normally be a gratuity of an amount not exceeding £3,560. Unemployability supplement plus age additions similar to invalidity allowance, may be payable to a disablement pensioner who, as a result of the relevant loss of faculty is incapable of work and likely to remain permanently so incapable. Increases for dependants at the same rates as for invalidity pension are also payable to a disablement pensioner who is entitled to unemployability supplement. The supplement cannot be paid at the same time as certain other benefits payable under the Social Security Act or out of public funds. Other increases of disablement benefit may be payable where the loss of faculty causes special hardship, *i.e.*, it prevents the beneficiary from undertaking his regular job or one of an equivalent standard of earnings; where there is a need for constant attendance; where there is exceptionally severe disablement and the need for constant attendance is likely to be permanent or where disablement is assessed at less than 100% and the beneficiary is in hospital for treatment for his injury or prescribed disease. Pensions for persons under 18 are at a reduced rate. When injury benefit was abolished for industrial accidents occurring and prescribed diseases commencing on or after 6 April 1983, a common start date was introduced for the payment of disablement benefit 90 days (excluding Sundays) after the date of the relevant accident or onset of the disease.

(*3*) *Death Benefit.* On the death of a person as the result of an industrial accident or a prescribed disease, certain dependants may qualify for benefit. Benefit for a widow is a pension normally of £45·95 weekly for the first 26 weeks and thereafter £33·40, depending on such factors as age, entitlement to a child's allowance and permanent incapacity for self-support. If the conditions for pension at the higher rate are not satisfied the widow may receive a pension of £9·86 a week. Child allowances may be payable to the widow, or other person, entitled to child benefit for children of the deceased. For widows, these allowances are usually at the rate of £7·95 a week for each child; for other persons, the rate is £0·30 for each child. An allowance of £1 is payable to a woman having care of a child of the deceased. Benefit for widowers, parents and certain other relatives takes the form of pensions, allowances or gratuities according to the relationship to, and degree of maintenance by, the deceased.

War Pensions. The number of beneficiaries in receipt of war (1914–18) pensions or allowances as at 25 Sept. 1981 was 33,000. The number of beneficiaries in receipt of war (1939–45 and later) pensions or allowances in payment as at 25 Sept. 1981 was 309,600. The estimated expenditure for both wars for 1981–82 was £482m. The expenditure is exclusive of administrative expenses.

National Insurance Fund. At 1 April 1980 the balance of the National Insurance Fund amounted to £4,625,775,000. Income during the period 1 April 1980 to 31 March 1981, consisting of contributions from insured persons and employers, payments from the Exchequer and interest on investments, etc., was £16,009·01m. Payments of benefit in respect of unemployment were £1,280,543,000; sickness, £595,806,000; invalidity, £1,150,104,000; maternity, £166m.; widows, £638m.; guardian's allowance and child's special allowance, £2·2m.; retirement pension, £10,541,251,000m.; death grants, £16,261,000m.; injury benefit, £45,925,000; disablement benefits, £281,819,000; death benefit, £42m. Included in these figures are the following estimated amounts of earnings-related supplement: unemployment benefit, £170m.; sickness benefit, £127m.; maternity allowance, £29m.; widow's benefit, £13m.; graduated retirement benefit, £165m. Administrative and other payments cost approximately £837,403,000. The balance at 31 March 1981 was £5,037,473,000.

From 1 April 1975 the National Insurance Reserve Fund and the Industrial Injuries Fund were merged with the National Insurance Fund. All basic scheme contributions payable under the 1975 Social Security Act are paid into the single fund out of which the existing range of benefits will continue to be financed. The new national insurance fund will continue to receive a Treasury Supplement set at a level of 18% of total contribution income.

Child Benefit. Child benefit is a tax-free cash allowance for all children. The weekly rate for each child is £5·85 from Nov. 1982. Child benefit is payable for all children under age 16 and for those under age 19 receiving full-time non-advanced education at a college or school. One Parent Benefit. This is a tax-free cash allowance for certain people bringing up children alone. It is payable for the first or only child in the family in addition to child benefit. The weekly rate from Nov. 1982 is £3·65.

Family Income Supplement. Family income supplement is payable to families with at least 1 dependent child where the head of the household is in remunerative work for at least 30 hours a week (24 hours for lone parents), and where the family's normal gross weekly income (but excluding child benefits) is below a prescribed amount. The prescribed amount for a 1-child family is £82·50, this amount being increased by £9 for each additional child in the family. The weekly rate of benefit payable is one-half of the difference between the prescribed amount and the family's normal income, subject to a maximum weekly payment of £21 for families with 1 child, increasing by £2 for each additional child. Benefit is usually payable for 52 weeks and is not affected by changes in circumstances. The prescribed amounts are the same for both 1- and 2-parent families.

Attendance allowance. This is a tax-free allowance for severely disabled people, including children aged 2 or over, who require a lot of help from another person. There are 2 rates, the higher rate of £26·25 a week for those who require attention or supervision by day and night, and the lower rate of £17·50 a week for those who need the attendance either by day or night. In addition to the medical requirements a simple test of residence and presence in Great Britain must also be satisfied.

Invalid Care Allowance. May be paid to those under pensionable age who stay at home to care for a person who is receiving attendance allowance or constant attendance allowance. In general married women do not qualify for this benefit. Current rate £19·70 a week, with increases for dependants.

Supplementary Benefit. Under the Supplementary Benefits Act, 1976, as amended by the Social Security Act 1980, benefit is payable to any persons in Great Britain aged 16 years or over (excluding persons at school or college or anyone directly involved in a trade dispute) who are not in full-time remunerative work and who are without resources, or whose resources (including national insurance benefits) need to be supplemented in order to meet their requirements. A person who is excluded from benefit under the normal rules may, nevertheless, receive payments to meet urgent need. The general standards by reference to which supplementary benefit is granted are determined by statutory regulations approved by Parliament. Persons who are dissatisfied with the amount of benefit granted to them may appeal to an independent Appeal Tribunal established under the Act.

During the financial year 1980–81 net payments on supplementary benefit amounted to £2,859m.

Newman, T. S., *Digest of British Social Insurance.* London, 1947 (and supplements, to date)

National Health. The National Health Service in England and Wales started on 5 July 1948 under the National Health Service Act, 1946. There is a separate Act for Scotland and also one for Northern Ireland, where the Health Services are run on similar lines to those in England and Wales.

The National Health Service, which is available to every man, woman and child, is a charge on the national income in the same way as the armed forces and other facilities.

Every person normally resident in this country is entitled to use any complete part of the services, and no insurance qualification is necessary.

Most of the cost of running the service is met from the national exchequer, *i.e.*, from taxes.

Since Sept. 1957 a small weekly National Health Service contribution has been payable by contributors and where applicable by their employers. For convenience this contribution is collected with the National Insurance contribution and for 1982–83 is estimated to be £1,618m. for Great Britain.

Organization. Under the provisions of the Health Service Act 1980, the administration of the National Health Service in England and Wales is organized under a system of regional and district health authorities accountable to the Secretary of State for the Social Services and the Secretary of State for Wales. In Scotland the National Health Service is administered under the National Health Service (Scotland) Act 1978, by 15 Health Boards and a Common Services Agency all accountable to the Secretary of State for Scotland.

There are 192 district health authorities in England responsible for the administration and development of health services in their district. Fourteen regional health authorities, each consisting of a number of complete health districts, are responsible for allocating resources between the district health authorities in their regions and for monitoring their performance. The regional authorities are responsible for developing strategic plans and priorities and for carrying out certain executive functions.

Services. The National Health Service broadly consists of hospital and specialist services, general medical, dental and ophthalmic services, pharmaceutical services, community health services and school health services. All these services are free of charge except for such things as prescriptions, spectacles, dentures and dental treatment, amenity beds in hospitals and for some of the community services, for which charges are made with certain exemptions.

The total cost of the Health and Personal Social Services (Great Britain) is estimated at £17,483m. for 1982–83 and the estimated net expenditure by the Exchequer (except for the Local Authority Personal Social Services, where the rates and the Exchequer grants are estimated at about £2,341m.) in 1982–83 is £12,651m.

The provisional number of abortions performed in 1981 under the provisions of the Abortion Act, 1967, was 162,454, of which 128,555 related to England and Wales residents. Of these 128,555 abortions, 70,021 (54·5%) were to single women, 42,427 (33%) were to married women, and 16,107 (12·5%) were to widowed, divorced or separated women and to women who did not state their marital status.

The number of abortion notifications received in Scotland in 1981 under the provisions of the Abortion Act 1967, was 8,975, of which 8,950 related to Scottish residents. Of these 8,975 notifications, 4,877 (54·3%) were to single women, 2,997 (33·4%) were to married women, and 1,101 (12·3%) were to widowed, divorced or separated women and to women who did not state their marital status.

In 1977 there were 26,810 general medical practitioners, 13,564 general dental practitioners and 219,900 qualified nurses and midwives. There were (1977) 469,849 allocated hospital beds.

Personal Social Services. Under the Local Authority Social Services Act 1970 and in Scotland the Social Work (Scotland) Act 1968 the welfare and social work services provided by local authorities were made the responsibility of a new local authority department—the Social Services Department in England and Wales, and Social Work Departments in Scotland headed by a Director of Social Work. The social services thus administered include: the fostering, care and adoption of children, welfare services and social workers for the mentally disordered, the disabled and the aged, and accommodation for those needing residential care services. In Scotland the social work departments' functions also include the supervision of persons on probation, of adult offenders and of persons released from penal institutions or subject to fine supervision orders.

The number of persons in residential and temporary accommodation provided by or on behalf of local authorities was as follows:

England and Wales (31 March)	Residential accommodation Adults
1977	135,000
1978	136,000
1979	135,000
1980	136,337
1981[1]	135,111

[1] Provisional.

Scotland	Residential accommodation Adults and Children	Temporary accommodation Adults	Temporary accommodation Children	Total Adults and Children
1979[1]	16,717	—	—	16,717
1980[1]	16,810	—	—	16,810
1981[1]	16,446	—	—	16,446

[1] Year ending 31 March.

England and Wales. Expenditure and income relating to the personal social services administered by local authorities (in £1,000 sterling):

Year ended 31 March	Gross current expenditure	Income from sales, fees and charges	Net current expenditure
1978	1,178,771	189,018	989,753
1979	1,335,252	214,757	1,120,495
1980	1,623,607	247,696	1,375,911
1981	1,997,767	294,710	1,703,057
1982[1]	2,214,750	327,152	1,887,598

[1] Provisional.

Scotland. The total local authority expenditure for 1979–80 in respect of residential accommodation and welfare services under the Social Work (Scotland) Act, 1968, was £231·7m. Central Government expenditure on social work totalled £9·5m.

Social Security Statistics 1980 (incorporating 1979). HMSO, 1980
Watkin, B., *The National Health Service.* London, 1978

DIPLOMATIC REPRESENTATIVES

Of the USA in Great Britain (Grosvenor Sq., London, W1A 1AE)
Ambassador: John J. Louis, Jr.

Of Great Britain in the USA (3100 Massachusetts Ave., Washington, D.C., 20008)
Ambassador: Sir Oliver Wright, GCVO, DSC.

Of Great Britain to the United Nations
Ambassador: Sir John Thomson, KCMG.

Books of Reference

The annual and other publications of the various Public Departments, and the Reports, etc. of Royal Commissions and Parliamentary Committees. (These may be obtained from HM Stationery Office.)
Allen, G. C., *British Industries and their Organization.* 4th ed. London, 1959
Bickmore, D. P., and Shaw, M. A. (ed.), *The Atlas of Great Britain and Northern Ireland.* OUP, 1963
Burn, D., *The Structure of British Industry.* 2 vols. CUP, 1958
Central Statistical Office. *Annual Abstract of Statistics.* HMSO.—*Monthly Digest of Statistics.* HMSO
Central Office of Information. *Britain: An Official Handbook.* HMSO, 1978.—*Britain in Brief.* 18th ed. HMSO, 1977
Demangeon, A., *The British Isles.* 3rd ed. London, 1952
Directory of British Associations. Beckenham, annual
Government Statistical Service. *Social Trends.* HMSO, 1979.—*Regional Statistics.* HMSO, 1979
Halsey, A. H., *Trends in British Society Since 1900.* London, 1972
History of the Second World War. HMSO, 1949 ff.

Jenkin, M., *British Industry and the North Sea.* London, 1981
Kendall, M. G. (ed.), *The Source and Nature of the Statistics of the United Kingdom.* 2 vols. London, 1952–1957
Mitchell, B. R., *Abstract of British Historical Statistics.* OUP, 1962
Oxford History of England. 15 vols. OUP, 1936 ff.
Stamp, L. D., and Beaver, S. H., *The British Isles: A Geographic and Economic Survey.* 4th ed., London, 1954
Woodward, Sir E. L., and Butler, R., *Documents on British Foreign Policy, 1919–39.* HMSO, 1957 ff.

Scotland

Scottish Council (Development and Industry). *Inquiry into the Scottish Economy, 1900–61.* Edinburgh, 1961
Scottish Office. *Scottish Economic Bulletin.* HMSO (quarterly).—*Scottish Abstract of Statistics.* HMSO (annual)
The New Scottish Local Authorities: Organisation and Management Structures. HMSO, 1973
Brand, J., *The National Movement in Scotland.* London, 1978
Campbell, R. H., *The Rise and Fall of Scottish Industry, 1707–1939.* Edinburgh, 1981
Donaldson, G. (ed.) *The Edinburgh History of Scotland.* 4 vols. Edinburgh, 1965–75
Drucker, N. and H. M., *The Scottish Government Year Book.* London, 1980
Grant, E., *Scotland.* [Bibliography] Oxford and Santa Barbara, 1982
Hogg, A., and Hutcheson, A. MacG., *Scotland and Oil.* 2nd ed. Edinburgh, 1975
Johnston, T. L., *Structure and Growth in the Scottish Economy.* London, 1971
Kellas, J. G., *The Scottish Political System.* 2nd ed. CUP, 1975
Meikle, H. W. (ed.), *Scotland: A Description of Scotland and Scottish Life.* London, 1947
Turnock, D., *Patterns of Highland Development.* London, 1970

Wales

Wales: The Way Ahead (Cmnd 3334.) HMSO, 1971
Wales: Employment and the Economy. Cardiff, 1972
Digest of Welsh Statistics. HMSO (annual)
Thomas, B. (ed.), *The Welsh Economy.* Cardiff, 1962
Williams, D., *A History of Modern Wales.* New ed. London, 1977
Williams, G., (ed.) *Social and Cultural Change in Contemporary Wales.* London, 1978

NORTHERN IRELAND

AREA AND POPULATION. Area (revised by the Ordnance Survey Department) and population at the census of 5 April 1981 were as follows:

District	*Population 1981*	*Area (Hectares)*
Antrim	45,303	40,527
Ards	57,598	36,779
Armagh	48,169	66,733
Ballymena	54,696	63,384
Ballymoney	22,932	41,687
Banbridge	29,831	44,131
Belfast	297,862	13,017
Carrickfergus	28,388	8,484
Castlereagh	61,107	8,441
Coleraine	47,524	47,763
Cookstown	26,323	51,207
Craigavon	71,049	27,989
Down	52,984	63,835
Dungannon	41,087	76,266
Fermanagh	51,973	169,952
Larne	29,475	33,744
Limavady	26,451	58,523
Lisburn	83,188	43,595
Londonderry	82,862	37,258
Magherafelt	30,781	56,186
Moyle	14,372	49,378
Newry and Mourne	72,615	88,589
Newtownabbey	71,917	15,108
North Down	65,692	7,241
Omagh	41,137	112,354
Strabane	34,912	86,090
Northern Ireland	1,490,228	1,348,261

Vital statistics for calendar years:

	Marriages	*Divorces*	*Births*	*Deaths*
1976	9,914	574	26,361	17,030
1977	9,696	569	25,437	16,921
1978	10,304	599	26,239	16,153
1979	10,214	757	28,178	16,811
1980	9,923	896	28,582	16,835

CONSTITUTION AND GOVERNMENT. The Northern Ireland Constitution Act 1973 as amended by the Northern Ireland Constitution (Amendment) Act 1973 and the Northern Ireland Assembly Act 1973 provide for a Northern Ireland Assembly of 78 members and a Northern Ireland Executive of not more than 11 members (including the Chief Executive Member). The Secretary of State appointed this full number to take office from 1 Jan. 1974. He may also, under the Amendment Act, appoint others to carry out particular functions in the Administration up to a total (including members of the Executive) of 15. This additional number were appointed.

Devolution of legislative and executive responsibility to the Northern Ireland Assembly and the new Administration under Section 2 of the Constitution Act was given effect by the Northern Ireland Constitution (Devolution) Order 1973 from 1 Jan. 1974 ('the appointed day'). On that day, Section 1 of the Northern Ireland (Temporary Provisions) Act 1972 expired and, with it, the power to legislate for Northern Ireland by Order in Council under that Act.

Power to make laws (to be known as Measures) in respect of 'transferred' matters, that is on matters other than those listed in Schedules 2 and 3 to the Constitution Act was vested in the Assembly subject to the overriding power of the UK Parliament to legislate on such matters and subject to Section 17 of the Constitution Act which declares void any provision which discriminates against any person or class of persons on the ground of religious belief or political opinion. The procedure for Measures is set out in the Standing Orders of the Assembly. All Measures require the approval of the Queen in Council before they become law. The first election of Members to the 78 seats in the Northern Ireland Assembly was held in 1973. The state of the parties following the election was: Social Democratic and Labour Party 19; Democratic Unionist Loyalist Coalition 8; Official Unionist 24; Northern Ireland Labour 1; Other Unionist 8; Alliance 8; Vanguard Unionist Coalition 7; Other Loyalist Coalition 2; Other Loyalist 1. Northern Ireland also returns 12 members of the UK House of Commons; however, under the terms of the House of Commons (Redistribution of Seats) Act 1979, the Boundary Commission published in April 1982 final recommendations for a scheme whereby the number of constituencies in the Province would be increased to 17.

On 28 May 1974 the Unionist members of the Administration resigned, as a result of which the Secretary of State terminated the appointments of members, and HM the Queen prorogued the Assembly for a period of 4 months (thus preventing it from legislating). Parliament subsequently enacted the Northern Ireland Act 1974 extending the prorogation of the Assembly and providing for its dissolution. The Act also reintroduced the power to legislate for Northern Ireland by Order in Council.

The Assembly was dissolved on 28 March 1975, and an election, provided for under the 1974 Act, of a Constitutional Convention took place on 1 May 1975. The Convention had the purpose of considering what provision for the government of Northern Ireland was likely to command the most wide-spread acceptance throughout the community there. The Convention was dissolved on 5 March 1976. Direct rule continues in being under the terms of the Northern Ireland Act 1974.

In Jan. 1980, the main political parties were invited by the Secretary of State to take part in a Conference with the object of seeking the highest level of agreement on the future government of the Province. In Oct. 1982 elections to new Assembly of 78 members elected by proportional representation took place. Results were: Official Unionists, 26; Democratic Unionists, 21; Social Democratic and Labour Party, 14; Alliance, 10; Sinn Fein, 5; Independent Unionst, 1; Ulster Popular Unionist Party, 1.

What began ostensibly as a Civil Rights campaign in 1968, escalated into a full-scale offensive designed to overthrow the State. This offensive was originally mounted by an illegal organization, the Irish Republican Army (not to be confused with the legitimate Army of the Republic of Ireland). At times countermeasures have required the services of over 20,000 regular troops, in addition to the Royal Ulster Constabulary, the RUC Reserve and the part-time Ulster Defence Regiment.

Secretary of State for Northern Ireland: Right Hon. James Prior, MP.

Local Government. Northern Ireland has a single-tier system of 26 district councils based on main centres of population.

The district councils are responsible for the provision of a wide range of local services including refuse collection and disposal, street cleansing, litter prevention, consumer protection, environmental health, miscellaneous licensing, the provision and management of recreational and cultural facilities, the promotion of tourist development schemes, the enforcement of building regulations and gas supply. They have in addition both a representative role in which they send forward representatives to sit as members of statutory bodies including the Northern Ireland Housing Council, the Fire Authority and the Area Boards for health and personal social services and education and libraries; and a consultative role under which the Department of Environment (NI) and the Northern Ireland Housing Executive, among others, have an obligation to consult them regarding the provision of the regional services for which these bodies are responsible.

Regional development strategy in Northern Ireland throughout the late sixties and early seventies was based on the *Matthew Report* of 1963, which marked the beginning of a new era in regional planning in the Province. This in turn was endorsed by the economic plan prepared by Professor Wilson in 1965, which modified and up-dated a number of the original Matthew proposals. The Northern Ireland Development Programme 1970-75 extended the scope of the regional strategy and basically identified two categories of interest: *(i)* centres of accelerated growth consisting of the greater Belfast area (including the Belfast Urban Area, Craigavon, Antrim, Bangor, Carrickfergus and Newtownards), Londonderry and Ballymena.

These were centres where a proportionately large expansion was deliberately planned and where population growth was to be actively encouraged. *(ii)* Eight key centres which were to be made as attractive as possible to potential new industry and where significant expansion was anticipated. The 8 centres were the provincial towns of Newry, Dungannon, Coleraine, Enniskillen, Omagh, Larne, Downpatrick and Strabane. This growth and key centre policy had a twofold purpose: to maintain a Development Stopline around Belfast and to encourage movement of population from the city and elsewhere to the major towns outside the Belfast Urban Area.

In 1975 the Development Programme of 1970 having run its full course, the Government published a discussion paper which outlined and evaluated 6 very broad options for the future development of the Province for the period 1975-95. Following comments from a wide variety of sources the Government announced its decision to adopt in principle the District Towns Strategy. Basically the strategy advocates that the growth and key centre strategy should be extended to embrace the major town in each local government district. A detailed exposition *Northern Ireland Regional Physical Development Strategy 1975-95* was published in May 1977.

While the physical strategy sets out the Government's aims and objectives on a regional basis, the details required to pursue these aims and objectives at local level are promulgated in Area Plans. These have been published for the Belfast Urban Area, the North Down, Londonderry, West Tyrone, Newry, Limavady, Armagh, East Antrim, East Tyrone, Magherafelt, Fermanagh and the north-east of the Province which incorporates the Coleraine–Portrush–Portstewart area. Work is continuing on the preparation of a plan for the Lisburn, Banbridge, Mourne, and Downpatrick areas. Statements of the Department's conclusions and decisions have been published on the Belfast Urban, North Down, Londonderry, Armagh,

Newry, West Tyrone, Limavady, East Antrim, East Tyrone, Magherafelt and the North East. Plans following consideration of the Reports of Public Inquiries held into objections to the Plans, and the latter 10 Plans have been adopted as statutory development plans under Article 7(2) of the Planning (NI) Order 1972. A public inquiry has been held into the Fermanagh Area Plan. A major review of the Belfast Urban Area Transportation Strategy has been carried out and a public inquiry held. A statement has been issued by the Department of the Environment (NI) indicating the future system of transport in Belfast.

Provisions in Part VII of the Planning (NI) Order 1972 enable the Department of the Environment (NI) to deal with areas requiring to be developed or redeveloped in overall schemes involving the participation of several agencies. Land when acquired is not normally developed by the Department itself but is disposed of to other agencies, in both public and private sectors, for the carrying out of their development. The Department is currently using these powers for two main purposes, the promotion of commercial redevelopment of certain town centre sites and the acquisition overall of large areas, principally in Belfast, which are in need of redevelopment and are proposed to be redeveloped for mainly other than housing purposes.

The legislative framework for planning in Northern Ireland is contained in the Planning (NI) Order 1972 and the Planning (Amendment) (NI) Order 1978. Under the 1972 Order the Department of the Environment (NI) is the sole planning authority for Northern Ireland. The Order includes procedures for the preparation of plans and development control, establishes a Planning Appeals Commission, contains provisions for the protection of buildings of special architectural or historic merit and trees and gives powers for the carrying out of town-centre redevelopment.

FINANCE. There exists a separate Northern Ireland Consolidated Fund from which is met the expenditure of Northern Ireland Departments. Its main sources of revenue are: *(i)* The Northern Ireland attributed share of UK taxes; *(ii)* A non-specific grant in aid of Northern Ireland's revenue, payable by the Secretary of State for Northern Ireland; *(iii)* Rates and other receipts of Northern Ireland Departments.

The general principle underlying the financial arrangements is that Northern Ireland should have parity of taxation and services with Great Britain.

Since the financial year 1980-81 the income of the Northern Ireland Consolidated Fund has been as follows (in £ sterling):

	1980–81	*1981–82*	*1982–83*
Attributed share of UK taxes	1,236,519,588[1]	1,475,213,755[2]	1,504,900,000[3]
Payments by UK Government:			
Grant in Aid	640,000,000	585,000,000	706,705,000
Refund of value added tax	15,880,250	18,274,933	20,000,000
Regional and district rates	133,150,000	153,950,000	171,000,000
Other receipts	190,547,879	255,517,656	253,649,000
Total	2,216,097,717	2,487,956,344	2,656,254,000

[1] Including final adjustment for 1978–79.
[2] Including final adjustment for 1979–80.
[3] Provisional.

The public debt at 31 March 1982 was as follows: Northern Ireland 7% Exchequer Stock 1982–84, £20m.; Ulster Savings Certificates, £149,259,000; Ulster Development Bonds, £2,452,000; borrowing from UK Government, £653,792,648; borrowing from Northern Ireland Government Funds, £211,820,209; borrowing from bank, £300,000; borrowing from building societies, £17m.; European Investment Bank Loan, £19,577,247; total, £1,074,201,104.

The above amount of public debt is offset by equal assets in the form of loans from Government to public and local bodies and of cash balances.

ENERGY AND NATURAL RESOURCES

Electricity. The planning, generation and distribution of electricity supplies are the responsibility of the Northern Ireland Electricity Service.

The installed capacity of the system is 2,015 mw largely provided from 4 thermal power-stations.

The total sales of electricity in Northern Ireland in the year ended 31 March 1982 amounted to 4,619m. units supplied to a total of 529,079 consumers.

Water Supplies and Sewerage. The Water Service Division of the Department of the Environment (NI) is responsible for water supply and sewerage. Over 665m. gallons of water a day are supplied throughout the Province. More than 90% of the population have a mains supply of water and about 85% live in property connected to public sewers.

The Department is also responsible for the conservation and planned development of water resources in Northern Ireland.

Minerals. The output of minerals (in 1,000 tonnes) during 1981 was approximately: Basalt and igneous rock (other than granite), 5,449; grit and conglomerate, 2,622; limestone, 2,281; sand and gravel, 3,738; and other minerals (rocksalt, flint, sandstone, diatomite, granite, chalk, clay and shale), 574.

Agriculture. Estimated gross output in 1981:

		Quantity (1,000)	*Value (£m.)*
Fat cattle	head	527	217·4
Calves	head	25	3·9
Store cattle	head	25	7·3
Exports of breeding livestock	head	6	1·2
Fat sheep and lambs	head	568	21·8
Fat pigs	head	1,137	66·6
Poultry (tonnes)		52	34·5
Eggs: for human consumption (dozen)		95,738	34·3
Wool (tonnes)		1,566	1·4
Milk (litres)		1,186,740	148·8
Potatoes	tonnes	278	18·7
Oats	tonnes	5	0·5
Barley	tonnes	63	6·7
Wheat	tonnes	2	0·2

		Quantity (1,000)	*Value (£m.)*
Grass seed	tonnes	—	—
Hay and straw	tonnes	12	0·6
Fruit	tonnes	26	3·3
Vegetables	tonnes	38	4·3
Mushrooms	tonnes	5	5·5
Flowers		—	2·0
Other items		—	30·8
Total receipts			609·6
Value of changes in stocks due to volume			−7·8
Gross output			601·8

Area (in 1,000 hectares) of crops at June census (1980 and 1981):

	1980	*1981*
Oats	4·0	3·4
Barley	51·6	51·0
Other cereals and pulses	1·9	1·4
Potatoes	15·1	12·5
Turnips, swedes, kale and cabbage[1]	0·8	0·8
Vegetables	1·2	1·2
Other crops	3·3	5·0
Fruit	2·5	2·4
Grass for mowing	264·2	252·8
Grass for grazing	510·1	501·2
Rough grazing (excluding common land)	199·6	197·7

[1] Stock feeding only.

Livestock (1,000) at June census (1980 and 1981):

	1980	*1981*
Dairy cows	270	270
Beef cows	224	205
Total cattle	1,507	1,436
Breeding ewes	539	575
Total sheep	1,061	1,139
Breeding sows	72	65
Total pigs	691	627
Total poultry	11,389	11,486

INDUSTRY AND TRADE

Industry. Industry makes a considerable contribution to the Northern Ireland economy. In 1980 employment in manufacturing and construction amounted to 131,650, some 28% of the total workforce. Of this number, 38,600 (29%) were engaged in the engineering and allied industries, which include shipbuilding and aircraft manufacture. The former predominance of shipbuilding has diminished, and the engineering sector now produces an impressive variety of goods: from textile machinery, air-conditioning plant and oilfield equipment to automobile and aero-engine components, data-processing and sound-reproduction equipment, and electronic components. The textile industry, with a workforce of 16,700, has traditionally been associated with linen, but man-made fibre production has brought diversification to the sector and now accounts for about a quarter of the total output of synthetic and artificial fibres in the UK. The related clothing and footwear trades employ 13,250 people. Taken together, food, drink and tobacco account for 18,350 jobs, the remainder of the manufacturing sector comprising a multiplicity of trades, such as chemicals and oil-refining, rubber and plastic goods, and furniture accounting for 19,800. The construction industry employs over 24,950 people. The Government offers special encouragement towards the establishment of new and the expansion of existing industry, including substantial grants towards capital investment and the provision of government-built factories at a low rent or on repayment terms. At 31 Dec. 1980 there were 173 new firms and 182 schemes of expansion by existing firms, giving employment to over 76,971 workers.

Labour. The main source of statistics in Northern Ireland is the census of employment which was conducted annually from 1971 to 1978 and then in 1981. This provides industrial analyses of employees distinguishing between full-time and part-time employees. The census is supplemented by a less detailed sample quarterly enquiry which since 1979 has been used to provide the main mid-year employment estimate. This showed that at June 1982 there were 451,350 jobs for employees in Northern Ireland; of which 239,750 were taken up by males.

Statistics of persons registered as unemployed in Northern Ireland are compiled monthly. The average rate of unemployment in Northern Ireland in 1981 was 18·3% compared with 13·7% in 1980. The average number registered as unemployed was 105,390. The Department of Economic Development provides an all-age guidance and placement service through a network of Employment Service Offices and Jobmarkets situated in the principal towns of Northern Ireland. They maintain registers of persons seeking employment (either full- or part-time) and those already in employment who wish to change their job. In 1981 the number of vacancies filled in Northern Ireland by the Employment Service was 17,020 (adults and young persons), and 13,152 were placed in centres of training.

Assistance is available to employers who transfer key workers temporarily or permanently to Northern Ireland from other countries or within Northern Ireland in connection with the establishment or expansion of an industrial undertaking.

The Department of Economic Development maintains a register of disabled persons who are in the employment field and under the provisions of the Disabled Persons (Employment) Acts (NI) 1945 and 1960, makes efforts to find suitable work for those who are unemployed. Employment rehabilitation courses are provided at the Employment Rehabilitation Unit at Mill Road, Newtownabbey and training courses at various locations are available to assist unemployed disabled persons to readjust themselves to working conditions and to enhance their prospects of obtaining suitable employment. Allowances are paid to persons attending these courses.

Enterprise Ulster is a direct labour organization whose objective is to recruit workers from the unemployed register. Work is carried out mainly for public bodies and projects are of a community and amenity nature such as play areas, parks, playing fields, etc. In Sept. 1982, 130 projects were in operation providing employment for 1,341 employees, of whom 214 were employed as part of the Youth Opportunities Programme. There are 12 Government Training Centres in Northern Ireland which provide over 3,000 training places and an annual output of over 5,000 trainees.

Government Training Centres contribute to the Youth Training Programme, having up to 2,400 places available for 16–17-year-olds who have been unable to find employment. A special six-month broad based modular course provides basic training in a wide variety of skills and the six-month craft skill courses provide initial apprentice training. The remaining places are reserved for adult trainees.

To supplement the Government Training Centres facilities, arrangements have been made for the use of spare training capacity in industry and commerce to attach people to firms for training courses. By this means a wide variety of training is made available and this has been further supplemented by extensive use of spare capacity in other training agencies and in Colleges of Further Education.

A comprehensive Youth Training Programme was introduced in the autumn of 1982 replacing the Youth Opportunities Programme. When fully operational the new Programme will cater for the vocational preparation needs of all 16- and 17-year olds whether in employment, in full-time education or unable to find work. All minimum age school leavers who cannot get a job are guaranteed a year's continuous full-time training under the Programme. In 1982–83 a total of 15,000 training places are being made available, mainly in Government Training Centres, Further Education Colleges, Work Preparation Units and with employers.

The Department of Economic Development administers two management training programmes aimed at developing management expertise in Northern Ireland. In 1981–82, 1,600 managerial posts were aided under the programme.

In the sphere of industrial relations an independent and statutory body entitled The Labour Relations Agency was established under the Industrial Relations (NI) Order 1976 with the general duty to promote the improvement of industrial relations and to encourage the extension, development and, where necessary, the reform of collective bargaining machinery. The Agency is empowered to undertake research and provide an advisory service on industrial relations matters and to act as a forum for discussion of matters of mutual concern to management and unions. It also has a range of specific functions in the industrial relations field, including the settlement of disputes concerning trade-union recognition. The Agency's major role is in relation to the provision of conciliation and arbitration services. This means that, supplementing the procedures within industry for the prevention and settlement of disputes, the Agency plays an important part as an impartial third party in helping the sides to clarify issues in dispute and to settle their differences by agreement. Where conciliation fails, the Agency may arrange, if the parties agree, for independent arbitration by one or more persons appointed by the Agency or by the Industrial Court. Occasionally a settlement is promoted by the appointment of a Court of Inquiry. However, the great majority of industrial disputes are settled without stoppage of work, and Northern Ireland's record of days lost due to industrial disputes bears favourable comparison with that of the rest of the UK.

The Fair Employment Agency for Northern Ireland was established under the Fair Employment (NI) Act 1976, with the duties of promoting equality of opportunity in employments and occupations as between persons of different religious beliefs (including people without any religious belief), of working for the elimination of religious and political discrimination (made unlawful by the Act) in employments and occupations, and of keeping under review patterns and trends of employment and occupations.

The Equal Opportunities Commission for Northern Ireland was established under the Sex Discrimination (NI) Order 1976 with the duties of working towards the elimination of sex discrimination in the fields covered by the Order, of promoting equality of opportunity between men and women generally and of keeping under review the working of the Order and equal pay legislation.

The Department of Economic Development is responsible for the administration of the Health and Safety at Work (NI) Order 1978 which came into force 1 May 1979. Existing statutory provisions including the Factories Act (NI) 1965 and the Office and Shop Premises Act (NI) 1966 together with many new provisions for the health, safety and welfare of persons at work are enforced by the Department's Health and Safety Inspectorate. The 1978 Order extends to all persons at work with the exception of private domestic employment and applies to over 40,000 employment situations. The 1978 Order lays duties on employers, employees, self-employed, manufacturers and suppliers of materials and persons having control of buildings. Employers and self-employed have duties in regard to persons not employed by them but who may be affected by their operations at work. Agricultural provisions are enforced by the Department of Agriculture and some existing statutory provisions under factories and shops legislation continue to be enforced by district councils with some additional duties.

COMMERCE. Northern Ireland has a substantial export trade with countries overseas, but as a large part of it is routed through Great Britain, separate details are not available. The main markets outside the UK are Ireland, USA, Saudi Arabia, Algeria, Japan, Romania, the EEC and EFTA. From 1975 no detailed trade figures of Northern Ireland were compiled.

Imports and exports, including trade with Great Britain (in £1m. sterling) for calendar years:

	1967	*1968*	*1969*	*1970*	*1971*	*1972*	*1973*	*1974*
Imports	552	660	728	829	892	937	1,304	1,734
Exports	507	596	669	745	843	917	1,175	1,368

In 1974, 74% of the total imports (by value) came from Great Britain or from foreign countries *via* Great Britain; 12% from Ireland. Of the exports, 82% (by value) went to Great Britain or to foreign countries *via* Great Britain; 13% to Ireland.

Principal imports in 1974 (including imports from Great Britain) were valued at: Textiles, fibres, yarns and fabrics, £341m.; machinery, £214m.; transport equipment, £158m.; petroleum and petroleum products, £115m.; chemicals, £90m.; manufactures of metal, fruit and vegetables, fresh and processed, £43m.

Principal exports in 1974 (including exports to Great Britain) were valued at: Textiles, fibres, yarns and fabrics, £485m.; machinery, £134m.; meat and meat preparations, £77m.; transport equipment, £65m.; clothing, £62m.

Tourism. Tourism earns a substantial amount of revenue for Northern Ireland and total spending by some 710,000 visitors in 1980 was estimated at £72m. Altogether tourism provides over 8,000 permanent jobs and some 3,000 temporary or seasonal jobs. The Northern Ireland Tourist Board plays a major role in promoting the development of tourist traffic in Northern Ireland.

The protection of scenic beauty, scientific and nature interest, and wildlife is fostered under the Amenity Lands Act (NI) 1965 and the Wild Birds Protection Acts (NI) 1931 to 1968 by the Department of the Environment for Northern Ireland, which is advised by the Ulster Countryside Committee, the Nature Reserves Committee and the Wild Birds Advisory Committee. Eight Areas of Outstanding Natural Beauty and 46 Areas of Scientific Interest have been designated, and in these areas special attention is given respectively to the amenity and scientific aspects of planning applications. Country Parks have been established at Crawfordsburn and Scrabo, Co. Down, and the Roe Valley and Ness Wood, Co. Londonderry, Castle Archdale, Co. Fermanagh. Land for further parks has been acquired at Redburn, Co. Down and The Birches in N. Armagh. The Lagan Valley between Belfast and Lisburn is being administered as Northern Ireland's first Regional Park. Thirty-seven National Nature Reserves have been declared, and steady progress is being made with the acquisition of further reserves. Nine areas have been designated as Bird Sanctuaries.

The Department is advised by the Historic Monuments Council on the exercise of its powers under the Historic Monuments Act (NI) 1971 in respect of the conservation of historic monuments and the preservation of objects of archaeological or historic interest. At present there are some 140 monuments in State care and over 450 are scheduled. The Department, advised by the Historic Buildings Council, is also responsible for listing buildings of special architectural or historic interest and for designating areas of similar interest the character or appearance of which it is desirable to preserve or enhance. To date some 5,500 buildings have been listed and 13 areas have been designated. Grants are payable by the Department to assist in the repair or maintenance of listed buildings and for schemes of enhancement in conservation areas.

COMMUNICATIONS

Road and Rail. All train services are operated by the Northern Ireland Railways

Co. Ltd which is a subsidiary of the Northern Ireland Transport Holding Co. The number of track miles operated is 357; passenger route miles, 210.In 1981-82 railways carried 5.4m. passengers. Most bus services are operated by two other subsidiaries, Ulsterbus Ltd and Citybus Ltd. Ulsterbus runs services outside the Belfast area (except for a few services provided by privately owned bus undertakings) while all the services within the Belfast area are run by Citybus.

The Department of the Environment (NI) administers a licensing system for professional hauliers with the objective of maintaining standards and conditions necessary for the safe operation of vehicles and fair competition between hauliers. The level of services provided and the rates charged by the industry are determined by the normal economic forces of supply and demand. At 31 March 1982 there were 1,777 professional hauliers and 3,125 vehicles licensed to engage in road haulage.

The number of motor vehicles licensed at 31 Dec. 1981 was 436,695, comprising private cars, 365,000; motor cycles, 14,550; hackney vehicles, 2,510; goods vehicles, 33,760; agricultural tractors, 7,660. In addition, there were 13,215 vehicles which were not subject to licence duty.

The Department of the Environment (NI) is responsible for the provision and maintenance of all public roads, bridges and street lighting in the Province, the provision and operation of car parks, and for the operation of the Strangford Lough Ferry. In addition to a Headquarters Unit the Roads Service of the Department operates through Divisional Offices in Ballymena, Belfast, Coleraine, Craigavon, Downpatrick and Omagh and smaller offices in other centres.

At 1 April 1979 the total mileage of roads was 14,652, graded for administrative purposes as follows: Motorway 69 miles; all purpose trunk, 338 miles; Class I, 1,040 miles; Class II, 1,760 miles; Class III, 2,947 miles; unclassified, 8,494 miles.

Aviation. Northern Ireland Airports Ltd is responsible for the operation of Belfast Airport. A major development programme, which will double the size of the terminal building and improve other operational facilities, is now under construction. In 1981, 1·3m. passengers and 17,738 tonnes of freight and mail were handled.

Scheduled passenger services operate between Belfast and 24 domestic airports throughout the UK.

Shipping. Passenger services operate between Belfast and Liverpool and between Larne and (i) Cairnryan and (ii) Stranraer. Conventional cargo services have given way in many cases to container, unit load and drive on/drive off services. The latter type of service now operates between Belfast, Larne and Warrenpoint to various ports in UK.

JUSTICE, RELIGION, EDUCATION AND WELFARE

Justice. The Lord Chancellor has responsibility for the administration of all courts in Northern Ireland through the Northern Ireland Court Service, and is responsible for the appointment of judges and resident magistrates.

The Court structure in Northern Ireland has 3 tiers–the Supreme Court of Judicature of Northern Ireland (comprising the Court of Appeal, the High Court and the Crown Court), the County Courts and the Magistrates' Courts. There are 25 Petty Sessions which when grouped together for administration purposes form 8 County Court Divisions and 4 Circuits.

The County Court has general civil jurisdiction subject to an upper monetary limit of £5,000. Appeals from the Magistrates' Courts lie to the County Court, while appeals from the County Court lie to the High Court. Circuit Registrars have jurisdiction to deal with most defended actions up to £500 and undefended actions up to £5,000. They also deal, by an informal arbitration procedure, with small claims whose value does not exceed £300. An appeal from the decision of a Registrar lies to the High Court.

Police. The police force consists of the Royal Ulster Constabulary, supported by the Royal Ulster Constabulary Reserve, a mainly part-time force.

Religion. The religious professions at the census of 1971 were: Roman Catholics,

477,919; Presbyterians, 405,719; Church of Ireland, 334,318 (including Church of England and Episcopal Church of Scotland); Methodists, 71,235; others and not stated, 230,449.

Education. Education in Northern Ireland is administered centrally by the Department of Education and locally by 5 education and library boards. The Department is concerned with the whole range of education from nursery education through to higher education and continuing education; for sport and recreation; for youth services; for the arts and culture (including libraries) and for community relations and community development. District councils are the main providers of sport, recreation and community facilities and the education and library boards have a responsibility where the facilities are intended primarily for education and youth service activities. The Department assists with grants as far as the district councils are concerned and meets the full cost in relation to education and library boards.

The 5 education and library boards which took over responsibility for the local administration of the education and library services on 1 Oct. 1973 are required to ensure that there are sufficient schools of all kinds to meet the needs of their area. They provide primary and secondary schools, special schools for handicapped pupils and institutions of further education. The boards also make contributions towards the cost of maintaining voluntary schools; award university and other scholarships; meet the tuition fees of the great majority of pupils attending grammar schools; provide milk and meals; free books and transport for pupils; enforce school attendance; regulate the employment of children and young people and secure the provision of recreational and youth service facilities. They are also required to develop a comprehensive and efficient library service for their areas. The following are the statistics for the 1980–81 academic year:

Universities. The Queen's University of Belfast (founded in 1849 as a college of the Queen's University of Ireland and reconstituted as a separate university in 1908) had 105 professors, 251 readers and senior lecturers, 474 lecturers and tutors and 6,248 full-time students.

The New University of Ulster at Coleraine, of which Magee University College, Londonderry, is now an integral part, had 25 professors, 47 readers and senior lecturers, 168 lecturers and demonstrators and 1,723 full-time students.

The Ulster Polytechnic is a central institution providing higher non-university education for the whole of Northern Ireland with a full-time academic staff of 558, 4,260 full-time and 2,798 part-time students on vocational and professional courses and 312 students on specialist teacher-training courses.

Secondary Education. 78 grammar schools with 58,896 pupils and 3,587 full-time teachers; 184 secondary (intermediate) schools with 105,339 pupils and 6,984 full-time teachers.

Primary Education. 1,048 primary schools with 191,689 pupils and 8,101 teachers; 79 nursery schools with 4,091 pupils and 144 teachers.

Further Education. 26 institutions of further education with 1,827 full-time and 1,692 part-time teachers and an enrolment of 12,825 full-time, 13,412 part-time day and 16,094 evening students on vocational courses; and nearly 43,000 students on non-vocational (mostly evening) courses.

Special Educational Treatment. 35 special schools, including hospital schools with 2,751 pupils and 335 teachers.

Teachers. There were 20,978 full-time teachers (8,484 men and 12,494 women) in grant-aided schools and institutions of further education. The minimum general teacher-training course is of 3 years' duration and there were 2,110 students (634 men and 1,476 women) in training; these included students following teacher-training courses at university establishments and at Ulster Polytechnic and Londonderry College of Technology.

Expenditure. Expenditure by the Department of Education in 1980–81 was £451·5m.

Health and Personal Social Services. Under the provisions of the Health and Personal Social Services (NI) Order 1972, the Department of Health and Social Services is responsible for the provision of integrated health and personal social services in Northern Ireland, designed to promote the physical and mental health of the people of Northern Ireland through the prevention, diagnosis and treatment of illness, and also to promote their social welfare. Four Health and Social Services Boards, Eastern, Northern, Southern and Western, established under the above Order, administer health and personal social services, as the Department directs, within their designated areas.

Social Security. The social security schemes in Northern Ireland are similar to those in force in Great Britain.

The system of social security established by the Social Security Acts 1975 to 1982, and the corresponding system established by the Social Security (NI) Acts 1975 to 1982, operate, by virtue of a reciprocal arrangement between Great Britain and Northern Ireland, as a single system throughout the UK. The National Insurance Joint Authority, consisting of the Secretary of State for Social Services and the Head of the Department of Health and Social Services for Northern Ireland is responsible under this reciprocal arrangement for making any necessary financial adjustments between the National Insurance funds of the two countries and also has responsibility for determining the administrative procedures necessary for the purpose of giving effect to the provisions of the reciprocal arrangement. There are comprehensive reciprocal agreements with the Isle of Man, and agreements covering reciprocity in respect of most benefits have been made by the Government of the UK, applying to the schemes in both Great Britain and Northern Ireland, with Australia, Austria, Belgium, Canada, Cyprus, Denmark, Finland, France, Germany (Fed. Rep.), Gibraltar, Guernsey, Ireland, Israel, Italy, Jamaica, Jersey, Luxembourg, Malta, Mauritius, the Netherlands, New Zealand, Norway, Portugal, Spain, Sweden, Switzerland Turkey and Yugoslavia. There are also limited agreements with Bermuda and the USA.

Since 1 April 1973 the reciprocal agreements between the UK and the other members of the EEC have been largely superseded by the Social Security Regulations of the Community.

These regulations apply to nationals of the Member States and Gibraltar (and to stateless persons and refugees living in the Member States) who are employed and self-employed workers moving within the Community.

National Insurance. During the year ended 31 March 1982, £25·8m. sickness benefit was paid to an average of 18,100 persons and £56·8m. unemployment benefit was paid to an average of 45,600 persons. Widows' benefits amounting to £24·8m. were paid to 15,200 persons and retirement pensions totalling £263·7m. were paid to an average of 196,100 persons. Invalidity pensions and allowances totalling £70·2m. were paid to approximately 32,500 persons. Accidents in respect of which claims to benefit are made occur at the rate of 130 per week and £0·9m. industrial injury benefit was paid in 1981–82 to an average of 750 persons. Industrial disablement benefit amounting to £8·7m. was paid to an average of 4,700 persons. Maternity benefit totalling £6·6m. was paid to approximately 25,000 persons. Receipts, including an item related to the financial adjustments mentioned above of the Northern Ireland Insurance Fund in the year ended 31 March 1982 were £480m. and payments were £485m.

Child Benefit. During the year ended 31 March 1982, £126m. was paid to an average of 218,500 families.

Supplementary Benefits. In 1981–82, £180m. was paid to an average of 151,500 persons.

Family Income Supplement. In 1981–82, £7m. was paid to an average of 10,700 persons.

Books of Reference

The annual and other publications of the various Departments and the Reports, etc., of Parliamentary Committees may be obtained from HM Stationery Office, Belfast.

Ulster Year Book, 1981. Belfast, HMSO, 1981
Census of Population Reports, Northern Ireland. Belfast, HMSO, 1971
Digest of Statistics. Belfast, HMSO (bi-annual)
Northern Ireland Development 1970–75. Belfast, HMSO, 1970
Social and Economic Trends. Belfast, HMSO (annual)
Who Makes What in Northern Ireland: A Trade Directory. Belfast, HMSO, 10th ed. 1979
Reports on the Census of Production of Northern Ireland. Belfast, HMSO, 1976
Re-organization of Secondary Education in Northern Ireland. Belfast, HMSO, 1976
The Statutes Revised: Northern Ireland. HMSO, 1982
Bell, G., *The Protestants of Ulster.* London, 1976
Bew, P., Gibbon, P. and Patterson, H., *The State in Northern Ireland, 1921–1972.* New York, 1980
Biggs-Davison, J., *The Hand is Red.* London, 1974
Boal, F. W. and Douglas, J. N. H., *Integration and Division.* London, 1982
Farrell, M., *Northern Ireland: The Orange State.* London, 1976
Flackes, W. D., *Northern Ireland: Political Directory 1968–79.* London, 1980
Heskin, K., *Northern Ireland: A Psychological Analysis.* Dublin, 1980
Hull, R. H., *The Irish Triangle.* Princeton Univ. Press, 1976
Lawrence, R. J., *The Government of Northern Ireland: Public Finance and Public Services.* OUP, 1965
Quekett, Sir A. S., *The Constitution of Northern Ireland.* 3 pts. Belfast, 1928–47
Rose, R., *Northern Ireland: A Time of Choice.* London, 1976
Wallace, M., *British Government in Northern Ireland: From Devolution to Direct Rule.* Newton Abbot, 1982
Watt, D. (ed.) *The Constitution of Northern Ireland.* London, 1981
Winchester, S., *Northern Ireland in Crisis: Reporting the Ulster Troubles.* New York, 1975

ISLE OF MAN

AREA AND POPULATION. Area, 227 sq. miles (572 sq. km); resident population census April 1981, 64,679. The principal towns are Douglas (population, 19,944), Ramsey (5,818), Peel (3,688), Castletown (3,141). Vital statistics, 1981: Births, 752; deaths, 979; marriages, 405. The number of Manx-speaking people was 284 in 1971 (165 in 1961 and 4,657 in 1901), all of whom were bilingual.

CONSTITUTION AND GOVERNMENT. The Isle of Man is administered in accordance with its own laws by the Court of Tynwald, consisting of the Governor, appointed by the Crown; the Legislative Council, composed of the Lord Bishop of Sodor and Man, the Attorney-General (who does not vote) and 8 members selected by the House of Keys, total 10 members; and the House of Keys, a representative assembly of 24 members chosen on adult suffrage with 12 months' residence for 5 years by the 6 'sheadings' or local sub-divisions, and the 4 municipalities. The Island is not bound by Acts of the Imperial Parliament unless specially mentioned in them.

A special relationship exists between the Isle of Man and the European Economic Community providing for free trade and adoption by the Isle of Man of the EEC's external trade policies with third countries. The Island remains free to levy its own system of rates and taxes.

The elections to the House of Keys, Nov. 1981, resulted in the return of 21 Independents and 3 Labour. Number of voters, 47,449.

An Executive Council to advise the Governor on all matters of government was set up under the Isle of Man Constitution Act, 1961. It consists at present of 5 members of the House of Keys and 3 of the Legislative Council.

Lieut.-Governor: Sir Nigel Cecil, KBE, CB (term of office began Sept. 1980).
Government Secretary: P. J. Hulme.
Government Treasurer: W. Dawson.

Flag: Red, with 3 steel-coloured legs armoured and spurred (knees and spurs, yellow) in the centre.

ECONOMY

Budget. Revenue is derived from customs duties, value added tax and from income tax. In 1982–83 the budget allowed for gross revenue and capital expenditure of £130,424,220. Income tax was 20p in the £. No death duties or surtaxes are levied. Company registration tax is levied at a flat rate of £250 on every company incorporated in the Isle of Man which trades and is controlled outside the island. A Land Speculation Tax applies at the same rate as income tax.

The Island currently makes an annual contribution to the UK Government of 2·5% of net 'common purse' receipts (share of customs and excise duties and VAT received by Treasury) towards the cost of defence and other common services provided by the UK Government. That contribution currently amounts to about £895,000.

Currency. Notes to the value of £20, £10, £5, £1 and 50p are issued by the Isle of Man Government. Annual minting of decimal coinage takes place, and in 1973, 1974, 1977 and 1979 and thereafter legal tender gold coins in half sovereign, sovereign, £2 and £5 pieces were issued. Commemorative crowns have also been issued since 1970, and silver and platinum decimal sets have been minted more recently. From 1978 onwards £5, £1, and 20p coins were minted for general circulation.

AGRICULTURE. The principal agricultural produce of the Island consists of oats, wheat, barley, potatoes, grasses, fatstock dairy products. The total area under grass and crops in 1981 was 78,853 acres and of rough grazings, 39,482 acres. The total area under cereals was 11,530 acres, including 1,903 under oats, 903 under wheat and 8,385 under barley or bere. There were also 1,084 acres under turnips and swedes, 698 under potatoes and 63,607 acres of grassland.

Livestock in 1981: 901 horses, 34,469 cattle, 116,430 sheep, 4,375 pigs and 77,845 poultry.

TOURISM. In 1980–81 tourism contributed 10% of national income and about 6,000 were employed in the industry during the summer season.

COMMUNICATIONS

Roads. There are 500 miles of good roads. The International TT Motor Cycle Races and cycle races take place annually. Omnibus services operate to all parts of the island.

Number of vehicles (31 March 1982): 27,496 cars, 3,894 goods vehicles and engineering plant, 1,111 agricultural vehicles, 2,881 motor cycles and scooters and 774 taxis and public service vehicles.

Railways. Several novel transport systems operate on the Island during the summer season, including 100-year-old horse-drawn trams, and the Manx Electric Railway, linking Douglas, Ramsey and Snaefell Mountain (2,036 ft). The Isle of Man Steam Railway also operates between Douglas and Port Erin.

Aviation. Ronaldsway Airport handles scheduled services operated by Manx Airlines, Dan-Air and Avair to and from London, Manchester, Belfast, Dublin, Glasgow, Liverpool, Blackpool, etc. Air taxi services also operate.

Shipping. Car ferries of the Isle of Man Steam Packet Co. link the Island with Liverpool throughout the year and similar services operate to Fleetwood, Ardrossan, Dublin and Belfast during the summer season.

Manx Line provides a roll-on roll-off service between Douglas and Heysham.

Broadcasting. The first constitutionally licensed commercial radio station in the British Isles, Manx Radio, is operated by Government on medium and VHF wavelengths from Douglas.

Newspapers. In 1982 there were 5 weekly newspapers.

JUSTICE AND EDUCATION

Police. The police force numbered 143 all ranks and 12 cadets in 1981.

Education. Education is compulsory between the ages of 5 and 15. In Jan. 1982 there were 37 primary schools with 5,532 pupils in attendance. The net expenditure on education for 1982–83 amounted to £15·7m.; in addition, capital expenditure of £0·4m. was made for school buildings. There are 7 secondary schools, 5 provided by the Board of Education (4,515 registered pupils), 1 direct grant school for girls (350 registered pupils), 1 independent public school for boys (402 registered pupils), 1 college of further education (364 full- and 3,292 part-time and evening pupils).

Books of Reference

Isle of Man Digest of Economic and Social Statistics, 1980. Isle of Man Government, 1980
A Report Comprising the Isle of Man Index of Retail Prices, the Family Expenditure Survey and a Cost of Living Comparison with the United Kingdom. 2nd ed. Isle of Man Government, 1980
A Businessman's Briefing 1982–83. Isle of Man Government 1982
Tynwald Companion 1982. Isle of Man Government, 1982
Manx Tourism 77. Isle of Man Government, 1977
Kinvig, R. H., *History of the Isle of Man.* Oxford, 1945.—*The Isle of Man: A Social, Cultural and Political History.* Liverpool Univ. Press, 1975
Mais, S. P. B., *Isle of Man.* London, 1954
Solly, M., *Anatomy of a Tax Haven. The Isle of Man and Manx Income Tax,* 2 vols. Douglas, 1980
Stenning, E. H., *Portrait of the Isle of Man.* London, 1958

CHANNEL ISLANDS

AREA. The Channel Islands are situated off the north-west coast of France and are the only portions of the 'Duchy of Normandy' now belonging to the Crown of England, to which they have been attached since the Conquest. They consist of Jersey (28,717 acres), Guernsey (15,654 acres) and the following dependencies of Guernsey–Alderney (1,962), Brechou (74), Great Sark (1,035), Little Sark (239), Herm (320), Jethou (44) and Lihou (38), a total of 48,083 acres, or 75 sq. miles (194 sq. km).

The climate is mild. Total rainfall (1981), Jersey, 1,034·4 mm; Guernsey, 903 mm. Temperature registered (1981): highest, Jersey, 28·1C.; Guernsey, 27·7C.; lowest, Jersey, –1·7C.; Guernsey, –0·4C.

CONSTITUTION. The Lieut.-Governors and Cs.-in-C. of Jersey and Guernsey are the personal representatives of the Sovereign, the Commanders of the Armed Forces of the Crown and the channel of communication between H.M. Government in the UK and the insular governments. They are appointed by the Crown and have a voice but no vote in the Assemblies of the States (the insular legislatures). The Secretaries to the Lieut.-Governors are their staff officers.

The Bailiffs are appointed by the Crown and are Presidents both of the Assembly of the States and of the Royal Courts of Jersey and Guernsey. They have in the States a casting vote.

LANGUAGE. The official languages are French and English, but English is gradually supplanting French. The language commonly used is English, but in the country districts of Jersey and Guernsey and throughout Sark some people also speak a Norman-French dialect; that of Alderney has died out.

TRADE. From 1958 the trade of the Channel Islands with the UK has been regarded as internal trade.

COMMUNICATIONS

Road. Omnibus services operate in all parts of Jersey and Guernsey.

Aviation. Scheduled air services are maintained by Air UK, Jersey European, British Midland, Aurigny Air Services, Dan-Air, Brymon Airways, Guernsey Airlines, NLM City Hopper and other companies between the islands and airports in the UK, Ireland, the Netherlands and France. During the summer months these services are greatly increased, both in the number of airports served and in the frequency of flights.

Shipping. Passenger and cargo steam services between Jersey, Guernsey and England are maintained by British Rail; between Guernsey, Jersey and England and St Malo by the Commodore Shipping Co.; between Guernsey, Jersey, Alderney and France by Condor Ltd (hydrofoil), and between Guernsey and Alderney and England and Guernsey and Sark by local companies.

Post and Broadcasting. Postal and overseas telephone and telegraph services are maintained by the respective Postal Administrations of each bailiwick. The local telephone services are maintained by the insular authorities. There were, in 1982, 32,700 subscribers in Jersey and 23,309 in Guernsey.

There is an independent television station in Jersey and a local radio station, BBC Radio Jersey, opened in 1982.

JUSTICE AND RELIGION

Justice. Justice is administered by the Royal Courts of Jersey and Guernsey, each of which consists of the Bailiff and 12 Jurats, the latter being elected by an electoral college. There is an appeal from the Royal Courts to the Courts of Appeal of Jersey and of Guernsey. A final appeal lies to the Privy Council in certain cases. A stipendiary magistrate in each, Jersey and Guernsey, deals with minor civil and criminal cases.

Church. Jersey and Guernsey each constitutes a deanery within the diocese of Winchester. The rectories (12 in Jersey; 10 in Guernsey) are in the gift of the Crown. The Roman Catholic and various Nonconformist Churches are represented.

Books of Reference

Ambrière, F., *Les Iles Anglo-Normandes.* Paris, 1971
Coysh, V., *The Channel Islands: A New Study.* Newton Abbot, 1977
Cruickshank, C., *The German Occupation of the Channel Islands.* London, 1975
Lempière, R., *Portrait of the Channel Islands.* London, 1970.–*History of the Channel Islands.* London, 1974
Lockley, R. M., *The Channel Islands.* London, 1968
Myhill, H., *Introducing the Channel Islands.* London, 1964
Uttley, J., *The Story of the Channel Islands.* London, 1966

JERSEY

POPULATION (census 1980), 76,100. In the year ended 31 Dec. 1981 there were 894 births and 929 deaths. The town is St Helier on the south coast.

CONSTITUTION. The States consist of 12 senators (elected for 6 years, 6 retiring every third year), 12 Constables (triennial) and 29 Deputies (triennial), all elected on universal suffrage by the people.

The island legislature is 'The States of Jersey'. The States comprises the Bailiff, the Lieut.-Governor, 12 Senators, the Constables of the 12 parishes of the island, 28 Deputies, the Dean of Jersey, the Attorney-General and the Solicitor-General.

They all have the right to speak in the Assembly, but only the 53 elected members (the Senators, Constables and Deputies) have the right to vote; the Bailiff has a casting vote. General elections for Senators and Deputies are held every third year. Except in specific instances, enactments passed by the States require the sanction of The Queen-in-Council. The Lieut.-Governor has the power of veto on certain forms of legislation.

Flag: White with a red diagonal cross. In the top centre of the flag a shield of the arms of Jersey ensigned with the Plantagenet Crown.

Lieut.-Governor and C.-in-C. of Jersey: Gen. Sir Peter Whiteley, GCB, OBE.
Secretary and ADC to the Lieut.-Governor: Lieut.-Cdr O. M. B. de Las Casas, MVO, OBE, RN (Retd).

Bailiff of Jersey and President of the States: Sir Frank Ereaut.
Deputy Bailiff: P. L. Crill, CBE.

ECONOMY

Budget (year ending 31 Dec. 1981). Revenue, £118,518,893; expenditure, £94,322,585; public debt, £759,230. The standard rate of income tax is 20p in the pound. No super-tax or death duties are levied. Parochial rates of moderate amount are payable by owners and occupiers.

Currency. The States issue bank-notes in denominations of £10, £5 and £1.

INDUSTRY AND TRADE

Industry. Principal activities: Tourism; total number of hotel and guesthouse bedrooms (1981), 7,873; expenditure of tourists (1981), £120m. Agriculture, total output (1981), £23m. Light industry, mainly electrical goods, textiles and clothing. Total exports (1980), £29m. Banking and finance, total bank deposits and balances due to parent companies by deposit-taking institutions (1981), £12,300m.

Commerce (1980). Principal imports: Machinery and transport equipment, £57·3m.; manufactured goods, £43·4m.; food, £40m.; mineral fuels, £21·5m.; chemicals, £15·1m., and miscellaneous, £53·6m. Principal exports (1980): Machinery and transport equipment, £28m.; food, £22·2m; manufactured goods, £15·6m., and miscellaneous, £24·1m.

COMMUNICATIONS

Aviation. The Jersey airport is situated at St Peter. It covers approximately 375 acres. Number of aircraft movements (1981) 25,032; number of passenger arrivals, 630,286.

Shipping (1981). All vessels arriving in Jersey from outside Jersey waters report at St Helier or Gorey on first arrival. There is a harbour of minor importance at St Aubin. Number of commercial vessels entering St Helier, 3,935; number of registered craft (of 15 ft and over), 1,531. Passengers arrived in 1981, 568,641.

EDUCATION (1981). There were 9 States secondary schools and 28 States primary schools; 4,355 pupils attended the primary schools, 4,369 the secondary schools. There were 9 private primary schools with 1,331 pupils and 6 private secondary schools with 981 pupils. Highlands College offers full- and part-time courses to Ordinary and National Certificate and Diploma levels or similar standards and, together with Les Quennevais Adult Community Centre, evening classes in technical and recreational subjects.

Books of Reference

Balleine, G. R., *Biographical Dictionary of Jersey.* London, 1948.—*A History of the Island of Jersey.* London, 1950.—*The Bailiwick of Jersey.* 3rd ed. London, 1970
Bois, F. de L., *The Constitutional History of Jersey.* Jersey, 1970

Carre, A. L., *English–Jersey Language Vocabulary*. Jersey, 1972
Le Maistre, F., *Dictionnaire Jersiais-Français*. Jersey, 1966
Powell, G. C., *Economic Survey of Jersey*. Jersey, 1971

States of Jersey Library: Royal Square, St Helier. *Librarian:* J. K. Antill, FLA.

GUERNSEY

POPULATION. Census population(1981) 53,313. Births during 1980 were 643; deaths, 614. The town is St Peter Port.

CONSTITUTION. The government of the island is conducted by committees appointed by the States.

The States of Deliberation, the Parliament of Guernsey, is composed of the following members: The Bailiff, who is President *ex officio;* 12 Conseillers; H.M. Procureur and H.M. Comptroller (Law Officers of the Crown), who have a voice but no vote; 33 People's Deputies elected by popular franchise; 10 Douzaine Representatives elected by their Parochial Douzaines; 2 representatives of the States of Alderney.

The States of Election, an electoral college, elects the Jurats and Conseillers. It is composed of the following members: The Bailiff (President *ex officio*); the 12 Jurats or 'Jurés-Justiciers'; the 12 Conseillers; H.M. Procureur and H.M. Comptroller; the 33 People's Deputies; 34 Douzaine Representatives; and (for the election of Conseillers) 4 representatives of the States of Alderney.

Since Jan. 1949 all legislative powers and functions (with minor exceptions) formerly exercised by the Royal Court have been vested in the States of Deliberation. Projets de Loi (Bills) require the sanction of The Queen-in-Council.

Flag: White with a red cross.

Lieut.-Governor and C.-in-C. of Guernsey and its Dependencies: Air Chief Marshal Sir Peter Le Cheminant, GBE, KCB, DFC.

ADC to the Lieut.-Governor: Capt. D. P. L. Hodgetts. *Secretary to the Lieut.-Governor:* R. J. Williams.

Bailiff of Guernsey and President of the States: C. K Frossard.
Deputy Bailiff of Guernsey: G. M. Dorey.

FINANCE (year ending 31 Dec. 1981). Revenue, £54,512,965 (including £1,859,563 for Alderney); expenditure, £64,318,956 (including £1,415,940 for Alderney). States' funded debt less sinking fund provisions, £955,893; note and coin issue, £24,550,582. The standard rate of income tax is 20p in the pound. States and parochial rates are very moderate. No super-tax or death duties are levied.

COMMERCE (1981). Principal imports: Coal, 20,133 tonnes; petrol and oils, 150,621,347 litres. Principal exports: Tomatoes (1981), £20,581,266; flowers and fern, £12,383,381; sweet peppers, £149,491; aubergines, £23,526; plants, £437,602.

COMMUNICATIONS

Aviation. The airport in Guernsey, situated at La Villiaze, has a landing area of approximately 124 acres and a tarmac runway of 4,800 ft. In 1981, 181,254 passengers arrived from places outside the Channel Islands.

Shipping. The principal harbour is that of St Peter Port, and there is a harbour at St Sampson's (used mainly for commercial shipping). In 1981 the number of ship tonnes gross entering and leaving Guernsey was 10,447,226. 147,635 passengers arrived from places outside the Channel Islands. Ships registered in Guernsey at 31

Dec. 1981 numbered 755 and 566 fishing vessels. Small craft registered, 4,100. In 1981, 10,310 yachts visited Guernsey.

EDUCATION. There are 2 public schools in the island: Elizabeth College, founded by Queen Elizabeth in 1563, for boys, and the Ladies' College, for girls. The States grammar schools provide for education up to University entrance requirements, and there are numerous modern secondary and primary schools and a College of Further Education. The total number of school children is 9,134. Facilities are available for the study of art, domestic science and many other subjects of a technical nature. There is also a convent school with boarding facilities for girls.

ALDERNEY. Population (census, 1971), 1,686 (1980 estimate, 2,000). The island has an airport. There are no public railways but a 3 km line carries minerals. The constitution of the island (reformed 1949) provides for its own popularly elected President and States (12 members), and its own Court. The town is St Anne's.

Flag: White with a red cross with the island badge in the centre.

President of the States: J. Kay-Mouat.
Clerk of the States: W. R. Jones, MA.
Clerk of the Court: P. J. Beer.

SARK. Population (census, 1971), 584 (1978 estimate, 600). The Constitution is a mixture of feudal and popular government with its Chief Pleas (parliament), consisting of 40 tenants and 12 popularly elected deputies, presided over by the Seneschal. The head of the island is the Seigneur. Sark has no income tax. Motor vehicles, except tractors, are not allowed.

Flag: White with a red cross and a red first quarter bearing two gold lions.

The Seigneur: J. M. Beaumont.
Seneschal: H. Carré, MBE.

Books of Reference

Carteret, A. R. de, *The Story of Sark.* London, 1956
Clark, L., *Sark Discovered.* London, 1956
Coysh, V., *Alderney.* Newton Abbot, 1974
Durand, R., *Guernsey, Present and Past.* Guernsey, 1933.—*Guernsey under German Rule.* London, 1946
Hathaway, Sybil, *Dame of Sark: An Autobiography.* London, 1961
Le Huray, C. P., *The Bailiwick of Guernsey.* London, 1952
Marr, L. J., *A History of Guernsey.* Guernsey, 1982
Robinson, G. W. S., *Guernsey.* Newton Abbot, 1977
Wood, A. and M. S., *Islands in Danger.* 2nd ed. London, 1957
Wood, J., *Herm, Our Island Home.* London, 1973

UNITED STATES OF AMERICA

Capital: Washington, D.C.
Population: 226·5m. (1980)
GNP per capita: US$11,360 (1980)

HISTORY. The Declaration of Independence of the 13 states of which the American Union then consisted was adopted by Congress on 4 July 1776. On 30 Nov. 1782 Great Britain acknowledged the independence of the USA, and on 3 Sept. 1783 the treaty of peace was concluded and was ratified by the USA on 14 Jan. 1784.

AREA AND POPULATION. Population of conterminous USA at each census from 1790 to 1950, and for USA including Alaska and Hawaii, from 1960. Residents of Puerto Rico, the Philippine Islands, Guam, American Samoa and the Virgin Islands of the USA, and persons in the military and naval service stationed abroad are not included in the figures of this table. Residents of Indian reservations are excluded prior to 1890.

	White	*Negroes* [1]	*Other races* [2]	*Total*	*Decennial increase %*
1790	3,172,464 [3]	757,208	—	3,929,672	—
1800	4,306,446	1,002,037	—	5,308,483	35·1
1810	5,862,073	1,377,808	—	7,239,881	36·4
1820	7,866,797	1,771,562	—	9,638,359	33·1
1830	10,537,378	2,328,642	—	12,866,020	33·5
1840	14,195,805	2,873,648	—	17,069,453	32·7
1850	19,553,068	3,638,808	—	23,191,876	35·9
1860	26,922,537	4,441,830	78,954 [4]	31,443,321	35·6
1870 [5]	33,589,377	4,880,009	88,985	38,558,371	22·6
1870 [5]	*34,337,292*	*5,392,172*	*88,985*	*39,818,449*	*26·6*
1880	43,402,970	6,580,793	172,020	50,155,783	30·1
1890	55,101,258	7,488,676	357,780	62,947,714	25·5
1900	66,809,196	8,833,994	351,385	75,994,575	21·0
1910	81,731,957	9,827,763	412,546	91,972,266	21·0
1920	94,820,915	10,463,131	426,574	105,710,620	14·9 [6]
1930	110,286,740 [7]	11,891,143	597,163	122,775,046	16·1 [6]
1940	118,214,870	12,865,518	588,887	131,669,275	7·3
1950	134,942,028	15,042,286	713,047	150,697,361	14·5
1960 [8]	158,831,732	18,871,831	1,619,612	179,323,175	18·5
1970	177,748,975	22,580,289	2,882,662	203,211,926	13·3
1980	189,079,281	26,504,985	10,961,539	226,545,805	11·4

[1] Seventeen southern states (including D.C.) in 1900 had 7,922,969 Negroes (89·7% of the total Negro population); in 1920, 8,912,231 (85·2%); in 1940, 9,904,619 (77%); in 1950, 10,225,407 (68%); in 1960, 11,311,607 (59·9%); in 1970, 11,969,961 (53%).

[2] 1870: 63,199 Chinese, 55 Japanese and 25,731 Indians; 1880, 105,465 Chinese, 148 Japanese and 66,407 Indians; 1890, 107,488 Chinese, 2,039 Japanese and 248,253 Indians; 1900, 89,863 Chinese, 24,326 Japanese and 237,196 Indians; 1910, 71,531 Chinese, 72,157 Japanese, 265,683 Indians and 3,175 other races; 1920, 61,639 Chinese, 111,010 Japanese, 244,437 Indians and 9,488 other races; 1930, 332,397 Indians, 74,954 Chinese, 138,834 Japanese and 50,978 other races; 1940, 333,969 Indians, 77,504 Chinese, 126,947 Japanese and 50,467 other races; 1950, 343,410 Indians, 141,768 Japanese, 117,629 Chinese, 110,240 other races; 1960, 523,591 Indians, 464,332 Japanese, 237,292 Chinese, 176,310 Filipino, 218,087 other races; 1970, 792,730 Indians, 591,290 Japanese, 435,062 Chinese, 343,060 Filipino, 720,520 other races.

[3] Made up of Anglo-Scottish, 89·1%; German, 5·6%; Dutch, 2·5%; Irish, 1·9%; French, 0·6%.

[4] 34,933 Chinese and 44,021 Indians.

[5] Enumeration in 1870 incomplete. Figures in italics represent estimated corrected population.

[*Footnotes continued on p. 1372.*]

Total population in 1980 at 226,504,825 comprised 110,032,295 males and 116,472,530 females; 166,965,380 were urban and 59,539,445 were rural. Negroes, 12,515,932 males and 13,972,286 females.

Estimated population, including Alaska and Hawaii, and armed forces overseas, on 1 July 1950, 152,271,000; 1955, 165,931,000; 1960, 180,671,000; 1965, 194,303,000; 1968, 200,706,000; 1969, 202,677,000; 1970, 204,878,000; 1971, 207,053,000; 1972, 208,846,000; 1973, 210,410,000; 1974, 211,901,000; 1975, 213,559,000; 1976, 215,142,000; 1977, 216,817,000; 1978, 218,059,000.

The age distribution by sex of the total population of the US (excluding armed forces overseas, US population abroad and outlying areas) at the 1980 census was as follows:

Age-group	*Male*	*Female*	*Total*
Under 5	8,353,244	7,987,808	16,341,052
5–9	8,498,857	8,087,108	16,585,965
10–14	9,369,552	8,995,619	18,365,171
15–19	10,762,578	10,413,597	21,176,175
20–24	10,655,133	10,646,657	21,301,790
25–34	18,386,611	18,715,524	37,102,135
35–44	12,573,340	13,064,790	25,638,130
45–54	10,975,005	11,858,540	22,833,545
55–59	5,491,484	6,096,239	11,587,723
60–64	4,687,919	5,383,337	10,071,256
65–74	6,794,488	8,858,382	15,652,870
75 and over	3,512,712	6,377,281	9,889,993
Total	110,060,923	116,484,882	226,545,805

The following table includes population statistics, the year in which each of the original 13 states ratified the constitution, and the year when each of the other states was admitted into the Union. Postal abbreviations for the names of the states are shown in brackets. Land area includes land temporarily or partially covered by water, and lakes, etc., of less than 40 acres. (For census population by states and regions in 1940 and 1950 *see* THE STATESMAN'S YEAR-BOOK, 1952, pp. 552 and 553.)

Geographic divisions and states		*Land area: sq. miles 1980*	*Census population 1 April 1970*	*Census population 1 April 1980*	*Pop. per sq. mile, 1980*
United States		3,543,883	203,235,298	226,545,805	63·9
New England		63,012	11,847,186	12,348,493	195·9
Maine (1820)	*(Me.)*	30,995	993,663	1,124,660	36·3
New Hampshire (1788)	*(N.H.)*	8,993	737,681	920,610	102·4
Vermont (1791)	*(Vt.)*	9,273	444,732	511,456	55·2
Massachusetts (1788)	*(Mass.)*	7,824	5,689,170	5,737,037	733·3
Rhode Island (1790)	*(R.I.)*	1,055	949,723	947,154	897·8
Connecticut (1788)	*(Conn.)*	4,872	3,032,217	3,107,576	637·8
Middle Atlantic		99,733	37,283,339	36,786,790	368·9
New York (1788)	*(N.Y.)*	47,377	18,241,266	17,558,072	370·6
New Jersey (1787)	*(N.J.)*	7,468	7,168,164	7,364,823	986·2
Pennsylvania (1787)	*(Pa.)*	44,888	11,793,909	11,863,895	264·3

[6] Between the 1910 census (15 April 1910) and the 1920 census (1 Jan. 1920), the period covered was 116 months (less than a full decade). Adjusting for this, the exact rate of increase for the decade was 15·4%. Similarly correcting for the 123 months between the 1920 and 1930 censuses, the true rate of increase was 15·7%.

[7] Figures for 1930 have been revised to include Mexicans (1,422,533), who were classified with 'Other Races' in the 1930 census reports.

[8] Figures for 1960 strictly comparable with those given for other years (*i.e.*, excluding Alaska and Hawaii) are: White, 158,454,956; Negroes, 18,860,117; other races, 1,149,163; total, 178,464,236; decennial increase, 18·4%.

Geographic divisions and states		*Land area: sq. miles 1980* [1]	*Census population 1 April 1970*	*Census population 1 April 1980*	*Pop. per sq. mile, 1980*
East North Central		243,961	40,252,678	41,682,217	170·8
Ohio (1803)	*(Oh.)*	41,004	10,652,017	10,797,630	263·3
Indiana (1816)	*(Ind.)*	35,932	5,193,669	5,490,224	152·8
Illinois (1818)	*(Ill.)*	55,645	11,113,976	11,426,518	205·3
Michigan (1837)	*(Mich.)*	56,954	8,875,083	9,262,078	162·6
Wisconsin (1848)	*(Wis.)*	54,426	4,417,933	4,705,769	86·5
West North Central		508,132	16,344,389	17,183,453	33·8
Minnesota (1858)	*(Minn.)*	79,548	3,805,069	4,075,970	51·2
Iowa (1846)	*(Ia.)*	55,965	2,825,041	2,913,808	52·1
Missouri (1821)	*(Mo.)*	68,945	4,677,399	4,916,686	71·3
North Dakota (1889)	*(N.D.)*	69,300	617,761	652,717	9·4
South Dakota (1889)	*(S.D.)*	75,952	666,257	690,768	9·1
Nebraska (1867)	*(Nebr.)*	76,644	1,483,791	1,569,825	20·5
Kansas (1861)	*(Kans.)*	81,778	2,249,071	2,363,679	28·9
South Atlantic		266,910	30,671,337	36,959,123	138·5
Delaware (1787)	*(Del.)*	1,932	548,104	594,338	307·6
Maryland (1788)	*(Md.)*	9,837	3,922,399	4,216,975	428·7
Dist. of Columbia (1791)	*(D.C.)*	63	756,510	638,333	10,132·3
Virginia (1788)	*(Va.)*	39,704	4,648,494	5,346,818	134·7
West Virginia (1863)	*(W. Va.)*	24,119	1,744,237	1,949,644	80·8
North Carolina (1789)	*(N.C.)*	48,843	5,082,059	5,881,766	120·4
South Carolina (1788)	*(S.C.)*	30,203	2,590,516	3,121,820	103·4
Georgia (1788)	*(Ga.)*	58,056	4,589,575	5,463,105	94·1
Florida (1845)	*(Fla.)*	54,153	6,789,443	9,746,324	180·0
East South Central		178,824	12,804,552	14,666,423	82·0
Kentucky (1792)	*(Ky.)*	39,669	3,219,311	3,660,777	92·3
Tennessee (1796)	*(Tenn.)*	41,155	3,924,164	4,591,120	111·5
Alabama (1819)	*(Al.)*	50,767	3,444,165	3,893,888	76·7
Mississippi (1817)	*(Miss.)*	47,233	2,216,912	2,520,638	53·4
West South Central		427,271	19,322,458	23,746,816	55·6
Arkansas (1836)	*(Ark.)*	52,078	1,923,295	2,286,435	43·9
Louisiana (1812)	*(La.)*	44,521	3,643,180	4,205,900	94·5
Oklahoma (1907)	*(Okla.)*	68,655	2,559,253	3,025,290	44·1
Texas (1845)	*(Tex.)*	262,017	11,196,730	14,229,191	54·3
Mountain		855,194	8,283,585	11,372,785	13·3
Montana (1889)	*(Mont.)*	145,388	694,409	786,690	5·4
Idaho (1890)	*(Id.)*	82,412	713,008	943,935	11·4
Wyoming (1890)	*(Wyo.)*	96,989	332,416	469,557	4·8
Colorado (1876)	*(Colo.)*	103,595	2,207,259	2,889,964	27·9
New Mexico (1912)	*(N. Mex.)*	121,335	1,016,000	1,302,894	10·7
Arizona (1912)	*(Ariz.)*	113,508	1,772,482	2,718,215	23·9
Utah (1896)	*(Ut.)*	82,073	1,059,273	1,461,037	17·8
Nevada (1864)	*(Nev.)*	109,894	488,738	800,493	7·3
Pacific		896,252	26,525,774	31,799,705	35·5
Washington (1889)	*(Wash.)*	66,511	3,409,169	4,132,156	62·1
Oregon (1859)	*(Oreg.)*	96,184	2,091,385	2,633,105	27·4
California (1850)	*(Calif.)*	156,299	19,953,134	23,667,902	151·4
Alaska (1959)	*(Ak.)*	570,833	302,173	401,851	0·7
Hawaii (1960)	*(Hi.)*	6,425	769,913	964,691	150·1

[1] Provisional.

Geographic divisions and states	*Land area sq. miles 1970*	*Census population 1 April 1970*	*Census population 1 April 1980*	*Pop. per sq. mile, 1980*
Outlying Territories, total	4,598	4,720,306	...	...
Puerto Rico (1898)	3,458	2,712,033	3,187,570	928
Virgin Islands (1917)	132	62,438	95,590	758
American Samoa (1900)	77	27,159	31,170[1]	...
Guam (1898)	209	84,996	105,820	521
Northern Marianas (1947)	184	9,640	16,500[1]	...
Trust Territory of the Pacific (1947)	533	81,300	117,500[1]	...
Midway Islands (1867)	2	2,220	2,256[1]	...
Wake Island (1898)	3	1,647	300	100
Johnston and Sand Islands (1858)	...	1,007	300[1]	...

[1] Estimate.

The 1970 census showed 8,733,770 foreign-born Whites. The 8 countries contributing the largest numbers who were foreign-born were Italy, 1,005,687; Germany, 830,498; Canada, 798,782; Mexico, 746,327; UK, 681,140; Poland, 547,010; USSR, 461,444; Ireland, 250,492.

Increase or decrease of native White, and foreign-born White, population from 1860 to 1970, by decades:

	Native White			*Foreign-born White*		
	Total	*Increase*	*Per cent increase*	*Total*	*Increase or decrease (–)*	*Per cent. change*
1860	22,825,784	5,513,251	31·8	4,096,753	1,856,218	82·8
1870	28,095,665	5,269,881	23·1	5,493,712	1,396,959	34·1
1880	36,843,291	8,747,626	31·1	6,559,679	1,065,967	19·4
1890	45,979,391	9,018,732[1]	24·5	9,121,867	2,562,188	39·1
1900	56,595,379	10,615,988	23·1	10,213,817	1,091,950	12·0
1910	68,386,412	11,791,033	20·8	13,345,545	3,131,728	30·7
1920	81,108,161	12,721,749	18·6	13,712,754	367,209	2·8
1930	96,303,335	15,195,174	18·7	13,983,405	270,651	2·0
1940	106,795,732	10,492,397	10·9	11,419,138	–2,564,267	–18·3
1950	124,780,860	17,985,128	16·8	10,161,168	–1,257,970	–11·0
1960	149,543,638	24,762,778	19·8	9,293,992	– 867,176	– 8·5
1970	169,385,451	19,841,813	13·3	8,773,770	– 560,222	6·0

[1] Exclusive of population specially enumerated in 1890 in Indian Territory and on Indian reservations.

Principal cities in 1910, 1960 and 1970:

	No. of cities [1]			*Combined population* [1]		
Cities with	*1910*	*1960*	*1970*	*1910*	*1960*	*1970*
250,000 or more	19	51	56	15,461,680	39,360,931	42,177,800
100,000–250,000	31	81	100	4,840,458	11,652,426	14,286,033
50,000–100,000	60	201	240	4,213,098	13,835,902	16,723,878
25,000–50,000	119	432	520	4,023,397	14,950,612	17,848,297
25,000 or more	229	765	916	28,504,450	79,799,871	91,036,008

[1] Exclusive of Honolulu (Hawaii) in 1910 and 1950 and San Juan (Puerto Rico) in 1910, 1950 and 1970.

The population of leading cities (with over 100,000 inhabitants) at the censuses of 1970 and 1980 were as follows:

Cities	*1 April 1970*	*1 April 1980*	*Cities*	*1 April 1970*	*1 April 1980*
New York, N.Y.	7,895,563	7,071,030	Detroit, Mich.	1,514,063	1,203,339
Chicago, Ill.	3,369,357	3,005,072	Dallas, Tex.	844,401	904,078
Los Angeles, Calif.	2,811,801	2,966,763	San Diego, Calif.	697,471	875,504
Philadelphia, Pa.	1,949,996	1,688,210	Phoenix, Ariz.	584,303	789,704
Houston, Tex.	1,233,535	1,594,086	Baltimore, Md.	905,787	786,775

Cities	1 April 1970	1 April 1980
San Antonio, Tex.	645,153	785,410
Indianapolis, Ind.	736,856	700,807
Honolulu, Hawaii	630,528	681,004
San Francisco, Calif.	715,674	678,974
Memphis, Tenn.	623,988	646,174
Washington, D.C.	756,668	637,651
San José, Calif.	459,913	636,550
Milwaukee, Wisc.	717,372	636,236
Cleveland, Ohio	750,879	573,822
Columbus, Ohio	540,025	564,871
Boston, Mass.	641,071	562,994
New Orleans, La.	593,471	557,927
Jacksonville, Fla.	504,265	540,898
Seattle, Wash.	530,831	493,846
Denver, Colo.	514,678	491,396
Nashville-Davidson, Tenn.	426,029	455,651
St Louis, Mo.	622,236	453,085
Kansas City, Mo.	507,330	448,159
El Paso, Tex.	322,261	425,259
Atlanta, Ga.	495,039	425,022
Pittsburgh, Pa.	520,089	423,959
Oklahoma City, Okla.	368,164	403,136
Cincinnati, Ohio	453,514	385,457
Fort Worth, Tex.	393,455	385,141
Minneapolis, Minn.	434,400	370,951
Portland, Oregon	379,967	366,383
Long Beach, Calif.	358,879	361,334
Tulsa, Okla.	330,350	360,919
Buffalo, N.Y.	462,768	357,870
Toledo, Ohio	383,062	354,635
Miami, Fla.	334,859	346,931
Austin, Tex.	253,539	345,496
Oakland, Calif.	361,561	339,288
Albuquerque, N. Mex.	244,501	331,767
Tucson, Ariz.	262,933	330,537
Newark, N.J.	381,930	329,248
Charlotte, N.C.	241,420	314,447
Omaha, Nebr.	346,929	313,911
Louisville, Ky.	361,706	298,840
Birmingham, Ala.	300,910	284,413
Wichita, Kans.	276,554	279,835
Sacramento, Calif.	257,105	275,741
Tampa, Fla.	277,714	271,523
St Paul, Minn.	309,866	270,230
Norfolk, Va.	307,951	266,979
Virginia Beach, Va.	172,106	262,199
Rochester, N.Y.	295,011	241,741
Akron, Ohio	275,425	237,177
St Petersburg, Fla.	216,159	236,893
Corpus Christi, Tex.	204,525	231,999
Jersey City, N.J.	260,350	223,532
Anaheim, Calif.	166,408	221,847
Baton Rouge, La.	165,921	219,486
Richmond, Va.	249,332	219,214
Fresno, Calif.	165,655	218,202
Colorado Springs, Colo.	135,517	215,150
Shreveport, La.	182,064	205,815
Lexington-Fayette, Ky.	108,137	204,165
Santa Ana, Calif.	155,710	203,713
Dayton, Ohio	243,023	203,588
Jackson, Miss.	153,968	202,895
Mobile, Ala.	190,026	200,452
Yonkers, N.Y.	204,297	195,351

Cities	1 April 1970	1 April 1980
Des Moines, Iowa	201,404	191,003
Grand Rapids, Mich.	197,649	181,843
Montgomery, Ala.	133,386	178,157
Knoxville, Tenn.	174,587	175,045
Lubbock, Tex.	149,101	173,979
Anchorage, Alaska.	48,081	173,017
Fort Wayne, Ind.	178,269	172,196
Lincoln, Nebr.	149,518	171,932
Spokane, Wash.	170,516	171,300
Riverside, Calif.	140,089	170,876
Madison, Wisc.	171,809	170,616
Huntington Beach, Calif.	115,960	170,505
Syracuse, N.Y.	197,297	170,105
Chattanooga, Tenn.	119,923	169,558
Columbus, Ga.	155,028	169,441
Las Vegas, Nev.	125,787	164,674
Salt Lake City, Utah	175,885	163,033
Worcester, Mass.	176,572	161,799
Warren, Mich.	179,260	161,134
Kansas City, Kans.	168,213	161,087
Arlington, Tex.	90,229	160,123
Flint, Mich.	193,317	159,611
Aurora, Colo.	74,974	158,588
Tacoma, Wash.	154,407	158,501
Little Rock, Ark.	132,483	158,461
Providence, R.I.	179,116	156,804
Greensboro, N.C.	144,076	155,642
Fort Lauderdale, Fla.	139,590	153,256
Mesa. Ariz.	63,049	152,453
Springfield, Mass.	163,905	152,319
Gary, Ind.	175,415	151,953
Stockton, Calif.	109,963	149,779
Raleigh, N.C.	122,830	149,771
Amarillo, Tex.	127,010	149,230
Hialeah, Fla.	102,452	145,254
Newport News, Va.	138,177	144,903
Bridgeport, Conn.	156,542	142,546
Huntsville, Ala.	139,282	142,513
Savannah, Ga.	118,349	141,634
Rockford, Ill.	147,370	139,712
Glendale, Calif.	132,664	139,060
Garland, Tex.	81,437	138,857
Paterson, N.J.	144,824	137,970
Hartford, Conn.	158,017	136,392
Springfield, Mo.	120,096	133,116
Fremont, Calif.	100,869	131,945
Winston-Salem, N.C.	133,683	131,885
Torrance, Calif.	134,968	131,497
Evansville, Ind.	138,764	130,496
Lansing, Mich.	131,403	130,414
Orlando, Fla.	99,006	128,394
New Haven, Conn.	137,707	126,109
Peoria, Ill.	126,963	124,160
Garden Grove, Calif.	121,155	123,351
Hampton, Va.	120,779	122,617
Erie, Pa.	129,265	119,123
San Bernadino, Calif.	106,869	118,794
Beaumont, Tex.	117,548	118,102
Pasadena, Calif.	112,951	118,072
Hollywood, Fla.	106,873	117,188
Macon, Ga.	122,423	116,860
Youngstown, Ohio.	140,909	115,436
Topeka, Kans.	125,011	115,266
Chesapeake, Va.	89,580	114,226
Lakewood, Colo.	92,743	112,860

Cities	1 April 1970	1 April 1980	Cities	1 April 1970	1 April 1980
Pasadena, Tex.	89,957	112,560	Allentown, Pa.	109,871	103,758
Independence, Mo.	111,630	111,806	Berkeley, Calif.	114,091	103,328
Cedar Rapids, Iowa	110,642	10,243	Waterbury, Conn.	108,033	103,266
Irving, Tex.	97,260	109,943	Davenport, Iowa.	98,469	103,264
South Bend, Ind.	125,580	109,727	Concord, Calif.	85,164	103,251
Sterling Heights, Mich.	61,365	108,999	Alexandria, Va.	110,927	103,217
Oxnard, Calif.	71,225	108,195	Stamford, Conn.	108,798	102,453
Ann Arbor, Mich.	100,035	107,316	Boise City, Idaho	74,990	102,160
Tempe, Ariz.	63,550	106,743	Fullerton, Calif.	85,987	102,034
Sunnyvale, Calif.	95,976	106,618	Albany, N.Y.	115,781	101,727
Elizabeth, N.J.	112,654	106,201	Pueblo, Colo.	97,774	101,686
Modesto, Calif.	61,712	106,105	Waco, Tex.	95,326	101,261
Bakersfield, Calif.	69,515	105,735	Reno, Nev.	72,863	100,756
Eugene, Oregon	79,028	105,624	Durham, N.C.	95,438	100,538
Livonia, Mich.	110,109	104,814	Roanoke, Va.	92,115	100,427
Portsmouth, Va.	110,963	104,577			

Vital Statistics: Vital statistics are based on records of births, deaths, fœtal deaths, marriages and divorces filed with registration officials of states and cities. Figures for the US include Alaska beginning with 1959 and Hawaii beginning with 1960.

Annual collection of mortality records from a national death-registration area was inaugurated in 1900. A national birth-registration area was established in 1915. These areas, which at their inception comprised 10 states and the District of Columbia, expanded gradually until 1933, when both the birth- and death-registration areas covered the entire continental US. Marriage and divorce statistics are compiled from reports furnished by state and local officials. Data on annulments are included in the divorce statistics. The marriage-registration area was established in 1957 with 29 states and 4 other areas. The divorce-registration area was established in 1958 with 14 states and 3 other areas. In Jan. 1972 the marriage-registration area included 41 states and 5 other areas, and the divorce-registration area included 29 states and one other area.

	Live births [1]	Deaths [2]	Marriages [3]	Divorces [4]	Maternal deaths [5]	Deaths under 1 year [6]
1900	—	343,217	709,000	56,000	—	—
1910	2,777,000	696,856	948,000	83,000	—	—
1920	2,950,000	1,118,070	1,274,476	170,505	16,320	170,911
1930	2,618,000	1,327,240	1,126,856	195,961	14,915	143,201
1940	2,559,000	1,417,269	1,595,874	264,000	8,876	110,984
1950	3,632,000	1,452,454	1,667,231	385,144	2,960	103,825
1960	4,257,850 [7]	1,711,982	1,523,000	393,000	1,579	110,873
1970	3,731,386	1,921,031	2,158,802	708,000	803	74,667
1977	3,326,632	1,899,597	2,178,367	1,091,000	373	46,975
1978	3,333,279	1,927,788	2,282,272	1,130,000	320	45,945
1979	3,494,398	1,913,841	2,331,337	1,181,000	336	45,665
1980 [8]	3,598,000	1,986,000	2,413,000	1,182,000	250	45,000
1981 [8]	3,646,000	1,987,000	2,438,000	1,219,000	...	42,700

[1] Figures through 1959 include adjustment for under-registration (the 1959 registered count was 4,244,796); beginning 1960 figures represent number registered.
[2] Excluding fœtal deaths and deaths among the armed forces overseas.
[3] Estimates for all years except 1970.
[4] Includes reported annulments. Estimated for all years.
[5] Deaths for 1979–80 (Ninth Revision, International Classification of Diseases, 1975). Deaths from complications of pregnancy, childbirth and the puerperium. Deaths for 1968–78 were classified according to the Eighth Revision, International Classification of Diseases, adopted, 1965. Deaths for 1958–67 were classified according to the Seventh Revision of the International Lists of Diseases and Causes of Death, those for 1949–57 according to the Sixth Revision and those for 1939–48, according to the Fifth Revision.
[6] Excluding fœtal deaths. [7] Based on a 50% sample. [8] Provisional.

The crude birth rate, based on total live-birth estimates per 1,000 total population, fell from 29·5 in 1915 to 18·4 in 1933; it rose to a peak of 26·6 in 1947—its highest for 25 years. This peak reflects demobilization (1945–46), the record marriage rate that followed, and the high levels of employment and income.

The decrease in the following 3 years was moderate. In 1951 the rate moved upward and levelled off in 1957 at about 25 per 1,000 population. Since 1957 the crude birth rate has declined every year to 18·4 live births per 1,000 population in 1966. The crude birth rate for 1979 was 15·9. Estimated number of illegitimate births in 1979 was 597,800, a ratio of 171·1 illegitimate births per 1,000 registered live births.

Deaths, excluding fœtal deaths (per 1,000 population), declined from 17·2 in 1900 to 10 in 1946. The death rate has been below 10 per 1,000 since 1947, fluctuating slightly from year to year, mainly under the impact of occurrences of outbreaks of severe respiratory diseases. Since the record low of 9·2 in 1954 the rate has changed only between 9·3 and 9·7. The rate for 1970, 9·5; for 1973, 9·4; for 1974, 9·2; for 1975, 8·9; for 1976, 8·9; for 1977, 8·8; for 1978, 8·8; for 1979, 8·7.

Leading causes of death, 1979, per 100,000 population: Diseases of heart, 333·1; malignant neoplasms, 183·3; cerebrovascular diseases, 77; accidents, 47·8. Suicides in 1979 were 11·9 per 100,000 population; homicides, 10·4.

The marriage rate per 1,000 population for selected years are: 1920, 12; 1932, 7·9; 1946, 16·4; 1951, 10·4; 1961, 8·5; 1969, 10·6; 1970, 10·6; 1971, 10·6; 1975, 10·1; 1976, 10; 1977, 10·1; 1978, 10·5; 1979, 10·6. The divorce rates per 1,000 population for selected years are: 1920, 1·6; 1946, 4·3; 1951, 2·5; 1961, 2·3; 1971, 3·7; 1976, 5; 1977, 5; 1978, 5·2; 1979, 5·4.

Maternal mortality rates (deaths of mothers from conditions associated with deliveries and complications of pregnancy, childbirth and the puerperium) per 100,000 live births, were 1915–19, 727·9 and thereafter declined: 493·9 for 1935–39; 376 for 1940; 207·2 for 1945; 83·3 for 1950; 47 for 1955; 37·1 for 1960; 31·6 for 1965; 21·5 for 1970; 12·8 for 1975; 11·2 for 1977; 9·6 for 1978; 9·6 for 1979. The 1979 rate for white women was 6·4 and for all other women 22·7. By state, the average maternal mortality rate for 1976–78 was highest for Wyoming (32·9) and lowest for Connecticut (3·7).

The infant mortality rates, per 1,000 live births were: 1915–19, 95·7; 1920–24, 76·7; 1925–29, 69; 1930–34, 60·4; 38·3 in 1945; 29·2 in 1950; 26·4 in 1955; 26 in 1960; 20 in 1970; 16·1 in 1975; 15·2 in 1976; 14·1 in 1977; 13·8 in 1978; 13·1 in 1979. In 1979 the rate for whites was 11·4; for all other, 21·8.

Immigration: The Immigration and Nationality Act, as amended by Public Law 95–412, establishes a worldwide numerical ceiling of 290,000 visas, with a maximum of 20,000 visas available for any one country. The visas are allocated under a system of 7 preference categories, 4 of which are designed to reunite close relatives of US citizens and resident aliens of the US, 2 for skilled and professional workers and 1 for refugees. Visa numbers not used in any of the preference categories are made available to qualified non-preference immigrants. Spouses, children and parents of US citizens are exempt from the numerical limitations.

During the year ended 30 Sept. 1979, 460,348 aliens became permanent residents of the US. Of the total immigrants admitted, 331,747 had obtained visas abroad and entered the US while 128,601 aliens who were already in the US had their status adjusted to that of permanent residents.

Immigrant aliens admitted to US for permanent residence, by country or region of birth.

Country or region of birth	*Immigrants admitted* 1976	1977[1]	1978	1979
All countries	398,613	462,315	601,442	460,348
Europe	72,411	70,010	73,198	60,845
Germany (GDR and FRG)	5,836	6,372	6,739	6,314
Greece	8,417	7,838	7,035	5,090
Italy	8,380	7,510	7,415	6,174
Poland	3,805	4,010	5,050	4,413
Portugal	10,511	9,657	10,445	7,085
Spain	2,254	2,487	2,297	1,933
UK	11,392	12,477	14,245	13,907
Yugoslavia	2,820	2,791	2,621	2,171
Other Europe	18,996	16,868	17,351	13,758

[1] Year ending 30 Sept.

Country or region of birth	Immigrants admitted 1976	1977[1]	1978	1979
Asia	149,881	157,759	249,776[1]	189,293
China and Taiwan	18,823	19,764	21,315	24,264
Hong Kong	5,766	5,632	5,158	4,119
India	17,487	18,613	20,753	19,708
Japan	4,258	4,178	4,010	4,048
Korea (North and South)	30,803	30,917	29,288	29,248
Philippines	37,281	39,111	37,216	41,300
Thailand	6,923	3,945	3,574	3,194
Other Asia	28,540	35,599	128,462	63,412
North America	142,307	187,345	220,778	157,579
Canada	7,638	12,688	16,863	13,772
Mexico	57,863	44,079	92,367	52,096
Cuba	29,233	69,708	29,754	15,585
Dominican Republic	12,526	11,655	19,458	17,519
Haiti	5,410	5,441	6,470	6,433
Jamaica	9,026	11,501	19,265	19,714
Trinidad and Tobago	4,839	6,106	5,973	5,225
Other West Indies	5,805	9,600	10,441	9,598
Central America	9,912	16,485	20,153	17,547
Other North America	55	82	34	90
South America	22,699	32,954	41,764	35,344
Colombia	5,742	8,272	11,032	10,637
Ecuador	4,504	5,302	5,732	4,383
Other South America	12,453	19,380	25,000	20,324
Africa	7,723	10,155	11,524	12,838
Australia and New Zealand	1,796	1,986	2,184	1,999
Other countries	1,796	2,106	2,218	2,450

[1] Year ending 30 Sept.

The total number of immigrants admitted from 1820 up to 30 Sept. 1979 was 49,125,313; this included 6,984,909 from Germany (GDR and FRG), and from Italy 5,300,387.

Aliens coming to the US for temporary periods of time are classified as non-immigrants. During the first 9 months of fiscal year 1979, a total of 7,060,082 non-immigrants were admitted. This is exclusive of multiple entry documents and excludes border crossers, crewmen and insular travellers. Tourists, primarily from Mexico, Japan, the UK, the West Indies, Germany (GDR and FRG) and Canada numbered 3,160,963. There were 992,025 aliens expelled during the first 9 months of fiscal year 1979. Of this number, 25,888 were deported and 966,137 were required to depart without formal orders of deportation.

In accordance with the Immigration and Nationality Act, 5,381,106 aliens reported their address in Jan. 1980. Of this total, 4,532,647 were permanent residents and 848,459 were aliens here temporarily. Of the permanent resident aliens who reported the best represented nationalities were the following: Mexico, 992,765; Canada, 301,085; Cuba, 279,100; UK, 273,521; Philippines, 223,743; Italy, 163,700; Germany (GDR and FRG), 147,647. Over 76% of the permanent resident aliens reported their states of residence as: California, 1,261,069; New York, 690,383; Texas, 411,163; Florida, 335,457; Illinois, 256,091; New Jersey, 238,883; Massachusetts, 152,916, and Michigan, 118,588.

In the year ended 30 Sept. 1979, 164,150 persons became US citizens through naturalization; this includes, 132,533 naturalized under the general provisions of 5-year residence in the US, 25,701 spouses and children of US citizens, 5,874 military and 42 who were naturalized under other provisions. Of the total, there were 13,313 former nationals of Cuba, 17,749 of the Philippines, 11,446 of China and Taiwan, 13,406 of Korea, 8,065 of UK, 7,296 of Italy, 8,046 of Mexico and 7,632 of Jamaica.

US Depart. of Commerce. *Population of the United States: Trends and Prospects, 1500–1990.* Washington, 1974

CONSTITUTION AND GOVERNMENT. The form of government of the USA is based on the constitution of 17 Sept. 1787.

By the constitution the government of the nation is composed of three co-ordinate branches, the executive, the legislative and the judicial.

The National Government has authority in matters of general taxation, treaties and other dealings with foreign Powers, foreign and inter-state commerce, bankruptcy, postal service, coinage, weights and measures, patents and copyright, the armed forces (including, to a certain extent, the militia), and crimes against the USA; it has sole legislative authority over the District of Columbia and the possessions of the US.

The 5th article of the constitution provides that Congress may, on a two-thirds vote of both houses, propose amendments to the constitution, or, on the application of the legislatures of two-thirds of all the states, call a convention for proposing amendments, which in either case shall be valid as part of the constitution when ratified by the legislatures of three-fourths of the several states, or by conventions in three-fourths thereof, whichever mode of ratification may be proposed by Congress. Ten amendments (called collectively 'the Bill of Rights') to the constitution were added 15 Dec. 1791; two in 1795 and 1804; a 13th amendment, 6 Dec. 1865, abolishing slavery; a 14th in 1868, including the important 'due process' clause; a 15th, 3 Feb. 1870, establishing equal voting rights for white and coloured; a 16th, 3 Feb. 1913, authorizing the income tax; a 17th, 8 April 1913, providing for popular election of senators; an 18th, 16 Jan. 1919, prohibiting alcoholic liquors; a 19th, 18 Aug. 1920, establishing woman suffrage; a 20th, 23 Jan. 1933, advancing the date of the President's and Vice-President's inauguration and abolishing the 'lame-duck' sessions of Congress; a 21st, 5 Dec. 1933, repealing the 18th amendment; a 22nd, 26 Feb. 1951, limiting a President's tenure of office to 2 terms, or to 2 terms plus 2 years in the case of a Vice-President who has succeeded to the office of a President; a 23rd, 30 March 1961, granting citizens of the District of Columbia the right to vote in national elections; a 24th, 4 Feb. 1964, banning the use of the poll-tax in federal elections; a 25th, 10 Feb. 1967, dealing with Presidential disability and succession; a 26th, 22 June 1970, establishing the right of citizens who are 18 years of age and older to vote.

National flag: Seven red and 6 white alternating stripes, horizontal; with a blue canton, extending down to the lower edge of the 4th red stripe from the top, and displaying 50 white 5-pointed stars, one for each state. The stars have one point directed vertically upward, and they are arranged in 6 rows of 5 each, alternating with 5 rows of 4 each. On the admission of additional states, stars are added, effective on 4 July following the date of admission. Congress, by law of 22 Dec. 1942, has codified 'existing rules and customs' pertaining to the display of the flag, for civilians.

National anthem: The Star-spangled Banner, 'Oh say, can you see by the dawn's early light' (words by F. S. Key, 1814; tune by J. S. Smith; formally adopted by Congress 3 March 1931).

National motto: 'In God we trust'; formally adopted by Congress 30 July 1956.

Presidency. The executive power is vested in a president, who holds office for 4 years, and is elected, together with a vice-president chosen for the same term, by electors from each state, equal to the whole number of senators and representatives to which the state may be entitled in the Congress. The President must be a natural-born citizen, resident in the country for 14 years, and at least 35 years old.

The presidential election is held every fourth (leap) year on the Tuesday after the first Monday in November. Technically, this is an election of presidential electors, not of a president directly; the electors thus chosen meet and give their votes (for the candidate to whom they are pledged, in some states by law, but in most states by custom and prudent politics) at their respective state capitals on the first Monday after the second Wednesday in December next following their election; and the votes of the electors of all the states are opened and counted in the presence of both Houses of Congress on the sixth day of January. The total electorate vote is one for each senator and representative.

If the successful candidate for President dies before taking office the Vice-President-elect becomes President; if no candidate has a majority or if the successful candidate fails to qualify, then, by the 20th amendment, the Vice-President acts as President until a president qualifies. The duties of the Presidency, in absence of the President and Vice-President by reason of death, resignation, removal, inability or failure to qualify, devolve upon the Speaker of the House under legislation enacted 18 July 1947. And in case of absence of a Speaker for like reason, the presidential duties devolve upon the President *pro tem.* of the Senate and successively upon those members of the Cabinet in order of precedence, who have the constitutional qualifications for President.

The presidential term, by the 20th amendment to the constitution, begins at noon on 20 Jan. of the inaugural year. This amendment also installs the newly elected Congress in office on 3 Jan. instead of—as formerly—in the following December. The President's salary is $200,000 per year, plus $50,000 to assist in defraying expenses resulting from official duties. Also he may spend up to $100,000 non-taxable for travel and $12,000 for official entertainment. The office of Vice-President carries a salary of $79,125, plus $10,000 allowance for travel.

The President is C.-in-C. of the Army, Navy and Air Force, and of the militia when in the service of the Union. The Vice-President is *ex-officio* President of the Senate, and in the case of 'the removal of the President, or of his death, resignation, or inability to discharge the powers and duties of his office', he becomes the President for the remainder of the term.

President of the United States: Ronald Reagan, of California, born at Tampico, Illinois, in 1911; Governor of California, 1967–75.

At the Presidential election on 4 Nov. 1980 total vote cast, including men and women in the armed services, was 86,513,296, of which Ronald Reagan (R.) received 43,901,812 (50·7%), James Earl Carter (D.) 35,483,820 (41%) and John Anderson 5,719,722 (6·6%). Electoral college votes: Reagan 489; Carter 49; Anderson 0.

PRESIDENTS OF THE USA

Name	*From state*	*Term of service*	*Born*	*Died*
George Washington	Virginia	1789–97	1732	1799
John Adams	Massachusetts	1797–1801	1735	1826
Thomas Jefferson	Virginia	1801–09	1743	1826
James Madison	Virginia	1809–17	1751	1836
James Monroe	Virginia	1817–25	1759	1831
John Quincy Adams	Massachusetts	1825–29	1767	1848
Andrew Jackson	Tennessee	1829–37	1767	1845
Martin Van Buren	New York	1837–41	1782	1862
William H. Harrison	Ohio	Mar.–Apr. 1841	1773	1841
John Tyler	Virginia	1841–45	1790	1862
James K. Polk	Tennessee	1845–49	1795	1849
Zachary Taylor	Louisiana	1849–July 1850	1784	1850
Millard Fillmore	New York	1850–53	1800	1874
Franklin Pierce	New Hampshire	1853–57	1804	1869
James Buchanan	Pennsylvania	1857–61	1791	1868
Abraham Lincoln	Illinois	1861–Apr. 1865	1809	1865
Andrew Johnson	Tennessee	1865–69	1808	1875
Ulysses S. Grant	Illinois	1869–77	1822	1885
Rutherford B. Hayes	Ohio	1877–81	1822	1893
James A. Garfield	Ohio	Mar.–Sept. 1881	1831	1881

Name	*From state*	*Term of service*	*Born*	*Died*
Chester A. Arthur	New York	1881–85	1830	1886
Grover Cleveland	New York	1885–89	1837	1908
Benjamin Harrison	Indiana	1889–93	1833	1901
Grover Cleveland	New York	1893–97	1837	1908
William McKinley	Ohio	1897–Sept. 1901	1843	1901
Theodore Roosevelt	New York	1901–09	1858	1919
William H. Taft	Ohio	1909–13	1857	1930
Woodrow Wilson	New Jersey	1913–21	1856	1924
Warren Gamaliel Harding	Ohio	1921–Aug. 1923	1865	1923
Calvin Coolidge	Massachusetts	1923–29	1872	1933
Herbert C. Hoover	California	1929–33	1874	1964
Franklin D. Roosevelt	New York	1933–Apr. 1945	1882	1945
Harry S. Truman	Missouri	1945–53	1884	1972
Dwight D. Eisenhower	New York	1953–61	1890	1969
John F. Kennedy	Massachusetts	1961–Nov. 1963	1917	1963
Lyndon B. Johnson	Texas	1963–69	1908	1973
Richard M. Nixon	California	1969–74	1913	—
Gerald R. Ford	Michigan	1974–77	1913	—
James Earl Carter	Georgia	1977–81	1924	—
Ronald Reagan	California	1981–	1911	—
		VICE-PRESIDENTS OF THE USA		
John Adams	Massachusetts	1789–97	1735	1826
Thomas Jefferson	Virginia	1797–1801	1743	1826
Aaron Burr	New York	1801–05	1756	1836
George Clinton	New York	1805–12 [1]	1739	1812
Elbridge Gerry	Massachusetts	1813–14 [1]	1744	1814
Daniel D. Tompkins	New York	1817–25	1774	1825
John C. Calhoun	South Carolina	1825–32 [1]	1782	1850
Martin Van Buren	New York	1833–37	1782	1862
Richard M. Johnson	Kentucky	1837–41	1780	1850
John Tyler	Virginia	Mar.–Apr. 1841 [1]	1790	1862
George M. Dallas	Pennsylvania	1845–49	1792	1864
Millard Fillmore	New York	1849–50 [1]	1800	1874
William R. King	Alabama	Mar.–Apr. 1853 [1]	1786	1853
John C. Breckinridge	Kentucky	1857–61	1821	1875
Hannibal Hamlin	Maine	1861–65	1809	1891
Andrew Johnson	Tennessee	Mar.–Apr. 1865 [1]	1808	1875
Schuyler Colfax	Indiana	1869–73	1823	1885
Henry Wilson	Massachusetts	1873–75 [1]	1812	1875
William A. Wheeler	New York	1877–81	1819	1887
Chester A. Arthur	New York	Mar.–Sept. 1881 [1]	1830	1886
Thomas A. Hendricks	Indiana	Mar.–Nov. 1885 [1]	1819	1885
Levi P. Morton	New York	1889–93	1824	1920
Adlai Stevenson	Illinois	1893–97	1835	1914
Garret A. Hobart	New Jersey	1897–99 [1]	1844	1899
Theodore Roosevelt	New York	Mar.–Sept. 1901 [1]	1858	1919
Charles W. Fairbanks	Indiana	1905–09	1855	1920
James S. Sherman	New York	1909–12 [1]	1855	1912
Thomas R. Marshall	Indiana	1913–21	1854	1925
Calvin Coolidge	Massachusetts	1921–Aug. 1923 [1]	1872	1933
Charles G. Dawes	Illinois	1925–29	1865	1951
Charles Curtis	Kansas	1929–33	1860	1935
John N. Garner	Texas	1933–41	1868	1967
Henry A. Wallace	Iowa	1941–45	1888	1965
Harry S. Truman	Missouri	1945–Apr. 1945 [1]	1884	1972
Alben W. Barkley	Kentucky	1949–53	1877	1956
Richard M. Nixon	California	1953–61	1913	—

[1] Position vacant thereafter until commencement of the next presidential term.

Name	*From state*	*Term of service*	*Born*	*Died*
Lyndon B. Johnson	Texas	1961–Nov. 1963 [1]	1908	1973
Hubert H. Humphrey	Minnesota	1965–69	1911	1978
Spiro T. Agnew	Maryland	1969–73	1918	—
Gerald R. Ford	Michigan	1973–74	1913	—
Nelson Rockefeller	New York	1974–77	1908	1979
Walter Mondale	Minnesota	1977–81	1928	—
George Bush	Texas	1981–	1924	—

[1] Position vacant thereafter until commencement of the next presidential term.

Cabinet. The administrative business of the nation has been traditionally vested in several executive departments, the heads of which, unofficially and *ex officio*, formed the President's Cabinet. Beginning with the Interstate Commerce Commission in 1887, however, an increasing amount of executive business has been entrusted to some 60 so-called independent agencies, such as the Veterans Administration, Housing and Home Finance Agency, Tariff Commission, etc.

All heads of departments and of the 60 or more administrative agencies are appointed by the President, but must be confirmed by the Senate.

The Cabinet consisted of the following (April 1982):

1. *Secretary of State* (created 1789). George P. Shultz; businessman, Secretary of Labor, 1969–70, Secretary of the Treasury, 1972–74; born 1920.

2. *Secretary of the Treasury* (1789). Donald Regan, of New York; Chairman of Merrill Lynch and Company, securities; born 1918.

3. *Secretary of Defense* (1947). Caspar Weinberger, Vice-President of the Bechtel Power Corporation; lawyer, former Secretary of Health, Education and Welfare; born 1918.

4. *Attorney-General* (Department of Justice, 1870). William French Smith, of California; lawyer; born 1917.

5. *Secretary of the Interior* (1849). James G. Watt, of Wyoming; lawyer; born 1938.

6. *Secretary of Agriculture* (1889). John R. Block, of Illinois; farmer; director of the Illinois Farm Bureau; born 1935.

7. *Secretary of Commerce* (1903). Malcolm Baldridge, of Connecticut; manufacturer; born 1922.

8. *Secretary of Labor* (1913). Raymond J. Donovan, of New Jersey; construction company executive; born 1930.

9. *Secretary of Health and Human Services* (1953). Margaret M. Heckler, of Massachusetts; lawyer and congresswoman; born 1931.

10. *Secretary of Housing and Urban Development* (1966). Samuel J. Pierce, of New York; lawyer; born 1922.

11. *Secretary of Transportation* (1967). Elizabeth H. Dole, of North Carolina; lawyer, Federal Trade Commissioner 1973–79, President's public liaison assistant, 1981; born 1936.

12. *Secretary of Energy* (1977). Donald P. Hodel, of Oregon; lawyer, undersecretary at the Department of the Interior 1978–81; born 1935.

13. *Secretary of Education* (1979). Terrel H. Bell, of Utah; born 1921.

Each of the above Cabinet officers receives an annual salary of $69,630 and holds office during the pleasure of the President.

Congress: The legislative power is vested by the Constitution in a Congress, consisting of a Senate and House of Representatives.

Electorate: By amendments of the constitution, disqualification of voters on the ground of race, colour or sex is forbidden. Accordingly, the electorate consists theoretically of all citizens of both sexes over 18 years of age, but the franchise is not universal. There are requirements of residence varying in the several states as to length from 6 months to 2 years and differing requirements as to registration. In 20 states the ability to read (usually an extract from the constitution) is required—in Alaska the ability to read English; in Hawaii, English or Hawaiian; in Louisiana, English or one's native tongue. In Alabama the voter must take an 'anti-Communist oath' and fill out a questionnaire to the satisfaction of the registrars. In some southern states voters are required to give a reasonable explanation of what they read. In most states convicts are excluded from the franchise, in some states duellists and fraudulent voters.

Legislation designed to discourage the rise of third parties has been adopted in a few states. In Illinois a new party must present a petition signed by at least 25,000 voters, including at least 200 in each of 50 of the 102 counties.

The method of balloting varies greatly. Seventeen states use different ballots for federal, state and local elections. In Delaware and South Carolina the various political parties furnish their own ballot-papers to the voters as he or she enters the polling-booth.

Senate: The Senate consists of 2 members from each state, chosen by popular vote for 6 years, one-third retiring or seeking re-election every 2 years. Senators must be no less than 30 years of age; must have been citizens of the USA for 9 years, and be residents in the states for which they are chosen. The Senate has complete freedom to initiate legislation, except revenue bills (which must originate in the House of Representatives); it may, however, amend or reject any legislation originating in the lower house. The Senate is also entrusted with the power of giving or withholding its 'advice and consent' to the ratification of all treaties initiated by the President with foreign Powers, a two-thirds majority of senators present being required for approval. (However, it has no control over 'international executive agreements' made by the President with foreign governments; such 'agreements', representing an important but very recent development, cover a wide range and are actually more numerous than formal treaties.) It also has the power of confirming or rejecting major appointments to office made by the President, but it has no direct control over the appointment by the President of 'personal representatives' or 'personal envoys' on missions abroad. Members of the Senate constitute a High Court of Impeachment, with power, by a two-thirds vote, to remove from office and disqualify any civil officer of the USA impeached by the House of Representatives, which has the sole power of impeachment.

The Senate has 15 Standing Committees to which all bills are referred for study revision or rejection. The House of Representatives has 22 such committees. In both Houses each Standing Committee has a chairman and a majority representing the majority party of the whole House; each has numerous sub-committees. The jurisdictions of these Committees correspond largely to those of the appropriate executive departments and agencies. Both Houses also have a few special Committees with limited duration; there are some Joint Committees.

House of Representatives: The House of Representatives consists of 435 members elected every second year. The number of each state's representatives is determined by the decennial census, in the absence of specific Congressional legislation affecting the basis. The states, in 1983, had the following representatives:

Alabama	7	Indiana	10	Nebraska	3	South Carolina	6
Alaska	1	Iowa	6	Nevada	2	South Dakota	1
Arizona	5	Kansas	5	New Hampshire	2	Tennessee	9
Arkansas	4	Kentucky	7	New Jersey	14	Texas	27
California	45	Louisiana	8	New Mexico	3	Utah	3
Colorado	6	Maine	2	New York	34	Vermont	1
Connecticut	6	Maryland	8	North Carolina	11	Virginia	10
Delaware	1	Massachusetts	11	North Dakota	1	Washington	8
Florida	19	Michigan	18	Ohio	21	West Virginia	4
Georgia	10	Minnesota	8	Oklahoma	6	Wisconsin	9
Hawaii	2	Mississippi	5	Oregon	5	Wyoming	1
Idaho	2	Missouri	9	Pennsylvania	23		
Illinois	22	Montana	2	Rhode Island	2		

The Supreme Court decided on 17 Feb. 1964, that the federal constitution requires congressional districts within each state to be substantially equal in population. By almost invariable custom the representative lives in the district from which he is elected.

Representatives must be not less than 25 years of age, citizens of the USA for 7 years and residents in the state from which they are chosen. The District of Columbia, Guam, American Samoa and the Virgin Islands have one non-voting delegate each. The House also admits a 'resident commissioner' from Puerto Rico, who has the right to speak on any subject and to make motions, but not to vote; he is elected in the same manner as the representatives but for a 4-year term. Each of the two Houses of Congress is sole 'judge of the elections, returns and qualifications of its own members'; and each of the Houses may, with the concurrence of two-thirds, expel a member. The period usually termed 'a Congress' in legislative language continues for 2-years, terminating at noon on 3 Jan.

The salary of a senator or representative, also that of a resident commissioner in Congress, is $60,662 per annum, with tax-free expense allowance and allowances for travelling expenses and for clerical hire. The salary of the Speaker of the House of Representatives is $79,125 per annum, with a taxable allowance.

No senator or representative can, during the time for which he is elected, be appointed to any *civil* office under authority of the USA which shall have been created or the emoluments of which shall have been increased during such time; and no person holding *any* office under the USA can be a member of either House during his continuance in office. No religious text may be required as a qualification to any office or public trust under the USA or in any state.

The 98th Congress (1983–84) was constituted (Jan 1983) as follows: Senate, 53 Republicans, 46 Democrats, 1 Independent; House of Representatives, 267 Democrats, 166 Republicans and 3 seats subject to re-election.

Indians: By an Act passed on 2 June 1924 full citizenship was granted to all Indians born in the USA, though those remaining in tribal units were still under special federal jurisdiction. Those remaining in tribal units constitute from one-half to three-fourths of the Indian population. The Indian Reorganization Act of 1934 gave the tribal Indians, at their own option, substantial opportunities to self-government and of self-controlled corporate enterprises empowered to borrow money, buy land, machinery and equipment; these corporations are controlled by democratically elected tribal councils; by 1945 roughly a third of the Indians had taken advantage of this Act. Recently a trend towards releasing Indians from federal supervision has resulted in legislation terminating supervision over specific tribes. Indian lands (1979) amounted to 51,801,865 acres, of which 41,874,797 was tribally owned and 9,927,068 in trust allotments. Indian lands are held free of taxes. Total Indian population at the 1980 census was 1,418,195, of which Oklahoma, Arizona, California and New Mexico accounted for 628,400.

State and Local Government: The Union comprises 13 original states, 7 states which were admitted without having been previously organized as territories, and 30 states which had been territories—50 states in all. Each state has its own constitution (which the USA guarantees shall be republican in form), deriving its authority, not from Congress, but from the people of the state. Admission of states into the Union has been granted by special Acts of Congress, either (1) in the form of 'enabling Acts' providing for the drafting and ratification of a state constitution by the people, in which case the territory becomes a state as soon as the conditions are fulfilled, or (2) accepting a constitution already framed, and at once granting admission.

Each state is provided with a legislature of two Houses (except Nebraska, which since 1937 has had a single-chamber legislature), a governor and other executive officials, and a judicial system. Both Houses of the legislature are elective, but the senators (having larger electoral districts usually covering 2 or 3 counties compared with the single county or, in some states, the town, which sends 1 representative to the Lower House) are less numerous than the representatives, while in 38 states their terms are 4 years; in 12 states the term is 2 years. Of the 4-year senates, Illinois, Montana and New Jersey provide for two 4-year terms and one 2-year term in each decade. Terms of the lower houses are usually shorter; in 45 states, 2 years.

Members of both Houses are paid at the same rate, which varies from $200 per biennium (New Hampshire) to $56,220 per biennium (California). The trend is towards annual sessions of state legislatures; in 1982, 36 were constitutionally required to meet annually (in 1939, only 4), the other 14 holding biennial sessions, 12 in the odd-numbered and 2 in the even-numbered years. Of these 14, 6 met annually in practice by invoking flexible constitutional powers to reconvene at intervals during the biennium.

The Governor has power to summon an extraordinary session, but not to dissolve or adjourn. The duties of the two Houses are similar, but in many states money bills must be introduced first in the Lower House. The Senate sits as a court for the trial of officials impeached by the other House, and often has power to confirm or reject appointments made by the Governor.

State legislatures are competent to deal with all matters not reserved for the federal government by the federal constitution nor specifically prohibited by the federal or state constitutions. Among their powers are the determination of the qualifications for the right of suffrage, and the control of all elections to public office, including elections of members of Congress and electors of President and Vice-President; the criminal law, both in its enactment and in its execution, with unimportant exceptions, and the administration of prisons; the civil law, including all matters pertaining to the possession and transfer of, and succession to, property; marriage and divorce, and all other civil relations; the chartering and control of all manufacturing, trading, transportation and other corporations, subject only to the right of Congress to regulate commerce passing from one state to another; labour; education; charities; licensing; fisheries within state waters, and game laws (apart from the hunting of migratory birds, which is a federal concern under treaties with Canada and Mexico). Taxes on income were left to the states until 1913, when the 16th amendment authorized the imposition of federal taxes on income without regard to apportionment.

The Governor is chosen by direct vote of the people over the whole state. His term of office varies in the several states from 2 to 4 years, and his salary from $35,000 (Arkansas, Delaware, Maine) to $85,000 (New York). His duty is to see to the faithful administration of the law, and he has command of the military forces of the state. He may recommend measures but does not present bills to the legislature. In some states he presents estimates. In all but one of the states (North Carolina) the Governor has a veto upon legislation, which may, however, be overridden by the two Houses, in some states by a simple majority, in others by a three-fifths or two-thirds majority. In some states the Governor, on his death or resignation, is succeeded by a Lieut.-Governor who was elected at the same time and has been presiding over the state Senate. In several states the Speaker of the Lower House succeeds the Governor.

The chief officials by whom the administration of state affairs is carried on (secretaries, treasurers, members of boards of commissioners, etc.) are usually chosen by the people at the general state elections for terms similar to those for which governors hold office. State employees, Oct. 1970, numbered 2,755,033, earning $1,612·1m. monthly; education accounted for 1·18m. employees (43%). Local government employees numbered 7,392,437, earning $4,294·2m. monthly.

Local Government. The chief unit of local government is the county, of which there were (1982) 2,992 with definite functions; in addition, Rhode Island has 5 'counties' which have no functions; Alaska does not have 'counties' as such and, since Oct. 1960, there has been no active county government in Connecticut. Louisiana has 64 'parishes'. The counties maintain public order through the sheriff and his deputies, who may, in a crisis, be drawn temporarily from willing citizens; in many states the counties maintain the smaller local highways; other functions are the granting of licences and the apportionment and collection of taxes. In a few states they also manage the schools.

The unit of local government in New England is the rural township, governed directly by the voters, who assemble annually or oftener if necessary, and legislate in local affairs, levy taxes, make appropriations and appoint and instruct the local officials (selectmen, clerk, school-committee, etc.). Townships are grouped to form counties. Where cities exist, the township government is superseded by the city government.

The **District of Columbia,** ceded by the State of Maryland for the purposes of government in 1791, is the seat of the US Government. It includes the city of Washington, and embraces a land area of 61 sq. miles. The Reorganization Plan No. 3 of 1967 instituted a Mayor Council form of government with appointed officers. In 1973 an elected Mayor and elected councillors were introduced; in 1974 they received power to legislate in local matters. Congress retains power to enact legislation and to veto or supersede the Council's acts. Since 1961 citizens have had the right to vote in national elections. On 23 Aug. 1978 the Senate approved a constitutional amendment giving the District full voting representation in Congress. This has still to be ratified.

The **Commonwealth of Puerto Rico, American Samoa, Guam and the Virgin Islands** each have a local legislature, whose acts may be modified or annulled by Congress, though in practice this has seldom been done. Puerto Rico since its attainment of commonwealth status on 25 July 1952, enjoys practically complete self-government, including the election of its governor and other officials. The conduct of foreign relations, however, is still a federal function and federal bureaux and agencies still operate in the island.

General supervision of territorial administration is exercised by the Office of Territories in the Department of Interior.

Congress and the Nation, 4 vols., Congressional Quarterly, Washington, from 1965—*Congressional Ethics,* Rev. ed., 1980.—*Congressional Quarterly Almanac,* annual

Constitution of the US, National and State. 2 vols. [with subsequent amendments]. Dobbs Ferry, 1962

Political profiles. 5 vols. New York, from 1978

Adrian, C. R., *State and Local Government.* 4th ed. New York, 1977

Barone, M. (ed.), *The Almanac of American Politics.* New York and London, Annual

Beloff, M., and Vale, V. (eds.), *American Political Institutions in the 1970s.* London, 1975

Berger, M., *Equality by Statute; The Revolution in Civil Rights.* Rev. ed. Gordon City, N.Y., 1968

Bone, H. A., *American Politics and the Party System.* 4th ed. New York, 1971

Cater, D., *Power in Washington.* London, 1964

Corwin, E. S., *Presidential Power and the Constitution.* Cornell Univ. Press, 1976

Dumbauld, E., *The Constitution of the United States.* Univ. of Oklahoma Press, 1965

Egger, R. A., *The President of the United States.* 2nd ed. New York, 1972

Ferguson, J. H., and McHenry, D. E., *Elements of American Government.* 6th ed. New York, 1963.—*The American Federal Government.* 12th ed. New York, 1973.—*The American System of Government.* 12th ed. New York, 1973

Fisher, L., *Presidential Spending Power.* Princeton Univ. Press, 1975

Hardin, C. M., *Presidential Power and Accountability: Towards a New Constitution.* Univ. of Chicago Press, 1974

Kelly, A. H., and Harbison, W. A., *The American Constitution, Its Origin and Development.* 4th ed. New York, 1970

Koenig, L. W., *The Chief Executive.* 3rd ed. New York, 1975

Levine, E. L., *An Introduction to American Government.* 2nd ed. New York, 1974

Maddox, R. W., and Fuquay, R. F., *State and Local Government.* 3rd ed. New York, 1975

Mayer, G. H., *The Republican Party, 1854–1966.* 2nd ed. OUP, 1967

Moe, R. C., *Congress and the President, Allies and Adversaries.* Pacific Palisades, 1971

Ogg, F. A., and Ray, P. O., *Introduction to American Government.* 12th ed. New York, 1962.—*Essentials of American National Government.* 10th ed. New York, 1969.—*Essentials of American State and Local Government.* 10th ed. New York, 1969

Pious, R. M., *The American Presidency.* New York, 1979

Pritchett, C. H., *The American Constitution.* 2nd ed. New York, 1968.—*The American Constitutional System.* New York, 1977

Redford, E. S., *Democracy in the Administrative State.* OUP, 1969

Ripley, R. B., *American National Government and Public Policy.* New York, 1974

Robinson, J. A., *State Legislative Innovation.* New York, 1973

Rossiter, C., *Parties and Politics in America.* Cornell Univ. Press, 1964

Scammon, R. M. (ed.), *America Votes. Handbook of Contemporary Election Statistics.* Pittsburg, 1975

Scheer, R., *America after Nixon: The Politics of the New World Order.* New York, 1975

Schlesinger, A. M., *Congress and the Presidency: Their Role in Modern Times.* Washington, 1967
Seymour-Ure, C., *The American President: Power and Communication.* London, 1982
Tugwell, R. G., *The Enlargement of the Presidency.* Garden City, N.Y., 1960.—*The Emerging Constitution.* New York, 1974
White, T. H., *The Making of the President.* New York, 1960.—*The Making of the President, 1964.* New York, 1965.—*The Making of the President, 1968.* New York, 1969

DEFENCE. The President is C.-in-C. of the Army, Navy and Air Force.

The National Security Act of 1947 provides for the unification of the Army, Navy and Air Forces under a single Secretary of Defense with cabinet rank. The President is also advised by a National Security Council and the Office of Civil and Defense Mobilization.

The major components of the Department of Defense are the Office of the Secretary of Defense and the Joint Chiefs of Staff, who provide immediate staff assistance and advice to the Secretary; the departments of the Army, Navy and Air Force, each separately organized under a civilian head (not of cabinet rank); and the unified and specified commands.

Army. *Secretary of the Army:* John Marsh.

Central Administration. The Secretary of the Army is the head of the Department of the Army. Subject to the authority of the President as C.-in-C. and of the Secretary of Defense, he is responsible for all affairs of the Department.

The Secretary of the Army is assisted by the Under Secretary of the Army, 4 Assistant Secretaries of the Army (Installations, Logistics and Financial Management; Research and Development; Manpower and Reserve Affairs, and Civil Works), the General Counsel, an Administrative Assistant, Chief of Legislative Liaison, Chief of Public Affairs and the Army Staff headed by the Chief of Staff, US Army. The office of the Under Secretary of the Army includes a Deputy Under Secretary (Operations Research).

The Chief of Staff is the principal military adviser of the Secretary of the Army, and performs his duties under the direction of the Secretary of the Army, except as otherwise prescribed by law, by the President or by the Secretary of Defense. He has supervision of all members and organizations of the Army. The Vice Chief of Staff assists and advises the Chief of Staff.

The Army General Staff is the principal element of the Army Staff and includes the offices of the Chief of Staff, Vice Chief of Staff, Director of Staff, the 4 Deputy Chiefs of Staff (Military Operations, Personnel, Logistics, and Research, Development and Acquisition), the Comptroller of the Army, the Assistant Chief of Staff for Intelligence, the Ballistic Missile Defense Program Manager and the Army Reserve Forces Policy Committee. Other elements of the Army Staff are the offices of the Judge Advocate General, Surgeon General, Adjutant General, Inspector General and Auditor General, Chief of Chaplains, Chief, Army Reserve, Chief, National Guard Bureau, and Chief of Engineers.

The Army consists of the Regular Army, the Army National Guard of the US, the Army Reserve and civilian workforce; and all persons appointed to or enlisted into the Army without component; and all persons serving under call or conscription, including members of the National Guard of the States, etc., when in the service of the US.

Department of the Army active authorized strength, including cadets, was (1982) 790,800, including 55,000 women, comprised, in major combat units, of 16 divisions and several separate brigades and regiments.

The US Army Forces Command, with headquarters at Fort McPherson, Georgia, commands the continental US Armies and all assigned Active Army and US Army Reserve troop units in the continental US, Alaska, Hawaii, Panama, Guam, Johnston Island, the Commonwealth of Puerto Rico, and the Virgin Islands of the USA. The headquarters of the continental US Armies are: First US Army, Fort George G. Meade, Maryland; Fifth US Army, Fort Sam Houston, Texas; Sixth US Army, Presidio of San Francisco, California. The US Army Training and Doctrine Command, with headquarters at Fort Monroe, Virginia, co-ordinates and integrates the total combat development effort of the Army as well as developing, managing and supervising the training of individuals of the US Army and authorized foreign nationals. The US Army Health Services Command, with headquarters at Fort Sam Houston, Texas, provides health services in the continental US for the US Army and provides professional education and training for medical personnel of the US Army and authorized foreign national personnel. The US Army Materiel Development and Readiness Command, with headquarters in Alexandria, Virginia, is responsible for all US Army operations dealing with equipment development, procurement, delivery, supply and maintenance. The US Army Communications Command, with headquarters at Fort Huachuca, Arizona, provides worldwide communication to the Department of the Army and supports the Defense Communications Systems. The US Army Military District of Washington, with headquarters at Fort McNair, Washington, D.C. provides support to the Department of the Army and the Department of Defense at the seat of Government.

Some 35% of the Army is deployed overseas. Two divisions two-thirds of which are located in the USA keep equipment in the Federal Republic of Germany and can be flown there in 48–72 hours. Headquarters of US Seventh and Eighth Armies are in Europe and Korea respectively.

Operational Commands and Weapons. The larger commands are the theater army and the corps. The typical theater army may consist of a variable number of corps; combat forces of armour and infantry; air defense artillery (*Nike-Hercules* and *Hawk* and short-range missile battalions); field artillery and Pershing missile battalions; combat support forces of aviation, engineer and signal elements; and combat service support forces. A typical corps consists of a variable number and mixture of infantry, mechanized infantry, armoured, airmobile, and airborne divisions; one or more separate infantry brigades; one or more armoured cavalry regiments; corps artillery (155-mm howitzer, 8-in. howitzer, 175-mm gun, *Lance* missile battalions); an air defense element of a size commensurate with the hostile air threat (*Nike-Hercules, Hawk* and *Chaparral/Vulcan* battalions), and a target acquisition unit; combat support and combat service support forces.

US Army Divisions have a common base (containing command, aviation divisional artillery, combat, combat support units and combat service support units) and a varying mixture of 'combat manoeuvre battalions' (usually 10 or 11 in number in 3 brigades) to make up airborne, infantry, armoured, mechanized infantry and air-mobile divisions. Divisions can in this way be 'tailored' to fit a variety of strategic or tactical situations. An infantry division, with about 16,900 men, may have 8 infantry battalions, an armoured battalion and a mechanized infantry battalion; a mechanized infantry division, with about 16,600 men, may have 6 mechanized infantry battalions and 4 armoured battalions; an armoured division, with about 16,900 men, may have 5 mechanized infantry battalions and 6 armoured battalions; an airborne division, with 13,000 men, may have 9 infantry (airborne) battalions.

Small arms include the M-16, which fires a 5·56-mm cartridge. The standard general-purpose machine-gun is the M-60 (23 lb.; 550 rounds of 7·63-mm per minute). Infantry weapons also include M-203 grenade launcher attachment for the M16A1 rifle, which fire a 40-mm grenade up to 400 metres, the *Tow* and *Dragon* anti-tank missile system, and the M-72 rocket, a light anti-tank weapon.

Combat vehicles of the US Army are the tank, armoured personnel carrier, armoured reconnaissance airborne assault vehicle and the armoured command and reconnaissance vehicle. The first-line tanks are the XM-1 Abrams tank, M-60A3 with 105-mm main armament. The M-60A2, a version of the M-60 series tank, fires both the *Shillelagh* missile and conventional ammunition. The standard armoured personnel carrier is the M-113A1; it carries a mechanized infantry squad. The M-113A1 is also being utilized as the ground scout vehicle in armoured cavalry regiments, squadrons and in scout platoons of armoured and mechanized infantry battalions. The M-551 'Sheridan' is an armoured reconnaissance airborne assault vehicle in armoured cavalry units and light armour battalions; it fires both *Shillelagh* missiles and conventional ammunition. Combat vehicles under development are mechanized infantry combat vehicle and armoured reconnaissance scout vehicle.

The approved calibres of artillery are: light, 105-mm howitzer, medium 155-mm howitzer; the heavy, 175-mm gun and 8-in. howitzer. The 4·2-in. mortars and the 81-mm mortar are used by combat manoeuvre elements. The 90-mm, 106-mm recoilless rifles are being replaced by the *Dragon* and *Tow* anti-tank missile systems which are the primary anti-tank weapons. *Chaparral* and *Vulcan*, forward-area air-defence weapons, provide the capability of low-altitude defence against high-performance aircraft.

The Army has two categories of missiles—surface-to-surface (field artillery) and surface-to-air (air defence artillery). Surface-to-surface missiles are: *Pershing II*, ballistic, nuclear warhead, range about 400 miles operational; *Lance*, guided, nuclear warhead, storable, liquid propellant, operational. Surface-to-air missiles, for air defence, are: *Nike-Hercules*, guided, field or fixed installation, nuclear warhead, operational; *Hawk*, homing type, low-to-mid-altitude, field, operational (an improved system has replaced the basic *Hawk*); *Chaparral*, infra-red homing, low-altitude, forward area, operational (improvements to the basic system are under development); *Redeye*, hand-held, infra-red homing, low-altitude, forward area, operational; *Patriot*, mid-to-high-altitude, replacement for *Hawk* and *Nike-Hercules*, under limited production; *Stinger*, hand-held infra-red homing, low-altitude, forward area, replacement for *Redeye* is under development. Anti-tank missiles are: *Tow*, tube launched, optically tracked, wire guided, anti-armour, forward area, operational; *Hellfire*, terminal homing under development.

The Army employs rotary- and fixed-wing aircraft as organic elements of its ground formations where their use is required on a full-time basis and their immediate and constant availability is essential. The front line commander exploits the benefits of aviation technology to perform traditional land battle tasks in the third dimension. This concept of airmobility for ground formation utilizes aerial vehicles as a highly integrated team to perform all five functions of land combat: reconnaissance, command and control, logistics and that inseparable combination, firepower and manoeuvre.

Enlistment, Terms of Service. Since 1974 the Army has operated a 'zero draft' system making it, in effect, an all-regular force. Terms of service may be 3, 4, 5 or 6 years. Men who enlist incur a 6-year obligation and must serve in the reserve any part of the period not served on active duty.

The Army National Guard is a reserve military component with a dual status and rôle. Enlistment is voluntary. The members are recruited by each state, but are equipped and paid by the federal government. Training is supervised by the active Army (FORSOM), and unit organization parallels that for the active army; training facilities are made available by the USA and each state. As the organized militia of the several states, the District of Columbia, Puerto Rico and the Territory of the Virgin Islands, the Guard may be called into service for local emergencies by the sovereigns in those jurisdictions; and may be called into federal service by the President to thwart invasion or rebellion or to enforce federal law. In its role as a reserve component of the Army, the Guard is subject to the order of the President in the event of national emergency. The Air Guard provide 100% of the air defence of Hawaii.

The Army Reserve is designed to supply qualified and experienced units and individuals in an emergency. US Army Forces Command is charged with the command, support and training supervision of US Army Reserve units. Members are assigned to one of 3 categories: the Ready, Standby or Retired Reserve. A limited number of Ready Reservists is subject to call by the President in case of national emergency without declaration of war by Congress. The Standby Reserve and the Retired Reserve may be called only after declaration of war or national emergency by Congress.

The Army Almanac. Dept. of the Army, Washington, D.C.
Forman, S., *West Point*. New York, 1950

Navy. *Secretary of the Navy:* John F. Lehman.

The Department of the Navy is administered under the Secretary of Defense by the Secretary of the Navy, assisted by the Under Secretary, the Deputy Under Secretary for Financial Management; 3 Assistant Secretaries, for Shipbuilding and Logistics; for Manpower and Reserve Affairs; and for Research, Engineering and Systems, as well as by the Chief of Naval Operations and the Commandant of the Marine Corps. The 3 divisions of the Department of the Navy are:

Navy Department, comprised of staff offices of the Secretary for Legislative Affairs, Information, the Judge Advocate General, Auditor General, Comptroller Program Appraisal, General Counsel, Naval Research; offices of the Chief of Naval Operations which include the Vice Chief, the Assistant Vice Chief/Director of Naval Administration, 6 Deputy Chiefs and 8 Directors; Naval Inspector Genn0 eral; the Surgeon General; and headquarters of the Chief of Naval Material, Bureau of Medicine and Surgery, and Bureau of Naval Personnel.

The Shore Establishment comprises commands dealing with air, electronic, facilities engineering, sea (including ordnance) and supply systems; and other commands: Naval Telecommunications, Naval Intelligence, Naval Security Group, Oceanography, Naval Education and Training, Naval Reserve, Naval Military Personnel, Civilian Personnel and Data Automation, as well as supporting establishment of the Marine Corps and Marine Corps Reserve.

The Operating Forces are the Military Sealift Command, U. S. Naval Forces Europe, the Atlantic and Pacific Fleet including Fleet Marine Forces; operating forces of the Marine Corps, and other Navy forces and commands not otherwise assigned.

Major shore activities include 8 shipyards, 30 air stations and facilities, 2 amphibious bases, 2 submarine bases and 12 naval stations and bases. By agreement dated 2 Sept. 1940, Britain granted leases for naval and air bases in Newfoundland, Bermuda, Bahamas, Jamaica, St Lucia, Trinidad, Antigua and Guyana; but these are not all now active.

Naval appropriations in recent fiscal years: 1975, $27,426m.; 1976, $31,480m.; 1977, $32,800m.; 1978, $39,639m.; 1979, $41,530m.; 1980, $47,084m.; 1981, $57,834m; 1982, $67,965m; and (planned FY) 1983, 88,022m.

The active personnel on duty on 1 Jan. 1983 was 547,315 Navy officers and enlisted men, plus 194,579 Marine Corp officers and men.

The following is a tabulated statement of US vessels listed on 31 Dec.:

Category	*1975*	*1976*	*1977*	*1978*	*1979*	*1980*	*1981*	*1982*
Multi-purpose aircraft carriers	15	15	15	15	15	15	15	15
Anti-submarine carriers	5 [1]	5 [1]	5 [1]	5 [1]	5 [1]	5 [1]	4 [1]	5 [1]
Helicopter carriers	7	9	9	10	11	12 [2]	12 [2]	25 [2]
Command ships	3 [3]	3 [3]	3 [3]	3 [3]	3 [3]	3 [3]	3 [3]	3 [3]
Nuclear powered submarines	107	108	109	113	115	118	124	129 [7]
Submarines (conventional)	15	15	15	13	10	10	8	6
Battleships	4	4	4	4	4	4	4	4
Cruisers	35 [4]	35 [4]	35 [4]	36 [4]	32 [4]	29 [4]	31 [4]	32 [4]
Destroyers	112 [5]	101 [5]	97 [5]	93 [5]	96 [5]	98 [5]	93 [5]	88 [5]
Frigates	71 [6]	65 [6]	65 [6]	65 [6]	69 [6]	67 [6]	77 [6]	82 [6]

[1] Comprises 1 training carrier and 4 anti-submarine warfare support carriers in reserve.

[2] Comprises 5 flat-top hangar/dock heavy amphibious assault ships and 7 lighter flat-top hangar ships and 13 lighter semi-flat-top amphibious transports dock.

[3] Includes 1 Middle East Flagship (converted amphibious transport dock).

[4] Includes 24 frigates (destroyer leaders, DLG) reclassified as cruisers in 1975.

[5] Includes 10 frigates (destroyer leaders, DLG) reclassified as destroyers in 1975. Of the 88 destroyers 41 are classified as DDG.

[6] Includes 65 escort ships reclassified as frigates on 1 July 1975.

[7] Includes 2 Trident (Ohio class) ballistic missile armed very large (see Table) vessels, 32 other ballistic missile submarines and 95 attack submarines.

The table below shows principal surface ships, guns under 3-in. calibre not given:

Completed	Name	Standard displacement Tons	Aircraft	Principal armament	Shaft horse-power	Speed Knots
		Multi-Purpose (Former Attack) Aircraft Carriers				
1982	Carl Vinson		90	Guided missiles	260,000 (nuclear power)	33
1977	Eisenhower	81,600	90	Guided missiles	260,000 (nuclear power)	33
1975	Nimitz	81,600	90	Guided missiles	260,000 (nuclear power)	33
1968	John F. Kennedy	61,000	85	Guided missiles	280,000	34
1965	America	60,300	85	Guided missiles	280,000	34
1962	Enterprise	75,700	84	Guided missiles	300,000 (nuclear power)	35
1962	Constellation	61,000	85	Guided missiles	280,000	34
1961	Kitty Hawk	61,000	85	Guided missiles	280,000	34
1959	Independence	60,000	80 to 75	Guided missiles	280,000	34
1957	Ranger	60,000	80 to 75	Guided missiles	280,000	34
1956	Saratoga	59,100	80 to 75	Guided missiles	280,000	34
1955	Forrestal	59,100	70	Guided missiles	260,000	33
1950	*Oriskany [1]	33,250	70	2 5-in. guns	150,000	33
1947	Coral Sea [2]	52,500	75	Guided missiles	212,000	33
1945	Midway [2]	51,000	75	Guided missiles	212,000	33
1944	*Bon Homme Richard [1]	33,100	70	4 5-in. guns	150,000	33

[1] In reserve (CVA) but standing by for reactivation. [2] Sister ship *Franklin D. Roosevelt* was stricken in 1977.

Anti-Submarine Support Aircraft Carriers [1]

Completed	Name	Standard displacement Tons	Aircraft	Principal armament	Shaft horse-power	Speed Knots
1944	*Bennington	33,000	45	4 5-in. guns	150,000	33
1944	*Shangri-La	33,000	45	4 5-in. guns	150,000	33
1943	*Hornet [3]	33,000	45	4 5-in. guns	150,000	33

[3] Sister ship *Intrepid* was stricken in 1981 to become a memorial ship.

Training Carrier

Completed	Name	Standard displacement Tons	Aircraft	Principal armament	Shaft horse-power	Speed Knots
1943	*Lexington	32,800	—	Removed	150,000	33

The 'Essex' class originally comprised 24 ships, the *Essex, Yorktown, Intrepid, Hornet, Franklin, Lexington, Bunker Hill, Wasp, Ticonderoga, Hancock, Randolph, Bennington, Bon Homme Richard, Shangri-La, Tarawa, Antietam, Boxer, Kearsarge, Lake Champlain, Leyte, Philippine Sea, Princeton, Valley Forge, Oriskany.* Only the above 6* now remain in reserve. For dates and other details of the 18 stricken during 1964–81, and of the 'Bogue' class, 'Commencement Bay' class, and other former aircraft carriers, see 1981–82 and earlier editions.

It is planned to relieve *Lexington* as Training Carrier (while she is in dockyard for refit) with the reactivated *Oriskany.*

Helicopter Carriers [2] *(Amphibious Assault Ships)*

Completed	Name	Standard displacement Tons	Aircraft	Principal armament	Shaft horse-power	Speed Knots
1981	Pelileu	39,300 (full load)	26 to 42 helicopters (or V/STOL aircraft)	3 5-in. guns; 2 missile launchers	140,000	24
1980	Nassau	39,300 (full load)	26 to 42 helicopters (or V/STOL aircraft)	3 5-in. guns; 2 missile launchers	140,000	24
1978	Belleau Wood	39,300 (full load)	26 to 42 helicopters (or V/STOL aircraft)	3 5-in. guns; 2 missile launchers	140,000	24
1977	Saipan	39,300 (full load)	26 to 42 helicopters (or V/STOL aircraft)	3 5-in. guns; 2 missile launchers	140,000	24
1976	Tarawa	39,300 (full load)	26 to 42 helicopters (or V/STOL aircraft)	3 5-in. guns; 2 missile launchers	140,000	24
1970	Inchon	17,000	20 to 26 helicopters (or V/STOL aircraft)	4 3-in. guns; 2 missile launchers	23,000	23
1968	New Orleans	17,000	20 to 26 helicopters (or V/STOL aircraft)	4 3-in. guns; 2 missile launchers	23,000	23
1966	Tripoli	17,000	20 to 26 helicopters (or V/STOL aircraft)	4 3-in. guns; 2 missile launchers	23,000	23
1965	Guam [1]	17,000	20 to 26 helicopters (or V/STOL aircraft)	4 3-in. guns; 2 missile launchers	23,000	23
1963	Guadalcanal	17,000	20 to 26 helicopters (or V/STOL aircraft)	4 3-in. guns; 2 missile launchers	23,000	23
1962	Okinawa	17,000	20 to 26 helicopters (or V/STOL aircraft)	4 3-in. guns; 2 missile launchers	23,000	23
1961	Iwojima	17,000	20 to 26 helicopters (or V/STOL aircraft)	4 3-in. guns; 2 missile launchers	23,000	23

[1] *Guam* was modified in 1971–72 as 'interim' sea control ship but reverted to the amphibious role in 1974.

[2] According to official statistics eleven of the 12 amphibious transports dock (the other is a command ship) of the Austin class; of 12,000 tons, and the two of the Raleigh class, each with a capacity of six helicopters, are now listed under the generic heading of helicopter carriers.

Completed	Name	Standard displacement Tons	Aircraft	Principal armament	Shaft horse-power	Speed Knots

Command Ships [1]

Completed	Name	Standard displacement Tons	Aircraft	Principal armament	Shaft horse-power	Speed Knots
1971	Mount Whitney	19,100 (full load)	1 helicopter	2 missile launchers; 4 3-in guns (twin)	22,000	23
1970	Blue Ridge					

[1] *Northampton*, originally heavy cruiser; and: *Wright*, originally light fleet aircraft carrier, converted into Command Ships were stricken from the Navy List in 1977–78.

The amphibious transport dock *Coronado* has been converted to a command ship to relieve *La Salle* as flagship of the Middle East Force.

Battleships

Completed	Name	Standard displacement Tons	Aircraft	Principal armament	Shaft horse-power	Speed Knots
1944	Missouri [1]	45,000		9 16-in.; 20 5-in.	212,000	33
	Wisconsin [1]					
1943	Iowa [1]					
	New Jersey [2]					

[1] All laid up in reserve since 1955–58 but reactivation scheduled in 1983 for recommissioning in 1985 and modernisation and conversion to cruise missile carrier (*Iowa*) followed by *Missouri* and *Wisconsin*, if approved.

[2] Reactivated in 1967 and commissioned 1968–69, reserve 1969 to July 1981. Reactivated Oct. 1981 and recommissioned Dec. 1982 for modernisation and conversion to cruise missile carrier.

Cruisers

Completed	Name	Standard displacement Tons	Aircraft	Principal armament	Shaft horse-power	Speed Knots
1961	Long Beach	14,200	—	1 twin 'Talos' and 2 twin 'Terrier'; guided missile launchers; 2 5-in.	80,000 (nuclear power)	30
1949	Salem*	17,000	—	9 8-in.; 12 5-in; 20 3-in.	130,000	33
1948	Des Moines					
1946	Albany	13,700	—	2 twin 'Tartar' launchers 2 5-in.	120,000	32
1945	Chicago	13,600	—			
1944	Oklahoma City	10,670	1 helicopter	Twin 'Talos' launchers 3 6-in. guns; 2 5-in.	100,000	31

* Sister ship *Newport News* was stricken from the Navy List on 31 July 1978, possibly to become a memorial.

Albany and *Chicago* were to have been disposed of in 1980 but in 1981 it was planned to retain these ships in reserve for a minimum of three years and *Oklahoma City* subsequently was similarly reprieved and restored to the Navy List.

For conversions and disposals of other cruisers of the 'Oregon City', 'Baltimore', 'Cleveland' and 'Juneau' classes see 1981–82 and earlier editions.

Cruisers, Former Frigates (Destroyer Leaders)

Completed	Name	Standard displacement Tons	Aircraft	Principal armament	Shaft horse-power	Speed Knots
1980	Arkansas	9,000	2 helicopters	2 twin 'Tartar/ASROC'; 2 5-in.	80,000 (nuclear power)	30
1978	Mississippi					
1977	Texas					
1976	Virginia					
1974	South Carolina	9,560	—	2 single 'Tartar'; 2 5-in.;	70,000 (nuclear power)	30
1973	California					
1967	Truxtun	8,200	1 helicopter	1 twin 'Terrier'; 1 5-in; 2 3-in.	60,000 (nuclear power)	30
1962	Bainbridge	7,600	—	2 twin 'Terrier'; 4 3-in.		
1964–67	9 Belknap Class [1]	6,570	—	1 twin 'Terrier'; 1 5-in; 2 3-in.	85,000	34
1962–64	9 Leahy Class [2]	5,670	—	2 twin 'Terrier'; 4 3-in.	85,000	34

[1] The 'Belknap' class comprises *Belknap, Biddle, Fox, Horne, Josephus Daniels, Jouett, Sterett, Wainwright* and *William H. Standley*.

[2] The 'Leahy' class comprises *Dale, England, Gridley, Halsey, Harry E. Yarnell, Leahy, Reeves, Richmond K. Turner* and *Worden*.

The 10 'Coontz' class comprises *Coontz, Dahlgren, Dewey, Farragut, King, Luce, Macdonough, Mahan, Preble* and *William V. Pratt*. They were reclassified from frigates (DLG) to destroyers (DDG) on 1 July 1975 when the later frigates above were reclassified as cruisers. See 1981–82 edition for earlier destroyer leader/frigates.

Capital (Strategic) Submarines

Class	*No.*	*Displacement (submerged) Tons*	*Missile Tubes (Vertical)*	*Nuclear Reactors*	*Shaft Horse-power*	*Speed Knots*
'726'	2	18,700	24 Trident	1	60,000	30 dived 20 surface
'640'	12	8,500	16 Poseidon	1	15,000	30 dived 20 surface
'616'	19	8,250	16 Poseidon	1	15,000	30 dived 21 surface
'608'	5 [1]	7,880	16 Polaris	1	15,000	30 dived 20 surface
'598'	5 [2]	6,888	16 Polaris	1	15,000	31 dived 20 surface

Completion:- '726' class in 1981–82 (five more to follow in 1983–85); '640' class 1965–67; '616' class in 1963–64; '608' class in 1961–63; '598' class in 1959–61. All these ballistic missile armed submarines also have four 21-inch torpedo tubes.

[1] This class reclassified as fleet submarines.

[2] Three of this class converted to fleet submarines and two laid up in reserve.

In addition to the above named ships there are 129 nuclear-powered submarines (including the ballistic missile armed vessels in the table), 6 conventionally propelled submarines, 84 destroyers, 82 frigates, 25 ocean minesweepers, 4 patrol vessels, 4 hydrofoil patrol craft, 4 fast patrol boats, 67 amphibious warfare ships, 64 landing craft, 30 replenishment ships, 70 sealift ships, 95 fleet support ships and auxiliaries, 100 minor landing craft and 1,100 service craft.

Ships under construction include 9 submarines of 18,700 tons submerged with nuclear power and ballistic missiles, 20 nuclear powered attack submarines of 6,900 tons submerged; the giant nuclear powered aircraft carrier *Theodore Roosevelt* and 2 sister ships each of 93,400 tons war load; 3 destroyers and 29 guided missile frigates.

Projected new construction includes 6 more 'Ohio' class nuclear powered deterrent or 'strategic' submarines; 6 more nuclear powered fleet or 'attack' submarines; 1 large aircraft carrier; 49 guided missile destroyers and 15 frigates.

Naval Aviation. The official figures given in the total aircraft inventory are: 6,184 flown by the Navy and the Marine Corps of which 5,577 are active and 4,940 are operating. There are 637 naval aircraft in the pipeline.

The US Coast Guard operates under the Department of Transportation in time of peace and as a part of the Navy in time of war or when directed by the President. The act of establishment stated the Coast Guard 'shall be a military service and branch of the armed forces of the United States at all times'. The Coast Guard did operate as part of the Navy during the First and Second World Wars. It also had some units serving in Vietnam. It comprises 250 ships including cutters of destroyer, frigate, corvette and patrol vessel types, powerful icebreakers, and paramilitary auxiliaries and tenders, plus some 600 small rescue and utility craft. It also maintains 40 fixed-wing aircraft and 100 helicopters. The Coast Guard missions include maintenance of aids to navigation, enforcement of maritime laws, enforcement of international treaties, environmental protection (especially waterway pollution), commercial vessel safety programmes, recreational boating safety, and search and rescue efforts. In the new construction programme are 10 cutters of frigate size and utility each capable of carrying a helicopter. The strength of personnel on 1 Jan. 1983 was 4,600 officers, 1,400 warrant officers and 28,000 enlisted men.

Air Force. *Secretary of the Air Force:* Verne Orr.

The Department of the Air Force was activated within the Department of Defense on 18 Sept. 1947, under the terms of the National Security Act of 1947. It is administered by a Secretary of the Air Force, assisted by an Under Secretary and 3 Assistant Secretaries (Research, Development and Logistics; Financial Management; and Manpower, Reserve Affairs and Installations). The USAF, under the administration of the Department of the Air Force, is supervised by a Chief of Staff, who is a member of the Joint Chiefs of Staff. He is assisted by a Vice Chief of Staff, Assistant Vice Chief of Staff, and 5 Deputy Chiefs of Staff (Manpower and Personnel; Programs and Evaluation; Research, Development and Acquisition; Operations, Plans and Readiness; and Logistics and Engineering).

The USAF consists of active duty Air Force officers and airmen, civilian employees, the Air National Guard and the Air Force Reserve. For operational purposes the service is organized into 12 major commands, 13 separate operating agencies and 6 direct reporting units. The Strategic Air Command, equipped with long-range bombers based both in the USA and overseas, and with intercontinental ballistic missiles, is maintained primarily for strategic air operations anywhere on the globe. Tactical Air Command is the Air Force's mobile strike force, able to deploy US general-purpose air forces anywhere in the world for tactical air combat operations. The Military Airlift Command provides air transportation of personnel and cargo for all military services on a worldwide basis; and is also responsible for Air Force audio-visual products, weather service, and aerospace rescue and recovery operations.

The other functional commands are the Air Force Systems Command, Air Force Logistics Command, Air Force Communications Command, Electronic Security Command, and Air Training Command.

The overseas commands are the Pacific Air Forces, the US Air Forces in Europe and the Alaskan Air Command. These commands conduct, control and coordinate offensive and defensive air operations according to tasks assigned by their respective theatre commanders. There are also a number of separate operating agencies which include the Air Force Accounting and Finance Center, Air Force Audit Agency, Air Force Commissary Service, Air Force Engineering and Services Center, Air Force Inspection and Safety Center, Air Force Intelligence Service, Air Force Office of Security Police, Air Force Manpower and Personnel Center, Air Force Medical Service Center, Air Force Service Information and News Center, Air Force Legal Services Center, Air Force Office of Special Investigations, and Air Force Test and Evaluation Center. The Air Force has several other direct reporting units, including the Air Force Academy, Air Force Reserve, Air National Guard, Aerospace Defense Center, the Albert F. Simpson Historical Research Center, and the Air Force Technical Applications Center.

Of the fighter and interceptor aircraft in service, the F-15 Eagle, F-5 Tiger II, F-16 Fighting Falcon, F-105 Thunderchief, F-106 Delta Dart, F-111 and F-4 Phantom II fly faster than the speed of sound in level flight and can carry a variety of armament. The E-3 Sentry is a large long-range airborne warning and control aircraft; the EF111A is a tactical electronics jamming aircraft produced by conversion of the F111A fighter. The subsonic A-7 Corsair II and the A-10 Thunderbolt II are close-support aircraft. Strategic bombers are the B-52 Stratofortress heavy bomber (to be supplemented by B-1B from mid-80s) and the 'swing-wing' FB-111A. The Strategic Air Command also operates the KC10A Extender and KC-135 Stratotanker for aerial refuelling, the SR-71 Blackbird and U-2 for strategic reconnaissance, and the TR-1 for tactical reconnaissance on behalf of Tactical Air Command. Current transport types include the C-141 StarLifter, the C-5 Galaxy and the turboprop-powered C-130 Hercules. Intercontinental ballistic missiles in USAF service are Titan II (to be retired, and replaced with MX from mid-80s) and Minuteman II and III.

In 1982, the Air Force had 580,800 personnel. Total 1982 aircraft strength was 9,314.

INTERNATIONAL RELATIONS

Membership. USA is a member of UN, OAS, NATO, OECD and the Colombo Plan.

ECONOMY

Budget. The budget covers virtually all the programmes of federal government, including those financed through trust funds, such as for social security, Medicare and highway construction. Receipts of the Government include all income from its sovereign or compulsory powers; income from business-type or market-orientated activities of the Government is offset against outlays. Budget receipts and outlays (in $1m.):

Year ending 30 June	*Receipts*[3]	*Outlays*[3]	*Surplus* (+) *or deficit* (–)
1945	45,216	92,690	–47,474
1950	39,485	42,597	– 3,112
1955	65,469	68,509	– 3,041
1960	92,492	92,223	+ 269
1970	192,807	195,652	– 2,845
1981 [1]	599,272	657,204	–57,932
1982	617,766	728,424	–110,658
1983 [2]	646,498	761,516	–115,018

[1] From 1977 the fiscal year changed from a 1 July–30 June basis to a 1 Oct.–30 Sept. basis.
[2] Estimate.
[3] From 1970, revised to include Medicare premiums and collections.

Budget receipts, by source, for fiscal years (in $1m.):

Source	*1981* [1]	*1982* [2]	*1983* [1 2]
Individual income taxes	285,917	298,111	293,792
Corporation income taxes	61,137	49,207	58,316
Social insurance taxes and contributions	182,720	201,132	215,720
Excise taxes	40,839	36,311	40,065
Estate and gift taxes	6,787	7,991	6,020
Customs	8,083	8,854	9,522
Miscellaneous	13,790	16,161	15,000
Adjustment for Senate Finance Committee Bill	...	...	8,063
Total	599,272	617,766	646,498

[1] From 1977, the fiscal year changed from a 1 July–30 June basis to a 1 Oct.–30 Sept. basis.
[2] Estimate.

Budget outlays, by function, for fiscal years (in $1m.):

Source	*1981* [1]	*1982* [1]	*1983* [1 4]
National defence [2]	159,765	187,397	221,502
International affairs	11,130	9,983	12,091
General science, space, and technology	6,359	7,096	7,636
Energy	10,277	4,844	4,151
Natural resources and environment	13,525	13,086	10,438
Agriculture	5,572	14,808	10,411
Commerce and housing credit	3,946	3,843	431
Transportation	23,381	20,589	19,886
Community and regional development	9,394	7,410	7,347
Education, training, employment and social services	31,402	25,411	23,783
Health	65,982	74,018	78,493
Income security	225,099	248,807	259,286
Veterans benefits and services	22,988	23,973	24,220
Administration of justice	4,698	4,648	4,646
General government	4,614	4,833	5,007
General purpose fiscal assistance	6,856	6,161	6,535
Interest	82,537	100,777	111,117
Allowances [3]	...	...	–4,687
Undistributed offsetting receipts	–30,320	–29,261	–40,777
Total budget outlays	657,204	728,424	761,516

[1] From 1977, the fiscal year changed from a 1 July–30 June basis to a 1 Oct.–30 Sept. basis.
[2] Includes allowances for civilian and military pay raises for the Department of Defense.
[3] Includes allowances for civilian agency pay raises and contingencies.
[4] Estimate.

Budget outlays, by agency, for fiscal years (in $1m.):

Agency	*1981* [1]	*1982* [1]	*1983* [1 2]
Legislative branch	1,209	1,362	1,514
The judiciary	637	705	840
Executive Office of the President	96	95	99
Funds appropriated to the President	7,010	6,073	7,017
Agriculture	26,030	36,213	29,578
Commerce	2,226	2,045	10,410
Defence—Military [3]	156,035	182,850	215,922
Defence—Civil	3,148	2,971	2,275
Education [4]	15,089	14,081	...
Energy [4]	11,797	7,705	...
Health and Human Services	226,987	251,269	272,878
Housing and Urban Development	14,033	14,491	12,982
Interior	4,262	3,793	2,662
Justice	2,682	2,584	2,743
Labour	30,084	30,736	26,230
State	1,897	2,185	2,470
Transportation	22,554	19,929	19,230
Treasury	92,633	110,521	123,759
Environmental Protection Agency	5,232	5,004	4,462
National Aeronautics and Space Administration	5,421	6,026	6,578
Veterans Administration	22,903	23,937	24,193
Other independent agencies:	...	...	12,865
Foundation for Education Assistance	18,089	19,973	21,889
Office of Personnel Management			
Postal Service	1,343	707	500
Railroad Retirement Board	5,308	5,733	350
All other	10,803	6,697	5,534
Allowances [5]	...	...	–4,687
Undistributed offsetting receipts	–30,306	–29,261	–40,777
Total budget outlays	657,204	728,424	761,516

[1] From 1977, the fiscal year changed from a 1 July–30 June basis to a 1 Oct.–30 Sept. basis.
[2] Estimate.
[3] Includes allowances for civilian and military pay raises for the Department of Defense.
[4] The Administration proposed in the 1983 Budget that the Departments of Education and Energy be eliminated and that their programmes be transferred to other agencies. Many of the Education programmes went to the proposed Foundation for Education Assistance.
[5] Includes allowances for civilian agency pay raises and contingencies.

National Debt: Gross federal debt outstanding (in $1m.), and *per capita* debt (in $1) on 30 June to 1970 and then on 30 Sept.:

	Public debt	*Per capita* [2]		*Public debt*	*Per capita* [2]
1919 [1]	25,485	243	1970	382,603	1,867
1920	24,299	228	1979	833,751	3,709
1930 [1]	16,185	132	1980	914,317	4,021
1940	50,696	382	1981	1,003,941	4,365
1950	256,853	1,687	1982 [3]	1,137,131	4,900
1960	290,862	1,610	1983 [3]	1,273,505	5,420

[1] On 31 Aug. 1919 gross debt reached its First World War (1914–18) peak of $26,596,702,000, which was the highest ever reached up to 1934; on 31 Dec. 1930 it had declined to $16,026m., the lowest it has been since the FirstWorld War. On the 30 Nov. 1941, just preceding Pearl Harbor, debt stood at $61,363,867,932. The highest Second World War debt was $279,764,369,348 on 28 Feb. 1946.
[2] *Per capita* figures, beginning with 1960, have been revised; they are based on the Census Bureau's estimates of the total population of the US, including Alaska and Hawaii.
[3] Estimate.

State and Local Finance: Revenue of the 50 states and all local governments (82,688 in 1982) from their own sources amounted to $416,433m. in fiscal year 1980–81; in addition they received $80,294m. in revenue from fiscal aid, shared revenues and reimbursements from the federal government, bringing total revenue from all sources to $506,728m. Of the revenue from state and local sources, taxes provided $244,514m., of which property taxes (mainly imposed by local governments) yielded $74,969m. or 31% of all tax revenue; and sales taxes, both general sales taxes and selective excises, provided $85,971m. (35%).

State tax revenue totalled $149,738m. in fiscal year 1981. Largest sources of state tax revenue are general sales taxes (imposed during 1980 by 45 states), motor fuel sales taxes (all states), individual income (44 states), motor vehicle and operators' licences (49 states), corporation income (46 states), tobacco products (all states) and alcoholic beverage sales taxes (all states).

General revenue of local units from own sources in fiscal year 1980–81 totalled $145,736m. In addition they received $111,443m. from state and federal aids. Property taxes provided 28% of total general revenue.

Total expenditures of state and local governments were $487,048m. in 1980–81, of which approximately 71% was for current operation. Education took $145,784m. in current and capital expenditure; highways, $34,603m.; welfare (chiefly public assistance), $54,121m., and health and hospitals, $36,101m. Capital outlays (construction, equipment and land purchases) totalled $67,596m.

Gross debt of state and local governments totalled $363,892m. or $1,606 *per capita* at the close of their 1980–81 fiscal year. Total cash and investment assets of state and local governments were $454,393m., about 23% being in cash and deposits, and the remainder in investments, mainly non-governmental securities.

US Bureau of the Census, *Governmental Finances in 1980–81.* Washington, 1982
American Economic Association, *Readings in Fiscal Policy.* Homewood, Ill., 1955
Brookings Institute and National Bureau of Economic Research, *Role of Direct and Indirect Taxes in the Federal Revenue System.* Washington, D.C., 1964

National Income. The Bureau of Economic Analysis of the Department of Commerce prepares detailed estimates on the national income and product of the United States. The principal tables are published monthly in *Survey of Current Business;* the complete set of national income and product tables are published in the *Survey* regularly each July, showing data for recent years. *The National Income and Product Accounts of the United States, 1929–1976: Statistical Tables* (1976) and the July 1982 *Survey* contain complete sets of tables from 1929 through 1979. The conceptual framework and statistical methods underlying the US accounts were described in *National Income, 1954.* Subsequent limited changes were described in *US Income and Output* (1958), and in *Survey of Current Business* (Aug. 1965, Jan. 1976 and Dec. 1980).

These latest figures [1] in $1,000m. for various years are as follows:

	1929 [2]	*1933* [3]	*1950*	*1960*	*1970*	*1980*	*1981*
I. Gross National Product	103·4	55·8	286·5	506·5	992·7	2,633·1	2,937·7
(*a*) Personal consumption expenditures	77·3	45·8	192·0	324·9	612·7	1,667·2	1,843·2
(*b*) Gross private domestic investment	16·2	1·4	53·8	75·9	144·2	402·3	471·5
(*c*) Net exports of goods and services	1·1	0·4	2·2	5·5	6·7	25·2	26·1
(*d*) Government purchases of goods and services	8·8	8·2	38·5	100·3	220·1	538·4	596·9
1. GNP *less* capital consumption allowances with capital consumption adjustment, indirect business tax and non-tax liability, business transfer payments, statistical discrepancy, *plus* subsidies less current surplus of government enterprises, equals:							
2. National Income	84·8	39·9	237·6	415·7	810·7	2,117·1	2,352·5
which, *less* corporate profits with inventory valuation and capital consumption adjustments, contributions for social insurance, wage accruals less disbursements, *plus* government transfer payments to persons, interest paid by government to persons and business less interest received by government, interest paid by consumers, personal dividend income, business transfer payments, equals:							

[1] The inclusion of statistics for Alaska and Hawaii beginning in 1960 does not significantly affect the comparability of the data.
[2] Peak year between First and Second World Wars. [3] Low point of the depression.

	1929[1]	*1933*[2]	*1950*	*1960*	*1970*	*1980*	*1981*
3. Personal income	85·0	47·0	227·2	402·3	811·1	2,160·4	2,415·8
whereof							
4. Personal tax and non-tax payments take	2·6	1·4	20·6	50·4	115·8	336·3	386·7
leaving							
5. Disposal personal income divided into	82·4	45·6	206·6	352·0	695·3	1,824·1	2,029·1
(*e*) Personal outlays[3]	79·1	46·5	194·7	332·3	639·5	1,717·9	1,898·9
(*f*) Personal saving	3·3	−0·9	11·9	19·7	55·8	106·2	130·2
IA. GNP in constant (1972) $s	315·7	222·1	534·8	737·2	1,085·6	1,474·0	1,502·6
(*a*) Personal consumption expenditures	215·1	170·5	337·3	452·0	672·1	930·5	947·6
(*b*) Gross private domestic investment	55·8	8·4	93·5	104·7	158·5	208·4	225·8
(*c*) Net exports of goods and services	3·7	0·4	5·9	7·7	3·9	50·6	42·0
(*d*) Government purchases of goods and services	41·0	42·9	98·1	172·8	251·1	284·6	287·1
II. National Income	84·8	39·9	237·6	415·7	810·7	2,117·1	2,352·5
composed of							
Compensation of employees	*51·1*	*29·5*	*154·8*	*294·9*	*612·0*	*1,598·6*	*1,767·6*
(*g*) Salaries and wages	50·5	29·0	147·0	271·9	548·7	1,356·1	1,494·0
(*h*) Supplements to wages and salaries	0·6	0·5	7·8	23·0	63·2	242·5	273·6
Proprietors' income[4]	*15·0*	*5·9*	*38·7*	*47·2*	*66·2*	*116·3*	*124·7*
(*i*) Farm[4]	6·1	2·5	13·7	11·7	14·3	19·4	24·0
(*j*) Business and professional[4]	8·9	3·3	25·0	35·5	51·9	96·9	100·7
Personal income from rents	*4·9*	*2·2*	*7·1*	*14·5*	*19·7*	*32·9*	*33·9*
Net interest	*4·7*	*4·1*	*3·0*	*11·4*	*41·4*	*187·7*	*235·7*
Corporate profits with inventory valuation and capital consumption adjustments	*9·0*	*−1·7*	*33·9*	*47·6*	*71·4*	*181·6*	*190·6*
(*k*) Tax liabilities	1·4	0·5	17·9	22·7	34·2	84·7	81·2
(*l*) Inventory valuation adjustment	0·5	−2·1	−5·0	−0·2	−6·6	−43·0	−24·6
(*m*) Capital consumption adjustment	−1·4	0·6	−4·0	−2·0	2·5	−17·8	−16·8
(*n*) Dividends	5·8	2·0	8·8	12·9	22·5	58·1	65·1
(*o*) Undistributed profits	2·8	−1·6	16·2	14·3	18·8	99·7	85·8

[1] Peak year between First and Second World Wars.
[2] Low point of the depression.
[3] Includes personal consumption expenditures, interest paid by consumers and personal transfer payments to foreigners (net).
[4] With inventory valuation and capital consumption adjustment.

Currency. Prior to the banking crisis that occurred early in 1933, the monetary system had been on the gold standard for more than 50 years. An Act of 14 March 1900 required the Secretary of the Treasury to maintain at a parity with gold all forms of money issued by the USA. For a description of these, *see* THE STATESMAN'S YEAR-BOOK, 1934, p. 491.

The old gold dollar had a par value of 49·32*d*., or $4·8666 to the £ sterling; it contained 25·8 grains (or 1·6718 grammes) of gold 0·900 fine. By the act of 12 May 1933 the President of the USA was given authority to reduce the gold content of the dollar by not more than 50% and by the Gold Reserve Act of 30 Jan. 1934 the minimum reduction which he could make was fixed at 40%; on 31 Jan. 1934 he fixed its value at 59·06%, or 15⁵⁄₂₁ grains of gold 0·900 fine. This was equal to a price for gold of $35 a fine oz. (old price, $20·67183). The President's power to alter the gold content of the dollar to 50% of its value, which was extended by Congress in 1937, 1939 and 1941, was not yet again extended in 1943.

The Par Value Modification Act (Public Law 92–268), enacted on 31 March 1972, authorized and directed the Secretary of the Treasury to take the steps necessary to establish a new par value of the dollar of $1 = 0·818513 gramme of fine gold or $38 per fine troy oz. of gold. The Secretary of the Treasury, pursuant to the statutory directive, proposed the new par value for the US dollar to the International Monetary Fund, which par value became effective on 8 May 1972.

In Public Law 93–110, enacted on 21 Sept. 1973, Congress amended the Par Value Modification Act of 1972, and authorized and directed the Secretary of the Treasury to take the steps necessary to establish a new par value of $1 equals 0·828948 Special Drawing Right or 1/42⁹⁄₁₀ of a fine troy ounce of gold. Pursuant to the statutory directive, the Secretary of the Treasury notified the International Monetary Fund that, effective 18 Oct. 1973, the par value of the dollar would be changed from 1/38 to 1/42⁹⁄₁₀ a fine troy ounce of gold. Expressed in terms of gold, the new par value of the dollar is 0·736662 gramme of gold per dollar, or $42.222 per fine troy ounce of gold. Expressed in percentage, the change in the par value of the dollar amounted to a reduction of 10% in the former gold content of the dollar. This is the equivalent to an 11·1% increase in the former dollar price of gold.

The USA, on 1 April 1978, accepted the second amendment to the Articles of Agreement of the International Monetary Fund. The par value of the dollar is no longer defined in terms of the Special Drawing Right and gold, and the USA is not obliged to establish and maintain a par value for the dollar.

At the time of the banking crisis in March 1933 gold payments by banks and the Treasury were suspended by the Government, and an embargo was placed on gold exports. Steps were taken to withdraw from circulation all gold coin and gold certificates and to prohibit the private ownership of all gold coin except for numismatic purposes. Public Law 93–373, 14 Aug. 1974, amended the Par Value Modification Act so as to provide for the termination of all governmental restrictions on private ownership of gold, including gold coins, no later than 31 Dec. 1974.

Currency in the USA for many years has comprised several varieties. Prior to May 1933 the legal tender qualities of the classes varied, but in that month all types of currency were made equally legal tender. Under the Coinage Act of 1965, all coins and currencies of the USA, regardless of when coined or issued, are legal tender for all debts, public and private.

Only two of the eight kinds of notes outstanding are now significant: Federal Reserve notes in denominations of $1, $2, $5, $10, $20, $50 and $100; and US notes in denominations of $100. The issue of *(a)* $500, $1,000, $5,000 and $10,000 Federal Reserve notes; of *(b)* silver certificates, and of *(c)* $5 and $2 US notes have been discontinued, although they are still in general circulation. The following issues were stopped many years ago and are in process of retirement: (1) Federal Reserve Bank notes; (2) National Bank notes; (3) Treasury notes of 1890; (4) fractional currency.

Federal Reserve notes are obligations of the USA and a first lien on the assets of the Federal Reserve Banks, through which they are issued. Each of the 12 banks issues them against the security of an equal volume of collateral.

Gold coins (of the old weight and fineness) were $20, $10, $5 and $2½ pieces called *double eagles, eagles, half-eagles* and *quarter-eagles.* The old eagle weighed 258 grains or 16·7181 grammes 0·900 fine, and therefore contained 232·2 grains or 15·0463 grammes of fine gold. Except for collector's holdings, these are no longer in circulation. The stock of gold bullion held by the Treasury on 31 Aug. 1982 was 264m. fine oz., valued at $11,100m.; stock of silver bullion was 38·7m. fine oz. (excluding 137·5m. fine oz. held for defence stockpile). Estimated stock of domestic coin on 30 June 1982 was $13,356m., including standard silver dollars and silver and other subsidiary coin.

The silver dollar weighs 412·5 grains or 26·7296 grammes 0·900 fine, and contains 371·25 grains or 24·0566 grammes of fine silver. Subsidiary, 0·900 fine, silver coins contain 347·22 grains of fine silver per dollar. These are the half-dollar, quarter-dollar and dime (one-tenth). Minor coins currently issued are the cupro-nickel 5-cent piece and the bronze 1-cent piece. Pursuant to the Coinage Act of 1965, Congress authorized the minting and issuance of new silver clad half-dollars containing 40% silver and cupro-nickel quarter-dollars and dimes containing no silver. In an amendment to the Coinage Act enacted on 31 Dec. 1970, Congress provided that all coins minted thereafter, including dollar and half-dollar coins, be made of cupro-nickel composition. However, a provision in the 1970 law permitted the coining of 1·500 inch dollar coins containing 40% silver. These dollar coins, which bear the likeness of the late President Eisenhower, are sold at premium price to coin collectors. In Oct. 1978 there was authorization of a new dollar bearing the likeness of suffragette Susan B. Anthony. The new dollars, which are 1·043 inches in diameter and weigh 8·1 grammes, replace the cupro-nickel Eisenhower dollars. In 1981 the Mint began producing 1-cent coins made of 97·6% zinc and 2·4%

copper (zinc and copper alloy blanks, barrel electro-plated with copper), pursuant to its authority under 31 USC 317(b) to alter the composition of the alloy of the 1-cent coin. In 1983 it was in the process of phasing out production of bronze cents and will shortly only be producing zinc cents.

Banking. On 31 Dec. 1979 there were 15,171 domestic banks doing a general deposit business with the public and having aggregate deposits of $1,241,596m. Of these, 4,448 with deposits of $594,970m. were national banks operating under charters granted by the federal government; the remaining banks, including trust companies and savings banks, were organized under the laws of the various states. Of the total number, 5,425 were members of the Federal Reserve System, namely, all the 4,448 national banks and 977 state banks admitted to membership.

The Federal Reserve System, established under an Act of 1913, comprises the Board of 7 Governors, the 12 regional Federal Reserve Banks with their 25 branches, the Federal Open Market Committee and the Federal Advisory Council. The 7 members of the Board of Governors are appointed by the President by and with the consent of the Senate. Each Governor is appointed to a full term of 14 years or an unexpired portion of a term, one term expiring every 2 years. No two may come from the same Federal Reserve District. The Board supervises the Reserve Banks and the issue and retirement of Federal Reserve notes; it designates 3 of the 9 directors of each Reserve Bank one of whom is designated Chairman; it passes on the admission of state banks to the System and has power to correct unsound conditions in State member banks or violations of banking law by them, including, if necessary, disciplinary action to remove officers and directors for unsafe or unsound banking practices or for continuous violations of banking laws; it also authorizes State member bank branches and approves mergers and consolidations if the acquiring, assuming or resulting bank is to be a State member; and it has power to control the expansion of bank holding companies and to require divestment of certain non-banking interests. The 12 members of the Federal Open Market Committee include the 7 members of the Board of Governors and 5 of the 12 Federal Reserve Bank presidents. The latter serve 1-year terms on the Committee in rotation except for the President of the Federal Reserve Bank of New York, who is a permanent member. The Federal Open Market Committee influences credit market conditions, money and bank credit, by buying or selling US Government securities; and it also supervises System operations in foreign currencies for the purpose of helping to safeguard the value of the dollar in international exchange markets and facilitating co-operation and efficiency in the international monetary system. The Board also influences credit conditions through powers to set member-bank reserve requirements, to approve discount rates at Federal Reserve Banks, and to fix margin requirements on stock-market credit.

The 12 Reserve Banks (one for each district) implement Federal Reserve policies, chiefly through their dealings with member banks, which, although outnumbered by non-member banks, hold about 73% of the country's total commercial banking deposits. The Reserve Banks hold bank reserves, advance funds to member banks, issue Federal Reserve notes, which are the principal form of currency in the US, act as fiscal agent for the Government and afford nation-wide cheque-clearing and fund transfer arrangements. They may issue notes, fully secured; discount paper for member banks; increase or reduce the country's supply of reserve funds by buying or selling Government securities and other obligations at the direction of the Federal Open Market Committee. Their capital stock is held by the member banks, but it carries no voting rights except in the election of directors.

Every member bank is required to subscribe to stock in the Reserve Bank of its district in an amount equal to 6% of its paid-up capital and surplus. Only one-half of the par value of the stock is paid in, the other half remaining subject to call by the Board of Governors. However, no call has been made for the second half of the subscription. The reserve balances which member banks must carry with Reserve Banks are based on the volume of their net demand and time deposits. The Board of Governors has the power to alter these requirements within limits. The Board of Governors also has authority to limit the rate of interest payable by member banks on time and savings deposits. Under provisions of the Defense Production Act of 1950 the Board of Governors prescribes regulations under which the Federal Reserve Banks act as fiscal agents of certain Government departments and agencies in guaranteeing loans made by banks and other private financing institutions to finance contracts for the procurement of materials or services which the guaranteeing agencies consider necessary for the national defence.

Under the Credit Control Act of 1969 the President is empowered to authorize the Board of Governors to institute selective credit controls when necessary to curb inflation.

Beginning in 1968, the Congress passed a number of consumer credit protection acts, the first of which was the Truth in Lending Act (and including the Equal Credit Opportunity Act), Home Mortgage Disclosure Act, Consumer Leasing Act and the Fair Credit Billing Act, for which it has directed the Board to write implementing regulations and assume partial enforcement responsibility. To manage these responsibilities the Board has established a Consumers Affairs Division. To assist it, the Board consults with a Consumer Advisory Council, established by the Congress as a statutory part of the Federal Reserve System.

Another statutory body, the Federal Advisory Council, consists of 12 members (one from each district); it meets in Washington four times a year (or oftener) to advise the Board of Governors on general business and financial conditions.

Banks which participate in the federal deposit insurance fund have their deposits insured against loss up to $40,000 for each depositor. The fund is administered by the Federal Deposit Insurance Corporation established in 1933; it obtains resources through annual assessments on participating banks.

All members of the Federal Reserve System are required to insure their deposits through the Corporation, and non-member banks may apply and qualify for insurance. On 31 Dec. 1979, 14,351 commercial banks with deposits of $1,085,739m. were members of the insurance fund. This insurance also covered 324 mutual savings banks with deposits of $132,338m. There were 496 uninsured banks comprising 357 commercial banks and trust companies and 139 mutual savings banks with deposits of $23,519m. (in 1975 this figure included mutual savings banks only).

There are also banks which operate solely in the field of agricultural credits under the Farm Credit Administration; Federal Home Loan Banks makes advances to financial associations and institutions upon the security of home mortgages.

US Board of Governors of the Federal Reserve System. *The Federal Reserve System Purposes and Functions.* 6th ed., 1974.—*Federal Reserve Bulletin.* Monthly.—*Annual Report.*—*Annual Statistical Digest.*—*The Federal Reserve Act, As Amended Through 1978*

Beckhart, B. H., *Federal Reserve System.* New York, 1972

Chandler, L. V., *Economics of Money and Banking.* 7th ed. New York, 1977

Clifford, A. J., *The Independence of the Federal Reserve System.* Philadelphia, 1965

Friedman and Swartz, *A Monetary History of the United States, 1867–1960,* National Bureau of Economic Research, New York, 1963

Horovitz, P. M., *Monetary Policy and the Financial System.* 4th ed. Englewood Cliffs, 1979

Maisel, S. J., *Managing the Dollar.* New York, 1973

Myers, M. G., *A Financial History of the United States.* Columbia Univ. Press, 1970

Timberlake, R. H., *The Origins of Central Banking in the United States.* Cambridge, Massachusetts, 1978

Young, R. A., *Instruments of Monetary Policy in the United States; the Role of the Federal Reserve System.* Washington, 1973

Weights and Measures. British weights and measures are usually employed, but the old Winchester bushel and wine gallon are used instead of the new or Imperial standards: *Wine gallon* = 0·83268 Imperial gallon; *Bushel* = 0·9690 Imperial bushel. Instead of the British cwt of 112 lb., one of 100 lb is used; the *short* or *net ton* contains 2,000 lb.; the *long* or *gross ton*, 2,240 lb.

ENERGY AND NATURAL RESOURCES

Minerals. Total value of non-fuel minerals produced in US (including Alaska and Hawaii) in 1981 was estimated at $25,173m. ($25,146m. in 1980). Details are given in the following tables.

Production of metallic minerals (long tons, 2,240 lb.; short tons, 2,000 lb.):

Metallic minerals	*1980 Quantity*	*Value ($1,000)*	*1981 Quantity*	*Value ($1,000)*
Bauxite (dried equiv.) tonnes	1,559,000	22,353	1,510	26,489
Copper (recoverable content), tonnes	1,181,116	2,666,931	1,538,160	2,886,440
Gold (recoverable content), troy oz.	969,782	594,050	1,377,946	633,359

	1980		1981	
Metallic minerals (contd.)	*Quantity*	*Value ($1,000)*	*Quantity*	*Value ($1,000)*
Iron ore (usable)[1], 1,000 long tons, gross	69,562	2,543,484	72,158	2,914,689
Lead (recoverable content), tonnes	550,366	515,189	445,535	358,821
Molybdenum (content of concentrate), 1,000 lb.	149,311	1,344,181	118,916	945,540
Silver (recoverable content), 1,000 troy oz.	32,329	667,278	40,685	427,943
Zinc (recoverable content), tonnes	317,103	261,671	312,418	306,879
Other metals	—	306,904	—	257,515
Total metals	—	8,922,000	—	8,758,000

[1]Excluding by-product iron sinter.

The two world wars and record levels of industrial production have hastened the depletion of once abundant supplies of metal and US is increasingly an importer. US is wholly or almost wholly dependent upon imports for industrial diamonds, bauxite, tin, chromite, nickel, strategic-grade mica and long-fibre asbestos; it imports the bulk of its tantalum, platinum, manganese, mercury, tungsten, cobalt and flake graphite, and substantial quantities of antimony, cadmium, arsenic, fluorspar, zinc and bismuth.

In 1981 precious metals were mined mainly in Idaho, Arizona, Nevada, Utah, Colorado and Montana (in order of combined output of gold and silver). US output of gold (troy oz.), 1930–39, 31,453,370; 1940–49, 24,171,646; 1950–59, 18,817,241; total 1792–1970, 316,620,436. Output of silver (troy oz.), 1930–39, 466,412,499; 1940–49, 434,656,631; 1950–59, 374,055,521; total 1792–1970, 4,701,429,507.

Statistics of important non-metallic minerals and mineral fuels are:

	1980		1981	
Non-metallic minerals	*Quantity*	*Value ($1,000)*	*Quantity*	*Value ($1,000)*
Boron minerals, short tons	1,545,000	366,760	1,481,000	435,387
Cement:				
00 short tons	71,612	3,613,332	68,197	3,515,600
Masonry, 1,000 short tons	3,040	188,456	2,738	161,819
Clays, 1,000 short tons	48,790	898,947	44,379	988,845
Gypsum, 1,000 short tons	12,376	103,059	11,497	98,101
Lime, 1,000 short tons	19,010	842,922	18,856	884,197
Phosphate rock, 1,000 tonnes	54,415	1,256,947	53,624	1,437,986
Potassium salts, 1,000 tonnes (K_2O equivalent)	2,217	353,862	1,908	328,900
Salt (common), 1,000 short tons	40,352	656,164	38,907	636,328
Sand and gravel, 1,000 short tons	792,700	2,289,000	754,800	2,290,000
Stone, 1,000 short tons	984,856	3,404,736	874,381	3,276,967
Sulphur (Frasch-process), 1,000 tonnes	7,400	720,511	5,910	715,683
Other non-metallic minerals	—	1,528,839	—	1,645,337
Total non-metallic minerals	—	16,224,000	—	16,415,000

	1977		1978	
Mineral fuels				
Coal: Bitum. and lignite, 1,000 short tons	678,685	13,189,481	...	...
Pennsylv. anthracite,[1] 1,000 short tons	6,228	209,234	...	...
Gas: Natural gas,[2] 1m. cu. ft	19,952,438	11,571,776	20,025,463	15,825,954
Natural gasoline and cycle products, 1,000 bbls of 42 gallons; L.P. gases, 1,000 bbls of 42 gallons	587,045	3,284,089	590,455	4,047,473
Petroleum (crude), 1,000 bbls of 42 gallons	2,976,180	24,229,540	3,009,265	25,790,732

[1] Includes a small quantity of anthracite mined in states other than Pennsylvania.
[2] Value at wells.

Minerals Yearbook. Bureau of Mines. Washington, D.C. Annual from 1932–33; containing the *Mineral Resources of the United States* series (1866–1931); from 1963 in 3 vols. *(Metals, Minerals, Fuels; Area Reports, Domestic; and Area Reports, International)*

Agriculture. Agriculture in the USA is characterized by its ability to adapt to widely varying conditions, and still produce an abundance and variety of agricultural products. From colonial times to about 1920 the major increases in farm production were brought about by adding to the number of farms and the amount of land under cultivation. During this period nearly 320m. acres of virgin forest were converted to crop land or pasture, and extensive areas of grass lands were ploughed. Improvident use of soil and water resources was evident in many areas.

During the next 20 years the number of farms reached a plateau of about 6·5m., and the acreage planted to crops held relatively stable around 330m. acres. The major source of increase in farm output arose from the substitution of power-driven machines for horses and mules. Greater emphasis was placed on development and improvement of land, and the need for conservation of basic agricultural resources was recognized. A successful conservation programme, highly co-ordinated and on a national scale—to prevent further erosion, to restore the native fertility of damaged land and to adjust land uses to production capabilities and needs—has been in operation since early in the 1930s.

Following the Second World War the uptrend in farm output has been greatly accelerated by increased production per acre and per farm animal. These increases are associated with a higher degree of mechanization; greater use of lime and fertilizer; improved varieties, including hybrid maize and grain sorghums; more effective control of insects and disease; improved strains of livestock and poultry; and wider use of good husbandry practices, such as nutritionally balanced feeds, use of superior sites and better housing. During this period land included in farms decreased slowly, crop land harvested declined somewhat more rapidly, but the number of farms declined sharply.

Some significant changes during these transitions are:

All land in farms totalled less than 500m. acres in 1870, rose to a peak of over 1,200m. acres in the 1950s and declined to 1,042m. acres in 1980, even with the addition of the new States of Alaska and Hawaii in 1960. The number of farms declined from 6·35m. in 1940 to 2·43m. in 1980, as the average size of farms doubled. The average size of farms in 1980 was 430 acres, but ranged from a few acres to many thousand acres. In 1978, 215,088 farms (128,254 in 1974) were less than 10 acres; 475,241 (379,543), 10–49 acres; 814,689 (827,884), 50–179 acres; 596,356 (616,098), 180–499 acres; 215,112 (207,297), 500–999 acres; 98,521 (92,712), 1,000–1,999 acres; 63,635 (62,225) 2,000 acres or more.

Farms operated by owners or part-owners, 1978, were 2,165,000 (87% of all farms), by all tenants, 314,000 (13%). The average size of farms in 1978 was 235 acres for full-owners, 792 acres for part-owners and 396 acres for tenants. Farms with white operators numbered 2,398,726, and those with operators who were black or of other races were 79,916. A higher proportion of blacks and operators of other races were tenants and operated a significantly smaller acreage than white operators.

In 1980 (with 1960 figures in parentheses) large-scale, highly mechanized farms with sales of agricultural products totalling $20,000 and over per farm made up 39% (8·6%) of all farms and accounted for 90% (48·3%) of the value of farm products sold. Farms selling between $19,999 and $2,500 worth of products per farm were 40% (44·8%) of all farms and sold 8·2% (43·3%) of all sales. The remaining 21% (46·6%) of all farms sold less than $2,500 worth of products per farm, 1·8% (8·4%) of total sales. Operators in every sales category received off-farm income, but operators selling less than $2,500 per year received 91·7% of their average income of $22,063 from non-farm sources in 1980.

A century ago three-quarters of the total US population was rural, and practically all rural people lived on farms. In April 1980 26% of the population was rural, and 6m. farm residents accounted for 3% of the total population.

Hired farm workers in 1980 averaged about 1·3m., and farm family workers, including operators, about 2·4m. In 1950 there were nearly 10m. farm workers. At that time each farm worker supplied farm products for 15 people; in 1974, 55 people, in 1977, 60 people and in 1980, 78 people.

Cash receipts from farm marketings and government payments (in $1m.):

	Crops	*Livestock and livestock products*	*Government payments*	*Total*
1932	1,996	2,752	—	4,748
1945	9,655	12,008	742	22,405
1950	12,356	16,105	283	28,744
1960	15,259	18,989	702	34,950
1970	20,976	29,563	3,717	54,256
1976	48,668	46,112	734	95,514
1977	48,650	47,639	1,819	98,108
1978	53,711	59,213	3,030	115,954
1979	63,394	68,522	1,375	133,291
1980	69,026	67,405	1,286	137,717

Realized gross farm income (including government payments), in $1m., was 141,581 in 1979, compared with 139,059 in 1980; net income of farm operators (only from farm sources), 32,081 (19,605). Farm-mortgage debt, on 1 Jan. 1981, was $84,100m.

US agricultural exports, fiscal year, totalled: 1972–73, $14,984m.; 1973–74, $21,608m.; 1974–75, $21,854m.; 1975–76, $22,760m.; 1976–77, $23,974m.; 1977–78, $27,290m.; 1978–79, $31,975m.; 1979–80, $40,481m.

Total area of farm land under irrigation in 1978 was 50,837,940 acres (302,674 farms).

Federal income taxes paid by farm people was $15m. in 1941, $1,365m. in 1948, $1,182m. in 1967, $3,434m. in 1971, $5,309m. in 1972, $8,364m. in 1973 and $8,277m. in 1974. Total taxes levied on farm real estate were $2,652m. in 1974, $2,855m. in 1975, $3,098m. in 1976, $3,039m. in 1977, $3,021m. in 1978 and $3,232m. in 1979.

According to census returns and estimates of the Economic Research Service, the acreage and specified values of farms has been as follows (area in 1,000 acres; value in $1,000):

	Farm area [1]	*Crop land available for crops*	*Value, land, bldgs, machinery, livestock*	*Value of products sold in preceding year*
1910	878,798	432,000	41,089,000	...
1930	986,771	480,000	57,815,000	9,609,924
1940	1,060,852	467,000	41,829,000	6,681,581
1950	1,158,566	478,000	99,366,000	22,051,129
1959	1,125,508	448,100	164,200,000	30,492,721
1969	1,063,346	459,048	206,751,000	44,519,658
1978	1,029,695	461,341	5,653,400,000	108,113,519

[1] Acreages are for the preceding year except for 1959.

The areas and production of the principal crops for 3 years were:

	1978			*1979*			*1980*		
	Harvested 1,000 acres	*Production 1,000 bu.*	*Yield per acre bu.*	*Harvested 1,000 acres*	*Production 1,000 bu.*	*Yield per acre bu.*	*Harvested 1,000 acres*	*Production 1,000 bu.*	*Yield per acre bu.*
Corn for grain	71,930	7,267,927	101·0	72,400	7,938,819	109·7	73,061	6,647,543	91
Oats	11,126	581,657	52·3	9,679	526,551	54·4	8,640	457,593	53
Barley	9,248	454,759	49·2	7,522	382,798	50·9	7,233	358,544	49·6
All wheat	56,495	1,775,524	31·4	62,454	2,134,060	34·2	70,853	2,369,666	33·4
Rice (cwt)	2,970	133,170	4,484	2,869	131,947	4,599	3,295	145,063	4,403
Soybeans for beans	63,663	1,868,754	29·4	70,566	2,267,901	32·1	67,856	1,817,097	26·8
Flaxseed	687	8,614	12·5	878	12,014	13·7	703	8,128	11·6
Cotton lint (bale)	12,400	10,856	420	12,831	14,629	547	12,989	11,125	411
Potatoes (cwt)	1,375	366,314	267	1,270	342,497	270	1,155	301,006	261
Tobacco (lb.)	964	2,024,820	2,101	827	1,526,549	1,845	915	1,772,001	1,936

Wheat. The chief wheat-growing states (1980) were (estimated yield in 1,000 bu.): Kansas, 420,000; Oklahoma, 195,000; N. Dakota, 179,650; Washington, 160,200; Texas, 130,000; Montana, 119,800; Nebraska, 112,100; Colorado, 109,900; Minnesota, 102,556; Idaho, 96,030; Missouri, 89,010; California, 85,500.

Cotton. Leading production, 1980, by state (in 1,000 bales, 480 lb. net weight) was: Texas, 3,305; California, 3,150; Arizona, 1,413; Mississippi, 1,150; Louisiana, 455; Arkansas, 450; Alabama, 275; Oklahoma, 216; Tennessee, 200; Missouri, 178.

Tobacco. Output (1,000 lb.) of the chief tobacco-growing states (92% of the crop) was, in 1980: N. Carolina, 763,665; Kentucky, 409,222; S. Carolina, 125,125; Tennessee, 112,544; Georgia, 110,550; Virginia, 108,919.

Fruit. A wide variety of fruits are grown; the chief products are as follows:

	1978		*1979*		*1980*	
	Production 1,000 tons	*Value $1,000*	*Production 1,000 tons*	*Value $1,000*	*Production 1,000 tons*	*Value $1,000*
Apples	3,798	781,350	4,072	883,384	4,353	821,827
Citrus Fruit	14,255	1,198,657	13,329	1,296,044	16,491	1,304,177
Grapes	4,567	1,005,794	4,989	1,180,025	5,576	1,323,152

Dairy produce. In 1980, production of milk was 128,425m. lb.; milkfat, 4,692m. lb.; cheese (not including cottage cheese), 3,983m. lb.; butter, 1,145m. lb.; eggs, 69,683m.

Livestock. Number of farm animals (in 1,000) on farms on 1 Jan.:

	1979	*1980*	*1981*
Cattle of all kinds	118,437	123,071	115,013
Sheep and lambs	365	12,687	12,942
Swine (hogs and pigs) [1]	60,356	67,353	64,520

[1] At 1 Dec. of previous year.

The value (in $1,000) was:

	1979	*1980*	*1981*
Cattle of all kinds	44,697,773	55,831,294	54,359,749
Sheep and lambs	890,970	992,127	904,488
Swine (hogs and pigs) [1]	5,023,454	3,774,920	4,822,265

[1] At 1 Dec. of previous year.

Total value of livestock, excluding poultry and goats and, from 1961, horses and mules (in $1m.) on farms in the USA on 1 Jan. was: 1930, 6,061; 1933 (low point of the agricultural depression), 2,733; 1970, 22,886; 1976, 29,483; 1977, 29,053; 1978, 31,952; 1979, 50,612; 1980, 60,598; 1981, 60,087.

In 1980 the production of shorn wool was 105·4m. lb. from 13·2m. sheep (average 1970–74, 320m. lb. from 18·2m. sheep); of pulled wool, 1m. lb. (1970–74, 10·1m. lb.).

Fact Book of US Agriculture. US Dept. of Agriculture, 1976

Forestry. In 1977 the US forest lands, including Alaska and Hawaii, capable of producing timber for commercial use, covered 482,485,900 acres (more than one-fifth of the land area), classified as follows: Saw-timber stands, 215,435,700 acres; pole timber stands, 135,609,900 acres, seedling and sapling stands, 115,032,100 acres; non-stocked and other areas, 16,408,200 acres. Ownership of commercial forest land is distributed as follows: Federal government, 99,410,400 acres; state, county, municipal and Indian, 36,311,200 acres; privately owned, 346,764,300 acres, including 115,777,100 acres on farms. Of the saw-timber stand (2,578,940m. bd ft) Douglas fir constitutes 514,317; Southern yellow pine, 321,563; Western yellow (ponderosa and jeffrey) pine, 192,638; other softwoods, 956,890; hardwoods, 593,532. In 1976 growing stock timber removals amounted to 14,229,023,000 cu. ft compared to net annual growth of about 21,664,316,000 cu. ft. Saw-timber removals amounted to 65,176,618,000 bd ft against an annual growth of 74,620,832,000 bd ft. The net area of the 154 national forests and other areas in USA and Puerto Rico administered by the US Department of Agriculture's Forest Service, including commercial and non-commercial forest land, was on 31 Dec. 1980, 190·15m. acres.

Fire takes a heavy annual toll in the forest; total area burned over in 1980 was 3,980,832 acres; 1,463,745,000 acres of land are now under organized fire-protection service. The area planted or seeded in forest and wind barrier nursery stock in the year ending 30 Sept. 1980 was 2,266,956 acres, an increase of 205,583 acres over the previous year.

Forest Statistics of the United States. Forest Service, US Dept. of Agriculture, 1977
Land Areas of National Forest System. Forest Service, US Dept. of Agriculture, 1981
Report of the Forest Service, 1980

Fisheries. The main fishing industries are in California (anchovy, tuna and sole); Alaska (notably salmon); Washington (salmon and halibut); Florida (the main source of turtles and sponges); Massachusetts, Maine, North Carolina and Oregon.

Total catch, 1975, 5,350m. lb. tons valued at $1,353m.

Tennessee Valley Authority. Established by Act of Congress, 1933, the TVA is a multiple-purpose federal agency which carries out its duties in an area embracing some 41,000 sq. miles, in 125 counties (aggregate population, about 7·9m.) in the 7 Tennessee River Valley states: Tennessee, Kentucky, Mississippi, Alabama, North Carolina, Georgia and Virginia. In addition, 76 counties outside the Valley are served by TVA power distributors. Its 3 directors are appointed by the President, with the consent of the Senate; headquarters are in Knoxville, Tenn. There were 39,899 employees in Oct. 1982.

In the 1930s and 1940s, the Tennessee Valley offered the world a model of the first effort to develop all resources of a major river valley under one comprehensive programme, the Tennessee Valley Authority. The multipurpose development of the Tennessee River for flood control, navigation, and electric power production was the first big task for TVA. But there were other needs; controlling erosion on the land, introducing better fertilizers and new farming practices, eradicating malaria, demonstrating ways electricity could lighten the burdens in the home and increase production on the farm, and a multitude of potential job-producing enterprises.

In the depression year, 1933, the average *per capita* income in the Valley was $168, compared with the national average of $375. Through the years, TVA has placed a strong emphasis on the economic development of the Valley. An abundant supply of reasonably priced power, combined with a reliable navigation system, has provided a strong incentive for industry to locate in the Valley. By 1980, the region's *per capita* income had multiplied over 44 times to $7,378, while the national average had increased 25 times.

Taming the Tennessee River has had two positive effects on the Valley: flood damages averted by river control now exceed $2,000m., and a navigable channel system 800 miles long, connecting with the American system of inland waterways, provides a readily accessible transportation system for industry. In 1980, over 29m. tons of barge-traffic travelled the TVA river system.

Another activity is experimentation in the development and manufacture of chemical fertilizers, accompanied by programmes designed to encourage proper fertilizer use in all parts of the United States and the world. TVA's National Fertilizer Development Center is recognized world-wide for its expertise in fertilizer technology. TVA also works closely with other federal agencies, and with state and local authorities in combating soil erosion, improving forest resources, improving agriculture, and in the development of local industries based on natural resources.

In recent years, attention has focused mainly on TVA's power programme. TVA supplies electric power to 160 local distribution systems serving 2·7m. customers. The power system originated with the water-power development of the Tennessee River, but has become predominantly a coal-fired system as power requirements have outgrown the region's hydro-electric potential. In fiscal year 1982, the TVA system generated 113,597m. kwh. Installed capacity in 1982 was 32·2m. kw, with another 4·8m. kw under construction at TVA's nuclear plants.

Because of the ever-increasing cost of energy in today's world, TVA has focused a good deal of its attention and resources on the research and demonstration of new and alternative energy sources. TVA is playing a lead rôle in the development of atmospheric fluidized bed combustion (AFBC) technology, an innovative process of burning high-sulphur coal cleanly and cheaply. TVA is continuing its research and demonstrations into solar energy, both for residential and commercial uses; energy from wood and waste products, and electric vehicle development. Other TVA activities include demonstration of effective ways of reclaiming strip-mined areas and development of new and improved methods of controlling air and water pollution.

Power operations are financially self-supporting from revenues. In 1981–82, power revenues were $3,964m., and net income $341m. Power facilities are financed from revenues and the sale of revenue bonds and notes, and TVA is repaying appropriations previously invested in power facilities. Other TVA resource development programmes continue to be financed from congressional appropriations, which amount to $129m. in 1981–82.

Annual Report of the TVA. Knoxville, 1934 to date
Clapp, G.R., *The TVA; An Approach to the Development of a Region*. Univ. of Chicago Press, 1955

Lilienthal, D. E., *TVA; Democracy on the March.* 20th Anniversary ed. New York and London, 1953
Owen, M., *The Tennessee Valley Authority.* New York, 1973
Tennessee Valley Authority. *Director of TVA Environment Programs, 1976.—Short History of the TVA.* Knoxville, Tennessee, 1973.—*TVA: The First Twenty Years* (ed. R. C. Martin), Univ. of Tennessee Press, 1956

INDUSTRY AND TRADE

Industry. The following table presents industry statistics of manufactures as reported at various censuses from 1909 to 1977 and from the Annual Survey of Manufactures for years in which no census was taken. The figures for 1958 to 1977 include data for some establishments previously classified as non-manufacturing. The figures for 1939, but not for earlier years, have been revised to exclude data for establishments classified as non-manufacturing in 1954. The figures for 1909–33 were previously revised by the deduction of data for industries excluded from manufacturing during that period.

The statistics for 1958, 1963, 1967, 1972 and 1977 relate to all establishments employing 1 or more persons anytime during the year; for 1950, 1956–57, 1959–62, 1964–66 and 1968–74 on a representative sample of manufacturing establishments of 1 or more employees; for 1929 through 1939, those reporting products valued at $5,000 or more; and for 1909 and 1919, those reporting products valued at $500 or more. These differences in the minimum size of establishments included in the census affect only very slightly the year-to-year comparability of the figures.

The annual Surveys of Manufactures carry forward the key measures of manufacturing activity which are covered in detail by the Census of Manufactures. The estimate for 1950 is based on reports for approximately 45,000 plants out of a total of more than 260,000 operating manufacturing establishments; those for 1956–57 on about 50,000, and those for 1959–62, 1964–66 and 1968–74 on about 60,000 out of about 300,000. Included are all large plants and representative samples of the much more numerous small plants. The large plants in the surveys account for approximately two-thirds of the total employment in operating manufacturing establishments in the US.

	Number of establishments	*Production workers (average for year)*	*Production workers' wages total ($1,000)*	*Value added by manufacture* [1] *($1,000)*
1909	264,810	6,261,736	3,205,213	8,160,075
1919	270,231	8,464,916	9,664,009	23,841,624
1929	206,663	8,369,705	10,884,919	30,591,435
1933	139,325	5,787,611	4,940,146	14,007,540
1939	173,802	7,808,205	8,997,515	24,487,304
1950	260,000	11,778,803	34,600,025	89,749,765
1960	...	12,209,514	55,555,452	163,998,531
1963	306,617	12,232,041	62,093,601	192,103,102
1964	...	12,403,300	65,838,900	206,193,600
1965	...	13,076,000	71,361,500	226,939,900
1966	...	13,826,500	78,256,400	250,880,100
1967	305,680	13,955,300	81,393,600	261,983,800
1968	...	14,042,500	87,485,400	285,016,200
1969	...	14,359,600	93,459,600	304,308,200
1970	...	13,258,000	91,609,000	300,227,600
1971	...	12,874,900	93,063,200	314,151,700
1972	320,710	13,527,900	105,501,800	353,994,000
1973	...	14,233,100	118,332,300	405,623,500
1974	...	13,970,900	124,983,200	452,468,400
1975	...	12,567,900	121,427,200	442,485,800
1976	...	13,051,200	137,564,600	511,470,900
1977	359,928	13,690,800	157,163,600	585,096,100
1978	...	14,228,700	176,416,800	657,412,000
1979	...	14,539,400	192,926,100	747,931,100

[1] For the period 1954–67 value added represents adjusted value added and for earlier years unadjusted value added. Unadjusted is obtained by subtracting cost of materials, supplies and containers, fuel, electricity and contract work from the value of shipments for products manufactured plus receipts for services rendered. Adjusted value added also takes into account value added by merchandizing operations plus net change in finished goods and work-in-process inventories between the beginning and end of the year.

For comparison of broad types of manufacturing, the industries covered by the Census of Manufactures have been divided into 20 general groups according to the *Standard Industrial Classification*. This was revised in 1972; 1967 figures are not therefore strictly comparable.

Code No.	Industry group	Census year	Production workers (average for year)	Production workers' wages, total ($1,000)	Value added by manufacture [1] ($1,000)
20.	Food and kindred products	1967	1,121,700	6,062,600	26,620,900
		1972	1,085,400	8,007,400	35,616,600
		1979	1,101,700	13,837,600	68,732,900
21.	Tobacco manufactures	1967	66,200	303,600	2,032,000
		1972	57,400	400,900	2,637,200
		1979	47,500	667,300	5,342,700
22.	Textile mill products	1967	828,200	3,556,600	8,153,000
		1972	836,200	4,807,200	11,718,000
		1979	732,400	6,942,300	18,216,200
23.	Apparel and related products	1967	1,200,000	4,340,600	10,064,400
		1972	1,198,300	5,461,100	13,487,500
		1979	1,129,500	7,937,900	21,709,700
24.	Lumber and wood products	1967	495,700	2,290,600	4,973,400
		1972	601,100	3,932,900	10,309,400
		1979	632,200	6,989,900	20,107,000
25.	Furniture and fixtures	1967	357,500	1,653,700	4,169,500
		1972	383,800	2,321,300	6,089,500
		1979	397,700	3,821,800	10,998,800
26.	Paper and allied products	1967	507,700	3,205,500	9,756,300
		1972	498,800	4,320,200	13,064,100
		1979	509,100	7,635,600	27,082,100
27.	Printing and publishing	1967	631,600	4,011,300	14,355,100
		1972	637,400	5,459,300	20,197,100
		1979	700,500	8,806,500	40,305,200
28.	Chemical and allied products	1967	541,400	3,555,200	23,550,100
		1972	525,000	4,753,900	32,413,900
		1979	552,000	8,849,900	70,356,000
29.	Petroleum and coal products	1967	99,400	786,400	5,425,800
		1972	97,900	1,064,000	5,793,100
		1979	106,200	2,188,700	28,865,400
30.	Rubber and plastics products, not elsewhere classified [2]	1967	410,100	2,312,500	6,799,500
		1972	486,800	3,605,000	11,653,300
		1979	592,900	6,938,700	23,112,400
31.	Leather and leather products	1967	293,300	1,147,000	2,626,500
		1972	240,400	1,230,800	2,917,200
		1979	206,600	1,542,400	4,248,500
32.	Stone, clay and glass products	1967	469,300	2,784,100	8,333,400
		1972	492,600	4,037,300	12,586,500
		1979	521,700	7,232,800	24,467,600
33.	Primary and metal industries	1967	1,041,500	7,457,300	19,978,200
		1972	922,700	9,202,400	23,258,100
		1979	952,000	18,174,700	51,005,900
34.	Fabricated metal products [2]	1967	1,056,900	6,541,600	18,042,600
		1972	1,148,000	9,544,400	26,945,800
		1979	1,286,400	17,552,700	56,892,600
35.	Machinery (except electrical)	1967	1,349,000	9,236,100	27,836,400
		1972	1,266,900	11,358,600	37,562,900
		1979	1,640,500	24,305,400	92,527,600
36.	Electrical machinery [2]	1967	1,323,800	7,607,000	24,587,000
		1972	1,160,800	8,822,600	30,583,600
		1979	1,337,400	16,592,800	66,476,300
37.	Transportation equipment [2]	1967	1,336,500	9,918,200	28,173,900
		1972	1,246,200	12,848,600	39,799,400
		1979	1,383,500	25,199,500	80,951,400
38.	Instruments and related products [2]	1967	265,900	1,569,000	6,418,400
		1972	292,000	2,237,100	10,583,700
		1979	370,800	4,561,700	24,598,100
39.	Miscellaneous manufacturing	1967	344,400	1,552,500	4,599,400
		1972	350,200	2,086,700	6,777,000
		1979	338,800	3,147,900	11,934,700

For footnotes see opposite

Iron and Steel: Output of the iron and steel industries (in net tons of 2,000 lb.), according to figures supplied by the American Iron and Steel Institute, was:

	Furnaces in blast 31 Dec.	Pig-iron (including ferro-alloys)	Raw steel	Steel by method of production[1] Open hearth	Bessemer	Electric[2]	Basic Oxygen
1932[3]	44	9,835,227	15,322,901	13,336,210	1,715,925	270,044	...
1939	195	35,677,097	52,798,714	48,409,800	3,358,916	1,029,067	...
1944[4]	218	62,866,198	89,641,600	80,363,953	5,039,923	4,237,699	...
1950	234	66,400,311	96,336,075	86,262,509	4,534,558	6,039,008	...
1960	114	68,566,384	99,281,601	86,367,506	1,189,196	8,378,743	3,346,156
1970	152	87,933,000	131,514,000	48,022,000	—	20,162,000	63,330,000
1979	...	89,011,000	136,341,000	19,158,000	—	33,927,000	83,256,000
1980	...	70,329,000	111,835,000	13,054,000	—	31,166,000	67,617,000
1981	...	75,096,000	120,828,000	13,452,000	—	34,145,000	73,231,000

[1] The sum of these 4 items should equal the total in the preceding column; any difference appearing is due to the very small production of crucible steel, omitted prior to 1950.
[2] Includes crucible production beginning 1950.
[3] Low point of the depression.
[4] Peak year of war production.

Wholesale price index of iron and steel mill products (1967 = 100) was: 1950, 59·4; 1960, 96·4; 1970, 114·3; 1977, 229·9; 1978, 254·4; 1979, 280·4; 1980, 302·7; 1981, 337·6.

Consumption of ore, 1981, was 106·25m. net tons, of which blast-furnaces took 88·1m. net tons; agglomerating plants, 17·81m. net tons; and steel producing furnaces, 378,000 net tons.

The iron and steel industry in 1981 employed 286,219 wage-earners (compared with 449,888 in 1960), who worked an average of 36·4 hours per week and earned an average of $15.45 per hour: total wages were $8,394m. and total salaries for 104,695 employees were $3,495m.

Annual Statistics Report. American Iron and Steel Institute

Labour. The American labour movement comprises about 203 national and international labour organizations plus a large number of small independent local or single-firm labour organizations. In 1980 total membership was approximately 23·9m., including 1·7m. Canadian workers affiliated with American labour organizations and under 120,000 others outside the USA. The American Federation of Labor (founded 1881 and taking its name in 1886) and the Congress of Industrial Organizations merged into one organization, named the AFL–CIO, in Dec. 1955, representing 16·8m. workers in 1980.

Unaffiliated or independent labour organizations, inter-state in scope, including those organizing coalminers, teamsters and government employees and railroad workers, had an estimated total membership excluding all foreign members (1980) of about 6·8m. Labour organizations represented approximately 20% of the labour force in 1980.

The Labor–Management Relations (Taft–Hartley) Act, 1947, applicable to industries affecting inter-state commerce, prohibits the closed shop, but permits union shop arrangements except where forbidden by state laws. Statutes regulating, restricting or prohibiting closed shop or other types of union security agreements are in effect in 20 states which ban all types of union security agreements (Alabama, Arizona, Arkansas, Florida, Georgia, Iowa, Kansas, Louisiana, Mississippi, Nebraska, Nevada, North Carolina, North Dakota, South Carolina, South Dakota, Tennessee, Texas, Utah, Virginia and Wyoming). Colorado and Wisconsin ban all-union agreements unless a certain percentage of employees have voted for them; in

---

[1] Figures represent adjusted value added. For definitions see footnote to previous table, p. 1,407.
[2] Figures for 1967 are not comparable to 1972 due to revisions in the Standard Industrial Classification System.

Hawaii an all-union agreement may be entered into unless a majority of employees votes against it. Thirteen states have acts to prevent industrial disputes between public utilities and their employees by means of compulsory arbitration or seizure; however, a number of these laws have been declared unconstitutional in so far as industries in inter-state commerce are concerned. Laws to restrict or regulate picketing or other strike activities have been enacted in over half the states. About one-half of the states also prohibit certain types of strikes, as 'sit down', jurisdictional or sympathy strikes.

The Employee Retirement Income Security Act of 1974 protects the interests of workers and their beneficiaries who are entitled to benefits from employee pension and welfare plans. The law requires disclosure of plan provisions and financial information and establishes standards of conduct for trustees and administrators of welfare and pension plans. It provides funding, participation and vesting requirements for pension plans and makes termination insurance available for most pension plans. The Department of Labor and the Internal Revenue Service share administration of the law. The pension plan termination insurance programme is administered by the Pension Benefit Guaranty Corporation.

The law does not require a company to establish a welfare or pension plan. But it does provide that any employee not covered by a pension plan, other than Social Security, may put aside a certain amount of his income, tax-free, to take care of his retirement needs.

Minimum wage laws governing private employers are in operation in 45 jurisdictions: 41 states, the District of Columbia, Guam, Puerto Rico and the Virgin Islands have minimum wage laws and minimum wage rates. As of 1 Aug. 1978, all but one of the laws cover men, women and, usually, minors. The exception covers only women and minors. The minimum wage rate under federal law is $3.35 per hour for employees who are engaged in commerce, in the production of goods for commerce or in certain enterprises which are engaged in commerce as well as federal employees.

A total of 2,568 strikes and lockouts occurred in 1981, involving 1·1m. workers and 24·7m. idle days; the number of idle days was 0·11% of the year's total working time of all workers.

There are 3 federal agencies which provide formal machinery for the adjustment of labour disputes: (1) The Federal Mediation and Conciliation Service, now an independent agency, whose mediation services are available 'in any labor dispute in any industry affecting commerce'; under Executive Order 11491, as amended, to federal agencies and organizations of federal employees involved in negotiation disputes; and in state and local government collective bargaining disputes when adequate dispute resolution machinery is not available to the parties. Its aim is to prevent and minimize work stoppages. (2) The National Mediation Board (1934) provides much the same facilities for the railroad and air-transport industries pursuant to the Railway Labor Act. (3) The National Railroad Adjustment Board (1934) acts as a board of final appeal for grievances arising over the interpretation of existing collective agreements under the Railway Labor Act; its decisions are binding upon both sides and enforceable by the courts.

The National Labor Relations Act, as amended by the Labor–Management Relations (Taft–Hartley) Act, 1947 (*see* THE STATESMAN'S YEAR-BOOK, 1955, p. 617), was amended by the Labor–Management Reporting and Disclosure Act, 1959, and again amended in 1974. The 1959 Act requires extensive reporting and disclosure of certain financial and administrative practices of labour organizations, employers and labour relations consultants. In addition, certain powers are vested in the Secretary of Labor to prevent abuses in the administration of trusteeships by labour organizations, to provide minimum standards and procedures for the election of union officers and to establish rules prescribing minimum standards for determining the adequacy of union procedures for the removal of officers. Other provisions impose a fiduciary responsibility upon union officers and provide for the exclusion of those convicted of certain named felonies from office for specified periods; more stringently regulate secondary boycotts and banning of 'hot' cargo agreements; put limitations upon organizational and recognition picketing and permit States to assert jurisdiction over labour disputes where the National Labor Relations Board declines to act. The Act also contains a 'Bill of Rights' for union members (enforceable directly by them) dealing with such things as equal rights in the nomination and election of union officers, freedom of speech and assembly subject to reasonable union rules, and safeguards against improper disciplinary action.

The Bureau of Labor Statistics estimated that in 1981 the total labour force was 110,812,000 (64·3% of those 16 years and over); the armed forces accounted for 2,142,000 and the civilian labour force for 108·67m., of whom 100,397,000 were employed and 8,273,000—or 7·6%—were unemployed. The following table shows employment by industry group and sex and percentage distribution of the total:

Industry Group	*Male*	*Female*	*Total*	*Percentage distribution*
Employed (1,000 persons):	57,397	43,000	100,397	100·0
Agriculture, forestry and fisheries	2,824	694	3,519	3·5
Mining	949	170	1,118	1·1
Construction	5,566	494	6,060	6·0
Manufacturing:				
Durable goods	9,798	3,368	13,166	13·1
Non-durable (including not specified)	5,108	3,543	8,651	8·6
Transportation, communication and other public utilities	4,875	1,758	6,633	6·6
Wholesale and retail trade	10,907	9,617	20,524	20·4
Finance, insurance and real estate	2,545	3,588	6,133	6·1
Business and repair services	2,794	1,344	4,138	4·1
Personal services	1,075	2,839	3,914	3·9
Entertainment and recreation services	671	436	1,107	1·1
Professional and related services	6,936	13,265	20,201	20·1
Public administration	3,348	1,884	5,233	5·2

Bureau of Labor Statistics, US Dept. of Labor. *Directory of National Unions and Employee Associations in the US.* 1979.—*Brief History of the American Labor Movement.* 1976.—*Analysis of Work Stoppages.* 1979.—*Employment and Earnings.* Monthly

A Guide to Basic Law and Procedures under the National Labor Relations Act, National Labor Relations Board, Washington, D.C., 1976

Brody, D., *Workers in Industrial America: Essays on the Twentieth-century Struggle.* New York, 1980

Lebergott, S., *Manpower in Economic Growth: The American Record Since 1800.* New York and London, 1963

Commerce. The subjoined table gives the total value of the imports and exports of merchandise by yearly average or by year (in $1m.):

	Exports Total	*Exports US mdse.*[1]	*General imports*		*Exports*[2] *Total*	*Exports*[2] *US mdse.*[1]	*General imports*[2]
1946–50	11,829	11,673	6,659	1977	121,293	119,086	151,534
1951–55	15,333	15,196	10,832	1978	143,766	141,228	176,052
1956–60	19,204	19,029	13,650	1979	182,025	178,798	210,285
1961–65	24,006	24,707	17,659	1980	220,786	216,672	245,262
1970	43,224	42,590	39,952	1981	233,739	228,961	260,982

[1] Excludes re-exports. [2] Includes US Virgin Islands trade with foreign countries.

For a description of how imports and exports are valued, see *Explanation of Statistics of Report FT990, Highlights of US Export and Import Trade,* Bureau of the Census, US Department of Commerce, Washington, D.C., 1946.

The 'most favoured nation' treatment in commerce between Great Britain and US was agreed to for 4 years by the treaty of 1815, was extended for 10 years by the treaty of 1818, and indefinitely (subject to 12 months' notice) by that of 1827.

Imports and exports of gold and silver bullion and specie in calendar years (in $1,000):

	Gold		Silver	
	Exports	Imports	Exports	Imports
1932	809,528	363,315	13,850	19,650
1940	4,995	4,749,467	3,674	58,434
1944	959,228	113,836	126,915	23,373
1955	7,257	104,592	8,331	72,932
1960	1,647	335,032	25,789	57,438
1965	1,285,097	101,669	54,061	64,769
1970	36,887	227,472	53,003	58,838
1975	429,278	406,583	104,086	274,106
1977	1,055,234	638,707	39,165	315,393
1978	1,024,912	857,488	54,594	324,714
1979	4,620,503	1,400,669	237,542	840,731
1980	2,787,431	2,508,520	1,326,878	1,336,009
1981	2,501,337	1,950,555	181,380	842,882

The domestic exports of US produce, including military, and the imports for consumption by economic classes for 3 calendar years were (in $m.):

	Exports (US merchandise)			Imports for consumption		
	1979	1980	1981	1979	1980	1981
Food and live animals	22,150	27,685	30,291	15,169	15,763	15,123
Crude materials	20,827	23,868	20,993	10,644	10,536	10,894
Machinery and transport equipment	70,528	84,708	95,736	53,728	60,631	69,247
Chemicals	17,305	20,713	21,187	7,489	8,600	9,259
Total	130,810	156,974	168,207	87,030	95,530	104,523

Leading exports of US merchandise are listed below for the calendar year 1981: Special category merchandise is included. Data for major subdivisions of certain classes are also given:

Commodity	$1m.
Machinery, total	95,736
Power generating machinery	9,465
Metalworking machinery	2,158
Agricultural machines and tractors	3,523
Office machines	9,810
Telecommunications apparatus	3,856
Electrical apparatus	11,494
Electrical power machinery and switchgear	2,495
Automobiles (and parts)	16,214
Aircraft (and parts)	14,738
Grains and preparations	19,457
Wheat (and flour)	8,073
Maize	8,014
Chemicals	21,187
Chemical elements and compounds	9,202
Plastic materials and resins	3,809
Soybeans	6,200
Cotton	2,260
Textiles and apparel	4,851
Tobacco and manufactures	1,458
Iron and steel-mill products	2,801
Non-ferrous base metals and alloys	2,046
Pulp, paper and products	2,315
Coal	6,006
Fruits, nuts and vegetables	3,314
Petroleum and products	3,696
Firearms of war and ammunition	2,165

Chief imports for 28 commodity classes for consumption for the calendar year 1981:

Commodity	$1m.
Petroleum and products	74,955
Petroleum	61,458
Petroleum products	13,497
Non-ferrous base metals	4,844
Copper	1,581
Aluminium	1,348
Nickel	878
Bauxite, crude	393
Tin	644
Pulp, paper and products	5,621
Newsprint	2,825
Wood pulp	1,754
Fertilizers	1,102
Sugar	2,141
Iron and steel-mill products	10,351
Cattle, meat and preparations	2,174
Automobiles and parts	26,241
Fish (and shellfish)	2,948
Fruit, nuts and vegetables	2,499
Alcoholic beverages	2,338

Commodity	$1m.
Wool and other hair	199
Metal manufactures	4,135
Diamonds (excl. industrial)	1,329
Rubber	778
Textiles and apparel	10,414
Clothing	7,397
Cotton fabrics, woven	604
Machinery, total	37,824
Electrical apparatus	9,125
Agricultural machines and tractors	1,280
Office machines	3,553
Coffee	2,623
Chemicals	9,259
Chemical elements and compounds	5,253
Uranium oxide	209
Plywood	702
Oils and oilseeds	387
Cocoa (and cacao beans)	466
Glass and pottery	1,329
Footwear	3,141
Toys and sports goods	2,170
Furs, undressed	168
Scientific/telecommunications apparatus	10,484
Artworks and antiques	2,056
Grains and animal feeds	375

Total trade beween the USA and the UK for 5 years (British Department of Trade returns, in £1,000 sterling):

	1978	*1979*	*1980*	*1981*	*1982*
Imports to UK	4,222,555	4,919,882	6,043,774	6,048,305	6,638,250
Exports and re-exports from UK	3,477,231	4,047,158	6,668,342	6,258,157	7,457,114

Imports and exports by continents, areas and selected countries for calendar years (in $1m.):

Area and country	*General imports 1980*	*General imports 1981*	*Exports incl. re-exports*[1] *1980*	*Exports incl. re-exports*[1] *1981*
Canada	41,030	45,912	35,395	39,564
20 American Republics	30,020	32,055	36,030	38,950
Western Europe	47,003	51,879	67,512	65,377
Western Hemisphere	78,329	84,967	74,114	81,667
Canada	41,030	45,912	35,395	39,564
20 American Republics	30,020	32,055	36,030	38,950
Central American Common Market	1,851	1,545	1,951	1,773
Costa Rica	357	366	498	373
El Salvador	428	259	272	308
Guatemala	435	348	552	559
Honduras	419	433	379	349
Nicaragua	211	140	250	184
Panama	330	296	699	844
Latin American FTA	26,797	29,011	32,274	35,260
Argentina	741	1,125	2,625	2,192
Brazil	3,716	4,470	4,344	3,798
Chile	515	603	1,354	1,465
Colombia	1,249	822	1,736	1,771
Ecuador	876	1,021	864	854
Mexico	12,634	13,799	15,145	17,789
Paraguay	81	48	109	108
Peru	1,385	1,222	1,172	1,486
Uruguay	97	158	183	163
Dominican Republic	788	926	795	772
Haiti	253	276	311	301
Bolivia	182	177	172	189
Venezuela	5,320	5,566	4,573	5,445
Bahamas	1,469	1,261	396	441
Netherlands Antilles	2,564	2,625	448	499
Jamaica	385	368	305	479
Trinidad and Tobago	2,383	2,216	680	688
Europe				
Western Europe	47,003	51,879	67,512	65,377
OECD Countries	46,537	51,423	66,654	64,548
European Economic Community[2]	36,742	41,647	54,601	52,363
Belgium and Luxembourg	1,924	2,297	6,661	5,764
Denmark	730	850	863	887

[1] 'Special category' exports are included in these totals.
[2] 1980 and 1981 figures include Greece.

Area and country	General imports 1980	General imports 1981	Exports incl. re-exports [1] 1980	Exports incl. re-exports [1] 1981
Europe (contd.)				
France	5,341	5,854	7,485	7,340
Germany (Fed. Rep.)	11,817	11,382	10,960	10,277
Ireland	417	498	836	1,025
Italy	4,390	5,191	5,511	5,360
Netherlands	1,924	2,370	8,669	8,595
UK	9,908	12,846	12,694	12,439
Greece	292	359	922	676
Turkey	175	261	540	789
EFTA countries	...	...	...	...
Austria	389	382	448	484
Norway	2,633	2,478	843	892
Portugal	279	238	911	1,074
Sweden	1,631	1,714	1,767	1,842
Switzerland	2,812	2,448	3,781	3,022
Finland	440	524	505	613
Iceland	200	198	79	71
Spain	1,235	1,534	3,179	3,397
Yugoslavia	447	438	756	648
Soviet bloc.	1,440	1,555	3,860	4,338
Poland	417	365	714	682
USSR	453	347	1,513	2,431
Asia [2] [3]	81,179	92,556	62,042	66,008
Near East	19,210	18,940	13,773	17,124
Egypt	539	397	1,874	2,159
Iran	456	64	23	300
Iraq	460	164	724	914
Israel	952	1,243	2,045	2,521
Kuwait	494	86	886	976
Lebanon	33	18	303	296
Saudi Arabia	12,648	14,392	5,768	7,327
Japan	30,890	37,655	20,790	21,823
Other Asia	29,598	33,544	23,571	23,353
Bangladesh	85	85	292	158
Hong Kong	4,711	5,389	2,686	2,635
India	1,104	1,202	1,689	1,748
Indonesia	5,217	6,022	1,545	1,302
Korea, Republic of	4,257	5,227	4,685	5,116
Malaysia	2,585	2,185	1,337	1,537
Singapore	1,921	2,114	3,033	3,003
Pakistan	128	174	642	492
Philippines	1,749	1,974	1,999	1,787
Sri Lanka	125	154	62	90
Thailand	816	946	1,263	1,170
Taiwan (Formosa)	6,900	8,072	4,337	4,305
Vietnam	[5]	[5]	1	10
China	1,062	1,895	3,755	3,603
Oceania	3,393	3,351	4,876	6,436
Australia	2,510	2,464	4,093	5,242
New Zealand and W. Samoa	703	717	599	940
Africa [4]	33,875	26,671	7,187	8,938
Algeria	6,576	5,038	542	717
Ethiopia	87	83	72	62
Libya	8,595	5,301	509	813
Morocco	35	36	344	429
Ghana	207	246	127	154
Liberia	128	113	113	128

[1] See note on previous page.
[2] Includes Egypt.
[3] Excludes Yemen (Aden) (formerly Southern Yemen), and Bahrain.
[4] Excludes Egypt. [5] Less than one-half of rounded unit.

Area and country	General imports 1980	General imports 1981	Exports incl. re-exports [1] 1980	Exports incl. re-exports [1] 1981
Africa (contd.)				
Nigeria	11,105	9,249	1,150	1,523
Kenya	54	52	141	150
Zaïre	418	423	155	141
South Africa, Republic of [2]	3,324	2,445	2,464	2,912

[1] See note on p. 1413. [2] Includes also South-West Africa (Namibia).

US Department of Commerce, Bureau of Census. Report FT 990, Highlights of US Export and Import Trade

Tourism. In 1981, 23·1m. tourists visited the USA and spent over US$12,000m. They came mainly from Canada (10·9m.), Mexico (3·8m.), Europe (3·5m.) and Asia (2·1m.). Approximately 22·9m. US tourists travelled abroad, mainly to Canada (11·3m.), Europe (3·8m.), Mexico (3·4m.) and the Caribbean and Central America (2·4m.).

COMMUNICATIONS

Roads. On 31 Dec. 1981 the total US public road[1] mileage, including rural and urban roads, amounted to 3,852,697 miles, of which 3,396,084 miles were surfaced roads. The total mileage cited includes 725,850 miles of rural roads under control of the states, 2,236,344 miles of local roads, 256,257 miles of federal park and forest roads, and 632,413 miles of urban roads and streets. Expenditures for construction and maintenance amounted to $30,895m. in 1980.

By the end of 1979, toll roads, financed by private capital through bond issues and administered by state toll authorities, totalled 4,685 miles (including some under construction) compared with 344 miles in 1940.

Motor vehicles registered in the calendar year 1981 were (Federal Highways Administration) 158,456,511, including 123,461,507 automobiles, 543,894 buses and 34,451,110 trucks.

Inter-city trucks (private and for hire) averaged 628,000m. revenue net ton-miles in 1979. Of the 543,894 buses in service in 1981, 432,813 were school buses. Inter-city service operated a total of 1,132m. bus-miles and carried a total of 360m. revenue passengers in 1978.

There were 49,268 deaths in road accidents in 1981.

[1] Public road mileage excludes that mileage not open to public travel, not maintained by public authority, or not passable by standard four-wheel vehicles. This excluded mileage was reported to the US Federal Highway Administration prior to 1981.

Railways. Railway history in the USA commences in 1828, but the first railway to convey both freight and passengers in regular service (between Baltimore and Ellicott's Mills, Md., 13 miles) dates from 24 May 1830. Mileage rose to 52,922 miles in 1870; to 167,191 miles in 1890, and to a peak of 266,381 miles in 1916, falling thereafter to 261,871 in 1925; 246,739 in 1940 and 222,164 in 1969 (these include some duplication under trackage rights and some mileage operated in Canada by US companies). The ordinary gauge is 4 ft 8½ in. (about 99·6% of total mileage). The USA has about 29% of the world's railway mileage.

In addition to the independent railroad companies, railway service is provided by two federally-assisted organizations, the National Railroad Passenger Corporation (Amtrak), and the Consolidated Rail Corporation (Conrail).

Amtrak was set up on 1 May 1971 to maintain a basic network of inter-city passenger trains with government assistance, and is responsible for almost all non-commuter services with 27,000 miles of route. From 1 Jan. 1983, an Amtrak commuter division took over from Conrail all commuter services not acquired by State of regional agencies.

Conrail is the organization established on 1 April 1976 to run freight services in the industrial north-east formerly operated by the bankrupt Penn Central, Reading, Lehigh Valley, Central of New Jersey, Erie Lackawanna, Lehigh & Hudson railroads, and Pennyslvania-Reading Seashore Lines.

The following table, based on the figures of the Interstate Commerce Commission, shows some railway statistics for 4 calendar years:

	1960	*1970*	*1980*[2 3]	*1981*[1 2]
Classes I and II Railroads				
Mileage owned (first main tracks)	223,779	204,621	157,078	150,131
Revenue freight originated (1m. short tons)	1,421	1,572	1,537	1,453
Freight ton-mileage (1m. ton-miles)	591,550	771,012	932,748	911,681
Passengers carried (1,000)	488,019	289,469	281,503	[4]
Passenger-miles (1m.)	31,790	10,786	6,557	[4]
Operating revenues ($1m.)	9,587	12,209	28,708	30,734
Operating expenses ($1m.)	7,135	9,806	26,761	28,476
Net railway operating income ($1m.)	1,055	506	1,364	1,336
Net income after fixed charges ($1m.)	855	126	2,029	3,070
Class I Railroads:				
Locomotives in service	40,949	27,086	28,240	27,571
Steam locomotives	25,640	—	—	—
Freight-train cars (excluding caboose cars)	1,721,269	1,423,921	1,101,343	1,066,786
Passenger-train cars	57,146	11,177	2,219	2,115
Average number of employees	1,220,784	566,282	458,996	436,397
Average wage per week ($1)	72.59	188.71	474.21	513.42

[1] Class I railroads only. From 1981, Class II railroads were no longer required to file annual reports.
[2] Data for National Railroad Passenger Corporation excluded.
[3] Data for St Louis–San Francisco Railway Co., who merged with Burlington Northern Inc. on 21 Nov. 1980, excluded from mileage owned, locomotives in service, and freight- and passenger-train cars.
[4] This data has been discontinued.

Aviation. In civil aviation there were, on 31 Dec. 1981, 764,192 certified pilots (including 179,912 student pilots) and 261,570 registered civil aircraft.

Airports on 31 Dec. 1981: Air carrier, 723; general aviation, 14,753. Of these airports, 12,427 were conventional land-based, while 485 were seaplane bases, 2,507 were heliports and 57 stolports (STOL—Short Take-Off and Landing).

Statistics from the Civil Aeronautics Board indicate that for 12 months ended June 1982 on US flag carriers in scheduled international service there were 20·2m. enplanements with 281m. aircraft miles (excluding all-cargo) for a total of 58,293m. revenue passenger-miles. The non-scheduled airlines had a total of 11,251m. revenue passenger-miles internationally and domestically. Domestically US scheduled airlines in 1982 had 269·8m. enplanements with a total of 2,348m. aircraft miles for 207,253m. revenue passenger-miles. (A revenue passenger-mile is one paying passenger carried per mile.)

Shipping. On 1 Sept. 1981 the US merchant marine included 859 sea-going vessels of 1,000 gross tons or over, with aggregate dead-weight tonnage of 24m. This included 309 tankers of 16·4m. DWT.

On 1 Sept. 1981 US merchant ocean-going vessels were employed as follows: Active, 535 of 19m. DWT, of which 225 of 6m. tons were foreign trade, 237 of 11m. tons in domestic trade and 73 of 1·8m. tons in other US agency operations. Inactive vessels totalled 5m. DWT; 59 of 2·6m. DWT privately owned were laid up and 265 of 2·8m. tons were in the National Defense reserve fleet. Of the total vessels in the US fleet, 577 of 21m. DWT were privately owned.

US exports and imports carried on dry cargo and tanker vessels in the year 1980 totalled 770m. long tons, of which 28·1m. long tons or 3·6% were carried in US flag vessels.

Post and Broadcasting. The telephone business is largely in the hands of the American Telephone and Telegraph Company (AT & T) and its telephone operating subsidiaries, which together are known as the Bell System. There are, however, many hundreds of smaller telephone companies having no common ownership affiliation with the Bell companies, but which connect with them for universal service, countrywide and worldwide. In addition, several new entrants have begun to compete with AT & T in the long-distance telephone market. The message telegraph and telex services are in the hands of The Western Union Telegraph Company, and the international record carriers, which compete with the telephone industry in providing leased private lines. Western Union also provides an intercity telephone service.

The number of telephones in service in the USA has increased in the period since 1945 at a much faster rate than has the population. Among principal reasons are the significant increase in the percentage of households with telephone service and the enormous growth in the number of extension telephones.

In marked contrast, the number of public telegrams has decreased by a substantial amount. Telegrams have lost favour due to shifts in user preference to the air-mail and to the telephone. The telex services of the telegraph company have also found broad acceptance in place of telegrams for business purposes. The following table contains key data items on a comparative basis for the domestic telephone and message telegraph services:

	1950	*1960*	*1970*	*1980*
All telephone systems:				
Total telephones	43,131,000	74,342,000	120,218,000	180,425,000
Bell System:				
Total telephones	35,343,400	60,735,100	96,561,000	141,674,000
Average daily telephone calls	140,782,000	219,093,000	368,363,000	580,230,000
Local	134,870,000	209,373,000	346,505,000	527,543,000
Long distance	5,912,000	9,720,000	21,858,000	52,687,000
Total plant in service ($1,000)	10,101,522	24,072,499	54,813,202	132,831,794
Total operating revenues ($1,000)	3,271,029	7,958,125	17,094,846	51,203,404
Employees, number	523,251	580,405	772,980	847,768
Western Union Telegraph Co.:				
Public telegrams for year	153,054,000	102,931,000	46,084,000	40,801,398
Total plant ($1,000)	294,451	398,023	1,029,149	2,101,007
Revenue from public telegrams ($1,000)	132,281	160,746	126,739	115,612
Total operating revenues ($1,000)	177,994	262,365	402,456	696,972
Employees, number	40,482	32,655	24,293	12,649

International communication services, providing overseas connexions with all parts of the world, are furnished principally by the American Telephone and Telegraph Company and three telegraph companies. The old submarine cable telegraph systems have all been abandoned in favour of using telegraph circuits derived from voice channels in the newer telephone ocean cables, which have also made inroads on the use of high-frequency radio. More recently, satellite communications facilities have been utilized not only for telephone and telegraph services but for television and data transmission as well.

International overseas telegrams, inbound to and outbound from the continental US, numbered 11·7m. in 1980 (12·5m. in 1978). This service has tended to decline in volume in recent years. It first lost ground to the air-mail and then to the telex and telephone services. For the US and its possessions the volume of international overseas telephone calls has grown enormously with the availability of the excellent voice-transmission qualities provided in the telephone ocean cables and in the satellite radio relays. Whereas international telephone calls were 990,000 in 1955, the last year in which there was no cable service available, there were 149·6m. such calls in 1980.

Postal business for the years ended 30 Sept. included the following items:

	1978	*1979*	*1980*	*1981*
Number of post offices, on 30 June [1]	30,518	30,449	30,326	30,242
Postal revenue ($1,000) [2]	14,133,056	16,106,085	17,142,760	19,133,041
Postal expenses ($1,000) [3]	16,219,619	17,529,303	19,412,587	21,369,139

[1] The US Postal Service was established 1 July 1971. Financial statements prior to that date are those of the Post Office Department. Such statements for 1968–71 have been restated to be in a format and on an accounting principle basis generally consistent with 1972.

[2] Operating revenue excludes government appropriations, operating reimbursements and other income.

[3] Operating expenses are stated net of operating reimbursements and exclude certain costs financed by revenue.

On 1 Jan. 1975 there were in the USA and Territories, 7,068 authorized commercial radio stations, 711 commercial television stations: of non-commercial stations 717 were for radio, 241 for television.

Cinemas. Cinemas increased from 17,003 in 1940 to 20,239 in 1950 and decreased to 12,187 in 1967.

Newspapers. Of the daily newspapers being published in the USA in 1971, 339 were morning papers with a circulation of 26,116,000, and 1,425 were evening papers with a circulation of 36,115,000. The 590 Sunday papers had a total circulation of 49·7m.

JUSTICE, RELIGION, EDUCATION AND WELFARE

Justice. Legal controversies may be decided in two systems of courts: the federal courts, with jurisdiction confined to certain matters enumerated in Article III of the Constitution, and the state courts, with jurisdiction in all other proceedings. The federal courts have jurisdiction exclusive of the state courts in criminal prosecutions for the violation of federal statutes, in civil cases involving the government, in bankruptcy cases and in admiralty proceedings, and have jurisdiction concurrent with the state courts over suits between parties from different states, and certain suits involving questions of federal law.

The highest court is the Supreme Court of the US, which reviews cases from the lower federal courts and certain cases originating in state courts involving questions of federal law. It is the final arbiter of all questions involving federal statutes and the Constitution; and it has the power to invalidate any federal or state law or executive action which it finds repugnant to the Constitution. This court, consisting of 9 justices who receive salaries of $60,000 a year (the Chief Justice, $62,500), meets from Oct. until June every year and disposes of about 3,380 cases, deciding about 380 on their merits. In the remainder of cases it either summarily affirms lower court decisions or declines to review. A few suits, usually brought by state governments, originate in the Supreme Court, but issues of fact are mostly referred to a master.

The US courts of appeals number 11 (in 10 circuits composed of 3 or more states and 1 circuit for the District of Columbia); the 97 circuit judges receive salaries of $42,500 a year. Any party to a suit in a lower federal court usually has a right of appeal to one of these courts. In addition, there are direct appeals to these courts from many federal administrative agencies. In the year ending 30 June 1976 more than 18,400 appeals were filed in the courts of appeals.

The trial courts in the federal system are the US district courts, of which there are 89 in the 50 states, 1 in the District of Columbia and 1 each in the territories of Puerto Rico, Virgin Islands, Canal Zone and Guam. Each state has at least 1 US district court, and 3 states have 4 apiece. Each district court has from 1 to 27 judgeships. There are 400 US district judges ($40,000 a year), who handle about 130,600 civil cases and 55,000 criminal defendants every year.

In addition to these courts of general jurisdiction, there are special federal courts of limited jurisdiction. The Court of Claims (7 judges at $42,500 a year) decides claims for money damages against the federal government in a wide variety of matters; the Customs Court (9 judges at $40,000 a year) determines controversies concerning the classification and valuation of imported merchandise; and the Court of Customs and Patent Appeals (5 judges at $42,500 a year) hears appeals from the Customs Court, the Tariff Commission and the Patent Office.

The judges of all these courts are appointed by the President with the approval of the Senate; to assure their independence, they hold office during good behaviour and cannot have their salaries reduced. This does not apply to the territorial judges, who hold their offices for a term of years. The judges may retire with full pay at the age of 70 years if they have served a period of 10 years, or at 65 if they have 15 years of service, but they are subject to call for such judicial duties as they are willing to undertake. Only 9 US judges up to 1974 have been involved in impeachment proceedings, of whom 3 district judges and 1 commerce judge were convicted and removed from office.

Of the 130,597 civil cases filed in the district courts in the year ending 30 June 1976, about 70,372 arose under various federal statutes (such as labour, social security, tax, patent, securities, antitrust and civil rights laws); 25,736 involved personal injury or property damage claims; 23,998 dealt with contracts; and 8,475 were actions concerning real property.

Of the 37,667 criminal cases filed in the district courts in the year ending 30 June 1974, about 1,900 were charged with alleged infractions of the immigration laws; 3,000, the transport of stolen motor vehicles; about 3,225 larceny and theft;

4,700, embezzlement and fraud; about 650, liquor laws, and 7,400 narcotics laws.

Persons convicted of federal crimes are either fined, released on probation under the supervision of the probation officers of the federal courts, confined in prison for a period of up to 6 months and then put on probation (known as split sentencing) or confined in one of the following institutions: 3 for juvenile and youths; 7 for young adults; 7 for intermediate term adults; 7 for short-term adults; 2 for females; 1 hospital and 15 community service centres. In addition, prisoners are confined in centres operated by the National Institutes of Mental Health. In addition, prisoner drug addicts may be committed to US Public Health Service hospitals for treatment. In 1972–73 about 1,500 of the federal prison population were placed on work release, that is, they were confined in community treatment centres at night and permitted to work at gainful employment during the weekdays. Prisoners confined in institutions operated by the US Bureau of Prisons for the year ending 30 June 1973, numbered 23,336.

The state courts have jurisdiction over all civil and criminal cases arising under state laws, but decisions of the state courts of last resort as to the validity of treaties or of laws of the US, or on other questions arising under the Constitution, are subject to review by the Supreme Court of the US. The state court systems are generally similar to the federal system, to the extent that they generally have a number of trial courts and intermediate appellate courts, and a single court of last resort. The highest court in each state is usually called the Supreme Court or Court of Appeals with a Chief Justice and Associate Justices, usually elected but sometimes appointed by the Governor with the advice and consent of the State Senate or other advisory body; they usually hold office for a term of years, but in some instances for life or during good behaviour. Their salaries range from $14,000 to $40,000 a year. The lowest tribunals are usually those of Justices of the Peace; many towns and cities have municipal and police courts, with power to commit for trial in criminal matters and to determine misdemeanours for violation of the municipal ordinances; they frequently try civil cases involving limited amounts.

The Federal Bureau of Investigation estimates the number of major crimes in the US and its possessions as follows:

Crime index classification	*1959–61 average*	*1975*
Murder	8,670	20,510
Forcible rape	15,860	56,090
Robbery	87,570	464,970
Aggravated assault	129,400	484,710
Burglary	789,300	3,252,100
Larceny over $50	464,300	5,977,700
Motor car theft	312,000	1,000,500
Total	1,807,100	11,256,600

The death penalty is illegal in Alaska, Hawaii, Iowa, Maine, Minnesota, Oregon, West Virginia, Wisconsin and Michigan; in North Dakota it is legal only for treason and first-degree murder committed by a prisoner serving a life sentence for first-degree murder, in Rhode Island only for murder committed by a prisoner serving a life sentence and in Vermont and New York for the murder of a peace officer in the line of duty and for first-degree murder by those who kill while serving a life sentence for murder. The death penalty, although still legal in most states, has fallen into disuse and has been abolished *de facto* in many states. The US Supreme Court has held the death penalty, as applied in general criminal statutes, to contravene the eighth and fourteenth amendments of the US constitution, as a cruel and unusual punishment when used so irregularly and rarely as to destroy its deterrent value.

In 1967 only 2 persons were executed under civil authority; both for murder. There were no executions 1968–76. In 1977 a convicted murderer requested that he should be executed and after a lengthy legal dispute the sentence was carried out at Utah state prison. In Jan. 1977, 350 prisoners were reported under sentence of death.

The total number of civilian executions carried out in the US from 1930 to 1967 was 3,859, including 1,751 white persons (20 women), 2,066 Negroes (12 women) and 42 persons of other races.

Federal 'Political' Crimes. Prosecutions for what may be loosely described as 'political' offences, or crimes directed towards the overthrow by violence of the federal government, which were somewhat numerous in the early 1950s, have declined sharply over the last 15 years and are now exceedingly rare. During the fiscal year 1975–76 the following number of defendants appeared in federal courts: Espionage, none; Subversive Activities Control Act, 1950, none; contempt of Congress, none.

A Guide to Court Systems. Institute of Judicial Administration. New York, 1960
The United States Courts (88th Congress, 1st Session, House Document No. 180). US Government Printing Office, 1975
The Challenge of Crime in a Free Society. Report of the President's Commission on Law Enforcement and Administration of Justice. US Government Printing Office, 1967
Blumberg, A. S., *Criminal Justice: Issues and Ironies.* 2nd ed. New York, 1973
Huston, L. A., *The Department of Justice.* New York, 1967
Huston, L. A., and others, *Roles of the Attorney General of the United States.* New York, 1968
McCloskey, R. G., *The Modern Supreme Court.* Harvard Univ. Press, 1972
McLauchlan, W. P., *American Legal Processes.* New York, 1977
Mayers, L., *The American Legal System.* Rev. ed. New York, 1964
Murphy, W. F., *Congress and the Court.* Univ. of Chicago Press, 1962
Walker, S. E., *Popular Justice.* New York, 1980
Warren, Charles, *The Supreme Court in United States History.* 2 vols. Rev. ed. Boston, Mass., 1960

Religion. *The Yearbook of American and Canadian Churches for 1982,* published by the National Council of the Churches of Christ in the USA, New York, presents the latest figures available from official statisticians of church bodies. The large majority of reports are for the calendar year 1980, or a fiscal year ending 1980. The 1980 reports indicated that there were 134,816,943 members with 336,281 local churches. There were 279,366 clergymen having local congregations. The principal religious bodies (numerically or historically) or groups of religious bodies are shown below:

Denominations	*Local churches*	*Total membership*
Summary:		
Protestant bodies	305,273	73,479,341
Roman Catholic Church	24,188	50,449,842
Jewish Congregations [1]	3,500	5,920,000
Eastern Churches	1,606	3,822,590
Old Catholic, Polish National Catholic and Armenian	436	923,985
Buddhists	60	60,000
Miscellaneous [2]	1,218	161,185
1980 totals	336,281	134,816,943 [3]

Protestant Church Membership	*Total membership*
Baptist bodies	
Southern Baptist Convention	13,600,126
National Baptist Convention, USA	5,500,000
National Baptist Convention of America, Inc.	2,668,799
National Primitive Baptist Convention	250,000
American Baptist Churches in the USA	1,600,521
American Baptist Association	1,500,000
Progressive National Baptist Convention	521,692
Conservative Baptist Association of America	225,000
Regular Baptist Churches	243,000
Free Will Baptists	227,888
Baptist Missionary Association of America	224,533
Christian Church (Disciples of Christ)	1,177,984
Christian Churches and Churches of Christ	1,063,254
Church of the Nazarene	484,276
Churches of Christ	1,600,000
The Episcopal Church	2,786,004
Latter-Day Saints:	
Church of Jesus Christ of Latter-Day Saints	2,811,000
Reorganized Church of Jesus Christ of Latter-Day Saints	190,087
Lutheran Bodies:	
Lutheran Church in America	2,923,260
The Lutheran Church-Missouri Synod	2,625,650

[1] Includes Orthodox, Conservative and Reformed bodies.
[2] Includes non-Christian bodies such as Spiritualists, Ethical Culture, Unitarian-Universalists.
[3] Care should be taken in interpreting membership statistics for the US Churches. Some statistics are accurately compiled and others are estimates. Also statistics are not always comparable.

Protestant Church Membership	*Total membership*
Lutheran Bodies *(contd.)*:	
The American Lutheran Church	2,353,229
Wisconsin Evangelical Lutheran Synod	407,643
Methodist Bodies:	
United Methodist Church	9,584,711
African Methodist Episcopal Church	2,050,000
African Methodist Episcopal Zion Church	1,134,178
Christian Methodist Episcopal Church	786,707
Pentecostal Bodies:	
Assemblies of God	1,732,371
Church of God in Christ, International	501,000
Church of God in Christ	425,000
Church of God (Cleveland, Tenn.)	435,012
United Pentecostal Church, International, Inc.	465,000
Presbyterian Bodies:	
United Presbyterian Church in the USA	2,423,601
Presbyterian Church in the US	838,485
Reformed Churches:	
Reformed Church in America	345,532
Christian Reformed Church	213,995
The Salvation Army	417,359
Seventh-day Adventists	571,141
United Church of Christ	1,736,244

Yearbook of American and Canadian Churches. Annual, from 1951. New York
Clarke, E. T., *The Small Sects in America.* Rev. ed. New York, 1949
Johnson, A. W., and Yost, F. H., *Separation of Church and State in the United States.* Minneapolis and London, 1949
Mead, F. S., *Handbook of Denominations in the US.* 6th ed. Nashville, 1975
Moehiman, C. H., *The Wall of Separation between Church and State.* Boston, 1951
Roemer, T., *The Catholic Church in the United States.* Rev. ed. New York, 1961
Sperry, W. L., *Religion in America.* London, 1945
Stokes, A. P., and Pfeffer, L., *Church and State in the US.* New York, 1964
Sweet, W. W., *The Story of Religion in America.* 2nd ed. New York, 1950

Education. Under the system of government in the USA, elementary and secondary education is committed in the main to the several states. Each of the 50 states and the District of Columbia has a system of free public schools, established by law, with courses covering 12 years plus kindergarten. There are 3 structural patterns in common use; the K8–4 plan, meaning kindergarten plus 8 elementary grades followed by 4 high school grades; the K6–3–3 plan, or kindergarten plus 6 elementary grades followed by a 3-year junior high school and a 3-year senior high school; and the K6–6 plan, kindergarten plus 6 elementary grades followed by a 6-year high school. All plans lead to high-school graduation, usually at age 17 or 18. Vocational education is an integral part of secondary education. In addition, some states have, as part of the free public school system, 2-year colleges in which education is provided at a nominal cost. Each state has delegated a large degree of control of the educational programme to local school districts (numbering 15,912 in autumn 1980), each with a board of education (usually 3 to 9 members) elected locally and serving mostly without pay. The school policies of the local school districts must be in accord with the laws and the regulations of their state Departments of Education. While regulations differ from one jurisdiction to another, in general it may be said that school attendance is compulsory between the ages of 7 to 16.

The Census Bureau estimates that in Nov. 1979 only 1m. or 0·6% of the 170m. persons who were 14 years of age or older were unable to read and write; in 1930 the percentage was 4·8. In 1940 a new category was established—the 'functionally illiterate', meaning those who had completed fewer than 5 years of elementary schooling; for persons 25 years of age or over this percentage was 3·3 in March 1981 (for the non-white population alone it was 8·1%); it was 0·7% for white and 0·7% for non-whites in the 25–29-year-old group. The Bureau reported that in March 1981 the median years of school completed by all persons 25 years old and over was 12·5, and that 17% had completed 4 or more years of college. For the 25–29-year-old group, the median school years completed was 12·8 and 21·3% had completed 4 or more years of college.

In the autumn of 1981, 12,372,000 students (5,975,000 men and 6,397,000 women) were enrolled in 3,253 colleges and universities; 2,595,000 were first-time students. Total enrolment in colleges and universities represents a number equal to 41·9 per 100 persons between the ages of 18 and 24.

Public elementary and secondary school revenue is supplied from the county and other local sources (about 43% in 1980–81), state sources (48%) and federal sources (about 9%). In 1980–81 expenditure for public elementary and secondary education totalled about $102,200m., including $92,000m. for regular day school programmes, $1,700m. for other programmes, $6,500m. for capital outlay and $2,000m. for interest on school debt. The current expenditure per pupil in average daily attendance was about $2,450. The total cost per pupil, also including capital outlay and interest, amounted to about $2,675. Estimated total expenditures, for private elementary and secondary schools in 1980–81 were $12,800m. In 1980–81 the 3,253 universities and colleges expended $64,053m. from current funds, of which $42,280m. was spent by institutions under public control. The federal government contributed 12·9% of total current-fund revenue; state governments, 30·7%; student tuition and fees, 21%; and all sources, 35·4%.

Vocational education below college grade, including the training of teachers to conduct such education, has been federally aided since 1918. During the school year 1979–80 enrolments in the vocational classes were: Agriculture, 879,000; distributive occupations, 961,000; health occupations, 834,000; home economics, 3,938,000; trade and industry, 3,216,000; technical education, 499,000; office occupations, 3·4m.; other programmes, 2,726,000. Federal support funds were $745,481,000.

Summary of statistics of regular schools (public and private), teachers and pupils in autumn 1981 (compiled by the US National Center for Education Statistics):

Schools by level	*Number of schools 1980–81*	*Teachers autumn 1981*	*Enrolment autumn 1981*
Elementary schools:			
Public	61,900	1,180,000	23,960,000
Private	16,771	190,000	3,600,000
Secondary schools:			
Public	24,500	990,000	16,230,000
Private	5,607	90,000	1,400,000
Higher education:			
Public	1,497	630,000	9,647,000
Private	1,734	230,000	2,725,000
Total	112,009	3,310,000	57,562,000

Most of the private elementary and secondary schools are affiliated with religious denominations. Of the children attending private elementary and secondary schools in 1980–81, 3,191,000 or 63·4% were enrolled in Roman Catholic schools.

During the school year 1979–80 high-school graduates numbered about 3,063,000 (1,503,000 boys and 1·56m. girls). Institutions of higher education conferred 935,140 bachelor's degrees for the academic year 1980–81, 469,883 to men and 465,257 to women; 295,739 master's degrees, 147,043 to men and 148,696 to women; 32,958 doctorates, 22,711 to men and 10,247 to women; and 71,956 first professional degrees, 52,792 to men and 19,164 to women.

During the academic year, 1980–81, 311,882 foreign students were enrolled in American colleges and universities. The percentages of students coming from various areas in 1980–81 were: South and East Asia, 30·4; Middle East, 27·2; Latin America, 16; Africa, 12·2; Europe, 8·1; North America, 4·7; Oceania, 1·3.

School enrolment, Oct. 1980, embraced 96% of the children who were 5 and 6 years old; 99% of the children aged 7–13 years; 93% of those aged 14–17, 46% of those aged 18 and 19, 31% of those aged 20 and 21, and 16% of those aged 22–24 years.

The US National Center for Education Statistics estimates the total enrolment in the autumn of 1982 at all of the country's elementary, secondary and higher educational institutions (public and private) at 57·32m. (57,842,000 in the autumn of 1981); this was 25·2% of the total population of the USA as of 1 Sept. 1981.

Enrolment at the elementary and secondary school level is expected to be down by 1·4% in autumn 1982 and total enrolment in the colleges and universities to rise by about 1%.

The number of teachers in regular public and private elementary and secondary schools in the autumn of 1982 is expected to decrease slightly to 2·43m. The average annual salary of the public school teachers was about $19,000 in 1981–82.

Digest of Education Statistics. Annual. Dept. of Education, Washington 20202, D.C. (from 1962)

American Junior Colleges. 6th ed. American Council on Education. Washington, 1963

American Universities and Colleges. 9th ed. American Council on Education. Washington, 1964

Ayer's Directory of Newspapers and Periodicals. Annual, from 1880. Philadelphia

Good, H. G., *History of American Education.* 2nd ed. New York and London, 1962

Hofstadter, R., and Smith, W., *American Higher Education: A Documentary History.* 2 vols. Univ. of Chicago Press, 1962

Health and Welfare. Admission to the practice of medicine (for both doctors of medicine and doctors of osteopathic medicine) is controlled in each state by examining boards directly representing the profession and acting with authority conferred by state law. Although there are a number of variations, the usual time now required to complete basic training is 8 years beyond the secondary school with up to 3 years of additional graduate training. Certification as a specialist may require between 3 and 5 more years of graduate training plus experience in practice. In academic year 1980–81 the 140 US schools (including 14 osteopathic and 126 medical) graduated 16,818 physicians. About 28% of first-year students were women. In Dec. 1981 the estimated number of active physicians (MD and DO—in all forms of practice) in the US, Puerto Rico and outlying US areas was 463,940 (1 active physician to 497 population). The distribution of physicians throughout the country is uneven, both by state and by urban–rural areas.

In 1980–81 the 60 dental schools graduated 5,550 dentists. Active dentists in Dec. 1981 numbered 129,330 (1 active dentist to 1,784 population).

In academic year 1980–81, there were 1,403 registered nursing programmes in the US and 74,890 graduates. In Dec. 1980 an estimated 1,164,000 registered nurses were employed full- or part-time (1 to 192 population).

Number of hospitals listed by the American Hospital Association in 1980 was 6,965, with 1,365,000 beds and 38,892,000 admissions during the year; average daily census was 1·06m. Of the total, 359 hospitals with 117,000 beds were operated by the federal government; 1,835 with 212,000 beds by state and local government; 3,339 with 693,000 beds by non-profit organizations (including church groups); 730 with 87,000 beds are proprietary. The categories of non-federal hospitals are 5,904 short-term general and special hospitals with 992,000 beds; 157 non-federal long-term general and special hospitals with 39,000 beds; 534 psychiatric hospitals with 215,000 beds; 11 tuberculosis hospitals with 2,000 beds.

Social welfare legislation was chiefly the province of the various states until the adoption of the Social Security Act of 14 Aug. 1935. This as amended provides for a federal system of old-age, survivors and disability insurance; health insurance for the aged and disabled; supplemental security income for the aged, blind and disabled; federal state unemployment insurance; and federal grants to states for public assistance (medical assistance for the aged and aid to families with dependent children generally) and for maternal and child-health and child-welfare services. The Social Security Administration of the Department of Health and Human Services has responsibility for the programmes—old-age, survivors and disability insurance, supplemental security income and aid to families with dependent children. The Health Care Financing Administration, an agency of the same Department, has federal responsibility for health insurance for the aged and disabled (Medicare) and medical assistance (Medicaid). The Department's Office of Human Development administers human development and social services programmes, and its Public Health Service is responsible for maternal and child-health services. Unemployment insurance is the responsibility of the Department of Labor.

The Social Security Act provides for protection against the cost of medical care through the two-part programme of health insurance for people 65 and over and for certain disabled people under 65, who receive disability insurance payments or who have permanent kidney failure (Medicare). During fiscal year 1981, payments totalling $28,907m. were made under the hospital insurance part of Medicare on behalf of 28·6m. people. During the same period, $12,345m. was paid under the voluntary medical insurance part of Medicare on behalf of 27·9m. people.

In 1981 about 115·6m. persons worked in employment covered by old-age, survivors and disability insurance.

In Dec. 1981 over 36m. beneficiaries were on the rolls, and the average benefit paid to a retired worker (not counting any paid to his dependants) was about $386 per month.

Benefits paid during calendar year 1981 totalled $140,800m., including $17,200m. paid to disabled workers and their dependants.

In Oct. 1981, over 11m. persons (adults and children) were receiving payments under aid to families with dependent children (average monthly payment, $288.51 per family). Total payments under aid to families with dependent children were $13,100m. for the calendar year 1981.

In Dec. 1981, about 4·1m. persons were receiving supplementary security income payments, including over 1·8m. persons aged 65 or over; 79,000 blind persons, and over 2·3m. disabled persons. Payments, including supplemental amounts from various states, totalled $8,600m. in 1981.

During the fiscal year 1981 federal appropriations for formula grants to states for maternal and child health services amounted to $221·4m.; for crippled children's services, $89·2m., and for child welfare services, 163m. In addition, federal funding for maternal and child health special projects was $25·3m., crippled children's special projects was $9·5m. and mental retardation special projects was $10m. Research, training and demonstration projects in the field of child welfare was $16·4m. Approximately $5m. was spent for research and $25m. for training in the fields of maternal and child health.

Burns, E. M., *Social Security and Public Policy.* New York, 1956 (Repr. 1976).—*Health Services for Tomorrow.* New York, 1973

Friedlander, W. A., *Introduction to Social Welfare.* 4th ed. New York, 1974

Grob, G. N., (ed.), *Social Problems and Social Policy Series.* 51 vols. New York, 1975

Grob, G. N., et al., (eds.), *Mental Illness and Social Policy: The American Experience.* 41 books. New York, 1973

Grod, F. P., *Public Health Law Manual.* New York, 1965

DIPLOMATIC REPRESENTATIVES

Of the United States in Great Britain (Grosvenor Sq., London, W1A 1AE)
Ambassador: John J. Louis, Jr.

Of Great Britain in the USA (3100 Massachusetts Ave., Washington, D.C., 20008)
Ambassador: Sir Oliver Wright, GCMG, GCVO, DSC.

Of the United States to the United Nations
Ambassador: Jeane Kirkpatrick.

Books of Reference

I. Statistical Information

Within the federal government of the USA, responsibilities for the collection, compilation, analysis and publication of statistics are decentralized among a number of agencies, with specified responsibilities for general-purpose statistics in particular areas. In addition, most agencies of the Government collect statistical data as a by-product of their administrative or operating responsibilities in specific fields. Responsibility for co-ordinating the decentralized statistical activities rests in the Office of Statistical Standards Bureau of the Budget, Washington 25, D.C., as a part of the Executive Office of the President. This Office reviews all proposed collections of statistical data to avoid duplication or overlapping; promotes the use of improved statistical techniques; develops standard definitions and classifications so that the data collected by different agencies are comparable; serves as liaison between federal agencies and international organizations and as an information centre on government statistical programmes. The Division does not itself collect or publish statistics.

The major general-purpose statistical agencies and their principal areas of responsibility are:

(1) Bureau of the Census in the Department of Commerce (A. Ross Eckler, Director). Decennial censuses of population and housing and quinquennial censuses of agriculture, manufactures and business; current statistics on population and the labour force, manufacturing activity and commodity production, retail and wholesale trade and services, foreign trade, and state and local government finances and operations.

(2) Bureau of Labor Statistics in the Department of Labor (Geoffrey H. Moore, Commissioner). Current statistics on employment, earnings, man-hours, labour turnover, industrial accidents, work stoppages, wage rates; collective bargaining agreements; construction; industrial productivity; wholesale prices, retail prices and urban consumers' price indexes; income and expenditures of urban families.

(3) Statistical Reporting Service and Economic Research Service in the Department of Agriculture. Statistics on crop and livestock production and inventories; crop forecasts; food processing and food consumption; farm population, labour and wages; farm management; farm ownership values, transfers; taxation and finance; prices farmers pay and receive; farm income; accidents; studies of land and water uses.

(4) National Center for Health Statistics in the Public Health Service, Department of Health, Education and Welfare (Theodore D. Woolsey, Chief). Current statistics on births, deaths, marriages and divorce.

(5) Bureau of Mines in the Department of the Interior (John F. O'Leary, Director). Statistics on production, consumption and stocks of metals and minerals, and on injuries in mineral industries.

Other agencies in which statistics are an important by-product of regulatory or other administrative functions include: Social Security Administration in the Department of Health, Education and Welfare; Internal Revenue Service in the Treasury Department; Federal Power Commission; Federal Trade Commission; Interstate Commerce Commission, and the Securities and Exchange Commission.

Among the more important statistical publications of a fairly general nature are:

Statistical Abstract of the United States, published by the Bureau of the Census, Department of Commerce. Annual. Important summary statistics on the industrial, social, political and economic organization of the USA, with a representative selection from most of the important statistical publications. *Survey of Current Business*, published by the Office of Business Economics, Department of Commerce. Monthly. Interpretative text and charts reviewing business trends, etc.; official estimates of national income. *Economic Indicators*, prepared by the Council of Economic Advisers and published by the Congressional Joint Committee on the Economic Report. Monthly. Tables and charts presenting current data on the total output of the economy; prices; employment and wages; production and business activity; purchasing power; money, banking and federal finance. *Monthly Labor Review*, published by the Bureau of Labor Statistics, Department of Labor. *Federal Reserve Bulletin*, published by the Board of Governors of the Federal Reserve System. Monthly. Current data on money and banking and selected other economic series. Federal Reserve indexes of industrial production, etc.; international financial statistics. *Treasury Bulletin*, published by the Office of the Secretary, Department of the Treasury. Monthly. Current coverage of federal fiscal statistics; international capital movements. *Minerals Yearbook*, published by the Bureau of Mines, Department of the Interior. Annual. *Agricultural Statistics*, published by the Department of Agriculture. Annual. *Crops and Markets*, published by the Bureau of Agricultural Economics in the Department of Agriculture. Monthly. Crop report and market statistics. *Foreign Agriculture*, published by the Office of Foreign Agriculture Service, Department of Agriculture. Monthly. Foreign agricultural production, foreign government policies relating to agriculture and international trade in agricultural products. *Vital Statistics of the United States*, published by the Public Health Service, US Department of Health, Education and Welfare. Monthly and Annual. Natality and mortality data tabulated by place of occurrence, with supplemental tables for Puerto Rico and the Virgin Islands; and tabulated by place of residence.

An annotated bibliography of about 100 periodical statistical publications is included in *Statistical Services of the United States Government*, a pamphlet issued by the Division of Statistical Standards, Bureau of the Budget, describing the general organization of the statistical system of the USA and the principal types of economic statistics.

II. Other Official Publications

Guide to the Study of the United States of America. General Reference and Bibliography Division, Library of Congress. 1960.

Historical Statistics of the United States, Colonial Times to 1957: A Statistical Abstract Supplement. Washington, 1960.—*Continuation to 1962 and Revisions,* 1965.

United States Government Manual. Washington. Annual.

The official publications of the USA are issued by the US Government Printing Office and are distributed by the Superintendent of Documents, who issued in 1940 a cumulative *Catalog of the Public Documents of the . . . Congress and of All the Departments of the Government of the United States.* This *Catalog* is kept up to date by *United States Government Publications, Monthly Catalog* with annual index and supplemented by *Price Lists.* Each *Price List* is devoted to a special subject or type of material, *e.g., American History* or *Census.* Useful guides are Schmeckebier, L. F., and Eastin, R. B. (eds.), *Government Publications and Their Use.* 2nd ed., Washington, D.C., 1961; Boyd, A. M., *United States Government Publications.* 3rd ed. New York, 1949, and Leidy, W. P., *Popular Guide to Government Publications.* 2nd ed. New York and London, 1963.

Treaties and other International Acts of the United States of America (Edited by Hunter Miller), 8 vols. Washington, 1929–48. This edition stops in 1863. It may be supplemented by *Treaties, Conventions . . . Between the US and Other Powers, 1776–1937* (Edited by William M. Malloy and others). 4 vols. 1909–38. A new Treaty Series, *US Treaties and Other International Agreements* was started in 1950.

Writings on American History. Washington, annual from 1902 (except 1904–5 and 1941–47).

III. Non-Official Publications

A. Handbooks

National Historical Publications Commission. *Guide to Archives and Manuscripts in the United States,* ed. P. M. Hamer. Yale Univ. Press, 1961

Adams, J. T. (ed.), *Dictionary of American History.* 2nd ed. 7 vols. New York, 1942

Dictionary of American Biography, ed. A. Johnson and D. Malone. 23 vols. New York, 1929–64.—*Concise Dictionary of American Biography.* New York, 1964

Current Biography. New York, annual from 1940; monthly supplements

Handlin, O., and others. *Harvard Guide to American History.* Cambridge, Mass., 1954

Herstein, S. R. and Robbins, N., *United States of America.* [Bibliography] Oxford and Santa Barbara, 1982.

Lord, C. L. and E. H., *Historical Atlas of the US.* Rev. ed. New York, 1969

Who's Who in America. Chicago, 1899–1900 to date; monthly Supplement. 1940 to date

B. General History

Barck, Jr, O. T., and Blake, N. M., *Since 1900: A History of the United States.* 5th ed. New York, 1974

Bellot, H. H., *American History and American Historians.* London, 1952, repr. 1974

Billington, R. A., *Westward Expansion.* 4th ed. New York, 1974

Carman, H. J., and others, *A History of the American People.* 3rd ed. 2 vols. New York, 1967

Commager, H. S. (ed.), *Documents of American History.* 8th ed. New York, 1966

Divine, R. A., *Since 1945: Politics and Diplomacy in Recent American History.* New York, 1975

Hicks, J. D., *The American Nation, A History of the United States from 1865.* 5th ed. Boston, 1971

Link, A. S., and Catton, W. B., *American Epoch: A History of the United States Since the 1890s.* 4th ed. New York, 1967

Morison, S. E., *The Oxford History of the American People.* OUP, 1968

Morison, S. E., with Commager, H. S., *The Growth of the American Republic.* 2 vols. 5th ed. OUP, 1962–63

Nicholas, H. G., *The Nature of American Politics.* OUP, 1980

Parkes, H. B., *The United States of America, A History.* 3rd ed. New York, 1968

Scammon, R. N. (ed.), *American Votes: A Handbook of Contemporary American Election Statistics.* Washington, D.C., 1956 to date (biennial)

Schlesinger, A. M., *The Rise of Modern America, 1865–1951.* 4th ed. New York, 1951.—*The Age of Roosevelt.* 4 vols. New York and London, 1957–62.—*A Thousand Days: John F. Kennedy in the White House.* New York and London, 1965

Snowman, D., *America Since 1920.* London, 1978

Watson, R. A., *The Promise and Performance of American Democracy.* 2nd ed. New York, 1975

C. Minorities

Bennett, M. T., *American Immigration Policies: A History.* Washington, D.C., 1963

Burma, J. J., *Spanish-speaking Groups in the US.* Duke University Press, 1954, repr. 1974

Frazier, E. F., *The Negro Family in the United States*. Chicago Univ. Press, 1966
McNickle, D., *The Indian Tribes of the United States*. OUP, 1962.—*Native American Tribalism*. OUP, 1973
Sklare, M., *The Jew in American Society*. New York, 1974
Wissler, Clark, *Indians of the United States*. Rev. ed. New York, 1966

D. Economic History
The Economic History of the United States. 9 vols. New York, 1946 ff.
Bining, A. C., and Cochran, T. C., *The Rise of American Economic Life*. 4th ed. New York, 1963
Dorfman, J., *The Economic Mind in American Civilization*. 5 vols. New York, 1946–59
Faulkner, H. U., *American Economic History*. 8th ed. New York, 1960
Friedman, M., and Schwartz, A. J., *A Monetary History of the United States, 1867–1960*. New York, 1963
Mund, V. A., *Government and Business*. 4th ed. New York, 1965

E. Foreign Relations
Documents on American Foreign Relations. Princeton, from 1948. Annual
The United States in World Affairs. 1931 ff. Council on Foreign Relations. New York, from 1932. Annual
Allison, G., and Szanton, P., *Remaking Foreign Policy: The Organizations Connection*. New York, 1976
Bartlett, R. (ed.), *The Record of American Diplomacy; Documents and Readings in the History of American Foreign Relations*. 4th ed. New York, 1964
Beloff, M., *The United States and the Unity of Europe*. London, 1963, repr. 1976
Bemis, S. F., *Diplomatic History of the US*. 4th ed. New York, 1955.—*Short History of American Foreign Policy and Diplomacy*. Rev. ed. New York, 1959.—*The United States as a World Power. A Diplomatic History*. Rev. ed. New York, 1955
Connell-Smith, G., *The United States and Latin America*. London, 1975
DeConde, A., *The American Secretary of State*. London, 1963, repr. 1976
Morgan, R., *The United States and West Germany, 1945–73*. OUP, 1975
Pratt, J. W., *A History of United States Foreign Policy*. 3rd ed. New York, 1972
Smith, R. F., *The United States and Cuba: Business and Diplomacy, 1917–1960*. New York, 1962
Spanier, J. W., *American Foreign Policy Since World War II*. 6th ed. London, 1973
Stebbins, R. P., and Adam, E. A., *Documents of American Foreign Relations, 1968–69*. New York, 1972
Stuart, Graham H., *Latin America and the United States*. 6th ed. New York, 1975
Wilcox, F. O., and Frank, R. A., *The Constitution and the Conduct of Foreign Policy*. New York, 1976

F. National Character
Coan, O. W., *America in Fiction, An Annotated List of Novels*. 5th ed. Stanford Univ. Press, 1967
Curti, M. B., *The Growth of American Thought*. 3rd ed. New York, 1964
Degler, C. N., *Out of Our Past: The Forces That Shaped Modern America*. Rev. ed. New York, 1970
Duigan, P., and Rabushka, A., (eds.) *The United States in the 1980s*. Stanford, 1980
Wish, H., *Society and Thought in America*. 2nd ed. 2 vols. New York [1962].—*Contemporary America*. 3rd ed. New York, 1961

National Library: The Library of Congress. Washington 25, D.C. *Librarian:* Lawrence Quincy Mumford, AB, MA, BS.

STATES AND TERRITORIES

For information as to State and Local Government, see under UNITED STATES, *pp.* 1385.

Against the names of the Governors and the Secretaries of State, (D.) stands for Democrat and (R.) for Republican.

Figures for the revenues and expenditures of the various states are those of the Federal Bureau of the Census unless otherwise stated, which takes the original state figures and arranges them on a common pattern so that those of one state can be compared with those of any other.

Official publications of the various states and insular possessions are listed in the *Monthly*

Check-List of State Publications, issued by the Library of Congress since 1910. Their character and contents are discussed in J. K. Wilcox's *Manual on the Use of State Publications* (1940). Of great importance bibliographically are the publications of the Historical Records Survey and the American Imprints Inventory, which record local archives, official publications and state imprints. These publications supplement those of state historical societies which usually publish journals and monographs on state and local history. An outstanding source of statistical data is the material issued by the various state planning boards and commissions, to which should be added the annual *Governmental Finances* issued by the US Bureau of the Census.

The Book of the States. Biennial. Council of State Governments, Lexington, 1953 ff.
State Government Finances. Annual. Dept. of Commerce, 1966 ff.

Regionalism
Jensen, M. (ed.), *Regionalism in America*. Univ. of Wisconsin Press, 1965
Odum, H. W., *American Regionalism, A Cultural–Historical Approach to National Integration*. New York, 1938
Visher, S. X., *Climatic Atlas of the USA*. Harvard Univ. Press., 1954

A. North-East
Gottman, J., *Megalopolis, the Urbanized North-eastern Seaboard of the US*. New York, 1964

B. The South
Clement, E., *A History of the Old South*. New York, 1949
Ezell, J. S., *The South Since 1865*. New York and London, 1963
Heseltine, W. B., and Smiley, D. L., *The South in American History*. 2nd ed. Englewood Cliffs, 1960
Sindler, A. P. (ed.), *Change in the Contemporary South*. Duke Univ. Press, 1963
Stephenson, W. H., and Coulter, E. M. (ed.), *A History of the South*. 10 vols. Louisiana State Univ. Press, 1947–67

C. The Middle West
Lynd, R. S. and H. M., *Middletown: A Study in Contemporary American Culture*. New York and London, 1929.—*Middletown in Transition: A Study in Cultural Conflicts*. New York and London, 1937
Nye, R. B., *Midwestern Progressive Politics, 1870–1938*. Michigan State Univ. Press, 1959

D. The West
Fogelson, R. U., *The Fragmented Metropolis: Los Angeles, 1850–1930*. Harvard Univ. Press, 1967
Fuller, G. W., *History of the Pacific Northwest*. 2nd ed. New York, 1938
Johansen, D. O., and Gates, C. M., *Empire of the Columbia: A History of the Pacific North-West*, New York, 1957
Parrish, P. H., *Before the Covered Wagon*. Portland, Oreg., 1931
Quiett, G. C., *They Built the West: An Epic of Rails and Cities*. New York and London, 001934
Scott, H. W., *History of the Oregon Country*. 6 vols. Cambridge, Mass., 1924
Winther, O. O., *The Great Northwest: A History*. 2nd ed., rev. New York, 1950

ALABAMA

HISTORY. Alabama, settled in 1702 as part of the French Province of Louisiana, and ceded to the British in 1763, was organized as a Territory, 1817, and admitted into the Union on 14 Dec. 1819.

AREA AND POPULATION. Alabama is bounded north by Tennessee, east by Georgia, south by Florida and the Gulf of Mexico and west by Mississippi. Area, 51,998 sq. miles, including 938 sq. miles of inland water. Census population, 1 April 1980, 3,893,888, an increase of 13·06% over that of 1970. Births, 1980, 61,497 (15·6 per 1,000 population); deaths, 35,348 (9); infant deaths (under 28 days), 512 (8·3 per 1,000 live births); marriages, 48,710 (12·3); divorces, 26,791 (6·8).

Population in 5 census years was:

	White	*Negro*	*Indian*	*Asiatic*	*Total*	*Per sq. mile*
1910	1,228,832	908,282	909	70	2,138,093	41·4
1930	1,700,844	944,834	465	105	2,646,248	51·3
1960	2,283,609	980,271	1,726	915	3,266,521	64·0
			All others			
1970	2,533,831	903,467	6,867		3,444,165	66·7
1980	2,872,621	996,335	24,932		3,893,888	74·9

Of the total population in 1980, 49% were male, 60% were urban and 65% were 21 years or older.

The large cities (1980 census) were: Birmingham, 284,413 (metropolitan area, 847,487; Mobile, 200,452 (443,536); Huntsville, 142,513 (308,593); Montgomery (capital), 178,157 (272,687); Tuscaloosa, 75,143 (137,541).

CLIMATE. Average temperature, 65·8°; average rainfall 53·3 inches. The growing season ranges from 190 days (north) to 298 days (south).

CONSTITUTION AND GOVERNMENT. The present constitution dates from 1901; it has had 410 amendments. The legislature consists of a Senate of 35 members and a House of Representatives of 105 members, all elected for 4 years. The Governor and Lieut.-Governor are elected for 4 years.

The state is represented in Congress by 2 senators and 7 representatives. Applicants for registration must take an 'anti-communist oath' and fill out a questionnaire to the satisfaction of the registrars. In the 1980 presidential election Reagan polled 654,192 votes, Carter, 636,730 and Anderson, 15,844.

Montgomery is the capital.

Governor: George C. Wallace (D.), 1983–86 ($50,000).
Lieut.-Governor: Bill Baxley (D.) ($400 a month plus daily allowances).
Secretary of State: Don Siegelman (D.) ($25,800).

BUDGET. The total receipts for the fiscal year ending 30 Sept. 1981 were $7,431·9m.; total expenditure was $6,896·3m.

The net long-term debt on 30 Sept. 1981 amounted to $906·8m.

Per capita income (1980) was $7,434.

ENERGY AND NATURAL RESOURCES

Minerals. Production of principal minerals (1981): Coal, about 23m. short tons; limestone, 18m. short tons. Total (non-fuel) mineral output (1981) was valued at $312m.

Agriculture. The number of farms in 1982 was 57,000, covering 12·3m. acres; average farm had 216 acres and was valued at $113,400.

Cash receipts from farm marketings, 1981: Crops, $989·1m.; livestock and products, $1,262m.; and total, $2,273·1m. Principal crops: soybeans, cotton, corn and peanuts; potatoes, tomatoes, hay and wheat are also important. In 1981, poultry accounted for the largest percentage of cash receipts from farm marketings; cattle and calves were second, hogs third, dairy products fourth. Soybeans are the most valuable crop.

Forestry. Area of national forest lands, Oct. 1982, 644,432 acres.

INDUSTRY. Alabama is predominantly industrial. In 1981, 6,448 manufacturing establishments employed 364,130 production workers, earning over $5,725m. Pig-iron, 1981, amounted to 2·5m. net tons.

TOURISM. In 1981 about 25m. travelled to or through Alabama from other states. Total income from tourism (including receipts from Alabama holiday-makers) was about $2,500m.

COMMUNICATIONS

Roads. Paved roads of all classes in 1981 totalled 57,730 miles; total highways, 88,020 miles.

Railways. In 1981 the railways had a length of 4,455 miles.

Aviation. In 1981–82 the state had 89 publicly owned and 27 privately owned licensed airfields, and 73 unlicensed private fields.

Shipping. The only port is Mobile, with a large ocean-going trade; imports (1981), 22·87m. tons; exports, 15,246,000 tons. The docks can handle 35 ocean-going vessels at once. The 9-ft channel of the Tennessee River traverses North Alabama for 200 miles; the Warrier–Tombigbee Waterway (476 miles) connects the Birmingham industrial area with Mobile and also with the Gulf Intracoastal Waterway; the Chattahoochee River 9-ft channel extends from the Gulf to Phenix City (Alabama). In 1971 a 9-ft channel was completed which connects Montgomery and Mobile through the Alabama River System. The Alabama State Docks also operates a system of 14 inland docks; there is 1 privately-run inland dock.

JUSTICE, RELIGION, EDUCATION AND WELFARE

Justice. The prison population on 1 Oct. 1982 was 8,419.

From 1927 to 1965 there were 153 executions (electrocution): 121 for murder, 25 for rape, 5 for armed robbery, 1 for burglary and 1 for carnal knowledge.

In 39 counties the sale of alcoholic beverage is permitted, and in 28 counties it is prohibited.

Religion. Chief religious bodies (in 1980) are: Southern Baptist Convention (about 1,182,018), Churches of Christ (113,919), United Methodist (about 344,790), Roman Catholic (106,123), African Methodist Episcopal Zion (139,714), Christian Methodist Episcopal (about 53,493) and Assemblies of God (48,610).

Education. In 1980–81 the 1,400 (estimated) public elementary and high schools required 31,548 teachers to teach 771,464 pupils enrolled in grades K-12. In 1982 there were 14 senior public institutions (13 4-year institutions and 1 upper-division college) with 102,065 students and 4,163 faculty members in 1981–82. The 21 junior colleges had 37,377 students and 996 teachers, 22 technical schools had 21,436 students and 815 teachers.

Health. In July 1982 there were 138 hospitals (20,758 beds) licensed by the State Board of Health. In 1980–81 hospitals for mental diseases had 2,582 beds. There were on average 1,563 beds occupied by cases of mental retardation.

Pensions and Security. In financial year 1981 Alabama paid supplements (to federal welfare payments) to a monthly average of 12,563 recipients of old-age assistance, receiving an average of $53.71 a month; 4,089 permanently and totally disabled, $57.01; 137 blind, $55.16. Combined state–federal aid to dependent children was paid to 60,394 families a month, average $107.91 per family per month.

Books of Reference

Alabama Official and Statistical Register. Montgomery. Quadrennial
Alabama Encyclopædia. Vol. I. Northport, 1965
Economic Abstract of Alabama. Center for Business and Economic Research, Univ. of Alabama, 1975
The Deep South in Transformation: A Symposium. Univ. of Alabama Press, 1964
Farmer, H., *The Legislative Process in Alabama.* Univ. of Alabama, 1949

ALASKA

HISTORY. Discovered in 1741 by Vitus Bering, its first settlement, on Kodiak Island, was in 1784. The area known as Russian America with its capital (1806) at Sitka was ruled by a Russo-American fur company and vaguely claimed as a Russian colony. Alaska was purchased by the United States from Russia under the treaty of 30 March 1867 for $7·2m. It was not organized until 1884, when it became a 'district' governed by the code of the state of Oregon. By Act of Congress approved 24 Aug. 1912 Alaska became an incorporated Territory; its first legislature in 1913 granted votes to women, 7 years in advance of the Constitutional Amendment.

Alaska officially became the 49th state of the Union on 3 Jan. 1959.

AREA AND POPULATION. Alaska is bounded north by the Beaufort Sea, west and south by the Pacific and east by Canada. It has the largest area of any state, being more than twice the size of Texas. The gross area (land and water) is 591,004 sq. miles; the land area is 570,833 sq. miles of which 86·6% was in federal ownership in 1978. Census population, 1 April 1980, was 401,851, including military personnel, an increase of 33·5% over 1970. Births, 1980, were 9,557 (23·8 per 1,000 population); deaths, 1,811 (4·5); infant deaths, 117 (12·3 per 1,000 live births); marriages, 5,361 (13·4); divorces, 3,517 (8·7).

Population in 5 census years was:

	White	*Negro*	*All Others*	*Total*	*Per sq. mile*
1940	39,170	...	33,354	72,524	0·13
1950	92,808	...	35,835	128,643	0·23
1960	174,649	...	51,518	226,167	0·40
1970	236,767	8,911	54,704	300,382	0·53
1980	309,728	13,643	78,480	401,851	0·70

Of the total population in 1980, 53·01% were male, 64·34% were urban and 68·57% were aged 21 years or over.

The largest city is Anchorage, which had a 1980 census population of 174,430. Other city area populations (1980), Fairbanks, 22,645; Juneau, 19,528; Sitka, 7,803; Ketchikan, 7,198. There are 11 major incorporated boroughs, of which the largest are Anchorage, Fairbanks-North Star (53,983), Kenai Peninsula (25,282), Juneau and Matanuska-Susitna (17,816).

CONSTITUTION AND GOVERNMENT. An important provision of the Enabling Act is that the state has the right to select 103·55m. acres of vacant and unappropriated public lands in order to establish 'a tax basis'; it can open these lands to prospectors for minerals, and the state is to derive the principal advantage in all gains resulting from the discovery of minerals. In addition, certain federally administered lands reserved for conservation of fisheries and wild life have been transferred to the state. Special provision is made for federal control of land for defence in areas of high strategic importance.

The constitution of Alaska was adopted by public vote, 24 April 1956. The state legislature consists of a Senate of 20 members (elected for 4 years) and a House of Representatives of 40 members (elected for 2 years). The state sends 2 senators and 1 representative to Congress. The franchise may be exercised by all citizens over 18 years of age.

The capital is Juneau. A new capital site near Anchorage was chosen in 1976.

In the 1980 presidential election Reagan polled 86,112 votes, Carter 41,842.

Governor: William Sheffield (D.), 1983–86 ($74,196).

Lieut.-Governor: Steve McAlpine (D.) 1983–86 ($69,240).

ECONOMY

Budget. Total state government revenue for the year ended 30 June 1981 (Annual Financial Report figures) was $4,232·2m. ($2,296·1m. from taxation, $314·1.m from federal sources). Total expenditure was $4,824·2m.

In 1976 a Permanent Fund was set up for the deposit of at least 25% of all mineral-related revenue. Cash and investment holdings at 30 June, 1982, $3,176·2m.

General obligation bonds at 30 June 1980, $809m.

Per capita income (1981) was $13,763.

Banking. Annual average assets, $2,418·9m., total deposits $1,932·2m.

ENERGY AND NATURAL RESOURCES

Oil and Gas. Commercial production of crude petroleum began in 1959 and by 1961 had become the most important mineral by value. Production: 1961, 6,327,000 bbls (of 42 gallons); 1965, 11m. bbls; 1976, 67m. bbls; 1977, 169m. bbls, value $989m. Estimate for 1978, the first full year of production for the Prudhoe Bay oilfield, 447m. bbls.; 1979 estimate, 511m. bbls., value $5,493·6m. Oil comes mainly from Prudhoe Bay, the McArthur River field and several Cook Inlet fields. Natural gas production, 1978, 167,168m. cu. ft, value 74·2m. Alaska receives 90%

of all royalties (12·5%) from oil, gas and coal production on federal lands and the full 12·5% royalty for oil and gas production in state lands (coal royalties are being negotiated). Revenue to the state from oil and gas production tax in 1980–81 was $1,170m., from corporate petroleum tax $860·1m. and from royalties $1,491·3m. In 1969, the state conducted a major competitive lease sale for the arctic coastal region where reserves are estimated to be as large as 50,000m. bbls. A further competitive lease sale for the Beaufort Sea was conducted in 1979.

Oil from the Prudhoe Bay arctic field is now carried by the Trans-Alaska pipeline to Prince William Sound on the south coast, where a tanker terminal has been built at Valdez.

Minerals. Value of production, 1981: sand and gravel (46·4m. short tons), $87·5m.; crushed stone (5·4m. short tons), $26·9m.; gold (134,000 troy oz.), $55m.; others, including silver, gemstones, lead, copper, tin, barite and platinum group minerals, $1·6m.

Agriculture. In some parts of the state the climate during the brief spring and summer (about 100 days in major areas and 152 days in the south-eastern coastal area) is suitable for agricultural operations, thanks to the long hours of sunlight, but Alaska is a food-importing area. In 1964, 1,959,440 acres were classified as agricultural land, 90% of this was unimproved pasture primarily government leases for grazing of sheep and beef cattle in south-west Alaska. In 1980 about 30,000 acres was cultivated. In 1980 (preliminary) there were 8,400 cattle, 1,100 milch cows, 1,800 hogs and 4,300 sheep stock.

Farm production in 1980: Milk, $2·1m.; eggs, $413,000; silage, $484,000; potatoes, $932,000.; hay, $952,000; beef and veal, $324,000; barley, $856,000; vegetables, $560,000.

There were about 25,000 reindeer in western Alaska in 1980, owned by individual Eskimo herders except for 750 at Nome owned by the Government.

Forestry. In south-eastern Alaska timber fringes the shore of the mainland and all the islands extending inland to a depth of 5 miles. The state's enormous forests could produce an estimated annual sustained yield of 1,500m. bd ft of lumber, nearly twice Alaska's record 1973 cut. Alaska has 2 national forests: the Tongass of 16·9m. acres and the Chugach of 5·9m. acres. An estimated total of 454m. bd ft was cut in 1980 on public lands, of which 453·7m. came from national forests and 33,800 from state forests. Total cut, including timber from private land and land held by the Bureau of Indian Affairs, about 563·7m. bd ft. Alaska has 2 large pulp-mills at Ketchikan and Sitka.

Fisheries. The catch for 1980 was 983·7m. lb. of fish and shellfish having a value to fishermen of $561·8m. This compares with 471m. lb. in 1971 with a value of $85·5m. Salmon remains the highest per unit value species, with a catch in 1980 of 511·7m. lb. valued to the fishermen at $268·5m.

INDUSTRY. Main industries with employment, 1981: Government, 54,800; trade, 31,165; services, 29,491; contract construction, 12,470; manufacturing, 11,655; mining including oil and gas, 7,925.

The major manufacturing industry was food processing, followed by timber industries. Total employment outside agriculture, 175,485. Total wages and salaries, $4,377,697,900.

TOURISM. About 690,000 tourists visited the state in 1982.

COMMUNICATIONS

Roads. Alaska's highway and road system, 1981, totalled 13,699 miles, including marine highway systems, local service roads, borough and city streets, national park, forest and reservation roads and military roads. Registered motor vehicles, 1981, 341,637.

The Alaska Highway extends 1,523 miles from Dawson Creek, British Columbia, to Fairbanks, Alaska. It was built by the US Army in 1942, at a cost of $138m.

The greater portion of it, because it lies in Canada, is maintained by the Canadian Government.

Railways. There is a railway of 111 miles from Skagway to the town of Whitehorse, the White Pass and Yukon route, in the Canadian Yukon region. The government-owned Alaska Railroad runs from Seward to Fairbanks, a distance of 471 miles. This is a freight service with only occasional passenger use. A passenger service operates from Anchorage to Fairbanks via Denali National Park in the tourist season.

Aviation. In 1982 the state had about 1,070 airports, of which about half were publicly owned. Commercial passengers by air from Alaska's largest international airports Anchorage and Fairbanks numbered 1·1m. at Anchorage and 273,512 at Fairbanks. General aviation aircraft in the state per 1,000 population was about ten times the US average.

Shipping. Regular shipping services to and from the US are furnished by 2 steamship and several barge lines operating out of Seattle and other Pacific coast ports. A Canadian company also furnishes a regular service from Vancouver, B.C. Freight handled at the Port of Anchorage, 1981 (short tons): Bulk petroleum, 365,999; vans, flats and containers, 1,154,060; cement and drilling mud, 32,497; vehicles, 39,822; total 1·65m.

A 1,000 nautical-mile ferry system for motor cars and passengers (the 'Alaska Marine Highway') operates from Seattle, Washington and Prince Rupert (British Columbia) to Juneau, Haines (for access to the Alaska Highway) and Skagway. A second system extends throughout the south-central region of Alaska linking the Cook Inlet area with Kodiak Island and Prince William Sound.

JUSTICE, RELIGION, EDUCATION AND WELFARE

Justice. There is no death penalty in Alaska.

Religion. Many religions are represented, including the Russian Orthodox, Roman Catholic, Episcopalian, Presbyterian, Methodist and other denominations.

Education. During 1980–81 there were 85,862 pupils at public schools, 3,900 at private schools. The Bureau of Indian Affairs schools had 2,668 pupils attending schools in the state. The University of Alaska (founded in 1922) had (1978) 4,382 students on the main campus, 3,341 at its branches in Anchorage and Juneau and 13,958 in community colleges. Other colleges had 674 students in 1978.

Health. In 1982 there were 28 acute care hospitals with 1,397 beds, of which 7 were federal public health hospitals; there was 1 mental hospital; there were 24 mental health clinics.

Welfare. Old-age assistance was established under the Federal Social Security Act; in 1982 aid to dependent children covered a monthly average of 6,617 households; payments, an average of $409 per month; aid to the blind and to the disabled was given to a monthly average of 2,170 persons receiving on average $185 per month. An average of 5,492 people per month received Medicaid.

Books of Reference

Statistical Information: Department of Commerce and Economic Development, Division of Economic Enterprise, Pouch EE, Juneau.

Alaska Economic Information. Reporting Service, Division of Economic Enterprise, Juneau 99811. Quarterly

Alaska Economy, The. Division of Economic Enterprise, Juneau. Annual

Alaskan Earthquake, preliminary report. Civil Defense Office (Army), Washington, 1964

Look North. Department of Economic Development, Juneau, 1970

Adams, B., *The Last Frontier.* New York, 1961

Gardey, J., *Alaska: The Sophisticated Wilderness.* London, 1976

Hulley, Clarence C., *Alaska Past and Present.* Portland, Oregon, 1970

Rogers, G. W., *Alaska in Transition: the south-east region.* Johns Hopkins Univ. Press, 1960.—*The Future of Alaska.* Johns Hopkins Univ. Press, 1962

Tourville, M., *Alaska, a Bibliography, 1570–1970.* 1971

State Library: Pouch G, Juneau. *Librarian:* Richard Engen.—Alaska Historical Library, Pouch G, Juneau. *Librarian:* Phyllis de Muth.

ARIZONA

HISTORY. Arizona was settled in 1752, organized as a Territory in 1863 and became a state on 14 Feb. 1912.

AREA AND POPULATION. Arizona is bounded north by Utah, east by New Mexico, south by Mexico, west by California and Nevada. Area, 113,909 sq. miles, including 346·6 sq. miles of inland water. Of the total area (72,680,320 acres) 32,336,577 were owned by the federal government in 1970, including 19,623,000 acres held by the Office of Indian Affairs. Census population on 1 April 1980 (preliminary) was 2,717,866, an increase of 53·4% over 1970. Births, 1981, 51,620; deaths, 21,318; infant deaths (1980), 684; marriages, 31,906; divorces, 20,819.

Population in 5 census years:

	White	*Negro*	*Indian*	*Chinese*	*Japanese*	*Total*	*Per sq. mile*
1910	171,468	2,009	29,201	1,305	371	204,354	1·8
1930	378,551	10,749	43,726	1,110	879	435,573	3·8
1960	1,169,517	43,403	83,387	2,937	1,501	1,302,161	11·3
				All others			
1970	1,604,498	53,344		117,557		1,775,399	15·6
1980	2,240,033	75,034		402,799		2,717,866	23·9

Of the population in 1980, 1,337,666 were male, 2,278,189 were urban and 1,820,909 were aged 20 and over.

The 1980 (preliminary) census population of Phoenix was 789,704; Tucson, 330,537; Scottsdale, 88,364; Tempe, 106,743; Mesa, 152,453; Glendale, 96,988.

CLIMATE. Average maximum temperature in July ranges from 80·8° in Flagstaff to 106° in Yuma; minimum (Jan.) ranges from 41·4° in Flagstaff to 67·4° in Yuma. The percentage of sunny days is high; rainfall fluctuates widely.

CONSTITUTION AND GOVERNMENT. The state constitution (1910, with now 70 amendments) placed the government under direct control of the people through the Initiative, Referendum and the Recall. The state Senate consists of 30 members, and the House of Representatives of 60, all elected for 2 years. Arizona sends to Congress 2 senators and 5 representatives. In the 1980 presidential election Reagan polled 529,688 votes, Carter 246,843, Anderson 76,952, Clark 18,784 and DeBerry 1,094.

The state capital is Phoenix. The state is divided into 15 counties.

Governor: Bruce Babbitt (D.), 1978– ($50,000).
Secretary of State: Rose Mofford (D.).

BUDGET. General revenues, year ending 30 June 1981 (US Census Bureau figures), were $1,984m. (taxation, $1,318·9m. and federal aid, $343m.); general expenditures, $2,176·1m. (education, $1,109·7m.; highways, $272·6m., and public welfare, $357·7m.).

Per capita income (1981) was $9,693.

NATURAL RESOURCES

Minerals. The mining industries of the state are important, but less so than agriculture and manufacturing. By value the most important mineral produced is copper. Production (1980): Copper (757,314 tonnes); gold (72,773 troy oz.) and silver (5,668 troy oz.) are both largely recovered from copper ore. Other minerals include sand and gravel (24,399 short tons), zinc and lead (401 tonnes). Total value of minerals mined in 1980 was $2,425,714.

Agriculture. Arizona, despite its dry climate, is well suited for agriculture along the water-courses and where irrigation is practised on a large scale from great reservoirs constructed by the US as well as by the state government and private interests. Irrigated area, 1978, 1·2m. acres. The wide pasture lands are favourable for the rearing of cattle and sheep, but numbers are either stationary or declining compared with 1920.

In 1981 Arizona contained 7,000 farms and ranches with 1·3m. acres (1979 estimate) of crop land, out of a total farm and pastoral area of 38·3m. acres. The average farm (1981) was estimated at 5,465 acres. Farming is highly commercialized and mechanized and concentrated largely on cotton (1,294 cotton farms 1978) picked by machines and by Indian, Mexican and migratory workers.

Area under cotton (1981), 632,600 acres; 1·6m. bales (of 500 lb.) of cotton were harvested in 1981.

Cash income, 1981, from crops, $943m.; from livestock, $786m. Most important cereals are grain sorghums and barley; other crops include oranges, grapefruit and lettuce. On 1 Jan. 1981 there were 1m. all cattle, 75,000 milch cows, 372,000 sheep and (1980) 66,950 swine. The wool clip in 1979 amounted to 2·57m. lb.

Forestry. The national forests in the state had an area (1980) of 11·27m. acres.

INDUSTRY. Manufacturing establishments (numbering 2,733 in 1981) had 161,200 production workers, earning $3,084m.; value of output $6,200m.

TOURISM. In 1981 total estimated tourist business in the state was $4,327m.

COMMUNICATIONS

Roads. In 1979 there were 51,100 miles of public roads and streets maintained by counties and cities, and 4,596 miles maintained by federal agencies.

Aviation. Airports, 1980, numbered 216, of which 94 were for public use.

JUSTICE, RELIGION, EDUCATION AND WELFARE

Justice. A 'right-to-work' amendment to the constitution, adopted 5 Nov. 1946, makes illegal any concessions to trade-union demands for a 'closed shop'.

The Arizona prisons 30 June 1980 held 4,360. There have been no executions since 1963; from 1930 to 1963 there were 38 executions (lethal gas) all for murder, and all men (28 whites, 10 Negro).

Religion. The leading religious bodies are Roman Catholics and Mormons (Latter Day Saints); others include Methodists, Presbyterians, Baptists and Episcopalians. No recent statistics of membership are available.

Education. School attendance is compulsory between the ages of 8 and 16 years, and instruction is free for pupils from 6 to 21 years of age. The enrolled pupils in 1981–82 in the elementary schools were 343,506 and public high schools had 159,686 pupils. Teachers for both elementary and high schools totalled 26,200. Teachers' salaries averaged (1981) $17,000. The state maintains 3 universities at Tucson, Tempe and Flagstaff and 17 junior colleges.

Health. In 1979 there were 80 hospitals reported by the State Department of Health; capacity 11,700 beds. Resident patients in mental hospitals on 30 June 1980 numbered 631.

Social Security. Old-age assistance (maximum depending on the programme) is given, with federal aid, to needy citizens 65 years of age or older. In June 1980, 2,300 people were receiving general assistance at an average of $105.29 a month; 18,875 families (52,642 recipients), $61.55 per recipient in aid to dependent children; in the supplemental payment programme 1,200 old persons received $86.38 per month; 6 blind, $61.17; 663 totally disabled, $36.44.

Books of Reference

Arizona Statistical Review. 36th ed. Valley National Bank, Phoenix, 1981

Federal Writers' Project. *Arizona: The Grand Canyon State.* 4th ed. New York, 1966
Comeaux, M. L., *Arizona: a Geography.* Boulder, 1981
Goff, J. S., *Arizona Civilization.* 2nd ed. Cave Creek, 1970
Mason, B. B., and Hink, H., *Constitutional Government of Arizona.* 6th ed. Tempe, 1979
Wyllys, R. K., *Arizona: The History of a Frontier State.* Phoenix, 1951

State Library: Department of Library, Archives and Public Records, Capitol, Phoenix 85007. *Director:* Sharon G. Womack.

ARKANSAS

HISTORY. Arkansas was settled in 1686, made a territory in 1819 and admitted into the Union on 15 June 1836. The name originated with the Quapaw Indian tribe. The constitution, which dates from 1874, has been amended 59 times.

AREA AND POPULATION. Arkansas is bounded north by Missouri, east by Tennessee and Mississippi, south by Louisiana, south-west by Texas and west by Oklahoma. Area, 53,187 sq. miles (1,109 sq. miles being inland water). Census population on 1 April 1980 was 2,286,435, an increase of 18·9% from that of 1970. Births, 1980, were 35,852 (15·4 per 1,000 population); deaths, 18,525 (9·6); infant deaths, 419 (11·7 per 1,000 live births); marriages, 27,673 (11·9); divorces 16,492 (7·1).

Population in 5 census years was:

	White	*Negro*	*Indian*	*Asiatic*	*Total*	*Per sq. mile*
1910	1,131,026	442,891	460	72	1,574,449	30·0
1930	1,375,315	478,463	408	296	1,854,482	35·2
1960	1,395,703	388,787	580	1,202	1,786,272	34·0
			All others			
1970	1,565,915	352,445	4,935		1,923,295	37·0
1980	1,890,002	373,768	22,335		2,286,435	43·9

Of the total population in 1980, 48·3% were male, 51·5% were urban, 65·1% were 21 years of age or older.

Little Rock (capital) had a population of 158,461 in 1980; Fort Smith, 71,626; North Little Rock, 64,288; Pine Bluff, 56,636; Fayetteville, 36,608; Hot Springs, 35,781; Jonesboro, 31,530; West Memphis, 28,138. The population of the largest standard metropolitan statistical areas: Little Rock–North Little Rock, 393,774; Fayetteville–Springdale, 178,609; Fort Smith (Arkansas portion), 132,064; Pine Bluff, 90,718.

GOVERNMENT. The General Assembly consists of a Senate of 35 members elected for 4 years, partially renewed every 2 years, and a House of Representatives of 100 members elected for 2 years. The sessions are biennial and usually limited to 60 days. The Governor and Lieut.-Governor are elected for 2 years. The state is represented in Congress by 2 senators and 4 representatives.

In the 1980 presidential election Reagan polled 402,945 votes, Carter 379,919.

The state is divided into 75 counties; the capital is Little Rock.

Governor: Bill Clinton (D.), 1983–84 ($35,000).
Lieut.-Governor: Winston Bryant (D.) ($14,000).
Secretary of State: Paul Riviere (D.) ($22,500).

FINANCE

Budget. The state's general revenue for the fiscal year 1980 was $2,897·5m., of which taxation furnished $1,495·3m. and federal aid, $835·8m. General expenditure was $2,742·3m., of which education took $1,084·5m.; highways, $406·4m., and public welfare, $322·3m.

Net long-term debt for the financial year 1980 was $1,984·1m.

Per capita income (1981) was $8,044.

Banking. In 1980 total bank deposits were $8,914·9m.

ENERGY AND NATURAL RESOURCES

Minerals. In 1979 crude petroleum amounted to 18·9m. bbls; natural gas, 132·4m. cu. ft; bromine brine, 234·7m. bbls; crushed stone, 14m. tons; sand and gravel 13·1m. tons. Arkansas produces about 90% of the country's supply of bauxite for aluminium; production 1978, 1·9m. tons dried bauxite equivalent. The state has a large coal area; 224,655 short tons were mined in 1979. Total mineral output in 1979 was valued at $667·9m.

Agriculture. In 1978 (Federal Census Report), 51,773 farms had a total area of 15·1m. acres; average farm was of 292 acres; 7·6m. acres were harvested cropland; 1,685,520 acres were irrigated.

The largest sources of income in 1980 were chickens including broilers ($669·1m.); soybeans ($659·8m.); cattle and calves ($289m.); rice ($508·6m.); eggs ($209·1m.) and cotton ($184m.). Cash farm income (1981) was $3,002·2m.; from crops, $1,531·2m., and from livestock, $1,471·1m.

Livestock on 1 Jan. 1981 included 2·2m. all cattle, 82,000 milch cows and 720,000 swine.

INDUSTRY. In Aug. 1982 total employment averaged 931,100 (77,000 agricultural, 194,600 manufacturing, 162,900 wholesale and retail trade, 128,100 government). The Arkansas Department of Labor estimated that 155,600 factory production workers earned an average $261·12 per week (38·8 hours). The most important manufacturing group was food and kindred products employing 36,600, followed by electric and electronic equipment (21,200) and lumber and wood products (18,000). Construction employed 31,600.

COMMUNICATIONS

Roads. Total road mileage, 74,857 miles. State-maintained highways (1 Jan. 1982) total 16,090 miles; local county highways, 49,346 miles; city streets, 9,421 miles. In 1981 there were 1,677,880 registered motor vehicles.

Railways. In 1979 there were in the state 5,308·4 miles of commercial railway.

Aviation. Two air carrier and 7 commuter airlines serve the state; there were, in 1982, 244 airports (78 publicly-owned and 166 private).

Waterways. There are 1,000 miles of navigable streams including the Kerr-McClellan Channel which bisects the state and gives access to the sea *via* the Mississippi River.

RELIGION, EDUCATION AND WELFARE

Religion. The most numerous religious bodies in the state are Baptist (601,200 members estimated in 1979), Methodist (219,398), Roman Catholic (53,555) and Assembly of God (26,910). Total known membership, all denominations, 976,867.

Education. In the school year 1980–81 elementary and secondary schools had 467,704 enrolled pupils and 22,365 classroom teachers. Average salaries of teachers in elementary and secondary schools was $12,993. Expenditure on elementary and secondary education was $801·5m.

An educational TV network began operating in 1966 with a full 12-hour-day telecasting.

Higher education is provided at 31 institutions: 9 state universities, 1 medical college, 12 private or church colleges, 9 community and junior colleges. Total enrolment in institutions of higher education, 1981–82, was 72,069.

There were (1981–82) 24 vocational-technical schools with 32,309 students, including extension class students. Total expenditure, 1981–82, $17·6m.

Social Welfare. In Nov. 1982, 37,940 persons were drawing old-age assistance at an average amount of $109·71 per month; 21,867 families (44,139 children),

$131·43 per family; 1,456 blind persons, $183·02; 33,712 totally and permanently disabled, $168·97.

There were 100 licensed hospitals (12,062 beds) in 1982, and 229 licensed nursing homes (23,308 beds).

State prisons in Nov. 1982 had 3,777 inmates (165 per 100,000 population).

Books of Reference

Directory of Arkansas Mineral Producers and Production. Arkansas Geological Commission, Little Rock

Current Employment Developments. Arkansas Employment Security Division, Little Rock

Arkansas State and County Economic Data. Industrial Research and Extension Center, Little Rock

Ferguson and Atkinson, *Historic Arkansas.* Little Rock, 1966

Fletcher, J. G., *Arkansas.* Univ. of N. Carolina, Chapel Hill, 1947

CALIFORNIA

HISTORY. California, first settled in July 1769, was from its discovery down to 1846 politically associated with Mexico. On 7 July 1846 the American flag was hoisted at Monterey, and a proclamation was issued declaring California to be a portion of the US, and on 2 Feb. 1848, by the treaty of Guadalupe–Hidalgo, the territory was formally ceded by Mexico to the US, and was admitted to the Union 9 Sept. 1850 as the thirty-first state, with boundaries as at present.

AREA AND POPULATION. Area, 158,706 sq. miles (2,407 sq. miles being inland water). In 1974 the federal government owned 45m. acres (45·03% of the land area); in 1975, 546,000 acres were under jurisdiction of the Bureau of Indian Affairs, of which 472,000 acres were tribal. Public lands, vacant in 1975, totalled 15,607,125 acres, practically all either mountains or deserts.

Census population, 1 April 1980, 23,667,902, an increase of 18·5% over 1970, making California the most populous state of the USA (New York: 17,557,288). Births in 1981, 420,418 (17·4 per 1,000 population); deaths, 184,732 (7·6); infant deaths, 4,270 (10·2 per 1,000 live births); marriages, 217,348 (9); divorces, dissolutions and nullities, 140,473 (5·8).

Population in 5 census years was:

	White	*Negro*	*Japanese*	*Chinese*	*Total (incl. all others)*	*Per sq. mile*
1910	2,259,672	21,645	41,356	36,248	2,377,549	15·0
1930	5,408,260	81,048	97,456	37,361	5,677,251	35·8
1960	14,455,230	883,861	157,317	95,600	15,717,204	99·0
1970	17,761,032	1,400,143	213,280	170,131	19,953,134	125·7
			All other			
1980	18,030,893	1,819,281	3,817,728		23,667,902	149·1

Of the 1980 population 49·3% were male, 91·3% were urban and 67·2% were 21 years old or older.

The largest cities with 1980 census population are:

Los Angeles	2,966,850	Anaheim	219,494	Fremont	131,945
San Diego	875,538	Fresno	217,289	Torrance	129,881
San Francisco	678,974	Santa Ana	204,023	Garden Grove	123,307
San José	629,546	Riverside	170,591	San Bernardino	118,794
Long Beach	361,334	Huntington Beach	170,505	Pasadena	118,550
Oakland	339,337	Stockton	149,779	Oxnard	108,195
Sacramento	275,741	Glendale	139,060		

Urbanized areas (1980 census): Los Angeles–Long Beach, 9,477,926; San Francisco–Oakland, 3,191,913; San Diego, 1,704,352; San José, 1,243,900; Sacramento, 796,266; San Bernardino–Riverside, 703,316; Oxnard–Ventura–Thousand Oaks, 378,420; Fresno, 331,551.

CONSTITUTION AND GOVERNMENT. The present constitution became effective from 4 July 1879; it has had numerous amendments since 1962. The Senate is composed of 40 members elected for 4 years—half being elected each 2 years—and the Assembly, of 80 members, elected for 2 years. Two-year regular sessions convene in Dec. of each even-numbered year. The Governor and Lieut.-Governor are elected for 4 years.

California is represented in Congress by 2 senators and 45 representatives.

In the 1980 presidential election Reagan polled 4,524,835 votes, Carter 3,083,652 and Anderson 739,832.

The capital is Sacramento. The state is divided into 58 counties.

Governor: George Deukmejian (R.), 1983–86 ($49,100).
Lieut.-Governor: Leo McCarthy (D.), 1983–86 ($42,500).
Secretary of State: March Fong Eu (D.) ($42,500).

BUDGET. For the year ending 30 June 1982 total revenues were $21,305m.; total expenditures were $21,609m. ($10,878m. for education, $7,300m. for health and welfare).

The long-term state debt (general obligation bonds outstanding) was $6,308m. on 31 Dec. 1981.

Per capita personal income (1981) was $11,923.

ENERGY AND NATURAL RESOURCES

Minerals. California is one of the three most important petroleum-producing states of the US (Texas and Louisiana being the other two); crude oil output was estimated at 341m. bbls in 1979. Output of natural gas was 343,000m. cu. ft; of natural gas liquids, (1977) 8,117,000 bbls. Gold output was 7·6m. troy oz.; asbestos (1978), 70,730 short tons; boron minerals, diatomite, tungsten, sand and gravel, salt, magnesium compounds, lead, zinc, copper and iron ore are also produced. The estimated value of all the minerals produced (other than petroleum) was $1,740m. in 1979.

Agriculture. Extending 700 miles from north to south, and intersected by several ranges of mountains, California has almost every variety of climate, from the very wet to the very dry, and from the temperate to the semi-tropical. Of the total surface area (100,313,600 acres), estimates (1971) show 5·9m. acres to be seriously eroded, 35·4m. acres moderately affected and 58·8m. with little or no erosion.

In 1981 there were 80,000 farms, comprising 34m. acres; average farm, 423 acres. Cotton, fruit, poultry and vegetables are important. Cash receipts, 1980, from crops, $9,390m.; from livestock and poultry, $4,149m. Cattle, dairy produce, cotton, grapes, hay, tomatoes (in that order) are the main sources of farm income.

Production of cotton lint, 1980, was 3m. bales (480 lb.); other field crops included sugar-beet (4·8m. short tons, 1978). Cereal crops include maize, 36m. bu.; wheat, 85·5m. bu., and rice, 26·2m. cwt in 1978. Principal crops (1978) include wine, table and raisin grapes (3,879,000 short tons); peaches (815,500 short tons); pears (288,200 short tons); apricots (123,000 short tons); prunes (131,000 short tons); plums, nectarines, avocados, olives and cherries. Citrus fruit crops were: Oranges, 47·1m. boxes; lemons, 47m. boxes; grapefruit, 8m. boxes.

On 1 Jan. 1981 the farm animals were: 909,000 milch cows, 4·7m. all cattle, 1·2m. sheep and 180,000 swine.

Forestry. Total forest area in 1975 was 36,549,000 acres, of which 16,299,000 acres was commercial forest. California ranks third to Oregon and Washington in volume of standing timber (278,000m. bd ft); total annual cut is about 4,731·3m. bd ft (1976). National forest service land in 1975 was 20·25m. acres.

Fishery. California ranks first as a fishing state (by value of fish caught). The catch in 1980 was 804m. lb.; leading species were anchovy, tuna and mackerel.

INDUSTRY. In 1979, manufacturing employed about 2m. The fastest-growing industries were instruments and related products, non-electrical machinery, electric and electronic equipment, transport equipment and fabricated metal products. The aerospace industry is important, as is also food-processing.

COMMUNICATIONS

Roads. In 1979 California had 52,400 miles of roads inside cities and 125,400 miles outside. In 1980 there were about 12m. registered cars and over 3m. commercial vehicles, leading all states in all items by a wide margin.

Railways. Total mileage of railways, 1 Jan. 1977, was 7,600 miles. There are 2 systems: Amtrack and Southern Pacific Railroad commuter trains. Amtrack carries about 900,000 passengers per year, Southern Pacific about 5m.

Aviation. In 1980 there were 311 public airports and 950 private airstrips.

Shipping. The chief ports are San Francisco and Los Angeles.

JUSTICE, RELIGION, EDUCATION AND WELFARE

Justice. State prisons, 31 Dec. 1978, had 19,116 inmates. From 1893 to 1942, 307 inmates were executed by hanging. From 1938 to 1976, 194 inmates were executed by lethal gas. No further death sentences were passed until 1980.

Religion. The Roman Catholic Church, with 2,483,411 adherents in 1954, is much stronger than any other single church; next are the Jewish congregations with an estimated 431,471 members, Methodists, Presbyterians and Baptists. There were 210,000 Episcopalians in 1973.

Education. Full-time attendance at school is compulsory for children from 6 to 16 years of age for a minimum of 175 days per annum, and part-time attendance is required from 16 to 18 years. In autumn 1980 there were 4m. pupils enrolled in elementary and secondary schools. Estimated expenditure on public schools, 1980–81, was $9,548m.

Community Colleges had 1,170,773 students in autumn 1978.

California has two publicly supported higher education systems: the University of California (1868) and the California State University and Colleges. In Jan. 1980, the University of California with campuses for resident instruction and research at Berkeley, Los Angeles, San Francisco and 6 other centres, had 121,489 full-time students. California State University and Colleges with campuses at Sacramento, Long Beach, Los Angeles, San Francisco and 15 other cities had 229,350 full-time students in Jan. 1980. In addition to the 28 publicly supported institutions for higher education there are 266 private colleges and universities which had a total estimated enrolment of 129,567 in the autumn of 1978.

Health. In 1979 there were 608 general hospitals; capacity, 114,400 beds. On 30 June 1980 state hospitals for the mentally disabled had 4,836 patients and state hospitals for the developmentally disabled had 8,522 patients.

Social Security. On 1 Jan. 1974 the federal government (Social Security Administration) assumed responsibility for the Supplemental Security Income/State Supplemental Program which replaced the State Old-Age Security. The SSI/SSP provides financial assistance for needy aged (65 years or older), blind or disabled persons. An individual recipient may own assets up to $1,500; a couple up to $2,250, subject to specific exclusions. There are federal, state and county programmes assisting the aged, the blind, the disabled and needy children. In Dec. 1980, 512,000 families with one or more children were receiving an average of $399 per month per family.

Books of Reference

California Statistical Abstract. 22nd. ed. Dept. of Finance, Sacramento, 1981
Economic Report of the Governor. Annual. Governor's Office, Sacramento
Arnold, R. K. (ed.), *The California Economy 1947–1980.* Menlo Park, 1961
Crouch, W. E., and others, *California Government and Politics.* 2nd ed. New York, 1960
Turner, H. A., and Veig, J. A., *The Government and Politics of California.* 2nd ed. New York, 1964

State Library: The California State Library, Library-Courts Bldg, Sacramento 95814.

COLORADO

HISTORY. Colorado was first settled in 1858, made a Territory in 1861 and admitted into the Union on 1 Aug. 1876.

AREA AND POPULATION. Colorado is bounded north by Wyoming, north-east by Nebraska, east by Kansas, south-east by Oklahoma, south by New Mexico and west by Utah. Area, 104,090 sq. miles (496 sq. miles being inland water). Federal lands, 1974, 23,974,000 acres (36% of the land area).

Census population, 1 April 1980, was 2,889,964, an increase of 680,368 or 30·8% since 1970. Births, 1981, were 52,104 (17·6 per 1,000 population); deaths, 19,360 (6·5); infant deaths, 517 (9·9 per 1,000 live births); marriages, 37,210 (12·5); dissolutions, 19,515 (6·6).

Population in 5 census years was:

	White	*Negro*	*Indian*	*Asiatic*	*Total*	*Per sq. mile*
1910	783,415	11,453	1,482	2,674	799,024	7·7
1930	1,018,793	11,828	1,395	3,775	1,035,791	10·0
1950	1,296,653	20,177	1,567	5,870	1,325,089	12·7
1970	2,112,352	66,411	8,836	10,388	2,207,259	21·3
			All others			
1980	2,570,615	101,702	216,517		2,888,834 [1]	27·7

[1] Preliminary.

Of the total population in 1980, 49·6% were male, 80·6% were urban; 68% were aged 20 years or older. Denver, the capital, had a 1980 census population of 492,365. Other cities with 1980 population: Colorado Springs, 215,150; Aurora, 158,588; Lakewood, 112,860; Pueblo, 101,686; Arvada, 84,576; Boulder, 76,685; Fort Collins, 65,092; Greeley, 53,006; Westminster, 50,211.

CONSTITUTION AND GOVERNMENT. The constitution adopted in 1876 is still in effect with (1982) 78 amendments. The General Assembly consists of a Senate of 35 members elected for 4 years, one-half retiring every 2 years, and of a House of Representatives of 65 members elected for 2 years. Sessions are annual, beginning 1951. The Governor, Lieut.-Governor, Attorney-General and Secretary of State are elected for 4 years. Qualified as electors are all citizens, male and female (except criminals and insane), 18 years of age, who have resided in the state and the precinct for 32 days immediately preceding the election. The state is divided into 63 counties. The state sends to Congress 2 senators and 6 representatives.

In the 1980 presidential election Reagan polled 652,264 votes, Carter 368,009 and Anderson 130,633.

The capital is Denver.

Governor: Richard D. Lamm (D.), 1983–86 ($60,000).
Lieut.-Governor: Nancy Dick (D.), 1983–86 ($32,500).
Secretary of State: Natalie Meyers (R.), 1983–86 ($32,500).

BUDGET. The state's total budget, 1981–82, is $2,518m., of which taxation and other revenue furnish $1,392m. and federal grants $791m. Education takes $1,202m.; health, welfare and rehabilitation, $598m., and highways, $289m. Total state and local taxes *per capita* (1981–82) were $990.

The state has no general debt. The net long-term debt (in revenue bond) on 30 June 1982 was $141m.

Per capita personal income (1981) was $11,215.

ENERGY AND NATURAL RESOURCES

Minerals. Colorado has a variety of mineral resources. Among the most important are crude oil, coal and molybdenum. The world's largest molybdenum mine is at Climax; the Climax and Henderson mines to date (1982) have provided about 40% of the western world's output. Mineral production by value in 1981: metals,

$763m.; petroleum and natural gas, $1,250m.; coal, $600m.; other non-metals, $202·7m. An estimated 28,000 people were employed in extracting petroleum and natural gas in 1982; 10,600 in metals and 6,500 in coal and non-metals.

Agriculture. Farms number about 27,200, with a total area of 35·8m. acres in 1980 (53·3% of the land area); 6,726,800 acres (1981) were harvested crop land; average farm, 1,345 acres (1978). Cash income, 1981, from crops (excluding sugar beet), $1,077m.; from livestock, $2,912m. In 1978 there were 3,518,166 acres under irrigation.

Production of principal crops in 1981: Maize for grain, 108·2m. bu. (from 790,000 acres); wheat, 86·9m. bu. (3·3m.); hay, 3·3m. tons (1·4m.); dry beans, 2·8m. cwt (190,000); potatoes, 13·9m. cwt (46,800); sugar-beet, 1·7m. tons (77,000); oats, barley and sorghums are grown, as well as fruit.

On 1 Jan. 1981 the number of farm animals was: 75,000 milch cows, 3m. all cattle, 710,000 sheep, 330,000 swine. The wool clip in 1981 yielded 7·6m. lb. of wool.

INDUSTRY. In 1981 1,280,300 were employed in non-agricultural sectors, of which 311,000 were in trade; 265,900 in services; 242,900 in government; 184,400 in manufacturing; 72,700 in construction; 81,500 in transport and public utilities; 42,300 in mining; the rest in finance, insurance and property. In manufacturing the biggest employers were non-electrical machinery, foods and kindred products, and printing. Value added by manufacturing was $8,400m. (1982 estimate).

TOURISM. In 1982 about 12m. people spent holidays in Colorado, of whom about 2·4% were Colorado residents. National parks, monuments and recreation areas had about 5·7m. visitors. Overall expenditure, $1,577m.; $36·3m. of this was from ski-ing holidays.

COMMUNICATIONS

Roads. The state highway system (1981) included 9,318 miles of highway. County roads totalled 67,572, and city streets, 7,634 miles. Total road mileage, 84,524, of which 9,892 miles are unmaintained county and city roads.

Railways. In 1982 there were in the state 3,322 miles of main-track and branch railway.

Aviation. There were (1982) 243 airports in the state. Of these, 71 are publicly owned and open to the public; 23 are privately owned and open to the public; 149 are private and not open to the public.

JUSTICE, RELIGION, EDUCATION AND WELFARE

Justice. State prisons on 27 Oct. 1982 had 3,209 inmates in the State Penitentiary, the State Reformatory and other institutions. In 1967 there was 1 execution; since 1930 executions (by lethal gas) numbered 47, including 41 whites, 5 Negroes and 1 other; all were for murder.

Colorado has a Civil Rights Act (1935) forbidding places of public accommodation to discriminate against any persons on the grounds of race, religion, sex, colour or nationality. No religious test may be applied to teachers or students in the public schools, 'nor shall any distinction or classification of pupils be made on account of race or colour'. In 1957 the General Assembly prohibited discrimination in employment of persons in private industry and in 1959 adopted the Fair Housing Act to discourage discrimination in housing. A 1957 Act permits marriages between white persons and Negroes or mulattoes.

Religion. In 1970 the Roman Catholic Church had 412,000 members; the 100 Protestant and independent churches totalled 404,000 members; the Jewish community had 26,000 members. Buddhism is among other religions represented.

Education. In autumn 1981 the public elementary and secondary schools had 544,174 pupils and 35,490 teachers and administrators; total instructional salaries averaged $19,577. Enrolments in universities and larger colleges, 1980, were: US Air Force Academy (Colorado Springs), 4,472 students; University of Colorado (Boulder), 21,878; University of Colorado (Denver), 9,101; University of Colorado (Colorado Springs), 4,787; University of Colorado (Medical Center), 1,363; Colorado State University (Fort Collins), 18,083; University of Denver (Denver), 8,259; Colorado School of Mines (Golden), 2,907; University of Northern Colorado (Greeley), 10,830; University of Southern Colorado (Pueblo), 4,682; Western State College (Gunnison), 3,120; Adams State College (Alamosa), 1,953; Metropolitan State College (Denver), 14,464; Colorado College (Colorado Springs), 1,954; Fort Lewis College (Durango), 3,260; Mesa College, 3,274.

Health. Approved hospitals, 1980, numbered 93 with 12,691 beds. In 1981, there were 23 public mental health centres and clinics with 79,000 patients and 2 public mental hospitals with 7,900.

Social Security. A constitutional amendment, adopted 1956, provides for minimum old age pensions of $100 per month, which may be raised on a cost-of-living basis ($352 for 1982); for a $5m. stabilization fund and for a $10m. medical and health fund for pensioners. Old-age assistance is available to citizens 60 years of age with assets not exceeding $1,000 (excluding home ownership). In 1981–82 an average of 24,200 persons were drawing an average of $105.06 per month.

Books of Reference

Directory of Colorado Manufacturers, 1982. Business Research Division, School of Business, Univ. of Colorado, Boulder, 1982

Economic Outlook Forum, 1982. Colorado Division of Commerce and Development, and the College of Business, Univ. of Colorado, Denver, 1981

State Library: Colorado State Library, State Capitol, Denver, 80203.

CONNECTICUT

HISTORY. Connecticut was first settled in 1634 and has been an organized commonwealth since 1637. In 1629 a written constitution was adopted which, it is claimed, was the first in the history of the world formed under the concept of a social compact. This constitution was confirmed by a charter from Charles II in 1662, and replaced in 1818 by a state constitution, framed that year by a constitutional convention.

AREA AND POPULATION. Connecticut is bounded north by Massachusetts, east by Rhode Island, south by the Atlantic and west by New York. Area, 5,018 sq. miles (147 sq. miles being inland water).

Census population, 1 April 1980 (preliminary), 3,107,576, an increase of 2·5% since 1970. Births (1980) were 34,069 (11 per 1,000 population); deaths, 26,597 (8·5); infant deaths, 343 (10 per 1,000 live births); marriages, 25,761 (8·3); divorces, 11,448.

Population in 5 census years was:

	White	*Negro*	*Indian*	*Asiatic*	*Total*	*Per sq. mile*
1910	1,098,897	15,174	152	533	1,114,756	231·3
1930	1,576,700	29,354	162	687	1,606,903	328·0
1960	2,423,816	107,449	923	3,046	2,535,234	517·5
			All others			
1970	2,835,458	181,177	15,074		3,031,709	629·0
1980	2,799,420	217,433	4,533	18,970	3,107,576	634·3

Of the total population in 1980, 1,498,005 persons were male, 2,449,774 persons were urban. Those 19 years old or older numbered 2,228,805.

The chief cities and towns, with census population 1 April 1980, are:

Bridgeport	142,546	New Britain	73,840
Hartford	136,392	Danbury	69,470
New Haven	126,109	Bristol	57,370
Waterbury	103,266	Meriden	57,118
Stamford	102,453	West Haven	53,184
Norwalk	77,767	Milford	50,898

Larger urbanized areas, 1980 census: Hartford, 726,114; Bridgeport, 395,455; New Haven, 417,592; Waterbury, 228,178; Stamford, 198,854.

CONSTITUTION AND GOVERNMENT. The 1818 Constitution was revised in June 1953 effective 1 Jan. 1955. On 30 Dec. 1965 a new constitution went into effect, having been framed by a constitutional convention in the summer of 1965 and approved by the voters in Dec. 1965.

The 1965 Constitution provides for 30 to 50 members of the Senate (instead of 24 to 36) and for 125 to 225 members of the House of Representatives, to be elected from assembly districts, rather than 2 or 1 from each town, as in the former constitution. The convention has added a new provision for a 3-day session following each regular or special session, solely to reconsider bills vetoed by the Governor.

The General Assembly consists of a Senate of 36 members and a House of Representatives of 151 members. Members of each House are elected for the term of 2 years (annual salary $9,500 first year, $7,500 second year; expenses $2,000 and mileage allowance). Legislative sessions are annual. The Governor and Lieut.-Governor are elected for 4 years. All citizens (with necessary exceptions and the usual residential requirements) have the right of suffrage.

Connecticut is one of the original 13 states of the Union. The state is represented in Congress by 2 senators and 6 representatives.

In the 1980 presidential election Reagan polled 677,210 votes, Carter 541,732.

The state capital is Hartford.

Governor: William A. O'Neill (D.), 1983–86 ($42,000).
Lieut.-Governor: Joseph J. Fauliso (D.), ($25,000).
Secretary of State: Julia Tashjian (D.) ($25,000).

BUDGET. For the year ending 30 June 1980 (state government figures) general revenues were $2,394,071,891 (taxation, $1,712m., and federal aid, $344·8m.); general expenditures were $2,393,636,000 (education, $636·6m., highways, $157·5m., and public welfare, $598·8m.).

The total net long-term debt on 31 Aug. 1980 was $1,944m.

Per capita income, 1980 federal estimate, was $11,445.

NATURAL RESOURCES

Minerals. The state has some mineral resources: sheet mica, sand, gravel, clays and stone; total production in 1980 was valued at $62·8m.

Agriculture. In 1978 the state had 4,560 farms with a total area of 500,369 acres; average farm was of 110 acres, valued at $2,227 per acre. Total cash income, 1980, was $254·8m., including $97·5m. from crops and $157·3m. from livestock and products (mainly from dairy products and poultry). Principal crops are hay, silage, forest, greenhouse and nursery products, tobacco, potatoes, sweet corn, tomatoes, apples, peaches, pears, vegetables and small fruit.

Livestock (1 Jan. 1980): 108,000 all cattle (value $70·7m.), 5,200 sheep ($387,000), 11,000 swine ($699,000) and 5·8m. poultry ($12m.).

Forestry. The state had (1980) 137,782 acres of state forest land, which is about 4·2% of the total land area.

INDUSTRY. Manufacturing establishments employed 417,560 production workers in Aug. 1980 who earned average weekly wages of $294.47; value added by manufacture (1977), $2,342m. Total non-agricultural employment in Aug. 1980 was 1,386,350.

COMMUNICATIONS

Roads. The state (1 Jan. 1981) maintains 4,035 miles of highways, all surfaced. Motor vehicles registered in 1979 numbered 2,229,000 (licences issued 1980, 1,688,373).

Railways. In 1981 there were 950 miles of railway track.

Aviation. In 1981 there were 61 airports (27 commercial including 5 state-owned, and 34 heliports).

JUSTICE, RELIGION, EDUCATION AND WELFARE

Justice. In 1981 there were no executions; since 1930 there have been 22 executions (19 by electrocution, 3 by hanging), including 19 whites and 3 Negroes, all for murder. The 6 community correctional centres, 1974, had 1,508 inmates; 5 correctional institutions had 1,136 inmates.

The Civil Rights Act makes it a punishable offence to discriminate against any person or persons 'on account of alienage, colour or race' and to hold up to ridicule any persons 'on account of creed, religion, colour, denomination, nationality or race'. Places of public resort are forbidden to discriminate. Insurance companies are forbidden to charge higher premiums to persons 'wholly or partially of African descent'. Schools must be open to all 'without discrimination on account of race or colour'.

Religion. The leading religious denominations (1980) in the state are the Roman Catholic (1·4m. members), United Churches of Christ, Protestant Episcopal, Jewish, Greek Orthodox, Methodist, Baptist, Presbyterian.

Education. Elementary instruction is free for all children between the ages of 4 and 16 years, and compulsory for all children between the ages of 7 and 16 years. In 1979 there were 715 public elementary schools, 170 middle schools and 142 high schools; enrolment was 304,637 (grades 1–6) and 289,120 (grades 7–12). The 17 state vocational technical schools had 527,152 students. Expenditure of the state Board of Education, 1978–79, was $267,154,300 grants in aid; local expenditure, $1,038,344,461. Average salary of teachers in public schools, 1978–79, $14,609.

Connecticut has 47 colleges, of which one state university, 4 state colleges, 5 state technical colleges and 12 regional community colleges are state funded. The University of Connecticut at Storrs, founded 1881, had 1,253 faculty and 22,407 students in 1980–81. Yale University, New Haven, founded in 1701, had 2,088 faculty and 9,626 students. Wesleyan University, Middletown, founded 1831, had 297 faculty and 2,775 students. Trinity College, Hartford, founded 1823, had 145 faculty and 2,007 students. Connecticut College, New London, founded 1915, had 203 faculty and 1,974 students. The University of Hartford, founded 1877, had 305 faculty and 9,836 students. The regional community colleges (2-year course) had 514 faculty and 34,082 students.

Health. Hospitals listed by the American Hospital Association, 1981, numbered 65, with 17,935 beds. The state operated one general hospital, one veterans' hospital, 8 hospitals for the mentally ill (2,450 patients in Jan. 1981), 2 training schools for the mentally retarded (and 12 regional centres), one chronic disease hospital (56 in-patients in Jan. 1981) and a state-aided institution for the blind.

Social Security. Disbursements during the year ending 30 June 1981 amounted to $10,751,924 for old-age assistance, and medical aid to the aged, $5,413,444. The average monthly number of cases, 1980–81, was 4,782. In other areas of welfare, there was an average of 47,096 cases for aid to families with dependent children; 889 cases for such aid where the parent is unemployed; 84 cases for aid to the blind; 6,357 for aid to the disabled; 1,411 for Connecticut Assistance and Medical Aid to the disabled.

Books of Reference

The Register and Manual of Connecticut. Secretary of State. Hartford. Annual

The Structure of Connecticut's State Government. Connecticut Public Expenditure Council. Hartford, 1973

Adams, V. Q., *Connecticut: The Story of Your State Government.* Chester, 1973
Smith, Allen R., *Connecticut, a Thematic Atlas.* Newington, 1974

State Library: Connecticut State Library, Capitol Avenue, Hartford, 06015. *State Librarian:* Clarence R. Walters.

DELAWARE

HISTORY. Delaware, permanently settled in 1638, is one of the original 13 states of the Union, and the first one to ratify the Federal Constitution.

AREA AND POPULATION. Delaware is bounded north by Pennsylvania, north-east by New Jersey, east by Delaware Bay, south and west by Maryland. Area 2,044 sq. miles (112 sq. miles being inland water). Census population, 1 April 1980 was 594,338, an increase of 46,234 or 8·4% since 1970. Births in 1981, 9,372; deaths, 5,169; infant deaths, 114; marriages, 4,561; divorces, 2,921.

Population in 5 census years was:

	White	*Negro*	*Indian*	*Asiatic*	*Total*	*Per sq. mile*
1910	171,102	31,181	5	34	202,322	103·0
1930	205,718	32,602	5	55	238,380	120·5
1960	384,327	60,688	597	410	446,292	224·0
			All others			
1970	466,459	78,276	3,369		548,104	276·5
1980	488,002	96,157	10,179		594,338	290·8

Of the total population in 1980, 48·4% were male, 70·7% were urban and 65·7% were 21 years old or older.

The 1980 census figures show Wilmington with population of 70,195; Newark, 25,241; Dover, 23,512; Elsmere Town, 6,493; Milford City, 5,356; Seaford City, 5,256.

CONSTITUTION AND GOVERNMENT. The present constitution (the fourth) dates from 1897, and has had 51 amendments; it was not ratified by the electorate but promulgated by the Constitutional Convention. The General Assembly consists of a Senate of 21 members elected for 4 years and a House of Representatives of 41 members elected for 2 years. The Governor and Lieut.-Governor are elected for 4 years.

With necessary exceptions, all adult citizens, registered as voters, who have resided in the state 1 year, and complied with local residential requirements, have the right to vote; those who have attained the age of 18 since 1900 must be able to read English and to write their names. Citizens resident for 3 months or over may vote for President and Vice-President only.

Delaware is represented in Congress by 2 senators and 1 representative, elected by the voters of the whole state.

In the 1980 presidential election Reagan polled 111,252 votes, Carter 105,754.

The state capital is Dover. Delaware is divided into 3 counties.

Governor: Pierre S. du Pont (R.), 1981–85 ($35,000).
Lieut.-Governor: Michael N. Castle (R.) ($16,600).
Secretary of State: Glenn C. Kenton (R.) ($44,800) (appointed by the Governor).

FINANCE. For the year ending 30 June 1982 general receipts were $1,624·6m., of which federal grants were $182·2m. General expenditure was $1,574·7m.

On 30 June 1982 the total debt was $539·2m.

Per capita income (1981) was $11,279.

ENERGY AND NATURAL RESOURCES

Minerals. The mineral resources of Delaware are not extensive, consisting chiefly of clay products, stone, sand and gravel. Value of mineral production in 1978 was $2m.

Agriculture. Delaware is mainly an industrial state, but about 1m. acres is in farms, which in 1981 numbered 4,000; average farm was of 186 acres and all farms were valued (land and buildings) at $1,255m.

Cash income, 1980, from crops and livestock, $333m., of which $237m. was from livestock and products. The chief crops are corn and soybeans.

INDUSTRY. In 1976–77 manufacturing establishments (numbering 619) employed 67,000 people, earning $1,141m.

COMMUNICATIONS

Roads. The state in 1981 maintained 4,655 miles of roads and streets and 1,371 miles of federally-aided highways. There were also 594 miles of municipal maintained streets. Vehicles registered in 1981, 443,511.

Railways. In 1981 the state had 290 miles of railway.

Aviation. Delaware had 17 airports, of which 12 were for general use in 1981.

JUSTICE, RELIGION, EDUCATION AND WELFARE

Justice. State prisons, 1 July 1981–30 June 1982, had daily average of 1,434 inmates. The death penalty was illegal from 2 April 1958 to 18 Dec. 1961. Executions since 1930 (by hanging) have totalled 12 (none since 1946).

Religion. Membership, 1979–80: Methodists, 60,489; Roman Catholics, 103,060; Episcopalians, 18,696; Lutherans, 10,000.

Education. The state has free public schools and compulsory school attendance. In Sept. 1981 the elementary and secondary public schools had 95,072 enrolled pupils and 5,458 classroom teachers. Appropriation for public schools (financial year 1982) was about $231·5m. Average salary of classroom teachers (financial year 1981), $19,290. The state supports the University of Delaware at Newark (1834) which had approximately 870 faculty members and 18,615 students in Sept. 1982, and Delaware State College, Dover (1892), with 144 faculty members and 2,151 students.

Health. In 1981 there were 15 hospitals (4,179 beds) listed by the American Hospital Association. During financial year 1982 patients in mental hospitals numbered 1,963.

Social Security. In 1974 the federal Supplemental Security Income (SSI) programme lessened state responsibility for the aged, blind and disabled. Provisions are also made for the care of dependent children in (June, 1978) 10,611 cases totalling 30,434 recipients ($73.36 per person); general assistance, 1,422 cases totalling 1,868 persons ($41.59 per person). The total state programme for the year ending 30 June 1978 was $13·5m. for the care of dependent children, $919,815 in general assistance and $603,698 for Supplemental Security Income. Total federal aid, $21m.

Books of Reference

Information: Division of Historical and Cultural Affairs, Hall of Records, Dover.

State Manual, Containing Official List of Officers, Commissions and County Officers. Secretary of State, Dover. Annual

The Delaware Economy, 1939–58. Bureau of Economic & Business Research, Univ. of Delaware, 1961

Topical History of Delaware. Division of Historical and Cultural Affairs. Dover, 1977

Dolan, P., *The Government and Administration of Delaware.* New York, 1956

Federal Writers' Project. *Delaware: A Guide to the First State.* Rev. ed. New York, 1955

DISTRICT OF COLUMBIA

HISTORY. The District of Columbia, organized in 1790, is the seat of the Government of the US, for which the land was ceded by the state of Maryland to the US as a site for the national capital. It was established under Acts of Congress in 1790 and 1791. Congress first met in it in 1800 and federal authority over it became vested in 1801.

AREA AND POPULATION. The District forms an enclave on the Potomac River, where the river forms the south-west boundary of Maryland. The area of the District of Columbia is 68·68 sq. miles, 6 sq. miles being inland water.

Census population, 1 April 1980 (preliminary), was 637,651, a decrease of 15·6% from that of 1970. Metropolitan statistical area of Washington, D.C.–Md–Va. (1980), 3m. Density of population in the District, 1980, 10,453 per sq. mile. Births, 1980, in the District were 17,835 (28·9 per 1,000 population); resident deaths, 9,165 (14·4); infant deaths, 522 (29 per 1,000 live births); marriages, 5,182 (8·1); divorces, 3,473 (5·4).

Population in 5 census years was:

	White	*Negro*	*Indian*	*Chinese and Japanese*	*Total*	*Per sq. mile*
1910	236,128	94,446	68	427	331,069	5,517·8
1930	353,981	132,068	40	780	486,869	7,981·5
1960	345,263	411,737	587	3,532	763,956	12,523·9
			All others			
1970	209,272	537,712	9,526		756,510	12,321·0
1980	171,796	448,229	17,626		637,651	10,453·3

GOVERNMENT. Local government, from 1 July 1878 until Aug. 1967, was that of a municipal corporation administered by a board of 3 commissioners, of whom 2 were appointed from civil life by the President, and confirmed by the Senate, for a term of 3 years each. The other commissioner was detailed by the President from the Engineer Corps of the Army. Reorganization Plan No. 3 of 1967 submitted by the President to Congress on 1 June 1967 abolished the Commission form of government and instituted a new Mayor Council form of government with officers appointed by the President with the advice and consent of the Senate. On 24 Dec. 1973 the appointed officers were replaced by an elected Mayor and councillors, with full legislative powers in local matters as from 1974. Congress retains the right to legislate, to veto or supersede the Council's acts. The 23rd amendment to the federal constitution (1961) conferred the right to vote in national elections; in the 1980 presidential election Carter polled 130,231 votes, Reagan, 23,313. On 23 Aug. 1978 the Senate approved a constitutional amendment giving the District full voting representation in Congress. In order to become part of the constitution the amendment must be ratified by 38 state legislatures within 7 years. It would give the District 2 senators and a number of representatives according to population.

BUDGET. The District's revenues are derived from a tax on real and personal property, sales taxes, taxes on corporations and companies, licences for conducting various businesses and from federal payments.

The District of Columbia has no bonded debt not covered by its accumulated sinking fund. *Per capita* personal income, 1980, $12,039.

INDUSTRY. The District's main industries are government service, food processing, printing and tourism. In 1981 the federal government employed 361,500 civilians; total employed, 1980, 1,633,000.

COMMUNICATIONS

Roads. Within the District are 340 miles of bus routes.

Railways. There is a rapid rail transit system including a town subway system.

Aviation. The District is served by 3 general airports; across the Potomac River in Arlington, Va., is National Airport, in Chantilly, Va., is Dulles International Airport and in Maryland is Baltimore—Washington International Airport.

JUSTICE, RELIGION AND EDUCATION

Justice. Since 1958 there have been no executions; from 1930 to 1957 there were 40 executions (electrocution) including 3 whites for murder and 35 Negroes for murder and 2 for rape.

Religion. The largest churches are the Protestant and Roman Catholic Christian churches; there are also Jewish, Eastern Orthodox and Islamic congregations.

Education. In 1980 there were 106,000 pupils in secondary and elementary schools. Expenditure on public schools, 1980, $279m. Higher education is given in Georgetown University, founded in 1795 by the Jesuit Order; George Washington University, non-sectarian founded in 1821; Howard University, founded in 1867; Catholic University of America, founded in 1884; American University (Methodist).

Books of Reference

Statistical Information: The Metropolitan Washington Board of Trade publications.
Reports of the Commissioners of the District of Columbia. Annual. Washington
Federal Writers' Project. *Washington, D.C.: A Guide to the Nation's Capital.* New York

FLORIDA

HISTORY. White men, probably Spaniards but possibly English, saw Florida for the first time in the period 1497–1512. Juan Ponce de Leon sighted Florida on 27 March 1513. Going ashore between 2 and 8 April in the vicinity of what is now St Augustine, he named the land 'Pasqua de Flores' because his landing was 'in the time of the Feast of Flowers'. The first permanent settlement in the entire US was made at St Augustine, 8 Sept. 1565. It was claimed by Spain until 1763, then ceded to England; back to Spain in 1783, and to the US in 1821. Florida became a Territory in 1821 and was admitted into the Union on 3 March 1845.

AREA AND POPULATION. Florida is a peninsula bounded west by the Gulf of Mexico, south by the Straits of Florida, east by the Atlantic, north by Georgia and north-west by Alabama. Area, 58,664 sq. miles, including 4,510 sq. miles of inland water. Census population, 1 April 1980 (preliminary), was 9,739,992, an increase of 43·4% since 1970. Births in 1980 were 131,923; deaths, 106,815; infant deaths, 1,904; marriages, 110,575; divorces, 71,409.

Population in 5 federal census years was:

	White	*Negro*	*All Others*	*Total*	*Per Sq. Mile*
1940	1,381,986	514,198	1,230	1,897,414	35·0
1950	2,166,051	603,101	2,153	2,771,305	51·1
1960	4,063,881	880,168	7,493	4,952,788	91·5
1970	5,719,343	1,041,651	28,449	6,789,443	125·6
1980	8,178,387	1,342,478	219,127	9,739,992	180·1

Of the population in 1980, 48% of the total were male; 84·3% were urban and 72·4% were 20 years of age or over.

The largest cities in the state (1980 census) are: Jacksonville, 540,898; Miami, 346,931; Tampa, 271,523; St Petersburg, 236,893; Fort Lauderdale, 153,256; Hialeah, 145,254; Orlando, 128,394; Hollywood, 117,188; Miami Beach, 96,298; Clearwater, 85,450; Tallahassee, 81,548; Gainesville, 81,371; West Palm Beach, 62,530; Largo, 58,977; Pensacola, 57,619.

CONSTITUTION AND GOVERNMENT. The 1968 Legislature revised the constitution of 1885. The state legislature consists of a Senate of 40 members, elected for 4 years, and House of Representatives with 120 members elected for 2 years. Sessions are held annually, and are limited to 60 days. The Governor is elected for 4 years, and can hold two terms in office. Two senators and 19 representatives are elected to Congress.

In the 1980 presidential election Reagan polled 2,046,951 votes and Carter 1,419,475.

The state capital is Tallahassee. The state is divided into 67 counties.

Governor: Robert Graham (D.), 1983–86 ($69,550).
Lieut.-Governor: Wayne Mixson (D.), 1983–86 ($60,455).
Secretary of State: George Firestone (D.), 1983–86 ($59,385).

FINANCE. There is no state income tax on individuals. For the year ending 30 June 1980 the state had a general revenue of $7,303·6m. General expenditure was $7,005m., of which education took $3,147·5m.; public welfare, $704·8m.; and highways, $947·3m.

Net long-term debt, 30 June 1980, amounted to $1,846·3m.

Per capita personal income (1980) was $8,546.

NATURAL RESOURCES

Minerals. Chief mineral is phosphate rock, of which marketable production in 1981 was 41·7m. tonnes, leading all states (Florida produces 78% of national and 30% of world demand). Total value of mineral production, 1979, $1,269·6m.

Agriculture. In 1980, 39,000 farms had a total acreage of 16m.; net income per farm was $25,200. Total cash receipts from crops and livestock (1980), $3,968m., of which crops provided $2,800m. Oranges, grapefruit, melons and vegetables are important. Other crops are soybeans ($68m.), sugar-cane, tobacco and peanuts. On 1 Jan. 1980 the state had 2·3m. cattle, including 187,000 milch cows and 370,000 swine.

The national forests area in Sept. 1980 was 1,097,930 acres.

Fisheries. Florida has extensive fisheries for oysters, shrimp, red snapper, crabs, mackerel and mullet. Catch (1980), 187·4m. lb. valued at $132·8m.

INDUSTRY. In 1980 there were 12,226 manufacturers. They employed 462,728 persons. Value added by manufacture (1977), $9,255·1m. The metal-working, lumber, chemical, woodpulp, food-processing and instruments industries are important.

TOURISM. During 1981 35·9m. tourists visited Florida. They spent $18,594m. making tourism one of the biggest industries in the state. There are 121 state parks, 4 state forests, 1 national park and 9 national forests. The state parks were visited by 13m. people in 1981, 1·2m. of them campers.

COMMUNICATIONS

Roads. The state (1979) had 96,300 miles of road and streets including 8,854 miles of primary federally-aided highways.

In 1979–80, 10·2m. vehicle licence plates were issued.

Railways. In 1979 there were 3,698 miles of railway.

Aviation. In 1981 Florida had 502 airports, including 140 public use airports of which 16 are international, 16 have air carrier service and 10 have scheduled commuter service. There are 4 public and 9 private seaplane bases.

JUSTICE, RELIGION, EDUCATION AND WELFARE

Justice. Since 1968 there has been 1 execution, by electrocution, for murder; from 1930 to 1968 there were 168 executions (electrocution), including 130 for murder, 37 for rape and 1 for kidnapping. State prisons, 30 June 1982, had 26,036 inmates.

Religion. The main Christian churches are Roman Catholic, Baptist, Methodist, Presbyterian and Episcopalian.

Education. Attendance at school is compulsory between 7 and 16.

In 1980–81 the public elementary and secondary schools had 1,496,321 enrolled pupils. State expenditure on public schools (1980–81) was $3,755·8m. The state maintains 28 community colleges with 339,161 enrollments in 1980.

There are 9 universities in the state system, namely the University of Florida at Gainesville (founded 1853) with 34,022 students in 1981; the Florida State University (founded at Tallahassee in 1857) with 22,551 students; the University of South Florida at Tampa (founded 1960) with 25,357 students; Florida A. & M. University at Tallahassee (founded 1887) with 5,404 students; Florida Atlantic University (founded 1964) at Boca Raton with 8,083 students; the University of West Florida at Pensacola with 5,432 students; the Florida Central University at Orlando with 12,902 students; the University of North Florida at Jacksonville with 4,763 students; Florida International University at Miami with 11,966 students.

Health. Hospitals, 1982, numbered 257 with 58,577 beds; there were 213 general, 23 special and 1 tuberculosis hospitals.

Social Security. From 1974 aid to the aged, blind and disabled became a federal responsibility. The state continued to give aid to families with dependent children and general assistance. Monthly payments 1981: aid to 4,200 blind averaged $168.50; aid to 187,280 dependent children averaged $60.59; aid to 126,500 disabled averaged $162.99; aid to 108,000 aged averaged $132.21.

Books of Reference

Florida Population: Summary of the 1980 Census. Univ. of Florida Press, 1981
Florida Statistical Abstract. Univ. of Florida Press, 1980
Florida Tourist Study. Florida Department of Commerce, Tallahassee. Annual
Historical Florida Economic Data 1970–80. Florida Dept. of Commerce, 1980
Report. Florida Secretary of State. Tallahassee. Biennial
Report of the Comptroller. Tallahassee, 1977–78. Biennial
Dimensions. Bureau of Business and Economic Research, Univ. of Florida, Gainesville. Monthly
Morris, Allen. *The Florida Handbook.* Tallahassee, 1977–78. Biennial
Raisz, E. J., and others, *Atlas of Florida.* Univ. of Florida Press, 1974

State Library: Gray Building, Tallahassee. *Librarian:* Barratt Wilkins.

GEORGIA

HISTORY. Georgia (so named from George II) was founded in 1733 as the 13th original colony; she became the 4th original state.

AREA AND POPULATION. Georgia is bounded north by Tennessee and North Carolina, north-east by South Carolina, east by the Atlantic, south by Florida and west by Alabama. Area, 58,910 sq. miles, of which 854 sq. miles are inland water. Census population, 1 April 1980 (preliminary), was 5,464,265. Births, 1980, were 95,980 (17·5 per 1,000 population); deaths, 43,519 (7·9); infant deaths, 1,208 (12·6 per 1,000 live births); marriages, 69,416 (12·7); divorces and annulments, 33,636 (6·2).

Population in 5 census years was:

	White	*Negro*	*Indian*	*Asiatic*	*Total*	*Per sq. mile*
1910	1,431,802	1,176,987	95	237	2,609,121	44·4
1930	1,837,021	1,071,125	43	317	2,908,506	49·7
1960	2,817,223	1,122,596	749	2,004	3,943,116	67·7
			All others			
1970	3,391,242	1,187,149	11,184		4,589,575	79·0
1980	3,948,007	1,465,457	50,801		5,464,265	92·7

Of the 1980 population, 2,641,030 were male, 3,406,171 were urban and those 20 years of age and over numbered 3,601,895.

The largest cities are: Atlanta (capital), with population, 1980 census, of 422,293 (urbanized area, 2,010,368); Columbus, 168,598 (238,593); Savannah, 133,672 (225,581); Macon, 116,044 (251,736); Albany, 74,471 (112,257).

CONSTITUTION AND GOVERNMENT. A new constitution was ratified in the general election of 2 Nov. 1976, proclaimed on 22 Dec. 1976 and became effective 1 Jan. 1977. The General Assembly consists of a Senate of 56 members and a House of Representatives of 180 members, both elected for 2 years. The Governor and Lieut.-Governor are elected for 4 years. Legislative sessions are annual, beginning the 2nd Monday in Jan. and lasting for 40 days.

Georgia was the first state to extend the franchise to all citizens 18 years old and above. The state is represented in Congress by 2 senators and 10 representatives.

Registered voters, 1976, numbered 2,178,623. At the 1980 presidential election Carter polled 890,955 votes, Reagan 654,168 and Anderson 36,055.

The state capital is Atlanta. Georgia is divided into 159 counties.

Governor: Joe F. Harris (D.), 1982–86 ($60,000).
Lieut.-Governor: Zell Miller (D.) ($28,846).
Secretary of State: Max Cleland (D.) ($38,400).

BUDGET. For the fiscal year ending 30 June 1980 general revenue was $5,194,061,000; general expenditure was $4,900,734,000.

On 30 June 1980 total liability was $1,404,635,000.

Estimated *per capita* personal income (1980), was $8,073.

NATURAL RESOURCES

Minerals. Georgia is the leading producer of kaolin. The state ranks first in production of crushed and dimensional granite, second in production of fuller's earth and marble (crushed and dimensional).

Mineral products, 1978, had a record value of $577m.

Agriculture. In 1978, 58,648 farms covered 37% of the land area; average farm was of 234 acres. For 1980 cotton output was 86,000 bales (of 480 lb.). Other crops, 1980, included tobacco, 110·5m. lb; corn, 54·6m. bu.; peanuts and pecans 52m. lb. Cash income, 1980, $2,705m: from crops, $1,173·4m.; from livestock, $1,503·3m.

On 1 Jan. 1981 farm animals included 1·9m. all cattle, including 130,000 milch cows and 2·3m. swine.

Forestry. The forested area in 1980 was 25m. acres.

INDUSTRY. In 1978 the state's manufacturing establishments had 392,900 production workers; the value added by manufacture was $13,944·6m.

TOURISM. In 1979 the tourist industry employed 182,370 earning $1,100m. Tourists spent $2,200m. and tax revenue was $95·9m.

COMMUNICATIONS

Roads. Total road mileage (1979) was 104,000 including 87,600 rural and 11,850 primary federal-aided. Motor vehicles registered, 1980, numbered 3,865,000.

Railways. In 1976 there were 5,417 miles of railways.

Aviation. Airports numbered 140 (107 publicly owned, 33 privately owned but open to the public) in 1977.

Shipping. The principal port is Savannah.

JUSTICE, RELIGION, EDUCATION AND WELFARE

Justice. State prisons, 1 Sept. 1977, had 11,800 inmates. Since 1964 there have been no executions. From 1924 to 1964 there were 415 executions (electrocution), including 75 whites and 268 Negroes for murder, 3 whites and 63 Negroes for rape and 6 Negroes for armed robbery.

Under a Local Option Act, the sale of alcoholic beverages (not including malt beverages and light wines) is prohibited in more than half the counties.

Religion. An estimated 78% of the population are church members. Of the total population, 74·3% are Protestant, 3·2% are Roman Catholic and 1·5% Jewish.

Education. Since 1945 education has been compulsory; tuition is free for pupils between the ages of 6 and 18 years. In 1980 public elementary and secondary schools had 1m. pupils and 56,200 teachers. Teachers' salaries averaged $15,900 (secondary) and $15,200 (elementary). Integration in public schools is now an accepted practice.

The University of Georgia (Athens) was founded in 1785 and was the first chartered State University in the US. Other institutions of higher learning include Georgia Institute of Technology (Atlanta), Emory University (Atlanta), Agnes Scott College (Decatur), Georgia College (Milledgeville), Georgia State University (Atlanta) and Mercer University (Macon). The Atlanta University Center, devoted primarily to Negro education, includes Clark College and Morris Brown College, co-educational, Morehouse, a liberal arts college for men, Interdenominational Theological Center, a co-educational theological school, and Spelman College, the first liberal arts college for Negro women in the US. Atlanta University serves as the graduate school centre for the complex. Wesleyan College near Macon is the oldest chartered women's college in the US. Total enrolment, 1980, was 184,200 in 76 institutions of higher education.

Health. Hospitals licensed by the Department of Human Resources, 1 July 1979, numbered 189 with 31,100 beds.

Social Security. In Dec. 1980, 71,100 persons were receiving SSI old-age assistance of an average $104 per month; 89,900 families were receiving as aid to dependent children an average of $133 per family; aid to 80,500 disabled persons was $163 monthly.

Books of Reference

Georgia History in Outline. Univ. of Georgia Press, Athens, 1978

Bonner, J. C., and Roberts, L. E., eds., *Studies in Georgia History and Government.* Reprint Company, Spartanburg, 1940 Repr.

Pound, M. B., and Saye, A. B., *Handbook on the Constitution of the U.S. and Georgia.* Univ. of Georgia Press, Athens, 1978

Rowland, A. R., *A Bibliography of the Writings on Georgia History.* Hamden, Conn., 1978

Saye, A. B., *A Constitutional History of Georgia, 1732–1968.* Univ. of Georgia, Athens, Rev. ed., 1970

State Library: Judicial Building, Capital Sq., Atlanta. *State Librarian:* John D. M. Folger.

HAWAII

HISTORY. The Hawaiian Islands, formerly known as the Sandwich Islands, were discovered by Capt. James Cook in Jan. 1778. During the greater part of the 19th century the islands formed an independent kingdom, but in 1893 the reigning Queen, Liliuokalani (died 11 Nov. 1917), was deposed and a provisional government formed; in 1894 a Republic was proclaimed, and in accordance with the request of the people of Hawaii expressed through the Legislature of the Republic, and a resolution of the US Congress of 6 July 1898 (signed 7 July by President McKinley), the islands were on 12 Aug. 1898 formally annexed to the US. On 14 June 1900 the islands were constituted as a Territory of Hawaii.

Statehood was granted to Hawaii on 18 March 1959.

AREA AND POPULATION. The Hawaiian Islands lie in the North Pacific Ocean, between 18° 50′ and 28° 15′ N. lat. and 154° 40′ and 178° 15′ W. long., about 2,090 nautical miles south-west of San Francisco. There are more than 20 islands in the group, of which 7 are inhabited. The land and inland water area of the state is 6,470 sq. miles, with census population, 1 April 1980, of 965,000, an increase of 195,087 or 25·4% since 1970; density was 150 per sq. mile.

The principal islands are Hawaii, 4,038 sq. miles (population, 1980, 92,206); Maui, 729 (71,337); Oahu, 608 (761,964); Kauai, 553 (39,117); Molokai, 261 (6,076); Lanai, 140 (2,125); Niihau, 73 (226); Kahoolawe, 45 (0). The capital Honolulu, on the island of Oahu, had a population in 1980 of 365,114 and Hilo on the island of Hawaii, 44,011.

Figures for racial groups, 1980, are: 318,608 White, 239,618 Japanese, 133,964 Filipinos, 115,962 Hawaiian, 56,260 Chinese, 17,948 Korean, 17,352 Negroes, 65,288 all others. Of the total, approximately 92% were citizens of the US.

Inter-marriage between the races is popular. Of the 10,376 persons married in the calendar year 1978, 37·9% married a wife or husband of a different race. Births, 1980, were 18,277; deaths, 5,190; infant deaths, 194; marriages, 11,670; divorces and annulments, 4,386.

CONSTITUTION AND GOVERNMENT. The constitution took effect on 21 Aug. 1959.

The Legislature consists of a Senate of 25 members elected for 4 years, and a House of Representatives of 51 members elected for 2 years. The constitution provides for annual meetings of the legislature with 60-day regular sessions. The Governor and Lieut.-Governor are elected for 4 years. The registered voters, 1982, numbered 405,005.

The state sends to Congress 2 senators and 2 representatives.

In the 1980 presidential election Carter polled 135,879 votes, Reagan, 130,112.

Governor: George R. Ariyoshi (D.), 1983–86 ($59,400).

BUDGET. Revenue is derived mainly from taxation of sales and gross receipts, real property, corporate and personal income, and inheritance taxes, licences, public land sales and leases. For the year ending 30 June 1980 state general fund receipts amounted to $1,049·7m.; special fund receipts, $710·4m., and federal grants, $65·2m. State expenditures were $1,815·8m. (education, $512·1m.; highways, $32·5m.; public welfare, $253·4m.; figures include both special and general funds).

Net long-term debt, 31 Dec. 1980, amounted to $2,224·2m.

Estimated *per capita* personal income (1980) was $10,101.

NATURAL RESOURCES

Minerals. Total value of mineral production, 1979, amounted to $63·9m. Cement shipped from plants amounted to 481,000 short tons; stone, 6·87m. short tons.

Agriculture. Farming is highly commercialized, aiming at export to the American market, and highly mechanized. In 1979 there were 4,300 farms with an acreage of 1·98m.

Sugar and pineapples are the staple crops. Income from crop sales, 1980, was $552m., and from livestock, $81m. The sugar crop was valued at $385·1m.; pineapples, $76·6m.; other crops, $90·5m.

Forestry. Commercial forests totalled 948,000 acres (1982); state lands, 1·4m. acres. Land held by the federal government totalled 402,900 acres in 1978.

INDUSTRY AND TRADE

Industry. In 1981 manufacturing establishments employed 23,700 production workers who earned an estimated $285·2m.; value added by manufacture was estimated at $782·9m.

Commerce. In 1979 imports of newsprint, fertilizer, lumber, feed, crude oil and other products from foreign countries such as Saudi Arabia, Indonesia and Japan exceeded $1,238·5m. In 1979 exports, primarily food and manufactures, amounted to $176·1m. About 68% of Hawaii's overseas trade is with the mainland USA.

Tourism. Tourism is an outstanding factor in Hawaii's economy. Tourist arrivals numbered 109,798 in 1955, and reached 3·92m. in 1980. Tourist expenditures, totalling $55m. in 1955, contributed $3,000m. to the state's economy in 1980.

COMMUNICATIONS

Roads. In 1980 there were 617,571 motor vehicles, and a total of 3,912 miles of highways (including 1,085 miles of federally assisted highways and federal highways in national parks).

Aviation. There were 10 commercial airports in 1980; passengers arriving from overseas numbered 4·3m., and there were 6·7m. passengers between the islands.

Shipping. Several lines of steamers connect the islands with the mainland USA, Canada, Australia, the Philippines, China and Japan. In 1978, 10,344 inbound vessels entered Hawaiian ports; cargo arriving, 1977, 9·5m. tons; passengers arriving, 14,073.

Post. There were 712,000 telephones at 1 Jan. 1981.

JUSTICE, RELIGION, EDUCATION AND WELFARE

Justice. There is no capital punishment in Hawaii.

Religion. The residents of Hawaii are mainly Christians, though there are many Buddhists. A sample survey in 1979 showed that 31% were Roman Catholic, 34% Protestant, 12% Buddhist, 2·5% Latter Day Saints.

Education. Education is free, and compulsory for children between the ages of 6 and 18. The language in the schools is English. In 1980–81 there were 230 public schools (165,094 pupils with 8,113 teachers) and 141 private schools (37,878 pupils and 2,211 teachers) ranging from kindergarten through the 12th grade. The University of Hawaii, founded in 1907, had 20,833 day students in 1979; total university and college attendance 1980–81, 49,871.

Social Security. During 1979 the state spent $244·9m., the federal government met 41% of this fund. In 1979 there were 25 non-military hospitals (2,850 beds in 1979) listed by the Department of Health. During 1980 the average number of persons served by major welfare programmes was 71,693. In early 1980, 6·6% of all welfare recipients were recent migrants to Hawaii.

Books of Reference

Government in Hawaii. Tax Foundation of Hawaii. Honolulu, 1980
Guide to Government in Hawaii. 7th ed. Legislative Reference Bureau. State of Hawaii, Honolulu, 1980
All About Hawaii: Thrum's Hawaiian Annual and Standard Guide. Honolulu, 1875 to date
Current Hawaiiana (quarterly bibliography). Hawaii Library Association, Honolulu
Allen, G. E., *Hawaii's War Years.* 2 vols. Hawaii Univ. Press, 1950–52
Day, A. Grove, *Hawaii and Its People.* New York, 1955.—and Stroven, C., *A Hawaiian Reader.* New York, 1961
Fodor, E., (ed.), *Hawaii, 1965.* New York, 1965
Fuchs, L. E., *Hawaii Pono: A Social History.* New York, 1961
Kamins, Robert M., *Hawaii's Revised Tax System.* Honolulu, 1957
Kuykendall, R. S., and Day, A. G., *Hawaii, A History.* Rev. ed. New Jersey, 1961
Mann, A. F., *Hawaii: The Fiftieth State: Government and Economy.* Honolulu, 1960
Morgan, J. R., *Hawaii.* Boulder, 1982
Pukui, M. K., and Elbert, S. H., *Hawaiian–English Dictionary.* Honolulu, 1957
Smith, Branford, *Yankees in Paradise: The New England Impact on Hawaii.* Philadelphia, 1956

IDAHO

HISTORY. Idaho was first permanently settled in 1860, although there was a mission for Indians in 1836 and a Mormon settlement in 1855. It was organized as a Territory in 1863 and admitted into the Union as a state on 3 July 1890.

AREA AND POPULATION. Idaho is bounded north by Canada, east by the Rocky Mountains of Montana and Wyoming, south by Nevada and Utah, west by Oregon and Washington. Area, 83,564 sq. miles, of which 1,153 sq. miles are inland water. In 1970 the federal government owned 33,979,389 acres (64% of the state area). Census population, 1 April 1980, 943,935, an increase of 32·4% since 1970.

Births, 1979, 19,919 (22 per 1,000 population); deaths, 6,386 (7·1); infant deaths, 202 (10·1 per 1,000 live births); marriages, 13,429 (14·8); divorces, 6,449 (7·1).

Population in 5 census years was:

	White	*Negro*	*Indian*	*Asiatic*	*Total*	*Per sq. mile*
1910	319,221	651	3,488	2,234	325,594	3·9
1930	438,840	668	3,638	1,886	445,032	5·4
1960	657,383	1,502	5,231	2,958	667,191	8·1
1970	693,375	3,655	5,413	2,526	713,008	8·5
			All others			
1980	901,641	2,716	39,578		943,935	11·3

Of the total 1980 population, 471,155 were male, 509,702 were urban and those 20 years of age or older 600,470.

The largest cities are Boise (capital) with 1980 census population of 102,160; Pocatello, 46,340; Idaho Falls, 39,734; Lewiston, 27,986; Twin Falls, 26,209; Nampa, 25,112.

CONSTITUTION AND GOVERNMENT. The constitution adopted in 1890 is still in force; it has had 87 amendments. The Legislature consists of a Senate of 35 members and a House of Representatives of 70 members, all the legislators being elected for 2 years. The Governor, Lieut.-Governor and Secretary of State are elected for 4 years. Voters are citizens, over the age of 18 years. The state is represented in Congress by 2 senators and 2 representatives.

In the 1980 presidential election Reagan polled 290,699 votes, Carter 110,192.

The state is divided into 44 counties. The capital is Boise.

Governor: John V. Evans (D.), 1983–86 ($50,000).
Lieut.-Governor: David Leroy (R.), 1983–86 ($14,000).
Secretary of State: Pete Cenarrusa (R.), 1983–86 ($37,500).

BUDGET. For the year ending 30 June 1982 (State Auditor's Office) general revenues were $406·6m. and general expenditures included education, $352·7m., transport, $129m., and public welfare, $187m.

Per capita personal income (1981) was $8,855.

NATURAL RESOURCES

Minerals. Production of the most important minerals (1980): Lead, 38,607 tonnes; silver, 13·7m. troy oz.; zinc, 27,722 tonnes; copper, 3,103 tonnes; gold, 24,140 troy oz. (1979). There is some tungsten, antimony and vadium. Non-metallic minerals include phosphate rock, barite, clay, garnet, gypsum, perlite, lime, cement, pumice, sand and gravel and dimension stone. Value of total mineral output was $522m. in 1980.

Agriculture. Agriculture is the leading industry, although a great part of the state is naturally arid. Extensive irrigation works have been carried out, bringing an estimated 3·5m. acres under irrigation; 83 reservoirs have a total capacity of 10·4m. acre-ft, 7·3m. acre-ft of which is primarily used for irrigation.

In 1982 there were 24,000 farms with a total area of 15·1m. acres (28% of the land area); average farm had 629 acres with land and buildings valued at approximately $753 per acre.

In 1982 there were 51 soil conservation districts, managed by local farmers and ranchers, covering most of the state.

Cash income, 1981, was $2,278m. ($1,322m. from crops and $956m. from livestock). The most important crops are potatoes and wheat—potatoes leading all states; in 1981 the production amounted to 84·5m. cwt, cash receipts $391m. Other crops are sugar-beet, alfalfa, barley, field peas, dry beans, onions and apples. On 1 Jan. 1982 the number of sheep was 498,000; milch cows, 168,000; all cattle, 1·85m.; swine, 150,000 (1 Dec. 1981).

Forestry. In 1981 a total of 20,635,700 acres (37·6% of the state's area) was in forests; 13,540,600 acres of this was commercial (non-reserved) forest. The volume of sawtimber in commercial forests was 139,600m. bd ft. The stumpage value of forest products was about $91m., and an additional $207m. was added by process. Ownership of commercial forests is 70% federal, 6·5% state and local government, 0·5% Indian, 22·3% private. Some 13,000 workers are involved in forestry.

INDUSTRY. In 1981 there were about 1,515 manufacturing establishments and they employed 53,000 production workers; value added by manufacture was $1,843m.

TOURISM. Money spent by travellers in 1981 was about $1,200m. Estimated state and local tax receipts from tourism, $42m. Jobs generated, 24,000 (pay-roll over $300m.).

COMMUNICATIONS

Roads. The state maintained in 1982, 4,971 miles of the total of 67,728 miles of public roads; 712,157 passenger vehicles were registered in 1981.

Railways. The state had (1982) 2,504 miles of railways (including 2 AMTRAK routes) operated by 7 companies.

Aviation. There were 85 municipally owned airports in 1982.

Shipping. Water transport is provided from the Pacific to Lewiston, by way of the Columbia and Snake rivers, a distance of 464 miles.

JUSTICE, RELIGION, EDUCATION AND WELFARE

Justice. The death penalty is mandatory for first degree murder, but has been used sparingly. Since 1926 only 3 men (white) have been executed, by hanging (2 in 1951 and 1 in 1957). The state prison system, 1 Oct. 1982, had 1,012 inmates.

Religion. The leading religious denomination is the Church of Jesus Christ of Latter Day Saints (Mormon Church), with 191,286 adherents; Roman Catholics have 53,104; Methodists, 19,017; Presbyterians, 14,130; Episcopalians, 5,000, and Lutherans, 4,602.

Education. In 1981–82 public elementary schools (grades K to 6) had 114,319 pupils and 5,199 classroom teachers; secondary schools had 90,205 pupils and 4,448 classroom teachers.

Average salary, 1981–82, of elementary and secondary classroom teachers, $16,080. The University of Idaho, founded at Moscow in 1889, had 379 professors in 1981–82 and 8,998 students. There are 9 other institutions of higher education; 5 of them are public institutions with a total enrolment (1981–82) of 21,514 (excluding vocational-technical colleges).

Social Welfare. Old-age assistance is granted to persons 65 years of age. In Aug. 1982, 1,027 persons were drawing an average of $90.79 per month; 6,385 families with 11,441 children were drawing an average of $242.51 per case (or $89.91 per eligible person); 25 blind persons, $76.24; 637 children were receiving $373.51 per child for foster care.

Health. In Aug. 1982 skilled nursing covered 4,391 beds; intermediate care, 4,580; mental intermediate care, 543.

Books of Reference

Biennial Report. Secretary of State. Boise
Idaho. Idaho First National Bank
Idaho Almanac. Division of Economic and Community Affairs, 1977
Idaho's Yesterdays. State Historical Society. Quarterly
Martin and Barber, *Idaho in the Pacific Northwest.* Boise, 1956

ILLINOIS

HISTORY. Illinois was first discovered by Joliet and Marquette, two French explorers, in 1673, and settled in 1720. In 1763 the country was ceded by the French to the British. In 1783 Great Britain recognized the title of the US to Illinois, which was organized as a Territory in 1809 and admitted into the Union on 3 Dec. 1818.

AREA AND POPULATION. Illinois is bounded north by Wisconsin, north-east by Lake Michigan, east by Indiana, south-east by the Ohio River (forming the boundary with Kentucky), west by the Mississippi River (forming the boundary with Missouri and Iowa). Area, 56,345 sq. miles, of which 700 sq. miles are inland water. Census population, 1980, 11,418,461, an increase of 2·71% since 1970. Births in 1980 were 186,578; deaths, 100,356; infant deaths, 2,693; marriages 110,667; divorces, 50,405.

Population in 5 census years was:

	White	*Negro*	*Indian*	*All others*	*Total*	*Per sq. mile*
1910	5,526,962	109,049	188	2,392	5,638,591	100·6
1930	7,295,267	328,972	469	5,946	7,630,654	136·4
1960	9,010,252	1,037,470	4,704	28,732	10,081,158	180·3
			All others			
1970	9,600,381	1,425,674	87,921		11,113,976	199·4
1980	9,225,575	1,675,229	517,657		11,418,461	203·0

Of the total population in 1980, 5,533,525 were male, 9,474,939 persons were urban and 7,743,162 were 20 years of age or older.

The most populous cities with population (1980 census), are:

Chicago	3,005,072
Rockford	139,712
Peoria	124,160
Springfield (cap.)	99,637
Decatur	94,081
Joliet	77,956
Aurora	81,293
Evanston	73,706
Waukegan	67,653
Elgin	63,798

Standard Metropolitan Statistical Area population (1980 census): Chicago, 7,102,378; East St Louis, 565,874; Peoria, 365,864; Rockford, 279,514; Springfield, 176,089; Decatur, 131,375.

CONSTITUTION AND GOVERNMENT. The present constitution became effective 1 July 1971. The General Assembly consists of a House of Representatives of 177 members, elected for 2 years and a Senate of 59 members who serve 2 terms of 4 years and 1 of 2 years during a decade. Sessions are annual. The Governor and Lieut.-Governor are elected as a team for 4 years; the Comptroller and Secretary of State are elected for 4 years. Electors are citizens 18 years of age, having the usual residential qualifications.

The state is divided into legislative districts, in each of which 1 senator and 3 representatives are chosen; for the election of the latter each elector has 3 votes, of which he may cast 3 for 1 candidate or distribute them equally among no more than 3 candidates.

Illinois is represented in Congress by 2 senators and 22 representatives.

In the 1980 presidential election Reagan polled 2,358,094 votes, Carter 1,981,413.

The capital is Springfield. The state has 102 counties.

Governor: James R. Thompson (R.), 1983–86 ($58,000).
Lieut.-Governor: George Ryan (R.), 1983–86 ($45,500).
Secretary of State: Jim Edgar, 1983–86 ($50,500).

BUDGET. For the year ending 30 June 1980 general revenues were $13,743·5m. and general expenditures were $14,363·2m.

Total net long-term debt, 1 July 1980, was $3,688m.

Per capita personal income (1980) was $9,799.

ENERGY AND NATURAL RESOURCES

Minerals. Chief mineral product is coal; 88 operative mines had an output (1977) of 58·2m. tons. Mineral production also included: Crude petroleum, 26·2m. bbls; fluorspar, 142,666 short tons. Total value of mineral products, 1977, was $1,581m.

Agriculture. In 1980, 105,000 farms had an area of 28·6m. acres; the average farm was 272 acres.

Cash receipts, 1979, from crops, $4,591·5m.; from livestock and livestock products, $2,368·4m. Illinois is a large producer of soybeans, the state's leading cash commodity. Output, 1979, was 374·2m. bu. Other crops were, in 1979, maize, 1,358m. bu.; wheat, 55·9m. bu; oats, 16·2m. bu. In Jan. 1980 there were 235,000 milch cows, 2·7m. all cattle, 190,000 sheep and 6·9m. swine (1979). The wool clip in 1979 was 1·3m. lb.

Forestry. National forest area under the US Forest Service administration, 1979, was 259,000 acres.

INDUSTRY AND TRADE

Industry. In 1977, 19,517 manufacturing establishments employed 1,286,200 workers, earning $18,740·8m.; value added by manufacture was $40,279m. Largest industry was machinery (excluding electrical).

Labour. In 1980 there were 4·89m. employees, of whom 1·2m. were in manufacturing, 1·1m. in trade, 944,000 in services, 764,000 in government.

COMMUNICATIONS

Roads. In 1979 there were 7·5m. passenger cars, 1·3m. trucks and buses, 924,372 trailers (1978) and 281,000 motor cycles registered in the state. In 1979 there were 17,604 miles of state administered roads. There were 4,291 miles of interstate or freeway roads.

Railways. There were 1978, 10,672 miles of main line railway.

Shipping. In 1974 the seaport of Chicago handled exports of 594,291 short tons and imports of 1·23m. short tons. Overseas grain exports were 481,424 short tons.

Aviation. There were (1979) 751 certified airports, 130 heliports and 569 restricted landing areas.

Post. In 1976 there were 9,110,273 telephones in the state.

JUSTICE, RELIGION, EDUCATION AND WELFARE

Justice. In 1980 there were no executions; since 1930 there have been 90 executions (electrocution), including 58 white men, 1 white woman and 31 Negro men, all for murder. In 1979 the total average daily prison population was 11,211.

A Civil Rights Act (1941), as amended, bans all forms of discrimination by places of public accommodation, including inns, restaurants, retail stores, railroads, aeroplanes, buses, etc., against persons on account of 'race, religion, colour, national ancestry or physical or mental handicap'; another section similarly mentions 'race or colour.'

The Fair Employment Practices Act of 1961, as amended, prohibits discrimination in employment based on race, colour, sex, religion, national origin or ancestry, by employers, employment agencies, labour organizations and others. These principles are embodied in the 1971 constitution.

Religion. Among the larger religious denominations are: Roman Catholic, Jewish, United Presbyterian Church, USA, Lutheran Church in America, Lutheran Church Missouri Synod, American Baptist, Disciples of Christ, and Methodist.

Education. Education is free and compulsory for children between 7 and 16 years of age. In 1980–81 there were 1,011 school districts. Public school elementary enrolments were 1,334,904 pupils and 59,865 teachers; secondary enrolments, 648,554 pupils and 32,373 teachers. Enrolment (1980–81) in non-public schools was 261,466 elementary and 91,690 secondary. Teachers' salaries, 1980–81, averaged $19,519. Total expenditure on public schools, 1979–80, $4,923m. Total enrolment in institutions of higher education (autumn 1979) was 611,412.

Colleges and universities with over 3,000 students:

Founded	*Name*	*Place*	*Control*	*Autumn 1980 Enrolment*
1851	Northwestern University	Evanston	Methodist	15,793
1857	Illinois State University	Normal	Public	19,000
1867	University of Illinois	Urbana	Public	61,000
1869	Chicago State University [1]	Chicago	Public	7,125
1869	Southern Illinois University	Carbondale	Public	27,255
1870	Loyola University	Chicago	Roman Catholic	14,909
1890	University of Chicago	Chicago	Non-Sect.	8,700
1895	Eastern Illinois University	Charleston	Public	9,600
1895	Northern Illinois University	DeKalb	Public	27,000
1897	Bradley University	Peoria	Non-Sect.	4,893
1898	DePaul University	Chicago	Roman Catholic	12,857
1899	Western Illinois University	Macomb	Public	11,030
1940	Illinois Institute of Technology [2]	Chicago	Non-Sect.	9,200
1945	Roosevelt University	Chicago	Non-Sect.	4,245
1961	Northeastern Illinois University [3]	Chicago	Public	10,061

[1] Formerly Illinois Teachers College (South).
[2] Illinois Institute of Technology formed in 1940 by merger of two older technical schools.
[3] Formerly Illinois Teachers' College (North).

Health. In 1980 hospitals listed by the American Hospital Association numbered 285, with 73,535 beds. In 1980 state institutions for the mentally retarded had 3,791 residents and state hospitals for the mentally ill, 4,368.

Social Security. In 1978, 41,967 persons were drawing old age assistance totalling $3·9m., 767,399 were drawing aid to dependent children totalling $60·4m., 1,623 persons blind assistance totalling $0·2m. and 85,429 persons assistance to the disabled totalling $13·3m.

Books of Reference

Blue Book of the State of Illinois. Edited by Secretary of State. Springfield. Biennial
Federal Writers' Project. *Illinois: A Descriptive and Historical Guide.* Rev. ed. Chicago, 1947
Angle, P. M., and Beyer, R. L., *A Handbook of Illinois History.* Illinois State Historical Society, Springfield, 1943
Pease, T. C., *The Story of Illinois.* 3rd ed. Chicago, 1965

The Illinois State Library: Springfield, Il.627567. *State Librarian:* Jim Edgar.

INDIANA

HISTORY. Indiana, first settled in 1732–33, was made a Territory in 1800 and admitted into the Union on 11 Dec. 1816.

AREA AND POPULATION. Indiana is bounded west by Illinois, north by Michigan and Lake Michigan, east by Ohio and south by Kentucky across the Ohio River. Area, 36,185 sq. miles, of which 253 sq. miles are inland water. Census population, 1 April 1980, was 5,490,224, an increase of 294,832 or 5·7% since 1970. In 1980 births were 88,420 (16·1 per 1,000 population); deaths 47,300 (8·6); infant deaths, 1,049 (11·9 per 1,000 live births); marriages 57,853 (10·5).

Population in 5 census years was:

	White	*Negro*	*Indian*	*Asiatic*	*Total*	*Per sq. mile*
1910	2,639,961	60,320	279	316	2,700,876	74·9
1930	3,125,778	111,982	285	458	3,238,503	89·4
1960	4,388,554	269,275	948	2,447	4,662,498	128·9
			All others			
1970	4,820,324	357,464	15,881		5,193,669	143·9
1980	5,004,394	414,785	71,045		5,490,224	152·8

Of the total in 1980, 2,665,805 were male, 3,525,298 were urban and 3,545,431 were 21 years of age or older.

The largest cities with population (census 1980) are: Indianapolis (capital), 711,539; Fort Wayne, 172,196; Gary, 151,953; Evansville, 130,496; South Bend, 109,727; Hammond, 93,714; Muncie, 77,216; Anderson, 64,695; Terre Haute, 61,125.

CONSTITUTION AND GOVERNMENT. The present constitution (the second) dates from 1851; it has had (as of Nov. 1978) 34 amendments. The General Assembly consists of a Senate of 50 members elected for 4 years, and a House of Representatives of 100 members elected for 2 years.

A constitutional amendment of 1970 allows the legislators to set the length and frequency of sessions, which are currently held annually. The Governor and Lieut.-Governor are elected for 4 years. The state is represented in Congress by 2 senators and 10 representatives.

In the 1980 presidential election Reagan polled 1,255,656 votes, Carter 844,197.

The state capital is Indianapolis. The state is divided into 92 counties and 1,008 townships.

Governor: Robert D. Orr (R.), 1981–85 ($48,000 plus expenses).
Lieut.-Governor: John Mutz (R.), 1981–85 ($34,000 plus expenses).
Secretary of State: Edwin Simcox (R.), 1978–82 ($34,000).

BUDGET. In the fiscal year 1979–80 (US Census Bureau figures) total revenues were $4,794·3m. ($882·7m. from federal government, $2,695·7m. from taxes), total expenditures were $4,866·8m. ($1,942m. for education, $574·5m. for public welfare and $645·2m. for highways).

Total long-term debt, on 30 June 1981, was $540·4m.

Per capita personal income (1980) was $8,924.

ENERGY AND NATURAL RESOURCES

Minerals. The state produced 28·6m. tons of limestone and 240,000 tons of dimension limestone in 1978; the output of coal was 23,942,000 short tons; petroleum, 5·42m. bbls (of 42 gallons). The total mineral output in 1978 was valued at $741·4m.

Agriculture. Indiana is largely agricultural, about 75% of its total area being in farms. In 1978, 95,000 farms had 17m. acres (average, 180 acres). Cash income, 1978, from crops, $1,921·5m.; from livestock and products, $1,556·7m.

The chief crops (1978) were maize (637·2m. bu.), winter wheat (31·78m. bu.), oats (8·91m. bu.), soybeans (140·42m. bu.), popcorn, rye, barley, hay (alfalfa, clover, timothy), lespedeza seed, mint, clover seed, apples, strawberries, tomatoes, water-melons and tobacco.

The livestock on 1 Jan. 1980 included 1·85m. all cattle, 200,000 milch cows, 155,000 sheep and lambs, 4·9m. swine, 21m. chickens. In 1979 the wool clip yielded 1·2m. lb. of wool from 163,000 sheep.

Forestry. The national forests area, 1 Oct. 1982, was 187,198 acres; 13 state forests and 2 state nurseries totalled 142,070 acres in June 1982.

INDUSTRY. Manufacturing establishments employed, in 1979, 750,124 workers, earning $12,713m. The steel industry is the third largest in the country.

COMMUNICATIONS

Roads. In 1979 there were 91,074 miles of highways, roads and streets, of which 66,313 miles were county highways and 11,183 miles state highways. Motor vehicles registered, 1981, 4,374,141.

Railways. In 1979 there were 5,269 miles of mainline railway and 2,796 miles of branch lines.

Aviation. Of airports, 1979, 130 were for public use, 350 were private and 1 was military.

JUSTICE, RELIGION, EDUCATION AND WELFARE

Justice. In 1963–80 there were no executions; since 1930 there have been 2 executions (electrocution), both for murder. State correctional institutions, 1 Oct. 1982, had 9,431 inmates.

The Civil Rights Act of 1885 forbids places of public accommodation to bar any persons on grounds not applicable to all citizens alike; no citizen may be disqualified for jury service 'on account of race or colour'. An Act of 1947 makes it an offence to spread religious or racial hatred.

A 1961 Act provided 'all . . . citizens equal opportunity for education, employment and access to public conveniences and accommodations' and created a Civil Rights Commission.

Religion. Religious denominations include Methodists, Roman Catholic, Disciples of Christ, Baptists, Evangelical United Brethren, Presbyterian churches, Society of Friends.

Education. School attendance is compulsory from 7 to 16 years. In 1980–81 public and parochial schools, had 1,150,883 pupils and 50,715 teachers. Teachers' salaries, grades 1–12, averaged $17,222. Total expenditure for public schools, 1980–81, $2,343·9m.

The principal institutions for higher education are (1977):

Founded	*Institution*	*Control*	*Teachers*	*Students (full-time)*
1824	Indiana University, Bloomington	State	3,223	77,948
1837	De Pauw University, Greencastle	Methodist	145	2,384
1842	University of Notre Dame	R.C.	780	8,556
1850	Butler University, Indianapolis	—	360	4,117
1859	Valparaiso University, Valparaiso	Evangelical Lutheran Church	343	3,537
1870	Indiana State University, Terre Haute	State	700	15,593
1874	Purdue University, Lafayette	State	2,376	40,997
1898	Ball State University, Muncie	State	881	17,547

Health. Hospitals listed by the Indiana State Board of Health (1981) numbered 120 (23,929 beds). On 30 June 1981, 11 state mental hospitals had 6,860 patients enrolled (4,764 present).

Social Security. Old-age assistance, assistance to the blind and to the disabled were transferred from state to federal programmes in June 1974. In July–Dec. 1981, state supplemental assistance and/or Federal Supplemental Security assistance was paid to an average of 14,096 elderly persons per month (total $8·1m.), 1,124 blind ($1·2m.) and 25,061 disabled ($23·8m.).

Books of Reference

Indiana State Chamber of Commerce. *Here is Your Indiana Government.* 18th ed. Indianapolis, 1977
Martin, J. B., *Indiana: An Interpretation.* New York, 1947

State Library: Indiana State Library, 140 North Senate, Indianapolis 46204. *Director:* C. Ray Ewick.

IOWA

HISTORY. Iowa, first settled in 1788, was made a Territory in 1838 and admitted into the Union on 28 Dec. 1846.

AREA AND POPULATION. Iowa is bounded east by the Mississippi River (forming the boundary with Wisconsin and Illinois), south by Missouri, west by the Missouri River (forming the boundary with Nebraska), north-west by the Big Sioux River (forming the boundary with South Dakota) and north by Minnesota. Area, 56,275 sq. miles, including 310 sq. miles of inland water. Census population, 1 April 1980, 2,913,387, an increase of 3·17% since 1970. Births, 1980, were 47,797; deaths, 27,096; infant deaths, 565; marriages, 27,474; dissolutions of marriages, 11,854.

Population in 5 census years was:

	White	*Negro*	*Indian*	*Asiatic*	*Total*	*Per sq. mile*
1870	1,188,207	5,762	48	3	1,194,020	21·5
1930	2,452,677	17,380	660	222	2,470,939	44·1
1960	2,729,286	25,354	1,708	1,022	2,757,537	49·2
			All others			
1970	2,782,762	32,596	10,010		2,825,368	50·5
1980	2,838,805	41,700	32,882		2,913,387	51·7

At the census of 1980, 1,416,195 were male, 1,624,547 were urban and 1,971,502 were 20 years of age or older.

The largest cities in the state, with their census population in 1980 are: Des Moines (capital), 191,003; Cedar Rapids, 110,243; Davenport, 103,264; Sioux City, 82,003; Waterloo, 75,985; Dubuque, 62,321; Council Bluffs, 56,449; Iowa City, 50,508; Ames, 45,775; Clinton, 32,828; Mason City, 30,144; Burlington, 29,529; Fort Dodge, 29,423; Ottumwa, 27,381.

CONSTITUTION AND GOVERNMENT. The constitution of 1857 still exists; it has had 37 amendments. The General Assembly comprises a Senate of 50 and a House of Representatives of 100 members, meeting annually for an unlimited session. Senators are elected for 4 years, half retiring every second year: representatives for 2 years. The Governor and Lieut.-Governor are elected for 4 years. The state is represented in Congress by 2 senators and 6 representatives. Iowa is divided into 99 counties; the capital is Des Moines.

In the 1980 presidential election Reagan polled 676,026 votes, Carter 508,672.

Governor: Terry Branstad (R.), 1983–86 ($60,000).
Lieut.-Governor: Robert Anderson (D.), 1983–86 ($18,000).
Secretary of State: Mary Jane Odell (R.) ($35,600).

BUDGET. For fiscal year 1980 state tax revenue was $1,733·6m. General expenditures were $903,627,943 for education, $84,247,368 for social services and human resources, and $30,741,006 for transport.

On 30 June 1979 the net long-term debt was $299·3m.

Per capita personal income (1980) was $9,178.

ENERGY AND NATURAL RESOURCES

Minerals. The leading products by value are cement (25·8m. tons in 1979) and limestone (29·6m. tons in 1979). Coalfields produced 696,230 tons in 1979. The value of mineral products, 1980, was $258·9m.

Agriculture. Iowa is the wealthiest of the agriculture states, partly because nearly the whole area (95·5%) is arable and included in farms. It has escaped large-scale commercial farming. The average farm (in 1979) was 281 acres.

In 1979, 121,000 farms had 34m. acres of farm land.

Cash farm income (1980 estimate) was $10,040m. (ranks second); from livestock, $5,487m., and from crops, $4,553m. Production of corn grain in 1980 was 1,460m. bu. Red meat production in 1980 totalled 6,520m. lb. On 1 Dec. 1980 livestock included swine, 16·1m. (leading all states); milch cows, 376,000; all cattle, 7·45m., and sheep and lambs, 408,000. The wool clip (1980) yielded 3·3m. lb. of wool.

INDUSTRY. In 1978 manufacturing establishments employed 246,600 people with annual payroll at $3,725·4m., value added by manufacture was $9,846m.

COMMUNICATIONS

Roads. On 1 Jan. 1980 number of miles of streets and highways was 112,080; there were 2·5m. licensed drivers and 2·9m. registered vehicles.

Railways. The state, 1980, had 6,900 miles of track, 8 Class I railways and 7 Class III railways.

Aviation. Airports (1980), numbered 355, including 131 lighted airports and 90 all-weather runways. There were almost 3,200 private aircraft.

JUSTICE, RELIGION, EDUCATION AND WELFARE

Justice. There is now no capital punishment in Iowa. State prisons, 12 Oct. 1981, had 2,598 inmates.

Religion. Chief religious bodies in 1980 were: Roman Catholic (542,698 members); United Methodists, 258,252; American Lutheran, 200,712 baptised members; United Presbyterians, 85,000; United Church of Christ, 50,679.

Education. School attendance is compulsory for 24 consecutive weeks annually during school age (7–16). In 1980–81 532,683 were attending primary and secondary schools; 51,880 pupils attending non-public schools. Classroom teachers (1980–81) numbered 32,828 with average salary of $15,150. Total expenditure on public schools in 1980–81 was $1,425,609,000. Leading institutions for higher education (1980–81) were:

Founded	*Institution*	*Control*	*Full-time Professors*	*Students*
1843	Clarke College, Dubuque	Independent	52	850
1847	University of Iowa, Iowa City	State	1,022	14,575
1847	Grinnell College, Grinnell	Independent	83	1,234
1852	Wartburg College, Waverly	American Lutheran	57	1,078
1853	Cornell College, Mount Vernon	Independent	53	1,129
1858	Iowa State University, Ames	State	1,253	18,639
1876	Univ. of Northern Iowa, Cedar Falls	State	536	8,184
1881	Drake University, Des Moines	Independent	206	3,777
1881	Coe College, Cedar Rapids	Independent	64	1,129
1894	Morningside College, Sioux City	Methodist	61	1,110

Health. In 1981, the state had 141 hospitals (about 20,476 beds). In July 1980 hospitals for mental diseases had 1,754 resident patients.

Social Security. Iowa has a Civil Rights Act (1939) which makes it a misdemeanour for any place of public accommodation to deprive any person of 'full and equal enjoyment' of the facilities it offers the public.

Old-age assistance was established in 1934 for citizens 65 years of age or older; in July 1981, 13,678 persons were drawing an average of $84.33 per month. Aid to dependent children, established 1974, was received by 38,621 families ($305.95 per family) representing 102,512 persons; aid to disabled was paid to 16,988 persons (average, $160.27); 1,039 recipients of aid to the blind averaged $160.07.

Books of Reference

Statistical Information: State Departments of Health, Public Instruction and Social Services; State Aeronautics, Commerce and Development Commissions; Crop and Livestock Reporting Services, Des Moines; Iowa Dept. of Transportation, Ames; Geological Survey, Iowa City; Iowa College Aid Commission.

Annual Survey of Manufactures. US Department of Commerce
Government Finance. US Department of Commerce
Official Register. Secretary of State. Des Moines. Biennial
Petersen, W. J., *Iowa History Reference Guide.* Iowa City, 1952

Iowa State Library: Des Moines 50319.

KANSAS

HISTORY. Kansas, settled in 1727, was made a Territory (along with part of Colorado) in 1854, and was admitted into the Union with its present area on 29 Jan. 1861.

AREA AND POPULATION. Kansas is bounded north by Nebraska, east by Missouri, with the Missouri River as boundary in the north-east, south by Oklahoma and west by Colorado. Area, 82,277 sq. miles, including 499 sq. miles of inland water. Census population, 1 April 1980, 2,363,208, an increase of 5·1% since 1970. Vital statistics, 1980: Births, 39,330 (16·7 per 1,000 population); deaths, 21,399 (9); infant deaths, 377 (9·6 per 1,000 live births); marriages, 24,928 (10·5); divorces 13,399 (5·6).

Population in 5 federal census years was:

	White	*Negro*	*Indian*	*Asiatic*	*Total*	*Per sq. mile*
1870	346,377	17,108	914	—	364,399	4·5
1930	1,811,997	66,344	2,454	204	1,880,999	22·9
1960	2,078,666	91,445	5,069	2,271	2,178,611	26·3
			All others			
1970	2,122,068	106,977	17,533		2,249,071	27·5
1980	2,167,752	126,127	69,329		2,363,208	28·8

Of the total population in 1980, 1,156,720 were male, 1,575,899 were urban and those 20 years of age or older numbered 1,620,368.

Cities, with 1980 census population, are Wichita, 279,352; Kansas City, 159,972; Topeka (capital), 115,996; Overland Park, 81,385; Lawrence, 52,003.

CONSTITUTION AND GOVERNMENT. The year 1861 saw the adoption of the present constitution; it has had 54 amendments. The Legislature includes a Senate of 40 members, elected for 4 years, and a House of Representatives of 125 members, elected for 2 years. Sessions are annual. The Governor and Lieut.-Governor are elected for 2 years. The right to vote (with the usual exceptions) is possessed by all citizens. The state is represented in Congress by 2 senators and 5 representatives.

The state was the first (of 42 states) to establish in 1933 a Legislative Council of

10 senators and 15 representatives to sit continuously between sessions for the study of legislative problems.

In the 1980 presidential election Reagan polled 566,812 votes, Carter 326,150.

The capital is Topeka. The state is divided into 105 counties.

Governor: John Carlin (D.), 1983–86 ($45,000).
Lieut.-Governor: Thomas Docking (D.), 1983–86 ($13,500).
Secretary of State: Jack H. Brier (R.) ($27,500).

BUDGET. For the year ending 30 June 1980 (US Census Bureau figures) general revenue was $2,418,808,000. General expenditures were $2,254,031,000.

Total net long-term debt, 30 June 1980, amounted to $438·14m.

Per capita personal income (1980) was $9,983.

ENERGY AND NATURAL RESOURCES

Minerals. Important minerals are coal, petroleum, natural gas, lead and zinc. Value of production (1980), $3,500m.

Agriculture. Kansas is pre-eminently agricultural, but sometimes suffers from lack of rainfall in the west. In 1978, 77,129 farms covered 91·2% of the land area; average farm, 619 acres.

Cash income, 1980, from crops was $2,525m.; from livestock and products, $3,361·7m.

Kansas is a great wheat-producing state. Its output in 1980 was 420m. bu. Other crops in 1980 (in bushels) were maize, 116·5m.; soybeans, 24m.; oats, 4·5m.; barley, 2·4m. The state has an extensive livestock industry, comprising, on 1 Jan. 1981, 123,000 milch cows, 6·45m. all cattle, 208,000 sheep and lambs 1·9m. swine. Wool clip (1978), 1,612,000 lb. from 219,000 sheep.

INDUSTRY. Employment distribution (1980): 18·6% in trade, 15·6% in manufacturing, 15·5% in government and 14·1% in services. Value added by manufacture in 1978 was $6,100m. The slaughtering industry, other food processing, aircraft, the manufacture of transport equipment and petroleum refining are important.

COMMUNICATIONS

Roads. The state in 1979 had 135,000 miles of roads and streets including 8,908 miles of primary federally-aided highways.

Railways. There were 7,621 miles of railway in 1974.

Aviation. There were 272 airports in 1969, of which 119 were public.

JUSTICE, RELIGION, EDUCATION AND WELFARE

Justice. There were 2,290 prisoners in state institutions, Jan. 1980. The death penalty (by hanging) for murder was abolished in 1907 and restored in 1935; there have been no executions since 1968; executions 1934 to 1968 have been 15 (all for murder).

For the various Civil Rights Acts forbidding racial or political discrimination, *see* THE STATESMAN'S YEAR-BOOK, 1955, p. 666. The 1965 Kansas Act against Discrimination declared that it is the policy of the state to eliminate and prevent discrimination in all employment relations, and to eliminate and prevent discrimination, segregation or separation in all places of public accommodations covered by the Act.

Religion. The most numerous religious bodies are Roman Catholic, Methodists and Disciples of Christ.

Education. In 1979–80 organized school districts had 1,801 elementary and secondary schools which had (1980) 423,000 pupils and 26,200 teachers. Average salary of public school teachers, $15,000 (elementary) and $15,100 (secondary). There were 52 institutions of higher education with 136,600 students.

Kansas has 6 state supported institutions of higher education: the University of Kansas, Lawrence, founded in 1865; Kansas State University of Agriculture and Applied Science, Manhattan (1863); Kansas State Teachers' College, Emporia (1865); Kansas State College of Pittsburg, Pittsburg (1903); Fort Hays State College, Hays (1901) and Wichita State University (1964), an associate of the University of Kansas. There is one municipal university, Washburn University, Topeka (1944).

Health. In 1979 the state had 164 hospitals (18,400 beds) listed by the American Hospital Association; hospitals had an average daily census of 13,101.

Social Security. In Dec. 1980, 92,100 persons received state and federal aid under programmes of aid to the aged or disabled and aid to dependent children. Total payments amounted to $114·9m. in 1980.

Books of Reference

Annual Economic Report of the Governor. Topeka
Directory of State Officers, Boards and Commissioners and Interesting Facts Concerning Kansas. Topeka, Biennial
Drury, J. W., *The Government of Kansas.* Lawrence, Univ. of Kansas, 1970
Zornow, W. F., *Kansas: A History of the Jayhawk State.* Norman, Okla., 1957

State Library: Kansas State Library, Topeka.

KENTUCKY

HISTORY. Kentucky, first settled in 1765, was originally part of Virginia; it was admitted into the Union on 1 June 1792 and its first legislature met on 4 June.

AREA AND POPULATION. Kentucky is bounded north by the Ohio River (forming the boundary with Illinois, Indiana and Ohio), north-east by the Big Sandy River (forming the boundary with West Virginia), east by Virginia, south by Tennessee and west by the Mississippi River (forming the boundary with Missouri). Area, 40,409 sq. miles, of which 740 sq. miles are water. Census population, 1980 3,660,777, an increase of 13·6% since 1970. Births in 1980, 59,550 (16·9 per 1,000 population); deaths, 33,765 (9·6); infant deaths, 590 (9·9 per 1,000 live births); marriages, 32,727 (9·3); divorces, 16,731 (4·7).

Population in 5 census years was:

	White	*Negro*	*All others*	*Total*	*Per sq. mile*
1930	2,388,364	226,040	185	2,614,589	65·1
1950	2,742,090	201,921	795	2,944,806	73·9
1960	2,820,083	215,949	2,124	3,038,156	76·2
1970	2,981,766	230,793	6,147	3,218,706	81·2
1980	3,379,006	259,477	22,294	3,660,777	92·3

Of the total population in 1980, an estimated 1,789,000 were male, 1,862,183 were urban and 2,359,614 were 21 years old or older.

The principal cities with census population in 1980 are: Louisville, 298,451 (urbanized area, 654,938); Lexington-Fayette, 204,165; Owensboro, 54,450; Covington, 49,563; Bowling Green, 40,450; Paducah, 29,315; Hopkinsville, 27,318; Ashland, 27,064; Frankfort (capital), 25,973.

CLIMATE. Kentucky has a temperate climate. Temperatures are moderate during both winter and summer, precipitation is ample without a pronounced dry season, and there is little snow during the winter. The average annual temperature ranges from 54° to 59°. Average annual rainfall ranges from 36 to 50 inches.

CONSTITUTION AND GOVERNMENT. The constitution dates from

1891; there had been 3 preceding it. The 1891 constitution was promulgated by convention and provides that amendments be submitted to the electorate for ratification. The General Assembly consists of a Senate of 38 members elected for 4 years, one half retiring every 2 years, and a House of Representatives of 100 members elected for 2 years. A constitutional amendment approved by the voters in Nov. 1979, changes the year in which legislators are elected from odd to even numbered years and establishes an organizational session of the legislature, limited to ten legislative days, in odd-numbered years. The amendment provides for regular sessions limited to 60 legislative days between the first Tuesday after the first Monday of Jan. and 15 April of even numbered years. The Governor and Lieut.-Governor are elected for 4 years. All citizens are (with necessary exceptions) qualified as electors; the voting age was in 1955 reduced from 21 to 18 years. Registered votes, Aug. 1981: 1,819,075. In the 1980 presidential election Reagan polled 635,274 votes, Carter 617,417.

The state is represented in Congress by 2 senators and 7 representatives.

The capital is Frankfort. The state is divided into 120 counties.

Governor: John Y. Brown, Jr. (D.), 1983–86 ($50,000).
Lieut.-Governor: Martha Layne Collins (D.) ($47,311).
Secretary of State: Frances Jones Mills (D.) ($47,311).

BUDGET. For the fiscal year ending 30 June 1982 revenues received within the five major operating funds amounted to $3,959m. Included in this figure are $2,098m. General Fund revenues and $804m. Federal revenues. Total expenditures amounted to $4,566m. including education, $1,719m.; public assistance, $859m.; and transport, $684m.

The general obligation bonded indebtedness on 30 June 1982 was $246m.

Per capita personal income (1981) was $8,420.

ENERGY AND NATURAL RESOURCES

Minerals. The principal mineral product of Kentucky is coal, 157·6m. short tons mined in 1981, value $4,608·6m. Output of petroleum, 6·5m. bbls (of 42 gallons); natural gas, 61,312m. cu. ft, value $61·8m.; stone, 32·1m. short tons, value $106m.; clay 360,000 short tons, value $2·4m.; sand and gravel, 7m. short tons, value $15·2m.. Total value of non-fuel mineral products in 1981 was $209,977,000. Other minerals include fluorspar, ball clay, lead, zinc, silver, cement, lime, and industrial sand and gravel.

Agriculture. In 1982, 103,000 farms had an area of 14·5m. acres. The average farm was 141 acres.

Cash income, 1981, from crops, $1,424m., and from livestock, $1,359m. The chief crop is tobacco: production, in 1981, 796·8m. lb., ranking second to N. Carolina in US. Other principal crops include corn, soybeans, wheat, barley, sorghum grain, hay, oats and rye.

Stock-raising is important in Kentucky, which has long been famous for its horses. The livestock in 1982 included 240,000 milch cows, 2·6m. cattle and calves, 25,000 sheep, 1m. swine.

Forestry. Total forests area, 1978, 12,160,800 acres. Total commercial forest land, 1978, 11,901,900 acres; 92% is privately owned.

INDUSTRY. In 1981 the state's 3,227 manufacturing plants had 199,800 production workers; value added by manufacture in 1978 was $10,800m. The leading manufacturing industries (by employment) are non-electrical machinery, electrical equipment, apparel and other fabric products and foods. Direct foreign investment in manufacturing by foreign investors was $107m. in 1981.

TOURISM. In 1981 tourist expenditure was $1,770m., producing over $110m. in tax revenues and generating 96,000 jobs. The state had (1981) 765 hotels and motels, 198 campgrounds and 43 state parks.

COMMUNICATIONS

Roads. In 1982 the state had over 69,000 miles of federal, state and local roads. There were over 2·7m. motor vehicle registrations in 1981.

Railways. In 1982 there were about 3,300 miles of railway.

Aviation. There are (1982) 117 aircraft landing areas and 2,000 registered aircraft in Kentucky. Seven airports served 5–6m. passengers with scheduled services in 1981.

Shipping. There is an increasing amount of barge traffic on 1,453·8 miles of navigable rivers. There are 7 river ports and 2 are being developed.

JUSTICE, RELIGION, EDUCATION AND WELFARE

Justice. There are 9 correctional institutions. Juvenile offenders are placed in custody of the Bureau for Social Services, Department for Human Resources, which maintains 9 institutions.

In 1981–82 the prisons had an average of 3,797 inmates. There has been no execution since 1962. A session of Congress in 1976 limited the death penalty to cases of kidnap and murder.

Total executions, 1911–62, were 162, including 76 whites and 86 Negroes; 144 were for murder, 7 for rape, 6 for criminal offences, 5 for armed robbery.

Religion. The chief religious denominations in 1980 were: Southern Baptists, with 883,096 members, Roman Catholic (365,277), United Methodists (234,536), Christian Churches and Church of Christ (81,222) and Christian (Disciples of Christ) (78,275).

Education. Attendance at school between the ages of 6 and 15 years (inclusive) is compulsory, the normal term being 175 days. In 1981–82, 21,060 teachers were employed in public elementary and 11,394 in secondary schools, in which 436,817 and 221,533 pupils enrolled respectively. Expenditure on elementary and secondary day schools in 1981–82 was about $1,356·8m.; public school classroom teachers' salaries (1981–82) averaged $17,294.

There were also 4,036 teachers working in private elementary and secondary schools with 73,084 students.

The state has 24 universities and senior colleges, 5 junior colleges and 13 community colleges, with a total (autumn 1981) of 135,461 students. Of these universities and colleges, 22 are state-supported, and the remainder are supported privately. The largest of the institutions of higher learning are (autumn 1981): University of Kentucky, with 23,441 students; University of Louisville, 20,302 students; Western Kentucky University, 13,174 students; Eastern Kentucky University, 13,394 students; Murray State University, 7,722 students; Morehead State University, 6,739 students; Northern Kentucky University, 8,835 students. Five of the several privately endowed colleges of standing are Berea College, Berea; Centre College, Danville; Transylvania University, Lexington; Georgetown College, Georgetown; and Bellarmine College, Louisville.

Health. In 1982 the state had 111 licensed general hospitals (15,949 beds), 10 psychiatric hospitals (1,482 beds) and 4 children's hospitals (264 beds).

Welfare. In June 1982 there were 240,903 persons receiving financial assistance; 91,348 of these persons received the Federal Supplemental Security Income (SSI); 37,373 of them were aged, 2,033 blind, 51,942 disabled. The average monthly SSI payment in each group is as follows: $116.15 to aged, $213.48 to blind and $194.60 to disabled. Also, in the all state funded Supplementation programme payments were made in June 1982 to 7,845 persons, of which 4,373 were aged, 103 blind and 3,369 disabled. The average State Supplementation payment was $108.99 to aged, $70.79 to blind and $120.49 to disabled.

In the Aid to Families with Dependent Children Programme as of June 1982, aid was given to 147,813 persons in 55,523 families. The average payment per person was $68.65, per family $183.26.

In addition to money payments, medical assistance, food stamps and social services are available.

Books of Reference

Kentucky 1983 Economic Statistics. 19th ed. Department of Economic Development, Frankfort, 1983

LOUISIANA

HISTORY. Louisiana was first settled in 1699. That part lying east of the Mississippi River was organized in 1804 as the Territory of New Orleans, and admitted into the Union on 30 April 1812. The section west of the river was added very shortly thereafter.

AREA AND POPULATION. Louisiana is bounded north by Arkansas, east by Mississippi, with the Mississippi River forming the boundary in the north-east, south by the Gulf of Mexico and west by Texas, with the Sabine River forming most of the boundary. Area, 52,453 sq. miles, including lakes, rivers and coastal waters inside 3-mile limit; land area, 44,873 sq. miles. Census population, 1 April 1980, 4,205,900, an increase of 15·5% since 1970. Births, 1979, 79,344 (19·7 per 1,000 population); deaths, 35,082 (8·8); infant deaths, 1,272 (15·5 per 1,000 live births); marriages, 41,347; divorces, 15,145.

Population in 5 census years was:

	White	*Negro*	*Indian*	*Asiatic*	*Total*	*Per sq. mile*
1910	941,086	713,874	780	648	1,656,388	36·5
1930	1,322,712	776,326	1,536	1,019	2,101,593	46·5
1960	2,211,715	1,039,207	3,587	2,004	3,257,022	72·2
			All others			
1970	2,541,498	1,086,832	12,976		3,641,306	81·1
1980	2,911,243	1,237,263	55,466		4,203,972[1]	93·5

[1] Preliminary.

Of the 1980 total, 2,039,894 were male, 2,885,535 were urban; those 20 years of age or older numbered 2,699,100.

The largest cities with their 1980 census population are: New Orleans, 557,482; Baton Rouge (capital), 219,486; Shreveport, 205,815; Lafayette, 81,961; Kenner, 66,382.

CONSTITUTION AND GOVERNMENT. The present constitution dates from 1974.

The Legislature consists of a Senate of 39 members and a House of Representatives of 105 members, both chosen for 4 years. Sessions are annual; a fiscal session is held in odd years. The Governor and Lieut.-Governor are elected for 4 years.

A Governor may serve a second consecutive term. Qualified electors are (with the usual exceptions) all registered citizens with the usual residential qualifications.

In the 1980 presidential election Reagan polled 792,853 votes, Carter 708,453.

The state sends to Congress 2 senators and 8 representatives. Louisiana is divided into 64 parishes (corresponding with the counties of other states).

Governor: David C. Treen (D.), 1980–84 ($73,440).
Lieut.-Governor: Robert Freeman (D.), 1980–84 ($63,367).
Secretary of State: James Brown (D.), 1980–84 ($60,169).

BUDGET. For the fiscal year ending 30 June 1981 (Louisiana State Budget Office figures) general revenues were $6,030,986,328, of which $1,419,048,091 were federal funds; total expenditures were $5,599,275,956 (education, $1,851,754,568; transport and development, $323,029,267; health, hospitals and public welfare, $1,464,853,279).

Per capita personal income (1980) was $8,458.

ENERGY AND NATURAL RESOURCES

Minerals. The yield in 1978 of crude petroleum was 534·4m. bbls. Rich sulphur mines are found in the state, and wells for the extraction of sulphur by means of hot water and compressed air are in operation; output, 1978, 2·1m. tonnes.

Louisiana is the USA's main salt producer. Output of salt (1978) was 13·5m. short tons valued at $97m. Total output of raw, non-fuel minerals in 1980 was valued at $455m.

Agriculture. The state is divided into two parts, the uplands and the alluvial and swamp regions of the coast. A delta occupies about one-third of the total area. Manufacturing is the leading industry, but agriculture is important. In 1978 there were about 35,500 farms with annual average sales of at least $1,000; average farm, 293 acres.

Cash income, 1978, from crops $980,969,000; from livestock, $438,782,000. Production of sugar-cane was valued at $109,647,000; rice, $179,539,000; sweet potatoes, $20·24m.; soybeans, $438,614,000; pecans, $7·8m.; cotton, $179·5m.; strawberries, $2·03m.

In 1979 the state contained 128,000 milch cows, 1·7m. all cattle, 13,000 sheep and 150,000 swine.

Forestry. Forests, 14·5m. acres, represent 47% of the state's area. Income from manufactured products exceeds $2,400m. annually. In 1980 pulpwood cut, 3,671,460 cords (value $5·7m.); sawtimber cut, 1,047m. bd ft.

INDUSTRY. The manufacturing industries are chiefly those associated with petroleum, chemicals, lumber, food, paper. Investment in manufacturing, 1977–80, about $8,000m.

TOURISM. Travellers spent an estimated $3,000m. in 1980 and generated over 75,000 jobs. State tax revenue, $90·3m. (nearly 4% of state tax revenue). New Orleans will be the site of the World's Fair in 1984.

COMMUNICATIONS

Roads. The state has more than 16,326 miles of public roads. In 1980, over 2m. automobiles were registered in the state.

Railways. In 1979 the railways in the state had a length of about 3,700 miles.

Aviation. There were, 1979, 240 commercial and private airports.

Shipping. In 1980 New Orleans was the first seaport of the US, handling 177·3m. tons of cargo. The Mississippi and other waterways provide 7,500 miles of navigable water.

JUSTICE, RELIGION, EDUCATION AND WELFARE

Justice. Prisons, Oct. 1981, had 8,308 inmates.

Since 1961 there have been no executions; total executions by electrocution since 1930 were 135.

Religion. The Roman Catholic Church is the largest denomination in Louisiana, with 1,316,441 members in 1979. The leading Protestant Churches are Southern Baptist, with (1979) 524,566 members; Methodist, (1979) 136,972.

Education. School attendance is compulsory between the ages of 7 and 15, both inclusive. In 1979–80 there were 1,490 public elementary and high schools which had 829,651 pupils with a current expenditure of $1,928 per pupil. Private schools had 154,296. In 1979–80, instructional staff had an average salary of $14,068.

There are 16 four-year public colleges and universities and 12 non-public four-year institutions of higher learning. There are 53 state trade and vocational-technical schools. Superior instruction is given in the Louisiana State University system with 55,915 students (1981). Tulane University in New Orleans had 10,050 students (1981). The Roman Catholic Loyola University in New Orleans had 4,500 students (1981). Dillard University in New Orleans (12,480 students in 1981) and the Southern University system (12,000 students in 1981) were formerly for Negroes.

Health. In 1982 the state had 156 licensed hospitals (25,410 beds); 3 mental hospitals cared for 12,381 patients.

Social Security. In Dec. 1980, assistance was being given to 76,457 elderly persons; 73,381 families with dependent children; 1,759 blind persons; 49,609 totally disabled persons; 4,095 general assistance cases and 1,023 Vietnamese and Cambodian refugees. Aid was from state and federal sources.

Books of Reference

Louisiana Almanac. New Orleans, 1979–80
The History and Government of Louisiana. Legislative Council, Baton Rouge, 1975
Louisiana State Agencies Handbook. Public Affairs Research Council of Louisiana. Baton Rouge, 1979
The State of the State: an Economic and Social Report to the Governor. Louisiana State Planning Office, New Orleans, 1978
Statistical Abstract of Louisiana. Division of Business and Economic Research, Univ. of New Orleans, 1977
Davis, E. A., *Louisiana, the Pelican State.* Louisiana State Univ. Press, Baton Rouge, 1975
Hansen, H., (ed.), *Louisiana, a Guide to the State.* Rev. ed. New York, 1971
Kniffen, F. B., *Louisiana, its Land and People.* Louisiana State Univ. Press, Baton Rouge, 1968

State Library: The Louisiana State Library, Baton Rouge, Louisiana. *State Librarian:* Thomas F. Jaques.

MAINE

HISTORY. After a first attempt in 1607, Maine was settled in 1623. From 1652 to 1820 it was part of Massachusetts and was admitted into the Union on 15 March 1820.

AREA AND POPULATION. Maine is bounded west, north and east by Canada, south-east by the Atlantic, south and south-west by New Hampshire. Area, 33,265 sq. miles, of which 2,269 are inland water. Of the state's total area, about 17·2m. acres (87%) are in timber and wood lots. Census population, 1 April 1980 1,125,027, an increase of 14·57% since 1970. In 1980 live births numbered 16,095; deaths, 10,857; infant deaths, 140; marriages, 14,351; divorces 6,239.

Population for 5 census years was:

	White	*Negro*	*Indian*	*Asiatic*	*Total*	*Per sq. mile*
1910	739,995	1,363	892	121	742,371	24·8
1930	795,185	1,096	1,012	130	797,423	25·7
1950	910,846	1,221	1,522	185	913,774	29·4
			All others			
1970	985,276	2,800	3,972		992,048	31·0
1980	1,109,850	3,128	12,049		1,125,027	36·3

Of the total population in 1980, 48·5% were male, 40·7% were urban and 60·5% were 21 years or older.

The largest city in the state is Portland with a census population of 61,572 in 1980. Other cities (with population in 1980) are: Lewiston, 40,481; Bangor, 31,643; Auburn, 23,128; South Portland, 22,712; Augusta (capital), 21,819; Biddeford, 19,638; Waterville, 17,779.

CLIMATE. Average maximum temperatures range from 56·3°F in Waterville to 48·3°F in Caribou, but record high (since *c.* 1950) is 103°F. Average minimum ranges from 36·9°F in Rockland to 28·3°F in Greenville, but record low (also in Greenville) is –42°F. Average annual rainfall ranges from 48·85″ in Machias to 36·09″ in Houlton. Average annual snowfall ranges from 118·7″ in Greenville to 59·7″ in Rockland.

CONSTITUTION AND GOVERNMENT. The constitution of 1820 is still in force, but it has been amended 143 times. In 1951, 1965 and 1973 the Legislature approved recodifications of the constitution as arranged by the Chief Justice under special authority.

The Legislature consists of the Senate with 33 members and the House of Representatives with 151 members, both Houses being elected simultaneously for 2 years. Apart from these legislators and the Governor (elected for 4 years), no other state officers are elected. The Justices of the Supreme Judicial Court give their opinion upon important questions of law and upon solemn occasions when required by the Governor, Senate or House of Representatives. The suffrage is possessed by all citizens, 18 years of age; persons under guardianship for reasons of mental illness have no vote. Indians residing on tribal reservations and otherwise qualified have the vote in all county, state and national elections but retain the right to elect their own tribal representative to the legislature.

In the 1980 presidential election Reagan polled 238,522 votes, Carter 220,974 and Anderson 53,327.

The state sends to Congress 2 senators and 2 representatives.

The capital is Augusta. The state is divided into 16 counties.

Governor: Joseph E. Brennan (D.), 1983–86 ($35,000).
Secretary of State: Rodney S. Quinn (D.), 1983–86 ($25,000).

BUDGET. For the financial year ending 30 June 1982 total general revenue was $1,260,287,000 and expenditure was $1,314,622,632.

Total net long-term debt on 30 June 1982 was $271·7m.

Per capita personal income (Sept. 1982) was $8,535.

NATURAL RESOURCES

Minerals. Minerals include sand and gravel, stone, lead, clay, copper, peat, silver and zinc. Mineral output, 1980, was valued at over $40m.

Agriculture. In 1981, 8,100 farms occupied 1·6m. acres; the average farm was 197 acres.

Cash receipts, 1981, $460·4m., of which $131·2 came from potatoes; Maine is the third largest producer of potatoes (about 8% of the country's total of 26m. cwt). Other important items include eggs ($108·5m.), dairy products ($102·4m.) and poultry ($56·2m.); these with potatoes provide 86·5% of receipts. Sweet corn, peas and beans, oats, hay, apples and blueberries are also grown. On 1 Jan. 1981 the farm animals included 57,000 milch cows, 76,000 all other cattle, 13,000 sheep, 10,000 swine.

Forestry. Lumber, wood turnings and pulp are important. In 1980 the cut of softwood was 782,071m. bd ft; hardwood, 140,902m. bd ft, and pulpwood, 3,368,344 cords. Spruce and fir, white pine, hemlock, white and yellow birch, sugar maple, northern white cedar, beech and red oak are the most important species cut. There were (1974) 16,894,300 acres of commercial forest (98% in private ownership). National forests comprise 37,500 acres; other federal, 35,800; state forests, 163,000 acres; municipal, 75,200 acres. Wood products industries are of great economic importance; in 1978 the paper, lumber and wood industries' production was valued at $2,379·5m. (54·5% of industrial production). There were (1980) 388 primary manufacturers and over 470 secondary.

Fisheries. In 1981, 245,423,026 lb. of fish and shellfish (valued at $108,020,818 were landed; the catch included 22,631,614 lb. of lobsters (valued at $47,236,000). 30·06m. lb. of sardines were packed in 1981 valued at $44m.

INDUSTRY. In 1980, 2,279 manufacturing establishments reported 112,829 workers, earning $1,554·3m.; gross value of production, $7,142·6m. (increase of 10·4% from 1979). Leading industry is paper with 47 plants, 18,076 workers and output valued at $2,434·5m. (34·1% of the state's total manufactures).

TOURISM. There are about 3·5m. visitors annually, generating about $6m. in business.

COMMUNICATIONS

Roads. In 1981 there were 21,940 miles of roads, of which 3,978 miles were state highways and 4,832 miles were state-aided; town streets and miscellaneous, 13,130 miles. In 1981, 1,784,299 motor vehicles were registered, including 608,684 passenger vehicles, 88,282 commercial vehicles and 39,854 motorcycles.

Railways. In 1980 there were nearly 2,000 miles of railway tracks.

Aviation. Commercially licensed airports, 1980, numbered 200, including 3 international, 2 county and 1 state; there were 2 military airports, 11 private landing strips (1 being state-owned), 14 licensed commercial seaplane bases and 3 registered non-commercial seaplane bases.

JUSTICE, RELIGION, EDUCATION AND WELFARE

Justice. The state's penal system in July 1982 held 573 adults in the State Prison, 369 in the Correctional Center and 355 juveniles in the Youth Center. There is no capital punishment. Inmates serving life sentences are eligible for parole consideration after 15 years, less remission for good conduct, provided they were imprisoned before the passage of a new Criminal Code by the 107th Maine Legislature, which abolished the parole system.

Religion. The largest religious bodies are: Roman Catholic (270,283 members), Baptists (36,808 members) and Congregationalists (40,750 members), and other Christian Churches (34,066 members).

Education. Education is free for pupils from 5 to 21 years of age, and compulsory from 7 to 17. In 1980–81 the 772 public schools (619 elementary, 103 secondary and 50 combined elementary and secondary) had 12,476 staff and 222,497 enrolled pupils. In 1980–81 there were 152 private schools with 1,108 teachers and 17,615 pupils. Public school teachers' salaries, 1980–81, averaged $14,462. Total public expenditure on public elementary and secondary education in 1980–81, $393,757,544.

The state University of Maine, founded in 1865, had (1981–82) 974 professors and 24,713 students at 7 locations; Portland campus is now called the University of Southern Maine; Bowdoin College, founded in 1794 at Brunswick, had 96 professors and 1,373 students; Bates College at Lewiston, 98 professors and 1,431 students; Colby College at Waterville, 118 professors and 1,675 students; Nasson College at Springvale, 32 professors and 505 students; Husson College, 42 professors and 1,432 students; Westbrook College at Westbrook, 38 professors and 1,012 students; Unity College at Unity, 18 professors and 322 students, and the University of New England (formerly St Francis College) at Biddeford, 20 professors and 1,116 students.

Health. In 1980 the state had 47 general hospitals (4,533 beds); 3 hospitals for mental diseases, acute and psychiatric care (476 beds); 133 nursing homes and 16 units in hospitals (8,555 beds).

Social Security. Supplemental Security Income (SSI) (maximum payment for single person, $294·30 per month) is administered by the Social Security Administration. It became effective on 1 Jan. 1974 and replaces former aid to the aged, blind and disabled, administered by the state with state and federal funds. SSI is supplemented by Medicaid for nursing home patients or hospital patients. State payments for SSI recipients for Jan. 1982 totalled $409,000, covering 20,700 cases. Aid to families with dependent children is granted where one or both parents are disabled or absent and income is insufficient; aid was being granted in Aug. 1982 to 16,306 families (29,975 children) with an average payment per family of $292·65 per month. Total aid under the programme, Aug. 1982, $4·8m. Payments under Maine Medical Assistance programme totalled $178m. for 1982. There is a programme of assistance for catastrophic illness. Child welfare services include basic child protective services, enforcing child support, establishing paternity and finding missing parents, foster home placements, adoptions; services in divorce cases and licensing of foster homes, day care and residential treatment services, and public guardianship. There are also protective services for adults.

Books of Reference

Maine Register, State Year-Book and Legislative Manual. Tower Publishing, Portland. Annual

Federal Writers' Project. *Maine, a Guide 'Down East'.* Courier Gazette, 1970

Banks, R., (ed.), *A History of Maine: a Collection of Readings on the History of Maine 1600–1970.* Kendall/Hunt, 1969

Banks, R., *Maine Becomes A State.* Wesleyan U.P., 1970

Day, C. A., *Farming in Maine, 1060–1940.* Univ. Maine Press, 1963

Rowe, W. H., *Maritime History of Maine.* Norton, New York, 1948

MARYLAND

HISTORY. Maryland, first settled in 1634, was one of the 13 original states.

AREA AND POPULATION. Maryland is bounded north by Pennsylvania, east by Delaware and the Atlantic, south by Virginia and West Virginia, with the Potomac River forming most of the boundary, and west by West Virginia. Chesapeake Bay almost cuts off the eastern end of the state from the rest. Area, 10,460 sq. miles, of which 623 sq. miles are inland water; in addition, water area under Maryland jurisdiction in Chesapeake Bay amounts to 1,726 sq. miles. Census population, 1 April 1980, 4,216,446, an increase since 1970 of 294,047 or 7·5%. In 1980 births were 52,284 (12·4 per 1,000 population); deaths, 33,337 (7·9); infant deaths, 673 (13 per 1,000 live births); marriages, 45,967 (10·9); divorces, 16,293 (3·9).

Population for 5 federal censuses was:

	White	*Negro*	*Indian*	*Asiatic*	*Total*	*Per sq. mile*
1920	1,204,737	244,479	32	413	1,449,661	145·8
1930	1,354,226	276,379	50	871	1,631,526	165·0
1960	2,573,919	518,410	1,538	5,700	3,100,689	314·0
			All others			
1970	3,194,888	499,479	28,032		3,922,399	396·6
1980	3,158,412	958,050	99,984		4,216,446	426·2

Of the total population in 1980, 2,042,558 were male, 3,386,026 persons were urban and those 20 years old or older numbered 2,889,816.

The largest city in the state (containing 19·1% of the population of the state) is Baltimore, with 786,775 in 1980; population of metropolitan area, 2,166,308. Maryland residents in the Washington, D.C., metropolitan area total more than 1m.; other cities (1978) are Dundalk (85,377); Towson (77,799); Silver Spring (77,496); Bethesda (71,621), Bome (37,323 in 1975), Hagerstown (37,233 in 1975), Annapolis (capital), 29,592. Incorporated places: Cumberland, 26,775; Cambridge, 11,476; Frederick, 25,464; Daithersburg, 25,930; Rockville, 43,441.

CONSTITUTION AND GOVERNMENT. The present constitution dates from 1867; it has had 125 amendments. The General Assembly consists of a Senate of 47, and a House of Delegates of 141 members, both elected for 4 years. Voters are citizens who have the usual residential qualifications.

At the 1980 presidential election Carter polled 726,161 votes, Reagan 680,606 and Anderson 119,537.

Maryland sends to Congress 2 senators and 8 representatives.

The state capital is Annapolis. The state is divided into 23 counties and Baltimore City.

Governor: Harry R. Hughes (D.), 1983–86 ($60,000).
Lieut.-Governor: J. Joseph Curran (D.), 1983–86 ($52,500).
Secretary of State: Patricia Holtz ($36,000).

BUDGET. For the fiscal year ending 30 June 1979 general revenues were $3,883,262,000 ($2,633,114,000 from taxation). General expenditures, $4,006,429,000, including $740,997,000 for education and $1,032,662,000 for public welfare and health; $678,421,000 for highways.

Total authorized long-term state debt, 30 June 1979 was $3,068,382,000. (Issued and outstanding, $2,154,075,000; authorized but not issued, $914,307,000.)

Per capita personal income (1980) was $10,460.

ENERGY AND NATURAL RESOURCES

Minerals. Value of mineral production, 1978, was $164·6m. Sand and gravel (13·3m. short tons) and stone (19·5m. short tons) account for over 59% of the total value. Coal is the leading mineral commodity by value followed by Portland cement, sand and gravel and stone. Output of coal was 2·9m. short tons, valued at $58m. Natural gas is produced from 2 fields in Garrett County; 88m. cu. ft in 1978. A third gas field in the same county is used for natural gas storage.

Agriculture. Agriculture is an important industry in the state. In 1980 there were approximately 16,400 farms with an area of 2·8m. acres (35% of the land area).

Farm animals, 1 Jan. 1980, were: Milch cows, 130,000; all cattle, 380,000; swine, 235,000 (1979); sheep and lambs, 20,000; chickens (not broilers), 2·15m. (1979). The most important crops, 1979, were: corn for grain, 58·9m. bu.; soybeans, 11·5m. bu.; tobacco, 26·4m. lb., and hay, 606,000 tons.

Cash receipts from farm marketings, 1980, were $906·3m.; from livestock and livestock products, $614·6m., and crops, $288·2m. Dairy products and broilers are important.

INDUSTRY. In 1978 manufactories had 169,700 production workers earning $2,218·8m.; value added by manufacture, $7,739·2m. Chief industries are food and kindred products, primary metal products, transport equipment, electrical and other machinery, chemicals and products, printing and publishing.

TOURISM. Tourism is one of the state's leading industries. In 1980 tourists spent over $2,000m.

COMMUNICATIONS

Roads. The state highway department maintained, 1 Jan. 1980, 5,239 miles of highways, of which 79 miles were toll roads. The 23 counties maintained 16,902 miles of highways, and the 159 municipalities (including the city of Baltimore) maintained 3,877 miles of streets and alleys. Total mileage, 1 Jan. 1980, of public highways, streets and alleys, 26,018 miles. In 1979, 2·2m. automobiles were registered.

Railways. Railways, in 1980, had 1,192 miles of line.

Aviation. There were, 1979, 39 commercially licensed airports.

Shipping. In 1979 Baltimore was the fourth largest US seaport in value of trade, eighth in tonnage handled.

JUSTICE, RELIGION, EDUCATION AND WELFARE

Justice. Prisons on 20 Oct. 1980 had 7,147 men and 214 women; the total equalled 177 per 100,000 population, a high rate, which may be explained by the fact that Maryland incarcerates domestic relations law violators in state prisons; state prisons also receive a considerable number of persons committed for misdemeanours by magistrates' courts of the counties as well as from Baltimore's court system.

Since 1930 there have been 68 executions (by lethal gas since 1957; earlier by hanging)—7 whites and 37 Negroes for murder, and 6 whites and 18 Negroes for rape. Last execution was June 1961.

Maryland's prison system has conducted a work-release programme for selected prisoners since 1963. All institutions have academic and vocational training programmes.

In accordance with the 1950 Supreme Court decisions declaring segregation unconstitutional, the University of Maryland and other public and private colleges admitted Negro students in Sept. 1956. Elementary and secondary schools accept the ruling, and gradual integration is under way in all counties under different methods.

Religion. Maryland was the first US state to give religious freedom to all who came within its borders. Present religious affiliations of the population are approximately: Protestant, 32%; Roman Catholic, 24%; Jewish, 10%; remaining 34% is non-related and other faiths.

Education. Education is compulsory from 6 to 16 years of age. In Sept. 1979 the public elementary schools (including kindergartens and secondary schools) had 777,725 pupils. Teachers and principals in the elementary and secondary schools numbered 44,648. Average salary of principals and teachers in elementary and secondary schools (1978–79) was $16,941. Current expenditure by local school boards on education, 1978–79, was $1,694·8m., of which the state's contribution was $600m.

In 1979 there were 31 degree-granting 4-year institutions and 19 2-year colleges. The largest two were the University of Maryland system, with 60,536 students (Sept. 1979) and Towson State College with 15,283 students (Sept. 1979).

Health. In Oct. 1979, 79 hospitals (22,047 beds) were licensed by the State Department of Health and Mental Hygiene.

The Maryland State Department of Health, organized in 1874, was in 1969 made part of the Department of Health and Mental Hygiene which performs its functions through its central office, 23 county health departments and the Baltimore City Health Department. For the financial year 1979 the department's budget was $739,367,064, of which $517,036,275 were general funds and $16,181,295 special funds appropriated by the General Assembly. The balance of the budget, $206,149,494, derives from federal funds.

During financial year 1979 Maryland's programme of medical care for indigent and medically indigent patients covered an average of 365,854 persons. The programme, which covers in-patient and out-patient hospital services, laboratory services, skilled nursing home care, physician services, pharmacy services, dental services and home health services, cost approximately $326·3m.

Social Security. Under the supervision of the Department of Employment and Human Resources, local social service departments administer public assistance for needy persons. In June 1980 families with dependent children received $15,204,233 (206,397 recipients, average actual monthly payment $72.17); general public assistance payments were $2,360,460 (21,628 recipients, average actual monthly payments $107.58); foster care of children cost $1,481,930 (7,731 recipients, average actual payment $193.77).

Books of Reference

Statistical Information: Maryland Department of Economic and Community Development, Annapolis, 21401.

Maryland Manual: A Compendium of Legal, Historical and Statistical Information Relating to the State of Maryland. Annapolis. Biennial

DiLisio, J. E., *Maryland.* Boulder, 1982

State Library: Maryland State Library, Annapolis. *Director:* Michael S. Miller.

MASSACHUSETTS

HISTORY. The first permanent settlement within the borders of the present state was made at Plymouth in Dec. 1620, by the Pilgrims from Holland, who were separatists from the English Church, and formed the nucleus of the Plymouth Colony. In 1628 another company of Puritans settled at Salem, forming eventually the Massachusetts Bay Colony. In 1630 Boston was settled. In the struggle which ended in the separation of the American colonies from the mother country, Massachusetts took the foremost part, and on 6 Feb. 1788 became the sixth state to ratify the US constitution.

AREA AND POPULATION. Massachusetts is bounded north by Vermont and New Hampshire, east by the Atlantic, south by Connecticut and Rhode Island and west by New York. Area, 8,284 sq. miles, 460 sq. miles being inland water. The census population 1 April 1980, was 5,737,037, an increase of 47,867 or 0·8% since 1970. Births, 1980 were 72,591 (12·7 per 1,000 population); deaths, 54,935 (9·6 per 1,000); infant deaths, 748 (10·4 per 1,000 live births); marriages, 46,273 (8); divorces, 16,487 (3·1).

Population at 4 federal census years was:

	White	*Negro*	*Other*	*Total*	*Per sq. mile*
1950	4,611,503	73,171	5,840	4,690,514	598·4
1960	5,023,144	111,842	13,592	5,148,578	656·8
1970	5,477,624	175,817	35,729	5,689,170	725·8
1980	5,362,836	221,279	152,922	5,737,037	732·0

Of the total population in 1980, 47·6% were male, 83·8% were urban and 32% were 21 years old or older.

In 1980 the population of the principal towns and cities was:

Boston	562,994	Fall River	92,574	Framingham	65,113
Worcester	161,799	Lowell	92,418	Lawrence	63,175
Springfield	153,319	Quincy	84,743	Waltham	58,200
New Bedford	98,478	Newton	83,622	Medford	58,076
Cambridge	95,322	Lynn	78,471	Weymouth	55,601
Brockton	95,172	Somerville	77,372	Chicopee	55,112

The largest of 10 standard metropolitan statistical areas, 1980 census were: Boston, 2,763,357; Springfield–Chicopee–Holyoke, 530,668; Worcester, 372,940.

CONSTITUTION AND GOVERNMENT. The constitution dates from 1780 and has had 116 amendments. The legislative body, styled the General Court of the Commonwealth of Massachusetts, meets annually, and consists of the Senate with 40 members, elected biennially, and the House of Representatives of 160 members, elected for 2 years. The Governor and Lieut.-Governor are elected for 4 years. The state sends 2 senators and 11 representatives to Congress.

At the 1980 presidential election Reagan polled 1,056,223 votes, Carter 1,053,800.

Electors are all citizens 18 years of age or older.

The capital is Boston. The state has 14 counties, 39 cities and 312 towns.

Governor: Michael S. Dukakis (D.), 1983–86 ($40,000).
Lieut.-Governor: John F. Kerry (D.) ($30,000).
Secretary of the Commonwealth: Michael J. Connolly (D.) ($30,000).

BUDGET. For the fiscal year ending 30 June 1982 the total revenue of the state was $7,514,324,721 ($4,637·5m. from taxes and $1,817·6m. from federal aid); general expenditures, $7,640,440,330m. ($505·4m. for education, $329·6m. for highway and transport construction and $1,974m. for public welfare).

The net long-term debt on 30 June 1982 amounted to $3,005·1m.

Per capita personal income (1981) was $11,128.

NATURAL RESOURCES

Minerals. There is little mining within the state. Total mineral output in 1981 was valued at $97m., of which most came from sand, gravel and stone.

Agriculture. On 1 Jan. 1980 there were 5,900 farms (11,179 in 1959) with an area of 680,000 acres.

Cash income, 1980, totalled $306·5m.; dairy, $79·3m.; greenhouse and nursery, $94·4m.; poultry, $2·3m.; vegetables, $23·5m.; tobacco, $10·8m.; cranberries, $30·6m.; other fruit, $15·3m.; potatoes, $4·1m.; all other, $46·2m.

Principal 1980 crops include cranberries, 1,185,000 bbls; apples, 2·4m. (42-lb. units); potatoes, 748,000 cwt, and tobacco, 2m. lb. On 1 Jan. 1980 farms in the state had 45,000 milch cows, 103,000 all cattle, 60,000 swine (Dec. 1979), 126,000 turkeys and 1·8m. chickens.

Forestry. State forests cover about 500,000 acres. Total forest land covers about 3m. acres. Commercially important hardwoods are sugar maple, northern red oak and white ash; softwoods are white pine and hemlock. About 240m. bd ft of timber are cut annually.

Fisheries. The 1981 catch amounted to 331·3m. lb. of finfish valued at $103m.; 28·5m. lb. of shellfish ($68m.); 9·8m. lb. of lobster ($25·7m.).

INDUSTRY. In 1981, 10,581 manufacturing establishments employed an average of 668,984 workers, who earned $12,078·3m.; value added by manufacture (1977) was $16,348·6m. The 3 most important manufacturing groups, based on employment, were electric and electronic equipment, machinery (except electrical), instruments and related products.

LABOUR. In 1980 the work force was 2,893,000. Changes in the industrial pattern have caused the loss of jobs in the shoe and textile industries. In 1981 there were 102 work stoppages involving 28,700 workers which resulted in 696,000 man-days idle.

COMMUNICATIONS

Roads. In Dec. 1981 the state had 33,772 miles of roads and streets and in 1981 registered 3·8m. motor vehicles.

Railways. In 1982 there were 1,310 miles of mainline railway.

Aviation. There were, in 1981, 52 aircraft landing areas for commercial operation, of which 26 were publicly owned.

Shipping. The state has 3 deep-water harbours, the largest of which is Boston (port trade (1980), 22,033,922 short tons). Other ports are Fall River and New Bedford.

JUSTICE, RELIGION, EDUCATION AND WELFARE

Justice. On 4 Nov. 1982 state penal institutions held 4,407 inmates. There have been no executions since 1947.

Religion. The principal religious bodies are the Roman Catholics, Jewish Congregations, Methodists, Episcopalians and Unitarians.

Education. A regulation effective from 1 Sept. 1972 makes school attendance compulsory for ages 6–16. In 1980–81 expenditure by cities and towns on public schools was $3,254m., including $214m. debt retirement and service payments. In 1980–81 there were 69,096 classroom teachers and 1,001,760 pupils.

Within the state there were (1981) 122 degree-granting institutions of higher learning (including 88 colleges and universities) with about 14,895 full-time teaching staff and about 404,850 students in 1979. Some leading institutions are:

Year opened	Name and location of universities and colleges	Students 1979
1636	Harvard University, Cambridge [1]	21,294
1793	Williams College, Williamstown [1]	2,034
1821	Amherst College, Amherst [1]	1,541
1837	Mount Holyoke College, South Hadley [2]	1,962
1843	College of the Holy Cross, Worcester [1]	2,531
1852	Tufts University, Medford [1,3]	6,796
1861	Mass. Institute of Technology, Cambridge [1]	9,053
1863	University of Massachusetts, Amherst [1]	24,012
1863	Boston College (RC), Chestnut Hill [1]	13,969
1865	Worcester Polytechnic Institute, Worcester [1]	3,367
1869	Boston University, Boston [1]	25,828
1870	Wellesley College, Wellesley [2]	2,233
1875	Smith College, Northampton [1]	3,016
1879	Radcliffe College, Cambridge [1]	2,320
1885	Springfield College, Springfield [1]	2,695
1887	Clark University, Worcester [1]	3,155
1894	University of Lowell [1]	10,703
1898	Northeastern University, Boston [1,4]	40,349
1899	Simmons College, Boston [2]	2,767
1948	Brandeis University, Waltham [1]	3,603

[1] Co-educational. [2] For women only. [3] Includes Jackson College for women. [4] Includes Forsyth Dental Center School.

Health. In 1980 the state had 186 hospitals (with 39,170 beds); average daily census, 38,799, of which 7,890 patients were in public and private mental hospitals and 4,270 patients were in institutions for the mentally retarded.

Social Security. The Department of Public Welfare had an appropriation of $1,818m. in 1981 and paid $514m. in aid to families with dependent children (average 140,000 families per month); other main items were general relief (average 22,422 cases), Supplemental Security Income (average 120,000 cases) and Medical Assistance (average 331,000 cases).

Books of Reference

Annual Reports. Massachusetts and US Boards, Commissions, Departments and Divisions, Boston, 1980

Manual for the General Court. By Clerk of the Senate and Clerk of the House of Representatives, Boston, Mass. Biennial

Levitan, D., and Mariner, E. C., *Your Massachusetts Government.* Boston, Mass., 1980

New England Board of Higher Education. *Facts.* Wenham, Mass., 1980–81

MICHIGAN

HISTORY. Michigan, first settled by Marquette at Sault Ste Marie in 1668, became the Territory of Michigan in 1805, with its boundaries greatly enlarged in 1818 and 1834; it was admitted into the Union with its present boundaries on 26 Jan. 1837.

AREA AND POPULATION. Michigan is divided into two by Lake Michigan. The northern part is bounded south by the lake and by Wisconsin, west and north by Lake Superior, east by the North Channel of Lake Huron; between the two latter lakes the Canadian border runs through straits at Sault Ste Marie. The southern part is bounded west and north by Lake Michigan, east by Lake Huron, Ontario and Lake Erie, south by Ohio and Indiana. Area, 58,527 sq. miles, of which 56,954 sq. miles are land area, 1,573 sq. miles are inland water. Census population, 1 April 1980, 9,258,344, an increase of 376,518 or 4·2% since 1970. In 1980 births were 145,162; deaths, 74,991; infant deaths, 1,851; marriages, 86,898; divorces, 45,047.

Population of 5 federal census years was:

	White	*Negro*	*Indian*	*Asiatic*	*Total*	*Per sq. mile*
1910	2,785,247	17,115	7,519	292	2,810,173	48·9
1930	4,663,507	169,453	7,080	2,285	4,842,325	84·9
1960	7,085,865	717,581	9,701	10,047	7,823,194	137·2
			All others			
1970	7,833,474	991,066	50,543		8,875,083	156·2
1980	7,868,956	1,198,710	190,678		9,258,344	162·7

Of the total population in 1980, 4,513,951 were male, 6,547,842 persons were urban and those 20 years old or older numbered 6,144,925.

Population of the chief cities (census of 1 April 1980) was:

Detroit	1,203,339	Westland	84,603	Troy	67,102
Grand Rapids	181,843	Kalamazoo	79,722	Wyoming	59,616
Warren	161,134	Taylor	77,568	Farmington Hills	58,056
Flint	159,611	Saginaw	77,508	Roseville	54,311
Lansing (capital)	130,414	Pontiac	76,715		
Sterling Heights	108,999	St Clair Shores	76,210		
Ann Arbor	107,316	Southfield	75,568		
Livonia	104,814	Royal Oak	70,893		
Dearborn	90,660	Dearborn Heights	67,706		

Larger standard metropolitan areas, 1980 census: Detroit, 4,344,139; Grand Rapids, 601,106; Flint, 521,541; Lansing, 467,584.

CONSTITUTION AND GOVERNMENT. The present constitution was adopted in April 1963 and became effective on 1 Jan. 1964. The Senate consists of 38 members, elected for 4 years, and the House of Representatives of 110 members, elected for 2 years. The Governor and Lieut.-Governor are elected for 4 years. Electors are all citizens over 18 years of age meeting the usual residential requirements. The state sends to Congress 2 senators and 18 representatives.

At the 1980 presidential election Reagan polled 1,915,225 votes, Carter 1,661,532 and Anderson 275,223.

The capital is Lansing. The state is organized in 83 counties.

Governor: James Blanch (D.), 1983–86 ($65,000).
Lieut.-Governor: Martha Griffiths (D.), 1983–86 ($45,000).
Secretary of State: Richard H. Austin (D.), ($60,000).

BUDGET. For the financial year ending 30 Sept. 1980, the general revenue was $8,598,770m. (taxation, $6,126,400m., and federal aid, $2,452,370m.); total revenue, $9,518,130m.; special revenue funds, $4,697,638m.; general expenditures, $9,933,024m.

Per capita personal income (1980 estimate) was $9,403.

ENERGY AND NATURAL RESOURCES

Minerals. Most important minerals by value of production are iron ore, petroleum and cement. Output (1980, preliminary): Iron ore, 16·3m. long tons ($652·6m.); Portland cement, 4,671,000 short tons ($228·5m.); petroleum, 33·9m. bbls ($664m.); copper, 35,000 short tons ($75·7m.); sand and gravel, 40·3m. short tons ($98·7m.); stone, 30·5m. short tons ($85·6m.); lime, 807,000 short tons ($37·6m.); natural gas, 159m. cu. ft ($386m.). Total value of natural salines, $182m. Mineral output in 1980 was valued at $2,530·7m.

Agriculture. The state, formerly agricultural, is now chiefly industrial. In 1980 it contained 65,000 farms with a total area of 11·4m. acres; the average farm was 175 acres. Cash income, 1979, from crops, $1,338m.; from livestock and products, $1,147·3m. Principal crops are maize (production, 1980, 247m. bu.), oats (20·1m. bu.), wheat (35·2m. bu.), sugar-beet (1·9m. tons); soybeans (30·4m. bu.), hay (3·8m. tons). On 1 Jan. 1981 there were in the state 124,000 sheep, 390,000 milch cows, 1·38m. all cattle, 830,000 swine, 8·2m. chickens and 45,000 turkey breeder hens. In 1980 the wool clip yielded 950,000 lb. of wool from 122,000 sheep.

Forestry. The forests of Michigan consist of 19,373,400 acres, about 52% of total state land area. About 18·9m. acres of this total is commercial forest, 67% of which is privately owned, 19% state forest, 13% national forest and 1% in various public ownerships. Three-fourths of the timber volume is hardwoods, principally hard and soft maples, aspen, oak and elm. Christmas trees are another important forest crop.

Michigan leads in the number of state parks and public campsites. There are 83 state parks and recreation areas, 6 state forests, 5 national forests and 3 national parks. There are 180 state forest campgrounds and 66 state game and wildlife areas.

INDUSTRY. Transport equipment and non-electrical machinery are the most important manufactures. The state ranks first in 19 manufacturing categories; among principal products are motor vehicles and trucks, cement, chemicals, furniture, paper, cereal, baby food and pharmaceuticals. Total labour force, 1980, 4,303,000, of which 1,028,000 are in manufacturing.

COMMUNICATIONS

Roads. State trunk-line mileage (31 July 1980) totalled, 9,500, all hard surfaced. Passenger car registrations, 18 Sept. 1981, 5,834,267.

Railways. On 1 Jan. 1980 there were 6,153 miles of railway and 383 active car-ferry routes.

Aviation. Airports (1980) numbered 205 licensed airports, 88 certified but not licensed and 23 air carrier airports.

JUSTICE, RELIGION, EDUCATION AND WELFARE

Justice. The 1963 Constitution provides that no person shall be denied the equal protection of the law; nor shall any person be denied the enjoyment of his civil or political rights or be discriminated against in the exercise thereof because of religion, colour or national origin. A Civil Rights Commission was established, and its powers and duties were implemented by legislation in the extra session of 1963. Earlier statutory enactments guaranteeing civil rights in specific areas are as follows. An Act of 1885, last amended in 1956, orders all places of public accommodation and resort, etc., to furnish equal accommodations without discrimination. An Act of 1941, as last amended, forbids the Civil Service in counties with population exceeding 1m. to discriminate against employees or applicants on the ground of political, racial or religious opinions or affiliations. An Act of 1881 incorporated into the school code of 1955 forbids any discrimination in school facilities. An Act of 1893 incorporated in the insurance code of 1956 prohibits insurance companies from discriminating between white and coloured persons.

In 1951 the legislature restored the unique one-man grand jury system abandoned in 1949.

Religion. There were 2,004,288 Roman Catholics in 1979; largest Protestant denominations, Lutherans, 500,000; United Methodists, 278,245; United Presbyterians, 155,864; Episcopalians, 63,873.

Education. Education is compulsory for children from 6 to 16 years of age. The operating expenditure for graded and ungraded public schools for the fiscal year ending 30 June 1980, was $3,905,187,158; total, including capital and debt expenditures, $4,681,147,904. In 1980 there were 575 school districts (elementary and secondary schools) with 1,910,385 pupils and 87,487 teachers. Teachers' salaries in 1980 averaged $19,663.

In the autumn of 1978 the 13 public 4-year institutions reported 236,035 students and the 54 non-public institutions reported 486,494 students. During fiscal year 1976–77 the public colleges had operating budgets financed by tuition and $484·8m. by state appropriations. The community colleges had an autumn enrolment (1978) of 187,649 students.

Universities and students (1978):

Founded	Name	Students
1817	University of Michigan	36,577
1849	Eastern Michigan University	18,655
1855	Michigan State University	46,567
1884	Ferris State College	10,208
1885	Michigan Technological University	7,130
1868	Wayne State University	33,423
1892	Central Michigan University	17,802
1889	Northern Michigan University	8,995
1903	Western Michigan University	22,447
1946	Lake Superior State College	2,401
1959	Oakland University	11,220
1960	Grand Valley State College	7,065
1965	Saginaw Valley College	3,706

Social Welfare. Old-age assistance is provided for persons 65 years of age or older who have resided in Michigan for one year before application; assets must not exceed various limits. In 1974 federal Supplementary Security Income (SSI) replaced the adults' programme. In 1980 aid was supplied to a monthly average of 455,022 dependent children in 218,814 families at $372·35 per family.

Health. In 1981 the state had 216 hospitals (40,217 beds) licensed by the state and 21 psychiatric hospitals.

In 1957 a programme came into force which provided for free medical care and hospital treatment for certain categories of persons. On 1 Oct. 1966 this programme was superseded by a more comprehensive programme called 'Medicaid' which, with federal support, disbursed in 1979–80, $1,071·6m. to an estimated 973,443 persons.

Books of Reference

Michigan Department of Economic Development. *Publications.* Lansing

Michigan Manual. Dept of State. Lansing. Biennial

Bureau of Business and Economic Research, Michigan State University. *Michigan Statistical Abstract.* East Lansing, 1981

Bald, F. C., *Michigan in Four Centuries.* 2nd ed. New York, 1961

Catton. B., *Michigan—a Bicentennial History.* Norton, New York, 1976

Lewis, F. E., *State and Local Government in Michigan.* Lansing, 1979

Dunbar, W. F., and May, G. S., *Michigan: A History of the Wolverine State.* Grand Rapids, 1980

Milliken, W. G., *Economic Report of the Governor 1981.* Lansing, 1981

Sommers, L. (ed.), *Atlas of Michigan.* East Lansing, 1977

State Library Services: Michigan Department of Education, Lansing 48909. *State Librarian:* Francis X. Scannell.

MINNESOTA

HISTORY. Minnesota, first explored in the 17th century and first settled in the 20 years following the establishment of Fort Snelling (1819), was made a Territory in 1849 (with parts of North and South Dakota), and was admitted into the Union, with its present boundaries, on 11 May 1858.

AREA AND POPULATION. Minnesota is bounded north by Canada, east by Lake Superior and Wisconsin, with the Mississippi River forming the boundary in the south-east, south by Iowa, west by South and North Dakota, with the Red River forming the boundary in the north-west. Area, 84,402 sq. miles, of which 4,854 sq. miles are inland water. Census population, 1 April 1980, 4,075,970, an increase of 7·1% since 1970. Births in 1980, 67,843 (16·6 per 1,000 population); deaths, 33,415 (8·2); infant deaths, 679 (10 per 1,000 live births); marriages, 37,625 (9·2); divorces, 15,274 (3·7).

Population in 5 census years was:

	White	Negro	Indian	Asiatic	Total	Per sq. mile
1910	2,059,227	7,084	9,053	344	2,075,708	25·7
1930	2,542,599	9,445	11,077	832	2,563,953	32·0
1960	3,371,603	22,263	15,496	3,642	3,413,864	42·7
			All others			
1970	3,736,038	34,868	34,163		3,805,069	47·6
1980	3,935,770	53,344	86,856		4,075,970	51·4

Of the 1980 population, 1,997,826 were male; 2,725,270 were urban; those 21 years of age or older numbered 2,656,947.

The largest cities are Minneapolis, 370,951; St Paul (capital), 270,230 (Minneapolis–St Paul standard metropolitan statistical area, 1,972,208 in 1970); Duluth, 92,811; Bloomington, 81,831; Rochester, 57,890.

CLIMATE. Average maximum temperature in July (Minneapolis–St. Paul) is 71·9°F; average minimum in Jan. is 12·2°F. Rainfall average is 0·73″ in Jan. (Minneapolis–St. Paul) and 3·94″ in June. Snow falls Oct. to May.

CONSTITUTION AND GOVERNMENT. The present constitution dates from 1858; it has had 94 amendments. The Legislature consists of a Senate of 67 members, elected for 4 years, and a House of Representatives of 134 members, elected for 2 years. The Governor and Lieut.-Governor are elected for 4 years. The state sends to Congress 2 senators and 8 representatives.

In the 1980 presidential election Carter polled 954,173 votes, Reagan 873,268.

The capital is St Paul. There are 87 counties, four containing less than 400 sq. miles, the largest being 6,092 sq. miles.

Governor: Rudy Perpich (D.), 1983–86 ($66,500).
Lieut.-Governor: Marlene Johnson (D.), 1983–86 ($38,000).
Secretary of State: Joan Anderson Growe (DFL.), 1983–86 ($36,000).

BUDGET. The general fund budget for the 1979–81 2-year period was $7,900m.; tax relief $760m., education $2,848m., public welfare $1,112m., transport $683m.

Net long-term debt, 30 June 1980, was $881m.

Per capita personal income (1979) was $8,865.

NATURAL RESOURCES

Minerals. The iron ore and taconite industry is the most important in the USA. Production of usable iron ore in 1981 was 50m. tons, value $2,062m. Other important minerals are sand and gravel, crushed and dimension stone, lime and manganiferous ore. Total value of mineral production, 1981, $2,151·9m.

Agriculture. Agriculture, including processing, is the leading industry. In 1982 there were 103,000 farms with a total area of 30·4m. acres (60% of the land area); the average farm was of 295 acres. Average value of land and buildings (1982) $348,800. Commercial farms in 1978 numbered 102,963; 12% of the farms were operated by tenant-farmers. Cash income, 1981, from crops, $3,520m.; from livestock, $3,390m. In 1981 Minnesota ranked first in oats, wild rice and timothy seed, and second in spring wheat, sugar-beet, red clover seed, non-fat dry milk, cheese, rye, processing sweet corn, turkeys and sunflower seed. Other important products are hay, butter, eggs, sheep, flaxseed, milch cows, milk, corn, barley, swine, cattle for market, soybeans, honey, potatoes, chickens, dry edible beans, and green peas for processing. Of livestock, cattle represents 13·7% of total farm income, swine 11·5% and milk 18·9%. Of crops, corn represents 17·3% and soybeans 14%. On 1 Jan. 1982 the farm animals included 3·88m. all cattle, 905,000 milch cows, 335,000 sheep and lambs, 4·3m. swine, 13·6m. chickens and 567,000 breeder hen turkeys. Turkey production, 1981, 25·7m. In 1981 the wool clip amounted to 2·25m. lb. of wool from 308,000 sheep.

Honey production (1981), 8·2m. lb; beeswax, 188,000 lb. About 95% of US commercial wild rice paddies are in Minnesota. Production from 16,000 acres

(1981), 2·3m. lb. of processed wild rice; production from natural stands, 1m. lb.

Forestry. Forests of commercial timber cover 13·69m. acres, of which 53·5% is government-owned. The value of forest products in 1980 was $1,917m.; $770·9m. of this was from pulpwood and $977·3m. from secondary manufacturing. Logging, pulping, saw-mills and associated industries employed 52,294 in 1980.

INDUSTRY. In 1977 there were 6,635 manufacturing establishments; they employed 330,300 production workers who earned $4,677m.; value added by manufacture was (1977), $9,245·3m.

TOURISM. Estimates for 1981 give approximately 8·5m. tourists (55% from outside the state), with a total expenditure of $2,256m.

COMMUNICATIONS

Roads. The state highway system (interstate and state trunk highways) covered 12,100 miles in 1981; total highway, road and street mileage, 130,800. In 1981, 2,092,170 passenger automobiles were registered.

Railways. There are 8 Class I railroads operating, with mainline mileage of 7,229 (total track miles, 7,510).

Aviation. Airports in 1980 numbered 593 (141 municipal, 27 privately owned for public use, 387 personal use, 11 public seaplane bases, 14 private, 74 for personal use).

JUSTICE, RELIGION, EDUCATION AND WELFARE

Justice. A Civil Rights Act (1927) forbids places of public resort to exclude persons 'on account of race or colour' and another section forbids insurance companies to discriminate 'between persons of the same class on account of race'. Contractors on public works may have their contracts cancelled if 'in the hiring of common or skilled labour' they are found to have discriminated on the grounds of 'race, creed or colour'. The state's penal reformatory system on 31 June 1971 held 2,144 men and women. There is no death penalty in Minnesota.

Religion. The chief religious bodies are: Lutheran with 1,112,495 members in 1970; Roman Catholic, 1,061,614; Methodist, 213,084. Total membership of all denominations, 3,044,055.

Education. In 1981, there were 51,720 kindergarten students, 318,852 elementary students, and 381,726 secondary students enrolled in 1,631 public schools. There were 6,588 kindergarten students, 51,405 elementary students and 33,084 secondary students enrolled in 553 private schools. There were 44,048 public school classroom teachers and 5,252 private. The average salary for a public classroom teacher was $18,161. Total public school expenditures for 1981 were $2,211m. and total revenues were $2,199m. Of the total revenues, $1,179m. came from State funds and $134m. came from Federal funds. The University of Minnesota at Minneapolis–St Paul, chartered in 1851 and opened in 1869, had a total enrolment in 1981 of 58,705 students. The 18 public community colleges (2-year) had a total enrolment of 34,894. Seven state universities (4-year) had 1981 enrolment of 41,361, State universities are at Bemidji, Mankato, Marshall, Moorhead, St Cloud, Winona, Minneapolis and St Paul.

Health. In 1980 the state had 165 general acute hospitals with 17,601 beds. Patients resident (average daily census) in institutions under the Department of Public Welfare included 1,520 mentally ill, 2,692 mentally retarded and 637 chemically dependent. There are 2 state nursing homes with (1979–80) a 753-bed capacity.

Social Security. On 1 Jan. 1974 the state administered programmes of old age assistance, aid to the disabled, and aid to the blind were given over to federal administration under the Supplemental Security Income (SSI) Programme. For some states, the new maintenance grants were less than under the state administered programmes. These states could establish a supplemental programme to correct the deficiency. The Minnesota Supplemental Aid (MSA) programme was later expanded to cover individuals who were not receiving SSI and to provide one-time payment for certain special needs such as major home repair, replacement of essential basic furniture or appliances, moving expenses and fuel and utility adjustments.

Books of Reference

Statistical Information: Current information is obtainable from the Department of Energy, Planning and Development (480 Cedar Street, St Paul 55101); non-current material from the Reference Library, Minnesota Historical Society, St Paul 55101. Demographic information (current) is available on request from the Office of State Demographer, DEP D, 101 Capitol Square Building, 550 Cedar Street, St Paul 55101.

Legislative Manual. Secretary of State. St Paul. Biennial
Minnesota Statistical Profile. Dept. of Energy, Planning and Development, Biennial
Blegen, T. C., *Minnesota: A History of the State.* Minnesota Univ. Press, 1963
Minnesota Agriculture Statistics. Dept. of Agric., St Paul. Annual
Manufacturers' Directory. Nelson Name Service, Minneapolis, Biennial

MISSISSIPPI

HISTORY. Mississippi, settled in 1716, was organized as a Territory in 1798 and admitted into the Union on 10 Dec. 1817. In 1804 and in 1812 its boundaries were extended, but in March 1817 a part was taken to form the new Territory of Alabama, leaving the boundaries substantially as at present.

AREA AND POPULATION. Mississippi is bounded north by Tennessee, east by Alabama, south by the Gulf of Mexico and Louisiana, west by the Mississippi River forming the boundary with Louisiana and Arkansas. Area, 47,689 sq. miles, 457 sq. miles being inland water. Census population, 1 April 1980, 2,520,638, an increase of 13·6% since 1970. Births, 1980, were 47,538; deaths, 22,911; infant deaths, 755; marriages, 28,043; divorces, 13,458.

Population of 6 federal census years was:

	White	*Negro*	*Indian*	*Asiatic*	*Total*	*Per sq. mile*
1910	786,111	1,009,487	1,253	263	1,797,114	38·8
1930	998,077	1,009,718	1,458	568	2,009,821	42·4
1950	1,188,632	986,494	2,502	1,286	2,178,914	46·1
1960	1,257,546	915,743	3,119	1,481	2,178,141	46·1
			All others			
1970	1,393,283	815,770	7,859		2,216,912	46·9
1980	1,615,190	887,206	18,242		2,520,638	53·0

Of the population in 1980, 1,213,878 were male, 1,192,805 were urban and 1,601,157 were 20 years old or older.

The largest city (1980) is Jackson, 202,895. Others are: Biloxi, 49,311; Meridian, 46,577; Hattiesburg, 40,829; Greenville, 40,613; Gulfport, 39,676; Pascagoula, 29,318; Columbus, 27,383; Vicksburg, 25,434; Tupelo, 23,905.

CONSTITUTION AND GOVERNMENT. The present constitution was adopted in 1890 without ratification by the electorate; it has since had 48 amendments.

The Legislature consists of a Senate (52 members) and a House of Representatives (122 members), both elected for 4 years, as are also the Governor and Lieut.-Governor. Electors are all citizens who have resided in the state 1 year, in the county 1 year, in the election district 6 months next before the election and have been registered according to law. In the 1980 presidential election Reagan polled 441,089 votes, Carter 429,281 and Anderson 12,036.

The state is represented in Congress by 2 senators and 5 representatives. The capital is Jackson; there are 82 counties.

Governor: William Forrest Winter (D.), 1980–84 ($53,000).
Lieut.-Governor: Bradford Johnson Dye (D.) ($34,000).
Secretary of State: Edwin Lloyd Pittman (D.) ($34,000).

BUDGET. For the fiscal year ending 30 June 1982 the general revenues were $1,195,416,360 (taxation, $1,107,474,774; federal aid, $57,982; other state resources, $87,883,604), and general expenditures were $1,233,098,506 ($703,862,812 for education, $80,000 for highways and $121,369,465 for public welfare).

On 1 Dec. 1982 the total net long-term debt was $1,133·8m.

Per capita personal income (1980) was $6,580 (lowest in US).

ENERGY AND NATURAL RESOURCES

Minerals. Petroleum and natural gas account for about 90% (by value) of mineral production. Output of petroleum, 1981, was 34,381,093 bbls and of natural gas 229,404,669m. cu. ft. There are 6 oil refineries. Value of oil and gas products sold 1981 was $1,807,679,550.

Agriculture. Agriculture is the leading industry of the state because of the semi-tropical climate and a rich productive soil. In 1982 farms with annual sales of $1,000 or more numbered 53,000 with an area of 14·5m. acres. Average size of farm was 274 acres. This compares with an average farm size of 138 acres in 1960.

Cash income from all crops and livestock during 1981, including government payments, was $2,265·7m. Cash income from crops was $1,382·5m. and from live-stock and products, $863·67m. The chief product is soybeans, cash income $467·2m. from 3·7m. acres. Cotton production (1981), 1·56m. bales of 480 lb. As a source of farm income, rice, corn, hay, wheat, sorghum, peanuts, pecans, sweet potatoes, peaches, other vegetables, nursery and forest products continue to contribute.

On 1 Jan. 1982 there were 1·95m. head of cattle and calves on Mississippi farms (twenty-first nationally). Milch cows and heifers which had calved totalled 97,000, beef cows and heifers that had calved, 953,000 (fifteenth nationally); hogs and pigs, 370,000 head (1 Dec. 1981), chickens (excluding broilers), 9·5m. (1 Dec. 1981). In 1981 cash income from livestock and products was 38·5% of total cash receipts. Of this total, $205·8m. was credited to cattle and calves. Cash income from poultry and eggs totalled $436·8m.; dairy products, $128·8m.; swine, $45·6m.

In 1982 there were 82 soil-conservation districts covering 26,342,406 acres.

Forestry. In 1981 income from forestry amounted to $467m.; output of logs, lumber, etc., was 1,218·2m. bd ft; pulpwood, 4,821,878 cords; distillate wood, 19,871 tons; turpentine gum, 1,205 bbls. There are about 16·5m. acres of forest (55% of the state's area). National forests area, 1982, 1·1m. acres.

INDUSTRY. In 1981 the 2,971 manufacturing establishments employed 220,670 workers, earning $3,000,328,756.

COMMUNICATIONS

Roads. The state in July 1982 maintained 10,175 miles of highways, of which 10,060 miles were paved. In 1981, 1,591,029 cars were registered.

Railways. The state in 1982 had 3,107·91 miles of railway.

Aviation. There were 77 public airports in 1982, 67 of them general. There were also 5 privately owned airports.

JUSTICE, RELIGION, EDUCATION AND WELFARE

Justice. In 1982 there were no executions; from 1955 to 1982 executions (by gas-chamber) totalled 31 (7 whites and 14 Negroes for murder, 9 Negroes for rape and 1 Negro for armed robbery). On 30 Sept. 1982 the state prisons had 5,150 inmates.

Religion. Southern Baptists in Mississippi (1981), 625,848 members; Methodists 202,879; Roman Catholics (1982), 96,300; Negro Baptists about 475,000.

The number of churches relative to the population is the highest in the US (one church per 289 persons; national average, 814).

Education. Attendance at school was compulsory until this was repealed by the Legislature in 1956. The public elementary and secondary schools in 1981–82 had 471,615 pupils and 25,255 classroom teachers.

In 1981–82, teachers' average salary was $14,135. The expenditure per pupil in average daily attendance, 1980–81, was $1,771.

There are 21 universities and senior colleges, of which 8 are state-supported. The University of Mississippi, at Oxford (1844), had, 1982–83, 441 instructors and 9,412 students; Mississippi State University, Starkville, 515 instructors and 12,049 students; Mississippi University for Women, at Columbus, 132 instructors and 1,894 students; University of Southern Mississippi, Hattiesburg, 537 instructors and 10,792 students; Jackson State University, Jackson, 334 instructors and 6,523 students; Delta State University, Cleveland, 188 instructors and 3,222 students; Alcorn State University, Lorman, 147 instructors and 2,442 students; Mississippi Valley State University, Itta Bena, 133 instructors and 2,238 students. State operational expenditure, 1981–82, for higher education was $215·7m.

Junior colleges had (1981–82) 49,403 students and 2,154 instructors. The state appropriation for junior colleges, 1981–82, was $39m.

Health. In 1982 the state had 117 acute general hospitals (13,015 beds) listed by the Mississippi Health Care Commission. In 1982, 14 hospitals with facilities for care of the mentally ill had 2,604 beds.

Social Security. Department of Public Welfare figures show (June 1982) 389 persons receiving State Mandatory Supplementation payments amounting to $6,039.86 or an average of $15.53 per case. The state Medicaid commission paid (1981–82) $293·8m. for medical services, including $29·9m. for drugs, $50m. for skilled nursing home care, $83·7m. for hospital services. There were 73,118 persons eligible for Aged Medicaid, 2,002 persons eligible for Blind Medicaid and 59,035 persons eligible for Disabled Medicaid benefits at 30 June 1982. In June 1982 49,668 families with 104,548 dependent children received $4,410,932 in the Aid to Dependent Children programme. The average payment was $88.81 per family or $42.19 per child.

Books of Reference

1980 Census of Population and Housing: Mississippi.
Mississippi Official and Statistical Register. Secretary of State. Jackson. Biennial
Bettersworth, J. K., *Mississippi: A History.* Rev. ed. Austin, Tex., 1964

Mississippi Library Commission: PO Box 3260 Jackson, MS. 39207. *Head of Information Services:* Sharman B. Smith.

MISSOURI

HISTORY. Missouri, first settled in 1735 at Ste Genevieve, was made a Territory on 1 Oct. 1812, and admitted to the Union on 10 Aug. 1821. In 1837 its boundaries were extended to their present limits.

AREA AND POPULATION. Missouri is bounded north by Iowa, east by the Mississippi River forming the boundary with Illinois and Kentucky, south by

Arkansas, south-west by Oklahoma, west by Kansas and Nebraska, with the Missouri River forming the boundary in the north-west. Area, 69,697 sq. miles, 752 sq. miles being water.

Census population, 1 April 1980, 4,917,444, an increase since 1970 of 5%. Births, 1980, were 80,770 (16·4 per 1,000 population); deaths, 50,504 (10·3); infant deaths, 970 (12·3 per 1,000 live births); marriages, 54,625 (11·1); divorces, 27,595 (5·6).

Population of 5 federal census years was:

	White	*Negro*	*Indian*	*Asiatic*	*Total*	*Per sq. mile*
1910	3,134,932	157,452	313	638	3,293,335	47·9
1930	3,403,876	223,840	578	1,073	3,629,367	52·4
1960	3,922,967	390,853	1,723	3,146	4,319,813	62·5
			All others			
1970	4,177,495	480,172	19,732		4,677,399	67·0
1980	4,346,267	514,274	56,903		4,917,444	71·0

Of the total population in 1980, 2,365,827 were male, 3,350,746 persons were urban and those 18 years of age or older numbered 3,554,203.

The principal cities (1980 census) are:

St Louis	453,085	University City	42,738	Gladstone	24,990
Kansas City	448,159	Joplin	38,893	Ferguson	24,740
Springfield	133,116	St Charles	37,379	Webster Groves	23,097
Independence	111,806	Cape Girardeau	34,361	Sedalia	20,927
St Joseph	76,691	Jefferson City	33,619	Overland	19,620
Columbia	62,061	Raytown	31,759		
Florissant	55,372	Kirkwood	27,987		

Metropolitan areas, 1980 estimate: St Louis, 2,418,879; Kansas City, 1,313,700.

CONSTITUTION AND GOVERNMENT. A new constitution, the fourth, was adopted on 27 Feb. 1945; it has been amended 26 times. The General Assembly consists of a Senate of 34 members elected for 4 years (half for re-election every 2 years), and a House of Representatives of 163 members elected for 2 years. The Governor and Lieut.-Governor are elected for 4 years. Missouri sends to Congress 2 senators and 9 representatives.

Voters (with the usual exceptions) are all citizens and those adult aliens who, within a prescribed period, have applied for citizenship. In the 1980 presidential election Reagan polled 1,074,181, Carter, 931,182 and Anderson 77,920.

Jefferson City is the state capital. The state is divided into 114 counties and the city of St Louis.

Governor: Christopher Bond (R.), 1981–85 ($55,000).
Lieut.-Governor: Kenneth Rothman (D.), 1981–85 ($30,000).
Secretary of State: James C. Kirkpatrick (D.) 1981–85 ($42,500).

BUDGET. For the year 1981 the total revenues from all funds were $4,237m. (federal revenue, $1,341m., general revenue, $2,124·2m.).

Total outstanding debt, 1980, was $3,262m.

Per capita personal income (1980) was $8,982.

NATURAL RESOURCES

Minerals. Principal minerals are lead (ranks first in USA), zinc (ranks second), clays, coal, iron ore, and stone for cement and lime manufacture. Value of production (1980) $1,056m.

Agriculture. In 1981 there 120,000 farms in Missouri covering 32m. acres. The average size of farms is 267 acres. Production of principal crops, 1981: Corn, 213·4m. bu.; soybeans, 159·1m. bu.; wheat, 89m. bu.; sorghum grain, 75·2m. bu.; oats, 1·1m. bu.; cotton, 168,000 bales (of 480 lb.). Cash receipts from farming, 1981, $4,179m. Export value of farm produce, $1,318m., to which soybeans contributed $607·8m.

Forestry. Forest land area, 1977, 12·9m. acres. Timber resources (sawtimber), 15,270m. bd ft.

INDUSTRY. The largest employer in 1980 was manufacturing, in which the transport equipment industry employed 65,102 workers. Other large industries are food and kindred products, electrical equipment and supplies, apparel and related products and non-electrical machinery, leather products, chemicals, paper, metal industries, stone, clay and glass. Retail trade employed 329,617 in 1980, 101,767 of them in eating and drinking places; wholesale trade employed 137,641.

LABOUR. The State Board of Mediation has jurisdiction in labour disputes involving only public utilities. The Prevailing Wage Law (1959) provides that no less than the local hourly rate of wages for work of a similar character shall be paid to any workmen engaged in public works. The Industrial Commission has authority to inspect records and to institute actions for penalties described in the Act. There is a state programme for industrial safety in hand, under the Federal Occupational and Health Act. In Aug. 1982 the estimated number of employed was 2,138,700, and 210,600 were unemployed. The unemployment rate was 9% (estimate).

COMMUNICATIONS

Roads. Federal and state highways, Jan. 1980, totalled 118,236 miles. In 1980 there were 3·4m. vehicles licensed in the state, of which 3,724 were private and commercial buses.

Railways. The state has 16 Class I railroads, operating approximately 3,820 miles of main-line track and 1,810 miles of branch-line track.

Aviation. In 1980 there were 116 public airports and 261 private airports.

Shipping. Ten carrier barge lines operate on 1,900 miles of navigable waterways, including the Missouri and Mississippi Rivers. Boat shipping seasons: Missouri River, March–end Nov.; Mississippi River, early March–mid-Dec.

Post and Broadcasting. There were 192 commercial radio stations and 24 TV stations in 1980. The number of telephones in 1979 was 3·79m.

Newspapers. There were (1982) 51 daily and 241 weekly newspapers.

JUSTICE, RELIGION, EDUCATION AND WELFARE

Justice. State prisons in 1979 had an average of 5,565 inmates. Of those committed, 70% are aged 17–29. There have been no executions since 1965 although the death penalty was reinstated in 1978; since 1930 executions (by lethal gas) have totalled 40, including 31 for murder, 6 for rape and 3 for kidnapping. The Missouri Law Enforcement Assistance Council was created in 1969 for law reform.

Religion. Chief religious bodies are Catholic, with 759,503 members, Southern Baptists (515,383), United Methodists (253,627), Christian Churches (121,827), Lutheran (107,763), Presbyterian (100,056). Total membership, all denominations, about 2·2m. in 1970.

Education. School attendance is compulsory for children from 7 to 16 years for the full term. In the 1980–81 school year, public schools (kindergarten through grade 12) had 844,648 pupils. Total expenditure for public schools in 1980–81, $1,947m. Salaries for teachers (kindergarten through grade 12), 1980–81, averaged $16,562. Institutions for higher education include the University of Missouri, founded in 1839 with campuses at Columbia, Rolla, St Louis and Kansas City, with 3,352 accredited teachers and 51,811 students in 1981. Washington University at St Louis, founded in 1857, and St Louis University (1818), are both private universities. Fourteen state colleges had 106,738 students in 1980. Private colleges had (1980) 57,816 students. Church-affiliated colleges (1980) had 28,783 students. Public junior colleges had 45,155 students. There are about 697 secondary and post-secondary institutions offering vocational courses. There were 234,400 students in higher education in autumn 1980.

Health. There were 8 state mental health hospitals and centres and 2 children's psychiatric hospitals in 1982, admitting 26,772 patients.

Social Security. In 1979 the number of recipients of medicare and medicaid was 338,000. The number of recipients of Aid to Dependent Children was 215,700 with an average monthly payment per family of $217 in 1980.

Books of Reference

Official Manual, Secretary of State, Jefferson City. Biennial
Annual Survey of Manufactures, U.S. Dept. of Commerce, Bureau of the Census
General Population Characteristics, Office of Comptroller and Budget Director, Jefferson City
Missouri Final Production Count, Office of Comptroller and Budget Director, Jefferson City
Missouri Corporate Planner, Division of Commerce and Industrial Development, Jefferson City

MONTANA

HISTORY. Montana, first settled in 1809, was made a Territory (out of portions of Idaho and Dakota Territories) in 1864 and was admitted into the Union on 8 Nov. 1889.

AREA AND POPULATION. Montana is bounded north by Canada, east by North and South Dakota, south by Wyoming and west by Idaho and the Bitterroot Range of the Rocky Mountains. Area, 147,045 sq. miles, including 1,657 sq. miles of water, of which the federal government, 1979, owned 27,741,000 acres or 29·7%. US Bureau of Indian Affairs administered 5·26m. acres, of which 2,204,000 were allotted to tribes. Census population, 1 April 1980, 786,690, an increase of 13·3% since 1970. Births, 1980, were 13,928 (17·7 per 1,000 population); deaths, 6,592 (8·4); infant deaths, 142 (11 per 1,000 live births); marriages, 8,367 (10·6); divorces 4,963 (6·3).

Population in 5 census years was:

	White	*Negro*	*Indian*	*Asiatic*	*Total*	*Per sq. mile*
1910	360,580	1,834	10,745	2,870	376,053	2·6
1930	519,898	1,256	14,798	1,239	537,606	3·7
1950	572,038	1,232	16,606	—	591,024	4·1
1970	663,043	1,995	27,130	1,099	694,409	4·7
1980	740,148	1,786	37,270	2,503	786,690	5·3

Of the total population in 1980, 392,625 were male, 416,402 persons were urban. Persons 20 years of age or older numbered 524,836.

The largest cities (1980) are Billings, 66,798; Great Falls, 56,725. Others, 1980: Butte-Silver Bow, 37,205; Missoula, 33,388; Helena (capital), 23,938; Bozeman, 21,645; Anaconda-Deer Lodge County, 12,518; Havre, 10,891; Kalispell, 10,648.

CONSTITUTION AND GOVERNMENT. A new constitution was ratified by the voters on 6 June 1972, and fully implemented on 1 July 1973; the Senate to consist of 50 senators, elected for 4 years, one half at each biennial election. The 100 members of the House of Representatives are elected for 2 years.

The Governor and Lieut.-Governor are elected for 4 years. Montana sends to Congress 2 senators and 2 representatives.

In the 1980 presidential election Reagan polled 206,814 votes, Carter 118,032.

The capital is Helena. The state is divided into 56 counties.

Governor: Ted Schwinden (D.), 1981–85 ($43,360).
Lieut.-Governor: George Turman (D.), 1981–85 ($31,077).
Secretary of State: Jim Waltermire (R.), 1981–85 ($28,685).

BUDGET. Total state revenues for the year ending 30 June 1980 were $1,153,208,000 ($435·7m. taxes); total expenditures were $1,004,971,000 ($279·3m. for education, $186·7m. for highways and $94·9m. for public welfare).

Total net long-term debt on 30 June 1980 was $146,063,000.

Per capita personal income (1979) was $7,684.

ENERGY AND NATURAL RESOURCES

Electricity. Electric power generated in July 1981 was 1,621 gwh., of which 1,286 gwh. was hydro-electric and 328 gwh. from coal-fired plants.

Minerals (1979). Output of crude petroleum, 30·29m. bbls; copper, 68,854 tonnes; sand and gravel, 7,012,000 short tons; phosphate rock, undisclosed; silver, 3,302,000 troy oz.; gold, 24,050 troy oz.; zinc, 104 tonnes; natural gas, 54,969,000 cu. ft; coal, 32,579,000 short tons. Value of total mineral production (1979), $1,085·7m., with petroleum ($393·6m.) the first, coal ($334·7m.) the second and copper ($143·3m.) the third most important commodity.

Agriculture. In 1980 there were 21,500 farms and ranches (50,564 in 1935) with an area of 62m. acres (47,511,868 acres in 1935). Large-scale farming predominates; in 1980 the average size per farm was 2,884 acres. Income from all farm marketings was $1,231·65m. in 1978 (crops, $548·9m.; livestock, $682·8m.). Irrigated area of total crop land harvested in 1979 was 1,685,000 acres or 19%; value of irrigated crops, $228·5m.

The chief crops are wheat, amounting in 1979 to 116·5m. bu., ranking sixth in US; barley, 40·56m. bu.; oats, 5·5m. bu.; sugar-beet, hay, potatoes, alfalfa, dry beans, flax and cherries. In 1980 there were 28,000 milch cows, 2·65m. all cattle; 209,000 swine.

The wool clip in 1979 was 4,017,000 lb. from 494,000 head of sheep.

Forestry. Total forest area (1977), 22·6m. acres. In 1979 there were 16·8m. acres within 11 national forests.

INDUSTRY. In 1981 manufacturing establishments numbering 612 had 17,264 production workers; value added by manufacture was (1978) $850·6m.

LABOUR (Aug. 1981). Work force, 403,700; total employed, 379,900; total non-agricultural workers, 336,100; agricultural workers, 43,800. Workers employed by major industry group: Mining, 8,500 (average net weekly earnings, $503.53); contract construction, 16,900 ($401.66); manufacturing, 23,600 ($369.8); transport and public utilities, 23,800 ($367.95; wholesale/retail trade, 77,000 ($214.66); finance/insurance/real estate, 13,000 ($163.52); services, 58,000 ($165.39); government, 65,100 (no income figures available). Average weekly earnings for all workers in private non-agricultural industries $254.44. Total unemployed 23,800 (5·9% of the work force in Aug. 1981 as compared to 7·2% nationally for that month).

There were 21 work stoppages in 1979 involving 2,400 workers, with a total of 46,300 man days idle during the year.

COMMUNICATIONS

Roads. In Jan. 1980 the state had 71,643 miles of public roads and streets including 11,695 miles of federally-aided highway. At 30 Sept. 1981 there were 410,283 passenger vehicles, 257,423 trucks and 34,030 motor cycles registered.

Railways. In Nov. 1981 there were 3,802 route miles of railway in the state.

Aviation. There were 121 airports open for public use in Dec. 1980, of which 117 were publicly owned.

JUSTICE, RELIGION, EDUCATION AND WELFARE

Justice. On 1 Nov. 1981 the Montana state prison held 690 inmates. Since 1943 there have been no executions; total since 1930 (all by hanging) was 6; 4 whites and 2 Negroes, for murder.

Religion. The leading religious bodies are (1978): Roman Catholic with 130,000 active members; Lutheran, 62,000; Methodist, 21,000 (church estimates).

Education. In Oct. 1980 public elementary and secondary schools had 155,193 pupils. Public elementary and secondary school teachers (9,139 full-time) had an average salary of $15,967. Total expenditure on public school education (1979–80) was $438·7m.; expenditure per pupil was $2,773. The Montana University system consists of the Montana State University, at Bozeman (autumn 1981: 11,187 students), the University of Montana, at Missoula, founded in 1895 (8,869), the College of Mineral Science and Technology, at Butte (1,992 students), Northern Montana College, at Havre (1,584), Eastern Montana College, at Billings (4,035) and Western Montana College, at Dillon (880).

Social Security. In Aug. 1981, 4,880 persons over age 65 were receiving in medical assistance an average of $588.69 per month; 271 blind persons, $230.31; 4,011 totally disabled, $550.52; 7,083 families (13,674 dependent children) receiving in aid-to-dependent children assistance an average of $237.33 per month. Aid was from state and federal sources.

Health. In July 1981 the state had 64 hospitals (3,534 beds) listed by the Montana Board of Health. Four centres for mental disease and development disorders had 1,027 beds and 769 patients.

Books of Reference

Montana Agricultural Statistics. U.S. Dept. of Agriculture, Montana Crop and Livestock Reporting Service. Biennial from 1946

Montana Employment and Labor Force. Montana Dept. of Labor and Industry. Monthly from 1971

Montana Federal-Aid Road Log. Montana Dept. of Highways and US Dept. of Transportation, Federal Highway Administration. Annual from 1938

Montana Vital Statistics. Montana Dept. of Health and Environmental Sciences. Annually from 1954

Statistical Report. Montana Dept. of Social and Rehabilitation Services. Monthly from 1947

Lang, W, L., and Myers, R. C., *Montana, Our Land and People.* 1979

Malone, M. P., and Roeder, R. B., *Montana, A History of Two Centuries.* Univ. of Washington Press, 1976

NEBRASKA

HISTORY. The Nebraska region was first reached by white men from Mexico under the Spanish general Coronado in 1541. It was ceded by France to Spain in 1763, retroceded to France in 1801, and sold by Napoleon to the US as part of the Louisiana Purchase in 1803. Its first settlement was in 1847, and on 30 May 1854 it became a Territory and on 1 March 1867 a state. In 1882 it annexed a small part of Dakota Territory, and in 1908 it received another small tract from South Dakota.

AREA AND POPULATION. Nebraska is bounded north by South Dakota, with the Missouri River forming the boundary in the north-east and the boundary with Iowa and Missouri to the east; south by Kansas, south-west by Colorado and west by Wyoming. Area, 77,355 sq. miles, of which 711 sq. miles are water. Census population, 1980: 1,569,825, an increase of 5·7% since 1970. Births, 1981, were 27,164 (17·2 per 1,000 population); deaths, 14,580 (9·2); infant deaths, 268 (9·9 per 1,000 live births); marriages, 14,363 (9·1): divorces, 6,769 (4·3).

Population in 5 census years was:

	White	*Negro*	*Indian*	*Asiatic*	*Total*	*Per sq. mile*
1910	1,180,293	7,689	3,502	730	1,192,214	15·5
1920	1,279,219	13,242	2,888	1,023	1,296,372	16·9
1960	1,374,764	29,262	5,545	1,195	1,411,330	18·3
			All others			
1970	1,432,867	39,911	10,715		1,483,791	19·4
1980	1,490,381	48,390	31,054		1,569,825	20·5

Of the total population in 1980, 48·8% were male,62·9% were urban 65·6% were 21 years of age or older. The largest cities in the state are: Omaha, with a census population, 1980, of 313,911; Lincoln (capital), 171,932; Grand Island, 33,180; North Platte, 24,509; Fremont, 23,979; Hastings, 23,045; Bellevue, 21,813; Kearney, 21,158; Norfolk, 19,449.

The Bureau of Indian Affairs, as of 30 June 1981, administered 65,000 acres, of which 22,000 acres were allotted to tribal control.

CONSTITUTION AND GOVERNMENT. The present constitution was adopted in 1875; it has been amended 176 times. By an amendment adopted in Nov. 1934 Nebraska has a single-chambered legislature (elected for 4 years) of 49 members—the only state in the Union to have one. The Governor and Lieut.-Governor are elected for 4 years. Amendments adopted in 1912 and 1920 provide for legislation through the initiative and referendum and permit cities of more than 5,000 inhabitants to frame their own charters. A 'right-to-work' amendment adopted 5 Nov. 1946 makes illegal the 'closed shop' demands of trade unions. Nebraska is represented in Congress by 2 senators and 3 representatives.

In the 1980 presidential election Reagan polled 413,338 votes, Carter 164,270 and Anderson 44,024.

The capital is Lincoln. The state has 93 counties.

Governor: Robert Kerrey (D.), 1983–86 ($40,000).
Lieut.-Governor: Donald F. McGinley (D.) ($32,000).
Secretary of State: Allen Beerman (R.) ($32,000).

BUDGET. For the fiscal year ending 30 June 1980 (US Census Bureau figures) the state's revenues were $1,506m. (taxation, $817m. and federal aid, $361m.); general expenditures were $1,341m. ($416m. for education, $265m. for highways and $191m. for public welfare).

The state has a bonded indebtedness limit of $100,000.

Per capita personal income (1981) was $10,366.

ENERGY AND NATURAL RESOURCES

Minerals. The total output of minerals, 1980, was valued at $271·8m., petroleum (6m. bbls) and sand and gravel (12m. tons) being the most important.

Agriculture. Nebraska is one of the most important agricultural states. In 1981 it contained approximately 65,000 farms, with a total area of 48m. acres. The average farm was 734 acres.

In 1980, 7·2m. acres were irrigated and 68,319 irrigation wells were registered.

Cash income from crops (1981), $2,855·2m., and from livestock, $3,520·8m. Principal crops, with estimated 1981 yield: Maize, 802·7m. bu. (ranking third in US); wheat, 106·2m. bu.; sorghums for grain, 164·8m. bu.; oats, 15·4m. bu.; soybeans, 82·7m. bu. About 953 farms grow sugar-beet for 5 factories; output, 1981, 1·9m. short tons. On 1 Jan. 1982 the state contained 7·3m. all cattle (ranking third in US), 122,000 milch cows, 225,000 sheep and 4·1m. swine.

Forestry. The area of national forest, 1980, was 352,000 acres.

INDUSTRY. In 1977 there were 1,969 manufacturing establishments. In 1978 61,400 production workers earned $786·5m. and value added by manufacturing was $2,821·8m. The chief industry is meat-packing, employing (1978), 8,200 (7,100 production workers) and value added was $258·3m.

COMMUNICATIONS

Roads. The state-maintained highway system embraced 9,885 miles in 1981; local roads, 96,270 miles. In 1981, 796,790 automobiles were registered.

Railways. In 1981 there were 7,342 miles of railway.

Aviation. Airports (1981) numbered 318, of which 112 were publicly owned.

JUSTICE, RELIGION, EDUCATION AND WELFARE

Justice. A 'Civil Rights Act' revised in 1969 provides that all people are entitled to a 'full and equal enjoyment of the accommodations, advantages, facilities and privileges' of hotels, restaurants, public conveyances, amusement places and other places. The state university is forbidden to discriminate between students 'because of age, sex, color or nationality'. An Act of 1941 declares it to be 'the policy of this state' that no trade union should discriminate, in collective bargaining, 'against any person because of his race or color'.

The state's prisons had, 19 Oct, 1982, 1,484 inmates (94 per 100,000 population). From 1930 to 1962 there were 4 executions (electrocution), 3 white men and 1 American Indian, all for murder, and none since.

Religion. The Roman Catholics had 332,000 members in 1982; Protestant Churches, 667,298; Jews, 7,500 members. Total, all denominations, 1,006,798 (unofficial figures).

Education. School attendance is compulsory for children from 7 to 16 years of age. Public elementary schools, autumn 1981, had 185,940 enrolled pupils.. Teachers' salaries, 1981–82, averaged $16,570. Estimated public school expenditure for year ending 30 Aug. 1981 was $632·6m. Total enrolment in 30 institutions of higher education, autumn 1981, was 93,513 students. The largest institutions were (1981):

Opened	*Institution*	*Students*
1867	Peru State College, Peru (State)	818
1869	Univ. of Nebraska, Lincoln (State)	24,786
1878	Creighton Univ., Omaha (RC)	5,766
1883	Midland Lutheran College, Fremont (Lutheran)	875
1887	Nebraska Wesleyan Univ. (Methodist)	1,183
1891	Union College, Lincoln (Seventh Day Adventist)	942
1894	Concordia Teachers' College, Seward (Lutheran)	1,068
1905	Kearney State College, Kearney (State)	7,004
1908	Univ. of Nebraska, Omaha (State)	14,023
1910	Wayne State College, Wayne (State)	2,233
1911	Chadron State College, Chadron (State)	1,909
1923	College of St. Mary	897
1966	Bellevue College, Bellevue (Private)	2,615

The state holds 1·52m. acres of land as a permanent endowment of her schools; permanent public school endowment fund in Aug. 1982 was $71·1m.

Health. In 1982 the state had 113 hospitals and 576 patients in mental hospitals.

Social Security. The administration of public welfare is the responsibility of the County Divisions of Welfare with policy-forming, regulatory, advisory and supervisory functions performed by the State Department of Public Welfare. In 1981 public welfare provided financial aid and/or services as follows: for 6,188 individuals who were aged, blind or disabled, with an average state supplement of $57.02; for 13,731 families with dependent children, with an average payment of $286.34 per family; for about 70,000 individuals who had medical needs, $1,708.91, per individual; for 1,768 children in need of child welfare services; for 3,307 children who were in need of crippled children's services and medical care. The amount of aid is based on need in accordance with State assistance standards; the programme of aid to families with dependent children is limited to a maximum maintenance payment of $293 for 1 child plus $71 for each additional child.

Books of Reference

Agricultural Atlas of Nebraska. Univ. of Nebraska Press, 1977
Climatic Atlas of Nebraska. Univ. of Nebraska Press, 1977
Economic Atlas of Nebraska. Univ. of Nebraska Press, 1977
Nebraska. A Guide to the Cornhusker State. Univ. of Nebraska Press, 1979
Nebraska Statistical Handbook, 1982–83. Nebraska Dept. of Econ. Development, Lincoln
Nebraska Blue-Book. Legislative Council. Lincoln. Biennial
Olson, J. C., *History of Nebraska.* Univ. of Nebraska Press, 1955

State Library: State Law Library, State House, Lincoln. *Librarian:* Larry D. Donelson.

NEVADA

HISTORY. Nevada, first settled in 1851, when it was a part of the Territory of Utah (created 1850), was made a Territory in 1861, enlarged in 1862 by an addition from Utah Territory and admitted into the Union on 31 Oct. 1864 as the 36th state. In 1866 and 1867 the area of the state was significantly enlarged at the expense of the Territories of Utah and Arizona.

AREA AND POPULATION. Nevada is bounded north by Oregon and Idaho, east by Utah, south-east by Arizona, with the Colorado River forming most of the boundary, south and west by California. Area 110,561 sq. miles, 667 sq. miles being water. The federal government in 1973 owned 60,908,872 acres, or 86·5% of the land area. Vacant public lands, 48,340,876 acres. The Bureau of Indian Affairs controlled 1·35m. acres in 1975, of which 1,062,047 acres have been assigned to Indian tribes.

Census population on 1 April 1980, 799,184, an increase of 310,446 or 63·5% since 1970. Births, 1980, were 13,156 (16·5 per 1,000 population); deaths, 6,408 (8); infant deaths, 157 (12 per 1,000 live births); marriages, 115,411 (144·5 per 1,000 population, largest of any state); divorces, 13,659 (17·1).

Population in 5 census years was:

	White	*Negro*	*Indian*	*Asiatic and all others*	*Total*	*Per sq. mile*
1910	74,276	513	5,240	1,846	81,875	0·7
1930	84,515	516	4,871	1,156	91,058	0·8
1960	263,443	13,484	6,681	1,670	285,278	2·6
1970	449,850	27,579	7,329	3,980	488,738	4·4
			All others			
1980	699,377	50,791	49,016		799,184	7·2

Of the total population in 1980, 404,372 were male, 681,682 were urban and 556,021 were 20 years of age or older.

The largest cities are Las Vegas, with population (1980 census) of 164,674; Reno, 100,756. Others (1980 preliminary): North Las Vegas, 39,196; Sparks, 38,114; Carson City, 30,807, and Henderson, 20,905. Clark County (Las Vegas, North Las Vegas and Henderson) and Washoe County (Reno and Sparks) together had 81% of the total state population in 1980.

CONSTITUTION AND GOVERNMENT. The constitution adopted in 1864 is still in force, with over 60 amendments. The Legislature meets biennially (and in special sessions) and consists of a Senate of 20 members elected for 4 years, half their number retiring every 2 years, and an Assembly of 40 members elected for 2 years. The Governor, Lieut.-Governor and Attorney-General are elected for 4 years. Qualified electors are all citizens with the usual residential qualification. Nevada is represented in Congress by 2 senators and 2 representatives. A Supreme Court of 5 members is elected for 4 years on a non-partisan ballot.

In the 1980 presidential election Reagan polled 155,017 votes, Carter 66,466 and Anderson 17,651.

The state capital is Carson City (population, 30,807 in 1980). There are 16 counties, 17 incorporated cities and towns, 44 unincorporated towns and 1 city-county (Carson City).

Governor: Richard Bryan (D.), 1983–86 ($50,000).
Lieut.-Governor: Bob Cashell (D.) ($8,000).
Secretary of State: William D. Swackhammer (D.) ($32,500).

BUDGET. For the fiscal year ending 30 June 1981 estimated state general fund revenues were $342·4m., including federal receipts; general expenditures were $334m. Education followed by human resources and public safety received the largest appropriations.

State bonded indebtedness on 30 June 1980, was $17·7m. The state has no franchise tax, capital stock tax, special intangibles tax, chain stores tax, stock transfer tax, admissions tax, estate tax, gift tax, income taxes or inheritance tax. The sales and use tax and gaming taxes are the largest revenue producers.

Per capita personal income (1980) was $10,723.

ENERGY AND NATURAL RESOURCES

Electricity. Electricity power stations supplied 8,463m. mwh. in 1978. There were about 316,484 private and commercial customers in 1979. There are 8 suppliers of natural gas producing 51,696,121 m.cu.ft in 1978.

Minerals. Production, 1980, in order of value was gold, barite, sand and gravel, silver. Other minerals are gypsum, iron ore, mercury, lime, lithium, petroleum, gemstones, lead, molybdenum, fluorspar, perlite, pumice, clays, talc, salt, tungsten, magnesite, diatonite and zinc. Value of mineral output for 1980, $386m.

Agriculture. In 1980, 2,000 farms had a farm area of 9m. acres (9·2m. in 1960). Farms averaged (1978) 4,500 acres. Area under irrigation (1979) was 1·3m. acres compared with 542,976 acres in 1959.

Gross income, 1980, from crops, livestock and government payments, $262·8m. Cattle, dairy products, hay, potatoes and sheep are the principal commodities in order of cash receipts. Average income per farm, $14,266 (estimate, 1978). Total value of crops produced, $75m., of which hay accounted for 17·1%. On 1 Jan. 1979 there were 15,000 milch cows, 280,000 beef cattle, 114,000 sheep and 8,000 swine.

Forestry. The area of national forests (1975) under US Forest Service administration was 5,051,938 acres.

INDUSTRY. The main industries are the service industry, especially tourism and legalized gambling, mining and smelting, livestock and irrigated agriculture, chemical manufacturing, and lumber processing. In 1981 there were 843 manufacturing establishments with 20,094 employees, earning $362m.; value added by manufacture (1977) was $498m.; value of shipments, about $800m.

Gaming industry gross revenue for financial year ending 30 June 1981, $2,463·1m. There were at the same time 1,300 licences in force.

LABOUR. In Oct. 1981 unemployment was 6·8% of the work force. All industries employed 425,000 workers. Main industries and employees, 1981: Mining, 7,900; contract construction, 25,300; manufacturing, 19,900; transport (except railways), public works and utilities, 25,100; interstate railways, 1,600; hotels, gaming and recreation, 116,800; other service industries, 58,200; retail trade, 71,800; government, 57,500.

COMMUNICATIONS

Roads. Highway mileage (federal, state and local) totalled 49,659 in 1973, of which 16,464 miles were surfaced; motor vehicle registrations at 1 Jan. 1982 numbered 757,609.

Railways. In 1973 there were 1,553 miles of main-line railway. Nevada is served by Southern Pacific, Union Pacific and Western Pacific railways, and Amtrac passenger service for Carlin, Elko, Reno and Sparks.

Aviation. There were (1974) 114 civil airports and heliports (1,307 civil aircraft registered); 16 scheduled airlines operated. During 1981 McCarren International Airport handled 9·5m. passengers and Cannon International Airport handled 2·3m. passengers.

Post. In 1976 there were 11 telephone exchanges with (1980), 787,232 telephones in service.

JUSTICE, RELIGION, EDUCATION AND WELFARE

Justice. Prohibition of marriage between persons of different race was repealed by statute in 1959.

A 1965 Civil Rights Act makes it illegal for persons operating public accommodations, employers of 15 or more employees, labour unions, and employment agencies to discriminate on the basis of race, colour, religion or national origin; a 1971 law makes racial discrimination in the sale or renting of houses illegal. A Commission on Equal Rights of Citizens is charged with enforcing these laws.

Between 1924 and 1967 executions (by lethal gas—the first state to adopt this method, in 1921), numbered 31. Capital punishment was abolished in 1972 and later re-introduced; there was 1 execution (by lethal gas) in 1979.

Prison population, 1976, was 953; men 902, women 51.

Religion. Roman Catholics are the most numerous religious group, followed by members of the Church of Jesus Christ of Latter-day Saints (Mormons) and various Protestant churches.

Education. School attendance is compulsory for children from 7 to 17 years of age. In Oct. 1979 the 184 public elementary schools, including kindergartens, had 93,516 pupils; there were 83 secondary public schools, including junior and high schools, with 45,997. Special schools for handicapped pupils had 8,221. There were 2,879 elementary teachers (average salary $15,283), 2,700 secondary teachers with an average salary of $15,392. There were 36 parochial and private schools. The University of Nevada, Reno, had, in 1979, 390 full-time instructors and 9,447 students (regular, non-degree and correspondent), and University of Nevada, Las Vegas, 300 instructors and 8,742 students. Two-year community colleges operate as part of the University of Nevada system in Carson City, Elko and Las Vegas. There were (1979) 19,175 students.

Health. In 1976 the state had 24 hospitals (3,064 beds) and 19 skilled nursing units (1,158 beds).

Social Security. Old-age assistance is granted to all 65 years of age or older who are in need, and have assets not over $750 ($1,500 for married couples); end of fiscal year 1974–75, total expenditure was $6,179,040 at an average of $140 each person per month, for 3,678 people. Families with dependent children received $7,613,458 at $45.52 monthly average per person. The blind received $328,440 at $170 for 161 people. Nevada is the only state without aid to the permanently and totally disabled.

Books of Reference

Information: Bureau of Business and Economic Research (Univ. of Nevada).

Handbook of the Nevada Legislature, 55th Session, 1969. Legislative Counsel Bureau. Carson City

Legislative Manual, State of Nevada, 55th Session, 1969. Legislative Counsel Bureau. Carson City

Political History of Nevada. Secretary of State. Carson City, 1965

Financing State and Local Government in Nevada. Legislative Counsel Bureau. Carson City 1960

Study of General Fund Revenues of the State of Nevada. Legislative Counsel Bureau. Carson City, 1966

Education, Manpower and Economic Data for Nevada. Nevada Employment Security Dept., Carson City, 1971

Bushnell, E., *The Nevada Constitution: Origin and Growth.* Univ. of Nevada Press, 2nd ed., 1968

Hulse, James W., *The Nevada Adventure, A History.* Univ. of Nevada Press, 2nd ed., 1969

Mack, E. M., and Sawyer, B. W., *Here is Nevada: A History of the State.* Sparks, Nevada, 1965

State Library: Nevada State Library, Carson City. *State Librarian:* Mildred J. Heyer.

NEW HAMPSHIRE

HISTORY. New Hampshire, first settled in 1623, is one of the 13 original states of the Union.

AREA AND POPULATION. New Hampshire is bounded north by Canada, east by Maine and the Atlantic, south by Massachusetts and west by Vermont. Area, 9,279 sq. miles, of which 286 sq. miles are inland water. Census population,

1 April 1980, 920,610, an increase of 24·8% since 1970. Births, 1980, were 12,330; deaths, 7,190; infant deaths, 101; marriages, 9,049; divorces, 4,471.

Population at 5 federal censuses was:

	White	*Negro*	*Indian*	*Asiatic*	*Total*	*Per sq. mile*
1910	429,906	564	34	68	430,572	47·7
1930	464,351	790	64	88	465,293	51·6
1960	604,334	1,903	135	549	606,921	65·2
			All others			
1970	733,106	2,505	2,070		737,681	81·7
1980	910,099	3,990	6,521		920,610	101·9

Of the total population in 1980, 448,462 were male, 480,325 were urban; those 20 years of age or older numbered 625,562.

The largest city of the state is Manchester, with a 1980 census population of 90,757. Other cities are: Nashua, 67,817; Concord (capital), 30,360; Portsmouth, 26,214; Dover, 22,265; Keene, 21,385; Rochester, 21,579; Berlin, 13,090; Laconia, 15,579; Claremont, 14,575; Lebanon, 11,052; Somersworth, 10,313.

CONSTITUTION AND GOVERNMENT. While the present constitution dates from 1784, it was extensively revised in 1792 when the state joined the Union. Since 1775 there have been 16 state conventions with 49 amendments adopted to amend the constitution.

The Legislature consists of a Senate of 30 members, elected for 2 years, and a House of Representatives, restricted to between 375 and 400 members, elected for 2 years. The Governor and 5 administrative officers called 'Councillors' are also elected for 2 years.

Electors must be adult citizens, able to read and write, duly registered and not paupers or under sentence for crime. New Hampshire sends to the Federal Congress 2 senators and 2 representatives.

In the 1980 presidential election Reagan polled 221,705 votes, Carter 108,864 and Anderson 49,693.

The capital is Concord. The state is divided into 10 counties.

Governor: John Sununu (R.), 1983–85 ($44,520).
Secretary of State: William M. Gardner (D.) ($31,270).

BUDGET. The state government's general revenue for the fiscal year ending 30 June 1980 (US Census Bureau figures) was $893m.; general expenditures, $889·4m.

Net long-term debt of state, 30 June 1980, was $899m.

Per capita personal income (1980) was $9,131.

NATURAL RESOURCES

Minerals. Minerals are little worked; they consist mainly of sand and gravel, stone, and clay for building and highway construction.

Agriculture. In 1978, there were 3,288 farms occupying 9·4% of the land area; average farm was 164 acres. The US Soil Survey estimates that the state has 164,167 acres of excellent soil, 486,615 acres of fair soil, 530,630 of poor soil and 3,843,798 of non-arable soil. Only 636,195 acres (11% of the total area) show moderate erosion.

Cash income, 1980, from crops and livestock, $99·2m. The chief field crops are hay and vegetables; the chief fruit crop is apples. On 1 Jan. 1975 animals on farms were 40,000 milch cows, 69,000 all cattle, 4,800 sheep, 8,700 swine, 1·8m. poultry, 28,000 turkeys and about 36,225 horses.

Forestry. In 1975 commercial forest land totalled 4,907,400 acres; national forest, 591,909 acres; state forests and parks, 72,353 acres; forest industry ownership, 793,400 acres.

INDUSTRY. In 1978, manufacturing establishments employed 78,400 production workers earning $773·3m., and value added by manufacture was $2,764·2m.; 54% of manufacturing employment is accounted for in durable goods.

Principal industries are, electrical machinery, non-electrical machinery, metal products, textiles and shoes.

COMMUNICATIONS

Roads. On 1 Jan. 1975 the length of state highways was 4,373 miles, of which the state maintained 4,155 miles and municipalities 218 miles. The length of town roads, urban and rural, totalled 7,918 miles. Motor vehicles registered, 1980, numbered 655,000.

Railways. In 1975 the length of railway in the state was 826 miles.

Aviation. There were 47 airports of which 14 were public.

JUSTICE, RELIGION, EDUCATION AND WELFARE

Justice. The state prison held 316 persons on 1 Jan. 1980. Since 1930 there has been only one execution (by hanging)—a white man, for murder, in 1939.

Religion. The Roman Catholic Church is the largest single body. The largest Protestant churches are Congregational, Episcopal, Methodist and United Baptist Convention of N.H.

Education. School attendance is compulsory for children from 6 to 14 years of age during the whole school term, or to 16 if their district provides a high school. Employed illiterate minors between 16 and 21 years of age must attend evening or special classes, if provided by the district.

In 1980 the public elementary and secondary schools enrolled 171,000 pupils. In 1975, 70 private and parochial elementary schools had 11,817 registered pupils and 20 secondary schools, 6,057. Public school salaries, 1979–80, averaged $13,342. Total expenditure on public schools in 1980 was estimated at $324m.

Total enrolment, 1980, in 25 institutions of higher education was 46,800 students. Dartmouth College, at Hanover was founded in 1769, the University of New Hampshire, at Durham was founded in 1866.

Health. In 1980 the state had 33 hospitals (4,680 beds). In 1975 mental hospitals had 1,260 patients, and there were 724 persons in institutions for the mentally retarded.

Social Security. The Division of Welfare handles public assistance for (1) aged citizens 65 years or over, (2) needy aged aliens, (3) needy blind persons, (4) needy citizens between 18 and 64 years inclusive, who are permanently and totally disabled, (5) needy children under 21 years, (6) Medicaid and the medically needy not eligible for a monthly grant.

In Dec. 1980, 2,100 persons were receiving SSI old-age assistance of an average $87 per month; 3,200 permanently and totally disabled, $166 per month; 8,600 families with dependent children, $271 per month.

Books of Reference

Morrison, L. S., *The Government of New Hampshire.* Concord, 1952
N.H. Register. State Year Book and Legislative Manual. Portland, Maine, 1965
Squires, J. D., *Granite State of the United States.* New York, 1956

NEW JERSEY

HISTORY. New Jersey, first settled in the early 1600s, is one of the 13 original states in the Union.

AREA AND POPULATION. New Jersey is bounded north by New York, east by the Atlantic with Long Island and New York City to the north-east, south by Delaware Bay and west by Pennsylvania. Area (US Bureau of Census), 7,787 sq. miles (319 sq. miles being inland water). Census population, 1 April 1980, 7,364,158, an increase of 2·3% since 1970. Births, 1979, were 95,672 (13 per 1,000 population); deaths, 65,495 (8·7); infant deaths, 1,223 (12·8 per 1,000 live births); marriages, 54,740 (7·5); divorces, 28,204.

Population at 5 federal censuses was:

	White	*Negro*	*Indian*	*Asiatic*	*All others*	*Total*	*Per sq. mile*
1910	2,445,894	89,760	168	1,345	—	2,537,167	337·7
1930	3,829,663	208,828	213	2,630	122	4,041,334	537·3
1960	5,539,003	514,875	1,699	8,778	2,427	6,066,782	739·5
1970	6,349,908	770,292	4,706	20,537	22,721	7,168,164	953·1
1980	6,127,090	924,786	8,394	103,842	200,046	7,364,158	979·1

Of the population in 1980, 3,532,719 were male, 6,556,697 persons were urban, 5,116,105 were 20 years of age or older.

Census population of the larger cities and towns in 1980 was:

Newark	329,248	Irvington	61,493	Parsippany-Troy Hills	49,868
Jersey City	223,532	Union City	55,593	Middleton	62,574
Paterson	137,970	Vineland	53,753	Union Township	50,184
Elizabeth	106,201	Passaic	52,463	Bloomfield	47,792
Trenton (capital)	92,124	Woodbridge	90,074	Atlantic City	40,199
Camden	84,910	Hamilton	82,801	Plainfield	45,555
Clifton	74,388	Edison	70,193	Hoboken	42,460
East Orange	77,025	Cherry Hill	68,785	Montclair	38,321
Bayonne	65,047				

Largest urbanized areas (1980) were: Newark, 1,963,000; Jersey City, 555,483; Paterson-Clifton-Passaic, 447,785; Trenton (NJ–Pa.), 305,678.

CONSTITUTION AND GOVERNMENT. The legislative power is vested in a Senate and a General Assembly, the members of which are chosen by the people, all citizens (with necessary exceptions) 18 years of age, with the usual residential qualifications, having the right of suffrage. The present constitution, ratified by the registered voters on 4 Nov. 1947, has been amended 27 times. In 1966 the Constitutional Convention proposed, and the people adopted, a new plan providing for a 40-member Senate and an 80-member General Assembly. This plan, as certified by the Apportionment Commission and modified by the courts, provides for 40 legislative districts, with 1 senator and 2 assemblymen elected for each. Assemblymen serve 2 years, senators 4 years, except those elected at the election following each census, who serve for 2 years. The Governor is elected for 4 years.

The state sends to Congress 2 senators and 14 representatives.

In the 1980 presidential election Reagan polled 1,546,557 votes, Carter 1,147,364 and Anderson 234,632.

The capital is Trenton. The state is divided into 21 counties, which are subdivided into 567 municipalities—cities, towns, boroughs, villages and townships.

Governor: Thomas H. Kean (R.), 1982–85 ($85,000).
Secretary of State: Jane Burgio ($60,000).

BUDGET. For the year ending 30 June 1982 (US Census Bureau figures) general revenues were $6,376·5m. (taxation $3,729·26m. and federal aid, $1,610·1m.); general expenditures were $6,539·5m. (education, $2,118·5m.; highways, $379·2m., and public welfare, $1,317·5m.).

Total net long-term debt, 30 June 1981, was $5,374,834,000.

Per capita personal income (1980) was $10,924.

NATURAL RESOURCES

Minerals. The chief minerals are stone ($63m., 1979) and sand and gravel ($45m.); others are zinc ($25m.), clay products ($559,000), peat ($549,000) and gemstones ($1,000). New Jersey is a leading producer of greensand marl, magnesium compounds and peat. Total value of mineral products, 1979, was $151·69.m.

Agriculture. Livestock raising, market-gardening, fruit-growing, horticulture and forestry are pursued. In 1980, 9,100 farms had a total area of 1m. acres; average farm had 109·9 acres valued at $2,998 per acre.

Cash income, 1980, from crops, $248·6, and livestock, $122·3m.

Leading crops are tomatoes (value, $14·26m., 1980), all corn ($22·26m.), peaches ($22·75m.), hay ($9·12m.), blueberries ($15·86m.), soybeans ($24·85m.).

Farm animals on 1 Jan. 1980 included 41,000 milch cows, 100,000 all cattle, 9,300 sheep and lambs and 69,000 swine.

INDUSTRY. In 1978 manufacturing establishments employed 798,100 workers, receiving $12,025·2m. in wages; value added by manufacture, $24,725·4m. The principal industries by value are: Chemicals and allied products, food and kindred products, electrical equipment and supplies, machinery (except electrical).

COMMUNICATIONS

Roads. In 1978 there were 33,249 miles of roads (municipal, 19,559 miles; state, 3,084 miles; county, 6,803 miles; others, 3,803 miles).

Railways. In 1979, the state had 1,576 route miles of railway.

Aviation. There were (1979) 266 airports, of which 30 were publicly owned.

JUSTICE, RELIGION, EDUCATION AND WELFARE

Justice. State prisons in Aug. 1981 had 7,932 inmates. Since 1930 executions (by electrocution) have totalled 74, including 47 whites, 25 Negroes and 2 other races, all for murder. There have been none since 1966.

The constitution of New Jersey forbids discrimination against any person on account of 'religious principles, race, color, ancestry or national origin'. The state has had, since 1945, a 'fair employment act', *i.e.*, a Civil Rights statute forbidding any employer, public or private (with 6 or more employees), to discriminate against any applicant for work (or to discharge any employee) on the grounds of 'race, creed, color, national origin or ancestry'. Trade unions may not bar Negroes from membership.

Religion. The Roman Catholic population of New Jersey in 1980 was 2,925,087. No official Protestant figures are available; estimates place Jewish population at 442,765 (1980).

Education. Elementary instruction is compulsory for all from 6 to 16 years of age and free to all from 5 to 20 years of age. In autumn 1979 public elementary schools had 798,329 and secondary schools had 489,930 enrolled pupils; public colleges in autumn 1980 had 252,102 students, including 111,137 in community colleges, and independent colleges had 67,220. The total cost of public schools, 1978–79, $3,296·9m. Average salary of all elementary and secondary classroom teachers in public schools 1979–80 was $17,159.

Rutgers, the State University (founded as Queen's College in 1766) had, in 1980, an opening autumn enrolment of 48,440 full- and part-time students. Princeton (founded in 1746) had 6,167 students. Fairleigh Dickinson (1941), had 19,076; Kean College, 13,237; Montclair State College, 15,829; Glassboro State College, 10,273; Trenton State College, 10,578.

Health. In 1980 the state had 135 hospitals (43,743 beds), listed by the American Hospital Association.

Social Security. In the financial year 1980 gross expenditure for all public assistance programmes was $613,804,321. Average monthly total of cases was $249,409 with an average grant per case of $205.

Books of Reference

Legislative District Data Book. Bureau of Government Research. Annual
Manual of the Legislature of New Jersey. Trenton. Annual
Boyd, J. P. (ed.), *Fundamentals and Constitutions of New Jersey, 1664–1954.* Princeton, 1964
Cunningham, J. T., *New Jersey: America's Main Road.* Rev. ed. New York, 1976
League of Women Voters of New Jersey. *New Jersey: Spotlight on Government.* Rutgers Univ. Press, 3rd ed., 1978
Lehne, R., and Rosenthal, A. (eds.), *Politics in New Jersey.* Rev. ed., Rutgers Univ. Press, 1979

State Library: 185 W. State Street, Trenton, N.J. 08625. *State Librarian:* Barbara F. Weaver.

NEW MEXICO

HISTORY. The first European settlement was established in 1598. Until 1771 New Mexico was the Spanish kings' 'Kingdom of New Mexico'. In 1771 it was annexed to the northern province of New Spain. When New Spain won its independence in 1821, it took the name of Republic of Mexico and established New Mexico as its northernmost department. When the war between the US and Mexico was concluded on 2 Feb. 1848 New Mexico was recognized as belonging to the US, and on 9 Sept. 1850 it was made a Territory. Part of the Territory was assigned to Texas; later Utah was formed into a separate Territory; in 1861 another part was transferred to Colorado, and in 1863 Arizona was disjoined, leaving to New Mexico its present area. New Mexico became a state in Jan. 1912.

AREA AND POPULATION. New Mexico is bounded north by Colorado, north-east by Oklahoma, east by Texas, south by Texas and Mexico and west by Arizona. Land area 121,593 sq. miles (258 sq. miles water). Public lands, administered by federal agencies (1975) amounted to 26·7m. acres or 34% of the total area. The Bureau of Indian Affairs held 7·3m. acres; the State of New Mexico held 9·4m. acres; 34·4m. acres were privately owned.

Census population, 1 April 1980, 1,302,894, an increase of 285,839 or 28% since 1970. Vital statistics, 1980: Births, 25,661 (20 per 1,000 population); deaths, 9,080 (7·1); infant deaths, 272 (10·6 per 1,000 live births); marriages, 16,324 (12·7); divorces, 10,444 (8·1).

The population in 5 census years was:

	White	*Negro*	*Indian*	*Asiatic*	*Total*	*Per sq. mile*
1910	304,594	1,628	20,573	506	327,301	2·7
1940	492,312	4,672	34,510	324	531,818	4·4
1960	875,763	17,063	56,255	1,942	951,023	7·8
1970	915,815	19,555	72,788	7,842 [1]	1,016,000	8·4
1980	1,165,930	24,020	106,119	6,825	1,302,894	10·7

[1] Includes unspecified races, 1970.

Of the 1980 total, 640,643 (preliminary) were male, 939,963 persons were urban; 884,987 were 18 years of age or older.

Before 1930 New Mexico was largely a Spanish-speaking state, but since 1945 an influx of population from other states has reduced the percentage of white persons of Spanish origin or descent to an estimated 37%.

The largest cities are Albuquerque, with population (Census, 1980) 331,767. Santa Fé (capital), 48,953; Las Cruces, 45,086; Roswell, 39,676; Farmington, 31,222.

CONSTITUTION AND GOVERNMENT. The constitution of 1912 is still in force with 73 amendments. The state Legislature, which meets annually, consists of 42 members of the Senate, elected for 4 years, and 70 members of the House of Representatives, elected for 2 years. The Governor and Lieut.-Governor are elected for 4 years. The state sends to Congress 2 senators and 3 representatives.

In the 1980 presidential election Reagan polled 250,779 votes, Carter 167,826.

The state capital is Santa Fé. For local government the state is divided into 33 counties.

Governor: Tony Anaya (D.), 1983–86 ($35,000).
Lieut.-Governor: Mike Runnells (D.), 1983–86 ($14.42 hourly rate).
Secretary of State: Clara Jones (D.), 1983–86 ($30,000).

BUDGET. For the year ending 30 June 1980 (US Census Bureau figures) general revenues were $2,514·3m. ($1,143m. from taxation and $554·3m. from federal government); general expenditures, $2,156m. (education, $924·2m.; highways, $252m., and public welfare, $166·4m.).

Long-term debt on 30 June 1980 was $1,888·8m.

Per capita personal income (1980) was $7,841.

ENERGY AND NATURAL RESOURCES

Minerals. New Mexico is the country's largest domestic source of uranium, perlite and potassium salts. Production of recoverable U_3O_8 was 15·3m. lb. in 1980; perlite, 544,000 short tons; potassium salts, 2·03m. short tons; petroleum, 74·3m. bbls (of 42 gallons); natural gas, 1,083,965m. cu. ft; natural gas liquids, 43m. bbls (of 42 gallons); copper, 155,261 tonnes; coal, 22·8m. short tons. The value of the total mineral output was $6,048m. An average of 29,500 persons were employed monthly in the mining industry in 1980.

Agriculture. New Mexico produces cereals, vegetables, fruit, livestock and cotton. Dry farming and irrigation have proved profitable in periods of high prices. There were 13,600 farms and ranches covering 46·7m. acres in 1981, average farm (or ranch) was valued (land and buildings) at $481,954 in the 1978 US Census of Agriculture; 3,862 farms and ranches were of 1,000 acres and over.

Cash income, 1980, from crops, $273m., and from livestock products, $850m. Principal crops are cotton (110,200 bales from 126,300 acres), hay (1·1m. tons from 310,000 acres) and grain sorghums (10·3m. bu. from 257,000 acres). Farm animals on 1 Jan. 1980 included 38,000 milch cows, 1·5m. all cattle, 650,000 sheep and 74,000 swine. National forest area (1980) covered 9·2m. acres.

INDUSTRY. Average monthly non-agricultural employment during 1980 was 462,300: 34,300 were employed in manufacturing, 124,500 in government. In 1977, 20,900 production workers earned $183·8m. during the year; value added by manufacture was $733·5m.

COMMUNICATIONS

Roads. The state, 1978, had 70,837 miles of road, of which the state maintained 12,692 miles. Motor vehicle registrations, 1980, 1,185,295.

Railways. In 1979 there were 1,964 miles of railway.

Aviation. There were 149 airports in Dec. 1980.

JUSTICE, RELIGION, EDUCATION AND WELFARE

Justice. The number of state prison inmates, average population 1981, was 1,479. The death penalty (by electrocution) has been imposed on 8 persons since 1933, 6 whites and 2 Negroes, all for murder. The last execution was in 1960.

Since 1949 the denial of employment by reason of race, colour, religion, national origin or ancestry has been forbidden. A law of 1955 prohibits discrimination in public places because of race or colour. An 'equal rights' amendment was made to the constitution in 1972.

Religion. There were (1975) approximately 356,530 Protestant Church members and 315,470 Roman Catholics.

Education. Elementary education is free, and compulsory between 6 and 17 years or high-school graduation age. In 1979–80 the 89 school districts had an estimated enrolment of 266,544 students in public elementary and secondary schools. Private and parochial schools had 20,416 pupils. There were 14,166 teachers receiving an average salary of $14,887. Public education expenditure was $646·8m.

The state-supported 4-year institutes of higher education are (1981):

	Faculty	*Students*
University of New Mexico, Albuquerque	768	22,902
New Mexico State University, Las Cruces	650	12,411
Eastern New Mexico University, Portales	140	3,761
New Mexico Highlands University, Las Vegas	123	2,257
Western New Mexico University, Silver City	64	1,578
New Mexico Institute of Mining and Technology, Sorocco	85	1,118

Health. In 1979 the state had 53 hospitals (5,273 beds).

Social Security. In June 1981, 14,775 persons were receiving federal supplemental security income for the disabled (average $175.84 per month); 10,129 persons were receiving old-age assistance (average $107.74 per month); 461 persons were receiving aid to the blind (average $171.83 per month); 56,157 people received aid to families with dependent children (average $65.98 per month).

Books of Reference

New Mexico Business (monthly; annual review in Jan.–Feb. issue). Bureau of Business and Economic Research, Univ. of N.M., Albuquerque

New Mexico Statistical Abstract: 1980. Bureau of Business and Economic Research, Univ. of N.M., Albuquerque, 1980

Muench, D., and Hillerman, T., *New Mexico.* Belding, Portland, Oregon, 1974

NEW YORK STATE

HISTORY. From 1609 to 1664 the region now called New York was claimed by the Dutch; then it came under the rule of the English, who governed the country until the outbreak of the War of Independence. On 20 April 1777 New York adopted a constitution which transformed the colony into an independent state; on 26 July 1788 it ratified the constitution of the US, becoming one of the 13 original states. New York dropped its claim to Vermont after the latter was admitted to the Union in 1791. With the annexation of a small area from Massachusetts in 1853, New York assumed its present boundaries.

AREA AND POPULATION. New York is bounded west and north by Canada with Lake Erie, Lake Ontario and the St Lawrence River forming the boundary; east by Vermont, Massachusetts and Connecticut, south-east by the Atlantic, south by New Jersey and Pennsylvania. Area, 49,108 sq. miles (1,731 sq. miles being water). Census population, 1 April 1980 (preliminary), 17,557,288, a decrease of 3·7% since 1970. Births in 1979 were 234,867; deaths, 162,966; infant deaths, 3,177; marriages, 115,912; divorces, 64,420 (includes all dissolutions).

Population in 5 census years was:

	White	*Negro*	*Indian*	*Asiatic*	*Total*	*Per sq. mile*
1910	8,966,845	134,191	6,046	6,532	9,113,614	191·2
1930	12,143,191	412,814	6,973	15,088	12,588,066	262·6
1960	15,287,071	1,417,511	16,491	51,678	16,782,304	350·2
			All others			
1970	15,834,090	2,168,949	233,828		18,236,967	380·3
1980	13,961,106	2,401,842	1,194,340		17,557,288	367·0

Of the 1980 population, 8,338,961 were male, 14,857,202 were urban; those 20 years of age or older numbered 12,232,284. Aliens registered in Jan. 1980 numbered 801,411.

The population of New York City, by boroughs, census of 1 April 1980 was: Manhattan, 1,427,533; Bronx, 1,169,115; Brooklyn, 2,230,936; Queens, 1,891,325; Staten Island, 352,121; total, 7,071,030. The New York metropolitan statistical area had, in 1980, 9,080,777.

Population of other large cities and incorporated places census, April 1980, was:

Buffalo	357,002	Troy	56,614	Auburn	32,548
Rochester	241,509	Binghampton	55,745	Poughkeepsie	29,757
Yonkers	194,557	White Plains	46,999	Watertown	27,861
Syracuse	170,292	Rome	43,826	Lindenhurst	26,919
Albany (capital)	101,767	Hempstead	40,404	Rockville Center	25,405
Utica	75,435	Freeport	38,272	Newburgh	23,438
Niagara Falls	71,344	Jamestown	35,775	Garden City	22,927
New Rochelle	70,345	Valley Stream	35,769	Massapequa Park	19,779
Schenectady	67,877	N. Tonawanda	35,760		
Mount Vernon	66,023	Elmira	35,327		

Other large urbanized areas, census 1980; Buffalo, 1·2m.; Rochester, 970,313; Albany–Schenectady–Troy, 794,298.

CONSTITUTION AND GOVERNMENT. The present constitution dates from 1894; a later constitutional convention, 1938, is now legally considered merely to have amended the 1894 constitution, which has now had 93 amendments. The Constitutional Convention of 1967 (4 April through 26 Sept.) was composed of 186 delegates who proposed a new state constitution; however this was rejected by the registered voters on 7 Nov. 1967. The Senate consists of 60 members, and the Assembly of 150 members, both elected every 2 years. The Governor and Lieut.-Governor are elected for 4 years. The right of suffrage resides in every adult who has been a citizen for 90 days, and has the residential qualifications; new voters must establish, by certificates or test, that they have had at least an elementary education.

The state is represented in Congress by 2 senators and 34 representatives.

In the 1980 presidential election Reagan polled 2,893,831 votes, Carter 2,728,372 and Anderson 467,801.

The state capital is Albany. For local government the state is divided into 62 counties, 5 of which constitute the city of New York. New York leads in state parks and recreation areas, covering 252,984 acres in 1979.

Cities are in 3 classes, the first class having each 175,000 or more inhabitants and the third under 50,000. Each is incorporated by charter, under special legislation. The government of New York City is vested in the mayor (Edward Koch), elected for 4 years, and a city council, whose president and members are elected for 4 years. The council has a President and 37 members, each elected from a state senatorial district wholly within the city. The mayor appoints all the heads of departments, except the comptroller, who is elected. Each of the 5 city boroughs (Manhattan, Bronx, Brooklyn, Queens and Richmond) has a president, elected for 4 years. Each borough is also a county bearing the same name except Manhattan borough, which, as a county, is called New York, and Brooklyn, which is Kings County.

Governor: Mario Cuomo (D.), 1983–86 ($85,000).
Lieut.-Governor: Alfred del Bello (D.), 1983–86 ($60,000).
Secretary of State: Gail Schaefer (D.), 1983–86 ($64,400).

BUDGET. The state's general revenues for the financial year ending 31 March 1982 were $16,142m. ($14,959m. from taxes); general expenditures were $16,126m. ($5,298m. for education, $8,049m. for social services, $1,893m. for transport).

Per capita personal income was $10,252 in 1980.

The assessed valuation in 1980 of taxable real property in New York City was $38,056m. The assessed valuation of the state was $86,741m.

ENERGY AND NATURAL RESOURCES

Minerals. Production of principal minerals in 1980: Sand and gravel (22,000 short tons), salt (5,500 short tons), zinc (33,629 tonnes), petroleum (824,296 bbls), natural gas (15,680m. cu. ft). The state is a leading producer of titanium concentrate, talc, abrasive garnet, wollastonite and emery. Quarry products include trap rock, slate, marble, limestone and sandstone. Value of mineral output in 1980 $497·9m.

Agriculture. New York has large agricultural interests. On 1 Jan. 1981 it had 49,000 farms, with a total area of 9·9m. acres; average farm was 202 acres.

Cash income, 1980, from crops and livestock, $2,420m. Dairying, with 18,500 farms, 1981, is an important type of farming with produce at a market value of $1,520m. Field crops comprise maize, winter wheat, oats and hay. New York (1981) ranks second in US in the production of apples, and maple syrup. Other products are grapes, tart cherries, peaches, pears, plums, strawberries, raspberries, cabbages, onions, potatoes, maple sugar. Estimated farm animals, 1981, included 1·95m. all cattle, 912,000 milch cows, 70,000 sheep, 165,000 swine and 10·6m. chickens.

INDUSTRY. In 1981 manufacturing establishments numbering 31,849 employed 1,439,872 workers whose average weekly earnings were $385. Leading industries were clothing, non-electrical machinery, printing and publishing, electrical equipment, instruments, food and allied products and fabricated metals.

COMMUNICATIONS

Roads. There were (1981) 109,485 miles of municipal and rural roads. The New York State Thruway extends 559 miles from New York City to Buffalo; in 1981 receipts from tolls amounted to $183,289,532. The Northway, a 176-mile toll-free highway, is a connecting road from the Thruway at Albany to the Canadian border at Champlain, Quebec.

Motor vehicle registrations in 1981 were 8·7m., most of which (7m.) were private passenger vehicles.

Railways. There were in 1981, 3,891 miles of Class I railways.

Aviation. There were 471 airports and landing areas in 1981.

Shipping. The canals of the state, combined in 1918 in what is called the Improved Canal System, have a length of 524 miles, of which the Erie or Barge canal has 340 miles. In 1981 the canals carried 807,925 tons of freight.

JUSTICE, RELIGION, EDUCATION AND WELFARE

Justice. The State Human Rights Law was approved 12 March 1945, effective 1 July, 1945. The State Division of Human Rights is charged with the responsibility of enforcing this law. The division may request and utilize the services of all governmental departments and agencies; adopt and promulgate suitable rules and regulations; test, investigate and pass judgment upon complaints alleging discrimination in employment, in places of public accommodation, resort or amusement, education, and in housing, land and commercial space; hold hearings, subpoena witnesses and require the production for examination of papers relating to matters under investigation; grant compensatory damages and require repayment of profits in certain housing cases among other provisions; apply for court injunctions to prevent frustration of orders of the Commissioner.

On 30 Dec. 1981, 25,600 persons were in state prisons.

In 1963–81 there were no executions. Total executions (by electrocution) from 1930 to 1962 were 329 (234 whites, 90 Negroes, 5 other races; all for murder except 2 for kidnapping).

In 1980 murders reported in New York were 2,225; total violent crimes, 179,981. Police strength (sworn officers) in 1980 was 55,222 (27,394 New York City).

Religion. The churches are Roman Catholic, with 6,367,576 members in 1981, Jewish congregations (about 2m. in 1981) and Protestant Episcopal (299,929 in 1980).

Education. Education is compulsory between the ages of 7 and 16. In autumn 1980 the public elementary schools (grades kindergarten to 6) enrolled 1,393,945 children, public secondary schools (grades 7 to 12) had 1,466,626 pupils; classroom teachers numbered 170,694 in public schools. Total expenditure on public schools in 1980–81 was $9,069,092,216. Teachers' salaries, 1980–81, averaged $21,316.

The state's educational system, including public and private schools and secondary institutions, universities, colleges, libraries, museums, etc., constitutes (by legislative act) the 'University of the State of New York', which is governed by a Board of Regents consisting of 15 members appointed by the Legislature. Within the framework of this 'University' was established in 1948 a 'State University' which controls 64 colleges and educational centres, 30 of which are locally operated community colleges. The 'State University' is governed by a board of 16 Trustees, appointed by the Governor with the consent and advice of the Senate.

Higher education in the state is conducted in 248 institutions (628,530 full-time students), of which 163 are under private control and 85 under public control.

In autumn 1980 the 248 institutions of higher education in the state had a total of 1,108,140 degree and non-degree credit students. Among them were:

Founded	*Name and place*	*Teachers*	*Students*
1754	Columbia University, New York	3,965	17,410
1795	Union University, Schenectady and Albany	178	2,071
1824	Rensselaer Polytechnic Institute, Troy	442	6,145
1831	New York University, New York	2,615	45,000
1846	Colgate University, New York	205	2,550
1846	Fordham University, New York	958	14,653
1847	University of the City of New York, New York	12,426	172,683
1848	University of Rochester, Rochester	1,549	11,159
1854	Polytechnic Institute of New York	242	4,583
1856	St Lawrence University, Canton	173	2,375
1857	Cooper Union Institute of Technology, New York	161	872
1861	Vassar College, Poughkeepsie	230	2,364
1863	Manhattan College, New York	291	3,498
1865	Cornell University, Ithaca	1,863	17,866
1870	Syracuse University, Syracuse	1,100	11,819
1948	State University of New York	13,228	372,415

The Saratoga Performing Arts Centre (5,100 seats), a non-profit, tax-exempt organization, which opened in 1966, is the summer residence of the New York City Ballet and the Philadelphia Orchestra—two groups which present special educational programmes for students and teachers.

Health. In 1981 the state had 278 hospitals (67,798 beds), 585 skilled nursing homes (62,435 beds) and 241 other institutions (24,302 beds). In 1980 mental health facilities had 27,309 patients and institutions for the mentally retarded had 18,577 patients.

Social Security. The federal Supplemental Security Income programme covered aid to the needy aged, blind and disabled from 1 Jan. 1975. In the state programme there were 1·35m. welfare recipients in 1978 (monthly average); average benefit, $125.43 per month; medical assistance went to 1,014,753 persons, average $230.80; aid to dependent children in 1978 went to 1,184,511 recipients, average benefits $121.77 per month.

Books of Reference

New York Red Book. Albany, 1979–80
Legislative Manual. Department of State, 1980–81
New York State Statistical Yearbook, 1979–80. Albany
Connery, R. and G. B., *Governing New York State: The Rockefeller Years.* Academy of Political Science, New York, 1974
Ellis, D. M., *History of New York State.* Cornell Univ. Press, 1967
Flick, A. (ed.), *History of the State of New York.* Columbia Univ. Press, 1933–37
Lincoln, C., *Constitutional History of New York 1809–1877.* Rochester, 1906
Rosenwhike, I., *Population History of New York City.* Syracuse Univ. Press, 1972
Thompson, J. H. (ed.), *Geography of New York State.* Syracuse Univ. Press, 1966
Wolfe, G. R., *New York: A Guide to the Metropolis.* New York Univ. Press, 1975

State Library: The New York State Library, Albany 12230. *State Librarian and Assistant Commissioner for Libraries:* Joseph Shubert.

NORTH CAROLINA

HISTORY. North Carolina, first settled in 1585 by Sir Walter Raleigh and permanently settled in 1663, was one of the 13 original states of the Union.

AREA AND POPULATION. North Carolina is bounded north by Virginia, east by the Atlantic, south by South Carolina, south-west by Georgia and west by Tennessee. Area, 52,669 sq. miles, of which 3,826 sq. miles are inland water. Census population, 1 April 1980, 5,874,429, an increase of 15·5% since 1970.

Births, 1979, were 83,782 (14·9 per 1,000 population); marriages, 45,064 (8); deaths, 46,640 (8·3); infant deaths, 1,270 (15·2 per 1,000 live births); divorces and annulments, 27,445 (4·9).

Population in 6 census years was:

	White	*Negro*	*Indian*	*Asiatic*	*Total*	*Per sq. mile*
1910	1,500,511	697,843	7,851	82	2,206,287	45·3
1930	2,234,958	918,647	16,579	92	3,170,276	64·5
1950	2,983,121	1,047,353	3,742	—	4,061,929	82·7
1960	3,399,285	1,116,021	38,129	2,012	4,556,155	92·2
			All others			
1970	3,901,767	1,126,478	53,814		5,082,059	104·1
1980	4,453,010	1,316,050	105,369		5,874,429	111·5

Of the total population in 1980, 2,852,012 were male, 2,818,794 were urban and 3,976,359 were 20 years old or older; 14·8% were non-white.

Cities (with census population in 1980) are: Charlotte, 310,799; Greensboro, 154,763; Winston-Salem, 131,211; Raleigh (capital), 148,299; Durham (1970), 95,438; High Point, 63,169; Asheville, 57,708; Fayetteville, 59,476.

CLIMATE. Climate varies sharply with altitude; the warmest area is in the south east round Southport and Wilmington; the coldest is Mount Mitchell (6,684 ft). Average temperatures: Coastal Plain 62°F; Piedmont 60°F; Mountains 55°F.

CONSTITUTION AND GOVERNMENT. The present constitution dates from 1971 (previous constitution, 1776 and 1868/76); it has had 12 amendments. The General Assembly consists of a Senate of 50 members and a House of Representatives of 120 members; all are elected by districts for 2 years. The Governor and Lieut.-Governor are elected for 4 years. The Governor may succeed himself but has no veto. There are 17 other executive heads of department, 8 elected by the people and 7 appointed by the Governor. All registered citizens with the usual residential qualifications have a vote.

The state is represented in Congress by 2 senators and 11 representatives.

In the presidential election of 1980 Reagan polled 915,018 votes, Carter 875,635 and Anderson 52,800.

The capital is Raleigh, established in 1792.

Governor: James B. Hunt, Jr (D.), 1977–85 ($55,104).
Lieut.-Governor: James C. Green (D.) ($45,636).
Secretary of State: Thad Eure (D.) ($45,636).

BUDGET. General revenue for the year ending 30 June 1981 was $3,023·8m. ($2,845·9m. from taxation). General expenditure was $3,154·1m. (education, $2,066·4m.; health, welfare and rehabilitation, $488·2m.).

On 30 June 1981 the net total long-term debt amounted to $853·2m.

Per capita personal income (1980) was $7,819.

NATURAL RESOURCES

Minerals. Mining production in 1980 was valued at $360·9m. Principal minerals were stone, sand and gravel, phosphate rock, feldspar, clay, mica, lithium minerals, olivine, kaolin and talc. North Carolina ranked first in the production of mica, feldspar, olivine and lithium minerals. It is also the leading producer of bricks. In 1980 North Carolina manufactured 800m. bricks valued at over $80m. or 13% of the total US production.

Agriculture. In 1981 there were 93,000 farms in North Carolina covering 11·7m. acres; average size of farms was 126 acres and average value (1 Feb. 1981), $167,400.

Income is primarily from tobacco, poultry, cattle, swine, maize, peanuts and soybeans. Cash income, 1980, from crops, was $2,000m. and from livestock, dairy and poultry and products, $1,436m.

North Carolina leads in production of tobacco (621·4m. lb., 1979). Production of maize, 1979, was 128,440 bu.; cotton, 43,000 lb.; peanuts, 378·5m. lb.; soybeans, 45m. bu. Also grown extensively are wheat, oats, barley, sweet potatoes, blueberries, hay, peaches and apples. On 1 Jan. 1980 farms had 145,000 milch cows, 1·08m. all cattle, 2·6m. swine and 7,500 sheep. Production of commercial broilers amounted to 377m. in 1979 (fourth highest in US).

Forestry. North Carolina is the second largest lumber-producing state in the South and the sixth largest in the US. Timber, covering 19·6m. acres (62·6% of land area), provided approximately $5,550m. income in forest industries and products in 1977. The area of forest lands in public ownership in 1974 was 1·7m. acres.

Fisheries. Commercial fish catch, 1980, amounted to 356m. lb.; value approximately $68·8m.

INDUSTRY. North Carolina's 9,668 industrial establishments in 1980 had 824,200 production workers. Value added (1977 estimate) was $18,105m. The leading industries are textile goods (leading all states), manufacture of cigarettes (about 55% of the US production, leading all states), chemicals, electronics and electrical machinery, processing of food crops and the manufacture of furniture and bricks (leading all states in both). Total receipts of the travel industry, $2,400m. in 1980. In 1980 new industrial investment was $1,252·8m. creating 16,856 new jobs; investment in expansion was $987·3m., creating 12,775.

COMMUNICATIONS

Roads. The state maintained, 1981, 76,032 miles of highways, comprising all rural roads and 4,388 miles of urban streets which are major thoroughfares. In Sept. 1981, 2,989,776 automobiles, 904,708 trucks and 572,550 other vehicles were registered.

Railways. The state in 1981 contained 4,000 miles of railway operating in 91 of the 100 counties.

Aviation. In 1981 there were 71 public airports of which 9 are served by major airlines and 5 by commuter airlines.

Shipping. There are 2 ocean ports, Wilmington and Morehead City.

JUSTICE, RELIGION, EDUCATION AND WELFARE

Justice. Total executions 1910–62, 362. Prison population at 28 Oct. 1980, 15,593.

Religion. Leading denominations are the Baptists (48·9% of church membership in 1974), Methodists (20·7%), Presbyterians (7·7%), Lutherans (3%) and Roman Catholics (2·7%). Total estimate of all denominations in 1974 was 2·58m.

Education. School attendance is compulsory between 6 and 16.

Public school enrolment, 1979–80, was 1,191,342; elementary and secondary schools numbered 2,035. Instructional staff consisted of 67,586 classroom teachers and administrators. Estimated total current expenditure for public schools, 1978–79, $1,706·9m., including $1,080·9m. from state, $403·4m. from local and $222·6m. from federal sources.

In autumn 1979 state-supported colleges and universities included 58 two-year community colleges with 95,670 students; 16 four-year colleges with 112,746 students. The 16 senior universities are all part of the University of North Carolina system, the largest campus being the University of North Carolina at Chapel Hill. This university was founded in 1789 and first opened in 1792. Its 1979–80 enrolment was 20,784 with a faculty of 1,736. The next three largest campuses are North Carolina State University in Raleigh (1887) with an enrolment of 19,516 and a faculty of 1,171, East Carolina University in Greenville (1907) with an enrolment of 12,874 and a faculty of 639; and the University of North Carolina at Greensboro (1891) with an enrolment of 9,925 and a faculty of 516. The total enrolment of public institutions of higher learning in 1979–80 was 254,859.

In addition to the state-supported institutions there were 8 private junior colleges with an enrolment of 4,866 and 30 private senior institutions with a total enrolment of 41,577. The largest of these are Duke University (1924) in Durham, a Methodist affiliated school with 8,140 students, and Wake Forest University (1834) in Winston-Salem, a Baptist school with 3,801 students. The total enrolment in private institutions for 1979–80 was 46,443.

Health. In Dec. 1980 the state had 158 hospitals (28,334 beds).

Social Security. In Dec. 1979 there were 881,381 persons receiving an average of $231.41 a month in social security benefits. Of that number 447,314 were retired, receiving an average of $265.70 a month; 89,380 were disabled ($294.39); 15,717 children of retired persons received $110.71 monthly; 39,678 children of disabled persons received $92.82 monthly; 84,934 widows and widowers received $191.34 monthly.

Books of Reference

North Carolina Manual. Secretary of State. Raleigh. Biennial
North Carolina: A Guide to the Old North State. Univ. of N.C., Chapel Hill, 1955
Corbitt, D. L., *The Formation of the North Carolina Counties.* Raleigh, 1969
Hobbs, S. H., *North Carolina: An Economic and Social Profile.* Univ. of N.C., Chapel Hill, 1958
Lefler, H. T., and Newsome, A. R., *North Carolina: The History of a Southern State.* Univ. of N.C., Chapel Hill, 1963

NORTH DAKOTA

HISTORY. North Dakota was admitted into the Union, with boundaries as at present, on 2 Nov. 1889; previously it had formed part of the Dakota Territory, established 2 March 1861.

AREA AND POPULATION. North Dakota is bounded north by Canada, east by the Red River (forming a boundary with Minnesota), south by South Dakota and west by Montana. Land area, 70,702 sq. miles, and 1,403 sq. miles of water. The Federal Bureau of Indian Affairs administered (1971) 850,000 acres, of which 153,000 acres were assigned to tribes. Census population, 1 April 1980, 652,717, an increase of 34,956 or 5·7% since 1970. Births in 1981 were 12,407 (19 per 1,000 population); deaths, 5,456 (8·4); infant deaths, 140; marriages, 6,204; divorces, 2,310.

Population at 5 census years was:

	White	*Negro*	*Indian*	*Asiatic*	*Total*	*Per sq. mile*
1910	569,855	617	6,486	98	577,056	8·2
1930	671,851	377	8,617	194	680,845	9·7
1960	619,538	777	11,736	274	632,446	9·1
			All others			
1970	599,485	2,494	15,782		617,761	8·9
1980	625,536	2,568	24,591		652,695[1]	9·2

[1] Preliminary.

Of the total population in 1980, 328,409 were male, 317,821 were urban and 419,224 were 21 years old or older. Estimated outward migration, 1970–80, 16,983.

The largest cities are Fargo with population (census), 1980, of 61,383; Grand Forks, 43,765; Bismarck (capital), 44,485, and Minot, 32,843.

CONSTITUTION AND GOVERNMENT. The present constitution dates from 1889; it has had 95 amendments. The Legislative Assembly consists of a Senate of 53 members elected for 4 years, and a House of Representatives of 106 members elected for 2 years. The Governor and Lieut.-Governor are elected for 4 years. Qualified electors are (with necessary exceptions) all citizens and civilized Indians. The state sends to Congress 2 senators elected by the voters of the entire state and 1 representative.

In the 1980 presidential election Reagan polled 193,695 votes, Carter 79,189 and Anderson 23,640.

The capital is Bismarck. The state has 53 organized counties.

Governor: Allen I. Olson (R.), 1981–85 ($65,000 plus expenses).
Lieut.-Governor: Ernest Sands (R.), 1981–85 ($9,700 plus expenses).
Secretary of State: Ben Meier (R.), 1981–85 ($48,000 plus expenses).

FINANCE. General revenue of state and local government year ending 30 June 1980, was $1,249m.; general expenditures, $1,201m., taxation provided $553m. and federal aid, $280m.; education took $427m.; highways, $198m., and public welfare, $98m.

Total net long-term debt (local government) on 30 June 1980, $826m.

Per capita personal income (1981) was $10,213.

ENERGY AND NATURAL RESOURCES

Minerals. The mineral resources of North Dakota consist chiefly of oil which was discovered in 1951. Production of crude petroleum in 1981 was 46m. bbls; of natural gas, 70,000m. cu. ft. Output (1981) of lignite coal was 17·4m. short tons. Total value of mineral output, 1980, $880m.

Agriculture. Agriculture is the chief pursuit of the North Dakota population. In 1982 there were 38,000 farms (61,963 in 1954) with an area of 42m. acres (41,876,924 in 1954); the average farm was of 1,097 acres. The greater number of farms are cash-grain or livestock farms with annual sales of $20,000–$39,999.

Cash income, 1981, from crops, $2,208·8m., and from livestock, $594m. North Dakota leads in the production of barley, sunflowers, flaxseed, durum, wheat. Other important products are sugar-beet, beans, potatoes, hay, oats, rye and maize.

The state has also an active livestock industry, chiefly cattle raising. On 1 Jan. 1982 the farm animals were: 92,000 milch cows, 2m. all cattle, 280,000 sheep and 230,000 swine. The wool clip yielded (1981), 2·2m. lb. of wool from 230,000 sheep.

Forestry. National forest area, 1977, 422,000 acres, of which 115,000 acres are federally owned or managed.

INDUSTRY. From 1970 to 1981 agricultural employment rose from 51,920 to 52,270; non-agricultural jobs rose from 148,910 to 263,650. Between 1970 and 1980, employment in manufacturing rose from 9,910 to 15,290, in trade from 43,890 to 66,290 and in government from 49,240 to 60,510.

COMMUNICATIONS

Roads. The state highway department maintained, in 1981, 7,220 miles of highway; local authorities, 95,938 miles, and municipal, 3,193 miles.

Car and truck registrations in 1980 numbered 645,441.

Railways. In 1980 there were 5,262 miles of railway.

Aviation. Airports in 1980 numbered 262, of which 107 were publicly owned.

JUSTICE, RELIGION, EDUCATION AND WELFARE

Justice. The state penitentiary, on 24 Jan. 1983, held 380 inmates. Of these, 32 were incarcerated at the North Dakota State Farm. There is no death penalty.

Religion. The leading religious denominations are the Roman Catholics, with 171,185 members in 1975; Combined Lutherans, 216,579; Methodists, 28,880; Presbyterians, 18,636.

Education. School attendance is compulsory between the ages of 7 and 16, or until the 17th birthday if the eighth grade has not been completed. In Sept. 1979 the public elementary schools had 76,000 pupils; secondary schools, 42,000 pupils. Average salary of teachers, 1970, was $6,375 in elementary and $7,263 in secondary schools. State expenditure on public schools, 1980, $427m. Private schools had 6,000 elementary pupils and 2,000 secondary pupils in 1980.

The university at Grand Forks, founded in 1883, had 9,440 students in 1982; the state university of agriculture and applied science, at Fargo, 8,079 students. Total enrolment in the 8 public institutions of higher education, 1980, 31,767.

Health. In 1982 the state had 60 hospitals (5,880 beds), and 79 nursing homes (5,100).

Social Security. In 1974 aid to the aged, blind and disabled was taken out of state programmes and included in federal programmes as Supplemental Security Income (SSI). In 1979 grants were made to 12,700 cases, including 8,800 families with dependent children. At Dec. 1979, 6,500 people received SSI assistance.

Books of Reference

North Dakota Growth Indicators, 1981. 19th ed. Economic Development Commission, Bismarck, 1982

North Dakota Industrial Location Facts. Economic Development Commission, Bismarck, 1981

North Dakota Blue Book. Secretary of State, Bismarck, 1981

Federal Writers' Project. *North Dakota: A Guide to the Northern State.* 2nd ed. OUP, New York, 1950

Goodey, R. B. (ed.), *Readings in the Geography of North Dakota.* North Dakota Studies, 1968

Robinson, E. B., *History of North Dakota.* Univ. of Nebraska Press, 1966

OHIO

HISTORY. Ohio, first settled in 1788, unofficially entered the Union on 19 Feb. 1803; entrance was made official, retroactive to 1 March 1803, on 8 Aug. 1953.

AREA AND POPULATION. Ohio is bounded north by Michigan and Lake Erie, east by Pennsylvania, south-east and south by the Ohio River (forming a boundary with West Virginia and Kentucky) and west by Indiana. Area, 41,330 sq. miles, of which 325 sq. miles are inland water. Census population, 1 April 1980 (preliminary), 10,797,419, an increase of 145,402 or 1·4% since 1970. In 1980 births numbered 169,359 (15·7 per 1,000 population); deaths, 97,779 (9); infant deaths, 2,020 (12 per 1,000 live births); marriages, 99,522 (9·2); divorces and annulments, 58,225 (5·4).

Population at 5 census years was:

	White	*Negro*	*Indian*	*Asiatic*	*Total*	*Per sq. mile*
1910	4,654,897	111,452	127	645	4,767,121	117·0
1930	6,335,173	309,304	435	1,785	6,646,697	161·6
1960	8,909,698	786,097	1,910	8,692	9,706,397	236·9
			All others			
1970	9,646,997	970,477	34,543		10,652,017	260·0
1980	9,597,266	1,076,734	123,419		10,797,419	263·5

Of the total population in 1980, 5,217,027 were male, 7,914,500 persons were urban. Those 20 years old or older numbered 7,294,471.

Census population of chief cities on 1 April 1980 was:

Cleveland	572,532	Hamilton	62,845	Cuyahoga Falls	43,710
Columbus	561,943	Lakewood	61,921	Mentor	42,065
Cincinnati	383,058	Kettering	61,223	Newark	41,200
Toledo	354,265	Euclid	59,896	Marion	37,040
Akron	236,820	Elyria	57,039	East Cleveland	36,957
Dayton	193,319	Cleveland Heights	55,563	North Olmsted	36,486
Youngstown	115,429	Warren	55,456	Upper Arlington	35,648
Canton	94,632	Mansfield	53,907	Lancaster	34,953
Parma	92,578	Lima	47,381	Garfield Heights	33,380
Lorain	75,339	Middletown	43,719	Zanesville	28,655
Springfield	72,098				

Urbanized areas, 1980 census: Cleveland, 1,895,997; Cincinnati, 1,392,394; Columbus (the capital), 1,088,973; Dayton, 826,891; Akron, 660,233; Toledo, 791,137; Youngstown-Warren, 529,887; Canton, 403,847.

CONSTITUTION AND GOVERNMENT. The question of a general revision of the constitution drafted by an elected convention is submitted to the people every 20 years. The constitution of 1851 had 105 amendments by 1978.

In the 112th General Assembly the Senate consisted of 33 members and the House of Representatives of 99 members. The Senate is elected for 4 years, half each 2 years; the House is elected for 2 years; the Governor, Lieut.-Governor and Secretary of State for 4 years. Qualified as electors are (with necessary exceptions) all citizens 18 years of age who have the usual residential qualifications. Ohio sends 2 senators and 21 representatives to Congress.

In the 1980 presidential election Reagan polled 2,206,545 votes, Carter, 1,752,414.

The capital (since 1816) is Columbus. Ohio is divided into 88 counties.

Governor: Richard Celeste (D.), 1983–86 ($50,000).
Lieut.-Governor: Myrl H. Shoemaker (D.), 1983–86 ($50,000).
Secretary of State: Sherrod Brown (D.), 1983–86 ($50,000).

BUDGET. For the year ending 30 June 1980 (Budget of the State of Ohio) total general revenue was $12,180·3m. and general expenditure was $11,397·4m.

The net long-term debt of the state on 30 June 1980 was $4,014·9m.

Per capita personal income (1980) was $9,462.

ENERGY AND NATURAL RESOURCES

Minerals. Ohio has extensive mineral resources, of which coal is the most important by value: output (1977) 46·6m. short tons, value $784·2m. Production of other minerals, 1977: Sand and gravel, 41·1m. short tons ($81·7m.); lime, 3·2m. short tons ($112·7m.); crude petroleum, 11·59m. bbls ($143·7m.); natural gas, 84·45m. cu. ft ($107·2m.); clay, 4·36m. short tons ($15·23m.); salt, 3·6m. short tons ($61·8m.); stone, 44·5m. short tons ($114m.).

Agriculture. Ohio is extensively devoted to agriculture. In 1981, 94,000 farms covered 16m. acres; all farms were valued at $28,143m.

Cash income 1980, from crop and livestock and products, $3,746·7m. The most important crops in 1980 were: Maize (440·7m. bu.),wheat (67·1m. bu.), oats (19·4m. bu.), soybeans (135·4m. bu.). The wool clip in 1976 yielded 3·35m. lb. from 423,000 sheep. On 1 Jan. 1981 there were 2m. swine 1·81m. all cattle and 310,000 sheep.

Forestry. State forest area, 1978, 170,000 acres including reclamation area.

INDUSTRY. In 1978, manufacturing employed an average of 1·36m. workers. The value added by manufacture was $47,641m. The largest industry was manufacturing of non-electrical machinery.

COMMUNICATIONS

Roads. The state (1977) maintained 19,458 miles of highway, including 1,303 miles of interstate highways and 241 miles on the Ohio Turnpike; there were 91,511 miles of country, township, city, park and forest development roads. Total miles of highway maintained by all government agencies (1977) 110,969.

Railways. The railroads had 7,400 route miles of track in 1978.

Aviation. Ohio had (1978) 719 airports and airfields, of which 212 are commercial and 527 private, 130 heliports and 2 seaplane bases. There were 6,600 licensed aeroplanes.

JUSTICE, RELIGION, EDUCATION AND WELFARE

Justice. A Civil Rights Act (1933) forbids inns, restaurants, theatres, retail stores and all other places of public resort to discriminate against citizens on grounds of 'colour or race'; none may be denied the right to serve on juries on the grounds of 'colour or race'; insurance companies are forbidden to discriminate between 'white persons and coloured, wholly or partially of African descent'.

A state Civil Rights Commission (created 1959) has general administrative powers to prevent discrimination because of race, colour, religion, national origin or ancestry in employment, labour organization membership, use of public accommodations and in obtaining 'commercial housing' or 'personal residence'. Ohio has no *de jure* segregation in the public schools.

The state's adult correctional institutions, 30 Oct. 1978, held 8,285 inmates (average daily count). Total executions (by electrocution) since 1930 were 170, all for murder. There have been no executions since 1963. The Department of Rehabilitation and Correction was created in July 1972, and has established probation services in 51 counties where services would otherwise be inadequate or non-existent.

Religion. Many religious faiths are represented, including (but not limited to) the Baptist, Jewish, Lutheran, Methodist, Presbyterian and Roman Catholic.

Education. School attendance during full term is compulsory for children from 6 to 18 years of age. In 1980 public schools had 2,025,000 enrolled pupils; elementary schools had 54,100 teachers; secondary schools had 45,200 teachers. Teachers' salaries averaged $16,800 (secondary) and $15,700 (elementary). Operating expenditure on elementary and secondary schools for 1980 was $3,839m. The state's universities and colleges had a total enrolment (1980) of 489,100 students; the following had 7,000 or more students, autumn 1977:

Founded	*Institutions*	*Enrolments*
1804	Ohio University, Athens (State)	13,021
1809	Miami University, Oxford (State)	14,759
1826	Case Western Reserve University, Cleveland	8,108
1850	University of Dayton (R.C.)	9,620
1870	University of Akron (State)	23,121
1872	Ohio State University, Columbus (State)	51,003
1872	University of Toledo (State)	16,933
1874	University of Cincinnati (State-affiliated)	32,952
1887	Sinclair Community College, Dayton	13,752
1908	Youngstown University (State)	15,696
1910	Bowling Green State University (State)	16,439
1912	Kent State University (State)	19,396
1962	Cuyahoga Community College (Municipal)	27,250
1964	Cleveland State University (State)	17,627
1964	Wright State University (State)	13,067

Health. In Oct. 1979 the state had 239 hospitals (63,600 beds) listed by the American Hospital Association. State hospitals for mental diseases and retardation had 5,478 patients.

Social Security. Public assistance is administered through 4 basic programmes: aid to dependent children, emergency assistance, Medicaid and general relief. Total public assistance expenditures during the year ending 30 June 1978 were $1,322·4m. In 1976–77 the number of persons receiving public assistance averaged 626,100 per month. Under the aid to dependent children programme $429·9m. provided assistance to an average of 526,434 recipients per month. Payments for Medicaid were $603·5m.; for social services, $189m.; for general relief, $78·4m., and emergency assistance, $21·6m. Recipients of general relief averaged 47,923 per month, emergency assistance, 30,585. Recipients of Medicaid during the year, 799,915.

Books of Reference

Official Roster: Federal State, County Officers and Department Information. Secretary of State, Columbus. Biennial

Rosebloom, E. H., and Weisenburger, F. P., *A History of Ohio.* State Arch. and Hist. Soc., Columbus, 1953

OKLAHOMA

HISTORY. An unorganized area in the centre of the present state was thrown open to white settlers on 22 April 1889. The Territory of Oklahoma, organized in 1890 to include this area and other sections, was opened to white settlements by runs or lotteries during the next decade. In 1893 the Territory was enlarged by the addition of the Cherokee Outlet, which fixed part of the present northern boundary. On 16 Nov. 1907 Oklahoma was combined with the remaining part of the Indian Territory and admitted as a state with boundaries substantially as now.

AREA AND POPULATION. Oklahoma is bounded north by Kansas, north-east by Missouri, east by Arkansas, south by Texas (the Red River forming part of the boundary) and, at the western extremity of the 'panhandle', by New Mexico and Colorado. Area 68,782 sq. miles, of which 1,137 sq. miles are water. Census population, 1 April 1980, 3,025,266, an increase of 465,803 or 18% since 1970. Births, 1980, were 52,065; deaths, 28,908; infant deaths 660; marriages, 46,509; divorces, including annulments, 24,226.

The population at 5 federal censuses was:

	White	*Negro*	*Indian*	*Asiatic*	*Total*	*Per sq. mile*
1910	1,444,531	137,612	74,825	187	1,657,155	23·9
1930	2,130,778	172,198	92,725	339	2,396,040	34·6
1960	2,107,900	153,084	68,689	1,414	2,328,284	33·8
			All others			
1970	2,280,362	171,892	106,999		2,559,253	37·2
1980	2,597,783	204,658	222,825		3,025,266	43·2

In 1980, 1,476,719 were male, 2,035,082 were urban and those 20 years of age or older numbered 2,052,729. In eastern Oklahoma the US Bureau of Indian Affairs is responsible for 14 Indian tribes, about 97,000 Indians on over 800,000 acres.

The most important cities with population, 1980 are Oklahoma City (capital), 403,213, Tulsa, 360,919; Lawton, 80,054; Norman, 68,020; Enid, 50,363; Midwest City, 49,559.

CONSTITUTION AND GOVERNMENT. The present constitution, dating from 1907, provides for amendment by initiative petition and legislative referendum; it has had 106 amendments.

The Legislature consists of a Senate of 48 members, who are elected for 4 years, and a House of Representatives elected for 2 years and consisting of 101 members. The Governor and Lieut.-Governor are elected for 4-year terms; the Governor can only be elected for two terms in succession. Electors are (with necessary exceptions) all citizens 18 years or older, with the usual qualifications.

The state is represented in Congress by 2 senators and 6 representatives.

In the 1980 presidential election Reagan polled 695,570 votes, Carter 402,026, Anderson 38,284 and Clark 13,828.

The capital is Oklahoma City. The state has 77 counties.

Governor: George Nigh (D.), 1983–86 ($70,000).
Lieut.-Governor: Spencer Bernard (D.), 1983–86 ($40,000).
Secretary of State: Jeanette B. Edmondson (D.), 1983–86 ($37,500).

BUDGET. Total revenue for the year ending 30 June 1981 (State Budget Office figures) was $3,982m. General revenue was $1,361m.

Bonded indebtedness for the year ending 30 June 1981, $1,169m.

Per capita personal income (1981) was $9,081.

ENERGY AND NATURAL RESOURCES

Minerals. Resources include petroleum, helium, natural gas, coal (bituminous), cement, granite, gypsum, olivestone, sand, gravel and some copper and silver. Production for 1981 was: Petroleum, 154,057,000 bbls; natural gas, 2,029,667m. cu. ft. In March 1981 there were 82,639 oilwells and 16,994 natural gaswells in production. Total value of mineral production, 1981, $8,677,798.

Agriculture. In 1980 the state had 73,000 farms with a total area of 35m. acres; average farm was 479 acres with an average gross income of $49,569. In 1980, there were 43,792 full-time farmers or ranchers, 25,719 part-owners and 10,019 tenants. Large-scale commercial farming is predominant.

The conservation and development of the renewable natural resources of the state has received close attention by local, county and state governments during the past 40 years. All of the land in the state is within the boundaries of one of the 88 conservation districts. Of the total surface (44m. acres), 92% is under a basic conservation plan prepared by the conservation district with assistance from the Soil Conservation Service. The Oklahoma Conservation Commission reported that good conservation measures by farmers, such as minimum tillage and crop residue management, are helping to conserve moisture and protect crops from erosion. Through Jan. 1980, 125 work plans had been approved for watersheds established in 1946 to aid flood control. In addition, 2,540 flood-prevention dams and 62 multi-purpose dams have been built or approved under this project. In 1981 there were 4 active Resource Conservation and Development Areas covering 16·8m. acres in 31 counties. Plans for 5 other areas covering another 32 counties have been submitted.

A trend of the last 40 years has been the conversion of arable land to grass; cattle and calves rank first in agricultural products, valued, 1981, at $1,460m.; winter wheat is second, at $845m.

Cash income from crops and livestock products 1981, $2,855m. The most valuable crop is winter wheat (production, 1981, 172m. bu.). Other crops (production, 1981) included hay (3·3m. tons), cotton (440,000 bales of 480 lb.), grain sorghums (22m. bu.) and peanuts (189m. lb.). On 1 Jan. 1982 the stock included 111,000 milch cows, 5·8m. all cattle, 105,000 sheep and lambs, 4·2m. farm chickens and 245,000 swine.

Forestry. There are nearly 10m. acres of forest, one half considered commercial. The forest products industry, concentrated in the southeastern counties, employs approximately 7,000 in over 100 manufacturing plants with an estimated combined annual payroll of $75m. Value of shipments of lumber and forest products in 1980 was over $50m.

INDUSTRY. The retail trade and service industries each employed 15% of the working population in 1981. Among other industries the most important by payroll employment (1982) were: mining (103,700); construction (49,300); transport and utilities (67,700); manufacturing (193,700); government (245,000); finance, insurance and property (58,800). In 1982 the civilian non-agricultural labour force averaged 1·2m.

COMMUNICATIONS

Roads. In 1982 there were 12,178 miles of inter-state, federal and state highway open, 81,304 miles of county roads, 15,458 miles of city streets, 487 miles of turnpike and 344 miles of park and forest roads. Motor vehicle registrations, 1980, 2,731,628.

Railways. In 1982 Oklahoma had 5,005 miles of railway operated by 12 companies.

Aviation. Airports, 1982, numbered 288, of which 131 were municipally owned. Seven cities were served by CAB-certificated airlines.

Shipping. The McClellan-Kerr Arkansas Navigation System provides access from east central Oklahoma to New Orleans through the Verdigris, Arkansas and Mississippi rivers. The main ports are Catoosa and Muskogee.

JUSTICE, RELIGION, EDUCATION AND WELFARE

Justice. Penal institutions, Oct. 1981, held 5,122 inmates. There are 9 correction centres and 9 community treatment centres.

The death penalty was suspended in 1966 and re-imposed in 1974. Since 1915 there have been 83 (52 whites, 27 Negroes, 4 other races) executions. Electrocution was replaced (1977) by lethal injection.

Religion. The chief religious bodies in 1980 were Baptists, 674,766; United Methodists, 248,635; Roman Catholics, 122,820; Churches of Christ, about 80,000; Assembly of God, 63,992; Disciples of Christ, 45,070; Presbyterian, 38,605; Lutheran, 33,664; Nazarene, 22,090; Episcopal, 21,500.

Education. In 1981–82 there were 611,246 pupils enrolled in elementary and secondary schools, 38,460 teachers at elementary schools and secondary schools had average salaries of $15,200. Total expenditure on public schools (1980–81), $1,028m.

In 1980–81, there were 3,415 special education units with 65,598 students in class.

The University of Oklahoma (founded at Norman in 1890) had 753 full-time faculty and 20,333 enrolled students in spring 1981; Oklahoma State University of Agriculture and Applied Science (founded in 1890 at Stillwater) had 718 full-time faculty and 20,739 students; Central State University (founded at Edmond in 1890) had 320 full-time faculty and 10,820 students. There are 10 other institutions of higher learning in the state system at the senior level and 14 junior colleges. Total enrolment in institutions of higher education, spring 1981, 154,266.

Health. In 1981 there were 134 hospitals (15,642 beds). In 1981 institutions for the mentally retarded had 1,828 inmates; the schools for deaf and blind had 234 children, 3 schools for delinquents, 862 children, 2 children's homes, 679 children.

Social Security. Public assistance, financial year 1981 was being drawn by 148,435 persons, receiving an average monthly payment of $930. This includes old age assistance, aid to families with dependent children, AFDC emergency, AFDC foster home care, aid to the blind and aid to the disabled. Medical payments were made for 234,393 persons, totalled $317·9m. and averaged $1,356.50 per person. Intermediate care was provided for 26,664 persons at an average of $5,914.05 per person. Non-technical medical care was provided for 10,129 persons at an average of $2,127.96 per person. A total of $29,954,310 was spent for vocational rehabilitation.

Books of Reference

Directory of Oklahoma. Dept. of Libraries, Oklahoma City
Chronicles of Oklahoma. State Historical Society, Oklahoma City (from 1921)
Statistical Abstract of Oklahoma, 1980. Centres for Economic and Management Research, Univ. of Oklahoma, Norman, 1980
Dale, E. E., and Aldrich, G., *History of Oklahoma.* New York, 1969

Debo, Angie, *Oklahoma.* Norman, 1949
McReynolds, Edwin C., *Oklahoma: A History of the Sooner State.* Rev. ed. Univ. of Oklahoma, Norman, 1964
Morgan, H. W., and Morgan, A. H., *Oklahoma: A Bicentennial History.* New York, 1977
Ruth, K., *et al.*, (eds.), *Oklahoma: A Guide to the Sooner State.* Rev. ed. Univ. of Oklahoma, Norman, 1957
Strain, J. W., *Outline of Oklahoma Government.* Central State Univ., Edmond, 1978

State Library: Oklahoma Dept. of Libraries, 200 N.E. 18th Street, Oklahoma City 73105. *State Librarian and State Archivist:* Robert L. Clark, Jr.

OREGON

HISTORY. Oregon was first settled in 1811 by the Pacific Fur Co. at Astoria, a provisional government was formed on 5 July 1834; a Territorial government was organized, 14 Aug. 1848, and on 14 Feb. 1859 Oregon was admitted to the Union.

AREA AND POPULATION. Oregon is bounded north by Washington, with the Columbia River forming most of the boundary, east by Idaho, with the Snake River forming most of the boundary, south by Nevada and California and west by the Pacific. Area, 97,073 sq. miles, 889 sq. miles being inland water. The federal government owned (1976) 32,370,216 acres (52·55% of the state area). Census population, 1 April 1980 (preliminary), 2,632,663, an increase of 541,278 or 26% since 1970. In 1980 births numbered 43,998 (16·7 per 1,000 population); deaths, 21,793 (8·2); infant deaths 556 (12 per 1,000 live births); marriages, 23,115 (8·8), and divorces, 17,925 (6·8).

Population at 5 federal censuses was:

	White	*Negro*	*Indian*	*Asiatic*	*Total*	*Per sq. mile*
1910	655,090	1,492	5,090	11,093	672,765	7·0
1930	938,598	2,234	4,776	8,179	953,786	9·9
1960	1,732,037	18,133	8,026	9,120	1,768,687	18·4
1970	2,032,079	26,308	13,510	13,290	2,091,385	21·7
1980	2,490,192	37,059	27,309	34,767	2,632,663	27·4

Of the total population in 1980, 1,296,355 were male, 1,787,912 persons were urban. Those 20 years and older numbered 1,817,059.

The US Bureau of Indian Affairs (area headquarters in Portland) administers (1976) 742,151·74 acres, of which 597,222·94 acres are held by the US in trust for Indian tribes, and 144,928·8 acres for individual Indians.

The largest towns, according to 1980 census figures, are: Portland, 364,246; Eugene, 104,673; Salem (the capital), 89,161; Corvallis, 40,960; Medford, 39,603; Springfield, 41,621; Beaverton, 30,582; Albany, 26,546. Metropolitan areas (1980): Portland, 1,236,294; Eugene-Springfield, 273,114; Salem, 249,655.

CONSTITUTION AND GOVERNMENT. The present constitution dates from 1859; some 80 items in it have been amended. The Legislative Assembly consists of a Senate of 30 members, elected for 4 years (half their number retiring every 2 years), and a House of 60 representatives, elected for 2 years. The Governor is elected for 4 years. The constitution reserves to the voters the rights of initiative and referendum and recall. In Nov. 1912 suffrage was extended to women.

The state sends to Congress 2 senators and 5 representatives.

In the 1980 presidential election Reagan polled 571,044 votes, Carter 456,890 and Anderson, 112,389.

The capital is Salem. There are 36 counties in the state.

Governor: Victor Atiyeh (R.), 1983–86 ($53,394 plus $1,000 monthly for expenses).

Secretary of State: Norma Paulus (R.) ($45,619).

BUDGET. Oregon has 2-year financial periods. General revenues for the biennium 1979–81 were $13,700,529,247 (federal funds, $1,216m.); general expenditures, $10,092,696,424 (education, $2,150·43m.; economic development and consumer services, $3,414m.; human resources, $2,195m.).

On 14 Oct. 1980 the outstanding bonded debt was $4,856,136,000.

Per capita personal income (1980) was $9,317.

ENERGY AND NATURAL RESOURCES

Electricity. Four privately owned utilities, 11 municipally owned utilities, 16 co-operatives and 4 utility districts provide electricity in the state. The privately owned companies serve 73·45% of the electricity. Private utilities sold 25,014,195,957 kwh. of electric power in 1979.

A federal agency, the Bonneville Power Administration, also markets electric power from 30 federal dams in the Pacific Northwest to 160 public and private utilities and large industrial plants. The dams, which are operated by the Army Corps of Engineers or the Bureau of Reclamation, had on 31 Dec. 1979 a total generating capacity of 17,926,788 kw. The Bonneville transmission network now covers the states of Oregon, Washington, Idaho, Western Montana, and parts of California, Nevada, Utah and Wyoming.

Minerals. Oregon's mineral resources include gold, silver, copper, lead, mercury, chromite, sand and gravel, stone, clays, lime, silica, diatomite, expansible shale, scoria, pumice and uranium. There is geothermal potential. Oregon is the only state producing nickel in the US. Value of mineral products, 1979, was $165m.

Agriculture. Oregon, which has an area of 61,557,184 acres, is divided by the Cascade Range into two distinct zones as to climate. West of the Cascade Range there is a good rainfall and almost every variety of crop common to the temperate zone is grown; east of the Range stock-raising and wheat-growing are the principal industries and irrigation is needed for row crops and fruits. In 1975 there were 2·18m. acres under irrigation

There were, in 1981, 35,000 farms with an acreage of 18m. (30% of the land area), including (1974) 5·3m. acres of total crop land; average farm size in 1981 was 517 acres; most are family-owned corporate farms.

Cash receipts from crops in 1980 amounted to $1,074·5m., and from livestock and livestock products, $537·3m. Principal crops are hay, wheat, potatoes, peppermint, ryegrass seed, pears, onions, snap beans, sweet corn and barley.

Livestock, 1 July 1980: Milch cows, 93,000; cattle and calves, 1·5m.; sheep and lambs, 350,000; swine, 100,000.

In 1979 the wool clip yielded 3·8m. lb.

Forestry. About 29·8m. acres is forested, almost half of the state. Of this amount, 24·2m. is commercial forest land suitable for timber production; ownership is as follows (acres): US Forestry service, 11·6m. (48%); Forest Industry, 5m. (22·8%); Small non-industrial landowners, 3·6m. (14·7%); US Bureau of Land Management, 2·2m. (9%); State of Oregon, 820,000 acres (3·4%) and other owners (city, county, Indian), 496,000 acres (2·1%). Oregon's commercial forest lands provide an annual harvest of 7,800m. bd ft of logs, as well as the benefits of recreation, water, grazing, wildlife and fish. Trees vary from the coastal forest of hemlock and spruce to the state's primary species, Douglas-fir, throughout much of western Oregon. In eastern Oregon, ponderosa pine, lodgepole pine and true firs are found. Here, forestry is often combined with livestock grazing to provide an economic operation. Along the Cascade summit and in the mountains of northeast Oregon, alpine species are found. Forest products manufacturing is Oregon's leading industry, and provides for 20% of the country's softwood lumber needs, 40% of its plywood and more than 25% of the hardboard. More than one-third of the economy depends directly or indirectly on timber industries; about 85,000 (1980) people are employed, the annual value of primary production is $4,420m., the payroll is $1,500m.

Fisheries. All food and shellfish landings in the calendar year 1980 amounted to 126m., valued at $56m. The most important are: tuna, crabs, bottom fish, shrimp.

INDUSTRY. During 1978, 5,696 manufacturing establishments reported to the Employment Division, average annual employment, 1978, 219,600 with pay of $3,359m.; value added by manufacture (1978), $7,100m.

TOURISM. In 1979, 13,520,033 out-of-state cars visited Oregon; the total 1979 income from tourism was estimated to be $1,082m.

COMMUNICATIONS

Roads. The state maintains (1980) 7,562 miles of primary and secondary highways, almost all surfaced; counties maintain 29,004 miles, and cities 7,391 miles; there were 79,436 miles in national parks and federal reservations. Registered motor vehicles, 31 Dec. 1979, totalled 2·5m.

Railways. The state had (1980) 19 common carrier railways with a total mileage of 4,428.

Aviation. In Oct. 1980 there were 5 public-use and 71 personal-use heliports; 4 public-use seaplane bases; 205 personal-use airports; 108 public-use airports including 37 state-owned airports.

Shipping. Portland is a major seaport for large ocean-going vessels and is 101 miles inland from the mouth of the Columbia River.

Post and Broadcasting. In Dec. 1980 there were 129 commercial radio stations and 13 educational radio stations. There were 12 commercial television stations and 6 educational television stations. There were also 5 campus limited radio stations and 1 subscription radio station.

Newspapers. In 1980 there were 21 daily newspapers with a circulation of 699,713 and 89 non-daily newspapers with a circulation of 349,849.

JUSTICE, RELIGION, EDUCATION AND WELFARE

Justice. There are 3 correctional institutions in Oregon, all in Salem. The Oregon State Penitentiary, on 1 Nov. 1980, held 1,682 males; the Women's Correctional Center had a resident population of 62; and the Oregon Correctional Institution, which is for first offenders, had a population of 747. The Oregon Correctional Division's Release Center in Salem held 190 inmates, 112 inmates were held in Oregon State Hospital wards and 329 inmates were on temporary leave or work release.

The sterilization law, originally passed in 1917, was amended in 1967. The amendments changed the number of persons on the Board of Social Protection from 15 to 7 and provided that the Public Defender would automatically represent all persons examined. The basis on which a person would be subject to examination by the Board are: *(a)* if such person would be likely to procreate children having an inherited tendency to mental retardation or mental illness, or *(b)* if such person would be likely to procreate children who would become neglected or dependent because of the person's inability by reason of mental illness or mental retardation to provide adequate care. Up to 1 July 1979, 941 men and 1,741 women have been sterilized.

Religion. The chief religious bodies are Catholic, Baptist, Lutheran, Methodists, Presbyterian and Mormon. Total membership, all denominations, 691,085 in 1971.

Education. School attendance is compulsory from 7 to 18 years of age if the twelfth year of school has not been completed; those between the ages of 16 and 18 years, if legally employed, may attend part-time or evening schools. Others may be excused under certain circumstances. On 30 June 1980 the 965 public elementary schools, 79 junior high schools and 232 standard senior high schools had 30,481 administrators and teachers; net enrolment was 494,635 (excluding transfers between districts), of whom 157,726 were high school pupils. Average salary for all classroom teachers, 1979–80, was $16,266. Total expenditure on elementary and secondary education (1979–80) was $1,380m.

Leading state-supported institutions of higher education (1980–81) included:

	Teachers	*Students*
University of Oregon, Eugene	878	17,488
University of Oregon Health Sciences Center:		
Medical School, Portland	364	1,502
Dental School, Portland		
Oregon State University, Corvallis	888	17,707
Portland State University, Portland	567	16,854
Oregon College of Education, Monmouth	163	3,150
Southern Oregon College, Ashland	216	4,760
Eastern Oregon College, La Grande	82	1,804
Oregon Institute of Technology, Klamath Falls	143	2,700

Largest of the privately endowed universities are Lewis and Clark College, Portland, with 1980–81 3,188 students; University of Portland, 2,746 students; Willamette University, Salem, 1,886 students; Reed College, Portland, 1,132 students, and Linfield College, McMinnville, 1,242 students. There are 13 community colleges and 1 area education district with an estimated enrolment of 275,000 students in 1980–81.

Health. In Oct. 1979 there were 97 licensed hospitals (11,496 beds) and 190 nursing homes with 16,147 beds. In Oct. 1979 there were 4 state hospitals for mentally ill and mentally retarded (2 for mentally ill, 1 for mentally retarded and 1 with both programmes). The average for the mentally ill in Oct. 1979 was 1,151 and for the mentally retarded 1,738.

Social Security. Old-age assistance is provided for all needy persons 65 years or older who meet certain eligibility requirements. In financial year 1979–80, 3,598 cases per month received average payments of $5.36 cash and $87.54 services. For the same period 98,278 persons in 36,166 families with dependent children received an average $279.74 per month; 552 blind recipients $38.56 cash and $62.52 services; 7,009 disabled $15.94 cash and $41.86 services; 4,501 general assistance cases $134.73 cash and $5.45 services.

Medical assistance and mental health costs averaged $14,494,000 per month.

A system of unemployment benefit payments, financed by employers, with administrative allotments made through a federal agency, started 2 Jan. 1938, and covers about 66,500 employers with average employment in 1979 of 1,024,535. By June 1980, $1,717m. in taxes had been paid into the trust fund plus $297·3m. in interest and reimbursed benefits. About $1,691m. has been paid in benefits which from July 1980 range from $38 to $138 weekly and up to $3,588 per year. About 38,406 state employees, 48,060 school employees, 5,507 community college employees and 18,879 political subdivision employees are participants in the public employees retirement programme. The same employees are covered under the federal old-age, survivors and disability insurance programme. Approximately 31,016 retired employees are receiving monthly benefit cheques.

Books of Reference

Oregon Blue Book. Issued by the Secretary of State. Salem. Biennial
Federal Writers' Project. *Oregon: End of the Trail.* Rev. ed. Portland, 1972
Atkeson, R., *Oregon.* Portland, 1968.—*Oregon Coast.* Portland, 1972
Baldwin, E. M., *Geology of Oregon.* Rev. ed. Dubuque, Iowa, 1976
Carey, C. H., *General History of Oregon, prior to 1861.* 2 vol. (1 vol. reprint, 1971) Portland, 1935
Corning, H. M. (ed.), *Dictionary of Oregon History.* New York, 1956
Dicken, S. N., *Oregon Geography.* 5th ed. Eugene, 1973.—with Dicken, E. F., *Making of Oregon: a Study in Historical Geography.* Portland, 1979
Dodds, G. B., *Oregon: A Bicentennial History.* New York, 1977
Friedman, R., *Oregon for the Curious.* 3rd ed. Portland, 1972
Highsmith, R. M. Jr. (ed.), *Atlas of the Pacific Northwest.* Corvallis, 1973
McArthur, L. A., *Oregon Geographic Names.* 4th ed., rev. and enlarged. Portland, 1974
Patton, Clyde P., *Atlas of Oregon.* Univ. Oregon Press, Eugene, 1976

State Library: The Oregon State Library, Salem. *Librarian:* Marcia Lowell.

PENNSYLVANIA

HISTORY. Pennsylvania, first settled in 1682, is one of the 13 original states in the Union.

AREA AND POPULATION. Pennsylvania is bounded north by New York, east by New Jersey, south by Delaware and Maryland, south-west by West Virginia, west by Ohio and north-west by Lake Erie. Area, 45,308 sq. miles, of which 420 sq. miles are inland water. Census population, 1 April 1980, 11,863,895, an increase of 63,129 or 0·5% since 1970. Births, 1981, 160,180; deaths, 119,611; infant deaths, 1,902; marriages, 92,644; divorces, 38,842.

Population at 5 census years was:

	White	*Negro*	*Indian*	*All others*	*Total*	*Per sq. mile*
1910	7,467,713	193,919	1,503	1,976	7,665,111	171·0
1930	9,196,007	431,257	523	3,563	9,631,350	213·8
1960	10,454,004	852,750	2,122	10,490	11,319,366	251·5
			All others			
1970	10,745,219	1,015,884	39,663		11,800,766	262·9
1980	10,652,320	1,046,810	164,765		11,863,895	264·3

Of the total population in 1980, 47·9% were male, 69·3% were urban and 68·1% were 21 years of age or older.

The population of the larger cities and townships, 1980 census, was:

Philadelphia	1,688,210	Scranton	88,117	Lancaster	54,725
Pittsburgh	423,938	Reading	78,686	Harrisburg	53,264
Erie	119,123	Bethlehem	70,419	Wilkes-Barre	51,551
Allentown	103,758	Altoona	57,078	York	44,619

Larger urbanized areas, 1980 census: Philadelphia (in Pennsylvania), 3,682,709; Pittsburgh, 2,263,894; Northeast, 640,396, Allentown–Bethlehem–Easton (in Pennsylvania), 551,052; Harrisburg, 446,576.

CONSTITUTION AND GOVERNMENT. The present constitution dates from 1968. The General Assembly consists of a Senate of 50 members chosen for 4 years, one-half being elected biennially, and a House of Representatives of 203 members chosen for 2 years. The Governor and Lieut.-Governor are elected for 4 years. Every citizen 18 years of age, with the usual residential qualifications, may vote. The state sends to Congress 2 senators and 23 representatives.

In the 1980 presidential election Reagan polled 2,261,872 votes, Carter 1,937,540 and Anderson 292,921.

The state capital is Harrisburg. The state is organized in counties (numbering 67), cities, boroughs, townships and school districts.

Governor: Richard Thornburgh (R.), 1979–86 ($75,000).
Lieut.-Governor: William W. Scranton (R.) ($54,500).

BUDGET. Total revenues for the year ending 30 June 1982 were $7,109·6m.; general fund expenditure, $7,376·2m. (education, $3,359·6m.; transport, $143·4m.; public welfare, $2,522·5m.; environment, $105·7m.).

On 30 June 1982 total net direct long-term debt amounted to $2,452·9m.

Per capita personal income (1981) was $10,370.

ENERGY AND NATURAL RESOURCES

Minerals. Pennsylvania is almost the sole producer of anthracite coal; its output reached a peak of 100,445,299 short tons in 1917 with a labour-force of 156,148 men. Production in 1981: Anthracite, 5·2m. tons, with about 3,200 men; bituminous coal, 76m. tons, with about 29,000 men; crude petroleum (1981), 3·61m. bbls; natural gas (1980), 97,439m. cu. ft. Total value of other minerals produced (1980), $342·3m., including $238m. for cement.

Agriculture. Agriculture, market-gardening, fruit-growing, horticulture and forestry are pursued within the state. In 1982 there were 61,000 farms with a total farm area of 8·9m. acres (4·7m. acres in crops); the average farm was 146 acres with average value per acre of $1,332. Cash income, 1981, from crops, $766m., and from livestock, $2,100m.

Pennsylvania ranks ninth in the production of tobacco (27·3m. lb., 1981 value $21·8m.) and leads in mushrooms (237·5m. lb., value $147·5m.). Other crops are winter wheat (9·72m. bu.), oats (20·01m. bu.), maize (134·4m. bu.), barley (4·1m. bu.) and potatoes (5·25m. cwt). On 1 Jan. 1982 there were on farms: 2·1m. cattle and calves, including 730,000 milch cows, 125,000 sheep, 750,000 swine. Milk production, 1981, was 8,965m. lb. valued at $1,299m., and eggs numbered 4,268m. valued at $213·4m. Pennsylvania is also a major fruit producing state; in 1981 apples totalled 400m. lb.; peaches, 65m. lb.; tart cherries, 8m. lb.; sweet cherries, 300 tons; and grapes, 61,000 tons. Other important items are soybeans (3·1m. bu.), vegetables for processing (109,000 tons), fresh vegetables (2·2m. cwt) and broiler-chickens (115·1m.).

Forestry. In 1979 national forest lands totalled 508,480 acres; state forests, 2,047,410 acres; state parks, 296,119 acres; state game land, 1,222,773 acres; game land leased but not owned by the state, 2,102,927 acres (co-operative and safety-zone programmes).

INDUSTRY. Pennsylvania leads in the production of iron and steel. Output of steel, 1981, 24·1m. net tons.

In 1979, 16,846 manufacturing establishments employed 1,400,270 workers (wages, $22,491m.).

COMMUNICATIONS

Roads. Highways and roads in the state (federal, local and state combined) totalled (1982) 118,575 miles. Registered motor vehicles for 1981 numbered 7,252,836 (including 5,416,765 passenger cars, 1,444,785 trucks, truck-tractors and trailers).

Railways. In Jan. 1978, 29 railways operated within the state with a line mileage of 7,788.

Aviation. There were (1979) 161 commercial airports, 3 public landing strips, 211 heliports and 370 airports for personal use.

Shipping. Trade at Delaware River ports (1980, short tons) imports, 57·9m., exports, 9·6m. Trade at Erie ports (1981): imports 50,004 short tons, exports 10,730 short tons.

Post and Broadcasting. Broadcasting stations comprised (1978) 37 television stations and 285 radio stations.

Newspapers. There were (1978) 116 daily and 322 weekly newspapers.

JUSTICE, RELIGION, EDUCATION AND WELFARE

Justice. No executions took place in 1963–82; since 1930 there have been 149 executions (electrocution), all for murder.

State prison population, on 31 Dec. 1981, was 9,420.

Religion. The chief religious bodies in 1977 were the Roman Catholic, with 3,717,667 members; Protestant, 3,150,920 (1971); and Jewish, 469,078. The 5 largest Protestant denominations (by communicants) were: Lutheran Church in America, 766,276; United Methodist, 728,915 (1971), United Presbyterian Church in the USA, 573,905 (1971); United Church of Christ, 257,138; Episcopal, 193,399 (1971).

Education. School attendance is compulsory for children 8–17 years of age. In 1981–82 the public kindergartens and elementary schools had 903,342 pupils; public secondary schools had 935,673 pupils. Non-public schools had 281,357 elementary pupils and 112,742 secondary pupils. Average salary, public school professional personnel, men $21,780; women $19,151; for classroom teachers, men $20,319, women $18,878.

Leading senior academic institutions included:

Founded	Institutions	Faculty (Autumn 1980)	Students (Autumn 1981)
1740	University of Pennsylvania (non-sect.)	3,509	22,246
1787	University of Pittsburgh	2,901	35,114
1832	Lafayette College, Easton (Presbyterian)	201	2,413
1842	Villanova University (R.C.)	660	10,753
1846	Bucknell University (Baptist)	224	3,314
1851	St Joseph's College, Philadelphia (R.C.)	282	5,578
1852	California State College	301	4,657
1855	Pennsylvania State University	4,275	63,800
1855	Millersville State College	329	6,239
1863	LaSalle College, Philadelphia (R.C.)	407	7,587
1866	Lehigh University, Bethlehem (non-sect.)	386	6,358
1871	West Chester State College	516	9,209
1875	Indiana University of Pennsylvania	661	12,391
1878	Duquesne University, Pittsburgh (R.C.)	456	6,628
1884	Temple University, Philadelphia	2,469	31,474
1885	Bryn Mawr College	157	1,850
1888	University of Scranton (R.C.)	205	4,542
1891	Drexel University, Philadelphia	678	12,594
1900	Carnegie-Mellon University, Pittsburgh	726	5,900

Health. In 1981 the state had 231 hospitals (53,029 beds) listed by the State Health Department, excluding federal hospitals and mental institutions. In 1978 the 32 mental hospitals had 11,079 patients (94 per 100,000 population); 60 institutions for the mentally retarded, 10,934 (93).

Social Security. During the year ending 30 June 1981 the monthly average number of cases receiving public assistance was: aid to families with dependent children, 630,588; blind pension, 5,127; general assistance, 176,906.

Payments for medical assistance for the year ending 30 June 1981 totalled $1,390·2m. Under the medical assistance programme payments are made for inpatient hospital care ($483·9m.); nursing care in home ($2·2m.); care in public institutions (nursing homes, mental institutions and geriatric centres) ($542·2m.); private nursing home care ($89·2m.); other medical care ($272·8m.).

Books of Reference

Pennsylvania Manual. Dept. of Property and Supplies, Division of Documents. Harrisburg. Biennial

Pennsylvania's Regions, A Survey of the Commonwealth. State Planning Board. Harrisburg, 1967

Pennsylvania Statistical Abstract. Dept. of Commerce, Harrisburg. Annual

Pennsylvania State Industrial Directory. New York. Annual

Carstens, A. H., *What to See in Pennsylvania.* 2nd ed. Cresco, 1965

Klein, P. S., and Hoogenboom, A., *A History of Pennsylvania.* New York, 1973

League of Women Voters of Pennsylvania, *Key to the Keystone State.* Philadelphia, 1972

Pennsylvania Chamber of Commerce, *Pennsylvania Government Today.* State College, Pa., 1973

Stevens, S. K., *Pennsylvania: Birthplace of a Nation.* New York, 1964.—*Exploring Pennsylvania: Geography History, Civics.* 3rd ed. New York, 1968

Wallace, P. A. W., *Pennsylvania: Seed of a Nation.* New York, 1962

Wilkinson, N. B., *Bibliography of Pennsylvania History.* Pa. Historical & Museum Commission. Harrisburg, 1957

RHODE ISLAND

HISTORY The earliest settlers in the region which now forms the state of Rhode Island were colonists from Massachusetts who had been driven forth on account of their non-acceptance of the prevailing religious beliefs. The first of the settlements was made in 1636, settlers of every creed being welcomed. In 1647 a patent was executed for the government of the settlements, and on 8 July 1663 a charter was executed recognizing the settlers as forming a body corporate and politic by the name of the 'English Colony of Rhode Island and Providence Plantations, in New England, in America'. On 29 May 1790 the state accepted the federal constitution and entered the Union as the last of the 13 original states.

AREA AND POPULATION. Rhode Island is bounded north and east by Massachusetts, south by the Atlantic and west by Connecticut. Area, 1,212 sq. miles, of which 158 sq. miles are inland water. Census population, 1 April 1980, 947,154 a decrease of 0·3% since 1970.

Births, 1981, were 12,430; deaths (excluding foetal deaths), 9,138; infant deaths (1980) 150; marriages (1980) 7,480; divorces (1980) 3,582.

Population of 5 census years was:

	White	*Negro*	*Indian*	*Asiatic*	*Total*	*Per sq. mile*
1910	532,492	9,529	284	305	542,610	508·5
1930	677,026	9,913	318	240	687,497	649·3
1960	838,712	18,332	932	1,190	859,488	812·4
1970	914,757	25,338	1,390	5,240	949,723 [1]	905·0
			All other			
1980	896,692	27,584	22,878		947,154	903·0

[1] Through tabulation errors there were 2,998 people unaccounted for, as to race and sex, in 1970.

Of the total population in 1980, 451,251 were male, 824,004 were urban and 665,054 were 20 years of age or older.

The chief cities and their population (census, 1980) are Providence, 156,304; Warwick, 87,127; Cranston, 71,992; Pawtucket, 71,204; East Providence, 59,980; Woonsocket, 45,914; Newport, 29,259; North Kingston (town), 21,938; Middletown (town), 17,216. The Providence–Pawtucket–Warwick Standard Metropolitan Statistical Area had a population of 914,110 in 1970.

CONSTITUTION AND GOVERNMENT. The present constitution dates from 1843; it has had 36 amendments. The General Assembly consists of a Senate of 50 members and a House of Representatives of 100 members, both elected for 2 years, as are also the Governor and Lieut.-Governor. Every citizen, 18 years of age, who has resided in the state for 30 days, and is duly registered, is qualified to vote.

Rhode Island sends to Congress 2 senators and 2 representatives.

At the 1980 presidential election Carter polled 198,342 votes, Reagan, 154,793.

The capital is Providence. The state has 5 counties (unique in having no political functions) and 39 cities and towns.

Governor: J. Joseph Garrahy (D.), 1982–84 ($42,500).
Lieut.-Governor: Thomas R. Diluglio (D.), 1982–84 ($30,500).
Secretary of State: Susan Farmer (R.), 1982–84 ($30,500).

BUDGET. For the fiscal year ending 30 June 1982 (Office of the State Controller) total revenues were $1,106·4m. (taxation, $6,645m., and federal aid, $302·3m.); general expenditures were $1,134·5m. (education, $212·3m.; highways, $63m.; and public welfare, $304·2m.).

Total net long-term debt on 30 June 1982 was $214·6m.

Per capita personal income (1981) was $10,466.

NATURAL RESOURCES

Minerals. The small mineral output, mostly stone, sand and gravel, was valued (1980) at $7·5m.

Agriculture. While Rhode Island is predominantly a manufacturing state, agriculture contributed $32·5m. to the general cash income in 1980. In 1978 it had 865 farms with an area of 75,791 acres (11·1% of the total land area), of which 36,632 acres were crop land; the average farm was 98·1 acres, valued (land and buildings) at $72,033.

Fisheries. The number of commercial fishermen in the state in 1970 (US census) was 310; value of all fish landed in 1980, $46·1m.

INDUSTRY. Total non-agricultural employment in 1981 was 400,500, of which 126,300 were manufacturing, 274,200 non-manufacturing. Manufacturing firms totalled 3,259; average weekly earnings for production workers in manufacturing, $238.26; value added by manufacture (1977), $2,737m. Principal industries are metals and machinery, textiles and jewellery–silverware.

COMMUNICATIONS

Roads. The state had (1 Jan. 1980) 5,758 miles of road, of which 1,313 were state-owned. In 1978, 605,000 motor vehicles were registered.

Railways. In 1977, 6 railways operated 135 line-miles.

Aviation. Of the 12 airports in 1980, 7 were state-owned and 5 privately owned. Theodore Francis Green airport at Warwick, near Providence, is served by 7 air-lines, and handled 1,004,464 passengers and 14m. lb. of freight in 1980.

Shipping. Waterborne freight through the Port of Providence (1980) totalled 6·4m. tons.

Broadcasting. There are 22 radio stations and 4 television stations in the state.

JUSTICE, RELIGION, EDUCATION AND WELFARE

Justice. The state's penal institutions, Nov. 1979, had 675 inmates (70 per 100,000 population).

The death penalty is illegal, except that it is mandatory in the case of murder committed by a prisoner serving a life sentence.

Religion. Chief religious bodies are (estimated figures Sept. 1975): Roman Catholic with 597,000 members; Protestant Episcopal (baptized persons), 50,000; Baptist, 22,500; Congregational, 12,000; Methodist, 10,000; Jewish, 24,000.

Education. In 1980–81 the 230 public elementary schools had 4,080 teachers and total enrolment of 68,275 pupils; about 15,000 pupils were enrolled in private and parochial schools. The 68 senior and vocational high schools had 4,134 teachers and 70,967 pupils. Teachers' salaries (1979–80) averaged $13,660. Local expenditure, for schools (including evening schools) in 1980–81 totalled $363·5m.

There are 11 institutions of higher learning in the state, including 1 junior college. The state maintains Rhode Island College, at Providence, with 800 faculty members, and 8,800 full-time students (1980), and the University of Rhode Island, at South Kingstown, with over 850 faculty members and over 14,000 students (including graduate students). Brown University, at Providence, founded in 1764, is now non-sectarian; in 1980 it had over 500 full-time faculty members and full-time students. Providence College, at Providence, founded in 1917 by the Order of Preachers (Dominican), had (1980) 218 professors and 3,800 students. The largest of the other colleges are Bryant College, at Smithfield, with 125 faculty and over 4,800 students, and the Rhode Island School of Design, in Providence, with about 100 faculty and 1,400 students.

Health. In 1982 the state had 24 hospitals (over 7,000 beds), including 4 mental hospitals.

Social Security. In Oct. 1978 aid to dependent children was being granted to 35,373 children in 17,186 families (52,559 persons), $264.06 per month, and general assistance to 7,119 persons at an average of $187.48 per month. (All other aid programmes were taken over by the federal government.)

Books of Reference

Rhode Island Manual. Prepared by the Secretary of State. Providence

Providence Journal Almanac: A Reference Book for Rhode Islanders. Providence. Annual
Rhode Island Basic Economic Statistics. Rhode Island Dept. of Economic Development. Providence, 1972

State Library: Rhode Island State Library, State House, Providence 02908. State Librarian: Elliott E. Andrews.

SOUTH CAROLINA

HISTORY. South Carolina, first settled permanently in 1670, was one of the 13 original states of the Union.

AREA AND POPULATION. South Carolina is bounded in the north by North Carolina, east and south-east by the Atlantic, south-west and west by Georgia. Area, 31,113 sq. miles, of which 909 sq. miles are inland water. Census population, 1 April 1980, 3,121,833, an increase of 20·5 since 1970. Births, 1981, were 51,908 (16·6 per 1,000 population); deaths, 25,138 (8·1); infant deaths, 809 (15·6 per 1,000 live births); marriages, 53,915 (17·3); divorces and annulments, 13,595 (4·4).

The population in 5 census years was:

	White	*Negro*	*Indian*	*Asiatic*	*Total*	*Per sq. mile*
1910	679,161	835,843	331	65	1,515,400	49·7
1930	944,049	793,681	959	76	1,738,765	56·8
1960	1,551,022	829,291	1,098	946	2,382,594	78·7
			All others			
1970	1,794,432	789,040	3,588		2,587,060	83·2
1980	2,150,507	948,623	22,703		3,121,833	100·3

Of the total population in 1980, 49% were male, 54·1% were urban and 55% were 25 years old or older.

Populations of large towns at the 1980 census (with those of associated metropolitan areas): Columbia (capital), 97,104 (395,775); Charleston, 69,296 (411,582); Greenville, 58,190; Spartanburg, 43,502 (Greenville–Spartanburg, 562,934).

CONSTITUTION AND GOVERNMENT. The present constitution dates from 1895, when it went into force without ratification by the electorate. The General Assembly consists of a Senate of 46 members, elected for 4 years (half retiring biennially), and a House of Representatives of 124 members, elected for 2 years. The Governor and Lieut.-Governor are elected for 4 years. Only registered citizens have the right to vote. South Carolina sends to Congress 2 senators and 6 representatives.

At the 1980 presidential election Reagan polled 441,841 votes, Carter 430,385 and Anderson 14,153.

The capital is Columbia.

Governor: Richard Riley (D.), 1983–86 ($60,000).
Secretary of State: John Tucker Campbell (D.), 1983–86 ($50,000).

BUDGET. For the fiscal year ending 30 June 1980 general revenues were $1,598m.; general expenditures were also $1,598m.

On 30 June 1980 the total bonded debt was $660m.

Per capita personal income (1981) was $8,050.

NATURAL RESOURCES

Minerals. Non-metallic minerals are of chief importance: value of mineral output in 1981 was $107m., chiefly from limestone for cement, clay, stone, sand and gravel. Production of kaolin, vermiculite, scrap mica and fuller's earth is also important.

Agriculture. In 1980 there were 35,000 farms covering a farm area of 6·5m. acres. The average farm was of 186 acres. Of the 33,412 farms of the 1978 census, there were 1,068 of 1,000 acres or more, average farm 188 acres; owners operated 19,339 farms; tenants 3,908. There were 2,044 farms with $100,000 or more in value of sales.

Cash receipts from farm marketing in 1980 amounted to $656m. for crops and $417m. for livestock. Chief crops are tobacco ($175m.), soybeans ($172m.), and corn ($87m.). Production, 1980: Cotton 77,000 bales; peaches, 355m. lb.; soybeans, 22·4m. bu.; tobacco, 125·5m. lb.; corn. 24·7m. bu. Livestock on farms, 1978: 690,000 all cattle, 575,000 swine, 7·6m. poultry.

Forestry. The forest industry is important; state and private forest land (1980), 12·5m. acres. National forests amounted to 578,724 acres.

INDUSTRY. A monthly average of 389,218 workers were employed in manufacturing in 1980, earning $5,710m.

Tourism is the second largest industry; tourists spend annually an estimated $2,188m.

COMMUNICATIONS

Roads. Total highway mileage in the combined highway system in 1982 was 39,695 miles. Motor vehicle registrations numbered 2m. in 1982.

Railways. In 1979 the length of railway in the state was 2,939 miles.

Aviation. There were, 1979, 72 airports and 1,700 registered aircraft.

Shipping. The state has 3 deep-water ports.

JUSTICE, RELIGION, EDUCATION AND WELFARE

Justice. In June 1980 penal institutions held 8,176 inmates of whom 7,469 were in state prisons.

Education. In 1980–81 the total public-school enrolment was 619,222; there were 455,747 white pupils and 163,475 non-white pupils. The total number of teachers was 34,309; average salary was $14,199.

For higher education the state operates the University of South Carolina, founded at Columbia in 1801, with, 1980, 33,129 enrolled students; Clemson University, founded in 1889, with 11,327 students; The Citadel, at Charleston, with 3,353 students; Winthrop College, Rock Hill, with 4,640 students; Medical University of S. Carolina, at Charleston 2,489 students; S. Carolina State College, at Orangeburg, with 3,437 students, and Francis Marion College, at Florence, with 2,703 students; the College of Charleston has 5,164 students and Lander College, Greenwood, 1,694.

There are also 428 private kindergartens, elementary and high schools with total enrolment of 54,047 pupils, and 25 private and denominational colleges and junior colleges with enrolment of 25,514 students.

Health. In 1980 the state had 181 hospitals and nursing homes and 102 intermediate care institutions licensed by the South Carolina Department of Health and Environmental Control.

Social Security. In 1981 there were 46,700 recipients of social security benefits per month. The average monthly expenditure in benefits was $120m.

Books of Reference

Reports of the South Carolina State Development Board. Columbia. Annual
South Carolina Legislative Manual. Columbia. Annual
South Carolina Statistical Abstract, 1980. South Carolina Budget and Control Board, Columbia, 1980

State Library: South Carolina State Library, Columbia.

SOUTH DAKOTA

HISTORY. South Dakota was first visited by Europeans in 1743 when Verendrye planted a lead plate (discovered in 1913) on the site of Fort Pierre, claiming the region for the French crown. Beginning with a trading post in 1794, it was settled from 1857 to 1861 when Dakota Territory was organized. It was admitted into the Union on 2 Nov. 1889.

AREA AND POPULATION. South Dakota is bounded north by North Dakota, east by Minnesota, south-east by the Big Sioux River (forming the boundary with Iowa), south by Nebraska (with the Missouri River forming part of the boundary) and west by Wyoming and Montana. Area, 77,116 sq. miles, of which 1,164 sq. miles are water. Area administered by the Bureau of Indian Affairs, 1980, covered 5m. acres (10% of the state), of which 2·6m. acres were held by tribes. The federal government, 1979, owned 3,492,000 acres or 7·1% of the total.

Census population, 1 April 1980, 690,178, an increase of 3·5% since 1970. Births, 1981, were 12,725 (18·4 per 1,000 population); deaths, 6,434 (9·3); infant deaths, 143 (11·2 per 1,000 live births); marriages, 8,662 (12·5); divorces, 2,772 (4).

Population in 5 federal censuses was:

	White	*Negro*	*Indian*	*Asiatic*	*Total*	*Per sq. mile*
1910	563,771	817	19,137	163	583,888	7·6
1930	669,453	646	21,833	101	692,849	9·0
1960	653,098	1,114	25,794	336	680,514	8·9
			All others			
1970	630,333	1,627	34,297		666,257	8·8
1980	638,955	2,144	49,079		690,178	9·0

Of the total population in 1980, 340,370 were male, 320,223 were urban and 441,851 were 21 years of age or older.

Population of the chief cities (census of 1980) was: Sioux Falls, 81,071; Rapid City, 46,340; Aberdeen, 25,973; Watertown, 15,632, Mitchell, 13,917; Brookings, 14,915; Huron, 13,000.

CONSTITUTION AND GOVERNMENT. Voters are all citizens 18 years of age or older who have complied with certain residential qualifications. The people reserve the right of the initiative and referendum. The Senate has 35 members, and the House of Representatives 70 members, all elected for 2 years; the Governor and Lieut.-Governor are elected for 4 years. The state sends 2 senators and 1 representative to Congress.

In the 1980 presidential election Reagan polled 198,343 votes, Carter 103,855 and Anderson 21,431.

The capital is Pierre (population, 1980, 11,973). The state is divided into 66 organized counties.

Governor: William Janklow (R.), 1983–86 ($49,025).
Lieut.-Governor: Lowell Hansen, 1983–86 ($6,800 plus expense allowance).
Secretary of State: Alice Kundert, 1983–86 ($33,275).

BUDGET. For the fiscal year ending 30 June 1980 general revenues were $895·7m. and expenditures, $818·1m. Taxes and fees from state sources furnished $681·2m. and federal receipts $235m.

Per capita personal income (1981) was $8,833.

NATURAL RESOURCES

Minerals. The mineral products include gold (267,392 troy oz. in 1980, second largest yield of all states), sand and gravel (100,000m. short tons), silver (51,000 troy oz.). Mineral products, 1980, were valued at $227·7m., of which gold accounts for $163·8m.

Agriculture. In 1978, 39,665 farms had an acreage of 45m.; the average farm had 1,123 acres. Farm units are large; at the 1978 census there were only 3,850 farms of 50 acres or less, compared with 10,264 exceeding 1,000 acres. 14,475 farms sold produce valued at $40,000 or over.

South Dakota ranks first in the US as producer of rye (3·2m. bu. in 1981) and second in flaxseed (2·25m. bu.) and oats (70·5m. bu.). The other important crops (1981) are maize (180·6m. bu.), and sunflower seeds (472·6m. lb.) The farm livestock on 1 Jan. 1982 included 3·9m. cattle, 780,000 sheep, 1·7m. swine. There are about 148,000 bee colonies; honey production (1981) 9·2m. lb.

Forestry. National forest area, 1980, 1,995,000 acres.

INDUSTRY. In 1980, manufacturing establishments numbered 668 and had 27,261 workers who earned 367·2m. Food processing is by far the largest industry with 27,261 workers and an annual payroll of $367·2m. Also significant are dairy, lumber and wood products, printing and publishing and machinery. Metal fabrication and the electronic components industry are rapidly growing.

COMMUNICATIONS

Roads. Total highway mileage was 17,056 in 1981. Registered passenger cars numbered 637,000 in 1981.

Railways. In 1981 there were 2,024·2 miles of railway in operation. The state owns 837·8 miles of track of which 435 miles is operating.

Aviation. In 1981 there were 69 general aviation airports and 9 air carrier airports.

JUSTICE, RELIGION, EDUCATION AND WELFARE

Justice. The State prisons had, in 1980, 635 inmates. The death penalty was illegal from 1915 to 1938; since 1938, one person has been executed, in 1949 (by electrocution), for murder.

Religion. The chief religious bodies are (1970): Lutherans with 162,243 members, Roman Catholics (138,250), Methodist (45,795), Disciples of Christ (22,374), Presbyterian (19,494), Baptist (16,055) and Episcopal (17,268).

Education. Elementary and secondary education are free from 6 to 21 years of age. Between the ages of 8 and 16, attendance is compulsory. In 1981–82 138,303 pupils were attending elementary and high (including parochial) schools (9,500 full-time equivalent classroom teachers).

Teachers' salaries (1980–81) averaged an estimated $13,636. Total expenditure on public schools (1980–81), $246·2m.

The School of Mines at Rapid City, established 1885, had, spring 1982, 2,571 students; the State University at Brookings, 6,903 students; the University of South Dakota, founded at Vermillion in 1882, 5,853 students; Northern State College, 2,676 students; Black Hills State College, 2,073 students; Dakota State College, 1,073 students; University of South Dakota, Springfield, 706 students. The 9 private colleges had 6,409 students. The federal Government maintains Indian schools on its reservations and 2 outside at Flandreau and Pierre.

Health. In 1982 the state Health Department listed 56 licensed hospitals (average size 63 beds).

Social Security. In financial year 1980–81, a monthly average of $312,351 was received by 3,673 aged persons; $23,859, by 139 blind; $545,403, by 3,938 disabled. Mandatory supplement to federal SSI payments were a monthly average of $1,519 to 49 aged; $159 to 4 blind; $2,047 to 70 disabled. An average of $1,444,899 was received by 18,429 recipients of aid to dependent children. Average monthly medical payments of $1,647,423 were made to 4,223 aged; $15,588, to 69 blind; $1,828,757, to 2,867 disabled. Food stamps were sold to a monthly average of 15,842 households; average monthly value, $1,697,446.

Books of Reference

Governor's Budget Report. South Dakota Bureau of Finance and Management. Annual
South Dakota Historical Collections. 1902–80
South Dakota Legislative Manual. Department of Finance, Pierre, S.D. Biennial
Berg, F. M., *South Dakota: Land of Shining Gold.* Hettinger, 1982
Karolevitz, Robert F., *Challenge: the South Dakota Story.* Sioux Falls, 1975
Milton, John R., *South Dakota; a Bicentennial History.* New York, W. W. Norton, 1977
Schell, H. S., *History of South Dakota.* 3rd ed. Lincoln, Neb., 1975

State Library: South Dakota State Library, State Library Building, Pierre, S.D., 57501. *State Librarian:* Clarence L. Coffindaffer.

TENNESSEE

HISTORY. Tennessee, first settled in 1757, was admitted into the Union on 1 June 1796.

AREA AND POPULATION. Tennessee is bounded north by Kentucky and Virginia, east by North Carolina, south by Georgia, Alabama and Mississippi and west by the Mississippi River (forming the boundary with Arkansas and Missouri). Area, 42,144 sq. miles (989 sq. miles water). Census population, 1 April 1980, 4,591,120, an increase of 665,102 or 16·9% since 1970. Vital statistics, 1981 (provisional): Births, 67,050 (14·5 per 1,000 population); deaths, 40,480 (8·8); infant deaths 846 (12·6 per 1,000 live births); marriages, 60,094 (26·1); divorces, 31,167 (13·5).

Population in 6 census years was:

	White	*Negro*	*Indian*	*Asiatic*	*Total*	*Per sq. mile*
1910	1,711,432	473,088	216	53	2,184,789	52·4
1930	2,138,644	477,646	161	105	2,616,556	62·4
1950	2,760,257	530,603	339	334	3,291,718	78·8
1960	2,977,753	586,876	638	1,243	3,567,089	85·4
			All others			
1970	3,293,930	621,261	8,496		3,923,687	95·3
1980	3,835,452	725,942	29,726		4,591,120	111·6

Of the population in 1980, 2,216,600 were male, 2,773,573 were urban and those 21 years of age or older numbered 3,026,398.

The cities, with population, 1980, are Memphis, 646,356; Nashville (capital), 455,651; Knoxville, 175,030; Chattanooga, 169,565; Clarksville, 54,777; Jackson, 49,131; Johnson City, 39,753; Murfreesboro, 32,845; Kingsport, 32,027; Oak Ridge, 27,662. Standard metropolitan areas (1980): Memphis, 810,043; Nashville, 850,505; Knoxville, 476,517; Chattanooga, 320,761; Johnson City–Bristol–Kingsport, 343,041; Clarksville, 83,342.

CONSTITUTION AND GOVERNMENT. The state has operated under 3 constitutions, the last of which was adopted in 1870 and has been since amended 22 times (first in 1953). Voters at an election may authorize the calling of a convention limited to altering or abolishing one or more specified sections of the constitution. The General Assembly consists of a Senate of 33 members and a House of Representatives of 99 members, senators elected for 4 years and representatives for 2 years. Qualified as electors are all citizens (with the usual residential and age (18) qualifications). Tennessee sends to Congress 2 senators and 9 representatives.

In the 1980 presidential election Reagan polled 787,761 votes, Carter 783,051 and Anderson 35,991.

For the Tennessee Valley Authority *see* pp. 1406–07.

The capital is Nashville. The state is divided into 95 counties.

Governor: Andrew Lamar Alexander (R.), 1983–86 ($68,226).

Secretary of State: Gentry Crowell (D.), ($46,524).

BUDGET. For 1979–80 total revenue was $4,028m.;general expenditure, $3,873·7m.

Total net long-term debt on 30 June 1980 amounted to $1,405·9m.

Per capita personal income (1980) was $7,720.

ENERGY AND NATURAL RESOURCES

Minerals. Coalfields cover about 5,000 sq. miles; output in 1975 was 8·2m. short tons valued at $140·3m. In 1975 Tennessee led the states in the production of clay (1·3m. short tons valued at $9m.), zinc (83,293 short tons) and pyrite and was an important producer of phosphate rock (2·3m. short tons). Other mineral products are copper, mica, cement, sand and gravel, limestone. Total value of mineral products in 1978 was $347·5m.

Agriculture. In 1978, 110,000 farms covered 14·6m. acres. The average farm was of 136 acres (only a few states had a smaller average) valued land and buildings, at $116,960.

Cash income (1980) from crops was $852·4m.; from livestock, $844·6m. Main crops were cotton and tobacco.

On 1 Jan. 1980 the domestic animals included 200,000 milch cows, 2·3m. all cattle, 12,000 sheep, 1·4m. swine.

Forestry. Forests occupy 13·16m. acres (50% of total land area). The forest industry and industries dependent on it employ about 40,000 workers, earning $150m. per year. Wood products are valued at over $500m. per year. National forest system land (1976) 620,000 acres.

INDUSTRY. The manufacturing industries include iron and steel working, but the most important products are chemicals, including synthetic fibres and allied products, electrical equipment and food. In 1978, manufacturing establishments employed 509,900 workers, who received wages of $5,863m.; value added by manufactures in 1978 was $14,046m.

TOURISM. 48m. out-of-state tourists spent $1,327m. in 1978. 90m. people travelled through the state in 1977. 8·6% of retail business is generated by tourists and travellers. There are 21,260 retail sales and service enterprises based on the tourist business. There are 146,180 people employed in industries directly connected with tourism.

COMMUNICATIONS

Roads. In 1977 there were 81,932 miles of municipal and rural roads, 38,312 miles of surfaced rural roads and 30,639 miles of unsurfaced rural roads. The state is served by 115 intrastate bus companies and 31 privately owned internal bus services.

Motor-vehicle registrations, 1981, totalled 2,842,452.

Railways. The state had (1975) 3,500 miles of track on 11 railways.

Aviation. The state is served by 11 major airlines. Airports, 1970, numbered 78 public airports and 72 private.

JUSTICE, RELIGION, EDUCATION AND WELFARE

Justice. There has been no execution since 1960; since 1930 there have been 22 whites and 44 Negroes executed (by electrocution) for murder and 5 whites and 22 Negroes for rape. A US Supreme Court ruling prohibits the use of capital punishment under present Tennessee law, except for first degree murder.

Prison population, 1 Jan. 1980, 6,626.

The law prohibiting the inter-marriage of white and Negro was declared unconstitutional by the US Supreme Court in June 1967.

Religion. The leading religious bodies are the Southern Baptists, Methodists and Negro Baptists.

Education. School attendance has been compulsory since 1925 and the employment of children under 16 years of age in workshops, factories or mines is illegal.

In 1980–81 there were 1,733 public schools with a net enrolment of 889,847 pupils. In 1981 49,021 teachers earned an average salary of $15,395·82. Total expenditure for operating county and city public schools (kindergarten to Grade 12) in 1980–81, $1,539·9m. Tennessee has 49 accredited colleges and universities, 18 2-year colleges and 28 vocational schools. The universities include the University of Tennessee, Knoxville (founded 1794), with 29,270 students in 1979; Vanderbilt University, Nashville (1873) with 7,373, Tennessee State University (1912) with 5,396, the University of Tennessee at Chattanooga (1886) with 7,106 and Fisk University (1866) with 1,154.

Health. In 1979 the state had 167 hospitals with 31,371 beds. There were 205 nursing homes in 1977.

Social Security. Old-age assistance was granted (1977) to 69,061 persons, who received an average of $78.4 per person; 1,824 blind persons, $137.54 per person; 63,772 disabled persons, $125.05 per person; 59,803 families with dependent children, $106.65 per family. Unemployment insurance, 69,288 persons receiving $65.76 each.

Books of Reference

Tennessee Dept. of Finance and Administration, Annual Report, 1971
Dept. of Education Annual Report for Tennessee, 1972
Survey of Current Business, 1972
Tennessee Blue Book. Secretary of State, Nashville
Tennessee Statistical Abstract, 1971. Knoxville, 1971

State Library: State Library and Archives, Nashville. *Librarian:* Miss K. Culbertson. *State Historian:* Dr S. Horn.

TEXAS

HISTORY. In 1836 Texas declared its independence of Mexico, and after maintaining an independent existence, as the Republic of Texas, for 10 years, it was on 29 Dec. 1845 received as a state into the American Union. The state's first settlement dates from 1686.

AREA AND POPULATION. Texas is bounded north by Oklahoma, north-east by Arkansas, east by Louisiana, south-east by the Gulf of Mexico, south by Mexico and west by New Mexico. Area, 266,807 sq. miles (including 4,790 sq. miles of inland water). Census population, 1 April 1980 (provisional), 14,228,383, an increase of 27% since 1970. Vital statistics for 1980: Births, 268,717 (18·9 per 1,000 population); deaths, 108,586 (7·6); infant deaths, 3,226 (12 per 1,000 live births); marriages, 187,118 (13·2); divorces, 97,161 (6·8).

Population for 5 census years was:

	White	*Negro*	*Indian*	*Asiatic*	*Total*	*Per sq. mile*
1910	3,204,848	690,049	702	943	3,896,542	14·8
1930	4,967,172	854,964	1,001	1,578	5,824,715	22·1
1960	8,374,831	1,187,125	5,750	9,848	9,579,677	36·5
			All others			
1970	9,717,128	1,399,005	80,597		11,196,730	42·7
1980	11,197,663	1,710,250	1,320,470		14,228,383	54·2

Of the population in 1980, 6,998,301 were male, 11,327,159 persons were urban. Those 20 years old and older numbered 9,357,309. A census report, 1980, showed, 2,985,643 persons of Spanish origin.

The largest cities, with census population in 1980, are:

Houston	1,554,992	Amarillo	149,167	Odessa	89,797
Dallas	901,450	Beaumont	118,031	Garland	138,749
San Antonio	783,296	Wichita Falls	93,543	Laredo	91,229
Fort Worth	382,349	Irving	109,575	San Angelo	72,655
El Paso	424,522	Waco	101,267	Galveston	61,601
Austin (capital)	343,390	Arlington	159,117	Midland	70,291
Corpus Christi	230,715	Abilene	98,231	Tyler	70,720
Lubbock	174,157	Pasadena	111,884	Port Arthur	61,106

Larger urbanized areas, 1980: Houston, 2,891,146; Dallas-Fort Worth, 2,964,342; San Antonio, 1,070,245.

CONSTITUTION AND GOVERNMENT. The present constitution dates from 1876; it has been amended 233 times. The Legislature consists of a Senate of 31 members elected for 4 years (half their number retire every 2 years), and a House of Representatives of 150 members elected for 2 years.

The Governor and Lieut.-Governor are elected for 4 years. Qualified electors are all citizens with the usual residential qualifications. Texas sends to Congress 2 senators and 27 representatives.

In the 1980 presidential election Reagan polled 2,510,705 votes, Carter, 1,881,147.

The capital is Austin. The state has 254 counties.

Governor: Mark White (D.), 1983–86 ($71,400).
Lieut.-Governor: William P. Hobby (D.), 1983–86 ($7,200).
Secretary of State: David Dean (R.) ($42,700).

BUDGET. In the fiscal year ending 31 Aug. 1980 general revenues were $12,924,347,000; general expenditures, $11,486,851,000. Texas is unique in the large revenue derived from the severance tax (*i.e.*, tax on the removal of oil, natural gas and sulphur from the soil or waters of the state).

Net long-term debt, 31 Aug. 1980, was $2,468,627,000.

Per capita personal income (1980) was $9,513.

ENERGY AND NATURAL RESOURCES

Minerals. Texas leads all states by a wide margin in the production of crude petroleum and related minerals. In 1975 Texas had 31% of proved US crude oil reserves. Production, 1980: Crude petroleum, 975,239,000 bbls. Other mineral products include natural gas, natural gasoline, butane and propane gases, helium, crude gypsum, granite and sandstone, salt and cement. Total value of mineral products in 1979, $23,283m., leading all states.

Agriculture. Texas is one of the most important agricultural states of the Union. In 1978 (census) it had 194,253 farms covering 82% of the land area; average farm was of 708 acres valued, land and buildings, at $386 per acre. Large-scale commercial farms, highly mechanized, dominate in Texas; farms of 1,000 acres or more in number far exceed that of any other state. But small-scale farming persists.

Soil erosion is serious in some parts. For some 97,297,000 acres drastic curative treatment has been indicated and for 51,164,000 acres, preventive treatment. In 1970 there were 188 soil-conservation districts embracing an area of 166·57m. acres, of which 144,366,000 acres were in farms and ranches.

Production, 1980: Cotton, 3,305,000 bales; maize (117m. bu.), wheat (130m. bu.), oats and barley (13·6m. bu.), soybeans (13·9m. bu.), peanuts, oranges, grapefruit, peaches, potatoes, sweet potatoes.

Cash income, 1980, from crops was $3,766·4m.; from livestock, $5,188m.

The state has a very great livestock industry, leading in the number of all cattle, 13·7m. on 1 Jan. 1981, and sheep, 2·36m.; it also had 320,000 milch cows, and 930,000 swine. The wool clip in 1977 amounted to 21·5m. lb.; mohair, 8·5m. lb.

Forestry. There were (1980) 23·3m. acres of forested land.

INDUSTRY. The 1978 survey showed manufacturing establishments employing 647,200 production workers earning $7,736·2m. Chemical industries along the Gulf Coast, such as the production of synthetic rubber and of primary magnesium (from sea-water), are increasingly important.

COMMUNICATIONS

Roads. In 1979 there were 264,900 miles of roads including 199,500 miles of rural roads. Motor registration in 1980, 10·2m.

Railways. The railways (1974) had a total mileage of 19,134 miles, of which 13,303 miles were main lines.

Aviation. Public airports, 1975, numbered 496, in addition, there were 725 private airports.

Shipping. The port of Houston, connected by the Houston Ship Channel (50 miles long) with the Gulf of Mexico, is the largest inland cotton market in the world.

JUSTICE, RELIGION, EDUCATION AND WELFARE

Justice. The prison system, Jan. 1980, held 26,522 men and women. Total executions from 1930 have been 298.

Texas has adopted 11 laws governing the activities of trade unions. An Act of 1955 forbids the state's payment of unemployment compensation to workers engaged in certain types of strikes.

Religion. The largest religious bodies are Roman Catholics, Baptists, Methodists, Churches of Christ, Lutherans, Presbyterians and Episcopalians.

Education. School attendance is compulsory from 7 to 17 years of age. In 1965–66 all public schools had completed or begun desegregation. The estimated total enrolment in public day schools in 1979–80 was 2,872,720.

In autumn 1979 public elementary schools (kindergarten through grade 6) had 2,004,224 enrolled pupils and secondary schools, 868,495 enrolled pupils; there were 162,426 classroom teachers. Teachers' salaries, 1980, estimate, averaged $15,200. Total public school expenditure, 1980, $5,256m.

The state maintains 127 institutions of higher learning with an estimated enrolment, Sept. 1977, of 725,016 students. The largest institutions, with faculty numbers and student enrolment, were:

Founded	*Institutions*	*Control*	*Students*
1845	Baylor University, Waco	Baptist	9,108
1852	St Mary's University, San Antonio	R.C.	3,286
1869	Trinity University, San Antonio	Presb.	3,538
1873	Texas Christian University, Fort Worth	Christian	6,159
1876	Texas A. and M. Univ., College Station	State	28,848
1876	Prairie View Agr. and Mech. Coll., Prairie View	State	5,146
1879	Sam Houston State University	State	10,749
1883	University of Texas, Austin	State	41,660
1890	North Texas State University	State	17,151
1891	Hardin-Simmons University, Abilene	Baptist	1,649
1895	University of Texas, Arlington	State	17,201
1899	East Texas State University	State	9,586
1899	South West Texas State University	State	14,670
1901	North Texas State University, Denton	State	17,151
1903	Texas Woman's University, Denton	State	8,915
1906	Abilene Christian College, Abilene	Church of Christ	4,220
1911	Southern Methodist University, Dallas	Methodist	8,678
1912	William Marsh Rice University, Houston	—	3,686
1913	University of Texas, El Paso	State	15,885
1923	Stephen F. Austin State University	State	10,446
1923	Texas Technical University, Lubbock	State	22,358
1924	College of Arts and Industries, Kingsville	State	6,600
1934	University of Houston, Houston	State	29,297
1947	Texas Southern University, Houston	State	9,510
1951	Lamar University	State	11,128

Health. In 1979, the state had 568 hospitals (80,083 beds) listed by the American Hospital Association; on 31 Dec. 1975 mental hospitals had 6,100 resident patients and institutions for the mentally retarded, 13,309 resident patients (1974).

Social Security. Aid is from state and federal sources. Old-age assistance (SSI) was being granted in Dec. 1980 to 146,800 persons, who received an average of $101 per month; aid was given to 320,000 dependent children (average payment per family, $109 per month).

Books of Reference

Texas Almanac. Dallas. Biennial
MacCorkle, S. A., and Smith, D., *Texas Government.* 7th ed. New York, 1974
Richardson, R. N., *Texas, the Lone Star State.* 3rd ed. New York, 1970

Legislative Reference Library: Box 12488, Capitol Station, Austin, Texas 78811. *Director:* James R. Sanders.

UTAH

HISTORY. Utah, which had been acquired by the US during the Mexican war, was settled by Mormons in 1847, and organized as a Territory on 9 Sept. 1850. It was admitted as a state into the Union on 4 Jan. 1896 with boundaries as at present.

AREA AND POPULATION. Utah is bounded north by Idaho and Wyoming, east by Colorado, south by Arizona and west by Nevada. Area, 84,899 sq. miles, of which 2,826 sq. miles are water. The federal government (1967) owned 35,397,274 acres or 67·1% of the area of the state. The area of unappropriated and unreserved lands was 23,268,250 acres in 1974. The Bureau of Indian Affairs in 1974 administered 3,035,190 acres, all of which were allotted to Indian tribes.

Census population, 1 April 1980 (preliminary), 1,461,037, an increase of 38% since 1970. Births in 1980 were 43,708 (29·9 per 1,000 population); deaths, 8,556 (5·9); infant deaths, 505 (11·5 per 1,000 live births); marriages, 17,074 (11·7); divorces, 7,957 (5·4).

Population at 5 federal censuses was:

	White	*Negro*	*Indian*	*Asiatic*	*Total*	*Per sq. mile*
1910	366,583	1,144	3,123	2,501	373,851	4·5
1930	499,967	1,108	2,869	3,903	507,847	6·2
1960	873,828	4,148	6,961	5,207	890,627	10·8
1970	1,031,926	6,617	11,273	6,230	1,059,273	12·9
1980	1,382,550	9,225	19,256	15,076	1,461,037	17·7

Of the total in 1980, 724,501 were male, 1,232,908 persons were urban; 860,304 were 20 years of age or older.

The largest cities are Salt Lake City (capital), with a population (census, 1980) of 162,960; Provo, 74,007; Ogden, 64,444; Bountiful, 32,877; Orem, 52,399; and Logan, 26,844.

CONSTITUTION AND GOVERNMENT. Utah adopted its present constitution in 1896 (now with 61 amendments). It sends to Congress 2 senators and 3 representatives.

The Legislature consists of a Senate (in part renewed every 2 years) of 30 members, elected for 4 years, and of a House of Representatives of 75 members elected for 2 years. The Governor is elected for 4 years. The constitution provides for the initiative and referendum. Electors are all citizens, who, not being insane or criminal, have the usual residential qualifications.

The capital is Salt Lake City. There are 29 counties in the state.

In the 1980 presidential election Reagan polled 439,687 votes, Carter 124,266.

Governor: Scott Matheson (D.), 1981–84 ($48,000).
Lieut.-Governor: David S. Monson (R.), 1981–84 ($33,500).
Attorney-General: David L. Wilkinson (R.) ($36,500).

BUDGET. For the year ending 30 June 1980 general revenue was $1,888·8m. while general expenditures were $1,754·8m.

The net long-term debt on 30 June 1980 was about $537m.

Per capita personal income (1980) was $7,649.

ENERGY AND NATURAL RESOURCES

Minerals The principal minerals are: copper, gold, petroleum, lead, silver and zinc. The state also has natural gas, clays, tungsten, molybdenum, uranium and phosphate rock. Total value of mineral production, 1980, $2,000m.

Agriculture. In 1978 Utah had 13,833 farms covering 20% of the total land area, of which about 2m. acres were crop land and about 300,000 acres pasture. About 1m. acres had irrigation; the average farm was of 760 acres.

Of the total surface area, 9% is severely eroded and only 9·4% is free from erosion; the balance is moderately eroded.

Cash income, 1980, from crops, $140m. and from livestock, $383·9m. The principal crops are: Barley, 10·8m. bu.; wheat (spring and winter), 8·9m. bu.; oats, 915,000 bu.; potatoes, 1·1m. cwt; hay (alfalfa, sweet clover and lespedeza), 2m. tons; maize, 1·5m. bu. In 1981 there were 660,000 sheep; 77,000 milch cows; 875,000 all cattle; 58,000 swine. The 1978 wool clip yielded 4·7m. lb. of wool; 936m. lb. of milk were produced; and 1·46m. chickens produced 335m. eggs.

Forestry. Area of national forests, 1970, was 9,088,986 acres, of which 8·01m. acres were under forest service administration.

INDUSTRY. In 1978 manufacturing establishments had 79,800 workers, and a payroll of $1,037·5m.; value added by manufacture was $2,380·2m. Leading manufactures by value added are primary metals, ordinances and transport, food, fabricated metals and machinery, petroleum products.

COMMUNICATIONS

Roads. The state has about 50,000 miles of highway. In 1980 there were 1,009,000 motor vehicles registered.

Railways. On 1 July 1974 the state had 1,734 miles of railways.

Aviation. There were (1971) 89 airports (51 municipal, 32 private, 6 commercial).

JUSTICE, RELIGION, EDUCATION AND WELFARE

Justice. The number of inmates of the state prison on 1 Jan. 1980 was 960. Since 1930 total executions have been 14 (13 by shooting, 1 by hanging—the condemned man has choice), all whites, and all for murder.

Religion. Latter-day Saints (Mormons) form about 73% of the church membership of the state, with approximately 829,990 members in 1974; their church is a substantial property-owner. There were (1970) about 50,483 Catholics. Most Protestant denominations are represented.

Education. School attendance is compulsory for children from 6 to 18 years of age. There are 40 school districts. Teachers' salaries, 1980, averaged $14,965. There were (autumn 1980) 333,000 pupils in public elementary and secondary schools. In 1980 estimated public school expenditure was $665m.

The University of Utah (1850) (21,487 students in 1978) is in Salt Lake City; the Utah State University (1890) (9,436 students) is in Logan. The Mormon Church maintains the Brigham Young University at Provo (1875) with 28,580 students. Other colleges include: Westminster College, Salt Lake City, 1,464 students; Weber State College, Ogden, 8,741; Southern Utah State College, Cedar City, 1,811; College of Eastern Utah, Price, 626; Snow College, Ephraim, 842; Dixie College, St George, 1,203; Utah Technical College, Salt Lake City, 5,644; Utah Technical College, Provo, 3,138; L.D.S. Business College, Salt Lake City, 1,035. Total higher education students, 1980, 94,000. A state bond of $70m. was approved in July 1975 for the University of Utah medical centre.

Health. In 1979, the state had 41 hospitals (5,121 beds) listed by the Utah Department of Social Services.

Social Security. The state department of public welfare provided assistance during Dec. 1980 to 43,700 persons receiving aid to dependent children at an average $314 per family per month; aid to the aged, the blind and disabled is provided from federal funds. Total expenditure of the department for assistance, welfare and administration, 1974–75, was $70,417,582 (state and federal aid).

Books of Reference

Compiled Digest of Administrative Reports. Secretary of State, Salt Lake City. Annual
Statistical Abstract of Government in Utah. Utah Foundation, Salt Lake City. Annual
A Statistical Abstract of Utah's Economy. Bureau of Economic and Business Research, Univ. of Utah, 1964
Utah Agricultural Statistics. Dept. of Agriculture, Salt Lake City. Annual
Utah: Facts. Bureau of Economic and Business Research, Univ. of Utah, 1975
Arrington, L., *Great Basin Kingdom: An Economic History of the Latter-Day Saints, 1830–1900.* Cambridge, Mass., 1958

VERMONT

HISTORY. Vermont, first settled in 1724, was admitted into the Union as the fourteenth state on 4 March 1791. The first constitution was adopted by convention at Windsor, 2 July 1777, and established an independent state government.

AREA AND POPULATION. Vermont is bounded north by Canada, east by New Hampshire, south by Massachusetts and west by New York. Area, 9,614 sq. miles, of which 341 sq. miles are inland water. Census population, 1 April 1980 (preliminary), 511,456, an increase of 15% since 1970. Births, 1980, were 7,640 (15 per 1,000 population); deaths, 4,312 (8·6); infant deaths, 63 (8·4 per 1,000 live births); marriages, 5,187 (10·2); divorces, 2,522 (5).

Population at 5 census years was:

	White	*Negro*	*Indian*	*Asiatic*	*Total*	*Per sq. mile*
1910	354,298	1,621	26	11	355,956	39·0
1930	358,966	568	36	41	359,611	38·8
1960	389,092	519	57	172	389,881	42·0
1970	442,553	761	229	787	444,732	48·0
1980	506,736	1,135	984	1,355	511,456	55·1

Of the population in 1980, 249,080 were male, 172,735 persons were urban; those 20 years of age or older numbered 343,666. The largest cities are Burlington, with a population in 1980 of 37,712; Rutland, 18,436; Barre, 9,824.

CONSTITUTION AND GOVERNMENT. The constitution was adopted in 1793 and has since been amended. Amendments are proposed by two-thirds vote of the Senate every 4 years, and must be accepted by two sessions of the legislature; they are then submitted to popular vote. The state Legislature, consisting of a Senate of 30 members and a House of Representatives of 150 members (both elected for 2 years), meets in Jan. in odd-numbered years. The Governor and Lieut.-Governor are elected for 2 years. Electors are all citizens who possess certain residential qualifications and have taken the freeman's oath set forth in the constitution.

The state is divided into 14 counties; there are 251 towns and cities and other minor civil divisions. The state sends to Congress 2 senators and 1 representative, who are elected by the voters of the entire state.

In the 1980 presidential election Reagan polled 94,628 votes, Carter 81,952.

The capital is Montpelier (8,241, census of 1980).

Governor: Richard Snelling (R.), 1983–86 ($44,850).
Lieut.-Governor: Peter Smith (R.) ($19,200).
Secretary of State: James Douglas (R.) ($24,380).

BUDGET. The general revenue for the year ending 30 June 1980 was $711·1m.; general expenditure was $675·9m.

Total net long-term debt, 1 July 1980, was $654,159,000.

Per capita personal income (1980) was $7,827.

NATURAL RESOURCES

Minerals. Stone, chiefly granite, marble and slate, is the leading mineral produced in Vermont, contributing about 60% of the total value of mineral products. Other products include asbestos, talc, peat, sand and gravel. Total value of mineral products, 1979, $49·5m.

Agriculture. Agriculture is the most important industry. In 1978 the state had 7,273 farms covering 29·6% of the land area; the average farm was of 241 acres. Cash income, 1980, from livestock and products, $352·8m.; from crops, $25·5m. The dairy farms produce about 1,958m. lb. of milk annually. The chief agricultural crops are hay, apples and maple syrup. In 1980 Vermont had 320,000 cattle, 8,000 sheep, 6,300 swine, 570,000 poultry.

Forestry. In 1973 there was cut 98m. bd ft hardwood and 87m. bd ft softwood. In addition, 142,139 cords of pulpwood and boltwood and 185m. bd ft of logs were produced.

National forests area (1972), 242,309 acres. In 1975 there were 34 state forests, and 41 state parks; total acreage 132,329.

INDUSTRY. In 1978, manufacturing establishments employed 31,500 production workers who earned $354·2m.; value added by manufacture was $1,382·7m.

COMMUNICATIONS

Roads. The state had 14,000 miles of roads in 1980, including 12,400 miles of rural roads. Motor vehicle registrations, 1980, 339,000.

Railways. There were, in 1973, 724 miles of main line railway, 277 of which was leased by the state to private operators.

Aviation. There were 23 airports, of which 10 were state operated, 3 municipally owned and 10 privately owned but open to public use.

Post and Broadcasting. In 1978 there were 329,812 telephones in use. There were (1975) 2 commercial television stations, 35 cable television companies franchised to serve 96 communities and 35 radio broadcasting stations.

JUSTICE, RELIGION, EDUCATION AND WELFARE

Justice. In Jan. 1980 there were 411 people in prison. The Vermont State Prison was closed in Aug. 1975 and prisoners transferred to federal prisons and community correction centres.

Religion. The principal denominations (1975) are Roman Catholic (with about 50,000 adult confirmed and 130,000 baptized), United Church of Christ (22,748), United Methodist (about 22,000), Protestant Episcopal (about 7,500), Baptist (about 7,000) and Unitarian–Universalist (2,054 in 1970).

Education. School attendance during the full school term is compulsory for children from 7 to 16 years of age, or to have completed the 10th grade. In 1979–80 the public elementary schools had 67,755 enrolled pupils; the public secondary schools had 30,583 pupils; the 64 private schools (1974) had 10,125 pupils. Full-time teachers for public elementary and secondary schools (1979–80) numbered 7,328. Teachers' salaries for 1980 averaged $12,750. The University of Vermont (1791) had 8,500 full-time students in 1973–74; Middlebury College (1800), 1,941 students; Norwich University (1834), 997 students; St Michael's College, 1,543 students; the 4 state colleges, 3,585 students. Total expenditure for education, 1978–79, was an estimated $1,976 per pupil, inclusive of capital outlay.

Health. In July 1979 the state had 18 general hospitals (2,717 beds), 2 mental hospitals and 1 T.B. hospital. There was 1 federal general hospital with 224 beds.

Social Security. Old-age assistance (SSI) was being granted in 1980 to 2,400 persons, drawing an average of $108 per month; aid to dependent children was being granted to 24,300 persons, drawing an average of $340 per family per month; and aid to the permanently and totally disabled was being granted to 5,200 persons, drawing an average of $192.

Books of Reference

Legislative Directory. Secretary of State, Montpelier. Biennial
Vermont Facts and Figures. Office of Statistical Co-ordination, Montpelier
Vermont Year-Book, formerly *Walton's Register*. Chester. Annual

State Library: Vermont Dept. of Libraries, Montpelier. *State Librarian:* John A. McCrossan.

VIRGINIA

HISTORY. The first English Charter for settlements in America was that granted by James I in 1606 for the planting of colonies in Virginia. The state was one of the 13 original states in the Union. Virginia lost just over one-third of its area when West Virginia was admitted into the Union (1863).

AREA AND POPULATION. Virginia is bounded north-west by West Virginia, north-east by Maryland, east by the Atlantic, south by North Carolina and Tennessee and west by Kentucky. Area, 40,767 sq. miles including 1,063 sq. miles of inland water. Census population, 1 April 1980, 5,346,818, an increase of 695,370 or 14·9% since 1970. In 1981 there were 79,278 births (14·6 per 1,000 population); 42,199 deaths (7·8); 1,000 infant deaths (12·6 per 1,000 live births); 61,410 marriages and 25,103 divorces.

Population for 5 federal census years was:

	White	*Negro*	*Indian*	*Asiatic*	*Total*	*Per sq. mile*
1910	1,389,809	671,096	539	168	2,061,612	51·2
1930	1,770,441	650,165	779	466	2,421,851	60·7
1960	3,142,443	816,258	2,155	4,725	3,966,949	99·3
			All others			
1970	3,761,514	861,368	25,612		4,648,494	116·9
1980	4,230,000	1,008,311	108,517		5,346,818	134·7

Of the total population in 1980, 49% were male, 66% were urban and 59% were 21 years of age or older.

The population (census of 1980) of the principal cities was: Norfolk, 266,979; Virginia Beach, 262,199; Richmond, 219,214; Newport News, 144,903; Hampton, 122,617; Portsmouth, 104,577; Alexandria, 103,219; Roanoke, 100,427; Lynchburg, 66,743.

CLIMATE. Average temperatures in Jan. are 41°F in the Tidewater coastal area and 32°F in the Blue Ridge mountains; July averages, 78°F and 68°F respectively. Precipitation averages 36″ in the Shenandoah valley and 44″ in the south. Snowfall is 5-10″ in the Tidewater and 25-30″ in the western mountains.

CONSTITUTION AND GOVERNMENT. The present constitution dates from 1971.

The General Assembly consists of a Senate of 40 members, elected for 4 years, and a House of Delegates of 100 members, elected for 2 years. The Governor and Lieut.-Governor are elected for 4 years. Qualified as electors are (with few exceptions) all citizens 18 years of age, fulfilling certain residential qualifications, who have registered. The state sends to Congress 2 senators and 10 representatives.

In the 1980 presidential election Reagan polled 989,609 votes, Carter 752,174 and Anderson 95,418.

The state capital is Richmond; the state contains 95 counties and 41 independent cities.

Governor: Charles S. Robb (D.), 1983–86 ($60,000).
Lieut.-Governor: Richard J. Davis (D.) $16,000.
Secretary of the Commonwealth: Laurie Naismith (D.) ($21,400).

BUDGET. General revenue for the year ending 30 June 1981 was $5,801·8m. (taxation, $3,006·5m., and federal aid, $2,795·3m.); general expenditures, $5,898·4m. ($1,722m. for education, $925m. for transport and $383·5m. for public welfare).

Total net long-term debt, 30 June 1981, amounted to $246,867,279.

Per capita personal income (1980) was $9,392.

ENERGY AND NATURAL RESOURCES

Minerals (1981). Coal is the most important mineral, with output of 41,977,807 short tons. Lead and zinc ores, stone, sand and gravel, lime and titanium ore are also produced. Total mineral output was 53m. tons.

Agriculture. In 1978 there were 57,000 farms with an area of 10m. acres; average farm had 175 acres and was valued at $163,918.

Income, 1980, from crops, $510m., and from livestock and livestock products, $949m. The chief crops (1980) are corn, hay and peanuts (137m. lb.), tobacco (107m. lb.).

Animals on farms on 1 Jan. 1981 included 173,000 milch cows, 1·8m. all cattle, 160,000 sheep and 750,000 swine (Dec. 1980).

Forestry. National forests, 1980, covered 1,617,000 acres.

INDUSTRY. The manufacture of cigars and cigarettes and of rayon and allied products and the building of ships lead in value of products. In 1977, 5,519 manufacturing establishments employed 395,000 workers; value added by manufacture was $10,882m.

TOURISM. Tourists spend about $3,000m. a year in Virginia, attracted mainly by the state's outstanding scenery, coastline and historical interest.

COMMUNICATIONS

Roads. The state highways system, 31 Dec. 1981, had 61,599 miles of highways, of which 8,954 miles were primary roads. Motor registrations, 1980, 3·58m.

Railways. In 1982 there were 3,705 miles of railways.

Aviation. There were, in 1980, 260 airports, of which 63 were publicly owned.

JUSTICE, RELIGION, EDUCATION AND WELFARE

Justice. Executions (by electrocution) since 1930 totalled 96. Prison population, 31 Dec. 1980, 8,581 in federal and state prisons.

Religion. The principal churches are the Baptist, Methodist, Protestant-Episcopal, Roman Catholic and Presbyterian.

Education. Elementary and secondary instruction is free, and for ages 6–17 attendance is compulsory. No child under 12 may be employed in any mining or manufacturing work.

In 1981 the 141 school districts had, in primary schools, 613,148 pupils and 35,617 teachers and in public high schools, 388,264 pupils and 26,094 teachers. Teachers' salaries (1980–81) averaged $15,553. Total expenditure on education, 1980–81, was $2,443m. The more important institutions for higher education (1981) were:

Founded	*Name and place of college*	*Staff*	*Students*
1693	William and Mary College, Williamsburg (State)	467	6,465
1749	Washington and Lee University, Lexington	168	1,634
1776	Hampden-Sydney College, Hampden-Sydney (Pres.)	65	731
1819	University of Virginia, Charlottesville (State)	1,429	16,452
1832	Randolph-Macon College, Ashland (Methodist)	75	899
1832	University of Richmond, Richmond (Baptist)	329	4,200
1838	Virginia Commonwealth University, Richmond	2,500	18,332
1839	Virginia Military Institute Lexington (State)	130	1,319
1865	Virginia Union University, Richmond	137	1,189
1868	Hampton Institute	235	3,220
1872	Virginia Polytechnic Institute and State University	2,795	22,729
1882	Virginia State College, Petersburg	236	4,310
1910	Radford College (State)	306	5,693
1930	Old Dominion University, Norfolk	796	16,353
1956	George Mason University (State)	761	13,293

Health. In 1980 the state had 134 hospitals (31,859 beds) listed by the American Hospital Association.

Social Security. In 1938 Virginia established a system of old-age assistance under the Federal Security Act; in March 1982 persons in 1,799 cases were drawing an average grant of $207.29; aid to permanently and totally disabled, 1,688 cases, average grant $215.49; aid to dependent children, 159,363 persons, average grant $84.76; general relief, 6,561 persons, average grant $146.73.

Books of Reference

Virginia Facts and Figures. Annual Division of Industrial Development, Richmond. Annual
Dabney, V., *Virginia, the New Dominion.* 1971
Friddell, G., *The Virginia Way.* Burda, 1973
Gottmann, J., *Virginia in our Century.* Charlottesville, 1969
Morton, R. L., *Colonial Virginia.* 2 vols. Univ. Press of Virginia, 1960
Rouse, P. *Virginia: a Pictorial History.* Scribner, 1975
Rubin, L. D., Jr., *Virginia: a Bicentennial History.* Norris, 1977

State Library: Virginia State Library, Richmond 23219. *State Librarian:* Donald Haynes.

WASHINGTON

HISTORY. Washington, formerly part of Oregon, was created a Territory in 1853, and was admitted into the Union as a state on 11 Nov. 1889. Its settlement dates from 1811.

AREA AND POPULATION. Washington is bounded north by Canada, east by Idaho, south by Oregon with the Columbia River forming most of the boundary, and west by the Pacific. Area, 68,139 sq. miles, of which 1,627 sq. miles are inland water. Lands owned by the federal government, 1977, were 12·4m. acres or 29·1% of the total area. Census population, 1 April 1980 (preliminary), 4,130,163, an increase of 730,994 or 21·4% since 1970. Births, 1980 were 67,518; deaths, 32,304; infant deaths, 143; marriages, 47,836; divorces and annulments, 28,733.

Population in 5 federal census years was:

	White	*Negro*	*Indian*	*Asiatic and others*	*Total*	*Per sq. mile*
1910	1,109,111	6,058	10,997	15,824	1,141,990	17·1
1930	1,521,661	6,840	11,253	23,642	1,563,396	23·3
1960	2,751,675	48,738	21,076	31,725	2,853,214	42·8
1970	2,351,055	71,308	33,386	53,420	3,409,169	51·2
1980	3,777,296	105,544	60,771	186,552	4,130,163	62·0

Of the total population in 1980, 2,051,369 were male, 3,037,765 persons were urban; 2,837,607 were 20 years of age or older.

There are 24 Indian reservations, the largest being held by the Yakima tribe. Indian reservations in Sept. 1979 covered 2,496,423 acres, of which 1,996,018 acres were tribal lands and 497,218 acres were held by individuals. Total Indian population, 1980, 60,771.

Leading cities are Seattle, with a population (1980 census) of 491,897; Spokane, 170,993; Tacoma, 158,101; Bellevue, 73,711. Others : Yakima, 49,826; Everett, 54,413; Vancouver, 42,834; Bellingham, 45,794; Bremerton, 36,208; Richland, 33,578; Longview, 31,052; Renton, 30,612; Edmonds, 27,526; Walla Walla, 25,618. Urbanized areas (1980 census): Seattle–Everett, 1,600,944; Tacoma, 482,692; Spokane, 341,058.

CONSTITUTION AND GOVERNMENT. The constitution, adopted in 1889, has had 63 amendments. The Legislature consists of a Senate of 49 members elected for 4 years, half their number retiring every 2 years, and a House of Representatives of 98 members, elected for 2 years. The Governor and Lieut.-Governor are elected for 4 years. The state sends 2 senators and 7 representatives to Congress.

Qualified as voters are (with some exceptions) all citizens 18 years of age, having the usual residential qualifications.

In the 1980 presidential election Reagan polled 865,244 votes, Carter 650,193 and Anderson, 185,073.

The capital is Olympia (population, 1980 census, 27,447). The state contains 39 counties.

Governor: John Spellman (R.), 1981–85 ($63,000).
Lieut.-Governor: John A. Cherberg (D.), 1981–85 ($28,600).
Secretary of State: Ralph Munro (R.), 1981–85 ($31,000).

BUDGET. For the 2-year budget period 1981–83 the state's total revenue is (projected) $13,545·2m.; general expenditure is (projected) $13,873·5m. (education, $6,150·7m.; transportation, $706·6m., and human resources, $3,636m.). State revenue in the period 1979–81 was $10,623·7m. and expenditure $10,857·8m.

Total net long-term debt on 30 June 1980 was $627,784,980.

Per capita personal income (1980) was $10,324.

ENERGY AND NATURAL RESOURCES

Minerals (1979). Production of principal minerals: Sand and gravel, 24·3m. short tons; cement, 1·7m. short tons; stone, 15·2m. short tons; coal, 4·6m. short tons (1981 estimate); clays, 343,300 short tons. Uranium ore is also mined but production figures are not disclosed. Total mineral output in 1977 was valued at $216m.

Agriculture. Agriculture is constantly growing in value because of more intensive and diversified farming and because of the 1m.-acre Columbia Basin Irrigation Project. Irrigated land in farms (1974) amounted to 1,286,412 acres.

In 1980 there were 37,800 farms with an acreage of 17m.; average farm was of 451 acres. Realized net income per farm in 1979 was $17,573.

Value of farm production, 1980, was $3,060m. (from field crops, $156m.; from speciality products, including flowers, bulbs, Christmas trees, $2,335·4m., fruit and vegetables, $533m., and from livestock, $496·6m.). Wheat, the leading farm commodity, was valued at $640·9m. Cattle and calves were valued at $383·5m. Other major commodities are milk ($374·2m.), apples ($288m.). Washington was the leading state in production of apples, hops and sweet cherries in 1979, and second in Irish potatoes, pears, asparagus, carrots, and mint oil.

On 1 Jan. 1980 animals on farms included 195,000 milch cows, 1·58m. all cattle, 65,000 sheep and 126,000 swine. The wool clip in 1978 amounted to 578,000 lb.

Forestry. Forests cover about 23m. acres, of which 9m. acres are national forest. In 1980, 3,841m. bd ft of timber was harvested; lumber production (1980) was 3,192m. bd ft; plywood, 7,512m. bd ft, and pulp wood (1979) 3,313,000 short tons. In 1980, 6,826m. bd ft of logs were shipped overseas from state ports.

Fisheries. Washington ranks second only to Alaska in the catch of salmon and halibut, and in the production of canned salmon. Value of food fish in 1978 was $221,898,000 processed value. Total weight of food fish caught, 153,583,801 lb., including salmon, 40·5m. lb.; shellfish, 28·8m. lb.; other marine fish, 81·1m. lb.

INDUSTRY. In 1977, 181,000 workers earned $2,385m.; value added by manufacture was $8,900m. Aircraft and aerospace manufacture, lumber and wood products, pulp and paper, plywood, food processing, machinery, metals, shipbuilding and chemicals are the major manufacturing industries.

With about 20% of potential water-power resources of US, the state is first in developed and potential hydro-electricity. Abundance of electric power has made Washington the leading producer of primary aluminium.

COMMUNICATIONS

Roads. The state (1979) maintained 6,920 miles of highway; the counties, 40,767 miles; municipalities, 9,888 miles. Motor vehicle registrations (1980), 3,566,639.

Railways. The railways had, in 1980, 6,057 miles.

Aviation. There were in 1979, 365 airports, 120 publicly owned. In 1978 Seattle–Tacoma Airport traffic was 8·3m. passengers, 48,000 tons of mail and 185,000 tons of freight and express.

JUSTICE, RELIGION, EDUCATION AND WELFARE

Justice. The average daily adult population in state prisons in Jan. 1982 was 4,674. Since 1963 there have been no executions; total 1930–63 (by hanging) was 47, including 40 whites, 5 Negroes and 2 other races, all for murder, except 1 white for kidnapping.

Religion. Chief religious bodies (1971) are the Roman Catholic (366,087), United Methodist (116,723), Lutheran (98,815), Presbyterian (75,818), Latter-day Saints (66,109), Episcopalian (56,319).

Education. Education is given free to all children between the ages of 5 and 21 years, and is compulsory for children from 8 to 15 years of age. In Oct. 1980 the 1,004 elementary schools had 16,785 classroom teachers and 370,597 pupils, 289 junior high and middle schools and 284 high schools had 14,771 classroom teachers and 369,985 pupils. In 1978–79 the average salary of teaching staff was $17,357. There were 2,629 teachers of handicapped children. The total expenditure on public elementary and secondary schools for the school year 1980–81 was $1,791·6m. In Oct. 1980 an estimated 472 private and parochial elementary and secondary schools had 54,600 elementary and high school pupils.

The University of Washington, founded 1861, at Seattle, had, autumn 1982, 34,769 students, and Washington University at Pullman, founded 1890, for science and agriculture, had 16,829 students. Twenty-seven community colleges had (1981) a total enrolment of 161,244 students (89,263 full-time equivalent).

Health. In 1981 the 2 state hospitals for mental illness had a daily average of 1,204 patients; schools for handicapped children, 1,999 residents in Sept. 1981.

In 1981 the state had 109 licensed general hospitals (13,201 beds), 3 licensed psychiatric hospitals (181 beds) and 3 alcoholism hospitals (174 beds).

Social Security. Old-age assistance is provided for persons 65 years of age or older without adequate resources (and not in need of continuing home care) who are residents of the state. In July 1981, 14,287 people were drawing an average of $130·93 per month; aid to 139,514 children in 52,781 families averaged $333·86 per family monthly; to 500 blind persons, $218·05 per person monthly; to 25,557 totally disabled, $216·59 monthly. 5,057 persons, under foster care, received payments of $366·11 per person. Total unemployment in 1981 averaged 176,000 (9·1% of the population). In June 1980 the unemployment insurance system covered 90·5% of employers (103,391). Benefits ranged from $41 to $150 per week and averaged $117·75 per week.

Books of Reference

Washington State Research Council. *Handbook: A Compendium of Statistical and Explanatory Information about State and Local Government in Washington.* 4th ed. Olympia, 1973.—*The Book of Numbers: A Statistical Handbook on Washington State Government.* Olympia, 1977

Washington (State) Office of Financial Management. *Pocket Data Book 1978*

Avery, M. W., *Washington, a History of the Evergreen State.* Univ. of Wash. Press, 1965.—*Government of Washington State.* Univ. of Wash. Press, revised ed. 1973

State Library: Washington State Library, Olympia. *State Librarian:* Roderick Swartz.

WEST VIRGINIA

HISTORY. In 1862, after the state of Virginia had seceded from the Union, the electors of the western portion ratified an ordinance providing for the formation of a new state, which was admitted into the Union by presidential proclamation on 20 June 1863, under the name of West Virginia. Its constitution was adopted by the voters almost unanimously on 26 March 1863.

AREA AND POPULATION. West Virginia is bounded north by Pennsylvania and Maryland, east and south by Virginia, south-west by the Sandy River (forming the boundary with Kentucky) and west by the Ohio River (forming the boundary with Ohio). Area, 24,282 sq. miles, of which 102 sq. miles are water. Census population, 1 April 1980 (preliminary), 1,949,644, an increase of 11·8% since 1970. Births, 1980, 29,438; deaths, 19,178; infant deaths, 347; marriages, 17,391; divorces, 10,275.

Population in 5 federal census years was:

	White	*Negro*	*Indian*	*Asiatic*	*Total*	*Per sq. mile*
1910	1,156,817	64,173	36	93	1,221,119	50·8
1940	1,614,191	114,893	18	103	1,729,205	71·8
1960	1,770,133	89,378	181	419	1,860,421	77·3
1970	1,673,480	67,342	751	1,463	1,744,237	71·8
1980	1,874,751	65,051	1,610	5,194	1,949,644	80·3

Of the total population in 1980, 945,408 were male, 705,319 were urban; those 20 years of age or older numbered 1,319,566.

The 1980 census population of the principal cities was: Huntington, 63,684; Charleston, 63,968. Others: Wheeling, 43,070; Parkersburg, 39,967; Morgantown, 27,605; Weirton, 24,736; Fairmont, 23,863; Clarksburg, 22,371.

CONSTITUTION AND GOVERNMENT. The present constitution was adopted in 1872; it has had 51 amendments.

The Legislature consists of the Senate of 34 members elected for a term of 4 years, one-half being elected biennially, and the House of Delegates of 100 members, elected biennially. The Governor is elected for 4 years and may succeed himself once. Voters are all citizens (with the usual exceptions) 18 years of age and meeting certain residential requirements. The state sends to Congress 2 senators and 4 representatives.

In the 1980 presidential election Carter polled 367,462 votes, Reagan 334,206 and Anderson 31,691.

The state capital is Charleston. There are 55 counties.

Governor: John D. Rockefeller IV (D.), 1981–85 ($50,000).
Secretary of State: A. James Manchin (D.) ($30,000).

FINANCE. Total revenues for the year ending 30 June 1980 were $3,608,262,063 ($1,004m. from general revenue fund, $694m. from federal funds, $324m. from state road fund, $215m. from special revenue fund); general expenditures were $3,638,672,449 (education, $758m.; highways, $646m.; public welfare, $379m.; other governmental costs, $417m.).

Bonds outstanding were $934,658,000 on 30 June 1980.

Estimated *per capita* personal income (1980) was $7,800.

ENERGY AND NATURAL RESOURCES

Minerals. 55% of the state is underlain with mineable coal; 96,408,980 short tons of coal were produced in 1980; coke (oven and bee-hive), 79,518,753 short tons. Petroleum output, 572,058m. bbls; natural gas production was 5,044,988 cu. ft. Salt, sand and gravel, sandstone and limestone are also produced. The total value of mineral output in 1980 was $5,111,274,000.

Agriculture. In 1980 the state had 20,000 farms with an area of 4·2m. acres; average size of farm was 210 acres and valued at $651 per acre. Livestock farming predominates.

Cash income, 1980, from crops was $75·8m.; from government payments, $2·5m., and from livestock and products, $182·2m. Total area of major crops harvested was 722,000 acres, chief crop being hay (595,000 acres); all corn, 96,000 acres. Apples (245m. lb.) and peaches (22m. lb.) are important fruit crops. Livestock on farms, 1 Jan. 1980, included 545,000 cattle, of which 37,000 were milch cows; sheep, 113,000; hogs, 56,000; chickens, 940,000 excluding broilers. Production, 1980, included 21·8m. broilers, 149m. eggs; 2·3m. turkeys.

Forestry. State forests, 1980, covered 79,307 acres; national forests, 1,647,146 gross acres; 75% of the state is woodland.

INDUSTRY. In 1980, 1,730 manufactories had 116,552 production workers who earned $2,167·9m. Value added by manufacture (estimate) was $3,660m. Leading industries are primary and fabricated metals, glass, chemicals, wood products, textiles and apparel, and machinery.

In 1980 average state employment was 757,000 who earned an average wage of $276·26 per week.

The first commercial coal liquefaction plant in the USA is being built near Morgantown with the co-operation of the governments of Fed. Rep. of Germany and Japan and the Gulf Oil Co.

COMMUNICATIONS

Roads. Total highways in 1980, 37,527 miles (state maintained, 33,436 miles; inter-state, 390 miles; national parks and other roads, 4,091 miles; West Virginia Turnpike, 87 miles). Registered motor vehicles, financial year ending 30 June 1980, numbered 1,140,673.

Railways. In 1980 the state had 3,941 miles of railway, all operated by diesel or electric trains.

Aviation. There were 42 licensed airports in 1980.

Post and Broadcasting. There are 65 AM radio stations, 41 FM radio stations. Television stations number 9 VHF and 3 UHF.

Newspapers. Daily newspapers number 25; weekly newspapers 78.

JUSTICE, RELIGION, EDUCATION AND WELFARE

Justice. The state court system consists of a Supreme Court and 31 circuit courts. The Supreme Court of Appeals, exercising original and appellate jurisdiction, has 5 members elected by the people for 12-year terms. Each circuit court has from 1 to 7 judges (as determined by the Legislature on the basis of population and case-load) chosen by the voters within each circuit for 8-year terms.

Effective on 1 July 1967, the West Virginia Human Rights Act prohibits discrimination in employment and places of public accommodations based on race, religion, colour, national origin or ancestry.

There are 8 penal and correctional institutions which had, on 30 June 1980, 1,590 inmates. In 1965 the State Legislature abolished capital punishment.

Religion. Chief denominations in 1980 were United Methodist (175,000 members, estimate), Baptists (141,000) and Roman Catholics (102,600).

Education. Public school education is free for all from 5 to 21 years of age, and school attendance is compulsory for all between the ages of 7 and 16 (school term, 200 days—180–185 days of actual teaching). The public schools are non-sectarian. During school year 1979–80 elementary schools had 13,574 instructional personnel and 230,120 pupils enrolled; secondary schools, 10,824 and 381,233 respectively. Average minimum salary of instructional personnel (1980–81) was $14,948. Total 1979–80 expenditures for public schools, $775,357,181.

Leading institutions of higher education in 1981:

Founded		*Full-time students*
1837	Marshall University, Huntington	11,482
	School of Medicine	401
1837	West Liberty State College, West Liberty	2,668
1867	Fairmont State College, Fairmont	5,262
1868	West Virginia University, Morgantown	19,874
	School of Medicine	1,437
1872	Concord College, Athens	2,174
1872	Glenville State College, Glenville	1,920
1872	Shepherd College, Shepherdstown	3,001
1891	West Virginia State College	4,368
1895	West Virginia Institute of Technology, Montgomery	3,343
1895	Bluefield State College, Bluefield	2,340
1901	Potomac State College of West Virginia Univ., Keyser	1,104
1972	West Virginia College of Graduate Studies	3,323
1976	School of Osteopathic Medicine, Lewisburg	231

In addition to the universities and state-supported schools, there are 3 community colleges (8,326 students in 1981), 10 denominational and private institutions of higher education (11,221 students in 1981) and 14 business colleges.

Health. In 1980–81 the state had 66 hospitals and 34 licensed personal care homes, 71 skilled-nursing homes and 6 mental hospitals.

Social Security. The Department of Welfare, originating in the 1930s as the Department of Public Assistance, is both state and federally financed. In the year ending 30 June 1981 day care for 5,288 children per month was provided; aid was given to 24,158 families with dependent children (average award, $173·05 per month); handicapped children's services conducted 134,640 examinations; 65,526 families per month received food stamps.

On 1 Jan. 1974 all blind, aged and disabled services were converted to the Federal Supplemental Security Income programme.

Books of Reference

West Virginia Blue Book. Legislature, Charleston. Annual, since 1916

West Virginia Statistical Handbook, 1974. Bureau of Business Research, W. Va. Univ., Morgantown, 1974

Bibliography of West Virginia. 2 parts. Dept. of Archives and History, Charleston, 1939

West Virginia History. Dept. of Archives and History. Charleston. Quarterly, from 1939

Cometti, Elizabeth, and Summers, F. P., *The Thirty-Fifth State.* Morgantown, 1966

Conley, P., and Doherty, W. T., *West Virginia History.* Charleston, 1974

Davis, C. J., and others, *West Virginia State and Local Government.* West Virginia Univ. Bureau for Government Research, 1963

Shetler, C., *Guide to the Study of West Virginia History.* Morgantown, 1960; *West Virginia Civil War Literature.* Morgantown, 1963

Williams, J. A., *West Virginia: A Bicentennial History.* New York, 1976

State Library: Division of Archives and History, Dept. of Culture and History, Charleston.

WISCONSIN

HISTORY. Wisconsin was settled in 1670 by French traders and missionaries. Originally a part of New France, it was surrendered to the British in 1763 and in 1783, when ceded to the US, became part of the North-west Territory. It was then contained successively in the Territories of Indiana, Illinois and Michigan. In 1836 it became part of the Territory of Wisconsin, which also included the present states of Iowa, Minnesota and parts of the Dakotas. It was admitted into the Union with its present boundaries on 29 May 1848.

AREA AND POPULATION. Wisconsin is bounded north by Lake Superior and Michigan, east by Lake Michigan, south by Illinois, west by Iowa and Minnesota, with the Mississippi River forming most of the boundary. Area, 56,153 sq. miles, including 1,727 sq. miles of inland water, but excluding any part of the Great Lakes. Census population, 1 April 1980 4,705,335, an increase of 6·5% since 1970. Estimated population (1982), 4,705,767. Births in 1981 (provisional) were 74,306 (15·8 per 1,000 population); deaths, 40,495 (8·6); infant deaths, 767 (10·3 per 1,000 live births); marriages, 41,115 (8·7); divorces and annulments, 18,459.

Population in 5 census years was:

	White	*Negro*	*All others*	*Total*	*Per sq. mile*
1910	2,320,555	2,900	10,405	2,333,860	42·2
1930	2,916,255	10,739	12,012	2,939,006	53·7
1960	3,858,903	74,546	18,328	3,951,777	72·2
1970	4,258,959	128,224	30,750	4,417,933	80·8
1980	4,442,598	182,593	80,144	4,705,335	86·4

Of the total population in 1980, 49% were male,64·2% were urban and 67% were 20 years old or older.

Population of the larger cities, 1980 census, was as follows:

Milwaukee	636,212	Appleton	59,032	Beloit	35,207
Madison	170,616	Oshkosh	49,678	Fond du Lac	35,863
Racine	85,725	La Crosse	48,347	Manitowoc	32,547
Green Bay	87,889	Sheboygan	48,085	Wausau	32,426
Kenosha	77,685	Janesville	51,071	Superior	29,571
West Allis	63,982	Eau Claire	51,509	Brookfield	34,035
Wauwatosa	51,308	Waukesha	50,319		

Population of larger urbanized areas, 1980 census: Milwaukee, 1,207,008; Madison, 213,678; Duluth–Superior (Minn.–Wis.), 132,585; Racine, 118,987; Green Bay, 142,747.

CONSTITUTION AND GOVERNMENT. The constitution, which dates from 1848, has 126 amendments. The legislative power is vested in a Senate of 33 members (1981 term: 19 Democrats, 14 Republicans), elected for 4 years, one-half elected alternately, and an Assembly of 99 members (1981 term: 59 Democrats, 40 Republicans, 1 vacancy) all elected simultaneously for 2 years. The Governor and Lieut.-Governor are elected for 4 years. All 6 constitutional officers serve 4-year terms.

Wisconsin has universal suffrage for all citizens over 18 years of age; but, as there is no official list of voters, the size of the electorate is unknown; 1,500,996 voted for Governor in 1978.

Wisconsin is represented in Congress by 2 senators and 9 representatives.

In the 1980 presidential election Reagan polled 1,088,845 votes, Carter 981,584 and Anderson 160,657.

The capital is Madison. The state has 72 counties.

Governor: Anthony S. Earl (D.), 1983–87 ($75,337).
Lieut.-Governor: James T. Flynn (D.), 1983–87 ($41,390).
Secretary of State: Douglas La Follette (D.), 1983–87 ($37,334).

BUDGET. For the year ending 30 June 1982 (Wisconsin Bureau of Financial Operations figures) total revenue for all funds was $8,321,973,874 ($3,744,196,082 from taxation and $1,564,269,614 from federal aid). General expenditure from all funds was $7,542,077,948 ($2,163,103,100 for education, $2,333,625,956 for human resources).

Per capita personal income (1981) was $10,035.

ENERGY AND NATURAL RESOURCES

Electricity. There were, Dec. 1981, 88 hydro-electric power plants (15 of them municipal, 58 private in Wisconsin; 15 private outside the state) operated by public utilities with a total installed capacity of 439,894 kw.; output, 1981, was 2,135,473m. kwh. The 15 outside plants are in Michigan; installed capacity 90,699 kw., output 525,720m. kwh.

Fossil fuel and nuclear plants numbered 26 (4 municipal); the former had a total installed capacity of 6,572,092 kw.; total output, (1981), 21,632,050m. kwh; the 2 nuclear plants had an installed capacity of 1,540,682 kw. and a total output (1981) of 10,103,260m. kwh.

There were also 34 internal combustion reciprocating plants (one in Michigan), with a total installed capacity of 107,676 kw. and a total output of (1981) 4,328m. kwh., and 17 internal combustion turbine plants with a total installed capacity of 1,286,450 kw.; total output was (1981) 189,575m. kwh.

There was a total of 165 plants, with a total installed capacity of 9,946,794 kw. and a total output of (1981) 34,064,686m. kwh.

Minerals. Sand and gravel, crushed stone, lime and taconite (iron ore) are the chief mineral products. Mineral production in 1981 was valued at $166·5m. This value included $50m. for sand and gravel, $43m. for crushed stone and about $17m. for lime. Value of all other minerals including lead, zinc, taconite, natural abrasives, peat, cement, gemstones, dimension stone and clay, $51m.

The large Forest County sulphide deposit (5,000 ft long, about 200 ft wide and over 1,500 ft deep and almost vertical) south of Crandon is estimated at over 77m. tons, averaging 5% zinc, 1% copper and lesser amounts of lead, silver and gold. The company owning the Crandon zinc-copper deposit initiated the process to acquire mine permits in 1982. In 1981, northern Wisconsin was explored for base metal deposits in Price, Forest, Lincoln, Rusk, and Marathon counties.

Agriculture. The total number of farms has declined in the last 47 years, but farms have become larger and more productive. On 1 Jan. 1982 there were 92,000 farms with a total acreage of 18·5m. acres and an average size of 201 acres, compared with 142,000 farms with a total acreage of 22·4m. acres and an average of 158 acres in 1959.

Cash income from products sold by Wisconsin farms in 1981 of $4,900m. was the highest on record, and included $3,800m. from livestock and livestock products and $1,100m. from crops.

Wisconsin ranked first among the states in 1981 in the number of milch cows, milk and butter production, output of American, both Brick and Munster, Italian and Blue Mold Cheese. Production of all cheese accounted for 36·9% of the nation's total. The state also ranked first in bulk whole condensed milk and bulk sweetened skim condensed milk, buttermilk, dry whey, condensed whey and lactose. In crops the state ranked first for snap beans for processing, green peas for processing, all hay and beets for canning, corn for silage, sweet corn for processing and cabbage for sauerkraut. Production of the principal field crops in 1981 included: Corn for grain, 378m. bu.; corn for silage, 11·7m. tons; oats, 52·6m. bu.; all hay, 11m. tons. Other crops of importance 18·1m. cwt of potatoes, 26m. lb. of tobacco, 1·03m. bbls of cranberries, 1·85m. cwt of cabbage, 1·8m. cwt of carrots and the processing crops of 594,220 tons of sweet corn, 60,120 tons of beets for canning, 125,460 tons of green peas and 214,110 tons of snap beans.

Forestry. In June 1982 national forests comprised 1·5m. acres; state forests, 415,264 acres; the county forests, 2·27m. acres. Wisconsin has an estimated 14·4m. acres of forest land (about 41·5% of land area) which consists of private (about 58%) and industrial forest. The production and remanufacture of wood and products is one of the state's most important industries.

INDUSTRY. Wisconsin has much heavy industry, particularly in the Milwaukee area. In 1982 the state ranked thirteenth in manufactured exports; non-electrical machinery was the major industrial group (23% of all manufacturing employment), followed by food processing, fabricated metals, electrical machinery, paper and products, transport equipment, primary metals and printing. Manufacturing establishments in 1982 provided 27% of all employment, 37·6% of all earnings; exports (1980) $3,800m. The total number of establishments was 8,627 in 1981; the biggest concentration is in the south-east.

TOURISM. The tourist-vacation industry ranks among the first three in economic importance. Approximately $6,203m. was spent in 1981 by tourists. The decline of lumbering and mining in the northern section of the state has increased dependency on the recreation industry. The Division of Tourism of the Department of Development spent $581,900 to promote tourism in financial year 1981–82.

COMMUNICATIONS

Roads. The state had on 1 Jan. 1982, 107,863 miles of highway. 72% of all roads in the state have a bituminous (or similar) surface. There are 11,948 miles of state trunk roads and 19,600 miles of county trunk roads.

In the year ending 30 June 1982 Wisconsin registered, 2,437,787 private motor cars.

Railways. On 1 Sept. 1981 the state had 5,160 road-miles of railway.

Aviation. There were, in 1982, 103 publicly operated airports. Fourteen airports were served by 10 major air carriers and 4 by commuter air carriers.

Shipping. With the opening of the St Lawrence Seaway in 1959, 14 Wisconsin ports became accessible to ocean-going vessels. Green Bay, Kenosha, Manitowoc, Marinette, Milwaukee, Sheboygan and Superior (one of the world's largest iron-ore and grain ports) have developed foreign waterborne commerce. Cargo is also carried by barge on the river Mississippi. Other ports handle mainly Great Lakes traffic.

JUSTICE, RELIGION, EDUCATION AND WELFARE

Justice. The state's penal, reformatory and correctional system on 30 June 1982 held 4,044 men and 153 women in the 10 institutions for adult and juvenile offenders; the probation and parole system was supervising 18,400 men and 3,468 women. Wisconsin does not impose the death penalty.

Religion. Wisconsin church affiliation, as a percentage of the 1980 population, was estimated at 32·2% Catholic, 20·06% Lutheran, 3·74% Methodist, 10·41% other churches and 32·6% un-affiliated.

Education. All children between the ages of 7 and 16 are required to attend school full-time to the end of the school term in which they become 16 years of age. Children living in a district with a vocational school must attend until 18. In 1982–83 the school grades kindergarten–8 had 493,100 pupils and 30,418 (full-time equivalent) teachers; school grades 9–12 had 344,991 pupils and 17,164 teachers. Grade kindergarten–8 teachers' salaries, 1981–82, averaged $19,387; grade 9–12 teachers, $19,895. Total cost per pupil was $2,823 in 1980–81.

In 1981–82 vocational, technical and adult schools had an enrolment of 515,832, and there were 6,333 faculty members in 1979–80. There is a school for the visually handicapped and a school for the deaf.

The University of Wisconsin, established in 1848, was joined by law in 1971 with the Wisconsin State Universities System to become the University of Wisconsin System with 13 degree granting campuses, 13 two-year campuses in the Center System, and the University Extension. The 26 campuses had, in 1982–83, 5,385 full-time professors and instructors, 475 part-time teachers, and 2,112 (full-time equivalent) teaching assistants. In autumn 1982, 159,868 students enrolled (10,867 at Eau Claire, 4,566 at Green Bay, 8,680 at La Crosse, 42,230 at Madison, 26,122 at Milwaukee, 11,221 at Oshkosh, 5,944 at Parkside, 5,433 at Platteville, 5,334 at River Falls, 9,045 at Stevens Point, 7,563 at Stout, 2,170 at Superior, 10,314 at Whitewater and 10,379 in the Center System freshman-sophomore centres). There are also several independent institutions of higher education. These (with 1982–83 enrolment) include 2 universities (12,696), 21 liberal arts colleges (16,337), 5 technical and professional schools (3,916), and 4 theological seminaries (509).

The total expenditure, 1981–82, for all public education (except capital outlay and debt service) was $3,714m.

The state maintains an educational broadcasting and television service.

Health. In May 1982 the state had 144 general and allied special hospitals (23,536 beds), 22 mental hospitals (2,380 beds), 6 treatment centres for alcoholism (285 beds), 1 rehabilitation centre (96 beds). Patients in state and county mental hospitals and institutions for the mentally retarded in July 1980 averaged 2,812.

Social Security. On 1 Jan. 1974 the US Social Security administration assumed responsibility for financial aid (Supplemental Security Income) to persons 65 years old and over, blind persons and totally disabled persons, who satisfy requirements as to need. Recipients receive a federal payment plus a federally administered state supplementary payment, except for those who reside in a medical institution. In July 1982, there were 62,231 SSI recipients in the state. In Nov. 1982 payment levels increased to $384 for a single individual, $434 for an eligible individual with an ineligible spouse, and $587.4 for an eligible couple. A special payment level of $481.50 for an individual and $930.20 for a couple may be paid with special approval for SSI recipients who are developmentally disabled or chronically mentally ill, living in a non-medical living arrangement not his or her own home. All SSI recipients receive state medical assistance coverage.

Under the Aid to Families with Dependent Children programme, 80,784 families constituting 241,865 persons received an average of $421.38 per family in Aug. 1982; there were then 3,710 county foster care cases, average cost per case of $193.49, and 295 state foster care cases, average $193.62. Medicaid in financial year 1982 cost $851·3m.

Books of Reference

Wisconsin Statistical Abstract. Wis. Dept. of Administration, State Bureau of Planning and Budget, Madison, 1979
Dictionary of Wisconsin Biography. Wis. Historical Society, Madison, 1960
Wisconsin Blue Book. Wis. Legislative Reference Bureau, Madison. Biennial
Current, R. N., *The History of Wisconsin,* Vol. II. State Historical Society of Wisconsin, Madison, 1976
Nesbit, R. C., *Wisconsin, A History.* State Historical Society of Wisconsin, Madison, 1973
Smith, Alice E., *The History of Wisconsin,* Vol. 1. State Historical Society of Wisconsin, Madison, 1973

State Information Agency: Legislative Reference Bureau, State Capitol, Madison, Wis. 53702. *Chief:* Dr H. Rupert Theobald.

WYOMING

HISTORY. Wyoming, first settled in 1834, was admitted into the Union on 10 July 1890. The name originated with the Delaware Indians.

AREA AND POPULATION. Wyoming is bounded north by Montana, east by South Dakota and Nebraska, south by Colorado, south-west by Utah and west by Idaho. Area 97,809 sq. miles, of which 820 sq. miles are water. The Yellowstone National Park occupies about 2,221,733 acres; the Grand Teton National Park has 310,350 acres. The federal government in 1979 owned 28,888,546 acres (46·1% of the total area of the state). The Federal Bureau of Land Management administers 17,546,188 acres.

Census population, 1 April 1980, 469,557, an increase of 41·25% since 1970. Births in 1980 were 10,546 (22 per 1,000 population); deaths, 3,215 (7); infant deaths, 104 (10 per 1,000 live births); marriages, 6,868; divorces, 4,003.

Population in 5 census years was:

	White	Negro	Indian	Asiatic	Total	Per sq. mile
1910	140,318	2,235	1,486	1,926	145,965	1·5
1930	221,241	1,250	1,845	1,229	225,565	2·3
1960	322,922	2,183	4,020	805	330,066	3·4
			All others			
1970	323,619	2,568	6,229		332,416	3·4
1980	446,488	3,364	19,705		469,557	4·8

Of the total population in 1980, 240,560 were male, 295,898 were urban and those over 21 years of age numbered 295,908.

The largest towns are Cheyenne (capital), with census population in 1980 of 47,283; Casper, 51,016; Laramie, 24,410; Rock Springs, 19,458.

CONSTITUTION AND GOVERNMENT. The constitution, drafted in 1890, has since had 43 amendments. The Legislature consists of a Senate of 30 members elected for 4 years, and a House of Representatives of 64 members elected for 2 years. The Governor is elected for 4 years.

The state sends to Congress 2 senators and 1 representative, elected by the voters of the entire state. The suffrage extends to all citizens, male and female, who have the usual residential qualifications.

In the 1980 presidential election Reagan polled 110,700 votes, Carter 49,427, and Anderson 12,072.

The capital is Cheyenne. The state contains 23 counties.

Governor: Ed Herschler (D.), 1983–86 ($55,000).
Secretary of State: Mrs Thyra Thomson (R.), 1983–86 ($37,500).

BUDGET. In the fiscal year ending 1 July 1982 (State Treasurer's figures) general revenues were $1,648,375,104; general expenditures were $1,193,991,439. Revenue Sharing Funds from federal government, $10·2m.

Per capita personal income (1981) was $11,780.

ENERGY AND NATURAL RESOURCES

Minerals. Wyoming is largely an oil-producing state. In 1981 the output of petroleum was valued at $2,319·7m.; natural gas, $671m. Other mining: Coal, $773·6m.; trona, $138·9m.; uranium, $80·9m.; other minerals mined include iron ore, feldspar, gypsum, limestone, phosphate, sand, gravel and marble, taconite, bentonite and hematite.

Value of mineral products in 1981 was $4,026·2m.

Agriculture. Wyoming is semi-arid, and agriculture is carried on by irrigation and by dry farming. In 1980 there were 9,100 farms and ranches; total land area 35m. acres.

Cash receipts, 1980, from crops, $126·4m.; from livestock and products, $524·3m. Principal commodities are wheat, cattle and calves, lambs and sheep, sugar-beet, barley, hay and wool. Animals on farms on 1 Jan. 1980 included 12,000 milch cows, 1·3m. all cattle, 1m. sheep and lambs and 30,000 swine.

INDUSTRY AND TRADE

Industry. In 1981–82 there were 570 manufacturing establishments. There were 458 mining establishments. A large portion of the manufacturing in the state is based on natural resources, mainly oil and farm products. Leading industries are food, wood products (except furniture) and machinery (except electrical). Casper is the most industrialized city, with 64 manufacturers and 145 mining companies. There were 3,200 new business incorporations in 1981. The Wyoming Industrial Development Corporation assists in the development of small industries by providing credit. Available capital, $3m.

Labour. Mining is the largest employer in the state with 41,500 workers in

1982. The total civilian labour force for June 1982 was 272,485; non-agricultural, 253,314. The average unemployment rate was 6·3% and average weekly earnings were $313.12 for manufacturing production workers.

Tourism. There are over 5m. tourists annually, mainly sportsmen. The state has the largest elk and pronghorn antelope herds in the world, 11 fish hatcheries and numerous wild game. Receipts from hunters and fishermen in 1981, $12,691,187.

COMMUNICATIONS

Roads. The roads in 1982 comprised 5,518 miles of federal highways, 343 miles of state highways and 921 miles of inter-state highway. There were (1980) 549,796 registered motor vehicles and 11 bus companies.

Railways. The railways, 1982, had a length of 2,528 mainline miles (Union Pacific, 1,194).

Aviation. There were 9 towns with regular scheduled services and 5 towns on jet routes in 1979.

JUSTICE, RELIGION, EDUCATION AND WELFARE

Justice. The state penitentiary in July 1979 held 437 male inmates. There are 2 other state correctional institutions. There have been 14 executions in Wyoming, 8 by hanging and 6 by lethal gas.

Religion. Chief religious bodies are the Roman Catholic (with 45,917 members in 1974), Mormon (28,954 in 1971) and Protestant churches (83,327 in 1974). There were 5,000 members of the Eastern Orthodox Church in 1972.

Education. In 1981–82 public elementary and secondary schools had 99,541 pupils. Enrolment in the parochial elementary and secondary schools was about 4,000. Approximately 7,655 public school teachers earned an average of $20,550. The average total expenditure per pupil for 1980–81 was $2,906.

The University of Wyoming, founded at Laramie in 1887, had in autumn 1981, 9,370 students. There are 2-year colleges at Casper, Riverton, Torrington, Cheyenne, Powell, Rock Springs and Sheridan with 25,097 students in 1980–81.

Social Welfare. In Jan. 1974 the federal government assumed many of the previous state programmes including old age assistance, aid to the blind and disabled. The state continues to administer over $5m. annually in emergency aid and aid to families with dependent children. In 1981 financial year, $7,118,545 was distributed in food stamps. Total state expenditure on public assistance and social services programmes, financial year 1981, $31m.

Health. In 1981 the state had 28 hospitals. There are 32 registered nursing homes.

Books of Reference

News of Big Wyoming. Cheyenne, 1975
Official Directory. Secretary of State. Cheyenne. Biennial
1981 Wyoming Data Handbook. Dept. of Administration and Fiscal Control. Division of Research and Statistics, Cheyenne, 1981
Brown, R. H., *Wyoming: A Geography.* Boulder, 1980
Davis, T. S., *A Study of Wyoming People.* Laramie, 1965
Larsen, T. A., *History of Wyoming.* Rev. ed. Univ. of Nebraska, 1979
Trachsel, H. H., and Wase, R., *The Government and Administration of Wyoming.* New York, 1953

OUTLYING TERRITORIES

Non-Self-Governing Territories: Summaries of Information Transmitted to the Secretary-General of the United Nations. Annual
Coulter, J. W., *The Pacific Dependencies of the United States.* New York, 1957
Perkins, W. T., *The United States and its Dependencies.* Leiden, 1962
Wiens, H. J., *Pacific Island Bastions of the US.* New York and London, 1962

GUAM

HISTORY. Magellan is said to have discovered the island in 1521; it was ceded by Spain to the US by the Treaty of Paris (10 Dec. 1898). The island was captured by the Japanese on 10 Dec. 1941, and retaken by American forces from 21 July 1944. Guam is of great strategic importance; substantial numbers of naval and air force personnel occupy about one-third of the usable land.

AREA AND POPULATION. Guam is the largest and most southern island of the Marianas Archipelago, in 13° 26′ N. lat., 144° 43′ E. long. The length is 30 miles, the breadth from 4 to 10 miles, and there are about 210 sq. miles (543 sq. km). Agaña, the seat of government is about 8 miles from the anchorage in Apra Harbour. The census on 1 April 1980 showed a population of 105,821, an increase of 20,825 or 25% since 1970; those of Guamanian ancestry numbered about 50,794; foreign-born, 28,572; density was 315 per sq. mile. On 1 July 1980 transient residents connected with the military were estimated at 20,000. The Malay strain is predominant. The native language is Chamorro; English is the official language and is taught in all schools.

CONSTITUTION AND GOVERNMENT. Guam's constitutional status is that of an 'unincorporated territory' of the US. Entry of US citizens is unrestricted; foreign nationals are subject to normal regulations. In 1949 the President transferred the administration of the island from the Navy Department (who held it from 1899) to the Interior Department. The transfer was completed by 1 Aug. 1950, on the passage of the Organic Act, which conferred full citizenship on the Guamanians, who had previously been 'nationals' of the US.

The Governor and his staff constitute the executive arm of the government. The Legislature is unicameral; its powers are similar to those of an American state legislature. At the general election of Nov. 1980, the Democratic Party won 10 seats and the Republicans 11. All adults 18 years of age or over are enfranchised. Guam returns one non-voting delegate to the House of Representatives.

Governor: Paul MacDonald Calvo (R.), 1978–82.

Lieut.-Governor: Joseph F. Ada (R.)

ECONOMY

Budget. At 30 June 1976 total assets were $43m.; federal grants $23·4m., taxes, $15m.: total liabilities were $45m.

Banking. Recent changes in banking law make it possible for foreign banks to operate in Guam; the first to obtain a licence was the First Commercial Bank of Taiwan.

ENERGY AND NATURAL RESOURCES

Water. Supplies are from springs, reservoirs and groundwater; 65% comes from water-bearing limestone in the north. The Navy and Air Force conserve water in reservoirs. The Water Resources Research Centre is at Guam University.

Agriculture. The major products of the island are sweet potatoes, cucumbers, water melons and beans. In 1979 there were 175 full-time and 150 part-time farmers. Livestock (1981) included 2,000 cattle, 14,000 hogs, and 190,000 laying hens. Commercial productions (1979) amounted to 3m. lb. of fruit and vegetables ($1·7m.), 1·2m. doz. eggs. There is an agricultural experimental station at Inarajan.

Fisheries. Fresh fish caught in 1980, 258,645 lb. About 16,000 people are active in inshore fishing, with a catch of 208,131 lb. Offshore fishing produced 26,224 lb., including 16,200 lb. of mackerel. Shrimp farming is being developed.

INDUSTRY AND TRADE

Industry. Guam Economic Development Authority controls three industrial estates: Cabras Island (32 acres); Calvo estate at Tamuning (26 acres); Harmon estate (16 acres). Industries include textile manufacture, cement and petroleum distribution, warehousing, printing, plastics and ship-repair.

Labour. In May 1978 the labour force was 30,000, of which 3,000 were unemployed.

Trade. Guam is the only American territory which has complete 'free trade'; excise duties are levied only upon imports of tobacco, liquid fuel and liquor. In the year ending 31 Dec. 1979 imports were valued at $445·8m. and accounted for 91% of trade.

Tourism. Tourism is developing; there were 1,900 visitors in 1964 and 272,681 in 1979, 190,810 of them from Japan.

COMMUNICATIONS

Roads. There are 419 miles of all-weather roads.

In 1976 there were 54,156 motor vehicles registered.

Aviation. Five commercial airlines (PANAM, Air Nauru, Japan Air Lines, Northwest Orient and Continental Air Micronesia) serve Guam.

Post and Broadcasting. Overseas telephone and radio dispatch facilities are available. In 1981 there were 27,982 telephones.

There are 4 commercial stations, a commercial television station, a public broadcasting station and a cable television station with 10 channels.

Newspapers. There is 1 daily newspaper and 4 weekly publications (all of which are of military or religious interest only).

JUSTICE, RELIGION, EDUCATION AND WELFARE

Justice. The Organic Act established a District Court with jurisdiction in matters arising under both federal and territorial law; the judge is appointed by the President subject to Senate approval. There is also a Supreme Court and a Superior Court; all judges are locally appointed except the Federal District judge. Misdemeanours are under the jurisdiction of the police court. The Spanish law was superseded in 1933 by 5 civil codes based upon California law.

Religion. About 96% of the Guamanians are Roman Catholics; others are Baptists, Episcopalians, Bahais, Lutherans, Mormons, Presbyterians, Jehovah's Witnesses and members of the Church of Christ and Seventh Day Adventists.

Education. Elementary education is compulsory. There are Chamorro Studies courses and bi-lingual teaching programmes to integrate the Chamorro language and culture into elementary and secondary school courses. There were, Sept. 1980, 28 elementary schools, 5 junior high schools, 3 senior high schools, one vocational-technical school for high school students and adults and 1 school for handicapped children. There were 15,849 elementary school pupils, 5,884 junior high and 4,323 senior high school pupils. Department of Education staff included 1,277 teachers. The Catholic schools system also operates 3 senior high schools, 3 junior high and 5 elementary schools. The Seventh Day Adventist Guam Mission Academy operates a school from grades 1 through 12, serving over 100 students. St John's Episcopal Preparatory School provides education for 200 students between kindergarten and the 9th grade. The University of Guam (an accredited institution) had 10,285 students, 1975–76. There is a vocational technical school for high school pupils and adults.

Health. There is a hospital, 8 nutrition centres, a school health programme and an extensive immunization programme. Emphasis is on disease prevention, health education and nutrition.

Books of Reference

Report (Annual) of the Governor of Guam to the US Department of Interior
Beardsley, C., *Guam Past and Present.* Rutland, Vt, 1964
Carano, P., and Sanchez, P. C., *Complete History of Guam.* Rutland, Vt, 1964

COMMONWEALTH OF PUERTO RICO

HISTORY. Puerto Rico, by the treaty of 10 Dec. 1898 (ratified 11 April 1899), was ceded by Spain to the US. The name was changed from Porto Rico to Puerto Rico by an Act of Congress approved 17 May 1932. Its territorial constitution was determined by the 'Organic Act' of Congress (2 March 1917) known as the 'Jones Act', which ruled until 25 July 1952, when the present constitution of the Commonwealth of Puerto Rico was proclaimed.

AREA AND POPULATION. Puerto Rico is the most easterly of the Greater Antilles and lies between the Dominican Republic and the US Virgin Islands. The island has a land area of 3,459 sq. miles and a population, according to the census of 1980, of 3,196,520, an increase of 475,537 or 17·5% over 1970. Of the population in 1970 about 529,000 were bilingual, Spanish being the mother tongue and (with English) one of the two official languages. Urban population (1980) 2,134,365 (66·8%).

Vital statistics (1980): Births, 75,982 (23·7 per 1,000 population); deaths, 20,486 (6·4); deaths under 1 year, 1,349 (17·8 per 1,000 live births).

Chief towns (1980) are: San Juan, 434,849; Bayamón, 196,207; Ponce, 189,046; Carolina, 165,954; Caguas, 117,959; Mayaguez, 96,193; Arecibo, 86,766.

The Puerto Rican island of Vieques, 10 miles to the east, has an area of 51·7 sq. miles and 7,662 inhabitants. The island of Culebra, with 1,265 inhabitants, between Puerto Rico and St Thomas, has a good harbour.

CONSTITUTION AND GOVERNMENT. Puerto Rico has representative government, the franchise being restricted to citizens 18 years of age or over, residence (1 year) and such additional qualifications as may be prescribed by the Legislature of Puerto Rico, but no property qualification may be imposed. Women were enfranchised in 1932 (with a literacy test) and fully in 1936. Puerto Ricans do not vote in the US presidential elections, though individuals living on the mainland are free to do so subject to the local electoral laws. The executive power resides in a Governor, elected directly by the people every 4 years. Fourteen heads of departments form the Governor's advisory council, also designated as his Council of Secretaries. The legislative functions are vested in a Senate, composed of 27 members (2 from each of the 8 senatorial districts and 11 senators at large), and the House of Representatives, composed of 51 members (1 from each of the 40 representative districts and 11 elected at large). Puerto Rico sends to Congress a Resident Commissioner to the US, elected by the people for a term of 4 years, but he has no vote in Congress. Puerto Rican men are subject to conscription in US services.

On 27 Nov. 1953 President Eisenhower sent a message to the General Assembly of the UN stating 'if at any time the Legislative Assembly of Puerto Rico adopts a resolution in favour of more complete or even absolute independence' he 'will immediately thereafter recommend to Congress that such independence be granted'.

For an account of the constitutional developments prior to 1952, *see* THE STATESMAN'S YEAR-BOOK, 1952, p. 742. The new constitution was drafted by a Puerto Rican Constituent Assembly and approved by the electorate at a referendum on 3 March 1952. It was then submitted to Congress, which struck out Section 20 of Article 11 covering the 'right to work' and the 'right to an adequate standard of living'; the remainder was passed and proclaimed by the Governor on 25 July 1952.

At the election on 4 Nov. 1980 the New Progressive Party (advocates of statehood), headed by Carlos Romero Barceló, polled 759,868 votes (47·2% of the total); the Popular Democratic Party, headed by Rafael Hernández Colon, polled 756,434 votes (47% of the total); the Independence Party (full independence by constitutional means), 87,275 (5·4% of the total); Partido Socialista Puertorriqueño (full independence), 5,225 votes (0·3% of the total).

Governor: Carlos Romero Barceló (New Progressive Party), 1980–84 ($35,000).

ECONOMY

Budget. Receipts and disbursements (US$) in central government fund for the year ending 30 June 1979 were:

Balance, 1 July 1979	4,568,220	Disbursements	2,884,461,765
Receipts	3,060,838,542	Balance, 1 July 1979	180,944,997
Total	3,065,406,762		

Assessed value of property, 30 June 1981, was $7,953·2m., and bonded indebtedness, $1,429·9m.

The US administers and finances the postal service and maintains air and naval bases. US payments in Puerto Rico, including direct expenditures (mainly military), grants-in-aid and other payments to individuals and to business totalled: 1975–76, $2,054·9m.; 1976–77, $2,176·1m.; 1977–78, $2,563·4m.; 1978–79, $2,814·4m.; 1979–80, $3,175·6m.; 1980–81, $3,405·3m.

Banking. Nineteen banks on 30 June 1982 had total deposits of $11,030·7m. and debits of $18,701m. Bank loans were $6,980·2m.

NATURAL RESOURCES

Minerals. Production: Cement (1982), 1m. short tons; stone (1980), 12·2m. short tons, value $44·3m. Total value of mineral production in 1979 was $142·1m.

Agriculture. In 1974 there were 47 'proportional profit' farms of 22,051 cords (about 22,704 acres) (mostly sugar-cane). The land had been bought from the big corporations by the Land Authority.

Production of raw sugar, 96 degrees basis, 1982 crop year, was 11,946 tons.

Livestock (1981): Cattle, 488,600; pigs, 230,311; goats, 212,151; and poultry, 7·5m.

COMMERCE. In 1981–82 imports amounted to $8,490·5m., of which $5,442m. came from US; exports were valued at $8,795·3m., of which $7,398·5m. went to US.

In 1981 the US took: Sugar, 53,402 short tons; tobacco and products, 5,871,015 lb.; rum, 25,828,424 proof gallons.

Puerto Rico is not permitted to levy taxes on imports.

Total trade between Puerto Rico and UK (British Department of Trade returns, in £1,000 sterling):

	1978	*1979*	*1980*	*1981*	*1982*
Imports to UK	29,266	40,807	33,002	29,085	2,345
Exports and re-exports from UK	23,291	18,332	16,970	19,819	5,371

COMMUNICATIONS

Roads. The Department of Public Works had under maintenance in June 1981, 6,920 miles of paved road. Motor vehicles registered 30 June 1981, 1,144,520.

Shipping. In fiscal year 1981–82, 7,906 American and foreign vessels of 44,299,793 gross tons entered and cleared Puerto Rico.

Post and Broadcasting. In 1981 there were 104 broadcasting stations and 10 television companies. There were (1981) 652,790 telephones.

Cinemas (1980). Cinemas numbered 151, with annual attendance of 8·4m.

Newspapers (1981). There are 5 main newspapers; 3 have a circulation of over 125,000.

JUSTICE AND EDUCATION

Justice. The Commonwealth judiciary system is headed by a Supreme Court of 7 members, appointed by the Governor, and consists of a Superior Tribunal with 11 sections and 89 superior judges, a District Tribunal with 38 sections and 98 district judges, and 37 municipal judges all appointed by the Governor. The police force (1982) consisted of 10,051 men and women.

Education. Education was made compulsory in 1899, but in 1981, 3·6% of the children still had no access to schooling. The percentage of illiteracy in 1976 was 8·7% of those 10 years of age or older. Total enrolment in public schools, 1981–82, was 711,748. Accredited private schools had 80,199 pupils. All instruction below senior high school standard is given in Spanish only.

The University of Puerto Rico, in Río Piedras, 7 miles from San Juan, had 51,159 students in 1981–82 and 4,838 in 4 Regional Colleges. Higher education is also available in the Inter-American University of Puerto Rico (34,479 students in 1981–82), the Catholic University of Puerto Rico (12,021), the Sacred Heart College (7,032) and the Fundacion Educativa Ana G. Méndez (13,307). These and other private colleges and universities had 83,374 students in 1981–82.

Books of Reference

Statistical Information: The area of Economic Research and Evaluation of the Puerto Rico Planning Board publishes: *(a)* annual *Economic Report to the Governor; (b) Statistical Yearbook* (since 1940–41); *(c) External Trade Statistics* (annual report); *(d) Economic Bulletin* (monthly); *(e) Reports on national income and balance of payments; (f) Socio-Economic Statistics* (since 1940); *(g) Puerto Rico Monthly Economic Indicators.* In addition there are annual reports by various Departments.

Annual Reports. Governor of Puerto Rico. Washington

Bird, A., *Bibliografia Puertorriqueña, 1930–45.* Social Science Research Centre, Univ. of Puerto Rico. 2 vols. 1946–47

Crampsey, R. A., *Puerto Rico.* Newton Abbot, 1973

Jones, C. F., and Pico, R. (eds.), *Symposium on the Geography of Puerto Rico.* Univ. of P.R. Press, 1955

Commonwealth Library: Univ. of Puerto Rico Library, Rio Piedras. *Librarian:* José Lázaro.

AMERICAN SAMOA

HISTORY. The Samoan Islands were first visited by Europeans in the 18th century; the first recorded visit was in 1722. On 14 July 1889 a treaty between the USA, Germany and Great Britain proclaimed the Samoan islands neutral territory, under a 4-power government consisting of the 3 treaty powers and the local native government. By the Tripartite Treaty of 7 Nov. 1899, ratified 19 Feb. 1900, Great Britain and Germany renounced in favour of the US all rights over the islands of the Samoan group east of 171° long. west of Greenwich, the islands to the west of that meridian being assigned to Germany (now the Independent State of Western Samoa, *see* p. 1598). The islands of Tutuila and Aunu'u were ceded to the US by their High Chiefs on 17 April 1900, and the islands of the Manu'a group on 16 July 1904. Congress accepted the islands under a Joint Resolution approved 20 Feb. 1929. Swain's Island, 210 miles north-north-west of the Samoan Islands, was annexed in 1925 and is administered as an integral part of American Samoa.

AREA AND POPULATION. The islands (Tutuila, Aunu'u, Ta'u, Olosega, Ofu and Rose) are approximately 650 miles north-east of Fiji. The total area of American Samoa is 76·1 sq. miles (197 sq. km); population, 1980, 32,395, nearly all Polynesians or part-Polynesians. The island's 3 Districts are Eastern (population, 1980, 17,339), Western (13,287) and Manu'a (1,740). There is also Swain's Island, with an area of 1·9 sq. miles and 29 inhabitants (1980), which lies 210 miles to the north west. Rose Island (uninhabited) is 0·4 sq. mile in area. In 1975 there were 1,154 births and 160 deaths.

CONSTITUTION AND GOVERNMENT. American Samoa is constitutionally an unorganized unincorporated territory of the US administered under the

Department of the Interior. Its indigenous inhabitants are US nationals and are classified locally as citizens of American Samoa with certain privileges under local laws not granted to non-indigenous persons. Polynesian customs (not inconsistent with US laws) are respected.

Fagatogo is the seat of the Government.

The islands are organized in 14 counties grouped in 3 districts; these counties and districts correspond to the traditional political units. On 25 Feb. 1948 a bicameral legislature was established, at the request of the Samoans, to have advisory legislative functions. With the adoption of the Revised Constitution of American Samoa, effective 1 July 1967, the legislature was vested with limited law-making authority. The lower house, or House of Representatives, is composed of 20 members elected by universal adult suffrage and 1 non-voting member for Swain's Island. The upper house, or Senate, is comprised of 18 members elected, in the traditional Samoan manner, in meetings of the chiefs.

Governor: Peter Tali Coleman.
Lieut.-Governor: High Chief Tufele Lia.

ECONOMY

Planning. The first formal Economic Development and Planning Office completed its first year in 1971. Much has been done to promote economic expansion within the Territory and a large amount of outside investment interest has been stimulated.

The Office initiated the first Territorial Comprehensive Plan. This plan when completed will, with periodic updating, provide a guideline to territorial development for the next 20 years. The planning programme was made possible under a Housing and Urban Development '701' grant programme.

The focus will be on physical development and the problems of a rapidly increasing population with severely limited labour resources.

Budget. The chief sources of revenue are annual federal grants from the US, and local revenues from individual and corporate income taxes, import duties, sale of utilities, rents and leases and liquor sales. During the fiscal year 1976 the Government had a revenue of $45·4m. including local appropriations of $3·9m. and federal appropriations of $41m.

Banking. The American Samoa branch of the Bank of Hawaii offers all commercial banking services. The Development Bank of American Samoa, government owned, is concerned primarily through loans and guarantees with the economic advancement of the Territory. The American Savings and Loan Bank has a branch in American Samoa.

ENERGY AND NATURAL RESOURCES

Electricity. Net power generated (1976) was 62·6m. kwh., of which 31·6m. kwh. was supplied to large power users and 16m. kwh. to householders. All the Manu'a islands have electricity.

Agriculture. There are virtually no public lands in American Samoa. Nearly all the land is owned by Samoans and with a few exceptions, cannot be sold except to persons having at least one-half Samoan blood. Of the 48,640 acres of land area, 11,000 acres are suitable for tropical crops, 1,000 acres for most temperate vegetables, 8,000 acres only to such crops as coconut and cacao with good conservation practice, 5,000 to controlled forestation and about 22,500 to indigenous and introduced forest with strict conservation measures; 1,000 acres are roads, building sites and villages. Principal crops are taro, bread-fruit, yams, bananas, coconuts, arrowroot and papayas.

Livestock (1981): Pigs, 8,000; goats, 8,000; poultry, 45,000.

INDUSTRY AND TRADE

Industry. Fish canning is important, employing the second largest number of people (after government). Attempts are being made to provide a variety of light industries. Tuna fishing and local inshore fishing are both expanding.

Commerce. In 1977 American Samoa exported goods valued at $81,232,067 and imported goods valued at $54,941,048. Chief exports are canned tuna, watches, pet foods and handicrafts. Chief imports are cement, lumber, rice, flour, fish, meat, fuel oil, sugar.

COMMUNICATIONS

Roads. There are about 45·2 miles of paved roads, 30·8 miles of unpaved and 5·4 miles of secondary roads. There are 12·7 miles of secondary unpaved roads maintained mainly on Tutuila. Motor vehicles registered, 1977, 4,127.

Aviation. PANAM operates between Western America, Honolulu, New Zealand, American Samoa, and Tahiti. South Pacific Island Airways and Polynesian Airlines operate daily services between American Samoa and Western Samoa. The islands are also served by Air New Zealand and UTA. Total landings at Pago Pago, 1977, 11,992.

Shipping. The harbour at Pago Pago, which nearly bisects the island of Tutuila, is the only good harbour for large vessels in Samoa. By sea, there is a twice-monthly service between Western America, New Zealand and Australia and regular service between US, South Pacific ports and Japan. In 1977, 779 vessels entered and 737 cleared Pago Pago harbour.

Post and Broadcasting. A commercial radiogram service is available to all parts of the world through 3 principal trunks, Hawaii, Fiji and Western Samoa. Commercial phone services are operated to all parts of the world on a 24-hour service. Number of telephones (June 1981), 5,918.

JUSTICE, EDUCATION AND WELFARE

Justice. Judicial power is vested in a High Court. Fifty-nine district courts, traffic courts and small claims courts are heard without record and appeals therefrom are tried, *de novo*, in the trial division of the High Court. The trial division also has original jurisdiction of all criminal and civil cases. The probate division has jurisdiction of estates, guardianships, trusts and other matters. The land and title division decides cases relating to disputes involving communal land and Matai title court rules on questions and controversy over family titles. The appellate division hears appeals from trial, land and title and probate divisions as well as having original jurisdiction in selected matters. The appellate court is the court of last resort. Two American judges sit with 5 Samoan judges permanently. In addition there are 8 temporary judges or assessors who sit occasionally on cases involving Samoan customs.

Education. Education is compulsory between the ages of 6 and 18. The Government (1978) maintains 24 consolidated elementary schools, 4 senior high schools with technical departments, 1 community college, special education classes for the handicapped and 100 Early Childhood Education Centres for pre-school children. Total elementary and secondary enrolment (1978), 7,492; in ECE schools, 1,505; classes for the handicapped, 102; total elementary and secondary classroom teachers, 435. Eight private schools had 1,820 students. Learning is by a variety of media including television.

Health. The Department of Health provides the only medical and dental care in American Samoa. It operates a general hospital (181 beds including 31 bassinets), 2 dispensaries on Tutuila, 4 dispensaries in the Manu'a group, 1 on Aunu'u and 1 on Swain's Island. A $3·5m. tropical medical centre was completed and placed in service in 1968. This now embraces the general hospital as well as out-patient clinics for surgery, obstetrics, gynaecology, emergencies, family practice, internal medicine, paediatrics; there are clinics for treatment of the eye, ear, nose and throat, dental and public health departments.

VIRGIN ISLANDS OF THE UNITED STATES

HISTORY. The Virgin Islands of the United States, formerly known as the Danish West Indies, were named and claimed for Spain by Columbus in 1493. They were later settled by Dutch and English planters, invaded by France in the mid-17th century and abandoned by the French *c.* 1700, by which time Danish influence had been established. St Croix was held by the Knights of Malta between two periods of French rule.

They were purchased by the United States from Denmark for $25m. in a treaty ratified by both nations and proclaimed 31 March 1917. Their value was wholly strategic, inasmuch as they commanded the Anegada Passage from the Atlantic Ocean to the Caribbean Sea and the approach to the Panama Canal. Although the inhabitants were made US citizens in 1927, the islands are, constitutionally, an 'unincorporated territory'.

AREA AND POPULATION. The Virgin Islands group, lying about 40 miles due east of Puerto Rico, comprises the islands of St Thomas (28 sq. miles), St Croix (84 sq. miles), St John (20 sq. miles) and about 50 small islets or cays, mostly uninhabited. The total area of the 3 principal islands is 132 sq. miles, of which the US Government owns 9,599 acres as National Park.

The population, according to the census of 1 April 1980, was 95,591, an increase of 33,123 or 53% since 1970. Population had slowly declined since 1835, when it stood at 43,000, but began to recover in the 1940s. Population of St Croix, 49,013; St Thomas, 44,218; St John, 2,360. About 20–25% are native-born, 35–40% from other Caribbean islands, 10% from mainland USA and 5% from Europe. St Croix has over 40% of Puerto Rican origin or extraction, Spanish speaking. In financial year 1980, live births were 2,552 and deaths, 548.

The capital and only city, Charlotte Amalie, on St Thomas, had a population (1980) of 11,756; there are two towns on St Croix. Christiansted with 2,856 and Frederiksted with 1,054.

CONSTITUTION AND GOVERNMENT. The Organic Act of 22 July 1954 gives the US Department of the Interior full jurisdiction; some limited legislative powers are given to a single- chambered legislature, composed of 15 senators elected for 2 years representing the two legislative districts of St Croix and St Thomas-St John.

The Governor is elected by the islanders. A new Constitution was under consideration in March 1979, but was rejected by the electorate; a further constitutional convention was held in 1980. A new document was submitted to the President of the United States and to Congress; it was approved and submitted to the Virgin Islands electorate and was defeated in a referendum in Nov. 1981.

For administration, there are 13 executive departments, 12 of which are under commissioners and the other, the Department of Law, under an Attorney-General. The US Department of the Interior appoints a Federal Comptroller of government revenue and expenditure.

The franchise is vested in residents who are citizens of the United States, 18 years of age or over. In 1982 there were 30,065 voters, of whom 23,188 participated in the local elections that year.

They do not participate in the US presidential election but they have a non-voting representative in Congress.

The capital is Charlotte Amalie, on St Thomas Island.

Governor: Juan Luis ($51,000).
Lieut.-Governor: Julio A. Brady ($47,000).

ECONOMY

Budget. Under the 1954 Organic Act finances are provided partly from local revenues—customs, federal income tax, real and personal property tax, trade tax, excise tax, pilotage fees, etc.—and partly from Federal Matching Funds, being the excise taxes collected by the federal government on such Virgin Islands products transported to the mainland as are liable.

Revenue for fiscal year ending 30 Sept. 1982, $225·6m., and expenditure $225·3m.

Currency and Banking. United States currency became legal tender on 1 July 1934. Banks are the Chase Manhattan Bank; the Bank of Nova Scotia; the First Federal Savings and Loan Association of Puerto Rico; Barclays Bank International; Bank of America; Citibank; First Pennsylvania Bank, Banco Popular de Puerto Rico, and the Royal Bank of Canada.

ENERGY AND NATURAL RESOURCES

Electricity. The Virgin Islands Water and Power Authority provides electric power from generating plants on St Croix and St Thomas; St John is served by power cable and emergency generator.

Water. Large de-salinization plants have been established, but rain-water remains the most reliable source. Every building must have a cistern to provide rain-water for drinking, even in areas served by mains (10 gallons capacity per sq. ft of roof for a single-storey house).

Agriculture. With the phasing out of the sugar-cane industry in St Croix, and the accelerated construction activities carried on in all three islands, the number of farms decreased, but there has recently been a revival of interest in food crops.

Land for fruit, vegetables and animal feed is available on St Croix, and there are tax incentives for development. Sugar has been terminated as a commercial crop and over 4,000 acres of prime land could be utilized for food crops.

Livestock (1981): Cattle, 6,739; goats, 6,463; pigs, 2,943; sheep, 3,224.

Fisheries. There is a fishermen's co-operative with a market at Christiansted. There is a shellfish-farming project at Rust-op-Twist, St Croix.

INDUSTRY AND TRADE

Industry. The main occupations on St Thomas are tourism and government service; on St Croix manufacturing is more important. Manufactures include textiles, pharmaceuticals, rum and fragrances. The Martin Marietta Alumina plant processes bauxite from Africa for refining in mainland USA. The Amerada Hess oil refinery has a capacity of 700,000 bbls per day.

The Virgin Islands offer liberal tax exemptions to persons, firms or companies prepared to invest $50,000 in new industries or in the promotion of tourism.

Commerce. Exports, calendar year 1981, totalled $5,068·2m. and imports $5,013·6m.

Total trade between the US Virgin Islands and UK (financial years, British Department of Trade returns, in £1,000 sterling):

	1978	*1979*	*1980*	*1981*	*1982*
Imports to UK	127	851	39	13	29
Exports and re-exports from UK	3,255	3,273	18,518	2,882	545

Tourism. Tourism is the most important business. There were about 1·3m. visitors in 1981 spending $317·5m.

About 691,000 tourists came on cruise ships which made more than 890 calls, mainly at St Thomas which has a good, natural deepwater harbour.

COMMUNICATIONS

Roads. The Virgin Islands have 531·6 miles of roads, and 40,388 motor vehicles were registered in 1981.

Aviation. There is a daily cargo and passenger service between St Thomas and St Croix. Hamilton Airport on St Croix can take all aircraft except Concorde. Harry S. Truman Airport on St Thomas takes 727-class aircraft. There are air connexions to mainland USA, other Caribbean islands, Latin America and Europe.

Shipping. The whole territory has free port status. There is an hourly boat service between St Thomas and St John.

Post and Broadcasting. All three Virgin Islands have a dial telephone system. In Nov. 1982 there were 48,000 telephones. Direct dialling to Puerto Rico and the mainland is now possible. Worldwide radio telegraph service is also available.

The islands are served by 7 radio stations, 4 television stations and 3 newspapers, 2 of them dailies.

RELIGION AND EDUCATION

Religion. There are churches of the Protestant, Roman Catholic and Jewish faiths in St Thomas and St Croix and Protestant and Roman Catholic churches in St John.

Education. Education is compulsory between the ages of 5½ and 16 years, inclusive. In 1981–82 there were 35 public schools (ranging from kindergarten to high schools); enrolment was 25,787; other schools had 7,093 pupils; the public school budget was $57·4m. In 1981 the College of the Virgin Islands had 2,608 registered students; 632 full-time undergraduates, 1,778 part-time undergraduates and 198 graduate students. The College is part of the United States land-grant network of higher education.

Books of Reference

Evans, L. H., *The Virgin Islands: From Naval Base to New Deal.* Ann Arbor, Mich., 1945
Jarvis, J. A., *The Virgin Islands and Their People.* Philadelphia, 1944
McGuire, J. W., *Geographic Dictionary of the Virgin Islands of the United States.* US Coast and Geodetic Survey. Special Publication No. 103. Washington, 1925
Reid, C. F., *Bibliography of the Virgin Islands of the United States.* New York, 1941

TRUST TERRITORY OF THE PACIFIC ISLANDS

HISTORY. Under the Treaty of Versailles (1919) Japan was appointed mandatory to the former German possessions north of the Equator. In 1946 the US agreed to administer the former Japanese-mandated islands of the Caroline, Marshall and Mariana groups (except Guam) as a Trusteeship for the United Nations; the trusteeship agreement was approved by the Security Council 27 April 1947 and came into effect on 18 July 1947. The Trust Territory was administered by the US Navy until 1951, when all the islands except Tinian and Saipan in the Marianas were transferred to the Secretary of the Interior. In 1962 the Interior Department assumed responsibility for them also. On 17 June 1975 the voters of the Northern Mariana Islands, in a plebiscite observed by the UN, adopted the covenant to establish a Commonwealth of the Northern Mariana Islands in Union with the USA. In April 1976 the covenant was approved by the US government and the administration of the Northern Marianas was separated from that of the rest of the Trust Territory; the group has a constitution and a constitutional government, installed 9 Jan. 1978. The rest of the Trust Territory is divided into 3 entities, each with its own constitution. The Marshall Islands, the Federated States of Micronesia (Yap, Kosrae, Truk and Ponape) and the Republic of Belau are all negotiating a status of free association with the US government. Free association will grant the USA the authority to control military and defence activities in return for federal government assistance and budget supports to the autonomous constitutional governments. Termination of the UN Trusteeship Agreement is contingent upon establishing a political status, either free association or independence, for the islands. Negotiations were proceeding in 1981.

AREA AND POPULATION. The Trust Territory extends from 1° to 22° N.

lat. and from 142° to 172° E. long. The area is generally known as Micronesia, or 'land of the small islands' (Guam, Kiribati and Nauru not part of the Trust Territory, are also ethnically and geographically Micronesian); total land area 708 sq. miles; population (1980 census), 116,974.

The census population of the 6 administrative districts as of Sept. 1980 was: Truk, 37,742; Ponape, 22,319; Marshall Islands, 31,042; Belau, 12,177; Yap, 8,172; Kosrae, 5,522. Nine different languages are spoken, each with variations; English is used in the schools and is the official language.

CONSTITUTION AND GOVERNMENT. Constitutional governments are functioning in the Mariana Islands (1978), the Marshall Islands (1979), the Federated States of Micronesia (1979) and the Republic of Belau (1981). Each of the 4 entities is autonomous from the other 3 but all are still legally under the single Trust Territory system. The citizens are Trust Territory citizens until the termination of the Trusteeship. Majuro is the capital of the Marshall Islands. Kolonia, Ponape, is the capital of the Federated States, Koror is the headquarters of Palau and Saipan is the capital of the Commonwealth of the Northern Marianas, as well as the US administrative headquarters.

High Commissioner: Adrian P. Winkel.

INDUSTRY. Tourism is the main source of income from overseas; industrial development is limited. There is some commercial fishing and agriculture, a coconut-processing plant and a tuna-packing plant.

COMMUNICATIONS

Aviation. The island groups are served by Continental Air Micronesia *via* Honolulu. Internal commuter airlines operate in Ponape, Yap, Marshalls, Belau and the Marianas. There are connexions to international routes at Guam and Hawaii.

JUSTICE, RELIGION, EDUCATION AND WELFARE

Justice. The Trust Territory Code, local constitutions and the Trusteeship Agreement are the foundations for law. Local police are responsible for enforcement. There is a Trust Territory High Court, constitutional courts and lesser courts. Local customs are recognized and protected in legal practice, when not in conflict with higher law.

Religion. Freedom of religion is guaranteed in the Trust Territory Code and all constitutions.

Education. Education is free and compulsory through elementary school (grades 1–8). There are public and private elementary and secondary schools and government post-secondary education.

Health. The public health system, which includes 6 district hospitals as well as other hospitals and clinics in outlying areas, is carried on by a staff consisting chiefly of trained Micronesian medical and dental officers and assistants under senior US doctors.

Books of Reference

Report to the United Nations Trusteeship Council, 1979. Dept. of State, Washington, D.C., 1980

Basic Information. High Commissioner's Office, Saipan

UNINCORPORATED TERRITORIES

Johnston Atoll. Two small islands 1,150 km south-west of Hawaii, administered by the US Air Force. Area, under 1 sq. mile; population, 1970 census, 1,007.

Midway Islands. Two small islands at the western end of the Hawaiian chain, administered by the US Navy. Area, 2 sq. miles; population, 1970 census, 2,220.

Wake Island. Three small islands 3,700 km west of Hawaii, administered by the US Air Force. Area, 3 sq. miles; population, 1970 census, 1,647.

UPPER VOLTA

République de Haute-Volta

Capital: Ouagadougou
Population: 7·29m. (1982)
GNP per capita: US$190 (1980)

HISTORY. A separate colony of Upper Volta was in 1919 carved out of the colony of Upper Senegal and Niger, which had been established in 1904. In 1932 it was abolished and most of its territory transferred to Ivory Coast, with small parts added to French Sudan and Niger, but it was re-constituted with its former borders on 4 Sept. 1947. Upper Volta became an autonomous republic within the French Community on 11 Dec. 1958 and reached full independence on 5 Aug. 1960.

On 3 Jan. 1966 the government of Maurice Yameogo was overthrown by a military *coup* led by Lieut-Col. Sangoulé Lamizana, who assumed the Presidency. Constitutional rule was resumed on 21 June 1970 but suspended from 8 Feb. 1974 until May 1978. In a further *coup* on 25 Nov. 1980, President Lamizana was overthrown and a Military Committee for National Recovery and Progress assumed power under Col. Saye Zerbo.

AREA AND POPULATION. Upper Volta is bounded north and west by Mali, east by Niger, south by Benin, Togo, Ghana and the Ivory Coast. The republic covers an area of 274,122 sq. km; population (census, 1975) 5,638,203. Estimate (1982) 7,285,000. Ouagadougou, the capital (172,661 inhabitants), Bobo-Dioulasso (115,063). The largest cities (estimates 1979) were: Koudougou (36,838), Ouahigouya (25,690), Kaya (18,402), Banfora (12,358). The principal ethnic groups are the Mossi (48%), Fulani (10%), Lobi-Dagari (7%), Mandé (7%), Bobo (7%), Sénoufo (6%), Gourounsi (5%), Bissa (5%), Gourmantché (5%).

CONSTITUTION AND GOVERNMENT. Following the *coup* of 25 Nov. 1980, the 1977 Constitution was suspended and the 57-member National Assembly dissolved. Supreme political power is now vested in a new 12-member People's Salvation Council (CSP), ruling through an appointed Cabinet composed in Jan. 1983 of:

President of CSP, Head of State, Minister for Defence and War Veterans: Maj. Jean-Baptiste Ouedraogo.

Prime Minister: Capt. Thomas Sankara.

Foreign Affairs and Co-operation: Michel Kafando. *Interior and Security:* Maj. Harouna Tarnarda. *Justice:* Mme. Marie-Louise Mignan. *Economy and Finance:* Pascal Sanou. *Planning:* Eugene Dondasse. *Rural Development:* Edouard Tapsoba. *Health:* Alain Ouedraogo. *Public Works and Town Planning:* Salikou Traoré. *Trade, Industrial Development and Mines:* Clement Bambara. *Labour, Social Laws and Civil Service:* Jean Bado. *Information, Posts and Telecommunications:* Adama Fofana. *Higher Education and Scientific Research:* Issa Tiendrebeogo. *Education, Arts and Culture:* Emmanuel Dadiuoari. *Youth and Sports:* Ibrahima Koné. *Transport, Environment and Tourism:* Frederic Korsaga. *Social and Women's Affairs:* Mme. Pauline Kambou Hien.

Secretaries of State: Justin Damou Barre *(Budget)*, Benjamin Bonkoungou *(Water Resources)*, Yacouba Jean Paul Sow *(Civil Service)*, Jean De Dieu Somda *(Government and Cabinet Affairs)*.

National flag: Three horizontal stripes of black, white, red.

Local government: There are 11 *départements* – Centre (capital, Ouagadougou), Centre-Est (Tenkodogo), Centre-Nord (Kaya), Centre-Ouest (Koudougou), Est (Fada N'Gourma), Hauts-Bassins (Bobo-Dioulasso), Komoé (Banfora), Nord

(Ouahigouya), Sahel (Dori), Sud-Ouest (Gaoua), and Volta Noire (Dédougou) – sub-divided into 80 *sous-préfectures*.

DEFENCE

Army. The Army consists of 3 infantry regiments, 1 reconnaissance squadron and support units; total strength (1983), 3,700.

Air Force. Creation of a small air arm to support the land forces began, with French assistance, in 1964. Equipment now comprises 2 HS.748 twin-turboprop freighters, 2 C-47s, 2 twin-turboprop Frégates, an Aero Commander 500, 1 Broussard and 2 Reims/Cessna Super Skymasters for transport and liaison duties. Personnel total about 75.

INTERNATIONAL RELATIONS

Membership. Upper Volta is a member of UN, OAU and is an ACP state of the EEC.

ECONOMY

Planning. The Third Development Plan 1977–81 aimed at an 8·4% average annual real growth in GDP.

Budget. Government revenue and expenditure balanced in 1981 at 46,164m. francs CFA.

Currency. The unit of currency is the *franc* CFA with a parity rate of 50 *francs* CFA to 1 French *franc*. In March 1983, £1 = 532 *francs*; US$1 = 363 *francs*.

Banking. The *Banque Centrale des Etats de l'Afrique de l'Ouest* is the bank of issue. The main commercial bank is the *Banque Internationale des Voltas*. In 1976 the savings banks had 668,146 depositors with 26,683,701 *francs* CFA to their credit.

ENERGY AND NATURAL RESOURCES

Electricity. Production of electricity (1980) was 140m. kwh.

Minerals. There are deposits of manganese near Tambao in the north, but exploitation is limited by existing transport facilities. Magnetite, bauxite, zinc, lead, nickel and phosphates have been found in the same area.

Agriculture. Production (1980, in tonnes): Sorghum, 559,118; millet, 329,831; maize, 98,297; groundnuts, 53,000; rice (paddy), 28,657; cotton, 56,039; sesame, 7,100. Rice and groundnuts are of increasing importance.

Livestock (1981): 2·8m. cattle, 1·9m. sheep, 2·9m goats, 70,000 horses, 200,000 donkeys.

INDUSTRY AND TRADE

Industry. In 1978 gross manufacturing (including energy) was 21,638 francs CFA, of which foodstuffs (7·17m. francs CFA), textiles (2·36m. francs CFA) and metal products (516m. francs CFA). In 1972 there were 91 industrial units.

Labour. In 1979 the labour force was 3,586,000 of whom 2,941,000 were engaged in agriculture, forestry and fishing. There were (1981) 4 trade unions.

Commerce. In 1980 imports totalled 75,614m. francs CFA and exports 19,076m. francs CFA. In 1977 the major exports were cotton (40%) and livestock (29%). In 1978 France provided 40%, the USA 12% and the Ivory Coast 11% of imports, while the Ivory Coast took 43%, Federal Republic of Germany 12% and UK 12%.

Total trade between Upper Volta and UK (British Department of Trade returns, in £1,000 sterling):

	1978	*1979*	*1980*	*1981*	*1982*
Imports to UK	4,496	338	2,819	2,864	1,289
Exports and re-exports from UK	914	1,234	1,039	5,311	2,166

Tourism. There were 43,724 tourists in 1979.

COMMUNICATIONS

Roads. The road system comprises 16,462 km, of which 4,460 km are national, 1,920 km departmental, 2,322 km regional and 7,760 km unclassified roads. There were 9,500 private cars and 10,100 commercial vehicles in 1975.

Railway. Ouagadougou is the terminus of the Abidjan-Niger railway, of which 517 km lie in Upper Volta. A 355-km extension to the manganese deposits at Tambao is planned with the first 107-km section to Kaya under construction.

Aviation. Ouagadougou and Bobo-Dioulasso are regularly served by UTA and Air Afrique and in 1977 dealt with 63,221 passengers and 3,802 tonnes of freight. Air Volta operates all internal flights to 47 domestic airports.

Post and Broadcasting. There were, in 1978, some 66 post offices and 3,564 telephones. There are radio stations at Ouagadougou and Bobo-Dioulasso and (1981) 90,000 receivers. The state television service, Voltavision, broadcasts 3 days a week in Ouagadougou; there were (1981) 5,500 receivers.

Newspapers. 3 daily newspapers are published in Ouagadougou.

JUSTICE, RELIGION, EDUCATION AND WELFARE

Justice. There are courts of first instance at Ouagadougou, Bobo-Dioulasso, Ouahigouya and Fada N'Gourma. The Supreme Court, High Court of Justice and Court of Appeal are all in Ouagadougou.

Religion. The majority of the population (53%) follow animist religions; 36% are Moslem and 11% Christian (mainly Roman Catholic).

Education. There were, in 1980, 185,759 pupils in 869 primary schools, 17,568 in secondary schools, and in 1979 there were 1,852 in technical schools and 495 students in teacher-training establishments. The Université d'Ouagadougou had 1,281 students.

Health (1976). There were 5 hospitals, 119 dispensaries with maternity units and 24 maternity units alone with a total of 3,623 beds. There were 107 doctors, 7 dentists, 11 pharmacists, 98 midwives and 1,193 nursing personnel.

A 10-year health programme started in 1979, providing for 7,000 village health centres, 515 district health centres, regional and sub-regional medical centres, 10 departmental hospitals, 2 national hospitals and a university centre of health sciences in Ouagadougou.

DIPLOMATIC REPRESENTATIVES

Of Upper Volta in Great Britain
Ambassador: Lieut-Col. Antoine Dakoure (accredited 14 July 1982; resides in Brussels).

Of Great Britain in Upper Volta
Ambassador: Michael Francis Daly (resides in Abidjan).

Of Upper Volta in the USA (2340 Massachusetts Ave., NW, Washington, D.C., 20008)
Ambassador: Tiemoko Marc Garango.

Of the USA in Upper Volta (PO Box 35, Ouagadougou)
Ambassador: Julius W. Walker, Jr.

Of Upper Volta to the United Nations
Ambassador: Aissé Mensah.

URUGUAY

Capital: Montevideo
Population: 2·9m. (1982)
GNP per capita: US$2,820 (1980)

República Oriental del Uruguay

HISTORY. The Republic of Uruguay, formerly a part of the Spanish Viceroyalty of Río de la Plata and subsequently a province of Brazil, declared its independence 25 Aug. 1825 which was recognized by the treaty between Argentina and Brazil signed at Rio de Janeiro 27 Aug. 1828. The first constitution was adopted 18 July 1830.

AREA AND POPULATION. Uruguay is bounded on the north-east by Brazil, on the south-east by the Atlantic, on the south by the Río de la Plata and on the west by Argentina. The area is 186,926 sq. km (72,172 sq. miles). The following table shows the area and the population of the 19 departments (capitals in brackets) as estimated in May 1975:

Departments	*Area sq. km*	*Population*	*Pop. per sq. km*
Artigas (Artigas)	11,378	57,528	4·6
Canelones (Canelones)	4,752	313,858	54·3
Cerro-Largo (Melo)	14,929	73,204	4·8
Colonia (Colonia)	5,682	110,820	18·5
Durazno (Durazno)	14,315	54,990	3·7
Flores (Trinidad)	4,519	24,684	5·2
Florida (Florida)	12,107	66,092	5·3
Lavalleja (Minas)	12,485	65,240	5·3
Maldonado (Maldonado)	4,111	75,607	14·9
Montevideo (Montevideo City)	664	1,314,129	2,102·4
Paysandú (Paysandú)	13,252	98,735	6·6
Río Negro (Fray Bentos)	8,471	49,816	5·5
Rivera (Rivera)	9,829	79,330	7·8
Rocha (Rocha)	11,089	59,952	5·0
Salto (Salto)	12,603	100,407	7·3
San José (San José)	6,963	88,281	11·4
Soriano (Mercedes)	9,223	80,114	8·4
Tacuarembó (Tacuarembó)	21,015	84,829	3·7
Treinta y Tres (Treinta y Tres)	9,539	45,680	4·5
Total	186,926	2,843,296	15·2

Estimated population in 1978 was 2,886,000. In 1980 Montevideo (the capital) had an estimated population of 1,314,129. Other cities (1975): Salto, 80,000; Paysandú, 80,000; Mercedes, 53,000.

CONSTITUTION AND GOVERNMENT. Since 1900 Uruguay has been unique in her constitutional innovations, all designed to protect her from the emergence of a dictatorship. The favourite device of the group known as the 'Batllistas' (a *Colorado* faction) which, until defeated at the 1958 elections, held the majority for over 90 years, has been the collegiate system of government, in which the two largest political parties were represented.

One such pattern lasted from 1917 to 1933, when it was abolished by a dictator who re-established the system of an individual President. Until 1951 Presidents were elected every 4 years and they selected their own Cabinet Ministers (*see* list of Presidents in THE STATESMAN'S YEAR-BOOK, 1956, p. 1493). In 1951, on the initiative of the 'Batllistas', the Constitution was amended: the individual presidency was abolished and the executive power vested in a National Council of Government of 9 members (6 from the majority and 3 from the minority parties).

As a result of a referendum held on 27 Nov. 1966, Uruguay returned to the presidential system. The President appoints a council of 11 Ministers; the Vice-President presides over the Senate and the General Assembly when this takes place. A new Constitution was rejected by referendum in Nov. 1980 and in Nov. 1983 an election took place to elect officials who will renegotiate a new draft Constitution prior to a general election in Nov. 1984.

President: Gregorio C. Alvarez (sworn in for a 3½-year term on 1 Sept. 1981).

The Cabinet in Dec. 1982 was as follows:

Interior: Gen. Yamandú Trinidad. *Foreign Affairs:* Dr Carlos A. Maeso. *Justice:* Dr Julio César Espínola. *Economy and Finance:* Cdr Walter Lusiardo Aznárez. *Transport and Public Works:* Francisco D. Tourreilles. *Public Health:* Luis A. Givogre. *Industry and Energy:* (Vacant). *National Defence:* Dr Justo M. Alonso Leguisamo. *Agriculture and Fisheries:* Carlos Mattos Moglia. *Education:* Dr Raquel Lombardo de la Betolaza. *Labour and Social Security:* Dr Luis A. Crisci. *Secretary to Presidency:* Dr Angel Mario Scelza.

Parliament was dissolved by Presidential decree on 27 June 1973. A new Constitution was being prepared in 1981 and general elections are due to be held in Nov. 1984.

National flag: Nine horizontal stripes of white and blue, a white canton with the 'Sun of May' in gold.

National anthem: Orientales, la patria ó la tumba (words by Francisco Acuña de Figueroa; music by Francisco José Deballi).

DEFENCE

Army. The Army is composed of the active army and its reserves. The active army is formed of volunteers, who contract for 1 year or 2 years' service. In 1983 there were 4 brigades of cavalry, 1 artillery and 3 infantry brigades, 5 engineer battalions and 1 air defence battalion. Peace-time strength, 22,000 men.

The reserve is formed by elements who, for some reason or other, retire from the active army. It is reckoned that about 120,000 men could be mobilized in case of war.

Navy. The Navy consists of 3 frigates (*ex*-US old destroyer escorts), 1 corvette (*ex*-US fleet minesweeper), 1 patrol vessel (*ex*-coastal minesweeper), 4 patrol craft, 6 coastal patrol launches, 1 transport, 1 training ship, 1 salvage vessel, 5 minor amphibious craft, 2 oilers and 3 tenders. Personnel in 1983: 3,500 officers and ratings including naval infantry (marines).

There is a small US-equipped naval air service of 30 aircraft and 7 helicopters.

Air Force. Organized with US aid, the Air Force has about 3,000 personnel and 110 aircraft, including 1 counter-insurgency squadron with 5 AT-33 armed jet trainers and 8 A-37B light strike aircraft, a reconnaissance and training squadron with 8 T-6Gs, 2 transport squadrons with 4 turboprop FH-227/F.27 Friendships, 6 Brazilian-built EMB-110 Bandeirantes (1 equipped for photographic duties), 12 C-47s, 5 CASA C-212 Aviocars and 5 Queen Airs, a search and rescue squadron with Cessna U-17A aircraft and light helicopters, and a number of Cessna 182 light aircraft for liaison duties. Basic training types are the T-41 and T-34, with 12 Argentinian-built Pucarás for advanced training.

INTERNATIONAL RELATIONS

Membership. Uruguay is a member of UN, OAS and LAIA (formerly LAFTA).

ECONOMY

Budget. The receipts and expenditure of the national accounts as approved by the National Council of Government (UR$1m.):

	1976	*1977*	*1978*	*1979*	*1980*	*1981*
Revenue	1,721,679	2,937,583	4,349,819	8,423,600	14,954,800	21,260,000
Expenditure	2,047,354	3,178,197	4,750,533	8,300,700	14,879,900	21,368,600

Now covering a 5-year period the budget is presented during the year following election of each new government; differences in actual annual income and expenditure and amendments to the budget (including new taxes) must be approved by Parliament each year-end; these usually come forward in July each year.

Expenditures in 1981 included: Salaries and social security payments, 68·9%; other current expenditure, 12·4%; subsidies and transfer payments, 4·5%; interests of public debts, 1·9%; and investments, 12·3%. Expenditure on public works is separately financed from specific revenues (*e.g.*, fuel tax). A law inaugurating income tax came into operation on 1 July 1961, but was repealed on 1 March 1974.

Foreign debt outstanding in Dec. 1981 was US$3,129m. Total reserves of the Banco Central in Dec. 1981 were US$840·8m.

Currency. There is no gold in circulation, but the monetary standard is gold, the theoretical gold coin being the *peso oro*, gold content of which was fixed, Dec. 1964, at 0·05924 gramme. It is equal to 100 *pesos.* The unit of currency is the *Nuevo Peso* (1,000 old pesos) of 100 *centésimos.* The actual circulating medium consists of paper notes issued by the Central Bank in *Nuevo Peso* denominations of 50, 100, 500 and 1,000 *Nuevo Peso*, and 1, 2, 5 and 10 coins.

In March 1982, US$ = 11·85 *pesos*; £1 = 21 *pesos.*

Banking. The Bank of the Republic (founded 1896), whose president and directors are appointed by the Government has a paid-up capital of N$1,852m. The Banco Central was inaugurated on 16 May 1967. Note circulation in Dec. 1980 was N$6,671m.

A state-owned National Insurance Bank *(Banco de Seguros del Estado)* has a monopoly of new insurance business of all kinds. The Bank re-insures much of its business in London.

Of the 36 banks in Uruguay the Bank of London and South America (British) has a main office and 16 branch agencies.

Weights and Measures. The metric system was adopted in 1862.

ENERGY AND NATURAL RESOURCES

Electricity. The supply of electricity for light, power and traction has been a State monopoly since 1897. In Jan. 1949 the first hydro-electric plant at the site of the dam of Rincón del Bonete was completed with an installed capacity of 144 megawatts. Another plant at Rincón de Baygorria on the Río Negro came into operation in 1960, with a capacity of 108 megawatts. Nine turbines of the Salto Grande hydro-electric dam were operating by Sept. 1981. Power output in Dec. 1981 was 3,349m. kwh.

Oil. An extension of the ANCAP refining plant, opened at Montevideo on 6 Dec. 1961, gives a capacity of 7,500 cu. metres daily of high-octane petrol and high-grade gas for domestic and industrial use.

Agriculture. Uruguay is primarily a pastoral country. Of the total land area of 46m. acres some 41m. are devoted to farming, of which 90% to livestock and 10% to crops. Some large *estancias* have been divided up into family farms; rural landlordism is much less than elsewhere. Uruguay is said to be the only Latin American country in which agricultural workers have the protection of a minimum-wage law. Animals and animal products constituted 39·6% of the exports in 1980. The 1966 census reported on 79,101 farms of all kinds, totalling 16·5m. hectares.

There were (1981) 11·3m. cattle, 20m. sheep, 530,000 horses, 450,000 pigs, 12,000 goats and 8m. poultry.

The wool clip in 1980–81 was 71,051 tonnes.

Agricultural products are raised chiefly in the departments of Paysandú, Río Negro, Colonia, San José, Soriano and Florida. The average farm is about 250 acres. The principal crops and their estimated yield (in tonnes) in 2 crop years were as follows:

	1980	1981		1980	1981
Wheat	429,500	306,600	Barley	71,100	102,900
Linseed	65,100	21,400	Maize	119,300	180,800
Oats	69,800	65,900	Rice	287,600	330,300

Uruguay is self-sufficient in rice, with a surplus for export. Three sugar refineries handle cane and (mainly) beet, their total production being approximately 90,000 tonnes, and approaching self-sufficiency.

Wine is produced chiefly in the departments of Montevideo, Canelones and Colonia, about enough for domestic consumption. The country has some 6m. fruit trees, principally peaches, oranges, tangerines and pears.

Forestry. In 1974 roundwood removals were 1,077,000 cu. metres, of which 1,001,000 cu. metres was softwood.

Fisheries. In 1980, the total catch was 115,900 tonnes. Exports were valued at US$46,431,000

INDUSTRY AND TRADE

Industry. In 1978 there were nearly 77,000 registered enterprises with 405,000 employees. These cover activities such as meat packing, oil refining, cement manufacture, foodstuffs, beverages, leather and textile maufacture, chemicals, light engineering and transport equipment. There are about 100 textile mills, but with the exception of half a dozen large plants, these are on the whole small.

The development of industry is an important economic policy objective and there is a liberal attitude to foreign investment for industrial promotion.

There are a number of public works programmes including airport modernization, port of Montevideo modernization, highways improvements, Montevideo sewage disposal, power production and transmission and telecommunications.

Trade Unions. Trade unions number about 150,000 members. About 1,036,000 (40%) population are classed as gainfully occupied.

Commerce. The foreign trade (officially stated in US$, with the figure for imports based on the clearance permits granted and that for exports on export licences utilized) was as follows (in US$1,000):

	1974	1975	1976	1977	1978	1979	1980
Imports	486·7	516·9	587·2	721·0	757	1,206	1,602·5
Exports	382·2	381·2	546·5	607·5	694	787	1,209·3

Of the imports in 1981 (in US$1m.) Brazil furnished 312·1; USA and Canada, 174·5; Argentina, 118·1; Federal Republic of Germany, 103·5; UK, 66·5; Middle East, 19·9; of the exports in 1981 Brazil took 169·5; Middle East, 146·7; Federal Republic of Germany, 123·1; Argentina, 114·7; USA and Canada, 103·3; Netherlands, 57·5; Italy, 55·9; UK, 53.

Principal imports and exports (in US$1,000):

Imports	1980	1981	*Exports*	1980	1981
Chemicals	...	139,300	Meat and meat products	155,400	213,600
Transport materials	237,000	210,600	Hides, furs and leather manufactures	139,500	138,300
Fuel and lubricants	420,200	447,800	Wool and manufactures	205,000	331,200
Machinery and accessories	241,400	291,100	Vegetable products	...	185,600

Total trade between Uruguay and UK (British Department of Trade returns, in £1,000 sterling):

	1978	1979	1980	1981	1982
Imports to UK	24,256	13,416	16,884	26,330	23,107
Exports and re-exports from UK	17,446	24,735	26,619	20,103	13,926

Tourism. There were 1,103,857 tourists in 1979 spending an estimated US$268m.

COMMUNICATIONS

Roads. The main highways, linking Montevideo with the interior, have a total length of 9,899 km, of which about 5,000 km are paved. Other roads, unpaved, are about 4,726 km. Considerable improvements, financed both internally and by international loans, have been carried out in the last few years.

Registered motor vehicles, 31 Dec. 1978, are estimated at 220,000 passenger cars and 92,150 trucks and buses.

Railways. The 4 principal railway systems, embracing 2,987 km, were all built by British capital amounting to £14,513,000. The Uruguayan Government in 1948 bought these railways for £7·15m., assuming control that year. The East Coast Railway (125·5 km) and 3 minor lines were already controlled by the State under a separate administration. In Oct. 1952 the railways were brought under a single administration and a major programme of track upgrading and rolling stock rehabilitation is being carried out. The total railway system open for traffic was (1980) 3,004 km of 1,435 mm gauge. In 1981 it carried 3·3m. passengers and 1·2m. tonnes of freight. In 1979 the 27 km line between Mercedes and Ombucito was opened, providing a direct route from Montevideo to Fray Bentos.

Aviation. Carrasco, 22·5 km from Montevideo, is the most important airport. US, Argentine, Brazilian, Chilean, Dutch, French, Fed. German, Scandinavian and Paraguayan airlines fly to and from Uruguay. The state-operated civil airline PLUNA runs services in the interior of the country and to Brazil, Paraguay and Argentina, and Spain.

Shipping. On 31 Dec. 1978 the 8 merchant vessels and 4 tankers under the Uruguayan flag had a GRT of 103,336. In 1979, 1,461 vessels cleared Montevideo, 50 being British. River transport (1,270 km) is extensive, its main importance being to link Montevideo with Paysandú and Salto.

Post and Broadcasting. The telegraph lines in operation have a total length of 12,083 km. The telephone system in Montevideo is controlled by the State; small companies operate in the interior. Telephone instruments, 1981, numbered 287,140. There are 1,277 post offices. Uruguay has 54 long-wave and 17 short-wave broadcasting stations. There are about 1m. wireless sets and 440,000 television receivers. There are 4 television stations in Montevideo and 11 in the interior. The State itself operates one of the most powerful sound broadcasting stations in South America. Colour television was inaugurated 1981.

Cinemas (1980). Cinemas numbered 85 with seating capacity of 47,000.

Newspapers (1981). There were 5 daily newspapers in Montevideo with aggregate daily circulation of about 210,000; most of the 25–30 provincial newspapers appear bi-weekly.

JUSTICE, RELIGION, EDUCATION AND WELFARE

Justice. The Ministry of Justice was created in 1977 to be responsible for relations between the Executive Power and the Judiciary and other jurisdictional entities. The Court of Justice is made up by 5 members appointed by the Council of the Nation at the suggestion of the Executive Power, for a period of 5 years. This court has original jurisdiction in constitutional, international and admiralty cases and hears appeals from the appellate courts, of which there are 4, each with 3 judges.

In Montevideo there are also 8 courts for ordinary civil cases, 3 for government *(Juzgado de Hacienda)*, as well as criminal and correctional courts. Each departmental capital has a departmental court; each of the 224 judicial divisions has a justice of peace court. In Sept. 1907 the death penalty was abolished, replaced by penal servitude for a period of 30–40 years.

Religion. State and Church are separated, and there is complete religious liberty. The faith professed by the majority of the inhabitants is Roman Catholic. The archbishop of Montevideo has 9 suffragan bishops in Salto, Melo, Florida, Minas, San José, Canelones, Tacuarembó, Mercedes and Maldonado.

Protestants numbered about 10,500 in 1957.

Education. Primary education is obligatory; both primary and superior education are free.

In 1979 there were 1,050 primary public schools with 364,910 pupils and approximately 10,300 teachers; in 1979, 249 secondary schools had 196,462 pupils. There are also evening courses for adults. Illiteracy is now confined largely to the older age groups.

The University of the Republic at Montevideo, inaugurated in 1849, has about 16,200 students; tuition is free to both native-born and foreign students; there are 10 faculties. There are 43 normal schools for males and females, and a college of arts and trades with about 33,000 students. There are also many religious seminaries throughout the Republic with a considerable number of pupils, a school for the blind, 2 for deaf and dumb and a school of domestic science.

Health. Hospital beds, 1981, numbered (estimate) 23,000; physicians numbered 5,600.

DIPLOMATIC REPRESENTATIVES

Of Uruguay in Great Britain (48 Lennox Gdns., London, SW1X 0DL)
Chargé d'Affaires: Adolfo Castells.

Of Great Britain in Uruguay (Calle Marco Bruto 1073, Montevideo)
Ambassador: Patricia M. Hutchinson, CMG, CBE.

Of Uruguay in the USA (1918 F St., NW, Washington, D.C., 20006)
Ambassador: Alejandro Vegh Villegas.

Of the USA in Uruguay (Calle Lauro Muller 1776, Montevideo)
Ambassador: Thomas Aranda, Jr.

Of Uruguay to the United Nations
Ambassador: Dr Juan Carlos Blanco.

Books of Reference

The official gazette is the *Diario Oficial*
Statistical Reports of the Government. Montevideo. Annual and biennial
Anales de Instruccion Primaria. Montevideo. Quarterly

Arcas, J. A., *Historia del siglo XX uruguayo, 1897–1943.* Montevideo, 1950
De Carlos, M., *La escuela púplica uruguaya.* Montevideo, 1949
Fernández Saldaña, J. M., *Diccionario Uruguayo de Biografias.* Montevideo, 1945
Finch, M.H.J., *A Political Economy of Uruguay Since 1870.* London, 1981
Fitzgibbon, R. H., *Uruguay, Portrait of a Democracy.* New Brunswick, NJ, 1954; London, 1956
Montañés, M. T., *Desarrollo de la agricultura en el Uruguay.* Montevideo, 1948
Pendle, G., *Uruguay.* 3rd. ed. Inst. of Int. Affairs, 1963
Porzecanski, A. C., *Uruguay's Tupamaros.* London and New York, 1973
Salgado, José, *Historia de la Republica O. del Uruguay.* 8 vols. Montevideo, 1943

National Library: Biblioteca Nacional del Uruguay, Guayabo 1793, Montevideo. It publishes *Anuario Bibliográfico Uruguayo.*

VANUATU

Capital: Vila
Population: 112,596 (1979)
GNP per capita: US$530 (1980)

Republic of Vanuatu

HISTORY. The group was administered for some purposes jointly, for others unilaterally, as provided for by Anglo-French Convention of 27 Feb. 1906, ratified 20 Oct. 1906, and a protocol signed at London on 6 Aug. 1911 and ratified on 18 March 1922. On 30 July 1980 the Condominium of the New Hebrides achieved independence and became the Republic of Vanuatu.

AREA AND POPULATION. The Vanuatu group lies roughly 500 miles west of Fiji and 250 miles north-east of New Caledonia. The estimated land area is 5,700 sq. miles (14,760 sq. km). The larger islands of the group are: Espiritu Santo, Malekula, Epi, Pentecost, Aoba, Maewa, Paama, Ambrym, Efate, Erromanga, Tanna and Aneityum. They also claim Matthew and Hunter islands.

There are 3 active volcanoes, on Tanna, Ambrym and Lopevi, respectively. Earth tremors are of common occurrence. Rainfall at Vila (the capital, population (1979) 14,000) averages 90 in. per annum.

The first complete census was taken in 1967. The total population was found to be 77,988, of whom 72,243 were Vanuatuans. Census, Jan. 1979, 112,596.

CONSTITUTION AND GOVERNMENT. General elections took place in Nov. 1975 to elect a 42-member Representative Assembly, replacing the former advisory council. Further general elections took place in Nov. 1979. A committee system was instituted and the Assembly chose its own President from its own members in 1977. The President replaced the Co-Presidents, who were the Resident Commissioners.

President: Ati George Sokomanu.
Prime Minister: Walter Hadye Lini, CBE.
Home Affairs and Deputy Prime Minister: F. Timakata. *Education:* D. Kalpokas. *Finance:* K. Kalsakau. *Health:* W. Korisa. *Transport, Communications and Public Works:* J. Naupa. *Agriculture, Forestry, Fisheries and Land:* S. Regenvanu.

Flag: Red over green, with a black triangle in the hoist, the three parts being divided by fimbriations of black and yellow, and in the centre of the black triangle a boar's tusk overlaid by two crossed fern leaves.

Language: The national language is Bislama; English and French are also official languages.

ECONOMY

Budget. The budget for 1980 (estimate): Revenue, 1,520m. Vatu; expenditure, 2,682m. NH francs. The main sources of revenue were import and export duties.

Currency. In 1982 a new currency, the *Vatu* was introduced

Banking. A Central Bank was established in 1980. Because of the absence of direct taxation, with the exception of an added value tax on sales of sub-divided land, there has been growing interest in Vanuatu as a finance centre and 500 overseas companies are using Vila and have contributed 450m. Vatu in invisible export earnings. There were 8 banks in Vila in 1980. There is a National Development Bank and a Central Bank operated by the government and branches of the Bank of Indochine et de Suez at Vila and Santo. Barclays Bank International has a branch in Vila and Santo. Other overseas banks are: ANZ Bank, New South Wales Bank and Hongkong and Shanghai Bank.

NATURAL RESOURCES

Minerals. The manganese mine, established at Forari on Efate by the Compagnie Française de Phosphates de l'Océanie, closed in 1968 but was reopened in 1970 by Southland Mining of Australia. Manganese exports, 1979, 25m. Vatu.

Agriculture. The main commercial crops are copra, cocoa and coffee. Yams, taro, manioc and bananas are grown for local consumption. A large number of cattle are reared on plantations, and an up-grading programme using pure-bred Charolais, Limousins and Illawarras has begun. A beef industry is developing.

Livestock (1981): Cattle, 95,000; goats, 8,000; pigs, 68,000; poultry, 154,000.

Forestry. An active forestry development programme is in progress and more than 26 plantations of South American hardwoods have been established.

Fisheries. The principal catch is tuna (1980, 10,000 tonnes) mainly exported to USA.

INDUSTRY AND TRADE

Industry. There is no heavy industry but there is increasing activity in light industry. Industries include a saw-mill, a soft drinks factory, meat canneries and a modern abattoir, and a fish-freezing plant. A few indigenous crafts, such as basketry, canoe-building and pottery, are practised. Subsistence fishing is done by the Vanuatuan, and a plant for freezing of tuna and bonito commenced operation in 1957. This plant, which is sited on Santo, freezes and packages for export to Japan and elsewhere, fish caught by Taiwanese and other vessels under contract to the British company running the plant. There are over 300 co-operative societies handling 85% of the distribution of goods in the islands.

Commerce. Imports and exports were (in 1m. Vatu):

	1978	*1979*	*1980*
Imports	3,691	4,276	4,220
Exports	2,682	2,851	1,759

In 1979 the main exports were: Copra, 39,821 tonnes, 1,505m. NH francs; fish, 7,623 tonnes, 831m. NH francs; beef, 750 tonnes, 135m. NH francs. Australia, France and Japan were the major sources of imports and principal imports were food and drink, manufactured goods and petroleum products.

Tourism. Tourism is a growing industry and in 1979 there were 30,454 visitors to Vanuatu.

COMMUNICATIONS

Roads. There are approximately 1,000 km of roads in Vanuatu, of these about 35 km are sealed, mostly on Efate Island. There were 7,000 registered motor vehicles in Vanuatu (1980).

Aviation. External air services are provided by Air Pacific, Solair and Air Vanuatu. Solair has a weekly service Honiara–Santo–Vila and return. Air Vanuatu has 2 services a week Sydney–Vila–Sydney, UTA (Unions de Transports Aériens) and Air Nauru. Air Pacific has two services a week Nandi–Vila–Honiara–Brisbane, and one Nandi–Vila–Noumea–Brisbane. UTA has daily flights from Noumea, and a weekly flight to Wallis. Air Nauru gives a weekly service Vila–Nauru. Inter-island flights are provided by Air Melanesiae. The principal airports are Bauer Field (for Vila) and Pekoa (for Santo). Seventeen smaller airfields provide an internal network. In 1977 there were 1,001 overseas aircraft arrivals in Vila, carrying 59,141 passengers.

Shipping. Several international shipping lines serve Vanuatu, linking the country with Australia, New Zealand, other Pacific territories notably Hong Kong, Japan, North America and Europe. The chief ports are Vila and Santo. In 1977, 394 vessels arrived including 48 cruise ships carrying 40,412 visitors. 92,340 tons of cargo were exported and 102,867 tons discharged. Small vessels provide frequent inter-island services.

Telecommunications. Internal telephone and telegram services are provided by the Posts and Telecommunications and Radio Departments. There are automatic telephone exchanges at Vila and Santo; rural areas are served by a network of tele-radio stations. In 1981 there were 3,000 telephones.

External telephone, telegram and telex services are provided by VANITEL, through their satellite earth station at Vila. There are direct circuits to Noumea, Sydney, Hong Kong and Paris and high quality communications are available on a 24-hour basis to most countries in the world. Air radio facilities are provided. Marine coast station facilities are available at Vila and Santo. Radio New Hebrides operates a broadcasting service 7 days a week in 3 languages, French, English and Pidgin. A new station was opened in April 1981.

JUSTICE, EDUCATION AND WELFARE

Justice. A study was being made in 1980 which could lead to unification of the judicial system.

Education. Primary and secondary education facilities are provided in both English and French. There is one technical training facility in Vila and students undergo higher (university) education either at the University of the South Pacific in Fiji, or University of Papua New Guinea or in France. Teacher training for both English and French language teachers is conducted in Vanuatu.

There were (1980) 115 French language primary and 3 secondary schools and 161 English language primary and 5 secondary schools.

Health. Medical care is provided through a network of 106 hospitals, health centres, clinics and dispensaries administered by the Government with the help of a number of voluntary agencies, and WHO. Public health measures and the control of communicable diseases are the responsibility of the public health administration. Local training schemes are devoted to basic community nurse training at hospitals in Vila, to rural health training and refresher courses at a special training health centre in North Efate, or by attachment to other suitable clinics and health centres, and to training of village sanitarians or health orderlies.

Malaria is still the most serious of the major endemic diseases which also include tuberculosis, leprosy, filariasis and venereal disease. During 1975–76 yaws recurred on some islands and there were epidemic outbreaks of dengue, influenza and gastro-enteritis.

For professional and technical education in medicine, nursing, X-ray, dentistry, laboratory work, health inspection, selected students or suitable in-service staff are awarded scholarships and fellowships for overseas training in Solomon Islands, Papua New Guinea, Fiji, New Zealand, Australia, New Caledonia and other countries.

DIPLOMATIC REPRESENTATIVES

Of Vanuatu in Great Britain
High Commissioner: Barak Teme Sope (accredited 4 June 1981).

Of Great Britain in Vanuatu (Melitco Hse., Rue Pasteur, Vila)
High Commissioner: R. B. Dorman.

Book of Reference

Annual Report 1968–69. HMSO

VATICAN CITY STATE

Stato della Città del Vaticano

HISTORY. For many centuries the Popes bore temporal sway over a territory stretching across mid-Italy from sea to sea and comprising some 17,000 sq. miles, with a population finally of over 3m. In 1859–60 and 1870 the Papal States were incorporated with the Italian Kingdom. The consequent dispute between Italy and successive Popes was only settled on 11 Feb. 1929 by three treaties between the Italian Government and the Vatican: (1) A Political Treaty, which recognized the full and independent sovereignty of the Holy See in the city of the Vatican; (2) a Concordat, to regulate the condition of religion and of the Church in Italy; and (3) a Financial Convention, in accordance with which the Holy See received 750m. lire in cash and 1,000m. lire in Italian 5% state bonds. This sum was to be a definitive settlement of all the financial claims of the Holy See against Italy in consequence of the loss of its temporal power in 1870. The treaty and concordat were ratified on 7 June 1929. The treaty has been embodied in the Constitution of the Italian Republic of 1947.

The Vatican City State is governed by a Commission appointed by the Pope. The reason for its existence is to provide an extra-territorial, independent base for the Holy See, the government of the Roman Catholic Church.

In 1930 the issue of Papal coinage was resumed, after a lapse of 60 years. In virtue of a special convention between the Vatican City and the Italian Government (last renewed in 1962), each state allows the currency of the other to circulate in its territory. The Vatican City has, however, given an undertaking that the total value of its coins issued in ordinary years will not exceed 100m. lire, 200m. lire in years of 'Sede vacante' or holy years, or 300m. in the year of the opening of a Council.

AREA AND POPULATION. The area of the Vatican City is 44 hectares (108·7 acres). It includes the Piazza di San Pietro (St Peter's Square), which is to remain normally open to the public and subject to the powers of the Italian police. It has its own railway station (opened Nov. 1932), postal facilities, coins and radio. Twelve buildings in and outside Rome enjoy extra-territorial rights, including the Basilicas of St John Lateran, St Mary Major, St Paul without the Walls and the Pope's summer villa at Castel Gandolfo. On 8 Oct. 1951 extra-territorial rights were also granted to a new Vatican radio station on Italian soil. *Radio Vaticana* is broadcasting an extensive service in 34 languages from transmitters in the Vatican City and in Italy.

The Vatican City has about 1,000 inhabitants.

CONSTITUTION. The Pope exercises the sovereignty and has absolute legislative, executive and judicial powers. The judicial power is delegated to a tribunal in the first instance, to the Sacred Roman Rota in appeal and to the Supreme Tribunal of the Signature in final appeal.

The Pope is elected by the College of Cardinals, meeting in secret conclave. The election is by scrutiny and requires a two-thirds majority.

Name and family	*Election*	*Name and family*	*Election*
Benedict XIV *(Lambertini)*	1740	Pius VI *(Braschi)*	1775
Clement XIII *(Rezzonico)*	1758	Pius VII *(Chiaramonti)*	1800
Clement XIV *(Ganganelli)*	1769	Leo XII *(della Genga)*	1823

Name and family	*Election*	*Name and family*	*Election*
Pius VIII *(Castiglioni)*	1829	Pius XI *(Ratti)*	1922
Gregory XVI *(Cappellari)*	1831	Pius XII *(Pacelli)*	1939
Pius IX *(Mastai-Ferretti)*	1846	John XXIII *(Roncalli)*	1958
Leo XIII *(Pecci)*	1878	Paul VI *(Montini)*	1963
Pius X *(Sarto)*	1903	John Paul I *(Luciani)*	1978
Benedict XV *(della Chiesa)*	1914	John Paul II *(Wojtyla)*	1978

Supreme Pontiff: **John Paul II** (Karol Wojtyla), born at Wadowice near Cracow, Poland, 18 May 1920. Archbishop of Cracow 1964–78, created Cardinal in 1967, elected Pope 16 Oct. 1978, inaugurated 22 Oct. 1978.

Pope John Paul II was the first non-Italian to be elected since Pope Adrian VI (a Dutchman) in 1522.

Secretary of State: Cardinal Agostino Casaroli (appointed May 1979).

Flag: Vertically yellow and white, with on the white the crossed keys and tiara of the Papacy.

ROMAN CATHOLIC CHURCH. The Roman Pontiff (in orders a Bishop, but in jurisdiction held to be by divine right the centre of all Catholic unity, and consequently Pastor and Teacher of all Christians) has for advisers and coadjutors the Sacred College of Cardinals, consisting in March 1983 of 138 Cardinals appointed by him from senior ecclesiastics who are either the bishops of important Sees or the heads of departments at the Holy See. In addition to the College of Cardinals, the Pope has created a ' Synod of Bishops'. This consists of the Patriarchs and certain Metropolitans of the Catholic Church of Oriental Rite, of elected representatives of the national episcopal conferences and religious orders of the world, of the Cardinals in charge of the Roman Congregations and of other persons nominated by the Pope. The Synod meets as and when decided by the Pope; its first session was held in the autumn of 1967 and its sixth session in Oct. 1980.

The central administration of the Roman Catholic Church is carried on by a number of permanent committees called Sacred Congregations, each composed of a number of Cardinals and diocesan bishops (both appointed for 5-year periods), with Consultors and Officials. Besides the Secretariat of State and the Council for Public Affairs of the Church (which deals with external relations) there are now 9 Sacred Congregations, viz.: Doctrine, Oriental Churches, Bishops, the Sacraments and Divine Worship, Clergy, Religious, Catholic Education, Evangelization of the Peoples and Causes of the Saints. There are also 3 Secretariats: for Christian Unity, Non-Christians and Non-Believers; a Prefecture of Economic Affairs, a Prefecture of the Pontifical Household and a Statistical Office. Furthermore, the Roman Curia contains 3 tribunals, the Apostolic Penitentiary, the Supreme Tribunal of the Apostolic Signature and the Sacred Roman Rota; and, lastly, various other councils and commissions dealing with the Laity, Justice and Peace, Women, the Family, the Revision of Canon Law, Social Communications, Migration, Tourism and Culture. The Pontifical Academy of Sciences was revived by Pius XI in 1936 with 70 members.

More than 2,500 Roman Catholic prelates and 99 observer-delegates from 27 other Christian Churches attended the Second Vatican Council which met 11 Oct. 1962 and 8 Dec. 1965. Sixteen Constitutions and Decrees were approved at the Council, and 7 commissions were set up to implement these decisions.

DIPLOMATIC REPRESENTATIVES

In its diplomatic relations with foreign countries the Holy See is represented by the Council for Public Affairs of the Church. It maintains permanent observers to the UN in New York and Geneva and to UNESCO and FAO. The Holy See is a member of IAEA and the Vatican City State is a member of UPU and ITU. It therefore attends as a member those international conferences open to State members of the UN and specialized agencies.

British Ambassador: Sir Mark Heath KCVO, CMG. *First Secretary:* R. J. Griffiths.
Apostolic Pro-Nuncio in Great Britain: Mgr Bruno Heim, Titular Archbishop of Xanto.

Books of Reference

Acta Apostolicæ Sedis Romanæ. Rome
Annuario Pontificio. Rome. Annual
L'Attivià della Santa Sede. Rome. Annual
The Catholic Directory. London. Annual
Codex Juris Canonici. Latest ed., 1948
Bilan du Monde: Encyclopédie catholique du monde chrétien. Tournai, 1964
Cardinale, Mgr. Igino, *Le Saint-Siège et la diplomatie.* Paris and Rome, 1962.—*The Holy See and the International Order.* Gerrards Cross, 1976
Hales, E. E., *The Catholic Church and the Modern World.* London, 1958
Mayer, F. *et al, The Vatican: Portrait of a State and a Community.* Dublin, 1980
Nichols, P., *The Politics of the Vatican.* London, 1968
Pallenborg, C., *Vatican Finances.* Harmondsworth, 1971

VENEZUELA

Capital: Caracas
Population: 14·63m. (1981)
GNP per capita: US$3,630 (1980)

Republica de Venezuela

HISTORY. Venezuela formed part of the Spanish colony of New Granada until 1821 when it became independent in union with Colombia. A separate, independent republic was formed in 1830.

AREA AND POPULATION. Venezuela is bounded north by the Caribbean, east by Guyana, south by Brazil, south-west and west by Colombia. The official estimate of the area is 912,050 sq. km (352,143 sq. miles); the frontiers with Colombia, Brazil and Guyana extend for 2,972 miles and its Atlantic coastline stretches for some 2,000 miles. Over half the population live in the valleys of Caracas and Valencia (once the capital). There are 20 states, 2 territories, the federal district and the federal dependencies (*i.e.* 72 islands in the Antilles); further states may be created from the territories. Bolívar, the largest state, has an area of 91,868 sq. miles; the other states are far smaller. The federal district embraces 745 sq. miles.

The language of the country is Spanish.

Population according to the 1971 census (estimate (1981) 14·63m.):

State	*Capital*	*Population*	*State*	*Capital*	*Population*
Anzoátegui	Barcelona	506,297	Portuguesa	Guanare	297,044
Apure	San Fernando	164,705	Sucre	Cumaná	469,006
Aragua	Maracay	543,170	Táchira	San Cristóbal	511,344
Barinas	Barinas	231,046	Trujillo	Trujillo	381,335
Bolívar	Ciudad Bolívar	391,665	Yaracuy	San Felipe	223,540
Carabobo	Valencia	659,339	Zulia	Maracaibo	1,229,037
Cojedes	San Carlos	94,351	Ter. Amazonas	Puerto Ayacucho	21,696
Falcón	Coro	407,957	Ter. Delta Amacuro	Tucupita	48,139
Guárico	San Juan	318,905	Federal District	Caracas	1,860,637
Lara	Barquisimeto	671,410	Federal Dependencies	—	463
Mérida	Mérida	347,095			
Miranda	Los Teques	856,272			
Monagas	Maturin	298,239			
Nueva Esparta	La Asunción	118,830		Total	10,721,522

The 1971 census excluded tribal Indians estimated at 31,800, of whom 20,000 are in Ter. Amazonas and 4,000 in Zulia. Excluding illegal immigrants, estimated (1979) at about 3m.

The 1971 population of Caracas was 1,035,499; Maracaibo 651,574; Barquisimeto, 330,815; Valencia, 367,154; Maracay, 255,134; San Cristóbal, 152,239; Ciudad Guyana, 143,540; Cabimas, 122,239; Maturín, 121,662; Baruta, 121,066; Cumaná, 119,751; Ciudad Bolívar, 103,728.

Vital statistics, 1979 (estimate): 484,700 births, 74,950 deaths. Life expectancy (1978) 66 years with 53% of population under 18 years.

CONSTITUTION AND GOVERNMENT. The constitution of 1958 provides for popular election for a term of 5 years of a President, a National Congress, and State and Municipal legislative assemblies, and guarantees the freedom of labour, industry and commerce. Aliens are assured of treatment equal to that extended to nationals.

Congress consists of a Senate and a Chamber of Deputies. At least 2 Senators are elected for each State and for the Federal District. Senators must be Venezuelans by birth and over 30 years of age. Deputies must be native Venezuelans over 21 years of age; there is 1 for every 50,000 inhabitants. The territories, on reaching the population fixed by law, also elect deputies. Voting (by proportional representation) is compulsory for men and women over 18. Owing to the high rate of illiteracy, voting is by coloured ballot cards.

The President must be a Venezuelan by birth and over 30 years of age; he has a qualified power of veto.

The following is a list of presidents since 1941:

	Took Office		*Took Office*
Gen. Isaias Medina Angarita	6 May 1941	Dr Edgard Sanabria	14 Nov. 1958[3]
Rómulo Betancourt	20 Oct. 1945	Rómulo Betancourt	13 Feb. 1959
Rómulo Gallegos	15 Feb. 1948	Raul Leoni	11 March 1964
Lieut.-Col. Carlos Delgado Chalbaud	24 Nov. 1948[4]	Rafael Caldera	11 March 1969
Dr G. Suárez Flamerich	27 Nov. 1950[2]	Carlos Andrés Pérez Rodríguez	12 March 1974
Col. Marcos Pérez Jiménez.	3 Dec. 1952[1]	Dr Luis Herrera Campíns	12 March 1979
Rear-Adm. Wolfgang Larrazábal Ugueto	23 Jan. 1958[2] [3]		

[1] Deposed. [2] Resigned. [3] Provisional. [4] Assassinated 13 Nov. 1950.

President: Luis Herrera Campins, elected 3 Dec. 1978 with 2,469,042 out of 5,412,673 votes, assumed office on 12 March 1979.

Foreign Minister: José Alberto Zambrano Velasco. *Finance Minister:* Arturo Sosa.

At the Congressional elections held in Dec. 1978, 88 of the 199 seats in the Chamber of Deputies were won by Acción Democrática, 64 by COPEI (the Social Christians) and 27 by other parties.

The city of Caracas is the capital. The 20 states, autonomous and politically equal, have each a legislative assembly and an elected governor. The states are divided into 156 districts and 613 municipalities. There are also 2 federal territories with 7 departments, and a federal district with 2 departments and 2 parishes. Each district has a municipal council, and each municipio a communal junta. The federal district and the 2 territories are administered by the President of the Republic.

National flag: Three horizontal stripes of yellow, blue, red, with an arc of 7 white stars in the centre, and the national arms in the canton.

National anthem: Gloria al bravo pueblo (1811; words by Vicente Salias, tune by Juan Landaeta).

DEFENCE

Army. All Venezuelans on reaching 18 years of age are liable for 2 years in the Armed Forces. The Army's established strength of approximately 27,000 all ranks, furnishes 1 cavalry battalion, 11 infantry and 2 mechanized battalions, 3 ranger battalions, 3 tank battalions and supporting engineering, artillery, anti-aircraft and supply services. There is a military academy for cadets, a school for staff studies and other technical training schools. Women can also be conscripted, as nurses, clerks, etc. Army aviation comprises 30 helicopters and 2 STOL transports.

Navy. Strength includes 3 diesel-powered patrol submarines (2 new built in Federal Republic of Germany and 1 very old *ex*-US submarine), 2 old destroyers (*ex*-US), 8 frigates built in Italy (6 new and 2 being refitted in Italy with diesel engines), 6 fast missile-armed patrol craft built in Britain in 1974–75, 21 coastal patrol craft, 1 tank landing ship, 2 medium landing ships, 1 transport landing ship (*ex*-repair ship), 12 minor landing craft, 1survey ship, 2 survey launches, 2 transports and 13 tugs. Coastal patrol boats operated by the National Guard now number 60.

New construction includes 3 corvettes to be ordered, 2 more submarines from the Federal Republic of Germany and 4 tank landing ships from Korea.

There is a naval academy and sail training ship for the training of officer cadets and a school of staff studies and various technical training schools. Personnel in

1983 totalled: 7,500 officers and men including 4,000 of the Marine Corps. Naval aviation comprises 6 S2E Trackers, shipborne helicopters and light aircraft for coastguard duties.

Air Force. Formed in 1920, the Air Force of some 4,800 officers and men is a small, but well-equipped service with a total of about 250 aircraft. There are 6 combat squadrons. One is equipped with 18 F-16A and 6 F-16B Fighting Falcons. Two others have 29 Canadair CF-5A fighter-bombers and 8 two-seat CF-5Ds. Two bomber squadrons are equipped with 20 modernized Canberra jet-bombers and a single reconnaissance Canberra. Another operational squadron has 15 OV-10E Bronco twin-turboprop counter-insurgency aircraft. A helicopter force consists of more than 40 Bell JetRangers, 212s, 214STs and 412s, UH-1B/D/H Iroquois and Alouette IIIs. Transport units are equipped with 12 C-123 Providers, 6 C-130H Hercules, 2 Aeritalia G222s, 1 HS.748 and 15 C-47s. Communications aircraft are Queen Airs and other types. T-34 Mentors are used for training, together with 23 T-2D Buckeye advanced jet trainers, which have a secondary attack role. A battalion of paratroops comes within Air Force responsibility. There is a staff college and a cadet academy.

National Guard, a volunteer force of some 15,000 under the Ministry of Defence, is broadly responsible for internal security. It includes customs and forestry duties among its tasks.

INTERNATIONAL RELATIONS

Membership. Venezuela is a member of UN, OAS, LAIA (formerly LAFTA), OPEC and the Andean Group.

ECONOMY

Planning. The sixth 5-year plan (1981–85) aims to achieve economic growth but with a reorientation of priorities towards social programmes: Education, housing and public services. There are 5 major projects: Caracas metro, Guri hydro-electric scheme, INOS water supply, major housing schemes and the Corpozulia coal and steel complex. These will cost Bs. 67,000m. over 5 years.

Budget. The revenue and expenditure for calendar years were, in Bs.1m., as follows:

	1974	*1975*	*1976*	*1977*	*1978*	*1979*
Revenue	42,799	41,270	43,143	51,179	44,480	50,588
Expenditure	40,059	40,266	44,571	50,694	44,273	51,236

Currency. The *bolívar* (Bs.) is divided into 100 *céntimos*. Gold coins, 100 (*pachanos*), 20 and 10 *bolívars* have been minted but are no longer in circulation; silver coins are 5 (*fuerte*), 2, 1 *bolívars*; nickel, 50 (*real*), 25 (*medio*) and 12·5 *céntimos* (*locha*), coppernickel, 5 *céntimos* (*puya*).

The bank-notes in circulation are 500, 100, 50, 20 and 10 bolívars. The circulation of foreign bank-notes is forbidden.

In March 1983, £ = Bs.6·32; US$1 = 4·39.

Banking. The major banks include: Banco Industrial de Venezuela, Banco de Venezuela, Banco nacional de Descuento, Banco Unión, Banco Mercantil y Agrícola, Banco de los Trabajadores de Venezuela, Banco Provincial SAICA, Banco Latino, Banco de Maracaibo, Banco Unido.

ENERGY AND NATURAL RESOURCES

Oil. The oil-producing region around Maracaibo, covering some 30,000 sq. miles, produces about three-quarters of Venezuelan petroleum. Deposits in the Orinoco region are likely to prove one of the largest heavy oil reserves in the world. Nationalization of the privately owned oil sector in 1976 has proved successful. New distribution channels have been established, with the result that the major transnational companies which took 80% of Venezuela's oil in 1976 handled only 50% in 1980. Oil production (1980) 114·4m. tonnes.

Proven reserves in mid-1979 stood at 18,500m. bbls, probable reserves at 15,000m. and possible at 102,000m. However, these are considered conservative estimates and new fields off-shore have estimated reserves of 6,000–40,000m. bbls. The Orinoco tar sands belt has reserves variously estimated at between 700,000m. bbls. and 3,000,000m. bbls.

Gas. Production (1978) 34,842m cu. metres.

Minerals. Bauxite is being exploited in the Guayana region by Bauxien, a state agency. There are important goldmines in the region south-east of Bolívar State, and new deposits have been discovered near El Callao (1959) and Sosa Méndez (1961) in the Guayana region. Output, 1977, amounted to 541 kg. Imports of 7,000 kg per annum are necessary for industrial purposes. Diamond output, from Amazonas territory, was 687,000 carats in 1977. Manganese deposits, estimated at several million tons, were discovered in 1954. Phosphate-rock deposits (yielding from 64 to 82% tricalcium phosphate) are found in the state of Falcón; reserves of 15m. tons of high-quality rock have been established. The state of Sucre has large sulphur deposits. Coal is worked in the states of Táchira, Aragua and Anzoátegui, production in 1977 being 115,000 tonnes. Coal proven reserves in Zulia (160m. tons) are to be developed to service a new thermal power station in the Maracaibo area. An important nickel deposit (at Loma de Hierro near Tejerías) is estimated to equal 600,000 tons of pure nickel. Saltmines are now worked by the Government on the Araya peninsula; output, 1964, 202,000 tonnes. Asbestos and copper pyrite are being exploited.

Iron ore is exploited in Bolívar State by the Orinoco Mining Co. and Iron Mines of Venezuela, subsidiaries respectively of the US Steel Corp. and the Bethlehem Steel Co. Proven reserves at the end of 1963 were 1,513m. tonnes. National output of iron ore, 1977, 14·4m. tonnes.

Agriculture. Venezuela is divided into 3 distinct zones—the agricultural, the pastoral and the forest zone. In the first are grown coffee, cocoa, sugar-cane, maize, rice, wheat (grown in the Andes), tobacco, cotton, beans, sisal, etc.; the second affords grazing for more than 6m. cattle and numerous horses; and in the third, which covers a very large portion of the country, tropical products, such as caoutchouc, balatá (a gum resembling rubber), tonka beans, dividivi, copaiba, vanilla, growing wild, are worked by the inhabitants. The 1981 livestock estimate showed cattle, 10·84m.; pigs, 2·3m.; goats, 1·4m.; sheep, 321,000; poultry, 40m. Area under cultivation is 5,530,898 acres. Agriculture is the weakest sector of the economy, accounting for only 6% of GDP and employing 16·3% of the national workforce. Over 50% of all farmers are engaged in subsistence agriculture and growth rates in agricultural production have not kept pace with the high population increase. Government has introduced a programme of price support, tax incentives and price increases but cattle farming is at present the only profit opportunity.

Production in tonnes in 1978: Coffee, 72,000; maize, 740,000; rice, 600,000, sugar-cane, 5·15m.

The coffee plantations number 62,673, covering 543,400 acres with 135m. bushes. The Venezuelan cocoa, from 13,000 plantations, is considered to be of high quality; it is grown chiefly in the states of Sucre and Miranda. The sugar industry has 6 government and 20 privately owned mills.

Forestry. Resources have been barely tapped; 600 species of wood have been identified. Output of roundwood timber, 1977, broadleaved, 8m. cu. metres.

Fisheries. The fishing industry is to be developed by the provision of port and processing facilities, research and training.

Total catch (1977) was 152·2m. tonnes.

INDUSTRY AND TRADE

Industry. Under the 5th National Plan, ending in 1980, a programme has been undertaken to establish the Guayana integrated industrial complex: by mid-1980, Bs.25,000m. had been invested. Plans involved expanding the capacity of the Guri dam to 9,000 mw as a power supply, raising steel capacity at the Sidor mill from 1·2m. to 4·8m. tonnes per annum (a new steel complex is also to be built in Zulia region) and establishing an integrated aluminium industry in the region.

Aluminio del Caroni (Alcasa) is to increase output from 54,000 to 120,000 tonnes per year, and a new facility, Venezolana de Aluminio (Venalum) is to be installed with a capacity of 280,000 tonnes per year, the largest in Latin America. An alumina factory, Interalumina, is to be built.

The shipbuilding industry is being developed and will become the largest in South America. Venezuela is the biggest and most advanced motor vehicle producer within the Andean Pact, with General Motors, Ford, Jeep, Rover, FIAV (Fiat) and Pegaso all having plants in the country.

Industrial development is concentrated in capital intensive areas where it can have a competitive advantage within the Andean Group, whereas in more labour intensive industries, the low labour costs of other member countries gives them an advantage. However, Venezuela currently produces 90% of its requirements of processed food, beverages, tobacco, clothing and textiles.

Labour. The labour force in 1979 was 4·2m. (including 1·25m. legal immigrants), some 32% of the total population (the low percentage is due to 55% of the population being under 20). 17% of the working population is in the primary sector, 27% in secondary and 56% in tertiary.

Job creation is a high priority in the 6th National Plan, with an aim of 200,000 new jobs per year. Unemployment increased from 4·8% to 6% in 1979. However, official statistics exclude the 3m. *indocumentados* (illegal immigrants) who find work on major construction projects such as the Guri dam.

Wages are the highest in Latin America, there is a high turnover of labour and a corresponding rate of absenteeism.

45% of the labour force is unionized. The most powerful confederation is the CTV (*Confederacion de Trabajadores de Venezuela*, formed 1947), which is dominated by the Accion Democratica party. Estimated membership, 1·1m., claims 2m. Comprises 68 regional and industrial federations with over 6,000 unions, including: FCV (peasants), 700,000; FETRACONS (construction workers), 1m.; FETRASALUD (health workers), 45,000; FETRAMETAL (metal workers and miners), 32,000; the very important FEDEPETROL (oil workers), 6,000; Federacion Venezolana de Maestros (teachers).

Other confederations are CUTV (*Confederacion Unitaria de Trabajadores Venezolanos*, formed 1963). Estimated membership, 40,000, claims 100,000. Comprises 8 regional and 5 industrial federations in 185 local unions; and, CODESA (*Confederacion de Sindicatos Autonomos de Venezuela*, formed 1964). Estimated membership, 10,000, claims 35,000. Dominated by COPEI party. Comprises 120 local unions, including textile, petrol distribution, public health and education workers' federations.

Commerce. Venezuela's exports and imports (in US$1m.):

	1978	*1979*	*1980*	*1981*
Exports	9,174	14,199	19,281	20,100
Imports	11,022	10,837	11,318	12,400

Main export markets in 1978 were USA (Bs.13,949m.), Netherlands Antilles (Bs.8,699m.) because of its oil refining and transhipment facilities, Canada (Bs.4,244m.), Puerto Rico (Bs.2,238m.), Italy (Bs.888m.) and Spain (Bs.715m.).

Principal imports are machinery and equipment, manufactured goods, chemical products, foodstuffs.

The USA supplied imports valued at Bs.17,940m. (40% of all imports) in 1978, followed by Federal Republic of Germany (Bs.4,785m), Japan (Bs.4,004m.), Italy (Bs.2,507m.) and the UK (Bs.1,677m.).

Total trade between UK and Venezuela (British Department of Trade returns, in £1,000 sterling):

	1978	*1979*	*1980*	*1981*	*1982*
Imports to UK	71,684	100,823	117,614	124,020	141,892
Exports and re-exports from UK	188,904	137,722	131,684	125,315	148,666

Tourism. 652,000 tourists visited Venezuela in 1977.

COMMUNICATIONS

Roads. There were, 1983, 61,000 km of road fit for traffic the year round; of these 20,000 km are paved. There are 10,097 km of high-speed 4-lane motorway type. The motorway system runs from Caracas to Puerto Cabello *via* Valencia and will shortly be linked direct with one from La Guaira to Caracas. Venezuela has received two World Bank loans for US$4·5m. and 30m. in connexion with this programme, for improvements of the express-ways in Caracas and for 2 roads in the south-west of the country.

Railways. Plans have existed since 1950 for large-scale railway construction but only the Puerto Cabello to Barquisimeto line (175 km–1,435 mm gauge) has been completed. A metro is under construction in Caracas the first section of which was opened in March 1983.

Aviation. The chief Venezuelan airlines are LAV (Líneas Aéreas Venezolanas), a government-owned concern, and AVENSA (Aerovías Venezolanas). Both operate numerous internal services. VIASA operates international routes in conjunction with KLM. There are also 3 specialist air freight companies. In all there are over 100 commercial aircraft in operation. In addition to Venezuelan international services, a number of US and Latin American and European lines operate services to Venezuela. British Caledonian operates twice-weekly flights between London and Caracas.

Shipping. Foreign vessels are not permitted to engage in the coasting trade, except by special concessions or by contract with the Government. La Guaira, Maracaibo, Puerto Cabello, Puerto Ordaz and Guanta are the chief ports. In Dec. 1978 the merchant fleet had an aggregate gross tonnage of 824,000; this included tankers of 368,000 gross tons.

The principal navigable rivers are the Orinoco and its tributaries Apure and Arauca, from San Fernando to Tucupita through Ciudad Bolívar, Puerto Ordaz and San Félix; San Juan from Carípito to the Gulf of Paria; and Esculante in Lake Maracaibo.

Post and Broadcasting. There were 847,318 telephones in 1978; 98,192 were in Caracas. An international telex service operates in the Caracas metropolitan zone. There is a submarine telephone link with USA.

There are 77 radio stations at Caracas, Maracaibo, Maracay and other towns. There are 3 television stations in Caracas (two privately owned), of which 2 cover, with relays, most of the country. In 1979 there were about 1·9m. homes with TV receivers.

Cinemas (1977). There were 563 cinemas and 25 drive-ins.

Newspapers (1976). There were 47 daily newspapers, 32 weeklies and 134 magazines.

JUSTICE, RELIGION AND EDUCATION

Justice. The Supreme Court, which operates in Divisions, each with 5 members, is elected by Congress for 5 years. The country is divided into 20 legal districts. They select their own President and Vice-President. The Federal Procurator-General is appointed for 5 years. There are lower federal courts.

Each state has a Supreme Court with 3 members, a superior court, or superior tribunal, courts of first instance, district courts and municipal courts. In the territories there are civil and military judges of first instance, and also judges in the municipios. Finally, there is an income-tax claims tribunal.

Religion. The Roman Catholic is the prevailing religion, but there is toleration of all others. There are 4 archbishops, 1 at Caracas, who is Primate of Venezuela, 2 at Mérida and 1 at Ciudad Bolívar. There are 19 bishops. In the state primary schools instruction is given only to those children whose parents expressly request it. Protestants number about 20,000.

Education. Elementary instruction is free and, from the age of 7 to 13 (the completion of the primary grade), compulsory. In 1974–75 Venezuela had 11,098 primary schools with (1976–77) 63,198 teachers and a total enrolment of 2,204,000 pupils. In 1976–77 there were 720,000 pupils in secondary schools and the number of students in higher education was 248,000 with 15,972 teaching staff. There were 14 universities. The education budget for 1982 was Bs. 8m.

DIPLOMATIC REPRESENTATIVES

Of Venezuela in Great Britain (1 Cromwell Rd., London SW7)
Ambassador: Néstor Coll (accredited 16 Dec. 1982).

Of Great Britain in Venezuela (Torre Las Mercedes, Avenida La Estancia, Chuao, Caracas 1060)
Ambassador: Hugh M. Carless, CMG.

Of Venezuela in the USA (2445 Massachusetts Ave., NW, Washington, D.C., 20008)
Ambassador: Marcial Perez-Chiriboga.

Of the USA in Venezuela (Avenida Francisco de Miranda and Avenida Principal de la Floresta, Caracas)
Ambassador: George Landau.

Of Venezuela to the United Nations
Ambassador: Manuel Perez Guerrero.

Books of Reference

Statistical Information: The following are some of the principal publications:
Dirección General de Estadística, Ministerio de Fomento, *Boletín Mensual de Estadística.—Anuario Estadístico de Venezuela, 1978.* Caracas, 1979
Banco Central, *Memoria Annual* and *Boletin Mensual*
Ministerio de Sanidad y Asistencia Social, Dirección de Salud Pública, *Anuario de Epidemiología y Asistencia Social*

Betancourt, R., *Venezuela's Oil.* London, 1978
Bigler, G. E., *Politics and State Capitalism in Venezuela.* Madrid, 1981
Buitrón, A., *Causas y Efectos del Exodo Rural en Venezuela.—Efectos Económicos y Sociales de las Inmigraciones en Venezuela.—Las Inmigraciones en Venezuela.* Pan American Union, Washington, D.C., 1956
Gil Yepes, J. A., *The Challenge of Venezuelan Democracy.* London, 1981
Lieuwen, E., *Venezuela.* Rev. ed. OUP, 1969
Lombard, J., *Venezuelan History: A Comprehensive Working Bibliography.* Boston, 1977
Salazar-Carrillo, J., *Oil in the Economic Development of Venezuela.* New York, 1976
Tugwell, F., *The Politics of Oil in Venezuela.* Stanford Univ. Press, 1975

VIETNAM

Capital: Hanoi
Population: 54m. (1981)
GNP per capita: US$170 (1978)

Công Hòa Xã Hôi Chu Nghĩa Viêt Nam—The Socialist Republic of Vietnam

HISTORY. The recorded history of Vietnam can be traced to Tonkin (now known as the northern part of Vietnam) at the beginning of the Christian era. Conquered by the Chinese (Han dynasty) in B.C. 111, the kingdom of Nam-Viet, as it was then called, broke free of Chinese domination in 939, though at many subsequent periods it again became a nominal vassal of the Chinese emperors.

By the end of the 15th century the Vietnamese had conquered most of the kingdom of Champa (in Annam, now known as the central part of Vietnam) and by the end of the 18th had acquired Cochin-China (now known as the southern part of Vietnam), formerly Cambodian territory.

French interest in Vietnam started in the late 16th century with the arrival of French and Portuguese missionaries. The most notable of these was Alexander of Rhodes, who, in the following century, romanized Vietnamese writing. At the end of the 18th century a French bishop and several soldiers of fortune helped to establish the Emperor Gia-Long (with whom Louis XVI had signed a treaty in 1787) as ruler of a unified Vietnam, known then as the Empire of Annam.

An expedition sent by Napoleon III in 1858 to avenge the death of some French missionaries led in 1862 to the cession to France of part of Cochin-China, and thence, by a series of treaties between 1874 and 1884, to the establishment of French protectorates over Tonkin and Annam, and to the formation of the French colony of Cochin-China. By a Sino-French treaty of 1885 the Empire of Annam (including Tonkin) ceased to be tributary to China. Cambodia had become a French protectorate in 1863, and in 1899, after extension of French protection to Laos in 1893, the Indo-Chinese Union was proclaimed.

In 1940 Vietnam was occupied by the Japanese and used as a military base for the invasion of Malaya. During the occupation there was considerable underground activity among nationalist, revolutionary and Communist organizations. In 1941 a nominally nationalist coalition of such organizations, known as the Vietminh League, was founded by the Communists.

On 9 March 1945 the Japanese interned the French authorities and proclaimed the 'independence' of Indo-China. In Aug. 1945 they allowed the Vietminh movement to seize power, dethrone Bao Dai, the Emperor of Annam, and establish a republic known as Vietnam, including Tonkin, Annam and Cochin-China, with Hanoi as capital. In Sept. 1945 the French re-established themselves in Cochin-China and on 6 March 1946, after a cease-fire in the sporadic fighting between the French forces and the Vietminh had been arranged, a preliminary convention was signed in Hanoi between the French High Commissioner and President Ho Chi Minh by which France recognized 'the Democratic Republic of Vietnam' as a 'Free State within the Indo-Chinese Federation'. Subsequent conferences convened in the same year at Dalat and Fontainebleau to draft a definitive agreement broke down chiefly over the question of whether or not Cochin-China should be included in the new republic. On 19 Dec. 1946 Vietminh forces made a surprise attack on Hanoi, the signal for hostilities which were to last for nearly 8 years.

An agreement signed by Emperor Bao Dai on behalf of Vietnam on 8 March 1949 recognized the independence of Vietnam within the French Union, and certain sovereign powers were forthwith transferred to Vietnam. The Paris agreements of 29 Dec. 1954 completed the transfer of sovereignty to Vietnam. Supreme authority in the military field remained with the French until the departure of the last French C.-in-C. in April 1956. Treaties of independence and association were initialled by representatives of the French and Vietnamese governments on 4 June 1954.

An agreement on the cessation of hostilities in Vietnam was reached on 20 July 1954 at the Geneva conference. The agreement was signed on behalf of the C.-in-C. of the French Forces in Indo-China and on behalf of the C.-in-C. of the People's Army of Vietnam. The Government of Vietnam did not sign the agreement.

The final declaration of the Geneva conference (21 July 1954) declared that general elections should take place in July 1956. These did not take place, and Vietnam remained divided until 1976.

In Paris on 27 Jan. 1973 an agreement was signed ending the war in Vietnam. After the US withdrawal, however, hostilities continued between the North and the South until the latter's defeat in 1975 . President Thieu resigned on 21 April. Gen. Duong Van Minh surrendered to the Communist forces on 30 April. 150,000–200,000 South Vietnamese fled the country, including the former President Thieu.

For details of the former Republic of Vietnam (South Vietnam), see THE STATESMAN'S YEAR-BOOK, 1975–76. After the collapse of President Thieu's regime the Provisional Revolutionary Government established an administration in Saigon on 6 June 1975 under the presidency of Huynh Tan Phat. A North–South conference on reunification of Nov. 1975 announced that agreement on 'the basic problems' had been reached. A general election was held on 25 April 1976 for a National Assembly representing the whole country. Voting was by universal suffrage of all citizens of 18 or over, except former functionaries of South Vietnam undergoing 're-education'. The unification of North and South Vietnam into the Socialist Republic of Vietnam took place formally on 2 July 1976. After previous US vetoes the new administration of President Carter indicated that it was not opposed to Vietnam's application to join the UN, and Vietnam was admitted unanimously and without a vote on 20 Sept. 1977. In June 1978 Vietnam was admitted to Comecon and in Nov. 1978 signed a 25-year treaty of friendship and co-operation with the USSR. Relations with China correspondingly deteriorated, an especially exacerbating factor being the successful Vietnamese military intervention in Kampuchea. On 17 Feb. 1979 China invaded North Vietnam, but claimed that its troops had all withdrawn by 19 March. Peace negotiations were commenced on 18 April 1979 but broken off by the Chinese on 6 March 1980. The Government announced it had suppressed an armed insurrection in the South in Nov. 1982.

AREA AND POPULATION. The country has a total area of 329,566 sq. km and is divided administratively into 36 provinces and 1 special area. Areas and populations (in 1,000) at the census of Oct. 1979 were as follows:

Province	*Sq. km*	*1979*	*Province*	*Sq. km*	*1979*
Lai Chau	17,408	322,077	Gia Lai – Kon Tum	18,480	595,906
Son La	14,656	487,793	Dac Lac	18,300	490,198
Hoang Lien Son	14,125	778,217	Phu Khanh	9,620	1,188,637
Ha Tuyen	13,519	782,453	Lam Dong	10,000	396,657
Cao Bang	13,731	479,823	Thuan Hai	11,000	938,255
Lang Son		484,657	Dong Nai	12,130	1,304,799
Bac Thai	8,615	815,105	Song Be	9,500	659,093
Quang Ninh	7,076	750,055	Tay Ninh	4,100	684,006
Vinh Phu	5,187	1,488,348	Long An	5,100	957,264
Ha Bac	4,708	1,662,671	Dong Thap	3,120	1,182,787
Ha Son Binh	6,860	1,537,190	Thanh Pho –		
Hanoi (city)[1]	597	2,570,905	Ho Chi Minh[1]	1,845	3,419,978
Hai Hung	2,526	2,145,662	Tien Giang	2,350	1,264,498
Thai Binh	1,344	1,506,235	Ben Tre	2,400	1,041,838
Hai Phong (city)[1]	1,515	1,279,067	Cuu Long	4,200	1,504,215
Ha Nam Ninh	3,522	2,781,409	An Giang	4,140	1,532,362
Thanh Hoa	11,138	2,532,261	Hau Giang	5,100	2,232,891
Nghe Tinh	22,380	3,111,989	Kien Giang	6,000	994,673
Binh Tri Thien	19,048	1,901,713	Minh Hai	8,000	1,219,595
Quang Nam – Da Nang	11,376	1,529,520	Vung Tau – Con Dao[2]	—	91,160
Nghia Binh	14,700	2,095,354			
				329,466	52,741,766

[1] Autonomous city. [2] Special area

At the census of Oct. 1979 the population was 52,741,766 (25,580,582 male; 19·7% urban).

Population (1981), 54m. (Ho Chi Minh 3·5m.; Hanoi, 2m. (1979); growth rate (1980) 2·9% per annum.

84% of the population are Vietnamese (Kinh). There are also over 60 minority groups thinly spread in the extensive mountainous regions. The largest minorities are (1976 figures in 1,000): Tay (742); Khmer (651); Thai (631); Muong (618); Nung (472); Meo (349); Dao (294). In 1981 0·5m. Vietnamese were living abroad, mainly in USA.

From 1979 to 30 Sept. 1982 22,132 persons emigrated legally. Between Apr. 1975 and Sept. 1982 a further 501,036 'boat people' succeeded in finding refuge aborad. (For previous details *see* THE STATESMAN'S YEAR-BOOK, 1981–82).

CONSTITUTION AND GOVERNMENT. A new Constitution was adopted in Dec. 1980. It states that Vietnam is a state of proletarian dictatorship and is developing according to Marxism–Leninism. The former, second, North Vietnamese Constitution dated from 1960 (the first was promulgated in 1946).

At the elections for the new National Assembly held on 26 April 1981. 613 candidates stood and 496 were elected. 70% of the candidates were standing for the first time.

Local government authorities are the people's councils, which appoint executive committees. Local elections were held in Ho Chi Minh City and the 38 provinces of the former South Vietnam on 5 May 1977.

The 1980 Constitution replaced the Presidency with the State Council, 'the standing organ of the National Assembly and presidium of the Republic'.

Chairman: Truong Chinh. *Vice-Chairmen:* Nguyen Huu Tho, Le Thanh Nghi, Chu Huy Man, Huynh Tan Phat. The *Prime Minister* is the Chairman of the Council of Ministers, Pham Van Dong.

Chairman of the National Assembly: Nguyen Huu Tho.

All political power stems from the Communist Party of Vietnam (until Dec. 1976 known as the Workers' Party of Vietnam), founded in 1930; it had 1m. members in Dec. 1979 (8·8% workers; 17% women). In April 1983 the Politburo consisted of Le Duan *(First Secretary)*; Truong Chinh; Pham Van Dong; Pham Hung *(Deputy Prime Minister and Minister of the Interior)*; Le Duc Tho; Gen. Van Tien Dung *(Minister of Defence)*; Vo Chi Cong; Gen. Chu Huy Man; To Huu *(First Deputy Prime Minister)*; Vo Van Kiet *(Deputy Prime Minister and Chairman, State Planning Commission)*; Do Muoi *(Deputy Prime Minister)* Le Duc Anh; Nguyen Duc Tam. Candidate members: Nguyen Co Thach *(Foreign Minister)*; Dong Si Nguyen *(Deputy Prime Minister)*. Ministers not in the Politburo include: Vo Nguyen Giap; Tran Quynh; Vu Dinh Lieu; Tran Phuong *(Deputy Prime Ministers)*; Chu Tham Phuc *(Finance)*; Le Khac *(Foreign Trade)*; Le Duc Thinh *(Home Trade)*; Dong Si Nguyen *(Transport)*; Mme. Nguyen Thi Binh *(Education)*; Nguyen Ngoc Triu *(Agriculture)*; Phan Hien *(Justice)*.

There are 2 puppet parties, the Democratic (founded 1944) and the Socialist (1946), which are unified with the trade and youth unions in the Fatherland Front.

National flag: Red, with a yellow 5-pointed star in the centre.
National anthem: 'Tien quan ca' ('The troops are advancing').

DEFENCE. Conscription is for 3 years at age 18.

Army. Estimated strength in 1983, 1m. organized in 48 infantry divisions (plus 2 training divisions), 2 artillery divisions, 1 armoured regiment, 1 AA division, about 15 independent infantry regiments and 35 independent artillery regiments. There are also 25 SAM regiments and 50 independent AA artillery regiments.

Navy. Before the North Vietnamese victory in 1975 the Navy comprised 3 old coastal escorts, 2 fast missile boats, 28 fast torpedo boats, 22 fast motor gunboats, 34 small patrol boats, 24 landing craft, 4 minesweeping boats, 10 tenders, 100 auxiliaries and 200 armed junks. It also had 10 Mi-4 SAR helicopters.

At least 1 frigate, several other major warships and a considerable number of auxiliaries were captured after the South Vietnamese surrender.

The fleet reportedly includes 4 new *ex*-Soviet escorts, 2 old frigates, 2 old corvettes, 1 minesweeper, 3 old submarine chasers, 8 fast missile boats, 8 fast torpedo boats, 8 fast gunboats, 4 patrol craft, 7 landing ships, 7 landing craft, 1 torpedo recovery vessel, 15 riverine craft, 24 minesweeping launches, 1 survey ship, 15 auxiliaries and 100 armed junks; but due to the lack of maintenance, spares and trials it is difficult to accurately assess the operational availability, fitness for sea or steaming capacity of this heterogeneous collection or the availability of trained personnel.

It is estimated that 3 missile craft, 6 torpedo boats, 22 gunboats, 4 minesweepers, 24 patrol craft, 25 coastguard cutters, 100 motor launches are non-operational together with 510 riverine craft, 125 landing craft, 30 monitors, 100 converted amphibious craft, 26 vedettes, 34 auxiliaries and 75 service craft.

Air Force. The Air Force, built up with Soviet and Chinese assistance, has about 25,000 personal and 450 combat aircraft (many stored), including modern US types captured in war. There are reported to be 2 squadrons of variable-geometry MiG-23s, 7 squadrons of MiG-17s, 4 squadrons of Su-7s and Su-20s, 2 or 3 squadrons of Northrop F-5A/Es and Cessna A-37s for attack duties; about 180 MiG-21 and 60 J-6 (Chinese-built MiG-19) interceptors; up to 70 C-130 Hercules, An-2, An-12, Li-2, An-24, and Il-14 transports; and a strong helicopter force with CH-47 Chinook, UH-1 Iroquois, Mi-4, Mi-6 and Mi-8 helicopters. Fighter pilots are trained in the USSR. 'Guideline', 'Goa' and 'Gainful' missiles are operational in large numbers.

INTERNATIONAL RELATIONS

Membership. Vietnam is a member of UN, Comecon and IMF.

ECONOMY

Planning. Long-term forward planning gives priority to creating self-sufficiency in agriculture before progressing to further industrialization. Targets for the second 5-year plan 1976–80) were not met. Growth in agriculture, 18·7%; industry, 17·3%. The third 5-year plan covers 1981–85. An agreement co-ordinating this plan with the current Soviet plan was signed with the USSR in July 1981.

Curtailment of imports, floods and resistance to new economic measures have contributed to a serious shortage of consumer goods, which it is hoped to correct by stimulating regional industry and utilizing the expertise of former businessmen. (For previous plans *see* THE STATESMAN'S YEAR-BOOK, 1976–77, p. 1473.)

Currency. The monetary unit is the *dong* = 10 *hao*, the *hao* = 10 *xu*. There are coins of 1, 2 and 5 *xu*, 1, 2 and 5 *hao*, 1 *dong*; and notes of 1, 2, 5, 10, 20, 30, 50 and 100 *dong*. In March 1983, £1 = 3·23 *dong*; US$1 = 2·18 *dong*.

Banking. The bank of issue is the National Bank of Vietnam (founded in 1951). There is also a Bank for Foreign Trade (Vietcombank). In 1980 this bank ceased all transactions with US banks.

ENERGY AND NATURAL RESOURCES

Electricity. In 1980, 368m. kwh. of electricity were produced. A hydro-electric power station with a capacity of 2m. kw. is being built at Hoa-Binh with Soviet assistance.

Minerals. North Vietnam is rich in anthracite, lignite and hard coal: total reserves are estimated at 20,000m. tonnes. Anthracite production in 1975 was 5m. tonnes. Coal production was 5·3m. tonnes in 1980. There are deposits of iron ore, manganese, titanium, chromite, bauxite and a little gold. Chromite production in 1962 was 35,000 tons. Reserves of apatite are some of the biggest in the world. Estimated production of phosphates in 1971, 1·1m. tonnes; salt, 150,000 tonnes. In 1973 and 1974 the former Vietnamese Government awarded concessions for offshore oil exploration but Western companies have pulled out of exploration in Vietnam as uneconomic. There are large limestone deposits in Kien Giang, Chau Doc and Thua Thien provinces. A recent geological survey reported on the prospects of valuable bauxite deposits. There is a small coal-bearing region at Nong-Son.

Agriculture. In 1980, 71% of the population was engaged in agriculture. . In the North in 1975 agricultural co-operatives were reorganized into larger units. (Previously there had been about 18,000 co-operatives, each comprising 200–400 households and averaging 200 hectares of land each.) In 1977 there were 15,200 co-operatives in the North averaging 300–500 hectares (less than 100 hectares in mountain regions) and a workforce of 1,000–2,000. There were 105 state farms employing in all 70,000 workers and with 55,000 hectares arable and 50,000 hectares of pasture. Other crops include maize, sugar-cane, sweet potatoes and cotton. The cultivated area in 1980 was 6·97m. hectares (5·54m. hectares for rice); in 1964, 2·4m. hectares were irrigated.

In the South to redress the disproportionate urbanization of the southern population during the war (40% of the population were living in Ho Chi Minh City by April 1975) resettlement of family units in rural areas began after the Communist take-over. Each family was allotted an average of 5,000 sq. metres of land, a dwelling and agricultural equipment. 1,000 sq. metres of this total are for private plots. Families are grouped by twenties in 'mutual aid and labour cells'. In 1972, 83,300 hectares produced 20,000 tonnes of rubber. In 1977 there were 74 state farms and a few experimental co-operatives.

Production in 1,000 tonnes in 1980: Soybeans (32), tea (21), rubber (45), cereals (13,520), maize (475), oil seed plants (595), tobacco (15·6), potatoes (684). (1979) sweet potatoes (from 380,000 hectares), sorghum (35) from 30,000 hectares), beans (45) from 93,000 hectares), coffee (15). The main crop is rice. Production was some 11·69m. tonnes in 1980, 4·4m. tonnes short of requirements.

Livestock (1980): Cattle 1·3m.; pigs, 9·4m.; goats, 200,000; poultry, 87·5m.

Animal products, 1980: Eggs, 1,129m., meat, 427,000 tonnes.

Forestry. 1,626,000 cu. metres of timber were produced in 1980.

Fisheries. Fishing is important, especially in Halong Bay. In 1976, 6m. tonnes of sea fish and 180,000 tonnes of freshwater fish were caught (representing only 83% of the planned target.)

INDUSTRY AND TRADE

Industry. Next to mining, food processing and textiles are the most important industries; there is also some machine building. Older industries include cement, cotton and silk manufacture. Local industries and handicrafts account for 50% of production.

Private businesses were taken over in 1978. Foreign firms, principally French, are continuing to function, but all US property has been nationalized. There is little heavy industry. Most industry is concentrated in the Ho-Chi-Minh area.

Production (1980, in 1,000 tonnes) iron, 125; steel, 106; sulphuric acid, 6,700; caustic soda, 4,500; mineral fertilizer, 260; pesticides, 18,400; paper, 54,000; sugar, 94,000, cement, 705. 1,500 tractors were built in 1980, and 621 railway coaches. Shoe productions, 200,000 pairs. Beer, 942,000 hectolitres.
Kenaf yarn production was 1,615 tons in 1972.

Labour. Average wage (1980) 40–60 dong per month. Non-agricultural workforce (1980) 3,587,000, of whom 2,238,000 in industry.

Commerce. USSR and Japan are Vietnam's main trading partners; others are Singapore and Hong Kong. Main exports are coal, farm produce, sea produce and livestock. Imports: technical equipment, industrial raw materials, foodstuffs and medical supplies. The Vietnamese Government recognizes a need for foreign aid and credit for the development of an industrial base. An aid agreement was reached with the USSR in Sept. 1981 for 5 years under which the USSR will participate in

40 construction projects and oil exploration in exchange for foodstuffs. By 1981 Sweden was the only Western country to give any significant aid. In 1982 Vietnam's total indebtedness was estimated at US$3,000m. In 1978 the IMF approved a virtually interest-free loan of US$90m. repayable over 50 years, but in July 1982 refused Vietnam's request for US$150m. in Special Drawing Rights until there are reforms in the economy. Foreign investments are encouraged and guaranteed for 15 years. Profits may be transferred and indemnities paid in the event of nationalization. In the case of foreign firms installed in Vietnam all capital may remain in foreign hands if goods are produced for export only; otherwise the Vietnamese Government will retain 51% of shares.

Trade between Vietnam and UK (British Department of Trade returns, in £1,000 sterling):

	1979	*1980*	*1981*	*1982*
Imports to UK	40	70	130	133
Exports and re-exports from UK	5,889	15,203	1,180	876

COMMUNICATIONS

Roads. In 1973 there were about 9,500 km of roads in the North. In 1970 there were 20,905 km of roads in the South. Of these, 5,908 km were asphalted.

Railways. 'Project Reunification', the rebuilding of the Hanoi–Ho Chi Minh City railway, is a major part of the new authorities' programme to repair and extend all communications systems and link them with the North. The Da Nang–Hue railway was reopened in 1975. Important sections of railway have been reconstructed rapidly since the cessation of hostilities in 1975, and through trains commenced running again between Hanoi and Ho Chi Minh City in Jan. 1977. The systems total 2,600 km.

Aviation. Civil Aviation of Vietnam operates internal services from Hanoi to Ho Chi Minh City, Cao Bang, Na Son and Dien Bien, Vinh and Hue, and from Ho Chi Minh City to Ban Me Thuot and Da Nang, Can Tho, Con Son Island and Quan Long.

Aeroflot (USSR) operate regular services from Ho Chi Min City to Moscow and from Hanoi to Moscow, Rangoon and Vientiane, Interflug (German Dem. Rep.) to Berlin, Moscow and Dacca and Air France to Paris.

Shipping. The major ports are Haiphong, which can handle ships of 10,000 tons, Ho Chi Minh City and Da Nang, and there are ports at Hong Gai and Haiphong Ben Thuy. There are regular services to Hong Kong, Singapore, Kampuchea and Japan. In 1953 there were 830 km of navigable waterways in the North and, in 1971, 4,783 km in the South.

Cargo is handled by the Vietnam Ocean Shipping Agency; other matters by the Vietnam Foreign Trade Transport Corporation.

Post and Broadcasting. In 1966 there were 1·4m. radios. There were 46,509 telephones in the South in 1974. There were 2m. TV sets in 1980.

Cinemas and theatres. 116 films were produced in 1980 (including 10 full-length). There were 145 theatres.

Newspapers and books. The Party daily is *Nhan Dan* ('The People') circulation, 1981: 200,000. The official daily in the South is *Giai Phong.* Two unofficial dailies, *Cong Giao Va Dan Toc* (Catholic) and *Tin Sang* (independent) are also published. 2,564 books were published in 1980 totalling 90·9m. copies.

JUSTICE, RELIGION, EDUCATION AND WELFARE

Justice. There are the Supreme People's Court, local people's courts and military courts. The president of the Supreme Court is responsible to the National Assembly, as is the Procurator-General, who heads the Supreme People's Office of Supervision and Control.

Religion. Taoism is the traditional religion but Buddhism is widespread. At a Conference for Buddhist Reunification in Nov. 1981, 9 sects adopted a charter for a new Buddhist church under the Council of Sangha. The Hoa Hao sect, associated with Buddhism, claimed 1·5m. adherents in 1976. Caodaism, a synthesis of Christianity, Buddhism and Confucianism founded in 1926, has some 2m. followers. There are some 5·3m. Roman Catholics headed by Cardinal Trinh Van Can, Archbishop of Hanoi and 13 bishops.

Education. Primary education consists of a 10-year course divided into 3 levels of 4, 3 and 3 years respectively. Numbers of pupils and students in 1980–81: nurseries, 2·66m.; primary schools, 12·1m.; complementary education, 2·19m.; vocational secondary education, 0·13m. In 1980–1 there were 92,913 nurseries. There were 11,400 schools and 280 vocational secondary schools, with 357,000 and 13,000 teachers respectively.

In 1980–81 there were 83 institutions of higher education (including 3 universities: (Hanoi, Ho Chi Minh City, Central Highlands University at Ban Me Thuot), 13 industrial colleges, 7 agricultural colleges, 5 economics colleges, 9 teacher-training colleges, 7 medical schools and 3 art schools, in all with 16,000 teachers and 159,000 students. In 1981 there were 5,000 Vietnamese studying in the USSR.

Health. In 1975 there were 1,996 hospitals and dispensaries and 93 sanatoria. There were some 13,300 doctors and dentists in 1980 and 197,000 hospital beds.

DIPLOMATIC REPRESENTATIVES

Of Vietnam in Great Britain (12–14 Victoria Rd, London, W8)
Ambassador: Dang Nghiem (accredited 5 Nov. 1982).

Of Great Britain in Vietnam (16 Pho Ly Thuong Kiet, Hanoi)
Ambassador: M. E. Pike.

Of Vietnam to the United Nations
Ambassador: Hoany Bich Son.

Books of Reference

Chen, J. H.-M., *Vietnam: A Comprehensive Bibliography.* London, 1973
Duiker, W. J., *The Communist Road to Power in Vietnam.* Boulder, 1981
Féray, P.-R., *Le Vietnam au Vingtième Siècle.* Paris, 1979
Goodman, A. E., *The Lost Peace: America's Search for a Negotiated Settlement of the Vietnam War.* Stanford Univ. Press, 1978
Hodgkin, T., *Vietnam: The Revolutionary Path:* London, 1981
Le Thanh Khoi, *Socialisme et Développement au Vietnam.* Paris, 1978
Le Van Hung, *Vietnamese–English Dictionary.* Paris, 1955
Lewy, G., *America in Vietnam.* OUP, 1979
Leitenberg, M., and Burns, R. D., *War in Vietnam.* 2nd ed. Oxford and Santa Barbara, 1982
Nguyen Tien Hung, C., *Economic Developments of Socialist Vietnam, 1955–80.* New York, 1977
Popkin, S. L., *The Rational Peasant: The Political Economy of Rural Society in Vietnam.* Berkeley, 1979
Viet Tran, *J'ai Choisi l'Exil.* Paris, 1979
Voronin, A. S. and Ognetov, I. A. *Sotsialisticheskaia Respublika V'etnam: Spravochnik.* (2nd ed). Moscow, 1981

BRITISH VIRGIN ISLANDS

Capital: Road Town
Population: 12,034 (1980)

HISTORY. The Virgin Islands were discovered by Colombus on his second voyage in 1493. The British Virgin Islands were first settled by the Dutch in 1648 and taken over in 1666 by a group of English planters.

AREA AND POPULATION. The British Virgin Islands form the eastern extremity of the Greater Antilles and, exclusive of small rocks and reefs, number 36, of which 16 are inhabited. The largest are Tortola (1980 population, 9,322), Virgin Gorda (1,443), Anegada (169) and Jost Van Dyke (136). Other islands in the group have a total population of 82; Marine population, 220; Institutional population, 662. Total area about 59 sq. miles (130 sq. km); population (1980), 12,034. Road Town, on the south-east of Tortola, is a port of entry; population, approximately 3,976.

CONSTITUTION AND GOVERNMENT. The Governor is responsible for defence and internal security, external affairs, the public service, and the courts. The Executive Council consists of the Governor, 1 *ex-officio* member who is the Attorney-General and 4 ministers in the Legislature. The Legislative Council consists of 1 *ex-officio* member who is the Attorney-General and 9 elected members, one of whom is the Chief Minister and Minister of Finance; the Speaker is elected from outside the Council.

Governor: David Robert Barwick, CBE, QC.
Chief Minister: H. Lavity Stoutt.
Flag: The British Blue Ensign with the arms of the Territory in the fly.

ECONOMY

Planning. The Peebles Hospital extension and the Virgin Gorda primary school have been formally opened, work on Road Town Primary School started in Sept., 1982, and there are continuing Youth and Community Development projects. Work on the Slaney Point Sewerage outfall is nearing completion. Phase I of the West End Harbour Extension Development is also nearing completion and the new Police Building on Virgin Gorda and the new Administration Building on Jost Van Dyke have been formally opened.

Budget. In 1983 revenue (estimate) was US$17,447,000 Capital expenditure (estimate) was US$ 16,670,063.

Currency. The unit of currency is the US dollar.

Banking. Barclays Bank International, the First Pennsylvania Bank, the Bank of Nova Scotia and the Chase Manhattan Bank have branches in the islands. There are also a large number of Trust Companies.

INDUSTRY AND TRADE

Industry. Agricultural production is now very limited with the chief products being livestock (including poultry), fish, fruit and vegetables. The export trade is carried on almost entirely with the Virgin Islands of the USA. The main industry is tourism and related activities, notably construction.

Livestock (1981): Cattle, 3,000; pigs, 3,000; sheep, 8,000; goats, 12,000.

Trade. In 1980 imports were US$36m. and exports US$1,087,000.

Tourism. There were 173,000 visitors in 1980.

COMMUNICATIONS

Roads. There were (1983) over 66 miles of roads and 3,000 licensed vehicles.

Aviation. Beef Island Airport, about 16 km from Road Town, is capable of receiving 48-seat turbo-prop aircraft. Air BVI operates internal services and external flights to the USVI, St Kitts, Antigua and Puerto Rico. Also, operating services to the BVI are Coral Air, Crown Air and LIAT.

Shipping. There are services to Europe and the USA, and daily services by motor launches to the US Virgin Islands.

Post and Broadcasting. There were (1983) over 2,000 telephones, and an external telephone service links Tortola with Bermuda and the rest of the world, and cable communications also exist to all parts of the world. Radio ZBVI transmits 10,000 watts and has stand-by transmitting facilities of 1,000 watts. Cable and Wireless, also, operates reception of approximately 7 television channels plus a number of FM stereo broadcasting stations.

RELIGION, EDUCATION AND WELFARE

Religion. There are Anglican, Methodist, Seventh-Day Adventist, Roman Catholic and Baptist Churches in the Territory. The Church of God is also represented.

Education. Primary education is provided in 16 government schools, one with a secondary division, 1 secondary school and 9 private schools. Total number of pupils (Dec. 1980) 2,748.

Secondary education to the GCE level and Caribbean Examination Council level is provided at the B.V.I. High School. Total pupils in Dec. 1980, 791.

In 1980 the total number of teachers in all the schools was 170.

Health. In 1982 there were 13 doctors and more than 50 hospital beds. Expenditure, 1983 was US$1,950,100.

Books of Reference

Dookhan, I., *A History of the British Virgin Islands.* Epping, 1975
Elkan, W., and Morley, R., *Employment in a Tourist Economy, British Virgin Islands*
Harrigan, N., and Varlack, P., *British Virgin Islands: A Chronology*

Library: Public Library, Road Town. *Librarian:* Miss Verna Penn, ALA.

WESTERN SAMOA

Capital: Apia
Population: 157,000 (1978)
GNP per capita: US$350 (1976)

Samoa i Sisifo

HISTORY. Western Samoa, a former German protectorate (1900 to the First World War), was administered by New Zealand from 1920 to 1961, at first under a League of Nations Mandate and since 1946 under a United Nations Trusteeship Agreement. In May 1961 a plebiscite held under the supervision of the United Nations on the basis of universal adult suffrage voted overwhelmingly in favour of independence as from 1 Jan. 1962, on the basis of the Constitution, which a Constitutional Convention had adopted in Aug. 1960. In Oct. 1961 the General Assembly of the United Nations passed a resolution to terminate the trusteeship agreement as from 1 Jan. 1962, on which date Western Samoa became an independent sovereign state.

Under a treaty of friendship signed on 1 Aug. 1962 New Zealand acts, at the request of Western Samoa, as the official channel of communication between the Samoan Government and other governments and international organizations outside the Pacific islands area. Liaison is maintained by the New Zealand High Commissioner in Apia, who is the only diplomatic representative accredited to the Government of Western Samoa.

AREA AND POPULATION. Western Samoa lies between 13° and 15° S. lat. and 171° and 173° W. long. It comprises the two large islands of Savai'i and Upolu, the small islands of Manono and Apolima, and several uninhabited islets lying off the coast. The total land area is 1,093 sq. miles (2,830·8 sq. km), of which 659·4 sq. miles (1,707·8 sq. km) are in Savai'i, and 431·5 sq. miles (1,117·6 sq. km) in Upolu; other islands, 2·1 sq. miles (5·4 sq. km). The islands are of volcanic origin, and the coasts are surrounded by coral reefs. Rugged mountain ranges form the core of both main islands and rise to 3,608 ft in Upolu and 6,094 ft in Savai'i. The large area laid waste by lava-flows in Savai'i is a primary cause of that island supporting less than one-third of the population of the islands despite its greater size than Upolu.

The population at the 1976 census was 151,983, of whom 109,765 were in Upolu (including Manono and Apolima) and 42,218 in Savai'i. The capital and chief port is Apia in Upolu (population 32,099 in 1976).

CONSTITUTION AND GOVERNMENT. The Constitution provides for a Head of State known as 'Ao o le Malo', which position from 1 Jan. 1962 was held jointly by the representatives of the two royal lines of Tuiaana/Tuiatua and Malietoa. On the death of HH Tupua Tamasese Mea'ole, CBE, on 5 April 1963, HH Malietoa Tanumafili II, CBE, became, as provided by the constitution, the sole Head of State for life. Future Heads of State will be elected by the Legislative Assembly and hold office for 5-year terms.

The executive power is vested in the Head of State, who appoints the Prime Minister and, on the Prime Minister's advice, the 8 Ministers to form the Cabinet which has general direction and control of the executive Government.

Parliament comprises the Head of State and the Legislative Assembly. The Legislative Assembly has 45 members elected from territorial constituencies on a franchise confined to matais or chiefs (of whom there are about 11,000) and 2 members elected on universal adult suffrage from the individual voters roll, which has replaced the old European roll (approximately 1,350 in 1971).

The Constitution also provides for a Council of Deputies. It may have 3 members. The only present member is the Hon. Tupua Tamasese Lealofi IV, who assumed the position in 1976.

The official languages are English and Samoan.

Head of State: HH Malietoa Tanumafili II, CBE.
Prime Minister: Tupuola Efi.
National flag: Red with a blue quarter bearing 5 white stars of the Southern Cross.

INTERNATIONAL RELATIONS

Membership. Western Samoa is a member of UN, the Commonwealth and is an ACP state of EEC.

ECONOMY

Budget. In 1980 budgeted revenue was $WS31·4m.; expenditure, $WS22·7m.; statutory expenditure, $WS3·1.

Currency. On 10 July 1966 Western Samoa changed over to decimal currency. The Western Samoa *talà* (dollar) is at parity with the NZ dollar, equally £0·50. Currency in circulation consists of Samoan Treasury notes and coins.

Banking. In 1959 the Bank of Western Samoa was established with a capital of $WS500,000, of which $WS275,000 was subscribed by the Bank of New Zealand and $WS225,000 by the Government of Western Samoa. In 1977 the Pacific Commercial Bank was established jointly by Australia's Bank of New South Wales and the Bank of Hawaii.

NATURAL RESOURCES

Agriculture. The main products are coconuts, cacao, taro and bananas.

Fisheries. The total catch (1977) was 1,270 tonnes.

INDUSTRY AND TRADE

Industry. Some industrial activity is being developed associated with agricultural products and forestry.

Commerce. In 1979, imports were valued at $WS52,794,811 and exports at $WS15,027,494. Principal exports were copra (18,517 tons; $WS8,728,038), cocoa (1,588 tons; $WS3,644,144), taro 126,030 cases, $WS1,186,543), timber (1,498,857 bd ft; $WS265,700), and bananas (33,454 cases; $WS151,919). Chief imports in 1979 included meat ($WS3,166,300), petroleum ($WS5,739,100) and machinery and transport equipment ($WS21,918,200).

Total trade between Western Samoa and UK (British Department of Trade returns, in £1,000 sterling):

	1977	*1978*	*1979*	*1980*	*1981*	*1982*
Imports to UK	776	567	837	572	90	107
Exports and re-exports from UK	609	719	619	710	431	285

Tourism. There were 26,114 visitors in 1977.

COMMUNICATIONS

Roads (1979). Western Samoa has over 246 miles of main roads, 251 miles of municipal secondary and village roads and 772 miles of plantation roads fit for light traffic.

A major road development programme has been under way including an all weather coastal road and a cross-island road, both for Upolu. A rural access roads programme to improve access to plantations is also underway. In 1979 there were 1,573 passenger cars and 2,203 commercial vehicles.

Aviation. Western Samoa is linked by daily air service with American Samoa, which is on the route of the weekly New Zealand–Tahiti and New Zealand–

Honolulu air services, with connexions to Fiji, Australia, USA and Europe. There are also services throughout the week to and from Tonga, Fiji, Nauru, the Cook Islands and New Zealand. Internal services link Upolu and Savai'i.

Shipping. Western Samoa is linked to Japan, USA, Europe, Fiji, Australia and New Zealand by regular shipping services. The newly established Pacific Forum Shipping Line has its headquarters in Apia.

Post and Broadcasting. There is a radio communication station at Apia. Radio telephone service connects Western Samoa with American Samoa, Fiji, New Zealand, Australia, Canada, USA and UK. Telephone subscribers numbered 5,066 in 1980.

Cinemas. In 1977 there were 10 cinemas with a seating capacity of 7,168.

Newspapers. In 1981, there were 8 weeklies, circulation 24,500 and 2 fortnightlies (14,500); all were in Samoan and English.

EDUCATION AND WELFARE

Education. In 1979 there were 153 primary, 150 intermediate and 39 secondary schools with a total of 51,792 pupils. There is also a trades training institute, a teacher-training college, a broadcasting training centre and a college of agriculture.

Health. In 1979 there were 30 hospitals (674 beds) and 65 doctors.

DIPLOMATIC REPRESENTATIVES

Of Great Britain in Western Samoa
High Commissioner: Sir Richard Stratton, KCMG (resides in Wellington, New Zealand).

Of Western Samoa in the USA and also to the United Nations
Ambassador: Maiava Iulai Toma.

Books of Reference

Statistical Year-Book. 1976
Economic Prospects. 1978
The Economy of Western Samoa. 1968
Clare, B. L., *A Review of Social, Labour and Economic Conditions in Western Samoa.* Apia, 1962, reprinted 1963.—*The Parliament of Western Samoa.* Rev. ed. Apia, 1964
Fox, J. W. (ed.), *Western Samoa.* Univ. of Auckland, 1963
Milner, G. B., *Samoan–English, English–Samoan Dictionary.* OUP, 1965

YEMEN ARAB REPUBLIC

Capital: San'a
Population: 7·7m. (1980)
GNP per capita: US$460 (1980)

al Jamhuriya al Arabiya al Yamaniya

HISTORY. On the death of the Iman Ahmad on 18 Sept. 1962, army officers seized power on 26–27 Sept., declared his son, Saif Al-Islam Al-Badr (Iman Mansur Billah Muhammad), deposed and proclaimed a republic. The republican régime was supported by Egyptian troops, whereas the royalist tribes received aid from Saudi Arabia. On 24 Aug. 1965 President Nasser and King Faisal signed an agreement according to which the two powers are to support a plebiscite to determine the future of the Yemen; a conference of republican and royalist delegates met at Haradh on 23 Nov. 1965, but no plebiscite was agreed upon. At a meeting of the Arab heads of state in Aug. 1967 the President and the King agreed upon disengaging themselves from the civil war in Yemen. At the time there were still about 50,000 Egyptian troops in the country, holding San'a, Ta'iz, Hodeida and the plains, whereas the mountains were in the hands of the royalist tribes. By the end of 1967 the Egyptians had withdrawn.

AREA AND POPULATION. In the north the boundary between the Yemen and Saudi Arabia has been defined by the Treaty of Taif concluded in June 1934. This frontier starts from the sea at a point some 5 or 10 miles north of Maidi and runs due east inland until it reaches the hills some 30 miles from the coast, whence it runs northwards for approximately 50 miles so as to leave the Sa'da Basin within the Yemen. Thence it runs in an easterly and south-easterly direction until it reaches the desert area near Nejran. The area is about 73,300 sq. miles (195,000 sq. km) with a population of 7,701,893, census 1980. There were 1,395,123 citizens working abroad mainly in Saudi Arabia and the United Arab Emirates not included in the census total. The capital is San'a with a population of 277,817.

The most important towns are the port of Hodeida (population, 126,386), and Ta'iz (119,572); other towns are Ibb, Yerim, Dhamar and the ports of Mokha and Loheiya.

CONSTITUTION AND GOVERNMENT. On 31 Oct. 1962, 13 April 1963, 17 April 1964, 9 May 1965 the revolutionary council issued 'interim' constitutions.

In Feb. 1979 fighting started between Yemen Arab Republic and the People's Democratic Republic of Yemen. A ceasefire was established in March and an agreement to unite the 2 countries was reached on 31 March 1979 and discussions to this end continued during 1982.

On 6 Feb. 1978 a 99-man People's Constituent Assembly was established.

President: Lieut.-Col. Ali Abdullah Saleh.

Prime Minister: Dr Abdel Karim Ali al-Iryani.

National flag: Three horizontal stripes of red, white, black, with a green star in the centre.

DEFENCE

Army. The Army consists of 10 infantry, 3 armoured, 1 parachute and 2 commando brigades, 7 artillery battalions and supports. Strength (1983): 30,000.

Navy. The Navy consists of 4 fast attack craft, 4 patrol craft and 4 very fast (50-knot) torpedo-boats (all 12 *ex*-Soviet). Personnel in 1983 numbered 300 officers and men.

Air Force. Built up with aid from both the USA and USSR, as well as Saudi Arabia, the Air Force is believed to be receiving many new Soviet aircraft. Current equipment includes 20 Su-22 fighter-bombers, 25 MiG-21 fighters, 12 MiG-17s, 16 F-5E/Bs, a total of 15 Il-14, C-47, An-24-26, C-130 Hercules and Skyvan transports, Mi-4, Mi-8 and Agusta-Bell JetRanger and 212 helicopters. Personnel (1982) about 1,500.

INTERNATIONAL RELATIONS

Membership. The Yemen Arab Republic is a member of UN and the Arab League.

ECONOMY

Planning. A development plan (1976–81) envisages expenditure of 16,500m. riyals. The largest allocations are for infrastructure development.

Budget. The budget for 1978–79 had estimated revenue, 3,013m. riyal; estimated expenditure, 4,384m. riyal.

Currency. The currency is the paper *riyal* of 100 rial. In March 1983, 6·74 *riyal* = £1 and 4·60 *riyal* = US$1.

ENERGY AND NATURAL RESOURCES

Oil. In 1977 there were plans to build a refinery.

Minerals. The only commercial mineral being exploited is salt and (1974) production was 1m. tonnes. Reserves (estimate) 25m. tonnes.

Agriculture. Wherever water-supply allows, and in general throughout the south-western part of the country, millet (*dhurra*) is grown as a subsistence crop. The traditional cultivation of coffee (no longer exported through Mokha) continues but is giving place to that of *qat* (*cathula edulis*), a narcotic shrub. Cotton (production, 1979, 1,000 tonnes) is grown in the Tihama, the coastal belt, round Bait al Faqih and Zabid (seat of a medieval university). Fruit is plentiful, especially fine grapes from the San'a district.

Livestock (1981): Cattle, 950,000; camels, 115,000; sheep, 3·2m.; goats, 7·5m.; poultry, 3·4m.

INDUSTRY AND TRADE

Industry. There is very little industry. In 1970 there were over 60 industrial enterprises employing 4,750. The largest is a textile factory at San'a. A cement factory with a capacity of 100,000 tonnes a year exists.

Commerce. Imports totalled 6,195m. riyals in 1977–78, the largest items being food and live animals. Exports totalled 35m. in 1977–78.

Total trade between Yemen Arab Republic and UK (British Department of Trade returns, in £1,000 sterling):

	1978	*1979*	*1980*	*1981*	*1982*
Imports to UK	7,331	2,305	469	966	1,340
Exports and re-exports from UK	48,498	49,169	36,428	31,599	52,593

COMMUNICATIONS

Roads. There were (1981) 19,223 km of roads of which 1,924 are asphalted.

Aviation. There are 3 international airports: San'a, Ta'iz and Hodeida.

Shipping. Hodeida, Mokha, Salif and Loheiya are the 4 main ports.

Post. There were about 90,350 telephones in 1981.

EDUCATION. There were (1980–81) 418,263 pupils at primary schools, 25,037 at intermediate, and 9,895 at higher secondary schools, and 2,450 at teacher-training establishments. In 1980–81 the University of San'a (founded in 1974) had 4,220 students.

DIPLOMATIC REPRESENTATIVES

Of Yemen Arab Republic in Great Britain (41 South St., London, W1Y 5PD)
Ambassador: Ahmed Daifellah Al-Azeib (accredited 16 Oct. 1982).

Of Great Britain in Yemen Arab Republic (23/25 Qasr al Jumhuri St., San'a)
Ambassador: J. F. Walker, CMG, MBE.

Of Yemen Arab Republic in the USA (600 New Hampshire Ave., NW, Washington, D.C., 20037)
Ambassador: Mohamad A. Al-Eryani.

Of the USA in Yemen Arab Republic (P.O. Box 1088, San'a)
Ambassador: David E. Zweifel.

Of Yemen Arab Republic to the United Nations
Ambassador: Muhammad Abdul Aziz.

Books of Reference

Heyworth-Dunne, G. E., *Al-Yemen. Social, Political and Economic Survey.* Cairo, 1952
Ingrams, H., *The Yemen.* London, 1963
Macro, E., *Yemen and the Western World, 1571–1964.* London, 1967
Peterson, J. E., *Yemen: The Search for a Modern State.* London, 1982
Stookey, R. W., *Yemen: The Politics of the Yemen Arab Republic.* Boulder, 1978

THE PEOPLE'S DEMOCRATIC REPUBLIC OF YEMEN

Capital: Aden
Population: 2m. (1980)
GNP per capita: US$420 (1980)

Jumhurijah al-Yemen al Dimuqratiyah al Sha'abijah—Southern Yemen

HISTORY. Between Aug. and Oct. 1967 the 17 sultanates of the Federation of South Arabia (*see* map in the STATESMAN'S YEAR-BOOK, 1965–66) were overrun by the forces of the National Liberation Front (NLF). The rulers were deposed, resigned or fled. At the same time the rival organization of FLOSY (Front for the Liberation of Occupied South Yemen) fought a civil war against NLF and harassed the British forces and civilians in Aden. In Nov. the UAR withdrew its support from FLOSY, and with the backing of the Army the NLF took over throughout the country.

The last British troops left Aden on 29 Nov., and on 30 Nov. the Southern Yemen People's Republic was proclaimed and the name subsequently changed to the People's Democratic Republic of Yemen.

AREA AND POPULATION. The People's Democratic Republic of Yemen is bounded north by Yemen Arab Republic and Saudi Arabia, east by Oman, south by the Gulf of Aden and west by the Yemen Arab Republic. The Republic covers an area of approximately 111,074 sq. miles (287,682 sq. km). The population was (estimate, 1980) 2m. The main towns are Aden (capital) (population, 264,326), including Shaikh Othman (30,000), Mukalla, (100,000) and Maalla (44,626).

The island of **Kamaran** in the Red Sea (area 70 sq. miles) was in British occupation from 1915 to 1967, when the inhabitants opted in favour of remaining with the Republic but Yemen Arab Republic occupied it in 1972.

The island of **Perim** was first occupied by the French in 1738. In 1799 the British took formal possession but evacuated the island the same year. It was re-occupied by the British in Jan. 1851 and was later used as a coaling station. In Nov. 1967 the inhabitants opted in favour of remaining with the Republic.

The island of **Socotra** lying to the east of the Horn of Africa in the Arabian sea (area 1,400 sq. miles) was formerly part of the Sultanate of Qishn and Socotra and became part of the Republic in 1967.

CONSTITUTION AND GOVERNMENT

An amended Constitution was approved by the Supreme People's Council on 31 Oct. 1978.

Meetings took place during 1981–82 between President Mohammed and the President Saleh of the Yemen Arabic Republic, to discuss further steps towards unification.

Cabinet at Jan. 1982 was composed as follows:
Secretary General of the Yemen Socialist Party, Chairman of the Presidium of

the Supreme People's Council and Prime Minister: Ali Nasser Mohammed.

First Deputy Prime Minister and Minister for Local Government: Brig. Ali Ahmed Nasser Antar. *Deputy Prime Minister and Minister of Fisheries:* Anis Hassan Yayha. *Deputy Prime Minister:* Ali Abdul Ar-razzaq Ba Dhib. *Defence:* Brig. Saleh Musleh Qassam. *Chairman of the State Security Committee:* Salih Munassanar As-Siyayli. *Foreign Affairs:* Salim Saleh Mohammed. *Interior:* Col. Mohammed Abdullah al-Battani. *Minister of State for the Council of Ministers:* Abdu Aziz Abdul Wali. *Finance:* Mahmood Said Madhi. *Health:* Dr Abdul Aziz Addali. *Constructions:* Haidar Abubaker Al Attas. *Labour and Civil Service:* Nasr Nasser Ali. *Culture and Tourism:* Rashid Mohammed Thabit. *Education:* Hassan Ahmed Asalami. *Communications:* Abdulla Mohammed Aziz. *Agriculture:* Mohammed Suleiman Nasser. *Industry:* Abdul Kader Bagamal. *Justice:* Khaled Fadhal Mansour. *Trade and Supply:* Ahmed Obeid al Fadhli. *Planning:* Dr Farag Bin Ghanem. *Housing:* Ahmed Mohammed Alqatabi.

National flag. Three horizontal stripes of red, white, black, with a blue triangle based on the hoist bearing a red star.

DEFENCE

Army. The Army, about 22,000 strong, consists of 11 infantry brigades, 1 mechanized and 1 marine brigade, and 1 surface-to-air missile regiment.

Navy. The Navy comprises 6 fast missile craft, 2 fast torpedo-boats, 2 fast attack craft, 2 anti-submarine patrol vessels, 1 gunboat, 1 fleet minesweeper, 3 inshore minesweepers, 1 tank landing ship, 3 medium landing ships and 3 minor landing craft, all transferred from the Soviet Navy and 6 very small British-built launches. Personnel in 1983 totalled 950 officers and men.

Air Force. Formed in 1967, the Air Force is now equipped mainly with aircraft of Soviet design. It has received about 50 MiG-21 fighters, 35 MiG-17 fighter-bombers, a few Il-28 twin-jet bombers, 30 Su-22 attack aircraft, 6 Mi-24 gunship helicopters, 4 An-24 twin-turboprop transports, about 25 L-39 jet trainers and about 8 Mi-8 and 6 Mi-4 helicopters. Personnel about 3,000.

INTERNATIONAL RELATIONS

Membership. The People's Democratic Republic of Yemen is a member of UN and the Arab League.

ECONOMY

Planning. The revised 5-year plan (1980–85) envisaged expenditure of 425m. dinars.

Budget. The budget of the Republic (in 1m. Yemeni dinars) for 1978 envisaged revenue at 54 and expenditure at 58·5.

Currency. The currency is the South Yemen *dinar* and is divided into 1,000 *fils*. Coins: 50, 25, 5, 1 *fils*; notes: 10, 5 and 1 *dinar*, 500 and 250 *fils*. In March 1983, £1 = 0.511 *dinars*; US$1 = 0·345 *dinars*.

Banking. The leading bank is the National Bank of Yemen. All foreign banks have been nationalized.

NATURAL RESOURCES

Agriculture. Agriculture is the main occupation of the people. This is largely of a subsistence nature, sorghum, sesame and millet being the chief crops, and wheat and barley widely grown at the higher elevations. Of increasing importance, however, are the cash crops which have been developed since the Second World War, by far the most important of which is the Abyan long-staple cotton, now the country's major export.

Owing to paucity of rainfall, cultivation is largely confined to fertile valleys and flood plains on silt, built up and irrigated in the traditional manner. These traditional methods are being augmented and replaced by the use of modern earth moving machinery and pumps. Irrigation schemes with permanent installations are in progress. Production (1979 in 1,000 tonnes): Millet, 70; wheat, 25; cotton lint and seed, 15; sesame, 4; barley, 2.

Livestock (1981): Cattle, 120,000; sheep, 987,000; goats, 1·35m.; poultry, 1·55m.

Fisheries. There is a thriving fisheries industry, fish being the Republic's major export after cotton.

INDUSTRY AND TRADE

Industry. Light industry is being established and paint, match and textile factories are in production.

Commerce. Trade is mainly transhipment and entrepôt, Aden serving as a centre of distribution to and from neighbouring territories. Transit trade is mainly in cotton piece-goods, grains, coffee, hides and skins, and cheap consumer goods.

In 1976 imports totalled 116m. dinar; exports and re-exports, 61·2m. dinar.

Total trade between Republic of Yemen and UK (British Department of Trade returns, in £1,000 sterling):

	1978	*1979*	*1980*	*1981*	*1982*
Imports to UK	208	2,713	5,685	7,272	26,631
Exports and re-exports from UK	29,030	18,920	25,425	31,480	35,577

COMMUNICATIONS

Roads. There are 1,150 miles of roads. Registered motor vehicles in 1972 numbered 19,373.

Aviation. Nine airlines operate scheduled services: Alyemda, Air-India, Ethiopian Airlines, Middle East Airlines, Yemen Airlines, Aeroflot, Saudi Airlines, Kuwait Airways, and Air Djibouti.

Shipping. Because of its favourable geographical position and its efficient service to ships, Aden used to be one of the busiest oil-bunkering ports in the world, handling some 550 ships a month.

Post. The automatic telephone system provided service to about 9,876 subscribers in 1973.

Radio telephone services are available with London (with extensions to Europe and America), Kenya (with extensions to Tanzania and Uganda), Bombay, Djibouti, Bahrain and Addis Ababa.

Cinemas (1971). There were 19 cinemas with a seating capacity of about 20,000.

EDUCATION. There were (1978, estimate) 281,900 primary school pupils and 39,300 secondary school pupils.

DIPLOMATIC REPRESENTATIVES

Of the People's Democratic Republic of Yemen in Great Britain (57 Cromwell Rd., London, SW7 2ED)
Chargé d'Affaires: Saeed Hadi Awad.

Of Great Britain in the People's Democratic Republic of Yemen (28 Shara Ho Chi Minh, Khormaksar, Aden)
Ambassador: Peter Williams.

Of the People's Democratic Republic of Yemen to the United Nations
Ambassador: Abdalla Saleh Ashtal.

The US Embassy in Aden was closed on 26 Oct. 1969 and UK acts as the protective power.

Books of Reference

Hickinbotham, Sir T., *Aden.* London, 1959
Ingrams, H., *Arabia and the Isles.* London
Stookey, R. W., *South Yemen.* Boulder, 1982
Thesiger, W., *Arabian Sands.* London, 1959

YUGOSLAVIA

Capital: Belgrade
Population: 22·43m. (1981)
GNP per capita: US$2,620 (1980)

Socijalistička Federativna Republika Jugoslavija— Socialist Federal Republic of Yugoslavia

HISTORY. On 29 Nov. 1945 Yugoslavia was proclaimed a republic. On 8 March 1947 King Peter II and the other members of the dynasty were deprived of their nationality and their property was confiscated.

The peace treaty with Italy, signed in Paris on 10 Feb. 1947, stipulated the cession to Yugoslavia of the greater part of the Italian province of Venezia Giulia, the commune of Zara and the island of Pelagosa and the adjacent islets.

By an agreement of 10 Nov. 1975 the city of Trieste ('Zone A') was recognized as Italian and the Adriatic coastal portion of the former Free Territory of Trieste ('Zone B') as Yugoslav. A free industrial zone was set up in the Fernetici–Sezana region on both sides of the frontier.

AREA AND POPULATION. Yugoslavia is bounded in the north by Austria and Hungary, north-east by Romania, east by Bulgaria, south by Greece and west by Albania, the Adriatic Sea and Italy. According to the census taken 31 March 1981 the population by republics was:

Federal Republics	*Area in sq. km*	*Population*
Bosnia and Herzegovina	51,129	4,124,008
Montenegro (Crna Gora)	13,812	584,310
Croatia	56,538	4,601,469
Macedonia	25,713	1,912,257
Slovenia	20,251	1,891,864
Serbia	88,361	9,313,677[1]
	255,804	22,427,585

[1] Serbia proper, 5,694,464; Vojvodina, 2,034,772; Kosovo, 1,584,441.

The federal capital is Belgrade (Beograd).

The population of the principal towns (census, 1971) and their conurbations (census, 31 March 1981) are as follows:

	Town	*Conurbation*
Serbia		
Belgrade (capital)	755,000	1,470,073
Niš	95,000	643,470
Kragujevac	71,180	164,823
Leskovac	50,000	159,001
Vojvodina		
Novi Sad (capital)	165,000	257,685
Subotica	97,000	154,611
Zrenjanin	72,000	139,300
Pančevo	61,000	123,791
Sombor	43,971	99,168
Vojvodina (contd.)		
Kikinda	38,000	69,854
Vršac	34,231	61,005
Senta	24,714	30,159
Bečej	27,000	44,243
Kosovo		
Priština (capital)	71,000	210,040
Croatia		
Zagreb (capital)	562,000	768,700
Rijeka-Sušak	129,000	193,044
Split	151,000	235,922

	Town	Conurbation		Town	Conurbation
Croatia (contd.)			*Bosnia and Herzegovina* (contd.)		
Osijek	95,000	158,790	Banja Luka	86,000	183,618
Karlovac	47,532	78,363	Mostar	62,000	110,377
Pula	47,414	77,278	*Macedonia*		
Slovenia			Skopje (capital)	308,000	506,547
Ljubljana (capital)	173,530	305,211	Bitolj	65,851	137,835
Maribor	97,167	185,699	Prilep	51,000	99,941
Kranj	27,209	66,879	*Montenegro*		
Bosnia and Herzegovina			Titograd (formerly Podgorica) capital)	55,000	132,290
Sarajevo (capital)	244,045	448,500			
Tuzla	53,825	121,717			

Population (1981 census) by ethnic group was *(i)* the 6 'leading nations': Serbs, 8,140,507; Croats, 4,428,043; Moslems, 1,999,890; Slovenes, 1,753,571; Macedonians, 1,341,598; Montenegrins, 579,043. *(ii)* of the 18 other 'nationalities': Albanians, 1,730,878; Hungarians, 426,867. 1,219,024 persons declared themselves 'Yugoslavs' (i.e. not wanting to be listed with any minority).

Vital statistics for calendar years:

	Live births	*Still-born*	*Deaths*	*Infantile deaths*	*Marriages*	*Divorces*
1979	380,615	...	190,459	12,241	177,305	21,268
1980	382,120	2,675	197,361	12,012	171,439	22,583

The Yugoslav (*i.e.*, South Slav) languages proper are Slovene, Macedonian and Serbo-Croat, the latter having 2 variants (Serbian and Croatian) which are regarded as constituting one language. There are claims, largely politically-motivated, that Croatian is a separate language and Macedonian a dialect of Bulgarian. Macedonian is and Serbian may be written in the Cyrillic alphabet. There are also substantial Albanian and Hungarian-speaking minorities. Art. 246 of the Constitution lays down that 'The languages of the nations and nationalities and their alphabets shall be equal throughout the territory of Yugoslavia'. In practice Serbo-Croat serves as a *lingua franca* throughout the country.

CLIMATE. Most parts have a central European type of climate, with cold winters and hot summers, but the whole coast experiences a Mediterranean climate with mild, moist winters and hot, brilliantly sunny summers with less than average rainfall. Belgrade. Jan. 29°F (–1·5°C), July 72°F (22°C). Annual rainfall 24·4″ (610 mm). Sarajevo. Jan. 31°F (–0·5°C), July 67°F (19·6°C). Annual rainfall 37·3″ (932 mm). Šibenik. Jan. 45°F (7°C), July 78°F (25·5°C). Annual rainfall 32·5″ (813 mm). Split. Jan. 47°F (8·5°C), July 80°F (26·5°C). Annual rainfall 28·1″ (703 mm). Zagreb. Jan. 32°F (0°C), July 72°F (22°C). Annual rainfall 34·6″ (865 mm).

CONSTITUTION AND GOVERNMENT. The Constitution passed on 31 Jan. 1946 declared the Federal Republic to be composed of 6 republics: Serbia, Croatia, Slovenia, Bosnia and Herzegovina, Macedonia and Montenegro.

On 13 Jan. 1953 a new Constitution (Fundamental Law) confirmed the management of all public affairs by the workers and their representatives (which was introduced in 1950) as the basis of the entire social, economic and political system of Yugoslavia.

The Constitution promulgated 7 April 1963 changed the name of the country into the Socialist Federal Republic of Yugoslavia, composed of the socialist republics of Bosnia and Herzegovina, Crna Gora (Montenegro), Croatia, Macedonia, Serbia and Slovenia (*i.e.*, now ranking in alphabetical order), and the 2 socialist autonomous provinces of Kosovo and Vojvodina within the framework of Serbia.

Under this Constitution, social self-government was exercised by the representative bodies of communes, districts, autonomous provinces, republics and the Federation and the rights to self-government and distribution of income proclaimed in 1953 were extended to those employed in public services. The former Council of Producers, in which only workers and employees engaged in economic production were represented, was replaced by Councils of Working Communities representing the working people employed in every field of social activity.

All the means of production and all natural resources are social property. Exceptions are peasants' holdings (up to 10 hectares of arable land) and handicrafts. Citizens may be owners of houses and dwellings for personal and family needs.

A new Constitution was proclaimed on 21 Feb. 1974. The political principle of this Constitution is the direct transfer of economic and political decision making power to the working people through the 'assembly system'. An assembly is defined (Art. 132) as 'a body of social self-management and the supreme organ of power within the framework of the rights and duties of its socio-political community'. Assemblies are based upon the work-place or community and take various forms depending upon the nature of employment. Art. 133 states, 'Working people in basic self-managing organizations and communities and in socio-political organizations shall form delegations for the purpose of the direct exercise of their rights, duties and responsibilities and of organized participation in the performance of the functions of the assemblies of the socio-political communities', and Art. 135, 'Candidates for members of delegations of basic self-managing organizations and communities shall be proposed and determined by the working people in these organizations and communities in the Socialist Alliance of the Working People ... or in trade union organizations'. At the apex of the assembly system is the federal legislature, the Assembly of the Socialist Federal Republic of Yugoslavia which has 2 Chambers: the Federal Chamber and the Chamber of Republics and Provinces.

The Federal Chamber consists of 30 delegates of self-managing organizations, communities and socio-political organizations from each Republic, and 20 delegates from each Autonomous Province. The Chamber of Republics and Provinces consists of 12 delegates from each Republican Assembly and of 8 delegates from each Provincial Assembly.

The Federal Executive Council consists of 29 ministers: a Chairman, who is prime minister, 14 members, 8 Federal Secretaries and 6 Chairmen of Federal Committees. Members of the Council are elected in conformity with the principle of equal representation of the Republics with corresponding representation of Autonomous Provinces.

The Chairman of the Council is elected by the Chambers of the Assembly of the SFRY at the proposal of the Presidency; Members, at the proposal of the candidate Chairman.

The State Presidency is elected every 5 years. It has 8 members representing the six republics and the two autonomous regions. The annual President is head of state.

Every citizen over the age of 18 has the suffrage (16 if employed). The last elections were held from Jan. to Apr. 1982.

Membership of the state Presidency and other government posts:

Bosnia and Herzegovina: Cvijetin Mijatović; *Croatia:* Mika Spiljak *(President until May 1984); Macedonia:* Lazar Koliševski; *Montenegro:* Vidoje Zarković; *Serbia:* Petar Stambolić *(President until May 1983); Slovenia:* Sergej Krajger; *Kosovo:* Fadilj Hodža; *Vojvodina:* Dušan Alimpić.

President of the Assembly of the SFRY: Raif Dizdarević (elected May 1982).

President of the Federal Executive Council (Prime Minister): Mrs. Milka Planinc. *Vice-Presidents:* Zvone Dragan; Borislav Srebrić; Mijat Suković.

Federal Secretary for Foreign Affairs: Lazar Mojsov; *Defence:* Adm. Branko Mamula; *Internal Affairs:* Stane Dolanc; *Finance:* Joze Florijanič; *Foreign Trade:* Milenko Bojanić; *Justice:* Borislav Krajina; *Information:* Mitko Calovski.

The League of Communists had 2,117,083 members in Nov. 1982. It is headed by a Presidium of 23 members led by Mitja Ribičič (till June 1983). *Secretary:* Nikola Stojanović (until June 1984).

National flag: Three horizontal stripes of blue, white, red, with a large red, yellow-bordered star in the centre.

National anthem: Hej, Slaveni, jošte živi reč naših dedova—O Slavs, our ancestors' words still live.

DEFENCE

The General People's Defence Law of 1969 bases Yugoslavia's defence on the principle of a nation in arms ready to wage partisan war against any invader.

Army. The Yugoslav Army comprises 8 infantry divisions, 8 armoured, 15 infantry, 1 mountain and 1 airborne brigade. Military service is for 15 months. Peace-time strength, 190,000 of which 140,000 conscripts.

Navy. The Navy comprises 7 diesel powered patrol submarines, 2 midget (2-man) submarines, 1 new *ex*-Soviet frigate, 16 fast missile boats, 15 fast torpedo boats, 3 patrol vessels, 6 fast attack craft, 4 minehunters, 20 patrol boats, 10 inshore minesweepers, 13 river minesweepers, 1 tank landing ship, 13 minelaying landing craft, 1 survey ship, 1 salvage vessel, 2 headquarters ships, 10 transports, 2 training ships, 21 minor landing craft, 4 ammunition carriers, 6 oilers, 3 water carriers and 12 tugs. Personnel in 1983 totalled: 1,500 officers and 12,500 ratings.

Air Force. The Air Force has about 250 combat aircraft and is organized in 2 Air Corps, with HQ at Zagreb and Zemun. There are 2 fighter divisions equipped primarily with about 125 Russian-built MiG-21s, 2 ground-attack divisions of locally-built Jastreb light jet attack aircraft (being replaced with Juper Galeb), and 2 squadrons of Jastreb jet reconnaissance aircraft. Transport units fly Il-14 and An-26 twin-engined aircraft, 4-turboprop An-12s, and a few other types in small numbers, notably Turbo-Porters and Yak-40s, Mystère 50s and Learjets for VIP duties. Training types are the nationally-designed UTVA-75 armed primary trainer, Galeb jet basic trainer and the T-33A jet advanced trainer (being replaced with Juper Galeb). A large number of Agusta-Bell 205, Gazelle, Mi-4 and Mi-8 helicopters are in service. 'Guideline' and 'Goa' surface-to-air missiles have been supplied by the USSR. Personnel number 45,000.

INTERNATIONAL RELATIONS

Membership. Yugoslavia is a member of UN and has special relationships with Comecon and OECD.

ECONOMY

Planning. A 5-year plan of economic development for 1981–85 envisages that industrial production should increase by 4·5–5%, and that of agriculture by 4·5%. Foreign indebtedness was officially acknowledged to be some £11,100m. in 1982. Austerity measures introduced in Oct. 1982 included petrol rationing and the obligation on Yugoslavs going abroad to deposit 5,000 dinars.

Budget. Revenue and expenditure (Federal, Republican, Provincial and Communal) for calendar years (in 1m. dinars):

	1974	*1975*	*1976*	*1977*	*1978*	*1979*
Revenue	82,302	107,191	148,824	165,875	168,487	224,500
Expenditure	81,492	106,545	148,204	165,832	168,487	222,356

Revenue for 1979 was composed of 102,028m. dinars in the federal budget, 81,520m. dinars in the republican budgets and in the budgets of the autonomous provinces, and 40,952m. dinars in other budgets.

Main items of distributed resources in 1979 (in 1m. dinars): Defence, 56,319; government, 44,215; investments in economy, 1,063; non-economic investments 8,523.

Currency. On 26 July 1965 the value of 1 *dinar*, divided into 100 *para*, was fixed at 0·710937 milligrammes of fine gold instead of 2·96224 milligrammes. A new *dinar*, equivalent of 100 old dinars, was introduced on 1 Jan. 1966. There are coins of 0·05, 0·1, 0·2, 0·5 and 1, 2, 5 and 10 *dinars*, and notes of 5, 10, 50, 100, 500 and 1,000 *dinars*. Circulation of notes and coins, as of 31 Dec. 1979, was 91,182m. *dinars*. The *dinar* was devalued by 30% in June 1980 and again by 20% in Oct. 1982. Inflation was 39·2% in 1980. In March 1983, £1 = 113 *dinars*; US$1 = 75·22 *dinars*.

Banking. The National Bank is the bank of issue. There are also republican National Banks, 115 (in 1980) 'internal banks', 160 'basic banks' and 9 'associated banks'. At 30 June 1982 total credits amounted to 2,108,300m. dinars. Savings deposits totalled 219,400m. dinars in 1982.

Weights and Measures. The metric weights and measures have been in use since 1883. The *wagon* of 10 tonnes is used as a unit of measure for coal, roots and corn. The Gregorian calendar was adopted in 1919.

ENERGY AND NATURAL RESOURCES

Electricity. Generation of electricity in 1981 (and 1980) was 60,364m. kwh. (59,435m.), of which 25,089m. kwh. (28,161m.) was hydro-electric.

Minerals. Yugoslavia has considerable mineral resources, including coal (chiefly brown coal), iron, copper ore, gold, lead, chrome, antimony and cement. The most important iron mines are at Vareš and Ljubija in Bosnia, and there are also considerable siderite and limonite iron ores between Prijedor, Sanski Most and Topusko. Copper ore is exploited chiefly at Bor (Serbia). The principal lead mines are at Trepča and Mežice. Chrome mines are in southern Serbia (Kosovo) and Macedonia (Skopje, Kumanovo). There are 2 antimony mines in western Serbia (Podrinje).

Mining output, in 1,000 tonnes, in 1981 (and 1980): Coal, 384 (388); lignite, 40,958 (36,949); bauxite, 3,249 (3,138); salt, 418 (377); manganese ore, 31 (30); iron ore, 4,794 (4,530); copper ore, 18,337 (19,559); lead and zinc ore, 4,365 (4,284); antimony ore, 67 (70); crude petroleum, 4,375 (4,229); pyrite concentrates, 652 (607); magnesite, 300 (262). In 1979, gold output was 4,323 kg; silver, 162,181 kg.

Agriculture. Yugoslavia, with a total area of 25,580,400 hectares, had a cultivated area of 9·9m. hectares in 1981. Agriculture is not collectivized, though private holdings are limited to 10 hectares.

Area (in hectares) and yield (in 1,000 tonnes) in 1981: Maize, 2·3m. (9,807); wheat, 1·4m. (4,349); barley, 0·3m. (720); rye, 54,000 (75); tobacco, 59,000 (63); (1979) hemp, 4,000 (35); sunflower, 257,119 (525); potatoes, 296,000 (2,724).

Livestock, Jan. 1981: 573,000 horses, 5·5m cattle, 7·4m. sheep, 7·9m. pigs.

The 1980 yield of fruit was as follows (in 1,000 tonnes): Apples, 483; pears, 115; grapes, 1,574; plums, 666; olives, 8; walnuts, 25; 8·2m. hectolitres of wine were produced.

There were, in 1977, 2,599,552 individual holdings and 856,872 peasant co-operatives. Total agricultural work force, 5·4m.; tractors, (1981) 415,655

Forestry. The forest areas of Yugoslavia consist largely of beech, oak and fir. Forest area in 1980: 9,227,000 hectares (2,357,000 in private hands). The gross timber cut in 1980 was 19,401,000 cu. metres.

Fisheries. In 1980 the landings of fish were (in tonnes): salt-water, 34,968; fresh-water, 23,428. The number of fishing craft was 227 motor vessels (9,588 GRT) and 1,176 sailing and rowing vessels.

INDUSTRY AND TRADE

Employment. In Dec. 1981 there were 5·8m. employed in the social sector (*i.e.*, excluding armed forces and self-employed) of whom 2·2m. were in manufacturing and mining, and 1·2m. in the social services. There were 808,623 unemployed. There were (1982) 5,485,000 trade union members.

Industry. The majority of industries are situated in the north-west part of the country.

Industrial output (in 1,000 tonnes) in 1980 (and 1981): Pig-iron, 2,425 (2,817); steel, 3,634 (3,976); cement, 9,400 (9,779); sulphuric acid, 1,190 (1,248); fertilizers, 2,370 (2,350); plastics, 438 (483). Fabrics (in 1m. sq. metres): Cotton, 390 (377); woollen, 92 (96). Sugar (1,000 tonnes), 758 (791). Motor cars (in 1,000s), 255 (242).

Commerce. Foreign trade, in 1m. dinars, for calendar years:

	1977	*1978*	*1979*	*1980*	*1981*
Imports	262,965	272,522	382,709	411,257	430,166
Exports	143,493	154,725	185,470	245,086	298,360

Imports to Yugoslavia, 1981, in 1m. dinars, from: Federal Republic of Germany, 66,691; USSR, 80,957; Italy, 35,242; Czechoslovakia, 17,901; UK, 12,357. Exports from Yugoslavia, 1981, in 1m. dinars, to: USSR, 99,471; Federal Republic of Germany, 23,667; Italy, 27,626; Czechoslovakia, 14,939; German Democratic Republic, 10,197.

The main imports (by value) in 1981 were (in 1m. dinars): Machinery, electrical goods, transport means and parts, 119,034; fuel and lubricants, 103,366; manufactured goods, 70,844; chemical products, 55,329; crude articles, 44,680; food, 21,066. The main exports: Machinery, electrical goods, transport means and parts, 85,073; fuel and lubricants, 5,980; manufactured goods, 65,905; chemical products, 37,587; crude articles, 15,118; foods, 25,317.

In Apr. 1980 a five-year agreement with the EEC was signed to help Yugoslav exports to the EEC and provide financial aid.

Total trade between Yugoslavia and UK (British Department of Trade returns, in £1,000 sterling):

	1978	*1979*	*1980*	*1981*	*1982*
Imports to UK	37,906	51,331	56,802	42,405	52,115
Exports and re-exports from UK	160,317	173,754	190,503	194,846	158,881

Tourism. In 1981, 6,616,000 (1980: 6,410,000) tourists visited Yugoslavia.

COMMUNICATIONS

Roads (1981). There were 59,481 km of asphalted roads and 37,283 km of macadamized roads. There were 2,568,000 passenger motor cars and 227,689 trucks and buses in 1981. The north–south highway is being converted to 6-lane motorway.

Railways. In 1981 Yugoslavia had 9,393 km of railway, of which 3,320 km are electrified, and ran 10,510 passenger-km and 25,720m. tonne-km of freight.

Aviation. The national airline, Jugoslovenski Aero Transport (Inex Adria-aviopromet, Panadria and Aviogenex) in 1981 flew on its home and international services, 55·9m. km and carried 5·1m. passengers and 78m. ton-km of freight; international services (without Panadria), 2·4m. passengers and 72·8m. ton-km of freight. The chief airfields are Belgrade, Zagreb, Ljubljana, Sarajevo, Skopje, Dubrovnik, Split, Titograd, Tivat, Pula and Zadar.

Shipping. In 1981 Yugoslavia possessed a total of 454 vessels of 2·5m. gross tons.

In 1981 vessels of 47·7m. net tons entered the ports of Yugoslavia.

In 1981 Yugoslavia had 1,267 river craft with 1,918 passenger capacity. The length of the navigable rivers amounted to 1,673 km, that of canals to 664 km. There are 2 navigable lakes: Skadar (391 sq. km, of which 243 in Yugoslavia) and Ohrid (348 sq. km, of which 230 in Yugoslavia). A Tisza-Danube canal system is under construction.

Pipeline. An oil pipeline runs from Krk to Pančevo.

Post and Broadcasting. There were 3,791 post offices and 1,698,748 telephone subscribers in 1981. *Jugoslovenska Radiotelevizija* consists of almost 250 main, relay and local stations operating on medium-waves and FM. *Radio Koper* also broadcasts commercial programmes in Italian for northern parts of Italy. National and regional TV programmes are broadcast. Advertisements are broadcast for maximum 170 minutes each week. Number of receivers in 1980: radio, 4·8m.; television, 4·4m.

Cinemas (1980). 1,278, seating 422,000

Theatres (1979–80). 397, seating (professional only), 25,751.

Newspapers (1980). There were 27 dailies, 2,865 other newspapers and 1,295 journals. There are no party newspapers but *Borba* and *Politika* enjoy semi-official status.

JUSTICE, RELIGION, EDUCATION AND WELFARE

Justice. There are county tribunals, district courts, supreme courts of the constituent republics and a Supreme Court. There are also self-management courts, including courts of associated labour. In county tribunals and district courts the judicial functions are exercised by professional judges and by lay assessors constituted into collegia. There are no assessors at the supreme courts.

All judges are elected by the socio-political communities in their jurisdiction. The judges exercise their functions in accordance with the legal provisions enacted since the liberation of the country.

The constituent republics enact their own criminal legislation, but offences concerning state security and the administration are dealt with at federal level.

Religion. Religious communities are separate from the State and are free to perform religious affairs. All religious communities recognized by law enjoy the same rights.

Serbia has been traditionally Orthodox and Croatia Roman Catholic. Moslems are found in the south as a result of the Turkish occupation. The 1953 percentage of the denominations was: Orthodox, 41·2%; Roman Catholic, 31·7%; Moslems, 12·3%; Protestants, 0·9%; without religion, 12·6%.

The Serbian Orthodox Church with its seat in Belgrade has 20 bishoprics within the country and 4 abroad, 3 in US and Canada and 1 in Hungary. The Serbian Orthodox Church numbers about 2,000 priests.

The Macedonian Orthodox Church with the Archbishop of Ohrid and Macedonia as its head in Skopje, has 4 bishoprics in the country and 1 abroad (American–Canadian–Australian). The Macedonian Orthodox Church numbers about 300 priests.

The Roman Catholic Church is divided into two provinces: Zagreb with 4 suffragan sees, and Sarajevo with 2 suffragan sees. In addition, the Roman Catholic Church has 4 archbishoprics, 10 independent bishoprics directly connected with the Vatican and 3 Apostolic Administrators. There is a National Conference of Bishops with the Archbishop of Zagreb, Cardinal Franjo Kuharič, at its head. The Roman Catholic Church has about 4,000 priests.

The Moslem Religious Union has 4 republic Superiorates in Sarajevo, Skopje, Titograd and Priština. The highest authority is the supreme synod of the Islamic Religious Community, which elects the Reis-ul-Ulema and the Supreme Islamic Superiorate.

The Moslem religious community has about 2,000 priests.

The Protestant churches covering 4 independent Lutheran Churches, numbering about 150,000 believers, the Reformed Christian Church, numbering about 60,000 believers, include also several much smaller churches of Baptists, Methodists, Adventists, Nazarenes, etc., numbering together about 100,000 believers. The Protestant churches have about 450 priests.

Also there are independent Old Catholic Churches with Synodal Council at Zagreb.

The Jewish religious community has about 35 communities making up a common league of Jewish Communities with its seat in Belgrade.

Education. Compulsory general education lasts 8 years, secondary 3–4 years. In 1980–81 there were 12,660 primary schools with 130,082 teachers and 2,808,575 pupils, 944 secondary schools (not including those covered by the reform programme) with 62,338 teachers and 329,621 pupils, 307 primary schools for adults with 30,830 pupils, and in 1980–81 585 secondary schools for adults with 47,577 pupils, 138 technical schools for adults with 10,309 pupils, 5 teacher training schools with 2,573 students.

Primary and secondary schools of ethnic minorities (1980–1): Albanian, 1,827; Hungarian, 230; Bulgarian, 63; Czech, 11; Slovak, 19; Italian, 39; Romanian, 38; Turkish, 75; Ukrainian, 6.

For higher and specialized education there were (1981–82) 358 faculties, academies and high schools with 24,596 professors and instructors and 402,037 students.

Social Welfare. In 1980 there were 32,850 doctors and dentists, and 133,399 hospital beds (10,508 psychiatric).

Health insurance benefits totalled 46,203m. dinars and pensions 88,580m. dinars in 1979.

DIPLOMATIC REPRESENTATIVES

Of Yugoslavia in Great Britain (5 Lexham Gdns., London, W8 5JJ)
Ambassador: Dragi Stamenković.

Of Great Britain in Yugoslavia (46 Generala Ždanova, Belgrade)
Ambassador: K. B. A. Scott, CMG.

Of Yugoslavia in the USA (2410 California St., NW, Washington, D.C., 20008)
Ambassador: Budimir Loncar.

Of the USA in Yugoslavia (50 Kneza Miloša, Belgrade)
Ambassador: David Anderson.

Of Yugoslavia to the United Nations
Ambassador: Miljan Komatina.

Books of Reference

Statistical Information: The Federal Statistical Office (Savezni Zavod za Statistiku; Kneza Miloša 20, Belgrade) was founded in Dec. 1944. *Director:* Franta Kornel. It publishes: *Indeks* (from April 1952, with English and French translations); *Statistički bilten* (1950 ff., with English or French translations); *Statistical Yearbook* (from 1954, with English, Russian and French translations); *Statistics of Foreign Trade of the SFR Yugoslavia* (annual, from 1946; half-yearly, from 1951); *Statistical Pocket-book* (from 1955; in 5 eds.: Yugoslav, English, French, Russian, German).

The Assembly of the SFR of Yugoslavia. Belgrade, 1974
The Constitution of the Socialist Federal Republic of Yugoslavia. Belgrade, 1974
Alexander, S., *Church and State in Yugoslavia since 1945.* CUP, 1979
Auty, P., *Yugoslavia.* New York, 1965.—*Tito: A Biography.* London, 1970
Carter, A., *Democratic Reform in Yugoslavia: The Changing Role of the Party.* Princeton Univ. Press and London, 1982
Dedijer, V., *et al., History of Yugoslavia.* New York, 1974
Denitch, B. D., *The Legitimation of a Revolution: The Yugoslav Case.* Yale Univ. Press, 1976
Djilas, M., *Memoir of a Revolutionary.* New York, 1973
Doder, D. *The Yugoslavs.* New York, 1978
Drvodelić, M., *Croatian or Serbian-English Dictionary.* 4th ed. Zagreb, 1978
Filipović, R., *English-Croatian or Serbian Dictionary.* Zagreb, 1980
Horton, J. J., *Yugoslavia.* [Bibliography] Oxford and Santa Barbara, 1978
Horvat, B., *The Yugoslav Economic System.* White Plains, 1976
Hunter, B., *Soviet–Yugoslav Relations, 1948–72: A Bibliography.* New York, 1976
Jambrek, P., *Development and Social Change in Yugoslavia.* Farnborough, Hants., 1975
Kotnik, J., *Slovensko–angleski slovar.* 4th ed. Ljubljana, 1959
Nord, L., *Nonalignment and Socialism: Yugoslavia's Foreign Policy in Theory and Practice.* Uppsala, 1974
Rusinow, D. I., *The Yugoslav Experiment, 1948–1974.* London, 1977
Ristić, Simić, Popović: *An English–Serbocroatian Dictionary.* 2 vols. Belgrade, 1956
Singleton, F., *Twentieth Century Yugoslavia.* London, 1976.–*The Economy of Yugoslavia.* London, 1982
Sirc, L., *The Yugoslav Economy under Self-Management.* London, 1979
Skerlj, R., *English–Slovene Dictionary.* 4th ed. Ljubljana, 1957
Stanković, S., *The End of the Tito Era: Yugoslavia's Dilemmas.* Stanford, 1981
Tito, J. B., *The Essential Tito.* New York, 1970
Wilson, D., *Tito's Yugoslavia.* CUP, 1979

ZAÏRE

Capital: Kinshasa
Population: 29·75m. (1982)
GNP per capita: US$220 (1980)

République du Zaïre

HISTORY. Until the middle of the 19th century the territory drained by the Congo River was practically unknown. When Stanley reached the mouth of the Congo in 1877, King Leopold II of the Belgians recognized the immense possibilities of the Congo Basin and took the lead in exploring and exploiting it. The Berlin Conference of 1884–85 recognized King Leopold II as the sovereign head of the Congo Free State.

The annexation of the state to Belgium was provided for by treaty of 28 Nov. 1907, which was approved by the chambers of the Belgian Legislature in Aug. and Sept. and by the King on 18 Oct. 1908. The law of 18 Oct. 1908, called the Colonial Charter (last amended in 1959), provided for the government of the Belgian Congo, until the country became independent on 30 June 1960. For subsequent history to 1977 *see* THE STATESMAN'S YEAR-BOOK, 1980–81, p. 1613.

AREA AND POPULATION. Zaïre is bounded north by the Central African Republic, north-east by Sudan, east by Uganda, Rwanda, Burundi and Lake Tanganyika, south by Zambia, south-west by Angola, north-west by Congo. There is a short Atlantic coastline between the two last-named.

The area of the republic is estimated at 2,344,885 sq. km (905,365 sq. miles). The population is composed of 3 ethnical groups: Negroes (Bantu, Sudanese, Nilotics), Pygmies and Hamites (in the east). In the census (1976) the population was 25,568,640. Estimate (1982) 29·75m. In 1982 there were about 325,000 refugees in Zaïre and 215,000 came from Angola.

The area (in sq. km) and populations (estimate) at 1 July 1976 of the regions are as follows, together with their capitals:

Region	*Sq. km*	*Population 1976*	*Chief town*	*Population 1976*
Bandundu	295,658	2,977,918	Bandundu (Banningville)	74,467 [1]
Bas-Zaïre	53,920	1,741,080	Matadi	162,396
Equateur	403,293	2,733,171	Mbandaka (Coquilhatville)	149,118
Haut-Zaïre	503,239	3,629,348	Kisangani (Stanleyville)	339,210
Kasai Occidental	156,967	2,817,717	Kananga (Luluabourg)	704,211
Kasai Oriental	168,216	2,078,403	Mbuji-Mayi (Bakwanga)	382,632
Kinshasa City	9,965	2,443,876	Kinshasa (Leopoldville)	2,443,876
Kivu	256,662	3,906,160	Bukavu (Costermansville)	209,051
Shaba	496,965	3,239,431	Lubumbashi (Elizabethville)	451,332
Total	2,344,885	25,567,104		

[1] 1970.

Other large towns: Kikwit, 172,450 in 1976; Likasi (Jadotville), 146,394 in 1970.

The most important languages are: Kiswahili in the east, Tshiluba in the south, Kikongo in the area between Kinshasa and the coast, while Lingala is spoken widely in and around Kinshasa and along the river; Lingala has become the *lingua franca* after French.

CONSTITUTION AND GOVERNMENT. Following amendments in 1971, 1974 and 1977, a new Constitution was promulgated in Feb. 1978. It established a single-chamber Parliament, the National Legislative Council, directly elected with 310 deputies, 1 for every 100,000 inhabitants; a President directly elected for 7 years. The supreme institution is the sole political party, the *Mouve-*

ment Populaire de la Révolution (MPR); its President is President of the Republic; its chief organ is the Congress which meets once every 5 years and in special session when necessary. It is summoned by the President. The *Bureau Politique* of the MPR is composed of 36 members all of whom are nominated by the President. The Executive Council (or Cabinet) is composed of State Commissioners; led by a First State Commissioner (or Prime Minister); all are appointed by the President.

Regional Commissioners, also appointed by the President, administer the Regions.

President: Mobutu Sese Seko (elected for a third term on 5 Dec. 1977).

Prime Minister: Kengo wa Donda.

Foreign Affairs: Kamanda wa Kamanda.

National flag: Green, with a yellow disc bearing an arm holding a flaming torch.

DEFENCE

Army. The country is divided in 9 military regions. Total strength (1983) approximately 22,000. Major units comprise 4 infantry brigades, 1 armoured brigade, 2 parachute battalions and 1 special force brigade. Supporting units include engineer, signal, transport and military police companies.

The *Gendarmerie Nationale* is a separate service with responsibility for security. Estimated strength (1982) 22,000 organized in 40 battalions.

Navy. The Navy consists of 3 flotillas, 1 coastal, 1 river and 1 lake, comprising 4 fast gunboats (*ex*-Chinese), 7 fast torpedo boats (4 *ex*-Chinese and 3 *ex*-North Korean), and 44 coastal patrol boats including 14 US-built and 29 French-built. Personnel in 1983 numbered 1,500 officers and men including marines.

Air Force. The Air Force has been built up with training assistance from Italy. In 1982 it had a squadron of Mirage 5 supersonic fighters, 20 Reims-Cessna Milirole observation and light attack aircraft, 13 Aermacchi MB.326GB and 6 MB.326K armed jet trainers, 6 C-130 Hercules and 3 DHC-5 Buffalo turboprop transports, 8 C-47 and 2 Caribou transports, 9 Super Frelon, Alouette and Puma helicopters, 23 SIAI-Marchetti SF.260MC basic trainers and a variety of other transport and training aircraft. Personnel, approximately 2,500.

INTERNATIONAL RELATIONS

Membership. Zaïre is a member of UN, OAU and is an ACP state of EEC.

ECONOMY

Budget. Revenue was envisaged at 5,070,820 zaïres in 1981, and expenditure, 5,571,501.

Currency. The currency unit, is the *zaïre*, divided into 100 *makuta*. Each *likuta* (plural *makuta*) is divided into 100 *sengi*. Bank-notes are issued in the following denominations: 10, 5 and 1 *zaïre*, 50, 20, 10 *makuta*. In March 1983, £1 sterling = 8·72 *zaïre*; US$1 = 5·89 *zaïre*.

Banking. The national bank is Banque du Zaïre. A development bank with state backing is the Société pour Finance et Développement (SOFIDE). Commercial banks operating in Zaïre are Banque de Paris et des Pays-Bas, Banque de Kinshasa, National & Grindlays Bank, Barclays Bank SZPRL, First National City Bank, Union Zaïroise de Banques, Banque Commerciale Zaïroise, Bank du Peuple, Caisse Nationale d'Epargne et de Crédit Immobilier and Banque Internationale pour L'Afrique au Zaïre.

Weights and Measures. The metric system was introduced by law on 17 Aug. 1910.

ENERGY AND NATURAL RESOURCES

Electricity. The installed generating capacity (1974) was hydro, 1,054 mw; thermal, 79 mw. Production (1978) 3,957m. kwh.

Minerals. In 1980 most of Zaïre's foreign exchange was derived from mining of copper (460,000 tonnes), zinc concentrates (172,000 tonnes), cobalt (14,500). The most important mining area is in the region of Shaba (formerly Katanga). The principal mining companies are the State-owned Gecamines which took over the interests of Union Minière du Haut Katanga in 1967; the Belgian Société Générale des Minerais; the Zaïre-Japanese Sodimiza; the international Société Minière de Tenke-Fungurume which started production in 1976; and 2 diamond companies, MIBA and British Zaïre Diamond Distributors. Production (1979) 11,225,000 metric carats. Offshore oil production began in Nov. 1975.; crude production (1980) was 6·6m. bbls.

Agriculture. Production (1979, in tonnes): Palm-oil, 170,000; coffee, 87,000; rubber, 27,000; cocoa beans, 5,000; tea, 5,000; rice (paddy), 230,000; sugar-cane, 700,000; onions, 10,000; bananas, 310,000; plantains, 1·4m.; mangoes, 172,000. Chief imports (1973) were maize (125,000), rice (52,000), wheat (129,300), meats (16,000). Chief exports (1975) were palm-oil (53,000), coffee (59,000), rubber (24,000), tea (4,600) and timber (49,000 cu. metres).

Livestock (1981): Cattle, 1·2m.; sheep, 753,000; goats, 2·8m.; pigs, 737,000; poultry, 15·5m.

Fisheries. The catch for 1978 was 100,000 tonnes, of which 98,700 tonnes was from inland waters.

INDUSTRY AND TRADE

Commerce. Imports in 1980 totalled 2,327·8m. zaïres, exports totalled 4,553·8m. zaïres. In 1980, 43% of the exports (by value) consisted of copper, 21% of cobalt and 10% of coffee. 22% of exports went to Angola and 13% to the USA, while 16% of imports came from Belgium, 10% from Federal Republic of Germany and 10% from the USA.

Total trade between Zaïre and UK (British Department of Trade returns, in £1,000 sterling):

	1977	*1978*	*1979*	*1980*	*1981*	*1982*
Imports to UK	59,246	98,471	67,006	52,585	17,986	15,801
Exports and re-exports from UK	18,234	20,658	22,246	27,629	22,452	20,557

Tourism. There were 40,948 visitors in 1975 spending US$5m.

COMMUNICATIONS

Roads. Of 150,000 km of roads only 20,600 km are of national importance and all roads are earth-surfaced. There were 177,931 motor vehicles registered in Dec. 1975. Of these, 95,978 were cars, 33,505 trucks, 2,989 buses, 9,153 motor cycles, and other types, 36,306.

Railways. The total length of public railways in 1979 was 5,169 km on 4 gauges, 858 km being electrified. The railways carried (1979) 1·3m. passengers and 1·9m. tonnes of freight.

Aviation. There are 2 international and 40 principal airports, and over 150 other landing strips.

Ten international airlines, including British Caledonian Airways, operate in and out of Kinshasa from Europe, Africa and the USA. The national airline Air Zaïre, with a fleet of 25 planes (Nov. 1975), operates on all the main internal routes as well as on international routes to Europe and other African cities. Internal feeder services are assured by the private charter company AMAZ. PANAM act as technical and managerial advisers to Air Zaïre.

Shipping. The Zaïre River and its tributaries are navigable for about 14,000 km. Regular traffic has been established between Kinshasa and Kisangani as well as Ilebo, on the Lualaba (*i.e.*, the river above Kisangani), on some tributaries and on the lakes. Zaïre has only 30 km of sea coast. The merchant marine in 1980 comprised 33 vessels with a total tonnage of 91,894 GRT.

Post and Broadcasting. In 1970 there were 351 post offices. Zaïre is included in the

Universal Postal Union and in the African Postal Union. Length of telegraph lines, 2,459 km. There were 15 broadcasting stations, 161 stations of wireless telegraphy and 206 telegraph offices; telephones numbered 30,284 in 1980. There is a ground satellite communications station outside Kinshasa. In 1977 there were 125,000 radio and 8,000 television receivers.

Cinemas (1974): 91 cinemas had a seating capacity of 23,300.

JUSTICE, RELIGION, EDUCATION AND WELFARE

Justice. A Justice Department was established in Jan. 1980 to replace the Judicial Council. There is a Supreme Court at Kinshasa, 9 Courts of Appeal and 32 courts of first instance.

Religion. There were, on 31 Dec. 1975, 2,637 foreign Catholic missionaries and 3,375 Catholic nuns. Numerous missionaries were massacred in 1964.

Roman Catholics in 1975 numbered 9m.; Protestants, 1·1m.; Moslems, about 115,000, and Jews, 1,520.

Education. In 1977–78 there were 3,818,934 pupils in primary schools, 458,776 in secondary schools, 84,995 in technical schools and 99,904 in teacher-training colleges. In 1971 all Institutes of Higher Education combined to form the National University of Zaïre, which 26,000 students were attending by 1976; in 1981 the National University was divided to form 3 Universities at Kinshasa, Kisangani and Lumumbashi.

Health. In 1973 there were 818 doctors, 22 dentists, 13 pharmacists, 1,235 midwives, 9,285 nursing personnel and 72,090 hospital beds.

DIPLOMATIC REPRESENTATIVES

Of Zaïre in Great Britain (26 Chesham Place, London, SW1X 8HH)
Ambassador: Matungulu N'Kuman Tavun.

Of Great Britain in Zaïre (Ave. de l'Equateur, Kinshasa)
Ambassador: J. M. O. Snodgrass, CMG.

Of Zaïre in the USA (1800 New Hampshire Ave., NW, Washington, D.C., 20009)
Ambassador: Kasongo Mutuale.

Of the USA in Zaïre (310 Ave. des Aviateurs, Kinshasa)
Ambassador: Peter D. Constable.

Of Zaïre to the United Nations
Ambassador: Kamanda wa Kamanda.

Books of Reference

Area Handbook for the Democratic Republic of the Congo (Kinshasa). US Government Printing Office, Washington, 1971
Atlas Général du Congo. Académie Royale, Brussels
Cornevin, R., *Histoire de Congo.* Paris, 1963
Ganshof van de Meersch, W. J., *Fin de la souveraineté Belge au Congo.* Brussels and The Hague, 1965
Gran, G., *Zaire: The Political Economy of Underdevelopment.* New York, 1979
Slade, R. M., *King Leopold's Congo: Aspects of the Development of Race Relations in the Congo's Independent State.* OUP, 1962

ZAMBIA

Capital: Lusaka
Population: 5·7m. (1980)
GNP per capita: US$560 (1980)

HISTORY. The independent Republic of Zambia (formerly Northern Rhodesia) came into being on 24 Oct. 1964 after 9 months of internal self-government following the dissolution of the Federation of Rhodesia and Nyasaland on 31 Dec. 1963.

By an Order in Council dated 4 May 1911 the two provinces of North-eastern and North-western Rhodesia were amalgamated under the name of Northern Rhodesia, with effect from 17 Aug. 1911.

By an Order in Council dated 20 Feb. 1924, the office of Governor was created, an executive council constituted and provision made for the institution of a legislative council which, since 1945, had an unofficial majority. On 1 April 1924 the British South Africa Company was relieved of the administration of the territory by the Crown.

AREA AND POPULATION. Zambia is bounded by Tanzania in the north, Malawi in the east, Mozambique in the south-east and by Zimbabwe and South West Africa (Namibia) in the south. The area is 290,586 sq. miles (752,620 sq. km).

The republic is divided into 9 provinces. Their names, headquarters, area (in sq. km) and estimated population in 1980 were as follows:

Province	*Headquarters*	*Area*	*Population*	*Province*	*Headquarters*	*Area*	*Population*
Copperbelt	Ndola	31,328	1,248,888	Eastern	Chipata	69,106	656,381
Luapula	Mansa	50,567	412,789	Southern	Livingstone	85,283	686,469
Northern	Kasama	147,826	677,894	N.-Western	Solwezi	125,827	301,677
Central (including Lusaka)	Kabwe	116,290	1,207,713	Western	Mongu	126,386	487,988

The seat of Government is at Lusaka (population, 1980, 538,469). The other important centres are Livingstone, the old capital (71,987), Ndola (282,439), Luanshya (132,164), Mufulira (149,778), Kitwe (314,794), Chililabombwe (61,928), Kalulushi (59,213) and Chingola on the Copperbelt (145,869); Kabwe, the oldest mining township (143,635); Chipata, centre of a tobacco farming area.

CONSTITUTION AND GOVERNMENT. The Constitution provides for a President, elected in the first instance by the General Conference of the ruling party, the United National Independence Party, and thereafter he is elected by the electorate. On 13 Dec. 1972 President Kaunda signed a new Constitution based on one-party rule.

The single political party is the United National Independence Party. Its full-time executive organ (headed by a Secretary-General) is the Central Committee, whose 24 members are elected by the General Conference of the Party. The Central Committee has precedence over the legislative body, the National Assembly, which is led by the Prime Minister and consists of 125 elected members and up to 10 nominated members, including a cabinet of 18 ministers.

Presidential elections were held in Dec. 1978 and on 16 Dec. President Kaunda was sworn in for a further 5-year term.

The Cabinet, as in Sept. 1982, was composed as follows:

President: Dr Kenneth David Kaunda.

Prime Minister: Nalumino Mundia. *Secretary of State for Defence and Security:* Grey Zulu. *Home Affairs:* Frederick Chomba. *Foreign Affairs:* Lameck Goma. *Legal Affairs and Attorney-General:* Gibson Chigaga. *General Education and Culture:* Mufaya Mumbuna. *Higher Education:* Remmy Chisupa. *Health:* Ben Kakoma. *Finance:* Kebby Musokotwane. *Commerce and Industry:* Clement Mwananshiku. *Mines:* Basil Kabwe. *Power, Transport and Communications:*

Rajah Kunda. *Works and Supply:* Haswell Mwale. *Labour and Social Services:* Frederick Hapunda. *Tourism:* Roger Sakuhuka. *Information and Broadcasting Services:* Mark Tambatamba. *Youth and Sport:* Gen. Kingsley Chinkuli. *Defence:* Wilson Chakulya. *National Guidance:* Arnold Simuchimba. *National Commission for Development and Planning:* Dr Henry Meebelo. *Agriculture and Water Development:* Unia Mwila. *Land and Natural Resources:* Fitzpatrick Chuula.

Flag: Green, with in the fly a panel of 3 vertical strips of dark red, black and orange, and above these a soaring eagle in gold.

The provinces are administered by Central Committee Members for the provinces who are responsible for the overall government and Party administration of their respective areas. The Members are assisted by a Political Secretary and a Permanent Secretary. Each district in all provinces is headed by a District Governor, and these are directly responsible to their respective provincial Political Secretaries.

DEFENCE

Army. The Army consists of 1 armed regiment, 1 armed reconnaissance battalion, 4 infantry battalions, 1 armoured car squadron, 1 artillery battery and supporting units. Strength, (1983) 12,500.

Air Force. Creation of the Zambian Air Force was assisted initially by an RAF mission. Equipment acquired in this period and still in use includes 5 twin-engined Caribou and 4 single-engined Beaver transports built in Canada. Training and expansion of the Air Force was next taken over by Italy, with the purchase of 23 Aermacchi M.B.326G armed jet basic trainers (of which 18 remain in service), 8 SIAI-Marchetti SF.260M piston-engined trainers and 28 Agusta-Bell 47G/205/212 Jet Ranger helicopters. Twelve J-6 (MiG-19) jet fighter-bombers and some CJ-6 primary trainers have since been acquired from China, a squadron of 16 MiG-21 fighters, 3 Yak-40 light jet transports and 6 Mi-8 helicopters from the Soviet Union, 6 SOKO Jastreb jet light attack aircraft and 6 Galeb jet trainers from Yugoslavia, 7 DHC-5 Buffalo twin-turboprop transports from Canada, 6 C-47s built in the USA, 10 Do 28D Skyservant light transports from Germany, 20 Supporter armed light trainers from Sweden.

INTERNATIONAL RELATIONS

Membership. Zambia is a member of UN, the Commonwealth, OAU and is an ACP state of EEC.

ECONOMY

Planning. A second 5-year development plan (1972-76) envisaged investment of K2,609m. and an economic growth rate of 6·8% per annum. The emphasis has been on rural development and an important goal is to achieve self-sufficiency in staple foodstuffs, particularly maize. The third development plan has been postponed from Jan. 1977 to Jan. 1980.

To promote industrial growth and to ensure greater Zambian participation in the economy the Government has, since 1968, taken a controlling interest in several companies, including the mines. Government's control of those companies in which it has a majority shareholding is exercised *via* the Zambian Industrial and Mining Corporation (ZIMCO) the holding company for the Industrial Development Corporation (INDECO) which controls all industrial and distributive concerns; the Mining Development Corporation (MINDECO) which holds the Government's 51% share in the mines.

Budget. Revenue and expenditure for 1981 (in K1m.): envisaged expenditure of 1,183 and income of 887.

Currency. Decimal currency was introduced on 16 Jan. 1968. The *Kwacha* (K) is divided into 100 *ngwee* (n). Notes of K20, K10, K5, K2 and K1 are in use. In March 1983, £1 = 1·77 *Kwacha*; US$1 = 1·19 *Kwacha*.

Banking. Barclays Bank International has 25 branches, 6 sub-branches and 17 agencies; Standard Bank has 18 branches and 17 agencies; National & Grindlays, 10 branches and 1 sub-branch; Zambia National Commercial Bank, 10 branches and 1 in London; the post office saving bank has branches throughout the republic.

The Finance Development Corporation (FINDECO) controls the building societies, all insurance companies, one commercial bank and has shares in a second one. The Agricultural Finance Corporation provides loans to farmers, co-operatives, farmers' associations, agricultural societies and such bodies as will further the agricultural industry.

ENERGY AND NATURAL RESOURCES

Electricity. The total installed capacity of hydro and thermal power stations, excluding Zambia's share of Kariba South, amounts to 855 mw and the energy consumption during 1978 amounted to some 5,626·3m. kwh. Zambia exports electricity to Zaïre, Zimbabwe and Angola.

The hydro stations are located at Mbala, Mansa, Kasama, Mulungushi, Lunsemfwa and Victoria Falls, Lusiwasi and Kafue Gorge. Work has started on the Kariba North Project. The thermal stations are located on the Copperbelt. A number of diesel power stations have been installed, mostly in the North-Western and Northern Provinces.

Minerals. The total value of minerals produced in 1978 was:

	Output (1,000 tonnes)	*Value (K1,000)*		*Output (1,000 tonnes)*	*Value (K1,000)*
Copper (blister)	26·6	23,292	Lead	12·7	4,734
Copper (electrolytic)	629·2	533,766	Coal	615·0	15,902
Zinc	34·4	16,360	Cobalt	1·6	35,342

Agriculture. Although 70% of the population is dependent on agriculture only 10% of GDP is provided by the industry. Principal agricultural products (1977) were maize, 693,000 tonnes; sugar, 71,203 tonnes; cotton, 8,929 tonnes; groundnuts, 7,229 tonnes; tobacco, 5,900 tonnes.

Livestock (1981): 2,225,000 cattle; 235,000 pigs; 50,000 sheep; 320,000 goats, and 12·5m. poultry.

INDUSTRY AND TRADE

Industry. In Dec. 1976 there were 32,500 persons employed in agriculture, forestry and fisheries; 64,360 in mining and quarrying; 43,080 in manufacturing; 50,270 in construction and 20,540 in transport and communications.

Commerce. In 1981 imports totalled US$1,040m., exports US$1,103m.

Total trade between Zambia and UK (British Department of Trade returns, in £1,000 sterling):

	1979	*1989*	*1981*	*1982*
Imports to UK	103,570	94,610	41,398	39,957
Exports and re-exports from UK	85,458	103,941	68,223	61,248

COMMUNICATIONS

Roads. There were (1978) over 4,588 km of tarred roads.

Railways. Zambia Railways are that part of the old Rhodesia Railways north of the Victoria Falls. In 1980 the total route-km was 1,297 km (1,067 mm gauge). In 1981 the Zambian railways (excluding Tan-Zam) carried 1·7m. passengers and 1·9m. tonnes of freight. The Tan–Zam railway, giving Zambia access to Dar es Salaam, was opened in 1975, comprising 892 km of route in Zambia.

The line, connecting with Zambia Railways at Kapiri Mposhi, was opened for traffic in Oct. 1975.

Aviation. There were (1978) 130 airports in Zambia (51 government owned). Lusaka is the principal international airport. Seven foreign airlines use Lusaka.

Post. There were (1978) 13 head post offices and 219 other post offices. On 1 Jan. 1980 there were 60,505 telephones.

Cinemas. In 1971 there were 28 cinemas with a seating capacity of 13,400.

Newspapers. There are 2 national daily papers: *The Times of Zambia* (circulation, 65,000) and *Zambia Daily Mail* (45,000).

JUSTICE, RELIGION, EDUCATION AND WELFARE

Justice. The Judiciary consists of the Supreme Court, the High Court and 4 classes of magistrates' courts; all have civil and criminal jurisdiction.

The Supreme Court hears and determines appeals from the High Court. Its seat is at Lusaka.

The High Court exercises the powers vested in the High Court in England, subject to the High Court ordinance of Zambia. Its sessions are held where occasion requires, mostly at Lusaka and Ndola.

All criminal cases tried by subordinate courts are subject to revision by the High Court.

Religion. Freedom of worship is one of the constitutional rights of Zambian citizens. Minority groups, such as the Asian community, are free to practise the religions of Hinduism and Islam, and the views of the leaders of these communities are respected by the Government. The Lumpa Church was banned in 1965 for security reasons, following considerable loss of life, but the Jehovah's Witnesses are allowed to continue their way of life despite the conflict of authority in their views and the views of politicians.

The Christian faith has largely replaced traditional African religion, and the Christian Churches number about 500,000 members and adherents. The Churches, founded mainly from the Western world, are slowly finding their autonomy—as illustrated by the United Church of Zambia (formerly British and French missions) and the Reformed Church of Zambia (formerly South African mission).

Education. In 1977 the primary school enrolments were 936,817, secondary school enrolments were 83,757 and 3,752 students were enrolled for teacher-training. In 1977 the University of Zambia had 3,111 full-time students. Government expenditure on education in 1981 (estimate) was K132·77m.

Health. In 1978 there were 82 hospitals and over 1,000 children's clinics served by 423 doctors.

DIPLOMATIC REPRESENTATIVES

Of Zambia in Great Britain (7–11 Cavendish Pl., London, W1N 0HB)
High Commissioner: Lieut.-Gen. Peter D. Zuze (accredited 24 June 1982).

Of Great Britain in Zambia (Independence Ave., Lusaka)
High Commissioner: John R. Johnson, CMG.

Of Zambia in the USA (2419 Massachusetts Ave., NW, Washington, D.C., 20008)
Ambassador: Putteho M. Ngonda.

Of the USA in Zambia (PO Box 31617, Lusaka)
Ambassador: Nicholas Platt.

Of Zambia to the United Nations
Ambassador: Paul Lusaka.

Books of Reference

General Information: The Director, Zambia Information Services, PO Box 50020, Lusaka.

Office of National Development and Planning, *First National Development Plan 1966–70*
Central Statistical Office, Lusaka, *Statistical Year-Book, 1973*
Laws of Zambia. 13 vols. Govt. Printer, Lusaka
Beveridge, A. A., and Oberschall, A. R., *African Businessmen and Development in Zambia.* Princeton Univ. Press, 1980
Bond, G. C., *The Politics of Change in a Zambian Community.* Univ. of Chicago Press, 1976

Kaunda, Kenneth D., *Zambia Shall be Free.* London, 1962.—*Humanism in Zambia.* Lusaka. 2 vols. 1967 and 1974.—*Zambia's Economic Revolution.* Lusaka, 1968.—*Zambia's Guidelines for the Next Decade.* Lusaka, 1968.—*Letter to my Children.* Lusaka, 1973
Mebeelo, H., *Reaction to Colonialism.* London, 1971
Mwanakatwe, J., *The Growth of Education in Zambia.* London, 1968
Roberts, A., *A History of Zambia.* London, 1977
Sklar, R. L., *Corporate Power in an African State.* Univ. of California Press, 1976
Schultz, J., *Land Use in Zambia.* Munich, 1976
Tordoff, W., *Politics in Zambia.* Manchester Univ. Press, 1974

ZIMBABWE

Capital: Harare (Salisbury)
Population: 7·7m. (1981)
GNP per capita: US$630 (1980)

HISTORY. Prior to Oct. 1923 Southern Rhodesia, like Northern Rhodesia, was under the administration of the British South Africa Co. In Oct. 1922 Southern Rhodesia voted in favour of responsible government. On 12 Sept. 1923 the country was formally annexed to His Majesty's Dominions, and on 1 Oct. 1923 government was established under a governor, assisted by an executive council, and a legislature, with the status of a self-governing colony. For the history of the period 1961–1979 including the period of unilateral declaration of independence *see* THE STATESMAN'S YEAR-BOOK, 1980–81, pp. 1623–25.

AREA AND POPULATION. Zimbabwe is situated between the northern border of the Transvaal and the Zambezi River and is bordered on the east by Mozambique and on the west by the republic of Botswana. The area is 150,699 sq. miles (390,308 sq. km). The capital is Harare (Salisbury). The total population was (1969 census) 5,099,340. Estimate (1981) 7·73m.

Population of main urban areas (1981 estimate): Bindura, 18,000; Bulawayo, 400,000; Masvingo (Fort Victoria) 24,000; Kadoma (Gatooma) 36,000; Gweru (Gwelo) 78,000; Chegutu (Hartley) 14,000; Marondera (Marandellas) 30,000; Kwekwe (Que Que) 62,000; Redcliffe, 20,000; Harare (Salisbury) 686,000; Zvishavane (Shabani) 21,000; Chinhoyi (Sinoia) 28,000; Mutare (Umtali) 74,000; Hwange (Wankie) 33,000.

Vital statistics (1980): Births, 3,657; deaths, 22,431. Many living in remote areas do not register births.

In 1979 the European birth rate was 11 per 1,000; the crude death rate, 9·1 per 1,000, and infant mortality, 14 per 1,000. Figures for Africans were estimated as follows (1969): Births, 52 per 1,000; deaths, 16 per 1,000.

CONSTITUTION AND GOVERNMENT. At the Commonwealth Conference held in Lusaka in Aug. 1979 agreement was reached for a new Constitutional Conference to be held in London and this took place between 10 Sept. and 15 Dec. 1979 at Lancaster House. It was attended by the various factions in Zimbabwe-Rhodesia, including Abel Muzorewa, Robert Mugabe and Joshua Nkomo, and was chaired by Lord Carrington. It achieved 3 objectives: (*i*) the terms of the Constitution for an independent Zimbabwe; (*ii*) terms for a return to legality: and (*iii*) a ceasefire. Lord Soames became Governor-General of Southern Rhodesia in Dec. 1979 and elections took place in March 1980.

Zimbabwe African National Union (ZANU, PF) won 57 of the 80 black seats, Zimbabwe African People's Party (ZAPU), 20 and United National Council (UANC), 3.

Rhodesia (Southern Rhodesia) became the Republic of Zimbabwe on 18 April 1980.

President: Canaan Banana.

The Cabinet in March 1983 was composed as follows:

Prime Minister and Minister of Defence: Robert Mugabe.

Deputy Prime Minister: Simon Muzenda. *National Supplies:* Enos Nkala. *Mines:* Tapfumaneyi Nyagumbo. *Youth, Sport and Recreation:* Ernest Kadungure. *Finance, Economic Planning and Development:* Dr Bernard Chidzero. *Trade and Commerce:* Richard Hove. *Labour and Social Services:* Kumbirai Kangai. *Justice:* Simbi Mubako. *Education and Culture:* Dzingai Mutumbuke. *Community Development and Women's Affairs:* Teurai Nhongo. *Agriculture:* Denis Norman. *Information, Post and Telecommunications:* Dr Nathan Shamuyarira. *Legal and Parliamentary Affairs:* Eddison Zvobgo. *Industry and Energy Development:* Simba

Makoni. *Foreign Affairs:* Dr Witness Mangwende. *Manpower Planning and Development:* Frederick Shava. *Roads and Road Traffic:* Daniel Ngwenya. *Local Government and Town Planning:* Enos Chikowore. *Natural Resources and Tourism:* Victoria Chitepo. *Lands, Resettlement and Rural Development:* Moven Mahachi. *Housing:* Simbarashe Mumbengegwi. *Transport:* Farai Masango. *Water Resources and Development:* Cephas Msipa. *Construction:* Dr Callistus Ndlovu. *Ministers of State in the Prime Minister's Office:* Emmerson Mnangagwa, Dr Sydney Sekeramayi *(Defence),* Jonas Anderson *(Public Service),* John Nkomo *(Deputy Prime Minister),* Tarisayi Ziyambi *(National Co-ordination).*

National flag: Seven horizontal stripes of green, yellow, red, black, red, yellow and green; on a white black-edged triangle in the hoist a red star surmounted by the Zimbabwe Bird in yellow.

The first municipal elections were held in Nov. 1980.

DEFENCE

Army. The strength (1983) of the Zimbabwe National Army was 48,859 consisting of 5 infantry brigades, 2 District Formation Headquarters and 13 Corps (including Armoured and Artillery Corps).

Air Force. The Zimbabwe Air Force (regular) has a strength of about 3,000 personnel and 162 aircraft in 8 squadrons, of which 2 are intended primarily for a training role. Headquarters ZAF and New Sarum ZAF station are in Harare; the second main base is at Thornhill, Gweru, with many secondary airfields throughout the country. Equipment includes 1 squadron of Canberra bombers with added underfuselage rocket racks; 1 squadron of Hunter FGA.9 fighter-bombers, supported by a squadron of Vampire FB.9 fighters and Vampire two-seater trainers used also in a strike role (being replaced with Hawks); a transport squadron with 6 turboprop CASA Aviocars, 4 twin-engined Islanders, a Cessna 421 and 12 C-47s; a squadron with 6 AL.60F5 Trojans for forward air control and 17 Reims/Cessna 337 Lynx attack aircraft; a squadron with 14 SIAI-Marchetti SF.260W Genet light attack aircraft and 17 SF.260C Genet trainers; a helicopter liaison/transport squadron with 49 Alouette II/IIIs, a helicopter casualty evacuation/transport squadron with 10 Bell 205s; and a squadron of 6 Cessna 185 light utility aircraft.

INTERNATIONAL RELATIONS

Membership. Zimbabwe is a member of UN, OAU and is an ACP state of EEC.

ECONOMY

Budget. Revenue and expenditure (in Z$1,000) for years ending 30 June:

	1978–79	*1979–80*	*1981–81*	*1981–82*	*1982–83*
Revenue	580,193	675,891	949,109	1,356,448	1,884,900
Ordinary expenditure:					
From revenue and loan funds	922,963	1,131,229	1,411,904	1,896,390	2,798,775

Receipts during the year ended 30 June 1982 were (in Z$1,000): Income and profits tax, 664,221; taxes on goods and services, 556,083; transfers (including pensions), 688,031.

The gross amount of the public debt outstanding in June 1982 was Z$2,227,341,353.

Currency. On 17 Feb. 1970 decimal currency was adopted. The unit of currency is the Zimbabwe *dollar* divided into 100 *cents*. In Sept. 1983, £1 = Z$1·43; US$1 = Z$0·97.

Banking. The Reserve Bank of Zimbabwe is the country's central bank; it became operative when the Bank of Rhodesia and Nyasaland ceased operations on 1 June 1965. It acts as banker to the Government and to the commercial banks and as agent of the Government for important financial operations. It is also the central note-issuing authority and co-ordinates the application of the Government's monetary policy.

The post office savings bank had Z$75·51m. fixed deposits at 31 Dec. 1982.

The 5 commercial banks are Barclays Bank of Zimbabwe Ltd, Grindlays Bank Ltd, Zimbabwe Banking Corporation Ltd, Standard Bank Ltd, Bank of Credit and Commerce Zimbabwe (Pvt) Ltd.

Weights and Measures. The metric system is in use but the US short ton is also used.

ENERGY AND NATURAL RESOURCES

Minerals. The total value of all minerals produced in 1981 was Z$393,519,815. Output (in 1,000 tonnes) and value (in Z$1,000):

	Output			*Value*		
	1979	*1980*	*1981*	*1979*	*1980*	*1981*
Asbestos	259·6	250·9	247·5	65,864	70,201	91,276
Gold (1,000 oz.)	386·0	367·0	355·3	80,912	144,875	117,381
Chrome ore	541·8	553·0	536·5	16,139	18,449	20,406
Coal	3,188·0	3,134·0	2,409·6	25,843	28,001	29,469
Copper	29·6	27·0	24·6	35,149	35,390	27,891
Nickel	14·6	15·1	13·1	45,077	55,571	51,734
Iron Ore	1,201·0	1,662·0	1,097·7	7,387	14,815	14,839
Silver (1,000 oz.)	977·0	949·0	841·0	7,259	13,004	5,997

Agriculture. The most important single food crop in Zimbabwe is maize, the staple food of a large proportion of the population; deliveries to the Grain Marketing Board in 1981 were 2,018,500. tonnes. The livestock industry is second to tobacco as regards its export potential. Sales of milk to the Dairy Marketing Board in 1980–81 were 150·6m. kg.

The country is suitable for the production of both citrus and deciduous fruits and fruit production is now well established.

In 1980–81 seed cotton production was 199,600 tonnes and irrigated wheat production (1981) was 183,380 tonnes.

Tea is grown in the Inyanga and Chipinge districts and production in 1981 was 9,661 tonnes. Coffee growing is of increasing importance (production, 1980-81, 5,100 tonnes) as is sugar; sugar exports (1981) were valued at about Z$45m. Other crops grown in substantial quantities include small grains (sorghums and millet), soya beans, groundnuts and vegetables. These crops form the basis of much subsistence farming undertaken by the African population.

Tobacco is the most important single product, amounting to about half the total agricultural output (by value). In 1965 tobacco accounted for Z$65m. out of a total agricultural output of Z$136m.; 1981, Z$126m.

Livestock (1981): Cattle, 4·9m.; pigs, 179,000; sheep, 439,000; goats, 1·22m.

INDUSTRY AND TRADE

Industry. The manufacturing industry has developed from the service and maintenance operations that initially provided the back-up needed by the mining and agricultural sectors, and it now supplies a comprehensive range of consumer goods and a growing number of capital goods to the local market. A high reputation for quality has been won by many manufacturers, including producers of clothing, footwear, furniture, radio equipment, steel sections, agricultural implements and pharmaceutical products.

The Customs Agreement with the Republic of South Africa was extended in March, 1982 pending further discussion. Zimbabwe has also entered into Trade Agreements with Zambia, Mozambique, Tanzania, Angola and Swaziland. There is a Customs Union with Botswana. In 1981 agriculture and forestry formed 17·8% and manufacturing 26·48% of the GDP.

Labour. The labour force (1983) was 2·5m.; 991,000 (40%) are employed in the formal sector; 750,000 (30%) are peasant cultivators. The remaining 750,000 are either self-employed in the informal sector or unemployed. Nearly 180,500 new job-seekers entered the employment market this year.

The major development in 1982 concerning employment services in Zimbabwe was that the Ministry of Labour and Social Services established the Department of Employment and Employment Development (DEED). The Department is now pursuing an active employment policy designed to achieve the following objectives: *(a)* To promote full, and gainful employment for every Zimbabwean of working age. *(b)* To ensure that the worker's capabilities and creativity are utilized to the greatest extent possible in order to maximise production, economic growth and development. *(c)* To ensure fair employment practices and equal opportunities in the employment market so that every Zimbabwean will have access to employment offices, career counselling, vocational training and promotion, irrespective of race, ethnic group, sex, religion, age, physical handicap and residence (urban, rural, density area, suburb). The major functions of the new Department are: *(a)* To provide nation-wide job placement services to all Zimbabweans. *(b)* To provide nation-wide career development programmes. *(c)* To register and monitor private employment agencies. *(d)* To promote employment creating programmes and projects.

Commerce. Imports and exports (in Z$1,000):

	1977	*1978*	*1979*	*1980*	*1981*
Imports	388,157	404,239	550,908	809,400	1,017,700
Exports	540,750	612,364	702,302	784,000	959,300

Principal imports in 1981 (in Z$1,000): Machinery and transport equipment, 372,400; petroleum products, 189,056; textiles, 67,394; chemicals, 48,424; steel products, 41,224; insecticides and disinfectants, 18,486; medicines and drugs, 16,216.

Principal exports in 1981 (in Z$1,000): Unmanufactured tobacco, 218,280; gold, 117,380; ferrochrome, 79,517; asbestos, 75,947; cotton lint, 60,299; nickel and nickel alloys, 46,787; raw sugar, 45,908; iron and steel, 42,638; maize, 34,738; copper, 18,317; clothing, 12,308; meat, 4,526.

Total trade between Zimbabwe and UK (British Department of Trade returns, in £1,000 sterling):

	1978	*1979*	*1980*	*1981*	*1982*
Imports to UK	234	325	28,632	38,331	62,584
Exports and re-exports from UK	1,146	1,497	16,209	45,314	95,019

Tourism. In 1981, 327,261 tourists visited Zimbabwe.

COMMUNICATIONS. The Minister of Transport and Power is responsible for the Government's relations with the Zimbabwe Railways and with Air Zimbabwe.

Roads. The Ministry of Roads and Road Traffic is responsible for the construction and maintenance of all State roads and bridges, and all bridges outside municipal areas. The Ministry assists and supervises junior road authorities who look after the secondary and tertiary roads. State roads are those connecting all the main centres of population, international routes, major links in the system and main roads serving rural communities. The total length of roads is approximately 85,000 km including surfaced, 12,000; gravel, 46,000; earth, 27,000.

Number of motor vehicles, 1982: Passenger cars, 219,000; commercial vehicles 17,000; motor cycles, 20,000; trailers, 29,000; tractors, 5,000.

Railways. Zimbabwe is served by the National Railways of Zimbabwe, which connect with the South African Railways to give access to the South African ports; with the Mozambique Railways to give access to the ports of Beira and Maputo; and with the Zambia railway system. In Sept. 1974 the National Railways of Zimbabwe opened another line from Rutenga to connect with South African Railways at Beitbridge. In 1982 there were 3,394 km (1,067 mm gauge) of railways including 335 km electrified. In 1979–80 National Railways of Zimbabwe carried 13·9m. tons of freight and 1·5m. passengers.

Aviation. Air Zimbabwe operates domestic services and also regular flights to Zambia, Kenya, Malawi, Botswana and South Africa, and to London, Frankfurt and Athens in Europe and also to Perth and Sydney in Australia in association with Qantas. The country is also served by British Airways, Kenya Airways, Ethiopian Airlines, Air Tanzania, Air Malawi, Zambian Airways, Mozambique Airlines, South African Airways, Air India, Air Botswana, the Royal Swazi Airlines, UTA French Airlines, Air Portugal, Swissair and Qantas. In 1979-80, 258,484,993 passenger-km were flown.

Shipping. Zimbabwe outlets to the sea are Maputo and Beira in Mozambique and the South African ports.

Post and Broadcasting. At Dec. 1982 there were 155 full post offices, 29 postal telegraph agencies and 27 postal agencies. In Dec. 1982 there were 242,252 telephones in Zimbabwe served by 97 exchanges; 1,282 telex connexions, served by 2 telex exchanges. Zimbabwe Broadcasting Corporation is an independent statutory body broadcasting general service in English and African service in English, Shona, N'debele and Nyanja and 3 regional commercial services in English on medium- and short-waves. Zimbabwe Television Ltd broadcasts one programme 45 hours a week *via* 7 transmitters. In June 1982 there were 82,000 television and 170,000 radio licences.

JUSTICE, RELIGION, EDUCATION AND WELFARE

Justice. The Supreme Court consists of the Chief Justice, the Judge President and at least one other judge of appeal. The High Court consists of a number of puisne judges. The Supreme Court considers appeals from the High Court and lower courts; the High Court has full jurisdiction, civil and criminal, over all persons and matters within Zimbabwe. The Judge President presides over the Supreme Court in the absence of the Chief Justice. The Courts sit at Harare and Bulawayo, and sittings of the High Court are held at three other principal towns three times a year.

Regional Courts, established in Harare and Bulawayo, are intermediate in jurisdiction between the magistrates' courts and the High Court, and have civil jurisdiction.

The tribal courts and District Commissioners' Courts of colonial days have now been replaced by a system of Primary Courts, comprising village courts and community courts. By 1982, 1,100 village and 50 Community Courts had been established. Village courts are presided over by officers selected for that purpose from the local population. They sit with two assessors, and apply customary law. They are not yet able to exercise criminal jurisdiction, but it is anticipated that this will soon come about.

Community Courts are presided over by a Presiding Officer, who is a Government Officer. They have a limited amount of criminal jurisdiction.

Religion. The largest religious groups are the Anglicans and Roman Catholics. Other denominations include Presbyterians, the Methodist Church in Zimbabwe and the United Methodist Church.

Education. Education is non-racial at all levels and not compulsory.

All primary schools offer free tuition; government secondary schools charge from Z$8–Z$18 per term. All instruction is given in English. There are also over 3,600 private primary schools and over 580 private secondary schools, all of which must be registered by the Ministry of Education and Culture.

There are 10 teachers' training colleges, 8 of which are in association with the University of Zimbabwe. In addition, there are 4 special training centres for teacher trainees in the Zimbabwe Integrated National Teacher Education Course.

The University of Zimbabwe provides facilities for higher education. In 1982 the total enrolment of full- and part-time students in the 9 Faculties of Agriculture, Arts, Commerce and Law, Education, Engineering, Medicine, Science, Social Studies and Veterinary Science, was 3,091. Of this 2,580 were full-time students.

Health. In 1982 there were 600 hospitals, clinics and health centres operated by the

Ministry of Health; 103 hospitals and clinics were operated by medical missions with 100% government grants-in-aid for recurrent expenditure. There was one medical practitioner for every 7,020 inhabitants in Zimbabwe

Social Services. It is a statutory responsibility of the government in many areas to provide: Processing and administration of war pensions and old age pensions; protection of children; administration of remand, probation and correctional institutions; registration and supervision of welfare organisations.

DIPLOMATIC REPRESENTATIVES

Of Zimbabwe in Great Britain (Zimbabwe Hse., 429 Strand, London, WC2R 0SA)
High Commissioner: R. T. Zwinoira.

Of Great Britain in Zimbabwe (Stanley Hse., Stanley Ave., Harare)
High Commissioner: Martin Ewans.

Of Zimbabwe in the USA (2852 McGill Terr., NW, Washington, D.C., 20008)
Ambassador: Edmund O. Z. Chipamaunga.

Of the USA in Zimbabwe (78 Enterprise Rd., Highlands, Harare)
Ambassador: Robert V. Keeley.

Books of Reference

Statistical Information: The Central Statistical Office, PO Box 8063, Causeway, Harare, Zimbabwe, originated in 1927 as the Southern Rhodesian Government Statistical Bureau. Ten years later its name was changed to Department of Statistics, and in 1948 it assumed its present title when it took over responsibility for certain Northern Rhodesian and Nyasaland statistics (which it relinquished in Dec. 1963 on the dissolution of the Federation). It publishes *Monthly Digest of Statistics.*

Akers, M., *Encyclopaedia Rhodesia.* Harare, 1973
Bowman, L. W., *Politics in Rhodesia: White Power in an African State.* OUP, 1974
Cann, L. H., *A History of Southern Rhodesia to 1934.* London, 1965
Caute, D., *Under the Skin: The Death of White Rhodesia.* London, 1983
Davies, D. K., *Race Relations in Rhodesia.* London, 1975
Good, R. C., *U.D.I.: The International Politics of the Rhodesian Rebellion.* London, 1973
Lardner-Burke, D., *Rhodesia: The Story of the Crisis.* London, 1966
Linden, I., *The Catholic Church and the Struggle for Zimbabwe.* London, 1980
Martin, D., and Johnson, P., *The Struggle for Zimbabwe.* London, 1981
Meredith, M., *The Past is Another Century: Rhodesia 1890–1979.* London, 1979
Morris-Jones, W. H., (ed.) *From Rhodesia to Zimbabwe.* London, 1980
Murphee, M. W. (ed.), *Education, Race and Employment.* Lichfield, 1975
O'Meara, P., *Rhodesia: Racial Conflict or Co-Existence.* Cornell Univ. Press, 1975
Palley, C., *The Constitutional History and Law of Southern Rhodesia, 1888–1965.* OUP, 1966
Palmer, R., *Land and Racial Domination in Rhodesia.* London, 1977
Pollak, K. and Pollak, O. B., *Rhodesia/Zimbabwe* [Bibliography] Oxford and Santa Barbara, 1979
Sithole, N., *Roots of a Revolution.* OUP, 1977
Stoneham, C., *Zimbabwe's Inheritance.* London, 1982.
Vambe, L., *From Rhodesia to Zimbabwe,* London, 1976
Windrich, E., *Britain and the Politics of Rhodesian Independence.* London, 1978
Wiseman, H. and Taylor, A. M., *From Rhodesia to Zimbabwe: The Politics of Transition.* Elmsford, N.Y., 1981

Reference Library: National Archives of Zimbabwe, PO Box 8043, Causeway, Harare.

PLACE AND INTERNATIONAL ORGANIZATIONS INDEX

PRODUCT INDEX